THE
OXFORD DICTIONARY OF
MUSIC

THE
OXFORD DICTIONARY
OF
MUSIC

MICHAEL KENNEDY

Oxford   New York

OXFORD UNIVERSITY PRESS

Oxford University Press, Walton Street, Oxford OX2 6DP

Oxford New York Toronto
Delhi Bombay Calcutta Madras Karachi
Kuala Lumpur Singapore Hong Kong Tokyo
Nairobi Dar es Salaam Cape Town
Melbourne Auckland

and associated companies in
Beirut Berlin Ibadan Nicosia

Oxford is a trade mark of Oxford University Press

First published 1985
Reprinted (with corrections) 1985, 1986, 1988

British Library Cataloguing in Publication Data

Kennedy, Michael, 1926–
The Oxford dictionary of music.
1. Music—Dictionaries
I. Title
780'.3'21 ML100

ISBN 0–19–311333–3

Library of Congress Cataloging in Publication Data

Kennedy, Michael, 1926–
The Oxford dictionary of music.
Rev. and enl. ed. of: The concise Oxford dictionary
of music. 3rd ed. 1980.
1. Music—Dictionaries. 2. Music—Bio-bibliography.
I. Kennedy, Michael, 1926–   . Concise Oxford
dictionary of music. II. Title.
ML100.K35 1985 780'.3'21 84–22803
ISBN 0–19–311333–3

Typeset by CCC, printed and bound in Great Britain by
William Clowes Limited, Beccles and London

In memory of my mother

PREFACE

THIS first edition of the *Oxford Dictionary of Music* is an enlargement and revision of the third edition of the *Concise Oxford Dictionary of Music* which appeared in 1980. I have added 500 new entries, completely rewritten another hundred, and have made some kind of minor amendment or correction to the majority. Work-lists, which were a new feature of the 1980 edition of the *Concise*, have been brought up to date in nearly all instances, and several of these have been completely rewritten, e.g. those for Chopin, Finzi, and Liszt. A change of style is that asterisks (indicating a separate entry) now occur against compositions only in the work-list, not in the preliminary essay. Dates of works are those of composition wherever possible. Where these have not been discovered, the date given is that of first performance or publication, whichever is the earlier.

The American nomenclature of whole-note, quarter-note, eighth-note, measure, etc. has again been preferred to the English semibreve, crotchet, quaver, bar, etc. Place names generally are given their modern spelling, and I have differentiated between St Petersburg, Petrograd, and Leningrad, and between Christiania and Oslo, etc. Where titles of foreign works are concerned my general policy is to give the chief entry under the name by which the work is best known, with a leaning towards the original-language title. This still leaves a broad middle group of disputable decisions. I have kept to the English titles of Russian works such as *Swan Lake*, since there is no excuse for *Le Lac des cygnes*. But *The Merry Widow* is preferred to *Die lustige Witwe*. For some opera titles I have given no English-title cross-reference, for example *Der Rosenkavalier*, *La Traviata*, *Così fan tutte*, *Il Trovatore*, and *Der Freischütz*. I regard *Le Nozze di Figaro* as a border-line case and list it under its original title. In the matter of transliteration of Russian names, I have (rather reluctantly) conformed to the growing usage Rakhmaninov and Skryabin, but too many record-labels and books prefer Chaliapin to Shalyapin, Diaghilev to Dyaghilev, and Tchaikovsky to Chaykovsky for any change to be anything but unnecessarily confusing.

I have followed Dr Percy Scholes's tradition by writing the whole dictionary myself in the hope this lends some continuity and consistency of style. But of course no one man is omniscient and I have been glad to avail myself of the chance to correct errors and omissions in the third edition of the *Concise Oxford Dictionary of Music*. The immense task of checking and revising has been lightened for me by the invaluable assistance of Joyce Bourne. Many kind people have sent me corrections and suggestions. I thank them all, but some must be mentioned individually. I say a special and wholehearted 'thank you' to Mr David Cummings of Wembley Park, who has also helped at the proof-stage, Professor D. K. McIntire of Indianapolis, and Mr Michael Keyton of Banff, Dallas. Their generous and unstinted help is deeply appreciated. To their names I add those of Mr Alfred H. Sommer of Wellesley, Maine; Mr George Thomas of Alphington, Victoria; Mr Alexander Brebane of Venice, Florida; Mr Paul E. Morrison of Rochester, Michigan; Mr Edward Veitch of the University of New Brunswick, Fredericton; Mr Fritz Spiegl of Liverpool; and Mr Rex Lister of Caterham.

I hope that readers of this new dictionary will continue to let me or the publishers know of defects which they notice. Some of the corrective letters I have received—particularly those from Mr John L. Disch of Seattle—have been so charming and witty that they made the commission of the error almost worth while!

MICHAEL KENNEDY

September 1984

ABBREVIATIONS

MANY of the abbreviations used in this dictionary are either in common use or are self-explanatory. Those used most frequently are listed below.

acc.	accompanying/accompanied (by)
acad.	academy
Amer.	America(n)
amp.	amplified
arr.	arranged (by, for)/arrangement (by, of)
art. dir.	artistic director
ass.	assistant
assoc.	associate/association
attrib.	attributed (to)
b	born
bar.	baritone
bass-bar.	bass-baritone
BBC	British Broadcasting Corporation
b.c.	basso continuo
BBC S.O.	BBC Symphony Orchestra
B.C.	Before Christ/British Columbia
Belg.	Belgium/Belgian
bn.	bassoon
BNOC	British National Opera Company
Braz.	Brazil/Brazilian
Brit.	Britain/British
BWV	Bach Werke-Verzeichnis
c.	*circa* (Latin = about)
Calif.	California
Cath.	Cathedral
C.B.	Companion of the Order of the Bath
C.B.E.	Commander of the Order of the British Empire
CBS	Columbia Broadcasting System
CBSO	City of Birmingham Symphony Orchestra
CEMA	Council for the Encouragement of Music and the Arts
cent.	century
cf.	*conferatur* (Latin = compare)
CG	Covent Garden (Royal Opera House), London
C.H.	Companion of Honour
ch.	chorus
Ch. Ch.	Christ Church, Oxford
choreog.	choreography/choreographed (by)/choreographer
cit.	citizen
cl.	clarinet

C.M.G.	Companion of the Order of St Michael and St George
coll.	college/collection
comp.	composed (by, in)/composition/competition
conc.	concerto
cond.	conductor (of)/conducted (by)
Conn.	Connecticut
cons.	conservatory
cont.	contralto
contrib.	contributor/contribution
coun.	council
counterten.	countertenor
C.V.O.	Commander of the Royal Victorian Order
Cz.	Czechoslovakia(n)
d	died
D	Deutsch catalogue number (Schubert works)
db.	double bass
D.B.E.	Dame Commander of the Order of the British Empire
ded.	dedicated (to)
Del.	Delaware
dept.	department
dir.	director (of)
D.Mus.	Doctor of Music
E.	East
ECO	English Chamber Orchestra
ed.	editor/edited (by)
edn.	edition
elec.	electronic
EMT	English Music Theatre
Eng.	England/English
ENO	English National Opera
ens.	ensemble
ENSA	Entertainments National Service Association
EOG	English Opera Group
esp.	especially
est.	established (in, by)/establishment
Eur.	Europe(an)
fest.	festival
Finn.	Finnish
fl.; *fl.*	flute; *floruit* (Latin = flourished)
f.p., f.ps.	first performance(s)/first performed (by, in)
Fr.	France/French
G.B.E.	Knight or Dame Grand Cross of the Order of the British Empire
G.C.V.O.	Knight or Dame Grand Cross of the Royal Victorian Order
gen.	general

gen. man.	general manager
Ger.	German(y)
Gr.	Greece/Greek
GSM	Guildhall School of Music and Drama, London
hn.	horn (French)
hon.	honorary
hp.	harp
hpd.	harpsichord
Hung.	Hungary/Hungarian
Ill.	Illinois
incid.	incidental (music)
incl.	include(d)/including
Ind.	Indiana
insp.	inspector
inst.	institute
instr.	instrument(s)/instrumental
int.	international
IoW	Isle of Wight
IRCAM	Institut de Recherche et de Co-ordination Acoustique-Musique
ISCM	International Society for Contemporary Music
I.S.M.	Incorporated Society of Musicians (Britain)
It.	Italy/Italian
K	Köchel catalogue number (Mozart works)
kbd.	keyboard
K.B.E.	Knight Commander of the Order of the British Empire
K.C.V.O.	Knight Commander of the Royal Victorian Order
La.	Louisiana
Lat.	Latin
ldr.	leader
lect.	lecturer/lectured
lib.	library
LPO	London Philharmonic Orchestra
LSO	London Symphony Orchestra
man.	manager
man. dir.	managing director
Mass.	Massachusetts
M.B.E.	Member of the Order of the British Empire
Md.	Maryland
Met.	Metropolitan Opera House, New York
mez.	mezzo-soprano
Mich.	Michigan
Mo.	Missouri
movt.	movement(s)
MS (S).	manuscript(s)

mus.	music/musical
mus. dir.	musical director
N.	North
narr.	narrator
nat.	national
N.B.C.	National Broadcasting Company of America
N.H.	New Hampshire
NJ	New Jersey
nr.	near
NSM	Northern School of Music, Manchester
N.S.W.	New South Wales, Australia
NY	New York
NY Met.	Metropolitan Opera House (or Company), New York
NY P.O.	New York Philharmonic Orchestra
N.Z.	New Zealand
ob.	oboe
obbl.	obbligato
O.B.E.	Officer of the Order of the British Empire
O.C.	Opera Company
O.M.	Order of Merit (Member of)
Op.	Opus
opt.	optional
orch.	orchestra/orchestral/orchestrated (by, for)
org.	organ/organist
Pa.	Pennsylvania
perc.	percussion
perf.	performer/performed (by)
pf.	pianoforte
Phil.	Philharmonic
picc.	piccolo
P.O.	Philharmonic Orchestra
posth.	posthumous(ly)
pres.	president
prin.	principal
prod.	produced (by, in)/producer/production
prof.	professor
prol.	prologue
pubd.	published (by, in)
RAM	Royal Academy of Music, London
R.C.	Roman Catholic
RCCO	Royal Canadian College of Organists
RCM	Royal College of Music, London
RCO	Royal College of Organists, London
reh.	rehearsal

rev.	revised/revision (by, in, for)
RFH	Royal Festival Hall, London
R.I.	Rhode Island
RLPO	Royal Liverpool Philharmonic Orchestra
RMA	Royal Musical Association (Britain)
RMCM	Royal Manchester College of Music
RNCM	Royal Northern College of Music, Manchester
RPO	Royal Philharmonic Orchestra
RSAMD	Royal Scottish Academy of Music and Drama
RSCM	Royal School of Church Music, London
RSM	Royal Schools of Music (Britain)
Russ.	Russia(n)
S.	South
S./San/St/Ste	Saint
SATB	soprano, alto (contralto), tenor, bass
sax.	saxophone
sec.	secretary
sch.	school
schol.	scholarship
SNO	Scottish National Orchestra
S.O.	Symphony Orchestra
soc.	society
sop.	soprano
Sp.	Spain/Spanish
S.P.N.M.	Society for the Promotion of New Music
str.	string(s)
str. qt(s).	string quartet(s)
suppl.	supplement
SW	Sadler's Wells (Theatre, Opera, Ballet), London
Swed.	Sweden/Swedish
sym.; syms.	symphony; symphonies
tb.	trombone
TCL	Trinity College of Music, London
tech.	technical/technician
ten.	tenor
Tenn.	Tennessee
th.	theatre
timp.	timpani
tpt.	trumpet
trans.	translated (by, for)/translation
transcr.	transcribed (by, for)/transcription
TV	television
U.C.L.A.	University of California, Los Angeles
unacc.	unaccompanied

univ.	university
USA	United States of America
v.; vv.	voice; voices
va.	viola(s)
var.	various/variation(s)
vc.	cello(s)
vib.	vibraphone
vn.	violin(s)
W.	West
WNO	Welsh National Opera
WoO	Werk ohne Opuszahl (work without opus number)
*	See separate entry for further information

DESIGNATION OF NOTES BY LETTERS

c''' to c''''

c'' to b''

c' to b'

c to b

C to B

C, to B,

A

A. Note of the scale (6th degree of natural scale of C). Hence A♭, A♭♭, A♮, A♯, A♯♯, A major, A minor, etc. A is note commonly used for tuning instr. (orchs. tune to the ob. A). a′ = 440 vibrations per second, internationally accepted since 1939, although some orchs. still accept a′ = 435 and (in USA) a′ = 445.

A (It.), **À** (Fr.). At, by, for, with, in, to, in the manner of, etc. For expressions beginning with A or À, e.g. *A cappella, A tempo,* see under their own entries.

'A 2' in orch. scores and parts directs (a) 2 instr. that normally play separate parts (e.g. the 2 ob. or 2 fl.) to play in unison, or (b) 2 or more instr. that normally play in unison (e.g. 1st vns.) to divide to play the separate parts provided for them.

A. Analytical term used to describe first section of a piece of music, i.e. *A B A = first section, different section, first section repeated, as in many songs.

A. Abbreviation for *accelerando* found particularly in Elgar's scores.

A.A.G.O. Associate of the *American Guild of Organists.

Ab (Ger.). Off. In org. mus., applied to a stop no longer required.

ABA. Term of analysis to describe form of a piece of mus., i.e. 1st section (A) followed by different section (B) followed by repeat of 1st section (A). Many permutations possible.

Abaco, Evaristo Felice dall' (*b* Verona, 1675; *d* Munich, 1742). It. violinist and composer at the Munich court; wrote sonatas and concs. for vn., vc., etc.

Abandonné (Fr.). Negligent (in such an expression as *Un rhythme un peu abandonné*—rhythm rather free-and-easy).

Abbà-Cornaglia, Pietro (*b* Alessandria, Piedmont, 1851; *d* Alessandria, 1894). It. composer and organist. Operas incl. *Isabella Spinola* (1877) and *Una partita di scacchi* (1892). Also wrote a requiem and chamber mus.

Abbado, Claudio (*b* Milan, 1933). It. cond. Studied pf. and comp., Verdi Acad., Milan, and cond. in Vienna. Won Koussevitzky Award at Berkshire Music Center, 1958, Mitropoulos prize, 1963. Cond. Berlin P.O. 1965 and at Salzburg Fest. 1965. Prin. cond., La Scala, Milan, 1968–86; regular cond., Vienna P.O. from 1970. Eng. début Manchester 1965. CG début 1968 (*Don Carlos*). Prin. cond. LSO 1979–88. Mus. dir., Vienna Opera from 1986.

Abbandono (It.). Abandon. Free, impassioned style. Hence the adverb *abbandonatamente,* vehemently.

A battuta (It.). With the beat, indicating return to strict tempo.

Abbassare (It.). To lower, e.g. to tune down a str. of an instr. of the vn. family to obtain a note normally outside its compass.

Abbatini, Antonio Maria (*b* Città di Castello, *c*.1609; *d* Città di Castello, *c*.1679). It. church musician and composer. Choirmaster at St John Lateran and other Roman churches. Helped to prepare new edn. of Gregorian hymns. Wrote several operas, incl. the comedy *Dal male il bene* (Rome, 1653).

Abbellimenti (It.). Ornaments, embellishments.

Abbreviations. Signs whereby writing-out of phrases or groups of notes may be abbreviated. For example, continued repetition of a note is indicated by crossing its stem with one or more strokes to show the required sub-division into smaller values (for triplets or groups of 6 the figures 3 or 6 are added above the notes); and a passage to be played in octaves may be written as a single line, with the words *con ottave* or *con 8ve*.

Abdämpfen (Ger.). To damp off. To mute, especially in connection with timp.

Abduction from the Seraglio, The (Mozart). See *Entführung aus dem Serail, Die.*

Abe, Komei (*b* Hiroshima, 1911). Japanese composer and cond. Studied vc. Tokyo Acad. of Mus., then in Ger. with Pringsheim (comp. 1933–6) and cond. with Rosenstock (1935–9). Prof. of comp., Kyoto Univ. of Arts 1969–74. Works incl.: *Theme and Variations,* orch. (1936), vc. conc. (1942), pf. conc. (1945), Sym. No. 1 (1957), No. 2 (1960), *Serenade* (1963), Sinfonietta (1965), *Variations on a Subject by Grieg,* brass ens. (1972); 9 str. qts. (1935–55), 2 fl. sonatas (1948, 1949), cl. quintet (1942), pf. sextet (1964), pf. sonatina (1970), choral mus., songs, film mus.

Abegg Variations. Schumann's Op. 1, for solo pf., comp. 1830. Written on a theme made out of the notes A–B♭ (Ger. B = Eng. B♭)–E–G–G, and ded. to his friend Meta Abegg.

Abel, Karl Friedrich (*b* Cöthen, 1723; *d* London, 1787). Ger. composer and player of viola da gamba. Pupil of J. S. Bach at Leipzig; orch. player under Hasse at Dresden 1748–58. Settled in London 1759, becoming chamber musician to Queen Charlotte. Associated with J. C. *Bach in promoting and directing subscription concerts 1764–82. Comps. incl. ov. to T. Arne's pasticcio *Love in a village* (1762), syms., ovs., sonatas, etc.

Abencérages, Les. Opera in 3 acts by Cherubini to lib. by V. J. E. de Jouy, based on Florian's novel *Gonzalve de Cordove* (f.p. Paris, 1813; revived Florence, 1957). Title refers to Moorish Abencer-agi warriors.

Abend (Ger.). Evening; **Abendlied.** Evening Song; **Abendmusik.** Evening mus. perfs., usually religious and specifically those by *Buxtehude at Lübeck on the 5 Sundays before Christmas, started in 1673. Continued after his death until 1810.

Abercrombie, Alexander (*b* London, 1949). Eng. pianist and composer. Studied RCM. Début London 1972. Gave f.ps. of pf. works by Finnissy, Xenakis, Skalkottas, etc.

Abert, Hermann (*b* Stuttgart, 1871; *d* Stuttgart, 1927). Ger. mus. scholar. His recasting (1919–21) of *Jahn's standard life of Mozart was very important. Prof. at Univs. of Leipzig (1920), Berlin (1923).

Aberystwyth. Hymn-tune by Joseph *Parry to which words 'Jesu, lover of my soul' are sung. Tune pubd. 1879. Words, by Charles Wesley, written in 1740 for his *Hymns and Sacred Poems*.

Abide With Me. Hymn, words written by Rev. Henry Francis Lyte (1793–1847) in 1820 after attending death-bed of friend at Pole Hore, near Wexford, and first pubd. in Lyte's *Remains* (1850). Tune, 'Eventide', comp. by organist William Henry Monk (1823–89) for these words for *Hymns Ancient and Modern* (1861). Descant by Vaughan Williams in *Songs of Praise* (1925). Among most popular hymns, nowadays particularly assoc. with FA Cup Final at Wembley where crowd sing it, movingly if incongruously, before teams come on to the pitch.

Ablösen (Ger.). To loosen from one another. There are various applications, e.g. to separate the notes (i.e. to play *staccato).

Abnehmend (Ger.). Off-taking, i.e. *Dimi-nuendo.

Abraham and Isaac. (1) Britten's Canticle II for alto, ten., and pf., text from Chester miracle play, comp. 1952 for Kathleen *Ferrier and Peter *Pears.

(2) Sacred ballad for bar. and chamber orch. by Stravinsky to Hebrew text. Comp. 1962–3 and ded. to 'people of the State of Israel'. F.p. Jerusalem 1964.

Abraham, Gerald (Ernest Heal) (*b* Newport, I. o. W., 1904). Eng. mus. critic and scholar, authority on Russ. mus.; ed. of *Monthly Musical Record*

1945–60. On BBC staff 1935–47, again 1962–7; first Prof. of Mus., Liverpool Univ. 1947–62. C.B.E. 1974. Author of *Concise Oxford History of Music* (1979).

Abram, Jacques (*b* Lufkin, Texas, 1915). Amer. concert pianist and teacher. Studied Curtis Institute, 1927–30 and at Juilliard Sch., NY, 1931–8. Schubert memorial award, 1938. Professional début Philadelphia 1938. Toured Europe 1951. Taught at Juilliard Sch. 1934–8, at Oklahoma Coll. for Women, Chickasha, 1955–60, and at Toronto Royal Cons. of Mus. from 1960.

Abravanel, Maurice (*b* Salonika, 1903). Gr.-born cond. Studied in Lausanne and Berlin (with Kurt *Weill). Début Paris 1932. Cond. at Zwickau and in opera houses in Berlin and Rome. Cond. at NY Met. 1936. Cond. of Utah S.O. 1947–79 Special sympathy for Eng. mus., notably that of Vaughan Williams.

Abruzzese (It.). A song or dance in the style of the Abruzzi district, to the E. of Rome.

Abschied (Ger.). Farewell. Hence *Abschiedsym-phonie* (No. 45 in F♯ minor) by Haydn. 6th and last movement of Mahler's *Das *Lied von der Erde* is named 'Der Abschied'.

Abschiedsymphonie (Farewell Symphony). Nickname of Haydn's Sym. No. 45 in F♯ minor, 1772 (Hob. I:45) because of the following incident: Prince Nikolaus, Haydn's employer, became so attracted to his lonely Esterháza Castle that he spent longer there each year. Except for Haydn, the court musicians could not have their families with them and grew depressed. Haydn comp. this sym. with a final adagio during which one player after another blew out the candle on his mus.-stand and crept away, leaving only 2 vns., Tomasini and Haydn. As they too were about to leave, the Prince is supposed to have taken the hint by saying: 'Well, if they all leave, we might as well go too'—and next day the court returned to Vienna.

Absil, Jean (*b* Bonsecours, Belgium, 1893; *d* Brussels, 1974). Belg. composer. Studied Brussels Cons. under Gilson. Prof. of harmony, Brussels Cons. 1930–59. Many comps., incl. 5 syms., 3 pf. concs., 2 vn. concs., 4 str. qts., and many instr. and choral works.

A.B.S.M.; A.B.S.M. (T.T.D.). Associate of the Birmingham School of Music (Teachers' Training Diploma).

Absolute Music. Instr. mus. which exists simply as such, i.e. not *'Programme Music', or in any way illustrative.

Absolute Pitch (Sense of). That sense which some people possess of the actual pitch of any note heard, as distinct from Relative Pitch, which implies the recognition of a note as being a certain degree of the scale or as lying at a certain interval above or below another note heard. The sense of relative pitch may readily be acquired by practice, but the sense of absolute pitch much less easily.

Absolute pitch is really an innate form of memory: the possessor retains in his or her mind (consciously or unconsciously) the pitch of some instr. to which he or she has been accustomed and instinctively relates to that pitch every sound heard. Many good musicians possess this faculty; as many others do not.

The possession of this sense is sometimes extremely useful, but may also prove an embarrassment, as, for instance, when a singer with absolute pitch is called upon to read mus. accompanied by an instr. tuned to what is to him or her 'the wrong pitch', necessitating a conscious transposition of the vocal line.

Abstossen (Ger.). (1) To detach notes from one another, i.e. to play *staccato.

(2) In org. playing, to cease to use a stop. (*Abgestossen* is the past participle.)

Abstract Music. Same as *Absolute Music. As used by Ger. writers (*Abstrakte Musik*), the term has a different meaning—mus. lacking in sensitivity, 'dry' or 'academic'.

Abt, Franz Wilhelm (*b* Eilenburg, 1819; *d* Wiesbaden, 1885). Ger. composer of vocal mus. and pf. pieces (over 600 opus nos.). Also Kapellmeister in various cities 1841–82.

Abu Hassan. *Singspiel in 1 act by Weber to lib. by F. K. Hiemer after tale in *1001 Nights*. Prod. Munich 1811; London (with mus. adapted) 1825; NY 1827.

Abwechseln, Abzuwechseln (Ger.). To change. Used of orch. instr. alternating with another in the hands of the same player, etc.

Abyngdon (Abingdon, Habyngton, etc.), **Henry** (*b* c.1418, *d* 1497). Eng. singer, organist, and composer (none of whose works has yet been found). Precentor of Wells Cath. First person known to have taken a mus. degree at Cambridge (B.Mus., 1464).

Academic Festival Overture (*Akademische Festouvertüre*). Brahms's Op. 80, f.p. 1881 at Breslau Univ. in acknowledgement of an honorary Ph.D. degree conferred on him there in 1879. Makes fantasia-like use of 4 Ger. student songs, *Wir hatten gebauet ein stattliches Haus* (We have built a stately house), *Der Landesvater* (The Land Father), *Was kommt dort von der Höhe* (What comes from afar), and *Gaudeamus igitur* (Therefore let us rejoice).

Academy of Ancient Music. London Soc. formed 1726 for perf. and study of vocal and instr. works. For some time dir. *Pepusch. Survived until 1792. Title revived in 1970: for early mus. ens. dir. by Christopher *Hogwood.

Academy of St Martin-in-the-Fields. Chamber orch. founded 1958 and so called because it gave concerts in the London church of that name. Dir. Neville *Marriner until 1978, then Iona Brown.

Academy of Vocal Music. Founded at St Clement Dane's, Strand, in 1725/6 and met fortnightly. Members incl. Pepusch, Greene, Bononcini, Geminiani, etc.

A Cappella (It.). In the chapel style, which in choral singing has come to mean unaccompanied. See *Cappella*.

Accardo, Salvatore (*b* Turin, 1941). It. violinist. Gave concerts as child; studied Naples Cons. and Siena (with Astruc). Professional début Naples, aged 13. First winner, Paganini Competition, 1958. Wide repertory, but particularly assoc. with mus. of Paganini, of whose long-lost E minor conc. he gave first modern perf.

Accarezzevole, accarezzevolmente (It.). Caressing, caressingly.

Accelerando, accelerato (It.). Accelerating, accelerated; i.e. getting gradually quicker.

Accent. (1) An emphasis on a particular note, giving a regular or irregular rhythmic pattern. For more detail, see *Rhythm*.

(2) The name is also applied to the simplest forms of plainsong tones (see *Plainsong*), i.e. very slightly inflected monotones.

Accento (It.). Accent; hence *accentato*, accented.

Accentuation. Emphasizing certain notes. In setting words to mus., coincidence of natural accents in text with mus. results in good accentuation.

Accentus (Lat.). (1) The part of the R.C. liturgy chanted only by the priest or his representative, as distinct from the *Concentus*, chanted by the congregation or choir.

(2) See *Accent* 2.

Acciaccato (It.). Broken down, crushed. The sounding of the notes of a chord not quite simultaneously, but from bottom to top.

Acciaccatura. A species of *grace note, indicated by a small note with its stem crossed through, viz.,

The prin. note retains its accent and almost all its time-value. The auxiliary note is theoretically timeless; it is just 'crushed' in as quickly as possible before the prin. note is heard. Some renowned pianists even play the 2 notes simultaneously, immediately releasing the Acciaccatura and retaining the prin. note.

Sometimes 2 or more small notes are shown before the prin. notes, and then they generally amount to Acciaccature (being in most cases perf.

on the 'crushed-in', or timeless and accentless, principle), although they have no strokes through their tails, and although the names *Double* or *Triple Appoggiatura* are often given them.

Note a combination of Acciaccatura with Spread chord:

perf. as though notated—

Although the Acciaccatura is theoretically timeless, it nevertheless must take a fragment of time from somewhere. In the cases shown above (which may be considered the normal ones) it takes it from the following note. In 2 other cases, however, time is taken from the preceding note: (1) when harmonically and in context it is clearly attached to that note rather than the following note; (2) when, in pf. mus., it appears in the bass followed by a chord in the left hand or in both hands—the composer's intention being to increase harmonic richness by sounding the bass note in a lower octave and then holding it by the pedal whilst the chord is played; in this case the chord (as a whole) is to be heard on the beat, the Acciaccatura slightly preceding it. See also *Mordent.*

Accidental. The sign indicating momentary departure from the key signature by the raising or lowering of a note by means of a sharp, flat, natural, etc. It holds good throughout the measure (bar) unless contradicted, and where it occurs attached to the last note of the measure and this note is tied to a note in the next measure, it holds good for that latter note also.

In some 20th-cent. mus. any accidental which occurs is understood to affect only the note before which it is placed, as was also often the case with mus. from the medieval period to the 17th cent.

Accompagnato (It.). Accompanied. In It. opera, from about the time of Cavalli, *recitativo accompagnato* meant a dramatic type of recit., fully written-out with ens. acc., as opposed to *recitativo secco*, notated with figured bass acc. only. In 18th-cent. opera, *acc. recit.* was normally reserved for the most important dramatic scenes and introduced the most brilliant arias.

Accompaniment. The term as sometimes used today implies the presence of a prin. perf. (singer, violinist, etc.) more or less subserviently supplied with a background by another perf. or perfs. (pianist, orch., etc.). This is not the original use of the word, which carried no suggestion of subservience, 'Sonata for Harpsichord with Violin Accompaniment' being a common 18th-cent. term.

However, to describe the orch. part of a Brahms conc. as a subservient acc. is obviously ridiculous. Equally, the pf. part of songs by such composers as Schubert, Wolf, Strauss, Fauré, and others is often of equal importance with the v. Thus, in the 20th cent., the art of pf. acc. has become highly developed, e.g. by Gerald *Moore, Benjamin *Britten, and many others.

Accompaniment to a Film Scene (*Begleitungsmusik zu einer Lichtspielszene*). Orch. work by Schoenberg, Op. 34, comp. Berlin 1929–30. F.p. Berlin 1930 cond. Klemperer; f.Eng.p. BBC broadcast 1931 cond. Webern. 3 movements are: *Drohende Gefahr* (Danger threatens), *Angst* (Anguish), *Katastrophe*. No specific film was in Schoenberg's mind, this being an example of 'pure' film mus.

Accoppiare (It.). To couple (org.). Hence *Accoppiato*, Coupled; *Accoppiamento*, Coupling (the noun).

Accord (Fr.). (1) Chord.
  (2) 'Tuning'.

Accordare (It.). To tune.

Accordato, accordati, accordata, accordate (It.). Tuned. (The word is sometimes used in a phrase indicating a particular instr. tuning, e.g. of the timps.) Hence *accordatura* (It.), Tuning.

Accorder (Fr.). To tune. Hence *Accordé*, Tuned.

Accordion (Accordeon). Small portable instr., shaped like a box, with metal reeds which are vibrated by air from bellows. The Accordion is similar in principle to the mouth org. but is provided with bellows and studs for producing the required notes (or, in the *Piano-Accordion*, a small kbd. of up to 3½ octaves). It is designed to be held in both hands, the one approaching and separating from the other, so expanding and contracting the bellows section, while melody studs or keys are operated by the fingers of the right hand and studs providing simple chords by those of the left hand. Invention credited to Damian of Vienna, 1829.

Accordo (It.). Chord.

Accoupler (Fr.). To couple (org.). So *accouplé*, coupled; *accouplement*, coupling, coupler (nouns); *accouplez*, couple (imperative).

Accursed Hunter, The (Franck). See *Chasseur maudit, Le.*

Acht (Ger.). (1) Eight.
  (2) Care.

Achtel, Achtelnote (Ger.). Eighth, Eighth-note, i.e. Quaver; hence *Achtelpause*, a quaver rest. *Achtstimmig*, in 8 vv. (or parts).

Achucarro, Joaquin (*b* Bilbao, 1936). Sp. pianist who studied in Madrid, Siena, and Saarbrücken. Début Masaveu, Spain, 1948. Won Liverpool Int. pf. competition, 1959, making London début same year.

Acis and Galatea. Masque, serenata, or pastoral in 2 acts by Handel to text by John Gay with additions by Pope, Dryden, and Hughes, based on Ovid's *Metamorphoses XIII*. Written and f.p. at Cannons, Edgware, seat of Earl of Carnarvon, later Duke of Chandos, May 1718; London f.p. 1732, when part of *Aci, Galatea e Polifemo*, comp. Naples, 1708, was incorporated. Rev. for larger forces and pubd. 1743. Contains bass aria *O ruddier than the cherry*. Lully, Haydn, and Hatton were among other composers of dramatic works on this subject.

Ackermann, Otto (*b* Bucharest, 1909; *d* Wabern, 1960). Romanian-born cond. (later Swiss citizen) who worked in most leading opera houses. Studied Bucharest Royal Acad. and Berlin Hochschule für Musik. Cond. Düsseldorf Opera 1927–32, Brno 1932–5, Berne 1935–46, Zürich 1948–53, Cologne 1953–8, Zürich 1958–60. Noted for interpretation of J. Strauss II and Lehár.

Ackté, Aïno (*b* Helsinki, Finland, 1876; *d* Nummela, 1944). Finn. sop., studied at Paris Cons. 1894–7, début Paris Opéra 1897 as Marguérite in *Faust*, London début 1907. First London Salome (1910), a role in which she won special acclaim. Dir., Finn. Nat. Opera, 1938.

Acoustic bass. Org. stop with 2 rows of pipes, those mentioned under **Quint*.

Acoustics. In its true sense, anything pertaining to the sense of hearing, but, as commonly used, firstly, the branch of physics concerned with the properties, production, and transmission of sound; and secondly, the quality of a building as regards its suitability for the clear hearing of speech or mus.

Sound is due to the vibrations of a source, such as a mus. instr., which are transmitted through the air to the ear-drum where they set up vibrations at the same rate.

The *pitch* of a sound depends on the speed of those vibrations, which if rapid produce a 'high' pitch and if slow a 'low' pitch. The rate of vibration per second is known as the 'frequency' of the note.

The *loudness* of a sound depends on the 'amplitude' of the vibrations; for instance, a vn. str. violently bowed will oscillate for a considerable distance on either side of its line of repose, thereby producing strong vibrations and a loud sound, whereas one gently bowed will only oscillate a short distance on each side and so produce small vibrations and a soft sound.

Smaller instr. produce more rapid vibrations and larger ones slower vibrations: thus the ob. is pitched higher than its relative the bn., likewise a vn. than a vc., a stopped str. than an 'open' str., a boy's v. than a man's v., etc. But other factors enter into the control of pitch. For instance, *mass* (the thinner str. of a vn. vibrate more quickly than the thicker ones and so possess a higher general pitch) and *tension* (a vn. str. tightened by turning the peg rises in pitch).

The varying *quality* of the sound produced by different instr. and vv. is explained as follows. Almost all vibrations are compound, e.g. a sounding vn. str. may be vibrating not only as a whole but also at the same time in various fractions which produce notes according to their varying lengths. These notes are not easily identifiable by the ear but are nevertheless present as factors in the tonal ens.

Taking any particular note of the harmonic series (as G, D, or B), the numbers of its harmonics double with each octave as the series ascends. The numbers attached to the harmonics represent also the ratios of the frequencies of the various harmonics to the fundamental. Thus if the frequency of the low G is 96 vibrations per second, that of the B in the treble stave (5th harmonic) is $5 \times 96 = 480$ vibrations per second.

Whilst these harmonics are normally heard in combination some of them may, on some instr., be separately obtained. By a certain method of blowing, a brass tube, instead of producing its first harmonic, or fundamental, can be made to produce other harmonics. By lightly touching a str. (i.e. a stopped str.), at its centre and then bowing it, it can be made to produce (in a peculiar silvery tone-quality) its 2nd harmonic; by touching it at a 3rd of its length it will similarly produce its 3rd harmonic, etc. (Harmonics are notated in str. parts as an 'o' above the note. 'Natural' harmonics are those produced from an open str.; 'artificial' harmonics those produced from a stopped str.).

The normal *transmission of sound* is through the air. The vibrations of a str., a drum-head, the vocal cords, etc. set up similar vibrations in the nearest particles of air; these communicate them to other particles, and so on, until the initial energy is gradually exhausted. This process of transmission of pressure to adjacent units of air creates what are known as *sound waves*: unlike waves created by water-motion, there is no forward movement, but each particle of air oscillates, setting up alternate pressure and relaxation of pressure which in turn produce similar effects on the human or animal ear-drum (= vibrations), so causing the subjective effect of 'sound'.

To judge pitch differences, or intervals, the human ear obeys a law of perception called the Weber-Fechner law, which states that equal increments of perception are associated with equal ratios of stimulus. Perception of the octave pitch is a 2:1 frequency ratio. In judging the loudness of sound there are 2 'thresholds', those of hearing and of pain. If the intensity of sound at the threshold of hearing is regarded as 1, the intensity at the pain threshold is 1 million million. Acousticians' scale of loudness, following the Weber-Fechner law, is logarithmic and based on a ratio of intensities 10:1. This is known as a *bel*. The range of loudness perception is divided into 12 large units. Each increment of a *bel* is divided into 10 smaller increments known as *decibels*, i.e. 1 *bel* = 10 *decibels*. A difference in loudness of 1 *decibel* in the middle range of hearing is about the smallest increment of change which the ear can gauge.

When 2 notes near to one another in vibration frequency are heard together their vibrations necessarily coincide at regular intervals and thus reinforce one another in the effect produced. This is called a *beat*. When the pf. tuner is tuning 1 str. of a certain note to another str. of the same note the beat may be heard to diminish in frequency until it gradually disappears with correct adjustment. When the rate of beating exceeds 20 per second, the sensation of a low bass note is perceived.

When 2 loud notes are heard together they give rise to a 3rd sound, a *Combination* or *Resultant Tone*, corresponding to the difference between the 2 vibration numbers: this low-pitched note is called a *Difference Tone*. They also give rise to a 4th sound (another Combination Tone—high and faint) corresponding to the sum of the 2 vibration numbers: this is called a *Summation Tone*.

There is *reflection of sound*, as of light, as we experience on hearing an echo. Similarly there are *sound shadows*, caused by some obstruction which impedes the passage of vibrations which reach it. However, unlike light vibrations, sound vibrations tend to 'diffract' round an obstruction, and not every solid object will create a complete 'shadow': most solids will transmit sound vibrations to a greater or lesser extent, whereas only a few (e.g. glass) will transmit light vibrations.

The term *Resonance* is applied to the response of an object to the sound of a given note, i.e. its taking up the vibrations of that note. Thus if 2 identical tuning-forks are placed in close proximity and one is sounded, the other will set up sympathetic vibrations and will also produce the note. The 1st fork is then a *Generator* of sound and the 2nd a *Resonator*. It is often found that a particular church window will vibrate in response to a particular organ note, and that a metal or glass object in a room will similarly respond to a certain vocal or instr. note.

This phenomenon is true resonance ('re-sounding') in the strict scientific sense of the word. There is also a less strict use of the word, which is sometimes applied to the vibration of floor, walls, and ceiling of a hall, not limited to a particular note, but in response to any note played or sung. A hall may either be too resonant for the comfort of performers and audience, or too little so—too 'dead' (a hall with echo is often described as 'too

resonant', but there is an obvious clear distinction to be made between the mere reflection of sounds and the sympathetic reinforcements of them). Reverberation time is defined as the time it takes for sound to fall 60 decibels (1 millionth of original intensity).

Materials of walls and ceiling should be neither too reverberatory nor too absorbent ('dead'). Acoustical engineers have worked out co-efficients of absorption for building materials, but absorption is rarely uniform throughout the whole spectrum of pitch. Only wood and certain special acoustic materials show nearly even absorption in the total frequency range. Amplifiers and loud-speakers can be used (as they nowadays often are) to overcome difficulties caused by original faulty design.

Action. The mechanism of a pf., org., or similar instr. which connects the kbd. and str., or the pipes and stops.

Action, Ballet d' (Pas d'). A ballet with a dramatic basis.

Act Tune (Curtain Tune, Curtain Music). A 17th- and 18th-cent. term for mus. between the acts of a play while the curtain was down, similar to an *entr'acte* or *intermezzo*.

Actus Tragicus. Name for Bach's church cantata No. 106, *Gottes Zeit ist die allerbeste Zeit* (God's Time is the best). It appears to have been written, probably in 1707, for an occasion of mourning on the death of some public personage.

Adagietto (It.). (1) Slow, but less so than *Adagio*.
(2) A short *adagio* comp. A famous example is the *Adagietto* for str. and harp, the 4th movement of Mahler's Sym. No. 5.

Adagio (It.). At ease. Slow (not so slow as *Largo*, but slower than *Andante*). A slow movement is often called 'an Adagio'. *Adagissimo*, Extremely slow. *Adagio assai*, very slow.

Adam, Adolphe (Charles) (*b* Paris, 1803; *d* Paris, 1856). Fr. composer and critic. Studied Paris Cons. and with *Boieldieu. Wrote 70 operas, mostly opéras comiques, of which best-known are *Le Postillon de Lonjumeau* (1836) and *Si j'étais roi* (1852). Also wrote church mus., songs, and several ballets, incl. *Giselle* (1841). Prof. of comp., Paris Cons. from 1849.

Adam, Theo (*b* Dresden, 1926). Ger. bass-bar. Opera début Dresden 1949. Member of Berlin Staatsoper from 1952. Bayreuth début 1952, CG début 1967 (Wotan), NY Met. 1969 (Sachs). Notable in Wagner roles but also as Strauss's Ochs, Beethoven's Pizarro, Berg's Wozzeck, and Mozart's Don Giovanni.

Adam de la Halle (de la Hale, de la Hèle) (*b* ?Arras, *c.*1231; *d* Naples, *c.*1288). Fr. troubadou.'. His *Le Jeu de Robin et Marion*, written for Fr. court at Naples, is regarded as precursor of opéra comique. Also wrote motets, chansons, and *Le Jeu d'Adam* (Arras, 1262).

Adam le Bossu (Adam the Hunchback). Identical with *Adam de la Halle.

Adamberger, Valentin (*b* Munich, 1743; *d* Vienna, 1804). Ger. ten., known in It. early in his career as Adamonti. Friend of Mozart, who greatly admired him and wrote for him the part of Belmonte in *Die Entführung aus dem Serail*.

Adamis, Michael George (*b* Piraeus, Greece, 1929). Gr. composer. Studied Athens Cons. 1947–59 and at Brandeis Univ., Mass., 1962–5, where he was assoc. with elec. mus. studio. Founded Athens Chamber Choir, 1958.

Adams, Stephen. See *Maybrick, Michael.*

A.D.C.M. Archbishop of Canterbury's Diploma in Church Mus., awarded only after examination to Fellows of the Royal Coll. of Organists who hold the Ch.M. (Choirmaster) diploma.

Added 6th, Chord of. In key of C, the chord F-A-C-D and similarly in other keys, i.e. the subdominant chord plus the 6th from the bass (major 6th added to major or minor triad), or, looked at from another viewpoint, the first inversion of the (diatonic) supertonic 7th. Frequently used by Delius, Mahler, and in jazz.

Addinsell, Richard (*b* Oxford, 1904; *d* Chelsea, 1977). Eng. composer. Trained Oxford, RCM, and Vienna. Wrote songs and film mus., of which outstanding example is *Warsaw Concerto*, skilful pastiche of romantic pf. conc., written for 1941 film *Dangerous Moonlight*. (See *Film Music*).

Additional Accompaniments. New or rev. accs. written by a later composer or ed. for mus. of the early masters, where perhaps only a figured bass is provided in the original. An extravagant example of such additions is found in the instr. parts Mozart wrote into Handel's *Messiah* for an occasion when no organ was available to provide the figured bass used in perf. of Handel's own time.

Addolcendo (It.). Becoming *dolce.

Addolorato (It.). Grieved, i.e. in a saddened style.

Adelaide. Song for high v. and pf. by Beethoven, Op. 46, comp. 1795/6 to poem by F. von Matthisson.

Adélaïde Concerto. Vn. conc. dubiously attrib. to the 10-year-old Mozart, supposedly ded. to the Princess Adélaïde, daughter of King Louis XV of France.

Adeney, Richard (*b* London, 1920). Eng. flautist. Studied RCM. Prin. flautist, LPO, 1941–50 and 1960–9; and in Melos Ens. and ECO.

Adeste Fideles (O come, all ye faithful). This hymn and tune probably date from the first half of the 18th cent. The late G. E. P. Arkwright

detected that the first part of the tune closely resembled a tune which appeared in a Paris *vaudeville* of 1744 (where it was described as 'Air Anglais') and suggested that it was probably an adaptation of some popular tune combined, in the hymn, with reminiscences of the air 'Pensa ad amare' from Handel's *Ottone* (1723). This view is supported by more recent researches, notably those of Dom John Stéphan, of Buckfast Abbey, Devon, who in 1947 discussed a newly-discovered MS. of the tune in the handwriting of John Francis Wade, a Lat. teacher and music copyist of Douai (*d* 1786). Stéphan believed this to be the 'first and original version', dating from 1740–43, and attrib. both words and mus. to Wade.

À deux cordes (Fr.). On 2 strings.

À deux mains (Fr.). For 2 hands.

À deux temps (Fr.). In 2/2 time.

Adieux Sonata. Fr. title (in full, *Sonate caractéristique; les adieux, l'absence et le retour*) given by publisher to Beethoven's Pf. Sonata No. 26 in E♭ major, Op. 81a, comp. 1809–10. Beethoven disapproved of the title, preferring the Ger. *Das *Lebewohl* (The Farewell). Ded. to Archduke Rudolph on his departure from Vienna for 9 months.

Adler, Guido (*b* Eibenschütz, Moravia, 1855; *d* Vienna, 1941). Austrian critic and musicologist; prof. of music history, Prague Univ., 1885–97. Succeeded *Hanslick as prof. of music history, Vienna Univ. 1898–1927. Author of books on Wagner (1904) and Mahler (1916), gen. ed. *Handbuch der Musikgeschichte* (1924).

Adler, Kurt (*b* Neuhaus, Cz., 1907; *d* Butler, NJ, 1977). Cz. cond., pianist, and scholar. Studied Vienna. Ass. cond. Berlin State Opera 1927–9; cond. Ger. Opera, Prague, 1929–32, Kiev Opera 1933–5. Settled in USA 1938. Ass. cond. and ch. master NY Met. 1943. On staff NY Met. 1943–73 (official début as cond. 1951).

Adler, Kurt Herbert (*b* Vienna, 1905). Austrian-born cond. and impresario. Studied Vienna Cons. Th. cond. in Vienna, Prague, etc. Ass. to Toscanini, Salzburg 1936. Went to USA as cond. Chicago Opera 1938–43. Ch. master, San Francisco Opera 1943, art. dir. 1953, gen. dir. 1956–82. Hon. C.B.E. 1980.

Adler, Larry (Lawrence Cecil) (*b* Baltimore, 1914). Amer. virtuoso on *harmonica (mouth org.). Has toured the world as mus.-hall artist and recitalist. Works written for him by Vaughan Williams, Gordon Jacob, Milhaud, Arnold, etc. Also writer for periodicals, reviews, etc. Settled in Eng. 1949.

Adler, Peter Herman (*b* Jablonec, 1899). Cz. cond. who became Amer. citizen. Studied in Prague with *Zemlinsky. Held posts in Bremen, Kiev, and Prague. Helped Fritz *Busch to found

New Opera Co., NY, 1941. Dir. NBC TV opera 1949–60. Cond., Baltimore S.O. 1959–68. NY Met. début 1972.

Adler, Samuel (*b* Mannheim, 1928). Amer. composer and cond. Attended Boston Univ., USA, 1946–8. Teachers have incl. Copland, Piston, Hindemith, and Koussevitzky. Prof. of comp., Eastman Sch. of Mus., 1966. Works incl. operas and syms.

Ad libitum (*Ad lib.*) (Lat.). Optional or At will, with regard to (a) Rhythm, tempo, etc.; (b) Inclusion or omission of some v. or instr.; (c) Inclusion or omission of some passage; (d) The extemporization of a cadenza.

Adni, Daniel (*b* Haifa, 1951). Israeli pianist. Studied Paris Cons. with Perlemuter. Début London 1970. Specialist in romantic repertory. Settled in Eng.

Adriana Lecouvreur. Opera in 4 acts by Cilea to lib. by Colautti from play of same name by Scribe and Legouvé (1849). Prod. Milan 1902; London 1904; NY 1907. Adriana was one of greatest 18-cent. Fr. tragic actresses, much admired by Voltaire.

Adson, John (*b* late 16th cent.; *d* London, 1640). Eng. composer, member of King's Musick under Charles I in 1625. Comp. *Courtly Masquing Ayres* for vns., consorts, and cornets in 5 and 6 parts (1611, another edn. 1621).

A due corde (It.). On two str.

Adventures of Mr Brouček, The (Janáček). See *Excursions of Mr Brouček, The.*

Adventures of the Vixen Bystroušky (Janáček). See *Cunning Little Vixen, The.*

Aeolian Harp (from Aeolus, the mythological keeper of the winds). An instr. consisting of a box about 3′ long, with catgut str. of different thicknesses but tuned in unison attached to its upper surface. It could be placed along a window ledge or elsewhere where the wind could catch it and set the str. in vibration, thereby producing harmonics which varied with the thickness of the str. and the velocity of the wind to give a chordal effect. The Aeolian harp was popular from the late 16th or early 17th cents. to the late 19th cent. Now made as a toy.

Aeolian mode. See *Modes.*

Aeolina. Mouth org. or harmonica, comprising metal plates enclosing free reeds.

Aeoline. Soft org. stop of 8′ length and pitch, supposed to imitate *Aeolian harp.*

Aeroforo (It.). *Aerophor.

Aerophone. Term for mus. instrs. which produce their sound by using air as principal vibrating factor. These instr. are subdivided according to whether air is unconfined by the instr. (bull-

roarer, motor horn, etc.) or enclosed within a tube (wind instr. proper). One of 4 classifications of instr. devised by C. Sachs and E. M. von Hornbostel and pubd. in *Zeitschrift für Ethnologie*, 1914. Other categories are *chordophones, *idiophones, and *membranophones, with *electrophones recently added.

Aerophor. Device (invented by Ger. flautist Bernhard Samuel and patented 1912) to help wind players. A small bellows, worked by foot, supplies wind by tube to a corner of the mouth, leaving the player free to breathe uninterruptedly through the nose. Richard Strauss called for its use in his *Festliches Präludium*, Op. 61, erroneously describing it as *Aerophon*, and in his *Alpensinfonie*, Op. 64.

Aevia. This 'word' consists of the vowels of 'Alleluia'. Used as an abbreviation in a similar way to *Evovae.*

Affetto (It.). Affection. Hence, *Affettuoso, affettuosa*, affectionate, with tenderness; *affettuosamente*, affectionately; *Affezione*, affection.

Affekt (Ger. 'fervour'). *Affektvoll*, full of fervour; *mit Affekt*, with warmth or passion.

Affretando (It. 'hurrying', 'quickening'). Instruction to increase tempo, implying also an increase in nervous energy.

Africaine, L' (The African Woman). Opera in 5 acts by *Meyerbeer to lib. by Scribe. Begun 1837, but work on it intermittent owing to constant alterations to lib., etc. Completed 1864. Meyerbeer died in Paris while supervising rehearsals. Orig. version lasts 6 hours. Prod. Paris, London, and NY 1865.

African Sanctus. Comp. by David *Fanshawe for 2 sop., pf., org., ch., and perc. incl. rock-kit drummer, cymbals, congas, timp., bass and ten. drums, tam-tam, tom-tom, amplified lead and rhythmic guitars, and tape recordings made in Africa. F.p. London 1972. Rev. version f.p. Toronto, Jan. 1978, f.p. in England BBC TV film. F. concert p. Worcester 1978.

Afternoon of a Faun, The (Debussy). See *Aprèsmidi d'une faune, Prélude à l'.*

Agazzari, Agostino (*b* Siena, 1578; *d* Siena, 1640). It. composer of church mus. Treatise *La musica ecclesiastica* (1638) discusses decrees of Council of Trent. Wrote influential treatise on thoroughbass.

Age of Anxiety, The. Sym. No. 2 by Leonard *Bernstein for pf. and orch. (Title from Auden poem.) F.p. Boston, Apr. 1949 cond. Koussevitzky, soloist Bernstein. As ballet, NY Feb. 1950.

Age of Gold, The (*Zolotoy vek.*). Ballet in 3 acts with mus. by Shostakovich, Op. 22, lib. A. Ivanovsky, choreog. E. Kaplan and V. Vaynonen. Comp. 1927–30. Prod. Leningrad 1930. Also suite for orch., 1929-32. Some of the mus. used in ballet *The Dreamers,* 1975.

Age of Steel, The (*Stalnoy skok*; Fr. *Le Pas d'acier*). Ballet in 2 scenes with mus. by Prokofiev (Op. 41, 1925), choreog. Massine, lib. Yakulov. Prod. Paris 1927. Symphonic suite contains 4 movements.

Aggiustamente, aggiustatamente (It.). Exact (in point of rhythm).

Agiatamente (It.). Comfortably, freely, i.e. with suitable liberty as regards speed, etc. (not to be confused with *Agitatamente*).

Agilement (Fr.), **agilmente** (It.). In an agile manner, implying speed and nimble execution. **Agilité** (Fr.), **agilità** (It.). Agility.

Agincourt Song. A famous 15th-cent. Eng. song commemorating the victory at Agincourt in 1415, for 2 vv. and 3-part ch. Used by Walton in his film music for *Henry V* (1944).

Agitato; agitatamente (It.), **agité** (Fr.), **agitirt, agitiert** (Ger.). Agitated, in an agitated manner. **Agitazione, agitamento** (It.). Agitation. Not to be confused with *Agiatamente*.

Agnesi, Luigi (Louis Agniez) (*b* Erpent, Namur, 1833; *d* London, 1875). Belg. bass especially celebrated for his singing in Rossini's operas.

Agnew, Roy (Ewing) (*b* Sydney, N.S.W., 1893; *d* Sydney, 1944). Australian pianist and composer of pf. sonatas and smaller pieces, also chamber and orch. mus., and songs. On staff N.S.W. State Cons., Sydney.

Agnus Dei (Lamb of God). Part of Ordinary of the *Mass. Many settings by various composers.

Agogic (from Gr. *Agoge*, melody). (1) An adjective indicating a variety of accentuation demanded by the nature of a particular mus. phrase, rather than by the regular metric pulse of the mus. The first note of a phrase, for instance, may be felt to suggest a slight lingering which confers the effect of an accent: similarly, a leap to note significantly higher or lower than the preceding notes, or a strong discord resolving to a concord, may convey an effect of accentuation (by means of lingering, pressure etc.) and there are other examples.
The complementary term to 'Agogic Accent' (accent of movement) is 'Dynamic Accent' (accent of force), which implies the normal and regular rhythmic accentuation of a piece of music.
(2) In a wider sense, 'Agogic' covers everything connected with 'expression', e.g. *rallentando, accelerando, rubato,* pause, accentuation as described above, etc.

Agon (Contest). Ballet for 12 dancers by Stravinsky, choreog. *Balanchine. Comp. 1953–7. F.p. as concert work Los Angeles, June 1957; as stage work by NY City Ballet, Dec. 1957.

Agostini, Paolo (*b* Vallerano, 1583; *d* Rome, 1629). It. maestro of Vatican chapel, 1626. Comp. church mus. incl. *Agnus Dei* in canon for 8 vv.

Agrell, Johan (Joachim) (*b* Löth, 1701; *d* Nuremberg, 1765). Swed. composer, violinist, and harpsichordist. At court in Kassel 1723–46. Kapellmeister, Nuremberg, from 1746. Wrote syms., concs., and many kbd. sonatas.

Agrémens (agréments) (Fr.). Grace notes.

Agricola, Alexander (*b* Flanders, *c.*1446; *d* Valladolid, 1506). Flemish composer in service of Fr. and It. royalty and aristocracy. Wrote masses, motets, songs, etc.

Agrippina. Opera in 3 acts by Handel to lib. by Grimani. Prod. Venice 1709.

A.G.S.M. Associate of *Guildhall School of Music and Drama (internal students only).

Agthe, Karl Christian (*b* Hettstedt, 1762; *d* Ballenstedt, 1797). Ger. organist and composer who wrote several *Singspiele. His son Wilhelm Johann (1790–1873) was a pianist, teacher, and composer for the pf.

Agujari, Lucrezia (*b* Ferrara, 1743; *d* Parma, 1783). It. operatic sop., much admired by Mozart, with remarkable range and compass. Début Florence 1764. Sang in London 1775–7. Because she was illegitimate, was known as 'La Bastardella' or 'Basterdina'. Retired on marriage, 1780.

Ägyptische Helena, Die (The Egyptian Helen). Opera in 2 acts, Op. 75, by R. Strauss to lib. by Hofmannsthal, comp. 1923–7, f.p. Dresden and NY Met. 1928. Rev. 1933.

Ahna, Pauline de (*b* Ingoldstadt, 1863; *d* Garmisch, 1950). Ger. sop. who married Richard *Strauss in 1894 and became notable exponent of his Lieder, many of which were written for her. Sang at Bayreuth. Created role of Freihild in Strauss's *Guntram,* Weimar 1894. Christine in Strauss's *Intermezzo* is a portrait of her, as (less directly) are several other of Strauss's operatic heroines. Known for her waspish tongue and massive (probably calculated) indiscretions; her coquettish nature is instrumentally portrayed in her husband's *Ein Heldenleben* and *Symphonia Domestica.*

Ahronovich, Yury (*b* Leningrad, 1932). Israeli cond. of Russ. birth. Studied Leningrad 1939 and after 1945. Violinist, but studied cond. with *Sanderling. Cond. Saratov P.O. 1956–7, Yaroslav S.O. 1957–64, Moscow Radio S.O. 1964–72. Left Russia 1972, settling in Israel. Opera début in Europe, Cologne 1973. CG début 1974 (*Boris Godunov*). Cond. Gürzenich Concerts, Cologne, from 1975.

Aiblinger, Johann Kaspar (*b* Wasserburg, 1779; *d* Munich, 1867). Ger. composer. Cond. of It. opera in Munich 1819–33. Comp. church mus.

and operas incl. *Rodrigo und Chimene* (based on *Le Cid*), 1821.

Aichinger, Gregor (*b* Regensburg, 1564; *d* Augsburg, 1628). Ger. organist and composer. Spent some years in It. and was influenced by Venetian sch., notably Gabrieli. His religious choral works are among the finest of their time in Ger.

Aida. Opera in 4 acts by Verdi to lib. by Ghislanzoni, being It. trans. from Fr. prose of Camille du Locle based on plot by Fr. Egyptologist Auguste Mariette Bey (Verdi had major hand in lib. and wrote words of final duet 'O terra, addio'). Metastasio's lib. *Nitteti* (1756) was major source of plot. Commissioned by Khedive of Egypt (but not, as is often said, for opening of either Suez Canal or Cairo Opera House). Comp. 1870. F.p. Cairo 1871, Milan 1872 (with extra aria for Aida), NY 1873, London 1876. Spelling Aïda, with diæresis, is incorrect in It.

Aiglon, L' (Fr. 'The Eaglet'). Rare example of opera by two composers, *Ibert writing the first and 5th acts and *Honegger the middle 3. Text by Cain after Rostand. Comp. 1935. (Prod. Monte Carlo 1937.)

Air. (1) Melody.
  (2) Comp. of melodious character. See also *Aria* and *Ayre*.

Airborne Symphony. Sym. for narrator, ten., bar., ch., and orch. by *Blitzstein to composer's text on evolution of flying. Comp. 1945, f.p. NY 1946 cond. *Bernstein.

Air de caractère (Fr.). In ballet, mus. for 'characteristic' occasions, such as an entry of warriors.

Air on the G String. The name given to an arr. for vn. and pf. by *Wilhelmj in 1871 of the 2nd movement (Air) of J. S. Bach's Suite No. 3 in D, in which the melody is transposed from D to C, the violinist playing on his lowest (G) str. Also heard in arr. for full str. orch., and for various other instr.

Ais (Ger.). A♯. **Aisis**, A♯♯.

Akademische Festouvertüre (Brahms). See *Academic Festival Overture*.

Akimenko (Akimyenko, etc.), **Fyodor Stepanovich** (*b* Kharkov, 1876; *d* Paris, 1945). Ukrainian composer, pupil of Rimsky-Korsakov. On staff St Petersburg Cons. Comp. opera *The Snow Queen*, ballet, orch. works, chamber mus.

Akkord (Ger.). Chord. Also a set of several different-sized instr. of one type.

Akkordieren (Ger.). To tune.

Al (It.). At the, to the, in the, in the style of, etc., i.e. the same as *A with the article added.

Ala and Lolly (Prokofiev). See *Scythian Suite*.

À la corde (Fr.). At the string. In str. playing, indication that the bow should be kept on the str., to ensure *legato* movement from note to note.

Alain, Jehan (*b* St Germain-en-Laye, 1911; killed Petit-Puy, nr. Saumur, 1940). Fr. organist and composer for org., pf., chamber combinations, etc.; in all, wrote 127 works. Pupil of Dupré (org.) and Dukas (comp).

Alain, Marie-Claire (*b* St Germain-en-Laye, 1926). Fr. organist. Studied Paris Cons. (Dupré for org., Duruflé for harmony). Début St Germain-en-Laye 1937. Org. prize, Geneva Competition, 1950. Worldwide tours as recitalist. Recorded complete org. works of Bach and of her brother Jehan.

Alalà. Plainsong-like type of Sp. folksong, in 4-line verses. The singer is at liberty to add melodic decorations to the vocal line.

Alaleona, Domenico (*b* Montegiorgio, 1881; *d* Montegiorgio, 1928). It. composer and teacher. His theories incl. splitting octave into unorthodox equal divisions and ways of combining the 12 notes of the chromatic scale into single chords.

A.L.A.M. Associate of the London Academy of Music.

Alan, Hervey (*b* Whitstable, 1910; *d* Croydon, 1982). Eng. bass-bar. in opera and oratorio. First sang with Glyndebourne co. at Edinburgh Fest. 1949, then regularly to 1960. Prof. of singing, RCM. Pres. I.S.M. 1969. O.B.E. 1974.

À la pointe d'archet (Fr.). At the point of the bow.

Alard, Jean Delphin (*b* Bayonne, 1815; *d* Paris, 1888). Fr. violinist and vn. teacher, author of a *Violin School*, and ed. and composer of vn. works. Among pupils was *Sarasate. Prof. of vn., Paris Cons., 1843–75.

Albanese, Licia (*b* Bari, 1913). It.-born sop. (Amer. citizen from 1945). Début Milan 1934, as Butterfly, and at CG 1937, NY Met. 1940–66. Recorded Mimi and Violetta with Toscanini.

Albani, (Dame) **Emma** (*b* Chambly, nr. Montreal, 1847; *d* London, 1930). Fr.-Canadian sop., born Marie Louise Cécilie Emma Lajeunesse, taking professional name from Albany, NY, where she spent early life. Studied in Paris and Milan. Début Messina 1870 in *La sonnambula*. CG début 1872. First CG Senta (*Fliegende Holländer*), 1877, first Desdemona at NY Met., 1894. Sang Isolde, CG 1896, retiring from stage a month later, but continuing to sing in oratorio. Retired to teach in 1911. D.B.E. 1925.

Albéniz, Isaac (Manuel Francisco) (*b* Camprodón, Catalonia, 1860; *d* Cambô-les-Bains, France, 1909). Sp. pianist and composer. After studying in Paris, Madrid, Leipzig, and Brussels, he followed Liszt's tour of Weimar, Prague and

Budapest, perfecting his piano technique with him. From 1880 toured widely, playing many of own pf. works, of which he comp. 250 between 1880 and 1892, most of them employing Sp. rhythmic and melodic idioms. For his Eng. banker patron F. Money-Coutts (Lord Latymer) he set 3 opera libs., *Henry Clifford* (Barcelona 1895), *Merlin,* and *Pepita Jiménez* (Barcelona 1896). Settled in Paris 1893, being influenced by Fauré and Dukas. His **Iberia,* 12 pf. pieces, was pubd. in 4 vols., 1906–9. Also wrote operettas, songs, orch. rhapsody *Catalonia,* pf. conc., and 5 pf. sonatas. *Iberia* was orch. by *Arbós, and *Suite española* by R. *Frühbeck de Burgos.

Albert, Eugen d' (really Eugène Francis Charles) (*b* Glasgow, 1864; *d* Riga, 1932). Scottish-born pianist and composer of Anglo-Fr. parentage, Ger. by adoption. Won scholarship at Nat. Training Sch. of Mus. (now RCM). Début London 1881; in same year won Mendelssohn Scholarship for study abroad at Vienna and under Liszt. Added fresh reputation as composer of operas, and wrote 2 pf. concs., vc. conc., sym., chamber mus., also ed. of pf. classics. Succeeded Joachim as dir., Berlin Hochschule für Musik, 1907. Of his 20 operas comp. 1893–1932, most successful were **Tiefland* (Prague 1903), *Die Abreise* (Frankfurt 1898), and *Die toten Augen* (Dresden 1916). 2nd of 6 wives was pianist Teresa *Carreño.

Albert Hall, Royal (London). See *Royal Albert Hall.*

Albert, Heinrich (*b* Lobenstein, Saxony 1604; *d* Königsberg, 1651). Ger. organist, poet and composer, cousin and pupil of *Schütz. Comp. words and mus. of hymns and secular songs. Pioneer of *basso continuo. His *Comödien-Musik* (1644) is early example of Ger. opera.

Albert Herring. Comic chamber opera in 3 acts, Op. 39, by Britten to lib. by Eric Crozier freely adapted from short story by Maupassant (*Le Rosier de Mme. Husson,* 1888). Prod. Glyndebourne 1947, Tanglewood, Mass., 1949.

Albert, Prince, Consort of Queen Victoria (*b* Rosenau, Ger., 1819; *d* Windsor, 1861). Trained in mus. by his father Ernest, Duke of Saxe-Coburg, who himself comp. opera. Patron of many Eng. mus. enterprises and friend of Mendelssohn. Wrote church mus. and some pleasant Lieder in style of Schubert and Mendelssohn.

Albert, Stephen (*b* NY, 1941). Amer. composer. Studied Eastman Sch., Rochester, and later with Milhaud, Rochberg, and others. Amer. Prix de Rome 1965–6, 1966–7. Works incl. *Bacchae,* ch. and orch. (1969), *Wolf Time,* sop. and instr., *Orchestrabook,* orch., *Voices Within,* orch. (1975), and chamber mus.

Alberti Bass. Simple (and often commonplace) acc. to a melody, consisting of 'broken chords',

viz., broken triads of which the notes are played in the order: lowest, highest, middle, highest. It takes its name from the It. composer who favoured it, Domenico *Alberti.

Alberti, Domenico (*b* Venice, 1710; *d* Rome, c.1740). It. composer of operas, songs, and of hpd. sonatas in which his use of the formula known as *Alberti Bass occurs frequently.

Albicastro, Henrico (Heinrich Weissenberg) **del Biswang** (*b* c.1680; *d* Holland, c.1738). Swiss composer and violinist of Ger. orig. who served in army and later worked in Netherlands. His 12 concs. à 4 are still played.

Albinoni, Tommaso (*b* Venice, 1671; *d* Venice, 1751). It. composer of instr. mus. and of 53 operas. Bach made use of several of his themes and used Albinoni bass parts for practice in thorough-bass. In recent years there has been keen interest in his concs. for str., *concerti grossi,* ob. and tpt. concs. The popular *Adagio* for org. and str. in G minor owes very little to Albinoni, having been constructed from a MS. fragment by the 20th-cent. It. musicologist, Remo Giazotto, whose copyright it is.

Alboni, Marietta (Maria Anna Marzia) (*b* Città di Castello, 1823; *d* Ville d'Avray, 1894). It. cont. So impressed Rossini that he taught her the cont. roles in his operas. Début Bologna 1842. Leading cont. CG 1847, becoming rival attraction to Jenny Lind, her salary being voluntarily raised overnight from £500 to £2,000 for the season. Sang in Paris and toured USA 1852. Sang with *Patti at Rossini's funeral, 1868. Retired 1872.

Alborada (Sp.). Dawn. Morning music (see also *Aubade*). This word has special application to a type of instr. mus. with a good deal of rhythmic freedom and often played on bagpipe (or rustic ob.) and small drum.

Alborado del gracioso (Aubade of the Clown). 4th of Ravel's pf. pieces entitled **Miroirs* (1905). Orch. 1918.

Albrecht, Gerd (*b* Essen, 1935). Ger. cond., pianist, and violinist. Studied Kiel Univ., Hamburg Univ., and Hamburg Acad. of Mus. Début Hamburg 1956. Won Hilversum Cond. Competition 1958. Coach and cond., Stuttgart Opera 1958–61. Opera cond. Mainz 1961–3, Lübeck 1963–6, Kassel 1966–72, Berlin (Deutsche Oper) 1972–9. Cond. Tonhalle orch., Zürich, 1975–80.

Albrechtsberger, Johann Georg (*b* Klosterneuberg, nr. Vienna, 1736; *d* Vienna, 1809). Austrian organist at Viennese court (1772) and cath. (1791); composer, but best remembered as comp. teacher (pupils incl. Beethoven) and as author of many theoretical works, incl. important textbook of comp. (1790, widely used in Eng. trans.).

Albright, William (*b* Gary, Indiana, 1944). Amer. composer. Studied Juilliard Sch., NY 1959–

62, and later at Paris Cons. with Messiaen. Ass. dir. of elec. mus. studio, Michigan Univ. 1970. Many comps. for org. and for jazz ens.

Albumblatt (Ger.). Album Leaf. Fanciful title for a brief instr. comp., usually for pf., and of a personal character (like an autograph in an album).

Albumblätter (Album-leaves). Title of 20 pf. pieces by Schumann (Op. 124, 1832–45, pubd. 1854).

Alceste (Gr. *Alkestis*). Opera in 3 acts by Gluck, lib. by Calzabigi, after Euripides. Prod. Vienna 1767, London 1795; Fr. version rev. by Gluck with text by Du Roullet, prod. Paris 1776. Preface to score contains Gluck's famous declaration on the nature of opera, which adumbrates mus.-drama. Other operas on this subject by Lully (1674), Schweitzer (1773), Boughton (1922), and Wellesz (1923), among others. Handel wrote a masque, *Alceste*, to a lib. by T. Smollett.

Alcina. Opera in 3 acts by Handel to lib. by Marchi after Ariosto's *Orlando furioso*. (Prod. CG 1735, revived London 1957.)

A.L.C.M. Associate of the London College of Music.

Alcock, (Sir) **Walter** (Galpin) (*b* Edenbridge, Kent, 1861; *d* Salisbury, 1947). Eng. organist. Ass. organist Westminster Abbey; organist of Chapels Royal (1902), and Salisbury Cath. from 1916 to death; composer of church mus. Knighted 1933. Played org. at coronations of Edward VII (1902) and George V (1911).

Alcuin (*b* York, *c*.735; *d* Tours, *c*.804). Friend and counsellor of Charlemagne at Aix-la-Chapelle; later Abbot of Tours. Author of treatise *De musica*.

Alcuno, alcuna, alcun' (plurals *alcuni, alcune,* etc.) (It.). Some.

Alda, Frances (née Davis) (*b* Christchurch, N.Z., 1883; *d* Venice, 1952). N.Z. operatic sop. who studied with Mathilde Marchesi in Paris where she made début as Manon in 1904. From 1908 to 1929 sang at NY Met., to whose dir., Gatti-Casazza, she was married 1910–28. Much given to litigation.

Aldeburgh Festival. Annual Fest. at Aldeburgh, Suffolk, since 1948, revolving largely round mus. and personality of Benjamin *Britten and his circle. Has superb concert-hall, The Maltings, at near-by Snape. Several Britten works had first perf. at Fest., incl. operas *A Midsummer Night's Dream* (1960) and *Death in Venice* (1973). Berkeley's *A Dinner Engagement* (1954), Walton's *The Bear* (1967), and Birtwistle's *Punch and Judy* (1968) were also f.p. at Aldeburgh. After Britten's death, *Rostropovich became one of art. dirs., as did Murray Perahia and Oliver Knussen.

Aldrich, Henry (*b* London, 1648; *d* Oxford, 1710). Eng. musician, theologian, and architect. Successively undergraduate, tutor, canon, and dean of Christ Church, Oxford, and twice Vice-Chancellor of the Univ. Comp. church mus. and catches, incl. 'Great Tom is cast'.

Aldrich, Richard (*b* Providence, R.I., 1863; *d* Rome, 1937). Amer. mus. critic. On *NY Tribune* 1891–1902, mus. critic of *NY Times* 1902–24. Books incl. *Guide to Parsifal* (1904) and *Guide to the Ring* (1905).

Aleatory Music (from Lat. *alea*, dice; hence the throw of the dice for chance). Synonym for *indeterminacy*, i.e. mus. that cannot be predicted before perf. or mus. which was comp. through chance procedures (statistical or computerized). The adjective 'aleatoric' is a bastard word, to be avoided by those who care for language.

Aleko. Opera in 1 act by Rakhmaninov, lib. by V. Nemirovich-Danchenko, based on Pushkin's poem *Tsygany* (*Gipsies*). Prod. Moscow 1893, NY 1926, London 1972.

Alessandro (Alexander). Opera in 3 acts by Handel to lib. by Paolo Rolli (London 1726). Revived as *Roxana*, with additions probably by another hand, London 1743.

Alexander Balus. Oratorio by Handel, text by Dr Thomas Morell. Comp. 1747. F.p. CG 1748.

Alexander Nevsky. Mus. by *Prokofiev for film dir. by S. Eisenstein (1938), later developed into cantata, Op. 78, with text by V. Lugovskoy and Prokofiev, for mez., ch., and orch. (f.p. Moscow 1939). Film mus. in adaptation for broadcast, f.p. Eng. 1941.

Alexander's Feast. Setting by Handel of Dryden's ode, with some changes and additions by Newburgh Hamilton, f.p. London 1736. Re-orch. by Mozart. Orig. setting for St Cecilia's Day, 1697, by Jeremiah Clarke.

Alexandre, Jacob (*b* Paris, 1804; *d* Paris, 1876). Fr. founder of Paris firm of harmonium makers. In 1874 introduced the *Alexandre Organ*.

Alexandrov, Alexander (Vasilyevich) (*b* Plakhino, 1883; *d* Berlin, 1946). Russ. composer, pupil of Rimsky-Korsakov. Cond. from 1928 of Red Army Song and Dance Ens. Comp. *Hymn of the Bolshevik Party*, adapted as Russ. nat. anthem, 1943.

Alexandrov, Anatoly (*b* Moscow, 1888; *d* Moscow, 1982). Russ. composer, studied with *Taneyev. Composer of operas, syms., pf. mus., and incidental mus. for many plays.

Alfano, Franco (*b* Posilippo, Naples, 1875; *d* San Remo, 1954). It. composer. Studied in Naples and Leipzig. Dir. of Bologna Cons. 1919–23, Turin 1924–39. Operas incl. *Risurrezione* (1902–3) and *Sakuntala* (1914–20; rewritten 1952). Completed

Puccini's *Turandot* (1926) from composer's sketches. Also wrote syms., str. qts., sonatas, etc.

Alfonso und Estrella. Opera in 3 acts (1821–2, D732) by Schubert to lib. by F. von Schober (Weimar 1854, Vienna 1882). Its ov., possibly revised, was used by Schubert as the ov. to *Rosamunde at the latter's f.p. in Dec. 1823.

Alford, Kenneth J. (real name Frederick Joseph Ricketts) (*b* Ratcliff, London, 1881; *d* Reigate, 1945). Eng. composer and bandmaster. Enlisted as bandboy 1895, playing cornet, pf., and organ. Student bandmaster at Kneller Hall 1904–8, bandmaster Argyll and Sutherland Highlanders 1908. Dir. of mus., Royal Marines 1927–40. Wrote under pseudonym, Alford being mother's maiden name. Considered to surpass Sousa in the quality of his march comps. These incl. *Colonel Bogey* (1914), *The Thin Red Line* (1925), *Dunedin* (1928), and *Eagle Squadron* (1942).

Alfred. Masque orig. in 2 acts about King Alfred by Thomas *Arne, with words by J. Thomson and D. Mallet, prod. Cliveden, Bucks., 1740. Contains song *Rule, Britannia!' Later revised extensively both as oratorio and opera in 3 acts, with much new material. Perfs. in Dublin 1744, 1756; London 1751, 1753, 1754, 1755, 1759, 1762, and 1773.

Alfvén, Hugo (*b* Stockholm, 1872; *d* Falun, 1960). Swed. composer, violinist, and dir. of mus. at Univ. of Uppsala (1910–39). Comp. 5 syms., choral works, and 3 Swed. Rhapsodies of which the first, *Midsummer's Vigil (Midsommarvaka)*, comp. 1904, is well known.

Algarotti, Francesco (*b* Venice, 1712; *d* Pisa, 1764). It. author of notable treatise, *Saggio sopra l'opera in musica* (1755) which made important criticisms of contemporary opera presentation and foresaw a th. not far short of Wagner's Bayreuth.

Aliquot Scaling. Arr., devised by the Blüthner firm, whereby the weak upper notes of a pf. are provided with sympathetic str. tuned an octave higher, thus increasing vol. of tone.

Alison (Allison), **Richard** (*fl.* late 16th and early 17th cents.). Eng. composer of madrigals and many instr. works, and compiler of famous book of metrical psalm tunes (1599).

Alkan (pseudonym of Charles Henri Valentin Morhange) (*b* Paris, 1813; *d* Paris, 1888). Fr. pianist, composer, and teacher. Studied Paris Cons. under Zimmermann from age 6, winning pf. prize at 10. His comps. for pf. (and for pedal-pf.) incl. chromatic harmonies well in advance of their time and are extremely difficult to perform.

Alkestis. Gr. tragedy by Euripides which has been the basis of many operas. See *Alceste*.

All', alla (It.). To the, at the, on the, with the, in the manner of.

Alla Breve (It.). Indicates 2/2 time when, in a measure of 4 beats, the tempo is so fast that the measure may be considered to have 2 beats. See also *Breve*.

Allant (Fr.). (1) Going, i.e. active, brisk.
(2) Going on, in sense of continuing, e.g. Debussy's *Allant grandissant*—Going on growing, continuing to grow (i.e. getting louder).

Allargando (It.). Enlarging. Getting slower and broadening, without loss of fullness in tone.

Alldis, John (*b* London, 1929). Eng. cond. and chorusmaster. Founded John Alldis Choir, 1962. On staff GSM. Chorusmaster, LSO 1966–9; cond., London Phil. Choir, 1969; Leeds Fest. Ch. 1975.

Alle (Ger.). All. Thus if 1 vn. has been playing alone all are now to enter. *Alle ersten* means all the first vns. and *Alle zweiten* all the 2nd.

Allegramente (It.). **Allègrement** (Fr.). Brightly, gaily.

Allegretto (It.). Moderately quick, pretty lively (but not so much as *allegro*). **Allegrezza.** Mirth, cheerfulness.

Allegri, Gregorio (*b* Rome, 1582; *d* Rome, 1652). It. priest, ten. singer, and composer among other things of a celebrated *Miserere* in 9 parts, long kept as exclusive possession of Sistine Chapel, where he served for the last part of his life. Mozart at the age of 14 secretly wrote out this work after 1 or 2 hearings.

Allegri Quartet. Brit. string quartet founded 1953 with Eli Goren (vn.), James Barton (vn.), Patrick Ireland (va.), William Pleeth (vc.). Peter Thomas succeeded Barton 1963. Re-formed 1968 with Hugh Maguire (leader), David Roth (vn.), Ireland, and Bruno Schrecker (vc.). In 1977 Peter Carter became leader and Prunella Pacey violist. Keith Lovell succeeded Pacey in 1983. In addition to classics, the Allegri has specialized in works by Brit. composers, e.g. Britten, Maconchy, LeFanu, and S. Forbes.

Allegro (It.). Merry, i.e. quick, lively, bright. Often used as the title of a comp. or movement in that style. The superlative is *Allegrissimo*.

Allegro Barbaro. Work for solo pf. by Bartók, comp. 1911 and f.p. by him in Budapest on 27 Feb. 1921. Orch. transcr. by Kenessey, 1946.

Alleluia. This Lat. form of Hebrew exclamation, meaning 'Praise Jehovah', was added to certain of the responds of the R.C. Church, suitably joyful mus. for it being grafted on to the traditional plainsong and, in time, itself becoming traditional.

Alleluiasymphonie. Title given to Haydn's Sym. No. 30 in C (Hob. I: 30), 1765. Incorporates part of a plainsong alleluia.

Allemand (Fr.). German.

Allemande (Almand, Almayne, Almain, etc.) (Fr.). The name of 2 distinct types of comp., both probably of Ger. origin.

(1) Dance, usually in $\frac{4}{4}$, but sometimes in duple time, much used by 17th- and earlier 18th-cent. composers as the first movement of the suite, or the first after a prelude. It is serious in character but not heavy, and of moderate speed: it is in simple *binary form.

(2) Peasant dance still in use in parts of Germany and Switzerland. It is in triple time, and of waltz-like character. Occasionally composers have called a comp. of this type a *Deutscher Tanz* (plural *Deutsche Tänze*), or simply *Deutsch* (plural *Deutsche*).

Allen, (Sir) **Hugh** (Percy) (*b* Reading, 1869; *d* Oxford, 1946). Eng. organist, cond., and teacher. Org. scholar Christ's College, Cambridge, organist at caths. of St Asaph (1897) and Ely (1898); then of New College, Oxford (1901–18). Prof. of mus., Oxford Univ. (1918–46), and general inspirer of Oxford mus. activities; Dir. RCM (1918–37). Cond., Bach Choir 1907–20. Knighted 1920, G.C.V.O. 1935.

Allen, Thomas (*b* Seaham Harbour, 1944). Eng. bar. Opera début with WNO 1969. CG début 1971. Glyndebourne début 1973 (Papageno). Fine interpreter of Britten's Billy Budd (WNO) and of Mozart's Don Giovanni (Glyndebourne). Many concert appearances in Orff, Berlioz, etc.

Allende y Saron, Pedró Humberto (*b* Santiago, Chile, 1885; *d* Santiago, 1959). Chilean composer and violinist, who also organized research into folk mus. Works incl. vn. conc., 12 *Tonadas* for pf. (3 of them orch.), and choral settings.

Allentamento, allentando (It.). Slowing.

Allin, Norman (*b* Ashton-under-Lyne, 1884; *d* Hereford, 1973). Eng. bass. Trained RMCM 1906–10. Became member of Beecham Opera Co. in 1916. Début CG 1919. Leading bass and dir. BNOC 1922–9. Member, Carl Rosa Co. 1942–9. Sang in first Glyndebourne *Figaro*, 1934. On staff RAM 1935–60 and RMCM 1938–42. C.B.E. 1958.

Allison, Richard. See *Alison, Richard.*

Allt, Wilfrid Greenhouse (*b* Wolverhampton, 1889; *d* London, 1969). Eng. organist and teacher. Ass. organist, Norwich Cath., 1910; organist St Giles's Cath., Edinburgh, 1915, and choral cond. in Edinburgh. Prin., TCL, 1944–65. Pres. RCO 1962–5.

All through the Night. The tune usually known outside Wales by this title is that of the Welsh folk-song *Ar Hyd y Nos.*

Alma Redemptoris Mater. See *Antiphons of the Blessed Virgin Mary.*

Almeida, Antonio de (*b* Paris, 1928). Fr. cond. Studied in Buenos Aires with *Ginastera. Later studied with Koussevitzsky and Szell. Held cond. posts in Portugal from 1956 and has toured Europe and USSR. Prin. guest cond. Houston S.O. 1969–71.

Almira. Opera in 3 acts (his first) by Handel to lib. by Feustking after It. text by G. Pancieri. Contains 41 Ger. and 15 It. airs. Prod. Hamburg 1705.

Alnaes, Eyvind (*b* Fredriksstad, 1872; *d* Oslo, 1932). Norweg. composer and organist best known for songs (often sung by *Flagstad) though he wrote syms. and a pf. conc.

Alpaerts, Flor (*b* Antwerp, 1876; *d* Antwerp, 1954). Belg. composer and cond. Studied at Antwerp Cons. where he later became prof. Wrote opera *Shylock* (1913), symphonic poems, and cantatas.

Alpensinfonie, Eine (An Alpine Symphony). Orch. comp. by Richard Strauss (Op. 64, 1911–15). 10th and last of his tone-poems. In 22 sections, it describes 24 hours in the mountains. Scored for very large orch. incl. wind and thunder machines. F.p. Berlin 1915, London 1923.

Alphorn, Alpenhorn (Ger.), **Cor des Alpes** (Fr.). The Alpine horn, a Swiss peasant instr. used for the evening calling of the cattle scattered over the summer pastures of the mountains (see also *Ranz des vaches*). It is made of wood and varies in length from about 7′ to 12′. It has a similar mouthpiece to that of the *cornet, and is restricted to notes of the harmonic series. Strauss wrote a part for Alphorn in *Daphne*, but it is usually played by tb. (except in Haitink's recording).

Alpine Symphony, An. See *Alpensinfonie, Eine.*

Als (Ger.). As, like, when, than.

Alsager, Thomas Massa (*b* 1779; *d* 1846). Eng. newspaper manager and amateur musician particularly devoted to furtherance of Beethoven's chamber mus. At his prompting *The Times* became first newspaper to employ professional mus. critics.

Al segno (It.). To the sign, meaning 'Go to the sign 𝄋'. This may mean '*Go back* to the sign', i.e. the same as *Dal segno*, or it may mean '*Continue* until you reach the sign'.

Alsop, Ada (*b* Darlington, 1915). Eng. sop. Specialist in oratorio, singing with all leading Brit. choral socs.

Also sprach Zarathustra (Thus spake Zoroaster). Tone-poem by Richard Strauss, Op. 30, comp. 1895–6 and f.p. Frankfurt 1896. Freely based on Nietzsche's epic prose poem of same name. Delius set 11 sections of poem in his *Mass of Life*.

Alt. (1) High. The note g″ marks the beginning of the range of vocal notes spoken of as in *alt*, and from g‴ as in *altissimo*.

(2) (Ger.). The alto (contralto) v.: prefixed to the name of an instr. (e.g. *Althorn*), it implies an alto pitch.

(3) (Ger.). Old.

Alta (It.). High, e.g. *Ottava alta*, High octave, i.e. one octave higher than written. Not to be confused with **alto*.

Altenberglieder (Songs by Altenberg). 5 songs to picture-postcard texts by Peter Altenberg (pseudonym of Richard Englander, 1862–1919), comp. by **Berg for v. and orch. (Op. 4). At f.p. in Vienna of 2 of the songs on 31 Mar. 1913, a riot seriously disrupted the concert. Not perf. complete until 1953 (Rome, cond. Horenstein).

Altenburg, Johann Ernst (*b* Weissenfels, 1734; *d* Bitterfeld, 1801). Ger. organist and virtuoso trumpeter who comp. works for the latter instr., incl. a conc. for 7 tpts., and wrote a treatise on tpt. playing (1795). His father Johann Caspar (*d* 1761) was also a noted trumpeter. Both had military careers.

Altenburg, Michael (*b* Alach, 1584; *d* Erfurt, 1640). Ger. theologian and composer, several of whose chorale melodies are still sung. Pubd. important colls. of sacred mus.

Altered Chord. Amer. synonym for Chromatic Chord.

Alternativo (It.). Name applied in early 18th-cent. mus. in dance style to a contrasting middle section (later called **Trio*). Sometimes used of a whole comp., apparently implying that the 2 sections may be alternated at will.

Altflügelhorn (Ger.). Another name for the **flügelhorn* in E♭.

Altgeige (Ger.). Alto fiddle, i.e. the **viola*.

Althorn (Ger.). The alto **saxhorn in E♭ and the **flügelhorn in E♭ are sometimes referred to as *althorns*.

Altissimo. See *Alt*.

Altiste (Fr.). (1) a player of the *alto*, i.e. of the **viola.

(2) An **alto singer.

Altmeyer, Jeannine (*b* Pasadena, 1948). Amer. sop. of Ger. parentage. Studied Mus. Acad. of Santa Barbara 1968–71, then with Lotte **Lehmann, and at Salzburg Mozarteum. NY Met. début 1971 (First Lady in *Die Zauberflöte*), Chicago 1972 (Freia in *Das Rheingold*). European début 1973, Salzburg Easter Fest. (Freia). Zürich Opera 1973–5, Stuttgart Opera 1975–9. Bayreuth début 1979 (Sieglinde). Sang role of Brünnhilde in **Janowski recording of *The Ring*.

Alto (It.). High. (1) Usually high type of falsetto male v., much used in Eng. church mus.; thus in SATB, A stands for alto.

(2) Low-register female v., usually referred to as **contralto.

(3) Applied to instr., the 2nd or 3rd highest of the family.

(4) (Fr.). **Viola.

Alto Clarinet. The **clarinet in E♭ and in F.

Alto Clef. Formerly used for alto v., now mainly used for viola. See *Clefs*.

Alto flügelhorn. The B♭ **flügelhorn, also in E♭.

Alto flute. The fl. in G, transposing instr. notated 4th above actual sound.

Alto Moderne. Also called 'Viole-ténor'. A large viola, played like the vc. and introduced in the 1930s by R. Parramon of Barcelona.

Alto oboe. The Eng. hn. (**cor anglais*), pitched in F, a 5th below the **oboe.

Alto Rhapsody. Name by which Brahms's Rhapsody for cont. solo, male ch., and orch. (Op. 53, 1869) is known in Eng. Text taken from Goethe's poem *Harzreise im Winter*. Ger. title of comp. is *Rhapsodie aus Goethes Harzreise im Winter*.

Alto saxhorn. The sop. **saxhorn in B♭ (or C), differing little from the B♭ cornet.

Alto saxophone. The E♭ sax., usually played in jazz (especially beautifully by Johnny Hodges of Duke Ellington's orch.).

Alto Staff. See *Great Staff*.

Alto Trombone. Obsolete type of **trombone, written for by Mozart, later replaced by ten. tb.

Altposaune (Ger.). **Alto trombone.

Altra, altre. See *Altro*.

Altra volta (It.). **Encore.

Altro, altri; altra, altre (It.). Another, others.

Alva, Luigi (*b* Lima, 1927). Peruvian ten., début Lima 1949, Milan 1954, Edinburgh 1957, CG 1960. Specializes in light, lyrical Mozart and Rossini roles.

Alvary, Max (Maximillian Achenbach) (*b* Düsseldorf, 1856; *d* Gross-Tabarz, Thuringia, 1898). Ger. ten. Studied with J. Stockhausen and Lamperti. Début Weimar. Sang Don José in *Carmen* at NY Met. 1885. Specialist in Wagnerian roles (Loge, Siegfried, Tristan, Tannhäuser). Bayreuth 1891. In CG *Ring* under Mahler, 1892.

Alwin, Karl (*b* Königsberg, 1891; *d* Mexico City, 1945). Ger. pianist, cond., and composer. Held various operatic posts before going to Vienna State Opera in 1920. At one time married to the sop. Elisabeth **Schumann. Arr. certain items by R. Strauss. Cond. first London perf. (1924) of 2nd version (1916) of Strauss's *Ariadne auf Naxos*. Cond., Nat. Opera, Mexico City, from 1941.

Alwyn, Kenneth (*b* London, 1925). Eng. cond. and composer. Studied RAM. Prin. cond. BBC Northern Ireland Orch. Assoc. cond. SW Th. Ballet 1952–6, Royal Ballet 1956–9.

Alwyn, William (*b* Northampton, 1905; *d* Southwold, 1985). Eng. composer, pianist, flautist, poet, translator, and painter. Studied RAM. Began career as orch. flautist with LSO. Prof. of comp., RAM, 1926–56. First orch. work (5 *Preludes for Orch.*) played at a Promenade Concert, 1927. 3 times chairman, Composers' Guild. Wrote much mus. for films, incl. wartime documentaries *Desert Victory* and *The Way Ahead*. Wrote several vols. of poetry and trans. Fr. poets. C.B.E. 1978. Prin. comps.:

OPERA: *Miss Julie* (1961–76).

ORCH.: Syms. No. 1 (1950), No. 2 (1954), No. 3 (1956), No. 4 (1960), No. 5 (1973); symphonic prelude *The Magic Island* (1953), *Festival March* (1952), *Conc. grosso* No. 1 (1952), No. 2, str. (1951), No. 3 (1964); *Elizabethan Dances* (1957), ob. conc. (1951), *Lyra Angelica*, conc. for harp and str. (1955), *Autumn Legend*, cor anglais and str. (1956), *Derby Day* (1962), *Sinfonietta* for str. (1970), No. 2 (1976).

CHAMBER MUSIC: Str. trio (1963); Str. qts. No. 1 in D minor (1955), No. 2 (*Spring Waters*) (1976); cl. sonata (1962); *Naiades*, fl. and harp sonata (1972); *Divertimento*, fl. (1940).

PIANO: *Fantasy Waltzes* (1956), *Sonata alla toccata* (1951), 12 *Preludes* (1959).

SONG CYCLES (all with pf.): *Mirages*, bar. (1974), 6 *Nocturnes*, bar. (1976), *A Leavetaking*, ten. (1977), *Invocations*, sop. (1978).

Alyabyev, Alexander (*b* Tobolsk, 1787; *d* Moscow, 1851). Russ. composer and precursor of nat. sch. Wrote famous song *The Nightingale*, utilized by Patti and others for lesson scene of Rossini's *Il barbiere di Siviglia*, and transcr. for pf. by Liszt.

Alzato, alzati; alzata, alzate (It.). Raised, lifted off (of a mute or mutes, etc.).

Alzira. Opera in prol. and 2 acts by Verdi to lib. by Cammarano based on Voltaire's play *Alzire* (1736). Comp. 1845. Prod. Naples 1845; revived Rome 1967, NY (concert) 1968, London (stage) 1970.

Am (Ger.). At the, on the, to the, by the, near the. As in *Am Meer*, by the sea.

Amabile (It.). Lovable, hence *amabilità*, lovableness.

Amadeus Quartet. Highly successful and admired Brit. str. qt. which gave its first London concert in Jan. 1948, though it had played, under various different titles, for a year before then. Membership remained constant, viz., Norbert Brainin, Sigmund Nissel (vns.), Peter Schidlof (va.), Martin Lovett (vc.). Britten's 3rd qt. (1975) comp. for them. Disbanded 1987 after Schidlof's

death. Brainin O.B.E. 1960, his three colleagues 1973.

Amahl and the Night Visitors. Opera in 1 act by *Menotti to his own lib. First TV opera (NBC NY 1951). First stage perf. Indiana Univ., Bloomington, 1952, NY 1952, BBC TV 1967. The Night Visitors are the Magi.

Amati. It. family of vn.-makers (also vas., vcs., and dbs.) at Cremona. Comprised Andrea (*c.*1505–*c.*1580) whose sons Antonio (*c.*1538–*c.*1595) and Girolamo (Geronimus) (1561–1630) made many changes. Nicola (1596–1684), son of Girolamo, is reckoned the greatest of the Amatis. Among his pupils were Stradivari and Guarneri. The last of the line was Nicola's son Girolamo (1649–1740).

Amato, Pasquale (*b* Naples, 1878; *d* NY, 1942). It. bar. Studied Naples Cons. Début Naples 1900. Career chiefly spent at NY Met. (1908–21), where he created role of the Sheriff in Puccini's *La fanciulla del West* (1910). Became teacher and dir. of univ. opera prods.

Amberley Wild Brooks. No. 2 of *2 Pf. Pieces* by *Ireland, comp. 1921.

Ambrosian Chant. Type of plainsong now lost, assoc. with St Ambrose, Bishop of Milan 374–397, who reorganized singing and tonality in the Christian church. See under *Modes* and *Plainsong*.

Âme (Fr.). Soul. The *sound-post of the vn., etc. The fanciful name doubtless comes from its importance to the whole tone-quality of the instr., which depends on its correct position. The Italians call it *anima*, which also means 'soul'.

Amelia goes to the Ball (*Amelia al ballo*). Comic opera in 1 act by *Menotti to It. lib. by composer (Eng. trans. by George Meade). Prod. Berlin and Philadelphia 1937, San Remo 1938, Liverpool 1956.

Ameling, Elly (Elisabeth) (*b* Rotterdam, 1938). Dutch sop. Studied The Hague Cons. and with Bernac. Début Amsterdam 1961. London début 1966, Amer. 1968. Specializes in Lieder and oratorio, being particularly fine in Bach cantatas and Passions, and Schubert songs.

Amen. So be it. The Hebrew terminal word of prayer in Jewish, Christian, and Mohammedan worship. It has been extended by composers, many times, into a long comp., e.g. the 'Amen Chorus' of Handel's *Messiah*. Shorter settings have been made for liturgical use, such as Gibbons's Threefold Amen and Stainer's Sevenfold Amen. The *Dresden Amen* comes from the Threefold Amen of the Royal Chapel of Dresden (common also throughout Saxony); its composer was J. G. *Naumann.

Amen Cadence. See *Cadence*.

America ('My Country, 'tis of thee'). Patriotic hymn with words by Rev. Samuel Francis Smith (1832) sung to tune of 'God save the King'. Also title of symphonic rhapsody (1928) by E. *Bloch.

American Academy (Rome). Building in Rome, formerly Amer. Sch. of Architecture, where winners of Amer. Rome Prize live. See *Prix de Rome*.

American Federation of Musicians. Trade-union organization for professional musicians in USA and Canada; founded 1895 and very active under the presidency (1942–58) of James C. Petrillo.

American Guild of Organists. Nat. assoc. of Amer. church orgs., founded 1896.

American in Paris, An. Orch. piece by *Gershwin, score of which incl. parts for 4 taxi-horns. F.p. NY 1928.

American Musical Terminology (compared with Brit.). Certain divergences between Amer. and Brit. mus. terminology sometimes cause confusion:

(1) NOTE and TONE. Such expressions as '3 tones lower', or 'the scale of 5 tones' have different meanings to the Amer. and the Brit. reader. A Brit. reader, finding these expressions in an Amer. book or journal, must be careful to understand by them '3 notes lower' and 'scale of 5 notes', while an Amer. reader finding such expressions in a Brit. book must interpret them as '3 whole-steps lower' or 'a scale of 5 whole-steps'.

(2) Eng. BAR = Amer. MEASURE, the former term being often reserved in Amer. for the actual bar-line.

(3) Eng. SEMIBREVE, MINIM, etc. = Amer. WHOLE-NOTE, HALF-NOTE, etc.

(4) Eng. NATURALS, e.g. the white keys of a pf., etc. = Amer. LONG KEYS.

(5) Eng. NATURAL NOTES (of brass instr.) = Amer. PRIMARY TONES.

(6) Eng. TO FLATTEN and TO SHARPEN = Amer. TO FLAT and TO SHARP.

(7) Eng. ORGAN (generally) = Amer. PIPE ORGAN (to distinguish from the various reed organs).

(8) Eng. GRAMOPHONE = Amer. PHONO-GRAPH.

(9) Eng. CONCERT-GIVING = Amer. CONCERTIZING.

(10) Amer. APPLIED MUSIC means perf. mus.; hence univ. courses in Applied Music are courses in instr. or vocal technique and interpretation.

(11) The Eng. term FOLK SONG is often used in the USA in a loose way, covering not only trad. peasant songs but also any songs which have become widely known by people in general.

(12) Eng. FIRST VIOLIN or *Leader* (of orch.) = Amer. CONCERT MASTER.

(13) Eng. CONDUCTOR (of orch.) = (often) Amer. LEADER (and Eng. *to conduct* = Amer. *to lead*).

(14) Eng. PART-WRITING = Amer. VOICE-LEADING.

(15) Eng. RECORD SLEEVE (container) = Amer. DISC (DISK) LINER.

American Organ. Called in USA the 'cabinet org.', this is a type of reed org. like the *harmonium in which air is sucked through reeds. Invented by workman in *Alexandre's factory but developed in Boston, Mass.

'American' Quartet. Name by which Dvořák's Str. Qt. in F, Op. 96, is generally known. Comp. in USA, 1893 and partly inspired by Negro melodies, hence its former names, now frowned on, of 'Negro' or 'Nigger' Qt.

American Society of Composers, Authors and Publishers ('ASCAP'). Founded 1914 to protect copyrights, perf. rights, etc. Headquarters in NY.

Amériques (New Worlds). Comp. for large orch. by *Varèse, instr. incl. cyclone whistle, fire siren, crow-call, etc. Comp. 1918–21. F.p. Philadelphia 1926.

Amfiparnaso, L'. *Comedia harmonica* by Orazio Vecchi. A string of pieces in madrigal style, in 3 acts with a prol.; not intended to be staged. (Prod. Modena 1594; pubd. 1597; revived Florence 1933, London 1946).

Amico Fritz, L' (Friend Fritz). Opera in 3 acts by Mascagni, lib. by P. Suardon (N. Daspuro), based on novel by Erckmann-Chatrian (1864). (Prod. Rome 1891; London and Philadelphia 1892; NY 1894).

Amid Nature (or *In Nature's Realm*, Cz. *V přírodě*). Ov. for orch., Op. 91, by Dvořák, comp. 1891, as first of cycle of 3 ovs. called *Nature, Life, and Love*, the others being *Carneval and *Othello. Also title of Dvořák's 5 chs. for mixed vv., Op. 63, to words by Hálek, comp. 1882.

Amis, John (*b* London, 1922). Eng. critic and administrator, with prin. reputation as presenter of mus. programmes on radio and TV. Studied to be professional singer and recorded ten. solo in Bernard Herrmann's *Moby Dick*. Secretary of Dartington Summer School 1948–79.

Ammerbach, Elias Nickolaus (*b* Naumberg, ?1530; *d* Leipzig, 1597). Ger. organist and composer. At Thomaskirche, Leipzig, from 1561. His *Orgel-oder Instrument-tabulatur* (1571) demonstrates progress in practice of tuning and kbd. fingering.

Amner, John (*b* Ely, 1579; *d* Ely 1641). Eng. composer and organist. Studied at Oxford. Org. of Ely Cath. for 31 years. Wrote much sacred mus. and some kbd. variations on a psalm-tune.

Amon, Johannes Andreas (*b* Bamberg, 1763; *d* Wallerstein, 1825). Ger. hn.-player and composer. Pupil of Punto. Dir. of mus. at Heilbronn 1789–1817. Composed syms., pf. conc., sonatas, ob. qts., fl. and va. conc., etc.

Amor brujo, El (Love, the Magician). Ballet in 1 act by Falla, based on Andalusian gipsy tale. Requires ballerina to sing as well as dance. Also exists as orch. suite (with cont.). The famous 'Ritual Fire Dance' occurs in it. *Brujo* means 'male witch' and the title is best trans. as 'Wedded by Witchcraft'. F.p. Madrid 1915; London in concert version 1921, as ballet 1931.

Amore (It.), **Amour** (Fr.). Love. A word often found in the names of certain forms of old instr., generally implying a lower pitch than the ordinary and a claim to sweeter tone, e.g. *va. d'amore*, *ob. d'amore*. In bowed instr. it also indicates the possession of *sympathetic strings.

Amore dei tre re, L' (The Love of the Three Kings). Opera in 3 acts by *Montemezzi to lib. adapted by Sem Benelli from his verse tragedy (1910). Prod. Milan 1913; NY and London 1914.

Amoyal, Pierre (*b* Paris, 1949). Fr. violinist. Studied Paris Cons., won Ginette Neveu Prize 1963, Paganini Prize 1964, Enescu Prize 1970. Pupil of *Heifetz in Los Angeles 1966–71. Returned to Paris, giving 4 perfs. of Berg conc. with *Solti and Orchestre de Paris, 1972. World-wide tours.

Amplifier. A piece of electrical equipment which 'amplifies', i.e. increases, the vol. of sound. Voltage-controlled amplifiers alter the vol. of the input signal. They can be used in *electronic music in conjunction with voltage-controlled oscillators and filters and a kbd. to function as a monophonic mus. instr.

Amram, David (*b* Philadelphia, 1930). Amer. hn.-player and composer. Played in jazz groups and sym. orchs. Studied comp. with Giannini and hn. with G. Schuller. First composer-in-residence with NY P.O. Works incl.: incid. mus. for chamber orch. for nearly 20 Shakespeare prods., opera *Twelfth Night* (1968), *Shakespearean Concerto, King Lear Variations*, incid. mus. to *Peer Gynt*, triple conc., vn. conc., cantata *A Year in our Land*, vn. sonata, str. qt., and songs.

A.Mus.L.C.M. Associate in Music [i.e. theory of mus.] of London College of Music.

A.Mus.T.C.L. Associate in Music, Trinity College of Music, London.

Amy, Gilbert (*b* Paris, 1936). Fr. composer and cond. Studied Paris Cons. 1955–60 under Messiaen and Milhaud. Cond. of *Domaine Musical*, Paris, 1967–73. Strongly influenced by Boulez and for 3 years attended Darmstadt summer courses. His comps. have moved from strict serialism to a more flexible use of the system and his later works, some employing tape, are of considerable poetic refinement. Prin. works:

ORCH: *Refrains* (1972), *Mouvements* (1958), *Inventions* (1959–61), *Diaphonies* (1962), *Iriade* (1963–4), *Chant pour orchestre* (1968), *Jeux et formes*, ob.

and chamber orch. (1971), *7 Sites*, 14 instr. (1975), *Eclos XIII*, 13 instr. (1976), *Adagio et Stretto* (1977–8).

VOCAL: *D'un Espace déployé*, sop., 2 pf., 2 orch. groups (1972–3); *Sonata pian'e forte*, sop., mez., 12 players (1974); *Après 'd'un désastre obscur'*, mez. and instr. (1976); *Shin'anim Sha'ananim*, mez., cl., vc., and ens. (1979); *Messe*, sop., cont., ten., bass, opt. children's ch., ch., and orch. (1982–3).

UNACC. CHORUS: *Récitatif, air et variation* (1970).

CHAMBER MUSIC: . . . *d'un Désastre obscur*, mez. and cl. (1976); *Jeux*, ob. (1976); pf. sonata (1957–60); *Epigrammes* (1961); *Quasi Scherzando*, vc. (1981).

An (Ger.). On, by, to, at, as in *An die Musik*, 'To Music'. In org. mus. it signifies that the stop in question is to be drawn.

Anacréon, ou L'amour fugitif. Opera-ballet in 2 acts by Cherubini, text by Mendouze. Prod. Paris 1803.

Anacreontic Society. Aristocratic mus. soc. in London 1766–94, meeting fortnightly during the season. Haydn attended a meeting. At each meeting, pres. sang constitutional song 'To Anacreon in Heaven'. See *Star-Spangled Banner*.

Anacrusis (plural *Anacruses*). Unstressed syllable at the beginning of a line of poetry or an unstressed note or group of notes at the beginning of a mus. phrase.

Analytical Notes. Another name for 'programme-notes', the descriptions of comps. which appear in annotated programmes. Possibly the earliest example is the programme of a Concert of Catches and Glees, given by Arne at Drury Lane Th. in 1768. It has a preface explaining the nature of the catch and the glee, and the various items are provided with historical interest. 15 years later (1783) Frederick the Great's Kapellmeister, J. F. Reichardt, founded in Potsdam a regular Tuesday perf. and provided in his programmes both the words of the songs and 'historical and aesthetic explanations enabling the audience to gain a more immediate understanding'.

John Ella, prominent in London mus. life as dir. of a chamber mus. organization, the Musical Union (1845–80), is often spoken of in Britain as the introducer of annotated programmes: he had been anticipated, but it was probably the utility of his analytical notes over a long period that formally est. the practice which from then on became widespread.

Some programme-notes have had a value beyond the occasion for which they were written, notably those by Sir George Grove for August Manns's orch. concerts at the Crystal Palace and those by Sir Donald *Tovey for the Reid concerts in Edinburgh.

Ančerl, Karel (*b* Tučapy, Bohemia, 1908; *d* Toronto, 1973). Cz. cond. Studied Prague Cons.

and with H. Scherchen in Berlin (1929–31). Cond. for Prague radio 1933–9. Sent to concentration camp by Nazis. Cond. Cz. Radio Orch. 1947–50, Cz. P.O., 1950–68; Toronto S.O., 1969–73.

Ancient Concert (Concert of Ancient Music). Important London subscription series (1776–1848). The royal and noble 'Directors' (e.g. George III, Prince Albert, Duke of Wellington) took turns to choose programmes. Another name was 'King's Concert' or, in Victorian times, 'Queen's Concert'. (Sometimes confused with *Academy of Ancient Music, 1726–92.) From 1804 the concerts were given in Hanover Sq. Rooms.

Ancora (It.). Still, yet; i.e. *Ancora forte*, still loud; *Ancora più forte*, even louder. Also used to mean 'Again', i.e. repeat. See also *Encore*.

Anda, Géza (*b* Budapest, 1921; *d* Zürich, 1976). Hung.-born pianist and cond. Pupil of Dohnányi and winner of Liszt Prize. Escaped from Hung. to Switzerland in 1943, becoming Swiss citizen 1955. World-wide reputation as interpreter of Mozart, Brahms, Beethoven, and especially Bartók.

Andaluz, andaluza (Sp.), **andalouse** (Fr.). Vaguely applied to several Sp. dances common in Andalusia, e.g. *Fandango, *Malagueña, and *Polo.

Andamento (It.). Going (i.e. running). A fugue subject of above average length, often of a running character. See also *Attacco*.

Andante (It., from *andare*, to go). Moving along, flowing (slowish but not slow). The word is often used for the title of a comp. *Andantino*. A diminution of *andante*. Some composers use it to mean a little slower than *andante*, but the commonly accepted modern usage means a little quicker.

Andante cantabile. (It.). Flowing and songlike. A direction often used by composers. To a large section of the public, however, it means one work, the 2nd movement, *andante cantabile*, of Tchaikovsky's Str. Qt. No. 1 in D (1871), Op. 11.

Andante favori. Publisher's title for Andante in F, pf. solo by Beethoven comp. 1804 and intended for the Sonata in C (Waldstein), Op. 53, but discarded and pubd. separately in 1806.

Andante spianato. (It.). Flowing and smooth. The title of Chopin's Op. 22 for pf. and orch., 1834. Linked by Chopin to a Polonaise in E♭ major.

An den Baum Daphne (To the Daphne Tree). Epilogue by R. Strauss to his opera *Daphne* (1936–7) for unacc. 9-part mixed ch., to words by J. Gregor, comp. 1943. This was the lib. for a choral finale to the opera which Strauss discarded in favour of an orch. transformation scene. He set the words later as this motet.

Anders, Peter (*b* Essen, 1908; *d* Hamburg, 1954). Ger. ten., specializing in lighter Mozart roles, notably at Berlin State Opera 1936–48, though later he sang Otello. CG début 1951 as Walther in *Die Meistersinger* under Beecham.

Andersen, Karsten (*b* Oslo, 1920). Norweg. cond. and violinist. Studied in Norway and It. Cond. and mus. dir. Stavanger 1945–64, Bergen from 1964. Chief cond. Iceland S.O. from 1973. Guest cond. of leading European orchs.

Anderson, Emily (*b* Galway, Ireland, 1891; *d* London, 1962). Eng. translator of the letters of Mozart and his family (1938) and of the letters of Beethoven (1961). Studied at Univs. of Berlin and Marburg and entered Brit. Foreign Office, being seconded to War Office 1940–3. O.B.E.

Anderson, Leroy (*b* Cambridge, Mass., 1908; *d* Woodbury, Conn., 1975). Amer. composer of light mus., notably *Sleigh Ride* and *Blue Tango*, but has also written more extended works.

Anderson, Lucy (née Philpot) (*b* Bath, 1797; *d* London, 1878). Eng. pianist, the first woman to play at a Phil. Soc. concert in London (29 April 1822, in a Hummel conc.). Teacher of Queen Victoria. Her husband, George Frederick Anderson (*b* London, 1793; *d* London, 1876) was a violinist and Master of the Queen's Musick, 1848–70.

Anderson, Marian (*b* Philadelphia, 1902). Amer. cont., mainly in concert repertory but became first black singer at NY Met. as Ulrica in *Un ballo in maschera*, 1955. Studied with Boghetti. Won competition to appear with NY P.O. 1925. Studied in Europe 1933–5, making début in London. Sang at inauguration of Pres. J. F. Kennedy, 1961.

Anderson, Ronald Kinloch (*b* Edinburgh, 1911; *d* London, 1984). Scot. pianist, teacher, writer, and record producer. Studied Edinburgh Univ. Début London 1938. Pianist in Robert Masters Qt. 1946–58, prof. of pf., TCL, 1946–63. Harpsichordist with Menuhin Fest. Orch. 1957–63. Producer of many gramophone recordings, incl. operas with Barbirolli and Karajan.

An die ferne Geliebte (To the Distant Beloved). Song-cycle by Beethoven, with pf. acc. (Op. 98, 1816), of 6 poems by Alois Jeitteles. Not to be confused with Beethoven's songs *An die fernen Geliebten* (1809, words by Reissig) and *An die Geliebte* (1811, words by J. L. Stoll, re-comp. 1814).

Andrade, Mario de (*b* Sâo Paulo, 1893; *d* Sâo Paulo, 1945). Brazilian musicologist, critic, and student of folk mus. Dir., Brazilian Dept. of Culture 1935–8. His book *Musica do Brasil* was pubd. 1941.

André, Franz (*b* Brussels, 1893; *d* Brussels, 1975). Belg. cond. Prin. cond. Belg. Radio S.O. 1935–58. On staff Brussels Cons. 1920–45.

André, Johann (*b* Offenbach-am-Main, 1741; *d* Offenbach-am-Main, 1799). Ger. composer, but best-known for publishing firm he founded in 1774. Among his own operas was the 4-act *Belmonte und Constanze, oder die Entführung aus dem Serail*, prod. Berlin 1781, the year before Mozart's setting of the same opera. His son, Johann Anton (1775–1842) in 1799 acquired entire mus. relicta of Mozart from the composer's widow and also pubd. Mozart's own thematic catalogue of his works from 1784 to 1791.

André, Maurice (*b* Ales, Gard, 1933). Fr. trumpeter. Studied Paris Cons. Début 1954. Prof. of tpt., Paris Cons., from 1967. Won Geneva Int. Competition 1955, Munich Int. Competition 1963. Soloist with leading orchs. Specialist in baroque and contemporary mus.

Andrea Chénier. Fr. Revolution opera in 4 acts by Giordano to lib. by Illica. Prod. Milan and NY 1896; London 1903.

Andreae, Volkmar (*b* Berne, 1879; *d* Zürich, 1962). Swiss cond. and composer. Dir. Zürich sym. concerts 1906–49, head of Zürich Univ. mus. dept. 1914–41. Cond. f.p. of Walton's *Portsmouth Point*, 1926. Comp. 2 operas, 2 syms., chamber mus.

Andreozzi, Gaetano (*b* Aversa, 1755; *d* Paris, 1826). It. composer, pupil of Jommelli. Wrote 43 operas and 6 str. qts.

Andrews, Herbert (Kennedy) (*b* Comber, Co. Down, 1904; *d* Oxford, 1965). Irish organist and scholar. Organist (1938–56) New College, Oxford, and univ. lecturer there. Author *Oxford Harmony*, Vol. 2, also books on Palestrina and Byrd.

Andrews, Hilda (Mrs. G. M. Lees) (*b* Birmingham, 1900; *d* Louth, Lincs., 1983). Eng. musicologist. Ed. of Byrd's *My Ladye Nevells Booke,* North's *Musicall Grammarian* (part of his *Memoires of Musick*), biography of Sir Richard *Terry, etc. Compiler of Catalogue of misc. MS. Mus. in King's (now Royal) Music Library.

Andriessen, Hendrik (*b* Haarlem, 1892; *d* Heemstede, 1981). Dutch composer and org., brother of Willem *Andriessen. Studied Amsterdam Cons. Organist at Haarlem and Utrecht between 1916 and 1938. Dir., Utrecht Cons. 1937–49, and Royal Cons., The Hague, 1949–57. Comp. principally org. and choral mus. but also operas, syms., and sonatas.

Andriessen, Louis (*b* Utrecht, 1939). Dutch composer, son of Hendrik *Andriessen, with whom he studied comp., later becoming pupil of Berio in Milan and Berlin. Comps. incl. th. and film scores and reflect influences of Cage, Stockhausen, and Stravinsky. Has made special critical study of Stravinsky. Mus. th. pieces incl. *Matthew Passion*, (1976), *Orpheus* (1977), *George Sand* (1980). Other works incl. *The 9 Symphonies of Beethoven*, orch. and ice-cream vendor bell (1970), *Symphonies of the Netherlands*, 2 or more wind bands (1974), and *Velocity*, orch. (1983).

Andriessen, Willem (*b* Haarlem, 1887; *d* Amsterdam, 1964). Dutch pianist and composer. Dir. of Amsterdam Cons. 1937–53. Composer of choral and orch. works.

Anerio, Felice (*b* Rome, *c*.1560; *d* Rome, 1614). It. church musician. Palestrina's successor as composer to Papal Chapel. Wrote 4 masses, spiritual madrigals, and secular canzonettas.

Anerio, Giovanni Francesco (*b* Rome, *c.* 1567; *d* Graz, 1630). It. composer and priest, brother of Felice *Anerio. Mus. dir. to King of Poland and later active in Rome. Composed masses, 83 motets, and many madrigals. More progressive than his brother.

Anfang (Ger.). Beginning. *Anfangs*, at the beginning. *Wie anfänglich*, as at the beginning. *Vom Anfang* is Ger. equivalent of *Da capo*.

Anfossi, Pasquale (*b* Taggia, nr. Naples, 1727; *d* Rome, 1797). It. composer of over 70 operas and then of church mus. when he became maestro of St John Lateran in 1792. Pupil of Piccinni. For Vienna prod. (1783) of his opera *Il Curioso indiscreto*, Mozart comp. 3 additional arias. Mus. dir., King's Th., London, 1782–6

Angeles, Victoria de los. See *De Los Angeles, Victoria.*

Angelica (It.), **angélique** (Fr.), **angel-lute** (Eng.). Instr. of the lute type popular *c*.1700. An archlute with long neck, 16 or 17 gut str. and 2 peg-boxes. Tuned diatonically.

Angelus. Prayer to the Virgin Mary offered at morning, noon, and evening at the sound of the Angelus bell. Also title of opera by Edward Naylor (1867–1934) which won Ricordi Prize and was prod. CG 1909.

Angerer, Paul (*b* Vienna, 1927). Austrian cond. and composer. Began career as orchestral violist. Kapellmeister, Bonn State Theatre 1964–6; opera dir. Salzburg Landestheater 1967–72. Harpsichordist and recorder-player in various baroque ens. Leader, S.W. Ger. Chamber Orch. since 1971. Comps. incl. va. conc., fl. conc., chamber works, and setting of Whitman's *Song of Myself.*

Anglais, Anglaise (Fr.). English. Term of variable meaning sometimes used by 18th-cent. composers as the title of a hornpipe or country dance; or of anything else thought to be Eng. in character.

Anglican Chant. Simple type of harmonized melody used in the Anglican Church (and nowadays often in other Eng.-speaking Protestant churches) for singing unmetrical texts, principally the Psalms and the Canticles (when these latter are not sung in a more elaborate setting). The main principle is that of the trad. *Gregorian tones, i.e. a short melody is repeated to each verse of the text (or sometimes to 2 or more verses; see below), the varying numbers of syllables in the different lines of the words being accommodated by the flexible device of a RECITING NOTE at the opening of each line—this being treated as timeless and so capable of serving as the vehicle for many or few syllables, while succeeding notes are sung in time and (normally) take one syllable each. The 1st part of the chant has 3 measures and the 2nd part 4.

Anhang (Ger.). A supplement, i.e. a Coda in the mus. sense, or in musicological terminology a section appended to a critical edn. of a work containing variant readings, material of doubtful attribution, etc.

Aniara. Opera in 2 acts by Blomdahl. Lib. by E. Lindegren based on H. Martinson's fantasy about space travel. (Prod. Stockholm and Edinburgh Fest. 1959.)

Anievas, Agustin (b NY, 1934). Amer. pianist of Sp.-Mexican descent. Studied Juilliard Sch., NY. Début NY 1959. Winner of Queen Elisabeth of the Belgians and Mitropoulos Int. prizes (1961).

Anima (It.). Soul, i.e. the sound-post of a vn., etc. (See also *Âme, Sound-post.*) *Con anima,* with feeling.

Animando (It.). Animating. *Animandosi,* becoming animated. *Animato* (It.)., *animé* (Fr.). Animated.

Animo, animoso (It.). Spirit, spirited, *Animosamente,* spiritedly.

Animuccia, Giovanni (b Florence, c. 1500; d Rome, 1571). It. composer. Predecessor of Palestrina as maestro of the Vatican and regarded as extraordinarily fertile innovator. Comp. *Laudi,* some of which were pubd. in 1563 and 1570.

Anna Bolena. Opera in 2 acts by Donizetti to lib. by Romani. Inaccurate but moving dramatization of life of Henry VIII's 2nd wife Anne Boleyn. (Prod. Milan 1830; London 1831; New Orleans 1839.) Revived for Maria *Callas at Milan, 1957, and at Glyndebourne 1965.

Anna Magdalena Books (J. S. Bach). 2nd and 3rd of the 3 colls. of kbd. pieces by Bach known as *Klavierbüchlein.* They were for the instruction of his 2nd wife Anna Magdalena and were pubd. 1722 and 1725.

Années de pèlerinage (Years of Pilgrimage). 23 pf. pieces by Liszt issued in 3 books as follows: Book 1 (1st Année, Switzerland). 1. *La Chapelle de Guillaume Tell.* 2. *Au lac de Wallenstadt.* 3. *Pastorale.* 4. *Au bord d'une source.* 5. *Orage.* 6. *Vallée d'Obermann.* 7. *Eglogue.* 8. *Le mal du pays.* 9. *Les Cloches de Genève.* Comp. 1848–54, pubd. 1855. Nos. 1–4, 6–8, and 9 based on *Album d'un Voyageur,* 1835–6; Book 2 (2nd Année, Italy). 1. *Sposalizio.* 2. *Il Penseroso.* 3. *Canzonetta del Salvator Rosa.* 4. *Sonetto 47 del Petrarca.* 5. *Sonetto 104 del Petrarca.* 6. *Sonetto 123 del Petrarca.* 7. *Aprés une*

lecture du Dante, fantasia quasi sonata. Comp. 1837–49, pubd. 1858. Book 3 (3rd Année). 1. *Angelus!* 2. *Aux cyprès de la Villa d'Este* (3/4). 3. *Aux cyprès de la Villa d'Este* (4/4). 4. *Les jeux d'eau à la Villa d'Este.* 5. *Sunt lachrymae rerum.* 6. *Marche funèbre.* 7. *Sursum corda.* Comp. 1866–77, pubd. 1883.

Annibali, Domenico (b Macerata, c. 1705; d Rome, 1779). It. male sop. assoc. with Handel operas in London 1736–7.

Annie Laurie. The poem is by William Douglas of Fingland (c. 1880), but has been much altered by various people, especially Lady John Douglas Scott (1810–1900, see *Loch Lomond*), who also wrote the air. First pubd. 1838.

Annunzio, Gabriele d' (b Pescara, 1863; d Vittoriale, 1938). It. poet and dramatist who was keen student of mus. Worked in Rome as mus. critic; in 1917 ed. *National Collection of Italian Music* with help of Pizzetti and Malipiero, among others. Debussy comp. incidental mus. for his play *Le Martyre de Saint-Sébastien* (1911) and Zandonai's *Francesca da Rimini* is based on another of his plays.

Anon in Love. Sequence of 6 love poems, anonymous 16th- and 17th-cent. lyrics, set for ten. and guitar in 1959 by Walton. F.p. Aldeburgh 1960 (Peter Pears and Julian Bream). Version for ten. and small orch. 1971.

Anreissen (Ger.). To tear at. Use a very forceful *pizzicato.*

Anschlag (Ger.). (1) Sometimes called a 'Double Appoggiatura' but consisting of the notes immediately below and above the prin. note.
(2) Touch (pertaining to a kbd. instr.).
(3) 'Attack', etc.

Ansell, John (b 1874; d Marlow, 1948). Eng. composer. Trained GSM. Mus. dir. various London ths. BBC 1925–30.

Ansermet, Ernest (b Vevey, Switzerland, 1883; d Geneva, 1969). Swiss cond. Studied mus. with E. *Bloch, among others. Became cond. at Kursaal, Montreux, 1911. Cond. for Diaghilev's Russian Ballet from 1915, touring widely. Cond. Buenos Aires S.O., 1924–7. In 1918 founded L'Orchestre de la Suisse Romande, of which he remained cond. until 1966. Noted as interpreter of Stravinsky (cond. several f.ps.), Ravel, and Debussy. Cond. f.p. of Britten's *The Rape of Lucretia,* Glyndebourne 1946. Taught mathematics in his youth at a Lausanne school, not (as is often stated) at the University.

Anstimmen (Ger.). To tune.

Anstrich (Ger.). Bow 'stroke'. (See also *Strich*).

Answer in Fugue. The 2nd entry of the main theme (subject) of a *fugue a 5th higher (or 4th lower) than the 1st is called the Answer. If subject and answer are identical it is a Real Answer; if the intervals are changed in the answer it is a Tonal Answer.

Antar. (1) Orch. work by Rimsky-Korsakov, Op. 9, first described as his Sym. No. 2 when it appeared in 1868. Rev. and re-orch. 1876 and 1897 and again in 1903 when it was designated 'oriental suite'. Based on an oriental tale by Sennkovsky.

(2) Opera by Gabriel *Dupont (1912–13).

Antarctic Symphony (Vaughan Williams). See *Sinfonia Antartica*.

Antecedent. In a *Canon the v. which first enters with the tune to be imitated is called the Dux or Antecedent.

Antechrist. Work for chamber ens. (incl. cowbell) by *Maxwell Davies. Comp. and f.p. 1967 (London, Pierrot Players, cond. composer).

Antheil, George (*b* Trenton, NJ, 1900; *d* NY, 1959). Amer. composer of Polish descent. Studied with Sternberg and Bloch. Caused furore in Europe in 1920s at his pf. recitals with his comps. called *Airplane Sonata* and *Mechanisms*. His *Ballet méchanique*, comp. 1923–4 and f.p. Paris 1926, was designed as film mus. but was rev. for the concert hall (scored for 8 pf., pianola, 8 xylophones, 2 doorbells, and sound of aeroplane propeller). For NY première in 1927 he doubled the pfs., added car-horns and anvils, and used a real propeller. A final rev. (1953) reduced the pfs. to 4 but incl. tape of a jet engine. Returned to USA 1933 and wrote Hollywood film scores from 1936. Became more conservative. Works incl. 6 syms., ballets, 3-act opera *Volpone* (1950–2), and 2 earlier 3-act operas, pf. conc., vn. conc., str. qts., and vn. sonatas. Also wrote detective stories, a study of the glandular abnormalities of criminals, and a daily column of advice to the lovelorn.

Anthem. The Eng.-speaking Protestant Churches' equivalent of the Latin motet, from which it sprang. An Anglican creation, with a place in the C. of E. liturgy. It constitutes in ordinary churches the one great occasion when the choir alone undertakes the duty of song, and when an elaborate vocal setting impossible and unsuitable in other parts of the service becomes proper and effective. It is usually but not necessarily acc. by organ, and frequently incl. passages for solo vv., individually or in combination. The anthems of Purcell and Blow are like cantatas. S. S. *Wesley was prolific composer of anthems nearer to the style favoured today.

The term is also less strictly used, as in the phrase 'National Anthem', to denote a solemn, hymn-like song.

Anticipation. The sounding of a note of a chord before the rest of the chord.

Antill, John (*b* Sydney, N.S.W., 1904; *d* Sydney, 1986). Australian composer and administrator on staff of Australian Broadcasting Commission.

Comp. operas and orch. works, and ballet *Corroboree* (1946) (based on aboriginal dances). C.M.G. 1981.

Antiphon (from Gr., 'sounding across'). (1) A versicle or phrase sung by one choir in reply to another.

(2) In the R.C. Church the antiphon is intoned or sung during the recitation of Divine Office, before and after the psalm or canticle, which is itself responsively sung by the singers divided into two bodies. The antiphon may serve to reinforce the meaning of the psalm, or to introduce a Christian application of the orig. Jewish text. The plainsong tune of the antiphon, though not the same as the 'tone' of the psalm, is in keeping with it as to mode, etc.

(3) Many antiphons now exist without psalms and are sometimes sung to comp. settings, rather than to the orig. plainsong, hence the Eng. word *'anthem', derived from 'antiphona'. Several composers have given the title *Antiphon* to a comp., e.g. Vaughan Williams in *5 Mystical Songs*.

Antiphonal, Antiphonary, Antiphoner. Properly, the R.C. Church's coll. of trad. plainsong *antiphons, but the word has come to be more comprehensively used as meaning the book containing all plainsong for the Divine Office, as distinct from the *Gradual, which contains the plainsong for the Mass.

Antiphonal Singing. When 2 parts of a choir (*Decani* and *Cantoris*) sing alternately, one answering the other. (Alternation between officiant and choir is 'responsorial'.) The term 'antiphonal' is generally used of the mus. effects drawn from groups of singers or instrumentalists stationed apart.

Antiphons of the Blessed Virgin Mary. There are 4, each with its season: (*a*) during Advent and until the Purification of the Virgin Mary, *Alma redemptoris mater*; (*b*) from then until Wednesday in Holy Week, *Ave regina coelorum*; (*c*) from then until Whitsun, *Regina coeli laetare*; (*d*) from the Octave of Whitsun until Advent, *Salve regina, mater misericordiae*.

Anvil. Perc. instr., imitating real anvil, used in many works, usually operas. In *Das Rheingold* Wagner uses 18 in 3 sizes to depict the activity in Nibelheim. In *Siegfried* Act I, Siegfried splits an anvil with the sword Nothung. Real anvils are used in *Il trovatore* (Verdi), *Benvenuto Cellini* (Berlioz), Mahler's 6th Sym., Bax's 3rd Sym., Walton's *Belshazzar's Feast*, and Britten's *The Burning Fiery Furnace*.

Anwachsend (Ger.). Growing. Swelling out in tone.

Apel, Willi (*b* Konitz, 1893). Amer. (Ger.-born) musicologist. Taught at various Ger. univs. and in 1936 settled in USA, joining staff of Harvard Univ. 1938–42 and becoming prof. of musicology, Indiana Univ., 1950–70. Pubd. many works, incl. *Harvard Dictionary of Music* (1944, rev. 1969). Has also written books on fugue, medieval harmony, and Gregorian chant.

Aperto (It.). Open. (1) Clear, distinct.
(2) Broad in style.

ApIvor, Denis (*b* Collinstown, Eire, 1916). Irish-born composer of Welsh parentage. Studied at choir schs. of Christ Church (Oxford) and Hereford, and under Hadley and Rawsthorne 1937–9. Works incl. 2 syms., operas *She Stoops to Conquer* (1943–7), *Yerma* (1959), *Ubu Roi* (1966); ballets *A Mirror for Witches* (1952), *Blood Wedding* (1953), and *Saudades* (1955); cantata *The Hollow Men* (T. S. Eliot, 1939–46) for bar., male ch., and orch., and concs. for cl., pf., and vn. Is qualified doctor of medicine.

Apollo Musagetes (Apollo, Leader of the Muses; Fr. *Apollon Musagète*). Ballet in 2 scenes by Stravinsky, scored for str. (1927–8). (Prod. Washington, Paris, London, 1928.) Choreog. Adolph Bolm for Washington, Balanchine for Paris (Diaghilev).

Apostel, Hans (Erich) (*b* Karlsruhe, 1901; *d* Vienna, 1972). Ger.-born Austrian composer. Studied with Schoenberg and Berg and settled in Vienna. Works incl. pf. conc., requiem, 2 str. qts., pf. pieces, songs, etc.

Apostles, The. Oratorio by Elgar, Op. 49, text compiled by Elgar from the Bible and other sources. Comp. 1901–3. For 6 soloists, ch., and orch. (F.p. Birmingham 1903, NY, London, and Cologne 1904.) See *Kingdom, The*.

Appalachia. 'Variations on an Old Slave Song' by Delius, for orch. with bar. solo and ch. First version comp. 1896, re-worked 1902–3. (F.p. Elberfeld 1904, London 1907.)

Appalachian Spring. Ballet by Copland, comp. 1943–4, choreog. Martha Graham, 1944. Scored for fl., cl., bn., 4 vn., 2 va., 2 vc., db., and pf. Fuller orch. version of suite and of ballet 1945.

Appassionata Sonata. Publisher's apt title for Beethoven's Pf. Sonata No. 23 in F minor, Op. 57, comp. 1804–5.

Appassionato, appassionata (It.). Impassioned; so *appassionatamente*, passionately; *appassionamento*, passion.

Appeldoorn, Dina (*b* Rotterdam, 1884; *d* The Hague, 1938). Dutch composer. Her works incl. symphonic poems, pf. pieces, and songs.

Appenzeller, Benedictine (*b* Oudenaarde, *c*.1500; *d* after 1558). Flemish composer. Wrote a 4-part *Nenia in memory of Josquin Desprès. Choirmaster to Netherlands regent 1537–after 1551. Composed nearly 50 *chansons*.

Appia, Adolphe (*b* Geneva, 1862; *d* Nyon, 1928). Swiss scenic artist who pioneered modern operatic trend for imaginative lighting and minimum of scenery. Designed *The Ring* for Bayreuth, 1899 and *Tristan* for Scala, Milan (Toscanini) 1923.

Applied Music. Amer. term for a study course in perf. as opposed to theory.

Appoggiando; appoggiato (It.). Leaning; leaned. (1) Each note passing very smoothly to the next (i.e. *portamento*).
(2) Stressed.

Appoggiatura (It.). Leaning Note. A grace note or species of ornament of which the exact interpretation has differed in various periods. In the 18th cent. the appoggiatura was often unwritten and left, e.g. in Handel and Mozart, to be inserted by the singer. Operatic appoggiatura was regarded as obsolete until its revival in certain operatic productions *c*.1960. Its harmonic application may be described as follows:

Properly an unprepared suspension (if such a contradictory term may be allowed) whether it be shown in full-sized type as a part of the chord in which it momentarily appears, or as a small note printed just before that chord. Having a harmonic status it is not an 'ornament' in the same sense as, for instance, the *Acciaccatura.

(a) With Ordinary and Dotted Notes.

The Appoggiatura is as important melodically as the note on which it 'leans', from which it takes normally half the time-value (two-thirds the time-value if the supporting note is dotted).

(b) With Tied Notes.

When the Appoggiatura 'leans upon' two tied notes, it normally takes the whole of the time-value of the first of these to itself.

(c) With a Chord.

As the Appoggiatura leans only upon one note of the chord the other notes are unaffected.

Apprenti Sorcier, L' (The Sorcerer's Apprentice). Symphonic poem ('Scherzo') by Dukas, f.p. Paris 1897, London and NY 1899. 'The Apprentice Sorcerer' would be a more accurate trans. Based on a poem by Goethe which, in turn, is based on a dialogue in Lucian (2nd cent. A.D.). The apprentice, in his master's absence, tries one of his spells and, to his consternation, cannot countermand it. In Disney film *Fantasia*, the apprentice was represented by Mickey Mouse.

Aprahamian, Felix (*b* London, 1914). Eng. mus. critic and organist of Armenian descent. On staff of *Sunday Times* since 1948. Authority on org. mus., Fr. mus., and works of Delius (mus. adviser, Delius Trust since 1961).

Après-midi d'un faune, Prélude à l' ('Prelude to the afternoon of a faun'). Tone-poem by Debussy, comp. 1892–4 and f.p. Paris 1894 (London 1904), being an orch. 'impression' of the poem by Mallarmé. He intended a set of 3 pieces, *Prélude, Interlude*, and *Paraphrase finale*, but only the first was written. It was the subject of a ballet by Nijinsky, Paris 1912, for Diaghilev.

A punta d'arco (It.). At the point of the bow (in str. playing).

Aquarelle (Fr.). Water-colour; sometimes musically applied to a piece of delicate texture, as in Eric *Fenby's arr. for str., as *Aquarelles*, of Delius's 2 wordless chs. 'To be sung of a summer night on the water'.

Arabella. Opera in 3 acts by R. Strauss to lib. by Hofmannsthal based on a combination of his short story *Lucidor* (1909) and his play *Der Fiaker als Graf* (The Cabby as Count) (1925). Their last collaboration. Comp. 1930–2. Prod. Dresden 1933, CG 1934, NY 1955. Rev. 1939 (Munich).

Arabesque (Fr., Eng.), **Arabeske** (Ger.). A florid element in Arabian architecture, hence a florid melodic section. The term is sometimes applied to a piece of instr. mus. (not always in an appropriate manner) as by Schumann for his pf. piece, Op. 18, or by Debussy to his *2 Arabesques* for pf.

Arada (Sp.). Ploughed land. A type of folk-song assoc. with ploughing.

Aragonesa (Sp.), **aragonaise** (Fr.). Sp. dance deriving from Aragon.

A.R.A.M., A.R.C.M., A.R.C.O., A.R.M.C.M. Assoc. of, respectively, *Royal Academy of Music, *Royal College of Music, *Royal College of Organists, *Royal Manchester College of Music.

Arányi, Jelly d' (*b* Budapest, 1893; *d* Florence, 1966). Hung.-born violinist, great-niece of Joachim. Trained at Royal High School for Mus., Budapest, under Hubay. Début Vienna 1909. Settled in London and became Brit. subject. Gave f.ps. (in London) with Bartók of Bartók's 2 vn. sonatas (1922 and 1923) both of which were ded. to her, as were Vaughan Williams's vn. conc. (1925) and Ravel's *Tzigane* (1924), in both of which she was also first soloist. Gave first Brit.

perf. of Szymanowski 1st Vn. Conc. (1930). Her sister was Adila *Fachiri.

Arbeau, Thoinot (pen-name of Jehan Tabourot) (*b* Dijon, 1520; *d* Langres, 1595). Fr. priest. Author of famous book on the dance, *Orchésographie* (1588–9) which also contained mus. illustrations. See *Capriol Suite*.

Arbós, Enrique (Fernández) (*b* Madrid, 1863; *d* San Sebastián, 1939). Sp. cond., composer, and violinist; pupil of Vieuxtemps and Joachim. Leader of Berlin P.O. and Boston S.O. Cond., Madrid S.O. from 1904. Settled in Eng. where he was on staff of RCM 1894–1916. Comp. opera and chamber mus. but best known for his orch. of several pieces from *Albéniz's *Iberia*: those he left unfinished were completed in 1954 by *Surinach.

Arcadelt (Arkadelt, Arcadet, Arcadente, etc.), **Jacob** (*b* c.1510; *d* Paris, 1568). Flemish composer attached to St Peter's and Sistine Chapel, Rome; then in Paris. Wrote church mus. but is chiefly remembered for secular madrigals, *chansons*, and motets, of which 5 books were pubd. before 1544.

Arcata (It.). Stroke of bow (in str. playing), often followed by the words *in giù* (down), or *in su* (up).

Arcato (It.). Bowed (after a passage of *pizzicato*).

A.R.C.C.O. Assoc. of the Royal Canadian College of Organists.

Archbishop of Canterbury's Degrees. By a custom begun in 13th cent. the Archbishop of Canterbury may confer degrees, among them a doctorate of mus., known as 'Canterbury' or 'Lambeth' degrees (Lambeth being site of the Archbishop's London palace). In 1936 he instituted a diploma in mus. granted on examination to F.R.C.O.s who hold a choirmaster's diploma. Those who pass become *A.D.C.M.s.

Archduke Trio. Beethoven's Pf. Trio in B♭, Op. 97 (1811). So nicknamed from ded. to Archduke Rudolph of Austria, who was pf. and comp. pupil of Beethoven.

Arched Viall. Instr. similar to a *Geigenwerk*, a kind of hurdy-gurdy, mentioned by Pepys in 1664 ('It will never do', he said).

Archet (Fr.). Bow (of a str. instr.).

Archi (It.). Bows (of str. instr.); the singular is *Arco.

Archlute. Large double-necked lute or *theorbo with extra bass strs.

Arco (plural *archi*) (It.). Bow. Used alone or as *coll' arco* (with the bow) after a passage marked *pizzicato* (plucked).

Arden muss Sterben (Arden must die). Opera in 3 acts by A. Goehr to Ger. lib. by Erich Fried based on anonymous play *Arden of Feversham* (1592). Prod. Hamburg 1967, London 1974 (in Eng. trans. by G. Skelton).

Arditi, Luigi (*b* Crescentino, 1822; *d* Brighton, 1903). It. composer and cond. Toured widely as cond. of opera cos., e.g. Mapleson's. Settled in Eng., conducting regularly at CG. Cond. f.p. in London of *Cavalleria Rusticana*. Remembered as composer for his waltz-song *Il bacio* (The Kiss).

Arend, Max (*b* Deutz, 1873; *d* Cologne, 1943). Ger. expert on mus. of Gluck and founder (1913) of Gluck Soc. Studied at Leipzig under Riemann.

Arensky, Anton (Stepanovich) (*b* Novgorod, 1861; *d* Terijoki, Finland, 1906). Russ. composer. Studied in St Petersburg with Rimsky-Korsakov. Prof. of harmony and counterpoint, Moscow Cons. 1882. Comp. 3 operas, 2 str. qts., and 2 syms., but best-known works are the pf. conc., pf. trio in D minor (in memory of the cellist Davidov), *Variations on a Theme of Tchaikovsky* for str., and many pf. pieces.

Aretino, Guido. See *Guido d'Arezzo*.

Arezzo. See *Guido d'Arezzo*.

Argento, Dominick (*b* York, Penn., 1927). Amer. composer. Studied Peabody Cons., Baltimore, with N. Nabokov and *Cowell, later at Eastman Sch. with *Hovhaness and *Hanson. Also studied in It. with Dallapiccola. Mus. dir., Hilltop Opera, Baltimore, 1958. Member of Dept. of Mus., Minnesota Univ., from 1958. Primarily interested in opera. Works incl.:

OPERAS: *Colonel Jonathan the Saint* (1958–60); *The Boor* (1957); *Christopher Sly* (1962); *The Masque of Angels* (1963); *The Shoemaker's Holiday* (1967); *Postcard from Morocco* (1971); *A Waterbird Talk* (1974); *The Voyage of Edgar Allan Poe* (1975–6); *Miss Havisham's Fire* (1978–9).
BALLETS: *The Resurrection of Don Juan* (1956); *Royal Invitation, or Homage to the Queen of Tonga* (1964).
ORCH: *From the Album of Allegra Harper, 1867* (suite from opera *Colonel Jonathan*) (1961); *Divertimento* for pf. and str. (1955); *Ode to the West Wind,* conc. for sop. and orch. (1956); *Suite, Resurrection of Don Juan* (1956); *Suite, Royal Invitation* (1964); *Variations (The Mask of Night)* (1965); *Bravo Mozart!* for vn., ob., hn., and chamber orch. (1969); *A Ring of Time* (1972).
CHORAL: *Revelation of St John the Divine*, for ten., male ch., brass, and perc. (1966); *A Nation of Cowslips*, 7 Keats songs for unacc. ch. (1968); *Tria Carmina Paschalia* for women's vv., harp, guitar (1970); *Jonah and the Whale*, oratorio for ten., bass, narrator, ch., and chamber ens. (1973).
SONG-CYCLES: *6 Elizabethan Songs*, ten. (or sop.) and baroque ens. (1958); *Letters from Composers, 7* songs for ten. and guitar (1968); *To be Sung Upon the Water*, for high v., pf., cl., and bass cl. (1972); *From the Diary of Virginia Woolf*, for medium v. and pf. (1974).

Argerich, Martha (*b* Buenos Aires, 1941). Argentinian pianist. Soloist with orch. in Buenos Aires at age of 8. Studied with V. Scaramuzzo, F. Gulda, N. Magaloff, and Michelangeli. 1st prize, Busoni Contest and Geneva international mus. competition 1957, 1st prize international Chopin competition, Warsaw, 1965. Soloist with world's leading orchs. Remarkable vitality and power in her performances. London début 1964.

Aria (It.). Air. From the time of A. Scarlatti in the 18th cent. onwards this has had the definite implication of a more or less lengthy and well-developed solo vocal piece in A-B-A form. The 19th-cent. operatic aria became more elaborate and complex. Arias used to be rather minutely classified as (a) *Aria cantabile*, slow and smooth; (b) *Aria di portamento*, in long notes and dignified, to be sung in *legato* style; (c) *Aria di mezzo carattere*, more passionate and with often elaborate orch. acc.; (d) *Aria parlante*, declamatory; (e) *Aria di bravura* (or *d'agilità*, or *d'abilità*), requiring great v.-control; (f) *Aria all'unisono*, with acc. in unison or octaves with the vocal part; (g) *Aria d'imitazione*, imitative of bird-song, hunting hns., etc.; (h) *Aria concertata* with elaborate acc.; and so on.

Ariadne. (1) Setting of poem by C. Day Lewis for sop. and orch. (1970) by *Maconchy (f.p. King's Lynn Fest. 1971).
(2) *Concertante* for ob. and 12 instrumentalists by *Crosse (f.p. Cheltenham Fest. 1972).

Ariadne auf Naxos (Ariadne on Naxos). Opera in prol. and 1 act by R. Strauss to lib. by Hofmannsthal. There are 2 versions. No. 1 was designed for perf. after Molière's play Le *Bourgeois Gentilhomme* (with incidental mus. by Strauss). F.p. Stuttgart 1912, London 1913. 2nd version substituted an operatic prol. for the play, f.p. Vienna 1916, London 1924, NY 1934. Many other composers have based operas on the Ariadne legend. Naxos is the island on which Ariadne, awaiting death, is consoled by Bacchus.

Arianna a Naxos (Ariadne on Naxos). Dramatic cantata by Haydn, for sop. and hpd. or pf. (Hob. XXVIb:2), comp. 1790.

Ariane et Barbe-bleue (Ariadne and Bluebeard). Fantasy-opera in 3 acts by Dukas to lib. based on Maeterlinck's play. (Prod. Paris 1907; NY 1911; London 1937.)

Arianna (Ariadne). Opera in prol. and 8 scenes by *Monteverdi to lib. by Rinuccini. Prod. Mantua 1608. Score now lost, only surviving part being *Lamento d'Arianna*.

Arienzo, Nicola d' (*b* Naples, 1842; *d* Naples, 1915). It. composer of operas prod. Naples and Milan, of which 2 (*Monzu Gnazio* and *I due mariti*) were in Neapolitan dialect. Also wrote syms. and concs.

Arietta (It.). A shorter and simpler *Aria. Usually lacks a middle section. Term sometimes applied to a piece of instr. mus.

Ariettes oubliées (Forgotten ariettas). Debussy's settings of 6 poems by Verlaine (1888). The songs' titles are: *C'est l'Extase langoureuse*; *Il Pleure dans mon coeur*; *L'Ombre des arbres*; *Chevaux de bois*; *Green*; *Spleen*.

Ariodante. Opera in 3 acts by Handel to It. libretto anonymously adapted from *Ginevra, Principessa di Scozia* by Antonio Salvi (Pratolino, 1705) based on Ariosto's *Orlando furioso* (canti V and VI). F.p. London (CG) 1735.

Arioso. (1) A recitative of the more melodious type.
(2) A short melodious passage at the beginning or end of an aria.
(3) A short air in an opera or oratorio.
(4) In instr. mus., a *cantabile passage.

Ariosti, Attilio (*b* Bologna, 1666; *d* ?England, 1729). It. composer, formerly monk who obtained dispensation to devote himself to mus. and occupied various court positions in Ger. and Austria; colleague in London of Bononcini and Handel as dir. of opera enterprise (Royal Academy of Music, 1719–27), and composer of 20 operas etc.; perf. on and composer for viola d'amore.

Arkadelt. See *Arcadelt, Jacob.*

Arkwright, Godfrey (Edward Pellen) (*b* Norwich, 1864; *d* Highclere, 1944). Eng. musicologist; ed. of comprehensive 'Old English Edition' in 25 vols. (1889–1902), and a quarterly, *The Musical Antiquary* (1909–13). Ed. of Purcell's church mus.

Arlecchinesco (It.). In the spirit of a Harlequinade.

Arlecchino (Harlequin). Opera in 1 act by Busoni, Op. 50, to his own lib. A 'theatrical capriccio', comp. 1914–16, prod. Zürich 1917, London (radio and TV) 1939, Glyndebourne (stage) 1954.

Arlésienne, L' (The Maid of Arles). Daudet's play, for which Bizet composed 27 items of incidental mus., Paris 1872 (later incorporating some of it into the ballet of *Carmen*). There are 2 orch. suites, the first arr. Bizet, the 2nd *Guiraud.

Armide. Opera in 5 acts by Gluck. Lib. by Quinault, based on Tasso's *Jerusalem Delivered.* (Prod. Paris 1777; Manchester, in concert version, 1860; NY 1910.) Among 40 operas based on Tasso's story are those by Lully, Handel, Jommelli, Salieri, Haydn, Rossini, and Dvořák.

Armonia, armonica (It.). (1) 'Harmony'.
(2) 'Wind band'.
(3) One of several names for the *hurdy-gurdy (also *armonie*).

Armstrong, Louis ('Satchmo') (*b* New Orleans, *c*.1898; *d* NY, 1971). Amer. jazz trumpeter and singer. From 1917 played on Miss. river boats. Joined King Oliver's Creole Jazz Band 1922. Played often with Fletcher Henderson's orch. 1924–5, then formed own band. Became world-famous as result of recordings in 1920s in which his virtuoso trumpet-playing and his idiosyncratic singing had enormous influence on jazz scene. Nickname 'Satchmo' a diminutive of 'Satchelmouth'. Visited Eng. and Europe in 1932 and 1934. Made many films and appeared with big bands in 'swing' era. Formed his All Stars 1947, touring Europe 1949, 1952, and 1956. Particularly remembered for his appearance with Bing Crosby and Frank Sinatra in film *High Society* (1956).

Armstrong, Richard (*b* Leicester, 1943). Eng. cond. Studied Cambridge Univ. On mus. staff CG 1966–8. Ass. cond. WNO 1968–73, mus. dir. 1973–86. Janáček Medal 1979. CG début 1982 (*Billy Budd*).

Armstrong, Sheila (Ann) (*b* Ashington, 1942). Eng. soprano. Studied RAM, winning a Ferrier scholarship, 1965. Opera début SW 1965 (Despina in *Così fan tutte*), Glyndebourne 1966 (Belinda in Purcell's *Dido and Aeneas*), CG 1973 (Marzelline in *Fidelio*). NY début 1973. Sang in f.p. of McCabe's *Notturni ed Alba*, 1970. Notable exponent of Elgar oratorios, Vaughan Williams's *Sea Symphony*, etc.

Armstrong, (Sir) Thomas (Henry Wait) (*b* Peterborough, 1898). Eng. organist and teacher. Studied Oxford and RCM. Organist Exeter Cath. 1928–33, Christ Church Cath., Oxford, 1933–55. Choragus and lecturer in mus., Oxford Univ., 1937–54. Prin., RAM, 1955–68. Composer of choral works, church mus., chamber mus., etc. Knighted 1957.

Arne, Michael (*b* London, *c.* 1740; *d* London, 1786). Eng. composer, illegitimate son of Thomas *Arne. Lived for a time in Hamburg. Comp. stage mus., etc.; his song *The Lass with a delicate air* is still heard.

Arne, Thomas (Augustine) (*b* London, 1710; *d* London, 1778). The leading Brit. composer of his day, notable for incidental mus. to plays, incl. Shakespeare's. His masque *Alfred* (1740) incl. song 'Rule, Britannia!' Operas incl. *Artaxerxes* (1762) and oratorio *Judith* (1761).

Arnell, Richard (Anthony Sayer) (*b* London, 1917). Eng. composer. Trained RCM 1935–9, studying comp. with Ireland. Lived in USA 1939–47. Comps. incl. 7 syms., ballet *Punch and the Child* (1947), symphonic portrait *Lord Byron*, pf. conc., vn. conc., str. qts., and 3 operas. On staff TCL 1948–64.

Arnim, Achim (really Ludwig Joachim) **von** (*b* Berlin, 1781; *d* Wiepersdorf, 1831). Ger. poet who can claim inclusion in a mus. dictionary because of his co-editorship with his future brother-in-law Clemens Brentano of the anthology of German folk poetry *Des knaben Wunderhorn* (Youth's Magic Horn), 1805–8, extracts from which have been set by several composers, notably Mahler. In 1811 he married Elisabeth (Bettina) *Brentano, a friend of Beethoven.

Arnold, Denis (Midgley) (*b* Sheffield, 1926; *d* Budapest, 1986). Eng. critic and teacher. Educated Sheffield Univ. (M.A., B.Mus.). Senior lecturer, Hull Univ., 1964–9; Prof. of Mus., Nottingham Univ. 1969–75; Prof. of Mus., Oxford Univ. from 1975. Author of books on Monteverdi and G. Gabrieli. Specialist on 16th- and 17th-cent. It. mus. Joint ed. *Music and Letters* 1976–80. Ed., *New Oxford Companion to Music*, 1983. C.B.E. 1983.

Arnold, Malcolm (Henry) (*b* Northampton, 1921). Eng. composer, trumpeter, and cond. Studied RCM 1938–40. Trumpeter in LPO 1941–2, BBC S.O. 1945, LPO (prin.) 1946–8. Studied in It. 1948–9. C.B.E. 1970. Works, in many genres, notable for melodic invention, colour, exuberance, and craftsmanship. One of post-1950 Eng. composers who has kept in touch with his audience without debasing his style or lowering his standards. Several film scores, incl. *The Bridge on the River Kwai*, 1957. Prin. works:

BALLETS: *Homage to the Queen*, Op. 42 (1953); *Rinaldo and Armida*, Op. 49 (1955); *Electra*, Op. 79 (1963).
ORCH: Syms: No. 1, Op. 22 (1951), No. 2, Op. 40 (1953), No. 3, Op. 63 (1954), No. 4, Op. 71 (1960), No. 5, Op. 74 (1961), No. 6, Op. 95 (1967), No. 7, Op. 113 (1973), No. 8, Op. 124 (1979); *Toy Symphony*, Op. 62 (1957); Sym. for Brass, Op. 123 (1979); Concs.; cl., No. 1, Op. 20 (1951), No. 2, Op. 115 (1974); fl., No. 1, with str., Op. 45 (1954), No. 2, Op. 111 (1972); guitar, Op. 67 (1961); harmonica, Op. 46 (1954); hn., No. 1, with str., Op. 11 (1947), No. 2, with str., Op. 58 (1956); ob. and str., Op. 39 (1952); org., Op. 47 (1954); pf. duet and str., Op. 32 (1950); 2 pf. (3 hands), Op. 104 (1969); va., Op. 108 (1971), 2 vn. and str., Op. 77 (1962), Fantasy on Theme of John Field, pf., Op. 116 (1975), Serenade, guitar and str., Op. 50 (1957); Serenade, Op. 26 (1950); Symphony for Str., Op. 13 (1947); Sinfonietta No. 1, Op. 48 (1956), No. 2, Op. 65 (1958), No. 3, Op. 81 (1964); A Grand Grand Ov. (3 vacuum cleaners, floor polisher, 4 rifles, and orch.) Op. 57 (1956); Anniversary Ov., Op. 99 (1968); *Beckus the Dandipratt*, Op. 5 (1948); The Fair Field Ov., Op. 110 (1972); Ov., Peterloo, Op. 97 (1968); *Tam O'Shanter*, Op. 51 (1955); Divertimento No. 2, Op. 24 (1952); English Dances, Set I, Op. 27 (1951), Set II, Op. 33 (1951); A Sussex Ov., Op. 31 (1951); Ov., The Smoke, Op. 21 (1948); 4 Scottish Dances, Op. 59 (1957); Suite, Homage to the Queen, Op. 42 (1953); Little Suite No. 1, Op. 53 (1956), No. 2, Op. 78 (1963), Little

Suite for brass band, No. 1, Op. 80 (1963), No. 2, Op. 93 (1966); Water Music, Op. 82b (1965); Concerto for 28 Players, Op. 105 (1970); Flourish, Op. 112 (1973); 4 Cornish Dances, Op. 91 (1966); Philharmonic Conc., Op. 120 (1976); 6 Variations on a Theme of Ruth Gipps, Op. 122 (1977).
CHORAL: Psalm 150, ch. and org., Op. 25 (1950); A John Clare Cantata, Op. 52 (1956); The Return of Odysseus, cantata, ch. and orch. (text by P. Dickinson), Op. 119 (1976).
CHAMBER MUSIC: Divertimento, fl., ob., cl., Op. 37 (1952); Vn. sonatas No. 1, Op. 15 (1947), No. 2, Op. 43 (1953); Quintet, fl., vn., va., hn., bn., Op. 7 (1944); Quintet, 2 tpts., hn., tb., tuba, Op. 73 (1963); Sonatina, recorder and pf., Op. 41 (1953); 3 Shanties, wind quintet, Op. 4 (1943); Trio, fl., va., bn., Op. 6 (1943); Pf. Trio, Op. 54 (1956); Str. Qts., No. 1, Op. 23 (1951), No. 2, Op. 118 (1975); ob. qt., Op. 61 (1957); Trevelyan Suite, wind ens., Op. 93 (1967); Fantasies for solo wind and brass (1965–7); Fantasy, guitar, Op. 107 (1970); Fantasy, harp, Op. 117 (1975); va. sonata, Op. 17 (1948); fl. sonatina, Op. 19 (1948); fl. sonata, Op. 121 (1977); ob. sonatina, Op. 28 (1951); cl. sonatina, Op. 29 (1951).
PIANO: Five by Ten, Books I–V (1952); Variations on a Ukrainian Folk Song, Op. 9 (1948); Children's Suite, Op. 16 (1948).

Arnold, Samuel (*b* London, 1740; *d* London, 1802). Eng. composer. Organist of Chapel Royal and Westminster Abbey; composer to CG Th., proprietor of Marylebone Gardens, cond. of *Academy of Ancient Music. Comp. many popular operas, church mus., etc.; ed. Handel's works in 36 vols. and a supplement to Boyce's Cathedral Music in 4 vols. Comp. 4 numbers in pasticcio The Maid of the Mill (London, 1765).

Aroldo (Harold). Opera in 4 acts by Verdi to libretto by Piave. Comp. 1856–7. Prod. Rimini 1857. Most of mus. is same as that for *Stiffelio (1850), though Act 4 was newly composed and lib. is new.

Aronowitz, Cecil (Solomon) (*b* King William's Town, S. Africa, 1916; *d* Ipswich, 1978). Eng. va. player of Russo-Lithuanian parentage. Studied RCM with Vaughan Williams and G. Jacob (comp.), and A. Rivarde (vn.). After war changed to va. Played in all London professional orchs. and was prin. violist of Boyd Neel Orch., London Mozart Players, and ECO. Founder member, Melos Ens. Frequent chamber mus. player. Prof. of va., RCM 1948–75; Head of Str. Sch., RNCM, 1975–7; Dir. of Str. Studies, Snape Maltings Sch. 1977–8.

Arpa (It.). Harp.

Arpa Doppia (It. 'double harp'). Name given in 16th-cent. Italy to both double-strung and triple-strung harp, probably because of increased range and size. Incl. in Monteverdi's *Orfeo* (1607).

Arpège (Fr., from *arpe*, 'harp'), **Arpeggio** (It., plural *arpeggi*). A chord 'spread', i.e. the notes heard one after the other from the bottom upwards, or sometimes from the top downwards, as on the harp.

Arpeggiare (It.). To play chords as arpeggios. (Present and past participles, *arpeggiando, arpeggiato*.)

Arpeggione (*Guitare d'amour*). Type of guitar-shaped 6-str. vc. with fretted fingerboard, played with a bow. Invented 1823 by G. Staufer. Schubert wrote a sonata for it in 1824 which is normally played on the vc. (also transcr. for va.).

Arraché (Fr.). Torn. Extreme form of *pizzicato*.

Arrangement or **Transcription**. Adaptation of a piece of mus. for a medium other than that for which it was orig. comp. Sometimes 'Transcription' means a rewriting for the same medium but in a style easier to play. (In the USA there appears to be a tendency to use 'Arrangement' for a free treatment of the material and 'Transcription' for a more faithful treatment. In jazz 'Arrangement' tends to signify 'orchestration'.)

Arrau, Claudio (*b* Chillán, Chile, 1903). Chilean pianist. Début Chillán 1908. Studied Santiago Cons., then from 1911 at Berlin with M. Krause. Début Berlin recital, 1914. Prof. of pf., Stern Cons., Berlin, 1925. Won Grand Prix de Genève 1927. London début 1922, USA 1923. Superb interpreter of Chopin, Liszt, Beethoven, Mozart, Schumann, and Brahms. Played all Bach's kbd. mus. in 12 recitals in Berlin, 1935–6.

Arriaga y Balzola, Juan Crisóstomo Jacobo Antonio de (*b* Rigoitia, Bilbao, 1806; *d* Paris, 1826). Sp. composer of great but unfulfilled talent. Opera *Los esclavos felices* (The Happy Slaves) prod. Bilbao, 1820. Studied Paris Cons. 3 str. qts. pubd. Paris, 1824. Also comp. sym.

Arrigo, Girolamo (*b* Palermo, 1930). Sicilian composer. Studied in Palermo 1950–4 (Bellini Cons.) and with Max Deutsch in Paris, 1954–7. Settled in Paris. Vocal mus., film scores, chamber works and *Orden*, a 'collage opera'. Also *Epitaffi* for ch. and orch. (1963), settings of Michelangelo.

Arroyo, Martina (*b* NY, 1936). Amer. sop. Early training in NY. Début NY 1958, then sang at Vienna State Opera and Deutsche Oper, Berlin. Substituted for *Nilsson as Aida at NY Met. 1965. CG début 1968 (Aida). Noted Verdi singer.

Ars Antiqua (Lat.). Old Art. The medieval W. European mus. style, based on plainsong and organum, employed by composers (notably Leonin and Pérotin) of the Notre Dame or Parisian sch. in the 12th and 13th cents. See *Ars Nova*.

Arsin et Thesin, Per. See *Canon*.

Ars Nova (Lat.). New art. The new style of mus. comp. in Fr. and It. in 14th cent. Name derived from tract (*c*.1320) by Philippe de Vitry. Restrictions of *Ars antiqua* were replaced by greater variety of rhythm, duple instead of triple time, and increased independence in part-writing. In Fr. *Machaut was finest exponent of *Ars nova* and in Italy G. da Cascia, J. da Bologna, and Landini. The It. madrigal was a later flowering of *Ars nova*.

Artaria. Austrian firm of mus. publishers founded in Mainz 1765, moving to Vienna 1766. Founders were cousins, Carlo Artaria (1747–1808) and Francesco Artaria (1725–97). Pubd. work by Haydn in 1780, leading to over 300 edns. of his comps. Mozart followed in 1781 and Beethoven in 1783. The firm also pubd. Boccherini, Clementi, Gluck, and Salieri. Firm closed 1858.

Artaxerxes. Thomas *Arne's most successful opera, in 3 acts. Lib. is Eng. trans. of Metastasio. (Prod. London 1762; Dublin 1765; NY 1828.) Many operas on this subject, e.g. by Hasse (1730), Galuppi (1749), Gluck (1741), Paisiello (1771), Piccinni (1762), Sacchini (1768), Cimarosa (1784), and Isouard (1794).

Art de toucher le clavecin, L' (The Art of playing the Harpsichord). Method by F. *Couperin (1716), with instructions and 8 illustrative comps. Known to have influenced Bach.

Articolato (It.), **articulé** (Fr.). Well-articulated; so *articolazione* (It.). Articulation.

Art of Fugue, The (J. S. Bach). See *Kunst der Fuge, Die*.

Art of Playing the Harpsichord (Couperin). See *Art de toucher le clavecin, L'*.

Artôt, Alexandre (Montagney, Joseph) (*b* Brussels, 1815; *d* Ville d'Avray, Paris, 1845). Belg. violinist. Made many world tours. Composer for vn. and for chamber combinations.

Artôt, Désirée (*b* Paris, 1835; *d* Berlin, 1907). Belg. mez., later sop. Studied with Pauline Viardot-García. Sang in opera in London 1859–66. In 1869 married Spanish bar. Mariano Padilla y Ramos, with whom she often sang. Their daughter Lola Artôt de Padilla (*b* Sèvres, 1876; *d* Berlin, 1933) was member of the Berlin Hofoper company from 1909 and sang the role of Oktavian at the first Berlin perf. of *Der Rosenkavalier*. Created Vreli in Delius's *A Village Romeo and Juliet*, Berlin 1907.

Arts Council of Great Britain. Independent body est. 1945 as successor to wartime Council for the Encouragement of Music and the Arts. Incorporated by Royal Charter 1946 'to preserve and improve standards of performance in the various arts'. New charter granted 1967. Annual grant-in-aid is provided through Dept. of Education and Science. Members, limited to 20, are appointed for periods not exceeding 5 years by the Minister responsible after consultation with the Secretaries of State for Scotland and Wales. Professional staff, under secretary-general, incl. mus. dir. Specialist advisory panels incl. one for mus. Subsidies are disbursed to many organizations, being channelled through certain independent bodies and regional arts assoc. Headquarters in London, but there are separate committees with executive powers for Scotland and Wales (Scottish and Welsh Arts Councils), each with dir. and ass. dirs. for individual arts, incl. mus.

Arundell, Dennis (Drew) (*b* London, 1898). Eng. actor, author, translator, and composer, but best known as opera producer. Educated Tonbridge and Cambridge (M.A., B.Mus.). Prod. first stage perf. of Handel's *Semele*, Cambridge 1925. Also Stravinsky's *The Soldier's Tale* (Cambridge, 1928), Honegger's *King David* (Cambridge, 1929), Purcell's *Fairy Queen* (1931), and Vaughan Williams's *The Pilgrim's Progress* (Cambridge 1954). Many prods. for SW Opera incl. Janáček's *Káťa Kabanová* (1951). Radio prods. of Stravinsky's *The Rake's Progress* and Benjamin's *Tale of Two Cities*. Eng. trans. of Ravel's *L'Enfant et les sortilèges* and Honegger's *Jeanne d'Arc au bûcher*.

A.S. *Al segno.*

As (Ger.). The note A♭.

Asaf'yev, Boris (*b* St Petersburg, 1884; *d* Moscow, 1949). Russ. composer, pupil of Lyadov and Rimsky-Korsakov. Chief reputation as composer of ballets, but wrote 10 operas and 5 syms. Under pseudonym Igor Glebov wrote criticism and books, incl. monograph on Stravinsky (1929).

Asas (Ases) (Ger.). The note A♭♭.

Ascanio in Alba. *Serenata teatrale* in 2 acts by boy Mozart to lib. by Parini (Milan, 17 Oct. 1771).

A.S.C.A.P. American Society of Composers, Authors and Publishers. Founded 1914.

Ascension, L' (The Ascension). Comp. in 4 movements by *Messiaen, for orch. (1933) and for org. (1934). The movements are 1. *Majesté du Christ demandant sa gloire à son Père*. 2. *Alléluias sereins d'une âme qui désire le ciel*. 3. *Alléluia sur la trompette, alléluia sur la cymbale*. 4. *Prière du Christ montant vers son Père*. 3rd movement of orch. version differs from that in the organ version, which is entitled *Transports de Joie d'une âme devant la gloire du Christ*. F.p. orch. version, Paris 1935.

Ashdown Ltd., Edwin. London mus. publishing firm (founded 1860), successors to Wessel and Stodart (dating from 1825).

Ashkenazy, Vladimir (*b* Gorky, 1937). Russ. pianist and cond. Studied at Moscow State Cons. with Lev Oborin. Winner Queen Elisabeth Prize, Brussels, 1956; joint winner Tchaikovsky competition, Moscow 1962. Toured USA 1958. London début 1963. Later settled in Eng., but now divides time between Iceland and Switzerland. One of finest pianists of post-1950 generation.

Ashton, Algernon (Bennet Langton) (*b* Durham, 1859; *d* London, 1937). Eng. composer, pianist, and teacher. Studied Leipzig Cons. with Reinecke, and with Raff at Frankfurt. Prof. of pf. RCM 1885–1910. Comp. 5 syms., concs., chamber mus. Also pubd. 2 vols. of his letters to the press on every possible subject. Known also for his exploration of London cemeteries, with frequent agitation for repair of tombstones of great men.

Ashton, (Sir) **Frederick** (William) (*b* Guayaquil, Ecuador, 1904). Eng. choreog. Associated with SW (now Royal) Ballet since 1936. Ballets incl. *Symphonic Variations, La Fille mal gardée, Façade, Horoscope, Ondine, Sylvia, Romeo and Juliet, Cinderella* (first 3-act ballet choreog. by Englishman), *Enigma Variations, A Month in the Country*. C.B.E. 1950, C.H. 1970, O.M. 1977. Knighted 1962.

Askenase, Stefan (*b* Lwów, Poland, 1896; *d* Cologne, 1985). Polish-born pianist, later Belg. citizen. Trained in Lwów and Vienna. Prof. of pf., Royal Cons., Brussels 1954–61. Noted Chopin player.

Asola, Giovanni Matteo (*b* Verona, ?1532; *d* Venice, 1609). It. composer. Cath. appointments in Treviso 1577, and Vicenza 1578. Became chaplain in Venice 1582. Influenced by Giovanni Gabrieli and Palestrina. Comp. book of madrigals for 2 vv. in strict canon throughout.

Aspull, George (*b* Manchester, 1813; *d* Leamington, 1832). Eng. pianist who gave f.p. in Eng. of Weber's *Konzertstück*.

Asrael. Title of Sym. in C minor, Op. 27, by *Suk, comp. 1906. Asrael is the Angel of Death. Begun as memorial to Dvořák, Suk's father-in-law, in 1904, became memorial also to Suk's wife who died 18 months after her father. Contains quotation from Dvořák's *Requiem*.

Assai (It.). Very, extremely (formerly synonymous with Fr. *assez*, but respective meanings have changed).

Assassinio nella cattedrale, L' (Murder in the Cathedral). Opera in 2 acts by Pizzetti to lib. adapted by A. Castelli from play by T. S. Eliot (1935). Prod. Milan 1958.

Assemble All Ye Maidens. No. 7 of Holst's 7 *Partsongs* Op. 44 for female vv. and str. to words by Robert Bridges, and often perf. separately. Has part for solo sop. F.p. London 1927.

Assez (Fr.). Enough, but the usual and best translation is 'fairly', e.g. *assez vite*, Fairly quick.

Associated Board of the Royal Schools of Music. Founded 1889, partly to combat effect of numerous spurious examining bodies, being a combination, for the conduct of local and sch. examinations, of the RAM, RCM, and also (since 1972) the RNCM, Manchester, and the RSAM.

Assoluto (It.). Absolute, free, alone. As in *prima donna (ballerina) assoluta.*

Aston (Ashton, Aystoun, etc.), **Hugh** (*b* c.1485; *d* 1558). Eng. composer of church and virginal mus., and pioneer of true instr. style. Master of choristers, St Mary Newarke Coll., Leicester 1525-48. Kbd. writing well in advance of his time.

Aston, Peter (George) (*b* Edgbaston, 1938). Eng. composer, cond., and teacher. Lecturer, York Univ. 1964-74. Prof. of music, Univ. of E. Anglia, since 1974. Cond. Aldeburgh Fest. Singers since 1975. Ed. complete works of George *Jeffreys. Works incl. *Sacrapane the Sorcerer*, children's opera (1969), *My Dancing Day*, cantata (1969), *5 Songs of Crazy Jane* (Yeats), for sop. solo (1960), *Haec Dies*, mixed vv. and org. (1971), *3 Pieces* for ob. (1968), and many choral works and part-songs.

Astorga, Baron d' (Emanuele Gioacchino Cesare Rincón) (*b* Augusta, Sicily, 1680; *d* ?Madrid, c.1757). Sp.-It. singer, harpsichordist, and composer, especially of chamber cantatas and of a *Stabat Mater* (f.p. London 1752). His opera *Dafni* was prod. Genoa 1709.

Atalanta in Calydon. 'Choral sym.' for vv. only by Bantock (Manchester 1912), poem by Swinburne (1865). Comp. 1911.

A.T.C.L. Associate of *Trinity College of Music, London.

Atempause (Ger.). Breath pause. Very slight pause on a weak beat in order to give greater effect to the following strong beat.

A tempo (It.). In time. Denotes reversion to speed at beginning of piece or movement after a deviation.

Athalia. Oratorio by Handel to lib. by S. Humphreys, after Racine. Rev. 1735 and 1756. (F.p. Oxford 1733).

Athalie. Mendelssohn's incidental mus. to Racine's drama (Op. 74; 1843-5). Ov. and *War March of the Priests* are the parts usually heard today.

Atherton, David (*b* Blackpool, 1944). Eng. cond. Studied Cambridge Univ. Début at CG 1968, Scala, Milan 1976, San Francisco 1978. Mus. dir. and founder London Sinfonietta 1968-73. Youngest ever cond. at Henry Wood Proms., 1968. Prin. cond. RLPO 1980-3. Mus. dir. San Diego S.O. from 1981.

Atkins, (Sir) **Ivor** (Algernon) (*b* Llandaff, 1869; *d* Worcester, 1953). Eng. organist, composer, and cond. Organist Worcester Cath. 1897-1950. Cond. Worcester Fests.; composer of choral works,

e.g. *Hymn of Faith*. Ed. with Elgar of Bach's *St Matthew Passion* (1911). Knighted 1921.

Atlántida (Atlantis). *Cantata escénica* by *Falla in prol. and 3 parts, text being poem by Jacinto Verdaguer adapted by Falla. Begun 1926 and left unfinished in 1946. Rev. and completed in first version by Ernesto *Halffter, Barcelona 1961 (staged Milan 1962), Edinburgh 1962. Halffter's 2nd (concert) version f.p. Lucerne 1976.

Atlas, Dalia (*b* Haifa, 1933). Israeli cond. and pianist. Studied Haifa Cons., Israel Acad. of Mus., and with Celibidache and Swarowsky. Cond., Haifa Chamber Orch. from 1963. Guest cond. BBC Northern S.O. from 1964, RLPO 1964, Houston S.O. 1976, and other leading orchs.

Atmosphères (Atmosphere). Work for orch. by *Ligeti, comp. 1961, f.p. Donaueschingen, cond. Rosbaud, 1961.

Atonal. Not in any key, hence atonality. *Schoenberg preferred the term pantonal, denoting synthesis of all keys. Atonality is usually applied where there is no tonal centre and the notes of the chromatic scale are used impartially: the 12 notes of the octave function independently, unrelated to a key centre. Atonality is foreshadowed in the mus. of Debussy and Skryabin, even Liszt, but can perhaps be dated from the finale of Schoenberg's 2nd str. qt. (1908). From atonality there developed the *twelve-note system. With atonality, consonances and dissonances of trad. harmony no longer apply.

A.T.S.C. Associate, Tonic Sol-fa College of Music.

Attacca (It.). Attack! (imperative). Used at the end of a movement to mean 'Start the next movement without a break'.

Attacco. Very short *motif* used as material for imitation or as fugue subject (see *Andamento*).

Attaignant, Pierre (*b* ?Donai, c.1494; *d* Paris, 1552). Fr. mus. printer and publisher. Experimented for years with music types. In 1527-8 produced *Chansons nouvelles* in a diamond-shaped notation, with staff segments attached, which required only one impression. This halved the printing time and led to cheap printed mus. From 1537 was official printer of the King's mus. First publisher to achieve a European distribution.

Attaque (Fr.). Attack. The *Chef d'attaque* in an orch. is the leader (Amer. 'Concert-master').

Atterberg, Kurt (*b* Gothenburg, 1887; *d* Stockholm, 1974). Swed. composer and writer on mus., subsidized by the Swed. Govt. Mus. critic, *Stockholms Tidningen* 1919-57. Composer of 5 operas, 5 concs., and 9 syms. of which the 6th won the £2,000 prize offered by Columbia Graphophone Co. in the centenary year of Schubert's death (1928). Sec. RAM, Stockholm, 1940-53.

Attey, John (d Ross-on-Wye, 1640). Eng. composer who pubd. a book of lute songs in 1622 (the last of such publications to appear).

At The Boar's Head. Opera in 1 act about Falstaff by Holst to lib. adapted by composer from Shakespeare's *Henry IV Parts 1 and 2*. Music based largely on folk tunes. Comp. 1924. (Prod. Manchester 1925; NY 1935).

Attila. Opera in 3 acts with prol., by Verdi to lib. by Solera. Verdi's 9th opera. Comp. 1845–6. (Prod. Venice 1846; London 1848; NY 1850). Revived in 1951 (concert perf.) after long neglect; staged Florence, 1962, SW 1963.

Attwood, Thomas (b London, 1765; d London, 1838). Eng. composer and org. Boy chorister in Chapel Royal; pupil in Vienna of Mozart; host and friend in London of Mendelssohn; org. St Paul's Cath., 1796–1838; composer of th. and church mus. One of first profs. at RAM, 1823. Founder-member of Philharmonic Soc., 1813.

Atzmon, Moshe (b Budapest, 1931). Hung.-born cond. Studied Tel Aviv Cons. and Acad. of Mus., and GSM. First prize, Liverpool Int. Cond. Competition, 1964. Chief cond., Sydney S.O. 1969–71. Cond. N. Ger. Radio S.O. 1972–6. Chief cond. Basle S.O. Guest cond. of world's leading orchs. Opera début, Berlin 1969.

Aubade (Fr., from *Aube*, dawn). Early morning music, likewise *Serenade—evening music.

Aubade Héroïque (Heroic dawn). Orch. work by *Lambert, f.p. 1942, inspired by composer's witnessing dawn invasion of The Hague by Ger. parachutists in 1940.

Auber, Daniel (François Esprit) (b Caen, 1782; d Paris, 1871). Fr. composer. Pupil of Cherubini. In youth, in business in London; then prominent in Paris as composer of instr. mus., and later of operas in which he collab. with the dramatist Scribe. Wrote in all 49 operas, of which the best known are *La Bergère châtelaine* (1820), *La Muette de Portici* (*Masaniello*) (1828), *Fra Diavolo* (1830), *Le Cheval de bronze* (1835), *Le Domino noir* (1837), *Les Diamants de la couronne* (1841), and *Manon Lescaut* (1856). From 1842 to 1870 was head of Paris Cons. and in 1852 mus. dir. to Napoleon III.

Aubert, Jacques (b Paris, 1689; d Belleville, 1753). Fr. violinist and composer of mus. for vn. and for the stage. Wrote several vn. sonatas with bass, 10 concs. for 4 vn. and bass, opera, and short pieces.

Aubin, Tony (Louis Alexandre) (b Paris, 1907; d Paris, 1981). Fr. composer and cond., pupil of Dukas. Won *Prix de Rome* 1930. Prof. of comp., Paris Cons., 1945. 2 syms., choral works, film mus., str. qt., etc.

Auden, W(ystan) **H**(ugh) (b York, 1907; d Vienna, 1973). Eng.-born poet (later Amer. citizen) and librettist. Wrote lib. for Britten's first opera *Paul Bunyan* (1941) and, with Chester Kallman, for Stravinsky's *The *Rake's Progress* (1951), and Henze's *Elegy for Young Lovers* (1961) and *The *Bassarids* (1966).

Audran, Edmond (b Lyons, 1840; d Tierceville, 1901). Fr. organist at Marseilles and composer first of church mus. and later (with great success) of comic operas such as *La Mascotte* (1880), and *La Poupée* (1896).

Auer, Leopold (b Veszprém, Hung., 1845; d Loschwitz, Dresden, 1930). Hung. violinist and teacher. Pupil of Joachim and others. Played in Ger. orchs. until in 1868 he became head of the vn. dept. of St Petersburg Cons., a post he held until 1917. Tchaikovsky dedicated his vn. conc. to him, but he refused it, saying the work was unplayable in its orig. form. Among his pupils were Heifetz, Zimbalist, and Elman.

Auf (Ger.). On, etc., e.g. *Auf der G* (like It. *Sul G*), means On the G (str.).

Auf einer Gondel (On a gondola). Title given by *Mendelssohn to 3 of his *Lieder ohne Worte*: Op. 19, No. 6 in G minor, Book I (1834); Op. 30, No. 12 in F♯ minor, Book II (1835), and Op. 62, No. 29 in A minor, Book VI (1843).

Aufforderung zum Tanz (Weber). See *Invitation to the Dance*.

Aufführung (Ger., from *Aufführen*, to perform). Performance. *Aufführungspraxis* is the practicalities of perf., particularly in relation to old mus. where a composer's directions were often lacking in explicit detail.

Auflage (Ger.). Edition.

Auflösen (Ger.). To loosen, release, etc. (1) To resolve a discord.
(2) In harp playing, to lower again a str. which has been raised in pitch. (Hence the noun *Auflösung, Auflösungszeichen*, release-sign).
(3) The sign for the natural (♮).

Aufschlag (Ger.). Up-beat (down-beat being *Niederschlag*).

Aufschnitt (Ger.). Slit, i.e. portion omitted, a cut (in a score, etc.).

Aufschwung (Ger.). Up-soaring, flight, e.g. *Mit Aufschwung*, in a lofty (impassioned) spirit.

Aufstieg und Fall der Stadt Mahagonny (Weill). See *Rise and Fall of the City of Mahagonny*.

Aufstrich (Ger.). Up-bow (in str. playing; down-bow being *Niederstrich*).

Auftakt (Ger.). Up-beat (down-beat being *Niederschlag*).

Aufzug (Ger.). Raising (of curtain). Act (of stage work).

Augengläser (Ger.). Eye-glasses. Word used by Beethoven on title-page of his duet for vn. and vc.—'mit 2 Augengläser obbligato', being a jocular reference to the 2 spectacled players for whom it was comp.

Augenlicht, Das (Eyesight). Setting by *Webern, Op. 26, for mixed ch. and orch. of text by Hildegard Jone. Comp. 1935. Pubd. 1938. F.p. London 1938, cond. Scherchen.

Augmentation and Diminution. In melodic parts, the respective lengthening and shortening of the time-values of the notes. Thus, in a fugue, the subject may (especially towards the end) appear in longer notes, a device which adds dignity and impressiveness.

Augmentation, Canon by. When the imitating vv. in a *canon are in longer notes than that which they are imitating. Canon by diminution is the reverse process.

Augmented Intervals. If any perfect or major *interval is increased by a semitone it becomes augmented. Thus:

Augmented 1st: C up to C♯
    ,,   2nd: C up to D♯
    ,,   4th: C up to F♯
    ,,   5th: C up to G♯, with harmonic implication of major 3rd, e.g. augmented 5th chord on C = C – E – G♯
    ,,   6th: C up to A♯.

Chords of augmented 6th are chromatic. The 3 most common are as follows (e.g. in key of C):

   (a)   (b)   (c)

(a) Chord of the Italian 6th: A♭ – C – F♯
(b) Chord of French 6th: A♭ – C – D – F♯
(c) Chord of the German 6th: A♭ – C – E♭ – F♯

The Ger. 6th is the commonest and serves as a convenient pivot for modulation, since it may be approached as based on the flattened submediant in one key, and quitted as based on the flattened supertonic in another (or vice versa); also, by enharmonic change (see *Interval*), it can be transformed into the chord of the Dominant 7th of another key, and so quitted (e.g. the Ger. 6th in key C (A♭ – C – E♭ – F♯) can be treated as the chord of the Dominant 7th in key D♭ (A♭ – C – E♭ – G♭)).

There are other possibilities.

Augmented 8th: C up to next C♯ but one.

Augmented Triad. A triad of which the 5th is augmented (and so in a diminished triad, the 5th is diminished).

Augusteo. Rome concert-hall, opened in 1908, built on the ruins of the mausoleum of Augustus.

Auld Lang Syne. The poem is a re-casting by Robert Burns (pubd. in final form 1794) of a popular song (probably orig. a folk-song) then current in various versions. The tune now current is sometimes stated to be by *Shield; something like it appeared in his opera *Rosina*, as a part of the ov. (CG 1783), where it is treated to imitate Scottish bagpipe mus. *Sir Alexr. Don's Strathspey* (issued possibly a year later than the perf. of Shield's opera) seems to have strong claim to be the orig.; it may have already been known to Shield, who was brought up at Durham, not far from the Scottish border. The air, like many Scots tunes, is based on the pentatonic scale. It has been proposed as the 'hidden theme' in Elgar's *Enigma Variations*, but the composer denied it.

Aulos. Ancient Gr. wind instr. with double reed, used to accompany the dithyramb in the orgiastic rites of Dionysus.

Auric, Georges (*b* Lodève, Hérault, Fr., 1899; *d* Paris, 1983). Fr. composer. Studied Paris Cons. and Schola Cantorum (pupil of d'Indy). Youngest member of *Les *Six*. Wrote for Diaghilev ballet in 1920s and worked as mus. critic. Gen. admin., Paris Opéra and Opéra Comique 1962–8. Works incl. operas, ballets (notably *Les Matelots*, 1925), film mus., orch. works, pf. sonata, songs etc.

Aurora's Wedding. The divertissement of the last act, perf. separately, of ballet *The Sleeping Beauty* (mus. by Tchaikovsky) supplemented by extra numbers based on Diaghilev's London prod. 1921. F.p. Paris 1922.

Aurresku. A type of Basque folk dance. The *zortziko forms part of it.

Aus den Sieben Tagen (From the Seven Days). 15 comps. by *Stockhausen (1968) for varying ens. for upwards of 3 musicians. Each piece has a verse or text to suggest a mood the players must create, a way of playing, combinations of both, etc., e.g. No. 14 *Goldstaub* (Gold Dust) for small ens.: 'Live completely alone for 4 days without food in complete silence, without much movement. Sleep as little as necessary, think as little as possible. After 4 days, late at night, without talking beforehand, play single sounds WITHOUT THINKING what you are playing. Close your eyes. Just listen.' The 15 items are 1. *Richtige Dauern* (Right Durations), about 4 players; 2. *Unbegrenzt* (Unlimited), ens.; 3. *Verbindung* (Union), ens.; 4. *Treffpunkt* (Rendezvous), ens.; 5. *Nachtmusik* (Night Music), ens.; 6. *Abwärts* (Downwards) ens.; 7. *Aufwärts* (Upwards), ens.; 8. *Oben und Unten* (High and Low), th. piece for man, woman, child, 4 instr.; 9. *Intensität* (Intensity), ens.; 10. *Setz die Segel zur Sonne* (Set sail for the Sun), ens.; 11. *Kommunion* (Communion), ens.; 12. *Litanei* (Litany), speaker or ch.; 13. *Es* (E♭), ens.; 14. *Goldstaub* (Gold Dust), small ens.; 15. *Ankunft* (Arrival), speaker or speaking ch.

Ausdruck (Ger.). Expression. Hence *ausdrucksvoll*, expressively.

Ausfüllgeiger (Ger.). Filling-out fiddler. A *Ripieno* violinist.

Ausgabe (Ger.). Out-giving. Edition.

Ausgehalten (Ger.). Held out, i.e. Sustained.

Aushalten (Ger.). To hold out, i.e. To sustain; so *aushaltungszeichen*, holding-out sign, i.e. pause.

Aus Italien (From Italy). Symphonic Fantasia in 4 movements by Richard Strauss, Op. 16, his first orch. work with pictorial background. Comp. 1886. F.p. Munich 1887. Finale quotes Denza's *Funiculì, Funiculà*.

Aus meinem Leben (From my Life; Cz. *Z mého života*). Sub-title of Smetana's Str. Qt. No. 1 in E minor (1876), an avowedly autobiographical work.

Austin, Frederic (*b* London, 1872; *d* London, 1952). Eng. bar. and composer. Opera début CG 1908 as Gunther in *The Ring* under Richter. Prin. bar., Beecham Opera. Sang Peachum in his own highly successful version of *The *Beggar's Opera*, 1920. Art dir., BNOC, 1924. Comp. sym., symphonic poem, choral works.

Austin, Richard (*b* Birkenhead, 1903). Eng. cond. Trained RCM under Boult and Sargent and in Milan 1922–6. Cond. Carl Rosa Opera and then Bournemouth Municipal Orch. 1934–40. Mus. dir. New Era Concert Soc. 1947–57. Prof. RCM from 1946. Son of Frederic *Austin.

Austin, Sumner (Francis) (*b* Anerley, Kent, 1888; *d* Oxford, 1981). Eng. bar. and opera prod. Carl Rosa 1919, then with O'Mara Opera Co. Sang at Old Vic and SW from 1920s to 1940. Prod. many SW operas, also first Eng. prod. of *Wozzeck at CG 1952.

Austral, Florence (née Wilson) (*b* Richmond, Melbourne, 1894; *d* Newcastle, N.S.W., 1968). Australian sop. Brünnhilde for BNOC in *Die Walküre*, CG 1922, and later in complete *Ring* cycles in London and on tour. Also a fine Isolde and Aida.

Austria. Name under which the Austrian 'Emperor's Hymn', comp. by Haydn, is found in many hymnals.

Auszug (Ger.). (1) Extract.
(2) Arrangement.

Authentic Cadence. See *Cadence*.

Authentic Modes. See *Modes*.

Autoharp. Type of easily-played *zither, played with the fingers or a plectrum. Chords are prod. by depressing keys.

Auxcousteaux (Hautcousteaux), **Artus** (*b* ?Amiens, 1590; *d* Paris, 1654). Fr. composer of church mus. and secular songs. Singer in chapel of Louis XIII 1613–27 and later dir. of mus., St Quentin Cath.

Auxiliary Note. This may be described as a variety of *Passing Note which, instead of passing on to another note, passes *back* to the note it has just left. Such a note may, like a Passing Note, be either diatonic or chromatic. Shakes, *Mordents, and Turns offer examples of the Auxiliary Note applied decoratively.

Avant-garde (Fr. 'vanguard'). Term used in the arts to denote those who make a radical departure from tradition. In 20th cent. mus., Stockhausen may be regarded as *avant-garde*, but not Shostakovich.

Aveling, Valda (*b* Sydney, N.S.W., 1920). Australian pianist, harpsichordist, and teacher. Studied N.S.W. State Cons., Sydney. Début Sydney 1938. Settled in Eng. Duo with Evelyn *Barbirolli, co-recitalist with Menuhin, Joan Sutherland, etc.

Ave Maria (Hail Mary). Prayer consisting partly of the biblical salutations of the Archangel Gabriel and Elizabeth to the Virgin Mary, and partly of matter added in the 15th cent. Many settings, that by Schubert being to a Ger. trans. of Walter Scott's poem from 'The Lady of the Lake' (1810). That known as by 'Bach-Gounod' is the first prelude from Bach's *Wohltemperierte Klavier* with Gounod's *Méditation* as counterpoint, the words having been added by someone else.

Ave Maris Stella (Hail, Star of the Sea). Hymn of R.C. Church.

Ave Regina Coelorum. See *Antiphons of the Blessed Virgin Mary*.

Ave Verum Corpus (Hail, true body). Hymn (anonymous and of unknown date) possessing its own plainsong and also frequently set by composers (Desprès, Byrd, Mozart, Cherubini, S. Wesley, Gounod, Elgar, etc.), such motet settings being frequently sung in the Roman office of Benediction. Translations sometimes begin *Jesu, Word of God Incarnate, Jesu, Blessed Word of God Incarnate,* or *Word of God Incarnate*.

Avidom, Menahem (orig. Mahler-Kalkstein) (*b* Stanislawow, Poland, 1908). Polish-born Israeli composer and sec.-gen. of Israel P.O. Studied in Beirut and Paris, settled Tel Aviv 1935. Wrote 9 syms., 5 operas, concs. Mus. critic, *Jerusalem Post* 1958–73.

Avison, Charles (*b* Newcastle upon Tyne, 1709; *d* Newcastle upon Tyne, 1770). Eng. composer; pupil in London of *Geminiani; organist of parish church of his native town from 1736; composer of 60 concs. for str. orch., 3 vols. of sonatas for hpd. and vn., and author of much-discussed *Essay on Musical Expression* (1752).

Avison Edition. Edn. of works by Brit. composers, prod. by certain publishers under the auspices of Soc. of Brit. Composers between 1905 and 1918.

Avoided Cadence. See *Cadence*.

Ax, Emanuel (*b* Lwów, 1949). Polish-born Amer. pianist. Studied Warsaw and Juilliard Sch., NY. Has lived in USA since 1961. 1st prize, 1st Rubinstein comp., Israel, 1974. NY début 1973, London 1977. Noted Chopin-player, also interpreter of Ravel, Bartók, and Schoenberg.

Axman, Emil (*b* Ratay, Moravia, 1887; *d* Prague, 1949). Cz. composer of 6 syms., sonatas, 4 str. qts., choral works. Pupil of Novák.

Ayre. Medieval spelling of 'Air', a type of Eng. song written by *Dowland and others, less contrapuntal than a madrigal, being more like a strophic song, with vocal or instr. (usually lute) acc., pubd. in a large book around which the performers could gather.

Ayrton, Edmund (*b* Ripon, 1734; *d* Westminster, 1808). Eng. organist and composer. Master of Children of Chapel Royal 1780–1805. His son William (*b* London, 1777; *d* London, 1858) was a mus. critic and a founder of the Philharmonic Soc.

B

B. 7th degree of natural scale of C. So B♭, B♭♭, B♮, B♯, B♯♯, B major, B minor etc. In Ger., B = B♭ and B♮ = B♭♭. The Eng. note B is represented in Ger. by H (hence composers can write fantasias on the name BACH, the notes being B♭-A-C-B♮. J. S. Bach himself used these notes in the unfinished final fugue of *The Art of Fugue*).

Baal Shem. Suite for vn. and pf. by Bloch, comp. 1923, subtitled '3 pictures of Chassidic Life'. Baal Shem Tov (Master of the Good Name) founded the Jewish sect of Chassidism in 17th cent. Movements are *Vidui* (Contrition), *Nigun* (Improvisation), and *Simchas Torah* (Rejoicing). Version with orch., 1939.

Babar le petit éléphant, Histoire de (Story of Babar the little elephant). Narration for v. and pf. by Poulenc to text by Jean de Brunhof. Comp. 1940–5. Version with orch. by *Francaix, 1962.

Babbitt, Milton (*b* Philadelphia, 1916). Amer. composer and mathematician. Studied at Princeton Univ. and with Roger *Sessions. On staff at Princeton since 1938, becoming Conant Prof. of Mus. His comps. developed from the 12-note system of Schoenberg and Webern, later employing elec. devices such as synthesizers and tape. Author of articles and monographs on Bartók qts., elec. mus., Varèse, and Schoenberg. Works incl.:

ORCH: *Relata I* (1965), *II* (1968); *Concerti*, vn., orch., tape (1974–6).
CHAMBER MUSIC: *Composition for 4 instruments* (1948); Str. Qts.: No. 1 (1950), No. 2 (1954), No. 3 (1969–70), No. 4 (1970); Woodwind Qt. (1953).
CHORAL: *Music for the Mass* (1941); 4 *Canons* (1969); *More Phenomena* (1977).
PIANO: *3 Compositions* (1947); *Partitions* (1957); *Post-Partitions* (1966); *Reflections*, with tape (1974).
ELECTRONIC: *Composition for Synthesizer* (1961); *Philomel*, sop., recorded sop., and syn. (1964); *Correspondences*, string orch. and syn. (1967); *Phenomena*, sop. and tape (1974).

Babell, William (*b* Canonbury, *c*.1690; *d* Canonbury, 1723). Eng. organist, harpsichordist, violinist, and composer for his instrs. Noted for his virtuoso hpd. arrs. of operatic arias and for the embellishments in his sonatas.

Babin, Victor (*b* Moscow, 1908; *d* Cleveland, Ohio, 1972). Russ.-born pianist and composer. Studied in Berlin with Schnabel and Schreker. Settled in USA 1937. Dir., Cleveland Institute of Mus. from 1961. Famous pf. duo with his wife,

Vitya *Vronsky, whom he married 1933. Works incl. 2-pf. conc., *Konzertstück* for vn. and orch., str. qt., songs, etc.

Babi-Yar. Sub-title of Shostakovich's Sym. No. 13 in B♭ minor, Op. 113, for bass, bass ch., and orch., to poems by Yevtushenko. Comp. and f.p. 1962. Babi-Yar was site of grave of thousands of Russ. Jews, murdered by Germans in World War II.

Baccaloni, Salvatore (*b* Rome, 1900; *d* NY, 1969). It. operatic bass (Rome 1922; La Scala 1926; CG 1928; Chicago 1930; Glyndebourne 1936–9; NY Met. 1940) outstanding as Leporello, Don Pasquale, Osmin, and similar comic roles.

Bacchanale (Fr., from Lat. *Bacchanalia*, a feast of dancing and singing in honour of Bacchus, god of wine). An orgiastic comp., as in the Venusberg scene of Wagner's *Tannhäuser* and in Saint-Saëns's *Samson et Dalila*.

Bacchetta (It.). Stick. (1) Drumstick. (2) Baton. The plural is *bacchette*—e.g. *bacchette di legno*, wooden drumsticks; *bacchette di spugna*, sponge-headed drumsticks.

Bacchus et Ariane (Bacchus and Ariadne). Ballet in 2 acts with mus. by *Roussel, choreog. Lifar, comp. 1930 and prod. Paris 1931. 2 orch. suites were extracted, the 2nd being the more popular.

Baccusi, Ippolito (*b* Mantua, *c*.1550; *d* Verona, 1609). It. madrigalist and church musician. Choirmaster, Verona Cath. from 1592. One of first composers to recommend instr. doubling of vocal parts.

Bacewicz, Grazyna (*b* Łódź, 1909; *d* Warsaw, 1969). Polish violinist and composer. Studied Warsaw Cons., Warsaw Univ., and in Paris with Nadia Boulanger. Vn. pupil of Flesch. Taught at Łódź Cons. 1934–5, 1945; Warsaw Acad. of Mus. 1966–9. Wrote 4 syms., 7 vn. concs., 7 str. qts., 2 vc. concs., va. conc., pf. conc., 5 vn. sonatas, 2 pf. quintets, etc.

Bach (Family). The Bach family lived from the early 16th cent. in the Thuringian duchies of Saxe-Weimar-Eisenach, Saxe-Coburg-Gotha, and Saxe-Meiningen and the principality of Schwarzburg-Arnstadt. Their profession was mus.—there are records that 53 Bachs held posts as organists, cantors, or town musicians over a span of 300 years. J. S. Bach himself compiled a genealogy of his family, which began, as far as his own line was concerned, with Veit Bach (*d* 1619), a miller with a passion for lute-playing. Other prin.

BACH 36

members of the family up to J. S. Bach's time were:

Hans Bach (*b* c.1550; *d* 1626). Violinist, son of Veit, and known as *Der Spielmann* (The Player). Carpet-weaver by trade. Johann Bach (*b* 1604; *d* 1673). Eldest son of Hans. Organist at Schweinfurt and Erfurt. Christoph Bach (*b* 1613; *d* 1661). 2nd son of Hans. Organist and composer. Town-musician at Eisenach. Heinrich Bach (*b* Wechmar, 1615; *d* Arnstadt, 1692). 3rd son of Hans. Arnstadt church organist for 51 years. Johann Christian Bach (*b* Erfurt, 1640; *d* Erfurt, 1682). Eldest son of Johann. Served under his father among town musicians of Erfurt but became first of family to settle at Eisenach where he married. Returned to Erfurt to succeed his father 1671. Johann Egidius Bach (*b* 1645; *d* 1716). 2nd son of Johann. Organist at Erfurt and composer of church mus., also va.-player. Georg Christoph Bach (*b* Eisenach, 1642; *d* 1697). Eldest son of Christoph. Cantor at Schweinfurt. Composer. Johann Christoph Bach (1) (*b* Arnstadt, 1642; *d* Eisenach, 1703). Eldest son of Heinrich. Became organist at Eisenach at age 23 in 1665. Considered by C. P. E. Bach as 'great and expressive' composer. Many elaborate and progressive vocal works, also instr. comps. 2 motets for double ch., *Herr nun Lassest* and *Ich lasse dich nicht* are extremely fine. Johann Michael Bach (*b* Arnstadt, 1648; *d* Gehren, 1694). Brother of preceding. Organist and parish clerk of Gehren from 1673 until his death. Maker of vns. and hpds. His motets have high merit. The youngest of his 5 daughters, Maria Barbara (*b* 20 Oct. 1684) became J. S. Bach's first wife. Johann Ambrosius Bach (*b* Erfurt, 1645; *d* Eisenach, 1695). 2nd (twin) son of Christoph. Played vn. and va. in addition to org. One of Erfurt *compagnie* of musicians from 1667 until Oct. 1671 when he succeeded his cousin, Johann Christian, at Eisenach. There the youngest of his 8 children, Johann Sebastian, was born on 21 Mar. 1685. Johann Christoph Bach (2) (*b* Erfurt, 1645; *d* Arnstadt, 1693). Twin brother of Johann Ambrosius. Court violinist at Arnstadt, where he was *Hofmusikus* and *Stadtpfeifer*. Johann Jakob Bach (*b* Wolfsbehringen, 1655; *d* Ruhla, 1718). Org. in Thal, cantor in Steinbach. Johann Bernard Bach (*b* Erfurt, 1676; *d* Eisenach, 1749). Son of Johann Egidius. Organist at Erfurt and Magdeburg. In 1703 succeeded cousin Johann Christoph (1) at Eisenach and became *Kammermusikus* in court orch. of Duke of Saxe-Eisenach. Instr. comps. admired and perf. at Leipzig by Johann Sebastian. Johann Nikolaus Bach (*b* Eisenach, 1669; *d* Eisenach, 1753). Eldest son of Johann Christoph (1). University and town organist at Jena from 1695 until death. Org.-builder and maker of hpds., to which he contributed some improvements. Comp. orch. suites, church mus. and opera. Johann Ludwig Bach (*b* Thal, 1677; *d* Meiningen, 1731). Son of Johann Jakob. Composer and Kapellmeister at Saxe-Meiningen. Johann Christoph Bach (3) (*b* Erfurt, 1671; *d* Ohrdruf, 1721).

Eldest son of Johann Ambrosius, and brother of Johann Sebastian. Pupil of Pachelbel at Erfurt. Organist at Ohrdruf. Taught his brother the klavier. Johann Jakob Bach (*b* Eisenach, 1682; *d* Stockholm, 1722). Son of Johann Ambrosius and brother of Johann Sebastian. Town musician at Eisenach. Entered Swed. army service in 1704 as oboist and in 1713 became *Hofmusikus* at Stockholm. It was for his joining the army that Johann Sebastian comp. the *Capriccio on the departure of his beloved brother* (BWV 992).

Bach, Carl (Karl) **Philipp Emanuel** (*b* Weimar, 1714; *d* Hamburg, 1788). Ger. composer. 5th child and 3rd son of J. S. *Bach. Intended for legal career but turned to mus. while at Frankfurt Univ. In 1738 became cembalist in Berlin at court of Frederick the Great, holding this post until 1767, when he succeeded *Telemann as dir. of church mus. at Hamburg. Applied unsuccessfully in 1750 to succeed his father at Leipzig. His achievement was to develop sonata-form and invest it with weight and imaginative quality, most evidently in his kbd. sonatas, of which there are over 200, but also in his sinfonias, concs. (over 50), and vn. sonatas. Also comp. 22 Passions, 2 oratorios, and many songs. Wrote celebrated treatise on klavier-playing.

Bach, Johann Christian (*b* Leipzig, 1735; *d* London, 1782). Ger. composer. 18th child and 11th (youngest) son of J. S. *Bach. Known as 'the English Bach'. Learned klavier-playing from his half-brother C. P. E. *Bach in Berlin. Went to Bologna in 1754 to study counterpoint with Padre *Martini. After becoming a Roman Catholic was appointed organist Milan Cath. in 1760. His 3-act opera *Artaserse* was prod. at Turin in 1760, followed by *Catone in Utica* in Naples the same year and *Alessandro nell'Indie* in 1762. These events were regarded in Milan as unduly frivolous, and Bach accepted offer from Signora Mattei, dir., King's Th., London, to succeed Cocchi as composer to the opera. His first London opera, *Orione*, prod. 1763. On this occasion cls. were first used in an Eng. orch. Later the same year his *Zanaida* was an equal success, and he was appointed music-master to Queen Charlotte. In 1764, when the boy Mozart visited London, Bach perf. a sonata with him. Also in 1764 he inaugurated a series of concerts with Karl Friedrich *Abel, who had been a pupil of J. S. Bach. These continued until 1782. His later operas met with less success. One of them, *Carattaco*, was on an Eng. subject which later attracted Elgar. On visits to Ger., Bach prod. his *Temistocle* in 1772 at Mannheim and his *Lucio Silla*, which Mozart had already set, in 1774. Comp. an opera for Paris, *Amadis de Gaule*, in 1779, and his last London opera, *La Clemenza di Scipione*, was successfully perf. in 1778. He died in debt, and was buried in a mass grave in St Pancras churchyard. Queen Charlotte helped to meet expenses arising from his debts and enabled his widow to return to Italy. His death went almost unnoticed by Londoners. There is a fine portrait of him by Gainsborough. Besides 11 operas, Bach wrote many instr. works—sinfonias, ovs., nearly 40 pf. concs., sonatas, qts., trios, marches, etc. Their felicitous scoring and melodic charm leave no doubt why Mozart admired Bach so much and why not only Mozart but also Haydn and Beethoven were fruitfully influenced by his work. Most of his church mus. was written before he left Italy.

Bach, Johann Christoph Friedrich (*b* Leipzig, 1732; *d* Bückeburg, 1795). Ger. composer. 16th child and 9th son of J. S. *Bach. Attended Leipzig Univ. and in 1750 appointed *Kammermusikus* to the court at Bückeburg; Konzertmeister 1756. In 1778 visited his half-brother Emmanuel in Hamburg and his brother Johann Christian in London. Comps. incl. 14 syms., 8 kbd. concs., sonatas, trios, oratorios, cantatas, secular songs.

Bach, Johann Sebastian (*b* Eisenach, 1685; *d* Leipzig, 1750). Ger. composer and organist. Son of Johann Ambrosius Bach, organist and town musician. J. S. Bach was orphaned at the age of 10 and went to live with his elder brother Johann Christoph at Ohrdruf where he had klavier and org. lessons. In 1700 was a chorister at St Michael's Church, Lüneburg, staying for 3 years, learning much from the organist-composer Georg Böhm. Organist at Arnstadt, 1703, and then Mühlhausen, 1707, when he married his cousin Maria Barbara Bach. In 1708 became organist in the Kapelle of the Duke of Saxe-Weimar, where he remained for 9 years, leaving in disappointment at not being appointed Kapellmeister in 1717. By this time he had comp. some of his finest org. works and church cantatas.

In 1717 appointed Kapellmeister at the court of Anhalt-Cöthen where the prince's interest was not in religious works but in instr. comps. From this period date his vn. concs., sonatas, suites, and Brandenburg concs. Also comp. many of his best klavier works at Cöthen, probably for his children's instruction. In 1720 his wife died and in Dec. 1721 he married Anna Magdalena Wilcken, 20-year-old daughter of the court trumpeter. Now dissatisfied with life at Cöthen, where the ruler's new wife showed little interest in mus., Bach applied for the cantorship at St Thomas's, Leipzig, in Dec. 1722. He was not selected, but the chosen candidate, Graupner, withdrew and Bach was appointed in May 1723, having in the meantime cond. his *St John Passion* in St Thomas's as evidence of his fitness for the post. Remained at St Thomas's for the rest of his life, not without several disputes with the authorities. During time there, comp. more than 250 church cantatas, the *St Matthew Passion*, Mass in B minor, *Christmas Oratorio*, *Goldberg Variations*, and many other works incl. his last, the unfinished *Die Kunst der Fuge* (Art of Fugue). In 1740 began

to have trouble with his eyesight and in the last year of his life was almost totally blind.

Bach was famous as an org. virtuoso. As a composer his reputation in his lifetime was restricted to a fairly narrow circle and his mus. was regarded by many as old-fashioned. His fame in no way approached that of, e.g., Telemann. His pubd. works today fill many vols., but in his lifetime fewer than a dozen of his comps. were printed, and for half a century after his death this position was only slightly improved until in 1801 the *Well-Tempered Klavier* was issued. The revival of interest in Bach's mus. may be dated from the Berlin perf. of the *St Matthew Passion* on 11 Mar. 1829, cond. Mendelssohn. Systematic publication of his works by the *Bach Gesellschaft began in 1850 to mark the centenary of his death. (See *Bach Revival*.)

Bach's supreme achievement was as a polyphonist. His N. Ger. Protestant religion was the root of all his art, allied to a tireless industry in the pursuit of every kind of refinement of his skill and technique. Sonata form was not yet developed enough for him to be interested in it, and he had no leaning towards the (to him) frivolities of opera. Although some of the forms in which he wrote—the church cantata, for example—were outdated before he died, he poured into them all the resources of his genius so that they have outlived most other examples. The dramatic and emotional force of his mus., as evidenced in the Passions, was remarkable in its day and has spoken to succeeding generations with increasing power. Suffice it to say that for many composers and for countless listeners, Bach's mus. is supreme—to quote Wagner: 'the most stupendous miracle in all music'. Prin. works:

ORCH: *Brandenburg Concertos Nos. 1–6 (*BWV1046–51); 7 *Concertos* for hpd. and str. (BWV1052–8), No. 1 in D minor, No. 2 in E, No. 3 in D, No. 4 in A, No. 5 in F minor, No. 6 in F, No. 7 in G minor; 3 concs. for 2 hpd. and str. (BWV1060–2), No. 1 in C minor, No. 2 in C, No. 3 in C minor; 2 concs. for 3 hpd. and str. (BWV1063–4), No. 1 in D minor, No. 2 in C (No. 1 arr. for vn., fl., ob., No. 2 for 3 vn. or fl., ob., vn.); conc. for 4 hpd. and str. in A minor (BWV1065, transcr. of Vivaldi conc. Op. 3 No. 10); conc. for fl., vn., hpd., str. (BWV1044), hpd., ob., str. (BWV1059), vn., str. in A minor (BWV1041, same work as BWV1058), vn., str. in E (BWV1042, same work as BWV1054), 2 vn. and str. in D minor (BWV1043, same work as BWV1062), vn., ob., str., in D minor (BWV1060, reconstr. of hpd. conc.); 4 *Suites* (BWV1066–9), No. 1 in C, No. 2 in B minor, No. 3 in D, No. 4 in D.

CHAMBER MUSIC: *Die *Kunst der Fuge* (The Art of Fugue) (BWV1080); *Das Musikalische Opfer* (The *Musical Offering) (BWV1079); 3 *Partitas*, solo vn. (BWV1002, 1004, 1006), No. 1 in B minor, No. 2 in D minor, No. 3 in E; 3 *Sonatas*, solo vn.

(BWV1001, 1003, 1005), No. 1 in G minor, No. 2 in A minor, No. 3 in C; 6 *Sonatas* for vn. and klavier (BWV1014–9), No. 1 in B minor, No. 2 in A, No. 3 in E, No. 4 in C minor, No. 5 in F minor, No. 6 in G; 6 *Sonatas* for vn./fl. and klavier (BWV1020–5), No. 1 in G minor, No. 2 in G, No. 3 in F, No. 4 in E minor, No. 5 in C minor, No. 6 in A; 4 *Sonatas* for 2 vn./2 fl./2 ob. and hpd. (BWV1036–9), No. 1 in D minor, No. 2 in C, Nos. 3 and 4 in G; 6 *Sonatas*, for fl. and hpd. (BWV1030–5), No. 1 in B minor, No. 2 in E♭, No. 3 in A, No. 4 in C, No. 5 in E minor, No. 6 in E; 3 *Sonatas* for viola da gamba (vc.) and klavier (BWV1027–9), No. 1 in G (same as BWV1039), No. 2 in D, No. 3 in G minor; sonata for fl. in A minor (BWV1013); 6 *Suites* for vc. (BWV1007–12), No. 1 in G, No. 2 in D minor, No. 3 in C, No. 4 in E♭, No. 5 in C minor, No. 6 in D.

KEYBOARD: *Capriccio* in B♭ (on the departure of a beloved brother) (BWV992); *Chromatic Fantasia and Fugue* in D minor (BWV903); 16 concs. for solo hpd. (BWV972–87), Nos. 1, 2, 3, 4, 5, 7 and 9 transcr. of Vivaldi, No. 3 of Marcello, Nos. 14 and 15 of Telemann; 6 *English Suites* (BWV806–11), No. 1 in A, No. 2 in A minor, No. 3 in G minor, No. 4 in F, No. 5 in E minor, No. 6 in D minor; *Fantasia* in A minor (BWV922); *Fantasia and Fugue* in A minor (BWV904); 6 *French Suites* (BWV812–17), No. 1 in D minor, No. 2 in C minor, No. 3 in B minor, No. 4 in E♭, No. 5 in G, No. 6 in E; *Fugue* in C (BWV952); *Goldberg Variations* (BWV988); 15 *Inventions* (2-part) (BWV772–86); 15 *Inventions* (3-part) (BWV787–801); *Italian Concerto* (BWV971); 6 *Partitas* (BWV825–30); 9 *Preludes for W. F. Bach* (BWV924–32); 6 *Preludes* (BWV933–8); 7 *Toccatas* (BWV910–16), No. 1 in F♯ minor, No. 2 in C minor, No. 3 in D, No. 4 in D minor, No. 5 in E minor, No. 6 in G minor, No. 7 in G; *Variations in the Italian Style* (BWV989); *Das Wohltemperierte Klavier* (The Well-Tempered Klavier), 48 preludes and fugues (BWV846–93).

LUTE: *Suites*: in A (BWV1007), in E minor (BWV996), in E (BWV1006a, transcr. from BWV1006, vn. Partita No. 3), in C minor (BWV997), in G minor (BWV995).

ORGAN: 6 concs. (BWV592–7), all transcr. from other composers, incl. Vivaldi); 4 *Duets* (BWV802–5); *Fantasia and Fugue* in C minor (BWV537), in G minor (BWV542); *Fantasias*, in C (BWV573), in C minor (BWV562), in G (BWV572); *Fugues*, in C minor (BWV574), in C minor (BWV575), in G (BWV577), in G minor (BWV578); *Passacaglia and Fugue* in C minor (BWV582); *Prelude and Fugue*: in A (BWV536), in A minor (BWV543), in A minor (BWV551), in B minor (BWV544), in C (BWV531), in C (BWV545), in C (BWV547), in C minor (BWV546), in C minor (BWV549), in D (BWV532), in D minor (BWV538), in D minor (BWV539), in E minor (BWV533), in E minor (*Wedge*) (BWV548), in E flat (BWV552), in F

minor (BWV534), in G (BWV541), in G (BWV550), in G minor (BWV535), in G minor (BWV542); 8 *Preludes and Fugues* (BWV553–60), No. 1 in C, No. 2 in D minor, No. 3 in E minor, No. 4 in F, No, 5 in G, No. 6 in G minor, No. 7 in A minor, No. 8 in B♭; 6 *Sonatas* (BWV525–30), No. 1 in E♭, No. 2 in C minor, No. 3 in D minor, No. 4 in E minor, No. 5 in C, No. 6 in G; *Toccata, Adagio, and Fugue* in C (BWV564); *Toccata and Fugue* in D minor (*Dorian*) (BWV538), in D minor (BWV565), in E (BWV566), in F (BWV540); *Trio* in D minor (BWV583), in G (BWV586).

CHORALE PRELUDES: *Orgelbüchlein* (Little Organ Book) (BWV599–644), containing 46 items; also many others of which only a brief selection is given here: *Ach, bleib bei uns* (BWV649), *Allein Gott in der Höh' sei Ehr* (BWV711), *An Wasserflüssen Babylon* (BWV653b), *Christum wir sollen Loben schon* (BWV696), *Ein' feste Burg* (BWV720), *Herr Jesu Christ, dich zu uns wend* (BWV709), *In dulci jubilo* (BWV729), *Jesu, meine Freude* (BWV713), *Jesus Christus, unser Heiland* (BWV688), *Komm, Gott Schöpfer* (BWV667), *Komm, heiliger Geist* (BWV652), *Kommst du nun, Jesu* (BWV650), *Liebster Jesu, wir sind hier* (BWV706), *Meine Seele erhebet den Herren* (BWV648), *Nun danket alle Gott* (BWV657), *Nun komm, der Heiden Heiland* (BWV659), *O Gott, du frommer Gott* (BWV767), *O Lamm Gottes unschuldig* (BWV656), *Schmücke dich, O liebe Seele* (BWV654), *Vater unser im Himmelreich* (BWV682/3, 737), *Vom Himmel hoch* (BWV700, 701 fughetta, 738, 769 canonic variations), *Wachet auf* (BWV645), *Wer nur den lieben Gott* (BWV647, 690, 691), *Wo soll ich fliehen hin* (BWV646).

CANTATAS: Merely a selection of these is given here, with dates of comp. where known: No. 4 *Christ lag in Todesbanden* (c.1707), No. 6 *Bleib bei uns* (1725), No. 10 *Meine Seele' erhebt den Herren* 1724, rev. 1744–50), No. 11 *Lobet Gott* (c.1735), No. 12 *Weinen, Klagen, Sorgen, Zagen* (1714), No. 20 *O Ewigkeit, du Donnerwort* (1724), No. 23 *Du wahrer Gott und Davids Sohn* (1723), No. 28 *Gottlob Nun geht das Jahr zu Ende* (1725), No. 29 *Wir danken dir, Gott* (1731), No. 34 *O ewiger Feuer* (? after 1742), No. 40 *Dazu ist erschiene der Sohn Gottes* (1723), No. 45 *Est ist dir gesagt* (1726), No. 51 *Jauchzet Gott* (1730), No. 60 *O Ewigkeit, du Donnerwort* (1723), No. 61 *Nun komm, der Heiden Heiland* (1714), No. 68 *Also hat Gott die Welt geliebt* (1725), No. 78 *Jesu, der du meine Seele* (1724), No. 80 *Ein' feste Burg ist unser Gott* (1724), No. 82 *Ich habe genug* (1727), No. 93 *Wer nur den lieben Gott* (1724), No. 95 *Christus der ist mein Leben* (1723), No. 106 *Gottes Zeit ist die allerbeste Zeit* (c.1707), No. 140 *Wachet auf* (1731), No. 143 *Lobe den herrn* (1735), No. 147 *Herz und Mund* (10th movement is *Jesu, bleibet meine Freude, Jesu, joy of man's desiring*) (1723), No. 197 *Gott ist unser Zuversicht* (c.1728), No. 201 *Der Streit zwischen *Phoebus und Pan* (?1729), No. 202 *Weichet nur, betrübte Schatten* (?1718–23), No.

208 *Was mir behagt* (?1713), No. 209 *Non sa che sia dolore* (after 1740), No. 211 *Schweigt stille, plaudert nicht* (*Coffee cantata, 1732), No. 212 *Mer hahn en neue Oberkeet* (*Peasant cantata, 1742). Canons for 2, 3, 4, and 7 voices (BWV1075, 1077, 1073, and 1078 respectively).

ORATORIOS etc: *Christmas Oratorio* in 6 parts (*Weihnachtsoratorium*) (BWV248, 1734); *Easter Oratorio* (BWV249, 1736); *Magnificat* in E♭ (BWV 243a, perf. Christmas Day 1723 incl. 4 Christmas texts), *Magnificat* in D (BWV243, rev. of *Magnificat* in E♭, c.1728–31, omitting Christmas texts); Mass in B minor (BWV232, 1724–49); Mass in G (BWV236, c.1738); Mass in G minor (BWV235, c.1737); 6 Motets (BWV225–230) 1. *Singet dem Herrn ein neues Lied*, 2. *Der Geist hilft*, 3. *Jesu meine Freude*, 4. *Fürchte dich nicht*, 5. *Komm, Jesu, komm*, 6. *Lobet den Herrn*; *St John Passion* (*Johannespassion*) (BWV245, 1723); *St Matthew Passion* (*Matthäuspassion*) (BWV244, 1727).

SONGS AND ARIAS: *Notebook (No. 2) of *Anna Magdalena Bach* (BWV508–18), contains 11 songs, the first being *Bist du bei mir* (With you beside me); Aria, *Gott lebet noch* (BWV461); *Jesus ist das schönste Licht* (BWV474); Aria, *Komm, süsser Tod* (BWV478); *O Jesulein süss* (BWV493); Song, *Vergiss mein nicht, mein allerliebster Gott* (BWV505).

Bach, Wilhelm Friedemann (*b* Weimar, 1710; *d* Berlin, 1784). Ger. composer. 2nd child and eldest son of J. S. *Bach. Possibly also favourite son, but one who sadly failed to justify parental hopes. First part of *The Well-Tempered Clavier* was written for his instruction. After Leipzig Univ., became a church organist in Dresden (he was regarded as one of the greatest organists of his day), and comp. many instr. works, such as kbd. concs. and sonatas. In 1746 resigned to become organist of the Liebfrauenkirche at Halle. In 1762 was invited to succeed Graupner at Darmstadt but does not seem to have taken up his duties. Left Halle in 1764. For the last 20 years of his life held no regular post, giving occasional org. recitals in Brunswick, Göttingen, and Berlin, and teaching. Befriended by his father's biographer, J. N. Forkel. Poverty led him to sell several of his father's MSS. and also to pass off some of his father's works as his own. In fact his own comps. have character and are today often played.

Bacharach, Burt (*b* Kansas City, 1928). Amer. composer and pianist. Studied McGill Univ., Montreal. Night club pianist and entertainer, accompanist to Marlene Dietrich. Composer, with lyrics by Hal David, of many popular songs and film scores. Best-known songs are *I'll never fall in love again*, *What's new pussycat?* and *Raindrops keep fallin' on my head* (from film *Butch Cassidy and the Sundance Kid*, 1970).

Bachauer, Gina (*b* Athens, 1913; *d* Athens, 1976). Gr. pianist of Austrian parentage. Trained

Athens Cons. and École Normale, Paris; teachers incl. *Cortot and *Rakhmaninov. Début Athens 1935. Recitalist and soloist at orch. concerts in Athens, Middle-Eastern centres, and Paris. London début 1947, NY 1950.

Bach Bow. A curved (convex) vn. bow invented by the violinist Emil *Telmányi as particularly suitable for performing the contrapuntal solo vn. mus. of J. S. Bach.

Bach Choir. Formed permanently in London in 1876 following success of first 2 complete Brit. perfs. in Apr. and May 1876 of Bach's Mass in B minor by group of amateurs assembled in 1875 under the choral direction of Otto *Goldschmidt, who remained cond. until 1885. His successors have been *Stanford, Walford *Davies, Hugh *Allen, *Vaughan Williams, *Boult, Reginald *Jacques and David *Willcocks. Gives 2 annual perfs. of *St Matthew Passion*; many modern works in its repertory. Choirs in several other cities and towns use the title preceded by their name, e.g. Oxford Bach Choir, Newcastle Bach Choir.

Bache, Walter (*b* Birmingham, 1842; *d* London, 1888). Eng. pianist and cond. Studied in Leipzig; from 1862 to 1865 in Rome was a pupil of Liszt. In 1871 in Florence had lessons from Bülow. For many years dir. concerts devoted to Liszt's mus. at which several of Liszt's works (*Faust Symphony*, both pf. concs., *St Elizabeth* etc.) were f.p. in London. Prof. of pf. RAM. His brother Francis Edward (*b* Birmingham, 1833; *d* Birmingham, 1858) was a composer and pianist of exceptional promise. Their sister Constance (*b* Birmingham, 1846; *d* Montreux, 1903) trans. Bülow's letters (1896).

Bachelet, Alfred (*b* Paris, 1864; *d* Nancy, 1944). Fr. composer. Winner of Prix de Rome, 1880, with cantata *Cléopatre*. His 3-act opera *Scemo* (Paris 1914) stimulated controversy at the time. Comp. songs, pf. pieces, and a ballet. Dir., Nancy Cons. from 1919.

Bach Gesellschaft (Bach Society). Ger. soc. founded 1850 to commemorate the centenary of the death of J. S. Bach by publishing complete critical edn. of his works based mainly on the coll. of his MSS. in Berlin. The project, urged by Robert Schumann in an article in the *Neue Zeitschrift für Musik* (xix, 87), was executed by Otto Jahn in assoc. with Schumann, Carl Friedrich Becker, Moritz Hauptmann, and the publishing firm of Breitkopf und Härtel. Issued 46 annual publications in 59 vols. between 1850 and 1900. The achievement was a vast feat of scholarship but, understandably, not without error. Some works definitely or probably not by Bach were incl.

With publication of the concluding volume on 27 Jan. 1900 the Society was wound up and the *Neue Bach Gesellschaft* founded under the presidency of Herman Kretzschmar, Prof. at Leipzig

Univ. Its objective was to publish Bach's mus. in practicable performing scores and to popularize it throughout Ger. by Bach fests. In 1904 the soc. began issue of a *Jahrbuch* (Yearbook), in which the latest Bach research is pubd., and in 1907 bought Bach's birthplace at Eisenach and made it a museum.

A Bach Soc. was founded in London 1849 to collect a library of Bach's comps. either printed or in MS. Under its auspices took place the first Eng. perfs. of *St Matthew Passion* (Hanover Sq. Rooms, London, 6 Apr. 1854) and *Christmas Oratorio* (London, 13 June 1864). 11 movements from the Mass in B minor were perf. on 24 July 1860. Soc. dissolved in Mar. 1870 and library given to RAM.

Bachianas Brasileiras. 9 pieces by *Villa-Lobos combining native Brazilian elements with the contrapuntal spirit of J. S. Bach's mus. They are: 1. for 8 vc. (1930); 2. for small orch. (1930); 3. for pf. and orch. (1938); 4. for pf. (1930–6) orch. 1941; 5. for v. and vcs. (1938); 6. for fl. and bn. (1938); 7. for orch. (1942); 8. for orch. (1945); 9. for str. or unacc. ch. (1944).

Bachmann, Anton (*b* Berlin, 1716; *d* Berlin, 1800). Ger. court musician who invented several improvements in construction of dbs. and vcs.

Bachmann, Karl Ludwig (*b* Berlin, 1743; *d* Berlin, 1809). Son of Anton *Bachmann. Noted solo va.-player in Berlin Royal Chapel. Later took over his father's business.

Bach Revival. In the half-century after J. S. Bach's death only a handful of his works were pubd., though these incl. C. P. E. Bach's edn. of the complete coll. of *Vierstimmige Choralgesänge* (Choral Songs for 4 Voices), issued by Breitkopf & Härtel (1784–7). Nevertheless, Mozart at the end of his life was a profound admirer of Bach, and at Bonn in 1780 Beethoven was instructed in the '48' preludes and fugues, then still in MS. The revival gathered momentum with publication in 1801 in 4 centres (Bonn, Zürich, Vienna, and Leipzig, with a London reprint of the Bonn edn.) of the *Well-Tempered Klavier* (*Wohltemperierte Klavier*) and the appearance in 1802 of Forkel's biography *Über Johann Sebastian Bachs Leben*. The *Magnificat* was pubd. in 1811, the *St Matthew Passion* in 1830, the Mass in B minor partially in 1833, fully in 1845, the *St John Passion* in 1830 (pf. score), vocal parts 1834; many cantatas, all the org. works, many works for klavier and much besides appeared between 1803 and 1850. In the matter of perf., the critic Johann Friedrich Rochlitz (1769–1842) stimulated interest by his articles in the *Allgemeine musikalische Zeitung*, which he founded in 1798, remaining ed. until 1818. Publication of the motets led to their perf. in the 1820s by the Berlin Singakademie under Carl Friedrich *Zelter. At his house Mendelssohn and the Devrients met to study Bach's mus. On 11 Mar. 1829 Mendelssohn cond. the first perf.

since Bach's day of the *St Matthew Passion* with the Singakademie. Two further perfs. followed within 5 weeks. In 1833 the Singakademie perf. the *St John Passion* and a much-cut Mass in B minor. Other leading Ger. mus. centres, incl. Leipzig, followed Berlin's lead.

In Eng., where it might have been thought that J. C. Bach would have encouraged study of his father's work, little was done until Samuel *Wesley's concerts of J. S. Bach's mus. in 1808 and 1809. William *Crotch also helped, but the main stimulus came from Mendelssohn's visits in 1829 and 1832, when he played Bach's org. works in St Paul's Cath. and elsewhere. In 1837 he had a section of the *St Matthew Passion* incl. in the Birmingham Fest. But it was not until the later 19th cent. that regular perfs. of Bach's mus. in Eng. began. Sterndale Bennett cond. first complete Eng. perf. of *St Matthew Passion* (in English) on 6 April 1854, in London. It was f.p. at Three Choirs Fest. 1871.

Bach Trumpet. High-pitched natural (i.e. unvalved) tpt. used in late 17th and 18th cents. J. S. Bach and Handel wrote ornate passages for it in certain comps. In the late 1880s valved versions were prod. on which such passages could be played, but virtuoso players today have recovered the art of playing the natural tpt. and need no such aids.

Back. The lower or rear part of the resonant box of str. instr. The strings are extended across the upper part, the belly or 'table'. The back has no sound holes; its primary function is to be reverberated by the air waves generated by the belly as it vibrates under the str. Usually made of maple, pear, or other hard wood.

Bäck, Sven-Erik (*b* Stockholm, 1919). Swed. composer, conductor, and violinist. Studied Royal Mus. Acad. Stockholm 1938–43; comp. pupil of Rosenberg and, in Rome 1951–2, of Petrassi. Member of several str. qts. Comp. 2 chamber operas, 3 str. qts., orch. works, elec. works.

Backer-Gröndahl, Agathe Ursula (*b* Holmestrand, Norway, 1847; *d* Ormøen, 1907). Norweg. pianist, pupil of Hans von *Bülow and Liszt, and popular composer of songs and pf. mus.

Backfall. (1) Part of an org., being the lever which connects the rods (stickers) to the kbd.
(2) 17th-cent. Eng. term for a type of upper *appoggiatura in lute and hpd. mus.

Backhaus (Bachaus), **Wilhelm** (*b* Leipzig, 1884; *d* Villach, Austria, 1969). Ger. pianist. Trained Leipzig Cons. and under d'Albert, etc. Made first concert tour age 16; later toured world. Prof. of pf., RMCM in 1905. Noted as Beethoven interpreter, recording most of the sonatas after his 80th birthday.

Bacon, Ernst (*b* Chicago, 1898). Amer. composer, cond., and critic. Works are mainly for v. with various accs. and incl. settings of Walt Whitman and Emily Dickinson. Also 4 syms., incl. 1 with narrator (No. 3, 1956), and 2-act 'music play' *A Tree on the Plains* (1940, rev. 1962). Has written over 250 songs.

Badajoz (*fl.* 15th–16th cent.). Sp. composer and organist. Choirmaster to John III of Portugal.

Badarczewska, Tekla (*b* Warsaw, 1834; *d* Warsaw, 1861). Polish composer of pf. pieces, among them *The Maiden's Prayer*, pubd. Warsaw 1856 and Paris 1859.

Badia, Carlo Agostino (*b* Venice, 1672; *d* Vienna, 1738). It. composer. First 'official composer' to the Viennese court, 1694. Comp. 25 operas, 42 oratorios, and other works.

Badinage, Badinerie (Fr.). Playfulness. Used as title of movement in 18th-cent. suite, e.g. *Badinerie* of J. S. Bach's Suite in B minor.

Badings, Henk (*b* Bandoeng, Java, 1907). Dutch composer. Began as engineer, but studied mus. with Pijper and joined staff of Rotterdam Cons. in 1934; co-dir., Amsterdam Lyceum 1937–41; dir., Hague Cons. 1941–5; dir., elec. mus. studio, Utrecht Univ., 1960–4; Prof. of comp., Musikhochschule, Stuttgart, 1962–72. Comps. incl. several operas and 14 syms., 25 concs., chamber mus., and elec. works. His Sonata No. 2 for 2 vn. (1963) is in 31-note scale and his ballet *Genesis* (1968) for 5 tone-generators.

Badura-Skoda, Paul (*b* Vienna, 1927). Austrian pianist. Trained Vienna Cons. 1945–8 and with Edwin *Fischer. Début Vienna 1948. Many recordings; specialist in Mozart and with musicologist wife Eva (*b* Munich, 1929) author of book on interpretation of his pf. mus. (1957, Eng. trans. 1962).

Bagatelle (Fr., Ger.). Trifle. So a short unpretentious instr. comp., esp. for pf. (Beethoven wrote 26 bagatelles, of which *Für Elise* is one). Dvořák's *Bagatelles* Op. 47 (1878) are for 2 vn., vc., and harmonium (or pf.).

Bagpipe Family. Forms of the bagpipe have existed for at least 3,000 years and it is known to many races in Europe and Asia. *Machaut (1300– 77) mentions bagpipes in a description of one of his own polyphonic works. Its essentials are that (*a*) It is a reed-pipe instr. and (*b*) Interposed between the medium supplying the wind and the reed-pipe is a bag serving as a reservoir and so preventing any undesired breaking of the flow of sound by the player's necessity to take breath.

Variable characteristics are: (*c*) The source of the wind-supply to the reservoir may be either by mouth or by a small bellows held under the arm. (*d*) The reed-pipe (*Chanter*) from which the various notes of the tune are obtained by means of a series of holes or keys may, or may not, be acc. by 1 or more other reed-pipes each confined to a single note (*Drones*), these being tuned to the

Tonic or Tonic and Dominant of the key of the instr. (*e*) The reed may be either single, like that of the cl. family, or double like that of the ob. family; in practice the chanter reed is usually (perhaps always) double, while the drone reeds vary in different types of instr.

The compass of nearly all bagpipes is limited to an octave but on some few types a 2nd octave can be obtained.

Brit. forms of the instr. are: 1. *Scottish Highland Bagpipe*, or *Great Pipe*, mouth-blown and possessing a conical-bore chanter and 3 drones (2 tuned to a′ and 1 to a). The tone is penetrating and best heard in the open air; the chanter scale is of D major but extends from a′ with a G♮ and with the C and F pitched between sharp and natural. 2. *Scottish Lowland Bagpipe* is much the same as the foregoing but bellows-blown. 3. *Northumbrian Bagpipe* is also bellows-blown but sweet and gentle in tone and normal as to scale (G major); it has usually 4 drones; its chanter pipes are endstopped, so that when the player closes all the finger-holes at once sound from them ceases, making possible a characteristic crisp staccato. 4. *Irish 'Union' Bagpipe* (the assertion that the word is a corruption of *Uillean* is unfounded). This is bellows-blown and sweet in tone; it has 3 drones. Its scale is nearly chromatic. Foreign terms for the bagpipe are: Fr. *musette*; Ger. *Dudelsack*, *Sackpfeife*; It. *piva*, *zampogna*; Sp. *gaita*.

Baguette (Fr.). Stick. In mus. usage (1) Drumstick (*baguettes de bois*, wooden drumsticks; *baguettes d'éponge*, sponge-headed drumsticks). (2) Stick of bow of vn., etc. (3) Conductor's baton.

Bahr-Mildenburg, Anna von. See *Mildenburg, Anna von*.

Bailey, Lilian (June) (*b* Columbus, Ohio, 1860; *d* London, 1901). Amer. sop. Studied in Paris 1878 with Pauline *Viardot-García and later in London with George *Henschel whom she married, 1881. Gave many recitals with her husband.

Bailey, Norman (*b* Birmingham, 1933). Eng. bass-bar. Studied in Vienna and made reputation in Austria and Ger. before SW début in 1967 (on tour) and in 1968 (London). Début CG 1969. Sang Hans Sachs at Bayreuth, 1969. NY début 1975, Met. 1976. Specialist in Wagner roles, e.g. Sachs, Dutchman, Wotan, Kurwenal. Has appeared with ENO, WNO, and Scottish Opera. C.B.E. 1977.

Baillie, (Dame) **Isobel** (Isabella) (*b* Hawick, Scotland, 1895; *d* Manchester, 1983). Scot.-born sop., noted for singing of oratorio (especially *Messiah*) and Lieder. Studied in Manchester with Sadler Fogg, later in Milan. Début, Hallé Concert, Manchester 1921, under name Bella Baillie, then at all chief Eng. Fests. Chosen by Toscanini for perfs. of Brahms's *Requiem*. One of 16 orig. singers in Vaughan Williams's *Serenade to Music* 1938. Amer. début 1933. Taught at RCM 1955–7, Cornell Univ. 1960–1, Manchester Sch. of Mus. from 1970. C.B.E. 1951, D.B.E. 1978. Autobiography pubd. 1982.

Baillot, Pierre (Marie François de Sales) (*b* Passy, nr. Paris 1771; *d* Paris, 1842). Fr. vn. virtuoso and composer of 9 vn. concs. Prof., Paris Cons. from 1795. Wrote *L'Art du violon* (1834).

Bainbridge, Simon (*b* 1952). Eng. composer. Studied RCM, comp. with J. Lambert, cl. with S. Fell. Teacher, RCM junior dept. Works incl. *Music to Oedipus Rex* (1969), *2 Pieces for Piano* (1969), *Heterophony* for orch. (1969–70), *Spirogyra* for chamber orch. (1970), wind quintet (1971), str. qt. (1972), *Interlude Music (Heterophons)* (1973, preliminary study for *Amoeba* for ens.), va. conc. (1977), *Landscapes and Woods*, sop. and ens. (1981).

Baines, William (*b* Horbury, Yorks., 1899; *d* York, 1922). Eng. composer and pianist. Mainly self-taught. Worked as cinema pianist. Few works pubd. in his lifetime, but his mother gave his musical effects to Brit. Mus. in 1960. Wrote sym. (1917), vn. sonata (1917), str. qt. (1917–18), songs, and a large number of piano pieces, incl. sonatas, *Paradise Gardens* (1918–19), *Coloured Leaves* (1918–21), *7 Preludes* (1918–19), *Twilight Pieces* (1921), and *8 Preludes* (1921).

Bainton, Edgar (Leslie) (*b* London, 1880; *d* Sydney, N.S.W., 1956). Eng. composer. Studied RCM under Stanford and Wood and then lived as pianist and dir. of Cons. in Newcastle upon Tyne 1912–34, having been prof. of pf. and comp. there from 1901. Dir., State Cons., Sydney, N.S.W. (1934–47). Comps. in many genres.

Baird, Tadeusz (*b* Grodzisk, Poland, 1928; *d* Warsaw, 1981). Polish composer. Studied at Warsaw State Music Acad. 1947–51 and Univ. 1948–52. Several of post-1956 works use 12-note procedures. Works incl.:

OPERA: *Tomorrow* (*Jutro*) (after J. Conrad) (1966).
ORCH: Syms: No. 1 (1950), No. 2 (1952), No. 3 (1968–9); *Sinfonietta* (1949); pf. conc. (1949); *Concerto for Orchestra* (1953); *Cassation* (1956); 4 *Essays* (1958); *Espressioni varianti*, vn. and orch. (1959); *Variations without a Theme* (1962); *Epiphany Music* (1963); *Sinfonia brevis* (1968); *Psychodram* (1972); ob. conc. (1973).
INSTR: *Colas Breugnon*, fl., chamber orch. (1951); 4 *Dialogues*, ob., chamber orch. (1964); 4 *Novelettes*, chamber orch. (1967).
VOCAL: 4 *Shakespeare Love Sonnets*, bar., chamber orch. (1956); *Exhortation*, narrator, ch., orch. (1960); *Erotica*, sop., orch. (1961); *Songs of Trouvères*, mez., fl., vc. (1964); 5 *Songs*, mez., chamber orch. (1967–8); *Goethe Letters*, bar., ch., and orch. (1970).

Bairstow, (Sir) **Edward** (Cuthbert) (*b* Huddersfield, 1874; *d* York, 1946). Eng. organist and composer. Held various organist's positions, incl. Leeds Parish Church (1906) and York Minster (1913 to death). V. trainer and choral cond. Wrote church mus. Prof. of mus., Durham Univ. from 1929. Knighted 1932.

Baiser de la fée, Le (The Fairy's Kiss). Ballet in 1 act by Stravinsky, mus. based on pf. pieces and songs by Tchaikovsky with linking passages by Stravinsky in Tchaikovsky's vein. Orch. 1928, rev. 1950. Scenario based on Andersen's *Ice Maiden*. Choreog. Nijinskaya. Prod. Paris 1928; London with choreog. by Ashton 1935. A *Divertimento* arr. from *Le Baiser de la Fée* was comp. 1934, rev. 1949.

Baker, George (*b* Birkenhead, 1885; *d* Hereford, 1976). Eng. bar. especially but not exclusively assoc. with the Gilbert and Sullivan operettas. Studied RCM and Milan. Also writer and adjudicator. BBC Overseas Music Dir. 1944–7. 2nd wife was sop. Olive Groves (*d* 1974). C.B.E. 1971.

Baker, (Dame) **Janet** (Abbott) (*b* Hatfield, Doncaster, 1933). Eng. mez. Sang in Leeds Phil. Choir (soloist in Haydn's *Nelson Mass* 1953). Studied with Hélène Isepp and Meriel St Clair. Joined Ambrosian Singers 1955; 2nd prize Kathleen Ferrier Competition 1956; opera début 1956 Roza in Smetana's *The Secret* with Oxford Univ. Opera Club. Glyndebourne Ch. 1956. Queen's Prize 1959. Wexford Fest. 1959. Sang leading roles with Handel Opera Soc. 1959; sang Dido in Purcell's *Dido and Aeneas*, cond. Anthony Lewis, Birmingham 1961, followed by roles in *Tamerlano* (1962), *Ariodante* (1964), *Orlando* (1966), *Admeto* (1968), also in Rameau's *Hippolyte et Aricie* (1965). Sang at Aldeburgh Fest. with Britten from 1962, giving f.p. of *Phaedra*, 1976. Sang Lucretia in EOG's Russ. tour 1964. Recorded Angel in Elgar's *Gerontius* with Barbirolli 1964. NY début 1966. CG début Hermia in Britten's *Midsummer Night's Dream* 1966. Sang Dorabella (*Così fan tutte*) with Scottish Opera 1967 followed by Berlioz's Dido (1969), Oktavian (1971), Composer in *Ariadne auf Naxos* (1975), Orpheus in Gluck's opera (1979); Diana in *La Calisto*, Glyndebourne 1970, followed by Penelope in *Il ritorno d'Ulisse in patria*, 1972. Sang Poppea for ENO in *L'incoronazione di Poppea* 1971, Mary Stuart (Donizetti) 1973, Charlotte in Massenet's *Werther*, 1977. Created role of Kate in Britten's *Owen Wingrave* (television 1971, CG 1973). Retired from operatic stage 1982, last appearance being as Orpheus in Gluck's opera at Glyndebourne. One of most intense and intelligent of contemporary singers, as impressive in operatic parts as in the realm of Lieder, Eng. and Fr. song, oratorio, and Mahler. C.B.E. 1970. Hamburg Shakespeare Prize 1971. D.B.E. 1976.

Baker, Richard (Douglas James) (*b* London, 1925). Eng. broadcaster and mus. presenter. Professional appearances on concert-platform as narrator in *King David* (Honegger), *Façade* (Walton), *Peter and the Wolf* (Prokofiev), *Survivor from Warsaw* (Schoenberg), etc. O.B.E. 1976.

Baker, Theodore (*b* NY, 1851; *d* Dresden, 1934). Amer. mus. scholar; after business training studied mus. in Leipzig; literary ed. (1892–1926) for G. Schirmer; books incl. *Biographical Dictionary of Musicians* (1900; 6th edn., 1978, 7th edn., 1984, both ed. N. Slonimsky).

Bakst, Ryszard (*b* Warsaw, 1926). Polish pianist and teacher. Trained Moscow State Cons. (pf. with Neuhaus). Taught at Warsaw State Acad. of Mus., 1953–68; RMCM, 1969–72; since 1972 RNCM, Manchester. Exponent of Chopin and Szymanowski.

Balakirev, Mily (Alexeyevich) (*b* Nizhny-Novgorod, 1837 (old style 1836); *d* St Petersburg, 1910). Russ. composer who made major contribution to development of nationalist school. Spent his formative years in the country home of Oulibichev, biographer of Mozart, where he studied in the library and had practical instruction with private orch. At 18 went to St Petersburg, where *Glinka, impressed by his nationalist ideals, encouraged him to continue his own work. From 1861 Balakirev became centre of a group of nationalistically inclined composers known as 'the *Five' (the others being Cui, Borodin, Mussorgsky, and Rimsky-Korsakov). In 1862 founded Free Sch. of Mus. At its sym. concerts Balakirev introduced many of the new works by his colleagues of 'the Five' and later those by Lyadov and Glazunov. Nervous breakdown led to his retirement from music 1871–6, during which period he worked as a railway official. From 1883 was mus. dir. to the Russ. court. Himself a fine pianist, his *Islamey*, like his other pf. works, is a brilliant virtuoso showpiece. Prin. works:

ORCH: Syms., No. 1 in C (1893–7), No. 2 in D minor (1900–08); *Overture on Spanish Themes* (1857, rev. 1886), *Overture on 3 Russian Themes* (1863–4, rev. 1884), *Overture on Czech Themes* (1867, rev. 1905); sym.-poem *Tamara* (1867–82).

PIANO: Oriental fantasy, *Islamey* (1869, rev. 1902), 6 mazurkas, 3 scherzos, 3 nocturnes, 4 waltzes, *Spanish Serenade*. Also many songs.

Balalaika. Russ. guitar, triangular in shape with (normally) 3 str., and a fretted fingerboard. Exists in various sizes. Assoc. with it, in balalaika bands, are the *Domra*, a somewhat similar instr. and the *Gusli*.

Balanchine (né Balanchivadze), **George** (*b* St Petersburg, 1904; *d* NY, 1983). Russ.-Amer. choreog. Thorough mus. training. Imperial Sch. of Ballet 1914–1921. Left Russ. 1924. After an appearance in Paris, was engaged by *Diaghilev as choreographer. Stravinsky's *Apollo Musagetes* had Balanchine choreog. for its first Paris perf. (1928). (Other Stravinsky works were later

choreog. by Balanchine, incl. *Orpheus, Jeu de Cartes, Baiser de la fée, Danses concertantes, Movements,* and *Agon*.) In 1932 became choreog. for Col. de Basil's Ballets Russes de Monte Carlo. In 1934 went to USA to create Amer. Ballet Co., début 1935. This was resident ballet at NY Met. 1935–8, when it was disbanded. Balanchine then worked as teacher and free-lance choreog. (incl. Hollywood films). Co-founder Ballet Soc. (1946) which became celebrated NY City Ballet, 1948, with Balanchine as art. dir. From this period dates his great and influential work for modern dance. Among ballets he choreog. were: *The Prodigal Son* (Prokofiev) 1929, *Ballet Imperial* (Tchaikovsky) 1941, *Night Shadow* (Bellini-Rieti) 1946, *La Valse* (Ravel) 1951, *Ivesiana* (Ives) 1954, *7 Deadly Sins* (Weill) 1958, *Slaughter on 10th Avenue* (Rodgers) 1968, *Duo Concertante* (Stravinsky) 1970. Among musicals he choreographed were: *On your Toes* (1936), *The Boys from Syracuse* (1938). Also worked as opera producer (Stravinsky's *Rake's Progress*, NY 1953; Tchaikovsky's *Eugene Onegin*, Hamburg 1962).

Balanchivadze, Andrey (*b* St Petersburg, 1906). Brother of G. *Balanchine and son of Meliton Balanchivadze, composer of first Georgian nat. opera. Andrey's works incl. 4 pf. concs., 2 syms., operas, ballets, and film mus. People's Artist of U.S.S.R., 1968.

Balart, Gabriel (*b* Barcelona, 1824; *d* Barcelona, 1893). Sp. violinist and composer. Cond. Barcelona Opera 1853–4. Wrote 5 syms., chamber mus., songs, and the zarzuela *Amor y Arte* (1868).

Balassa, Sándor (*b* Budapest, 1935). Hung. composer. Studied Bartók Cons., Budapest. Mus. dir. Hung. Radio. Comps. incl. *Requiem for Lajos Kassák* (1969); *Xenia* (1970); *Iris* (1971) for orch.; wind quintet; Legend for mixed ch.; *Tabulae* for chamber orch. (1973); *3 Fantasies* for orch. (1984).

Balbi, Lodovico (*b* Venice, 1545; *d* Venice, c.1604). It. church musician and composer in Verona, Padua, and Venice. Also comp. madrigals.

Baldi, Antonio (*fl.* 1722–35). It. counter-ten. who sang in London 1725–8 in operas by Handel (*Alessandro, Ottone, Scipione, Radamisto,* and *Serse*), and Bononcini.

Baldwin Company. Pf. makers of Cincinatti. Founded 1862 by Dwight Hamilton Baldwin. Factories also in Canada, Eng., and W. Ger. Developed electronic org. 1947.

Balfe, Michael (William) (*b* Dublin, 1808; *d* Rowney Abbey, Herts., 1870). Irish composer, violinist, and bar. Lived for a time in Paris and Berlin and prod. his operas there and in St Petersburg. Sang Figaro in Rossini's *Il Barbiere de Siviglia* in Paris, 1827, and sang at La Scala, Milan, with *Malibran in 1830s. Sang Papageno in *The Magic Flute* in Eng. at Drury Lane, 1838. First opera, *I rivali di se stessi*, was prod. Palermo 1829.

His *Falstaff* was prod. London 1838 and his greatest success *The *Bohemian Girl* in 1843. Cond. of opera at His Majesty's, London, 1845–52.

Balkwill, Bryan (Havell) (*b* London, 1922). Eng. cond. Trained RAM. On cond. staff CG 1959–65; WNO 1963–7; SW (mus. dir.) 1966–9; Glyndebourne 1950–8; and posts in N. Amer.

Ball, (Sir) **George Thomas Thalben.** See *Thalben-Ball, George Thomas.*

Ball, Eric (*b* Bristol, 1903). Eng. composer, cond., and arranger, principally of works for brass band. Also adjudicator of band competitions. Assoc. for many years with C.W.S. (Manchester) Band. Arr. Elgar's *Enigma Variations* for brass band (f.p. Warwick, 1984).

Ball, Ernest R. (*b* Cleveland, Ohio, 1878; *d* Santa Ana, Calif., 1927). Amer. popular composer, 3 of whose songs were in the regular repertory of John *McCormack, namely *Mother Machree, When Irish Eyes are Smiling,* and *Little Bit of Heaven.*

Ballabile (It.). In a dance style.

Ballad. (1) Properly a song to be danced to (It. *Ballare,* to dance) but from the 16th cent. or earlier the term has been applied to anything singable, simple, popular in style, and for solo v.
(2) The word 'ballad' was in the 19th cent. also attached to the simpler type of 'drawing-room song'—sometimes called 'Shop Ballad', possibly to distinguish it from those hawked by the ballad-seller on broadsheets. Hence the Eng. 'Ballad Concerts' inaugurated by the mus. publisher, John Boosey, in 1867.
(3) Self-contained narrative song, such as Loewe's *Edward* or Schubert's *Erlkönig.* Also applied to certain narrative operatic arias, e.g. Senta's ballad in Wagner's *Der fliegende Holländer.*
(4) Term applied in jazz to sentimental song.

Ballade (Fr.). Ballad. A term given by *Chopin to a long, dramatic type of pf. piece, the mus. equivalent of a poetical ballad of the heroic type. He wrote 4—G minor, Op. 23; F major, Op. 38; A♭ major, Op. 47; and F minor, Op. 52. Brahms, Liszt, Grieg, Fauré, and others later used the title.

Ballad Horn. Type of Saxhorn. Different makers apply the name to different varieties, but generally understood as alto hn. in E♭ or C with cup mouthpiece and 3 piston valves.

Ballad Opera. Opera with spoken dialogue and using popular tunes of the day provided with new words. Form originated in England with Allan Ramsay's *The Gentle Shepherd* (1725), but the success in 1728 of Gay's *The *Beggar's Opera* started the vogue for this type of entertainment which lasted for nearly 30 years. Charles Coffey's *The Devil to pay* (1731) was adapted in Ger. in 1743 as *Der Teufel ist los* and est. the *Singspiel* tradition which culminated in Mozart's *Die Entführung aus dem Serail.* There are also wider

definitions of the genre; and in the 20th cent. Vaughan Williams's *Hugh the Drover* (1914) is described as a 'romantic ballad opera' by the composer although it has no spoken dialogue and does not exclusively comprise traditional tunes.

Ballata (It.). One of poetic forms in It. secular songs of 14th and early 15th cents., the others being madrigal and caccia. Form comprised *ripresa* (refrain), two *piedi, volta,* and *ripresa.* Landini was prolific comp. of *ballate.* Was used by Dufay and then lost its appeal.

Ballerina, Ballerino (It.). Ballet dancer—female and male respectively, hence *prima ballerina,* the leading female dancer of the co., and *prima ballerina assoluta,* the undisputed leading female dancer of the co.

Ballet. Entertainment in which dancers, by use of mime, etc., perform to mus. to tell a story or to express a mood. The ballet was largely developed in the courts of Fr. and It. during the 16th and 17th cents. and especially in that of Louis XIV (reigned 1643–1715), where *Lully was in charge of the mus. The ballets of this period were danced by the court itself and were very formal (gavottes, minuets, chaconnes, etc.), heavy dresses being worn, with wigs, high heels, and other trappings of court life. But the first ballet is generally held to have been the *Balet comique de la Royne* given in Paris in 1581.
Even in the days of the ballerina Camargo (1710–70), who introduced many innovations, dress was ample, skirts still falling below the knees; however, she introduced a more vigorous style involving high jumps. J. G Noverre (1727–1810) banished the conventions hitherto ruling as to the use of mythological subjects, set order of dances, elaborate dresses, etc., and thus made himself the founder of the dramatic ballet, or *ballet d'action.* He est. the 5-act ballet as an entertainment in its own right; collab. with Gluck and Mozart in operatic ballets, and wrote an important treatise on the ballet. Other great masters of this period were Dauberval (1742–1806), Gaetano Vestris (1729–1808), and Pierre Gardel (1758–1840). Vestris was the founder of a family of *maîtres de ballet,* active in 3 generations (1747–1825), and of several important ballerinas. The Italian choreographer Salvatore Vigano (1769–1819), for whom Beethoven wrote *Die Geschöpfe des Prometheus,* continued Noverre's work.
By the end of the 18th cent. the ballet had almost discarded the last of its stately court influences and had developed gymnastic virtuosity, although movement was still mainly confined to the legs and feet. Dancing on the *pointe* (on the tips of the toes) came in only about 1814; it calls for arduous practice, requires special shoes, and carries a danger of dislocation; Marie Taglioni (career from 1822 to 1847) was its first notable exponent. The Romantic Movement introduced

into the ballet an attempt at ethereal informality. Costumes grew shorter and the skin-tight *Maillot*, named after its Parisian inventor, was daringly introduced.

From the mid-19th cent., spectacular ballets, of a realistic and topical character, became common, and much effective ballet mus. was written, esp. by Fr. composers: Adam's *Giselle* (1841) has remained a classic and the appearance of Delibes's *Coppélia* (1870) marks an epoch.

Ballet as an integral part of opera was at its height of popularity in the first half of the 19th cent. Some of the operas of Rossini and Donizetti incl. ballets, and Verdi, bowing to the demands of Paris, where a ballet was *de rigueur* in opera, incl. ballets in many of his operas for that capital, even writing ballet mus. for *Otello* for its Paris prod. (1894). The high priest of ballet-in-opera was Meyerbeer, and even Wagner had to introduce ballet into *Tannhäuser* to placate his Paris audiences (but enraged the blades of the Jockey Club by refusing to place it, as was customary, in the 2nd act, by which time they would have finished their coffee and cigars). The extent of the Parisian 'craze' can be judged from the fact that Berlioz's orchestration of Weber's *Invitation to the Dance (Aufforderung zum Tanz*, 1819) was commissioned for the 1841 prod. of *Der Freischütz*, and dances from Bizet's incidental mus. to *L'Arlésienne* were interpolated into *Carmen*.

Fr. influence on the Russ. Imperial court ths. also created a tradition of ballet in St Petersburg and Moscow to which national traditions were added. Both cities had long had their royal schs. of ballet where technique was highly polished but there was little of mus. worth for them to dance until the masterpieces of Tchaikovsky: *Swan Lake* (1876), The *Sleeping Beauty* (1889), and *Nutcracker* (1892). The outstanding choreog. was Marius Petipa (*b* Marseilles, 1818; *d* Gurzuf, Crimea, 1910) who was principal ballet master in St Petersburg from 1862 to 1903.

The 20th cent. saw reforms and revolutionary tendencies in the development of ballet which may be identified principally but not wholly with two individuals. The Amer. Isadora Duncan (1878–1927) was inspired by Gr. classicism and by the natural movements of the birds, the waves, etc., thereby rejecting many conventional choreographical formulae. She toured Russ. and was seen by the young dancer Mikhail *Fokine (1880–1942) who was also working to free ballet from its 19th-cent. conventions, having been deeply impressed by the visit of Siamese dancers to Russ. in 1900. He achieved his ambition in collab. with the impresario and opera producer Serge *Diaghilev (1872–1929). Taking advantage of the Franco-Russ. entente and realising that radical reforms would not be allowed in the imperial ths., Diaghilev est. his Russian Ballet (Ballets Russes) in Paris, 1909, bringing together choreogs. such as Fokine, and dancers such as *Nijinsky, Pavlova, and Karsavina. Ballet scores were com-

missioned from 'progressive' contemporary composers, e.g. Ravel (*Daphnis et Chloé*), Stravinsky (*Fire-Bird*, *Petrushka, The *Rite of Spring*), Strauss (*Josephslegende*), and Debussy (*Jeux*). The artists Bakst and Picasso were among those commissioned to design scenery. Ballet mus. ceased to be wholly subservient to the dancers' demands. The impact of these Diaghilev prods. on Paris, London, Berlin, and other cities was electrifying and exercised considerable influence on all the arts. Diaghilev introduced 1-act ballets, making an evening from 2 or 3 short ballets. In this way there came about the ballet based on the Polovtsian Dances from Borodin's *Prince Igor*, the famous *Spectre de la rose* (to the Weber-Berlioz *Invitation to the Dance*) and, as a vehicle for Nijinsky, a ballet to the mus. of Debussy's *Prélude à l'après-midi d'un faune*. Diaghilev frequently used re-workings of mus. not comp. for dancing as the basis of successful ballets, the most famous being Les *Sylphides* (1909), from Chopin pieces. Other composers treated in this way were Rossini, Cimarosa, Scarlatti, and Handel. Stravinsky was adept at these re-workings, as can be heard from *Pulcinella* (Pergolesi) and Le *Baiser de la fée* (Tchaikovsky). After the 1914–18 war, Stravinsky continued for a time to collaborate with Diaghilev but other composers who wrote ballets for him were Satie (*Parade*), Falla (*Three-Cornered Hat*) and Prokofiev (*Chout, Le Pas d'acier*, and *L'*Enfant prodigue*). Most of the outstanding figures of ballet between 1918 and 1939 came from the Diaghilev co., Serge Lifar, Léonide Massine and George *Balanchine among them. The virtuosity of dancers and the constantly developing art of choreogs. has successfully brought a vast range of non-ballet mus. into the ballet th. Examples of scores to which ballets have been devised incl. Strauss's *Till Eulenspiegel*, Tchaikovsky's 5th Sym., Brahms's 4th Sym., Berlioz's *Symphonie fantastique*, Elgar's *Enigma Variations* and Mahler's Das *Lied von der Erde*. Nevertheless the comp. of orig. ballet scores has prospered. Tchaikovsky's heir was undoubtedly Prokofiev, whose *Cinderella* and *Romeo and Juliet*, for the Bolshoy Ballet, are superb, and distinguished scores have been written for ballet by Bartók, Copland, Shostakovich, Henze, Hindemith, Britten, and others.

In Brit. ballet was imported after the days of the masque, but the impetus provided by the Diaghilev co. led to the formation of the Camargo Soc. in 1930, of whom the leading lights were the economist Maynard Keynes (married to Lydia Lopokova), his doctor brother Geoffrey Keynes, and Ninette de *Valois. Among its first prods. was Vaughan Williams's *Job*, the first large-scale modern ballet score (though it is designated 'a masque for dancing') by a Brit. composer. The Camargo Soc. became the Vic-Wells Ballet, under the aegis of Lilian *Baylis at the Old Vic and SW, later the SW Ballet, and eventually the Royal Ballet (based on CG). Leading figures assoc. with

Brit. ballet have incl. Constant *Lambert, Frederick *Ashton, John Cranko, Antony Tudor, Anton Dolin, Alicia Markova, Robert Helpmann, Marie Rambert, Margot Fonteyn, Rudolf Nureyev, and Kenneth MacMillan. Beside the Royal Ballet, leading cos. working regularly in Brit. are London Festival Ballet, Ballet Rambert, and the Northern Ballet Th. Orig. ballet scores by Brit. composers incl. Bliss's *Checkmate and *Miracle in the Gorbals, Britten's *Prince of the Pagodas, Walton's The Quest, Arnold's *Homage to the Queen and Solitaire, and Maxwell Davies's Salome.

In Europe after Diaghilev, and contemporary with him, leading influences in varying degrees were the Paris-based Ballets Suédois, under Rolf de Maré (1886–1964), the Ger. choreog. Kurt Jooss's Ballets Jooss, (for which the mus. was written by one composer, Frederick Cohen (1904–67)), Rudolf von Laban (1879–1958), Mary Wigman (1886–1973), Ida Rubinstein (c.1885–1960), Emile Jaques-Dalcroze (1865–1950) and Maud Allan (1883–1956). There has been a vigorous expansion of ballet and ballet potentialities in the USA. Ex-Diaghilev associates such as Balanchine worked there and other pioneers of ballet there incl. Ruth St Denis (1877–1968), Ted Shawn (1891–1972), and Adolph Bolm (1884–1951). Later the chief figures were Mary Wigman and especially Martha Graham (b 1894), Paul Taylor (b 1930), and Louis Horst (1884–1964) who was director of the Denishawn Sch. 1915–25 and mus. dir. for the Graham co. 1926–48. Amer. composers have been prolific in writing mus. specifically for dancing and while ballet has invaded the popular Broadway musicals such as On Your Toes, Oklahoma!, and Kiss Me, Kate, avant-garde ballet developments have kept pace with those in music. The collab. between the composer John *Cage and the choreog. Merce Cunningham (b 1919) pioneered new forms of presenting ballet as, to quote Cage, 'an activity of movement, sound, and light', using non-sequential, non-mimetic movement. The aleatory trend in mus. has had its parallel in ballet, where all formal organization has been thrown overboard. Elec. scores have become commonplace, and slide and film projections are used. As mus. is now prod. without instr. or performers, ballet can be prod. without dancers, by means of electrocybernetic devices. Mention should also be made, if briefly, of the influence on ballet of jazz, Latin-Amer. mus., African tribal dances, and the stylized ballets of China and Japan.

Ballet de Cour (Fr.). Fr. Court ballet of the 17th cent. The Balet comique de la royne, comp. for the marriage festivities of the Duc de Joyeuse and the sister of the queen of Fr. in 1581 is considered the first of its kind. Numerous other ballets were comp. for the Fr. court up to the 1670s, when they were gradually superseded by Lully's operas.

Ballet Russe de Monte Carlo. Ballet co. formed in 1932, and orig. called Ballets Russes de Monte Carlo, in effort to continue *Diaghilev's work. It was headed by Colonel Wassili de Basil and René Blum, with Fokine, Massine, and Balanchine as choreogs. Later de Basil split away from Blum and Massine and his co. disbanded in Paris in 1947, though it was revived for a year in London, 1951. The Blum-Massine co., under the name Ballet Russe de Monte Carlo, went to USA at outbreak of World War II where it toured N. Amer. until disbandment in 1962.

Ballets Russes (Russian Ballet). See under Ballet and Diaghilev.

Balletomane. 20th-cent. term meaning one who is extremely enthusiastic about ballet, hence also 'balletomania'.

Ballett (Ballet). A form of *madrigal orig. so called because the performers also danced to the tune. Thought to have been invented by the It. 16th-cent. composer Gastoldi who in 1591 pubd. Balletti a cinque voci with instructions for dancing and instr. accs. In Eng. the ballett was popularized by *Morley and *Weelkes, whose first colls. were pubd. respectively in 1595 and 1598. Balletts differ from madrigals in their regular rhythm and (an indispensable feature) the singing of 'fal-lal-la' between the clauses.

Balliff, Claude (b Paris, 1924). Fr. composer and teacher. Studied at Bordeaux 1942–51, Paris Cons. (under Messiaen) and Berlin Hochschule (with Blacher). Taught in Berlin and Hamburg 1955–1958. Worked at Fr. radio's Groupe de Recherches Musicales 1959–61. Teacher at Reims Cons. 1965–8, prof. of analysis Paris Cons. from 1971. Author of book on Berlioz (1968). Works incl.:

ORCH: Voyage de mon oreille (1957); Fantasio (1957, rev. 1976); Ceci et cela (1959–65); A cor et à cri (1962); Poème de la felicité (1978).

INSTR: Antienne No. 1 à la Ste. Vierge, 6 singers, 8 instr. (1952, rev. 1956); 3 str. qts. (1955, 1958, 1959); 2 str. trios (1956, 1959); vn. sonata (1957); 4 quintets (1952–60); Phrases sur le souffle, alto, 8 instr. (1958); quintet for fl., ob., str. trio (1958); fl. sonata (1958); Mouvement pour 2, fl., pf. (1959); double trio for fl., ob., vc., and vn., cl., hn. (1961); Imaginaire I, fl., cl., tpt., tb., vn., vc., harp (1963).

PIANO: Sonatas: Nos. 1–5 (1957–60).

ORGAN: 4 Sonatas (1956).

CHORAL: Requiem, 8 solo vv., 5 ch., orch. (1953–68); Prières, ch. (1971); Chapelet, ch. (1971).

Balling, Michael (b Heidingsfeld-am-Main, 1866; d Darmstadt, 1925). Ger. cond. who began as violist. Founded mus. sch. in N.Z., 1892. Ass. cond. at Bayreuth, 1896–1924. Cond., Karlsruhe Opera, 1903–9. Cond. Wagner's Ring in Eng. with Denhof Co., Edinburgh, 1910. Cond., Hallé Orch., 1912–14; mus. dir., Darmstadt from 1919.

Ballo (It.). Ball, dance; so tempo di ballo, which can mean (a) At a dancing speed, or (b) A dance-style movement.

Ballo in Maschera, Un (A Masked Ball). Opera in 3 acts by Verdi to lib. by Somma based on Scribe's lib. for Auber's *Gustave III ou Le Bal masqué*. Prod. Rome 1859, NY and London 1861. Events of the opera are based on assassination of King Gustavus III of Sweden in 1792. The Naples censor forbade regicide on the opera stage and ordered Verdi to adapt his mus. to a new lib. He refused, but Rome agreed to stage the opera if the locale was moved outside Europe. Verdi and Somma thereupon changed Sweden to Boston, Mass., before the War of Independence. In 1952 at CG the action was replaced in Sweden and the characters resumed their orig. (and historical) names. These, with the Boston version equivalents in brackets, are: Gustavus (Riccardo, Earl of Warwick); Count Ankarstroem (Renato); Mme Arvidson (Ulrica); Count Ribbing (Samuel); Count Horn (Tom). Only the heroine, Amelia, and the page Oscar were unaffected by the change. Other operas on this subject are *Auber's *Gustave III* (Paris 1833), *Gabussi's *Clemenza di Valois* (Venice 1841), and *Mercadante's *Il reggente* (Turin 1843).

Balsam, Artur (*b* Warsaw, 1906). Polish-born pianist. Educated Lódź Cons. and Berlin Hochschule. Début Lódź 1918. Settled in USA, where he has taught at various academies. Distinguished chamber-mus. player.

Baltsa, Agnes (*b* Lefkas, 1944). Greek mezzo-soprano. Studied Athens Acad., winning first Callas Scholarship. Frankfurt Opera 1968–71, making début as Cherubino. Sang Oktavian in Vienna 1970. Deutsche Oper, Berlin, from 1970. La Scala début 1976, Amer. début 1971 (Houston), CG 1976, NY Met. 1979. Outstanding Carmen, Composer (*Ariadne auf Naxos*), Dorabella, and Dido in Berlioz's *Les Troyens*. Sang Romeo in revival of Bellini's *I Capuleti e i Montecchi* at CG, 1984.

Baltzar, Thomas (*b* Lübeck, *c*.1630; *d* London, 1663). Ger.-born violinist and the most accomplished up to his period heard in Eng., according to Evelyn and Anthony Wood. Appointed leader of band of Charles II, 1661. Some comps. survive.

Bamberg Symphony Orchestra. Orch. based in Bamberg, Bavaria, founded 1946 from the Prague Deutsche Philharmonie. Prin. conds. have incl. Herbert Albert (1947–8), Eugen Jochum (1948–9), Joseph Keilberth (1949–68), Jochum (1969–78), James Loughran (1978–83), Witold Rowicki (1983–6), Horst Stein from 1986.

Bamberger, Carl (*b* Vienna, 1902). Austrian-born cond. and teacher. Studied Vienna Univ., cond. opera in Danzig, Darmstadt, and Russia 1924–31, before settling in USA in 1937. Mus. dir., spring fest., Columbia, S.Car., 1942–50. Cond. Montreal Chamber Concerts 1950–2. Founder-cond. Mannes College Orch. 1938–75. Author of book on conducting.

Bamboo Pipe. Simple instr. of the *recorder type, introduced into Amer. schs. in the 1920s and later into those of Brit., the players usually making their own instr. Vaughan Williams wrote a *Suite* (1939) for treble, alto, ten., and bass pipes.

Bamboula. (1) Primitive Negro tambourine in use in the West Indies.
(2) Dance to which this is the acc.

Bampton, Rose (*b* Lakewood, Ohio, 1908). Amer. operatic sop. (at first mez.). Trained Curtis Institute. Début NY Met. 1932, member of Met. 1932–50. CG 1937. Buenos Aires 1942–50. Taught at Juilliard Sch. from 1974.

Banalités (Banalities). Song-cycle by Poulenc to 5 poems by Guillaume Appollinaire, comp. 1940. Titles are: *Chanson d'Orkenise, Hôtel, Fagnes de Wallonie, Voyage à Paris, Sanglots*.

Banchieri, Adriano (*b* Bologna, 1568; *d* Bologna, 1634). It. composer, organist, and theorist. Org., S. Michele, Bosco, and of Monte Oliveto, where in 1613 he became abbot. His *L'organo suonarino*, pubd. Venice 1605, contains first precise rules for accompanying from a figured bass. In *Moderna practica musicale* (Venice 1613) he discusses alterations necessary because of the influence of figured bass on ornaments in singing. Comp. much church mus., also 'Intermedi' for comedies. His *La pazzia senile* (1598), regarded as almost the first comic opera, is a sequence of madrigals, in the Vecchi manner, based on the *commedia dell'arte* character Pantaloon. He was pioneer of fantasies for instr. ens.

Band. A numerous body of instr. players, e.g. brass, dance, military, steel, and perc. bands. Rarely now applied to full sym. orch except affectionately (Hallé Band). Also applied to sections of the orch., e.g. str. band and, particularly, wind band. Thus when Berlioz in his *Requiem* and Walton in *Belshazzar's Feast* require extra brass 'bands', they mean brass sections, not a full complement *à la* Black Dyke Mills.

Bandoneon. Argentinian type of *Accordion. Instead of a kbd. it has buttons producing single notes.

Bandora. Eng. wire-str. mus. instr. similar to lute invented by John Rose of Bridewell in 1561. A bass instr.with sonorous quality of sound, it was used to acc. the v. by such composers as J. *Mundy and *Peerson and works for solo bandora survive. Orig. had 6 courses but a 7th was added in 17th cent. Name possibly derived from Sp. *bandurria*.

Bandurria. Sp. type of flat-backed guitar, known as early as 14th cent. as *mandurria*. 3-course (sometimes 4 or 5) instr. shaped like *rebec and played with plectrum.

Banfield, Raffaello de (*b* Newcastle upon Tyne, 1922). It. composer whose works incl. 2 operas based on stories by Tennessee Williams, *Lord Byron's Love Letter* and *Orpheus Descending*.

Banister, John (*b* London, *c*.1625; *d* London, 1679). Eng. violinist, member of the band of Charles II, becoming leader in 1662. Dismissed for financial irregularities, 1667. Composer and said to be Britain's first organizer of public concerts (in London, 1672).

Banjo. Instr. of the same general type as the *guitar, but the resonating body is of parchment strained over a metal hoop and it has an open back. There are from 4 to 9 str. (usually 5 or 6), passing over a low bridge and 'stopped' against a fingerboard, which is often without *frets; one is a *melody string* (thumb string, or *chanterelle*), the others providing a simple chordal acc. Some examples have gut str. (played with the fingertips) and others wire str. (played with a plectrum). Used by Gershwin in *Porgy and Bess* and by Delius in *Koanga*. The origin of this instr. is supposed to be Africa, and it was in use among the slaves of S. USA; then, in the 19th cent., it became the accepted instr. of 'Negro *Minstrels' and in the 20th found a place in jazz bands. These last sometimes used a *Tenor Banjo*, with a different scheme of tuning (resembling that of the vn. family). The *Zither Banjo* is of small size and has wire str.

Banjolin. Instrument of the banjo type, but with a short, fretted neck, like that of a mandoline. It has 4 single (or pairs of) str., played with a plectrum.

Banks, Don (Donald Oscar) (*b* Melbourne, 1923; *d* Sydney, N.S.W., 1980). Australian composer. Studied Melbourne Univ. Cons. of Mus., 1947–9, then privately with Seiber (London 1950–2) and Dallapiccola (Florence 1952–3). Worked in Australia as jazz pianist and arranger. Several film scores. Met Milton *Babbitt in 1952 and has followed his excursions into elec. mus. Mus. dir., Goldsmiths' College, London Univ., 1969–71. Head of comp. and elec. music studies, Canberra Sch. of Mus. from 1974. Prin. works incl. concs. for vn. (1968), hn. (1965), *Settings from Roget* for jazz singer and jazz qt. (1966), *Assemblies* for orch. (1966), *Tirade*, mez., pf., harp, perc. (1968), Psalm 70, sop. and chamber orch., *Divisions* for orch., *Nexus*, orch. and jazz quintet, *Commentary*, pf. and tape, *Prospects* (1973).

Banner of St George, The. Ballad for ch. and orch., Op. 33 by Elgar. Text by Shapcott Wensley. Comp. 1896–7. F.p. London 1897.

Bantock, (Sir) Granville (*b* Westbourne Park, London, 1868; *d* London, 1946). Eng. composer, cond., and educationist. Trained at RAM 1889–93, toured as cond. of a theatrical co. and became mus. dir. at New Brighton, nr. Liverpool, where he gave remarkable concerts of mus. by contemporary Brit. composers. Was among first Eng. champions of mus. of Sibelius, whose 3rd Sym. is

ded. to him. From 1900 Prin. of Sch. of Mus. in Birmingham and from 1908 Prof. of Mus., Birmingham Univ.; in 1934 became Chairman of Corporation of TCL. Knighted 1930.

His orch. mus. is extremely brilliantly scored in a romantic manner but has not held its place in the repertory apart from occasional perfs. of his ov. *Pierrot of the Minute* and his tone-poem after Browning *Fifine at the Fair*. Prolific composer of part-songs for competitive fests., and his most ambitious works were 2 unacc. choral syms. *Atalanta in Calydon* (Manchester 1912) and *Vanity of Vanities* (Liverpool 1914) and a 3-part setting for cont., ten., and bass soloists, ch., and orch. of *Omar Khayyám* (1906, 1907, 1909). Other comps. incl.:

STAGE: *Caedmar*, opera (1893); *The Pearl of Iran*, opera (1894); *Eugene Aram*, unfinished opera (1896); *Hippolytus*, incid. mus. (1908); *Electra*, incid. mus. (1909); *The Great God Pan*, ballet (1915); *Salome*, incid. mus. (1918); *The Seal-Woman*, opera (1924); *Macbeth*, incid. mus. (1926).

ORCH: *Elegiac Poem*, vc. and orch. (1898); *Helena Variations* (1899); *English Scenes* (1900); Tone-poems: *Dante* (1901, rev. as *Dante and Beatrice*, 1910), *Fifine at the Fair* (1901), *Hudibras* (1902), *The Witch of Atlas* (1902), *Lalla Rookh* (1902); *Sapphic Poem*, vc. and orch. (1906); ov. *The Pierrot of the Minute* (1908); *From the Scottish Highlands*, str. (1913); *Dramatic Poem*, vc. and orch. (1914); *Hebridean Symphony* (1915); *Pagan Symphony* (1923–8); *Celtic Symphony*, str., 6 hps. (1940); *Overture to a Greek Comedy* (1941); *The Funeral* (1946).

CHORUS AND ORCH: *The Fire Worshippers*, soloists, ch., and orch. (1892); *The Blessed Damozel*, reciter and orch. (1892); *The Time Spirit*, ch. and orch. (1902); *Ferishtah's Fancies*, v. and orch. (1905); *Sappho*, v. and orch. (1906); *Sea Wanderers*, ch. and orch. (1906); *Omar Khayyám*, cont., ten., bass, ch., and orch. (1906–9); *Song of Liberty*, ch. and orch. (1914); *Song of Songs*, soloists, ch., and orch. (1922); *Pagan Chants*, v. and orch. (1917–26); *The *Pilgrim's Progress*, soloists, ch., and orch. (1928); *Prometheus Unbound*, ch. and orch. (1936); *Thomas the Rhymer*, v. and orch. (1946).

UNACC. VOICES: Mass in B♭, male vv. (1903); *Atalanta in Calydon*, sym. for ch. (1911); *Vanity of Vanities*, sym. for ch. (1913); *A Pageant of Human Life*, sym. for ch. (1913); 7 *Burdens of Isaiah*, male vv. (1927); 5 *Choral Songs and Dances from The Bacchae*, female vv. (1945).

CHAMBER MUSIC: Str. qt. (*c*.1899); *Pibroch*, vc., hp. (1917); va. sonata (1919); vc. sonata (1924); 3 vn. sonatas (1929, 1932, 1940); 2 vc. sonatas (1940, 1945).

Also many pf. pieces, 40 song-cycles, nearly 50 solo songs, works for brass band.

Bar, Bar Line. The vertical line marked on a stave to denote the point of metrical division is actually the bar but in modern usage has come to be called the bar line, while the space between such lines is the bar itself. Thus, '3 beats to the bar'. In Amer. parlance, a bar is called a measure, and a bar means a bar line. 2 vertical lines close together are, in Eng., a double bar, not double bar line.

Barbarie, Orgue de. Small mechanical org. played by turning a handle, at one time commonly found in Eng. streets.

Barber, Samuel (*b* West Chester, Penn., 1910; *d* NY, 1981). Amer. composer. Played pf. and vc. at age 6. At 14 entered Curtis Institute, Philadelphia, as one of first charter students, studying comp. under Scalero, pf. under Isabelle Vengerova, and singing under Emilio de Gogorza. In 1928 formed a lasting and fruitful friendship with Gian Carlo *Menotti. From 1933 his comps. began to be played, notably his setting of Arnold's *Dover Beach*, in which he sang the bar. part, and his Vc. Sonata, in which he played the pf. In 1935 won a Pulitzer scholarship and in 1936 the Amer. Academy's *Prix de Rome*. His first Sym. was given its f.p. in Rome that year. Toscanini cond. f.ps. of his *Adagio for Strings* (orig. the slow movement of his str. qt.) and the first *Essay for Orchestra* in 1938 and in subsequent years f.ps. of his works were given in NY, Boston, and Philadelphia under Walter, Koussevitzky, Leinsdorf, Mitropoulos, Ormandy, and Mehta. His 4-act opera *Vanessa*, to lib. by Menotti, was perf. at the NY Met. in 1958 and another opera *Antony and Cleopatra* was commissioned for the opening of the new Metropolitan in the Lincoln Center, NY, in Sept. 1966.

Barber's mus. is in the European traditional line rather than specifically 'American'. Conservative in idiom, it is melodic, elegant, and brilliant. His lyricism is best heard in *Knoxville: Summer of 1915*, for sop. and orch., and his romanticism in *Dover Beach*, the Vc. Sonata, and the Sym. No. 1. His Pf. Sonata, first played by Horowitz, is a bravura work. The operas met with a poor initial response, but the concs. and songs are highly effective. Prin. works:

OPERAS: *Vanessa* (1957), *A Hand of Bridge* (1958), *Antony and Cleopatra* (1966, rev. 1974).
BALLETS: *Medea* (1946), *Souvenirs* (1952).
ORCH: Sym. No. 1 (1936), No. 2 (1944), *Overture to School for Scandal* (1933); *Music for a Scene from Shelley* (1937), *Essay No. 1* (1937), *No. 2* (1942), *No. 3* (1978); *Adagio for Strings* (1938) (orch. from Str. Qt. Op. 11).
VOCAL AND CHORAL: *Dover Beach* (bar. with str. qt. or str. orch.) (1933), *Knoxville: Summer of 1915*, sop. and orch. (1947), *Prayers of Kierkegaard* (1954), *Andromache's Farewell* (1962), and many solo songs, incl. *Hermit Songs* (1953) and *The Lovers*, song-cycle of 9 poems of Neruda (1971).
CONCERTOS: Vn. (1940), Vc. (1945), Pf. (1962), *Capricorn Concerto* (for chamber orch.) (1944).

CHAMBER MUSIC: Cello Sonata (1932), *Excursions* for Pf. (1944), Piano Sonata (1949), String Quartet (1936), *Summer Music* (woodwind quintet) (1956).

Barber of Bagdad, The (Cornelius). See *Barbier von Bagdad, Der.*

Barber of Seville, The (Rossini; also Paisiello). See *Barbiere di Siviglia, Il.*

Barber's Shop Music. One of the regular haunts of mus. in the 16th and 17th cents. was the barber's shop. Here customers awaiting their turn found some simple instr. on which they could strum. The barbers themselves, waiting between customers, took up the instr. and thus came to possess some repute as performers. In Eng. lit. of the 16th and 17th cents. allusions to barbers as musicians are numerous.

The mus. proclivities of barbers ceased in Eng. in the earlier part of the 18th cent. The tradition was maintained longer in Amer. where 'barber-shop harmony', implying a rather banal style of close harmony singing, has enjoyed a 20th-cent. revival.

Barbican. District in City of London where arts and conference centre is situated. Arts centre, opened in 1982 at a cost of £143 million, includes concert-hall, theatre and studios, lending and reference library, art gallery, sculpture court, and cinema. *Guildhall School of Music and Drama housed on the site since 1977.

Barbier von Bagdad, Der (The Barber of Bagdad). Comedy-opera in 2 acts by Cornelius to his own lib. based on *1001 Nights.* (Prod. Weimar, under Liszt, 1 perf. 1858; NY and Chicago 1890; London 1891). Most perfs. since 1884 have been of a rev. and re-orchestration by *Mottl.

Barbiere di Siviglia, Il (The Barber of Seville). 2-act opera buffa by Rossini, to lib. by Sterbini based on Beaumarchais. To differentiate it from Paisiello's opera of the same name it was called *Almaviva, ossia L'inutile precauzione* (Almaviva, or the Useless Precaution) at its f.p. (Rome 1816). Perf. London 1818, NY 1819. The famous ov. had already been used by Rossini for 2 other operas (*Aureliano in Palmira* and *Elisabetta, Regina d'Inghilterra*).

Paisiello's opera is in 4 acts to a lib. by Petrosellini. Prod. St Petersburg 1782, London 1789. Several modern revivals. Operas on this subject were also comp. by Elsperger (1783), Benda (1785), Schulz (1786), Morlacchi (1816), and Graffigna (1879).

Barbieri, Fedora (*b* Trieste, 1920). It. mez. who made operatic débuts in Trieste and in Florence, 1941. Sang in opera cos. at Rome 1941–2, Milan (La Scala) 1943, Florence 1945. CG 1950 and 1957–8. NY Met. 1950–4 (début as Eboli in *Don Carlos*) and 1956–75.

Barbirolli, (Lady) **Evelyn** (née Rothwell) (*b* Wallingford, 1911). Eng. oboist and teacher. 2nd wife of Sir John *Barbirolli whom she married 1939. Trained at RCM. Oboist, CG Touring Orch. 1931–2, Scottish Orch. 1933–7, Glyndebourne Opera Orch. 1934–8, LSO 1935–9. Thereafter soloist and recitalist, member of various ens. Gave f.p. in modern times of Mozart's oboe concerto (K314), Salzburg, 1948. Author of several books on ob. technique. Prof. of ob., RAM, from 1971. O.B.E. 1984.

Barbirolli, (Sir) John (Giovanni Battista) (*b* London, 1899; *d* London, 1970). Eng. cond., of It.-Fr. parentage. Studied at TCL and RAM, being prominent as cellist. First public appearance as conc. soloist, London 1911. Member of Queen's Hall Orch. 1916. Served in army 1918. After war, free-lance cellist and member of str. qt. Formed own str. orch. to conduct, 1924. Appointed staff cond., BNOC, 1926. Cond at CG 1929 and became prin. cond. CG touring co. 1929–33. Cond., Scottish Orch., Glasgow 1933–6, NY Phil.-Sym. Orch. 1936–42. Returned to Eng. 1943 as cond., Hallé Orch., Manchester, where he remained until his death, lifting the orch. to new heights and taking it on several foreign tours. Also prin. cond., Houston S.O. 1961–7. Guest cond. of orchs. throughout the world, esp. Berlin P.O., Boston S.O., and Chicago S.O., etc. Famed interpretations of Mahler, Elgar, Vaughan Williams, Sibelius, Puccini, and Verdi, but successful in remarkably wide repertory. Also arr. mus. by Purcell, Corelli, Pergolesi, and Elizabethan composers for orch. and as ob. concs. for his wife Evelyn *Barbirolli whom he married 1939. Knighted 1949, C.H. 1969. Hon. Freeman of Manchester, 1958.

Barcarolle (Fr. from It.; Ger. *Barkarole*). Boat song or an instr. comp. with a steady rhythm (in compound duple or compound quadruple time) reminiscent of songs of the Venetian gondoliers or *barcaruoli*.

Barcarolle from *Les Contes d'Hoffmann*. Retrieved by Offenbach from his much earlier opera, *Die Rheinnixen*, 1864 (a failure). In this it figured as a Goblin's Song.

Bard, The (Barden). Tone-poem for orch., Op. 64, by *Sibelius, comp. 1913, rev. 1914. F.p. Helsinki 1913, cond. Sibelius. F.p. in England 1935 (broadcast, cond. Boult), (public 1938, cond. Beecham).

Bardgett, Herbert (*b* Glasgow, 1894; *d* Leeds, 1962). Scot. choral trainer and cond. Nottingham Harmonic Soc.; ch. master Huddersfield Choral Soc., Hallé Choir, Leeds Fest.

Bardi, Count Giovanni (*b* Florence, 1534; *d* Rome, 1612). It. nobleman in whose palace in Florence a group of poets and musicians met regularly in the later years of the 16th cent., this giving rise to what are considered to have been the first operatic perfs. He wrote at least 2 libs. and comp. madrigals. See *Camerata*.

Barenboim, Daniel (*b* Buenos Aires, 1942). Israeli pianist and cond. Taught pf. by his mother, then his father. Début Buenos Aires 1949. Family moved to Israel 1952. Mus. training at S. Cecilia Acad., Rome. Studied privately with Edwin Fischer and Nadia Boulanger, also attended Igor Markevitch's cond. classes at Salzburg Mozarteum. Début as conc. soloist, Paris 1955, in London 1956 (with RPO cond. Josef Krips), and NY 1957 (with Stokowski). Has several times given recital series of all Beethoven pf. sonatas (Israel, S. Amer. 1960, London 1967, 1970, NY 1970). Worked as cond.-soloist with ECO 1966 and cond. New Philharmonia Orch. 1967, Hallé and LSO (US tour) 1968, Berlin Phil. Orch. 1969, NY P.O. 1970. Mus. dir. Orchestre de Paris 1975–89. Has recorded Berlioz orch. and choral works. Début in opera, Edinburgh Fest. 1973 (*Don Giovanni*). Cond. *Tristan und Isolde*, Bayreuth, 1981. Married cellist Jacqueline *du Pré, 1967, and settled in Eng., pursuing highly successful career both as pianist and cond. Has acc. Janet Baker and Fischer-Dieskau in recitals and is chamber-mus. player with Zukerman, Perlman, and (until 1976) Piatigorsky. Awarded Bruckner Medal.

Bärenhäuter, Der (The Lazybones). Opera in 3 acts by Siegfried *Wagner to his own lib. Prod. Munich, 1899.

Bärenreiter-Verlag (Kassel). Ger. publishers. Founded Augsburg 1924 by Karl Vötterle. Emphasis on early mus.; many musicological publications including the monumental encyclopedia, *Die Musik in Geschichte und Gegenwart* ed. *Blume. Moved to Kassel, 1927.

Bargiel, Woldemar (*b* Berlin, 1828; *d* Berlin, 1897). Ger. pianist, composer, and teacher, stepbrother of Clara *Schumann. Prof. of pf., Cologne Cons. 1858–74, when he went to Berlin as prof. of pf. at Hochschule. Comp. sym., chamber mus., and pf. pieces, much influenced by Schumann.

Baring-Gould, Sabine (*b* Exeter, 1834; *d* Lew Trenchard, Devon, 1924). Eng. author, folk-song collector, and rector. Compiled (with Rev. H. Fleetwood Shephard) *Songs and Ballads of the West* (1889–91). Wrote words of popular hymns (e.g. *Onward, Christian Soldiers*, 1865).

Bariolage (Fr.). Rapid alternation of open and stopped str. in vn.-playing. The word means 'odd mixture of colours'.

Baritone. Male v. roughly midway in compass between ten. and bass and sometimes combining elements of both. Normal range from A–f♯'. But in It. and Fr. opera bars. are sometimes required to sing up to a♭'. The bass-bar. (e.g. Wagner's Wotan and Hans Sachs) has a range A♭–f'.

Baritone Horn. See *Saxhorn*.

Barker, John (Edgar) (*b* Twickenham, 1931). Eng. cond. Worked at Glyndebourne Opera

1958–9. Has cond. Wagner's *Ring* in London and on tour for ENO. Chorusmaster, CG, from 1978.

Barlow, Alan (*b* St Neots, 1927). Eng. cond. Studied at GSM and Salzburg Mozarteum. Prin. cond., Jacques Orch. 1967–71. Ed. suite from Elgar's mus. for *Arthur*.

Barlow, David (Frederick) (*b* Rothwell, Northants., 1927; *d* Newcastle upon Tyne, 1975). Eng. composer and teacher. Studied Cambridge Univ., RCM with Jacob, and in Paris with Boulanger. Senior lecturer Newcastle upon Tyne Univ. from 1968. Comps. include 2 syms., prelude *The Tempest*, church operas *David and Bathsheba* (1969) and *Judas* (1974), and chamber mus.

Barlow, Howard (*b* Plain City, Ohio, 1892; *d* Bethel, Conn., 1972). Amer. cond. Début Peterborough, New Hampshire, 1919. Cond. of CBS Sym. Orch. 1927–47.

Barlow, Wayne (*b* Elyria, Ohio, 1912). Amer. composer and author. Studied Eastman Sch. of Mus. 1930–7, having comp. lessons from Howard Hanson, among others. In 1935 studied comp. with Schoenberg at Univ. of Southern California. Taught at Eastman from 1937, becoming dir. of elec. mus. studio. Comps. incl. religious choral works, orch. works (*Sinfonietta*, sax. conc.), and works incorporating pre-recorded tape (*Sonic Pictures*, 1971; Psalm 97, 1971; *Dialogues*, 1969; and *Moonflight*, 1970).

Bärmann, Heinrich Joseph (*b* Potsdam, 1784; *d* Munich, 1847). Ger. clarinettist for whom Weber's cl. works were comp. Prin. cl. of Munich Court Orch. Comp. especially for combinations incl. his instr. His son Karl (*b* Munich, 1811; *d* Munich, 1885), composer and clarinettist, toured with him and succeeded him in court orch. Wrote *Clarinet Method*. Karl's son, also Karl (*b* Munich, 1839; *d* Boston, Mass., 1913) was pianist and pupil of Liszt. Settled Boston 1881.

Barnard, Charlotte Alington (Claribel) (*b* Louth, Lincs., 1830; *d* Dover, 1869). Eng. composer of songs, pubd. under her pseudonym, popular in their day but now represented solely by *Come back to Erin* (1866).

Barnard's Collection. Valuable and distinguished coll. of mus. in use in Brit. cath. services in the 17th cent., made by the Rev. John Barnard, a canon of St Paul's Cath. during Charles I's reign. Mus. is in 10 parts for each side of the ch., and incl. works by Tallis, Byrd, Gibbons, Morley, Weelkes, and others.

Barnby, (Sir) **Joseph** (*b* York, 1838; *d* London, 1896). Eng. organist, cond., and composer, whose finest service to mus. was during his period as organist at St Anne's, Soho, 1863–71, when he gave yearly perfs. of Bach's *St John Passion*. Cond. f.ps. in England of Dvořák's *Stabat Mater* (1883) and Wagner's *Parsifal* (in concert version, 1884). Precentor, Eton College, 1875. Prin., GSM,

1892–6. Knighted 1892. Among his many comps., sacred and secular, the chief survivor has been the part-song *Sweet and Low*.

Barn Dance. Amer. rural meeting where dances are performed, perhaps taking its name from the festivities usual in the building of a new barn. But in Britain the name was applied in the late 1880s to a particular dance also known as the Military Schottische.

Baroque (Fr.). Bizarre. Term applied to the ornate architecture of Ger. and Austria during the 17th and 18th cents. and borrowed to describe comparable mus. developments from about 1600 to the deaths of Bach and Handel in 1750 and 1759 respectively. It was a period in which harmonic complexity grew alongside emphasis on contrast. So, in opera, interest was transferred from recit. to aria, and in church mus. the contrasts of solo vv., ch., and orch. were developed to a high degree. In instr. mus. the period saw the emergence of the sonata, the suite, and particularly the concerto grosso, as in the mus. of Corelli, Vivaldi, Handel, and Bach. Most baroque mus. uses *continuo. By 'baroque organ' is meant the 18th-cent. type of instr., more brilliant in tone and flexible than its 19th-cent. counterpart. Note that 18th-cent. writers used 'baroque' in a pejorative sense to mean 'coarse' or 'old-fashioned' in taste'.

Barraine, Elsa (*b* Paris, 1910). Fr. composer, pupil of Dukas at Paris Cons. Won *Prix de Rome* 1929. Her works incl. 2 syms. (1931, 1938), cantatas, th. and film mus.

Barraqué, Jean (*b* Puteaux, Seine, 1928; *d* Paris, 1973). Fr. composer. Studied with *Messiaen 1948–51. Member of French Radio's *Groupe de Recherches musicales* 1951–3. Serialist composer, developing 'proliferating series' (e.g. 2 series producing a 3rd). Complex polyphonic writing is combined with irregular rhythms. Opposed to aleatory methods. Works incl. Pf. Sonata (1952), Cl. Conc. (1968), and group of works comp. after 1956 part of, or related to, large-scale dramatic cycle *The Death of Virgil*.

Barraud, Henry (*b* Bordeaux, 1900). Fr. composer. Studied Paris Cons. 1926–7; expelled because his comps. were considered 'a bad influence' and worked under Dukas, Aubert, etc. In charge organization of mus., Paris Int. Exposition, 1937. Mus. dir., Paris Radio, 1944–65. Comps. incl. syms., opera, oratorio *Le Mystère des Saints Innocents* (1946–7), pf. conc. (1939), fl. conc. (1962), *Symphonie concertante* for tpt. (1966), *Études* for orch. (1967), *Rapsodie dionysienne*, orch. (1962), *Une saison en enfer*, orch. (1969), saxophone qt. (1972), *Te Deum*, ch., 16 winds (1955), and *La Divine Comédie* (Dante), 5 solo vv., orch. (1972).

Barré (Fr.). Barred. Method of playing a chord on the guitar, etc., with one finger laid rigidly (like a bar) across all the str. raising their pitch equally.

Barrel Organ. Popular misusage has conferred this term on the *street piano. The real barrel org., formerly used in churches, was a genuine automatic pipe-org. in which projections on a hand-rotated barrel brought the required notes into play. It was restricted to a no. of predetermined tunes, like a musical box.

Barrett, Thomas A. See *Stuart, Leslie.*

Barri, Odoardo (really Edward Slater) (*b* Dublin, 1844; *d* London, 1920). Irish composer of Eng. drawing-room songs (e.g. *The Boys of the Old Brigade*, 1874).

Barrington, Daines (*b* London, 1727; *d* London, 1800). Eng. lawyer who wrote essays and books on mus. and musicians incl. *Crotch, Mornington, Mozart, The Wesleys*; in 1773 pubd. *Experiments and Observations on the Singing of Birds.*

Barrington, Rutland (really George Rutland Fleet) (*b* Penge, 1853; *d* London, 1922). Eng. bass singer. Début 1873. Joined D'Oyly Carte Co. and from 1877 a leading Gilbert and Sullivan exponent.

Barrios, Angel (*b* Granada, 1882; *d* Madrid, 1964). Sp. violinist; composer for orch. and the stage, also of guitar mus.

Barry, John (*b* York, 1933). Eng. composer of film mus. Studied with Francis Jackson (York Minster) and Bill Russo, Amer. arranger and composer. Has had much success with scores for films and TV.

Barsanti, Francesco (*b* Lucca, *c.*1690; *d* London, 1772). It. fl. and ob. player who settled in London 1714, playing in opera orchs. Then in Scotland, returning London 1743 and playing va. in orchs. Chamber comps. incl. recorder sonatas.

Barshay, Rudolf (*b* Labinskaya, 1924). Russ. cond. Studied Moscow Cons. Founder and cond. Moscow Chamber Orch. 1956–76. Left Russia 1976 and settled in Israel. Arr. Shostakovich's 8th str. qt. for str. orch. Prin. cond. Bournemouth S.O. from 1982.

Barstow, Josephine (Clare) (*b* Sheffield, 1940). Eng. sop. Studied Birmingham Univ. and London Opera Centre. Début Opera for All, 1964. Has sung at CG and with ENO, WNO, and Scottish Opera as well as overseas. CG début 1969. Created Denise and Gayle in Tippett's *The Knot Garden* and *The Ice Break*, Young Woman in Henze's *We Come to the River*. Fine Salome, Jenůfa, etc. Sang Gutrune in *Ring*, Bayreuth 1983. C.B.E. 1985.

Bartered Bride, The (*Prodaná Nevěsta*; Ger. *Die verkaufte Braut*). Opera in 3 acts by Smetana to lib. by Karel Sabina. (Prod. Prague 1866; Chicago 1893; London 1895; NY Met. 1909). 1st version was in 2 acts, with ov. and 20 nos. (1863–6), rev. with ballet added 1866; further rev. 1869; 3 acts, with additions, 1870; fifth and final vers., with recitatives replacing spoken dialogue, 1870.

Barth, Christian Samuel (*b* Glauchau, Saxony, 1735; *d* Copenhagen, 1809). Ger. oboist, who comp. concs. for the instr. Studied Leipzig under J. S. Bach and became oboist in orchs. at Weimar, Hanover, Kassel, and Copenhagen. His son, Friedrich Phillipp Karl August (*b* Kassel, 1774; *d* Copenhagen, 1804) was also an oboist and wrote concs. for ob., fl., and 2 hn.

Barth, Hans (*b* Leipzig, 1897; *d* Jacksonville, Florida, 1956). Ger.-born pianist and composer. Taken to USA at age 10. Became known as recitalist, etc., and held various teaching positions. Comps. incl. opera, 2 syms., etc., some employing microtones. Invented quarter-tone pf. for which he wrote 2 concs., 10 *Études*, and quintet.

Barth, Richard (*b* Grosswanzleben, Saxony, 1850; *d* Marburg, 1923). Ger. violinist (left-handed). Pupil of Joachim. Cond. of Hamburg P.O. 1894 and from 1908 dir. of Hamburg Cons. Author of book on Brahms's mus. (1904). Comp. chamber mus.

Barthélemon, François Hippolyte (*b* Bordeaux, 1741; *d* London, 1808). Fr. violinist and composer. Settled London 1764 as orch. leader at the opera and remained there with exception of continental tours and residence in Dublin 1771–3. Comps. incl. 6 syms., concs., and several operas (*The Judgment of Paris* 1768, *Belphegor* 1778, etc.), and ballets. Also wrote well-known tune to Bishop Ken's Morning Hymn ('Awake my soul and with the sun'). Particularly admired for his playing of Corelli's vn. sonatas.

Bartlet (Bartlett), John (*fl.* 1606–10). Eng. lutenist and composer of songs of the ayre type. Coll. pubd. 1606.

Bartlett, Ethel (*b* Epping Forest, 1896; *d* S. Barbara, Calif., 1978). Eng. pianist. Trained at RAM. Married fellow-student Rae *Robertson and with him est. int. reputation in interpretation of mus. for 2 pf. Settled in USA and in later years was teacher. Pianist with *Barbirolli (vc.) in his recitals in 1920s.

Bartók, Béla (*b* Nagyszentmiklós, Hungary (now Romania), 1881; *d* NY, 1945). Hung. composer, pianist, and folklorist. Parents were musical and mother gave him his first pf. lessons. In 1894 at Bratislava (then Pozsony) studied with the cond. Laszlo Erkel until 1899 when he entered Budapest Royal Acad. of Mus. In 1902 heard a perf. of Strauss's *Also sprach Zarathustra* which stimulated his powers of comp. to such a degree that he wrote his nationalistic tone-poem *Kossuth* in 1903. By this time was travelling abroad as solo pianist in mus. by Liszt and other kbd. virtuosi. In 1905 began systematic exploration of Hungarian peasant mus. and in 1906, with his fellow-composer Kodály, pubd. a coll. of 20 folk-songs. In 1907 became prof. of pf. at the Budapest RAM. For the next decade, while his mus. was badly received in his own country, continued systematic coll. of

Magyár folk-songs. In 1917 his ballet *The Wooden Prince* was successfully prod. in Budapest and led to the staging in the following year of his 1-act opera *Duke Bluebeard's Castle* (1911). In 1922 and 1923 his first 2 vn. sonatas had their f.ps. in London, and in 1923 comp. the *Dance Suite* to celebrate the 50th anniv. of the union of Buda and Pest. During the 1920s resumed career as pianist, composing several works for his own use. In 1934 was given a salaried post in the Hung. Acad. of Sciences in order that he could prepare his folk-song coll. for publication. In the spring of 1940, in view of political developments in Hungary, emigrated to USA. This was not a happy time for him; his health began to fail, his mus. was infrequently perf., and there was little demand for his services as a pianist. Nevertheless the Koussevitzky Foundation commissioned the *Concerto for Orchestra*, Yehudi Menuhin a solo vn. sonata, and William Primrose a va. conc. (left unfinished but completed by Tibór *Sérly). He died from leukaemia.

Bartók's mus. is a highly individual blend of elements transformed from his own admirations: Liszt, Strauss, Debussy, folk-mus., and Stravinsky. Perhaps his greatest achievement lies in his 6 str. qts. in which formal symmetry and thematic unity were successfully related. But the melodic fertility and rhythmical vitality of all his mus. have ensured its consistent success since his death. Prin. comps.:

STAGE: *Duke Bluebeard's Castle (A kékszakállú herceg vára)*, Op. 11, 1-act opera (1911, rev. 1912, 1918); *The *Wooden Prince (A fából faragott királyfi)*, Op. 13, 1-act ballet (1914–17); *The *Miraculous Mandarin (A csodálatos mandarin)*, Op. 19, 1-act pantomime (1918–19, orchd. 1923, rev. 1924, 1926–31).

ORCH: *Kossuth*, sym.-poem (1903); *Rhapsody*, pf. and orch., Op. 1 (1904); *Suite No. 1*, Op. 3 (1905, rev. c.1920), No. 2 (small orch.), Op. 4 (1905–7, rev. 1920, 1943); Vn. Conc. No. 1. (1907–8; 1st movt. rev. as No. 1 of *2 Portraits*), No. 2 (1937–8); *2 Portraits*, Op. 5 (No. 1 1907–8, No. 2 orch. 1911); *2 Pictures*, Op. 10 (1910); *Romanian Dance*, Op. 11 (1911); *4 Pieces*, Op. 12 (1912, orchd. 1921); *Suite* (3 dances), *The Wooden Prince* (1921–4); *Suite*, *The Miraculous Mandarin* (1919, 1927); *Dance Suite* (1923); Pf. Conc. No. 1 (1926), No. 2 (1930–1), No. 3 (1945); *Rhapsody*, vn. and orch., No. 1 (1928), No. 2 (1928, rev. 1944); *Transylvanian Dances* (1931); *Hungarian Sketches* (1931); *Hungarian Peasant Songs* (1933); *Music for Strings, Percussion and Celesta* (1936); *Divertimento*, str. (1939); 2-pf. Conc. (arr. of Sonata for 2 pf. and perc.) (1940); *Concerto for Orchestra* (1942–3, rev. 1945); Va. Conc. (completed from draft by Sérly) (1945).

VOICE(S) AND ORCH: *3 Village Scenes*, women's vv. (1926); *Cantata Profana (The 9 Enchanted Stags)*, ten., bar., double ch., and orch. (1930); *5 Hungarian Folk Songs*, low v. (1933).

CHORUS: *Evening*, male vv. (1903); *4 Old Hungarian Folk Songs*, male vv. (1910, rev. 1912); *5 Slovak Folk Songs*, male vv. (1917); *5 Hungarian Folk Songs* (1930); *5 Székely Songs*, male vv. (1932); *27 Traditional Choruses*, children's and women's vv. (1935); *From Olden Times*, male vv. (1935).

CHAMBER: Pf. Qt. (1898); Pf. Quintet (1903–4, rev.? 1920); Str. Qt. No. 1, Op. 7 (1908), No. 2, Op. 17 (1915–17), No. 3 (1927), No. 4 (1928), No. 5 (1934), No. 6 (1939); Vn. Sonatas, No. 1 (1921), No. 2 (1922); *Rhapsody* No. 1, vn. and pf. (1928, also orch. vers.), No. 2 (1928, rev. 1945, also orch. vers.); *Rhapsody*, vc. and pf. (1928); *44 Duos*, 2 vn. (1931); Sonata for 2 pf. and 2 perc. (1937, orch. 1940); Sonata for unacc. vn. (1944); *Contrasts*, vn., cl., and pf. (1938).

PIANO: *3 Klavierstücke*, Op. 13 (1897); *Scherzo (Fantasie)*, Op. 18 (1897); *Scherzo* in B♭ minor (1900); *12 Variations* (1900–01); *4 Pieces* (1903); *Rhapsody*, Op. 1 (1904, also orch. vers.); *14 Bagatelles*, Op. 6 (1908); *10 Easy Pieces* (1908); *85 Pieces for Children* (1908–9, rev. 1945); *2 Romanian Dances*, Op. 8a (1909–10, No. 1 orch. 1911); *7 Sketches*, Op. 9b (1908–10); *4 Dirges*, Op. 9a (1909–10, No. 2 orch. as No. 3 of *Hungarian Sketches*, 1931); *3 Burlesques*, Op. 8c (1908–11, No. 2 orch. as No. 4 of *Hungarian Sketches*, 1931); *Allegro barbaro* (1911); *Sonatina* (1915, orch. as *Transylvanian Dances*, 1931); *Romanian Dances* (1915, orch. 1917); *Suite*, Op. 14 (1916); *3 Hungarian Folk Tunes* (c.1914–18); *15 Hungarian Peasant Songs* (1914–18, Nos. 6–12, 14–15 orch. 1933); *3 Studies*, Op. 18 (1918); *8 Improvisations on Hungarian Peasant Songs*, Op. 20 (1920); *Dance Suite* (1925, arr. of orch. work); Sonata (1926); *Out of Doors* (1926); *9 Little Pieces* (1926); *Mikrokosmos*, 6 vols. containing 153 'progressive pieces' (1926, 1932–9).

Also many Solo Songs, editions of Italian kbd. mus., etc.

Bartoletti, Bruno (*b* Sesto Fiorentino, 1926). It. flautist and cond., particularly of opera. Début Florence 1953. Mus. dir. Rome Opera 1965–73, cond. Maggio Musicale Orch. 1957–64. Introduced several 20th cent. operas to It. repertory. Amer. début Chicago 1956. Prin. cond. Chicago Lyric Opera from 1964 (art. dir. from 1975).

Bartolozzi, Bruno (*b* Florence, 1911; *d* Fiesole, 1980). It. violinist and composer. Student 1926–30 at Cherubini Cons. where he taught from 1965. Comps. incl. Conc. for Orch., vn. conc., str. qt., and vocal works. Author of book *New Sounds for Woodwind*.

Bartós, Jan Zdeněk (*b* Dvůr Králové nad Labem, Cz., 1908; *d* Prague, 1981). Cz. composer and violinist. Studied Prague Cons. Violinist in orchs. and as soloist 1929–31. Teacher of comp. and theory, Prague Cons., from 1958. Works incl. 2 operas, va. conc., hn. conc., 4 syms., ballets, choral works, and chamber mus.

Baryton. Str. instr. rather like viola da gamba but with sympathetic str. There are many works by Haydn for it, because his patron, Prince Nikolaus Esterházy, played it. Use revived in 2nd half of 20th cent.

Barzun, Jacques (*b* Créteil, Val-de-Marne, 1907). Fr.-born historian, critic, and musicologist. Settled in USA 1919. Lecturer at Columbia Univ., NY, 1927, Prof. 1945, Provost 1958–67. Authority on Berlioz, about whom he has written extensively.

Baskische Trommel (Ger.). Basque drum, i.e. tambourine.

Basques. Various Basque dances. *Pas de Basque* (Fr.) is sometimes a general term with the same meaning, but it may indicate a particular dance of the Basque peasantry—one with very varied rhythms.

Bass. (1) Lowest male voice—see *basso*.
(2) Lowest note or part in a chord.
(3) Lowest regions of mus. pitch.
(4) Lowest of a family of instr., as shown in entries below.
(5) Colloquialism for (in sym. orchs.) the db., and (in military and brass bands) the bombardon.

Bassanello. Obsolete woodwind instr., first mentioned in 1577, related to *shawm. Made in 3 sizes, bass, tenor, and alto. 7 finger-holes and reed set on a crook. Legend that it was invented by the composer Giovanni Bassano or Bassani is suspect.

Bassani, Giovanni Battista (*b* Padua, *c*.1657; *d* Bergamo, 1716). It. violinist, composer, and organist. Choirmaster, Ferrara Cath. from 1677, later at Bergamo, 1712. Wrote oratorios, masses, operas, and sonatas.

Bassarids, The. Opera seria with intermezzo in 1 act by Henze to lib. by W. H. Auden and Chester Kallman based on *The Bacchae* of Euripides. Comp. 1965. (Prod. Salzburg 1966 in Ger. trans. by M. Bosse-Sporleder; Santa Fe 1968 (in orig. Eng.); London (broadcast) 1968. ENO 1974 (cond. and prod. Henze).)

Bass-bar. In a bowed instr. the strip of wood glued under the belly along the line of the lowest str. and supporting one foot of the bridge.

Bass-baritone. See *Baritone*.

Bass Clarinet. One of cl. family, pitched in B♭, an octave below the sop. cl. In Eng. and Fr. instrs. its range extends to E♭ (sounding D♭). Earliest extant examples made in 1793. Meyerbeer wrote for it, later Wagner, Mahler, Schoenberg, and Stravinsky. See *Clarinet*.

Bass Clef. Sometimes called the F clef: the F below middle C as the top line but one of the staff.

Bass Drum. Large drum of indefinite low pitch. In most orchs. is mounted on a large, wheeled rack so that drum can be tilted at any desired angle.

Basse chantante (Fr.). Basso cantante (It.). Lyric bass, sometimes of bar. quality.

Basse chiffrée, basse continue (Fr.). Figured bass. See *Basso continuo*.

Basse danse (Fr.). An early dance type which became extinct in the 16th cent. when supplanted by the *Pavan. It was probably the ancestor of other dances which survived it (see also *Branle*). The first word meaning 'low', it has been supposed that the name indicated humble origin, or (more plausibly) that it arose from the fact that the feet were generally kept low, i.e. were glided, not lifted (see *Haute Danse*). The time is generally simple duple, but sometimes triple, and occasionally a mixture of the 2. Sometimes the mus. falls into 3 parts: (*a*) *Basse Danse,* (*b*) *Retour de Basse Danse* (Return of the Basse Dance), and (*c*) *Tordion* (or *Tourdion*). Attaingnant pubd. colls. of *basses danses* in 1529 and 1530.

Basse d'harmonie (Fr.). *Ophicleide.

Basset Horn. Alto cl. in F, whole tone higher than E♭ alto cl., with a total possible compass of 4 complete octaves. Invented *c*.1765 and used by Mozart in *Requiem, Die Zauberflöte,* and *La Clemenza di Tito.* He first used it 1781 in the *Serenade* in B♭ (K 361). Beethoven (*Prometheus*) and Mendelssohn (*Scottish Symphony*) wrote for it, but after 1850 it was replaced by the E♭ alto cl. Richard Strauss revived it in his operas *Elektra* (1906–8) and *Daphne* (1936–7), and for his 2 wind sonatinas comp. 1943 and 1945. A transposing instr. in F. Name is said to derive from a Bavarian term for small bass, and the basset-hound was named after the sound it makes. The It. term *corno di bassetto* was adopted by Bernard *Shaw as his pseudonym when writing mus. criticism.

Bassettflöte (Ger.). A 17th- and 18th-cent. name for a recorder of low pitch. Sometimes called *Bassflöte*.

Bassett Nicolo. An alto reed-cap shawm in F with extension keys and a 9-note range.

Bassflicorno (Flicorno basso). Large size of It. variety of saxhorn or flügelhorn called *Flicorno. Others are *Flicorno basso grave* and *Flicorno contrabasso*.

Bassflöte. See *Bassettflöte*.

Bass Flute. Fl. in C, pitched one octave below the ordinary fl. (not, as sometimes miscalled, the *alto fl. in G). Also an org.-stop, 8′ length and pitch. See *Flute*.

Bass Horn. Obsolete brass instr. made in 3 sizes, alto, bass, and db., but only the bass was much used; now supplanted by bass tuba.

Bass Oboe. Term used to denote baritone oboe.

Bass-Saite (Ger.). Bass string. Lowest str. on any (bowed or plucked) instr.

Bass Saxhorn. One of brass wind instr. made by *Sax. In B♭, E♭, and double B♭.

Bass Staff. See *Great Staff*.

Bass Trombone (Ger. *Bassposaune*). Brass instr. with a range to F or E below the ten. tb. B♭. See *Trombone*.

Bass Trumpet (Ger. *Basstrompete*). Wind instr., made of brass. Really a valve tb. Pitched in C, therefore not a transposing instr. See *Trumpet*.

Bass Tuba. Brass instr. of the *tuba family of which there are the following: E♭ bass tuba or E♭ bombardon; F bass tuba; and B♭ bass tuba or B♭ bombardon. Vaughan Williams wrote a conc. for bass tuba. See *Tuba*.

Bass Viol. Member of the *viol group of str. instr. Often called *viola da gamba, 'leg viol', because it is held as the vc. is.

Basso (It.; plural *bassi*). Low male v., bass, normally ranging from E–e'/f'.

Basso continuo (It.). Continuous bass. Figured bass from which in concerted mus. of the 17th and 18th cents. the cembalist or organist played. Doubled the lowest v. part. Term often shortened to *continuo*. To 'play the *continuo*' does not mean to play a particular instr., but to play this variety of bass.

Basson (Fr.). *Bassoon.

Basson russe (Fr.). Russian bassoon, a variety of *bass horn.

Bassoon (It. *fagotto*). Bass member of the double reed (ob.) family, pitched in C, with range from B♭' upwards for about 3½ octaves. Made of wood and with conical bore. Dates from 1660s. Modern instrs. made by Heckel (Ger.), Buffet-Crampon (Fr.), and Fox (Amer.). Often used for comic effect but its capacity for melancholy has not been overlooked by composers. Also an org. reed stop of 8' length and pitch.

Bassoon, Double. See *Double Bassoon*.

Bassoon, Russian. See *Basson russe*.

Basso ostinato (It.). Obstinate bass, i.e. *Ground bass.

Basso profondo. Bass v. of exceptionally low range.

Bastardella, La. See *Agujari, Lucrezia*.

Bastianini, Ettore (b Siena, 1922; d Sirmione, 1967). It. bar., outstanding in Verdi. Began career as bass at Ravenna (1945). Raised voice to bar., making 2nd début 1951. NY Met. 1953–66. CG 1962. Sang role of Prince Andrey in Prokofiev's *War and Peace*, Florence 1953.

Bastien und Bastienne. *Singspiel* in 1 act by the 12-year-old Mozart to lib. by Friedrich Wilhelm Weiskern, after Favart's parody on Rousseau's *Le *Devin du village* (1752). (Prod. in the garden-th. of Mesmer, the introducer of mesmerism, Vienna, 1768; not again perf. until Berlin 1890; London 1894; NY 1916.)

Bat, The (Strauss). See *Fledermaus, Die*.

Bataille, Gabriel (b ?Brie, c.1575; d Paris, 1630). Fr. lutenist at court of Louis XIII. Comp. ballets, lute pieces, and chansons with lute acc.

Bate, Stanley (Richard) (b Plymouth, 1911; d London, 1959). Eng. composer and pianist. Comp. pupil of Vaughan Williams, Hindemith, and Nadia Boulanger. In USA 1946–50. Comp. 4 syms., concs., chamber mus., incidental mus., and 7 ballets.

Bateson, Thomas (b c.1570; d Dublin, 1630). Eng. organist and composer of madrigals. Organist of Chester Cath. and Christ Church Cath., Dublin. Pubd. 2 sets of madrigals, 1604 (29 items) and 1618 (30). Contrib. to The *Triumphs of Oriana*.

Bath, Hubert (b Barnstaple, 1883; d Harefield, 1945). Eng. composer of stage, film, and other (chiefly light) mus. Studied RAM 1901–4 (pf. with Beringer, comp. with Corder). Was for some years in charge of park bands in London. Wrote first sym. for brass band, *Freedom*, and opera based on G. du Maurier's *Trilby*.

Batka, Richard (b Prague, 1868; d Vienna, 1922). Austrian critic and mus. scholar of Cz. ancestry. Ed. periodical *Der Merker* and the *Notebooks of Anna Magdalena Bach*. Admirer of Mahler and Strauss. Taught history of opera at Vienna Acad. 1909–14.

Baton (Fr.). The stick used by conds. for beating time and securing expressive playing. The accurate orig. of its use is undiscoverable, but it is said that in the 15th cent. in the Sistine Choir at Rome the maestro di cappella beat time with a roll of paper called 'sol-fa'. Lully's death is alleged to have been the result of an injury to his foot caused by accidentally striking it with a heavier-than-usual cane he was using to thump out the beat on the floor. During the 18th cent. perfs. were dir. from the kbd. and early in the 19th cent. by the first violinist waving his bow at his colleagues when he was not playing. The use of a baton began in Ger. in the 19th cent. Beethoven appears to have cond. with a baton and so did Mendelssohn. Then followed the virtuoso conds. such as Wagner and Bülow. The length of the stick varies, some conds. (e.g. Richter and Boult) using a long baton. Generally, however, a light, short baton is preferred with which the cond. can indicate more than merely the beats of the bar; hence 'stick technique'. Some conds. abjure the baton and use their hands only (and, of course, their eyes).

Battaglia di Legnano, La (The Battle of Legnano). Opera in 3 acts by Verdi, his 13th, to lib. by S. Cammarano. (Prod. Rome 1849; Cardiff 1960.)

Batten, Adrian (*b* Salisbury, 1591; *d* London, 1637). Eng. composer. Singer in choirs of Westminster Abbey 1614–26, St Paul's Cath. 1626–37. Wrote anthems and services. Collected 16th-cent. church mus. in *Batten Organ Book.*

Batterie (Fr.). Battery. (1) The perc. instr.
(2) Any rhythmic formula for the drums such as those used in the army for signalling.
(3) Striking instead of plucking str. of guitar.

Battishill, Jonathan (*b* London, 1738; *d* Islington, 1801). Eng. organist, th. musician, and composer for church, stage, and glee clubs. His anthem, *O Lord, look down from Heaven,* still often sung. (Elgar provided an orch. accompaniment for it, Worcester Fest. 1923.)

Battistini, Mattia (*b* Rome, 1856; *d* Rieti, 1928). It. *bel canto* operatic bar. of great dramatic force and vocal agility. His v. could encompass a high A♮ and Massenet re-wrote the ten. role in *Werther* for him. Début Rome 1878, London 1883. Repertory of over 80 operas. Never sang in USA. Kept his vocal powers till he was over 70.

Battle Hymn of the Republic. Poem by Julia Ward Howe (1819–1910) written 1862, first line being 'Mine eyes have seen the glory of the coming of the Lord', sung to the tune of *John Brown's Body.* Last verse beginning 'He is coming like the glory of the morning on the wave' is not in orig., authorship being unknown.

Battle of Prague. Pf. piece, with *ad lib* vn., vc., and drum, by Franz *Kotzwara. Comp. 1788, it was long a favourite in Eng.

Battle of the Huns (Ger. *Hunnenschlacht*). Symphonic poem for orch. by Liszt, 1856–7, inspired by a fresco by Kaulbach.

Battle Symphony (or Battle of Victoria, or Wellington's Victory). Eng. title for Beethoven's *Wellingtons Sieg, oder die Schlacht bei Vittoria,* Op. 91, a piece of programme-mus. illustrating the Eng. defeat of Napoleon's troops at Vitoria in Sp. in 1812. Comp. 1813 for perf. by Beethoven's friend Maelzel's panharmonicon but actually perf. by a live orch. at 2 Viennese concerts in Dec. 1813 in aid of Austrian soldiers wounded in the Battle of Hanau. The tunes *Rule, Britannia!, Malbrouck s'en va-t-en guerre,* and *God Save the King* are incorporated, and the work was ded. to the Prince Regent. 'Vittoria' in the title was Beethoven's mistake for *Vitoria.* The work was the cause of a rift with Maelzel.

Batton, Désiré Alexandre (*b* Paris, 1798; *d* Versailles, 1855). Fr. composer. Pupil of Cherubini. Wrote 7 operas and became teacher at Paris Cons.

Battre (Fr.). To beat: *battre à deux temps,* to beat 2 in a measure.

Battuta, A (It.). To the beat—same as *A tempo,* i.e. return to normal speed (after a *rallentando* or *accelerando*).

Baudo, Serge (*b* Marseilles, 1927). Fr. conductor. Studied at Paris Cons. (cond. with Fourestier). Début 1950 at Concerts Lamoureux. Cond. Orch. Nationale and radio orch. Cond., Nice-Côte d'Azur Orch. 1959–62. Cond., Paris Opéra 1962–5. La Scala début 1970, NY Met. 1970–1 season. Cond., Orchestre de Paris, 1967–9, art. dir., Rhône-Alpes P.O. from 1969. Cond. f.ps. of Messiaen's *Et exspecto resurrectionem mortuorum* (Chartres, 1965), Milhaud's *La Mère coupable* (Geneva, 1965), and Dutilleux's vc. conc. (Aix, 1970).

Baudrier, Yves (*b* Paris, 1906). Fr. composer; co-founder of group '*Jeune France*', formed 1936. Works incl. *Le Musicien dans la cité* for orch. (1937).

Bauer, Harold (*b* New Malden, Surrey, 1873; *d* Miami, 1951). Eng.-born pianist. From age 9 made frequent public appearances as violinist; then, 1892, as pianist (London newspaper notices show him within 3 weeks in that year as leader of str. qt., solo violinist, and pf. recitalist). After study with Paderewski appeared as pianist throughout Europe and USA, settling in NY. US début Boston 1900. Known principally as Beethoven interpreter, but did much for Fr. pf. mus. (Debussy, Ravel, Franck).

Bauerncantate (Bach). See *Peasant Cantata.*

Bauernleier (Ger.). *Hurdy-gurdy.

Bauernlied (Ger.). Peasant song or ballad.

Bauld, Alison (*b* Sydney, N.S.W., 1944). Australian composer. Studied Sydney Univ. and York Univ., and with Lutyens and H. Keller. Mus. dir., Laban Centre for Dance, London Univ., 1975–8. Works incl. *Exiles,* mus.-th. (1974), *Inanna,* tape for ballet (1975), *In a Dead Brown Land,* mus.-th. (1971, rev. 1972), *Mad Moll,* sop. (1973), *I Loved Miss Watson,* sop. and pf., with tape (1977), *One Pearl II* for sop., alto fl., and str. (1976, rev. of *One Pearl,* 1973), *Van Diemen's Land,* unacc. ch. (1976), *The Busker's Story,* alto sax., bn., tpt., vn., db. (1978), *Banquo's Buried,* sop. and pf. (1982).

Baur, Jürg (*b* Düsseldorf, 1918). Ger. composer and teacher. Educated Cologne. Dir. of Robert Schumann Cons., Düsseldorf, 1965–71. In 1971 succeeded Zimmermann as teacher of comp. at Cologne Musikhochschule. Comps. incl. works for org., sym., concs., chamber mus., sonata for 2 pf., and song-cycles.

Bautista, Julián (*b* Madrid, 1901; *d* Buenos Aires, 1961). Sp. composer and teacher. Studied Madrid

Cons., where he also taught, 1936–9; works incl.
3 str. qts., ballet, chamber mus., and *Sinfonia breve*
(1956).

Bavarian Highlands, Scenes from the. 6 choral
songs by Elgar, Op. 27. Texts, in style of Bavarian
folk-songs, by C. A. Elgar. Pf. acc. 1895, orch.
1896. Three (*The Dance, Lullaby,* and *The Marks-men*) arr. for orch. alone by Elgar.

Bavarian Radio Symphony Orchestra.
Founded in Munich 1949, with Eugen Jochum
as cond. until 1961. Rafael Kubelik was cond.
from 1961 to 1981; Colin Davis prin. cond. from
1984. Has toured frequently and made many
recordings.

Bax, (Sir) **Arnold** (Edward Trevor) (*b* Streatham,
London, 1883; *d* Cork, 1953). Eng. composer
who was Master of the King's (Queen's) Musick
1942–53. Studied RAM, 1900–5. Knighted 1937.
Was himself a brilliant pianist and wrote fluently
and perceptively for the kbd. Felt a special
sympathy with Irish subjects, particularly Yeats's
poetry, and with the Irish land and seascapes,
hence the intensely picturesque and romantic
flavour of his mus. Also much influenced by
Russ. mus. after his visit to Russ. in 1910. Only
stage works were for ballet, incl. *The Truth About
the Russian Dancers* (1920), a play by Barrie in
which the central non-speaking part of the
ballerina was created and choreog. by Karsavina
when prod. 1920 by Gerald du Maurier, with
Paul Nash décor.

Although a prolific composer, Bax's mus. has
never est. itself in the forefront. His 7 syms.,
luxuriantly scored and full of romantic melody,
contain too much good mus. ever to deserve total
neglect, but are only intermittently perf. in the
concert-hall, the public seeming to prefer the
more concise tone-poems. The chamber mus. is
less diffuse in form and is beautifully written for
the instr., while there are also some exquisite
short choral pieces. Bax's autobiography, *Farewell,
My Youth* (1943), is one of the best books by a
composer. Prin. works:

ORCH: Syms.: No. 1 in E♭ (1921), No. 2 in E
minor and C (1924–5), No. 3 in C (1929), No. 4
in E♭ (1930–1), No. 5 in E minor (1931–2), No.
6 in C minor (1934), No. 7 in A♭ (1939);
Symphonic Variations (1905–6); **In the Faery Hills*
(1909); *The *Garden of Fand* (1913); *The Happy
Forest* (1914–21); *Spring Fire* (1913); *Symphonic
Variations,* pf. and orch. (1917); **Tintagel* (1917–
19); *November Woods* (1917); *Phantasy,* viola,
orch. (1920); *Summer Music* (1920); *Northern
Ballad* No. 1 (1927), No. 2 (1933–4); *Overture to
a Picaresque Comedy* (1930); *Winter Legends,* pf.,
orch. (1929–30); *The Tale the Pine Trees knew*
(1931); vc. conc. (1932); *London Pageant* (1937–
8); vn. conc. (1938); concertante for pf. (left-hand) (1948–9); *Coronation March* (1953).

VOICE(S) AND ORCH: *Fatherland,* ten., ch., orch.
(1907); *Enchanted Summer* (1910); *6 Songs from*
The Bard of the Dimbovitza, mez., orch. (1914); *Of
a Rose I Sing* (1920); *To The Name Above Every
Name* (1923); *St Patrick's Breastplate* (1923);
Walsinghame, ten., ch., orch. (1926); *The Morning
Watch* (1935–6).

UNACC. VOICES: *Mater Ora Filium* (1921); *This
Worlde's Joie* (1922); *The Boar's Head* (1923); *I
sing of a maiden* (1923); *5 Greek Folk Songs* (1944);
What is it like to be young and fair? (**Garland for
the Queen*) (1953).

CHAMBER MUSIC: Str. Qts.: No. 1 in G (1916), No. 2
(1924–5), No. 3 in F (1936); Pf. trio (1904); Str.
quintet in G (1906–7); Pf. Quintet in G minor
(1915); *Ballade,* vn., pf. (1916); *Folk Tale,* vc., pf.
(1916); *Elegiac Trio,* fl., va., harp (1916); harp
quintet (1919); va. sonata (1922); ob. quintet
(1922); *Nonet,* fl., ob., cl., harp, str. quintet
(1930); vc. sonatina (1933); cl. sonata (1934);
Trio, pf., vn., va. (1946); *Legend-sonata,* vc., pf.
(1943); Vn. sonatas: No. 1 (1910, rev. 1915), No.
2 in D (1915).

PIANO: *Valse de Concert* (1904); *Moy Mell* (2 pf.)
(1908–17); *2 Russian Tone-Pictures* (1911); *Toc-cata* (1913); *The Maiden with the Daffodil* (1915);
In a Vodka Shop (1915); *A Mountain Mood* (1915);
Dream in Exile (1916); *Romance* (1918); *On a May
Evening* (1918); *What the Minstrel told us* (1919);
Lullaby, A Hill Tune, Country Tune (1920);
Mediterranean (1920, orch. 1921); *Hardanger* (2
pf.) (1927); Sonatas: No. 1 in F♯ minor (1910,
rev. 1917–21), No. 2 in G (1919), No. 3 (1926),
No. 4 (1932).

SONGS: *A Celtic Song-Cycle* (1904); *A Christmas Carol*
(1909); *3 Chaucer Roundels* (1914); *Parting* (1916);
5 Traditional French Songs (1920); *5 Irish Songs*
(1921); *3 Irish Songs* (incl. *Rann of Exile*) (1922).

Bayer, Joseph (*b* Vienna, 1852; *d* Vienna, 1913).
Austrian violinist, composer, and conductor.
Studied Vienna Cons.; later was violinist in court
opera orch. Dir. of ballet, Vienna Court Opera,
1885–98. Comp. 22 ballets, incl *Die Puppenfee*
(1888), also some operettas.

Bayle, François (*b* Tamatave, Madagascar, 1932).
Fr. composer. Studied under Messiaen at Paris
Cons. 1959. Worked with Pierre **Schaeffer* at
comp. studio of *Groupe de Recherches Musicales*
1960–2 and was its dir. from 1966. Several film
scores. Most of his works are **musique concrète,*
e.g. *L'Oiseau chanteur, Galaxie, Espaces inhabitables,*
and *L'Expérience humaine.*

Baylis, Lilian (*b* London, 1874; *d* London, 1937).
Eng. th. man. and impresario. From 1898 until
her death was man. of the **Old Vic, of which her
aunt, Emma Cons, was lessee. Staged Shakespeare
there, also opera and ballet (with Ninette de
**Valois). In 1931 re-opened SW Th., to which she
transferred the opera and ballet cos. C.H. 1929.

Bayreuth. Town in Bavaria, Ger., where Wagner
built his home, **Wahnfried, and also his long-planned fest. th. to house perfs. of *Der *Ring des
Nibelungen.* First fest. 1876, cond. Hans Richter.

Th. holds *c*.1,800 and has wonderful acoustics. Innovation was covered orch. pit. *Parsifal* f.p. there, 1882. Fests. of Wagner's operas held regularly (with wartime interruptions) since 1892, the successive dirs. having been members of the Wagner family. Although Beethoven's 9th Sym. has been perf. in the th., so far no opera by any composer but Wagner has been prod. there.

Bazelon, Irwin (*b* Evanston, Ill., 1922). Amer. composer. Studied De Paul Univ. and with Milhaud and Bloch. Has written much incidental mus. for th., cinema, and TV. Author of book on film mus. Works incl. *De-Tonations,* brass quintet and orch. (1978); woodwind quintet (1975); *Concatenations,* perc. qt. and va. (1976); *Sound Dreams,* fl., cl., va., vc., pf., solo perc. (1977); *Imprints,* pf. (1978); *Junctures for Orchestra,* with sop. (1979); *Symphony No. 7,* 'ballet for orch.' (1980); *Spires,* tpt. and orch. (1981); *Suite,* marimba (1983); *Quintessentials,* wind quintet (1983).

Bazzini, Antonio (*b* Brescia, 1818; *d* Milan, 1897). It. violinist and composer. After career as vn. virtuoso became prof. of comp., Milan Cons., 1873 and dir., 1882. One of leaders of It. non-operatic revival. Comp. 6 str. qts., 2 quintets, tone-poem *Francesca da Rimini,* also celebrated vn. solo, *Ronde des lutins* (Dance of the Elves) (1852).

Bazzini, Francesco (*b* Lovere, Brescia 1593; *d* Bergamo, 1660). It. organist, composer, and player of *theorbo, for which he wrote sonatas. Also comp. oratorio and canzonettas.

BBC (British Broadcasting Corporation). The first Brit. broadcasting station was opened at Writtle, Chelmsford, in 1920 by the Marconi Co. In 1922 4 Brit. electrical manufacturers formed the Brit. Broadcasting Co. which began transmitting from 2LO at Savoy Hill on 15 Nov. of that year. The first mus. broadcast, by an orch. of 9 players, was on 25 Nov. 1922. In Jan. 1923 Act I of *Die Zauberflöte* was relayed from CG, being so successful that 20 other operatic relays followed shortly, incl. those of *Siegfried* and *Le Nozze di Figaro.* The first studio opera prod. was of Gounod's *Roméo et Juliette* in Oct. 1923. The importance of mus. as a staple element of broadcasting was recognized by the appointment in May 1923 of a Mus. Controller, the first being Percy *Pitt. In 1924 the BBC, amid opposition and controversy, sponsored 6 public sym. concerts in London. On 1 Jan. 1927 the private co. became a public monopoly with the issue of a Royal charter constituting the British Broadcasting Corporation, its revenue coming from licence-holders. In the same year the BBC assumed financial responsibility for the London Promenade Concerts and its mus. patronage extended to the commissioning of new works and the sponsorship of important perfs. of contemporary mus. A logical outcome was the formation in 1930 of the BBC S.O., offering permanent

contracts to over 110 players. Adrian *Boult, who had succeeded Pitt as controller of mus. in 1930, was appointed cond., a post he held until 1950. Regional sym. orchs. were later formed in Glasgow, Manchester, Birmingham, Cardiff, and Belfast.

With the inauguration of a TV service on 2 Nov. 1936 the BBC quickly seized the chance to televise opera, and in the three years 1936–9 nearly 30 operas were prod. for TV, incl. *La serva padrona, Pagliacci, Gianni Schicchi,* and the first staged perf. in Britain of Busoni's *Arlecchino.* During the war the BBC's role as a dispenser of mus. of all kinds intensified. Arthur *Bliss succeeded Boult in 1942 as mus. dir., and was himself succeeded in 1944 by Victor *Hely-Hutchinson. Successive dirs. (or controllers) have been Steuart *Wilson 1947–50, Herbert Murrill 1950–2, R. J. F. Howgill 1952–9, William *Glock 1959–73, Robert Ponsonby 1973–85, John Drummond from 1985.

A major broadcasting development was the formation in Sept. 1946 of the 3rd Programme, designed for 'cultivated tastes and interests'. Music made up 50% of its output and the opportunities for broadcasting a wide range of mus. were almost limitless. In Mar. 1965 the 3rd Programme underwent changes, incl. the emergence of the Mus. Programme which ran continuously for nearly 12 hours a day. In 1970 the 3rd Programme and Mus. Programme became Radio 3. TV has also developed mus. series of its own, reaching enormous audiences. Among operas specially commissioned by BBC TV were Bliss's *Tobias and the Angel* (1960), and Britten's *Owen Wingrave* (1971).

BBC Philharmonic Orchestra. Regional symphony orchestra based in Manchester which adopted this name in 1983 having previously been BBC Northern S.O. Developed from Northern Wireless Orchestra, founded 1931, and renamed BBC Northern Orch. 1934. Chief conds. have incl. Sir Charles Groves, John Hopkins, George Hurst, Bryden Thomson, Raymond Leppard, and Edward Downes.

BBC Singers. Unacc. ch. (present strength 28 full-time professional singers) formed 1924 as Wireless Chorus. Changed name to BBC Chorus 1935, present title 1973. 1st cond. was Stanford *Robinson. 1934–61 cond. was Leslie Woodgate. Other conds. Peter Gellhorn and John Poole.

BBC Symphony Orchestra. Chief orch. of the BBC, formed 1930 with 114 (later 119) players on permanent contract. Has given f.ps. of many works by Brit. composers. Guest conds. have incl. the world's leading exponents, notably *Toscanini. Chief conds. since inception: Adrian *Boult 1931–50; Malcolm *Sargent 1950–7; Rudolf *Schwarz 1957–62; Antal *Dorati 1962–6; Colin *Davis 1967–71; Pierre *Boulez 1971–75; Rudolf *Kempe 1975–6; Gennady *Rozhdestvensky 1978–81; John *Pritchard from 1981. Other BBC sym. orchs. are the Philharmonic (based in Manchester), Scottish (based in Glasgow), and Welsh (based in Cardiff). The BBC Symphony Chorus was formed 1928 as National Chorus (at its 1st concert, 23 Nov. 1928, *Bantock cond. f.p. of his *Pilgrim's Progress*). Name changed to BBC Chorus 1932, to BBC Choral Society 1935, to present title 1977. Up to 1976, ch. master was dir. of *BBC Singers, but in that year separate appointment (Brian Wright) was made.

B Dur (Ger.). The key of B♭ major (not B major). See *B*.

Be (Ger.). The flat sign ♭.

Beach, Mrs. H. H. A. (*née* Amy Marcy Cheney) (*b* Henniker, New Hampshire, 1867; *d* NY, 1944). Amer. pianist and composer. Her performing career was cut short by her marriage in 1885, after which she concentrated on comp., but she resumed it in 1910 when her husband died. Wrote numerous songs, pf. conc. (1899), vn. sonata, Mass in E♭ (1891), *Gaelic Symphony* (1896), *The Canticle of the Sun* (1925), *Christ in the Universe* (1931), and opera *Cabildo* (1932).

Beach, John Parsons (*b* Gloversville, NY, 1877; *d* Pasadena, Calif., 1953). Amer. composer, regarded as one of the first modernists. Graduated New Eng. Cons. and spent 7 years in Paris from 1910. Comps. incl. 2 short stage works, 2 ballets, orch. and chamber mus.

Bean, Hugh (Cecil) (*b* Beckenham, 1929). Eng. violinist. Studied RCM with *Sammons 1938–57 and Brussels Cons. with Gertler 1952–3. Leader, Philharmonia and New Philharmonia Orch. 1957–67. Ass. leader, BBC S.O. 1967–9. Active in chamber mus. (Music Group of London) and as conc. soloist. Prof. of vn., RCM from 1954. C.B.E. 1970.

Bean, (Thomas) **Ernest** (*b* Colne, 1900; *d* Dorking, 1983). Eng. orch. concert administrator and lecturer. Secretary and gen. man., Hallé Concerts Society, Manchester, 1944–51; gen. man., Royal Festival Hall, London, 1951–65. C.B.E. 1965.

Bearbeitet (Ger.). Worked-over, i.e. Arranged. *Bearbeitung*, *arrangement.

Beard, John (*b* 1716; *d* Hampton, 1791). Eng. ten. assoc. with Handel operas and oratorios. Ten. parts of *Israel in Egypt, Messiah, Samson, Judas Maccabaeus*, and *Jephtha* were written with Beard in mind. Also sang Macheath in *The *Beggar's Opera*. Man., CG Th., 1761–7.

Beard, Paul (*b* Birmingham, 1901). Eng. violinist. Taught by father and played in public 1907. Spa orch., Scarborough, 1920; Leader, CBSO 1922–32, LPO 1932–6, BBC S.O. 1936–62. Prof. of vn. GSM and also taught at RAM. O.B.E. 1952.

'Bear' Symphony (*L'Ours*). Nickname for Haydn's Sym. No. 82 in C (Hob.I:82), 1786, first of Paris syms., because the bagpipe-like theme of the finale suggests the perf. of a bear-leader, or because of a 'growling' theme in the same movement.

Bear, The. Comic opera in 1 act—extravaganza by *Walton to lib. by Paul Dehn adapted from play (vaudeville) by Chekhov (1888). Prod. Aldeburgh 1967. Also set by Jacobo *Ficher, 1952.

Bearded Gamba. See *Gamba* (organ stop).

Beat. (1) Unit of measurement of rhythmic pulse of mus. (i.e. waltz has 3 beats to the measure), as indicated in time signature. In ⁴₄ time each quarter-note (crotchet) is one beat, but in more complicated signatures much depends on the tempo selected. E.g. in ¹²₈ time there are 12 beats to a measure if taken very slowly, or else one for each dotted crotchet.
(2) The cond.'s action corresponding to the required rhythmic pulse.
(3) When 2 notes near to each other in vibration frequency are heard together their vibrations necessarily coincide at regular intervals and thus reinforce each other. This periodical reinforcement is known as a beat and is made use of in pf.-tuning.
(4) Name given variously to ornament in early mus., sometimes applied to a *mordent and sometimes to *acciaccatura. Still other references imply a 'reversed shake' by this term.
(5) Term in jazz, basically meaning the rhythmical pulse of the mus., but also meaning jazz in a generic sense, e.g. 'the beat is black' = Negro jazz.

Béatitudes, Les (The Beatitudes). Oratorio by Franck, comp. 1869–79, based on Sermon on the Mount, for soloists, ch., and orch. (F.p. Paris 1879, privately; first complete public perf. Paris 1893. Glasgow 1900; Cardiff 1902.)

Beatitudes, The. Cantata by *Bliss, 1961, for sop., ten., ch., org., and orch., biblical text being interspersed with poems. F.p. Coventry Cath. 1962.

Beatles, The. Vocal and instr. Eng. pop group (guitars and drums) who attained worldwide popularity and critical acclaim during 1960s, chiefly in songs by 2 of the members, John Lennon (*b* Liverpool, 1940; *d* NY, 1980) and Paul McCartney (*b* Liverpool, 1942). Formed and named in Liverpool *c*.1957 by Lennon, with McCartney and George Harrison (*b* Liverpool, 1943). Played at Casbah and Cavern Clubs, Liverpool, until invited to Hamburg, 1960, where 2 extra members were Stuart Sutcliffe (electric bass guitar) and Pete Best (drums). Sutcliffe died 1962. Best was replaced by Ringo Starr (orig. Richard Starkey, *b* Liverpool, 1940). Group's nat. popularity as qt. (Lennon, McCartney, Harrison, and Starr) began 1962 under management of Brian Epstein (*b* Liverpool, 1935; *d* London, 1967), followed by highly successful tours of USA and elsewhere. Term 'Beatlemania' coined to describe adulation accorded them, not only by the young. Among songs written by Lennon and McCartney were *Please, please me, She loves you, Yesterday, Eleanor Rigby, Yellow submarine,* and *Hey Jude.* Each of group became M.B.E., 1965. Group made several films; record sales were phenomenal. Ceased performing together 1969, partnership being later legally dissolved. McCartney formed new group called 'Wings', Lennon settled in USA where he was shot dead, Harrison continued to record, performing only rarely, and Starr continued to record and to perform in films.

Beatrice di Tenda. Opera in 2 acts by Bellini, lib. by Romani. Prod. Venice 1833, London 1836, Paris 1841, New Orleans 1842. Revived Catania 1935.

Béatrice et Bénédict (Beatrice and Benedick). Opera in 2 acts by Berlioz, with lib. considerably adapted by the composer from Shakespeare's comedy *Much Ado about Nothing* (1599–1600). Comp. 1860–2. Prod. Baden-Baden 1862; Glasgow 1936; Washington, DC, 1964. His last work.

Beaumarchais, Pierre Augustin Caron de (*b* Paris, 1732; *d* Paris, 1799). Fr. playwright and musician. An accomplished flautist and harpist, his mus. fame rests, however, on his authorship of the plays *Le Barbier de Séville* (1772, perf. 1775) and its sequels *La Folle Journée, ou Le Mariage de Figaro* (1781, perf. 1784), and *La Mère Coupable* (perf. 1792). The first play was originally intended as a comic opera, with mus. by Beaumarchais adapted from Sp. airs. Librettist of *Tarare*, opera in 5 acts by Salieri (1787). *The Barber of Seville* was set as an opera by Paisiello (1782) and Rossini (1816) and also by F. L. Benda (1776) and Isouard (*c.*1796), *The Marriage of Figaro* by Mozart (1786), and *La Mère Coupable* by Milhaud (1964–5).

Beautiful Galathea, The (*Die schöne Galatea*). Operetta by Suppé, prod. Vienna 1865, of which ov. is still often heard. Libretto by P. Henrion.

Beaux Arts Trio. Amer. pf. trio who gave their f.p. at Berkshire Mus. Fest., 1955, and since then have won international reputation, esp. in Haydn, Beethoven, and Schubert. Original members were Menahem Pressler, pf. (*b* Magdeburg, 1923), Daniel Guilet, vn., and Bernard Greenhouse, vc. (*b* Newark, NJ, 1916). Guilet was succeeded in 1968 by Isadore Cohen (*b* NY, 1922). Pressler studied with Egon Petri. Prof. of mus., Indiana Univ. since 1958. Cohen was member of Juilliard Quartet 1958–66. Greenhouse studied with Casals.

Bebend (Ger.). Trembling, i.e. **Tremolo.*

Be-Bop. Jazz development of the 1940s, primarily for small groups of instrumentalists, such as a rhythm section of 4 or 5 players with some solo instr. Scat singing was a feature. Be-bop used highly complex chord sequences often at very fast tempi. Specially assoc. with the alto saxophonist Charlie Parker. It had a marked effect on the jazz techniques of drumming and pf.-playing.

Bebung (Ger.). Trembling. A tremolo effect obtained by a rapid shaking movement of the finger on a str. of a bowed instr. or on a key of a clavichord (see also *Bebend*).

Bec (Fr.), **becco** (It.). Mouthpiece of cl. *Flûte à bec* is Fr. for recorder.

Bécarre (Fr.). The natural sign.

Bechstein, Friedrich Wilhelm Carl (*b* Gotha, 1826; *d* Berlin, 1900). Ger. pf. manufacturer. After working in pf. factories in Ger., Fr., and Eng., founded his own firm in Berlin, 1853. Branches were est. in Fr., London (1879), and Russ. London recital hall built in 1901 was named Bechstein Hall, though re-named Wigmore Hall in 1917 after the street in which it stands.

Beck. Short for *Becken*, cymbals.

Beck, Conrad (*b* Lohn, Schaffhausen, Switzerland, 1901). Swiss composer. Zürich Cons. 1921–4, studying with V. **Andreae. Lived in Paris 1923–32, studying orch. with Ibert. Mus. dir. Basle Radio, 1938–66. Works incl. syms., concs. for str. qt. and orch., vn. and chamber orch., fl., va., cl., concertinos for pf., for cl., bn., and orch., ob. and orch.; 5 str. qts.; cantatas, *La Mort d'Oedipe* (1928), *Die Sonnenfinsternis* (1967); chamber cantata on sonnets of Louiza Labé (1937); and ballet *Der Bär* (1937).

Beck, Karl (*b* 1814; *d* Vienna, 1879). Austrian ten. who created the role of Lohengrin, Weimar, 1850.

Becken (Ger.). **Cymbals.

Becker, Günther Hugo (*b* Forbach, Ger., 1924). Ger. composer and teacher. Comp. lessons from Fortner between 1949 and 1956, privately and at Detmold Mus. Acad. Taught in Gr. 1956–68. In 1969 in Essen founded elec. instr. ens. *Gruppe MHz*, re-named (1971) Live-Electronic Ensemble Folkwang, Essen. Prof. of comp., Düsseldorf Cons. from 1973.

Becker, Hugo (*b* Strasbourg, 1863; *d* Geiselgasteig, 1941). Ger. cellist, student of (among others) Piatti. Member of Heermann Qt. 1890–1906. Taught during that time at Frankfurt Cons. From 1910 prin. vc. teacher, Berlin Hochschule. Cellist in trios with Schnabel and Flesch, and Ysaÿe and Busoni. Comp. vc. conc. (1898) and short pieces.

Becker, John Joseph (*b* Henderson, Kentucky, 1886; *d* Wilmette, Illinois, 1961). Amer. composer. Mus.B. degree from Wisconsin Cons., Milwaukee. Prof. of comp., North Texas College, 1906–14; dir. of mus., Univ. of Notre Dame, 1918–28; chairman of fine arts dept., St Thomas College, St Paul, 1928–33. While at St Paul his romantic-impressionist style as composer changed into more radical and dissonant idiom after assoc. with Cowell, Ives, Ruggles, and Riegger. Several of his later works carry message of social protest. From 1943, dir. of mus. and composer in residence, Barat College, Lake Forest, Ill. Comp. 7 syms. between 1915 and 1954, the last being unfinished; 2 pf. concs., va. conc., hn. conc.; 7 *Soundpieces* for various chamber combinations; *The Snow Goose* (orch.); 1-act opera *Deirdre of the Sorrows* (1945).

Beckus the Dandipratt. Concert-ov. by Malcolm *Arnold, pubd. 1948. A dandipratt is an urchin.

Beckwith, John (*b* Victoria, B.C., 1927). Canadian composer. Studied Toronto Univ. and with Nadia *Boulanger in Paris 1950–2. Instructor in mus. theory, Toronto Royal Cons. 1955–65. Member of mus. faculty, Toronto Univ. since 1952, dean 1970. Works incl. 1-act opera *The Night Blooming Cereus* (1953–8), *A Message to Winnipeg* (1960), *Wednesday's Child* (1962), *Circle, With Tangents* (1967, for hpd. and 13 str.) and *The Sun Dance* (1968). Several of his works are described as 'collages' and employ narrators.

Bedford, David (Vickerman) (*b* London, 1937). Eng. composer and teacher. Studied RAM with Berkeley, and privately, 1960, in Venice with Luigi *Nono. Was member of pop group 'The Whole World'. Prin. works:

MUSIC THEATRE: *The Rime of the Ancient Mariner* (school opera, 1975–6); *The Ragnarok* (1982–3) (school opera, part of trilogy with *The Death of Baldur* (1979) and *Indiof's Saga* (1980)).

ORCH: *This One for You* (1965); *Gastrula* (1968); *Star's End*, rock instr. and orch. (1974); Sym. for 12 mus. (1981); *Sun Paints Rainbows on the Vast Waves* (1982); *The Valley-Sleeper, The Children, Snakes and the Giant* (1982).

CHORUS AND ORCH: *Dream of the 7 Lost Stars* (1964–5); *Star Clusters, Nebulae, and Places in Devon* (1971); *12 Hours of Sunset* (1974); *The Odyssey*, sop., girls' vv., instr., elec. (1976); *Song of the White Horse* (1977); *The Way of Truth*, ch., elec. (1978).

UNACC. CHORUS: 2 Poems (Patchen) (1963), *The Golden Wine is Drunk* (Dowson) (1974).

INSTR. ENSEMBLE: *Piece for Mo* (1963), *Five* (1967), *Pentomino*, wind quintet (1968), *The Garden of Love* (1970), *The Sword of Orion* (1970), *With 100 Kazoos* (1971), *Nurse's Song with Elephants* (1971), *Jack of Shadows*, va. solo and small orch. (1973), *A Horse, His Name was Hunry Fencewaver Walkins*, acoustic guitar and chamber ens. (1973), *Pancakes, with Butter, Maple Syrup and Bacon and the TV Weatherman*, brass quintet (1973), *Variations on a Rhythm by Mike Oldfield*, perc. (3 players, 84 instr.) (1973).

VOICE AND INSTR: *Music for Albion Moonlight*, sop. (1965), *That White and Radiant Legend*, sop. and speaker (1966), *The Tentacles of the Dark Nebula*, ten. (1969), *When I Heard the Learn'd Astronomer*,

ten. (1972), *Holy Thursday with Squeekers*, sop. (1972).

INSTR: *18 Bricks Left on April 21st*, 2 electric guitars (1967); *Piano Piece I* (1966), *II* (1968); *'You Asked for It'*, acoustic guitar (1969); *Spillihpernak*, va. (1972); wind sextet (1981); *SPNM Birthday Piece*, str. qt. (1983).

VOICE AND ACC: *O Now the Drenched Land Wakes*, bar. and pf. duet; *Come In Here, Child*, sop. and amplified pf. (1968); *Because He Liked to be at Home*, ten. (also plays recorder) and harp (1974); *On the Beach at Night*, 2 ten., pf., chamber org. (1978).

Bedford, Steuart (*b* London, 1939). Eng. cond. and pianist, particularly assoc. with Eng. Mus. Th. and Aldeburgh Fest. Studied RAM and Oxford Univ. On Glyndebourne mus. staff 1965–6. Cond. début SW 1967 (*The Beggar's Opera*). Prof. at RAM from 1965. Cond. f.p. Britten's *Death in Venice*, 1973, and *Phaedra*, 1976. Arr. orch. suite from *Death in Venice* (Aldeburgh 1984).

Bédos de Celles, Dom Francis (*b* Caux, 1709; *d* Saint-Denis, 1779). Fr. Benedictine, org. builder and author of important book, *L'Art du facteur d'orgues* (The Art of the Organ-builder, 1766–8).

Bedyngham, John (*b* ?Oxford, 1422; *d* London, 1459 or 1460). Eng. composer. Comp. motets *Manus Dei, Salva Jesu,* and *Vide dire,* also *O rosa Bella, Beata es Virgo Maria,* and *Mi verry joy.* Influential on Continent, though unlikely he worked there. Music survives largely in foreign sources.

Beecham, (Sir) Thomas (*b* St Helens, 1879; *d* London, 1961). Eng. cond. and impresario. First appearance was as cond. of Hallé Orch. at St Helens, 1899. Educated Rossall School and Wadham College, Oxford. Early ambition to be composer, but took up cond. instead. Came to the fore about 1905 when he founded New Sym. Orch. In 1910, with backing of his father, the industrialist Sir Joseph Beecham, staged season of opera at CG at which Strauss's *Elektra* had first Eng. perf., also Delius's *A *Village Romeo and Juliet*. Thereafter there was hardly a feature of Eng. mus. life with which Beecham was not closely, often controversially, and always artistically involved. Assoc. with most leading Brit. orchs. Founded LPO 1932, and RPO 1946. In decade preceding World War II was art. dir. of Royal Opera House, CG. Cond. many Amer. orchs. Ardent champion of Delius, about whom he wrote a book, and notable interpreter of Mozart, Haydn, Sibelius, Strauss, and Fr. composers of 19th cent. Thrice married. Knighted 1915, 2nd baronet 1916, C.H. 1957.

Beecke, Ignatz von (*b* Wimpfen, 1733; *d* Wallerstein, 1803). Ger. army officer and Kapellmeister. Pupil of Gluck. His pf.-playing was excellent and, with Schubart, developed new techniques. Played Mozart's conc. for 2 pf. with the composer at Frankfurt, 1790. Friend of Gluck. Comp. operas, oratorio, syms., concs., and pf. sonatas.

Beer Barrel Polka ('Roll out the barrel'). Tune composed by Jaromír Vejvoda (b 1902) and pubd. in Prague, 1934. as *Lost Love* (*Škoda Lásky*). Acquired Eng. title when pubd. in NY, 1939. Became very popular with Servicemen in 2nd World War.

Beer, Jakob Liebmann. Real name of Giacomo *Meyerbeer.

Beeson, Jack (Hamilton) (b Muncie, Ind., 1921). Amer. composer. Studied Toronto Univ. and Eastman Sch., also had informal comp. lessons from Bartók. Accompanist and cond. of opera workshop, Columbia Univ. 1944–8. MacDowell prof. of mus., Columbia Univ. since 1967, head of mus. dept., 1968–72. Comps. incl. Sym. in A (1959) and 6 operas, *Jonah* (1950), *Hello Out There* (1953), *The Sweet Bye and Bye* (1956), *Lizzie Borden* (1965), *My Heart's in the Highlands* (1969), and *Captain Jinks of the Horse Marines* (1975).

Bee's Wedding, The. Fanciful name for Mendelssohn's *Lieder ohne Worte* No. 34 in C for solo pf. (Book VI, Op. 67, No. 4, *Spinnerlied*). Sometimes known as *Spinning Song*. Comp. 1845.

Beethoven, Ludwig van (b Bonn, 1770; d Vienna, 1827). Ger. composer and pianist who radically transformed every mus. form in which he worked. His paternal family were of Flemish stock, his grandfather having emigrated to Bonn where he became Court Singer to the Elector. Beethoven's father also became Court Singer, but was a coarse, drunken man, hopeful of exploiting his 2nd child Ludwig's mus. talents. Beethoven's early mus. education came from his father and several mediocre teachers. In 1779 he became a pupil of Christian Gottlob Neefe and his ass. as court organist in 1784. In 1786 he visited Vienna and may have extemporized for Mozart. On return to Bonn he found an understanding patron in Count Waldstein. For 4 years he was a violist in the court th. orch. in addition to other duties. In 1792 Haydn, visiting Bonn, saw some of Beethoven's early comps. and invited him to study with him in Vienna. There, despite his brusque and often uncouth manner, he was patronized by the aristocracy and lived for 2 years (1794–6) in the home of Prince Lichnowsky. His fame was entirely that of a virtuoso improviser at the kbd. Lessons from Haydn proved unsatisfactory and Beethoven went for theory to Schenk and later to Albrechtsberger and Salieri. His Op. 1, 3 pf. trios, was pubd. 1795 and had immediate success.

Apart from occasional visits to the countryside Beethoven passed the rest of his life in Vienna. For 30 years he prod. mus. of all kinds in a steady flow. His first public appearance in Vienna was as soloist in his B♭ major pf. conc. in 1795. His 3rd

Symphony (the *Eroica*), besides being a work of revolutionary import because it greatly extended the possibilities of symphonic form, was significant because it was originally ded. to Napoleon Bonaparte. Beethoven erased the dedication when he heard that Napoleon had proclaimed himself emperor. In 1805 his only opera *Fidelio*, originally called *Leonore*, was performed but withdrawn for rev. after 3 perfs. and given the following year in a 2-act version. His 5th and 6th (*Pastoral*) Syms. were f.p. at the same concert in 1808 and the 7th appeared in 1813, the year before the successful prod. of the further rev. *Fidelio*. In 1817 and 1818 he began work on his 9th Sym., which departed from all precedent by including a choral finale for solo vv., ch., and orch., and the *Missa Solemnis*. These were perf. in 1824. From 1824 to 1826 he comp. the last 5 of his 17 str. qts.

Beethoven's mus. may have sometimes been misunderstood in his lifetime but it was never neglected. However, his personal eccentricities and unpredictability were to grow, principally because of his discovery in 1798 that he was going deaf. It was not until 1819 that conversation with him was possible only by writing in a notebook, but in the intervening 20 years his affliction, though it varied in intensity, steadily worsened. Perhaps this is also why he never married, though he loved several women, and one in particular, the still unidentified 'Immortal Beloved' (Maynard Solomon, in his *Beethoven*, 1977, gives convincing but not incontrovertible reasons for believing that she was Antonie Brentano, wife of a Frankfurt merchant. She lived from 1780 to 1869. Beethoven dedicated the *Diabelli Variations* to her.) An indication of the esteem in which Beethoven was held is that in 1815 Vienna conferred its honorary freedom on him. When he died, his funeral at Währing was a nat. occasion. His grave is now in the Central Friedhof, Vienna.

Beethoven's significance in the history and development of mus. is immense. He emancipated and democratized the art, composing out of spiritual inner necessity rather than as provider of virtuoso display material. He was not a quick or facile worker—his sketchbooks show how he laboriously developed an idea from sometimes banal beginnings to the final version. His mastery of structure and of key relationships was the basis on which he worked a revolution in the handling of sonata-form. It is to Beethoven that we owe the full emergence of the symphony as a repository for a composer's most important ideas. He expanded the coda from a formal conclusion to a climactic splendour; he transformed the minuet into the tempestuous, exultant scherzo; he was the first to use 'motto-themes' as a consistent formal device. In his slow movements, mus. expressed a mystical exaltation which even Mozart had never approached. In the str. qt. and the pf. sonata also, Beethoven extended the medium to a vastly increased technical and expressive degree (though in the case of the pf. it was not until his last sonatas that his technical use of the instr. went beyond that of his predecessors). It is probably true to say that today his mus. is the most frequently performed of any composer's. Among the most important of his many comps. are:

SYMPHONIES: No. 1 in C, Op. 21, comp. 1799–1800, f.p. Vienna, 2 April 1800, cond. P. Wranitzky; pubd. 1801. No. 2 in D, Op. 36, comp. 1801–2, f.p. Vienna, 5 Apr. 1803, cond. Beethoven; pubd. 1804. No. 3 in E♭ (*Eroica*), Op. 55, comp. 1803–4, f.pub.p. Vienna, 7 Apr. 1805; pubd. 1806. No. 4 in B♭, Op. 60, comp. 1806, f. public p. Vienna, 15 Nov. 1807, cond. Clement; pubd. 1808. No. 5 in C minor, Op. 67, comp. 1804–8, f.p. Vienna, 22 Dec. 1808, cond. Beethoven; pubd. 1809. No. 6 in F (*Pastoral*), Op. 68, comp. 1807–8, f.p. Vienna, 22 Dec. 1808, cond. Beethoven; pubd. 1809. No. 7 in A, Op. 92, comp. 1811–2, f.p. Vienna, 8 Dec. 1813, cond. Beethoven; pubd. 1816. No. 8 in F, Op. 93, comp. 1812, f.p. Vienna, 27 Feb. 1814, cond. Beethoven; pubd. 1816. No. 9 in D minor (*Choral*), Op. 125, comp. 1817–23, f.p. Vienna, 7 May 1824, cond. Beethoven; pubd. 1826. *Battle Symphony*, Op. 91, comp. 1813, f.p. Vienna, 8 Dec. 1813, cond. Beethoven; pubd. 1816.

CONCERTOS: *Piano*: No. 1 in C, Op. 15 (really No. 2 in order of comp.), comp. 1795–8, f.p. (presumed) Vienna, 2 April 1800, soloist Beethoven, cond. Wranitzky; pubd. March 1801. No. 2 in B♭, Op. 19 (really No. 1 in order of comp.), comp. 1794–5, f.p. Vienna, 29 Mar. 1795, soloist Beethoven; pubd. Dec. 1801. No. 3 in C minor, Op. 37, comp. 1800–1, f.p. Vienna, 5 Apr. 1803, soloist Beethoven; pubd. 1804. No. 4 in G, Op. 58, comp. 1805–6, f.p. Vienna, 22 Dec. 1808, soloist Beethoven; pubd. 1808. No. 5 in E♭ (nicknamed *'Emperor'* but not by Beethoven), Op. 73, comp. 1809, f.p. Leipzig, Dec. 1810, soloist F. Schneider, f. Vienna p. 12 Feb. 1812, soloist Czerny; pubd. 1811. Vn. conc. Op. 61, arr. for pf. by Beethoven in 1807 and pubd. 1808. *Violin*: Vn. Conc. in D, Op. 61, comp. 1806, f.p. Vienna, 23 Dec. 1806, soloist Franz Clement; pub. 1809. *Piano, violin, and cello*: Triple conc. in C, Op. 56, comp. 1804, f.p. 1808; pubd. 1807.

PIANO SONATAS (32 in number): Nos. 1, 2 and 3, Op. 2, No. 1 in F minor, No. 2 in A major, No. 3 in C major (1794–5); No. 4, Op. 7, in E♭ (1796); Nos. 5, 6 and 7, Op. 10, No. 1 in C minor, No. 2 in F major, No. 3 in D major (1798); No. 8, Op. 13, *Pathétique* in C minor (1799); Nos. 9 and 10, Op. 14, No. 1 in E major, No. 2 in G major (1799); No. 11, Op. 22, in B♭ (1800); No. 12, Op. 26, in A♭ (1800–1); Nos. 13 and 14, Op. 27, No. 1 in E♭, No. 2 in C♯ minor (*Moonlight*), both described as *quasi una fantasia* (1800–1); No. 15, Op. 28, in D major (*Pastorale*)

(1801); Nos. 16, 17 and 18, Op. 31, No. 1 in G major, No. 2 in D minor, No. 3 in E♭ (1801–2); Nos. 19 and 20, Op. 49, No. 1 in G minor, No. 2 in G major (1802); No. 21, Op. 53, in C major (*Waldstein*) (1804); No. 22, Op. 54, in F major (1804); No. 23, Op. 57, in F minor (*Appassionata*) (1804–5); No. 24, Op. 78, in F♯ major (1809); No. 25, Op. 79, *Sonatina* in G major (1809); No. 26, Op. 81a, in E♭ (*Lebewohl*, usually known as *Les *Adieux*) (1809–10); No. 27, Op. 90 in E minor (1814); No. 28, Op. 101, in A major (1816); No. 29, Op. 106, in B♭ (*Hammerklavier*) (1817–18); No. 30, Op. 109, in E major (1820); No. 31, Op. 110, in A♭ (1821); No. 32, Op. 111, in C minor (1821–2).

OTHER PIANO WORKS: Sonata in D for 4 hands, Op. 6 (1797); 7 *Bagatelles*, Op. 33 (1782–1802); 6 Variations in F major on orig. theme, Op. 34 (1802); 15 Variations in E♭ and fugue on theme from *Prometheus* (known as *Eroica Variations*) Op. 35 (1802); 32 Variations in C minor (1806–7); 6 Variations in D, Op. 76 (1810); Fantaisie in G minor, Op. 77 (1810); 11 *Bagatelles*, Op. 119 (1821); 33 Variations on a Waltz by *Diabelli, Op. 120 (1819–23); 6 *Bagatelles*, Op. 126 (1823–4); *Grosse Fuge* in B♭ Op. 133 (arr. Beethoven for pf. duet, Op. 134) (1826). *Rondo a capriccio* in G ('Rage over a lost Groschen'), Op. 129 (1825–6).

CHAMBER MUSIC: *String Quartets*: Op. 18, Nos. 1–6 in F major, G major, D major, C minor, A major, B♭ (1798–1800); Nos. 7, 8 and 9, Op. 59, Nos. 1–3 in F major, E minor, C major (the *Rasoumovsky* qts., ded. to Count *Rasoumovsky, Russian ambassador in Vienna, a keen qt. player); (comp. 1806); No. 10, Op. 74, in E♭ (known as *Harp*; 1809); No. 11, Op. 95, in F minor (1810); No. 12, Op. 127, in E♭ (1822–5); No. 13, Op. 130, in B♭ (1825–6; present finale replaces *Grosse Fuge*, Op. 133); No. 14, Op. 131 in C♯ minor (1825–6); No. 15, Op. 132, in A minor (1825); No. 16, Op. 135 in F major (1826); Op. 133, in B♭ (*Grosse Fuge*), orig. finale of Op. 130 (1825). *String Quintets*; Op. 4, in E♭ (1795–6), arr. of Octet for wind instr. (comp. 1792–3, pubd. 1830 as Op. 103); Op. 29 in C major (1800–1); Op. 104, in C minor, arr. by Beethoven in 1817 of his pf. Trio, Op. No. 1 No. 3 (1792–4). *Piano Trios*: Op. 1, Nos. 1–3, in E♭, G major, and C minor (1792–4); Op. 38, in E♭ (with vn. or cl.), arr. by Beethoven of his Septet, Op. 20 (1820–3); 14 Variations in E♭, Op. 44 (1802–3); Op. 70, Nos. 1–2, in D major and E♭ (1808); Op. 97, in B♭ (*Archduke*) (1810–11); Variations on 'Ich bin der Schneider *Kakadu', Op. 121a (*Kakadu*) (c.1798). *String Trios*: Op. 3 in E♭ (pre-1794) transcribed for vc. and pf., Op. 64; Op. 8, *Serenade* in D major (1796–7); Op. 9, Nos. 1–3, in G major, D major, and C minor (1797–8); *Piano Quintet* (pf., ob., cl., hn., bn.), Op. 16, in E♭ (1796), arr. for pf. qt. (1796, pubd. 1801); *Septet* (vn., va., vc., cl., hn., bn., and db.), Op. 20 in E♭ (1799–1800). *Violin Sonatas* (but note that Beethoven described them as sonatas for pf. and vn.): Op. 12, Nos. 1–3, in D major, A major and E♭ (1797–8); Op. 23, in A minor (1800); Op. 24, in F major (*Spring*) (1800–1); Op. 30, Nos. 1–3, in A major, C minor, and G major (1801–2); Op. 47, in A major (*Kreutzer*) (1802–3); Op. 96, in G major (1812, rev. 1815). *Cello Sonatas*: Op. 5, Nos. 1–2, in F major and G minor (1796); Op. 69, in A major (1807–8); Op. 102, Nos. 1–2, in C major and D major (1815). *Miscellaneous*: *Serenade* in D major, Op. 25, fl., vn., va. (1801); *Sextet* in E♭, Op. 81b, 2 hn., str. (?1795); *Trio* in B♭, Op. 11, pf., cl. or vn., vc. (1797); *Sonata* in F major, Op. 17, hn., pf. (1800); *Variations* for vc. and pf.: in G major, WoO 45, on 'See the conqu'ring hero comes' from *Judas Maccabaeus* (1796), in F major, Op. 66, on 'Ein Mädchen oder Weibchen' from *Die Zauberflöte* (1796), and in E♭, WoO 46, on 'Bei Männern, welche Liebe fühlen' from *Die Zauberflöte* (1801).

ORCHESTRAL (excl. Symphonies): *Overtures*: *Coriolan*, Op. 62 (1807); *Die Weihe des Hauses* (*Consecration of the House*), Op. 124 (1822); *Leonora No. 1*, Op. 138 (1805), *Leonora No. 2* (1805), *Leonora No. 3* (1806); *Fidelio* (1814). For details see under *Fidelio*; *Overture* and 9 items of incidental mus. for *Egmont* (Goethe), Op. 84 (1809–10); *Overture* and 8 items of incidental mus. for *Die *Ruinen von Athen* (Kotzebue), Op. 113 (1811); *Overture* and 9 items of incidental mus. for *König Stephan* (Kotzebue), Op. 117 (1811); *Ov.* in C (*Namensfeier*), Op. 115 (1814–15); *Ov.*, introduction, and 16 Nos. for ballet *Die Geschöpfe des *Prometheus*, Op. 43 (1800–1).

OPERA: *Fidelio*, Op. 72 (1805, rev. 1806 and 1814).

CHORAL: *Cantata on the death of the Emperor Joseph II* (1790); *Cantata on the accession of Emperor Leopold II* (1790); *Christus am Ölberge*, oratorio, Op. 85 (1803); Mass in C major, Op. 86 (1807); *Mass in D major (*Missa Solemnis*), Op. 123 (1819–22); *Choral Fantasia (pf., ch., and orch.), Op. 80 (1808); *Meeresstille und Glückliche Fahrt* (*Calm Sea and Prosperous Voyage*), Op. 112 (1814–15); *Der glorreiche Augenblick* (The Glorious Moment), cantata, Op. 136 (1814).

SOLO VOICE: (Songs, etc.): Scena and aria 'Ah! Perfido!', sop. and orch., Op. 65 (comp. 1796); *Adelaide*, Op. 46 (1795); *An die Hoffnung*, Op. 32 (1805); *An die ferne Geliebte (To the distant beloved), song-cyle for ten. and pf. (words by A. Jeitteles), Op. 98 (1816); 25 Scot. songs, with acc. for pf. trio, Op. 108 (1815–16); 12 Scot. songs, with acc. for pf. trio, Op. 108 (1815–16); 12 Scottish songs (pubd. 1841).

Beggar's Opera, The. First and most popular of ballad operas. In 3 acts, arr. and adapted by Christoph Pepusch to a lib. by John Gay (London, Jan. 1728; NY Dec. 1750). Its 69 tunes are mostly derived from popular ballads of the day. The plot deals with London low life, the 'hero' being the highwayman Macheath and the heroine Polly, and is a satire on contemporary politics and on It.

operatic conventions. 20th-cent. vogue dates from London revival at Lyric, Hammersmith, in version re-orchestrated and re-harmonized by Frederic *Austin which ran from June 1920 for 1,463 perfs. Other versions by E. J. *Dent (Birmingham 1944), *Britten (Cambridge 1948), *Bliss (film, 1953), and Muldowney (1982). Milhaud's 3-act *L'Opéra des gueux* (1937) is an arr. of *The Beggar's Opera*. The Gay-Pepusch sequel *Polly*, dating from 1729, was banned by the Lord Chamberlain for nearly 50 years. See also *Weill, Kurt.*

Beggar Student, The (Millöcker). See *Bettelstudent, Der.*

Beglarian, Grant (*b* Tiflis, USSR, 1927). Russ.-born Amer. composer who received his early mus. education in Teheran, Iran. Went to USA in 1947 and continued training at Michigan Univ. (1947–51, 1954–8). Studied comp. with R. L. Finney and va. with Paul Doktor. Founded Music Book Associates in NY, 1961. Dir. young composers' project, Ford Foundation 1961–9. Appointed dean of sch. of performing arts, Univ. of S. California, 1969. Comps. incl. vn. sonata, vc. sonata, Sym., *Divertimento for orchestra* (1957–8), cantata '. . . . And All the Hills Echoed' (1968), *Fables, Foibles, and Fancies* (1971), *Diversions*, va., vc., orch. (1972) and Sinfonia for str. (1974).

Begleiten (Ger.). To accompany. Hence *Begleitung*, accompaniment; *Begleitend*, accompanying.

Beherrscher der Geister, Der (Weber). See *Ruler of the Spirits, The.*

Behrens, Hildegard (*b* Land Oldenburg, 1937). Ger. sop. Studied to be lawyer, then took up singing as pupil of Prof. Leuwen at Freiburg Mus. Acad. Opera début 1971, Deutsche Oper am Rhein, Düsseldorf, where she sang wide variety of roles from Fiordiligi in *Così fan tutte* and Musetta in *La Bohème* to Marie in *Wozzeck* and title-role of *Káťa Kabanová*. Sang Leonore in *Fidelio*, Zürich 1975. CG Début 1976 (Leonore), NY Met. 1976 (Giorgetta in *Il Tabarro*), Salzburg Fest. 1977 (Salome). Bayreuth Fest. 1983 (Brünnhilde).

Beier, Franz (*b* Berlin, 1857; *d* Kassel, 1914). German opera composer. Held several posts as Kapellmeister and ch. master. Operas incl. *Der Posaunist von Speikingen* (Kassel 1889) and *Der Gaunerkönig* (Kassel 1890).

Beinum, Eduard van (*b* Arnhem, Holland, 1900; *d* Amsterdam, 1959). Dutch cond. Began career in Haarlem 1926–31; 2nd cond., Concertgebouw Orch. of Amsterdam 1931–8, then associate to *Mengelberg whom he succeeded as chief cond. 1945. London début, LPO 1946. Took Concertgebouw Orch. on Amer. tour 1954. Prin. cond. LPO 1949–51. Cond. Los Angeles P.O. 1956–9.

Beisser (Ger.). Biter i.e. *Mordent.

Beklemmt, beklommen (Ger.). Oppressed, heavy of heart. Most famous use of this instruction is by Beethoven in middle section of cavatina of Str. Qt. in B♭ major, Op. 130, where mus. modulates into C♭.

Belaieff. See *Belyayev, Mitrofan*.

Bel Canto (It.). Beautiful singing, beautiful song. A term covering the remarkable qualities of the great 18th-cent. and early 19th-cent. It. singers, and suggesting rather perf. in the lyrical style, in which tone is made to tell, than in the declamatory style. Beauty of tone and legato phrasing, with faultless technique, were the prin. ingredients.

Belcke, Christian Gottlieb (*b* Lucka, Altenberg, 1796; *d* Lucka, 1875). Ger. flautist, for many years in Leipzig Gewandhaus Orch. Comp. fl. concs. and fantasias.

Belcke, Friedrich August (*b* Lucka, Altenberg, 1795; *d* Lucka, 1874). Ger. trombonist of great virtuosity. Member of Berlin royal band 1816–58. Comp. concs. and études for tb.

Belfagor. Lyric comedy in prol., 2 acts, and epilogue by *Respighi to lib. by C. Guastalla after Hauptmann. Prod. Milan 1923.

Belisario. Opera in 3 acts by Donizetti, to his own lib. Prod. Venice 1836, London 1837, Paris 1843.

Bell. (1) This popular and ubiquitous mus. instr. varies in weight from over 100 tons to a fraction of an ounce. For public bells the most usual bell metal is a bronze of 13 parts copper to 4 parts tin: the shape and proportions are the result of very intricate calculations in order to secure good tone and tuning—the latter not only of the *Strike Note* with its attendant overtones but also of the deep tone which persists after these have died away, i.e. the *Hum Note*, which should be an octave below the Strike Note.

There are 2 chief ways of sounding ordinary church bells, *Chiming* (the clapper moved mechanically just sufficiently to strike the side of the bell) and *Ringing* (in which the bell is swung round full circle).

A *Ring* of church bells may consist of any number from 5 to 12. With 5 bells 120 variations of order, or *Changes*, are possible; with 12 bells they number almost 480 millions. *Change Ringing* by hand-ropes, a characteristic British practice, is a still popular hobby. Various standard Changes are described by various traditional names, as 'Grandsire Triples', 'Bob Major', or 'Oxford Treble Bob'. Dorothy L. Sayers's detective story *The Nine Tailors* (1934) hinges on bell-ringing most ingeniously.

On the continent of Europe 'rings' are unknown but the *Carillon* is there an ancient institution—esp. in Belgium and Holland. This consists of a series of anything up to 70 bells played by skilful artists from a manual and pedal console somewhat similar to that of an organ but more cumbrous. Tunes and simple accompanying harmonies can be perf. At the hours and their halves and quarters the carillon is set in operation by clockwork. There are now some carillons in Britain and in the USA.

(2) *Tubular Bells* are often used in the orch. and are also now used (electrically operated from a kbd.) in church towers. They are cylindrical metal tubes of different lengths, suspended in a frame and played by being struck with a hammer.

(3) Handbells are small bells with handles: they are arr. in pitch order on a table and played by several performers, each in charge of several bells. They are used for the practice of change ringers and also as an entertainment.

(4) A term to describe the open end of a wind instr. from which the sound comes.

Bell, William Henry (*b* St Albans, 1873; *d* Gordon's Bay, Cape Province, 1946). Eng. composer, org., and violinist. Studied RAM where he became prof. of harmony 1903–12. Went to Capetown 1912 to become prin., S. African College of Mus. in 1919, becoming dean of faculty of mus., Capetown Univ., until retirement 1935. Comp. operas, syms., hymns, va. conc., chamber mus.

Bellaigue, Camille (*b* Paris, 1858; *d* Paris, 1930). Fr. mus. critic, from 1885 for *Revue des deux mondes*. Biographer of Mendelssohn, Gounod, Mozart, and Verdi.

Bell Anthem. Purcell's *Rejoice in the Lord alway* (1684–5). The name (which dates from the composer's lifetime) alludes to the pealing scale passages of the instr. introduction.

Belle Hélène, La (Beautiful Helen). Opéra-bouffe in 3 acts by Offenbach to lib. by Meilhac and Halévy. Prod. Paris 1864; London, 1866; Chicago 1867. Successfully revived in Paris 1960 and later in London by SW Opera (now ENO).

Belletti, Giovanni Battista (*b* Sarzana, 1813; *d* Sarzana, 1890). It. bar. assoc. with Jenny *Lind. Studied Bologna. Début in Stockholm 1839 in Rossini's *Il barbiere di Siviglia*. Sang with Lind in Donizetti, Meyerbeer, and Rossini operas in Sweden, Eng. (1848 début), and USA. In the USA his tours with Lind were arr. by Barnum. Retired 1862.

Bellezza, Vincenzo (*b* Bitonto, Bari, 1888; *d* Rome, 1964). It. cond. Studied Naples Cons. Début San Carlo, Naples, 1908, in *Aida*. Cond. at NY Met. 1926–35, CG 1926–30 and 1935–6. Cond. at Melba's farewell, CG 1926 and at first London perf. of Puccini's *Turandot*. Rome Opera after 1935. Re-visited London 1957 and 1958.

Bell'haver, Vincenzo (*b* Venice, 1530; *d* Venice, 1587). It. organist and composer. 2nd organist of St Mark's, Venice, 1586, succeeding Andrea

Gabrieli. Comp. madrigals, his 2nd book being pubd. in Venice, 1575.

Belli, Giulio (*b* Longiano, *c*.1560; *d* Imola, 1621). It. composer and teacher. Choirmaster in churches in Venice, Forlì, Montagnana, Padua, and Imola. Comp. masses, motets, canzonets, and madrigals.

Bellincioni, Gemma (*b* Monza, 1864; *d* Naples, 1950). It. sop. who created Santuzza in *Cavalleria rusticana* (1890) and title-role in *Fedora* (1898). Début in Naples, 1879. Was first It. Salome. Wife of ten. Roberto Stagno, the first Turiddù, who was also her teacher.

Bellini, Vincenzo (*b* Catania, Sicily, 1801; *d* Puteaux, nr. Paris, 1835). It. composer. Educated San Sebastiano Cons., Naples, where he studied under *Zingarelli. Perf. of his first opera, *Adelson e Salvini*, at cons. in 1825 led to commission for opera for San Carlo, Naples; and this in its turn led to a commission from La Scala, Milan, which resulted in *Il pirata*, a vehicle for the expressive lyrical style of the ten.*Rubini. This opera was then prod. in Paris and initiated Bellini's fame outside It. Another success was his setting of Vaccai's version of the Romeo and Juliet story, *I Capuleti e i Montecchi*, prod. Venice 1830 with Pasta in the *travesti* role of Romeo. Recent revivals have shown this to be one of Bellini's masterpieces. However, its popularity was eclipsed by *La Sonnambula* (Milan 1831), in which *Malibran appeared throughout Europe. Less than a year later came *Norma*; its sop. title-role was first sung by Pasta and succeeding exponents have included Grisi, Tietjens, Lilli Lehmann, Callas, and Sutherland. His last opera, *I Puritani*, was written for Paris (on the advice of Rossini) where its first cast in 1835 was led by Grisi, Rubini, Tamburini, and Lablache. Seven of his operas have libretti by Felice Romani.

Bellini's vocal style requires superb legato allied to great florid agility. His long elegant melodies, of which *Casta diva* from *Norma* is a supreme example, were admired by, and influenced, Berlioz. Wagner, too, was attracted by Bellini's operas and noted the close alliance between mus. and lib. For a period, Bellini was out of fashion, being regarded as merely a composer of display pieces, but a new generation of great singers has restored them to favour, revealing their dramatic force and melodic beauty.

Operas: *Adelson e Salvini* (Naples 1825); *Bianca e Gernando* (Naples 1826; rev. as *Bianca e Fernando*, Genoa 1828); *Il *pirata* (Milan 1827); *La straniera* (Milan 1829); *Zaira* (Parma 1829); *I *Capuleti e i Montecchi* (Venice 1830); *La *sonnambula* (Milan 1831); *Norma* (Milan 1831); *Beatrice di Tenda* (Venice 1833); *I *puritani* (Paris 1835). He also comp. songs and instr. works, incl. an ob. conc.

Bell Lyra. Portable form of glockenspiel. It is mounted on a rod held perpendicularly in the left hand whilst the right hand holds the beater.

Bellman, Carl Michael (*b* Stockholm, 1740; *d* Stockholm, 1795). Swed. poet and composer. His series of lyrics, 'Fredmans Epistlar' and 'Sanger', are set mostly to the then fashionable popular Fr. melodies.

Belloni, Gioseffo (*b* Lodi, *c*.1575; *d* after 1606). It. composer of church mus., some of it pubd. at Augsburg *c*.1610.

Bellows and Tongs. One of the burlesque means of mus.-making common in the 18th cent. Presumably the sound evoked was merely that of adroit rhythmic tapping.

Bell Rondo (It. *Rondo alla campanella*). Finale of vn. conc. in B minor by Paganini, containing bell-like effect. Liszt twice used same theme, in his *Grande Fantaisie de bravoure sur 'La Clochette'* (1832) and in *La campanella* (from the 6 *Transcendental studies of execution based on Paganini*, 1838).

Bells, The (*Kolokola*). Choral sym., Op. 35, by Rakhmaninov for sop., ten., and bar. soloists, ch., and orch. Comp. 1913, f.p. St Petersburg 1913, cond. Rakhmaninov; f. Eng. p. Liverpool 1921, cond. Wood. Rev. version 1936, f.p. Sheffield 1936, cond. Wood. Text is adaptation by Konstantin Balmont of E. A. Poe's poem.

Bells of Aberdovey. This is not a Welsh folksong, as claimed in many books of such songs, but appears to be the comp. of *Dibdin. He pubd. it in 1785, when it was sung in his Drury Lane opera *Liberty Hall*, and it appeared many times subsequently in vols. of his songs, not figuring in any of the numerous Welsh colls. before 1844.

Bells of Corneville (Planquette). See *Cloches de Corneville*.

Bells of Zlonice, The. A sym. in C minor by Dvořák, comp. 1865. Orig. his Op. 3, it was lost and not recovered until 1923. Pubd. 1961, it is the longest of his orch. works (*c.* 55 mins.).

Belly. The upper surface of a str. instr., over which the str. are stretched. Also the soundboard of pf.

Belshazzar. Oratorio by Handel. (F.p. London 1745.) Text by Charles Jennens.

Belshazzar's Feast. (1) Cantata by *Walton for bar., ch., and orch. to text compiled from biblical sources by O. Sitwell, comp. 1929–31; f.p. Leeds Fest., 1931, cond. Sargent.

(2) Incidental mus. by Sibelius for play by Hjalmar Procopé, from which he provided 4-movement suite for small orch. (1906).

Belyayev, Mitrofan (Petrovich) (*b* St Petersburg, 1836; *d* St Petersburg, 1904). Russ. mus. publisher. Son of wealthy timber merchant, but trained as musician. Enthusiastic sponsor of 'new' nationalist school of Russian composers. Founded his publishing house at Leipzig, 1885, and sponsored concerts in St Petersburg. Russian composers gathered at his St Petersburg house every Friday from 1891, hence 16 pieces for str. qt. known as 'Les Vendredis' (Fridays) written in his honour in collab. by Borodin, Rimsky-Korsakov, Glazunov, Lyadov, and others. Firm moved to Bonn, then to Frankfurt. Absorbed by C. F. Peters, 1971.

Bemberg, Hermann-Emmanuel (*b* Paris, 1859; *d* Berne, 1931). Fr. composer, pupil at Paris Cons. of Dubois and Massenet. His 4-act opera *Elaine* was a success at CG (with Melba in the cast) in 1892 and NY 1894. Other works incl. comic opera *Le Baiser de Suzon* (1888), cantata *La Mort de Jeanne d'Arc* (1886), and many songs.

Bémol (Fr.), **bemolle** (It.). Flat (♭).

Beňačková, Gabriela (*b* Bratislava, 1947). Cz. soprano. Studied at Bratislava Cons. and in Italy. Opera début Prague 1970 (Natasha in Prokofiev's *War and Peace*). Member Prague Nat. Th., but guest artist at world's leading opera houses, particularly in Janáček operas. Opera début outside Cz., Dublin 1975 (*The Bartered Bride*), Moscow 1977 (Tatyana), Vienna 1978 (Jenůfa), CG 1979 (Tatyana).

Benatzky, Ralph (*b* Moravské-Budejovice, 1884; *d* Zürich, 1957). Cz. composer of nearly 100 operettas, many film scores, and songs. Lived for some years in USA. Wrote title-song and much of the score of *White Horse Inn* (*Im weissen Rössl*, Berlin 1930).

Benda. Bohem. mus. family active in the 18th cent., 4 of them being the sons of a weaver and peripatetic musician. 3 of these were:
(1) František (Franz) (*b* Staré-Benátky, 1709; *d* Potsdam, 1786). Chorister in Prague, then became violinist and moved to Dresden. In 1732 obtained a place at the Berlin court of Crown Prince of Prussia, later Frederick the Great. In 1771 became Frederick's Konzertmeister, accompanying him in fl. conc. Works incl. trio sonatas, vn.concs., 6 vn. sonatas, and 2 books of vn. *études*.
(2) Jiří Antonin (Georg) (*b* Jungbunzlau, 1722; *d* Köstritz, Thuringia, 1795). Skilled oboist and kbd.-player. Went to Berlin in 1740 for lessons from his brother ((1) above). Violinist in royal band from 1742. Became Kapellmeister to Duke of Gotha in 1748. Spent 2 years in It. after 1764; on return wrote his *Ariadne auf Naxos* (1774) which earned him the claim to have invented *melodrama. Another melodrama, *Medea*, followed, also *Romeo und Julie* (1776). Retired 1778.
(3) Josef (*b* Staré-Benátky, 1724; *d* Berlin, 1804). Violinist, succeeded his brother František as leader of Frederick the Great's orch.
Several sons of the above also achieved mus. distinction, usually in Prussian court bands. Jiři's son, Friedrich Ludwig (*b* Gotha, 1752; *d* Königsberg, 1792) comp. an oratorio, church cantatas, 3 operas incl. *Der Barbier von Sevilla* (1776) and 3 vn. concs. František's eldest son, Friedrich Wil-

helm Heinrich (*b* Potsdam, 1745; *d* Potsdam, 1814) was a fine violinist, playing in the Berlin court band from 1782, and comp. 2 operas, *Alceste* (1786) and *Orpheus* (1785), an operetta, *Das Blumenmädchen*, a cantata *Pygmalion*, and instr. works.

Bender, Paul (*b* Driedorf, 1875; *d* Munich, 1947). Ger. bass. Début Breslau 1900; but after his début there in 1903 closely assoc. with Munich Opera. CG début 1914 (Amfortas in first Eng. stage perf. of *Parsifal*). Distinguished exponent of roles of Wotan, Sachs, Osmin, and Baron Ochs and of ballads of J. Loewe. Became teacher at Munich Mus. Sch.

Bendl, Karel (*b* Prague, 1838; *d* Prague, 1897). Boh. composer of nationalist works in the model of Smetana. Operas incl. *Lejla, Bretislav and Jikta*, and *The Montenegrins* (*Cernohorci*). Also comp. sacred and secular choral works.

Benedicite. (1) *The Song of the Three Holy Children* (Shadrach, Meshach, and Abednego) while in Nebuchadnezzar's fiery furnace. It is not in the Hebrew version of the book of Daniel, but comes from the Septuagint, or early Gr. translation of the Old Testament. It is one of the canticles of the Anglican service.
(2) Work by Vaughan Williams, for sop., ch., and orch. Comp. 1929 (prod. Leith Hill Fest. 1930); combines text of the canticle with a poem by J. Austin (1613–69).

Benedict, (Sir) Julius (*b* Stuttgart, 1804; *d* London, 1885). Ger.-born composer and cond., naturalized Eng. Son of a banker, he had lessons from Hummel who introduced him to Weber, in whose house he lived as pupil and protégé 1821–4 and by whom he was taken to meet Beethoven in 1823. Appointed cond., Vienna Kärntnerthor Th. 1823–5. Went to work at San Carlo, Naples, 1825, where several of his operas were perf., and to Paris in 1834, where the singer *Malibran suggested he should visit London. From 1835 lived in Eng. He cond. opera seasons at Lyceum, Drury Lane, and Her Majesty's Th. In 1848 cond. *Elijah* when Jenny Lind first sang in oratorio and later dir. most of her Amer. concerts. Cond., Norwich Fest., 1845–78, Liverpool Phil. Soc. 1867–79. Of his operas, oratorios, cantatas, syms., and concs., only the opera *The Lily of Killarney* (1862) is still occasionally perf. Knighted 1871. Wrote important biog. of Weber (1881).

Benedictus. (1) In the R.C. Mass, the *Benedictus qui venit*, i.e. simply the words 'Blessed is he that cometh in the name of the the the Lord', which complete the *Sanctus* section of the *Mass.
(2) The song of Zacharias (Luke I. 68 et seq.). 'Blessed be the Lord God of Israel', which is sung daily at *Lauds in R.C. churches and in the Eng. Prayer Book occurs in the Order for Morning Prayer.

Beneplacito, Beneplacimento (It.). Good pleasure. Preceded by the words *A suo* (At one's) this has the same sense as *Ad libitum.

Benet, John. See *Bennet, John.*

Benevoli, Orazio (*b* Rome, 1605; *d* Rome, 1672). It. composer of Fr. extraction. Choirmaster in var. Roman churches, 1624–43. At Austrian court 1643–5. Choirmaster at Vatican from 1646. Wrote contrapuntal church mus., incl. anthems for 48 vv.

Ben-Haim, Paul (orig. Frankenburger) (*b* Munich, 1897; *d* Tel Aviv, 1984). Israeli composer and cond. Studied Munich, where he was ass. cond. at State Opera 1920–4. Cond. at Augsburg opera 1924–31. Emigrated to Tel Aviv 1933. After formation of State of Israel in 1948 became Pres., Israeli Composers' Assoc., Dir., Jerusalem Acad. of Mus. 1949–54. Traditional Jewish and Arab melodies of the Near East flavour his works, which incl. 2 syms., vc. conc. (1962), pf. sonatina, pf. conc., and oratorio *Thanksgiving from the Desert.*

Beni Mora. Oriental Suite in E minor, Op. 29 No. 1 for orch. by Holst in 3 movements. Comp. 1909–10 after visit to Algeria and rev. 1912. F.p. London 1912.

Benjamin, Arthur (*b* Sydney, N.S.W., 1893; *d* London, 1960). Australian composer and pianist. Studied RCM (comp. with Stanford after 1911). Prof. of pf. at Sydney Cons. 1919–21, then returned to Eng. in similar post at RCM. Comps. incl. sym., vn. conc., ob. conc., film mus., the 2-pf. piece *Jamaican Rumba* (1938), and 4 operas, *The *Devil Take Her* (1931), *Prima Donna* (1933 prod. 1949), *A *Tale of Two Cities* (1949–50, prod. 1957), and *Tartuffe* (1959–60, prod. 1964).

Benjamin, George (*b* London, 1960). Eng. composer and pianist. Began pf. lessons at 7 and comp. when he was 9. Studied comp. and pf. with P. Gellhorn in London from 1974 and with Messiaen and Y. Loriod in Paris. Entered Paris Cons. 1977, King's Coll., Cambridge, 1978–82 (comp. with A. Goehr). Gave f.p. of Britten's *Sonatina Romantica*, Aldeburgh Fest. 1983. Works incl.:

ORCH: *Altitude*, brass band (1977); *Ringed by the Flat Horizon* (1979–80); *At First Light*, chamber orch. (1982).
VOCAL: *A Mind of Winter*, sop. and small orch. (1981).
CHAMBER MUSIC: Vn. Sonata (1976–7); Octet, fl. (picc.), cl., perc., celesta, str. (1978); *Flight*, fl. (1979); *Duo*, vc. and pf. (1980).
PIANO: Pf. sonata (1977–8); *Sortilèges* (1981); *Meditation on Haydn's Name* (1982).

Benjamin Cosyn's Virginal Book. A MS. coll. of mus., chiefly for virginals, made 1622–43 by Benjamin *Cosyn. It is now in the Brit. Museum. Pubd. 1923.

Bennet, John (*fl.* late 16th–early 17th cent.). Eng. (probably Lancastrian) composer of madrigals, whose first book, pubd. 1599, refers in preface to his youth. Remembered for *All creatures now are merry-minded*, his contribution to The *Triumphs of Oriana*, in which it is No. 4, and *Weep, O mine eyes*. Not to be confused with John Benet (*fl.* ?c.1420–50), Eng. composer of sacred mus. in style of Dunstable.

Bennett, Joseph (*b* Berkeley, Glos., 1831; *d* Berkeley, 1911). Eng. organist who became mus. critic, chiefly of the *Daily Telegraph*, 1870–1906. Author of libs. for leading Brit. Victorian composers, incl. *The Golden Legend* for Sullivan.

Bennett, Richard Rodney (*b* Broadstairs, 1936). Eng. composer and pianist. Studied RAM 1953–6 with Lennox Berkeley and Howard Ferguson, then with Boulez in Paris for 2 years. A fluent composer, absorbing influences of jazz, atonality, and traditional harmony and structures, he has had success in many spheres incl. films, for which he has comp. over 35 scores (*Far From the Madding Crowd* a notable example). Prof. of comp., RAM, 1963–5. C.B.E. 1977. Settled in NY, 1979. Prin. works incl.:

OPERAS: *The Ledge* (1961); *The *Mines of Sulphur* (1963–5); *Penny for a Song* (1966); *Victory* (1968–9).
BALLET: *Jazz Calendar*, for chamber ens. (1963–4); *Isadora* (1981).
ORCH: *Nocturnes* (1962); *Aubade* (1964); Syms.: No. 1 (1965), No. 2 (1967); *Suite* for small orch. (1966); *Concerto for Orchestra* (1973); *Serenade* (1976); *Commedia III* for 10 instr. (1973); *Music for Strings* (1977); *Anniversaries* (1982).
CONCERTOS: Pf. (1968); ob. and str. (1969–70); guitar (1970); va. (1973); vn. (1975); *Actaeon* (*Metamorphosis I*) for hn. (1977); db. (1978); *Sonnets for Orpheus*, vc. and orch. (1979); hpd. (1980); *Memento*, fl. and str. (1983).
VOICE(S) AND ORCH: *The Approaches of Sleep* (1960); *London Pastoral*, ten. and chamber orch. (1962); *Crazy Jane*, sop., cl., vc., pf. (1968–9); *Jazz Pastoral*, v. and jazz orch. (1969); *Sonnet Sequence*, ten. and str. (1974); *Spells*, sop., ch., and orch. (1974); *Love Spells* (2nd and 5th movements from preceding), sop., and orch. (1974); *5 Sonnets of Louise Labé*, sop. and ens. (1984).
CHAMBER MUSIC: *Winter Music*, fl. and pf. (1960); ob. sonata (1962); solo vn. sonatas: No. 1 (1955), No. 2 (1964); Str. Qts.: No. 1 (1952), No. 2 (1953), No. 3 (1960), No. 4 (1964); wind quintet (1967–8); *5 Impromptus* for guitar (1968); *Commedia II*, fl., vc., pf. (1972); *IV*, brass quintet (1973); *Scena II*, solo vc. (1973); Ob. Qt. (1975); *Travel Notes, Book 1*, str. qt. (1975); *Travel Notes, Book 2*, wind qt. (1976); *Scena III*, cl. (1977); hn. sonata (1978); vn. sonata (1978); *Metamorphoses*, str. octet (1980); *6 Tunes for the Instruction of Singing Birds*, fl. (1981); *Music for String Quartet*

(1981); sonatina for cl. (1981); *After Syrinx*, ob. and pf. (1982).

VOICE AND PIANO (or other instr.): *The Music that her Echo is*, ten. and pf. (1967); *A Garland for Marjory Fleming*, sop. and pf. (1969); *Time's Whiter Series*, counter-ten. and lute (1974); *The Little Ghost Who Died for Love*, sop. and pf. (1976); *Vocalese*, sop. and. pf. (1981).

PIANO: Sonata (1954); *Fantasy* (1962); *5 Studies* (1962–4); *Capriccio*, 4 hands (1968); *Scena I* (1973); *4-Piece Suite*, 2 pianos (1974); *Kandinsky Variations*, 2 pf. (1977); *Impromptu* (1981); *Noctuary* (*Variations on a Theme of Joplin*) (1981).

VOICES: *Letters to Lindbergh*, female vv. and pf. duet (1982); *Puer nobis* (1980); *Nonsense* (*7 Poems of Mervyn Peake*) (1979); *Devotions* (1971); *The House of Sleep*, 6 male vv. (1971); *Nowell, Nowell Tidings True* (1962).

Bennett, Robert Russell (*b* Kansas City, 1894; *d* NY, 1981). Amer. composer and arranger. Taught by his parents and later studied comp. with Carl Busch. In late 1920s studied for 4 years in Paris with Nadia Boulanger. At 16 began to earn living by orchestrating and arranging scores for Broadway mus. comedies and the list of works to which he has applied his talent proves his succcess. It incl. *Rose-Marie* (1924), *Showboat* (1927), *On Your Toes* (1936), *Oklahoma!* (1943), *Carmen Jones* (1943), *Carousel* (1945), *Annie Get Your Gun* (1946), *South Pacific* (1948), *Kiss Me Kate* (1948), *The King and I* (1951), *My Fair Lady* (1956), and *The Sound of Music* (1959). But perhaps his most famous arr. is the symphonic suite from Gershwin's *Porgy and Bess*. His own comps. incl. *Abraham Lincoln Symphony* (1931), *Hollywood* for orch. (1937), *Concerto Grosso* for wind (1957), and Sym. (1963). In 1935 he comp. a 3-act opera, *Maria Malibran*.

Bennett, (Sir) William Sterndale (*b* Sheffield, 1816; *d* London, 1875). Eng. composer, pianist, and teacher. Chorister at King's, Cambridge, at 7 and went 2 years later to newly founded RAM in London. Learned vn., pf., and comp. (with *Crotch). Later was taught by Cipriani *Potter. A pf. conc. written when he was 16 was heard a year later by Mendelssohn, who invited him to Ger. For 3 more years stayed at the RAM, composing 5 syms. and 3 more pf. concs. In one of these was soloist at a Phil. Soc. concert at the age of 19. In 1836 visited Leipzig where he became a friend of Schumann, who praised his work highly. Played his own concs. at Gewandhaus concerts. After marriage in 1844, career restricted to Eng., where he took on several demanding executive and admin. duties such as cond. of Phil. Soc. (1856–66), founder of Bach Soc., and, also in 1856, prof. of mus., Cambridge Univ. In 1866 became prin., RAM. Knighted 1871.

Whether Schumann's praise was extravagant is difficult to judge, since little of Sterndale Bennett's instr. music is now played. Undoubtedly his powers as a composer were lessened by the load

of official work he undertook. In his lifetime his most popular works were the pastoral cantata *The May Queen* (Leeds Fest. 1858) and the oratorio *The Woman of Samaria* (Birmingham Fest. 1867). Other works incl. ov. *The Naiads*. Schumann's *Symphonic Studies* are ded. to him. Conducted f. Eng. p. of Bach's *St Matthew Passion*, 1854.

Benoit, Peter (Léopold Léonard) (*b* Harlebeke, Flanders, 1834; *d* Antwerp, 1901). Belg. composer, one of the chief promoters of the Flemish mus. movement, in the interests of which he founded a sch. of mus. at Antwerp, 1867, remaining dir. until his death. Wrote articles and pamphlets, and comp. choral works to libs. in the Flemish language. Amongst works are a *Rubens Cantata* (*Flanderens Kunstroem*) (1877), calling for huge resources, incl. bells of Antwerp Cath.

Benoliel, Bernard (John) (*b* Detroit, 1943). Amer. composer and pianist. Studied Detroit and Michigan Univ. and with S. Wolpe. Settled in Eng. Secretary, Vaughan Williams Trust, from 1978. Works incl. *5 Poems of Emily Dickinson*, ch. (1968), *The Black Tower*, sop. and chamber ens. (1968), str. qt. (1969), sym. (1972–3), *With St Paul in Albion*, amplified vc., org. (1974).

Bent, Ian (David) (*b* Birmingham, 1938). Eng. musicologist and univ. lecturer specializing in medieval mus. Studied Cambridge Univ. 1958–65. Lecturer in mus., King's College, London Univ. Prof. of mus., Nottingham Univ. from 1975.

Bentzon, Niels (Viggo) (*b* Copenhagen, 1919). Danish composer. Studied Royal Danish Cons. Comp. several ballets, an opera *Faust III*, 5 pf. concs., many pf. sonatas, 13 syms., 2 vn. concs., vc. conc., 9 str. qts., *Symphonic Variations*, fl. conc. Some of works use 12-note system, and he is also influenced by jazz.

Benvenuto Cellini. Opera in 2 acts by Berlioz (Op. 23) to lib. by Léon de Wailly and A. Barbier, loosely based on Cellini's autobiography. Comp. 1834–7. Prod. Paris 1838, London 1853 (revived 1976). Rev. in 3 acts after Weimar perfs. in 1852. Berlioz withdrew the opera because of its failure. Some of the mus. is used in the ov. *Carnaval romain*. Cellini is subject of operas by Schlösser, Lachner, Diaz, and Saint-Saëns, among others.

Bequadro (It.). The natural sign, (♮).

Berberian, Cathy (*b* Attleboro, Mass., 1925; *d* Rome, 1983). Amer. sop. and singer-actress. Studied Columbia Univ. and in Milan. Specialized in *avant-garde* works, notably those of her former husband Luciano *Berio. Also teacher, composer, and writer.

Berceuse (from Fr. *Bercer*, to rock to sleep). A lullaby or an instr. comp. (in compound duple time) suggesting such. The popular pf. piece of this name, and in this style, by Chopin, is his Op. 57 in D♭ major (1844).

Berceuse de Jocelyn. See *Godard, Benjamin.*

Berceuse Élégiaque. Piano piece by Busoni, comp. 1909 and added to *Elegien* (1907). Orch. version, Op. 42, comp. 1909, sub-titled 'The man's lullaby at his mother's coffin'. F.p. NY 1911.

Bereite Vor (Ger.). Make ready, prepare (an organ stop).

Berenice. Opera in 3 acts by Handel to lib. by Antonio Salvi already used by Perti. Prod. London 1737. Well-known minuet occurs in the ov.

Berezovsky, Nikolay (also spelt Berezowsky) (*b* St Petersburg, 1900; *d* NY, 1953). Russ.-born violinist in Moscow and then in NY P.O. 1923–9. Cond., composer of 4 syms., concs. for vn., va., and vc., and chamber mus.

Berg, Alban (*b* Vienna, 1885; *d* Vienna, 1935). Austrian composer whose output, though small, is among the most influential and important of the 20th cent. One of 4 children of a well-to-do family, had little formal mus. education but comp. romantic songs when he was 15. In 1904 began private comp. lessons with *Schoenberg and decided to devote his life to mus., giving up a job in the Civil Service. With his friend and fellow-pupil *Webern, entered the *avant-garde* artistic life of Vienna—the Sezession artists, the poet Peter Altenberg, the painter Kokoschka—but the dominating figure was *Mahler. Some of his songs were perf. at a concert by Schoenberg pupils in Vienna, Nov. 1907, the pf. variations a year later, and the str. qt. in 1911. When 2 of the 5 *Altenberglieder* with orch. were perf. in Vienna in Mar. 1913, cond. Schoenberg, the concert was interrupted until order was restored. In May 1914 Berg attended a perf. of Büchner's play *Wozzeck* and determined to make an opera of it. Military service delayed work, but the mus. was eventually finished in 1922 and was perf. in Berlin, Dec. 1925. It caused a furore but its success with the public was never in doubt, despite critical polemics. In the next decade Berg's powers were at their height and he comp. the Chamber Conc. (1925), the *Lyric Suite* for str. qt. (1926), and the concert aria *Der Wein* (1929). In 1929 began adaptation of 2 Wedekind plays as an opera lib. called *Lulu.* By 1934 he had completed the mus. in short score and begun full instrumentation. In the spring of 1935 began vn. conc. commissioned by Louis *Krasner. Impelled by news of the death of the beautiful 18-year-old Manon Gropius, daughter of Mahler's widow by her 2nd marriage, worked unwontedly quickly and finished the conc. in Aug. 1935, dedicating it 'to the memory of an angel'. 4 months later he too died, through blood poisoning from an insect-bite. It has recently been established that several of Berg's works, incl. the *Lyric Suite, Lulu,* and the Violin Concerto, contain mus. cryptograms referring to his love for Frau Hanna Fuchs.

Berg has become, to the general public, the most acceptable of the so-called '12-note' or 'dodeca-phonic' composers, probably because he never was an orthodox atonalist. His work is nearer to the Mahler idiom than to the Schoenbergian. In *Wozzeck* atonality is very freely used and applied to a highly formal structure, each scene being in a particular mus. form (variations, passacaglia, fugue, etc.). From the *Lyric Suite* onwards, Berg used 12-note procedures nearer to, but still significantly different from, the Schoenberg method. Technical methods notwithstanding, however, it is the emotional content of Berg's mus. which has awoken a ready response in listeners, particularly the Vn. Conc., which quotes the Bach chorale *Es ist genug* at its climax. Prin. comps.:

OPERAS: *Wozzeck* (1917–22); *Lulu* (1929–35); Act 3 realized from short score by *Cerha (1978–9).

ORCH: *Three Pieces,* Op. 6 (1913–14); 3 movements from *Lyric Suite* arr. for str. orch. (1928); *Chamber Concerto* for pf., vn., and 14 wind instr. (1923–5); Vn. Conc. (1935).

VOICE AND ORCH: *7 Early Songs* (1905–8, orch. 1928), 5 *Altenberglieder* (1912), *3 Fragments from Wozzeck,* Op. 7 (f.p. Frankfurt 1924), *Der Wein* (1929), *Lulu-Symphonie* (1934).

CHAMBER MUSIC: *Variations on an Original Theme* for pf. (1908), Pf. Sonata (1907–8), Str. Qt., Op. 3 (1910), *4 Pieces* for cl. and pf. (1913), *Lyric Suite* for str. qt. (1925–6), *Adagio* from *Chamber Concerto* arr. for vn., cl., and pf. (1935).

SONGS: *7 Early Songs* (1905–8), *4 Songs,* Op. 2 (1909–10), and about 70 early songs.

Berg, Natanaël (*b* Stockholm, 1879; *d* Stockholm, 1957). Swed. composer of 5 operas, concs., symphonic poems, ballets, and chamber mus. By profession an army veterinary surgeon.

Bergamasque (Fr.), **Bergamasca** (It.), **Bergomask** (Eng.). Tune and chord sequence from Bergamo, It., found as ground bass in 16th and 17th cents. Also a peasant's dance from Bergamo. Composers have used the term with little significance, e.g. Debussy's *Suite Bergamasque* (1890, rev. 1905) for pf.

Berganza (orig. Vargas), **Teresa** (*b* Madrid, 1935). Sp. mez. Studied with Lola Rodrigues Aragón. Début Madrid 1955. Sang at Aix-en-Provence 1957, La Scala, Milan, 1957–8. Notable for her singing of Rossini, as in *La Cenerentola.* Glyndebourne 1958–9, London CG 1960.

Berger, Arthur (*b* NY, 1912). Amer. composer and writer on mus.; pupil of Piston and Milhaud. Some years as teacher and mus. journalist in NY, then on staff of Brandeis Univ., becoming prof. of mus., 1962. Works incl. orch. and choral mus., and chamber mus. Author of book on *Copland (1953).

Berger, Erna (b Dresden, 1900). Ger. operatic sop. Début Dresden 1925. Sang at Bayreuth 1929–33; CG début 1934. Notable Mozart singer, esp. of Queen of the Night in *Die Zauberflöte*. Sang in opera until 1955, when became teacher. Pupils incl. Rita *Streich. Retired 1968.

Berger, Francesco (b London, 1834; d London, 1933). Eng. pianist, composer, teacher, and secretary of the Phil. Soc., 1884–1911. Studied at Leipzig under Moscheles.

Berger, Jean (b Hamm, 1909). Ger. (naturalized Amer.) composer long resident in Fr., then in USA. Studied at Heidelberg and Vienna Univs. 1928–32. From 1932 to 1946 was choral cond. and accompanist. Works incl. *Brazilian Psalm* for ch. (1941), *Vision of Peace* for ch. (1948), *The Pied Piper*, play with mus. (1968). Ed. of Bolognese 17th-cent. mus., e.g. by Torelli, Perti, etc.

Berger, Theodor (b Traismauer, Austria, 1905). Austrian composer. Studied Vienna Acad. 1926–32 with Franz Schmidt and *Korngold. Works incl. *Homeric Symphony* (1948), vn. conc. (1954), and *Concerto-manuale* for 2 pf., metallophone, marimbaphone, perc., and str. (1951).

Bergerette (from Fr. *berger*, shepherd). A shepherd's song or dance or simple comp. supposed to be in the style of such. Popular in Fr. in 18th cent.

Berglund, Paavo (Allan Engelbert) (b Helsinki, 1929). Finn. cond. Studied Sibelius Acad., Helsinki. Violinist in Finn. Radio S.O. 1949–56, ass. cond. 1956–62, prin. cond. 1967–71. Prin. cond. Bournemouth S.O. 1972–9, Helsinki P.O. 1975–9.

Bergman, Erik (Valdemar) (b Uusikaarlepyy, Finland, 1911). Finn. composer. Studied Sibelius Acad., Helsinki, 1931–8, and 12-note techniques with Vladimir Vogel in Switzerland 1949–50. Prof. of comp., Helsinki Acad., from 1963. Works incl. setting of Rubaíyat of Omar Khayyám for bar., male ch., and orch. (1953), *Aubade* for orch. (1958), concertino da camera (1961), *The Birds* (*Fåglarna*) for vocal soloists, perc., and celesta (1962), *Noa*, bar., vv., and orch. (1976), and vn. conc. (1983–4).

Bergmann, Carl (b Ebersbach, 1821; d NY, 1876). Ger. cond. and cellist. Emigrated to NY 1850 and joined orch. of Ger. émigré musicians. Cond. in Boston, Mass., 1852–4. In 1855 he cond. for NY Phil., alternating with associates until 1866 when he became sole cond. until his death. Prominent champion in USA of Wagner and Liszt.

Bergmann, Walter (George) (b Hamburg, 1902). Ger. continuo player and recorder virtuoso. Studied Leipzig Cons. Settled in Eng. as teacher and ed.

Bergonzi, Carlo (b Cremona, c.1683; d Cremona, 1747). It. maker of vns. in style of his master, Stradivarius; succeeded by his son and nephews.

Bergonzi, Carlo (b Polisene, Parma, 1924). It. ten. Studied Parma. Began career as bar. at Lecce 1948 as Figaro in *Il barbiere di Siviglia*. Second début, as ten., at Bari 1951 as Andrea Chénier. London 1953, Chicago 1955, NY Met. 1956, CG 1967.

Bergsma, William (b Oakland, Calif., 1921). Amer. composer. Trained Stanford Univ. and Eastman Sch.; pupil of *Hanson and B. Rogers. On staff Juilliard Sch. 1946–63; Prof. Washington Univ., Seattle, from 1963. Comps. incl. opera, *The Wife of Martin Guerre* (1955), ballet *Paul Bunyan* (1937), vn. conc. (1966), 2 syms., and chamber mus.

Beringer, Oscar (b Furtwangen, Baden, 1844; d London, 1922). Ger.-born pianist. Spent childhood in Eng. to which his father fled 1849. Studied Leipzig 1864–6 and Berlin under Tausig. Appointed prof. at Tausig's Berlin Sch. for pianists, 1869. In 1873 returned to London, founding pf. sch. which survived until 1897. Gave f.p. in England of Brahms's 2nd conc., London, 14 Oct. 1882. Prof. RAM from 1885. Composer of pf. pieces.

Berio, Luciano (b Oneglia, now Imperia, It., 1925). It. composer. Studied with Ghedini at Milan Acad. until 1951, then serial techniques with *Dallapiccola at Tanglewood. In 1955 with *Maderna founded elec. studio at It. Radio, remaining until 1961. Went to USA 1963, teaching in California and from 1965 at Juilliard Sch., returning to It. in 1971. Comps. are influenced by serialism, elec. devices, and indeterminacy. Has developed individually the 'collage' technique, borrowing extracts from other composers or imitating stylistic characteristics. Examples are *Sinfonia*, in which Berio quotes material from Mahler's 2nd Sym., Wagner's *Das Rheingold*, Ravel's *La Valse*, and Strauss's *Der Rosenkavalier*, and *Laborintus II*, where street cries and interjections are blended with references to madrigals and to jazz. Another collage is *Recital I (for Cathy)*, one of several works (e.g. *Epifanie* and *Sequenza 3*) written for his former wife, the sop. Cathy *Berberian. His *Sequenza* series for various instr. is largely aleatory. In *Circles* the singer may perform either the notated pitches or the approximations: the choice is hers. While in Milan in his youth Berio cond. a small touring opera co. and has remained enthusiastic about the th., though his works for it have so far been extremely unconventional. Prin. works:

THEATRE: *Passaggio*, *messa in scena* for sop., 2 ch., and orch. (1962–3); *Opera* (3 acts) for 10 actors, sop., ten., bar., orch. (1960–70, rev. 1977); *Allez Hop*, mimed tale, for mez., 8 mimes, dancers, and orch. (1952–9, 1968); *I trionfi del Petrarca*, ballet (1974); *Un Re in Ascolto*, 2-act opera (1979–83); *Duo*, bar., 2 vns., ch., orch. (1982).

ORCH: *Nones* (1954–5); *Allelujah I* (1955–7), II (1956–8); *Divertimento* (collab. *Maderna)

(1957); *Quaderni I–III* from *Epifanie* (1959–63); *Chemins IIB* (1969); *Bewegung I* (1971); *Still* (1973); *Eindrücke* (1973–4); *Encore* (1978); *Entrata* (1980); *Suite da 'La vera storia'* (1981); *Accordo*, for 4 wind bands (1981).

CHAMBER ORCH: *Variazioni* (1954–5); *Différences* (1958–9); *Tempi Concertati* (1958–9); *Linea* (1973–4).

SOLO INSTR. AND ORCH: *Corale on Sequenza VIII*, vn., 2 hns., str. (1981); 2-pf. conc. (1972–3); '*Points on the Curve to Find . . .*', pf. and 23 instr. (1973–4); *Il Ritorno degli Snovidenia*, vc. and 30 instr. (1976–7); Pf. conc. (1977); *Chemins I* (from *Sequenza II*), harp and orch. (1965); *Chemins II* (from *Sequenza VI*) va. and 9 instr. (1967–8); *Chemins IIC*, bass cl. and orch. (1972); *Chemins III* (from *Chemins II*), va. and orch. (1968–9); *Chemins IV* (from *Sequenza VII*), ob. and str. (1975); *Serenata*, fl. and 14 instr. (1957); *Concertino*, cl., vn., harp, celesta, and str. (1950); *Voci*, va. and orch. (1984).

VOICE(S) AND ORCH. OR ENS: *Laborintus II*, vv., instr., reciter, tape (1965); *Bewegung II*, bar. and orch. (1971); *Sinfonia*, 8 vv. and orch. (1968–9); *Coro*, 40 vv. and instr. (1974–6); *Epifanie*, sop. or mez. and orch. (1959–61, rev. 1965); *Ora*, sop., mez., and chamber ens. (1971); *Magnificat*, 2 sop., mystic ch., and ens. (1949); *A-Ronne*, radiophonic documentary for 8 actors (1974), version for 8 vv. and tape (1975); 11 *Folk Songs*, mez. and orch. (1975), version for mez. and 7 players (1964); *Recital I (for Cathy)*, mez. and 17 instr. (1972); *Calmo (in memoriam Bruno Maderna)*, sop. and ens. (1974); *El mar la mar*, mez. and 7 players (1952); *O King*, mez. and 5 players (1967); *Circles*, female v., harp, and 2 perc. (1960); *Chamber Music*, female v., cl., vc., harp (1953); *Agnus*, 2 sop., 3 cl. (1970); *Cries of London*, 6 vv. (1973–4), 8 vv. (1975).

INSTR: *Opus Number Zoo*, 5 wind instr. (1950–1); Str. Qt. (1956); *Sincronie*, str. qt. (1963–4); *Autre Fois*, lullaby canon for Stravinsky (1971); 2 *Pieces*, vn. and pf. (1951); *Gesti*, fl. (1966); *Duetti per due violini* (1979–82).

PIANO: *Memory*, 2 pf. (1970); 5 *Variations* (1952–3); *Rounds* (1967) for hpd. (1965); *Wasserklavier* (1965); *Erdenklavier* (1968).

*SEQUENZA series: I, fl. solo (1958); II, harp solo (1963); III, female v. (1965); IV, pf. (1966); V, tb. (1967); VI, va. (1967); VII, ob. (1969); VIII, vn. (1975–7); IX, perc. (1978–9); IX A, cl. (1980); IX B, alto-sax. (1981). II arr. with orch. as *Chemins I* (1965); VI arr. for va. and 9 instr. as *Chemins II* (1967), for orch. as *Chemins IIB* (1969), and for bass cl. and orch. as *Chemins IIC* (1972); VII arr. for ob. and str. as *Chemins IV* (1975).

ELECTRONIC: *Mutations* (1954); *Perspectives* (1956); *Moments* (1957); *Theme* (homage to Joyce) with v. of C. Berberian (1958); *Visage*, with v. of C. Berberian (1961); *Chants parallèles* (1975).

Bériot, Charles Auguste de (*b* Louvain, 1802; *d* Brussels, 1870). Belg. violinist and composer, also mechanic, landscape painter, and sculptor. Married the singer *Malibran in 1836. Prof., Brussels Cons. 1843, retiring 1852 when sight failed. Wrote 10 vn. concs., a no. of pieces for 2 vn., etc., and also a *Violin School* which enjoyed much popularity.

Bériot, Charles Wilfrid de (*b* Paris, 1833; *d* Sceaux-en-Gatinais, 1914). Son of C. A. de *Bériot. Pianist (pupil of *Thalberg) and, as Prof., Paris Cons., teacher of Granados, Ravel, and others. Comp. 4 pf. concs.

Berkeley, (Sir) **Lennox** (Randall Francis) (*b* Boar's Hill, Oxford, 1903). Eng. composer. Studied mus. in Paris with Nadia Boulanger 1927–32. On BBC mus. staff 1942–5. Prof. of comp., RAM, 1946–68. C.B.E. 1957. Knighted 1974. His works are outstanding in quality and fastidious of workmanship. Prin. comps.:

OPERAS: *Nelson (1953), A *Dinner Engagement (1954), *Ruth (1956), Castaway (1966).

ORCH: *Mont Juic (suite in collab. with *Britten, 1937); *Serenade for Strings* (1939); Syms., No. 1 (1940), No. 2 (1956–8, rev. 1976), No. 3 (1969), No. 4 (1976–8); *Divertimento* (1943); *Nocturne* (1946); *Sinfonietta* (1950); *Suite from Nelson* (1955); *Suite, A Winter's Tale* (1960); *Partita* (1965); *Windsor Variations* (1969); *Antiphon*, str. (1973); *Voices of the Night* (1973); *Suite for Strings* (1974).

CONCERTOS: *Introduction and Allegro*, 2 pf. (1938); vc. (1939, f.p. 1983); pf. (1947); 2 pf. (1948); fl. (1952); 5 *Pieces*, vn. and orch. (1961); vn. and chamber orch. (1961); *Dialogue*, vc. and chamber orch. (1970); *Sinfonia concertante* for ob. (1973); guitar (1974).

VOICE(S) AND ORCH: *Domini est Terra* (1937); 4 *Poems of St Teresa of Avila*, cont. and str. (1947); *Stabat Mater* (1947); *Colonus' Praise* (1949); *Batter my Heart* (1962); *Signs in the Dark*, ch. and str. (1967); *Magnificat* (1968); 4 *Ronsard Sonnets*, Set 2, ten. and orch. (1963; also with chamber orch.).

CHORAL: *Gibbons Variations* (1951); *Crux fidelis* (1955); *Salve Regina* (1955); *Missa brevis* (1960); *Justorum Animae* (1963); Mass for 5 vv. (1964); 3 *Latin Motets* (1972); *Hymn for Shakespeare's Birthday* (1972); *Herrick Songs* (1974); *The Lord is My Shepherd* (1975); *The Hill of the Graces* (1975); *Judica Me* (1978); *Ubi Caritas* (1978); *Magnificat and Nunc Dimittis* (1980).

VOICE AND PIANO (or other instr.): *How Love Came In* (1935); 5 *Songs* (1939–40); 5 *De La Mare Songs* (1946); *The Lowlands of Holland* (1947); 3 *Greek Songs* (1951); 4 *Ronsard Sonnets Set 1*, 2 ten. (1952, rev. 1977); 5 *Poems of W. H. Auden* (1958); *Autumn's Legacy* (1962); *Songs of the Half Light* (with guitar) (1964); *Chinese Songs* (1971); 5 *Housman Songs* (1978); *Una and the Lion*, cantata for sop., recorders, hpd., viola da gamba (1979); *Sonnet*, high v. and pf. (1982).

CHAMBER MUSIC: Str. Qts., No. 1 (1935), No. 2 (1942), No. 3 (1970); recorder sonatina (1940);

vn. sonatina (1942); str. trio (1943); va. sonata (1945); *Elegy* and *Toccata*, vn. and pf. (1950); hn. trio (1954); sextet for cl., hn., str. (1955); guitar sonatina (1957); ob. sonatina (1962); *Diversions*, ob., cl., bn., hn., vn., va., vc., pf. (1964); ob. qt. (1967); *Introduction and Allegro*, db. and pf. (1971); *Duo*, vc. and pf. (1971); *In Memoriam Igor Stravinsky*, str. qt. (1971); pf. and wind quintet (1975); fl. sonata (1978).

PIANO: *5 Short Pieces* (1936); *3 Pieces* for 2 pf. (1938–40); *3 Impromptus* (1935); *4 Concert Studies, Set 1* (1940); sonata (1945); *6 Preludes* (1945); *3 Mazurkas and Scherzo* (1949); sonatina, pf. duet (1954); *Concert Study in E* (1955); sonatina, 2 pf. (1959); *Improvisation on a theme of Falla* (1960); *4 Concert Studies, Set 2* (1972); *Prelude and Capriccio* (1978); *Bagatelle*, 2 pf. (1981); *Mazurka* (1982).

Berkeley, Michael (*b* London, 1948). Eng. composer; son of Lennox *Berkeley. Studied Westminster Cath. Choir Sch., RAM, and with Lennox Berkeley and Richard Rodney *Bennett. BBC Radio 3 announcer 1976–9. Works incl.:

ORATORIO: *Or Shall We Die?*, sop., bar., ch., and orch. (1982).

ORCH: *Meditations*, str. (1976); ob. conc. (1977); *Fantasia Concertante*, chamber orch. (1977); *Uprising*, sym. (1980); *Chamber Sym.* (1980); *Flames* (1981); Suite, *Vision of Piers the Ploughman* (1981); *Gregorian Variations* (1981–2); vc. conc. (1982).

VOICE AND INSTR: *The Wild Winds*, sop. and small orch. (1978); *At the Round Earth's Imagin'd Corners*, sop., bar., ch., org., optional tpt. (1979–80); *Wessex Graves*, ten. and hp. (1981).

CHAMBER MUSIC: Str. trio (1978); *Étude de Fleurs*, vc., pf. (1978–9); vn. sonata (1979); *American Suite*, rec. or fl. and bn. or vc. (1979–80); str. qt. (1980–1); guitar sonata (1982); cl. quintet (1983).

ORGAN: *Ricercare* (1978); sonata (1979).

Berlin, Irving (orig. Israel Baline) (*b* Tyumen, Russia, 1888). Russ.-born Amer. composer of highly successful popular mus.—an instinctive composer, since his technical knowledge was rudimentary. Among his songs, many for films and mus. comedies, are *Alexander's Ragtime Band* (1911), *God Bless America, Easter Parade, White Christmas, Putting on my Top Hat, This is the Army, What'll I do?*, and *Always* (1925). Wrote the words (lyrics) for almost all his songs.

Berlin Philharmonic Orchestra. One of the world's major orchs., founded 1882. Among prin. conds. have been Franz Wüllner, Karl Klindworth, Hans von Bülow, Richard Strauss, Artur Nikisch (1895–1922), Wilhelm Furtwängler (1922–45), Leo Borchard (1945), Sergiù Celibidache (1945–51), and Herbert von Karajan (from 1954). The Philharmonic Hall was destroyed during 1939–45 war and replaced by a fine modern hall in 1963.

Berlinski, Herman (*b* Leipzig, 1910). Ger. composer. Studied Leipzig Cons. 1928–32 and in 1933 went to Paris where he studied pf. with Cortot and comp. with Nadia Boulanger, 1934–8. Escaped to USA, 1940, and entered Seminary College of Jewish Mus., NY, 1953–60. Early works influenced by Schoenberg and Hindemith but experiences as a refugee from Nazis led to his concentration on Jewish sacred and secular mus.

Berlioz, (Louis) **Hector** (*b* La Côte-St André, Grenoble, 1803; *d* Paris, 1869). Fr. composer, cond., and critic. His life, especially as related by himself in his marvellous *Memoirs*, reads like a novel. Son of a provincial doctor, he showed early liking for mus., learning the fl. and flageolet, and later the guitar, but never the pf. Intended for a medical career, in 1821 went to Paris medical sch. In 1822 applied for mus. lessons and began to compose an opera. An oratorio followed in 1823, when he became a private pupil of *Le Sueur. In 1826 entered Paris Cons. to study with Reicha and LeSueur, 1826–8. In 1827 saw Kemble's co. in *Hamlet* at the Odéon and was stricken 'like a thunderbolt' with a passion both for Shakespeare and for the Irish actress who played Ophelia, Harriet Smithson. In the first 5 months of 1830, comp. the *Symphonie fantastique*, sub-titled 'Episodes in the life of an artist' and dealing autobiographically with his passion for Miss Smithson. It was perf. on 5 Dec. In Dec. 1832 at last met Miss Smithson and married her 10 months later. Over the next decade some of his greatest works were comp., incl. *Harold in Italy*, the *Symphonie funèbre et triomphale*, the dramatic sym. *Roméo et Juliette*, the *Grand' Messe des morts (Requiem)* and the opera *Benvenuto Cellini*. Though some of these works were commissions (and Paganini gave him 20,000 francs for *Harold in Italy*, although he never played the va. solo), Berlioz supplemented his income by writing mus. criticism, a chore he detested but accomplished brilliantly. In 1841 his marriage broke up and he formed a liaison with the singer Marie Recio. They toured Ger. in 1843, and in the ensuing years he travelled frequently, visiting Russia and also paying 4 visits to London. Dramatic cantata *La Damnation de Faust* was a failure in Paris, 1846, and *Te Deum*, comp. 1849–50, was not perf. until 1855. From 1856 to 1858 engaged on enormous opera *Les Troyens*, for which he wrote the lib., basing it on Virgil's *Aeneid*. This work, Berlioz's masterpiece, was on too large a scale and efforts to have it staged at the Opéra failed. Eventually, having divided it into 2 parts, *La Prise de Troie* and *Les Troyens à Carthage*, he saw the 2nd part prod. at the Théâtre-Lyrique, Paris, in Nov. 1863. It was withdrawn after 22 perfs., a failure which broke Berlioz's spirit. In 1860–2 completed his last work, the comic opera *Béatrice et Bénédict*, based on Shakespeare.

For nearly 100 years after his death, Berlioz's true qualities were obscured by his image as the

'Romantic artist' *par excellence*. His extravagances in his scores, no longer very remarkable but ahead of their time, diverted critical attention, even among his admirers, from the classical purity of his melody and the Beethovenian grandeur of his command of dramatic contrasts. Today, the opera *Les Troyens*, the *Grand' Messe des morts* and the *Nuits d'été* (forerunner of Mahler's song-cycles with orch.) are recognized for their poetry and originality. Principal compositions:

STAGE: *Les Francs Juges*, Op. 3 (1826, rev. 1829, 1833); **Benvenuto Cellini*, Op. 23 (1834–7); *Les *Troyens* (1856–8); **Béatrice et Bénédict* (1860–2); **Lélio* (monodrama, 1831).

ORCH: Ovs.: *Waverley*, Op. 1 bis (1827–8); *Les *Francs-Juges*, Op. 3 (1826); *Le Roi Lear*, Op. 4 (1831); *Le *Corsaire*, Op. 21 (1831); *Rob Roy* (1832); *Le *Carnaval romain*, Op. 9 (1844); **Harold en Italie*, for va. and orch., Op. 16 (1834); **Symphonie fantastique* Op. 14 (1830); *Rêverie et caprice*, for vn. and orch., Op. 8 (1839); **Symphonie funèbre et triomphale* (ch. ad lib.), Op. 15 (1840).

VOICES AND ORCH: **Grand' Messe des morts* (*Requiem*), Op. 5 (1837); *La *Mort de Cléopâtre* (1829); **Roméo et Juliette*, dramatic sym., Op. 17 (1838–9); *La *Damnation de Faust*, Op. 24 (1828–46); *L'*Enfance du Christ*, oratorio, Op. 25 (1850–4); *Te Deum*, Op. 22 (1849–50); *Les *Nuits d'été* (with pf. or orch.), Op. 7 (1840–1, pf.; 1843–56, orch.).

Berman, Lazar (*b* Leningrad, 1930). Russ. pianist. Début Leningrad 1934. Pupil of Alexander Goldenweiser and at Moscow Cons. of Richter and V. Sofronitsky. London début 1958, NY 1976. Specialist in 19th-cent. composers.

Bernacchi, Antonio Maria (*b* Bologna, 1685; *d* Bologna, 1756). It. alto castrato. Pupil of Pistocchi. Sang in Ger. and studied counterpoint in Munich. It. opera début Genoa 1703. From 1709 to 1736 sang in most It. cities, and sang regularly in Munich 1720–7. London début 1716. Engaged as prin. singer by Handel for London season 1729–30. Sang in f.ps. of Handel's *Lotario* and *Partenope*. Retired 1736 and founded singing sch. in Bologna.

Bernac, Pierre (really Pierre Bertin) (*b* Paris, 1899; *d* Avignon, 1979). Fr. bar., distinguished as recitalist and teacher (Gérard *Souzay among his pupils). Gave first recital 1925. Frequently assoc. with composer *Poulenc, his accompanist in concerts throughout Europe and USA. Several Poulenc song-cycles written for him, incl. *Tel jour, telle nuit*.

Bernard, Anthony (*b* London, 1891; *d* London, 1963). Eng. cond., pianist, and composer. Studied under Holbrooke and Ireland. Cond. with BNOC. Organist, pf. accompanist, and cond. at Shakespeare Memorial Th., Stratford-on-Avon (1932–42), of London Chamber Singers and of London

Chamber Orch., which he founded in 1921, reviving much old mus. Cond. of Dutch Chamber Orch., The Hague, 1922–6.

Bernardi, Mario (*b* Kirkland, Ontario, 1930). Canadian-It. cond. and pianist. Studied Venice and Toronto Royal Cons. Mus. dir. SW 1966–8. Cond. Nat. Arts Centre Orch., Ottawa, 1969–82.

Bernardi, Steffano (*b* Verona, *c*.1585; *d* ?Salzburg, 1635). It. church musician. Choirmaster, Verona Cath. 1615–22. Later, Kapellmeister Salzburg Cath. Comp. masses, motets, madrigals, and instr. works.

Bernasconi, Antonia (*b* Stuttgart, ?1706; *d* Munich, 1784). It. operatic sop. for whom Gluck is said to have written *Alceste*, in which she sang in Vienna 1767. Sang Aspasia in the child Mozart's *Mitridate* in Milan 1770–1. Also sang in London 1778 and again in Vienna 1781.

Bernauerin, Die (The Wife of Bernauer). A 'Bavarian piece' by *Orff, to his own lib., for speaker, sop., ten., ch., and orch. Comp. 1944–5. Prod. Stuttgart 1947.

Berners, Lord (Gerald Hugh Tyrwhitt-Wilson) (*b* Apley Park, Bridgnorth, Shropshire, 1883; *d* Faringdon, Berks., 1950). Eng. composer, also painter, author, and diplomat. Studied music in Dresden and Vienna but pursued career as diplomat 1909–20, mainly in Rome. Early works pubd. under name Gerald Tyrwhitt. Had advice and lessons in Rome from Casella and Stravinsky. Marked gift for mus. satire and parody, as exemplified in his *3 Little Funeral Marches* for pf. (1916), *Fragments psychologiques* for pf. (1915), *3 Orchestral Pieces* (1916), *Fantaisie espagnole* for orch. (1918–19), and *Valses bourgeoises*, 2 pf. (1919). Set Mérimée's *Le Carrosse du Saint-Sacrément* as 1-act opera (prod. Paris 1924). His best-known work is the ballet *The *Triumph of Neptune* (London, 3 Dec. 1926). Other ballets were *Luna Park* (1930 Cochran revue), *A Wedding Bouquet* (London 1936), which has choral parts to words by Gertrude Stein, *Cupid and Psyche* (1939), and *Les Sirènes* (1946). Also wrote *L'Uomo dai Baffi*, for solo woodwind, pf., str. (1918), *3 Songs in the German manner* (1920), *3 Chansons* (1919–20), *3 Sea Shanties* (1921), and pf. piece **Portsmouth Point* (1920). Succeeded to barony 1918. Autobiography *First Childhood* highly recommended. Comp. mus. for film *Nicholas Nickleby* (1946), and other film scores. Also wrote novel *Far from the Madding War*.

Bernhard, Christoph (*b* ?Kolberg, 1628; *d* Dresden, 1692). Ger. singer and composer. Went to Dresden, with recommendation to Schütz, where his fine ten. v. induced the Kurfürst to send him to It. for further tuition. In Rome, became friend of *Carissimi. Later returned to Dresden, worked in Hamburg 1664–74, returned to Dresden 1674, becoming Kapellmeister 1681.

Church comp. show mastery of counterpoint, notably hymn *Prudentia prudentiana*, 1669.

Bernier, René (*b* St Gilles, Belg., 1905; *d* Brussels, 1984). Belg. composer and teacher. Studied Brussels Cons. Active in Belgian mus. education from 1945, teaching at Liège and Mons. Comps. incl. ballets, choral works, and *Hommage à Sax*, concertino for alto sax., 1958.

Bernstein, Leonard (*b* Lawrence, Mass., 1918). Amer. composer, cond., and pianist. Educated Boston Latin Sch. and at Harvard Univ. 1935–9. In 1939 entered Curtis Institute, Philadelphia, studying cond. with *Reiner. Already his outstanding talent had led a friend to say 'Lenny is doomed to success'. In summers of 1940–3 studied at Tanglewood summer sch., Boston, becoming ass. to *Koussevitzky and was also noticed by *Rodzinski, who invited him to become ass. cond. of NY Phil. Sym. Orch. 1943–4; début Nov. 1943, deputizing for Bruno Walter. Cond. NY City Center Orch., 1945–8, presenting adventurous programmes. Taught at Tanglewood 1951–5 in orch. and cond. dept.; part-time prof. of mus., Brandeis Univ. 1951–5. Career as opera cond. began at Tanglewood, 1946, in Amer. première of Britten's *Peter Grimes*. Cond. his own *Trouble in Tahiti* at Brandeis, 1952, and Cherubini's *Medea* (with Callas) at La Scala, Milan, 1953, returning there to cond. *La Sonnambula* for *Callas. Début NY Met. 1964, Vienna 1966.

In 1957–8 appointed joint prin. cond. (with *Mitropoulos) of NY P.O., becoming sole cond. 1958–69, the first Amer.-born holder of the post. Guest cond. many of world's leading orchs., notably Vienna P.O., Israel P.O., and LSO. In 1969 was made 'laureate conductor for life' of NY P.O.

Bernstein's outstanding quality as a musician is his catholic taste. Hence his comps. are markedly eclectic, bearing influences of Gershwin, Jewish ritual mus., Mahler, Stravinsky, Villa-Lobos, and Copland. (In 1941 he worked for a popular mus. publisher, making arrs. and jazz transcrs.). His first sym., *Jeremiah* (1941–44) won 1944 NY Music Critics' Award and in that year his ballet *Fancy Free* was perf. in NY. Later the same year his musical *On the Town* began a long run. Other musicals have been *Wonderful Town* (1953), *Candide* (1956), and the very successful *West Side Story* (1957). His most famous film mus. was for *On the Waterfront* (1954), from which he arr. a suite. He has comp. 2 other syms., The *Age of Anxiety*, for pf. and orch. (1947–9), and *Kaddish*, for female narrator, sop., ch., boys' ch., and orch. (1961–3). Also notable are *Chichester Psalms* (1965) and his *Mass* (1970–1) described as 'theatre piece for singers, players, and dancers' to lib. by himself and Stephen Schwartz. He is also an outstanding TV mus. educator and a persuasive writer.

Béroff, Michel (*b* Epinal, Vosges, 1950). Fr. pianist. Trained Nancy Cons. and Paris Cons. Début Paris 1966, London 1968. Specialist in pf. works of Messiaen.

Berry, Walter (*b* Vienna, 1929). Austrian bassbar. Studied at Vienna Acad., then made début at Vienna Opera 1950 in small roles. Sang Masetto in *Don Giovanni* there 1953, later the Count in *Figaro*. Sang regularly at Salzburg Fest. after 1952, creating roles in 20th cent. works by Einem, Liebermann, and Egk. London début (Festival Hall) 1954, CG 1976 (Barak in Strauss's *Die Frau ohne Schatten*), NY Met. 1966. Fine exponent of roles of Figaro, Ochs, Wozzeck, and Wotan. Distinguished concert-hall career.

Bersag Horn or Bersaglieri Bugle. Bugle with a single valve, lowering the pitch by a 4th. Made in different sizes: sop. in B♭, cont. in E♭, ten. in B♭, bar. in B♭, and bass in F. Became popular with bugle bands during 1914–18 war. Presumably of It. origin (*Bersaglieri* = a sharpshooter corps of It. army).

Berté, Heinrich (*b* Galgócz, 1857; *d* Vienna, 1924). Hung. composer of ballets, notably *Der Karneval in Venedig* (Vienna, 1900), and operettas of which the best-known is *Das Dreimäderlhaus* (1916, Vienna) based on Schubert melodies and depicting (mainly fictitious) scenes from Schubert's life. Amer. version arr. Romberg prod. in 1921 as *Blossom Time* and Eng. version arr. G. H. Clutsam as *Lilac Time* (1922).

Bertin, Louise Angélique (*b* Les Roches, 1805; *d* Paris, 1877). Fr. cont., pianist, and composer of operas *Le loup-garou* (Paris 1827), *Faust* (1831), and *L'Esmeralda* (1836, for which Hugo adapted lib.).

Bertini, Gary (*b* Brichevo, Bessarabia, 1927). Israeli cond. and composer. Studied Tel Aviv, Milan Cons. 1946–7, and Paris Cons. 1951–4. Founder and cond. Israel Chamber Orch. from 1965, prin. guest cond. SNO from 1970. Cond. Detroit S.O. 1981–3, Cologne Radio S.O. from 1983. Guest cond. Scottish Opera. Head, cond. class, Israel Acad. of Mus. from 1958. Mus. dir. Jerusalem S.O. from 1977. Comps. incl. incidental mus., ballets, vn. sonata, hn. conc.

Bertini, Henri Jérôme (*b* London, 1798; *d* Meylan, Grenoble, 1876). Eng.-born composer for pf., and especially of pf. studies which have long been used by teachers. Worked in Paris 1821–59.

Berton, Henri Montan (*b* Paris, 1767; *d* Paris, 1844). Fr. violinist, composer, and teacher. Violinist in Opéra orch. from 1782. Prof. of harmony Paris Cons., 1795–1818, when he succeeded Méhul as prof. of comp. Cond., Opéra-Comique 1807–9. Besides sacred mus. and instr. works, comp. over 40 operas (some in co-operation with Méhul, Spontini, Paër, and Boieldieu) of which best-known were *Les Rigueurs du cloître* (1790), a 'rescue opera' which was an exemplar for *Fidelio*, and *Montano et Stéphanie* (1799). Wrote pamphlets attacking Rossini.

Bertoni, Ferdinando Gasparo (*b* Salò, Venice, 1725; *d* Desenzano, Brescia, 1813). It. composer, pupil of Padre *Martini. Organist St Mark's Venice, 1752–85. Comp. *Orfeo* (1776) to same lib. as Gluck. Several visits to London to conduct his own operas (of which he wrote about 50). Became cond. at St Mark's 1785 on death of *Galuppi.

Bertrand, Antoine de (*b* c.1540; *d* Toulouse, c.1580). Fr. composer. Comp. notable 4-part settings of Ronsard Sonnets, using half-modal, half-tonal harmonic idiom.

Berutti, Arturo (*b* San Juan, 1862; *d* Buenos Aires, 1938). Arg. composer. Studied with *Reinecke at Leipzig, then in Paris and Milan. From 1896 worked in Buenos Aires, composing instr. works and operas of strong nat. character. Operas incl. *Taras Bulba* (1895) and *Pampa* (1897).

Berwald, Franz (Adolf) (*b* Stockholm, 1796; *d* Stockholm, 1868). Swed. composer (mainly self-taught), and violinist. Studied in Berlin where he comp. opera *Der Verräter*. Lived for time in Vienna, where opera *Estrella di Soria* was comp., also orch. works. Returned to Sweden, where his work was unfavourably received, so went back to Vienna, where Jenny Lind sang in his opera *Ein Ländlisches Verlobungsfest in Schweden* (A Swedish country betrothal, 1847). His chamber mus. is rewarding, also his 4 syms., of which only No. 1 in G minor (*Sérieuse*) was perf. in his lifetime. No. 3 in C major (*Singulière*) (1845) has become relatively popular. The best-known of his operas is the last, *Queen of Golconda*, 1864. Also wrote vn. conc. (1820), pf. conc. (1855), 3 str. qts. (1818, 1849, 1849), 2 pf. quintets (1853, c.1850–7), and Septet in B♭ (?1828).

Bes (Ger.). The note B♭♭.

Bésard, Jean Baptiste (*b* Besançon, 1567; *d* ?S. Ger., after 1617). Fr. amateur composer and lutenist. Worked variously in Rome, Cologne, and Augsburg. Author of books on medicine, history, and philosophy. Pubd. 2 vols. of lute mus., incl. own comps., 1603 and 1617.

Besch, Anthony (John Elwyn) (*b* London, 1924). Eng. opera producer for Glyndebourne, ENO, Scottish Opera, NY City Opera, San Francisco Opera, and others.

Besozzi. It. family of orch. musicians specializing in woodwind, particularly ob. Headed by Alessandro (*b* Parma, 1702; *d* Turin, 1793) who comp. several trio sonatas, etc. Second generation settled in Paris where the last member, Louis Désiré (*b* Versailles, 1814) died in 1879.

Besson, Gustave Auguste (*b* Paris, 1820; *d* Paris, 1875). Fr. maker of mus. instr. Prod. a new cornet when only 18. Many inventions to improve valve-mechanism of cornet, most successful being 'prototype system' of construction with conical steel mandrels. Also invented db. cl., and family of 'cornophones' to reinforce orch. hns. Branch factory opened London 1851.

Best, William Thomas (*b* Carlisle, 1826; *d* Liverpool, 1897). Eng. organist, recognized as the greatest concert organist of his time, the chief centre of his activities being St George's Hall, Liverpool, 1855–94. Assoc. for 21 years with Handel fests. in London. Arr. many works for his instr. Ed. Bach's org. works, and wrote books on organ-playing. Gave first recital on Royal Albert Hall organ, 1871.

Bestimmt (Ger.). (1) Decided (in style). (2, applied to a particular line in the score) Prominent.

Besuch der Alten Dame, Der (Einem). See *Visit of the Old Lady, The.*

Bethlehem. Choral-drama by *Boughton. Lib. based on medieval Coventry Play. (Prod. Street, Somerset, 1915).

Bethlehem, Penn. Known for its fests., which began in 1742 with Moravian settlers. Since 1900 fest. has been given by Bethlehem Bach Choir, with orch. recruited from leading Amer. orch. musicians.

Betonung (Ger.). Accentuation.

Betrothal in a Nunnery (Prokofiev). See *Duenna, The.*

Bettelstudent, Der (The Beggar Student). Operetta in 3 acts by *Millöcker to lib. by F. Zell and R. Genée. Prod. Vienna 1882, NY 1883, London 1884.

Betz, Franz (*b* Mainz, 1835; *d* Berlin, 1900). Ger. bass-bar. Studied Karlsruhe, début Hanover 1856. Created role of Hans Sachs in Wagner's *Meistersinger*, Munich 1868, and sang Wotan at first Bayreuth Fest. 1876. First Berlin Falstaff (Verdi).

Bevignani, Enrico (*b* Naples, 1841; *d* Naples, 1903). It. cond. and composer. Spent much of his career in London. Répétiteur at Her Majesty's Th. 1863–9. Cond., CG 1869–87 and 1890–6, NY Met. 1894–1900. Cond. first London perfs. of *Aida* (1876) and *Pagliacci* (1893). Patti insisted on his conducting for her whenever possible.

Bevin, Elway (*b* 1554; *d* Bristol, 1638). Welsh composer, and organist of Bristol Cath. from 1589. Wrote book on mus. theory. Pupil of *Tallis.

Bevington and Sons. Eng. firm of org.-builders founded in London 1794 by Henry Bevington. Built orgs. of St Martin-in-the-Fields, London, and St Patrick's Cath., Dublin.

Beweglich (Ger.). Agile. So *Beweglichkeit*, agility.

Bewegt. (1) Moved, i.e. speeded. (2) Moved, i.e. emotionally. **Bewegter.** Quicker. **Bewegung.** (1) Rate of motion, speed. (2) Emotion. (3) Commotion.

Beydts, Louis (b Bordeaux, 1895; d Caudéran, 1953). Fr. composer of operettas and instr. mus. Wrote mus. for film *La Kermesse Heroïque.*

Beyschlag, Adolf (b Frankfurt-am-Main, 1845; d Mainz, 1914). Ger. cond. and composer. Worked in Cologne, Treves, and Frankfurt, also in Belfast, Manchester (with Hallé), and Leeds (cond. Phil. Soc.). Went to Berlin as teacher, 1902. Pubd. treatise on ornamentation, Leipzig, 1908.

Bezekirsky, Vasily (b Moscow, 1835; d Moscow, 1919). Russ. violinist and composer. Many tours abroad as soloist. Leader, Imperial Th., Moscow, orch. 1871–91. Prof. of vn., Moscow Cons. of Phil. Soc. 1882–1902. Comp. orch. works incl. vn. conc. and wrote cadenzas for concs. of Beethoven and Brahms.

Bialas, Günter (b Bielschowitz, 1907). Ger. composer and teacher. Studied at Breslau Univ. 1925–7, Berlin Acad. of Church and Sch. Mus. 1927–33. Taught mus. theory at Breslau Univ. 1940–1. In 1947 taught in Weimar; teacher of comp. N.W. Ger. Acad. of Mus., Detmold, 1948–59 (prof. from 1950), Munich Municipal Sch. of Mus. from 1959. Comps. incl. 3 operas, Conc. for Orch. (1938), va. conc. (1940), fl. conc. (1947), vn. conc. (1947), cl. conc. (1961), vc. conc. (1962), choral works, songs, 3 str. qts., and vn. sonata.

Bianca (It.). White. Half-note or minim.

Bianca und Giuseppe. Opera in 4 acts by Kittl (prod. 1848) memorable only because lib. is by Wagner, who adapted König's novel for his own use in 1836 but did not set it.

Bianchi, Francesco (b Cremona, 1752; d Hammersmith, 1810). It. composer of over 80 operas and oratorios. Worked at It. Opera in Paris under Piccinni, 1775. From 1785 to 1797 was 2nd organist at St Mark's, Venice. Went to London 1794. Wrote opera *Inez de Castro* for It. début of Elizabeth *Billington. Cond. in Dublin, 1797–1801. Among operas are *Semiramide* (1790), *Acis and Galatea* (1792), and *Alzira* (1801). Took own life.

Biancolli, Louis Leopold (b NY, 1907). Amer. mus. critic, chiefly for *World-Telegram and Sun* 1928–66. Programme annotator NY Phil. 1941–1949. Author of several books, incl. biography of Kirsten Flagstad (1952).

Bibalo, Antonio (b Trieste, 1922). It. composer who settled in Norway. Studied with E. *Lutyens. Has concentrated principally on opera. Comps. in this genre incl. *The Smile at the foot of the ladder* (based on story by Henry Miller, comp. 1958–62), *Miss Julie* (based on Strindberg's play, comp. 1973, rev. with orch. reduced to pf. and str. qt.

1983–4), and *Ghosts* (based on Ibsen's play, comp. 1981).

Bibelorgel, Bibelregal (Ger.). A type of Regal, a reed org. which came into use in the 15th cent. and remained popular into the 17th. In appearance it was a small, portable, single-manual org. of small compass, but the pipes (all short) were at first all reed-pipes, the reeds being of that type called 'Beating Reeds' (see *Reed*): later flue pipes were sometimes added. The Bible Regal folded in 2 like a book.

Biber, Heinrich Ignaz Franz von (b Wartenberg, Bohemia, 1644; d Salzburg, 1704). Ger.-Bohemian violinist and composer, becoming Kapellmeister at Salzburg, 1684. Prolific composer for vn., also wrote operas, chamber mus., tpt. conc., and 'Nightwatchman' Serenade (for 2 vn., 2 va., and continuo).

Biblical Songs. 10 settings for v. and pf. by Dvořák, comp. 1894 as his Op. 99, of passages from the Psalms. Nos. 1 and 5 orch. Dvořák.

Biches, Les. (The Hinds; colloq. The Little Darlings). Ballet in 1 act with ch., incorporating 17th-cent. texts, comp. by Poulenc in 1923 and prod. Monte Carlo 1924. Scenario by composer, choreog. Nijinskaya. Suite (re-scored) 1940.

Bicinium (Lat.). A 2-v. song.

Biene, August van (b Holland, 1850; d Eng., 1913). Dutch cellist. Went to London as child and played in streets; discovered by *Costa. Comp. popular *The Broken Melody* and played it (in mus. halls, etc.) over 6,000 times.

Biggs, (Edward George) **Power** (b Westcliff-on-Sea, 1906; d Boston, Mass., 1977). Eng.-born concert organist (Amer. citizen 1937). Studied RAM. Specialized in reviving neglected classical works, often on reconstructions of old instr. Commissioned works from Amer. composers.

Bigophone, Bigotphone. Improved *mirliton introduced by Bigot, a Frenchman, in the 1880s. Often made up to resemble the various brass instr.

Bihári, János (b Nagyabony, 1764; d Pest, 1827). Hung. violinist and composer credited with composing the *Rákóczy March, although version of the tune already existed.

Bilitis, Chansons de (Debussy). See *Chansons de Bilitis.*

Billings, William (b Boston, Mass., 1746; d Boston, 1800). One of first Amer.-born composers, he abandoned tanning for mus. Wrote much church mus., including 'fuguing pieces', essays in imitative counterpoint. Comp. patriotic songs.

Billington, Elizabeth (b London, 1765; d Venice, 1818). Eng. sop. with European reputation. Daughter of Carl Weichsel, Ger.-born oboist at King's Th., London. Child prodigy as pianist and composer. Studied with J. C. Bach. In 1783 married James Billington, db. player, with whom she also studied. Began opera career in Dublin, 1783, as Polly in *Beggar's Opera*. Sang in Naples 1794 in Bianchi's *Inez di Castro*. Paisiello, Paër, and Himmel wrote operas for her. First Eng. Vitellia in Mozart's *La clemenza di Tito*, London 1806. Retired 1817, living in Venice from 1817. Painted by Reynolds.

Billroth, Theodor (*b* Bergen, Isle of Rügen, 1829; *d* Abazzia, 1894). Prussian surgeon and amateur musician, famous as close friend of Brahms in Vienna from 1867. Many of Brahms's chamber works received private f.ps. at his soirées. Correspondence with Brahms pubd.

Billy Budd. Opera, orig. in 4 acts, by Britten, Op. 50, to lib. by E. M. Forster and Eric Crozier from Melville's story. Comp. 1950–1, prod. London 1951, NY (TV) 1952. Rev. in 2 acts for BBC radio prod., broadcast Nov. 1960. F. stage p. of this verson, CG 1964, Chicago 1970. Subject also of opera by *Ghedini (Venice 1949).

Billy the Kid. Ballet in 1 act, mus. by Copland, to lib. by Kirstein, choreog. Loring; comp. for Ballet Caravan 1938 (Chicago). Subject was 'Wild West' gunman (William Bonney). Concert Suite for orch., and pf. suite, 1938.

Binary Form. Literally, a form in 2 sections. Simple binary form, as in an 18th-cent. kbd. suite, has no strong contrast of material. The first section opens in the Tonic key and then (subject to an exception shortly to be mentioned) modulates, as it ends, into the key of the Dominant. The 2nd section then opens in that 2nd key and, before it ends, modulates back to the 1st. There are, then, 2 distinct main cadences, or points of rest, the 1st in the Dominant and the 2nd in the Tonic. The exception just referred to occurs if the piece is in a minor key, when the 1st section sometimes ends in the relative major. This form is unsuitable for very long pieces, since the variety offered to the listener is almost entirely confined to details of treatment and the element of key, the thematic material employed throughout being the same. Since the deaths of Bach and Handel, this form has been little used. It developed into compound binary form, another name for *Sonata form.

Binchois, Gilles de Bins (*b* ?Mons, *c*.1400; *d* Soignies, 1460). Franco-Flemish composer and organist. Regarded as one of major composers of early part of 15th cent. Probably trained as chorister and thought to have been soldier in service of Earl of Suffolk in Eng. occupation army in France. In 1420s joined Burgundian court chapel. Provost of collegiate church of St Vincent, Soignies, from 1452. Most of his surviving secular songs are rondeaux. Church mus. incl. a *Te Deum*, several settings of the *Magnificat, Credo*, and *Gloria*, but no complete *Mass* survives.

Bind. See *Tie or Bind*.

Binet, Jean (*b* Geneva, 1893; *d* Trélex-sur-Nyon, 1960). Swiss composer of choral, orch., and chamber works; pupil of Jaques-Dalcroze and Bloch. Taught in USA and Belg.

Bing, (Sir) **Rudolf** (Franz Joseph) (*b* Vienna, 1902). Austrian-born impresario. Studied Vienna Univ., then worked in concert agency 1923–7. At Darmstadt State Th., 1928–30, and Charlottenburg-Berlin Opera 1930–3, under Carl *Ebert. Went to Eng. (naturalized 1946) and was manager, *Glyndebourne Opera 1935–9 and 1946–9. First dir., *Edinburgh Festival, 1947–9. Gen. man. NY Met., 1950–72. C.B.E. 1956. K.B.E. 1971.

Binge, Ronald (*b* Derby, 1910; *d* Ringwood, Hants, 1979). Eng. composer of light orch. works such as *Elizabethan Serenade, Spitfire, Thames Rhapsody*, also alto sax. conc. and film mus. Began career as cinema organist. Became arr. in 1935 for Mantovani, whose post-1945 'singing strings' style was his creation.

Biniou (Fr.). Bagpipe.

Binkerd, Gordon Ware (*b* Lynch, Nebraska, 1916). Amer. composer; studied at Eastman Sch. 1940–1 and Harvard Univ. 1946–9 (comp. with W. Piston). Prof. of comp., Illinois Univ., 1949–71. Comps. incl. 3 syms., 2 str. qts., and a song-cycle and choral work, both to words by Hardy.

Binns, Malcolm (*b* Gedling, Nottingham, 1936). Eng. pianist. Studied RCM. London début 1957. Prof. of pf., RCM, 1962–9. Specialist in perf. of works on instr. of the period in which they were composed.

Biondi, Giovanni Battista (*b* Cesena, *fl.* 1605–30). It. Minorite friar known to have worked in Bologna and in Brisighella, near Faenza. Comp. 19 vols. of motets, masses, psalms, etc. pubd. in Venice 1606–30.

Birch, John (Anthony) (*b* Leek, Staffs, 1929). Eng. organist and choirmaster. Studied RCM. Organist, Chichester Cath. from 1958; prof. of org., RCM from 1959.

Bird Organ (or Serinette). Simple form of the *'Orgue de Barbarie', intended by reiteration of a short tune to teach captive birds to sing. (Serin, Fr. = the domestic canary.)

Birds, The (*Gli uccelli*). Suite for small orch. by *Respighi. Based on 17th- and 18th-cent. bird-pieces for lute and for hpd. In 5 movements: *Prelude, Dove, Hen, Nightingale*, and *Cuckoo*. (F.p. São Paulo, Brazil, 1927.)

Birmingham. City in West Midlands, Eng., with splendid mus. tradition. Fest. was held there triennially, with occasional breaks, from 1768 to 1912. *Costa cond., 1849–82; Mendelssohn's *Elijah* f.p. 1846 and Gounod's *Rédemption* 1882. *Richter became cond. 1885. Byrd's Mass in 5 parts was revived 1900. Most significant fest. f.ps.

were of Elgar works: *The Dream of Gerontius* (1900), *The Apostles* (1903), *The Kingdom* (1906), *The Music Makers* (1912). Sibelius cond. f.p. in England of his 4th Sym., 1912. CBSO was founded 1920 with Appleby Matthews as cond. (though first concert cond. Elgar). Conds. since then have been *Boult 1924–30, *Heward 1930–1943, *Weldon 1943–51, *Schwarz 1951–7, *Panufnik 1957–9, *Rignold 1960–8, *Frémaux 1969–78, *Rattle from 1980. Birmingham Sch. of Mus. developed slowly until appointment of *Bantock as prin., 1900. Orig. part of Birmingham and Midland Institute and formally constituted in 1886 but now part of City of Birmingham Polytechnic and in new building since 1973. Pupils have incl. Julius Harrison, Frank Mullings, and Clarence Raybould. Other prins. have been A. K. Blackall (1934–45), Christopher Edmunds (1945–57), Steuart *Wilson (1957–60), Gordon *Clinton (1960–73), and L. Carus from 1973. At univ., Peyton Chair of Mus. was founded 1905 with Elgar as first prof. Succeeded by Bantock (1908), other incumbents being V. Hely-Hutchinson, J. A. Westrup, A. Lewis, and I. Keys.

Birtwistle, Harrison (Paul) (*b* Accrington, 1934). Eng. composer. As clarinettist, entered RMCM 1952, studying comp. with Richard *Hall. While still a student was one of Manchester New Music Group (with A. *Goehr, P. *Maxwell Davies and J. *Ogdon), performing *avant-garde* works. Leaving RMCM in 1960, spent a year at RAM. From 1962 to 1965 was dir. of mus., Cranborne Chase Sch. In USA 1966–8, first year as visiting fellow, Princeton Univ. With Maxwell Davies formed *Pierrot Players in London for perf. of new chamber mus. involving theatrical elements (named after *Pierrot Lunaire*). Received commissions for works from many organizations and rapidly moved into forefront of Eng. composers of his generation. Music marked by genuine lyrical impulse built on dramatic use of ostinato and repeated thematic fragments. A strong poetic feeling pervades all his work. Prin. comps.:

OPERA AND DRAMATIC: *Punch and Judy* (1966–7); *Down by the Greenwood Side* (1968–9); *The Mask of Orpheus*, (1973–5, 1981–4); *Bow Down* (1977); *Yan Tan Tethera*, TV opera (1983–4).

BALLET: *Frames, Pulses and Interruptions* (1977).

ORCH: *Chorales* (1960–3); *3 Movements with Fanfares* (1964); *Nomos* (1967–8); *An Imaginary Landscape* (1971); *The Triumph of Time* (1972); *Melencolia I* (1976); *Still Movement*, 13 solo str. (1984).

INSTRUMENTAL (without v.); *Refrains and Choruses*, wind quintet (1957); *The World is Discovered*, chamber ens. (1960); *Tragoedia*, wind quintet, hp., str. qt. (1965); *Verses for Ensembles*, wind quintet, brass, perc. (1969); *Some Petals from the Garland*, chamber ens. (1969); *Medusa*, ens. (1969–70, rev. 1980); *Dinah and Nick's Love Song*, 3 sop. sax., hp., or 3 cor. ang., hp. (1972); *Tombeau, in mem. Igor Stravinsky*, fl., cl., hp., str.

qt. (1972); *Chorales from a Toyshop* (1974); *Silbury Air*, chamber ens. (1977); *Carmen Arcadiae Mechanicae Perpetuum*, chamber ens. (1977); *For O, For O, the Hobby Horse is Forgot*, 6 perc. players (1976); *Pulse Sampler*, ob. and claves (1981).

INSTRUMENTAL (with vv.): *Monody for Corpus Christi* (1959); *Entr'actes and Sappho Fragments*, sop. and ens. (1964); *Cantata*, sop. and ens. (1969); *Nenia on the Death of Orpheus*, sop. and ens. (1970); *Prologue*, ten. and ens. (1970); *The Fields of Sorrow*, 2 sop., ch., and ens. (1971, rev. 1972); *Meridian*, mez., ch., and ens. (1970–1); *La Plage*, sop., 3 cl., pf., marimba (1972); . . . *agm* . . . , 16 solo vv. and 3 instr. ens. (1978–9).

UNACC. VOICES: *Description of the Passing of a Year*, ch. (1963); *On the Sheer Threshold of the Night*, 4 solo vv. and 12-part ch. (1980).

BRASS BAND: *Grimethorpe Aria* (1973).

ELECTRONIC: *4 Interludes from a Tragedy*, cl. and tape (1968–9); *Chronometer*, 8-track tape (1971–2).

CHAMBER MUSIC: *Verses*, cl., pf. (1965); *Linoi*, cl., pf. (1968), with tape and dancer added (1969), cl., pf., vc. (1973); cl. quintet (1980); *Deowa*, sop., cl. (1983); *Duets for Storab*, 2 fl. (1983).

INCIDENTAL MUSIC: *Hamlet* (1975).

Bis (Fr.). Twice. (1, at a concert) 'Encore!'. (2, in a score) Repeat the passage.

Bisbigliando (It. 'Whispering'). Effect used on harp. Constantly repeated notes are played *pianissimo* in upper and middle registers. Involves both hands playing adjacent strings set to same pitch with the pedals.

Biscroma (It.). The 32nd note or demisemiquaver.

Bishop, (Sir) **Henry** (Rowley) (*b* London, 1786; *d* London, 1855). Eng. composer and cond., pupil of F. *Bianchi. Engaged in 1810 to cond. and compose for CG. Founder member and dir., London Phil. Soc., 1813. Left CG 1824, becoming mus. dir. Drury Lane. 'Adapted' other composers' operas for Eng. stage, incl. Mozart's *Figaro* and *Don Giovanni*. Prof. of mus. Edinburgh Univ. 1841–3, Oxford Univ. 1848–55. Knighted 1842, first musician to be thus honoured. Of his large output only 2 songs effectively survive, *Home, Sweet Home* and *Lo, Here the Gentle Lark*.

Bishop-Kovacevich, Stephen (*b* Los Angeles, 1940). Amer. pianist of Yugoslav parentage, living in Eng. Studied with Lev Shorr; début 1951 (San Francisco). Studied with Myra *Hess in London, 1959, début Wigmore Hall, 1961. Int. tours as recitalist and in concs. Dedicatee and first player of Richard Rodney Bennett's conc.

Bispham, David (Scull) (*b* Philadelphia, 1857; *d* NY, 1921). Amer. operatic and concert bar. Pupil of Lamperti in Milan. Eng. début 1891 in Messager's *La Basoche*; sang Kurwenal in *Tristan* under Mahler, Drury Lane, 1892; NY Met. début as Beckmesser in *Die Meistersinger*, 1896. Determined advocate of opera in English.

Bissex. 12-str. guitar, invented 1770 by Van-hecke, with 6 str. over the finger-board and the rest sympathetic.

Bist du bei mir (With you beside me). Aria by J. S. Bach from Anna Magdalena Bach notebook (1725) written on 2 staves only, with v. part and unfigured bass.

Bitonality. The use of 2 keys simultaneously, as in the works of Stravinsky, Vaughan Williams, Holst, and many other 20th-cent. composers. See *Tonality* and *Polytonality*.

Bittner, Julius (*b* Vienna, 1874; *d* Vienna, 1939). Austrian composer. Trained as lawyer, but turned to mus. and comp. operas, songs, chamber mus., etc., as well as editing a mus. journal. Operas incl. *Das höllisch Gold* (1916) and *Das Veilchen* (1934).

Bizet, (Alexandre Césare Léopold), known as **Georges** (*b* Paris, 1838; *d* Bougival, 1875). Fr. composer. Studied Paris Cons., pupil of Halévy (whose daughter he married). Won Grand Prix de Rome 1857, in which year his *Docteur Miracle* was perf. In Rome comp. an *opéra-bouffe Don Procopio* (prod. Monte Carlo 1906) and a choral sym. *Vasco da Gama*, also his *Te Deum* (1858). On return to Paris comp. several operas, none of which had much success. They were *Les Pêcheurs de perles* (The Pearl Fishers) (1863), *La Jolie Fille de Perth* (The Fair Maid of Perth) (1866), and *Djamileh* (1871). In the early 1860s, comp. a 5-act opera *Ivan IV* which he later abandoned, using some of the mus. in other works, but which was prod. in a mutilated edn. after World War II as *Ivan le Terrible*. Other operas which exist either in incomplete or fragmentary form are *La Coupe du Roi de Thule* (1868), *Grisélidis* (1870–1), which incl. mus. later used in *L'Arlésienne* and *Carmen* (Flower Song), and *Don Rodrigue* (1873). Had more success in his lifetime with non-operatic works such as *Souvenirs de Rome* (perf. 1869, pubd. 1880 as suite *Roma*), the *Petite Suite, Jeux d'enfants* (1871), and incidental music to *L'Arlésienne* (1872). In 1873 began work on an opéra-comique *Carmen,* prod. Paris 1875 and coolly received, though it has since become one of the most popular operas ever written.

A brilliant pianist, Bizet also comp. for that instr. and his songs and church mus. are of high quality. A Sym. in C, 1855, of felicitous youthful charm, was disinterred in 1933 and f.p. in Basle cond. Weingartner, 26 Feb. 1935. If Bizet's fame rests largely on *Carmen,* all his pubd. work has colour, melody, and brilliant aptness of orchestra-tion. But in practically all of Bizet's work, incl. *Carmen,* there are musicological pitfalls for the unwary writer who has not consulted the work of authorities such as Winton *Dean concerning spurious edns., additions, and interpolations.

Prin. works:
OPERAS: *Le *Docteur Miracle* (1856); *Don Procopio* (1858–9); *La Prêtesse* (?1861); *Ivan IV* (?1862–

3, rev. 1864–5); *Les *Pêcheurs de perles* (The Pearl Fishers) (1863); *La *jolie fille de Perth* (The Fair Maid of Perth) (1866); *Djamileh* (1871); *Carmen* (1873–4).

INCIDENTAL MUSIC: *L'*Arlésienne* (play by A. Dau-det) (1872).

ORCH: *Overture* (*c.* 1855); Sym. in C (1855); *Scherzo et Marche funèbre* (1860–1); *Roma*, sym. (1860–8, rev. 1871); *Marche funèbre* (1868–9); *Petite Suite* (1871, orch. of Nos. 2, 3, 6, 11, and 12 from *Jeux d'Enfants,* pf. duet 1871); *L'*Arlésienne,* Suite No. 1 (1872. Suite No. 2 is by *Guiraud); *Patrie,* ov. (1873).

CHORAL: *Valse in G,* 4 vv., orch. (1855); *La Chanson du Rouet,* solo v., 4 vv., pf. (1857); *Clovis et Clotilde,* cantata (1857); *Te Deum,* sop., ten., 4 vv., orch. (1858); *Vasco de Gama,* ode-symphony (1859–60); *La Mort s'avance,* 4 vv., orch. (1869).

PIANO: *Grande Valse de Concert in E♭, Nocturne in F* (1854); *3 Esquisses Musicales* (1858); *Chants du Rhin* (1865); *Variations Chromatiques de Concert* (1868); *Nocturne in D* (1868); *Jeux d'Enfants* (Children's Games), 12 pieces, pf. duet (1871).

SONGS: *Vieille Chanson* (1865); *Après l'hiver* (1866); *Feuilles d'Album,* 6 songs (1866); *Chants des Pyrénées,* 6 folk-songs (1867); *Berceuse* (1868); *La Coccinelle* (1868); *Absence* (1872); *Chant d'Amour* (1872); *Sérénade: O, quand je dors* (1870); 12 extracts from unperf. stage works all fitted with new words (pubd. 1886).

Bizony, Celia (*b* Berlin, 1904). Ger.-born v. teacher, composer, and harpsichordist. Studied Geneva and Vienna. Co-founder Musica Antica e Nuova, Cambridge, 1942–8. Lecturer and teacher in Canada 1949–55. Prof., GSM and lecturer, Morley College, London, 1956–69. Mus. dir., Musica Antica e Nuova, London, from 1956. Comp. part-songs, str. qt., hpd. pieces. Wrote short history of Bach family.

Bjoner, Ingrid (*b* Kraakstad, Norway, 1927). Norwegian sop. Studied Oslo Cons. and Frankfurt Hochschule für Musik. Début Oslo 1957 (Donna Anna in *Don Giovanni*). Wuppertal Opera 1957–9, Düsseldorf 1959–61, Munich from 1961. Guest singer, leading opera houses and fests.

Björling, Jussi (Johan) (*b* Stora Tuna, Sweden, 1911; *d* Island of Siar Oe, 1960). Swed. ten., taught by father. Early public appearances in male v. qt. with father and 2 brothers. Studied Royal Opera Sch., Stockholm. Début Stockholm 1930 as Don Ottavio in *Don Giovanni.* London début 1939. NY Met. 1938–59 (excluding war).

Blacher, Boris (*b* Niu-chang, China, 1903; *d* Berlin, 1975). Ger. composer. Studied mus. in Irkutsk, Siberia, and at Charbin, China, where he worked in the opera house, 1919. Moving to Berlin 1922, studied architecture and mathemat-ics, and comp., after 1924, with Friedrich Koch. Taught at Dresden Cons. 1938–9. In 1945 became prof. of comp., Berlin Hochschule and dir., 1953–1970. Prolific composer in many forms, Blacher's mus. is basically tonal, though he has used the 12-note method, and he developed (in *Ornamente*, Op. 37, for pf., 1950) a rhythmical process called 'variable metres' whereby systematic changes of metre are planned according to mathematical relationships. Employed jazz styles in early works and elec. devices in later ones (after 1962). Works incl.:

OPERAS: *Fürstin Tarakanowa* (1940; also orch. suite); *Romeo und Julia* (1943); *Die Flut* (1946); *Die Nachtschwalbe* (1947); *Preussisches Märchen* (1949); *Rosamunde Floris* (1960); *Zwischenfälle bei einer Notlandung*, 'reportage' for elec. instr. and singers (1965); *200,000 Taler* (1969); *Yvonne, Prinzessin von Bergund* (1972); *Das Geheimnis des entwendeten Briefes* (1974).
BALLETS: *Harlekinade* (1939); *Das Zauberbuch von Erzerum* (on themes of Flotow) (1941; rev. as *Der erste Ball*, 1950); *Chiarina* (1946); *Lysistrata* (1950; also orch. suite); *Hamlet* (1949; also orch. suite); *Der Mohr von Venedig* (based on *Othello*) (1955); *Demeter* (1963); *Tristan* (1965; also orch. suite).
ORCH: *Kleine Marschmusik* (1932); *Kurmusik* (1933); *Divertimento*, str. (1935); *Divertimento*, wind (1936); *Geigenmusik*, vn., orch. (1936); *Concertante Musik* (1937); Sym. (1938); *Hamlet*, sym.-poem (1940); Conc. for str. (1940); *Partita*, str., perc. (1945); *Variations on a Theme of Paganini* (1947); Pf. Conc. No. 1 (1947), No. 2 (1952); Vn. Conc. (1948); Conc. for cl., bn., hn., tpt., hp., str. (1950); *2 Inventions* (1954); Va. Conc. (1954); *Fantasy* (1955); *Homage to Mozart* (1956); *Music for Cleveland* (1957); *Variations on a Theme of Clementi*, pf., orch. (1961); *Konzertstück*, wind quintet, str. (1963); Vc. Conc. (1964); *Collage* (1968); Conc. for tpt. and str. (1970); Cl. Conc. (1971); *Stars and Strings*, jazz ens., str. (1972); *Poème* (1974); *Pentagramm*, str. (1974).
CHORAL: *Der Grossinquisitor*, oratorio after Dostoyevsky (1942); *Träume vom Tod und vom Leben*, cantata, ten., ch., orch. (1955); *Die Gesänge des Seeräubers O'Rourke und seiner Geliebten Sally Brown*, sop., female cabaret singer, bar., speaker, speaking ch., orch. (1958); *Requiem*, sop., bar., ch., orch. (1958).
VOICE(S) AND INSTR: *Jazz-Koloraturen*, sop., alto sax., bn. (1929); *Francesca da Rimini*, sop., vn. (1954); *13 Ways of Looking at a Blackbird*, sop. or ten., str. (1957); *3(6+x) oder For Seven*, sop., perc., db. (1973).
CHAMBER MUSIC: Str. qts., No. 1 (1930), No. 2 (1940), No. 3 (1944), No. 4 (*Epitaph*) (1951), No. 5 (*Variationem über einem divergierenden c-moll-Dreiklang*) (1967); vc. sonata (1940); vn. sonata (1941); solo vn. sonata (1951); *4 Studies* for hpd. (1967); pf. trio (1970); quintet, fl., ob., str. trio (1973); *Tchaikovsky-Variations*, vc., pf. (1974).
PIANO: 2 sonatinas (1940); *3 Pieces* (1943); *Ornamente* (1950); sonata (1951); 24 Preludes (1974).

ELEC: *Multiple Raumperspektiven*, pf., elec. (1962); *Glissierende Deviationen*, tape (1962); *Der Astronaut*, tape (1963); *Elektronisches Scherzo*, tape (1965); *Ariadne*, duodrama, 2 speakers, elec. (1971).

Blachut, Beno (*b* Ostrava-Vitkovice, 1913; *d* Prague, 1985). Cz. ten. Studied Prague 1935–9. Opera début Olomouc, 1938, as Jenik in Smetana's *The Bartered Bride*. Member, Prague Nat. Th. from 1941. One of finest singers of Janáček and Smetana operatic roles.

Black Dyke Mills Band. Brass band, founded 1855, in connexion with mills of same name in village of Queensbury, Yorkshire. Has always held high place in band world, frequently winning Brit. nat. championships and other prizes, and touring both sides of the Atlantic.

Blackford, Richard (*b* London, 1954). Eng. composer and cond. Studied with *Lutyens and at RCM. Ass. to Henze in It. 1975. Founded mus.-th. workshop at London Acad. of Mus. and Dramatic Art, 1977. Works incl. opera for children *Sir Gawain and the Green Knight* (1977); *Inamorata—6 Sappho Fragments* for sop., harp, and str. sextet (1976), *Concerto for 7* (1976), *Sinfonie Poliziane* for 3 orch. groups (1977), and *Pietà* for orch. (1977).

Black Key Étude. No. 5 (in Gb major) of Chopin's 12 *Grandes Études* for pf. (Op. 10; pubd. 1833). The right hand confines itself to the black keys.

Black Knight, The. Sym. for ch. and orch. by Elgar, his Op. 25. Comp. 1889–93. Setting of Longfellow's trans. of Uhland. (F.p. Worcester Choral Soc. 1893; London, 1895).

Blackshaw, Christian (*b* Cheadle Hulme, 1949). Eng. pianist. Studied RMCM 1965–70, Leningrad Cons. 1970–2, RAM 1972–4. Début, London 1969. 1st prize Casella Int. Pf. Competition, Naples, 1974.

Black, Stanley (*b* London, 1913). Eng. composer, pianist, and cond., esp. of film mus. Studied Matthay Sch. of Mus. Cond., BBC Dance Orch. 1944–52; mus. dir. ABC Pictures, 1958–63; prin. cond. BBC Northern Ireland Orch., 1968–9; ass. cond. Osaka P.O. 1971; N.Z. Proms 1972. O.B.E. 1986.

Bladder-Pipe. Instr. similar to *bagpipe which existed from 13th to 16th cents. and was sometimes called *Platerspil*. Attempted to combine bagpipe's continuous air flow with a means of stopping and starting more easily, thus making some kind of tonguing and articulation possible. This it did by using elastic animal bladder which expelled air down the pipe by its own elasticity instead of, as in the bagpipe, by arm pressure on animal skin.

Blades, James (*b* Peterborough, 1901). Eng. percussion-player. Prof. of timp. and perc. RAM.

Former member, ECO, Melos Ens., etc. Author of books on perc. instr. and technique. O.B.E. 1972.

Blagrove, Henry (Gamble) (b Nottingham, 1811; d London, 1872). Eng. violinist. Studied in Ger. with Spohr 1832–4. On return to Eng. formed qt., establishing first regular series of chamber concerts in London, 1835. Leader of many British orchs. of his time.

Blagrove, Richard (Manning) (b Nottingham, 1826; d London, 1895). Brother of Henry ★Blagrove. Noted va. player, and propagandist, as composer and executant, for the concertina.

Blake, David (Leonard) (b London, 1936). Eng. composer. Studied Cambridge Univ. and Ger. Acad. of Arts, Berlin, with Eisler. Lecturer in mus., York Univ., 1964–71, senior lecturer from 1971, prof. from 1981. Also cond. and pianist with his ensemble Lumina. Early works in tonal idiom influenced by Bartók and Mahler, later adopted 12-note system, but later evolved a freer, more relaxed style, the vn. conc. being deeply romantic in style and spirit. Prin. works:

OPERA: *Toussaint L'Ouverture*, 3 acts (lib. by T. Ward) (1974–6, rev. 1982).
ORCH: *Chamber Symphony* (1966), *Metamorphoses* (1971), vn. conc. No. 1 (1976), No. 2 (1983), *Sonata alla Marcia* (1978).
VOCAL AND CHORAL: *3 Choruses to Poems by Frost* (1964), *Beata L'Alma*, sop. and pf. (1966), *Lumina*, soloist, ch., and orch. (1969), *The Bones of Chuang Tzu*, bar. and pf. (1972), bar. and chamber orch. (1973); *In Praise of Krishna*, sop. and 9 instr. (1973); *Toussaint Suite*, mez., bar., orch. (1977); *Toussaint: Song of the Common Wind*, mez., orch. (1977); *From the Mattress Grave*, 12 Heine poems for sop. and 11 instr. (1978), *The Spear*, mez., speaker, ch., cl., tpt., va., pf. (1982), *Change is Going to Come*, mez., bar., ch., and 4 players (1982), *Rise, Dove*, bar. and orch. (1982).
CHAMBER MUSIC: Str. Qt. No. 1 (1961–2), No. 2 (1973), No. 3 (1982), *Sequence*, 2 fl. (1967), Nonet for wind (1971, rev. 1978), *Scenes* for vc. (1972), *Arias*, cl. (1978), cl. quintet (1979–80), *Cassation*, wind octet (1979), *Capriccio*, wind, str., pf. (7 players) (1980).

Blake Watkins, Michael. See *Watkins, Michael Blake.*

Blanche (Fr.). White. The half-note or minim.

Blanik (Smetana). See *Má Vlast.*

Blasinstrumente (Ger.). Blowing instruments, i.e. wind instr.

Blasis, Carlo de (b Naples, 1797; d Cernobbio, L. Como, 1878). It. ballet dancer and choreog. on whose system classical training is still based. Dir., Royal Acad. of Dance, Milan, 1837–53. Worked in London and Paris. Created 90 ballets, some

with own mus. Father was composer and sister operatic sop.

Blasmusik (Ger.). Blowing mus., i.e. mus. of wind instr.

Blaukopf, Kurt (b Czernowitz, 1914). Austrian musicologist and writer. Studied with S. Wolpe and H. Scherchen in Vienna, 1932–7 and with Tal in Jerusalem 1940–2. Prof. of mus. sociology, Vienna Hochschule für Musik from 1963. Ed., *Phono*, 1954–65. Author of two books on Mahler (1969, Eng. trans. 1973, and 1976, Eng. trans. 1976).

Blavet, Michel (b Besançon, 1700; d Paris, 1768). Fr. flautist and composer of operas, fl. sonatas, and ballets. Probable that several of ★Leclair's fl. sonatas were written for him.

Blech (Ger.). Sheet metal, i.e. the Brass. *Blechmusik*, brass band.

Blech, Harry (b London, 1910). Eng. violinist and cond. Trained TCL and RMCM. Member Hallé Orch., and then BBC S.O. 1930–6. Founder and leader, Blech Str. Qt. 1933–50. Founded London Wind Players 1942, London Symphonic Players 1946, London Mozart Players 1949 (mus. dir. until 1984). O.B.E. 1964, C.B.E. 1984.

Blech, Leo (b Aachen, 1871; d Berlin, 1958). Ger. cond. and composer. Studied Berlin Hochschule, 1890. First cond. posts in Aachen and Prague; from 1906 Kapellmeister, Royal Berlin Opera, becoming Generalmusikdirektor 1913–23, working for much of that period with R. Strauss, of whose operas he cond. several f.ps. in Berlin. Brief spell in Vienna, then cond. (jointly with ★Kleiber) Berlin State Opera 1926–37, until removal by Nazis. Cond. Riga 1937–41 and Stockholm 1941–1946. Returned to Berlin Städtische Oper 1949–53. Composer of 5 operas, symphonic poems, and other works.

'Bleeding chunks'. Phrase sometimes used by writers on mus. when referring to operatic extracts played out of context in the concert-hall. It is a quotation from a programme-note by Sir Donald ★Tovey on Bruckner's 4th Sym. in his *Essays in Musical Analysis*, Vol. II (1935), p. 71. Tovey wrote: 'Defects of form are not a justifiable ground for criticism from listeners who profess to enjoy the bleeding chunks of butcher's meat chopped from Wagner's operas and served up on Wagner nights as *Waldweben* and *Walkürenritt*'.

Bleiben (Ger.). To remain. In org. mus., *Bleibt* (remains) means that the stop in question is to remain in use.

Blessed Damozel, The (*La Damoiselle élue*). Cantata (*poème lyrique*) by Debussy for sop., women's ch., and orch., comp. 1887–8 on G. Sarrazin's trans. of D. G. Rossetti's poem (1850). Re-orchestrated 1902.

Blessed Virgin's Expostulation, The. Song for sop. or treble by *Purcell, comp. 1693 to text by Nahum Tate beginning 'Tell me some pitying angel'.

Blest Pair of Sirens. Ode for ch. and orch. by Parry, f.p. 1887. Words from Milton's *At a Solemn Musick.*

Blind Man's Buff. Th. piece by *Maxwell Davies, masque for sop. (or treble), mez., and mime, and stage band. Text by composer from Büchner's *Leonce und Lena*, and other sources. F.p. London 1972 (Josephine Barstow, Mary Thomas, Mark Fourneaux, BBC S.O., cond. *Boulez).

Bliss, (Sir) **Arthur** (Drummond) (*b* London, 1891; *d* London, 1975). Eng. composer, conductor, and administrator. Studied counterpoint with Charles *Wood at Cambridge Univ. Mus.B. 1913. Pupil of Stanford at RCM 1913–14. Served in Royal Fusiliers 1914–17, Grenadier Guards 1917–18. From 1919 earned reputation of being *enfant terrible*, influenced in such works as *Madame Noy* and *Rout* by Stravinsky, Satie, etc. Wrote incid. mus. for Nigel Playfair, 1919. Cond., Portsmouth Philharmonic Soc. 1921. His *Colour Symphony* was commissioned for the 1922 Three Choirs Fest. on Elgar's suggestion. Went to Santa Barbara, Calif., 1923–5, working as cond. Returned to Eng. 1925, writing a series of chamber works for virtuosi soloists and ensembles. His *Morning Heroes* (1930) was perf. at 1930 Norwich Fest., one of its movts. being a setting of a war poem by Wilfred Owen. *Music for Strings* followed in 1935. In 1934–5 he wrote the mus. for Korda's H. G. Wells film *Things to Come* and in 1937 his ballet *Checkmate* was produced at S.W. Two other important ballet scores, *Miracle in the Gorbals* (1944) and *Adam Zero* (1946), followed. His piano concerto was first performed at the 1939 New York World Fair. From 1939 to 1941 he taught at Berkeley in California, but on return to Eng. became BBC dir. of mus., 1942–4. An opera, *The Olympians*, to a lib. by J. B. Priestley, failed to win approval at its 1949 CG première, but he wrote an opera for television, *Tobias and the Angel*, in 1960 to a lib. by Christopher Hassall. In 1950 he was knighted and in 1953 became Master of the Queen's Music, a post he filled with flair and energy. Among the best of his later works were the vn. conc. (for Campoli) and the orch. *Meditations on a Theme by John Blow* (both 1955) and the vc. conc. (1970). K.C.V.O. 1969. C.H. 1971.

Bliss's early Stravinskyan phase gave way to works in a bold, post-Elgarian style, vigorous and rich in texture but lacking the inner poetry of his model. Some of his best music is to be found in his chamber works, notably the cl. quintet, written for Frederick Thurston, and the ob. quintet, for Léon Goossens. His sense of drama and of vivid musical imagery found their truest outlet in his ballet scores and in the excellent *Things to Come* suite. Prin. works:

OPERAS: *The *Olympians* (1948–9); *Tobias and the Angel* (1960); *The *Beggar's Opera* (1952–3, version of Gay-Pepusch work for film).

BALLETS: *Checkmate* (1937); *Miracle in the Gorbals* (1944); *Adam Zero* (1946); *The Lady of Shalott* (1958).

ORCH: *2 Studies* (1920); *Mêlée Fantasque* (1921, rev. 1937 and 1965); *A *Colour Symphony* (1921–2, rev. 1932); *Introduction and Allegro* (1926, rev. 1937); *Hymn to Apollo* (1926, rev. 1965); *Music for Strings* (1935); Processional, with org. (1953); *Meditations on a Theme by John Blow* (1955); *Edinburgh Overture* (1956); *Metamorphic Variations* (1972); *2 Contrasts*, str. (1972, arr. from Str. qt. No. 2).

CONCERTOS: 2 pianos (1924, rev. 1925–9 and 1950), also arr. for 2 pianos (3 hands) in 1968; pf. (1938–9); vn. (1955); vc. (1970).

CHORAL: *Pastoral*: *Lie strewn the white flocks*, mez., ch., and orch. (1928), *Morning Heroes*, sym. for orator, ch., and orch. (1930); *A Song of Welcome*, sop., bar., ch., and orch. (1954); *The *Beatitudes*, sop., ten., ch., and orch. (1961); *Mary of Magdala*, cont., bar., ch., and orch. (1962); *The Golden Cantata*, ten., ch., and orch. (1963); *The World is charged with the grandeur of God*, ch. and wind (1969); *2 Ballads*, women's vv. and orch. (1971).

UNACC. VOICES: *Aubade for Coronation Morning* (1953); *Seek the Lord* (1956); *Birthday Song for a Royal Child* (1959); *Stand up and bless the Lord your God* (1960); *Cradle Song for a Newborn Child* (1963); *O Give Thanks* (1965); *River Music* (1967); *Lord, who shall abide in Thy Tabernacle* (1968); *A Prayer to the Infant Jesus* (1968); *Ode for Sir William Walton* (1972); *Prayer of St Francis of Assisi* (1972); *Put thou thy trust in the Lord* (1972); *Sing, Mortals!* (1974); *Shield of Faith* (1974).

VOICE AND ENS.: *Madam Noy*, sop. (1918); *Rhapsody*, sop., ten. (1919); *Rout*, sop. (1920); *2 Nursery Rhymes*, sop. (1920); *The Women of Yueh*, sop. (1923–4); *Serenade*, bar. (1929); *The Enchantress*, scena for cont. (1951); *Elegiac Sonnet*, ten. (1954); *A Knot of Riddles*, bar. (1963).

BRASS AND MILITARY BAND: *Kenilworth Suite* (1936); *The First Guards* (1956); *Belmont Variations* (1963); *The Linburn Air* (1965); and many ceremonial fanfares for royal and other occasions.

CHAMBER MUS.: Str. qt. (1914, withdrawn), str. qt. (1923–4? MS.), No. 1 in B♭ (1941), No. 2 (1950); *Conversations*, fl., alto fl., ob., cor ang., vn., va., vc. (1920); pf. quintet (1919, unpubd.); ob. quintet (1927); cl. quintet (1932).

INCID. MUS. (STAGE AND RADIO) AND FILM MUS.: *As You Like It* (1919); *King Solomon* (1924); *Things to Come* (1934–5); *Conquest of the Air* (1937); *Caesar and Cleopatra* (1944); *Men of Two Worlds* (1945); *Christopher Columbus* (1949); *Summer Day's Dream* (1949).

PIANO: *Bliss* (1923); *Masks* (1924); *Toccata* (c.1925); *Interludes* (1925); *Suite* (1926); *The Rout Trot* (1927); *Study* (1927); *Sonata* (1952); *Miniature*

Scherzo (1969); *Fun and Games*, 2 pf. 3 hands (1970); *Triptych* (1970); *A Wedding Suite* (1974). SOLO SONGS: *The Tramps* (c. 1916); *3 Romantic Songs* (1921); *3 Songs* (1923, rev. 1972); *When I was One and Twenty* (1923); *Ballads of the 4 Seasons* (1923); *3 Jolly Gentlemen* (1924); *The Fallow Deer at the Lonely House* (1924); *A Child's Prayer* (1926); *Rich or Poor* (1925–6); *Simples* (1932); *7 American Poems* (1940); *Auvergnat* (1943); *Angels of the Mind*, song-cycle, 7 songs (1969); *Tulips* (1970).

Blitheman, John (*b* c.1525; *d* London, 1591). Eng. organist of Queen Elizabeth's Chapel Royal from 1553; composer of church mus. and virginals mus.—the latter important for its influence on his successor in the organistship, his pupil John *Bull.

Blitzstein, Marc (*b* Philadelphia, 1905; *d* Fort-de-France, Martinique, 1964). Amer. composer and pianist. Scion of a wealthy family, his work reflected his radical political outlook. Studied Curtis Institute, 1924–6, in Paris with Boulanger 1926, and Berlin with Schoenberg 1927. Returning to USA during depression, decided to compose for the popular th. and prod. perhaps his finest work, The *Cradle Will Rock* (1936). Never repeated its success, though his adaptation of Brecht's *Threepenny Opera* (1952) was acclaimed. Served 1942–5 with US Air Force in Eng. and comp. *Airborne Symphony* (1945). After he abandoned Parisian neo-classicism, his work was based on diatonicism laced with jazz and popular influences, in the manner made more familiar by *Bernstein. Other works incl.:

OPERAS: *Triple-Sec* (1928), *No For An Answer* (1940), *I've Got the Tune* (1937), *Regina* (1949), *Juno*, based on O'Casey's *Juno and the Paycock* (1958).

BALLETS: *Cain* (1930), *The Guests* (1949).

ORCH.: works incl. pf. conc. and mus. for th. and films.

Bloch, Ernest (*b* Geneva, 1880; *d* Portland, Oregon, 1959). Swiss-born composer (naturalized Amer.). First mus. instruction from Jaques-Dalcroze. Comp str. qt. and sym. before age 15. Brussels Cons. 1897, studying with Ysaÿe, followed by spells at Frankfurt with Knorr and Munich with Thuille. Went to Paris 1903. From this period date the symphonic poem *Winter—Spring* (1904–5) and the opera *Macbeth*, prod. Paris 1910, in which the influence of Mussorgsky and Debussy can be detected together with Bloch's hallmarks of frequent changes of tempo and key, use of modality, cyclic form, and propensity for open 5ths and 4ths. The next few years saw some works of Jewish inspiration, the *Israel Symphony* (1912–16), *Trois poèmes juifs* for orch. (1913), *Psalm 22* for bar. and orch. (1914), and *Schelomo*, rhapsody for vc. and orch. (1916). This distinctive and powerful Jewish element in Bloch's mus. sprang from a deep spiritual impulse and not from external application. He said that

the Jewish heritage as related in the Old Testament moved him powerfully. In 1915 became prof. of comp. at Geneva Cons., but went to USA in 1916 as cond. for the dancer Maud Allan. He became and remained Amer. citizen, 1924. Taught in NY 1917–20, first director, Cleveland Institute of Mus. 1920–5, head of San Francisco Cons., 1926–1930. From 1930–9 lived principally in Geneva and Rome. In this period comp. symphonic suite for orch. *Evocations* (1937), the *Sacred Service* (*Avodath Hakodesh*) for bar., ch., and orch. (1930–1933), pf. sonata (1935), *Voice in the Wilderness*, vc. and orch. (1936), and vn. conc. (1938). In 1941 returned to USA and settled at Agate Beach, Oregon. For a time was prof. of mus. at Univ. of Calif. in Berkeley. In last 20 years of his life comp. the *Concerto Grosso* No. 2 for str. qt. and str. (1953), Symphony in E♭ (1954–5), *Concerto symphonique*, pf. and orch. (1948), *Suite hébraique*, va. and orch. (1953), str. qts. Nos. 2–5 (1946,1951, 1954, 1956), and 2nd pf. quintet (1957). Among his earlier works are some of his masterpieces, e.g. *Suite* for va. and pf. or orch. (1919), Pf. Quintet (1921–3), *Baal Shem* for vn. and pf. or orch. (1923), and *Concerto Grosso* No. 1 for str. and pf. (1924–5). Also wrote *America*, epic rhapsody (1926) and *Helvetia*, symphonic fresco (1929).

Block Flute (Ger. *Blockflöte*). Recorder or flageolet, so called after its 'block' or fipple; also an org. stop.

Block, Michel (*b* Antwerp, 1937). Belg. pianist. Childhood in Mexico, where he made début at 16 with Mexican Nat. Orch. Studied Juilliard Sch., NY, 1954. NY début 1959.

Blockx, Jan (*b* Antwerp, 1851; *d* Antwerp, 1912). Belg. composer; pupil and follower of *Benoit, whom he succeeded in 1901 as dir. of Royal Flemish Cons., Antwerp. Propagandist for Flemish nat. movement. Wrote 8 operas to Fr. and Flemish texts, incl. *Thyl Uylenspiegel* (1900).

Blom, Eric (Walter) (*b* Berne, 1888; *d* London, 1959). Eng. critic and scholar. Active as writer of annotated programmes; London mus. critic *Manchester Guardian* 1923–31; *Birmingham Post* 1931–46; *Observer* 1949–59; ed. *Everyman's Dictionary of Music* (1946, rev. 1954), *Grove's Dictionary of Music and Musicians*, 5th edn. (1954); *Music and Letters*, 1937–50 and 1954–9; *Master Musicians* series. Author of book on Mozart. C.B.E. 1955.

Blomdahl, Karl-Birger (*b* Växjö, Sweden, 1916; *d* Kungsängen, 1968). Swed. composer, pupil of Hilding Rosenberg, studied in Fr. and It. 1946–7. Prof. of comp., Swedish Royal Acad. of Mus., 1960—4, dir. of mus., Swedish Radio, from 1965. Pioneered elec. mus. studio. After a Hindemithian early phase, adopted serial techniques and, later, elecs. First opera *Aniara* (Stockholm 1959) is set in a spaceship. Prin. works incl.:

OPERAS: *Aniara (1959), Herr von Hancken (1962–4).

ORCH: Concerto Grosso (1944), Sym. No. 1 (1943), No. 2 (1947), No. 3 (*Facets*) (1948), Va. Conc. (1941), Vn. Conc. (1947), Chamber Conc. (1952–3), Sisyphos, choreographic suite (1954), Minotauros, choreographic suite, (1957), Altisonans (tape) (1966).

CHORAL: In the Hall of Mirrors (I splegnarnes sal) for soloists, reciter, ch., and orch. (1951–2).

CHAMBER MUSIC: Trio (1938), Str. qt. (1939), Str. trio (1945), etc.

Blondel (de Nesle) (*fl.* 12th cent.). Fr. trouvère (minstrel), 22 of whose songs survive. Said to have discovered where King Richard I was imprisoned by Duke of Austria.

Blossom Time. Amer. version of operetta *Das Dreimäderlhaus* by Berté.

Blow, John (*b* Newark, Notts., 1649; *d* Westminster, 1708). Eng. composer and organist. One of first choirboys of Chapel Royal after Restoration in 1660. Organist, Westminster Abbey, 1668–79, when his pupil Purcell succeeded him, and 1695–1708. Also Master of Choristers, St Paul's Cath., 1687–1703. Wrote over 100 anthems, 13 services, many secular songs, and the masque *Venus and Adonis.* *Bliss comp. *Meditations on a Theme by John Blow.*

Bluebeard's Castle (Bartók). See *Duke Bluebeard's Castle.*

Blue Bells of Scotland (properly 'Bell', not 'Bells'). This song, of unknown origin, first appears at the end of the 18th or beginning of the 19th cent., sung by the London actress, Mrs Jordan (an Irishwoman), at Drury Lane Th.

Blue Bird, The. Part-song for mixed ch., with sop. solo, by *Stanford, Op. 119 No. 4, comp. 1911, setting of poem by Mary Coleridge (1861–1907).

Blue Danube, On The Beautiful (*An der schönen blauen Donau*). Concert waltz, Op. 314, by Johann *Strauss II, known in Eng. simply as *The Blue Danube.* F.p. Vienna 1867. Orig. with ch. part.

Blues. Slow *jazz song of lamentation, generally for an unhappy love affair. Usually in groups of 12 bars, instead of 8 or 16, each stanza being 3 lines covering 4 bars of music. Tonality predominantly major, but with the flattened 3rd and 7th of the key (the 'blue notes'). Harmony tended towards the plagal or subdominant.

The earlier (almost entirely Negro) history of the Blues is traced by oral tradition as far back as the 1860s, but the form was popularized about 1911–14 by the Negro composer W. C. Handy (*St Louis Blues, Basin Street Blues*). Composers such as Gershwin, Ravel, Copland, and Tippett have used the term to indicate a Blues-type mood rather than a strict adherence to the form. Among notable blues singers were Bessie Smith and Billie Holiday (though Holiday's main repertoire was pop music).

Blum, Robert (Karl Moritz) (*b* Zürich, 1900). Swiss composer. Studied Zürich Cons. 1919–22 and later with Busoni at Prussian State Acad., Berlin. Cond. at Baden from 1925. Teacher at Zürich from 1945. Composer of much film and incidental mus. but also of 6 syms., conc. for orch., choral works, triple conc. (vn., ob., tpt.), and va. conc.

Blume, Friedrich (*b* Schlüchtern, 1893; *d* Schlüchtern, 1975). Ger. musicologist. After studying medicine, philosophy, and mus. at Eisenach, Munich, Berlin, and Leipzig, embarked on distinguished career as ed. of early mus. and writer of scholarly studies on a wide variety of mus. subjects. Prof. of musicology, Kiel Univ. 1935–58. From 1943 directed the preparation of the encyclopedia *Die Musik in Geschichte und Gegenwart*, which began to appear in 1949. Authority on Bach and Mozart.

Blumenfeld, Harold (*b* Seattle, 1923). Amer. composer. Studied Eastman Sch., 1941–3, Yale 1946–9 (comp. with Hindemith) and Zürich Univ. 1948–9. Prof., Washington Univ. in St Louis since 1951. Comps. incl. opera *Amphitryon 4* (1956–62), TV opera *The Road to Salem* (1966–1969), *Songs of War* (Sassoon poems) (1970), *Elegy for the Nightingale* (choral work, 1954), and orch. suites, etc.

Blumenstück (Flower-piece). Pf. solo in D♭ major, Op. 19, by Schumann, comp. 1839.

Blüthner. Pf.-making firm, founded Leipzig 1853.

Blyth, Alan (*b* London, 1929). Eng. critic, broadcaster, and author. Studied Oxford Univ. Contributor to *The Times* 1963–77, *Musical Times*, *Opera* (ass. ed. 1967–84), esp. on operatic subjects. Member of mus. staff of *Daily Telegraph* from 1977. Author of monographs on Colin Davis and Janet Baker. Ed. *Opera on Record* 1, 2, and 3 (1979, 1983, 1984), *Remembering Britten* (1981).

Blyton, Carey (*b* Beckenham, 1932). Eng. composer. Studied zoology but decided to follow mus. career, entering TCL 1953. Bantock comp. prize 1954. Studied Copenhagen 1957 with Jersild. Prof. of harmony, TCL, 1963–73. Mus. ed., Faber Mus., 1964–71. Comps. incl. orch. suite *Cinque Port*, ov. *The Hobbit*, works for sax. qt. and for guitar, cantatas, song-cycles, madrigals, chamber mus., and vocal pieces such as *Lyrics from the Chinese, Lachrymae*, and *Symphony in Yellow.*

B Moll (Ger.). The key of B♭ minor (not B minor; see *B*).

B.N.O.C. See *British National Opera Company.*

Boatswain's Mate, The. Opera in 1 act by Ethel *Smyth to her lib. based on W. W. Jacobs's story. (Prod. London 1916).

Boatwright, Howard (*b* Newport News, Virginia, 1918). Amer. composer, studied with Hindemith at Yale (1945–8). Teacher of mus. theory, Yale, 1948–64, dean of mus. sch., Syracuse Univ. from 1964. Works incl. *The Woman of Trachis* (1955), cl. qt. (1958), *St. Matthew Passion* (1962), *Canticle of the Sun* (1963), *Ship of Death* (1966).

Bobillier, Marie. See *Brenet, Michel.*

Boccaccio. Opera in 3 acts by Suppé to lib. by F. Zell and R. Genée. Prod. Vienna 1879, Boston and NY 1880.

Bocca chiusa (It.). Closed mouth, i.e. a wordless humming (in choral mus.).

Boccherini, Luigi (*b* Lucca, 1743; *d* Madrid, 1805). It. cellist and composer. Famous in teens as virtuoso cellist. Contemporary of Haydn and resembling him in ideals, methods, and general spirit. Settled in Madrid in 1769, remaining until 1787. Appointed 'composer of his Chamber' by Friedrich Wilhelm II of Prussia. Returned to Spain 1797, when he then lacked a patron and died in poverty. Comp. opera, 30 syms., 11 vc. concs., 91 str. qts., 154 quintets (various combinations), guitar qts., 60 trios, church mus., etc. The famous Minuet is from the String Quintet in E major, Op. 13, No. 5. Boccherini's mus., which combines harmonic adventurousness with melodic profundity, is well worth detailed study.

Bocchino (It.). Mouthpiece of a wind instr.

Bocedization. 16th-cent. Flemish system of naming notes of scale (Bo-Ce-Di, etc.), somewhat on principle of tonic sol-fa. Introduced by Hubert *Waelrant.

Bochsa, (Robert) **Nicolas Charles** (*b* Montmédi, 1789; *d* Sydney, N.S.W., 1856). Fr. composer and harpist, author of a famous harp method and leader of a colourful life. Studied Paris Cons. 1806. Revolutionized way of playing the harp. Harpist to Napoleon 1813 and to Louis XVIII 1816. Wrote 8 operas for Opéra Comique between 1813 and 1816. Fled from France 1817, was tried *in absentia* for forgeries and sentenced to 12 years' imprisonment. Settled in London. Dir., Lent oratorios from 1823. First gen. sec. and prof. of harp RAM from 1822. Dismissed 1827. Cond., King's Th., London, 1826–30. In 1839 ran away with singer Anna Bishop, wife of Henry *Bishop, after touring provinces as her accompanist. Spent rest of his life on tour abroad (except in Fr.). Composed *Requiem* in 15 movts., 1816, commissioned for ceremony of reinterment of the beheaded Louis XVI's remains. Contains anticipations of Berlioz's *Symphonie funèbre et triomphale.* Also comp. sym. (1821), 5 harp concs., and many chamber works involving harp.

Bodanzky, Artur (*b* Vienna, 1877; *d* NY, 1939). Austrian cond. Trained Vienna Cons. as violinist, then took various humble conducting posts. Ass.

to Mahler at Vienna Opera 1903–4. Cond. first Brit. perf. of *Parsifal*, CG, 1914. Then at NY Met. from 1915 until his death, apart from brief break in 1928. Notorious for the cuts he made in Wagner's *Ring* cycle.

Bode, Johann Joachim Christoph (*b* Barum, Brunswick, 1730; *d* Weimar, 1793). Ger. composer, bassoonist, and oboist. Mus. teacher and ed., Hamburg, 1757–78, later becoming printer and publisher. Comp. syms., bn. conc., vc. conc., vn. conc., and songs.

Boehm, Theobald (Boehm System, Boehm Flute) (*b* Munich, 1794; *d* Munich, 1881). Ger. flautist and composer, remembered principally for the system whereby he replaced the clumsily-placed holes of his instr. by keys enabling the cutting of the holes in their proper acoustical positions, yet leaving them in easy control of the fingers. He made his first 'ring key' fl. in 1832, while a player in Munich court orch., and in 1847 brought out an improved metal fl. with 15 holes and 23 levers and keys. This system has been adapted for ob., cl., and bn. Boehm was also a goldsmith and ironmaster. From 1833 to 1846 he superintended reorganization of Bavarian steel industry.

Boëllmann, Léon (*b* Ensisheim, Upper Alsace, 1862; *d* Paris, 1897). Fr. organist and composer, pupil of *Gigout. From 1881 organist of Paris church of St Vincent de Paul; wrote org. mus. and mus. for other instr., incl. *Symphonic Variations* for vc. and orch.

Boesmans, Philippe (*b* Tongeren, 1936). Belg. composer and pianist. Studied Liège Cons. and privately with *Pousseur, 1962. Mus. prod. for Belg. radio from 1961. From 1971 collab. with Pousseur at Liège elec. mus. studios. Works incl. opera *La Passion de Gilles* (Brussels 1983), *Sonances*, 2 pf. (1964), *Impromptu*, 23 instr. (1965), *Sym.*, pf. (1966), *Verticales*, orch. (1969), *Upon la mi*, sop., hn., 11 instr., elec. (1971), *Intervalles*, orch. (1973), *Multiples*, 2 pf., orch. (1974), *Eléments/Extensions*, pf., ens. (1975).

Boësset, Antoine (*b* Blois, 1586; *d* Paris, 1643). Fr. court musician, being master of royal mus. from 1613 and holding other royal posts simultaneously. Pubd. 9 vols. of airs (1617–42), also masses and motets.

Boethius, Anicius Manlius Torquatus Severinus (*b* Rome, *c.*475; *d* Pavia, *c.*525). Roman philosopher and mathematician who wrote *De institutione musica*, a 5-vol. treatise on Gr. mus.

Boettcher, Wilfried (*b* Bremen, 1929). Ger. cond. and cellist. Studied Hamburg and Paris (with *Fournier). Prin. cellist, Hanover Opera 1956–8. Prof. of vc., Vienna Acad. of Mus. 1958. Founder and dir. Vienna Soloists 1959. Prof. of vc. and chamber mus., Hamburg Acad. 1965. Cond. Hamburg S.O. 1967–71. Guest cond. of several Brit. orchs.

Boeuf sur le toit, Le (The Ox on the Roof). Pantomimic divertissement with mus. by Milhaud to lib. by Cocteau. Prod. Paris 1920 as mus.-hall spectacle, later as ballet.

Bogatyryov, Anatoly (Vasilyevich) (*b* Vitebsk, 1913). Russ. composer. Studied at Minsk Cons. where he eventually became dir. Composer of 2 operas, syms., and cantatas.

Bogen (Ger.). (1) Bow. So *Bogenstrich*, bow stroke. (2) Short for **Krummbogen*. (3) The **Tie* or Bind. (4) *Bogen* form. The design of e.g. a movement of a sym. which can be likened to the curve of a bow.

Bohème, La (Bohemian Life). (1) Opera in 4 acts by Puccini to lib. by Giacosa and Illica, based on H. Murger's novel *Scènes de la vie de Bohème* (1847–9). Comp. 1894–5. Prod. Turin 1896, Manchester (in Eng.) and Los Angeles 1897, San Francisco and NY 1898, London 1899.
(2) Opera by Leoncavallo, also founded on Murger's novel but using different episodes. Prod. Venice 1897.

Bohemian Girl, The. Opera in 3 acts by Balfe to lib. by Alfred Bunn based on a ballet-pantomime *The Gipsy* by Saint-Georges and orig. from Cervantes's *La Gitanella*. Prod. London 1843, NY 1844. Incl. songs *I dreamt that I dwelt in marble halls* and *When other lips*. Revived by Beecham, Liverpool and London, 1951.

Bohemian String Quartet. See *Czech Quartet*.

Bohemia's Meadows and Forests, From (Smetana). See *Má Vlast*.

Böhm, Georg (*b* Goldbach, 1661; *d* Lüneburg, 1733). Ger. organist and composer. Worked in Hamburg, 1693–8. Org., Johanniskirche, Lüneburg, 1698–1733. Influenced Bach, whom he knew, through his suites, preludes, and fugues. Also comp. hymns, Passions, and chorale preludes.

Böhm, Karl (*b* Graz, 1894; *d* Salzburg, 1981). Austrian cond. Studied Graz and Vienna Cons. First post at Graz 1917, becoming chief cond. 1920. At Munich Opera 1921–7. Generalmusikdirektor Darmstadt 1927–31, Hamburg 1931–4, Dresden 1934–42, Vienna 1943–5. Dir. of rebuilt Vienna State Opera 1955–6. Regular cond. Salzburg, Vienna, Bayreuth. London début, CG 1936; NY 1957. Specialist in mus. of R. Strauss. Cond. f.ps. of *Die schweigsame Frau* (1935) and *Daphne* (1938), both Dresden.

Bohnen, Michael (*b* Cologne, 1887; *d* Berlin, 1965). Ger. bass-bar. Début as Kaspar in *Der Freischütz*, Düsseldorf, 1910. Berlin Court Opera 1913–21. NY Met. 1923–32 where he sang Jonny in NY première of Křenek's *Jonny spielt auf*. Berlin Deutsches Oper 1933–45. Intendant, Berlin Städtische Oper, 1945–7.

Boieldieu, François Adrien (*b* Rouen, 1775; *d* Jarcy, 1834). Fr. composer. First 2 operas, to libs. by his father, were prod. in Rouen in 1793 and 1795. Went to Paris in 1795, soon having operas staged there. First major success in 1800 with *Le *Calife de Bagdad*, but Cherubini asked him 'Are you not ashamed of such undeserved success?' and took him as pupil, the first result (another success) being *Ma Tante Aurore* (1803). From 1803 to 1811 cond. of Imperial Opera, St Petersburg. Returning to Paris 1811, comp. *Jean de Paris* (1812), his biggest success until *La *Dame blanche* (The White Lady) 1825, which is based on two Scott novels (*The Monastery* and *Guy Mannering*). Last years were haunted by ill-health and money troubles. Also composed chamber mus., concs. for harp and for pf., and was prof. of pf., Paris Cons., 1798–1803, prof. of comp. 1817–26.

Bois (Fr.). Wood. *Avec le bois d'archet*, play with the wood of the bow, not the hair (same as **col legno*); *Les bois*, the woodwind; *Baguette de bois*, wooden-headed drumstick.

Boismortier, Joseph Bodin de (*b* Thionville, 1689; *d* Roissy-en-Brie, 1755). Fr. composer of 3 opéra-ballets, cantatas, works for recorder, bn. conc., and pieces for the then fashionable hurdy-gurdy. Remembered chiefly, however, for his many works for fl., and for composing the first Fr. solo concerto (conc. for vc., bn., or viol, 1729).

Boîte (Fr.). Box, i.e. swell box of org.

Boîte à joujoux, La (The box of toys). Children's ballet in 4 scenes by Debussy, comp. 1913 for pf. to scenario and choreog. by André Hellé, and f.p. Paris 1919. Version for orch. sketched 1914 and completed 1918–19 by **Caplet*, f.p. Paris 1923.

Boito, Arrigo (baptized Enrico) (*b* Padua, 1842; *d* Milan, 1918). It. composer and poet, son of It. painter and Polish countess. Fame chiefly rests on superb libs. for Verdi's last operas, *Otello* (1886) and *Falstaff* (1893). First collab. with Verdi in 1862 on *The Hymn of the Nations*, after which there was coolness between them until he rev. the existing lib. of *Simone Boccanegra* in 1880–1. Studied mus. in Milan and went to Paris on a government travelling scholarship, 1862, with **Faccio*. Met Hugo, Berlioz, Verdi, and Rossini there. Returning to It., espoused cause of mus. reform and redress of neglect of Ger. classics. Comp. opera **Mefistofele* 1866–7. F.p. in Milan 1868 was attended by much publicity about its revolutionary nature; this led to a riot in La Scala between traditionalists and reformers and eventually to the opera's withdrawal on police orders. Rev. version, perf. Bologna 1875, was acclaimed. Wrote libs. for Faccio's *Amleto* (1865), Catalani's *La Falce* (1875), and Ponchielli's *La Gioconda* (1876, under the anagrammatic pseudonym Tobia Gorrio). Also trans. into It. the texts of Beethoven's 9th Sym. and Wagner's *Rienzi* and *Tristan*. Only other pubd. opera, **Nerone*, was begun in 1877 and left unfinished. Completed and rev. by Toscanini, Smareglia, and Tommasini, and prod, Milan 1924. Received hon. doctorates of mus. from both Cambridge and Oxford and was dir., Parma Cons. 1889–97. Correspondence with Verdi is of great interest.

Bolcom, William Elden (*b* Seattle, 1938). Amer. composer. Studied Univ. of Washington 1949–58 and then at Paris Cons. 1959–61 with Milhaud and Messiaen, and at Stanford Univ. 1961–4. Has worked as teacher (at Sch. of Mus. of Univ. of Michigan at Ann Arbor) and critic. Comps. admit wide range of influences, from serialism to collage. They include several str. qts., *Session 2* for vn. and va. (1966), *Black Host* for organ, perc., and tape (1967), 14 *Piano Rags* (1967–70), *Dark Music* for timp. and vc. (1970), *Open House*, ten. and chamber orch. (1975). One of his highly praised works is the *Songs of Innocence and Experience* (48 Blake poems), for 9 solo vv., 2 ch., unacc. ch., children's ch., and orch. (1981–3, f.p. Stuttgart, 1984).

Bolero. Sp. dance in simple triple time, almost same as *Cachucha* but danced by a couple or several couples. Acc. is of (or incl.) the dancers' own vv. and castanets, sometimes with added guitars and tambourines. Introduced *c*.1780.

Boléro. Ballet in 1 act by *Ravel, choreog. Nijinskaya, comp. for Ida Rubinstein in 1928 (prod. Paris Opéra, Nov. 1928). Mus. consists of repetition of theme, in C major almost throughout, in unvarying rhythm and gradual crescendo. Its immense popularity made Ravel world-famous. Later also choreog. Lifar (1941), Béjart (1961), and others.

Bolet, Jorge (*b* Havana, 1914). Cuban-born pianist, now Amer. citizen. Studied Curtis Institute, Penn., 1926–32, later with Godowsky and Rosenthal. European début Amsterdam 1935, Amer. début Philadelphia 1937. Mus. dir. US Army G.H.Q. Tokyo, 1946, when he directed Japanese première of Sullivan's *The Mikado*. Prof. of mus., Indiana Univ. 1968–77, then head of piano dept., Curtis Inst. Soundtrack pianist in film biography of Liszt, *Song Without End* (1960). Outstanding player of Liszt.

Bolshoy Theatre (Russ., 'Great Theatre'), Moscow. Oldest th. in Moscow, home of the Bolshoy opera and ballet cos. Orig. named Petrovsky and built by Englishman (Maddox) in 1780. Destroyed by fire in 1805. Bolshoy Petrovsky opened 1825, but in 1853 its interior was burnt out. Restored by Cavos and reopened in 1856. Seats approx. 2,000 people. Stage is half as wide again as that of CG. There was also a Bolshoy Theatre in St Petersburg, 1783–1859.

Bolt, John (*b* 1564; *d* Louvain, 1640). Eng. virginalist and composer. Fled from Eng. because he was papist and became organist in Brussels 1608–11, thereafter at Louvain.

Bolt, The (*Bolt*). Ballet (choreographic spectacle) in 3 acts, mus. by Shostakovich, Op. 27, lib. by V. Smirnov, choreog. Lopokov. Prod. Leningrad 1931. Also orch. suite 1931.

Bomarzo. Opera ('gothic melodrama of sex and violence') in 2 acts (15 scenes with instr. interludes) by *Ginastera, to lib. by Manuel Mujica Láinez based on his novel. Bomarzo is 16th-cent. It. nobleman. Prod. Washington and NY 1967, Buenos Aires 1972, London 1976 (Eng. trans. by Lionel Salter). Ginastera's cantata *Bomarzo* (1964) for narrator, bar., and orch. is derived from the same literary source by Láinez but is distinct musically.

Bombard. A type of *shawm—but in 14th and 15th cent. was applied in Fr. and Eng. to alto-pitched shawm. Name was probably taken over from an artillery piece of the same name. (The word is derived from the Lat. *bombus*, drone or buzz.)
Note that the *Bombardon has nothing in common with it, being a brass instr., as is the It. *Bombarda*, euphonium.

Bombarda (It.). Euphonium.

Bombarde, Bombardon. Powerful org. *Reed Stop*, often in pedal department and sometimes of 32′ pitch.

Bombardon. (1) Form of bass tuba with 3 piston valves, in B♭, C, CC, F, or E♭. Replaced by *Sax's E♭ or BB♭ bass tubas, 1842 (double letter indicates specimens with wider bore). (2) It. term for bass shawm.

Bonavia, Ferruccio (*b* Trieste, 1877; *d* London, 1950). It.-born violinist and mus. critic. Studied vn., etc. in Milan. For 10 years was member of Hallé Orch., Manchester, under Richter, at same time writing for *Manchester Guardian* on mus. subjects. From 1920 until death a mus. critic of London *Daily Telegraph*. Wrote book on Verdi, and comp. str. mus. (qt., octet, etc.).

Bonci, Alessandro (*b* Cesena, 1870; *d* Viserba, 1940). It. ten. Opera début as Fenton in *Falstaff*, Parma 1893. First visit to London 1900, NY 1906. Especially effective in Bellini, Donizetti, and Rossini.

Bond, Capel (*b* Gloucester, 1730; *d* Coventry, 1790). Eng. composer and org. Dir. and organist first Birmingham Fest., 1768. Pubd. 6 concs., incl. tpt. and bn., in 1766 and 6 anthems in 1769.

Bond, Carrie Jacobs (née Jacobs) (*b* Janesville, Wisc., 1862; *d* Glendale, Calif., 1946). Amer. song composer, among her most popular being 'Just a-wearyin' for you' and 'The end of a perfect day' (of which over 5 million copies were sold).

Bondeville, Emmanuel (*b* Rouen, 1898). Fr. composer and administrator. Art. dir. Radiodiffusion Française 1937–45, dir., Monte Carlo Opera 1945–9, Paris Opéra-Comique 1949–52, and Paris Opéra 1952–70. Comps. incl. *Madame Bovary*, opera (1951), *L'École des Maris*, lyric comedy (1935), *Symphonie lyrique* (1957), *Symphonie choréographique* (1965).

Bonduca, or The British Heroine. Incidental mus. by Purcell to a play adapted from Beaumont and Fletcher on the story of Boadicea (1695).

Bones. Two pieces of animal rib bone held between the fingers and rhythmically clacked— the 19th-cent. 'nigger *minstrel' equivalent of the castanets.

Bongos. Small Cuban drums, bucket-shaped vessels cut out of solid wood, bound with brass, and having strong vellum heads. 2 of them are fixed together by a bar of metal. They are played with the thumb and fingers by dance-band musicians and have been used in comps. by John *McCabe, Varèse, Orff, and Boulez.

Bonini, Severo (*b* Florence, 1582; *d* Florence, 1663.). It. organist and composer of madrigals, motets, and a setting of Rinuccini's *Lamento d'Arianna* (1613). One of first to use monodic style. Author of important treatise *Prima parte de' discorsi e regole sovra la musica* (First part of discourses and rules about music), completed 1649–50.

Bonmarché (Bonmarchié), **Jean de** (*b* ?Douai, *c.*1520–5; *d* ?Madrid, 1570). Belg. composer. Master of choristers, Cambrai Cath. from 1560. From 1565 master of Royal Chapel of Philip II of Spain. Comp. many masses and motets.

Bonne Chanson, La (The Good Song). (1) Settings by *Fauré in 1892–3, Op. 61, of 9 poems by Verlaine, namely *Une Sainte en son auréole ; Puisque l'aube grandit ; La Lune blanche luit dans les bois ; J'allais par des chemins perfides ; J'ai presque peur en vérité ; Avant que tu ne t'en ailles ; Donc ce sera par un clair jour d'été ; N'est ce pas? ; L'hiver a cessé*.

(2) Tone-poem by *Loeffler comp. 1901 and f.p. Boston 1902. Also inspired by Verlaine.

Bonnet, Joseph (Élie Georges Marie) (*b* Bordeaux, 1884; *d* nr. Quebec, 1944). Fr. organist and composer. Pupil of Guilmant; at 22 organist of St Eustache, Paris; toured widely in Europe and Amer. Organ comps. have wide popularity.

Bonnie Annie. Folk tune to which words of 'John Peel' were later fitted by J. W. Graves.

Bononcini, Antonio Maria (*b* Modena, 1677; *d* Rome, 1726). It. composer. Brother of Giovanni *Bononcini and said to be the more talented. Comp. at least 17 operas and 39 cantatas. Was also cellist.

Bononcini, Giovanni (*b* Modena, 1670; *d* Vienna, 1747). It. composer and cellist. Usually spelt his name Buononcini. Elder son of G. M. *Bononcini. Studied in Bologna. Worked in Rome from 1692 and scored success throughout It. with opera *Il trionfo di Camilla* (1696). Went to

Vienna 1697 and was court composer there 1700–11, but also spent time in Rome and Berlin. Invited to London in 1720 to work at newly-founded Royal Acad. of Mus. with Handel as dir. Enjoyed great favour, esp. with the Marlborough family who paid him £500 p.a. Several operas prod. in London over next decade, most successful being *Astarto* (1720, rev. of 1714 Rome version). In 1721 contrib. act to *Muzio Scevola*, the other 2 being by Amadei and Handel. In 1722 wrote anthem for Duke of Marlborough's funeral in Westminster Abbey. In 1732 left Eng. for Fr., scorning to answer an accusation of plagiarism. Lived rest of his life in Paris, Vienna, and Venice. Comp. nearly 50 operas, also masses, oratorios, many cantatas for solo voice, and a large amount of chamber mus.

Bononcini, Giovanni Maria (*b* Montecorone, nr. Modena, 1642; *d* Modena, 1678). It. composer. Head of family of musicians. Employed at court of Duke of Modena. Wrote operas, masses, cantatas, sonatas, etc. Pubd. treatise on mus. 1673.

Bonporti (Buonporti), **Francesco Antonio** (*b* Trento, 1672; *d* Padua, 1748). It. violinist and composer of instr. mus. Comp. 10 'Inventions' for vn. and figured bass, 1712 (Bach's use of word apparently taken from this), also vn. sonatas and minuets.

Bontempi (really Angelini), **Giovanni Andrea** (*b* Perugia, 1624; *d* Brufa, nr. Perugia, 1705). It. musician. Sang as castrato in St Mark's, Venice, 1643–50, when he went to Dresden. Befriended by Schütz, becoming associate Kapellmeister with him in 1656. Wrote 3 operas and several theoretical treatises. Settled in It., 1680, becoming choirmaster Spello 1686.

Bonynge, Richard (*b* Sydney, N.S.W, 1930). Australian cond. and pianist. Studied Sydney Cons., RCM. Cond. début, Rome 1962. Specializes in late 18th- and early 19th-cent. *bel canto* operas, many of them vehicles for his wife, the sop. Joan *Sutherland. CG début 1964, NY Met. 1970. Mus. dir., Australian Opera 1976–84. C.B.E. 1977.

Boobams. Perc. instr. of definite pitch made of lengths of bamboo each having an end covered by a plastic membrane which is struck by the finger or a soft-headed hammer. Pitch determined by length of tubes. Name is an inversion of bamboos.

Boogie-Woogie (or Boogie). Jazz style of pf.-playing originating in early years of 20th cent. but becoming popular from about 1928. One of first exponents was Negro jazz pianist Clarence 'Pine Top' Smith. Prin. feature is ostinato bass in broken octaves.

Boosey & Hawkes, Ltd. London mus. publishers and instr. manufacturers. Boosey founded 1816; Hawkes 1865. Amalgamation 1930. Catalogue incl. works by R. Strauss, Stravinsky, Bartók, Britten, Ginastera, and many young composers. Specialists in brass band mus. Subsidiary cos. in USA, Fr., Ger. Major manufacturer of wind instr. Published magazine *Tempo* from 1939.

Bord. Paris pf.-making firm; est. 1843 and taken over by Pleyel 1934.

Bordes, Charles (*b* La Roche-Corbon, Indre-et-Loire, 1863; *d* Toulon, 1909). Fr. composer. Pupil of César Franck. Organist of Paris church of St Gervais, where he founded a choral body for the perf. of Renaissance church mus. under the name of 'Les Chanteurs de St Gervais' (later an independent body); with Guilmant and d'Indy founded also the Société Schola Cantorum for the study of church mus. (1894), which led to est. of Schola Cantorum of Paris as mus. sch. (1896). Collected and pubd. early church mus. and Basque folk tunes, and comp. mus. for pf., orch., etc. From 1905, at Montpellier, organized perfs. of Rameau operas.

Bordoni, Faustina (*b* Venice, 1700; *d* Venice, 1781). It. mezzo-soprano. Brought up under protection of A. and B. Marcello and taught singing by M. Gasparini. Début Venice 1716. Sang in Venice until 1725 in operas by Albinoni, Lotti, etc. Ger. début Munich 1723, Vienna 1725. First sang in London 1726 in Handel's *Alessandro*. Created 4 other Handel operatic roles 1727–8. Her rivalry with Cuzzoni led to a fight between them on stage in 1727. Returned to It. 1728–32. Married comp. *Hasse in 1730 and thereafter sang chiefly in his operas after he became Kapellmeister at Dresden 1731. Retired from stage 1751. Voice was of exceptional brilliance, with accurate intonation and capable of intense dramatic expression.

Bore. Interior of tube of wind instr. Determines length and proportions of air column and pitch of lowest note obtainable. In brass instr. length of bore is variable by use of valves, in woodwind by opening and closing sideholes.

Borg, Kim (*b* Helsinki, 1919). Finn. bass singer and composer. Studied chemistry and mus., Helsinki. Début Helsinki 1947, in opera at Åarhus 1951. Frequent visits to USA and Eng. Recorded Elgar's *Dream of Gerontius* with Barbirolli. Comp. songs.

Borge, Victor (*b* Copenhagen, 1909). Danish pianist and entertainer. Studied Copenhagen Cons., Berlin Univ. and with Egon Petri. Début Copenhagen 1922. Best known as humorist, dealing amusingly with mus. quirks and oddities.

Borghi, Giovanni Battista (*b* Camerino, 1738; *d* Loreto, 1796). It. organist and composer of at least 25 operas, incl. *Piramo e Tisbe* (1783) and *La Morte di Semiramide* (1791). Studied in Naples. Choirmaster, Macerata Cath. 1759–78, Loreto 1778–96. Also wrote much sacred mus.

Borgioli, Dino (*b* Florence, 1891; *d* Florence, 1960). It. ten. Début, Milan 1914, London 1925 (as Edgardo in *Lucia di Lammermoor*). Often sang at CG and Glyndebourne (1937–9), his Mozart and Rossini style being much admired. Law graduate, also a painter.

Borgström, Hjalmar (*b* Christiania, 1864; *d* Oslo, 1925). Norweg. composer and critic. Wrote 2 syms., pf. conc., vn. conc., tone-poem *John Gabriel Borkman* (1905), and chamber mus.

Bori, Lucrezia (orig. Lucrecia Borja y Gonzalez de Riancho) (*b* Valencia, 1887; *d* NY, 1960). Sp. sop. Trained in Milan. Début Rome 1908 as Micaela in *Carmen*. Sang Manon Lescaut opposite Caruso in Paris 1910. First It. Oktavian, Milan 1911. Début NY Met. 1912 as Manon. Career interrupted by throat operation 1915, but resumed 1919. Member of NY Met. co. 1921–36 and of board of dirs. from 1935.

Boris Godunov. Opera in 4 acts, with prol., by *Mussorgsky to his own lib. based on Pushkin's poetic drama, *The Comedy of the Distress of the Muscovite State, of Tsar Boris, and of Grishka Otrepyev* (1826) and Karamzin's *History of the Russian Empire* (1829). Orig. version comp. 1868–9, rev. 1871–2, 3 scenes prod. St Petersburg 1873 and complete opera 1874, but withdrawn after 25 perfs. Cut, re-orchestrated, and rev. by Rimsky-Korsakov after Mussorgsky's death and thus prod. St Petersburg 1896. This version rev., with some cuts restored, 1906, prod. NY and London 1913. Orig. versions of 1869 and 1872 pubd. Leningrad 1928 in edn. prepared by Prof. Pavel Lamm of Moscow and perf. Leningrad 1928, London (SW) and Paris 1935. The 1869 version had 7 scenes which were altered and re-arranged and an extra (Kromy Forest) scene added. Musicological controversy rages on the 'correct' version to use, but there is a growing tendency to prefer the Mussorgsky orchestration. In 1975 David Lloyd-Jones pubd. an edn., for which he had the use of MS. sources unknown to Lamm, which also corrects errors of detail and transcr. in Lamm. Vol. I of Lloyd-Jones contains Mussorgsky's 1872 version of prol. and 4 acts and Vol. II the 1869 version of Act 2, the discarded 'St Basil' scene, with variants and other scenes. A re-orch. version by Shostakovich exists (1940, prod. Leningrad 1959). Title-role inseparably assoc. with *Chaliapin and *Christoff.

Borkh, Inge (orig. Ingeborg Simon) (*b* Mannheim, 1921). Ger.-born Swiss sop. Began career as actress 1937, then vocal training in Milan and Salzburg. Début Lucerne 1940. Int. career followed success in Menotti's *The Consul* in Lucerne 1952. US début San Francisco 1953, London 1955 in concert perf. of *Elektra*, at CG 1959 in *Salome*. Renowned for dramatic Strauss roles and Verdi's Lady Macbeth, esp. as member of Stuttgart Opera.

Bořkovec, Pavel (*b* Prague, 1894; *d* Prague, 1972). Cz. composer. Studied privately with J. B.

Foerster and Křička and at Prague Cons. with Suk. In 1920s was a leading figure in Czech neoclassic sch. Taught comp. Prague Acad. 1946–64. Comps. incl. 3 syms. (1926–7, 1955, 1959), 2 sinfoniettas (1947, 1969), 2 pf. concs. (1931, 1950), vn. conc. (1933), vc. conc. (1951), opera *Tom Thumb* (1945–7), *Dreams*, 7 songs for low v. and orch. (1962), chamber mus., etc.

Borodin, Alexander (Porfiryevich) (*b* St Petersburg, 1833; *d* St Petersburg, 1887). Russ. composer, one of the group known as 'The *Five'. Illegitimate son of Russ. prince. Showed childhood talent for mus. and science, composing pf. pieces and fl. conc. Entered medical profession, graduating in 1855 from Acad. of Medicine and Surgery, St Petersburg. Studied science in Heidelberg and elsewhere 1859–62. Appointed ass. prof. of chemistry, Acad. of Medicine 1862. Meeting with *Balakirev 1862 persuaded him to devote leisure to serious study of mus. while continuing his scientific work, which incl. foundation of School of Medicine for Women, where he lectured from 1872 to his death. His 1st sym. was prod. 1869, but he had already tasted failure with comic opera *The Bogatyrs* in 1867. His Sym. No. 2 in B minor was also a failure at f.p. 1877, the year in which he visited Liszt at Weimar. Liszt in 1880 ensured a perf. of the 1st Sym. at Baden-Baden which initiated Borodin's popularity outside Russia. In 1869 his friend Stasov suggested an opera on the subject of *Prince Igor*. This appealed to Borodin's nationalism, but difficulties with the lib., plus the interruptions from his scientific career, made comp. slow and the work, Borodin's masterpiece, was never finished, but was completed by Rimsky-Korsakov and Glazunov. Melodic and harmonic originality of Borodin's style are best heard in *Prince Igor*, but the 2nd sym., the 2 str. qts., and the tone-poem *In the Steppes of Central Asia* (1880) ensure his survival.

Prin. works:

OPERA: *Prince Igor* (unfinished, completed by *Rimsky-Korsakov and *Glazunov) (1869–70, 1874–87).
ORCH: Syms.: No. 1 in E♭ (1862–7), No. 2 in B minor (1869–76), No. 3 in A minor (1885–6, unfinished, completed and orch. by Glazunov); tone-picture *In the Steppes of Central Asia (V sredney Azii) (1880); Nocturne from 2nd Str. Qt., orch. Sargent.
CHAMBER MUSIC: Str. Qts.: No. 1 in A major (1877–9), No. 2 in D (1881–7); Pf. Quintet in C minor (1862).
PIANO: *Petite Suite* (1885), orch. Glazunov; Scherzo in A♭; *Polka, Requiem, Dead March*, and *Mazurka* in coll. *Paraphrases on theme of *Chopsticks* (1880).

Boroni (Buroni), **Antonio** (*b* Rome, 1738; *d* Rome, 1792). It. composer and choirmaster. Studied under Padre *Martini and at Naples. Followed Jommelli as Kapellmeister at Stuttgart 1771–7. Choirmaster, St Peter's, Rome, 1778–92.

Comp. 21 operas, masses, motets, and contrib. with J. C. Bach to a book of odes pubd. in London 1775.

Borowski, Felix (*b* Burton, Westmorland, Eng., 1872; *d* Chicago, 1956). Eng.-born composer, violinist, and teacher, of Polish and Brit. parentage (later Amer. citizen). Studied Cologne Cons. Went to USA 1897 as teacher at Chicago Mus. Coll., becoming pres. 1916–25. Pres., Civic Music Assoc., 1926–32. Wrote mus. criticism for Chicago *Sun* and other papers. Comp. 3 syms., pf. conc., ballets, opera, and 3 org. sonatas.

Borre, Borree, Borry. Old Eng. spellings of *Bourrée.

Borri, Giovanni Battista (*b* Bologna, *fl.* 1665–88). It. composer who worked principally in Bologna. Comp. oratorio *La Susanna*, mass and other church mus., and instr. works such as *sinfonie a tre* (2 vn. and vc.).

Borsdorf, (Friedrich) **Adolph** (*b* Dittmansdorf, Saxony, 1854; *d* London, 1923). Ger. hn. player who studied in Dresden but in 1879 settled in Eng. where he joined CG orch. and became 1st hn. in Richter's London orch. Later with Scottish Orch., Queen's Hall Orch. and LSO. Superb technician but especially noted for beauty of phrasing in such works as Brahms's hn. trio. As a teacher at RCM (from 1882) and RAM (from 1897) trained whole generation of English hn.-players, incl. his son Oscar.

Bortkevich, Sergey (Eduardovich) (*b* Kharkov, 1877; *d* Vienna, 1952). Russ. composer. Studied St Petersburg and Leipzig. Lived in Berlin 1901–14. Left Russia after revolution, living in Istanbul, Berlin, and Vienna. Comps. (in late 19th-cent. Ger. idiom) incl. 3 pf. concs. (1 for left hand), vn. conc., vc. conc., and symphonic poem *Othello*.

Bortnyansky, Dmitry (Stepanovich) (*b* Glukhov, Ukraine, 1751; *d* St Petersburg, 1825). Russ. composer who studied in Moscow and in St Petersburg under Galuppi. When Galuppi left Russia, Empress Catherine gave Bortnyansky funds to follow him to Venice in 1768; later studied in Bologna, Rome, and Naples. His operas *Creonte* and *Quinto Fabio* were performed respectively in Venice (1776) and Modena (1778). On return to Russia in 1779, became dir. of Empress's church choir (re-named Imperial Kapelle in 1796) which he reformed and for which he comp. large amount of mus. His sacred works were pubd. in 10 vols. in St Petersburg under editorship of Tchaikovsky (1885).

Boschi, Giuseppe Maria (*fl.* 1698–1744). It. bass. Sang at Venice 1707 in operas by Lotti. In London 1710–11, creating role of Argante in Handel's *Rinaldo*. In Dresden 1717–20. From 1720 to 1728 sang in London in all 32 operas prod. by Handel's Royal Academy, incl. 13 by Handel, 7 by Bononcini, and 6 by Ariosti. Returned to Venice

1729 and became member of choir of St Mark's. His wife was the cont. Francesca Vanini (d Venice, 1744).

Borwick, Leonard (b Walthamstow, 1868; d Le Mans, 1925). Eng. pianist, pupil of Clara Schumann at Frankfurt 1883–9, making début there 1889. London début 1890. Played Brahms's D minor conc. in Vienna under Richter 1891. After 1912 took up pf. works of Debussy and Ravel, making pf. versions of the former's *L'Après-midi d'un faune* and *Fêtes*.

Bösendorfer. Viennese pf.-making firm, founded 1828 by Ignaz Bösendorfer (b Vienna, 1796; d Vienna, 1859) and carried on by son Ludwig from 1859. *Bösendorfersaal* (concert-room) opened 1872. Taken over by Jasper Corp., 1966.

Boskovich, Alexander (Urijah) (b Cluj, Transylvania, 1907; d Tel Aviv, 1964). Romanian-born Israeli composer, cond., and pianist. Studied Vienna Acad. 1924–9 and in Paris with Dukas, Boulanger, and Cortot. Cond. Cluj State Opera 1930–8. Emigrated to Palestine 1938, teaching at Tel Aviv Acad. 1945–64. Mus. critic, Israeli newspaper *Ha'aretz* 1955–64. Comps. incl. Suite, *The Golden Chain* (1937), vn. conc. (1942), ob. conc. (1943, rev. 1960), *Semitic Suite* for orch. (1946–7), *Daughter of Israel*, cantata (1960), *Concerto da camera*, vn. and 10 instr. (1962), and *The Hidden Light* (*Ha'or haganuz*), oratorio (1964).

Boskovsky, Willi (b Vienna, 1909). Austrian violinist and cond. Educated Vienna Acad. Joined Vienna P.O., 1933, co-leader 1939–71. Cond. of celebrated New Year's Day Vienna concerts of Strauss waltzes. Cond. Vienna Strauss Orch. from 1969.

Bossa-nova. Brazilian term that first appeared in 1959 in a song 'Desafinado' by Jobim which was extremely complex in melody and harmony, but its innovation was its radical change in the rhythmic structure of the samba. In 1960 bossa-nova became associated with social protest. 'Bossa' in Rio slang means 'shrewdness'.

Bossi, Marco Enrico (b Salò, Lake Garda, 1861; d at sea, 1925). It. organist, teacher, and composer, one of chief figures in revival of non-operatic It. mus. at end of 19th cent. Studied Bologna and Milan 1871–81. Organist and choirmaster, Como Cath. 1881–91; prof. of org. and theory, Naples Cons., 1891–5. Dir. Liceo Benedetto Marcello, Venice, 1896–1902, dir. Liceo Musicale, Bologna, 1902–12, dir. Academy of St Cecilia, Rome, 1916–23. Wrote large body of works, incl. 3 operas, org. conc., and chamber mus., but best known are 3 choral works, *Canticum Canticorum* (Leipzig 1900), *Il paradiso perduto* (Augsburg 1903), and *Giovanna d'Arco* (Cologne 1914). His son Renzo (b Como, 1883; d Milan, 1965) was also organist, composer, and cond.

Boston Symphony Orchestra. One of great orchs. of world, founded at Boston, Mass., 1881 by Henry Lee Higginson who endowed it with a million dollars. First concert 22 Oct. 1881, cond. by Sir George *Henschel who was cond. 1881–4. He was succeeded by Wilhelm *Gericke 1884–9, *Nikisch 1889–93, Emil *Paur 1893–8, Gericke 1898–1906, Karl *Muck 1906–8, Max *Fiedler 1908–12, Muck 1912–18, Henri *Rabaud 1918–19, Pierre *Monteux 1919–24, Serge *Koussevitzky 1924–49, Charles *Munch 1949–62, Erich *Leinsdorf 1962–9, William *Steinberg 1969–72, Seiji *Ozawa from 1973. Koussevitzky's 25-year tenure was outstanding for its encouragement of new works both by Amer. composers and by est. composers such as Prokofiev, Stravinsky, and Bartók.

Bote and Bock. Ger. mus. publishing firm, founded in Berlin in 1838 by Eduard Bote and Gustav Bock. Remained in Bock family until 1935 when it was reorganized as limited co. under direction of Robert Lienau, dir. of R. & W. Lienau. Wiesbaden branch, 1948. Publisher of mus. of many Ger. composers incl. Reger, Blacher, and Einem.

Bottesini, Giovanni (b Crema, Lombardy, 1821; d Parma, 1889). It. virtuoso of db. which he took up because there was a vacancy at Milan Cons. in 1835 only for a db. student. Extraordinary mastery of the instr. soon acknowledged. Settled in Havana, Cuba, as prin. db. of orch. there. First played in London 1849. Used 3-str. *basso da camera* made by Testore of Milan, with a bow more like that for a vc. Was successful opera cond. in Paris 1855–7 and in London 1871. Dir. of opera ths. at Palermo, 1861–3, Barcelona, and Cairo. Cond. f.p. of Verdi's *Aida*, Cairo, 1871. Comp. many pieces for db., several operas, and an oratorio *The Garden of Olivet* (Norwich, 1887).

Bouche fermée (Fr.). Closed-mouth singing, i.e. humming.

Bouchés, Sons (Fr.). Stopped notes in hn. playing (see also *Gestopft* and *Schmetternd*).

Boucourechliev, André (b Sofia, 1925). Bulg.-born composer and pianist, Fr. citizen since 1956. Studied Sofia State Acad. 1946–9, École Normale de Musique, Paris, 1949–51, Saarbrücken Cons. 1955 (pf. with Gieseking), and at Darmstadt summer courses 1958–62. Has worked for radio in Milan and Paris. Teacher of pf. École Normale 1954–60. Mus. critic of various Fr. publications since 1957. Author of books on Schumann, Chopin, Beethoven, and Stravinsky. Comps. incl. pf. sonata (1959), *Texte I* (tape, 1959), *Texte II* (tape, 1960), *Musiques nocturnes*, cl., harp, pf. (1966), *Archipel 1* for 2 pf., 2 percussionists (1967), *Archipel 2*, str. qt. (1968), *Archipel 3*, pf., 6 percussionists (1969), *Archipel 4*, pf. (1970), *Archipel 5*, 6 instr. (1970); *Ombres*, str. (1970); *Faces*, orch. (1972); pf. conc. (1974–5). The *Archipel* works are in open form, generally perf. in 2 or more versions per concert. In *open form the sequence and/or structure of some parts of a work can be varied by the performers.

Bouffons (or *Mattachins*, or *Matassins*). Old sword dance of men wearing armour of gilded cardboard.

Bouffons, Querelle des. 'War of the Comedians' in Paris, 1752–4. A quarrel over an opera by *Destouches led to the invitation to Paris of troupe of It. comedians, who made much stir with their perf. of Pergolesi's intermezzo *La *serva padrona*. The Fr. literary and mus. world split into 2 factions, favouring respectively It. and Fr. opera (as exemplified by Rameau). Rousseau and Diderot joined the controversy on the It. side.

Boughton, Rutland (*b* Aylesbury, 1878; *d* London, 1960). Eng. composer. Studied RCM under Stanford and Walford Davies 1900–1. Early orch. works perf. 1901 and 1902. From 1904 to 1911 on staff of Birmingham Midland Institute of Mus. Choral work, *Midnight* (1907), perf. Birmingham Fest. 1909. Inspired by Wagner's theory of mus. drama, conceived idea of an Eng. Bayreuth at Glastonbury for perf. of series of mus. dramas, based on the Arthurian legends, by himself, with Reginald Buckley as librettist. First fest. held 1914 when his The *Immortal Hour* (1912–13) was perf. In 1916 his *Bethlehem* (1915) and parts of *The Birth of Arthur* (1908–9) were perf. In 1920 the Glastonbury Players perf. *The Immortal Hour* and other works at the Old Vic, London, preceding f.p. at Glastonbury in Aug. of the complete *Birth of Arthur* and *The Round Table* (1916). In 1922 his *Alkestis* (1920–22), a 3-act setting of Gilbert Murray's trans. of Euripides, was perf. at Glastonbury and, in 1926, *The Queen of Cornwall* (1923–4), based on Hardy's verse-play. Greatest success came in 1922 with the long London run of Birmingham Repertory Th.'s prod. of *The Immortal Hour*, with Gwen Ffrangcon-Davies. *Alkestis* was prod. CG 1924. In 1934 *The Lily Maid* was prod. in London. In 1943–4 Boughton wrote the mus. drama *Galahad*, followed in 1945–6 by *Avalon*. Also comp. 3 syms. (1904, 1927, 1937) and other instr. works. His daughter Joy (1913–63) was a talented oboist.

Boulanger, Lili (Juliette Marie Olga) (*b* Paris, 1893; *d* Mézy, 1918). Fr. composer, sister of Nadia *Boulanger. Studied at Paris Cons. 1912 with G. Caussade and P. Vidal, winning 1st *Grand Prix de Rome* in 1913 (the first woman to do so) with cantata *Faust et Hélène*. Career constantly interrupted by ill-health, but comps. show exceptional gifts. They incl. mus. for Maeterlinck's *Princesse Maleine*, 2 symphonic poems, 2 Psalms with orch., str. qt., etc.

Boulanger, Nadia (Juliette) (*b* Paris, 1887; *d* Paris, 1979). Fr. composer and cond. but principally known as outstandingly influential teacher of comp. At Paris Cons. won 1st prizes in harmony, counterpoint, fugue, org., and acc.

Studied comp. with Fauré. Awarded 2nd *Grand Prix de Rome* 1908 for cantata *La Sirène*. Teacher at Paris Cons. from 1946, at École Normale de Musique, Paris, 1920–39, in USA 1940–6, and at Amer. Cons., Fontainebleau, from 1921 (dir. 1950). The list of her pupils, many of them private, is long and incl. many distinguished composers, esp. Americans (Copland, Harris, Thomson, Carter, and Piston). Eng. pupils incl. Lennox Berkeley and Hugo Cole. Frequent visitor to USA, studied at Juilliard Sch., etc. Was among first in 20th cent. to rediscover Monteverdi madrigals, making famous 78 r.p.m. records. Noted cond. of Fauré's *Requiem*. First woman to cond. complete concert of Royal Phil. Soc., London, 4 Nov. 1937. Cond. Boston S.O. (1938), NY P.O. (1939), and Hallé Orch. (1963). Cond. f.p. of Stravinsky's *Dumbarton Oaks Concerto*, Washington D.C., 1938. Hon. C.B.E. 1977.

Boulevard Solitude. Opera in 7 scenes by *Henze to lib. by G. Weil after W. Jöckisch, being modernized version of Prévost's *Manon Lescaut*. Prod. Hanover 1952, London 1962. Santa Fe 1967.

Boulez, Pierre (*b* Montbrison, 1925). Fr. composer and cond. Intended for career in engineering, went to Paris Cons. in 1942, studying comp. with Messiaen until 1945. Studied counterpoint with Andrée Vaurabourg-Honegger and 12-note technique with René Leibowitz. In 1946 became mus. dir. and cond. of Barrault-Renaud co. at Théâtre Marigny, Paris, travelling with them to N. and S. Amer. and European cities during next 10 years. In 1953, with Barrault's help, founded the Concerts Marigny, later re-named Domaine musical when the venue was moved to the Odéon in 1959. In this series Boulez introduced to Paris audiences not only works by Schoenberg, Webern, and Berg, but mus. of his contemporaries. At this time, est. contacts with Maderna and Stockhausen and joined teaching staff at the Int. summer sch. for new mus., Darmstadt. In early 1960s comp. engagements increased and dir. several major European orchs., incl. the Vienna P.O. at Salzburg, 1962. Cond. first Fr. p. of Berg's *Wozzeck*, Paris 1963. In 1963 visiting prof. at Harvard Univ.; made Amer. conducting début with Cleveland Orch. 1964. In 1966 cond. *Parsifal* at Bayreuth and in same year severed connection with Paris life as a protest over a ministerial appointment. Guest cond. BBC S.O. in London 1964 and in USA in 1965 and on its Russ. tour in 1967. Gave up conductorship of Domaine musical, 1967. Prin. guest cond., Cleveland Orch., 1969–70 and chief cond. of the BBC S.O. 1971–5 and NY P.O. 1971–7. His BBC period was notable for remarkable perfs. of 20th cent. music, especially Schoenberg, Webern, and Debussy. Cond. centenary cycle of Wagner's *Ring* at Bayreuth, 1976. From 1976 dir. Fr. Govt.'s research institute into techniques of modern comp. (IRCAM). Cond. first complete perf. of Berg's *Lulu*, Paris, 1979.

Boulez's importance and originality as an *avant-garde* composer were evident from the first. He came to prominence with the *Sonatine* for fl. and pf. and the Pf. Sonata No. 1. The cantata *Le visage nuptial*, to poems by René Char made use of choral speech, spoken glissandi, crying, and whispering. Boulez's orthodox use of serialism is found in *Structures I* for 2 pf. *Le Marteau sans maître*, to text by Char (f.p. Baden-Baden June 1955, cond. Rosbaud) made him a celebrity. His most ambitious work to date is *Pli selon pli* for sop. and orch. This 5-part portrait of Mallarmé developed from *Improvisation sur Mallarmé*. These are now flanked by 2 outer movements, *Don* and *Tombeau*, all 5 containing extracts from Mallarmé sung or declaimed in many ways. There are elements of indeterminacy in the 3 sections of the improvisations. The work has constantly been radically rev., in accordance with Boulez's view that a comp. is never finished.

Boulez experimented with *musique concrète* in early 1950s and combined it with elec. sounds in *Poésie pour pouvoir* (1958). His use of indeterminacy dates from about 1957 with the 3rd Pf. Sonata, the 5 movements of which can be played in any order except for the 3rd which must be central. Like Mahler and Richard Strauss, Boulez has pursued parallel careers as cond. and composer. Prin. comps.:

ORCH: *Strophes* (1957), re-comp. as *Don* (1960–2); *Doubles* (1958), expanded as *Figures-Doubles-Prismes* (1964); *Livre pour Cordes* (1968–); . . . *explosante fixe* . . . , unspecified forces (1971), fl., cl., tpt. (1972), fl., cl., tpt., hp., vibraphone, vn., va., vc., elec. (1973, rev. 1974); *Mémoriales* (1973–5); *Rituel in memoriam Bruno Maderna* (1974–5); *Notations* (rev. of early pf. pieces, 1981); *Répons*, 24 players, 6 instr. soloists, elec. (1981).

ENS: *Le Visage nuptial* (Char), sop., alto, chamber orch. (1946), rev. sop., alto, women's ch., orch. (1950–1); *Éclat*, 15 instr. (1965), expanded as *Éclats/Multiples* (1970, in progress); *Domaines*, cl., 21 instr. (1968).

VOCAL: *Le *Soleil des Eaux* (Char), mus. for radio play (1948), rev. as cantata for sop., ten., bass, chamber orch. (1950), rev. sop., ten., bass, ch., orch. (1958), rev. sop. and ch. (1965); *Le *Marteau sans Maître* (Char), alto, alto fl., guitar, vib., xylorimba, perc., va. (1952–4, rev. 1957); *Improvisations sur Mallarmé* I, sop., hp., bells, vib., perc. (1957), alternative version 1962, II, sop., celesta, hp., pf., bells, vib., perc. (1957), III, sop., orch. (1959) 2nd. version (1983); *Tombeau*, sop., orch. (1959, rev. 1962); *Don*, sop., orch. (1960–2); *Pli selon pli* (*Don, Improvisation sur Mallarmé I–III, Tombeau*) (1957–62); *e.e.cummings ist der dichter*, 16 solo vv., 24 instr. (1970–).

INCIDENTAL MUSIC: *Ainsi parla Zarathoustra* (1974).

PIANO: Sonatas: No. 1 (1946), No. 2 (1948), No. 3 (1955–7); *Structures*, Book I, 2 pf. (1952) complete (1953), Book II, 2 pf. (1956–61).

CHAMBER MUSIC: *Sonatine*, fl., pf. (1946); *Livre pour quatuor*, str. qt. (1948–9, rev. as *Livre pour Cordes*, 1968–); *Messagesquisse*, 7 vc. (1977).

TAPE: *Etudes I, sur un son*, II, *sur sept sons*, 1-track tape (1952); *Symphonie Méchanique*, 1-track tape (1955).

Boult, (Sir) **Adrian** (Cedric) (*b* Chester, 1889; *d* Hampstead, 1983). Eng. cond. Began mus. education at Christ Church, Oxford, under H. P. *Allen. At Leipzig Cons. 1912–13. While there studied Nikisch's methods of conducting. Came into prominence 1918–19 with outstanding perfs. of works by Elgar, Vaughan Williams, and Holst, all of whom became close friends. Teaching staff RCM 1919–30. Cond. London season of Diaghilev ballet and operas at CG. Toured Europe introducing Brit. mus. to foreign audiences. Championship of Eng. composers was dominant but not exclusive element in his career. Cond., CBSO 1924–30. Appointed mus. dir., BBC, 1930–42, and chief cond., BBC S.O., 1931–50. Prin. cond. LPO 1951–7. Guest cond. of world's leading orchs. Returned to RCM staff 1962–6. Author of handbook on conducting and of autobiography. Knighted 1937. C.H. 1969. Retired 1979.

Bourdon. (1) Dull-toned pedal stop found on every org., however small; end-plugged; 8' length and 16' pitch.

(2) Lowest str. on the lute or vn.

(3) Very large and deep-toned bell.

(4) Drone str. of hurdy-gurdy.

(5) Drone pipe of bagpipe.

Bourgault-Ducoudray, Louis Albert (*b* Nantes, 1840; *d* Vernouillet, Paris, 1910). Fr. composer and scholar. Student at Paris Cons. under Thomas; then cond. of a Paris choral body which revived comps. of Palestrina, Bach, and others. Prof. of History of Mus. at Cons., 1878–1908. In 1874 went to Greece on official mission, and studied folk mus. on which he became authority. Pubd. colls. of folk-songs from Greece, Brittany, Scotland, and the Middle East. Comp. 5 operas and choral works, incl. *Stabat Mater*.

Bourgeois, Derek (David) (*b* Kingston-on-Thames, 1941). Eng. composer. Studied Cambridge Univ. and RCM (1963–5). Lecturer in mus., Bristol Univ., from 1971. Comps. incl. syms., concs., cantatas, str. qt., vn. sonatas, variations for 2 db. and orch., brass quintets, org. sym., etc.

Bourgeois Gentilhomme, Le (The would-be gentleman). *Comédie-ballet* in 5 acts by Molière (Jean-Baptiste Poquelin), written in 1670 for court of Louis XIV. Mus. for f.p. comp. by *Lully. In 1912, for his Op. 60 (the first version of *Ariadne auf Naxos*), R. Strauss comp. incidental mus. for adaptation by Hofmannsthal (*Der Bürger als*

Edelmann). Some of Lully's mus. was quoted. In 1916, for second version of *Ariadne auf Naxos*, the play was abandoned and Strauss expanded the incid. mus. in 1917 to 17 items for a further adaptation of *Le bourgeois gentilhomme* by Hofmannsthal. This was f.p. Berlin, 9 April 1918, prod. by Max Reinhardt. From this Strauss arr. a Suite for orch. comprising: 1. *Overture*, 2. *Minuet*, 3. *The fencing master*, 4. *Entrance and dance of the tailors*, 5. *Minuet of Lully*, 6. *Courante*, 7. *Entrance of Cléonte* (after Lully), 8. *Prelude, Act 2 (Intermezzo)*, 9. *The Dinner (Table music and dance of the kitchen boy)*. Nos. 1–4 and 8–9 are from the 1912 mus., Nos. 5–7 from the 1917 reworking. F.p. of Suite, Vienna 1920; f. Eng. p. Manchester 1921.

Bourgeois, Louis (*b* Paris, *c*.1510; *d* Paris, *c*.1561). Fr. church musician, in Geneva 1541–57 where he played leading part in compiling Genevan Psalter. Developed a system of sight-reading. Pubd. settings of 83 psalms, 1561.

Bourguignon, Francis de (*b* St Gilles, 1890; *d* Brussels, 1961). Belg. composer and pianist. Accompanist to Melba in Australia. Comp. sym., concs., chamber mus. Taught harmony at Brussels Cons. 1939–55.

Bournemouth Symphony Orchestra. Title adopted in 1954 by Bournemouth Municipal Orch., founded 1893 by Dan *Godfrey and famous for its encouragement of mus. by Eng. composers. Godfrey was succeeded, 1934, by Richard Austin. Other conds.: Rudolf Schwarz 1946–51, Charles Groves 1951–61, Constantin Silvestri 1961–9, George Hurst 1969–71, Paavo Berglund 1972–9, Uri Segal 1980–3, Rudolf Barshai from 1983.

Bourrée (Fr.; Old Eng. *Borry, Borree,* etc.). A lively dance style very like the gavotte, in quadruple time beginning with an up-beat. It is sometimes found in the classical suite in a ternary arrangement: (a) 1st Bourrée, (b) 2nd Bourrée, (c) 1st Bourrée again.

Boutade (Fr.). Improvised dance or other comp.

Boutique fantasque, La. (The Fantastic Toyshop). Ballet in 1 act with mus. arr. from Rossini's *Soirées musicales*, and other pieces, by *Respighi to lib. by Derain. Choreog. Massine. Prod. London 1919.

Bovicelli, Giovanni Battista (*b* Assisi, *fl.* 1592–4). It. singer at Milan Cath. and author (1594) of important work on vocal figuration and ornamentation.

Bow. Flexible stick with horsehair (usually) stretched across it, used to produce sound vibrations from strings of vn., va., vc., db., and other str. instr. Until 17th cent. bow was convex. As vn. technique developed, new forms of concave bow were devised, with hairs kept in place and at an even spread by means of metal ferrule through which hair passed as it left the nut, or 'frog' at

one end of the bow. Prin. developer of modern bow was François *Tourte, *c*.1785.

Bowed Lyre. Instr. known in Middle Ages by variety of names—cruit, crot, rota, rotta, crwth, crouthe, chorus, and others—of which the Welsh *crwth has survived longest. The bowed lyre was made from one piece, the yoke's resonator and pillars being hollowed out and the soundboard added. Fitted with plain pegs which required a tuning key.

Bowen, (Edwin) **York** (*b* Crouch End, 1884; *d* London, 1961). Eng. composer and pianist. At RAM 1898–1905 and later on staff. Best known for short pf. pieces but wrote sym. (1912), 3 pf. concs. (1904, 1906, 1908), vn. conc. (1920), and va. conc.

Bower, (Sir) **John Dykes** (*b* Gloucester, 1905; *d* Orpington, 1981). Eng. organist. Studied Cambridge Univ. Organist Truro Cath. (1926), New Coll., Oxford (1929), Durham Cath. (1933), St Paul's Cath., London (1936–67). Prof. of organ, RCM, 1936–69. Knighted 1968.

Bowing. (1) Style or method in which bow is applied to str. of instr.
(2) Marking of score (often by cond.) to indicate to the player which notes should be played to an up (V) or down (Π) stroke of the bow.
(3) Particular types of bowing technique incl. *spiccato, sautillé, staccato, ricochet, saltato, col legno.*

Bowles, Paul (Frederic) (*b* NY, 1910). Amer. composer. Studied with *Copland and *Thomson. Collector of folk mus. in Sp., N. Africa, C. and S. America, results influencing his exotic and colourful mus. Has comp. much chamber mus., 3 operas (2 to texts by Lorca), 5 ballets, incl. *Yankee Clipper* (1936), film mus. and much th. mus. (for plays by Tennessee Williams, Saroyan, Koestler, and Hellman). Also successful as novelist (e.g. *The Sheltering Sky*, 1949).

Bowman, James (Thomas) (*b* Oxford, 1941). Eng. counterten. Studied Oxford Univ. Début London 1967 as Oberon in Britten's *A Midsummer Night's Dream*, a role he has made his own. His perf. led Britten to compose the Voice of Apollo in *Death in Venice* for him (Aldeburgh 1973). Has sung with EOG, Early Music Consort, Glyndebourne, CG, ENO, Scottish Opera, etc. Has sung many of the castrato roles in Handel operas.

Boyce, Bruce (*b* London, Ontario, 1910). Canadian bar. Prof. RAM from 1956. Many opera perfs., also Bach Passions and Delius works with Beecham.

Boyce, William (*b* London, 1711; *d* London, 1779). Eng. composer and organist. Boy chorister, St Paul's Cath., then pupil of Maurice Greene. Organist of Oxford Chapel, Vere Street, 1734, and became known as composer of masques and oratorios. Organist, St Michael's, Cornhill, 1736, also becoming composer to Chapel Royal. Appointed cond., 3 Choirs Fest., 1737. Organist, Allhallows the Great and Less, Thane Street, 1749. D.Mus., Oxford, 1749. Succeeded Greene as Master of the King's Musick, 1755. Organist, Chapel Royal, 1758. Resigned from St Michael's 1768, dismissed from Allhallows 1769. Increasing deafness, which had first manifested itself in his youth, caused him to give up other posts c.1770. Retired to Kensington to edit a coll. of English Cathedral Music, a task projected by Greene who bequeathed to Boyce the material he had collected. Boyce's 3 vols. remained in use for almost 150 years. His comps. incl. masques, odes, ovs., church anthems and services, trio sonatas, and 8 syms., of which the modern revival is due to the researches and enthusiasm of Constant *Lambert. The song *Heart of Oak was comp. by Boyce in 1759 for the pantomime Harlequin's Invasion.

Boyd, Anne (b Sydney, N.S.W., 1946). Australian composer. Studied N.S.W. Cons. and Sydney Univ. (comp. with *Sculthorpe). Went to Eng. 1972, studying at York Univ. with Mellers and Rands. Lecturer in mus. Sussex Univ. 1975–7. Head of Mus. Dept., Hong Kong Univ. from 1980. Works incl.: The Voice of the Phoenix (1971) (orch., incl. amplified instr. and optional synthesizer); As Far As Crawls the Toad (1970, rev. 1972), th. piece for 5 young percussionists; 2 str. qts. (1968, rev. 1971, and 1973); The Rose Garden (1971), th. piece for singing actress, ch., and chamber ens.; The Metamorphoses of the Solitary Female Phoenix (1971), wind quintet, pf., perc.; As it leaves the Bell (1973), pf., harp, perc.; Summer Nights (1976), alto and str., perc., harp; As All Waters Flow (1976), 5 female vv., chamber ens.; As I Crossed a Bridge of Dreams (1975), 12 unacc. vv.; Anklung (1974), pf.; Bencharong (1976), str.; The Death of Captain Cook, oratorio, sop., ten., bar., ch., and orch. (1978); The Little Mermaid, children's opera (1978); The Beginning of the Day, children's opera (1980); Anklung 2, vn. (1980).

Boyden, David (Dodge) (b Westport, Conn., 1910). Amer. musicologist and expert on str.instr. Studied Columbia Univ., Hartt Sch. of Mus., Harvard Univ. Teacher at Univ. of Calif. 1938–75. Author of book on counterpoint and history of vn.-playing (1965).

Boyhood's End. Cantata for ten. and pf. by *Tippett on texts by W. H. Hudson. Comp. 1943.

Bozay, Attila (b Balatonfiizfo, Hungary, 1939). Hung. composer. Studied with Farkas at Budapest Acad. 1958–62. Mus. influenced by serialism and folk-derived rhythms in manner of Bartók. Works incl. Papirszeletek (Paper Slips), song-cycle (1962); wind quintet (1962); str. qts. No. 1 (1964), No. 2 (1971); Variations for pf. (1964); Pezzo concertato for va. and orch. (1966); Pezzo sinfonico for orch. (1967); Labyrinth, ens. (1973).

Bozza, Eugène (b Nice, 1905). Fr. composer and cond. Studied Paris Cons. (1st Grand Prix de Rome

1934). Prin. cond. Opéra-Comique 1939–48. Composer of 3 operas, 4 syms., oratorio, vn. conc., pf. conc., and mus. for wind ens.

Br. Short for Bratsche(n) (Ger.), i.e. viola(s).

Brabançonne, La. Belg. nat. anthem. Written and comp. at time of 1830 demonstration in Brussels which led to separation of Belg. from Holland. Author of words was Fr. actor then in Brussels, named Jenneval, and composer was François van *Campenhout. Name comes from 'Brabant'.

'Braccio' and 'Gamba'. All *viols were held downwards and to them was given the general name of Viole da gamba, i.e. 'leg-viols', a description afterwards restricted to latest survivor of the family, bass viol.
The smaller members of the vn. family were held on the shoulder, and, by analogy, all members of this family (incl. even those which from their size had to be held downwards) came to be called Viole da braccio, i.e. 'arm-viols'. Later this term became limited to the alto vn., i.e. the va. (still in Ger. called Bratsche).

Brace. Perpendicular line, with bracket, joining the staves in scores.

Bradbury, Colin (James) (b Blackpool, 1933). Eng. clarinettist. Studied RCM, and prof. there from 1963. Début 1951. Prin. cl., BBC S.O. from 1960.

Bradbury, Ernest (b Leeds, 1919). Eng. critic and lecturer. Studied with *Bairstow. Chief mus. critic Yorkshire Post 1947–84.

Brade, William (b 1560; d Hamburg, 1630). Eng. composer and violinist who lived mainly on continent, working at Danish court 1594–6, 1599–1606, and 1620–2, and intermittently in Hamburg, Berlin, and elsewhere. Comps. incl. suites, dances, and ovs.

Bradshaw, Susan (b Monmouth, 1931). Eng. pianist and critic. Studied RCM and in Paris with *Boulez. Specialist in contemporary works.

Braga, Francisco (b Rio de Janeiro, 1868; d Rio, 1945). Brazilian composer, cond., and teacher. In 1890 studied at Paris Cons. with Massenet. Cond. sym. concerts in Rio 1908–33. Comp. operas Jupira (Rio 1899) and Anita Garibaldi (1901, unfinished), symphonic poems, etc.

Braga, Gaetano (b Giulianova, Abruzzi, 1829; d Milan, 1907). It. cellist and composer. After touring widely, lived mainly in Paris and London. Comp. 9 operas, 2 vc. concs., 2 syms., and a very popular song, 'Angel's Serenade'. Also wrote vc. method.

Braga-Santos, Joly (b Lisbon, 1924). Portuguese composer and cond. Studied Lisbon Cons. 1934–43, Venice Cons. 1948 (cond. with H. *Scherchen). Studied elec. mus. in Switzerland

1957–8. Cond., Oporto Radio S.O., 1955–9. Comps., some of them atonal, incl. 6 syms., 3 operas, va. conc., double conc. (vn. and vc.), *Requiem for Pedro de Freitas-Branco* (1964).

Braham (orig. Abraham), **John** (*b* London, 1774; *d* London, 1856). Eng. ten., pupil of Leoni. Début aged 13 at CG. Became pf. teacher until 1794 when he took up singing again at Bath. Engaged by *Storace for Drury Lane 1796. Sang in oratorios and at Three Choirs Fests. Sang in Fr. and It. with Nancy (Anna) Storace. Reappeared CG 1801. Following custom of time, wrote mus. of his own part in several operas in which he appeared. For Lyceum opera *The Americans* (1811), comp. *The Death of Nelson*, which remained most popular item in his repertory. Sang part of Max in English in Weber's *Der Freischütz*, 1824, and created role of Sir Huon in Weber's *Oberon*, 1826. His v., regarded as unequalled in It. opera and in Handel, deepened in the 1830s and he sang bar. roles of William Tell at Drury Lane in 1838 and Don Giovanni a year later. Toured America unsuccessfully in 1840. Last appearance was in London, Mar. 1852, when he was 78.

Brahms, Johannes (*b* Hamburg, 1833; *d* Vienna, 1897). Ger. composer and pianist. Son of db. player in Hamburg State Th. In childhood was taught vn. by father, pf. by Otto Cossel, and comp. by Eduard Marxsen. Public début as pianist, Hamburg, September 1848. Earned living by teaching and by playing at theatres, for dances, and in taverns frequented by prostitutes. In 1853 engaged to acc. Hung. vn. virtuoso *Reményi on a concert tour. While in Hanover met *Joachim, who was impressed by youth's comps. and gave him letters of introduction to Liszt and Schumann. Latter hailed him as genius in an article entitled *Neue Bahnen* (New Paths) in the *Neue Zeitschrift für Musik* of 28 Oct. 1853. After Schumann's death in 1856, Brahms became pf. teacher to Princess Friederike and choral cond. at little court of Lippe-Detmold 1857–60, unexacting duties which left him time for comp. In 1860 signed famous manifesto opposing 'new music' methods adopted by Liszt and his followers and thereafter was regarded as the polar opposite to Wagnerian sch. in Ger. mus. His first pf. conc. had been a failure at its f.p. in Leipzig on 27 Jan. 1859 and it was not until nearly 10 years later, with *Ein Deutsches Requiem*, that he achieved a major success. In 1862 first visited Vienna, where he lived for most of next 35 years. From 1863–4 was cond. of Vienna Singakademie and in 1872 succeeded Rubinstein as art. dir. of Gesellschaft der Musikfreunde, holding post until 1875. Thereafter his life was uneventful except for comp. of major works and tours as pianist. Brahms was a master in every form of comp. except opera, which he never attempted. He eschewed programme-mus. and wrote in the classical forms, yet his nature was essentially romantic. His 4 syms. are superb examples of his

devotion to classical mus. architecture within which he introduced many novel thematic developments. In the chamber mus. practically every work is a masterpiece; his 4 concs. are indispensable features of concert life, and his songs, numbering nearly 200, are closely based on Ger. folk-songs but are polished and refined to a highly sophisticated degree. His prin. comps. are:

SYMPHONIES: No. 1 in C minor, Op. 68 (f.p. Karlsruhe, 6 Nov. 1876, cond. Dessoff); No. 2 in D major, Op. 73 (f.p. Vienna, 30 Dec. 1877, cond. Richter); No. 3 in F major, Op. 90 (f.p. Vienna, 2 Dec. 1883, cond. Richter); No. 4 in E minor, Op. 98 (f.p. Meiningen, 25 Oct. 1885, cond. Bülow).

CONCERTOS: Pf., No. 1 in D minor, Op. 15 (f.p. Leipzig, 27 Jan. 1859, Brahms soloist); No. 2 in B♭ major, Op. 83 (f.p. Budapest, 9 Nov. 1881, Brahms soloist); Vn., in D major, Op. 77 (f.p. Leipzig, 1 Jan. 1879, cond. Brahms, Joachim soloist); Vn. and Vc. in A minor, Op. 102 (f.p. Cologne, 15 Oct. 1887, soloists Joachim (vn.), R. Hausmann (vc.), cond. Brahms).

CHAMBER MUSIC: Str. Sextets No. 1, B♭ major, Op. 18 (1860), No. 2 in G major, Op. 36 (1864–5); Str. Qts., Op. 51, No. 1 in C minor, No. 2 in A minor (1859–73), No. 3 in B♭ major, Op. 67 (1875); Str. Quintets, No. 1 in F major, Op. 88 (1882), No. 2 in G major, Op. 111 (1890); Cl. Quintet in B minor, Op. 115 (1891); Pf. Qts., No. 1 in G minor, Op. 25 (1861), No. 2 in A major, Op. 26 (1861), No. 3 in C minor, Op. 60 (1855–75); Pf. Quintet in F minor, Op. 34 (1864); Pf. Trios, No. 1 in B major, Op. 8 (1853–4, second version 1890). No. 2 in C major, Op. 87 (1880–2), No. 3 in C minor, Op. 101 (1886); Hn. Trio in E♭ major, Op. 40 (1865); Vc. Sonatas, No. 1 in E minor, Op. 38 (1862–5), No. 2 in F major, Op. 99 (1886); Vn. Sonatas, No. 1 in G major, Op. 78 (1878–9), No. 2 in A major, Op. 100 (1886), No. 3 in D minor, Op. 108 (1886–8); Cl. (or Va.) Trio in A minor, Op. 114 (1891); Cl. (or Va.) Sonatas, Op. 120, No. 1 in F minor, No. 2 in E♭ major (both 1894); Scherzo in C minor, vn., pf. (1853).

MISC. ORCH: *Serenades*, No. 1 in D, Op. 11 (1857–8), No. 2 in A, Op. 16 (1857–60, rev. 1875), *Hungarian Dances, *Variations on a Theme by Haydn, Op. 56a (1873), *Akademische Festouvertüre, Op. 80 (1880), *Tragic Ov., Op. 81 (1880–1).

PIANO: Sonatas, No. 1 in C major, Op. 1 (1852–3), No. 2 in F♯ minor, Op. 2 (1852), No. 3 in F minor, Op. 5 (1853); Scherzo in E♭ minor, Op. 4 (1851), *Variations on a Theme by R. Schumann, Op. 9 (1854), *Variations and Fugue on a Theme by Handel, Op. 24 (1861),*Hungarian Dances (21 pf. duets) (1852–69), *Variations on a Theme by Paganini*, Op. 35 (1862–3), *Variations on a Theme by Haydn*, Op. 56b (two pianos) (1873), *Liebeslieder Waltzes, Op. 52, 18 waltzes for SATB and pf. 4 hands (1868–9), Op. 52a (without vocal parts) (1874), Pf. Quintet in F minor, Op. 34, arr. for 2 pf. as Op. 34a; rhapsodies, intermezzos, and studies.

CHORUS AND ORCH: Ein *Deutsches Requiem, sop., bar., ch. and orch., Op. 45 (1857–68), *Rinaldo, ten., male ch., and orch., Op. 50 (1863–8), Rhapsody for cont., male ch., and orch., Op. 53 (1869), *Schicksalslied, ch. and orch., Op. 54 (1871), *Triumphlied, ch. and orch., Op. 55 (1870–1), *Nänie, ch. and orch., Op. 82 (1880–1), *Gesang der Parzen, ch. and orch., Op. 89 (1882).

ORGAN: 11 Choral Preludes, Op. 122 (pubd. 1896 in 2 books) Bk. I: 1, Mein Jesu, der du mich. 2, Herzliebster Jesu. 3, O Welt, ich muss dich lassen. 4, Herzlich tut mich erfreuen. Bk. II: 5, Schmücke dich, O liebe Seele. 6, O wie selig seid ihr doch, ihr Frommen. 7, O Gott, du frommer Gott. 8, Es ist ein Ros' entsprungen. 9, Herzlich tut mich verlangen. 10, O Welt, ich muss dich lassen (II); Fugue in A♭ minor (1856); Prelude and Fugue in A minor (1856); Prelude and Fugue in G minor (1857).

PART-SONGS etc.: 4 Part-Songs, Op. 17, women's vv., 2 hns., harp (1860); 7 Marienlieder, Op. 22, mixed ch.; Ps. XIII, Op. 27, women's vv., pf. (1859); 2 Motets, Op. 29, unacc. ch. (1860); Geistliches Lied (Lass dich nur nichts dauern), Op. 30, ch., org. or pf. (1856); 3 Quartets, Op. 31, solo vv., pf. (1859–63); 3 Sacred Ch., Op. 37, unacc. women's vv. (1859–63); 5 Soldatenlieder, Op. 41, unacc. male ch. (1861–2); 3 Lieder (incl. Abendständchen), Op. 42, unacc. mixed ch. (1859–61); 12 Lieder und Romanzen, Op. 44, unacc. women's vv. (1859–63); 7 Lieder, Op. 62, unacc. (1874); 3 Quartets, Op. 63, 4 solo vv., pf. (1862–74); 2 Motets, Op. 74, unacc. (1863–77); 4 Quartets, Op. 92, solo vv., pf. (1877–84); 6 Lieder und Romanzen, Op. 93a, unacc. (1883–4); Tagelied, Op. 93b, unacc. (1884); 11 *Zigeunerlieder, Op. 103, 4 vv., pf. (1887); 5 Lieder, Op. 104, unacc. (1888); Deutsche Fest- und Gedenksprüche, Op. 109, unacc. double ch. (1886–8); 3 Motets, Op. 110, unacc. (1889); 6 Vocal Quartets, Op. 112, unacc. (1889–91); 13 Canons, Op. 113, women's vv., pf. (1863–90); also 14 Ger. Folksongs, unacc. (1864); 14 Volks-Kinderlieder, vv., pf. (pubd. 1858).

SONG-CYCLES: Die schöne *Magelone, Op. 33, v. and pf., 15 Romanzen from Magelone (L. Tieck, 1773–1853): 1, Keinen hat es noch gereut. 2, Traun! Bogen und Pfeil. 3, Sind es Schmerzen, sind es Freuden. 4, Liebe kam aus fernen Landen. 5, So willst du des Armen. 6, Wie soll ich die Freude. 7, War es dir? 8, Wir müssen uns trennen. 9, Ruhe, Süssliebchen. 10, So tönet denn. 11, Wie schnell verschwindet. 12, Muss es eine Trennung geben. 13, Geliebter, wo zaudert dein irrender Fuss. 14, Wie froh und frisch. 15, Treue Liebe dauert lange. (1861–8); *Vier ernste Gesänge, Op. 121, low v. and pf. (orch. by Sargent): 1, Denn es gehet dem Menschen. 2, Ich wandte mich und sahe. 3, O Tod, wie bitter. 4, Wenn ich mit Menschen- und mit Engelszungen redete (1896).

SONGS: Brahms published over 200 songs, from his Op. 3 (1852–3) to his Op. 107 (1886). Among the best known, with poets' names, are: Abenddämmerung (Schack), Op. 49, No. 5 (1868), Am Sonntag Morgen (Heyse), Op. 49, No. 1 (1868), An eine Aeolsharfe (Mörike), Op. 19, No. 5 (1859), Auf dem Kirchhofe (Liliencron), Op. 105, No. 4 (1886), Blinde Kuh (Kopisch), Op. 58, No. 1 (1871), Botschaft (Daumer), Op. 47, No. 1 (c.1860), Dein blaues Auge (Groth), Op. 59, No. 8 (1873), Es liebt sich so lieblich (Heine), Op. 71, No. 1 (1877), Feldeinsamkeit (Allmers), Op. 86, No. 2 (1877–8), Geistliches Wiegenlied (Geibel), with va. obb., Op. 91, No. 2 (1884), Gestillte Sehnsucht (Rückert), with va. obb., Op. 91, No. 1 (1884), Immer leise (Ling), Op. 105, No. 2 (1886), Der Jäger (Halm), Op. 95, No. 4 (1884), Kein Haus, keine Heimat (Halm), Op. 94, No. 5 (1884), Komm bald (Groth), Op. 97, No. 5 (1884), Der Kranz (Schmidt), Op. 84, No. 2 (1881), Lerchengesang (Candidus), Op. 70, No. 2 (1877), Liebestreu (Reinick), Op. 3, No. 1 (1853), Das Mädchen spricht (Gruppe), Op. 107, No. 3 (1886), Die Mainacht (Hölty), Op. 43, No. 2 (1868), Mein Herz ist schwer (Geibel), Op. 94, No. 3 (1884), Mit vierzig Jahren (Rückert), Op. 94, No. 1 (1884), Die Nachtigall (Reinhold), Op. 97, No. 1 (1884), Nachtigallen schwingen (Fallersleben), Op. 6, No. 6 (1853), O kühler Wald (Brentano), Op. 72, No. 3 (1876–7), Salome (Keller), Op. 69, No. 8 (1877), Sapphische Ode (Schmidt), Op. 94, No. 4 (1884), Sonntag (Uhland), Op. 47, No. 3 (c.1865), Ständchen (Kugler), Op. 106, No. 1 (1886), Steig auf, geliebter Schatten (Halm), Op. 94, No. 2 (1884), Therese (Keller), Op. 86, No. 1 (1877), Vergebliches Ständchen (trad.), Op. 84, No. 4 (1881), Verzagen (Lemcke), Op. 72, No. 4 (1877); also several duets and 7 vols. containing 49 Ger. folk-song settings.

Braille, Louis (b Coupvray, Paris, 1809; d Coupvray, 1852). Fr. inventor of 'Braille'. Blind from age of 3, developed Braille system of mus. notation for blind, perfecting it by 1834. Attempts to standardize method for int. use began at Cologne in 1888 but were not finally agreed until 1929.

Brailowsky, Alexander (b Kiev, 1896; d NY, 1976). Amer. pianist of Russ. birth, pupil in Vienna of *Leschetizky, 1911, and later of Busoni. Début Paris 1919, NY 1924. Specialist in Chopin.

Brain, Aubrey (b London, 1893; d London, 1955). Eng. player of French hn. Studied RCM. Prin. hn. of several orchs. incl. BBC S.O. 1930–45. Prof. RAM 1923–55. His brother Alfred (b London, 1885; d Los Angeles, 1966), regarded by some as an even finer player, was for many years first hn. of Henry Wood's Queen's Hall Orch., until in 1923 he went to USA becoming prin. hn. of Los Angeles P.O. and manager of Hollywood Bowl concerts.

Brain, Dennis (b London, 1921; d Hatfield, 1957). Eng. player of French hn., son of Aubrey *Brain, with whom he studied at RAM. Prin hn., RPO from 1946 and later of Philharmonia Orch., freqent conc. soloist, and founder of Dennis Brain Wind Ens. Regarded as finest virtuoso of his day. Britten, Hindemith, and others comp. works for him. Killed in car crash.

Brain, Leonard (b London, 1915; d London, 1975). Eng. player of ob. and cor anglais, son of Aubrey *Brain. Studied RAM. Played in RPO 1946–73. Member, Dennis Brain Wind Ens. Prof. of oboe, RAM, from 1963.

Brainin, Norbert (b Vienna, 1923). Austrian-born violinist. Studied Vienna Cons. Settled in London 1938, studying with *Flesch and *Rostal. Founded *Amadeus Quartet 1947. O.B.E. 1960.

Braithwaite, Nicholas (Paul Dallon) (b London, 1939). Eng. cond. Son of Warwick *Braithwaite. Studied RAM, Vienna Acad. of Mus. Cond. début, BBC Scottish S.O. 1966. Ass. cond., Bournemouth S.O., 1967–70, ass. prin. cond., SW Opera, 1971–1974. Guest cond. leading sym. orchs. Cond. Glyndebourne Touring Opera 1977–81. Prin. cond. Göteborg Opera from 1981, Manchester Camerata from 1984.

Braithwaite, Warwick (b Dunedin, N.Z., 1896; d London, 1971). New Zealand cond. Studied RAM 1916–19. Cond. with *O'Mara Opera Co. 1919–22, *BNOC 1922. Mus. dir. BBC Wales, 1924–32. Cond., *Sadler's Wells Opera, 1932–40, Scottish Orch. 1940–6, CG 1950–2, prin. cond. SW Ballet 1948–52. Cond. Nat. Orch. of N.Z. 1953–4, Nat. Opera of Australia 1954–6, *Welsh National Opera 1956–60, SW Opera 1960–8.

Brandenburg Concertos. Bach's 6 'Concerti Grossi' for various combinations. Dedicated to Christian Ludwig, Margrave of Brandenburg (1721) but it appears they were never played for him. They are as follows:
(1) F Major. 2 hns., 3 ob., and bn., str. (incl. *Violino Piccolo*, i.e. small vn.), hpd.
(2)† F Major. In 2 groups, plus Continuo—(a) Concertino: tpt., fl., ob., vn.; (b) Ripieno: str.; (c) hpd.
(3) G Major. 3 groups of str. (each vn., va., vc., db., and hpd.
(4)† G Major. In 2 groups, plus Continuo—(a) Concertino: vn. and 2 fl.; (b) Ripieno: str.; (c) hpd.
(5)† D major. In 2 groups, plus Continuo—(a) Concertino: hpd., fl., vn.; (b) Ripieno: str. (no 2nd vns.); (c) hpd. for the continuo.
(6) B♭ Major. (No vns.) 2 va., 2 viole da gamba, vc., hpd.
It will be seen that the 3 marked † are true Concerti Grossi in the traditional style of contrasting groups. No. 3 has only 2 movements and there is considerable scholastic speculation on the 'missing' middle movement. Presumably the

works were comp. for Cöthen court orch. Bach's title for them was *Concerts avec plusieurs instruments.*

Brandt, Michel (b Rennes, 1934). Fr. cond. Studied Paris Cons. and École Normale de Musique. Début, Åarhus, Denmark. Cond. Biel-Solothurn 1961–4, Cologne Opera 1964–71. Lecturer, RNCM, Manchester, from 1973. Guest cond., Manchester Camerata and other orchs.

Branle (Bransle, etc.; from *branler*, to sway). Rustic round-dance of Fr. origin, at one time carried out to singing of dancers. Popular at court of Louis XIV but had earlier been taken up in Eng. (Shakespeare calls it 'Brawl'; Pepys 'Brantle'). Mus. usually in simple duple time.

Brannigan, Owen (b Annitsford, 1908; d Newcastle upon Tyne, 1973). Eng. bass singer. Studied GSM. Début Newcastle 1943. Created several roles in Britten operas, i.e. Swallow (*Peter Grimes*), Collatinus (*Rape of Lucretia*), Supt. Budd (*Albert Herring*), Noye (*Noye's Fludde*), Bottom (*A Midsummer Night's Dream*). Also distinguished in oratorio and Gilbert and Sullivan, with special affection for and knowledge of N. Country folk-songs. Glyndebourne début 1947, CG 1948. O.B.E. 1964.

Brant, Henry Dreyfuss (b Montreal, 1913). Amer. (Canadian-born) composer, flautist, pianist, and organist. Studied McGill Univ. Cons., 1926–9 and Institute of Mus. Art, NY, 1929–34, Juilliard Sch. 1932–4. Private comp. studies with Riegger and Antheil. Earned living in 1930 as orchestrator for *Kostelanetz and Benny *Goodman. Later comp. and cond. for radio, films, and ballet in NY and Hollywood. Teacher at Columbia Univ. (1945–52), Juilliard (1947–54), Bennington Coll., Vermont, from 1957. Disciple of *Ives. Comps. are markedly experimental, employing spatial effects. His *Antiphony 1* (1953), using 5 separated orch. groups, anticipated Stockhausen's *Gruppen.* Other works incl. syms., sonatas, ballets (*The Great American Goof, City Portrait*), cantata *December, Millennium 2* for sop., bass, and perc., *Kingdom Come* for 2 orchs. and org., *Verticals Ascending* for 2 orch. groups and 2 conds., etc.

Bransle, Brantle. See *Branle.*

Brass. This term, technically used, covers wind instr. formerly made of that metal, some of which, however, are now sometimes made of other metals; it does not incl. instr. formerly of wood but now sometimes of metal, e.g. fl., nor does it incl. metal instr. with reed mouthpieces, e.g. sax. and sarrusophone. Each instr. possesses a mouthpiece of the nature of a cup or funnel to be pressed against the player's lips, which vibrate within it something like the double reed of the ob. family. The shape of this mouthpiece affects the quality of the tone, a deep funnel-shaped mouthpiece (e.g. hn.) giving more smoothness, and a cup-shaped mouthpiece (e.g. tpt.) more brilliance. The shape of the bell with which the tube ends also affects the character of the tone as does the nature of the tube's bore, i.e. cylindrical or conical.

'Natural' brass instr., playing merely the notes of the harmonic series of their 'fundamental' note, are no longer in artistic use, a system of valves having been introduced which makes it possible instantaneously to change the fundamental note of the instr. and so to have at command the notes of another whole harmonic series. However, composers sometimes ask for a 'natural' sound, e.g. Vaughan Williams in his *Pastoral Symphony* (2nd movement) and Britten in his *Serenade*. And the 'natural' hn. is often used today for 18th-cent. mus. The tbs. have always formed a class apart, as they possess a sliding arrangement by which the length of the tube can be changed and a fresh fundamental, with its series of harmonics, quickly obtained.

Usual brass section of orch. comprises 4 hn., 3 tpt., 2 ten. and 1 bass tb., 1 tuba, with additions as specified.

Brass Band. This type of combination is found all over Europe and in countries settled by Europeans, but highest standard of perf. is possibly reached in N. of Eng., especially Lancashire and Yorkshire, where its popularity is great. Usual constitution in Brit. is cornets, flügelhorn, saxhorns, euphoniums, tbs., and *bombardons, with perc. Saxs. (not strictly a brass instr.) are sometimes incl.

All the wind instr. of the brass band except the bass tb. are scored for as transposing instr. Their keys being B♭ and E♭, their notation shows, respectively, 2 flats less (or 2 sharps more) than the sounding effect, or 3 flats less (or 3 sharps more). With exception of bass tbs. and perc. all are notated in treble clef: except E♭ cornet, where the sound is a minor third higher than the notation, all the sounds are lower, the intervals of the discrepancy ranging from a 2nd below (B♭ cornet) to 2 octaves and a second below (B♭ bombardon). Thus a brass band score is rather puzzling to an unaccustomed reader.

Many 20th-cent. Eng. composers (e.g. Elgar, Holst, Vaughan Williams, Ireland, Bliss, Bantock, Howells, Birtwistle and Bourgeois) have written for brass bands, as has Henze. There is also a distinguished line of 'brass band composers', including Percy Fletcher, Cyril Jenkins, Hubert Bath, Denis Wright, Kenneth Wright, Eric Ball, Gilbert Vinter, and Edward Gregson. The 'brass band movement' in Brit. has a history (almost a folklore) stretching back to the start of the 19th cent. It derived partly from the old city 'waits' and partly from the military wind bands, of which there were many during the Napoleonic Wars. After Waterloo (1815) men left the army, but the musicians continued playing in civilian life. Brass instruments were comparatively cheap, and the bands flourished as hobbies among the

working-class population in the manufacturing towns of Lancs. and Yorks. (though also in Cornwall and elsewhere). Brass band competitions began c.1818 but developed fully c.1840. Among the most celebrated championships are the British Open (formerly held at Belle Vue, Manchester) and the National (held in London). It was for the latter in 1930 that Elgar comp. his *Severn Suite. Bands are frequently named after an industrial firm or colliery as well as after a place. Among the most celebrated have been Bacup, Black Dyke Mills, Besses o' th' Barn, Wingate's Temperance, Foden's Motor Works, St Hilda Colliery (reputedly the greatest of all), Creswell Colliery, Brighouse and Rastrick, Munn and Felton's, Fairey Aviation, CWS Manchester, GUS Footwear, Grimethorpe Colliery, Cory, Carlton Main Frickley, and Hammond's Sauce Works—names of industrial poetry! Among notable band impresarios, arrangers, and conductors mention should be made of Henry Geehl, William Rimmer, William Halliwell, Eric Ball, Walter Hargreaves, Elgar Howarth, J. H. Iles, Alexander Owen, John Gladney, Edwin Swift, Roy Newsome, Maj. Peter Parkes, the Wrights (Denis, Frank, and Kenneth), and the Mortimers (Alex, Fred, Harry, and Rex).

Bratsche (Ger.). Viola (see *Braccio and Gamba*). So *Bratschist,* viola player.

Braunfels, Walter (*b* Frankfurt-am-Main, 1882; *d* Cologne, 1954). Ger. pianist and composer, pupil of *Leschetizky. Dir. of Hochschule für Musik, Cologne, 1925–33 and 1946–50. Wrote 7 operas, pf. conc., Mass, and Te Deum.

Brautlied (Ger.). Bridal song.

Brautwahl, Die (The Bridal Choice). Opera by Busoni, Op. 45, to his own lib. based on E. T. A. Hoffmann. Prod. Hamburg 1912.

Bravington, Eric (*b* Ealing, 1920; *d* 1982). Eng. trumpeter and orch. administrator. Studied RCM. Joined LPO 1939, prin. tpt. 1948–59 when he became man. dir. of the orch until 1980.

Bravo (It.). Brave, fine. Exclamation of approval which therefore has no need to alter, though purists would insist on *brava* for a woman performer, *bravi* for male performers, and *brave* for female performers. Superlative form is *bravissimo.*

Bravoure (Fr.). (1) Bravery, gallantry.
  (2) Same as *Bravura.*

Bravura (It.). Courage, or swagger. A *bravura* passage calls for a brilliant and extrovert display of vocal or instr. technique.

Brawl, Brawle. Old Eng. name for *Branle.*

Break. (1) Place in the v. range where the registers change.
  (2) The permanent change in the male v. which occurs at puberty.

(3) A term in jazz meaning an improvised solo passage, in the style of a *cadenza.

Bream, Julian (Alexander) (*b* London, 1933). Eng. guitarist and lutenist. Won RCM exhibition aged 12 and studied pf. and vc. there; later given special scholarship as student of guitar. Début Cheltenham 1947, London 1950. Also a lutenist and has ed. and transcr. much early mus. for his instrs. Britten, Walton, Henze, and Tippett have comp. works for him. O.B.E. 1964, C.B.E. 1985.

Brecher, Gustav (*b* Eichwald, 1879; *d* aboard ship, 1940). Ger.-Boh. cond. and composer. Cond. opera in Hamburg, Leipzig, Cologne, and Frankfurt 1924–33. Comp. symphonic poem *Rosmersholm* (1895) and other works.

Brecht, Bertolt (*b* Augsburg, 1898; *d* Berlin, 1956). Ger. dramatist and theatrical producer whose radical outlook had enormous influence before and after Nazi régime in Ger. After 1948 his Berliner Ens. fathered a sch. of realistic theatrical experiment. He provided libs. for several mus. works by Kurt *Weill, chief among them *Die *Dreigroschenoper* (Threepenny Opera) (1928) and *Aufstieg und Fall der Stadt Mahagonny* (*Rise and Fall of the City of Mahagonny) (1927–9). Also wrote libs. for Hindemith, Eisler, Wagner-Regény, Dessau, and Sessions.

Breeches Part. See *Travesti*.

Brehme, Hans (*b* Potsdam, 1904; *d* Stuttgart, 1957). Ger. composer and pianist. Teacher at Stuttgart Hochschule für Musik 1928–45 and 1949–57. Comp. 3 operas, 2 syms., cl. conc., 2 pf. concs., chamber mus. incl. several works for accordion.

Breit (Ger.). Broad. Sometimes the equivalent of *Largo,* and sometimes applied to bowing, e.g. *Breit gestrichen,* broadly bowed.

Breitkopf and Härtel. Ger. firm of mus. publishers founded Leipzig 1719 by Bernhard Christoph Breitkopf (1695–1777) as book publishers. His son Johann Gottlieb (1719–94) invented system of movable mus. type in 1750 enabling publication in 1756 of full score of an opera pseudonymously comp. by Princess of Saxony. Breitkopf family severed connection in 1800, dir. being transferred to Gottfried Christoph Härtel (1763–1827) who concentrated on mus. and prod. complete edns. of Mozart (17 vols., 1798–1816), Haydn (12 vols., 1800–6), Clementi, and Dussek. He also founded *Allgemeine musikalische Zeitung.* By 1874 firm's catalogue listed over 14,000 works, incl. complete edns. of Beethoven, Mendelssohn, Schumann, Schubert, Chopin, Liszt, Wagner, and Berlioz, and edns. of earlier composers such as Palestrina, Schütz, Victoria, Lassus, and Sweelinck. In 20th cent. many important composers have been added to their lists. Firm is now divided between East Germany (Leipzig) and West Germany (Wiesbaden).

Brema, Marie (*née* Minny Fehrman) (*b* Liverpool, 1856; *d* Manchester, 1925). Eng. mez. (Ger. father, Amer. mother). Did not begin serious mus. study until after marriage in 1874. Studied with Henschel, 1890; sang in London 1891 under name Bremer (allusion to father's birthplace, Bremen). Later that year appeared as Lola in London at first Eng. perf. of *Cavalleria Rusticana.* Sang Ortrud in *Lohengrin* at Bayreuth 1894, Fricka in *The Ring* 1896, Kundry in *Parsifal* 1897. Amer. tour 1894 singing Ortrud, Brangäne, and Brünnhilde. Thereafter specialized in Wagner, singing Brünnhilde in *Götterdämmerung* under Richter in Paris 1902. Created part of Angel at f.p. of Elgar's *Dream of Gerontius* 1900. In 1910 promoted 2 seasons of opera at Savoy, London, singing Gluck's *Orpheus* and producing all the works. From 1913 until her death was prof. of singing and dir. of opera class at RMCM.

Brendel, Alfred (*b* Wiesenberg, Moravia, 1931). Austrian pianist. Studied Vienna Acad. of Mus., and with Edwin *Fischer. First recital, Graz 1948. Toured with Vienna Chamber Orch. 1951. Début with Vienna P.O., Salzburg, 1960. Played all Beethoven sonatas, London 1962. Amer. début 1963. Thereafter built worldwide reputation through tours and recordings. Settled in London, 1974. Admired principally for playing of Mozart, Beethoven, Schubert, Schumann, and Liszt, but is frequent performer of Schoenberg's pf. conc. Has written essays on several composers and comp. pf. mus.

Brenet, Michel (really Antoinette Christine Marie Bobillier) (*b* Lunéville, 1858; *d* Paris, 1918). Fr. musicologist. Author of biographies of Ockeghem, Palestrina, Handel, Grétry, etc., an historical dictionary of mus. (posthumous), and many other works of research.

Brentano, Elisabeth (Bettina) (*b* Frankfurt-am-Main, 1785; *d* Berlin, 1859). Friend of Goethe and later of Beethoven. Her hysterical nature led her to invent letters she said she received from Goethe, and only one letter to her from Beethoven, though revealing an affectionate relationship, has been authenticated. In 1811, married poet A. von *Arnim who collab. with her brother Clemens (1778–1842) in editing the folk-anthology *Des Knaben Wunderhorn.*

Bretón, Tomás (*b* Salamanca, 1850; *d* Madrid, 1923). Sp. composer. Played vn. in cafés as child. Studied Madrid Cons. and in Paris, Rome, and Vienna on special grants. Became cond. of Madrid Opera and, in 1903, dir. of Madrid Cons. Like *Albéniz fought for the cause of Sp. mus. nationalism, his special contribution being artistic treatment of the operatic form of the *Zarzuela. Also wrote 9 operas, orch. works incl. vn. conc., and oratorio.

Brett, Philip (*b* Edwinstowe, Notts, 1937). Eng. musicologist and writer. Studied King's Coll., Cambridge, 1955–62, with Thurston Dart. Collab. with Dart in rev. Fellowes's *English Madrigalists*. Also rev. 2 vols. of Byrd's works and ed. new vols. Teacher at Univ. of Calif., Berkeley, from 1966 (assoc. prof. from 1971). Author of book on Britten's *Peter Grimes* (1983).

Breuning. Ger. family remembered for its connection with Beethoven who at 18 became mus. teacher in Bonn to 2 of the 4 children of a widow, Hélène Breuning. He became almost an adopted son. His closest friend was perhaps the 2nd son, Stephan (1774–1827), to whom the vn. conc. is ded. Letters from Beethoven to various members of the family are pubd.

Bréval, Lucienne (*b* Männedorf, 1869; *d* Neuilly, 1935). Swiss-born sop. (real name Berthe Agnes Lisette Schilling), naturalized Fr. Studied Geneva and Paris Cons. Opera début Paris 1892, London 1899, NY 1901. Noted for Wagnerian roles at Paris Opéra, but created title roles in Massenet's *Grisélidis* and in Fauré's *Pénélope*.

Breve (▷◁). Double whole-note. Formerly the short note of mus., but as the longer notes have fallen into disuse and shorter ones been introduced it has become the longest (twice the length of the semibreve or whole-note). *Alla breve* means (it is not clear why) 'Take the minim as your beat-unit' (the same effect may be indicated by the time-signature $\frac{2}{2}$, or ₵, or sometimes $\frac{4}{2}$). Still occurs in vocal mus., but rarely in instr. scores where it has been replaced by 2 tied whole-notes.

Brevi, Giovanni Battista (*b* Bergamo, *c.*1650; *d* Milan, after 1725). It. church musician and organist in Milan and Bergamo. Comp. motets, ariettas, and cantatas pubd. between 1693 and 1725.

Bréville, Pierre Onfroy de (*b* Bar-le-Duc, Meuse, 1861; *d* Paris, 1949). Fr. composer, pupil of Dubois and Franck. Teacher at Schola Cantorum, also mus. critic. Comp. chamber mus., pf. works, incidental mus. for Maeterlinck's *Les sept princesses*, but best known for 3-act lyric drama *Eros vainqueur*, prod. Brussels 1910, Paris 1932.

Brewer, (Sir) (Alfred) Herbert (*b* Gloucester, 1865; *d* Gloucester, 1928). Eng. organist, cond., and composer assoc. in all 3 capacities with Gloucester meeting of 3 Choirs Fest. Chorister Gloucester Cath. 1877–80, org. schol. Exeter College, Oxford, 1883. Studied RCM 1883–5. Organist, Bristol Cath., 1885, St Michael's, Coventry, 1886–92. Mus. master Tonbridge Sch. 1892–6. Organist and choirmaster Gloucester Cath. 1896–1928. Knighted 1926. Comps. incl. cantatas *Emmaus* (1901, some of it scored by Elgar) and *The Holy Innocents* (1904).

Brewer, Thomas (*b* London, 1611; *d c.* 1660–70). Eng. composer of songs, glees, and mus. for viols.

Brian, Havergal (*b* Dresden, Staffs., 1876; *d* Shoreham-by-Sea, 1972) (christened William, adopted name Havergal in 1899). Eng. composer. Mainly self-taught and did not devote himself wholly to mus. until he was 23. Was Manchester mus. critic of *Musical World* 1905, attending Richter's Hallé concerts. His *English Suite* for orch. was cond. by Wood 1907, and Beecham cond. 2 of his works at Hanley 1908. His ov. *Dr. Merryheart* was perf. at Birmingham in 1913 and taken up by Wood. Other orch. works were cond. by Ronald, Godfrey, Bantock, and others, but none est. themselves in the permanent repertory. He comp. 32 syms. but was 78 years old before any was perf., this being No. 8 in a BBC broadcast, 1954. The 18th was perf. in London in 1962 and the 32nd in Jan. 1971 on the eve of his 95th birthday. The BBC undertook to broadcast all the syms. to mark the centenary of Brian's birth, and a movement developed to try to remedy the neglect he had suffered in his life. His largest work was the *Gothic Symphony* (No. 1), comp. 1919–27, for an orch. of 180, with 4 brass groups and 4 large mixed choirs. This was f.p. in London in 1961 and again in 1966 to mark his 90th birthday. Prin. works:

OPERAS: *The Tigers* (1916–18, orch. 1918–29); *Turandot* (?1949–51); *The Cenci* (1952); *Faust* (?1954–6); *Agamemnon* (1957).

ORCH.: Syms.: No. 1 in D minor (*The *Gothic*), SATB soloists, ch., children's ch., brass band, orch. (1919–27), No. 2 in E minor (1930–1), No. 3 in C♯ (1931–2), No. 4 (*Das Siegeslied*), sop., ch., and orch. (1932–3), No. 5 (*Wine of Summer*), bar. and orch. (1937), No. 6 (*Sinfonia tragica*) (1947–8), No. 7 in C (1948), No. 8 in B♭ minor (1949), No. 9 in A minor (1951), No. 10 in C minor (1953–4), No. 11 (1954), No. 12 (1957), No. 13 in C (1959), No. 14 in F minor (1960), No. 15 in A (1960), No. 16 (1960), No. 17 (1960–1), No. 18 (1961), No. 19 in E minor (1961), No. 20 (1962), No. 21 in E♭ (1963), No. 22 (*Symphonia brevis*) (1964–5), No. 23 (1965), No. 24 in D (1965), No. 25 in A minor (1965–6), No. 26 (1966), No. 27 in C (1966), No. 28 in C minor (1967), No. 29 in E♭ (1967), No. 30 in B♭ minor (1967), No. 31 (1968), No 32 in A♭ (1968); *Dr Merryheart*, comedy ov. (*c.* 1911–12); *English Suite* No. 3 (1919), No. 4 (1921), No. 5 (1953); Vn. Conc. No. 2 in C minor (1934–5); *The Tinker's Wedding*, comedy ov. (1948); *Elegy*, sym.-poem (1954); Vc. Conc. (1964); *Concerto for Orchestra* (1964); *Ave atque Vale* (1968).

CHORUS AND ORCH: *Psalm 23*, op. 9, ten., ch., and orch. (1901, reconstructed 1945); *Requiem for the Rose*, women's vv. and orch. (or pf.) (1911); *Prometheus Unbound* (1937–44, lost).
Also many choral songs and solo songs.

Bridge. (1) In str. instr., the piece of wood that supports the str. and communicates their vibrations to the belly.

(2) A term, usually 'bridge passage', in comp., meaning a short section which links together— perhaps by a key change—2 important sections of a large-scale sym. or similar work.

Bridge, Frank (*b* Brighton, 1879; *d* Eastbourne, 1941). Eng. composer, conductor, violinist, violist, and teacher. Studied RCM, comp. pupil of Stanford 1899–1903. Played vn. and va. in several str. qts., incl. Joachim, Grimson, and English. Was a member of the last-named until 1915. Also cond. of New S.O. and of opera during Marie Brema's 1910–11 season at the Savoy. Cond. at CG 1913 and many BBC studio concerts in 1930s. Visited USA 1923, under sponsorship of Elizabeth Sprague Coolidge, to cond. own works. Was noted teacher, but his only composition pupil was Benjamin *Britten, who first went to him for lessons at the age of 14.

Bridge's early songs, chamber mus., and orch. works such as *The Sea* are in an idiom familiar to British audiences from the works of Bax, Ireland, and Delius. However, the impact of the First World War on one of deeply held pacifist convictions wrought a significant change and the piano sonata of 1921–4 showed a tougher harmonic idiom, with a more radical approach which in the 3rd and 4th str. qts. came near to the atonality of the Second Viennese School. Yet Bridge never wholly severed his 'Englishness', as can be heard in the orch. tone-poem *Enter Spring* (1927). His detachment from the 'establishment' figures in the Eng. mus. of his day led to his being regarded as an outsider and to the almost complete neglect of such major works as the *Phantasm* for pf. and orch. (1931) and the vc. conc. *Oration* (1930). It was not until his works were rehabilitated by his former pupil Britten at Aldeburgh Festivals that a new generation had its interest in him stimulated, leading to many more performances and recordings. Prin. comps.:

OPERA: *The Christmas Rose* (1918–29).

ORCH.: *Coronation March* (1901); *3 Orchestral Pieces* (1902); *Isabella* (1907); *Dance Rhapsody* (1908); *Suite*, str. (1910); *The *Sea* (1910–11); *Dance Poem* (1913); *Summer* (1914); *Lament*, str. (1915); *Sir Roger de Coverley*, str. (also str. qt.) (1922); *Enter Spring* (1927); *There is a willow grows aslant a brook* (1928); **Oration*, concerto elegiaco, vc. and orch. (1930); *Phantasm*, pf. and orch. (1931); *Rebus Overture* (1940); *Allegro Moderato*, str. (1941, unfinished, last 21 bars orch. Anthony Pople 1979).

CHAMBER MUSIC: Pf. Trio (1900); *Scherzo Phantastick*, str. qt. (1901); str. qt. in B♭ (1901); pf. qt. in C minor (1902); *Phantasie String Quartet* (1905); *3 Idylls*, str. qt. (1906); *Phantasie Piano Trio* (1907); *Allegro appassionato*, va. and pf. (1908); *Phantasie Piano Quartet* (1910); *Elégie*, vc. and pf. (1911); pf. quintet (1904–7); str. sextet (1906–12); vc. sonata (1913–17); str. qt. (1915); *Sally in our Alley, Cherry Ripe*, str. qt. (1916); Str. Qt. No. 3 (1925–6, rev. 1927); Trio, rhapsody, 2 vn., va.

(1928); pf. trio No. 2 (1929); vn. sonata (1932); Str. Qt. No. 4 (1937).

VOCAL: *Music when soft voices die*, SATB (1904); *A Prayer*, ch. and orch. (1916); *A Litany*, 3-part ch. (1918); *Evening Primrose*, 2-part ch. (1923); *Golden Slumbers*, 3-part ch. (1923).

SOLO SONGS: *Blow, blow, thou winter wind* (1903); *Tears, idle tears* (1905); *Love is a rose* (1907); *Love went a-riding* (1914, also orch. acc.); *Go not, happy day* (1916); *Blow out, you bugles* (1918, also orch. acc.); *Journey's End* (1925).

PIANO: *Capriccio* Nos. 1 and 2 (1905); *3 Sketches* (1906); *3 Pieces* (1912); *Lament* (1915, also for str.); *4 Characteristic Pieces* (1915); *Sally in our Alley, Cherry Ripe*, Pf. duet (1916, also for str. qt.); *Fairy Tale Suite* (1917); sonata (1921–4); *In Autumn* (1924); *4 Pieces* (1925); *Winter Pastoral* (1925); *Berceuse* (1929).

ORGAN: *3 Pieces* (1905); *Organ Pieces*, Book 1 (1905), Book 2 (1912); *In memoriam C.H.H.P.* (1918); *Minuet* (1939); *Prelude* (1939); *Processional* (1939).

Bridge, (Sir) (John) **Frederick** (*b* Oldbury, Worcs., 1844; *d* London, 1924). Eng. composer, cond., and organist. Boy chorister, Rochester Cath. Organist, Manchester Cath., 1869–75, prof. of harmony, Owens College, Manchester, 1872–5. Deputy organist, Westminster Abbey, 1875–82, organist, 1882–1918. Cond., Royal Choral Soc., 1896–1922. First Prof. of Mus., Univ. of London, 1903. Arr. mus. at 2 coronations (1902 and 1911) and for Queen Victoria's diamond jubilee service (1897). Comp. mainly oratorios. Knighted 1897.

Bridgetower, George Augustus Polgreen (*b* Biala, Poland, 1778; *d* Peckham, 1860). Violinist (mulatto, having African father). Début Paris 1789. From then lived mainly in London, but also Rome and Paris. Was violinist in service of Prince of Wales at Brighton and played in Haydn-Salomon concerts, London 1791. Beethoven's 'Kreutzer' Sonata comp. for him and first played by him and composer, Vienna 1803. Quarrel caused Beethoven to transfer ded. to Fr. violinist Rodolphe *Kreutzer.

Bridgewater, (Ernest) **Leslie** (*b* Halesowen, Worcs., 1893; *d* Hong Kong, 1975). Eng. pianist and composer. Mus. dir. various ths. Light mus. section BBC 1935–42. Comp. pf. conc. and incidental mus. for stage and films.

Brigg Fair. 'English Rhapsody' for orch. by Delius, being variations on Lincolnshire folk-song introduced to Delius by *Grainger. Comp. 1907. (F.p. Liverpool, Jan. 1908, cond. Bantock).

Brighenti (Brighetti), **Maria** (*b* Bologna, 1792; *d* ?). It. operatic singer, début Bologna 1814. Created Rosina in Rossini's *Il barbiere di Siviglia* (Rome 1816). Rossini then wrote *La Cenerentola* for her (Rome 1817). Retired 1836.

Bright, Dora Estella (Mrs. Knatchbull) (*b* Sheffield, 1863; *d* Babington, Som., 1951). Eng.

pianist and composer. Trained RAM. First woman to be invited to compose work for Phil. Soc. (*Fantasia* in G for pf. and orch. 1892) and said to be first pianist to give a recital entirely devoted to Eng. mus. Comp. 3 operas, 2 pf. concs.

Brindisi (It.). Toast. Jovial song to acc. the drinking of a health. A famous operatic example is 'Libiamo' in Act I of Verdi's *La traviata*.

Brindle, Reginald Smith. See *Smith Brindle, Reginald.*

Brinsmead, John and Sons, Ltd. London pf.-makers. Est. 1835 by John Brinsmead (*b* Wear Giffard, Devon, 1814; *d* London, 1908). His younger son Edgar Brinsmead (*d* London, 1907) wrote *History of the Pianoforte* (1870; 2nd ed. 1879).

Brio (It.). Vigour, spirit, fire. So the adjective *Brioso. Con brio,* spiritedly.

Brisé (Fr.). Broken. Applied (a) to a chord played in arpeggio fashion, or (b) to str. mus. played in short, detached movements of the bow. The *style brisé* was the characteristic arpeggiated style of 17th-cent. Fr. lute mus., which in turn influenced the kbd. mus. of the later clavecinistes.

British Council. Govt.-sponsored organization formed 1935 to spread in foreign countries interest in Brit. and its cultural activities. Centres in various parts of the world, with libraries, help towards perf. of British plays and mus. It sponsors exhibitions and tours by Brit. artists, actors, and musicians, and occasionally sponsors recordings. It receives a considerable govt. grant.

British Federation of Music Festivals. Founded 1921 as assoc. of amateur competitive mus. fests. in Brit. and the Commonwealth. Organizes summer schs.

British Grenadiers. Orig. words date from end of 17th cent., but a later version now sung includes an allusion to Battle of Waterloo (1815). Origin of tune unknown; earliest copy dates from c.1740. Regimental march of the Grenadier Guards.

British Institute of Recorded Sound. Organization founded 1948 by Patrick Saul and incorporated 1951 in London for preservation of recordings of all kinds, which are then made available for study.

British National Opera Company. Formed 1921 by singers and instrumentalists of Sir Thomas *Beecham's opera co., disbanded when financial difficulties compelled Beecham's temporary withdrawal from mus. scene. F.p. at Bradford in Feb. 1922, opera being *Aida.* Dir. was Percy *Pitt, succeeded 1924 by Frederic *Austin. Most of its work was in the provinces, with short seasons at CG and His Majesty's Th. Repertory was wide, embracing Wagner, Debussy, the Italians and several Eng. works, e.g. Vaughan

Williams's *Hugh the Drover* and Holst's *The *Perfect Fool* and *At the Boar's Head.* Co. incl. most of leading British singers and conds. of day, Barbirolli, Boult, Harty, and Sargent among the latter, and Allin, Radford, Labbette, Turner, Mullings, Heming, and Nash among former. Co. ceased to exist, crippled by entertainment tax, in 1929, but was re-named Covent Garden English Company, with Barbirolli as mus. dir., in Sept. 1929 and survived in that form for another 3 seasons.

Britten, (Edward) **Benjamin** (Lord Britten of Aldeburgh) (*b* Lowestoft, 1913; *d* Aldeburgh, 1976). Eng. composer, pianist, and cond. His birth on St Cecilia's Day, 22 Nov., was a happy augury for the career of one of Britain's greatest composers. Essentially a vocal composer, his operas and song-cycles won wide int. acceptance. He never abandoned the principles of tonality and was a 'modern' composer who reached a mass audience and a conservative whose originality no radical would sensibly deny. He shared with his predecessors Parry, Vaughan Williams, and Holst, an intense interest in the work of amateurs and children. His brilliant gifts as a pianist and cond., coupled with the virtuoso nature of his inventiveness, also led him to compose mus. for great performers such as the cellist Rostropovich and the singers Vishnevskaya, Fischer-Dieskau, and Janet Baker. The greatest personal influence on his mus. was his friendship with the tenor Peter *Pears, for whom he comp. many operatic and vocal roles.

Britten's mus. gifts became apparent at an early stage. In sch. holidays he had lessons from Harold *Samuel (pf.) and Frank *Bridge (comp.); the influence of Bridge in particular was strong and lasting. Britten was at RCM 1930–3, but found mus. atmosphere uncongenial and resented official refusal to allow him to study with Berg in Vienna. Studied pf. with Benjamin and comp. with Ireland. His astonishing early works were pubd., incl. the *Sinfonietta* and *A Boy was Born,* and his song-cycle with orch. *Our Hunting Fathers* (Auden) was perf. at Norwich Fest. 1936. He worked for the G.P.O. Film Unit, writing mus. for a dozen short documentaries, the best known being *Coal Face* and *Night Mail* (both 1936). In 1937, for the Boyd Neel String Orch.'s concert at the Salzburg Fest., he wrote the *Variations on a Theme by Frank Bridge.* He and Pears followed their friend the poet Auden to N. Amer. in 1939, staying until 1942. While in NY, f.ps. of his Vn. Conc. (1939) and *Sinfonia da Requiem* (1940) were given in Carnegie Hall under Barbirolli. Returning to Eng., Britten settled at Aldeburgh, Suffolk. His opera *Peter Grimes* was perf. at SW on 7 June 1945, a day of importance for Eng. mus. comparable with the f.p. of Elgar's *Enigma Variations* in June 1899. His interest in chamber opera led in 1947 to foundation of the EOG (later *English Music Theatre) and his desire for a fest.

rooted in Eng. village life and the work of amateurs yet capable of enticing int. performers led to the *Aldeburgh Festival, first held in 1948. Thereafter his career was uneventful outwardly except for the prolific output of works of all kinds, in many of which he took part as cond. or pianist. He excelled not only in his own mus.: as an accompanist in Schubert he was 2nd to none, he played and cond. Mozart superbly, and cond. major works by Bach, Mahler, Elgar, Schumann, and others. The Aldeburgh Fest. also featured neglected works by composers whom Britten and his colleagues deemed to deserve reappraisal. After a severe heart operation in 1973 his activities were much reduced. C.H. 1953, O.M. 1965. First composer to be created life peer (Lord Britten of Aldeburgh, 1976). (Lord Berners was a hereditary peer.)

A major strength of Britten's art, which contributes to the dramatic effectiveness of his operas, is his gift for finding the apt, simple, quickly memorable, and not thereafter easily forgotten phrase to illustrate a point or situation. Another feature is his uncanny ability to capture the imagination and interest of children. Such works as *Let's Make an Opera*, *Noye's Fludde*, and *Saint Nicolas* testify to this. He was much preoccupied with themes of innocence destroyed, of the persecution of the 'outsider' in society (stemming from his own pacifism and conscientious objection to war service), and of cruelty. These themes found their most impressive outlet in the operas *Billy Budd*, *The Turn of the Screw*, and *Owen Wingrave*, the two last being adaptations by Myfanwy Piper of Henry James. If these, and such works as the great *War Requiem*, represent the dark side of his musical personality, the 1953 Coronation opera *Gloriana* (a failure at first), his splendid *Midsummer Night's Dream*, the comedy *Albert Herring*, and a host of choral and instrumental works such as the pf. conc., the *Cantata Academica*, and the *Spring Symphony* show a capacity for joy. He invented a new genre of music theatre in the 3 church parables, the first (*Curlew River*) being an adaptation of a Japanese Noh play; his song-cycles, to Eng., Fr., It., Ger., and Russ. texts are magnificent word-settings; his 5 canticles are works of original insights; and his instrumental works, in particular the str. qts. and vc. suites, explore and stretch the players' capacities without ceasing to be musical. Few composers have caught the public's imagination in their lifetime as vividly as did Britten; each new work was eagerly awaited and absorbed. Intensely practical, he won the devoted admiration of the artists for whom he wrote, and on his several visits to the Soviet Union formed a firm friendship with Shostakovich who ded. his 14th Sym. to him. If it is his operas, particularly *Peter Grimes*, with its evocation of early 19th cent. Aldeburgh, which dominate his output, it is a mistake to overlook his genius in non-vocal forms. Prin. works are:

OPERAS: **Paul Bunyan* (1940–1, rev. 1974); **Peter Grimes* (1945); *The *Rape of Lucretia* (1946); **Albert Herring* (1947); *The *Beggar's Opera* (new version of Gay's opera, 1948); **Let's Make an Opera* (1949); **Billy Budd* (1951, rev. 1960); **Gloriana* (1953); *The *Turn of the Screw* (1954); **Noye's Fludde* (1958); *A *Midsummer Night's Dream* (1960); **Owen Wingrave* (1971); **Death in Venice* (1973; orch. suite arr. S. Bedford, 1984).

CHURCH PARABLES: **Curlew River* (1964); *The *Burning Fiery Furnace* (1966); *The *Prodigal Son* (1968).

BALLET: *The *Prince of the Pagodas* (1956).

ORCH: *Sinfonietta* (1932); *A *Simple Symphony* (1934); *Soirées musicales* (arr. of Rossini, 1936); **Variations on a Theme of Frank Bridge* (1937); **Mont Juic* (suite of Catalan dances composed jointly with L. Berkeley (1937)); *Canadian Carnival* (1939); *Young Apollo*, pf., str. qt., str. orch. (1939, withdrawn until 1979); *Overture, Paul Bunyan* (1940, rev. 1974, orch. C. Matthews 1977); **Sinfonia da Requiem* (1940); *An American Overture* (1941–2, f.p. 1983); *Matinées musicales* (arr. of Rossini, 1941); *Prelude and Fugue* for str. (1943); *Four *Sea Interludes*, *Passacaglia* from *Peter Grimes* (1944); **Young Person's Guide to the Orchestra* (*Variations and Fugue on a Theme of Purcell*) (1946); *Occasional Overture* (1946); *Men of Goodwill* (*Variations on a Christmas Carol*) (1947); *Ov., The Building of the House* (with ch. ad. lib.) (1967); *Suite on English Folk Tunes* (*A Time There Was* . . .) (1974); *Lachrymae*, va. and str. (1976, arr. of 1950 work for va. and pf.); *The Prince of the Pagodas*, concert suite arr. from 1956 ballet by Lankester (1979).

CONCERTOS: Pf. (1938, rev. 1945); Vn. (1939, rev. 1958); *Diversions on a Theme*, pf. left-hand (1940, rev. 1954); *Scottish Ballad*, 2 pf. (1941); Vc. Sym. (1963).

BRASS: *Russian Funeral*, brass and perc. (1936).

CHORAL: *Hymn to the Virgin* (1930, rev. 1934); *A Boy Was Born* (1933, rev. 1955); *Friday Afternoons* (children's vv.) (1933–5); *Te Deum* (1934); *Advance Democracy* (1938); *Ballad of Heroes* (1939); *AMDG*, 4 prayers and holy songs of G. M. Hopkins, for unacc. ch. (1939); **Ceremony of Carols*; **Hymn to St Cecilia* (1942); *Rejoice in the Lamb* (1943); *Festival Te Deum* (1944); **Saint Nicolas* (1948); **Spring Symphony* (1949); *Five Flower Songs* (1950); *Missa Brevis* (boys' vv.); **Cantata Academica* (1959); *Jubilate Deo* and *Venite* (1961); **War Requiem* (1961); *Cantata Misericordium* (1963); *Voices for Today* (1965); *The Golden Vanity* (boys' vv.) (1966); *Children's Crusade* (1968); *Sacred and Profane* (1975); *Welcome Ode* (young people's ch. and orch.) (1976).

SOLO VOICE AND ORCH: *Quatre chansons françaises* (1928); **Our Hunting Fathers* (1936); *Les *Illuminations* (1938–9); **Serenade* (1943); **Nocturne* (1958); **Phaedra* (1975).

SOLO VOICE AND PIANO (unless otherwise indicated): *3 Early Songs* (1922–6); *4 Cabaret Songs* (1937);

*On This Island (1937); *Seven Sonnets of Michelangelo (1940); Folk-Song Arrangements, Vol. I British (1945), II French (1946); III British (1948); 9 *Holy Sonnets of Donne (1945); *Canticle I, My Beloved is Mine (1947); A *Charm of Lullabies (1947); Canticle II, *Abraham and Isaac (1952); *Winter Words (1953); Canticle III, Still Falls the Rain (with hn. and pf.) (1954); Songs from the Chinese (v. and guitar) (1957); 6 *Hölderlin Fragments (1958); Songs and Proverbs of William Blake (1965); The *Poet's Echo (1965); Who are these Children? (1969); Canticle IV, Journey of the Magi (1971); Canticle V, The Death of St Narcissus (1974); A Birthday Hansel (v. and harp) (1975); 8 Folk Song Arrangements (v. and harp) (1976).

CHAMBER WORKS: Elegy, va. (1926); Rhapsody, str. qt. (?date); Quartettino, str. qt. (1930); Phantasy String Quintet (1932); Phantasy Oboe Quartet (1932); 2 Insect Pieces, ob. and pf. (1935, Op. posth., f.p. 1979); Suite for vn. and pf. (1934–5); 3 Divertimenti, str. qt. (1936); Temporal Variations, ob. and pf. (1936); Reveille, vn. and pf. (1937); Str. Qt. No. 1 (1941), No. 2 (1945), No. 3 (1975); Str. Qt. in D (1931, rev. 1974); Lachrymae, va. and pf. (1950); 6 *Metamorphoses after Ovid, ob. (1951); Vc. Sonata (1961); Suite No. 1 for vc. (1964), No. 2 (1967), No. 3 (1971); Gemini Variations (fl., vn., and pf. 4 hands) (1965).

PIANOFORTE: 5 Waltzes (Waltzes) (1923–5, rewritten 1969); Holiday Diary (1934); Sonatina Romantica (1940, f.p. Aldeburgh 1983); Night Piece (Notturno) (1963).

TWO PIANOS: Introduction and Rondo alla burlesca (1940); Mazurka Elegiaca (1941).

INCIDENTAL MUSIC FOR FILMS, PLAYS AND RADIO: Coal Face, Night Mail (1936); The Ascent of F6, Love from a Stranger (1937); Hadrian's Wall (1938); The Sword in the Stone (1938; concert suite for chamber ens. ed. C. Matthews); Johnson Over Jordan (1939); The Rescue (1943); This Way to the Tomb, The Duchess of Malfi (1945); The Dark Tower (1946), and others.

Britten, Improvisations on an Impromptu of Benjamin. Orch. work by *Walton, comp. 1969, f.p. San Francisco 1970. Theme taken from Britten's pf. conc.

Britten, Sinfonia in Memoriam Benjamin. Work for 17 wind instr. by *Fricker, 1976–7. F.p. in England, Aldeburgh 1978.

Britton, Thomas (b Higham Ferrers, Northants., 1651; d London, 1714). Eng. coal merchant, organizer of concerts in London in which the young *Handel took part with *Pepusch and others. Known as 'the small-coal man'.

Brixi, František (Franz) **Xaver** (b Prague, 1732; d Prague, 1771). Cz. composer and organist of Prague Cath. from 1759. Prolific composer of masses, oratorios, and requiems, also org. concs. and other secular works.

Broadcast Music Inc. (BMI). Amer. performing right soc. owned by the broadcasting and TV industry. Founded 1940 by broadcasters in NY.

Broadwood, Rev. John (b 1798; d Lyne, 1864). Eng. clergyman and folklorist. Member of pf. firm family and one of earliest collectors of Eng. folk-songs. His Old English Songs of Surrey and Sussex was pubd. 1843.

Broadwood, John & Sons Ltd. London firm of pf. makers, orig. founded in 1728 by Burkat *Shudi, whose daughter married John Broadwood (1732–1812), hpd. maker in the firm. Broadwood became Shudi's partner 1770. Firm re-named John Broadwood & Son in 1795, & Sons 1807. Earliest Broadwood grand built 1781.

Broadwood, Lucy Etheldred (b Melrose, 1858; d London, 1929). Eng. folk-song collector. Niece of Rev. John *Broadwood, whose interest in folk-song she pursued. Pubd. Sussex Songs 1889, being an expanded reprint of her uncle's Old English Songs, and English County Songs (with J. A. *Fuller Maitland) 1893. Founder-member of Folk Song Soc. 1898, serving as its hon. sec. 1904–8 and 1914–18. Encouraged *Vaughan Williams to collect folk-songs.

Brockway, Howard (b Brooklyn, 1870; d NY, 1951). Amer. composer and pianist. Studied in Berlin 1890–5. Then various important educational positions Baltimore and NY. Comp. orch. and chamber works, etc., and collected Kentucky mountain tunes.

Brod, Max (b Prague, 1884; d Tel Aviv, 1968). Cz. novelist, critic, and composer. Trans. *Janáček's operas into Ger. and wrote his biography (1924). Went to Palestine 1939. Comp. requiem, songs, and chamber mus.

Brodsky, Adolph (b Taganrog, Russia, 1851; d Manchester, 1929). Russ. violinist and teacher. Studied in Vienna under *Hellmesberger. Joined staff of Moscow Cons. and later Leipzig. Gave f.p. of Tchaikovsky vn. conc., Vienna, 1881. From 1890 to 1894 was leader of NY S.O. Leader of Hallé Orch., Manchester, 1895, but on Hallé's death in Oct. 1895 succeeded him as Prin., RMCM, holding this post until 1929. Brodsky Qt. concerts were notable feature of Eng. mus. life; Elgar ded. his Str. Qt. in E minor to the Brodsky team. Among many famous Brodsky pupils was Arthur *Catterall.

Broken Cadence. Interrupted *cadence.

Broken Chord. A chord in which the notes are played one after the other, or a group followed by another group, instead of simultaneously.

Broken Consort or Broken Music. A consort which contained both str. and woodwind instr., as opposed to a whole consort (all str. or all woodwind).

Broken Melody. Comp. for vc. by A. van *Biene.

Broken Octave. Began as device for reducing expenditure on organs and other kbd. instr. On orgs. the lowest octave was complete from C to C, except that the lowest C♯ was replaced by a more useful note, the A from below. See also *Short Octave*.

Broman, Sten (*b* Uppsala, 1902). Swed. composer and violist. Also mus. critic in Malmö 1930–66. Has written 9 syms., *Concerto for Orchestra*, 4 str. qts., and an *Academic Festival* ov.

Bronfman, Yefim (*b* Tashkent, 1958). Russian-born pianist. Studied with his mother and, after emigration to Israel in 1973, at Rubin Acad. of Mus., Tel Aviv. Studied with Rudolf Serkin in USA 1976–8. Appeared with most of the leading Amer. orchs. London début 1981.

Bronsart, Hans von (Bronsart von Schellendorff) (*b* Berlin, 1830; *d* Munich, 1913). Ger. pianist, composer, and opera administrator. Intendant, Hanover Opera 1867–87, Weimar 1887–95. Comp. pf. conc. played by *Bülow and other pf. and orch. works and chamber mus.

Bronze Horse, The (*Le Cheval de bronze*). Opera by Auber to lib. by Scribe. F.p. Paris and London 1835, NY 1837.

Brook Green Suite. Suite for str. orch. and optional woodwind, by Holst. Comp. 1933.

Brook, Peter (Stephen Paul) (*b* London, 1925). Eng. producer. Produced Shakespeare at Stratford, 1945. Dir. of productions CG 1948–9, an appointment ended by the furore over his 1949 prod. of Strauss's *Salome*. Prod. *Faust* NY Met. 1953. His 1982 'compressed' vers. of *Carmen* in Paris—*The Tragedy of Carmen*—was controversially successful.

Broqua, Alfonso (*b* Montevideo, 1876; *d* Paris, 1946). Uruguayan composer. Studied with d'Indy in Paris 1898–1904, then returned to Montevideo. Wrote in nationalist style. Comp. opera, several song-cycles for v. and guitar, and pieces for solo guitar.

Brosa, Antonio (*b* Canonja, Sp., 1894; *d* Barcelona, 1979). Sp. violinist who settled in Eng., 1914. Founded Brosa Qt. 1925 (disbanded 1938). Soloist début, London 1926. In USA 1940–6. Gave f.p. of *Britten's Vn. Conc., NY 1940.

Brott, Alexander (*b* Montreal, 1915). Canadian violinist, cond., and composer. Trained McGill Cons. (later on staff) and Juilliard Sch., NY. Leader, McGill Qt., Les Concerts Symphoniques, etc. Comps. incl. vn. conc. (1950), symphonic suite *From Sea to Sea* (1947), symphonic poems, and chamber mus.

Brott, Boris (*b* Montreal, 1944). Canadian cond. Son of Alexander *Brott. Studied McGill Univ. and with Monteux, Markevich, Bernstein, and A. Brott. Début as violinist, Montreal 1949, as cond. Mexico 1958. Ass. cond. Toronto S.O. 1963–5;

cond. Northern Sinfonia, Newcastle, 1964–8; BBC Welsh S.O. 1972–9; mus. dir. and cond., Lakehead S.O., 1968–72.

Brouček, The Excursions of Mr (Janáček). See *Excursions of Mr Brouček, The*.

Brouwenstijn, Gré (*b* Den Helder, 1915). Dutch sop. Stage début Amsterdam 1940 in *Die Zauberflöte*. First CG appearance 1951 as Aida. Bayreuth 1954–6, Glyndebourne 1959. A distinguished Leonora in *Fidelio*. Retired from stage 1971.

Brower, Leo (*b* Havana, 1939). Cuban composer and guitarist. Studied guitar with I. Nicola and later at Juilliard Sch., NY 1959–60 (comp. with Persichetti and Wolpe) and at Hartt College. Taught harmony, counterpoint, and comp., Nat. Cons., Havana, 1961–7. Dir., experimental dept. of Cuban film industry since 1969. Comps. influenced by *Xenakis, *Nono, and *Henze. His *Sonograma I* was first mus. by Cuban to use *indeterminacy. Has written over 40 film scores, works for solo guitar, guitar conc. (1972), and elec. comp. *Homenaje a Lenin*.

Brown, Christopher (Roland) (*b* Tunbridge Wells, 1943). Eng. composer. Studied King's College, Cambridge, and RAM (under Berkeley). Also in Berlin under Blacher. On staff RAM from 1969. Early works were mainly religious, but increasingly has developed impressive command of instr. style. Works incl.:

ORCH: *Triptych* (1978); *The Sun Rising: Threnody* (1977); *Sonata for Strings* (1974); *Sinfonia* (1971); Org. Conc. (1979); *Festival Variations*, str. (1981).
VOICE(S) AND ORCH: *Soliloquy* (1976); *David*, cantata for bar. soloists, ch., and orch. (1970); *3 Mediaeval Lyrics*, sop., ten., ch., and orch. (1973); *The Snows of Winter* for vv. and chamber ens. (1971); *Chauntecleer*, sop., ten., bar., ch., and orch. (1979); *Magnificat*, SATB soloists, ch., and orch. (1980); *The Vision of Saul*, sop., ten., counterten., bar., ch., orch. (1983); *Tres Cantus Sacri*, ch. and chamber orch. (1984).
CHORAL: *Hymn to the Holy Innocents*, chamber cantata (1965); *Aubade* (1968); *Gloria* (1968); *Laus Creatorum* (1969); *4 Motets* (1970); *3 Mediaeval Carols* (1969–73); *Hodie Salvator Apparuit* (1970); *Oundle Jubilate* (1972); *Even Such is Time* (1977).
CHAMBER MUSIC: *Chamber Music* (cl., hn., vn., vc., pf.) (1974, rev. 1979); Str. Qt. No. 2 (1975); Trio (fl., bn., pf.) (1975); *All Year Round*, ten. and guitar (1976).

Brown, David (Clifford) (*b* Gravesend, 1929). Eng. writer and scholar. Studied Sheffield Univ. 1949–52. Studied Russ. while on national service 1952–4. Schoolteacher 1954–9, mus. librarian London Univ. 1959–62. On staff Southampton Univ. from 1962. Author of 3-vol. biog. of Tchaikovsky. Biographies of Glinka (1974), Wilbye (1974), and Weelkes (1969).

Brown, Earle (*b* Lunenburg, Mass., 1926). Amer. composer. Studied at Schillinger House Sch. of Mus., Boston, 1946–50. Worked with *Cage in NY 1952–5 on project for mus. for magnetic tape. Influenced by visual arts, esp. sculpture of Calder and paintings of Pollock. His *25 Pages* (1953) for 1–25 pf. uses *'open form' and space-time notation, e.g. pitches and durations are specified but, clefs being absent, the pages can be played either way up. On faculty Cologne Cons. 1966. His *Available Forms I* was commissioned by Darmstadt, 1961, and *Available Forms II* (1962) by Rome Radio Orch. Other works:

ORCH: *Modules 1 and 2* (1966), *Module 3* (1969), *Time Spans* (1972), *Cross Sections and Color Fields* (1973–5).
CHORAL: *New Piece: Loops* (1972); *From Here* (1963).
INSTR. ENS: *Transients* (1976); *Event—Synergy II* (1967–8); *Sign Sounds* (1972); *Centering* (1973); *Novara* (1962); *Syntagm III* (1970); *Times Five* (1963).
CHAMBER MUSIC: Str. qt. (1965); *Music*, vn., vc., pf. (1952); *Corroboree*, 3 or 2 pf. (1964).

Browne, (William Charles) **Denis** (*b* Leamington Spa, 1888; *d* Achi Baba, Turkey, 1915). Eng. composer and critic. Studied at Cambridge Univ., becoming friend of E. J. *Dent. After spell as schoolteacher, wrote mus. criticism for *The Times*, 1913–14, and *New Statesman*, 1914. Wrote several beautiful songs, which suggest that his death in action robbed Eng. mus. of a rich talent. His works incl. a ballet *The Comic Spirit, God is Our Strength* for unacc. ch. (1912), 2 Tennyson settings (*Move Eastward, Happy Earth* and *The Snowdrop*) (c.1909), and the songs *Arabia* (de la Mare), *Epitaph on Salathiel Pavy* (Jonson), *Diaphenia* (H. Constable), and *To Gratiana Dancing and Singing* (Lovelace).

Browning, John (*b* Denver, Col., 1933). Amer. pianist. Studied Juilliard Sch., NY. Début Denver 1943. Queen Elisabeth Int. Competition Prize, 1956. Gave f.p. of Barber's pf. conc. 1962. Soloist with world's leading orchs.

Brownlee, John (Donald Mackenzie) (*b* Geelong, 1901; *d* NY, 1969). Australian bar. Début CG as Marcello in *La Bohème* on night of *Melba's farewell, 8 June 1926. Paris Opéra, 1927–36. Glyndebourne 1935–9 (where he was a famous Don Giovanni), NY Met. 1937–56. Staff of Manhattan Sch. of Mus., NY, from 1953, pres. 1958–69.

Bruch, Max (*b* Cologne, 1838; *d* Friedenau, 1920). Ger. composer and cond. Studied in Cologne with F. *Hiller and *Reinecke, returning as teacher 1858–61. Cond. of various concert organizations in Berlin and Bonn and of Liverpool Phil. Soc. 1880–3 (an unhappy period). Dir. Orchesterverein, Breslau, 1883–90, prof. of comp. Berlin Hochschule 1892–1910, among his pupils for a brief period being *Vaughan Williams.

Cond. Scottish Orch. 1898–1900. His comps. incl. 3 operas (one of them, *Hermione*, Berlin 1872, based on Shakespeare's *The Winter's Tale*), 3 syms. (1870, 1870, 1887); many choral works (by which he is best known in Ger.), 3 vn. concs. (No. 1 in G minor, 1868, No. 2 in D minor, 1878, No. 3 in D minor, 1891), *Scottish Fantasia* for vn. and orch. (1880), *Kol Nidrei*, vc. and orch. (1881), conc. for 2 pf. (1912), and 2 str. qts. (1859, 1860).

Bruckner, Anton (*b* Ansfelden, 1824; *d* Vienna, 1896). Austrian composer and organist. Son of village schoolmaster, showed precocious mus. talent but had no expert teaching until aged 11. Was choirboy at St Florian's monastery, 1837–40, and in 1840 began training in Linz as a schoolmaster, mus. remaining an absorbing sideline. Persisted with org. studies and became a virtuoso of the instr., especially in art of improvisation. In 1845 returned to St Florian as ass. teacher, but continued his mus. studies. In 1848 became 'provisional' organist. For some years had been composing org. and choral mus., but 1849 saw the first recognizably Brucknerian work, the *Requiem* in D minor. In 1851 became official organist of St Florian and in 1855 was appointed organist of Linz Cath. Also in 1855 decided to study harmony and counterpoint with Simon *Sechter in Vienna, lessons which continued until 1861. In 1862 studied orchestration in Linz with Otto Kitzler, cellist and cond., who also introduced him to Wagner's mus. From this period, 1863–9, came 3 Masses and 3 syms. In 1868 moved to Vienna, where he was to live for the next 28 years, to succeed Sechter as prof. of harmony and counterpoint at the Cons.

Continued in demand as an improviser on the org., visiting Paris in 1869 to play in Notre Dame and London in 1871 to play at the new Albert Hall. In 1865 first met Wagner in Munich at the première of *Tristan* and their friendship grew. The 3rd Sym. of 1873 was ded. to Wagner. Though this was a matter of personal delight to Bruckner it made him the butt of Viennese mus. politics at the period of great hostility between the supporters of Brahms and of Wagner and ensured him the critical hostility of *Hanslick. In 1875 became lecturer in harmony and counter-point at Vienna Univ. During 1871–6 wrote Syms. Nos. 2–5, following this with a 3-year spell of rev. F.p. of 3rd Sym. in 1877 was fiasco. From 1879 to 1887 worked on Syms. Nos. 6–8 and *Te Deum*. F.p. of No. 4 in 1881 was first considerable success with Viennese public. In 1883, while working on the Adagio of Sym. No. 7, heard of Wagner's death: he referred to the coda of that movement as 'funeral music for the Master'. Success of the first 2 perfs. of No. 7 under *Nikisch (1884) and *Levi (1885) launched int. recognition, but Bruckner received severe blow in 1887 when Levi rejected score of No. 8 with several bitter criticisms. Began another period of rev. with the advice of friends, and the 8th Sym.

was not played until 1892 when, under *Richter, it had a triumphant reception.

In the last 5 years of his life Bruckner enjoyed greater financial reward than before and received several state and university honours. But his health deteriorated and he worked on his 9th (actually 11th) Sym. from 1891 until the day he died (11 Oct. 1896), leaving 200 pages of the finale of No. 9 in sketch form only.

Bruckner's personal character has for too long been misrepresented as boorish and simple-minded. He did have a child-like religious faith, which lies at the root of all his mus., and a becoming modesty. But the composer of those superbly organized and complex syms., most of them over an hour in duration, was no simpleton. He was a late starter as a composer because of his determination to master his technique and recognition only came late in his lifetime. The 'Wagnerian' tag on his syms. led to their being regarded as elephantine monsters, but they are now widely recognized as being in the Austrian tradition of Schubert's last sym. and are admired for their combination of contrapuntal splendour with intense melodic beauty and grandeur (but not extravagance) of orchestration. His Masses, also on a symphonic scale, are equally splendid, and in all his mature church mus. there is the radiance of a devout believer and the technical dexterity of a composer whose mastery of vocal polyphony stemmed from intimate study of Palestrina and his sch.

A peculiarly complex problem exists over the various versions of Bruckner's syms. caused by his proclivity for revisions, often at the behest of well-meaning friends who urged him to cut and reorchestrate works in order to have them perf. and pubd. Since 1934, first under the editorship of Robert *Haas and later of Leopold *Nowak, the Int. Bruckner Soc. has pubd. the 'original' edns. of the syms. Even here confusion arises because there are discrepancies in some of the syms. ed. by both Haas and Nowak. The general tendency today is to return to Bruckner's first thoughts. For this reason the following list of the syms. is in some detail:

Symphony in F minor. Comp. 1863.
Symphony in D minor (designated by Bruckner as 'No. 0'). Comp. 1863–4, rev. 1869 (some authorities insist 'comp. 1869'). F.p. Klosterneuburg, 12 Oct. 1924. Publication: Ed. Nowak 1968.
No. 1 in C minor. Comp. 1865–6, rev. 1868, 1877, 1884 (foregoing known as 'Linz Version'). Major rev. ('Vienna version') 1890–1. F.p. 9 May 1868 Linz, cond. Bruckner; 13 Dec. 1891 Vienna, cond. Richter. Publication: 1893 (Eberle); Linz and Vienna versions ed. Haas 1934, Linz version ed. Nowak 1953. (Nowak ed. mainly corrects misprints.)
No. 2 in C minor. Comp. 1871–2, rev. 1873; 1876–7 version 2 (cuts and alteration). F.p. 26

Oct. 1873, Vienna, cond. Bruckner; version 2, 20 Feb. 1876, Vienna, cond. Bruckner. Publication: 1892 (Eberle), ed. Haas 1938, version 2 ed. Nowak 1965. Haas ed. restores many of Bruckner's 1876–7 cuts.
No. 3 in D minor. Comp. 1873, rev. 1874; thorough rev. (excising several Wagner quotations) 1876–7 (version 2). Another thorough rev. (version 3) 1888–9. F.p. 16 Dec. 1877 (version 2) Vienna, cond. Bruckner; 21 Dec. 1890 (version 3) Vienna, cond. Richter. F.ps. of 1873 version, 1 and 2 Dec. 1946, Dresden, cond. Keilberth. Publication: 1878 (Rättig, version 2), 1890 (Rättig, version 3); ed. Nowak (version 3) 1959.
No. 4 in E♭ major ('Romantic'). Comp. 1874 (version 1). Major rev. (new scherzo) 1878, new finale 1879–80, minor rev. 1881, 1886 (version 2); major cuts and alterations by F. *Löwe 1887–8 (version 3). F.p. 20 Feb. 1881, Vienna, cond. Richter (version 2); 22 Jan. 1888, Vienna, cond. Richter (version 3); f.p. version 1: 20 Sept. 1975, Linz, cond. Wöss (but scherzo alone was perf. 12 Dec. 1909, Linz, cond. A. Göllerich). Publication: 1896 (Doblinger); ed. Haas (version 2) 1936 and 1944; ed. Nowak (version 2) 1953.
No. 5 in B♭ major. Comp. 1875–6, minor rev. 1877–8. F.p. 8 April 1894, Graz, cond. F. *Schalk (spurious version by Schalk); orig. version 20 Oct. 1935, Munich, cond. Hausegger. Publication: 1899 (Doblinger); ed. Haas 1936, ed. Nowak 1951 (little discrepancy).
No. 6 in A major. Comp. 1879–81. F.p. 11 Feb. 1883, Vienna, cond. Jahn (2nd and 3rd movements only); 26 Feb. 1899, Vienna, cond. Mahler (with severe cuts); 14 March 1901, Stuttgart, cond. Pohlig (complete). Publication: 1899 (Doblinger); ed. Haas 1936, ed. Nowak 1952 (minor discrepancies.).
No. 7 in E major. Comp. 1881–3. F.p. 30 Dec. 1884, Leipzig, cond. Nikisch. Publication: 1885 (Gutmann); ed. Haas 1944, ed. Nowak 1954. (Discrepancies affect dynamic and tempo markings, deleted by Haas, restored as 'authentic' by Nowak.)
No. 8 in C minor. Comp. 1884–7 (version 1). Thorough revision, inc. rev. coda of 1st movement, new trio, major cuts and changes of scoring, 1889–90 (version 2). F.p. 18 Dec. 1892, Vienna, cond. Richter (version 2). F.p. (version 1) 2 Sept. 1973 (BBC broadcast), Bournemouth S.O., cond. Schönzeler. Publication: 1892 (Lienau, version 2); ed. Haas 1935 (version 2), ed. Nowak 1955 (version 2). (Haas restores several cuts).
No. 9 in D minor. First 3 movements comp. 1891–4 (sketches date from 1887), sketches for finale 1894–6. F.p. 11 Feb. 1903, Vienna, cond. Löwe (in spurious Löwe version), 2 April 1932, Munich, cond. Hausegger (orig.). Publication: 1903 (Universal); ed. Orel 1934, ed. Nowak 1951 (almost identical). Completion of finale in version prepared (1979–83) by William Carra-

gan, prof. of physics at Hudson Valley Community Coll., Troy, NY, perf. by American S.O. cond. Moshe Atzmon, 8 Jan. 1984. (In 1979 Carragan, assisted by Paul Nudelman, made pf. score of finale based on Orel's edn. of sketches but with coda added. This was perf. in NY 1979). Other works incl.:
ORCH: *Overture* in G minor (1863); *4 Orchestral Pieces* (1862).
CHORAL: Masses, No. 1 in D minor (1864, rev. 1876, 1881–2); No. 2 in E minor (wind band acc.) (1866, rev. 1869, 1876, 1882); No. 3 in F minor (1867–8, rev. 1876–7, 1881, 1890–3); *Te Deum* (ch. and orch.) (1884), Mass in F (1844), *Requiem* in D minor (1849), *Missa solemnis* in B♭ (1852), *Ave Maria* (1861), *Pange lingua* (1868), *Abendzauber* (1878), *Os justi* (1879), *Ave maria* (1882), *Vexilla Regis* (1892), *Germanenzug* (male ch. and brass band) (1863), *Helgoland* (male ch. and orch.) (1893).
CHAMBER: Str. Quintet in F major (1879), *Intermezzo* for str. quintet (1879).

Brueggen, Frans (*b* Amsterdam, 1934). Dutch virtuoso of the recorder, also cond. Prof. of recorder and transverse fl., Hague Royal Cons. Visiting prof., Univ. of Calif., 1974.

Bruhns, Nikolaus (*b* Schwabstedt, Schleswig, 1665; *d* Husum, 1697). Ger. organist and composer. Pupil of *Buxtehude. Wrote choral works and org. pieces.

Brüll, Ignaz (*b* Prossnitz, Moravia, 1846; *d* Vienna, 1907). Austrian pianist and composer. Visited London 1878, playing at 20 concerts. Comp. sym., 2 pf. concs., vn. conc., sonata for 2 pf., and 10 operas, of which best known is *Das goldene Kreuz* (Berlin 1875).

Brulles, Gaces (*fl.* 13th cent.). Fr. composer of *chansons*.

Brumel, Antoine (*b* c.1460; *d* c.1515). Flemish composer. Wrote sacred mus. and *chansons*. Held posts in Paris, Lyons, and Ferrara. First of great Renaissance composers of Fr. origin.

Bruneau, (Louis Charles Bonaventure) Alfred (*b* Paris, 1857; *d* Paris, 1934). Fr. composer and critic. Studied Paris Cons. under Massenet. His 2nd opera *Le Rêve,* in 4 acts based on Zola, was a success in 1891, being regarded as very 'advanced' harmonically. Followed by *L'Attaque du moulin* (1893) in which Zola collab. directly as librettist, as he did for *Messidor* (1897), *L'Ouragan* (1901), and *L'Enfant-Roi* (1905). Comp. 13 operas, several employing Wagnerian principles, also ballet, orch. works, and songs. Worked as mus. critic and wrote several books.

Brunskill, Muriel (*b* Kendal, Cumbria, 1900; *d* Bishops Tawton, Devon, 1980). Eng. cont. Trained by Blanche *Marchesi. Début London 1920. In BNOC 1922–7. Late in career sang frequently in Gilbert and Sullivan operas.

Brunswick, Mark (*b* NY, 1902; *d* London, 1971). Amer. composer, studied at various periods under Rubin Goldmark, Bloch, Boulanger, and Sessions. Prof. of Mus., City College of NY, 1946–67. Comps. incl. syms., chamber mus., and unfinished opera *The Master Builder* (Ibsen).

Bruscantini, Sesto (*b* Porto Civitanova, Macerata, 1919). It. bar. Studied in Rome. Début La Scala 1949; Glyndebourne 1951. Sang Verdi's Falstaff with Scottish Opera, Glasgow 1976. Amer. début Chicago 1961. Produced Verdi's *Un giorno di regno,* Wexford 1981.

Brushes, Wire. Used to produce particular effect from snare drum, cymbals, etc., esp. in jazz.

Bruson, Renato (*b* Este, nr. Padua, 1936). It. baritone. Studied at Padua. Opera début Spoleto 1961 (Luna in *Il Trovatore*). Scala début 1972 in Donizetti's *Linda di Chamounix.* NY Met. 1968–9. Brit. début Edinburgh Fest. 1972. CG 1976 (Ankarstroem in Verdi's *Un Ballo in Maschera*). Outstanding Falstaff in Giulini–Eyre prod. for San Francisco 1982.

Brustad, Bjarne (*b* Christiania, 1895; *d* Oslo, 1978). Norweg. composer, cond., and violinist. Studied in Berlin, 1915–16, with Carl *Flesch. Prin. viola Oslo P.O. 1929–43. Teacher of comp., Oslo Cons. from 1937. Works incl. opera *Atlantis,* syms., vn. concs., and chamber mus.

Brustwerk (Ger.). Choir Organ.

Brydon, Roderick (*b* Edinburgh, 1939). Scot. cond. Studied Edinburgh Univ. and mus. academies in Siena and Vienna. Operatic work with ENO and especially Scottish Opera. Ass. cond. SNO. Art. dir. *Scottish Chamber Orch. from 1974.

Brymer, Jack (*b* South Shields, 1915). Eng. clarinettist. Prin. cl. RPO 1947–63, BBC S.O. 1963–71, LSO from 1971. Soloist and chamber mus. player. Prof. RAM 1950–9. Popular broadcaster. O.B.E. 1960.

Bryn-Jones, Delme (*b* Brynamman, Wales, 1934). Welsh bar. Studied GSM. Début Glyndebourne, CG, and WNO 1963. San Francisco 1967.

Bryn-Julson, Phyllis (Mae) (*b* Bowdon, N. Dakota, 1945). Amer. sop. of Norweg. parentage. Trained as pianist, but at prompting of Gunther *Schuller studied singing at Tanglewood. Début with Boston S.O. Oct. 1966, in Berg's *Lulu-Symphonie.* Eng. début, London 1975 (Boulez's *Pli selon pli*). Sang in Amer. f.p. of *Sessions opera *Montezuma* (Boston 1976). Has made reputation in contemp. mus. because of her perfect pitch, range of 3 octaves, and ability to sing accurately in quarter-tones.

Bryson, Ernest Robert (*b* Liverpool, 1867; *d* St Briavels, Glos., 1942). Eng. composer of opera (*The Leper's Flute,* Glasgow, 1926), syms., and chamber works.

Bucchi, Valentino (*b* Florence, 1916; *d* Rome, 1976). It. composer. Studied Florence Univ. and Cherubini Cons. (comp. with *Dallapiccola). Has worked as critic and teacher. Comp. operas, syms., and religious choral mus.

Buccina. Roman wind instr., made of metal, varying from 8' to 12' long. Its notes were of the natural or 'bugle' scale.

Buchbinder, Rudolf (*b* Leitmeritz, 1946). Austrian pianist. Studied Vienna Acad. of Mus. London début 1962.

Buch der hängenden Gärten, Das (The Book of the Hanging Gardens). Settings for solo v. and pf. by Schoenberg of 15 poems by Stefan George (Op. 15; 1908). F.p. Vienna, Jan. 1910.

Buchner, Hans ('Hans von Constanz') (*b* Ravensburg, Württemberg, 1483; *d* 1538). Ger. organist and composer for his instr. Constanz Cath. 1512–26. Was also organ-builder.

Budapest Quartet. Hung. string quartet founded 1917 by players from Budapest Opera Orch. (Emil Hauser, Imre Poganyi, Istvan Ipolyi, and Harry Son). First played in London 1925. By 1936 membership was Russ. and Ukrainian (1st vn. Joseph Roisman). Under Roisman, quartet became noted for brilliance of style and made many recordings. Settled in USA 1938, being quartet-in-residence at Library of Congress until 1962, when they moved to State Univ. of NY at Buffalo. Recorded all Beethoven's quartets three times. Last public appearance 1967.

Budden, Julian (Midforth) (*b* Hoylake, 1924). Eng. writer, administrator, and musicologist. Studied Oxford Univ., RCM, and TCL. BBC mus. producer 1956, chief prod. of opera 1970–6, mus. organizer, external services from 1976. Authority on Verdi.

Buffa, Buffo (It.). Gust, Puff. The term has come to mean comic, thus *basso buffo*, comic bass in opera. *Opera buffa*, comic opera, is opposite of *opera seria*.

Buffet d'orgue. (Fr.). Organ case.

Buffoon, The (*Prokofiev*). See *Chout*.

Bugle. Valveless brass or copper instr. of treble pitch, with wide tube of conical bore, moderate-sized bell, and cup-shaped mouthpiece. Notes are merely a few of those of the harmonic series, normally in B♭, and it is mainly a means of military signalling or (in bugle bands) simple acc. of marching.

Bugle à clefs. *Keyed Bugle.

Bühnenfestspiel, Bühnenweihfestspiel. Wagner's Ger. terms respectively for (a) *Der Ring des Nibelungen,* a 'stage-festival-play', and (b) *Parsifal,* a 'stage-consecrating festival-play'.

Buisine (Fr. corruption of Lat. *buccina*). Medieval straight tpt. over 6' long, made in jointed sections often with flared bell.

Bull, John (*b* ?Radnor, *c*.1562; *d* Antwerp, 1628). Eng. composer and virginalist. Choir-boy in Queen Elizabeth I's Chapel Royal; organist, Hereford Cath. 1582–5 and then Chapel Royal; D.Mus., Oxford and Cambridge, and first Gresham Public Reader in Mus., London 1597. Left Eng. for Belg. 1613 becoming organist, Chapel Royal, Brussels, and of Antwerp Cath., 1617 until his death. Friend of *Sweelinck.

His importance is as a highly skilled performer on and ingenious composer for the virginals. He ranks as one of the founders of kbd. perf. and the kbd. repertory. He contributed to *Parthenia,* 1611. One of his comps. is called *God Save the King* but bears no resemblance to the nat. anthem; however, another untitled piece by Bull is a possible source of this melody.

Bull, Ole Bornemann (*b* Bergen, Norway, 1810; *d* Lysøen, Bergen, 1880). Norweg. violinist and composer. In emulation of Paganini, toured widely as virtuoso recitalist. Convinced patriot, frequently played Scandinavian melodies, earning large sums and founding in USA in 1852 a Norweg. colony and in the capital of his own country a mus. conservatory (both of which schemes proved abortive). Wrote 2 vn. concs. Encouraged Grieg.

Buller, John (*b* London, 1927). Eng. composer. Worked as architectural surveyor until 1959 when he studied comp. with Anthony Milner. Came to notice in 1970s with series of works based on James Joyce's *Finnegans Wake.* Works incl.: *The Cave,* fl., cl., tb., vc., tape (1970); *2 Night Pieces* from 'Finnegans Wake', for sop., fl., cl., pf., vc. (1971); *The Melian Debate,* ten., bar., fl., cor anglais, hn., tpt., hp., vc. (1971); *Finnegan's Floras,* ch., perc., pf. (1972); *Poor Jenny,* fl., perc. (1973); *Le Terrazze,* 14 instr., tape (1974); *Familiar,* str. qt (1974); *The Mime of Mick, Nick, and The Maggies,* sop., ten., bar., ch., orch. (1975–6); *Proença,* mez., elec. guitar, orch. (1977); *The Theatre of Memory,* orch. (1980–1); *Sonnet,* mez., fl., str. qt. (1983); *Towards Aquarius,* ens. (1983).

Bullock, (Sir) Ernest (*b* Wigan, 1890; *d* Aylesbury, 1979). Eng. organist and educator. Studied with *Bairstow. Sub-organist, Manchester Cath., 1912–15. Organist, Exeter Cath. 1919–27, Westminster Abbey 1928–41. Prin., RSAM, and Prof. of Mus., Glasgow Univ. 1941–52; dir., RCM 1953–60. Comp. org. mus. and songs. Knighted 1951. In charge of mus., Coronation of George VI, 1937.

Bull Roarer. See *Thunder Stick.*

Bülow, Hans (Guido) Freiherr **von** (*b* Dresden, 1830; *d* Cairo, 1894). Ger. cond. and pianist. Pf. pupil of Friedrich *Wieck. Became law student but abandoned it for mus. under influence of f.p.

of Wagner's *Lohengrin* at Weimar. Went to Zürich for instruction from Wagner. Pf. pupil of Liszt, 1851. First concert tour of Ger., 1853. Prin. pf. prof., Stern-Marx Cons., Berlin, 1855–64, during which time developed conducting potentialities in addition to making many tours as concert pianist. Married Liszt's daughter Cosima, 1857. Chief cond., Munich Royal Opera, 1864, and there cond. f.p. of Wagner's *Tristan und Isolde* (1865) and *Die Meistersinger von Nürnberg* (1868) to the composer's immense satisfaction. In 1869 left Munich because of Wagner's affair with Cosima; they were divorced the next year. First visit to London 1873, to USA 1875–6. In 1880 became court cond. to Duke of Meiningen and made the court orch. finest in Europe for disciplined playing. Resigned 1885, handing over to his protégé Richard *Strauss. Cond. Berlin P.O. 1887–93. In 1888 became cond. of opera and concerts in Hamburg. Comp. orch. and pf. works and pubd. edn. of Beethoven sonatas. Gave f.p. of Tchaikovsky's 1st pf. conc. (Boston, 25 Oct. 1875).

Bumbry, Grace (*b* St Louis, 1937). Amer. mez., later sop. Studied with Lotte *Lehmann, 1955–8. Début Paris Opéra 1960 as Amneris in *Aida*. Basle Opera 1960–3. Sang at Bayreuth 1961, being first black singer to do so. NY début 1962. CG début 1963, Salzburg 1964. Remarkable Carmen and Salome.

Bunting, Edward (*b* Armagh, 1773; *d* Dublin, 1843). Irish organist and pianist renowned for his coll. of over 300 Irish folk tunes, harp mus., etc., pubd. in 3 sections, 1796, 1809, and 1840.

Buonaccordo (It.). Child's toy pf. or spinet.

Buonamici, Giuseppe (*b* Florence, 1846; *d* Florence, 1914). It. pianist, studied Munich Cons. under Bülow. Prof. of pf., Istituto Musicale, Florence, from 1873. Ed. Beethoven sonatas and other classics.

Buononcini. See *Bononcini, Giovanni*.

Buonporti. See *Bonporti, Francesco Antonio*.

Burden, or Burthen. (1) A recurring line after each stanza of a ballad, etc.
   (2) Drone or bass of *bagpipe.

Burgmüller, Johann Friedrich (*b* Regensburg, 1806; *d* Beaulieu, Fr., 1874). Ger. composer remembered chiefly for his mus. for the ballet *La Péri*.

Burgon, Geoffrey (*b* Hambledon, 1941). Eng. composer. Studied GSM (with *Wishart) and with *Berkeley. Played tpt. in jazz groups and orchs. Original and imaginative user of all the influences and procedures at the disposal of the 20th-cent. composer. High reputation as composer of incid. music for television, e.g. *Brideshead Revisited* and *Tinker, Tailor, Soldier, Spy*. Works incl.:

MUSIC THEATRE: *Epitaph for Sir Walter Raleigh* (1968); *Joan of Arc* (text by Susan Hill) (1970).
BALLETS: *The Golden Fish* (1964); *Ophelia* (1964); *The Calm* (1974); *Running Figures/Goldberg's Dream* (1975); *Persephone* (1979); *Songs, Lamentations and Praises* (1979).
ORCH.: Conc. for str. (1963); *5 Pieces for Str.* (1967); *Gending* (1968); *Alleluia Nativitas* (1970); *Cantus Alleluia* (1973); *Brideshead Variations* (1981); *The World Again* (1982–3).
VOICES AND ORCH.: *Acquainted with Night*, counterten., str., harp, perc. (1965); *Think on Dredful Domesday* (1969); *Magnificat* (1970); *The Golden Eternity* (1970); *Requiem* (1976); *Veni Spiritus*, sop., bar., ch., and orch. (1978–9); *Orpheus*, sop., ten., bar., bass, male ch., and orch. (1982).
VOICE(S) AND PIANO or ENSEMBLE: *Cantata on Mediaeval Latin Texts*, counterten., fl., ob., bn. (1964); *Hymn to Venus*, mez. and pf. (1966); *5 Sonnets of Donne* (1967); *Worldes Bliss*, counterten. and ob. (1971); *This Endris Night*, ten., female vv., brass (1972); *Canciones del Alma*, 2 counterten. and 13 solo str. (1975); *The Fall of Lucifer*, ten., bar., counterten., ch., and ens. (1977); *Hymn to St Thomas*, ch. and str. (1980).
CHORAL: *3 Elegies* (1964); *Short Mass* (1965); *Farewell Earth's Bliss*, 6 solo vv. (1966); *A Prayer to the Trinity* (1972); *The Fire of Heaven* (1973); *Dos Coros* (1975); *But Have Been Found Again* (1983).
CHAMBER MUSIC: *Chamber Dances* (1981–2); Ob. qt. (1980); *Sanctus Variations*, 2 tpts., org. (1980).

Burian, Emil František (*b* Pilsen, 1904; *d* Prague, 1959). Cz. composer and actor; studied Prague Univ. (comp. with J. B. *Förster) 1920–7. Sometime dir., Brno Nat. Th. Comps. incl. operas, jazz opera, 8 str. qts., wind quintet, etc.

Burkhard, Paul (*b* Zürich, 1911; *d* Tosstal, 1977). Swiss composer, pianist, and cond. Studied Zürich Cons. Cond. radio orch. Beromünster, 1945–57. Successful operettas incl. *Tic-Tac* (1941) and *Der schwarze Hecht* (The Black Jack) (1939) which was rev. 1948 as *Feuerwerk* (Firework) and contained the popular 'O mein Papa'.

Burkhard, Willy (*b* Évilard sur Bienne, Switzerland, 1900; *d* Zürich, 1955). Swiss composer, pianist, and cond. Studied at Cons. of Berne, Leipzig, and Munich, and then became teacher of comp. and pf. in Berne. Comp. opera *Die schwarze Spinne* (The Black Spider) (Zürich 1949), 2 syms., cantatas, 2 vn. concs., oratorio *Das Gesicht Jesajahs* (The Vision of Isaiah) (Basle 1936), str. qts., vc. sonata, organ mus.

Burla (It.). Jest. So *burlando*, jestingly; *burletta*, a mus. farce, etc.

Burlesco, Burlesca (It.). Burlesque, jocular (see also *Burla*). So the adverb, *burlescamente*.

Burleske (Burlesque). Work for pf. and orch. in D minor by R. Strauss, comp. 1885–6, rev. 1890. F.p. Eisenach, 1890.

Burlesque (Fr.; It. *burlesca*; Ger. *Burleske*). Humorous form of entertainment involving an element of parody or exaggeration. Applied in 18th cent. to mus. works in which comic and serious elements were contrasted. In Eng. word usually means a dramatic work ridiculing stage conventions, while in Amer. it means a variety show, often involving strippers.

Burletta (It.). Type of Eng. mus. farce which had a vogue in late 18th/early 19th cent.

Burney, Charles (*b* Shrewsbury, 1726; *d* London, 1814). Eng. organist (London churches, King's Lynn, finally Chelsea Hospital); minor composer; author of History of Music (4 vols., 1776–89), of 2 books narrating his travel experiences in Fr., It., Ger., etc., also of a life of Metastasio. Friend of and greatly esteemed by Johnson, Garrick, Reynolds, Burke, and other leaders of politics, science, art, literature, and social life of his period. Father of the novelists Fanny and Sarah Harriet Burney, of the writer on South Sea exploration, Admiral James Burney (one of Cook's officers in his circumnavigation), and of the Gr. scholar, Charles Burney, jun.

Burning Fiery Furnace, The. 2nd parable for church perf., Op. 77, by Britten to lib. by W. Plomer based on Book of Daniel. Prod. Aldeburgh Fest. (Orford Church) 1966.

Burrell, Mary (1850–98). Daughter of Sir John Banks, Regius Prof. of Medicine, Trinity College, Dublin; wife of Hon. Willoughby Burrell (after her death Lord Gwydyr). Amassed enormous coll. of Wagner documents of every kind; planned complete life of Wagner but only immense first vol. was pubd., covering 21 years (1898). Other material now at Philadelphia (Catalogue pubd. 1929).

Burrowes, Norma (Elizabeth) (*b* Bangor, Co. Down, 1944). Irish sop. Studied RAM. Singer in opera, Lieder, and oratorio. CG début 1970 (Fiakermilli in *Arabella*), Salzburg and Wexford, 1971. Title-role in Janáček's The Cunning Little Vixen, Glyndebourne 1975.

Burrows, (James) **Stuart** (*b* Pontypridd, 1933). Welsh tenor. Was schoolteacher until winning tenor comp. at Royal Nat. Eisteddfod 1959. Opera début with WNO 1963 (Ismaele in *Nabucco*). CG 1967, S. Francisco 1967, Vienna 1970 (Tamino in *Die Zauberflöte*), NY Met. 1971. Particularly noted as Mozart singer.

Burt, Francis (*b* London, 1926). Eng. composer. Studied comp. with Howard *Ferguson at RAM 1948–51 and in Berlin with Boris *Blacher 1951–4. Lived in Vienna from 1956. Prof of comp., Vienna Hochschule für Musik from 1973. Comps. incl. opera *Volpone* (Ben Jonson) (1952–8), *Iambics* for orch. (1953), *Espressione orchestrale* (1958–9) and *Und Gott der Herr sprach*, mez., bar., bass, ch.,

and orch. (1983) and many works for Ger. and Austrian ths. and TV.

Burthen. See *Burden*.

Busch, Adolf (Georg Wilhelm) (*b* Siegen, Westphalia, 1891; *d* Guilford, Vermont, 1952). Ger.-born violinist and composer. Studied at Cologne with Willy *Hess. Violin prof. Berlin Hochschule 1918. Founded qt. 1919. Settled in Basle 1927, taking Swiss nationality 1935. Went to USA 1939. His qt. made many famous recordings. Noted for sonata recitals with his son-in-law, the pianist Rudolf *Serkin. Comp. sym., concs., sonatas.

Busch, Fritz (*b* Siegen, Westphalia, 1890; *d* London, 1951). Ger. cond., brother of A. *Busch. Studied Cologne Cons. (cond. with F. *Steinbach). Opera house appointments at Riga 1909, Aachen 1912, Stuttgart 1918, succeeding Fritz *Reiner at Dresden, 1922. His period at Dresden revived glories of *Schuch era. Cond. f.ps. of R. Strauss's *Intermezzo (1924) and Die ägyptische Helena (1928). Left Ger. 1933, working in Buenos Aires 1933–6 and 1941–5 and at NY Met. 1945–49. In England best known as first cond. of *Glyndebourne Opera 1934–9, returning in 1950 and 1951. Also had long assoc. with Danish Radio S.O. and Stockholm P.O.

Bush, Alan (Dudley) (*b* London, 1900). Eng. composer, cond., and pianist. Studied RAM 1918–22 and privately with John *Ireland 1922–7. Teacher at RAM since 1925. In 1929–31 studied at Berlin Univ. Had pf. lessons from *Moiseiwitsch and *Schnabel. Many of his works reflect his Communist sympathies but are held in high esteem for their mus. qualities by listeners of all political persuasions. Major works are:

OPERAS: *The Press-Gang* (1946); *Wat Tyler (1948–50) (Leipzig 1953, London 1974); The Spell Unbound (1953); Men of Blackmoor (1954–5) (Oxford 1960, Weimar 1965); The Ferryman's Daughter (1961); The Sugar Reapers (1961–4) (Leipzig 1966); Joe Hill: the Man Who Never Died (1965–8) (Berlin 1970).

ORCH: Syms., No. 1 in C (1939–40), No. 2 'Nottingham' (1949), No. 3 'Byron' (1959–60), No. 4 'Lascaux' (1982–3); Pf. Conc., with bar. and male ch. (1934–7); Vn. Conc. (1948); Concert Suite for vc. and orch. (1952); English Suite for str. (1946); Dorian Passacaglia and Fugue (1959); Variations, Nocturne and Finale on an English Sea Song, pf. and orch. (1960); Time Remembered for chamber orch. (1968); Africa, pf. and orch. (1971–2); Liverpool Overture (1972).

CHAMBER: Str. Qt. in A minor (1923); Dialectic for str. qt. (1929); 3 Concert Studies for pf. trio (1947); Serenade for str. qt. (1969); pf. sonata (1971); Suite of Six for str. qt. (1975); 24 Preludes, pf. (1977).

Bush, Geoffrey (*b* London, 1920). Eng. composer, teacher, and writer. Chorister, Salisbury Cath.,

1928–33. Lecturer, Oxford Univ., Extra-Mural Dept., 1947–52, London Univ. from 1952. Works incl. operas, concs., 2 syms., *Music for Orchestra*, ov. *Yorick*, pf. pieces, songs, and *Twelfth Night* for ten., ch., and orch. Ed., pf. and chamber mus. of Sterndale Bennett 1972.

Busnois, Antoine (*b* c.1430; *d* Bruges, 1492). Fr. composer. May have been pupil or colleague of *Ockeghem. Was for long in service of Charles the Bold (who became Duke of Burgundy in 1467) and after Charles's death in 1477 served his daughter Mary of Burgundy until her death in 1482. Moved to Bruges and became *rector cantoriae* at the church of St Sauveur. Regarded as one of leading composers of his day, ranking next to Ockeghem, with whom he shared a penchant for elaborate melody, the use of canon, and lively rhythms. His *Missa L'homme armé* is one of earliest based on this secular tune, but some of his most original work is to be found in his *chansons*, of which over 60 survive. For some of these he wrote the words. His motet *Anthoni usque limina* has a part for a tenor who sings the note D in imitation of a bell. Its text has a reference to his name in the line '. . . in omnibus noys'. His three-part setting of an It. text, the motet *Fortunata desperata*, was a model for Josquin *Desprès, and the melodies of some of his *chansons* were used in Masses by his contemporaries just as he had used *L'homme armé*.

Busoni, Ferruccio Benvenuto (*b* Empoli, 1866; *d* Berlin, 1924). It. composer, cond., and pianist. Son of clarinettist and pianist. First public pf. recital, Trieste, at age 7. Studied comp. at Graz, 1880–1 and Leipzig 1886. Teaching posts at Helsinki 1889, Moscow 1890, Boston, Mass., 1891–4. After 1894 settled mainly in Berlin. Although his brilliance as a pianist earned him most fame, from 1898 concentrated on comp. and also est. master classes at Weimar in 1901 and 1902 which broke new ground as meeting-places for young composers and performers. From 1902–9 cond. orch. concerts in Berlin at which contemporary works were perf. From 1913–15 dir. of Liceo Rossini, Bologna, but disagreements with the municipal authorities over reforms ensured failure. Lived in Zürich from 1915, refusing to enter the belligerent countries, but returned to Berlin 1920. Resumed pianist career despite failing health.

Busoni's pf.-playing, of virtuoso quality, was also notable for its grandeur and poetry. His mus. found mixed favour in his lifetime but has become increasingly admired for its visionary nature and for its anticipation of many of the devices and styles of 'advanced' composers. Deriving from the impressionistic late works of Liszt, it ventured into harmonic and rhythmic territory that became the preserve of *Webern, *Bartók, and *Messiaen. His earlier works, in a classical-romantic style, are best represented by the Vn. Sonata in E minor, the Vn. Conc., and

the Pf. Conc. (in 5 movements, with male ch. in finale). His change in style dates from the *Elegies* for pf. of 1907. His most elaborate work was his opera *Doktor Faust*, begun 1916 and left incomplete. His writings were both progressive and influential, particularly the *Entwurf einer neuen Ästhetik der Tonkunst* (Trieste, 1907). Prin. works:

OPERAS: *Die *Brautwahl* (The Bridal Choice) (1908–11); *Arlecchino* (1914–16); *Turandot* (1917, orig. incid. mus. 1911); *Doktor Faust* (1916–24, completed. by P. Jarnach).

ORCH: *Symphonic Suite* (1883); *Konzertstück*, pf., orch. (1890); *Concert-Fantasy*, pf., orch. (1888–9), rev. as *Symphonisches Tongedicht*, orch. (1893); *Suite No. 2* (1895, rev. 1903); vn. conc. (1896–7); *Comedy Overture* (1897, rev. 1904); pf. conc. (male ch. in finale) (1903–4); *Turandot Suite* (1904); *Berceuse élégiaque* (1909, orig. for pf.); *Symphonic Nocturne* (1912); *Indianische Fantasie*, pf., orch. (1913); *Rondò Arlecchinesco* (1915); *Indianisches Tagebuch* (Book II) (1915); cl. concertino (1918); *Divertimento*, fl., orch. (1920); *Tanzwalzer* (1920).

VOICE AND ORCH: *Ave Maria*, bar., orch. (1882); *Unter den Linden*, sop., orch. (1885, 1893); *Zigeunerlied*, bar., orch. (1923); *Schlechter Trost*, low v., orch. (1924).

CHAMBER: Str. Qt. No. 1 in C minor (1880–1), No. 2 in D minor (1887); Vn. Sonata No. 1 in E minor (1890), No. 2 in E minor (1898); *Little Suite*, vc., pf. (1886); *Bagatelles*, vn., pf. (1888); *Serenata*, vc., pf. (c.1882); *Elegy*, cl., pf. (1920).

PIANO: *Prelude and Fugue in C minor* (1878); *24 Preludes* (1879–80); *3 Pieces* (1884); *Study in Form of Variations* (1884); *5 Pieces* (1887); *Élegien* (7 pieces) (1907–9; No. 7, *Berceuse*, comp. 1909 and orch. as *Berceuse élégiaque*); *Christmas Night* (1909); Sonatinas: No. 1 (1910), No. 2 (1912), No. 3 (1916), No. 4 (1917), No. 5 (transcr. of Bach) (1919), No. 6 (on *Carmen*) (1920); *Indianisches Tagebuch* (Book I) (1915); *Fantasia contrappuntistica* (based on Bach), 1st version (1910), 2nd version (1910), 3rd version (1912), 4th version, arr. 2 pfs. (1921); *3 Albumblätter* (1917–21); *Klavierübung* (1st edn. in 5 parts, 1917–22; 2nd edn. in 10 parts, 1925).

Also songs and many transcr. and arr. of Bach, Beethoven, Bizet, Chopin, Cornelius, Liszt, Mozart, Schoenberg, Schubert, and Wagner. His transcr. of J. S. Bach's *Chromatic Fantasia* dates from 1911.

Busser, Henri Paul (*b* Toulouse, 1872; *d* Paris 1973). Fr. composer, organist and cond., pupil of Gounod, Franck, and Widor at Paris Cons. and at 21 won *Prix de Rome*. In 1902 became cond. at the Opéra-Comique, at the Opéra 1905. Prof. of comp., Paris Cons. 1931–49. Wrote several operas incl. *Jane Grey* (1891), *Colomba* (1921), *Les Noces corinthiennes* (1922), and *Le Carrosse du Saint-Sacrement* (1948). Orch. Debussy's *Petite Suite, Printemps*, and other works.

Bussotti, Sylvano (b Florence, 1931). It. composer. Studied vn. as a child but pursued career as composer. Studied under Max Deutsch in Paris 1957–8. Prizewinner at I.S.C.M. festival and Venice Biennale. Influenced by Webern and serialism, later by John *Cage. Operas incl. *Lorenzaccio* (1972) and *Nottetempo* (1976). Other works incl.: *La Passion selon Sade*, vv., instr., narrator (1966), *5 Piano Pieces for David Tudor* (1959), *Torso*, v. and orch. (1963), *Rara Requiem* (1969). Some of these are in graphic score. Also a painter.

Buths, Julius (b Wiesbaden, 1851; d Düsseldorf, 1920). Ger. cond. and pianist. After conducting at Elberfeld, 1879–90, moved to Düsseldorf, 1890–1908, where he became mus. dir., Lower Rhine Fest. Cond. several now famous contemporary works by, among others, Mahler, Delius, and Strauss, but most notably Elgar's *Dream of Gerontius*, which he trans. into Ger. and prod. at Düsseldorf in 1901 and 1902. Soloist in f.p. of Delius's pf. conc. at Elberfeld, 1904 (cond. *Haym).

Butt, (Dame) Clara (b Southwick, 1872; d North Stoke, Oxon, 1936). Eng. cont. Studied Bristol and, from 1890, at RCM. Sang title-role of Gluck's *Orfeo* in 1892 at Lyceum with conspicuous success but thereafter pursued career on concert platform except for an *Orfeo* with Beecham at CG, 1920. Toured British Empire in ballad recitals with husband Kennerley *Rumford. First singer of Elgar's *Sea Pictures, Norwich 1899, and of the song version of *Land of Hope and Glory*, 1902. Also sang in his *Spirit of England*, 1916. D.B.E. 1920.

Butterworth, Arthur (Eckersley) (b Manchester, 1923). Eng. composer, cond., and trumpeter. Studied RMCM. Trumpeter in SNO 1949–54, Hallé Orch. 1955–61. Cond., Huddersfield P.O. from 1964. Works incl. 3 syms., several works for brass band, *Trains in the Distance*, ch. and orch. Arr. Elgar's *Introduction and Allegro* (str.) for brass band (1976).

Butterworth, George (Sainton Kaye-) (b London, 1885; d Pozières, Battle of Somme, 1916). Eng. composer. Educated Eton and Trinity College, Oxford. At Oxford influenced by H. P. *Allen and began collecting folk-songs, leading to friendship with *Vaughan Williams and Cecil *Sharp. Was excellent folk-dancer. Comps., few in number, suggest he might have achieved greatness. Left several fine settings of Housman's 'Shropshire Lad' poems, with orch. rhapsody, *A Shropshire Lad* (Leeds 1913) based on theme of his song 'Loveliest of Trees'. Orch. idyll *The Banks of Green Willow* f.p. London 1914. Song-cycle *Love Blows as the Wind Blows* (W. E. Henley) was composed 1911–12, being 4 songs for voice with pf. or str. qt. but was revised in 1914 as 3 songs with orch. Posthumously awarded Military Cross. Vaughan Williams's *A London Symphony* is ded. to his memory.

Butting, Max (b Berlin, 1888; d Berlin, 1976). Ger. composer. Studied Munich Univ. and Cons. Early specialist in comp. for radio. Inactive 1933–45; mus. dir., E. Berlin radio 1948. Comp. opera, 10 syms., pf. conc., 10 str. qts., etc.

Button. Pin at the end of a vn., etc., which bears the pull of the str.

Buxtehude, Dietrich (Diderik) (b Oldesloe, Holstein, 1637; d Lübeck, 1707). Danish organist and composer. In 1668 appointed organist, Marienkirche, Lübeck, from which his fame as a player spread through Europe. Instituted in 1673 ambitious mus. perfs. in assoc. with church services. Known as *Abendmusiken* (evening concerts), they were held annually on the 5 Sundays before Christmas. Such was Buxtehude's fame that J. S. Bach walked 200 miles from Arnstadt to hear him play. Comp. many works for org. (which influenced Bach), and trio sonatas. His vocal music, most of it to sacred texts, is as important as his organ works. He wrote 20 cantatas; his other vocal comps. may be categorized as concertos, chorales, and arias. His arias suggest the influence of Monteverdi, with a strong preference for strophic form over the *da capo* aria.

Buzuk. Turkish instr. resembling long-necked lute, having 4 str. passing over a movable bridge, a fingerboard twice as long as the soundboard, a small oval body, and rounded back.

BWV, *Bach Werke-Verzeichnis* (Index to Bach's Works). The initials, preceding nos., which indicate the catalogue nos. of J. S. Bach's works in the thematic index (*Thematisch-Systematisches Verzeichnis der musikalischen Werke von Johann Sebastian Bach*) compiled and ed. by Wolfgang *Schmieder (1950). Now accepted as standard means of numbering his works, e.g. *St John Passion* is BWV245.

Byrd, William (b probably Lincoln, 1543; d Stondon Massey, Essex, 1623). Eng. composer. Pupil of *Tallis. Organist, Lincoln Cath., 1563. From 1572 hon. organist, Chapel Royal jointly with Tallis. In 1575 he and Tallis jointly pubd. a coll. of motets, *Cantiones sacrae*, dedicated to Queen Elizabeth I. Little is known of Byrd's life apart from various lawsuits over property and the fact of his Roman Catholicism, from the consequences of which he seems to have been protected at a time of anti-Papism by his fame as a composer and by friends in high places. In his motets and masses, Byrd showed himself the equal of his Fr. and It. contemporaries as a contrapuntist. He was an innovator in form and technique in his liturgical works, the finest of which is the Great Service. His madrigals are also of exceptional quality, and there is superb mus. in his solo songs and songs for the stage. In his *Fancies* and *In Nomines* for str. instr. he est. an Eng. instr. style of comp., but perhaps even more significant was his mus. for virginals, in which he developed variation form. Prin. comps.:

SACRED WORKS: Masses, No. 1 in 3 v.-parts, No. 2 in 4, No. 3 in 5. Motets: *Cantiones* (with Tallis, 1575. Contains 17 items by Byrd); **Cantiones Sacrae*, Book I, 1589 (29 motets), Book II, 1591 (32 motets); **Gradualia*, Book I, 1605 (63 motets), Book II, 1607 (45 motets). *Preces, Psalms and Litany*; Short Service; Great Service; 12 verse anthems; 10 psalms.

SECULAR: Madrigals, sonnets; *Songs of sundrie natures* (1589), containing 47 songs; solo songs, canons and rounds.

INSTRUMENTAL: 14 *Fantasies*; 8 *In Nomines*; 9 pieces in *In Nomine* style on plainsong melodies.

KEYBOARD: Over 120 pieces in various colls., incl. **My Ladye Nevells Booke,* transcr. 1591, and **Parthenia* (1611).

Byzantine Music. Christian liturgical song (often highly ornamented) of the E. Roman Empire (capital Byzantium = Constantinople = Istanbul), founded AD 330 by Constantine the Great and destroyed 1453 with the Fall of Constantinople. It appears to derive from an ancient source common to it and to the plainsong of the W. Church. The various forms of notation are also a subject for special study.

C

C. First note of the natural scale, thus C♭, C♭♭, C♮, C♯, C♯♯, C major, C minor. *In C* means either (1) in the key of C major or (2) indicates a non-transposing instr., e.g. tpts. in C. Middle C is the C in about the middle of the pf. and is notated on the line below the treble staff. C clefs indicate position of middle C, e.g. alto and ten. clefs and sop. clef (obsolete). In SCTB, C = contralto.

C.A. **Coll' arco.*

Cabaca. Round or pear-shaped gourd covered with beads and with a handle. Some have beads inside to rattle. Is used in Lat. American dance bands and by several 20th cent. composers.

Cabaletta (Cabbaletta, Cavaletta) (It., from *cavata*, extraction). A term with a number of meanings: (1) Short aria of simple and much reiterated rhythm, generally with repeats. (2) Type of song in rondo form, sometimes with variations. (3) Recurring passage in a song, first appearing simply and then varied (some authorities make a triplet acc. a necessary qualification for the title). (4) Final section of elaborate operatic duet or aria in which mus. often settles down to a steady rhythm, e.g. 'Ah! non giunge' in *La *sonnambula*.

Caballé, Montserrat (*b* Barcelona, 1933). Sp. sop. Studied Barcelona Cons. from age 9. Opera début Basle 1956, First Lady in *Die Zauberflöte*. Glyndebourne 1965, NY Met. 1965. Notable for singing of Bellini, Donizetti, and early Verdi, but successful also in R. Strauss, Puccini, and Mozart. CG début 1972 as Violetta.

Cabanilles, Juan Bautista José (*b* Algemesí, 1644; *d* Valencia, 1712). Sp. composer. Organist, Valencia Cath. from 1665. Org. comps. pubd. in 4 vols. 1927–52.

Cabaret. Term applied to places of entertainment such as night clubs and to the mus. entertainment provided there. Though it had 18th cent. forerunners, cabaret in the modern sense began in 1881 when the 'Chat Noir' opened in Paris. From this milieu arose the great *diseuse* Yvette Guilbert (1885–1944). With her own form of *Sprechgesang* and eloquent movements of limbs and body, she intensified the meaning of words sung to simple tunes. In Ger. the leading cabaret was the 'Überbrettl', founded by Ernst von Wolzogen (librettist of Strauss's *Feuersnot*) in 1901. Schoenberg cond. there and comp. some *Brettllieder*. Political satire was a prin. feature of the cabaret of the 1920s and 1930s in Ger., where Kurt Weill and Hanns Eisler were protagonists. This period was captured by Christopher Isherwood in his novel *Goodbye to Berlin* (1939) (re-named *Cabaret*

for the stage and film). In Eng., cabaret tended to be more genteel and like an intimate revue, but something of the Ger. spirit was emulated by W. H. Auden in his *The Ascent of F6* (1936), the songs being set to mus. by Britten (e.g. 'Tell me the truth about love').

Cabezón, Antonio de (*b* Castrillo de Matajudíos, nr. Burgos, 1510; *d* Madrid, 1566). Sp. composer, blind from birth, one of first to compose for the kbd. Organist and harpsichordist to Kings of Spain. Mus. ahead of its time, as shown by variations on popular melody *El caballero*.

Cabinet Organ. Amer. nomenclature for what in Eng. is called Amer. org. This resembles the **Harmonium, but the air is sucked through the reeds instead of being forced through them and the tone is less pungent. There is no 'Expression' device and so where other means than the player's feet can be applied for operating the bellows, a pedal-board like that of an organ can be built in as part of the instr. Invented by worker in Alexandre's Paris factory but developed in Boston, Mass.

Caccia (It.). Chase, hunt, e.g. *alla caccia*, in hunting style. In **Ars nova* 2 vv. 'chased' each other in strict canon, the text often dealing with hunting. See **Oboe (da caccia)* and **Corno da caccia*.

Caccini, Giulio (*b* Rome, *c.*1548; *d* Florence, 1618). It. singer, composer, and lutenist. Taken to Florence by Cosimo I de' Medici, *c.*1565. One of members of **Camerata, some of his mus. was incl. in Peri's *Euridice* to Rinuccini's lib. which he then also set in rivalry in 1600. Also composed opera *Il rapimento di Cefalo*, perf. Florence 1600. Canzonets and madrigals published in *Le nuove musiche* (New Music) 1602, marking change to monodic style. His daughter Francesca was a celebrated singer.

Cachucha. Andalusian dance for a single performer in triple time. Its mus. is not unlike that of the **bolero*.

Cadéac, Pierre (*fl.* 1538–56). Fr. composer of church mus. and *chansons*. His music was sung in Venice and Kraków, as well as in Ger. and Sp. Best known for *chanson Je suis dehéritée*.

Cadence or Close. Any melodic or harmonic progression which has come to possess a conventional association with the ending of a comp., a section, or a phrase.

The commonest harmonic cadences are: (a) Perfect Cadence (or Full Close). Chord of the

Dominant followed by that of Tonic. (b) Interrupted Cadence. Chord of the Dominant followed by that of Submediant. (c) Imperfect Cadence (or Half Close). Chord of the Tonic or some other chord followed by that of Dominant. (d) Plagal Cadence. Chord of the Subdominant followed by that of Tonic.

To any of the Dominant chords above mentioned the 7th may be added. Any of the chords may be taken in *inversion, but if that is done in the case of the Perfect Cadence its effect of finality (i.e. its 'perfection') is lost.

The term Phrygian Cadence is applied by various writers to (i) in major key a cadence ending on the chord of the Dominant of relative minor (e.g. in Key C major E–G♯–B), or (ii) any sort of Imperfect Cadence (Half Close) in minor mode, or (iii) first inversion of Subdominant chord followed by Dominant chord (e.g. in Key C the chord A–C–F followed by the chord G–B–D). (It seems best to confine the name to the cadence (i) above, which is fairly common in J. S. Bach and for which no other name is available, whereas (ii) and (iii) are simply varieties of the Imperfect Cadence.)

For the cadence employing the *Tierce de Picardie see under that term.

Other terms are:

Abrupt Cadence = Interrupted Cadence (see above). Amen Cadence = Plagal cadence (see above). Authentic Cadence = Perfect Cadence (Full Close; see above). Avoided Cadence = Interrupted Cadence (see above). Broken Cadence = Interrupted Cadence (see above). Church Cadence = Plagal Cadence (see above). Complete Cadence = Perfect Cadence (Full Close; see above). Deceptive Cadence = Interrupted Cadence (see above). Demi-Cadence = Imperfect Cadence (Half Close; see above). Dominant Cadence = Imperfect Cadence (Half Close; see above). Evaded Cadence = Interrupted Cadence (see above). False Close = Interrupted Cadence (see above). Greek Cadence = Plagal Cadence (see above). Half Cadence = Half Close (see *Imperfect Cadence*, above). Inverted Cadence = A Perfect or Imperfect Cadence (Full Close or Half Close; see above) with its latter chord inverted. (Some confine the name to

the Perfect Cadence thus changed; others extend it to all cadences having either chord, or both, inverted.) Irregular Cadence = Interrupted Cadence (see above). Mixed Cadence. The term is used in 2 ways—both of them superfluous. (1) A 'mixing' of the Plagal and Imperfect Cadences, consisting of Subdominant-Dominant, this being merely the Imperfect Cadence in one of its commonest forms. (2) A mixing of the Plagal and Perfect Cadences, consisting of the Perfect Cadence preceded by the Subdominant—making 3 chords, instead of the usual 2. This is merely the Perfect Cadence led up to in one of its commonest manners and should not require any special name. Radical Cadence = any cadence of which the chords are in root position, i.e. the roots of the chords in the bass. Semi-Perfect Cadence = Perfect Cadence (see above) with the 3rd or 5th of the Tonic in the highest part. Surprise Cadence = Interrupted Cadence (see above). Suspended Cadence = A hold-up before the final cadence of a piece, as that in a conc. (or, in former times, an aria) for the solo performer to work in a *cadenza.

The above definitions accord with Brit. terminology. Amer. usage is different and inconsistent.

Cadenza (It.). A flourish (properly, improvised) inserted into the final cadence of any section of a vocal aria or a solo instr. movement. The conventional final cadence consists, harmonically, of 3 chords, the 2nd inversion of the Tonic Chord, and the Dominant and Tonic Chords in root position (i.e. $\frac{6}{4}$ $\frac{5}{3}$ on the Dominant bass, followed by $\frac{5}{3}$ on the Tonic bass). The interpolated cadenza begins on the first of these chords, the orch. joining in again only when the soloist, after a display of vocal or instr. virtuosity, indicates by a long trill that he or she is ready to be rejoined in the final chords or in any passage elaborated out of them.

In the operatic aria conventional practice admitted 3 cadenzas—one at the end of each of its sections (see *Aria*), the most elaborate being reserved to the last. The term *melisma* has been used for the vocal cadenza.

From the time of Mozart and Beethoven in instr. mus. the tendency grew for the composer to write out the cadenza in full, although Mozart's and Beethoven's cadenzas are often still rejected by soloists who substitute cadenzas by other hands (e.g. by Busoni, Reinecke, etc.). In Beethoven's and Brahms's vn. concs. the cadenza was left to the performer's invention, but Joachim and Kreisler (and others) provided written-out cadenzas which are generally used. Schumann in his pf. conc. and Mendelssohn in his vn. conc. began the trend, general now, of integrating the cadenza into the comp. There are many fine examples of acc. cadenzas (e.g. Elgar's Vn. Conc.). Sometimes the cadenza assumes the importance of, effectively, an extra movement (e.g. Shostakovich's First Vn. Conc., Walton's Vc. Conc.). Of course, with the growth of *aleatory procedures, the improvised cadenza has come back into its own.

Cadenzato (It.). Cadenced, i.e. rhythmic.

Cadman, Charles Wakefield (b Johnstown, Penn., 1881; d Los Angeles, 1946). Amer. composer, organist, and mus. critic. Specialist in mus. of Amer. Indians, using it in his own works which incl. several operas, orch. comps., and many songs.

Caffarelli (Gaetano Majorano) (b Bitonto, 1710; d Naples, 1783). It. mezzo-soprano castrato. Studied in Naples under Porpora. Début Rome 1726. Sang in prin. It. opera-houses from 1729 but chiefly in Naples, where he was appointed to royal chapel. Sang in London 1737–8, creating title-roles in Handel's *Faramondo* and *Serse*. Sang in Fr. 1754, Lisbon 1755, Madrid 1756. Temperamental artist who was once imprisoned for making obscene gestures during a performance. Retired with a fortune and bought a dukedom, an estate, and a palace.

Cage, John (b Los Angeles, 1912). Amer. composer, pianist, and writer. Studied with *Cowell and *Schoenberg. From 1937 developed interests in dance and perc. In 1938 invented the 'prepared pf.' by inserting various objects, from rubber-bands to hatpins, between the str. to create new effects. Settled in NY 1942, beginning long assoc. with Merce Cunningham Dance Co. as mus. dir. Study of oriental philosophies led to his utilization of 'chance' in his mus., as in *Music of Changes* (1951). In 1952 he prod. his first piece involving tape, *Imaginary Landscape V*, and in the same year came *4'33"* in which the performer makes no sound.

The particular elements of Cage's *avant-garde* outlook are: use of any kind of environmental sounds or noises; use of 'chance', as in *Music of Changes* where the selection process involves tossing a coin; abandonment of formal structures; use of silence; use of a wide range of elec. and visual techniques. Books incl. *Silence* (1961), *A Year from Monday* (1967), and *For the Birds* (1981). Works incl.:

ORCHESTRA: Conc. for prepared pf. and orch. (1951); Concert for pf. (1957–8); *Atlas Eclipticalis* (1961–2); *Cheap Imitation* (1972, orch. version of pf. solo); *Etcetera* (1973); *Score (40 drawings by Thoreau)* and *23 Parts* (for any instr. and/or vv., 1974); Quartets I–VIII (24, 41, or 93 instrs., 1976); *30 Pieces for 5 Orchestras* (1981).
PERCUSSION AND ELECTRONIC: *Construction I in Metal* for perc. sextet (1939); *Imaginary Landscape I* for 2 variable speed gramophone turntables, frequency recordings, muted pf. and cymbal (1939); *Imaginary Landscape II (March)* for perc. quintet (1942); *Imaginary Landscape III* for perc. sextet (1942); *Amores* (1943); *Imaginary Landscape IV (March No. 2)* for 12 radios, 24 players and cond. (1951); *Imaginary Landscape V*

(1952); *Speech* for 5 radios with news reader (1955); 27'10.554" for percussionist (1956).
CHAMBER MUSIC: 3 pieces for fl. duet (1935); Str. Qt. (1950); *4'33"* (silent, for any instr. or combination of instr.) (1952); *Variations I–VI* for any no. of players and sound-producing means (1958–66); HPSCHD for 7 hpd. soloists and 51 or any no. of tape machines (1967–9); *30 Pieces for Str. Qt.* (1984).
PIANO SOLO: *Metamorphosis* (1938); 7 Haiku (1952); *Music of Changes* (1951, in 4 vols.); *Music for Piano* (1952–6, several works); 0'00" to be perf. in any way by anyone (1962); *Cheap Imitation* (1969, orch. version 1972); *Étude Australes*, 32 studies in 4 books (1974–5).
PREPARED PIANO: *Bacchanale* (1938); *Meditation* (1943); *Sonatas and Interludes* (1946–8); *Music for Marcel Duchamp* (1947).
MISCELLANEOUS: Cl. Sonata (1933); *Music for Carillon* Nos. 1–5 (1952–67); *Les Chants de Maldoror pulverisés par l'assistance même* (1971).
VOICE: 5 Songs for cont. and pf. (e.e. cummings) (1938); *The Wonderful Widow of Eighteen Springs* for v. and closed pf. (Joyce) (1942); *Song Books, Solos for voice 3–92* (1970); *62 Mesostics re Merce Cunningham* (1971, unacc.); *Hymns and Variations* (12 amp. vv., 1978); *Litany for the Whale* (2 vv., 1980).
TAPE, AUDIO-VISUAL etc.: *Water Music* (1952); *Fontana Mix* (1958); *Where are we going? And what are we doing?* (1960); *Rozart Mix* (1965); *Bird Cage* (12 tapes, 1972); *Lecture on the Weather* (12 perf., 1975).

Cahier, Mme Charles (b Nashville, Tenn., 1870; d Manhattan Beach, Calif., 1951). Amer. mez., born Sarah-Jane Layton Walker. Studied in Paris with J. *de Reszke and in Berlin with Amalie Joachim. Début in opera, Nice 1904. Vienna Opera 1907–11, NY Met. 1911–13. Taught at Curtis Institute. Soloist in f.p. in 1911 (Munich) of Mahler's *Das Lied von der Erde*.

Cahill, Teresa (Mary) (b Maidenhead, 1944). Eng. sop. Studied pf., then singing at London Opera Centre. Début Glyndebourne 1970, CG 1970. Milan début 1976. Won John Christie award 1970.

Ça Ira! (That will succeed). This expression, many times repeated, made up about half the words of a revolutionary song (later the official song of the Revolution) said to have originated on 5 Oct. 1789 when the Fr. mob marched to Versailles to bring the King and the royal family to Paris, and which became the mus. acc. to almost every incident of the Terror. The tune adopted was that of a popular contredanse, called *Carillon national*, by a th. violinist of the day, Bécourt. See also *Carmagnole*.

Cairns, David (Adam) (b Loughton, Essex, 1926). Eng. critic and writer. Studied Oxford Univ. (1945–8) and Princeton Univ. (1950–1). One of founders of Chelsea Opera Group, 1950. Authority on Berlioz, translating and editing the *Memoirs*

(1969, rev. 1977). Mus. critic *Financial Times*, 1962–7, *New Statesman*, 1967–70, *Sunday Times* from 1973 (chief critic from 1983). Worked for record company, 1967–72. His brilliant essays on mus. subjects were published under title *Responses* (1973).

Caisse (Fr.). Box, hence drum.

Caisse claire (Fr.). Clear drum, i.e. Snare drum, otherwise *side drum*.

Caisse grosse (Fr.). Large drum, i.e. *Bass drum.

Caisse roulante (Fr.). Rolling drum, i.e. *Tenor drum.

Caisse sourde (Fr.). Dull drum, i.e. *Tenor drum; see also *Caisse roulante*.

Caix d'Hervelois, Louis de (*b* Paris, *c*.1670; *d* Paris, 1760). Fr. performer on and composer for the viola da gamba, some of whose works are now sometimes perf. by cellists. Wrote 5 books of pieces for viola da gamba, 3 books of fl. sonatas.

Calando (It.). Lowering. *Diminuendo*, with also *rallentando*.

Calcando (It.). Trampling. Much the same as *accelerando*, i.e. quickening gradually.

Caldara, Antonio (*b* Venice, *c*.1670; *d* Vienna, 1736). It. composer, pupil of *Legrenzi. Imperial chamber-composer at Vienna court 1714, ass. Kapellmeister to *Fux from 1716. Comp. 87 operas, over 40 oratorios, masses, and other church mus., incl. Christmas Cantata, and songs, of which *Come raggio di sol* is well known. Among his many operas was the first setting of Metastasio's libretto *La Clemenza di Tito* (Vienna, 1734).

Caldwell, Sarah (*b* Maryville, Miss., 1924). Amer. opera producer, administrator, and conductor. Studied vn. at New England Cons. Staged Vaughan Williams's *Riders to the Sea* at Tanglewood 1947. Head of Boston Univ. opera workshop 1952–60. Founded Boston Opera Co. 1957. Responsible for f. Amer. ps. of Prokofiev's *War and Peace*, Nono's *Intolleranza*, and Schoenberg's *Moses und Aron*. First woman cond. at NY Met., 1976 (*La Traviata*). Has cond. NY P.O., Boston S.O., etc.

Calife de Bagdad, Le (The Caliph of Bagdad). Opera in 1 act by Boieldieu to lib. by C.H. d'A. de Saint-Just. Prod. Paris 1800; London 1809; New Orleans 1806.

Calinda, La. Orch. interlude by Delius in his opera *Koanga* (1896–7); it is a dance named after a Negro dance imported to Amer. by African slaves.

Calino Castureme (*Caleno custureme*). Tune mentioned by Shakespeare in *Henry V* (Act IV, sc. 4). It is to be found in the *Fitzwilliam Virginal Book. In *A Handefull of Pleasant Delites*, 1584, the words 'Caleno Custureme' are interpolated between every 2 lines of the poem 'When as I view your comly grace'. Possibly a perversion of the Irish 'Cailín, ó cois t Suire, mé' (I am a girl from the banks of the river Suir).

Caliph of Bagdad, The (Boieldieu). See *Calife de Bagdad, Le*.

Calisto, La. Opera in 2 acts by *Cavalli to lib. by G. Faustini, prod. Venice 1651, and revived at Glyndebourne 1970 in a realization by Raymond *Leppard.

Callas, (Cecilia Sophia Anna) **Maria** (Kalogeropoulos) (*b* Manhattan, NY, 1923; *d* Paris, 1977). Amer.-born sop. of Gr. parentage. Studied Athens Nat. Cons. from 1936 with Sp. coloratura sop. Elvira de Hidalgo. Début Athens 1940 in Suppé's *Boccaccio*, Leonore in *Fidelio*, and Tosca. It. début Verona, 1947, in *La gioconda*. Among her roles at this time were Isolde, Brünnhilde (*Die Walküre*), Kundry, and Turandot. Potentialities recognized by cond. Tullio *Serafin when, in 1948, she was singing Brünnhilde in Venice. Prima donna engaged as Elvira for next opera, Bellini's *I puritani*, fell ill and Serafin suggested Callas as substitute. Her singing of a *bel canto* role in the powerful, dramatic way the composer intended was a revelation. Not since Lilli Lehmann had a sop. encompassed Wagnerian roles and the coloratura repertory. With Serafin and de Sabata, Callas revived operas wholly or relatively neglected in It. for over a century, incl. Rossini's *Armida* and *Il turco in Italia*, Cherubini's *Medea*, Spontini's *La vestale*, Donizetti's *Anna Bolena*, and Bellini's *Il pirata*, thereby changing the face of the post-1945 opera repertory. First sang at La Scala, Milan, April 1950. From then until 1958 reigned supreme there, earning title *La divina* in her vivid portrayals of Norma, Violetta, and Tosca, working with de Sabata, Giulini, Bernstein, and Karajan as conds., and the producers Visconti and Zeffirelli. Voice not beautiful but musicianship was impeccable, insight remarkable, and acting ability exceptional, so that she presented her roles as organic wholes. Her Norma, Tosca, and Violetta were unforgettable examples of dramatic opera singing-acting, linking her in this branch of her art to the legendary names of Malibran and Schröder-Devrient. Sang at CG 1952–3 (*Norma*), 1957–9, and 1964. Amer. début at Chicago, 1954, and at NY Met. 1956 (*Norma*). Private life was lived in the glare of publicity inseparable from such a magnetic personality. Retired from stage 1965 (last perf. was as Tosca at CG 5 July 1965) but continued to record and gave some concerts in 1973 and 1974. Also worked as producer and teacher.

Caller Herrin'. Poem by Lady Nairne (1766–1845) written *c*.1821 to fit tune of a hpd. piece comp. *c*.1798 by Nathaniel *Gow in which he incorporated Edinburgh fishwives' traditional cry with bells of St Andrew's Church.

Calligrammes. Song-cycle by Poulenc to 7 poems by Guillaume Apollinaire, comp. 1948. Titles are: *L'Espionne, Mutation, Vers le Sud, Il pleut, La Gâce exilée, Aussi bien que les cigales, Voyage.*

Calliope. Amer. term for steamblown mechanical organ.

Calmato, Calmando (It.). Calmed; calming.

Calm Sea and Prosperous Voyage (Meeresstille und glückliche Fahrt). Poems by Goethe set by several composers incl. (1) Beethoven, Op. 112, for SATB and orch., comp. 1815, pubd. 1823. (2) Song by *Reichardt (1752–1814). (3) Song (*Meeresstille* section only) by Schubert (D216), comp. 1815. (4) Concert-ov. by Mendelssohn, Op. 27, 1832, f.p. 1836. Theme from this is quoted by Elgar in 13th (*Romanza*) of his *Enigma Variations.

Calore (It.). Heat. Passion. So the adjective *caloroso*.

Calvé, Emma (orig. Rosa Calvet) (*b* Decazeville, 1858; *d* Millau, 1942). Fr. operatic sop. particularly noted for perf. as Carmen. Studied in Paris. Début Brussels 1881, Milan 1887, CG 1892 after further study with Mathilde Marchesi. NY Met. 1893, where first sang Carmen. Created roles of Anita in Massenet's *La Navarraise* and Suzel in Mascagni's *L'amico Fritz*. Retired 1910.

Calvocoressi, Michel Dimitri (*b* Marseilles, 1877; *d* London, 1944). Fr.-born mus. critic of Gr. parentage. Career in Paris as mus. critic, author, and lecturer on mus.; settled in London. Early student of Russ. mus. and assoc. with Diaghilev opera enterprise; wrote books on Mussorgsky, Schumann, Glinka, Liszt, and other mus. subjects; provided many trans. of Russ. libs., contributed in various languages to mus. journals.

Calypso. W. Indian folk dance, but better known in its sung form. Began among slaves on plantations. Forbidden to talk, they chanted news and opinions to a tom-tom rhythm, using a *patois*. Today, especially in Trinidad, is used as a way of commenting on politics, scandal, and sport. Among best-known examples are the cricket calypsos, such as 'Cricket, lovely cricket', with its references to the bowling of Ramadhin and Valentine in the Test matches of 1950 when, at Lord's, W. Indies beat England for the first (but not the last!) time in England.

Calzabigi, Raniero de (*b* Leghorn, 1714; *d* Naples, 1795). It. writer of libs. for Gluck's *Orfeo, Alceste,* and *Paride ed Elena.* Pubd. ed. of *Metastasio's works. Ran lottery in Paris in partnership with Casanova.

Camargo. See *Ballet.*

Cambert, Robert (*b* Paris, *c*.1628; *d* London, 1677). Fr. harpsichordist and organist; colleague in Paris of the Abbé Pierre Perrin who in 1669 obtained monopoly for perf. of opera in Fr. language, Cambert's *Pomone* (1671) being earliest

Fr. opera. On Lully taking over the monopoly in 1672, Cambert went to Eng. where he founded a Royal Academy of Music, which soon failed. Only fragments of his compositions remain.

Cambini, Giovanni (Gioacchino) (*b* Leghorn, 1746; *d* Bicêtre, nr. Paris, 1825). It. composer, violinist, and violist, associated with Paris Concert Spirituel. Comp. syms., over 140 qts., concs., operas, and shorter pieces.

Cambio, Perissone (*fl.* 16th cent.). Fr. composer who lived in Venice, where he was a singer at St Mark's. Works incl. mass, madrigals, and canzonas.

Cambridge University. Eng. univ. which has conferred mus. degrees (Bachelor of Music, Doctor of Music) since 1463. Formal examinations were instituted by Sterndale Bennett, 1857. The Professors of Mus. have been—1684 Nicolas Staggins; 1705 Thos. Tudway; 1730 Maurice Greene; 1755 John Randall; 1799 Charles Hague; 1821 J. Clarke-Whitfield; 1836 Thomas A. Walmisley; 1856 W. Sterndale Bennett; 1875 G. A. Macfarren; 1887 C. V. Stanford; 1924 Charles Wood; 1926 E. J. Dent; 1946 Patrick Hadley; 1962 Thurston Dart; 1965 Robin Orr; 1976 Alexander Goehr.

Camden, Archie (Archibald Lewis) (*b* Newark, Notts., 1888; *d* Wheathampstead, Herts., 1979). Eng. bassoonist. Trained RMCM. Member Hallé Orch. 1906–33 (prin. bn. from 1914), BBC S.O. 1933–45, RPO 1946–7. Soloist and recitalist. Prof. of bn. RMCM 1914–33. Cond. London Stock Exchange Orch. O.B.E. 1969.

Camden Festival. Annual festival founded in 1954 as the St Pancras Festival. Special feature is production of operas outside standard repertory, e.g. Brit. stage premières of Haydn's *Orfeo ed Euridice* (1955) and *Il Mondo della Luna* (1960), Verdi's *Un giorno di regno* (1961), Donizetti's *Maria Stuarda* and Verdi's *Il corsaro* (1966), Massenet's *Sappho* (1967), Rimsky-Korsakov's *Mozart and Salieri* (1968), Storace's *Gli equivoci* (1974), Meyerbeer's *L'Etoile du Nord* and Donizetti's *Torquato Tasso* (1975), Delius's *Fennimore and Gerda* (1979) and *Margot-la-Rouge* (1984), Cavalli's *Eritrea,* Pacini's *Maria Tudor* (1983), Lecocq's *Dr Miracle* (1984), and Vivaldi's *Juditha triumphans* (1984). Concert perfs. were given of Strauss's *Feuersnot* (1978), Walton's *Troilus and Cressida* (1982), J. C. Bach's *Adriano in Siria* (1982), Shostakovich's *Lady Macbeth of Mtsensk* (1984).

Camera (It.). Chamber—as opposed to hall, opera-house, etc. (For *Cantata da camera,* see *Cantata*; for *Concerto da camera,* see *Concerto*; for *Sonata da camera,* see *Sonata.*) *Musica di camera* (It.). Chamber mus.

Camerata (It.). Society. Group of poets and musicians who met in houses of Florentine aristocrats *Bardi and *Corsi from about 1580 and from whose discussions opera was developed.

Among them were composers Galilei, *Peri, *Caccini, and Cavalieri. Bardi wrote lib. for Peri and Caccini. The group evolved the monodic *stile rappresentativo* of which the first example (now lost) was Peri's *dramma per musica, Dafne*. Various modern chamber-mus. organizations use word *Camerata* in their title.

Cameron, Basil (*b* Reading, 1884; *d* Leominster, 1975). Eng. cond. Studied Berlin Hochschule für Musik 1902–6. At early stage of his career called himself Basil Hindenburg because conds. with Eng. names then received few engagements. Cond. Torquay Municipal Orch. 1913–14, Hastings 1923–30, Harrogate 1924–30, San Francisco S.O. 1930–2, Seattle 1932–8. Ass. cond. Henry Wood Promenade Concerts from 1940. C.B.E. 1957.

Cameron, Douglas (*b* Dundee, 1902; *d* London, 1974). Scot. cellist. Studied RAM. Member, Blech String Qt. Played in several leading Brit. orchs., being prin. cellist of Beecham's RPO. Prin. cellist BBC S.O. O.B.E. 1974.

Cameron, John (Ewen) (*b* Coolamon, N.S.W., 1920). Australian bar. Studied Sydney Cons. Settled in Brit. 1949. Opera at CG (début 1949 as Germont *père* in *La traviata*), Glyndebourne, and many concert appearances.

Camidge. Eng. family of organists spanning nearly 200 years. John (*b* York, 1735; *d* York, 1803), organist, York Minster 1756–99 and composer for hpd. His son Matthew (*b* York, 1758; *d* York, 1844), organist, York Minster 1799–1842, composer of org. mus. His son John (*b* York, 1790; *d* York, 1859), organist, York Minster 1842–8. His son Thomas Simpson (*b* York, 1828; *d* York, 1912), organist, York Minster 1848–59. His son John (*b* York,1853; *d* York, 1939), organist, Beverley Minster 1875–1933.

Camilleri, Charles (Mario) (*b* Hamrun, Malta, 1931). Maltese composer and cond. Studied Malta and Toronto Univ. Cond. Canadian Broadcasting Corporation 1960–5. Comp. incl. 1-act opera *Melita* (1968), *Maltese Dances* for orch., *Maqam*, pf. and orch., *Zeitgeist*, orch., ob. concertante, accordion conc., pf. trio, vc. sonata, and *Missa Mundi* for organ.

Cammarano, Salvatore (*b* Naples, 1801; *d* Naples, 1852). It. poet, dramatist, and librettist. Had plays staged when he was 18. Wrote first lib. in 1834 (for Vignozzi). In 1835 first collab. with *Donizetti. Among the many libs. he wrote for him were those of *Lucia di Lammermoor* and *Belisario*. In 1841 wrote *Alzira* for Verdi, following it with *La battaglia di Legnano, Luisa Miller*, and most of *Il Trovatore* (he died before completing the last). Also wrote libs. for Pacini and Mercadante.

Campana; Campane (It.). Bell; bells, e.g. those used in the orch.

Campana sommersa, La (The Submerged Bell). Opera in 4 acts by *Respighi to lib. by Guastalla based on play by G. Hauptmann. Prod. Hamburg 1927, NY Met. 1928.

Campanella (It.). Little bell. (The plural, *campanelle,* is sometimes used for *Glockenspiel.)

Campanella, La. Transcr. for pf. by Liszt of the *Rondo alla campanella* (Ronde à la clochette; *Bell rondo) from Paganini's Vn. Conc. in B minor. Liszt first used theme in *Grand Fantaisie sur La Clochette* (La campanella) of 1831–2, rev. in *Six grandes études d'après les caprices de Paganini* (1838, rev. 1851).

Campanello di Notte, Il (The Night Bell). Opera in 1 act by Donizetti (sometimes also known as *Il campanello dello Speziale*) to text by composer. Prod. Naples 1836, London 1837.

Campanetta (It.). *Glockenspiel.

Campbells are Coming, The. This popular Scot. tune first appeared in print in 1745, at which time it was used as a country dance under the title *Hob and Nob*, but about the same period also found with its present title. Many contradictory statements about its origin.

Campenhout, François van (*b* Brussels, 1779; *d* Brussels, 1848). Belg. ten., violinist, and composer. Comp. operas, ballets, and church mus., but remembered chiefly as composer of Belg. nat. anthem, *La *Brabançonne*.

Campiello, Il (The Square). Opera in 3 acts by *Wolf-Ferrari to lib. by Ghisalberti based on Goldoni's comedy. Prod. Milan 1936.

Campion (Campian), **Thomas** (*b* Witham, Essex, 1567; *d* Witham, 1620). Eng. composer, lawyer, and physician. Pubd. first *Book of Ayres*, in a group by *Rosseter, 1601, following it with 4 more (1610–12) in which he wrote both mus. and words, with lute acc. Wrote several masques for perf. at court, critique of Eng. poetry, and treatise on counterpoint (1613)—a prototype 'Elizabethan man', proficient in all the arts.

Campoli, Alfredo (*b* Rome, 1906). It.-born violinist. Studied with father. Settled in Eng. as a child. London début at age 11. Made reputation in light mus., running his own orch., but after 1945 devoted himself to the conc. repertory, notably in Elgar and Bliss. Amer. début 1953 (NY).

Campra, André (*b* Aix-en-Provence, 1660; *d* Versailles, 1744). Fr. composer. Dir. of mus. at several caths., incl. Notre Dame de Paris 1694–1700. First stage work was *opéra-ballet L'Europe galante* (Paris 1697). Created the form *opéra-ballet*. Comp. many more operas and *opéra-ballets*, incl. *Tancrède* (1702) and *Idoménée* (1712). Also wrote much church mus. incl. *Requiem* (c.1722).

Canale. Another name for *psaltery.

Canaries (or *Canarie,* or *Canary*). Old dance in rhythm something like *gigue but with all its phrases beginning on first beat of the measure with a note a beat and a half long. So called in 17th cent. because it imitated Canary Is. rituals.

Can-Can (or *Chahut*). Boisterous (and supposedly indecorous) Parisian dance of quadrille pattern. Best-known example is Offenbach's from *Orpheus in the Underworld.*

Canción (Sp.). Song. There are diminutives— *Cancioncica, Cancioncilla, Cancioncita.* The *Canción danza* is a Sp. dance-song.

Cancrizans. See *Canon.*

Candide. Comic operetta by Leonard *Bernstein, to lib. by Lillian Hellman adapted from Voltaire. Prod. Boston, Oct. 1956.

Caniglia, Maria (*b* Naples, 1906; *d* Rome, 1979). It. sop. Début Turin 1930; Milan 1930–42; at CG 1937, 1939, and 1950; NY Met. 1938–9. A famous Tosca.

Canino, Bruno (*b* Naples, 1935). It. pianist and composer. Studied at Milan Cons. Won prizes at int. pf. comps. at Bolzano and Darmstadt. Specialist in contemp. mus., notably works by Donatoni and Bussotti. Often accompanied Cathy *Berberian. Member of Trio di Milano. Prof. of mus., Milan Cons. from 1961. Works incl. chamber concs. and str. qts.

Cannabich, Johann Christian (*b* Mannheim, 1731; *d* Frankfurt, 1798). Ger. violinist, composer, and cond. Trained under *Stamitz. In 1759 became leader of Mannheim orch., becoming dir. 1775. Dir., court mus. at Munich, 1778. Mozart praised his conducting. Wrote operas, ballets, syms., sinfonie concertanti, and chamber mus. His son Karl (*b* Mannheim, 1771; *d* Munich, 1806) succeeded him as dir. of Munich orch. 1800.

Cannon, (Jack) **Philip** (*b* Paris, 1929). Eng. composer and cond. Studied Dartington Hall with Imogen Holst and RCM with Vaughan Williams and Gordon Jacob. Lecturer, Sydney Univ. 1957–9; prof. of comp. RCM from 1960. Works incl. operas *Morvoren* (Cornish for 'mermaid'), *Dr Jekyll and Mr Hyde,* and *The Man from Venus;* pf. concertino; str. qt. (1964); Sym. (*Oraison funèbre de l'âme humaine*); *The Temple* (1974), unacc. ch.; pf. trio (*Lacrimae mundi*); *Son of Man,* 'European choral symphony' in Lat., Eng., Fr., and Ger. for ten., bar., ch., and orch.; *Son of God,* unacc. ch.; *Son of Science,* cantata; *Spring,* symphonic study; 5 *Chansons de Femme,* sop. and harp; *Fleeting Fancies,* unacc. ch.; *3 Rivers,* ten. and pf.; *Carillon* for organ; cl. quintet; *Te Deum,* ch. and organ (1975); *Lord of Light,* oratorio, soloists, ch., semi-ch., organ, orch. (1980).

Canntaireachd. Curious Scot. Highland bagpipe notation, in which syllables stand for recognized groups of notes.

Canon. (1) Strictest form of contrapuntal imitation. The word means 'rule' and, musically, it is applied to *counterpoint in which one melodic strand gives the rule to another, or to all the others, which must, at an interval of time, imitate it, note for note. Simple forms of choral canon are the *Catch and the *Round. There are varieties of canon, as follows:

Canon at the Octave in which the vv. (human or instr.) are at that pitch-interval from one another. *Canon at the Fifth,* or at any other interval, is similarly explained.

A Canon for 2 vv. is called a *Canon 2 in 1* (and similarly with *Canon 3 in 1,* etc.). A *Canon 4 in 2* is a double canon, i.e. one in which 2 vv. are carrying on 1 canon whilst 2 others are engaged on another.

Canon by Augmentation has the imitating vv. in longer notes than the one that they are imitating. *Canon by Diminution* is the reverse.

Canon Cancrizans is a type in which the imitating v. gives out the melody backwards ('Cancrizans' from Lat. *Cancer* = crab; but crabs move sideways). Other names for it are *Canon per recte et retro* (or *Rectus et Inversus*) and *Retrograde Canon.*

A *Perpetual Canon* or *Infinite Canon* is a Canon so arranged that each v., having arrived at the end, can begin again, and so indefinitely as in *Three blind mice.* The converse is *Finite Canon.*

Strict Canon in which the intervals of the imitating v. are exactly the same as those of the v. imitated (i.e. as regards their quality of major, minor, etc.).

In *Free Canon* the intervals remain the same numerically, but not necessarily as to quality (e.g. a major 3rd may become a minor 3rd).

That v. in a canon which first enters with the melody to be imitated is called *Dux* (leader) or *Antecedent,* and any imitating v. is called *Comes* (companion) or *Consequent.*

In *Canon by Inversion,* (also styled *al rovescio*), an upward interval in the *Dux* becomes a downward one in the *Comes,* and vice versa. *Canon per Arsin et Thesin* has the same meaning, but also another one, i.e. Canon in which notes that fall on strong beats in the *Dux* fall on weak beats in the *Comes,* and vice versa.

Choral Canon in which there are non-canonic instrumental parts is *Accompanied Canon.*

Passages of canonic writing often occur in comps. that, as wholes, are not canon. In addition to actual canonic comp. there exists a great deal of comp. with a similar effect but which is too free to come under that designation, being mere *Canonic Imitation.*

(2) Name for *psaltery (or *canale*).

Cantabile (It.). Singable, singingly, i.e. with the melody smoothly perf. and well brought out. Critics frequently write of a performer's *cantabile* style, meaning a lyrical 'singing' style. (For Aria Cantabile see *Aria.*) **Cantando** (It.), singing.

Cantata (It.). Sung. Term with different meanings according to period:

(1) In early 17th cent., often a dramatic madrigal sung by one v., with lute acc. or basso continuo. The form became very popular in It. later in 17th cent., being perf. by several vv., some cantatas being comp. of recit., others of a succession of arias. The *cantata da camera* was secular, the *cantata da chiesa* (developed by *Carissimi) sacred. A prolific exponent of the cantata was A. *Scarlatti, who wrote 600 for solo v. and continuo, 60 for v. and instrs., and several chamber cantatas for 2 vv.

(2) During 18th cent., became more theatrical, comprising a *ritornello, aria* on two contrasted themes, and concluding *ritornello,* and acc. by str. In Ger. the form was found mainly in the church, written for soloist(s), ch., organ, and orch. on biblical text. *Telemann, *Schütz, and *Handel wrote in this style but were overshadowed by *Bach who wrote nearly 300 church cantatas as well as secular cantatas which resemble a short opera (*Coffee Cantata* and *Peasant Cantata*).

(3) From Bach's model there developed the cantata of the 19th cent. which was usually on a sacred subject and was, in effect, a short oratorio. Secular cantatas on an elaborate scale are Elgar's *King Olaf* and *Caractacus.* In the 20th cent. the term has acquired a much looser meaning. Walton's *Belshazzar's Feast* and Vaughan Williams's *Sancta Civitas* are described by their composers as oratorios, but could equally well be classified as cantatas. Britten's *Cantata academica* is for soloists, ch., and orch., while Stravinsky's *Cantata* is for 2 soloists, women's ch., and 6 instr.

Cantata. Setting by Stravinsky for sop., ten., female ch., 2 fl., 2 ob., cor anglais, and vc. of anon. 15th- and 16th-cent. Eng. poems (incl. 'Lyke Wake Dirge' and 'Westron Wind'). Comp. 1951–2. F.p. Los Angeles 1952; London 1953.

Cantata Academica (Carmen Basiliense). Choral work, Op. 62, by Britten, comp. 1959 for 500th anniv. of Basle Univ. For SATB soloists, ch., and orch. F.p. Basle 1960. Lat. text, compiled from Univ. Charter and orations in praise of Basle, by Bernhard Wyss.

Cantata Profana (*A Kilenc csodaszarvas;* The 9 Enchanted Stags). Work by Bartók for double ch., ten. and bar. soloists, and orch., comp. 1930 and f.p. London (BBC broadcast) 25 May 1934.

Cantatrice (It.). Female singer.

Cante flamenco. Type of melody popular in Andalusia and used in both song and dance. A branch of *Cante hondo. The significance of the word *Flamenco* (Flemish) is much disputed. See also *Flamenco.*

Cante hondo or **Cante jondo** (Sp.). Deep song. Traditional Andalusian song, with a good deal of repetition of the note, much melodic decoration, and the use of some intervals that do not occur in

the accepted European scales. The Phrygian *cadence is much used and the acc. is usually by guitar, played by another performer.

Cantelli, Guido (*b* Novara, 1920; *d* Orly, Paris, 1956). It. cond. Studied Milan Cons. Début Novara (Teatro Coccia) 1943. Guest cond. La Scala, Milan, after 1945. Invited by Toscanini to guest-cond. NBC Orch., NY, 1949. Edinburgh Fest. 1950. Appointed mus. dir. of La Scala, Milan, a few days before death in air crash.

Canteloube de Malaret, Marie-Joseph (*b* Annonay, 1879; *d* Paris, 1957). Fr. composer. Pupil of Schola Cantorum of *d'Indy, whose biography he wrote (1949). Wrote 2 operas but best known as collector of Fr. folk-songs, hence the *Chants d'Auvergne,* 9 songs for v. and pf. or orch. taken from the 4 vols. he pubd., 1923–30.

Canterbury Degrees. See *Archbishop's Degrees.*

Canterbury Pilgrims, The. (1) Opera in 3 acts by Stanford to lib. by G. A. A'Beckett based on Chaucer's poem. Prod. London 1884.

(2) Opera in 4 acts by *de Koven to lib. by MacKaye after Chaucer. Prod. NY Met. 1917.

(3) Cantata by George Dyson based on Chaucer (modernized text) f.p. Winchester 1931 (ov. *At the Tabard Inn* 1946).

Canti carnascialeschi (It.). Carnival Songs (singular is *canto carnascialesco*). Processional madrigals of an early simple variety, with several stanzas to the same mus., something like the Eng. Ayre but with the tune in the ten. Part of social life of Florence in the 15th and 16th cents.

Canticle. (1) A Bible hymn (other than a psalm) as used in the liturgy of a Christian church. In the R.C. Church the Canticles drawn from the New Testament are called the *Evangelical Canticles* or *Major Canticles,* in distinction from those drawn from the Old Testament, which are called the *Minor Canticles.*

(2) Concert work with (usually but not exclusively) religious text, particularly favoured by Britten (see below).

Canticles. Name given by Britten to 5 of his comps. I (1947) Op. 40, is a setting of a poem by Francis Quarles (*My beloved is mine*) and is subtitled 'In Memory of Dick Sheppard' (a former vicar of St Martin-in-the-Fields, London); II (1952) *Abraham and Isaac,* Op. 51, on a text from a Chester miracle play, for cont., ten., and pf.; III (1954) *Still Falls the Rain,* Op. 55, for ten., hn., and pf., poem by Edith Sitwell; IV (1971) *Journey of the Magi,* Op. 86, for counterten., ten., bar., and pf., poem by T. S. Eliot; V (1974) *The Death of St Narcissus,* Op. 89, for ten. and harp, poem by Eliot.

Canticum Sacrum (ad honorem Sancti Marci nominis) (Sacred song (to the honour of the name of St Mark)). Comp. by Stravinsky in 5 movements, with introductory ded., for ten., bar., ch., and orch. Comp. 1955. F.p. Venice (St Mark's) 1956.

Canti di Prigionia (Songs of Imprisonment). Work by *Dallapiccola, comp. 1938–41 as a protest against Mussolini's adoption of Hitler's racial policies (Dallapiccola's wife was Jewish), for ch., 2 pf., 2 harps, and perc. 3 movements are: 1, *Preghiera di Maria Stuarda*, 2, *Invocazione di Boezio*, 3, *Congedo di Girolamo Savonarola*.

Cantiga. Sp. or Port. folk-song; also type of medieval religious song, of which most celebrated examples are probably contained in the 420 *Cantigas de Santa Maria* (Songs of the Virgin Mary), compiled 1250–80 by Alfonso the Wise, King of Sp.

Cantilena (It.; Fr. *cantilène*). Cradle song. (1) Smooth, melodious (and not rapid) vocal writing (used operatically esp. in relation to R. Strauss) or perf.
(2, now obsolete). Short song.
(3) In choral mus., the part carrying the main tune.
(4) Type of *solfeggio in which all the notes of the scale appeared.

Cantillation. Chanting in free rhythm, in plainsong style. The term is most used in connexion with Jewish liturgical mus.

Cantiones sacrae (Sacred Songs). Term used by many composers, incl. (1) Motets by William *Byrd. Book I (1589) contains 29 for 5 vv., Book II (1591) 20 for 5 vv. and 12 for 6 vv. In 1575 Byrd and Tallis jointly pubd. vol. of *Cantiones sacrae* of which 17 were by Byrd.
(2) Comp. by John *Gardner for sop., ch., and orch., to biblical text, f.p. Hereford 1952.

Canto (It.). Song, melody. So *Col Canto*, With the song, i.e. the accompanist to take his time throughout from the performer of the melody. Also *marcato il canto*, bring out the tune.

Canto fermo (It.). See *Cantus firmus*.

Cantor. (1) The precentor or dir. of the mus. in a Ger. Protestant church (as J. S. Bach was at Thomaskirche, Leipzig).
(2) The leading singer in a synagogue.

Cantoris (Lat.). Of the singer, i.e. precentor. That side of the choir of a cath., etc., on which the precentor sits but now normally the north side. Opposite of *decani*.

Cantrell, Derrick (Edward) (*b* Sheffield, 1926). Eng. organist. Studied Oxford Univ. Master of Mus., Chelmsford Cath. 1953–62; organist, Manchester Cath. 1962–77. Prof. of org. RMCM and RNCM from 1963.

Cantus (Lat.). Song. In the 16th and 17th cents. applied to the uppermost v. in choral mus.

Cantus choralis. See *Chorale*. For **Cantus figuratus, Cantus mensuratus,** and **Cantus planus,** see *Plainsong*.

Cantus firmus (Lat.). Fixed song. A melody, usually taken from plainsong, used by composers in 14th–17th cents. as the basis of a polyphonic comp. and against which other tunes are set in counterpoint. Also, in 16th cent., the upper v.-line of a choir. Sometimes referred to as *canto fermo*. See *Conductus*.

Canyons aux Étoiles, Des (From Canyons to the Stars). Work by *Messiaen for pf., hn., and orch., comp 1970–4, f.p. NY, 1974.

Canzona, canzone (It., plural *canzoni*). (1) Type of troubadour song in the characteristic form AAB (also known as *canzo* or *canso* (Provençal)).
(2) Designation for several types of 16th-cent. It. secular vocal mus., some similar to the madrigal, others to the popular *villanella*.
(3) In 18th- and 19th-cent. mus., a song or instr. piece of lyrical character, e.g. *Voi che sapete* from Mozart's *Le nozze di Figaro*.
(4) 16th- and 17th-cent. instr. comp. which developed from lute and kbd. arrs. of Fr.-Flemish *chansons* of Janequin, Sermisy, Josquin Desprès, etc. It. composers wrote orig. comps. on these models either for organ (*canzona d'organo*), or for instr. ens. (*canzona da sonar*), which led in turn to the 17th-cent. sonata and kbd. fugue. Notable composers of the kbd. canzona, which throughout its development retained characteristic sectional form and quasi-fugal use of imitation, incl. G. Cavazzoni, A. Gabrieli, C. Merulo, Frescobaldi, Froberger, and J. S. Bach; while sectional variety and contrast of the ens. canzona exploited by G. Gabrieli and Frescobaldi.

Canzonet, canzonetta. Diminutive of *Canzona. In late 16th and 17th cents., a short, polyphonic, dance-like vocal piece, unacc. or (later) with instr. acc.; later applied to a light, flowing kind of simple solo song. Tchaikovsky called the slow movt. of his vn. conc. a *canzonetta*.

Caoine. Irish funeral song, acc. by wailing (Eng. spelling is 'Keen').

Cape, Safford (*b* Denver, Col., 1906; *d* Brussels, 1973). Amer. cond., specialist in medieval mus. Settled in Brussels 1925. Founded Pro Musica Antiqua for perf. of early mus., 1933. Also comp. chamber mus.

Capell, Richard (*b* Northampton, 1885; *d* London, 1954). Eng. critic and author. Studied Lille Cons. Mus. critic of London *Daily Mail* (1911–31) and of *Daily Telegraph* (1931–54). Owner and ed. of quarterly *Music and Letters* from 1936. Wrote *Schubert's Songs* (1928) and trans. lib. of R. Strauss's *Friedenstag* (Day of Peace) 1938. Served 1914–18 war and as war correspondent 1939–45 war, writing *Simiomata* (Jottings) about Greece 1944–5. O.B.E. 1946.

Capella. See *Cappella.*

Capelle (Fr.). Same as Ger. *Kapelle.

Capellmeister. See *Kapellmeister.*

Capet, Lucien (*b* Paris, 1873; *d* Paris, 1928). Fr. violinist, composer, and teacher at Paris Cons. Wrote str. qts. and vn. sonata but memorable chiefly as founder and leader of the Capet Qt. which existed, with varying membership, from 1893 until Capet's death, apart from an interlude 1899–1903 and again 1914–18.

Capilupi, Geminiano (*b* Modena, 1573; *d* Modena, 1616). It. composer, pupil of *Vecchi whom he succeeded as choirmaster, Modena Cath., 1604. Wrote madrigals, motets, etc.

Capitán, El. March by *Sousa, also an operetta by him to lib. by C. Klein with lyrics by T. Frost. Prod. Boston and NY 1896, London 1899.

Caplat, Moran (*b* Herne Bay, 1916). Eng. administrator and actor. Joined staff at Glyndebourne 1945 becoming gen. admin. 1949–81. C.B.E. 1968.

Caplet, André (*b* Le Havre, 1878; *d* Paris, 1925). Fr. cond. and composer. Studied Paris Cons. (*Prix de Rome* 1901). Cond. Boston, Mass., Opera Co. 1910–14; CG 1912. Friend of Debussy whose *Children's Corner* and *Pagodes* he orch. and whose *Le Martyre de Saint-Sébastien* he cond. at its f.p. 1911. Comp. orch. works, chamber mus., choral works, and songs.

Capo, Capotasto, capo d'astro, capodastro (It.); **Capodastère** (Fr.), **Kapotaster** (Ger.). Head of the touch, i.e. the 'nut', or raised portion of the top of the fingerboard of a str. instr., which 'touches' the str. and defines their length at that end. Another name is *Barre* (Fr.). A movable capotasto has sometimes been used (esp. in guitar playing) which can be placed at any point on the str. (in vc. playing the thumb acts as such and in the 18th cent. was sometimes so called). In USA the name *capotasto* is reserved for this type.

Cappella. (It.). Chapel. *A cappella* or *alla cappella* (applied to choral mus.) meaning in church style, i.e. unaccompanied (like 16th-cent. and other church mus.). A rarer sense of these expressions makes them synonymous with *alla *breve.*

Cappuccilli, Piero (*b* Trieste, 1929). It. baritone. Studied in Trieste. Official début Teatro Nuovo, Milan, 1957 in *Pagliacci* (Tonio). Scala début 1964, CG 1967 (*La Traviata*), Chicago 1969. One of outstanding Verdi bar. of his generation.

Capriccio (It.); **caprice** (Eng. and Fr.). (1) Term applied to some 16th-cent. It. madrigals and, later, to a kind of free fugue for kbd. instr., and later to any light quick comp.
(2) In early 18th cent. sometimes used for *'Cadenza'.

(3) *A capriccio* means According to the fancy (caprice) of the performer, hence a comp. which has unexpected and orig. effects. Stravinsky and Janáček both wrote works for pf. and orch. which they called *Capriccio,* Janáček's being for left hand only and wind ens. (comp. for the Cz. pianist Otakar Hollmann). 2nd movement of Haydn's Sym. No. 86 (Hob.I:86) is called *Capriccio,* unusual in a sym.

Capriccio. R. Strauss's last opera, comp. 1940–1, styled a 'conversation piece', written in 1 act but usually perf. in 2-act Munich version. Lib. by Clemens *Krauss, incorporating elements by Hans Swarowsky, Josef Gregor, S. Zweig, and Hofmannsthal, and loosely based on Casti's comedy *Prima la musica, poi le parole* (1786). Prod. Munich 1942, London CG 1953, NY 1954. F.p. of version in Eng. trans., Glyndebourne Touring Co. 1976.

Capriccio Burlesco. Orch. work by Walton, commissioned for 125th anniv. of NY P.O. and f.p. by that orch., cond. *Kostelanetz, 1968. London 1969.

Capriccio espagnol. See *Spanish Caprice.*

Capriccio italien. See *Italian Caprice.*

Capriccioso (It.), **capricieux** (Fr.). Capricious, hence in a lively, informal, whimsical style. So the adverb *capricciosamente. La Capricieuse* is by Elgar (Op. 17) for vn. and pf., comp. 1891.

Caprice. See *Capriccio.*

Caprioli (or **Caproli**), **Carlo** (*b* Rome, *c*.1615; *d* Rome, *c*.1692). It. composer, thought to be one of the originators of the cantata. Comp. operas, oratorio, and songs.

Capriol Suite. Suite for str. orch. by Peter *Warlock, comp. 1926, later arr. for full orch. Its 6 movements are based on old Fr. dances from *Arbeau's *Orchésographie* (1589), 'Capriol' being a character in the book.

Capuana, Franco (*b* Fano, 1894; *d* Naples, 1969). It. cond. Début Brescia 1919. Cond. San Carlo, Naples, 1930–7, Scala, Milan, 1937–40, 1946–52 (mus. dir. from 1949). First to cond. opera at CG after World War II (*La traviata*, 5 Sept. 1946). Specialist in Wagner and Strauss. Cond. first It. perf. of Janáček's *Jenůfa*, Venice 1941.

Capuleti e i Montecchi, I (The Capulets and the Montagues). Opera in 4 parts by Bellini to lib. by Romani freely adapted from the It. sources of Shakespeare's *Romeo and Juliet.* Prod. Venice 1830, London 1833, New Orleans 1847.

Capuzzi, Giuseppe Antonio (*b* Brescia, 1755; *d* Bergamo, 1818). It. violinist and composer, pupil of Tartini. Visited London 1796. Comp. operas, chamber mus., cantatas, and orch. works, incl. conc. for db. and conc. for violone.

Cara, Marchetto (*b* Verona, late 15th cent.; *d* Mantua, *c*.1527). It. composer of **frottole* and works for lute. Was in service of Gonzaga court from about 1490 until his death.

Carabella, Ezio (*b* Rome, 1891; *d* Rome, 1964). It. composer. Studied Milan and Rome. Comp. comic opera, operettas, sym., and other orch. works, and film mus.

Caractacus. Several composers have written mus. based on the Brit. King or chieftain who put up almost the last resistance to the Romans, but the best-known work is Elgar's dramatic cantata, Op. 35, for sop., ten., bar., and bass soloists, ch., and orch. to text by H.A. Acworth. F.p. Leeds 1898, London 1899.

Caradori-Allan, Maria (Caterina Rosalbina) (*b* Milan, 1800; *d* Surbiton, 1865). It.-born sop. who settled in Eng. Début London 1822 in *Le Nozze di Figaro* (Cherubino). Successful career in opera, but chief claims to fame are as sop. soloist in first London perf. Beethoven's 9th Sym. 1825, and in f.p. of Mendelssohn's *Elijah*, Birmingham 1846. She was duettist with **Malibran at Manchester Fest. 1836 when the latter collapsed, dying 9 days later.

Carapetian, Armen (*b* Isphahan, Persia, of Armenian parents, 1908). Persian-Amer. musicologist. Educated Teheran, then Sorbonne and Harvard Univ. Also studied vn. under Capet and comp. under Malipiero. In 1944 founded Institute of Renaissance and Baroque Mus., Rome, superseded by the American Institute of Musicology of which he was dir. Ed works of **Brumel.

Cardew, Cornelius (*b* Winchcombe, Glos., 1936; *d* London, 1981). Eng. composer and guitarist. Chorister, Canterbury Cath. 1943–50. Studied RAM 1953–7 as pupil of H. Ferguson. Studied elec. mus., Cologne 1957–8, becoming ass. to **Stockhausen 1958–60. Also studied in Rome with **Petrassi 1964–5. Prof. of comp. RAM, from 1967. His early pf. works are in the style of early Boulez and Stockhausen, but later comps. follow a **Cage-like indeterminacy, e.g. *Treatise* (1963–7), a graphic score of nearly 200 pages containing no instructions to the performer. Formed Scratch Orch. 1969. Works incl. Str. Trio (1957); 2 *Books of Study for Pianists* (1958); *Octet '61* (1961) for unspecified instr.; 3 *Winter Potatoes* (1965) for pf.; *The Great Learning* (parts 1–7, 1968–70) for various perf.; *The East is Red*, vn. and pf. (1972); *Piano Album*, pf. (1973); *The Old and the New*, sop., ch., and orch. (1973); *Thälmann Variations*, pf. (1974); *Vietnam Sonata*, pf. (1976).

Cardillac. Opera in 3 acts by Hindemith to lib. by Ferdinand Lion based on E.T.A. Hoffmann's *Das Fräulein von Scuderi* (1818). Prod. Dresden 1926. Concert perf. London 1936. Rev. version, also with new lib. by composer, Zürich 1952. F. London stage p. 1970 (SW), Santa Fe 1967. Cardillac is name of prin. character.

Cardoso, Fray Manuel (*b* Fronteira do Alemtejo, 1566; *d* Lisbon, 1650). Portuguese composer and organist. Wrote masses, motets, and other church mus. influenced by Palestrina.

Cardus, (Sir) (John Frederick) **Neville** (*b* Rusholme, Manchester, 1888; *d* London, 1975). Eng. critic and essayist, also writer on cricket. Chief mus. critic *Manchester Guardian* 1927–40, *Sydney Morning Herald* 1941–7, rejoined *Guardian* 1951 but wrote occasionally for other newspapers. Author of book on Mahler's first 5 syms., 2 vols. of autobiography, and several colls. of mus. and cricket essays. C.B.E. 1964, knighted 1967.

Carestini, Giovanni (*b* Filottrano, nr. Ancona, 1705; *d* Filottrano, *c*.1760). It. castrato (cont.) singer. After successes on continent 1721–33, went to London where Handel engaged him for opera prods. in 1734. Returned to Venice 1735 and was active for another 20 years.

Carewe, John (*b* Derby, 1933). Eng. cond. Studied GSM, then with W. Goehr, Deutsch, Boulez, and with Messiaen at Paris Cons. Founded New Mus. Ens. 1957. Staff, Morley Coll., 1958–66. Cond. BBC Welsh S.O. 1966–71. Mus. dir. Brighton Phil. Soc. from 1974.

Carey, (Francis) **Clive** (Savill) (*b* Sible Hedingham, Essex, 1883; *d* London, 1968). Eng. bar. Trained RCM (on staff 1946–53). Toured with **English Singers, sang in opera at Old Vic from 1920, prof. of singing, Adelaide, 1924–8, Melbourne 1942–5, worked as producer at SW 1933, and comp. incidental mus. for plays. Active in Eng. folksong movement. C.B.E. 1955.

Carey, Henry (*b* ?Yorkshire, *c*.1690; *d* Clerkenwell, 1743). Eng. composer, poet, and playwright. Wrote successful burlesques of It. opera and cantatas, and songs, incl. 'Sally in our alley' *c*.1715 (of which he also wrote the words).

Carezzando, carezzevole (It.). Caressing; caressingly.

Carillon. (1) See Bell.
(2) Org. stop; a **Mixture of 3 ranks (12th, 17th, 22nd): chiefly in USA.

Carillon. Recitation with orch. by Elgar, Op. 75, to poem by Belg. writer E. Cammaerts, comp. Nov. 1914 as tribute to Belgium. Can be perf. without narrator.

Carissimi, Giacomo (*b* Marini, Rome, 1605; *d* Rome, 1674). It. composer, one of early masters of oratorio form. Choirmaster Assisi 1628–9, Collegio Germanico, 1629–74. Oratorios incl. *Lucifer, Job, Baltazar, Jephte* (1650), *Judicium Salomonis*; motets, and recits. (e.g. *Abraham and Isaac*). Adapted Monteverdi's operatic innovations to sacred drama. His *Missa 'L'Homme armé'* was last of its kind. In 1656 was appointed choirmaster to Queen Christina of Sweden when she established her court in Rome.

Carl Rosa Opera Company, Royal. Eng. opera co. founded 1875 in Dublin and London by Ger. violinist Karl August Nicolaus Rose who settled in Eng. in 1866 and became known as Carl *Rosa. Rosa died in 1889, when co. became touring organization and was accorded title 'Royal' by Queen Victoria in 1893. 1923–50 dir. H.B. Phillips. After various dissensions, Arts Council withdrew subsidy in 1958 and co. became defunct, and attempt to revive it failed in 1960. Policy was opera in English and co. provided invaluable training-ground for many singers. Gave f.p. in England of Massenet's *Manon* (1885), Puccini's *La Bohème* (1897), and Giordano's *Andrea Chénier* (1903).

Carlton, Nicholas (*fl.* early 16th cent.). Eng. composer. His 'Verse for 2 to play on 1 org.' (or virginals) is among earliest examples of 4-hand mus. for kbd. instr.

Carlton, Richard (*b c.*1558; *d c.*1638). Eng. composer of madrigals and contributor to *The *Triumphs of Oriana* ('Calm was the Air', in 5 parts). Vicar of Norfolk churches.

Carmagnole, La. Originally name of short coat, worn in north It. district of Carmagnola, and imported into Fr. by workmen from that district. The insurgents of Marseilles in 1792 introduced it to Paris, where it became identified with the Revolution. A round dance of the time was given the name, and a song with the refrain, 'Dansons la Carmagnole, vive le son du canon', to a very catchy air, became identified with activities during Reign of Terror. Authorship of words and mus. unknown.

Carman's Whistle. Tune to be found, with variations by Byrd, in *Fitzwilliam Virginal Book. It is that of a ballad pubd. 1592. A carman was a carter.

Carmelites, The (Poulenc). See *Dialogues des Carmélites, Les.*

Carmen (Lat.). (1) Tune, song, strain, poem.
   (2, in 14th- and 15th-cent. parlance; plural *carmina*.) V. part of a comp. (as distinguished from the instr. parts), or uppermost part of a choral comp.

Carmen. Opera (*opéra-comique*) in 4 acts by Bizet to libretto by Meilhac and Halévy after Mérimée *nouvelle* (1845). Comp. 1873–4. Sometimes perf. with orig. spoken dialogue replaced by recitatives composed by Ernest Guiraud. Prod. Paris 1875, Vienna (with Guiraud recit.) 1875, London and NY 1878. The famous *Habañera* may have been inspired (consciously or unconsciously) by a *chanson havanaise* by, or collected by, Sebastian *Yradier, Sp. composer (1809–65).

Carmichael, Hoagy (Hoagland Howard) (*b* Bloomington, Ind., 1899; *d* Rancho Mirage, Calif., 1981). Amer. composer of songs and lyrics, pianist, film actor, and singer. Songs incl. *Two* *Sleepy People, Stardust, Little Old Lady, Georgia on My Mind, Lazy Bones, Rockin' Chair, The Nearness of You,* and *I Get Along Without You Very Well.*

Carmina Burana (cantiones profanae) (Songs of Beuren, profane songs). Scenic cantata by Carl *Orff, with optional mimed action, in 25 movements for sop., ten., and bar. soloists, boys' choir, ch., and orch. (14 movements for ch.). Lat. text—student songs about wine, women, and love—based on poems in Lat., Old Ger. and Old Fr. from MS. dated 1280 found in Benedictine monastery of Beuren. First part of Orff's trilogy *Trionfi*. Prod. Frankfurt 1937, London 1960.

Carmirelli, Pina (*b* Varzi, It., 1914). It. violinist and teacher at Accademia di S. Cecilia, Rome. Concert career began 1937. Champion of mus. of Boccherini, founding Boccherini Quartet (1949) and Carmirelli Quartet (1954). Ed. of Boccherini's instr. works.

Carnaval (Carnival). Schumann's pf. comp. Op. 9, comp. 1834–5 and sub-titled *Scènes mignonnes sur quatre notes* (dainty scenes on 4 notes), the notes being A–S–C–H (a♭–E♭–C–B). Asch was the home-town of a girl with whom he was in love and its 4 letters were the only 'musical' letters of his name. Each of the 21 pieces has a descriptive title, e.g. *Papillons.* Orch. version by Glazunov and others used for Fokine ballet (St Petersburg 1910).

Carnaval à Paris (Carnival in Paris). 'Episode for orchestra', Op. 9, by *Svendsen, pubd. 1879.

Carnaval des animaux, Le (The Carnival of Animals). 'Grand zoological fantasy' by Saint-Saëns. Orig. chamber version for 2 pf., str. quintet, fl., cl., and xylophone, but also for 2 pf. and orch. Comp. 1886 but perf. forbidden in composer's lifetime. Pubd. 1922. 14 movements, of which No. 13 is the famous *Le Cygne* (The Swan).

Carnaval de Venise (Carnival in Venice). Paganini's Op. 10, comp. in or before 1829, was a set of variations for unacc. vn. on *Le Carnaval de Venise,* being the popular Venetian song 'O mamma mia'. Other composers, e.g. *Benedict, have also used the theme. A. *Thomas wrote an opera *Le Carnaval de Venise,* prod. 1857.

Carnaval Romain, Le ('The Roman Carnival'). 'Ouverture caractéristique' by Berlioz, comp. and f.p. 1844, derived from material in his opera *Benvenuto Cellini* (1834–7).

Carnegie Hall. Largest concert-hall in NY, seating *c.*3,000, and, until 1962 when the Phil. (now Avery Fisher) Hall, Lincoln Center, opened, home of the city's prin. orch. concerts. Architect, W. B. Tuthill. Opened May 1891, Tchaikovsky being among guest conds. Called 'Music Hall' until 1898, when renamed in honour of industrialist Andrew Carnegie (1835–1919), who had provided most of the money to build it.

Carner, Mosco (*b* Vienna, 1904; *d* Cornwall, 1985). Austrian-born cond. and critic. Studied Vienna Univ. under Adler. Settled London 1933, working as cond. and as London correspondent for some continental papers. Contrib. criticism to many Eng. newspapers and periodicals. Author of several books, notably *Puccini* (1958, 2nd edn. 1974) and *Alban Berg* (1975).

Carneval (Carnival). (1) Ger. title by which Dvořák's ov. *Karneval* is usually known. His Op. 92, comp. 1891, with **Amid Nature* and **Othello* it formed a cycle, **Nature, Life and Love.* F.p. in this form, Prague and NY 1892. Now usually played separately. Orig. title was *Bohemian Carnival.*

(2) Ov., Op. 45, by Glazunov (1894).

Carol (Fr. *Noel*; Ger. *Weihnachtslied*). In medieval times a round dance with mus. acc., but soon developed into a song for 2 or 3 vv. usually (but not necessarily) to a text dealing with the birth of Christ. All Christian nations, Western and Eastern, have carols, some of them evidently of pagan origin but taken over and adapted in early days of Christianity. The nature of the carol varies: it may be dramatic, narrative, or lyrical.

One of oldest printed Eng. Christmas carols is the *Boar's Head Carol,* sung as the traditional dish is carried in on Christmas Day at Queen's College, Oxford; it was printed in 1521. This is but one of a large group of carols assoc. with good cheer as an element in Christmas joy.

With the growth of the Christmas season as a public holiday which became increasingly commercialized, the carol grew in popularity and, concomitantly, in vulgarity so that some 19th-cent. carols are of inferior standard, but the best of them have achieved a place alongside the folk-carols and 17th-cent. Ger. carols which were revived by the late 19th-cent. folk-song movement. A fine selection is sung annually in Eng. on Christmas Eve at King's College, Cambridge. Vaughan Williams wrote a **Fantasia on Christmas Carols,* **Hely-Hutchinson A Carol Symphony,* and Britten a **Ceremony of Carols.*

Caroso, Fabritio (*b* Sermoneta, *c.*1521–35; *d* after 1605). It. scholar and composer of lute mus. His book *Il ballarino* was pubd. Venice, 1581, being enlarged in 1600 as *Nobiltà di dame.* It is important source for 16th-cent. dance steps and mus.

Carpenter, John Alden (*b* Park Ridge, Ill., 1876; *d* Chicago, 1951). Amer. composer who, like **Ives, combined mus. with successful business career. Studied pf. and, at Harvard, mus. theory. Made name with orch. suite *Adventures in a Perambulator* (Chicago 1915). Comp. 3 ballets, *Birthday of the Infanta* (Chicago 1919), *Krazy-Kat,* using jazz idioms (Chicago 1922), and *Skyscrapers* (NY 1926). Other works incl. 2 syms., tone-poem *Sea Drift,* vn. conc., str. qt., pf. quintet, and songs.

Carrée (Fr.). Square. Double whole-note or breve.

Carreño, (Maria) **Teresa** (*b* Caracas, 1853; *d* NY, 1917). Venezuelan pianist, taught by her father. Début NY at age 9. Studied with **Gottschalk and Anton **Rubinstein. Toured Europe 1865–75, when she became operatic sop. and, for a brief spell, cond. Returned to pf. 1889, consolidating reputation as leading woman player of her day. Her 4 husbands incl. d'**Albert.

Carreras, José (Maria) (*b* Barcelona, 1946). Sp. ten. Studied Barcelona. Début 1956 in Falla's *Retablo de Maese Pedro.* Prof. début Barcelona. London début 1971 (concert perf. *Maria Stuarda*), CG 1974. NY City Opera 1972, Met. 1974, Milan 1975.

Carrillo, Julián (*b* Ahualulco, Mexico, 1875; *d* San Angél, 1965). Mexican composer. Studied in Mexico 1885–90, and at Leipzig and Ghent (1899–1904) with Reinecke and Nikisch. In his teens showed exceptional interest in fractional divisions of the accepted intervals and coined term *sonido 13* (13th sound) for the first 2-octave harmonic on the vn.'s 4th str., this being for him the first pitch outside the traditional 12 semitones to the octave. Gave concerts to demonstrate potentialities of microtonal intervals and invented special instrs., incl. the *octavina* (8th-tones) and *arpa citera* (16th-tones). In 1926 his microtonal works were championed by **Stokowski, who cond. the *Sonata casi-fantasia* (in 4ths, 8ths, and 16ths), and in the 1930s Stokowski and Carrillo toured Mexico with the Sonido 13 Orch. In 1947 built a pf. tuned in 3rds of a whole tone. Comps. divide into 3 periods: traditional tuning up to 1911, atonal from 1911 to 1922, and in *Sonido 13* idiom thereafter. They incl. operas, syms., str. qts., vn. conc., and pf. mus. His *Horizontes* (1950) employs a small orch. tuned in 4th, 8ths, and 16ths, combined with conventionally tuned orch.

Carrodus, John (Tiplady) (*b* Keighley, 1836; *d* London, 1895). Eng. violinist, pupil of **Molique. Leader of several London orchs. incl. CG, 1869–95. Comp. for vn. His 5 sons were musicians; at Hereford Fest. 1894 they and their father played in the orch.

Carroll, Ida (Gertrude) (*b* Manchester, 1905). Eng. mus. educationist and db. player. Secretary, Northern Sch. of Mus., Manchester, 1926, acting prin. 1956–8, prin. 1958–72, becoming dean of management RNCM. Retired 1976. Comp. pieces for db. O.B.E. 1964.

Carse, Adam (A. von Ahn Carse) (*b* Newcastle upon Tyne, 1878; *d* Great Missenden, 1958). Eng. composer and author. Studied RAM; mus. master Winchester College 1909–22, then prof. of harmony, RAM, 1922–40. Comp. orch. works, chamber mus., and educational mus., and author of valuable treatises on orchestration. Made collection of 350 old wind instruments, presented to Horniman Museum, London.

Carte, Richard D'Oyly. See *D'Oyly Carte, Richard.*

Carter, Elliott (Cook) (*b* NY, 1908). Amer. composer. Encouraged by *Ives, who recommended him to Harvard where he studied with *Piston and had lessons from Holst. From 1932 to 1935 studied in Paris with *Boulanger. Has taught at various Amer. univs. His music is uncompromising and challenging, its harsh brilliance enhanced by compelling intellectual qualities. Early works were neo-classical in style but a new harmonic structure and treatment of rhythm became apparent in the *Piano Sonata* (1945–6). With the *Cello Sonata* (1948) he developed 'metric modulation' whereby a new tempo is established from development of a cross-rhythm within the old tempo. The listener has a clear impression of the simultaneous existence of 2 tempos. The 3 Str. Qts. have been described as the most significant comps. in the medium since Bartók. His writings on many subjects were collected into one vol. (NY 1977). Prin. works:

BALLETS: *Pocahontas* (1937–9); *The Minotaur* (1947).
ORCH: *Prelude, Fanfare, and Polka* (1938); Sym. No. 1 (1942, rev. 1954); *Holiday Overture* (1944, rev. 1961); *Elegy*, str. (1946); *Variations* (1955); *Double Concerto*, hpd., pf., 2 chamber orchs. (1961); pf. conc. (1964–5); Conc. for Orch. (1969); *Symphony of 3 Orchestras* (1976–7); *Triple Duo*, chamber ens. (1982–3).
VOICE & ENS: *Syringa*, cantata for mez., bass, and 11 instrs. (1978); *A *Mirror on Which to Dwell*, sop. and ens. (1975); *In Sleep, In Thunder*, ten. and ens. (1982).
CHORUS: *To Music* (1937); *Heart Not So Heavy as Mine* (1938); *The Defence of Corinth* (1942); *The Harmony of Morning* (1944); *Musicians Wrestle Everywhere* (1945); *Emblems* (1947).
CHAMBER MUSIC: *Canonic Suite*, 4 sax. (1939, rev. for 4 cl. 1955–6); *Pastorale*, cor anglais, va., cl., pf. (1940); *Elegy*, va. or vc. and pf. (1943, rev. 1961; arr. str. qt. 1946, str. 1952); woodwind quintet (1948); vc. sonata (1948); *8 Études and a Fantasy*, woodwind qt. (1949–50); Str. Qts., No. 1 (1951), No. 2 (1958–9), No. 3 (1971); *2 Pieces for 4 Kettledrums* (1950, rev. 1966); Sonata, fl., ob., vc., hpd. (1952); *Duo*, vn. and pf. (1973–4); brass quintet (1974); *Changes*, guitar (1983).
PIANO: Sonata (1945–6); *Night Fantasies* (1980).
VOICE & PIANO: *Voyage* (1943); *The Line Gang* (1943).

Carulli, Ferdinando (*b* Naples, 1770; *d* Paris, 1841). It. guitarist and composer for his instr. of over 300 works, incl. concs., duos, etc. Wrote treatise on guitar playing.

Caruso, Enrico (*b* Naples, 1873; *d* Naples, 1921). It. ten., regarded as one of the greatest there has been. Studied with Vergine and Lombardi. Début Naples 1894. Created tenor roles in Cilea's *Adriana Lecouvreur* and Giordano's *Fedora. Int. fame after *Bohème* with Melba at Monte Carlo

1902. CG début same year in *Rigoletto*. Début NY Met. 1903. Between then and 1920 sang 36 roles and appeared over 600 times at Met. First ten. to make records, his recording career extending 1902–20 and royalties in his lifetime amounting to nearly £500,000. Though not flawless stylistically, his v. was of sumptuous resonance, mellow and almost baritonal, with an exquisite *mezza voce*. Created Dick Johnson in *La *fanciulla del West* (NY Met. 1910).

Carvalho, Eleazar de (*b* Iguatu, Ceará, Brazil, 1915). Brazilian cond. and composer. Studied Nat. Sch. of Mus., Brazil. Tuba-player, later cond., at Rio Municipal Th. Member, Brazilian S.O., ass. cond. 1941. Went to USA 1946, studying with Koussevitzky. Guest cond. leading Amer. orchs. Cond., St Louis S.O. 1963–8. Returned to Brazil 1971. Works incl. operas, symphonic poems, and chamber mus.

Carvalho, João de Sousa (*b* Estremoz, 1745; *d* Alentejo, 1798). Portuguese composer of operas, kbd. mus., etc. Studied in Naples, 1761. One of few Port. composers of opera in 18th cent. Taught Port. royal family.

Cary, Tristram (Ogilvie) (*b* Oxford, 1925). Eng. composer and percussionist. Studied TCL 1948–50. Began interest in elec. mus. 1944 and was producing *musique concrète* by 1949. Founded own elec. studio, first in Brit., and prod. scores for several films and BBC TV and radio drama. Teacher at RCM where in 1968 founded elec. studio.

Caryll, Ivan (Felix Tilkin) (*b* Liège, 1861; *d* NY, 1921). Belg.-Amer. composer of mus. comedies such as *The Duchess of Danzig* (1903) and *Our Miss Gibbs* (1909). Also had th. orch. (Elgar's *Sérénade lyrique*, 1899, is ded. 'to Ivan Caryll's Orchestra'.)

Casa (It.). Box. Any drum of a large size, hence *gran cassa*, bass drum, and *cassa rullante*, ten. drum.

Casadesus. Of this large family of Fr. musicians, the best-known are: Robert Marcel (*b* Paris, 1899; *d* Paris, 1972). Pianist and composer. Studied Paris Cons. Notable Mozart player. Wrote syms., pf. concs., 24 pf. preludes, and chamber mus. His son Jean (*b* Paris, 1927; *d* Renfrew, Ontario, 1972) was also a pianist. Went to USA 1939 and studied at Princeton Univ. Début 1946 with Philadelphia Orch. in Ravel conc. Winner Geneva competition 1947. Many tours. Killed in car crash.

Casali, Giovanni Battista (*b* Rome, 1715; *d* Rome, 1792). It. composer, choirmaster St John Lateran, Rome, 1759–92. Wrote operas and church mus. Taught *Grétry.

Casals, Pablo (Pau, in the Catalan form) (*b* Vendrell, Catalonia, 1876; *d* Rio Piedras, Puerto Rico, 1973). Sp. cellist, cond., composer, and pianist. Vc. pupil of J. Garcia in Barcelona and later studied at Madrid Cons. Began career in

Barcelona cafés and Paris ths. Prof. of vc., Barcelona Cons. 1897–9. Soloist at Lamoureux Concerts, Paris, and Crystal Palace, London, 1899. First US tour 1901. Thenceforward brilliant career as world's foremost cellist. Formed notable trio with *Cortot and *Thibaud. Founded Casals Orch., Barcelona 1919. Went into voluntary exile from Sp. 1939 in protest against Franco régime, vowing never to return while Spain was under totalitarian rule (a vow he kept). In 1950 founded Prades Fest. in French Pyrenees. Settled in Puerto Rico, 1956, founding fest. there. In Oct. 1971 cond. his *Hymn to the United Nations* (Auden) at the U.N. headquarters, NY. Comp. vc. pieces, orch. works, and oratorio *El pessebre* (The Manger).

Casavola, Franco (*b* Modugno, 1891; *d* Bari, 1955). It. composer, pupil of Respighi. Joined 'Futurist' movement 1920, composing for 'noise-machines' of *Russolo. In 1927 reverted to more conventional means, producing comic opera *Il gobbo del Califfo* (1929).

Casella, Alfredo (*b* Turin, 1883; *d* Rome, 1947). It. composer, cond., pianist, and author. Entered Paris Cons. 1896, studying with Fauré. On return to It. in 1915 became champion of all that was new in the arts and headed It. section of I.S.C.M. Anticipated tastes of a later epoch by interest in It. baroque mus., particularly Vivaldi. His own mus. reflected restless and questing mind. Early works influenced by Mahler, whose mus. he cond. in Paris in the early 1900s. Tempted by atonality but after 1920 identified himself with neo-classicism. Comps. incl.:

BALLETS: *Il convento veneziano* (1912), *La Giara* (1924).
OPERAS: *La donna serpente* (1928–31), *La favola d' Orfeo* (1932), *Il deserto tentato* (1937).
ORCH: Syms: No. 1 (1905), No. 2 (1908–9 unpubd.), No. 3 (1940), *Italia Suite* (1909), *Pupazzetti* (1919), *Scarlattiana,* pf. and orch. (1926), Vn. Conc. (1928), *Concerto romano* (organ) (1926), Conc. for pf., vn., and vc. (1933), Vc. Conc. (1934–5), *Conc. for Orch.* (1937); conc. for pf., timp., perc., str. (1943), songs, and pf. pieces (incl. 2 series entitled *À la manière de . . .* (In the style of . . . (1911 and 1913), 2nd series collab. Ravel.)

Casini, Giovanni Maria (*b* Florence, 1652; *d* Florence, 1719). It. organist and scholar. Organist, Florence Cath. from 1685. Comp. org. works and church mus. Had hpd. with 4 octaves div. into 31 notes.

Casiolini, Claudio (*b* Rome, 1670; *d* ?). It. composer of motets and masses in style of *Palestrina. Choirmaster S. Lorenzo in Damaso, Rome.

Casken, John (*b* Barnsley, 1949). Eng. composer. Studied at Birmingham Univ. with Joubert and Dickinson and in Warsaw with Dobrowolski 1971–2. Lecturer, Birmingham Univ. 1973–9,

Huddersfield Polytechnic 1979–81, Durham Univ. from 1981. Featured composer at Bath Fest. 1980 where his mus. created a strong impression through its individuality, while suggesting to critics the influences of Debussy and Tippett. Prin. works incl.:

ORCH: *Arenaria,* fl. and 13 players (1976); *Tableaux des Trois Ages* (1976–7); Pf. Conc. (1980–1); *Masque,* ob., 2 hns., str. (1982); *Erin,* db. and small orch. (1982–3); *Orion over Farne* (1984).
ENSEMBLE: *Kagura,* 13 wind instr. (1972–3); *Music for the Crabbing Sun,* fl., ob., vc., hpd. (1974); *Music for a Tawny-Gold Day,* va., alto sax., bass cl., pf. (1975–6); *Amarantos,* 9 players (1977–8); *Melanos,* tuba and 7 players (1979); *Eructavit,* 10 instr. (1982); *Fonteyn Fanfares,* 12 brass instr. (1982).
VOICE AND INSTR: *Ia Orana, Gauguin,* sop., pf. (1978); *Firewhirl,* sop. and 7 players (1979–80).
CHAMBER MUS: *Music for Cello and Piano* (1971–2); *Jadu,* 2 vc. (1973); *Fluctus,* vc., pf. (1973–4); *Thymehaze,* alto rec., pf. (1976); *À Belle Pavine,* vn. and tape (1980); str. qt. (1981–2); *Taerset,* cl., pf. (1982–3).
ORGAN: *Ligatura* (1979–80).

Cassadó, Gaspar (*b* Barcelona, 1897; *d* Madrid, 1966). Sp. cellist and composer. Studied at Barcelona Cons. and with *Casals in Paris in 1910. Int. career began in 1918. Toured extensively as solo cellist and in chamber mus. Prof. at Siena Acad. Wrote vc. conc., str. qts., pf. trio, and *Rapsodía Catalana.*

Cassation (It. *cassazione*). 18th-cent. instr. comp. (several by Mozart) similar to divertimento and serenade and often to be perf. outdoors.

Casse-noisette (Tchaikovsky). See *Nutcracker.*

Cassette (Fr.). Little box. Literally the small package into which a commercial tape-recording is packed but in a wider sense the automatic-rewinding tape itself. Record-playing equipment now generally provides facilities for playing cassettes. Many disc recordings are also issued in cassette form.

Cassilly, Richard (*b* Washington D.C., 1927). Amer. ten. Studied Baltimore. Prin. ten. Hamburg State Opera from 1967. CG début 1968. NY City Opera 1955–66. Milan 1970. Has also appeared with Vienna State Opera, San Francisco, Scottish Opera. His roles include Otello, Siegmund, Peter Grimes, Troilus, Laca, and Aaron

Cassirer, Fritz (*b* Breslau, 1871; *d* Berlin, 1926). Ger. cond. and writer. Studied in Munich and Berlin. Held opera posts in Lübeck, Elberfeld, and Berlin. Cond. f.p. of Delius's operas *Koanga* (Elberfeld 1904) and *A *Village Romeo and Juliet* (Berlin 1907) and f.p. in Eng. of Delius's *Appalachia* (London, 1907). Selected words from Nietzsche's *Also sprach Zarathustra* for Delius's *Mass of Life.*

Castanets (Fr. *castagnettes,* It. *castagnette*). Perc. instrs. consisting of 2 cup-shaped wooden clappers clicked rhythmically together by Sp. dancers, to whose hands they are attached. In orch. use, they are mounted on a handle which is shaken.

Castello, Dario (*fl.* early 17th cent.). It. maestro of instr. mus. at St Mark's, Venice, 1629. Comp. sonatas for vv. and instr. and for hpd. or spinet with vn., tpt., and bn.

Castelnuovo-Tedesco, Mario (*b* Florence, 1895; *d* Hollywood, Calif., 1968). It. composer, pupil of *Pizzetti. Assoc. with progressive faction in It. mus. led in 1920s by *Casella. Settled in USA 1939. Devotee of Shakespeare. Operas incl. *La mandragola* (1921–5), *Aucassin et Nicolette* (1938), *All's Well That Ends Well* (1958), *Il Mercanto di Venezia* (1961). Comp. ballets, oratorios (*Ruth* 1949, *Song of Songs* 1963) and orch. works incl. *Concerto Italiano,* vn. and orch. (1926) and 2 further vn. concs. (1933, 1939), 2 pf. concs. (1928, 1939), guitar conc. (1939), conc. for 2 guitars, *American Rhapsody* (1943), ovs. to Shakespeare's plays (1931–42). Much chamber mus. incl. guitar quintet and guitar sonata. His songs incl. *33 Shakespeare Songs,* setting in Eng. of all the song-texts in the plays.

Castiglioni, Niccolò (*b* Milan, 1932). It. composer and pianist. Studied Verdi Cons., Milan, (pf. with Gulda, comp. with *Ghedini) and later with *Blacher at Salzburg. Early works influenced by Mahler, later by Boulez. Settled in USA 1967. Comps. incl. *Synchromie* for orch. (1962–3), *Solemn Music II* for sop. and chamber orch. (1964–5), Sym. in C for ch. and orch. (1968–9), *Alef* for solo ob. (1971); *Inverno in-ver,* chamber orch. (1972); *Quodlibet,* pf. and chamber orch. (1976).

Castillane (Sp.). Dance of the Province of Castile.

Castor et Pollux (Castor and Pollux). Opera in prol. and 5 acts by Rameau to lib. by Pierre Joseph Bernard. Prod. Paris 1737 (rev. without prol. and with new Act I 1754); Glasgow 1927; NY 1937.

Castrato (It.). Castrated. Male sop. or cont. whose v. was preserved by castration before puberty. In great demand in It. opera in 17th and 18th cent., the voice being brilliant, flexible, and often sensuous. Gualberto, a castrato, sang title-role in Monteverdi's *Orfeo* (1607). Other famous castrati were Senesino, Farinelli, Caffarelli, Guadagni, and Velluti. Castrati survived in Vatican chapel and Roman churches until 20th cent. Recordings exist of Alessandro Moreschi (1858–1922), male sop. of Sistine Chapel. Wagner wanted the male soprano D. Mustafà to sing Klingsor in *Parsifal.*

Castro, Juan José (*b* Avellaneda, 1895; *d* Buenos Aires, 1968). Argentinian composer and cond. Studied Paris 1920 with d'Indy. Cond. posts in Buenos Aires, Havana, Montevideo, and Melbourne. Dir. Puerto Rico Cons. 1959–64. Cosmopolitan composer with nationalistic flavour

and use of serialism. His several operas incl. *Proserpina y el extranjero* (Proserpine and the Stranger) (Milan 1952) and 2 based on plays by Lorca, *La zapatera prodigiosa* (1943) and *Bodas di sangre* (Blood Wedding) (1952). Also 5 syms., pf. conc., vn. conc., orch. suites, choral works. His brother José Maria (*b* Buenos Aires, 1892; *d* Buenos Aires, 1964) was also cond. and composer.

Castrucci, Pietro (*b* Rome, 1679; *d* Dublin, 1752). It. violinist, pupil of Corelli. Settled in London 1715 becoming leader of Handel's opera orch. until 1737. Invented 'violetta Marina' for which instr. Handel wrote solos in *Orlando* and *Sosarme.* Went to Dublin 1750.

Catalán (Sp.), **Catalane** (Fr.). Type of Sp. dance from Catalonia.

Catalani, Alfredo (*b* Lucca, 1854; *d* Milan, 1893). It. composer. Studied Paris (1872) and Milan. Friend of *Boito who wrote lib. for *La Falce* (Milan 1875). Operas show affinity with Ger. romantics, e.g. Weber and Marschner, and were *Elda* (1876, rev. 1889 as *Loreley*), *Dejanice* (1883), *Edmea* (1886), and *La *Wally* (1891), the last-named being the best and most popular of his works, highly esteemed by Toscanini.

Catalani, Angelica (*b* Sinigaglia, 1780; *d* Paris, 1849). It. sop. Début Venice 1797, London 1806. First singer in London of Mozart's Susanna in *Le nozze di Figaro,* 1812. Managed Paris Théâtre des Italiens 1814–17. Retired from stage 1819 but continued concert work until 1828. In her day extremely highly paid. Founded singing sch., Florence.

Catalogue Aria. Nickname for Leporello's aria in Act I Sc. 2 of Mozart's *Don Giovanni* in which he recounts to Donna Elvira a list of the Don's amorous conquests in various countries, ending each instalment with the words 'but in Spain, a thousand and three (*mille e tre*)'. This aria was probably modelled on a similar one in Gazzaniga's *Don Giovanni,* the rapid singing of a list of items being a popular feature of 18th-cent. comic opera.

Catalogue d'oiseaux. Work by Messiaen for solo pf. in 7 books, comp. 1956–8, based on birdsong as noted and remembered by the composer. F.p. Paris 1959 (Loriod).

Catch. A type of *round; but the term is now often used in a less general sense which confines its application to such rounds as, in the singing, afford a laugh by the way the words are heard, as for instance in the one *Ah, how Sophia,* which in the singing suggests 'Our house afire', the later line 'Go fetch the Indian's borrowed plume' similarly suggesting 'Go fetch the engines!'. Restoration specimens are more amusing and much more indecent. A Catch Club (Noblemen and Gentlemen's Catch Club) was founded in London in 1761 and still exists.

Cathédrale engloutie, La (The submerged cathedral). Pf. piece by Debussy, No. 10 of his *Préludes,* Book I, comp. 1910. Based on cath. of Ys, with its legend of underwater bells and chanting. F.p. Debussy, Paris 1910. Quoted by Debussy in his vc. sonata, 1915. Orch. version by Büsser, f.p. Paris 1927.

Catiline Conspiracy, The. Opera in 2 acts by *Hamilton to lib. by comp. based on Ben Jonson's *Catalina* (1611). Comp. 1972–3. Prod. Stirling 1974.

Catterall, Arthur (*b* Preston, 1883; *d* London, 1943). Eng. violinist. Taught by father from age 4. Played Mendelssohn conc. at Manchester th. at age 8. Entered RMCM 1893 as pupil of Willy Hess and later of *Brodsky. First played in Hallé Orch. 1900. Played in Bayreuth orch. 1902. Soloist at Hallé concert with Richter 1904. Leader of Queen's Hall Orch., 1905–14, Hallé Orch. 1914–25, BBC S.O. 1930–6. Prof. of vn., RMCM, 1910–29. Led own str. qt. 1911–25. Frequent conc. soloist (gave f.p. of *Moeran conc. 1942).

Catulli Carmina (Songs of Catullus). Scenic cantata by *Orff, successor to his *Carmina Burana,* and 2nd part of his trilogy *Trionfi.* 1943 rev. of much earlier work, f.p. Leipzig 1943, Cambridge 1948. For soloists, ch., 4 pf., 4 timp., and up to 12 percussionists. Setting of 12 Lat. poems by Catullus, with opening and closing Lat. choruses by Orff.

Caucasian Sketches. Symphonic suite for orch., Op. 10, by *Ippolitov-Ivanov. Comp. 1894, f.p. Moscow 1895. 4 movements are: *In the Mountain Pass; In the Village; In the Mosque; March of the Sirdar.*

Caurroy, François Eustache de (*b* Gerberoy, 1549; *d* Paris, 1609). Fr. composer and canon of Saint Chapelle, Paris, becoming court composer to Fr. Kings. His *Mass for the Dead* was perf. at Fr. royal funerals until 18th cent. Wrote church and instr. mus.

Causton (Caustun), **Thomas** (*d* London, 1569). Eng. composer of church mus. Member of Chapel Royal from *c*.1550. His anthems and services were published in Day's *Certaine Notes* (1565).

Cavaillé-Col, Aristide (*b* Montpellier, 1811; *d* Paris, 1899). Fr. organ-builder, most prominent of his family. Went to Paris 1833, built organ for basilica of St Denis. Also built org. for Madeleine. His orgs. in Eng. incl. that for Manchester Town Hall. Estimated to have built nearly 500 organs. The great school of Fr. organ composers from Franck to Messiaen was motivated by his instruments.

Cavalieri, Emilio de' (*b c*.1550; *d* Rome, 1602). It. composer who was at the Medici Court in Florence and a member of *Camerata. One of first to use *Basso continuo.* Wrote at least 4 early mus.-dramas to texts by Guidiccioni and a morality-play, forerunner of oratorio, *La *rappresentazione di anima e di corpo* (The Representation of Soul and Body) to a text by Manni, f.p. 1600.

Cavalieri, Katharina (*b* Währing, Austria, 1760; *d* Vienna, 1801). Austrian sop. who studied with *Salieri. Spent most of her career in Vienna. Mozart wrote Constanze in *Die Entführung* for her and the aria 'Mi tradi', added to Elvira's part in *Don Giovanni* for its Vienna première.

Cavalleria rusticana (Rustic Chivalry). Opera in 1 act by *Mascagni to lib. by Menasci and Targioni-Tozzetti based on play by Verga adapted from his short story. Won prize for 1-act opera in competition organized by *Sonzogno, 1889. Prod. Rome 1890, London 1891. Usually perf. as double bill with *Leoncavallo's *Pagliacci,* hence the vernacular 'Cav. and Pag.'.

Cavalli (Caletti-Bruni), **Pietro** (Pier) **Francesco** (*b* Crema, 1602; *d* Venice, 1676). It. composer of operas, possibly pupil of *Monteverdi. Between *c*.1635 and 1670 about 40 of his operas were prod. in Venice. Twice visited Paris, his *Serse* (Venice 1654) being given there 1660 as part of Louis XIV's marriage festivities. Operatic importance lies in enlargement of dramatic potentialities and command of comic possibilities. Operas incl. *Didone* (1641), *L'Egisto* (1643), *Giasone* (Jason) (1649), *La Doriclea* (1645), *Oristeo* (1651), *Scipiano Africano* (1664), *Statira, Principessa di Persia* (1655), *La virtù de'strali d'amore* (1642), *L'Erismena,* *L'Ormindo* (1644), *La *Calisto* (1651), *Eritrea* (1652), *Orione* (1653), *Serse* (1654), *Ercole amante* (1662), *Mutio Scevola* (1665), and *Pompeo magno* (1666). *L'Ormindo* and *La Calisto* were revived successfully at Glyndebourne in realizations by Raymond *Leppard which are sometimes some way removed from the original score. Cavalli was also an org. and composer of church mus. (e.g. *Vespers of the Annunciation* (1675) and a *Requiem*) and instr. pieces.

Cavatina (It.). (1) Operatic solo aria in regular form and in one section instead of the classical aria's 3, without repetition of words or phrases, e.g. *Porgi amor* from Mozart's *Le nozze di Figaro.* Also used of song-like air incl. in a long *scena.

(2) Song-like instr. piece, e.g. Raff's *Cavatina* and the *Cavatina* movement of Beethoven's Str. Qt. in B♭, Op. 130. 3rd movement of Vaughan Williams's 8th Sym. (1955) is a *Cavatina* for str.

Cavendish, Michael (*b c*.1565; *d* London, 1628). Eng. composer of madrigals and lute mus. Madrigal 'Come, gentle swains' is in *The *Triumphs of Oriana.*

Cawston. See *Caustun, Thomas.*

Cazden, Norman (*b* NY, 1914; *d* Bangor, Mne., 1980). Amer. composer and pianist. Studied Juilliard Sch. 1927–39 (comp. with *Wagenaar) and later at Harvard with Piston and Copland. Piano recitalist, also worked for radio stations and dance cos. Many comps., several based on folk mus. collected in Catskill Mts., incl. sym., pf. sonatas, str. qt., brass sextet.

Cazzati, Maurizio (*b* Lucera, *c.*1620; *d* Mantua, 1677). It. composer and org. Choirmaster at Bergamo 1653–7, Bologna 1657–73, and Mantua 1673–7. Wrote religious mus. and instr. works.

CB. Short for *Contrabassi,* i.e. str. dbs.

C Clef. See *Clef.*

C Dur (Ger.). Key of C major.

Cebell (cibell). Eng. dance, used by Purcell and others, similar to a fast gavotte. So called because based on an air assoc. with the goddess Cybèle in Lully's opera *Atys* (1676).

Cebotari, Maria (*b* Kishinev, Bessarabia, 1910; *d* Vienna, 1949). Austro-Russ. sop. Actress at Moscow Art Th. 1926. Studied singing in Berlin. Opera début Dresden 1931 as Mimì. In Dresden co. 1931–41, also Berlin 1936–44, Vienna 1946–9. Début CG 1936 with Dresden co., sang there with Vienna Opera 1947. Created role of Aminta in R. Strauss's *Die schweigsame Frau* (1935). Appeared in films.

Ceccato, Aldo (*b* Milan, 1934). It. cond. Studied Milan; ass. to *Celibidache at Siena Acad. 1961–3. Début Milan 1964, Wexford 1968, Chicago 1969, CG 1970, Glyndebourne 1971. Prin. cond. Detroit S.O. 1973–7.

Cecilia, Saint (martyred in Sicily *c.* A.D. 176). Patron saint of mus., commemorated annually on 22 Nov. Her assoc. with mus. is very obscure, apparently dating from 15th cent. (There is a theory that it arose from the misreading of an antiphon for her day.) First recorded mus. fest. in her honour *c.*1570 at Evreux, Normandy; earliest recorded date of a Brit. mus. celebration 1683. Innumerable paintings and stained glass windows depict her playing the org.—always one of many centuries later than A.D. 176. Many comps. in her honour, outstanding examples being Purcell's *Ode for St Cecilia's Day* (1692) and Britten's *Hymn to St Cecilia* (1942).

Cédez (Fr.). Give way, i.e. Diminish the speed (present and past participles *cédant, cédé*).

Celere (It.). Quick, speedy. Hence *celerità,* speed; *celeramente,* with speed.

Celesta (It., Fr. *céleste*). Small kbd. instr. not unlike glockenspiel. Invented in Paris by Auguste Mustel in 1886. Series of steel plates (suspended over wooden resonators) which are struck by hammers when keys are depressed, giving ethereal bell-like sound. Range of 4 octaves upwards from middle C. Used in 1892 by Tchaikovsky in 'Dance of the Sugar-Plum Fairy' in *Nutcracker* ballet. Many others have used it since, notably *Bartók in *Music for Strings, Percussion and Celesta.* First used in sym. by Mahler in his 6th (1903–5).

Celeste (Fr.). (1) Type of soft pedal on old-fashioned pfs., interposing a strip of cloth between the hammers and strings.

(2) The *Voix Céleste* stop on the organ.

Celestial Railroad, The. Fantasy for pf., 1924, by *Ives, arr. from 2nd movement of his Sym. No. 4.

Celibidache, Sergiu (*b* Iasi, Romania, 1912). Romanian cond. and composer. Studied Berlin Hochschule and Univ. Cond. Berlin P.O. 1945–51. London début 1948. Taught cond. at Siena. Author of study of Josquin *Desprès. Comp. 4 syms. and pf. conc. Has spent much time with radio orchs., e.g., S. Ger. Radio (Stuttgart) from 1959 and Stockholm 1962–71. Insists on heavy rehearsal schedule and dislikes recordings.

Cello. Short for *Violoncello. It used to be spelled with a preliminary apostrophe, but *cello* is now accepted as standard, like piano.

Cello Symphony. Britten's Op. 68—in full, Sym. for Cello and Orch.—comp. 1963 for, and ded. to, *Rostropovich, who gave f.p. in Moscow 1964, the composer conducting. F.p. in England, Aldeburgh 1964.

Celtic Harp. See *Clàrsach.*

Celtic Requiem. Work by *Tavener for sop., children's ch., mixed ch., and orch., comp. 1969 and f.p. London 1969.

Cembalo. See *Clavicembalo.*

Cendrillon (Cinderella). Opera in 4 acts by Massenet to lib. by Henri Cain. Prod. Paris 1899, NY Met. 1912, London (with puppets) 1928.

Cenerentola, La (Cinderella). Opera in 2 acts by Rossini to lib. by Ferretti. Prod. Rome 1817, London 1820, NY 1826. There are other Cinderella operas by Laruette, Steibelt, *Massenet and Wolf-Ferrari. Also ballets by Prokofiev and J. Strauss II.

Cento, Centon, Centone. A medley of tunes. See *pasticcio.*

Central Park in the Dark in the Good Old Summertime (or A Contemplation of Nothing Serious). Work for chamber orch. by *Ives, comp. 1906.

Ceòl beag (Gaelic). Little music. That part of Scottish Highland bagpipe repertory comprising marches, *strathspeys, and *reels. (See also *Ceòl mor* and *Ceòl meadhonach.*)

Ceòl Meadhonach (Gaelic). Middle music. That part of Scottish Highland bagpipe repertory comprising folk songs, lullabies, croons, and slow marches. (See also *Ceòl beag* and *Ceòl mor*).

Ceòl Mor (Gaelic). Big music. That part of Scottish Highland bagpipe repertory comprising salutes, gatherings, and laments, also tunes comp.

in memory of some historical event. (See also *Ceòl beag* and *Ceòl meadhonach*.)

Ce qu'on entend sur la montagne (What one hears on the Mountain; Ger. *Bergsymphonie*, Mountain Symphony). Symphonic poem for pf. by Liszt comp. 1848–9, scored for orch. by *Raff 1849 and by Liszt 1850, rev. 1854. Based on Victor Hugo's *Feuilles d' automne*, No. 5.

Ceremony of Carols, A. Settings by Britten, Op. 28, of carols (in 11 movements) for treble vv. and harp, comp. 1942 at sea on voyage back to U.K. Also arr. for SATB and harp or pf. by Julius Harrison.

Cererols, Joan (*b* Martorell, 1618; *d* Montserrat, 1676). Sp. Catalan composer, connected for most of his life with Montserrat Abbey where he was dir. of choir for over 30 years. His works show adventurous technique and incl. *Requiem, Magnificat, Ave maris stella, Regina coeli*, etc.

Cerha, Friedrich (*b* Vienna, 1926). Austrian composer and violinist. Studied Vienna Acad. and Univ. Founded instr. ens. 'Die Reihe' 1958. Prof., Vienna Acad. 1969, teaching new mus. and elec. comp. Orch. Act III of Berg's *Lulu* (from composer's short score) for first complete perf., 1979. Works incl.:

OPERA: *Baal* (1974–9); *Netzwerk* (1981).

ORCH: *Spiegel I*, for orch., *II* for 55 str., *III-VII* for orch. (1960–71); *Fasce* (1960–72); *Langegger Nachtmusik I* (1969), *II* (1971); *Intersecazioni I* for vn. and orch. (1959), *II* (1959–72); Sym. (1975); Conc. for vn., vc., orch. (1975); Conc. for fl., bn., orch. (1982).

CHAMBER ORCH: *Catalogue des objets trouvés* (1968–9); *Symphonies for wind and drums* (1964); *Curriculum*, for wind (1972); *Movements I–III* (1960); *Enjambements* (1959).

VOICE(S) AND ORCH: *Exercises*, bar., speaker, chamber orch. (1962–8); *Baal-Gesänge*, bar. and orch. (1982); *Requiem für Hollensteiner*, speaker, bar., ch., and orch. (1983).

UNACC. CHORUS: *Verzeichnis*, 16 vv. (1969).

Cernikof, Vladimir (*b* Paris, 1882; *d* London, 1948). Franco-Russian pianist, studied Geneva and Berlin. Début Mülhausen, 1905 and London 1908. Settled in London, touring widely.

Certon, Pierre (*b* c.1510; *d* Paris, 1572). Fr. composer. Wrote over 200 *chansons, chansons spirituelles*, 8 masses, Magnificat, and many motets. Clerk, Notre Dame de Paris 1529–32, next 40 years at Sainte Chapelle, mostly as master of choirboys.

Cervelat (cervelas, Fr.; It. *cervellate*). The *rackett.

Ces (Ger.). The note C♭.

Ceses (Ger.). The note C♭♭.

Cesti, Pietro Antonio (*b* Arezzo, 1623; *d* Florence, 1669). Orig. friar, believed to have studied with

*Carissimi. Released from vows, became mus. dir. Medici Court, Florence, 1643. In 1666 became vice-Kapellmeister at Vienna imperial court. Operas rank with Cavalli's in importance. They incl. *Orontea* (Venice 1649), *Cesare amante* (Venice 1651), *La Dori* (Innsbruck 1657), *Il Tito* (Venice 1666) and *Il pomo d'oro* (Vienna 1668).

Ceterone. The bass *cittern, dating perhaps from 1524 but certainly from end of 16th cent. Monteverdi's *Orfeo* (1615 ed.) lists '2 ceteroni'. Had a number of additional unstopped bass str. and was particularly suitable for *continuo.

Cetula. It. medieval instr. identified by scholars as ancestor of the cittern, a derivative of the lyra. Described c.1487 as having '4 brass or steel strings usually tuned a tone, a 4th and back again a tone, and it is played with a quill'.

Chabrier, (Alexis) **Emmanuel** (*b* Ambert, Puy-de-Dôme, 1841; *d* Paris, 1894). Fr. composer, pianist, and cond. Largely self-taught and was civil servant until 1880. After visiting Sp. wrote orch. rhapsody *España*, 1883. Became ass. ch.-master to Lamoureux in Paris 1884–5. Fervent admirer of and propagandist for Wagner. Works incl. operas *L'Étoile* (1877), *Une Education manquée* (1879), *Gwendoline* (1885), *Le *Roi malgré lui* (1887) and *Briséis* (unfinished); *Joyeuse Marche*, orch. (1888); pf. pieces and songs (incl. *Ballade des gros dindons*, 1889).

Cha Cha Cha. Ballroom dance originating in Cuba c.1952. Development of mambo. Name derives from rhythm—2 crotchets, 3 quavers, quaver rest. Steps are glided, with rocking of hips as in rumba.

Chaconne (Fr.; Eng. chacony, It. Ciaccona, Sp. Chacona; from Basque chocuna pretty). A musical form almost indistinguishable from *Passacaglia. Both were orig. dances of 3-in-a-measure rhythm, and the mus. of both was erected on a *ground bass. In some specimens this bass theme passes into an upper part. In others while there is no actual ground bass the mus. falls into a number of quite short sections similar to those written over a ground bass. Lully, Rameau, and other composers of their period and a little later, often ended an opera with a movement of this type (e.g. Gluck's *Orfeo*). A universally known *Chaconne* is that by Bach which closes the 2nd Partita (D minor) for solo. vn.—often played without its companion movements. Purcell's aria *When I am laid in earth* (Dido and Aeneas) is a chaconne, so are Beethoven's *32 Variations in C minor* for piano, the finale of Brahms's Sym. No. 4 (usually called a passacaglia), and the last movement of Britten's Str. Qt. No. 2 (*Chacony*).

Chadwick, George (Whitefield) (*b* Lowell, Mass., 1854; *d* Boston, 1931). Amer. composer, organist, and cond. Gave up business for mus. and at 23 went to Munich and Leipzig to study. Returned to Boston 1880, becoming teacher, org., and choral cond. Joined staff New England Cons. 1882, becoming dir. 1897 until his death. Comp. opera *Judith* (1900), 3 syms., several symphonic poems incl. *Tam O'Shanter* (1911), 5 str. qts., and choral works.

Chagall Windows, The. Orch. work by *Mc-Cabe inspired by Marc Chagall's stained-glass windows in synagogue of Hadassah Hospital, Hebrew Univ., Jerusalem, representing 12 tribes of Israel. Comp. 1974, f.p. Manchester 1975.

Chagrin, Francis (really Alexander Paucker) (*b* Bucharest, 1905; *d* London, 1972). Romanian-born composer and cond. resident in Eng. for many years. Studied Zürich and Paris with Boulanger, Dukas, and in London with Seiber. Founded 1943 Committee (now Society) for the Promotion of New Mus. (S.P.N.M.). Comp. and cond. for over 200 films. Cond. for various ballet cos. Works incl. *King Stag, Volpone, Lamento appassionato*, pf. conc., and 2 syms.

Chahut. See *Can-Can*.

Chains, Iron. Required by Schoenberg among perc. instr. in his *Gurrelieder*, 1900–11.

Chair Organ. Term applied to small organ in Eng. in 17th and 18th cents. Used in conjunction with 'great organ'. Originally separate, they were incorporated but played on different manuals.

Chaliapin (Shalyapin), **Fyodor** (Ivanovich) (*b* Kazan, 1873; *d* Paris, 1938). Russ. bass singer. Of humble orig., having little mus. training before joining provincial opera co. 1890. Sang in St Petersburg 1894, then joined Mamontov's private opera co. in Moscow 1896, singing Ivan in Rimsky-Korsakov's *Maid of Pskov* and especially Boris Godunov in Mussorgsky's opera, role with which he became inseparably assoc. Milan début 1901, NY Met. 1907, London 1913 in Beecham season. NY Met 1921–9. Created title-role of Massenet's *Don Quichotte*. Gave frequent recitals. Superb actor-singer.

Chalumeau (Fr.). Reed. Simple rustic reed-pipe, ancestor of *clarinet, with 6 to 8 finger-holes. Also applied to *shawm and to double-reed bagpipe chanter. Also wind instr. that came into use in 17th and 18th cents. Term used to describe lowest register of cl.

Chamberlain, Houston Stewart (*b* Portsmouth, 1855; *d* Bayreuth, 1927). Eng.-born writer, naturalized Ger. Educ. Cheltenham College. In 1870 went to Stettin and conceived intense admiration for Ger. culture. Lived Dresden 1885–9 and Vienna 1889–1908. Wrote *Foundations of the 19th Century* (1899–1901). Married Wagner's daughter Eva 1908 and lived at Bayreuth, publishing several books on Wagner and ed. of letters.

Chamber Music (It. *Musica da camera*, Ger. *Kammermusik*). A term orig. intended (as Burney puts it *c*.1805) to cover such mus. as was not intended 'for the church, the theatre, or a public concert room'. As now used it has lost any implication as to place of perf. and excludes, on the one side, solo vocal mus. and mus. for a single instr. (or for a solo instr. acc. by another), and, on the other, orch. and choral mus., etc., incl. merely instr. mus. for 2, 3, 4, or more instr., played with a single instr. to a 'part', all the parts being on equal terms. Thus it comprises duet sonatas for vn. and pf. or vc. and pf., sonatas for a wind instr. and pf., trios for str. or for 2 str. instr. and pf., qts. for str. or for 3 str. instr. and pf., instr. qts., sextets, septets, and octets, etc. Of all these types the most important is the str. qt.: the instrs. employed in it are 2 vn., va., and vc., the db. having very rarely a place in chamber mus. (two outstanding exceptions being Schubert's 'Trout' Pf. Quintet and Dvořák's Str. Quintet, Op. 77).

The modern conception of chamber mus. may be said to date from Haydn. For a century and more before his time nearly all mus. was supplied with a figured bass guided by which a harpsi-chordist extemporized a background: in earlier times we find something more like our idea of chamber mus. in 16th-cent. mus. for viols.

Most composers have contributed to the now abundant repertory of chamber mus., and so far have we departed from the early 19th-cent. idea of the meaning of the term that 'Chamber Concerts' are common. Such concerts date effec-tively from the 1830s when the Müller Brothers Str. Qt. began touring Europe with a fine classical repertory. Since that period there have been many world-famous str. qts., pf. trios, and other groups. Despite much concert-room perf., how-ever, chamber mus. still retains some right to its name, since it is often treated as 'the music of friends' and is much practised privately.

The term *Chamber Music* (*Kammermusik*) was used by *Hindemith for 7 comps. between 1921 and 1927; these incl. a pf. conc., vc. conc., va. conc., viola d' amore conc., and organ conc., the orch. in most cases comprising at least 12 players, sometimes more. His wind quintet, 1922, he called *Kleine* (Little) *Kammermusik*.

Chamber Opera. Term applied to operas with comparatively small no. of singers and orch. players, e.g. Britten's *The Rape of Lucretia* and *The Turn of the Screw*, but there is no question of such works being perf. in a room instead of a th. R. Strauss's *Ariadne auf Naxos* is strictly a chamber opera, but is perf. at CG, NY Met., and Vienna State Opera.

Chamber Orchestra. Small-sized orch. capable of playing in a room or small hall, but term is elastic and works for chamber orch. of symphonic proportions are written.

Chamber Symphony (*Kammersymphonie*). Title of 2 works by Schoenberg for small orch. No. 1 in E major, Op. 9, for 15 solo instr., comp. 1906, f.p. Vienna 1907. Also exists in simplified arr. by Webern (1922) and 2 orch. versions by Schoenberg (1922 and 1935). No. 2, Op. 38a, was begun 1906, completed 1939, f.p. NY 1940. Other composers have used this title, e.g. *Schreker, and others have preferred the term Chamber Concerto, e.g. *Berg and Hugh *Wood.

Chambonnières, Jacques Champion de (*b* Paris, *c*.1602; *d* Paris, 1672). Fr. composer and harpsichordist. His father was harpsichordist to Louis XIII as he himself became to Louis XIV, who ennobled him. Regarded as founder of Fr. hpd. sch. Pubd. 2 books of *Pièces de clavecin* (1670), ed. in modern times by T. Dart, 1969.

Chaminade, Cécile (*b* Paris, 1857; *d* Monte Carlo, 1944). Fr. pianist and composer. Pupil of Godard. Began composing at 8. From 1875 regularly gave pf. recitals, incl. her own comps. Eng. debut 1892. Comp. *opéra-comique*, ballet, orch. suites, *Konzertstück* for pf. and orch., *Les Amazones* for ch. and orch., many songs, and pf. pieces of graceful *salon* variety.

Champêtre (Fr.). Rustic. Hence *Danse champêtre*, a peasant dance in the open air; *fête champêtre*, a picnic.

Chance. See *Aleatory*.

Chandos Anthems. 12 anthems on religious texts comp. by *Handel between 1717 and 1718 when he was dir. of mus. for the Earl of Carnarvon, later the Duke of Chandos, at his palace, Cannons, near Edgware, Middlesex (not far from London). They are short cantatas for 3-part ch. acc. by obs., str., and org. In No. 6 (*As pants the hart*) Handel used Ger. chorale as *cantus firmus*.

Change-Ringing. Practice, virtually confined to Britain, of ringing church bells by teams each member pulling the rope controlling one bell. See *Bell*.

Changes. Nocturnal cycle, Op. 17, by *Crosse, comp. 1965, for sop., bar., children's ch., and orch. F.p. Worcester 1966. Title refers both to transience of nature and to bell-ringing.

Changing Note or Nota Cambiata (It.). Idiomatic melodic formula, salient characteristic of which is leap of a third away from an unessential note. Earliest form (in the polyphonic age) was a 3-note figure, (*a*). This was soon joined and eventually superseded by a 4-note idiom, (*b*). In the harmonic age of counterpoint (from Bach and Handel onwards) a variety of other changing note figures appear, (*c*) (*d*) (*e*).

In USA the term *Cambiata* is in common use for 'changing note'. Also when the leap of 3rd is in the dir. opposite to that of the step-wise movement the term *Échappé*, is sometimes used, and, where the movement is back to the orig. note, the term *Returning Tone*.

Chanot. Family of Fr. vn.-makers. François (*b* Mirecourt, 1787; *d* Brest, 1823) invented a pear-shaped vn. with flat belly and no sound-post. His brother Georges (*b* Mirecourt, 1801; *d* Courcelles, 1873) set up his business in Paris in 1823 and his son Georges (*b* Paris, 1831; *d* London, 1893) began his own business in London in 1858.

Chanson (Fr.). Song. A term with many applications, especially: (1) Any sort of simple verse-repeating song. (2) Type of song, for several vv. or for one v. with acc., that grew up in Fr. and north It. in 14th cent. and flourished until end of 16th—really a kind of early madrigal of the 'ayre' type. The *chanson de geste* was an heroic verse chronicle set to mus., of the 11th and 12th cents.

Chansons de Bilitis. 3 settings by Debussy, 1897–8, for v. and pf. of prose-poems by Pierre Louÿs. They are *La Flûte de Pan, La Chevelure* and *Tombeau des Naïades*. Orch. version 1926 by *Delage. Incidental mus. for 2 fl., 2 harps, and celesta to acc. recitation of poems, 1900; arr. *Boulez for reciter, 2 harps, 2 fl., and celesta 1954.

Chant. See *Anglican Chant*. For Gregorian chant see *Plainsong*.

Chantant (Fr.). Singing. In a singing style. Sometimes the past participle is used, *chanté* (sung).

Chanter. See *Bagpipe*.

Chanterelle (Fr.). Highest str. of vn., etc. (See *Banjo*.)

Chants d'Auvergne (Songs of the Auvergne). Series of traditional dialect songs of the Auvergne collected by *Canteloube and pubd. between 1923 and 1930. Best-known is suite of 9 for sop. and orch. (or pf.) drawn from series 1 to 4, being 1. *Baïlèro*, 2. *L'Aio dè rotso* (Spring Water), 3. *Ound 'onorèn gorda?* (Where shall we go to graze?), 4. *Obal din lou Limouzi* (Down there in Limousin), 5. *La delaïssàdo* (The forsaken girl), 6. *Lo Fiolairé* (The spinning girl), 7. *Passo pel prat* (Come through the meadow), 8. *Brezairola* (Cradle Song), 9. *Chut, chut* (Hush, hush).

Chanty. See *Shanty*.

'Chaos instead of music' (*Sumbur vmesto muzyki*). Notorious article published in *Pravda* on 28 January 1936, followed by another 10 days later, attacking Shostakovich's opera *Lady Macbeth of the Mtsensk District* and leading to its withdrawal from the stage. Believed to have been dictated by Stalin, who had left a performance of the opera in a rage over its alleged dissonance and immorality.

Chapelle (Fr.). See *Kapelle*.

Chapel Royal. No one institution was more useful in fostering Eng. musicianship and promoting the development of Eng. mus. than the Chapel Royal—by which must be properly understood not a building but a body of clergy and musicians (like Ger. **Kapelle*) whose principal duty was to arrange and perform divine service in the sovereign's presence.

Existing records go back to 1135. During reign of Edward IV (1461–83) the Chapel consisted of 26 chaplains and clerks, 13 minstrels (a very wide term), 8 choirboys and their master, and a 'Wayte', or mus. night-watchmen, sounding the hours nightly. Under Richard III (1483–5) a press-gang system was authorized (though the practice of pressing seems to have existed earlier); this remained in operation for about 2 centuries; representatives of the Chapel were entitled to listen to all the best cath. choirs, and rob them of any boys whose vv. marked them out as fit to sing before the King. Under *Henry VIII (1509–47), a practical musician, the mus. staff of the Chapel rose to 44 (32 Gentlemen and 12 Children) and remained at this strength under Edward VI (1547–53) and Mary (1553–8). Under Elizabeth I (1558–1603) and James I (1603–25), the Chapel's personnel incl. Tye, Tallis, Byrd, Gibbons, Morley, Tomkins, and Bull. These brought church mus. to a level not exceeded even by the musicians of the Sistine Chapel at Rome; they developed the Eng. madrigal, and laid foundations of artistic kbd. music. The artistically-minded Charles I (1625-49) established the King's Band (6 recorders, 3 fl., 9 ob. and sackbuts, 12 vn., and 24 'lutes and voices', plus trumpets, drums and pipes). He appointed Nicholas *Lanier as 'Master of the Musick' as from 30 Nov., 1625. With the death of Charles I in 1649 the Chapel ceased. Cromwell was a lover of mus. and retained a small body of domestic musicians, but did not maintain a princely state, and, of course, did not approve of choirs as an inst. of public worship. In 1660 Charles II recalled the Chapel. A talented choirboy, Pelham Humfrey, was sent abroad to learn foreign styles; a younger boy, Purcell, without going abroad, was very apt to learn, and these youths and others, as they matured, largely trained by Captain Henry *Cooke, were quickly able to put to good use the new resources (such as the band of 24 fiddlers in church) with which the King had provided himself. Purcell, from 1677 to his death in 1695, was 'Composer in Ordinary' to the Chapel.

Under William and Mary, Anne, and the Georges, less was heard of the Chapel. George III had musicians in his employ beyond those of his Chapel; he spent little time in London, and when at Windsor had no need of his 'Chapel Royal', in the technical sense, since the Chapel of St George,

in Windsor Castle, had its own distinct staff, as it still has. The great days, then, were over, but a line of orgs. continued. Some clever boys, incl. Sullivan, still received training in the Chapel.

Today the 'Chapel Royal' consists of a body of clergy, choirmen, and boys ('Priests in Ordinary', 'Gentlemen', and 'Children'), and the org. charged with the conduct of the Sunday services. Their place of duty is chiefly the chapel of St James's Palace, but they have other places of duty incl. Buckingham Palace.

By the end of George III's reign the King's Band had almost ceased to exist. George IV maintained a private wind band and so did Victoria after her accession in 1837. The Prince Consort enlarged it to a small orchestra. In 1893 the 'Queen's Band' was constituted, unifying the private band and the state band, but Edward VII (1901–10) only required the musicians for state functions and abandoned concerts. Under George V (1910–35) they were never used, though the 24 musicians nominally still belonged to the royal household. Four survivors played in the orch. at the coronation (1937) of George VI (1936–52). Today the post of Master of the Queen's Music is an honour for a distinguished musician, with no real duties.

Chapí y Lorente, Ruperto (*b* Villena, Alicante, 1851; *d* Madrid, 1909). Sp. composer. Studied Madrid Cons. and became regimental bandmaster. Comp. many *zarzuelas, orch. works incl. sym., cantatas, chamber mus.

Chappell, William (*b* London, 1809; *d* London, 1888). Eng mus. publisher. Founded Musical Antiquarian Soc. (1840) to publish works of early Eng. composers. Ed. *Popular Music of the Olden Time* (2 vols. 1855–9; new edn. by H. E. Woodridge 1893).

Chappell & Co. Ltd. London mus. publishers, pf. makers, etc. Founded 1810 by Samuel Chappell (1776–1834). Firm was largely responsible for building of St James's Hall, London, ran ballad concerts, was lessee of Queen's Hall, London, and sponsor of New Queen's Hall Orch. After 1st World War, its dominant interest was light music (musicals and film music), band music, and educational, but has recently accepted work of some important composers, e.g. Sebastian Forbes and Stephen Dodgson. Now part of Philips organization.

Chapple, Brian (*b* London, 1945). Eng. composer. Studied RAM with L. Berkeley. Influenced by Messiaen, has used serial technique but is one of group of Eng. composers who have moved to a more tonal idiom in the 1970s. Works incl.: *Green and Pleasant*, for orch. (1973), pf. conc. (1977), *Veni Sancte Spiritus*, double ch. (1974), *In ecclesiis*, sop. and ch. (1976), *Summoned by Bells*, pf. and alarm clocks (1968), *Concert Piece*, 2 pf. qts. (1969), *5 Blake Songs*, ten. and pf. (1972), *Light breaks out where no sun shines*, sop. and pf. (1978),

Cantica, sop., ten., ch., orch. (1978), *Venus Fly-Trap*, chamber ens. (1980), *Delphine*, orch. (1980), 5 Shakespeare songs, 6 male vv. (1981), *5 Carols*, women's vv., pf. (1982), *Little Sym.*, str. (1983).

Characteristic Piece (Ger. *Charakterstück*). Imprecise term occasionally applied by composers to shorter instr. comp. (esp. for pf.); the equivalent of *Stimmungsbild* (Ger.), Mood-picture.

Charivari (Fr.). Extemporized mus. of a violent kind made with any household utensils etc., that lie to hand, generally before the house of a person who has incurred communal disapprobation. Equivalents are *Rough Music* (Eng.); *Chiasso* (It.). Uproar; or *Scampanata* (It.). Bell ringing; *Katzenmusik* (Ger.). Cat Music; *Shivaree, Calthumpian Concert* (Amer). In USA also means 'musical' teasing of newly-weds.

Charleston. A fast *fox-trot named after Charleston, S. Carolina, popularized in NY, 1922, in Negro revues, by Cecil Mack and Jimmy Johnson; it then had a short but widespread vogue in ballrooms and dance-halls. The dance-step was characterized by 2 twists on each foot, with one kicked sharply backwards.

Charm of Lullabies, A. Songs by Britten for mez. and pf., Op. 41, comp. 1947. Poems by Blake, Burns, Green, Randolph, and Philip.

Charpentier, Gustave (*b* Dieuze, 1860; *d* Paris, 1956). Fr. composer, pupil of Massenet at Paris Cons., winning Prix de Rome, where he wrote *Impressions d' Italie* for orch. (1890, arr. as ballet 1913). Had great success with opera *Louise (Paris 1900) but its successor *Julien* (1913) failed. Wrote cantata *La Vie du poète* (1892). Founded in 1902 Conservatoire Populaire where working girls like Louise could learn mus. and dancing.

Charpentier, Marc-Antoine (*b* Paris, ?1645; *d* Paris, 1704). Fr. composer. Studied in Rome with *Carissimi. On return to Fr. became *maître de musique* and court singer to Duchess of Guise until her death in 1688. In about 1670 began long association with Molière's theatrical co. Wrote prologue and *intermèdes* for *Le malade imaginaire* (1673). Never held a court post but in 1698 became master of the music of Sainte-Chapelle, for which he wrote many of his finest religious motets and oratorios. His early style was Italian based, but he soon adopted a Fr. tone of voice. His mus. is noted for harmonic richness and colour contrasts, also for the vividness of his word-painting. Comp. 17 operas, incl. *Médée* (Paris 1693). His other th. pieces (*intermèdes* and incid. mus.) are notable for lightness of texture and for wit and humour.

Chasins, Abram (*b* NY, 1903). Amer. pianist and composer. Studied pf. with *Hofmann and *Godowsky, comp. with R. *Goldmark. On staff Curtis Institute 1926–35. Mus. dir. of NY radio station (WQXR) 1949–65. Author of several

books. Comps. incl. 2 pf. concs., *Parade* (1931), *Rush Hour in Hong Kong* (pf.), etc.

Chassé (Fr.). In ballet, the 'chasing' away of one foot by a touch from the other.

Chasse, Cor de (Fr.). Hunting horn.

Chasse, La (Fr.). The Hunt. Nickname for Haydn's Sym. in D, No. 73 (Hob.I:73); reference is to the final movement. Comp. 1780–1.

Chasseur Maudit, Le (The Accursed Hunter). Symphonic poem by Franck (1881–2), based on ballad by G. A. Bürger.

Chatburn, Thomas (*b* Blyth, 1941). Eng. composer. Studied Univ. of Wales, RMCM, and Princeton Univ. Studied in USA with Sessions and Babbitt. Lecturer in mus. Oxford Polytechnic. Works incl. pieces for ch. and jazz orchs., and *Study and Prayer* for small orch. (1978).

Chausson, Ernest (*b* Paris, 1855; *d* Limay, 1899). Fr. composer. Law student; entered Paris Cons. 1879 to study with Massenet, but left to transfer to Franck. Best-known works are *Poème de l'amour et de la mer*, v. and orch., Op. 19 (1882–90, rev. 1893); *Poème*, vn. and orch., Op. 25 (1896); *Chanson perpetuelle*, v. and orch., Op. 37 (1898); pf. qt., Op. 30 (1897); sym. in B flat, Op. 20 (1889–90); Conc. for pf., vn., and str. qt., Op. 21 (1889–91). Of his 3 operas, only *Le roi Arthus* has been staged (Brussels 1903).

Chavez, Carlos (*b* Mexico City, 1899; *d* Mexico City, 1978). Mex. composer and cond. Travelled in Europe and USA 1922–8. Cond. Mexico S.O. 1928–48. Dir., Nat. Cons. of Mexico 1928–34. Founder and dir., Mexican Nat. Institute of Fine Arts 1947–52. Dir., composers' workshop, Nat. Cons. 1960–5. Comps. incl. 7 syms., pf. conc., vn. conc., opera *The Visitors* (lib. by Kallman) (1953–6), ballet *Caballos de Vapor* (Horse Power) (1926–7). Nationalist style but rarely used folk material.

Chaykovsky. See *Tchaikovsky, Pyotr*.

Che (It.). Who, which.

Checkmate. Ballet in 1 act by *Bliss to his own lib., choreog. N. de Valois. Prod. by SW co., Paris 1937; then over 100 perfs. in Britain; as Suite, NY 1939.

Chef d'attaque (Fr.). Leader of the attack. Orch. leading vn. (Eng.), or concert-master (Amer.).

Chef d'orchestre (Fr.). Conductor.

Chekker. 14th-cent. name for an unidentified instr. which may have been a *clavichord.

Chélard, Hippolyte André Jean Baptiste (*b* Paris, 1789; *d* Weimar, 1861). Fr. composer and violinist. Studied Paris Cons. (Prix de Rome). Opera *Macbeth* (lib. by Rouget de Lisle) prod. Paris Opéra 1827. Settled Munich 1830. Cond. Ger. opera in London 1832–3 and later worked in Weimar. Other operas incl. *Die Hermannschlacht* (Munich 1835).

Chelsea Opera Group. Opera co. founded 1950 to give concert perfs., usually in orig. language. Gave early opportunities to many young British singers, conds., and musicians who later achieved fame, e.g. Colin Davis, Thomas Hemsley, Bernard Keeffe, John Carol Case, Heather Harper, Roger Stalman, Peter Glossop, James Loughran, Alberto Remedios, Sheila Armstrong, Pauline Tinsley, Derek Hammond-Stroud, Sarah Walker, and Roger Norrington. F.p. (*Don Giovanni*) organized by Colin Davis, David Cairns, and Stephen Gray, was given in Oxford. Among operas perf. have been *Fidelio*, Menotti's *The Telephone*, Mozart's *Zaide* and *Idomeneo*, Hugo Cole's *The Tunnel*, Rossini's *Guillaume Tell* and Verdi's *Don Carlos* (both in Fr.), Berlioz's *Les Troyens*, Weber's *Euryanthe*, Mussorgsky's *Boris Godunov* (orig. version), Strauss's *Feuersnot*, Dvořák's *The Jacobin*, and Janáček's *Jenůfa*.

Cheltenham Festival. Annual summer mus. fest. held (usually in July) in spa of Cheltenham, Eng. Begun in 1945 as a fest. of Brit. contemporary mus. but scope widened in 1969 to embrace contemporary mus. of other nationalities. Many post-1945 Brit. chamber works, concs., and syms. (hence the expression 'a Cheltenham Symphony') received f.ps. at the fest., many of them from Hallé Orch., cond. Barbirolli, who gave bulk orch. concerts 1947–61. First dir. G.A.M. Wilkinson, 1944–69. Since 1969 programme dir. has been John *Manduell..

Cheminée du roi René, La (King René's Chimney). Suite by Milhaud for fl., ob., cl., bn., and hn., 1939. Title refers to street in Aix-en-Provence commemorating 15th-cent. monarch.

Chemin-Petit, Hans (*b* Potsdam, 1902; *d* Berlin, 1981). Ger. composer and cond. Studied Berlin Hochschule, becoming prof. there 1929 and ass. dir. 1965–8. Dir. Magdeburg Cath. choir 1939–44 and from 1944 of Berlin Phil. Choir. Comps. incl. opera *König Nicolo* (1959), org. conc. (1963), 2 syms. (1932, 1949), choral works, and chamber mus.

Cherkassky, Shura (Alexander Isaakovich) (*b* Odessa, 1911). Russ.-born pianist, Amer. citizen. Pupil of J. *Hofmann. Settled USA 1922. Studied Curtis Institute. First extensive European tours after 1945.

Cherniavsky, Mischel (*b* Uman, S. Russia, 1893; *d* Dieppe, 1982). Russ.-born cellist, later Brit. citizen. Studied with *Popper. Member of pf. trio 1900–23 with brothers Leo and Jan, thereafter solo performer in concs. and recitals.

Cherry Ripe. Setting by C. E. *Horn early in 19th cent. of poem by Herrick (1648).

Cherubini, (Maria) **Luigi** (Carlo Zanobi Salvadore) (*b* Florence, 1760; *d* Paris, 1842). It. composer. Studied in It. Comp. quantity of church mus. by age of 16. Visited London in 1784 producing 2 operas there. Settled in Paris 1788 where his new, Gluck-inspired operatic style revolutionized Fr. stage. Under a cloud because of Napoleon's disfavour, went for a time to Vienna where he met Beethoven who was strongly influenced (esp. in *Fidelio*) by Cherubini's operas, 4 of which he heard in Vienna. Visited London 1815, writing Sym. while there. Became prof. of comp. Paris Cons. 1816, dir. 1821–41. His Masses are deservedly famous. Among his nearly 30 operas were: *Quinto Fabio* (1779, rev. 1783, Rome), *Armida* (Florence 1782), *Adriano in Siria* (Leghorn 1782), *Lo sposo di tre* (Venice 1783), *La finta principessa* (London 1785), *Giulio Sabino* (London 1786), *Ifigenia in Aulide* (Turin 1788), *Démophoön* (Paris 1788), *Lodoïska* (Paris 1791), *Médée (Paris 1797), Les *Deux Journées (Ger. *Der Wasserträger*, Eng. *The Water Carrier*) (Paris 1800), *Anacréon (1803), *Faniska* (Vienna 1806), *Les *Abencérages* (Paris 1813), *Bayard à Mezières* (1814). His *Requiem* No. 2, in D minor, still frequently performed, was written in 1836 and f.p. at the Paris Cons. in 1838. His *Requiem* in C minor was comp. in 1816 and f.p. in St Denis 1817. He also wrote 6 str. qts.

Chester, J. & W. Ltd. Eng. firm of mus. publishers founded in Brighton 1874, transferred to London 1915, specializing in Russ. and contemporary foreign composers. Pubd. journal *The Chesterian* from 1915 to 1961. Since 1957 linked with Hansen and other Scandinavian publishers.

Chest of Viols. Any complete set of 6 viols of different sizes (so called because they were usually stored in a specially built chest or cupboard).

Chest Voice. Lowest register of human v., others being 'head' and 'middle', so called because the notes seem to come from singer's chest.

Chetham's School of Music. School in Manchester founded 1653 by Humphrey Chetham as charitable foundation for boys. In 1969 became first Brit. co-educationl sch. basing admission solely on mus. audition. Has 275 pupils. Specialist mus. education given within framework of full academic curriculum.

Chevalet (Fr.). Trestle. Bridge of bowed instr., etc.

Chevé, Emile J. M. See *Galin-Paris-Chevé*.

Chevillard, Camille (Paul Alexandre) (*b* Paris, 1859; *d* Chatou, 1923). Fr. cond. and composer, son of leading Fr. cellist. In 1886 became ass. cond. to *Lamoureux, succeeding him 1899. Prof. at Cons. 1907. Cond. Paris Opéra 1914. Wrote orch. and chamber mus.

Cheville (Fr.). Peg, e.g. of str. instr.

Chevreuille, Raymond (*b* Brussels, 1901; *d* Montignies-le-Tilleul, 1976). Belg. composer. Studied Brussels Cons. Dir. of mus. programmes, Brussels radio 1956–63. Comps. incl. 6 str. qts., 8 syms., 3 pf. concs., 2 vc. concs., 3 vn. concs., hn. conc., cl. conc., etc.

Chiaro, chiara (It.). Clear, unconfused. Hence *Chiaramente,* clearly, distinctly; *chiarezza,* clarity, distinctness.

Chiave (It.). Clef.

Chica (Sp.). Early form of *Fandango.

Chicago Musical College. Division of Roosevelt Univ. since 1954 when it merged with univ.'s sch. of mus. Offers degrees of B. Mus. and M. Mus. Founded as Chicago Acad. of Mus. 1867 by Florenz Ziegfeld Sr. Changed name 1872. Rudolph Ganz was dir., later pres., 1930–54.

Chicago Opera Company. Several cos. have used this title, the first in 1910 with Campanini as dir. Leading light was sop. Mary Garden, who was art. dir. 1921–2. Co. re-formed as Civic Opera Co. 1922–32, with Giorgio Polacco as cond. (1918–30). Singers like Frida Leider and Eva Turner in co. at this time. New opera house opened 1929, but depression closed co. 1932. Visiting cos. until 1954 when Carol Fox (*b* Chicago, 1926; *d* Chicago, 1981) formed Lyric Opera of Chicago.

Chicago Symphony Orchestra. 3rd oldest sym. orch. in USA. Founded 1891 by Theodore Thomas as the Chicago Orch. Re-named Theodore Thomas Orch. 1906, then present name 1912. Conds.: Thomas 1891–1905; Frederick Stock 1905–42; Désiré Defauw 1943–7; Artur Rodzinski 1947–8; Rafael Kubelik 1950–3; Fritz Reiner 1953–63; Jean Martinon 1963–9; Georg Solti from 1969. First tour of Europe 1971.

Chichester Psalms. Choral work by Leonard Bernstein for counterten., ch., and orch. Text in Hebrew. Written for Chichester Cath., where perf. in July 1965. Orig. scoring is for organ, harp, and perc.

Chiesa (It.). Church. Hence Aria da Chiesa (an aria for church use); Cantata da Chiesa (see *Cantata*); Concerto da Chiesa (see *Concerto*); Sonata da Chiesa (see *Sonata*).

Chifonie. Another name for *hurdy-gurdy.

Chilcot, Thomas (*b* ?Bath, *c*.1700; *d* Bath, 1766). Eng. org.; composer of settings of Shakespeare songs, and kbd. works.

Childhood of Christ, The (Berlioz). See *Enfance du Christ, L'*.

Child of our Time, A. Oratorio by *Tippett for sop., cont., ten., and bass soloists, ch. and orch. Comp. 1939–41, f.p. 1944. Lib. by composer based on persecution of Jews begun after assassination of Nazi official Vom Rath by Jewish boy Grynspan at Ger. Legation, Paris, autumn 1938. Uses Negro spirituals in manner of Bach's chorales in his Passions.

Child, William (*b* Bristol, 1606; *d* Windsor, 1697). Eng. composer and organist. Organist Chapel Royal, in reign of Charles I, also serving Charles II at Restoration. Comp. hymns, anthems, church services, mus. for viols, and catches.

Children's Corner. 6 pf. pieces by Debussy (1906–8) ded. to his daughter. With Eng. titles (explained by influence of Eng. governess)— *Doctor Gradus ad Parnassum* (see *Gradus ad Parnassum*); *Jimbo's Lullaby* ('Jimbo' is composer's mistake for 'Jumbo'); *Serenade for the Doll*; *Snow is Dancing*; *The Little Shepherd*; *Golliwogg's Cakewalk*. Orch. by *Caplet, 1911.

Children's Overture, A. Orch. work by *Quilter, 1914, based on nursery-rhymes. Intended as ov. to play 'Where the Rainbow Ends', for which Quilter wrote incid. mus., but not used.

Chilingirian, Levon (*b* Nicosia, 1948). Cypriot violinist. Studied RCM and with M. Parikian. First prize, BBC Beethoven Competition 1969 and Munich Int. Competition 1971. Sonata duo with Clifford Benson. Founder and leader *Chilingirian Quartet from 1971.

Chilingirian Quartet. Formed 1971, led by L. *Chilingirian, coached by S. Nissel (*Amadeus Quartet) and Hans *Keller. Resident qt. Liverpool Univ. 1973–6. Tours of Europe and Scandinavia. NY début 1977, followed by US tour.

Chime Bells. Small medieval bells related to modern cymbals. Had a high central dome.

Chinese Crash Cymbal. This differs in shape from the normal *cymbal. The cup is much shallower and its edge turns up. It is made of a special alloy peculiar to the Chinese, and when struck with a drum stick gives a brilliant crash.

Chinese Temple Block. See *Korean Temple Block*.

Chinese Wood Block. Oblong block of wood, 7″ or 8″ long, with slots cut in it. Struck with stick of a snare drum gives a hard, hollow tone. Other names are *Clog Box* and *Tap Box*. Used in jazz and by 20th-cent. composers, e.g. Lambert in *Rio Grande*.

Ching, James (*b* Thornton Heath, Surrey, 1900; *d* 1962). Eng. pianist. Studied Oxford, RAM and RCM, Berlin, and Leipzig. Founded own pf. sch. and wrote books on pf. technique.

Chiroplast. Hand-rest for pf. practice, once a part of the *Logier system's equipment.

Chisholm, Erik (*b* Glasgow, 1904; *d* Rondebosch, S. Africa, 1965). Scot. cond., pianist, and composer. Studied with Tovey and Pouishnoff (pf.). Cond. Glasgow Grand Opera Soc. 1930–9, giving Brit. première of several operas, e.g. Berlioz's *Béatrice et Bénédict* and *Les Troyens,* and reviving

Mozart's *Idomeneo* and *La Clemenza di Tito*. Prof. of mus., Cape Town Univ. 1945–65, where his opera pioneering continued. Comp. 4 operas, ballets, 2 pf. concs., vn. conc., 2 syms., chamber mus.

Chistu. Basque mus. instr. similar to the Renaissance *tabor pipe.

Chitarra. It. name for *guitar. Hence *chitarriglia*, a smaller higher-pitched type of Sp. guitar; *chitarrino*, 17th-cent. name for small 4-course guitar; *chitarra battente*, 5-course metal-strung guitar with fixed metal frets and played with plectrum.

Chittarone. Largest of the lute family, developed in It. during 16th cent. Larger than its close relative the *theorbo, both being designed as accompanying instr. and to improve on the bass register of the lute. However a solo repertory exists. Stringing was variable, 6 double course and 8 single basses being the most usual. Mentioned by *Caccini in his *Le nuove musiche* (1602).

Chiuso, Chiusa (It.). Closed, stopped, with special reference to the *horn.

Chladni, Ernst (Florenz Friedrich) (b Wittenberg, 1756; d Breslau, 1827). Ger. scientist who made important acoustic researches. Invented Clavicylinder, kbd. instr. with glass cylinder, worked by pedal and revolving against strips of wood, glass, or metal activated by keys.

CHM. Choirmaster's diploma of *Royal College of Organists.

Ch.M. Choirmaster's diploma of Amer. Guild of Organists or of Royal Canadian College of Organists.

Chocolate Soldier, The (*Der tapfere Soldat*, The Valiant Soldier). Operetta by O. *Straus to lib. by L. Jacobson and R. Bernauer based on G. B. Shaw's play *Arms and the Man* (1894). Prod. Vienna 1908, NY 1909, London 1910.

Choeur (Fr.). Chorus, choir. But *Grand choeur*, besides meaning Large Chorus and Full Choir, means Full Organ (or a comp. for such).

Choir or **Chorus.** (1) A *Mixed Voice Choir* (or Chorus) is one of both women and men.
  (2) A *Male Voice Choir* is (usually) of men only, but may be of boys and men.
  (3) A *Double Choir* is one arr. in 2 equal and complete bodies, with a view not merely to singing in 8 parts but also to responsive effects.
  (4) Architecturally, the choir is that part of a cath. which, in a church other than a cath., is called the chancel.
  (5) *Chorus* tends to be used for secular bodies, but there are many exceptions.

Choir Organ (or choir). Division of org. consisting of soft stops suitable for acc. of choir.

Choke Cymbals. 2 ordinary *cymbals fixed face to face on a rod, with a device by which their pressure one on the other can be adjusted, according to the tone-quality desired. They are played with a drumstick, giving a short, sharp crash.

Chop, Max (b Grenszen, 1862; d Berlin, 1929). Ger. composer and scholar. Turned to mus. from law. Comp. 2 pf. concs., orch. suites, songs, etc. Mus. critic and ed. Analyst of Liszt symphonic poems and Wagner operas. First to write monograph on Delius (1907).

Chopin, Fryderyk (Franciszek) (Frédéric François), (b Zelazowa Wola, 1810; d Paris, 1849). Polish composer and pianist (Fr. father, Polish mother). Began pf. studies with Zywny 1816 and played conc. by *Gyrowetz in Warsaw 1818. In 1822 began studies in harmony and counterpoint with Joseph Elsner, dir. of Warsaw Cons. In 1825 his *Rondo* in C minor was pubd. as Op. 1, though it was far from being his first comp. The next year, entered Warsaw Cons. as full-time mus. student, leaving in 1829. While student, wrote *Krakowiak* Rondo. In 1829 comp. his conc. in F minor and gave 2 concerts in Vienna. Played the conc. in Warsaw twice in Mar. 1830 and later in year played E minor conc. Left home late in 1830, travelling via Dresden and Prague to Vienna and giving many concerts. In Stuttgart heard that the Russians had captured Warsaw. Arrived Paris Sept. 1831; became pf. teacher to aristocracy, gradually renouncing public career and concentrating on composing. Became friend of most of outstanding musicians of day. In an essay taking the form of a discussion between Florestan and Eusebius, Schumann hailed the *Là ci darem variations*, Op. 2, with the words 'Hats off, gentlemen! A new genius!' In 1836 Chopin met Fr. novelist George Sand and lived with her 1838–47. From 1836 the first signs of the tuberculosis that was to kill him appeared and the rest of his life was a constant struggle with sickness. After break with George Sand, gave a concert in Paris early in 1848 but left for London after the revolution, in need of money. Gave concerts in Manchester, Glasgow, Edinburgh, and London and returned to Paris to die in Oct. 1849.
  Although Chopin's pf. mus. is beset with romantic stories and nicknames, he himself insisted on its existence only as absolute mus., hence the rather severe titles which refer only to mus. forms and are never picturesque, as in Schumann and Liszt. His own playing was both powerful and rhythmically subtle, with astonishing evenness of touch. Taking the name 'nocturne' from John *Field, he transformed the form, as he did everything, by harmonic imagination and melodic distinction. There are bold, prophetic passages in his mus., ornamentation derived from his admiration for It. opera, and, in his Polish works such as the mazurkas and polonaises, a raw

passion elemental in its strength. The Victorian conception of Chopin as a consumptive drawing-room balladeer of the kbd., a conception connived at by lesser pianists, has long been exposed as a false trail leading hearers away from the true, poetic, heroic Chopin. Prin. comps.:

PIANO SONATAS: C minor, Op. 4 (1828); B♭ minor, Op. 35 (1839, Funeral March 1837); B minor, Op. 58 (1844).

PIANO AND ORCH.: Conc. No. 1 in E minor, Op. 11 (1830); No. 2 in F minor, Op. 21 (1829–30); Variations on Là ci darem la mano, Op. 2 (1827); Grande Fantaisie on Polish Airs, Op. 13 (1828); *Krakowiak Rondo, Op. 14 (1828); Andante Spianato (1834); Grande Polonaise brillante in E flat, Op. 22 (1830–1).

SOLO PIANO: Ballade in G minor, Op. 23 (1831–5), in F major/A minor, Op. 38 (1836–9), in A♭, Op. 47 (1840–1), in F minor, Op. 52 (1842); Scherzo in B minor, Op. 20 (1831–2), in B♭ minor/D♭, Op. 31 (1837), in C♯ minor, Op. 39 (1839), in E, Op. 54 (1842); 12 Études, Op. 10 (1829–32), 12 Études, Op. 25 (1832–6); 3 Nocturnes, Op. 9 (1830–1), 3 Nocturnes, Op. 15 (1830–3), 2 Nocturnes, Op. 27 (1835), 2 Nocturnes, Op. 32 (1836–7), 2 Nocturnes, Op. 37 (1838–9), 2 Nocturnes, Op. 48 (1841), 2 Nocturnes, Op. 55 (1843), 2 Nocturnes, Op. 62 (1846), 2 Nocturnes, Op. 72 (1827, 1830); 24 Preludes, Op. 28 (1836–9), Prelude in C♯ minor, Op. 45 (1841); Valses, in A♭ (1827), in E (1829), in E♭ (1829–30), in E minor (1830), in E♭ (1840), in E♭, Op. 18 (1831), 3 Valses, Op. 34 (1831–8), in A♭, Op. 42 (1840), 3 Valses, Op. 64 (1846–7), 2 Valses, Op. 69 (1835, 1829), 3 Valses, Op. 70 (1829–41); Polonaises, in G minor (1817), in B♭ (1817), in A♭ (1821), in G♯ (1822), 2 Polonaises, Op. 26 (1834–5), 2 Polonaises, Op. 40 (1838–9), Polonaise in F♯, Op. 44 (1840–1), Polonaise in A♭, Op. 53 (1842), 3 Polonaises, Op. 71 (1825–8); Polonaise Fantaisie in A♭, Op. 61 (1845–6); 4 Mazurkas, Op. 6 (1830), 5 Mazurkas, Op. 7 (1831), 4 Mazurkas, Op. 17 (1834), 4 Mazurkas, Op. 24 (1834–5), 4 Mazurkas, Op. 30 (1836–7), 4 Mazurkas, Op. 33 (1837–8), 4 Mazurkas, Op. 41 (1838–40), 3 Mazurkas, Op. 50 (1842), 3 Mazurkas, Op. 56 (1843), 3 Mazurkas, Op. 59 (1845), 3 Mazurkas, Op. 63 (1846), 4 Mazurkas, Op. 67 (1835, 1846, 1849), 4 Mazurkas, Op. 68 (1827–49); Berceuse, in D♭, Op. 57 (1843–4); Barcarolle in F♯, Op. 60 (1845–6); Boléro, Op. 19 (1833); 3 Écossaises, Op. 72 (1826); Fantasie in F minor, Op. 49 (1841); Fantasie Impromptu in C♯ minor, Op. 66 (1835); 3 Impromptus, A♭, Op. 29 (1837), F♯, Op. 36 (1839), G♭, Op. 51 (1842); Allegro de concert, Op. 46 (1832–41); Tarantelle In A♭, Op. 43 (1841).

2 PIANOS: Rondo in C, Op. 73 (1828).

CHAMBER MUSIC: Piano Trio in G minor, Op. 8 (1828–9); vc. sonata in G minor, Op. 65 (1845–6); Introduction and Polonaise in C, vc. and pf., Op. 3 (1829–30); Grand Duo in E on themes

from Meyerbeer's Robert le Diable, vc. and pf. (1832).

SONGS: 17 Polish Songs (1829–47).

Chopsticks (Fr. Côtelettes, cutlets; Ger. Koteletten Walzer). Anonymous quick waltz tune for pf. first pub. London 1877 as 'the celebrated Chop Waltz'. It is perf. with 2 outstretched forefingers or with the flat hands held perpendicularly, the notes being struck by their sides (i.e. with the outsides of the little fingers), with a tonic-dominant vamping bass part and an occasional touch of *glissando. The name therefore refers to chopping and to Chinese eating utensils. There is a coll. of comps. based on a similar tune— Paraphrases, by Borodin, Cui, Lyadov, Rimsky-Korsakov, and Liszt (1877).

Choragus. (1) In Ancient Gr., leader of ch.
(2) An official peculiar to the Univ. of Oxford. When the Lectureship or Professorship in Mus. was founded and endowed by William Heather in 1626, he laid it down that a subordinate official, called Choragus, was to conduct practices of mus. twice a week. The office still exists (but not with that duty).

Choral (Ger.), **Chorale** (Eng.). (1) Metrical hymn-tune characteristic of the Ger. Reformed Church and sung in unison. Martin Luther (1483–1546) wished to restore the congregation's role in church services and wrote simple devotional words to tunes familiar either as folk-songs or as old ecclesiastical melodies (i.e. plainsong chants). A famous example is Ein' feste Burg ist unser Gott (A Safe Stronghold our God is still). But the Ger. word Choral orig. belonged to the unreformed Church and means the ecclesiastical Plainsong, the Cantus choralis. Properly, the 'Choral' in the Ger. R.C. Church is that part of the plainsong sung by more than one v. (the 'Concentus' as distinguished from the 'Accentus'), but this distinction of terminology is not always observed.

The first Lutheran chorales had not the regular rhythms that they later took on. They had often a mixture of duple and triple time and, indeed, a good deal of the free rhythm of plainsong. With Lutheran chorales, as with Genevan, Eng., and Scot. hymn tunes, the melody was at first in the ten. During the 17th cent. it gradually became usual to place it in the treble, as today. 4-part settings of chorales were made by many musicians in the 16th, 17th, and 18th cents.

The repertory of the Ger. chorale may be said to have been completed in Bach's day. He comp. only about 30, but he made 400 reharmonizations of existing chorale melodies and used some of them with memorable effect in his settings of the *Passions.
(2) The term is used in USA as a synonym for choir or chorus, e.g. Robert Wagner Chorale.

Choral Fantasia. (1) Beethoven's Op. 80, in C minor, for solo pf., ch., and orch., comp. 1808. Comprises variations on Beethoven's song Gegen-

liebe (1794–5), a melody which resembles that of prin. theme of finale of his 9th Sym., for which this Fantasia seems to have been a preliminary experiment. Text is poem by Christoph Kuffner.

(2) Holst's Op. 51, for sop., ch., org., brass, perc., and str., to words by Robert Bridges (1844–1930), comp. 1930. F.p. Gloucester Fest. 1931.

Choral Prelude or **Chorale Prelude** (Ger. *Choral Vorspiel*). From the custom of playing org. preludes and interludes to the chorale grew the technique of 2 special forms of comp., one based upon a treatment of the chorale melody, often taken line by line and surrounded by other melodic parts woven together into elaborate *counterpoint, and the other not reproducing the chorale intact but suggesting it to the minds of the hearers by taking its first few notes as the theme to be elaborated. For a north Ger. congregation, to whom the melodies were all known from childhood, such a piece of organ mus. had great interest and significance.

Among the composers who helped to develop this form were Sweelinck (1562–1621), Scheidt (1587–1654), Pachelbel (1653–1706), Buxtehude (1637–1707), Reinken (1623–1722), and Böhm (1661–1733). Such of Bach's forebears as were orgs. also took their part in the working out of the form, and he himself crowned the labours of all his predecessors and contemporaries.

In addition to the Chorale Preludes of Bach there are certain early works which he called *Chorale Partitas*, the word Partita here, as with certain other composers, having not the usual sense of a suite but of an air with variations. The no. of variations corresponds to the number of the verses of the hymns, and each variation seems to be designed to re-express the thought of the corresponding verse. Since Bach many other Ger. composers have written chorale preludes, Brahms's last comp., Op. 122, being a set of 11.

To some extent the same form was cultivated in Eng. Purcell has a Voluntary on the Old Hundredth that, in its way, is on the lines of the Bach Chorale Prelude.

Choral Symphony. A sym. in which a ch. is used at some point. By general usage *the* Choral Sym. means Beethoven's Sym. No. 9 in D minor, Op. 125, in which the finale is a setting for 4 soloists, ch., and orch. of Schiller's 'Ode to Joy'. But Holst wrote a *Choral Symphony* (to poems by Keats, f.p. 1925), and there are many syms. since Beethoven which use soloists and ch. in one or more movements, e.g. Vaughan Williams's *A Sea Symphony*, Britten's *Spring Symphony*, Mahler's Syms. Nos. 2, 3, and 8, and Shostakovich's 2nd and 13th Syms. Bantock's *Atalanta in Calydon* is a choral sym. for vv. alone.

Choral Vorspiel. See *Choral Prelude*.

Chord. Any simultaneous combination of notes, but usually of not fewer than 3. The use of chords is the basic foundation of harmony.

Chording. (1) A choir-trainer's term for bad and good intonation of the notes sounded together in chords.

(2) Spacing of the intervals in a chord.

(3) In USA the term means the improvised strumming of accompanimental chords on a banjo, etc.

Chordophone. Term for mus. instr. which produce sound by means of str. stretched from one point to another. Simple chordophones are various types of zither; composites are lutes, lyres, rebecs, violins, guitars, harps, etc. One of 4 classifications of instr. devised by C. Sachs and E. M. von Hornbostel and pubd. In *Zeitschrift für Ethnologie*, 1914. Other categories are *membranophones, *idiophones, and *aerophones, with *electrophones recently added.

Choreographic Poem. An orch. work designed for ballet but also self-sufficient because it has something of the quality and form of a tone-poem, e.g. Ravel's *La Valse* (1920), described on the score as *poème choréographique*.

Choreography. (1) The system of describing dances, esp. in ballet, by signs for the steps, written alongside the melodies. An early method was *Arbeau's, described in his *Orchésographie* (1588–9). The term choreography was introduced by Lefeuillet in 1699. Today one speaks of a ballet having been 'choreographed' by its creator.

(2) The visual comp. of the ballet.

Chorist-Fagott. Name for the bass (double) curtal, forerunner of the bn., because it was often used for doubling the bass line in church mus.

Chorley, Henry Fothergill (*b* Blackley Hurst, Lancs., 1808; *d* London, 1872). Eng. mus. critic for the *Athenaeum* weekly magazine 1831–68, influential in his time. Also wrote novels, plays, and libs. for operas by Sullivan, Benedict, and Wallace.

Chôros. A sequence of 14 works by Villa-Lobos, comp. between 1920 and 1929, for various instr. ranging from solo guitar to 2 pf. and orch. and incorporating S. Amer. rhythms and popular melodic characteristics.

Chorus. (1) See *Choir* or *Chorus*.

(2) Old name for *Bagpipe.

(3) Old str. instr.—generally the *crwth.

Chorus Reed. Any org. reed stop not intended for solo use.

Chorzempa, Daniel (*b* Minneapolis, 1944). Amer. organist, pianist, and composer. Educated Minnesota Univ. and Cologne (elec. studio). Int. reputation as org. virtuoso. Authority on *Reubke.

Chotzinoff, Samuel (*b* Vitebsk, 1889; *d* NY, 1964). Russ.-Amer. pianist and critic. Settled in USA at 17, becoming accompanist to Zimbalist and Heifetz. Critic for NY *World*, then for NY

Post. Taught at Curtis Institute. Persuaded Toscanini to become cond. of NBC Sym. Orch. in 1936 and became NBC dir. of mus. and, in 1951, producer of NBC TV operas, commissioning Menotti's *Amahl and the Night Visitors*. Wrote several books.

Chout (Fr. spelling of Russ. *Shut*, buffoon). Ballet by Prokofiev (The Buffoon who out-buffooned seven buffoons), his Op. 21. First version 1915, rev. 1920. Prod. *Diaghilev, Paris 1921. Based on A. Afanasyev's Russ. tales. Symphonic suite 1922.

Christie, John (*b* Eggesford, 1882; *d* Glyndebourne, 1962). Eng. org. builder and schoolmaster. Married sop. Audrey *Mildmay 1931, and founded in 1934 annual summer fest. of opera in opera house built at his home *Glyndebourne, near Lewes, Sussex. C.H. 1954. His son George (*b* Glyndebourne, 1934) succeeded him as chairman of the Glyndebourne Fest. and was knighted in 1984. In John Christie's memory, the Worshipful Company of Musicians has, since 1965, enabled the award of an annual scholarship for a promising member of the Glyndebourne company to study abroad. Holders have included Ryland Davies, Richard Van Allan, Jill Gomez, Teresa Cahill, Ian Caley, Linda Esther Gray, Elizabeth Gale, John Rawnsley, Anthony Rolfe Johnson, Fiona Kimm, Kate Flowers, and Helen Walker.

Christmas Concerto. Name of *Corelli's Concerto Grosso in G minor, Op. 6, No. 8, for str. and continuo (1712). It was intended as a *concerto da chiesa* (for church use) and was inscribed *fatto per la notte di Natale* (made for Christmas Night). Torelli's 12 Concerti Grossi Op. 8 (1709) for str. and continuo are entitled *con un pastorale per il Santissimo Natale*, this 'pastoral for the most holy night of Christmas' being No. 6, also in G minor.

Christmas Oratorio. Choral work by Bach for soloists, ch., and orch., text by Picander and Bach, being biblical story of the Nativity with commentary. Comprises 6 cantatas designed for perf. in Leipzig on 3 days of Christmas fest., New Year's Day, New Year's Sunday, and Epiphany. Some of the mus. was comp. for secular words. Schütz also wrote a Christmas Oratorio (1664). Ger. title is *Weihnachts-Oratorium*.

Christoff, Boris (*b* Plovdiv, Bulgaria, 1914). Bulgarian bass. Orig. lawyer. Studied singing in Rome and Salzburg. Opera début Rome 1945, CG 1949. Chicago Opera 1958–63. Notable interpreter of Mussorgsky's Boris and Verdi's King Philip.

Christopher Columbus (*Christophe Colomb*). (1) Opera in 2 acts (27 scenes) by Milhaud to lib. by Paul Claudel. Comp. 1928. Prod. Berlin 1930. Paris (concert version) 1936. Uses cinema screen. Operas on this subject also by Ottoboni, Morlacchi, and Egk.

(2) Early ov. by Wagner intended for play by Apel, f.p. Leipzig 1835.

(3) Incidental mus. by Walton (unpubd.) for radio play by Louis MacNeice broadcast BBC Oct. 1942.

Christou, Jani (*b* Heliopolis, Egypt, 1926; *d* Athens, 1970). Gr. composer. Educated Alexandria and Cambridge Univ. Studied comp. with H. F. *Redlich, also psychology with Jung. Employed serialism and 12-note technique 1948–58, then became interested in elec. sounds, establishing elec. workshop in Athens. Invented form of notation to incorporate stage action. Comps. incl. syms.; *Tongues of Fire* and *Mysterion* (oratorios); and works involving tape and aleatory procedures.

Christus. (1) Oratorio by Liszt for soloists, ch., and orch., comp. 1862–7, f.p. Budapest 1873.

(2) Oratorio, Op. 97, by Mendelssohn, text by Chevalier Bunsen, begun 1844, unfinished. F.p. of 8 nos., Birmingham 1852.

(3) The part of Christ in Bach's *St Matthew Passion* is often denominated thus.

Christus am Ölberge (Christ on the Mount of Olives). Oratorio by Beethoven, Op. 85, for sop., ten., bass, ch., and orch., comp. 1803. Lib. by Franz Xaver Huber. F.p. Vienna 1803. English version entitled *En Gedi* changes subject to story of David.

Chromatic (derived from Gr. *chromos* = colour). The chromatic was one of the 3 classifications of Gr. scales. In modern mus. it refers to notes not belonging to the diatonic scale. They are indicated by *chromatics*. The *chromatic scale* is 12 ascending or descending semitones (sharps ascending, flats descending). *Chromatic chords* incl. one or more notes not in the diatonic scale of the prevailing key of the relevant passage.

Chromatic Fantasia and Fugue. Hpd. work by Bach, comp. 1720–3 at Cöthen.

Chromatic Harp. Harp built by Pleyel 1897 with a str. for every semitone, thus needing no pedals.

Chromaticism. (1) The use of chromatic intervals and chromatic chords.

(2) A style of composing using chromatic harmony. *Gesualdo in 16th cent. used advanced chromaticism. Bach's experiments in chromaticism were based on diatonic principles. The age of Romanticism explored chromaticism further because of need for emotional expression, hence the chromatic elements in Wagner's *Tristan und Isolde* and later works. See also *Atonal*.

Chronochromie (Time-colour). Orch. work by Messiaen in 7 sections: *Introduction, Strophe I, Antistrophe I, Strophe II, Antistrophe II, Epode, Coda*. Comp. 1960. F.p. Donaueschingen, 16 Oct. 1960, cond. Rosbaud. *Epode* is written for 18 str., each playing a different birdsong.

Chrysander, (Karl Franz) **Friedrich** (*b* Lübthen, Mecklenburg, 1826; *d* Bergedorf, 1901). Ger. critic and mus. historian. Authority on Handel, editing complete works for Ger. Handel Soc. and writing biography (1858–67; never completed). Worked also on other musicological subjects, publishing or editing works of Palestrina, Schütz, Carissimi, Corelli, Couperin, and J. S. Bach, and discovering autograph of Bach's B minor Mass.

Chueca, Federico (*b* Madrid, 1846; *d* Madrid, 1908). Sp. composer of *zarzuelas, most of them in one act. Best-known is *La gran via* (1886), written in collab. with Valverde. His march *Càdiz* was Sp. nat. anthem under monarchy.

Chung, Kyung-Wha (*b* Seoul, Korea, 1948). Korean violinist, sister of Myung-Wha *Chung and Myung-Whun *Chung. Studied privately in Korea and at Juilliard Sch., NY. Début aged 9, Seoul, in Mendelssohn conc. NY début with NY P.O., 1968, European début with LSO, London, 1970. Brilliant int. career. Recordings of Sibelius, Walton, Elgar, and Stravinsky concs., among others.

Chung, Myung-Wha (*b* Seoul, Korea, 1944). Korean cellist, sister of Kyung-Wha *Chung and Myung-Whun *Chung. Studied Juilliard Sch., NY, and Univ. of S. Calif. (master-class with *Piatigorsky). Soloist with leading orchs. Plays trio with sister and brother.

Chung, Myung-Whun (*b* Seoul, Korea, 1953). Korean pianist and cond., brother of Kyung-Wha *Chung and Myung-Wha *Chung. Studied Mannes Sch. of Mus. and Juilliard Sch., NY. Début, Seoul 1960, as pianist; as cond. 1971. 2nd prize Tchaikovsky pf. competition, Moscow, 1974. Soloist with leading orchs. Ass. cond., Los Angeles P.O. 1978.

Church, John (*b* Windsor, 1675; *d* London, 1741). Eng. composer and chorister, Gentleman of Chapel Royal. Wrote anthems and songs.

Church Music Society (British). Founded 1906. Its objects are the encouragement of a high standard in the choice and perf. of mus. in worship. Predominantly Anglican in membership. See also *Royal School of Church Music.*

Chute de la Maison Usher, La (The Fall of the House of Usher). Opera in 3 scenes planned by Debussy based on Edgar Allan Poe but left incomplete. Work on it extended from 1908 to 1917. What survives is complete text and vocal score of scene 1 (prologue) and part of scene 2. F.p. New Haven, 1977.

Ciaia, Azzolino Bernardino della (*b* Siena, 1671; *d* Siena, 1755). It. composer, organist, and org.-designer. Wrote masses, cantatas, and instr. works.

Ciampi, Legrenzio Vincenzo (*b* Piacenza, 1719; *d* Venice, 1762). It. composer of operas and instr.

pieces. Worked in London 1748–56. His opera *Gli tre cicisbei ridicoli* incl. song 'Tre giorni son che Nina' often attrib. Pergolesi.

Cibber, Susanna (Maria) (*b* London, 1714; *d* London, 1766). Eng. singer and actress; sister of Thomas *Arne and 2nd wife (1734) of Theophilus Cibber. Début 1732, frequently singing Polly in *The Beggar's Opera*. Greatly admired by Handel, in whose *Messiah* she first sang the cont. arias (Dublin 1742). Gave up singing for acting 1746.

Ciccolini, Aldo (*b* Naples, 1925). It.-born Fr. pianist. Studied Naples Cons. Début 1942. Prof. of pf., Naples Cons., 1947. NY début 1950. Has specialized in works of Satie. Prof. of pf., Paris Cons., from 1971.

Ciconia, Johannes (*b* Liège, *c.* 1373; *d* Padua, 1412). Belg. composer of choral mus., also theorist. Importance was his combination of French Ars Nova and It. styles. Trained in Liège. Went to It. in cardinal's service, living and working there for some years.

Cid, Le. Opera in 4 acts by Massenet to lib. by d'Ennery, Gallet, and Blau, based on play by Corneille (1637). Prod. Paris 1885. Ballet mus. very popular. Operas on this subject also by Farinelli, Aiblinger, and Cornelius.

Cifra, Antonio (*b* probably nr. Terracina, 1575; *d* Loreto, 1629). It. composer, disciple of Palestrina. Held many important church mus. positions in It. and comp. over 200 motets, and madrigals, chamber mus., and org. mus.

Cigány (Hung; Ger. *Zigeuner*). Gipsy. What are called *Cigány Bands* consist normally of str., cl., and dulcimer.

Cigna (orig. Sens), **Gina** (*b* Angères, 1900). Fr.-It. sop.; studied Paris Cons. Début Milan 1927 (as Genoveffa Sens) in *Rheingold*, CG 1933, NY Met. 1936–8. Famous interpreter of Turandot in Puccini's opera. Became singing teacher 1948.

Cikker, Ján (*b* Banská Bystrica, Cz., 1911). Cz. composer. Studied Prague Cons. and Prague Acad. of Mus. (comp. with Novák). Studied cond. with Weingartner, Vienna 1936–7. Works incl. str. qts., symphonic poems, and operas incl. *Resurrection* (*Vzkriesenie*) (Tolstoy) 1962, *Mr Scrooge* (Dickens) 1963, and *Coriolanus* (1972).

Cilea, Francesco (*b* Palmi, Calabria, 1866; *d* Varazza, 1950). It. composer. Studied Naples Cons. First opera, *Gina* (1889), prod. while he was student. Other operas incl. *La tilda* (1892), *L'Arlesiana* (1897), *Adriana Lecouvreur* (1902), and *Gloria* (1907). From 1896 to 1904 prof. of comp., Florence Mus. Institute, dir. Palermo Cons. 1913–16, dir. Naples Cons. 1916–35.

Cima, Giovanni Paolo (*b c.*1570). It. composer and organist. Wrote masses, motets, and sonatas for vn., viola da gamba and org., hpd., etc. Early user of medium of trio sonata. Wrote treatise on counterpoint 1622.

Cimarosa, Domenico (*b* Aversa, Naples, 1749; *d* Venice, 1801). It. composer. Studied in Naples, where he wrote first of his 65 operas. Pupil of Fenaroli and Piccinni. Worked in Rome and Naples until 1787 when he went to St Petersburg as court composer. In 1791 succeeded Salieri as court Kapellmeister in Vienna, writing *Il *matrimonio segreto* there. Returned to Naples 1793 as choirmaster to the king. Sentenced to death 1799 for supporting French republican army but reprieved on condition he left Naples. Other operas incl. *Artaserse* (1784) and *Le astuzie femminili* (1794). Also wrote oratorios, church mus., and sonatas.

Cimbalom (Hung.). *Dulcimer. It is a large concert instr. (horizontal str. struck with hammers) used in popular mus., by *Kodály in his opera *Háry János*, and by Debussy and other composers, incl. Stravinsky (in *Renard* and *Ragtime*). First comp. to use it in symphonic mus. was *Mosonyi. Stravinsky's interest was stimulated by the Hung. player, Aladar Racz. In the 1970s Márta Fábián has played works written for her by Jozsef Soproni and by György Ránki (a conc. for cimbalom and chamber ens., 1978).

Cimbasso (It.). Narrow bore tuba in B♭, used in Verdi opera scores up to *Aida* (1871).

Cincinnati Symphony Orchestra. Founded 1895. First regular cond. Frank van der Stucken, 1896–1907. Orch. suspended 1907–9 because of labour dispute. Stokowski cond. 1909-12; Ernst Kunwald 1912–17; Ysaÿe 1918–22; Fritz Reiner 1922–31; Eugene Goossens 1931–47; Thor Johnson 1947–58; Max Rudolf 1958–70; Thomas Schippers 1970–77; Michael Gielen from 1980. Concerts given in Mus. Hall since 1930s (renovated 1970).

Cinderella. (1) Various operas have been written based on Perrault's fairy-tale. See *Cenerentola, La* (Rossini) and *Cendrillon* (Massenet).
(2) (*Zolushka*). Ballet, with songs, by Prokofiev, comp. 1940-4, f.p. Moscow 1945. Also ballet by J. Strauss II.

Cinelli (It.). Cymbals.

Cinesi, Le (The Chinese Ladies). 'Opera serenade', or divertissement, in 1 act by Gluck, to text expanded from lib. written by Metastasio for Caldara. Comp. 1754 for visit by Maria Theresa and Francis I to court of Gluck's employer, Prince von Hildburghausen.

Cipher, Ciphering. Continuous sounding of a note on the org. because of some mechanical defect.

Circles. Work by *Berio for female v., harp, and 2 percussionists to text by e. e. cummings from his 'poems 1923–54'. Comp. 1960.

Circus Polka (for a young elephant). Pf. piece comp. 1942 by *Stravinsky for Barnum and Bailey Circus to be danced by troupe of young elephants who gave f.p. in 1942 to arr. for wind band scored by David Resksin. Composer's version for sym. orch. f.p. Cambridge, Mass., 1944; f.p. in England, London 1952.

Cis (Ger.). The note C♯.

Cisis (Ger.). The note C♯♯.

Citole. Scholars are still uncertain just which medieval instr. was described by this term, but it seems possible that it was a forerunner of the Renaissance *cittern, a kind of *lyra.

Cittern. Renaissance instr. something between a lyre and a guitar, but with metal str., a flat back, and pear-shaped body. Played with a quill plectrum. Name derived from Gr. *kithara* (lyre), and the cittern was known as *cistra* (Fr.), *Cister* (Ger.), and *Cithren* (Eng.). In It. where it was developed it was called the *cetra*. Used as a solo instr. and in *broken consort. Not to be confused with *gittern. From late 17th cent. gave way to guitar but survived into early 20th cent. as folk instr. in Switz. and Ger.

City Center, New York. Home of enterprising opera and ballet cos., the former (NY City Opera) founded 1944 to provide high-standard opera at moderate prices. Housed in Lincoln Center since 1964. First mus. dir. László Halász 1944–51, then Joseph Rosenstock 1951–6, Erich Leinsdorf 1956, Julius Rudel 1957–79. Co. has given premières of several Amer. operas, also first Amer. perfs. of Bartók's *Duke Bluebeard's Castle, Orff's Der Mond, and Strauss's Die schweigsame Frau. Several fine singers have begun careers with co. incl. Beverly *Sills, (dir. since 1979) and Placido Domingo.

City of Desolation, The. Cantata, Op. 7, for sop., ch., and orch. by A. *Milner, comp. 1955.

Civil, Alan (*b* Northampton, 1929). Eng. hn.-player and composer. Pupil of Aubrey *Brain. Member of RPO 1953–55, Philharmonia Orch. 1955–66, prin. hn. BBC S.O. Prof. of hn. RCM. Member of several chamber groups. Comp. sym. for brass and perc. (1950), wind quintet (1951), wind octet (1951), hn. trio (1952). O.B.E. 1985.

Clair de Lune (Moonlight). (1) 3rd movement of Debussy's *Suite bergamasque* for pf.; exists in several other arrs., none by Debussy.
(2) Song by Debussy (poem by Verlaine), No.4 of his *Fêtes galantes*, in orig. version (1882).
(3) Song by Fauré, his Op. 46 No. 2, same poem as (2).

Claque (Fr.). Smack, clap. Members of the audience at (usually) an opera-house but also in the concert-hall who are engaged by a performer, often at considerable expense, to applaud, call for encores, and generally show enthusiasm. Claques are highly organized, under leadership of a *chef *de claque*, and exert considerable influence. The claque appears to have developed in Paris *c.* 1820 and then to have spread to It. and to Vienna, and eventually to all the famous opera houses.

Clarabel, Clarabella, or **Claribel Flute.** Org. stop much the same as **Hohlflöte.*

'Claribel'. See *Barnard, C. A.*

Claricembalo, Clarichord. Misspellings (apparently) of **Clavicembalo* (Harpsichord) and **Clavichord.*

Clari, Giovanni Carlo Maria (*b* Pisa, 1667; *d* Pisa, 1754). It. composer. Studied at Bologna. Choirmaster, Pistoia Cath., 1703–24. His madrigals are notable for their daring modulations. Comp. operas and church mus., making advanced use of fugue in the latter. Best known for secular vocal duets and trios with continuo, comp. after 1730 and mainly fugal.

Clarinet. Single-reed woodwind instr. with cylindrical tube developed *c.*1690 by J. C. Denner of Nuremberg, who, by adding 2 keys to the **chalumeau*, increased that instr.'s range by over 2 octaves. It was not playable in all keys until 1843 when Klose adapted the Boehm fl. key system to the cl. The first composer to use the cl. in a sym. was Mozart.

As the reed blocks one end of the tube, the pipe acts as a 'stopped' one, sounding an octave lower than it would have done if left open. Like other cylindrical tubes the cl. overblows at the interval not of its first upper partial, the interval of an octave (as the fl. and ob. do), but at its 2nd (the interval of a 12th). The notes of the instr.'s first octave are obtained in the normal way and the gap of a 5th before the overblowing begins has to be filled by additional side-holes which leave the tone weaker at this point and the fingering somewhat more awkward. All members of the family have great powers of *pianissimo* and of *crescendo* and *diminuendo*—greater than those of any other wind instr. Double, triple, and flutter **tonguing* are possible.

Varieties of cl. incl.:

(*a*) Clarinet in C, B♭, or A—The normal treble instr. The existence of these 3 pitches was to enable the composer to use any key without creating undue difficulty for the player (*see Transposing instrument*). The B♭ clarinet is a transposing instr., sounding a tone lower than written. The A clarinet sounds a minor 3rd lower than written. The C instr. is now not much used, on account of inferior tone, but figures in the scores of classical composers. It is not a transposing instr. (*b*) Bass Clarinet. Its range lies an octave below that of one of the above (usually of that of the B♭ instr.). It differs somewhat in shape, its lower end being curved upwards and ending in a bell, and its upper one continued by a tube bent downwards to reach the player's mouth. Except in military band mus. it is treated as a transposing instr., its mus. being notated either in the treble clef and a 9th higher than the sound (Fr. method), or in the bass clef a 2nd above the sound (Ger. Method).

(*c*) High E♭ Clarinet, a 4th above the B♭ instr. It is found in all military bands and occasionally figures in orch. scores, e.g. Richard Strauss's *Alpensinfonie*. It is a transposing instr., its mus. being notated a minor 3rd lower than the sound. (*d*) High D Clarinet. This serves the same purpose as the E♭ Cl., but is much rarer. It is a transposing instr., being written for a tone lower than the sound. R. Strauss uses it in *Symphonia Domestica* and with outstanding effect in *Till Eulenspiegel*. (*e*) Alto Clarinet—in E♭ and F. The E♭ is practically a military band instr. and, even so, rare. The F instr. is practically a modernized **Basset Horn*. Both are written for in the treble clef and are transposing instr. (*f*) Pedal Clarinet, or Contrabass Clarinet, or Double-Bass Clarinet. Almost entirely a military band instr. Its part is written a 9th higher than the sound. (The word 'pedal' had no reference to any part of the construction and the origin of its use is not very clear.) (*g*) 3 obscure modern instr. related to the cl. family by possessing a single reed are the *Clarina*, the *Heckelclarina* or *Heckelclarinette*, and the *Holztrompete*. All were invented to represent the shepherd-boy's pipe in Act III of Wagner's *Tristan und Isolde*, but have not displaced customary use of the **cor anglais*.

Note that the old Eng. spelling 'clarionet' is obsolete.

Clarinet Flute. Org. flue stop, end-plugged; 4' length and 8' pitch; slightly reedy in quality.

Clarinet Stop. Reed stop smoother than ob.; 8' pitch or occasionally 16'.

Clarino. Term applied to the high, brilliant tpt. and hn. parts in baroque mus., probably because the **clarion* was used for high-register playing.

Clarion. Org. stop like **Trumpet* but of 4' pitch.

Clarion (Fr. *claron*). Medieval short tpt. (2' or 3' long), used particularly by armies because it was easier to carry than the longer **buisines* and its high-pitched notes (hence **clarino*) could be more easily heard.

Clark, Edward (*b* Newcastle upon Tyne, 1888; *d* London, 1962). Eng. cond. and administrator. For some time connected with **Diaghilev*. With BBC, in various capacities 1923–36. Esp. interested in contemporary developments in comp. and was responsible for the f.ps. or f. broadcast ps. of many important works. Pres. Brit. section of I.S.C.M. from 1945. Husband of Elisabeth **Lutyens*.

Clarke, Douglas (*b* Reading, 1893; *d* Warwick, 1962). Anglo-Canadian composer, cond., and teacher. Studied Cambridge Univ., studied comp. with Holst and Vaughan Williams. Cond. Winnipeg Male Voice Ch. 1927–9; Dean of Faculty of Mus. McGill Univ., Montreal, 1930–55; cond. Montreal S.O. 1930–41. Returned to Eng. 1958. Comp. orch. and other works.

Clarke, Henry Leland (*b* Dover, N.H., 1907). Amer. composer. Educated Harvard Univ. Studied comp. 1929–31 with N. Boulanger in Paris and later with Holst. Held several teaching posts, incl. Univ. of California, Vassar Coll., and Univ. of Washington. Many comps. in wide range of fields incl. *Gloria in 5 Official Languages of the United Nations* (1950) for ch. and orch.

Clarke, Jeremiah (*b* London, *c*.1670; *d* London, 1707). Eng. composer and organist. Pupil of *Blow. Joint org. (with Croft) of Chapel Royal 1704. Comp. setting of Dryden's *Alexander's Feast*, cantatas, anthems, odes, and hpd. pieces. In his 'Choice lessons for the Harpsichord or Spinet' (pubd. 1700) there occurs 'The Prince of Denmark's March', better known in its arr. as the *Trumpet Voluntary*. Shot himself supposedly because of unhappy love affair.

Clarke, Rebecca (*b* Harrow, 1886; *d* NY, 1979). Eng. composer, violist, and violinist. Entered RAM 1902 to study vn. Later, in 1908, became Stanford's first woman comp. student at RCM and was encouraged by him to take up va. From 1911 played in various chamber groups with the d'*Arányi sisters, Myra *Hess, and *Suggia. Comp. 58 songs and part-songs and 24 instr. chamber works. Song 'Shy One' (Yeats) was often sung by Gervase *Elwes. Prin. works incl. va. sonata (1918–19), pf. trio (1920–1). Wrote only one work (a setting of Blake's *The Tiger*, 1933) after 1930 until she settled in USA 1939, when she comp. more instr. works and some songs. Married James *Friskin, the pianist, in 1944.

Clàrsach. The ancient small Celtic harp, revived in Scotland during the 20th cent.

Classical. Term which, applied to mus., has vague rather than specific meaning: (1) Mus. comp. roughly between 1750 and 1830 (i.e. post-Baroque and pre-Romantic) which covers the development of the classical sym. and conc. (2) Mus. of an orderly nature, with qualities of clarity and balance, and emphasising formal beauty rather than emotional expression (which is not to say that emotion is lacking). (3) Mus. generally regarded as having permanent rather than ephemeral value. (4) 'Classical music' is used as a generic term meaning the opposite of light or popular mus.

Classical Symphony. Title of Prokofiev's Sym. No. 1 in D, Op. 25, comp. 1916–17, f.p. Petrograd 1918 cond. composer. Deliberately written in style of Haydn. The gavotte was used by Prokofiev again in his *Romeo and Juliet* ballet mus.

Clausula. (1) *Cadence. Some medieval terms are *Clausula vera*, Perfect cadence; *Clausula falsa*,

Interrupted cadence; *Clausula plagalis*, Plagal cadence; etc.

(2) Section of medieval *organum in which textless contrapuntal parts are heard in strict rhythm with chant tune on which organum is based.

Clavecin. Fr. name for hpd., shortening of *clavecinon*, first used 1611.

Claves. Cuban perc. instr., being round sticks of hard wood 7″ or 8″ long. The player holds one over the upturned fingernails of his left fist and beats it with the other held lightly in the right hand. Used in dance bands but taken up by 20th-cent. composers incl. *Birtwistle, Copland, Varèse, and *McCabe.

Clavicembalo (It.). Clavicymbal. The It. word for *harpsichord. It derives from *clavichordium*, found in Ger. poem of 1404 which lists the instr. of courtly love. The It. is occasionally corrupted to *gravicembalo* and regularly shortened to *cembalo*. The Fr. form is *clavecinon*, shortened to *clavecin* (1611).

Clavichord. Small kbd. instr. developed in 14th cent. from the *monochord sometimes called *clarichord* or *manichord* or *chekker*. The early clavichord used the same str. to produce 2, 3, or 4 notes by stopping the str. at different points along its length. There was a bridge for each note which was brought into contact with the str. from pressure on a key on the kbd. The bridge also sounded the str., producing a very soft attack. Because of this process of stopping the str., the early clavichord was known as *gebunden*, or fretted. (*Gebunden* means 'bound', and the frets on some early instr. were cords bound round the fingerboard.) Because some notes employed the same str. they could not be played simultaneously, but by the 17th cent. the proportion of str. to keys increased until in the early 18th cent. some clavichords were unfretted (*bundfrei*). Essentially an instr. for private practice, being too soft in tone for concert use, and is used in this way by orgs. In 20th cent. *Howells has composed for it.

Clavicytherium. Upright version of hpd., developed in 15th and early 16th cents. A rare surviving example is in the coll. of the RCM.

Clavier. See *Klavier*.

Clavier des bombardes (Fr.). That organ manual having *Trumpet* and *Tuba*.

Clavier de Récit (Fr.). *Swell Organ*.

Clavierübung. See *Klavierübung*.

Clavicymbal. Eng. form of It. *Clavicembalo*, i.e. *harpsichord.

Claviorganum. Combination of org. and hpd. developed in 16th cent. and known in Fr. as *clavecin organisé* and in It. as *claviorgano*. The org. pipes were laid horizontally inside the chest.

Clay, Frédéric Emes (b Paris, 1838; d Great Marlow, 1889). Eng. composer. Studied with Molique in Paris. Wrote over a dozen operettas prod. in London between 1859 and 1883. His cantata *Lalla Rookh* (1877) contains the song 'I'll sing thee songs of Araby'. Also wrote popular ballads 'She wandered down the mountainside' and 'The Sands of Dee'.

Clear Flute. Organ stop much like *Waldflöte.

Clef (Lat. *clavis*, Fr. *clef*, key). Symbol normally placed at the beginning of every line of mus. to indicate the exact location of a particular note on the staff; also placed at any point where new clef begins to operate. The *Treble Clef* places the note G above middle C on the second line (the G clef); the *Bass Clef* fixes the note F below middle C on the second line (descending) (F clef); the *Alto Clef*, on the middle line, fixes middle C and is used for the va; the *Tenor Clef* fixes middle C on the fourth line (ascending) and is used for vc. and bn. parts above the bass staff. The *Soprano Clef*, fixing middle C on the first line, is obsolete, but is found in medieval mus. and in some works well into 19th cent. In the following example middle C is represented in five different ways:

Returned to London 1785, composing several syms., pf. conc., and coll. of 100 studies, *Gradus ad Parnassum*, which remains a foundation of pf. technique. Comp. over 100 piano sonatas, some of them valued highly by Beethoven, whom Clementi met in 1807. Among pupils were Field, Moscheles, Kalkbrenner, and Cramer. Also went into the business of making pfs., becoming partner in London firm, Clementi & Co., which in 1832 became Collard & Collard. Clementi's early sonatas were written for the hpd., but after 1780 his allegiance was to the piano, His influence on subsequent piano composers was immeasurable.

Clemenza di Tito, La (The Clemency of Titus). Opera in 2 acts by Mozart (his last, K621) to lib. by Metastasio, altered by Mazzolà. Comp. for coronation of Emperor Leopold II as King of Bohemia. Prod. Prague 1791, London 1806. About 20 other composers, incl. Caldara (1734) and Gluck (1752), set Metastasio's text.

Cleobury, Nicholas (Randall) (b Bromley, 1950). Eng. cond., organist, pianist, and harpsichordist. Studied Oxford. Ass. organist Chichester Cath. 1971–2, Christ Church, Oxford, from 1972.

G or TREBLE CLEF On 2nd line up fixing that as Treble G	F or BASS CLEF On 2nd line down, fixing that as Bass F	C (SOPRANO) CLEF On 1st line, fixing that as middle C	C (ALTO) CLEF On 3rd line, fixing that as middle C	C (TENOR) CLEF On 4th line, fixing that as middle C

Clemens (non Papa). Name applied to Jacob (Jacques) Clement (b Middelburg, c.1510; d Dixmuide, c.1556). Flemish composer. First Kapellmeister to Emperor Charles V in Vienna. Wrote masses, motets, and *chansons*, pubd. in Louvain, 1555–80, and 4 books of psalms set to popular Flemish melodies (Antwerp 1556–7). Nickname variously explained as distinguishing him from Pope Clement VII or from Flemish poet Jacobus Papa who also lived in Ypres, but the probability is that it was a joke.

Clement, Franz (b Vienna, 1780; d Vienna, 1842). Austrian violinist. Public début 1789, followed by tours of Ger. and Eng. Cond., Theater an der Wien, Vienna, 1802–11. Soloist, f.p. of Beethoven's vn. conc. 1806; cond. f.p. of Beethoven's 4th Sym. 1807.

Clementi, Muzio (b Rome, 1752; d Evesham, 1832). Eng. pianist and composer of It. birth. Child prodigy as organist and composer. In 1766 went to Eng. under patronage of Peter Beckford. London début as pianist and composer 1775. Cond. It. opera in London 1777–8 and in 1781 began his tours of Europe in which he engaged with other pianists (incl. Mozart) in public tests of skill in improvisation, sight-reading, etc.

Cond., Oxford Schola Cantorum from 1973. Ass. cond. Kent Opera and Glyndebourne. Cond. Eng. Bach Fest. Ch. Ch.-master, Glyndebourne Opera, 1977–9. Cond. Opera North's revival of Delius's *A Village Romeo and Juliet*, 1984.

Cleopatra. Dramatic scene for sop. (or high v.) and orch. by Iain *Hamilton. F.p. Cheltenham Fest. 1978.

Cléopâtre, La Mort de (Berlioz). See *Mort de Cléopâtre, La*.

Clérambault, Louis Nicolas (b Paris, 1676; d Paris, 1749). Fr. org. and composer for kbd. instr. and v. His books of Fr. cantatas are the best of their period. Organist St Sulpice, Paris, later of St Jacques. Wrote 5 books of cantatas, 20 in all, pubd. 1710, 1713, 1716, 1720, and 1726. Another 5 cantatas were pubd. separately. Also comp. 3 pieces for strs. under title *Simphonie-sonata*. His *premier livre d'orgue* comprises 2 suites of 14 pieces.

Cleve, Halfdan (b Kongsberg, 1879; d Oslo, 1951). Norweg. composer of 5 pf. concs., songs, pf. pieces.

Cleveland Orchestra. Amer. orch. founded 1918. Conds: Nikolay Sokoloff 1918–33; Artur

Rodzinski 1933–43; Erich Leinsdorf 1943–4; Georg Szell 1946–70; Lorin Maazel 1972–82; Christoph von Dohnányi from 1984. Home since 1931 Severance Hall (acoustically renovated 1960).

Cliburn, Van (Harvey Lavan) (*b* Shreveport, La., 1934). Amer. pianist. Taught by his mother from age 3 until 1951 when he went to Rosina Lhévinne at Juilliard Sch. First recital at age 4; played Tchaikovsky first conc. at Houston 1946. NY début 1948. In 1958 won Tchaikovsky Competition, Moscow. Est. Cliburn Int. piano comp. at Fort Worth, Texas, 1962.

Cliffe, Frederick (*b* Lowmoor, Yorks., 1857; *d* London, 1931). Eng. composer, pianist, and organist. Prof. of pf., RCM 1883, remaining over 40 years on faculty. Comp. 2 syms., symphonic poem, vn. conc., and songs.

Clinton, (Francis) **Gordon** (*b* Broadway, Worcs., 1912). Eng. bar. Studied RCM. Career mainly in concert-hall for 35 years. Prin., Birmingham Sch. of Mus. 1960–73. Prof. of singing, RCM.

Cloches (Fr.). Bells, e.g. those used in the orch.

Cloches de Corneville, Les (The Bells of Corneville). Opera in 3 acts by Planquette to lib. by Clairville and Gabet. Prod. Paris and NY 1877, London 1878 (as *The Chimes of Normandy*).

Clock Symphony (*Die Uhr*). Nickname of Haydn's Sym. in D, No. 101 (Hob.I;101), comp. 1794 in London. So called because of 'tick-tock' acc. to first subject of 2nd movement. This movement was separately pubd. in Vienna 1798 in pf. arr. as 'Rondo, Die Uhr'.

Clog Box. See *Chinese Wood Block*.

Close. The same as *Cadence*.

Close Harmony. Harmony in which the notes of a chord are close together. In close harmony singing the vv. are distributed within the compass of an octave.

Cloud Messenger, The. Ode for ch. and orch., Op. 30, by Holst to text by Holst founded on Sanskrit poem of *Kalidasa*. Comp. 1910, rev. 1912. F.p. London 1913.

Cluster. Term used in connection with chords, meaning chords of which the constituents are a major or minor 2nd apart. In US, called 'tone-cluster'. Kbd. clusters, i.e. a group of adjacent notes played together with the forearm flat, were first demonstrated by the Amer. composer *Cowell in 1913, but *Ives had also used the same idea.

Clutsam, George Howard (*b* Sydney, N.S.W., 1866; *d* London, 1951). Australian composer, pianist, and critic, settled in London 1889. Accompanist to Melba. Perpetrated with *Berté Eng. version of *Das Dreimäderlhaus* as *Lilac Time* (1923).

Cluytens, André (*b* Antwerp, 1905; *d* Paris, 1967). Belg. cond. Studied Antwerp Cons. Cond. Antwerp Opera 1927–32, Lyons from 1935, Paris Opéra from 1941, Opéra Comique 1947, Société des Concerts du Cons. 1949. First Gallic cond. at Bayreuth, 1955–58, 1965. London début 1958.

Coates, Albert (*b* St Petersburg, 1882; *d* Cape Town, 1953). Eng. cond. and composer, born in Russ. of Eng. parents (not Anglo-Russian, as often stated). Studied Leipzig Cons. 1902 (cond. classes with Nikisch). Cond. opera at Leipzig, Elberfeld, and Dresden. London début 1910 (LSO), CG 1914 (*Tristan*). Cond. of opera at St Petersburg 1911–18 during which time became close friend of Skryabin. Returned to Eng. 1919, conducting opera with Beecham, BNOC, Leeds Fest., etc. Also cond. much in USA. Settled in S. Africa 1946. Comps. incl. operas *Samuel Pepys* (1929) and *Pickwick* (1936). As a cond. was at his best in Russ. mus. and Wagner, but cond. f.ps. of Vaughan Williams's rev. *London Symphony* (1920), Bax's 1st Symphony (1922), and Holst's *Choral Symphony* (1925).

Coates, Eric (*b* Hucknall, Notts., 1886; *d* Chichester, 1957). Eng. composer and violist. Entered RAM 1906, studying va. with *Tertis and comp. with *Corder. Member of several str. qts. Prin. va., Queen's Hall Orch. 1912. Gave up orch. playing 1919. Comps. in light vein, distinguished by finished craftsmanship, impeccable orchestration, and personal melodic flavour. They incl. several orch. suites—*From the Countryside* (1915); *Summer Days* (1919); *Cinderella* (1929); *From Meadow to Mayfair* (1929); *London* (1932); *London Again* (1936); *The Three Elizabeths* (1944); *The Three Bears* (1926). Also *Saxo-Rhapsody* (1937); *The Jester at the Wedding*; *By the Sleepy Lagoon* (1939); *Calling All Workers* (1940); *The Dam Busters March* (1942), and many songs incl. 'Bird Songs at Eventide' (1926). The *London Suite's* 3rd movement is the march 'Knightsbridge', long famous as introductory music to BBC radio feature 'In Town Tonight'.

Coates, John (*b* Girlington, Yorks., 1865; *d* Northwood, 1941). Eng. ten., orig. bar. Sang bar. roles with D'Oyly Carte Opera Co. 1894. Début as ten. 1899. Sang Faust in Gounod's opera CG 1901. Member of Moody-Manners and Beecham opera cos., singing Tristan and Siegfried. Also achieved eminence in choral works, notably Elgar's *Dream of Gerontius*.

Cobbett, Walter Willson (*b* Blackheath, 1847; *d* London, 1937). Eng. businessman and amateur violinist whose love of chamber mus. led him to promote many chamber concerts and to institute prizes both for playing and comp. Commissioned many works by Brit. composers in the Elizabethan fantasia-form, preferring the spelling 'Phantasy', hence the 'Phantasy' qts., quintets, and trios by Bridge, Vaughan Williams, Bax, Goossens, Ireland, Britten, etc. Endowed Cobbett Medal for services to chamber mus. and ed. *Cyclopedic Survey of Chamber Music* (1929, rev. 1963).

Cocardes (Cockades). 3 songs for v. and pf. by Poulenc to texts by Cocteau. Comp. 1919. Titles are: *Miel de Narbonne, Bonne d'enfant, Enfant de troupe.*

Cockaigne (In London Town). Concert-ov., Op. 40, by Elgar, comp. 1900–1 and ded. to 'my friends the members of British orchestras'. Title refers to imaginary land of idleness and luxury from which word 'Cockney' is said to be derived.

Cocteau, Jean (*b* Maisons-Lafitte, 1889; *d* Milly-la-forêt, 1963). Fr. poet, novelist, and playwright, often assoc. with mus. as librettist or propagandist. Wrote scenario for Satie's *Parade* (1917) and libs. for Honegger's *Antigone*, Stravinsky's *Oedipus Rex*, Milhaud's *Le Pauvre Matelot*, and Poulenc's *La Voix humaine*, among others.

Coda (It.). Tail. Orig. a section of a movement added at the end to clinch matters rather than to develop the mus. further. However, in the syms. of Mozart, Haydn, and especially Beethoven, the coda came to have integral formal significance, becoming at times 2nd development section and sometimes containing new material. Later composers have increased and extended this tendency.

Codetta (It.). Little tail. (1) Short or less important coda, often at the end of a section of a movement.
(2) In a fugue, an episodical passage occurring in the exposition between appearances of the subject.

Coelho, Manuel Rodrigues (*b* 1583; *d* 1635). Portuguese composer and org. at Chapel Royal, Lisbon, 1603–23. His *Flores de Música* (Lisbon, 1620) was the first book of instr. pieces to be printed in Portugal. It contains 24 *tientos* (ricercari), and 4 variations on a Lassus *chanson*, all for kbd.

Coelho, Ruy (*b* Alcacer do Sal, Portugal, 1892). Portuguese composer, cond., pianist, and critic. Studied Lisbon Cons., Berlin (with Humperdinck, Bruch, and Schoenberg) and Paris Cons. Comps. influenced by Portuguese folk and popular mus. They incl. 19 operas, 11 ballets, an oratorio (*Fatima*), 2 pf. concs., 5 *Symphonias camoneanas*, 2 vn. sonatas, etc.

Coertse, Mimi (*b* Durban, 1932). S. African sop. Studied in S. Africa and Vienna. Début Naples 1955. Joined Vienna Opera 1956. Début CG 1956, later Glyndebourne.

Coffee Cantata (*Kaffeecantate*). Nickname for humorous cantata by Bach (BWV 211, 1732) sometimes perf. as opera. Lib., by Picander, refers to the growing fondness for coffee at the time it was comp.

Cogli, Coi (It.). With the (plural).

Cohen, Harriet (*b* London, 1895; *d* London, 1967). Eng. pianist. Studied RAM. Won reputation as advocate of early kbd. mus. and of modern Eng. composers. Bax ded. to her his *Symphonic Variations* for pf. and orch. (1917) and his *Concertante* for orch. and pf. (left hand) (f.p. 1950), the latter written for her when she had injured her right hand. The pf. concs. by Vaughan Williams (f.p. 1933) and Fricker (1952–4) were ded. to and f.p. by her. Also considerable chamber-mus. player. C.B.E. 1938.

Cohen, Raymond (Hyman) (*b* Manchester, 1919). Eng. violinist. Studied RMCM. At 15 became youngest ever to play in Hallé Orch. of which he was member 1934–40. After war service adopted career as chamber-mus. player and conc. soloist, but led RPO 1960–6. Winner of first Carl Flesch int. award 1945.

Cohen, Robert (*b* London, 1959). Eng. cellist, son of Raymond *Cohen. Studied GSM with W. Pleeth. Solo début, London 1971. Recorded Elgar conc. 1978. Won Piatigorsky comp., Tanglewood, and made Amer. début 1979. Plays in trio with father (vn.) and his mother Anthya Rael (pf.).

Col, coll', colla, colle (It.). With the, e.g. *col basso*, with the bass; *colla voce*, with the voice (indication to accompanist to be subservient, i.e. as to the time details).

Colas Breugnon. Name under which *Kabalevsky's opera *The Craftsman of Clamecy* (*Master iz Clamesy*) Op. 24, is usually known outside Russ. In 3 acts, to lib. by V. Bragin based on R. Rolland's novel *Colas Breugnon*. Prod. Leningrad 1938. Rev. 1953 and in 1969, final rev. being given Op. No. 90.

Colascione. European version of Eastern long-necked lute, first made in It. in early 16th cent. Had 2 or 3 single or double courses made of metal, though sometimes of gut, and 24 movable frets.

Colbran, Isabella (*b* Madrid, 1785; *d* Bologna, 1845). Sp. sop., considered to be finest dramatic coloratura of her day. Début Paris 1801, Milan 1807. Engaged for Naples, 1811, where she became impresario's mistress but left him in 1815 to live with *Rossini, who married her in 1822 (they later separated). Rossini wrote *Elisabetta, Regina d'Inghilterra* for her and she created the leading sop. roles in his *Otello, Semiramide, Mosè*, and other operas. Also comp. songs.

Cold, Ulrik (Thestrup) (*b* Copenhagen, 1939). Danish bass-baritone. Studied in Copenhagen, making début there 1963. Kassel Opera 1969–71. Dir., Royal Th., Copenhagen, from 1975. Fine singer of Falstaff, King Marke, and Gurnemanz.

Cole, Hugo (*b* London, 1917). Eng. composer and writer; studied RCM with R. O. Morris and Howells and in Paris with Boulanger. Works incl. operas, opera-cantata *Jonah*, hn. conc., str. qts. Mus. critic of the *Guardian*.

Cole, Nat King (Coles, Nathaniel Adams) (*b* Montgomery, Alabama, 1917; *d* Santa Monica, Calif., 1965). Amer. singer and jazz pianist. Had his own band in Chicago. Formed King Cole Trio 1939–51. After a best-selling record of 1947 he concentrated on singing (to the detriment of his jazz reputation). Among his most popular recordings were 'Nature Boy' and 'Answer me'.

Coleman, Ornette (*b* Fort Worth, Texas, 1930). Amer. jazz composer and saxophonist. Began to play alto sax. in 1944, tenor sax. in 1946. Influenced by Charlie *Parker. Played in bebop, blues, and rhythm bands in Southern States before settling in New Orleans in 1948. In 1950 joined Pee Wee Crayton band in Fort Worth. In Los Angeles studied harmony and theory and by 1958 was regarded as one of jazz's major innovators. Attended Lenox Sch. of Jazz, Mass., 1959, and led quartet in NY 1958–62, then forming trio. Caused controversy 1960 with his recording *Free Jazz* (Coleman and 7 other musicians) in which improvisation was taken almost to anarchic limits. Semi-retired 1963 to learn tpt. and vn. Reappeared in 1965 and then toured Europe. Style noted for free improvisation based on melodic shapes over a pedal-point rather than on succession of chords. Relied greatly on intuition and at times approached atonality. Gunther Schuller wrote *Abstraction*, a serial comp., for Coleman and augmented str. qt. Coleman's own mus. includes *Lonely Woman* and *Turnaround*. His major piece of symphonic mus. is *Skies of America* (1972) for jazz qt. and orch. (recorded with LSO with solo alto sax. only). This was followed in 1977 by *Dancing in Your Head* and in 1979 by *Of Human Feelings* which explored 'funk-jazz', a development dating from about 1970 features of which incl. a repetitive bass line, a hint of Latin rhythms, and complex rhythmic relationships.

Coleridge-Taylor, Avril (Gwendolen) (*b* South Norwood, 1903). Eng. cond. and composer, daughter of S. *Coleridge-Taylor. Studied GSM and TCL. Active in many fields of conducting, some but not all connected with her father's works. Worked in S. Africa 1952–5. Comps. incl. pf. conc., orch. works, chamber mus., and songs.

Coleridge-Taylor, Samuel (*b* London, 1875; *d* Croydon, 1912). Eng. composer, son of Sierra Leone physician and Eng. mother. Entered RCM as vn. student 1890 but studied comp. with Stanford 1892–7. His cl. quintet, Op. 10, was played in 1897 in Berlin by Joachim's qt. and his *Ballad* in A minor at 1898 Gloucester Fest. (thanks to Elgar's encouragement). In Nov. 1898 his cantata *Hiawatha's Wedding Feast* was perf. at RCM. This was first of 3 works based on Longfellow's poem. The *Death of Minnehaha* followed in 1899 and *Hiawatha's Departure* in 1900. Success of these works led to many demands for fest. comps. Later works were *Meg Blane*

(Sheffield 1902), *The Atonement* (Hereford 1903), *Kubla Khan* (London 1906), and *A Tale of Old Japan* (London 1911), but none achieved the success of *The Song of Hiawatha* Trilogy. Also wrote sym., *Symphonic Variations on an African Air* (1906), vn. conc. (1912), chamber mus., pf. solos, and songs.

Colgrass, Michael (*b* Chicago, 1932). Amer. composer and percussionist. Educated Univ. of Illinois. In 1956 worked in NY as free-lance percussionist, being specially concerned with th. work. Works incl. *Percussion Music* (1953), *Chant* for ch. and vibraphone (1954), *Seventeen* for full orch. (1960), Wind Quintet (1962), *Virgil's Dream* for 4 actor-singers, 4 mime-musicians (Brighton Fest. 1967), *The Earth's a Baked Apple* for ch. and orch. (Boston 1969), *Nightingale Inc.*, opera (1971), *Auras*, hp. and orch. (1976–7), and *Theatre of the Universe*, solo vv., ch., and orch. (1976–7).

Colista, Lelio (*b* Rome, 1629; *d* Rome, 1680). It. composer remembered for his influence on Purcell, who quotes from his works in his introduction to Playford's *Introduction to the Skill of Music* (1694).

Coll', colla, colle (It.). See *Col*.

Colla, Giuseppe (*b* Parma, 1731; *d* Parma, 1806). It. composer and choirmaster. Comp. several operas, incl. *Tolomeo* (Milan 1773), in which his wife Lucrezia *Agujari ('La Bastardella') was a great success.

Collage (Fr.). A putting-together of independent styles in juxtaposition either simultaneously or successively. The separate styles usually consist of contrasting rhythm, melody, or harmony. For a true collage the juxtaposition must be of coherent sections which are the product of separate mus. elements, e.g. the many examples in the mus. of Charles *Ives, where dissonances are not resolved but treated as a normal situation. The term is borrowed from the visual arts, and literally means 'glueing together'.

Coll'arco (It.). With the bow; i.e. after a passage marked *pizzicato*. (Sometimes shortened to *c.a.*).

Colla parte (It.). With the part, **colla voce** (It.), with the voice. An indication to an accompanist carefully to take his tempos and rhythm from the soloist.

Colla punta dell' arco (It.). With the point of the bow.

Collegium Aureum. Ger. ensemble founded 1964 by Franzjosef Maier to record baroque and early classical mus. Has toured Russia and Japan. Pioneered recordings using original and authentic instrs., incl. one of Beethoven's *Eroica* Symphony.

Collegium Musicum (Lat. 'musical guild'). In 16th cent. term applied to groups of enthusiasts concerned with perf. of mus. From these grew concert-giving societies performing under noble patronage or in the informal surroundings of a coffee-house. J. S. Bach wrote many works for perf. at a collegium musicum.

Col legno (It.). With the wood. Striking the str. with the stick of the bow, instead of playing on them with the hair.

Colles, Henry Cope (*b* Bridgnorth, 1879; *d* London, 1943). Eng. mus. critic. Studied RCM and Oxford Univ. Mus. critic for *The Times* 1905–43 (chief critic from 1911), ed. of 3rd and 4th edns. of *Grove's Dictionary of Music*, and author of several books incl. history of RCM (1933) of which he was member of staff.

Collier, Marie (*b* Ballarat, 1927; *d* London, 1971). Australian sop. Début Melbourne 1954 as Santuzza; CG 1956. Possessed dramatic acting powers and richly expressive v. Sang Tosca, Cressida (in Walton's *Troilus and Cressida*), and was notable exponent of Emilia Marty in Janáček's *The Makropoulos Affair*. Created Hecuba in Tippett's *King Priam* (1962). NY Met. début 1967 in Levy's *Mourning Becomes Electra*.

Collingwood, Lawrance (Arthur) (*b* London, 1887; *d* Killin, Perthshire, 1982). Eng. cond. and composer. Studied GSM, then went to St Petersburg as ass. to Albert *Coates. Cond. opera in London (Old Vic and SW; mus. dir. latter 1940–7). Comps. incl. opera *Macbeth* (SW 1934) and *Death of Tintagiles* (after Maeterlinck, concert version SW 1950), also pf. conc., pf. qt., pf. sonatas. For nearly 50 years made gramophone recordings, 'producing' many of them. Cond. Elgar's last recording session, 1934. C.B.E. 1948.

Collins, Anthony (*b* Hastings, 1893; *d* Los Angeles, 1963). Eng. va. player and then cond. and composer. Studied RCM after 1914–18 war, then prin. va. LSO and CG orch. Left orch. playing 1936 to become cond. Founded London Mozart Orch. Worked in USA 1936–45. Comp. operas, 2 vn. concs., syms. for str., film mus. Orch. Schubert's *Grand Duo*.

Colofonia (It.). See *Colophony*.

Colonel Bogey. Military march comp. by 'Kenneth *Alford' in 1914. Popularity attributable not only to splendid tune, but to improvised words and to its use (whistled) in the film *The Bridge on the River Kwai* (1957).

Colonna, Giovanni Paolo (*b* Bologna, 1637; *d* Bologna, 1695). It. composer. Studied with *Carissimi and *Benevoli. Held org. posts in Rome and, from 1674, Bologna. Wrote opera *Amilcare* (1693) and a quantity of church mus.

Colonne, Edouard (Judas) (*b* Bordeaux, 1838; *d* Paris, 1910). Fr. cond. and violinist. Studied Paris Cons. Leader of Paris Opéra Orch. 1858–67. In 1873 founded series of orch. concerts, eventually to be known as the Concerts Colonne, at which he championed young Fr. composers and the

mus. of Berlioz. Toured as cond. in Eng., Russ., and USA. Concerts continued after his death organized by the Société des Concerts Colonne.

Colophony (Fr. *colophane*; It. *colofonia*; Ger. *Kolophon*). Rosin for bow of str. instr., so called after Colophon, Asia Minor, whence best rosin comes.

Colorato, colorata, or **figurato, figurata** (It.). Treated in the manner of *Coloratura. See also *Musica figurata*.

Coloratura. Word derived from the Ger. *Koloratur*. The elaborate and agile ornamentation of a melody, either extemporized or written, with runs, cadenzas, trills, roulades, and the like. Hence a *coloratura soprano* is one whose v. is flexible enough to cope with these demands.

Colour (Tone-colour). It is impossible for mus. to convey colours, but it is customary to speak of 'colouring' or 'tone-colour' where variations of *timbre* or tone are prod. by different intensities of the overtones of sounds. 'Shade' is perhaps a more accurate term, since the differences are often those of 'darker' or 'lighter' sound. But in his tone-poem *Prometheus: The Poem of Fire*, Op. 60, *Skryabin introduced a colour kbd. to project colours on to a screen, intended to convey the mood of the mus. The colour-organ was used for this purpose.

Colour Symphony. Orch. work by Bliss, f.p. Gloucester Fest. 1922. The movements are entitled *Purple, Red, Blue,* and *Green,* the colours being interpreted through their heraldic assocs.

Colpo (It.). Stroke, e.g. *Colpo d'arco,* a stroke of the bow.

Combattimento di Tancredi e Clorinda, Il (The combat of Tancred and Clorinda). Dramatic cantata by Monteverdi to text by Tasso (verses 52–68 of Canto XII of *Gerusalemme liberata*). Prod. Venice (Palazza di Girolamo Mocenigo) 1624. Pub. 1638 in *Madrigali guerrieri e amorosi*. Monteverdi's description of f.p. shows that this could be claimed as early example of 'music theatre'. A narrator comments upon the action, which is acted or danced by Tancred and Clorinda. A feature of the score is the earliest-known use of the str. *tremolo,* or *stile concitato,* to express excitement, and the str. *pizzicato* (but see *pizzicato*). Scoring is for 4 viols with contrabass and hpd.

Combination Pedals. See *Composition pedals*.

Combined Counterpoint. See *Counterpoint*.

Come (It.). As, like, as if; *come prima,* as at first; *come stà,* as it stands; *come sopra,* as above.

Comédie-ballet. Fr. musico-dramatic entertainment devised by Molière and Lully in late 17th cent. Their first collab. was in *Le mariage forcé* (1664), their last *Le bourgeois gentilhomme* (1670).

Mus. and dance were regarded as complementary to the main plot; the sub-plots were carried on in the *intermèdes*.

Comedy on the Bridge (*Komedie na mostě*). Opera for radio in 1 act by Martinů to his own lib. based on V. K. Klicpera. Prod. Prague Radio 1937, London (stage) 1965.

Comes. See *Canon*.

Come ye Sons of Art. Ode by *Purcell for the birthday of Queen Mary, wife of William III, in 1694 for sop., counterten., bass, ch., and orch. Contains aria 'Sound the trumpet'.

Comic Opera. An imprecise term, though by it most people today would understand an opera with a comic element. *Opéra bouffe* or *opera buffa* means comic opera but has a specific meaning, as has opéra comique.

Comissiona, Sergiu (*b* Bucharest, 1928). Romanian-born cond. (Amer. citizen). Studied Mus. Acad., Romania, and cond. with *Silvestri. Cond. Romanian State Ens. 1948–55. Cond. Romanian State Opera 1955–9; Haifa S.O. and Israeli Chamber Orch. 1958–66; Göteborg S.O. 1966–72; Ulster Orch. 1967–9; Baltimore S.O. 1969–76; Pittsburgh S.O. 1976–8; American S.O. 1978–82; Houston S.O. from 1984. London début (LSO) 1960, CG début (ballet) 1962, CG opera début 1974 (Rossini's *Il barbiere di Siviglia*), NY 1977 (*La fanciulla del West*).

Comma. A minute interval such as that resulting when a rising succession of untempered 5ths (see *Temperament*) and a similar succession of octaves arrive at what is ostensibly the same note, but is not really quite such.

Commedia per musica (It.). Comedy for Music. Term used in It. in 18th cent. for comic opera. Note that Strauss and Hofmannsthal called their 18th-cent. comedy of manners, *Der Rosenkavalier*, a 'comedy for music'.

Common Chord. A *triad of which the 5th is perfect. In *Major Common Chord* the 3rd is major and in *Minor Common Chord* it is minor.

Common Time. Another name for ₄ time. The C sometimes used instead of the figures ₄ does not stand for 'common': it dates from the period when triple time (called 'perfect') was indicated by a full circle and quadruple time (called 'imperfect') by a broken circle.

Community Singing. Any occasion when a number of people sing together is 'community singing', but the term today usually means a crowd's singing at a meeting or at a sporting occasion (notably the F.A. Cup Final at Wembley or a rugger int. at Cardiff Arms Park).

Comodo (It.). Leisurely, convenient, i.e. without any suspicion of strain, e.g. *tempo comodo*, at a

comfortable, moderate speed. So the adverb, *comodamente*.

Compact discs. See *Gramophone (Phonograph) Recordings*.

Compass. The range of a v. or instr. from the highest to the lowest note obtainable; or the extreme limit of the notes obtainable. The usual classification of vv. according to compass takes account of 6 ranges, with their distinctive qualities, the average vv. in these ranges extending an octave to a 10th below and above the following notes:

(male alto a
note or two less)

Compère, Loyset (*b* Hainaut, *c*.1440; *d* St Quentin, 1518). Flemish composer, possibly a pupil of Ockeghem; later canon and chancellor of the cath. of St Quentin and an important composer of church mus.

Competitions, Musical. The urge to compete is basic to human nature and musicians are no exception. Reports of mus. contests go back to ancient times but the modern form developed in the late 18th cent. in Great Britain. Brass band contests began early in the 19th cent. but even more widespread were the choral competitions and those between individual instrumentalists. From 1904 these have been organized by what is now the Brit. Federation of Mus. Fest., apart from the Welsh *eisteddfodau*. Similar competitions, mainly involving amateurs, are firmly est. in many other countries. Other forms of mus. competition on a high professional (and commercial) level have developed, incl. competitions for composers, conds., and for instrumentalists (notably the Moscow Tchaikovsky pf. competition, the Leeds pf. competition, the Carl Flesch award for violinists, the Mitropoulos prize for conds., the Queen Elisabeth of Belgium competition, the BBC's 'Young Musician of the Year', and numerous others). Undoubtedly the most famous mus. competitions are those involving Tannhäuser and Wolfram in the Hall of Song at the Wartburg Castle in Wagner's *Tannhäuser* (Act II) and the song contest on the banks of the River Pegnitz at Nuremberg in Act III Sc. 2 of Wagner's *Die Meistersinger von Nürnberg*—both events being based on reality. In lighter vein there is the annual Eurovision song contest, promoted by European TV organizations, to discover the best 'pop song' of the year according to the votes of an int. jury.

Complete Cadence. See *Cadence*.

Composer's Counterpoint. See *Counterpoint*.

Composers' Guild of Great Britain. Brit. organization founded 1944 and affiliated to Soc. of Authors. Exists to protect the interests of composers. First pres. Vaughan Williams. Publishes journal *Composer* since 1958. In 1967 founded British Music Information Centre.

Composition Pedals (combination pedals). Organ pedals to facilitate rapid changing of tonecolour effects by means of adjustment pistons which bring instantly into action selected groups of stops instead of their having to be operated individually by hand.

Compound Binary Form. Same as *Sonata Form*.

Compound Intervals. Those greater than an octave, e.g. C to the D a 9th above it, which may be spoken of as a major 9th or as a compound major 2nd. See *Interval*.

Compound Time. Each beat in a measure consists of a dotted note or its equivalent (in contrast to simple time where each beat consists of a complete note). Can be duple, triple, or quadruple, each related to corresponding simple time. Thus 3/4 (simple triple) has 3 quarter-note (crotchet) beats to a measure; 9/8 (compound triple) has 3 dotted quarter-note (crotchet) beats. So called because a measure is made up of a mixture (or *compound*) of 2, 3, or 4 main beats, each beat having 3 subdivisions. See also *Simple Time* and *Time Signature*.

Compter (Fr.). To count. *Comptent*, count (plural), indicates in an orch. score that the instr. in question are silent for the moment and are merely 'counting their bars' until re-entry.

Compton, John (Haywood) (*b* Newton Burgoland, Leics., 1876: *d* Ealing, 1957). Eng. organbuilder. Worked for organ firms in Sheffield and Nottingham 1898–1911. In 1912 established his own co. in Nottingham. Built electric-action organs with much use of extension, the best being for Davis Th., Croydon, Southampton Guildhall, Downside Abbey, and St Bride's, Fleet St. Also built cinema orgs. Pipe-organ section of firm taken over by Rushworth and Dreaper 1964; elec. section went to J. and J. Makin Organs 1970.

Computers in Music. Elec. computers have so far been used in two ways by composers: (a) to aid pre-compositional calculations and (b) to produce elec. sound. They have also been used to analyse works, to study comp. styles, and to prod. systems of notation. Among the first composers to use a computer was the Amer. Lejaren *Hiller, who used the Illiac computer to 'compose' a piece of mus. by feeding into it a programme comprising Fux's rules for 16th-cent. modal counterpoint and others relating to 20th-cent. serialism. The result was the *Illiac Suite for String Quartet* (1957).

Excluded from the programme were all notes that broke the rules, so the computer chose at random from the remaining possibilities. In later Hiller works, such as *Computer Cantata* (1963), notes and intervals were not chosen at random but according to weighted probabilities, e.g. a note was chosen according to the implications of the previously chosen note. Another composer, *Xenakis, used the computer for sound effects rather than for comp. processes. In his *Metastaseis* for orch. (1953–4) the computer calculates glissandi at different speeds.

A computer works musically by producing 'waveforms'. Recent developments involving the 'digital analogue converter' mean that waveforms can be created which perfectly simulate instr. sounds. The present tendency is to use computers in assoc. with *synthesizers as a memory bank, capable of producing any required sounds, memorizing the composer's sequence of events, and playing the finished work whenever required. This information is fed to the computer by a teletype kbd. or special manual controller.

Comte Ory, Le (Count Ory). *Opera buffa* in 2 acts by Rossini to lib. by Scribe and Lestre-Poirson. Prod. Paris 1828, London 1829, NY 1831. One of Rossini's 2 Fr. operas. It uses much mus. comp. in 1825 for a stage cantata, *Il viaggio a Reims*. Revived Florence 1952 and Glyndebourne 1954.

Comus. Masque by John Milton prod. at Ludlow Castle 1634 with mus. by Henry *Lawes, who himself took the part of the Attendant Spirit. New mus. was provided for an adapted version of the poem by Thomas *Arne in 1738. In 1942, for a ballet in which some of Milton's verse was spoken, Lambert arr. mus. by Purcell. Another ballet, with mus. by Handel and Lawes arr. E. Irving, was prod. 1946. Hugh *Wood's *Scenes from Comus* for sop., ten., and orch. was comp. and f.p. London 1965.

Concentus. See *Accentus*.

Concert. A perf. of mus. in public by a fairly substantial no. of performers (but not a stage performance or as part of a religious service). A perf. by 1 or 2 performers is usually called a recital. A pre-requisite of concerts, except on certain special occasions, is that people should pay to attend them, and this seems to have begun in England in the middle of the 17th cent. Historians point to the Whitefriars concerts arr. by John *Banister in 1672 as the 'first' in Eng., but perhaps that is only because we have a printed record of them. Thomas *Britton also financed concerts in Clerkenwell 1678–1714. More important were the Bach-Abel concerts which began in Spring Gardens, London, in 1764. With the opening of the Hanover Square Rooms in 1775 the way was open for such major events as Haydn's concerts on his 2 visits to London. Thereafter concerts became an accepted way of life. The Phil. Soc. was founded 1813, and in several provincial cities concert socs. were formed. Other developments incl. the Promenade Concerts, so called because people could stand or walk about at them, which originated in the 18th-cent. pleasure gardens, but found their most abiding form in 1895 when Henry Wood began his famous series at Queen's Hall and which, under BBC sponsorship, are still held from mid-July to mid-September in the Royal Albert Hall, London.

Public concerts for an audience of subscribers began in Frankfurt, Ger., in 1712 and in Hamburg in 1721. What were to become the Leipzig Gewandhaus concerts were founded by 16 businessmen meeting in an inn in 1743 (much as Manchester's concerts began in the 1770s when a group of flautists met regularly in a tavern, hence the 'Gentlemen's Concerts'). The *Concert Spirituel* was founded in Paris, 1725, but 'progressive' works were given at the *Concert des Amateurs*, cond. *Gossec, which in 1780 became the *Concert de la Loge Olympique* (because the venue was also a Masonic Lodge). In 1786 this organization commissioned 6 syms.—the 'Paris' syms.—from Haydn. In Vienna there was so much mus. in private houses or in the ths. that no regular concerts were given until 1782 (in the open air: Mozart played at them).

Concertant(e) (Fr.). In concerted form; a term preferred to sonata or suite by Stravinsky to describe the nature of his *Duo Concertant* for vn. and pf. (1932).

Concertante (It.). (1) In the nature of a conc., thus a *Sinfonia Concertante* is a work for solo instr(s). and orch. in a form nearer to that of sym. than conc.

(2) The concertante instr. in the old *concerto grosso* were those which played the solos, as distinct from the *ripieno* instr., which played in the *tuttis*. Many 20th-cent. composers have used the term to indicate that while a solo instr(s). is/are used, the work is not formally organized like a conc.

Concertata, Aria. See *Aria*.

Concertato (It.). Concerted. Another name for the *concertino* or *concertante* group in baroque mus. which contained the solo instrs. or vv. to contrast with the *ripieno*.

Concert Band. An Amer. band, comprising woodwind, brass, and perc., similar to the Brit. military band. Schoenberg's *Theme and Variations* Op. 43a (1943) is for concert band, so is Hindemith's Sym. in B♭ (1951).

Concerted. A perf. of mus. by 2 or more instrumentalists on reasonably equal terms. In opera an ens. is sometimes called a 'concerted number'.

Concert Flute. (1) Org. stop, sometimes on principle of *Harmonic Flute*; usually on Solo Manual; generally 4′ pitch.

(2) See *Flute*.

Concertgebouw Orchestra of Amsterdam. Dutch sym. orch. which plays in the Concertgebouw (Dutch, 'concert building') built Amsterdam, 1888, though the Concertgebouw Soc. was founded 5 years earlier. The first cond. was Willem *Kes, but the orch. became internationally famous under his successor *Mengelberg, cond. 1895 to 1945. Conds. since then have incl. Eduard van *Beinum 1945–59, Bernard *Haitink and Eugen *Jochum jointly 1961–4, Haitink since 1964.

Concertina. Small instr. with bellows similar to *accordion but with hexagonal ends and studs (no kbd.). The bellows are opened and closed by the hands, the pressure created causing metallic reeds to vibrate when selected by operation of the studs by the player's fingers. Made in SATB sizes, each with range of approx. an octave. Said to have been invented by Charles Wheatstone, 1829. First to play it at a public concert was Giulio Regondi (1822–72), who lived in Eng. from 1831 and toured Europe as concertina player 1846. He wrote 2 concs. and shorter pieces for it.

Concertino. (1, in older usage) The solo instr. group in the Concerto Grosso (see also *Concertante*; *Concerto*).

(2, in more modern usage) A shorter and lighter conc. for solo instr. and orch., e.g. Weber's cl. concertino, Op. 26.

Concertino Pastorale. Work for str. orch. in 3 movements by John Ireland, comp. 1939 for Boyd Neel Orch. Movements entitled *Eclogue*, *Threnody*, and *Toccata*.

Concertmaster (Amer.; Ger. *Konzertmeister*). The *leader of an orch.

Concerto (It.). Concert, concerted performance. A work in which a solo instr(s). is contrasted and blended with the orch. Earliest publication using name 'concerto' is *Concerti di Andrea et di Gio. Gabrieli* (Venice, 1587). Viadana's *Cento Concerti ecclesiastici*, comp. in the 1590s, developed into church concs. (*concerti da chiesa*) and there were also in the 17th cent. vocal *concerti da camera* (chamber concs.) which were adapted as purely instr. works by *Torelli. Monteverdi's Book 7 of madrigals is called *Concerto*. From Torelli came the *concerto grosso as comp. by *Corelli and *Handel. But the conc. for an individual player as opposed to a *concertino* group was developed by J. S. Bach in his hpd. concs., but note that his *Italian Concerto* is written for a single performer (though the effect of contrast is supplied by the effective use of the 2 manuals). Handel's organ concs. were also an important development, he being among the first to provide a *cadenza in which the soloist could display his skill by extemporization. Mozart est. the style of the modern instr. conc., composing nearly 50 for various instr. combinations. Concs. are usually in

3 movements, but there are many exceptions. A significant change since the 19th cent. has been for the composer to write out the cadenzas and sometimes (e.g. Elgar's Vn. Conc.) to acc. them with the orch. Thus the conc. has grown according to the increasing virtuosity of soloists. See also *Concerto for Orchestra*.

Concert of Ancient Music, also known as 'Ancient Concert', or 'King's Concert'. London series under royal and aristocratic management, 1776–1849, with attempts at revival in 1867 and 1870. No mus. less than 20 years old in programmes. (Not to be confused with Academy of Ancient Music.)

Concerto for Orchestra. A comp. like a conc. but not for one particular soloist, though individual members or sections of the orch. may have important solo (concertante) roles. The form is a 20th-cent. development. Famous examples are by Bartók, Tippett, Kodály, Gerhard, Lutosławski, Petrassi, and others.

Concerto Grosso (It.). Great concerto. Early form of *concerto at its zenith in the 17th and 18th cents., though the term has been used by 20th-cent. composers, e.g. Bloch, Schoenberg, and Vaughan Williams, for works based on earlier models. The works were antiphonal, i.e. a small body of str. (*concertino, concertato,* or *concertante*) was heard in alternation, contrast and combination with a larger group (*ripieno*). These were in several movements, roughly similar to the 18th-cent. ov. or suite. The most celebrated early concerti grossi are those by *Corelli (1712) (*Concerti grossi con duoi violini e violoncello di concertino obbligati*) and those by Handel (1740). J. S. Bach's *Brandenburg Concertos* Nos. 2, 4, and 5 are traditional concerti grossi.

Concert Overture. An independent 1-movement orch. work to open a concert, but not the ov. to an opera. Many concert ovs. are in sonata-form, others are practically symphonic-poems, e.g. one of the first of the genre, Mendelssohn's *The Hebrides*, and among later examples, Elgar's *Cockaigne* and *In the South.*

Concert Pitch. (1) The *pitch internationally agreed in 1960 by which the note a′ has 440 vibrations per second, but see *A.*
(2) One speaks of someone being at 'concert pitch', meaning keyed-up and alert, on top form.

Concert Spirituel (Fr. 'Sacred concert'). Series of concerts founded in Paris in 1725 by A. D. Philidor, the oboist, to perform sacred works and instrumental mus. Later secular works with Fr. texts were permitted. Twenty-four concerts a year were given during periods, e.g. Lent, when other perfs. were forbidden. Ended in 1790.

Concertstück. See *Konzertstück.*

Concierto de Aranjuez (Aranjuez Concerto). Conc. for guitar and orch. by Rodrigo, comp.

1939, f.p. Barcelona 1940. Arr. for harp and orch. by composer.

Concord (Consonance). Chord which seems satisfactory in itself, or an interval that can be so described, or a note which is part of such a chord or interval. The opposite is *discord (dissonance). What constitutes a concord is not strictly laid down and must often depend on individual assessment. However, concordant intervals comprise all perfect intervals and all major and minor 3rds and 6ths.

Concordant Intervals. See *Interval.*

Concord Sonata. Work for pf., with solos for va. and fl., by *Ives, full title *Sonata No. 2 (Concord Mass., 1840–1860)*. Comp. 1911–15. F.p. New Orleans 1920. Movements are entitled 1. *Emerson*, 2. *Hawthorne*, 3. *The Alcotts*, 4. *Thoreau*, in honour of the Concord group of writers whom Ives admired. Early example of use of *clusters.

Concrete Music. See *Musique Concrète.*

Conducting. The art (or method) of controlling an orch. or operatic perf. by means of gestures, this control involving the beating of time, ensuring of correct entries, and the 'shaping' of individual phrasing. (For a discussion of the history of the use of the baton see under that entry.) The advance of the cond. as one of the most important and idolized of musicians dates from early in the 19th cent. and is parallel with (and perhaps a consequence of) the development of the expressive, Romantic elements in mus. François *Habeneck, conductor at Paris Opéra 1824–47, also founded in 1828 the Société des Concerts du Conservatoire at which he introduced Beethoven's syms. to Paris and cond. Berlioz's works, but he never used a full score, conducting from a copy of the first vn. part (and presumably from a memory of the full score). Berlioz himself was one of the first to conduct from a full score, and Spohr, one of the best of the early 'modern' conds., probably used a pf. reduction since he is credited with the invention of 'cue' letters and nos. in scores as aids to rehearsal. Mendelssohn was an excellent cond., not only of his own mus. Perhaps the first virtuoso cond. as the term is now understood was Wagner. From him stems the great tradition of 'interpretation', whereby a cond. is not merely responsible for the technical excellence of the perf. but also for projecting his personal attitude to the composer's intentions. He was followed by *Bülow, Anton Seidl, Hermann Levi, Hans Richter, Franz Wüllner, Felix Mottl, and others. After Wagner came a trio of composer-conds., Mahler, R. Strauss, and Weingartner, who dominated European mus. until the coming of Furtwängler, Walter, Klemperer, Kleiber, Krauss, and many besides, the most illustrious being Toscanini. The first English conds. to win wide acceptance were Frederic Cowen, Henry Wood, and Thomas Beecham.

With the development of recording, conducting ceased to be an ephemeral calling—the interpretations were preserved and can be studied and compared. There is no explanation, beyond the obvious one of psychological personality, for the way in which a cond. can, often with a minimum of rehearsal, impose his own style on an orch. he may not have encountered before, often completely changing the quality of sound or tone-colour even when the orch. is used to regular perf. under another permanent cond. Nor is there an explanation why some (not all) conds. differ vastly in their artistic approach to the recording-studio and the public hall.

There are many examples of long assoc. between a cond. and an orch., e.g. Amsterdam Concertgebouw (Mengelberg), Suisse Romande (Ansermet), Boston S.O. (Koussevitzky), Philadelphia (Ormandy), Chicago (Stock), Hallé (Barbirolli), Cleveland (Szell), NBC (Toscanini), Berlin Phil. (Furtwängler and Karajan).

Conductus. Metrical Latin song, sacred or secular, originating in France in 12th cent. Superseded in 13th cent. by motet. Usually for 2 or 3 vv.

Confessions of a Justified Sinner. Opera in 3 acts by Thomas *Wilson to lib. by John Currie, after novel by James Hogg (1824). Prod. York (Scot. Opera) 1976, cond. Norman Del Mar.

Conjunct Motion. See *Motion.*

Conlon, James (*b* NY, 1950). Amer. cond. Studied Juilliard Sch., NY. While student, cond. *Boris Godunov* at Spoleto Fest., Italy. Début NY Met. 1976–7 season; CG début 1979 (*Don Carlos*). Cond. Rotterdam P.O. from 1983.

Connolly, Justin (Riveagh) (*b* London, 1933). Eng. composer. Studied RCM with Fricker and Boult. Prof. of theory and comp. RCM since 1966. Taught at Yale Univ. 1963–6. Comps. incl. *The Marriage of Heaven and Hell* (Blake) for soloists, ch., and orch.; *Antiphonies* for 36 players; *Cinquepaces* (brass quintet); *Poems of Wallace Stevens I* for sop. and 7 players (1967), *II* for sop., cl., and pf. (1970); *Rebus* for orch. (1970); *Anima*, va. and orch. (1974); *Diaphony*, org. and orch. (1977); various chamber works under titles *Triad* and *Tesserae*; *Ceilidh*, for 4 vn. (1976); *Regeneration*, ch. and brass (1977); *Sestina B*, hpd., fl., ob., cl., vn., and vc. (1972, rev. 1978); *Sentences* (Traherne), ch., brass, org. (1979); *Chimaera*, dancer, alto, bar., ch., pf., perc., and vc. (1979, rev. 1981); *Obbligati V*, vn., va., vc., str. (1981); *Tesserae F*, solo bass cl. (1981); *Fourfold from the Garden Forking Path*, 2 pf. (1983); *Annéad, Night Thoughts*, pf. (1983); Brahms's *Variations on a Theme of R. Schumann*, Op. 23, arr. for 9 wind instr. (1983).

Conradi, August (*b* Berlin, 1821; *d* Berlin, 1873). Ger. composer, cond., and organist. Friend of Liszt at Weimar where he helped him in preparation of his early orch. scores. Kapellmeister at Berlin (twice), Stettin, Düsseldorf, and Cologne.

Comp. 5 syms., str. qts., vaudevilles, and 8 operas (incl. *Rübezahl*, 1846).

Consecration of the House, The (*Die Weihe des Hauses*). Title of Ger. play by C. Meisl perf. at the opening of the Josephstadt Th., Vienna, 1822. Beethoven comp. an ov. in C major, Op. 124, and an item of incidental mus. Since the play was an adaptation of Kotzebue's play *Die *Ruinen von Athen* for which he had comp. incidental mus. in 1811, Beethoven rearr. his mus. for that for *Die Weihe des Hauses*, but wrote a new ov.

Consecutive. Applied to harmonic intervals of the same size which succeed one another in the same parts or vv. Academic condemnation was reserved for *consecutive fifths* and *consecutive octaves*. In both intervals, the component notes are in the closest relationship to each other so that if they are used consecutively, they may both sound as one. Many 20th-cent. composers use consecutive 5ths to splendid effect. *Hidden fifths* are consecutive 5ths believed to be implied, i.e. the progression in similar *motion of two parts to a perfect 5th (or octave) from such an interval in the same 2 parts in the previous chord, so that it may be imagined there is also an intermediate 5th (or octave).

Conservatory (Fr. *Conservatoire*, Ger. *Konservatorium*). School of mus. training and instruction. Name derived from It. *conservatorio*, a sch. in Naples, Venice, and elsewhere where children were 'conserved' and educated in mus. and other matters.

Consolations. 6 pieces (nocturnes) for solo pf. by Liszt, comp. 1849–50. The best-known is No. 3.

Console. All that part of the machinery of an org. which is in front of and on each side of the player and by which he operates, i.e. the manuals, pedal board, mus. stand, stop handles, swell pedals, composition pedals, pistons, and levers, etc.

Con sordino (It.). With *mute.

Consort. An old spelling of 'concert', meaning a concerted perf. by any body of performers. A *Whole Consort* was one in which all the instr. were of one family; a *Broken Consort* one in which there was a mixture.

Constant, Marius (*b* Bucharest, 1925). Romanian-born composer and cond. living in Fr. Educated Bucharest Cons. and Paris Cons. Studied comp. with Messiaen, Boulanger, and Honegger. Pres. and mus. dir. Ars Nova 1963–71, a Paris orch. for perf. of modern mus. Mus. dir., Fr. Radio, 1953, 1963–7. Comps. incl. 24 *Preludes* for orch. (1958); *Turner*, 3 *Essays* for orch. (1961); *Chants de Maldoror* (1962) for dancer-cond., narrator, 23 improvisers, 10 vc.; *Paradise Lost* (ballet by Roland Petit) (1967); *Chaconne et Marche Militaire* for orch. (1968); *14 Stations* for perc. (1970); *Equal* for 5 percussionists (1970); *Strings*, 12 str. and elec. guitar (1972); *Faciebat anno 1972*, orch.

(1972); *Piano personnage*, ens. (1973); *For Clarinet* (1974); *Le jeu de Ste Agnes*, stage (1974).

Construction in Metal. 3 works by *Cage for perc. instr., No. 1 for sextet (1939), Nos. 2 and 3 (1940 and 1941) for qt.

Consul, The. Opera in 3 acts by Menotti to his own lib. Prod. Philadelphia 1950, London 1951. Deals with plight of refugees in modern totalitarian state. The consul, who never appears, represents bureaucratic red tape.

Conte (Fr.). Tale. Sometimes used as title for picturesque piece of instr. mus.

Contes d'Hoffmann, Les (Offenbach). See *Tales of Hoffmann, The*.

Conti, Francesco Bartolomeo (*b* Florence, 1681; *d* Vienna, 1732). It. composer and theorbist. Appointed to court of Vienna 1701. Comp. oratorios, serenades, over 50 cantatas, and 30 operas incl. one on Don Quixote (Vienna 1719).

Continuo. See *Basso continuo*.

Contra- (*Kontra-, Contre-*). Respectively It., Ger., and Fr. prefixes to names of instr. signifying lower in pitch (by about an octave). Thus *contrebasse* is Fr. for db., *contrebasson* Fr. for double-bn. In mus. It. these are *contrabasso* and *contrafagotto*, though in correct modern It. they should be *contrabbasso* and *controfagotto*. The Eng. *contrabass* is another name for a bass viol. To use it as the trans. of *contrabasso* is not strictly correct since the correct counterpart of the prefix is 'counter-'. But no one would know what you were talking about if you said 'counterbassoon', since the Eng. term is 'double-bassoon' and the Amer. 'contra-bassoon'.

Contradanza. See *Country Dance*.

Contraltist. A *castrato with a v. of cont. range.

Contralto (It.). The lowest of the ranges of female v., with a normal range g–e". Originally term meant a male singer, falsetto or castrato, being derived from 'contr' alto', abbrev. of contratenor altus.

Contrapunctus. Made-up Latin for *counterpoint and used by J. S. Bach instead of 'fugue' as a heading for the movements of his *Die *Kunst der Fuge*.

Contrapuntal. The adjective of *Counterpoint.

Contrary Motion. See *Motion*.

Contrasts. Work for vn., cl., and pf. in 2 movements by Bartók, comp. 1938 for jazz clarinettist Benny Goodman who, with Szigeti and Endre Petri, gave f.p. NY 9 Jan. 1939. The violinist uses 2 instr., the 2nd being tuned G♯,-D,-A,-E♭ (*scordatura*) for 30 bars.

Contredanse. See *Country Dance*.

Converse, Frederick Shepherd (*b* Newton, Mass., 1871; *d* Westwood, Mass., 1940). Amer. composer. Studied comp. with *Rheinberger in Munich, a Sym. in D minor being played at his graduation. His 1-act opera *The Pipe of Desire* (Boston 1906) was first Amer. opera to be staged at NY Met. (1910). Wrote several more operas, 6 syms., orch. pieces incl. *The *Mystic Trumpeter* (1904), and *Flivver Ten Million* (1926), a fantasy to celebrate the manufacture of the 10 millionth Ford car, vn. conc. (1902), choral works, chamber mus., and pf. works.

Cook, (Alfred) **Melville** (*b* Gloucester, 1912). Eng. organist. Pupil of Sumsion; ass. organist, Gloucester Cath. 1932; organist, Leeds Parish Church 1937–56, Hereford Cath. 1956–66; cond. Winnipeg Phil. Choir 1966–7. On mus. staff McMaster Univ., Hamilton, Ont., from 1973.

Cook, Brian Rayner (*b* London, 1945). Eng. bar. Studied RCM. Recital début, London 1970. Specializes in oratorio, songs, etc.

Cooke, Arnold (Atkinson) (*b* Gomersal, Yorks., 1906). Eng. composer. Studied Cambridge Univ. 1925–9 and with Hindemith at Berlin Hochschule für Musik 1929–32. Prof. of harmony and comp. RMCM 1933–8 and at TCL from 1947. Comps. incl.:

OPERAS: *Mary Barton* (1949–54); *The Invisible Duke* (1 act), (1975–6).
BALLET: *Jabez and the Devil* (1959–60).
ORCH: 6 syms. (1946–7, 1963, 1967–8, 1973–4, 1978–9, 1983–4), ob. conc. (1954), 2 cl. concs. (1955, 1981–2), vn. conc. (1958), vc. conc. (1974).
CHAMBER MUSIC: 4 str. qts.; 2 vc. sonatas (1941, 1979–80), ob. qt. (1948), str. trio (1950), vn. sonata No. 1 (1938), No. 2 (1951), ob. sonata (1957), cl. sonata (1959), hn. quintet (also exists as hn. trio) (1956), *Concertante Quartet*, 4 cl. (1976).
VOICES: *5 Part-Songs* (1959), *Song on May Morning* (1966), *The Sea Mew*, song-cycle for bar., fl., ob., str. qt. (1980).
ORGAN: Sonata No. 1 (1971), No. 2 (1980).

Cooke, Deryck (Victor) (*b* Leicester, 1919; *d* Croydon, 1976). Eng. critic, broadcaster, and musicologist. Studied music Cambridge Univ. under Hadley and Orr, 1938–40, 1946–7. On BBC staff 1947–59 and after 1965. Wrote important book, *The Language of Music*. Made perf. version from chaotic MS. score of *Mahler's 10th Sym. (f.p. 1964, rev. 1972). Authority on Bruckner, Delius, and Wagner (esp. *The Ring*, first part of his projected study of which was posthumously pubd. in 1979, as *I Saw the World End*).

Cooke, Henry (*b c*.1616; *d* Hampton Court, 1672). Eng. bass singer and choirmaster. Choirboy in Chapel Royal; later joined the royalist forces and became captain; at Restoration returned to

Chapel Royal as Master of the Children, among whom were Pelham Humfrey, John Blow, and Henry Purcell. Was favourably known not only as their teacher but as composer for stage and church, as actor and as singer.

Coolidge, Elizabeth Sprague (b Chicago, 1864; d Cambridge, Mass., 1953). Amer. pianist, composer, and patron of mus. Founder of chamber mus. fests. (Pitsfield, Mass.; then Washington D.C.). Coolidge Foundation (1925) was founded to sponsor the fests. and to commission works from leading 20th-cent. composers (e.g. Stravinsky, Bartók, Pizzetti, Prokofiev, Dallapiccola, Crumb). Gave generous private sponsorship to Schoenberg and Frank Bridge.

Cooper, Emil (b Kherson, Russia, 1877; d NY, 1960). Russ.-born cond. Studied Odessa, Vienna (Hellmesberger), Moscow (Taneyev). Début Odessa 1896, Kiev 1900. Cond. f.p. of Rimsky-Korsakov's The *Golden Cockerel, Moscow 1909, and its f.p. in London 1914. Cond. first Russ. perfs. of Wagner's Ring and Meistersinger. Cond. for Diaghilev ballet, Paris 1909. Cond. Leningrad P.O. 1921–2. Left Russia 1922. Cond. at Chicago Opera 1929–32, and at NY Met. 1944–50, where he introduced Britten's Peter Grimes.

Cooper, Gerald (Melbourne) (b London, 1892; d London, 1947). Eng. musicologist and ten., who promoted concerts of old and modern mus. in London 1922–30 and in later years. Ed. popular edn. of extracts from Purcell. Hon. Sec., Royal Phil. Soc. 1929–32, and sometime chairman of Brit. section of I.S.C.M.

Cooper, Imogen (b London, 1949). Eng. pianist, daughter of Martin *Cooper. Studied with Kathleen *Long until 1961, then at Paris Cons. as pupil of Jacques Ferrier and Yvonne Lefébure. Won a Premier Prix 1967, then studied with *Brendel. Won Mozart Prize 1969. Many solo recitals and concs. with leading orchs. Amer. début Los Angeles, 1984.

Cooper, John. See Coprario, Giovanni.

Cooper, Joseph (b Bristol, 1912). Eng. pianist. Studied with Petri. Lecture-recitalist, also chairman of TV mus. quiz. Assisted Vaughan Williams in adapting pf. conc. to double pf. conc., 1946.

Cooper, Martin (Du Pré) (b Winchester, 1910; d Richmond-on-Thames, 1986). Eng. critic. Studied in Vienna with Egon Wellesz. Mus. critic of Daily Telegraph 1950–76 (chief critic from 1954). Mus. critic London Mercury 1935–9, Daily Herald 1946–50. Ed., Musical Times 1952–5. Author of books on Gluck, Bizet, French music, and Beethoven (The Last Decade). C.B.E. 1972.

Coperti (It.). Covered. Term used of drums muted by being covered with a cloth.

Copla. (1) Sp. popular poem and song in short stanzas (see Seguidilla), sometimes extemporized. (2) A solo movement in a *Villancico.

Copland, Aaron (b Brooklyn, NY, 1900). Amer. composer, pianist, and cond., of Russ. parentage (name was originally Kaplan). First Amer. composer whose mus. was recognized outside USA as distinctively nat. Studied mus. theory in 1917 with Rubin *Goldmark but in 1921 went to Paris as Nadia *Boulanger's first full-time Amer. student. On return to USA, wrote Sym. for Organ and Orch. (1923–4) for Mlle Boulanger's Amer. début as organist. F.p. in 1925 gained him notoriety as apostle of dissonance, the cond. (Damrosch) remarking: 'If he can write like that at 23, in 5 years he'll be ready to commit murder'. Led to a Boston commission (Music for the Theater, for orch., 1925) from Koussevitzky, who also cond. f.p. of pf. conc., 1927. In both works jazz elements were introduced to purge what Copland felt was the 'too European' flavour of his mus. Abandoned jazz in 1930, adopting a more austere style in the Pf. Variations (1930) and Short Symphony (1932–3). At the same time, concerned with widening gap between modern and contemporary composers, wrote some works in a more accessible, popular style. Visited Mexico several times in the 1930s and in 1936 prod. his highly successful El salón México, orch. fantasy on popular Mexican tunes. Other works in this style incl. ballets Billy the Kid (1938), Rodeo (1942), and Appalachian Spring (1944). In later years Copland has prod. little mus., preferring to conduct.

Copland has always worked hard on the promotional side of Amer. mus. as lecturer and teacher (head of the comp. faculty at Berkshire Mus. Center 1940–65). He has toured the world as cond. and ambassador for his country's mus.; co-founded (with *Sessions) a series of NY concerts of new Amer. works 1928–31, founded a publishing press, and was active with the League of Composers. In 1937 he founded the Amer. Composers' Alliance. He received the Congressional Medal of Honour 1977, Presidential Medal of Freedom 1964, Gold Medal of Amer. Acad. 1956, and Pulitzer Prize for Mus. 1944. He has written several books. Prin. comps.:

STAGE: Ballets: *Billy the Kid (1938); *Rodeo (1942); *Appalachian Spring (1944). Opera: The *Tender Land (1952–4, rev. 1955).

ORCH: Sym. for Organ (1924) (version without organ is Sym. No. 1 1928); Music for the Theater (1925); Pf. Conc. (1926); Symphonic Ode (1928–9, rev. 1955); Short Symphony (Sym. No. 2) (1932–3); Statements (1932–5); Suite: *Billy the Kid (1938); *El salón México (1933–6); *Quiet City (1939); Suite from film mus. Our Town (1940); A *Lincoln Portrait for speaker and orch. (1942); *Fanfare for the Common Man (1942); Music for the Movies (1942); Suite, *Rodeo (1943); Suite, *Appalachian Spring (1945); Sym. No. 3 (1944–6); cl. conc. (1947–8); Orchestral Variations (1957, orch. version of Pf. Variations);

Connotations (1962); *Music for a Great City* (1964); *3 Latin-American Sketches* (1972); *Inscape* (1967).
CHORAL: *The House on the Hill* (1925); *In the Beginning*, mez. and unacc. ch. (1947); *Canticle of Freedom* (1955, rev. 1965).
CHAMBER MUSIC: *As it fell upon a day*, for sop., fl., and cl. (1923); 2 pieces for str. qt. (1923 and 1928, also for str. orch.); *Vitebsk* (Study on a Jewish Theme), pf. trio (1928); Vn. sonata (1943); pf. qt. (1950); Nonet for str. (1960); *Duo* for fl. and pf. (1971); *Threnody* (in memoriam Stravinsky), fl. qt. (1971).
PIANO: *The Cat and the Mouse* (1920); *Piano Variations* (1930, orch. version 1957); Sonata (1939–41); *Fantasy* (1952–7). Also pf. suites from *Billy the Kid* and *Our Town*.
Also songs, incl. *12 Poems of Emily Dickinson* (1950) and *Old American Songs* (1950–2), and film mus. incl. *Of Mice and Men* (1939), *Our Town* (1940), *The Red Pony* (1948) and *The Heiress* (1949) (Hollywood 'Oscar').

Coppel (Ger.). Coupler (organ).

Coppélia, ou La Fille aux yeux d'émail (*Coppelia, or The Girl with enamel eyes*). Ballet in 3 acts with mus. by Delibes to lib. by Nuitter and Saint-Léon, choreog. Saint-Léon, prod. Paris 1870. Based on story by E. T. A. Hoffmann (*Der Sandmann*). Many other choreographic versions.

Coppola, Piero (*b* Milan, 1888; *d* Lausanne, 1971). It. cond. and composer. Studied Milan Cons. Int. career as conductor overshadowed his comps., somewhat like *Casella's bolder style. They incl. 2 operas, sym., and chamber mus.

Coprario, Giovanni (John Cooper) (*b c.*1575; *d* London, 1626). Eng. composer and viol player. Visited It. *c.*1600, changing name to Giovanni Coprario (or Coperario) and retaining this on return. Comp. str. fantasias, masques, anthems, and suites. Taught mus. to Charles I and to the *Lawes brothers. His *Funeral Teares* (1606) and *Songs of Mourning* (1613), 7 songs written at death of James I's eldest son, Henry, are among earliest Eng. song-cycles. Some time before 1617 he wrote his *Rules How to Compose*. Was in service of Cecil family.

Coprifuoco, coprifoco (It.). Curfew. Occasional title for instr. comp., sometimes with bell effect.

Coq d'Or, Le (Rimsky-Korsakov). See *Golden Cockerel, The.*

Cor (Fr.). Properly *horn but the term forms a part of the name of several instr. which are not hns., e.g. *cor anglais.

Cor anglais (Fr.). English horn. Neither Eng., nor a hn., but an alto ob. pitched a 5th below oboe. A transposing instr., being written a 5th higher than it sounds. Compass from e upwards for about 2½ octaves. The reed is inserted in a metal tube which is bent back. Invented by Ferlandis of Bergamo in 1760. Not much used

before 19th-cent. Romantic composers, but there are several famous solos for it, e.g. Wagner's *Tristan und Isolde*, Act III; in slow movement of Franck's Sym., and in Sibelius's *The Swan of Tuonela*. Also organ reed stop of 8' pitch but sometimes 16'.

Corant, coranto. See *Courante.*

Corda, Corde (It.). String, strings. (1, pf. mus.) *Una corda*, 1 string, i.e. use the 'soft' pedal which causes the hammers (on a pf.) to strike only 1 str. per note instead of 3. Cancelled by term *tre corde* (3 str.) or *tutte le corde* (all the str.). (2, Vn. mus., etc.) *Corda vuota*, empty string, i.e. *open string.

Corde (Fr.). String.

Corde à jour, Corde à vide (Fr.). *Open string.

Cor de chasse (Fr.). Hunting horn. 17th-cent brass instr. developed from combination of tightly-coiled helical hn. and crescent-shaped hn.

Cor de nuit (Fr.). Night-horn, i.e. watchman's horn. Org. flue stop; end-plugged; of 4' length and 8' pitch; of very characteristic tone quality.

Corder, Frederick (*b* London, 1852; *d* London, 1932). Eng. composer and teacher. Studied RAM and in Cologne with Hiller. Founded Soc. of Brit. Composers (1905–18) to promote Brit. mus. Prof. of comp. RAM for many years. Opera *Nordisa* prod. London 1887. Trans. into Eng. libs. of Wagner's *Ring, Tristan, Lohengrin, Die Meistersinger* and *Parsifal* (helped by his wife).

Cor des Alpes. See *Alphorn.*

Cor d'harmonie (Fr.). Horn, with or without valves.

Corelli, Arcangelo (*b* Fusignano, nr. Milan, 1653; *d* Rome, 1713). It. violinist and composer. Spent much of his youth in Ger. as virtuoso violinist, returning to Rome 1682: from 1684 was under patronage of Cardinal Pamphili, and from 1690 under that of Cardinal Ottoboni. Lived in cardinal's palace and died a rich man with a fine art coll. His importance as a composer lies in his sonatas da camera and concerti grossi from which the solo sonata and the orch. concs. of Handel and Bach evolved. They are beautiful in themselves, notably the *Christmas Concerto. His works are grouped under 6 opus nos.
  1. *12 Sonatas a tre*; 2. *12 Sonatas da camera a tre*; 3. *12 Sonatas a tre*; 4. *12 Sonatas da camera a tre*; 5. *12 Sonatas for vn. or vn. and cembalo* (also arr. as concerti grossi by *Geminiani). 6. *12 Concerti grossi*.

Corelli, Franco (*b* Ancona, 1921). It. ten. Studied Milan, Florence, and Spoleto. Début Spoleto 1951 as Don José in *Carmen*, Milan 1953 (with Callas), CG 1957, NY Met. 1961. V. of heroic quality in roles such as Manrico (*Trovatore*) and Calaf (*Turandot*).

Corelli, Variations on a Theme of. Work for solo pf. by Rakhmaninov, Op. 42, comp. and f.p. 1931 (Montreal). Theme is 'La folia'.

Corena, Fernando (*b* Geneva, 1916; *d* Lugano, 1984). Swiss-It. bass. Studied Milan. Début Milan 1937. Opera début Trieste 1947 in *Boris Godunov*. NY Met. 1953, CG 1960, Vienna 1963.

Corfini, Jacopo (*b* Padua, 1540; *d* Lucca, 1591). It. composer and organist (Lucca Cath. from 1557). Wrote madrigals, motets, *concerti da chiesa*, etc.

Corigliano, John (*b* NY, 1938). Amer. composer. Studied with Luening and Creston. Ass. dir. mus. C.B.S. TV 1961–72. Teacher at Lehman Coll., NY, from 1972. Works incl. vn. sonata (1963), *Elegy* for orch. (1966), cl. conc. (1977), incidental mus., and *The Naked Carmen* (arr. of Bizet's *Carmen* for rock and pop groups and Moog synthesizer).

Coriolan (Coriolanus). Ov., Op. 62, by Beethoven comp. in 1807 for revival in Vienna of H. von Collin's play *Coriolan* (not Shakespeare's).

Cori spezzati (It. 'Divided choirs'). Singers placed in different parts of a building; also the mus. written for them.

Cor mixte. See *Corno Alto* and *Corno Basso*.

Cornago, Johannes (*fl. c.*1455–85). Sp. composer of masses, motets, and *villancicos. Active at court of Naples, where most of his works were composed. His courtly love-songs are especially fine. Known to have returned to Spain.

Cornamuse. Obsolete instr. extant during 16th cent. Term frequently means bagpipe (Fr. *cornemuse*) but It. *cornamusa* sometimes refers to a *crumhorn and sometimes to a different instr., like a soft crumhorn.

Cornelius, Peter (*b* Mainz, 1824; *d* Mainz, 1874). Ger. composer and writer. Studied Berlin 1845–52. His delightful comic opera *Der Barbier von Bagdad* was produced by Liszt at Weimar, 1858, but controversy caused by Cornelius's advocacy of the Liszt-Wagner 'New Music' led to its withdrawal and to Liszt's resignation as court cond. Became prof. of harmony, Munich Cons., and spent some time with Wagner. Wrote 2 other operas, *Der Cid* (Weimar 1865) and *Gunlöd* (unfinished, completed by Bausznern, prod. 1891). Wrote many beautiful vocal works and songs incl. the Christmas hymn known in Eng. as 'Three Kings from Persian Lands afar' but orig. *Die Könige* from the *Weihnachtslieder* (1856).

Cornelius, Peter (*b* Labjerggaard, 1865; *d* Snekkersten, 1934). Danish ten. Studied Copenhagen and Berlin. Début as bar., Copenhagen 1892; as ten., Copenhagen 1899. Sang at Bayreuth 1906 and at CG 1907–14. Was Siegfried in the *Ring* perfs. cond. Richter at CG 1908 and 1909.

Cornemuse (Fr.). Type of bagpipe.

Cornet or **Cornet à pistons** (Fr.). An instr. of brass (or other metal), of partly cylindrical and partly conical bore, with a cup-shaped mouthpiece. Like both tpt. and hn. it operates on the harmonic series filling in the gaps by the use of 3 valves which, singly or in combination, lengthen the tube so giving new fundamentals of 1 semitone to 6 lower, and consequently as many new harmonic series. Its tone is of a quality between that of the hn. and that of the tpt. Owing to the width of its bore it has great flexibility. Double and triple tonguing are possible. Like the tpt. as found in most Brit. orchs. it is constructed so that its primary key can be either B♭ or A, as desired: this removes some of the difficulties of playing in the extreme flat and sharp keys, as in the one case the player is eased of 2 flats and in the other 3 sharps. There is also a cornet in E♭, almost exclusively for wind-band use. In all these 3 keys the cornet is a *transposing instr., its mus. being written respectively a tone or minor 3rd higher, or a minor 3rd lower.

The cornet's first orch. appearance seems to have been in Rossini's opera *William Tell*, in 1829, and cornets are used by Berlioz in several works, incl. the *Symphonie Fantastique*, by Bizet, and by Tchaikovsky in *Francesca da Rimini*. By the 1890s it had almost displaced the tpt. in the orch., but is now seldom found in the orch. or in dance bands, and is now chiefly used in brass and military bands where a sop. cornet in E♭ is also used. But some 20th-cent. composers specify its use where they want its particular tone-quality, e.g. Vaughan Williams in *London Symphony*, Lambert in *Rio Grande*, and Arnold in *Beckus the Dandipratt*.

Cornet, Peeter (*b* Brussels, *c.*1575; *d* Brussels, 1633). Flemish composer and court organist at Brussels, 1603–1626. Wrote org. pieces in the Venetian style; also influenced by the Fr. and Eng. schools, and by Sweelinck and Scheidt.

Cornet Stop. Org. stop of *Mixture type: usually of 4 or 5 ranks. *Mounted Cornet* is one placed high on its own sound-board so as to be well heard.

Cornett. Renaissance wind instr., spelt usually with double 't' to avoid confusion with the band *cornet. Name means 'little horn'. Heyday approx. 1500–1600. Hybrid form, combining brass cup-mouthpiece technique with woodwind finger technique, and was admired for its versatility of tone: as loud as a tpt., agile as a vn., and flexible as a v. 3 varieties, curved, straight, and mute, all in different sizes. Mute prod. an exquisitely soft tone. Curved was most popular form and was used as a virtuoso instr., particularly by Monteverdi in his *Vespers* and *Orfeo*. All cornetts were in G with a range of 2 octaves. *Cornettino* developed for very high parts, pitched in C or D, and there were alto cornetts in F and the large ten. cornett in C. The cornett was displaced by baroque tpt. and baroque ob. *See* also *serpent* and *ophicleide*.

Cornish, William. See *Cornyshe, William*.

Corno (It.). Properly **horn*, but the term forms a part of the name of several instr. that are not hns. (e.g. *corno inglese*, **cor anglais*).

Corno alto and **corno basso** (It.). High horn and low horn. (1) Old names for hn. players who specialized in the high and low registers respectively. (In early 19th-cent. Fr. there was a middle category, *cor mixte*.)
(2) In modern scores the terms are used to distinguish, e.g. the horn in B♭ which transposes down one tone, and that which transposes down a 9th.

Corno a macchina (It.). Valve horn.

Corno a mano (It.). Hand horn. The natural Fr. hn.

Corno a pistoni (It.). Valve hn.

Corno basso. See *Corno alto*.

Corno cromatico (It.). Chromatic hn., i.e. Valve hn.

Corno da caccia. Hunting hn.

Corno di bassetto (It.). (1) The **basset horn*.
(2) Pseudonym of Bernard Shaw for his mus. criticisms in *The Star* 1889–90; he used it again in articles he contrib. to the same paper in 1896 and 1897.
(3) Org. stop much like cl. stop.

Corno dolce. Soft org. stop generally of fl. (not hn.) type; 8′ length and pitch (occasionally 16′).

Corno inglese (It.). **Cor anglais*.

Cornopean. Organ stop like **Trumpet* but softer.

Corno ventile (It.). Valve hn.

Cornyshe (Cornish), **William** (*b* E. Greenwich, *c*.1465; *d* Hylden, Kent, 1523). Eng. composer and actor. Member of Chapel Royal 1496. Master of children, Chapel Royal, 1509. Organized mus. at masques, pageants, and banquets for Henry VIII and supervised mus. at Field of Cloth of Gold 1520. Wrote part-songs, notable for inventiveness and jovial humour, and church mus.

Coro (It.). Choir, chorus. *Gran coro,* in org. mus., means 'full org'.

Cor-oboe. Org. flue stop of 8′ length and pitch, and somewhat reedy quality.

Coronation Concerto. Nickname of Mozart's pf. conc. No. 26 in D, K537, perf. Frankfurt, 1790, on occasion of coronation of Leopold II but comp. 1788 and previously perf. by Mozart in 1789.

Coronation Mass. Mozart's Mass in C, K317, comp. 1779. So nicknamed, apparently, from some assoc. with the annual crowning of a statue of the Virgin, nr. Salzburg.

Coronation Ode. Choral work, Op. 44, for 4 soloists, ch., and orch. by Elgar to words by A. C. Benson. Commissioned for CG gala perf. for Coronation of Edward VII, June 1902 (cancelled because of King's illness). F.p. Sheffield Fest. Oct. 1902. Finale is ***'Land of Hope and Glory', to melody from trio of **Pomp and Circumstance March* No. 1.

Coronation of Poppea, The (Monteverdi). See *Incoronazione di Poppea, L'.*

Corps de Ballet (Fr.). The ballet troupe (excluding principals) of any particular th.

Corps de réchange (Fr.). **Crook of a brass instr.

Corps glorieux, Les (The Glorious Hosts). Work for org. by **Messiaen*, comp. 1939, in 7 movements:
1. *Subtilité des corps glorieux.* 2. *Les Eaux de la grace.* 3. *L'Ange aux parfums.* 4. *Combat de la mort et de la vie.* 5. *Force et agilité des corps glorieux.* 6. *Joie et clarté des corps glorieux.* 7. *Mystère de la Sainte Trinité.*

Corranach (also Coronach). (1) Highland Scot. and Irish funeral dirge.
(2) Person performing such a dirge.

Corregidor, Der (*The Mayor*). Opera in 4 acts by Hugo Wolf to lib. by Rosa Mayreder based on story by Alarcón, *El sombrero de tres picos* (The Three-Cornered Hat) 1874, on which **Falla's* ballet was also to be based. Prod. Mannheim 1896, London 1934. Eng. trans. by Gerald **Larner,* Manchester 1966.

Corrente. See *Courante*.

Corrette, Michel (*b* Rouen, 1709; *d* Paris, 1795). Fr. composer. Organist at Jesuit College, Paris, 1750–9. Comps. incl. conc. for hpd., fl., hurdy-gurdy, and org., sonatas for bn., vc., and vn., much church mus., and works for org. solo.

Corsaire, Le (*The Corsair*). Concert-ov., Op. 21, by Berlioz, based on Byron's poem. First drafted in 1831, then rev. Nice 1844 under title *The Tower at Nice.* Perf. thus in Jan. 1845 and again rev. 1855. At one point called *Le Corsaire rouge,* Fr. title of Fenimore Cooper's *The Red Rover.*

Corsaro, Il (*The Corsair*). Opera in 3 acts by Verdi to lib. by Piave based on Byron's poem. Prod. Trieste 1848. Revived London 1966.

Corsi, Jacopo (*b* Florence, 1560; *d* Florence, 1602). It. nobleman in whose house in Florence the **Camerata* met, as also in **Bardi's*. Comp. 2 songs (the only surviving part) in Peri's *Dafne,* perf. in Corsi's house, in 1598. In 1600 was responsible for prod. of Peri's *Euridice.*

Cor simple (Fr.). Natural hn.

Corta, corte, corti. See *Corto.*

Corteccia, Francesco di Bernardo (b Florence, 1502; d Florence, 1571). It. org. and composer. Choirmaster at ducal court in Florence 1540–71. Wrote madrigals, etc. Joint composer with Striggio of wedding mus. for Franceso de' Medici and Joanna of Austria, 1565.

Cortèges (Funeral processions). Fantasy ov. for orch. by *Rawsthorne, f.p. London 1945.

Corto, corta, corti, corte (It.). Short.

Cortot, Alfred (b Nyon, Switz., 1877; d Lausanne, 1962). Swiss-born pianist and cond. long resident in Fr. Studied Paris Cons. Début as pianist Paris 1896. Keen Wagnerian, went to Bayreuth and became ass. cond. to Richter and Mottl 1898–1901. Cond. first Paris perf. of Götterdämmerung 1902. Became cond. of orch. concerts of Société Nationale 1904. From 1905 played in celebrated pf. trio with *Thibaud and *Casals. On staff Paris Cons. 1907–17, succeeding *Pugno as prof. of pf. In 1919 founded École Normale de Musique. One of 3 conds. of Orchestre Symphonique de Paris, founded 1928. Ed. pf. works of Chopin, Schumann, and Liszt and wrote several books. Arrested 1944 on charges of collab. with Nazi occupation forces but released.

Cosaque (Fr.). Cossack dance in simple duple time with continual accelerando.

Così fan tutte, ossia la scuola degli amanti (Women are all the same, or The School for Lovers). Opera in 2 acts by Mozart (K588) to lib. by da Ponte. Prod. Vienna 1790, London 1811, NY 1922. History of this opera is of special interest. Today it is regarded by many critics as Mozart's greatest and was a success at its first appearance, being repeated 10 times in 1790 and perf. at Prague, Dresden, Leipzig, and Frankfurt before Mozart died. After about 1830 it became a rarity for about 60 years, when it was re-est. through the advocacy of R. Strauss, Mahler, and, later, Beecham. This neglect may have been because the plot was considered (by Beethoven among others) to be immoral, but a mus. reason may have been that the chief sop. role of Fiordiligi was long regarded as unsingable: it was written for Adriana del Bene who was a brilliant high coloratura but also commanded a very low register. The opera requires carefully rehearsed ens. work.

Cosma, Edgar (b Bucharest, 1925). Romanian cond. and composer. Cond. Romanian film mus. orch. 1950–8; Ulster Orch. 1969–74. Comps. incl. str. qt., pf. trio, pf. sonata.

Cossotto, Fiorenza (b Crescentino di Vercelli, 1935). It. mez. Studied Turin Cons. Début La Scala, Milan, 1957 in f.p. of Poulenc's Les Dialogues des Carmélites. Sang Leonora in La favorite, Milan 1961. Début CG 1959 in Medea (with Callas), NY Met. 1968 as Amneris in Aida. Also recitalist, and distinguished exponent of Verdi Requiem.

Cossutta, Carlo (b Trieste, 1932). It. ten. Studied Buenos Aires. Début Buenos Aires 1956 (in La traviata). CG début 1964. NY Met. from 1973, Milan etc. Noted Otello, Manrico, and Turiddu.

Costa, Mary (b Knoxville, Tenn., 1930). Amer. sop. Studied Southern Calif. and made TV commercials. Deputized for Schwarzkopf, Hollywood Bowl 1958. Sang at Glyndebourne, San Francisco, and Cincinnati Opera Houses. Début NY Met. as Violetta in La traviata 1964.

Costa, (Sir) Michael (Andrew Agnus) (orig. Michele Andrea Agniello) (b Naples, 1808; d Hove, 1884). It.-born cond. and composer, naturalized Brit. Studied Naples Cons. Wrote 4 operas for Naples 1826–9. Went to London 1829 to conduct *Zingarelli cantata and settled there, taking leading part in many mus. activities. Maestro al piano King's Theatre 1830, cond. and mus. dir. 1833–46. Cond. Phil. Soc. 1846–54, Birmingham Fest. 1849–82, Handel Fest. 1857–80, Royal It. Opera, CG 1847–69 and 1871–9. Knighted 1869. Comp. 3 syms., cantatas, operas incl. Don Carlos (London 1844), and oratorios Eli (Birmingham 1855) and Naaman (Birmingham 1864). Opinions differ on Costa's merits as a cond., but he was certainly a superb orch. trainer.

Costeley, Guillaume (b Fontanges, 1531; d Évreux, 1606). Fr. composer of Chansons, repubd. 1896. Pres. of soc. in honour of St. Cecilia, formed c.1571, which est. a mus. contest at Évreux. Experimented with microtonal comp. First comp. to call a work an 'air'.

Cosyn, Benjamin (b c.1570; d ?London, after 1652). Eng. organist and composer. Org., Dulwich Coll. 1622–4 and Charterhouse 1626–43. Compiled Virginal Book of 90 pieces, incl. 32 of his own and others by Bull, Gibbons, Tallis, and Byrd. Influenced by Bull.

Côtelettes. See Chopsticks.

Cotillon (Fr. 'Under-petticoat'). Elaborate ballroom dance popular in 19th cent. as final dance of the evening. It was a type of *country dance, perf. by any no., all imitating the leading couple, who chose their figures out of a large number available. The mus. was simply that of various waltzes, mazurkas, etc. In earlier centuries was akin to quadrille.

Cotrubas, Ileana (b Galati, Romania, 1939). Romanian sop. Studied Bucharest and Vienna Acad. of Mus. Début Bucharest Opera 1964 (Yniold in Debussy's Pelléas et Mélisande), then operatic appearances in Vienna, Salzburg, Berlin, and Frankfurt. Glyndebourne 1969 (Mélisande) and 1970 (La Calisto). CG 1971 (Tatyana). Chicago from 1973, Milan 1974. Noted Mozart singer.

Coulisse (Fr.). Groove, Sliding-piece, etc. (1) Slide of tb. and slide tpt. (2, followed by the words à accorder) Tuning slide of a wind inst.

Counterpoint. The ability, unique to mus., to say 2 things at once comprehensibly. The term derives from the expression *punctus contra punctum*, i.e. 'point against point' or 'note against note'. A single 'part' or 'voice' added to another is called 'a counterpoint' to that other, but the more common use of the word is that of the combination of simultaneous parts or vv., each of significance in itself and the whole resulting in a coherent texture. In this sense Counterpoint is the same as *Polyphony.

The art of counterpoint developed gradually from the 9th cent. onwards and reached its highest point at the end of the 16th cent. and beginning of the 17th cent. When, at a later date, attempts were made to formulate rules for students of the art they were based on the practice of that period of culmination. The chief theorist responsible for the formulation of those rules was *Fux whose *Gradus ad Parnassum* of 1725 is a book which still shows its influence in modern textbooks of *Strict counterpoint* (or Student's Counterpoint), a form of training intended to be preparatory to the practice of Free Counterpoint (or Composer's Counterpoint).

In Strict Counterpoint the processes are studied under 5 heads, the result of an analysis which dissects the practice of the art into 5 *Species*. Following the practice of early composers a *Cantus firmus* (fixed song) is employed, i.e. a short melody, set by the master, against which another melody is to be written by the student— or, it may be, several such melodies. It is usually set out with one note to a measure (bar).

The Species are as follows:

I. The added v. proceeds at the same pace as the *cantus firmus*, i.e. with 1 note to a measure.
II. The added v. proceeds at twice (or 3 times) the pace of the *cantus firmus*, i.e. with 2 or 3 notes to a measure.
III. The added v. proceeds at 4 (or 6) times the pace of the *cantus firmus*, i.e. with 4 notes to a measure.
IV. The added v. proceeds (as in Species II) at the rate of 2 notes to 1, i.e. 2 to a measure; but the second note is tied over to the first note of the following measure, i.e. *Syncopation is introduced.
V. (Sometimes called *Florid Counterpoint.*) The added v. employs a mixture of the processes of the other 4 species and also introduces shorter notes (quavers).

The use of Strict Counterpoint as a method of study has tended to decline, its 'rules' being felt to be too rigid.

Combined Counterpoint (strict or free) is that in which the added vv. are different species. *Invertible Counterpoint* is such as permits of vv. changing places (the higher becoming the lower, and vice versa). *Double Counterpoint* is Invertible Counterpoint as concerns 2 vv. *Triple Counterpoint* is that in which 3 vv. are concerned, which are capable of changing places with one another, so making 6 positions of the v. parts possible. *Quadruple and Quintuple Counterpoint* are similarly explained, the first allowing of 24 positions and the second of 120.

Imitation is common in contrapuntal comp.— one v. entering with a phrase which is then more or less exactly copied by another v. When the Imitation is strict it becomes *Canon.

In the 20th cent. there have been no new contrapuntal procedures but composers have made much freer and more daring use of traditional forms. In particular they have concentrated on what is known as *Linear Counterpoint*, i.e. on the individual strands of the texture rather on thematic and rhythmic relationships rather than on harmonic implications. *Linear* harmony is the opposite of *vertical* harmony, i.e. confluences. With the blurring or virtual elimination of the boundaries between consonance and dissonance a much wider range of confluences is open to the composer.

Countersubject. In *Fugue, in addition to the subject, there is often a *countersubject* appearing in the exposition and probably later also. This is a melodic acc. to the answer and subject and is generally in double counterpoint. The v. which has just given out the subject or answer then proceeds to the countersubject while the next v. gives out the answer or subject, and so on.

Countertenor. High male v. not to be confused with male alto, falsetto, or *castrato and with a strong, almost instr. purity of tone. Was popular in Handel's and Purcell's lifetimes and has been revived in 20th cent. largely thanks to artistry of Alfred *Deller. Several modern composers, incl. Britten in his opera *Midsummer Night's Dream*, have written parts for counterten. With the search for authenticity in perf. of early mus., it has reclaimed many roles in baroque works long since assigned to conts. or tens.

Count of Luxemburg, The (Der Graf von Luxemburg). Operetta in 3 acts by Lehár (1909) to libretto by A. M. Wilner and R. Bodanzky. F.p. Vienna 1909.

Country Dance (Eng.), **Contredanse** (Fr.), **Contradanza** (It.), **Kontretanz** (Ger.). This type of dance is of Brit. origin. Its various foreign names have come about from a plausible false etymology ('counter-dance'—one in which the performers stand opposite to one another—as distinguished from a round dance). Both Mozart and Beethoven wrote *Kontretänze*. No. 7 of Beethoven's 12 *Kontretänze* contains the theme used also in the finale of the *Eroica* Sym. and other works. The term is generic and covers a whole series of figure dances deriving from the amusements of the Eng. village green. Such dances became popular at the court of Queen Elizabeth I, and during the Commonwealth were systematically described by *Playford in his *English Dancing Master*. In early years of the 19th cent. the waltz and quadrille drove the country dance out of the English ballroom (with the exception of the popular example known as *Sir Roger de Coverley*); the folk-dance movement of the 20th cent., however, brought it into considerable use again. Scotland has throughout retained a number of its country dances.

Country Gardens. Eng. country dance-tune to which *The Vicar of Bray* is nowadays sung, but perhaps best known in *Grainger's arr. for pf. (1908–18) and 2 pf. (1918) orch. by L. Artok.

Coup d'archet (Fr.). Bow-stroke or bowing.

Coup de glotte (Fr.). Blow of the glottis. In v. prod., a method, thought by many to be harmful, of attacking a note by closing the false vocal cords (2 membranes above the true vocal cords) and quickly opening them to release the tone. If the release is too abrupt, a cough will be the result.

Coupé (Fr.). In ballet, a step like the *Chassé* but the displaced foot goes into the air.

Couperin, François (*b* Paris, 1668; *d* Paris, 1733). Fr. composer, harpsichordist, and organist, the most distinguished of his family and thus known as 'Couperin le Grand'. Taught by his father Charles and by Thomelin. Became organist of St Gervais, Paris, in 1685, holding post until his death. In 1693 succeeded Thomelin as organist of Royal chapel, with the title 'organiste du Roi' (Louis XIV). In 1717 became 'ordinaire de la musique de la chambre du Roi', acknowledgement of his special position in the court. On almost every Sunday Couperin and colleagues gave chamber concerts for the king, for which he comp. what he called 'Concerts'. These are in the form of suites and may have been intended for the hpd., of which he was a virtuoso, but were probably perf. on vn., viol, ob., bn., and hpd. (*clavecin*). Couperin was greatly influenced by *Corelli and introduced into Fr. the Italian's trio-sonata form, himself publishing in 1726 *Les Nations*, a set of 4 Suites (*Ordres*) for 2 vn. and hpd. Also comp. 'grand trio sonata' sub-titled *Le Parnasse, ou l'Apothéose de Corelli*. In 1716 pubd. famous book *L'*Art de toucher le clavecin*, containing instructions for fingering, methods of touch, and execution of *agréments* (ornamentation) in performing his hpd. pieces. This had strong influence on Bach. His 4 pubd. vols. of hpd. works contain over 230 pieces which proclaim him a supreme master of the kbd. Most have picturesque or descriptive titles and are like miniature tone-poems. This perhaps is a clue to their appeal to Richard Strauss, who orchestrated several Couperin pieces. Prin. works:

CHAMBER MUSIC: *Quatre Concerts Royaux* (1722); *Les Goûts-Réunis ou Nouveaux Concerts* (10 *Concerts* incl. the 'Corelli' Grand Trio, 1724); *Les Nations* (4 *Ordres* for 2 str. and hpd. 1726); *Concert instrumental* ('in memory of the immortal Lully', 1725).

HARPSICHORD: *Pièces de Clavecin*, Book 1 (5 *Ordres*, 1713), Book 2 (7 *Ordres*, 1717), Book 3 (7 *Ordres*, 1722), Book 4 (8 *Ordres*, 1730).

ORGAN: 42 *Pièces d'orgue consistantes en deux Messes* (1690). Also songs and religious works.

Couperin, Louis (*b* Chaumes, *c*.1626; *d* Paris, 1661). Fr. composer and organist, first of his family to be organist at St Gervais (from *c*.1650). Also played vn. and comp. instr. works, incl. 132 pieces for hpd. Uncle of F. *Couperin.

The Couperin family were professional musicians in Paris from late in the 16th cent. to the middle of the 19th. Members were organists at St Gervais for over 170 years. François (*le grand*) and Louis were the most illustrious of the clan, but others deserving mention were: Margaret-Louise Couperin (*b* Paris, 1676 or 1679; *d* Versailles, 1728), singer and harpsichordist, who is known to have sung mus. by her cousin François; Armand-Louis Couperin (*b* Paris, 1727; *d* Paris, 1789), composer, organist, and harpsichordist. Org. at St Gervais. Well known for his gifts in improvisation and for some pleasant hpd. pieces. Killed in Paris street when knocked down by a horse; Gervais-François Couperin (*b* Paris, 1759; *d* Paris, 1826), son of Armand-Louis, composer and organist. By 1790 was org. of several Paris churches, incl. St Gervais. Played for Napoleon, but comp. a work called *Louis XVIII ou le retour du bonheur en France*.

Couple. To arrange, by means of a mechanism called a coupler, that the pedal org. can have 1 or more of the manuals connected with it so that the effect of its stops is reinforced. 2 manuals can be connected in the same way (e.g. the Swell may be joined with the Great). There are 'super-octave' and 'sub-octave' couplers which duplicate the notes played, an octave higher or lower (on the same stop). Couplers are 4′, 8′, and 16′.

Couplet. (1) Episode in the early Fr. rondo (e.g. by Couperin).

(2) Same as *Duplet, i.e. 2 in the time of 3.

(3) The 2-note slur ♩♪—the 2nd note of which should be slightly curtailed ♩♪ ♪ .

(4) Stanza of a poem, the mus. being repeated for each stanza.

Coupure (Fr.). Cut. Portion omitted, e.g. in orch. score.

Courante (Fr.), **corrente** (It.), **coranto, corant.** Running. Fr. dance, at height of popularity in 17th cent., which spread to It. The mus. based on it falls into 2 classifications.

(a) It. variety, in a rapid tempo and in simple triple time. (b) Fr. variety, similar to the above, but with a mixture of simple triple and compound duple rhythms, the latter pertaining especially to the end of each of the 2 sections. Occasionally in Bach's kbd. examples the conflicting rhythms are found together, one in each hand.

In classical suite the courante followed the allemande (see *Pavan* and *Galliard*). Occasionally it was, in turn, followed by 'Doubles', i.e. variations on itself.

Course. Term used of str. instrs., particularly lute family, guitar, etc., meaning a group of strs. tuned in unison or in the octave and plucked simultaneously so as to give extra loudness. In 16th cent., lutes had double-courses on lower strs. The single str. g″ is called a course, thus lutes had 11 strs. in 6 courses. Bass-course is single or double str. running alongside fingerboard without crossing the frets and does not vary in pitch.

Courtois, Jean (*fl.* 16th cent.). Fr. composer. Choirmaster to Archbishop of Cambrai 1539. Wrote masses, motets, and secular songs.

Cousu, Antoine de (*b* Amiens, *c.*1600; *d* St Quentin, 1658). Fr. singer and church musician. His book *La Musique universelle* (1658) inveighs against hidden 5ths and octaves (see *Consecutive*).

Covent Garden. Generally used name for London theatre of which full title is Royal Opera House, Covent Garden (since 1892). So called because site in Bow Street was orig. church property, a convent garden. First th. built there 1732 by John *Gay and used mainly for plays, though 3 of Handel's operas were given there for the first time. Destroyed by fire 1808. 2nd theatre opened 1809, still mixing plays and opera, but became Royal Italian Opera 1847, retaining title until 1892. Destroyed by fire 1856. 3rd, and present building opened 1858. During 1939–45 was used as dance hall but re-opened 1946 with resident opera and ballet cos. which were re-named Royal Ballet in 1957 and Royal Opera 1969. Between 1924 and 1939 prin. opera conds. at CG were Bruno Walter and Beecham. From 1946 to 1951 Karl *Rankl was mus. dir., being succeeded by Rafael *Kubelik 1955–8, Georg *Solti 1961–71, Colin *Davis 1971–86, Bernard *Haitink from 1987. Gen. Administrators: David *Webster 1944–70, John Tooley 1970–87, Jeremy Isaacs from 1988. Famous manager-impresarios of the past incl. Frederick Gye 1849–77, and Sir Augustus Harris 1888–96.

Coward, (Sir) **Henry** (*b* Liverpool, 1849; *d* Sheffield, 1944). Eng. choral cond. Largely self-taught but became Oxford Univ. Mus.B. 1889, Mus.D. 1894. Founded Sheffield Musical Union 1876. Est. of Sheffield Fest. 1895 enabled him to set new standards of choral singing in works of Handel, Bach, and Elgar. Cond. choirs at Leeds, Glasgow, Preston, and Newcastle upon Tyne. Toured N. Amer. 1908 and 1911, also Australia and S. Africa. Advocate of *tonic sol-fa system. Knighted 1926.

Coward, (Sir) **Noël** (*b* Teddington, 1899; *d* Blue Harbour, Jamaica, 1973). Eng. actor, playwright, and composer. No formal mus. training. Author and composer of several successful mus. shows and plays with mus., e.g. *Bitter-Sweet* (1929), *Private Lives* (1930), *Conversation Piece* (1934), *Operette* (1938), and several revues in which his songs such as 'Mad Dogs and Englishmen' were perf. (most effectively in his own light bar.). Knighted 1970.

Cowbell. As perc. instr., this is the ordinary Central European cowbell with the clapper removed. It is fixed to a drum and struck with the stick of a snare drum. Used by R. Strauss in *Eine Alpensinfonie*, by Mahler in his 6th Sym., and by Elgar in The *Starlight Express*.

Cowell, Henry (Dixon) (*b* Menlo Park, Calif., 1897; *d* Shady, NY, 1965). Amer. composer and pianist, one of those remarkable pioneering figures who belong naturally to the *avant-garde*. Began to play vn. at age 3 and to compose at 11. In 1912 devised pf. technique known as *clusters (tone-clusters) in which adjacent notes are played simultaneously with the forearm or flat of the hand. Had 100 comps. to his credit when he began formal training in 1914 at Univ. of Calif. with Charles Seeger, who encouraged him to codify the unorthodox rules he was making for himself. This resulted in his book *New Musical Resources* (1919). In the 1920s his recitals attracted notoriety among the public not only because of clusters but because he pioneered other unusual uses of the piano such as plucking the strings or muting them with cardboard or metal. Made 5 tours of Europe between 1923 and 1933, earning friendship of Bartók, Berg, and Schnabel, and studied in Berlin with Schoenberg. In 1922 17 of his cluster pieces were pubd. Cowell also invented new methods of notation to indicate his intentions and was co-inventor with Theremin in 1931 of early elec. instrument called the *rhythmicon*, which could reproduce exactly the complicated rhythmic combinations in his work. Cowell was also one of the first composers—in the 1930s—to bring an element of indeterminacy into his works, suggesting that parts of them could be assembled by the performers in any order and repeated at will, with some measures to be improvised.

Deeply interested in mus. of other cultures, introducing Eastern instr. in combination with conventional Western ones, e.g. Indian jalatarang and tablas. Studied Persian folk mus. and in his *Ongaku* reproduced Japanese quarter-notes and third-notes. At the other extreme, explored early Amer. mus. culture in a series of works called *Hymn-and-Fuguing-Tunes*. It is not surprising that such an original man should have been friend, companion, and biographer of Charles *Ives or that he should have devoted so much time and energy to lecturing, teaching, writing, and generally promoting new Amer. mus. Most of his teaching was done as dir. of mus. at the New School for Social Research, NY 1928–63, and at Columbia Univ. 1949–65. Among his pupils were *Gershwin and *Cage. His list of comps. is very long. Among them are:

ORCH: 21 Syms., incl. No. 3 (*Gaelic*, 1942), No. 11 (*Seven Rituals of Music*, 1953), No. 13 (*Madras*, 1957–8), No. 16 (*Icelandic*, 1963); *Synchrony* (1931); *American Melting Pot* (1939); *Shoonthree* (1941); *Hymn-and-Fuguing Tunes* Nos. 2, 3, 5, 10, and 16; 2 Concs. for Koto and orch. (2nd, 1964); *Ongaku* (1957); *Variations for Orch.* (1956), conc. for perc.

OPERA: *O'Higgins of Chile* (1949).

Also chamber mus. (5 str. qts.), songs, pf. solos, band works, choral, and org. pieces.

Cowen, (Sir) **Frederic** (Hymen) (*b* Kingston, Jamaica, 1852; *d* London, 1935). Eng. composer and cond. Comp. operetta at age 8, becoming pupil of Goss and Benedict in same year. Pf. recitalist at 11. Studied Leipzig Cons. with Reinecke and Moscheles, and, in 1867, at Stern Cons., Berlin, where he concentrated on cond. Cond. Phil. Soc., London, 1888–92 and 1900–07, Hallé Orch. 1896–99, Liverpool P.O. 1895–1913, Scottish Orch. 1900–10, Handel Triennial Fests. 1902–23 and several other choral socs. Comp. several operas, 6 syms., and other orch. works incl. *The Butterfly's Ball* (1901), 3 oratorios, 9 cantatas, and various other works. Today best remembered by his setting of Longfellow's 'Onaway, awake beloved' (*Hiawatha*). Knighted 1911.

Cowhorn. Ancient signalling instrument for calling cattle which by 10th cent. had 2 or 3 fingerholes so that simple melodies could be played. Used by Britten in *Spring Symphony* (1949).

Cowie, Edward (*b* Birmingham, 1943). Eng. composer and painter. Began to compose at age of 11. Chorister, Gloucester Cath. 1955–7. Studied at Morley Coll. with Fricker, 1961, privately with A. Goehr 1964–8, and at Southampton Univ. 1970–1, Leeds Univ. 1971–3. Worked in Poland 1971, being encouraged by Lutoslawski. Lect., Lancaster Univ. 1973. Visited USA 1977. Guest prof. of mus., Kassel Univ. 1979, prof. of creative arts, Univ. of Wollongong, N.S.W., 1983, composer-in-residence RLPO 1983–6. Deeply interested in ornithology. Has painted oils and watercolours; his Choral Sym. (1981–2) was inspired by paintings by Turner. Also fascinated by Australian criminal Ned Kelly, making him the basis of several works, incl. an as yet unfinished opera. Prin. works:

OPERAS: *Commedia*, Op. 12 (1976–8); *Kelly*, Op. 23 (begun 1980).

MUSIC THEATRE: *Kate Kelly's Roadshow*, Op. 27, mez. and ens. (1982).

ORCH: *Leviathan*, sym.-poem, Op. 4 (1975); *L'Or de la trompette d'été*, Op. 9, 18 str. (1977); *Concerto for Orchestra*, Op. 19 (1979–80); *Leonardo*, Op. 20, chamber orch. (1980–1); Sym. No. 1 (*The American*), Op. 21 (1980–1), No. 2 (*The Australian*), Op. 28 (begun 1982).

CONCERTOS: Conc. for bass cl. and tape, Op. 1b (1969); Clarinet Conc. No. 2, Op. 5 (1975); Pf. Conc., Op. 8 (1976–7); hp. conc., Op. 26 (1981–2).

BRASS: *Somnus ei inductus*, Op. 2b, 4 tb. (1973); *Cathedral Music* (sonata for symphonic brass), Op. 10 (1977).

VOICE(S) & INSTR: *Endymion Nocturnes*, Op. 2. ten., str. qt. (1973, version for ten., hn., str. 1981); *Shinko-Kinshu*, Op. 3, high v., ens. (1968, rev. 1972); *Leighton Moss*, Op. 4b, ch. and chamber orch. (1974–5); *Gesangbuch*, Op. 6, 24 vv., 12 instr. (1973–6); *A Charm of Finches*, sop., 3 fl. (1978); *Columbine*, Op. 13, sop., chamber orch. (1979); *Brighella's World*, Op. 14, bar., pf. (1979); *Kelly Choruses*, Op. 23b, vv., hp. (1981); *Choral Symphony* (*Symphonies of Rain, Sea, and Speed*), Op. 24, bar., ch., orch. (1981–2).

UNACC. VOICE(S): *Dungeness Choruses*, Op. 1 (1970); *Gesangbuch*, Op. 6b (unacc. version, 1976); *Madrigals*, 12 vv. (1980–1); *Missa brevis* (*Mass for Peace*), Op. 29b (1983); *Ancient Voices*, 4 vv. (1983).

CHAMBER MUSIC: Str. Qts.: No. 1 (1973), No. 2, Op. 11 (1977), No. 3, Op. 31 No. 1 (1983), No. 4 (*Australia II*), Op. 31 No. 2 (1983); *Kelly Passacaglia*, str. qt. (1980); *Harlequin*, Op. 15, hp. (1980); *Commedia Lazzis*, Op. 17, guitar (1980); *Kelly-Nolan-Kelly*, Op. 22, cl. in A (1980).

PIANO(S): *Piano Variations*, Op. 7 (1976); *The Falls of Clyde*, Op. 16, 2 pf. (1980); *Kelly Variations*, Op. 22b (1980).

Cox and Box. Operetta in 1 act by *Sullivan to lib. by F. C. Burnand after farce *Box and Cox* by Maddison Morton. Prod. London 1867, NY 1875.

Cox, David Harold (*b* Southsea, Hants, 1945). Eng. composer and teacher. Studied Birmingham Univ. 1964–70 with Joubert, Crosse, and Dickinson. On mus. staff, Sheffield Univ. from 1970. Works incl. opera *Disappearing Act* (1968), *Orpheus in the Underworld*, female v. and pf. (1976), hn. trio (1978), ob. sonata (1975), cl. trio (1972), 2-pf. sonata (1974), pf. sonata (1970), *Variations on a Theme by Mozart*, solo cl. (1978), *The Presage*, unacc. ch. and elec. tape (1977).

Cox, David (Vassall) (*b* Broadstairs, 1916). Eng. composer, pianist, and critic. Studied RCM under Howells. Mus. organizer, BBC External Services 1956–76. Comps. incl. many choral and vocal works, opera *The Children in the Forest*. Author of book on Debussy.

Cox, Frederic (Robert) (*b* London, 1905; *d* Altrincham, 1985). Eng. singing teacher, singer, and composer. Studied Oxford Univ. Studied singing in Paris 1924–30, Milan from 1931. London début as ten. and composer 1938. Served in Home Office 1939–45 (O.B.E.). Worked in London 1946–9 with Joseph Hislop. Prof. of singing, RMCM, 1949–53, Prin. 1953–70 (Prin. Emeritus 1970). Head of Vocal Dept., TCL 1970–5. Chairman, London Orchestras Concert Board, 1970–5. Singing teacher at RNCM, Manchester, 1975–84. One of most distinguished singing teachers of his time. Pupils incl. John Mitchinson, Joseph Ward, Ryland Davies, Anne Howells, Elizabeth Harwood, Sandra Browne, Ann Murray, and many more. During his 17 years as Prin., opera prods. at RMCM achieved a standard which attracted int. attention and admiration.

Cox, Jean (b Gadsden, Alabama, 1932). Amer. tenor. Studied New England Cons. of Mus. and in Rome. Début New Eng. Opera Th. as Lensky in *Eugene Onegin* 1953. Sang in Kiel 1953–4 and Brunswick 1955–9, then Mannheim Opera. Début Bayreuth 1956, returning 1967–9 and as Siegfried 1970–5.

Cox, John (b Bristol, 1935). Eng. opera producer. Studied Oxford Univ. Opera début as producer, SW *L'Enfant et les sortilèges* (Ravel). Dir., Music Th. Ens. 1967–70. Dir. of Prod., Glyndebourne, 1971–81. Gen. admin. Scottish Opera from 1982. Notable Strauss and Mozart prods. Has worked in world's leading opera houses.

Cracovienne. See *Krakowiak*.

Cradle will Rock, The. Opera-musical in 1 act by *Blitzstein (1936) to his own lib. on conflict between steel magnate and trade union. Prod. NY 1937.

Craft, Robert (Lawson) (b Kingston, NY, 1923). Amer. cond., musicologist, and author. Studied Juilliard Sch. and Berkshire Music Center, also cond. pupil of Monteux. Skilled interpreter of mus. of Webern, Schoenberg, Berg, and especially of Stravinsky with whom he was on terms of intimate friendship, collaborating with him in recordings and in 6 vols. of conversations and memoirs. Advised Stravinsky to compose in serial technique. Has also written *Stravinsky: Chronicle of a Friendship* (1972). Conducted Amer. première of Berg's *Lulu* (3-act version), Santa Fe 1979, having cond. the 2-act version there in 1963.

Craig, Charles (b London, 1920). Eng. ten. Studied with Beecham. Concert début with Beecham 1952. Opera début 1953 with Carl Rosa; CG 1959 (Pinkerton); prin. tenor SW 1956–9. Has sung at all leading opera houses. Noted for his interpretation of title-role in Verdi's *Otello* and of Siegmund in *Die Walküre*.

Cramer, Johann Baptist (b Mannheim, 1771; d London, 1858). Ger.-born pianist, composer, and teacher, descendant of distinguished mus. family, most of whom worked in Eng. Came to London when 1 year old and became pupil of *Clementi, making début as pianist in his early teens. Toured Europe 1788–91. High reputation in London as pf. teacher; pubd. first book of *Studies* (eventually composing 84) in 1804. These *Studies* are still in use, having survived his 105 sonatas and 9 concs. In 1824, with 2 partners, founded publishing firm of J. B. Cramer and Co., remaining until 1842. (After Cramer's death this firm added manufacture of pfs. to its activities.) Founder-

member and dir., Phil. Soc. 1813, and one of orig. partners of *Chappell & Co., who issued his *Studies* from 1812.

Cranmer, Philip (b Birmingham, 1918). Eng. teacher and composer. Studied RCM. BBC staff accompanist, Birmingham 1948–50, Birmingham Univ. 1950–4; Prof. of Mus., Queen's Univ., Belfast, 1954–70, Manchester Univ. 1970–5. Secretary, Associated Board, Royal Schs. of Mus. from 1974.

Crash Cymbal. See *Chinese Crash Cymbal*.

Crawford, Robert (Caldwell) (b Edinburgh, 1925). Scot. composer and critic. Studied with Hans *Gál, Edinburgh and at GSM with *Frankel. Won Fest. of Brit. Arts Council prize 1951 with str. qt. Other works incl. pf. sonatas, variations for str. orch., sinfonietta, incidental mus. for BBC.

Crawford (Seeger), **Ruth** (b East Liverpool, Ohio, 1901; d Chevy Chase, Md., 1953). Amer. composer. At Amer. Cons., Chicago, 1920–9 as student and teacher. Studied comp. NY 1929 with Charles Seeger, whom she married. Transcr. several thousand Amer. folk-songs from recordings in Library of Congress and wrote pf. acc. for over 300. Comps. incl. Str. Qt. (1931), Vn. Sonata (1927), 9 pf. preludes (1924–8), and other works.

Craxton, Harold (b London, 1885; d London, 1971). Eng. pianist and teacher. Studied with Tobias *Matthay. Taught at Matthay's Pf. Sch. 1914–40 and at RAM 1919–61. Noted accompanist. Ed. Beethoven sonatas (with Tovey) and Chopin for Associated Board of RSM. O.B.E. 1960.

Craxton, Janet (b London, 1929; d London, 1981). Eng. oboist. Daughter of Harold *Craxton. Studied RAM 1945–8 and Paris Cons. 1948–9. Prin. ob. Hallé Orch. 1949–52, London Mozart Players 1952–4, BBC S.O. 1954–63, London Sinfonietta from 1969. Prin. oboe, Royal Opera Orch., 1980–1. Also frequent soloist and recitalist. Prof. of ob. RAM.

Crazy Jane. Work for sop., cl., vc., and pf. by Richard Rodney Bennett, comp. 1968–9, f.p. (TV) 1970.

Creation, The (*Die Schöpfung*). Oratorio for sop., ten., bass, ch., and orch. by Haydn, comp. at suggestion of *Salomon to text by unknown Eng. author trans. into Ger. by Baron Gottfried van Swieten who also provided a re-trans. into Eng. (later modified). F.p. Vienna 1798, London 1800, Boston, Mass. (complete) 1819. Contains famous sop. aria 'With verdure clad' and ch. 'The heavens are telling the glory of God'.

Création du monde, La (The Creation of the World). Ballet in 1 act, mus. *Milhaud, lib. Cendrars, choreog. Börlin. Prod. Paris 1923. Later choreog. de Valois, MacMillan, and others.

Creation Mass (*Schöpfungsmesse*). Name for Haydn's Mass No. 11 in B♭, comp. 1801, because there is a quotation from *The Creation* in the *Qui tollis*.

Creatures of Prometheus, The (Beethoven). See *Prometheus, Die Geschöpfe des*.

Crecquillon, Thomas (*b* c.1490; *d* ?Béthune, 1551). Fr.-Flemish composer. Choirmaster to Emperor Charles V. Wrote over 200 *chansons*, over 100 motets, 12 masses, and other church mus. Regarded as one of leading composers of post-Josquin Desprès generation.

Crécelle (Fr.). Rattle.

Credo (I believe). Section of the Proper of the *Mass frequently set by composers. Operatically speaking, the 'Credo' refers to Iago's aria in Act II of Verdi's *Otello* in which he states his belief in a cruel god.

Creighton, Robert. See *Creyghton, Robert*.

Crembalum. *Jew's harp.

Cremona. (1) Org. stop much like *Clarinet.
   (2) It. town where lived several famous makers of str. instr., e.g. *Stradivarius, *Guarnerius, and *Amati.

Creole Music. Indigenous mus. of Lat. Amer. Has distinctive rhythms, and melodies often acc. by a short bass phrase much repeated with slight changes. The *castanets are used.

Crescendo (It., abbreviation *cresc*.). Growing. Directive used by composers to indicate that a passage should gradually increase in loudness. Sometimes the direction is *crescendo poco a poco*, meaning to increase the loudness by degrees (little by little) or *subito crescendo* (suddenly increasing in loudness). One also speaks of 'a crescendo', meaning a striking example of this feature such as is found frequently in the mus. of Rossini. According to Dr *Burney, the device was first used in Terradellas's opera *Bellerofonte* (London 1747): it was much exploited in the orch. mus. of J. *Stamitz and his colleagues at the Mannheim court as the celebrated 'Mannheim crescendo'. (Some writers betray their lack of mus. knowledge by using the phrase 'rising to a crescendo', which is obvious nonsense.) The opposite is *diminuendo*. See *Hairpins*.

Crescendo Pedal. An org. device which gradually brings into action all the stops.

Crescent. Turkish instr. comprising small bells hung from an inverted crescent. Also known as *'Jingling Johnny'.

Crescentini, Girolamo (*b* Urbania, 1762; *d* Naples, 1846). It. mez. castrato. Studied in Bologna. Sang in Sarti opera in Padua 1782. Visited London 1784, being coolly received, and spent next 10 years in major European opera houses, his repertory being chiefly opera by Zingarelli, Mayr, Cimarosa, and Gazzaniga. Lived in Paris 1806–12 as singing teacher to Napoleon's family. Retired 1812 and returned to It., teaching at Naples Cons. Also a composer.

Crespin, Régine (*b* Marseilles, 1927). Fr. sop. Studied Paris Cons. Début Mulhouse 1950 as Elsa in *Lohengrin*, Paris 1951 in same role. Bayreuth 1958 as Kundry in *Parsifal*, Glyndebourne 1959 as Marschallin in *Rosenkavalier* (same role CG 1960, NY Met. 1962). Mez. roles since 1977.

Cresswell, Lyell (*b* Wellington, N.Z., 1944). N.Z. composer. Studied Victoria Univ. of Wellington, and Toronto Univ. Settled in Brit. 1972. Taught at Aberdeen Univ. 1973–4, Glasgow Univ. 1976–7. Mus. organizer, Chapter Arts Centre, Cardiff, 1978–80. Works incl. vn. conc.; conc. for 2 orchs.; *Translations*, sop., ch., orch., and tape; 4 *Sentimental Songs*, sop., pf., bamboo chimes, bag of wooden clothes pegs; *Wagner is a Fink*, brass band; *Music for Skinheads*, 3 percussionists; 3 str. qts.; *Salon*, orch; *O! for Orchestra*, orch.; *Taking a Line for a Walk*, elec. tape; vc. conc.

Creston, Paul (orig. Giuseppe Guttoveggio) (*b* NY, 1906; *d* San Diego, 1985). Amer. composer and organist of It. origin. Self-taught in harmony and comp. Organist St Malachy's, NY, 1934–67. Prof. of mus., Cent. Washington State Coll., 1968–75. Comps. incl.:

ORCH.: 5 syms. (1941–56); *Walt Whitman* (1952); *Pavane Variations* (1966); Concertos: sax. (1941), harp (*Poem*) (1945), tb. (*Fantasy*) (1947), pf. (No. 1 1949, No. 2 1962), 2 pf. (No. 1 1951, No. 2 1968), vn. (No. 1 1956, No. 2 1960), accordion (1958); *Jubilee*, band, (1971).
Also choral works, chamber mus., songs, pf. pieces.

Creyghton (Creighton), **Robert** (*b* c.1636; *d* Wells, 1734). Canon and precentor of Wells Cath. from 1674. Wrote anthems and settings of church services. Prof. of Greek, Cambridge Univ., 1666–72.

Creyghtonian Seventh. Mannerism of *Creyghton, i.e. preceding final perfect cadence by subdominant chord with added 7th (e.g. in key C, F-A-C-E).

Cricket and Music. Although cricket is a quasi-religion for many inhabitants of the British Commonwealth, it has had relatively few adherents among the great Eng. composers. Elgar preferred horse-racing, Vaughan Williams took no interest in it, and Britten played it well at school but forsook it for lawn tennis. The keenest cricketer-composer was probably Bax, though Delius watched Yorkshire on several occasions. Among conductors, Beecham played for Rossall School 1st XI and Barbirolli was a keen spectator at Lord's and Old Trafford. A former captain of England, A. L. Lewis, was leader of the Nat. Youth Orch. of Wales. Peter *Warlock in 1929

composed a song *The Cricketers of Hambledon.*
Cricket features in many school, music-hall, and
revue songs, and the *Ranjitsinhji Waltz* by C. T.
West (1897) celebrated one of the most graceful
batsmen ever to play for Eng. and Sussex. The
most prolific batsman of the 1928–48 era, the
Australian D. G. (Sir Donald) Bradman, was
celebrated in 1930 in a song *Our Don Bradman.*
He was a good pianist and also composed the
mus. for a song *Every Day is a Rainbow Day For
Me* (only too true from his opponents' standpoint)
by Jack Lumsdaine (1930). Probably the best-
known cricket song is Egbert Moore's West
Indian *calypso, *Cricket, Lovely Cricket,* which
marked the first West Indies victory in a Test
Match in Eng., at Lord's in 1950. The most
famous alliance between cricket and music was
in the person of the critic and essayist Neville
*Cardus, but he omitted to write the words and
mus. of a cricket song. David Rayvern Allen's *A
Song for Cricket* (London 1981) is a documentary
record of all musical 'cricketana'.

Cries of London. Orig. the calls of street salesmen
(hawkers) in selling their wares; over 150 have
been collected. Some Eng. composers, e.g. Gibbons and Weelkes, incorporated these mus. cries
into their works. The 20th-cent. composer *Berio
has written a work called *Cries of London* and
Vaughan Williams incorporates a reminiscence
of the lavender-seller's cry into his *London
Symphony.*

Cristofori, Bartolomeo di Francesco (*b* Padua,
1655; *d* Florence, 1731). It. hpd.-maker who, in
Florence, 1700, constructed a *gravicembalo col
piano e forte* (hpd. with softness and loudness).
This was a forerunner of the modern pf.: he
substituted the blows of a series of hammers for
the hpd. plucking of the str. By 1720 he improved
it by graduating the force of the fall of the
hammers and by putting a damper above instead
of under the str. The compass was over 4 octaves.
Only 3 Cristofori pfs. survive, so far as is known
(in NY, Leipzig, and Rome).

Critic, The, or An Opera Rehearsal. Opera in 2
acts by Stanford, his Op. 144, to lib. by L. C.
James based on Sheridan's comedy (1779). Prod.
London 1916.

Criticism, Musical. The profession of writing
about the aesthetics, history, and evolution of
mus. and of reviewing mus. comps. and perfs. in
newspapers, periodicals, books, and on the radio
and TV. No one can say exactly when criticism
began, but in the sense understood today it
developed parallel with the spread of the printed
word. By its nature, criticism is controversial and
often resented, but there are several examples of
a critic's, or group of critics', championship of a
composer or a branch of comp. which has had
beneficial results (e.g. the revival of interest in
Mahler since *c.*1950). The first periodical devoted
to mus. was Mattheson's *Critica musica,* founded

in Hamburg 1722. In Fr. the first was *Journal de
musique française et italienne* in 1764, though the
pamphlets written during the *Querelle des *Bouffons* 1752–4 perhaps count as criticism. In Eng.
the *New Musical and Universal Magazine* was
founded in 1774. The last vol. of *Burney's
History of Music, 1789, abounds in candid criticism
of composers and performers of his day.
    The first professional critic was probably J. F.
Rochlitz (1769–1842), ed. of the *Allgemeine
Musikalische Zeitung* in Leipzig, and champion of
Bach. Journalism in Ger. daily papers began with
F. Rellstate, who wrote for the Berlin *Vossische
Zeitung* 1803–13, but the first newspaper to
appoint a professionally-trained musician as critic
was *The Times* of London, through the influence
of one of its managers, Thomas Alsager, a musical
enthusiast. Eng. criticism in the 19th cent. was
dominated by J. W. *Davison of *The Times* (1846–
79) and H. F. *Chorley, of the *Athenaeum* (weekly)
from 1833 to 1868. One of the first men to write
about mus. and musicians not as an expert but as
a fine journalist was Heinrich Heine in the 19th-
cent. *Allgemeine Zeitung* of Augsburg. There have
been many examples of composers who wrote
criticism, notably Robert Schumann in the *Neue
Zeitschrift für Musik* (in which he advanced the
causes of Chopin, Berlioz, and Brahms), Berlioz
in the *Journal des Débats* from 1835 to 1863
(although the outstanding critic of the day in Fr.
was F. J. *Fétis, who founded the *Revue musicale*),
Wolf (in the *Wiener Salon-Blatt*), Weber, Wagner,
and Debussy (under the pseudonym *Monsieur
Croche*). In Vienna, where critical polemics reach
a high voltage, the most illustrious and historically
significant critic was Eduard *Hanslick, the
'Bismarck of music criticism' (Verdi), known for
his extreme partisanship in the divergence of
views on Wagner and Brahms. This resulted in
his being immortalized by his opponent Wagner
as Beckmesser in *Die Meistersinger* (Wagner
originally called the character Hanslich). Nevertheless Hanslick is still highly readable.
    In the USA several critics have achieved a
reputation beyond the local sphere of their
activities, notably Philip Hale of Boston, and
(from NY), Lawrence Gilman, H. E. Krehbiel,
Olin Downes, and Richard Aldrich. Outstanding
among Brit. mus. critics of the past have been
Bernard Shaw (the most entertaining of all),
Ernest *Newman, a Wagner authority, Neville
*Cardus, and H. C. *Colles.

Croce, Giovanni (*b* Chioggia, *c.*1558; *d* Venice,
1609). It. composer and priest, pupil of *Zarlino.
Choirmaster St Mark's, Venice, from 1603. Wrote
madrigals, also motets and other church mus.

Croche (Fr.). Hook. The 8th-note or quaver (not
the crotchet).

Croche, Monsieur. Pseudonym under which
*Debussy wrote some of his mus. criticisms,

himself making a selection in 1917 called *Monsieur Croche anti-dilettante* (pubd. 1921).

Croft, William (*b* Nether Ettington, Warwicks., 1678; *d* Bath, 1727). Eng. composer and organist. By 1700 had collab. with Blow and others in *Ayres for the Harpsichord or Spinet*. Organist, St Anne, Soho, 1700–12, Chapel Royal, 1707, and master of the children and composer to Chapel Royal from 1708. Organist, Westminster Abbey from 1708. Comp. many fine anthems and a Burial Service, also hpd. works, cantatas, vn. sonatas, and songs. Also wrote hymn-tune 'St Anne' to which is sung 'O God, our Help in Ages Past'.

Croiza (Conelly), **Claire** (*b* Paris, 1882; *d* Paris, 1946). Fr. mez. Opera début Nancy 1905. Sang for many years at Th. de la Monnaie, Brussels, where her repertory incl. Charlotte in Massenet's *Werther*, Klytemnestra in Strauss's *Elektra*, Pénélope in Fauré's opera, and Carmen, Erda, and Dido (Berlioz's *Les Troyens*). Taught at École Normale, Paris, from 1922 and at Paris Cons. from 1934, her pupils incl. Souzay and Micheau. Greatly admired by Fr. composers for her sensitive artistry. Sang Angel in Elgar's *Dream of Gerontius* at f. Paris p. 1906.

Croma (It.). 8th-note or quaver.

Cromatico, cromatica, cromatici, cromatice (It.). Chromatic. The *Corno cromatico* is the Valve Hn.

Cromorne. (1) On Fr. org. a delicate type of cl. stop.
  (2) Fr. name for the *crumhorn (not encountered until 17th cent.).

Crook. Detachable accessory section of tubing applied to the mouthpiece of brass instr. such as hns. and tpts. to lengthen the instr.'s tube and thus to give it a different basic key. (Players generally carried 10 or 12 crooks.) Natural tpts. or hns., without valves or slides, could play only the notes of the harmonic series, the crook enabling the player to transpose the fundamental note. Thus for a hn.-player, with all parts written in C, to play in D, he would fit a D crook. The introduction of *valves from c.1850 almost eliminated the need for crooks. The term is applied also to the bent metal tube connecting the body of the bn. with the reed, and to comparable detachable bent tubes at mouthpieces of cls. and saxs.

Crooks, Richard (*b* Trenton, NJ, 1900; *d* Portola Valley, Calif., 1972). Amer. ten. NY début 1922. Concert-hall reputation before turning to opera in which he made début as Cavaradossi in *Tosca* in Hamburg, 1927; Philadelphia 1930; NY Met. 1933–43 (début there as Des Grieux in *Manon*). Also popular singer of Irish ballads in manner of *McCormack.

Croon. To sing softly to a baby, but the wider usage since 1930s means to sing softly, and often sentimentally, with a dance band. Practitioners are known as 'crooners', the most eminent being Bing Crosby.

Crosby, Bing (Harry Lillis) (*b* Tacoma, 1904; *d* Madrid, 1977). Amer. singer and actor. One of Rhythm Boys who sang with Paul Whiteman Orch. 1926–30 and appeared in film *The King of Jazz* (1930). Successful radio career as solo singer from 1931. Made many other films, incl. *Holiday Inn* (1942) in which he sang 'White Christmas' and those in which he had a comedy partnership with Bob Hope and Dorothy Lamour. For his part as priest in *Going My Way* (1944) he won a Motion Picture Academy Award. Influenced by Al Jolson and developed a very personal intimate style of crooning.

Cross-accent. Variation of expected accentuation of notes by shifting beat to a point ahead of or behind its normal point in a rhythmic pattern. If this is maintained for some time it becomes *syncopation.

Cross-Fingering. On woodwind instr., fingering the ascending or descending scale in a manner contrary to the normal order of lifting or lowering successive fingers.

Cross, Joan (*b* London, 1900). Eng. sop. and opera producer. Studied St Paul's Girls' Sch., London, and TCL (as violinist). Joined Lilian *Baylis's Old Vic opera ch. 1924, graduating to leading roles. Prin. sop., SW Opera 1931–46. Début CG 1931 and sang there 1947–54. Founder member *English Opera Group 1946–54. Est. Nat. Sch. of Opera, being dir. 1948–64. Has prod. operas at SW, CG, Oslo, Amsterdam, and Toronto. Dir., Phoenix Opera Co. Joint translator (with E. *Crozier) of Smetana's *The Bartered Bride*. Created five roles in Britten operas: Ellen Orford in *Peter Grimes* (1945), Female Chorus in *The Rape of Lucretia* (1946), Lady Billows in *Albert Herring* (1947), Elizabeth I in *Gloriana* (1953), and Mrs Grose in *The Turn of the Screw* (1954). With Anne Wood, founded Opera School 1948 which in 1955 became Nat. Sch. of Opera. C.B.E. 1951.

Cross-rhythm. Regular shift of some beats in a metric pattern to points ahead of or behind their normal positions, e.g. division of 9/8 into 2 + 2 + 2 + 3 quavers.

Crosse, Gordon (*b* Bury, 1937). Eng. composer. Studied Oxford Univ. 1958–63 with B. Rose and Wellesz, and at Accademia di S. Cecilia, Rome, with Petrassi 1962. Tutor, extra-mural dept., Birmingham Univ. 1964–6 and in mus. dept. 1966–9. Fellow in Mus., Essex Univ., 1969–76. Works incl.:

OPERAS: *Purgatory* (1969); *The Grace of Todd* (1969); *The Story of Vasco* (1974).

MUSIC DRAMA: *Wheel of the World* (1972); *World Within*, speaker, sop., chamber ens. (1977).
ORCH: *Elegy* (1959); Concerto da camera (Vn. Conc. No. 1) (1962); Sym. I (1964); *Ceremony*, vc. and orch. (1966); vc. conc. (1979); Vn. Conc. No. 2 (1969); *Some Marches on a Ground* (1970); *★Ariadne*, ob. and 12 players (1972); *Epiphany Variations* (1975–6); *Play Ground* (1977); *Wildboy*, concertante for cl. and 8 players (1977); *Thel*, fl., 2 str. septets, 2 hns. (1978); Studies for Str. Qt., set 2 (1977); Sym. No. 1 for chamber orch. (1976 rev. of Sinfonia Concertante, 1965); *Dreamsongs*, small orch. (1979); *Elegy and Scherzo alla marcia* (adapted from str. qt.) (1981).
CHORAL: *★Changes*, sop., bar., ch., and orch. (1965); *The Covenant of the Rainbow*, ch. and org. (1968); *Harvest Songs*, ch. and orch. (1980); *Dreamcanon I*, ch., 2 pfs., perc. (1981).
VOCAL: *For the Unfallen*, ten., hn., str. (1968); *Memories of Morning, Night*, mez. and orch. (1971); *The New World*, 6 poems by Ted Hughes for v. and pf. (1978).
CHAMBER MUSIC: Str. qt. (1980); *Wave Songs*, vc., pf. (1983).
FOR CHILDREN: *★Meet My Folks!* (poems by Ted Hughes) for speaker, children's ch. and instr. (1964); *Potter Thompson* (A. Garner), mus. drama for solo vv., children's ch., and orch. (1974); *Holly from the Bongs* (A. Garner), Nativity opera (1974).

Crossley, Ada (*b* Tarraville, Gippsland, Australia, 1874; *d* London, 1929). Australian cont. Pupil in London of ★Santley; in Paris of Mathilde ★Marchesi. Melbourne début 1892; London 1895. Reputation chiefly in oratorio.

Crossley, Paul (Christopher Richard) (*b* Dewsbury, 1944). Eng. pianist. Studied Oxford Univ. Pupil of Fanny ★Waterman in Leeds, later of Yvonne ★Loriod in Paris. Début Tours 1968. Specialist in Romantics (Liszt, Brahms, etc.) and in sonatas of Tippett whose 3rd sonata (Bath Fest. 1973) was comp. for him.

Crossley-Holland, Peter (Charles) (*b* London, 1916). Eng. musicologist, composer, and writer on mus. Studied RCM (comp. with Ireland). BBC mus. staff 1948–63. Special study of Welsh folk mus. and authority on oriental mus. Comps. incl. cantata *The Sacred Dance*. Prof. of mus., U.C.L.A. from 1972.

Crotales (Fr.). Perc. instr. Ancient Gr. *crotalum* was rattle or clapper similar to castanets, consisting of wooden or metal shells struck together. The modern version, employed by Ravel and others, consists of small cymbals of thick metal tuned to a definite pitch.

Crotchet (♩) (Fr. *Noire*; Ger. *Viertelnote*; It. *semiminima*). The 'Quarter-Note', i.e. a quarter the time-value of the whole-note or semibreve.

Crotch, William (*b* Norwich, 1775; *d* Taunton, 1847). Eng. organist, teacher, and composer. Child prodigy, giving org. recitals in London when 4, a pupil-ass. organist of King's and Trinity Colleges, Cambridge, at 11, wrote oratorio at 14; organist Christ Church Cath., Oxford, at 15, took B.Mus. at 19, became Oxford prof. of mus. at 22 (1797) and D.Mus. 1799. First Prin., RAM, 1822–32. Comp. prolifically in many genres. His ch. *Lo, star-led chiefs* from the oratorio *Palestine* (1812) is still heard as an anthem.

Crown Imperial. March by Walton comp. for coronation of George VI in 1937. Score is headed by line from poem 'In Honour of the City' by Dunbar (1465–1520) 'In beautie beryng the crone imperiall'. F.p. Westminster Abbey, 12 May 1937, cond. Boult. Also arr. for military band, pf., and organ. See also *Orb and Sceptre*.

Crown of India, The. Masque, Op. 66, by Elgar, for cont. and bass soloists, ch., and orch. to words by H. Hamilton. Written to celebrate Delhi Durbar 1911 and f.p. London 1912. Also orch. suite, 1912.

Crozier, Eric (John) (*b* London, 1914). Eng. writer and opera producer. BBC TV producer 1936–9. Closely assoc. with ★Britten, being co-founder of EOG 1946. Librettist of Britten's *Albert Herring, Let's Make an Opera*, and (with E. M. Forster) *★Billy Budd*, and of Berkeley's *★Ruth*. Co-trans. (with Joan ★Cross) of Smetana's *The Bartered Bride* (1943). Prod. f.p. of *Peter Grimes* in London 1945 and in Tanglewood 1946, and of *Rape of Lucretia*, Glyndebourne 1946.

Crucifixion, The. Oratorio for ten. and bass soloists, ch., org., and orch. by ★Stainer, comp. 1887 to text written by J. S. Simpson, with selections from the Bible. Congregation may join in 5 hymns (omitted in some perfs.).

Crucifixus. See *Mass*.

Cruft, Adrian (Francis) (*b* Mitcham, 1921; *d* London, 1987). Eng. composer, cond., and teacher. Studied RCM with Jacob and Rubbra. Played db. in London orchs. 1947–69. Prof., RCM, from 1962. Chairman, Composers' Guild 1966. Comps. incl. Partita for orch., *Divertimento* for str., *Prospero's Island*, cantata *Alma Redemptoris Mater*, other choral works, and songs.

Cruft, Eugene (John) (*b* London, 1887; *d* London, 1976). Eng. db. player. Studied RCM. In Beecham Orch. 1909, prin. db. BBC S.O. 1929–49, CG Orch. 1949–52, Bath Fest. Orch. 1959–65. Prof. of db. RCM 1946–57. Organized coronation orchs. 1937 and 1953. Assoc. with many chamber orchs. O.B.E.

Cruft, John (Herbert) (*b* London, 1914). Eng. oboist and administrator. Trained RCM. Mus. dir., Arts Council 1965–78. Oboist LPO 1937–9, Orchestre de la Suisse Romande 1939–40, LSO 1946–9, prof. of ob. RCM 1947–9, Secretary, LSO 1949–59, dir. of mus., Brit. Council 1959–61, of drama and mus. 1961–5.

Crüger, Johannes (*b* Gross-Breesen, Prussia, 1598; *d* Berlin, 1662). Ger. composer and cantor. Cantor and org., St Nicholas, Berlin, from 1622 till death. Wrote text-book on throroughbass. Comp. masses, motets, concs., and hymn-tunes. In vol. of hymn-tunes pubd. 1644 occur the famous chorales *Nun danket alle Gott, Schmücke dich, o liebe Seele,* and *Jesu, meine Freude,* all used later by Bach.

Crumb, George (Henry) (*b* Charleston, West Virginia, 1929). Amer. composer. Studied Berkshire Mus. Center and Berlin 1955–6. Has held various teaching posts. His mus. is highly individual. Early influence was Webern, and has developed interest in new sonorities combined with a comp. technique which is sometimes fragmented and sometimes aleatory. This is not employed for freakish effect and his presentation of his ideas remains comprehensible, as in his 1972 fantasy-pieces for amplified pf. called *Makrokosmos which employ many unusual pf. methods with poetic results. His other works incl.:

ORCH: *Variazioni* (1959); *Echoes of time and the River* (1967, also as mus. th. 1970); *Star-Child* (1977).
INSTRUMENTAL: *Night music I*, sop., pf., celesta, perc. (1963), *Night Music II*, vn. and pf. (1964); *3 Madrigals, Book I* sop., vibraphone, bass, *Book II* fls., picc., perc. (1965), *Book III* sop., harp, perc., *Book IV* sop., fl., harp, bass, perc. (1969); *Eleven Echoes of Autumn,* vn., fl., cl., pf. (1965); *Night of the Four Moons* (1969); *Black Angels,* 'electric' str. qt. (1970); *Ancient Voices of children,* sop. and instr. ens. (1970); Str. Qt. (1954); *Dream Sequence,* vn., vc., pf., perc. (1976); *4 Nocturnes,* vn., pf. (1977–8); Vc. Sonata (1955); *5 Pieces* for pf. (1962).
Several of Crumb's works are settings of the poems of Lorca.

Crumhorn (Old Eng. *crump*; Fr. *cromorne*; Ger. *Krummhorn*). Earliest and most common of Renaissance *reed-cap instr., the name meaning 'curved horn'. Characteristic shape is like a fish-hook. Name first occurred in 1489 describing an org.-stop in Dresden, and this implied that the instr. had been in use for some time. Survived in Fr. until the middle of the 17th cent. Standard consort of crumhorns was alto (in G), 2 tens., and bass. Sop. crumhorn (*stortina*) was a rarity but occurs in music by *Corteccia. Crumhorns had 7 finger-holes with 3 extension keys for low notes. With revival of interest in early music, crumhorns have been manufactured since the 1950s.

Crusell, Bernhard Henrik (*b* Uusikaupunki, Finland, 1775; *d* Stockholm, 1838). Finnish composer, cond., teacher, and virtuoso player of cl. for which he wrote 3 concs. and 3 qts. Was clarinettist in military band at age of 12. Studied comp. with Vogler, Berton, and Gossec. Also

comp. opera and translated Fr., Ger., and It. operas for the Swed. stage.

Cruz, Agostinho da (*b* Braga, *c.*1590; *d* Coimba, *c.*1633). Portuguese composer, organist, and viol player. Wrote instr. pieces and viol method (1629).

Cruz, Ivo (*b* Corumba, Brazil, 1901). Portuguese composer and cond. Studied Munich 1925–30. Founder of several mus. bodies in Lisbon incl. Lisbon P.O. 1936. Dir. Nat. Cons., Lisbon, 1938–71. Comps. incl. *Lusitanian Themes* for orch. (1928); Portuguese Conc. No. 1 for pf. and orch. (1945), No. 2 (1946); *Sinfonia de Amadis* for orch. (1952); *Sinfonia de Queluz* for orch. (1964); chamber mus., and songs.

Crwth. Welsh medieval instr., the most developed form of *bowed lyre, with 6 str., a central fingerboard, and the bridge acting as a sound-post.

Crystal Palace. Glass building designed by J. Paxton to house Great Exhibition of 1851 in Hyde Park, London. Later removed to S. London suburb of Sydenham and became home of Crystal Palace concerts cond. *Manns, 1855–1901, notable for adventurous nature of programmes, also of triennial Handel Fests. from 1857. Destroyed by fire 1936.

Csárdás. Hungarian dance, often misspelt *Czardas*, in 2 parts; slow introductory *lassú* followed by excited main section in duple time, *friss*. The mus. has a wild, gipsy flavour. Liszt was one of first composers to use the *csárdás* as the basis for comps. The form of the *csárdás* is also used vocally, a famous example being sung by Rosalinde at Orlofsky's party in Act II of *Die *Fledermaus.*

Csárdásfürstin, Die (Princess Csárdás; usually known in Eng. as The Gipsy Princess). Operetta in 3 acts by Kálmán to lib. by L. Stein and B. Jenbach, comp. 1915, prod. Vienna 1921.

Cuckoo. Simple 2-note wind instr., imitating call of the bird, used in Toy Syms.

Cuckoo, The (Le Coucou). Hpd. piece by *Daquin, comp. 1735.

Cuckston, Alan (*b* Horsforth, 1940). Eng. performer on early kbd. instr. Studied Cambridge Univ. Pupil of Thurston *Dart. Dir. of mus., Leeds Polytechnic. Continuo player with leading chamber orchs.

Cudmore, Richard (*b* Chichester, 1787; *d* Manchester, 1840). Eng. instrumentalist. Violinist at It. Opera, London, then settled in Manchester as leader of Gentlemen's Concerts until 1840. In Liverpool played concs. for vn., pf., and vc. in one concert. Comp. concs. for vn. and pf.

Cudworth, Charles (*b* Cambridge, 1908; *d* Cambridge, 1977). Eng. musicologist, teacher, and critic. Librarian, Pendlebury Library of Mus., 1946–58. Authority on baroque and pre-classical mus.

Cue. (1) Last few notes of another instr. part which immediately precede entrance or re-entrance after a lengthy rest of the instr. (or v.) on whose mus. the cue is written
(2) When instrumentation is condensed, orch. parts of eliminated instrs. are 'cued' in with the parts of suitable alternative instrs.
(3) Cue nos.: the system of letters and/or nos. in a score which enable cond. to rehearse certain sections by indicating exact place in the score, e.g. '3 bars before letter D'.

Cuénod, Hugues (Adhemar) (*b* Coiseaux, 1902). Swiss ten. Studied Basle and Vienna. Taught at Geneva Cons. then began concert career, later entering opera. Débuts, Milan 1951, CG and Glyndebourne 1954. Specialist in roles such as Astrologer in *Golden Cockerel* and Sellem (which he created) in *The Rake's Progress*. Sang in Mozart's *Le Nozze di Figaro* in Glyndebourne's 50th anniversary season, 1984.

Cui, César (Kyui, Tsezar Antonovich) (*b* Vilna, 1835; *d* Petrograd, 1918). Russ. composer. Son of Fr. army officer. Studied mus. with *Moniuszko but studied military engineering at univ., becoming Lieut.-Gen. of engineers and authority on fortifications. On meeting *Balakirev shared his nationalist mus. ideals and with him joined group known as 'the Five' or the 'Mighty Handful' (the others were Borodin, Mussorgsky, and Rimsky-Korsakov). Although a prolific composer, his biggest contribution to the cause of the Five was through his excellent and witty writings. Comp. ov. for *Dargomyzhsky's *The Stone Guest* and made a version of Mussorgsky's incomplete *Sorochintsy Fair* (prod. St Petersburg, 1917). Prin. comps.: 15 operas, 2 scherzos for orch., 3 str. qts., vn. sonata, choral mus., many songs, and pf. pieces.

Cuivre (Fr.). Copper, brass. *Les Cuivres* are the brass instr. of the orch.

Cuivré (Fr.). Brassy, i.e. (in hn. mus., etc.) the tones are to be forced, with a harsh, ringing timbre.

Culshaw, John (Royds) (*b* Southport, 1924; *d* London, 1980). Eng. writer, and administrator. Worked for Decca Records 1946–54, Capitol Records, USA, 1954–5, Decca 1955–67, being assoc. with stereophonic developments. Prod. first complete recording of Wagner's *Ring* (with Solti conducting), 1958–64. Head of Mus. BBC TV 1967–75. Author of book on Rakhmaninov. O.B.E. 1966.

Cummings, Henry (*b* Dublin, 1906). Irish bar., teacher, and adjudicator. Studied RAM and with John *Coates and Plunket Greene. Career in oratorio and on stage. Prof. of v. RAM.

Cummings, Keith (*b* Perth, W. Australia, 1906). Australian va. player. Studied RMCM. Member Hallé Orch. 1933–6, LSO 1937–41, Blech Qt. 1941, and soloist and chamber-mus. player in many other organizations. Prof. of va. TCL.

Cummings, William Hayman (*b* Sidbury, 1831; *d* London, 1915). Eng. organist, ten., and musicologist. Org. Waltham Abbey 1847. Sang at Birmingham Fest. 1864 and became noted for perf. in Bach Passions. Prof. of singing RAM 1879–96, Prin., GSM 1896–1910. Ed. 3 vols. of Purcell Soc. of which he was a founder. Wrote biography of Purcell. Comp. cantata *The Fairy Ring*. While at Waltham, adapted theme from Mendelssohn's *Festgesang* to hymn 'Hark! the herald angels sing'.

Cum sancto Spiritu. See *Mass*.

Cundell, Edric (*b* London, 1893; *d* London, 1961). Eng. cond., composer, and teacher. Began career as hn.-player, CG. Teaching staff TCL from 1919 and travelled widely as adjudicator. Prin. GSM 1938–59. Cond. opera at SW, Robert Mayer concerts for children, etc. Comp. symphonic poems, pf. conc., chamber mus. C.B.E. 1949.

Cunningham, George (Dorrington) (*b* London, 1878; *d* Birmingham, 1948). Eng. organist. Trained RAM. Organist of Alexandra Palace, London (1901), Birmingham Town Hall (1924–48); cond. City of Birmingham Choir; also held church positions. Pres. RCO 1938.

Cunning Little Vixen, The (*Příhody lišky Bystroušky*). Opera in 3 acts by Janáček to lib. by himself based on novelette by Rudolf Těsnohlídek (1882–1928) orig. written as captions for drawings by Stanislav Lolek. Comp. 1921–3. Prod. Brno 1924, London 1961; NY 1964. (Title sometimes trans. as 'The Sly Little Vixen', but 'Cunning' seems to be generally accepted. A better title would be *Adventures of the Vixen Sharp-Ears*.)

Cupid and Death. Masque by James Shirley prod. 1653 with mus. by, probably, Christopher *Gibbons; rev. 1659 with mus. by C. Gibbons and Matthew *Locke.

Cupo (It.). Dark, sombre.

Curlew River. Parable for church perf., Op. 71, by Britten to text by W. Plomer after a Japanese Noh play *Sumidagawa*, by Juro Motomasa (1395–1431). Prod. Aldeburgh Fest. (Orford Church) 1964, Katonah, NY, 1966.

Curlew Sign. Pause mark invented by *Britten for his church parable *Curlew River* (1964) where there is no cond. This sign, when placed over a note or rest, indicates that the singer or instrumentalist must listen and wait until the other performers have reached the next barline or meeting-point. Thus the note or rest may be longer or shorter than its written value.

Curlew, The. Song-cycle by *Warlock, on 4 poems by Yeats, for ten., fl., cor anglais, and str. qt., comp. 1920–1, f.p. London 1921, rev. 1922.

Curtain Music or **Curtain Tune.** See *Act Tune.*

Curtal (Curtall). Renaissance wind instr., ancestor of the bn., developed in mid-16th cent. Had double reeds, single U-tube, and conical bore. Name comes from Lat. *curtus*, short and, like *bombard*, was borrowed from artillery, the curtal being a variety of short-barrelled cannon. Bass curtal was known in Eng. as double curtal and had 2 keys (little finger and thumb). There were also the great bass curtal (an octave below the bass), and sop., alto, and ten. sizes.

Curtin, Phyllis (*b* Clarksburg, West Virginia, 1922). Amer. sop. Studied NY and Boston. Début with New England Opera Th. 1946. Joined NY City Opera 1953. Début Vienna 1960, NY Met. 1961 (as Fiordiligi in *Così fan tutte*). Sang Walton's Cressida in NY 1955-6. Sang role of Cathy in *Floyd's *Wuthering Heights* NY 1959.

Curtis, Alan (Stanley) (*b* Mason, Mich., 1934). Amer. musicologist, harpsichordist, and cond. Studied Michigan Univ. and Univ. of Illinois, also in Amsterdam 1957–9, with Gustav Leonhardt. On staff Univ. of Calif., Berkeley, from 1960, becoming prof. in 1970. Authority on Sweelinck and on authentic interpretation of mus. of 16th–18th cents. Has cond. own edns. of baroque operas, e.g. *Cesti's *Il Tito* at Innsbruck, 1983.

Curtis Institute, Philadelphia. Sch. of mus. founded and endowed in 1924 by Mrs Mary Louise Bok (later Mrs. Zimbalist) in memory of her father Cyrus H. K. Curtis. Tuition fees abolished 1928. Dir. from 1926 was the pianist Josef *Hofmann, who retired 1938, followed by

Randall *Thompson 1938–40, Efrem *Zimbalist 1941–68, Rudolf *Serkin 1968–76; John de Lancie from 1977. Long list of distinguished teachers and visiting professors.

Curtis, Natalie (*b* NY, 1875; *d* Paris, 1921). Amer. pianist, pupil of Friedheim and Busoni, who became interested in mus. of Amer. Indians and collected 200 songs, pubd. in *The Indians' Book* (1907). Later explored negro mus., publishing *Negro Folk Songs* (4 series 1918–19). Wife of artist Paul Burlin.

Curved Line, Various uses of (see below).

Curwen. Eng. family of mus. publishers and educationists. John Curwen (*b* Heckmondwike, 1816; *d* Manchester, 1880) was a Congregational minister. Adopted *tonic sol-fa system of Sarah Glover and resigned his ministry in 1864 to promote tonic sol-fa movement. Founded pub. firm J. Curwen and Sons in 1863. His son John Spencer Curwen (*b* London, 1847; *d* London, 1916) continued the tonic sol-fa work. J. S. Curwen's nephew, John Kenneth Curwen (*b* London, 1881; *d* Gerrards Cross, 1935) supervised the pub. firm and added to its catalogue Holst's *Planets*, Vaughan Williams's *Pastoral Symphony* and *Hugh the Drover*, and works by Bantock, Smyth, and Varèse. Published journal *The Sackbut* (1920–34), at one time edited by Philip Heseltine. In 1971 catalogue was divided between Faber Music and Roberton Publications.

Curzon, (Sir) **Clifford** (Michael) (*b* London, 1907; *d* London, 1982). Eng. pianist. Entered RAM 1919, studying with Charles Reddie. In 1923 was a soloist in Bach triple concerto at Promenade Concert cond. by Wood. In 1928 studied with Schnabel in Berlin, and in 1930 moved to Paris

---

Curved Line, Various uses of.

The Tie or Bind

The 2 notes become 1 (see *Tie or Bind*).

The Slur, or Legato (or Bowing Mark)

All the notes affected by the curve are to be played smoothly. In str. mus. they are to be played in a single bow movement.

The Phrase Mark

See *Phrase.*

The Syllable Mark

The mark is to make clearer the fitting of the notes to the syllables.

*The *Portamento Mark*

Instead of jumping cleanly the singer is to slide from the one note to the other, taking all intervening pitches en route. The same effect is possible on bowed instr., but here a wavy line is sometimes the indication.

for studies with Landowska and N. Boulanger. In 1931 married Amer. harpsichordist Lucille *Wallace. Returned to Eng. 1932. Amer. début 1939. Though often playing Romantics such as Liszt and Tchaikovsky, increasingly concentrated on Schubert, Beethoven, and especially Mozart. Gave f.p. of Rawsthorne's 2nd pf. conc. (1951) and played pf. duets with Britten. C.B.E. 1958. Knighted 1977.

Cushion Dance (Ger. *Kissentanz*, or *Polstertanz*). An old dance in which a participant chose a partner by dropping a cushion before him or her, who then knelt on it and bestowed a kiss on the cushion-bearer.

Cusins, (Sir) William (George) (*b* London, 1833; *d* Remonchamps, Ardennes, 1893). Eng. cond., organist, and composer. Studied RAM and Brussels. Début 1849 as pianist, then organist of Queen's private chapel, and violinist in CG orch. On staff RAM from 1851. Cond., Phil Soc. 1867–83, continuing to tour widely as pianist. Comp. oratorio, pf. conc., and ovs. Knighted 1892. Master of the Queen's Musick 1870–93.

Cutner, Solomon. See *Solomon*.

Cutting, Thomas (*fl.* 17th cent.). Eng. lutenist and composer. Worked in Denmark 1607–11. Possibly a member of same family as Francis Cutting (*fl.* 1583–*c*.1603), composer of a quantity of lute mus.

Cuzzoni, Francesca (*b* Parma, *c*.1698; *d* Bologna, 1770). It. sop., pupil of Lanzi. Probable début Parma 1716, then sang in Venice and Turin. London début, King's Th. 1723 in Handel's *Ottone*. Remained in Handel's opera co. (Royal Academy) until 1728, singing a leading role in all his operas. Her rivalry with Faustina Bordoni led to their fighting on the stage in 1727 during Bononcini's *Astianatte*. Sang in Vienna 1728–9 and then returned to It., where she sang in several of Hasse's operas. In 1739 returned to Ger. and in 1750 to London, where she was arrested for debt. Farewell appearance London 1751. Last years spent in prison and in poverty. Contemporary accounts leave no doubt of her greatness as an artist, especially in Handel.

Cycle. (1) Name for series of items written to be perf. as a group and sometimes linked thematically either musically or by subject, esp. song-cycle (Ger. *Liedercyclus*). In opera the greatest cycle (4 operas) is Wagner's *Der Ring des Nibelungen*.

(2) A complete vibration in mus. acoustics.

(3) Any of systems of equal temperament in which tonal material is obtained by dividing octave into number of equal intervals.

Cyclic Form. Formal structure of a comp. in which one mus. theme is heard, sometimes in a varied form, in more than one movement. Early examples occur in Handel, Vivaldi, Mozart, and Haydn, but it was developed by Beethoven e.g.

in his *Pathétique* Sonata and 5th Sym. The *idée fixe* of Berlioz and *leitmotiv* of Wagner are akin to cyclic form, as are the thematic transformations of Liszt and R. Strauss. But the most emphatic uses of cyclic form occur in the works of Franck and in the Sym. No. 1 of Elgar.

Cylinder or rotary valve. A special type of valve in brass instr., in much use in some European countries but in Brit. and USA applied only to the Fr. hn. The term is sometimes used for any kind of valve, e.g. It. *Trombone a Cilindri* (valve tb.).

Cymbalon. See *Cimbalom*.

Cymbals. Perc. instrs. consisting of plate-shaped discs made of brass or other metal with leather handles. Played by being held one in each hand and clashed together; or fixed on a stand enabling the foot to do the clashing; or one can be fixed to the side of a big drum and the other clashed on to it; or they can be rattled at their edges; or one cymbal can be struck with a drumstick (or wire brush) or a roll perf. on it with drumsticks. *Antique cymbals*, specified in some scores (e.g. Debussy's *L'Après-midi d'un faune*), are tuned to a definite pitch. Ordinary cymbals have no definite pitch but one may sound higher than another. See *Choke cymbals*, *Chinese crash cymbals*, and *Sizzle cymbals*.

Cymbel. Org. stop; a brilliant type of *Mixture*.

Cymbelstern. See *Zimbelstern*.

Czárdás. See *Csárdás*.

Czar und Zimmermann (Lortzing). See *Zar und Zimmermann*.

Czech Philharmonic Orchestra. Founded as independent body in 1901 having previously been orch. of Prague Nat. Opera. Achieved worldwide reputation through tours and recordings during conductorship of Václav *Talich 1919–41. Among his successors have been Rafael *Kubelik 1941–8, Karel *Ančerl 1950–68, and Václav Neumann from 1968.

Czech Quartet. Cz. string quartet formed in 1891 by pupils of Hanuš *Wihan at Prague Cons. First concert 1892. Visited Russ. 1895 and Brit. 1896. Last tour Holland 1931. Disbanded 1933. Orig. members were Karel Hoffmann (1872–1936), Josef *Suk (1874–1935), Oskar Nedbal (1874–1930), and Otto Berger (1873–97). Nedbal was replaced 1906 by Jiří Herold (1875–1934) and Berger in 1894 by Wihan (1855–1920). Wihan was replaced 1914 by Ladislav Zelenka (1881–1957). Gave 1,000th concert in 1902. Specialized in Smetana, Dvořák, and Beethoven, but played many modern qts. incl. those by Reger, Pfitzner, Schoenberg, Ravel, etc.

Czernohorsky (Černohorský), **Bohuslav** (*b* Nimburg, 1684; *d* Graz, 1742). Cz. composer and choirmaster. Taught Gluck and Tartini. Worked in Padua and Prague. Comp. preludes, toccatas, and fugues for org., *Regina coeli* for sop., and other church mus., but the bulk of his work was lost in a fire at a Prague convent, 1754.

Czerny, Karl (*b* Vienna, 1791; *d* Vienna, 1857). Austrian pianist, teacher, and composer. Pf. pupil 1800–3 and friend of Beethoven, who admired him. Also influenced by *Hummel and *Clementi. Was popular teacher at age 15. Pupils incl. 10-year-old Liszt. Indefatigable composer and arranger, works numbering more than 1,000 and incl. examples of every form from operas to pf. solos, but best known for his instructive studies. Arr. operas, oratorios, and syms. for pf(s). (incl. arrs. of Rossini's *Semiramide* and *William Tell* ovs. for 8 pf., 4 hands each). Contrib. to *Hexameron.

Czerny-Stefańska, Halina (*b* Kraków, 1922). Polish pianist. Studied Warsaw. Joint winner Chopin Int. Competition 1949. Int. tours.

Czerwenka, Oskar (*b* Linz, Austria, 1924). Austrian bass. Opera début Graz 1947; joined Vienna Opera 1951. NY Met. 1960. Has sung at Salzburg (1953) and Glyndebourne (1959). Repertory of over 70 parts.

Cziffra, György (*b* Budapest, 1921). Fr. pianist of Hung. birth. First public perf. at 5 in circus. Studied Budapest 1930 with Dohnányi and had successful career in Hung. and Europe 1933–41. Prisoner of war and again imprisoned for political beliefs 1950–3. Won Liszt Prize 1955. Escaped from Hung. during 1956 uprising, settling in Fr. Virtuoso interpreter of 19th cent. repertory.

Czimbal, Czimbalom, Czimbalon. See *Cimbalom*.

Czyz, Henryk (*b* Grudziadz, Poland, 1923). Polish cond. and composer. Studied Poznań and Toruń. Cond. début 1948, Polish Nat. Radio Orch. Cond. f.p. of Penderecki's *St Luke Passion*, 1966. Prin. cond. Düsseldorf Opera. 1971–4. Comp. syms., operas, and film mus.

D

D. The name of the 2nd degree of natural scale of C. Thus D♭, D♭♭, D♮, D♯, D♯♯, D major, D minor. *In D* indicates either 'in the key of D major' or, of transposing instr., that the written note C sounds D.

D. Abbreviated prefix to nos. in the O.E. *Deutsch thematic catalogue of Schubert's works, and now generally used to identify them; e.g. the Str. Quintet in C major (D956).

d. Tonic Sol-fa symbol for first degree (tonic) of scale, pronounced *doh*.

Da (It.). Of, from.

Da capo (It., abbreviates to D.C.). From the head. A term meaning 'Repeat from the beginning until you come to the word *Fine* (end), or the pause mark (⌒)'. Sometimes the expressions *da capo al segno* (From the beginning to the sign) or *da capo al fine* (From the beginning to the word *Fine*) are encountered; these are occasionally followed by *e poi la coda*, meaning that having arrived at the place indicated, the coda should immediately follow.

A *da capo* aria is one in which the first part is repeated.

Daddi, Joao Guilherme (*b* Oporto, 1814: *d* 1887). Portuguese pianist and composer of light operas.

Daffner, Hugo (*b* Munich, 1882; *d* Dachau, 1936). Ger. composer and critic. Comp. pupil of Thuille and Reger. His 3 operas incl. *Macbeth*. Wrote 2 syms., 2 str. qts., and sonatas for pf., vn., and vc. Mus. critic *Allgemeine Zeitung*, Königsberg, 1907–10. Author of books incl. one on Mozart pf. concs.

Dafne. Opera in prol. and 6 scenes by *Peri to lib. by Ottavio Rinuccini. Comp. 1594–8. Generally supposed to be the earliest opera, but the mus. is lost. Prod. in *Corsi's house, Florence, 1598. (See *Camerata*.) The same lib. was also set by Corsi himself (2 fragments survive), *Gagliano (1607), and Schütz (lost, 1627). Operas on the same theme were comp. by A. Scarlatti (1700), *Astorga (1709), Mulé (1928), and R. Strauss (1936–7, see under *Daphne*).

Dalayrac, Nicolas-Marie (*b* Muret, Haute Garonne, 1753; *d* Paris, 1809). Fr. composer. Trained as lawyer. Wrote nearly 60 *opéras comiques*, among them *Nina* (1786), *Azémia* (1786), *Les deux petits Savoyards* (1789), and *Camille* (1791). Also wrote str. qts., vn. duos, and songs.

d'Albert. See *Albert, Eugen d'*.

Dalberto, Michel (*b* Paris, 1955). Fr. pianist. Studied Paris Cons. 1968–75 (with Perlemuter, Trouard, and Hubeau). Winner, 1st Mozart comp., Salzburg 1975; winner Leeds pf. comp. 1978. Recitalist and concert soloist.

Dalby, (John) Martin (*b* Aberdeen, 1942). Scottish composer. Violist in Nat. Youth Orch. Studied RCM., then 2 years in Italy. On BBC mus. staff in London 1965–71, Glasgow Univ. 1971–2. Head of Mus. BBC Scotland from 1972. Compositions incl.:

ORCH:*Waltz Overture* (1965), *Sym.* (1970), *Concerto Martin Pescatore*, strings (1971), *The Tower of Victory* (1973), va. conc. (1974), *El Ruisenor* (1979), *Chamber Sym.* (1982), *Nozze di Primavera* (1984).

CHAMBER & INSTR: Ob. sonatina (1969), *Commedia*, cl., vn., vc., pf. (1969), *Whisper Music* (1971), *Cancionero para una Mariposa*, 9 instr. (1971), str. quintet (1972), *Yet Still She is the Moon*, brass septet (1973), *Unicorn*, vn. and pf. (1975), *Aleph*, 8 instr. (1975), *Almost a Madrigal*, wind and perc. (1977), *Man Walking*, octet for wind and str. (1980).

VOCAL & CHORAL: *The Fiddler*, sop. or ten. and vn. (1967), *Cantica*, sop. or ten., cl., va., pf. (1969), *The Keeper of the Pass*, sop. and instr. (1971), *Orpheus*, ch., narrator, and 11 instr. (1972), *Cantigas del Cancionero*, 5 solo vv. (1972), *El Remenso del Pitido*, 12 solo vv. (1974), *Ad Flumina Babyloniae*, motet (1975), *Call for the Hazel Tree*, ch. and elec. (1979), *Antoinette Alone*, mez., pf. (1980).

Dalcroze. See *Jaques-Dalcroze, Émile*.

Dale, Benjamin (James) (*b* London, 1885; *d* London, 1943). Eng. composer. Studied RAM, of which he was later Warden, 1937. Comps. incl. pf. sonata (1902), cantatas, and several works for va.

Dalibor. Opera in 3 acts by Smetana to E. Spindler's Cz. trans. of Ger. text by Joseph Wenzig. Comp. 1865–7, rev. 1870. Prod. Prague 1868, Chicago 1924, Edinburgh 1964, London 1976.

Dallam. Eng. family of org.-builders. Thomas Dallam (*fl.* early 17th cent.) built org. at Worcester Cath., 1613; his son Robert (1602–65) built orgs. of York Minster and Durham Cath.

Dallapiccola, Luigi (*b* Pisino d'Istria, 1904; *d* Florence, 1975). It. composer and pianist. At the time of his birth, Pisino was in the Austro-Hungarian empire, being transferred to It. in

1918 (now in Yugoslavia). Because Dallapiccola's father was suspected in 1917 of It. nationalism, the family was forcibly moved to Graz where Dallapiccola learned to admire opera and where he conceived the passionate love of liberty which inspires several of his works. In 1922 he entered the Cons. Cherubini, Florence, studying comp. under Frazzi. In 1924 a perf. of Schoenberg's *Pierrot Lunaire* made a deep impression on him, in addition to his existing passion for Debussy, Monteverdi, and Gesualdo. In the late 1920s he taught, gave pf. recitals, and in 1934 joined the pf. staff of the Cons. Cherubini. Travelling abroad he met Berg, Malipiero, and Casella. He fell out of favour with the authorities because of his opposition to Fascism, but after 1945 he spent a considerable time in the USA.

Known as the principal (and probably the first) It. composer to adopt 12-note methods, Dallapiccola also remained a lyrical, thoroughly It. composer. But he did not adopt *dodecaphony until he was nearly 40. His early works, such as the first pair of *Cori di Michelangelo Buonarroti il Giovane* (1933), reflect his interest in the Italian madrigalists. The later pairs (1934–6) combine the influence of Busoni with his own typically sensuous warmth. The culmination of this period of his work was the *Canti di prigionia* (1938–41).

In 1942 he adopted serialism, but never the purely academic variety. His natural It. aptitude for elaborate polyphony led him, in such works as *Piccola musica notturna* (1954), to use the all-interval row. His opera *Il prigioniero* (1944–8) exemplifies his unorthodoxy in using several different note-rows and ignoring other standard serial procedures. From about 1956 his music showed a Webernian intricacy in its textures and angularity, yet was never wholly devoid of the lyricism and colour of his earlier phases. Prin. comps.:

OPERAS: *Volo di notte* (Night Flight) 1 act, lib. by composer after Saint-Exupéry (comp. 1937–9, prod. 1940); *Il *prigioniero* (The Prisoner) (1944–8); **Job* (1950); *Ulisse* (prol. and 2 acts, lib. by composer after Homer, comp. 1959–68, prod. 1968).
BALLET: *Marsia* (comp. 1942–3, prod. Venice 1948).
CHORUS AND ORCH: *6 Cori di Michelangelo Buonarroti il Giovane* in 3 pairs: 1 (1933), for unacc. mixed ch., 2 (1934–5), for women's vv. and 17 instr., 3 (1935–6), for ch. and orch.; 3 *Canti di prigionia* (Songs of Imprisonment) (1938–41); *Requiescant* (1957–8): *Canti di Liberazione* (1951–55).
SOLO VOICE AND ORCH: *Partita* for orch. (sop. solo in finale) (1930–2); 3 *Laudi* for high v. and 13 instr. (1936–7); *Liriche Greche* (Greek Lyrics): I, *Five Sappho Fragments*, for v. and 15 instr. (1942), II, *Two Anacreontic Lyrics*, for v., Eb cl., cl. in A, va., pf. (1944–5), III, *6 Songs of Alcaeus*, for v. and 11 instr. (1943): *An Mathilde*, for sop. and orch. (1955); *Concerto per la notte di Natale dell'anno

1956, for chamber orch. with sop. (1957): *4 liriche di Antonio Machado* for sop. and chamber orch. (orig. version for sop. and pf., 1948) (1964); *Commiato*, for sop. and chamber orch. (1972).
ORCH: *Piccolo Concerto per Muriel Couvreux*, for pf. and chamber orch. (1939–41); *Variations* (1954) (adapted from *Quaderno musicale di Annalibera* for pf., 1952); *Tartiniana*, divertimento for vn. and chamber orch. (1951); *Piccola musica notturna* (1954) (also arr. for chamber ens., 1961); *Dialoghi* for vc. and orch. (1960).
INSTR.: *Ciacona, Intermezzo, e Adagio*, vc. (1945).
SONGS: *Rencesval* for bar. (1946); *4 Liriche di Antonio Machado* for sop. (1948).

Dal Monte, Toti (Antonietta Meneghel) (*b* Mogliano Veneto, 1893; *d* Treviso, 1975). It. sop. Début Milan 1916, then continued studies with Pini-Corsi. Sang Gilda in *Rigoletto* cond. Toscanini, Milan 1921. Regular operatic appearances in It., also Chicago 1924–8, NY Met. 1924–5, CG 1926. Became teacher.

Dal segno (It.). From the sign, i.e. return to the sign *S.*, and repeat thence to the word *Fine* (end), or to a double bar with a pause sign (⌢) above it.

Daman. See *Damon, William*.

Damase, Jean-Michel (*b* Bordeaux, 1928). Fr. composer and pianist. Studied Paris (*Grand Prix de Rome*). Wrote 7 ballets, incl. *La Croqueuse de diamants* (The Diamond Cruncher) 1950, pf. concs., vn. conc., harp concertino, vc. sonata, wind quintet, etc.

Dame blanche, La (The White Lady). Opera in 3 acts by Boieldieu, to lib. by Scribe, based on Scott's *The Monastery* (1820) and *Guy Mannering* (1815). Prod. Paris 1825, London 1826, NY 1827.

Damnation de Faust, La (The Damnation of Faust). Dramatic cantata (*légende dramatique*) in 4 parts for sop., ten., and bass soloists, ch. and orch., Op. 24, by Berlioz, sometimes perf. in operatic form. Text by Berlioz and A. Gandonnière after G. de Nerval's Fr. version of Goethe. F.p. Paris, Opéra-Comique, 6 Dec. 1846. F. p. in England, Manchester, 5 Feb. 1880 cond. Hallé. Comp. was completed 1846, incorporating earlier *Huit Scènes de Faust* (1828). See also *Rákóczy March*.

Damon (Daman), **William** (*b* Liège, *c*.1540; *d* London, 1591). Walloon composer, employed in Eng. at Queen Elizabeth's court; comp. anthems, lute mus. etc., and pubd. notable coll. of metrical psalm tunes (1579).

Damp. To check the vibrations of an instr. (e.g. kettledrum) by touching it in some way. See also *Piano*.

Dampers. See *Piano*.

Dämpfer (Ger.). *Mute. Mit Dämpfern*, with mutes.

Dämpfung. Muting, or (pf.) soft-pedalling.

Damrosch, Frank (Heino) (*b* Breslau, 1859; *d* NY, 1937). Ger.-born Amer. cond. Went to USA with father, Leopold, in 1871. Chorusmaster NY Met. 1885–91. Cond. and founder of several NY choral socs. Founded Institute of Musical Art, 1905, remaining dir. until it was merged with *Juilliard Sch., 1926.

Damrosch, Leopold (*b* Posen, 1832; *d* NY, 1885). Ger. cond., composer, and violinist. Doctor of medicine, Berlin, 1854, but turned to mus. Violinist in Weimar court orch. under Liszt 1855–9, cond. Breslau P.O. 1859–60. Went to NY 1871 and played increasingly important role in US mus. life. Co-founder and first cond. NY Oratorio Soc. (1873) and NY Sym. Soc. (1878). Organized and cond. Ger. opera season at NY Met. 1884–5 which incl. f. complete US p. of *Die Walküre*.

Damrosch, Walter (Johannes) (*b* Breslau, 1862; *d* NY, 1950). Ger.-born Amer. cond. and composer, younger son of Leopold *Damrosch. Pupil of Bülow. Succeeded father, 1885, as cond. NY Oratorio Soc. and ass. cond. Ger. opera, NY Met. Cond. first concert perf. in USA of *Parsifal*, 1896. Formed opera co. 1895 which until its disbandment in 1900 toured USA performing mainly Wagner's operas, with singers who incl. Sucher, Gadski, Klafsky, Melba, Alvary, and Bispham. Returned to Met. 1900–3. In 1903 reorganized NY Sym. Soc. as permanent orch., remaining cond. until merger with NY P.O. in 1928. Introduced many 20th-cent. works to USA and cond. f. ps. in USA of Bruckner's 3rd and Mahler's 4th syms. Comp. 4 operas, incl. *The Scarlet Letter* (1896) and *Cyrano de Bergerac* (1913), choral works incl. *The Canterbury Pilgrims*, and *Dunkirk*, for bar., male ch., and orch. (1943).

Danby, John (*b* London, *c*.1757; *d* London, 1798). Eng. organist of Sp. Embassy chapel, London; comp. many fine glees, e.g. *Awake, Aeolian Lyre*. Won 8 prizes from *Catch Club.

Danby, Nicholas (Charles) (*b* London, 1935). Eng. org. Studied RCM. Org. prof. GSM and RCM. Organist Jesuit Church, Farm Street, London, since 1967.

Dance. In every age and among every race dancing has existed either as recreation or as a religious manifestation or as both.
In Europe all countries have their traditional ('folk') dances. Those of England are numerous, falling into three classes—for men alone the Sword Dance and the Morris Dances and for men and women together the Country Dances.
There has always been a tendency for some peasant dances to pass into wider use, their steps and music then becoming sophisticated. Some typical examples are *Allemande, Bergomask, Bourrée, Branle, Canaries, Chaconne and Passacaglia, Courante, Dump, Gavotte, Hay, Jig, Minuet, Passamezzo, Passepied, Pavan and Galliard, Rigaudon, Sarabande, Volta.* The rhythms and styles of some of the above, from the 16th cent. onwards, supplied conventional models for instrumental compositions (see *Suite*). The Dances later popular in social circles (some of them of rustic origin) were the *Minuet* and the Eng. *Country Dance* (17th cent.); *Cotillon* and *Écossaise* (18th cent.); *Waltz, Quadrille, Polka, Schottische, Mazurka, Barn Dance* (19th cent.); and some of these also were taken as models by instrumental composers.
In the 20th cent. the dance has become synonymous with ballet, but the pattern of previous centuries has continued and modern dances such as the foxtrot, quickstep, and rumba have influenced composers. Dance Companies such as those of Merce Cunningham and Martha Graham in the USA have been of significant importance. Dance has also been harnessed to the electronic experiments of the *avant-garde*. See *Ballet*.

Dance before the Golden Calf. Climax (mainly orch.) of Act 2 of Schoenberg's opera *Moses und Aron*.

Dance of Death. See (1) *Danse macabre*; (2) *Totentanz*.

Dance of the Blessed Spirits. A slow dance episode in Act 2 of Gluck's *Orfeo ed Euridice*, characterized by a beautiful fl. solo.

Dance of the Comedians. Dance episode in Act 3 of Smetana's The *Bartered Bride* featuring the clowns and tumblers of the travelling circus.

Dance of the Hours. Episode, frequently played as separate orch. piece, in Act 3 of Ponchielli's *La gioconda*. It is an entertainment staged by one of the characters for his guests and symbolizes the conflict between darkness and light.

Dance of the Seven Veils. Popular title for Salome's dance before Herod in Strauss's *Salome*. For orch. alone, and often perf. as concert item.

Dance of the Sylphs. Orch. episode, often played separately, in Berlioz's *La *Damnation de Faust* where it forms part of Faust's dream on the banks of the Elbe.

Dance of the Tumblers. Episode in Act 3 of Rimsky-Korsakov's The *Snow Maiden* in which acrobats dance for the Tsar Berendey.

Dance Rhapsody. Name given by Delius to 2 orch. works. No. 1, comp. 1908, was f.p. at Hereford Fest. 8 Sept. 1909, cond. composer. No. 2, comp. 1916, was f.p. London, 23 Oct. 1923, cond. Wood. Also title of orch. work by Bridge (1908).

Dances of Galánta. Orch. suite by *Kodály comp. 1933 for 80th anniv. of Budapest Phil. Soc. Based on gipsy tunes collected in Hung. market town of Galánta.

Dance Suite (*Táncszvit*). Orch. work by Bartók comp. 1923 to celebrate 50th anniv. of merging of Buda and Pest. F.p. Budapest 19 Nov. 1923, cond. Dohnányi. Also pf. version.

Dancla, Jean Baptiste Charles (*b* Bagnères-de-Bigorre, 1817; *d* Tunis, 1907). Fr. violinist, composer, and teacher. Prin. violinist, Société des Concerts du Conservatoire, Paris, 1841–63. Prof., Paris Cons. 1860–92. Wrote 4 syms., 6 vn. concs., 14 str. qts., and 3 books. Brother Arnaud (1819–62) was cellist.

Danco, Suzanne (*b* Brussels, 1911). Belg. sop. Studied Brussels Cons. Début Genoa 1941 as Fiordiligi. Sang Ellen Orford in Britten's *Peter Grimes* at first Milan perf. 1947 and Marie in *Wozzeck* at Naples 1949. Edinburgh Fest. 1948. CG 1951. Also exponent of Fr. songs and Ger. Lieder.

Dandelot, Georges (*b* Paris, 1895; *d* St Georges de Didon, 1975). Fr. composer. Studied Paris Cons. with Widor, Dukas, and Roussel. Teacher, École Normale de Musique, Paris, from 1919 and prof. at Paris Cons. 1942. Works incl. operas, ballets, oratorio *Pax* (1937), sym. (1941), pf. conc. (1934), *concerto romantique* for vn. and orch. (1944).

Dandrieu, Jean-François (*b* ?Paris, *c*.1682; *d* Paris, 1738). Fr. composer. Infant prodigy. Held several organists' posts. Members of royal chapel from 1721. Wrote many hpd. pieces in style of Couperin, one of which was famous battle piece, *Les caractères de la guerre*.

Danican. See *Philidor*.

Daniel. See *Danyell, John*.

Daniel, Ernö (*b* Budapest, 1918). Hung.-Amer. pianist and cond. Studied Liszt Acad., Budapest, later with Dohnányi (comp.) and Monteux and Szell (cond.). Eur. reputation as pianist in works of Liszt, Bartók, and Dohnányi. Went to USA 1949 (citizen 1954), cond. Santa Barbara S.O. 1960–7. Also teacher and writer.

Daniel-Lesur. See *Lesur, Daniel*.

Daniel, The Play of. See *Play of Daniel, The*.

Danks, Harry (*b* Dudley, 1912). Eng. violist, pupil of *Tertis. Prin. va. BBC S.O. 1946–78. Specialist on 16th- and 17th-cent. viols and viola d'amore.

Dankworth, John (Philip William) (*b* London, 1927). Eng. jazz musician and composer. Studied RAM 1944–6. Formed jazz orch. 1953. Comp. much film mus. and works combining jazz and symphonic musicians, e.g. *Improvisations*, with *Seiber 1959, str. qt. 1971, pf. conc. 1972. Frequent appearances as accompanist to wife, Cleo Laine. C.B.E. 1974.

Dannreuther, Edward (George) (*b* Strasbourg, 1844; *d* Hastings, 1905). Alsatian pianist and writer. At age 5 went to Cincinnati where mus. education began. Leipzig Cons. 1859–63 under Moscheles. Début as pianist in London 1863, then settled there. Ardent Wagner enthusiast; founded Wagner Soc. 1872, was host to Wagner on his visit to London 1877 to conduct several concerts. Wrote several books on Wagner and his theories. Promoted chamber concerts in his home 1874–93. Gave f. Eng. ps. of pf. concs. by Grieg, Liszt (A major), and Tchaikovsky (No. 1).

Danon, Oskar (*b* Sarajevo, 1913). Yugoslav cond. and composer. Studied Prague Cons. Cond. Sarajevo Opera and P.O. 1938–41. Dir. Belgrade Opera and P.O. 1945–59. Chicago 1962; Edinburgh Fest. 1962. Comp. choral works, ballet, symphonic scherzo, etc.

Danse macabre (Dance of Death). Symphonic poem by Saint-Saëns, Op. 40, comp. 1874 (pf. transcr. by Liszt 1877). Based on poem by Henri Cazalis in which Death the Fiddler summons skeletons from their graves at midnight to dance. Orig. conceived as a song, in which form it exists. See also *Totentanz*.

Dante Sonata. Pf. comp. by Liszt, No. 7 of the *seconde année* of the *Années de pèlerinage*, its full title being *Fantaisie, quasi Sonate: 'D'Après une lecture de Dante'*. First played by Liszt 1839, rev. 1849. Version by *Lambert for pf. and orch. 1940 as basis for ballet *Dante Sonata*.

Dante Symphony. Orch. work by Liszt (*Symphony to Dante's Divina Commedia*) comp. 1855–6 and f.p. 1857. In 2 movements, ending with Magnificat sung by women's ch. (of which there are 2 versions).

Dantons Tod (Danton's Death). Opera in 2 parts by *Einem, Op. 6, to lib. by *Blacher and composer, after Büchner's drama (1835). Comp. 1944–6. Prod. Salzburg 1947.

Danyel(l) (Daniel), **John** (*b* Wellow, Som., 1564; *d* *c*.1626). Eng. lutenist and member of Queen Elizabeth's Chapel Royal. B.Mus., Oxford, 1603. His fancies and galliards for lute show advanced use of chromaticism for his time. His 20 songs for lute, viol, and v. were pubd. 1606.

Danza (It.). *Dance.

Danza española (Sp.). Spanish dance (in some parts of S. America applied to a particular type, generally in simple duple rhythm).

Danzi, Franz (*b* Schwetzingen, 1763; *d* Karlsruhe, 1826). Ger. composer (pupil of Vogler) and cellist. Kapellmeister, Stuttgart 1807–12, Karlsruhe from 1812. Friend and patron of *Weber, putting several of his operas into production. One of first opera conductors to conduct from rostrum rather than from keyboard. Comp. 11 operas, incl. one on subject of *Turandot*, vc. concs., hn. conc., and several works for wind quintet.

Daphne. Opera (bucolic tragedy) in 1 act by R. Strauss to lib. by Gregor. Comp. 1936–7. Prod. Dresden 1938, Santa Fe 1964, Leeds (Opera North) 1987.

Daphnis et Chloé. Ballet (choreographic sym.) by Ravel in 3 scenes, choreog. Fokine, comp. 1909–12 to commission from *Diaghilev, prod. Paris 1912, London 1914. 2 concert suites arr. Ravel, No. 1, 1911, No. 2, 1913. Score incl. part for wordless ch.

Da Ponte, Lorenzo (Emanuela Conegliano) (*b* Ceneda, nr. Venice, 1749; *d* NY, 1838). It. poet and librettist for many composers but especially for Mozart's *Le nozze di Figaro*, *Don Giovanni*, and *Così fan tutte*. In Vienna was poet to the court opera but left in 1791. Worked in London 1792–1804 teaching It. and acting as poet to It. Opera. Went to NY 1805, working as tobacco dealer and grocer. Worked with Manuel García 1825 to institute It. opera season in USA and with Montressor on similar venture 1832–3. Teacher of It., Columbia Univ. 1826–37. Wrote entertaining memoirs (1823–7).

Daquin (d'Aquin), **Louis Claude** (*b* Paris, 1694; *d* Paris, 1772). Fr. organist and composer. Child prodigy. Organist, Fr. Chapel Royal, 1739. Comp. many hpd. works, best-known being *Le Coucou* (The *Cuckoo) (1735), and solo works for org., also church mus.

D'Arányi, Jelly. See *Arányi, Jelly d'*.

Dargason. Eng. folk-tune, used from the 16th cent. onwards for a country dance. Also used for the folk-song *It was a maid of my country*. *Holst, in his *Suite No. 2* for military band (1911), combines the Dargason with *Greensleeves* in the finale, later transposing the movt. for strings in his *St Paul's Suite* (1912–3).

Dargomyzhsky, Alexander (*b* Tula, 1813; *d* St Petersburg, 1869). Russ. composer and pianist. Studied mus. as youth but was civil servant until 1843, though he studied comp. seriously after meeting *Glinka in 1834. His first opera *Esmeralda* (based on Hugo) was completed 1840 but not prod. until 1847, when it failed. *Rusalka* (based on Pushkin) was prod. with success in 1856. He wrote several orch. works, incl. *Baba Yaga*, and in 1864–5 visited Fr., Eng., and Belgium. Inspired by the nationalist ideals of 'the Five', he began another Pushkin opera, *The *Stone Guest*, on the Don Juan legend, making use of declamatory 'mezzo-recitative'. This was left unscored and unfinished. *Cui completed 2 scenes and the opera was scored by Rimsky-Korsakov and prod. St Petersburg 1872. Also wrote nearly 100 songs.

Darke, Harold (Edwin) (*b* London, 1888; *d* Cambridge, 1976). Eng. organist, cond., and composer. Pupil at RCM of *Parratt and *Stanford. Organist of St Michael's, Cornhill, 1916–66, with wartime break as organist King's Coll.,

Cambridge, 1941–5. Organ prof. RCM 1919–69. D.Mus., Oxford. C.B.E. 1966. Founded St Michael's Singers to perform Bach cantatas, Byrd's Great Service and works by Parry, Vaughan Williams, etc. Comp. cantatas (*Ring Out, Ye Crystal Spheres*, *An Hymn of Heavenly Beauty*, etc.), org. works, songs, pf. pieces, and notable setting of carol *In the Bleak Midwinter*.

Darlow, Denys (*b* London, 1921). Eng. org., cond., and composer. Pupil of *Darke. Founder, 1951, and cond. Tilford Bach Fest. Comp. choral mus., song-cycle, anthems, and songs.

Darmstadt. City in W. Ger. with musical tradition dating from 17th cent. Operatic activity was especially vital under Grand Duke Ludwig I (1790–1830), when the court conductor was *Vogler. Later *Rinck was organist for 41 years. Among 20th cent. opera conds. at Darmstadt have been Weingartner, Balling, Böhm, E. Kleiber, and Szell. But the most significant development has been the city's association with *avant-garde* contemporary mus. The International Summer Courses for New Music were instituted in 1946 by Wolfgang Steinecke, who directed them until his death in 1961. The courses were held annually up to 1970, and now every two years. They cover composition and interpretation and incl. f.ps. of works. Lecturers have incl. Křenek, Fortner, Hába, Adorno, Leibowitz, Messiaen, Varèse, Kolisch, Berio, Babbitt, Cage, Henze, Kontarsky, Ligeti, Maderna, Nono, Pousseur, Stockhausen, and Xenakis.

Darnton, (Philip) **Christian** (*b* Leeds, 1905; *d* Hove, 1981). Eng. composer. Pupil of Corder, Dale, and H. Craxton, later of Charles Wood and Rootham at Cambridge 1923–6. Entered RCM 1927. Works incl. 3 syms., cantata *Jet Pilot*, pf. conc., opera *Fantasy Fair*, va. conc., film and th. mus.

Dart, (Robert) **Thurston** (*b* Kingston-upon-Thames, 1921; *d* London, 1971). Eng. organist, harpsichordist, and musicologist. Studied RCM 1938–9, London Univ. (B.A. in mathematics), and Cambridge. Prof. of mus. Cambridge Univ. 1962–4, London Univ. from 1964. Undertook research into early mus., publishing many articles on subject and conducting fine recordings. Influential teacher.

Dartington Summer School. Annual combination of coaching, festival, and holiday lasting four weeks each August at Dartington Hall, arts and education college near Totnes, Devon. Began in 1948 at Bryanston Sch., Dorset, moving to Dartington 1953. Dir. William *Glock 1948–79, Peter *Maxwell Davies 1979–84, Gavin Henderson from 1985. Leading composers and performers instruct and lecture students, who vary from the professional to the enthusiastic amateur.

Das (Ger.). The.

185   **DAVIES**

Daser, Ludwig (*b* Munich, *c.*1525; *d* Stuttgart, 1589). Ger. composer. Kapellmeister at Munich 1552–63 when replaced by *Lassus. Kapellmeister, Stuttgart 1572–89. Wrote *Passion á 4* (1578), motets, masses, hymns, etc.

Daughter of the Regiment, The (Donizetti). See *Fille du régiment, La*.

David. Opera in 5 acts and 12 scenes by *Milhaud to lib. by Lunel, commissioned by Koussevitzky Foundation to mark 3,000th anniv. of Jerusalem. Comp. 1952. Prod. Jerusalem, concert version, 1954, Milan, stage, 1955, Hollywood Bowl 1956.

David, Félicien (César) (*b* Cadenet, 1810; *d* St Germain-en-Laye, 1876). Fr. composer. Chorister in Aix Cath. and at 18 2nd cond. of th. there. Studied Paris Cons. 1830. In 1831 joined Saint-Simonist movement and travelled in Middle East, where he collected oriental melodies which later influenced his mus. Paris success with symphonic ode *Le Désert*, 1844, which in its exotic oriental tone-colours influenced Bizet, Gounod, and Delibes. His operas incl. *La Perle du Brésil* (1851), *Lalla Roukh* (1862), and *Le Saphir* (1865). Also wrote oratorios, chamber mus., 4 syms., pf. pieces, and songs.

David, Ferdinand (*b* Hamburg, 1810; *d* nr. Klosters, Switz., 1873). Ger. violinist and composer. Pupil of Spohr. Début at 15 with Leipzig Gewandhaus Orch. Leader of nobleman's private str. qt. in Estonia 1829–35. Appointed leader, Leipzig Gewandhaus Orch. 1836, prof. of vn. Leipzig Cons. 1843. Visited Eng. 1839 and 1841. Advised Mendelssohn on technicalities for his Vn. Conc. and was soloist at f.p. 1845. Taught Joachim and Wilhelmj.

Dávid, Gyula (*b* Budapest, 1913; *d* Budapest, 1977). Hung. composer. Studied with Kodály, and became professional cond. Taught at Budapest Acad. of Mus. Comps. incl. 4 syms. (1947, 1957, 1960, 1970), va. conc. (1950), *Sinfonietta* (1961), 4 wind quintets, str. qt., and incidental mus.

David, Johann Nepomuk (*b* Eferding, 1895; *d* Stuttgart, 1977). Austrian composer, organist and teacher. Studied Vienna 1920–3. Held many academic posts incl. dir. of Mozarteum, Salzburg, 1945–8, and prof. of comp., Stuttgart Hochschule für Musik 1948–63. Ed. works by J.S. Bach and Mozart. Own works influenced by Baroque composers until he turned to serialism in 1953. Many choral works and org. pieces, sonata for 3 vc., conc. for vn., vc., and orch., 8 syms., org. conc., 2 vn. concs., and 3 concs. for str.

Davidde Penitente (David the Penitent). Cantata (K469) by Mozart for 3 soloists, ch., and orch. Comp. 1785 with material from unfinished Mass in C minor (K427) (1782–3).

Davidoff, Karl (*b* Goldingen, 1838; *d* Moscow, 1889). Russ. cellist and composer. Prin. cellist Leipzig Gewandhaus Orch. 1859–62, St Peters-burg Opera orch. from 1862. Prof. of vc. St Petersburg Cons. from 1863, becoming dir. 1876–87. Comps. incl. 4 vc. concs.

Davidovsky, Mario (*b* Medanos, Buenos Aires, 1934). Argentinian composer who settled in NY, 1960. Associate dir. elec. mus. centre, Princeton, and Columbia Univ. 1964. Held later teaching posts in NY. Comps. incl. orch. works, chamber mus., and elec. works. His *Synchronism No. 6* (from Nos. 1 to 8) for pf. and elec. sound won *Pulitzer Prize 1971.

Davidsbündler (Ger.). Adherents of the League of David. The *Davidsbund* was an imaginary soc. of artists invented by Robert Schumann to fight the philistines of art in the pages of his magazine *Neue Zeitschrift für Musik*. Some members represented Schumann's friends under fanciful names, e.g. Wieck (Master Raro), Mendelssohn (Felix Meritis), Stephen Heller (Jeanquirit), Clara Schumann (Chiara, Chiarina, Zilia), and Schumann himself (Florestan and Eusebius, representing the two sides of his nature, fiery and gentle). Other names were taken from the writings of Jean Paul Richter. The *Davidsbündlertänze* (Dances of the Adherents of the League of David) are 18 'characteristic pieces' for pf. by Schumann, Op. 6, comp. 1837, rev. 1850.

Davie, Cedric Thorpe (*b* London, 1913; *d* Dalry, Kirkcudbrightshire, 1983). Scottish composer, organist, and pianist. Studied RAM, RCM with R.O. Morris and Vaughan Williams, and abroad with Kilpinen and E. Petri. Joined staff, Royal Scottish Acad. of Music, then Master of Mus., St Andrews Univ., 1945–73, Prof. of Mus., 1973–8. Comp. opera *Gammer Gurton's Needle*, sym., *Fantasy on Scottish Tunes*, str. qt., vc. sonatina, incidental mus. for *The Thrie Estaites*, films, and TV. O.B.E. 1955.

Davies, Ben (Benjamin Grey) (*b* Pontardawe, 1858; *d* Bath, 1943). Welsh ten. Studied RAM 1878–80. Début Birmingham 1881 in *The Bohemian Girl*. Sang with Carl Rosa and other opera cos. but after 1894 was chiefly to be heard in concerts and oratorio, particularly Handel Fests. at which he last sang in 1926.

Davies, David Ffrangçon. See *Ffrangçon-Davies, David*.

Davies, Dennis Russell (*b* Toledo, Ohio, 1944). Amer. conductor. Début as pianist Toledo 1961, then studied Juilliard Sch. Cond. début 1968 in NY. Cond. Berio's *Opera* in Santa Fe 1970. Mus. dir. St Paul Chamber Orch. 1973. Cond. *Der fliegende Holländer* Bayreuth 1978. Mus. dir. Württemberg State Opera, Stuttgart, 1978–87. Has cond. f.ps. of works by Cage, Carter, Feldman, Berio, etc., with NY chamber orch. Ensemble.

Davies, Fanny (*b* Guernsey, 1861; *d* London, 1934). Eng. pianist. Studied Leipzig Cons. 1882 and Frankfurt Cons. 1883–5 with Clara Schumann. Début London 1885, thereafter assoc. in chamber mus. with musicians such as Joachim, Casals, and Piatti. Had repertory of 30 concs. High Ger. reputation as interpreter of Brahms and Schumann. First to play Debussy preludes in Eng. Elgar's *Concert Allegro* was written for her.

Davies, Hugh (Seymour) (*b* Exmouth, 1943). Eng. composer. Studied Oxford Univ. with Rubbra. Ass. to Stockhausen 1964–6 and member of his elec. mus. studio. In 1967 became dir., elec. mus. workshop, London Univ. Comps. are mainly elec., e.g. Quintet (1967–8) for 5 performers, 5 microphones, sine/square wave generator, 4-channel switching unit, potentiometers, 6 loudspeakers.

Davies, (Albert) **Meredith** (*b* Birkenhead, 1922). Eng. cond. and organist. Studied RCM and Acad. of St Cecilia, Rome. Cond. Bach Choir 1947, organist and master of choristers St Albans Cath. 1947–9, organist, Hereford Cath. 1949–56, assoc. cond. CBSO 1957–60, mus. dir. EOG 1962–4, cond. Vancouver S.O. 1964–71, BBC Training Orch. 1969–72. Shared, with composer, conducting of f.p. of Britten's *War Requiem* (Coventry, 1962). Guest cond. leading Brit. orchs., also at CG, SW, Aldeburgh, and other fests. Prin., TCL from 1979. C.B.E. 1982.

Davies, Peter Maxwell. See *Maxwell Davies, Peter.*

Davies, Ryland (*b* Cwm, Ebbw Vale, 1943). Welsh ten. Studied RMCM under F.R. Cox. Ricordi opera prize; Glyndebourne Christie Scholarship 1965. Début WNO 1964 as Almaviva, Glyndebourne 1965 (Major Domo in *Der Rosenkavalier*), Scottish Opera 1966, CG since 1969, Salzburg 1970, San Francisco 1970, NY Met. 1975.

Davies, Tudor (*b* Cymmer, S. Wales, 1892; *d* Penault, Mon., 1958). Welsh ten. Trained RCM. CG début as Rodolfo in *La Bohème* with BNOC 1921. First professional singer of title-role in Vaughan Williams's *Hugh the Drover*. Prin. ten. Old Vic and SW, 1931–41, Carl Rosa 1941–6. Also sang at Paris Opéra and in USA.

Davies, (Sir) (Henry) **Walford** (*b* Oswestry, 1869; *d* Wrington, 1941). Welsh composer and organist. Org. pupil of Parratt. Studied RCM with Parry and Stanford. Taught counterpoint RCM 1895–1903. Organist, Temple Church, London, 1898–1918. Cond. Bach Choir 1903–7. Mus. dir. RAF 1917 (comp. its march). Prof. of mus. Univ. of Wales 1919–26. Organist St George's Chapel, Windsor, 1927. Master of the King's Musick 1934–41. One of first popular broadcasters on mus. Apart from RAF march, best-known comps. are *Solemn Melody* for org. and str. (1908) and hymn *God be in my head*. Knighted 1922. Comps. incl. cantatas *The Temple* (1902) and *Everyman* (1904), Sym. (1911), church mus., and songs.

Davis, Andrew (*b* Ashridge, 1944). Eng. cond., organist, and harpsichordist. Educated King's Coll., Cambridge (org. scholar) and Acad. of St Cecilia, Rome. Studied cond. with Franco Ferrara. Assoc. cond. BBC Scottish S.O. 1970–2, assoc. cond. New Philharmonia Orch. 1974, prin. cond. and mus. dir. Toronto S.O. from 1975, prin. guest cond. Royal Liverpool P.O. 1974–6. Has cond. opera at Glyndebourne incl. Strauss's *Intermezzo, Capriccio,* and *Die schweigsame Frau.*

Davis, (Sir) **Colin** (Rex) (*b* Weybridge, 1927). Eng. cond. Studied RCM (cl.). Early cond. engagements with Chelsea Opera Group. Assoc. cond. BBC Scottish S.O. 1957–9; CG début with Royal Ballet 1960, with opera co. 1965 (*Le Nozze di Figaro*). Cond. SW Opera 1958–65 (mus. dir. from 1961); cond. BBC S.O. 1967–71; chief cond. and mus. dir. Royal Opera, CG, 1971–86; cond. Bavarian Radio S.O. from 1984. Début Glyndebourne 1960 (*Die Zauberflöte*). Guest cond. Minneapolis S.O. 1960 and other Amer. orchs., particularly Boston S.O. Début NY Met. 1967 (*Peter Grimes*). Notable exponent of Berlioz, Mozart, Stravinsky, Tippett, and Sibelius. Cond. f.p. of Tippett's *The Knot Garden* (CG 1970). First Briton to cond. at Bayreuth Fest. (1977, *Tannhäuser*). C.B.E. 1965. Knighted 1980. Hamburg Shakespeare Prize 1984.

Davis, Miles (Dewey) (*b* Alton, Ill., 1926). Amer. jazz trumpeter and flügel horn player. Began playing at 13. Went to NY, playing with Charlie Parker and Billy Eckstine. After success at Newport Jazz Fest. 1955 formed own quintet which lasted until 1957. In 1960s and 1970s led series of small groups. Noted for restraint and lyricism of his playing and for his consistently progressive approach.

Davison, James William (*b* London, 1813; *d* Margate, 1885). Eng. mus. critic on *The Times* 1846–79. Friend of Mendelssohn and antipathetic to Wagner. Husband of pianist Arabella *Goddard.

Davy, John (*b* Upton-Hellions, Exeter, 1763; *d* London, 1824). Eng. composer and violinist. Articled to William Jackson, org. of Exeter Cath.; then went to London where became prominent as composer of light th. mus. Some of his songs, e.g. *The Bay of Biscay*, have survived. Violinist at CG.

Davy, Richard (*b* c.1467; *d* c.1507). Eng. composer of motets, part-songs, and fine setting of *St Matthew Passion*—probably written and perf. after his appointment in 1491 as choirmaster of Magdalen College, Oxford.

Dawson, Peter (*b* Adelaide, 1882; *d* Sydney, N.S.W., 1961). Australian bass-bar. Studied in London 1902 with *Santley. Début CG 1909 but became better known for singing of popular ballads, e.g. Kipling's *The Road to Mandalay* and *Boots*, which he comp. under pseudonym J. P.

McCall. These overshadowed his excellent ability in operatic arias and Lieder, always sung in Eng. and preserved by recordings. Began recording 1904; sold 13 million records.

Dazu (Ger.). Thereto, i.e. (in org. playing) the stops mentioned are now to be added to the others.

D.C. Abbreviation for *Da Capo.

Dead March in Saul. Popular name for the funeral march from Handel's oratorio *Saul* (1739) which is used on state occasions such as the funeral of a sovereign. See also *Funeral Marches.*

Dean Paul, Lady. See *Poldowski.*

Dean, Stafford (Roderick) (b Kingswood, Surrey, 1937). Eng. bass. Studied RCM. Opera début, SW 1964. Prin. bass SW Opera Co. 1964–70. CG début 1969. Many appearances at Glyndebourne, Munich, WNO, Scottish Opera etc.

Dean, Winton (Basil) (b Birkenhead, 1916). Eng. mus. scholar and writer. Educated King's Coll., Cambridge. Authority and author of books on Bizet, Handel, and other composers. His *Handel's Dramatic Oratorios and Masques* (1959) is a major work of scholarship.

Dearnley, Christopher (Hugh) (b Wolverhampton, 1930). Eng. organist. Studied Oxford Univ. 1948–52 with Rubbra and H. K. Andrews. Ass. org. Salisbury Cath. 1954, org. from 1957. Org., St Paul's Cath. from 1968. Authority on church mus. of late 17th and early 18th cents.

Deas, (James) **Stewart** (b Edinburgh, 1903; d 1985). Scottish teacher, writer, cond., and organist. Studied Edinburgh Univ. and with Tovey; in Berlin, 1926–8, and in Basle with Weingartner. Cond. Edinburgh Opera Co. 1931–3. Dir. of mus., S. African Coll. of Mus. and prof. of mus. Capetown Univ. 1936–8. Prof. of mus., Sheffield Univ. 1948–69. Founded Sheffield Bach Soc. 1950. Mus. critic at various times for *Glasgow Evening Times, The Scotsman* and *Country Life.* Wrote book *In Defence of Hanslick.*

Death and the Maiden. (Der Tod und das Mädchen). Song (D531) comp. by Schubert in Feb. 1817, a setting of poem by Matthias Claudius (1740–1815). The theme of the pf. introduction to the song was used again by Schubert in 1824 in his Str. Qt. No.14 in D minor (D810) where it is the theme for the 2nd movement set of variations.

Death and Transfiguration (Strauss). See *Tod und Verklärung.*

Death in Venice. Opera in 2 acts by Britten, Op. 88, to lib. by Myfanwy Piper based on Thomas Mann's novella, *Der Tod in Venedig* (1912). F.p. Aldeburgh 16 June 1973, CG 18 Oct. 1973. NY Met. 1974. Orch. suite arr. S. *Bedford, Aldeburgh 1984.

Debain, Alexandre François (b Paris, 1809; d Paris, 1877). Fr. manufacturer of kbd. instr. Est. factory 1834. Invented *harmonium (c.1842), antiphonal (1846), and harmonicorde (1851).

De Bériot. See *Bériot, Charles August de.*

Deborah. Oratorio by Handel to lib. by S. Humphreys, after *Judges* V. Mus. taken partly from earlier works. F.p. London 1733.

De Burgos, Rafael Frühbeck. See *Frühbeck de Burgos, Rafael.*

Debussy, Achille-Claude (b St Germain-en-Laye, 1862; d Paris, 1918). Fr. composer and critic. As a child he had little formal education but his mus. tendencies were channelled into pf. lessons, those with Verlaine's mother-in-law, Mme Mauté de Fleurville, leading to his entry into the Paris Cons. in 1872. His reputation there was that of an erratic pianist and a recalcitrant in matters of harmony and theory. In 1880 and 1881 he went for summer employment to Russia as pianist to Tchaikovsky's patron, Mme von Meck. Failing to win the *Prix de Rome* in 1883, he succeeded in 1884 with the cantata *L'Enfant prodigue.* He spent 2 years at the Villa Medici, Rome, where he met Liszt, Verdi, and Boito, and heard *Lohengrin.* He went to the Bayreuth fests. of 1888 and 1889, but an even greater mus. influence was that of hearing the Javanese *gamelan at the 1889 Paris Exposition. Other influences of these years were his friendship with the painters of what became known as the 'Impressionist' movement and, even more important, with writers and poets such as Mallarmé and the 'symbolists'. But after 1889 he could not share the symbolists' idolatry of Wagner, recognising his greatness but also the fact that he represented a 'dead end' for other composers. He cultivated a distinctively Fr. mus. outlook, eventually styling himself 'musicien français'. Other significant events in his life were his study in 1889 of the score of *Boris Godunov and his acquaintance from 1891 with Erik *Satie.

In 1893 Debussy began work on an opera based on Maeterlinck's play *Pelléas et Mélisande,* a task that was to occupy him for nearly 10 years. In 1893 his str. qt. was perf., and in 1894 his orch. *Prélude à l'après-midi d'un Faune* caused a scandal because of its alleged 'formlessness'. He followed this with his 3 *Nocturnes,* orig. planned for solo vn. and orch., perf. 1900 and 1901. They are ded. to Rosalie (Lily) Texier, whom he married in 1899 but deserted 5 years later for Mme Emma Bardac, a singer and wife of a banker, whom he married in 1908. Their child was born in 1905, the year in which the symphonic sketches *La Mer* were f.p. *Pelléas* had been successfully prod. at the Opéra-Comique in 1902, to the fury of Maeterlinck who publicly wished it 'emphatic failure'. Debussy's remaining orch. works were the set of 3 *Images* comp. between 1905 and 1912, and the ballet *Jeux* for Diaghilev (1913). In 1910 he developed cancer and was a semi-invalid when war broke out in 1914. He wrote some mus.

inspired by patriotic sentiments and completed 3 sonatas before his death.

Debussy was among the greatest and most important of 20th-cent. composers both by reason of his own achievement and by the paths he opened for others to explore, hence the homage to him paid by later composers such as Boulez, Messiaen, Webern, Bartók, Stravinsky, and many others. His use of block chords, of harmony with a modal flavour and based on the whole-tone scale, the delicate colours of his orchestration, his technique of 'layering' sounds, the declamatory yet wholly lyrical style of his vocal writing, especially in *Pelléas*, all proclaim him an innovator of the first degree who revolutionized comp. for the pf. and for the orch. In general Debussy's effects are understated, his aim being for a 'sonorous halo' of sound. But the label of 'impressionist', while accurate, has tended to obscure the strong sense of form which underlies all his works. Prin. comps.:

STAGE: *Pelléas et Mélisande* (opera, 1893–5, 1901–2); *Jeux* (ballet, 1912–13); *Khamma* (ballet, 1911–12, orch. *Koechlin, 1912–13); *La *boîte à joujoux* (children's ballet, 1913, orch. Caplet); incidental mus. to *King Lear* (1904); incidental mus. for *Le *Martyre de Saint Sébastien* by D'Annunzio (1911); *La *Chute de la Maison Usher* (1908–17, unfin. opera).

ORCH.: *Printemps* (1887); *Prélude à L'*Après-midi d'un faune* (1892–4); 3 *Nocturnes* (1897–9); *La *Mer* (1903–5); 3 *Images* (1905–12); *Fantaisie* for pf. and orch. (1889); *Rapsodie* for sax. and orch. (1901–8); *Danse sacrée et danse profane* for harp and str. (1904); *Berceuse héroïque* (1914, also for pf.).

PIANO: 2 *Arabesques* (1888–91); *Suite bergamasque* (1890, rev. 1905); *Pour le Piano* (1896–1901); *Estampes* (1903); *L'*Ile joyeuse* (1904); *Images* I (1905), *Images* II (1907); *Children's Corner* (1906–08); 12 *Préludes*, Book I (1910), Book II (1912–13); 12 *Études* (Books I and II, 1915).

PIANO DUET: *Petite Suite* (1886–9); *Marche écossaise* (1891) (orch. version by Debussy); 6 *Épigraphes antiques* (1914).

TWO PIANOS: *Lindaraja* (1901); *En blanc et noir* (1915).

CHAMBER MUSIC: Str. Qt. (1893); *Première rapsodie* for cl. and pf. (1901–8); *Syrinx* for fl. (1913); Vc. sonata (1915); Sonata for fl., va., and harp (1915); vn. sonata (1916–17).

SONGS: *Mandoline* (1880–3); *Cinq poèmes de Baude-laire* (1887–9); *Ariettes oubliées* (1888); *Fêtes galantes* I (1882, rev. 1891–2) and II (1904); *Proses lyriques* (1892–3); *Chansons de Bilitis* (1897–8); *Trois ballades de Villon* (1910) (also with orch. acc.); *Trois ballades de Mallarmé* (1913).

CHORAL: *L'*Enfant prodigue*, cantata for sop., ten., bar., ch., orch. (1884, rev. 1906–8); *La Damoiselle élue* (*The *Blessed Damozel*) cantata for sop., women's ch., and orch. (1887–8, re-orch. 1902);

3 *Chansons de Charles d'Orléans* for unacc. SATB (1898–1908).

ARRANGEMENTS: Orch. of 2 of Satie's *Gymnopédies* 1896; pf. transcrs. of Wagner, Schumann, Gluck, Raff, Saint-Saëns, and Tchaikovsky.

Début (Fr.). Beginning. First public appearance.

Decani (Lat.). Of the dean, i.e. that side of the choir of a cath., etc., on which the Dean sits, now normally the south side. In church mus., passages marked *decani* must be taken by the singers on that side. See also *cantoris*.

Deceptive cadence. Same as Interrupted cadence, i.e. chord of the dominant followed by that of submediant.

Decibel. Logarithmic unit which expresses difference between different intensities of sound-levels or differently-powered electric signals.

Décidé (Fr.), **deciso** (It.). Decided. With decision (i.e. firmly, not flabbily). So the It. superlative, *decisissimo*.

Decimette. A comp. for 10 performers.

Decoration Day. 2nd movement of Ives's *New England Holidays* for orch., sometimes played separately. Comp. 1912.

Decrescendo; decresciuto (It.). Decreasing, decreased, i.e. getting gradually softer.

Decsényi, János (*b* Budapest, 1927). Hung. composer. Studied Budapest Cons. and Acad. On staff Hung. radio from 1951. Works incl. ballets, cantatas, and chamber mus.

Dedler, Rochus (*b* Oberammergau, 1779; *d* Vienna, 1882). Ger. composer of the Passion Play mus. used at Oberammergau.

Deering (Dering), **Richard** (*b* Kent, *c.* 1580; *d* London, 1630). Eng. composer and organist. Studied in It. Pubd. some of oldest known comps. with basso continuo (Antwerp 1597). Org., Eng. nuns' convent in Brussels 1617. Org. at court of Charles I 1625. Comps. incl. anthems, motets, mus. for viols, and choral pieces based on London street cries.

De Fabritiis, Oliviero (Carlo) (*b* Rome, 1902; *d* Rome, 1982). It. conductor and composer. Studied Rome Cons. Début Rome 1920. Worked in Salerno and Rome, then was art. secretary Rome Opera House 1932–43. In 1938 began summer perfs. at Baths of Caracalla. Cond. many opera perfs. in which Gigli sang. Brit. début Edinburgh Fest. 1963 (San Carlo co. in *Adriana Lecouvreur*). CG début 1965 (*Simon Boccanegra*). Comp. songs and other vocal mus.

Défauw, Désiré (*b* Ghent, 1885; *d* Gary, Ind., 1960). Amer. (Belg.-born) violinist and cond. London début 1910. Formed Allied Str. Qt. (which incl. L. *Tertis) 1914–18. Prof. at Antwerp Cons. Cond. Défauw concerts and Brussels Cons.

orch. (1926–40). Est. Orchestre nationale de Belgique 1937. Went to USA 1939. Cond., Chicago S.O. 1943–7. Returned to Belgium 1949 but then went back to USA as cond. Gary S.O. 1950–8.

De Fesch, William (*b* Alkmaar, 1687; *d* London, ?1757). Flemish composer, organist, cellist, and violinist. Choirmaster, Antwerp, 1725–31. Settled in London 1733. Wrote oratorios, masses, concs., and songs.

De Gaetani, Jan (*b* Massillon, Ohio, 1933). Amer. mez. Studied Juilliard Sch., making NY début 1958. Specialist in contemporary mus. Gave f.ps. of Crumb's *Ancient Voices of Children* (1970) and Maxwell Davies's *Stone Litany* (1973). Teacher at Eastman Sch., Rochester.

Degeyter. See *Internationale*.

Degree. A note's classification regarding its position in the scale. When a note is 3 degrees from another, the interval separating them is a 4th. The notes of the major scale are called the 1st, 2nd, etc. degrees of the scale, returning to the first degree. Alternative names for the 7 degrees are tonic, supertonic, mediant, subdominant, dominant, submediant, and leading-note.

De Greef, Arthur. See *Greef, Arthur de*.

Degrees and Diplomas in Music. (1) BRITISH UNIVERSITY DEGREES. The degrees in music given by Brit. and Irish universities are Bachelor ('B.Mus.' or 'Mus.B.') Master of Music (M.Mus.), and Doctor ('D.Mus.' or 'Mus.D'). Universities which confer a M.Mus. degree are Birmingham, Bristol, Cambridge, Durham, East Anglia, Edinburgh, London, Newcastle upon Tyne, and Surrey.

In several universities it is possible to obtain by research in musical subjects the degree of Litt.M., Litt.B., Litt.D., Ed.M., and Ph.D. (or M.Litt, B.Litt., D.Litt., M.Ed., and D.Phil.)—Bachelor and Doctor of Letters, and Doctor of Philosophy. At Reading, music may be studied with physics for B.Sc.

By an old custom dating from the 13th cent., the Archbishop of Canterbury (by virtue of his former office of Legate of the Pope) has the power to grant degrees, and he sometimes exercises this power by conferring the doctorate of music. These degrees are known as 'Canterbury Degrees' (D.Mus. Cantuar.) or (from the Archbishop's London palace, from which they are issued) 'Lambeth Degrees'.

Various universities in the Commonwealth confer musical degrees, their requirements being not so much standardized as those of British universities.

At some Brit. universities music can now be taken as one of the subjects for a degree in Arts. Through the Council for National Academic Awards, some polytechnics and colleges of technology award a B.A. degree for music.

(2) DIPLOMAS. The diploma-conferring bodies in the list now to be given are recognized as genuine public bodies. Their diplomas are usually graded as follows: (*a*) Associateship, (*b*) Licentiateship (not always present), (*c*) Fellowship. This is not quite invariable, however; for instance, the Royal Academy of Music confers Licentiateship upon external or internal candidates. Fellowship is reserved by some institutions as a purely honorary distinction.

ROYAL ACADEMY OF MUSIC (founded 1822). F.R.A.M. (limited to 150 distinguished past students); Hon. R.A.M. (honorary members); A.R.A.M.; L.R.A.M. (open to non-students and with the differentiation, 'teacher' or 'performer'); SPECIAL DIPLOMA of the Teachers' Training Course.

ROYAL COLLEGE OF MUSIC (founded 1883, succeeding the National Training Coll. of Music, founded 1873). F.R.C.M. (honorary, limited to 50); Hon. R.C.M. (distinguished non-students); Hon. A.R.C.M. (distinguished past students); A.R.C.M. by examination, open to non-students and with the differentiation, 'teacher' or 'performer'); M.Mus. R.C.M. ('Master of Music'— severe and varied tests; open to non-students); Teachers' Training Course certificate awarded to selected students from certain colleges for a 1-year course.

ASSOCIATED BOARD The R.A.M. and R.C.M. combine, under the title 'Royal Schools of Music, London' with also Royal Northern College and Royal Scottish Academy), to confer in the Commonwealth the diploma, formerly known as 'L.A.B.' (Licentiate of the Associated Board), now entitled 'L.R.S.M., London'. This is the Overseas equivalent of L.R.A.M. and A.R.C.M.

ROYAL COLLEGE OF ORGANISTS (founded 1864), A.R.C.O.; F.R.C.O., with an additional (optional) diploma entitling the candidate to add the letters Ch.M. (i.e. 'Choirmaster'). In 1936 the Archbishop of Canterbury instituted a Diploma in Church Music to the examination for which he admits only F.R.C.O.s holding the Ch.M. diploma, who on passing his examination become A.D.C.M.s.

TRINITY COLLEGE OF MUSIC (founded 1872 and a teaching school of music in Univ. of London). A.T.C.L.; L.T.C.L.; F.T.C.L. (these in executive subjects—as Teacher or Performer); A.Mus.T.C.L.; L.Mus.T.C.L. (these in theoretical subjects). G.T.C.L.; Hon. F.T.C.L. Hon. T.C.L. (F.T.C.L. awarded also for orig. composition.)

GUILDHALL SCHOOL OF MUSIC AND DRAMA (founded 1880). A.G.S.M. (internal students); L.G.S.M. (internal and external students); F.G.S.M. (honorary—limited to 100); G.G.S.M. (internal students); Hon. G.S.M. (honorary—limited to 100).

ROYAL MANCHESTER COLLEGE OF MUSIC (founded 1893). A.R.M.C.M. (after a 3 years' course and examination) and F.R.M.C.M. (honorary only) also Hon.R.M.C.M. This college was amalgamated in 1972 into Royal Northern College of Music.

ROYAL NORTHERN COLLEGE OF MUSIC, MANCHESTER (founded 1972, being amalgamation of R.M.C.M. and Northern School of Music). G.Mus.R.N.C.M.; G.R.N.C.M.; P.P.R.N.C.M. (Professional Performance Course).

BIRMINGHAM SCHOOL OF MUSIC (founded 1887). A.B.S.M.; A.B.S.M. (T.T.D.), Teacher's Training Diploma; L.B.S.M.; G.B.S.M. (after Graduate Course); F.B.S.M. (honorary).

ROYAL SCOTTISH ACADEMY OF MUSIC (founded 1929). Dip. R.S.A.M. and (in musical education) Dip.Mus.Ed. R.S.A.M. (both after a full course in the Academy and examination).

LONDON COLLEGE OF MUSIC. (Founded 1887). Diplomas include A.L.C.M., L.L.C.M., F.L.C.M., G.L.C.M. A.Mus.L.C.M., L.Mus.L.C.M.

ROYAL MILITARY SCHOOL OF MUSIC (Kneller Hall). Graduation is indicated by the letters p.s.m., meaning 'passed school of music'.

BANDSMAN'S COLLEGE OF MUSIC. This examining body was instituted in 1931 with unpaid officials and described as 'The National Institutions of the Brass Band Movement'. It awards, after examination, 3 diplomas, B.B.C.M. ('Bandmaster'), A.B.C.M., and L.B.C.M.

OVERSEAS SCHOOLS OF MUSIC. Some of the universities in different parts of the Commonwealth, having schools of music attached, grant a diploma. The Royal Canadian College of Organists grants diplomas of A.R.C.C.O. and F.R.C.C.O.

(3) AMERICAN DEGREES. The number of universities, colleges, schools of music, etc., conferring music degrees is well over 700, of which over half are at bachelor level only. The oldest undergraduate degrees are B.A. and B.Mus. Many music courses are for 4 years, most of them involving practical work such as conducting. Degrees in theory, musicology, and performance in some universities are Master of Music (M.M.) and Master of Music Education (M.M.E.). There are also D.M.A. (Doctor of Musical Arts) and M.M.A.

(4) AMERICAN DIPLOMAS. The U.S.A., fortunately, does not possess the bewildering variety of diploma-conferring institutions of Britain, nor are alphabetical distinctions of any kind so much valued. The Amer. Guild of Organists (1896) confers diplomas of Associateship and Fellowship—A.A.G.O. and F.A.G.O.: when the examination as choirmaster is passed the letters Ch.M. may be added.

Degrigny, Nicolas. See *Grigny, Nicolas de*.

Dehors (Fr.). (1) Outside, as in *en dehors*, from the outside.

(2) Prominent. Applied musically to a melody which the composer intends to be particularly prominent.

Deidamia. Opera in 3 acts by Handel (his last), to lib. by Rolli. Comp. 1740, prod. London 1741. Revived London 1955 and subsequently in Ger.

Deirdre of the Sorrows. (1) Opera by Karl *Rankl, based on Synge's play, which won Fest. of Britain prize, 1951, but was not prod.

(2) Lyric drama in 1 act by John J. Becker (1945).

Dekany, Béla (*b* Budapest, 1928). Hung.-born violinist. Studied Franz Liszt Acad. of Mus., Budapest, and Vienna Acad. of Mus. Début Budapest 1947. Formed Dekany Qt. in Holland 1960. Leader, BBC S.O. from 1969.

De Koven, Henry Louis Reginald (*b* Middletown, Conn., 1859; *d* Chicago, 1920). Amer. composer and cond. Family moved to Eng. in 1872 and he studied at Oxford, Stuttgart, Vienna, and Paris (with Delibes). Returned to USA where he became successful composer of light operas, mus. critic, and founder and cond. of Washington P.O. (1902–5). Wrote 2 operas, *The Canterbury Pilgrims* (NY Met. 1917) and *Rip Van Winkle* (Chicago and NY 1920). Operettas incl. *Don Quixote* (1889) and *Robin Hood* (1890). Comp. over 400 songs, pf. sonata, and ballets.

Delage, (Charles) **Maurice** (*b* Paris, 1879; *d* Paris, 1961). Fr. composer, pupil of Ravel. Student of Indian mus. and wrote *Quatre poèmes hindous* for v. and orch. Orch. version of *Debussy's *Chansons de Bilitis* 1926.

Delalande, Michel Richard. See *Lalande, Michel de*.

Delannoy, Marcel François Georges (*b* La Ferté-Alain, 1898; *d* Nantes, 1962). Fr. composer. Trained as architect, self-taught in mus. but helped and advised by *Honegger. Comp. operas, ballet, ballet-cantatas, 2 syms., str. qt., pf. conc.

de Lara, Isidore. See *Lara, Isidore de*.

Delibes, (Clément Philibert) **Léo** (*b* St Germain-du-Val, nr. Le Mans, 1836; *d* Paris, 1891). Fr. composer and organist. Studied at Paris Cons. 1848–52. Became accompanist at Théâtre Lyrique, 1853. First operetta, *Deux Sous de Charbon*, 1855, led to series of popular short works in this genre. 2nd chorusmaster at Opéra 1865. Wrote ballets *Coppélia* (1870) and *Sylvia* (1876), and 3 works for the Opéra Comique, *Le Roi l'a dit* (1873), *Jean de Nivelle* (1880), and *Lakmé* (1883). A 4-act opera, *Kassya*, was left unfinished, completed by Massenet and staged 1893. Wrote incidental mus. for *Le Roi s'amuse* (1882) and 15 songs, best-known being *Les Filles de Cadiz*. Org., St Jean-St François, 1862–71. Prof. of comp., Paris Cons. 1881. Name frequently misspelt 'Délibes'.

Delicato (It.). Delicate. So *delicatamente* delicately; *delicatissimo*, as delicately as possible; *delicatezza*, delicacy.

Délié (Fr.). Untied. (1) The notes separated from each other, i.e. staccato.

(2) Unconstrained in style.

(3) Supple (fingers).

Delirio (It.). Frenzy. So *delirante*, frenzied.

Delius, Fritz later **Frederick** (Theodor Albert) (*b* Bradford, Yorks., 1862; *d* Grez-sur-Loing, Fr., 1934). Eng. composer, 4th of 14 children of a Ger. couple who had settled in Eng. to engage in the wool trade. The father, Julius Delius, was a mus. lover, helping to organize Hallé concerts in Bradford and entertaining musicians like Joachim and Piatti in his home, but implacably opposed to mus. as a career for his son, despite Fritz's talent and aptitude. The youth tried to accede to his father's wishes by entering business, but he had no gift for textile commerce and in 1884 went to Florida to manage an orange-plantation at Solano Grove. The oranges were neglected while Delius studied mus. with Thomas F. Ward, a Jacksonville organist. A year later he himself set up as a vn. teacher first in Jacksonville, then at Danville, Virginia, eventually taking an organist's post in NY. The Negro melodies he heard in Florida deeply influenced him, as can be heard in *Appalachia*. By now his father was prepared to allow him to enter the Leipzig Cons. (1888). Academic tuition held no attractions, however, and Delius went to live in the Paris of the 90s where his circle incl. Gauguin, Ravel, Munch, and Strindberg. Already, on a holiday in Norway in 1887, he had become a close friend of *Grieg and deeply attached to Scandinavian life and literature.

His *Florida* suite was perf. privately in Leipzig, 1888. While in Paris he comp. an opera, *The Magic Fountain* (1894–5, f.p. BBC studio broadcast 1977), songs, the first Vn. Sonata, the tone-poem *Over the Hills and Far Away* (begun *c*.1893), and another opera, *Koanga* (1896–7). In 1899 a concert of his works was given in London which encouraged him to complete his orch. nocturne *Paris: the Song of a Great City*. This was perf. at Elberfeld, 1901, cond. by Hans *Haym and a year later in Berlin under Busoni. Haym also cond. f.p. of the Pf. Conc., in Elberfeld 1904, with Julius Buths as soloist. Haym, together with Fritz *Cassirer, was Delius's earliest champion, being followed some years later in England by Wood and, in particular, *Beecham. Until about 1904 Delius pubd. his works under the name Fritz Delius.

From 1897, Delius lived at Grez-sur-Loing, near Fontainebleau with the artist Jelka Rosen, whom he married in 1903. From 1900 to 1902 he worked on 2 operas, *A Village Romeo and Juliet*, and *Margot-la-Rouge*, and revised *Appalachia* (begun *c*.1896). His reputation in Ger. was greater at this time than in his native land but the balance was corrected from 1907 with f.ps. in England of a series of works: 1907: Pf. Conc. (London, soloist, Szanto, cond. Wood); 1908: *Paris* (Liverpool, cond. Beecham), *Life's Dance* (first version) (London, cond. Arbós), *Brigg Fair* (Liverpool, cond. Bantock), *Sea Drift* (Sheffield, cond. Wood); 1909: *A Mass of Life* (London, cond. Beecham), *In a*

Summer Garden (first version) (London, cond. Delius), *Dance Rhapsody No. 1* (Hereford, cond. Delius).

In 1908–10 he comp. his last opera *Fennimore and Gerda*, prod. Frankfurt 1919. During the 1914–18 war he left Grez for Eng. for a time, composing *Dance Rhapsody No. 2*, vn. sonata, vc. sonata, conc. for vn. and vc., str. qt., vn. conc., *Eventyr*, and a *Requiem* (text by H. Simon) 'dedicated to the memory of all young artists fallen in the war'. This last work was perf. in 1922 and was so savagely criticized for its 'atheism' that it remained unperf. again for over 40 years. Shortly after the war he wrote a vc. conc. and the incidental mus. to Flecker's play *Hassan* (1923). In 1922 Delius developed the first signs of progressive paralysis, said to have resulted from syphilis contracted in Paris in 1890s, although medical research has cast doubt on this theory. Four years later he became blind and helpless. From 1928 he was enabled to continue composing through the assistance of a young Yorkshire musician, Eric *Fenby, who offered his services as amanuensis. Among the works comp. in this period were *A Song of Summer*, the 3rd vn. sonata, *Songs of Farewell*, *Fantastic Dance*, and an *Idyll* based on material from *Margot-la-Rouge*. In 1929 Delius was made a C.H. and went to London to attend a fest. of 6 concerts of his mus. organized by Beecham. He died 5 years later, being buried at Grez, but in May 1935 was reinterred at Limpsfield, Surrey.

Delius's mus. is chromatic in harmony and belongs in form and spirit to the post-Wagnerian world of Chausson, Debussy, Strauss, and Mahler. He is *par excellence* the composer-poet of regret for time past, of the transience of human love, but there is also a vigorous ecstatic elation in sections of *A Mass of Life* and the *Song of the High Hills*. Though he despised the classical procedures, his sonatas and concs. succeed because of the way in which he adapted his rhapsodic manner to suit his own version of sonata form. The exquisite orch. scoring of such short works as *On hearing the first cuckoo in spring* and the intermezzo, *Walk to the Paradise Garden*, from *A Village Romeo and Juliet*, have ensured him a regular place in the Eng. repertory, and his songs and unacc. choral works are also very fine.

Prin. works:

OPERAS: **Irmelin* (1890–2); The **Magic Fountain* (1894–5, rev. 1898); **Koanga* (1896–7, rev. 1898); A **Village Romeo and Juliet* (1900–1); **Margot-la-Rouge* (1901–2); **Fennimore and Gerda* (1908–10).
ORCH: *Florida Suite* (1886–7, rev. 1889); *Sleigh Ride*; *Marche Caprice* (1888; *Sleigh Ride* orch. 1889, *Marche Caprice* rev. 1890); *Summer Evening* (1890); *Paa Vidderne* (On the Mountains), sym.-poem (1890–1, rev. 1892); *Over the Hills and Far Away* (?1893–?7); *La *Calinda* (from *Koanga*, 1896–7, arr. Fenby 1938); **Life's Dance* (1899,

rev. 1901 and 1912); *Paris: the Song of a Great City* (1899); *Appalachia* (with ch. and bar.) (1896; 1902–3); *Intermezzo: *Walk to the Paradise Garden* (1906, addition to *A Village Romeo and Juliet*); *Brigg Fair: an English Rhapsody* (1907); *In a Summer Garden* (1908, rev. 1913); *Dance Rhapsody* No. 1 (1908), No. 2 (1916); 2 *Mood Pictures for small orch.*: *On hearing the first cuckoo in spring* (1911–13), *Summer Night on the River* (1911); *North Country Sketches* (1913–14); *Air and Dance*, str. (1915); *Eventyr* (1917); 2 *Aquarelles* (arr. for str. by Fenby, 1938, from 2 unacc. ch. 1917); *A Song before Sunrise* (1918); *A Song of Summer* (1930); *Fantastic Dance* (1931); *Prelude to Irmelin* (1931).

VOICES AND ORCH.: *Maud* (Tennyson), song cycle for v. and orch. (1891), *Appalachia* (1896; 1902–3), *Zarathustra's Night Song*, bar., male ch., orch. (1898), *Sea Drift* for bar., ch., and orch. (1903–4), *A *Mass of Life* for SATB soloists, double ch., and orch. (1904–5), *Cynara* for bar. and orch. (1907, rev. 1928–9), *Songs of Sunset* for mez., bar., ch., and orch. (1906–8), *Song of the High Hills* for ch. and orch. (1911), *Arabesk* for bar., ch., and orch. (1911), *Requiem* for sop., bar., ch., and orch. (1914–16), *A Late Lark* (Henley) for v. and orch. (1921–5), *Songs of Farewell* for double ch. and orch. (1930), *Idyll: Once I passed through a populous city* for sop., bar., and orch. (1930–2).

INCIDENTAL MUSIC: *Folkeraadet* (Parliament), play by G. Heiberg (1897); *Hassan*, play by James Elroy Flecker (1920–3).

MELODRAMA: *Paa Vidderne*, speaker and orch. (poem by Ibsen, 1859–60, set to Ger. trans., *Auf dem Hochgebirge*, by L. Passarge). Comp. 1888.

VOICE(S) AND PIANO: 5 *Songs from the Norwegian* (1888), 7 *Songs from the Norwegian* (1889–90, No. 3 with Eng. words, 1930, known as *Twilight Fancies*), 3 *English Songs* (Shelley) (1891), 2 *Songs* (Verlaine) (1895), 7 *Danish Songs* (1897), 5 *Songs* (4 to poems by Nietzsche) (1898), 2 *Songs* (1900), *Summer Landscape* (1902), *The nightingale has a lyre of gold* (Henley) (1910), *I-Brasil* (1913), *On Craig Dhu* (1907), *Midsummer Song* (1908), *Wanderer's Song* (1908), *To be sung of a summer night on the water* (unacc.) (1917, arr. for str. by Fenby as 2 *Aquarelles*, 1938), *The Splendour Falls* (unacc.) (1923).

CONCERTOS: Pf. (first version in 3 movements 1897, rev. 1898; rev. in 1 movement 1906–7), Vn. and vc. (1915, f.p. 1920, arr. for vn. and va. by Tertis 1934–5), Vn. (1916, f.p. 1919 Sammons, Boult), Vc. (1921, f.p. 1923 Frankfurt), *Caprice and Elegy* for vc. and chamber orch. (1930, also for vc. and pf. or va. and pf. 1931), *Suite* (incl. *Pastorale*) for vn. and orch. (1888), *Légende* for vn. and orch. (1895).

CHAMBER MUSIC: Str. Qt. (1916, scherzo added 1919, incorp. themes from abandoned 1888 str. qt. 3rd movement, *Late Swallows*, arr. for str. by Fenby 1963, other 3 movements 1977 with title *Sonata for Strings*); Vn. Sonata (1892, unpubd.), No. 1 (1905–14, f.p. 1915), No. 2 (f.p.

1924, arr. for va. by Tertis), No. 3 (1930, arr. for va. by Tertis); Vc. Sonata (1916).

PIANO: *Zum Carnival* (1886), 3 *Preludes* (1923), 5 *Pieces* (1923).

Della Casa, Lisa (*b* Burgdorf, nr. Berne, 1919). Swiss sop. Studied singing at 15 in Zürich with Margarete Haeser. Début Solothurn-Biel 1941 as Butterfly, Salzburg 1947 (becoming member of Vienna State Opera), Glyndebourne 1951. Noted in Vienna, London, and NY for Mozart and especially for R. Strauss (*Arabella, Der Rosenkavalier*, and the *Four Last Songs*).

Deller, Alfred (George) (*b* Margate, 1912; *d* Bologna, 1979). Eng. counterten. Trained in parish church choir, but self-trained when he found he was true counterten. Lay clerk Canterbury Cath. 1940–7; joined St Paul's Cath. Choir 1947. Soloist at Morley College concerts cond. Tippett. Formed Deller Consort 1950 for authentic perf. of baroque mus. Deller's artistry almost solely responsible for revival of counterten. v. and its use in Purcell, Handel, Monteverdi, etc. Created role of Oberon in Britten's *Midsummer Night's Dream*, 1960. O.B.E. 1970. Son Mark Deller (*b* St. Leonards, 1938) is also counterten.

Dello Joio, Norman (*b* NY, 1913). Amer. composer, pianist, and organist. Son of NY organist and choirmaster, was influenced from childhood by Gregorian chant and It. opera. Studied Inst. of Mus. Art 1936 and Juilliard Sch. 1939–41. Pupil of Wagenaar and Hindemith (1940–1). Organist, St Ann's Church, NY, 1934–40. Mus. dir. Loring Dance Players 1941–3. Prof. of comp., Mannes Coll. 1956–72, prof. of mus., Boston Univ. from 1972. His mus. is noted for melodic content rather than for adventurous technique, and he displays a natural gift for opera and ballet (several works for Martha Graham). Prin. works incl.:

OPERAS: *The Ruby* (1953), *The Trial at Rouen* (1955, rev. 1958 as *The Triumph of St Joan*), *Blood Moon* (1961).

ORCHESTRAL: *Sinfonietta* (1940), *To a Lone Sentry* (1943), *Concert Music* (1945), *Serenade* (1948), *New York Profiles* (1949), *Air Power* (1957), *Five Images* (1967), *Homage to Haydn* (1969), *Satiric Dances*, band (1975), *Colonial Variations* (1976).

BALLETS: *On Stage!* (1946), *Diversion of Angels* (1948), *The Triumph of St Joan* (1951, rev. as *Seraphic Dialogue*, 1955), *Time of Snow* (1968).

CONCERTOS: Fl. and str. (1939), 2 pf. (1941), harmonica (1944), harp (1945), concertante for cl. (1949), *Fantasy and Variations* for pf. (1961), *Lyric Fantasies*, va. and str. (1973), *Notes from Tom Paine*, pf. and band (1975).

CHORAL: *Mystic Trumpeter* (1943), *Psalm of David* (1950), *Song of Affirmation* (1952), *Prayers of Cardinal Newman* (1960), *Songs of Walt Whitman* (1966), *Mass* (1968), *Evocations* (1970), *Mass* (1976).

CHAMBER MUSIC: Vc. Sonata (1937), Vn. Sonata (1938), Trio (1944); also 3 pf. sonatas (1943, 1944, 1948), songs, and incidental mus. for TV.

Del Mar, Norman (René) (b Hampstead, 1919). Eng. cond. and hn.-player. Studied RCM. Hn.-player in Beecham's RPO, becoming ass. cond. 1947–8. Founded Chelsea S.O. 1944, giving perfs. of works then little known in Eng., e.g. Busoni's pf. conc. and Mahler's 2nd Sym. Prin. cond. EOG 1948–56. Cond. Yorkshire S.O. 1954–5. Cond. BBC Scottish S.O. 1960–5. Prof. GSM 1952–60. Guest cond. of leading orchs. Cond. f.p. of Britten's Let's Make an Opera, 1949. Author of 3-vol. survey of mus. of R. Strauss. C.B.E. 1975. His son Jonathan (b London, 1951) is also a cond.

Del Monaco, Mario (b Florence, 1915; d Mestre, Venice, 1982). It. ten. Sang in opera at Mondalfo at age of 13. Mainly self-taught. Début Pesaro 1939, Milan 1941 (Pinkerton), CG 1946 (with San Carlo co.), NY Met. 1950–8. Verdi's Otello among his prin. roles.

De Los Angeles, Victoria (Victoria Gomez Cima) (b Barcelona, 1923). Sp. sop. Studied Barcelona Cons. Début while student in Monteverdi's Orfeo. Sang Countess in Figaro, Barcelona 1945. Winner Geneva int. fest. 1947. Eng. début, BBC 1949 in Falla's La Vida breve. CG 1950, NY 1950. Notable interpreter of Mimi, Butterfly, Carmen, Dido, etc., also of Mozart and Wagner roles.

Delsarte, François Alexandre Nicolas Chéri (b Solesmes, 1811; d Paris, 1871). Fr. ten. and singing teacher. Created system known as 'Delsarte method' by which singers were taught to match the emotion of the text with their facial expression (a method prone to unfortunate distortion).

Del Tredici, David (b Cloverdale, Calif., 1937). Amer. composer and pianist. Studied at Berkeley and NY. Turned to comp. 1958, encouraged by Milhaud. Studied with Sessions. Works incl: Night Conjure-Verse, 2 Joyce poems for sop., mez. or counterten., wind, and str. qt. (1965); Syzygy, 2 Joyce poems for sop., hn., and chamber orch. (1966); The Last Gospel, amplified sop., rock group, ch., and orch. (1967); Pot-Pourri, amplified sop., rock group, ch., and orch. (1968); The Lobster Quadrille, extract from In Wonderland for folk group and orch. (1969, rev. 1974); Vintage Alice, text from L. Carroll, amplified sop., folk group, and chamber orch. (1972); Adventures Underground (Carroll), amplified sop., folk group, and orch. (1973); In Wonderland (Carroll) Part I, A Scene with Lobsters, amplified sop., folk group, and orch. (1969–74), Part II, amplified sop. and orch. (1975); Final Alice (Carroll), amplified sop., folk group, and orch. (1976); Annotated Alice, amplified sop., folk group, and orch. (1976); Child Alice, orch., in 4 parts: In memory of a summer day, Happy Voices, All in the golden afternoon, and Quaint Events (1977–81, f.p. Aspen 1984).

De Luca, Giuseppe (b Rome, 1876; d NY, 1950). It. bar. Studied Rome. Début Piacenza 1897. La Scala, Milan, 1903–10, creating role of Sharpless in Madama Butterfly. CG début 1907. NY Met. 1915–35 and 1939–40. First Gianni Schicchi 1918. Became teacher at Juilliard Sch. NY, and gave last NY recital in Nov. 1947.

De Lucia, Fernando (b Naples, 1860; d Naples, 1925). It. tenor. Studied Naples, making opera début there 1885 in Faust. Became exponent of verismo heroes (Turiddù, Canio, etc.). Sang in f.p. of Mascagni's L'amico Fritz (Rome, 1891). London début 1887 (Drury Lane), CG 1892. Retired 1917, but sang at Caruso's funeral, 1921. Made over 400 recordings.

Démancher (Fr., from manche, neck). (1) To move the left hand along the neck of a str. instr.
(2) To move the left hand closer to the bridge of a str. instr.

Demantius, Christoph (b Reichenberg, 1567; d Freiberg, 1643). Ger.-Bohemian composer of church mus. (incl. St John Passion for 6 vv., 1631), and quodlibets, dances, villanelles, etc. Works influenced by Italian methods.

Demessieux, Jeanne Marie-Madeleine (b Montpellier, 1921; d Paris, 1968). Fr. organist and composer. Trained Montpellier Cons. and Paris Cons., then spent 5 years studying with Marcel *Dupré. First recital Paris 1946, London 1947, and Edinburgh 1948, Amer. début 1953. Won praise for remarkable powers of improvisation. Organist of Saint-Esprit, Paris, from age 12. Prof., Liège Cons., 1952. Org., Madeleine, from 1962.

Demetrio e Polibio. Opera in 2 acts by Rossini to lib. by Vincenza Mombelli. His first opera, written in 1806 when he was 14. Orch. for str. only. Prod. Bologna 1812, Manchester (RMCM) 1969.

Demi-cadence. Same as Imperfect Cadence (Half Close), i.e. chord of the tonic or other chord followed by that of dominant.

Demi-jeu (Fr.). Half-play, i.e. at half power (in org. and harmonium mus., etc.).

Demi-pause (Fr.). Half-rest, minim rest.

Demisemiquaver (♬). The Thirty-second note, i.e. $\frac{1}{32}$ the time-value of the whole-note or semibreve. See Note Values.

Demi-ton (Fr.). Semitone.

Demi-voix (Fr.). Half voice, i.e. half the vocal power (It. mezza voce).

Demus, Jörg (b St Pölten, 1928). Austrian pianist. Studied Vienna, 1940–5, and with Michelangeli, Kempff, and Gieseking. Début Vienna 1943. Foreign tours after 1947. Won Busoni Prize, Bolzano, 1956. Has collection of historical kbd. instrs.

Demuth, Norman (b S. Croydon, 1898; d Chichester, 1968). Eng. composer, cond., author, and teacher. Studied RCM. On staff of RAM from 1929. Wrote 5 operas, 4 syms., 2 pf. concs., vn. conc., va. conc., alto sax. conc., ballet *Planetomania*. Wrote books on Ravel, Roussel, Dukas, Franck, and Gounod.

Denhof Opera Company. Short-lived but significant body formed in 1910 by Ernst Denhof, Ger.-born resident of Edinburgh, to give provincial perfs. of Wagner's *Ring* in Eng. *Balling cond. f.ps. in Edinburgh, 1910, followed in 1911 by tours to Leeds, Manchester, and Glasgow, and to these cities again in 1912 plus Hull and Liverpool. Repertory by now incl. *Elektra* (in Eng.) and *Meistersinger*, with *Pelléas* and *Rosenkavalier* added in 1913, in which year co. ran into financial trouble in Manchester, being rescued and absorbed by Beecham's co. (Scotland did not hear a complete *Ring* cycle again until 1971.)

Denison, John (Law) (b Reigate, Surrey, 1911). Eng. hn. player and concert administrator. Trained RCM. Hn. player in BBC S.O., LPO, and CBSO 1934–9; ass. mus. dir., Brit. Council 1946–8; mus. dir., Arts Council from 1948; gen man. Royal Festival Hall, 1965–70; dir., South Bank Concert Halls 1971–6. C.B.E. 1960.

Denisov, Edison (b Tomsk, 1929). Russ. composer. Trained as mathematician but persuaded by Shostakovich to study mus. at Moscow Cons. 1951–6. Taught at Moscow Cons. from 1960. Worked at Experimental Studio of Elec. Mus., Moscow, 1968–70. Student of Russ. folk-mus. Comps. incl. conc. for fl., ob., pf., and perc.; *Crescendo e Diminuendo* for hpd.; *Tears (Plachi)* for sop., pf., 3 percussionists; *Ode* for cl., pf., perc.; *Romantic Music* for ob., harp, str. trio; str. trio; wind quintet; *Peinture* for orch., 2 syms., vc. conc., pf. conc., cl. sonata, and vc. sonata.

Denner, Johann Christoph (b Leipzig, 1655; d Nuremberg, 1707). Ger. instr.-maker. In attempting to improve the Fr. *chalumeau he invented the *clarinet c.1690. Subject of opera by Weigmann *Der Klarinettenmacher* (1913).

Dent, Edward (Joseph) (b Ribston, Yorks., 1876; d London, 1957). Eng. scholar, teacher, and author. Educated Eton and Cambridge. Prof. of mus., Cambridge Univ. 1926–41. Active in many Eng. operatic ventures and esp. as translator of libs. (notably for Mozart operas); his prods. of Mozart operas in his own trans. at Cambridge from 1911 contributed largely to their re-evaluation in Eng. In 1919 he helped found Brit. Mus. Soc. (disbanded 1933) and in 1922 organized a fest. of contemporary chamber mus. in Vienna from which developed the *International Society for Contemporary Music. Dent became first pres., 1923–37. Ed. *The Beggar's Opera*, 1944. Contrib. to many encyclopaedias and dictionaries, critic, and author of books *Alessandro Scarlatti* (1905),

Mozart's Operas (1913), and *Ferruccio Busoni* (1933).

Denza, Luigi (b Castellammare di Stabia, Naples, 1846; d London, 1922). It. composer, pupil of *Mercadante at Naples Cons. Wrote opera and 600 popular songs, best-known being *Funiculi, Funicula*, 1880, comp. for opening of Naples funicular railway. Settled in London 1879. Prof. of singing, RAM, 1898–1922.

Denzler, Robert (b Zürich, 1892; d Zürich, 1972). Swiss cond. and composer. Studied Zürich (with*Andreae) and Cologne Cons. Ass. cond. Bayreuth 1911–12. Chief cond. Zürich Opera 1915–27 and 1934–47 and Berlin State Opera 1927–32. Cond. f.ps. of 2-act version of Berg's *Lulu* (1937) and Hindemith's *Mathis der Maler* (1938).

Déploration (Fr.). A poem of mourning, and therefore its musical setting. Term generally confined to Renaissance comps. written in memory of a composer, e.g. Andrieu's for Machaut, Ockeghem's for Binchois, and Josquin Desprès's for Ockeghem.

De profundis (Out of the depth). Psalm 129 in the Vulgate (following the Septuagint) and 130 in the Eng. Authorized and Revised versions (following the Hebrew). It is one of the 7 Penitential Psalms (see *Psalm*) and, attached to its traditional plainsong, has a place in the Office of the Dead of the R.C. Church. It has been set by composers many times.

Der (Ger.). (1) The (masc. sing.) (2) Of the (fem. sing.).

De Reszke, Édouard (b Warsaw, 1853; d Garnek, 1917). Polish bass, brother of Jean *de Reszke. Studied Warsaw and It. Joined Paris Opéra, making début as the King in first Paris *Aida* cond. Verdi. London CG 1880, Chicago 1891. Stalwart of NY Met. 1891–1903. Notable in Wagner, first in It. then in Ger. (King Marke, Sachs, Hagen). Retired 1903. Orig. name Edward Mieczyslaw.

De Reszke, Jean (b Warsaw, 1850; d Nice, 1925). Polish ten., brother of Édouard *de Reszke. Studied Warsaw and It. Début (as bar.), Turin and London 1874 (singing Alfonso in *La Favorite*). His brother persuaded him he was really a ten. and after further study from 1876 he sang *Robert le Diable* in Madrid 1879. After 5 fallow years he had a great success in Massenet's *Hérodiade* (Paris, 1884) and *Le Cid* (1885). Sang Faust at 500th Paris perf. in 1887 (with Édouard as Mephistopheles). CG début 1888, returning nearly every year until 1900. NY Met. 1891–1901. Late in career sang Wagner roles of Lohengrin, Walther, Tristan, and Siegfried. Retired 1902, and taught in Paris and Nice. Regarded as one of greatest operatic tens. Orig. name Jan Mieczyslaw.

De Reszke, Joséphine (b Warsaw, 1855; d Warsaw, 1891). Polish sop., sister of above. Début

Venice 1874. Paris Opéra 1875–84. Début CG 1881 as Aida. Retired 1885 on marriage.

Dering, Richard. See *Deering, Richard.*

D'Erlanger, Baron Frédéric (*b* Paris, 1868; *d* London, 1943). Eng. (naturalized) composer (of Ger. and Amer. parents). Studied in Paris. Wrote several operas, incl. *Inez Mendo* (CG 1897) and *Tess* (based on Hardy's novel, Naples 1906, CG 1909 with Destinn), *Requiem* (1931), vn. conc., and chamber mus. Banker by profession and financial supporter of CG between the wars.

Dermota, Anton (*b* Kropa, 1910). Yugoslav ten. Studied at Laibach and Vienna. Début Vienna 1936, appearing mainly there and at Salzburg for the rest of his career, notably in Mozart roles. Sang Florestan in *Fidelio* at reopening of Vienna State Opera, 1955.

Dernesch, Helga (*b* Vienna, 1939). Austrian sop. Studied Vienna Cons. Member of Berne Opera 1961–3, Wiesbaden 1963–6, Cologne 1966–9. Bayreuth Fest. 1965–9, Salzburg Easter Fest. 1969–73. Scottish Opera début 1968 (Gutrune), later singing Leonore in *Fidelio* and the Marschallin. CG 1970 (Sieglinde), Chicago 1971 (*Fidelio*), Vienna 1972 (*Fidelio*). Outstanding in Strauss and Wagner. Mez. roles from 1979.

Des (Ger. singular; Fr. plural). Of the. Also (Ger.), the note D♭.

De Sabata, Victor (*b* Trieste, 1892; *d* S. Margherita, 1967). It. cond. and composer. Studied Milan Cons. Cond. Monte Carlo Opera where he cond. f.p. of Ravel's *L'Enfant et les Sortilèges* (1925). Cond. La Scala, Milan, 1930–57, latterly as art. dir. Cond. Bayreuth (*Tristan*) 1939. Took Scala Co. to CG 1950. Frequent guest cond. of concerts and opera throughout world. Wrote 2 operas, 3 symphonic poems, and other works.

De Saram, Rohan (*b* Sheffield, 1939). Sri Lankan cellist. Studied in Florence with Cassado and later with Casals in Puerto Rico. After European recitals made Amer. début in NY, 1960. Settled in Eng. 1972, joining teaching staff of TCL. Wide repertory from Haydn to Xenakis, specializing in contemp. works. Cellist of Arditti String Quartet.

Descant. Like *'Faburden' a puzzling term because at different periods used with different significances, chief of which are as follows: (1) A term, usually spelt *Discant*, for a form of the 12th cent. part-writing known as *organum. (2) A part extemporized by a singer to a non-extemporized part sung by another singer. (3) The art of composing or singing part-music. (4) The soprano part in choral music. (5) In modern hymn singing, a freely written or improvised soprano part added to a hymn tune while the tune itself is sung by the rest of the choir or by the congregation.

Descant Viol. The treble viol. See *Viol.*

Deses (Ger.). The note D♭♭.

Desiderio (It.). Desire. Hence *con desiderio*, longingly.

Desmond, Astra (*b* Torquay, 1893; *d* Faversham, 1973). Eng. mez. Educated Westfield College, London (B.A.), and studied singing under Blanche *Marchesi. First London recital 1915. Sang title-role in Boughton's *Alkestis* 1922. Became notable exponent of Eng. mus., esp. Elgar and Vaughan Williams, but also sang in 12 languages and wrote books on songs of Grieg, Dvořák, Sibelius, and Schumann. Prof. of singing, RAM 1947–63. C.B.E. 1949.

Désormière, Roger (*b* Vichy, 1898; *d* Paris, 1963). Fr. cond. and composer. Studied Paris Cons. Cond. Diaghilev Ballet 1925–30. Opéra-Comique 1937, becoming mus. dir. 1944–6. Cond. *Pelléas* at CG 1949. Retired 1950.

Desprès (Desprez, des Pres), **Josquin** (*b* ?Picardy, *c*.1440; *d* Condé-sur-l'Escaut, Hainaut, 1521). Fr.-Flemish composer. Possibly a pupil of *Ockeghem. From *c*.1459 to 1504 was in It., first as singer in Milan Cath. and employee of Sforza family. Went to Rome in 1484 in service of Cardinal Ascanio Sforza and as member of papal chapel. Became choirmaster at Ferrara, 1503. Returned to Low Countries 1504, after outbreak of plague, where he became provost of church at Condé. Regarded as most gifted and influential composer of his time. He was no radical innovator but successfully developed existing and unexplored techniques. Was particularly successful in giving dramatic emphasis to the texts he set by means of word-rhythms and imitation. Although his early masses used a *cantus firmus, later ones employed parody techniques and were sometimes based on a motto theme or a series of canons. Similarly in motets he abandoned a plainchant *cantus firmus* in favour of imitative devices. Some of his *chansons* were on erotic and frivolous texts and he was one of the first to appropriate tunes from court and theatre for his serious works. His work was so popular that many forgeries were published. He wrote 18 masses (the best-known being *Ave Maris Stella, L'homme armé*, and *Pange lingua*), nearly 100 motets, and over 70 secular works.

Dessau, Paul (*b* Hamburg, 1894; *d* E. Berlin, 1979). Ger. composer and cond. Studied Klindworth-Scharwenka Cons., Berlin, 1910–12. Opera coach, Hamburg, 1913–14. Cond. Cologne Opera 1918–23, Berlin State Opera 1926. Lived in Paris 1933–9, USA 1939–45, then returned to Ger. Close assoc. of Brecht, having written incidental mus. to the plays *Mutter Courage* (1946), *Der gute Mensch von Sezuan* (1947), *Mann ist Mann* (1951), etc. Other works incl. 5 str. qts.; *Deutsches miserere*, choral work to text by Brecht; operas *Die Verurteilung des Lukullus* (The Trial of Lucullus, lib. by Brecht, 1949), *Puntila* (lib. after Brecht,

1957–9), *Lanzelot* (1969), *Einstein* (1971–3); *In memoriam Bertolt Brecht*, for orch. (1957), *Requiem für Lumumba*, sop., bar., speaker, ch., and ens. (1963), 2 syms. (1926, 1934, rev. 1962), 3 *Orchestermusik* (1955, 1967, 1973), and many songs.

Destinn, Emmy (Ema Kittl) (*b* Prague, 1878; *d* Budějovice, 1930). Cz. sop. Trained as violinist but her vocal prowess was noticed and she studied with Marie Loewe-Destinn, whose name she adopted. Début Berlin 1898 (Santuzza) remaining at Court Opera until 1908. Sang at CG 1904–14, 1919, and NY Met. 1908–16, 1919–21. Senta in first Bayreuth *Fliegende Holländer*, 1901; Diemut in Strauss's *Feuersnot* 1901 and first Berlin Salome 1906. First Butterfly at CG 1905 (with Caruso) and Tatyana in *Eugene Onegin* 1906. Created role of Minnie in Puccini's *La fanciulla del West* 1910. In 1914–18 war adopted name Ema Destinnová; was interned on her Bohem. estate for duration. Returned to Met. and CG 1919 as Aida. Retired from stage 1921 but sang in London at concert cond. by Wood in 1928.

Destouches, André-Cardinal (*b* Paris, 1672; *d* Paris, 1749). Fr. composer. Studied with *Campra. Superintendent, Paris Opéra, 1713, dir. 1728–30. Best-known work is 3-act opera *Issé*, heroic pastorale prod. Fontainebleau 1697. It was one of his operas that sparked off the 'Querelle des *Bouffons'.

Détaché (Fr.). Detached, i.e. Staccato. (1) *Grand Détaché*, Staccato with a full bow for each note. (2) *Petit détaché*, Staccato with the point of the bow for each note. (3) *Détaché sec*, same as *Martelé* (hammered).

Detached Console. Placed at a distance from the org. so that the player can hear the full effect as his listeners hear it. In electric orgs. such a console may be movable.

Detroit Symphony Orchestra. Founded 1914 with Weston Gales as cond. 1914–18, followed by Ossip *Gabrilowitsch 1918–35. Victor Kolar and guest conds. succeeded the latter, but after difficult times the orch. disbanded 1949. Reorganized 1952, with Paul *Paray as cond. 1952–63, Sixten Ehrling 1963–73, Aldo Ceccato 1973–7, Antal Dorati 1977–81; Gary Bertini 1981–3; Günther Herbig from 1984. First European tour 1979.

Dettingen Te Deum and Anthem. Comp. by Handel, to celebrate Brit. defeat of Fr. at Dettingen, nr, Frankfurt, 1743. First sung at Chapel Royal, St James's, Nov. 1743. Anthem's text begins 'The King shall rejoice'.

Deuteromelia (Gr.). 'Second honey.' 2nd coll. of Eng. rounds and catches pubd. 1609 by T. *Ravenscroft. See *Pammelia*.

Deutsch, Otto Erich (*b* Vienna, 1883; *d* Vienna, 1967). Austro-Eng. mus. scholar and art critic.

Studied in Vienna and Graz. Wrote book on Schubert 1905 and biog. 1913–14. Worked at Vienna Univ. art-history library 1909–12. Mus. lib. to A. van *Hoboken 1926–35. Went to Eng. 1939, settling in Cambridge. Naturalized 1947, returned to Vienna 1952. Ed., Brit. Union Catalogue of Early Mus. 1946–50. Author of books on Handel (1955), Haydn, Schumann, and Beethoven, but his masterpieces are his books on Schubert. These incl. an edn. of all documents, pictures, and relevant material (1914, Eng. edn. 1946) and a thematic catalogue (1951, rev. by others 1978) which gave all Schubert's works D nos. Also wrote documentary biography of Mozart (1961, Eng. edn. 1963).

Deutsche Motette (German Motet). Motet by R. Strauss, Op. 62, for sop., alto, ten., and bass soloists and 16-part unacc. mixed ch., to words by Rückert, comp. 1913, rev. 1943.

Deutscher Tanz, Deutsche Tänze (Ger.). German dance(s). Peasant dance from Ger. and Switzerland, like slow waltz. Adopted particularly by Mozart and Schubert.

Deutsches Requiem, Ein (A German Requiem). Choral work, Op. 45, by Brahms for sop. and bar. soloists, ch., and orch. Comp. 1861–68, though what is now 2nd movement was comp. in 1857. So called because text is not that of the R.C. Liturgy but consists of passages selected by Brahms from Luther's trans. of the Bible. 7 movements. First 3 movements perf. Vienna, Dec. 1867. 2nd perf. Bremen Cath. 10 Apr. 1868, with 3 movements added. A month later he inserted new 5th movement, *1hr habt nun Traurigkeit*, for sop., in memory of his mother, *d* Feb. 1865. First complete perf. Leipzig 18 Feb. 1869, cond. Reinecke.

Deutschland über Alles. (Ger. 'Germany beyond everything' or 'Germany before everything'), known also as the *Deutschlandlied* ('Germany Song'). A poem of aspiration for the unity of the Ger. peoples written in the period which preceded the 1848 revolutionary disturbances, by August Heinrich Hoffmann (generally called Hoffmann von Fallersleben, 1798–1874). Sung to the tune Haydn wrote (or adapted, for there is a similar tune in Telemann) as Austrian national anthem, the *Emperor's Hymn*. Nat. anthem of German Fed. Republic from 1922 until 1945. Reinstated 1950 with 3rd verse ('Einigkeit und Recht und Freiheit', 'Unity and Right and Freedom') replacing the 1st with its controversial reference to 'über Alles'.

Deux (Fr.). Two. *À deux*, for 2 vv. or instr., or (sometimes) short for 'À *deux temps'. In orch. mus., however, this expression has 2 opposite meanings: (*a*) 2 separate instr. parts are now merged in 1 line of mus.; (*b*) 1 instr. part is now divided, the players becoming 2 bodies.

Deux Journées, Les (The Two Days). Opera in 3 acts by Cherubini to lib. by J.-N. Bouilly. Generally known in Britain as *The Water Carrier*, and in Ger. as *Der Wasserträger*. Prod. Paris 1800, London 1801, New Orleans 1811.

Deux Pigeons, Les (The Two Pigeons). Ballet in 3 acts by Messager, lib. by H. Régnier and Mérante, choreog. Mérante. Prod. Paris 1886. New version choreog. Ashton, London 1961.

Deux temps (Fr.). Two beats (1) In $\frac{2}{2}$ time.
(2) *Valse à deux temps* has the following varied meanings; (*a*) In normal Waltz ($\frac{3}{4}$) time with 2 dance steps to a measure, on the first and 3rd beats; (*b*) In $\frac{6}{4}$ or $\frac{6}{8}$ time, with steps on the first and 4th 'beats'; (*c*) Having 2 values of beat, as in Gounod's *Faust* where 2 waltzes are combined, one of them in $\frac{3}{4}$ time and the other in $\frac{3}{2}$, 2 measures of the $\frac{3}{4}$ being heard against 1 measure of the $\frac{3}{2}$ and thus rhythmically conflicting.

Development (also called *Free Fantasia,* or *Working-out.* Fr. *Développement*; Ger. *Durchführung*, i.e. 'Through-leading'; It. *Svolgimento*, i.e. 'Unfolding'). The treatment of the detailed phrases and motifs of a previously heard theme ('subject') in such a way as to make new passages, often of a modulatory nature. The second section of sonata form, coming between exposition and recapitulation, is the development. With the expansion of the symphony, the development section became increasingly complex and important. Beethoven departs from convention in his 3rd Symphony by introducing new thematic material in this section. There is also a development in **fugue*.

Devienne, François (*b* Joinville, 1759; *d* Charenton, 1803). Fr. woodwind player and composer. Prof., Paris Cons. Played bn., ob., and fl., composing many works for fl. and writing a method for it (1794). Also comp. 11 operas and much chamber mus.

Devil and Daniel Webster, The. (1) Opera in 1 act by Douglas *Moore to lib. by Stephen Vincent Benét based on his own story. Prod. NY 1939.
(2) Film score by *Herrmann from which he prod. 5-movement suite. F.p. Philadelphia.

Devil in Music. See *Tritone*.

Devils of Loudun, The (*Diably z Loudun*). Opera in 3 acts by *Penderecki to his own lib. based on John Whiting's play (1961) from A. Huxley's novel (1952), in Ger. trans. by Erich Fried. Prod. Hamburg 1969, Santa Fe 1969, London (ENO) 1973.

'Devil's Trill' Sonata (*Trillo del Diavolo* or *Sonata del Diavolo*). Nickname of Vn. Sonata in G minor by *Tartini, comp *c*.1714, which has a long trill in the last of its 4 movements. The legend is that Tartini dreamed he had made a deal with the Devil to whom he gave his vn. The Devil played a solo so beautiful that Tartini awoke and tried to

play what he had heard. He failed but comp. the 'Devil's Trill'. The sonata was found by *Baillot (1771–1842) and first pub. in *L'Art du violon* (1798, 1801) by Cartier. Legend is subject of ballet *Le Violon du diable* with mus. by Pugni, Paris 1849.

Devil Take Her, The. Comic opera in prol. and 1 act by A. Benjamin to lib. by A. Collard and J.B. Gordon. Prod. London 1931.

Devin du village, Le (The Village Soothsayer). Opera (*intermède*) in 1 act by *Rousseau to his own lib. Prod. Fontainebleau 1752, Paris 1753, London 1766, NY 1790. Lib. of Mozart's *Bastien *und Bastienne* is based on a parody.

De Vito, Gioconda (*b* Martina Franca, Lecce, 1907). Eng. violinist of It. birth. Studied in Pesaro and Rome. Won international competition Vienna 1932. Prof. of vn., Accademia di S. Cecilia, Rome. Visited London 1947 to make records. Public début 1948 (LPO). Specialist in standard repertory, notably Brahms concerto. Retired 1961.

D'Hardelot. See *Hardelot, Guy de*.

Diabelli, Antonio (*b* Mattsee, Salzburg, 1781; *d* Vienna, 1858). Austrian composer and publisher. Went to Vienna in 1803 as teacher of pf. and guitar and as proof-reader. Entered publishing 1818, founded Diabelli and Co., publishing works by Beethoven, Schubert, and Czerny. Wrote operetta, masses, pf. pieces, and songs. See *Diabelli Variations*.

Diabelli Variations. Beethoven's Thirty-Three Variations on a Waltz by Diabelli, Op. 120, for pf., comp. 1819–23. The publisher *Diabelli commissioned 50 composers to write a variation apiece on his theme and was delighted to receive 33 from Beethoven, immediately recognizing the work as a major masterpiece. Among the other composers who responded to Diabelli's request were Liszt (aged 11), Schubert, Drechsler, Schenk, Czerny, Kalkbrenner, Pixis, Moscheles, Stadler, Sechter, Hoffmann, and Archduke Rudolph.

Diabolus in musica (Lat.). The devil in mus., i.e. the *tritone. Term is derived from various prohibitions on using this awkward interval.

Diaghilev, Serge (Dyagilev, Sergey) (Pavlovich) (*b* Selistchev, Novgorod, 1872; *d* Venice, 1929). Russ. impresario. Studied law at St Petersburg, 1890–7, but gravitated into journalism and art criticism. Art. adviser to Maryinsky Theatre 1899–1901. In 1907 organized Paris concerts of Russ. mus. and prod. of *Boris Godunov* with *Chaliapin. In 1909 he was invited to present a season of Russ. opera and ballet in Paris, scoring a major triumph with the ballet, for which he engaged the dancer Nijinsky, choreographer Fokine, and the painters Bakst and Benois. From this season the sensational Ballets Russes developed, transforming the ballet world. Diaghilev directed the co. until his death, surviving financial crises and personal quarrels which threatened to tear it apart. Over the years he called on an astonishing range of talents, not only among dancers (Nijinsky, Karsavina, Massine, Sokolova, Dolin, etc.) but choreographers (Fokine, Nijinsky, Massine, Nijinskaya, Balanchine), designers (Bakst, Benois, Matisse, Picasso, Utrillo, Derain) and composers (scores commissioned from Ravel, Stravinsky, Falla, Debussy, Prokofiev, Milhaud, Satie, Strauss, Poulenc, Auric, Lambert, and Berners). See *Ballet*.

Dialogue. (1) Vocal work, mainly from medieval times to 17th cent., in which echo, alternation, or contrast suggested spoken dialogue.

(2) Spoken dialogue is used in some types of opera, e.g. Fr. *opéra comique*, Ger. *Singspiel*, Sp. *zarzuela*, and Eng. ballad opera (and the operas of Gilbert and Sullivan). In Beethoven's *Fidelio* there is spoken dialogue and *melodrama. In some cases spoken dialogue has been replaced by accompanied recitative comp. by someone else (e.g. Guiraud for Bizet's *Carmen*). There are examples of a brief spoken passage used in opera to great dramatic effect, e.g. in Britten's *Peter Grimes*.

Dialogues des Carmélites, Les. (The Carmelites' dialogues). Opera in 3 acts by Poulenc to lib. by Georges Bernanos adapted from novel *Die letzte am Schafott* (The Last on the Scaffold) by G. von le Fort (1931) and film scenario by Bruckenberger and Agostini. Comp. 1953–6. Prod Milan, Paris, and San Francisco 1957, CG 1958. Known in Eng. as *The Carmelites*.

Diamand, Peter (*b* Charlottenburg, 1913). Dutch administrator, born an Austrian. Studied law Berlin Univ. Secretary to *Schnabel 1934–8. Ass. to dir. Netherland Opera 1946–8, dir. Holland Fest. 1947–65. Dir. Edinburgh Fest. 1966–78. Gen. man. RPO 1978–81. Hon. C.B.E. 1972.

Diamond, David (Leo) (*b* Rochester, NY, 1915). Amer. composer. Studied Cleveland Institute of Mus., 1927–9, Eastman Sch. of Music 1930–4 (comp. with Bernard Rogers). Sym. in one movement perf. at Eastman Sch. 1931. Studied with *Sessions in NY 1935. Went to Paris and studied with *Boulanger 1936–7. Juilliard Award 1937, Guggenheim Fellowship 1938, 1941, Amer. Acad. in Rome Award 1942. Lived in Florence 1953–65. Head of comp. dept., Manhattan Sch. of Mus., NY, 1965–7. His mus. owes something to his admiration for Ravel and Stravinsky and is strongly contrapuntal. He adopted serialism in the 1950s. Works incl. 8 syms. (1940–60), *Psalm* for orch. (1936), *Elegy in Memory of Ravel* (1938), *Rounds* for str. (1944), *Timon of Athens* (1949), *The World of Paul Klee* (1957), 2-pf. conc., pf. conc., 3 vn. concs. (1936–67), vc. conc., 11 str. qts., pf. qt., pf. quintet, vn. sonata, *L'Ame de Debussy* (song-cycle), vc. sonata,

Choral Symphony: To Music (male soloists, ch., and orch.) (1967), songs, etc.

Diapason (Gr.). Through all. (1) Greek name for the octave.

(2) The name of certain org. stops which are the foundation tone of the instr. and are either 'open' or 'stopped' according to whether the ends of the pipes are clear or plugged (plugged stops are lower in pitch by an octave). *Open diapason*, 8′, is the chief manual stop. There are also *stopped diapason*, *horn diapason*, and *diapason phonon* in which the lips of the pipes are leathered to refine the tone.

(3) In Fr., *diapason normal* is a standard indication of pitch: A = 440 vibrations per sec.

Diapente (Gr.). The interval of the perfect 5th.

Diaphone. Org. stop (open diapason) invented by Robert Hope-Jones (1859–1914) which was actuated by vibratory apparatus to increase loudness.

Diaphony. Gr. term for dissonance, applied to form of *organum. Some define it as a freer form, admitting other intervals than the perfect ones, others consider it to be a later form, admitting of contrary motion, part-crossing, etc.

Diary of One who Disappeared (*Zápisník zmizelého*). Song-cycle by Janáček, comp. 1917–19, for ten., cont. (or mez.), 3 women's vv., and pf. Setting of 22 anonymous poems, No. 13 being represented by a pf. solo (*intermezzo erotico*). All the vv. are heard only in No. 9, women's vv. only in No. 10, ten. and cont. in No. 11, the remainder being for ten. F.p. Brno 1921, f.p. in England, London 1922. Eng. trans. by Bernard Keeffe.

Diatonic. The *Diatonic Scales* (see *Scale*) are those of the major and minor keys, and diatonic passages, intervals, chords, and harmonies are those made up of the notes of the key prevailing at the moment. The *Modes must also be considered diatonic. See also *Chromatic*.

Dibdin, Charles (*b* Southampton, 1745; *d* London, 1814). Eng. composer, impresario, and singer. Choirboy, Winchester Cath. 1756–9. From 1764 in London wrote words and mus. of many popular 'musicals'. In 1789 began 'table entertainments' at which he sang his own songs. Th. manager 1796–1805. Best-known songs are 'The Bells of Aberdovey' from *Liberty Hall* (Drury Lane 1785) and the beautiful 'Tom Bowling' from table entertainment *The Oddities* (Lyceum 1789).

Dichterliebe (Poet's Love). Cycle of 16 songs for v. and pf. by Schumann, Op. 48 (1840), being settings of Heine.

Dichtung (Ger.). Poem. Hence *symphonische Dichtung*, symphonic poem. R. Strauss used the term *Tondichtung*, tone-poem.

Dickie, Brian (James) (*b* Newark, 1941). Eng. opera dir. Art. dir., Wexford Fest. 1967–74. On

Glyndebourne staff since 1962, gen. admin. from 1982.

Dickie, Murray (*b* Bishopton, nr. Glasgow, 1924). Scottish operatic ten. and producer. Studied Vienna, London, and Milan. Début London 1947, CG 1948–52, Vienna State Opera since 1952 (Kammersänger).

Dickinson, Meriel (*b* Lytham St Annes, 1940). Eng. mez. Studied RMCM and Vienna Acad. Member BBC Ch. 1963–4, solo recitalist and oratorio.

Dickinson, Peter (*b* Lytham St Annes, 1934). Eng. composer and pianist. Studied Cambridge Univ., Juilliard Sch. NY. Extra-mural staff tutor in mus. Birmingham Univ., 1966–70. Prof. of mus., Keele Univ., 1974–84. Works include:

THEATRE: *Vitalitas*, ballet (1959; orch. of *Variations* for pf. 1957); *The Judas Tree*, 5 speaking parts, 2 tens., ch., and orch. (1965).

ORCH: *Monologue*, strs. (1959); *5 Diversions* (1969); *Transformations, Homage to Satie* (1970); org. conc. (1971); conc. for str., perc., and electronic org. (1971); pf. conc. (1978–84).

VOCAL: *4 Auden Songs*, sop. or ten. and pf. (1956); *Dylan Thomas Song Cycle*, bar. and pf. (1959); *4 Poems of Alan Porter*, counterten. and hpd. (1968); *Extravaganzas*, v. and pf. (1969); *e. e. cummings Song Cycle*, mez. and pf. (1965 rev. 1970); *Winter Afternoons* (Emily Dickinson), cantata for 6 solo vv. and db. (1971); *Surrealist Landscape*, counterten., pf., and tape (1973); *Lust*, for 6 vv. (1974); *Schubert in Blue*, mez. and pf. (1977).

CHORAL: *Martin of Tours*, ten., bar., ch., and pf. duet (1966); *The Dry Heart*, 5 Alan Porter poems for unacc. ch. (1967); *Outcry*, contralto, ch., orch. (1969); *Late Afternoon in November*, 16 solo vv. (1975).

CHURCH: 2 Motets (1963); *Magnificat and Nunc Dimittis*, vv. and org. (1963); *Mass* (1965); *Mass of the Apocalypse*, 16 solo women's vv., 4 perc. players (1984).

CHAMBER MUSIC: *Juilliard Dances* (1959); vn. sonata (1961); *Fanfares and Elegies*, 3 tpts., 3 tbs., org. (1967); *Translations*, recorder, va. da gamba, hpd. (1971); *Hymns, Blues, and Improvisations*, str. qt., pf., and tape (1973); Str. Qt. No. 1 (1958, rev. 1974), No. 2, with tape or pf. (1975).

PIANO: *Variations* (1957); *5 Forgeries*, pf. duet (1963); *5 Diversions* (1963); *Paraphrase II* (1967).

ORGAN: *Dirge* (1963); *Carillon* (1964); *Paraphrase I* (1967).

Dickson, Joan (*b* Edinburgh, 1921). Scot. cellist. Studied RCM, then Paris with *Fournier, Rome with *Mainardi. London début 1953. Prof. RCM from 1968. Member Edinburgh Str. Qt. 1953–8. Soloist with leading orchs.

Diction. Properly, verbal phrasing, or skill in the choice of words, but used in context of singing to denote clear and correct enunciation.

Didjeridu. Australian aborigines' wind instr., straight (over 3 ft. in length), end-blown, and capable of producing a variety of sounds, such as trills, croaks, gurgles, and imitations of birds and animals. The player can breathe through the nose without interrupting the sound he is making.

Dido and Aeneas. Opera in prol. and 3 acts by Purcell to lib. by Nahum Tate, after Book 4 of Virgil's *Aeneid*. F.p. Josias Priest's sch. for young gentlewomen, Chelsea, in 1689 or 1690. Staged in London *c*.1700 and *c*.1704 and not again until RCM 1895 (Lyceum Th.). F.p. in NY 1923 (at Hotel Plaza). Several versions survive, the score held by St Michael's College, Tenbury, being accepted as standard. Another important version was found at Tatton Hall, Cheshire. *Dido's Lament, When I am laid in earth*, occurs in Act 3.

Dido's Lament. Aria for Dido at end of Act 3 of Purcell's *Dido and Aeneas*, beginning with words 'When I am laid in earth'. Orch. arr. is played annually at Remembrance Day service at Cenotaph, London.

Die (Ger.). The.

Diepenbrock, Alfons (*b* Amsterdam, 1862; *d* Amsterdam, 1921). Dutch composer, mainly self-taught. Influential teacher. Wrote chiefly church mus. (2 settings of *Te Deum*, a *Stabat mater*, etc.) and incidental mus. to plays. Befriended and admired by *Mahler.

Dieren, Bernard van (*b* Rotterdam, 1887; *d* London, 1936). Dutch composer, long resident in Eng. Trained as scientist, but began to write mus. criticism and in 1909 settled in London as correspondent for several European periodicals. Mainly self-taught as composer but studied in Ger., 1912. His works became the subject of a cult among leading Brit. intellectuals of the 1920s, e.g. Sitwells, Gerald Cooper, Heseltine, Gray, and others. Successive efforts to persuade his contemporary public and later generations of his genius have made little ground, the mus. being less novel than is suggested. Works incl. *The Tailor* (comic opera) (1917), *Symphony on Chinese Themes* (with vv.) (1914), *Serenade*, 6 str. qts., solo vn. sonata, songs. Wrote book on Epstein (1920) and vol. of criticism, *Down Among the Dead Men* (1935).

Dièse (Fr.). Sharp.

Dies Irae (Day of Wrath). A section of the Requiem Mass. The poem is probably by Thomas of Celano (*d c*.1250). The plainsong tune has frequently been introduced into instr. mus., as in Berlioz's *Symphonie fantastique*, Saint-Saëns's *Danse macabre*, Rakhmaninov's *Paganini Rhapsody*, etc. Settings of the Requiem by Verdi, Berlioz, and others contain vivid depictions of the *Dies Irae*.

Diesis (It.). (1) Sharp.

(2) In acoustical theory the minute interval between the sum of 3 major 3rds (in perfect tuning) and an octave.

Dies Natalis (Lat. 'Birthday'). Cantata, Op. 8, by *Finzi, for sop. or ten. and str., composed between 1926 and 1939, f.p. 1940. It is in 5 movements, the 1st instrumental, the 2nd a setting of a prose passage from *Centuries of Meditations* by T. Traherne (1638–74), and the last 3 being settings of Traherne poems.

Dieupart, Charles (François) (*b* 1670; *d* London, *c*.1740). Fr. violinist, harpsichordist, and composer. Taught in London and played for It. opera at Drury Lane. Pubd. *Six Suittes de Clavecin* (1701). The gigue from first suite may have been model of Bach's prelude in his first *English Suite*.

Differential Tone (or Resultant Tone). In acoustics: (1) When two loud notes are played, another, lower, note may sometimes be heard which corresponds to the difference in vibration between the original 2 notes.
(2) When a note higher than the original 2 may be heard which corresponds to the sum of their vibrations.

Digital. Any one of the keys comprising the kbd. of a pf. or similar instr. For digital recording, see *Gramophone Recordings*.

Digitorium. A small portable apparatus for the use of kbd. players wishing to strengthen their fingers. It usually had no more than 5 keys and these had strong springs so that considerable force was required to depress them. Invented by Myer Marks about the middle of the 19th cent.

Dilkes, Neville (*b* Derby, 1930). Eng. cond. Studied privately. Founded Midland (now Eng.) Sinfonia 1961. Mus. dir. Corby Grammar Sch. 1955–65, cond. Kettering S.O. 1958–63, Opera da camera 1961–7.

Dillon, James (*b* Glasgow, 1950). Scottish composer. As a boy, played in pipe band. Studied medieval, Renaissance, and non-Western mus. Awarded Kranichsteiner prize, Darmstadt 1982. His mus. was featured at Bath and La Rochelle fests., 1984.
Works incl.: *Babble*, 40 vv. (1974–6); *Dillug Kefitsah*, pf. (1976); *Cumha*, 12 str. (1976–8); *Incaain*, 16 vv. (1977); *Ariadne's Thread*, va. (1978); *Crossing Over*, cl. (1978); *Ti-re-Ti-ke-Dha*, solo drum (1979); . . . *Once Upon a Time*, 10 instr. (1980); *Spleen*, pf. (1980); *Who do you Love*, v. and 8 instr. (1980–1); *Evening Rain*, solo v. (1981); *Parjanya-Vata*, vc. (1981); *Come Live with Me*, mez. and 4 instr. (1981); *A Roaring Flame*, v. and contrabass (1981–2); *Time Lag Zero*, v. and va. (1982); *East 11th St. NY 10003*, perc. (6 players) (1982); str. qt. (1983); *Zone* (. . . . *de azul*), 8 instr. (1983); *Le Rivage*, wind quintet (1984); *Sgothan*, fl. (1984).

Diluendo (It.). Dissolving, i.e. dying away.

Dilungando (It.). Lengthening.

Diminished Intervals. Perfect or minor intervals which are reduced chromatically by a semitone are diminished intervals. For practical purposes this term is useful only when applied to the diminished 5th (semitone less than perfect 5th) and diminished 7th (semitone less than minor 7th).

Diminished Triad. A *triad of which the 5th is diminished.

Diminuendo (It.). Diminishing, i.e. gradually getting quieter.

Diminution. Shortening of the time-values of the notes of melodic parts. Opposite of *Augmentation. In *Canon by Diminution* the imitating vv. are in shorter notes than the one they are imitating.

Dimitrij. Opera in 3 acts by Dvořák to lib. by Marie Červinková-Riegrová based on writings by Mikovec and on Schiller's *Demetrius*. Comp. 1881–2, prod. Prague 1882. Rev. version prod. Prague 1885; further rev. 1894–5. Brit. f.p. Nottingham 1979.

Di Molto (It.). Of much, i.e. Very. Augments the word to which it is applied, e.g. *allegro di molto*, very fast.

D'India, Sigismondo. See *India, Sigismondo d'*.

D'Indy, (Paul Marie Théodore) **Vincent** (*b* Paris, 1851; *d* Paris, 1931). Fr. composer and teacher. Though musically trained in boyhood his family wanted him to enter law. In 1872 he sent a pf. qt. to *Franck, who agreed to teach him. As a member of Franck's class at the Paris Cons. he imbibed not only Franck's teaching, but also his lofty and idealistic attitude to art. To supplement his studies, d'Indy in 1872 became 2nd perc. player in the Colonne Orch., and from 1875–9 was ch.-master of the Concerts Colonne. Public début as composer 1874. In 1876 he attended the first Bayreuth Fest., having been introduced to Wagner's mus. by *Duparc in 1869, and became fervent enthusiast of *The Ring*. Keenly interested in education, d'Indy in 1894 accepted invitation from *Bordes to join him and Guilmant in founding the Schola Cantorum for the study of church mus. In 1900 this became a general mus. sch. at which d'Indy taught comp. until his death, becoming sole dir. in 1911. His teaching methods are described in his 3-vol. *Cours de Composition*, written in assoc. with A. Sérieyx. His pupils incl. Satie, Auric, Roussel, Turina, and Roland-Manuel. D'Indy was also active in assisting Lamoureux to introduce Wagner's works to Paris, was a champion of Debussy, and revived the mus. of Monteverdi, Rameau, Gluck, and Bach. He wrote several books (incl. biography of Franck), toured as cond. abroad, ed. old mus. (incl. several Monteverdi operas), and pubd. colls. of folksongs. His comps. are characterized by rich orchestration, a vein of folk-like melody, and often employ Franck's 'cyclic method'. Chief among them are:

OPERAS: Le Chant de la cloche (1879–83), Fervaal (1889–95), L'Étranger (1898–1901), La Légende de Saint-Christophe (1908–15), Le Rêve de Cynias (1922–3).
ORCH: La Forêt enchantée (1878), Wallenstein, trilogy (1874–82), *Symphonie sur un chant montagnard français (Symphonie Cévenole) (1886), Istar (1896), 2nd Sym. (1902–3), Jour d'été à la montagne (1905), Le Poème des rivages (1920–1).
CHAMBER MUSIC: 3 str. qts., vc. sonata, vn. sonata, pf. quintet, str. sextet.
PIANO: Promenades, Schumanniana, Menuet sur le nom de Haydn, Conte de fées.
CHORAL: Sainte Marie-Magdaleine, cantata (1885), Sur la Mer (1888), Deus Israël (1896).

Dinner Engagement, A. 1-act comic opera by Lennox Berkeley to lib. by Paul Dehn. Prod. Aldeburgh 1954.

Dinorah, ou le pardon de Ploërmel. 3-act opera by Meyerbeer to lib. by Barbier and Carré. Prod. Paris and London 1859, New Orleans 1861. Contains the coloratura sop. 'Shadow Song'.

Dioclesian (The Prophetess or the History of Dioclesian). Semi-opera by Purcell (1690). Dialogue by T. Betterton, adapted from Beaumont and Massinger.

Diplomas. See Degrees and Diplomas.

Dippel, (Johann) **Andreas** (b Kassel, 1866; d Hollywood, Calif., 1932). Ger. ten. and impresario. Member of opera cos. in Bremen 1887–92 and Vienna 1893–8. Début CG 1897, NY Met. 1890. At NY Met. 1890–1908, becoming joint man. with *Gatti-Casazza 1908–10. Man., Chicago Opera, 1910–13. Sang over 150 roles and was famous for ability to replace indisposed colleague at very short notice.

Direct. The sign ∿ at the end of a page or line (in older mus.) to give warning of the next note.

Dirge (Lat. naenia). Burial or memorial song, often with character of funeral march. Shakespeare's Dirge for Fidele (Cymbeline) has been set by several composers incl. Vaughan Williams (1922) and Finzi (1942). The 15th cent. Lyke-wake Dirge was set by Stravinsky (Cantata 1952), Britten (Serenade 1943), and Whittaker (1924).

Dirge for Two Veterans. (1) Setting of text from Whitman's Drum Taps (1865) by Holst for male vv., brass, and perc. Comp. 1914.
(2) Setting of same text for ch. and orch. by Vaughan Williams, comp. 1911 and incorporated into his cantata Dona nobis pacem (1936) as 4th movement.

Dirigent, dirigieren (Ger.). 'Conductor', 'to conduct'.

Dis (Ger.). The note D♯.

Disc (Amer. Disk). Gramophone record.

Discant. Same as *Descant.

Discography. A list of gramophone recordings, either of those of the mus. of a particular composer, or those made by an individual artist, orch., or instr. combination. When an artist has recorded for several cos. and in several countries, these can require considerable and valuable research. A discography is becoming a standard feature of many books on music.

Discord. A chord which is restless, jarring to the ear, requiring to be resolved in a particular way if its presence is to be justified by the ear (or the note or interval responsible for producing this effect).

Disis (Ger.). The note D♯♯.

Disjunct Motion. A note which moves to another note or an adjacent note by a leap. See Motion.

Dissonance. See Discord.

Dissonanzen Quartett (Les Dissonances). Ger. and Fr. nicknames for Mozart's Str. Qt. No. 19 in C major, K465, comp. 1785. The introduction contains remarkable use of dissonance.

Di Stefano, Giuseppe (b Molta Santa Anastasia, nr. Catania, 1921). It. tenor. Studied in Milan. Début 1946 Reggio Emilia as Des Grieux in Massenet's Manon. La Scala début 1947, NY Met. 1948 (Duke in Rigoletto). Brit. début Edinburgh Fest. 1957, CG 1961 (Cavaradossi). Sang often with *Callas, making recordings with her, and partnering her on her 1973–4 concert tour.

Distler, Hugo (b Nuremberg, 1908; d Berlin, 1942). Ger. composer and organist whose work was stigmatized by the Nazi régime as 'degenerate art'. Studied Leipzig. Organist of Jakobikirche, Lübeck, 1931–7. Teacher at Stuttgart Musikhochschule, 1937–40. Berlin Hochschule für Musik from 1940. Comp. org. works and choral mus., also hpd. conc. (1935) and str. qt. (1939–40). Committed suicide.

Distratto, Il (The Distraught Man). Nickname for Haydn's sym. in C major, No. 60 in Breitkopf edn. of syms. 6 movements are derived from Haydn's incidental mus. (1774) for J. F. Regnard's play Le Distrait (Ger. Der Zerstreute), revived at Esterház that year.

Dital Harp. Obsolete instr. invented in 1798 by Edward Light, a teacher of guitar: it was at first called Harp Guitar. By 'dital' is meant a finger-key (actually played by the thumb): each dital raised the pitch of a string by a semitone. Another name was Harp Lute, the appearance of the instr. suggesting the body of a lute continued upwards by that of a small harp.

Dithyramb (from Gr. *dithyrambos*). In ancient Greece an intoxicated song in honour of the god Dionysus; in modern usage applied to a comp. of wild, passionate character.

Dittersdorf, Karl Ditters von (orig. Karl Ditters) (*b* Vienna, 1739; *d* Neuhof, 1799). Austrian composer and violinist. As boy, in private orch. of nobleman who paid for his education. Kapellmeister to various princes, esp. to Prince-Bishop of Breslau 1770–95. Ennobled 1773. Prolific composer, works incl. 40 operas (incl. *The Marriage of Figaro* (c.1789) and *The Merry Wives of Windsor* (1796)), c.120 syms. (incl. 12 syms. after Ovid's *Metamorphoses*), 35 concs., 12 str. quintets, 14 str. trios, 17 vn. sonatas, 30 pf. sonatas, and quantities of church mus.

Div. Abbreviation for **Divisi.*

Diversions. Occasional synonym for variations.

Divertimenti by Mozart. Mozart's comps. to which he gave the title Divertimento are: E♭ (K113), D major (K131), D major (str. qt., K136), B♭ (str. qt., K137), F major (str. qt. K138), E♭ (K166), B♭ (K186), C major (K187), C major (K188), D major (K205), F major (K213), B♭ (K240), F major (K247), D major (K251), E♭ (K252), F major (K253), B♭ (pf. trio, K254), B♭ (K270), B♭ (K287), F major (K288), E♭ (K289), D major (K334), E♭ (str. trio, K563), E♭ (K Anh.226), B♭ (K Anh.227).

Divertimento (It.). Amusement. (1) An 18th-cent. suite of movements of light, recreational mus., sometimes for open-air perf., for a small no. of players. Mozart wrote 25, calling them Divertimenti or sometimes serenades or cassations. In the 20th cent. composers use the term to denote a not-too-serious work.
    (2) Fantasia on airs from operas, etc.

Divertissement (Fr.). Amusement. The same as **divertimento*, with the additional meaning of an entertainment of dances and songs inserted in an 18th-cent. stage spectacle or sometimes in a ballet or opera (as in Gounod's *Faust* or Delibes's *Coppélia*). The term is also applied to a suite of dances unconnected by a story. Ibert's *Divertissement* is an orch. work derived from mus. for the film *The Italian Straw Hat*.

Dives and Lazarus, 5 Variants of. Work by Vaughan Williams for str. and harp(s) comp. 1939 for NY World Fair. F.p. NY 1939. *Dives and Lazarus* is Eng. folk-song.

Divina Commedia, Symphony to (Liszt). See *Dante Symphony*.

Divine Office. The Canonical Hours of the RC Church (*Matins, Lauds, Prime, Terce, Sext, None, Vespers*, and *Compline*: these are daily said by all the clergy and in cath. and monastic churches are daily said or sung). Also *Matins* and *Evensong* in the Church of England.

Divine Poem, The (*Bozhestvennaya poema*). Title of Skryabin's Sym. No. 3 in C minor, Op. 43, comp. 1902–4, f.p. Paris 1905, NY 1907, London 1913. Illustrates his theosophical ideas; the 3 movements are entitled *Struggles, Delights,* and *Divine Play.*

Divisi (It.). Divided, often abbreviated to 'div.'. Term used, for instance, where orch. str. parts are written in double (or more) notes, and the players, instead of individually attempting to play all the notes of each chord, are to divide themselves into 2 (or more) groups to perform them.

Divisions. (1, 17th and 18th cent.) The splitting up of the notes of a tune into shorter notes, i.e. a form of variation; this was especially common in viol playing and was extemporized.
    (2) Long vocal runs, as in Bach, Handel, and other 18th-cent. composers. Obsolete term.

Division Viol. Small bass viol for the playing of popular sets of (often extemporized) variations.

Dixieland. Style of instr. jazz-playing from c.1912, also called 'New Orleans' or 'classic' style. Had elements of ragtime and blues with own distinctive improvisation. Dixieland bands were divided into 2 sections, one providing rhythm and harmony, the other melody and extemporization. The melody section consisted of tpt. or cornet, cl., and tb. (and, later, sax.); the rhythm section of pf. and/or banjo, trap drums, and sousaphone, tuba, or plucked db. Outstanding Dixieland performers were Louis Armstrong, Kid Ory, King Oliver, Sidney Bechet, Jelly Roll Morton, and Earl Hines.

Dixon, (Charles) **Dean** (*b* NY, 1915; *d* Zug, Switz., 1976). Amer. cond., one of the first blacks to achieve fame as a symphonic cond. Trained Juilliard Sch. and Columbia Univ. Début NY Town Hall 1937, NY P.O. 1942, and then other leading orchs. Founded Amer. Youth Orch. 1944. In 1949 cond. in Scandinavia. Cond. Israel P.O. 1950–1. Mus. dir. Gothenburg S.O. 1953–60, Hesse Radio S.O. 1961–74, Sydney S.O. 1964–7. British début 1963 with BBC S.O. Series of concerts with leading Amer. orchs. after 1970.

Djamileh. 1-act opera by Bizet to lib. by L. Gallet based on Alfred de Musset's poem *Namouna* (1832). Prod. Paris 1872, Manchester 1892, London 1893.

Do. The name for **Ut* or C in the Romance languages, introduced by G. M. **Bononcini*, 1673. See *Doh*.

Dobbs, Mattiwilda (*b* Atlanta, 1925). Amer. coloratura sop. Studied pf. for 10 years, then turned to singing at 17 and studied with Lotte Leonard in NY 1946–50. Studied with **Bernac* in Paris 1950–2, winning Geneva Fest. first prize 1951 and appearing in concerts in Scandinavia, Fr., etc. Opera début as Stravinsky's Nightingale, Holland Fest. 1952. First black singer to appear at

La Scala, Milan, 1953. Outstanding Zerbinetta in Strauss's *Ariadne auf Naxos*, Glyndebourne 1953. CG début 1954. Member of NY Met. co. from 1957.

Dobrowen, Issay (Alexandrovich) (*b* Nizhny Novgorod, 1891; *d* Oslo, 1953). Russ.-born cond., pianist, and composer. Studied in Moscow with Taneyev and Vienna with Godowsky. Début as cond. Moscow 1919 (Bolshoy 1921). Worked at Dresden with Fritz Busch, cond. first Ger. perf. of *Boris Godunov* (Dresden, 1922). Worked in Vienna, Sofia, and Budapest, frequent visitor to USA. Cond. Göteborg S.O. 1939, Stockholm Royal Opera from 1941. Comps. incl. concs. for pf. and vn. Became Norweg. citizen in 1930s.

Dobrowolski, Andrzej (*b* Lemberg, now Lwów, 1921). Polish composer and teacher. Studied Kraków Sch. of Mus. 1945–51 (org., singing, cl., theory with Lobaczewski, and comp. with Malawski). Worked for Polish radio experimental studio. From 1954 teacher at Warsaw Acad. Works incl. sym. vars. (1949), sym. (1955), bn. conc. (1953), wind trio (1955), *Music for Orch. I* (1969), *II* (1971), *III* (1972–3), *IV* (1974), *V* (1979); *Music for Magnetic Tape No. 1* (1963) (reproduced on p. 223), songs, and *musique concrète*.

Docteur Miracle, Le (Doctor Miracle). Operetta in 1 act by Bizet to lib. by Battu and Halévy. Prod. Paris 1857, London 1957, also 1-act operetta by Lecocq, prod. Paris 1857, the day before Bizet's, both works being entries in competition sponsored by Offenbach and being adjudged joint winners. F. Eng. stage p. of Lecocq, London 1984.

Doctor of Music. Highest mus. degree in Brit., Commonwealth, and USA. According to individual univ. style, abbreviated to D.Mus., Mus.D., or Mus. Doc.

Dodecaphonic (Gr.). 12 sounds. Adjective describing the system of comp. with 12 notes (dodecaphony). In the dodecaphonic scale the 12 notes are considered to be of equal status and are so treated. See *Atonal* and *Note-row*.

Dodge, Charles (*b* Ames, Iowa, 1942). Amer. composer. Studied Univ. of Iowa 1960–4, Columbia Univ. 1964–70. Specialist in elec. and computer-programmed mus. Works incl. *Changes* (computer-synthesized sounds on tape), *Earth's Magnetic Field* (elec. on tape), and *Humming* (computer-synthesized vocal and elec. sounds on tape).

Dodgson, Stephen (*b* London, 1924). Eng. composer. Studied under R.O. Morris and others. Works incl. sym., pf. qt., guitar concs., songs, and pf. pieces. Sym. for wind (1974); *Epigrams from a Garden*, cont. and cls. (1977). Frequent broadcaster.

Dods, Marcus (*b* Edinburgh, 1918; *d* Henley-on-Thames, 1984). Scot. cond. Cond. at SW 1951–8.

Frequent cond. of ballet, TV opera, West End musicals, film mus., etc.

Doglia (It.). Sorrow. So *doglioso*, sorrowful; *dogliosamente*, sorrowfully.

Doh. In Tonic sol-fa the spoken name for the tonic (first degree) of the scale. *Doh* sharpened becomes *de*.

Dohnányi, Christoph von (*b* Berlin, 1929). Ger. conductor. Grandson of Ernö *Dohnányi. Studied Munich 1948–51. Ass. cond. to Solti, Frankfurt Opera 1952. Gen. mus. dir. Lübeck 1957–63, Kassel 1963–6, Frankfurt 1968–77, Hamburg 1977–84. Chief cond. W. Ger. Radio S.O. 1964–70, Cleveland Orch. from 1984. Brit. début 1965 (LPO), CG 1974 (*Salome*). Cond. f.ps. of Henze's *Der junge Lord* (Berlin 1965) and *Die Bassariden* (Salzburg 1966).

Dohnányi, Ernö (Ernst von) (*b* Pozsony, now Bratislava, 1877; *d* NY, 1960). Hung. composer, pianist, and cond. Studied pf. and harmony with Karoly Forstner (cath. organist) 1885–94; entered Budapest Acad. 1894. Also studied with d'Albert. Concert pianist of int. repute 1897–1908. London début 1898 (Richter concert). Prof of pf., Berlin Hochschule, 1908. Dir. Budapest Cons. 1919. Dir. Hungarian radio 1931, Hochschule 1934. Cond. Budapest P.O. 1919–44. Settled in USA 1949 at Florida State Univ., Tallahassee, as prof. of pf. and comp. His mus. has nationalist flavour but much less than that of Bartók and Kodály. Prin. works:

OPERAS: *Tante Simona* (Dresden 1913), *The Tower of Voivod* (Budapest 1922), *The Tenor* (Budapest 1929).

ORCH: Sym. in D minor (1900–01), in E (1943–4, rev. 1953–6), pf. conc. No. 1 (1897–8), No. 2 (1946–7), vn. conc. No. 1 (1914–15), no. 2 (1949–50), *Suite* in F# minor (1908–9), *Variations on a Nursery Song* for pf. and orch. (1913).

CHAMBER MUSIC: 3 str. qts., 2 pf. quintets, vc. sonata, vn. sonata, sextet (1935).

PIANO: 4 *Klavierstücke*, 4 *Rhapsodies*, *Variations*, *Passacaglia*, and *Ruralia Hungarica* (1923, orch. 1924).

Doktor Faust. Opera in 2 prols., interlude, and 3 scenes by Busoni to his own lib., comp. 1916–24, the final scene being completed by *Jarnach. Prod. Dresden (Busch) 1925, London (concert) 1937, NY (concert) 1964.

Doktor, Paul (Karl) (*b* Vienna, 1919). Austrian-born violist. Studied va. with father, Karl Doktor (violist in Busch Qt. for over 30 years). Vienna State Acad. of Mus. until 1938. Prin. violist Lucerne S.O. 1940–7. Won Geneva Int. Fest. 1942. Went to USA 1947. Lecturer, violist in resident qt., Univ. of Michigan 1948–51; prof. of va., Mannes College of Mus., NY 1952. Summer faculty Colorado College from 1957. On staff

Juilliard Sch. from 1971. Soloist with leading orchs., ed. of va. mus.

Dolcan (Org. stop). Same as *Dolce.

Dolce (It.). Sweet (with the implication of 'soft' also). Hence *dolcissimo*, very sweet; *dolcemente*, sweetly; *dolcezza*, sweetness.

Dolce or **dolcan** (org. stop). Soft open metal *diapason; pipes are of inverted conical shape; 8' length and pitch.

Dolente (It.). Doleful, sorrowful. So the adverb *dolentemente* and the superlative *dolentissimo*.

Doles, Johann Friedrich (*b* Steinbach, 1715; *d* Leipzig, 1797). Ger. composer and court musician. Pupil of Bach at Leipzig from 1739. Cantor, Thomas-schule, Leipzig, 1756–89 and mus. dir. of 2 prin. Leipzig churches. Comp. church mus., hpd. sonatas, and songs in light operatic style.

Dollarprinzessin, Die (The Dollar Princess). Operetta in 3 acts by *Fall, to lib. by A.M. Willner and F. Grünbaum based on comedy by Gatti-Trotha. Prod. Vienna 1907, London and NY 1909.

Dolly. Pf. suite by Fauré, Op. 56, comp. 1894–7, for 4 hands. 6 movements are: *Berceuse, Mi-a-ou, Le Jardin de Dolly, Kitty-valse, Tendresse,* and *Le Pas espagnol.* Orch. version by *Rabaud, 1906.

Dolmetsch, Arnold (*b* Le Mans, 1858; *d* Haslemere, 1940). Swiss musician and maker of old instr. Studied vn. in Brussels with *Vieuxtemps, later going to RCM, London. Taught vn. Dulwich Coll. 1885–9. Restored old instrs., made his first lute 1893, clavichord 1894, harpsichord 1896. Worked on early kbd. instr. at Chickering's pf. factory, Boston, Mass., 1902–9; in charge Gaveau's hpd. dept., Paris, 1911–4. Settled in Eng. at Haslemere, Surrey, 1917, establishing workshop for manufacture and repair of clavichords, hpds., viols, lutes, recorders, etc., and founding (1925) annual fest. at which old mus. was perf. by himself and his family on authentic instr.

Dolmetsch, Carl (Frederick) (*b* Fontenay-s-Bois, 1911). Eng. recorder-player, son of Arnold *Dolmetsch. Studied with his father and at 15 was a virtuoso, touring the world. Also makes recorders and plays vn. and lute. Ed. of recorder mus. Dir., Haslemere Fest. since 1940. C.B.E. 1954.

Dolore (It.). Sorrow, dolour, pain. Hence *doloroso*, dolorous, painful, and the adverb, *dolorosamente*.

Dolzflöte (Ger.). Same as It. *Flauto dolce*, i.e. a soft-toned org. stop of fl. tone.

Domanínska (Kobáskova, Vyčichlová), **Libuše** (*b* Brno, 1924). Cz. soprano. Studied at Brno Cons. Début Brno Opera, becoming a principal in the co. Outstanding exponent of Janáček heroines. Joined Prague Nat. Th. 1955, visiting Edinburgh Fest., Holland Fest., and Helsinki. Sang at Vienna Opera 1958–68.

Domestic Symphony (Strauss). See *Symphonia domestica.*

Domgraf-Fassbänder, Willi (*b* Aachen, 1897; *d* Nuremberg, 1978). Ger. bar., father of Brigitte *Fassbaender. Studied Aachen, making operatic début there 1922 as the Count in Mozart's *Figaro*. Prin. lyric bar., Berlin State Opera 1928–45. Sang Mozart's Figaro at opening night of Glyndebourne Opera, 1934. Chief producer, Nuremberg Opera, 1953–62. On retirement became dir. of opera studies, Nuremberg Cons.

Dominant. (1) 5th degree of major or minor scale, thus if the key is B (major or minor) the dominant is F♯. Chords built on this note are *dominant chords*, the most important being the *dominant seventh* which is a chord consisting of the common chord of the dominant with the minor 7th from its root added, e.g. in key C it is G–B–D–F. Like all intervals of a 7th, the dominant 7th is a discord. It normally resolves on the Tonic or Submediant chord, the note constituting the 7th falling a semitone, allowing the 3rd (i.e. the leading note of the scale) to rise to the tonic. More rarely the 7th can remain as a note common to the following chord, usually the 1st or 2nd inversion of the subdominant. The three inversions of the Dominant Seventh chord are, of course, in common use.

(2) See *Modes.*

Dominant Cadence. Same as Imperfect Cadence, or Half Close.

Domingo, Placido (*b* Madrid, 1941). Sp. tenor. Lived in Mexico from 1950, studying pf., cond. with Markevich and singing at Mexico Nat. Cons. Début as baritone 1957 in zarzuela. Opera début as ten. 1960 (Alfredo in *La traviata*). Member of Israeli Nat. Opera 1962–5. Amer. début 1961 (Dallas, as Arturo in *Lucia di Lammermoor*). NY Met. début 1968 (*Adriana Lecouvreur*), Scala, Milan 1969 (as Ernani), CG 1971 (Cavaradossi). Sang his first Otello Hamburg 1975. Outstanding exponent of lyrical and heroic roles of It. opera, but also a fine Walther in *Die Meistersinger*. Has also cond. opera, incl. *Die Fledermaus* at CG, 1983.

Dominguez, Oralia (*b* S. Luis Potosi, Mexico, 1928). Mexican mez. Studied Mexico Nat. Cons. Operatic début, Nat. Opera of Mexico. Has sung since 1953 at world's leading opera houses, also concerts and recitals. CG début 1955 as Sosostris in f.p. of Tippett's *The Midsummer Marriage*. Has sung Mrs Quickly in *Falstaff* at CG and Glyndebourne (1967–8).

Dominicus Mass, or **Pater Dominicus Mass.** Mozart's Mass in C, K66 (1769). Written for the first celebration of mass by a young priest who had taken that name.

Domnich, Heinrich (*b* Würzburg, 1767; *d* Paris, 1844). Ger. virtuoso hn.-player. Prof. of hn. Paris Cons. 1795–1817. Comp. concs. and romances for hn. Wrote first definitive tutor for the hn. (Paris, 1807).

Domp(e). See *Dump.*

Domra. Russ. instr., like *balalaika, played by plucking. Has convex back like *mandolin.

Dona nobis pacem (Give us peace). (1) Part of the *Mass.

(2) Cantata by Vaughan Williams to text selected from the Bible, Whitman, and a parliamentary speech by John Bright. Comp. 1936, except for movt. *Dirge for Two Veterans* (1911). F.p. Huddersfield 1936, London 1936 (broadcast), 1938 (public).

Donath, Helen (Helen Erwin) (*b* Corpus Christi, Texas, 1940). Amer. sop. Pupil of Paola Novickova. Member of Cologne Opera under Sawallisch 1962–3. Sang in Hanover 1963–4, Salzburg Fest. 1967, San Francisco Opera, Vienna Opera. Frequent recitalist in Lieder and concert-hall choral works. Husband is Klaus Donath, mus. dir. Darmstadt Opera.

Donato, Anthony (*b* Prague, Nebraska, 1909). Amer. composer and violinist. Studied Eastman Sch. of Mus. Has held several teaching posts. Comps. incl. 2 syms., 3 str. qts., 2 vn. sonatas, hn. sonata.

Donato (Donati), **Baldassare** (*b* Venice, *c.*1530; *d* Venice, 1603). It. composer and church musician. Maestro di cappella, St Mark's, Venice, from 1590, having been singer there since 1550. Wrote madrigals and motets.

Donatoni, Franco (*b* Verona, 1927). It. composer. Studied Verdi Cons., Milan, 1946–8, Martini Cons., Bologna, 1948–51, Accademia S. Cecilia, Rome, 1952–3 (with Pizzetti). Teacher since 1953 in various It. cons. Comps. incl. 4 str. qts., concertino for perc., str., and brass, *Sinfonia* for str., 3 *Improvisations* for pf., *Doubles* for hpd., *Doubles II* for orch., *Souvenir* for 15 instr.

Donaueschingen. Town in W. Germany with a mus. tradition going back to 17th cent. but notable especially for foundation in 1921 of first fest. devoted exclusively to contemporary mus. Fest. programmes 1921–6 planned mainly by Hindemith and Joseph Haas and incl. works by Křenek and Hába. In 1926 fest. was moved to Baden-Baden, with emphasis on chamber opera, and in 1930 to Berlin, where competition from New Mus. fest. proved too great. In 1950 fest. was revived in collab. with S.W. Ger. Radio, Baden-Baden, using radio orch. under Rosbaud and, from 1964, Ernest Bour. Among composers brought to the fore at post-1950 fests. are Boulez, Stockhausen, Xenakis, Nono, Ligeti, Berio, Fortner, Penderecki, and Henze. F.ps. there incl. Hindemith's *Kammermusik No. 1* (1922), Webern's *6 Songs*, Op. 14 (1924), Schoenberg's *Serenade*, Op. 24 (1924), Boulez's *Poésie pour pouvoir* (1958),

Messiaen's *Chronochromie* (1960), and Stockhausen's *Mantra* (1970).

Don Carlos. 5-act opera by Verdi, to French lib. by Méry and du Locle after Schiller's play, comp. 1866, prod. Paris 1867, London CG 1867, NY 1877. This orig. version was heavily cut in Paris; the f.p. of the uncut score was in a BBC studio production in 1973, cond. by John Matheson. There was a stage perf., omitting only the ballet *La Pérégrina,* in Boston, Mass., 1975. In 1882–3 Verdi reduced it to 4 acts by omitting Act I (the 'Fontainebleau scene'), and in 1886 he restored orig. Act I to the 4-act rev. It. version is properly known as *Don Carlo.* In recent years both 5- and 4-act versions have been perf. and tendency has grown to sing it in Fr. rather than in It. trans.

Done, William (*b* Worcester, 1815; *d* Worcester, 1895). Eng. organist and cond. Organist Worcester Cath., 1844–95, also cond. at 3 Choirs Fests. in that period.

Don Giovanni (*Il dissoluto punito, ossia Il Don Giovanni*; The Rake punished, or Don Giovanni). *Dramma giocoso* in 2 acts by Mozart (K527) to lib. by da Ponte based on the Don Juan legend as told in Bertati's play (1775). Comp. 1787. Prod Prague 1787, Vienna 1788 (with extra material), London 1817, NY 1826. See also *Don Juan.*

Donington, Robert (*b* Leeds, 1907). Eng. author, composer, musicologist, and authority on old instr. Studied with A. *Dolmetsch, R. O. Morris, and Wellesz. Expert player of viola da gamba; worked with Dolmetsch at Haslemere. Played in Eng. Consort of Viols 1935–9, London Consort 1950–60, Donington Consort 1956–61. Prof. of mus. at several Amer. univs. 1961–71. Comp. 12-note works. Several books on early mus. but most famous books are his *Wagner's 'Ring' and its Symbols* (1963), a detailed exposition of the psychological basis of *Der Ring des Nibelungen*; and two major books on performance practice in early mus., *The Interpretation of Early Music* (London, 1963) and *Performer's Guide to Baroque Music* (London, 1973). O.B.E. 1979.

Donizetti, Gaetano (*b* Bergamo, 1797; *d* Bergamo, 1848). It. composer, principally of operas. Pupil of *Mayr at Bergamo and of Padre Mattei at Bologna. Because of parental opposition to mus. career, he joined the Austrian army, composing in his off-duty spells. His opera *Enrico di Borgogna* was prod. Venice, 1818, and his 4th opera, *Zoraida di Granata* was so successful in Rome in 1822 that he obtained his release from the army. In the next 8 years he wrote nearly 30 operas which were perf. throughout It. His first int. success was with *Anna Bolena* (1830), and this was followed by the comedy *L'Elisir d'Amore* (1832), and by his masterpiece *Lucia di Lammermoor* (1835). For Paris, 1840, he comp. the light-hearted *La Fille du Régiment* and the large-scale *La Favorite.* His last success was also in Paris, with

Don Pasquale in 1843. Donizetti was prof. of counterpoint at Naples Cons. 1835–7, becoming dir. in 1837. He became paralysed and mentally unbalanced as a result of syphilis in 1844.

Donizetti's ability to write at great speed has prejudiced attitudes to the quality of his work; so has the fact that he wrote specifically for a generation of great singers such as Grisi, Mario, Lablache, and Tamburini. However, though he catered for their ability and agility, the tendency to underrate the melodic and dramatic content of his operas has only recently been corrected by a more discriminating willingness to recognise Donizetti's brilliance as a rival in comic opera to Rossini; and to acknowledge the debt, in the form of recognizable borrowings, owed to him by Verdi, who clearly appreciated his dramatic mastery. Recently several of Donizetti's lesser-known operas have been revived and found to have unsuspected merit. He also wrote church mus., 12 str. qts., and some orch. works. A list of his operas follows:

Enrico di Borgogna, Una follia (1818); *Il falegname di Livonia, Le nozze in villa* (1819); *Zoraida di Granata, La zingara, La lettera anonima, Chiara e Serafina* (1822); *Il fortunato inganno, Alfredo il Grande* (1823); *L'ajo nell'imbarazzo, Emilia di Liverpool* (1824); *Alahor in Granata, Elvida, Gabriella di Vergy* (1826); *Olivo e Pasquale, Il borgomastro di Saardam, Le convenienze ed inconvenienze teatrali, Otto mesi in due ore* (1827); *Alina, regina di Golconda, Gianni di Calais, Il Giovedi Grasso, L'esule di Roma* (1828); *Il Paria, Elisabetta, o Il castello di Kenilworth* (1829); *Il diluvio universale, I pazzi per progetto, Imelda de' Lambertazzi, *Anna Bolena* (1830); *Gianni di Parigi, La Romanziera, Francesca di Foix* (1831); *Fausta, Ugo, conte di Parigi, L'*elisir d'amore, Sancia di Castiglia* (1832); *Il furioso, Parisina, Torquato Tasso, *Lucrezia Borgia* (1833); *Rosmonda d'inghilterra, *Maria Stuarda, Gemma di Vergy* (1834); *Marino Faliero, *Lucia di Lammermoor* (1835); *Belisario, Il campanello di notte, L'assedio di Calais, Betly* (1836); *Roberto Devereux, Pia de' Tolomei* (1837); *Poliuto, Maria di Rudenz* (1838); *Le *Duc d'Albe* (1839); *La *Fille du régiment, La *Favorite* (1840); *Adelia, o La Figlia dell'arciere, Rita, ou le mari battu, Maria Padilla* (1841); *Linda di Chamounix, Caterina Cornaro* (1842); *Maria di Rohan, *Don Pasquale, Dom Sébastien, roi de Portugal* (1843).

Don Juan. (1) The legend of the libertine Don Juan has been the basis of many plays since that of Tirso di Molina in 1630, and of many operas, Mozart's *Don Giovanni* being the best-known. Other composers who have treated the subject incl. Melani, Gazzaniga, Fabrizi, Federici, Dibdin, Pacini, Dargomyzhsky, Delibes, Alfano, and Goossens.

(2) Tone poem, Op. 20, by Richard Strauss, based on poem by Lenau, comp. 1888, f.p. Weimar 1889.

(3) Ballet-pantomime in 3 acts, music by Gluck, lib. by Calzabigi, based on Molière. Prod. Vienna 1761.

Donna Diana. Opera in 3 acts by *Rezniček to lib. by composer based on Moreto's comedy *El Lindo Don Diego* (1654). Prod. Prague 1894. Rev. 1908 and 1933.

Donohoe, Peter (*b* Manchester, 1953). Eng. pianist. Studied at Chetham's Sch. of Mus., RMCM, and RNCM. Studied with Deryck Wyndham 1966–76 and then with Yvonne Loriod in Paris. Recital début, Manchester. Joint silver medal, Moscow Tchaikovsky Comp. 1982.

Don Pasquale. 3-act opera buffa by Donizetti to lib. by Ruffini and composer based on Anelli's *Ser Marc' Antonio* (1810) and ultimately derived from Ben Jonson's *Epicene*. Prod. Paris and London 1843, New Orleans 1845.

Don Quichotte (Don Quixote). Opera in 5 acts by Massenet to lib. by Henri Cain after Le Lorrain's play based on Cervantes's novel. Comp. 1908–9. Prod. Monte Carlo 1910, London 1912, NY 1914.

Don Quichotte à Dulcinée. 3 songs for v. and pf. by Ravel to poems by Paul Morand. Comp. 1932–3 (his last work). Also version for v. and orch. Written for a film starring Chaliapin.

Don Quixote. (1) Cervantes's novel, pubd. in 2 parts (1605, 1615), has been the inspiration of many mus. works. Operas on the subject have been comp. by Förtsch, Conti, Boismortier, Paisiello, Piccinni, Salieri, Hubaček, García, Mendelssohn, Mercadante, Donizetti, Macfarren, Clay, Jaques-Dalcroze, Heuberger, and Falla. Incidental mus. to a play by D'Urfey was written by Purcell, 1694–5.

(2) Tone-poem, Op. 35, by R. Strauss, comp. 1896–7, f.p. Cologne 1898. Introduction, theme and 10 variations, and finale, with solo parts for vc. and va. Sub-titled *Fantastische Variationen über ein Thema ritterlichen Charakters* (Fantastic Variations on a theme of knightly character).

(3) Ballets on the subject are also numerous, including Petipa's of 1869 with mus. by Minkus. More recent ballet mus. has been composed by Petrassi (1947), Ibert (1950), and *Gerhard (1950, SW, choreog. N. de Valois).

Donska, Maria (*b* Lódź, 1912). Polish pianist. Studied in Berlin with *Schnabel, later at RCM, London. Prof. of pf., RCM.

Dopo (It.). After.

Doppel (Ger.). Double.

Doppel B or **Doppel-be** (Ger.). Double flat.

Doppelchor (Ger.). Double chorus.

Doppelfagott (Ger.). Double Bassoon.

Doppelflöte (Ger.). Double flute. Wooden org. stop; sometimes end-plugged pipes: generally 8′ pitch (name comes from pipes having 2 mouths, one on each side, producing a loud and pure fl. tone).

Doppelfuge (Ger.). Double fugue.

Doppelkreuz (Ger.). Double sharp.

Doppelschlag (Ger.). Double stroke, i.e. the *turn (ornament).

Doppeltaktnote (Ger.). Double-measure-note, or two-bar note. The Breve, or Double Whole-note.

Doppelt so schnell (Ger.). Twice as fast.

Doppio (It.). Double. So *Doppio diesis, Doppio bemolle,* double sharp, double flat; *Doppio movimento,* double speed (i.e. twice the preceding speed).

Doppione. Rare medieval double-bore reed-cap wind instr., though experts have discovered that it was later blown directly. Had parallel conical bores, each with a basic set of 7 finger-holes.

Doppler, (Albert) **Franz** (*b* Lemberg, 1821; *d* Baden, nr. Vienna, 1883). Austrian flautist, cond., and composer. First fl., Pest Opera orch. 1847–58, Vienna Opera orch. from 1858. Prof. of fl., Vienna Cons. from 1865. Cond. ballet at Vienna Opera. Comp. 7 operas, ballets, fl. concs., etc.

Doppler, Karl (*b* Lemberg, 1825; *d* Stuttgart, 1900). Austrian flautist, composer, and cond., brother of above. Cond. at Pest Opera and at Vienna Opera 1862–5. Court cond., Stuttgart, 1865–98. Comp. operas, ballets, and fl. mus.

Dorabella. The 10th (Intermezzo) of Elgar's *Enigma Variations.* Mus. portrait of Dora Penny (Mrs Richard Powell), nickname being reference to *Così fan tutte.* Mrs Powell's book *Edward Elgar: Memories of a Variation* (London 1937) gives interesting domestic glimpses of the composer.

Dorati, Antal (*b* Budapest, 1906). Hung.-born cond. and composer (Amer. citizen since 1947). Studied Budapest Acad. and Univ., and Vienna Univ. Early career as opera cond. in Budapest (début 1924), Dresden, and Munster, then 2nd cond. Ballet Russe de Monte Carlo 1935–7, cond. orig. Ballet Russe 1938–41, and Ballet Th. 1941–5. Prin. cond. Dallas S.O. 1945–9, Minneapolis S.O. 1949–60, BBC S.O. 1962–6, Stockholm P.O. 1966, National Sym. of Washington D.C. 1970–6, RPO 1975–8, Detroit S.O. 1977–81. Comp. sym., vc. conc., cantata, ballet, and str. qt. Arr. ballet mus. Cond. recording with Philharmonia Hungarica of complete Haydn syms. and several Haydn operas. Hon. K.B.E. 1983.

Dorfmann, Ania (*b* Odessa, 1899). Russ. pianist. Studied in Paris. European tours 1920–6; later career mainly in USA. Teacher at Juilliard Sch. from 1966.

Dorfmusikanten Sextett (Mozart). See *Musical Offering.*

Dorian Mode. The Mode represented by the white keys of the pf. beginning at D. See *Modes.*

Dorian (Doric) Toccata and Fugue. Name given to a Toccata and Fugue in D minor by Bach because orig. copy omitted key-signature and thus suggested Dorian Mode.

Dorward, David (Campbell) (*b* Dundee, 1933). Scot. composer. Studied St Andrews Univ., RAM. Joined mus. staff, BBC Scotland, 1962. Works include 1-act opera *Tonight, Mrs Morrison,* sym., vc. conc., vn. conc., str. qts., songs, etc.

Dot, Dotted Note. Mark in notation. (1) Placed above a note indicates *staccato. (2) Placed after a note lengthens it by half. But in music up to and including Bach and Handel the addition intended was merely *approximately* half, something being left to the decision of the performer, e.g. a dotted quaver and a semiquaver in one part, played against a triplet of quavers in another part, might accommodate itself to that latter rhythm,

being rendered thus

Also in a very slow movement ♩. ♪ might be rendered ♩·· ♪. It was, indeed, to meet this latter case that the DOUBLE DOT (the second dot adding half the value of the first one) was in 1769 introduced by Mozart's father, Leopold Mozart.

Doublé (Fr.). The *turn (ornament).

Double. (1) (Fr.). A variation, especially one with elaborate ornamentation. Similar to Eng. 'division'.

(2) Indicates a lower octave, e.g. double bassoon plays an octave below bassoon.

(3) Singers who perform two roles in one work and instrumentalists who play more than one instr. in a comp. e.g. fl. doubles piccolo.

Double Action. The mechanism of a *harp invented by *Érard, so called to distinguish it from earlier models on which pitches could be raised only by a semitone.

Double Appoggiatura. See *Acciaccatura.*

Double Bar. The double perpendicular line marking the end of a comp. or of some section thereof. (It may or may not coincide with a single bar line and if it does not do so has no rhythmic function.) Usually reinforced when they mark the end of the work. With dots on either side of the lines they indicate that the previous or subsequent section is to be repeated.

Double Bass (or Contrabass). Largest and lowest-pitched of bowed string instruments, derived from the *Violone. Formerly had 3 strings but now generally has 4, usually tuned at the interval of a 4th. Compass from E just over an octave below bass stave upwards for nearly 3 octaves. Some instruments have 5 strings, extra string sounding B below bottom E. Generally an orchestral instrument, but occasionally used in chamber music and very occasionally as solo concerto instrument. Used in jazz and dance bands, mostly pizzicato.

Double-Bass Clarinet. Also known as pedal cl., or contrabass cl., in BB♭. Mainly used by military bands. Part written 9th higher than sounds.

Double Bassoon (Contrabassoon; Fr. 'Contrebassoon'; Ger. 'Kontrafagott'). Wind instr. octave deeper than *bassoon and notated octave higher than it sounds, though Wagner and Debussy sometimes wrote for it at pitch. Some baroque examples were made but standard modern design is Heckel's (1876). Conical bore tube is 18′ long, with 5 parallel sections connected by 4 U-bends. Crook fits into metal tube. Brahms scored for it in his 1st Sym. In Strauss's *Salome* there is a long solo for the instr. when Jokanaan descends into his cell.

Double-Bass Saxhorn. In B♭ or C. Almost identical with B♭ bass tuba, but with range complete at bottom. Sometimes treated as *transposing instr.

Double-Bass (Contrabass) **Trombone.** Pitched an octave below ten. tb.

Double-Bass (Contrabass) **Tuba.** One of the tuba family, pitched an octave below ten. tuba. Has wide conical bore and cup-shaped mouthpiece. Wagner used one to strengthen the bass of his 8-part harmony by doubling it an octave lower.

Double-Bass Viol. Also known as Violone or Consort Viol. Sounded an octave below bass viol. See *Viol*.

Double-bémol (Fr.). Double flat.

Double C. Sometimes used to indicate the note C, 2 lines below the bass stave.

Double Choir (or Chorus). Ch. arranged in 2 equal and complete bodies with a view not merely to singing in 8 parts but also to responsive effects, etc. Much used by Venetian composers of 16th and 17th cents.

Double Concerto. A conc. with 2 prin. instr., either of the same kind, as in double pf. conc., or different, as in Brahms's conc. for vn. and vc. Also

used to denote use of 2 orchs. (generally str.), e.g. Tippett's Conc. for double str. orch.

Double Counterpoint. Invertible *counterpoint concerning 2 vv. (permitting vv. to change places, the higher becoming lower and vice versa).

Double-croche (Fr.). Double-hook, i.e. semiquaver or 16th-note.

Double-Curtal. 16th-cent. instr., being a larger or different size of the *curtal or dulcian, ancestor of the bn. In Eng. it meant the bass curtal.

Double-dièse (Fr.). Double sharp.

Double Dot. See *Dot*.

Double English Horn. Org. stop of *Hope-Jones invention: 16′ *chorus reed.

Double Flat. The sign ♭♭ when placed before a note, indicates that its pitch is lowered a whole-step or tone. The resultant note has a simpler enharmonic name, e.g. on the pf., A♭♭ is G♮. See *Inflection of notes*.

Double Fugue. A *fugue with 2 subjects. There are 2 types: (1) in which the subjects appear from the start, and (2) in which the first subject is treated for a time, the other then appearing and being similarly treated, after which the 2 are combined.

Double-handed. Term applied to band of players that is convertible from wind to str. or to full orch; or to an instrumentalist who can play 2 different instr.

Double Harp. Early form of harp which had only 2 rows of str., diatonically tuned. Intermediate semitones could be obtained only by shortening the length of a str. with the thumb while plucking it with a finger. Not the same as *Double Action* Harp.

Double Horn. Valve *horn pitched in both F and B♭ alto.

Double Octaves. In pf.-playing, octaves played simultaneously in both hands.

Double Open Diapason. *Diapason org. stop of 16′ pitch.

Double Organ. (1, obsolete). Either one with a full kbd., descending to 8′ C or 12′ G, or one with 2 manuals.

(2, modern, sometimes used in USA). Org. with separate 'sanctuary' division.

Double Pedal. Harmonic *pedal in which 2 notes are held, generally tonic and dominant.

Double Reed. Wind instr. such as ob., cor anglais, Heckelphone, bn., and double bn., whose mouthpiece consists of 2 pieces of cane between which air is blown so that the 2 reeds vibrate against each other.

Double-sharp. The sign x which, placed before a note, raises it by a whole-step or tone. As with *Double-flat, the resultant note can be more simply named, e.g. F x is G♮ on the pf. See *Inflection of Notes.*

Double Stopping. Term used of str. instr., to indicate stopping and playing on 2 str. simultaneously to produce a 2-part effect. Also used, loosely, when one or both of the str. are 'open'.

Double Suspension. Harmonic term, when 2 notes of a chord are held over as a momentary discordant part of the following combination. Resolved by moving to notes which form real part of 2nd chord.

Double Tonguing. Fast method of articulation while playing wind instr. such as fl. and piccolo. Obtained by alternation of the sounds T and K or D and G when the mouth is applied to the embouchure. See *Tonguing.*

Double Virginals. A virginals of which the kbd. descended to C below bass stave.

Double Whole-Note. Amer. term for the *Breve.

Doubling. Term meaning (1) Duplication of a melody by several performers, e.g. 'the solo soprano's part is doubled by the oboe'.
(2) Duplication of instr. by one player, the commonest orch. example being the doubling of piccolo by one of the flautists, i.e. the 2nd flautist plays piccolo instead of fl. when required.

Douçaine. Medieval reed instr. about which information is very scanty, but it is thought to have been of ten. pitch and soft in tone.

Douglas, Nigel (*b* Lenham, Kent, 1934). Eng. ten. Studied Oxford and Vienna Mus. Acad. Prin. ten. Zürich Opera House from 1964; Vienna Volksoper 1964–8, Scottish Opera 1968–71, WNO 1971. Expert on Viennese operetta. Frequent broadcaster of mus. talks.

Douglas, (Richard) **Roy** (*b* Tunbridge Wells, 1907). Eng. composer, arranger, and mus. ed. Orch. of Chopin for ballet *Les Sylphides* used by many cos. Worked closely with Vaughan Williams 1944–58, and wrote book about their assoc. *Working with RVW* (1972). Comp. and arr. of mus. for brass band.

Doux, Douce (Fr.). Sweet. *Doucement,* sweetly.

Dowland, John (*b* London, ?1563; *d* London, 1626). Eng. composer, singer, and lutenist. From 1580 to 1584 was in service of Brit. Ambassador to Paris where he became R.C. Mus.B. Oxon 1588. Lutenist at courts at Brunswick, Hesse, Venice, Florence, and Nuremberg, 1595. Lutenist to King of Denmark 1598–1606. Returned to London 1606; musician to James I 1612. Though noted in his day as a virtuoso lutenist and singer, he is now recognized as a great composer, whose songs melodically and harmonically advanced the

'art song'. His printed songs numbered 87 of which 84 appeared in 4 vols. (3 *Books of Songs or Ayres,* 1597, 1600, 1603, and *A Pilgrims Solace,* 1612), and 3 in his son Robert's *Musical Banquet,* 1614. Among his finest songs are *Awake, Sweet Love; Come again Sweet Love; Fine Knacks for Ladies; Flow my Tears; Flow not so fast, ye Fountains; In Darkness let me Dwell; Sweet, stay awhile; Weep ye no more, sad Fountains; Welcome black night.* Among his other comps. are the *Lachrimae of 1604, which contains 21 instr. items incl. the celebrated *Semper Dowland semper dolens,* and many pieces for solo lute. These include *Walsingham, Loth to Depart, My Lady Hunsdons Puffe, Queen Elizabeths Galliard,* and *Dowlands Adew.*

Down-Beat. Downward movement of cond's. stick or hand, in particular when indicating first beat of the bar. See also *Up-beat.*

Down by the Greenwood Side. Dramatic pastoral by *Birtwistle to lib. by Michael Nyman for sop., mime and speech, and chamber ens. Comp. 1969.

Downes, Edward (*b* Birmingham, 1924). Eng. cond. and hn.-player. Studied Birmingham Univ. and RCM, later with H. *Scherchen. Ass. cond. Carl Rosa Opera 1950–1; staff cond. CG 1951–69. First Eng. cond. after 1945 to conduct full *Ring* cycle (1967); mus. dir. and chief cond. Australian Opera 1972–6. Trans. Russ. libs., e.g. *Khovanshchina and *Katerina Izmaylova.* Guest cond. leading sym. orchs. Prin. cond., BBC Philharmonic from 1980. Cond. f.p. of Maxwell Davies's *Taverner,* 1972, and first opera perf. in Sydney Opera House (*War and Peace,* 28 Sept. 1973). C.B.E. 1986.

Downes, Ralph (William) (*b* Derby, 1904). Eng. organist. Studied RCM. Lecturer Princeton Univ., NJ, 1928–35; organist London Oratory from 1936; designed many important orgs. incl. for Royal Festival Hall. Prof. RCM from 1954. C.B.E. 1969.

Doxologia, Doxology (from the Gr. *Doxa,* 'Glory', and *Logos* 'Discourse'). Any liturgical formula of praise, as the *Gloria patri* ('Glory be to the Father', etc., i.e. the 'Lesser Doxology', or 'Doxologia parva', used at the end of the Psalms), or the *Gloria in excelsis Deo* ('Glory to God in the highest'—the 'Greater Doxology', or 'Doxologia magna').
The 'Greater Doxology' is a part of the Roman Mass (sung to differing plainsong according to the feast); properly it should be left to the priest until the words 'Et in terra pax', when the choir should enter, but composers such as Bach, Mozart, and Beethoven have ignored this. In its Eng. wording the 'Greater Doxology' is a part of the Anglican Communion Service.

D'Oyly Carte, Richard (*b* London, 1844; *d* London, 1901). English impresario and producer of light operas, who brought together the librettist

Gilbert and the composer Sullivan for *Trial by Jury*, 1875. Partnership so successful he built theatre, the Savoy, which opened 1881 with *Patience*. His attempt to launch English grand opera with Sullivan's *Ivanhoe*, 1891, failed. His widow Helen (*d* 1913) continued management of 'Savoy operas', followed by son Rupert (1876–1948) and granddaughter Bridget. The Gilbert and Sullivan operas were generally presented in Britain professionally by the D'Oyly Carte Opera Co. until 1982 (they were known more widely as 'D'Oyly Carte operas' than as 'Savoy operas') but the D'Oyly Carte's exclusive ownership of them ended with expiry of Sullivan's copyright in 1950 and other opera companies have produced them, e.g. Sadler's Wells.

Draghi, Antonio (*b* Rimini, *c*.1635; *d* Vienna, 1700). Austrian composer and administrator of It. birth. Worked in Venice, went to Vienna 1658. Kapellmeister to Viennese court from 1682. Comp. operas, oratorios and cantatas, numerous serenades, etc.

Draghi, Giovanni Battista (*b c*.1640; *d* London, 1708). It. harpsichordist and composer who settled in Eng. and became organist to Charles II's queen, Catherine of Braganza, and mus.-teacher of the future Queen Anne. Wrote incid. mus. and songs for plays by Shadwell, Tate, Apra Behn, etc.

Dragonetti, Domenico (*b* Venice, 1763; *d* London, 1846). It. virtuoso on db. Largely self-taught. In orch. of St Mark's Venice, at age 18. Went to London 1794, playing in opera orch. and giving nationwide recitals with cellist *Lindley. Twice visited Vienna, where he knew Haydn and Beethoven. Played db. in f.p. of Beethoven's 9th Sym. Comp. solos for db. At 82 in 1845 led db. section in Bonn Beethoven Fest.

Dragoni, Giovanni Andrea (*b* Meldola, *c*.1540; *d* Rome, 1598). It. composer and pupil of Palestrina. Choirmaster at St John Lateran 1576–98. Comp. madrigals and motets.

Dramatic. (1) Applied to sop., ten., etc., a singer with a powerful vocal style suitable for forceful operatic roles.
   (2) Applied strictly to mus., this adjective signifies mus. written for the stage, but the much more general meaning is mus. of strongly theatrical spirit and effect, e.g. Tchaikovsky's 4th Sym., Berlioz's *Symphonie Fantastique*, Strauss's *Don Juan*, Beethoven's *Appassionata Sonata*, etc.

Dramaturg. Official at Ger. opera houses who adapts libs., edits programmes, works as press officer, and sometimes produces.

Drame Lyrique (Fr.). Lyric drama, i.e. serious opera. Debussy thus described his *Pelléas et Mélisande*.

Dramma Giocoso (It.). Comic drama. 18th-cent. It. term for comic operas containing tragic features. Used by Mozart to describe *Don Giovanni* and by Haydn for several of his operas.

Dramma per musica (It.). Drama through music. 17th- and 18th-cent. It. term for serious opera.

Drängend (Ger.). Urging forward, hurrying.

Drawstop. The part of an *organ which operates a row of pipes. See *Stop*.

Drdla, František (Franz) (*b* Žd̓ár nad Sázavou, Moravia, 1869; *d* Gastein, 1944). Cz. composer and violinist. Member of Vienna court opera orch. Comp. 2 operettas, pf. pieces, and songs, but best known for pieces for vn. and pf. such as *Serenade* and *Souvenir*.

Dream of Gerontius, The. Setting by Elgar, Op. 38, for mez., ten., bass, ch., semi-ch., and orch. of Cardinal J. H. Newman's poem (1866). Comp. 1900 (some sketches 1896). F.p. Birmingham 1900, cond. Richter. F. London p. 1903. Although frequently described and classified as an oratorio, this is not a term Elgar approved in this connection and does not appear on the score.

Dreigroschenoper, Die (The Threepenny Opera). Opera in prol. and 8 scenes by *Weill, text being a modern interpretation of Gay's *The Beggar's Opera* based on a trans. by Elisabeth Hauptmann with lyrics (some from Kipling and Villon) by Bertolt Brecht. Prod. Berlin 1928, NY 1933, London 1956. Eng. trans. and adaptation by *Blitzstein prod. Brandeis, Mass., 1952, and NY 1954.

Drei Pintos, Die (The Three Pintos). Comic opera in 3 acts left unfinished by Weber and completed by Mahler. Weber began work in 1820 on lib. by Theodor Hell (Karl Winkler) based on story *Der Brautkampf* by C. Seidel. Work on mus. for *Preciosa* and the commissioned operas *Euryanthe* and *Oberon* prevented Weber composing for *Die drei Pintos* beyond 1821. On his death in 1826, he left sketches for 7 out of 17 numbers, a total of 1,700 bars of which only 18 were scored. In 1826 these were taken to Meyerbeer, who kept them until 1852 but did nothing with them. In 1887 Weber's grandson invited Mahler, then 2nd cond. at Leipzig Opera, to complete the work, which he undertook by using Weber's sketches and extending the opera to 21 numbers in length by inserting other pieces by Weber and sections comp. by himself based on Weber's themes. The result is a remarkable example of posthumous collaboration. Prod. Leipzig 1888, cond. Mahler; London 1962.

Dresden. City in E. Germany (Saxony) with long mus. tradition. Its archives mention an organist in 1370 and from about 1420 three wind players were instructed to play on 29 major church fests. At the court mus. first achieved prominence *c*.1540. In the 18th cent. artistic life at court was on a grand scale and among the court composers and Kapellmeisters of that era were Zelenka, Lotti, Hasse, and J. S. Bach (who held the title 1736–50 but was active only in Leipzig at this period). By the end of the cent. Dresden's reputation for It. opera was high. A German Opera was founded in 1817 with Weber as cond. Weber's ideals were continued 17 years after his death by Wagner, whose own *Rienzi* was produced in Dresden in 1842, followed by *Der fliegende Holländer* 1843 and *Tannhäuser* 1845. The Royal Saxon Opera House, designed by Gottfried Semper, was opened 1841. This was burned down 1869 and his second building was opened 1878. Dresden's most illustrious operatic period dates from the appointment as cond. in 1882 of Ernst von Schuch. He championed Wagner's later operas and those of Richard Strauss whose *Feuersnot* (1901), *Salome* (1905), *Elektra* (1909), and *Der Rosenkavalier* (1911) had their f.ps. under Schuch. After Schuch the opera was cond. by Fritz Reiner (1914–21), but it was Fritz Busch (1922–33) who revived its glories and continued the Strauss assoc. with f.ps. of *Intermezzo* (1924) and *Die ägyptische Helena* (1928). He also cond. new operas by Hindemith (*Cardillac*, 1926) and Busoni (*Doktor Faust*, 1925). Driven out by the Nazis, Busch was succeeded by Karl Böhm, although Clemens Krauss cond. the f.p. of Strauss's *Arabella* in 1933. Under Böhm (1934–42), Strauss's *Die schweigsame Frau* (1935) and *Daphne* (1938) were first performed, also Sutermeister's *Romeo und Julia* (1940). Böhm was succeeded by Karl Elmendorff (1943–4). The opera house was bombed in 1945 and rebuilt 1948. Cond. from 1945 to 1950 was Joseph Keilberth. His successors were Rudolf Kempe (1950–3), Franz Konwitschny (1953–5), Lovro von Matačić (1956–8), Otmar Suitner (1960–4), Kurt Sanderling (1964–7), Martin Turnovsky (1967–8), Siegfried Kurz (1971–5), and Herbert Blomstedt from 1975. Operas given f.ps. in Dresden since 1945 incl. Blacher's *Die Flut* (1947), and U. Zimmermann's *Levins Mühle* (1973). The opera dir. from 1973 was Harry Kupfer.

Orch. mus. in Dresden has been provided by two orchs., the venerable Staatskapelle (which plays for the opera) and the Philharmonic. The Staatskapelle dates its origins to the 16th cent. and has had various guises. One of them, from 1923, was as the Saxon State Orch. cond. by Busch and later by Böhm. The Philharmonic was founded in 1871, though under another name. Its conds. incl. Strauss, Bülow, Nikisch, Mottl, and Edwin Lindner. Its greatest period, which incl. fests. of modern mus., was under Paul van Kempen (1934–42). After 1945 conds. incl. Heinz Bongartz (1947–64), H. Förster (1964–7), Kurt Masur (1967–72), Günther Herbig (1972–7), and Herbert Kegel from 1977.

Other composers beside Wagner to have lived in Dresden were Schumann (1844–50), who cond. the Liedertafel and founded a choir, and Rakhmaninov (1906–9).

Dresden Amen. Setting of *Amen* comp. by J. G. *Naumann (1741–1801) in Threefold Amen of Royal Chapel of Dresden. Quoted by Mendelssohn in his *Reformation Sym.* (1830–2) and by Wagner in *Parsifal* (1878–82).

Drew, David (*b* London, 1930). Eng. mus. critic and publisher. Mus. critic *New Statesman*, 1959–67, ed. *Tempo* 1971. Specialist in Messiaen, Weill, Stravinsky, Gerhard, and other 20th cent. figures. On staff Boosey and Hawkes from 1975.

Drigo, Riccardo (*b* Padua, 1846; *d* Padua, 1930). It. composer and cond. Cond., St Petersburg court opera from 1878, chief. cond. Maryinsky Th. 1886–1917. Wrote operas and ballets, latter incl. *Les Millions d'Arlequin* (1900), from which the *Serenade* is well-known. *Valse bluette* was a popular salon piece.

Drone. Pipe or pipes sounding continuous note of fixed pitch as a permanent bass, e.g. of bagpipes. Hence *drone bass* applied to orch. mus.

Droit, droite (Fr.). Right, e.g. *main droite*, right hand. But *droit* as a noun means right in another sense, e.g. *Droits d'exécution*. Performing Rights.

Drouet, Louis Francois Philippe (*b* Amsterdam, 1792; *d* Berne, 1873). Fr. flautist. Played in public at age 7. Taught King of Holland 1807–10; solo flautist to Napoleon 1811. Founded fl. factory in London 1818–19. Court mus. dir. Coburg 1836–54. Wrote many works for fl., incl. 10 concs.

Druckman, Jacob (*b* Philadelphia, 1928). Amer. composer. Studied Juilliard Sch. 1949–54, 1955–6, with Wagenaar and Mennin, also in Paris and at Columbia-Princeton Elec. Mus. Center (1965–6). Dir. Yale Univ. Sch. of Mus. elec. studio 1971–2. Pulitzer Prize 1972 for *Windows*, f.p. Chicago S.O. cond. Maderna. Works incl. conc. for str. (1951), ballet mus., 2 str. qts., *Valentine*, db. solo (1969), *The Sound of Time* for sop. and orch. (1965), and *Animus* I, II, III, and IV (1966, 1968, 1969, 1977), for instr. and tape, *Lamia*, sop. and orch. (1974), *Chiaroscuro*, orch. (1976), *Other Voices*, brass quintet (1976), va. conc. (1978), *Aureole*, orch. (1979), *Prism*, 3 pieces for orch. after Charpentier, Cavalli, and Cherubini (1980).

Drum. Percussion instrument of several kinds consisting of hollow wood or metal cylinder over which a skin is stretched (the drumhead). Sound is obtained by striking the skin with a stick. Among the leading types of drum are: (1) KETTLEDRUM (It. *timpano*; plur. *timpani*. The spelling 'tympani' is incorrect). Tuned to a definite pitch. A bowl of metal with, stretched over its open end, a membrane of which the tension can be increased or decreased by turning screws (in Machine Drums) or by some mechanical method. The playing is by means of 2 drumsticks, with heads of material which varies according to the tone-quality desired. Up to and including Beethoven the orch. player had 2 kettledrums normally tuned to the tonic and dominant (Doh and Soh) of the key in use; nowadays he has usually 3, and sometimes more. Both repeated notes and rolls are played. Forms of 'muffling' (= muting, see *Mute*) are possible, such as placing a cloth over the drumhead. Most composers up to and including Mozart notated for the kettledrums as one of the *'transposing instruments', the part being written in key C (i.e. the notes shown being C and G) and the actual pitch of the 2 notes being indicated at the outset by some such indication as timpani in D, A (according to the key of the piece). The current method is to show the actual notes to be played with all sharps and flats indicated. The use of pedals for mechanical tuning is widespread and enables *glissando effects. In mounted military bands the kettledrum is used, one being slung on each side of the horse. Introduction of the kettledrum into the orch. is generally attributed to Lully in his opera *Thésée* (1675).

(2) SIDE DRUM or SNARE DRUM. Of indefinite pitch. A small cylindrical drum with parchment at each end, one end having strings (*snares*) across it, to add a rattling effect and so increase the brilliance of the tone, the other end being left clear for the use of 2 drumsticks. It can be muted by placing a handkerchief or a wooden wedge between the snares and the parchment.

(3) TENOR DRUM. Larger than the *side drum and without snares. It is rarely used in the sym. orch.

(4) BASS DRUM. Indefinite and low pitch. Large and shallow, used in the sym. orch., military band, and dance band (in which the drumstick is often worked by a pedal). Played with skinheads perpendicular.

(5) TRAP DRUM. Drum equipment used in dance bands and theatre pit, comprising *bass drum with *cymbal attached, both being played with foot pedal. Drummer thus has both hands free to play snare drum.

Drum Mass (Haydn). See *Paukenmesse*.

Drum Roll Symphony (Haydn). See *Paukenwirbel*.

D.S. Abbreviation for *Dal segno*.

DSCH. Personal motto, derived from letters of his name, by Dmitri Shostakovich, notated as D-E♭-C-B. Occurs in several of his works, incl. 8th str. qt., 10th and 15th Syms., and 1st Vn. Conc.

Dub. Old Eng. for *tabor.

Dubensky, Arkady (*b* Vyatka, Russia, 1890; *d* Tenafly, NJ, 1966). Russ.-born violinist and composer. Studied Moscow Cons. Leader, Moscow Imperial Opera Orch. for 9 years. Went to NY 1921, joining NY S.O. until merger with NY P.O. of which he became member until 1953. Comp. for unusual combinations, e.g. *Fugue* for 18 vn., *Fugue* for 4 bn., *Suite* for 9 fl., Ov. for 18 toy tpt., *Fantasy on Negro Themes* for tuba and orch., tb. conc., concerto grosso for 3 tb., tuba, and orch. Also wrote operas, str. qts., and works for conventional orch. forces.

Dubois, (François Clément) **Théodore** (*b* Rosnay, 1837; *d* Paris, 1924). Fr. composer, organist, and teacher. Studied Paris Cons. under A. Thomas. Followed Saint-Saëns as organist of Madeleine 1877–1906. Prof. of harmony, Paris Cons. 1871–90, dir. 1896–1905. Resigned after protests over exclusion by jury incl. Dubois, of Ravel from entering for *Prix de Rome* for 4th time. Wrote operas, ballet, oratorios, cantatas, orch. works, incl. 3 syms., 2 pf. concs., and vn. conc.

Ducasse. See *Roger-Ducasse, Jean J. A.*

Duc d'Albe, Le (The Duke of Alba). (1) 4-act opera by Donizetti, to lib. by Scribe, written for Paris 1839 but not prod. Score recovered at Bergamo 1875, completed by Salvi, and prod. as *Il duca d'Alba*, Rome 1882. Scribe altered lib. and re-sold it to Verdi in 1853 as *Les *Vêpres siciliennes*, Verdi only discovering 30 years later that it had been used by Donizetti.

(2) Opera, *Il Duca d'Alba*, by Pacini to lib. by Piave, 1842.

Dudelkastensack, or **Dudelsack** (Ger.). Bagpipe.

Due (It.). Two. (1) *A due*, either (*a*) div. between 2 instr. or vv., or (*b*) 2 instr. or vv. to join in playing the same line.

(2) *Due corde*. Two strings, i.e. in vn. mus., etc., divide the passage over 2 str.

Due Foscari, I (The Two Foscari). 3-act opera by Verdi to lib. by Piave, based on Byron's drama (1821). Comp. 1843–4. Prod. Rome 1844, London and Boston, Mass., 1847.

Duenna, The, or The Double Elopement. (1) 3-act opera comp. and compiled by Thomas Linley senior and junior to text by Sheridan. Prod. London 1775, NY 1786.

(2) 4-act opera by Prokofiev, to his own lib. based on Sheridan with verses by Mira Mendelson, and sometimes known as *Betrothal in a Nunnery*. Comp. 1940–1, prod. Leningrad 1946, London, 1980.

(3) 3-act opera by *Gerhard to his own lib. after Sheridan. Comp. 1945–7, rev. 1950. BBC broadcast 1949. Prod. (concert) Wiesbaden 1951.

Duet (Fr. *duo*; Ger. *Duett*; It. *duo* or *duetto*). Any combination of 2 performers (with or without acc.), or a comp. for such, as in pf. duet.

Dufay, Guillaume (*b* c.1400; *d* Cambrai, 1474). Fr. composer. Choirboy at Cambrai Cath. Went to It. in his twenties and fled from Bologna to Rome in 1428, staying until 1433. Sang in the papal chapel. Met *Binchois in 1434. Returned to Cambrai 1439. His connection with the Burgundian court is now thought to have been unlikely. Was most acclaimed comp. of 15th cent. Nearly 200 of his works have survived incl.

8 complete Masses and 84 songs. Use of a secular *cantus firmus* such as 'L'homme armé' in a Mass possibly originated with him. Was basically a conservative comp., but his warm harmonies and expressive tunes anticipate the Renaissance. Undoubtedly his melodic clarity stemmed from his It. years. Composed the earliest Requiem Mass, now lost.

Dukas, Paul (*b* Paris, 1865; *d* Paris, 1935). Fr. composer. Studied Paris Cons. 1882–9, 2nd *Prix de Rome* 1888. Early works influenced by Wagner. Scored major success in 1897 with orch. scherzo *L'Apprenti Sorcier*. Perhaps his finest work is his opera *Ariane et Barbe-Bleu*, (Paris, 1907) based like Debussy's *Pelléas* on a Maeterlinck play and finding, like Debussy, symbolic and emotional depths in the text which are luminously translated into mus. Also wrote ballet *La Péri* (1912), and pf. sonata (1901) said to be the first by a major Fr. composer. Prof. of orch., Paris Cons. 1910–13, of comp., 1928–35. Wrote much criticism. Pubd. very little mus. after 1920 and destroyed his unpubd. works before he died. Aided Saint-Saëns in completion of Guiraud's opera *Frédégonde*, orchestrating first 3 acts. Ed. several Rameau operas. Prin. works:

OPERA: *Ariane et Barbe-Bleu* (1899–1906).
BALLET: *La* ★ *Péri* (1911–12).
ORCH: Ov. *Polyeucte* (1892); Sym. in C (1896); *L'*★*Apprenti Sorcier* (1897); *La Péri*, suite.
PIANO: Sonata in E♭ minor (1899–1901), *Variations, Interlude et Final (sur un thème de Rameau)* (1903), *Prélude élégiaque* (1908), *La Plainte au loin du faune* (1920).
CHAMBER MUSIC: *Villanelle* (hn. and pf.).
SONG: *Sonnet de Ronsard* (1924).

Duke Bluebeard's Castle (*A kékszakállú herceg vára*). Opera in 1 act, Op. 11, by Bartók, comp. 1911, to lib. by Béla Balázs, for sop. and bar. Rev. 1912 and 1918. First perf. Budapest 1918, NY 1952, London 1957.

Duke, Vernon. See *Dukelsky, Vladimir*.

Dukelsky, Vladimir (*b* Parfianovka, 1903; *d* Santa Monica, Calif., 1969). Russ.-born composer (Amer. citizen). Studied comp. with Glière at Kiev Cons. Ballet *Zéphyr et Flore* prod. Diaghilev, 1925. Wrote several other ballets, operas, 3 syms., oratorio, pf. conc., vn. conc., vc. conc., pf. sonata, hpd. sonata. Under name Vernon Duke wrote mus. for musical comedies, films, etc. Best-known song *April in Paris*.

Dulcet. Org. stop: a ★Dulciana of 4′ length and pitch.

Dulcian. Alternative name for the ★curtal.

Dulciana. Soft org. stop usually in Brit. of ★diapason class, and in USA of str.-toned class.

Dulciana Mixture. Org. ★Mixture stop of soft tone, generally on Swell or Echo manual.

Dulcimer. Old instr. A shallow closed box over which are stretched wires to be struck with 2 wooden hammers held in the player's hands. Still in use in E. Europe for traditional mus. (known in Hung. as *cimbalom*). In USA is wrongly applied to plucked zither-like folk-instr.

Dulcitone. Kbd. instr. similar to ★celesta, but with steel tuning forks instead of steel plates. In Fr. known as *typophone*. Used by ★d'Indy in *Chant de la Cloche*.

Dumbarton Oaks Concerto. Name given to Stravinsky's Conc. in E♭ for chamber orch. (15 instr.) because it received its f.p. in May 1938 (cond. by N. Boulanger) at Dumbarton Oaks, the estate in Washington D.C. of Mr & Mrs R. W. Bliss who commissioned this 'little concerto in the style of the Brandenburg Concertos'.

Dumka (plural *Dumky*). A type of Slavonic folk-ballad, Ukrainian in orig., in which elegiac and fast tempi alternate. Term was used by ★Dvořák for movements in his str. sextet and pf. quintet. His *Dumky* Trio is the nickname for his pf. trio, Op. 90, comprising 6 *dumka* movements. His Pf. Sonata, Op. 35 (1876) is also known as the *Dumka*.

Dump, Dumpe. Title given to some Eng. kbd. pieces of the 16th and early 17th cents., often in variation form and possibly elegiac in intention ('down in the dumps', for example, means 'in a depressed mood'). *My Ladye Careys Dompe* is a typical (though anonymous) example.

Dunayevsky, Isaak (*b* Lokhvitsa, 1900; *d* Moscow, 1955). Russ. composer of popular mus. Pupil of J. Akhron. First Soviet composer to adopt jazz idiom. Wrote many songs, also operettas, ballets, orch. works, and str. qt.

Dunhill, Thomas (Frederick) (*b* London, 1877; *d* Scunthorpe, 1946). Eng. composer and writer. Studied RCM with Stanford. Ass. mus. master, Eton College, 1899–1908. Comps. incl. sym., operetta *Tantivy Towers* (lib. by A. P. Herbert, prod. London 1931), *Elegiac Variations* for orch., vn. sonata, pf. qt., 2 pf. trios, many songs incl. *The Cloth of Heaven* (Yeats). Wrote several books, subjects incl. Mozart's str. qts., Elgar, and chamber mus.

Duni, Egidio Romoaldo (*b* Matera, 1708; *d* Paris, 1775). It. composer. Wrote over 12 It. operas, then settled in Fr., composing 20 Fr. operas in the *opéra comique* style. These incl. *La Fille mal gardée* (1758), *Les Deux Chasseurs* (1763), and *La Clochette* (1766).

Dunstable (Dunstaple), **John** (*b* c.1390; *d* London, 1453). Eng. composer, astrologer, and mathematician. Leading Eng. composer of first half of 15th cent. Enjoyed European reputation, attested by discovery of his works in early It. and Fr. colls. Was member of households of John, Duke of Bedford and Humphrey, Duke of Gloucester, the latter a noted patron of the arts.

Travelled to Europe and was given land holdings in Normandy. Influenced *Dufay and *Binchois. Probably first to write instr. acc. for church mus. Wrote masses, isorhythmic motets, etc. Buried in St Stephen's, Walbrook, London.

Duo (It.). Two. (1) Duet, usually but not exclusively instr.

(2) 2 performers, or a work written for them. In USA a *duo*-pianist is member of a 2-pf. duo.

Duodrama. A work for 2 actors to speak to orch. acc. Mozart admired the form.

Duparc, Elisabeth ('Francesina') (d ?1778). Fr. soprano trained in It. Opera engagement London 1736. Sang in Handel's *Faramondo* and *Serse* in 1738 and thenceforward was almost exclusively a Handel singer, being his leading sop. from 1738 to 1745. Sang in *Messiah*, April 1745.

Duparc, (Marie Eugène) **Henri** (Fouques) (b Paris, 1848; d Mont-de-Marsan, 1933). Fr. composer. Intended for law but studied pf. and comp. with *Franck. Extremely self-critical, destroying most of his early works. His 16 songs, orig. in idiom and foretelling impressionism, are models of sensitivity to the poetic text combined with melodic inspiration and a harmonic style based on Wagner. They were comp. between 1868 and 1884. After 1885 he wrote nothing owing to an incurable nervous disease. His output is as follows:

SONGS: (with pf. acc., but † = orch. version provided by Duparc): †*Chanson triste* (1868 or 9); *Soupir* (1869); *Romance de Mignon* (1869); *Sérénade* (1869); *Le galop* (1869); †*Au pays où se fait la guerre* (?1869–70, orig. title *Absence*); †*L'Invitation au voyage* (1870); †*La vague et la cloche* (1871, comp. for orch., with pf. acc. supplied later first by d'Indy then by Duparc); *Elégie* (1874); *Extase* (1874, ?rev. 1884); †*Le Manoir de Rosemonde* (1879 or 82); *Sérénade Florentine* (?1880–1); †*Phidylé* (1882); *Lamento* (1883 or 5); †*Testament* (1883 or 5); †*La Vie antérieure* (1884).

VOCAL: *La fruite*, sop., ten., pf. (1871); *Benedicat vobis Dominus*, motet, STB (1882).

ORCH: *Poème Nocturne* (1874, orig. in 3 movts., but only No. 1, *Aux Étoiles*, survives); *Lénore*, sym.-poem (1875).

PIANO: *5 Feuilles volantes* (?1867–9).

Duplet. Pair of notes of equal time-value, written where number of beats cannot be divided by 2. See *Irregular rhythmic groupings*.

Duple Time. Where the primary division is into 2 e.g. $\frac{2}{4}$ as distinct from triple time (primary division into 3) or quadruple (division into 4). See *Time Signature*.

Duplex-Coupler Piano. Pf. invented 1921 by *Moór. Has 2 manuals, the upper tuned an octave higher. These are placed so that the hand can easily move from one to the other or play on both together. Thus, scales in 10ths are played as scales in 3rds as on a normal pf. The manuals can be instantly coupled, so that scales in octaves can be played as scales in single notes.

Duplex Instruments (Brass). These exist in 2 types: (a) Those planned to produce 2 qualities of tone by the provision of 2 bells of different bore, and (b) Those planned to play in either of 2 different keys (i.e. from either of 2 different *fundamental notes) without change of quality of tone (e.g. the double hn. in F and B♭) by the provision of double lengths of valve tubing.

Duplex Scaling. System by which those portions of pf. str. which are normally dumb, lying beyond each end of the vibrating portion, are left free and tuned so as to correspond with some of the harmonics of the main note of the str. See *Aliquot scaling*.

Dupont, Gabriel (b Caen, 1878; d Le Vésinet, nr. Paris, 1914). Fr. composer. Pupil of *Widor at Paris Cons. Won Sonzogno Prize in Italy with 2-act opera *La Cabréra*. Wrote other operas, chief among them *Antar* (1912–13, prod. Paris 1921). Ill-health affected career. Also wrote symphonic poems, str. qt., and group of 14 pf. pieces, *Les heures dolentes*.

Duport, Jean Louis (b Paris, 1749; d Paris, 1819). Fr. cellist and composer. Pupil of his brother Jean Pierre *Duport. Court cellist in Berlin 1792–1806, court musician to ex-King of Spain at Marseilles, 1807–12. Prof. of vc., Paris Cons. 1812–15. Wrote 6 vc. concs. and many solo pieces, also still-important method, *Essai sur le doigter du violoncelle et la conduite de l'Archet*.

Duport, Jean Pierre (b Paris, 1741; d Berlin, 1818). Fr. cellist. Member of court orch., Berlin, 1773–1811, dir. of court concerts 1787–1806. Beethoven's 2 vc. sonatas Op. 5 may have been written for him and f.p. in Berlin by Beethoven and Duport, 1796.

Dupré, Desmond (John) (b London, 1916; d nr. Tonbridge, 1974). Eng. lutenist, guitarist, and viol player. Studied RCM. Lute-song duo with Alfred *Deller from 1950, touring widely. Many solo recitals. Member of Morley Consort, Jaye Consort of Viols, Musica Reservata, etc.

Du Pré, Jacqueline (b Oxford, 1945; d London, 1987). Eng. cellist. Studied GSM with W. *Pleeth, also with *Tortelier in Paris, and *Rostropovich in Moscow. Suggia award, Queen's Prize. Public début at age 7. Début recital Wigmore Hall 1961. Festival Hall début 1962 in Elgar's conc., with which she became closely identified, playing it also on first NY appearance, 1965, and recording it with Barbirolli and with her husband, Daniel *Barenboim, whom she married 1967. Perf. in chamber mus. trio with Barenboim and P. *Zukerman. Career halted 1972 by illness. O.B.E. 1976.

Dupré, Marcel (b Rouen, 1886; d Meudon, nr. Paris, 1971). Fr. organist and composer. Studied

Paris Cons., being pupil of Guilmant and Widor. Organist, St Vivien, Rouen, at age 12. Ass. organist to Widor at St Sulpice, Paris, from 1906; succeeded him 1934. London début 1920, NY 1921. Noteworthy improviser. Prof. of org., Paris Cons. 1926–54. Ed. org. works of Bach, Handel, Schumann, Liszt, Franck, etc. Comp. sym., vn. sonata, cantatas, and many org. works incl. 2 org. syms., org. conc., and *poèmes symphoniques*.

Dur (Ger.). 'Major' (key), e.g. *Dur Ton, Dur Tonart*, major key; *A dur*, A major.

Duramente (It.). With hardness, harshness, sternness.

Durand. Fr. mus. publishers (Durand, Schoenewerk, & Cie) founded 1869 in Paris by mus. critic Auguste Durand (1830–1909). Became Durand et Fils 1891. Complete editions of Rameau begun 1894 (ed. Saint-Saëns). Pubd. editions of Chopin by Debussy and of Schumann by Fauré. Composers in firm's list incl. Debussy, Ravel, Saint-Saëns, Milhaud, Poulenc, d'Indy, Messiaen, Ibert, and others.

Durante, Francesco (*b* Frattamaggiore, 1684; *d* Naples, 1755). It. composer and teacher. Comp. church mus., hpd. concs. and sonatas, concs. for str., songs, etc. Pupils incl. Jommelli, Paisiello, Pergolesi, and Piccinni.

Durch (Ger. 'Through'). **Durchaus** 'Throughout.' **Durchkomponiert** or **durchcomponiert** ('through-composed'). Applied to songs of which the music is different for each stanza of the poem, i.e. the opposite of *strophic; but use of the term has been widened to mean a composition which has been 'fully worked out', 'thoroughly composed', as opposed to something that seems episodic or patchy. **Durchdringen** ('through-forcing') 'Penetrating', 'shrill'. **Durchführung** ('through-leading') *'Development'. **Durchweg** (1) 'Throughout', 'altogether'. (2) 'Generally', 'nearly always'.

Durey, Louis (*b* Paris, 1888; *d* St Tropez, 1979). Fr. composer. Studied privately. In 1917 joined Milhaud, Honegger, and others under leadership of Satie as 'les nouveaux jeunes', becoming *Les *Six* in 1920. Abandoned them in 1921. Works incl. chamber mus. and songs. After 1945 became Progressist, one of group of Fr. composers who wrote mus. of deliberate 'mass appeal' in accordance with Communist doctrines on art.

Durkó, Zsolt (*b* Szeged, 1934). Hung. composer. Studied Budapest Acad. with Farkas up to 1960, then attended Petrassi's master-classes in Rome 1961–3. Broke away from influence of Kodály, all his work being atonal. Works incl. *Altamira*, ch. and orch. (1967–8), *Burial Prayer*, oratorio, ten., bar., ch., and orch. (1967–72), *Moses*, opera (1977), *Organismi*, vn., orch. (1964), *Fioriture* (1965–6), *Turner Illustrations*, orch. (1976), *Chamber Music*, 2 pf., 11 str. (1973), Str. qt. No. 1

(1966), No. 2 (1969, rev. 1970), *Dwarfs and Giants*, pf. (1974), *Impromptus in F*, fl. and ens. (1984).

Duruflé, Maurice (*b* Louviers, 1902; *d* Paris, 1986). Fr. composer and organist. Comp. pupil of Dukas, org. pupil of Gigout at Paris Cons. Organist, St Étienne-du-Mont, Paris, from 1930. Ass. to M. *Dupré at Paris Cons. from 1942, prof. of harmony 1943–69. Works incl. *Requiem*, Op. 9, *3 Dances for Orch.*, *Messe-cum jubilo*, motets, and org. works.

Dušek, František (*b* Chotěboř, 1731; *d* Prague, 1799). Bohem. pianist and composer, pupil of Wagenseil. Prominent teacher in Prague. Close friend of Mozart. Comp. syms., chamber mus.

Dušek (Dussek), **Jan Ladislav** (*b* Čáslav, 1760; *d* St Germain-en-Laye, 1812). Bohem. pianist and composer. Began career as virtuoso pianist in Malines, 1779, then had comp. lessons from C. P. E. Bach in Hamburg 1782. Visited Ger., Russia, Fr., and It. as pianist; settled in London 1789–99, appearing with Haydn. Served various royal patrons after 1803, the last being Talleyrand (Prince of Benevento). Prolific composer, works incl. 28 pf. sonatas, 15 pf. concs., conc. for 2 pf., pf. trios, ballad-opera, mass, 38 vn. sonatas, 16 fl. sonatas, etc. (much of it worth exploring).

Dušek, Josepha (née Hambacher) (*b* Prague, 1754; *d* Prague, 1824). Bohem. sop., composer, and pianist, wife of František *Dušek. Friend of Mozart who wrote concert aria *Bella mia Fiamma* (K528, 1787), for her. First singer of Beethoven's *Ah, perfido!* Op. 65, 1796, also probably written for her.

Dushkin, Samuel (*b* Suwalki, Poland, 1891; *d* NY, 1976). Amer. violinist of Polish birth, pupil of Auer and Kreisler. European début 1918. Gave f.p. 1924 of orch. version of Ravel's *Tzigane*. Stravinsky wrote vn. conc. for him, 1931, f.p. Berlin that year, also *Duo Concertant*, of which he and Stravinsky gave f.p. Berlin 1932.

Dutilleux, Henri (*b* Angers, 1916). Fr. composer. Studied piano and theory at Douai Cons. while schoolboy. Paris Cons. 1933–8 (comp. with Busser). Won *Prix de Rome* 1938. Joined French Radio 1943, becoming dir. of mus. productions 1945–63. Prof. of comp., École Normale de Musique 1961, Paris Cons. 1970. Regarded as natural successor to Ravel and Roussel. Works incl. ballet *Le Loup* (1953), 2 syms. (1950 and 1958–9), *Métaboles* (1964), *Tout un monde lointain*, vc. and orch. (1968–70), pf. sonata (1947), ob. sonata (1947), *Thus the Night*, str. qt. (1975–6), and songs.

Dutoit, Charles (*b* Lausanne, 1936). Swiss violist and cond. Studied vn., va., comp., and cond. in Switz., It., and USA. Began career as violist in orch. but also guest cond. of Suisse Romande Orch. Chief cond. Berne S.O. 1967–77, Montreal

S.O. from 1978. Eng. début 1966, especially assoc. with RPO. Visits to N. and S. America and Japan.

Duval, Denise (b Paris, 1921). Fr. sop. Début Paris 1947 as Butterfly. Created Blanche in Poulenc's *Dialogues des Carmélites* (1957). First Brit. performer of Poulenc's *La Voix humaine*, Edinburgh Fest. 1960. Sang Mélisande, Glyndebourne 1962. Retired 1965.

Dux. The v. in a canon which first enters with the melody to be imitated. Also called Antecedent. See also *Comes*.

Dux, Claire (b Witkowicz, 1885; d Chicago, 1967). Polish sop. Opera début Cologne 1906 as Pamina. Berlin Opera 1911–18. CG début 1913 as first Eng. Sophie in *Rosenkavalier*. Chicago Opera 1921–3. Retired on marriage.

Dvořák, Antonín (b Nelahozeves, Bohemia, 1841; d Prague, 1904). Cz. (Bohem.) composer. Son of a village butcher, Dvořák as a child helped in the shop and also showed talent as a violinist. At 14 he was sent to relatives in Zlonice to learn Ger.; while there he was taught va., org., pf., and counterpoint by A. Liehmann. From 1857 to 1859 he attended the Org. Sch., Prague, leaving to become va. player in a band and later in the orch. of Prague Nat. Th., 1866–73, playing under Smetana. At this time he comp. several works which he later destroyed or withdrew, the most significant being a song-cycle *Cypress Trees* from which he drew themes in later years (for the Vc. Conc., for example). The cycle was a tale of disappointed love, the result of Dvořák's disappointment that a girl he adored married someone else. (He later married her sister.) Like most young composers of the time, his natural tendencies were complicated by the inescapable influence of Wagner. His first opera, *Alfred* (1870) was Wagnerian in tone. 3 years later he had his first major success with a cantata, *Hymnus*, which enabled him to give up his orch. playing. In 1874 his Sym. in E♭ won him an Austrian nat. prize, Brahms being on the jury. 2 years later the Moravian duets won him the same prize, and Brahms recommended them to the publisher Simrock. The nationalist element in such works as the *Slavonic Rhapsodies* – the results of Smetana's beneficial influence – earned Dvořák increasing recognition and requests for new works e.g. from Joachim for a vn. conc. and from Hans *Richter for a sym. Both Richter and *Bülow championed his mus. in their concerts. In 1884 he paid the first of 9 visits to England and cond. his *Stabat Mater* which had scored a tremendous success the previous year under *Barnby. His popularity in Britain was immediate and sustained both as comp. and cond., and he was financially successful enough to be able to buy an estate in S. Bohemia. Several of his works were written for or first perf. in Eng., e.g. the Sym. in D minor (No. 7), comp. for the Phil. Soc. (1885), the cantata *The Spectre's*

Bride (Birmingham, 1885), the oratorio *St Ludmila* (Leeds, 1886), the Sym. in G major (No. 8) (Phil. Soc. 1888), and the *Requiem* (Birmingham, 1891). Cambridge made him Hon. D.Mus. in 1891 and in the same year he was appointed prof. of comp. at Prague Cons. The Cons. granted him leave to accept the invitation of Mrs Jeanette Thurber, founder in 1885 of the Nat. Cons. of Mus., NY, to become dir. of the cons. He remained in Amer. for 3 years, a fruitful period in which he wrote some of his finest works, incl. the 'New World' Sym., the Vc. Conc., the Biblical Songs, the str. qt. Op. 96, and the pf. quintet. His art seems to have been intensified by a combination of the influence of Negro melodies and of a deep homesickness. He returned to his teaching post in Prague in 1895, becoming dir. of Prague Cons. in 1901. His pupils incl. his son-in-law *Suk, and *Novák. In his last years he devoted his creative energies to symphonic poems and to operas.

Dvořák's mus. is a particularly happy result of the major influences on his art: Wagner, Brahms, and folk mus. His innate gift for melody was Schubertian and his felicitous orchestration, often reflecting natural and pastoral elements, is of an art that conceals art. But a tendency to regard him as blithely naïve would be both unjust and misleading, for his mastery of form and his contrapuntal and harmonic skill are the manifestations of a powerful mus. intellect. The nationalist feeling in his mus. is beautifully integrated into classical structures and his use of Cz. dances and songs, such as the furiant, polka, *skočná* (reel), *dumka*, and *sousedská* (slow waltz), is in no way bizarre. His syms., the vc. conc., and perhaps above all his chamber mus. show the best side of his work; the operas, apart from *Rusalka*, are only just beginning to travel outside Czechoslovakia; and the choral works which won him such a following in late Victorian Eng. are due for rehabilitation. For many years it was customary to credit him only with the 5 syms. pubd. in his lifetime, but the 4 early examples have now been accepted into the canon and the whole series is numbered chronologically. Prin. works:

OPERAS: *Alfred* (unpubd.) (1870); *King and Collier* (*Král a uhlíř*) (1871, totally re-composed 1874, rev. 1887), Op. 14; *The Pig-headed Peasants* (*Tvrdé palice*) (1874), Op. 17; *Vanda*, (1875, rev. 1879, 1883) Op. 25; *The Peasant a Rogue* (*Šelma sedlák*) (1877), Op. 35; *Dimitrij* (1881–2, several revs.), Op. 64; *The *Jacobin* (1887–8, rev. 1897), Op. 84; *Kate and the Devil* (*Čert a Káča*) (1898–9), Op. 112; *Rusalka*, (1900) Op. 114; *Armida* (1902–3), Op. 115.

SYMPHONIES: No. 1 in C minor (*The *Bells of Zlonice*) (1865) (no Op. no., recovered 1923, pubd. (1961)); No. 2 in B♭ (1865) (no Op. no.); No. 3 in E♭ (1873), (no Op. no. but orig. Op. 10); No. 4 in D minor (1874, (no Op. no. but orig. Op. 13, pubd. (1912)); No. 5 in F major (1875, rev. 1887), Op. 76 (orig. Op. 24 and formerly No. 3);

No. 6 in D major (1880), Op. 60 (formerly No. 1); No. 7 in D minor, (1884–5) Op. 70 (formerly No. 2); No. 8 in G major, (1889) Op. 88 (formerly No. 4); No. 9 in E minor (*From the *New World*) (1893), Op. 95 (formerly No. 5).

ORCH: Symphonic poems: *The Water sprite (Vodník)*, Op. 107 (1896), *The *Noonday Witch (Polednice)*, Op. 108 (1896), *The Golden Spinning Wheel (Zlatý Kolovrat)*, Op. 109 (1896), *The *Wood Dove (Holoubek)*, Op. 110 (1896); *Heroic Song*, Op. 111 (1897); Ovs.: *My Home*, Op. 62a (1882), *Hussite (Husitská)*, Op. 67 (1883), Cycle, *Nature, Life and Love* comprising *Amid Nature, Op. 91, *Carneval*, Op. 92, and *Othello, Op. 93 (1891–2); *Serenade* in E major for str., Op. 22 (1875), *Suite in D (Czech)*, Op. 39 (1879), *Serenade* in D minor for wind, vc., and bass, Op. 44 (1878), 3 *Slavonic Rhapsodies* in D, G minor, and A♭, Op. 45 (1878), 8 *Slavonic Dances*, 1st series, Op. 46 (1878), 8 (2nd series) Op. 72 (1886), *Legends*, Op. 59 (1881), *Scherzo capriccioso*, Op. 66 (1883), *Symphonic variations*, Op. 78 (1877, orig. Op. 40).

SOLOIST AND ORCH: Vc. conc. in A major (1865, with pf. acc. only. Orch. Raphael 1928, Burghauser 1975, vc. part ed. Sádló), *Romance* for vn., Op. 11 (1873–7, arr. of *andante con moto* of str. qt. in F minor, Op. 9, of 1873), pf. conc. in G minor, Op. 33 (1876), *Mazurka* for vn., Op. 49 (1879), Vn. conc. in A minor, Op. 53 (1879–80), *Rondo* for vc., Op. 94 (1893), *Forest Calm*, for vc. (1891), Vc. conc. in B minor, Op. 104 (1894–5).

CHAMBER MUSIC: String quartets: F minor, Op. 9 (1873), A minor, Op. 12 (1873), A minor, Op. 16 (1874), D minor, Op. 34 (1877), E♭, Op. 51 (1878–79), C major, Op. 61 (1881), E major, Op. 80 (1876, orig. Op. 27), F major (the *'American'), Op. 96 (1893), A♭, Op. 105 (1895), G major, Op. 106 (1895). Also several without Opus no. incl. *Cypresses* (Cypřiše), (1887); String quintets: G major, Op. 77, with db. (1875, orig. Op. 18), E♭, Op. 97 (1893); String sextet: A major, Op. 48 (1878); Piano Trios: B♭, Op. 21 (1875), G minor, Op. 26 (1876), F minor, Op. 65 (1883), E minor (*Dumka*) Op. 90 (1890–1); Piano Quartets: D major, Op. 23 (1875), E♭, Op. 87 (1889); Piano Quintet: A major, Op. 81 (1887); *Bagatelles (Maličkosti)* for 2 vn., vc., and harmonium (or pf.), Op. 47 (1878); *Terzetto* for 2 vn. and va., Op. 74 (1887); Violin Sonata: F major, Op. 57 (1880); vn. sonatina in G, Op. 100 (1893).

CHORAL: *Stabat Mater*, Op. 58 (1876–7, orig. Op. 28), *The *Spectre's Bride*, Op. 69 (1884), *St Ludmila*, Op. 71 (1885–6), Mass in D, Op. 86 (1887, rev. 1892), *Requiem*, Op. 89 (1890), *The American Flag*, Op. 102 (1892), *Te Deum*, Op. 103 (1892), *Hymn of the Czech Peasants (Hymna ceského rolnictva)*, Op. 28 (1885), with 4-hand acc., *Hymnus*, Op. 30 (1872, orig. Op. 4), *Amid Nature (V přírodě)* 5 ch., Op. 63 (1882).

SONGS: Cycle, *Cypress Trees*, 18 songs to words by Pflager (1865), unpubd. in orig. form but pubd.

as 4 *Songs*, Op. 2, 8 *Love Songs*, Op. 83 (1888) and *Cypress Trees* for str. qt; 5 *Evening Songs*, Op. 31 (1876), 3 *Modern Greek Songs*, Op. 50 (1878), 7 *Gipsy Songs*, Op. 55 (1880; No. 4 is *Songs my Mother taught me)*, 4 *Songs*, Op. 82 (1887–8), 10 *Biblical Songs*, Op. 99 (1894, Nos. 1 and 5 are orch.).

PIANO: *Silhouettes*, Op. 8 (1879), *Dumka and Furiant*, Op. 12 (1884), *Dumka*, Op. 35 (1876), *Theme and Variations*, Op. 36 (1876), *Scottish Dances*, Op. 41 (1877), 4 *Pieces*, Op. 52 (1880), 8 *Waltzes*, Op. 54 (1879–80; Nos. 1 and 4 arr. for str. qt.), 6 *Mazurkas*, Op. 56 (1880), *Poetic Tone Pictures (Poetické nálady)*, Op. 85 (1889), *Suite in A*. Op. 98 (1894, arr. for orch.), 8 *Humoresques*, Op. 101 (1894; No. 7 is the famous one), *Éclogues* (1880), *Album Leaves* (1881).

PIANO DUETS: 16 *Slavonic Dances*, Opp. 46 and 72 (2 sets of 8; also for orch.), *Legends*, Op. 59 (1881, also for orch.), *From the Bohemian Forest (Ze Šumavy)*, Op. 68 (1884).

Dvořákova, Ludmila (b Kolín, 1923). Cz. soprano. Studied at Prague Cons. 1942–9. Opera début Ostrava 1949 (as Káťa Kabanová). Bratislava Opera 1952–4, Prague 1954–60, Berlin State Opera from 1960 (début as Oktavian). First sang Brünnhilde in Berlin 1962, Isolde in Karlsruhe 1964. Vienna début 1965, NY Met. 1966 (*Fidelio*). Sang Brünnhilde in *Ring* cycles CG 1966–71. Bayreuth début 1965 (Gutrune), later singing Brünnhilde and Kundry there.

Dwarf, The (Zemlinsky). See *Zwerg, Der*.

Dykes, John Bacchus (b Hull, 1823; d Ticehurst, Sussex, 1876). Eng. church composer, precentor of Durham Cath., and Vicar. His popular hymn tunes incl. *Nearer My God to Thee*, *Eternal Father, strong to save*, *Our blest Redeemer*, *Holy, holy, holy*, *Jesu, Lover of my Soul*, and *Lead, Kindly Light*.

Dykes Bower, John. See *Bower, John Dykes*.

Dynamics. The gradations of vol. in mus., e.g. *forte, piano, crescendo*, etc.

Dyson, (Sir) **George** (b Halifax, Yorks., 1883; d Winchester, 1964). Eng. composer, teacher, and organist. Studied RCM. Spent 1904–8 in It. and Ger. on Mendelssohn Scholarship. From 1908–37 was mus. master at a succession of Eng. schs. incl. Rugby and Winchester. Dir., RCM, 1937–52. Comps. incl. Sym. in G (1937), cantatas *In Honour of the City* (1928), *The *Canterbury Pilgrims* (1931), *St Paul's Voyage to Melita* (1933), and *Quo Vadis* (1939); vn. conc. (1942). Knighted 1941, K.C.V.O. 1953.

Dzerzhinsky, Ivan (b Tambov, 1909; d Leningrad, 1978). Russ. composer whose operas were upheld as models when Shostakovich was in disgrace with Soviet authorities for his *Lady Macbeth of the Mtsensk District*. They incl. *Quiet Flows the Don* (1935), *Virgin Soil Upturned* (1937), *Blood of the People* (1941), *Grigory Melekhov* (1967). Also 3 pf. concs., symphonic poem, songs, etc.

E

E. Note of the scale: 3rd degree of natural scale of C. Thus, E♮, E♭♭, E♯, E♯♯. Keys of E major and E minor, E♭ major and E♭ minor. E♭ is also indication of *transposing instr. (e.g. the E♭ cl.) on which written note C sounds as E♭.

E (It.). And.

Eadie, Noël (b Paisley, 1901; d London, 1950). Scottish sop. Début London, CG 1926, BNOC 1928. Chicago Opera 1931–2, Glyndebourne 1935–6, SW, and other cos.

Eames, Emma (b Shanghai, 1865; d NY, 1952). Amer. sop. Studied in Boston, Mass., later in Paris with M. Marchesi. Paris Opéra 1889–91, making début as Juliette in Gounod's Roméo et Juliette. Début CG and NY Met. 1891. Member of Met. co. until 1909. Last stage appearances Boston 1911, thereafter recitals. Sang Mrs. Ford in Amer. première of Verdi's Falstaff, 1895.

Ear, Playing by. The ability to play an instr. intuitively, without instruction, or to improvise without a score.

Early Music. Term by which is generally understood mus. comp. from earliest times up to and incl. mus. of Renaissance period. With growth of interest in mus. of this period and especially the use of authentic instrs. in perf., various 'early mus.' consorts and ens. were formed. The periodical Early Music has been pubd. quarterly in London since 1973.

Early Music Consort. Group of musicians founded by David *Munrow in 1967 to perform Renaissance and other early mus. on orig. instrs. such as rebec, sackbut, shawm, curtall, etc. Many recordings.

Easdale, Brian (b Manchester, 1909). Eng. composer. Studied RCM. Comps. incl. operas Rapunzel (1927), The Corn King (1935), and The Sleeping Children (1951); also pf. conc. (1938), song-cycles, and th. mus.

East (Easte, Est, Este), Michael (b c.1580; d Lichfield, 1648). Eng. composer and organist. Organist, Lichfield Cath. Wrote madrigals, anthems, and mus. for viols. His 5-part madrigal Hence Stars is in The *Triumphs of Oriana. Also wrote madrigal called O metaphysical tobacco (1606).

East (Easte, Est, Este), Thomas (b c.1550; d London, 1608). London mus. publisher. Issued Byrd's psalms, sonnets, and songs (1588), works by other madrigalists, and 4-part settings of psalms (1592).

Eastman School of Music. Dept. of Univ. of Rochester, NY. Founded 1919 through munificence of George Eastman (1854–1932), inventor of Kodak photographic process, and opened in 1921. Dir. 1924–64 was Howard *Hanson.

Easton, Florence (b South Bank, Yorks, 1882; d NY, 1955). Eng. sop. Studied RAM 1900–1 and in Paris. Opera début Moody-Manners Co., Newcastle upon Tyne; 1903. Joined Savage Co., 1904–5, 1906–7. Member Berlin Royal Opera 1907–13. Hamburg Opera 1912–16, Chicago 1915–17, NY Met. 1917–29 and 1935–6. CG 1927 and 1932; SW 1934. Repertory of 150 very varied roles in 4 languages and could learn a new score in 12 hours. Retired 1936. Resplendent Brünnhilde with Melchior in Siegfried, CG 1932.

Eastwood, Thomas (Hugh) (b Hawley, 1922). Eng. composer. Studied in Turkey, then in Berlin with *Blacher and E. *Stein. Worked for Brit. Council in Ankara and Berlin 1947–54. On council of S.P.N.M. 1959–70. Works incl. 2 operas (one of them Christopher Sly), cantatas, chamber mus., songs, and incidental mus. for plays incl. John Osborne's Look Back in Anger (1956). Made new realization of *Love in a Village for BBC (1964).

Eathorne, Wendy (b Four Lanes, Cornwall, 1939). Eng. sop. Studied RAM. Specialist in oratorio and Lieder, also opera.

Eben, Petr (b Žamberk, Cz., 1929). Cz. composer and pianist. Studied Prague Acad. of Mus. 1948–54. Comps. incl. oratorio Apologia Sokratus (1964), pf. conc. (1961), song cycles, chamber mus., Mutationes, org. (1980), and motets.

Eberl, Anton (b Vienna, 1765; d Vienna, 1807). Austrian composer and pianist. Kapellmeister, St Petersburg, 1796–1802. Friend of Mozart, with whose widow he made a concert-tour of Ger. Wrote 5 operas, syms., pf. concs., pf. works, chamber mus., etc.

Eberlin, Johann (Ernst) (b Jettingen, 1702; d Salzburg, 1762). Ger. composer, mainly of church mus. Court organist to Archbishop of Salzburg from 1754. Wrote org. toccatas and fugues, 21 oratorios, masses, motets, etc.

Ebert, Carl (b Berlin, 1887; d Santa Monica, Calif., 1980). Ger.-born operatic producer and impresario. Actor in Frankfurt and Berlin 1915–27. Dir., Darmstadt State Th. 1927–31, Berlin State Opera 1931–3. Producer, Glyndebourne Fest. from 1st season in 1934 to 1939, and 1947–59. Organized Turkish Nat. Opera 1937–47, dir., opera dept. Univ. of S. Calif. 1948–54. Returned to Berlin State Opera 1954–61; NY Met. 1959–62. Set new standards of ens. and detailed rehearsal in Verdi and Mozart. C.B.E. 1960.

Ebert, Peter (*b* Frankfurt, 1918). Ger. opera producer, son of Carl *Ebert. Has worked at Glyndebourne, Rome, Venice, Wexford, Los Angeles, and Copenhagen. Chief producer Hanover State Opera and Deutsche Oper am Rhein 1954–64; dir. of prods. Scottish Opera 1965–75; gen. administrator Scottish Opera 1977–80.

Ebony Concerto. For cl. and orch. by *Stravinsky. Comp. 1945 for jazz musician Woody Herman who was soloist with his band at f.p. in NY 1946. Jazz slang for cl. is 'ebony stick'.

Eccard, Johannes (*b* Mühlhausen, 1553; *d* Berlin, 1611). Ger. composer, pupil at Munich of *Lassus. Held several court posts, finally becoming Kapellmeister to Kurfürst of Brandenburg, Berlin, 1608. Wrote many motets and chorales.

Eccles, John (*b* London, *c*.1668; *d* Hampton Wick, 1735). Eng. composer. Prolific writer of th. mus., incl. Congreve's *The Way of the World* and masque *The Judgement of Paris*. Collab. with Purcell on *Don Quixote* (1694–5). Master of King's Band 1700. Pubd. 100 songs in 1710.

Eccles (Eagles), **Solomon** (*b* London, 1618; *d* London, 1682). Eng. composer and performer on virginals and viol. On becoming Quaker *c*.1660 publicly burned his mus. and instrs., later accompanying George Fox to W. Indies.

Ecclesiastical Modes. See *Modes*.

Échappé. See *Changing Note*.

Échelle (Fr.). Ladder, i.e. Scale (*Gamme* is the more usual word for the mus. scale). **Échelette** (Fr.). Little ladder, i.e. *Xylophone.

Echo Cornet. Organ stop of gentle tone (see *Cornet Stop*).

Echo Gamba. A soft type of organ stop.

Echoklavier (Ger.). Echo-keyboard. *Choir Organ (not Echo Organ).

Echo Organ. An org. manual with very soft stops to give an echo effect.

Eckhardt-Gramatté, Sophie-Carmen (Sonia) (*b* Moscow, 1899; *d* Stuttgart, 1974). Russ.-Fr. composer, violinist, and pianist. Studied Paris Cons. with d'Indy, also vn. with Thibaud and Huberman, comp. in Berlin with Max Trapp. Career as solo violinist and pianist from age 11, but later concentrated on comp. Works incl. 3 pf. concs., vn. conc., conc. for orch., triple conc. (tpt., cl., bn.), bn. conc., 2 syms., 3 str. qts., 6 pf. sonatas, and other chamber works. Settled in Canada 1953.

Éclat (Fragment). Work for chamber orch. (15 instr.) by Boulez, comp. 1965. F.p. Los Angeles

1965, London 1966. Expanded and rev. 1970 as *Éclat/Multiples*, f.p. London 1970, but regarded as 'work in progress'.

Eclecticism. Term frequently used to describe a composer's conscious use of styles alien to his nature, or from a bygone era. Also used pejoratively when applied to mus. in which the composer, thought to be lacking originality, has freely drawn on other models.

Eclogue. Short pastoral poem (sometimes used as title of a piece of mus.).

Écossaise. A type of contredanse (see *Country Dance*) in duple time. The orig. of the name is a mystery, since there appears to be nothing Scottish about the character of the mus. It is not the same as the *Schottische.

Ed (It.). 'And' (version of *E as used before a vowel). Thus the title of Bellini's opera may be given as *I Capuleti e (ed) i Montecchi*.

Edelmann, Otto (*b* Brunn am Gebirge, 1917). Austrian bass. Studied Vienna Acad. Début Gera 1937. Joined Vienna Opera 1947, also regular visitor to NY Met. and San Francisco. Bayreuth début 1951 as Sachs. Notable Ochs in *Der Rosenkavalier*.

Eden and Tamir. Israeli piano duo formed 1952 by Bracha Eden (*b* Jerusalem, 1928) and Alexander Tamir (*b* Vilnius, 1931). Both studied at Rubin Acad., Jerusalem until 1952 and at Aspen in 1955 with Vronsky and Babin. Début Israel 1954, NY 1955, London 1957. Have revived many two-piano works by Clementi, Dussek, and Hummel. Gave f. Amer. p. of Lutoslawski's *Paganini Variations* and f. public. p. of pf. duet version of Stravinsky's *Rite of Spring*.

Edgar. 4-act opera by Puccini to lib. by F. Fontana after A. de Musset's verse-drama *La Coupe et ses lèvres* (1832). Comp. 1884–8. Prod. Milan 1889; NY 1956. Rev. 3-act version f.p. Ferrara 1892. Further rev. 1901, 1905.

Edinburgh Festival. 3-week annual int. fest. of the arts held in Scottish capital Aug.–Sept., with strong emphasis on opera, concerts, and recitals. Founded 1947 with Rudolf Bing as dir.; he was succeeded by Ian Hunter 1949–55, Robert Ponsonby 1955–60, Earl of Harewood 1961–5, Peter Diamand 1966–78, John Drummond 1979–83; Frank Dunlop from 1984. Many distinguished visiting cos. have supplied opera, incl. Glyndebourne, Stuttgart, Stockholm, Hamburg, Prague, Belgrade, Scala, Florence, Deutsche Oper, Bavarian State, and Scottish. Visiting orchs. and soloists incl. virtually all the most celebrated. Several works have had f.ps. at fest. A feature is the very lively 'fringe', events outside the official programme, some of which have 'stolen the show'.

E Dur (Ger.). The key of E major.

Edwards, Richard (*b* Somerset, 1524; *d* London, 1566). Eng. composer, poet, and scholar. Master of the Children of the Chapel Royal from 1561. Best known for his madrigal *In going to my naked bed*. His *Damon and Pythias* (1564) has been described as early 'mus. drama'.

Edwards, Ross (*b* Sydney, N.S.W., 1943). Australian composer. Studied at N.S.W. Cons. and Univs. of Sydney and Adelaide. Studied comp. with Meale, Sculthorpe, Maxwell Davies, and Veress. Went to London 1969. Returned to Australia 1972. Taught in mus. dept., Univ. of Sydney. Lect., N.S.W. Cons. from 1976. Comps. incl.: *5 Carols*, women's or boys' vv. (1967); *Mountain Village in a Clearing Mist*, orch. (1973); *5 Little Piano Pieces* (1976); *Shadow D-Zone*, fl., cl., perc., pf., vn., vc. (1977); *The Tower of Remoteness*, cl., pf. (1978); *Laikan I*, 6 players (1979), *II*, 6 players (1981); *Ab estasis foribus*, unacc. ch. (1980); *Maninya*, alto v. and vc. (1981); *Kumari*, pf. (1981).

E.F.D.S.S. *English Folk Dance and Song Society.

Egdon Heath. Orch. work, Op. 47, by Holst, comp. 1927 and inspired by the Dorset landscape described as 'Egdon Heath' in Thomas Hardy's *The Return of the Native* (1878). Sub-titled 'Homage to Thomas Hardy'. Commissioned by NY S.O. which gave f.p. 1928. F.p. in England, Cheltenham 1928, cond. Holst, and London 10 days later (all these perfs. were in Feb.).

Egge, Klaus (*b* Gransherad, Norway, 1906; *d* Oslo, 1979). Norweg. composer and critic. Studied Oslo Cons. and privately with *Valen, later attending Berlin Hochschule für Musik. Later works use a form of serial technique. Comps. incl. 5 syms., 2 pf. concs., vn. conc., vc. conc., ballet *Fanitullen*, choral works, and chamber mus.

Eggen, Arne (*b* Trondheim, 1881; *d* Baerum, 1955). Norweg. composer and organist. Cond. Drammen orch. Works incl. org. pieces and vn. sonatas but best-known for his songs.

Egk, Werner (*b* Auchsesheim, Bavaria, 1901; *d* Inning, Bavaria, 1983). Ger. composer and cond. Mainly self-taught. Cond. for Bavarian radio 1930–3 and at Berlin State Opera 1937–41. Dir., Berlin Hochschule für Musik 1950–3. Very active on behalf of performing rights, etc. Controversial figure, his opera *Peer Gynt* being banned by Nazis because of its satire on régime, but he wrote mus. for Berlin Olympic Games 1936. Colouristic and rhythmical features of his work derive from admiration for Stravinsky. Works incl.:

OPERAS: *Columbus* (1933 radio, 1942 stage), *Die Zaubergeige* (1935, rev. 1954), *Peer Gynt* (1938), *Circe* (1945, rev. 1966 as *17 Tage und 4 Minuten*), *Irische Legende* (after Yeats, 1955, rev. 1970), *Der Revisor* (after Gogol's *The *Government Inspector*, 1957), *Die Verlobung in San Domingo* (1963).

BALLET: *Joan von Zarissa* (1940), *Abraxas* (1947–8), *Ein Sommertag* (1950), *Die chinesische Nachtigall* (1953), *Casanova in London* (1969).

ORCH: *Geigenmusik*, vn. and orch. (1936), *Olympische Festmusik* (1936), *Französische Suite* (after Rameau, 1949), *Variations on a Caribbean Theme* (1959), *Orchestra Sonata No. 2* (1969), *Spiegelzeit* (1979).

VOICE AND ORCH: *Variations on an Old Viennese Song* for coloratura sop. (for singing-lesson scene in *Il barbiere di Siviglia*) (1938), *La Tentation de Saint Antoine* for mez., str. qt. (1947, rev. for mez., str. qt., and str. 1952), *Chanson et Romance* for coloratura sop. (1953).

CHORAL: *Furchtlosigkeit und Wohlwollen*, oratorio (1931, rev. 1959), *Mein Vaterland* (1937).

Egmont. Ov. and 9 items of incidental mus., Op. 84, by Beethoven to Goethe's historical drama about the Flemish aristocrat Egmont who defied Philip of Spain and was beheaded in 1567. Comp. 1809–10.

Eguale (It.). Equal. So *egualità*, *egualezza*, equality; *egualmente*, equally. *Voci eguali*, *equal voices.

Egyptian Helen, The (Strauss). See *ägyptische Helena, Die*.

Ehrling, Sixten (*b* Malmö, 1918). Swed. cond. and pianist. Studied Stockholm Cons., and in Paris, Dresden, and London. Prin. cond. Stockholm Royal Opera 1953–70, Detroit S.O. 1963–73. Cond. of *Ring* at NY Met.

Eichner, Ernst (*b* Arolsen, 1740; *d* Potsdam, 1777). Ger. composer and bassoonist. Worked in Paris and London 1770–3, then in Potsdam court orch. Noted composer of Mannheim sch., writing 31 syms., also concs. and chamber mus.

Eighteen-Twelve (1812). Concert-ov., Op. 49, by Tchaikovsky, comp. 1880, commemorating Napoleon's retreat from Moscow in 1812 and incorporating *La Marseillaise* and the Tsarist nat. anthem. Orig. idea was for perf. in a Moscow square with large orch., military band, cath. bells, and cannon fire. Sometimes still perf. with cannon (esp. at Royal Albert Hall popular Tchaikovsky evenings).

Eight-foot. Term in org. mus. for sound of normal pitch, the lowest pipe of normal pitch being theoretically 8′ in length.

Eighth Note. The quaver in Amer. terminology.

Eight Songs for a Mad King (Maxwell Davies). See *Songs for a Mad King, 8*.

Eimert, Herbert (*b* Bad Kreuznach, 1897; *d* Cologne, 1972). Ger. composer and theorist. Studied Cologne High School for Mus. 1919–24 and at Cologne Univ. until 1930, graduating in musicology. Worked for Cologne Radio 1927–33. Mus. critic *Kölnische Zeitung* 1936–45. Founder-dir., elec. mus. studio, Cologne, 1951–62. Co-ed. *Die Reihe* 1955–62. Prof. and dir. elec. mus.

studio, Cologne Hochschule für Musik 1965–71. Assoc. with Stockhausen and Ger. *avant-garde* in propounding theories of elecs. Works incl. 2 str. qts. (1925, 1944), *Tanzmusik*, sax., fl., mechanical instr. (1926), *Glockenspiel*, tape (1953), and other works on tape. Author of textbooks on atonality, 12-note technique, and elec. music.

Eine kleine Nachtmusik (Mozart). See *Kleine Nachtmusik, Eine.*

Einem, Gottfried von (*b* Berne, 1918). Austrian composer. Studied comp. with *Blacher 1941–3. Ch. coach Berlin State Opera 1938–43; one of Salzburg Fest. administrators 1948–66; lecturer Vienna Konzerthaus Gesellschaft 1946–66; teacher of comp., Vienna Acad. 1963–72. Essentially a tonal composer, Einem has had considerable success in the opera house where his melodic gifts and command of colour have been well deployed. Works incl.:

OPERAS: *Dantons Tod* (1944–6), *Der *Prozess* (1950–2), *Der Zerrissene* (1961–4), *Der Besuch der Alten Dame* (The *Visit of the Old Lady*, 1970), *Kabale und Liebe* (1970–5), *Jesu Hochzeit* (1978–9).
BALLETS: *Prinzessin Turandot* (1942–3), *Rondo vom goldenen Kalb* (1950), *Glück, Tod und Traum* (1953), *Medusa* (1957).
ORCH: *Capriccio* (1943), *Concerto for Orch.* (1943), *Meditations* (1954), pf. conc. (1955), *Symphonische Szenen* (1956), *Ballade* (1957), *Dance-Rondo* (1959), *Philadelphia Symphony* (1960), *Nachtstück* (1960), vn. conc. (1966–7), *Hexameron* (1969), *Bruckner Dialog* (1971), *Wiener-Symphonie* (1976), *Ludi Leopoldini* (1980).
CHORAL: *Hymnus an Goethe*, for cont., ch., and orch. (1949), *Von der Liebe*, high v. and orch. (1961), *Kammergesänge* (1965), *Rosa mystica*, bar., orch. (1972), and songs.
CHAMBER: Vn. sonata (1949), 2 pf. sonatinas (1947), 3 str. qts. (1975, 1977, 1980), solo vn. sonata (1975), wind quintet (1976).

Ein' feste Burg (A Safe Stronghold). Luther's setting of Ps. 46 in his own trans.; tune adapted by him from a plainsong melody. Quoted by several composers, e.g. in Meyerbeer's *Les Huguénots*, Mendelssohn's *Reformation Sym.*, and Wagner's *Kaisermarsch.*

Einstein, Alfred (*b* Munich, 1880; *d* El Cerrito, Calif., 1952). Ger. scholar and writer (from 1945 Amer. citizen). Ed. *Zeitschrift für Musikwissenschaft* 1918–33; mus. critic *Berliner Tageblatt* 1927–33. Ed., 9th–11th edns. Riemann's *Musiklexikon* (1919, 1922, 1929). Lived in London and It. 1933–9; settled in USA 1939. Prof. of mus., Smith Coll., Northampton, Mass., 1939, later teaching at other Amer. univs. Rev. Köchel's Mozart catalogue 1937. Books incl. *History of Music* (1917, and many later edns.), *Gluck* (1936), *Mozart, his character, his work* (1945), *The Italian Madrigal* (1949), *Schubert* (1951). Not to be confused with his cousin the physicist Albert Einstein.

Einstimmig (Ger.). One-voiced, i.e. for one part.

Eis (Ger.). The note E♯.

Eisenberg, Maurice (*b* Königsberg, 1902; *d* NY, 1972). Ger.-Amer. cellist and teacher. Studied Peabody Cons., Baltimore, then in Berlin with Becker and in Spain with Casals. Début with Philadelphia Orch. 1916, later becoming its prin. cellist. Member of Menuhin Trio. Prof. of vc., École Normale, Paris, 1929–39, Juilliard Sch. from 1964.

Eisis (Ger.). The (theoretical) note E♯♯.

Eisler, Hanns (*b* Leipzig, 1898; *d* Berlin, 1962). Ger. composer. Studied Vienna Cons., being pupil of Schoenberg 1919–23. His Marxist beliefs led him from 1927 to a more 'popular' style, and he wrote political marching-songs, chs., and th. mus. in collab. with Brecht. Exiled in 1933, he worked in Paris, London, Copenhagen, and USA, settling in Hollywood 1938 where he taught at the Univ. of S. Calif. and worked on films with Chaplin. He wrote (in Eng.) the book *Composing for the Films* (1947). McCarthy drive against Communists in 1947 led to a deportation order, but he left peacefully in 1948, to live in Vienna and Berlin. In 1952 he settled in E. Ger. organizing workers' choirs and writing popular songs (incl. the DDR anthem). Nevertheless many of his comps. were in advanced 12-note technique. Works incl. 600 songs, mus. for 40 plays and over 40 films. The following have words by Brecht: *Die Massnahme* (1930), *Deutsche Sinfonie* (1935–9), *Lenin-Requiem* (1937), *Die Teppichweber von Kujan-Bulak* (1957), *Solidaritätslied* (1930), *Kinderlieder* (1951), *Die Mutter* (Gorky and Brecht, 1931), *Die Rundköpfe und die Spitzköpfe* (1934–6), *Galileo Galilei* (1946), *Die Gesichte der Simone Machard* (1946), *Schweyk im zweiten Weltkrieg* (1957).

Also *Kleine Sinfonie* (1932), *5 Orchestral Pieces* (1938), *Chamber Symphony* (1940), Str. Qt. (1937), *Nonet* (1939), *Theme and Variations* for pf. (1940), Septet (variations on Amer. nursery songs) (1941), Pf. Quintet (1944), Septet No. 2 (1947), Pf. Sonatas (1924 and 1943), *Ernste Gesänge* (bar. and orch.) (1962).

Eisteddfod (Welsh, 'Session', from *eistedd*, 'to sit'. Plural *Eisteddfodau*). The nat. Welsh gathering of bards, dating in its present form from 1817, though it is said to date back, in one form or another, as far as the 7th cent., with a suspension throughout the entire 18th cent. and a few years before and after it. It now takes place annually (in Aug.) in various Welsh towns. Degrees of *Ofydd* (Ovate), *Bardd* (Bard), and *Pencerdd* (Chief Musician) are conferred on candidates who pass various tests and there is a strong choral and competitive side to the gathering. Many local *Eisteddfodau* exist in the form of competitive fests. An int. *Eisteddfod*, at which choirs and dancers from all over the world compete, has been held annually in Llangollen since 1947.

Eitner, Robert (*b* Breslau, 1832; *d* Templin, Berlin, 1905). Ger. musicologist and composer. Prin. achievement, begun 1882, was his *Biographisch-bibliographisches Quellen-Lexikon der Musiker und Musikgelehrten* (10 vols., 1900–4).

Ek, Gunnar (*b* Åsarum, 1900; *d* Lund, 1981). Swed. composer and cellist. Studied Stockholm Cons. Cellist in Stockholm Orch. 1928–37. Composer of syms., *Swedish Fantasy* for orch., pf. conc., and *Doomsday Cantata*.

Elder, Mark (Philip) (*b* Hexham, 1947). Eng. conductor and bassoonist. Studied Bryanston (prin. bn. in Nat. Youth Orch.) and Cambridge Univ. Ass. to R. *Leppard at Glyndebourne 1970 and chorusmaster 1970–2. Début with RLPO, 1971. Australian Opera 1972–4 (début in Sydney in *Nabucco*). ENO 1974, becoming ass. cond.; prin. cond. from 1979. CG début 1976 (*Rigoletto*). Cond. f.p. of Blake's *Toussaint*, London, 1977. Cond. *Die Meistersinger* at Bayreuth, 1981. Impressive cond. of Strauss; guest cond. of leading orchs.

Electric Action. Means of permitting air to enter an org. pipe by electrical device, after key has been depressed.

Electric Guitar. *Guitar, used in pop groups or jazz bands, connected by wire to electrical apparatus which amplifies or modifies the sound. Used in Tippett's *The Knot Garden*, Stockhausen's *Gruppen*, and Boulez's *Domaines*.

Electric Musical Instruments. Instrs. in which the use of elec. devices such as valves and photo-cells determines or affects the actual sound of the note prod. Before the full-scale development of *electronic music several different electric instr. were pioneered. Chief among these were the *Sphaerophon, the *Theremin, the *Trautonium, the *Ondes Martenot, the *Hellertion, the *Electronde, and the *Rhythmicon.

Electric Organ. Organs of various makes (most notably by the Hammond Instr. Co. of Chicago) which work on an electro-magnetic principle. Their tone is prod. not from pipes but by means of rotating discs with electro-magnetic pick-ups. They are popular as domestic instr.

Electrochord. Trade name of elec. instr. resembling a pf., in which the str. are set vibrating by hammers. There is no soundboard, vibrations being picked up electrically and amplified through a loudspeaker. Variations of tone-quality and vol. can be controlled.

Electrofonic Violin. Semi-elec. instr. developed in 1938 by Marshall Moss, leader of the Nat. S.O., Washington, and William Bartley, an engineer. The vn., which has no sound-board, is played in the usual way, the mechanically-prod. vibrations being picked up by electro-magnets or a microphone and amplified through a loudspeaker. Similar instr., and a vc., was developed by Vierling, and there is a 5-string electric vc. by Karapetov.

Electronde. Elec. instr. developed by Martin Taubman in 1933. On similar lines to *theremin, but by pressing a switch at the same time as moving his hand over the antenna, the player can obtain a staccato effect. It also enables playing of rapid passages.

Electronic Music. Mus. prod. by elec. means, the resulting sounds being recorded on tape. At first the term applied strictly to sounds synthesized electronically, to differentiate from *musique concrète*, which was assembled from normal mus. and everyday sounds. But by now it covers both groups. Attempts to produce elec. sounds began in the USA and Canada in the 1890s. Early in the 20th cent., experiments were made in Ger. by Fischinger; and in USSR in the 1930s elec. mus. was prod. by the use of photo-electric techniques rather than by oscillator. In fact, the development of elec. mus. has proceeded step by step with the invention of equipment: telephone, loudspeaker, microphone, tape, film sound-track, oscillator, gramophone recording, etc.

For composers, an important milestone was reached with experiments at Bonn Univ. in 1949–50 followed by a public perf. at Darmstadt in 1951. The first elec. mus. studio was est. 1951 by W. Ger. Radio, Cologne, dir. by Herbert *Eimert. Other studios were set up in Milan, Tokyo, London, Warsaw, Brussels, Munich, Eindhoven, Paris, and at Columbia Univ., NY.

In the 1950s the comp. of elec. works was a slow and laborious business, chiefly because of the comparatively primitive equipment in the early studios. A comp. consisting of hundreds of predetermined and separately recorded sounds which would last a few minutes could take weeks to assemble on the final tape. The equipment in the early studios generally comprised: (a) *Sine-Tone Generators*. Sine-tones are pure sounds which have no harmonics and are on a single frequency of even dynamic level. To build a complex tone at least 8 generators were needed. (b) *White Sound Generator*. White sound comprises all audible frequencies sounding together. (c) *Square Wave Generator*. Square waves are richly harmonic and produce contrasts to sine-tones. (d) *Filters*. Devices which, as their name implies, can 'filter' sound, or extract a single sine-tone from the white sound. Filters are classified according to their frequency-response characteristics, i.e. low-pass, high-pass, band-pass, and band-stop. For example, the band-pass filter passes only the sound-waves within a specified band of frequencies grouped round a centre frequency. (e) *Ring modulator*. Used to combine several sound signals so that the sound output comprises the sums and differences of all the input-frequency components. (f) *Variable speed tape recorders*. Varying speeds of playing the tape are used to speed up or slow down specific effects. (g) *Dynamic suppressor*. A device which allows signals to be cut out below a selected level of dynamics, thus introducing a 'chance' element.

Among the most celebrated elec. pieces composed in the 1950s were Eimert's *Fünf Stücke*, Stockhausen's *Gesang der Jünglinge* (which incl. a boy's v., fragmented and superimposed upon itself, thereby creating a bridge with *musique concrète*), Křenek's *Spiritus Intelligentiae Sanctus*, Berio's *Mutazioni*, and Maderna's *Notturno*. But it should be remembered that in 1939–42 John *Cage's first 3 *Imaginary Landscapes* incl. the use of records played at different speeds, audio oscillators, and an amplified wire coil.

Dobrowolski: *Music for Magnetic Tape No. 1*

MUZYKA NA TAŚMĘ MAGNETOFONOWĄ Nr 1

ANDRZEJ DOBROWOLSKI (1963)

Elec. mus. was revolutionized in the 1960s by the invention of voltage-controlled sound *synthesizers*, especially the model developed in 1964–5 by the American Robert A. *Moog. This instr. dispensed with the drudgery of tape-splicing and cutting. It not only presented composers with a complete spectrum of new sounds, but could be made to play itself in a remarkable variety of sounds which could be recurrent or otherwise, as required. By the fitting of a control device known as a *sequencer*, the synthesizer can be used by a composer to memorize a long and complicated mus. compilation and play it 'live' without recording or tape-editing. Because of the synthesizer's astonishing imitative qualities, its use has been commercialized and vulgarized, but its potentiality as a serious instr. is still being explored and awaits a Wagner to exploit it to the full. Its main working principle, greatly over-simplified, is that the oscillators used as sound sources are also used to 'control' each other. Some synthesizers have a kbd., often with its own tuned oscillator, or set to act as a voltage control.

The sequencer is a small variety of the other revolutionary device also introduced in the 1960s, *digital computer synthesis*. Control by digital computer means that the equipment the composer uses is supplied with a 'memory'. For example, a work comp., or 'programmed', for voltage-controlled equipment by means of punched paper tape has an intrinsic major problem in that the system has no way of storing information until it is needed; everything must be supplied in detail each time it is required. The computer memorizes all this information. The disadvantages of a computer are those inherent in 'programming', and it remains to be seen whether a supreme work of art will evolve by this system. The advantages of elec. mus. for th., radio, and film incidental mus. are obvious, and so far it is in these fields that the best results have been achieved.

Notation of elec. mus. obviously bears no relation to conventional mus. notation, and since the principal feature of an elec. work is that it is predetermined and mechanically produced, notation as a guide to performers is unnecessary. But 'live' elec. mus. is a developing art-form, and graphic directions in pitch (frequency) etc. are provided in 'realization' scores which provide all the technical data necessary to reproduce the piece. 'Representational' scores, for the score reader, are slightly less fearsome. An illustration of a typical elec. score or graph will perhaps give the reader a better idea of what is involved.

Among composers who have prod. elec. works are: Cage, Berio, Stockhausen, Wuorinen, Blacher, Boulez, Babbitt, Pousseur, Badings, Varèse, Davidovsky, Ligeti, Takemitsu, Penderecki, Xenakis, and many others.

Interested readers who wish for fuller and more technical information than can be provided here are referred to Reginald Smith Brindle's *The New Music* (London, 1975), to which this entry acknowledges its indebtedness.

See also *Computers in music.*

Electrophone. Term for mus. instr. which produce sound by electronic means, either by oscillation or by electromagnetic or electrostatic methods. Does not cover instr. in which tone is conventionally produced and then electronically modified (e.g. electric guitar, piano, double bass). Classification added to four devised by C. Sachs and E. M. von Hornbostel and pubd. in *Zeitschrift für Ethnologie*, 1914, i.e. *aerophones, *chordophones, *idiophones, and *membranophones.

Elegia, elegiaco (It.). *Elegy, elegiac.

Elegy, Élégie (Fr.). A song of lament for the dead or for some melancholy event, or an instr. comp. with that suggestion, such as Elgar's *Elegy for Strings* and Fauré's *Élégie.*

Elegy for Young Lovers. Opera in 3 acts by Henze to lib. (in Eng.) by Auden and Kallman. Comp. 1959–61. Prod. Schwetzingen 1961, Glyndebourne 1961.

Elektra. Opera in 1 act by R. Strauss to lib. by Hofmannsthal based on Sophocles' *Electra*. Comp. 1906–8. Prod. Dresden 1909, NY and London 1910.

Elevatio (Lat.), **Elevation** (Eng.). Mus. (choral or organ) perf. during the Elevation of the Host in the R.C. Church.

Elgar, (Sir) **Edward** (William) (*b* Broadheath, Worcester, 1857; *d* Worcester, 1934). Eng. composer and cond. He was the son of a mus.-shop proprietor in Worcester who was also an organist, pf.-tuner, and teacher. He showed an early aptitude for mus., learning the org., vn., and other instr. He hoped, on leaving school at 15, to go to Leipzig Cons. but his father could not afford to send him, so after a brief spell in a solicitor's office, he helped his father in the shop and became his ass. organist at St George's R.C. Church, Worcester. Soon he was playing the vn. in several local orchs. or chamber groups and became cond. of several. With his brothers and friends he formed a wind quintet, for which he comp. several works. His first comps. had been written during childhood, incl. mus. for a play written and prod. by the Elgar children, *The Wand of Youth*, which he adapted as 2 orch. suites in 1907–8. In 1877 he went to London for vn. lessons from *Pollitzer but abandoned them when he realized he would not become a virtuoso. He played in the 2nd vns. in the 3 Choirs Fest. orch. at Worcester in 1878. The following year he became bandmaster at the county lunatic asylum at Powick where members of the staff played weekly for dances. Elgar made several arrs. of operatic arias for concerts there and also comp. a series of quadrilles. In 1882 he joined the 1st vns. in a Birmingham orch. cond. by W.

Stockley, who incl. Elgar's *Sérénade mauresque* in a concert in 1883. For the next 6 years, until his marriage in 1889, Elgar was in demand locally in many mus. capacities but he was unknown outside the Midlands apart from a perf. of his *Sevillana* at a Crystal Palace concert in May 1884. After his marriage to a general's daughter, Elgar gave up his work in Malvern and Worcester and went to London, but met with no success there. He returned to Malvern a year later to resume his teaching and other activities. In the meantime, however, the 1890 3 Choirs Fest. at Worcester had commissioned a work from him, the concert-ov. *Froissart*. In 1893 he comp. a secular cantata, *The Black Knight*, which was the first of a series of choral works taken up by the great Midlands choral socs. Its successors were *King Olaf* (1896), *The Light of Life* (1896), and *Scenes from the Bavarian Highlands* (1896). For Queen Victoria's Diamond Jubilee in 1897 Elgar comp. an *Imperial March* which *Manns cond. at the Crystal Palace and which the Queen requested should be incl. in the State Concert marking the Jubilee. Its success led to a commission from the Leeds Fest., the result being the large-scale cantata *Caractacus* (1898). At this time, Elgar was still earning his living as a vn. teacher; his first large-scale London success came in 1899 when *Richter cond. the f.p. of the *Variations on an Original Theme (Enigma)*, one of Elgar's greatest and best-known works. A few months later Clara Butt sang the *Sea Pictures* at the Norwich Fest. Commissioned to write a big choral work for the 1900 Birmingham Fest., Elgar, a Catholic, chose to set Newman's poem *The Dream of Gerontius*. The f.p. was a failure, but the worth of the mus. was recognized and 2 Düsseldorf perfs. followed, after the 2nd of which Richard Strauss hailed Elgar as the foremost Eng. composer of the day. From that day there developed an Elgar vogue on the Continent, and several conds. such as Weingartner, Strauss, Steinbach, and Busoni incl. his works in their programmes. The neglect of the previous 25 years in Eng. was forgotten (though not by Elgar) overnight as he became the most talked-about composer of the day. From 1901 until 1914 were the years of greatest acclaim for Elgar in his lifetime, and he responded with a succession of splendid works incl. the *Cockaigne* ov., the oratorios *The Apostles* and *The Kingdom*, 2 syms., a vn. conc. (for *Kreisler), the *Introduction and Allegro* for str., the choral ode *The Music Makers*, and the symphonic study *Falstaff*. The 1st Sym. (1908) in particular had an astonishing initial success, being perf. 100 times in just over a year in cities as far apart as Manchester, Vienna, St Petersburg, Rome, and Budapest. However, the work which had made him a household name was No. 1 of a set of *Pomp and Circumstance* Marches, f.p. 1901. The splendid tune of the trio section caught the ear of King Edward VII who suggested that it should be set to words. When in 1902 it emerged in the *Coronation Ode* as *Land of*

Hope and Glory it soon became clear that Elgar had comp. an alternative nat. anthem. Elgar was knighted in 1904 at age 47, and in 1911 became a member of the O.M. He visited the USA to cond. his own works and spent several periods in It. From 1905 to 1908 he was Peyton Prof. of Mus., Birmingham Univ. He was appointed cond. of the LSO for 1911–12 and in 1912 moved from Hereford to a large house in Hampstead.

During the 1914–18 war Elgar wrote several patriotic works, including the recitation with orch. *Carillon*, the symphonic prelude *Polonia*, and the Binyon settings *The Spirit of England*. He also wrote incidental mus. for a children's play, *The Starlight Express*, and a ballet *The Sanguine Fan*. In 1918–19 he wrote 3 chamber works, a vn. sonata, str. qt., and pf. quintet, and a vc. conc. These were to be his last major works. In 1920 his wife died and for the last 14 years of his life he wrote hardly anything that was not concocted from earlier sketches. In this last period he prod. incidental mus. for 2 plays, *Arthur* and *Beau Brummel*, a 5th *Pomp and Circumstance* march, the *Nursery Suite*, and the *Severn Suite*. He was at work on a Ben Jonson opera, *The Spanish Lady*, and a 3rd sym. at the time of his death. In 1923 he returned to live in Worcestershire and often appeared throughout the country as cond. of his own works. He became Master of the King's Musick in 1924 and was created a baronet in 1931. He was the first great composer to realize the possibilities of the gramophone and from 1914 to 1933 made many recordings of his own mus. which are important historical documents, the most celebrated being that of the vn. conc. made in 1932 with the 16-year-old *Menuhin.

Elgar's greatness as a composer lies in his ability to combine nobility and spirituality of utterance with a popular style. Side by side with his large-scale works are dozens of lighter pieces distinguished by melodic charm and fine craftsmanship. Learning entirely by the practical experiences of his youth, he became one of the supreme masters of the orch., but his command of choral effects in his masterpiece *The Dream of Gerontius* is no less wonderful. His harmonic language derives from Schumann and Brahms coloured by the Wagnerian chromaticism endemic to his generation, the whole being lightened by a gracefulness akin to Bizet and Saint-Saëns. Like his personality, his mus. veers from extrovert warmth and geniality to a deep introspective melancholy. His prin. works are:

ORCH: *Froissart*, Op. 19 (1890), *Serenade* for str. in E minor, Op. 20 (1892); *Sursum Corda*, Op. 11 (1894); *Imperial March*, Op. 32 (1897); *Enigma Variations*, Op. 36 (1898–9); *Pomp and Circumstance Marches*, Op. 39, No. 1 in D major, No. 2 in A minor (1901), No. 3 in C minor (1904), No. 4 in G major (1907), No. 5 in C major (1930); *Cockaigne*, Op. 40 (1901); *In the South (Alassio)*, Op. 50 (1904); *Introduction and*

Allegro for str., Op. 47 (1905); *The *Wand of Youth* Suites Nos. 1 and 2, Opp. 1a and 1b (1907 and 1908); Sym. No. 1 in A♭ major, Op. 55 (1907–8); *Elegy* for str., Op. 58 (1909); Vn. Conc. in B minor, Op. 61 (1909–10); *Romance* for bn., Op. 62 (1910); Sym. No. 2 in E♭ major, Op. 63 (1903–11); *Coronation March*, Op. 65 (1911); *Suite, Crown of India*, Op. 66 (1912); *Falstaff*, Op. 68 (1902–13); *Sospiri* for str., harp, and organ, Op. 70 (1914); *Polonia*, Op. 76 (1915); Vc. Conc. in E minor, Op. 85 (1918–19); *Empire March* (1924); *Severn Suite*, Op. 87, for brass band (1930), for orch. (1932); *Nursery Suite* (1931).

VOICES AND ORCH: *The *Black Knight*, cantata, Op. 25 (1889–93); *Scenes from the *Bavarian Highlands*, Op. 27 (1896); *The *Light of Life (Lux Christi)*, oratorio, Op. 29 (1896); *Scenes from the Saga of *King Olaf*, cantata, Op. 30 (1894–6); *The *Banner of St George*, ballad, Op. 33 (1896–7); *Caractacus*, cantata, Op. 35 (1898); *The *Dream of Gerontius*, Op. 38 (1899–1900); *Sea Pictures*, song-cycle for mez. and orch., Op. 37 (1897–9); *Coronation Ode*, Op. 44 (1902); *The *Apostles*, oratorio, Op. 49 (1901–3); *The *Kingdom*, oratorio, Op. 51 (1901–6); 3 Songs with orch., Op. 59 (1909–10); *The *Music Makers*, choral ode, Op. 69 (1902–12); *The *Spirit of England*, Op. 80 (1915–17).

PART-SONGS AND CHURCH MUSIC: *Ave, verum corpus*, Op. 2, No. 1 (1887); *Ecce sacerdos magnus*, ch. and organ (1888); *My love dwelt in a northern land* (1889); *Spanish Serenade*, Op. 23 (1891, with orch. 1892); *Te Deum and Benedictus*, Op. 34 (1897); *The Sword Song*, from *Caractacus* (1898); *To her beneath whose steadfast star* (1899); *Weary Wind of the West* (1902); 5 *Part-Songs from the Greek Anthology*, Op. 45 (1902); *Evening Scene* (1905); 4 *Part-Songs*, Op. 53 (1907); *The Reveille*, Op. 54 (1907); *Angelus*, Op. 56 (1909); *Go, Song of Mine*, Op. 57 (1909); *O hearken thou*, offertory, Op. 64 (Coronation 1911); *Great is the Lord* (Psalm 48), Op. 67 (1912); *Give Unto the Lord* (Psalm 29), Op. 74 (1914); 2 *Choral Songs*, Op. 71 (1914); *Death on the Hills*, Op. 72 (1914); 2 *Choral Songs*, Op. 73 (1914); *The Wanderer* and *Zut, zut, zut* (1923).

CHAMBER MUSIC: *Promenades* for wind quintet (1878); *Harmony Music* for wind quintet (1879); *Allegretto on GEDGE*, vn. and pf. (1885); *Salut d'Amour*, Op. 12, for pf. solo, for vn. and pf., for orch., and in many other arrs. (1888–9); *Liebesahnung*, vn. and pf. (1889); *La Capricieuse*, Op. 17, vn. and pf. (1891); *Very Easy Melodious Exercises in the 1st Position*, Op. 22, for vn. (1892); *Études caractéristiques*, Op. 24, for vn. (1882–92); *Chanson de Nuit, Chanson de Matin*, Op. 15, Nos. 1 and 2, for vn. and pf. (later orch.) (No. 1 pubd. 1897, No. 2 pubd. 1899); Vn. Sonata in E minor, Op. 82 (1918); Str. Qt. in E minor, Op. 83 (1918); Pf. Quintet, Op. 84 (1918–19).

PIANO SOLOS: *Rosemary (Douce Pensée)* (1882, orch. 1914); *May Song* (1901, orch. 1928); *Concert*

Allegro, Op. 46 (1901); *Dream Children*, Op. 43 (1902); *Skizze* (1903); *In Smyrna* (1905); *Echo's Dance* (from *Sanguine Fan*) (1917); *Sonatina* (1889, rev. 1930); *Adieu* (1932); *Serenade* (1932).

THEATRE (incl. recitations): Incidental mus., funeral march, and song for *Grania and Diarmid* (Yeats and Moore), Op. 42 (1901); *The *Crown of India*, masque, Op. 66 (1902–12); *Carillon*, Op. 75, reciter and orch. (1914); incidental mus. for *The *Starlight Express* (Blackwood and Pearn), Op. 78 (1915); *Une voix dans le désert*, Op. 77, reciter and orch. (1915); *The *Sanguine Fan*, ballet, Op. 81 (1917); *Le drapeau belge*, Op. 79, reciter and orch. (1917); incidental mus. to *Arthur* (Binyon) (1923); incidental mus. to *Beau Brummel* (Matthews) (1928).

ORGAN: 11 Vesper Voluntaries, Op. 14 (1889–90); Sonata in G major, Op. 28 (1895); Sonata No. 2, Op. 87a (arr. by Atkins of *Severn Suite*) (1932–3).

SOLO SONGS: *Through the long days* (1885); *The Wind at Dawn* (1888); *Queen Mary's Song* (1889); *Like to the Damask Rose* (1893); *Shepherd's Song* (1893); *Rondel* (1894); *After* (1895); *Love Alone Will Stay* (incorporated into *Sea Pictures* as *In Haven*) (1897); *Pipes of Pan* (1900); *In the Dawn; Speak, Music* (1902); *Land of Hope and Glory* (1902); *Pleading* (1908); *The Torch; The River* (1909–10); *The Fringes of the Fleet* (1917); and many more.

SHORT PIECES FOR SMALL ORCH: *Cantique*, Op. 3 (1912 orch. of 1897 organ solo *Adagio solenne*); *Rosemary* (1914 orch. of 1882 pf. solo); *Sevillana*, Op. 7 (1884); *Salut d'Amour*, Op. 12 (1888); 3 *Bavarian Dances*, Op. 27 (Nos. 1, 3, and 6 of *From the Bavarian Highlands*) (orch. 1897); *Minuet*, Op. 21 (1899 orch. of 1897 pf. solo); *Chanson de Nuit; Chanson de Matin*, Op. 15, Nos. 1 and 2 (1901 orch.); *Sérénade lyrique* (1899); *Dream Children*, Op. 43 (1902); *Carissima* (1913); *Minuet (Beau Brummel)* (1928); *Mina* (sketched for pf. 1932, orch. 1933).

TRANSCRIPTIONS FOR ORCH: J.S. Bach: *Fugue in C minor* (Elgar Op. 86) f.p. London 1921; *Fantasy in C minor*, f.p. Gloucester 1922; Handel: *Overture in D minor*, f.p. Worcester 1923; Chopin: *Funeral March from Pf. Sonata in B♭ minor*, 1933.

UNCOMPLETED: Sym. No. 3, Op. 88 (begun *c.*1932); *The *Spanish Lady*, opera, Op. 89 (begun *c.*1932); Pf. Conc., Op. 90 (sketches date from 1909).

Elias, Brian (*b* Bombay, India, 1948). Eng. composer. Studied RCM with Bernard Stevens and H. Searle, and privately with Lutyens. Works incl. *La Chevelure*, sop. and chamber ens. (1967); *ELM*, sop., ten., pf. (1969); 5 *Pieces for Right Hand*, pf. (1969); *Piece*, vc. (1970); *Peroration*, solo sop. (1973); *Proverbs of Hell*, unacc. ch. (1975); *Tzigane*, vn. (1978); *Somnia*, ten. and orch. (1979); *At the Edge of Time*, ten. and pf. (1982); vn. conc. (1984); *L'Eylah* (1984).

Elijah (*Elias*). Oratorio, Op. 70, by Mendelssohn to text selected from the Bible by Julius Schrubring. For sop., cont., ten., bass, and treble soloists, boys' ch., ch., and orch. Comp. 1846, f.p. Birmingham 1846, Hamburg 1847, NY 1851.

Elinson, Iso (*b* Mogilev, 1907; *d* London, 1964). Russ.-born pianist, became Brit. subject. Studied Petrograd Cons. Pupil of Blumenfeld. Recitalist esp. in Chopin, Schubert, Beethoven, and soloist with orch. Prof. of pf. RMCM 1944–64.

Elisabetta, Regina d'Inghilterra (Elizabeth, Queen of England). Opera in 2 acts by Rossini to lib. by Giovanni Schmidt, after C. Federici's play (1814) based on Sophia Lee's novel *The Recess* (1783–5). Prod. Naples 1815, London 1818. First opera in which Rossini provided orch. acc. for all the recitatives. Ov. is same as for *Aureliano in Palmira* and *Il Barbiere di Siviglia*. Much of the mus. is taken from earlier operas, incl. *Sigismondo* (1814). First opera Rossini comp. for Isabella *Colbran, whom he later married.

Elisir d'amore, L' (The Elixir of Love). Comic opera in 2 acts by Donizetti to lib. by Romani after Scribe's lib. *Le Philtre* for Auber (1831). Prod. Milan 1832, London 1836, NY 1838.

Elizalde, Federico (*b* Manila, 1907; *d* Manila, 1979). Sp. composer, cond., and pianist. Studied under Bloch and Halffter. From 1926 to 1929 was in Eng. where he influenced development of jazz, particularly by his arrangements for a band at the Savoy Hotel 1927–9. Cond., Manila S.O., 1930. President, Manila Broadcasting Co., 1948. Comps. incl. opera *Paul Gauguin*, pf. conc., vn. conc., *Music for 15 soloists*, etc.

Ella, John (*b* Leicester, 1802; *d* London, 1888). Eng. writer, violinist, and impresario. Pupil of *Fétis. Dir. of mus. society at London home of Lord Saltoun, 1826–46. Founded and dir. chamber mus. concerts known as the *Musical Union* 1845–80, writing series of analytical notes. Critic of *Morning Post* 1828–42, *Athenaeum* 1831–4, and other journals.

Ellington, Duke (Edward Kennedy) (*b* Washington, D.C. 1899; *d* NY, 1974). Amer. composer, pianist, and jazz-band leader. One of the most influential figures in the history of jazz. From 1927 to 1932 his band established its fame at the Cotton Club, NY. Later it toured Europe (1933 and 1939), attracting and influencing several composers; though re-formed several times, some of its members remained with Ellington for over 30 years. Among his most celebrated players were Johnny Hodges (sax.), Barney Bigard (cl.), Cootie Williams (tpt.), Lawrence Brown (tb.), and Harry Carney (bar. sax.). Wrote about 6,000 comps., among best-known being *Mood Indigo, Solitude, Caravan, Sophisticated Lady, Black and Tan Fantasy, Creole Love Call*, and *Black, Brown, and Beige*.

Ellis, David (*b* Liverpool, 1933). Eng. composer and administrator. Studied RMCM 1953–7. Comps. awarded Royal Philharmonic prize, RCM patrons' award, and Morley College opera prize.

Joined staff of BBC, Manchester, 1964 with responsibility for BBC Northern S.O. (now BBC Philharmonic) programmes. Head of Mus., BBC North, 1978–86. Prin. works:

OPERA: *Crito*, Op. 21 (1963).

ORCH: Sym. No. 1, Op. 38 (1973); *Sinfonietta*, Op. 13 (1953); *L*, Op. 41 (1977); vn. conc., Op. 22 (1958); pf. conc., Op. 27 (1962); *Dance Rhapsody*, Op. 28 (1963); *Elegy*, Op. 30 (1966); *Fanfares and Cadenzas*, Op. 31 (1968).

CHAMBER ORCH: *February Music*, Op. 43, vc. and chamber orch. (1977); *Diversions*, Op. 39 (1974); *In Nomine* (1963); *Sequentia III (Tenebrae)*, Op. 32 (1970); *Circles* (1979); *Capriccio 'The Bear'* (1981).

STRING ORCH: *Dewpoint*, Op. 10, sop. and cl. (1955); *Diversions on a Theme of Purcell*, Op. 16 (1956); *Concert Music*, Op. 24 (1960); *Solus*, Op. 37 (1973).

CHORAL: *Crux fidelis (Sequentia I)*, Op. 26, ten., ch., and orch. (1962); *Magnificat and Nunc Dimittis*, ch. and org. (1964); *Sequentia in tempore Natali Sacri*, Op. 29, ch. and ens. (1964); *Psalm 115*, ch., brass, and org., Op. 33 (1970); *Carols for an Island Christmas*, Op. 34, ch. and ens. (1971); *An Image of Truth*, Op. 35, bass, ch., and orch. (1974); *Sequentia IV (Visions)*, Op. 36, ten., bar., ch., org., and perc. (1972); *Sequentia V (Genesis)*, Op. 40, ch. and orch. (or org.) (1975).

CHAMBER MUSIC: String Trio, Op. 9 (1954); wind quintet, Op. 17 (1956); Sonata for db., Op. 42 (1977).

PIANO: Sonatina, Op. 2 (1953); Sonata, Op. 12 (1956).

Ellis, Osian (*b* Ffynnongroew, 1928). Welsh harpist and singer. Studied RAM. Member of Melos Ens. Former prin. harpist LSO. Many recitals, tours, and recordings. Britten wrote Harp Suite in C, Op. 83, for him. C.B.E. 1971.

Elman, Mischa (*b* Talnoye, Russia, 1891; *d* NY, 1967). Russ.-Amer. violinist (Amer. citizen from 1923). Child prodigy. Studied under *Auer at St Petersburg Cons. Professional début Berlin 1904, London 1905. First played in NY 1908, thereafter maintaining brilliant int. reputation.

Elmendorff, Karl (*b* Düsseldorf, 1891; *d* in the Taunus, 1962). Ger. cond. Studied Cologne. Held cond. posts in Munich, Düsseldorf, and Berlin. Bayreuth Fest. 1927–42. Cond. Dresden State Opera, 1942–5, Wiesbaden 1948–56.

Eloy, Jean-Claude (*b* Mont-Saint-Aignan, nr. Rouen, 1938). Fr. composer. Studied Paris Cons. 1950–61 with *Milhaud and *Martenot, and with *Boulez in Basle 1961–2. Visited USA 1964 and 1967–9. Worked at elec. mus. studio, Cologne, 1972. Works incl. *Stèle pour Omar Khayyám* for sop., harp, pf., and perc. (1960), *Étude III* (Sym. No. 1) (1962), *Equivalences* for 18 instr. (1963), *Poly-chronies* I and II for wind and perc. (1964), *Macles* I/II, 6 groups of instr. (1967), *Faisceaux-Diffractions* for 28 instr. (1970), *Kamak-*

ala, for 3 ens. and 3 ch. (1971), *Shanti*, 6 solo vv., instrs., elec. (1972–3, rev. as *Vers l'étendue*, orch. 1974), *Kshara-akshara*, sop., ch., 3 orch. groups (1974).

El Salón México. Orch. work by *Copland based on popular Mexican themes. Comp. 1933–6, f.p. Mexico S.O. 1937. Also arr. by composer for solo pf.

Elsner, Joseph Xaver (*b* Grottkau, 1769; *d* Warsaw, 1854). Silesian composer, largely self-taught. Kapellmeister, Lemberg, 1792–9. Cond. in Warsaw from 1799, in charge of opera until 1824 and becoming dir. of Cons. 1821–30. Taught Chopin. Comp. 20 operas, 8 syms., ballet, concs., etc.

Elwell, Herbert (*b* Minneapolis, 1898; *d* Cleveland, 1974). Amer. composer and critic. Studied with *Bloch in NY and *Boulanger in Paris. Mus. critic, Cleveland *Plain Dealer* 1932–65. Head of comp., Cleveland Institute of Mus. 1928–45. Teacher of comp. Oberlin Cons. from 1945. Works incl. ballet *The Happy Hypocrite* (1925), 2 str. qts., *Lincoln: Requiem aeternam* (1947), *Introduction and Allegro* for orch. (1942), etc.

Elwes, Gervase (Cary) (*b* Northampton, 1866; *d* Boston, Mass., 1921). Eng. ten. Studied mus. Vienna, Munich, Paris, and London, but did not become professional musician until 1903, having begun diplomatic career. Soon in demand for Lieder recitals and as notable exponent of Evangelist in Bach's *St Matthew Passion* and of Gerontius in Elgar's choral masterpiece. Gave recitals in Ger., partnered by the pianist Fanny Davies. First singer of Vaughan Williams's *On Wenlock Edge* (1909). Sang ten. songs in f.p. in England of Mahler's *Das Lied von der Erde* (1914). Fund est. in his memory is now the *Musicians' Benevolent Fund.

Embellishments. See *Ornaments*.

Embouchure. (1) In brass and some woodwind playing, the mode of application of the lips, or their relation to the mouthpiece.
   (2) (Fr.). The *mouthpiece of a brass instr.

Emerald Isle, The. Posthumous comic opera in 2 acts by Sullivan, begun 1900 and completed by Edward German. Lib. by Basil Hood. Prod. Savoy Th. 1901.

Emicon. Elec. instr. invented in USA, 1931, producing notes from the air in a graded chromatic scale. Kbd. controls accurate tuning.

Emmanuel, (Marie François) **Maurice** (*b* Bar-sur-Aube, 1862; *d* Paris, 1938). Fr. composer and scholar. Studied Paris Cons. under Delibes and *Bourgault-Ducoudray. Prof. of mus. history Paris Cons. 1909–36. Authority on Gr. mus., about which he wrote extensively. Comp. 2 operas, 2 syms., str. qt., and suite on popular Gr. airs for vn. and pf.

E moll (Ger.). The key of E minor.

'Emperor' Concerto. Nickname by which Beethoven's Pf. Conc. No. 5 in E♭ major, Op. 73, is known in Eng. and USA. Not known when or by whom this title was conferred, but it is not inapt.

'Emperor' Quartet (*Kaiserquartett*). Nickname for Haydn's Str. Qt. in C major, Op. 76 No. 3, because the slow movement is a set of variations on the tune he wrote for the *Emperor's Hymn.

Emperor's Hymn (*Gott erhalte Franz den Kaiser*, i.e. God preserve the Emperor Francis). Tune found in many hymn-books under the name *Austria*. The nat. hymn of Austria from the time of comp. of the tune by Haydn in 1797 to the creation of the Republic in 1918. Thereafter the tune was officially retained, but other words adopted, *Sei gesegnet ohne Ende* (Thine be never-ending blessings) by Ottokar Kernstock. The orig. words were by Lorenz Leopold Haschka (1749–1827). Haydn, whose instructions were to compose something approaching in merit the Eng. nat. anthem, took a folk melody of his childhood, which probably suggested itself to him as fitting metrically and rhythmically the opening lines, and altered and extended its later part. For the application of the tune in Ger. see *Deutschland über Alles*.

Emperor Waltz (Strauss). See *Kaiser-Walzer*.

Empfindung (Ger.). Feeling, sentiment; hence *Empfindungsvoll*, feelingly.

Enchaînez (Fr.). Chain together, join up (i.e. next movement to be played without break).

Enchanted Lake, The (*Volshebnoye ozero*). Symphonic poem by *Lyadov, comp. 1909.

Encina (Enzina), **Juan del** (*b* Salamanca, 1468; *d* Léon, *c*.1530). Sp. composer and poet. Served 2nd Duke of Alba, 1492–8, then worked in Rome. Archdeacon of Málaga 1509–17, prior of Léon from 1519. Wrote several eclogues (pastoral plays) and a large no. of songs for 3 or 4 vv. His *Cancionero*, 1495, was an anthology of plays and poems.

Encore (Fr.). Again. In Eng. has been adopted as the word of demand for the repetition of a perf. (properly, perhaps, of the same piece, but often used of a return to the platform to give additional perf., either of the same or another piece). Also used as verb (to encore).
   Although a Fr. word, *encore* entered the Eng. language as a corruption of It. *ancora* (with the same meaning), which, from the early 18th cent. onwards, was used by audiences at the It. Opera in London (together with the words *altra volta*, another time). The Fr. use *bis* (Lat., twice; verb *bisser*).

End-Plugged. Term for org. flue pipes with a stopper at the top which lowers their pitch by an octave.

Energia (It.). Energy. *Energico*, energetic.

Enescu, George (Enesco, Georges) (*b* Liveni-Virnav, Romania, 1881; *d* Paris, 1955). Romanian composer, violinist, and cond. First public recital as violinist at age 7. Studied Vienna Cons. under Hellmesberger and R. Fuchs, then at Paris Cons. under Massenet and Fauré. Concert of his works in Paris 1897. Frequent appearances as cond. (until 1951), and as sonata recitalist with Cortot. His vn. pupils incl. Menuhin, Grumiaux, and Gitlis. His comps. use Romanian folk-idioms and are also influenced by late romanticism. They incl.: *Oedipe* (4-act opera, 1921–31); Sym. No. 1 (1905), No. 2 (1912–14), No. 3, with ch. and pf. solo (1916–21), No. 4 (1934), No. 5, ten., ch., and orch. (1941); *Symphonie concertante* for vc. and orch. (1901); 2 *Romanian Rhapsodies* (1901); 3 vn. sonatas (1897, 1899, 1926); 2 vc. sonatas (1898, 1935); 2 pf. sonatas (1924, 1933–5); 2 pf. quintets (1895, 1940); 2 str. qts. (1916–20, 1950–3); 2 pf. qts. (1909, 1943–4); *Chamber symphony* for 12 instr. (1954); and songs.

Enfance du Christ, L' (The Childhood of Christ). Oratorio, Op. 25, by Berlioz for soloists, ch., and orch., comp. 1850–4. F.p. Paris 1854, Manchester 1880. Text by composer.

Enfant et les Sortilèges, L' (The Child and the Spells). *Fantaisie lyrique* in 2 parts by Ravel, to lib. by Colette. Comp. 1920–5. Prod. Monte Carlo 1925, San Francisco 1930, Oxford 1958.

Enfant prodigue, L' (The Prodigal Son). (1) Cantata by Debussy, comp. 1884, for sop., ten., and bar. soloists, ch., and orch. It won Debussy the *Prix de Rome*. F.p. Paris 1884 with acc. for 2 pf. Orch. rev. 1906 and 1908.
(2) Opera by Auber, 1850.
See under *Prodigal Son* for Prokofiev ballet and Britten church parable.

En-Gedi (In the wilderness). F. X. Huber's lib. for Beethoven's oratorio *Christus am Ölberge* (1803) was replaced in Eng. by new text by H. Hudson, changing story to that of 'David in the Wilderness' in view of 'objectionable nature' of orig. words.

Engel, Karl (*b* Theiedewiese, 1818; *d* Kensington, 1882). Ger. pianist and writer. Studied under Hummel. Settled London, *c*.1845, where he formed valuable library and coll. of ancient instr. Among his writings are *Introduction to the Study of National Music* (1866) and *Researches into the Early History of the Violin Family* (1883).

Engelstimme (Ger.). Angel-voice. The *Vox Angelica* stop on the organ.

Englisches Horn (Ger.). English horn, i.e. *Cor anglais*.

English Chamber Orchestra. Orig. name was Goldsbrough Orch., founded 1948 by Arnold Goldsbrough and Lawrence Leonard to perf.

*baroque mus. Present name adopted 1960 when repertory was expanded to cover mus. of all periods written for 'Mozart-sized' ens. Assoc. with *Aldeburgh Fest. since 1961, playing in premières of Britten's *Midsummer Night's Dream*, *Owen Wingrave*, church parables, and Cello Sym. Has also given f.ps. of works by Maw, Birtwistle, Tavener, Richard Rodney Bennett, etc. No prin. cond., but has worked closely with Britten, Leppard, Barenboim, Davis, Zukerman, and others. Many recordings. Worldwide tours, incl. Japan, the Americas, Europe, Israel, etc.

English Fingering. The (obsolete) 'Eng.' system of marking printed pf. mus. with the composer's or ed.'s suggested *fingering, whereby a cross represented the thumb and the figures 1 to 4 the fingers (as opposed to 'continental' system using 1 for thumb and 2 to 5 for fingers).

English Folk Dance and Song Society. Amalgamation in 1932 of Folk Song Society (founded 1898) and Eng. Folk Dance Soc. (1911), with general aim of preserving songs and dances of Brit. people. H.Q. in Cecil Sharp House, London, where library and archives are housed. Holds annual fest. in London, but regional branches are also active.

English Horn. See *Cor anglais*.

English Hymnal, The. Coll. of Eng. hymns and tunes pubd. 1906 (rev. 1933) ed. by Percy Dearmer with *Vaughan Williams as mus. ed. Incl. several hymn tunes by Vaughan Williams and others by his Eng. contemporaries, several being adaptations of folk-songs.

English Lyrics. Title given to 12 sets of songs (74 in all) for v. and pf. by *Parry, all settings of Eng. poetry. 1st set (4 songs) 1881–5, 2nd (5) 1881–5, 3rd (6) 1895, 4th (6) 1897, 5th (7) 1902, 6th (6) 1902, 7th (6) 1907, 8th (6) 1907, 9th (7) 1909, 10th (6) 1909, 11th (8) pubd. 1920, 12th (7) pubd. 1920. The last 2 sets were selected and ed. by Dr Emily Daymond.

English Madrigal School. First complete edn. of Eng. madrigals, 1588–1624, transcr., scored, and ed. by Dr E. H. *Fellowes and pubd. in 36 vols., 1913–24.

English Music Theatre. Title from 1976 of former English Opera Group, founded by Britten, Eric Crozier, and John Piper in 1946 to perf. chamber operas old and new. Closely connected with Britten's operas, but also gave f.ps. of Walton's *The Bear* and Birtwistle's *Punch and Judy*. Has toured abroad widely, incl. USSR (1964). From 1961 administered and financed by CG. Re-formed 1976 under joint dir. of Colin Graham and Steuart Bedford with aim of longer season and to embrace opera, operetta, musicals, and less conventional works, all generalized as 'music theatre'. Ceased to exist 1980.

English National Opera. See *Sadler's Wells*.

English Opera Group. See *English Music Theatre*.

English Singers, The. Title of group of 6 singers specializing in Eng. madrigals and folk-song arrs. who gave 1st concert in 1920. Visited Prague 1922 and later toured in Berlin, Vienna, Holland, and the USA. Orig. members were Flora Mann, Winifred Whelen, Lillian Berger, Steuart Wilson, Clive Carey, and Cuthbert Kelly. In 1924 Nellie Carson, Norman Stone, and Norman Notley replaced Whelen, Wilson, and Carey, and there were further changes before final disbandment.

English Suite, An. Suite in G in 7 movements for str. orch. by Parry. The 5th (*Pastoral*) movement dates from 1890, some from 1914 and other parts from 1916. Left unfinished and put in final form by Dr Emily Daymond. Pubd. 1921, f.p., in public 1922.

English Suites. Set of 6 kbd. suites by Bach, pubd. posthumously. Title seems to have arisen from the existence of MS. copy (in the possession of Bach's youngest son, Johann Christian) describing the work as *fait pour les Anglais* ('made for the English'). See also *French Suites*; *German Suites*.

Englund, (Sven) **Einar** (*b* Ljugarn, Gotland, Sweden, 1916). Finn. composer, cond., and writer. Studied Sibelius Acad., Helsinki, 1933–41 (comp. with Palmgren, pf. with Paavola) and Tanglewood, 1949 (with Copland). Cond., pianist, and reviewer for Finn. radio and TV from 1950; mus. critic, Helsinki *Hufvudstadsbladet* from 1957. Taught comp. at Sibelius Acad. from 1958. Works incl. 3 syms. (1946, 1948, 1970), vc. conc. (1954), pf. sonatina (1968), film mus., etc.

Enharmonic Intervals. Those *intervals which differ from each other in name but not in any other way (so far as modern kbd. instr. are concerned). For example: C to G♯ (augmented 5th) and C to A♭ (minor 6th). Hence *enharmonic change*, the change of a note in a part, e.g. from D♯ to E♭.

Enigma Variations (*Variations on an Original Theme (Enigma)*). Elgar's Op. 36 for full orch. F.p. London, 19 June 1899; finale rev. for 3rd perf. Sept. 1899. The 'Enigma' is the theme itself, probably representing Elgar, but he said 'through and over the whole set another and larger theme "goes", but is not played'. Identity of this 2nd theme, if it exists, has never been established despite many ingenious guesses. The work is ded. 'to my friends pictured within', each variation being a mus. sketch. Initials or pseudonyms disguise the individuals but their identities are: 1. C.A.E. (Lady Elgar); 2. H.D.S.-P. (Hew Steuart-Powell); 3. R.B.T. (R.B. Townshend); 4. W.M.B. (W. Meath Baker); 5. R.P.A. (Richard P. Arnold); 6. Ysobel (Isabel Fitton); 7. Troyte (A. Troyte Griffith); 8. W.N. (Winifred Norbury); 9. Nimrod (A. J. Jaeger); 10. Dorabella (Dora Penny); 11. G.R.S. (G. R. Sinclair, but more accurately his bulldog Dan); 12. B.G.N. (Basil G. Nevinson); 13. *** (Lady Mary Lygon); 14. E.D.U. (Elgar). Also 1-act ballet by *Ashton, f.p. CG 1968 (uses orig. ending to finale). Arr. for brass band by Eric *Ball, 1984.

Enlevez (Fr.). Take up, i.e. remove (e.g. pedal or mute).

En Saga (A Saga). Symphonic poem by Sibelius, Op. 9, 1892, rev. 1901.

Ensalada (Sp.). Salad. Comical Sp. 16th-cent. choral pieces, using combination of texts in various languages.

Ensemble (Fr.). Together. (1) Any combination of performers, but especially a small group playing individual parts.
(2) The quality in perf. implying the greater or lesser exhibition of the co-operative spirit, e.g. unanimity of attack, balance of tone, etc., thus giving rise to such expressions as 'good ens.', 'poor ens.', etc.
A *morceau d'ensemble* (e.g. in an operatic context) is a piece in which several performers combine.

Entführung aus dem Serail, Die. (The Abduction from the Seraglio). Opera (Singspiel) in 3 acts by Mozart (K384) to Ger. lib. by Gottlob Stephanie adapted from C. F. Bretzner's lib. for André's *Belmont und Constanze* (1781). Comp. 1781–2. Prod. Vienna 1782, London 1827, NY 1860. In 19th cent. was sung in It. in Eng.

Entr'acte (Fr.). Between the acts. Strictly the interval between the acts of a play or opera, but in mus. parlance refers to the piece of orch. mus. played at such times, e.g. Schubert's entr'actes for *Rosamunde*.

Entrada (Sp.). Same as *Entrée*.

Entrée (Fr.). Entrance. (1) A 17th- and 18th-cent. term for an instr. piece before a ballet.
(2) An act in an *opéra-ballet* of which every act is self-contained (corruption of *entremets*, 'side-dish', old title for a kind of masque).
(3) The opening moment of any part of a work.

Entremont, Philippe (*b* Rheims, 1934). Fr. pianist and cond. Studied with Marguérite Long and at Paris Cons. Winner Belgian State Competition, Brussels, 1951. Specialist in Fr. mus. but wide repertory. Mus. dir. Vienna Chamber Orch. from 1976, cond. New Orleans P.O. 1980–5, cond. Denver S.O. from 1986.

Envelope. Term in elec. mus. for those characteristics of amplitude which determine the growth and decay of a signal.

Éolides, Les (The Breezes). César Franck's first symphonic poem, comp. 1876, based on poem by Lecomte de Lisle describing flight of the breezes, daughters of Aeolus, over the southern lands. F.p. Paris 1877.

Epicedium. Dirge or lament, e.g. Purcell's *The Queen's Epicedium*, 1695.

Epilogue. A concluding piece: in opera, for example, sometimes addressed directly to the audience, as in Stravinsky's *The Rake's Progress*. Term has been used as description of movements in their syms. by Vaughan Williams and Bax.

Episode. In comps. designed on one of the regular patterns, a section containing thematic material of secondary importance is sometimes called an episode. It can also contain new material. In *Rondo form, the contrasting sections between returns of the main material are sometimes called episodes. In *Fugue form, an episode follows the exposition and is a passage of connective material, usually a development of a theme from the exposition, leading to another entry or series of entries of the subject. One function of the fugal episode is to effect modulation to various related keys so that later entries may take advantage of this variety.

Epitaffio per García Lorca (Epitaph for García Lorca). Work by *Nono, comp. 1951–3, in 3 parts: 1. *Espana en la corazón*, sop., bar., small ch., and instr. 2. *Y su sangre ya viene cantando*, fl. and small orch. 3. *Memento*, female speaker, speaking choir, ch., and orch.

Epithalamium (Lat., Eng. epithalamion). A marriage song or wedding hymn. Vaughan Williams's cantata *Epithalamion* (1957) has words selected from Spenser's poem of that name.

Éponge, Baguette d' (Fr.). Sponge-headed drumstick.

Epstein, Julius (*b* Agram, 1832; *d* Vienna, 1926). Croatian pianist, prof. at Vienna Cons. 1867–1901. Taught Mahler and recognized his genius even as a boy.

Equale, equali (Old It.). (1) Equal.
(2) 18th-cent. term for a funeral qt. of instr. of the same kind, usually tbs.; or mus. for such, e.g. Beethoven's 3 *Equali* (1812) in D minor, D major, and B major), 2 of which, with vocal parts added by Seyfried, were perf. at Beethoven's funeral.

Equal Temperament. See *Temperament*.

Equal Voices (It. *Voci eguali*; Lat. *Voces aequales*; Ger. *Gleiche Stimmen*). A choral comp. is said to be for 'equal vv.' when it is for vv. of the same kind, generally for 2 sop. or 3 sop. (sch. mus. and mus. for women's choirs). In such mus., in fairness to the vv. of the performers, the parts are usually so arr. that sometimes one v. and sometimes another is at the top. Occasionally the term is less correctly used as implying 'for children's vv.' (unmixed with adults) or 'for women's vv.' (unmixed with men's), or vice versa.

Érard, Sébastien (*b* Strasbourg, 1752; *d* La Muette, 1831). Fr. founder of firm of pf. and harp manufacturers. Went to Paris 1768, built first Fr. pf. 1777. Est. firm with his brother in Paris 1779. Opened London branch 1786 working there until

1796, in which year he made his first grand pf. Patented improvements to pf. and harp. Succeeded by nephew Pierre Érard (1796–1855). London branch closed 1890. Amalgamated with Gaveau, 1960.

Erb, Donald James (*b* Youngstown, Ohio, 1927). Amer. composer. Studied Kent State Univ., Ohio, Cleveland Institute of Mus., and in Paris with Boulanger. Teacher at Cleveland Institute. Comps. incl. several works involving tape and synthesizers, but many works employ more conventional means.

Erb, Karl (*b* Ravensburg, 1877; *d* Ravensburg, 1958). Ger. ten. Début with Stuttgart Opera 1907, Munich opera 1913–25. Created title-role in *Pfitzner's *Palestrina* 1917. CG 1927. Retired from stage 1930. Noted exponent of Evangelist in Bach's *St Matthew Passion*.

Erbach, Christian (*b* Algesheim, *c*.1570; *d* Augsburg, 1635). Ger. composer of motets and songs. Organist, Augsburg, from 1602.

Erbse, Heimo (*b* Rudolstadt, 1924). Ger. composer. Studied Weimar 1945–7 and Berlin 1950–2 (comp. with *Blacher). From 1947 to 1950 was opera producer and coach. Comps. incl. 2 syms., operas *Julietta* and *Der Herr in Grau*, wind qt., pf. sonata, ballet *Ruth*, fl. sonata, and choral and orch. works.

Erede, Alberto (*b* Genoa, 1909). It. cond. Studied in Genoa, Milan, and Basle, then with *Weingartner 1929–31 and in Dresden with Fritz *Busch. Début Rome 1930. Cond. at Glyndebourne 1938–9, NY 1939. Cond., New London Opera Co. 1946, NY Met. 1951–5, Deutsche Oper am Rhein 1956–62. Guest cond. CG and Scottish Opera.

Erickson, Robert (*b* Marquette, Mich., 1917). Amer. composer. Lessons in comp. 1936 from *Křenek. Teacher at San Francisco Cons. 1957–66 and at Univ. of Calif., San Diego, from 1966. Began as 12-note composer but changed course in 1957 with his Str. Qt. No. 2 where he showed new interest in qualities of sound. This interest in sonorities and combinations of tempi led him to introduce improvisation into his *Chamber Concerto* (1960) and pf. conc. (1963). He began to use tape in 1964, employing *musique concrète processes. Works comp. in this idiom incl. *Ricercar* for 3 db. (1967), *Pacific Sirens* (1968) for 10–14 instr. on tape, *High Flyer* for amplified fl. (1969), etc.

Erkel, Ferenc (*b* Gyula, 1810; *d* Budapest, 1893). Hung. composer. Cond. Budapest Nat. Th. from 1838. Founder and cond. Budapest Phil. and professor, Hung. Nat. Acad. of Mus. One of first Hung. 'nationalists', striving to est. nat. opera. His first opera, *Bátori Mária* (1840), was followed by *Hunyádi László* (1844) and by *Bánk Bán* (1844–52, prod. 1861) which is traditionally perf. on nat. holiday. Other operas are *Dozsa* (1866),

György Brankovics (1874), and *King István* (1874–84).

Erlanger, Camille (pseudonym Frédéric Regnal) (*b* Paris, 1863; *d* Paris, 1919). Fr. composer. Studied Paris Cons. with Delibes. Works incl. *Requiem* for double ch. and several operas (*Le Juif polonais*, 1900; *Le Fils de l'étoile*, 1904; *Bacchus triomphant*, 1909; *Le Barbier de Deauville*, 1917).

Erlebach, Philipp Heinrich (*b* Esens, Friesland, 1657; *d* Rudolstadt, 1714). Ger. composer who was for 33 years Kapellmeister in Rudolstadt. Among surviving works are 6 sonatas for vn., bass viol, and cont. (1964), 2 vols. of songs (1697, 1710), and sacred mus.

Erleichterung (Ger.). An 'easing', i.e. a simplified version.

Erlih, Devy (*b* Paris, 1928). Fr. violinist. Studied Paris Cons. Début 1944 with Pasdeloup Orch. Frequent tours as conc. soloist.

Erlkönig (The Erl-King). Ballad by Goethe, the Erl-King being a King of all the spirits who appears to a child and entices him to death. Poem comes from Goethe's ballad-opera *Die Fischerin* (1782) and 1st mus. setting was an 8-bar melody written by Corona Schröter, actress who played the fisherwoman at the f.p. It was then set by Reichardt, Klein, and Zelter, but the best-known settings (for v. and pf.) are those by Schubert (D328), 1815, and Loewe, 1818. Sketches of an abandoned Beethoven setting exist. Special importance of Schubert's setting is the difficult and vivid acc., which revolutionized the art of acc. for composers and pianists.

Ernani. 4-act opera by Verdi to lib. by Piave based on Hugo's novel *Hernani* (1830). Comp. 1843. Prod. Venice 1844, London 1845, NY 1847.

Erniedrigen (Ger.). To lower (pitch).

Ernst, Heinrich Wilhelm (*b* Brünn (Brno), 1814; *d* Nice, 1865). Moravian violinist and composer. Studied Vienna Cons. and modelled his style on that of *Paganini. Lived in Paris 1832–8, toured Europe 1838–44. Frequent visitor to London after 1843, settling there in 1855. Comp. vn. concs. and other pieces for his instr. Viola soloist in Berlioz's *Harold en Italie*, with comp. conducting, on several occasions.

Ernste Gesänge, Vier (Four Serious Songs) (Brahms). See *Vier Ernste Gesänge*.

'Eroica' Symphony (*Sinfonia Eroica*). Sym. No. 3 in E♭ major, Op. 55, by Beethoven, comp. 1803–4, f.p. 1804, f.pub.p. 1805. Orig. called *Bonaparte*, this title being erased by Beethoven on hearing that Napoleon had proclaimed himself emperor. On publication it bore the title *Sinfonia Eroica, composta per festeggiare il Sovvenire di un grand Uomo* (Heroic Symphony, composed to celebrate the memory of a great man). Finale is set of variations on theme taken from Beethoven's ballet *Die Geschöpfe des *Prometheus* (1801).

Eroica Variations. Title given (not by Beethoven) to his Pf. Variations in E♭ major, Op. 35, comp. 1802, based on theme from his ballet *Die Geschöpfe des *Prometheus*, 1801, also used in *Eroica Sym. Sometimes known as *Prometheus Variations*. Theme is used again for No. 7 of 12 *Kontretänze* for orch., WoO 14, pubd. 1803.

Erotikon (Gr.). Love-song.

Erst, erste (Ger.). First.

Ersterbend (Ger.). Dying away.

Erste Walpurgisnacht, Die (The First Walpurgis Night). Mus. by Mendelssohn, Op. 60 (comp. 1831, rev. 1842) to Goethe's ballad, for soloists, ch., and orch. Walpurgis Night is spring fest. when witches ride to the Brocken in Harz Mountains.

Erwartung (Expectation, Suspense). Monodrama in 1 act by Schoenberg, Op. 17, to lib. by Marie Pappenheim, for sop. and orch. Comp. 1909. Prod. Prague 1924 (cond. Zemlinsky), London and Washington D.C. 1960 (but Schoenberg cond. a BBC concert perf. in London 1931).

Erweitert (Ger.). Widened, broadened (i.e. slower and with steadiness).

Erzähler (Ger., 'narrator'). (1) The Evangelist in settings of the Passion.
(2) Soft organ-stop of 8′ length and pitch, invented by Skinner of Boston, Mass., giving octave above the fundamental.

Es (Ger.). The note E♭.

Escales (Ports of call). Orch. suite by Ibert, comp. 1922. The 3 ports are said to be Palermo, Tunis, and Valencia.

Eschenbach, Christoph (*b* Breslau, 1940). Ger. pianist and cond. Studied Musikhochschule, Cologne and Hamburg. World-wide tours as conc. soloist and recitalist. London début 1966. Gave f.p. of Henze's 2nd pf. conc. (Bielefeld, 1968). Début as cond. 1973. Cond. Tonhalle Orch., Zürich, from 1982. CG début 1984 (*Così fan tutte*).

Escher, Rudolf George (*b* Amsterdam, 1912; *d* DeKoos, 1980). Dutch composer. Studied Rotterdam 1934–7 (comp. with *Pijper). In 1960–1 worked in Delft studio for elec. mus. and similar studio at Utrecht State Univ. Writer on Ravel and Debussy. Comps. incl. *Le Tombeau de Ravel* (1952), 2 syms., *Summer Rites at Noon* for 2 orchs. facing each other (1962–9), Owen's *Strange Meeting*, bar. and pf. (1952).

Esclarmonde. Opera (*opéra romanesque*) in 4 acts and prol. by Massenet to lib. by Alfred Blau and Louis de Gramont based on medieval romance *Parthenopoeus*. Comp. for Amer. sop. Sibyl Sanderson, who first sang title-role. Prod. Paris 1889, New Orleans 1893, CG 1983.

Escobar, Luis Antonio (*b* Villapinzón, Colombia, 1925). Colombian composer and diplomat. Studied Nat. Univ. of Colombia 1944–7, Peabody Cons., Baltimore, with N. Nabokov 1947–50, and in Salzburg and Berlin 1951–3 with *Blacher. Teacher of comp. etc. at Cons. of Colombia Nat. Univ. 1954–7. Founded Colombia Phil. 1966. Dir., cultural div., Ministry of Nat. Education 1960–3, 2nd Secretary, Colombian Embassy, Bonn, 1967–70. Works incl. 5 pf. sonatinas, sym., pf. conc., ballet *Avirama, Cánticas de cantas colombianas* for ch. and orch., *Juramento a Bolivar* (symphonic poem), 2 str. qts., etc.

Escobar, Pedro de (*b* Oporto, *c*.1465; *d* ?Evora, after 1535). Portuguese composer of sacred and secular mus. Maestro di cappella, Seville 1507–14. Renowned contrapuntist.

Eses (Ger.). The note E♭♭.

Eshpay, Andrey (Yakovlevich) (*b* Kozmodemyansk, 1925). Russ. composer and pianist. Studied Moscow Cons. 1948–56 (pf. with Sofranitsky, comp. with Myaskovsky and Khachaturian). Taught comp. Moscow Cons. 1963–70. Works incl. 3 syms., *Concerto for Orch.*, pf. conc., vn. conc., 2 vn. sonatas, film mus., etc.

Eskdale, George (*b* Tynemouth, 1897; *d* London, 1960). Eng. trumpeter. Trained *Kneller Hall. Then in chief London orchs. (LSO from 1932) and on staff RAM from 1938.

Es moll (Ger.). The key of E♭ minor.

Espagne (Fr.). Spain. **Espagnol, espagnole** (Fr.), **Espagn(u)olo, espagn(u)ola** (It.). Spanish. Used in titles of works such as *Rapsodie espagnole* (Ravel), *Symphonie espagnole* (Lalo).

España (Spain). Orch. rhapsody by *Chabrier, f.p. 1883, in which Sp. tunes and rhythms are quoted. He visited Sp. 1882–3.

Espansiva, Sinfonia (Expansive Symphony). Title of *Nielsen's 3rd sym., Op. 27, comp. 1910–11, f.p. Copenhagen 1912. F. Brit. p., London 1962.

Esplá, Oscar (*b* Alicante, 1886; *d* Madrid, 1976). Sp. composer, mainly self-taught, being trained as engineer. Won competition in Vienna 1911, then devoted himself to comp. Mus. influenced by (but does not directly quote) Sp. folk-tunes, using 'Levantine' scale of his own devising. Dir., Madrid Cons. 1936–9, Esplá Cons., Alicante, from 1958. Comp. operas, ballet, symphonic poems, choral works, chamber mus.

Esposito, Michele (*b* Castellammare, Naples, 1855; *d* Florence, 1929). It. composer and pianist. Studied Naples Cons., then lived in Paris 1878–82. In 1882 became prof. of pf., Royal Irish Acad. of Mus., Dublin. Founded and cond. Dublin

Orch. Soc. 1899. Hon.D.Mus., Dublin, 1917. Works incl. operetta *The Postbag* (1902), cantata *Deirdre* (1897), *Irish Symphony* (1902), str. qt., vc. sonata, etc. Mentor of Hamilton *Harty.

Espressione (It.). Expression. **Espressivo.** Expressively.

Esquisse (Fr.). *Sketch.

Esquivel, Barahona Juan de (*b* Ciudad Rodrigo, *c*.1563; *d* Ciudad Rodrigo, after 1613). Sp. composer and church musician. Choirmaster, Ciudad Rodrigo Cath. 1608–13. Ranked by some as equal of Victoria.

Esraj. Indian mus. instr. played with a bow and having 4 melodic str. and 10 to 15 sympathetic understr. Tone like a vn. but with more resonance. Fingerboard has 20 movable frets.

Essential Note. An actual note of a chord, as distinct from a passing note, suspension, appoggiatura, etc. These latter are 'Unessential Notes'.

Esser, Karl Michael von (*b* Aix-la-Chapelle, *c*.1736; *d c*.1783). Ger. composer, violist, and player of viola d'amore. Wrote 12 syms., viola d'amore conc., vn. duets.

Essex, Kenneth (*b* Hinckley, Leics., 1920). Eng. violist. Studied RAM. Prin. violist with several chamber orchs. Extra va. in quintets with *Amadeus and other str. qts.

Esswood, Paul (Lawrence Vincent) (*b* West Bridgford, 1942). Eng. counterten. Studied RCM. Lay vicar, Westminster Abbey choir 1964–71. Début 1965 (*Messiah*). Opera début 1968 (Berkeley, Calif.). Founder of Pro Cantione Antiqua singers.

Estampes (Engravings). 3 pieces for pf. by Debussy comp. 1903. Movements are *Pagodes* (Pagodas), *Soirée dans Grenade* (Evening in Granada) and *Jardins sous la pluie* (Gardens in the rain). F.p. as complete set Paris 1904. No. 1 orch. Caplet, No. 2 orch. Büsser.

Estampie (Fr.), **Estampida** (Provençal). Type of troubadour tune for dancing, sometimes with words, in form of a *rondeau.

Esterháza. A castle on the S. side of the Neusiedlersee in Austria (now Hungary) which was opened in 1766 as a seat of the Esterházy family. It stood in marshy country and was very isolated, but it contained an opera house and a marionette th. Scene of f.ps. of many works by Josef Haydn, who was engaged in 1761 by Prince Paul Anton Esterházy (1711–62) and became Kapellmeister in 1766 under his successor Prince Nicolaus (1714–90).

Esther. Oratorio by Handel to text by S. Humphreys after Racine. F.p. as masque *Haman and Mordecai*, 1720, at Cannons but expanded into concert oratorio 1732. 1st Eng. oratorio.

Estinguendo (It.). Extinguishing, i.e. dying away.

Estinto (It.). Extinct. As soft as possible.

Estrada, Carlos (*b* Montevideo, 1909; *d* Montevideo, 1970). Uruguayan composer and cond. Studied in Montevideo and at Paris Cons. (comp. with Roger-Ducasse and Büsser, cond. with Wolff and Paray). Founded Montevideo S.O. 1959. Taught harmony Montevideo Univ. 1950–6. Works incl. oratorio *Daniel* (1942), 2 syms. (1951, 1967), mus. drama *L'Annonce faite à Marie* (1943), and many shorter pieces.

Estribillo (Sp.). A choral movement at the beginning or end of a **Villancico.

Estro armonico, L' (Harmonious Inspiration). Title of Vivaldi's Op. 3, 12 concs. for various instrs., pubd. Amsterdam 1711, 6 of which were transcr. by J. S. Bach. Comprised conc. in D for 4 vn. (RV549), in G minor for 2 vn. and vc. (RV578), in G for vn. (Bach BWV978, RV310), in E minor for 4 vn. (RV550), in A for 2 vn. (RV519), in A minor for vn. (RV356), in F for 4 vn. and vc. (RV567), in A minor for 2 vn. (Bach BWV593, RV522), in D for vn. (Bach BWV972, RV230), in B minor for 4 vn. and vc. (Bach BWV1065, RV580), in D minor for 2 vn. and vc. (Bach BWV596, RV565), in E for vn. (Bach BWV976, RV265).

Eternal Father, Strong to Save. Hymn, words by William Whiting (1825–78), written in 1860 and pubd. in *Anglican Hymn Book* (1868) in orig. version beginning 'O thou who bidd'st the ocean deep'. Revs. appeared in *Hymns Ancient and Modern* 1861 and appendix to *Psalms and Hymns* 1869. Known as 'the Navy's hymn'. Tune by J. B. *Dykes.

Et Exspecto Resurrectionem Mortuorum (And I look forward to the resurrection of the dead). Orch. work by *Messiaen for woodwind, brass, metal perc. Comp. 1964. Commissioned by French Govt. and ded. to memory of dead of two World Wars. F.p. Sainte-Chapelle, Paris, 1965, cond. Baudo, later in Chartres Cath. in presence of Gen. de Gaulle.

Et incarnatus est. See *Mass*.

Et in Spiritum Sanctum. See *Mass*.

Et in unum Dominum. See *Mass*.

Etler, Alvin (*b* Battle Creek, Iowa, 1913; *d* Northampton, Mass., 1973). Amer. composer and oboist. Studied Cleveland Institute of Mus. 1931–6 and Yale Univ. Sch. of Mus. 1942–4 (with Hindemith). Oboist, Indianapolis S.O. 1938–40. Held various teaching posts. From 1968 chairman, Hampshire Coll. elec. workshop. Works incl. sym., 2 str. qts., 2 wind quintets, conc. for orch., conc. for vn. and wind quintet, conc. for wind quintet and orch., brass quintet, conc. for str. qt. and orch., etc.

Étoile du Nord, L' (The North Star). 3-act opera by Meyerbeer to lib. by Scribe. Prod. Paris 1854, London 1855, New Orleans 1855. Incorporated 6 items from Meyerbeer's opera *Ein Feldlager in Schlesien* (1844, rev. as *Vielka*, 1847).

Eton College Manuscript (Eton Choir Book). A book of choral mus. at Eton College, dating from between 1490 and 1504.

Étouffer (Fr., imperative *étouffez*; past participle *étouffé*). To stifle, i.e. to damp, e.g. with vn. mute, pf. pedal, etc. *Étouffoir*, damper (pf. pedal).

Et resurrexit. See *Mass*.

Étude (Fr.). Study. Comp. intended as a basis for the improvement of the performer's technique. In pf. mus. the term is especially applied to a short piece restricted to the exploitation of one kind of passage. Masterpieces of this kind suitable for public perf. as well as private practice were written by Chopin and Debussy.

Études d'exécution transcendante (Fr., 'Transcendental Studies'). 12 pieces for solo pf. by Liszt, comp. 1851 and based on his *24 Grandes Études* of 1837 and *Mazeppa* of 1840. The titles are 1, *Preludio*, 2, in A minor, 3, *Paysage*, 4, *Mazeppa*, 5, *Feux follets*, 6, *Vision*, 7, *Eroica*, 8, *Wilde Jagd*, 9, *Ricordanza*, 10, in F minor, 11, *Harmonies du soir*, 12, *Chasse-neige*.

Études d'exécution transcendante d'après Paganini (Transcendental Studies after Paganini). Transcr. for pf. by Liszt, 1838, of 6 of *Paganini's vn. caprices, incl. *La *Campanella*. Rev. and reissued 1851 as *Grandes Études de Paganini*.

Études symphoniques (Symphonic Studies). Schumann's Op. 13 for pf. solo with orig. title *Etuden im Orchester-Charakter von Florestan und Eusebius*, comp. 1834–7, rev. 1852, first pubd. 1837, ded. to Sterndale *Bennett. The first version contained 12 studies; in 1852, Schumann omitted Nos. 2 and 9 and rewrote finale. Wieck's 1862 edn. restored Nos. 2 and 9. 5 further variations, orig. suppressed, have since been discovered and are included in some perfs.

Etwas (Ger.). Some, something, somewhat.

Eugene Onegin (Evgeny Onyegin). 3-act opera by Tchaikovsky to lib. by composer and K. S. Shilovsky based on Pushkin's poem (1831). Comp. 1877–8. Prod. Moscow 1879, London 1892, NY Met. 1920 (but concert perf. NY 1908).

Eulenburg, Ernst (*b* Berlin, 1847; *d* Leipzig, 1926). Ger. mus. publisher. Studied Leipzig Cons. Founded firm in Leipzig 1874, taking over in 1892 the series of miniature scores, *Kleine Partitur-Ausgabe*, pubd. by Albert *Payne, and later Donajowski's edition.

Eulenburg, Kurt (*b* Berlin, 1879; *d* London, 1982). Son of E. *Eulenburg. Succeeded as head of firm 1926, enlarging no. of miniature scores and publishing scholarly edns. by *Blume, *Einstein, and others. Went to Switzerland 1939. Opened new London co. 1939, with branch in Zürich. Settled in London 1945. Edn. acquired by *Schott 1957, but retained identity. On Eulenburg's retirement in 1969, Roger Fiske was ed. 1969–76, succeeded by Philip Cranmer.

Eulenspiegel, Till (Strauss). See *Till Eulenspiegel*.

Euphonium. (1) Member of the tuba family of brass instrs., being a tenor tuba in B♭. Mainly used in brass and military bands, many solos for euphonium having been written.

(2) Instr. invented by Chladni in 1790, made of glass plates and rods and with a pleasant but soft tone.

Eurhythmics. Method invented by *Jaques-Dalcroze for expressing rhythmical aspect of mus. through gymnastic exercises.

Euryanthe. 3-act opera by Weber to lib. by Helmina von Chézy after 13th-cent. Fr. romance. Comp. 1822–3. Prod. Vienna 1823, London 1833, NY Met. 1887. Because of weaknesses of lib. various attempts have been made to renovate *Euryanthe*, but it is best perf. as Weber left it, flaws and all.

Evans, David (Emlyn) (*b* Newcastle Emlyn, Wales, 1843; *d* London, 1913). Welsh composer. Pubd. 2-vol. coll. of 500 Welsh airs (1896), dictionary of Welsh musicians (1887), and comp. anthems, cantatas, and part-songs.

Evans, Edwin (*b* London, 1871; *d* London, 1945). Eng. critic. Educated Lille and Luxembourg. Musically self-educated except for lessons from his father (also a writer on mus. and translater of Wagner's *Opera and Drama*). Took up financial journalism, but turned to mus. 1901 and became expert on Russ. composers. Champion of Debussy and young Eng. composers. Critic, *Pall Mall Gazette* 1914–23. Worked with Ballets Russes. Critic, *Daily Mail* from 1933. Wrote biography of Tchaikovsky, many essays, transls. of *Louise* and *Pelléas et Mélisande*. Succeeded *Dent as president of ISCM, 1938.

Evans, (Sir) Geraint (Llewellyn) (*b* Pontypridd, 1922). Welsh bar. and opera producer. Studied GSM and in Hamburg and Geneva. Début CG 1948, becoming one of leading int. bars., his best roles incl. Falstaff, Figaro, Papageno, Wozzeck, Beckmesser, and Leporello. Glyndebourne 1950–61. Début San Francisco 1959, Milan 1960, Vienna 1961, Salzburg 1962. C.B.E. 1959. Knighted 1971. Last opera perf. CG 4 June 1984 (Dulcamara in *L'Elisir d'Amore*).

Evans, Nancy (*b* Liverpool, 1915). Eng. mez. Studied with Maggie *Teyte and John Tobin. Début Liverpool 1933, London 1934. Alternated with Kathleen Ferrier as Lucretia in first prod. of Britten's *The Rape of Lucretia*, Glyndebourne 1946.

Created role of Nancy in Britten's *Albert Herring* 1947. Also notable concert career.

Evans, Peter (Angus) (*b* West Hartlepool, 1929). Eng. teacher and musicologist. D.Mus., Univ. of Durham. Mus. master, Bishop Wordsworth's Sch., Salisbury, 1951–2; lecturer, Durham Univ. 1953–61; prof. of mus., Southampton Univ. since 1961. Cond., Southampton Phil. Soc. Author of *The Music of Benjamin Britten* (1979).

Evening Hymn. Song by Purcell to words by Fuller, 1688, beginning 'Now that the sun hath veiled his light'. Arr. for v. and str. by Vaughan Williams 1912.

Evenings in the Orchestra (*Les Soirées de l'orchestre*). Entertaining and instructive coll. of criticisms and essays by Berlioz, pubd. in Paris in 1853 and in Eng. trans. by Jacques *Barzun, 1956.

Eventail de Jeanne, L' (Jeanne's Fan). Ballet in 10 nos. choreog. Y. Franck and A. Bourgat, commissioned in 1927 for her Paris ballet school by Jeanne Dubost, who gave the 10 leaves of her fan to 10 composers, asking each to compose a no. Those participating were Ravel, Ferroud, Ibert, Roland-Manuel, Delannoy, Roussel, Milhaud, Poulenc, Schmitt, and Auric. Ravel's 1-minute *Fanfare* is marked *Wagneramente*.

Eventyr (Once Upon a Time). Ballad for orch. by Delius after Asbjörnsen's fairy tales. Comp. 1917, f.p. 1919 cond. Wood.

Everyman. (1) Oratorio by Walford *Davies based on medieval mystery play, Leeds 1904.

(2) Incidental mus. for small orch. by Sibelius, 1916, for prod. of Hofmannsthal's version of *Everyman* (*Jedermann*).

(3) 6 monologues for bar. or cont. and pf. or orch. from Hofmannsthal's *Jedermann* by Frank *Martin, 1943.

Evirato (It.). Unmanned. 18th-cent. type of male singer whose boy-sop. v. had been preserved by castration. Same as *Castrato.

Evovae or **Euouae.** This 'word' consists of the vowels of 'seculorum, Amen', being the last words of the Gloria Patri (see *Doxologia*), and is used as a name for the cadential endings of the Gregorian Psalm tones. These letters are often placed under the notes of the plainsong as an abbreviation of the words they represent.

Ewing, Maria (*b* Detroit, 1950). Amer. mez. Studied Cleveland Inst. of Mus., 1968–70, with Eleanor Steber and Jennie Tourel. Opera début 1973, Ravinia Fest. NY Met. début 1976 (Cherubino), La Scala, Milan, 1976 (Mélisande), Glyndebourne 1978 (Dorabella).

Excursions of Mr Brouček, The (*Výlety pana Broučka*). Opera in 2 parts by Janáček. Lib. of Part 1, *Mr Brouček's Excursion to the Moon*, adapted from satirical novel (1887) by S. Čech (1846–

1908) by V. Dyk, K. Mašek, Z. Janke, F. Gellner, J. Mahen, and F. S. Procházka; Part 2, *Mr Brouček's Excursion to the XVth Century*, adapted from S. Čech's satirical novel (1888) by Procházka. Comp. 1908–17. It is now believed that Janáček himself wrote large part of lib. of Part 1. F.p. Prague 1920; f.Brit.p. Edinburgh, 1970; London 1978.

Execution of Stepan Razin, The (*Kazn' Stepana Razina*). Cantata by Shostakovich, Op. 119, to text by Yevtushenko, for bass, ch., and orch. Comp. 1964, f.p. Moscow 1964.

Exercise. (1) An instr. passage purely for technical practice and with little or no artistic interest.
(2) In the 18th cent., a kbd. suite such as D. Scarlatti's early sonatas, pubd. as *Esercizii*.
(3) Comp. submitted by candidates for certain univ. mus. degrees.

Expert, Henri (*b* Bordeaux, 1863; *d* Tourettes-sur-Loup, 1952). Fr. musicologist. Studied Paris and with *Franck. Joint founder, 1903, *Société d'Études Musicales*. Specialist in mus. of Fr. Renaissance period, publishing 23 vols. and 5 subsidiary sections.

Exposition. (1) In sonata form, the first section of a comp. in which the prin. themes are expounded before they are developed.
(2) In fugue the first statement of the subject by all the 'voices' in turn.

Expression. That part of a composer's mus. such as subtle nuances of dynamics which he has no full means of committing to paper and must leave to the artistic perception and insight of the executant. All he can do is to indicate speed and the kind of mood to be expressed by means of conventional mus. terms written on the score. A large part of the cond.'s art is the imparting of expressive qualities to the perf.

Expressionism. Term borrowed from painting, generally assoc. with work of the early 20th-cent. Ger. artists of the Munich 'Blaue Reiter' group led by Kandinsky. Prin. characteristics were avoidance of representational forms and interest in psychological impulses. These were musically reflected in works of Schoenberg, Webern, and Berg. But, like *impressionism, the term is vague.

Expression Stop. A stop in a harmonium or other reed org. When drawn, the passage of the air is made to short-circuit the reservoir through which it otherwise passes, and this gives the feet great control over degrees of force and accent.

Exsultate, Jubilate (Rejoice, be glad). Motet by Mozart (K165) for sop., orch., and org., comp. 1773. 3rd movt. is famous setting of 'Alleluia'. Orig. comp. for castrato Venanzio *Rauzzini.

Extemporization. See *Improvisation*.

Extension Organ. Same as unit org., i.e. built on the principle of saving space and money by making a comparatively small no. of pipes produce something of the effect of a larger number by 'borrowing'. The pipes of an 8' stop may, for example, be made to do duty also for a 4' by a connexion which draws on them an octave higher throughout (as in cinema orgs.).

Extravaganza (from It. 'stravaganza'). A mus. work which intentionally caricatures conventional procedures, such as Mozart's *Ein musikalische Spass* (A *Musical Joke), and especially a 19th-cent. Eng. form of stage entertainment with mus.

Eybler, Joseph Edler von (*b* Schwechat, 1765; *d* Vienna, 1846). Austrian composer. Pupil of *Albrechtsberger. Vice-Kapellmeister, Viennese Imperial court, from 1804 until he succeeded Salieri in 1824 as Kapellmeister. Comp. opera, oratorio, masses, requiem, syms., pf. solos, and other works. Friend of Mozart, whom he nursed in last illness. Asked by Mozart's widow to complete the *Requiem* but did not finish the task.

Eysler, Edmund (*b* Vienna, 1874; *d* Vienna, 1949). Austrian composer of operettas, incl. *Bruder Straubinger* (1902), *Künstlerblut* (1906), *Das Zirkuskind* (1911).

Ezcudantza. Basque fest. dance for 2 performers with acc. of pipe and tabor, and sometimes of v.

F

F. Note of the scale, 4th degree of natural scale of C. Thus F♭, F♭♭, F♮, F♯, F♯♯. Keys of F major and F minor, F♯ major, F♯ minor. 'In F' is also an indication of *transposing instr. on which written note C sounds as F (e.g. hn., F tpt.). The F clef is the bass clef.

F. Prefix given to numbers in the catalogue of Vivaldi's works by Antonio Fanna. Superseded by that of *Ryom.

f. Abbreviation of *forte* (It., 'loud', 'strong'), hence degrees of increasing loudness, *ff* (fortissimo) and *fff* (sometimes more).

Fa. The 4th degree of the major scale, according to the system of vocal syllables derived from Guido d' Arezzo, and so used (spelt *Fah*) in *Tonic Sol-fa (also in that system the 6th degree of the minor scale; see *Tonic Sol-fa*). In many countries, however, the name has become attached to the note F, in whatever key this may occur.

Faber, Heinrich (*b* Lichtenfels; *d* Ölsnitz, 1552). Ger. mus. theorist, graduate of and prof. of mus. at Wittenberg Univ. Author of Lat. compendium of mus. (1548) later trans. into Ger. by *Vulpius (Halle, 1608).

Faber Music. Mus. publishing branch of book publishers Faber & Faber; est. 1964, becoming separate co. 1966. Catalogue incl. mus. by Britten, Holst, Arnold, G. Benjamin, R. Smalley etc.

Fabritius, Albinus (*b* Görlitz; *d* ?Bruck an der Mur, 1635). Ger. composer of motets, secular songs, and dances.

Faburden (Eng.), **Fauxbourdon** (Fr.), **Falsobordone** (It.). Literally, false bass, or drone. This term has had a surprisingly large number of different applications at different periods.

(1) In very early use, the acc. in parallel 3rds and 6ths of a plainsong melody.

(2) In 15th cent., any added part to such a plainsong melody, both parts moving at the same rate. Apparently used especially of such passages interpolated among unison singing of the plainsong, e.g. in the psalms.

(3) About the same period, also used of the same kind of liturgical singing as that mentioned under (2), but without plainsong in any of the vv. (This is sometimes spoken of as 'free' Faburden as distinct from the previous type, spoken of as 'strict'.)

(4) A sort of chanting in which the whole of a phrase was declaimed on one chord, except that the cadence was harmonized as such. (The same

mus. was used for every verse of a psalm, etc., as is done today with the Anglican Chant.)

(5) Sometimes applied to a sort of monotoning.

(6) A drone bass, such as that of a bagpipe.

(7) In 16th- and 17th-cent. Eng. usage, sometimes applied to the ten. part of a metrical psalm tune, etc., which part then usually carried the melody.

(8) A refrain to the verses of a song.

(9) Nowadays (as with Descant) the word is used in Brit. for a freely-written sop. part added to a hymn tune while the tune itself is sung by the ten. vv. of the ch. or by the congregation, or (more commonly in recent years) for a 4-part .harmonization with the tune in the ten.—this last a revival of the old English practice.

When this word is used in old mus. treatises or in the modern mus. historical works any of the above senses may be intended.

Façade. 'Entertainment' by *Walton, being acc. for small chamber ens. (6 players) to poems by Edith Sitwell declaimed in notated rhythm by a speaker or speakers. Comp. 1921, f.p. (private) 1922, (public) 1923. This version has been several times rev. with many substitutions of items. Final pubd. version (1951) contains 21 items. 8 unpubd. nos. perf. under title *Façade Revived*, London 1977, 3 of these were rejected before publication and 3 others (nos. 4, 6, 7) substituted by composer; rev. and re-worked version perf. 1979 as *Façade II*. Prin. revs. of *Façade I* 1926, 1928, 1942. Also arr. by composer for larger orch. (without poems) as 2 Suites (No. 1, of 5 items, f.p. London 1926; No. 2, of 6 items, f.p. NY and London 1938). Also arr. as ballet, with choreog. by Gunter Hess, f.p. Hagen, Westphalia, 1929; with choreog. by Frederick *Ashton f.p. London 1931 (7 items), extra item 1935, 2 further addns. 1940; Ashton ballet of work with reciter and chamber ens. f.p. Snape, Suffolk, and London 1972. Many arrs. by others of items from *Façade* for a variety of combinations.

Faccio, Franco (*b* Verona, 1840; *d* Monza, 1891). It. cond. and composer. Studied Milan Cons. 1856–61. Served in Garibaldi's army 1866. Prof. of harmony, Milan Cons. 1868. Chief cond. Scala, Milan, from 1871. Cond. f. It. p. of Verdi's *Aida* (1872) and f.p. of *Otello* (1887). Cond. 1st Wagner opera in It. (*Lohengrin*, 1873) and 1st London *Otello* (1889). Comp. operas *I profughi Fiamminghi* (Milan 1863), *Amleto* (lib. by *Boito, Genoa 1865), cantata *Le Sorelle d'Italia* (text by Boito, 1861), 3 syms., str. qt., and songs.

Fach (Ger.). Fold, as in *Zweifach*, twofold, *Dreifach*, threefold, etc. Most commonly used to indicate a division of, e.g., the 1st vns. of an orch., but there is an org. application indicating the no. of ranks in a mixture stop; and in an operatic context it denotes the proper range of parts in Ger. operas.

Fachiri, Adila (*née* d'Arányi) (*b* Budapest, 1886; *d* Florence, 1962). Hung.-born violinist, sister of Jelly d'*Arányi. Studied under *Hubay, Budapest Cons., and in Berlin 1905–7 with *Joachim (her great-uncle). Foreign tours with her sister. Eng. début Haslemere 1909. Settled and married in Eng., continuing to appear as orch. soloist and in chamber mus.

Facile (Fr.). Easy. **Facilement** (Fr.), **Facilmente** (It.). Easily, i.e. fluently and without an effect of striving.

Facilità (It. 'facility'). (1) Ease, fluency.
(2) Simplification, as of a virtuoso solo passage brought within the range of less skilled performers.

Fackeltanz (Ger.). 'Torch dance', more often a torchlight procession to mus. Spontini, Meyerbeer, and others have comp. these dances, which were usually part of a wedding or similar celebration.

Fado. A type of popular Portuguese song and dance with guitar acc., apparently dating from *c.* 1850.

Fa fictum. A term used in connexion with the *Hexachords—the note B flattened (in the Soft Hexachord).

Fagan, Gideon (*b* Somerset West, S. Africa, 1904; *d* Cape Town, 1980). S. African cond. and composer. Studied S.A. Coll. of Mus. and RCM. Cond. BBC Northern Orch. 1939–42, Johannesburg Orch. 1949–52. Mus. dir. S. African Broadcasting Corp. 1963–6, lecturer Univ. of Cape Town 1967–73. Cond. several London musicals. Comps. incl. *Afrikaans Folktune Suite.*

F.A.G.O. Fellow of the American Guild of Organists.

Fagott (Ger.), **fagotto** (It.), **fagote** (Sp.). (1) The *bassoon. The name derives from *fagotto* (It., 'bundle of sticks'), possibly applied jokingly to the *phagotum*, a kind of bagpipe invented by Canon Afranio of Ferrara in 1521. In the 16th cent. the word *fagotto* covered a range of instr., such as the *curtal or *dulcian which are forerunners of the modern bn.
(2) Organ stop, same as bn.

Fah. See *Fa.*

Fair at Sorochinsk, The (Mussorgsky). See *Sorochintsy Fair.*

Fairfax, Bryan (Lancelot Beresford) (*b* Sydney, 1930). Australian cond. and violinist. Studied N.S.W. Cons., Sydney, then in London with

Rostal. Violinist Hallé Orch. 1954–6. Studied cond. Vienna Acad. 1956–7 (with Swarowsky). Founded Polyphonia Orch. 1961 for perf. of new or rarely heard mus. Cond. f.p. of Brian's *Gothic Symphony*, 1961, concert perf. of Britten's *Gloriana*, London 1963 (on night of composer's 50th birthday), and f.Brit.pub.p. of Nielsen's *Sinfonia espansiva* (1962).

Fair Maid of Perth, The (Bizet). See *Jolie Fille de Perth, La.*

Fairy Queen, The. Semi-opera, but really a succession of masques, by Purcell in prol. and 5 acts, to lib. (by E. Settle?) based on Shakespeare's *A Midsummer Night's Dream* (which is not quoted). Prod. London 1692, London 1911 (Morley Coll., cond. Holst), Cambridge (stage) 1920, San Francisco 1932. Score was lost by 1700 but found in library of RAM, 1901. 1st work staged at CG after World War II.

Fairy's Kiss, The (Stravinsky). See *Baiser de la fée, Le.*

Falkner, (Sir) (Donald) **Keith** (*b* Sawston, Cambs., 1900). Eng. bar. and administrator. Trained at New Coll., Oxford, and RCM, also in Berlin, Paris, and Vienna. Sang in opera (BNOC) but best known as oratorio soloist. On retirement became teacher. Brit. Council mus. officer for It. 1946–50; teacher at Cornell Univ. 1950–60; dir., RCM, 1960–74. Knighted 1967.

Fall, Leo (*b* Olomouc, 1873; *d* Vienna, 1925). Austrian composer. Studied Vienna Cons. Th. cond., Berlin, Hamburg, and Cologne. Comp. 2 operas, but greatest success with operettas, e.g. *Der Rebell* (1905), *Der Fidele Bauer* (1907), *Die *Dollarprinzessin* (1907), *Brüderlein fein* (1909), *The Eternal Waltz* (London 1911), *Die Rose von Stamboul* (1916) and *Madame Pompadour* (1922).

Falla, Manuel de (Manuel Maria de Falla y Matheu) (*b* Cádiz, 1876; *d* Alta Gracia de Córdoba, Argentina, 1946). Sp. composer and pianist. He was taught the pf. by his mother and harmony by 2 local musicians. In Madrid he continued pf. studies with José Tragó, but his ambition was to be a composer and he wrote 2 *zarzuelas, the first of which was prod. in 1902. Falla then studied comp. in Madrid for 3 years with *Pedrell, who imparted the doctrine that a nation's mus. should be based on folk-song. However, it was to the spirit rather than to the letter of Sp. folk-mus. which Falla turned. In 1905 he won the Madrid Acad. of Fine Arts prize for the best lyrical drama by a Sp. composer with his 2-act opera *La Vida Breve* (but it was not perf.). In the same year he won the Ortiz y Cusso prize for Sp. pianists. For 2 years he taught the pf. in Madrid and in 1907 went to Paris, where he became the friend of and was greatly influenced by Dukas, Ravel, and Debussy. Ricardo *Viñes played the *4 Spanish Pieces* for pf. in Paris in 1908, and Falla himself introduced them to London at his début there in

1911. *La Vida Breve* was produced in Nice and Paris in 1913 and in Madrid in 1914. The ballet-pantomine *El Amor brujo* followed in 1915. In 1916 he completed his most ambitious and successful concert work (begun in Paris 1909), the *Noches en los Jardines de España* (Nights in the Gardens of Spain) for pf. and orch. Falla's fame was est., however, in 1919 by Diaghilev's prod. in London of the ballet *El Sombrero de Tres Picos* (Tricorne, or The *Three-Cornered Hat). In 1919 Falla also completed his major work for solo pf., *Fantasia Bética*, dedicated to Arthur *Rubinstein. Bética was the Roman name (Baetica) for Andalusia. After World War I, Falla's style was less colourfully but no less inherently Sp.—it is truer to say that the popular Andalusian folk element was succeeded by a re-creation of the severer style of the early Sp. polyphonic masters. From this period come the chamber opera (based on an incident in *Don Quixote*) *El Retablo de Maese Pedro* (*Master Peter's Puppet Show), f.p. 1923, and the hpd. conc. (1926) ded. to Wanda *Landowska. In 1926 he began work on an enormous 'scenic cantata *Atlántida* which was left unfinished and was completed by *Halffter. In 1939, after cond. 4 concerts in Buenos Aires, he settled in Argentina. Prin. comps.:

OPERAS: *La *Vida Breve* (1904–5), *Fuego Fatuo* (based on Chopin) (1918–19), *El Retablo de Maese Pedro* (1919–22).
BALLETS: *El *Amor Brujo* (1915), *El Sombrero de Tres Picos* (1917–19, being rev. version of *El Corregidor y la Molinera*, 1917).
ORCH: **Noches en los Jardines de España* (1909–16) for pf. and orch., Suites Nos. 1 and 2 from *El Sombrero de Tres Picos*.
PIANO: *Cuatro Piezas Españolas* (4 Spanish Pieces), (1907–8); **Fantasia Bética* (1919); *Homenajes* (Homages) 1. *Fanfare on the name of *Arbós*, 1933, orch. 1938; 2. *A Claude Debussy (elegia de la guitarra)*, also for guitar as *Homenaje a Debussy*, 1920, orch. 1939; 3. *Rapel de la Fanfare*, 1941; 4. *A Paul Dukas (Spes Vitae)* 1935, orch. 1939; 5. *Pedrelliana*, 1938. **Ritual Fire Dance, Dance of Fear, Pantomime, Récit du Pêcheur*, arr. by Falla from ballet *El Amor Brujo*; Suite from 7 *Spanish Popular Songs*, arr. by Falla; *Dance of Miller's Wife* and *Miller's Dance*, from *El Sombrero de Tres Picos*, arr. Falla.
CHAMBER MUSIC: *Psyche* for mez., fl., harp, vn., va., vc. (1924); conc. for hpd. (or pf.), fl., ob., cl., vn., and vc. (1923–6).
CHORAL AND VOCAL: **Atlántida*, scenic cantata, unfinished (completed by Halffter); *3 Melódies*, v. and pf. (1909); *Siete Canciones Populares Españolas* (7 Spanish Popular Songs) for v. and pf. (1914–5); *Soneto a Córdoba*, v. and harp (1927); *Balada de Mallorca* (after Chopin), mixed ch. (1933).
ARRS. BY OTHERS: *La Vida Breve*: 2 *Spanish Dances*, pf. solo and pf. duet, arr. Samazeuilh; 1st *Spanish Dance*, vn. and pf., arr. Kreisler; 2 *Spanish Dances*,

orch. Chapelier; 7 *Spanish Popular Songs*, orch. by Halffter; Suite for vn. and pf. arr. P. Kochanski; for vc. and pf., arr. M. Maréchal.

Fallows, David (Nicholas) (*b* Buxton, 1945). Eng. musicologist. Studied Cambridge Univ. 1964–7, King's Coll., London, 1967–8, Univ. of Calif. at Berkeley, 1970–3. Has held academic posts at Studio der frühen Musik, Munich, 1968–70, Univ. of Wisconsin-Madison 1973–4, and Manchester Univ. from 1976. Wrote on many medieval subjects and on tempo and expression marks in *The New Grove Dictionary of Music & Musicians* (1980). Many articles on his special subjects. Writes mus. criticism for the *Guardian*. Author of *Dufay* (1982).

False Accent. When the accent is removed from 1st beat of a bar to 2nd or 4th.

False Close. See *Cadence*.

False Relation. In harmony, the appearance of a note with the same letter-name in different parts (or 'voices') of contiguous or the same chords, in one case inflected (♯ or ♭) and in the other uninflected (e.g. F♮ and F♯). Amer. term is 'cross-relation'.

Falsetto (It.). Singing method used by males, particularly tens., to achieve a note or notes higher than comes within the normal range of their v. Often used for comic effect, e.g. Falstaff imitating the Merry Wives in Verdi's opera.

Falsobordone (It.). Same as Eng. **Faburden**).

Falstaff. (1) Comic opera in 3 acts by Verdi (his last) to lib. by Boito after Shakespeare's *The Merry Wives of Windsor* and *King Henry IV*, Parts 1 and 2. Comp. 1889–92. Prod. Milan 1893, CG 1894, NY Met. 1895. Operas on same subject incl. those by *Dittersdorf (1796), *Salieri (1798), *Balfe (1838), *Nicolai (*Die lustigen Weiber von Windsor*, 1849), and Vaughan Williams (*Sir John in Love*, 1924–8).
(2) Symphonic study in C minor, with 2 interludes, Op. 68, for orch. by Elgar. Comp. 1902–13. F.p. Leeds Oct. 1913, f. London p. Nov. 1913.

Fanciulla del West, La (The Girl of the Golden West). 3-act opera by Puccini to lib. by Civinini and Zangarini based on Belasco's play *The Girl of the Golden West* (1905). Comp. 1908–10. F.p. NY Met. 1910; CG and Rome 1911.

Fancy. Eng. 16th- and 17th-cent. equivalent of *Fantasia.

Fandango. A lively Sp. dance believed to be of S. Amer. origin. It is in simple triple or compound duple time, and of ever-increasing speed, with sudden stops during which the performers (a single couple) remain motionless, and with intervals during which they sing. Acc. is normally by guitar or castanets. There is a fandango in Mozart's *Figaro*.

Fanfare. (1, Eng.) Flourish of tpts., or other instrs. in imitation of them, as a means of proclamation, such as a military signal.

(2, Fr.). Brass band (as distinct from *Harmonie*, a band of mixed brass and woodwind).

Fanfare for the Common Man. Orch. work by *Copland, comp. 1942 as one of series of wartime fanfares commissioned by Eugene Goossens, who cond. f.p. with Cincinnati S.O., March 1943.

Fanny Robin. Opera in 1 act by Harper to his own lib. derived from Hardy's *Wessex Poems* (1898) and *Far From the Madding Crowd* (1874). Comp. 1974, prod. Edinburgh (Scottish Opera) 1975.

Fanshawe, David (*b* Devon, 1942). Eng. composer. Studied with John Lambert, then at RCM. Has devoted much time to research into African folk mus. and into that of Iraq and Tonga. Works incl. *Escapade I* and *II* for pf., *Fantasy on Dover Castle*, orch., *Requiem for the Children of Aberfan* orch., *African Sanctus* (orig. version 1972, rev. 1977), and *Salaams*, tone-poem (1978).

Fantasia (It.), **Fantaisie** (Fr.), **Fantasie** (Ger.). Fantasy or Fancy. Generally a comp. in which form is of secondary importance, although the 16th-cent. It. fantasia was an instr. comp. in strict imitation of a vocal motet. In Eng. in the 16th and 17th cents. the term 'fancy' was used for comps. for both kbd. and str. instr., notably consorts of viols. Such comps. were usually contrapuntal and in several sections often with a common theme, thus being an early form of variations. In the 20th cent. the chamber mus. patron *Cobbett revived the form, preferring the spelling Phantasy. Sweelinck and Bach used the term fantasia for their organ comps. in which the character of the mus. suggested an improvisational character or the play of free fancy. In the 19th cent. the term was applied by Schumann, Chopin, and others to short mood pieces, e.g. Schumann's *Fantasiestücke*. Other meanings of the word are: (1) a comp. comprising a string of tunes, e.g. from an opera, as in Liszt's pf. fantasies on operatic arias.

(2) Development section in sonata-form, i.e. free fantasia.

(3) Title of film first shown in 1940, made by Walt Disney, in which cartoons (some merely abstract patterns) were set to famous pieces of music played by the Philadelphia Orch. conducted by Stokowski. The items were: J. S. Bach's *Toccata and Fugue in D minor* (transcr. Stokowski); Tchaikovsky's *Nutcracker Suite*; Ponchielli's *Dance of the Hours*; Beethoven's *Pastoral Symphony*; Dukas's *L'Apprenti sorcier*; Stravinsky's *The Rite of Spring*; Mussorgsky's *Night on the Bare Mountain*; and Schubert's *Ave Maria*. See *Film Music*.

Fantasia Bética. Work for pf. by Falla, completed 1919 and ded. to Arthur Rubinstein who commissioned it and gave f.p. in NY 1920. Baetica was Roman name for Andalusia.

Fantasia Concertante on a Theme of Corelli. Work for str. by *Tippett, comp. 1953 for Edinburgh Fest. on tercentenary of Corelli's birth. Str. div. into concertino (2 solo vn. and vc.), conc. grosso (half remaining body), conc. terzo (other half). Theme taken from Corelli's Conc. Grosso Op. 6 No. 2, and work quotes Bach's *Fugue on themes of Corelli*.

Fantasia Contrappuntistica. Work for solo pf. comp. by Busoni in 3 versions between 1910 and 1912. Sub-titled *Preludio al Corale 'Gloria al Signori nei Cieli' e fuga a quattro soggetti obbligati sopra un frammento di Bach*. Arr. for 2 pf., 1921. Adapted for org. by work's dedicatee Wilhelm Middelschulte. Based on Bach's Contrapunctus XVIII from *The Art of Fugue*, in desire to complete Bach's unfinished fugue. Busoni created 4th subject (Bach having comp. only 3), and added 5th.

Fantasias on an In Nomine by John Taverner. 2 works for orch. by *Maxwell Davies, comp. as studies for his opera *Taverner*. 1st, comp. 1962; 2nd, comp. 1964 (f.p. London 1965, cond. John Pritchard).

Fantasia on a theme by Thomas Tallis. Comp. by Vaughan Williams for double str. orch. and str. qt., f.p. Gloucester 1910, London 1913 (rev.). Tallis's theme is No. 3 ('Why fumeth in fight') of 9 psalm tunes comp. 1567 for Archbishop Parker's Psalter.

Fantasia on a theme of Handel. Comp. for pf. and orch. by *Tippett, comp. 1939–41, f.p. London 1942 by Phyllis Sellick, cond. Walter Goehr.

Fantasia on British Sea Songs. Compilation of trad. and other songs made by Henry J. *Wood for concert on 21 Oct. 1905 to celebrate centenary of Nelson's victory at Trafalgar and which became (and remains) traditional finale to Last Night of London Promenade Concerts, with the audience joining in (singing, clapping, and foot-stamping). In 9 sections: 1, *Naval Bugle calls*. 2, *The anchor's weighed* (solo tpt., solo tb.). 3, *The saucy Arethusa* (solo euphonium). 4, *Tom Bowling* (Dibdin) (solo vc.). 5, *Hornpipe, Jack's the lad* (solo vn., solo fl., solo piccolo). 6, *Farewell and adieu, ye Spanish ladies* (4 tbs.). 7, *Home, sweet home* (Bishop) (solo cl., solo ob.). 8, *See, the conquering hero comes* (Handel) (solo hns.). 9, *Rule, Britannia!* (Arne) (org. and full orch.). For some years the Fantasia was cut, but the practice recently has been to give it in full. Bringing a solo cont. into *Rule, Britannia!* was Sargent's departure from Wood's score.

Fantasia on Christmas Carols. Comp. by *Vaughan Williams for bar., ch., and orch. Founded on traditional carols: 1. The truth sent from above. 2. Come all you worthy gentlemen. 3. On Christmas night. 4. There is a fountain; with fragments of others. F.p. Hereford 1912, London 1913.

Fantasia on 'Greensleeves'. Arr. by Ralph Greaves for strs. and harp (or pf.) with optional fl.(s) of interlude from Vaughan Williams's opera *Sir John in Love*, middle section being based on folk-song *Lovely Joan*. Several other arrs., none by Vaughan Williams, exist.

Fantasiestücke (Fantasy Pieces). 8 pieces for solo pf., Op. 12, by Schumann, 1837–8, with descriptive titles. 3 further *Fantasiestücke* described only by key-signatures were pubd. as Op. 111 (1851).

Fantaisies Symphoniques. Sub-title of 6th Sym. by Martinů, f.p. Boston 1955.

Farandole (Fr.). Lively Provençal dance in ⅜ time in which, to the acc. of *galoubet* and *tambourin*, the participants danced through the streets holding each other by the hands or by a handkerchief. The *farandole* in Bizet's incidental mus. to *L'*Arlésienne* is based on an authentic Provençal dance-tune but is not in ⅜.

Farewell, Manchester. Jacobite song played while the Young Pretender's army left Manchester in 1745, tune being a hpd. piece, *Felton's Gavotte*, comp. *c*.1740 by Rev. William *Felton, of Hereford.

Farewell Symphony. See *Abschiedsymphonie.*

Farina, Carlo (*b* Mantua, *c*.1600; *d c*.1640). It. violinist and composer. One of earliest writers of virtuoso vn. mus. (pubd. 1626–8). Worked at Dresden court 1625-32.

Farinelli (Carlo Broschi) (*b* Andria, 1705; *d* Bologna, 1782). It. castrato singer. Studied with Porpora. Début Naples, 1720. In 1727 was defeated in public exhibition of vocal skill by Bernacchi, who then taught him. Sang in Vienna and in London, where he joined Porpora's opera co. which was in competition with Handel's. Sang in Madrid, 1737, where Philip V offered him 50,000 francs a year to stay, which he did for 25 years, singing each night to the king. Was instrumental in est. It. opera in Madrid. Left Spain on Charles III's accession in 1759, living in Bologna in some splendour, collecting pictures and playing hpd. and va. d'amore.

Farkas, Ferenc (*b* Nagykanizsa, 1905). Hung. composer. Studied Budapest Acad. of Mus. 1922–8 (with Weiner and Siklós) and S. Cecilia Acad., Rome, 1929–31, with Respighi. Worked as composer and cond., film studios in Vienna and Copenhagen 1933–6. Prof. of comp., Kolozsvár Cons., 1941–3, dir. 1943–4. Dir. Székesfehérvár Cons., 1946–8. Prof. of comp., Budapest Acad. 1949–75. Comps. incl. 2 operas, ballet, choral works, concs. (incl. one for baryton or va. da gamba), chamber mus., and songs.

Farkas, Ödön (*b* Jászmonostor, 1852; *d* Kolozsvár, 1912). Hung. composer. Studied Pest Mus. Acad. Wrote 7 operas, sym., 5 str. qts.,

songs, and choral mus., all of strong Hung. character.

Farmer, John (*fl.* late 16th cent.). Eng. madrigal composer. Organist, Christ Church, Dublin. Lived in London from 1599. Contrib. to *The *Triumphs of Oriana.

Farnaby, Giles (*b* Truro, 1563; *d* London, 1640). Eng. composer of madrigals, mus. for virginals, canzonets, psalm-tunes, etc. Over 50 of his virginals pieces are included in *Fitzwilliam Virginal Book*; among the best-known are *His dreame*, *A Toye*, and *Loth to depart*. In 1592 contributed to *East's book of psalms; his canzonets for 4 vv. were pubd. 1598.

Farncombe, Charles (*b* London, 1919). Eng. cond. Studied Royal Sch. of Church Mus. (Canterbury) and RAM. Founder, Handel Opera Soc., 1955, and dir. since then. Chief cond. Royal Court Th., Drottningholm, from 1970. C.B.E. 1977.

Farnon, Robert (Joseph) (*b* Toronto, 1917). Canadian composer and cond. Trumpeter in CBC orch. 1936–42; cond. Canadian Army orch., 1943–6. Settled in Brit. Comp. and arr. much mus. for films, radio, TV, etc.

Farrant, Richard (*b c*.1530; *d* London, 1580). Eng. composer and organist of St George's Chapel, Windsor; member of Chapel Royal. Composer of anthems and songs.

Farrar, Ernest (Bristow) (*b* Lewisham, 1885; *d* in action nr. Le Cateau, Cambrai, 1918). Eng. composer and organist. Studied at Durham Univ. from 1904, also at RCM 1905–9, comp. with Stanford, org. with Parratt. Friend of Frank *Bridge. Org., Eng. church, Dresden, 1909, then St Hilda's, South Shields, 1910–12 and Christ Church, Harrogate, 1912–16. While at Harrogate gave lessons from 1914 to *Finzi. Enlisted in army 1915; commissioned in Devonshire Regiment 1918. Killed at Battle of Epéhy Ronssoy, Somme Valley, 18 Sept. 1918. Comp. prize in his memory founded at RCM (later twice won by *Britten), but now amalgamated with Sullivan Prize. Bridge's pf. sonata (1921–4) is dedicated to his memory. Works (dates given are either of publication or f.p.) incl.:

ORCH: Rhapsody No. 1 *The Open Road*, after Whitman (1909), No. 2 *Lavengro*, after Borrow (1913); sym.-poem *The Forsaken Merman*, after Arnold (1914); *Variations on an Old British Sea Song*, pf., orch. (1915); *English Pastoral Impressions*, suite (1915); *3 Spiritual Studies*, str. (1925); *Heroic Elegy 'For Soldiers'*, orch. (1918).
CHORAL: 3 Partsongs, mixed ch. (1907); 2 Partsongs, male vv. (1909); *The Blessed Damozel*, low v., ch., orch. (1907); *Margaritae Sorori*, unacc. ch. (1916); *Out of Doors*, Whitman suite for ch. and orch. (*c*.1911); *A Song of St Francis*, unison,

pf. (1919); *Summer* (C. Rossetti), women's vv. and pf. or sop. and orch. (1918).
CHAMBER MUSIC: Vn. Sonata (lost); *Celtic Suite*, vn., pf. (1910); *Celtic Impressions*, str. qt. (?).
PIANO: *Valse caprice* (1913); *Miniature Suite* (1913); *Shadow Dance* (1922); *3 Pieces* (1915–27, pubd.); *3 Pieces* (1916); *2 North Country Sketches* (1920).
ORGAN: *Fantasy Prelude* (1908); *3 Chorale Preludes* (1920); *A Wedding Piece* (1925); *Elegy* (1925); *6 Pieces* (1926).
SONGS: *3 Songs* (1906); *Vagabond Songs*, bar., orch. (1911); *Brittany* (1914); *O Mistress Mine* (1921); *2 Elizabethan Love Songs* (1921).

Farrar, Geraldine (*b* Melrose, Mass., 1882; *d* Ridgefield, Conn., 1967). Amer. sop. Studied in Boston, Mass., and then in Berlin with Graziani. Début, Berlin Court Opera, 1901, as Marguérite in *Faust*. Became pupil of Lilli *Lehmann. Sang at Monte Carlo 1904–6. Sang Mimi and Gilda to Caruso's Rodolfo and Duke on several occasions. Début at NY Met. 1906; sang Butterfly at its first Met. perf. Member of Met. co. until 1922, singing nearly 500 times. Created roles of Amica (Mascagni) at Monte Carlo 1905, Goose-Girl in *Königskinder* (Humperdinck) in NY 1910, and *Suor Angelica* (Puccini) in NY 1918. Also appeared in many films.

Farruca. An Andalusian dance of gipsy origin. *Falla, in his ballet *The Three-Cornered Hat,* uses the *farruca* for the Miller's Dance.

Fasano, Renato (*b* Naples, 1902; *d* Rome, 1979). It. cond., pianist, and composer. Founder and cond., 1947, of Collegium Musicum Italicum which in 1952 became I Virtuosi di Roma, chamber ens. specializing in old mus. Dir., Rome Cons., 1960–72.

Fasch, Carl (Friedrich Christian) (*b* Zerbst, 1736; *d* Berlin, 1800). Ger. composer, son of J. F. *Fasch. Studied vn. and clavier. Accompanist to Frederick the Great from 1756, dir. court opera 1774–6. In 1790 held choral rehearsals which led to foundation of Berlin *Singakademie*. Beethoven twice visited Fasch in 1796, improvising for his pupils. Works inc. oratorio, mass, and other church mus.

Fasch, Johann (Friedrich) (*b* Buttlestädt, 1688; *d* Zerbst, 1758). Ger. composer. Studied Thomasschule, Leipzig, 1701–7. Founded Leipzig Collegium Musicum which later became the Gewandhaus concerts. Court Kapellmeister, Zerbst, from 1722. Comp. 4 operas, concs., sonatas, trios, church mus., etc.

Faschingsschwank aus Wien (Viennese Carnival Pranks). Pf. comp. (*Fantasiebilder*) by Schumann, Op. 26, comp. 1839. In 5 movements.

Fassbaender, Brigitte (*b* Berlin, 1939). Ger. mez., daughter of Willi *Domgraf-Fassbänder. Studied with her father and at Nuremberg Cons. Début Munich 1961, London CG 1971 (Oktavian), San Francisco 1970, Salzburg 1973, NY Met. 1974 (Oktavian). Member of Bavarian State Opera since 1961. Specializes in *travesti* roles.

Fassung (Ger.). Drafting. *Neue Fassung,* new version.

Fate (Janáček). See *Osud*.

Fauré, Gabriel (Urbain) (*b* Pamiers, 1845; *d* Paris, 1924). Fr. composer and organist. From 1854 to 1866 studied at École Niedermeyer, Paris, under *Niedermeyer and Saint-Saëns. Organist, St Sulpice, Paris, 1870, St Honoré; choirmaster from 1877 at the Madeleine, organist 1896–1905. Prof. of comp., Paris Cons. 1896, dir. 1905–20. Pupils incl. Ravel, N. Boulanger, Enescu, Schmitt, Koechlin, and Roger-Ducasse. Fauré's music was slow to gain recognition outside Fr., but he is now acknowledged as one of the greatest of Fr. composers, a master of the song-cycle, a poet of the kbd., and a profound composer of chamber mus. His delicate and elegant but by no means harmonically unadventurous style has an unsuspected strength and emotional appeal. His opera *Pénélope* is regarded by many as a masterpiece. His best-known work is the *Requiem,* comp. between 1877 and 1890, but it did not achieve general popularity until after World War II despite the earlier advocacy of Nadia *Boulanger. Prin. works:

OPERAS: *Prométhée*, Op. 82 (1900); *Pénélope* (1913); *Masques et Bergamasques* (divertissement) (1919).
INCIDENTAL MUSIC: *Caligula* (Dumas), Op. 52 (5 movements, 1888); *Shylock* (Haraucourt after Shakespeare), Op. 57 (6 movements), (1889); *Pelléas et Mélisande* (Maeterlinck), Op. 80 (1898); *Le Voile du bonheur* (Clémenceau), Op. 88 (1901).
ORCH: *Ballade,* pf. and orch., Op. 19 (1881); *Pavane* (with optional ch.) Op. 50 (1887); Suite, *Shylock,* Op. 57 (1889); Suite, *Pelléas et Mélisande,* Op. 80 (4 items) (1901); *Fantaisie* in G major, pf. and orch., Op. 111 (1919); Suite, *Masques et Bergamasques,* Op. 112 (4 items) (1919); Suite *Dolly,* Op. 56 (orch. Rabaud, 1906).
CHORAL: *Cantique de Racine,* Op. 11 (1876); *La Naissance de Vénus,* Op. 29 (1882); *O Salutaris: Maria, Mater Gratiae,* Op. 47, Nos. 1 and 2 (1887); *Requiem,* Op. 48, for sop. and bar. soloists, ch., org., and orch. (1877, 1887–90, orch. 1900); *Ecce fidelis servus,* Op. 54, motet (1890); *Tantum ergo,* Op. 55 (1890); *Salve Regina; Ave Maria,* Op. 67, Nos. 1 and 2 (1895).
SONGS AND SONG-CYCLES (v. and pf.): *Sylvie, Après un rêve, Hymne, Barcarolle,* Op. 7, Nos. 1–4, (No. 2 orch. Busser 1925) (*c.*1865); *Nell, Le Voyageur, Automne,* Op. 18, Nos. 1–3 (No. 3 orch. Busser 1925) (1880); *Les Berceaux, Notre Amour, Le Secret,* Op. 23, Nos. 1–3 (No. 2 orch. Busser 1925) (1882); *2 Mélodies,* Op. 27 (1883); *Aurore, Fleur jetée, Les pays des rêves, Les Roses d' Ispahan,* Op. 39, Nos. 1–4 (1884); *Les Présents, *Clair de Lune,* Op. 46, Nos. 1–2 (1887); *Larmes, Au*

cimitière, *Spleen, La Rose, Op. 51, Nos. 1–4 (1889); 5 Mélodies (Verlaine), Op. 58 (1891) (sometimes known as 5 Chansons de Venise); La *Bonne Chanson (Verlaine cycle), Op. 61, Nos. 1–9 (1892–3); Prison, Soir, Op. 83, Nos. 1–2 (c.1895); Le Parfum impérissable, Arpège, Op. 76, Nos. 1–2 (No. 1 orch. Busser 1924) (1897); 3 Mélodies, Op. 85 (1902); Le Plus Doux Chemin, Le Ramier, Op. 87, Nos. 1–2 (1904); Le Don silencieux, Op. 92 (1906); Chanson, Op. 94 (1907); Vocalise (1907); La Chanson d'Eve (Lerberghe cycle), Op. 95, Nos. 1–10 (1906–10); Le *Jardin clos (Lerberghe cycle), Op. 106, Nos. 1–8 (1914–15); Mirages (Brimont cycle), Op. 113, Nos. 1–4 (1919); C'est la Paix! Op. 114 (1919); L'*Horizon chimérique (Mirmont cycle), Op. 118, Nos. 1–4 (1921).

CHAMBER MUSIC: Sonata for pf. and vn., No. 1 in A, Op. 13 (1876), No. 2 in E minor, Op. 108 (1916); Pf. Qt. No. 1 in C minor, Op. 15 (1879), No. 2 in G minor, Op. 45 (1886); Pf. Quintet No. 1 in D minor, Op. 89 (1903–6), No. 2 in C minor, Op. 115 (1919–21); Sonata No. 1 in D minor for pf. and vc., Op. 109 (1917), No. 2 in G minor, Op. 117 (1921); Pf. Trio in D minor, Op. 120 (1922–3); Str. Qt. in E minor, Op. 121 (1923–4); Berceuse for pf. and vn., Op. 16 (1879) (also for vn. or vc. and orch.); Elégie for pf. and vc., Op. 24 (1883) (also with orch.); Romance for vn. and pf., Op. 28 (1882); Romance in A for vc. and pf., Op. 69 (1894); Andante for pf. and vn., Op. 75 (1894); Papillon for vc. and pf., Op. 77 (1897) (also for str. quintet or vn. and pf.); Sicilienne for vc. and pf., Op. 78 (1893); Fantaisie for fl., and pf., Op. 79 (1898) (orch. Aubert 1958); Sérénade for vc. and pf., Op. 98 (1908).

PIANO: 3 Romances sans paroles, Op. 17 (1863); Impromptus: No. 1 In Eb, Op. 25 (1882), No. 2 in F minor, Op. 31 (1883), No. 3 in Ab, Op. 34 (1883), No. 4 in Db, Op. 91 (1905), No. 5 in F# minor, Op. 102 (1909), No. 6, Op. 86 bis (see Harp); Nocturnes: 3 Nocturnes, Op. 33, No. 1 in Eb minor, No. 2 in B major, No. 3 in Ab (1883); No. 4 in Eb, Op. 36 (1884), No. 5 in Bb, Op. 37 (1884), No. 6 in Db, Op. 63 (1894), No. 7 in C# minor, Op. 74 (1897), No. 8 in Db (8th of Pièces brèves, Op. 84 (1898–1902)), No. 9 in B minor, Op. 97 (1908), No. 10 in E minor, Op. 99 (1908), No. 11 in F# minor, Op. 104, No. 1 (1913), No. 12 in E minor, Op. 107 (1915), No. 13 in B minor, Op. 119 (1921); Barcarolles: No. 1 in A minor, Op. 26 (1882), No. 2 in G major, Op. 41 (1885), No. 3 in Gb, Op. 42 (1885), No. 4 in Ab, Op. 44 (1886), No. 5 in F# minor, Op. 66 (1894), No. 6 in Eb, Op. 70 (1895), No. 7 in D minor, Op. 90 (1905), No. 8 in Db, Op. 96 (1908), No. 9 in A minor, Op. 101 (1910), No. 10 in A minor, Op. 104, No. 2 (1913), No. 11 in G minor and No. 12 in Eb, Op. 105, Nos. 1 and 2 (1914–15), No. 13 in C major, Op. 116 (1921); Valses-Caprices: No. 1 in A, Op. 30 (1883), No. 2 in Db, Op. 38 (1884), No. 3 in Gb, Op. 59 (1891), No. 4 in Ab, Op. 62 (1894); Mazurka in Bb, Op. 32

(1883); Thème et variations, Op. 73 (1896) (orch. Inghelbrecht 1955); 8 Pièces brèves, Op. 84 (1898–1902); 9 Préludes, Op. 103 (1910).

PIANO DUET (4 hands): *Dolly, Op. 56 (1894–7) (orch. Rabaud 1906); *Souvenirs de Bayreuth (with *Messager) (pubd. 1930).

HARP: Impromptu, Op. 86 (1904) (rearr. for pf. as Impromptu No. 6, Op. 86 bis (1913)); Une Châtelaine en sa tour, Op. 110 (1918) (arr. Durand for pf.).

Faust. (1) Opera in 5 acts by Gounod to lib. by Barbier and Carré based on Goethe's poem (1808, 1832). Prod. Paris 1859, London 1863, Philadelphia 1863, NY Met. 1883 (inaugural opera).
(2) Singspiel in 2 acts by Spohr to lib. by J. K. Bernard not based on Goethe, comp. 1813, prod. Prague 1816; rev. 1852 as 3-act opera, prod. London 1852 and 1984.

Faust, Doktor (Busoni). See Doktor Faust.

Faust, Le Damnation de (Berlioz). See Damnation de Faust, Le.

Faust Overture, A (Eine Faust Ouvertüre). Concert ov. by Wagner, orig. intended as 1st movement of a Faust Sym., comp. 1840, f.p. Dresden 1844. Rev. 1855.

Faust, Scenes from Goethe's. Ov. and 6 other movements for soloists, ch., and orch. by Schumann, comp. 1844–53.

Faust Symphony, A (Eine Faust-Symphonie). Sym. by Liszt in 3 character studies (in drei Charakterbildern) based on Goethe's poem, with ad lib male-v. choral ending. Comp. 1854–7, f.p. 1857, rev. 1880. 3 movements entitled Faust, Gretchen, and Mephistopheles.

Faust, 2 Episodes from Lenau's. 2 orch. works by Liszt, comp. before 1861, inspired by poem about Faust by Lenau. Titles are The Night Ride and Dance in the Village Inn, the latter being the *Mephisto Waltz No. 1, later transcr. for pf. solo and pf. duet.

Fauxbourdon (Fr.). Literally 'false bass'. Way of singing improvised polyphony in 15th cent. mus., particularly that by Burgundian composers. Plainsong melody in treble is acc. by two lower parts, one in parallel sixths, the other a fourth below melody. Similar to but not identical with Eng. *faburden and derivation one from another is disputed.

Favart, Charles-Simon (b Paris, 1710; d Belleville, 1792). Fr. librettist and impresario. Stage-manager at Opéra Comique (which was called Salle Favart after him) and from 1758 to 1762 its dir. Wrote over 150 opera libs. for composers incl. Grétry, Gluck, and Philidor.

Favola d'Orfeo, La (The Legend (Fable) of Orpheus). (1) Favola in musica in prol. and 5 acts by Monteverdi to lib. by Striggio. Prod. Mantua 1607. Rev. in concert version arr. *d'Indy, Paris

1904, London 1924; staged Paris 1911 and Oxford 1925. Also ed. by *Malipiero, Orff, Westrup, Hindemith, Stevens, Leppard, and others.

(2) 1-act opera by Casella, 1932.

Favola in (or per) Musica (It., 'fable for music'). 17th-cent. term for opera lib. of mythological or legendary character.

Favorite, La (The Favourite). 4-act opera by Donizetti to lib. by Royer, Vaëz, and Scribe. Prod. Paris 1840, New Orleans and London 1843. Also perf. under titles *Dalila, Leonora di Guzman,* and *Riccardo e Matilda,* as well as *La Favorita* (It.). It is a rev. of *L'Ange de Nisida,* in 3 acts by same librettists, comp. 1839 and unperformed.

Fayrfax, Robert (b Deeping Gate, Lincs., 1464; d St Albans, 1521). Eng. composer and organist. Member of Chapel Royal; attended Field of the Cloth of Gold, 1520. Comp. masses, motets, other church mus., and songs.

F.B.S.M. Fellow of the Birmingham Sch. of Mus.

Fedora. 3-act opera by Giordano to lib. by Colautti after Sardou's play (1882). Prod. Milan 1898, London and NY Met. 1906.

Feen, Die (The Fairies). 3-act opera by Wagner (his 1st) to lib. by composer after Gozzi's comedy *La donna serpente* (1762). Comp. 1833–4. Prod. Munich 1888, Birmingham 1969.

Feierlich (Ger. 'solemn', 'festive'). Expression mark used by Bruckner in his syms. and by Wagner for Siegfried's funeral march in *Götter-dämmerung.* Term is assoc. with public celebrations, 'solemn' for religious occasions, 'festive' for secular.

Feldman, Morton (b NY, 1926; d Buffalo, NY, 1987). Amer. composer. Studied comp. with Riegger and Stefan Wolpe. Later was influenced by the theories and ideas of *Cage, Earle *Brown, Christian Wolff, and David Tudor. Used indeterminacy and graphic notation in his mus. from *Projections* (1950–1). Another major influence was the painting of Jackson Pollock and W. de Kooning, and Feldman said that he tried, in sound, to emulate the world of their art. Low dynamic levels and occasional use of oscillators are also features of his work. Prin. comps.:

OPERA: *Neither* (S. Beckett) (1977).

ORCH: *Marginal Intersection* (1951); *Intersection I* (1951); *11 Instruments* (1953); *Atlantis* (1958); *Out of Last Pieces* (1958); *Structures* (1960–2); *In Search of an Orchestration* (1969); *On Time and the Instrumental Factor* (1969); *The Viola in My Life IV* (1971); *Cello and Orchestra* (1972); *String Quartet and Orchestra* (1973); *Piano and Orchestra* (1975); *Orchestra* (1976); *Oboe and Orchestra* (1976); *Flute and Orchestra* (1977–8); *Violin and Orchestra* (1979); *The Turfan Fragments* (1980); vn. conc. (1984).

CHORUS AND ORCH: *Chorus and Instruments I* (1963), *II* (1967); *Chorus and Orchestra I* (1972), *II* (1972); *Elemental Procedures* (1976).

INSTR. ENS: *Projections II* (1951), *V* (1951); *Durations V* (1961); *2 Pieces for 6 Instruments* (1964); *Ixion* (1965); *False Relationships and the Extended Ending* (1968); *Between Categories* (1969); *Madame Press Died Last Week at Ninety* (1970); *The Viola in My Life I and II* (1972); *Routine Investigations* (1976); *Why Patterns* (1978).

INSTR. ENS. AND VOICE(S): *For Franz Kline* (1962); *Vertical Thoughts V* (1965); *Journey to the End of Night (after Céline)* (1963); *The O'Hara Songs* (1963); *I met Heine in the Rue Fürstemberg* (1971); *The Rothko Chapel* (1971–2); *Voice and Instruments I* (1972), *II* (1974); *Voices and Instruments I* (1972), *II* (1972).

CHAMBER MUSIC: *Projection I–V* (1950–1); *Structures,* str. qt. (1951); *3 Pieces,* str. qt. (1956); *2 Instruments* (1958); *Durations I–IV* (1960–2); *De Kooning* (1963); *Vertical Thoughts I–IV* (1963); *The Viola in My Life III* (1970); *3 Clarinets, Cello and Piano* (1971); *Voice, Violin and Piano* (1976); *Spring of Chosroes* (1978); *String Quartet* (1979), No. 2 (1983); *Trio* (1980); *For John Cage* (1982).

PIANO(S): *Illusions* (1950); *2 Intermissions* (1950); *Intersection II and III* (1951, 1953); *Intermission, 5 pfs.* (1952); *Extensions III* (1952), *IV, 3 pfs.* (1960); *Piano Pieces* (1952–77); *2 Pieces,* 2 pf. (1954); *Piano Three Hands* (1957); *Piece,* 4 pf. (1957); *Piano Four Hands* (1958); *Last Pieces* (1963); *Vertical Thoughts I,* 2 pf. (1963); *2 Pieces,* 3 pf. (1966); *Pianos and Voices I,* 5 pf. (1971), *II,* 5 sop., 5 pf. (1972); *Piano* (1977); *Triadic Memories* (1981).

SOLO INSTR(S): *Intersection IV,* vc. (1964); *The King of Denmark,* perc. (1964); *Principal Sound,* org. (1980).

UNACCC. VOICE(S): *Christian Wolff in Cambridge* (1963); *Only,* 1 v. (1977); *3 Voices,* 3 sops. or v. and tape (1982).

Feldpartita or **Feldpartia** (Ger., 'field suite'). Suite for perf. in the open air by a military band. Haydn wrote 6 *Feldpartien.*

Feldpfeife (Ger., 'field pipe'). Renaissance version of the fife, or military fl., used in the Swiss infantry's fife-and-drum corps. Shrill sound due to narrow bore.

Fellowes, E(dmund) **H**(orace) (b London, 1870; d Windsor, 1951). Eng. musicologist and ed. Minor canon of St George's Chapel, Windsor, from 1900, and choirmaster 1924–7. Ed. complete works in 36 vols. of the *English Madrigal School* (pubd. 1913–24, rev. 1956 by Dart as *The English Madrigalists*), the *English School of Lutenist Song-Writers* (32 vols., 1920–32, partly rev. 1959–66 by Dart as *The English Lute-Songs*), and the complete works of * Byrd (20 vols., 1937–50, rev. 1962 by Dart, Brett, and Elliott). Also wrote books on the Eng. madrigalists, Byrd, and Gibbons. C.H. 1944.

Felsenstein, Walter (*b* Vienna, 1901; *d* East Berlin, 1975). Austrian opera producer and actor. Studied in Graz and at Vienna Burgtheater. Opera producer at Cologne (1932–4), Frankfurt (1934–6), Zürich (1938–40), and Schiller Th., Berlin (1940–4). Producer and Intendant, Berlin Komische Oper from 1947, setting new standards in imaginative and totally integrated prod. techniques, particularly in Janáček's *The Cunning Little Vixen*, Mozart's *Don Giovanni*, Bizet's *Carmen*, Offenbach's *Les Contes d' Hoffmann*, and Verdi's *La traviata*.

Felton, William (*b* Drayton, 1715; *d* Hereford, 1769). Eng. composer, organist, harpsichordist, and Anglican clergyman (vicar-choral, Hereford Cath.). His popular hpd. gavotte was adapted for the song *'Farewell Manchester'.

Feminine. Term used in such phrases as *feminine cadence* and *feminine ending* to denote relative weakness, e.g. the final chord is reached on a 'weak' beat of the bar. Second subjects in sonata-form are sometimes described as 'feminine', meaning gentler than the first subject. This is a hangover from the age when women were regarded as the weaker sex.

Fenby, Eric (William) (*b* Scarborough, 1906). Eng. organist, composer, and teacher. His unique claim to fame is that, at the age of 22 and totally unknown, he volunteered to go to Grez-sur-Loing to act as amanuensis to the blind and paralysed *Delius. Several of Delius's late works were dictated to Fenby, a laborious and sometimes acrimonious process recorded in Fenby's book *Delius as I knew him*. Also arr. some of Delius's mus., and since the composer's death in 1934 has been active in writing about it, and in working for the Delius Trust. Comps. incl. a sym. and the ov. *Rossini on Ilkla Moor*. Prof. RAM from 1964. Mus. dir. North Riding Training Coll. 1948-62. Art. dir. Delius centenary fest. 1962. O.B.E. 1962.

Fenice, Teatro La. Prin. and extremely beautiful Venetian opera house. Opened 1792, destroyed by fire 1836, rebuilt 1837, restored 1854 and 1938. Among operas f.p. there are Rossini's *L'Italiana in Algeri* and *Semiramide*, Bellini's *I Capuleti e i Montecchi*, Verdi's *Ernani*, *Rigoletto*, *La traviata*, and *Simone Boccanegra*, Stravinsky's *The Rake's Progress*, Britten's *The Turn of the Screw*, and Prokofiev's *The Fiery Angel*.

Fennimore and Gerda. Opera by Delius to his own lib., being '2 episodes in the life of *Niels Lyhne* in 11 pictures after the novel by J.P. Jacobsen'. Comp. 1908–10. Prod. Frankfurt 1919; London 1968, St Louis 1981. Intermezzo often perf. as concert item is derived from material in last scene.

Ferdinand III, Emperor of Austria (*b* Graz, 1608; *d* Vienna, 1657). Reigned from 1637. Est. It. opera in Vienna. Comp. *Drama musicum* (1649), Mass, motets, and other church mus. Monte-

verdi's 8th book of Madrigals (1638) is dedicated to him.

Ferencsik, János (*b* Budapest, 1907; *d* Budapest, 1984). Hung. cond. Studied Budapest Cons. Coach at Hung. State Opera 1927, cond. 1930. Mus. assistant at Bayreuth Fest. 1930–1. Cond. Vienna State Opera 1948–50, thereafter chief cond. Hung. State Opera and State Orch. London début 1957 (LPO), Amer. 1962.

Ferguson, Howard (*b* Belfast, 1908). N. Irish composer, pianist, and teacher. Studied pf. with Harold Samuel, 1922, and at RCM (comp. with R. O. Morris). Prof. at RAM 1948–63. Comps. incl. pf. conc., pf. sonata, Partita for orch., 2 vn. sonatas, octet for wind and str., *Amore Langueo* (soloist, ch., and orch.). Exercises in score-reading (with R. O. Morris).

Ferial. The word comes from the Lat. *feria*, 'feast day', but has by etymological perversity come to mean an ordinary day, as distinguished from a feast. Hence the application of 'Ferial Use' to liturgy and mus.

Fermata (It.), **Fermate** (Ger.). A pause ⌒. (Sometimes the use is a special one—the pause mark in a conc. which indicates the point at which the *cadenza begins.)

Fermer (Fr., 'to close'; past participle *fermé*). Used in org. mus. as indication to (1) close the swell box, or (2) put a particular stop out of action.

Fermo (It.). 'Fixed', in style of perf., as in *canto fermo*.

Ferne Klang, Der (The Distant Sound). 3-act opera by *Schreker to his own lib. Prod. Frankfurt 1912, BBC studio 1957.

Ferneyhough, Brian (*b* Coventry, 1943). Eng. composer. Studied Birmingham Sch. of Mus. 1961–3, and at RAM 1966–7 with L. Berkeley. Played in and comp. for brass bands. Studied in Holland with Ton de *Leeuw 1968–9. Emigrated to Switzerland 1969, studying at Basle Cons. with Klaus *Huber. Based in W. Ger. since 1973. Mus. of extreme complexity; elec. devices employed in some works. Works incl.: Sonatina for 3 cl. and bn. or bass cl. (1963); *Prometheus* for wind sextet (1965, rev. 1967); Sonata for 2 pf. (1966); 3 Pieces for pf.; *Sonatas* for str. qt. (1967); *Epicycle* for 20 str. (1968); *Missa brevis* for 12 vv. (1969); *Cassandra's Dream Song*, for solo fl. (1971); *Sieben Sterne* for org. (1969–70); *Firecycle Beta* for orch. (1969–71); *Transit* for 6 vv. and chamber orch. (1972–4, rev. 1975); *Time and Motion Study III* for 16 vv. with perc. and elecs. (1974); *Time and Motion Study II* for vc., tape, and elecs. (1973–6); *Unity Capsule* for solo fl. (1975–6); *Time and Motion Study I* for bass cl. (1971–7); *Funérailles* for str. sextet, db., and harp (1969–77); *La Terre est un homme* for orch. (1977–8); 2nd str. qt. (1979–80); *Lemma-Icon-Epigram*, pf. (1981); *Superscriptio*, piccolo (1981); *Carceri d'Invenzione I*, chamber orch. (1982).

Fernflöte (Ger., 'distant flute'). Soft metal org. stop of 8′ length and pitch.

Fernwerk (Ger. 'distant work'). Echo Manual of org.

Ferrabosco, Alfonso (*b* Bologna, 1543; *d* Bologna, 1588). It. composer, son of Domenico Ferrabosco who was maestro di cappella at Basilica Vaticana, Rome, from 1546. Settled in Eng. *c.*1560, entering service of Elizabeth I. In It. 1569–71. Left Eng. 1578 to enter service of Duke of Savoy. Comp. madrigals, motets, and lute pieces. In contest with *Byrd, each set plainsong *Miserere* in 40 different ways.

Ferrabosco, Alfonso (*b* Greenwich, *c.*1575; *d* Greenwich, 1628). Son of above. Violinist in service of James I. Comp. mus. for several of Jonson's masques. Was made 'Composer of King's Music' to Charles I. Skilled player of lyra viol, for which he wrote fantasies. His 3 sons, Alfonso, Henry, and John, were also musicians in royal service, John becoming organist of Ely Cath.

Ferrari, Luc (*b* Paris, 1929). Fr. composer. Studied Versailles Cons. 1946–8, École Normale de Musique, Paris, 1948–50 (under Honegger). Joined *Groupe de Musique Concrète* at Fr. Radio, 1958, and on its dissolution that year re-formed it, with *Schaeffer, as *Groupe de Récherche Musicale* of which he was a dir. until 1966. Prof. at Rheinische Musikschule, Cologne, 1964–6. Comps. mainly on tape.

Ferras, Christian (*b* Le Touquet, 1933; *d* Paris, 1982). Fr. violinist. Studied at Nice with Bistesi, and with Calvet at Paris Cons. Paris début as conc. soloist 1946. Appeared as conc. soloist and recitalist in all leading mus. centres. Gave f. Eng. p. of Fricker's *Rapsodia Concertante,* Cheltenham 1954.

Ferrier, Kathleen (Mary) (*b* Higher Walton, Lancs., 1912; *d* London, 1953). Eng. cont. Began mus. career as pianist and accompanist in N. of Eng. competitive fests. Worked as telephone switchboard operator. Entered singing competition, Carlisle 1937, winning Rose Bowl. Studied singing with Thomas Duerdon, Dr J. E. Hutchinson, and Roy Henderson. London début in *Messiah,* Westminster Abbey 1943, after which she rose rapidly to a leading position among Brit. singers in Elgar's *Gerontius,* Bach's *St Matthew Passion,* and other works. Opera début as Lucretia in Britten's *The Rape of Lucretia,* Glyndebourne 1946. Sang Gluck's *Orfeo,* Glyndebourne 1947. Became noted exponent of Mahler's *Das Lied von der Erde* under batons of Walter and Barbirolli, and frequently appeared in recitals with Britten and Pears. The beauty of her v., combined with a warm and humorous personality, endeared her to audiences, and her early death from cancer was

profoundly and widely mourned. Last appearance was at CG 1953 in *Orfeo,* cond. Barbirolli. C.B.E. 1953. Royal Phil. Soc. Gold Medal, 1953.

Fes (Ger.). The note F♭. **Feses, F♭♭.**

Fesca, Friedrich (Ernst) (*b* Magdeburg, 1789; *d* Karlsruhe, 1826). Ger. violinist and composer. *Konzertmeister* at Karlsruhe from 1815. Wrote 2 operas, 3 syms., 16 str. qts., and church mus. His son, Alexander Ernst (*b* Karlsruhe, 1820; *d* Brunswick, 1849) comp. 4 operas and some chamber mus.

Festa, Costanzo (*b c.*1490; *d* Rome, 1545). It. composer. Choirmaster at Vatican. Comp. masses, motets, and other church mus., his *Te Deum* still being sung at election of new Pope. Also wrote madrigals, one known in Eng. as *Down in a Flowery Vale.*

Festal. Applied in the distinction of ecclesiastical feast days from ordinary, or *Ferial days.

Feste Romane (Roman Festivals). Orch. work by Respighi comp. 1928 and f.p. NY 1929 cond. Toscanini. In 4 sections entitled *Circus Maximus, The Jubilee, The October Festival,* and *Epiphany.*

Festgesang (Festive Hymn). Work for 2 male ch. and brass by Mendelssohn to words by Prof. Prölss of Freiberg, comp. for fest. at Leipzig 1840 in honour of invention of printing by Gutenberg and f.p. in open market-place. (*Lobgesang* was comp. for same occasion.) 2nd no. of *Festgesang* was adapted by W. H. Cummings to words of hymn *Hark, the herald angels sing'.

Festin de l'araignée, Le (The Spider's Banquet). Ballet-pantomime with mus. by *Roussel to scenario by G. de Voisins and choreog. by Staats. Prod. Paris 1913. Orch. suite (1912).

Festing, Michael (Christian) (*b* London, *c.*1680; *d* London, 1752). Eng. violinist and composer. Pupil of *Geminiani. First public appearance 1724. Played in King's Th. orch. 1727; dir. of the It. Opera from 1737. Mus. dir., Ranelagh Gardens 1742–52. Comp. concs., cantatas, and vn. solos.

Festivals (from Lat. *festivalis,* 'festival'). The Eng. derivative 'festival' has come to be applied to gatherings in which one or several of the arts is celebrated. Its first mus. use was possibly the Fest. of the Sons of the Clergy which, from 1698, used an orch. as part of what was really only an elaborate church service. The oldest Eng. fest. in the truer sense is the 3 Choirs Fest., alternating annually between the cath. cities of Gloucester, Hereford, and Worcester. In the 19th cent. the emphasis was on choral mus., and the Handel Fest., the Birmingham, Leeds, Sheffield, and Norwich Fests. flourished. Abroad, the Haydn Fests. in Austria and the 1845 Beethoven Fest. in Bonn were outstanding events. Other famous continental fests. are those at Bayreuth (devoted exclusively to Wagner) and Salzburg (based on

Mozart, but with wider scope). Since the end of the 1939–45 war, fests. have developed alongside the growth of tourism. Almost any attractive town (and several unattractive ones) has considered establishing a fest. as a means of attracting visitors. Among the best and longest est. are those at Edinburgh, Cheltenham, Bath, Harrogate, Aldeburgh, York, Haslemere, Holland, Aix-en-Provence, Spoleto, Berkshire (Boston, Mass.), Hollywood Bowl, Ravinia Park (Chicago), etc. Some fests. have a theme (one particular composer or one type of mus.); others are just a random coll. of artistic events.

Festivo (Festive). No. 3 of Sibelius's 1st set of *Scènes historiques* for orch., Op. 25, comp. 1899, rev. 1911.

Festspiel (Ger., 'Festival-play'). A term applied to certain mus. stage works, or works in which mus. has some part. Wagner extended the term in the title to his *Ring* tetralogy, which he called a *Bühnenfestspiel* (Stage-festival-play) and still further in the title of *Parsifal,* described as a *Bühnenweihfestspiel* (Stage-consecration festival-play).

Fêtes galantes. Two sets of songs for v. and pf. by Debussy to poems by Verlaine. The first version, comp. 1882, comprised *Pantomime, En sourdine, Mandoline, Clair de Lune,* and *Fantoches,* but three of the songs were revised in 1891–2 and were pubd. in 1903 as Set I (*En sourdine, Fantoches* and *Clair de Lune*). Set II, comp. 1904, comprises *Les ingénus, Le faune,* and *Colloque sentimental.* No. 2 of Set II orch. Roland-Manuel 1923, No. 3 orch. Beydts 1929. *Mandoline* and *Pantomime* were issued separately.

Fétis, François (Joseph) (b Mons, 1784; d Brussels, 1871). Belgian critic, historian, composer, and organist. Studied Paris Cons. Org., Douai 1813–18. Prof. of comp., Paris Cons., 1821, librarian 1826–30. Founded and ed. *Revue musicale* 1827–33. Dir., Brussels Cons. from 1833. Reputation est. by *Biographie universelle des musiciens* (8 vols., 1835–44, 2nd edn. 1860–5; suppl. by Pougin, 2 vols., 1878–80). Also author of vols. of history, theoretical works, and biographies of Paganini and Stradivari. Comp. 7 operas, 2 syms., 3 pf. quintets, sonatas, church mus., etc.

Feuermann, Emanuel (b Kolomyja, Lwów, 1902; d NY, 1942). Austrian cellist. Public début at age 11. Teacher of vc. at Cologne Cons. 1917–23, at Berlin Hochschule 1929–33. Settled in USA 1938 becoming Amer. cit. Frequent soloist with leading orchs.

Feuersnot (Trial by fire). 1-act opera by R. Strauss to lib. *(Singgedicht)* by E. von Wolzogen based on Flemish legend. Comp. 1900–1. Prod. Dresden 1901, London 1910, Philadelphia 1927.

Feux d'artifice (Fireworks). Title of pf. prelude by Debussy, last of the 2nd book of 12 (1912–13).

Févin, Antoine de (b?Arras, c.1473; d Blois, c.1512). Fr. composer. High contemporary reputation as composer of church mus., incl. several masses.

Février, Henry (b Paris, 1875; d Paris, 1957). Fr. composer, pupil of Massenet and Pugno at Paris Cons. Comp. several operas incl. *Monna Vanna* (1909) and *Gismonda* (1918).

ff. Abbreviation for **fortissimo,* very loud. Composers occasionally use *fff* and even more.

Ffrangçon-Davies, David (Thomas) (b Bethesda, 1855; d London, 1918). Welsh bar. Originally a clergyman, he took up singing, trained at GSM, and made stage début in opera in London, 1890. Toured USA and Canada 1896–8. High reputation in oratorio. Teacher, RAM 1903–7. Illness cut short career 1907. His daughter Gwen (b 1891) began her career as a sop., singing in *Boughton's *Immortal Hour,* and later became a leading actress.

Fg. Abbreviation for **Fagott* (Ger.), bassoon.

F.G.S.M. Fellow of Guildhall Sch. of Mus. and Drama.

Fiala, Joseph (b Lochovice, 1754; d Donaueschingen, 1816). Cz. composer, oboist, and cellist. Studied in Prague. Oboist in court band at Oettingen-Wallerstein, 1774–7, during which time he pubd. 6 str. qts. Went to Munich 1777, meeting Mozart, of whom he became close friend. Played in Archbishop of Salzburg's orch. 1778–85, and in Vienna 1785–90. Kapellmeister at Donaueschingen from 1792. Works incl. 12 str. qts., syms., pieces for wind band, duos, and sonatas.

Fiato (It., 'breath'). Wind instr. are *stromenti a fiato.*

Fibich, Zdeněk (Antonin Václav) (b Všebořice, 1850; d Prague, 1900). Cz. composer. Studied with his mother and in Vienna, Prague, and Leipzig (1865–7) under Moscheles and E. F. Richter. Taught piano in Paris 1868–9. Returning to Prague, worked as theatre cond., but lived mainly from compositions. Was first Romantic Cz. composer, in this respect standing apart from Dvořák, Smetana, and Janáček. Among his most remarkable achievements are his concert and stage melodramas, the most ambitious ever written, especially the trilogy *Hippodamia* (1888–91), and his 376 *Moods, Impressions and Reminiscences* for solo piano (1892–9), a 'diary' of his love for his piano pupil, the writer Anežka Schulzová (1868–1905). His operas include *Bukovin* (1870–1), *Blaník* (1874–7), *Nevěsta mesinská* (The Bride of Messina) (1882–3), *Bouře* (The Tempest, after Shakespeare) (1893–4), *Hedy* (1894–5), *Šárka* (1896–7), and *Pád Arkuna* (The Fall of Arkona) (1898–9). Wrote much incidental music, 3 syms., several sym.-poems, chamber mus., and over 200 songs. His sym.-poem *At Twilight* (V podvečer) (1893) contains the celebrated *Poem.*

Ficher, Jacobo (*b* Odessa, 1896; *d* Buenos Aires, 1978). Russ. composer and violinist. Studied St Petersburg/Petrograd Cons. 1912–17. In 1923 settled in Argentina, founding contemporary mus. group, conducting, and after 1956 teaching comp. at Nat. Cons., Buenos Aires. Comp. incl. 2 Chekhov chamber operas, *The *Bear* (1952) and *Proposal of Marriage* (1956), 3 pf. concs., 8 syms., sax. qt., fl. conc., 7 pf. sonatas, wind quintet, 4 str. qts., etc.

Fiddle. Colloquial term for any kind of bowed instr., especially the vn., or in reference to its use as a 'folk' instr. (as in Mahler's 4th Sym. where a solo vn., specially tuned, is instructed to play *wie ein Fiedel* ('like a fiddle', in folk style). Also name for the medieval ancestor of the vn.

Fiddle Fugue. Nickname for org. fugue in D minor by Bach (because it was arr. from an earlier version for solo vn., 1720).

Fidelio, oder Die eheliche Liebe (Fidelio, or Married Love). Opera in 2 acts by Beethoven, Op. 72, to lib. by Josef Sonnleithner based on Bouilly's *Léonore, ou L'Amour conjugal*. F.p. in orig. 3-act version, Vienna 1805. Reduced to 2 acts by Stefan von Breuning 1806, prod. Vienna 1806. Further rev., and lib. rev. by G. F. Treitschke, 1814, prod. Vienna 1814, London 1832, NY 1839. Orig. 1805 version, under title *Leonore*, reconstructed in edn. by E. Prieger, 1905. Of the 4 ovs., *Fidelio* (comp. for 1814 revival but not ready for f.p.) is now used in the th. *Leonora* No. 2 is thought to have been comp. 1804–5, No. 3 in 1806, and No. 1 in 1807 for a projected Prague perf. It is now customary to perform No. 3 as an entr'acte before final scene. Bouilly's lib. was also the basis of *Gaveaux's *Léonore* (Paris 1798), *Paër's *Leonora* (Dresden 1804), and *Mayr's *L'Amor coniugale* (Padua 1805).

Fiedler, Arthur (*b* Boston, Mass., 1894; *d* Boston, 1979). Amer. cond. Studied with his father, member of Boston S.O., then in Berlin with the violinist Willy Hess. Joined Boston S.O. as violinist 1915, later violist. Formed Boston Sinfonietta, conducting it in Boston and on tour. In 1930 became cond. of Boston 'Pops' concerts, spreading their fame through recordings.

Fiedler, (August) **Max** (*b* Zittau, 1859; *d* Stockholm, 1939). Ger. cond., trained Leipzig Cons. 1877–80. Taught at Hamburg Cons. from 1882, becoming dir. 1903–8. Cond., Hamburg Phil. from 1904; Boston S.O. 1908–12; mus. dir. in Essen 1916–34. Comp. sym., ov., and pf. quintet.

Field, John (*b* Dublin, 1782; *d* Moscow, 1837). Irish pianist and composer. Pupil in Dublin of Giordani, making début aged 9. In London became pupil of *Clementi, whose pfs. he exhibited and who took him to Fr., Ger., and Russia, where he settled in St Petersburg in 1803, becoming teacher and touring Europe as virtuoso pianist. His importance as a composer for the pf.

has only latterly been recognized. He invented the style and name *Nocturne* for short pieces, composing 19. Wrote 7 pf. concs., 4 sonatas, and other works. Schumann and Liszt admired his work, and Chopin developed the Nocturne form.

Field-Hyde, Margaret (*b* Cambridge, 1905). Eng. sop. and violinist. Studied singing with her father, a pupil of *García, and in Frankfurt and Paris. Début 1928 in Cambridge revival of Purcell's *King Arthur*. Specialist in Purcell and Bach, but also in works by Lutyens and other contemporaries. Founded Golden Age Singers 1950, touring Europe and USA with them.

Fiery Angel, The (*Ognenny Angel;* sometimes known as *The Flaming Angel*). Opera in 5 acts by Prokofiev to his lib. based on novel by V. Bryusov (1908). Comp. 1919–23, rev. 1926–7. F.p. Paris (concert) 1954, staged Venice 1955, London and NY 1965. Prokofiev's 3rd Sym. uses themes from the opera.

Fiesco, Giulio (*b* Ferrara, *c*.1519; *d* Modena, *c*.1586). It. madrigal composer and lutenist.

Fife. Ancient side-blown instr. like a high-pitched fl., frequently used in military bands. Modern drum and fife bands incl. low-pitched fls.

Fifteenth. A high-pitched *Diapason org. stop sounding 2 octaves above the note played; 2′ length and pitch on manuals, 4′ on pedals.

Fifth. Interval consisting of 3 whole-tones and a semitone, so-called because no. of notes from one extreme of the interval to the other in the diatonic scale is 5. A perfect 5th is the distance from, for example, C to G. From C up to G♭ is a diminished fifth, and from C up to G♯ is an augmented fifth. See *Consecutive Fifth*.

'Fifths' Quartet (Quintenquartett). Name for Haydn's Str. Qt. in D minor, Op. 76, No. 2 (1797–8) because it begins with melodic leaps of a 5th.

Figural, figured (Eng.); **figuré** (Fr.); **figurato** (It.); **figural, figuriert** (Ger.). Florid. (1) A 'figured chorale', is one in which the melody is acc. by quicker notes in the other parts.

(2) In solo vocal mus. the word implies *Coloratura*.

Figuralmusik. See *Musica figurata*.

Figurato, figurata (It.). Same as *colorato, colorata,* i.e. treated in the manner of *Coloratura*.

Figure. (1) In mus. structure, this word usually carries the same meaning as *Motif*. A 'figure of accompaniment' refers to the mus. cell from which a certain type of song acc. may be evolved.

(2) In dancing the word implies a set of movements by the dancers as a body, forming a distinct division of the whole. This element is prominent in a *Figure Dance*, as opposed to a *Step Dance*, in which it is largely absent.

Figured Bass. See *Basso continuo*.

Filare la voce, filar il tuono (It.), **filer la voix (le son)** (Fr.). To draw out the voice (tone). The *messa di voce*; or sometimes understood to mean the holding of a long note without any dynamic fluctuation.

Fille aux cheveux de lin, La (The girl with the flaxen hair). Pf. piece by Debussy, No. 8 of his *Préludes*, Book I. Comp. Jan. 1910, f.p. London 1910. Based on poem by Leconte de Lisle.

Fille de Madame Angot, La (Mme Angot's Daughter). 3-act operetta by Lecocq to lib. by Clairville, Siraudin, and Koning, after Maillot's vaudeville *Madame Angot* (1796). Prod. Brussels 1872, London 1873, NY 1873.

Fille du Régiment, La (The Daughter of the Regiment). 2-act opera by Donizetti to lib. by V. de Saint-Georges and Bayard. Prod. Paris 1840, London 1843, New Orleans 1847.

Fille mal gardée, La (The Unchaperoned Girl). 2-act ballet to lib. by Dauberval orig. to medley of Fr. songs and airs. Prod. Bordeaux 1789. For 1828 revival in Paris, Hérold provided new score, using some of orig. tunes, extracts from Rossini and Donizetti operas, and his own mus. Mus. for 1864 Berlin version comp. by Hertel. For 1960 London revival to Ashton choreog., John Lanchbery prepared new score based mainly on Hérold but with Hertel's 'Clog Dance'.

Film Music. Mus. written to acc. action in documentary and feature films. In the days of silent films a pianist or small orch. in the cinema pit provided a mus. commentary on the action, usually by a selection of appropriate popular operatic and orch. items. But the first piece of 'original' film mus. was written by Saint-Saëns (Op. 128) for H. Lavedan's film *L'Assassinat du Duc de Guise*, 1908.

An ambitious development for its day was the silent film made in 1924 of Strauss's *Der Rosenkavalier*. For this, mus. from the opera was adapted for th. orch., with some additional items for extra scenes. With the advent of the 'talkie' and the development of the sound-track, the opportunities for the use of illustrative mus. were gradually seized and exploited by composers. In Hollywood, the capital of the cinema industry, mus. for many films was written by Erich *Korngold and later by Miklós *Rózsa. Distinguished film music was written by Bernard *Herrmann for Welles's *Citizen Kane* and for a series of Hitchcock films, notably *Psycho*. Fr. composers such as *Auric wrote for films, and in Britain practically all the leading composers—Britten, Walton, Vaughan Williams, Rawsthorne, Bax, Ireland, Alwyn, Arnold, Richard Rodney Bennett, and many others—have written film mus. Some of the greatest film mus. was written by Prokofiev for Eisenstein's *Alexander Nevsky*, and Shostakovich and Khachaturian have also written effective film scores. Walton's *Henry V*

and Vaughan Williams's *Scott of the Antarctic* are highly regarded. Mention should also be made of the scores by Michel Legrand, John Barry, and Burt Bacharach, while Addinsell's clever pastiche of a romantic pf. conc., the 'Warsaw' Conc. from *Dangerous Moonlight*, perhaps made a wider audience aware of the potency of film music. There have been examples of brilliant use in a film of mus. which was not written specially for it, e.g. Rakhmaninov's C minor pf. conc. in *Brief Encounter*; Mozart's C major pf. conc. No. 21, K467 (2nd movement) in *Elvira Madigan*, and the Adagietto from Mahler's 5th sym. in *Death in Venice*. And there is Schoenberg's *Accompaniment to a Film Scene,* Op. 34 (1930), comp. for no particular film or scene.

Filter. Elec. device permitting selective transmission of specified frequencies of the input signal by attenuating, or filtering out, unwanted frequencies.

Filtz, (Johann) **Anton** (*b* Eichstätt, 1733; *d* Mannheim, 1760). Ger.-Bohemian composer and cellist. Pupil of Stamitz. Prin. cellist in famous Mannheim orch. Wrote over 40 syms., concs. for vc. and fl., chamber mus., etc.

Fin (Fr.). End.

Fin (It.). Same as **Fino*.

Final. (1) (Eng.). The note on which the modal scale ends (see *Modes*), as on the keynote of the major or minor scale.
  (2) (Fr.). **Finale*.

Finale (It.). End. The last movement of a work in several movements, i.e. sym., conc., suite, sonata, etc. Also the ens. ending an act of an opera.

Finck, Herman (*b* London, 1872; *d* London, 1939). Eng. composer and cond. Studied GSM. At 16 was pianist and violinist at Palace Th., London, becoming cond. there 1900. Mus. dir. Drury Lane 1922–31. Comp. comic operas, such as *Katinka*, and th. mus. Best known for his short piece *In the Shadows* (1910).

Finck, Hermann (*b* Pirna, 1527; *d* Wittenberg, 1558). Ger. organist and composer of motets, etc. Wrote treatise *Practica Musica* (1556).

Fine, Irving (*b* Boston, Mass., 1914; *d* Natick, Mass., 1962). Amer. composer and critic. Studied Harvard Univ. 1933–9 and in Paris with *Boulanger. Ass. prof. of mus., Harvard, 1939–50. Chairman, sch. of creative arts, Brandeis Univ., from 1950. Mus. tended towards neo-classicism; in his last years he was attracted by 12-note technique. Works incl. Sym. (1962), *Music for Modern Dance* (1941), 3 *Choruses from Alice in Wonderland* (1942), *Mutability*, 6 songs for mez. and pf. (1952), *The Hour Glass* for ch. and orch. (1949), vn. sonata, str. qt., etc.

Fine, Vivian (*b* Chicago, 1913). Amer. composer. Studied pf. at Chicago Mus. Coll. 1919–22 and at Amer. Cons., Chicago, 1925–31, later studying comp. with *Sessions 1934–42 and orchestration with George Szell, 1943. Has held several teaching posts, and from 1931 championed modern pf. mus. Her works incl. pf. conc., str. qt., vn. sonata, *Alcestis* (ballet for Martha Graham), and *A Guide to the Life Expectancy of a Rose* for sop., ten., and chamber ens.

Fingal's Cave (The Hebrides) (*Die Hebriden (Fingals Höhle)*). Ov. in B minor, Op. 26, by Mendelssohn, who is said to have invented the prin. theme while on a visit to the Hebrides and the island of Staffa in 1829. (In fact he jotted down the theme in a letter written before he went to Staffa. The orig. version was called *The Lonely Island*.) Comp. 1830, rev. 1832. After rev. the work was f.p., as *The Isles of Fingal*, London, CG 1832. It is in effect a descriptive tone-poem.

Finger Board. In a str. instr., the long strip of hard wood over which the str. are stretched.

Finger, Gottfried (*b* Olomouc, *c*.1660; *d* Mannheim, 1730). Moravian composer who settled in England at royal court 1687–1704 when he became musician to Queen of Prussia. Kapellmeister, court of Gotha, from 1717. Wrote operas, th. mus., concs., sonatas, etc.

Fingering (of kbd. instr.). Since the end of the 18th cent., this has been standardized on something like modern principles. Before this period there was a good deal of passing of the 3 middle fingers over one another and comparatively little use of the thumb and little finger; this was partly due to the fall of the keys being much shallower than with modern instr. The pf. killed finger-crossing, since it demanded an actual blow (properly a blow by pressure—one sufficient to *throw* the hammer at the strings, yet so exactly controlled as to throw it with either the greater force required by a fortissimo or the lesser required by a pianissimo).

Clementi firmly est. the modern principles of fingering: his use of the thumb was the same as ours, except that he did not use it on the black keys, as is sometimes done today. These modern principles incl. the division of a scale into 2 groups of 3 and 4 notes respectively, with the thumb as the pivot between them, the playing of arpeggio passages on the basis of the octave, some adaptation of fingering to the hand of the individual player, the planning of the fingering of a passage by working backwards from the point at which it is ultimately to arrive, and the division of such a passage into 'physical groups' as units, each of these being considered as a chord.

Organ fingering follows much the same principles as pf. fingering but, as the nature of the instr. generally calls for a perfect legato, more substitution of finger is required, a key often being depressed by one finger and then held by another, so freeing the first for use on another key.

See also *English fingering*.

Finite Canon. A *canon which is not repeated, the converse of 'perpetual' or 'infinite' canon.

Finlandia. Short work for orch., Op. 26, by Sibelius. Comp. 1899 as final tableau of nationalist pageant to raise money for a press pension fund in Helsinki. Rev. 1900 and f.p. Helsinki, July 1900. Its patriotic fervour, though no folk-song material was used, led to its adoption as a symbol of Finnish nat. aspirations. F.p. in Eng. 1905 (Liverpool, cond. Bantock).

Finney, Ross Lee (*b* Wells, Minn., 1906). Amer. composer and teacher. Studied mus. at Univ. of Minnesota, with Boulanger in Paris 1927–8, with Berg in Vienna 1931–2, and with Roger Sessions intermittently 1929–48. Taught at Smith Coll., 1929–47. Prof. of mus., Univ. of Michigan from 1949, where he est. elec. mus. studio. Since 1950 he has combined in his mus. tonalism with 12-note and serial techniques. Works incl. 4 syms., 8 str. qts., vn. sonatas, vc. sonatas, pf. qt., pf. quintets, str. quintets, 2 pf. concs., vn. conc., and choral pieces.

Finnila, Birgit (*b* Falkenberg, Swed., 1931). Swed. mez. Studied with Roy Henderson, RCM. Exponent of Wagner, Mahler, Brahms, etc. Prof. début Göteborg 1963.

Finnissy, Michael (*b* London, 1946). Studied at RCM with Bernard Stevens and Humphrey Searle and later with R. Vlad in Rome. Formed mus. dept. at London Sch. of Contemporary Dance, teaching there 1969–74. Works incl.:

MUSIC THEATRE: *Circle, Chorus, and Formal Act*, bar., women's ch., perc., ch., 6 sword-dancers, 4 mimes, small ens. (1973); *Mysteries*: 1. *The Parting of Darkness from Light*, 2 ten., 2 bar., bass. 2. *The Earthly Paradise*, mez., ten., bass, 2 actors, ens. 3. *The Great Flood*, ten., 4 actors, 4 actresses, 2 instr., 3 perc. 4. *The Prophecy of Daniel*, sop., bar., actor, ch., hp., perc. 5. *The Parliament of Heaven*, 3 sop., mez., ten., 2 actors, 3 ch., children's ch., ens. 6. *The Annunciation*. 7. *The Betrayal and Crucifixion of Jesus of Nazareth*. 8. *The Deliverance of Souls*, 2 sop., mez., 2 ten., 2 bar., bass, 4 ch., children's ch., orch. (1972–9); *Bouffe*, for a person alone on stage (1975); *Mr Punch*, speaker, 5 instr., perc. (1976–7); *Vaudeville*, mez., bar., 2 mimes, 6 instr., perc. (1983).

ORCH: *Song II* and *IV* (1963–9); *Song X* (1968–75); *Offshore* (1975–6); *Pathways of Sun and Stars* (1976); *Sea and Sky* (1979–80).

VOICE(S) AND INSTR: *Le dormeur du val*, mez. and 8 instr. (1963–8); *From the Revelations of St John the Divine*, sop., fl., str. sextet (1965–70); *Horrorzone*, sop., fl., hn., pf. duet (1966–71); *Song III*, sop., 4 instr. (1963–9); *Folk-Song Set*, sop. and 9 instr. (1969–70, rev. 1975–6); *Song XI*, sop., cl. (1968–75); *Jeanne d'Arc*, sop., ten., vc., small orch.

(1967–71); *Babylon*, mez. and ens. (1971); *World*, 2 sop., cont., ten., bar., bass, orch. (1968–74); *Tsuru-Kame*, sop., 3 chorus sop., instr., and dancers (1971–3); *Commedia dell' incomprehensibile Potere che alcune Donne hanno sugli Uomini*, sop., counterten., vc., cembalo (1973–5); *Orfeo*, vv. and instr. (1974–5); *Medea*, vv. and instr. (1973–6); *Mine Eye awake*, sop., pf. (1977); *Gorō*, ten. and 6 instr. (1978); *Sir Tristran*, sop., cl., pf., vn., va., vc. (1978); *. . . fairest noonday . . .*, ten., pf. (1979); *Talawva*, mez., instr. (1979); Pf. Conc. No. 5, pf., mez., and ens. (1980); *Green Bushes*, cont., pf. (1980); *Duru-duru*, mez., fl., pf., 1 perc. (1981); *Warara*, ten., fl., cl., 2 perc. (1982); *Anninnia*, sop., pf. (1982); *Whitman*, vv., instr. (1980–3); *Botany Bay*, mez., fl., cl. or ob. (1983); *Soda Fountain*, sop., mez., cont., ten., 2 pairs of cymbals (1983); *Ngano*, mez., ten., ch., fl., 2 perc. (1983–4).

UNACC. VOICES: *Cipriano*, 10 vv. (1974); *Tom Fool's Wooing*, 14 vv. (1975–8); *Kelir*, 6 vv. (1981); *Australian Sea Shanties I* (1983).

INSTR. ENS: *Afar*, 7 instr. (1966–7); *As when upon a tranced summer night*, 3 vc., pf., 2 perc. (1966–8); *Song VI*, fl., ob., vc., cembalo (1963–8); *Piece to honour Igor Stravinsky*, fl., va., hp. (1971); *Transformations of the Vampire*, cl., vn., va., 3 perc. (1968–71); *n*, 1–4 instr. (1969); *Evening*, 6 instr. and perc. (1974); Pf. Conc. No. 1 (1975), No. 2 (1975–6), No. 3 (1978), No. 7 (1981); *Lost Lands*, 5 instr. (1977); *Long Distance*, pf. and 14 instr. (1977–8); *Alongside*, 13 instr. and perc. (1979); *Kagami-Jishi*, fl., hp. (1979); *Lord Melbourne*, sop., cl., pf. (1980); *Nobody's Jig*, str. qt. (1980–1); *Jiseī*, vc. and 5 instr. (1981); *Keroiylu*, ob., bn., pf. (1981); *Aijal*, fl., ob. or cl., 1 perc. (1982); *Banumbirr*, fl., cl., vn., vc., pf. (1982); *Tya*, 11 instr. and perc. (1982); *Mississippi Hornpipes*, vn., pf. (1982); *Ouraa*, 10 instr. and perc. (1982–3); *Australian Sea Shanties II*, recorder consort (1983); *Cātana*, 8 instr. and perc. (1984).

SOLO VOICE: *Song I*, sop. (1963–9); *Songs XIV, XV*, sop. (1968–75); *Song XVI*, sop. (1976); *Ohi! ohi! ohi!*, mez. (1978); *Mountainfall*, mez. (1978); *Moon's goin' down*, solo instr. (or v.) (1980).

PIANO: *Song V* (1963–9); *Songs VII–IX* (1963–8); *Autumnall* (1968–71); *Snowdrift* (1972); *Wild Flowers*, 2 pf. (1974); *Ives* (1974); *Verdi Transcriptions* (1974); *English Country Tunes* (1977); *all. fall. down.* (1977); *Kemp's Morris*, pianist wearing morris bells (1978); *Piano Studies* (1976–8); *Fast Dances, Slow Dances* (1978–9); *Grainger* (1979); Pf. Conc. No. 4 (1978–80); *Boogie-Woogie* (1980); *Nancarrow* (1980); Pf. Conc. No. 6 (1980–1); *Liz* (1980–1); *Free Setting* (1981); *Reels* (1980–1); *White Rain*, pf. or clavichord (1981); *Rushes* (1981); *Hikkai* (1982–3); *Australian Sea Shanties III* (1983); *Tango* (1984).

SOLO INSTR: *Piece to honour Igor Stravinsky*, fl. (1967); *Song XII*, bass cl. (1968–75); *Song XIII*, vn. (1968–75); *Alice I*, db., *II*, vc., *III*, vc. and 1 perc. (1970–5); *Ru Tchou*, perc. (1975); *Song XVII*, guitar (1976); *Song XVIII*, db. (1976); *All the trees they are so high*, vn. (1977); *Doves Figary*, vc. (1976–7); *Runnin' Wild*, ob. (or sax.) (1978); *Sikangnuqa*, fl. (1979); *Pavasiya*, ob. (1979); *Hinomi*, perc. (1979); *Stomp*, pf. accordeon (1981); *Andimironnai*, vc. (1981); *Yalli*, vc. (1981); *Terekemme*, cembalo (1981); *Marrngu*, cl. (1982); *Nasiye*, guitar (1982); *Dilok*, ob. and 1 perc. (1982); *Gerhana*, perc. (1982); *Cirit*, cl. (1982); *Uzundara*, cl. (1983); *Sepevi*, db. (1982–3); *Ulpirra*, bass fl. (1982–3); *The Eureka Flag*, picc. (1983).

Fino (It.). As far as, e.g. *Fino al segno*, As far as the sign ($).

Finta giardiniera, La (The Feigned Gardener's Girl). Opera buffa in 3 acts (K196) by Mozart to lib. attrib. Petrosellini, written for *Anfossi (1774), and altered by Coltellini. Prod. Munich 1775, NY 1927, London 1930.

Finta semplice, La (The Feigned Simpleton). Opera buffa in 3 acts (K51) by Mozart to lib. by Coltellini, after lib. by Goldoni first set by Perillo (1764). Prod. Salzburg 1769, London (Paumgartner ed.) 1956, Boston, Mass., 1961.

Finzi, Gerald (Raphael) (*b* London, 1901; *d* Oxford, 1956). Eng. composer. Studied mus. with Ernest *Farrar at Harrogate, 1914–16, and with *Bairstow at York, 1917–22. Studied counterpoint with R. O. Morris in London, 1925, and taught comp. at RAM 1930–33. After marriage in 1933, he retired to isolated life in countryside, building his own house at Ashmansworth, nr. Newbury. Formed Newbury String Players, 1939. Worked in Ministry of War Transport, 1941–5. For the Newbury players he revived and ed. many 18th cent. works by Eng. composers such as Boyce, Stanley, and Mudge. Also worked to obtain publication of mus. by Ivor *Gurney, whom he never met. Was collector of rare books and grower of rare apples.

His works, some of them spread over many years and constantly revised, can be broadly linked to the Eng. tradition of Elgar and Vaughan Williams, but the influence on him of these composers can be overstressed. His settings of Eng. poetry, particularly of Thomas Hardy, have a distinctive individuality, with musical imagery to match the verbal. Nor would it be just to describe him as a miniaturist, for such works as *For St Cecilia*, the *Intimations of Immortality*, and the cello concerto show an ability to handle larger forms. Through Parry, he reached back to J. S. Bach in the vocal style of his masterpiece, the cantata *Dies Natalis*; and the same fluent imaginative vision gives an unfading emotional power to his Shakespeare song-cycle *Let us Garlands Bring* and to his touching Christmas work *In terra pax*. Prin.works:

ORCH: *Introit*, vn. and orch. (1925, rev. 1935, 1942); *New Year Music* (1926, rev. c.1946); *Eclogue*, pf. and str. (1920s, rev. 1940s); *Romance*, str. (1928); *The Fall of the Leaf* (1929, rev. 1939–41, orch. completed by H. Ferguson); cl. conc., str. (1948–9); *Grand Fantasia and Toccata*, pf. and orch. (*Fantasia* 1928, rev. 1953, *Toccata* 1953); vc. conc. (1951–5).

CHORAL: *Lo, the full final sacrifice*, with org. (1946, orch. 1947); *Intimations of Immortality*, ten., ch., and orch. (1936–8, 1949–50); *For St Cecilia*, ten., ch., and orch. (1947); *Magnificat*, with org. (1952, orch. 1956); *In terra pax*, sop., bar., ch., str., hp., cymbals (1954, full orch. 1956).

SOLO VOICE AND ORCH. OR ENSEMBLE: *By Footpath and Stile*, bar., str. qt. (1921–2); *Dies Natalis*, sop. (or ten.) and str. (1926, 1938–9); *Farewell to Arms*, ten. and str. or small orch. (1925–44); 2 *Milton Sonnets*, ten. (or sop.) and small orch. (*c.*1928).

UNACC. VOICES: *3 Short Elegies*, SATB (1926); *7 Part-songs*, SATB (1934–7); *White-flowering days* (in *A Garland for the Queen*), SATB (1953).

VOICE(S) AND PIANO: *A Young Man's Exhortation*, 10 songs (Hardy), ten. and pf. (1926–33); *Earth and Air and Rain*, 10 songs (Hardy), bar. and pf. (1928–36); *Before and After Summer*, 10 songs (Hardy), bar. and pf. (1938–49); *Let Us Garlands Bring*, 5 songs (Shakespeare), bar. and pf. (also with orch.) (1929–42); *Let us now praise famous men*, male vv. and pf. (1952); *Till Earth Outwears*, 7 songs (Hardy), sop. or ten. and pf. (1927–55); *I said to Love*, 6 songs (Hardy), bar. and pf. (1928–56).

Fiocco, Gioseffo-Hectore (*b* Brussels, 1703; *d* Brussels, 1741). Belgian-born It. composer and harpsichordist. Choirmaster, Antwerp Cath. 1731–7; dir. of mus. Ste-Gudule, Brussels, from 1737. Comp. organ mus. and works for hpd.

Fioritura (It.). Flowering (pl. *fioriture*). In 17th and 18th cents., the vocal decoration of the melody of an operatic aria, etc., usually extemporized during perf. by the singer. Also a common practice in vn. and kbd. playing.

Fipple. The block of wood which canalizes the air (i.e. plugs the mouthpiece) in woodwind instr. of the *recorder family, known therefore as 'fipple flutes'.

Firebird, The (*Zhar-Ptitsa*, Fr. *L'Oiseau de Feu*). Ballet (*conte dansé*) in 1 act and 3 scenes by Stravinsky, comp. 1909–10 and orig. choreog. by Fokine, with later versions by Bolm, Balanchine, Lifar, Cranko, and Béjart. Prod. Paris 1910 (Diaghilev Ballet Russe). Based on Russ. fairy-tales. Mus. had 19 sections. Suite, 1911, with orch. as for ballet, had 5 movements; rev. and re-orch. (also 5 movements), 1919; further rev. with orch. as 1919 but with 10 movements, 1945.

Fires of London, The. Instr. ens. founded 1970 by Peter Maxwell Davies after reorganization of *Pierrot Players. Has given f.ps. of most major works by *Maxwell Davies since that date.

Fireworks. Fantasy, Op. 4, for large orch. by Stravinsky. Comp. 1908, f.p. St Petersburg 1909.

Fireworks Music (Music for the Royal Fireworks). Suite of 8 movements by Handel for wind band, comp. for and played at fireworks display in Green Park, London, to mark Peace of Aix-la-Chapelle, 1749. Later Handel added str. parts. Arr. for modern orch. by *Harty and by *Mackerras.

Firkušný, Rudolf (*b* Napajedlá, Moravia, 1912). Amer. pianist of Cz. birth. Studied pf. and comp. (with Janáček) at Brno Cons., later at Prague Cons. with Karel and Suk. Début Prague 1922, London 1933, NY 1938. Worldwide tours. Settled in USA. Taught at Berkshire Mus. Center, Juilliard Sch. of Mus. Comp. pf. conc., str. qt., pf. pieces, songs.

First. In orch. parlance this term implies leadership of a section (e.g. 1st cl., or prin. cl.) in addition to, often, a part higher in pitch. The 1st vn. is leader of the orch., but the 1st vns. are a section div. from the 2nd vns. In choral terms a higher-pitched part.

First Inversion. That in which the 3rd of a chord becomes the bass, e.g. common chord C–E–G becomes E–G–C or E–C–G.

First Post. Brit. Army bugle-call sounded at 9.30 p.m. which calls all men back to barracks. See also *Last Post*.

First Subject. (1) The 1st melody, motif, or theme in a *sonata-form movement, in the tonic key. (2) 1st of the 2 themes of a double fugue.

First Walpurgis Night (Mendelssohn). See *Erste Walpurgisnacht*.

Fis (Ger.). The note F♯. **Fisis**, F♯♯.

Fischer, Annie (*b* Budapest, 1914). Hung. pianist. Studied at Franz Liszt Cons. and with Székely and Dohnányi. Début Budapest 1922. Winner, Int. Liszt Competition, Budapest, 1933. Worldwide tours as conc. pianist and recitalist.

Fischer, Edwin (*b* Basle, 1886; *d* Zürich, 1960). Swiss pianist and cond. Studied under Huber and Krause. Teacher at Stern Cons., Berlin, 1905–14. Cond. posts in Lübeck 1926–8 and Munich 1928–32. Formed chamber orch., directing it from the kbd. in concs. Specialist in, and writer about, mus. of Bach. whose kbd. works he ed. Comp. of pf. works.

Fischer, Ivan (*b* Budapest, 1951). Hung. conductor. Studied at Bartók Cons., Budapest, and Vienna Acad. (with Swarowsky). Had cond. engagements in Milan, Florence, Budapest, Vienna before winning Rupert Foundation comp. in Eng. 1976. Joint mus. dir. Northern Sinfonia 1979–82. Opera début Zürich 1977 (*Don Giovanni*). Brit. opera début, Kent Opera 1982 (*Agrippina*), Royal Opera 1983 (Manchester, *La*

Clemenza di Tito). Mus. dir. Kent Opera from 1984.

Fischer, Johann (*b* nr. Schlackenwerth, Bohemia, *c.*1665; *d* Rastatt, 1746). Ger. composer. Kapellmeister to Markgraf of Baden. Wrote klavier suites, and 20 preludes and fugues for org. in different keys.

Fischer, Johann (Christian) (*b* Freiburg in Breisgau, 1733; *d* London, 1800). Ger. oboist. Played in Court orch. at Dresden from 1764. Went to London, 1768, becoming member of Queen's band and playing at Bach-Abel concerts. Married Gainsborough's daughter 1780. Returned to Continent on disappointment at not being made Master of King's Band 1786. Returned to London 1790. Mozart wrote variations on his Minuet (1773).

Fischer-Dieskau, Dietrich (*b* Berlin, 1925). Ger. bar. and cond. Studied Berlin Hochschule für Musik. Teachers incl. Georg Walter and, after 1945, Hermann Weissenborn. Stage début Berlin State Opera, 1948, as Posa in *Don Carlos*. Rapidly became one of world's leading singers, outstanding in Lieder and in wide range of operatic roles from the Count in *Figaro* to Falstaff, Wozzeck, Don Giovanni, Sachs, and Mittenhofer in Henze's *Elegy for Young Lovers*. Eng. début 1951 with Beecham in Delius's *Mass of Life.* NY début 1955. CG début 1965, as Mandryka in Strauss's *Arabella.* Bayreuth 1954–6, and has sung at most leading fests. Vienna State Opera from 1957. 1st singer of bar. role in Britten's *War Requiem,* Coventry 1962. Took up cond. 1973. Author of books on Schubert and relationship between Nietzsche and Wagner.

Fišer, Luboš (*b* Prague, 1935). Cz. composer. Studied Prague Cons. 1952–6 and Prague Acad. of Mus. Arts 1956–60. Comps. incl. pf. sonatas, chamber conc., *15 Prints after Dürer's Apocalypse* (orch.), *Requiem.*

Fisher, Sylvia (Gwendoline Victoria) (*b* Melbourne, 1910). Australian sop. Studied Melbourne Cons. Début Melbourne 1932. Début CG 1948 as Leonore in *Fidelio,* becoming co.'s leading sop. until 1958 in roles such as Isolde, the Kostelnička in *Jenůfa,* Sieglinde, and the Marschallin. Chicago Opera 1959. Sang with EOG 1963–71 in Britten operas and with SW Co. (later ENO), notably with latter as Elizabeth I in Britten's *Gloriana.*

Fiske, Roger (Elwyn) (*b* Surbiton, 1910; *d* Kendal, 1987). Eng. musicologist and critic. Studied Oxford and RCM. On BBC mus. staff 1939–59. Gen. ed. Eulenburg miniature scores 1969–76. Author of several books.

Fistoulari, Anatole (*b* Kiev, 1907). Russ.-born cond., Brit. citizen since 1940s. Cond. ballet in Paris 1933 and toured with Ballets Russes de Monte Carlo. Settled in Eng. 1940; prin. cond. LPO 1943–4. Toured USSR with LPO 1956. Guest cond. of world's leading orchs.

Fitelberg, Grzegorz (*b* Dynaburg, Latvia, 1879; *d* Katowice, 1953). Polish cond., violinist, and composer. With *Szymanowski and others, founded 'Young Poland' group of composers in Berlin 1905. Cond. Warsaw P.O. 1907, Vienna Opera 1911–14, Petrograd and Moscow 1914–20. Returned to Warsaw P.O. 1923–34. Permanent cond. Polish Radio S.O. 1934–9 and from 1947. Comp. 2 syms., vn. conc., symphonic poem, vn. sonata, etc.

Fitelberg, Jerzy (*b* Warsaw, 1903; *d* NY, 1951). Polish composer, son of above. Studied in Berlin, emigrating to Paris 1933 and then to USA 1940. Wrote 5 str. qts. (Coolidge Prize 1936 for No. 4), sym., 2 vn. concs., vc. conc., 2 pf. concs., wind quintet, vn. sonata, and other chamber works.

Fitzwilliam Virginal Book. Remarkable MS. coll. of early 17th-cent. Eng. mus. for kbd. by (mostly) Eng. composers, comprising 297 pieces. Coll. orig. made by Francis Tregian in 17th cent. Bears present title because it became property of the mus. antiquarian Richard, Viscount Fitzwilliam (1745–1816) who bequeathed it, together with the annual interest on £100,000, to Cambridge Univ. where it is preserved in Fitzwilliam Library. Pubd. 1894–9 in edn. by *Fuller Maitland and Barclay *Squire.

Five, The. Name given to group of 5 Russ. composers, Balakirev, Borodin, Cui, Mussorgsky, and Rimsky-Korsakov, who est. a 'national' sch. of comp. in 19th cent. In Russia they were known as *moguchaya kuchka,* 'the mighty handful', a term invented by the critic Stasov in 1867.

Five Tudor Portraits. Choral suite in 5 movements by Vaughan Williams for mez., bar., ch., and orch. Comp. 1935. Texts are from the poetry of John Skelton (1460–1529) incl. 'The Tunning of Elinor Rumming' and the 'Lament for Philip Sparrow'. F.p. Norwich 1936, London 1937.

Fixed-Doh. System of sight-singing in which the note C, in every key in which it occurs, is called *doh,* D called *ray,* etc. See *Movable-doh.*

Fjeldstad, Øivin (*b* Oslo, 1903). Norweg. cond., composer, and vn. teacher. Début as violinist 1921, as cond. 1931. Chief cond. Norwegian State Opera 1958–60, Oslo P.O. 1962–9.

Flageolet. (1) Late 16th-cent. instr. of end-blown fl. type, with 4 finger-holes and 2 thumb-holes, 'invented' by Sieur de Juvigny of Paris, *c.*1581. The name has also been applied to earlier instr. of the end-blown fipple type of pipe. Handel wrote for the true flageolet in *Rinaldo.*

(2) Soft organ stop of 2′ length and pitch.

(3) *Flageolet notes* is a term applied to harmonics on a str. instr., produced by light stopping of the str. at natural points of vibration, and so called because the resultant high thin sound is said to resemble that of the flageolet.

Flagstad, Kirsten (Malfrid) (*b* Hamar, Norway, 1895; *d* Oslo, 1962). Norweg. sop., one of the greatest of Wagnerian singers. Studied singing in Christiania, making début there in 1913 at Nat. Th. in *Tiefland*. Sang wide range of roles in opera and operetta in Scandinavia up to 1932 but was virtually unknown elsewhere until glowing reports of her Isolde in Oslo led to her engagement in small roles at 1933 Bayreuth Fest. Sang Gutrune and Sieglinde at Bayreuth 1934. Début NY Met. as Sieglinde 1935, later singing Brünnhilde and Kundry. CG début as Isolde 1936. Her int. standing as leading exponent of Wagner's great female roles was thereafter unchallenged until her retirement from the stage in 1953. Gave f.p. of Strauss's *Vier letzte Lieder*, London 1950 (Furtwängler cond.). Sang Purcell's Dido at Mermaid Theatre, London, 1951. Dir., Norweg. State Opera 1958–60. Fine exponent of Grieg songs.

Flam. Rhythmic 2-note figure in side-drum playing, 'open' or 'closed' according to whether the 1st or 2nd note is on the accented beat.

Flamenco. Very rhythmical Sp. dance style, particularly Andalusian. See *Cante flamenco*. The 'flamenco' style of guitar-playing, rhythmical and improvisatory, is the opposite of the 'classical'.

Flanagan, William (*b* Detroit, 1923; *d* NY, 1969). Amer. composer and critic. Studied at Eastman Sch. of Mus., later with *Copland and *Diamond. Promoted recitals of Amer. song with Ned *Rorem. Wrote incidental mus. for 4 plays by Albee. Wrote th. and mus. criticism for NY *Herald Tribune*, etc. Works incl. opera *Bartleby* (prod. NY 1961), *Notations* for orch., song-cycles incl. *The Weeping Pleiades* (Housman), and choral mus.

Flat (♭). The sign which, placed before a note, lowers its pitch by a semitone. In Britain, the verb 'to flatten' (past participle 'flattened') is in use; in USA, 'to flat' ('flatted').
(2) 'Flat' singing or playing is that which departs from correct intonation on the downward side.

Flat Twenty-first. Rank in an organ Mixture stop, sounding 2 octaves and a minor 7th above normal (i.e. interval of minor 21st or compound minor 7th).

Flautando, flautato (It., 'fluting', 'fluted'). The prod. of fl.-like notes from the vn., etc., either by bowing near the finger-board with the point of the bow, or by the use of *Harmonics.

Flautina. A *Gemshorn* org. stop of 2' length and pitch.

Flautist. A fl.-player. Flutist is an older term; 'flautist' is derived from the It. *flauto* and, in Britain, has been retained as a hangover from the 18th-cent. domination of It. mus. and musicians.

Flauto (It., 'flute', plural *flauti*). In printed scores since Haydn's time *flauto* implies the side-blown fl. (*flauto traverso*). The small version of this is the *flauto piccolo*, usually called *piccolo. In earlier periods *flauto* sometimes meant the *recorder. J. S. Bach wrote *flauto piccolo* to indicate a small recorder; if he wanted the side-blown flute he wrote *flauto traverso*. For history of fl., see under *flute*.

Flauto dolce. Org. stop; much the same as *dolce* but more fl.-like.

Flauto Traverso (It., 'transverse flute'). (1) The side-blown fl., as opposed to the end-blown variety.
(2) Org. stop of 4' length and pitch.

Flea, Song of the. See *Song of the Flea*.

Flebile; flebilmente (It.). Mournful; mournfully.

Flecha, Mateo (the younger) (*b* Prades, *c*.1530; *d* Lérida, 1604). Sp. composer of church and secular choral mus. Worked at imperial court in Prague and Vienna. His uncle, Mateo Flecha the elder (1481–1553), was also court musician to the imperial family.

Fledermaus, Die (The Bat). Operetta in 3 acts by J. Strauss II to lib. by Haffner and *Genée after *Le Réveillon* (1872) by Meilhac and Halévy, this being based on *Das Gefängnis* (The Prison, 1851) by R. Benedix. Comp. 1874. Prod. Vienna and NY 1874, London 1876. Eng. versions under titles *The Gay Rosalinda* and *The Merry Countess*. Filmed (1955) as *Oh, Rosalinda!*

Fleisher, Leon (*b* San Francisco, 1928). Amer. pianist and cond. Début at age 7. Studied with *Schnabel 1938–9. Appeared in San Francisco 1943, NY 1944, with *Monteux conducting. 1st prize Brussels Queen Elisabeth competition 1952. Career as pianist halted by illness 1964 but resumed 1982, though in the meantime he had played works for left hand. Début as cond., NY 1970.

Flesch, Carl (*b* Moson, Hung., 1873; *d* Lucerne, 1944). Hung. violinist, pupil of Marsick. Prof. of vn., Bucharest Cons. 1897–1902, Amsterdam Cons. 1903–8. Taught in Berlin from 1908. Chief vn. prof. Curtis Institute, Philadelphia, 1924–8. Ed. of vn. mus. Author of famous method and of several books on vn.-playing. Prize awarded in his memory since 1945.

Flessibile, flessibilità (It.). Flexible, flexibility.

Fleury, André (*b* Neuilly-sur-Seine, 1903). Fr. org. and composer. Pupil of M. Dupré and Vierne. Organist, St Augustin, Paris, 1930–49. Prof. of org. École Normale de Musique, Paris, from 1943; prof. Dijon Cons. and org. Dijon Cath. 1949–71. Org. St. Eustache, Paris, from 1971. Wrote syms. for org. and other works.

Fleury, Louis François (b Lyons, 1878; d Paris, 1926). Fr. flautist, for whom several composers wrote works, including Debussy (*Syrinx*). Frequent visitor to Eng.

Flexatone. Novelty instr., patented 1922, producing a weird tremolo. A flexible metal sheet is suspended in wire frame with handle. On each side of the metal sheet is a wooden knob on a spring of steel. Performer shakes the instr. so that knobs hit sides of metal. Pitch may be altered by varying pressure on metal sheet. Used by Schoenberg in his *Variations*, Op. 31, *Von Heute auf Morgen*, and *Moses und Aron*, by Khatchaturian (pf. conc.), and by Henze and Penderecki, among others.

Flicorno. It. variety of *saxhorn and *flügelhorn used in military bands. There are 3 sizes: *flicorno basso* (*Bassflicorno*), *flicorno basso grave*, and *flicorno contrabasso*.

Fliegende Holländer, Der (The Flying Dutchman). Opera in 3 acts by Wagner, comp. 1841, to his own lib. based on the legend. Prod. Dresden 1843, London 1870, Philadelphia 1876. Orig. intended to be in 1 act, it has in recent years been so perf. (e.g. by ENO and Opera North).

Fliessend (Ger.). Flowing. So **fliessender**, more flowing.

Flight of the Bumble Bee, The. Orch. interlude in opera *The *Legend of Tsar Saltan* (1900) by Rimsky-Korsakov in which a prince becomes a bee and stings his villainous relatives. Many arrs. (some highly spurious) for variety of solo instr.

Flonzaley Quartet. Str. qt. founded by patron E. J. de Coppet of NY, in 1902, and named after his residence near Lausanne. Orig. membership A. Betti, A. Pochon, U. Ara and I. d'Archambeau. Toured Europe 1904. 1st NY concert 1905. L. Bailly replaced Ara, 1917, and was replaced by F. d'Archambeau, 1924. I. d'Archambeau replaced by N. Moldavan 1924. Disbanded 1928 (London) after giving 3,000 concerts, mostly in USA.

Flood, The. Mus. play for 3 speakers, ten., and 2 basses, ch., and orch. by *Stravinsky to lib. chosen and arr. by Robert Craft from *Genesis*, and York and Chester cycles of mystery plays. Comp. 1961–2. F.p. on TV (CBS) 1962, f. stage p. Hamburg 1963. See also Britten's *Noye's Fludde*.

Flood, (William Henry) **Grattan** (b Lismore, Ireland, 1859; d Enniscorthy, 1928). Irish organist and writer. Noted collector of Irish folk-tunes; ed. *Moore's Irish Melodies* and wrote memoir of John *Field (Dublin, 1920).

Florid. Descriptive term for melody embellished by ornaments and trills, either improvised or comp.

Florid Counterpoint. The 5th species of strict counterpoint in which the added v. employs

mixture of the processes of the other 4 species and also introduces shorter notes (eighth-notes).

Flos Campi (Flower of the Field). Suite by Vaughan Williams for solo va., mixed ch. (wordless), and small orch. F.p. London 1925 (soloist Lionel *Tertis). Each of the 6 movements is prefaced by a Latin quotation from *The Song of Solomon*.

Floss der Medusa, Das (The Raft of the Medusa). 'Popular and military oratorio' (or cantata) by Henze, to lib. by Ernst Schnabel, for narrator, sop., bar., ch., boys' ch., and orch. Based on historical (1816) event, the subject of Géricault's painting, when the Fr. frigate *Medusa* ran aground, its officers escaping in the boats and leaving the crew to their fate on an improvised raft. Henze's avowedly political and class-conscious work was cause of a famous fracas involving students and police in Hamburg, 1968, which caused cancellation of première. F.p. Vienna 1971, London 1977.

Flothuis, Marius (Hendrikus) (b Amsterdam, 1914). Dutch composer, musicologist, and critic. Studied pf. with A. Koole, pf. and theory with Hans Brandts Buys (1928–37). Ass. man., Concertgebouw Orch., 1937–42 and 1953–5, art. dir. 1955–74. Mus. critic Amsterdam *Het Vrije Volk* 1945–53. Prof. of musicology, Utrecht Univ. from 1974. Author of books on Monteverdi, Mozart, Eng. composers, etc. Composer of concs. for fl., vn., hn., pf., and cl., vn. sonata, *Hymnus* for sop. and orch., cantatas, song cycles, str. qt., etc.

Flotow, Friedrich von (b Teutendorf, 1812; d Darmstadt, 1883). Ger. composer. Studied mus. under Reicha in Paris 1828–30. Lived mostly in Paris and Vienna. Wrote ballets, chamber mus., and 30 operas of which only *Martha* (1847) and *Alessandro Stradella* (1844) seem to have outlived him.

Flotter (Fr., 'to float', present participle *flottant*, 'floating'). An undulating movement of the bow in str. playing.

Flourish. (1) A tpt. call of the fanfare type.
(2) In a more general sense any florid instr. passage.

Flower, (Sir) (Walter) **Newman** (b Fontmell Magna, Dorset, 1879; d Blandford, 1964). Eng. writer and publisher. Author of books on Handel, Sullivan, and Schubert. Collected mus. autographs and portraits. Chairman, Cassell & Co. (publishers). Knighted 1938.

Flowers o' the Forest. Scottish lament, orig. words of which are lost, but many lines were incorporated into an 18th-cent. version by Jane Elliott. A new set of words was written c.1765 by Mrs Cockburn to a different tune but is now generally sung to old tune. The flowers are young men, the Forest a district of Selkirk and Peebles: the poem commemorates their death in battle.

The tune, played by pipers, is a regular and moving feature of the Remembrance Day ceremony at the Cenotaph in Whitehall, London.

Floyd, Carlisle (b Latta, S. Carolina, 1926). Amer. composer. Studied at Spartanburg and Syracuse Univ. Private pf. tuition from *Firkušný. Works incl. several operas, notably *Susannah* (1955), *Wuthering Heights* (1958), *The Passion of Jonathan Wade* (1962), *Of Mice and Men* (1970), and *Bilby's Doll* (1976).

Flue-Pipe. Org. pipe into which the air enters directly, i.e. not striking a reed. See *Organ*.

Flügel (Ger., 'wing'). The grand pf., formerly the hpd.

Flügelhorn (Ger.). Brass wind instr. with cup-shaped mouthpiece and wide conical bore. Bell held forward. Types are (1) Sop. in E♭ (rare). (2) Alto in B♭, same compass as cornet in B♭ but mellower in tone. (3) Ten. in E♭ (sometimes called *Altflügelhorn* or *Althorn*) or sometimes in F. (2) is the type used in Brit. brass bands and sometimes in orch. comp., e.g. by Vaughan Williams in his 9th Sym. (1956–8).

Flute (It. *Flauto*, Fr. *Flûte*, Ger. *Flöte*). Wind instr. of ancient origin formerly made of wood but now of silver and other metals. From medieval times 2 methods of producing sound were used: (a) blowing across a round mouth-hole as on the panpipes or transverse (side-blown) fl.; (b) blowing into a whistle mouthpiece (end-blown) as on the *recorder or *flageolet. The word fl. was used indiscriminately to denote both types during medieval times, but in the baroque period fl. or *flauto specifically meant the end-blown recorder. The modern fl. is descended from the Ger. (transverse) fl. Whereas today it is cylindrical in bore, stopped at one end, until the early 19th cent. it was conical. The player's breath sets in vibration the column of air inside the tube. Acoustically the tube acts as an open one; the mouth-hole serves to prevent its acting as stopped and thus sounding an octave lower. The body orig. had one thumb-hole and from 4 to 8 finger-holes. The 1st key was added in 1677, the 2nd in 1726 by *Quantz, fl. teacher of Frederick the Great. The great fl. virtuoso of the Bavarian Court Orch., Theobald *Boehm, used an 8-key fl., but revolutionized the instr. in 1832 with his 'ring key' system. In 1847 he produced a 15-hole metal instr. with 23 keys and levers. See *Alto flute, Bass flute*.

Flûte-à-bec (Fr., 'beaked flute'). *Recorder or *flageolet.

Flûte à cheminée (Fr., 'Chimney flute'). Same as *Rohrflöte.

Flute amabile. Org. stop, same as *Flûte d'amour*.

Flûte à pavillon (Fr., 'tented flute'). Org. stop of 8' or 4' length and pitch; each pipe ends in a sort of bell-tent structure.

Flûte d'amour (Fr., 'love flute'). (1) Flute pitched a third lower than regular fl.

(2) Soft org. stop, in Britain, of 8' or 4' length and pitch, and in USA of 2' length and 4' pitch (being end-plugged).

Flûte harmonique (Fr.). (1) *Mouth org.

(2) An org. stop.

Flute stop (on org.). See *Doppelflöte, Fernflöte, Flauto traverso, Flûte d'amour, Grosseflöte, Harmonic Flute, Hohlflöte, Rohrflöte, Spitzflöte, Waldflöte, Zauberflöte*.

Flutist. Player of the flute (Amer. usage). See *Flautist*.

Flutter-Tonguing (Ger. *Flatterzunge*). *Tonguing in the playing of wind instr. is the interruption of the flow of air by a motion of the tongue to produce certain effects. Flutter-tonguing—chiefly on the fl. but possible on the cl. and some brass—consists of a trilling of the letter R while playing a chromatic scale. It was introduced by R. Strauss and Mahler (e.g. in the latter's *Das Lied von der Erde*).

Flying Dutchman, The (Wagner). See *Fliegende Holländer, Der*.

Foggin, Myers (b Newcastle upon Tyne, 1908; d Chichester, 1986). Eng. pianist, cond., and teacher. Studied RAM. Prof. of pf. RAM 1936–49, cond. People's Palace Ch. and Orch. Soc. 1936–49, dir. of opera RAM 1948–65. Prin. TCL 1965–79. Chairman, Royal Phil. Soc. from 1968.

Fogliano, Lodovico (b Modena, ? ; d Modena, c. 1539). It. composer and theorist. Wrote *Musica theorica* (1529) defining rules on uses of 3rds and 5ths.

Fokine, Mikhail (Mikhaylovich) (Michel) (b St Petersburg, 1880; d NY, 1942). Russ. dancer and choreog. Member of Maryinsky Th. Started to teach 1902. Choreog. *The Dying Swan* for Pavlova 1907. Engaged as chief choreog. 1909 by *Diaghilev who recognized his genius as a reformer of ballet methods. Among his greatest ballets were *Les Sylphides, Sheherazade, Firebird, Petrushka, Daphnis et Chloé*, and *Josephslegende*. After break with Diaghilev, worked as freelance, settling in NY 1923.

Foldes, Andor (b Budapest, 1913). Hung.-born pianist and composer. Studied Budapest Acad. with Dohnányi. Won Int. Liszt Prize, Budapest, 1933. Authoritative exponent of mus. of Bartók with whom he worked. Toured Europe until 1939 when he settled in USA, becoming Amer. citizen 1948. Author of books on pf. technique. Some pf. comps.

Foli, Signor (Allan James Foley) (b Cahir, Tipperary, 1835; d Southport, 1899). Irish-Amer. bass singer. Studied Naples. Début Catania 1862 in Rossini's *Otello*, London 1865. Sang in over 60 operas in London. Appeared in USA, Russia, and

Austria. Sang Daland in f. London p. of Wagner's *Der fliegende Holländer* (Drury Lane, 1870).

Folía, La (Sp., 'The Folly'; It. *La Follia*). A type of wild Portuguese dance. One particular melody used for the dance attained wide popular currency in the 16th, 17th, and 18th cents., being first mentioned by Salinas in 1577, and subsequently used by numerous composers as an ostinato basis for variations. The best-known set is by *Corelli in his 12th sonata for vn. and hpd., 1700. Other composers to use the melody incl. Vivaldi, Frescobaldi, Lully, Pergolesi, Geminiani, Bach, Grétry, Cherubini, Liszt, Nielsen, and Rakhmaninov.

Folk Music. Term covering folk-songs and folk dances. Folk-songs are songs of unknown authorship passed orally from generation to generation, sung without acc., and often found in variants (of words and tune) in different parts of a country (or in different countries). Folk-songs were generally found among the country-dwellers, but with the increase of urbanization and industrialization they spread to the towns and factories. In the 19th and early 20th cents. the fear that with the advance of modern life the old customs were dying out led to a major campaign of song coll., in Eng. by Cecil *Sharp, Vaughan Williams, Maud Karpeles, Mrs Leather, Anne Gilchrist, Frank Kidson, and many others; in Hungary by Kodály and Bartók, and similarly in other countries. Many composers have made use of folk-songs in their comps., from Renaissance times to Haydn, Grieg, Dvořák, Tchaikovsky, Bartók, Vaughan Williams, and others. Although folk-songs enshrine the nat. characteristics of their country of origin, they have int. similarities. Most of them are modal. Like every generic term, folk-song is susceptible to many conflicting interpretations, and readers are referred to several important books on the subject. It is also impossible to predict how folk-song may develop in future centuries. It may well be that the popular songs of the 20th cent. by named composers may become (indeed already have become) the folk-songs of a new age. Folk dance is a type of dance which has developed by itself without aid from choreogs., is connected with traditional life, and is passed from one generation to the next.

Fomin, Evstigney (Ipatovich) (*b* St Petersburg, 1761; *d* St Petersburg, 1800). Russ. composer. Studied with Padre Martini in Bologna 1782. Coach at Imperial Th., St Petersburg, 1786. Composed several operas in 'national' style, and also *Orpheus and Eurydice* (1792) and *The Americans* (1800).

Fonds d'orgue. 'Foundation Tone' and also 'Foundation Stops' of an org. *Jeux de Fonds* means the Foundation Stops (i.e. all the stops except the Mutation and Mixture stops).

Fontaine, Pierre (*b* ?1390; *d* c.1450). Fr. composer of *chansons*. Singer in Papal chapel.

Fontana, Giovanni Battista (*b* Brescia, ? ; *d* Padua, c.1630). It. violinist and composer of vn. sonatas. Regarded as a leading figure in the development of the solo sonata.

Fontane di Roma (It., 'Fountains of Rome'). Symphonic poem for orch. by Respighi, comp. 1914–16, in 4 sections, each depicting the sensations of the composer in contemplating 4 of the city's most famous fountains, Vale Giulia at dawn, Tritone in mid-morning, Trevi at noon, and Villa Medici at sunset. F.p. Rome 1917, NY 1919, London 1921.

Foot. Unit of length for measuring vibrating air-column, and therefore a measure of pitch. An air-column of 8′ vibrates at twice the speed of a 16′ column, and thus emits a note an octave higher. Organ stops are classified by the sound which will be emitted if the note representing 8′ C is struck. An 8′ stop sounds the note itself, 16′ the note an octave below, 32′ the note 2 octaves below. A 4′ stop sounds the note an octave above, 2′ 2 octaves above, 1′ 3 octaves above.

Foote, Arthur William (*b* Salem, Mass., 1853; *d* Boston, 1937). Amer. composer and organist. Recipient of 1st M.A. conferred at Harvard Univ. for work in mus. Organist, First Unitarian Church, Boston, 1878-1910. A founder of Amer. Guild of Organists, president 1909–12. Comps. incl. orch. suites, vc. conc., cantata *The Farewell of Hiawatha*, chamber mus., vocal works, songs, pf. pieces, and org. mus. Author of books on harmony and fugue.

Forbes, Robert (Jaffrey) (*b* Stalybridge, 1878; *d* Manchester, 1958). Eng. pianist, cond., and teacher. Trained at RMCM 1897–1900, joining staff as accompanist 1903. Frequent pf. partner of *Brodsky in sonatas. Prin., RMCM 1929–53. Guest cond. Hallé Orch. with which he also appeared as solo pianist. Opera cond. C.B.E. 1948.

Forbes, Sebastian (*b* Amersham, 1941). Eng. composer and organist. Studied RAM and King's Coll., Cambridge. Producer for BBC 1964–7. Organist, Trinity Coll., Cambridge, 1968. Works incl. sym., str. qts., trio, pf. quintet, opera, songs, choral mus., org. sonata, sonata for 8 instr. (pf., fl., ob., cl., hn., vn., va., vc., 1978). Son of W. *Forbes.

Forbes, Watson (*b* St Andrews, 1909). Scottish va. player. Studied at RAM and in Cz. with Sevčik. Prof. of chamber mus. RAM from 1956, of va. from 1958. Member Aeolian Qt. from 1932, Head of BBC Mus., Scotland, 1964. Has made many arrs. and transcrs. for va.

Ford, Thomas (*b* c.1580; *d* Westminster, 1648). Eng. composer and lutenist. Musician to Prince Henry, 1611; later one of lutes and voices in service of Prince Charles (later King Charles I), with whom he remained until 1642. His 19 anthems were pubd. 1614 and his *Musicke of Sundrie Kindes* (for voices and bass viols) in 1607.

Forelle, Die (Schubert). See *Trout, The.*

Forgotten Rite, The. Orch. 'prelude' by John Ireland, 1913. The unspecified rite is assoc. with the Channel Islands.

Forkel, Johann Nicolaus (*b* Meeder, 1749; *d* Göttingen, 1818). Ger. organist and writer. Dir. of mus., Göttingen Univ. from 1778, cond. *Akademie* concerts 1779–1815. Wrote several theoretical books, but his *chef d'oeuvre* was 1st biography of J. S. Bach (Leipzig 1802). Composer of cantatas, oratorios, and instr. works.

Form. The structure and design of a composition. Whereas in the 16th and 17th cents. instr. comps. were usually very brief (e.g. a movement in a kbd. suite of Byrd or Purcell), by the 19th cent. they were frequently long (e.g. a sonata or sym. movement of the later Beethoven, Bruckner, and Mahler). This implies an enormous growth in the understanding of the principles of form and in mastery of the application of those principles. In general, however, despite continuous experimentation the mus. forms so far devised can be classified into no more than 6 categories, all of them exploiting the idea of contrast plus variety both in the domain of content (Thematic Material) and in that of Key (combinations of these are, of course, possible, e.g. in Simple Ternary Form each section can be in Binary Form, and so on).

(1) SIMPLE BINARY FORM (e.g. in the movements of Bach's kbd. suites) has no strong contrast of material. The 1st section opens in the Tonic key and then modulates, as it ends, into the key of the Dominant (or in the case of a minor key, sometimes the relative major). The 2nd section then opens in that 2nd key and, before it ends, modulates back to the 1st. There are, then, 2 distinct main cadences, or points of rest, the 1st in the Dominant (or relative major), and the 2nd in the Tonic. This form, although it sometimes attained fairly considerable dimensions in the 18th cent., is unsuitable for very long pieces, since the variety offered to the listener is almost entirely confined to details of treatment and the element of key, the thematic material employed throughout being the same. This form has been little used since *c*.1750.

(2) TERNARY FORM. This is one of the most commonly used forms for short comps. It consists of a first section (more or less complete and self-contained), a 2nd section, contrasting as to mus. material and key (normally in the Dominant or the Tonic Minor or Relative Major), and then the first section repeated. See *ABA*.

(3) COMPOUND BINARY FORM (also known as SONATA FORM, because often employed in the first or some other movement or movements of a Sonata; and as FIRST MOVEMENT FORM for the same

reason). This derives historically from Simple Binary Form but has developed into something more resembling Ternary Form. Like Simple Binary it falls into 2 sections, of which the 1st modulates to the Dominant and the 2nd takes us back to the Tonic. But the sections have become elaborated as follows:

1st Section. Strain I (*First Subject*) in Tonic key; followed by Strain II (*2nd Subject*) in Dominant key. Those 2 strains (or Subjects) are generally contrasted in character. This section is called the *Exposition.*

2nd Section. Some *Development* (also called 'Working-out' or 'Free Fantasia') of the material in the previous section, followed by a repetition (*Recapitulation*) of that section, but this time with both subjects in the Tonic key so that the piece may end in the key with which it opened.

Further details may incl. (a) a *Bridge Passage*, leading (in both sections) from the First Subject to the Second; (b) a closing passage (Coda), at the end of each section.

A tendency towards the evolution of Simple Binary Form into Compound Binary Form may be observed in some of Bach's movements, but its first real exploitation is connected with the name and fame of his son, C. P. E. Bach, and its further exploitation and elaboration with the names of Haydn, Mozart, Beethoven, and their contemporaries. This form is still in frequent use, but 20th-cent. composers have modified it in detail.

(4) RONDO FORM. This may be considered an extension of Ternary Form. If the 3 sections of that form are indicated by the formula A, B, A, then the Rondo Form must be indicated by A, B, A, C, A, D, A, or some variant of this. (The sections B, C, D, etc. are often spoken of as *Episodes*.)

SONATA-RONDO FORM, as its name implies, offers a combination of Compound Binary and Rondo Forms. The general plan is as follows: *1st Section.* Subject I, Subject II in another key, Subject I repeated. *2nd Section.* Development of the previous Subject-material. *3rd Section.* Subject I and Subject II again, but the latter this time in the same key as Subject I.

Sometimes the Development above mentioned is replaced by new material. And there are other variants.

(5) AIR WITH VARIATIONS. This form, which from the 16th cent. to the present day has been popular with composers of every class from the most trivial to the most serious, consists, as the name implies, of one theme (or 'Subject'), first played in its simplicity and then many times repeated with elaborations, each variation thus taking on its own individuality.

There are very many types of comp. to which distinctive names are given, each representing not a 'Form' but rather a style in which one of the above forms is presented; such as the Nocturne, the Gavotte, the Barcarolle, the Konzertstück, and others.

With the development of elec. mus. and the use of *aleatory techniques in 20th-cent. comps., the use of form is stretched to meet whatever the composer may wish to do. Infinite flexibility would seem to be the guiding principle in works of this kind.

(6) See *Fugue*.

Formalism. Alleged fault in comp. by Soviet Union composers for which Prokofiev, Shostakovich, and others were officially criticized, esp. in 1948. The criticism is of too much intellectual emphasis on form as opposed to content, with the suggestion also that the mus. is too 'modern' and discordant.

Forqueray, Antoine (*b* Paris, *c*.1672; *d* Mantes, 1745). Fr. player of viola da gamba, and composer. At age 5, played to Louis XIV, and entered king's service as chamber musician 1689. Retired to Mantes 1728. One of greatest viol virtuosi of his day, rival to *Marais. Comp. *c*.30 viol pieces, pubd. in 5 suites. His son, Jean-Baptiste Antoine (*b* Paris, 1699; *d* Paris, 1782) was also a viol player of some renown, in service of king and Prince de Conti.

Forrester, Maureen (Katherine Stewart) (*b* Montreal, 1930). Canadian cont. Studied in Berlin. Début Montreal 1953. Recital tour of Europe 1955. Sang in Mahler's 2nd Sym. at Bruno Walter's invitation, NY 1957, later recording this with him. Noted as Mahler interpreter, also as Angel in Elgar's *Dream of Gerontius*.

Förster, Josef (Bohuslav) (*b* Dětenice, 1859; *d* Novy Vesteč, 1951). Cz. composer, organist, and critic. Prof. of piano at Hamburg Cons. from 1901 and critic for several Hamburg papers 1893–1903, during which period he was perceptive champion and friend of *Mahler. Prof. of comp. at New Vienna Cons. and critic of *Die Zeit* 1910–18. Prof. of comp., Prague Cons. 1918–22, dir. 1922–31. Works incl. 5 syms., 6 suites, 2 vn. concs., vc. conc., 4 symphonic poems, 6 operas, chamber mus., and songs.

Forsyth, Cecil (*b* Greenwich, 1870; *d* NY, 1941). Eng. violist, cond., composer, and musicologist. Studied RCM under Parry and Stanford. Violist in London orchs. Settled in NY 1914. Comps. incl. operas, va. conc., setting of Keats's *Ode to a Nightingale* for bar. and orch., masses, part-songs, chamber mus., and songs. Author of several books incl. *History of Music* (1916, with Stanford) and valuable treatise on orchestration (1914).

Forte (It.). 'Strong', i.e. loud (abbreviation *f*). So *fortissimo*, 'very strong' (abbreviation *ff*, or *fff*); *fortemente*, 'strongly'.

Fortepiano (It.). Same as *pianoforte, but the term has come to be used to denote the late 18th-cent./early 19th-cent. instr. known to Haydn, Hummel, Beethoven, and Schubert.

For the Fallen. 3rd movement of Elgar's choral work *Spirit of England, but perf. 1916 before work as a whole was completed and still often perf. separately. Words by Laurence Binyon.

Fortissimo (It.). Very loud. See *Forte*.

Fortner, Wolfgang (*b* Leipzig, 1907; *d* Heidelberg, 1987). Ger. composer, cond., and teacher. Studied Leipzig Cons. (comp. with H. Grabner). Taught theory and comp. at Church Music Institute, Heidelberg, 1931–54; prof. of comp. N. W. Ger. Mus. Acad., Detmold, 1954–7, and at State Mus. Sch., Freiburg im Breisgau from 1957. Founded Heidelberg Chamber Orch. 1935. Dir. of *Musica Viva* series in Heidelberg, Freiburg, and Munich. Early music influenced by Hindemith and Stravinsky; he adopted 12-note method in mid-1940s. Comps. incl. operas (among them *Bluthochzeit* (Blood Wedding), after Lorca (1957), *In Seinem Garten liebt Don Perlimplin Belisa*, chamber opera after Lorca (1962), and *Elisabeth Tudor* (1972)), sym., 4 str. qts., organ conc., concs. for pf. (1943), vn. (1947), vc. (1951), *Fantasy on the Name BACH* for 2 pf. and orch. (1950), *Movements* for pf. and orch. (1953), oratorio *Isaaks Opferung* (1952), ballet *Die Weisse Rose* (1950; after Wilde's *Birthday of the Infanta*), *Variations* for solo vc. (1975), pf. trio (1978), 4th str. qt. (1979), *Immagini*, sop. and str. (1979); *Variations* for chamber orch. (1980); *Petrarca-Sonette*, for unacc. ch. (1980); *Madrigal* for 12 vcs. (1980).

'Forty-eight, The' (Bach). See *Wohltemperierte Klavier, Das*.

Forza del Destino, La (The Force of Destiny). 4-act opera by Verdi to lib. by Piave based on Spanish drama *Don Alvaro* (1835) by the Duke of Rivas. Comp. 1861–2 for Imperial Th., St Petersburg, where f.p. was given in 1862. Prod. Rome (as *Don Alvaro*) 1863, NY 1865, London 1867. For 1869 Milan prod. Verdi made extensive revs. and added ov. Lib. rev. by Ghislanzoni.

Foss, Hubert (James) (*b* Croydon, 1899; *d* London, 1953). Eng. pianist and ed. Joined staff of OUP 1921 becoming head of mus. dept. on its foundation in 1924. Pubd. mus. of several Eng. composers, notably Walton and Vaughan Williams. Wrote book about Vaughan Williams (1950).

Foss (orig. Fuchs), **Lukas** (*b* Berlin, 1922). Ger.-born Amer. composer and cond. Studied in Berlin and Paris before settling in USA, 1937, where he studied at Curtis Institute (comp. with Scalero, cond. with Reiner). Became student of Koussevitzky and Hindemith. Pianist, Boston S. O. 1944–50. Worked in Rome 1950–2. Prof. of comp., Univ. of California, from 1953. Cond. Buffalo P.O. 1963–70. Mus. dir. Milwaukee S.O. from 1981. Foss's mus. is both traditional and experimental, the latter employing indeterminacy though scores are wholly notated. In his *Baroque Variations*, on themes by Bach, Handel, and Scarlatti, the method of 'composition by deletion' is used in an effective and sophisticated manner. Works incl.:

OPERAS: *The Jumping Frog of Calaveras County* (after Mark Twain) (1950); *Griffelkin* (TV, 1955); *Introductions and Goodbyes* (1959).
BALLET: *Gift of the Magi* (1945).
ORCH: Sym. (1945), Pf. Conc. No. 1 (1944), No. 2 (1951), Ob. conc. (1950), Vc. Concert (vc., orch., and tape) (1967), *Baroque Variations* (1967), *Paradigm* for perc., guitar and 3 other optional instr. (1968), *Time Cycle* for sop. and orch. (1960).
CHORAL: *The Prairie* (1944), *Parable of Death* (1953), *Psalms* (1957), *Round a Common Centre*, v. and ens. (1979).
CHAMBER MUSIC: *Echoi*, for cl., vc., perc., pf. (1961–3), *Elytres*, for fl., vns., pf., harp, perc. (1964), *Cave of the Winds*, woodwind quintet with multiphones (1972).

Foster, Lawrence (*b* Los Angeles, 1941). Amer. cond. of Romanian origin. Studied cond. in Los Angeles, at Bayreuth master classes, and with Walter and Böhm. Début 1960 with Young Musicians' Foundation Début Orch., which he cond. for 4 years. Assoc. cond. Los Angeles P. O. 1966. Eng. début 1967 with ECO, since then being frequent visitor. CG début 1976, revival of Walton's *Troilus and Cressida*. Cond. Houston S.O. 1971–8. Chief cond. Monte Carlo Opera 1978–81, gen. mus. dir. Duisburg from 1981. Cond. f.p. of Birtwistle's *The Triumph of Time* (1972).

Foster, Muriel (*b* Sunderland, 1877; *d* London, 1937). Eng. mez. Studied RCM. Became closely assoc. with mus. of Elgar, singing Angel in *Dream of Gerontius* in Düsseldorf and Worcester 1902, at f. London p. 1903, and many other times. Sang in f.ps. of *The Apostles* (1903) and *The Kingdom* (1906), gave f.p. of song-cycle Op. 59 (1910), and of *The Music Makers* (1912). Also notable Bach singer. Illness compelled premature retirement.

Foster, Stephen (Collins) (*b* Pittsburgh (Lawrenceville), 1826; *d* NY, 1864). Amer. composer. Mainly self-taught in mus. Wrote over 200 songs, several of which have come to be regarded almost as Amer. folk-songs. Though a Northerner, several of his songs capture the Southern plantation spirit in an authentic and eloquent manner. Among the best-known are: *Oh! Susanna* (*c*.1845), *Camptown Races* (1850), *Old Folks at Home* (1851), *Massa's in de Cold, Cold Ground* (1852), *My Old Kentucky Home* (1853), *Jeanie with the light brown hair* (1854), *Come where my love lies dreaming* (1855), *Old Black Joe* (1860), and *Beautiful Dreamer* (1864, posth.).

Foulds, John (Herbert) (*b* Manchester, 1880; *d* Calcutta, 1939). Eng. composer and cellist. Son of a professional bassoonist. Studied pf. at 4 and

started to compose at 7. Became orch. cellist at 14 and until 20 played in theatre bands in Manchester region. Joined Hallé Orch. under Richter in 1900. In 1906 was Eng. composer-delegate to Essen Mus. Fest., where he met Mahler and Strauss, and in 1910 went to Munich for f.p. of Mahler's 8th Sym. Comp. incid. mus. for plays produced by Lewis Casson. Moved in 1912 to London, where he met and eventually married the actress, musician, and writer Maud MacCarthy (1882–1967). Mus. dir., YMCA National Council 1918–23. From 1919 to 1921 he worked on his *World Requiem*, for soloists, ch., and orch. This ambitious work was perf. in Royal Albert Hall at Armistice Night commemoration ('Festival of Remembrance') in 1923 and for 3 subsequent years. In 1924 wrote incid. mus. for Shaw's *Saint Joan*. In 1927 Foulds went abroad, returning in 1930. Unable to obtain more than a few perfs., he went to India in 1935 to study folk music. In 1937 he was appointed dir. of mus. for All-India radio in Delhi. Formed radio orch. and Indo-European orch. of traditional Ind. instr. In 1939 was transferred to Calcutta to organize mus. at newly established radio station, but died from cholera after only a few days in new post.

Foulds's mus. was perhaps too eclectic to survive but a body of opinion exists which makes high claims for it. Like *Ives he was a tireless experimenter and was ahead of his time in Eng. mus. in working in microtonalities. The modal pf. mus., the str. qt. *Quartetto Intimo*, the Vc. Sonata, and several songs are splendid mus. and deserve to emerge from oblivion. Prin. works:

ORCH: *Epithalamium*, Op. 10 (1905); *Apotheosis*, Op. 18 (1908); *Holiday Sketches*, Op. 16 (1909); *Mirage*, Op. 20 (1910); *Keltic Suite*, Op. 29 (1911); *Music-Pictures No. 3*, Op. 33 (1912); *3 Mantras*, Op. 61b (*c*.1923); *Dynamic Triptych*, pf. and orch. (1927–30); *April-England* (orch. of pf. piece) (1932); *Hellas*, double str. orch., hp., perc., Op. 45 (1915–32); *Chinese Suite*, Op. 95 (*c*.1938).
CHORUS AND ORCH: *The Vision of Dante*, Op. 7 (1904–08); *World Requiem*, Op. 60 (1919–21).
CHAMBER MUSIC: *Music-Pictures*, Op. 30, pf. trio (1912); *Aquarelles*, Op. 32, str. qt. (1912); *Vc. sonata*, Op. 6 (1905, rev. 1927); Str. Qts. (at least 9) (1896–1933), *Quartetto Intimo*, Op. 89 (1933).
PIANO: *Lyrics*, Op. 1 (1900); *Variazioni ed Improvvisati*, Op. 4 (1905); *Gandharva-Music*, Op. 49 (1915); *Essays in the Modes*, Op. 78 (1928).
MISC: *The Tell-Tale Heart*, Op. 36, dramatic monologue for reciter and orch. (or pf.) (1912).
SONGS: *Mood Pictures*, Op. 51 (1917); *Lyra Celtica*, cont. and orch. (unfinished).

Foundation. In organ parlance this word is used in 2 different senses. (1) *Foundation Tone* is that of all the more dignified stops (Diapason, the more solid of the Fl. stops etc.).
(2) *Foundation Stops* are all the stops except the Mutation and Mixture stops.

Fountain of Arethusa, The. No. 1 of *Myths* (*Mity*), 3 Poems for vn. and pf. by Szymanowski, Op. 30 (1915).

Fourestier, Louis (*b* Montpellier, 1892; *d* Boulogne-Billancourt, 1976). Fr. cond. and composer. Studied Paris Cons. with Leroux and Gédalge. Cond. in Marseilles and Bordeaux, then Opéra-Comique, Paris, 1927–32 and Paris Opéra 1938–45. NY Met. 1946–8. Prof. of cond., Paris Cons. 1945–63. Comp. cantatas, symphonic poem, str. qt., etc.

Four Last Songs. (1) See *Vier letzte Lieder* (Strauss). (2) For v. and pf. by Vaughan Williams, comp. between 1954 and 1958 to words by Ursula Vaughan Williams. Title given by publisher, songs being intended by composer as part of 2 cycles. Individual titles: *Procris, Tired, Hands, Eyes, and Heart*, and *Menelaus*. F.p. as cycle 1960.

Fournet, Jean (*b* Rouen, 1913). Fr. cond. and flautist. Worked for Fr. Radio and was mus. dir., Opéra-Comique, Paris, 1944–57. Cond. Rotterdam P.O. 1968. Prof. of cond., École Normale de Paris, 1944–62.

Fournier, Pierre (*b* Paris, 1906; *d* Geneva, 1986). Fr. cellist. Studied Paris Cons. Début 1925. Worldwide tours as recitalist and conc. soloist. Chamber mus. partner of Szigeti, Primrose, and Schnabel. Master-class teacher, Paris Cons. 1941–9.

Four Rustics, The (Wolf-Ferrari). See *Quattro rusteghi, I*.

Four Saints in Three Acts. Opera in 4 acts by Virgil *Thomson to lib. by Gertrude Stein. Comp. 1928. Prod. Hartford, Conn., and NY 1934.

Four Seasons, The (*Le quattro Stagioni*). 4 vn. concs. by Vivaldi, No. 1 in E (Spring), RV269, No. 2 in G minor (Summer), RV315, No. 3 in F (Autumn), RV293, No. 4 in F minor (Winter), RV297. They are first 4 of 12 vn. concs. of Op. 8, *Il cimento dell' armonia e dell' inventione* (The contest between harmony and invention), pubd. Amsterdam 1725. Nos. 9 and 12 also exist as ob. concs. Fl. transcr. of whole work by James Galway.

Four Serious Songs (Brahms). See *Vier ernste Gesänge*.

Four Temperaments, The (1) Sub-title of *Nielsen's Sym. No. 2 in C minor, Op. 16 (*De Fire Temperamenter*), 1901–2, inspired by a painting of that name, each movement being descriptive of one of the medieval 'temperaments' of human character: choleric, phlegmatic, melancholic, sanguine.
(2) Sub-title of Hindemith's *Theme and Variations* for str. and pf., 1940, each of the 4 variations denoting a temperament, in the order melancholic, sanguine, phlegmatic, choleric. Also ballet (f.p. NY, 1944).

Fourth. Interval in melody or harmony in which there are 4 steps in the major or minor scale from one extreme to the other (incl. the bottom and top notes). Perfect 4th is the distance from C up to F or from G to C; a semitone more gives the augmented 4th (e.g. C up to F$\sharp$).

Fou Ts'ong (*b* Shanghai, 1934). Chinese pianist. Studied at Warsaw Cons. Début Shanghai 1953. Brit. début 1959. Settled in Eng., but int. tours.

Fox Strangways, Arthur Henry (*b* Norwich, 1859; *d* Dinton, Salisbury, 1948). Eng. critic and author. Mus. master Wellington Coll., 1893–1901. Mus. critic, *Times* 1911–25, *Observer* 1925–39. Founder and 1st ed. *Music and Letters* 1920–37. Authority on Indian mus. Joint biographer. (with M. *Karpeles) of Cecil Sharp. Trans. (with S. *Wilson) of Lieder of Schubert, Brahms, and Wolf.

Fox-trot. Amer. ballroom dance (and the mus. for it) of a kind of march-like ragtime, slow or quick. From *c*.1913 it spread to ballrooms all over the world. The *Charleston* and *Black Bottom* are varieties of it. In several of his works, Peter *Maxwell Davies has made use of the fox-trot for nostalgic and ironic effect.

F.R.A.D. Fellow of the Royal Academy of Dancing (founded 1927; chartered 1936).

Fra Diavolo (Brother Devil). Opéra-comique in 3 acts by Auber to lib. by Scribe. Prod. Paris 1830, London and NY 1831.

Frager, Malcolm (*b* St Louis, 1935). Amer. pianist. Trained in St Louis, NY, and at Amer. Cons., Fontainebleau (1952). Recital début 1941, conc. début St Louis 1945. NY début 1952. Winner of several int. competitions incl. Queen Elisabeth, Brussels, 1960. Tours of Europe and Russia.

F.R.A.M. Fellow of the Royal Academy of Music.

Franc (Le Franc), **Guillaume** (*b* Rouen, *c*.1505; *d* Lausanne, 1570). Huguenot composer, precentor successively at the Calvinist caths. of Geneva and Lausanne, and ed. of a book of metrical psalms (1565).

Française. Old round dance in triple or compound duple time. Very popular in the 1830s.

Françaix, Jean (*b* Le Mans, 1912). Fr. composer and pianist. Studied comp. with *Boulanger and pf. with Isidor Philipp. Frequent soloist in his own works, which are marked by wit and elegance. Wrote mus. for Sacha Guitry films. Comps. incl. operas (notably *La Main de Gloire*, 4 acts, prod. 1950), ballets, sym., sym. for str., pf. concertino, pf. conc., chamber mus. (incl. sax. qt.), pf. pieces, songs, oratorio *L'Apocalypse de Saint Jean* (1939), conc. for 2 harps and str. (1979), vn. conc. (1970), cl. quintet (1978), *Theme and Variations*, cl. and str. (1978), 6 *Impromptus*, fl. and bn. (1978), Ballet, *Les Demoiselles de la nuit* (1948), Vn. conc. No. 2 (1979), bn. conc. (1980), and *L'Horloge de Flore*, ob. and orch. (1959).

Francesca da Rimini. The story of the adulterous lovers Paolo and Francesca in Canto V of Dante's *Inferno* has been the basis of several comps.:

(1) Symphonic fantasy by Tchaikovsky, Op. 32, 1876, based on picture by Doré.

(2) Opera in 4 acts by Zandonai to lib. by T. Ricordi after play by d'Annunzio (1902), prod. Turin and London 1914, NY Met. 1916.

(3) Opera in prol., 2 scenes, and epilogue by Rakhmaninov to lib. by M. Tchaikovsky, prod. Moscow 1906.

(4) Symphonic poem by H. Hadley f.p. Boston 1905. Also operas on the subject by Goetz, Pierné, Thomas, *Nápravník, and several other composers.

Francescatti, (René) **Zino** (*b* Marseilles, 1902). Fr. violinist (It.-born father). Début at 5, played Beethoven conc. at 10. Toured Brit. 1926 with Ravel. Settled in USA. Soloist with world's leading orchs.

Francesch, Homero (*b* Montevideo, 1947). Uruguayan pianist. Début 1963. Studied Munich, 1967, with Maria Hindemith-Landes, and Munich Cons. with Steurer. Henze wrote his *Tristan* for him. London début 1974.

Francesina. See *Duparc, Elisabeth*.

Franchetti, Alberto (*b* Turin, 1860; *d* Viareggio, 1942). It. composer, pupil of Rheinberger at Munich Cons. His considerable wealth enabled him to stage his 9 operas which incl. *Germania* (1902, CG 1907), *Cristoforo Colombo* (1892), *La figlia di Jorio* (1906), and *Notte de Legenda* (1915). Wrote sym. and chamber mus.

Franchomme, Auguste (Joseph) (*b* Lille, 1808; *d* Paris, 1884). Fr. cellist. Played in Fr. th. orchs. in youth. With Alard and *Hallé founded series of Paris chamber concerts. Prof. of vc., Paris Cons. from 1846. Played in duos with Mendelssohn and Chopin. Wrote vc. conc. and other vc. pieces.

Franci, Carlo (*b* Buenos Aires, 1927). It. cond. and composer. Pupil of Petrassi (comp.) and Previtali (cond.). Cond. Rome Opera and NY Met., also Radio Eireann S.O. 1955-7. Wrote opera and instr. works.

Franck, César (Auguste Jean Guillaume) (*b* Liège, 1822; *d* Paris, 1890). Belg.-born composer (Fr. cit. from 1870). He toured Belgium as a pianist at the age of 13. In 1835 he went to Paris, studying harmony with Reicha and was at the Paris Cons. from 1837 to 1842. On leaving the Cons. he concentrated on comp. and settled in Paris in 1844. In 1858 he became organist of the church of Sainte-Clotilde, Paris, where his outstanding ability as an improviser drew listeners from far and wide, incl. Liszt who in 1866 likened his skill to that of Bach. He was prof. of org. at the Cons. from 1872. Throughout these years as teacher and organist, his comps. were ignored by the general public. His pupils, led by *d'Indy,

organized a concert of his works in Jan. 1887, which, although poorly perf., pleased the uncomplaining composer, who subsequently wrote 3 of his finest works. The Sym. was received with incomprehension in 1889, but there was an enthusiastic response to the Str. Qt. He became Chevalier du Légion d'Honneur in 1885.

In his early works Franck was influenced by the opéra-comique composers such as Grétry. His middle years were dominated by works of religious character, his oratorio *Les Béatitudes* occupying him for 10 years. In his later works he developed 'cyclic form' whereby a theme, modified or varied, recurs in each section of the work. His symphonic poems date from the late 1870s and the *Variations Symphoniques* for pf. and orch. from 1885. Franck's harmonic idiom, no doubt influenced by Wagner and by the org.-loft, has a pungent individuality which exerted a powerful sway not only over his pupils but over a much later generation, e.g. *Messiaen. His work also played a large part in restoring French taste to 'pure music', thereby opening the way for Debussy, Ravel, and others. Prin. comps.:

OPERAS: *Le Valet de Ferme*, opéra-comique (1851–2), *Hulda* (1882–5), *Ghisèle* (1889–90, orch. by Chausson, d'Indy, and others).

ORCH: *Les *Éolides* (1876), *Le *Chasseur maudit* (1882), *Les Djinns* (1884, pf. and orch.), *Variations Symphoniques* (1885, pf. and orch.), *Psyché* (1887–8, with ch.), Sym. in D minor (1886–8).

CHORAL: *Ruth*, biblical eclogue for soloists, ch., and orch. (1843–6); *La Tour de Babel*, oratorio (1865); *Les *Béatitudes*, oratorio (1869–79); *Rédemption*, for sop., ch., and orch. (1871–2, orch. item and male ch. added 1874); *Rebecca* (1881); *Messe solennelle*, for bass and org. (1858); Mass for 3 vv. (STB) with org., harp, vc., and db. (1860); 3 *Offertories*, for soloist, ch., org., and db.; *Panis angelicus*, for ten., org., harp, vc., and db. (1872).

CHAMBER MUSIC: Pf. Trio (1834); *Trois Trios Concertants*, pf., vn., and vc. (1841–2); 4th *Trio Concertant* (1842); Pf. Quintet (1878–9); Sonata for pf. and vn. (1886, also arr. for pf. and vc. and for pf. and fl.); Str. Qt. in D major (1889).

ORGAN: 6 *Pièces pour Grand Orgue* (1862); 44 *Petites Pièces* (1863); 3 *Pièces pour Grand Orgue* (incl. *Pièce heroique*) (1878); *Andantino* (1889); 3 *Chorals* (1890).

PIANO: *Souvenirs d'Aix-la-Chapelle* (1843); *Fantasia on 2 Polish Airs* (1845); *Prélude, Choral, et Fugue*, (1884); *Prélude, Aria et Final* (1886–7).

Also songs and works for harmonium incl. *L'Organiste*, 59 pieces for harmonium (1889–90).

Franck, Melchior (*b* Zittau, *c.*1579; *d* Coburg, 1639). Saxon composer. Kapellmeister to Duke of Coburg from 1603. Wrote songs, instr. works, and church mus.

Francoeur, François (*b* Paris, 1698; *d* Paris, 1787). Fr. composer and violinist. Twice manager of Paris Opéra (1757–67, 1772–5). Court musician. Wrote vn. sonatas, operas, and ballets. Collab. with F. *Rebel.

François, Samson (b Frankfurt, 1924; d Paris, 1970). Fr. pianist. Public début at age 6. Studied Nice Cons., in Italy and Belgrade, and in Paris with Cortot. Winner of several int. prizes. World tours. Fine exponent of Mozart and Debussy.

Francs Juges, Les (The judges of the secret court). Ov., Op. 3 by Berlioz, comp. 1826 to opera in 3 acts (libretto by H. Ferrand). 1st version of opera composed 1826, expanded in 1829, and recast in 1833 as 1-act intermezzo, *Le cri de guerre de Brisgaw*. Ov. and 6 numbers survive.

Frank, Alan (Clifford) (b London, 1910). Eng. publisher, ed., writer, and clarinettist. Joined OUP staff 1927, music ed. 1948, head of mus. dept. 1954–75.

Frankel, Benjamin (b London, 1906; d London, 1973). Eng. composer and cond. Watchmaker's apprentice. Studied mus. in Ger., returning to London (GSM) 1923. Worked as café musician and as jazz-band violinist, leader, and orchestrator (orch. of Coward's *Operette* and many C. B. Cochran revues). On staff GSM 1946. Many of his more serious comps. are in 12-note system. Wrote mus. for over 100 films. Prin. works:

ORCH: Vn. Conc. (1951), *Concertante Lirico* for str. (1953), *Serenata Concertante*, pf. trio and orch. (1961), va. conc. (1967), *Pezzi Melodici* for chamber orch. (1972), Syms., No. 1 (1958), No. 2 (1962), No. 3 (1964), No. 4 (1966), No. 5 (1967), No. 6 (1969), No. 7 (1969), No. 8 (1972).
CHAMBER MUSIC: Str. Trio (1944), Solo vn. sonata No. 1 (1944), No. 2 (1962), Str. Qts., No. 1 (1944), No. 2 (1945), No. 3 (1947), No. 4 (1948), No. 5 (1965), *3 Poems* for vc. and pf. (1950), pf. qt. (1953), *Bagatelles* for 11 instr. (1959).
VOCAL: *The Aftermath*, ten., tpt., str. (1947), 8 *Songs*, medium v. and pf. (1959).
OPERA: *Marching Song* (1972–3), 3 acts, lib. by Hans Keller after play by John Whiting. Completed in short score only. F.p. BBC broadcast 1983 in ed. by Buxton Orr.

Frankenstein, Alfred (b Chicago, 1906; d San Francisco, 1981). Amer. critic of mus. and art. Educated Chicago Univ., where he was on staff 1932–4. Mus. critic *San Francisco Chronicle* 1934–65. Found and pubd. (1939) sketches by V. Hartmann which inspired Mussorgsky's *Pictures at an Exhibition* and ed. illustrated edn. of score (1951).

Frankfurt Group. Group of Eng. composers (Norman O'Neill, Roger Quilter, Cyril Scott, and Balfour Gardiner) who were pupils of Iwan *Knorr at Frankfurt Hoch Cons. in late 1890s.

Frankl, Peter (b Budapest, 1935). Hung.-born pianist (Brit. citizen from 1967). Studied Liszt Acad., Budapest. 1st prize in pf. competitions in Paris 1957, Munich 1957, Rio de Janeiro 1959. Frequent conc. soloist. Member of chamber mus. trio with György Pauk (vn.) and Ralph Kirshbaum (vc.).

Franklin, David (b London, 1908; d Evesham, 1973). Eng. bass, discovered as amateur by John Christie 1934. Studied Vienna with Jani Strasser. Début Glyndebourne 1936. Leading bass CG 1947–50. Notable Ochs in *Rosenkavalier*. Also concert work (*Gerontius*, etc.). Throat ailment caused retirement 1951. Thereafter worked as effective broadcaster, lecturer, and writer. Librettist of *Tate's *The Lodger*.

Franquin, Merri (b Lançon, 1848; d Paris, 1934). Fr. trumpeter. Prof. of tpt., Paris Cons. Invented 5-piston tpt. Author of tpt. method.

Franz, Robert (Robert Franz Knauth) (b Halle, 1815; d Halle, 1892). Ger. composer. Studied at Dessau 1835–7. A set of his songs was highly praised by Schumann in 1843 and won the attention of Mendelssohn, Liszt, and others. Appointed org. at Halle, becoming mus. dir. of Halle Univ. Retired 1868 because of severe illness; thereafter ed. works of Bach and Handel, supplying additional accs., and comp. some choral mus. His reputation rests on his 300 Lieder, which some enthusiasts rank alongside those of Schubert and Schumann.

Frauenliebe und -Leben (Woman's Love and Life). Song-cycle for sop. or mez. and pf., Op. 42, by Schumann, being settings of 8 poems by Adalbert von Chamisso. Comp. 1840.

Frau ohne Schatten, Die (The Woman without a Shadow). Opera in 3 acts by R. Strauss to lib. by Hofmannsthal. Comp. 1914–18. Prod. Vienna 1919, San Francisco 1959, London 1967.

F.R.C.C.O. Fellow of the Royal Canadian College of Organists.

F.R.C.M. Fellow of the Royal College of Music.

F.R.C.O. Fellow of the Royal College of Organists.

Freccia, Massimo (b Florence, 1906). It. cond. and composer. Studied Florence Cons. and cond. under F. *Schalk in Vienna. Cond., Budapest S.O. 1933. Amer. début 1938. Cond. New Orleans S.O. 1944–51, Baltimore S.O. 1952–9; chief cond. Radio-televisione Italiana (RAI) Orch., Rome, 1959–63. Guest cond. of many other orchs.

Frederick the Great (Friedrich II, King of Prussia) (b Berlin, 1712; d Potsdam, 1786). Ger. sovereign (reigned 1740–86) who was also composer, flautist, and patron of mus. Pupil of Hayne and *Quantz. Est. court orch. Berlin 1740, and opera house 1742. Employed C. P. E. Bach as harpsichordist from 1740, and J. S. Bach visited the court at Potsdam, 1747, the *Musical Offering being the result (based on theme supplied by Frederick). Other notable musicians in Frederick's service incl. the Graun brothers and *Quantz. Comp. syms., opera, marches, arias, etc.

Fredigundis. Opera in 3 acts by F. *Schmidt to lib. by B. Warden and I. M. Welleminsky after Felix Dahn. Comp. 1916–21. Prod. Berlin 1922.

Fredman, Myer (b Plymouth, 1932). Eng. cond. On staff Glyndebourne Opera 1959–74; mus. dir. Glyndebourne Touring Opera 1968–74. Guest cond. BBC, LPO, RPO, ECO, and other orchs. Mus. dir. Adelaide Opera from 1975.

Free Canon. Form of *canon in which the intervals of the imitating v. remain the same numerically, but not necessarily as to quality (e.g. a major 3rd may become a minor 3rd).

Free Counterpoint. See *Counterpoint.*

Freed, Isadore (b Brest-Litovsk, 1900; d Rockville Center, NY, 1960). Russ.-born cond. and pianist. Emigrated to USA as child, studied Pennsylvania Univ. and Philadelphia Cons. Pf. pupil, 1924, of Josef *Hofmann. Studied comp. with *Bloch, 1918–21, and with *d'Indy, 1929–30. Cond. Concert Spirituel, Paris, 1930–3. On faculty Hartt Coll. of Mus., Hartford, Conn., 1944–60. Comps. incl. opera, ballet, 2 syms., vn. conc., vc. conc., va. rhapsody, 3 str. qts., choral works, and pf. pieces.

Free Fantasia. Same as 'Development' in Compound Binary Form, etc. See also *Form* (3).

Frei aber Froh (Ger., 'Free but happy'). Brahms's personal motto, the initial letters of which (F-A-F) he used as the basic thematic structure of his 3rd Sym. (1883).

Freischütz, Der (The Freeshooter). 3-act opera by Weber to lib. by Friedrich Kind after a story by Apel and Laun in *Gespensterbuch* (1811). Comp. 1817–21. Prod. Berlin 1821, London 1824, NY 1825.

Freitas, Frederico de (b Lisbon, 1902). Portuguese composer and cond. Studied Nat. Cons., Lisbon, 1919–24. Founder and cond. Lisbon Choral Soc. 1940–7, cond. Oporto S.O. 1949–53. Comps. incl. opera, sym., vn. sonata, str. qt., ballets, and choral works.

Freitas Branco, Luís de (b Lisbon, 1890; d Lisbon, 1955). Portuguese composer. Studied in Lisbon and in Berlin with Humperdinck. Taught at Lisbon Cons. and held govt. posts from which he was removed between 1939 and 1947 because of his protests over persecution of artists in Ger. and It. Comp. 4 syms., concs. for vn., pf., and vc., chamber mus., choral works. Wrote educational books.

Freitas Branco, Pedro de (b Lisbon, 1896; d Lisbon, 1963). Portuguese cond. and composer, brother of Luis *Freitas Branco. Founded Portuguese Opera Co. 1926. Cond. state sym. orch.

from 1934. Cond. Venice Biennale 1943. Guest cond. in Fr., Ger., Sp., Eng. (Hallé Orch. etc.).

Frémaux, Louis (b Aire sur Lys, 1921). Fr. cond. Studied Paris Cons. Cond. Nat. Orch. Monte Carlo 1956–65, Rhône-Alpes P.O. 1968–71, prin. cond. and mus. dir. CBSO 1969–78; prin. cond. Sydney S.O. 1979–81.

Fremstad, Olive (Olivia Rundquist) (b Stockholm, 1871; d Irvington, NY, 1951). Swed. sop. (later Amer. citizen). Her family emigrated to USA when she was in her early teens, when she expected to become pianist, having made recital début at age 12. Opera début Boston 1890 in Sullivan's *Patience.* Went to NY 1890, becoming cont. soloist at St Patrick's Cath. Studied in Berlin 1893 with Lilli Lehmann, who convinced her she was sop. or mez. Soloist 1895 in Schumann's *Paradise and the Peri* at Cologne Fest., leading to engagement with Cologne Opera, début as Azucena. Bayreuth 1896, London 1902, Munich Opera 1900–3, NY Met. 1903 as Sieglinde, cond. Mottl. Increasingly specialized in Wagner roles e.g. Kundry and Brünnhilde, of which she was one of greatest interpreters, but sang Carmen opposite Caruso 1906 and Salome in the single perf. at NY Met. 1907 (also first Paris Salome, 1907). Sang Isolde at Mahler's Met. début, 1908. Farewell appearance at Met. 1914, but sang opera at Boston and Chicago, and gave final recital, NY 1920.

French Horn. Coiled brass wind instr. (tube over 11′ in all) of conical ¼″ bore, with funnel-shaped mouth-piece and bell of 11–14″ diameter. The hn. was one of the earliest primitive instrs., being used for military purposes and esp. for hunting. The modern hn. was developed in Fr. (hence the name). It has existed in 2 forms: (a) *Natural, but with *crooks.* This is the instr. for which the older classical composers wrote and is said to have been introduced into the orch. by Lully in his comedy-ballet *La Princesse d'Elide,* Paris 1664. A notational convention existed whereby if notes occurred low enough to demand the use of the bass clef, they were written an octave lower than that pitch demanded. All parts were written as if in the key of C, with sharps and flats inserted as accidentals. Certain notes not in tune with the modern tempered scale were modified by the insertion of a hand in the bell ('stopped notes'). (b) *With valves.* The Fr. hn. was equipped with rotary valves in about 1827 and this instr. gradually displaced (a). Schumann was among the first to specify its use, and Wagner abandoned (a) in and after *Lohengrin* (1848). Traditionally the valved hn. is pitched in F, but other pitches exist. Compass is from B′ upwards for about 3½ octaves. The 'double hn.' pitched in both F and B♭ alto, is normally used today. The valves act much as the old crooks did but of course more speedily. Notation is without key signature, written a perfect 5th higher than it is intended to sound. There is a modern tendency to use a key signature, which, from the use of the F pitch, necessarily has a flat less or sharp more than the actual key. The hn.'s place in the sym. orch. has grown in importance since the 19th cent., composers such as Mahler and Strauss sometimes specifying 8 hns. Orch. parts assume that the higher notes will be played by the odd-numbered players, the lower by the even. Many hn. concs. have been written (e.g. by Mozart, Strauss, Hindemith), and it is also employed in chamber works (notably Brahms's Hn. Trio). The Fr. hn. is also used in military bands, but not in brass bands where the term is colloquially used to denote the ten. saxhorn.

French Overture. 17th and 18th-cent. form of the piece of orch. mus. played before an opera or oratorio (see *Overture*). It was orig. developed by Lully, and was in 3 movements, slow, quick, slow.

French Sixth. A type of *augmented 6th, containing an augmented 6th, major 3rd, and augmented 4th (taking key C as example: A♭-C-D-F♯).

French Suites. Name (possibly unauthorized) given to a set of 6 kbd. suites by Bach, comp. c.1722. See also *English Suites, German Suites*.

Freni, Mirella (b Modena, 1935). It. sop. Studied with Campogalliani. Début Modena as Micaela in *Carmen* 1955. Netherlands Opera 1959–60. Glyndebourne (Zerlina) 1960. CG début 1961 (Nannetta), Milan 1963 (Mimi), NY Met. from 1965. Many appearances Vienna and Salzburg in operas cond. *Karajan.

Frescobaldi, Girolamo (b Ferrara, 1583; d Rome, 1643). It. composer and organist. Held post at Antwerp, becoming organist at St Peter's, Rome, 1608–28 (30,000 are said to have attended his f.p. there, an indication of his reputation as a virtuoso). Organist at Florentine court 1628–33, returning to St Peter's thereafter. Comp. motets and madrigals, but prin. achievements were his toccatas, fugues, ricercari, and capriccios for org. and hpd. His mus. had strong influence on Ger. mus. through his pupil *Froberger.

Frets. Strips of wood or metal (orig. cords) on the fingerboard of certain str. instrs. e.g. guitar, viol, lute (though not vn. family). They indicate the length of str. required to produce a given note—the player presses his finger against a fret to shorten the vibrating length of str.

Fretta (It.). Haste. Hence *frettevole, frettoso, frettoloso, frettolosamente,* 'hurried'.

Fretwell, Elizabeth (b Melbourne, 1922). Australian sop. Début Australian Nat. Opera 1947 as Senta. Sang with Dublin Grand Opera 1954. Prin. sop. SW Opera from 1955, becoming a famous Violetta. First Brit. Ariadne in Strauss's opera. Notable exponent of Britten roles. O.B.E. 1977.

Freund, Marya (b Breslau, 1876; d Paris, 1966). Fr. (Polish-born) sop. and teacher. Began as vn. student of Sarasate but switched to singing, studying under Stockhausen etc. Début 1909. Became authoritative interpreter of contemporary composers; one of 1st to sing 12-note works. Created part of Wood Dove in Schoenberg's *Gurrelieder* (1913), was speaker in 1st Fr. and Eng. perfs. of *Pierrot Lunaire* (but not at f. Berlin p.). Sang in new works by Satie, Bloch, Milhaud, Szymanowski, Poulenc, and others. Teacher in Paris for over 30 years.

Frick, Gottlob (b Abronn, 1906). Ger. bass singer. Studied Stuttgart Cons., joined ch. of Stuttgart Opera 1927. Solo roles from 1934 at Coburg, Dresden 1940–50, Berlin Städtische Opera 1950–3, Munich and Vienna from 1953. Début CG 1951, NY Met. 1962. Noted for Wagner roles. Bayreuth 1957–64. Retired 1971 but continued to make occasional appearances.

Fricker, Peter Racine (b London, 1920). Eng. composer. Studied RCM, later with *Seiber. Served RAF 1941–6. Won Clements Prize 1947 with wind quintet, and Koussevitzky award with his Sym. No. 1 (f.p. cond. Barbirolli, Cheltenham 1950). Won Arts Council Fest. of Britain award for young composers, 1951, with vn. conc. Prof. of comp., RCM 1956–64, dir. of mus., Morley Coll., 1953–64, composer-in-residence Univ. of Calif. (S. Barbara) since 1964. One of 1st post-1945 Eng. composers to develop individual style derived from influences of Bartók, Stravinsky, and Schoenberg. Prin. comps.:

ORCH: Sym. No. 1 (1949), No. 2 (1950–1), No. 3 (1960), No. 4 (1966), No. 5 (1975–6), *Prelude, Elegy, and Finale* for str. (1949), *Dance Scene* (1954), *Litany,* for double str. orch. (1955), *3 Scenes* (1966), *7 Counterpoints* (1967); *Sinfonia in memoriam Benjamin *Britten* (for 17 wind instr.) (1976–7).

CONCERTOS: Vn. (1949–50), cor anglais and str. (or pf.) (1950), 3 pf., str., and timp. (1951), va. (1952), pf. (1952–4), vn. No. 2 (*Rapsodia Concertante*) (1952–4), *Toccata* for pf. (1958–9), *Laudi Concertati,* org. and orch. (1979).

VOICE AND INSTR: *Night Landscape,* sop. and str. trio (1947), *3 Sonnets by Cecco Angiolieri,* ten. and 7 instr. (1947), *Tomb of St Eulalia,* elegy for countertenor, va. da gamba, hpd. (1955), *Cantata,* ten. and chamber orch. (1962), *O Longs désirs,* 5 songs for sop. and orch. (1963), *The Day and the Spirits,* sop. and harp (1966–7), *Some Superior Nonsense,* ten. and chamber ens. (1968), *The Roofs,* coloratura sop. and perc. (1970), *Come, sleep,* cont., alto fl., bass cl. (1972).

CHORAL: *Madrigals* (a cappella) (1947), *Musick's Empire,* ch. and small orch. (1955), *The *Vision of Judgement,* oratorio for sop., ten., ch., and orch. (1957–8), *Ave Maris Stella* (1967), *Magnificat* (1968), *Whispers at these Curtains,* bar., ch., boys' ch., orch. (1984).

CHAMBER MUSIC: Wind Quintet (1947), Str. Qt. No. 1 (1947), No. 2 (1952–3), No. 3 (1975), Vn. Sonata (1950), Hn. Sonata (1955), Vc. Sonata (1956), Octet (1957–8), *Serenade* No. 1 (1959), No. 2 (1959), 4 *Dialogues*, ob. and pf. (1965), *Fantasy*, va. and pf. (1966), *Paseo*, for guitar (1970).

PIANO: *Variations* (1957–8), 12 *Studies* (1961), Episodes I (1967–8), II (1969); *Anniversary* (1978).

2 PIANOS: Sonata (1977).

ORGAN: *Sonata* (1947), *Choral* (1956), *Ricercare* (1965), 6 *Pieces* (1968), *Toccata* (1968), *Praeludium* (1970).

Fricsay, Ferenc (b Budapest, 1914; d Ermatingen, Switz., 1963). Hung. cond. Studied with Kodály and Bartók. Cond. at Szeged 1933–9. Prin. cond. Budapest Opera 1939–45. Cond. f.ps. of *Einem's Dantons Tod*, Salzburg 1947, and Orff's *Antigonae*, Salzburg 1949. Cond. Berlin Städtische Opera 1948–52, Munich Opera 1956–8, Deutsche Oper, Berlin, from 1961. Prin. cond. RIAS Orch., Berlin, from 1948. Mus. dir. Bavarian State Opera 1956–8. Brit. début, Edinburgh Fest. 1950. Guest cond. of many orchs. Amer. début Boston S.O. 1953.

Frid, Géza (b Máramaros-Sziget, 1904). Hung.-born pianist and composer (Dutch citizen 1948). Studied Budapest Acad. 1912–24, working with Kodály and Bartók. Settled in Amsterdam 1929. Comps. incl. sym., pf. conc. (with ch.), pf. sonata, str. qts.

Fried, Oskar (b Berlin, 1871; d Moscow, 1941). Ger. cond., hn.-player, and composer. Guest cond. of most leading European orchs., specially active in Berlin. Champion of Delius, Mahler, and others among his contemporaries. His comps. incl. opera *Die vernarrte Prinzess, Verklärte Nacht*, mez., ten., orch. (1901), and *Das trunkene Lied*, sop., cont., bass, ch., and orch. (1904).

Friedenstag (Day of Peace). 1-act opera by R. Strauss to lib. by J. Gregor based on Calderón's play *La Rendención de Breda* (1625). Comp. 1935–6. Prod. Munich 1938. F. Eng. p. BBC broadcast 1971.

Friedheim, Arthur (b St Petersburg, 1859; d NY, 1932). Ger pianist, composer, and teacher. Educated St Petersburg Univ., later cond. th. orchs. in Ger. Studied for 8 years with Liszt, becoming his friend and secretary. Lived and worked in USA 1891–5. Prof. of pf., RMCM 1903–4. Cond. in Munich, 1908–10, returning to USA. Settled in NY 1914 but became prof. of pf., Canadian Acad., Toronto, 1921. Ed. complete works of Chopin, transcr. Liszt works, and comp. operas and pf. concs.

Friedman, Ignaz (b Podgórze, nr. Kraków, 1882; d Sydney, N.S.W., 1948). Polish pianist and composer. Pupil of Leschetizky. Toured in Europe and USA, living in Berlin until 1914, then in Copenhagen and, from 1940, in Australia. Ed. Chopin's works. Comp. chamber mus. and songs.

Friedrich, Götz (b Naumburg, 1930). Ger. opera producer. Studied in Weimar and joined *Felsenstein at the Komische Oper, Berlin, 1953. First prod. *Così fan tutte* 1958, dir. of prods. 1968. Chief prod. Hamburg from 1973. Prod. *Tannhäuser* at Bayreuth 1972. Prin. prod. CG from 1976 and has staged there *The Ring* (1974–6), *Der Freischütz* (1977), *Idomeneo* (1978), and *Lulu* (1981). An avowed Marxist, his political leanings are reflected in his prods. Deutsche Oper, Berlin, from 1980. Married to soprano Karan Armstrong (b 1941).

Friend, Rodney (b Huddersfield, 1939). Eng. violinist. Studied RAM and RMCM. Début as conc. soloist London 1962 (Hallé, Barbirolli). Leader, LPO 1964–76. Concertmaster (leader) NY P.O. 1976–9 (1st Englishman to hold this post). Leader, BBC S.O. from 1980.

Friml, Rudolf (b Prague, 1879; d Hollywood, 1972). Cz. composer who settled in USA 1906. Studied Prague Cons. First visited USA 1901 as pianist with Jan *Kubelik. Played his pf. conc. with NY S.O. and comp. pf. works and chamber mus. Fame rests on series of popular operettas: *The Firefly* (1912), *Katinka* (1915), *Rose Marie* (1924), and *The Vagabond King* (1925).

Friskin, James (b Glasgow, 1886; d NY, 1967). Scottish pianist. Studied RCM (pf. with Dannreuther, comp. with Stanford). Settled in USA 1914, devoting most of time to teaching and to recitals of Bach's mus., in which he specialized. Taught at Institute of Mus. Art, NY, and Juilliard Sch. for a total of 50 years.

F.R.M.C.M. Fellow of the Royal Manchester College of Music.

Froberger, Johann Jacob (b Stuttgart, 1616; d Héricourt, 1667). Ger. composer and organist. Organist at court of Vienna 1637, but spent next 4 years in Italy as pupil of *Frescobaldi. Visited Belgium, Germany, Holland, France, and England before returning to Vienna as court org. 1653–8. Comp. much for org. and hpd. (toccatas, capriccios, ricercari, etc.).

'Frog' Quartet. (Ger. *Froschquartett*). Nickname of Haydn's Str. Qt. in D major, Op. 50, No. 6 (1787) because of the 'croaking' theme in the finale.

Froissart. Concert-ov., Op. 19, by Elgar comp. for and f.p. at Worcester Fest. 1890. Title refers to passage in Scott's *Old Mortality* in which Claverhouse speaks of his enthusiasm for the historical romances and *Chronicles* of the Fr. writer Jean Froissart (1337–1410). Score is headed by Keats quotation 'When chivalry lifted up her lance on high'.

From Bohemia's Meadows and Forests (Z *Českych Luhu a Haju*). The 4th symphonic poem of Smetana's *Má Vlást*, often played separately.

From My Life (Z *mého života*; Ger. *Aus meinem Leben*). Title of Smetana's 2 str. qts. (E minor, 1876, and D minor, 1882–3) though it has become customary to apply it only to No. 1. Autobiographical character of this qt. culminates in sustained high E in finale depicting whistling in composer's ear which in 1874 heralded his deafness.

From Stone to Thorn. Work by *Maxwell Davies for mez. and instr. ens. to poem by George Mackay Brown. F.p. Oxford 1971, with Mary Thomas (mez.) cond. composer.

From the Bavarian Highlands (Elgar). See *Bavarian Highlands, Scenes from the.*

From the Diary of Virginia Woolf. Song-cycle of 8 songs for medium v. and pf. by *Argento with text from V. Woolf: 1. *The Diary*, 2. *Anxiety*, 3. *Fancy*, 4. *Hardy's Funeral*, 5. *Rome*, 6. *War*, 7. *Parents*, 8. *Last Entry*. Comp. 1974. F.p. Minneapolis, 1975 (Janet Baker and Martin Isepp).

From the House of the Dead. See *House of the Dead, From the.*

Frosch (Ger., 'frog'). The nut of the vn. bow. *Am Frosch*, 'at the nut'.

Frottola (It., plural *frottole*). A late 15th- and early 16th-cent. popular unacc. It. choral form, a type of simple *madrigal similar to the Eng. ayre. The same mus. was sung to each verse and the tune was invariably in the highest part.

F.R.S.C.M. Fellow of the Royal School of Church Music.

Frühbeck de Burgos, Rafael (b Burgos, 1933). Sp. cond. Studied Bilbao Cons. and Madrid Cons. 1950–3, then Acad. of Mus., Munich, until 1958. Prin. cond. Bilbao orch. 1958–62, Madrid Nat. Orch. 1962–77, Düsseldorf S.O. 1966–71, Montreal S.O. 1975–6. Guest cond., prin. European and Amer. orchs., incl. Nat. S.O. of Washington from 1980.

Frumerie, Per (Gunnar Fredrik de) (b Nacka, Stockholm, 1908). Swed. composer and pianist. Studied Stockholm Cons. and in Vienna and Paris. Prof. of pf., Stockholm Cons., from 1962. Works incl. opera, ballet, symphonic variations, 2 pf. concs., vn. conc., pf. pieces, 2 vn. sonatas, 3 str. qts., songs, etc.

Fry, William (Henry) (b Philadelphia, 1813; d Santa Cruz, 1864). Amer. composer, mus. critic, and author. Mainly self-taught. In 1845 wrote *Leonora*, regarded as first significant Amer. opera. From 1846 spent 6 years in London and Paris as correspondent of NY *Tribune*, meeting Berlioz and others. On return to NY as mus. critic of *Tribune*, championed Amer. composers. Wrote another opera, syms., church mus., etc.

F.T.C.L. Fellow of Trinity College of Music, London.

F.T.S.C. Fellow of the Tonic Sol-fa College of Music.

Fuchs, Carl (b Offenbach, 1865; d Manchester, 1951). Ger. cellist. Studied in Frankfurt and St Petersburg (under Davidov). Prin. cellist Hallé Orch., Manchester, 1887–1914. Prof. of vc. RMCM 1893–1914 and 1921–42. Member of Brodsky Qt. 1895–1926. Pubd. a vc. method (3 vols.) 1906.

Fuchs, Johann (Nepomuk) (b Frauenthal, 1832; d Vöslau, 1899). Austrian cond. and composer. Vienna Opera from 1880. Dir., Vienna Cons. from 1893. Wrote opera *Zingara* (1872).

Fuchs, Joseph (b NY, 1900). Amer. violinist. Studied Institute of Mus. Art, NY. Début 1920. Concertmaster, Cleveland Orch. 1926–40. Career as soloist began 1943. Frequent chamber mus. player, often with sister Lillian (b 1910, va. player and composer for that instr.) Prof. of vn. Juilliard Sch. from 1946. Toured Russ. 1965.

Fuchs, Robert (b Frauenthal, 1847; d Vienna 1927). Austrian composer and teacher, brother of Johann Nepomuk *Fuchs. Studied Vienna Cons. and was prof. of harmony and counterpoint there 1875–1912. (Mahler and Wolf were among his pupils.) Wrote 2 operas, 5 syms., 5 serenades, mass, chamber mus., songs.

Fuchsova, Liza (b Brno, 1913; d London, 1977). Cz. pianist. Studied Brno Cons. and Prague Cons. Début with Czech. P.O. Settled in London 1939. Member of Dumka Trio. Excelled in chamber mus. Teacher in later years.

Fuenllana, Miguel de (b Navalcarnero, Madrid, c.1500; d ?Valladolid, c.1579). Blind Sp. composer and vihuela virtuoso. Pubd. *Orphénica Lyra* (1554), containing orig. works and transcrs. of vocal works, etc. Served at Sp. royal court during 1560s.

Fuga (Lat., It. 'Flight'). Since mid-17th cent. this term has meant It. equivalent of *Fugue. From Middle Ages to early 17th cent. denoted strict imitation or an individual point of imitation.

Fuga alla giga (Fugue in Jig-style). A fugue in G by J. S. Bach for org., so called from its rhythmic nature.

Fugara. Org. stop; a rather rougher toned variety of *Gamba.

Fugato. A passage in fugal style. See *Fugue.*

Fughetta. A short *Fugue.

Fugue (Fr. 'fugue', Ger. 'Fuge', It. 'fuga'). Type of contrapuntal comp. for particular no. of parts or 'voices' (described thus whether vocal or instr., e.g. fugue in 4 parts, fugue in 3 vv.). The point of fugue is that the vv. enter successively in imitation of each other, the 1st v. entering with a short melody or phrase known as the *Subject* (different from sonata-form 'subject' in that it is merely melodic and short). When all the vv. have entered, the *Exposition* is over. Then (normally) there comes an Episode or passage of connective tissue (usually a development of something that has appeared in the exposition) leading to another entry or series of entries of the Subject, and so on until the end of the piece, entries and episodes alternating.

Contrasts of key constitute an important element in fugal construction. In the Exposition the Subject first appears, naturally, in the tonic key; the 2nd v. to enter with it does so a 5th higher (or 4th lower), i.e. in the dominant key, the name *Answer* now being attached to it; the 3rd is a repetition of the Subject (in a higher or lower octave) and so on, Subject and Answer, Tonic and Dominant keys, thus appearing alternately, according to the no. of 'voices' engaged. One function of the Episodes is to effect modulation to various related keys, so that the later entries may have the advantage of this variety, but once the Exposition is over it is not considered necessary that further series of entries shall always alternate as to keys in the Subject-Answer manner.

In addition to the Subject there is often a *Countersubject* appearing in the Exposition and probably later in the Fugue. It is of the nature of a melodic acc. to the Answer and Subject (generally in double *counterpoint). The v. which has just given out the Subject or Answer then goes on to the Countersubject whilst the next v. is giving out the Answer or Subject and so on.

Sometimes in later entries there is overlapping of the Subject, each v., as it gives out, not waiting for the previous v. to finish it but breaking in, as it were, prematurely. This device, which is called *Stretto*, tends to increase the emotional tension of the entry in which it occurs.

Occasionally, after the Exposition (and possibly before the 1st Episode) there is a *Counter-Exposition*, much like the 1st Exposition in that the same 2 keys are employed. Appearances of the Subject (in the Exposition or elsewhere) are sometimes separated by something of the nature of the Episode, but shorter, called a *Codetta*.

There exist 2 types of Fugue with 2 subjects (or *double fugue*), one in which the 2 Subjects appear together from the outset, and another in which the 1st Subject is treated for a certain time, the other then appearing and being likewise treated, after which both are combined. In choral fugues (e.g. in an oratorio movement) there is sometimes a free instr. part, an *accompanied fugue*. The device of *pedal is often employed in fugue, especially near its close.

There are cases in which, instead of the Answer being an exact replica of the Subject (*Real Answer*), it is slightly changed in 1 or 2 of its intervals (*Tonal Answer*), resulting respectively in a *Real Fugue* and a *Tonal Fugue* (an absurdity since the tonal treatment may not extend beyond the exposition).

A shortened type of fugue is sometimes called a *fughetta*. A passage in fugal style, not in itself an actual fugue, is called *fugato*.

The above descriptions are of the academic fugue form, but the great composers have, naturally, varied it, e.g. Bach in *Die Kunst der Fuge*. Superb fugues occur in many works, e.g. Beethoven's *Grosse fuge* for str. qt., Op. 133, in Elgar's *Introduction and Allegro* for str., and in many choral comps. Fugue-form is also used effectively in opera, e.g. the finale of Act 2 of Wagner's *Die Meistersinger von Nürnberg* and the finale of Verdi's *Falstaff*.

Fuguing tune. An 18th-cent. type of hymn-tune in which 1 or more vv. fell silent and then came in with an imitation of some preceding v. Popular in USA, particularly those by *Billings.

Fujikawa, Mayumi (*b* Asahikawa, Japan, 1946). Japanese violinist. Studied with her father and at Toho Cons., Tokyo, and later in Belgium. Pupil of Leonid *Kogan in Nice 1968–70. Won Vieuxtemps grand prix, Verviers, 1970. London début 1975 (with LSO cond. Previn). Plays in pf. trio with Michael Roll (pf.) and Richard Markson (vc.).

Fuleihan, Anis (*b* Cyprus, 1900; *d* Stanford, Calif., 1970). Cyprian-born Amer. composer, cond., pianist, and teacher. Settled in USA 1915, début as pianist NY 1919. Comp. ballets for Bolm and Denishaw cos. in 1920s. Prof. of mus., Indiana Univ. 1947–52, dir., Nat. Cons., Beirut, 1953–60. Cond. Tunis orch. 1963–5. Returned to USA as teacher at Illinois Univ. Comps. incl. opera, 2 syms., 3 *Cyprus Serenades*, 3 vn. concs., 2 pf. concs., concs. for vc., bn., *Theremin, fl., and va., 5 str. qts., fl. sonata, vn. sonata, vc. sonata, va. sonata, 4 pf. sonatas, songs.

Full Anthem. Anglican church anthem sung by full choir throughout, as opposed to *verse anthem*.

Full Close. Perfect *cadence, i.e. chord of the dominant followed by that of the tonic.

Fuller, Donald (*b* Washington, D.C., 1919). Amer. composer. Pupil of Wagenaar, Milhaud, and Copland. Comps. incl. sym., cl. trio, pf. sonata, 2-pf. sonata, songs.

Fuller Maitland, John (Alexander) (*b* London, 1856; *d* Carnforth, 1936). Eng. critic, ed., and harpsichordist. Studied pf. Started career as mus. critic, *Pall Mall Gazette*, 1882–4, chief critic of *Times* 1889–1911. One of founders of Folk Song Soc. 1898, having collaborated with L. *Broadwood in *English County Songs*, 1893. Ed. 2nd edn. *Grove's Dictionary of Music and Musicians* (1904–10). Ed. (with W. Barclay *Squire) *Fitzwilliam Virginal Book* (1894–9). Also wrote books on Schumann, Brahms, Joachim, J. S. Bach, and 19th-cent. Eng. mus.

Füllflöte (Ger.). A 'full-toned' (i.e. loud) fl. stop on the org.

Fülligstimmen (Ger., 'full-toned voices'). Org. stops of loud tone.

Full mixture. Org. *Mixture stop of which pipes are of Diapason scale.

Full Orchestra. The orch. of the normal 4 main sections (str., woodwind, brass, perc.) at concert-hall strength.

Full Organ. As an indication in org. music, directs the player to use Great coupled to Swell, with all the louder stops on both manuals.

Füllstimme (Ger., 'filling-voice'). (1) A middle strand in the texture of a choral or instr. comp. which may be considered purely accessory.
(2) An additional orch. part (see *Ripieno*).
(3) The Mixture stop of an org.

Full to Mixtures. Org. composers' term meaning use all loud stops except Reeds.

Fulton, (Robert) **Norman** (*b* London, 1910; *d* Birmingham, 1980). Eng. composer. Studied RAM 1928–33. BBC staff 1936–60. Prof. of harmony RAM 1966. Comps. incl. 2 syms., pf. conc., vn. conc., va. sonata, songs.

Functional analysis. Form of analysis of a comp., without words, simply by musical extracts showing its structural features and thematic developments, invented for radio by Hans *Keller because he believed that writing or talking about music distorts the music (though he has valuably done a lot of both).

Fundamental. A chord in which the lowest note is that from which the chord is derived. *Fundamental Bass* is the imaginary bass of a passage, consisting not of its actual bass notes but of the roots of its chords, i.e. the bass of its chords when in root position.

Fundamental Discord. A discordant chord of which the discordant note forms a real part of the chord, i.e. not a mere suspension, anticipation, or retardation. Or the discordant note itself (e.g. dominant 7th, etc.).

Fundamental Note. The primary note of the harmonic series.

Funèbre (Fr.), **Funebre** (It.). Funeral. *Marche funèbre*, funeral march.

Funeral March of a Marionette (*Convoi funèbre d'une marionette*). Light-hearted piece by Gounod comp. as pf. solo 1872 and orch. 1879.

Funeral Marches. Among the best known of these (all of them in some public use on occasions of mourning) are the following: (1) Handel's *Dead March in Saul* (from the oratorio of that name); (2) The 2nd movement of Beethoven's 3rd Sym. (*Eroica*); (3) The 3rd movement of Chopin's 2nd pf. sonata (in B♭ minor, Op. 35); (4) Chopin's *Marche funèbre*, Op. 72b in C minor.

There are also (5) Beethoven's March 'sulla morte d'un eroe' (on the death of a hero), which is a movement in his pf. sonata in A♭, Op. 26; (6) Mendelssohn's *Song without Words* No. 28, in E minor (the title *Funeral March* not, however, authentic); (7) Siegfried's Funeral March from Wagner's *Götterdämmerung*; (8) Grieg's Funeral March for Nordraak (military band, but scored also by Halvorsen for orch.); (9) Berlioz's *Funeral March for the Last Scene of 'Hamlet'* (Op. 18, No. 3, 1848). Several symphonic movements (e.g. Elgar's 2nd Sym. *Larghetto* and various examples in the works of Mahler) have the character if not the title of funeral marches.

Fünf (Ger.). Five. *Fünfstimmig*, '5-voiced', i.e. in 5 parts.

Funiculì, funiculà. Song comp. by *Denza, 1880, in honour of the opening of the Naples funicular railway. Quoted by R. Strauss, who was apparently under the impression that it was a genuine folk-song, in *Aus Italien*, 1886.

Fuoco (It.). Fire, e.g. *con fuoco*, with a combination of force and speed. (But *focoso*, fiery.)

Für Elise (For Elise). Bagatelle in A minor for pf. by Beethoven, comp. *c*.1810. Autograph score is inscribed 'Für Elise am 27 April zur Erinnerung von L. v. Bthvn'. Theory put forward by Max Unger that 'Elise' may have been copyist's misreading of Therese (von Brunswick) with whom Beethoven was in love and among whose papers the score was discovered. Pubd. 1867.

Furia (It.). Fury. So *furioso, furibondo*, furious; *furiosamente*, furiously.

Furiant. A rapid Bohemian dance of decided yet frequently-changing rhythm. Dvořák used the title for several movements, but in some of his examples the rhythm remained unchanged.

Furniture, fourniture (in org. terminology). A powerful *Mixture Stop*.

Furore (It.). (1) Fury.
(2) Enthusiasm.

Furtwängler, Wilhelm (*b* Berlin, 1886; *d* nr. Baden-Baden, 1954). Ger. cond. and composer. Studied in Munich with Rheinberger and Schillings. Cond. th. orchs. in Zürich, Strasbourg, and Lübeck 1905–15. Mannheim Opera 1915–20. Tonkünstler Orch., Vienna, 1919–24. Leipzig Gewandhaus Orch. 1922–28, Berlin P.O. 1922 (for most of the rest of his life), Vienna P.O. 1924 (prin. cond. 1927–28, 1933–54). Bayreuth Fest. 1931, 1936, 1937, 1943, 1944, 1951 (Beethoven's 9th Sym. only). London début 1924, NY 1925, CG opera début 1935 (*Tristan*). Regularly cond. Salzburg Fest. and perfs. of Wagner's *Ring* at the Scala, Milan. In concert-hall gave memorable perfs. of the classics, Bruckner, Tchaikovsky, Strauss, etc., and championed music of Stravinsky and other 20th cent. composers. Cond. f.ps. of

Bartók's 1st pf. conc. (Frankfurt 1927), Schoenberg's *Variations*, Op. 31 (Berlin 1928), Hindemith's sym. *Mathis der Maler* (Berlin 1934), and Strauss's *Vier letzte Lieder* (London 1950). Controversy over his position during Nazi régime led to withdrawal of his appointment as cond. NY P.-S.O., 1936 and as cond. of Chicago S.O. 1949. Cleared of pro-Nazi activities 1946 and resumed his int. career, visiting London several times. One of the great masters of the art of cond. Comp. 3 syms., pf. conc., and chamber mus.

Futurism. Artistic movement which began in 1909 when *Marinetti published his futurist manifesto in a Paris newspaper. Aim was to emphasize dynamic force and motion in industrial soc. Musically this meant all kinds of noise, and special instr. were invented, such as exploders, thunderers, and whistlers. Prominent in the movement were Francesco Pratella (1880–1955), who composed for a standard orch. and Luigi Russolo (1885–1947), a painter, who wanted every kind of sound to be mus. material. 2 of his works, perf. London 1914, were *The Awakening of a Great City* and *A Meeting of Motorcars and Aeroplanes.* Movement petered out *c.*1918, but left its mark.

Fux, Johann Joseph (*b* Hirtenfeld, nr. Graz, 1660; *d* Vienna, 1741). Austrian composer, organist, and theorist. Organist in Vienna 1696, court composer 1698–1705, choirmaster St Stephen's Cath. 1705, vice-Kapellmeister 1713, Kapellmeister 1715. His *Gradus ad Parnassum* (Vienna 1725) formulated rules for counterpoint. Wrote over 400 works, incl. 19 operas, 14 oratorios, *c.*80 masses, instr. partitas, etc.

G

G. Note of the scale: 5th degree of natural scale of C. Thus G♭, G♭♭, G♮, G♯, G♯♯. Keys of G major and G minor. 'In G' signifies either in key of G major or *transposing instr. on which written note C sounds as G (e.g. alto flute in G).

G. In Fr. org. mus., *grand orgue*, i.e. 'Great Org'.

G. Letter prefix to lists of works by Beethoven and Liszt compiled for *New Grove Dictionary of Music and Musicians* (1980).

Gabrieli, Andrea (*b* Venice, *c*.1510; *d* Venice, 1585). It. organist and composer. Org. St Mark's, Venice 1566–86. Comp. psalms, motets, madrigals, and org. works. Pupils incl. *Hassler, *Sweelinck, and his nephew Giovanni *Gabrieli.

Gabrieli (Gabrielli), **Domenico** (*b* Bologna, 1651; *d* Bologna, 1690). It. cellist and composer of a dozen operas, oratorios, and instr. pieces.

Gabrieli, Giovanni (*b* Venice, *c*.1554; *d* Venice, 1612). It. composer and organist, nephew of A. *Gabrieli whose pupil he was. Organist, St Mark's, Venice, from 1585. One of the great Venetian composers of motets with instr. accs. His mus. made use of the special antiphonal effects of vv. and brass obtainable in St Mark's. Comps. incl. *Canzone* for various combinations; 2 sets of *Sacrae symphoniae* (1597 and 1615), the first set containing the celebrated *Sonata pian' e forte alla quarta bassa*; concertos; and many motets incl. *Angelus ad pastores, O magnum mysterium, Exaudi Deus, Hodie Christus natus est, Jubilate Deo, Regina coeli, Sancta et immaculata virginitas*, etc. Pupils incl. *Schütz and Praetorius.

Gabrieli Quartet. Brit. qt. formed in 1966. Members are Kenneth Sillito (*b* Newcastle upon Tyne, 1939) and Brendan O'Reilly (*b* Dublin, 1934) (who in 1969 replaced Claire Simpson), vns., Ian Jewel (*b* London, 1944), va., and Keith Harvey (*b* Liverpool, 1938), vc. Début London 1967. Wide repertory, incl. many 20th cent. works.

Gabrilowitsch, Ossip (Salomonovich) (*b* St Petersburg, 1878; *d* Detroit, 1936). Russ.-born pianist, composer, and cond. (Amer. citizen). Studied St Petersburg Cons. 1888–94, with Anton Rubinstein (pf.) and Lyadov and Glazunov (comp.), and in Vienna with *Leschetizky (pf.) 1894–6. Début Berlin 1896, followed by European tours and Amer. début 1900. Took up cond. *c*.1905 in Vienna and Paris. Friend of Mahler. Cond. Konzertverein Orch., Munich, 1910–14. Settled NY, 1914, début there as cond. in 1917. Cond., Detroit S.O., 1918–35. Continued annual recital tours of USA as pianist. Comp. pf. pieces, songs, etc.

Gabussi, Giulio Cesare (*b* Bologna, *c*.1555; *d* Milan, 1611). It. composer. Became choirmaster at Forli Cathedral and, in 1583, at Milan. In Warsaw 1601–2, then returned to duties in Milan. Wrote motets and madrigals.

Gabussi, Vincenzo (*b* Bologna, 1800; *d* London, 1846). It composer and teacher. Studied in Bologna. Opera *I furbi al cimento* perf. Modena, 1825. Settled in London 1825, teaching upper-class amateurs. His *Ernani* (Paris 1834) was a failure. Wrote 100 vocal duets and over 30 solo songs.

Gade, Niels (Vilhelm) (*b* Copenhagen, 1817; *d* Copenhagen, 1890). Danish composer, organist, and violinist. Royal stipend enabled him to travel to It. and Ger. Became friend of Mendelssohn in Leipzig; ass. cond. of Gewandhaus concerts 1844–6, cond. 1847–8. Returned to Copenhagen, becoming court Kapellmeister 1861. Visited Eng. 1876 to conduct his cantata *The Crusader* at Birmingham Fest. His comps., influenced by Mendelssohn and Schumann, are of persuasive charm and skill. They incl. 8 syms., ovs., suites, vn. conc., opera-ballet *The Fairy Spell*, str. qt., pf. trio, str. quintet, str. octet, str. sextet, pf. pieces, cantatas, and songs.

Gafori, Franchino (*b* Lodi, 1451; *d* Milan, 1522). It. priest and mus. theorist. From 1484 at Milan Cath. Wrote *Practica musicae* (Milan, 1496).

Gagliano. 18th-cent. Neapolitan family of vn. makers. Chief members were Alessandro, active up to *c*.1730, his sons Gennaro and Niccolò and grandsons Ferdinando and Giuseppe.

Gagliano, Marco da (*b* Florence, 1582; *d* Florence, 1643). It. composer, one of the founders of opera. Educated as priest. Maestro di cappella, S. Lorenzo, 1608. His opera *Dafne* (1607, prod. Mantua 1608) was rated highly by *Peri; its preface anticipated Gluck in advocating dramatic reality as more important than singers' whims. Collab. with Peri on *Il medoro* (1616, lost). *Dafne* and last opera, *La flora* (1628), survive. Also comp. madrigals, motets, etc.

Gagnebin, Henri (*b* Liège, 1886; *d* Geneva, 1977). Belg.-born composer and organist of Swiss parentage. Studied Schola Cantorum, Paris, 1908–16, with d'Indy (comp.) and Vierne (org.), and in Berlin 1905–6. Organist, Église de la Redemption, Paris, 1910–16, and St-Jean, Lausanne, 1916–25. Teacher at Lausanne Cons. 1918–25; dir., Geneva

Cons. 1925–57, dean of pf. faculty 1957–61. Founder, Geneva int. perf. competition 1938. Comps. incl. 3 syms. (1911, 1921, 1955); oratorios, *St Francis of Assisi, Les Vanités du monde, Les Mystères de la foi*; 3 str. qts., wind octet, brass quintet, pf. sonata, vc. sonata, fl. trio, str. trio, etc.

Gaîté parisienne (Parisian gaiety). Ballet in 1 act to Rosenthal's arr. of mus. by Offenbach, lib. Comte Etienne de Beaumont, choreog. Massine. Prod. Monte Carlo 1938. Some characters taken from Offenbach's *La *Vie parisienne*.

Gál, Hans (*b* Brunn, Vienna, 1890; *d* Edinburgh, 1987). Austrian-born composer, pianist, and writer. Educated Vienna Univ. Début as pianist 1910. Lecturer, Vienna Univ. 1919–28. Dir., Mainz municipal coll. of mus. 1929–33. Cond., Vienna Concert Orch. and Bach Soc. 1933–8. Settled in Edinburgh 1938, lecturer Edinburgh Univ. 1945–65. Author of books on Brahms, Wagner, Schubert, and Vienna. Comps. incl. 5 operas, 4 syms., *Lilliburlero: Improvisations on a Martial Melody* for orch. (1946), vn. conc., vc. conc., concertinos for pf. and str. and vn. and str., 2 str. qts., pf. qt., pf. trio, str. trio, choral mus., pf. pieces. O.B.E. 1964.

Galant (Fr., Ger.). Courtly. 18th-cent. term to describe elegant style (Fr. *Style galant*; Ger. *Galanter Stil*) favoured by, for example, J. C. Bach, the Stamitzes, and early Mozart.

Galanterien (Ger.), **galanteries** (Fr.). In the classical *suite 3 movements which were not looked upon as essential to the scheme but rather as interpolations of light relief. They usually comprised any of the following: minuet, gavotte, bourrée, passepied, loure, polonaise, air.

Galilei, Vincenzo (*b* S. Maria a Monte, *c*.1520; *d* Florence, 1591). It. composer and lutenist. Associate of members of *Camerata from which first opera perfs. developed. Pubd. 2 books of madrigals and 1 of lute pieces. Also mus. theorist: author of *Dialogo della musica antica e della moderna* (1581). His *Il fronimo* (1568, rev. 1584) is a valuable treatise on lute-playing. His son Galileo Galilei was the great astronomer.

Galin-Paris-Chevé. Fr. sight-singing system, devised by Pierre Galin (1786–1821), Aimé Paris (1798–1866), Nanine Paris (*d* 1868), and Émile J. M. Chevé (1804–64), on movable-doh lines and with a practical device for acquiring the sense of time-values of notes. See also *Tonic Sol-fa*.

Galliard (It. *Gagliarda*; Fr. *Gaillard*). Lively dance, from 15th cent. or earlier, in simple triple time. Featured a group of 5 steps, and was therefore sometimes called *Cinque passi* (It.), *Cinque pas* (Fr.), and *Cinque pace* or *Sink-a-pace* (Eng.). Often paired and contrasted with the slower *pavan, this assoc. being the origin of the *suite. Vaughan Williams's *Job* contains a modern galliard.

Galli-Curci, Amelita (*b* Milan, 1882; *d* La Jolla, Calif., 1963). It. sop. Studied pf., harmony, and comp. at Milan Cons. but was self-taught as a singer. Début as Gilda in *Rigoletto* at Trani, 1906. Amer. début, also as Gilda, Chicago 1916. Chicago Opera 1916–24. NY Met. 1921–30. Brilliant agility in coloratura roles such as Gilda, Violetta, and Elvira in *I puritani*. Retired 1937. Never sang in opera in Brit., but gave recitals.

Galliera, Alceo (*b* Milan, 1910). It. cond. and composer. Teacher of comp. Milan Cons., 1932. Cond. début, Rome 1941. Guest cond. of many orchs. and of opera at La Scala, Milan. Resident cond., Carlo Felice opera house, Genoa, 1957–60, subsequently resident cond. Orch. Municipale de Strasbourg from 1964. Comps. incl. ballet, orch. mus., chamber works, and songs.

Gallus. See *Händl, Jacob*.

Gallus, Joannes (*fl* 16th cent.). Dutch composer and contrapuntist, also known as Jehan le Cocq. Maestro di cappella to Duke of Ferrara, *c*.1534–41. Church mus. survives.

Galop or **Galopade.** 19th-cent. ballroom round dance in simple duple time, with a change of step, or hop, at the end of every mus. phrase. Koenig's *Posthorn Galop* f.p. in Eng., 1844. Galops have been included in 20th cent. Soviet ballets.

Galpin, Francis William (*b* Dorchester, 1858; *d* Richmond, Surrey, 1945). Eng. clergyman and authority on ancient mus. instrs. Books incl. catalogue of European instrs. in Metropolitan Museum, NY (1902), study of instrs. of American Indians, history of sackbut, etc. In 1946 the Galpin Soc. was formed in London to continue his work.

Galuppi, Baldassare (*b* Island of Burano, nr. Venice, 1706; *d* Venice, 1785). It. composer. Pupil of Lotti. From 1728 comp. several operas for It. ths. Visited London 1741, with considerable success. Ass. choirmaster of St Mark's, Venice, 1748, choirmaster 1762. Visited St Petersburg 1766–8. His 112 operas incl. *Adriano in Siria* (1740), *Didone abbandonata* (1741), *Scipione in Cartagine* (1742), *Il filosofo di campagna* (1752), *Il re pastore* (1762), and *Ifigenia in Tauride* (1768). Also wrote oratorios, church mus., hpd. sonatas. Browning's poem *A Toccata of Galuppi's* refers to an imaginary comp.

Galway, James (*b* Belfast, 1939). Irish flautist. Studied RCM (with John Francis), GSM (with G. Gilbert), and Paris Cons. (with Crunelle). Private study with *Rampal. Flautist, SW Orch. 1960–5. Prin. flautist, LSO and RPO, then Berlin P.O. 1969–75. After 1975 soloist with orchs. and chamber groups. O.B.E. 1977.

Gamba (It.). Leg. (1) Abbreviation of *viola da gamba*.
  (2) Str.-toned org. stop of 8′ (sometimes 4′ or 16′) length and pitch. Metal pipes often taper towards top and sometimes widen again into an inverted bell (*Bell Gamba*). The *Bearded Gamba* is a

variety with a small roller before the mouth of each pipe.

Gambler, The (*Igrok*). Opera in 4 acts, Op. 24, by *Prokofiev to lib. by composer based on Dostoyevsky's short story (1866). Comp. 1915–17, rev. 1927–8. Prod. Brussels 1929, NY 1957, Edinburgh 1962. Orch. suite *4 Portraits*, Op. 49, f.p. Paris 1932.

Gamblers, The. Unfinished opera by Shostakovich, planned as Op. 63, to lib. by composer based on comedy *The Gamblers* by Nikolai Gogol (1832) for six male solo vv. and large orch. Begun 1941, abandoned 1942 when not quite eight of 25 scenes were completed. F.p. (concert) Leningrad 1978, cond. Rozhdestvensky. Completed by Krzysztof Meyer, 1981. Scherzo of Va. Sonata (1975) uses mus. from *The Gamblers*.

Gamelan. Type of orch. found in S.-E. Asia, particularly Indonesia (e.g. Java). Incl. str. and woodwind instrs., but is notable for range of perc. such as gongs, drums, chimes, marimbas, etc. The visit of a Javanese gamelan to the Paris Exposition of 1889 had a marked influence on *Debussy.

Game of Cards (Stravinsky). See *Jeu de cartes*.

Gamme (Fr.). Scale.

Gamut. (1) Properly, the note G at the pitch now indicated by the lowest line of the bass staff. Greek G or 'gamma' was used for its designation, and as the note just mentioned was the 'Ut' ('Doh') of the lowest *hexachord, this portmanteau word was adopted as a name for it.

(2) By extension, the word came to be used as a comprehensive name for the whole series of hexachords as displayed in writing.

(3) By a further extension it came to mean 'scale' in general (Fr. *gamme*).

(4) Also came to mean the whole range of mus. sounds from the lowest to the highest; and to be applied in a metaphorical way to a singer's or actor's range, e.g. 'He covered the whole gamut of tragic expression'.

Ganz (Ger.). Quite, whole, e.g. *ganzer Bogen*, whole bow; *gänzlich*, completely.

Ganz, Wilhelm (*b* Mainz, 1833; *d* London, 1914). Ger. pianist and cond. Settled in London 1850. Accompanist for Jenny Lind and other singers and violinists. Cond. orch. concerts at which he gave first complete London perfs. of Berlioz's *Symphonie fantastique* (April 1881) and Liszt's *Dante Symphony*. Prof. of singing, GSM.

Ganze, Ganze Note (Ger.). Same as *Ganzetaktnote*.

Ganze Pause (Ger.). Whole-note (semibreve) rest.

Ganzetaktnote (Ger.). Whole-measure note, or whole-bar note, i.e. the whole-note, or semibreve.

Gapped. Term applied to a scale, indicating inclusion of intervals of more than a tone's distance, e.g. the *pentatonic scale.

García, Manuel del Populo Vicente (*b* Seville, 1775; *d* Paris, 1832). Sp. ten., composer, and singing teacher. Choirboy, Seville Cath., at age 6. Sang in Paris 1808 and 1819–23, Naples 1811–16, creating role of Almaviva in Rossini's *Il barbiere di Siviglia,* and London 1817–19. Returned to London 1823, founding singing sch. Est. It. opera co. in NY 1825–6, giving US première of Mozart's *Don Giovanni* with da Ponte in audience. Took co. to Mexico 1827–8 where bandits robbed him of all his earnings (some £6,000). Returned to Paris first as a singer, then teacher. Comp. 97 operas. Pupils incl. his daughters Maria *Malibran and Pauline *Viardot.

García, Manuel Patricio Rodriguez (*b* Zafra, Madrid, 1805; *d* London, 1906). Sp. bass and singing teacher, son of above. Trained in singing by his father, going to USA in 1825 where he sang Figaro in *Il barbiere di Siviglia* in NY. From 1829 devoted himself to teaching. Prof. of singing, Paris Cons. 1847–50. First to make scientific study of v. production. Invented laryngoscope, 1855. Pubd. *Mémoire sur la voix humaine* (1840) and *Traité complet de l'art du chant* (1840, trans. into It., Ger., and Eng.). Settled in London 1848, becoming prof. at RAM until 1895. Pupils incl. Jenny Lind, Stockhausen, Santley, and Mathilde Marchesi.

García, Maria Felicitá. See *Malibran, Maria Felicitá.*

García, Pauline. See *Viardot-García, Pauline.*

Gardelli, Lamberto (*b* Venice, 1915). Swed. cond. and composer of It. birth. Studied Pesaro and Rome. Répétiteur, Rome Opera, with *Serafin. Opera début as cond. Rome 1944 (*La Traviata*). Stockholm Opera 1946–55; Budapest Opera 1961–5. Glyndebourne début 1964; NY Met. 1966–8; CG début 1969. Comp. 4 operas. Prin. cond. Munich Radio S.O. from 1983.

Garden, Mary (*b* Aberdeen, 1874; *d* Inverurie, 1967). Amer. sop. of Scot. birth. Taken to USA as a child, having first singing lessons in Chicago. Sent by patron to Paris in 1895 where teachers incl. M. Marchesi. Befriended by Amer. sop. Sibyl *Sanderson who sent her to Carré, dir. of Opéra-Comique. Studied title-role of Charpentier's *Louise* and took over from the indisposed Mme Rioton midway through a perf. in April 1900. Created role of Mélisande in Debussy's opera, 1902, at composer's request. Further successes followed in operas by Massenet, Saint-Saëns, Leroux, and Erlanger. CG 1902–3. Joined Manhattan Opera, NY, 1907–10; then Chicago Opera from 1910, becoming dir. 1919–20 and remaining until 1931.

Garden of Fand, The. Symphonic poem by *Bax, comp. 1913, f.p. Chicago 1920. Fand is a heroine in Irish legend and her garden was the sea. Used for ballet *Picnic at Tintagel* by Ashton, NY 1952.

Gardiner, (Henry) **Balfour** (*b* London, 1877; *d* Salisbury, 1950). Eng. composer. Studied at Frankfurt. Mus. master, Winchester Coll. Promoted concerts of contemporary Eng. mus. 1910–20, and was especial champion of *Holst. Comp. sym., *Shepherd Fennel's Dance* for orch. (after Hardy), *News from Whydah* for ch. and orch., chamber mus., and songs.

Gardiner, John Eliot (*b* Fontmell Magna, Dorset, 1943). Eng. cond. Studied at Camb. Univ., then at London Univ. with Thurston Dart and with N. Boulanger in Paris. Founded Monteverdi Choir 1964, Monteverdi Orch. 1968. Prof. début 1966. Has made new edns. of Monteverdi's *Vespers* 1967, and Rameau's *Dardanus, Les Fêtes d'Hébé,* and *Les Boréades.* Cond. f. staged p. of *Les Boréades,* Aix 1982. SW début 1969 (*Zauberflöte*), CG 1973 (Gluck's *Iphigénie en Tauride*). Mus dir. Lyons Opera from 1982.

Gardner, John (Linton) (*b* Manchester, 1917). Eng. composer and pianist. Dir. of mus. Repton School 1939–40. Mus. staff, CG 1946–52; tutor, Morley Coll. 1952–76, dir. of mus. 1965–9; dir. of mus. St Paul's Girls' School 1962–75; prof. of comp., RAM from 1956. Comps. incl. operas *The Moon and Sixpence* and *Tobermory* (1-act, 1977); orch: sym. (Cheltenham 1951), *Variations on a Waltz by Nielsen* (1952), pf. conc. (1957), *An English Ballad* (1969); chamber mus.: str. qt. (1939), ob. sonata (1953), *Sonata da chiesa,* 2 tpt. and organ (1976, rev. 1977); choral: *Jubilate Deo* (1947), *Ballad of the White Horse,* bar., ch., and orch. (1959), *A Latter Day Athenian Speaks* (1962), *Cantiones sacrae* (1952), Mass in C (1965), *Cantata for Christmas* (1966), *Proverbs of Hell* (1967), *Cantata for Easter* (1970), *The Entertainment of the Senses,* 5 singers and 6 players (words by Auden and Kallman) (1974). Also th. and film scores. C.B.E. 1976.

Garland for the Queen, A. Collection of songs for unacc. mixed ch. by 10 Brit. composers to texts by 10 contemporary Brit. poets written to celebrate coronation of Elizabeth II in 1953 (in emulation of *The *Triumphs of Oriana* in Elizabeth I's reign). Works and composers (with poets' names in parentheses) were: *Aubade for Coronation Morning,* Bliss (Henry Reed); *What is it Like to be Young and Fair?,* Bax (C. Bax); *Dance, Clarion Air,* Tippett (Fry); *Silence and Music,* Vaughan Williams (Ursula Wood); *Spring at this Hour,* Berkeley (P. Dehn); *The Hills,* Ireland (J. Kirkup); *Inheritance,* Howells (De la Mare); *White Flowering Days,* Finzi (Blunden); *Canzonet,* Rawsthorne (MacNeice); and *Salutation,* Rubbra (Hassall). F.p. London, 1 June 1953.

Gascogne, Mathieu (*fl.* 16th-cent.). Fr. composer of masses, *chansons,* motets, etc.

Gaspard de la nuit. Set of 3 pf. pieces by *Ravel, comp. 1908: 1. *Ondine,* 2. *Le Gibet,* 3. *Scarbo.* Composite title taken from prose-ballads by A. Bertrand, sub-titled *Fantaisies à la manière de Rembrandt et de Callot* (1842).

Gasparini, Francesco (*b* Camaiore, 1668; *d* Rome, 1727). It. composer, pupil of Corelli and Pasquini. Choirmaster at Venice 1701–13; maestro di cappella St Lorenzo in Lucina, Rome, 1717–25; maestro di cappella St John Lateran, Rome, from 1725 but did not assume post because of illness. Wrote oratorios, cantatas, church mus., and many operas, incl. *Amleto* (1705) which is not based on Shakespeare's play. Wrote treatise (1708) on hpd. acc.

Gassmann, Florian Leopold (*b* Brüx, Bohemia, 1729; *d* Vienna, 1774). Ger.-born composer. Pupil of *Martini in Bologna. Court musician in Venice from 1742. Ballet composer, Vienna Opera, from 1762, court Kapellmeister from 1772. Comp. over 20 operas, incl. *La contessina* (1770), 33 syms., and much chamber mus. Taught *Salieri.

Gastoldi, Giovanni Giacomo (*b* Caravaggio, *c.*1555; *d* Mantua, 1622). It. composer of madrigals and church mus. Choirmaster, ducal chapel at Mantua from *c.*1581.

Gatti, Guido (Maggiorino) (*b* Chieti, 1892; *d* Turin, 1973). It. critic and scholar. Leading mus. figure in Turin until *c.*1940. Founded and ed. review *Il pianoforte* 1920 (re-titled *La rassegna musicale* 1928) until its demise 1962. Dir.-Gen Teatro di Torino 1925–31. Sec.-gen. Florence Maggio Musicale from 1933. Instrumental in persuading leading It. composers to write film mus. Ed. of several periodicals, contributor to many dictionaries.

Gatti-Casazza, Giulio (*b* Udine, 1868; *d* Ferrara, 1940). It. impresario. Succeeded father as dir. of municipal th., Ferrara, 1893; dir. of La Scala, Milan, 1898–1908, working with *Toscanini and helping to popularize Wagner in It. trans. Dir. NY Met. 1908–35, when he staged over 5,000 perfs. of 177 works. Took Toscanini to NY with him, thus inaugurating the cond.'s Amer. career.

Gatty, Nicholas (Comyn) (*b* Bradfield, 1874; *d* London, 1946). Eng. composer. Studied RCM. Mus. critic *Pall Mall Gazette* 1907–14. Wrote several operas incl. 2 after Shakespeare, *The Tempest* and *Macbeth,* also choral works, vn. sonata, str. qt., songs, etc.

Gaul, Alfred (Robert) (*b* Norwich, 1837; *d* King's Norton, 1913). Eng. organist, composer, and cond. Cond., Walsall Phil. Soc. from 1887. Comp. oratorios and cantatas, etc., best-known being *The Holy City* (1882).

Gaultier, Denis (*b* Marseilles, 1603; *d* Paris, 1672). Fr. composer of mus. for lute, mostly suites of stylized dances with fanciful titles, such as *Le Rhétorique des dieux* (c.1652), and of other instr. pieces.

Gauntlett, Ambrose (b London, 1890; d London, 1978). Eng. cellist and player of viola da gamba. Trained GSM and RAM. Prin. cellist CG orch., later of BBC S.O. 1935–47.

Gauntlett, Henry John (b Wellington, Salop, 1805; d London, 1876). Eng. organist and composer. Trained as lawyer. Organist, Southwark 1827. Lecturer, London Institute 1837–43. Expert in Gregorian chant. Designed orgs., initiating several reforms. Said to have comp. several thousand hymn tunes, among them *Once in Royal David's City* (1849).

Gavazzeni, Gianandrea (b Bergamo, 1909). It. cond., composer, and critic. Studied Milan Cons. (comp. with Pizzetti). In 1930s wrote opera, ballet, oratorio, vc. conc., and vn. conc., then devoted more time to writing and cond., eventually giving up composing and discouraging perfs. of his works. Cond., La Scala, Milan, NY Met. 1976; Glyndebourne 1965.

Gaveaux, Pierre (b Béziers, 1760; d Paris, 1825). Fr. composer and ten. From 1792 about 30 of his operas were prod. at Opéra-Comique, incl. *Léonore* (1798) to a lib. which was prin. source of lib. for Beethoven's *Fidelio*. Wrote revolutionary hymn *Le Réveil du peuple* (1795).

Gavotte. Old Fr. dance in common time beginning on 3rd beat of the bar. Originated in Pays de Gap where the inhabitants were known as 'gavots'. Popularized at court of Louis XIV, where Lully comp. several examples. Became optional movement of baroque suite. Some examples by 20th-cent. composers, e.g. Prokofiev in his *Classical Symphony* and Schoenberg in his Suite for String Orch.

Gay, John (b Barnstaple, 1685; d London, 1732). Eng. poet, playwright, and th. manager. Wrote lib. for Handel's *Acis and Galatea,* and for *The *Beggar's Opera* (1728) and its sequel *Polly* (1729). Built first CG th., 1732.

Gayane (*Gayeneh*). Ballet in 4 acts, mus. by *Khachaturian, lib. Derzhavin, choreog. Anisimova. Comp. 1940–2, rev. 1952 and (with new plot) 1957. Prod. Leningrad 1942. Earlier version, *Happiness,* prod. Erevan 1939. Contains famous 'Sabre Dance'. Also 3 orch. suites.

Gazza ladra, La (The Thievish Magpie). Opera in 2 acts by Rossini to lib. by Gheradini after comedy *La Pie voleuse,* 1815, by d'Aubigny and Caigniez. Prod. Milan 1817, London 1821, Philadelphia 1827. Though the opera was not revived until 1965 in Florence, the ov., in Rossini's most brilliant style, has remained popular.

Gazzelloni, Severino (b Roccasecca, 1919). It flautist. Studied Rome, where he made début 1945. Prin. fl., It. Radio S.O. Renowned for

playing *avant-garde* works by (*inter alia*) Maderna, Boulez, Berio, Nono, and Haubenstock-Ramati. Also specialist in baroque mus.

G.B.S.M. Graduate of Birmingham School of Music.

G Clef. See *Great Staff.*

Gebrauchsmusik (Ger.). Utility music. Term applied in 1920s to works (by Hindemith, Weill, Křenek, and others, influenced by the poet Brecht) which were directed to some social or educational purpose instead of being 'art for art's sake'. Later disowned by Hindemith.

Gebunden (Ger.). Bound. Used musically in the sense of 'tied' or 'slurred'.

Gedackt, Gedeckt (Ger.). Covered. Soft organ stop approaching fl. quality. The name comes from end-plugged pipes of 8′, 16′, 4′ (occasionally 2′) pitch.

Gedämpft (Ger.). Damped. When applied to str. and brass instr., it means 'muted'; to drums, 'muffled'; and to pf., 'soft-pedalled'.

Gedda, Nicolai (b Stockholm, 1925). Swed. ten. of Russ. descent. Studied with his father, then at Stockholm Acad. Operatic début Stockholm 1951 in Sutermeister's *Rote Stiefel,* leading to appearances in Paris and London (CG 1954). Member NY Met. since 1957. Has sung most leading lyrical ten. roles in opera repertory and also specialized in operetta by Lehár, etc. Also frequent singer of Lieder and oratorio (has recorded Elgar's *Dream of Gerontius*).

Geddes, John Maxwell (b Glasgow, 1941). Scot. composer. Studied RSAM and in Copenhagen with Bentzon (1967). Works incl. sym., *Portrait of a City* for orch., ob. sonata, *Apt* for solo va., etc.

Gedeckt. See *Gedackt.*

Geehl, Henry (Ernest) (b London, 1881; d Beaconsfield, 1961). Eng. composer, cond., and pianist. Teacher at TCL from 1918. Had special interest in composing and arranging for brass band. Orch. Elgar's *Severn Suite* (1930) for brass band from composer's pf. score.

Gehend (Ger.). Going. Same as *andante.*

Geige (Ger., plural *Geigen*). Fiddle. Originally any bowed instr., now the vn.

Geigen (Principal). Organ stop; a slightly str.-toned diapason of 8′ (sometimes 4′) length and pitch.

Geigenwerk. Obsolete kbd. instr. invented in Nuremberg 1575 by Hans Haiden. A type of hurdy-gurdy with brass and steel str. activated by 5 or 6 parchment-covered wheels set in motion by treadle.

Geiringer, Karl (b Vienna, 1899). Amer. musicologist and writer of Austrian birth. Studied mus. history in Vienna with G. *Adler and in Berlin with Kretzschmar. Curator of collections of Vienna Gesellschaft der Musikfreunde 1930–8. Ed. rare works by Haydn, Brahms, Schubert, Schumann, etc. From 1940 resident of USA. Prof. of mus. history and theory, Boston Univ., 1941–62. Prof. of mus. Univ. of California, Santa Barbara, 1962–72. Books incl. biographies of Haydn (1946, rev. 1961, 1982), and Brahms (1934), *The Bach Family* (1954), *Structure of Beethoven's Diabelli Variations* (1964), and *Johann Sebastian Bach* (1966).

Geister Trio (Ghost Trio). Name for Beethoven's Pf. Trio in D major, Op. 70 No. 1, comp. 1808. Mysterious atmosphere of slow movement, which has a theme intended for a projected *Macbeth* opera, gave rise to nickname.

Gekkin. Japanese str. instr. with circular body like banjo. Has 9 frets and 4 strs., tuned in pairs.

Geliot, Michael (*b* London, 1933). Eng. opera and th. producer. Art. dir. WNO 1969–77. Translator of Mozart's *Die Zauberflöte* and *Le Nozze di Figaro,* and Weill's *Mahagonny.* Opera productions for SW, Scot. Opera, CG, Munich, Cassel, Zürich, Barcelona, etc.

Gellenflöte. (Ger.). *Clarinet.

Gellhorn, Peter (*b* Breslau, 1912). Ger.-born cond., pianist, and composer. Studied Berlin Univ. and Mus. Acad. Settled in Eng. Mus. dir. Toynbee Hall, London, 1935–9; ass. cond. SW Opera 1941–3; cond. Royal Carl Rosa Opera 1945–6; on cond. and mus. staff CG 1947–53; cond. and ch. master Glyndebourne, 1954–61 and from 1974; dir., BBC Chorus 1961–72. Co-founder and mus. dir., Opera Barga, Italy, 1967–9.

Geminiani, Francesco (*b* Lucca, 1687; *d* Dublin, 1762). It. violinist and composer. Pupil of Corelli and Scarlatti. In Naples opera orch. 1711–14. Lived in London from 1714, with intervals in Dublin 1733–40 and 1759–62, and Paris 1749–55. His *Art of Playing the Violin* (London 1751) was first vn. method ever to be pubd. Also wrote *Art of Accompaniment* (1754) and *Art of Playing the Guitar* (1760). Comp. 42 concerti grossi, over 40 vn. sonatas, 6 vc. sonatas, ballet *La foresta incantata* (Paris 1754), etc.

Gemshorn (Ger.). Chamois horn. (1) Obsolete medieval type of fl. with sharply-tapering conical bore, made from animal horn (cow, ox, or goat, rather than chamois). Disappeared from use in mid-16th cent.

(2) Light-toned organ stop with conical pipes, usually 4′ length and pitch.

Gendron, Maurice (*b* Nice, 1920). Fr. cellist and cond. Studied Nice and Paris Cons. Début London 1945 (f. Eur. p. of Prokofiev's vc. conc., Op. 58). Played at Aldeburgh Fests. World-wide tours as conc. soloist and recitalist. Master classes in Fr.

and Ger. Ass. cond. Bournemouth Sinfonietta 1971–2.

Genée, Franz (Friedrich Richard) (*b* Danzig, 1823; *d* Baden, 1895). Ger. composer and cond. Th. cond. in various cities from 1848; cond. at Theater an der Wien, Vienna, 1868–78. Comp. over a dozen operettas, librettist of others incl. *Die *Fledermaus.*

Generalbass (Ger.). See *Basso continuo.*

General Pause. Rest or pause for all the executants.

General William Booth Enters into Heaven. (1) Song by *Ives to words by Vachel Lindsay, for v. and pf., 1914, also for bass soloist, ch., and chamber orch. Pubd. in collection *19 Songs.*

(2) For ten., male vv., and chamber orch., 1932, by Philip *James.

Genoveva. Opera in 4 acts, Op. 81, by R. Schumann, lib. R. Reinick adapted from plays by Tieck (1799) and Hebbel (1843). Prod. Leipzig 1850, London 1893.

Gentele, Goeran (*b* Stockholm, 1917; *d* Sardinia, 1972). Swed. impresario and opera dir. Began career as actor, play producer, and film dir. Staged Menotti's *Consul* for Stockholm Royal Opera, 1952, joined staff 1953, gen. man. 1963–71 during which period the co. visited Eng., Ger., and Can. Appointed gen. man., NY Met. 1970, but was killed in car crash on eve of first season of prods.

Gentlemen's Concerts. Series of concerts in Manchester begun as gathering of amateur flautists *c.*1770. Concert hall built 1777. Gave enterprising programmes but declined in 1840s. Revived by appointment of Charles *Hallé as cond. 1850, but subsequently overshadowed by foundation of Hallé's own concerts and orch. 1858. Survived until 1920.

Gentle Shepherd, The. Scot. ballad opera in 5 acts to lib. by Allan Ramsay who selected traditional airs as mus. (1728) for what was orig. (1725) a comedy without songs. Prod. Edinburgh 1729, London 1730.

Genzmer, Harald (*b* Blumental, Bremen, 1909). Ger. composer. Studied with *Hindemith in Berlin. Breslau Opera 1934–7. Prof. of comp. Hochschule für Musik, Freiburg, 1946–56, Akademie der Tonkunst, Munich, 1957. Made special study of elec. instr. the *Trautonium for which he wrote 2 concs. (1939, 1952). Other works incl. Bremen Symphony, Sym. No. 1, Concerto for Orchestra, Music for strings, concs. for pf., vc., fl. (2), and ob., choral works, str. qt., harp septet, 2 fl. sonatas, 2 vn. sonatas, recorder sonata, suite for Trautonium and pf., etc. His Mass in E (1953) is highly regarded.

Gerhard, Roberto (*b* Valls, Tarragona, 1896; *d* Cambridge, 1970). Composer and pianist of Swiss parentage who identified himself with Sp. mus. and eventually became Eng. citizen. Studied with Granados (pf.) and Pedrell (comp.) in Barcelona 1915–22, and with Schoenberg in Vienna and Berlin, 1924–8. Returned to Barcelona to teach 1929 but moved to Eng. during Sp. Civil War.

Influenced at first by Debussy and Ravel, Gerhard became a Schoenberg pupil on the strength of his 7 *Hai-Ku* for sop., wind, and pf. (1922). His wind quintet (1928) was basically serial but not 12-note and, despite the influence of Schoenberg, his mus. of this date remained tonal in essence and had a distinctive Sp. melodic and rhythmic flavour. On settling in Cambridge in 1940 he seemed to expand as a composer, this period of his development culminating in the 3-act Sheridan opera *The Duenna* (1947, rev. 1950) where a Sp. idiom is combined with tonal, bitonal, and serial harmonic styles. For 3 years Gerhard reassessed his attitude to Schoenbergian methods and studied the serial opinions of *Hauer and A. Habá. His pf. conc. (1951) was consistently 12-note but was not 'strict' and drew on early Sp. kbd. styles. In a series of splendidly individual works from 1952 onwards, Gerhard adopted Habá's 'athematicism'. Sometimes, as in his 3rd Sym. ('Collages'), he combined orch. sound with elect. tape. All his mus. has imaginative genius and colour, its fundamentally lyrical and original nature never being sacrificed to doctrinaire procedures. Prin. works:

OPERA: *The *Duenna* (after Sheridan) (1945–7, rev. 1950) (BBC broadcast 1949, concert perf. Wiesbaden 1951).

BALLETS: *Ariel* (1934), *Soirées de Barcelone* (1936–8), *Alegrías* (1942), *Pandora* (1944), *Don Quixote* (1940–1).

ORCH: *Hommaje a Pedrell*, sym. (1941); vn. conc. (1942–3); pf. conc., with str. (1951); Sym. No. 1 (1952–3), No. 2 (1957–9, recomp. as *Metamorphoses* 1967–8), No. 3 ('Collages') (1960), No. 4 ('New York') (1967); hpd. conc. with str. and perc. (1955–6); *Concerto for Orchestra* (1965); *Epithalamion* for orch. (1966); *Hymnody* for 11 players (1963); *Leo*, chamber sym. for 10 players (1969).

VOICE(S) AND INSTR: *L'Infantament meravellos de Shahrazada*, sop. and pf. (1917); 7 *Hai-Ku*, v. and 5 instr. (1922); *The Akond of Swat*, v. and perc. (1954); *The Plague* for speaker, ch., and orch. (after Camus) (1963–4).

CHAMBER MUSIC: Pf. Trio (1918); Va. Sonata (1950); Str. Qt. No. 1 (1950–5), No. 2 (1960–2); Nonet for 8 wind instr. and accordion (1956); *Libra*, fl., cl., vn., guitar, pf., perc. (1968); vc. sonata (1956).

INCIDENTAL MUSIC: *Cristóbal Colón* (Madariaga, BBC 1943); *Don Quixote* (Linklater, BBC 1940); *Conquistador* (MacLeish, BBC 1953); and for several Shakespeare plays.

Gerhardt, Elena (*b* Leipzig, 1883; *d* London, 1961). Ger. mez. (orig. sop.). Studied Leipzig Cons. and with A. Nikisch, who later often acted as her accompanist. Début 1903. Rejected opera in favour of the recital platform, becoming outstanding exponent of Ger. Lieder, esp. Wolf, Brahms, Schubert, R. Strauss. Eng. début 1906, Amer. 1912. Settled in London 1934, becoming teacher.

Gericke, Wilhelm (*b* Schwanberg, 1845; *d* Vienna, 1925). Austrian cond. and composer (under pseudonym Wenzel Ecker). Studied under Dessoff at Vienna Cons. Th. cond., Linz, from 1865; 2nd cond. Vienna Opera from 1874. Succeeded Brahms as cond. of Gesellschaft Konzerte, Vienna, 1880. Cond. Boston S.O. 1884–9, returning to Vienna but resuming Boston post 1898–1906, when he retired. Comp. operetta, requiem, orch. mus., songs, etc.

German Dance. See *Deutscher Tanz*.

German, (Sir) Edward (German Edward Jones) (*b* Whitchurch, Salop, 1862; *d* London, 1936). Welsh composer. Studied RAM 1880–4; played in th. orchs., soon becoming cond. Mus. dir., Globe Th. from 1888, writing incidental mus. for Shakespeare's plays which made him famous. Greatest success was patriotic operetta *Merrie England* (1902). Knighted 1928. Prin. works:

LIGHT OPERAS: *The *Emerald Isle* (1901, completion of *Sullivan's last work), *Merrie England* (1902), *A Princess of Kensington* (1902), *Tom Jones* (1907), *Fallen Fairies* (1909).

ORCH: Syms. No. 1 (1887, rev. 1890) and No. 2 ('Norwich', 1893), *Welsh Rhapsody* (1904), *Theme and 6 Diversions* (1919).

THEATRE MUSIC: *Richard III* (1889), *Henry VIII* (1892), *Romeo and Juliet* (1895), *Nell Gwyn* (1900).

Germani, Fernando (*b* Rome, 1906). It. org., composer, and scholar. Trained Rome Cons. and Papal Institute of Church Mus. Organist St Peter's, Rome, 1948–59. Head of org. studies, Curtis Institute, Philadelphia, 1936–8. London début 1936. First org., St Peter's, Rome, 1948–59. World-wide recital tours. Ed. of *Frescobaldi's org. works (1936) and author of an org. method (1942–52).

German Requiem, A (Brahms). See *Deutsches Requiem, Ein*.

German Sixth. Type of *augmented 6th chord.

German Suites. Unauthorized title for the set of 6 kbd. partitas by J.S. Bach. See also *French Suites*; *English Suites*; *Klavierübung*.

Gershwin, George (*b* Brooklyn, NY, 1898; *d* Hollywood, Calif., 1937). Amer. composer and pianist. Son of Russ. Jewish migrants who went to USA *c*.1893 (family name Gershovitz). Pf. lessons 1913 from Charles Hambitzer; later studied theory and harmony with Edward Kilenyi for whom he wrote a str. qt. (1919). In 1914 left school to work as pianist and 'song plugger' for Remick, a publisher of popular mus. Wrote his first song in 1916 and his first Broadway musical, *La La Lucille*, in 1919. For the next 14 years a Gershwin musical was a feature of NY theatrical life. His first outstanding 'hit' was the song *Swanee* (1919), which became assoc. with Al Jolson. In 1924 he enjoyed success in a new genre, that of applying jazz idioms to concert works, when his *Rhapsody in Blue* for pf. and orch. had its f.p. From then until the end of his life he produced larger-scale works alongside the songs (many with words by his elder brother Ira (Israel)) he wrote for musicals and, after 1931, films. The Pf. Conc. of 1925 was followed by *An American in Paris*, a second Rhapsody, the Cuban Overture, and in 1935 by the opera *Porgy and Bess* which is still the only opera by an Amer. composer to become est. in the repertory.

Gershwin's melodic gift was phenomenal. His songs contain the essence of NY in the 1920s and have deservedly become classics of their kind, part of the 20th-cent. folk-song tradition in the sense that they are popular mus. which has been spread by oral tradition (for many must have sung a Gershwin song without having any idea who wrote it). His larger-scale works, melodically remarkable as might be expected, suffer from his haphazard mus. education and lack of grounding in counterpoint, theory, etc. (*Rhapsody in Blue* was orchestrated by Ferde *Grofé, but Gershwin himself scored the later works.) He went for lessons to Rubin Goldmark, Henry Cowell, and Joseph Schillinger, and there can be little doubt that had he lived longer he would have progressed to considerable symphonic achievement. As it is, his mixture of the primitive and the sophisticated gives his mus. an individuality and appeal which show no sign of diminishing. Prin. works:

OPERAS: *Blue Monday* (1-act; item in *George White's Scandals* 1922 but withdrawn after 1 perf.; retitled *135th Street* and revived Miami 1970); *Porgy and Bess* (1934–5).
ORCH: *Rhapsody in Blue* (pf. and orch.) (1924); Pf. Conc. in F major (1925); *An *American in Paris* (1928); Second Rhapsody (pf. and orch.) (1931); Cuban Overture (1932); '*I Got Rhythm' Variations* (pf. and orch.) (1934).
MUSICALS: *The Passing Show of 1916*, *La La Lucille* (1919), *George White's Scandals* (1920–4), *Sweet Little Devil* (1924), *Primrose* (1924), *Lady Be Good* (1924), *Song of the Flame* (1925), *Tell Me More* (1925), *Tip Toes* (1925), *Oh, Kay* (1926, lyrics by P.G. Wodehouse), *Strike up the Band* (1927, 1930), *Funny Face* (1927), *Rosalie* (1928), *Treasure Girl* (1928), *Show Girl* (1929), *Girl Crazy* (1930), *Of Thee I Sing* (1931, lyrics by George F. Kaufman), *Pardon my English* (1933), *Let 'em eat Cake* (1933).
FILMS: *Delicious* (1931), *Shall We Dance?*, *A Damsel in Distress* (1937), *The Goldwyn Follies* (1938), *The Shocking Miss Pilgrim* (1946), *Kiss Me, Stupid* (1964).
PIANO: 3 Preludes (1926) (transcr. for vn. and pf. by Heifetz).

SONGS: Among the best of hundreds of songs are *Swanee*, *The Man I Love*, *Embraceable You*, *I Got Rhythm*, *Fascinating Rhythm*, *'S Wonderful*, *Lady Be Good*, and *Love Walked In*. The popular *Summertime* is from *Porgy and Bess*.

Gertler, André (*b* Budapest, 1907). Hung. violinist. Studied Budapest Acad., pupil of Hubay and Kodály. Frequently gave recitals with Bartók as pianist. Settled in Brussels where he founded Gertler Qt., 1931–51. On staff Brussels Cons. 1940–54. Conc. soloist with leading orchs. Prof., Cologne Acad. of mus. 1954–9, Hanover Acad. from 1964. Brother of painter Mark Gertler.

Gervaise, Claude (*fl.* 16th cent.). Fr. composer and viol player. Edited books of *Danceries* and composed 46 *chansons*. Employed as editor by *Attaignant.

Ges (Ger.). G♭. *Geses*, G♭♭.

Gesamtkunstwerk (Ger.). Unified work of art. Wagner's term for a dramatic work in which drama, music, poetry, song, and paintings should be united into a new and complete art-form. This theory is expounded in his *Das Kunstwerk der Zukunft* (The Art-work of the Future, 1849).

Gesang der Jünglinge (Song of the Young Boys). Elec. comp. (on tape) by *Stockhausen, 1955–6, comprising spoken and sung boy's v. so altered and multiplied by various devices that it sounds to be many vv., with elec. sounds added.

Gesang der Parzen (Song of the Fates). Ballad, Op. 89, by Brahms for 6-part ch. and orch., comp. 1882. Text by Goethe.

Geschöpfe des Prometheus, Die (Beethoven). See *Prometheus, Die Geschöpfe des*.

Gesellschaft der Musikfreunde, Wien (Society of Friends of Music, Vienna). Founded 1813, through efforts of Joseph von Sonnleithner, with Beethoven's friend and pupil, Archduke Rudolph, as patron, to perf. oratorios in the Riding School, but later had own home. Also founded cons., library, and museum. A choral soc., Singverein, of over 300 members, was founded 1858, and an Orchesterverein in 1860. Gesellschaft concerts were cond. by members until 1851 when Hellmesberger was appointed. Successors incl. Brahms, *Gericke, Richter, Franz Schalk, and Furtwängler. The soc. archives contain priceless manuscripts by Beethoven (*Sinfonia Eroica*), Haydn, Mozart, Schubert, Schumann, Brahms, Wagner, and Johann Strauss II. Also possesses Beethoven's ear-trumpet.

Gestopft (Ger.). Stopped. (1) 'Stopped' hn. notes are those prod. with the bell of the instr. more or less closed by the hand.
(2) An equivalent for *gedämpft*.

Gesualdo, Don Carlo, Prince of Venosa (*b* Naples, *c*.1560; *d* Gesualdo, Avellino, 1613). It. composer and lutenist. Pubd. 4 books of madrigals from 1594 to 1596 when at court of the Estensi at Ferrara. Returned to Naples 1597. Two further books of madrigals pubd. 1611; these contain harmonic complexity and modernity far in advance of his contemporaries: in the 20th cent., for example, these madrigals inspired and fascinated Stravinsky. Also wrote motets and religious songs. In 1590 murdered his first wife and her lover, an event which is explored in a book on Gesualdo by Cecil *Gray and Philip *Heseltine (1926).

Geteilt, getheilt (Ger.). Divided, e.g. of vns., corresponding to *divisi*. Sometimes abbreviated as *get*.

Gevaert, François (Auguste) (*b* Huysse, 1828; *d* Brussels, 1908). Belgian historian and composer. Wrote operas and operettas. Mus. dir., Paris Opéra 1867–70. Dir., Brussels Cons. 1871–1908, succeeding *Fétis. Pubd. treatise on orchestration, 1885.

Gewandhaus (Ger.). Cloth hall. Leipzig's concert hall. Concerts began in Bach's time, being held in a private house, then in an inn. In 1781 they moved to the Gewandhaus, where they were given until 1885, when a new hall was built.

Gewöhnlich (Ger.). Usual. Used in scores to countermand previous indication that the instr. concerned was to play in some unusual way, e.g. the vn. after it has been playing *am Griffbrett* (near the fingerboard).

Gezogen (Ger.). Drawn. (1) Drawn out, sustained. (2) Same as *portamento*.

G.G.S.M. Graduate of Guildhall School of Music.

Ghedini, Giorgio (Federico) (*b* Cuneo, 1892; *d* Nervi, 1965). It. composer. Studied at Turin Cons. and Bologna Cons. Ass. cond. Teatro Regio, Turin. Prof. of harmony and comp. Turin Cons. to 1937, Parma Cons. 1938–41, Milan Cons. 1941–51. Ed. works by Monteverdi, A. and G. Gabrieli, Frescobaldi, Schütz, etc. 8 operas incl. *Re Hassan* (1938), *Billy Budd* (1949), and *L'ipocrita felice* ('The Happy Hypocrite', Max Beerbohm, 1956). Also wrote sym., *Concerto dell' albatro*, *Canzoni* for orch.; pf. conc., double vc. conc., 2 vn. concs., va. conc.; chamber mus., choral works, and songs.

Gheyn, Matthias van den (*b* Tirlemont, 1721; *d* Louvain, 1785). Flemish organist and composer. Carilloneur at Louvain from 1741. Wrote org. works, hpd. sonatas, etc.

Ghiaurov, Nicolai (*b* Velingrad, Bulgaria, 1929). Bulgarian bass. Played vn., cl., tb., and pf. by age of 14. Studied Sofia Mus. Acad. from 1948 and at Moscow Cons. Opera début Sofia 1955 (Don Basilio in Rossini's *Il barbiere di Siviglia*). Member of Bolshoy Opera from 1956. Vienna début 1962. Frequent guest singer at Milan, CG, Salzburg, NY

Met., especially in *Boris Godunov* and as King Philip in Verdi's *Don Carlos*.

Ghiselin, Jean (*d* c.1508). Flemish composer of masses, songs, motets, etc. May have been pupil of *Ockhegem. Connected with court at Ferrara from c.1490 to 1505 but was singer at church in Florence 1492–3. In 1503 went to Paris to escort Josquin *Desprès to Ferrara on his appointment as maestro di cappella. Pubd. vol. of masses 1503. In 1504–5 Ghiselin, Obrecht, and Desprès worked in Ferrara. Returned to Netherlands 1505. Comps. noted for technical skill.

Ghislanzoni, Antonio (*b* Lecco, 1824; *d* Caprino-Bergamasco, 1893). It. writer. Trained as bar. Ed. *Gazzetta musicale*, Milan; author of at least 80 opera libs., incl. that for Verdi's *Aida*.

Ghost Trio (Beethoven). See *Geister Trio*.

Giacomelli, Geminiano (*b* Piacenza, c.1692; *d* Loreto, 1740). It. composer. Wrote 19 operas, incl. *Cesar in Egitto* (Milan 1735). Choirmaster, court of Parma 1719–27 and 1732–7, Piacenza 1727–32.

Giannini, Vittorio (*b* Philadelphia, 1903; *d* NY, 1966). Amer. composer. Studied Milan Cons. and Juilliard Sch. (pupil of R. Goldmark). Wrote 8 operas incl. *The Taming of the Shrew*, *The Scarlet Letter*, *Beauty and the Beast*, and *The Servant of Two Masters*, also 5 syms., conc. grosso for str.; *Stabat Mater*, *Requiem* (Vienna 1937); conc. for pf., 2 pf., org., vn.; str. qt., pf. quintet, pf. sonata, etc.

Gianni Schicchi. 1-act opera by Puccini to lib. by Forzano based on incident in Dante's *Inferno*. Comp. 1917–18. Prod. NY Met. 1918, Rome 1919, London 1920. The 3rd of Puccini's *Trittico*, the others being *Il *tabarro* and *Suor Angelica*.

Gianoncelli, Bernardo (*d* before 1650). It. composer and lutenist in first half of 17th cent.; one of last It. composers for lute. Little known biographically. In 1650 his widow pubd. *Il liuto di Bernardo Gianoncelli* in his memory (only surviving copy in Biblioteca Nazionale Marciana, Venice). Contains several suites, arr. according to key. Best-known piece was *Bergamasca*, of which a lute arr. by Chilesotti was pubd. 1891. Also orch. version by *Respighi. Opening theme of *Bergamasca* used by BBC Radio 3 to introduce programme 'Homeward Bound'.

'Giant' Fugue. Nickname for Bach's organ fugue in D minor in Part III of the *Klavierübung*. So-called because of giant-like strides of a pedal figure:

Giardini, Felice de (*b* Turin, 1716; *d* Moscow, 1796). It. violinist and composer. Chorister, Milan Cath. Played in opera orchs. in Rome and Naples. Toured Ger. and Eng. 1750, settling in latter as leader of orch. at It. Opera, which he managed from 1756–65. Leader of orch. at 3 Choirs Fest. 1770–6. Left Eng. 1784, returning 1790 to start comic opera co. in London. It failed and he took it to Moscow. Wrote operas, 54 vn. sonatas, 12 vn. concs., 18 str. qts., etc.

Gibbons, Christopher (*b* Westminster, 1615; *d* Westminster, 1676). Eng. composer and organist, second son of O. *Gibbons. Organist Winchester Cath. 1638; Westminster Abbey, Chapel Royal and private organist to Charles II, 1660. Wrote str. fantasies, anthems, masques, etc.

Gibbons, Orlando (*b* Oxford, 1583; *d* Canterbury, 1625). Eng. composer, organist, and virginalist. Entered choir of King's Coll., Cambridge, 1596. Organist Chapel Royal from 1604. Mus. B. Cambridge Univ. 1606. Chamber musician to King, 1619, organist Westminster Abbey from 1623. Composer of noble church mus., incl. many anthems (e.g. *This is the Record of John*), motets and madrigals (e.g. *The Silver Swan*), 40 kbd. pieces, incl. contribution to *Parthenia*, 30 fantasies for viols, several pavans and galliards, and 3 *In nomines*. One of the greatest of the early Eng. composers. His father, William, brothers Edward, Ellis, and Ferdinando, and son Christopher *Gibbons were musicians.

Gibbs, (Cecil) **Armstrong** (*b* Great Baddow, 1889; *d* Chelmsford, 1960). Eng. composer. Studied RCM with Charles Wood and Vaughan Williams. On staff RCM 1921–39. Comp. opera, incidental mus., cantatas, church mus., but best known for waltz *Dusk* and for his many songs, several being settings of Walter De la Mare (such as the popular *Five Eyes*).

Gibet, Le (The Gallows). Second of 3 pf. pieces by Ravel under title *Gaspard de la Nuit*, 1908.

Gibson, (Sir) **Alexander** (Drummond) (*b* Motherwell, Scotland, 1926). Scot. cond. Studied Glasgow Univ., RCM, Salzburg Mozarteum, and Acad. Chigiana, Siena. Répétiteur and ass. cond., SW Opera 1951–2, ass. cond. BBC Scot. S.O. 1952–4, staff cond. SW Opera 1954–7, mus. dir. 1957–9. Prin. cond. Scot. Nat. Orch. 1959–84. Founded Scottish Opera 1962, mus. dir. 1962–87. C.B.E. 1967. Knighted 1977.

Gielen, Michael (Andreas) (*b* Dresden, 1927). Ger.-Argentinian composer, cond., and pianist. Studied Buenos Aires, where he perf. all Schoenberg's pf. works. Mus. staff, Teatro Colón, Buenos Aires, 1947–51. Joined staff of Vienna State Opera 1951, becoming resident cond. 1954–60. Chief cond. Royal Swed. Opera, Stockholm, 1960–5. Cond. W. Ger. Radio Orch., Cologne, 1965–9. Mus. dir., Nat. Orch. of Belg. 1969–72; mus. dir. Netherlands Opera from 1972. NY début 1971.

Mus. dir., Frankfurt Opera, 1977–87. Chief guest cond., BBC S.O. from 1979. Mus. dir., Cincinnati S.O. 1980–6. Cond. Baden-Baden Radio S.O. from 1986. Particularly noted for championship of contemp. music. Comps. incl. chamber cantatas, choral works, and chamber mus.

Gieseking, Walter (Wilhelm) (*b* Lyons, 1895; *d* London, 1956). Ger. pianist. Studied Hanover Cons. Début 1912 followed by int. tours. London début 1923. NY 1926. Especially renowned for playing of Debussy and Ravel, but also for Beethoven and Brahms. Comp. pf. pieces and songs.

Giga. See *Gigue.*

Gigault, Nicolas (*b* ?Paris, *c*.1627; *d* Paris, 1707). Fr. organist and composer. Org. at four Paris churches (St Honoré 1646–52, St Nicolas-des-Champs 1652–1707, St Martin-des-Champs from 1673, Hôpital du St Esprit from 1685) and owned large collection of instr., both keyboard and stringed. Regarded as equal of Couperin as executant. His *Livre de musique* (1683) contains 20 noëls with variations, the earliest known example of this genre.

Gigg, Gigge. Old Eng. spellings of *Jig or *Gigue.*

Gigli, Beniamino (*b* Recanati, 1890; *d* Rome, 1957). It. ten. Studied Rome with Rosati. First prize int. contest, Parma, 1914. Début Rovigo 1914, followed by appearances in Berlin, Dresden, Turin, Rome, Madrid, and Monte Carlo. Milan début 1918 with Toscanini. NY Met. 1920–32, 1938–9; CG 1930–1, 1938–9, 1946. Still sang superbly on tour of USA 1955. Excelled as Rodolfo (*Bohème*), Duke of Mantua (*Rigoletto*), and Cavaradossi (*Tosca*). Sang Ruggero in Puccini's *La rondine* at NY Met. 1928.

Gigout, Eugène (*b* Nancy, 1844; *d* Paris, 1925). Fr. organist and composer. Studied under Saint-Saëns at École Niedermeyer, Paris, becoming prof. there 1863–85 and 1900–5. Organist St Augustin, 1863, touring widely and becoming known for brilliant improvisations. Founded own org. sch. 1885. Prof. of org., Paris Cons., from 1911. Comp. many works for org.

Gigue, Giga (Fr., It.). Jig. (1) A lively rustic Eng., Scot., and Irish dance type (see Jig), usually in compound duple or triple time, with the characteristic rhythm ♩ ♪♪ ♪ etc. Eng. virginalists were first to use the *gigue*, which was introduced to the Continent by *Froberger, 1657, though the term had appeared in 1648 in a lute piece by Ebner. Pieces in gigue style were absorbed into the suite as the customary closing movements: in Bach's gigues the 2 halves of binary form often opened in something like fugal style, the subject of the first half being often inverted as that of the 2nd half. (Occasionally Bach applied the term 'gigue' loosely to a piece in simple duple or quadruple time.)

(2) Medieval name for str. instr.

Gigues (Debussy). See *Images*.

Gilbert, Anthony (*b* London, 1934). Eng. composer. Studied Morley Coll., 1958–62 (harmony, etc. with A. *Milner, comp. with Walter *Goehr). Lecturer in comp. Goldsmiths' Coll., London Univ., 1969–73. Ed. of contemporary mus. Schott's, London, from 1965. Course tutor in comp. RNCM from 1973. Comps. incl. Sinfonia for chamber orch. (1965); *Regions* for 2 chamber orchs. (1966); *9 or 10 Osannas* for cl., hn., vn., vc., pf. (1967); *Spell Respell* for elec. basset cl., pf. (1968); *Mother*, for chamber ens. and elec. devices (1969); *The Scene Machine*, 1-act opera, lib. G. McBeth (1970, prod. Cassel 1971, SW 1972); *The Incredible Flute Music*, fl. and pf. (1968); *String quartet with piano pieces* (1972); *Cantata* (1972); Symphony (1973); *Canticle I*, for brass and cls. (1973), *Canticle II* for 6 male vv. (1974); *Ghost and Dream Dancing (Studies for Orch. I)* (1974); *Inscapes* for sop., reader, 2 reeds, and percussionist (1975); *Crow-Cry* for orch. (1976–7); *Welkin* for sch. orch. (1976); *The Chakravaka Bird*, song-drama for radio (1976–7); *Treatment of Silence*, solo vn., and tape (1978); *Towards Asavari*, pf. and small orch. (1978); *Long White Moonlight*, sop. and db. (1980); *Calls Around Chungmori*, ens. and audience (1980); *Vasanta With Dancing*, chamber ens. (1981).

Gilbert, Geoffrey (Winzer) (*b* Liverpool, 1914). Eng. flautist and teacher. Studied RMCM. Hallé Orch. 1930–3; LPO 1933–9, 1945; BBC S.O. 1948–52; RPO 1957–63; prof. of fl. TCL 1947–65, GSM 1948–69, RMCM 1959–69; cond. in residence Stetson Univ., Florida, 1966–9, prof. of fl. and dir. of instr. studies from 1969. O.B.E. 1977.

Gilbert, Henry (Franklin Belknap) (*b* Somerville, Mass., 1868; *d* Cambridge, Mass., 1928). Amer. composer. Studied Boston, comp. pupil of *MacDowell. Great interest in folk music and Negro melodies. Works incl. *Comedy-Overture on Negro Themes* (1905), *3 American Dances* (1911), *Negro Rhapsody* (1913), symphonic prol. *Riders to the Sea* (1915), ballet *Dance in Place Congo* (1918).

Gilbert, Kenneth (*b* Montreal, 1931). Canadian harpsichordist and organist. Studied at Montreal Cons., then in Paris with Duruflé, N. Boulanger, and Leonhardt. Church org. in Montreal 1955–67. London début 1968. Ass. prof., Laval Univ., Quebec, from 1969. Ed. of F. Couperin's *Pièces de clavecin*.

Gilbert, (Sir) W(illiam) S(chwenk) (*b* London, 1836; *d* Harrow Weald, 1911). Eng. poet and playwright, librettist of 14 operettas (the 'Savoy Operas') with *Sullivan from 1871 to 1896. Knighted 1907.

Gilels, Emil (*b* Odessa, 1916; *d* Moscow, 1985). Soviet pianist, pupil of Heinrich Neuhaus. Studied in Odessa, début there 1929. First prize Brussels pf. competition 1938. Début in Paris and London

1954, Philadelphia 1955. Brilliant interpreter of Prokofiev sonatas, and also of classics.

Giles, Nathaniel (*b* ?Worcester, *c*.1558; *d* Windsor, 1634). Eng. composer and organist. Organist of Worcester Cath. 1581–5, then of St George's, Windsor, from 1585, and Chapel Royal from 1597. Comp. church mus.

Gillis, Don (*b* Cameron, Missouri, 1912; *d* Columbia, S. Carolina, 1978). Amer. composer. Studied at, and later taught at, Texas Christian Univ. Played tb. in jazz bands. Worked as composer, arranger, and trombonist, Fort Worth Radio, Texas, 1932–5. Programme dir. and producer NCB, NY, 1944–54, working with Toscanini. His comps. are in a popular and traditional style, influenced by jazz, hymns, dances, and Sibelius, Strauss, etc. Composer of 10 syms. and Sym. No. $5\frac{1}{2}$ ('for fun'), 2 pf. concs., *The Crucifixion* (oratorio), str. qts., comic operas.

Gilly, Dinh (*b* Algiers, 1877; *d* London, 1940). Fr. bar. Studied Paris Cons. Début Paris 1899, Paris Opéra 1902–8, NY Met. 1909–14, CG 1911. Settled in Eng., appearing with Beecham, Carl Rosa, and Brit. Nat. opera cos. Founded singing sch. in London with wife, Edith Furmedge.

Gilman, Lawrence (*b* Flushing, NY, 1878; *d* Franconia, New Hampshire, 1939). Amer. critic, author, and journalist. Mus. critic *Harper's Weekly* 1901–13, *NY Herald Tribune* 1923–39. Programme-annotator NY Phil. Soc. and Philadelphia Orch. 1921–39. Author of books on MacDowell, Strauss's *Salome*, Wagner, and Toscanini.

Gilson, Paul (*b* Brussels, 1865; *d* Brussels, 1942). Belg. composer and critic. Studied Brussels Cons. 1887–9 with Gevaert. Mus. critic *Le Soir* 1906–14, founded *La Revue musicale belge* 1924. Strong influence on younger school of Belg. composers 1920–40. Inspector gen. of Belg. sch. mus. 1908–30. Comp. operas, cantatas, orch. works, and chamber mus.

Gimel. See *Gymel*.

Ginastera, Alberto (*b* Buenos Aires, 1916; *d* Geneva, 1983). Argentinian composer. Studied at Williams Cons., Buenos Aires, 1928–35, and Nat. Cons. 1936–8. Ballet suite *Panambi* performed in Buenos Aires 1937. Guggenheim fellowship 1942. Lived in NY 1945–7. Returned to Argentina 1948 to teach and compose (though falling foul of Peron régime). Founded various mus. schs., incl. Centre for Advanced Mus. Studies, Buenos Aires, of which he became dir. 1962–9. Settled in Geneva 1971. His mus. was in a nationalistic idiom up to about 1958 when he adopted more advanced procedures incl. serialism (first apparent in the 1952 pf. sonata), microtones, and aleatory rhythms. His operas have attracted wide attention. Works incl.:

OPERAS: *Don Rodrigo*, 3 acts (prod. Buenos Aires, 1964), *Bomarzo*, 2 acts (prod. Washington

1967, London 1976), *Beatrix Cenci*, 2 acts (prod. Washington 1971).

BALLETS: *Panambi* (1934–6), *Estancia* (1941).

ORCH: Suite, *Panambi* (1937), *Ollantay* (1947), *Variaciones concertantes* (1953), *Pampeana No. 3* (1954), *Concerto per corde* (1965), *Estudios sinfónicos* (1967), *Glosses sobre temes de Pau Casals* (1976–8), *Iubilum* (1980).

CONCERTOS: pf. No. 1 (1961), No. 2 (1972), vn. (1963), harp (1956), vc. No. 1 (1968), No. 2 (1980).

CHURCH AND ORCH: Ps. 150 (1938), *Turbae ad Passionem Gregorianam*, 3 singers, boy's ch., ch., and orch. (1974).

VOICE AND ORCH: *Cantáta para América mágica* for sop. and perc. (1960), *Sinfonia, 'Don Rodrigo'* for sop. and orch. (1964), cantata *Bomarzo* for narrator, bar., and orch. (1964, distinct from opera of same name), *Milena* for sop. and orch. (1971), *Serenata*, vc., bar., and chamber orch. (1973).

CHAMBER MUSIC: Duo for fl. and ob. (1945); Str. Qts., No. 1 (1948), No. 2 (1958), No. 3 (1973, with sop.); pf. sonatas, No. 1 (1952), No. 2 (1981), No. 3 (1982); pf. quintet (1963); *Puneña No. 2 'Hommage à Paul Sacher'*, vc. (1976); guitar sonata (1976); vc. sonata (1979); *Variations and Toccata sopra 'Aurora Lucis Rutilat'*, org. (1980).

Gioconda, La (The Joyful Girl). Opera in 4 acts by *Ponchielli, lib. 'Tobia Gorrio' (Arrigo Boito), based on Hugo's *Angelo, Tyran de Padoue* (1835). Prod. Milan 1876, CG and NY Met. 1883. Contains in Act 3 Sc. 2 the ballet 'Dance of the Hours'.

Giocoso (It.). Jocose, merry, playful. So the adverb *giocosamente.*

Gioia, Gioja (It.). Joy. So *gioiante, gioioso; gioiosamente,* joyful.

Gioielli della Madonna, I (The Jewels of the Madonna). Opera in 3 acts by *Wolf-Ferrari, lib. Golisciani and Zangarini. Prod. Berlin 1911 in version by H. Liebstöckl, Chicago and CG 1912, Genoa 1913, Wexford 1981.

Giordani (Giordano), **Giuseppe** (b Naples, c.1753; d Fermo, 1798). It. composer popularly called Giordanello. Ch.-master Fermo from 1791. Wrote operas, church mus., instr. works, and, it is believed, the popular song *Caro mio ben.*

Giordani (Giordano), **Tommaso** (b Naples, c.1733; d Dublin, 1806). It. composer and cond. Began career as singer. Settled in London 1753, active as opera impresario and composer of over 50 operas. Comp. songs for f.p. of Sheridan's *The Critic* (1779). Settled in Dublin 1782.

Giordano, Umberto (b Foggia, 1867; d Milan, 1948). It. composer. Studied Naples Cons. First success 1892 in Rome with opera *Mala vita*, an example of the *verismo* sch. which he continued to exploit. Later successes were *Andrea Chenier

(1896), *Fedora* (1898), and *Madame Sans-Gêne* (1915).

Giorno di regno, Un (King for a Day). Comic opera in 2 acts by Verdi to lib. by Romani orig. written (as *Il finto Stanislao*) for Gyrowetz in 1818. Comp. 1840. Prod. Milan 1840, NY 1960, London 1961, Wexford 1981.

Giovanna d'Arco (Joan of Arc). Opera in 4 acts by Verdi, lib. Solera based on Schiller's *Die Jungfrau von Orleans* (1801). Comp. 1844–5. Prod. Milan 1845, NY (concert) and London 1966.

Giovanelli, Ruggiero (b Velletri, Rome, 1560; d Rome, 1625). It. composer. Succeeded *Palestrina in 1594 as maestro di cappella, St Peter's, Rome. Member of Sistine Choir, 1599. Wrote madrigals, 12-part Mass, and other church mus.

Giovanni da Cascia (da Firenze) (*fl.* 14th cent.). It. composer of madrigals, canzonets, etc., at Verona.

Gipps, Ruth (b Bexhill-on-Sea, 1921). Eng. composer, cond., oboist, and pianist. Studied RCM with Vaughan Williams, R. O. Morris, and Gordon Jacob (comp.), Kendall Taylor (pf.), and Leon Goossens (ob.). Oboist in professional orchs. and concert pianist until 1952, ch.-master City of Birmingham Choir, 1948–50; cond. London Repertoire Orch. from 1955; founder and cond. Chanticleer Orch. from 1961. Prof. at RCM from 1967. M.B.E. 1981. Comps. incl. 4 syms; concs. for pf., vn., vn. and va., ob., hn., and double bn; cantata *Goblin Market*; tone-poem for wind instrs.; *Magnificat*; and *The Cat* for 2 soloists, ch., orch.

Gipsy Baron, The (Strauss). See *Zigeunerbaron, Der.*

Gipsy Princess, The (Kálmán). See *Csárdásfürstin, Die.*

Gipsy Songs, Seven. For ten. and pf. by Dvořák, Op. 55, to words by Heyduk, comp 1880. 1. *My Song Resounds.* 2. *My Triangle is Singing.* 3. *Silent the Woods.* 4. *Songs my Mother Taught me.* 5. *Sound the Fiddle.* 6. *Clean Cotton Clothes.* 7. *To the Heights of Tatra.*

Girl I left behind me, The. The words can be traced back to the end of the 18th cent.; so can the tune, sometimes known as *Brighton Camp.* It is played in the Brit. Army on occasions of departure.

Girl of the Golden West, The (Puccini). See *Fanciulla del West, La.*

Gis (Ger.). G♯. *Gisis,* G♯♯.

Giselle, ou Les Wilis (Giselle, or the Wilis). 'Fantastic ballet' in 2 acts, mus. *Adam, choreog. Coralli and Perrot, f.p. Paris 1841. Lib. based on legend recounted by Heine. Carlotta Grisi danced first Giselle. F.p. London, Vienna, St Petersburg 1842. Modern prods. are based on Petipa's last St

Petersburg prod. of 1884. The Wilis are the ghosts of girls who die before their intended marriages.

Gitano, gitana (Sp.). Gipsy.

Gitlis, Ivry (*b* Haifa, 1922). Israeli violinist. Gave first public concert at age of 8. Studied École Normale de Paris 1932–5, then with Enescu, Flesch, and Thibaud. Début with Brit. orchs. after Second World War. Won Thibaud Prize 1951. Début with Israel P.O. 1952. Settled in Paris. Noted for playing of contemporary mus.

Gittern. Medieval forerunner of guitar, heyday being 14th cent.

Giù (It.). Down, e.g. *arcata in giù*, 'down-bowed'.

Giuditta. Opera in 3 acts by *Lehár, lib. Knepler and Löhner. Prod. Vienna 1934, with *Tauber. Lehár's only opera.

Giuliani, Mauro (*b* Bisceglie, 1781; *d* Naples, 1829). It. guitar virtuoso. Self-taught. Lived in Vienna 1806–19, during which time he knew Beethoven. Toured Russ. and Eng. before settling in Naples. Comp. over 200 works for guitar.

Giulini, Carlo Maria (*b* Barletta, 1914). It. cond. Studied Accademia di Santa Cecilia, Rome. Mus. dir. It. Radio 1946–51. Opera début Bergamo 1950 (*La traviata*). Scala, Milan, 1951–6. Brit. début 1955 at Edinburgh Fest. when he cond. the Glyndebourne Co. in Verdi's *Falstaff*. Later cond. many London concerts with Philharmonia Orch. (memorable perfs. of Verdi *Requiem*) and was guest cond. Hallé Orch. 1968. CG 1958–67 (incl. celebrated *Don Carlos* 1958) and 1982 (*Falstaff*). Joint cond. Chicago S.O. (with *Solti) 1969–72. Cond. Los Angeles P.O. 1978–84.

Giulio Cesare (Julius Caesar). (1) Opera in 3 acts by Handel, lib. N.F. Haym. Prod. London 1724, Northampton, Mass., 1927.
   (2) Opera in 3 acts by *Malipiero, lib. composer, based on Shakespeare's play. Prod. Genoa 1936.
   (3) Other operas on this subject by Cavalli, Sartorio, Freschi, Keiser, and others.

Giustamente (It.). With exactitude i.e. unvarying speed and rhythm.

Giustiniana. Type of love song popular in 15th and 16th cents. named after poet Leonardo Giustiniani (*c*.1385–1446).

Giusto (It.). Just, strict. *Allegro giusto* means either a strict allegro or a moderate allegro (neither too fast nor too slow). *Tempo giusto* means either 'strict' time or 'suitable' time.

Glagolitic Mass (*M'sa Glagolskaja*). Mass for sop., cont., ten., bass, ch., and orch. by Janáček, comp. 1926, f.p. Brno 1927, Norwich 1930. Text adapted from Ordinary of the Mass by Miloš Weingant. Movements entitled: Kyrie (*Gospodi pomiluj*); Gloria (*Slava*); Credo (*Věruju*); Sanctus (*Svet*); Agnus Dei (*Agneče Božij*). Vernacular version of Ordinary was taken by Janáček from church magazine. He mistakenly called Old Slavonic language of time of St Cyril and St Methodius (9th cent.) 'glagolitic', which properly refers only to Old Slavonic script and alphabet. Mus. contains important org. part.

Glanville-Hicks, Peggy (*b* Melbourne, Victoria, 1912). Australian-born composer (Amer. citizen 1948). Comp. lessons at 15 from Fritz Hart. Studied Melba Cons. 1929–31 and RCM (comp. with Vaughan Williams, pf. with A. Benjamin and C. Lambert). Later studied with Wellesz in Vienna and Boulanger in Paris. Lived in NY 1942–59, organizing concerts of modern mus. and working as critic of *NY Herald Tribune* 1948–58. Went to live in Greece 1959. Her mus. combines serialism with the use of oriental and ancient modes. Comps. incl.:

OPERAS: *Caedmon; The Transposed Heads* (after T. Mann); *Nausicaa* (lib. R. Graves and A. Reid; prod. Athens 1961).
BALLETS: *Saul and the Witch of Endor; Tragic Celebration; A Season in Hell; Postman's Knock; The Masque of the Wild Man.*
ORCH: *Sinfoniettas Nos. 1 and 2, Spanish Suite, Sinfonia Pacifica, Gymnopédies 1–3, Etruscan Concerto* for pf. and chamber orch., *Concerto romantico* for va. and orch., fl. conc.
CHAMBER MUSIC: Sonata for pf. and 5 percussionists, harp sonata, *Concertino da camera* for fl., cl., bn., pf., str. qt. *Letters from Morocco* for ten. and chamber orch., *Concertino antico* for harp and str. qt.
Also songs and film mus.

Glasenapp, Carl (Friedrich) (*b* Riga, 1847; *d* Riga, 1915). Ger.-Russ. teacher and writer. Authority on Wagner. Wrote 2-vol. life and works of Wagner 1876–7, rewritten in 6 vols. (1894–1911, Eng. trans. by Ashton Ellis); also ed. Bayreuth letters and archives for publication.

Glass Dulcimer. Strips of glass struck with hammers. Occasionally provided with mechanism and kbd.

Glass Armonica (Ger. Glasharmonika). Obsolete mus. instr., also known as 'musical glasses', comprising either (a) drinking glasses filled with water to different heights in order to leave a larger or smaller area of glass free to vibrate, and so to produce different notes; or (b) glass basins, graduated in size, fixed to a spindle revolved by pedal mechanism, the bottoms of the basins running in a trough of water, so as to be kept permanently damp. Sound is produced by rubbing the rims of the glasses with a wet finger. Gluck performed in London on the first type, Mozart on the second, for which he and Beethoven wrote mus. Donizetti wrote a part for glass harmonica in Lucia's Mad Scene in *Lucia di Lammermoor*, the alternative being fl.; and R. Strauss used it in his opera *Die Frau ohne Schatten*. George *Crumb revived the instr. in last movement of his *Black Angels* for electric str. qt. Bruno Hoffmann is the 20th cent. virtuoso of the instr.

Glass, Philip (*b* Baltimore, 1937). Amer. composer. Studied fl. at Peabody Cons. at age of 8. Studied mathematics and philosophy, Univ. of Chicago. At Juilliard Sch. 1958–62, then in Paris with N. Boulanger 1964–6. Working on a film in Paris with Ravi Shankar awakened interest in non-Western mus. Under this influence, divised a style whereby within a strong diatonic framework, his work was based on 5 or 6 notes with no harmonic change but powerful rhythmical steadiness. This produced a mus. similar to that of Steve Reich and Terry Riley although he did not then know their work. The result has been called *‘minimalist’ music, because there was maximum repetition of a minimum amount of material. In 1968 founded Philip Glass Ensemble, comprising keyboards (incl. elec. org.) and wind instr. His works incl. the operas *Einstein on the Beach* (Avignon, 1976), *Satyagraha* (Rotterdam, 1980), *The Photographer* (Amsterdam, 1982), and *Akhnaten* (Stuttgart 1984, NY 1984, London 1985), the film score *Koyaanisqatsi* (1982); and instr. works, *Strung Out*, amplified vn. (1967), *Music in Similar Motion* (1969), *Music with Changing Parts* (1970), *Music in 12 Parts* (1971–4), *Another Look at Harmony* (1974).

Glazunov, Alexander (Konstantinovich) (*b* St Petersburg, 1865; *d* Paris, 1936). Russ. composer. Pupil of Rimsky-Korsakov 1880–1. Balakirev cond. his first sym. in 1882, the work being hailed as a precocious masterpiece. Glazunov later met Liszt at Weimar and was influenced by his and Wagner's mus. Became dir. of St Petersburg Cons. 1905 after which his comps. became fewer. Left Russia 1928, visited USA 1929, then lived in Paris. Cosmopolitan rather than nationalist in mus. style. Works incl.:

BALLETS: *Raymonda* (1896–7), *The *Seasons* (1899).
ORCH: Syms. No. 1 (1881), No. 2 (1886), No. 3 (1892), No. 4 (1893), No. 5 (1895), No. 6 (1896), No. 7 (1902), No. 8 (1907), No. 9 (unfinished 1909, perf. Moscow 1948); *Suite caractéristique* (1887), *Stenka Razin* (1885), *The Sea* (1890), *Carneval* ov. (1894), *Chopiniana* (1895), *Scènes de ballet* (1895), vn. conc. (1904), pf. conc. No. 1 (1911), No. 2 (1917), Sax. conc. (1934).
CHAMBER MUSIC: 7 str. qts., str. quintet.
Also pf. pieces and songs.

Glee. A choral comp. in a number of short self-contained sections, each expressing the mood of some particular passage of the poem set, the mus. predominantly harmonic (i.e. in blocks of chords), rather than contrapuntal. Properly it is for solo male vv. (unacc.). It flourished *c*.1750–*c*.1830, during which time a remarkable series of able composers, such as Samuel Webbe, made lavish contributions to the repertory, but subsequently gave way gradually to the *part-song. It is a purely Eng. form, and was much fostered by the popularity of glee clubs. (In USA this name has been applied to univ. mus. clubs with more general aims.)

Gli, glie (It.). ‘The’ (plural).

Glière, Reinhold (Moritsovich) (*b* Kiev, 1875; *d* Moscow, 1956). Russ. composer and cond. Studied Kiev 1891–4, Moscow Cons. 1894–1900 (comp. with Arensky, Taneyev, and Ippolitov-Ivanov). Later studied in Berlin, 1905–7. Dir. and prof. of comp., Kiev Cons. 1913–20, then taught at Moscow Cons. His ballet *The Red Poppy* was one of first ‘social realism’ works of Soviet régime. The conservative-nationalist nature of his idiom was much to liking of official party arbiters of taste. Works included 3 syms., 4 str. qts., *March of the Red Army* for wind instrs. (1924), operas *Shakh Senem* (1923–5) and *Rachel* (1943), ballets *The Red Poppy* (1926–7, rev. 1949) and *The Bronze Horseman* (1948–9), harp conc. (1938), vc. conc. (1945–6), and 123 songs, 175 pf. pieces, and much chamber mus.

Glinka, Mikhail (Ivanovich) (*b* Novospasskoye, Smolensk, 1804; *d* Berlin, 1857). Russ. composer, regarded as founder of nat. sch. and the first Russ. composer to be accepted outside Russia. Son of wealthy landowner. During general education in St Petersburg from 1817 had pf. lessons from John *Field. Also studied vn. and harmony. Worked in Ministry of Communications 1824–8 but gave recitals as amateur singer. In 1828 began serious study of comp. with Zamboni. Went to Milan 1830 where homesickness led him to contemplate writing a truly nat. opera, then to Vienna and Berlin 1833, studying comp. with Siegfried Dehn. Returned to St Petersburg to compose opera *A Life for the Tsar*, successfully prod. 1836. Appointed Kapellmeister, Imperial Chapel 1837. His second opera *Ruslan and Lyudmila* was prod. 1842. In 1844 visited Paris, meeting Berlioz, travelling on to Sp. where the folk-dance rhythms fascinated him. Returned to Russ. 1847, but made several more foreign journeys. Works incl.:

OPERAS: *A *Life for the Tsar* (*Ivan Susanin*) (1834–6); *Ruslan and Lyudmila* (1837–42).
ORCH: *Jota aragonesa*; *Kamarinskaya*; *Night in Madrid*; *Valse fantaisie*.
CHAMBER MUSIC: Str. qt. (1830); Sextet for pf. and strs. (1832); *Trio pathétique*, pf., cl., bn. (1832). Also pf. and vocal works.

Glissando (bastard It. from Fr. *glisser*, to slide). (1 pf., harp, xylophone, vibraphone, etc.) The drawing of a finger down or up a series of adjacent notes.
(2, bowed insts.) Passing all or part of the way from one note to another on the same str., in much the same way as above and with much the same effect—with the difference that the pitches passed through, instead of representing the fixed tones and semitones of a scale, are infinite in

number. Tb. can also perform a satisfactory glissando.

Globokar, Vinko (*b* Anderny, Fr., 1934). Fr.-born Yugoslav trombonist and composer. Studied Ljubljana Cons. 1949–54 (tb. with Karas), Paris Cons. 1955–9 (tb. with Lafosse and Masson), and comp. with Leibowitz, 1959–63, and Berio, 1965. Prof. of tb. at Cologne Musikhochschule from 1968. By remarkable virtuosity extended range of tb. into *avant-garde* mus., making the instr., as has been said, not only talk but sing, scream, weep, and laugh. Prin. works:

ORCH: *Plan*, 5 instr. (1965); *Fluide*, 12 instr. (1967); *Étude pour Folklora* I, 19 soloists (1968), II, full orch. (1968); *La Ronde* (1970); *Ausstrahlungen*, soloists and 20 players (1971); *Laboratorium*, ens. (1973); *Material zur Diskussion eines historischen Instr.*, orch. (1974).

CHORAL: *Voie*, narrator, ch., and orch. (1965–6); *Traumdeutung*, 4 ch. and instr. (1967); Concerto grosso, 5 solo instr., 23 orch. players, and ch. (1969–70).

VOICE & INSTR: *Accord*, sop. and 5 instr. (1966); *Airs de voyages vers l'intérieur*, 8 vv., 2 instr., elec. (1972); *Carrousel*, 4 vv., 16 instr. (1977).

INSTR: *Discours I–VI*, for various instr. (1967–82); *Correspondences*, 4 instr. (1969); *Drama*, pf., perc. (1971); *Atemstudie*, ob. (1972); *Notes*, pf. (1972); *Limites*, vn., va., (1973); *Voix instrumentalisée*, cl. (1973); *Toucher*, perc. (1973); *Dédoublement*, cl. (1975).

Glock, (Sir) **William** (Frederick) (*b* London, 1908). Eng. critic, administrator, and pianist. Organ scholar Gonville and Caius Coll., Cambridge, 1919–26. Studied pf. with*Schnabel in Berlin, 1930–3. Mus. critic *Daily Telegraph* 1934, *Observer* 1934–45, *New Statesman* 1958–9. Dir., summer sch. of mus., Bryanston, 1948–52, Dartington Hall 1953–79. Founder and ed. *The Score* 1949–61. Controller of mus. BBC 1959–72, achieving catholic expansion of repertory, bringing Boulez to conduct BBC S.O., and extending scope and range of Henry Wood Promenade Concerts. Chairman, British section ISCM 1954–8. Artistic dir., Bath Fest. 1976–84. C.B.E. 1964. Knighted 1970.

Glocke(n) (Ger.). Bell(s). In orch. scores means tubular bells.

Glockenspiel (Ger.). Play of bells. Perc. instr. of tuned metal bars, with compass of 2 to 3 chromatic octaves, emitting brittle bell-like sound when played with kbd. or (more commonly) by small hand-held hammers. Orch. glockenspiel is played in horizontal position; in military bands it is carried vertically, bars being mounted in lyre-shaped frame (hence alternative name bell-lyra). First used 1739 by Handel in *Saul* (where he called it a carillon) and later by Mozart in *Die Zauberflöte* (1791). K. Salomon wrote glockenspiel conc., 1948.

Gloria in Excelsis Deo (Lat.). 'Glory to God in the highest'. The 'Doxologia Magna' (see *Doxologia*), an amplification of the song of the angels announcing the birth of Christ. It occurs in the Roman Mass and in the Communion Service of the Anglican Church.

Gloriana. Opera in 3 acts, Op. 53, by Britten, lib. W. Plomer after L. Strachey's *Elizabeth and Essex*. Commissioned by CG for coronation of Elizabeth II, who attended f.p. at CG on 8 June 1953, 6 days after her coronation. Cincinnati (concert) 1956, f. Amer. stage p. San Antonio 1984 (ENO tour).

Glossop, Peter (*b* Sheffield, 1928). Eng. bar. Opera début SW, 1952, in ch. Member SW Opera, 1952–62, CG 1962–5, thereafter guest singer at leading opera houses. Won int. competition for young singers, Sofia, 1961; Verdi gold medal, Parma, 1964. CG début 1962, Milan 1965, NY Met. 1967, Vienna 1968.

Glotte, Coup de. See *Coup de glotte*.

Glover, Jane (Alison) (*b* Helmsley, Yorks., 1949). Eng. cond. and musicologist. Studied Oxford Univ. At Wolfson Coll., Oxford, from 1975. Has ed. and cond. operas by Cavalli and Monteverdi. Art. dir., London Mozart Players from 1984. Chorus dir. Glyndebourne 1980–4. Prof. cond. début Wexford 1975 (Cavalli's *Eritrea*). Cond. Britten's *A Midsummer Night's Dream*, Glyndebourne Touring Opera 1981, Mozart's *Don Giovanni* at Glyndebourne 1982. Mus. dir., Glyndebourne Touring Opera 1982–5.

Gluck, Alma (orig. Fiersohn, Reba) (*b* Bucharest, 1884; *d* NY, 1938). Amer. soprano of Romanian birth. Studied singing in NY after marriage. Opera début with Met. company in 1909 (Sophie in *Werther*). Member of Met. company 1909–12. Studied with Sembrich in Berlin and from 1913 appeared mainly as concert singer. Noted for purity of vocal tone. Her second husband was the violinist Efrem Zimbalist (married 1914).

Gluck, Christoph Willibald von (*b* Erasbach, 1714; *d* Vienna, 1787). Ger. composer. Went to Prague Univ. in 1732 to study mus. and philosophy, also learning vc. In 1736 travelled to Vienna under protection of Prince Lobkowitz. Joined private orch. of Prince Melzi, with whom he went to Milan 1737. There he studied with *Sammartini and wrote his first opera *Artaserse*, 1741, 7 more following up to 1744. Travelled with Prince Lobkowitz to London 1745, composing 2 operas prod. 1746, meeting Handel, and giving 2 concerts as performer on *glass armonica. After 1746 travelled in Austria and Denmark and again visited Prague and Naples. In 1754 Empress Maria Theresa appointed him opera Kapellmeister to court th. in Vienna, a post which required him to compose in the more lively and flexible style of the fashionable Fr. opéras comiques. During 1755–61 he was closely assoc. with Durazzo (court th. Intendant), Quaglio (scene-painter), Angiolini (dancer), and the poet Calzabigi, with whom he evolved his operatic 'reforms' in which the singers' claims were subjugated to those of the drama, with *recitativo accompagnato* ousting the more formal *secco* recit. His ballet *Don Juan* (1761) and opera *Orfeo* (1762) embodied these principles which reached full expression in *Alceste* (1767), an anticipation of Wagner's music-drama. Gluck set forth his operatic creed in the preface to *Alceste*.

He resigned his Vienna court post in 1770 and in 1773 went to Paris, having been contracted to compose *Iphigénie en Aulide* for the Opéra. Its prod. in 1774 was followed by a slightly rev. Fr. version of *Orfeo* and 2 years later of *Alceste*. Jealousy of Gluck's success in Paris led to an engineered quarrel with the It. composer *Piccinni, who was asked to set the same lib. on which Gluck was known to be working. Gluck destroyed his sketches but composed *Armide* (1777), followed by *Iphigénie en Tauride* (1778). In 1779 he returned to Vienna and retired, living in a grand manner and dying after defying his doctor by drinking a post-prandial liqueur. The simplicity and sublimity of Gluck's melodies, supported by a vivid dramatic sense, have ensured the survival of a large proportion of his mus. Works incl.:

OPERAS: *Artaserse* (Milan 1741), *La caduta dei giganti* and *Artemene* (London 1746), *La Semiramide riconosciuta* (Vienna 1748), *La contesa dei Numi* (Copenhagen 1749), *La clemenza di Tito* (Naples 1752), *Le *Cinesi* (1754), *La danza* (Vienna 1755), *Il rè pastore* (Vienna 1756), *Orfeo ed Euridice* (Vienna 1762), *Telemaco* (Vienna 1765), *Paride ed Elena* (Vienna 1770), *Iphigénie en Aulide* (Paris 1774), *Orphée* (Paris 1774), *Alceste* (Vienna 1767, Paris 1776), *Armide* (Paris 1777), *Iphigénie en Tauride* (Paris 1778), *Echo et Narcisse* (Paris 1779).

OPÉRAS COMIQUES: *L'Île de Merlin* and *La Fausse Esclave* (Vienna 1758), *La Cythère assiégée* (Schwetzingen 1759), *L'Arbre enchanté* (Vienna 1759), *La Rencontre imprévue* (Vienna 1764).

BALLETS: *Don Juan* (Vienna 1761), *Semiramide* (Vienna 1765).

MISC: *De Profundis* (ch.), 6 sonatas a tre (London 1746), 9 syms. (Vienna 1753).

Glückliche Hand, Die (lit. The Blessed Hand; The Knack). Drama with mus. in 1 act by Schoenberg, Op. 18, lib. composer. Comp. 1910–13. Prod. Vienna 1924, Philadelphia and NY Met. 1930, London 1962 (concert perf.). Contains mimed parts for man and woman. Use of coloured lights also has fundamental importance.

Glyndebourne. House and estate near Lewes, Sussex, in grounds of which the owner, John *Christie, built opera house with (as it was thought) eccentric idea of staging ideal perfs. of opera in beautiful setting. Inspiration for enterprise was Christie's wife, the soprano Audrey *Mildmay. First Glyndebourne Fest. began on 28 May 1934 with Mozart's *Le nozze di Figaro*, followed the next evening by *Così fan tutte*. Fritz Busch was the cond. with Carl *Ebert as producer and, later, Rudolf *Bing as administrator, a team which set new standards for Brit. opera. In 1939 the th. was enlarged to seat 600 instead of 300; today over 800 can be accommodated. While mus. considerations have always been paramount, Glyndebourne has also always had a special significance because of the beauty of the gardens. The tradition of a long dinner interval, during which visitors can picnic in the grounds or dine in the restaurant, is a big social attraction, so that what began as a risky venture lasting a few days is now a fully booked-up annual season extending from May to early August.

After the war Glyndebourne re-opened in 1946 with Britten's *Rape of Lucretia*. There were no perfs. in 1948 and 1949 but Glyndebourne presented operas at the *Edinburgh Fest. from 1947 to 1951. On Busch's death in 1951, Vittorio *Gui became chief cond. He was succeeded in 1960 by John *Pritchard who first joined the mus. staff in 1947 and retired in 1977, being succeeded by Bernard *Haitink. When Ebert retired in 1959, Gunther Rennert became chief producer. He was succeeded by John *Cox 1971–83 and by Sir Peter *Hall from 1984. Although Glyndebourne's basic diet is the operas of Mozart, it has also staged *Don Pasquale* and several Rossini operas (under Gui) including successful revivals of *Le Comte Ory*, *La Cenerentola*, and *L'italiana in Algeri*. The first Eng. performance of Verdi's *Macbeth* was at Glyndebourne 1938. A speciality has been made of Richard Strauss's operas, with *Der Rosenkavalier* (in a reduced orchestration exclusively made by Strauss for Glyndebourne), *Ariadne auf Naxos*, *Capriccio*, *Intermezzo*, *Die schweigsame Frau*, and *Arabella*. The prod. of *Idomeneo* restored Mozart's opera seria to general circulation. Among adventurous prods. have been Stravinsky's *The Rake's Progress*, Busoni's *Arlecchino*, Gluck's *Alceste*, Henze's *Elegy for Young Lovers*, Donizetti's *Anna Bolena*, Cavalli's *L'Ormindo* and *La Calisto*, Monteverdi's *L'incoronazione di Poppea* and *Il ritorno d'Ulisse in patria*, Maw's *Rising of the Moon*, Britten's *Midsummer Night's Dream*, Prokofiev's *Love for 3 Oranges*, Janáček's *The Cunning Little Vixen*, and Knussen's *Where the Wild Things Are*. The policy of engaging the most suitable singers has meant that many of the world's great operatic artists have sung at Glyndebourne, which also has a penchant for discovering a rising star some years before everyone else. Scrupulous attention is also paid to sets and lighting, with the engagement of such artists as Oliver Messel, Osbert Lancaster, John Piper, and David Hockney. In 1968 the Glyndebourne Touring Co. was formed to make an autumn tour (usually to Oxford, Bristol, Norwich, Southampton, and Manchester) with some of the Sussex productions sung by casts specially recruited to give opportunities to the best of young Brit. singers. Just as the RPO or LPO (since 1964) is engaged for Glyndebourne itself, the touring co. has used the Northern Sinfonia, Bournemouth Sinfonietta and, from 1987, London Sinfonietta.

G. Mus. R.N.C.M. Graduate, with honours, of the *Royal Northern College of Music, Manchester.

Gnecchi, Vittorio (*b* Milan, 1876; *d* Milan, 1954). It. composer. Studied Milan Cons. Operas incl. *Cassandra* (1905) and *La rosiera* (1910). Latter said to be first opera to use quarter-tones. Accused R. Strauss of plagiarism because of resemblance between themes in *Cassandra* and *Elektra* (1908).

G.O. In Fr. org. mus., *grand orgue*, i.e. 'great org.'.

Gobbi, Tito (*b* Bassano del Grappa, 1913; *d* Rome, 1984). It. bar. and opera producer. Studied law, then became singer, studying in Rome. Début Gubbio 1935 as Rodolfo in *Sonnambula*, San Francisco 1948, Salzburg and CG 1950, NY Met. 1956. Outstanding actor as well as singer: notable for interpretations of Wozzeck, Scarpia, Rigoletto, Macbeth, Iago, Falstaff, and Boccanegra. Début as producer, Chicago and CG 1965. Repertory of 100 operas.

Godard, Benjamin (Louis Paul) (*b* Paris, 1849; *d* Cannes, 1895). Fr. composer and violinist. Studied Paris Cons. 1863. Cond. Concerts Modernes, Paris 1885–6. Wrote 2 vn. concs., pf. conc., syms., and 8 operas, (from which only the *Berceuse* for sop. from *Jocelyn* (1888) seems to have survived). Some of the instr. works are still played.

God bless the Prince of Wales. Song with words written in Welsh by Ceiriog Hughes and mus. by Henry Brinley Richards (1817–85). They were pubd. together in 1862. F.p. London 14 Feb. 1863 by Sims Reeves, preparatory to wedding of Prince of Wales on 10 March.

Goddard, Arabella (*b* St Servan, 1836; *d* Boulogne, 1922). Fr.-born pianist of Eng. origin. Pupil of Thalberg, Kalkbrenner, and J.W. Davison (mus. critic of *The Times*) whom she married 1859. London début 1850. Among first to play Beethoven's last sonatas in London. Retired 1880.

Godefroid, Dieudonné (Joseph Guillaume Félix) (*b* Namur, 1818; *d* Villers-sur-mer, 1897). Belg. harpist and composer. Trained Paris Cons. 1832–5. Wrote 2 operas, oratorio, and harp pieces. His brother Jules Joseph (*b* Namur, 1811; *d* Paris, 1840) was also harpist and composer.

Godfrey, (Sir) **Daniel** (Dan) (Eyers) (*b* London, 1868; *d* Bournemouth, 1939). Eng. cond. (son, grandson, and nephew of military bandmasters). Studied RCM. Conducted military bands 1890, opera in S. Africa 1891–2. Engaged at Bournemouth in 1893 to form municipal orch. to give sym. concerts. These he cond. until 1934, introducing many new works to Brit. audiences and making the concerts a particular forum for the f.ps. of works by Brit. composers. Knighted 1922. See *Bournemouth Symphony Orch.*

Godowsky, Leopold (*b* Soshly, nr. Vilna, 1870; *d* NY, 1938). Polish-born pianist and composer (Amer. citizen 1891). Studied Berlin Hochschule für Musik and with Saint-Saëns 1887–90. Toured USA 1884 and again in 1890, after which he became a pf. teacher in Philadelphia and, in 1894, dir. of pf. sch. at Chicago Cons. Returned to Berlin 1900–9, teaching and touring as recitalist. Dir., Master sch. of pf.-playing, Vienna, 1909. Returned to USA 1912. Career ended by illness 1930. Comps. incl. *53 Studies on Chopin Études*, *Triakontameron* (30 pf. pieces each comp. on a different day), the *Java Suite* (12 pieces), 3 symphonic metamorphoses for orch., and numerous pf. transcrs.

God Save The Queen (King). The tune of the Brit. 'National Anthem' must long have been the best-known tune in the world, having at one time or another been borrowed by about 20 countries as that of their official nat. song. The popularity of the words and tune in Brit. seems to date from the time of the landing of the Young Pretender, 1745, when they were introduced in London th. and widely taken up, being sung on several successive nights at Drury Lane and Covent Garden theatres in Sept. of that year. The authorship of both words and tune is obscure, but it existed in some form before 18th cent.

The tune is in rhythm and style a galliard. There is a Geneva tune of this type with some phrases resembling those in God Save The Queen; it was introduced in 1603 at a banquet celebrating the first anniversary of the unsuccessful attempt of the Duke of Savoy to seize the city (the 'Escalade'). An Eng. Christmas carol printed in 1611, *Remember, O thou Man*, shows similar resemblances. Much stronger resemblances are seen in a kbd. piece by John *Bull, (though in the minor), and his name is sometimes attached to the tune. The earliest known source is in a vol. of songs, *Harmonia anglica*, issued by John Simpson in London in 1744.

In the Amer. colonies and the USA the tune has at different times been sung to many different sets of words, e.g. *God Save America, God Save George Washington, God Save the Thirteen States*, etc. The present words *My country, 'tis of Thee*, date from 1831 and are the work of the Rev. Samuel Francis Smith. The name usually given to the tune is *America*.

Many composers, incl. Beethoven, Weber, Marschner, Paganini, Brahms, Donizetti, etc., have introduced the tune into their comps. or based works on it.

Gods go a-begging, The. Ballet in 1 act to mus. by Handel arr. *Beecham, choreog. Balanchine, prod. Diaghilev's Ballet Russe, London, 1928. Later choreog. by N. de Valois 1936, Lichine 1937. Also orch. suite.

Godunov, Boris (Mussorgsky). See *Boris Godunov*.

Goehr, Alexander (*b* Berlin, 1932). Eng. composer, son of Walter *Goehr. Studied RMCM 1952–5 (comp. with Richard Hall) where he was contemporary of Maxwell Davies, Birtwistle, and Ogdon, and in Paris (1955–6) with Messiaen and Yvonne Loriod. On mus. staff BBC 1960–8; composer-in-residence New England Cons. 1968–9; assoc. prof. of mus. Yale Univ. 1969–70; prof. of mus. Leeds Univ., 1971–6; prof. of mus. Cambridge Univ. from 1976. Dir., Leeds Fest., 1975. Goehr's mus. employs serialism but rejects elec. devices. He is among leaders of group of Eng. composers influenced by 2nd Viennese Sch. and his mus. can be described as essentially radical-conservative in idiom. Works incl.:

OPERA: *Arden muss sterben* (Arden must die) (1966); *Die Wiedertäufer* (The Anabaptists) (1984–5).
ORCH: Fantasia (1954, rev. 1958), *Hecuba's Lament* (1959–61), vn. conc. (1961–2), *Little Symphony* (1963), *Little Music for Strings* (1963), *Pastorals* (1965), *3 Pieces from Arden Must Die* (1967), *Romanza* for vc. and orch. (1968), *Konzertstück* for pf. and orch. (1969), *Symphony in 1 Movement* (1969–70), Conc. for 11 instrs. (1970), pf. conc. (1971), *Chaconne for 19 wind instrs.* (1974), *Metamorphosis/Dance* (1974), *Fugue on Psalm IV*, str. (1976), *Romanza on Psalm IV*, str. (1976), *Sinfonia* (1980), *Deux Études* (1981).
BALLET: *La belle dame sans merci* (1958).
MUSIC THEATRE: *Triptych*, 3-part th. piece for actor, 2 mimes, 5 singers, instr. group, 1. *Naboth's Vineyard* (1968), 2. *Shadowplay* (1970), 3. *Sonata about Jerusalem* (1970).
CHORAL AND VOCAL: *The Deluge*, cantata after da Vinci for sop., alto, fl., hn., tpt., harp, and strs. (1957–8); *Sutter's Gold*, cantata for bar., ch., and orch. (1959–60); *2 Choruses* (Milton and Shakespeare) (1962); *5 Poems and an Epigram of William Blake*, ch., tpt. (1964); *Orpheus Songs* for sop. (1971); Psalm IV for sop., alto, women's ch., va., and organ (1976); *Babylon the Great is fallen*, ch. and orch. (1979); *Das Gesetz der Quadrille*, bar., pf. (1979); *Behold the Sun*, concert aria for sop., vib., ens. (1981).
CHAMBER MUSIC: Pf. sonata (1951–2); *Suite* for fl., cl., hn., harp, vn., va., vc. (1961); *3 Pieces* for pf. (1964); pf. trio (1966), Str. Qt. No. 1 (1956–7), No. 2 (1967), No. 3 (1975–6); *Nonomiya* for pf. (1969); *Paraphrase* for cl. (1969); *Lyric Pieces* for wind septet and db. (1974); *Prelude and Fugue*, 3 cl., (1978); *Lento e Sostenuto*, str. qt. (1956–7, rev. 1983, orig. slow movt. of Str. Qt. No. 1).

Goehr, Walter (*b* Berlin, 1903; *d* Sheffield, 1960). Ger.-born cond. and composer. Pupil of Schoenberg at Prussian Acad. of Arts, Berlin. Cond. Berlin radio 1925–31, composing for it opera *Malpopita*. Settled in Eng. 1933. Mus. dir., Columbia Graphophone Co. 1933–9. Cond. BBC Th. Orch. 1945–8. On staff Morley Coll., London. Ed. Monteverdi's *Vespers* (York 1954) and *L'incoronazione di Poppea*. Wrote scores for radio, films, and th. Orch. Mussorgsky's *Pictures from an Exhibition*. Cond. f.ps. of Britten's *Serenade* (1943), Tippett's *A Child of Our Time* (1944), Seiber's *Ulysses* (1949), and A. Goehr's *The Deluge* (1959); and f.Brit. p. of Mahler's 6th Sym. (BBC 1950).

Goetz, Hermann (*b* Königsberg, 1840; *d* Hottingen, Zürich, 1876). Ger. composer. Studied at Stern Cons., Berlin, 1860–2. Org. at Winterthur 1863–7, moving to Zürich where he comp. his successful opera *The Taming of the Shrew* (prod. 1874). His sym. was also much admired and is convincing evidence of a rare talent prematurely cut short. Works incl.:

OPERAS: *Der widerspenstigen Zähmung* (The *Taming of the Shrew*) (1868–72); *Francesca da Rimini* (1875–6, completed by Ernst Frank).
ORCH: Sym. in F (1873); *Frühlingsouvertüre*; pf. conc.; vn. conc.
CHAMBER MUSIC: Pf. Trio; Pf. Qt; Pf. Quintet. Also songs and pf. pieces.

Goeyvaerts, Karel (August) (*b* Antwerp, 1923). Belg. composer and musicologist. Studied at Antwerp Cons. 1942–7 and with Messiaen and Milhaud at Paris Cons. 1947–50. His sonata for 2 pfs. (1951) laid foundations of total serialism and isolated note writing. Invited by Stockhausen to work in elec. studios of W. Ger. Radio, Cologne. Abandoned mus. career 1958 to work for Belg. airline Sabena but continued to comp. In 1970 went to work for Inst. of Psychoacoustics and Elec. Mus., Ghent. Comps. incl. mixed media pieces, works for elec. tape, and for medieval ens.

Goff, Thomas (Robert Charles) (*b* London, 1898; *d* London, 1975). Eng. builder of clavichords and hpds. Began business in partnership with J. C. Cobby 1933, later opening his own London headquarters. His particular achievement has been to adapt tone and dynamics to modern concert hall requirements. Adopted clavichord design of Herbert Lambert of Bath.

Gold and Silver (Ger. *Gold und Silber*). Waltz by Lehár comp. for gold and silver ball given by Prince Metternich, Jan. 1902.

Goldberg, Johann (Gottlieb Theophilus) (*b* Danzig, 1727; *d* Dresden, 1756). Ger. organist, composer, and klavier player. Said to have been pupil of Bach 1742–3. Chamber musician to Count Brühl 1751–6. Wrote 2 kbd. concs., 6 fl. trios, etc. Bach gave him a copy of his 30 vars. for hpd., but the story that they were commissioned by him is doubtful.

Goldberg, Szymon (*b* Włocławek, Pol., 1909). Pol.-born violinist and cond. (Amer. citizen 1953). Studied with *Flesch in Berlin. Début Warsaw 1921. Leader, Dresden P. O. 1925–9, Berlin P.O.

1929–34. Member of trio with *Hindemith and *Feuermann 1930–4. Settled in London and USA. Duo with Lili Kraus 1935–40. Member of fest. pf. qt., Aspen, Colorado, 1951–65. Solo concert violinist from 1955. Cond. Netherlands Chamber Orch. from 1955. Cond. Manchester Camerata 1977–9.

'Goldberg' Variations. 30 variations on an orig. theme for 2-manual hpd., by Bach. Nickname arose from story, now thought to be untrue, that they were commissioned by the Russ. ambassador to Saxony, Count Keyserlingk, for J. G. T. *Goldberg to play. Bach gave Goldberg a copy of the work.

Gold Coast Customs. Setting of poem by Edith Sitwell by H. *Searle for speakers, men's ch., winds, 2 pf., and perc., comp. 1947–9.

Golden Age, The (*Zolotoy vek*). Ballet in 3 acts with mus. by Shostakovich, choreog. Kaplan and Vaynonen. Prod. Leningrad 1930. Also orch. suite, Op. 22a.

Golden Cockerel, The (*Zolotoy petushok*). Opera (his 14th and last) in 3 acts by Rimsky-Korsakov, lib. Belsky after Pushkin's poem (1834). Prod. Moscow 1909, London 1914, NY Met. 1918. Comp. 1906–7, but perf. was banned in the composer's lifetime because of the opera's satire on autocracy. The indefensible habit of referring to it by the Fr. title *Le Coq d'or* arose from the prod. by Diaghilev in Paris, 1914, when all the roles were enacted by dancers while singers sat at the sides of the stage.

Golden Legend, The. Cantata by Sullivan for soloists, ch., and orch. to text based on Longfellow's poem. Comp. for Leeds Fest. 1886.

'Golden' Sonata. Nickname, but not the composer's, for Purcell's Sonata in F for 2 vns., va. da gamba, and org. or hpd., No. 9 of 10 sonatas posthumously pubd. 1697.

Goldmark, Károly (*b* Keszthély, Hung., 1830; *d* Vienna, 1915). Hung. composer and violinist, son of a cantor. Studied Vienna Cons. 1847. After playing in th. orchs., settled in Vienna 1850 as composer, teacher, and critic. His tuneful, colourful mus. is remembered today chiefly through his *Rustic Wedding* sym. Comp. 6 operas incl. *Die *Königin von Saba* (The Queen of Sheba) (1875) and *Ein Wintermärchen* (A Winter's Tale, after Shakespeare) (1908), Sym. in E♭ (properly suite) *Die ländliche Hochzeit* (*Rustic Wedding), ov. *Sakuntala*, 2 vn. concs., str. qt., vc. sonata, etc.

Goldmark, Rubin (*b* NY, 1872; *d* NY, 1936). Amer. composer, nephew of K. *Goldmark. Studied NY and Vienna Cons., later with Dvořák at Nat. Cons. of Mus., NY. Dir., Colorado Coll. Cons. 1895–1901. Teacher of pf. and theory in NY 1902–24; dir. of comp. dept., Juilliard Sch. 1924–36. Pupils incl. Copland, Chasins, and

Gershwin. Wrote *Requiem* for orch., *Hiawatha*, *Negro Rhapsody*, and several chamber works.

Goldschmidt, Berthold (*b* Hamburg, 1903). Ger.-born composer and cond. (Brit. cit. from 1947). Studied Hamburg Univ. and Berlin Hochschule für Musik (comp. with Schreker) 1922–5. Ass. cond. Berlin State Opera 1926–7. Cond. Darmstadt Opera 1927–9. Cond. in Leningrad 1931. Artistic adviser Berlin State Opera 1931–3. Settled in Eng. 1935. Cond. Glyndebourne co. in Verdi's *Macbeth* at first Edinburgh Fest. 1947. Guest cond. various Brit. orchs. Aided and advised Deryck *Cooke in preparing perf. version of Mahler's 10th sym., and cond. 1st complete perf. London 1964. Comp. 2 operas, of which *Beatrice Cenci* (1949–50) won a Fest. of Britain prize but was not perf. Sym., *Sinfonietta*, vn. conc., cl. conc., 2 str. qts., pf. sonata.

Goldschmidt, Otto (*b* Hamburg, 1829; *d* London, 1907). Ger.-born pianist, composer, and cond. Pupil of Mendelssohn at Leipzig Cons. In 1851 visited USA as accompanist for Jenny *Lind, whom he married 1852. Settled in London 1858, becoming vice-prin. RAM 1866. Founded and cond. London Bach Choir 1875. Comp. oratorio *Ruth*, pf. conc., songs, part-songs, etc.

Goldstone, Anthony (*b* Liverpool, 1944). Eng. pianist. Studied Cambridge Univ. and RMCM, later with Maria Curcio. Début Manchester 1965, RMCM orch. cond. Barbirolli. Won int. prizes in Munich and Vienna. London début 1968. Was member of pf. trio with Ralph Holmes (vn.) and Moray Welsh (vc.).

Golliwogg's Cakewalk. 6th item of Debussy's *Children's Corner* suite for pf. (1906–8).

Golschmann, Vladimir (*b* Paris, 1893; *d* NY, 1972). Fr.-born cond. of Russ. parentage (Amer. citizen 1947). Founded Golschmann concerts, Paris, 1919, for perf. of contemporary mus. Cond. for Diaghilev ballets. NY début 1924. Prin. cond. St Louis S.O. 1931–56, Denver S.O. 1964–70.

Goltermann, Georg (Eduard) (*b* Hanover, 1824; *d* Frankfurt, 1898). Ger. cellist, cond., and composer. 2nd cond., Frankfurt state th. 1853, 1st cond. 1874. Comp. sym., vc. conc., and other works for vc.

Goltz, Christel (*b* Dortmund, 1912). Ger. sop. Studied Munich. Member, Dresden State Opera 1936–50. Début CG 1951, NY Met. 1954. Created title-role in Liebermann's *Penelope* (Salzburg 1954). Repertory of over 120 parts. Noted for her Salome, Elektra, Marie (*Wozzeck*), and Tosca.

Gombert, Nicolas (*b* S. Flanders, *c*.1495; *d* after 1560). Flemish composer, believed to have been pupil of Josquin *Desprès. In court service of Charles V until 1540; later worked at Tournai. Comp. motets, masses, and songs.

Gomes, Antonio Carlos (*b* Campinas, 1836; *d* Belém, 1896). Brazilian composer. After 2 of his operas had been prod. in Rio, he was given govt. scholarship, 1864, to study in Milan where several of his operas were prod. (and admired by Verdi). Operas incl. *Il Guarany* (1870), *Fosca* (1873), *Salvator Rosa* (1874), *Maria Tudor* (1879), *Lo Schiavo* (1889), and *Condor* (1891). Also wrote cantatas, songs, and pf. pieces. Dir., Belém Cons. in 1896.

Gomez, Jill (*b* New Amsterdam, Brit. Guiana, 1942). W. Indian-born sop. Studied RAM and GSM. Opera début Cambridge 1967. Glyndebourne Touring Co., 1968. Sang Mélisande in Debussy's opera, Glyndebourne 1969. Created Flora in Tippett's The *Knot Garden*, CG 1970. ENO début 1984 (Governess). Has sung with English Opera Group, Scottish Opera, WNO, Kent Opera; also concert career, esp. in certain contemporary works (e.g. McCabe's *Notturni ed alba*).

Gondola Song. (1) A *barcarolle type of comp., supposed to recall the singing of Venetian gondoliers at their work. It is generally in $\frac{6}{8}$ or other compound time.
   (2) Name given by Mendelssohn to 3 of his *Songs without words* (No. 6 in G minor, No. 12 in F♯ minor, and No. 29 in A minor), and also to another pf. piece, *Auf einer Gondel* (On a Gondola) in A major, 1837.

Gondoliers, The, or The King of Barataria. Operetta by Sullivan, lib. Gilbert. Prod. London 1889, NY and Capetown 1890.

Gong. Perc. instr., also called tam-tam, of Chinese origin, being a large round sheet of metal turned up at the edge to form a kind of dish. Struck with felt mallet. Of indefinite pitch, but Puccini in *Turandot* and Vaughan Williams in his 8th Sym. require tuned gongs.

Goodall, (Sir) **Reginald** (*b* Lincoln, 1901). Eng. cond. Studied pf. and vn., RCM. Further study Munich and Vienna. Became ass. to Albert Coates with BNOC at CG. Ass. cond. Royal Choral Soc. 1936–9. Cond. at SW Opera from 1944. Cond. f.p. of Britten's *Peter Grimes*, June 1945. Cond. Glyndebourne 1946. On mus. staff of CG from 1946, but went abroad to assist Furtwängler, Krauss, and Knappertsbusch. Cond. *Tannhäuser*, SW, 1960. Overdue recognition as a Wagner cond. came in 1968 when he cond. SW *Mastersingers*. This was followed by hugely successful cycles, in Eng., of *The Ring* from 1973. Cond. *Parsifal* at CG 1971, *Tristan* with WNO (recorded) 1979, *The Valkyrie* (WNO 1984). C.B.E. 1975. Knighted 1985.

Good Friday Music (*Karfreitagzauber*). The mus. in Wagner's *Parsifal* Act 3, Sc. 1 as Parsifal is anointed in preparation for his entry into the castle of the Grail. Sometimes perf. as separate concert piece.

Good-Humoured Ladies, The (*Les femmes de bonne humeur*). Choreog. comedy in 1 act to mus. by D. Scarlatti arr. by V. *Tommasini, choreog. Massine. Prod. Rome 1917.

Goodman, Benny (*b* Chicago, 1909; *d* NY, 1986). Amer. clarinettist and jazz musician. Joined band in NY 1928, forming his own in 1934 (called in Chicago a 'swing band', thus giving the term wide currency). Appeared as soloist with NY P.O. (cond. Barbirolli) in Mozart conc. Bartók's *Contrasts* and Copland's and Hindemith's concs. were written for him. Recorded Mozart cl. quintet with Budapest Quartet, 1938.

Goose of Cairo, The (Mozart). See *Oca del Cairo, L'*.

Goossens, Eugene (*b* Bruges, 1845; *d* Liverpool, 1906). Belg. cond. Pupil of Fétis at Brussels Cons. Cond. of opera in Belgium, Fr., and It., then in Eng. from 1873. Cond. Carl Rosa Opera 1883–93. Organist St Anne's R.C. Church, Liverpool.

Goossens, Eugene (*b* Bordeaux, 1867; *d* London, 1958). Fr.-born cond., son of above. Lived in Eng. from 1873. Worked with father for Carl Rosa, then prin. cond. of various other cos. Prin. cond. Carl Rosa 1899–1915. Cond. for Beecham co. from 1917.

Goossens, (Sir) **Eugene** (*b* London, 1893; *d* Hillingdon, 1962). Eng. cond., violinist, and composer, son of above. Studied Bruges Cons., Liverpool Coll. of Mus., and RCM (comp. with Stanford). Violinist in Queen's Hall Orch. 1911–15. Ass. cond. to Beecham 1916–20. Cond. f. Eng. concert p. of Stravinsky's *The Rite of Spring*, London 1921. Cond. opera and ballet CG 1921–3. Went to USA, becoming cond. Rochester P.O. 1923–31 and Cincinnati S.O. 1931–47. Cond. Sydney S.O., N.S.W., and dir., N.S.W. Cons. 1947–56. Knighted 1955.

Comps. incl.:

OPERAS: *Judith (1 act, lib. Arnold Bennett, CG 1929); *Don Juan de Manara* (4 acts, lib. by Bennett, CG 1937).

ORCH: *Sinfonietta* (1922); ob. conc. (1927); Sym. No. 1 (1940), No. 2 (1942–4).

CHORAL: *Silence* (1922), *Apocalypse*, oratorio (1950–4).

CHAMBER MUSIC: *Phantasy* for str. qt. (1915); str. qts. No. 1 (1915), No. 2 (1942); pf. quintet (1919); concertino for str. octet (1930).

Goossens, Leon (*b* Liverpool, 1897). Eng. oboist, brother of above. Trained RCM. Prin. oboist Queen's Hall Orch. 1913, later at CG. Prin. ob. LPO from its formation, 1932–9. Then free-lance as soloist and chamber mus. player. Prof. of oboe RAM 1924–35, RCM 1924–39. Brilliant virtuoso for whom several composers—e.g. Elgar, Vaughan Williams, Gordon Jacob, and Eugene Goossens—wrote works. C.B.E. 1950.

Goossens, Marie (Henriette) (*b* London, 1894). Eng. harpist, sister of above. Studied RCM. Début Liverpool 1910. Prin. harpist CG, Diaghilev Ballet seasons, Queen's Hall Orch. 1920–30, LPO 1932–9, LSO 1940–59, London Mozart Players from 1972. Prof. of harp, RCM 1954–67. O.B.E. 1984.

Goossens, Sidonie (*b* Liscard, Cheshire, 1899). Eng. harpist, sister of above. Studied RCM. Prin. harpist BBC S.O. 1930–80. Prof. of harp, GSM from 1960. M.B.E. 1974. O.B.E. 1981.

Gopak (Hopak). A lively Russ. folk dance in duple time.

Górecki, Henryk (Mikolaj) (*b* Czernice, 1933). Polish composer. Studied at Katowice Cons. 1955–60 and in Paris with Messiaen. His mus., initially influenced by Webernian serialism and later by clusters, has never made use of elec. instr. and has developed a highly individual style, going back for inspiration to 14th cent. Polish chants, to Palestrina's polyphony, and to the richness of the Wagnerian orch. Works incl.: Sym. No. 1, str., perc. (1959), No. 2 (*Kopernikowska*), sop., bar., ch., and orch. (1972), No. 3 (*Sorrowful Songs*), sop., orch. (1976); *Scontri*, orch. (1960), *Old Polish Music*, orch. (1969); conc. for 5 instr. and str. qt. (1957); *Genesis*: I *Elementi*, str. trio (1962), II *Canti strumentali*, 15 instr. (1962), III *Monodramma*, sop., metal perc., 6 db. (1963); *Muzyczka* I, 2 tpt., guitar (1967), II, 4 tpt., 4 tb., 2 pf., perc. (1967), III, vas. (1967), IV, cl., tb., vc., pf. (1970); pf. sonata (1956); sonata for 2 vns. (1957); *Cantata* for org. (1968).

Gorr, Rita (Marguérite Geirnaert) (*b* Ghent, 1926). Belg. mez. Studied in Ghent and Brussels. Début Antwerp 1949 as Fricka. Strasbourg Opera 1949–52. Won Lausanne int. competition 1952, then joined Paris Opéra. Début Bayreuth 1958 (Fricka), CG 1959, NY Met. 1962 (Amneris).

Goss, (Sir) John (*b* Fareham, 1800; *d* Brixton, 1880). Eng. organist and composer. Pupil of *Attwood, succeeding him as organist of St Paul's Cath., London, 1838. Comp. anthems, glees, etc. Knighted 1872.

Goss, John (*b* London, 1894; *d* Birmingham, 1953). Eng. bar. Particularly active in 1920s as interpreter of songs of Warlock and other Eng. composers. Lived in Vancouver, BC, 1940–50.

Gossec, François (Joseph) (*b* Vergnies, 1734; *d* Passy, 1829). Belg. composer. Boy chorister Antwerp Cath. Self-taught in comp. Went to Paris 1751 where he was helped by *Rameau for whose patron's private band he comp. first Fr. syms. from 1754. Also comp. str. qts. for Prince de Condé, whose service he entered 1762–9. Dir., Concert Spirituel 1773–7. 2nd cond. at Opéra 1780–2. Organized and dir. École Royale de Chant 1784–95, when it became the Nat. Cons. Prof. of comp. at Paris Cons. 1795–1815. Comp. about 30 syms., 20 operas, church and choral

mus. (incl. many pieces in favour of the Revolution), and ballets.

Gothic Symphony. Havergal *Brian's 1st Sym., comp. 1919–27, in 4 movements, the last of which is setting of *Te Deum* for 4 vv., ch., children's ch., 4 brass bands, and very large orch. F.p. London 1961; f.p. with complete forces required, Hanley 1978.

Gotovac, Jakov (*b* Split, 1895; *d* Zagreb, 1982). Yugoslav composer and cond. Studied in Split and at Vienna Acad. Cond. Croatian Opera, Zagreb, 1923–57. Comps. for orch., ch., and chamber groups, also folk-influenced opera *Ero the Joker* (*Ero s onoga svijeta*, 1935), which he cond. in London 1955.

Götterdämmerung (Twilight of the Gods). Mus. drama in prol. and 3 acts by Wagner to his own lib. The final opera in his tetralogy *Der *Ring des Nibelungen*. Comp. 1869–74. Prod. Bayreuth 1876, London 1882, NY Met. 1888.

Gottschalk, Louis Moreau (*b* New Orleans, 1829; *d* Tijuca, Brazil, 1869). Amer. pianist, cond., and composer. Went to Paris 1842, studying with *Hallé and Berlioz. His pf. début in 1844 was praised by Chopin. On return to USA toured widely, playing and conducting his own sentimental and naive mus. for unsophisticated audiences who enjoyed his virtuoso panache and his arrs. of nat. airs. Wrote 2 syms., 2 operas, pf. pieces such as *The Dying Poet* (1863–4).

Goudimel, Claude (*b* Besançon, *c*.1514; *d* Lyons, 1572). Fr. composer. Comp. masses and motets, then became Protestant and wrote hymn-tunes and secular songs. Died in St Bartholomew's Day massacre.

Gould, Glenn (Herbert) (*b* Toronto, 1932; *d* Toronto, 1982). Canadian pianist, composer, and writer. Trained Toronto Royal Cons. Début at age of 14; Washington D.C., and NY 1955, European tour 1957, first appearing as soloist with Karajan and Berlin P.O. London 1958. Toured USSR. Exceptionally wide repertory, from 16th-cent. kbd. works to jazz.

Gould, Morton (*b* Richmond Hill, NY, 1913). Amer. comp., cond., and pianist. Studied Institute of Mus. Art, NY. Member of Radio City Mus. Hall staff. Worked for NBC and CBS broadcasting systems. His mus. contains popular Amer. mus., jazz, and more formal structures. Brilliant orchestrator. Works incl.:

ORCH: *Little Symphony* (1939); Syms. No. 1 (1942), No. 2 (*Marching Tunes*) (1944), No. 3 (1947); pf. conc. (1937); vn. conc. (1938); *American Symphonette* No. 1 (*Swing*) (1935), No. 2 (1936), No. 3 (1937), No. 4 (*Latin American*) (1940); *Lincoln Legend* (1940); va. conc. (1943); va. concertette (1943); *Concerto for Orchestra* (1944); *Minstrel Show* (1946); Conc. for tap dancer and orch. (1952); *Jekyll and Hyde Variations* (1957); *St*

Lawrence Suite (1958); Prisms (1962); Venice, audiograph for 2 orch. (1966); Columbia (1966); Vivaldi Gallery, for str. qt., div. orch. (1967); Troubadour Music, 4 guitars, orch. (1968); Symphony of Spirituals (1976).
BALLETS: Interplay (1943); Fall River Legend (1947); Fiesta (1957).
Also chamber works, and much mus. for films and TV.

Gounod, Charles François (b Paris, 1818; d St-Cloud, 1893). Fr. comp., cond., and organist. Studied Paris Cons. with Halévy, Paër, and Le Sueur. Won Grand Prix de Rome 1839; impressed by Rome and made special study of Palestrina. Became organist at Paris church and studied for priesthood but eventually decided to devote himself to comp. Wrote several operas from 1851 but had no real success until Faust in 1859, which became and remained one of the most popular of all operas. Later operas were less successful, though Roméo et Juliette survives. Also wrote many choral works and lived in Eng. 1870–5, becoming first cond. of what is now Royal Choral Soc. His oratorios La Rédemption and Mors et vita were comp. for the Birmingham and Norwich Fests. of 1882 and 1885. Gounod's mus. has considerable melodic charm and felicity, with admirable orchestration. He was not really a master of the large and imposing forms, in this way perhaps being a Fr. parallel to Sullivan. Works incl.:

OPERAS: Sapho (1851; La Nonne sanglante (1854); Le Médecin malgré lui (1858); *Faust (1859); La Colombe (1860); Philémon et Baucis (1860); La Reine de Saba (1862); *Mireille (1864); *Roméo et Juliette (1867); Cinq Mars (1877); Polyeucte (1878); Le Tribut de Zamora (1881).

ORATORIOS: La Rédemption (1868–81); Mors et Vita (1885).

CANTATAS: Marie Stuart (1837); Gallia (1871).

CHURCH MUS.: Messe a tre (1841); Messe solennelle (1849); Messe à Ste Cécile (1855); Messe à Jeanne d'Arc (1887); three Requiems; Stabat Mater, Te Deum, Magnificat, etc.

ORCH: Sym. No. 1 in D, No. 2 in E♭; Petite Symphonie in B♭, for 9 wind instrs. (1885).

MISC: Funeral March of a Marionette (for pf., 1872, orch. 1879); Méditation sur le prélude de Bach for sop., pf., vn., and organ (1889, known as Gounod's *Ave Maria, being 1st prelude of Bach's '48' with counterpoint melody by Gounod, entitled Méditation, to which someone fitted the words of the Ave Maria); many songs.

Government Inspector, The (Der Revisor). Opera in 5 acts by *Egk to his own lib. based on play by Gogol (1836). Prod. Schwetzingen 1957.

Gow, Nathaniel (b Inver, Dunkeld, 1763; d Edinburgh, 1831). Scot. composer, trumpeter, and violinist, member of family of musicians. Leader of Edinburgh Assembly orch. from 1791, providing mus. for dancing. Became publisher

1796, issuing 'collections' of dance-mus. Wrote *Caller Herrin' as hpd. piece in about 1800, the words being added by Lady Nairne about 1823.

Goyescas (Los majos enamorados) (Sp. 'Goya-like works', or 'Youth in Love'). (1) 2 sets of pf. pieces, 7 in all. by *Granados, inspired by paintings of Goya, comp. 1911, f.p. 1914. Titles are 1. Los requiebros (Loving words), 2. Coloquio en la reja (A conversation through the grating), 3. El fandango del candil (Kitchen fandango), 4. Quejas o la maja y el ruisenor (Lament, or The Love-sick Girl and the Nightingale), 5. El amor y la muerte (Love and death), 6. Epilogo: la serenada del espectro (Epilogue: The ghost's serenade), 7. El pelele (The worthless man).
(2) Opera in 3 scenes by Granados, amplified and scored from the above pf. pieces, with Sp. lib. by F. Periquet. Prod. NY Met. 1916, London 1951. See also Maja y el ruisenor.

G.P. (1) *General Pause, of 1 or 2 bars for all performers. (2) (Fr.). Grand et positif, i.e. great and choir organs to be coupled.

G.P.R. (Fr.). Grand-positif-récit, i.e. great, choir, and swell organs to be coupled.

G.R. (Fr.). Grand récit, i.e. great and swell organs to be coupled.

Grabu, Louis (Grabut, Lewis) (d after 1694). Fr. comp. and violinist. Settled in Eng. after 1665, becoming Master of the Musick to Charles II. Comp. mus. for Dryden's Albion and Albanius (1685) and other plays.

Grace Notes. *Ornaments in vocal and instr. mus., indicated in very small notation.

Gradual. (1) The Respond sung in the service of the Mass between the Epistle and Gospel.
(2) The book containing the Concentus of the traditional plainsong of the Mass, i.e. it is the choir's (or congregation's) mus. companion to the Missal—in which last the only mus. is the *Accentus or priest's parts.

Gradualia. Motets by William Byrd. Book I (1605) contains 32 for 5 vv., 20 for 4, and 11 for 3; Book II (1607) contains 9 for 6 vv., 17 for 5, and 19 for 4.

Gradus ad Parnassum (Steps to Parnassus (the abode of the muses)). (1) Title of treatise on *counterpoint by J. J. *Fux, 1725.
(2) Series of 100 studies by *Clementi, pub. 1817 (50 ed. *Bülow; complete series ed. Vogrich, 1898).
(3) 1st piece in Debussy's Children's Corner is called Dr Gradus ad Parnassum (a parody of a Clementi study).

Graf, Herbert (b Vienna, 1903; d Geneva, 1973). Austrian (later Amer.) opera producer and impresario, son of Max *Graf. Studied Vienna Univ. with G. *Adler. Stage dir. at opera houses in Münster, Breslau, Frankfurt, and Basle. Went to

USA 1934, staged opera in Philadelphia 1934–5, NY Met. 1936–60, head of opera dept. Curtis Institute from 1949. Dir., Zürich Opera, 1960–3, Geneva Opera from 1965. Regular prod. at Salzburg and Verona. CG *Parsifal* 1959. Author of books on opera.

Graf, Max (*b* Vienna, 1873; *d* Vienna, 1958). Austrian critic. Taught at Vienna Acad. of Mus. Lived in NY 1939–45. Author of books on Wagner, etc.

Graffman, Gary (*b* NY, 1928). Amer. pianist. Studied Curtis Institute and Columbia Univ., later with *Horowitz and *Serkin. Début Philadelphia 1947, Europe 1956, followed by worldwide tours. Leventritt Award 1949.

Graf von Luxemburg, Der (Lehár). See *Count of Luxemburg, The.*

Graham, Colin (*b* Hove, 1931). Eng. stage dir. and designer, opera producer. Art dir. *Eng. Mus. Th. from 1976; dir. of prods., *Eng. Opera Group 1961–75; assoc. dir. of prod. ENO 1967–75, dir. 1978–80., art. dir., Aldeburgh Fest. from 1966. Close assoc. with operas of Britten, notably the premières of the 3 church parables. Opera prods. for Glyndebourne, CG, Scottish Opera, Berlin, NY Met., etc. Librettist of *Penny for a Song* (R. R. Bennett).

Graham, Martha (*b* Allegheny, 1894). Amer. dancer, choreog., teacher, and ballet co. dir. Began studying at Denishawn 1916, member of Denishawn Dancers till 1923. Founded own co. 1929. Developed own technique and became leading exponent of modern dance in USA, exerting enormous influence and producing many famous pupils. Comps. who wrote ballets for her co. incl. Hindemith, Hunter Johnson, Copland, Chávez, Barber, Menotti, Schuman, Dello Joio, Hovhaness, and Seter.

Grainger, Percy (Aldridge) (*b* Brighton, Victoria, 1882; *d* White Plains, NY, 1961). Australian-born composer and pianist (Amer. citizen 1919). Studied in Melbourne, later in Frankfurt 1894–1900, becoming pupil of *Busoni in Berlin. Came to notice in London, 1900, and then toured extensively. In London in 1906 he was befriended by *Grieg, who greatly admired his playing and invited him to Norway to make a special study of the pf. conc. in A minor, a work of which he remained a notable interpreter. Collected and ed. Eng. folksongs, incl. *Brigg Fair*, collected at N. Lincs. mus. competition fest. at Brigg, 1905. His arr. of it was admired by *Delius, whose orch. rhapsody was based on this tune. Delius and Grainger remained close friends. Grainger's NY début was in 1915, after which the USA became his home. Although best-known as a composer for his lighter works such as *Shepherd's Hey*, usually based on traditional tunes, his folksong arrs. for ch., e.g. *Shallow Brown*, are original and impressive and won the admiration of Britten.

He was a lifelong experimenter and something of an eccentric, a very lively and stimulating figure. Prin. works:

ORIGINAL: KEYBOARD: *Over the Hills and Far Away*, 2 pf. (1916–18); *Colonial Song*, pf. (1914); *Handel in the Strand*, pf. (1930), 2 pf. (1947); *Hill Song No. 1*, 2 pf. (1921), *No. 2*, 2 pf. (1907); *Mock Morris*, pf. (1910), 2 pf. (1910); *Suite, In a Nutshell*, 2 pf. (1916); *The Warriors*, 2 pf., 6 hands (1922); *Walking Tune*, pf. (*c*.1905).

CHAMBER: *Colonial Song*, pf. trio (1912); *Handel in the Strand*, pf. trio (1911–12); *Hill Song No. 1*, 22 instr. (1921, rev. 1923), *No. 2*, 22 wind/cymbal (1907, rev. 1911, 1940–6); *Mock Morris*, str. sextet (1910), vn., pf. (1910); *Walking Tune*, wind quintet (1900–5).

ORCH: *Colonial Song* (1905–12, rev. *c*.1928); *Handel in the Strand*, str. (1932); *Mock Morris*, str. (1910), orch. (1914); *Suite, In a Nutshell* (1905–16); *The Warriors*, 3 pf., orch. (1912–16).

LARGE WIND ENS: *Colonial Song*, band (1918); *Over the Hills and Far Away*, band, pf. (1916–9); *Hill Song No. 2*, band (1901, rev. 1911, 1940–6); *Marching Song of Democracy*, band (1948).

VOCAL AND CHORAL: *Colonial Song*, sop., ten., hp., orch. (1905–12, rev. 1914); sop., ten., pf. trio (1912); *Danny Deever*, male vv., orch./bar., male vv., pf. (1903, 1922–4); *Marching Song of Democracy*, ch., org., orch. (1901–17); *Recessional*, ch. (1905, 1929).

FOLK-SONG SETTINGS: KEYBOARD: *Country Gardens*, pf. (1908–18), 2 pf. (1918) orch. by L. Artok; *Green Bushes*, 2 pf., 6 hands (1919); *Irish Tune from Co. Derry* (*Londonderry Air*), pf. (1911); *Lincolnshire Posy*, 2 pf. (1937–8); *Molly on the Shore*, pf. (1918), 2 pf. (1947); *My Robin is to the Greenwood Gone*, pf. (1912); *Shepherd's Hey*, pf. (1911), 2 pf. (1947); *Spoon River*, pf. (1919–22), 2 pf. (1932, rev. 1946).

CHAMBER AND INSTR: *Early One Morning* (1901, 1939–40); *Green Bushes* (1905–6, rev. 1921); *Irish Tune from Co. Derry*, str. and hn. (1913); *Molly on the Shore*, str. qt. (1907, rev. *c*.1911), vn., pf. (1914); *My Robin is to the Greenwood Gone*, 2 wind, 6 str. (1904, 1912), pf. trio (1912); *Shepherd's Hey*, 11 or 12 instr. (1908–9); *Spoon River*, 2 pf., harmonium (1929).

ORCH: *Irish Tune from Co. Derry*, str. (1913); *Molly on the Shore*, str. (1907, rev. *c*.1911), orch. (1914); *Shepherd's Hey*, orch. (1912–3); *Ye Banks and Braes*, orch. (1932).

LARGE WIND ENS: *Irish Tune from Co. Derry*, band (1917); *Lincolnshire Posy*, band (1906–37); *Molly on the Shore*, band (1920); *Shepherd's Hey*, band (1918); *Spoon River*, band (1933); *Ye Banks and Braes*, band (1949).

VOCAL AND CHORAL: *Bold William Taylor* (1908); *Brigg Fair* (1906, rev. 1911); *Died for Love* (1906–7); *Early One Morning* (1901, 1939–40); *I'm Seventeen Come Sunday* (1905–12); *Irish Tune from Co. Derry* (1902, 1920); *Shallow Brown* (1910, rev. 1923–5); *Six Dukes Went A-Fishin'*

(1905, 1910–12); *Sir Eglamore* (1904, rev. 1912–3); *Pretty Maid Milking Her Cow* (1920); *Lost Lady Found* (1905–10); *Men of Harlech* (1904); *Three Ravens* (1902, rev. 1943–9); *Willow, Willow* (1898–1911); *Ye Banks and Braes* (1901).

Gramm, Donald (*b* Milwaukee, 1927; *d* NY, 1983). Amer. bass-bar. Studied Wisconsin Coll. of Mus. and Cons. 1935–44, Chicago Mus. Coll. 1944–9. Opera début Chicago 1944. NY City Opera 1952, NY Met. 1964, Glyndebourne 1975 (*The Rake's Progress*). Sang in many European fests. and opera houses. Was Moses in US première of Schoenberg's *Moses und Aron*, Boston 1966.

Gramophone. Monthly magazine specializing in reviews and news of recordings and technical equipment. Founded by Compton Mackenzie (1883–1972) in April 1923.

Gramophone (Phonograph) Recordings. The idea of recording sound by attaching a needle to a membrane vibrating in sympathy, and by allowing its point to mark a plate travelling at a fixed speed, dates from as early as the beginning of the 19th cent., the object being to add to acoustical knowledge about the differences in the vibrations evoked by sounds of various pitches and timbres. The Amer. Edison, in 1877 constructed such an apparatus, with the intention that it should be used in a 'dictating machine': this he called *The Phonograph—the Ideal Amanuensis*, and the records, on wax cylinders, he called phonograms. The vv. of many celebrities of the day were crudely preserved in this way (e.g. Gladstone, Irving, Tennyson) and in 1878 Lily Moulton, an amateur singer, sang into Edison's device. Other musicians, incl. Brahms, made recordings in the 1880s.

Emile Berliner, a Ger.-born citizen of the USA, had by 1888 obtained patents for important improvements—a circular plate of a shellac mixture instead of a waxed cylinder, and a horizontal motion of the needle instead of a perpendicular one (i.e. a motion making lateral impressions on the sides of a spiral track instead of the previous 'hill and dale' impressions), and his principles were in time developed and universally adopted. The patented title for the instr. which played Berliner's discs was 'gramophone', but the less accurate 'gramophone' was adopted.

The flat disc record led to a boom among commercial cos. for preserving the vv. of celebrated singers. The first singer to record commercially and to make a reputation thereby was the Russian sop. Maria Mikhailova. Soon Calvé, Van Rooy, Plançon, Kirkby-Lunn, Albani, Maurel, and Ben Davies were recorded, but it was the ten. *Caruso who 'made' the gramophone record. Instrumentalists, too, were recorded, among them Grieg, Sarasate, Joachim, and Pugno. The historical importance of these discs is obvious,

and many of them have been transferred on to modern records and tapes.

So far the processes used had been purely 'acoustic', the result of the direct action of sound vibrations. The human v. could be fairly satisfactorily and faithfully recorded by this means, but attempts to record orch. mus. were crude and primitive. In 1925 appeared the earliest electrically made records, in which the vibrations had been received by means of a microphone and converted into electrical vibrations, causing, in turn, mechanical vibrations in a steel or fibre needle travelling over the recording disc. It was found that by the use of electric-made records operating at the standard speed of 78 revolutions per minute, very much more faithful reproductions could be secured, and the acoustic-made record in time disappeared from the market. The motive power of the Edison and early Berliner instrs. had been supplied by a handle turned by the operator. This was superseded by a clock-spring device, which in the more expensive instrs. was, in turn, superseded by electric power obtained by plugging to the domestic electric circuit: such instrs. also reproduced the sounds by electric means, reversing the above process of electrical recording. The new apparatus was very commonly combined with one for the reception of radio broadcasting, and called a radiogram. During the 1920s and 1930s recordings of most of the world's great orchs. and chamber groups were made, the perf. of great artists such as Rakhmaninov, Kreisler, and Heifetz were preserved, and the composers Elgar and Strauss cond. their own mus. for the gramophone. Whole operas were issued, and the significance of the gramophone as an educative force and as a means of widening the public's repertory became apparent.

A great disadvantage of the 78 rpm record was that comps. were dissected into sides lasting less than 5 minutes. An opera could run to 40 or more sides. It was in 1948 that (in the USA) all the problems inherent in trying to combine a narrower groove and slower speed without loss of 'high fidelity' throughout the greater part of the range of audible frequencies were satisfactorily solved.

This was when the Columbia co. announced the long-playing (LP) disc. Attempts to introduce LPs had been made in 1904 and 1931, but the 1948 version offered an average of 23 mins. per side at 33 rpm, with the advantages of records made from non-breakable material, with greatly improved recording techniques, and with light-weight pick-ups and sapphire and diamond needles. At first there was some resistance and a 'battle' between 33 and 45 rpm (for short items). In Brit., Decca was the first firm to market LPs (1950), the EMI group not following until 1952. However, the artistic advantage of being able to record a whole opera on 6 or 8 sides, a Mozart sym. on 1 side, and to offer complete recitals by singers and instrumentalists on 1 record revolutionized the industry and listening habits. The standards of recording improved constantly with the advent of the record 'producer' who, like an opera producer, governed the whole recording process. It could be argued that the remarkable growth of the public appetite for the mus. of Mahler is partly due to the fact that LPs enabled his vast syms. to be recorded easily. The rise of the LP was paralleled by the growth of high-fidelity—'Hi-fi'—reproductive equipment—the coupling of amplifier, speakers, pick-up, and needle-cartridge instead of the mass-produced radiogram.

The other great single factor in LP recording was the use of magnetic tape instead of wax or acetate for the orig. recording process. Experiments with tape were made, esp. in Ger., in the late 1930s and early 1940s. Tape enables long stretches of mus. to be recorded without a break; it also enables flaws and errors to be corrected by the re-recording of the offending bar or two, so that a final recording may be, and often is, a compilation of the best of several 'takes', skilfully ed. The next 'recording revolution' was in 1958 with the introduction of stereophonic (as opposed to monophonic) sound, whereby the sound of instrs. or singers was as realistically 'placed' as in the hall or opera house. Eventually 'stereo' replaced 'mono' entirely; and demands for still more realistic and spectacular sound led in the 1970s to 'quadraphonic' recordings (which means that the engineers have fed four independent signal channels into the master tape).

In 1979 recordings made by the even more accurate *digital* tape process appeared on the market from Decca. This system of recording on tape differs from the conventional magnetic system in measuring the shape of the changes in air pressure (sounds) so that the sounds received through the microphone are stored in a computer as a series of numbers (digits). No matter how often the numbers are re-converted into sounds they cannot become distorted. Thus the tape recording is more accurate, has less background noise and no speed variations, and can be re-recorded without loss in quality. In some digital systems the shapes are measured 40,000 times a second.

In 1983 the *compact disc* was introduced, bringing exceptional clarity and dynamic range into recording. It is the first sound reproduction system to dispense with contact between disc and stylus or between cassette and tape-recorder heads. Thus any hiss or hum is eliminated, also any damage to the grooves. The compact disc has a coating of acrylic plastic to protect it from scratches or other damage.

The rotating disc is played by a small low-powered laser which directs a beam of infra-red light on to it, translates a reflected message as a digital code and converts it into sound. The laser's collection and transference of the recorded message is achieved by a technology derived from computers. During recording, a machine makes a series of sound 'samples' at the rate of 44,000 per second. These are converted into a binary code (noughts and ones). This code is inscribed in the form of billions of microscopic pits on the surface of the disc in a spiral 2½ miles long (the disc has a diameter of 4.7 inches). The laser reads the code by focusing on the line of dots as the disc rotates. When the laser fixes on one of the pits, its beams scatter. When it hits the reflecting surface between the pits, it shines back to produce a pattern which re-creates the original binary code. The code is converted into electrical impulses and passed through amplifiers to the speakers in the normal way. The process was pioneered independently by Philips and the Sony Corporation of Japan, who joined in 1980 to produce the first players for the European market.

Of less commercial success at first was the issue of recordings as tapes instead of discs (mono from 1951, stereo from 1956 in the USA). These did not appeal to the public until the introduction of the automatic cassette in 1965. Soon the sales of cassettes threatened to rival those of discs.

Alongside the enormous expansion of recording has developed the 'literary' side of the gramophone, not only expert reviewing, but the specialized compilation of lists of recordings made by individual artists, these being known as *discographies.

Granados, Enrique (Granados y Campina) (*b* Lérida, 1867; *d* at sea, 1916). Sp. comp. and pianist. Studied Barcelona (comp. with Pedrell). In Paris 1887–9 for pf. lessons from de Bériot. Founded Soc. of Classical Concerts, Barcelona, 1900, and his own pf. sch. Academia Granados, 1901. Famous as brilliant pianist especially of his own comps. These pf. pieces are elegant and poetic; so are his songs, many of them in the style of 18th-cent. tonadillas. Best-known of his orch. comps. is the Intermezzo from his opera *Goyescas*. He and his wife were drowned when the liner *Sussex* was torpedoed by a Ger. U-boat in the Eng. Channel. Prin. works:

OPERAS: *Maria del Carmen* (1898), *Petrarca, Picarol* (1901), *Follet* (1903), *Gaziel* (1906), *Liliana* (1911), *Goyescas* (1914–15).
ORCH: Suites: *Elisenda* (c.1910), *Navidad, Suite Arabe, Suite Gallega; La Nit del mor*, symphonic poem; *Serenata; Tres danzas españolas* (orch. de Grignon).
VOICE AND PIANO: *Colección de canciones amatorias; Colección de tonadillas, escritas en estilo antiguo*, etc.
PIANO: *10 Sp. Dances* (1892–1900); *6 Pieces on Sp. Popular Songs; Rapsodia Aragonesa; Escénas Romanticas; 7 valses poéticos; Bocetos; 6 Studies in Expression; *Goyescas* (1911).

Gran Cassa (It.). Big box, i.e. bass drum.

Gran coro (It.). Full organ.

Grand chœur (Fr.), sometimes abbreviated to *Gd. chœur* or *Gd. Ch.* 'Large Choir', or 'Full Organ'.

Grand Duke, The, or The Statutory Duel. Comic opera by Sullivan, lib. Gilbert, their last and unsuccessful collaboration. Prod. London and Berlin 1896, NY 1937.

Grand Duo. Sub-title given by publisher in 1838 to Schubert's Sonata in C major for pf., 4 hands (1824, D813) comp. at Zseliz. Once thought to be piano version of a 'lost' symphony, but this theory is totally discredited by recent scholarship. Orch. versions by Joachim and Anthony Collins.

Grande Duchesse de Gérolstein, La. *Opéra bouffe* in 3 acts by Offenbach, lib. Meilhac and Halévy. Prod. Paris, NY, and London 1867.

Grande sonate pathétique. Fr. title given by Beethoven to his pf. sonata in C minor, Op. 13, comp. 1798–9.

Grandezza (It.). Grandeur, dignity. **Grandioso** (It.). With dignity.

Grandi, Alessandro (*b* ?1575; *d* Bergamo, 1630). It. composer of motets, madrigals, and church mus. Choirmaster at Ferrara Cath. in 1615. In 1617 he was vice-maestro di cappella to Monteverdi at St Mark's, Venice; and from 1627 he worked at Bergamo.

Grand jeu (Fr.). Full organ (or harmonium, of which a combination stop is so named).

Grand Macabre, Le (The Great Macabre). Opera in 2 acts by *Ligeti, lib. M. Meschke and comp., freely adapted from M. de Ghelderode. Prod. Stockholm 1978, cond. Elgar Howarth who also cond. f. Eng. p. ENO 1982 (trans. by G. Skelton).

Grand' Messe des Morts (High Mass for the Dead). Fr. title of *Berlioz's Requiem Mass, Op. 5, for ten., boys' ch., ch., and orch., commissioned 1836 and f.p. Paris, Dec. 1837.

Grand Opera. Imprecise term, generally taken to mean either (a) opera in which every note of the lib. is sung, i.e. no spoken dialogue, or (b) 'serious' opera as distinct from operetta. *Grand opéra* (Fr.) means an epic or historical work in 4 or 5 acts, using the ch. and incl. a ballet.

Grand orchestre (Fr.). (1) Full orchestra.
 (2) Large orchestra.

Grand orgue (Fr.). (1) Full organ or Great Organ (see *Organ*).
 (2) Pipe Organ—as distinct from Reed Organ, i.e. from American organ or cabinet organ.

Grand Prix de Rome. 1st prize in the *Prix de Rome* contest of the Fr. Acad. of Fine Arts.

Grand staff, or **Grand stave.** See *Great Staff*.

Grange, Philip (*b* London, 1956). Eng. composer. Attended Dartington Summer School of Mus. 1975–81, receiving guidance from Maxwell Davies and Hans Keller. Studied at York Univ.

1976–9 (comp. with David Blake and privately with Maxwell Davies, cl. with Alan Hacker). Works incl. *3 Piano Pieces* (1976); pf. sonata (1978); *Cimmerian Nocturne*, chamber ens. (1979); Sextet for wind quintet and pf. (1980); *3 Pieces*, cl. and orch. (1981); *The Kingdom of Bones*, mus. th. (1982–3); *Nocturnal Image*, vc., pf. (1984).

Grania and Diarmid. Play by W. B. Yeats and George Moore for which Elgar wrote incidental mus. Op. 42, Dublin Gaiety Th., 21 Oct. 1901. Most frequently played item is the *Funeral March*, f. London p. 1902.

Graphic Scores. Scores by 20th-cent. *avant-garde* composers which employ drawn visual analogues in order to convey the composer's intentions with regard to the required sounds and textures. Earliest example is thought to have been *Feldman's *Projections* 1950–1. Some graphic scores indicate distinct mus. parameters, as in Feldman, Stockhausen, and Ligeti. Others deliberately omit any notational sign or mus. indication, seeking only to stimulate the performer's creativity. Examples by Bussotti and Earle Brown are often pictorially delightful if musically enigmatic. (See example from Logothetis's *Agglomeration* on facing page.)

Grappelli, Stephane (*b* Paris, 1908). Fr. jazz violinist. Had classical training and turned to jazz in late 1920s. Formed Quintet of the Hot Club of France 1934 with the guitarist Django Reinhardt. Lived in Eng. 1940–8. In 1973 formed popular partnership with *Menuhin, resulting in recordings, later with Nigel *Kennedy.

Graubart, Michael (*b* Vienna, 1930). Austrian-born comp., cond., teacher, and flautist. Studied Manchester Univ., and privately with Seiber (comp.), Gilbert (fl.), and Lawrence Leonard (cond.). Freelance flautist 1953–7. Cond. amateur orchs. and choirs from 1953. Teacher and cond. at Morley Coll. from 1966, dir. of music from 1969. Ed. of works by Monteverdi, Dufay, and Pergolesi. Comps. incl. va. concertino, *Aria* for orch., and works incorporating elec. tape.

Graun, Karl (Heinrich) (*b* Wahrenbrück, Saxony, *c.*1704; *d* Berlin, 1759). Ger. ten. and comp. Sang as ten. at Brunswick Opera 1725, but became 2nd Kapellmeister there 1726 and wrote several operas. Entered service of Crown Prince Frederick at Rheinsberg 1735. When Frederick (the Great) became King, Graun was made cond. of Berlin Royal Opera, 1740, for which he wrote 26 It. operas, incl. *Rodelinda* (1741) and *Eʒio* (1755), and dramatic cantatas. Also wrote Passion-cantata *Der *Tod Jesu* (1755). Instr. works incl. hn. conc.

Graupner, Christoph (*b* Kirchberg, 1683; *d* Darmstadt, 1760). Ger. comp. Pupil of Kuhnau. Court cond. at Darmstadt from 1712. Wrote 9 operas, 113 syms., 50 concs., kbd. works, and over 1,000 pieces of church mus.

Logothetis: *Agglomeration*

Grave (It., Fr.). (1, as a term of expression), slow and solemn.

(2, as a term of pitch), low.

(3, in Fr. org. mus.) *octaves graves* means sub-octave coupler.

Grave Mixture. Org. *mixture stop* of 2 ranks (12th and 15th).

Graves, Alfred (Perceval) (*b* Dublin, 1846; *d* Harlech, 1931). Irish poet, folksong collector, and sch. inspector. Collab. with Stanford in publication of Irish folksongs, many of which he collected, incl. the Co. Kerry tune for which he wrote the words *Father O'Flynn*. Provided first two sets of words for tune *Londonderry Air.* Father of poet Robert Graves.

Gravicembalo (It., probably corruption of *clavicembalo*). The hpd.

Gray, Alan (*b* York, 1855; *d* Cambridge, 1935). Eng. org. and comp. Mus. dir. Wellington Coll. 1883–92. Organist, Trinity Coll., Cambridge, 1892–1912. Pupils incl. Vaughan Williams. Cond. Cambridge Univ. Music Soc. Comps. incl. cantatas *Arethusa* (1892), *The Vision of Belshazzar* (1896), *Song of Redemption* (1898). Also *Coronation March,* chamber mus., and org. pieces.

Gray, Cecil (*b* Edinburgh, 1895; *d* Worthing, 1951). Scot. comp. and critic. Studied Edinburgh Univ. and in Birmingham with *Bantock. Settled in London 1915. Joint ed. with Philip *Heseltine of periodical *The Sackbut.* Mus. critic *Nation and Athenaeum* 1925–30, *Daily Telegraph* 1928–32, *Manchester Guardian* 1932. Wrote 3 operas to his own libs.: *Deirdre, Temptation of St Anthony,* and *The Trojan Women.* His reputation rests on his books, which incl. *A Survey of Contemporary Music* (1924), *Carlo Gesualdo, Musician and Murderer* (with P. Heseltine) (1926), *History of Music* (1928), *Sibelius* (1931), *Peter Warlock* (1934), *Predicaments* (1936), and *Contingencies* (1947).

Gray, Linda Esther (*b* Greenock, 1948). Scottish soprano, pupil of Eva *Turner. John Christie award 1973. Opera début as Mimi with Glyndebourne Touring Opera, 1972. Sang Elektra in Mozart's *Idomeneo,* Glyndebourne 1974, Paris 1976. ENO début 1978 (Micaela in *Carmen,* then Aida, Tosca, and Isolde). Isolde with WNO, cond. Goodall, 1979. Amer. début Dallas 1981 (Sieglinde in *Die Walküre*). Also sings in oratorio, etc.

Gray, Stephen (*b* Guildford, 1923). Eng. pianist, oboist, and administrator. Founder, Chelsea Opera Group 1950. Gen. manager LPO 1957–9, Philharmonia Orch. 1959–64, Royal Liverpool P.O. 1964–87. O.B.E. 1987.

Grazia; grazioso; graziosamente (It.). Grace; graceful; gracefully.

Great Organ (Great). Chief division (manual and its controlled equipment) of an org. Full org. is always played from the Great kbd. coupled to other divisions.

Great Staff or **Great Stave** (or grand staff or stave). Notational device introduced by mus. pedagogues for the purpose of explaining the clefs—

The two staves in common use are brought near together. It suffices then to place between them one extra line for Middle C ('middle' in a double sense: in the middle of this diagram, as it is in the middle of the piano kbd.). The C clef is placed on this line. The treble (or G) clef now comes 2 lines above and the Bass (or F clef) 2 lines below.

The Treble Staff, Bass Staff, Soprano Staff (in some choral use in Ger. still), the *Alto Staff* (in use in older choral mus., in mus. for the viola, etc.) and the *Tenor Staff* (in use in the older choral mus., for the tb., etc.) are seen as sections of the 'Great Staff', with Middle C as the pivot.

G   Soprano Staff   Alto Staff   Tenor Staff

F

Greaves, Terence (*b* Hodthorpe, Derbyshire, 1933). Eng. comp., pianist, and teacher. Royal Signals Staff Band 1952–7. On staff Birmingham Sch. of Mus. 1962–73 (dir. of studies 1970–3); dean of development RNCM from 1973.

Grechaninov, Alexander (Tikhonovich) (*b* Moscow, 1864; *d* NY, 1956). Russ. composer. Pf. pupil of Safonov, Moscow Cons., and comp. pupil of Rimsky-Korsakov, St Petersburg Cons. Left Russia for Fr. 1925, settled in USA 1939 becoming Amer. citizen 1946. Comps. in traditional idiom showing no sign of modern influences. Master of choral mus. Works incl. operas, cantatas, 5 syms., fl. conc., 4 str. qts., vn. sonata, vc. sonata, cl. sonata, 258 songs, 14 vocal qts., masses, and pf. pieces.

Greef, Arthur de (*b* Louvain, 1862; *d* Brussels, 1940). Belg. pianist and composer. Studied with Liszt at Weimar. Prof. at Brussels Cons. from 1885. Toured widely. Especial champion of mus. of his friend Grieg. Comp. sym., works for pf. and orch., and songs.

Green. Poem by Verlaine set for v. and pf. by Debussy, 1887–8, as No. 5 of *Ariettes oubliées*, and by Fauré, 1891, as No. 3 of 5 *Mélodies*, Op. 58.

Green, Gordon (*b* Barnsley, 1905; *d* London, 1981). Eng. pianist and teacher. Studied RMCM and privately with *Petri. Prof. of pf., RMCM and RNCM from 1945, RAM from 1962. John *Ogdon among pupils. O.B.E. 1981.

Green, Samuel (*b* 1740; *d* Isleworth, 1796). Eng. org. builder. Built instrs. in Canterbury, Rochester, and Salisbury Caths., also in many churches.

Greenbaum, Hyam (*b* Brighton, 1901; *d* Bedford, 1942). Eng. cond. and violinist. Member of Queen's Hall Orch. and Brosa Qt. Cond. BBC TV Orch. 1936–9, BBC Revue Orch. 1939–42.

Greenberg, Noah (*b* NY, 1919; *d* NY, 1966). Amer. cond. and mus. ed., specializing in medieval and Renaissance mus. Founded NY Pro Musica 1952 to perf. early mus. in authentic fashion. In 1958 revived medieval drama *The Play of Daniel*, touring Europe with it in 1960.

Greene, Harry Plunket (*b* Old Connaught House, Co. Wicklow, 1865; *d* London, 1936). Irish bass-bar. Studied Stuttgart, Florence, and London. Sang in London concerts from 1888, opera from 1890, but later confined himself to songs and oratorio. 1st interpreter of songs, some written for him, by Parry, Stanford, and Vaughan Williams. 1st singer of bass parts in Elgar's *Dream of Gerontius*, 1900. Later became teacher. Wrote biography of Stanford and *Interpretation in Song* (1924).

Greene, Maurice (*b* London, 1696; *d* London, 1755). Eng. comp. and organist. Organist of St Paul's Cath., London, 1718, and Chapel Royal, 1727. Master of the King's Musick, 1735. Prof. of mus., Cambridge Univ. from 1730. Began great collection of Eng. cath. mus. which he bequeathed to *Boyce, who completed and pubd. it. Comp. anthems (best-known *Lord let me know my end*), oratorios, org. pieces, opera, and songs.

Greensleeves. Old Eng. tune twice mentioned by Shakespeare in *The Merry Wives of Windsor* and by other writers of this and later periods. It is first referred to in the Stationers' Co. Register in 1580, when it is called 'a new Northern Dittye', but there is evidence that it is of earlier date. There seem to be many ballads to the tune, also some examples of its conversion to sacred use, as, for instance (again in 1580), 'Green Sleeves moralized to the Scripture'. During the Civil War of the 17th cent. 'Greensleeves' was a party tune, the Cavaliers setting many political ballads to it. From this period the tune is sometimes known as *The Blacksmith*, under which name Pepys alludes to it (23 April 1660). The tune is sung by Mistress Ford in Act 3 of Vaughan Williams's opera *Sir John in Love* (based on *The Merry Wives*) to the words printed in *A Handefull of Pleasant Delites*, 1584. An orch. fantasia from the opera is frequently played. The tune is also used by *Holst in his *St Paul's Suite* for strs. and in his *Suite No. 2* for military band.

Gregor, Bohumil (b Prague, 1926). Cz. conductor. Studied Prague Cons. Ass. cond. Brno Opera, 1949–51, mus. dir. Ostrava Opera 1958–62, cond. Prague Nat. Th. 1962–6, Stockholm Opera 1966–9, Hamburg Opera 1969–72. Specialist in operas of Janáček. Brit. début Edinburgh Fest. 1964 (*From the *House of the Dead*), Amer. début, San Francisco 1969 (**Jenůfa*).

Gregor, Joseph (b Czernowitz, now Cernăuti, 1888; d nr. Vienna, 1961). Austrian writer and librettist. Studied th. prod. with Max Reinhardt and mus. with Robert Fuchs. On staff Vienna Nat. Library from 1918, founding theatrical archive 1922 and motion-picture archive 1929. Wrote 3 opera libs. for Richard Strauss, *Friedenstag*, *Daphne*, and Die *Liebe der Danae*. Wrote books on Viennese th. history, also on Strauss and Clemens Krauss. Correspondence with Strauss pubd. 1955.

Gregorian Chant. Solo and unison plainsong choral chants assoc. with Pope Gregory I which became the fundamental mus. of the R.C. Church. See *Plainsong*.

Gregorian Tones. The 8 plainsong melodies prescribed for the psalms in the R.C. Church, one in each of the 8 modes. They have alternative endings (or 'inflexions') so as to connect properly with the various following *antiphons. The *Tonus Peregrinus* is additional to the 8.

Gregson, Edward (b Sunderland, 1945). Eng. comp. Studied RAM 1963–7 with Alan Bush. Lecturer in mus. at Goldsmiths' Coll. Works mainly for brass band, incl. brass quintet, *3 Dance Episodes* for brass octet and perc., *Essay*, *The Plantagenets*, *Concerto Grosso*, *Prelude and Capriccio*, *March Prelude*, tuba conc., tpt. conc., tb. conc., and *Metamorphoses*.

Greindl, Josef (b Munich, 1912). Ger. bass. Studied Munich where he made début 1935. Berlin Staatsoper 1942–8, Städtische Oper from 1948, Vienna Staatsoper from 1956. Bayreuth 1943, leading bass from 1951. Guest appearances (esp. in Wagner) in London, USA, It. Prof. of singing, Vienna Hochschule from 1973.

Grelots (Fr.). Little bells (e.g. sleigh bells, sometimes used in the orch.).

Grenadiere, Die beiden (The Two Grenadiers). Song for v. and pf. by R. Schumann, to poem by H. Heine (1797–1856), being No. 1 of *Romanzen und Balladen*, Vol. II, Op. 49 (1840). Also set by Wagner for v. and pf., 1840.

Gresham Professorship. In the will of Sir Thomas Gresham (c.1519–79), founder of London Royal Exchange, provision was made for 7 professorships in various subjects and for a lecture on mus. John *Bull was first mus. prof. (1596–

1607). Later incumbents have incl. Sir Frederick Bridge, Sir Walford Davies, and Peter Latham.

Gretchen am Spinnrade (Gretchen at the Spinning-wheel). Song for v. and pf. by *Schubert to text from Goethe's *Faust*, comp. 19 Oct. 1814 (D 118).

Grétry, André Ernest Modeste (b Liège, 1741; d Montmorency, Paris, 1813). Belg. composer. Comp. mass for 4 vv. 1759, thereby winning patronage enabling study in Rome 1761–5. His intermezzo *La Vendemmiatrice* was successfully prod. 1765. Visited Geneva, where he met Voltaire, and returned to Paris 1767. In Paris his *opéras comiques*, from *Le Tableau parlant*, 1769, quickly found favour. During the next 35 years he wrote some 50 operas, of which the best were *Zémire et Azor* (1771), *L'Amant jaloux* (1778), *L'Épreuve villageoise* (1784), *La Caravane du Caire* (1783) and *Panurge dans l'île des lanternes* (1785). His finest work is said to be his most serious opera, *Richard Cœur de Lion* (1784). Also comp. requiem, motets, str. qts., 6 pf. sonatas, fl. conc., and songs. His melodic gift was immense, but his lack of mastery of harmony and counterpoint was a permanent defect. Wrote several treatises. Standard edn. of his works in 42 vols. financed by Belg. Govt. from 1883.

Grieg, Edvard (Hagerup) (b Bergen, 1843; d Bergen, 1907). Norweg. composer, cond., and pianist. (Great-grandfather was Scotsman named Greig.) Early tuition from mother, who was gifted pianist. On advice of violinist Ole *Bull, went to study at Leipzig Cons., working so hard that his health was permanently impaired. Settled in Copenhagen, being encouraged (but not taught) by *Gade. In 1865–6 visited Rome where he comp. his concert ov. *In Autumn* which later won Stockholm Acad. of Mus. prize. Married his cousin, the sop. Nina Hagerup in 1867, she being the inspiration and interpreter of many of his songs. Settling in Christiania (Oslo), became teacher and cond. His comps. earned admiration of Liszt, whom he met in Rome 1870 where Liszt played Grieg's pf. conc. from MS. at sight. In 1874 Grieg received life annuity from Norweg. Govt. and was asked by Ibsen to write incidental mus. to *Peer Gynt*. This had its f.p. in 1876 and made Grieg a nat. figure. He was a great favourite in Eng., where he and his wife gave recitals. He received Hon.D.Mus. Cambridge 1894 and Oxford 1906. Befriended Delius and Percy Grainger. Grieg's mus. eschews the larger forms of opera and sym. (he wrote a sym. in 1864 but forbade perfs. after a few had been given, though this edict has been posthumously ignored) but within his chosen scale it is deeply poetic, superbly fashioned, and, in the songs especially, emotionally passionate. His nationalist idiom transcends local boundaries by reason of the strong individuality of his work. Comps. incl.:

INCIDENTAL MUSIC: *Sigurd Jorsalfar (Bjørnson), Op. 22 (1872); *Peer Gynt (Ibsen), Op. 23 (1874–5, rev. 1885, 1891–2).

ORCH: In Autumn, concert ov., Op. 11 (1866); *Peer Gynt, suite No. 1 from incid. mus., Op. 46 (1874–5, rev. 1885, 1891–2), suite No. 2, Op. 55 (1874–5, rev. 1891 and 1892); 3 pieces from incid. mus. for *Sigurd Jorsalfar, Op. 56 (1872, rev. 1892); *Lyric Suite (orch. of 4 items from Op. 54 for pf.) (1904); pf. conc., Op. 16 (1868, rev. 1906–7); 2 Elegiac Melodies (Heart's Wounds and Last Spring), Op. 34 (version for str. of 2 songs from Op. 33); *Holberg Suite for str., Op. 40 (1884) (also for pf.); 2 Melodies for str., Op. 53; (1891); 2 Norwegian Melodies for str., (1869), orch. (1895), Op. 63; 4 Symphonic Dances, Op. 64 (orch. of work for pf., 4 hands) (1896–7); Sym. (1863–4, withdrawn by composer but perf. Oslo 1980 and recorded).

CHORUS AND ORCH: Before the Cloister Gate, soloists and women's ch., Op. 20 (1871); Olaf Trygvason, for soloists and ch., Op. 50 (1873, rev. 1889).

VOICE AND ORCH: Bergliot, reciter and orch., Op. 42 (1871, orch. 1885); The Mountain Thrall, bar., 2 hns., str., Op. 32 (1877–8); 6 Songs, v. and orch. (incl. 'Solvejg's Song' from Peer Gynt) (1870–80, rev. 1891–4).

CHAMBER MUSIC: Vn. Sonata, No. 1 in F, Op. 8 (1865), No. 2 in G, Op. 13 (1867), No. 3 in C minor, Op. 45 (1886–7); Str. Qt. in G minor, Op. 27 (1877–8); vc. sonata in A minor, Op. 36 (1883).

PIANO: 4 Pieces, Op. 1 (1861); 4 Humoresques, Op. 6 (1865); sonata in E minor, Op. 7 (1865); Lyric Pieces, Book 1 (8 items), Op. 12 (1867), Book 2 (8 items), Op. 38 (1883), Book 3 (6 items), Op. 43 (1884), Book 4 (7 items), Op. 47 (1885–8), Book 5 (6 items), Op. 54 (1891) (those orch. as Lyric Suite are No. 1, Shepherd's Boy, 2, Norwegian Rustic March, 3, Nocturne, and 5, March of the Dwarfs), Book 6 (7 items), Op. 57 (1893), Book 7 (6 items), Op. 62 (1895), Book 8 (6 items), Op. 65 (1897) (No. 6 *Wedding Day at Troldhaugen, also for orch.), Book 9 (6 items), Op. 68 (1898), Book 10 (6 items), Op. 71 (1901); Sketches of Norwegian Life, Op. 19 (1870–1); Ballade in G minor, Op. 24 (1875–6); 4 Albumblätter, Op. 28 (1878); Holberg Suite, Op. 40 (1884); 6 Songs transcr. for pf., Op. 52 (incl. 'Solvejg's Song' as No. 4); 19 Norwegian Folk Tunes, Op. 66 (1896); Norwegian Peasant Dances, Op. 72 (1902–3); Moods, Op. 73 (1903–5).

PIANO (4 HANDS): 2 Symphonic Pieces, Op. 14 (1863–4); 4 Norwegian Dances, Op. 35 (also orch.) (1881); 2 Waltz Caprices, Op. 37 (1883); Symphonic Dances, Op. 64 (also orch.) (1897).

SONGS: Grieg's songs, numbering over 120, were pubd. as follows: 4 Songs, Op. 2; 6 Songs, Op. 4; 4 Songs, Op. 5; 4 Songs and Ballads, Op. 9; 4 Songs, Op. 10; 4 Songs, Op. 15; 8 Songs, Op. 18; 4 Songs, Op. 21; 3 Songs from Peer Gynt (1. Solvejg's Song, 2. Solvejg's Cradle Song. 3. Peer Gynt's Serenade) Op. 23; 5 Songs, Op. 25; 4

Songs, Op. 26; 12 Songs, Op. 33; 5 Songs, Op. 39; 4 Songs, From Fjeld and Fjord, Op. 44; 6 Songs (Ger. words), Op. 48; 6 Songs, Op. 49; 5 Songs, Op. 58; 6 Songs, Op. 59; 5 Songs, Op. 60; 7 Children's Songs, Op. 61; *Haugtussa (The Mountain Maid), cycle of 8 songs, Op. 67 (1895); 5 Songs, Op. 69; 7 Songs, Op. 70. The best-known individual titles with opus numbers are: Hope (or Ambition), Op. 26, No. 3; 'Neath the Roses, Op. 39, No. 3; Autumn Song, Op. 18, No. 3; A Dream, Op. 48, No. 6; Eros, Op. 70, No. 2; The First Meeting, Op. 21, No. 4; From Monte Pincio, Op. 39, No. 5; The Hut, Op. 18, No. 4; I love thee, Op. 5, No. 3 (1864); Spring, Op. 33, No. 2; The Swan, Op. 25, No. 1; With a Water Lily, Op. 25, No. 3.

Grier, (Hugh) **Christopher** (b Derby, 1922). Eng. mus. critic. B.Mus. King's Coll., Cambridge. Mus. officer, Brit. Council, Scandinavia, 1947–9. Mus. critic, Scotsman, 1949–63. Prof. at RCM. Broadcaster. Freelance critic since 1970.

Griffes, Charles (Tomlinson) (b Elmira, NY, 1884; d NY, 1920). Amer. composer. Studied at Stern Cons., Berlin, with Humperdinck 1903–7. On return to USA taught at boys' school in Tarrytown, NY from 1908 until his death. His mus. was beginning to be recognized as important just before he died. Much influenced by Fr. mus. impressionists, he also used Japanese and Amer.-Indian themes and oriental scales. In his later works, polymetric and polytonal features occur. Prin. works:

ORCH: Nocturne (1919); The *White Peacock (orch. in 1919 of No. 1 of 4 Roman Sketches for pf. of 1915); Poem for fl. and orch. (1918); The *Pleasure Dome of Kubla Khan (symphonic poem after Coleridge arr. from pf. piece of 1912) (1917).

DRAMATIC: The Kairn of Koridwen, dance-drama for 5 woodwinds, celesta, harp, pf. (1916); Shojo, Japanese dance-pantomime for 4 woodwinds, strs., harp, perc. (1917).

VOICE AND PIANO: Tone Images, mez. (Wilde and Henley) (1912); 3 Songs (1916); 3 Poems of Fiona MacLeod for sop. (also with orch.) (1918).

PIANO: 3 Tone Pictures (1911–12); The Pleasure Dome of Kubla Khan (1912, orch. 1917); Fantasy Pieces (1912–14); 4 Roman Sketches (1915–16); Sonata (1917–18).

CHAMBER MUSIC: 2 Sketches Based on Indian Themes, for str. qt. (c.1918).

Griffiths, Paul (b Bridgend, Glam., 1947). Eng. music critic. Studied Oxford Univ. Freelance critic from 1971. Chief mus. critic The Times from 1982. Contributor (especially on late 20th cent. subjects) to New Grove Dictionary of Music and Musicians (1980) and New Oxford Companion to Music (1983). Author of monographs on Boulez, Cage, Maxwell Davies, and Ligeti, and A Concise History of Modern Music (1978), The String Quartet (1983), and Bartók (1984).

Grigny, Nicolas de (b Rheims, 1672; d Rheims, 1703). Fr. organist (Rheims Cath. from 1695), comp. of *Pièces d'Orgue*, admired by Bach.

Griller, Sidney (Aaron) (b London, 1911). Eng. violinist. Studied RAM. Founded Griller Str. Qt. 1928 (disbanded 1961), resident qt. at Univ. of Calif. 1949–61. Head of str. dept., Royal Irish Acad., Dublin, 1963–73. Prof., RAM from 1964. C.B.E. 1951.

Grinke, Frederick (b Winnipeg, 1911; d Ipswich, 1987). Canadian violinist. Studied with Adolf Busch and Flesch, also RAM. Member of Kutcher Qt. for 6 years, leader of Boyd Neel Orch. 1937–46, later becoming soloist and teacher. Champion of Eng. mus., notably that of Vaughan Williams, Rubbra, Berkeley. C.B.E. 1979.

Grisi, Carlotta (b Visinada, 1819; d St Jean, Switz., 1899). It. dancer. Contract at Paris Opéra 1841, creating divertissement in Donizetti's *La favorite* with Petipa and title-role in *Giselle*. London début 1836. Most admired ballerina of her time. Cousin of the sisters Grisi (below).

Grisi, Giuditta (b Milan, 1805; d Robecco, nr. Cremona, 1840). It. mez. Studied Milan. Début Vienna 1826. Bellini wrote role of Romeo for her in *I Capuleti e i Montecchi*.

Grisi, Giulia (b Milan, 1811; d Berlin, 1869). It. sop., sister of Giuditta, who taught her. Début in Bologna 1828, Milan 1831. Created Juliet opposite her sister in Bellini's *I Capuleti e i Montecchi* and Adalgisa in *Norma*. Sang regularly in Paris 1832–49, creating roles of Elvira in *I puritani* and Norina in *Don Pasquale*. London début 1834, singing there every season except 1842, until 1861. US début 1854. One of great singers of her day.

Grist, Reri (b NY, 1932). Amer. sop. Studied privately in USA and Europe. Began career in Broadway musicals (*Carmen Jones* and *West Side Story*). Début with NY City Opera, 1959, and Santa Fe Opera. Queen of Night in *Die Zauberflöte* at Cologne, 1960; Zerbinetta in *Ariadne auf Naxos*, Salzburg. Guest appearances in opera at Milan, Chicago, Munich, Glyndebourne, and CG 1962, NY Met. 1966, San Francisco, Holland Festival, and Buenos Aires.

G.R.N.C.M. Graduate of the *Royal Northern College of Music, Manchester.

Grofé, Ferde (Ferdinand Rudolf von Grofe) (b NY, 1892; d Santa Monica, Calif., 1972). Amer. composer, cond., and arranger. Violist in Los Angeles S.O. for 10 years, also played pf. and vn. in th. bands. Work as arranger admired by the band-leader Paul Whiteman, who engaged him to arr. the symphonic jazz which was attracting attention. Thus he orchestrated *Gershwin's Rhapsody in Blue* (1924). Wrote several works in popular symphonic idiom e.g. *Mississippi Suite*, *Hollywood Suite*, and, most popular of all, *Grand Canyon Suite* (1931), cond. Toscanini.

Groot, Cor de (b Amsterdam, 1914). Dutch composer and pianist. Studied Amsterdam Cons. Won Vienna int. pf. contest 1936. Composer of ballet, 2 pf. concs., 2-pf. conc., and solo pieces.

Gros, grosse (Fr.). Great, large. In the case of an org. stop this means of low pitch, e.g. 16′ instead of 8′.

Gross, grosse (Ger.). Great, large. *Grösser*, greater.

Grosse caisse (Fr.). big box, i.e. *bass drum (It. *gran cassa*).

Grosseflöte (Ger.). Large flute. (1) The normal fl. (2) Metal org. stop of 8′ length and pitch.

Grosse Fuge (Great Fugue). Fugue in B♭ major for str. qt. by Beethoven. Intended as finale of his Str. Qt. No. 13 in B♭ major, Op. 130, comp. 1825–6. After f.p. in March 1826, the publisher Artaria persuaded Beethoven to substitute a less onerous finale, so the fugue was detached and pubd. as separate work, Op. 133, in 1827. Beethoven made arr. for pf., 4 hands, Op. 134. In recent times, some qts. have restored it as finale of Op. 130. Although it is customary to refer to it by its Ger. title, Beethoven wrote the title in Fr., *Grande Fugue tantôt libre tantôt recherché*.

Grosse Orgelmesse (Great Mass with Organ). Popular name for Haydn's Mass No. 2 in E♭, 1766, in which the org. has an important part. See also *Kleine Orgelmesse*.

Grosses Orchester (Ger.). Full orch.

Grosse Trommel (Ger.). Great drum, i.e. *bass drum.

Grossi, Carlo (b Vicenza, c.1634; d Venice, 1688). It. composer of operas, cantatas, and church mus. Choirmaster at churches in Modena, Vicenza, and Mantua. Org. in Venice 1664–7.

Gros tambour (Fr.). Great drum. Same as *grosse caisse, i.e. *bass drum.

Ground Bass (It. *Basso ostinato*, 'obstinate bass'). Short thematic motif in bass which is constantly repeated with changing harmonies while upper parts proceed and vary. Originated in *cantus firmus* of choral mus. and became popular in 17th cent., particularly in Eng., as a ground for variations in str. mus. Hence the no. of 'Divisions on a ground'. Examples exist by Byrd, Purcell, Frescobaldi, Carissimi, and Cavalli. See *Chaconne*.

Groupe de Recherches Musicales (Group for musical research). Elec. mus. studio (the 1st), est. at Fr. Radio in 1951 by Pierre *Schaeffer, which has exerted wide influence on composers invited to work there, e.g. Messiaen, Boulez, Stockhausen, Berio, and Xenakis.

Grout, Donald Jay (b Rock Rapids, Iowa, 1902). Amer. musicologist and teacher. Studied Syracuse Univ. and Harvard Univ. Taught at Harvard 1936–42; assoc. prof. of mus., Univ. of Texas

1943–5; prof. of mus. Cornell Univ. 1945–70. Books incl. *A Short History of Opera* (1947, rev. 1965), *History of Western Music* (1960, rev. 1973). Editor of operas of A. Scarlatti.

Grove, (Sir) George (*b* Clapham, 1820; *d* Sydenham, 1900). Eng. writer on mus. and teacher. Trained as civil engineer, constructing several railway stations and also taking part in building of Crystal Palace, of which he was secretary 1852–73. From 1856 became increasingly involved in mus., writing programme notes for Crystal Palace concerts for 40 years. Went with Sullivan to Vienna in 1867 on successful quest for missing items of Schubert's *Rosamunde* mus. and at the same time propounding the now disproved theory of a 'lost' *Gastein* sym. by Schubert. In 1873 began work on compilation of vast **Grove's Dictionary of Music and Musicians*, pubd. in 4 vols. at intervals from 1879 to 1889. First dir. of RCM 1882–94. Knighted 1883. Also wrote *Beethoven and his Nine Symphonies* (1884). Among his other activities were building lighthouses in W. Indies, founding Palestine Exploration fund, ed. biblical dictionary, primer of geography, and *Macmillan's Magazine* (1868–83).

Groven, Eivind (*b* Laerdal, Telemark, 1901; *d* Oslo, 1977). Norweg. composer and authority on Norweg. folk mus. Composed 2 syms., choral works, pf. pieces. Author of treatise on tuning according to natural intervals (1948).

Groves, (Sir) Charles (Barnard) (*b* London, 1915). Eng. cond. Studied RCM. Ch. master at BBC 1938–42. Assoc. cond. BBC Th. Orch. 1942–4. Cond. BBC Northern Orch., Manchester, 1944–51, Bournemouth S.O. 1951–61, WNO 1961–3, Royal Liverpool P.O. 1963–77, ENO 1978–9. O.B.E. 1958, C.B.E. 1968. Knighted 1973.

Grove's Dictionary of Music and Musicians. Largest and most far-ranging mus. dictionary pubd. in Eng. 1st compiled and ed. by George *Grove (1879–89, 4 vols.); 2nd edn. ed. J. A. *Fuller Maitland (1904–10, 5 vols.); 3rd edn. ed. H. C. Colles (1927, 5 vols.); 4th edn. ed. H. C. Colles (1940, 5 vols.+suppl.); 5th edn. ed. Eric Blom (1954, 9 vols.+suppl.); 6th edn. ed. Stanley Sadie (1980, 20 vols., title changed to *The New Grove Dictionary of Music and Musicians*). Always pubd. by Macmillan and Co., London.

Grové, Stefans (*b* Bethlehem, Orange Free State, 1922). S. African composer. Studied S. African Coll. of Mus. with W. H. *Bell, later with W. *Piston at Harvard. Teacher at Peabody Cons., Baltimore, 1957–72, then at Univ. of Pretoria. Works incl. *Elegy for Strings, Sinfonia Concertante* for orch., sym., vn. conc., cl. sonata, pf. trio, fl. sonata, etc.

Growing Castle, The. Chamber opera in 2 acts by *Williamson, for 4 singers and chamber ens., to his own lib. based on Strindberg's *Dream Play*. Prod. Dynevor Fest. 1968.

G.R.S.M. Graduate of the *Royal Schools of Music.

Gr. Tr. Abbreviation for **Grosse Trommel* (Ger.), bass drum.

Gruber, H(einz) **K**(arl) (*b* Vienna, 1943). Austrian composer, db. player, and bar. In Vienna Boys' Choir, 1953–7. Studied at Vienna Hochschule für Musik 1957–63, followed by private study with G. von Einem 1963–4. Db. player in Die Reihe ens. from 1961. Prin. db., Tonkünstler Orch. 1963–9. Co-founder of 'MOB Art and Tone ART' ens., 1968–71. Joined Austrian Radio S.O. 1969. Soloist in *Frankenstein!!*, Liverpool 1978. Works incl.:

ORCH: *Manhattan Broadcasts*, light orch. (1962–4); *Frankenstein!!*, pan-demonium for bar. chansonnier and orch. (1976–7); *Phantom-Bilder*, small orch. (1977); Vn. Conc. (1977–8); *Charivari* (1981); *Rough Music*, conc. for perc. and orch. (1982).

ENS: *Die Vertreibung aus dem Paradies (The Expulsion from Paradise)*, for speakers and 6 solo instr. (1966, rev. 1979); *3 MOB Pieces*, for 7 instr. and perc. (1968, rev. 1977); *Frankenstein!!*, ens. version for bar. and 12 players (1979).

BRASS BAND: *Demilitarized Zones* (1979).

CHORAL: *5 Kinderlieder*, unacc. female vv. (1965, rev. 1980).

CHAMBER MUSIC: *4 Pieces*, solo vn. (1963); *6 Episodes from a Discontinued Chronicle*, pf. (1967); *Castles in the Air*, pf. (1981).

Gruenberg, Erich (*b* Vienna, 1924). Austrian-born violinist and cond. (Brit. cit. from 1950). Trained Jerusalem Cons. Settled in London 1946. Leader Boyd Neel Orch., Stockholm P.O. 1956, LSO 1962–5, RPO 1972. Frequent chamber-music player in str. qts. and pf. trios. Champion of contemp. vn. concs.

Gruenberg, Louis (*b* nr. Brest-Litovsk, now Brest, 1884; *d* Los Angeles, 1964). Russ.-born Amer. comp. and pianist. Studied NY, then in Berlin with Busoni. Début as pianist with Berlin P.O., 1912. Gave up concert touring for comp. on return to USA. Head of comp. dept., Chicago Mus. Coll., 1930–3. Comps. strongly influenced by jazz. Success with opera *The Emperor Jones* (based on O'Neill play), NY Met. 1933. His vn. conc. was written for Heifetz. Also wrote film scores. Comps. incl.: *The Emperor Jones* (1933), *Green Mansions* (for radio) (1937), *Volpone* (1945), operas; 5 syms. (1919–48), *The Hill of Dreams* for orch. (1921), *Jazz Suite* (1929), 2 pf. concs., vn. conc. (1944), 2 vn. sonatas, str. qt., pf. quintet, pf. pieces incl. *Jazzberries, 6 Jazz Epigrams*, etc.

Gruhn, Nora (*b* London, 1905). Eng. sop. and teacher. Studied RCM. Cologne Opera 1930–1, CG 1929–32, SW 1932–6, 1945–8.

Grumiaux, Arthur (*b* Villers-Perwin, Belg., 1921; *d* Brussels, 1986). Belg. violinist. Studied Brussels and Paris. Début Brussels 1940, career then interrupted by war. Début in London 1945, then worldwide career as leading soloist. Prof. of vn., Brussels Cons., from 1949. Became a baron 1973.

Grümmer, Elisabeth (*b* Niederjeutz, Alsace-Lorraine, 1911; *d* Berlin, 1986). Ger. sop. Began career as actress in Aachen. Singing début there 1940. Sang opera in Duisburg and Prague. Berlin Städtische from 1946, Deutsche Oper, Berlin, from 1961. Début CG 1951, Bayreuth from 1957. Notable in Wagner, Mozart, and Strauss.

Grundstimmen (Ger.). Ground voices: foundation-stops of an org.

Grunebaum, Hermann (*b* Giessen, 1872; *d* Chipstead, Surrey, 1954). Ger.-born cond. and teacher. Studied Frankfurt and Berlin. Début Coblenz 1893. Went to London, becoming ch.-master at CG 1907–33. Chief coach BNOC. Head of opera class RCM 1924–46. Cond. f.p. of Holst's *Savitri* at London Sch. of Opera 1916. Father of Nora *Gruhn.

Grünewald, Gottfried (*b* Eibau, 1675; *d* Darmstadt, 1739). Ger. singer at Hamburg Opera from 1703; ass. cond. at Darmstadt from 1712. Toured as virtuoso on *pantaleon. Comp. opera and organ mus.

Gruppen (Groups). Comp. for 3 orchs. by *Stockhausen, 1955–7, each placed in a different part of the hall and each playing different mus. F. Brit. p. 1967.

Gruppetto (It.). Grouplet. The turn, a type of ornament in vocal and instr. mus. *Gruppetto* implies a 4-note figure, the note above, the note itself, the note below, and the note itself. This figure is perf. *after* the note itself or *instead of it*, according to whether the turn sign is placed *after* the note itself or *over* it.

The inflection of the upper or lower note of the turn (in either form) is shown by the placing of a sharp, flat, natural, etc., sign above or below.

When the *gruppetto* occurs after the note the taste of the performer governs the division of the time

available. The general principle seems to be that the *gruppetto* is to be perf. fairly rapidly. To bring this about, the first example just given (if occurring in a slow tempo) might be treated thus:

whilst in a very quick tempo it might be treated as follows (indeed there might be no time to treat it in any other way):

The number of different examples given in different textbooks is very large, and no 2 textbooks quite agree, but the above statement gives the chief general principles accepted by all. They also apply, of course, to the Inverted Turn, which begins with the *lower* auxiliary note, instead of the upper one.

G.S.M. *Guildhall School of Music and Drama.

G string (vn.). The lowest str., possessing a rich tone. Composers sometimes direct that a passage should be played entirely on that str. Bach's so-called 'Air on the G string' is really the 2nd movement from his 3rd orch. suite in D, rearr. by *Wilhelmj in 1871 as a vn. solo in the key of C, the melody transposed down a 9th, and with pf. acc.

Guadagni, Gaetano (*b* Lodi, *c*.1725; *d* Padua, 1792). It. castrato, cont., later sop. Début Parma 1747. Joined buffa co. which visited Eng. 1748, remaining there and in Dublin until 1755. Handel engaged him to sing in *Messiah* 1750, and *Samson*. After studying with Conti in Lisbon, created role of Orpheus in Gluck's *Orfeo ed Euridice,* Vienna 1762, and *Telemaco*, 1765. Several arias in *Messiah*, incl. 'But who may abide', were transposed or rewritten for him by Handel.

Guajira. Sp. dance, with rhythm constantly alternating between $\frac{6}{8}$ and $\frac{3}{4}$. Also found in varied form in Cuba where it is a narrative folk-song.

Guaracha, Guarracha. Sp. and Mexican folk dance in 2 sections respectively in triple and duple time. Dancer usually accompanies himself on guitar.

Guarneri (Guarnerius). It. family, makers of vns., vcs., etc. in 17th and 18th cents. Founder was Andrea (*b* Cremona, *c*.1626; *d* Cremona, 1698), fellow-pupil with *Stradivari of Nicola *Amati.

His sons were Pietro Giovanni (b Cremona, 1655; d Mantua, 1720) who settled as vn.-maker in Mantua, and Giuseppe Giovanni Battista (b Cremona, 1666; d Cremona c.1739) who developed an individual style. But most celebrated of family was Bartolomeo Giuseppe (b Cremona, 1698; d Cremona, 1744), nephew of Andrea, and known as 'del Gesù', from the letters I.H.S. on his labels. Regarded as 2nd only to Stradivari. Revived early Brescian sch. traditions, making instrs. with rich, powerful tone. One was owned by *Paganini, who bequeathed it to city of Genoa.

Guarneri Quartet. Amer. str. qt. formed 1964 in Vermont at suggestion of Alexander Schneider. Members are Arnold Steinhardt (b Los Angeles, 1937) and John Dally (b Madison, Wisc., 1936) vns., Michael Tree (b Newark, NJ, 1935) va., and David Soyer (b Philadelphia, 1925) vc. Visited London 1970 to perf. all Beethoven's quartets, which it has also recorded.

Guarnieri, Camargo Mozart (b Tiété, São Paulo, 1907). Brazilian comp. and cond. Went to Paris 1938, studying comp. and orch. with *Koechlin. Returned to São Paulo, becoming cond. of Phil. Soc. and prof. at Cons. Colourful mus. using Brazilian folk mus. at times. Comps. incl. opera, 3 syms., *Dansa Brasileira* for orch., *Brasiliana*, suite for orch., 2 pf. concs., 2 vn. concs., 2 str. qts., pf. pieces, songs.

Gueden, Hilde (b Vienna, 1917). Austrian sop. Studied Vienna Cons. Worked in operetta at 16. Opera début as Cherubino, Zürich 1939. Went to Munich Staatsoper 1942 on recommendation of Strauss and Clemens Krauss. Also sang in Rome and Florence 1942–5. Salzburg Fest. 1946, joined Vienna Staatsoper 1947, CG début 1947 during visit of Vienna co. Kammersängerin, Vienna Opera, 1950. Début NY Met. 1951. Sang Anne in Amer. première of Stravinsky's *Rake's Progress* 1953. Specializes in Strauss roles (Daphne, Sophie, etc.), Mozart, Verdi, but equally at home in Weill and Lehár.

Guédron (Guesdron), **Pierre** (b Beauce, Normandy, c.1570; d Paris, 1619 or 1620). Fr. singer, later composer, to chapel of Henry IV; subsequently master of mus. to Louis XIII. Comp. court ballets, etc. which in dramatic sense anticipated those of Lully; and pubd. 5 books of *Airs de cour* (1608–20). Work in general tended in same direction as that of the Florentine *Camerata.

Guerre des bouffons. See *Bouffons, Querelle des.*

Guerrero, Francisco (b Seville, 1528; d Seville, 1599). Sp. comp. Pupil of brother Pedro *Guerrero. Held various church posts in Sp., Portugal, and It., until in 1574 he was made choirmaster of Seville Cath. after 23 years as assistant. Wrote much church mus. and secular madrigals.

Guerrero, Pedro (b Seville, c.1520). Sp. comp. of madrigals, motets, and lute pieces. Elder brother and teacher of Francisco *Guerrero.

Guest, Douglas (Albert) (b Mortomley, Yorks., 1916). Eng. organist and composer. Studied RCM. Dir. of mus., Uppingham Sch. 1945–50, org., Salisbury Cath. 1950–7, org. Worcester Cath. 1957–63, dir. of mus. Westminster Abbey 1963–81, prof. RCM from 1963. Comp. *Missa brevis*, 1957.

Guest, George (Howell) (b Bangor, N. Wales, 1924). Welsh org. and cond. Studied St John's Coll., Cambridge. Fellow and org. St John's Coll., Cambridge. Under his guidance, the St John's Choir has become one of the finest in the world, with a continental rather than Eng. style.

Gui, Vittorio (b Rome, 1885; d Florence, 1975). It. cond. and composer. Studied S. Cecilia Acad., Rome. Début Rome, 1907, in *La Gioconda*. Ass. to Toscanini, Milan, 1923–5 and 1932–4. Cond. Florence Orch. from 1928–40, helped to found (1933) Maggio Musicale Fiorentino. CG début 1938. Cond., Glyndebourne Opera 1952–60, after which 'artistic counsellor'. Last cond. at Glyndebourne in 1964. Noted for revivals of rare Rossini operas. Comp. operas, sym. poems, and author of critical essays.

Guido d'Arezzo (b Paris, c.995; d Avellano, after 1033). It. theorist, teacher, and monk who reformed mus. notation. Long resident in Arezzo, hence his name. Pubd. his theories in *Micrologus* (1025). Inventor of *solmization, whereby names 'ut', 're', 'mi' etc. were used as indications of relative positions of notes of the scale; and of the 'Guidonian Hand', an aid to memory in which tips and joints of the fingers are given names of various notes. See *Hexachords*.

Guildhall School of Music and Drama. Mus. acad. est. 1880 by Corporation of City of London in warehouse at Aldermanbury. Moved in 1887 to new premises in Blackfriars, when number of students had risen in 7 years from 62 to 2,700. Buildings extended in 1898 and 1970. In 1977 moved to present building in *Barbican Arts Centre. Name changed to add 'and Drama' in 1935. Full-time courses. First prin. Weist-Hill 1880–92, followed by Sir Joseph Barnby 1892–6, W. H. Cummings 1896–1910, Sir Landon Ronald 1910–38, Edric Cundell 1938–59, Gordon Thorne 1959–65, Allen Percival 1965–78, John Hosier from 1978.

Guillaume Tell (William Tell). Opera in 4 acts by Rossini (his last) to lib. by de Jouy and Bis after Schiller's play (1804) based on the legend. Prod. Paris 1829, London 1830 (in version adapted by Planché and Bishop) and 1839 (orig. version), NY 1831. Operas on same subject by Grétry (1791) and B. A. Weber (1795).

Guillemain, Gabriel (b Paris, 1705; d Chaville, nr. Paris, 1770). Fr. violinist and comp. of trio syms. in It. style, str. qts., vn. sonatas, hpd. pieces. Violinist in Marchioness de Pompadour's court orch., 1747–50.

Guilmant, Félix Alexandre (b Boulogne, 1837; d Meudon, nr. Paris, 1911). Fr. organist and composer. Studied under Lemmens in Paris and Brussels. Organist, La Trinité, Paris, 1871–1901. Toured in England, USA, and Europe. Co-founder of Schola Cantorum, where he became organ prof. Also prof. of org. Paris Cons., from 1896. Comp. org. syms., 8 sonatas (1874–1909), and other works.

Guiraud, Ernest (b New Orleans, 1837; d Paris, 1892). Fr. comp. and teacher. Studied Paris Cons., winning *Grand Prix de Rome*, 1859 (as his father had done in 1827). 1st opera, *Le Roi David*, prod. New Orleans 1852. On staff Paris Cons. from 1876, prof. of comp. from 1880. Wrote treatise on instrumentation. Comp. several operas, the last, *Frédégonde*, being completed by Saint-Saëns (1895), ballet *Gretna Green*, and other works, but remembered today because he comp. the recits. for Bizet's *Carmen* and completed orchestration of Offenbach's *Les Contes d'Hoffmann*. Compiled Suite No. 2 from Bizet's *L'Arlésienne*.

Guitar (Fr. *Guitare*, Sp. *Guitarra*). Stringed instr., plucked and fretted, of ancient origin, its 16th-cent. ancestor being the Sp. *vihuela de mano*. Not unlike a lute but with flat or slightly rounded back. Now has 6 courses, tuned E–A–d–g–b–e'. Became very popular in 19th cent: first great virtuoso of int. fame was Fernando Sor, 1778—1839; while such composers as Boccherini, Berlioz, and Paganini played and comp. for the instr. Present-day revival initiated by Spaniard Francisco Tárrega (1852–1909), and popularity has continued in 20th cent. with emergence of virtuosi such as Segovia, John Williams, and Julian Bream. Concs. have been written for guitar by Villa-Lobos, Ponce, Castelnuovo-Tedesco, Stephen Dodgson, Arnold, and Richard Rodney Bennett. Also used in popular mus. (skiffle, pop, folk, etc.) and in jazz (especially electric guitar (connected to amplifier) and bass guitar). See *Hawaiian guitar*.

Gulda, Friedrich (b Vienna, 1930). Austrian pianist. Studied Vienna. 1st prize Geneva int. contest 1946. Worldwide reputation as recitalist. Also jazz player, having comp. several jazz pieces.

Gundry, Inglis (b Wimbledon, 1905). Eng. composer, teacher, and barrister. Studied Oxford and RCM (pupil of Vaughan Williams and Gordon Jacob). Lecturer on mus., Workers' Educational Assoc., and at univs. from 1946. Works incl. 5 operas, ballet, orch. works, and Phantasy str. qt. (Cobbett Prize 1937).

Gung'l, Joseph (b Zsàmbèk, Hung., 1810; d Weimar, 1889). Hung. composer and bandmaster. Formed own band in Berlin 1843, touring Europe and visiting USA 1849. Kapellmeister to Emperor of Austria from 1876. Comp. over 300 dances and marches.

Guntram. Opera in 3 acts by R. Strauss (his 1st) to his own lib. Comp. 1892–3. Prod. Weimar 1894. Rev. 1940 for Weimar revival, also Berlin 1942. F. Eng. p. BBC broadcast 1981.

Guridi, Jésus (b Vitoria, Sp., 1886; d Madrid, 1961). Sp. composer and organist of Basque origin. Studied under d'Indy at Paris Schola Cantorum. On return to Sp. became org. prof. and later dir. of Madrid Cons. Collected Basque folk-tunes and based many of his comps. on them, incl. operas, zarzuelas, choral works, and organ pieces.

Gurlitt, Manfred (b Berlin, 1890; d Tokyo, 1973). Ger. composer and cond. Studied with Humperdinck and Karl Muck. Cond. at Essen 1911–12, Augsburg 1912–14, and Bremen 1914–27. His comps. were banned by the Nazis. Went to Japan 1939, forming Gurlitt Opera Co. Works incl. 9 operas (incl. *Wozzeck*, 1920, prod. 1928), *Goya Symphony* (1938), *Shakespeare Symphony* (choral) (1954), pf. quintet, chamber conc., songs, etc.

Gurney, Ivor (b Gloucester, 1890; d Dartford, 1937). Eng. composer, organist, and poet. Chorister, Gloucester Cath. 1900, pupil of *Brewer. Ass. org. 1906–11. Won scholarship to RCM 1911, studying comp. under Stanford. Joined army 1915, gassed at Passchendaele 1917. Wrote poetry, setting several of his own poems to mus. as well as poetry by Housman, etc. Song-cycles, of touching beauty and promise, incl. *Ludlow and Teme*, for ten., str. qt., and pf., and *The Western Playland* for bar., str. qt., and pf. Other songs incl. *Desire in Spring* and *Severn Meadows*. Returned to RCM 1919 but declared insane 1922.

Gurrelieder (Songs of Gurra). Work by Schoenberg, comp. 1901–3 and 1910–11 and given no Op. no., being setting for 5 soloists, speaker, 3 male chs., mixed ch., and orch. of a Ger. trans. from the Danish of poems by J. P. Jacobsen. (Gurra is castle where the 14th-cent. heroine Tove lives.) Mus. is in Schoenberg's Wagnerian style but foreshadows his maturity. Requires huge orch. incl. 10 hn., 8 fl., 4 Wagner tubas, 6 timp., and iron chains. F.p. Vienna 1913, cond. F. Schreker; London (broadcast) 1928. The *Song of the Wood Dove* (*Lied der Waldtaube*) was arr. by Schoenberg for v. and chamber orch. 1922.

Gusla (gusle, guzla). Ancient 1-str. bowed instr. still popular in some Slavonic regions (not to be confused with *gusli*).

Guslar. A player on the *gusli*.

Gusli (Guslee). Ancient Russ. instr. of the zither family (not to be confused with *gusla*). Imitated by Rimsky-Korsakov in his opera *Sadko*.

Gutheil-Schoder, Marie (b Weimar, 1874; d Bad Ilmenau, 1935). Ger. sop. Studied Weimar, début there 1891. Engaged for Vienna Opera by Mahler, 1900, remaining until 1926. Sang Oktavian in *Rosenkavalier* CG 1913 (her only London appearance). Outstanding actress, hence success in *Elektra, Carmen*, etc. Created role of The Woman in Schoenberg's *Erwartung* (Prague, 1924).

Gutierrez, Horacio (*b* Havana, 1948). Cuban pianist. Studied Los Angeles, then Juilliard Sch., NY 1967–70. Début Havana 1959. Soloist in concs. with leading US and European orchs. 2nd prize Tchaikovsky competition 1970.

Guy, Barry (*b* London, 1947). Eng. composer and db. player. Studied GSM (comp. with Buxton Orr and Patric Standford). Prin. db. player in several chamber orchs. Founder and artistic dir., London Jazz Composers' Orch. Works incl. *Incontri*, vc. and orch. (1969–70), 'D', 15 solo str. (1972), *Anna*, amplified db. and orch. (1974), *Songs from Tomorrow*, orch. (1975), *Eos*, db. and orch., (1977), 3 str. qts., *Play* for chamber ens. (1976), *Voyages of the Moon*, db. and orch. (1983), *Bitz*, septet (1984).

Gymel, Gimel (from Lat. *gemellus*, twin). The word has been used in mus. in 3 senses, all with the idea of twinship. (1) Style of singing alleged to have been common in parts of Britain as early as the 10th or 11th cents. Whilst one body of singers took the tune of a song another body would extemporize a part in 3rds beneath it.

(2) Type of comp. found in the 14th and early 15th cents. in which, whilst the main tune, or *cantus firmus, was sung in a lower v., 2 upper vv. sang an acc. in which they moved independently of the other v. but in 3rds with one another.

(3) In 16th-cent. choral mus. the word *Gymel* on a vocal part means that the singers of that part are here divided (same as *divisi*). The restoration of the status quo is then indicated by the word *semel*.

Gymnopédies. 3 pf. pieces by *Satie, comp. 1888. Nos. 1 and 3 orch. by Debussy 1896, No. 2 by Roland-Manuel and also by Herbert Murrill. Title refers to Ancient Greek annual fest. in Sparta in honour of Apollo, the Gymnopaidiai being choral dances perf. by naked men and boys div. by age into 3 choruses.

Gyrowetz (Jiroveč), **Adalbert** (*b* Budějovice, 1763; *d* Vienna, 1850). Bohemian composer. His work was admired by Mozart in Vienna in 1785. Studied in Naples and Paris, lived in London 1789–92. Was of much assistance to Haydn, whom he idolised, during his two visits to Eng. Kapellmeister and Intendant of Vienna court ths. 1804–31. Compd. 30 operas (incl. *Hans Sachs*), 25 ballets, 40 syms., 45 str. qts., pf. sonatas, etc.

H

H (Ger.). B♮, *H dur* being key of B major and *H moll* key of B minor.

Haas, Joseph (*b* Maihingen, 1879; *d* Munich, 1960). Ger. composer. Studied comp. with *Reger in Munich 1904–8. Taught comp. at Stuttgart Cons. 1911–21, Munich 1921–50. One of founders of *Donaueschingen Fest., 1921. Wrote biography of Reger (1949). Works incl. operas *Tobias Wunderlich* and *Die Hochzeit des Jobs*; oratorios *Das Lebensbuch Gottes, Das Lied von der Mutter, Das Jahr im Lied,* and *Die Seligen*; vn. sonata, str. qt., and other choral mus. and song-cycles.

Haas, Karl (Wilhelm Jacob) (*b* Karlsruhe, 1900; *d* London,1970). Ger.-born cond. and musicologist. Studied Heidelberg and Munich Univ. Mus. adviser Karlsruhe and Stuttgart radio. Settled in Eng. 1939. Founded London Baroque Ens. 1941 to perform then unfamiliar mus. from baroque period. Public début, Nat. Gallery, 1943, last concert 1966. Ed. works of Cherubini, Boccherini, Haydn, etc.

Haas, Monique (*b* Paris, 1906). Fr. pianist. Studied Paris Cons. Began concert career 1927. Worldwide tours. Specialist in Ravel and other contemporary works. Taught at Paris Cons.

Haas, Robert (Maria) (*b* Prague, 1886; *d* Vienna, 1960). Ger.–Cz. cond. and musicologist. Studied Prague, Vienna, Berlin. Ass. to G. *Adler in Vienna 1909, cond. th. orchs. 1910–13. Mus. librarian Vienna State Library, 1920–45. Prof. Vienna Univ. 1930. Ed. works by Monteverdi etc., but best known for his editorship of complete edn. of Bruckner's works from 1932 to 1949 when he was succeeded by *Nowak. Haas restored the syms. nearer to the form in which Bruckner intended they should be heard. Author of books on Vienna Opera (1926), Mozart (1933), and Bruckner (1934).

Hába, Alois (*b* Vizovice, 1893; *d* Prague, 1973). Cz. composer. Studied with Novák at Prague Cons. 1914–15 and with Schreker in Vienna and Berlin 1918–22. Worked in Vienna as proofreader for Universal Edition, thereby learning Schoenberg's works. Studied oriental music and also Moravian folk-mus. Became prin. propagator of *microtonal mus., founding and directing dept. of ¼-tone and ⅙-tone mus. at Prague Cons. 1924–51. Wrote comps. in ¼-tones, ⅓-tones, and some in ⅙-tones. Developed harmonic theory in ¼-tone, ⅙-tone, and 12-tone systems. ¼-tone and ⅙-tone instrs. (3 types of pf., harmonium, cls., and tpts.) were made for him. Folk music also influenced

his works, and his 12-note works, while never abandoning tonality, are on Schoenbergian principles. Works incl.: Operas *Matka* (The *Mother) in ¼ tones (1927–9, rev. 1964), *Přiid Královtsvi Tvé* (*Nezaměstnani*) (Thy Kingdom Come (The Unemployed)) in ⅙ tones (1932–42), and *Nová Země* (The New Land) (1935–6); 16 str. qts., some in ¼, ⅙ and ⅗ tones; fantasias for vc. and for pf. in ¼ tones; vn. conc. (1954); va. conc. (1956); symphonic fantasia *Cesta Života* (The Way of Life) (1934); and *Fantasia* for nonet (1932, 12-tone) and ⅓ tone, 1932.

Hába, Karel (*b* Vizovice, 1898; *d* Prague, 1972). Cz. composer and violist, brother of Alois *Hába. Studied Prague Cons. 1918–23 (comp. with Novák). Ed., Cz. nat. radio journal 1929–50. Violist Cz. P.O. 1929–36. Like his brother's, his works employ microtones. They incl. str. qts; vc. conc.; vn. conc.; operas *Jánošík* and *Stará historie* (Old History); 2 syms.; choral works; and chamber mus.

Habañera (Fr. *Havanaise*). Slow Cuban (orig. African) song and dance (Habana = Havana), which became very popular in Sp. It is in simple duple time and dotted rhythm. Famous examples are the habañera in Bizet's opera *Carmen* ('L'Amour est un oiseau rebelle') which is an adaptation of a popular song by *Yradier, and the Habañera for 2 pfs. by Ravel, later incorporated in his *Rapsodie espagnole* for orch.

Habeneck, François (Antoine) (*b* Mézières, 1781; *d* Paris, 1849). Fr. cond., composer, and violinist. Studied Paris Cons. 1st vn. in Paris Opéra orch. 1815, dir. 1821–4, and cond. 1824–47 (chief cond. from 1831). Ass. prof. of vn., Paris Cons. 1808–16, teaching special class 1825–48. Founded Société des Concerts du Conservatoire 1828, conducting it until 1848 and introducing Beethoven's syms. to Fr. Cond. f.ps. of some works by Berlioz incl. the Requiem.

Hackbrett (Ger.). Chopping board, i.e. *dulcimer.

Hacker, Alan (*b* Dorking, 1938). Eng. clarinettist. Studied at RAM and later in Paris, Vienna, and Bayreuth. On staff RAM 1959. Member of LPO 1959–66 and was founder-member of *Pierrot Players 1967. Founded Matrix 1971. On staff York Univ. Has restored basset-clarinet to playing of Mozart, and given f.ps. of works by Boulez, Goehr, Birtwistle, Blake, and Maxwell Davies.

Hadley, Patrick (Arthur Sheldon) (*b* Cambridge, 1899; *d* King's Lynn, 1973). Eng. composer.

Studied Cambridge and RCM. Taught at RCM 1925–62. Prof. of mus., Cambridge Univ., 1946–62. Comps., influenced by folk mus., Eng. poetry, Vaughan Williams, and Delius, mainly for vv. and orch. They incl.: *Ephemera,* for sop. or ten. and chamber orch. (1929); *Scene from Hardy's The Woodlanders* for sop. and orch. (1926); *The Trees so high* for bar., ch., and orch. (1931); *La Belle Dame sans merci* for ten., ch., and orch. (1935); *The Hills* for soloists, ch., and orch. (1944); *Scene from Shelley's The Cenci* for sop. and orch. (1951); and *Fen and Flood* for soloist, ch., and orch. (1954). Also many songs.

Hadow, (Sir) **William** (Henry) (*b* Ebrington, 1859; *d* London, 1937). Eng. educator, writer, and composer. Studied mus. at Darmstadt 1882. Lecturer on mus. Oxford Univ. 1890–9; prin., Armstrong Coll., Newcastle upon Tyne, 1909–19; vice-chancellor, Sheffield Univ. 1919–30. Comp. chamber mus. and songs. Books incl. *Studies in Modern Music* (1892, 1894, new edn. 1926), *English Music* (1931). Gen. ed. *Oxford History of Music,* Vol. V (*The Viennese Period*), 1904. Knighted 1918.

Haebler, Ingrid (*b* Vienna, 1929). Austrian pianist. Studied Vienna, Salzburg, and Geneva. Won Munich int. competition 1954. Specialist in Mozart concs. and Schubert sonatas. Mozart medal, Vienna, 1971.

Haendel, Ida (*b* Chelm, Poland, 1924). Polish-born violinist. Studied Warsaw Cons. and with Flesch and Enescu. Début London 1937. Settled in Eng., but toured worldwide. In 1952 left Eng. to live in Canada. Toured Russia 1966.

Haffner Serenade. Nickname of Mozart's Suite in D major, K250, comp. 1776 for a marriage in the Salzburg family of Haffner.

Haffner Symphony. Nickname of Mozart's Sym. No.35 in D major, K385, arr. from a serenade (but not the D major, K250) written for the Haffner family in 1782.

Hageman, Richard (*b* Leeuwarden, Holland, 1882; *d* Beverly Hills, Calif., 1966). Dutch-born Amer. composer and cond. Studied Brussels Cons. Ass. cond. Amsterdam Royal Opera, 1898, chief cond. 1900. Went to USA 1907. Cond. at NY Met. 1912–21 and 1935–6. Wrote opera *Caponsacchi* (prod. Freiburg 1932 and NY Met. 1937), film mus., songs, etc.

Hahn, Reynaldo (*b* Carácas, 1874; *d* Paris, 1947). Fr. composer and cond. Studied Paris Cons. 1886, comp. with Massenet. His operas incl. 2 special successes, *Ciboulette* (1923) and *Mozart* (1925). Though he wrote ballets, operetta, a cantata, pf. conc., and incidental mus., he is best remembered by his elegant and charming songs incl. *Si mes vers avaient des ailes.* Dir., Paris Opéra, 1945–6.

Hairpins. Nickname for the signs < and > which represent *crescendo and *diminuendo.

Haitink, Bernard (*b* Amsterdam, 1929). Dutch conductor. Studied vn. and cond. at Amsterdam Cons. Violinist in Netherlands Radio P.O., becoming prin. cond. 1957. Guest cond. Concertgebouw Orch. 1958–60, becoming joint prin. cond. (with *Jochum) 1961, prin. cond. from 1964. Amer. début 1958 (Los Angeles), Brit. début 1959 (visit with Concertgebouw Orch.). Prin. cond. LPO 1967–79 (art. dir. from 1970). Brit. opera début, Glyndebourne 1972 (*Die Entführung*), CG 1977 (*Don Giovanni*). Mus. dir. Glyndebourne Opera 1977–87. NY Met. début 1982 (*Fidelio*). Mus. dir. CG from 1987. Specialist in syms. of Mahler and Bruckner. Hon. K.B.E. 1978.

Halb, Halbe (Ger.). Half. *Halbe, Halbenote, Halbe Taktnote,* half-note (minim); *Halbe-pause,* half-rest (minim rest).

Halbprinzipal (Ger.). Half Diapason, i.e. 4′ Principal (org. stop).

Halbsopran (Ger.). Mezzo-soprano.

Halbtenor (Ger.). Baritone.

Hale (Halle), Adam de la. See *Adam de la Halle.*

Halek, Václav (*b* Prague, 1937). Cz. composer. Studied Prague Cons. Comps. incl. 2 pf. concs., 2 str. quintets, sym., tb. conc., vn. and pf. conc., *Battle for Peace* for org. and strs., choral works.

Halévy (orig. Lévi), **Jacques** (François Fromental Elias) (*b* Paris, 1799; *d* Nice, 1862). Fr. composer. Pupil of Cherubini at Paris Cons., also studied in It. *Grand Prix de Rome* 1819. Achieved fame with opera *La *Juive.* Taught at Paris Cons. from 1827. *Chef du chant* Paris Opéra 1829–45. Comp. over 30 operas, several ballets, cantatas, and songs.

Half Cadence. See *Cadence.*

Half Close. See *Cadence.*

Halffter, Cristóbal (*b* Madrid, 1930). Sp. composer and cond. Studied with C. del Campo and A. Tansman. Works for Sp. radio. Teacher of comp. and theory, Madrid Cons. 1960–7 (dir. 1964–6). Guest cond. of leading orchs. Works incl.:

ORCH: *Sequences* (1965); Sym. for 3 groups of instrs. (1963); *Anillos* (1967–8); 5 *Microforms* (1960); *Requiem por la Libertad Imaginada* (1971); *Elegies for death of 3 Spanish poets* (1974–5); vc. conc. (1974); *Fibonaciana,* fl. conc. (1969); vn. conc. (1979); *Tiento* (1980); *Fantasia on a Theme of Handel,* str. (1981); *Sinfonia ricercata,* org. and orch. (1982); *Versus* (1983).

CHORAL: *Yes Speak Out Yes,* U.N.O. cantata, sop., bar., ch., orch. (1968); *In exspectatione resurrectionis Domini,* bar., male ch., and orch. (1965); *Symposion,* bar., ch., orch. (1968); *In memoriam Anaick,* reciter, ch., and orch. (1967); *Jarchas de dolor de Ausencia,* 12 vv. (1979).
Also chamber mus. and songs.

Halffter (Escriche), **Ernesto** (*b* Madrid, 1905). Sp. composer and cond. Pupil of *Falla. Lived in

Portugal until he founded chamber orch. in Seville. Works incl. *The Death of Carmen* (1977), orch. pieces, pf. mus., etc. Completed Falla's *Atlántida.*

Halffter (Escriche), **Rodolfo** (*b* Madrid, 1900). Sp.-born composer (Mexican cit. from 1939), brother of Ernesto *Halffter. Mainly self-taught with help from Falla. Influenced by Schoenberg. Settled in Mexico 1939. Composed orch. works and chamber mus.

Half-note (♩). Half the time-value of the whole-note or semibreve. Known in Eng. usage as 'minim' (from Lat. *minima*). See also *Rests; Names of Notes.*

Haliř, Karl (*b* Hohenelbe, 1859; *d* Berlin, 1909). Cz. violinist. Studied Prague Cons. and with Joachim in Berlin. Leader of several Ger. orchs. 2nd violinist in Joachim Qt. 1897–1907.

Halka (Helen). Opera in 4 (orig. 2) acts by Moniuszko to lib. by Wolski after Wójcicki's story *Góralka*. F. (concert) p. Wilno 1848; (rev. version) Warsaw 1858; NY 1903; London 1961.

Hall, Ernest (*b* Liverpool, 1890; *d* London, 1984). Eng. orch. trumpeter. Trained RCM, becoming prof. of tpt., 1924–70. 3rd tpt. LSO 1911, prin. tpt. 1924–30; prin. tpt. BBC S.O. 1930–50.

Hall, Marie (Paulina) (*b* Newcastle upon Tyne, 1884; *d* Cheltenham, 1956). Eng. violinist. Pupil of Elgar, Kruse, and Sevčik. Début Prague 1902, London 1903. Gave f.p. of Vaughan Williams's *The Lark Ascending* 1920.

Hall, (Sir) **Peter** (*b* Bury St Edmunds, 1930). Eng. theatrical producer. Dir., Oxford Playhouse 1954–5; man. dir. Royal Shakespeare Co. 1960–8; dir., Nat. Th. from 1973. Art. dir. Glyndebourne from 1984. First opera prod., Gardner's *The Moon and Sixpence,* SW 1957. Produced Wagner's *Ring* at Bayreuth 1983. His other prin. opera prods. have been: CG: Schoenberg's *Moses and Aaron* (1965), Mozart's *Die Zauberflöte* (1966), Tippett's *The Knot Garden* (1970), Tchaikovsky's *Eugene Onegin* (1971), Wagner's *Tristan und Isolde* (1971); Glyndebourne: Cavalli's *La Calisto* (1970), Monteverdi's *Il Ritorno d'Ulisse in Patria* (1972), *L'Incoronazione di Poppea* (1984), Mozart's *Le Nozze di Figaro* (1973), *Don Giovanni* (1977), *Così fan tutte* (1978), Beethoven's *Fidelio* (1979), Britten's *A Midsummer Night's Dream* (1981), Gluck's *Orfeo* (1982). NY Met.: Verdi's *Macbeth* (1982). C.B.E. 1963. Knighted 1977.

Hall, Richard (*b* York, 1903; *d* Horsham, 1982). Eng. composer, teacher, and poet. No formal mus. education beyond a few lessons from *Bairstow. Played vc. and org. Org., Dorchester Abbey, Oxon, 1923. Org. scholar Peterhouse, Cambridge Univ., 1923–8. Ordained in C. of E. Precentor, Leeds Parish Church 1926–36. Left church 1936, chiefly because of growing interest

in Eastern religion and philosophy. Mus. adv., Lancs. Community Council 1936–40. Prof. of harmony and comp., RMCM, 1938–56. Influential teacher, pupils incl. Maxwell Davies, A. Goehr, Birtwistle, D. Wilde, and A. Butterworth. Dir. of mus. Dartington Hall 1956–65, founding Dartington Str. Qt. Ordained as Liberal Catholic priest 1959. Minister, Unitarian Church, Moretonhampstead 1965–7, Horsham 1967–76, Billinghurst 1968–76. Pubd. 7 books of poetry 1970–5. Comps., influenced by Delius, Skryabin, Schoenberg, and Berg, incl. 5 syms.; pf. conc.; 2 str. qts.; 19 pf. sonatas (1934–5); vc. conc.; *Lyric Pieces,* orch. (1946); sym.-poem *Lemura ; Creator Spiritus,* vv. and orch.; *Rhapsody,* for org. and str. (1929); orch. fantasy *The Sheep Under the Snow;* songs, etc.

Hallé, (Sir) **Charles** (orig. Halle, Karl) (*b* Hagen, Ger., 1819; *d* Manchester, 1895). Ger.-born pianist and cond. Child prodigy pianist. Studied Darmstadt 1835; went to Paris 1836 to improve pf. technique, becoming friend of Chopin, Liszt, and Berlioz. Début in Paris in pf. trio with Alard and Franchomme, 1840. Concert tour of Ger. 1842, London 1843. Instituted first Paris series of chamber concerts 1847. Settled in Eng. 1848. First pianist to play complete series of Beethoven pf. sonatas in London (also in Manchester and Paris). Invited to settle in Manchester, 1848, where he lived for the rest of his life. Founded chamber concerts in Manchester 1848–9, choral soc. 1850, became cond. of *Gentlemen's Concerts orch. 1849, cond. his first concert 1850. Founded his own series of orch. concerts Jan. 1858, thereby inaugurating what are still known as the *Hallé Orch. and Hallé Concerts. Regularly appeared as soloist in concs. and as recitalist. Annual visits to London, Edinburgh, etc. Champion of new works, esp. those of Berlioz. Cond. f.p. in Eng. of *Symphonie Fantastique, L'Enfance du Christ,* and *La Damnation de Faust.* Cond. opera seasons in Manchester 1854–5, London 1860–1. Cond. Bristol Festival 1873–93. Toured Australia 1890 and 1891 and S. Africa 1895 with 2nd wife, the violinist Wilhelmina Norman-*Neruda. 1st Prin., RMCM 1893–5. Knighted 1888.

Hallelujah Chorus. Usually taken to mean one particular ch. out of many which exist, i.e. that which closes Part II of Handel's *Messiah.* At one of the 3 London perfs. in CG Th. in 1743, the whole assembly, led by George II, rose to its feet as the ch. opened, and remained standing to the end, thus establishing a tradition which is still maintained by Brit. audiences.

Hallén, Anders (Johan Andreas) (*b* Gothenburg, 1846; *d* Stockholm, 1925). Swed. composer, cond., and critic. Studied with Reinecke in Leipzig, Rheinberger in Munich. Cond. Gothenburg Mus. Union 1872–8 and 1883–4, Stockholm P.O. 1884–92, Royal Opera 1892–7, Malmö P.O. 1901–07. Prof. of comp. Stockholm Cons. from

1907. Comp. 3 operas, *Missa solemnis*, cantatas, symphonic poems, and songs, etc.

Hallé Orchestra. Manchester's prin. sym. orch., founded 1858 by Charles *Hallé, after success of series of orch. concerts at 1857 Art Treasures Exhibition. Hallé remained cond. (and proprietor and prin. pf. soloist) until death in 1895. In interregnum Frederic *Cowen was cond. until 1899 when Hans *Richter took up post offered to him in 1895. Concerts managed from 1898 by non-profit-making Hallé Concerts Soc. (today with considerable financial support from Arts Council, private patronage, and local govt.). Richter left in 1911 and was succeeded in 1912 by Michael *Balling who remained until 1914. No permanent cond. appointed until Hamilton *Harty, 1920–33. During decade 1933–43, Beecham and Sargent, with others, were conds. Orch. reconstituted 1943 on annual basis giving many more concerts and John *Barbirolli was appointed cond., retaining post until his death in 1970. Succeeded 1971 by James *Loughran who resigned 1983 and was succeeded (1984) by Stanislaw *Skrowaczewski. Among works f.p. by Hallé are Elgar's 1st Sym. (1908) and Vaughan Williams's 7th and 8th syms. (1953 and 1956). Orch. gives regular series in Sheffield and Bradford, tours throughout Britain, and has made many overseas tours.

Halling. A popular solo Norweg. dance, presumed to have originated in the Hallingdal. The mus. is in simple duple time, and the steps are remarkably vigorous. Acc. played on 'Hardanger fiddle', vn. strung with 4 stopped and 4 sympathetic str.

Halm, Hans (*b* Munich, 1898; *d* Munich, 1965). Ger. musicologist. Dir., mus. section, Munich State Library from 1938. After death of *Kinsky, completed and pubd. his thematic catalogue of Beethoven's works (1955).

Halsey, Louis (Arthur Owen) (*b* London, 1922). Eng. cond. Studied King's Coll., Cambridge. Founded and cond. Elizabethan Singers 1953–66, Louis Halsey Singers from 1967, Thames Chamber Choir from 1964. Mus. producer, BBC, from 1963.

Hambourg, Mark (*b* Bogutchar, 1879; *d* Cambridge, 1960). Russ.-born pianist, later Brit. citizen. Début with Moscow P.O. 1888, then pupil of *Leschetizky in Vienna. Many world tours.

Hambraeus, Bengt (*b* Stockholm, 1928). Swed. composer and organist. Studied Upsala Univ. 1947–56 and at Darmstadt summer courses with Fortner, Messiaen, and Křenek. Joined staff, Swedish Broadcasting Corporation, 1957: dir. of chamber mus. 1965–8, prod. dir. 1968–72. Prof., McGill Univ., Montreal, from 1972. Has comp. at elec. studios in Cologne, Milan, and Munich.

Hamburg. N. German city and port with long mus. tradition. Famous figures in its church mus. history who held office of Musikdirektor der Hauptkirchen incl. Sartorius (1604–37), Selle (1638–63), Telemann (1721–67), C. P. E. Bach (1767–88), and C. F. G. Schwencke (1788–1822). In 17th cent. Hamburg was leading centre of N. German org. mus. Schnitger (1648–1719) was important org. builder and among distinguished organists were the Praetorius brothers, Reincken, and Lübeck. Became opera centre in 1678. Keiser, who moved to Hamburg in 1695, wrote over 50 operas for the company he directed from 1703 to 1706, with Handel as apprentice. Telemann wrote several operas for Hamburg. In 19th cent., Bernhard Pollini (Pohl) from 1874 established a Wagnerian reputation and engaged Mahler as cond. (1891–7). Later conds. incl. Klemperer (1910–12), Pollak (1917–31), and Böhm (1931–4). Opera house bombed 1943, rebuilt 1955. Conds. after 1945 incl. Arthur Gruber (1946–50), Leopold Ludwig (1951–71), and Christoph von Dohnányi (1977–84). Producers such as Günther Rennert and intendants such as Tietjen (1954–9) and R. Liebermann (1959–73) lifted Hamburg to a leading place in European opera. Orch. concerts developed *c.*1660. C. P. E. Bach arr. concerts from 1768 for the next 20 years. Hamburg Philharmonic Orch. gave first concert in Jan. 1829 but was eclipsed from 1886 by concerts given by the opera orch. under Hans von Bülow. But Muck from 1922 transformed the playing until, when he retired in 1933, the orch. was merged with the opera orch. under joint cond. of Jochum and Schmidt-Isserstedt. After 1945 conds. incl. Keilberth and Sawallisch. In 1945 Schmidt-Isserstedt became chief cond. of Hamburg radio orch. which later toured Eng., Russ., and USA. Known as North German Radio S.O. from 1951. Gave f.p. (concert) of Schoenberg's *Moses und Aron*, 1954. Atzmon was chief cond. 1972–9, Tennstedt 1979–82, Wand from 1982.

Hamburger, Paul (*b* Vienna, 1920). Austrian-born pianist and critic. Studied Vienna State Acad. Settled in Eng. Worked with EOG 1953–6, Glyndebourne Opera 1956–62. Frequent accompanist and chamber mus. player. Has contributed to pubd. symposiums on Britten, Mozart, and Chopin. Translator of Hollander's *Janáček*.

Hamerik (orig. Hammerich), **Asger** (*b* Copenhagen, 1843; *d* Frederiksburg, 1923). Danish composer and pianist. Pupil of Gade and Bülow. In Paris 1864–9 was helped and taught by Berlioz. Went to Italy 1869, opera *La Vendetta* prod. Milan 1870. Dir. of Cons., Peabody Institute, Baltimore, 1871–98, founding sym. concerts there. Returned to Copenhagen 1900. Comp. 8 syms., 5 suites, 3 other operas, chamber mus., etc.

Hamerik, Ebbe (*b* Copenhagen, 1898; *d* Copenhagen, 1951). Danish composer and cond. Son of Asger *Hamerik, with whom he studied. Cond.,

Danish Royal Opera 1919–22. Comp. 5 syms., several operas, and chamber mus.

Hamilton, Iain (Ellis) (*b* Glasgow, 1922). Scot. composer and pianist. Trained in London as engineer but won scholarship to RAM in 1947, studying comp. with *Alwyn and pf. with H. Craxton. Cl. Quintet perf. 1949; 2nd Sym. (1951) won Koussevitzky award. Lecturer, Morley Coll. 1952–9, London Univ. 1955–60. Prof. of mus., Duke Univ., N. Carolina, 1961–81, becoming chairman, mus. dept. 1966. Returned to Eng. 1981. Early works showed influences of Bartók and Hindemith, and in the *Sinfonia* he used serial procedures. Growing interest in vocal and operatic mus. has eased tendency to austerity in his mus. Prin. works:

OPERAS: *Rondo*, 1-act opera buffa; *Agamemnon*, 2-act (1967–9); *Royal Hunt of the Sun*, 2-act (1967–9); *Pharsalia* 1-act, (1968); The *Catiline Conspiracy* (1972–3); *Tamburlaine* (1976); *Anna Karenina* (1978); *Dick Whittington* (1980–1); *Lancelot* (1982–3).

BALLET: *Clerk Saunders* (1951).

ORCH: *Variations* for str. (1948); Sym. No. 1 (1950), No 2 (1951), No. 3 (*Spring*) (1981), No. 4 in B (1981); ov. *Bartholomew Fair* (1952); cl. conc. (1950); pf. conc. No. 1 (1949), No. 2 (1960 rev. 1967); *Sinfonia Concertante* for vn., va., and orch. (1950); vn. conc. No. 1 (1952); conc. for jazz tpt. (1958); *Scottish Dances* (1956); ov. *1912* (1958); *Sinfonia* for 2 orch. (1958–9); *Sonata per orchestra da camera* (1956); *Arias* for small orch. (1962); *Cantos* for orch. (1964); org. conc. (1964); *Jubilee* (1964); *Circus* for 2 tpt. and orch. (1969); *Voyage* for hn. and orch. (1970); *Alastor* (1970); *Amphion*, vn. conc. No. 2 (1971); *Commedia: Concerto for Orch.* (1972–3); *Aurora* (1975); The *Alexandrian Sequence*, chamber orch. (1976).

CHORAL: The *Bermudas* for bar., ch., and orch. (1956); *Nocturnal* for 11 solo vv. (1959); *Epitaph For This World and Time* for 3 ch., 3 organs (1970); *Te Deum; The Descent of the Celestial City*, vv. and org. (1972); The *Golden Sequence*, ch. and org. (1973); *To Columbus*, ch., brass, and perc. (1975); *Requiem*, unacc. ch. (1980); *Mass in A*, unacc. ch. (1980); *Vespers*, ch., 2 pf., hp., perc. (1980); The *Morning Watch*, ch. and 10 winds (1981); *St Mark Passion*, SATB soloists, ch., and orch. (1982).

VOICE AND ORCH: *Cinque Canzone d'Amore*, ten. and orch. (1957); *Dialogues*, coloratura sop. and small orch. (1965); *Pharsalia*, dramatic commentary for bar. and chamber ens. (1968); *Cleopatra*, dramatic scene for sop. and orch. (1978); *La Ricordanza*, ten. and orch. (1981).

CHAMBER MUSIC: Cl. quintet No. 1 (1948); str. qt. (1949); va. sonata (1951); fl. qt. (1951); cl. sonata (1954); pf. trio (1954); octet for str. (1954); vc. sonata No. 1 (1958); sextet (1962); brass quintet (1964); 2nd str. qt. (1965); sonata for 3 winds (1966); *5 Scenes*, tpt. and pf. (1966); fl. sonata (1966); vc. sonata No. 2 (1974); cl. quintet No. 2

(*Sea Music*) (1974); *Hyperion*, pf., cl., hn., vn., vc. (1977); *Spirits of the Air*, bass tb. (1977); octet (1983–4).

ORGAN: *Fanfares and Variants* (1960); *Aubade* (1965); *Threnos—in time of war* (1966); *Roman Music* (1973); *Vision of Canopus* (1975).

PIANO: Sonata No. 1 (1951 rev. 1971), No. 2 (1973), No. 3 (1978); *3 Pieces* (1955); *Nocturnes with cadenzas* (1963); *Palinodes* (1972).

SONGS: *Spirit of Delight*, song-cycle, sop. and bar. (1978); *Love is Life's Spring*, sop., pf. (1982).

Hamlet. Shakespeare's play (1600–1) has inspired operas and orch. mus. e.g. (1) Opera in 5 acts by Ambroise Thomas to lib. by Barbier and Carré, prod. Paris 1868, London 1869, NY 1872. (2) Opera (*Amleto*) by *Faccio to lib. by Boito, prod. Genoa 1865. (3) Sym. poem by Liszt, comp. 1858 as prelude to play. (4) Fantasy-ov. Op. 67a by Tchaikovsky, 1888, and incidental mus. (16 items) Op. 67b, 1891. (5) Opera in 3 acts by *Searle to his own lib., prod. Hamburg 1968, London 1969. (6) Ballets on the subject have used mus. by Tchaikovsky, Clerico, Gallenberg, Blacher, and Shostakovich. (7) Other operas on the subject by Gasparini, D. Scarlatti, Mercadante, Grandi, and Szokolay among others. (8) Film music by Shostakovich and Walton.

Hammerich. See *Hamerik, Asger*.

Hammerklavier Sonata. Title generally applied solely to Beethoven's Pf. Sonata No. 29 in B♭ major, Op. 106, comp. 1817–18, but in a letter written in Jan. 1817 Beethoven said he had decided to use the word 'Hammerklavier' (Ger., 'pianoforte') on all his pf. mus. with Ger. titles, adding 'this is to be clearly understood once and for all'.

Hammerstein, Oscar (*b* Stettin, 1846; *d* NY, 1919). Ger.-Amer. impresario and businessman. Settled in NY 1863, making fortune from inventions such as cigar-making machine. From 1890 built and managed various ths. In 1906 built Manhattan Opera House, NY, engaging superb singers and producing adventurous repertory, incl. first NY perfs. of *Louise, Pelléas et Mélisande, Salome*, and *Elektra*. In 1908 built Philadelphia Opera House, run in assoc. with his NY co. The Met. in 1910 bought his interests and stipulated he should not produce opera in the US for 10 years. So in London he built London Opera House (Stoll, Kingsway), opening in 1911 but failing after 2 seasons. Built Lexington Opera House, NY, in 1913, but the Met. legally restrained him from producing opera there.

Hammerstein, Oscar (II) (*b* NY, 1895; *d* Doylestown, Penn., 1960). Amer. librettist and producer, grandson of above. Collab. with Kern (notably in *Show Boat*, 1927), Romberg, Friml, and most notably with Richard Rodgers in *Oklahoma! (1943), Carousel (1945), South Pacific (1949), The King and I (1951) and The Sound of Music (1959).

Wrote lib. for *Carmen Jones* (1943), the brilliant adaptation of *Carmen* as an Amer. musical.

Hammond, (Dame) **Joan** (Hood) (*b* Christchurch, N.Z., 1912). New Zealand sop. Studied Sydney Cons. and played vn. in Sydney S.O. for 3 years. Début as singer 1929. Later studied singing in Vienna (1936) and in London with Dino Borgioli. Singing début London 1938 (*Messiah*) and in opera in Vienna 1938. Later career in opera houses in London, Vienna, Moscow, and Netherlands, repertory incl. *Aida, Fidelio,* and some Wagner. Member Carl Rosa Co. 1942–5. Sang with NY City Opera 1949. Sang title-role in f.p. in Eng. trans. of Dvořák's *Rusalka*, 1959. Worked as journalist in Australia, also excellent golfer. O.B.E. 1953, C.B.E. 1963, C.M.G. 1972, D.B.E. 1974. Retired 1965.

Hammond Organ. Type of elec. org. invented and manufactured by Hammond Organ Co., Chicago (first introduced 1933). Usually has 2 manuals and pedal kbd. Sound is prod. and controlled by electricity in simulation of pipe-org. Inventor, Laurens Hammond, also produced the Solovox, the Chord Organ, and the Nova-chord.

Hammond-Stroud, Derek (*b* London, 1929). Eng. bar. Studied with Elena *Gerhardt and Gerhard *Hüsch. Prin. bar. SW Opera 1961–71, CG from 1971. Noted for his Alberich in ENO *Ring* cycle and for Faninal in *Der Rosenkavalier*. O.B.E. 1987.

Hampel, Anton Joseph (*b* 1700; *d* Dresden, 1771). Ger. hn.-player. In Dresden court orch. from, probably, 1731 where he was first to develop method of playing chromatic scale by hand-stopping. In about 1753 devised way of inserting crooks into body of horn rather than at the mouthpiece. Wrote hn. concertos.

Hanacca, Hanakisch (Ger.; Fr. *Hanaise*). A Moravian dance in simple triple time; a sort of quick polonaise.

Handbells. Small bells attached to the hands by leather straps and played by striking them together. Used for practice by change ringers.

Handel, George Frideric (orig. Händel, Georg Friederich) (*b* Halle,1685; *d* London,1759). Ger.-born composer and organist (naturalized Eng. from 1726). Son of a barber-surgeon who opposed mus. as his son's career though he permitted lessons from *Zachau, organist and composer. Handel studied law at Halle Univ., turning to full-time mus. when his father died. He went to Hamburg in 1703 where he joined the opera house under the composer Reinhard *Keiser, playing 2nd vn. in the orch. His first opera *Almira*, written because Keiser lost interest in the lib., which Handel took over, was prod. there in 1705, being followed by 3 others. In 1706 Handel went to Italy in a prince's retinue, meeting Corelli, the Scarlattis, and other leading figures, and rapidly

attaining mastery of It. style in opera, chamber mus., and vocal mus. He was acclaimed as a genius, the rival of his It. contemporaries. His opera *Agrippina* was produced in Venice in 1709. The following year he was appointed court cond. in Hanover and was also invited to write an opera (*Rinaldo*) for London, where he quickly realized the possibilities for his own success and, after settling his affairs in Hanover, settled there permanently.

For the next 35 years Handel was immersed in the ups and downs of operatic activity in London where the It. *opera seria* was the dominant force. In 1712 he received a pension of £200 a year for life from Queen Anne, this being increased to £600 by King George I, his former ruler in Hanover, for whom in 1717 he comp. the famous *Water Music* suite. From 1717 to 1720 Handel was resident comp. to the Earl of Carnarvon (Duke of Chandos from April 1719) at his palace of Cannons in Edgware. The 11 *Chandos Anthems* were the chief fruit of this appointment. In 1719 Handel, in assoc. with G. *Bononcini and *Ariosti, was a mus. dir. of the so-called Royal Acad. of Mus. (not a coll. but a business venture to produce It. opera). Handel travelled abroad to engage singers and in the 8 years until the acad. closed because of lack of support he comp. 14 operas, among them *Radamisto, Rodelinda, Admeto,* and *Tolomeo*. In 1727, for the coronation of George II, Handel wrote 4 anthems, incl. *Zadok the Priest*, which has been sung at every Brit. coronation since then.

The success of Gay's *The Beggar's Opera* and imitative works was the prin. cause of the falling-away of support for Handel's co. He went to It. to hear operas by composers such as Porpora and Pergolesi and to engage the leading It. singers. Back in London in partnership with Heidegger at the King's Theatre, Handel wrote *Lotario* (1729), *Partenope* (1730), and *Orlando* (1733). In 1734 he moved to the new CG Th., but he recognized that the popularity of It. opera was declining and began, somewhat unwillingly, to develop the genre of dramatic oratorios which is perhaps his most orig. contribution to the art of mus. *Esther* (1732 in rev. form) and *Acis and Galatea* are typical examples. Ironically, released from the conventions of *opera seria*, Handel's dramatic gifts found wider and more expressive outlets in the oratorio form. Scores contain stage directions and the use of ch. and orch. became more dramatic and rich. He cond. several oratorio perf. in London, 1735, playing his own org. concs. as entr'actes. Nevertheless he continued to write operas and between 1735 and 1740 comp. *Ariodante, Alcina, Berenice, Serse,* and *Deidamia*.

In 1737 Handel's health cracked under the strain of his operatic labours and he had a stroke. Following his recovery, he wrote a series of oratorios, incl. *Messiah*, prod. Dublin, 1742. By this work his name is known throughout the world, yet it is something of an oddity in Handel's work since he was not a religious composer in the accepted sense. But its power, lyricism, sincerity, and profundity make it one of the supreme mus. creations as well as an outstanding example of devotional art. It was followed by *Samson, Judas Maccabaeus,* and *Solomon.* The success of these works made Handel the idol of the Eng., and that popularity dominated Eng. mus. for nearly 150 years after his death. It was not until Handel's operas were revived in Ger. in the 1920s that the perspective was corrected and the importance of that branch of his art was restored. Superb as are Handel's instr. comps. such as the *concerti grossi,* sonatas, and suites, it is in the operas and oratorios that the nobility, expressiveness, invention, and captivation of his art are found at their highest degree of development. He did not revolutionize operatic form but he brought the novelty of his genius to the genre as he found it. The scene-painting and illustrative qualities of his orchestration are remarkable even at a period when naive and realistic effects were common currency.

For the last 7 years of his life Handel was blind, but he continued to conduct oratorio perfs. and to revise his scores with assistance from his devoted friend John Christopher Smith. His works were pubd. by the Ger. *Handel Gesellschaft* in a complete edn. (1859–94) of 100 vols., ed. *Chrysander, and a new edn., the *Hallische Handel-Ausgabe,* is in progress. Prin. comps.:

OPERAS: Hamburg: *Almira, Nero* (lost), (1705), *Florindo e Dafne* (lost) (1707); Florence: *Rodrigo* (1707); Venice: *Agrippina* (1709); London: *Rinaldo* (1711), *Il pastor fido* (1712; 2nd version with ballet *Terpsicore,* 1734); *Teseo* (1712); *Silla* (1714); *Amadigi* (1715); *Radamisto* (1720); *Muzio Scevola, Floridante* (1721); *Ottone, Flavio* (1723); *Giulio Cesare, Tamerlano* (1724); *Rodelinda* (1725); *Scipione, Alessandro* (1726); *Admeto, Riccardo I* (1727); *Siroe, Tolomeo* (1728); *Lotario* (1729); *Partenope* (1730); *Poro* (1731); *Ezio, Sosarme* (1732); *Orlando* (1733); *Arianna,* (1734); *Ariodante,* *Alcina* (1735); *Atalanta* (1736); *Arminio, Giustino,* *Berenice* (1737); *Faramondo,* *Serse* (1738); *Imeneo* (1740); *Deidamia* (1740).

DRAMATIC ORATORIOS: Rome: *La Resurrezione, Trionfo del Tempo* (1708); Naples: *Aci, Galatea e Polifemo* (1709); Hamburg: *Der für die Sünde der Welt gemartete und sterbende Jesus* (Brockes Passion) (?1716); London: *Haman and Mordecai* (masque 1720, later rev. as *Esther* in 1732); *Acis and Galatea* (1718; rev. 1732 incorporating part of 1709 work, and 1743); *Deborah* (1733); *Athalia* (1733); *Alexander's Feast* (1736); *Saul,* *Israel in Egypt, Ode for St Cecilia's Day* (1739); *L'Allegro, il Pensieroso ed il Moderato* (1740); *Messiah* (1741); *Samson, Joseph* (1743); *Semele,* *Belshazzar, Hercules* (1744); *Occasional Oratorio,* *Judas Maccabaeus* (1746); *Alexander Balus,* *Joshua* (1747); *Solomon, Susanna* (1748); *Theodora, Alceste* (1749); *Choice of Hercules* (1750);

Jephtha (1752); *Triumph of Time and Truth* (1757).

CANTATAS AND CHAMBER DUETS: Handel comp. 100 of the former and 20 of the latter. Among the best known are *Silete Venti,* sop. and instr. (1729); *La terra è liberata* (*Apollo e Dafne*), sop. and instr. (c.1708); and *O numi eterni* (*La Lucrezia*), sop. and continuo (1709).

CHURCH MUSIC: *Gloria Patri* (1707); *Utrecht Te Deum and Jubilate* (1712–13); *Dettingen Te Deum* (1743); 11 *Chandos Anthems* (1717–18); 4 *Coronation Anthems* (1727: *The King Shall Rejoice; Let thy hand be strengthened; My heart is inditing; *Zadok the Priest*); *The Ways of Zion do Mourn,* funeral anthem for Queen Caroline (1737).

VOCAL: *Birthday Ode for Queen Anne* (1713); 9 *German Arias* (1729).

INSTRUMENTAL AND CHAMBER MUSIC: 6 *Concerti Grossi* for str., woodwind, and continuo, Op. 3 (1734); 12 *Concerti Grossi* for str. and optional wind, Op. 12 (1740); 5 *Concerti* for orch. (1741); 6 *organ concerti,* Op. 4 (1738); 6 *organ concerti,* Op. 7 (1760); 6 *organ concerti* (1740); 15 chamber sonatas (fls., recorders), Op. 1 (1724); 3 *concerti a due cori;* 2 ob. sonatas; 12 fl. sonatas; 6 trio sonatas; 9 trio sonatas, Op. 2 (1722–33); 7 trio sonatas, Op. 5 (1739); va. da gamba sonata; 8 *suites de pièces* for hpd. (1720); 8 *suites de pièces* (1733); 6 *Fugues* (1736). See also *Harmonious Blacksmith.*

ORCH.: *Water Music* (c.1717); *Music for Royal *Fireworks* (1749).

Handel Opera. Founded 1955 as Handel Opera Society by Charles *Farncombe, at suggestion of E. J. *Dent, to revive interest in Handel's operas. First prod. was *Deidamia,* 1955, at St Pancras Town Hall. Moved in 1959 to Sadler's Wells Th. Has revived over 20 Handel works, many for the first time since Handel's lifetime. Name changed to Handel Opera 1977. Singers appearing with the company have incl. Richard Lewis, Geraint Evans, James Bowman, Janet Baker, Joan Sutherland, and Anna Reynolds.

Handford, Maurice (*b* Salisbury, 1929; *d* Warminster, 1986). Eng. cond. and hn.-player. Studied RAM. Prin. hn. Hallé Orch. 1949–61. Assoc. cond. Hallé Orch. 1966–71. Staff cond. CBSO, prin. cond. Calgary P.O. 1971–5.

Hand Horn. The 'Natural' *French horn, i.e. without valves, which can produce only the notes of the harmonic series, together with some obtained by placing the hand in the bell of the instr.

Händl, Jacob (*b* Krain, 1550; *d* Prague, 1591). Ger. composer. Kapellmeister at Olmütz, c.1579, later cantor in Prague. Wrote 16 masses, many motets, and other church mus. Handel's *Funeral Anthem* is based on a Händl motet. Also known as Gallus.

Handley, Vernon (George) (*b* Enfield, 1930). Eng. cond. Studied GSM. Début 1961 Bournemouth S.O. Prof., RCM 1966–72. Guest cond. of most Brit. orchs. Cond. Ulster Orch. from 1985. Specialist in Eng. mus.

Hand Organ. *Barrel Organ. The word 'Hand' distinguishes it from the 'Finger Organ' (played from a kbd.).

Handy, W(illiam) **C**(hristopher) (*b* Florence, Alabama, 1873; *d* NY, 1958). Amer. composer whose parents had been slaves. Studied org. but was only allowed to play sacred mus. Left home at 18 to become vagrant musician, playing tpt. in brass bands. Became co-proprietor of mus. publishing business in Memphis. Among works he published were his own *Memphis Blues* (1912) and *St Louis Blues* (1914). Known as 'father of the blues'.

Hanff, Johann Nikolaus (*b* Wechmar, 1665; *d* Schleswig, 1711). Ger. organist and composer for his instr. Influenced J. S. Bach.

Hannikainen, Tauno (*b* Jyväskylä, 1896; *d* Helsinki, 1968). Finnish cond. and cellist. Studied Helsinki Cons. and in Paris with Casals. Prin. cellist Helsinki Orch. 1916–19; cond. Finnish opera orch. 1922–7. Settled in US 1940. Cond., Duluth S.O. 1942–6, ass. cond. Chicago Civic S.O. 1947–50. Cond., Helsinki City S.O. 1951–63. Visited Eng. as guest cond., Hallé Orch.

Hanover Square Rooms. Formerly London's prin. venue for concerts, built by Gallini, J. C. *Bach, and K. F. *Abel and opened in 1775 with a Bach-Abel subscription concert. *Salomon est. concerts there in 1786 at which , in 1791–2 and 1794–5, Haydn's 12 Salomon syms. were introduced. From 1833–69 the Phil. Soc.'s concerts were given there. Closed 1874.

Hänsel und Gretel. Opera in 3 acts by *Humperdinck to lib. by Adelheid Wette (his sister) based on story by brothers Grimm in *Kinder und Hausmärchen* (1812–14). Prod. Weimar 1893 (R. Strauss cond.); London 1894; NY 1895.

Hansen. Danish publishers of mus., founded 1853 by Jens Wilhelm Hansen. At first published educational mus., but later issued works by Gade and other Danish composers. Branch opened in Leipzig 1887 (closed during Second World War) and a Swedish branch, Nordiska Musikforlag, in 1915. New Ger. branch established 1951 in Frankfurt and in 1957 assoc. began with London firm of J. & W. Chester. Composers in Hansen list incl. Nielsen, Holmboe, Backer-Grøndhal, Svendsen, Sinding, Alfvén, Rosenberg, Bäck, Sibelius, and Kilpinen. Recently some Lutoslawski has been published by them.

Hans Heiling. Opera in prol. and 3 acts by *Marschner to lib. by Devrient. Prod. Berlin 1833, Oxford 1953, Wexford, 1983.

Hanslick, Eduard (*b* Prague, 1825; *d* Baden, nr. Vienna, 1904). Austrian critic and writer of Cz.

descent. Studied mus. with Tomášek and law at Prague and Vienna Univs. Deeply impressed by Wagner's *Tannhäuser* in Dresden, 1845, about which he wrote long critical article. Settled in Vienna 1846, contributing articles on mus. and in 1848 becoming mus. ed. of *Wiener Zeitung*, while working as civil servant. Mus. critic *Die Presse* 1855–64, *Die Neue Freie Presse* 1864–95. His book *Vom Musikalisch-Schönen (Beauty in Music)* was pubd. 1854. Lecturer in history and aesthetics of mus., Vienna Univ., 1856–95 (prof. from 1861). His *Beauty in Music* aligned him with the purist Leipzig school, represented by Mendelssohn, Schumann, and Brahms, against the Weimar school of Liszt and Wagner whose 'music of the future' had to comprise elements other than mus. His early admiration of Wagner changed to critical hostility with his review of *Lohengrin* in Vienna in 1858. Wagner's reaction was such that in the orig. poem of *Die Meistersinger* the character of Beckmesser was called Veit Hanslich. But those who regard Hanslick merely as the bigoted opponent of Wagner, Strauss, Bruckner, etc. should read his criticism, which is among the best and most penetrating ever written.

Hanson, Howard (Harold) (*b* Wahoo, Nebraska, 1896; *d* Rochester, NY, 1981). Amer. composer and educator, of Swed. descent. Studied comp. with Goetschius in NY. Won Amer. *Prix de Rome*, 1921, spending 3 years at Amer. Acad. in Rome. In 1924 became dir. of Eastman Sch. of Mus., Rochester, NY, holding this post for 40 years. Est. Amer. fests. at Rochester in 1925 at which hundreds of works by Amer. composers have received f.ps. Dir. of Institute of Amer. Mus., Rochester Univ., from 1964. Known as 'the American Sibelius', his mus. reflects a similar romantic outlook firmly rooted in tonality, His book *Harmonic Materials of Modern Music* (NY 1960) shows his grasp of contemporary technical devices. Prin. works:

ORCH: Syms., No. 1 (*Nordic*) (1921), No. 2 (*Romantic*) (1930), No. 3 (1938), No. 4 (*Requiem*) (1943), No. 5 (*Sinfonia Sacra*) (1955), No. 6 (1968), No. 7 (*Sea*), with ch. (1977); *Lux aeterna*, symphonic poem with va. obbl. (1923); organ conc. (1926); *Pan and the Priest*, symphonic poem with pf. obbl. (1926); pf. conc. (1948); *Mosaics* (1958); *Summer Seascape* (1958); *Summer Seascape II* (1966); *Bold Island Suite* (1961).

OPERA: *Merry Mount* (3 acts, NY Met. 1933).

CHORAL: *Lament for Beowulf*, ch, and orch. (1925); *Heroic Elegy*, ch. and orch. (1927); *3 Songs from Drum Taps*, vv. and orch. (1935); *Song of Democracy*, soloists, ch., and orch. (1957); *Song of Human Rights*, cantata (1963); *New Land, New Covenant*, oratorio (1976).

CHAMBER MUSIC: pf. quintet (1916); str. qt. (1923). Also works for pf. and songs.

Happy Birthday to You. Song composed by Mildred Hill of Louisville, Kentucky, and published by Clayton F. Summy, head of Chicago mus. publishing firm (est. 1888). Popular as choral greeting on birthdays. Used—not knowing it was Summy's copyright—by Stravinsky as basis for his short *Greetings Prelude*, comp. for Monteux's 80th birthday, 1955.

Happy Prince, The. Opera in 1 act by *Williamson for children's and women's vv., pf. duet, perc., and optional str. quintet, to his own lib. based on Oscar Wilde's fairy-tale. Prod. Farnham Fest., 1965.

Harawi, chant d'Amour et de Mort. Song-cycle by Messiaen for sop. and pf. (1945), one of 3 of his works inspired by Tristan and Isolde legend (the others being 5 *Rechants and *Turangalîla). F.p. Brussels 1946.

Hardelot, Guy d' (Mrs. W. I. Rhodes, *née* Helen Guy) (*b* Hardelot, Boulogne, 1858; *d* London, 1936). Fr. composer. Studied Paris Cons. Toured USA with Calvé, 1896. After marriage, settled in London. Wrote many songs (incl. *Because*, 1902) which went into repertory of Melba, Calvé, Plançon, Maurel, and others.

Harewood, George (Henry Hubert Lascelles), **7th Earl of** (*b* London, 1923). Eng. opera administrator, writer, and ed. Enthusiasm for opera stimulated in It. when prisoner of war. Assoc. with EOG from its inception. Founded magazine *Opera* 1950 (ed. 1950–3). Board of dir. CG 1951–3, contr. of opera planning 1953–60. Dir., Leeds Fest. 1958–74; dir., Edinburgh Fest. 1961–5. Man. dir. SW Opera (ENO) 1972–85. Ed., 8th, 9th, and 10th edns. of *Kobbé's Complete Opera Book*, 1954, 1976, and 1987. K.B.E. 1987.

Harfe (Ger.). Harp.

Hark, the Herald Angels Sing. Hymn orig. written by Charles Wesley (1743) beginning 'Hark, how all the welkin rings'. G. Whitefield incl. it in his *Collection* of 1753, substituting the familiar first line. It was further altered in other hymn publications in 1760, 1774, and 1775. In 1782 it was added to the suppl. of Tate and Brady. Dr. W. H. Cummings, organist of Waltham Abbey, fitted the tune of the 2nd no. of Mendelssohn's *Festgesang* to the words for his choir and pubd. the adaptation in 1856. It soon became very popular. Mendelssohn thought the tune would 'never do to sacred words'.

Harmonica. Name given at different times to various mus. instrs. Today its prin. meaning is the mouth-organ, a small wind instr. invented in 1830s with metal reeds, 1 to each note, which is held against the lips and moved from side to side according to the note desired. The term also meant mus. glasses (see *Glass armonica*).

Harmonic Bass. Org. stop; same as *Acoustic Bass*.

Harmonic Flute. Org. stop usually of 8′ length but 4′ pitch, pipes being pierced at half-length: silvery tone.

Harmonic Piccolo. Org. stop of 4′ length and 2′ pitch—on principle of *Harmonic Flute*.

Harmonics. The lowest tone of the harmonic series (the 'fundamental') is the 1st harmonic, the next lowest the 2nd harmonic, and so on. These other tones are the 'upper partials' or 'overtones', at fixed intervals above the fundamental, an octave, then a perfect 5th, etc. On str. instrs., 'playing in harmonics' refers to harmonics other than the 1st, i.e. the overtones. To obtain these, the str. must be set vibrating in fractions of its length. On an open str. the result is a natural harmonic; on a 'stopped' str. (a finger used to stop and another lightly placed) it is an artificial harmonic. In brass instrs. harmonics are produced by varying the method of blowing. Every note of normal mus. instr. is a combination of the fundamental and certain upper partials. The only exception is the tuning-fork.

Harmonic Trumpet. Org. stop (see *Trumpet*) embodying (in upper pipes, at any rate) constructional principle of *Harmonic Flute; 8′ pitch.

Harmonie (Fr., Ger., 'harmony'). *Harmonie, Musique d'Harmonie, Harmoniemusik,* etc. means (1) a band of woodwind, brass, and perc. instr., as distinct from *Fanfare,* a band of brass and perc.; or (2) the wind instr. of an orch.

Harmonie, Basse d' (Fr.). *Ophicleide.

Harmonie, Cor d' (Fr.). Valveless Fr. hn. See *Hand horn.*

Harmonie, Trompette d' (Fr.). The ordinary modern *trumpet.

Harmonie der Welt, Die (The Harmony of the World). Opera in 5 acts by Hindemith to his own lib. based on life of 17th-cent. astronomer Johannes Kepler (author of *De harmonia mundi*). Comp. 1956–7 (earlier sketches). Prod. Munich 1957. Preceded by orch. sym. in 3 movements comp. 1951, f.p. Basle 1952, f. Brit. p. Edinburgh 1953 cond. Furtwängler.

Harmonielehre (Ger.). Study, teaching, and theory of *Harmony.

Harmoniemesse (Wind-band Mass). Popular name for Haydn's Mass No. 12 in B♭, of 1802, which makes a fuller, but not exclusive, use of wind instr. than is common in Haydn's Masses.

Harmoniemusik (Ger.). Mus. for wind instr.

Harmonious Blacksmith, The. Nickname for air and variations in Handel's 5th hpd. suite in E in the 1st set of 8 suites (1720). The name was bestowed after Handel's death and has no connection with the circumstances of the work's comp.

Harmonium. Small portable example of the reed org. family dating from early 19th cent. Perfected by Debain of Paris *c*.1842, but the instr. made by Alexandre achieved wider popularity. It is blown by 2 pedals operated by left and right foot working in alternate strokes to drive air through bellows. Used as substitute for org. to acc. hymns etc., but has been used by Dvořák in his *Bagatelles* (with 2 vn. and vc.) and by R. Strauss in *Ariadne auf Naxos*.

Harmony. The simultaneous sounding (i.e. combination) of notes, giving what is known as vertical mus., contrasted with horizontal mus. (*Counterpoint). Composers, in much the greater proportion of their mus., maintain in their minds some melody which ranks as the principal one, and which they intend the listener to recognize as such, whilst other melodies which are combined with it, or chords with which it is acc., rank as subsidiary.

The word *chord may be defined as any combination of notes simultaneously perf., and even when the main process in the composer's mind is a weaving together of melodic strands he has to keep before him this combinational element, both as regards the notes thus sounded together and the suitability of one combination to follow and precede the adjacent combination.

At different periods composers have given more attention to 1 or the other of the 2 aspects of their work: (a) the weaving together of melodic strands and (b) the chords thus brought into existence from point to point.

The former aspect of the result is the *Contrapuntal* element (see *Counterpoint) and the latter the *Harmonic* element. In less elaborate mus. (as, for instance, a simple song with pf. acc.) the contrapuntal element may be unimportant or even non-existent. Counterpoint necessarily implies also harmony, but harmony does not necessarily imply counterpoint.

Over a long period the resources of harmony may be said to have widened: new combinations introduced by composers of pioneering spirit have been condemned by unaccustomed ears as ugly, have then gradually come to be accepted as commonplace, and have been succeeded in their turn by other experimental combinations. The following definitions concern traditional and basic harmonic procedures:

(*a*) DIATONIC HARMONY: Harmony which confines itself to the major or minor key in force at the moment. CHROMATIC HARMONY: Harmony which employs notes extraneous to the major or minor key in force at the moment.

(*b*) OPEN HARMONY: Harmony in which the notes of the chords are more or less widely spread. CLOSE HARMONY: Harmony in which the notes of the chords lie near together.

(*c*) PROGRESSION: The motion of one note to another note or one chord to another chord.

(*d*) TRIAD: A note with its 3rd and 5th (e.g. C–E–G). COMMON CHORD: A Triad of which the 5th is perfect. MAJOR COMMON CHORD: A Common Chord of which the 3rd is major. MINOR COMMON CHORD: A Common Chord of which the 3rd is minor.

AUGMENTED TRIAD: A Triad of which the 5th is augmented. DIMINISHED TRIAD: A Triad of which the 5th is diminished.

(*e*) ROOT of a chord. That note from which it originates. (For instance, in the common chord C–E–G we have C as the root, to which are added the 3rd and 5th.) INVERSION of a chord: The removal of the root from the bass to an upper part. FIRST INVERSION: That in which the 3rd becomes the bass (e.g. E–G–C or E–C–G). SECOND INVERSION: That in which the 5th becomes the bass (e.g. G–E–C or G–C–E). THIRD INVERSION: In a 4-note chord that inversion in which the fourth note becomes the bass. (For instance, in the chord G–B–D–F the form of it that consists of F–G–B–D or F–B–G–D, etc.) FUNDAMENTAL BASS: An imaginary bass of a passage, consisting not of its actual bass notes but of the roots of its chords, i.e. the bass of its chords when uninverted.

(*f*) CONCORD. A chord satisfactory in itself (or an interval that can be so described; or a note which forms a part of such an interval or chord). CONSONANCE: The same as *Concord*. DISCORD: A chord which is restless, requiring to be followed in a particular way if its presence is to be justified by the ear (or the note or interval responsible for producing this effect). See, for instance, the examples given under *Dominant* (*Seventh*) and *Diminished* (*Seventh*). DISSONANCE: The same as *Discord*. RESOLUTION: The satisfactory following of a discordant chord (or the satisfactory following of the discordant note in such a chord). SUSPENSION: A form of discord arising from the holding over of a note in one chord as a momentary (discordant) part of the combination which follows, it being then resolved by falling a degree to a note which forms a real part of the second chord. DOUBLE SUSPENSION: The same as the last with 2 notes held over.

(*g*) ANTICIPATION: The sounding of a note of a chord before the rest of the chord is sounded. RETARDATION: The same as a Suspension but resolved by *rising* a degree.

PREPARATION: The sounding in one chord of a concordant note which is to remain (in the same 'part') in the next chord as a discordant note. (This applies both to Fundamental Discords and Suspensions.) UNPREPARED SUSPENSION: A contradiction in terms meaning an effect similar to that of Suspension but without 'Preparation'.

FUNDAMENTAL DISCORD: A discordant chord of which the discordant note forms a real part of the chord, i.e. not a mere Suspension, Anticipation, or Retardation. Or the said discordant note itself (e.g. *Dominant Seventh, Diminished Seventh,* etc.).

PASSING NOTE: A connecting note in one of the melodic parts (not forming a part of the chord which it follows or precedes).

(*h*) FALSE RELATION: The appearance of a note with the same letter-name in different parts (or 'voices') of contiguous chords, in one case inflected (sharp or flat) and in the other uninflected.

(i) PEDAL (or 'Point d'Orgue'): The device of holding on a bass note (usually Tonic or Dominant) through a passage including some chords of which it does not form a part. INVERTED PEDAL: The same as the above but with the held note in an upper part. DOUBLE PEDAL: A pedal in which two notes are held (generally Tonic and Dominant).

From Wagner onwards the resources of harmony have been enormously extended, and those used by composers of the present day often submit to no rules whatever, being purely empirical, or justified by rules of the particular composer's own devising. Among contemporary practices are:

Bitonality—in which two contrapuntal strands or 'parts' proceed in different keys.

Polytonality—in which the different contrapuntal strands, or 'parts', proceed in more than one key.

Atonality—in which no principle of key is observed.

Microtonality—in which scales are used having smaller intervals than the semitone.

In the 20th cent. greater freedom in the treatment of the above procedures has developed, together with a much wider application of dissonance. Chords of 7th, 9th, 11th, and 13th are treated as primary chords, and there has been a return to the use of pentatonic scales, medieval modes, and the whole-tone scale. A prin. revolution *c.*1910 was the abandonment of the triad as the prin. and fundamental consonance. Composers such as Bartók, Stravinsky, Schoenberg, and Webern widened the mus. spectrum of tone-colour by showing that any combination of notes could be used as a basic unresolved chord. The tritone has been used as the cause of harmonic tensions in place of tonic-dominant relationships. Another 20th-cent. harmonic feature is the 'layering' of sound, each layer following different principles of organization. Milhaud produces bitonal passages from two layers in different tonalities.

Since 1950 much mus. has been comp. in which harmony has hardly any place, for example in some of the serial works of Boulez and Stockhausen. Where non-pitched sounds are used, harmony no longer exists and its place is taken by overtones, densities, and other concomitants of 'clusters', etc.

In amplification of this entry see *Added Sixth, Augmented, Consecutive, Counterpoint,* and *Chromatic Intervals.*

Harnoncourt, Nikolaus (*b* Berlin, 1929). Ger. cond. and musicologist. Studied Vienna Acad. of Mus. Cellist in Vienna S.O. 1952–69. Founder-member Concentus Musicus of Vienna 1954, reviving early mus. on orig. instr. Ed. of perf. edns. of Monteverdi's *Il ritorno d'Ulisse in Patria* and *L'incoronazione di Poppea* and of Bach choral works.

Harold en Italie (Harold in Italy). Sym. (No. 2) for orch., with solo va., by Berlioz, Op. 16, inspired by Byron's *Childe Harold.* After a Paris concert of Berlioz's mus. in Dec. 1833, Paganini asked Berlioz for a va. work in which he could display his Stradivarius instr. Berlioz sent him the 1st movement which Paganini rejected because it gave him too little to play. The work was completed in 4 movements and f.p. Paris 1834, solo va. C. *Urhan.

Harp. This instr., of very ancient lineage, can be simply defined as an open frame over which is stretched a graduated series of str., set in vibration by plucking with the fingers. In the modern orch. harp the series is not normally chromatic, as it is in the pf., having merely 7 different notes with the octave, these being in the major scale of B (treated for convenience as that of C♭). There are 7 pedals, each affecting one note of this foundational scale; each pedal works to 2 notches, and by depressing it to its first or 2nd notch, respectively, the vibrating lengths of all the relevant strings are simultaneously shortened by fractions representing a semitone and a tone: thus all keys become possible, and by depressing all the pedals together the pitch of the complete instr. can be raised from C♭ (the normal key) to C♮ or C♯. The usual compass is 5½ octaves from C. Chords are normally played in more or less rapid succession of their notes, in the form understood by the word *arpeggio* (It. *arpa,* Harp). The typical 'sweeping' (*glissando*) action of the hand may be used in many kinds of scale (but evidently not in the chromatic scale, nor in any other scale passage employing more than 8 notes to the octave). In addition, of course, single str. may be plucked individually or in small groups.

The instr. described above is the *double-action* harp, introduced by Érard (*c.*1810), the word 'double' marking its differences from its predecessors on which the pitches could be raised only a semitone.

One earlier form of the harp is the *Welsh harp* or *telyn,* with 3 rows of str., the 2 outer rows (tuned in unison or octaves) giving the diatonic scale and the inner row the intermediate semitones: a simple modulation was effected by touching one of the inner str.

The harp has been much used as a solo instr. in Wales from time immemorial and in Eng. domestically during the Victorian period. It was a frequent member of the early 17th-cent. orch. but in later times was rarely found again in orch. use until the 19th cent. when the great Romantic orchestrators—Berlioz, Wagner, Strauss, Mahler, Elgar, etc.—made effective use of it. In the 20th cent. it has been used in chamber mus. (e.g. by Debussy and Ravel). There are several harp concs.

See also *Chromatic Harp, Double Harp, Clarsach, Dital Harp, Aeolian Harp.*

Harper, Edward (James) (*b* Taunton, 1941). Eng. composer, pianist, and cond. Studied Christ

Church, Oxford. Lecturer, Faculty of Mus., Edinburgh Univ., dir., New Music Group of Scotland. Comps. incl. pf. conc. (1969), *Ricercari in memoriam Luigi Dallapiccola* for chamber ens. (1975), *Fantasias* I (chamber orch.) and II, for 11 solo str. (1976), sonata for chamber orch. (1971), opera *Fanny Robin* (1974), *7 poems by e.e. cummings*, sop. and orch. (1977), Sym. (1978–9), quintet for fl., cl., vn., vc., pf. (1974), *Chester Mass*, ch. and orch. (1979), cl. conc. (1981–2), *Intrada after Monteverdi*, chamber orch. (1982), *Hedda Gabler*, opera (1984–5).

Harper, Heather (*b* Belfast, 1930). Irish sop. Studied TCL. Sang in BBC Chorus. Opera début Oxford 1954 as Lady Macbeth. Sang The Woman in first Brit. stage perf. of Schoenberg's *Erwartung*, 1960. Glyndebourne début 1957, CG 1962, Bayreuth 1967 (Elsa). Roles incl. Arabella in Strauss's opera, Ellen Orford in Britten's *Peter Grimes*, and Elsa in *Lohengrin*. Sang in f.p. of Britten's *War Requiem*, 1962 and Tippett's 3rd Sym. 1972. C.B.E. 1965. Retired from stage 1984.

Harp Quartet. Name for Beethoven's Str. Qt. No. 10 in E♭ major, Op. 74, comp. 1809, because of harp-like pizzicato arpeggios in 1st movement.

Harpsichord Family (Virginals, Spinet, Harpsichord). The *harpsichord* is a wing-shaped kbd. instr. in which the str. are plucked mechanically. It was developed during the 15th cent., the earliest surviving example (in the Victoria and Albert Museum, London) having been made in Bologna in 1521, but there are illustrated representations of the instr. dating from nearly a century earlier, and a reference in a Ger. poem of 1404 to the *clavicimbalum*, the earliest recorded use of the name from which the It. word *clavicembalo* is derived. The hpd. is fundamentally a mechanized *psaltery*. Each key operates a mechanical device known as the 'jack', equipped with a small leather or quill plectrum attached to a pivoted tongue. When the key is released the jack descends and, by positioning of a spring, the tongue pivots back, allowing the plectrum to pass the str. silently on its return. When the jack is back in its orig. position, a felt damper silences the vibration of the str. Very few contrasts of tone or dynamics are possible, variation in finger touch having little effect.

Italy was the home of the first important sch. of hpd. makers; at the end of the 16th cent., however, Antwerp became the centre of activity, particularly for the family of Ruckers. Their aim was to give the players some tonal contrast, a typical Ruckers single-manual instr. having a compass of four octaves from C and two sets of strings, one 8′ and one 4′. Hand stops in the right-hand side of the case brought one or both sets of jacks into contact with the strings. Ruckers also prod. a 2-manual hpd., the lower manual a 4th below the upper. From the 17th cent. to the end of the 18th, the hpd. was the indispensable supporting basis for continuo in almost every instr. combination, as well as being a popular domestic instr. With the development of the pf., the hpd. fell into semi-oblivion during the 19th cent., but in the 20th it has been revived both by modern composers, several of whom—e.g. Falla and McCabe—have written concs. for it, and in the authentic perf. of baroque mus. The *Dolmetsch family played a major part in the revival, and there are several distinguished modern hpd. manufacturers. 20th cent. virtuosi have incl. Wanda *Landowska and Ralph *Kirkpatrick.

Virginal or *Virginals*. This plucked kbd. instr. was first mentioned *c*.1460. The origin of the name is not, as is generally supposed, Eng. nor has it anything to do with Elizabeth I, but it is widely accepted that the name derives from the fact that young ladies were regularly depicted playing the instr. The main differences from the hpd. are in the oblong shape of the soundbox, the placing of the str. parallel to the kbd. instead of at right-angles, and the existence of 2 bridges. Sometimes one sees references to 'double virginals' or 'a pair of virginals'. The origins of these terms are obscure, since a double-manual virginal was extremely rare; a likely explanation is that they referred to the instr.'s compass. Eng. virginal mus. of the 17th cent. is of major importance; colls. of it incl. the *Fitzwilliam Virginal Book*, *My Ladye Nevells Booke*, and *Benjamin Cosyns Virginal Book*. The earliest pubd. coll. was *Parthenia* (1611).

Spinet. This resembles the virginals in having one str. to a note, but differs from it in being not rectangular but wing-shaped in an uneven 6 sides with the longest containing the kbd. It has a 4-octave compass. The str. either run roughly parallel to the kbd. as with the virginals, or diagonally in front of the player. (In the *Clavicytherium*, however, a rarer form than that described above, the str. ran perpendicularly like those of an upright pf.) The spinet was in use from the later 15th cent. to the end of the 18th.

Harrell, Lynn (*b* NY, 1944). Amer. cellist. Studied Juilliard Sch., NY, Curtis Institute, Penn., master classes with Piatigorsky and Casals. Début recital, NY 1960. Prin. cellist Cleveland Orch., 1965–71. Soloist since 1971, appearing with major Amer., Brit., and European orchs. Brit. début was 1975, with LSO.

Harrhy, Eidwenn (*b* Trowbridge, Wilts., 1949). Welsh soprano. Studied RMCM, singing in *Così fan tutte* 1970 and winning Imperial League of Opera prize. After study in London and Paris and concert appearances, made strong impression in Handel operas in 1974. CG début 1974 (Wellgunde) and ENO 1977 (Adèle in Rossini's *Le Comte Ory*). Has sung often with WNO, Opera North, Kent Opera, and Glyndebourne Touring Opera.

Harris, (Sir) **Augustus** (*b* Paris, 1852; *d* Folkestone, 1896). Eng. impresario. Son of CG stage-manager. Ass. manager to Mapleson. Manager, Drury Lane, 1879–94, managing Carl Rosa opera seasons there 1883–7. Formed opera co. 1887, engaging de Reszke, Maurel, Melba, etc. Manager, CG from 1888, achieving brilliant success, paying careful attention to production details. Introduced opera in its orig. language to CG and was sturdy champion of Wagner's operas, presenting *Ring* cycles at CG 1892, cond. Mahler. Knighted 1891.

Harris, Renatus (*b* France, *c*.1652; *d* Salisbury, 1724). Eng. org.-builder (of 39 instr.). His grandfather (Renatus), father (Thomas), and sons (Renatus and John) were also org.-builders.

Harris, Roy (Ellsworth) (*b* Lincoln County, Nebraska, 1898; *d* Santa Monica, Calif., 1979). Amer. composer. Studied Univ. of Calif., Berkeley, 1919. Private mus. pupil of Arthur Farwell, Modest Altschuler, and Arthur Bliss. From 1926 to 1929 studied in Paris with Nadia Boulanger. His 1st sym., cond. Koussevitzsky in Boston, 1934, earned him the reputation as America's leading symphonist, confirmed by 3rd sym. in 1939. Taught at many colls., incl. Juilliard Sch. and Cornell Univ., becoming composer-in-residence at Univ. of Calif. His music is basically diatonic and consonant, its rugged rhythmic qualities and falling intervals, combined with a melodic flavour of hymn-tunes and folk-tunes, making him an Amer. counterpart of Janáček, without the Czech's genius. Prin. works:

ORCH: Syms.: No. 1 (*Symphony 1933*) (1934), No. 2 (1936), No. 3 (1939), No. 4 (*Folksong*, with ch.) (1940), No. 5 (1943), No. 6 (*Gettysburg Address*) (1944), No. 7 (1952), No. 8 (*San Francisco*) (1962), No. 9 (*Polytonality*) (1963), No. 10 (*Abraham Lincoln*) (1965), No. 11 (1968); *American Portraits* (1929); *When Johnny Comes Marching Home* (1935); *Prelude and Fugue* for str. (1936); *Farewell to Pioneers* (1936); *Time Suite* (1937); *Ode to Friendship* (1944); pf. conc. No. 1 (1945); accordion conc. (1946); conc. for 2 pf. (1947); *Kentucky Spring* (1949); pf. conc. No. 2 (1953); *Ode to Consonance* (1957); *Elegy* (1958); *Horn of Plenty* (1964); conc. for amplified pf. (1968).

CHORAL: *Songs for Occupations* (unacc.) (1934); *Symphony for Voices* (unacc.) (1936); *Challenge 1940*, bar., ch., and orch. (1940); *Cantata*, ch., organ, brass (1943); *Mass* for male ch. and organ (1943); *Psalm 150* (1955); *Give me the splendid silent sun*, bar. and orch. (1959); *Canticle to the Sun*, cantata (1961).

CHAMBER MUSIC: *Songs for a Rainy Day* for str. qt. (1925); str. qts. No. 1 (1930), No. 2 (1933), No. 3 (1939); pf. trio (1934); pf. quintet (1937).

Harris, (Sir) William (Henry) (*b* London, 1883; *d* London, 1973). Eng. organist and composer. Studied RCM under Parratt (org.) and Stanford (comp.). Organist, New Coll., Oxford, 1919–28, Ch. Ch., Oxford, 1928–33, St George's Chapel, Windsor, 1933–61. Cond., Oxford Bach Choir 1926–33. Prof. of org. and harmony RCM, 1923–

53. Dir. of mus. studies, Royal Sch. of Church Mus., 1956–61. Comp. *The Hound of Heaven* for bar., ch., and orch., church mus., and org. works. K.C.V.O. 1954.

Harrison, Beatrice (*b* Roorkee, India, 1892; *d* Smallfield, Sussex, 1965). Eng. cellist. Studied RCM. Début with Queen's Hall Orch. 1907, then studied in Berlin with Hugo Becker. Frequently played in recitals with her violinist sister May (1891–1959). Delius's double conc. was written for them. Notable exponent of Elgar conc., which she recorded with composer. Gave f.p. of Delius's vc. sonata, 1918, and f. Eng. p. of his vc. concerto, 1923. In early BBC broadcasts played vc. in Surrey wood to acc. of nightingale. Her sister studied at RCM and with Auer in St Petersburg. London début in Mendelssohn conc.

Harrison, Julius (Allen Greenway) (*b* Stourport, 1885; *d* Harpenden, 1963). Eng. composer, cond., and writer. Studied with Bantock at Birmingham and Midland Institute. Cond. opera CG 1913. In Paris 1914 to help Nikisch and Weingartner prepare Wagner perfs. Conducted for Beecham Co. and BNOC (1922–7). Cond. Scottish Orch. 1920–3. Cond., Hastings Municipal Orch. 1930–40 (doing splendid work for Brit. mus.). Prof of comp. RAM. Works, influenced by Elgar, incl. Mass in C and *Requiem*; cantata *Cleopatra*; suite *Worcestershire Pieces*; *Cornish Sketches* for str., *Bredon Hill* for vn. and orch., str. qt., songs, etc. Contributor to various books on mus.; specialist on Brahms.

Harrison, Lou (*b* Portland, Oregon, 1917). Amer. composer and teacher. Studied San Francisco State Coll. and with Henry *Cowell. Organized concerts with John *Cage. Taught at Mills Coll., 1936–9. Studied with Schoenberg 1941. Went to NY 1943, writing mus. criticism and working as copyist and ballet composer. Ed. some of *Ives's mus., incl. 3rd Sym. of which he cond. f.p. 1947. Later taught in N. Carolina and took many jobs not connected with mus. His works reflect his busy and restless outlook: they combine Schoenbergian and aleatory procedures, use quarter-tones, call for extraordinary devices for producing unusual sounds, and emulate medieval polyphony and gamelan rhythms. Comps., in many genres, incl. opera *Rapunzel*, str. sextet *Schoenbergiana*, vn. conc., sym., *Young Caesar* (puppet opera), several ballets, chamber mus., and songs.

Harrison, Sidney (*b* London, 1903; *d* London, 1986). Eng. pianist, teacher, and writer. Studied GSM. Prof. of pf., GSM 1927–65, RAM from 1965. Outstanding broadcaster. First to give televised pf. lesson (1950).

Harrowing of Hell, The. Cantata, Op. 9, for ten. and bass soloists and ch. by A. *Milner, comp. 1956.

Harsányi, Tibor (*b* Magyarkanisza, 1898; *d* Paris, 1954). Hung. composer, pupil of Kodály. Settled in Paris 1923. Wrote operas, ballets, sym., vn. conc., chamber works, etc.

Hart, Fritz (*b* London, 1874; *d* Honolulu, 1949). Eng. conductor and composer. Studied RCM 1893–6, becoming friend of Holst, Vaughan Williams, and Hurlstone. Became th. cond. and went in 1908 to Australia. Dir., Melbourne Cons. from 1915. Cond. Melbourne S.O. 1928. Prof. of mus., Univ. of Hawaii 1936–42. Cond. Honolulu S.O. 1932–49. Wrote 20 operas, 514 songs, sym. (1934), 3 vn. sonatas, 2 str. qts., and choral works. Style influenced by Eng. folk-song.

Hartig, Heinz Friedrich (*b* Kassel, 1907; *d* Berlin, 1969). Ger. composer. Studied in Kassel, Berlin, and Vienna, and with Blacher. From 1948 cond. mus. for Brecht prods. in Berlin. Teacher at Berlin Hochschule from 1951. Works incl. Mass to text by Dylan Thomas, oratorio *Wohin?* employing tape with conventional forces, chamber opera *Escorial*, and ballet *Das Tor*. Also concs. for pf., for vn., and for guitar, songs with orch., and chamber mus.

Hartmann, Johan Peter Emilius (*b* Copenhagen, 1805; *d* Copenhagen, 1900). Danish composer. Dir., Copenhagen Cons. from 1867. Comp. syms., vn. conc., and several operas, incl. *Ravnen* (The Raven) (1832, text by Hans Christian Andersen).

Hartmann, Karl Amadeus (*b* Munich, 1905; *d* Munich, 1963). Ger. composer. Studied Munich Acad. of Mus. with Joseph Haas, 1923–7, and later with Hermann *Scherchen and *Webern. Works perf. in 1930s but he withdrew from public life because of opposition to Nazi régime. After 1945 organized Musica Viva concerts of new works in Munich. His mus. is very much of its time, with marked polyphonic tendencies and showing traces of such varied influences as Bruckner, Berg, Stravinsky, and Blacher. Comp. 8 syms. (No. 1 for cont. and orch. to text by Whitman) between 1936 and 1962; also 2 str. qts. (1933 and 1945–6), opera *Des Simplicius Simplicissimus Jugend* (Cologne 1949, comp. 1934–5), vn. conc., pf. conc., va. conc.

Hartmann, Rudolf (*b* Ingolstadt, 1900). Ger. opera producer and impresario. Chief resident producer Altenberg 1924, Nuremberg 1928–34 and 1946–52; Berlin State Opera 1934–8. Specially assoc. with cond. Clemens Krauss and operas of R. Strauss at Munich 1938–44 and 1953–67. Author of *Richard Strauss, the Staging of his Operas and Ballets* (Fribourg 1980, Eng. trans. 1981).

Harty, (Sir) (Herbert) **Hamilton** (*b* Hillsborough, Co. Down, 1879; *d* Brighton, 1941). Irish composer, cond., organist, and pianist. Church organist at age 12, later holding posts in Belfast and Dublin. Helped by *Esposito. Settled in London 1900 where he quickly won attention as composer and as brilliant pf. accompanist. Gradu-

ally his conducting took priority. Cond. opera at CG and LSO concerts. Appointed permanent cond. Hallé Orch. 1920, holding post until 1933 and re-establishing orch. as one of finest in Europe. Cond. LSO and other orchs. from 1933. Comps. incl. pf. quintet, *Irish Symphony*, vn. conc., pf. conc., *Ode to a Nightingale* for sop. and orch., sym.-poems *With the Wild Geese* and *The Children of Lir*, cantata *The Mystic Trumpeter* for ch. and orch., also modern orchestrations of Handel's *Water Music* and *Fireworks Music*. Knighted 1925.

Harvey, Jonathan (Dean) (*b* Sutton Coldfield, 1939). Eng. composer and teacher. Cellist in Nat. Youth Orch. Studied Cambridge and Glasgow Univs. and with Erwin Stein and Hans Keller. Impressed Stockhausen at Darmstadt 1966, and studied with *Babbitt 1969–70. On staff, mus. dept., Southampton Univ. 1964–77, Sussex Univ. from 1977 (prof. from 1980). Comps., some of which use tape, incl.:

CHURCH OPERA: *Passion and Resurrection* (1981).

ORCH.: Sym. (1966); *Benedictus* (1970); *Persephone Dream* (1972); *Inner Light III* (1975); *Smiling Immortal* (ballet), chamber orch. and pre-prepared tape (1977); *Whom Ye Adore* (1981); *Bhakti*, chamber ens. and quad. tape (1982); *Easter Orisons*, str. (1983).

INSTR. AND CHAMBER: *Dialogue*, vc. and pf. (1965); *Variations*, vn. and pf. (1965); *4 Images after Yeats*, pf. (1969); *Inner Light I*, instr. and tape (1973); pf. trio (1971); *Round the Star and Back*, pf. and ens. (1974); str. qt. (1977); *Album*, wind quintet (1978); *Be(com)ing*, cl., pf. (1979); *Concelebration*, fl., cl., vc., pf., perc. (1979, rev. 1980); *Modernsky Music*, 2 ob., bn., hpd. (1981); *Curve with Plateaux*, vc. (1982); *Nataraja*, fl., pf. (1983).

VOCAL AND ORCH: *Cantata I* (1965), *Cantata IV—Ludus Amoris*, sop., ten., speaker, ch. and orch. (1969); *Cantata VI*, ch. and str. (1970); *Cantata VII—On Vision*, sop., ten., speaker, chamber group, and tape (1971); *Inner Light II*, vv., ens., and tape (1977); *Hymn*, ch. and orch. (1979).

VOICE AND INSTR: *Angel Eros*, v. and str. qt. (1973); *Cantata II—3 Lovescapes*, sop. and pf. (1967); *Cantata III*, sop. and chamber ens. (1969); *Cantata V—Black Sonnet*, 4 singers and wind quintet (1970); *The Dove Descending*, ch. and org. (1975); *Correspondences*, mez. and pf. (1975); *Cantata X—Spirit Music*, sop., 3 cl., and pf. (1975); *Magnificat and Nunc Dimittis*, ch. and org. (1978); *Resurrection*, ch. and org. (1981).

TAPE: *Time-Points*, magnetic tape (1970); *Veils and Melodies*, 3 prepared tapes (1978); *Mortuos plango, Vivos voco*, computer-manipulated concrete sounds (1980).

UNACC. VOICES: *I Love the Lord* (1976); *O Jesu, Nomen dulce*, motet (1980).

ORGAN: *Toccata*, with pre-rec. tape (1980).

Harvey, Trevor (Barry) (*b* Freshwater, I.o.W., 1911). Eng. cond., critic, and broadcaster. Worked for BBC (ass. ch. master) 1935–42. Free-lance cond. from 1946. Cond. Sir Robert Mayer children's concerts 1951–73, Brit. Youth Orch. 1960–72.

Harwood, Basil (b Woodhouse, Glos., 1859; d London, 1949). Eng. composer and organist. Pupil of Reinecke in Leipzig. Organist, Ely Cath., 1887–92, Christ Church, Oxford, 1892–1909. Composer of org. sonatas and many church anthems, etc.

Harwood, Elizabeth (b Barton Seagrave, 1938). Eng. sop. Studied RMCM 1955–60. Successful career in concert hall and opera house. Won Ferrier Prize 1960. Opera début Glyndebourne 1960. SW 1961–5. CG début 1967 (in *Arabella*). Guest singer at Salzburg, Aix, and Vienna fests. NY Met. début 1976 (Fiordiligi in *Così fan tutte*). Particularly fine Strauss singer.

Háry János (John Háry). Opera in prol., 5 parts, and epilogue by Kodály to lib. by Paulini and Harsányi after poem by Garay. Prod. Budapest 1926, NY 1960, London 1967. Orch. suite of 6 movements drawn from opera f.p. NY 1927, cond. Mengelberg.

Haskil, Clara (b Bucharest, 1895; d Brussels, 1960). Romanian pianist, later Swiss citizen. Studied in Bucharest, Vienna, and at Paris Cons. with Cortot and Fauré, later in Berlin with Busoni. Début Bucharest 1904. Concert career began in 1910. Exponent of classical and early romantic composers.

Hasler. See *Hassler, Hans.*

Hassan, or The Golden Journey to Samarkand. Play by James Elroy Flecker (1884–1915) for the 1st prod. of which in Darmstadt 1923 Delius comp. incid. mus. incl. songs, dances, and choral episodes. The *Intermezzo* and *Serenade* exist in several arrs. and there is a *Suite* arr. Fenby 1933.

Hasse, Johann (Adolph) (b Bergedorf, 1699; d Venice, 1783). Ger. composer. Sang at Hamburg Opera as ten. 1718–19, then at Brunswick where his opera *Antioco* was prod. 1721. Went to Naples 1724, studying with Porpora and A. Scarlatti and writing several popular operas. Married singer Faustina *Bordoni. Dir., Dresden court opera 1731–63, also visiting London and It. Most of his MSS. destroyed in siege of Dresden. Moved to Vienna 1763, composing operas to Metastasio librettos in opposition to Gluck and eventually setting almost all Metastasio's opera texts. Lived in Venice from 1775. Despite nationality, It. by style and inclination. Wrote over 100 operas, also masses, oratorios, sinfonias, etc. Hearing Mozart's *Ascanio in Alba* in 1771 said: 'This boy will cause us all to be forgotten'.

Hasselmans, Alphonse (Jean) (b Liège, 1845; d Paris, 1912). Belg.-born harpist (Fr. citizen from 1903). Prof. of harp, Paris Cons. from 1884. Virtuoso player who composed many pieces for

the instr. His son Louis (b Paris, 1878; d San Juan, Puerto Rico, 1957) was a cellist and cond. Cond. of Fr. repertory at NY Met. 1922–37.

Hassler (Hasler), **Hans** (Leo) (b Nuremberg, 1562; d Frankfurt-am-Main, 1612). Ger. composer and organist. Studied in Venice with A. *Gabrieli. Organist at Augsburg 1586–1600, Nuremberg 1601–08, Dresden from 1608. Wrote It. *canzonette, cantiones sacrae,* madrigals, masses, and motets.

Haubenstock-Ramati, Roman (b Kraków, 1919). Austrian composer (Polish-born). Studied Kraków Univ. Mus. dir., Radio Kraków 1947–50. Dir., state mus. library and prof. of mus., Tel Aviv Acad. Worked at Fr. Radio *musique concrète* studio, 1957. Settled in Vienna 1957–68. Composer of several elec. works. Much concerned with new methods of notation. Organized 1st exhibition of graphic scores, Donaueschingen 1959. Works incl. opera *America* (based on Kafka); Symphony 'K', *Les Symphonies de timbres, Petite musique de nuit, Psalm* for orch., *Nocturnes I and II* for orch., chamber mus., and choral pieces.

Hauer, Josef Matthias (b Wiener Neustadt, 1883; d Vienna, 1959). Austrian composer. Self-taught. Met Schoenberg 1919. In 1919, independently of Schoenberg, developed 12-note system and wrote his first 12-note piece, *Nomos*. Method based on 44 combinations (tropes) of 12 notes of the octave, each subdivided into 6-note groups. Works incl. operas *Die schwarze Spinne* and *Salambo* (comp. 1929, f.p. Vienna 1983), oratorio *Wandlungen,* pf. conc., vn. conc., Hölderlin songs, 3 str. qts. From 1939 all his works bore the title *Zwölftonspiel* (12-note piece).

Haug, Hans (b Basle, 1900; d Lausanne, 1967). Swiss composer and cond. Cond., Swiss Radio orch., Lausanne, 1935–8, Zürich 1938–43. Wrote 8 operas, incl. *Tartuffe* (1937), oratorio *Michelangelo,* sym., vn. conc., pf. conc., guitar conc., 3 str. qts.

Haugtussa (Norweg. The Mountain Maid). Song-cycle for sop. and pf., Op. 67, by Grieg, comp. 1895, being settings of 8 poems by Arne Garborg written in archaic Norweg. and pubd. 1895. The songs are 1. *Det syng* (The Singing), 2. *Veslerny* (Little Maid), 3. *Blaaberri* (Bilberry slopes), 4. *Mote* (Meeting), 5. *Elsk* (Love), 6. *Killingsdans* (Kidlings' dance), 7. *Vond dag* (Evil Day), 8. *Ved gjaetle-bekken* (By the brook).

Hauk, Minnie (orig. Mignon Hauck) (b NY, 1851; d Tribschen, Lucerne, 1929). Amer. mez. Studied New Orleans and NY. Début Brooklyn 1866, CG 1868. First Amer. and London Carmen, but also famous as Norma, Amina, and other *bel canto* roles. Sang at NY Met. 1890–1. Formed own opera co., but after one year retired to live with husband in Wagner's villa Tribschen. After war became blind and poor; supported by funds from Amer. opera enthusiasts.

Haunted Ballroom, The. Ballet in 1 act, mus. and lib. by Geoffrey Toye, choreog. by de Valois. Prod. London 1934.

Hauptstimme (Ger.). Prin. v. or part.

Hauptthema (Ger.). Prin. subject of a comp.

Hauptwerk (Ger., 'chief work'). Great Organ.

Hausegger, Siegmund von (*b* Graz, 1872; *d* Munich, 1948). Austrian composer and cond. Cond. Hamburg Phil. 1910–18, Konzertverein, Munich, from 1920. Dir., Munich Acad. of Mus. 1920–34. Wrote operas, symphonic poems, songs, etc.

Hausmann, Robert (*b* Rottleberode, 1852; *d* Vienna, 1909). Ger. cellist. Pupil of Müller and Piatti. Member of Count Hochberg's qt., Dresden, 1872–6; of Joachim Qt. 1879–1907. Prof. of vc. Berlin Hochschule from 1876. Gave f.p. of Brahms's 2nd vc. sonata, Op. 99, in 1886 and, with Joachim, of Brahms's Double Concerto (Cologne 1887).

Hausmann, Valentin (*fl.* 16th cent.). Ger. organist and composer. Organist at Gerbstädt, near Merseburg. Comp. secular songs, dances, church mus., instr. pieces, etc.

Hautboy. Obsolete Eng. name for *oboe, derived from Fr. *hautbois* ('loud wood') from which the It. *oboe* was derived.

Hautcousteaux. See *Auxcousteaux, Artus.*

Haute Danse (Fr., 'High Dance'). An old general term covering any dance in which the feet were lifted, as distinguished from the *Basse Danse,* in which they were kept close to the floor.

Havanaise (Fr.). Same as *Habañera.*

Hawaiian Guitar. Type of guitar introduced by Portuguese which has distinctive str. tunings. The str. are 'stopped' with a small moveable metal bar which goes across all str., in order to obtain the characteristic portamento effect.

Hawes, William (*b* London, 1785; *d* London, 1846). Eng. composer, cond., and violinist. Chorister, Chapel Royal, 1795–1801. Violinist, CG orch. 1802–5. Gentleman, Chapel Royal, 1805, master of choristers 1817. From 1812, master of choristers, St Paul's Cath. Dir. of Eng. opera at Lyceum Th., 1824–36. Adapted many operas for Eng. stage, incl. Mozart's *Così fan tutte* and *Don Giovanni.* Introduced Weber's *Der Frei-schütz* to Eng., 1824, adding some airs of his own. Wrote glees and madrigals.

Haydn, Franz Joseph (*b* Rohrau, 1732; *d* Vienna, 1809). Austrian-born composer of pure Ger. stock. The son of a farmer-wheelwright, Haydn showed immediate mus. precocity and at the age of 5 was given into the care of a Hainburg schoolmaster called Franck, who taught him the rudiments of mus. At 8 went to Vienna as choirboy at St Stephen's. When his v. broke at 17, he lived in poverty as a teacher and became accompanist and servant to the It. composer and teacher *Porpora. He worked for two aristocratic patrons in 1750s, and in 1761 was engaged as vice-Kapellmeister at Eisenstadt by Prince Paul Esterházy. Haydn remained with the Esterházy household for 30 years, for both Prince Paul and his successor Prince Nikolaus, who reigned from 1762 to 1790, were passionate mus.-lovers. In 1766 Nikolaus built the palace of Esterháza (modelled on Versailles) on the south side of the Neusiedlersee, spending the greater part of each year in this isolated home. Haydn's art benefited from this seclusion. 'There was no one near to confuse me, so I was forced to become original', he said. His duties were numerous; besides administrative work and caring for the court musicians, he cond. the orchestra, arr. and dir. operatic perfs., played in chamber mus., and produced a stream of works in many genres, incl. incidental mus. for plays, to please his patron. Haydn's fame spread from Esterháza throughout Austria, Ger., and It. as his syms. were pubd. Fr. edns. of his works began to appear in the 1760s and later in London. In 1785 he was commissioned by Cadiz to compose an oratorio without words on the Saviour's 7 Last Words, and by the Parisian soc. Concert de la Loge Olympique to compose 6 syms. By this time he had become friends with Mozart, for whom he had the highest admiration. Their works from this date (1781) betray mutual influence. Haydn's life at Esterháza ended in 1790 when Prince Nikolaus died and his successor dismissed the musicians, though leaving Haydn his salary and title. Haydn left the castle for Vienna where he accepted an invitation from the impresario J. P. *Salomon to visit London. He stayed in England from 1 Jan. 1791 to the middle of 1792, being fêted, lionized, and entertained by royalty. He comp. syms. 93–98 on this visit, when he was deeply impressed by the 1791 Handel Fest. in Westminster Abbey. In July 1791 the hon. degree of D.Mus. was conferred on him by Oxford Univ. On his return to Vienna he bought a house there and accepted Beethoven as a pupil, an uneasy relationship for both great men. In 1794 he visited Eng. again, having been commissioned by Salomon to write 6 new syms. This 2nd visit lasted from Feb. 1794 to Aug. 1795 and was even more successful artistically and, especially, financially than the first.

The Esterházy family had now reconstituted their mus. est., but Haydn comp. only for special occasions and was allowed to concentrate on his work as a composer. Between 1796 and 1802 he wrote 6 magnificent settings of the Mass. In 1797 he comp. his *Gott erhalte Franz den Kaiser,* which was adopted as Austria's nat. anthem. But his chief pre-occupation at this time was his oratorio *Die Schöpfung* (The Creation), f.p. privately in Vienna, 1798. This was followed by *Die Jahres-zeiten* (The Seasons), f.p. 1801. From then on,

Haydn's health began to fail and, though he made several more public appearances, he died during the Fr. occupation of Vienna.

If Haydn's life was comparatively uneventful, his vast output of mus. is notable for the number of delights and surprises contained in almost every work. Yet though the number and magnitude of Haydn masterpieces are constantly amazing, his mus. for long failed to exert as powerful a sway over the public as that of Mozart and Beethoven. He is regarded as the 'father' of the sym. (which he was not) and of the str. qt., but some treasurable Haydn lies in his vocal mus., in his oratorios, masses, and in his operas (which are still in process of re-discovery). In all his mus. his inventive flair seems inexhaustible. He delighted in exploiting the capabilities of solo instr. and virtuoso performers, and every genre in which he worked he enlarged, extended, and re-shaped. The syms. are a remarkable example of his development of a particular form, hallmarked by deep feeling, drama, elegance, wit, and, in the final 12, a Mozartian perfection of all these qualities combined. But much the same can be said of the qts. and masses; nor should the kbd. sonatas be overlooked.

The cataloguing of Haydn's works has been the object of considerable scholarship. It was begun in 1766 by Haydn himself, aided by the Esterházy court copyist Joseph Elssler, whose son Johann (1769–1843) later became Haydn's copyist and faithful servant. Haydn worked on this list until about 1805. Pohl prepared a MS. catalogue, and for the Breitkopf and Härtel complete edn. Mandyczewski assembled his list of 104 syms. (omitting 3 now acknowledged as such). Modern scholarship, led by H. C. Robbins *Landon, has amended this list, and a thematic catalogue has been ed. by *Hoboken in which works are given Hob. nos. in the manner of Köchel's Mozart catalogue.

Haydn's works are too numerous to be listed in full detail. The following is a concise list of the prin. comps.:–

OPERAS: 20 were comp., some of the first being lost. The extant 15 incl. *La Canterina* (1766), *Lo Speziale* (1768), *Le Pescatrici* (1769), *L'Infedeltà delusa* (1773), *L'Incontro improvviso* (1775), *Il *Mondo della Luna* (1777), *La vera constanza* (1778), *L'*isola disabitata* (1779), *La fedeltà premiata* (1780), *Orlando Paladino* (1782), *Armida* (1783), *Orfeo ed Euridice* (1791); also 5 puppet operas incl. *Philemon und Baucis* (1773) and *Dido* (1776).

MASSES: No. 1 in F (*Missa brevis*) (1750), No. 2 in Eb (*Grosse Orgelmesse*) (1766), No. 3 in C (*St Cecilia*) (1776), No. 4 in G (1772), No. 5 in Bb (*Kleine Orgelmesse*) (c.1775), No. 6 in C (*Mariazellermesse*) (1782), No. 7 in C (*In tempore belli*— *Paukenmesse*) (1796), No. 8 in Bb (*Heiligmesse*) (1796), No. 9 in D minor (*Nelson*) (1798), No. 10 in Bb (*Theresienmesse*) (1799), No. 11 in Bb (*Schöpfungsmesse*) (1801), No. 12 in Bb (*Harmoniemesse*) (1802). Also Mass in G (c.1750).

CANTATAS AND ORATORIOS: *Stabat Mater* (1767); *Applausus* (1768); *Il Ritorno di Tobia* (1774–5); *Die sieben letzten Worte unseres Erlösers am Kreuz* (The *Seven Last Words of Our Saviour on the Cross, 1st version (str. qt.) 1785, 2nd version 1796); *Die Schöpfung* (The *Creation*) (1797–8); *Die Jahreszeiten* (The *Seasons*) (1798–1801).

SYMPHONIES: Nos. 1–5 (1757); No. 6 in D (*Le *Matin*), No. 7 in C (*Le Midi*), No. 8 in G (*Le soir*) (c.1761); No. 9 in C (c.1762); No. 10 in D (c.1761); No. 11 in Eb (c.1760); No. 12 in E, No. 13 in D (1763); No. 14 in A, No. 15 in D (1764); No. 16 in Bb, No. 17 in F, No. 18 in G, No. 19 in D, No. 20 in C (all before 1766, prob. 1761–2); No. 21 in A, No. 22 in Eb (*The *Philosopher*), No. 23 in G, No. 24 in D (1764); No. 25 in C (c.1761–3); No. 26 in D minor (*Lamentatione*) (c.1770); No. 27 in G (c.1760); No. 28 in A, No. 29 in E, No. 30 in C (*Alleluja*), No. 31 in D (*Horn Signal*) (1765); No. 32 in C, No. 33 in C (c.1760); No. 34 in D minor (c.1766); No. 35 in Bb (1767); No. 36 in Eb (c.1761–5); No. 37 in C (c.1757); No. 38 in C (*Echo*) (c.1766–8); No. 39 in G minor (c.1768); No. 40 in F (1763); No. 41 in C (c.1769); No. 42 in D (1771); No. 43 in Eb (*Merkur*), No. 44 in E minor (*Trauer*) (c.1771); No. 45 in F♯ minor (*Abschied*), No. 46 in B, No. 47 in G (1772); No. 48 in C (*Maria Theresia*) (c.1768–9); No. 49 in F minor (*La *Passione*) (1768); No. 50 in C (1773); No. 51 in Bb, No. 52 in C minor (c.1771–3); No. 53 in D (L'*Impériale*) (c.1780); No. 54 in G, No. 55 in Eb (*Der *Schulmeister*), No. 56 in C (1774); No. 57 in D (1774); No. 58 in F, No. 59 in A (*Feuersymphonie*) (c.1776–8); No. 60 in C (*Il *Distratto*) (1774); No. 61 in D (1776); No. 62 in D, No. 63 in C (*La *Roxolane*) (c.1780); No. 64 in A (c.1775); No. 65 in A (c.1771–3); No. 66 in Bb, No. 67 in F, No. 68 in Bb, No. 69 in C (*Laudon*) (c.1778); No. 70 in D (1779); No. 71 in Bb, (c.1779–80); No. 72 in D (c.1763–5); No. 73 in D (*La *Chasse*) (1780–1); No. 74 in Eb (1780); No. 75 in D (1779); No. 76 in Eb, No. 77 in Bb, No. 78 in C minor (1782); No. 79 in F, No. 80 in D minor, No. 81 in G (1783–4); No. 82 in C (*Bear*) (1786); No. 83 in G minor (*La *Poule*) (1785); No. 84 in Eb (1786); No. 85 in Bb (*La *Reine*) (1785); No. 86 in D (1786); No. 87 in A (1785); No. 88 in G, No. 89 in F (c. 1787); No. 90 in C, No. 91 in Eb (1788); No. 92 in G (*Oxford*) (1789); No. 93 in D, No. 94 in D (*Surprise*), No. 95 in C minor, No. 96 in D (*Miracle*) (1791, London); No. 97 in C (1792, London); No. 98 in Bb (c.1792, London); No. 99 in Eb (1793, Austria); No. 100 in G (*Military*), No. 101 in D (*Clock*), No. 102 in Bb (1794, London); No. 103 in Eb (*Paukenwirbel*, Drum Roll), No. 104 in D (*London*) (1795, London).

CONCERTOS: Vc. in C (c.1765), in D (1783); Klavier in D (c.1784), Klavier and str. in G; hn. No. 1 in D (1762), No. 2 in D (c.1764); 2 hn. and str. in Eb; for *lira organizzata* No. 1 in C, No. 2 in G,

No. 3 in G, No. 4 in F, No. 5 in F (*c*.1786); organ conc. (1756); for tpt. in E♭ (1796); for vn. No. 1 in A, No. 2 in C, No. 3 in G (*c*.1765); for vn., pf., and str. in F (1766); *Sinfonia Concertante* in B♭ for ob., bn., vn., vc. (1792).

STRING QUARTETS: Op. 1 (6 qts., 1760); Op. 2, nos. 7–12 (1755–60); Op. 9 (6 qts., 1771); Op. 17, nos. 25–30 (1771); Op. 20, nos. 31–6 (1772); Op. 33, nos. 37–42 (1781); Op. 42, no. 43 (1758); Op. 50, nos. 44–9 (*c*.1787); Op. 51, nos. 50–6 (1785, 7 *Last Words from the Cross*); Op. 54, nos. 57–9 (*c*.1788); Op. 55, nos. 60–2 (*c*.1788); Op. 64, nos. 63–8 (*c*.1790); Op. 71, nos. 69–71 (1793); Op. 74, nos. 72–4 (1793); Op. 76, nos. 75–80 (*c*.1797); Op. 77, nos. 81–2 (*c*.1799); Op. 103, No. 83 (1802–3).

KEYBOARD: 60 sonatas (*c*. 1761–94), *Variations* in F minor (1793).

CHAMBER MUSIC: 32 pf. trios; 6 sonatas for klavier and vn.; fl. qts; lute qt; divertimentos for str. trio; str. trios; 126 *baryton trios; 32 pieces for mechanical clocks; and *Notturnos* for lira organizzata.

SOLO CANTATAS: *Arianna a Naxos* for mez. (1789); *Berenice che fai* (1795).

VOCAL: Qts. and trios (1796 and 1799); *Alfred—Chorus of the Danes* (1796); 12 Canzonettas to Eng. words for solo v. and pf. (1794–5) incl. *My mother bids me bind my hair, Spirit's Song, Piercing Eyes, She never told her love*; 450 arrs. of Brit. folksongs (1791–1805).

Haydn, (Johann) **Michael** (*b* Rohrau, 1737; *d* Salzburg, 1806). Austrian-born composer, brother of Franz Joseph *Haydn. Chorister, St Stephen's, Vienna, 1745–55, also deputy organist. Court mus. and Konzertmeister to Archbishops of Salzburg 1763 to end of his life. Wrote 40 syms., vn. concs., hn. concs., tpt. conc., hpd.-and-va. conc., fl. concs., str. quartets, operas, masses, and vast amount of other church mus. *Weber and *Diabelli were among his pupils. His *Requiem* in C minor was perf. at his brother's funeral.

'Haydn' Quartets. Name customarily given to set of 6 str. qts. by Mozart (No. 14 in G, K387 (1782), No. 15 in D minor, K421 (1783), No. 16 in E♭, K428 (1783), No. 17 in B♭, *Hunt*, K458 (1784), No. 18 in A, K464 (1785), No. 19 in C, *Dissonanzen*, K465 (1785)), because he ded. them to Haydn, who played 1st vn. in perfs. at Mozart's house. (Mozart played the va.).

Hayes, William (*b* Gloucester, 1707; *d* Oxford, 1777). Eng. composer and organist. Organist, Worcester Cath., 1731–4, Magdalen Coll., Oxford, 1734–42, prof. of mus., Oxford Univ., 1742–77. Comp. cantatas, catches, glees, church mus.

Haym, Hans (*b* Halle, 1860; *d* Elberfeld, 1921). Ger. cond. Studied singing and pf. at Munich. Mus. dir. Elberfelder Gesangverein, 1890. Friend and champion of Delius, cond. f.p. of *Paris* (Elberfeld 1901), unpubd. 1st version (1897) of

pf. conc. (Elberfeld 1904), and f. complete p. in Ger. of *Mass of Life*, 1909.

Haym, Nicola (Francesco) (*b* Rome, 1678; *d* London, 1729). It. cellist, composer, and librettist, of Ger. parentage, who took leading role in establishing It. opera in London. Played violone in private orch. in Rome under Corelli 1694–1700. From 1701 to 1711 was in London as chamber musician to Duke of Bedford. Played cello in orch. when Clayton's *Arsinoe* was first all-sung opera in It. style to be given at Drury Lane. Wrote lib. for Handel's *Teseo* (1713) and *Radamisto* (1720) and between 1723 and 1728 wrote 8 more libs. for him, viz. *Ottone, Flavio* (1723), *Giulio Cesare, Tamerlano* (1724), *Rodelinda* (1725), ? *Admeto* (1727), *Siroe, Tolomeo* (1728). From 1718 was string bass player in service of Duke of Chandos at Cannons, playing in Handel oratorios. Comp. oratorios, anthems, etc.

Head, Michael (Dewar) (*b* Eastbourne, 1900; *d* Cape Town, 1976). Eng. composer, singer, and pianist. Prof. of pf. RAM, from 1927. Comps. incl. cantata, light operas, works for ob., and many songs (in which he acc. himself).

Headington, Christopher (John Magenis) (*b* London, 1930). Eng. composer, pianist, and writer. Studied at RAM, later with L. Berkeley. Joined BBC mus. staff 1964. Comps. incl. pf. preludes, pf. sonatas, vn. conc., 2 str. qts., song-cycles, etc.

Head Voice. Method of vocal tone prod. in high register, so called because singer experiences sensation of v. vibrating in the head.

Hear my Prayer (*Hör mein Bitten*). Hymn by Mendelssohn for sop. solo, choir, and org. (also orch.) comp. 1844 for Bartholomew's concerts in Crosby Hall, London, where f.p. 1845.

Heart of Oak (*not* 'Hearts of Oak'). This bold patriotic song comes from a pantomime, *Harlequin's Invasion*, written by Garrick in 1759, the mus. being supplied by *Boyce. It is a topical song, alluding to 'this wonderful year' (the victories of Minden, Quiberon Bay, and Quebec).

Heart's Assurance, The. Song-cycle for high v. and pf. by *Tippett on poems by Sidney Keyes and Alun Lewis. Commissioned by Peter Pears. Comp. 1950–1. F.p. London 1951 (Pears and Britten).

Heather. See *Heyther, William*.

Hebden, John (*fl.* 1740–50). Eng. cellist, bassoonist, and composer. Prin. cellist in London th. orchs. Comp. 6 concerti grossi for str. which were ed. R. Wood in 1980 and revived, after 200 years of neglect, by the Scottish ens. Cantilena. Also wrote 6 solos for fl. and continuo.

Hebrides, The (Mendelssohn). See *Fingal's Cave*.

Hecht, Eduard (*b* Durkheim, 1832; *d* Manchester, 1887). Ger. composer, cond., and teacher. Went to Paris 1851; settled Manchester 1854, becoming chorus-master of Hallé Choir and ass. cond. of Hallé's concerts. Cond. of several Manchester choral socs. Lecturer, Owens Coll. (now Univ.) from 1875. Comp. sym., cantatas, str. qts., songs.

Heckel, Johann Adam (*b* Adorf, 1812; *d* Biebrich, 1877). Ger. instr-maker. Founded own firm at Biebrich, 1831. Worked on improvements to bn. and cl. Son Wilhelm (1856–1909) invented *heckelphone 1904.

Heckelclarina. Rare type of cl. invented by Ger. firm of Heckel expressly for shepherd's pipe part in Act 3 of Wagner's *Tristan und Isolde* (cor anglais is usually preferred).

Heckelphone. Bass ob. (octave lower than ob.) made by Ger. firm of Heckel in 1904. Used by R. Strauss in *Salome* and *Elektra* and by Delius, as 'bass oboe' in *Dance Rhapsody No. 1, Fennimore and Gerda, Songs of Sunset, Arabesk,* and *Requiem.*

Hedges, Anthony (John) (*b* Bicester, 1931). Eng. composer, pianist, writer, and teacher. Studied Oxford and RAM. Lecturer RSAM 1957–62, Hull Univ. from 1962 (senior lecturer from 1967). Comps. incl. opera, orch. mus., choral works, anthems, chamber mus., partsongs, and ballet.

Hedley, Arthur (*b* Newcastle upon Tyne, 1905; *d* Birmingham, 1969). Eng. scholar and writer. Studied Durham Univ. and Paris Sorbonne. Specialist in mus. of Chopin, about whom he wrote book and many articles.

Heel. That end of the bow of a str. instr. at which it is held, as distinguished from the other end, which is called 'point'.

Heger, Robert (*b* Strasbourg, 1886; *d* Munich, 1978). Ger. composer and cond., studied with Schillings in Munich. Cond. début Strasbourg 1907; opera cond. Nuremberg 1913–21, Vienna 1925–33, Berlin 1933–50, Munich from 1950. Cond. many times at CG 1925–35, esp. operas of Strauss, and cond. f. Brit. p. of Strauss's *Capriccio* 1953. Comp. 5 operas, incl. *Lady Hamilton* (1951), 3 syms., vn. conc., vc. conc., cantatas, and songs.

Heifetz, Jascha (*b* Vilna, Lithuania, 1901). Russ.-born violinist (Amer. citizen from 1925). Lessons at 3 from father, public début in Vilna at 5. Entered St Petersburg Cons. at 8 as pupil of *Auer. While still student played concs. with Berlin P.O. under Nikisch, and in Vienna and Leipzig. Family went to USA 1917, where Heifetz made début in that year. Thereafter worldwide reputation as among very greatest violinists. Commissioned Walton conc., 1939. In later years played principally in chamber mus.

Heiligmesse (Holy Mass). Popular name, derived from the special treatment of the words 'Holy, holy' in the Sanctus, for Haydn's 8th Mass in B♭, 1796.

Heiller, Anton (*b* Vienna, 1923; *d* Vienna, 1979). Austrian composer, organist, and harpsichordist. Prof. of org., Vienna Acad. 1945. Composer of chamber sym., 5 masses, radio ballad *François Villon*, etc.

Heinze, (Sir) **Bernard** (Thomas) (*b* Shepparton, Victoria, 1894; *d* Sydney, N.S.W., 1982). Australian cond. and teacher. Studied Melbourne Univ., RCM, in Paris under *d'Indy, and in Berlin with Willy *Hess. Returned to Australia 1923. Prof. of mus., Melbourne Univ., 1925–57, dir. State Cons., N.S.W. 1957–66. Cond. Melbourne S.O. 1933–49. Knighted 1949.

Heldenleben, Ein (A Hero's Life). Orch. tone-poem, Op. 40, by R. Strauss. Comp. 1897–8, f.p. 1899 in Frankfurt (though ded. to Mengelberg and Concertgebouw Orch. of Amsterdam). In the 5th of the 6 sections, the 'Hero's Works of Peace', Strauss quotes from several of his own comps.

Heldentenor (Ger., 'heroic tenor'). Ten. with powerful v. of wide range capable of such parts as Huon in Weber's *Oberon*, Bacchus in Strauss's *Ariadne auf Naxos*, and most of the Wagner ten. parts.

Helffer, Claude (*b* Paris, 1922). Fr. pianist. Pupil of R. Casadesus until 1939. After war studied harmony and comp. with Leibowitz. Début Paris 1948. Specialist in 20th-cent. pf. mus., having given f.ps. of works by Amy. Has recorded complete solo pf. music of Schoenberg, also works by Boulez and Barraqué.

Helicon. Form of bass tuba made so that it may be wrapped round the player's body and rest on the shoulder (useful when played on the march). So called because of helical (spiral) shape. Largely displaced by modified version, *Sousaphone.

Heliogabalus Imperator. Tone-poem ('allegory for music') by Henze (1972) after Enzensberger. F.p. Chicago (cond. Solti) 1972.

Heller, Stephen (*b* Pest, 1813; *d* Paris, 1888). Hung. pianist and composer. Studied in Vienna. Settled in Paris 1838. Friend of Liszt, Chopin, Hallé, and Berlioz. Visited Eng. 1850 and 1862. Wrote well over 100 short pf. pieces and items of chamber mus.

Hellertion. Elec. instr. developed in Frankfurt in 1936 by Bruno Helberger and Peter Lertes. Similar to *theremin, but with a guide kbd. and pedals to regulate vol. and tone-quality. Range of nearly 6 octaves, capable of 4-part harmony, and able to simulate human v. and some instrs. Played by pressure on 4 leather bands stretched across front, which sets up a current.

Hellflöte (Ger.). Clear flute (an org. stop).

Helliwell, Clifton (*b* Farnworth, 1907). Eng. pianist and teacher. BBC mus. staff as accompanist 1929–61; staff of RMCM 1961–72; head of kbd. studies RNCM 1972–8.

Hellmesberger, Joseph (*b* Vienna, 1828; *d* Vienna, 1893). Austrian violinist, cond., and teacher. Father and brother were also violinists. Pupil of father. Cond., Vienna Gesellschaft concerts 1851–9, prof. of vn., Vienna Cons. 1851–77, dir., Vienna Cons. 1851–93. Founder and leader, Hellmesberger Qt., 1849–91.

Hellmesberger, Joseph (*b* Vienna, 1855; *d* Vienna, 1907). Austrian violinist and composer, son of above. 2nd vn. in Hellmesberger Qt. from 1875, succeeding as leader 1891. Prof. of vn., Vienna Cons. from 1878. 2nd cond., Vienna Opera 1899. Cond. Vienna P.O. 1901–3. Court cond. Stuttgart 1904–5. Comp. 10 operettas.

Helm, Everett (*b* Minneapolis, 1913). Amer. composer and writer. Studied at Harvard Univ. with W. Piston and H. Leichtentritt. Later had comp. lessons from *Malipiero (1936–7) and Vaughan Williams (1937–8). In 1941 worked with Milhaud at Mills Coll. Holder of various teaching posts. Active as mus. critic from 1948. Works incl. opera, sym. for str., 2 pf. concs., 2 str. qts., 2 pf. sonatas, db. conc., etc.

Helmholtz, Hermann (Ludwig Ferdinand) **von** (*b* Potsdam, 1821; *d* Charlottenburg, 1894). Ger. authority on acoustics (also medical man and prof. of physiology at various univs.). Most famous work is *Sensations of Tone* (1863, Eng. trans. by A. J. Ellis, 1875).

Heltay, László (István) (*b* Budapest, 1930). Brit. cond. of Hung. birth. Studied at Liszt Acad., Budapest, with Kodály and Bárdos. On staff Budapest Radio 1952–6. Left for Eng. 1956. Founded Schola Cantorum, Oxford, 1960. Brit. cit. 1962. Dir. of mus., Merton Coll., Oxford, 1962–4. Ass. cond. New Zealand B.C. S.O. 1964–6. Dir. of mus., Gardner Centre, Sussex Univ. from 1968. Founded Brighton Fest. Chorus.

Hely-Hutchinson, (Christian) **Victor** (*b* Cape Town, 1901; *d* London, 1947). S. African-born composer, cond., pianist, and administrator. Studied RCM and as pupil of Tovey. On BBC staff from 1926, becoming head of mus., Midlands Region (Birmingham) from 1933. Prof. of mus., Birmingham Univ. 1934–44. Dir. of mus., BBC, 1944–7. Works incl. *A Carol Symphony*, pf. quintet, va. sonata, and settings of Edward Lear's *Nonsense Songs*.

Hemidemisemiquaver (♬). The 64th note (i.e. 1/64th of a semibreve in value).

Heming, Percy (*b* Bristol, 1883; *d* London, 1956). Eng. bar. Studied RAM and with *Henschel, later in Dresden with Grose. Opera début, London 1915 in Gounod's *Roméo et Juliette*. Prin. bar. BNOC from 1922. SW 1933–5. Ass. art. dir.

(to Beecham), CG 1937, art. dir. CG Eng. Co. 1937–9. Art. adviser, CG 1946–8. Notable Amfortas, Scarpia, etc.

Hemiola or **Hemiolia**. This rhythmic device consists of superimposing 2 notes in the time of 3, or 3 in the time of 2, e.g.:

A rhythmic device much used in cadential progressions by composers up to and including the baroque period.

Hemmings, Peter (William) (*b* Enfield, 1934). Eng. administrator and singer. Ed. Cambridge Univ. Repertory, planning man., SW Opera 1959–65, gen. man. New Opera Co. 1957–65; gen. administrator Scottish Opera 1962–77; dir. Australian Opera 1977–80. Man. dir. LSO 1981–4. Dir. Los Angeles Opera from 1984.

Hempel, Frieda (*b* Leipzig, 1885; *d* Berlin, 1955). Ger. sop. Entered Leipzig Cons. as pianist, going to Stern Cons., Berlin, on decision to become singer. Début Breslau, then Berlin 1905 and Schwerin 1905–7. Berlin Opera 1907–12. London début CG 1907, NY Met. 1912. 1st Berlin and NY Marschallin in *Der Rosenkavalier*, 1911 and 1913. Retired from opera 1921 (Chicago), continuing to give concerts.

Hemsley, Thomas (Jeffrey) (*b* Coalville, 1927). Eng. bar. Stage début London 1951 as Aeneas to Flagstad's Dido. Prin. bar., Aachen Opera 1953–6, Deutsche Oper-am-Rhein 1957–63, Zürich opera 1963–7. Glyndebourne from 1953, Bayreuth 1968–70, guest singer CG, Scottish Opera, ENO etc. Notable Beckmesser. Also sings in oratorio, cantatas, Lieder recitals, etc.

Henderson, Roy (Galbraith) (*b* Edinburgh, 1899). Scottish bar. Studied RAM. Début Queen's Hall, London, 1925. Opera début CG 1929 as Donner in *Rheingold*. Member Glyndebourne co. 1934–9 (Papageno, Almaviva, etc.). Noted in concert and recital work. Retired 1952. Prof. of singing RAM 1940–74. Private pupils incl. Kathleen *Ferrier. Cond. of several choirs, incl. Nottingham Oriana Choir 1936–52. C.B.E. 1970.

Henry, Pierre (*b* Paris, 1927). Fr. composer. Studied Paris Cons. 1937–47. Comp. pupil of Messiaen and Boulanger. Dir., Groupe de Recherches de Musique Concrète, Fr. Radio, 1950–8, working with Pierre *Schaeffer. Founded 1st private elec. studio in Fr. at Apsome, 1958. Works incl. *Le Voile d'Orphée* (1953), *La Reine verte* (1963), *Messe de Liverpool* (1967), *Gymkhana* (1970), all with elecs.

Henry VIII (*b* Greenwich, 1491; *d* Windsor, 1547). Eng. king (from 1509). Talented musician and composer. Attrib. to him are 17 songs, several pieces for viols, masses, and motets. The anthem *O Lord, the Maker of All Things,* however, is not by Henry, as was long supposed, but by W. Mundy.

Henry VIII. (1) Opera in 4 acts by Saint-Saëns to lib. by Détroyat and Silvestre. Prod. Paris 1883, CG 1898.

(2) Incidental mus. to Shakespeare's play by Sullivan, 1878, and by *German, 1892.

Henry Watson Music Library. Prin. mus. library in Manchester, part of the corporation's Central Reference Library. Basis was coll. of 5,000 books and many more scores handed over in 1899 by Henry Watson (*b* Burnley, 1846; *d* Salford, 1911), organist, cond., and teacher at RMCM, to Manchester Corporation and since greatly expanded.

Henschel, (Sir) **George** (orig. Isidor Georg) (*b* Breslau, 1850; *d* Aviemore, Scotland, 1934). Ger.-born bar., pianist, cond., and composer. Brit. citizen from 1890. Public début as pianist, Berlin 1862. Leipzig Cons. 1867–70. Sang Hans Sachs in concert perf. of *Die Meistersinger,* Munich 1868. Berlin Royal Cons. 1870–4. London début 1877. 1st cond. Boston S.O. 1881–4. Prof. of singing, RCM 1886–8. Cond., London Symphony Concerts 1886–96. Cond. Scottish Orch. 1891–5. Acc. himself as singer. Continued to broadcast and record until past 70. Comp. 3 operas, str. qt., choral works, songs, etc. Knighted 1914.

Henselt, Adolf von (*b* Schwabach, Bavaria, 1814; *d* Warmbrunn, Silesia, 1889). Ger. pianist and composer. Pupil of Hummel (pf.) at Weimar and of Sechter (comp.) at Vienna. Went to St Petersburg 1838, becoming court pianist and teacher of Royal family. No tours after 1838 yet acclaimed as one of greatest pianists. Comp. pf. conc., 2 sets of 12 Studies, pf. pieces, etc.

Hen, The (Haydn). See *Poule, La.*

Hen Wlad fy Nhadau. See *Land of my Fathers.*

Henze, Hans Werner (*b* Gütersloh, Westphalia, 1926). Ger. composer and cond. Studied at Brunswick State Mus. Sch. 1942–4, Heidelberg 1946. Studied privately with *Fortner, 1946–8. Studied Schoenberg's 12-note system with *Leibowitz at Darmstadt 1948. Mus. dir. Hessian State Opera's ballet, Wiesbaden, 1950. Settled in Italy 1953. Politically Henze moved in the 1960s to the extreme Left and many of his works after that date reflect revolutionary ideals and dogmas. Henze's mus. style is bewilderingly diverse, reflecting his fertile imaginative gifts and his refusal to be 'tied down' by formulae. As much a Fr. or It. composer as a Ger. one, he can adopt at will Schoenbergian, Stravinskyan, or aleatory styles. Sensuous lyricism, rich and delicate tone-colours, and easy mastery of choral writing are among the prin. features of his work. Prin. works:

OPERAS AND MUSIC THEATRE: *Das Wundertheater* (1-act, after Cervantes, for actors and orch., 1948;

new version for singers 1964); *Boulevard Solitude (1951); *König Hirsch (1952–5; reduced version as *Il Re Cervo,* 1962); *Der *Prinz von Homburg* (after Kleist) (1958); *Elegy for Young Lovers (1959–61); *Der *junge Lord (1964); *Das ende eine Welt* (1964, stage version of radio opera, 1953); *Ein Landarzt* (1964, stage version of radio opera, 1951); *The *Bassarids (1965); *Moralities* (3 scenic cantatas to Auden text, 1967); *Der langwierige Weg in die Wohnung der Natascha Ungeheuer* (The Tedious Way to the Place of Natasha Ungeheuer) (1971); *La Cubana* (vaudeville, 1973); *We Come to the River (1974–6); *Don Chisciotte della Mancia* (version of Paisiello, 1976); *Pollicino* (children's opera, 1979); *Il Ritorno di Ulisse in Patria* (realization of Monteverdi, 1980–2); *The English Cat* (lib. by E. Bond) (1983).

RADIO OPERAS: *Ein Landarzt* (Kafka) (1951); *Das Ende einer Welt* (1953).

BALLETS: *Ballett-Variationen* (1949, *Suite* 1949); *Rosa Silber* (1950, *Suite* 1950); *Maratona* (1956, *Suite* 1956); *Undine (1956–71, 2 Suites 1958); *Tancredi* (1964 rev. of *Pas d'action* 1952, *Suite* 1952); *Orpheus* (1978).

CHAMBER BALLETS: *Jack Pudding* (1949, *Suite* 1949); *Die schlafende Prinzessin* (arr. of Tchaikovsky for small orch. 1951); *Labyrinth* (1951, choreog. fantasy for orch. 1950); *Der Idiot* (1952); *Des Kaisers Nachtigall* (after Andersen, 1959, *Suite* 1959).

INCIDENTAL MUSIC: *Der tolle Tag* (Beaumarchais) (1951); *Les Caprices de Marianne* (Musset/Ponnelle) (1962); *Der Frieden* (Aristophanes/Hacks) (1964).

ORCH.: Syms.: No. 1 (for chamber orch. 1947, rev. 1963), No. 2 (1949), No. 3 (1949–50), No. 4 (1955), No. 5 (1962), No. 6, for 2 chamber orch. (1969), No. 7 (1982–4); *Symphonic Interludes from Boulevard Solitude* (1953); *Quattro Poemi* (1955); *Antifone* (1960); *Los Caprichos* (1963); *Symphonic Interludes from Der junge Lord* (1964); *3 Symphonic Studies* (1955–64); *The Hunt of the Maenads* (from *The Bassarids*) (1965); *Telemanniana* (1967); *Heliogabalus Imperator (1971–2); *Tristan, preludes for pf., orch., tape (1973); *Ragtimes and Habañeras,* brass band (1975); *Suite from Pollicino* (1979); *2 Dramatic Scenes from Orpheus* (1979); *Barcarola* (1983).

CHAMBER ORCH: *Sinfonie* (1947, rev. for full orch. as Sym. No. 1, 1963); *Symphonic Variations* (1950); *Sonata for Strings* (1957–8); *3 Dithyrambs* (1958); *4 Fantasies* (3 movts. from *Chamber Music 1958* with new *Adagio*), 8 instr. (1963); *In memoriam: Die weisse Rose* (1965); *Fantasia für Streicher* (1966, from film mus. for *Der junge Törless*); *Fragments from a Show* (from *Natasche Ungeheuer*), hn., 2 tpt., tb., tuba (1971); *Suite from film mus. Katharina Blum* (1975); *Amicizia,* cl., tb., vc., pf., perc. (1976); *Aria de la folia española,* orch., also chamber orch. (1977); *Apollo trionfante,* wind, perc., db. (1979); *Arien des Orpheus,* guitar, hp., hpd., str. (1979); *Canzona,* ob., 3 vas., vc., pf., hp. (1982); *I Sentimenti di Carl*

P. E. Bach (transcr. of *Fantasia* for pf. and vn., 1787), fl., hp., str. (1982); *Cinque piccoli concerti* (interludes from *The English Cat*), 8 instr. (1983); *Sonata* for 6 (1984).

CONCERTOS: Chamber Conc., pf., fl., str. (1946); vn. conc. No. 1 (1947), No. 2, vn., bass-bar., 33 instr., tape (1971); concertino, pf., wind, perc. (1947); pf. conc. No. 1 (1950), No. 2 (1967); *Jeux des Tritons* (from *Undine*), pf., orch. (1956–7/ 1967); *Ode to the West Wind*, vc., orch. (1953); *Concerto per il Marigny*, pf., 7 instr. (1956); Double Conc., hp., ob., str. (1966); db. conc. (1966); *Compases para preguntas ensimismadas*, va., 22 players (1969–70); *Il Vitalino raddoppiato*, vn., chamber orch. (1977); *Musik*, vc., chamber orch. (1977); *Le Miracle de la Rose*, cl., 13 instr. (1981).

VOICE AND INSTR: *Ein Landarzt*, monodrama, bar., orch. (1951–64, see also RADIO OPERA); *Whispers from Heavenly Death* (Whitman), high v., 8 instr. (or pf.) (1948); *The Reproach* (*Der Vorwurf*) (Werfel), aria for bar., tpt., tb., str. (1948); *Apollo and Hyacinth*, alto, 9 instr. (1949); *5 Neopolitan Songs*, mez. or bar., chamber orch. (1956); *Nocturnes and Arias, sop., orch. (1957); *Chamber Music 1958* (Hölderlin), ten., guitar, 8 instr. (1958); *3 Hölderlin Fragments*, v., guitar (1958); *Ariosi* (Tasso), sop., vn., and orch. (or pf. 4 hands) (1963); *Being Beauteous* (Rimbaud), coloratura sop., hp., 4 vc. (1963); *Essay on Pigs*, bar., chamber orch. (1968); *El Cimarrón*, bar., fl., guitar, perc. (1969–70); *Voices* (22 songs), mez., ten., 15 instr. (1973); *The King of Harlem*, mez., instr. ens. (1979); *3 Auden Poems*, v., pf. (1982–3).

CHORAL: *5 Madrigals*, ch., 11 instr. (1947); *Lullaby of the Blessed Virgin*, boys' ch., 9 instr. (1948); *Chorus of the Captured Trojans* (from Goethe's *Faust II*), ch., orch. (1948, rev. 1964); *Novae de Infinito Laudes*, cantata, 4 solo vv., ch., small orch. (1962); *Cantata della Fiaba Estrema*, sop., small ch., 13 instr. (1963); *Choral Fantasia* (Bachmann), chamber ch., tb., 2 vc., db., org., perc., timp. (1964); *Muses of Sicily*, conc. for ch., 2 pf., wind, timp. (1966); *Das *Floss der Medusa*, oratorio for sop., bar., speaker, ch., 9 boys' vv., orch. (1968); *Jephte* (realization of Carissimi's oratorio, 1650), 3 sop., alto, ten., 2 bass, 6 vv., instr. (wind, hp., perc., guitar, banjo, mandolin) (1976); *Canzoni für Orpheus*, unacc. ch. (1980).

CHAMBER MUSIC: Str. Qts.: No. 1 (1947), No. 2 (1952), No. 3 (1975–6), No. 4 (1976), No. 5 (1976); vn. sonata (1946); sonatina, fl., pf. (1947); *Chamber Sonata*, pf., vn., vc. (1948, rev. 1963); *Serenade*, vc. (1949); *Quintet*, fl., ob., cl., hn., bn. (1952); *3 Tentos* (from *Chamber Music 1958*), guitar (1958); *Der junge Törless*, fantasia (after work for str. orch.), str. sextet (1966, trans. of *Fantasia für Streicher*); *Memorias de El Cimarrón*, guitar (1970); *Carillon, Récitatif, Masque*, mandolin, guitar, hp. (1974); *Royal Winter Music* (2 sonatas on Shakespearean characters), guitar (1975–6 and 1979); *L'Autunno*, wind quintet, fl.,

cl., ob., hn., bn., with interchangeable instr. (1977); va. sonata (1979); *Capriccio*, vc. (1983).

KEYBOARD: *Variations*, pf. (1949); pf. sonata (1959); *Lucy Escott Variations*, pf. or hpd. (1963); *6 Absences*, hpd. (1961); *Divertimenti*, 2 pf. (1964); *Toccata senza Fuga* from *Orpheus*, org. (1979); *Euridice*, hpd. (1981).

Heptatonic. Scale or mode based on seven pitches to the octave.

Herabstrich (Ger.). Down-bow, in vn. and va. playing. **Heraufstrich** is up-bow.

Herbage, Julian (Livingston) (*b* Woking, 1904; *d* London, 1976). Eng. musicologist and writer. Career in th. before joining BBC 1927–46 (ass. dir. of mus. 1940–6). Helped to plan and produce Promenade concerts until 1961. Ed. and cond. works by Locke, Purcell, Bach, Arne, and Handel. Wrote books and essays on Handel's *Messiah*, Sibelius, Bax, and Tchaikovsky. With wife Anna Instone (*b* Cardiff, 1912; *d* London, 1978), presented BBC's weekly *Music Magazine* on radio 1944–73.

Herbert, Victor (*b* Dublin, 1859; *d* NY, 1924). Irish-born (Amer. citizen) composer, cond., and cellist. Studied Stuttgart Cons.; prin. cellist Stuttgart court orch. 1883–6. Went to USA 1886, becoming prin. cellist, NY Met. orch., and in other orchs. Also appeared as soloist and cond. military bands. First operetta, *Prince Ananias* (NY 1894) was success and was followed by over 30 others, incl. *Naughty Marietta* (1910) and *Sweethearts* (1913). Wrote 2 operas, *Natoma* (1911) and *Madeleine* (1914). Cond., Pittsburgh S.O. 1898–1904. Also comp. symphonic poem *Hero and Leander*, 2 vc. concs., *Irish Rhapsody*. etc.

Herbig, Günther (*b* Ústí nad Labem, Cz., 1931). Cz.-born Ger. cond. Studied at Weimar State Acad. of Mus. Cond. Dresden P.O. 1972–7, Berlin S.O. 1977–83. Eng. début 1973, London. Chief guest cond., BBC Northern S.O. (now BBC Philharmonic) 1980–4. Cond. Detroit S.O. from 1984.

Herman, Woody (Woodrow Charles) (*b* Milwaukee, 1913; *d* Los Angeles, 1987). Amer. jazz saxophonist, clarinettist, and composer. Formed own band 1936, re-formed 1946, 1947 and 1950. Worldwide tours. Comps. incl. *Blues in the Night* and *At the Woodchoppers' Ball*. Stravinsky wrote his *Ebony Concerto for him, 1945.

Hérodiade (Herodias). Opera in 4 acts by Massenet to lib. by P. Milliet and 'H. Grémont' (G. Hartmann) after story by Flaubert (1877). Prod. Brussels 1881, New Orleans 1892, London 1904 (under title *Salome*).

Hérold, (Louis Joseph) **Ferdinand** (*b* Paris, 1791; *d* Les Ternes, Paris, 1833). Fr. composer. Entered Paris Cons. 1806, studying with Adam and Méhul. *Grand Prix de Rome* 1812. 1st opera prod.

Naples 1815. Returned to Paris 1815, composing 12 operas and several ballets in 14 years. Gained biggest success with *Zampa (1831) followed by Le Pré aux Clercs (1832). Among his ballets were La *Fille Mal Gardée (1828) and La Belle au Bois dormant (1829). Also comp. 2 syms., 3 str. qts., 4 pf. concs., and pf. pieces.

Herrmann, Bernard (b NY, 1911; d Hollywood, 1975). Amer. composer and cond. Studied Juilliard Sch. of Mus. under B. Wagenaar. Foundercond. New Chamber Orch. 1931–4. Mus. dir. CBS 1934–40, cond.-in-chief CBS S.O. 1942–59. Champion of Ives's mus. and also of Eng. composers—not only Elgar and Vaughan Williams, but Rubbra, Brian, Bax, Cecil Gray, and Cyril Scott. Also an enthusiast for Raff. Lived in London for several months each year. Wrote successful scores for Orson Welles and Hitchcock films. His opera Wuthering Heights and other comps. have an expressive and lyrical warmth which compensate for some lack of originality. Comps. incl.:

OPERA: *Wuthering Heights (1940–52).
ORCH: Sym. No. 1 (1940); vn. conc. (1937); For the Fallen (1943); Suite, The *Devil and Daniel Webster (1941); *Welles Raises Kane (1942); Sinfonietta, str. (1935).
CHORAL: *Moby Dick, cantata for 2 ten., 2 basses, ch. and orch. (1936–8); Johnny Appleseed (1940).
CHAMBER MUSIC: Echoes for str. qt. (1932); Aubade (1933).
FILMS: Citizen Kane, The Devil and Daniel Webster, The Snows of Kilimanjaro, The Magnificent Ambersons, Jane Eyre, Marnie, Psycho, Jason and the Argonauts, Beneath the Twelve-Mile Reef, Fahrenheit 451.

Herstrich (Ger.). A bow movement towards the player, i.e. the down stroke in vc. and db. playing. See also Hinstrich.

Hertel, Johann Wilhelm (b Eisenach, 1727; d Schwerin, 1789). Ger. violinist and composer. Studied with F. *Benda. Kapellmeister at Schwerin from 1754. Wrote 36 sym., several conc., pf. sonatas, etc.

Hertz, Alfred (b Frankfurt, 1872; d San Francisco, 1942). Ger.-born cond. Studied at Hoch Cons., Frankfurt. Début Halle 1891. Held various cond. posts in Ger.; in 1902 went to USA (becoming Amer. citizen). Cond. of Ger. opera at NY Met. 1902–15, during which time he cond. f. stage p. of *Parsifal outside Bayreuth in 1903, thereby infringing Bayreuth copyright and ensuring that no Ger. opera house again employed him. Cond. 1st US perfs. of Strauss's Salome and Rosenkavalier and f.p. of several Amer. operas. Cond. CG 1910. Cond. San Francisco S.O. 1915–29. First to conduct at Hollywood Bowl, July 1922.

Herunterstimmen (Ger.). 'To tune down' a str. to (nach) a specified note.

Herunterstrich (Ger.). Down-bow in vn. and va. playing.

Hervé (pen-name of Florimond Ronger) (b Houdain, 1825; d Paris, 1892). Fr. composer, singer, and organist. Pupil of Auber. Org., St Eustache, Paris, 1845–53. Cond. several th. orchs. in Paris and appeared as singer and actor, sometimes in his own works. Wrote over 100 operettas, incl. Don Quixote et Sancho Pança, Le Petit Faust, and Cléopâtre. Cond. at Empire Th., London, from 1886. Also wrote 'heroic symphony' The Ashanti War (London 1874).

Herz, Henri (Heinrich) (b Vienna, 1803; d Paris, 1888). Austrian composer and pianist. Studied Paris Cons., becoming prof. of pf. there 1842–74. Worldwide tours as pianist and soloist in his own works (incl. 8 concs.). Est. pf. factory in Paris. Contrib. to *Hexameron.

Herzogenberg, Heinrich von (Baron von Herzzogenberg-Peccaduc) (b Graz, 1843; d Wiesbaden, 1900). Austrian pianist and composer. Pupil of Dessoff at Vienna Cons. Dir., Bach-Verein, Leipzig, 1875—85. Prof. of comp. Berlin Hochschule für Musik 1885. Dir., Meisterschule für Komposition, Berlin, 1888–92 and 1897–1900. Wrote 3 syms., 3 oratorios, mass, requiem, chamber mus., etc.

Hes (Ger.). The note B♭. (Usually, however, the Germans call this note B; see H above.)

Heseltine, Philip. See Warlock, Peter.

Hess, (Dame) **Myra** (b London, 1890; d London, 1965). Eng. pianist. Studied at GSM and, from 1902, at RAM with Tobias *Matthay. Début 1907, London (Beethoven 4th conc., cond. Beecham). Thereafter one of England's leading pianists, especially in mus. of Schumann, Beethoven, Mozart, and Bach. Her transcription of chorale from Bach's church cantata No. 147 under title 'Jesu, joy of man's desiring' was immensely popular. During World War II, founded and dir. series of lunchtime recitals at Nat. Gallery, London, which played important role in sustaining morale. C.B.E. 1936, D.B.E. 1941.

Hess, Willy (b Mannheim, 1859; d Berlin, 1939). Ger. violinist. Lived in USA 1865–72, making début with Theodore *Thomas Orch. Studied in Berlin with *Joachim 1876–8. Leader, opera orch., Frankfurt, 1878–86. Prof. of vn., Rotterdam Cons. 1886–8. Leader, Hallé Orch. 1888–95; prof of vn. RMCM 1893–5, Cologne Cons. 1895–1903 (also leader of Cologne Gürzenich Concerts and Qt.), RAM 1903–4. Leader, Boston S.O. 1904–10. Prof. of vn. Berlin Hochschule 1910–28 and leader of Halif Qt., Darmstadt 1931–3.

Heuberger, Richard (Franz Joseph) (b Graz, 1850; d Vienna, 1914). Austrian composer, cond., and critic. Cond. Vienna Singakademie 1878–81, Männergesangverein 1902–9. Mus. critic in

Munich and Vienna 1881–1901. Prof., Vienna Cons. from 1902; ed. of various periodicals. Comp. 3 operas, sym., cantata, partsongs, and 6 operettas incl. *Der *Opernball* (The Opera Ball, 1898),

Heure espagnole, L' (The Spanish Hour). Opera (*comédie musicale*) in 1 act by *Ravel to lib. based on his own comedy by Franc-Nohain. Comp. 1907–9. Prod. Paris 1911, London 1919, Chicago 1920.

Heward, Leslie (Hays) (*b* Liversedge, 1897; *d* Birmingham, 1943). Eng. cond. and composer. Chorister, Manchester Cath., 1910, ass. organist 1914. Studied RCM 1917. Mus. dir., Westminster Sch. 1920. Cond. opera for BNOC. Mus. dir. S. African Broadcasting Corporation and cond. Cape Town Orch., 1924–7. Cond. CBSO 1930–43.

Hexachord. A group of 6 consecutive notes regarded as a unit for purposes of singing at sight—somewhat as the octave is in 'movable-doh' systems. It was introduced (or perfected) by *Guido d'Arezzo in the 11th cent. and was still widely current up to the 17th.

There were 3 different Hexachords, the *Hard* one beginning on G, the *Natural* one beginning on C, and the *Soft* one beginning on F. It will be realized that these overlapped in their range, and that a singer reading a piece of mus. might have to pass from one to another if its compass extended beyond one of those sets of 6 notes.

The names of the notes were taken from the opening syllables of 6 lines of a Lat. hymn, which syllables happened to ascend a degree with each succeeding line. These names were *Ut, Re, Mi, Fa, Sol,* and *La.* Letter names were also then in use for the notes, but these were *absolute* names, as they are still, whereas the hexachordal names were *relative* to the group in use at the moment, as their successors the modern Tonic sol-fa names are relative to the *key in use at the moment: the Sol-fa system (on its pitch side) may, indeed, be looked upon as a modernization of the hexachordal system, which served well in the period of simple modal mus. (see *Modes*) but was incapable of application to the increasing complexities of a key system.

To the Hexachords Guido added the device of The Guidonian Hand.

In the 20th cent. the term is applied to a coll. of 6 pitch classes considered either simultaneously or as a succession, esp. in reference to segments of 12-note rows. Unconnected with medieval term.

Hexameron (Six Days). 6 variations for pf. on march from Bellini's *I Puritani*, each written by a different composer-pianist — Liszt, Thalberg, Pixis, Herz, Czerny, and Chopin — with introduction, connecting links, and finale by Liszt. F.p. Paris charity concert 1837, the composers sitting at a pf. apiece and each playing his own variation. Liszt later added orch. acc. and played whole series at recitals.

Hexatonic. Mode or scale based on system of six different pitches to the octave, as in *Whole-tone scale.

Heyther (Heather), **William** (*b* Harmondsworth, *c*.1584; *d* Westminster, 1627). Eng. musician. Gentleman of Chapel Royal from 1615. Founded mus. lecture at Oxford Univ. 1626–7.

Heyworth, Peter (Lawrence Frederick) (*b* NY, 1921). Amer.-born Eng. mus. critic. Studied Balliol Coll., Oxford. Mus. critic of the London *Observer,* from 1955. Biographer of *Klemperer.

Hiawatha. Cantata in 3 parts by *Coleridge-Taylor, text from Longfellow's poem of this title. Part 1, *Hiawatha's Wedding Feast,* f.p. London 1898, Part 2, *The Death of Minnehaha,* f.p. Hanley 1899, Part 3, *Hiawatha's Departure,* f.p. London 1900 (as part of f. complete p. of trilogy). Frequently perf. in pageant form.

Hidalgo, Elvira de (*b* Aragón, 1892; *d* Milan, 1980). Sp. sop. Début Naples 1908 as Rosina in Rossini's *Il barbiere di Siviglia*. Début NY Met. 1910, BNOC 1924. Became teacher at Athens (pupils incl. *Callas), and Ankara.

Hidden Fifths (or Octaves). The progression in similar motion of 2 parts to perfect 5th (or octave) from such an interval in the same 2 parts in the previous chord, so that a pedant might find a 5th (or octave) in intermediate hiding (e.g. C-G in ten. and sop. proceeding to A-E in next chord).

Hildegard of Bingen (*b* Bemersheim, 1098; *d* Rupertsberg, 1179). Ger. abbess, mystic, and writer. Took veil at 15. Became superior at Benedictine monastery of Disibodenberg 1136. *C*.1147 founded monastery on the Rupertsberg, near Bingen, Rhine Valley. Wrote lyrical poetry from 1140, setting it to her own mus., much of it of strong individuality and complexity. She collected it together in 1150s under title *Symphonia armonie celestium revelationum*. Her morality play, *Ordo Virtutum*, a kind of pre-opera, representing the struggle for the soul between 16 virtues and the devil, contains 82 melodies. Edn. of her mus., ed. by J. Gmelch, pubd. Düsseldorf 1913.

Hill, Alfred (*b* Melbourne, 1870; *d* Sydney, N.S.W., 1960). Australian cond., composer, violinist, and teacher. Studied at Leipzig Cons., playing in Gewandhaus Orch. Settled in N.Z. where he collected Maori mus., using it in his comps. Prof. of harmony and comp., N.S.W. Cons. 1915–35. Works incl. 8 operas, 10 syms., cantata *Hinemoa, Maori Rhapsody,* 17 str. qts., songs, etc. O.B.E 1953, C.M.G. 1960.

Hill, Thomas (Henry) **Weist** (*b* London, 1828; *d* London, 1891). Eng. violinist and cond. Pupil of Sainton at RAM. First to play Mendelssohn conc. in USA. 1st Prin., GSM 1880–92.

Hill & Son, W. Firm of London org.-builders, later W. Hill & Son & Norman & Beard. Founded

1755 by John Snetzler. William Hill became partner in 1825, firm changing name to his in 1838. Built orgs. in York Minster, Ely, Worcester, and Manchester Caths., Birmingham Town Hall, etc.

Hill & Sons, W. E. London firm of vn. makers and dealers founded by Joseph Hill (1715–84).

Hillbilly Songs. The traditional songs (largely of European origin) of the primitive peoples of the mountain regions (e.g. Appalachians) of the S.-E. parts of the USA.

Hiller, Ferdinand (*b* Frankfurt, 1811; *d* Cologne, 1885). Ger. pianist, cond., and composer. Pupil of Hummel, with whom he visited Beethoven on his deathbed, 1827. Lived in Paris 1828–35; 1st to play Beethoven's 5th pf. conc. in Paris. Held cond. posts in Frankfurt, Düsseldorf, and Cologne. Founded Cologne Cons., 1850, becoming dir. until 1884. Cond. of It. opera in Paris 1852–3. Wrote 6 operas, 2 oratorios, 3 syms., 3 pf. concs., vn. conc., cantatas, chamber mus., and pf. pieces.

Hiller (Hüller), **Johann Adam** (*b* Wendisch-Ossig, 1728; *d* Leipzig, 1804). Ger. composer. Studied in Dresden and Leipzig. Settled in Leipzig 1758, becoming cond. of several organizations. Regarded as founder of the *Singspiel, which he based on the Ger. *Lied*. First of these was *Der Teufel ist los* (The Devil is at large), 1766, followed by 11 others. Also wrote church mus.

Hiller, Lejaren (*b* NY, 1924). Amer. composer. Had lessons at Princeton Univ. from Sessions and Babbitt. Worked as research chemist; experimented in composition with computers, collaborating with Leonard Isaacson with whom in 1957 he produced *Illiac Suite* (named after the computer). This was first computer-composition. Dir., experimental mus. studio, Illinois Univ. 1958–68; prof of comp., State Univ. of NY, Buffalo, from 1968. Works incl. pf. conc. (1949); *Computer Cantata* (1963); *7 Electronic Studies* (1963); *Rage over the Lost Beethoven* (1972); many works for stage, films, and television.

Hilton, John (*b* *c*.1560; *d* Cambridge, 1608). Eng. composer and organist (Trinity Coll., Cambridge). Wrote anthems and madrigals, later incl. *Fair Oriana, Beauty's Queen* in The *Triumphs of Oriana*.

Hilton, John (*b* ?Cambridge, 1599; *d* London, 1657). Eng. composer and organist (St Margaret's, Westminster), son of above. Comp. church mus., Ayres of *ballett type, etc., and 'Catch that Catch Can', coll. of rounds, canons, and catches (1625).

Himmel, Friedrich Heinrich (*b* Treuenbrietzen, 1765; *d* Berlin, 1814). Ger. composer. Studied Dresden and in It. Court Kapellmeister, Berlin, 1795. Visited Russia, England, and Austria. Wrote operas and operettas (Ger. and It.), sym., pf. conc., and church mus. incl. anthem *Incline Thine Ear*.

Hindemith, Paul (*b* Hanau, 1895; *d* Frankfurt, 1963). Ger.-born composer, cond., violist, and teacher. Studied comp. at Hoch Cons., Frankfurt, 1913–17, under Arnold Mendelssohn and Bernhard Sekles, and vn., va., and cond. under F. Bassermann. Became 1st violinist in Frankfurt Opera orch. 1915 and Rebner Qt. Served in Ger. Army 1917–19, but continued to compose and to play in str. qt. Returned to opera orch. Left Rebner Qt. 1921. Two 1-act operas, *Mörder, Hoffnung der Frauen* and *Das Nusch-Nuschi* were cond. by Fritz Busch, Stuttgart 1921 and by Ludwig Rottenberg (whose daughter, Gertrud, Hindemith married in 1924) in Frankfurt 1922 (with a 3rd opera *Sancta Susanna*). These works, later disowned as prentice pieces, had a *succès de scandale*. His 2nd str. qt. was perf. Donaueschingen 1921, by qt., with Hindemith as violist, led by Licco Amar. This led to the permanent est. of the Amar Qt., which played only modern works. Hindemith left the Frankfurt Opera orch. in 1923, concentrating on his work with the Amar Qt. and as a member of the selection committee for Donaueschingen fests.

In 1927 Hindemith became teacher of comp. at Berlin Hochschule für Musik. Among his pupils were Franz *Reizenstein, Walter *Leigh, and Arnold *Cooke. Also working in Berlin were 2 conds. who had championed Hindemith's mus., *Furtwängler at the Phil. and *Klemperer at the *Kroll Opera. In 1929, because of pressure of work, Hindemith disbanded the Amar Qt. His satirical opera *Neues vom Tage* (News of the Day) was prod. in Berlin under Klemperer in summer 1929 (the 1st opera to incl. a sop. singing in her bath); and his cantata *Lehrstück*, to a text by Brecht, created a scandal at the 1929 Baden-Baden Festival. In Oct. 1929 Hindemith made his 1st visit to London, where he was soloist in the f.p. of *Walton's va. conc., having met Walton at Salzburg in 1923.

In 1933, the year Hitler came to power, Hindemith began work on an opera on the subject of the painter Matthias Grünewald, a medieval artist with a social conscience. He arr. 3 interludes as a suite, which he called the *Mathis der Maler* (Matthias the Painter) Sym. These were performed by the Berlin P.O. under Furtwängler in Mar. 1934 and were an immediate success. But official criticism of his mus. now began to be voiced publicly. (Hitler had once been shocked by the sop.-in-the-bath scene in *Neues vom Tage*.) Furtwängler wrote an article in Nov. 1934 defending Hindemith and opposing his 'political denunciation'. As a result of the ensuing controversy, the Nazis forbade prod. of the *Mathis* opera. In 1935 Hindemith accepted an invitation from Turkey to est. a mus. sch. On his return from Ankara, he found the régime friendlier towards him and a Frankfurt première for *Mathis* seemed possible. But in 1936, after 'demonstrative' applause for *Kulenkampff's playing of the new vn. sonata, Goebbels banned all further perfs. of

Hindemith's mus. After a further spell in Turkey in 1937, Hindemith resigned from the Berlin Hochschule and sailed for NY. In May 1938 *Mathis der Maler* was staged in Zürich, but mention of the event was forbidden in Ger. newspapers. In Feb. 1940 he again sailed for the USA, this time to stay indefinitely. He was appointed visiting prof. of the theory of mus. at Yale Univ., and also was head of advanced comp. at the Berkshire summer fest. at Tanglewood, where his pupils in 1940 incl. Lukas *Foss and Leonard *Bernstein. In 1945 he became an Amer. citizen. He returned to Europe in 1947, visiting Italy, Holland, Belgium, Eng., Ger., Austria, and Switzerland where he renewed friendship with Furtwängler. In 1949–50 he spent a year at Harvard Univ. as Norton Prof., giving the Charles Eliot Norton lectures, later pubd. as *A Composer's World*. In 1951 he accepted a teaching post at Zürich Univ., dividing his time with his duties at Yale, but in 1953 resigned from Yale and returned to Europe, conducting Beethoven's 9th Sym. at the 1953 Bayreuth Fest.

Hindemith is invariably associated with the term *Gebrauchsmusik* (utility mus.) but this is a misleading and drab name for his attitude to his art, which was that audiences should participate as well as listen. In his Berlin teaching days, therefore, he comp. works which could be used for teaching and would also provide material for amateurs. His title for this type of work was *Sing-und Spielmusik* (Music to Sing and Play). Examples are his children's opera *Wir bauen eine Stadt* (Let's Build a Town—echoed years later by Britten in *Let's Make an Opera*)—and *Plöner Musiktag* (A Day of Music in Plön), which is a series of instr. and choral pieces written for schoolchildren in Schleswig-Holstein.

Like his friend Walton, Hindemith began as an *enfant terrible* and ended by being regarded by the *avant-garde* as an ultra-conservative. He rejected the extremist methods of the *avant-garde* (but this did not prevent him from writing for an early elec. instr., the *trautonium). His early works show the influences of Strauss and Reger, succeeded by Stravinsky and Bartók. As his style developed, his rhythmic drive and partiality for contrapuntal textures grew more evident, coupled with a reticent lyricism. This lyricism grew more evident at the time of *Mathis der Maler*, while his harmonic idiom was based on well-controlled dissonant tensions. Tonality was the firm basis of all his comps. The severe reaction against his mus., which eventually slackened, was as unjust as it was unthinking. The best of his mus. occupies an important place in the history of 20th-cent. comp. Prin. works:

OPERAS: *Mörder, Hoffnung der Frauen* (Murder, the Hope of Women), 1-act, text by Kokoschka, Op. 12 (1919); *Das *Nusch-Nuschi*, 1-act, text by Blei, Op. 20 (1920); *Sancta Susanna*, 1-act, text by Stramm, Op. 21 (1921); **Cardillac*, Op. 39 (1926, new version 1952); **Hin und Zurück*, Op. 45a (1927); **Neues vom Tage* (1928–9, new version 1953); **Mathis der Maler* (1933–5); *Die *Harmonie der Welt* (The Harmony of the World), (1956–7); *The *Long Christmas Dinner* (*Das lange Weihnachtsmahl*) (1960). Also realization of Monteverdi's *Orfeo* (1943).

THEATRE PIECES: *Tuttifäntchen*, mus. for children's Christmas play (1922); *Lehrstück* (Lesson on Consent), cantata to text by Brecht (1929); *Wir bauen eine Stadt*, children's opera (1930).

BALLETS: *Der Dämon*, Op. 28 (1922); **Nobilissima Visione* (1938); *Hérodiade* (1944).

CHORUS AND ORCH: *Das Unaufhörliche* (The Perpetual), oratorio for sop., ten., bar., and bass, ch. and orch., text by G. Benn (1931); Requiem **When Lilacs Last in the Dooryard Bloom'd* (text by Whitman) for mez., bar., ch., and orch. (1946); *Ite, angeli veloces* (Go, flights of angels), cantata to text by Claudel in 3 parts: I, *Triumphgesang Davids*, for alto, ten., ch., orch., wind band, and spectators (1955), II, *Custos quid de nocte*, for ten., ch., and orch. (1955), III, *Cantique de l'espérance*, for mez., ch., orch., wind band, and spectators (1953); *Mainzer Umzug*, sop., ten., bar., ch., and orch. (1962).

ORCH: *Lustige Sinfonietta*, Op. 4 (1916); Dance Suite, *Das Nusch-Nuschi*, Op. 20 (1921); *Concerto for Orchestra*, Op. 38 (1925); *Concert Music* for pf., brass, and harps, Op 49 (1930); *Concert music* for str. and brass, Op. 50 (1930); *Philharmonic Concerto* (1932); Sym., **Mathis der Maler* (1934); *Symphonic Dances* (1937); Suite **Nobilissima Visione* (1938); *The *Four Temperaments*, theme and vars. for str. and solo pf. (1940, perf. as ballet 1944); Sym. in E♭ (1940); **Symphonic Metamorphosis of Themes by Carl Maria von Weber* (1940–3); *Symphonia Serena* (1946); *Sinfonietta* in E (1949–50); Sym. in B♭ for concert band (1951); Sym. *Die *Harmonie der Welt* (1951); *Pittsburgh Symphony* (1958); *March* (1960).

**KAMMERMUSIK SERIES: No. 1 for small orch. Op. 24 (1922); *Kleine Kammermusik* for wind quintet Op. 24 No. 2 (1922); No. 2 (pf. conc. with 12 instr.) Op. 36 No. 1 (1924), No. 3 (vc. conc. with 10 instr.) Op. 36 No. 2 (1925), No. 4 (vn. conc.) Op. 36 No. 3 (1925), No. 5 (va. conc.) Op. 36 No. 4 (1927), No. 6 (va. d'amore conc.) Op. 46 No. 1 (1927), No. 7 (organ conc.) Op. 46 No. 2 (1927).

CONCERTOS (besides those above): *Concert Music* for va. and large chamber orch., Op. 48 (1930); *Concert Piece* for trautonium and str. (unpubd.) (1931); *Der *Schwanendreher*, for va. and small orch., based on folk-songs (1935); **Trauermusik* for va. and str. (1936); Vn. Conc. (1939); Vc. Conc. (1940); Pf. Conc. (1945); Cl. Conc. (1947); Hn. Conc. (1949); Conc. for woodwinds, harp, and orch. (1949); Conc. for tpt., bn., and str. (1949); Organ Conc. (1962).

VOICE AND ORCH: *Die *junge Magd*, 6 Trakl songs for cont., fl., cl., str. qt., Op. 23 No. 2 (1922); *Das *Marienleben*, 15 Rilke songs for sop. and pf., Op. 27 (1922–3; rev. version 1948, begun 1936; version with orch. Nos. 1–4 1938, Nos. 5–6 1959); *Die Serenaden*, cantata for sop., ob., va., vc., Op. 35 (1924).

CHAMBER MUSIC: 3 *Pieces* for vc. and pf., Op. 8 (1917); Str. Qt. No. 1, Op. 10 (1918), No. 2, Op. 16 (1920), No. 3, Op. 22 (1921), No. 4, Op. 32 (1923), No. 5 (1943), No. 6 (1945); Vn. sonata in E♭, Op. 11 No. 1, in D, Op. 11 No. 2 (1918); Va. sonata in F, Op. 11 No. 4, for solo va. Op. 11 No. 5, vc. sonata Op. 11 No. 6 (1919); solo va. sonata Op. 25 No. 1, va. d'amore sonata Op. 25 No. 2, solo vc. sonata Op. 25 No. 3, va. sonata (unpubd.) Op. 25 No. 4 (1922); cl. quintet Op. 30, solo va. sonata (unpubd.) Op. 31 No. 4, *Canonic sonata* for 2 fl. Op. 31 No. 3 (1923); sonatas for solo vn. Op. 31 Nos. 1 and 2 (1924); str. trio Op. 34 (1924); 3 Pieces for cl., tpt., vn., db., pf. (1925); trio for pf., va., heckelphone (or tenor saxophone) Op. 47 (1929); 14 *Easy Duets* for 2 vn. (1931); str. trio (1933); Scherzo for va. and vc. (1934); vn. sonata in E (1935); fl. sonata (1936); bn. sonata, 3 *Easy Pieces* for vc. and pf.; qt. for cl., vn., vc., pf.; ob. sonata (1938); va. sonata in C, vn. sonata in C, cl. sonata, harp sonata, tpt. sonata (1939); cor anglais sonata, tb. sonata, *A Frog he went a-courting*, vars. for vc. and pf. (1941); sax. sonata (1943); vc. sonata, septet for wind instr. (1948); db. sonata (1949); sonata for 4 hn. (1952); tuba sonata (1955); octet (1957–8).

PIANO: *Tanzstücke*, Op. 19 (1920); *Suite 1922* (1922); *Klaviermusik*, Op. 37 (part I 1925, Part II 1926); Mus. for film *Vormittagsspuk* for player-pf. (unpubd.) (1928); pf. sonata No. 1 in A, No. 2 in G, No. 3 in B♭ (1936); sonata (4 hands) (1938); sonata for 2 pf. (1942); *Ludus Tonalis* (1942).

ORGAN: Organ sonatas Nos. 1 and 2 (1937), No. 3 (1940).

VOCAL: 8 Lieder for sop. and pf., Op 18 (1920); 6 *Songs on Old Texts*, unacc. ch., Op. 33 (1923); 4 3-part choruses for boys (1930); 2 *Hölderlin Songs* (1933); 4 *Hölderlin Songs* (1935); 5 *Songs on Old Texts*, unacc. ch. (rev. version to Eng. texts of 6 Songs, 1923, Nos. 1, 2, 3, and 6, with new song *Wahre Liebe*, 1937); 3 *Choruses* for male vv., 6 *Chansons* for ch., *Variations on an Old Dance Song* for male vv. (1939); *La Belle Dame Sans Merci* for v. and pf., 7 Songs to Eng. texts (1942); *Sing on There in the Swamp*, v. and pf. (1943); *To music* (1944); *Apparebit repentina dies*, ch. and brass (1947); 2 Songs to words by Oscar Cox for v. and pf. (1955); 12 *Madrigals* for ch. (1958); Mass for unacc. ch. (1963). 13 *Motets* for sop. or ten. and pf. (comp. in following order: No. 8 (1940–41), No. 13 (1943), Nos. 2 and 11 (1944), Nos. 5 and 7 (1958), Nos. 3, 4, 6, 9, 10 (1959), Nos. 1 and 12 (1960).

COMMUNAL AND EDUCATIONAL MUSIC: *Spielmusik* for str., fls., obs., Op. 43, No. 1; *Lieder für Singkreise* (Songs for Group Singing) for unacc. ch., Op. 43 No. 2 (1926); *Schulwerk für Instrumental-Zusammenspiel* (Educational Music for Instrumental

Ensembles) for str., Op. 44 (1927); *Sing-und Spielmusik für Liebhaber und Musikfreunde* (Music to Sing and Play, for Amateurs and Music-lovers), Op. 45, *Frau Musica* for 2 solo vv., ch. and str., Op. 45 No. 1 (1928, as *In Praise of Music* 1943); *Plöner Musiktag* (1932).

BOOKS: *The Craft of Musical Composition (Unterweisung im Tonsatz)* Vol. I, *Theoretical* (1935-7), Vol. II, *Exercises in 2-part writing* (1938–9), Vol. III, *3-part Writing* (posth.); *A Concentrated Course in Traditional Harmony* (1942–3); *Elementary Training for Musicians* (1945–6); *A Composer's World: Horizons and Limitations* (Norton Lectures, Harvard 1949–50; pubd. in Eng. 1950, in Ger. as *Komponist im seiner Welt*, 1953); *Johann Sebastian Bach, Heritage and Obligation* (Frankfurt Lecture, 1950).

Hindemith, Variations on a Theme of. Orch. work by *Walton comp. 1962–3 to commission by Royal Phil. Soc. for its 150th anniversary concert. Theme is from 2nd movement of Hindemith's vc. conc. (1940) and 7th var. quotes 4 bars from *Mathis der Maler*. F.p. London 1963, cond. composer.

Hingston, John (*d* London, 1688). Eng. composer and organist. In choir of York Minster, 1618, and possibly pupil of O. Gibbons. Organist to Cromwell 1654–8. From 1660 keeper of orgs. to Charles II. Purcell was his apprentice in 1673.

Hinrichsen, Max (*b* Leipzig, 1901; *d* London, 1965). Ger.-born publisher. Joint man. dir. Peters Edition, Leipzig, 1931–7. Went to London 1937, founding Peters Edition, London, and Hinrichsen Edition. Contributed valuably to revival of early Eng. organ and choral mus. Authority on J. S. Bach.

Hinstrich (Ger., 'away-stroke'). The up-bow on vc. and db. (see also *Herstrich*).

Hin und Zurück (There and Back). Opera (*Sketch mit Musik*) in 1 act by *Hindemith to lib. by M. Schiffer based on Eng. revue sketch. Prod. Baden-Baden 1927. Tanglewood 1940, London 1958. The plot and, in part, the mus. go into reverse at the half-way point.

Hipkins, Alfred (James) (*b* London, 1826; *d* London, 1903). Eng. pianist and scholar, authority on ancient instrs. In 1840 joined firm of *Broadwood & Sons, London. Tuned Chopin's pfs. in Eng. 1848. One of first to revive study of hpd. and clavichord. Wrote books about them. Left coll. of instrs. to RCM. Also expert on standard of pitch.

Hirt (Ger.). 'Herd', 'Herdsman'. *Hirtenlied*, 'Herdsman's Song', etc.

Hirt auf dem Felsen, Der (Schubert). See *Shepherd on the Rock, The.*

His (Ger.). The note B♯. *Hisis*, the (probably theoretical) note B♯♯.

Hislop, Joseph (*b* Edinburgh, 1884; *d* Lundin Links, 1977). Scot. ten. and teacher. Studied Stockholm, making début at Royal Opera 1914, before further study in It. Début CG 1920 as Rodolfo in *La Bohème*. Distinguished operatic career. Taught at RAM and GSM and in Stockholm (1936–49).

Histoire du Soldat, L' (The Soldier's Tale'). Work in 2 parts by Stravinsky 'to be read, played, and danced'. Comp. 1918 to Fr. text by C. F. Ramuz based on Russ. tale. Orch. of 12 instrs., 2 speaking parts, 2 danced parts (no singers). Prod. Lausanne 1918, NY 1928, London (concert 1920). Also suite of 8 movements with orig. orch. or of 5 movements for vn., cl., and pf. (Lausanne 1919).

Histoires naturelles (Natural histories). Song-cycle for v. and pf. by Ravel to poems by Jules Renard, comp. 1906, f.p. Paris 1907. 1. *Le Paon* (The Peacock), 2. *Le Grillon* (The Cricket), 3. *Le Cygne* (The Swan), 4. *Le Martin-pêcheur* (The kingfisher), 5. *La Pintade* (The guinea-fowl). Orch. version by M. Rosenthal.

Hitschiriki. Japanese instr. like a bamboo fl., with 7 finger-holes and 2 thumb-holes. Shrill tone.

Hityokin. Japanese vertical fl. made of bamboo.

H.M.S. Pinafore, or The Lass that loved a Sailor. Comic opera by Sullivan to lib. by Gilbert. Prod. London (Opéra Comique), Boston, and San Francisco 1878; NY and Philadelphia 1879.

Hob. Abbreviated prefix to nos. in the *Hoboken catalogue of Haydn's works.

Hoboe (Hoboy). Name sometimes given to the *oboe.

Hoboken, Anthony van (*b* Rotterdam, 1887; *d* Zürich, 1983). Dutch musicologist. In 1927 founded Vienna nat. archive of photographs of mus. MSS. Compiler of definitive catalogue of Haydn's works, 1st vol. appearing 1957. Works are given 'Hob.' nos., followed by Roman numeral and Arabic figure, e.g. Hob IV. 6.

Hobrecht. See *Obrecht, Jacob.*

Hochschule, Berlin. In full the Staatliche Akademische Hochschule für Musik, formerly the Royal High School for Mus. Founded 1869, with Joachim as dir.

Hochzeit des Camacho, Die (The Wedding of the Camacho). Comic opera in 2 acts by Mendelssohn, Op.10, to lib. based on an episode in *Don Quixote*. Comp. 1825, prod. Berlin 1827.

Hochzeitsmarsch (Ger.). Wedding March.

Hocket ('hiccough'; Lat. *hoquetus*, Fr. *hoquet*, It. *ochetto*). Device in medieval vocal mus. whereby rests were inserted into vocal parts, even in the middle of words, to intensify expressive effect.

Hoddinott, Alun (*b* Bargoed, 1929). Welsh composer. Studied Univ. Coll., S. Wales, and with A. *Benjamin. Lecturer, Cardiff Coll. of Mus. and Drama 1951. Lecturer, Univ. Coll., S. Wales, 1959–65, Reader 1965–7, Prof. of Mus. since 1967. Arnold Bax Medal 1957. C.B.E. 1983. Comps. are strongly structured, romantic in feeling, and deeply serious. Serialist technique used without strict formal adherence. Prin. works:

OPERAS: *The Beach of Falesá* (3 acts, lib. by Glyn Jones based on story by R. L. Stevenson, prod. Cardiff 1974); *The Magician* (1 act, lib. by John Morgan, prod. Cardiff 1976 — previously as *Murder the Magician* on TV 1976); *The *Rajah's Diamond* (1978–9) (1 act, lib. by Myfanwy Piper, prod. TV 1979); *The Trumpet Major* (3 acts, lib. by Myfanwy Piper based on T. Hardy, 1981).

ORCH: Syms., No. 1 (1955), No. 2 (1962), No. 3 (1968), No. 4 (1969), No. 5 (1973), No. 6 (1984); *Fugal Overture* (1953); *Nocturne* (1953); *Serenade for Strings* (1958); *4 Welsh Dances* (1958); *Folk-Song Suite* (1962); Ovs., *Jack Straw* (1964), *Pantomime* (1966); *Variants* (1966); *Night Mus.* (1967); *Sinfoniettas*, No. 1 (1968), No. 2 (1969), No. 3 (1970), No. 4 (1971); *Concerto Grosso No. 1* (1965), No. 2 (1966); *Fioriture* (1968); *Divertimento* (1969); *Investiture Dances* (1969); *The Sun, the Great Luminary of the Universe* (1970); *Aubade* (1972); *The Hawk is set free* (1972); *The Floore of Heav'n* (1973); *Landscapes* (1975); *Lanterne des Morts* (1981).

CONCERTOS: Cl. (1954); harp (1958); pf., No. 1 with wind and perc. (1960), No. 2 (1969), No. 3 1966); va. (1958); vn. (1961); organ (1967); hn. (1969); ob. (1971); *Aubade and Scherzo*, hn. and str. (1965); *Nocturne and Dance*, harp and orch. (1959); *Nocturnes and Cadenzas*, vc. and orch. (1969); *Ritornelli*, tb., wind, and perc. (1974); *The Heaventree of Stars*, vn. and orch. (1980); *Doubles*, ob., hpd., str. (1982).

CHORAL: Cantata *Dives and Lazarus*, sop., bar., ch., and orch. (1965); *Black Bart*, ballad, ch. and orch. (1969); *Eryri*, ch. and orch. (1969); *4 Welsh Folk Songs*, vv. and orch. or pf. (1965); *The Tree of Life*, sop., ten., ch., organ, and orch. (1971); cantata *Sinfonia Fidei*, sop., ten., ch., and orch. (1977).

CHAMBER MUSIC: Str. qt. (1966); pf. quintet (1972); septet (1956); sextet (1960); divertimento for ob., cl., hn., bn. (1963); vn. sonatas, No. 1 (1969), No. 2 (1970), No. 3 (1971), No. 4 (1976); harp sonata (1964); cl. sonata (1967); vc. sonata No. 1 (1970), No. 2 (1977); hn. sonata (1971); suite for harp (1967); pf. trio (1981).

PIANO: Sonatas, No. 1 (1959), No, 2 (1962), No. 3 (1965), No 4 (1966), No. 5 (1968), No. 6 (1972).

SONGS: *A Contemplation Upon Flowers*, 3 songs for sop. and orch. (1976); *Landscapes*, 5 songs for high v. and pf. (1975); *Roman Dream*, scena for sop. and instr. ens. (1968); *Ancestor Worship*, songcycle (1972).

Hodgson, Alfreda (*b* Morecambe, 1940). Eng. mez. Studied at Northern Sch. of Mus., Manchester, first as cellist. Début Liverpool 1961, London 1963. Several appearances in opera, but mainly heard in oratorio, Mahler, Elgar, etc.

Hodie (Lat. 'On this day'). Christmas cantata for mez., ten., bar., boys' vv., ch., and orch. by Vaughan Williams, f.p. Worcester 1954. Orig. title *This Day (Hodie)*, the composer preferring *Hodie*, which has been generally adopted. Text, selected by composer, incl. settings of words from Bible, Milton, Herbert, Hardy, Drummond, Coverdale, Ballet, and Ursula Vaughan Williams.

Hoengen, Elisabeth (*b* Gevelsberg, 1906). Ger. mez. Studied Berlin Univ. and Hochschule. Opera début Wuppertal 1933. Düsseldorf opera 1935–40, Dresden 1940–3, Vienna State Opera from 1943. Sang at CG, London, 1947, 1959–60. NY Met. 1951–2. Teacher at Vienna Acad. 1957–60. Specialist in dramatic roles (Herodias, Ortrud, etc.).

Høffding, Finn (*b* Copenhagen, 1899). Danish composer. Studied under Joseph Marx. Teacher of comp., Copenhagen Cons. 1931, prof. 1949, dir. 1954. Works incl. 5 operas, incl. *The Emperor's New Clothes*, after Andersen, 4 syms., ob. conc., 2 str. qts., wind quintet, ob. sonata.

Hoffman, Grace (*b* Cleveland, Ohio, 1925). Amer. mez. Studied Manhattan Sch. of Mus., NY, and in It. Member of Zürich Opera. 1953–5. Bayreuth 1957–70. NY Met. 1958. CG début 1959 (Eboli).

Hoffman, Irwin (*b* NY City, 1924). Amer. cond. and violinist. Studied Juilliard Sch. Cond. Vancouver S.O. 1952–64, ass. cond. Chicago S.O. 1964–70, cond. Belg. Radio and TV S.O. 1972–6.

Hoffman, Ludwig (*b* Berlin, 1925). Ger. pianist. Studied Vienna, Berlin, and Cologne. Début Cologne 1953. He served on many int. pf. competition juries.

Hoffmann, Bruno (*b* Stuttgart, 1913). Ger. player of and composer for *Glass armonica. Début London 1938 when he revived Mozart's quintet (K617). His name for the instr. is 'glass harp'.

Hoffmann, E(rnst) **T**(heodor) **A**(madeus) (orig. Wilhelm, but adopted name Amadeus in homage to Mozart) (*b* Königsberg, 1776; *d* Berlin, 1822). Ger. writer, mus. critic, composer, and cond. Had mus. lessons while studying law. Was th. cond. from 1808 at Bamberg, Leipzig, and Dresden. Comp. 10 operas, incl. *Undine* (Berlin 1816), ballet, sym., mass, pf. sonatas, etc. Best known for his essays and tales, which have remarkable bizarre humour. His character, the Kapellmeister Kreisler, inspired Schumann's *Kreisleriana*. He himself is the hero of Offenbach's *Les Contes d'Hoffmann*.

Hoffmann, Karl (*b* Smichov, 1872; *d* Prague, 1936). Cz. violinist. Founded Bohemian Str. Qt. 1892. Prof. of vn., Prague Cons., from 1922.

Hoffmann, Leopold (*b* Vienna, 1738; *d* Vienna, 1793). Austrian composer. Kapellmeister, St Stephen's Cath., Vienna, from 1772 (Mozart assisted him in 1791). Wrote sym., concs., church mus., etc.

Hoffmeister, Franz Anton (*b* Rothenburg, 1754; *d* Vienna, 1812). Austrian composer and mus. publisher. Mus.-dealer in Vienna 1784-98; founded Bureau de Musique, Leipzig, 1800, with Kühnel. Returned to Vienna 1805, becoming active as composer. Wrote many works for fl., cl., and str., over 65 syms., operas, songs, church mus., etc.

Hoffnung, Gerard (*b* Berlin, 1925; *d* Hampstead, 1959). Ger.-born artist, humorist, and tuba-player. Settled in Britain as child; educated Highgate, and Hornsey Sch. of Art. Contrib. as freelance artist to various publications from 1940. Made series of illustrations, 1949, to Ravel's *L'Enfant et les sortilèges*. Founded Hoffnung Mus. Fests. at which various witty mus. parodies were perf. Drew series of amusing drawings of mus. subjects. Soloist in London, 1958, in Vaughan Williams's tuba conc.

Hofhaimer, Paul (*b* Radstadt, 1459; *d* Salzburg, 1537). Austrian organist and composer. Organist Imperial Chapel Innsbrück, 1480–1519., Salzburg Cath. from 1526. Wrote much org. mus., of which little survives, and several 4-part songs.

Hofmann, Josef (Józef Kazimierz) (*b* Podgorze, Kraków, 1876; *d* Los Angeles, 1957). Polish-born pianist and composer (Amer. citizen from 1926). Son of a pianist-conductor and opera singer, showed prodigious talent and made début as pianist at 6, appearing as soloist with Berlin P.O. at 9. Toured Europe, made NY début at 11. Amer. tour halted midway by action of soc. for prevention of cruelty to children, enforcing unwilling retirement until he was 18. Returned to Europe to study with Moszkowski and Anton Rubinstein. Returned to platform 1894, followed by regular world tours. Settled principally in USA from 1898. Dir. of Curtis Institute, Philadelphia, 1926–38. One of greatest players of Chopin, Liszt, and romantics. Comp. sym., 5 pf. concs., pf. sonatas, and many pf. pieces. Sometimes used pseudonym 'Michel Dvorsky'.

Hofmann, Peter (*b* Marienbad, 1944). Ger. tenor. Studied Karlsruhe Hochschule. Début Lübeck 1972 (Tamino), member Stuttgart Opera from 1973. Siegmund in the 1976 centenary prod. of *The Ring* at Bayreuth and CG. Sang Parsifal at CG 1979 and Salzburg Easter Fest. 1980. San Francisco 1977 (Siegmund); Lohengrin at NY Met. 1980 and with CG in Manchester 1981. Sings Tristan in 1983 recording with Bernstein.

Hofmannsthal, Hugo von (*b* Vienna, 1874; *d* Rodaun, nr. Vienna, 1929). Austrian author, poet, and playwright. With Max Reinhardt, founded Salzburg Fest. in 1920. Librettist for several works of Richard Strauss: the operas *Elektra* (1906–8), *Der Rosenkavalier* (1909–10), *Ariadne auf Naxos* (1912, 2nd version 1916), *Die Frau ohne Schatten* (1914–18), *Die ägyptische Helena* (1924–7), and *Arabella* (1928–32), the ballet *Josephslegende* (1913–14), *Der Burger als Edelmann* (*Le Bourgeois Gentilhomme*) (1912 and 1917); ed. with Strauss of Beethoven's ballet *Die Geschöpfe des Prometheus*; cantata *Tüchtigen stellt das schnelle Glück* (1914). Also librettist for Wellesz's *Alkestis* (1922–3).

Hofoper (Ger., 'Court opera'). Title given up to 1918 to the Court or Royal opera houses in many Ger. and Austrian cities, e.g. Vienna Hofoper, which became *Staatsoper (State Opera) in 1919.

Hogwood, Christopher (Jarvis Haley) (*b* Nottingham, 1941). Eng. harpsichordist and conductor. Studied hpd. with Rafael Puyana and Gustav Leonhardt. Founder-member with David *Munrow of Early Music Consort, 1967. Frequent broadcaster. Founder and dir., Academy of Ancient Music, from 1973. Author of books on the trio sonata, 1979, and on Handel, 1985.

Hohlflöte (Ger., 'hollow flute', i.e. hollow-sounding fl.). Metal or wooden org. stop of 8′ length and pitch.

Holberg Suite (*Holbergiana*; Ger. *Aus Holbergs Zeit*, From Holberg's Time). Pf. suite in 5 movements by Grieg comp. 1884 and orch. for str. in same year, both versions Op. 40. Written to celebrate bicentenary of birth of Norweg. dramatist Ludvig Holberg (1684–1754).

Holborne, Anthony (*d* ?London, 1602). Eng. composer. Pub. *The Cittharn Schoole* (1597, modern edn. by Kanazawa 1973) containing 57 pieces for cittern and bass viol; and *Pavans, Galliards, Almans, and other Short Aires* (1599).

Holborne, William (*d* after 1602). Brother of Anthony. 6 of his airs are incl. in *The Cittharn Schoole*.

Holbrooke, Joseph (Josef Charles) (*b* Croydon, 1878; *d* London, 1958). Eng. composer and pianist. Mus.-hall pianist at age of 12. Studied RAM 1893–6 under Corder (comp.) and F. Westlake (pf.) Pianist-cond. for travelling pantomime 1899. After perf. of his tone-poem *The Raven* (1900) his works were much in demand at Eng. fests., but did not hold their place and are rarely heard. Comp. trilogy of Celtic operas 1911–15. Controversial writer (e.g. *Contemporary British Composers* 1925) and frequent polemicist against 'Establishment'. Prin. works:

OPERAS: *Pierrot and Pierrette* (1909); trilogy, *The Cauldron of Anwen* comprising *The Children of Don* (1911), *Dylan* (1914), and *Bronwen* (1915).

ORCH: Symphonic poems, *The Raven* (1900), *Ulalume* (1904), *Queen Mab* (1904), *Byron*, with ch. (1906), *Apollo and the Seaman*, with ch. (1908), *Variations on Three Blind Mice*, vn. conc. Also much chamber mus., pf. pieces, songs, part-songs, etc.

Hold, Trevor (*b* Northampton, 1939). Eng. composer and poet. Studied Nottingham Univ. Lecturer on mus. Aberystwyth and Liverpool Univs., later on staff of Leicester Univ. Works incl.: *Gunpowder Plot Music* for orch.; ov. *My Uncle Silas*; *Rondo* for str. orch.; *Requiescat*, for speaker, ch., brass sextet; *The Falcon*, church drama; *The Pied Piper*, entertainment for children; *Early One Morning*, high v. and guitar; *Cinquefoils* for pf. quintet.

Hölderlin-Fragmente, Sechs (Six Hölderlin Fragments). Setting by Britten, Op. 61, for v. and pf. of 6 poems by German poet Hölderlin. Comp. 1958.

Holidays Symphony (Ives). See *New England Holidays*.

Höller, Karl (*b* Bamberg, 1907). Ger. composer. Teacher at Hoch Cons., Frankfurt, 1937–45, Munich Cons. 1946–72. Composer of 2 syms., *Variations on a Theme of Sweelinck* for orch., 2 vn. concs., 2 vc. concs., org. conc., 6 str. qts., 8 vn. sonatas, film mus.

Höller, York (Georg) (*b* Leverkusen, 1944). Ger. composer. Studied at Cologne Musikhochschule 1963–8 (with Zimmermann and A. Kontarsky). Répétiteur, Bonn municipal th., 1968–9. Worked with Eimert at Cologne elec. studio. Comps. incl.:

ORCH: *Topic* (1967); Pf. Conc. (1970); *Chroma* (1972–4); *Arcus* (1978); *Umbra* (1979–80); *Mythos* (1979–80).

CHAMBER MUSIC: Vc. sonata (1969); *Epitaph*, vn., pf. (1969); *Antiphon*, str. qt. (1977); *Moments musiceaux*, fl., pf. (1979).

ELECTRONIC: *Horizont* (1972); *Tangens* (1973); *Klanggitter* (1976).

PIANO: *5 Pieces* (1964); *Diaphonie*, 2 pf. (1965); *Sonate informelle* (1968).

Holliger, Heinz (*b* Langenthal, Switz., 1939). Swiss oboist and composer. Studied Berne Cons. and Basle Cons., 1955–9, Paris Cons. 1962–3, (ob. with Cassagnaud and Pierlot, pf. with Yvonne Lefébure, comp. with Veress and Boulez). 1st ob., Basle Orch. 1959–64. Prof. of ob., Freiburg Musikhochschule, 1966. Works written for him by Berio, Huber, Křenek, Henze, Penderecki, Stockhausen, etc. His own comp. incl. *Erde und Himmel*, cantata for ten. and 5 instr.; *Elis*, 3 nocturnes for pf. (1961); *3 Liebeslieder* for alto and orch.; *Schwarzgewebene Trauer* for sop. and 3 instr.; *4 Bagatelles* for sop. and pf. (1963); *Glühende Rätsel* for alto and instr. (1964); *Der magische Tänzer*, for 2 singers, 2 dancers, 2 actors, ch., orch., tape (1965); *Trio* for ob., va., harp (1966);

Siebengesang for ob., orch., vv., amplifiers (1967); *h* for wind quintet (1968); *Dona nobis pacem* for 12 unacc. vv. (1968–9); *Pneuma* for 34 winds, organ, perc., radios (1970); *Cardiophonie*, for 1 wind player (1971); Str. Qt. (1974–5); *Atembogen* for orch. (1975); *Chaconne*, vc. (1976); *NOT 1*, monodrama for sop. and elec. (1980).

Hollingsworth, John (Charles) (*b* Enfield, 1916; *d* London, 1963). Eng. cond. Studied GSM. Assoc. cond. R.A.F. S.O. 1940–5. Cond. much film mus., also ballet and opera at CG from 1950. Assoc. cond., Henry Wood Proms 1949–63.

Holloway, Robin (*b* Leamington Spa, 1943). Eng. composer. Studied St. Paul's Cath. Choir Sch., Cambridge Univ., and Oxford Univ. Ass. lecturer in mus., Cambridge Univ. from 1974. One of most gifted and interesting of younger school of Eng. composers, with a richly romantic style owing something to Strauss but not merely backwards-looking. Works incl.:

OPERA: *Clarissa* (1975).

ORCH: Concertino No. 1 (1964, new finale 1968–9), No. 2 (1967, menuetto added 1974), No. 3 (*Homage to Weill*) for 11 players (1975); *Concerto for Orchestra* (1966–9); *Second Concerto for Orchestra* (1979); *Divertimento No. 1* (amateur orch.) (1968); *Scenes from Schumann*, 7 paraphrases (1969–70); *Domination of Black*, sym. poem (1973–4); *Romanza*, vn. and small orch. (1976); *Idyll*, small orch. (1979–80); *Aria (Dark Air)*, chamber orch. (1979–80); *Sonata*, hn. and orch. (1979–80); *Adagio and Rondo*, hn. and orch. (1979–80); *Serenata Notturna*, 4 hn., small orch. (1982); *Second Idyll*, small orch. (1983).

ENS: *Garden Music*, 8 players (1962, rev. 1967); Conc. for organ and wind (1965–6); *Fantasy-Pieces*, on Heine *Liederkreis* of R. Schumann, for 13 players (1971); *Evening with Angels*, 16 players (1972); *Divertimento No. 2*, wind nonet (1972); *The Rivers of Hell*, 7 players (1977); *Serenade* in C, octet (1979); *Ode*, 4 winds and str. (1980); *Showpiece* (Concertino No. 4), 14 players (1982–3).

VOICE(S) AND ORCH: *The Wind Shifts*, 8 poems of W. Stevens, high v. and str. (1970); *Cantata on the Death of God*, sop., ten., bass soloists, speaker, ch., org., orch. (1972–3); *Sea Surface Full of Clouds*, cantata, sop., cont., counterten., ten. soloists, small ch., chamber orch. (1974–5); *Clarissa Symphony*, sop., ten., orch. (1976, 1981); *Brand*, ballad for solo vv., ch., org., orch. (1981).

VOICE(S) AND ENS: *3 Poems of William Empson*, mez. and ens. (1964–5); *Music for Eliot's 'Sweeney Agonistes'*, 3 or 4 speakers and 5 players (1965); *In Chymick Art*, cantata, sop., bar., 9 players (1965–6); *Melodrama*, 3 poems of S. Plath, speaker., male ch., ens. (1967); *Divertimento No. 3* (*Nursery Rhymes*), sop., wind quintet (1977); *Conundrums (Divertimento No. 4)*, sop., wind quintet (1977, 1979); *Moments of Vision*, speaker, vn., vc., pf., perc. (1984).

UNACC. CHORUS: *The Consolation of Music* (1967–71–77); *5 Madrigals* (1973); *Hymn for Voices*, (1977); *He-She-Together* (1978).

SONG-CYCLES AND SONGS: *4 Housman Fragments*, sop., pf. (1965–6); *4 Poems of Stevie Smith*, unacc. sop. (1968–9); *Banal Sojourn*, 7 Stevens poems, high v. and pf. (1971); *Georgian Songs*, 10 songs, bar. and pf. (1972); *5 Little Songs about Death* (S. Smith), unacc. sop. (1972–3); *★Lights Out*, 4 songs for bar. and pf. (1974); *In the Thirtieth Year*, 5 songs for ten. and pf. (1974); *Author of Light*, 4 songs for cont. and pf. (1974); *The Leaves Cry*, 2 songs for sop. and pf. (1974); *This is Just to Say*, ten., pf. (1977); *The Blue Doom of Summer*, v. and harp (1977); *Willow Cycle*, ten., harp (1977); *From High Windows*, 6 poems by P. Larkin, for bar. and pf. (1977); *Killing Time*, unacc. sop. (1978); *The Noon's Repose*, 3 songs for ten. and harp (1978–9); *Wherever We May Be*, 5 songs by R. Graves, for sop. and pf. (1980–1); *The Lovers' Well*, bass-bar. and pf. (1981); *Women in War*, revue for 4 female vv. and pf. (1982).

CHAMBER MUSIC: *3 Slithy Toves*, 2 cl. (1978); sonata for vn. solo (1981); *Suite for Saxophone* (1982).

BRASS BAND: *From Hills and Valleys* (1983).

Hollreiser, Heinrich (*b* Munich, 1913). Ger. cond. Began career with opera posts in Wiesbaden, Darmstadt, and Mannheim. In 1942 at Munich Staatsoper. Mus . dir. Düsseldorf Opera 1945–52, Vienna 1952–61, Berlin 1961–4. Bayreuth début 1973 (*Tannhäuser*). Cond. f. Ger. p. of Britten's *Peter Grimes* (Hamburg, 1947).

Hollweg, Werner (Friedrich) (*b* Solingen, 1936). Ger . ten. Studied Detmold Acad. of Mus. Début Vienna 1962. Int. career in opera and concert-hall.

Hollywood Bowl. Natural open-air amphitheatre (65 acres) near Los Angeles, Calif., purchased in 1919 and in which since 1922 concerts of the Los Angeles P.O. are given annually for 9 weeks from July to September. Seats 25,000 and has remarkable acoustics.

Holmboe, Vagn (*b* Horsens, Jutland, 1909). Danish composer. Studied Royal Cons., Copenhagen, 1926–30 (comp. with ★Høffding) and in Berlin 1931 with E. Toch. In 1930s collected Romanian and Danish folk music. Teacher Royal Danish Institute for Blind 1940–49, mus. critic *Politiken* 1947–55. Teacher at Royal Danish Cons. 1950–65. Comps. incl. 11 syms., 3 operas, *Requiem for Nietzsche*, 3 chamber syms., 14 str. qts. (1926–75), 13 concs., 14 motets.

Holmès (orig. Holmes), **Augusta** (Mary Anne) (*b* Paris, 1847; *d* Paris, 1903). Irish-born composer (under pseudonym Hermann Zenta) who lived in Paris. Studied comp. with ★Franck 1875. Wrote syms., symphonic poems, 4 operas, and choral works.

Holmes, Ralph (*b* Penge, 1937; *d* Beckenham, 1984). Eng. violinist. Studied RAM with David

Martin, then in Paris with Enescu. London début 1951 with RPO. Amer. début 1966 (NY, Houston S.O. and Barbirolli). Prof. of vn., RAM, from 1964. Had all major 20th cent. vn. concs. in his repertoire. Also played in chamber mus.

Holst, Gustav (Theodore) (*b* Cheltenham, 1874; *d* London, 1934). Eng. composer of Swed. descent. Trained as a pianist, his father being a pf. teacher. In 1892 he became organist and choirmaster at Wyck Rissington, Glos. His operetta *Lansdowne Castle* was prod. in Cheltenham in 1893, after which his father sent him to the RCM to study comp. under Stanford and the org. under Hoyte. At the same time he learned the tb., his pf.-playing being handicapped by chronic neuritis in the arm. In coll. holidays he played the tb. on seaside piers in the White Viennese Band. He left the RCM in 1898, having formed there a lifelong friendship with Vaughan Williams which extended to frank and detailed criticism of each other's comps. He worked as a trombonist in the Carl Rosa Opera 1898–1900 and Scottish Orch. from 1900 to 1903 and learned a smattering of Sanskrit in order to be able to trans. hymns from the *Rig Veda* which he wished to set to mus. His *Cotswolds Symphony* (unpubd.) was perf. in Bournemouth 1902 by Dan *Godfrey and in 1905 his *Mystic Trumpeter* was perf. at the Queen's Hall. In 1903 he became mus. teacher at a Dulwich girls' sch., holding this post until 1920, and in 1905 he became dir. of mus. at St Paul's Girls' Sch., Hammersmith, retaining this appointment until his death. At this time, too, like Vaughan Williams he became deeply interested in Eng. folksong, and in 1907 became mus. dir. at Morley Coll., holding this post until 1924. At all the schs. where he taught he raised both standards and taste. In 1908 he went on holiday to Algeria (bicycling in the desert), the direct mus. result of which was an orch. suite *Beni Mora*. On return he comp. his chamber opera *Savitri*. In 1911 he cond. at Morley College the f. modern p. of Purcell's *The Fairy Queen*, and in 1913 began work on a large-scale orch. suite *The Planets*, sketching *Mars* just before World War I began in 1914. In that year he set Whitman's *Dirge for 2 Veterans* for male vv., brass, and drums. At this time he went to live in Thaxted, Essex, where in 1916 he organized a Whitsuntide Fest., singing and performing mus. by Bach, Byrd, Purcell, and Palestrina. Later that year *Savitri* was prod. in London and in 1917 Holst began his choral work *The Hymn of Jesus*. He was unfit for war service, but in 1918 was offered the post of YMCA mus. organizer among the troops in the Near East. As a parting present a wealthy friend, Balfour Gardiner, arranged a private perf. of *The Planets* in Queen's Hall, cond. Adrian Boult. The f. public p. was in 1919 and was Holst's first major public success. On return to Eng. later in 1919 he was appointed prof. of mus. at University Coll., Reading, and joined the teaching staff of the

RCM. His comic opera *The Perfect Fool* was perf. at CG in 1923 while Holst was conducting at a fest. at the Univ. of Michigan at Ann Arbor. In 1924 he comp. his *Choral Symphony* on poems by Keats which was f.p. at the 1925 Leeds Fest., the same year that his 1-act Falstaff opera *At the Boar's Head* was staged by the BNOC. The ill-health from which he had always suffered in some degree plagued him more after he fell from a platform while rehearsing at Reading in 1923 and comp. became an arduous burden. But in 1927 he wrote his tone-poem *Egdon Heath* (the title given by Thomas Hardy to a stretch of countryside in Dorset), to a commission from the NY S.O. This was followed in 1929 and 1930 by *12 Songs by Humbert Wolfe*, the Double Conc., an opera *The Wandering Scholar*, the *Choral Fantasia* (perf. 1931 at the Gloucester 3 Choirs Fest.), and the prelude and scherzo, *Hammersmith*, for orch. These works gave promise of a new, richer, and more lyrical phase, as did the *Brook Green Suite* and *Lyric Movement* of 1933. But in 1934, after an operation, Holst died in the plenitude of his powers. His mus., while owing something to folk-song influence and to the madrigalian tradition of Byrd and Weelkes, is intensely orig. and has a visionary quality similar to that found in Vaughan Williams but expressed with more austerity and greater natural technical facility. His *Planets* suite, now a popular orch. showpiece, is markedly eclectic, but its finest movements, *Mars*, *Venus*, *Saturn*, and *Neptune*, show varied aspects of Holst's style. His genius as a teacher and his feeling for the community spirit engendered by mus. also contributed to the outstanding part he played in Eng. mus.-making in the first 2 decades of the 20th-cent. Prin. works:

OPERAS: *Savitri, Op. 25 (1908); The *Perfect Fool, Op. 39 (1918–22); *At the Boar's Head, Op. 42 (1924); The *Wandering Scholar, Op. 50 (1929–30).

BALLET: *The Lure* (1921, ed. for orch. by I. Holst and C. Matthews, 1981).

ORCH: *Suite de Ballet in E♭, Op. 10 (1899); A Somerset Rhapsody, Op. 21b (1906–7); 2 Songs Without Words, Op. 22 (1906); *Beni Mora, Oriental Suite in E minor, Op. 29 No. 1 (1910, rev. 1912); Suite No. 1 in E♭, Op. 28a, for military band (1909), Suite No. 2 in F, Op. 28b (1911); Invocation, vc. and orch. (1911); *St. Paul's Suite, Op. 29 No. 2, for str. (1912–13); Japanese Suite, Op. 33 (1915); Suite, The *Planets, Op. 32 (1914–16); Ballet mus. from The Perfect Fool, Op. 39 (1918); A Fugal Overture, Op. 40 No. 1 (1922); Fugal Concerto, Op. 40 No. 2, for fl., ob. (or 2 vn.), and str. (1923); *Egdon Heath, Op. 47 (1927); A Moorside Suite, for brass band (1928); Conc. for 2 vn. and orch., Op. 49 (1929); Hammersmith, Op. 52, prelude and scherzo for military band and for orch. (1930–1); Capriccio, jazz-band piece (1932, ed. Imogen Holst 1967); *Brook Green Suite for str. and optional woodwind

(1933); *Lyric Movement* for va. and orch. (1933); *Scherzo* (from unfinished sym.) (1933–4).

CHORAL: 5 *Part-Songs* Op. 9a (1899–1900); *Ave Maria*, Op. 9b, for female vv. (1900); 5 *Part-Songs*, Op. 12 (1902–3); *King Estmere*, Op. 17, Old English ballad for ch. and orch. (1903): *The *Mystic Trumpeter*, Op. 18, scena for sop. and orch. (1904, rev. 1912); *Songs from 'The Princess'*, Op. 20a, for female vv. (1905); 3 *Choral *Hymns from the Rig Veda*, Op. 26 No. 1, for ch. and orch. (1908–10), Op. 26 No. 2 (3 Hymns) for female vv. and orch. (1909), Op. 26 No. 3 (4 Hymns) for female vv. and harp (1910), Op. 26 No. 4 (4 Hymns) for male vv. and orch. (1912); *Hecuba's Lament*, Op. 31 No. 1, for cont., female ch., and orch. (1911); *The *Cloud Messenger*, Op. 30, ode for ch. and orch. (1910, rev. 1912); 2 *Psalms* for ch., str., and org. (1912); *Hymn to Dionysus*, Op. 31 No. 2, for female ch. and orch. (1913); **Dirge for 2 Veterans*, for male vv., brass, and perc. (1914); **This have I done for my true love*, Op. 34, for unacc. ch. (1916); 6 *Choral Folksongs*, Op. 36, for unacc. ch. (1916); 3 *Festival Choruses*, with orch. (1916); *The *Hymn of Jesus*, Op. 37, for 2 ch., semi-ch., and orch. (1917); **Ode to Death*, Op. 38, for ch. and orch. (1919); *I vow to thee, my country*, unison song with orch. (to central melody from *Jupiter*, No. 4 of *The Planets*) (1921); *First Choral Symphony*, Op. 41, for sop., ch., and orch. (1923–4); 2 *Motets*, Op. 43, for unacc. ch. (1924–5); 7 *Part-Songs*, Op. 44, (to poems by Bridges) for female vv. and str. (1925–6)—No. 7 is **Assemble, all ye maidens*; *The Golden Goose*, Op. 45 No. 1, choral ballet with orch. (1926); *The Morning of the Year*, Op. 45 No. 2, choral ballet with orch. (1926–7); **Choral Fantasia*, Op. 51, for sop., ch., org., brass, and str. (1930); 12 *Welsh Folksongs* for unacc. ch. (1930–1); 6 *Choruses*, Op. 53 (to words trans. from Lat. by Helen Waddell) for male vv. and str. (or org., or pf.) (1931–2); 6 *canons*, (to words trans. from Lat. by H. Waddell) for equal unacc. vv. (1932).

SOLO SONGS: 4 *Songs*, Op. 4, for v. and pf. (1896–8); 6 *songs*, Op. 15, for bar. and pf. (1902–3); 6 *Songs*, Op. 16, for sop. and pf. (1903–4); 9 **Hymns from the Rig Veda*, Op. 24, for v. and pf. (1907–8); 4 *Songs*, Op. 35, for v. and vn. (1916–17); 12 *Songs by Humbert Wolfe*, Op. 48, for v. and pf. (1929); 2 *Canons* (to words trans. from Lat. by H. Waddell) for 2 equal vv. and pf. (1932).

CHAMBER MUSIC: 6 *Instrumental pieces* (variously for 2 vn., vn. (or vc.), and pf.) (1902–3); wind quintet (1903); *Terzetto* for fl., ob., and va. (1925).

PIANO: 2 *Pieces* (1901); *Toccata* (1924); *Chrissemas Day in the Morning*, Op. 46 No. 1 (1926); 2 *Folksong Fragments*, Op. 46 No. 2 (1927); *Nocturne* (1930); *Jig* (1932).

Holst, Henry (*b* Copenhagen, 1899). Danish violinist. Studied Royal Danish Cons., Copenhagen, and later in Berlin with Willy Hess. Début

Copenhagen 1919. Leader, Berlin P.O. 1923–31. Prof. of vn. RMCM 1931–46, 1950–3, RCM 1946–54, Royal Danish Cons. from 1953; guest prof. Tokyo 1961–3. Frequent conc. soloist. Gave f. Eng. p. of Walton conc. 1941.

Holst, Imogen (Clare) (*b* Richmond, Surrey, 1907; *d* Aldeburgh, 1984). Eng. cond., ed., and writer. Daughter of Gustav **Holst. Educated St Paul's Girls' Sch. and RCM. Ed. several of her father's works and cond. them for recordings. Mus. dir., arts centre, Dartington Hall, 1943–51. Dir. of Aldeburgh Fest. and for several years mus. ass. to **Britten. Author of biography and other books about Gustav Holst, also on Britten and Byrd. C.B.E. 1975.

Holy Boy, The. No. 3 of 4 *Preludes* for pf. by **Ireland, comp. 1913–5. Orch. for str. 1941, for str. qt. 1941; arr. for org. (by Alec Rowley) 1919, for brass ens. (by R. E. Stepp) 1950, for v. and pf. (poem by Herbert S. Brown) 1938, for unacc. ch. 1941, for str. qt. 1941.

Holy Sonnets of John Donne. Setting of 9 Donne sonnets for high v. and pf. Op. 35, by Britten. Comp. 1945 after visit to Ger. concentration camps.

Holzbauer, Ignaz (*b* Vienna, 1711; *d* Mannheim, 1783). Austrian composer. Mus. dir. Vienna court th. 1745, court Kapellmeister, Stuttgart 1751, Mannheim 1753. Comp. about 40 syms., several operas, chamber works, and much church mus. Admired by Mozart. His opera *Günther von Schwarzburg* (1776) used recit. instead of spoken dialogue.

Holzblasinstrumente (Ger., 'wood-blown instruments'). The woodwind.

Holzflöte (Ger.). 'Wooden flute' (org. stop).

Holztrompete (Ger.). (1) Wooden tpt., or Alphorn; Swiss folk instr. for playing simple tunes. (2) Wooden instr. with bell of cor anglais, one valve, and cup mouthpiece invented to play shepherd's tune in Act 3 of Wagner's *Tristan und Isolde* (nevertheless, a cor anglais is usually employed for this passage).

Homage March. See *Huldigungsmarsch*.

Homage to the Queen. Ballet in 1 act, mus. by Malcolm Arnold, choreog. Ashton, prod. London 1953 on night of Queen Elizabeth II's Coronation.

Home, Sweet Home. Melody by Henry **Bishop, comp. 1821 for album of nat. airs, described as 'Sicilian'. In 1823, with words by J. H. Payne (1791–1852), incorporated in Bishop's opera *Clari*. Tune occurs, altered, in Donizetti's *Anna Bolena*, leading to action by Bishop for 'piracy and breach of copyright'.

Homme Armé, L' (The Armed Man). Old Fr. folk-song used by Dufay, Palestrina, and more than 20 other composers in 15th, 16th, and 17th cents. as a *cantus firmus in their Masses, which then became known by this title. *Maxwell Davies, in the 20th cent., wrote *Missa super 'L'Homme Armé'* for speaker and ens. (1968).

Homophone. 2 harp str. tuned to produce the same note.

Homophony (Gk., 'Same-sounding'). Term applied to mus. in which the parts or vv. move 'in step' with one another, instead of exhibiting individual rhythmic independence and interest, as in *Polyphony*. Many modern hymn-tunes are homophonic, whereas Bach's settings of Ger. chorales and many Handelian choruses are polyphonic.

Honegger, Arthur (*b* Le Havre, 1892; *d* Paris, 1955). Swiss composer. Studied Zürich Cons. 1909–11, Paris Cons. 1911 (comp. with Widor, orchestration with d'Indy). Member of group of Fr. composers known as Les *Six from 1920. His *Le Roi David* won him wider fame in 1921, but this was eclipsed in 1924 by f.p. of his representation of a locomotive in *Pacific 231*. From these works he moved nearer to a neo-romantic style with overtones of baroque influence from his admiration for Bach. His mus. remained tonal and often has strong emotional impact, as in his dramatic oratorio, based on a Claudel 'mystery play', *Jeanne d'Arc au bûcher*. His syms. were championed by the cond. Charles *Munch. He visited the USA several times and despite ill-health taught in his last years at the École Normale in Paris. Prin. works:

THEATRE: *Le *Roi David*, dramatic psalm (1921); *Judith*, biblical opera (1925); *Antigone* (1927); *Amphion*, ballet-melodrama, speaker, bar., 4 female vv., ch., orch. (1929); *Jeanne d'Arc au bûcher*, stage oratorio (1934–5); *L'*Aiglon*, 5-act opera with *Ibert (1935); *Charles le téméraire* (1943–4).

ORCH: *Pastorale d'Été* (1920); *Chant de Joie* (1923); *Pacific 231* (1923); concertino for pf. and orch. (1924); *Rugby* (1928); vc. conc. (1929); Syms., No. 1 (1929–30), No. 2 for str. and tpt. (1941), No. 3 (*Liturgique*) (1945–6), No. 4 (*Deliciae basiliensis*) (1946), No. 5 (*Di tre re*) (1951); *Mouvement symphonique* No. 3 (1932–3); *Nocturne* (1936); *La Construction d'une cité* (with Milhaud) (1937); Concerto da camera for fl., cor anglais, and str. (1948); *Monopartita* (1951).

VOICE AND ORCH: *Chanson de Ronsard*, with fl. and str. (1924); 3 *Chansons populaires* (1926).

CHORAL: *Cantique des Cantiques* (1926); *Les Cris du Monde* (1930–1); *La Danse des Morts* (Claudel), solo vv., ch., orch. (1938); *Chant de libération* (1944); *Une Cantate de Noël* (1941/1953).

CHAMBER MUSIC: Str. qts., No. 1 (1916–17), No. 2 (1936), No. 3 (1936–7); Sonatas for pf. and vn., No. 1 (1916–18), No. 2 (1919); va. sonata (1920); vc. sonata (1920); vn. sonatina (1932); vn. sonata (1940).

BALLETS: *Les *Mariés de la Tour Eiffel* (with Les Six) (1921); *L'appel de la montagne* (1945).
Also incidental mus. for plays, mus. for films (incl. *Mayerling*, 1935, and *Pygmalion*, 1938), radio mus., many songs, and pf. pieces.

Hook, James (*b* Norwich, 1746; *d* Boulogne, 1827). Eng. composer and organist. Organist and composer Marylebone Gardens 1769–73, Vauxhall Gardens 1774–1820. Wrote oratorio, org, conc., pf. sonatas, cantatas, and over 2,000 songs, best-known being *Sweet Lass of Richmond Hill*.

Hopak. See *Gopak*.

Hope-Jones, Robert (*b* Hooton Grange, Cheshire, 1859; *d* Rochester, NY, 1914). Eng. org. builder. Started own business 1889. Settled in USA 1903, founded Hope-Jones Organ Co. 1907, selling patents and plant in 1910 to Wurlitzer. Invented several electrical and tonal devices.

Hopf, Hans (*b* Nuremberg, 1916). Ger. ten. Studied Munich with Paul Bender. Opera début 1936. Munich Opera 1949. CG 1951–3, 1963, NY Met. 1952–5. Sang at Bayreuth and Salzburg Fest.

Hopkins (orig. Reynolds), **Antony** (*b* London, 1921). Eng. composer, pianist, and educator. Studied RCM 1939–42. Mus. dir. Intimate Opera Co., 1952, writing several chamber operas for it. Composer of mus. for films, radio, and th. His series 'Talking About Music' has been regular and valuable contribution to educational radio for many years. Works incl. operas *Lady Rohesia* (1948), *Three's Company* (1954), ballet *Café des Sports*, and pf. mus. C.B.E. 1976.

Hopkins, Edward (John) (*b* Westminster, 1818; *d* London, 1901). Eng. organist and composer. Organist, Temple Church 1843–98. Wrote church mus. Authority on org. construction and, with *Rimbault, author of *The Organ, its History and Construction* (1855 and subsequent edns.).

Hopkins, John (Raymond) (*b* Preston, 1927). Eng. conductor and administrator. Studied vc. at RMCM 1943–6 and cond. at GSM 1947–8. Salzburg Mozarteum 1949. Apprentice cond. Yorkshire S.O. 1948–9, ass. cond. BBC Scottish Orch. 1949–52, cond. BBC Northern Orch. 1952–7. Went to N.Z. 1957 as cond. Nat. Orch. In 1963 became dir. of mus. Australian Broadcasting Commission until 1973 when he was appointed dean of Sch. of Mus., Victoria Coll. of Arts, Melbourne. O.B.E. 1970.

Hopkinson, Francis (*b* Philadelphia, 1737; *d* Philadelphia, 1791). Amer. composer, harpsichordist, poet, and politician (one of signatories of Declaration of Independence, 1776). Wrote 1st surviving piece of mus. by an American, the song *My days have been so wondrous free* (1759). Hpd. pieces, pub. 1788, dedicated to George Washington.

Hoquet. Same as *Hocket.

Horenstein, Jascha (*b* Kiev, 1898; *d* London, 1973). Russ.-born cond. Studied in Vienna; pupil of F. Busch and F. Schreker. Cond. Vienna S.O. 1923, then worked in Berlin and at Düsseldorf Opera from 1929. After 1933 worked in Fr., Russ., Poland, and Belg. Amer. début 1940. Frequent guest cond. of Brit. orchs. CG début 1961 (*Fidelio*). Fine interpreter of Mahler and Bruckner.

Horizon Chimérique, L' (The Fanciful Horizon). Song-cycle of 4 songs by Fauré, Op. 118, to poems by J. de la Ville de Mirmont, comp. 1921, f.p. 1922.

Horn. (1) See *Horn Family*.
  (2) Org. stop like *Trumpet* but fuller and smoother in tone.

Horn, Charles Edward (*b* London, 1786; *d* Boston, Mass., 1849). Eng. composer and singer, son of Karl F. *Horn. Actor-singer in London from 1809. Settled in USA 1833, producing ballad-operas in NY. Returned to Eng. 1843, but settled finally in Boston from 1847. Comp. oratorios, operettas, and songs incl. *Cherry Ripe*.

Horn diapason. 8′ org. stop of str.-like tone ('Horn' being a misnomer).

Horn Family. Brass instr. The modern hn. is an intricately coiled tube of over 11′; it is of $\frac{1}{4}$″ bore at one end but widens gradually until it terminates in a large bell of 11″–14″ diameter: the mouth-piece is funnel-shaped. All these details differentiate it from the *trumpet. The principle on which the notes are obtained is that of all brass instr.
  There are 2 main forms of the hn.: the *Natural Horn* and the *Valve Horn*. The Natural Horn is restricted, at any given moment, to one pitch of the harmonic series; the Valve Horn can at will be switched from the harmonic series at one pitch to that of another, so making any note of the chromatic scale instantaneously available. Its technique is more difficult to acquire than that of any other instr. in the orch.
  The *basset-horn and *cor anglais are not horns but reed instruments.
  See *French horn*.

Horn, Karl Friedrich (*b* Nordhausen, 1762; *d* Windsor, 1830). Ger. organist and composer. Settled in London 1782. Mus.-master to Queen Charlotte 1789–83, to Princess Augusta 1793–1811. Organist St George's Chapel, Windsor, from 1823. Comp. pf. sonatas. Ed., with Samuel Wesley, of Bach's *Wohltemperierte Klavier* (1810–13). Author of treatise on thoroughbass.

Horne, Marilyn (*b* Bradford, Penn., 1934). Amer. mez. Studied Univ. of S. California. Dubbed singing v. (for Dorothy Dandridge) in film of *Carmen Jones*, 1954. Opera début as Hata in *The Bartered Bride*, Los Angeles 1954. Member of Gelsenkirchen opera co. 1956–60. Sang Marie in

Berg's *Wozzeck*, San Francisco 1960; NY début 1962 in *Beatrice di Tenda*. NY Met. début 1970 (Adalgisa in *Norma*). CG 1965 (*Wozzeck*). Appeared in series of 19th cent. *bel canto* operas in partnership with Joan *Sutherland, beginning in NY in 1961 in *Beatrice di Tenda* (concert perf.) and incl. *Semiramide* and *Les Huguenots*. Repertory extends from Handel to Wagner.

Hornpipe. The word has 2 meanings: (1) An obsolete instr., consisting of a wooden pipe with a reed mouthpiece (a single 'beating' reed), and, at the other end, a hn. as 'bell'. Common in the Celtic parts of Brit.
  (2) A dance once popular in the Brit. Isles only, to which that instr. was orig. the usual acc. Properly a solo dance; earlier examples of the mus. are in simple triple time, but by the end of the 18th cent. this had changed to simple duple. This dance was later chiefly kept up by sailors. Purcell, Handel, and others wrote hornpipes.

Horn Signal. Nickname for Haydn's Sym. in D major, 1765, No. 31 in Breitkopf edn. (Hob. I: 31). So called because of calls written for 4 horns in slow movement.

Horoscope. Ballet in 1 act, lib. and mus. by Constant Lambert, choreog. Ashton. Comp. 1937. Prod. London 1938. Orch. suite.

Horovitz, Joseph (*b* Vienna, 1926). Austrian-born composer, cond., and teacher. Settled in Eng. in 1938. Educated Oxford and RCM. Ass. dir. Intimate Opera Co. 1952–63, ass. cond. Glyndebourne 1956, prof. of comp., RCM from 1961. Composer of two 1-act operas, 11 ballets, vn. conc., tpt. conc., chamber mus. Arr. of witty parodies for Gerard *Hoffnung's mus. fests. in London.

Horowitz, Vladimir (*b* Kiev, 1903). Russ.-born pianist (Amer. cit. 1944). Studied Kiev Cons. until 1921. Début Kharkov 1921, followed by study with Felix Blumenfeld. Toured Europe. Amer. début 1928. London début 1928. Settled in US, marrying Toscanini's daughter. Career as int. virtuoso of highest rank interrupted by illness 1936–39. From 1953 played only for recordings. Returned to concert-platform, NY 1965.

Horsley, Colin (*b* Wanganui, N.Z., 1920). New Zealand pianist. Studied RCM. Début Manchester with Hallé Orch. 1943. Gave f.p. of L. Berkeley's pf. conc. 1948. Taught at RAM and RMCM. Frequent tours. O.B.E. 1963.

Horst, Louis (*b* Kansas City, 1874; *d* NY, 1964). Amer. pianist, cond., composer, and teacher. Closely assoc. with modern US dance. Cond. for Denishawn Co. 1915–26, mus. dir. for Martha Graham 1926–48. Teacher of dance comp. in NY 1928–64. Scores for Graham incl. *Frontier* and *Celebration*.

Horszowski, Mieczyslaw (*b* Lwów, 1892). Polish-born pianist (Amer. citizen 1948). Studied with *Leschetizky in Vienna. Début Warsaw 1901. Toured Europe, frequently partnering the cellist Casals. Settled NY 1940. On staff Curtis Institute from 1942. Played at Aldeburgh Fest. 1984.

Horton, John (William) (b Nottingham, 1905). Eng. author, organist, and teacher. Studied Durham Univ. Worked for BBC 1937–47; sch. mus. inspector 1947–67. Author of books on Grieg, Brahms, Mendelssohn, and César Franck.

Hotter, Hans (b Offenbach-am-Main, 1909). Austrian bass-bar. Began as organist and choirmaster, turned to opera. Début Opava 1929. Sang in Prague 1932–4 and Hamburg 1934–7, then joined Vienna and Munich Operas. CG début 1947, NY Met. 1950–4. Bayreuth Fest. from 1952. Outstanding Wotan in Wagner's *Ring*; created Strauss roles of Commandant in *Friedenstag* and Olivier in *Capriccio*. Sang Jupiter in unofficial Salzburg f.p. of Strauss's *Die *Liebe der Danae*, 1944. Prod. *Ring* at CG 1962–4. Sang his last Wotan in Paris, 1972.

Hotteterre, Jacques (-Martin) ('le Romain') (b Paris, 1674; d Paris, 1763). Fr. flautist, bassoonist, and instr. maker, best known of Fr. family of woodwind instr. makers, composers, and performers active in 17th and 18th cents. Called himself 'le Romain' probably because of visit to It. in his youth. By 1708 was bassoonist in Grands Hautbois and flautist in 'chamber of the king'. Much sought-after as teacher. The flutes he made are magnificent instrs. Wrote *Principes de la flûte traversière* (1707, Eng. trans. 1968), *L'art de préluder sur la flûte traversière* (1719), and *Méthode pour la musette* (1737). Pubd. 2 books of suites for fl. and bass (1708, 1715).

Housatonic at Stockbridge, The. 3rd movement of Ives's *Three Places in New England* for orch., sometimes played separately.

House of the Dead, From The (Z Mrtvého Domu). Opera in 3 acts by Janáček to his own lib. based on Dostoyevsky's novel (1862) about his experiences in prison. Comp. 1927–8. Prod. Brno 1930, Edinburgh 1964, London 1965. Part of orch. prelude was taken by Janáček from unfinished vn. conc. (1927–8) to be called *Pilgrimage of the Soul* (Putováné dušičky). Problem arises over final 17 bars of this opera inserted by O. Zitek, B. Bakala, and O. Chlubna at the f.p. (1930) which is choral and optimistic; Janáček's orig. ending was more realistic, with an orch. epilogue of 27 bars, and this has been restored in perfs. cond. by Mackerras and Armstrong.

Houston Symphony Orchestra. Founded in Houston, Texas, 1913 with Julian Paul Blitz as cond., succeeded 1916 by Paul Berge until 1917. Reorganized 1930, with Frank St Leger as cond. 1931–5, Ernst Hoffmann 1936–47. Hoffmann increased size and standards of orch. Cond. after him were Efrem Kurtz 1948–54, Beecham 1954–

5, Stokowski 1955–60, Barbirolli 1961–7, Previn 1967–9, Foster 1971–8, Comissiona art. adv. 1980, cond. from 1984.

Hovhaness, Alan (b Somerville, Mass., 1911). Amer. composer, cond., and organist of Armenian and Scot. descent. Studied New England Cons. and at Tanglewood with Martinů. Worked in Boston 1940–7, taught at Boston Cons. 1948–52, then settled in NY. Prolific composer, deeply interested in Eastern mus. style, which embraces aleatory procedures as in *Lousadzak* (Coming of Light) 1944, combines Western elements with modal harmony, Eastern rhythms, and the exotica of Chinese and Balinese instrs. Works incl. 52 syms., operas, *Mysterious Mountain* for orch., *Fantasy on Japanese Woodprints* for xylophone and orch. (1965), *And God Created Great Whales* (1970) for humpbacked whale solo (on tape) and orch., choral works, chamber mus., etc.

Howard, Ann (b Norwood, 1936). Eng. mez. Studied in London and Paris. Opera début London 1964 in *Zigeunerbaron*. Leading roles with ENO, CG, Scottish and Welsh Opera, and in Canada and USA. Specialities Carmen, Fricka, Azucena, and Hélène (Offenbach).

Howard, Leslie (John) (b Melbourne, Victoria, 1948). Australian pianist and composer. Studied in Australia, It., and London. Début Melbourne 1967, London 1975. On teaching staff Monash Univ. 1970–3. Notable Liszt exponent. Composer of opera, hn. sonata, etc.

Howarth, Elgar (b Cannock, Staffs., 1935). Eng. conductor, composer, and trumpeter. Studied at Manchester Univ. and RMCM. Trumpeter in Vesuvius Ens. and Philip Jones Brass Ens. Prin. tpt., RPO 1963–8. Guest cond. London Sinfonietta from 1969, dir. from 1973. Cond. f.p. of Ligeti's *La grand macabre*, Stockholm 1978, and London première, ENO 1982. Has often cond. and comp. for brass band.

Howell, Dorothy (b Handsworth, 1898; d Worcester, 1982). Eng. composer and pianist. Studied RAM under McEwen and Matthay. Prof. of harmony and comp. RAM 1924–70. Comp. incl. symphonic poem, pf. conc. (1923), ballet, chamber mus., and songs.

Howell, Gwynne (Richard) (b Gorseinon, 1938). Welsh bass. Studied RMCM (part-time) from 1963. Joined SW Opera 1968, début as Monterone in *Rigoletto*. CG début 1970 (*Salome*). Sang in f.p. of Maxwell Davies's *Taverner*, 1972. Fine singer in oratorio and concert repertoire.

Howells, Anne (Elizabeth) (b Southport, 1941). Eng. mez. Studied RMCM where in 1963 she sang Eros in f. Eng. p. of Gluck's *Paride ed Elena*. Glyndebourne ch. 1964–7. Début CG as Flora in *La Traviata* 1967. Amer. début 1972 (Chicago). NY Met. 1975. Leading roles at CG, ENO, Scottish Opera, WNO, Milan, Wexford, Chicago, etc.

Howells, Herbert (Norman) (*b* Lydney, Glos., 1892; *d* London, 1983). Eng. composer, organist, and teacher. Studied with Brewer at Gloucester 1905–11, RCM 1912–16 (comp. with Stanford). *Mass in Dorian Mode* perf. Westminster Cath. 1912. Sub-organist, Salisbury Cath., 1917. Several comp. perf. at 3 Choirs Fests. in 1920s. Succeeded Holst as dir. of mus., St Paul's Girls' Sch., 1936–62, prof. of mus., London Univ., 1954–64. On staff RCM from 1920. Frequent adjudication at mus. fests. Organist, St John's Coll., Cambridge, 1941–5. His work, influenced by Elgar and Vaughan Williams, has strong individuality, at its finest in the *Missa Sabrinensis* and at its most eloquent in the *Hymnus Paradisi*, where some affinity with the choral writing of Delius may be detected. One of few 20th cent. composers to write for clavichord. The pieces in his two major works for it are musical portraits of friends, incl. Herbert Lambert, Thomas Goff, Vaughan Williams, Finzi, etc. C.B.E. 1954, C.H. 1972. Prin. works:

ORCH: *Merry-Eye* and *Puck's Minuet* (1917–20); *Procession* (1922); *Pastoral Rhapsody* (1923); pf. conc. (1924); *Elegy for Strings* (1937); vc. conc. (1937); *Concerto for Strings* (1938); *Pageantry Suite* (brass band, 1934); *Music for a Prince* (1948).
CHORAL: *Sir Patrick Spens*, ch., orch. (1918); *3 Carol-Anthems*, ch. (1918–20; No. 2 is *A Spotless Rose*); *A Kent Yeoman's Wooing Song* for 2 soloists, ch., and orch. (1933); *Requiem*, unacc. ch. (1936); *Hymnus Paradisi* for sop., ten., ch., and orch. (1938, f.p. 1950); *Missa Sabrinensis*, for sop., cont., ten., bar., double ch., and orch. (1953); *Inheritance* (1953, in *Garland for the Queen*); *St. Paul's Service* (1954); *An English Mass* (1956); *Take him, earth, for cherishing* (motet on the death of Pres. Kennedy) (1964); *The Coventry Mass*, ch. and org. (1964).
VOICE AND ACC: 4 *French Chansons*, v. and pf. (1918); *In Green Ways*, v. and pf. (1915, rev. with orch. 1928); *King David*, v. and pf. (1921); *Sine Nomine*, soloists, organ, and orch. (1922).
CHAMBER MUSIC: Pf. Qt. in A minor (1916); *Phantasy Quartet* (1917); *Rhapsodic Quintet*, cl. and str. (1919); *In Gloucestershire* (str. qt.) (1924); cl. sonata (1946).
ORGAN: 3 Rhapsodies (1917); 2 organ sonatas, *De Profundis* (1960); *Fugue, Chorale, and Epilogue*; *Sarabande for the Morning of Easter*.
CLAVICHORD: *Lambert's Clavichord*, 12 pieces (1926–7); *Howells's Clavichord*, 20 pieces (1955–61).
Also about 65 songs incl. several settings of De la Mare, of which *King David* (1921) is a favourite.

Howes, Frank (Stewart) (*b* Oxford, 1891; *d* Oxford, 1974). Eng. mus. critic. Educated St John's Coll., Oxford. Staff mus. critic for *The Times* 1925–60 (chief critic from 1943). Chairman, Eng. Folk Dance and Song Soc. 1938–45 and ed. of its journal 1927–46. Author of books on Vaughan

Williams, Walton, Eng. mus. renaissance, and aesthetics. Lecturer at RCM. C.B.E. 1954.

Hrotta. Another name for the *Crwth.

Hubay, Jenö (*b* Budapest, 1858; *d* Budapest, 1937). Hung. violinist, composer, and cond. Studied with his father Karl Hubay (1828–85), composer, cond., and vn. teacher. Public début at 11; entered Berlin Hochschule 1871, studying for 5 years with Joachim. Paris début 1878. Prof. of vn., Brussels Cons. 1882–6, Pest Cons. 1886–1919, dir. Budapest Acad. 1919–34. Led str. qt. Pupils incl. Szigeti, Telmányi, and Jelly d'Arányi. Comp. 8 operas, incl. *Der Geigenmacher von Cremona* (1893) and *Anna Karenina* (1915), 4 syms., incl. *Dante Symphony* (ch.), 4 vn. concs., chamber mus., etc.

Huber, Hans (*b* Eppenburg, 1852; *d* Locarno, 1921). Swiss composer. Studied Leipzig Cons. 1870–4. Taught Basle Mus. Sch. 1889–1918 (dir. from 1896). Wrote 9 syms. (incl. *William Tell and Böcklin*), 4 pf. concs., vn. conc., 2 pf. quintets, 5 pf. trios, 9 vn. sonatas, 5 operas, oratorio, cantatas, etc.

Huber, Klaus (*b* Berne, 1924). Swiss composer and violinist. Studied Zürich Cons. 1947–9, then privately with Willy Burkhard and (1955–6) with *Blacher. Taught vn. Zürich Cons. 1950–60, harmony at Basle Cons. from 1961. Comps. incl. *Turnus*, for orch. and tape (1974), *Litania instrumentalis* for orch., *Tenebrae* for orch., *Moteti cantiones* for str. qt., *Noctes intelligibilis lucis* for ob. and hpd. (1961), *Tempora*, conc. for vn. and orch., *Psalm of Christ*, bar. and ens., *Invention and Chorale*, orch., *Jot oder Wann kommt der Herr Zurück*, opera, and several other chamber works.

Huberman, Bronislaw (*b* Czestochowa, 1882; *d* Nant-sur-Cosier, 1947). Polish violinist. Pupil of Michalowicz and C. Grigorovich. Début in Vienna aged 10; played Brahms conc. in composer's presence at 14; London début 1894. Int. career, based on Vienna until 1936. Founded Palestine (now Israel) S.O. 1936.

Hucbald (*b c.*840; *d* Saint-Amand, Tournai, 930). Fr. monk, remembered for his treatise *De harmonica institutione* (? *c.*880) which describes the gamut and the modes.

Huddersfield Choral Society. Amateur choir founded in Huddersfield, Yorkshire, in 1836. Regular concerts given since 1881. During 1930s had 400 members, but has since been reduced to 230. Has sung at most Brit. fests. and made many recordings. Its *Messiah* perf. is renowned. First overseas tour to Netherlands, 1928. Vienna Mus. Fest. 1958, Boston, Mass. 1965. Has also visited Berlin, Brussels, and Lisbon. At one time had its own orch. but now sings with independent orchs. Sir Henry Coward and Sir Malcolm Sargent were conductors for over 30 years each. Other conds. have incl. John Pritchard (1973–80) and Owain

Arwel Hughes. Its chorus-masters have incl. Herbert Bardgett, Eric Chadwick, and Douglas Robinson. For centenary in 1936 Vaughan Williams wrote *Dona Nobis Pacem.*

Hughes, Arwel (*b* Rhosllanerchrugog, 1909). Welsh composer and cond. Studied RCM with Vaughan Williams. On staff BBC in Wales from 1935 (head of music, BBC Wales 1965–71). Cond. BBC Welsh Orch. 1950. Comp. opera *Menna* (1950–1), suite for orch., 3 str. qts., oratorio, etc. O.B.E. 1969.

Hughes, Herbert (*b* Belfast, 1882; *d* Brighton, 1937). Irish composer and critic. Studied RCM. Collected and arr. many Irish folk-songs. Mus. critic, *Daily Telegraph*, 1911–32.

Hughes, Owain Arwel (*b* Cardiff, 1942). Welsh cond., son of Arwel *Hughes. Studied Univ. Coll., Cardiff, and RCM (under Boult and Harvey Philips). Professional career began 1968. Studied with *Haitink in Amsterdam and *Kempe in London. Guest cond., WNO and ENO. Mus. dir., Royal Nat. Eisteddfod of Wales, 1977.

Hughes, Spike (Patrick Cairns) (*b* London, 1908; *d* Brighton, 1987). Eng. writer, composer, and broadcaster, son of Herbert *Hughes. Studied in Vienna with Wellesz 1923–5. For a time led jazz band. Mus. critic *Daily Herald* 1933–6. Jazz critic of *The Times* 1957–67. Comps. incl. light music, film scores, etc. His *Cinderella* (1938) was first opera specially comp. for television. Author of books on operas of Mozart, Puccini, and Verdi, history of Glyndebourne Opera (1965, rev. 1981), and 2 vols. of entertaining autobiography.

Hugh the Drover, or Love in the Stocks. Opera in 2 acts by Vaughan Williams to lib. by Harold Child. Comp. 1910–14, rev. 1924 and 1956. Prod. London 1924, Washington 1928.

Huguenots, Les. Opera in 5 acts by *Meyerbeer to lib. by Scribe and Deschamps. Prod. Paris 1836, New Orleans 1839, London 1842.

Huldigungsmarsch (Ger., 'Homage March'). (1) By Wagner, 1864, in honour of his patron, King Ludwig II of Bavaria. Orig. for military band. Orch. version, partly scored by Raff, f.p. at laying of foundation stone at Bayreuth, 1872.
  (2) By Liszt, in honour of Grand Duke of Saxe-Weimar. For pf., 1853, scored by Raff 1853; rev. and re-scored by Liszt 1857.
  (3) By Grieg, Op. 56, No. 3, in the *Sigurd Jorsalfar* mus., also known as 'Triumphal March'.

Hull, (Sir) **Percy** (Clarke) (*b* Hereford, 1878; *d* Farnham, 1968). Eng. organist and cond. Ass. organist to Sinclair at Hereford Cath., 1896–1914; organist, 1919–49; cond. 3 Choirs Fests. Knighted 1947.

Hullah, John Pyke (*b* Worcester, 1812; *d* London, 1884). Eng. composer, organist, and educator. Propagator from 1840 of Wilhem's fixed-doh method of sight-singing. Prof. of vocal mus., Queen's Coll. and Bedford Coll., London, 1844–74, Inspector of Training Schools UK from 1872. Comp. operas (1 to lib. by Dickens), church mus., part-songs, and songs.

Hume, Tobias (*b* ?c.1569; *d* London, 1645). Eng. composer and army officer. His *First Part of Ayres* for lyra-viol was pub. 1605, with fanciful titles such as 'Tickle me quickly' and the instruction, thought to be the first recorded use of *col legno*, to 'drum this with the back of the bow'. In 1607 his *Captaine Humes Poeticall Musicke* constituted the largest pubd. repertory of solo lyra-viol music to that date.

Humfrey (Humphrey), **Pelham** (*b* London, 1647; *d* Windsor, 1674). Eng. composer. Chorister of Chapel Royal 1660–4, then studied with Lully in Paris. Gentleman of Chapel Royal 1667, Master of the Children 1672. Taught Purcell. Comp. incidental mus. to Shakespeare's *The Tempest*, sacred and secular songs, anthems, and other church mus.

Hummel, Johann Nepomuk (*b* Pozsony, 1778; *d* Weimar, 1837). Austrian pianist and composer. Lived and studied pf. with Mozart 1785–7. Début Vienna 1787 at Mozart concert. Toured Holland and Britain studying in London with *Clementi. In Vienna, 1793, studied comp. with *Albrechtsberger and *Salieri. Kapellmeister to Prince Esterházy 1804–11. Kapellmeister at Stuttgart 1816–18, then at Weimar 1819–37. Toured extensively, conducting the Ger. Opera in London, 1833. Pubd. pf. sch. 1828. Comp. numerous works incl. pf. concs. and sonatas, bn. conc., mandolin conc., operas, oratorios, and much chamber mus. Mus. has melodic grace and abundant craftsmanship. Pf. writing influenced Chopin. His relationship with Beethoven fluctuated but they were reconciled at Beethoven's death-bed. Was pall-bearer at Beethoven's funeral and played at his memorial concert. Schubert dedicated his last 3 pf. sonatas to him (but publisher altered the dedications after Schubert's death).

Humoresque (Fr.), **Humoreske** (Ger.). Title given by some composers to a lively and capricious (sometimes a little sad) instr. comp. Famous examples are by Dvořák (particularly No. 7 of his 8 *Humoresques* for pf., Op. 101, 1894), and Schumann, for pf., Op. 20, 1839. Mahler orig. conceived his 4th Sym. as a 'symphonic Humoresque'.

Humperdinck, Engelbert (*b* Siegburg, 1854; *d* Neustrelitz, 1921). Ger. composer. Studied Cologne Cons. 1872–6 under F. Hiller and later at Munich. Met Wagner in It. 1879 and was invited to assist in preparation for prod. of *Parsifal* at Bayreuth. Taught theory, Barcelona Cons., 1885–6. Prof. of harmony, Hoch Cons., Frankfurt, 1890–6, also acting as mus. critic for *Frankfurter*

Zeitung. His opera *Hänsel und Gretel*, which effectively uses a Wagnerian idiom for a fairytale, was a success at Weimar, 1893, and subsequently elsewhere ever since. His other operas failed to emulate its success. Dir., Berlin Akademische Meisterschule for comp. from 1900. Prin. works:

OPERAS: **Hänsel und Gretel* (1893); *Dornröschen* (1902); *Die Heirat wider Willen* (1905); **Königskinder* (1910); *Die Marketenderin* (1914); *Gaudeamus* (1919).

INCIDENTAL MUSIC: *Merchant of Venice* (1905); *The Winter's Tale* and *The Tempest* (1906); *As You Like it* (1907); *Lysistrata* (1908); *The Miracle* (1911); *The Blue Bird* (1912).

SONGS: *Kinderlieder*.

Humphrey, Pelham. See *Humfrey, Pelham*.

Hungarian Dances (*Ungarische Tänze*). 21 pf. duets by Brahms pubd. in 4 vols. between 1852 and 1869. 3 were orch. by him, and he arr. some for pf. solo (Nos. 1–10).

Hungarian Rhapsodies. 19 comps. for pf. by Liszt, comp. 1846–85. Of·these 12 were orch., some by Franz Döppler. The *Hungarian Fantasia* for pf. and orch. is based on No. 14. There are discrepancies between the numbering of pf. and orch. versions.

Hunnenschlacht (Battle of the Huns). 11th of Liszt's 12 symphonic poems. Comp. 1856–7, f.p. Weimar 1858. Inspired by Kaulbach's mural of legend of battle in the air between ghosts of slain Huns and Romans after Battle of Chalons in 451.

Hunt, Donald (Frederick) (*b* Gloucester, 1930). Eng. cond., organist, and composer. Studied RCO and RCM and with Herbert **Sumsion*. Ass. organist Gloucester Cath. 1948–54, dir. of mus. Leeds Parish Church 1957–74, organist Worcester Cath. from 1975. Composer of church mus., org. sonata, carols, etc.

Hunt Quartet. Nickname for Mozart's Str. Qt. No. 17 in B♭ (K458, 1784), ded. to Haydn, and so called because of the 1st subject of 1st movement.

Hunt, The (Haydn). See *Chasse, La*.

Hunt, Thomas (*fl.* early 17th cent.). Eng. composer of church mus., etc. Contributed madrigal *Hark, did you ever hear so sweet a singing?* to *The *Triumphs of Oriana* (1601).

Hunter, Rita (*b* Wallasey, 1933). Eng. sop. Joined SW ch. 1954. Studied with Clive Carey, Eva Turner, and Redvers Llewellyn. CG début (3rd Norn) 1963. Prin. sop. SW from 1965. Prin. sop., ENO, the Brünnhilde of their Eng. *Ring* cycle, 1970. NY Met. début 1972 (Brünnhilde in *Die Walküre*). C.B.E. 1980.

Hüpfend (Ger., 'hopping'). In str. playing, 'with springing bow', i.e. **spiccato*.

Hurd, Michael (John) (*b* Gloucester, 1928). Eng. composer, cond., author, and teacher. Studied Oxford. Comps. incl. operas, cantatas, church mus., chamber mus., songs. Books on Britten, Elgar, Vaughan Williams, Gurney, opera, sea shanties, soldiers' songs; author of *The Oxford Junior Companion to Music* (1979).

Hurdy-gurdy (*organistrum, symphonia, chifonie, organica lyra, vielle à roue* 'wheel fiddle'). A portable medieval str. instr., shaped like a viol, dating (in Europe) from early 12th cent. 1st str. instr. to which kbd. principle was applied. The instr. is hung round the player's neck or strapped to the body at an angle which lets the keys fall back under their own weight. Bowing action replaced by wheel cranked by a handle. Outer rim of wheel, coated with resin, makes all str. resonate at once, providing a continuous drone like a bagpipe. Fingering is also mechanized, the same str. being stopped at different points to produce required scale. Orig. required 2 players, but during 13th cent. improvements enabled solo perf., thus transforming its use from a cumbersome instr. to one capable of providing dance mus. By 14th cent. there were 6 str. and a kbd. compass of 2 chromatic octaves. Application of the term to any instr. worked by turn of a handle, e.g. barrel-org., street pf., is incorrect. See *Lira organizzata*.

Hurford, Peter (John) (*b* Minehead, 1930). Eng. organist and composer. Studied RCM and Cambridge Univ. 1948–52. Début, London (Festival Hall) 1957. Master of the Mus., St Albans, from 1958. Comps. incl. church mus. and org. suites. O.B.E. 1984.

Hurlstone, William (Yeates) (*b* London, 1876; *d* London, 1906). Eng. composer and pianist. Studied RCM 1894–8 with Stanford (comp.) and Dannreuther (pf.). Soloist in own pf. conc., London, 1896. Wrote much chamber mus., ballad *Alfred the Great*, and *Fantasie-Variations on a Swedish Air* (1903) for orch. Prof. of counterpoint RCM, from 1905.

Hurst, George (*b* Edinburgh, 1926). Eng. cond. of Romanian and Russ. parentage. Studied pf. with J. Isserlis, then entered Royal Cons., Toronto. Studied cond. with Monteux. Cond., York S.O. Penn., 1950–55, London début 1953 (with LPO); ass. cond., LPO 1955–7. Prin. cond., BBC Northern S.O. 1958–68; Bournemouth S.O. 1969–71; art. adviser and cond. Bournemouth Sinfonietta to 1978, then free-lance.

Hurtig (Ger.). **Allegro*, i.e. nimble, quick.

Hurwitz, Emanuel (*b* London, 1919). Eng. violinist and cond. Studied RAM. Leader, Aeolian Str. Qt. from 1970. Leader, Melos Ens. 1956–72, ECO 1947–69, New Philharmonia Orch. 1969–71. Cond. N.W. Youth Chamber Orch. from 1976. Frequent player in various chamber ens. C.B.E. 1978.

Husa, Karel (*b* Prague, 1921). Amer. composer and cond. of Cz. birth. Studied Prague Cons.

1941–5 and in Paris 1946–51 with Boulanger and Honegger (comp.) and Cluytens and Fournet (cond.). Cond. of various orchs. in Prague and Paris. Ass. prof. Cornell Univ. Mus. Dept. 1954–61, prof. from 1961. Comps. incl.:

ORCH: 3 *Frescoes* (1947); pf. concertino (1949); Sym. No. 1 (1953); *Portrait* for str. (1953); *4 Easy Pieces* for str. (1955); *Fantasies* (1956); *Poem* for va. and orch. (1959); *Mosaïques*; *Elegy and Rondo* for alto sax. and orch. (1961); *Serenade* for wind quintet and str. (1963); Conc. for brass quintet and str. (1965); *Music for percussion* (1966); Conc. for alto sax. and band (1967); *Music for Prague* (1968); *The Steadfast Tin Soldier*, speaker, orch. (1974).

CHAMBER MUSIC: Str. Qts. No. 1 (1948), No. 2 (1953), No. 3 (1968); vn. sonatina (1945); *Evocations of Slovakia* for cl., va., and vn. (1951); wind trio (1966); pf. sonata (1949); vn. sonata (1972–3).

Hüsch, Gerhard (*b* Hanover, 1901; *d* Munich, 1984). Ger. bar. Début Osnabrück 1923. Sang in opera in Bremen 1924–7, Cologne 1927–30, and Berlin 1930–42. Début CG 1930. Particularly noted for Lieder singing.

Hutchings, Arthur (James Bramwell) (*b* Sunbury-on-Thames, 1906). Eng. teacher, author, and composer. Prof. of mus. Durham Univ. 1947–68, Exeter Univ. 1968–71. Author of books on Schubert, Delius, Mozart's pf. concs., and church mus. Contrib. to many reference books.

Hüttenbrenner, Anselm (*b* Graz, 1794; *d* Ober-Andritz, 1868). Austrian composer. Studied in Vienna with *Salieri. Acquainted with Beethoven and Schubert.

Huygens, Constantijn (*b* The Hague, 1596; *d* The Hague, 1687). Dutch composer and perf. on a variety of instr., incl. viol, lute, org., theorbo, and guitar. Visited London 1618 and twice thereafter. Comp. nearly 900 instr. and vocal pieces.

Hyde, Walter (*b* Birmingham, 1875; *d* London, 1951). Eng. ten. Studied RAM with G. Garcia. Sang Siegmund in Richter's Eng. *Ring*, CG 1908. Sang regularly at CG 1908–32, with Beecham Co. and later with BNOC. First Eng. Sali in Delius's *A Village Romeo and Juliet*.

Hydraulis. Ancient instr., also known as water org., said to have been invented by Gr. Ktesibios *c.*250 BC Resembled small modern org. Kbd. operated by series of levers, each with a return mechanism, pressed down by fingers to obtain required notes. Water was used to stabilize wind pressure. In 4th cent. AD hydraulic mechanism was replaced by bellows, enabling much louder tone. See also *Organ.*

Hymn. Song of praise to the deity or a saint. Particularly assoc. with Anglican church where words and melodies of hymns are especially popular for congregational singing. Books of hymns and hymn-tunes of special significance are *Hymns Ancient and Modern* (1861 and many subsequent edns.), *The Yattendon Hymnal* (Bridges, 1899), *The English Hymnal* (1906, rev. 1933, mus. ed. Vaughan Williams, in which some folk tunes were adapted as hymn-tunes), and *Songs of Praise* (1925, rev. 1931, mus. ed. Vaughan Williams and Martin Shaw). In Eng. hymn-books, tunes are given an identifying title such as a Latin translation, or the name of a town or village, e.g. Down Ampney (Vaughan Williams's birthplace) is title of his *Come down, O love divine*.

Hymnen (Anthems). Comp. by *Stockhausen which exists in 3 versions, incl. one for elec. instr. and *musique concrète*, and one with added soloists, (both 1966–7). A shorter version with orch. was made in 1969. The anthems are nat. anthems.

Hymn of Jesus, The. Work for 2 ch., women's semi-ch., and orch., Op. 37, by Holst to words trans. by Holst from the apocryphal Acts of St John. Comp. 1917. F.p. London 1920, cond. Holst.

Hymns from the Rig Veda. 23 settings by Holst of his trans. of words from the Sanskrit. There are 5 sets: *9 Hymns* for solo v. and pf., Op. 24, 1907–8; *3 Choral Hymns*, Group I, for ch. and orch., Op. 26, 1908; *3 Choral Hymns*, Group II, for women's vv. and orch., Op. 26, 1909; *4 Choral Hymns*, Group III, for women's vv. and harp, Op. 26, 1909–10; *4 Choral Hymns*, Group IV, for men's vv., str., and brass, Op. 26, 1912.

Hymn to St Cecilia. Setting of text by W. H. Auden for unacc. 5-part ch. by Britten, Op. 27. Comp. 1942. F.p. London 1942.

Hymn to St Magnus. Work by *Maxwell Davies for sop. and chamber ens. F.p. London 1972, cond. composer.

Hymnus Amoris (Hymn of Love). Cantata, Op. 12, by Nielsen, comp. 1896 to Danish text by A. Olrik, Latin text by J. L. Heiberg, for sop., ten., bar., and bass soloists, children's ch., mixed ch., male ch., and orch. F.p. Copenhagen 1897, cond. Nielsen; f. Eng. p. Birmingham 1959.

Hymnus Paradisi (Hymn of Paradise). Requiem by *Howells for sop. and ten. soloists, ch., and orch. to texts selected by him from Latin Mass for the Dead, Psalm 23, Psalm 121, the Burial Service, and the Salisbury Diurnal (trans. G. H. Palmer). Comp. 1938 in memory of his son, but not released for perf. until 1950 (Gloucester Fest.). Some of the themes in *Hymnus Paradisi* were first employed in Howells's *Requiem* for unacc. ch., comp. in 1936. The *Requiem* was reassembled from MS. and perf. in 1980.

I

I (It.). The (masc. plural).

Ibéria. No. 2 of Debussy's *Images* for orch. Comp. 1905–8, f.p. 1910, Paris. In 3 sections: 1. *Par les Rues et par les chemins* (By highways and byways); 2. *Les Parfums de la nuit* (Night Scents); 3. *Le Matin d'un jour de fête* (Morning of festival day). This evocation of Sp. was written by a composer who went to Sp. for one day in his life—to see a bullfight.

Iberia. 4 books (1906–09) containing 12 pf. pieces by *Albéniz, several being orch. by *Arbós.

Ibert, Jacques (François Antoine) (*b* Paris, 1890; *d* Paris, 1962). Fr. composer. Studied Paris Cons. 1909–13. Dir., Fr. Acad., Rome, 1937–55, ass. dir. Paris Opéra and Opéra-Comique 1955–7. Works, light and witty in style, incl.:

OPERAS: *Angélique* (1926); *Le Roi d'Yvetot* (1928); *Gonzague* (1930); *L'*Aiglon* (with Honegger, 1935).

BALLETS: *L'*Eventail de Jeanne* (with 9 other composers, 1927); *Le Chevalier errant* (1935).

ORCH: *Escales* (1922); *Divertissement* (1930, adaptation from mus. for Lebiche's play *Un Chapeau de paille d'Italie* (The Italian Straw Hat)); fl. conc. (1934); concertino da camera for alto sax. (1935); *Louisville Concerto* (1953); Sym. No. 2 ('Bostoniana') (1955–61).

CHAMBER MUSIC: *Capriccio* for 10 instr. (1938); Str. qt. (1937–42); Trio for vn., vc., harp (1942).

VOICE AND PIANO (or ORCH.): *Le Petit Âne blanc* (The Little White Donkey) (1940, from *Histoire No. 2* for pf., 1922).

Ice Break, The. Opera in 3 acts by *Tippett to his own lib., comp. 1973–6. Prod. CG 1977, Kiel 1978 (as *Wenn das Eis bricht*).

Idée fixe (Fr.). Fixed idea. Term used by *Berlioz, in his *Symphonie fantastique* and elsewhere, for what is in essence a *leitmotiv* or *motto-theme. Berlioz borrowed the term from medicine, where it means 'a delusion that impels towards some abnormal action'.

Idiophone. Term for mus. instr. which produce sound from their own substance, e.g. castanets, cymbals, bells, etc. Can be struck, plucked, blown, or vibrated by friction. One of 4 classifications of instr. devised by C. Sachs and E. M. von Hornbostel and pubd. in *Zeitschrift für Ethnologie*, 1914. Other categories are *aerophones, *chordophones, and *membranophones, with *electrophones recently added.

Idomeneo, Re di Creta, ossia Ilia ed Idamante (Idomeneus, King of Crete, or Ilia and Idamante).

Opera seria in 3 acts by Mozart (K366) (comp. 1780–1) to It. lib. by G.B. Varesco, after Danchet's lib. for *Campra's *Idoménée* (1712) and the ancient legend. For Vienna private perf. in 1786 Mozart made additions to the score incl. new sop. aria *Non temer, amato bene* (K490), now sung in many modern perfs. Prod. Munich 1781, Karlsruhe 1917, Dresden 1925, Glasgow 1934, Tanglewood 1947, Glyndebourne 1951, NY 1951, London 1962 (1st CG prod. 1978). For revival at Vienna, 1931, R. Strauss ed. (liberally) the score and added mus. of his own, with text rewritten by L. Wallerstein, and Wolf-Ferrari ed. the work for Munich, 1931. Many textual and other special musicological problems attend this opera. For details, see W. Mann's *The Operas of Mozart* (1977).

Idyll. In literature a description (prose or verse) of happy rural life, and so sometimes applied to a mus. comp. of peaceful pastoral character (e.g. Wagner's *Siegfried Idyll*).

Idyll: Once I Passed through a Populous City. For sop., bar., and orch. by Delius to text by Whitman. Comp. 1930–2, containing re-working of parts of early opera, *Margot-la-rouge* (1901–2).

Igloi, Thomas (George) (*b* Budapest, 1947; *d* London, 1976). Hung.-born cellist. Studied RAM and with Fournier and Casals. Début London 1969. Winner, BBC vc. competition 1969, Casals int. vc. competition, Florence, 1971; soloist with leading orchs.

Il (It.). The (masc. sing.).

Île joyeuse, L' (The Island of Joy). Pf. piece by Debussy comp. 1904 and inspired by one of Watteau's 2 pictures, *L'Embarquement pour Cythère*, which delicately depicted early 18th-cent. scene of party about to embark for the island sacred to Venus.

Iliffe, Barrie (John) (*b* Westcliff, 1925). Eng. concerts administrator. Concerts manager, RLPO, 1951–5, orch. manager, Philharmonia 1955–6, Cape Town Orch. 1956–8, London Mozart Players 1961–3, gen. manager New Philharmonia 1964–5. Head of Mus., Brit. Council since 1966.

Illica, Luigi (*b* Piacenza, 1857; *d* Piacenza, 1919). It. playwright and librettist. Wrote, or helped to write, over 80 opera libs., among them (with Giacosa) those for Puccini's *Manon Lescaut, La Bohème, Madama Butterfly*, and *Tosca*; also for Catalani's *La Wally*, Mascagni's *Iris*, and Giordano's *Andrea Chénier*.

Illuminations, Les (The Illuminations). Song-cycle for high v. and str. orch., Op. 18, by Britten, comp. 1938–9, text being 9 prose-poems by Fr. poet Arthur Rimbaud written 1872–3 (*Les Illuminations* and *Poèmes en prose*). F.p. London, 1940 (Nos. 5 and 7 perf. separately in Birmingham and London 1939).

Images (Pictures). Title given by Debussy to 2 works: (1) *Images* for orch. (*Gigues*, 1909–12, orch. *Caplet; *Ibéria*, 1905–8, and *Rondes de Printemps*, 1905–9). First perf. as triptych, Paris 1913 cond. Pierné. (2) 2 sets for solo pf., set 1 (1905) containing *Reflets dans l'eau, Hommage à Rameau, Mouvement*; set 2 (1907) containing *Cloches à travers les feuilles, Et la lune descend sur le temple qui fut,* and *Poissons d'or*.

Imaginary Landscape. Title of 5 perc. works by *Cage in which he also developed his interest in unusual and elec. sounds. No. 1 (1939) is for two variable speed gramophone turntables, frequency recordings, muted pf., and cymbal; No. 2 (*March*) is for perc. quintet (1942); No. 3 (1942) for perc. sextet; No. 4 (*March No. 2*) for 12 radios, 24 players, and cond. (1951); No. 5 (1952) is a score for making a recording on tape using any 42 gramophone records.

Imbrie, Andrew (Welsh) (*b* NY, 1921). Amer. composer and pianist. Studied pf. with Leo Ornstein 1930–42, later with R. Casadesus. Studied comp. privately with *Sessions 1938–48. Taught at Univ. of Calif. from 1948 (prof. from 1960). *Prix de Rome* 1947, working in Rome 1947–51, 1953–4. Works incl. opera (*Christmas in Peebles Town*, 1962–3), 4 syms., vn. conc., 3 pf. concs., fl. conc., *Legend* for orch., chamber sym., vc. sonata, 4 str. qts., pf. sonata, *Psalm 42* for male ch. and org., *Drum Taps* for ch. and orch.

Imitation. Compositional device in part-writing involving repetition by one v. of more or less the phrase previously stated by another v. In *Canon* and *Fugue*, imitation is according to a strict regulated pattern.

Imitazione, Aria d'. See *Aria*.

Immortal Hour, The. Mus. drama in 2 acts by *Boughton to own lib. based on works of 'Fiona Macleod' (William Sharp). Prod. Glastonbury 1914, London 1922, NY 1926.

Imperfect Cadence. See *Cadence*.

'Imperfect' Time. See *Common Time*.

Impériale, L' (The Imperial). Nickname for Haydn's Sym. in D major, No. 53 in Breitkopf edn., comp. *c*.1780. Name first used in 19th-cent. Paris catalogue of Haydn syms. for unknown reason.

Imperial Mass. Another name for Haydn's *Nelson Mass*.

Impresario, The(*Der Schauspieldirektor*). Comedy with mus. in 1 act (K486) by Mozart to lib. by G. Stephanie. Prod. Vienna 1786, London 1857, NY 1870.

Impressionism. Term used in graphic art from 1874 to describe the work of Monet, Degas, Whistler, Renoir, etc., whose paintings avoid sharp contours but convey an 'impression' of the scene painted by means of blurred outlines and minute small detail. It was applied by musicians to the mus. of Debussy and his imitators because they interpret their subjects (e.g. *La Mer*) in a similar impressionistic manner, conveying the moods and emotions aroused by the subject rather than a detailed tone-picture. To describe Debussy's harmony and orchestration as impressionist in the sense of vague or ill-defined is to do them a severe injustice. Some of the technical features of musical impressionism included new chord combinations, often ambiguous as to tonality, chords of the 9th, 11th, and 13th being used instead of triads and chords of the 7th; *appoggiatura* used as part of the chord, with full chord included; parallel movement in a group of chords of triads, 7ths, and 9ths, etc.; whole-tone chords; exotic scales; use of the modes; and extreme chromaticism.

Impromptu (Fr.). Literally 'improvised' or 'on the spur of the moment', but in 19th cent., name given to short piece of instr. mus., often in song-like form, e.g. those by Schubert, Chopin, and Schumann. In 20th cent., term has been used by Britten for rev. 3rd movement of his pf. conc.

Improvisation (or extemporization). A perf. according to the inventive whim of the moment, i.e. without a written or printed score, and not from memory. It has been an important element in mus. through the centuries, viz. (1) from the 12th to the 17th cents., in vocal descant when a part was improvised by one singer to a notated part sung by another. (2) in 17th and 18th cents. in the *'divisions' of viol players, i.e. the improvised decoration of the notes of a tune by shorter notes. Also the kbd. player's improvisation of the figured bass. (3) In the 18th cent. the filling-in of the preludes to kbd. suites which Handel and others often indicated merely as a series of chords from which the perf. was to develop his material. (4) From 18th cent., the *cadenza in concs. (sometimes written out, but often left to the virtuoso to invent). (5) In 18th and early 19th cents., the kbd. perfs. by which Bach, Mozart, Beethoven, Hummel, Clementi, and others enthralled their audiences by brilliant displays of improvisation. (6) The same as (5) by organists such as Bruckner and Widor, this practice still being fairly common among organists. (7) In jazz, improvisation by solo instrumentalists is part of the idiom's attraction. (8) *Aleatory or indeterminate features of 20th-cent. works are of an improvisatory nature. (9) The term is sometimes used as the title of a notated work which is intended to convey an impression of improvisation.

In Alt (It.). Notes are *in alt* which are in the octave immediately above the top line of the treble stave; the next octave is *in altissimo*.

In a Summer Garden. Rhapsody for large orch. by Delius, comp. 1908. F.p. London 1909, rev. version Edinburgh 1913. The garden was Delius's own at Grez.

Inbal, Eliahu (*b* Jerusalem, 1936). Israeli cond. Studied Paris Cons. under Fourestier and at Hilversum and Siena. Won Cantelli int. competition for conds. 1963. Chief cond. Frankfurt Radio S.O. from 1974. Opera début cond. Strauss's *Elektra*, Bologna 1969.

Incalcando (It.). Warming-up, i.e. getting faster and louder.

Incidental Music. Mus. written for atmospheric effect or to accompany the action in a play. It was provided 'incidentally' as far back as Gr. drama. Purcell wrote much incidental mus. for the th. of his day, and there are dozens of superb examples since the early 19th cent., e.g. Beethoven's for Goethe's *Egmont*, Mendelssohn's for Shakespeare's *A Midsummer Night's Dream*, Grieg's for Ibsen's *Peer Gynt*, Bizet's for Daudet's *L'Arlésienne*, Sibelius's for Maeterlinck's *Pelléas et Mélisande*, Walton's for Shakespeare's *Macbeth*, etc. Music for films and TV is also in a sense 'incidental music'.

Incoronazione di Poppea, L' (The Coronation of Poppaea). Opera in prol. and 3 acts by Monteverdi (his last) to a lib. by Busenello after Tacitus. Prod. Venice 1642, Naples 1651, Paris, concert version ed. d'Indy, 1905, stage 1913, Northampton, Mass., 1926, Oxford 1927. First opera on an historical, other than biblical, subject. In the 20th cent. there have been several edns., incl. those by Křenek, d'Indy, Benvenuti, Malipiero, Ghedini, W. Goehr, Harnoncourt, Curtis, and R. Leppard (first version f.p. Glyndebourne 1962, London 1971; second version f.p. Glyndebourne 1984). New edn. by Roger Norrington for Kent Opera 1974. In some respects this was the first 'modern' opera by virtue of its treatment of human emotions and personalities and its anticipation of a *leitmotiv* technique of comp.

Incorporated Society of Musicians. Assoc. of professional musicians founded in 1882. Meetings are held regularly in regional branches, and an annual conference is held in one of the large cities of the U.K. Examinations conducted by the soc. were dropped in 1928.

Incredible Flutist, The. Ballet with mus. by Walter *Piston. Prod. 1938. Concert suite from the ballet f.p. 1940.

Indes galantes, Les (The courtly Indies). Opéra-ballet in prol. and 3 *entrées* by *Rameau to lib. by Louis Fuzelier. Prod. Paris 1735, with 4th *entrée* 1736, NY 1962. Each *entrée* tells a love-story from a different part of the world: 1. *Le Turc généreux* (The generous Turk). 2. *Les Incas de Pérou* (The Incas of Peru). 3. *Les Fleurs, feste Persane* (The Flowers, Persian festival). 4. *Les Sauvages* (The Savages).

Indeterminacy. Much the same as *aleatory, but specially the principle by which a decision of the performer of a comp. replaces a decision of the composer.

India, Sigismondo d' (*b* Palermo, *c*.1582; *d* ? Modena, before 1629). It. composer and singer. Said to be of noble birth and spent 1600–10 travelling in It., visiting several courts. Probably met Monteverdi in Mantua 1606. Dir. of chamber mus. to the Duke of Savoy in Turin, 1611–23, during which period most of his mus. was written. Moved to Modena 1623–4, then to Rome where in 1625 his sacred opera *Sant' Eustachio* was perf. in Cardinal Maurizio's palace. Returned to Modena 1626. Regarded as most important composer of secular vocal mus. in early 17th cent. It. after Monteverdi. Collections of his works were pubd. in Milan and Venice from 1609 to 1623. Blended styles of Marenzio, Wert, Gesualdo, and Monteverdi into a rich polyphonic style of his own, with daring harmonies and treatment of dissonance.

Indianische Fantasie (Indian Fantasy). Busoni's Op. 44 for pf. and orch. Comp. 1913. Based on Amer. Indian themes.

Indianisches Tagebuch (Indian Diary). Work by Busoni, Book I being for pf. solo and Book II for orch. Comp. 1915.

Indian Queen, The. Semi-opera in 5 acts by Purcell, with text by Dryden and R. Howard about rivalry between Mexicans and Peruvians. Prod. London 1695, the final masque in Act V being by Daniel Purcell.

In dulci Jubilo (In sweet joy). 14th-cent. Ger. macaronic carol; Eng. version *c*. 1540. Popular setting for solo vocal octet and 5-pt. chorus by Robert L. Pearson dates from 1834.

Indy, Vincent d'. See *D'Indy, Vincent*.

Inextinguishable, The (*Det uudslukkelige*). Title of Sym. No. 4 by Carl *Nielsen, comp. 1915–16. F.p. Copenhagen 1 Feb. 1916; f.p. in England London, 22 June 1923, cond. Nielsen.

Infinite Canon (Perpetual Canon). Canon in which each v., having reached the end, begins again, and so indefinitely.

Inflection. In plainsong, the general name given to such parts as are not in monotone, i.e. incl. intonation, mediation, and ending, and excl. the recitation.

	♯	✕	♭	♭♭	♮
English	sharp	double sharp	flat	double flat	natural
German	Cis Dis Eis Fis Gis Ais ★His (The sign is called *Kreuz*)	Cisis Disis Eisis Fisis Gisis Aisis ★Hisis (The sign is called *Doppelkreuz*)	Ces Des Es Fes Ges As ★B (The sign is called *Be*)	Ceses Deses Eses Feses Geses Ases ★Bes (The sign is called *Doppel-Be*)	The sign is called *Quadrat* or *Auflösungszeich- en* (release- sign)
French	dièse	double-dièse	bémol	double-bémol	bécarre
Italian	diesis	doppio diesis	bemolle	doppio bemolle	bequadro

Inflection of Notes.

SHARP
Raising the note a half-step or semitone
♯

DOUBLE SHARP
Raising the note a full-step or tone
✕

FLAT
Lowering the note a half-step or semitone
♭

DOUBLE FLAT
Lowering the note a full-step or tone
♭♭

After a Sharp or Flat the Natural Sign ♮ restores the note to its normal pitch.
After a Double Sharp or Double Flat the Sign ♯ or ♭ (or ♮♯ or ♮♭) changes the pitch of the note to that of a single sharp or flat.
After a Double Sharp or Double Flat the Sign ♮ (rarely given ♮♮) restores the note to its normal pitch.
Any of these various signs is understood to affect not only the note before which it immediately occurs, but also, unless contradicted, any other notes on that same line or space of the staff throughout the measure (bar), and if the last note of the measure is thus inflected and is tied to the same note at the opening of the next measure, that latter also is understood to be included in the inflection.
Additions are made to the names of the notes as shown above.
Because of several irregularities in the Ger. names it has been thought best to set these out in full. Notice particularly the names marked ★.

Ingegneri, Marco Antonio (*b* Verona, *c.*1547; *d* Cremona, 1592). It. composer and church musician. Pupil of V. ★Ruffo. Choirmaster, Cremona Cath. from 1579. Comp. masses, motets, 8 books of madrigals, and 27 Responsoria for Holy Week. Taught ★Monteverdi.

Ingham, Steve (*b* London, 1951). Eng. composer. Studied at York Univ. 1972–5, later with Donald Erb in Indiana and with Ferneyhough in Ger. 1977–80. Northern Arts composer fellow, Newcastle upon Tyne Univ., 1980–2, lect. in mus.

1984. Comps. incl. *Ein frohlich Wesen*, orch. (1980), *Élégie*, str. qt. (1981), and *Indiana Suite*, small orch. (1982).

Inghelbrecht, Désiré (Émile) (*b* Paris, 1880; *d* Paris, 1965). Fr. cond. and composer. Cond. Swedish Ballet in Paris and London. Ass. cond. Pasdeloup concerts. Ass. cond. Opéra-Comique 1924, cond. 1932; cond. Paris Opéra 1945–50. Cond. Fr. Nat. Radio Orch. Author of several books. Comp. opera, ballet (*El Greco*), choral, orch., and chamber mus.

Inglott, William (*b* 1554; *d* Norwich, 1621). Eng. composer and organist. Organist, Norwich Cath. from 1608. Comp. a *Te Deum*, pieces for virginals, madrigals, etc.

In Honour of the City. Cantata by ★Dyson, setting of poem by William Dunbar (1465–1520), f.p. Lincoln 1928.

In Honour of the City of London. Cantata for ch. and orch. by ★Walton, setting of poem by William Dunbar, f.p. Leeds 1937; f. London p. Dec. 1937, cond. Walton.

In modo di (It.). In the manner of.

Innig (Ger.). Inmost, heartfelt. So the noun *Innigkeit*. Word frequently used by Eng. mus. critics to describe mystical or spiritual passages in the mus. of, for instance, Beethoven and Bruckner.

In nomine (In the name). A type of contrapuntal instr. comp. by 16th-cent. Eng. comps., usually for consort of viols but sometimes for lute or kbd. based on a version of a piece of plainchant. First used by ★Taverner, when he comp. an instr. piece based on the theme to which he set the words 'In nomine Domini' in his *Gloria Tibi Trinitas* Mass. This set a fashion, and the name 'In nomine' was adopted for this type of piece.

Insanguine, Giacomo (*b* Monopoli, Bari, 1728; *d* Naples, 1795). It. composer, sometimes called Monopoli. Comp. several operas, incl. *Didone abbandonata* (1769), and church mus.

Institut de recherche et de co-ordination acoustique-musique. Laboratories and elec. studios, part of the Georges Pompidou Centre, Paris, inaugurated 1977 under directorship of *Boulez, for experiment and research into modern compositional techniques. Known as I.R.C.A.M.

Instrumentation. Writing of mus. for particular instrs., especially referring to composer's knowledge of what is practicable on various instrs. Also used in sense of *orchestration.

Instruments, Musical. Objects or devices for producing mus. sound by mechanical energy or electrical impulses. They can be classified as: (1) Str. (plucked or bowed). (2) Wind (played by blowing direct into the mouthpiece or through a reed). (3) Perc. (of determinate or indeterminate pitch). (4) Elec. Note that the pf., though it has str., is percussive in its mechanism, so is not easily classified. For the classifications of instr. by C. Sachs and E. M. von Hornbostel pubd. in 1914, see *aerophones, chordophones, idiophones,* and *membranophones,* with *electrophones* as additional category. For the Sachs-Hornbostel introduction to their classifications, see *New Grove,* Vol. 9, pp. 241–5.

Intavolatura (It.). Entablature. Term denoting 'scoring' used in Elizabethan period. Referred to arr. of madrigals for kbd. perf.

Intégrales. Work for small orch. and perc. by *Varèse, comp. 1924–5, f.p. NY 1925.

Intendant (Ger.). Superintendent. Administrative dir. (not necessarily artistic or mus. dir.) of a Ger. opera house or th.

Interlude. Piece of mus. played between other pieces, such as an org. passage played between verses of a hymn, or between the acts of a play, or between scenes in an opera (e.g. the *Sea Interludes* in Britten's *Peter Grimes*). Also used as a title of a mus. work without above connotations.

Intermezzo (Intermedio) (It.; Fr. *Intermède*). In the middle. This word has undergone several changes in application, viz., (1) Originally, in 16th-cent. It., a mus. entertainment interpolated between sections of more serious fare, such as songs or madrigals, or between the acts of a play. Earliest recorded was at Florence 1539. In France, the *intermèdes* were sometimes on a sumptuous scale and sometimes comprised ballet only. Those by Lully for Molière's plays preceded or followed the comedy in addition to separating its acts and in some cases had nothing to do with the plot, e.g. the *Ballet des Nations* which concluded *Le bourgeois gentilhomme* (1670). (2) With the development of opera seria, based invariably on mythological legends, the *intermezzo* became popular because of its contrasted, more realistic, and topical, often comic, characters. At the beginning of the 18th cent., comic characters were admitted into opera seria in scenes near the end of an act, thus forming a separate plot, an *intermezzo*. Most popular of these *intermezzi* was Pergolesi's *La serva padrona* (The maid as mistress) (1733). From this form developed *opera buffa. (3) By the 19th cent. the word had come to be applied in the same sense as *interlude; and for a short orch. piece inserted into an opera to denote a lapse of time, as in Mascagni's *Cavalleria Rusticana,* or summarizing events as in the 'Walk to the Paradise Garden' in Delius's *A Village Romeo and Juliet.* (4) A short movement in a sym., conc., or sonata, e.g. the slow movement of Schumann's pf. conc. (5) Short independent pf. pieces by Brahms, Schumann, etc.

Intermezzo. 'Bourgeois comedy with symphonic interludes' in 2 acts by R. Strauss, comp. 1917–23 to his own lib. (based on a marital incident in his life, the two main characters being portraits of himself and his wife Pauline). Prod. Dresden 1924, Vienna 1927, NY 1963, Edinburgh 1965, Glyndebourne 1974.

Internationale. Socialist song composed by P. Degeyter (1848–1932) to words by Eugène Pottier, a Lisle woodworker. Was official anthem of Communist Russia until 1 Jan. 1944. Not the same as *The Red Flag.*

International Folk Music Council. Organization formed in London in 1947 at conference representing 28 countries. First pres. Vaughan Williams, succeeded 1958 by Maud *Karpeles. Devoted to int. research into folk mus., arranges fests., etc.

International Musical Society. Soc. devoted to musicological research, having about 20 nat. sections which combined for purposes of publication and conferences. Founded 1899 in Leipzig, terminated 1914 by World War I. Work carried on by *International Musicological Society.

International Musicological Society (International Society for Musical Research). Founded 1927 to resume and continue the work of the *International Musical Society. Headquarters at Basle. Publishes journal, *Acta Musicologica.*

International Society for Contemporary Music. Soc. founded after fest. by young Viennese composers in Salzburg in 1922, under first presidency of E. J. *Dent. Many nat. sections. Annual fest. held each year at a different place, at which the works of contemporary composers of all nationalities are given a hearing. Works to be played are chosen by int. jury. Known as I.S.C.M.

Interpretation in mus. is merely the act of perf., with the implication that in it the performer's judgement and personality have a share. Just as there is no means by which a dramatist can so write his play as to indicate to the actors precisely how they should speak his lines, so there is no means by which a composer can indicate to a performer the precise way in which his mus. is to be sung or played—so that no 2 performers will adopt the same slackenings and hastenings of speed (incl. *Rubato*), the same degree of emphasis on an accented note, and so forth. The matter is further complicated by composers' latitude in use of metronome markings as applied to a term such as *allegro* or *moderato* (e.g. varying in one work from ♩ = 160 to ♩ = 100 for *allegro*). Thus there is no 'right' or 'wrong' interpretation in the strict sense, but in matters of style and taste, a performer's 'interpretation' may be felt by listeners to be out of sympathy with, or a distortion of, the composer's intentions.

Interrupted Cadence. Chord of the dominant followed by that of sub-mediant.

Interval. The 'distance' between 2 notes is called an 'interval', i.e. the difference in pitch between any 2 notes. The 'size' of any interval is expressed numerically, e.g. C to G is a 5th, because if we proceed up the scale of C the 5th note in it is G.

The somewhat hollow-sounding 4th, 5th, and octave of the scale are all called *Perfect*. They possess what we may perhaps call a 'purity' distinguishing them from other intervals. The other intervals, in the ascending major scale, are all called *Major* ('Major 2nd', 'Major 3rd', 'Major 6th', 'Major 7th').

If any Major interval be chromatically reduced by a semitone it becomes *Minor*; if any Perfect or Minor interval be so reduced it becomes *Diminished*; if any Perfect or Major interval be increased by a semitone it becomes *Augmented*.

Enharmonic Intervals are those which differ from each other in name but not in any other way (so far as modern kbd. instruments are concerned). As an example take C to G♯ (an augmented 5th) and C to A♭ (a minor 6th).

Compound Intervals are those greater than an octave, e.g. C to the D an octave and a note higher, which may be spoken of either as a major 9th or as a compound major 2nd.

Inversion of Intervals is the reversing of the relative position of the 2 notes defining them. It will be found that a 5th when inverted becomes a 4th, a 3rd becomes a 6th, and so on. It will also be found that perfect intervals remain perfect (C to G a perfect 5th; G to C a perfect 4th, etc.), while major ones become minor, minor become major, augmented become diminished, and diminished become augmented.

Every interval is either *Concordant* or *Discordant*. The Concordant comprise all perfect intervals and all major and minor 3rds and 6ths; the Discordant comprise all augmented and diminished intervals and all 2nds and 7ths. It therefore follows that all Concordant intervals when inverted remain Concordant and all Discordant intervals remain Discordant.

Musical examples of Intervals are as follows:

N.B. The intervals marked * have little beyond a theoretical existence.

In the Faery Hills (*An Sluagh Sidhe*). Symphonic poem by Bax, comp. 1909, f.p. London 1910. The Faery Hills are in Co. Kerry, Ireland. One of 3 tone-poems comp. under the composite title *Eire*.

In the South (Alassio). Concert-ov. (tone-poem) by Elgar, Op. 50, f.p. London 1904. Sketched at Alassio, the work being an impression of It., its landscape and its imperial past.

In the Steppes of Central Asia (*V sredney Azii*, In Central Asia). 'Orchestral picture' by *Borodin, comp. 1880 to acc. *tableau vivant* at exhibition marking Alexander II's silver jubilee. Represents approach and passing of a caravan.

Intimate Letters (*Listy důvěrné*). Sub-title of Janáček's Str. Qt. No.2, comp. in 22 days 1928; so called because it is autobiographical in content, the letters concerned being those he wrote to Kamilla Stoesslová between 1917 and 1928 (he wanted to call it 'Love Letters'). F.p. Brno 1928; f.p. in England 1936 (broadcast).

Intolleranza 1960 (Intolerance 1960). Opera in 2 parts for 5 singers, mime, ch., and orch. by *Nono to his own lib. based on an idea by A. M. Ripellino. Comp. 1960–1. Prod. Venice 1961.

Intonation. (1) The opening phrase of a *plainsong melody, perhaps so called because it was often sung by the precentor alone, giving the pitch and (in the Psalms) the 'tone' of what was to follow.
(2) The act of singing or playing in tune. Thus we speak of a singer or instrumentalist's 'intonation' as being good or bad.

Intoning. The singing upon one tone or note, as is done by the clergy in parts of the Roman, Anglican, and other liturgies.

Intrada. The It. equivalent of the Fr. *Entrée*. Used as name for a movement by 18th-cent. composers and also in 20th cent. (e.g. in Vaughan Williams's *Concerto Grosso*).

Introduction. The beginning of a piece of mus., sometimes but not necessarily thematically linked to what follows (as in Elgar's *Introduction and Allegro for Strings*). Many syms., especially among those by Haydn, Mozart, and Beethoven, have extensive slow introductions to the first movement.

Introduction and Allegro. (1) Elgar's Op. 47, for str. qt. and str. orch., comp. 1905 (theme sketch 1901) and f.p. London 1905. Contains melody inspired by hearing Welsh singers on a distant hillside.
(2) *Bliss wrote an *Introduction and Allegro* for full orch. (1926).
(3) Ravel's Septet (1905) is entitled *Introduction and Allegro* for hp., fl., cl., str. qt.

Introit. Part of the Proper of the Mass. Initial chant, usually comprising antiphon with one verse and the Gloria patri. Also organ piece which replaces all or part of the sung Introit.

Invention. Name given by J. S. Bach to 15 of his shorter kbd. comps. in 2 parts or 'voices', incl. in his *Klavierbüchlein*, 1720. They are highly contrapuntal, being largely in the nature of imitation. Each works out some short melodic motif. Bach also left another 15 comps. in the same style, now known as his '3-part Inventions', to which he gave the title 'Symphonies'. The term was used before Bach's day for short vocal or instrumental pieces by Dowland, Janequin, and Negri, among others. It has occasionally been revived in the 20th cent., e.g. by Blacher and Berg.

Inventionshorn, Inventionstrompete (Ger.). Invention Horn, Invention Trumpet. The prefix 'Inventions' has been used to characterize several novelties. The *Inventionshorn* was the work of Charles Clagget (1740–c.1795) who united 2 instr., one in D and the other in Eb, in such a way that the player had both at command and could thus gain the advantage of the full chromatic scale. Clagget's work, patented 1788, was made possible by the invention, by the hn. player Hampel of Dresden, of curved sliding crooks called 'inventions', hence the name. The term *Inventionstrompete* seems to have been applied not only to the tpt. equivalent of the *Inventionshorn* but also to 2 earlier novelties, a short horn in F with crooks for every key down to Bb, and the 'Italian Trumpet' (coiled into horn shape).

Inversion. Literally, the turning upside down of a chord, interval, counterpoint, theme, or pedal point. A chord is said to be inverted when not in its 'root position'. For inversion of intervals, see *Interval*.

Inversion, Canon by. See *Canon*.

Inverted Cadence. See *Cadence*.

Inverted Mordent. See *Mordent*.

Inverted Pedal. See *Harmony*.

Inverted Turn. See *Gruppetto*.

Invertible Counterpoint. See *Counterpoint*.

Invisible City of Kitezh, The (*Skazaniye o nevidimom grade Kitezhe i deve Fevronii*; The legend of the invisible city of Kitezh and of the maid Fevronia). Opera in 4 acts by Rimsky-Korsakov to lib. by V. Belsky. Comp. 1903–5. Prod. St Petersburg 1907, London (concert) 1926.

Invitation to the Dance (*Aufforderung zum Tanz*). Title of Rondo Brillant in Db, Op. 65, for pf. by Weber (1819), representing a ballroom scene. Arr. for small orch. by *Lanner, c.1828. Often heard in arr. for orch. by Berlioz (1841), and sometimes, much altered, in one by Weingartner. Adopted by Diaghilev's Russian Ballet as mus. for *Le Spectre de la rose.*

In Windsor Forest. Cantata for ch. and orch. by Vaughan Williams containing 5 items adapted from his opera *Sir John in Love.* F.p. London 1931.

Ioannidis, Yannis (*b* Athens, 1930). Gr. composer. Studied pf. at Athens Cons. 1946–55, then organ, comp., and hpd. at Vienna Acad. 1955–9. Settled in Caracas and became Venezuelan cit. 1968. Prof. of harmony, Caracas Cons. 1971–6. Returned to Athens 1976. Several orch. works, incl. *Tropic* (1968) and *Orbis,* pf. and orch. (1975–6), also chamber mus. and songs.

Iolanta (Tchaikovsky). See *Yolanta.*

Iolanthe, or The Peer and the Peri. Operetta in 2 acts by Sullivan to lib. by Gilbert. Prod. London and NY 1882.

Ionian Mode. See *Modes.*

Ionisation. Work for perc. instr. by *Varèse comp. 1929–31, f.p. NY, 1933.

Iphigénie en Aulide (Iphigenia in Aulis). Opera in 3 acts by Gluck to lib. by Du Roullet after Racine's play based on Euripides. Prod. Paris 1774, Philadelphia 1935. Gluck used 3 nos. from *Don Juan* in this score. Also opera by Jommelli (1751).

Iphigénie en Tauride (Iphigenia in Tauris). Opera in 4 acts by Gluck to lib. by Guillard after Euripides. Prod. Paris 1778, London 1796, NY Met. 1916 (in version by R. Strauss, 1889–90). Ger. version 1781. Also opera by Jommelli (1771).

Ippolitov-Ivanov, Mikhail (Mikhaylovich) (*b* Gatchina, 1859; *d* Moscow, 1935). Russ. composer and cond. Studied St Petersburg with Rimsky-Korsakov. Head of Tiflis Cons. 1883–93. Reputation est. with *Caucasian Sketches* for orch. 1894. Prof. of comp. and harmony, Moscow Cons. 1893–1935 (dir. 1905–22). Cond., Bolshoy Opera from 1925. Wrote patriotic songs and marches such as *Song of Stalin.* Comp. 6 operas, the best of which (*The Last Barricade,* 1933–4) dealt with a Revolutionary subject. Added 3 acts to Mussorgsky's unfinished opera *The Marriage* (1931). Comp. sym., symphonic poem, 2 str. qts., vn. sonata, cantatas, songs, etc.

I.R.C.A.M. See *Institut de Recherche et de Coordination Acoustique-Musique.*

Ireland, John (Nicholson) (*b* Bowdon, Ches., 1879; *d* Washington, Sussex, 1962). Eng. composer and pianist. Studied RCM 1893–1901 (comp. with Stanford, pf. with Cliffe). Org., St Luke's, Chelsea, 1904–26. Prof. of comp. RCM 1923–39, pupils incl. Britten, Bush, Searle, and Arnell. He made his reputation with chamber mus. and with pieces for pf. solo in which his understanding of the instr. is paramount. His songs are in the best Eng. tradition and are typical of Ireland's style, which owes more to French influences than to English and has an individual restraint and austerity which is highly attractive. He did not compose syms. or large-scale choral works, but his orch. tone-poems and ovs. are colourfully scored and his pf. conc., with its racy jazz interludes, is among the best in the genre by an Eng. composer. Prin. works:

ORCH: *Tritons,* symphonic prelude (*c.*1905); *Bagatelle* (orig. for vn. and pf. 1911, arr. for orch. 1916); *Concertino Pastorale* for str. (1939); pf. conc. in E♭ (1930); *Epic March* (1942); *The *Forgotten Rite,* prelude (1913); *Legend* for pf. and orch. (1933); *A London Overture* (orig. for brass) (1936); *Mai-Dun,* symphonic rhapsody (1920–1); *The Overlanders,* suite arr. Mackerras from film mus. (1946–7); *Satyricon,* ov. (1946); *Downland Suite* for str. (1932).

CHORUS AND ORCH: *Vexilla Regis* (1898); *Greater Love Hath No Man,* motet (1912, orch. 1924); *These Things Shall Be,* cantata for bar. (or ten.), ch., and orch. (1936–7).

BRASS BAND: *Downland Suite* (1933); *Comedy Overture* (1934, orch. as *A London Overture* 1936); *Maritime Overture* (1944).

VOICES: *Greater Love Hath No Man* (sometimes called *Many Waters cannot quench Love*), motet for treble, bar., ch., and org. (1912, with orch. 1924); *The *Holy Boy,* unacc. carol (orig. pf. prelude 1913–5, arr. for vv. 1941, for org. 1919, for v. and pf. 1938, for brass (by Robert E. Stepp) 1950, for str. 1941); *Adam Lay Ybounden,* unacc. carol (1956); *Man in his labour rejoiceth,* with pf. (1947); *Island Praise,* unacc. male vv. (1955).

CHAMBER MUSIC: Sextet for cl., hn., str. qt. (1898); Str. qts.; No. 1 in D minor (1895), No.2 in C minor (1897); *Phantasy Trio* in A minor (1908); Piano Trio in E (1917); *Bagatelle* for vn. and pf. (1911, arr. for orch. 1916); Vn. Sonata No.1 in D minor (1908–9, rev. 1917), No.2 in A minor (1915–17); Vc. Sonata in G minor (1923, arr. for va. by *Tertis, 1941); *Fantasy Sonata* for cl. and pf. (1943); *The Holy Boy* (arr. for str. qt. 1941).

PIANO: Sonata in E minor (1918–20); sonatina (1926–7); *Decorations* (3 pieces incl. *The Island Spell*) (1921); 4 Preludes (No.3 is *The Holy Boy*) (1913–15); *Rhapsody* (1915); 3 *London Pieces* (No.1 is *Chelsea Reach*) (1917–20); *Merry Andrew* (1918); *The Towing-Path* (1918); *Summer Evening* (1919); 2 *Pieces* (*For Remembrance* and *Amberley Wild Brooks*) (1921); *Equinox* (1922); *Prelude* in E♭ (1924); *Ballade of London Nights* (*c.*1929, pubd. 1968); *Greenways* (3 *Lyric Pieces*) (1937); *Sarnia: An Island Sequence* (3 pieces) (1940–1); 3 *Pastels* (1941).

SONGS AND SONG-CYCLES: 5 *Songs of a Wayfarer* (*c.*1905–11); *Sea Fever* (1913); *The Holy Boy* (orig. pf. piece, 1913, arr. as song to poem by H.S. Brown 1938); *I Have Twelve Oxen; If there were Dreams to sell* (1918); *The *Land of Lost*

Content (6 Housman poems) (1920–1); 3 *Hardy Songs* (cont.) (1925); 5 *Poems by Thomas Hardy* (bar.) (1926); *We'll To The Woods No More* (3 Housman poems) (1926–7); 6 *Songs Sacred and Profane* (1929–31).

Iris. Opera in 3 acts by Mascagni, to lib. by Illica. Prod. Rome 1898; rev. version Milan 1899, Philadelphia 1902, London 1919.

Irische Legende (Irish Legend). Opera in 5 scenes by *Egk to his own lib. based on Yeats's *The Countess Cathleen* (1892). Prod. Salzburg 1955. (Rev. 1970).

Irish Symphony. (1) Sub-title of Stanford's Sym. No.3 in F minor, Op. 28, comp. 1887.

(2) Title of sym. by *Harty, based on Irish folk-songs; popular scherzo 'The Fair Day' often played separately. Comp. 1904, rev. 1915 and 1923.

(3) Title of Sym. in E minor by Sullivan, 1864–6.

Irmelin. Opera in 3 acts by Delius to his own lib. Comp. 1890–2, prod. Oxford 1953. The orch. prelude, frequently played separately, was comp. 1931.

Irregular Cadence. See *Cadence*.

Irregular Rhythmic Groupings.

(Duplets, Triplets, Quadruplets, etc.) Various combinations are possible other than those shown below, and it is hardly possible to list them or to lay down rules. When an irregular combination occurs the performer should observe the other notes of the measure, and he will quickly realize into what fraction of the measure the irregular grouping is to be fitted.

Irving, (Kelville) **Ernest** (*b* Godalming, 1878; *d* Ealing, 1953). Eng. cond., particularly of th. and film mus. Mus. dir., Ealing film studios 1935–53, engaging several leading Brit. composers to write film mus. Dedicatee of Vaughan Williams's *Sinfonia Antartica*.

Irving, Robert (Augustine) (*b* Winchester, 1913). Eng. cond. Studied RCM. Ass. cond. BBC Scottish Orch. 1945–8, mus. dir. SW (later Royal) Ballet 1949–58, NY City Ballet from 1958.

Isaac (Isaak), **Heinrich** (*b* Brabant, *c.*1450; *d* Florence, 1517). Flemish composer. From 1485 to 1493 in service of Lorenzo de' Medici at Florence as org., choirmaster, and teacher of his children. Court composer at Innsbruck 1497. Returned to Florence 1502 and also served at Ferrara. Comp. much church mus. and many secular songs. Wrote mus. for a religious drama by Lorenzo, many of whose poems he also set. Regarded as one of major figures of the *Desprès era.

Isaacs, Edward (*b* Manchester, 1881; *d* Manchester, 1953). Eng. pianist and composer. Studied RMCM and in Berlin, Vienna, and Leipzig. Débuts Berlin and Manchester 1904. Dir., Manchester mid-day concerts 1923–53. Blind for almost last 30 years of his life. Wrote pf. conc., pf. trio, etc.

Duplet or Couplet	Two in the time of three:
Triplet (see also under 'Sextolet' below)	Three in the time of two:
Quadruplet	Four in the time of three:
Quintuplet	Five in the time of four—or of three:
Sextolet or Sextuplet (and Double Triplet)	Six in the time of four: (really a triplet) If a grouping of 3+3 is desired it should be written as below: (really a double triplet)
Septolet, or Septuplet, or Septimole	Seven in the time of four—or of six:

Isaacs, Leonard (*b* Manchester, 1909). Eng. pianist and administrator, son of Edward *Isaacs. Studied RCM, and with Cortot and Petri. Joined staff of BBC 1936, becoming mus. programme organizer 1948–50 and head of mus. for 3rd Programme. Prof. of mus., Univ. of Manitoba, 1963.

Isador, Michael (*b* Philadelphia, 1939). Amer. pianist. Studied Paris Cons., Juilliard Sch., NY, and with Ilona Kabos in London 1962–5. Début Philadelphia 1951. Taught at Univ. of Calif. and San Francisco Cons. 1965–8, Univ. of Capetown 1969–71. Settled in Eng. 1975.

Islamey. Oriental fantasy for pf. by *Balakirev, 1st version, comp, 1869, 2nd version, comp. 1902. Orch. by Casella 1907.

I.S.C.M. *International Society for Contemporary Music.

Isepp, Martin (Johannes Sebastian) (*b* Vienna, 1930). Austrian-born pianist and harpsichordist. Studied Oxford and RAM. On staff Glyndebourne Opera from 1957 (chief coach 1973); taught at Juilliard Sch., NY, 1973–6. Accompanist to several leading singers, notably Janet Baker.

Isle of the Dead, The (*Ostrov myortvykh*). Symphonic poem Op. 29 by Rakhmaninov, comp. 1909 and inspired by Böcklin's painting of that name (*Insel der Toten*). F.p. Moscow 1909.

I.S.M. *Incorporated Society of Musicians (Britain).

Isola disabitata, L' (The Desert Island). Opera (*azione teatrale*) by Haydn to lib. by Metastasio. Prod. Esterháza 1779, Washington D.C. 1936, Wexford 1982.

Isometric (from Gr. *isos,* equal). Having the same rhythm in every v. or part (i.e. proceeding in chords rather than in freely moving counterpoint).

Isorhythm (from Gr. *isos,* equal). Term coined in 1904 by F. Ludwig to describe the principle found in medieval mus., *c.*1300–1450, whereby the same rhythmic pattern recurs in successive repetitions of the melody. It was usually applied to the ten. part of a motet which would consist of a short repeated rhythmic pattern; the melody in the ten. part was also often repeated but not in synchronization with the rhythmic repetition. Rhythmic repetition was known as *talea*, melodic as *color*. In the mus. of Machaut and de Vitry, the rhythmic pattern was not repeated in the same note values but in proportional diminution, e.g. original values were halved or reduced by a third. Nor did these composers confine isorhythm to the ten. parts but extended it to upper vv., especially in hocket. Eng. composers at the end of the 14th cent. developed isorhythm in all vv., so that it took two appearances of the *talea* to accommodate one of the *color*.

Isouard, Nicolò (*b* Malta, 1775; *d* Paris, 1818). Maltese composer, known sometimes as Nicolò. Studied pf. in Paris, completing studies in Naples. 1st opera prod. Florence 1794. Returned to Paris 1799, becoming popular opera composer in rivalry to Boieldieu. Of over 35 operas prod. in 16 years, the best was *Cendrillon* (1810), but also set *Il Barbiere di Siviglia* (*c.*1796). Comp. sacred works, airs, and romances.

Israel in Egypt. Oratorio by Handel, to Biblical text probably compiled by him. Comp. 1738, f.p. London 1739. Famous for its superb double choruses. The ch. *Egypt was glad* was borrowed, unacknowledged, from a canzona by *Kerll— indeed, up to a third of the music was taken from other composers.

Israel Philharmonic Orchestra. Formerly known as Palestine S.O., founded in 1936 by *Huberman. Toscanini cond. first concert, December 1936. Since 1951 has made frequent tours. Chief conds. have incl. Jean Martinon, Paul Kletzki, and, since 1968, Zubin Mehta, but many guest conds. Based in Tel Aviv.

Israel Symphony. For 2 sop., 2 cont., bass, and orch. by Bloch. Comp. 1912–16; f.p. NY 1916.

Istel, Edgar (*b* Mainz, 1880; *d* Miami, 1948). Ger. composer and musicologist. Studied Munich Univ. (comp. with *Thuille). Writer and teacher in Munich 1900–13; lecturer in Berlin 1913–19; worked in Sp. 1920–36, leaving there for Eng. and then (1938) USA. Comp. several operas and choral works; author of several books on Wagner, also on Cornelius, Paganini, comic opera, etc.

Istesso (It.). Same. Used in such connexions as *L'istesso tempo,* 'The same speed'—usually meaning that, though the nominal value of the beat has changed, its actual time duration is to remain the same: for instance, the former beat may have been ♩ (say in 4 time) and the new one ♩. (say in 6 time) and these are to have the same time value.

Istomin, Eugene (*b* NY, 1925). Amer. pianist of Russ. parentage. Studied Curtis Institute 1939 with Horszowski and Serkin. Début with Philadelphia Orch., 1943. Prades Fest. with Casals 1950. Played in pf. trio with Isaac Stern and Leonard Rose.

Istrumento d'acciaio (It.). Instrument of steel. Mozart's name for his *glockenspiel in *Die Zauberflöte.*

Italiana in Algeri, L' (The Italian girl in Algiers). Comic opera in 2 acts by Rossini to lib. by Anelli. Prod. Venice 1813, London 1819, NY 1832.

Italian Caprice. Orch. work by Tchaikovsky, Op. 45, comp. 1880, often known by mixed It.-Fr. title *Capriccio italien.*

Italian Concerto. Instr. comp. by Bach for solo hpd. with 2 manuals, pubd. in 2nd section of *Klavierübung, 1735. He seems to have used the term to draw attention to the facts that there are (a) passages of alternation and contrast, and (b) 3 movements, so resembling the It. *concerto grosso*.

Italian Girl in Algeria, The (Rossini). See *Italiana in Algeri, L'*.

Italian Serenade *(Italienische Serenade)*. Work for str. qt. by Wolf, 1887. Later arr. for orch. (1892) and ed. Reger.

Italian Sixth. See *Augmented Intervals*.

Italian Song-book (Wolf). See *Italienisches Liederbuch*.

Italian Symphony. Title given by Mendelssohn to his Sym. No.4 in A major, Op. 90. Begun in It. 1830–1 and completed 1833 but not pubd. until 1847 (it was his 3rd sym. in order of comp.). F.p. London 1833.

Italienisches Liederbuch (Italian Songbook). 46 songs for v. and pf. by *Wolf, all being settings of poems trans. from the It. by Paul von Heyse (1830–1914) and pubd. in 1860 under title *Italienisches Liederbuch*. Wolf's songs were comp. in 2 parts, Book I of 22 songs 1890–1, Book 2 of 24 songs in 1896. Some were later orch. by Wolf, others by Reger.

Iturbi, José *(b* Valencia, 1895; *d* Los Angeles, 1980). Sp. pianist and cond. Studied Valencia and Paris Cons. Head of pf. dept., Geneva Cons. 1919–23. London début 1923, Philadelphia 1928. Began active cond. career 1933 in Mexico City and NY. Mus. dir. Rochester P.O. 1935–44. Appeared in several films.

Ivan IV. Correct name of opera in 4 (orig. 5) acts by Bizet to lib. by F. H. Leroy and H. Trianon orig. written for Gounod. Comp. ?1862–3, rev. 1864–5. Efforts to have it prod. having failed, Bizet withdrew it. Incomplete MS. of score passed to Paris Cons. in 1929. Private stage perf. of this version was given at Mühringen Castle, Württemberg, 1946 under title *Ivan le Terrible*. Completed and rev. (reduced to 4 acts) by Henri Busser, perf. Bordeaux 12 Oct. 1951, Cologne 1952. Bizet used portions of score in other works. Perf. of orig. version broadcast by BBC 1975.

Ivanhoe. Opera in 5 acts by Sullivan (his only 'grand opera') to lib. by J. Sturgis after Scott's novel (1819). Comp. 1890. Prod. London 1891 (run of 160 perfs.), Berlin 1895.

Ivan Susanin. Orig. title of Glinka's opera *A *Life for the Tsar* by which it is now known in Communist and some other countries.

Ivan the Terrible (Rimsky-Korsakov). See *Maid of Pskov, The*.

Ives, Charles (Edward) *(b* Danbury, Conn., 1874; *d* NY, 1954). Amer. composer, one of the most extraordinary and individual figures in the history of Western mus. In his works, many of the innovatory and radical procedures adopted by younger *avant-garde* composers are anticipated or foreshadowed in some degree. His father was a town bandmaster who experimented with tone clusters, polytonality, quartertones, and acoustics, inspiring similar interests in his son. What fascinated George Ives, and later his son, was the clash of rhythm and tone resulting from two bands playing different tunes at a parade, or from his wife whistling at her housework and a boy elsewhere practising the pf. He would make Charles sing in a key different from the acc. 'to stretch our ears'.

At 14 Charles became organist at Danbury Baptist Church, composing in 1891 his *Variations on 'America'*. He entered Yale Univ. in 1894, studying org. with Dudley Buck and comp. with Horatio Parker (with whose conventional outlook Ives soon grew weary). Ives wrote his first sym. while at Yale, played the org. at Centre Church on the Green, and tried out some of his comps. on the local th. orch. In 1898 he graduated and moved to NY as a clerk in an insurance co., taking up several organist posts. In 1907 he and a friend formed their own insurance agency, which became very successful. Ives divided his time between business and mus., working long hours and damaging his health. He worked on a 2nd Sym. from 1900 to 1902 and a 3rd from 1904–11. Mahler was interested in this latter work but died before he could conduct it. From 1910 to 1918 Ives was at his most prolific, working on several comps. simultaneously. In 1918 he was seriously ill, sustaining cardiac damage; he gradually reduced his business activities, retiring in 1930, and he comp. little new after 1917, devoting the rest of his life to revising his comps. and thereby contributing to the chaotic state of his MSS., which led to untold difficulties in perf. He planned a *Universe Symphony* in which several different orchs., with huge choirs, were to be stationed in valleys, and on top of mountains.

In 1919 Ives decided to publish some of his mus., without copyright or performing rights. The vast *Concord Sonata* and 114 songs were issued in this way. The 1st perf. in NY of orch. mus. by Ives was in Jan. 1927 when Eugene Goossens cond. 2 movements from the 4th Sym. It was a failure. However, Ives's mus. was beginning to attract champions, among them the lecturer Henry Bellamann, the French pianist Robert Schmitz, and the composers and conds. Henry *Cowell, Wallingford *Riegger, Carl *Ruggles, Nicolas *Slonimsky and, later, Bernard *Herrmann and Lou *Harrison. Slonimsky bravely cond. perfs. of *Three Places in New England* in Boston, NY, and Los Angeles from 1930–2 and later cond. Ives works in Europe. Slonimsky also made the first Ives recording (1934) and Herrmann cond. the first Ives broadcast (*c*.1933). The pianist John Kirkpatrick devoted nearly 10 years to mastering the complexities of the *Concord Sonata* in consultation with Ives and played it in NY and elsewhere in 1939, arousing considerable enthusiasm. (It was f.p. in New Orleans in 1920.) In 1947 the 3rd Sym., perf. in NY that year, won the Pulitzer Prize, to Ives's dismay (he gave the prize money away). The 4th Sym. was not heard in its entirety until 11 years after Ives's death, when Stokowski cond. it.

Ives's mus. is sometimes called primitive but is in fact highly sophisticated. It is, like it or not, entirely honest mus., the outpouring of its stubborn and unusual creator, who delighted in pointing out that he had written most of his works before those by Stravinsky and Hindemith which some critics claimed had influenced him. The juxtaposition of incongruous elements, derived from the Danbury bands, occurs even in his earliest works. His *Psalm 67* of 1893 is in 2 keys throughout. Even in the Dvořákian 1st Sym. the use of tonality is remarkably free and unconventional. Jazz is drawn upon in his first pf. sonata; in the psalm settings for choir of 1896–1900 occur whole-tone scales, a 12-note row, tone clusters, polytonality, and polyrhythms. Aleatory procedures are anticipated in *The Unanswered Question* where the cond. is told to cue in various parts at will. In several of the orch. works the memory of the 2 bands playing different marches in different keys and tempi is vividly re-created. He 'borrowed' consistently from popular sources such as songs and hymns, or from other composers—over 170 such sources have been positively identified by scholars. Prin. works:

ORCH: *New England Holidays* (sometimes called *Holidays Symphony*): 1. *Washington's Birthday*. 2. *Decoration Day*. 3. *Fourth of July*. 4. *Thanksgiving and/or Forefathers' Day* (with ch.) (1904–13); *Orchestral Set No. 1* (*Three Places in New England*) (1908–14); *Orchestral Set No. 2* (1909–15); *Robert Browning Overture* (1908–12); *The *Unanswered Question* (1906); *Over the Pavements* (1906); *Central Park in the Dark in the Good Old Summertime* (1906); *The Gong on the Hook and Ladder* (or *Firemen's Parade on Main Street* (1911); *Rainbow* (1914, as song 1921); *Hymn* (arr. for orch. 1921); *Largo Cantabile* (1921); *Set* for th. or chamber orch. (1906–11); *Tone Roads No. 1* (1911), No. 3 (1915); Sym., No. 1 in D minor (1895–8), No. 2 (1900–02, some sketches earlier), No. 3 (*The Camp Meeting*) (1904–11), No. 4 (1910–16, with ch. in finale); *Variations on 'America'* (orch. arr. by W. Schuman). [Dates of comp. of the syms. are approximate, since Ives himself said he was not sure when he wrote them.]

CHORAL: *The Circus Band* (1894), bass soloist, ch., and orch.; *December* (1912–13), ch. and orch.; *Duty* (c.1912), ch. and orch.; *Easter Carol* (1892), ch. and orch.; *General William Booth Enters Into Heaven* (1914), bass soloist, ch., and orch. (also v. and pf.); *Lincoln The Great Commoner* (ch. and orch. 1912, v. and pf. 1914); *Majority* (ch. and orch. 1914–15, v. and pf. 1921); *The New River* (1911, rev. 1913 and ? 1921), ch. and orch.; *On The Antipodes* (1904), ch. and orch. 1915, v. and pf. 1923; *Psalm 14* (c.1897), *Psalm 25* (c.1897), *Psalm 54* (c.1896), *Psalm 67* (1898), *Psalm 100* (c.1898), *Psalm 135* (c.1899), *Psalm 150* (1896), for unacc. ch., orch., and org. or orch., *Psalm 90* (1896–1901, 1923–4), for sop., ten., ch., and orch; *Serenity* (ch. and orch. 1909, v. and pf. 1919); 3 *Harvest Home Chorales* (c.1898–1912), ch. and orch. or ch., brass, and org.; *Vita* (ch. and orch. or org. 1912, v. and pf. 1921); *Walt Whitman* (ch. and orch. 1913, v. and pf. 1921); *An Election, or Nov. 2, 1920* (male vv. or unison ch. and orch. 1920, v. and pf. 1921).

CHAMBER MUSIC (incl. v. and chamber ens.): *Song for Harvest Season*, mez. and brass quintet (c.1893); *The Children's Hour*, mez. and ch. orch. (1901); *Chromatimelodtune* for brass qt. and pf. (1909, 1913, 1919); *From the Steeples and the Mountains*, brass quintet (1901); *The Indians*, mez. and chamber orch. (1912), v. and pf. (1921); *Largo*, vn., cl., and pf. (1901); Vn. Sonata No.1 (1903–8), No. 2 (1903–10), No. 3 (1902–14), No. 4 (1892–1906, 1914–15); Str. Qt. No. 1 (*A Revival Service*) (1896), No. 2 (1907–13); Pf. Trio (1904–11).

PIANO: Over 20 *Studies* for pf., incl. Nos. 2, 5, 6, 7, 8, and 9 (*The Anti-Abolitionist Riots*), Nos. 15, 18, 20, 21 (*Some South-Paw Pitching*), No. 22 (*Twenty-Two*), and No. 23 (*Baseball Take-off*) (1907–9); 5 *Take-Offs* (*Seen and Unseen, Rough and Ready, Song without (good) Words, Scene Episode, Bad Resolutions and Good*) (1906–7); Sonata No. 1 (1901–9), No. 2 (*Concord, Mass. 1840–1860*) with solos for va. and fl. (1911–15); *3-Page Sonata* (1905); 6 *Protests* (*Varied Air and Variations*) (1916); 3 *Quarter-Tone Piano Pieces* for 2 pf. (1923–4); *Celestial Railroad*, arr. from 2nd movt. of 4th Sym. (c.1924).

ORGAN: *Prelude, Adeste Fideles* (1897); *Variations on a National Hymn, 'America'* (c.1891, also arr. for orch. by W. Schuman).

SONGS: Pubd. in the following colls.: 3 *Songs*; 4 *Songs*; 7 *Songs*; 9 *Songs*; 10 *Songs*; 11 *Songs and 2 Harmonizations*; 12 *Songs*; 13 *Songs*; 14 *Songs*; 19 *Songs*; 34 *Songs*; *Sacred Songs*.

Ivogün, Maria (Ilse Kemperer) (*b* Budapest, 1891; *d* Berlin, 1987). Hung. sop. Studied Vienna. Member of Munich Opera 1913–25. Created role of Ighino in Pfitzner's *Palestrina*, Munich 1917. CG début 1924 as Zerbinetta in Strauss's *Ariadne auf Naxos* (a role in which Strauss described her as 'without rival'), Berlin Municipal Opera 1925–34. Devoted herself to teaching after retirement (pupils incl. Elisabeth Schwarzkopf and Rita Streich).

Iwaki, Hiroyuki (*b* Tokyo, 1932). Japanese cond. Studied Tokyo Univ. Début Tokyo 1956. Chief cond. Melbourne S.O., mus. dir. and cond. N.H.K. S.O., Japan.

J

Jabo (Sp., in old Sp. *Xabo*). A solo dance in a slow triple rhythm.

Jacchini, Giuseppe Maria (*b* Bologna, *c*.1663; *d* Bologna, 1727). It. cellist and composer. Studied cello with Domenico Gabrielli (*b* Bologna, 1651; *d* Bologna, 1690). Cellist in orch. S. Petronio 1689–96 and 1701–27. Famous for tpt. and str. sonatas. Wrote pioneering solo vc. sonata.

Jack. See *Harpsichord*.

Jackson, Francis (Alan) (*b* Malton, 1917). Eng. organist, composer, and cond. Studied Durham Univ. and with *Bairstow. Organist Malton church 1933–40; organist and master of the mus., York Minster 1946–82. Frequent recitalist. Comps. incl. monodramas (speaker, ch., and orch.), org. sonatas, *Variations on a Theme by Vaughan Williams*, sym. in D minor (orch.), and numerous org. pieces, anthems, canticles, etc. O.B.E. 1978.

Jacob, Gordon (*b* London, 1895; *d* Saffron Walden, 1984). Eng. composer, teacher, and cond. Studied RCM under Stanford, Boult, and Howells. On staff RCM as prof. of theory, comp., and orchestration 1926–66. Author of textbooks on orchestration and its technique. Transcr. for full orch. and brass band Vaughan Williams's *English Folk-Song Suite*, orig. for military band, and for full orch. his *Variations* for brass band. Comps. incl. 2 syms. (1929, 1944), sinfonietta (1942), 2 va. concs. (1925, 1979), 2 pf. concs. (1927, 1957), bn. conc. (1947), hn. conc. (1951), vn. conc. (1953), 2 ob. concs. (1933, 1956), cl. conc. (1980), ballets, and numerous arrs. C.B.E. 1968.

Jacobi, Frederick (*b* San Francisco, 1891; *d* NY, 1952). Amer. composer, cond., and pianist. Studied NY with R. Goldmark (comp.) and at Berlin Hochschule. Ass. cond. at NY Met. 1913–17. Studied mus. of Pueblo Indians, living among them in New Mexico and Arizona. Indian themes and Jewish liturgical mus. are the main influences on his works. Taught at Juilliard Sch., NY, 1936–50. Comp. opera *The Prodigal Son* (1943–4), 2 syms., *Indian Dances* for orch., *Sabbath Evening Service*, *Ode to Zion*, vc. conc., pf. conc., vn. conc., 3 str. qts., pf. pieces, songs, etc.

Jacobin, The (*Jakobín*). Opera in 3 acts by Dvořák to lib. by M. Červinková-Riegrová. Comp. 1887–8. Prod. Prague 1889, London 1947.

Jacobs, Arthur (David) (*b* Manchester, 1922). Eng. mus. critic, ed., and translator. Mus. critic *Daily Express* 1947–52, then freelance critic for var. newspapers. Deputy ed. *Opera* magazine 1962–71; ed. *British Music Yearbook* 1971–80; ed. *A New Dictionary of Music* (1958, rev. 1967, 1973, 1977), *Choral Music* symposium 1963. Wrote *A Short History of Western Music* (1972), *Arthur Sullivan, a Victorian Musician* (1984), and contrib. to many other books and publications. Librettist of *Maw's *One-Man Show* (1964) and translator of over 20 opera libs. Lecturer in mus. history, etc., at RAM from 1964. Head of mus. dept., Huddersfield Polytechnic, 1979–85 (prof. from 1984). Visiting lecturer to several Amer. univs.

Jacobs, Robert L(ouis) (*b* Melbourne, Victoria, 1904). Australian writer and teacher. Studied privately in Vienna and Berlin. Extra-mural lecturer, London Univ. 1947–72. Author of books on Wagner, harmony, etc.; contrib. to encyclopedias.

Jacobson, Maurice (*b* London, 1896; *d* Brighton, 1976). Eng. composer and publisher. Studied RCM with Stanford and Holst. Mus. reader to J. Curwen & Sons from 1923, becoming dir. 1933, chairman 1950–72. Comps. incl. cantatas *The Hound of Heaven*, *The Lady of Shalott*, Symphonic Suite for Str., chamber mus., etc. Arr. several works by Vaughan Williams. O.B.E. 1971.

Jacotin, Jacques (*b* 1445; *d* Antwerp, 1529). Flemish composer whose identity is speculative. His *chansons* were pubd. by Attaignant. Also composed sacred mus.

Jacques, Reginald (*b* Ashby-de-la-Zouch, 1894; *d* Stowmarket, 1969). Eng. cond. and composer. Organist, Queen's Coll., Oxford. Cond. Oxford Harmonic Soc. 1923–30, Oxford Orch. Soc. 1930–6, London Bach Choir 1932–60. 1st mus. dir. of CEMA (later Arts Council) 1940–5. Founded Jacques Orch. 1936, remaining cond. Author of books on school mus. and v. training. C.B.E. 1954.

Jaeger, August (Johannes) (*b* Düsseldorf, 1860; *d* London, 1909). Ger. musician who settled in Eng. in 1878, working for printer of maps in the Strand, London. Joined staff of mus. publishers, Novello, in 1890, becoming head of publishing office. Was responsible for seeing works by Novello composers into print, especially those by Elgar, whose greatness he recognized. Became intimate friend of Elgar, their correspondence having since been pubd. Immortalized in Elgar's *Enigma Variations* as 'Nimrod' (Nimrod in the Bible was a hunter; *Jäger* = hunter in Ger.). To say, as is sometimes committed to print, that he was 'Elgar's publisher' is inaccurate.

Jahn, Otto (b Kiel, 1813; d Göttingen, 1869). Ger. archaeologist, philologist, and writer on mus. Held professional posts in Greifswald, Leipzig, and Bonn. Author of *Life of Mozart* (1st edn., 4 vols. Leipzig 1856–9, 2nd edn., 2 vols. 1867, 3rd edn. 1889–91, 4th edn. 1905–7. Eng. trans. 1882). Collected material for biographies of Haydn and Beethoven which was passed, respectively, to Pohl and Thayer. One of founders in 1850 of *Bach Gesellschaft.

Jahreszeiten, Die (Haydn). See *Seasons, The.*

Jakobsleiter, Die (Jacob's Ladder). Unfinished oratorio by Schoenberg, comp. 1917–22, for sop., 3 tens., 2 basses, speaking ch., ch., and orch., to his own text. Scoring completed by Winfried Zillig. F.p. (1st part) Hamburg 1958; (completed version) Vienna 1961; f.p. in England, London 1965.

Jalas, Jussi (b Jyväskylä, 1908). Finn. cond. Cond. at Finn. Nat. Th. 1930–45, cond. Helsinki Nat. Opera from 1945. Guest cond. in Eng., USA, and Europe. Son-in-law of Sibelius.

Jaleadas (Sp.). The 'Seguidillas Jaleadas' dance (see Seguidilla) is a vigorous form, showing the influence of the *cachucha.

Jaleo (in old Sp., *Xaleo*). Sp. solo dance in slow triple time.

Jalousieschweller (Ger.). Venetian-blind swell. The org. swell pedal.

Jamaican Rumba. Short piece for 2 pf. by Arthur Benjamin, pubd. in 1938. Arr. for many other combinations, particularly small orch.

James, Ifor (b Carlisle, 1931). Eng. hn.-player and cond. Hn.-player in Hallé, RLPO, and other orchs. Member, Philip Jones Brass Ens. Cond. of brass bands.

James, Ivor (b London, 1882; d London, 1963). Eng. cellist. Studied RCM, where later he was prof. of vc. and chamber mus. from 1919. Member of Eng. Str. Qt. 1909–25, Menges Qt. from 1931. C.B.E. 1953.

James, Philip (b Jersey City, NJ, 1890; d Southampton, NY, 1975). Amer. composer and cond. Studied Coll. of City of NY. Comp. pupil of R. Goldmark. Cond. operettas of Victor Herbert 1919–22. Faculty of Mus. NY Univ. 1923 (head of dept. 1933–55). Won NBC prize 1932 for satirical suite *Station WGZBX*. Works incl. ballet *Judith* (1927), ov. *Bret Harte*, 2 syms., symphonic poems, choral works (incl. *General William Booth Enters Into Heaven*), chamber mus.

Jam Session. Informal perf. by jazz musicians improvising collectively.

Janáček, Leoš (b Hukvaldy, E. Moravia, 1854; d Ostrava, 1928). Cz. composer, cond., organist, and teacher. Although he was 47 when the 20th cent. began, he is essentially a 20th-cent. com-poser. His father was a choirmaster. At 11, Janáček entered the Augustinian monastery, Brno, as a choirboy, studying mus. with Pavel Křížkovský. In 1872 he became a junior master at Brno teachers' training coll., and was at the Prague Organ Sch., 1874–6. He went to Leipzig and Vienna in search of fame and fortune but returned disappointed to Brno as mus. master at the training coll. His early comps. met with little success, but he became deeply involved with Moravian folk music, working with Bartoš on editing, harmonizing, and performing folk-songs. He also founded Brno Organ Sch. in 1881, becoming dir. and remaining as organizer until 1919. In 1894 he began work on his 3rd opera, *Jenůfa*, which was perf. in Brno with considerable success in January, 1904, the year of his 50th birthday. He had every right to expect it would then be staged in Prague, but some years earlier he had severely criticized a comp. by Karel Kovařovic who was now head of the Prague Opera. He refused to hear *Jenůfa* and it took Janáček's friends until 1916 to have the work accepted for Prague—even then, Kovařovic insisted on 'editing' it himself, for which he received a royalty. Nevertheless the opera was a triumph, as it was in Max Brod's Ger. version in Vienna and Cologne in 1918. This success at the age of 62, coupled with the formation of the Cz. republic, was a tremendous creative spur to Janáček and in the last 10 years of his life he produced a series of works full of originality, vitality, and power. The opera *The Excursions of Mr Brouček* (1917) and the orchestral rhapsody *Taras Bulba* (1918) were followed by the song-cycle *The Diary of One Who Disappeared*, the operas *Káťa Kabanová* and *The Cunning Little Vixen*, the concertino for pf. and chamber orch., the *Sinfonietta*, 2 str. qts., the wind sextet *Mládí*, the *Glagolitic Mass*, and 2 more operas, *The Makropulos Affair* and *From the House of the Dead*. Mus. history can offer few, if any, parallels with this upsurge of sustained inspiration—an inspiration partly derived from his unconsummated love for a young married woman whom he met in 1917 and to whom he wrote over 600 letters.

Janáček's early works belong to the 19th-cent. world of Dvořák and Smetana. But in his maturity, from *Jenůfa* onwards, his individual style developed. His works are based on short bursts of melody, strongly rhythmical, like vocal exclamations, these deriving from his fascination by speech-rhythms. He noted in sketch-books phrases he overheard in town and countryside, particularizing the moods in which they were spoken. The melodic fragments undergo sudden changes of tonality and mood, being built by simple but unusual means to strong emotional climaxes. His harmonic language, however, was in no way innovatory. His staple fare in this respect comprised common chords, 7ths, 9ths, and the whole-tone scale, but what is unusual is his spacing and juxtaposition of chords. His orchestration is equally striking and unusual, often seeming harsh and raw but invariably being apt and effective. He liked to use instr. at the extremes of their range.

Janáček's operas have held their place in the repertory since they were first perf. in Europe but only since the 1950s has the Eng. public been awakened to their originality and beauty, largely through the efforts of the cond. Charles *Mackerras, who has also purged the scores of corruptions and accretions by other hands. The emotional range of the operas is wide: jealousy, hatred, love, and guilt are explored in *Jenůfa* and *Káťa Kabanová*, nature and the eternal round of the seasons in the fantasy *The Cunning Little Vixen*, satire in *The Excursions of Mr Brouček*, and harsh reality in *The Makropulos Affair* and the extraordinary *From the House of the Dead*—yet in all these disparate works the principal element is a compelling faith in humankind and its grip on life. Prin. works:

OPERAS: *Šárka* (text by Zeyer) (1887–8, rev. 1918 and 1924); *The Beginning of a Romance (Počátek Románu)* (1891, prod. 1894); *Her Foster-Daughter (Její Pastorkyňa*, known as *Jenůfa*) (1894–1903, rev. before 1908); *Fate (*Osud*)* (1903–5, rev. 1906–7); *The *Excursions of Mr Brouček (Výlety pana Broučka)* (1908–17); *Káťa Kabanová (Katya Kabanova)* (1919–21); *The *Cunning Little Vixen (Příhody lišky Bystroušky)* (1921–3); *The *Makropulos Affair (Věc Makropulos)* (1923–5); *From the *House of the Dead (Z Mrtvého Domu)* (1927–8).
ORCH: *Suite for Strings* (1877); *Idyll for strings* (1877); *Suite* (c.1891); *Lachian Dances (Lašske tance)* (1889–90); overture *Jealousy (Žárlivost)* (1894); ballad *The Fiddler's Child (Šumařovo Dítě)* (1912); rhapsody *Taras Bulba* (1915–18); symphonic poem *The Ballad of Blanik (Balada blanická)* (1920); *Sinfonietta* (1926); symphonic poem *Danube (Dunaj)* (1923–8, completed by O. Chlubna).
CHORUS AND ORCH: *Lord, have mercy on us (Hospodine pomiluj ny)* for double ch., solo qt., wind orch., organ, harp (1897); *Amarus*, solo, ch., and orch. (c.1897, rev. 1901, 1906); *At the Inn of Solan (Na Solani Čarták)* male ch., solo, and orch. (1901); *The Eternal Gospel (Věčné Evangelium)* solo, ch., and orch. (1914–15); *Glagolitic Mass (Glagolská mše)* sop., alto, ten., bass, ch., organ, and orch. (1926); *Nursery Rhymes (Říkadla)* 9 vv., pf., and 11 instr. (1925, rev. 1927).
CHORUS: *Ploughing (Oriani)* male ch. (1876); *The Wild Duck (Kačena Divoka)* (c.1885); 4 *Choruses*, male vv. (1886); *The Wreath (Vinek)* for 4 male ch. (1904); 4 *Moravian Choruses* for male vv. (1904); *Songs of the Hradčany (Hradčanské Piškičky)* 3 ch. for women's vv. (1916); *Diary of One Who Disappeared (Zápisník Zmizelého)* song-cycle for ten., cont., 3 women's vv., and pf. (1917–19); *Wolf Tracks (Vlčí stopa)*, sop., women's ch., and pf. (1916); *Kaspar Rucky*, women's ch. (1916); *Teacher Halfar (Kantor Halfar)* male

vv. (1906, rev. 1917); *The Czech Legions (České Legie)* male ch. (1918); *The Wandering Madman (Potulny šilenec)* sop., male ch. (1922).
CHAMBER MUSIC: *Dumka*, vn. and pf. (c.1880); *Fairy Tale (Pohádka)* vc. and pf. (1910, 2nd version 1923); vn. sonata (1914, rev. 1921); Str. Qt. No. 1 (*Kreutzer Sonata*) (1923), No. 2 (*Intimate Letters (Listy důvěrné)* (1928); *Youth (*Mládi*)*, wind sextet (1924); concertino for pf. and chamber orch. (c.1925); *Capriccio* for pf. (left hand) and chamber orch. (c.1926).
PIANO: *Vallachian Dances* (1888); *National Dances of Moravia* for pf. (4 hands), Books 1 and 2 (1891), Book 3 (1893); *On an Overgrown Path (Po zarostlém Chodníčku)* 15 short pieces (7 orig. for harmonium) (1901–8); *Sonata 1:x:1905* (A street scene; *Z ulice)* (the day a worker was killed by a soldier for demonstrating for a Cz. univ. in Brno); *In the Mists (V mlhách)* (1912); *Moravian Dances*, 2 books (1912); *In the Threshing House* (1913).
SOLO VOICE: *Song of Spring*, v. and pf. (1897); *Folk Poetry of Hukwald*, 13 songs for v. and pf. (1899); *A Garland of Moravian Folk Songs*, 53 songs coll. by Bartoš and Janáček, with pf. acc. by Janáček, Book 1 (1892), 2 (1901).

Janáček Quartet. Cz. str. qt. formed 1947 by students of Brno Cons. First public concert, Brno, Oct. 1947. Adopted name Janáček Qt. after Prague début 1949. Toured Poland 1949, Middle East 1955, W. Berlin 1956. First visit to Brit. 1958. Original members were Jiří Trávníček, (*b* Vlaštovičky, 1925; *d* Brno, 1973) and Miroslav Matyás (*b* Brno, 1924), vns.; Jiří Kratochvíl (*b* Ivančice, 1924), va.; and Karel Krafka (*b* Znojmo, 1921), vc. Trávníček was succeeded by Bohumil Smejkal (*b* Brno, 1935); Matyás by Adolf Sýkora (*b* Brno, 1931) in 1952. Has made close study of Janáček's two qts., also those by Bartók, Shostakovich, Britten, and Novák. Always performs from memory.

Janequin (Jannequin), **Clément** (*b* Châtellerault, nr. Poitiers, c.1485; *d* Paris, 1558). Fr. composer. Studied for priesthood. Choirmaster, Angers Cath. from 1537. Comp. over 250 *chansons*, some of which were pubd. by Attaignant. Settled in Paris 1549, becoming *compositeur du roi*. Entered Paris Univ. as a student when over 70. Wrote two Masses based on two of his *chansons*. Introduced bird-song and other programmatic effects. His *Le bataille de Marignan* (1515) imitates sword-clashes, warriors' cries, and other sounds.

Janiewicz (Yaniewicz), **Feliks** (*b* Wilno, 1762; *d* Edinburgh, 1848). Polish violinist and composer. Visited Vienna 1785, meeting Haydn and Mozart; then 3 years in It.; Paris 1787–90. Visited Eng. 1792, playing in London, Bath, Liverpool, and Manchester. Took part in Haydn's London concerts 1794. Settled in Liverpool 1800, founding publishing firm 1803. One of founders of Phil. Soc., London. Lived in Edinburgh from

1815, retiring in 1829. Comp. vn. concs., chamber mus., etc.

Janigro, Antonio (*b* Milan, 1918). It. cellist and cond. Studied Milan Cons. and École Normale de Musique, Paris. Début 1934. Worldwide reputation as solo cellist. Head of advanced vc. class, Zagreb Univ. 1939–53; cond. Zagreb radio-TV orch. 1954–64; founder of chamber ens., *I solisti di Zagreb* (12 musicians) 1954, cond. until 1967; cond. Angelicum Orch., Milan, 1965–7; cond. Saar chamber orch. from 1968; head of advanced vc. class Schumann Cons., Düsseldorf, from 1965.

Janis (orig. Yanks), **Byron** (*b* McKeesport, Penn., 1928). Amer. pianist. Début Pittsburgh 1937. Studied with Adele Marcus and Horowitz. Soloist with NBC S.O. 1943, recital début, NY 1948. European début, Amsterdam 1952; toured USSR 1960 and 1962.

Janissary Music (Ger. *Janitscharenmusik*). Term once used for the imitation-Turkish mus. produced by triangle, cymbals, and bass drum as in Mozart's *Die Entführung aus dem Serail*. The Janissaries were the Sultan's bodyguard, disbanded 1826, who had a band.

Janko Keyboard. Pf. kbd., invented in 1882 by Paul von Janko (*b* Totis, 1856; *d* Constantinople, 1919), with 6 manuals, each giving a whole-tone series of notes. The finger keys of each kbd. were on one level; the kbds. were arr. so that the hands could move easily over all 6 as over the keys of a typewriter. The span of the octave was reduced and large chords were easy. Won praise from Liszt and Anton Rubinstein but never became popular.

Jannaconi, Giuseppe (*b* Rome, 1741; *d* Rome, 1816). It. composer. Succeeded Zingarelli as choirmaster, St Peter's, Rome, 1811. Wrote 32 masses, 52 psalm-settings, many motets, etc.

Janowitz, Gundula (*b* Berlin, 1937). Ger. soprano. Studied at Styrian Cons., Graz. Début Vienna State Opera 1960 as Barbarina in *Le Nozze di Figaro*. Bayreuth Fest. 1960. Sang Countess in *Figaro* at re-opening of Paris Opéra 1973. CG début 1976 (Donna Anna), Glyndebourne 1964. Noted Lieder singer.

Janowski, Marek (*b* Warsaw, 1939). Polish-born cond. (now W. Ger. cit.). Studied Cologne High Sch. of Mus. and in Siena. Ass. cond. in Aachen, Cologne, and Düsseldorf opera houses, later guest cond. Cologne, Hamburg, Munich, Paris, and Berlin Opera. Mus. dir. Freiburg Opera 1973–5, Dortmund 1975–9. Cond. Radio France from 1984. Also guest cond. Berlin P.O. etc. London début 1969 (Brit. première of Henze's *Der junge Lord* with Cologne Opera). Amer. opera début 1983 (San Francisco), NY Met. 1984 (*Arabella*). Art. adv. RLPO 1983–6. Cond. first compact disc recording of Wagner's *Ring*.

Janssen, Herbert (*b* Cologne, 1892; *d* NY, 1965). Ger.-born bar. (Amer. citizen 1946). Studied Cologne and Berlin. Début Berlin 1922, CG 1926 (annual visits until 1939). Member of NY Met. 1939–52. Singer of Wagnerian roles such as Gunther, Kothner, Amfortas, and Kurwenal.

Janssen, Werner (*b* NY, 1899). Amer. composer and cond. Studied Univ. of Calif. Cond. début Rome 1931. Amer. début with NY P.O. 1934. Cond. Baltimore S.O. 1937–9, Janssen S.O. of Los Angeles 1940–52, Utah S.O. 1946–7, Portland S.O. 1947–9, San Diego P.O. 1952–4. Comps. incl. *Louisiana Suite* (1929–30), *Dixie Fugue* (1932), 2 str. qts., film mus.

Japanese Fiddle. A 1-str. instr. sometimes seen in the hands of Eng. street perfs., etc.

Jaques-Dalcroze, Émile (*b* Vienna, 1865; *d* Geneva, 1950). Swiss composer and teacher. Studied Geneva, Vienna (with Bruckner), and Paris. On staff Geneva Cons. 1892, developing his *gymnastique rythmique*, known as **'Eurhythmics'*, exercises for expressing rhythmical aspects of mus. by physical movements. Influence on ballet. Taught method 1910–14 at Hellerau, Dresden. Founded Institut Jaques-Dalcroze in Geneva 1915. Wrote several books on subject. Comp. 5 operas (incl. *Sancho Panza*, 1896), operetta, 2 vn. concs., 3 str. qts., pf. pieces, etc.

Jardin clos, Le (The Enclosed Garden). Song-cycle of 8 songs by Fauré, Op. 106, to poems by Charles van Lerberghe, comp. 1914–15.

Jarnach, Philipp (*b* Noisy, 1892; *d* Börnson, 1982). Fr.-born Catalan composer. Studied in Paris 1912–14. Taught at Zürich Cons. 1915–21. Mus. critic, *Börsen-Kurier*, Berlin, 1922–7. Studied with **Busoni, whose opera **Doktor Faust* he completed. Prof. of comp., Cologne Cons. 1927–49; dir., Hamburg Cons. 1949–59. Composer of orch. and choral works, str. qt., unacc. vn. sonatas, 2 pf. sonatas, etc.

Järnefelt, Armas (*b* Viborg (now Viipuri), 1869; *d* Stockholm, 1958). Finnish-born composer and cond., naturalized Swed. 1910. Cond. Viipuri orch. 1898–1903, Helsinki opera 1903–7, Royal Opera, Stockholm, 1907–32, Helsinki opera 1932–6. Brother-in-law of **Sibelius. Said to have introduced Wagner's mus. to Finland. Comps. incl. **Praeludium* for orch. (1907), *Berceuse*, pf. pieces, etc.

Jarred, Mary (*b* Brotton, Yorks., 1899). Eng. cont. Member, Hamburg Opera 1929–32, later at CG. Notable also for singing in oratorio.

Jarrett, Keith (*b* Allentown, Pa., 1945). Amer. jazz pianist and composer of Scottish-Irish and Hungarian descent. Child-prodigy pianist. In early teens toured with Fred Waring and his Pennsylvanians. Studied Berklee Sch. of Mus., Boston. Was offered schol. to study with N. Boulanger in Paris but went instead to NY where he formed his own jazz group and occasionally played with a Miles Davis band. His solo piano improvisations embrace classical and jazz history, rarely with direct quotations, and he has been classified with the 'back to romanticism' movement of Rochberg and Del Tredici. Has been soloist in pf. concs. by Hovhaness and McPhee. Comps. incl. *Ritual* for pf. and *The Celestial Hawk*, a pf. conc.

Järvi, Neeme (*b* Tallin, Estonia, 1937). Estonian-born conductor. Studied Tallin and Leningrad Cons. (with Mravinsky). Début at Kirov Th. (*Carmen*). Dir., Estonian Opera 1963. Won 1st prize, Accademia di St Cecilia, Rome, 1971. Emigrated to USA 1980. Prin. guest cond. CBSO 1981–4, prin. cond. SNO from 1984.

Jazz (etymology obscure). A term, which came into general use *c*.1913–15, for a type of mus. which developed in the Southern States of USA in the late 19th cent. and came into prominence at the turn of the century in New Orleans, chiefly (but not exclusively) among black musicians. Elements which contributed to jazz were the rhythms of W. Africa, European harmony, and Amer. 'gospel' singing. Before the term *Jazz* was used, ragtime was the popular name for this genre. Ragtime lasted from *c*.1890 to *c*.1917. It was an instr. style, highly syncopated, with the pf. predominant (though a few rags had words and were sung). Among the leading exponents of the pf. rag were Scott *Joplin, Jelly Roll Morton, and J. P. Johnson, with the cornettists Buddy Bolden and King Oliver. Some rags were notated (e.g. Joplin's *Maple Leaf Rag*) but the majority were improvised. About 1900 also, the 'blues' craze began. 'Blues' implies a largely vocal form and a depressed frame of mind on the part of the perf. The form originated from Negro spirituals, and made use of a blend of major and minor harmony, and non-tempered scale intervals. In instr. blues the prominent instrs. were tpt., cornet, cl., sax., or tb. A leading figure of the blues era was the black composer W. C. *Handy whose *Memphis Blues* (1909) and *St Louis Blues* (1914) are jazz classics. Outstanding blues singers have been Bessie Smith and, later, Billie Holiday.

The subsequent history of jazz has embraced a diversity of styles, e.g. *Dixieland*, from *c*.1912, which borrowed elements from both ragtime and blues and made a feature of group improvisation led by the trumpeter. The principal Dixieland musicians included the trumpeters King Oliver and Louis *Armstrong, the trombonists Kid Ory and Jack Teagarden, the saxophonist Sidney Bechet, the pianists Jelly Roll Morton and Earl Hines. In the 1920s, jazz became more sophisticated as it spread to New York, Paris, and London and became a social 'rage'. The jazz arranger emerged and with him the bigger band: harmony became more conventional, melodies were played by a full instr. section with the solos as central display-pieces, like cadenzas. These 'big

bands' had marked individual styles. Paul Whiteman popularized 'symphonic jazz' using vns. and elaborate arrs. At the other extreme was the Negro style of Duke *Ellington, the first great jazz composer. A 'Chicago' style revived smaller bands and more improvisation (its star was the trumpeter Bix Beiderbecke).

The 1930s coincided with the style known as 'swing'. The swing bands—led by such virtuoso instrumentalists as Benny *Goodman (cl.), Jimmy Dorsey (alto sax.), Gene Krupa (drums), Glenn *Miller (tb.), Tommy Dorsey (tb.), Artie Shaw (cl.)—concentrated on precision, arr., and good ens. work. Though Ellington's band was influenced by swing, its members were such superb players and such strong individualists that improvisation still played a large part in his comps. Swing yielded in the 1940s to 'be-bop', principally for smaller groups of perhaps 7 players. Rhythm was the prime feature of be-bop, allied to scat singing (vocalizing to nonsense syllables). Tempi were fast and great virtuosity was needed. The dominant player was the alto saxophonist Charlie *Parker (1920–55). Also important were Dizzy Gillespie (trumpeter), Stan Getz (tenor saxophonist), and Kenny Clarke and Max Roach (drummers). 'Be-bop' was later re-christened 'modern jazz'. Among its derivatives were 'cool' jazz, led by Getz and Miles Davis, and by Shorty Rogers (tpt.) and Lennie Tristano (pf.). In the 1960s 'free jazz' was pioneered but the jazz scene was overshadowed by the emergence of 'pop' and the pop groups, e.g. the *Beatles, the *Rolling Stones, and many others, these comprising usually a vocalist, guitarist(s), and perc. 'Hard rock' was a development from this period, and elec. instrs. were commandeered, as in other branches of mus.

The influence of jazz on so-called 'serious music' has been widespread and beneficial. Ives composed ragtime pieces for th. orch. as early as 1902; Debussy in 1908 wrote the *Golliwogg's Cakewalk*; Ravel used the blues in his vn. sonata, and both his pf. concs. are jazz-influenced; Stravinsky wrote ragtime pieces and composed the *Ebony Concerto* (1945) for Woody Herman; Hindemith, Poulenc, Weill, Křenek, Lambert, and Copland all used jazz features, as did Berg in *Lulu*. Duke Ellington and Bill Russo are among the leading composers of jazz, while those who have written works throwing a bridge between jazz and symphonic forms incl. Gershwin, Rolf Liebermann, Leonard Bernstein, Gunther Schuller, Richard Rodney Bennett, and John Dankworth.

Jazz Calendar. Ballet in 7 parts, mus. by Richard Rodney *Bennett, choreog. Ashton, comp. 1963–4, prod. CG 1968. Based on rhyme 'Monday's Child is Fair of Face' . . . etc.

Jeanne d'Arc au bûcher (Joan of Arc at the Stake). (1) Dramatic oratorio for 4 speakers, 3 sops., cont., ten., bass, ondes Martenot, ch., and orch. by Honegger to text by Claudel. Comp.

1935. F.p. Basle 1938; f.p. in England, London, BBC 1947, staged 1954; San Francisco 1954.

(2) Scena for mez. and pf. by Liszt, 1845.

Jeffreys, George (b c.1610; d Weldon, Northants, 1685). Eng. composer. Thought to have studied in Italy. Org. to Charles I at Oxford during Civil War. In 1646 became steward to Sir Christopher Hatton at Kirby, Northants, remaining until death. Worked as amateur composer, only one work being published in lifetime. Wrote mainly church mus., influenced by It. Baroque, particularly Monteverdi and Gesualdo. Collected works ed. Peter *Aston, from 1970. Works incl. 35 Eng. anthems, over 70 Latin settings, secular songs, str. fantasias (1629), and mus. for plays (1631).

Jehan, Marie-Thérèse (b St Gildas-des-Bois, 1944). Fr. organist. Studied Paris, début 1957. Recitals throughout Europe.

Jeji Pastorkyňa (Janáček). See *Jenůfa*.

Jelinek, Hanns (b Vienna, 1901; d Vienna, 1969). Austrian composer. Mainly self-taught but studied with Schoenberg, Berg, and Schmidt. Comps., in 12-note idiom, incl. *Symphonia brevis* for orch., and 5 other syms., *12-Note Primer* for pf., *Prometheus* (Goethe) for v. and orch. Wrote treatise on 12-note comp. (1952–8).

Jemnitz, Sándor (b Budapest, 1890; d Balatonföldvár, 1963). Hung. composer. Studied Budapest Acad., in Leipzig with Reger and Straube, and in Berlin (1921–4) with Schoenberg. Returned to Hung. 1916. Mus. critic, *Népszava* of Budapest, 1924–50. Prof. at Bartók Cons., Budapest, from 1951. Wrote books about Mendelssohn, Chopin, and Mozart. Comps. incl. 3 vn. sonatas, tpt. qt., 2 str. trios, conc. for str. orch., sonatas for several solo instr. (e.g. 5 for pf., 3 for vn., and for vc., harp, va., fl., org., tpt., db., etc.).

'Jena' Symphony. Name given to orch. work found by F. *Stein in 1909 at Jena, Ger., and long attrib. to Beethoven. H. C. Robbins Landon in 1957 est. it was comp. by Friedrich *Witt.

Jenkins, John (b Maidstone, 1592; d Kimberley, Norfolk, 1678). Eng. composer. Musician in service of Charles I and Charles II but mainly in private service in Norfolk. Wrote many Fancies for viols or org., 12 sonatas for 2 vns., str. bass, and continuo (org. or theorbo) (1660), light pieces called rants, and songs, catches, etc.

Jenkins, Newell (Owen) (b New Haven, Conn., 1915). Amer. conductor and scholar. Studied in Munich (with Orff) and NY. Début as cond., Freiburg 1935 (*Dido and Aeneas*). Founded Yale Opera Group, New Haven, 1940. Cond., Bologna Chamber Orch. 1948–53. Founder and dir., Piccola Accademi a Musicale, Florence, 1952. Founder, Clarion Concerts, NY, 1956. Expert on music of Sammartini, J. M. Kraus, and Cherubini.

Jensen, Adolf (b Königsberg, 1837; d Baden-Baden, 1879). Ger. composer and pianist. Worked in Russia and Denmark until 1860. Comp. over 150 songs, unfinished opera *Turandot*, cantatas, chs., etc.

Jenůfa. Opera (Moravian music drama) in 3 acts by Janáček. This is title by which it is known outside Czechoslovakia, where it retains its orig. title of *Her Foster-daughter* (*Její Pastorkyňa*). Lib. by composer based on story by G. Preissová. Comp. 1894–1903, rev. 1906, 1911, 1916. Prod. Brno 1904, Prague 1916, Vienna 1918, NY Met. 1924, London 1956. Orig. version of ov., comp. 1894, was pubd. in 1906 as independent orch. piece *Jealousy* (*Žárlivost*). Since 1916 opera has usually been performed in edn. with re-orch. by Prague cond. Kovařovic, but Mackerras and others have restored orig. scoring.

Jephte. (1) Oratorio by *Carissimi to Lat. text based on biblical words. For 6 vv. and continuo; comp. 1650. Version by Henze for 7 solo vv., 6 vv. ch., 4 fl., perc., hp., guitar, mandolin, banjo, 1976.

(2) Oratorio (*Jephtha*) by Handel to text by Morell based on Bible. F.p. London 1752.

Jeremiah. Sym. No. 1 by Leonard Bernstein for orch. with mez. soloist in last movement to words from *Book of Jeremiah*. F.p. Pittsburgh, Jan. 1944, cond. Bernstein, with Jennie Tourel.

Jeremiáš, Jaroslav (b Písek, 1889; d České Budějovice, 1919). Cz. composer and cond. Studied Prague Cons. and with Novák. Comp. opera *Stary Krae* (The Old King) (1912), oratorio *Jan Hus* (1915), tone-poem, songs, etc.

Jeremiáš, Otakar (b Písek, 1892; d Prague, 1962). Cz. composer, brother of Jaroslav *Jeremiáš. Studied Prague Cons. and with Novák. Dir. of mus. sch. at Budějovice 1918–30. Chief cond. Prague Radio 1930–45, dir. Prague Opera 1945–7. Comp. 2 syms., operas *The Brothers Karamazov* (1928) and *Till Eulenspiegel* (1949), cantatas, chamber mus., etc.

Jerger, Alfred (b Brno, 1889; d Vienna, 1976). Austrian bar. Studied Vienna. Began career as cond., Passau 1913; singing début 1917. Munich Opera 1919–21, Vienna 1921 remaining as leading bar. until 1953. Created roles of The Man in Schoenberg's *Die glückliche Hand*, Vienna 1924, and Mandryka in Strauss's *Arabella*, Dresden 1933 and CG 1934. After retirement was prod. at Vienna Volksoper and teacher at Acad.

Jeritza, Maria (orig. Mizzi Jedlitzka) (b Brno, 1887; d Orange, NJ, 1982). Cz. sop. Studied Brno. Opera début as Elsa in *Lohengrin* at Olmütz, 1910. Engaged 1912 for Vienna Volksoper. Created role of Ariadne in Strauss's *Ariadne auf Naxos*, Stuttgart 1912. Member, Vienna Court (State) Opera 1913–32, 1949–52, creating role of the Empress in Strauss's *Die Frau ohne Schatten*. NY Met. 1921–

32, where she was first Amer. Jenůfa, Turandot, Marietta in Korngold's *Die tote Stadt*, and Helen (in Strauss's *Die ägyptische Helena*). Sang at CG 1925–6 (début as Tosca). Of striking personal beauty and acting ability.

Jerusalem. (1) Setting for unison ch. by C. H. *Parry of Blake's poem. Comp. and f.p. 1916. Orch. by Elgar for Leeds Fest. 1922.
(2) Oratorio by H. H. Pierson, Norwich Fest. 1852.

Jérusalem. Fr. version by Verdi, 1847, of his opera I *Lombardi alla prima crociata* (1842), made for Paris with lib. re-fashioned by Vaëz and Royer. Contains some new mus.

Jerusalem, Siegfried (*b* Oberhausen, 1940). Ger. tenor. Began career as bassoonist in various Ger. orchs. Opera début Stuttgart 1975. Regular appearances in Vienna, Hamburg, and Bayreuth since 1977 in Wagnerian roles of Lohengrin, Siegmund, Parsifal, and Walther.

Jesu, Joy of Man's Desiring. Eng. name for chorale *Jesu, bleibet meine Freude* in J. S. Bach's church cantata No. 147, *Herz und Mund und Tat und Leben*, orig. orch. for tpt., ob., str., and org. but best known in pf. transcr. by Myra *Hess of choral arr. by Hugh P. Allen with poem by Robert Bridges. Chorale melody is *Werde Munter* by Johann Schop, 1641.

Jeu (Fr.; plural *Jeux*). (1) Game, play, etc.
(2) Stop (org.), e.g. *Jeux d'anche*, Reed Stops; *Jeux de fonds*, Foundation Stops (see *Fonds d'Orgue*); *Grand jeu* or *Plein jeu*, Full Org.

Jeu de cartes (Card Game). Ballet 'in 3 deals' with lib. and mus. by Stravinsky, comp. 1936, choreog. Balanchine, prod. NY Met. 1937. Also orch. suite.

Jeu de clochettes (Fr.). Play of little bells, i.e. *Glockenspiel.

Jeune, Claude le (*b* Valenciennes, *c*.1530; *d* Paris 1600). Fr. composer of psalm-settings and many secular *chansons* and instr. pieces.

Jeune France, La (Fr.). Young France. Group of Fr. composers formed in Paris in 1936 to re-establish then unfashionable idea of 'a personal message' in comp. Members were *Baudrier, *Jolivet, *Lesur, and *Messiaen.

Jeunesse d'Hercule, La (The Youth of Hercules). Symphonic poem by Saint-Saëns, Op. 50, 1877.

Jeunesses Musicales (Fr.). Musical Youth. Int. organization formed in Belg., 1946 as *La Fédération internationale des jeunesses musicales*, later with over 30 member-nations. Aim to spread love of mus. among youth of all lands. Arr. congresses and exchange-visits.

Jeux (Games). Ballet (*poème dansée*) by Debussy comp. in 1912–13 and f.p. Paris 1913 by Diaghilev's co. with choreog. by Nijinsky. The scenario, also by Nijinsky, involves a game of tennis.

Jeux d'eau (Fountains). Work for solo pf. by Ravel, comp. 1901, f.p. Paris 1902.

Jeux d'enfants (Children's Games). Suite of 12 pieces for pf. duet comp. by Bizet in 1871. Nos. 2, 3, 6, 11, and 12 were orch. by Bizet as *Petite Suite d'Orchestre* and perf. Paris 1873. 5 were orch. also by Karg-Elert (nos. 6, 3, 4, 11 and 12 in order of perf.) and nos. 6, 3, 2, 11 and 12 were arr. by H. Finck.

Jewels of the Madonna, The (Wolf-Ferrari). See *Gioielli della Madonna, I*.

Jewess, The (Halévy). See *Juive, La*.

Jewish Music. It is apparent from the Old Testament and from archaeological discoveries that instr. and vocal mus. has always played a part in Jewish life, both on sacred and secular occasions. After the destruction of the Second Temple, instr. mus. was banned as a token of mourning, but the *shofar was retained as the ritual horn and decorative bells were attached to the curtain covering the Ark. Instr. mus was later permitted at weddings and festive events. The oldest element of synagogue mus. is still the cantillation of biblical texts, from which synagogue prayer chants derived. These chants were orally transmitted from generation to generation by cantor-composers. In the middle of the 19th cent. cantorial schools were founded as moves towards a printed repertory began. 19th-cent. Jewish liturgical composers incl. Solomon Sulzer (1804–90), Samuel Naumburg (1815–80), Hirsch Weintraub (1811–81), and Boruch Schorr (1823–1904). In the 20th cent., liturgical services have been comp. by Paul Ben-Haim, *Bloch, *Milhaud, and *Castelnuovo-Tedesco.

Jew's Harp (Fr. *rebube, guimbarde*; Ger. *Trumpel*). One of the simplest and most widely distributed instr., being found throughout Europe and Asia. It consists of a tiny iron frame, open at one end, in which end a single strip of metal vibrates. The frame is held between the teeth, and the strip then twanged by the finger. The strip, in itself, is obviously capable of producing only one note, but the harmonics of this note become available by resonance, through various shapings of the cavity of the mouth. Thus tunes can be played.
The origin of the name is unknown and seems to be unconnected with Jewry. The name 'Jew's Trump' was recorded in 1545.

Jig. (1) A dance once popular in Eng., Scot., and Ireland, in the last of which its popularity was of longest duration. For its general character and music see *Gigue*.
(2) In the late 16th and 17th cents., the term was applied to a lively song and dance item, of comic character, used to terminate theatrical perfs.

(3) Title of last movement of an 18th-cent. orch. suite. See *Gigue*.

Jílek, František (*b* Brno, 1913). Cz. cond., pianist, and composer. Cond. début Nat. Th., Brno, later working in Prague, Helsinki, Florence, Leipzig, etc. Prof. of cond., Janáček Acad. of Mus. Arts. Dir. of opera, Brno State Th. Authority on Janáček.

Jingling Johnny (Fr. *pavillon chinois* or *chapeau chinois*). Perc. instr., now obsolete, also known as 'Turkish Crescent' or 'Turkish Jingle'. Used in military bands. It comprised a long stick surmounted by a tent-shaped construction, with an inverted crescent lower down the stick, small bells and the like being suspended from both of these. Used by Berlioz in his *Symphonie funèbre et triomphale*.

Jirák, Karel (Boleslav) (*b* Prague, 1891; *d* Chicago, 1972). Cz. composer and cond. Pupil of Novák in Prague and Foerster in Vienna. Cond. at Hamburg Opera 1915–18, prof. of comp., Prague Cons. 1920–30, mus. dir. Cz. radio 1930–45. Settled in USA 1948, joining faculty of Chicago Mus. Coll. Comp. opera, 6 syms., 7 str. qts., song-cycles, etc.

Joachim, Joseph (*b* Kitsee, 1831; *d* Berlin, 1907). Hung. violinist and composer. Gave first concert at age of 7. Studied in Vienna 1839–43 under Hellmesberger and Boehm. Went to Leipzig Cons. 1843, where he was welcomed by the dir., Mendelssohn, playing at *Gewandhaus concerts and, in 1844, in London. Returned to Leipzig, studying with Mendelssohn and David. In 1849 became leader of Weimar court orch., under Liszt, and leader and soloist to the King of Hanover 1853–66. In 1868 went to Berlin as head of the new *Hochschule für ausübende Tonkunst*, forming *Joachim Quartet following year. Frequent visitor to England (hon. Mus.D., Cambridge, 1887). Superb interpreter of classical conc., especially that by Beethoven (for which he wrote cadenzas). Dedicatee and first player of Brahms's conc., and dedicatee of Dvořák's conc., which he refused to play. Was close friend of Brahms until rift when his marriage broke up and Brahms sided with Frau Joachim (the singer Amalie Weiss). This rift was healed by Brahms's Double Conc. Comp. 3 vn. concs. (incl. *Hungarian Concerto*), 5 ovs., songs, etc. Orchestrated Schubert's *Grand Duo* (1855).

Joachim Quartet. Str. qt. founded in Berlin in 1869 by Joseph *Joachim, who was 1st vn. 1869–1907. Other members were: 2nd vn., E. Schiever 1869–72, H. de Ahna 1872–92, J. Kruse 1892–7, K. *Halíř 1897–1907; va., H. de Ahna 1869–72, E. Rappoldi 1872–7, E. Wirth 1877–1907; vc., W. Müller 1869–79, R. Hausmann 1879–1907. Annual series of concerts in Berlin from 1869. Visits to Vienna, Budapest, Rome, Paris, and London (1900). Halíř led the qt. during Joachim's illness in 1907, and formed his own qt. after Joachim's death.

Job. (1) Masque for dancing in 9 scenes and epilogue by Vaughan Williams, founded on Blake's *Illustrations of the Book of Job*. Comp. 1927–30. F.p. (concert) Norwich 1930, (ballet) London 1931.
(2) Oratorio by Parry, f.p. Gloucester 1892.
(3) Opera (*sacra rappresentazione*) in 1 act by Dallapiccola, text by composer from *Book of Job*, comp. 1950, f.p. Rome 1950.

Jochum, Eugen (*b* Babenhausen, 1902; *d* Munich, 1987). Ger. cond. Studied Augsburg and Munich Acad. Opera coach at Munich 1924–5, Kiel 1926–7. Cond. Kiel opera 1927–9. Chief cond., Duisburg 1930. Cond. for Berlin radio and State Opera 1932–4. Mus. dir. Hamburg State Opera 1934–45, Hamburg P.O. 1934–49. Founder and chief cond. Bavarian Radio Sym. Orch. 1949–61. Joint chief cond. Concertgebouw Orch., Amsterdam, 1961–4, then chief cond. Bamberg S.O. 1969–78. Regular visitor to Eng. as cond. of LPO. Cond. laureate LSO 1975.

Jodelling (Yodelling; from Ger. *Jodel*). A type of vocal expression common in Switzerland and the Tyrol, which employs an alternation of normal v. production with falsetto in simple rhythmic tunes.

Johannesburg Festival Overture. Ov. by *Walton written for 70th anniv. of city of Johannesburg, 1956. F.p. Johannesburg, cond. Sargent, 1956.

Johannesen, Grant (*b* Salt Lake City, 1921). Amer. pianist. Studied with Petri and Casadesus. Début with NY P.O., 1944. Several tours of Europe and USSR. Dir., Cleveland Institute of Mus.

Johansson, Bengt (Viktor) (*b* Helsinki, 1914). Finnish composer and cond. Studied Sibelius Acad., Helsinki; mus. supervisor Finnish Radio from 1952, début as cond. 1952. Lecturer in mus. history, Sibelius Acad. since 1960. Comps. incl. opera *The Castle*, *Requiem* (1962), *3 Electronic Études*, *3 Classic Madrigals* (1967), *Cantata humana* (1969).

John (João) **IV, King of Portugal** (*b* Villa-Viçosa, 1603; *d* Lisbon, 1656). Patron of mus. and composer of church mus. such as well-known *Crux fidelis*. Wrote defence of 'modern music' 1649.

Johnny strikes up (Křenek). See *Jonny spielt auf*.

John of Fornsete (*b* Forncett, Norfolk; *d* 1238 or 9). Eng. monk at Reading Abbey where he kept the records and hence is credited as being composer of *Sumer is icumen in*.

Johnson, Edward (*fl.* 1570–1602). Eng. composer of madrigals, virginals pieces (3 in *Fitzwilliam Virginal Book*) and psalm-tunes. Contrib. 6-part madrigal *Come, blessed byrd*, to The *Triumphs of Oriana*.

Johnson, Edward (b Guelph, Ontario, 1878; d Guelph, 1959). Canadian ten. and opera administrator. Studied NY, where he made début 1908 in O. Straus's *Waltz Dream*. Studied in Florence with Lombardi for 2 years. It. début Padua 1912 as Andrea Chénier. Sang first It. Parsifal at Scala, Milan, under Toscanini 1914. Prin. ten. roles in Milan, Rome, Buenos Aires, Rio, and Madrid 1914–19. Chicago Opera 1919–21, NY Met. 1922–34. First Met. Pelléas, 1925. Gen. man. NY Met. 1935–50.

Johnson, Graham (b Bulawayo, 1950). Rhodesian-born Eng. pianist. Studied RAM 1967–72, and later with G. Parsons. Début, London 1972. Art. dir. *Songmakers' Almanac from 1976. Accomp. to Schwarzkopf, de los Angeles, Baker, etc.

Johnson, Hunter (b Benson, N. Carolina, 1906). Amer. composer. Studied Univ. of N. Carolina, 1924–6, Eastman Sch. of Mus. 1927–9. Head of comp. dept., Michigan Univ. 1929–33. Won Amer. *Prix de Rome* 1933, going to Europe for 2 years' study. Teacher at Manitoba Univ. 1944–7, Cornell Univ. 1948–53. Illinois Univ. 1959–65, Texas Univ. 1966–71. Comps. incl. sym. (1932), pf. conc. (1936), *Concerto for Orchestra* (1944), ballet *Letter to the World* (1940, suite for chamber orch., 1952, for full orch. 1959), and *Deaths and Entrances* (1943), chamber mus., etc.

Johnson, John (b c.1540; d c.1595). Eng. composer and lutenist at court of Elizabeth I from 1579. Developed lute duet. Earliest of major lutenists of period.

Johnson, Robert (b London, c.1583; d London, 1633). Eng. composer and lutenist. Appointed as one of King's Musicians 1604. Composed instr. pieces, catches, and songs. His settings of *Full Fathom Five* and *Where the Bee Sucks* from Shakespeare's *The Tempest* are thought to have been comp. for the orig. production.

Johnson, Robert Sherlaw (b Sunderland, 1932). Eng. composer and pianist. Studied Durham Univ. 1950–3, RAM 1953–7, and in Paris 1957–8 with Boulanger (comp.) and Février (pf.). Lecturer, Leeds Univ., 1961–5, York Univ., 1965–70. Lecturer, Oxford Univ. from 1970. Specialist in mus. of *Messiaen and author of book on him. Works incl. opera *The *Lambton Worm* (1978); *Songs of Love and Springtime*, sop. and pf.; *Carmen Vernalia*, sop. and chamber orch. (1972); *Praises of Heaven and Earth*, sop., pf., and tape (1969); *Green Whispers of Gold*, sop., pf., and tape (1971); *Festival Mass of the Resurrection*, ch. and orch.; *The Resurrection of Fêng-Huang*, sop., unacc. ch. (1968); *Where the Wild Things Are*, sop. and tape; *Triptych*, for fl., cl., va., vc., pf., and perc. (1973); 3 pf. sonatas (1963, 1967, 1976); 2 str. qts., cl. quintet (1974); *7 Short Piano Pieces* (1968); *Asterogenesis* for pf. (1973); *Anglorum Feriae*, sop., ten., ch., orch. (1977).

Johnston, Benjamin (b Macon, Georgia, 1926). Amer. composer. Studied Cincinnati Cons., Univ. of Calif., Mills Coll., Univ. of Illinois, and Columbia-Princeton Elec. Mus. Center. Pupil of John Cage 1959–60. Comps., which use microtones, serialism and indeterminacy, incl. 4 str. qts., dance-opera, sonata for microtonal pf., and 2 *Oboes and 2 Tablas and 2 Banyas*, using 142–tone *just-intonation scale.

Johnstone, Maurice (b Manchester, 1900; d Harpenden, 1976). Eng. composer, cond., and administrator. Studied RMCM and RCM. Secretary to Beecham 1932–5, mus. staff BBC in London and Manchester 1935–60 (head of mus. programmes 1953–60). Works incl. *Tarn Hows* for orch. (1949), *The Oak and the Ash*, orch. (1953), *Dover Beach* for bar. and orch. (1943), mus. for brass band.

Jolie Fille de Perth, La (The Fair Maid of Perth). Opera in 4 acts by Bizet to lib. by St Georges and Adenis, based on Scott's novel (1823). Comp. 1866. Prod. Paris 1867, Manchester and London 1917.

Jolivet, André (b Paris, 1905; d Paris, 1974). Fr. composer. Studied harmony at Paris Univ. with Paul Le Flem, 1927–32, comp. with Varèse 1928–30. One of founders of *Jeune France group 1936. Cond. and later mus. dir. Comédie-Française 1943–59, prof. of comp., Paris Cons. 1965–70. Interested in and influenced by oriental mus. and unusual instr. sonorities. Prin. works:

ORCH: Syms., No. 1 (1953), No. 2 (1959), No. 3 (1964), *5 Danses rituelles* (1939), *Symphonie des danses* (1940), *Guignol et Pandore* (1943), Conc. for Ondes Martenot (1947), concertino for tpt., str., pf. (1948), fl. conc. (1949), pf. conc. (1950), harp conc. (1952), bn. conc. (1954), tpt. conc. No. 2 (1954), *Suite transocéane* (1955), *3 Interludes de la vérité de Jeanne* (1956), *Suite française* (1957), perc. conc. (1958), *Les amants magnifiques*, variations on Lully (1960), Sym. for str. (1961), vc. conc. No. 1 (1962), No. 2 (1966), *Heptade* for tpt. and perc. (1971), vn. conc. (1972).

STAGE: *Dolorès, ou le miracle de la femme laide*, opera (1942); *Ariadne*, ballet (1964–5).

VOICE AND ORCH: *3 Chants des hommes*, bar. (1937), *Les Trois Complaintes du soldat* (1940), *Songe à nouveau rêvé*, sop. (1970).

CHORUS: Kyrie (1938), *La Tentation dernière de Jeanne d'Arc* (1941), Mass, *Uxor tua* (1962), *Le Coeur de la matière* (1965).

CHAMBER MUSIC: Str. qt. (1934), *Pastorales de Noël*, fl., bn., harp (1943), *Poèmes intimes*, v. and pf. or chamber orch. (1944), *Chant de Linos*, fl., vn., va., vc., harp (1944), *Serenade*, wind quintet (1945), *Suite rapsodique*, vn. (1965), *Cérémonial en hommage à Varèse* for 6 percussionists (1968).

PIANO: *Mana* (1935), Sonata No. 1 (1945), No. 2 (1957).

Also incidental mus., songs, etc.

Jommelli, Niccolò (*b* Aversa, Naples, 1714; *d* Naples, 1774). It. composer. Studied Naples. Comp. first opera 1737. Worked in Rome and Bologne 1740–1. Visited Vienna 1749, forming friendship with *Metastasio, most of whose texts he subsequently used, several of them more than once. Kapellmeister to Duke of Württemberg, Stuttgart, 1753–69, composing 17 operas. Returned to Naples 1769, but his work no longer found favour. Comp. over 80 operas and much church mus. Anticipated Gluck in use of dramatic recit. and in abandonment of *da capo* arias unless they had dramatic point. Among his operas were: *L'errore amoroso* (1737), *Merope* (1741), *Ifigenia in Aulide* (1751), *La clemenza di Tito* (2 versions, 1753 and 1765), *Ifigenia in Tauride* (1771).

Jones, Daniel (Jenkyn) (*b* Pembroke, 1912). Welsh composer and cond. Studied RAM and in Vienna. O.B.E. 1968. Works incl. 10 syms., vn. conc., operas *The Knife* and *Orestes*, oratorio *St Peter*, cantata *The Country Beyond the Stars*, incidental mus. for *Under Milk Wood* (Dylan Thomas), 8 str. qts., str. trio, sonata for 3 kettledrums.

Jones, Geraint (Iwan) (*b* Porth, 1917). Welsh organist, cond., harpsichordist. Début Nat. Gallery 1940. Founder, Geraint Jones Singers and Orch. 1951. Dir. Lake District Fest. since 1960. Dir. Int. Org. Fest., Manchester, 1978.

Jones, (Dame) **Gwyneth** (*b* Pontnewynydd, 1936). Welsh sop. Studied RCM and at Siena and Zürich. Notable Leonore in *Fidelio* with WNO, Oktavian in *Der Rosenkavalier* at CG. Frequent guest appearances at Vienna Opera since 1966, Rome, Munich, Milan, San Francisco. Sang Brünnhilde in *Der Ring des Nibelungen* at centenary Bayreuth Fest. 1976. NY début 1966 (concert), Met. 1972 (Sieglinde). C.B.E. 1976, D.B.E. 1986.

Jones, Parry (*b* Blaina, Monmouth, 1891; *d* London, 1963). Welsh ten. Studied RCM, Italy, and with John Coates. Became prin. ten. with Beecham and D'Oyly Carte cos. 1915–19. Prin. ten. Carl Rosa Opera 1919–22, BNOC 1922–8, then CG Eng. (touring) Co. Sang at CG 1946–55. Sang in first Eng. concert perfs. (BBC) of *Wozzeck* (1934) and *Mathis der Maler* (1939). Notable career in oratorio (*Gerontius*, etc.). O.B.E. 1962.

Jones, Philip (*b* Bath, 1928). Eng. tpt. player. Studied RCM with Ernest Hall. Prin. tpt. in most leading Brit. orchs. incl. CG, RPO (1956–60), Philharmonia (1960–4), LPO (1964–5), New Philharmonia (1965–7) and BBC S.O. (1968–71). Founder and dir. Philip Jones Brass Ens. 1951. Taught at RNCM, Manchester 1973–6. O.B.E. 1977.

Jones, Robert (*b c.*1485; *d c.*1535). Eng. composer and singer. Member of Chapel Royal. Comps. incl. songs and church mus. (Mass and *Magnificat*).

Jones, Robert (*b c.*1570; *d c.*1615). Eng. composer and lutenist. Wrote 5 sets of 'songs and ayres' and set of madrigals. Contributed *Fair Oriana to The *Triumphs of Oriana* (1601).

Jones, Sidney (*b* London, 1861; *d* London, 1946). Eng. composer of operettas, notably *The Geisha*, prod. London and NY 1896. Son of bandmaster. Became cond. Prince of Wales Th., London, for which he wrote *A Gaiety Girl* (1893) and other musical comedies. Cond. Empire Th. from 1905 to retirement in 1916.

Jongen, Joseph (*b* Liège, 1873; *d* Sart-Lez Spa, 1953). Belg. composer and teacher. Studied Liège Cons. (*Prix de Rome* 1897). Joined staff, Liège Cons. 1898, becoming prof. of harmony 1911. Prof. of counterpoint Brussels Cons. 1920, dir. 1925–39. Comps. incl. sym., vn. conc., vc. conc., pf. conc., harp conc., 3 str. qts., opera, cantata, etc.

Jongen, Léon (*b* Liège, 1884; *d* Liège, 1969). Belg. composer and pianist, brother of Joseph. Studied Liège Cons. (*Prix de Rome* 1913). Succeeded brother as dir., Brussels Cons. 1939. Comp. operas, cantatas, *Rhapsodia Belgica* for vn. and orch., vn. conc., and film mus.

Jongleur (Fr., 'juggler'). Medieval Fr. mus. entertainer or wandering minstrel who sang, played an instr., and was juggler and acrobat. See *Meistersinger*, *Ménestrel*, and *Minnesinger*.

Jongleur de Notre Dame, Le (Our Lady's Juggler). (1) Opera in 3 acts by Massenet to lib. by M. Léna from Anatole France's story *L'Étui de Nacre* (1892), this being based on medieval miracle play. Prod. Monte Carlo 1902, London 1906, NY 1908.
(2) Masque by *Maxwell Davies for mime, bar., chamber ens., and children's band, f.p. St Magnus Fest., Orkney, 1978.

Jonny spielt auf (Johnny strikes up). Opera in 2 parts (11 scenes) by *Křenek, Op. 45, to his own lib. Comp. 1925–6. Prod. Leipzig 1927, NY Met. 1929, Leeds 1984. First opera to use jazz, Johnny being a Negro jazz player.

Joplin, Scott (*b* Texarkana, Texas, 1868; *d* NY, 1917). Black Amer. composer and ragtime pianist. Played pf. in brothels of St Louis and Chicago before settling in NY in 1907. Pf. rags incl. *Maple Leaf Rag*, *The Entertainer*, and *Wall Street Rag*. Also wrote the first ragtime operas, *A Guest of Honor*, to his own lib., and *Treemonisha* (pubd. 1911). The latter received a single perf. without scenery in 1915 and its failure contributed largely to the composer's death. Revival of popular enthusiasm for Joplin's mus. in mid-1970s due largely to efforts of Amer. pianist and musicologist Joshua Rifkin.

Jordá, Enrique (*b* San Sebastian, 1911). Amer. cond. of Sp. birth. Studied Madrid Univ. and in Paris with Paul Le Flem and M. Dupré. Début Paris 1938. Cond. Madrid S.O. 1940–5, Cape

Town S.O. 1948–54, San Francisco S.O. 1954–63, Antwerp P.O. from 1970.

Joseph. (1) Oratorio by Handel (*Joseph and His Brethren*) perf. London 1744.

(2) 3-act opera by *Méhul, to lib. by Duval. Prod. Paris 1807, Philadelphia 1828, London (concert) 1841, CG (rev. Weingartner) 1914.

(3) Oratorio by Macfarren, 1877 Leeds Fest.

Joseph I, Emperor of Austria (*b* Vienna, 1678; *d* Vienna, 1711). Patron of mus. and composer of vocal and instr. items.

Josephs, Wilfred (*b* Newcastle upon Tyne, 1927). Eng. composer. Studied dentistry at Newcastle Univ. and mus. with Arthur Milner. At GSM 1954–7, Paris (with Max Deutsch) 1958. Won 1st Milan int. comp. competition in 1963 with *Requiem*. Prolific composer of mus. for TV and films. Works incl.:

ORCH: 9 syms.; 2 pf. concs.; vn. conc.; conc. for 2 vn.; vc. conc.; ob. conc.; *Aeolian Dances*; *Monkchester Dances*; *Canzonas on a Theme of Rameau* (str.); *Variations on a Theme of Beethoven*; *Polemic* (str.); *Saratoga Concerto*; ov. *The 4 Horsemen of the Apocalypse*; comedy ov. *The Ants*; *Elegy for Strings*; *Concerto a Dodici*, wind ens.; *Meditatio de Beornmundo*, va. and small orch.; conc. da camera, vn., hpd., str.; conc. for 4 pf. and perc. (1979); va. conc. (1983).

CHORAL AND VOCAL: *Requiem*; *Mortales*, soloists, ch., and orch.; *Nightmusic*, v. and orch.; *Death of a Young Man*, bar. and pf. or chamber orch.

THEATRE: *The Nottingham Captain* (mus. th.); *The Appointment* (TV opera); *King of the Coast* (children's musical); *Rebecca* (opera, 1983).

CHAMBER MUSIC: 3 str. qts.; str. quintet; 2 vn. sonatas, pf. quintet, hn. trio, sonata for brass quintet, solo vc. sonata, str. trio, pf. trio (1978–9).

Josephslegende (The Legend of Joseph). Ballet in 1 act with mus. by R. Strauss to lib. by H. Kessler and H. von Hofmannsthal, choreog. Fokine. Comp. 1913–4. Prod. Paris (Diaghilev) and London, 1914, with Massine as Joseph. Also symphonic fragment for orch., 1947, f.p. Cincinnati 1949.

Joshua. Oratorio by Handel. Text by Rev. T. Morell. F.p. London 1748.

Josquin Des Près. See *Desprès, Josquin.*

Jota, La. A lively dance in triple time from N. Spain. It is perf. by one or more couples, acc. by a guitar player who also sings, and castanets.

Joubert, John (*b* Cape Town, 1927). S. African composer. Studied S. Africa Coll. of Mus. and RAM, London. Lecturer in mus. at Hull Univ. and Birmingham Univ. Comps. incl. syms., pf. conc., vn. conc., *Déploration* (1978), operas *Silas Marner* (1961) and *Under Western Eyes* (1968),

church mus., *The Magus*, soloists, ch., orch. (1976), *Herefordshire Canticles* (1979), choral works, etc.

Joyce, Eileen (*b* Zeehan, Tasmania, 1912). Australian pianist and harpsichordist. At recommendation of Percy Grainger, studied Leipzig Cons. under Teichmuller and Schnabel. London début Prom. concert under Sir Henry Wood. Soloist with all leading orchs. C.M.G. 1981.

Jubilate. Psalm 100 in Authorized Version of Bible (Ps. 99 in Latin Psalter). Used in Anglican service as alternative to Benedictus. Has been set to mus. by many composers, incl. G. Gabrieli, Purcell, and Britten.

Judas Maccabaeus. Oratorio by Handel to text by Rev. T. Morell based on biblical incidents. Comp. in summer of 1746 on commission from Frederick, Prince of Wales, to celebrate Eng. victory over Young Pretender at Culloden and return of victorious general, Duke of Cumberland, to London. (Part 3 contains ch. *See the Conquering Hero Comes.*) Prod. London 1747.

Judd, Terence (*b* London, 1957; *d* Beachy Head, 1979). Eng. pianist. Studied RCM. Won Nat. Junior Pf. Competition 1967. 1st prize Brit. Liszt Pf. Competition 1976. 4th place Tchaikovsky Competition, Moscow, 1978.

Judenkünig, Hans (*b* Schwäbisch Gmünd, *c*.1450; *d* Vienna, 1526). Austrian composer and lutenist. Wrote 2 lute-books, with mus. in Ger. tablature, which were manuals of self-instruction.

Judith. (1) Oratorio by Parry, f.p. Birmingham Fest. 1888.

(2) Opera in 3 acts by *Honegger to lib. by R. Morax, prod. Monte Carlo 1926.

(3) Opera in 1 act by E. Goossens to lib. by Arnold Bennett, prod. London and Philadelphia 1929.

(4) Oratorio by Thomas Arne, words by Bickerstaffe, f.p. London 1761.

Juditha Triumphans (Judith triumphant). Oratorio (RV644) by Vivaldi to lib. by Cassetti, f.p. Venice 1716, f. stage ps. Schwetzingen 1981, London 1984.

Juilliard Quartet. Amer. str. qt. founded in 1946 by William Schuman when pres. of Juilliard Sch. of Mus., NY. Specializes in contemporary mus., but has also recorded and given several cycles of all the Beethoven qts. Membership has altered more than once except for the 1st vn. Robert Mann (*b* Portland, Oregon, 1920).

Juilliard School. Amer. mus. coll. est. in NY in 1905 as Inst. of Mus. Art. In 1923 reorganized under foundation incorporated 1920 under will of Augustus D. Juilliard, NY cotton merchant, who left around 20 million dollars for the development of Amer. mus. The composer William Schuman was pres. 1945–62, Peter Mennin 1962–83, Joseph W. Polisi from 1984. In

Nov. 1969 the Sch. moved to its own building as a constituent part of the Lincoln Center for the Performing Arts. This building has 4 auditoria, incl. opera th. Name changed from Juilliard School of Mus. to Juilliard Sch. because of est. of dance dept. in 1952 and drama division in 1968.

Juive, La (The Jewess). Opera in 5 acts by Halévy to lib. by Scribe. Prod. Paris 1835, New Orléans 1844, NY 1845, London 1846.

Juke boxes. Automatic coin-operated machines for playing gramophone records, orig. installed in Amer. inns, etc., and common in Britain in the last few decades. (Name derived from 'jouke'; local inns in southern states of USA being called 'jouke joints', perhaps from Old Eng. *Jowken*, to rest or sleep).

Julien. Opera in prol. and 4 acts by Charpentier to his own lib. Sequel to **Louise*. Prod. Paris 1913, NY 1914.

Julietta, or The Key of Dreams. Opera in 3 acts by Martinů to his own lib. based on the novel *La Clé des songes* (1930) by Georges Neveux. Comp. 1936–7. Prod. Prague 1938, London 1978.

Julius Caesar (Handel). See *Giulio Cesare*.

Jullien (Julien), **Louis** (Georges Maurice Adolph Roch Albert Abel Antonio Alexandre Noé Jean Lucien Daniel Eugène Joseph-le-brun Joseph-Barème Thomas Thomas Thomas-Thomas Pierre Arbon Pierre-Maurel Barthélemi Artus Alphonse Bertrand Dieudonné Emanuel Josué Vincent Luc Michel Jules-de-la-Plane Jules-Bazin Julio César) (*b* Sisteron, 1812; *d* Paris, 1860). Fr. cond., composer, and impresario. Sponsored at his baptism by 35 members of local Phil. Soc., each of whom contrib. a name. Studied Paris Cons. under Halévy. Early ventures led to insolvency; fled to London where he promoted opera and promenade concerts 1838–59 with his own orch. which he cond. in highly flamboyant style. Employed what today would be called 'publicity gimmicks'. Comp. an opera *Pietro il Grande* (CG 1852). Toured USA 1853–4. Lost all his mus. in CG fire 1856, investments failed 1857. Returned to Paris 1859, was arrested for debt, released, and then put in asylum where he died. Pioneer in use of the baton. Notwithstanding his indulging in such showmanship as being handed a jewelled baton on a silver salver, he had the best players in London in his orch. and was a serious figure in the popularization of mus.

Jumping Frog of Calaveras County, The. Opera in 1 act by Lukas *Foss to lib. by J. Karsavina after story by Mark Twain. Prod. Bloomington, Ind., 1950.

June, Ava (*b* London, 1931). Eng. soprano. Member of SW chorus 1953, becoming prin. sop. 1957. CG début 1958 (in Verdi's *Don Carlos*). Has sung with WNO and in San Francisco (her Amer. début, as Ellen Orford in *Peter Grimes*), but has sung mainly with ENO, roles incl. Marschallin, Gloriana, Sieglinde, the *Figaro* Countess, Violetta, Tatyana, Butterfly, and Kaťa Kabanová.

Jung, Manfred (*b* Oberhausen, 1945). Ger. tenor. Bayreuth ch. 1970–3, début as soloist Dortmund 1974. Member Düsseldorf Opera from 1977. Sang Siegfried in *Götterdämmerung*, Bayreuth 1978; also in TV version of Chéreau's prod. of *The Ring*. Sang Tristan and Parsifal, Salzburg Easter Fest. 1980. Returned to Bayreuth 1983 as Siegfried in Solti-Hall *Ring*.

Junge Lord, Der (The Young Lord). Comic opera in 2 acts by Henze to lib. by I. Bachmann after fable *Der Scheik von Alexandria und seine Sklaven* (1827) by W. Hauff. Comp. 1964. Prod. Berlin 1965, London 1969.

Junge Magd, Die (The Young Servant). 6 songs by Hindemith to poems by Trakl, set for alto v., fl., cl., and str. qt. His Op. 23 No. 2. Comp. 1922, f.p. Donaueschingen 1922.

Juon, Paul (*b* Moscow, 1872; *d* Vevey, 1940). Ger. composer of Russ. birth. Studied Moscow Cons. under Arensky and Taneyev. Settled in Berlin. Prof. of comp. Berlin Hochschule 1906–34. Comp. sym. (1903), chamber sym., 3 vn. concs., triple conc., and 3 str. qts.

'Jupiter' Symphony. Nickname for Mozart's Sym. No. 41 in C major, K551 (1788). Not known why or when name originated, but possibly first used in programme of Phil. Soc. of London concert cond. *Bishop on 26 March, 1821. Mozart's son F. X. Mozart said that the nickname was coined by the impresario *Salomon.

Jürgens, Jürgen (*b* Frankfurt am Main, 1925). Ger. conductor. Studied in Frankfurt and Freiburg. Dir. of Hamburg Monteverdi Choir 1955. Joined staff of Hamburg Univ. 1960, becoming mus. dir. 1966. Editor of works by Monteverdi and A. Scarlatti. His choir's repertory ranges from Ockeghem and Monteverdi to Henze.

Jurinac, Sena (Srebrenka) (*b* Travnik, Yugoslavia, 1921). Austrian sop. of Yugoslav birth. Studied Zagreb, début there 1942 as Mimi in *La Bohème*. Member, Vienna State Opera from 1945. London début 1947 with Vienna State Opera. Glyndebourne 1949–56 (memorable Composer and Oktavian in Strauss's *Ariadne auf Naxos* and *Rosenkavalier*). San Francisco 1959. In latter part of her career sang Kostelnička in Janáček's *Jenůfa*.

Just Intonation. System of instr. tuning whereby a single scale, usually C, was determined according to ratio of its notes. Those far removed from C would be severely out of tune, hence the introduction of equal temperament as substitute for this 'natural' non-tempered scale.

K

K. Abbreviated prefix given to nos. in (1) *Köchel catalogue of Mozart's works; the letter is followed by a numeral, e.g. K491 (C minor pf. conc.).
(2) *Kirkpatrick catalogue of Domenico Scarlatti's works.

K. Anh. Köchel Anhang, the appendix to Köchel's catalogue of Mozart's works, some of which have the suffix K. Anh. followed by a number. In the main, works of dubious attribution are confined to the appendix.

Kabalevsky, Dmitry (Borisovich) (*b* St Petersburg, 1904; *d* Moscow, 1987). Russ. composer and pianist. Moved to Moscow 1918, studying pf. at Skryabin Mus. Institute 1919–25. Worked as pf. teacher and silent-cinema pianist 1922–5. Studied Moscow Cons. 1925–9 (comp. with Catoire and Myaskovsky). His pf. conc. 1929 won him fame in Soviet Union. In 1932, when Union of Soviet Composers was formed, he helped to organize Moscow branch, thereafter holding various administrative posts and writing many articles on Soviet mus. and composers. His output in the next 5 years was prolific, incl. 3 syms., the 3rd of which was a requiem for Lenin. Ass. prof. of comp., Moscow Cons. from 1932, prof. from 1939. During World War II he wrote numerous patriotic works, having joined Communist party in 1940. His post-war works reflected the official policy of 'Socialist realism'. His works comp. specially for young musicians are regarded as of particular significance. The West knows his instr. works better than his operas and operettas which are perf. in Russia. Prin. works:

OPERAS: *The Craftsman of Clamecy* (known in West as *Colas Breugnon*) (1936–8, rev. 1953, 1969); *Into the Fire* (*Before Moscow*) (1942); *The Taras Family* (incorporating much of *Into the Fire*) (1947, 2nd version 1950, 3rd version 1967); *Nikita Vershinin* (1954–5); *Spring Sings* (1957); *In the Magic Forest* (1958); *The Sisters* (1967).
ORCH AND CHORAL: Syms.: No. 1 in C♯ minor (1932), No. 2 in C minor (1934), No. 3 in B♭ minor (*Requiem* with ch.) (1933), No. 4 in C minor (1954); *The Comedians*, suite (1940); *Suite for Jazz Orch.* (1940); *Parade of Youth*, with ch. (1941); *The Mighty Homeland*, 2 soloists and ch. (1941–2); *The People's Avengers*, suite for ch. and orch. (1942); Suite, *Romeo and Juliet* (1956); *Song of Morning, Spring, and Peace*, children's ch. (1957–8); *Leninists*, 3 ch. and orch. (1958–9); *Spring*, symphonic poem (1960); *Requiem*, mez., bar., double ch., and orch. (1962); *Of the Homeland*, children's ch. and orch. (1965); *Letter to the 30th Century*, oratorio (1972).

CONCERTOS: Pf., No. 1 in A minor (1928), No. 2 in G minor (1935), No. 3 in D major (1952), *Rhapsody* for pf. and orch. (1963); Vn. conc. in C major (1948); Vc. conc. No. 1 in G minor (1948–9), No. 2 in C major (1964).
CHAMBER MUSIC: Str. Qts. No.1 in A minor (1928), No. 2 in G minor (1945); vc. sonata (1962).
PIANO: Sonata No.1 in F major (1927), No. 2 in E♭ major (1945), No. 3 in F major (1946); *4 Preludes* (1927–8); *30 Children's Pieces* (1938–9); *24 Preludes* (1943–4).
SONGS: *3 Poems of A. Blok* (1927–8); *8 Songs for children's ch.* (1932); *7 Merry Songs* (English nursery-rhymes) (1944–5); *10 Shakespeare Sonnets* (1953–5); *5 Romances* (1963–4).
Also th. and film mus.

Kabeláč, Miloslav (*b* Prague, 1908; *d* Prague, 1979). Cz. composer. Studied Prague Cons. 1928–34. Cond. Prague Radio 1932–41, head of mus. 1945–57, prof. of comp. Prague Cons. 1958–62. Works incl. 8 syms. (some with org. and vv.), cantatas, chamber mus., org. pieces.

Kaddish. Jewish mourners' prayer. Set by *Josephs in his Requiem and by *Bernstein as 3rd Sym.

Kadosa, Pál (*b* Léva, Hungary (now Czechoslovakia), 1903; *d* Budapest, 1983). Hung. composer and pianist. Studied Budapest Acad. 1921–7 (pf. with A. Székely, comp. with Kodály). Taught pf. at Fodor Cons. 1927–43. Prof. and dean of pf. faculty, Budapest Acad. from 1945. Works incl. 2 operas, 8 syms., 4 pf. sonatas, 4 pf. concs., va. conc., conc. for str. qt. and orch., 3 str. qts., etc.

Kaffeecantate (J. S. Bach). See *Coffee Cantata*.

Kagel, Mauricio (*b* Buenos Aires, 1931). Argentinian-born composer, cond., and teacher. Studied literature and philosophy at Buenos Aires Univ., mus. privately. Choral coach and cond. at Teatro Colón, 1955–6. Moved to Cologne 1957, working at elec. studio. Has worked in th. as composer and dir. of his own works since 1963. His mus. uses tape and elec. procedures; also he has demanded 'screams and yells' from singers and the sound of balls thrown on a kettle-drum. In his later works, visual and theatrical elements ('mixed media') have predominated. Many of the scores involve *indeterminacy. Works incl.: Str. Sextet (1953); *Tower Music*, for pre-recorded *concrète* and instr. sounds for 24 groups of loudspeakers, with light projections (1953); *Anagrama* (1957–8); *Heterophonie* (1959–60); *Antithèse*, for actor, elec., and audience sounds (1962); *Diaphonie*, for 2 projectors, ch., and orch. (1962–4); *Tremens*, scenic montage (1963–5); *Kommentar und Extempore,* soliloquies with gestures (1965–7); *Music for Renaissance Instruments* (1965–7); Str. Qt. (1966–8); *Variations without Fugue,* orch. (1971); *Programm, Gespräche mit Kammermusik,* vv. and ens. (1971–2); *Kantrimusik, Pastorale für Stimmen und Instrumente* (1973–5); *Dressage,* 3 perc. instr. (1977); th. piece *Ex-Position,* with gymnasts (1978); *Rhythm-machines,* for gymnasts or dancers, 2 perc., rhythm-generators (1978); *Chorbuch* (1978) (arr. of 53 Bach chorales for amplified mixed ch. and pf.); *Die Erschöpfung der Welt (The Exhaustion of the World),* mus. theatre for 6 solo vv., 6 actors, 2 chs., and orch. (1974–8).

Kahnt, Christian Frederik (*b* Leipzig, 1823; *d* Leipzig, 1897). Ger. mus. publisher. Founded his firm at Leipzig 1851. Pubd. works by Liszt and Mahler. Firm moved to Bonn 1950 and then to Wasserburg.

Kaim, Franz (*b* Kirchheim, 1856; *d* Munich, 1935). Ger. patron of mus. who founded Kaim concerts in Munich 1893, building hall and starting orch. (Kaim Orch.). Works by Mahler and Strauss were perf. at Kaim concerts which, in 1908, were absorbed by new Konzertverein. The orch. in 1924 became the Munich P.O.

Kaisermarsch (Emperor March). Orch. work by Wagner, comp. 1871 to celebrate Ger. victory in Franco-Prussian War of 1870 and election of Wilhelm I as Ger. emperor. F.p. Berlin 1871.

Kaiserquartett (Haydn). See *Emperor Quartet.*

Kaiser-Walzer (Emperor Waltz). Waltz, Op. 437, by Johann Strauss II, comp. 1888 in honour of Emperor Franz Josef to mark 40th anniversary of his accession. Arr. for chamber ens. 1925 by *Schoenberg.

Kajanus, Robert (*b* Helsinki, 1856; *d* Helsinki, 1933). Finn. cond. and composer. Studied Oslo, Leipzig, and Helsinki. Founded Helsinki Phil. Soc., 1882, cond. Helsinki P.O. until 1932. Taught mus. at Helsinki Univ. 1897–1926 (prof. from 1908). Friend and interpreter of Sibelius, several of whose syms. he cond. for early recordings. Comp. syms., cantatas, hymns, etc.

Kakadu Variations. Variations on 'Ich bin der Schneider Kakadu' for pf. trio, Op. 121a, by Beethoven, probably comp. in 1798 but not pubd. until 1824. Song is by Wenzel Müller from mus. play *Die Schwestern von Prag* (The Sisters from Prague), (1794). Kakadu is Ger. for cockatoo, but in this case refers to a character in the play.

Kalabis, Viktor (*b* Červený Kostelec, Cz., 1923). Cz. composer. Studied Charles Univ., Prague, 1945–9 and Prague Acad. 1948–52. Man., mus. dept., Prague Radio since 1953. Works incl. 4 syms., symphonic variations for orch., vc. conc., vn. conc., pf. conc., *Concerto for Orchestra,* conc. for chamber orch. ('Homage to Stravinsky'), 2 str.

qts., vc. sonata, sonata for vn. and hpd., tb. sonata, cl. sonata, hn. sonata, songs, etc.

Kalevala (from *Kaleva,* Finland). Finn. nat. epic, transmitted orally over several centuries, on which Sibelius based several works. In 1835 Elias Lönnrot published an edn. of 12,000 verses and in 1849 a 2nd edn. of 23,000 verses in trochaic verse, unrhymed, divided into 50 cantos or runes. This has been trans. into Swed., Ger., Eng., and Fr. Sibelius works which draw on it incl. *Kullervo, *Pohjola's Daughter,* and the *Lemminkäinen works.

Kalichstein, Joseph (*b* Tel Aviv, 1946). Israeli pianist. Studied Juilliard Sch., NY. Début NY, 1967. Thereafter int. concert career.

Kalinnikov, Vasily (Sergeyevich) (*b* Govt. of Orel, 1866; *d* Yalta, 1901 (old calendar 1900)). Russ. composer and cond. Ass. cond. Moscow It. Opera 1893–4. Ill-health compelled resignation. Comp. 2 syms., cantata, str. qt., etc.

Kalisch, Alfred (*b* London, 1863; *d* London, 1933). Eng. mus. critic and librettist. Orig. a barrister, began writing on mus. 1894, working for various papers. Strong champion of R. Strauss in Eng.; trans. libs. of *Salome, Elektra, Der Rosenkavalier* (much bowdlerized), and *Ariadne auf Naxos.* Also trans. lib. of Mascagni's *Iris.*

Kalkbrenner, Friedrich (Wilhelm) (*b* Kassel, 1785; *d* Enghien-les-Bains, 1849). Fr. pianist, teacher, and composer of Ger. extraction. Studied Paris Cons. 1798–1802. Lived in London 1814–23. Joined pf.-making firm of *Pleyel in Paris, 1824, establishing himself as renowned teacher, whose classes Chopin attended. Wrote pf. method. Comp. 4 pf. concs., 13 pf. sonatas, and much chamber mus.

Kalliwoda, Johann Wenzel (Jan Václav) (*b* Prague, 1801; *d* Karlsruhe, 1866). Cz. composer and violinist. Studied Prague Cons. For over 30 years Kapellmeister at court of Donaueschingen. Comp. 7 syms., str. qts., ob. conc., song-cycle *Das deutsche Lied.*

Kallman, Chester (*b* Brooklyn, NY, 1921; *d* Athens, 1975). Amer. poet and librettist. Joint librettist with Auden for Stravinsky's *The Rake's Progress* and Henze's *The Bassarids* and *Elegy for Young Lovers.* Also joint translator, with Auden, of *Die Zauberflöte.* Trans. libs. of Verdi's *Falstaff,* Donizetti's *Anna Bolena* and Mozart's *Die Entführung aus dem Serail.*

Kálmán, Emmerich (Imre) (*b* Siófok, 1882; *d* Paris, 1953). Hung. composer who settled in Vienna until 1938. In Paris 1938–40, USA 1940–6. Wrote successful operettas, e.g. *Tatárjárás* (The Gay Hussars) (1908); *Fräulein Susi* (1915); *Die Csárdásfürstin* (The Gipsy Princess) (1915); *Gräfin Mariza* (Countess Maritza) (1924); *Die Zirkusprinzessin* (The Circus Princess) (1926).

Kalmus, Alfred (August Uhlrich) (*b* Vienna, 1889; *d* London, 1972). Eng. mus. publisher of Austrian birth. Studied law at Vienna Univ. and mus. under G. Adler. Joined mus. publishers Universal Edition in Vienna, 1909. Went to London 1936 and opened branch of Universal Ed. Unceasing champion of 20th century composers, incl. Schoenberg, Berg, Webern, Bartók, Janáček, Berio, Boulez, Stockhausen, Birtwistle, David Bedford, and Hugh Wood.

Kalomiris, Manolis (*b* Smyrna, 1883; *d* Athens, 1962). Gr. composer and pianist. Studied Athens, Constantinople, and Vienna Cons. (1901–6). Taught piano Kharkov Cons. 1906–10, pf. and harmony Athens Sch. of Mus. 1911–19. Founded Hellenic Sch. of Mus. 1919, being dir. until 1926 when he founded Nat. Sch. of Music which he directed until 1948. Comps., some of which use Gr. folk-song, incl. operas *The Master Builder* (1915) and *The Shadowy Waters* (1950–2), sym.-poems, other orch. works, pf. conc., pf. preludes, vn. sonata, etc.

Kamarinskaya (Wedding Song). Orch. fantasia on 2 Russ. folk-songs by Glinka, comp. 1848 in Warsaw. Title refers to Russ. dance. Version generally played contains revs. by Glazunov and Rimsky-Korsakov.

Kaminski, Heinrich (*b* Tiengen, 1886; *d* Ried, nr. Benediktbeuren, 1946). Ger. composer and cond. Studied in Berlin. Works, in markedly polyphonic style, incl. opera *Jürg Jenatsch*, 2 str. qts., str. quintet, cl. qt., church mus.

Kaminski, Joseph (*b* Odessa, 1903; *d* Gedera, Israel, 1972). Russ.-born violinist and composer. Studied Warsaw, Vienna, and Berlin. Went to Tel Aviv 1935, becoming leader Palestine S.O. 1937–69. Wrote vn. conc., tpt. concertino, etc.

Kammer (Ger.). Chamber. So *Kammercantate,* Chamber Cantata (see *Cantata*); *Kammerduett, Kammertrio,* Chamber Duet, Chamber Trio (i.e. for a room rather than a concert hall); *Kammerconcert, Kammerkonzert,* either Chamber Concert, or Chamber Concerto; *Kammermusik,* Chamber Music; *Kammersymphonie,* Chamber Symphony.

Kammermusik (Chamber Music). Title given by *Hindemith to 7 instr. works comp. between 1922 and 1927: No. 1 for small orch., No. 2 (pf. conc.), No. 3 (vc. conc.), No. 4 (vn. conc.), No. 5 (va. conc.), No. 6 (viola d'amore conc.), No. 7 (org. conc.).

Kammersänger(in) (Ger.). Chamber Singer. Esteemed honorary title bestowed by Ger. and Austrian govts. on distinguished singers.

Kamu, Okko (*b* Helsinki, 1946). Finn. cond., composer, and violinist. Studied Sibelius Acad. 1952–67. Début as violinist early 1950s, in str. qt. 1965, as cond. 1968–9. Violinist in Helsinki P.O. 1965–6, leader Finn. Nat. Opera Orch. 1966–9, 3rd cond. at Nat. Opera 1968–9. Guest cond.

Royal Swedish Opera 1969–70. Cond. Finn. Radio S.O. 1970–7. Chief cond. and mus. dir. Oslo P.O. 1975–9. Chief cond. Helsinki P.O. from 1979. Guest cond. of Brit. orchs. (London début 1970, New Philharmonia). Won Karajan cond. competition 1969. Composer of film mus., songs for children, etc.

Kanawa, Kiri te. See *Te Kanawa, Kiri.*

Kantele. Finnish variety of *Gusli, plucked with the fingers.

Kapell, William (*b* NY, 1922; *d* nr. San Francisco, in air crash, 1953). Amer. pianist of Russ. and Polish parentage. Studied Philadelphia Cons. NY début 1941. Brilliant virtuoso with deep musical sensibility. Never played in Eng.

Kapelle (Ger.). Chapel. A term at one period applied to the whole staff of clergy, musicians, etc., attached to a royal chapel or the like. In time it came to be used for any organized body of musicians employed at court, etc., and from this it ultimately became a designation for any orch. body, from sym. orch. to dance band.

Kapellmeister (Capellmeister) (Ger.). The dir. or cond. of a *Kapelle. Kapellmeistermusik* became, sometimes unfairly, a derogatory term applied to mus. 'composed to order'.

Kapr, Jan (*b* Prague, 1914). Cz. composer, pianist, and teacher. Studied Prague Cons. Mus. dir. Prague Radio 1939–46, prof. of comp. Janáček Acad., Brno, 1961–70. Works incl. 8 syms., 7 str. qts. (one with bar. solo), 3 pf. sonatas, cl. concertino.

Karajan, Herbert von (*b* Salzburg, 1908). Austrian cond. Studied (to become pianist) Salzburg Mozarteum and Vienna Univ. and Cons. Début Salzburg Landestheater 1927 in *Fidelio.* Cond. Ulm Opera 1929–34; Aachen 1934–42; Berlin State Opera 1938–45; art. dir. Vienna State Opera 1957–64. Cond. at Bayreuth 1951–2, Salzburg Fests. Founded Salzburg Easter Fest. 1967. Cond. Berlin P.O. since 1954. Assoc. also with Philharmonia Orch., Orchestre de Paris (1969–70), and La Scala, Milan. One of outstanding conds. of post-1945 era, his career having been halted up to 1947 because of his Nazi affiliations. Also opera producer on stage and film.

Karel, Rudolf (*b* Pilsen, 1880; *d* Terezín, 1945). Cz. composer. Comp. pupil of Dvořák. Prof. of comp. and orch., Prague Cons., 1923–41. Wrote 2 operas, sym., symphonic poems (incl. *The Demon,* 1920), oratorio *Resurrection,* cantatas, chamber mus., etc. Died in Ger. concentration camp.

Karelia. Ov. and suite for orch., Opp. 10 and 11 by Sibelius, comp. 1893. Karelia is province in southern Finland.

Karfreitagzauber (Wagner). See *Good Friday Music.*

Karg-Elert (orig. Karg), **Sigfrid** (b Oberndorf-am-Neckar, 1877; d Leipzig, 1933). Ger. composer, pianist, and organist. Studied Leipzig Cons., becoming prof. there 1919, succeeding Reger. Best known for strikingly orig. org. comps. Works incl. pf. conc., 5 pf. sonatas, 28 pf. preludes, vc. sonata, vn. sonata, str. qt., chamber sym., org. sonata, *66 Chorale Improvisations* for org. (1908–10), *Fantasia and Fugue* in D for organ, *20 Preludes and Postludes* for org., 2 sonatas for harmonium, *Scènes pittoresques* for harmonium, choral works. Arr. Elgar's syms. for pf. solo.

Karłowicz, Mieczyslaw (b Wiszniewe, 1876; d Tatra Mountains, 1909). Polish composer. After spells in Heidelberg, Prague, and Dresden, settled in Warsaw, studying vn. Gave up career as violinist because of bad health, concentrated on comp., studying in Berlin 1895–1901 with Urban. Dir., Warsaw Mus. Soc. from 1905. In 1907 settled at Zakopane, at foot of Tatra Mountains. Died in avalanche. Works incl. sym. ('Revival', *Odrodzenie*) (1902); vn. conc. (1902); and several sym.-poems, incl. *Stanislaw i Anna Oświecimowie*. Strongly supported 'Young Poland' group of Szymanowski, Fitelberg, and Szeluto. His sym.-poems, in an individual style derived from Wagner and Strauss, reflect Schopenhauerian obsessions with love, death, and pantheism.

Karpeles, Maud (b London, 1885; d London, 1976). English folk-song collector, ed., and scholar. With sister Helen, was one of folk dancing team who illustrated Cecil *Sharp's lectures. Assoc. with Sharp's folk-song collecting from 1903, she went with him in 1916 to Appalachian Mts., collecting songs which had travelled to N.Amer. with early immigrants. Also went alone to Newfoundland 1929 and 1930 to collect songs there. Held many administrative folk-song posts, incl. hon. secretaryship *English Folk Dance and Song Society. In 1947 she founded International Folk Music Council, attending its conferences in many countries, first as secretary and later pres. Wrote biography of Cecil Sharp and ed. many colls. of folk-songs. O.B.E. 1961.

Karr, Gary (Michael) (b Los Angeles, 1941). Amer. double-bass player. Début recital NY 1962, also soloist with NY P.O. European tour 1964. Has commissioned concertos from Henze and Schuller.

Kars, Jean-Rodolphe (b Calcutta, 1947). Austrian pianist. Studied Paris Cons. 1958–64 and with Katchen. London début 1967. Winner of 1968 Messiaen Comp., Royan.

Kassern, Tadeusz (Zygfryd) (b Lwów, 1904; d NY, 1957). Polish composer. Studied in Lwów and Poznán, later in Paris. Sought asylum in USA 1948, teaching in NY. Works incl. operas, conc. for str., conc. for sop. and orch., pf. sonatas, fl. conc., db. conc., choral mus.

Káťa Kabanová (Katya Kabanova). Opera in 3 acts by Janáček to his own lib. based on the play *The Storm* (*Groza*) (1859) by A. N. Ostrovsky (1823–86) in Cz. trans. by V. Červinka. Comp. 1919–21. Prod. Brno 1921, London 1951, Cleveland, Ohio, 1957. (This was first Janáček opera to be staged in London, but a Brno perf. had been broadcast in 1948.)

Katchen, Julius (b Long Branch, NJ, 1926; d Paris, 1969). Amer. pianist. Studied NY. Début 1937 with Philadelphia Orch. Settled in Paris and had int. career as virtuoso with wide repertory.

Kate and the Devil (*Čert a Káča*). Opera in 3 acts by Dvořák to lib. by A. Wenig. Comp. 1898–9. Prod. Prague 1899, Oxford 1932.

Katerina Izmaylova. Title given to rev. version (1956) of Shostakovich's 4-act opera *Lady Macbeth of the Mtsensk District* (*Ledi Makbet Mtsenskovo uyezda*), comp. 1930–2 as Op. 29. Lib. by A. Preys and composer, after story (1865) by N. Leskov. Prod. Moscow 1934, Cleveland, Ohio, 1935, London (concert) 1936. Rev. version, Op. 114, Moscow 1963, London CG, 1963, San Francisco 1964. Orig. version was unperf. in USSR after Jan. 1936 when Soviet newspaper *Pravda* attacked it as 'leftist' and discordant, but there were prods. in Venice 1947 and Düsseldorf 1959.

Katin, Peter (Roy) (b London, 1930). Eng.-born pianist (now Canadian cit.). Début London 1948. Noted as interpreter of Chopin, Rakhmaninov, and Tchaikovsky.

Katz, Mindru (b Bucharest, 1925; d Istanbul, 1978). Romanian pianist. Studied Bucharest Royal Acad. Début with Bucharest P.O. 1947. Début in West (Paris) 1957, London début 1958. Settled in Israel 1959. On staff Rubin Acad. of Mus., Tel Aviv Univ., 1962 (prof. from 1972).

Kaun, Hugo (b Berlin, 1863; d Berlin, 1932). Ger. composer. Studied Berlin Hochschule 1879–80, by which time he had comp. 160 works. Lived in Milwaukee, Wisconsin, 1887–1902, during which time he comp. the symphonic poems *Minnehaha* and *Hiawatha*. Returned to Berlin as teacher 1902. Comp. 4 operas, 3 syms., symphonic poem *Sir John Falstaff*, 3 pf. concs., choral works, chamber mus., etc.

Kay, Ulysses Simpson (b Tucson, Arizona, 1917). Amer. composer. Studied with Hanson and B. Rogers at Eastman Sch. of Music and later with *Hindemith at Yale. Won *Prix de Rome* and worked in It. 1949–52. Prof. of mus., Lehman Coll. of City Univ., NY, from 1968. Works incl. 4 operas, ob. conc., *Concerto for Orchestra*, *Suite* for orch., sym., ballet *Dance Calinda*, cantata *Song of Jeremiah*, 3 str. qts., pf. sonata, fl. quintet, etc.

Kazoo (Fr. *mirliton*). Children's mus. instr., consisting of a short tube with membrane at each end, played by humming or singing into a side-hole to produce effect similar to comb-and-paper.

Kb. (Ger.). Abbreviation for *Kontrabass,* i.e. the db.

Keeffe, Bernard (*b* London, 1925). Eng. cond. Prof. of cond. TCL. Noted broadcaster and introducer of televised mus. Made Eng. trans. of Janáček's *Diary of One who Disappeared.*

Keel Row (Keel = boat). Song of unknown orig. which first appeared in print in *A Collection of Favourite Scots Tunes* (Edinburgh, *c.*1770) but is principally assoc. with Newcastle and Tyneside district. Quoted by Debussy in the 3rd movement (*Gigues*) of his ★*Images* for orch.

Keen (Irish *Caoine*). Irish funeral song acc. by wailing (keening). Reproduced in Vaughan Williams's opera ★*Riders to the Sea.*

Keene, Christopher (*b* Berkeley, Calif., 1946). Amer. cond. Founded own opera co. while at Univ. of Calif., staging two of Britten's operas. Worked as ass. to Kurt Adler at San Francisco Opera. Ass. to Menotti, Spoleto Fest. 1968. NY City Opera from 1970, conducting ★Ginastera's *Don Rodrigo*; art. supervisor from 1982. Mus. dir. Syracuse S.O. 1975–84. Cond. f.p. of Villa-Lobos's *Yerma,* Santa Fe, 1971. NY Met. début 1971.

Keilberth, Joseph (*b* Karlsruhe, 1908; *d* Munich, 1968). Ger. cond. Studied Karlsruhe, joined town's opera co. as répétiteur 1925, becoming cond. Mus. dir. 1935–40. Cond., Ger. P.O., Prague, 1940–5. Mus. dir. Dresden State Opera 1945–50; cond. Bavarian State Opera, Munich, 1951–68 (dir. from 1959); art. dir. Hamburg P.O. 1950–9, cond. Bamberg S.O. 1949–68. Bayreuth Fest. 1952–6. Notable Strauss interpreter. Died while cond. *Tristan.*

Keiser, Reinhard (*b* Teuchern, 1674; *d* Hamburg, 1739). Ger. composer. Pupil at Thomasschule, Leipzig. At court of Brunswick 1694 where he succeeded ★Kusser. Moved to Hamburg 1696, achieving success with opera *Mahumet II.* In next 40 years comp. over 100 operas for Hamburg, becoming dir. of the opera 1703–7. Visited Copenhagen, Ludwigsburg, etc., returning to Hamburg 1724. Cantor of cath. 1728. Regarded at one time as greatest orig. genius Ger. had prod. His operas contain magnificent florid arias and instrumentation which was emulated by ★Handel, who was violinist and harpsichordist for Keiser at Hamburg. Keiser's operas incl. *Der hochmütige, gestürzte und wieder erhabene Croesus* (1710, rev. 1730, modern edn. 1912, rev. 1958), *Die Römische Unruhe* (1705), *Die verdammte Staat-Sucht* (1705), *Fredegunda* (1715), and *Der Lächerliche Prinz Jodelet* (1726). Keiser also wrote dramatic and striking oratorios, and settings of the Passions, incl. *Der blutige und sterbende Jesus* (1704), and *St Mark Passion* (1717).

Kéler-Béla (Adalbert von Keler) (*b* Bártfa, 1820; *d* Wiesbaden, 1882). Hung. violinist, bandmaster, composer, and cond. Worked in Vienna, Berlin, and Wiesbaden. Wrote waltzes and light mus. of brilliant character.

Kell, Reginald (Clifford) (*b* York, 1906; *d* Frankfort, Kentucky, 1981). Eng. clarinettist. Studied RAM 1929–32. Prin. cl. Beecham's LPO 1932–6 and CG orch. 1932–6, LSO 1936–9, Liverpool P.O. 1942–5, and Philharmonia 1945–8. Went to USA 1948. Prof. at Aspen Mus. Fest., Colorado, 1951–7. Returned to Eng. 1971, but died in USA. Prof. cl., RAM, 1935–9 and 1958–9. Noted for artistic use of vibrato. Published Kell method, NY 1968.

Keller, Hans (*b* Vienna, 1919; *d* Hampstead, 1985). Austrian-born violinist, violist, mus. critic, and author (naturalized Eng., 1948). Member of BBC mus. division 1959–79. Joint ed. of book on Britten. Contrib. to many periodicals. Authority on Assoc. football. See *Functional Analysis.*

Kelley, Edgar (Stillman) (*b* Sparta, Wisconsin, 1857; *d* NY, 1944). Amer. composer, organist, and author. Studied Chicago and Stuttgart. Organist in San Francisco and Oakland, mus. critic, San Francisco *Examiner* 1893–5. Worked in San Francisco 1880–6 and 1892–6, coming into contact with Chinese and their mus. Acting prof. and orch. cond., Yale Univ. Sch. of Music 1901–02. Taught in Berlin 1902–10, returning to USA to teach comp. at Cincinnati Cons. Works incl. incidental mus. to *Macbeth* and *Ben Hur*; 2 syms. (No.1 *Gulliver—His Voyage to Lilliput,* Op. 15; No. 2 *New England*); pantomime suite *Alice in Wonderland; Pilgrim's Progress*; pf. quintet; str. qt., etc.

Kelly, Bryan (*b* Oxford, 1934). Eng. composer, pianist, and cond. Studied RCM 1951–5 with Jacob and Howells, then Paris with Boulanger. Taught at RSAM. Prof. of comp. RCM from 1962. Has written several works for children. Prin. comps.:

ORCH: *Latin Quarter Overture* (1955), *Music for Ballet* (1957), *The Tempest Suite,* str. (1964), *Cookham Concertino* (1969), ob. conc. (1972), guitar conc. (1978), Sym. (1983); for brass band: *Divertimento* (1969), *Edinburgh Dances* (1973), *Andalucia* (1976), *Concertante Music* (1979).

CHAMBER MUSIC: *3 Pieces,* vn. and pf. (1959), *Aubade, Toccata, and Nocturne,* guitar (1964), *2 Concert Pieces,* cl. and pf. (1964), *Zodiac,* cl., pf. (1978), *Suite parisienne,* brass quintet (1979).

CHORUS AND ORCH: *Tenebrae Nocturnes,* ten., ch., and orch. (1965), *The Shell of Achilles,* ten. and orch. (1966), *Stabat Mater,* sop., bass, ch., and orch. (1970), *At the round earth's imagined corners,* ten., ch., str. (1972), *Let there be light,* sop., narrator, ch., and orch. (1972–3), *Latin Magnificat,* ch. and wind instr. (1979).

VOCAL: *Magnificat and Nunc Dimittis* ('Latin American'), ch. and org. (1965), *Sleep Little Baby,* carol, SATB (1968), *O Be Joyful* (Caribbean Jubilate), ch. and org. (1970), *Abingdon Carols,* unacc. ch. (1973), *Te Deum and Jubilate,* ch. and org. (1979).

KEYBOARD: Pf. sonata (1971); *Prelude and Fugue*, org. (1960); *Pastorale and Paean*, org. (1973).

CHILDREN: *Herod, do your worst*, nativity opera (1968); *On Christmas Eve*, suite of carols for vv. and pf. (1968); *The Spider Monkey Uncle King*, opera pantomime (1971); *Half a Fortnight*, unison vv., pf., perc. (1973).

Kelly, Frederick (Septimus) (*b* Sydney, N.S.W., 1881; *d* in action, Beaucourt-sur-Ancre, 1916). Australian composer and pianist. Studied Frankfurt under Knorr, 1903–8, then in London. As adviser to Classical Concert Soc., London, promoted contemporary mus. Comp. pf. pieces and other small works.

Kelly, Michael (*b* Dublin, 1762; *d* Margate, 1826). Irish ten. and composer. Studied with Arne and later with Rauzzini. Début Dublin 1779 in Piccinni opera, then further study in Naples. Sang for 4 years at Vienna Court Opera, becoming friend of Mozart and creating roles of Basilio and Curzio in *Le Nozze di Figaro*, 1786. Sang in London 1787; actor-man. King's Th., London, 1793. Comp. mus. for plays and songs. Retired 1811. Wrote amusing and informative *Reminiscences* (1826; ed. R. Fiske, 1975).

Kelterborn, Rudolf (*b* Basle, 1931). Swiss composer and cond. Studied in Basle, Salzburg (cond. with Markevich), and Detmold (comp. with Fortner). Taught at Basle and at Detmold (1960–8). Prof. of comp. Zürich Musikhochschule from 1968. Works incl. 2 operas, incl. *Ein Engel kommt nach Babylon* (An Angel comes from Babylon) (1977), oratorio *Die Flut*, 3 syms. (incl. No.3, *Espansioni*, for orch., bar., and tape), 3 str. qts., 2 chamber syms., octet, etc.

Kemble, Adelaide (*b* London, 1814; *d* Warsash, Hants., 1879). Eng. sop. Concert début London 1835. Went to It. to study with *Pasta. Opera début as Norma, Venice 1839. Sang same role in Eng. at CG, 1841. Retired 1843 on marriage to E. J. Sartoris.

Kemp, Barbara (*b* Kochem an der Mosel, 1881; *d* Berlin, 1959). Ger. sop. Studied Strasbourg, début there 1903. Leading sop. Berlin Opera 1913–31. NY Met. 1922–4. Bayreuth Fest. (Senta and Kundry) 1914–27. Wife of Max von *Schillings. Became stage dir. in Berlin in 1930s.

Kemp, Ian (*b* Edinburgh, 1931). Scottish musicologist and teacher. Studied at Cambridge Univ. with R. Orr and P. Hadley. Worked for Schott's 1954–64. Lect. in mus. Aberdeen Univ. 1964–71, Cambridge Univ. 1972–6. Prof. of mus. Leeds Univ. 1977–81, Manchester Univ. from 1981. Author of books on Tippett and Hindemith, ed. Vol. 13 *New Berlioz Ed.*

Kempe, Rudolf (*b* Niederpoyritz, Dresden, 1910; *d* Zürich, 1976). Ger. cond. Studied Dresden with F. *Busch. Began career as oboist in Dortmund, becoming prin. oboist Leipzig Gewandhaus Orch.

1929–36. Répétiteur and junior cond. Leipzig Opera 1936–42. Cond. début Leipzig 1935, Lortzing's *Der Wildschütz*. Cond. opera Chemnitz 1945–8, Weimar 1948–9, Dresden 1949–53, Munich 1952–4. CG début 1953 with Munich company. NY Met. 1954–6. Bayreuth from 1960 incl. new prod. of *Der Ring des Nibelungen*. Cond. *Ring* cycles at CG 1955–9. Succeeded Beecham as chief cond. RPO 1961–3, art. dir. from 1964, prin. cond. for life from 1970. Cond. Delius centenary fest. 1962. Art. dir. Tonhalle Orch., Zürich, 1965–72, Munich P.O. 1967. Prin. cond. BBC S.O. 1975–6. Recorded complete orch. works of R. Strauss.

Kempen, Paul van (*b* Zoeterwoude, Leyden, 1893; *d* Hilversum, 1955). Dutch cond. and violinist. Leader, Concertgebouw Orch. under *Mengelberg. Cond. Dresden P.O. 1934–42. Cond. Berlin State Opera 1940, Aachen Opera 1942. Chief cond. Hilversum Radio from 1949, and in Bremen from 1953.

Kempff, Wilhelm (Walter Friedrich) (*b* Jüterbog, 1895). Ger. pianist and composer. Trained by his father and by Barth and Kahn in Potsdam and Berlin. Reputation grew from 1916 as virtuoso pianist. Dir., Stuttgart Hochschule für Musik, 1924–9. Noted for playing of Beethoven and classics. Comp. opera *King Midas*, 2 syms., vn. conc., pf. conc., chamber mus., and choral works.

Kennedy Center for Performing Arts. Arts centre in Washington, D.C., opened in 1971 and named in honour of late President J. F. Kennedy (assassinated 1963). Contains concert hall seating 2,700, opera house (2,300), and drama th. First event was *Bernstein's *Mass* (Sept. 1971).

Kennedy, Michael (*b* Chorlton-cum-Hardy, Manchester, 1926). Eng. critic, author, and journalist. On staff of *Daily Telegraph* in Manchester from 1941 (northern ed. from 1960); staff mus. critic from 1950. Author of histories of Hallé Orch. (1960 and 1983), RMCM (1971), and biog. studies of Vaughan Williams (1964), Elgar (1968, rev. 1982), Barbirolli (1971), Mahler (1974), Strauss (1976), and Britten (1981). Ed., *Concise Oxford Dictionary of Music* (3rd. ed. 1980), *Oxford Dictionary of Music* (1st ed. 1985). O.B.E. 1981.

Kennedy, Nigel (*b* Brighton, 1956). Eng. violinist. Studied Yehudi Menuhin Sch. (initially as pianist). Went to Juilliard Sch., NY, 1972. Début London 1977. Rapidly went to forefront of Eng. violinists. Toured Hong Kong and Australia as soloist with Hallé Orch., 1981. Amer. tour 1985. Regarded as one of finest exponents of Elgar conc. Regular jazz/improvisation concerts with S. *Grappelli.

Kennedy-Fraser, Marjory (*b* Perth, 1857; *d* Edinburgh, 1930). Scots singer and collector of folk-songs. As child, toured as accompanist to father, the singer David Kennedy (1825–86).

Studied singing in Milan and with M. Marchesi in Paris. When widowed, taught singing and in 1905 visited Outer Hebrides, where she began coll. of folk-songs which she arr. and pubd. for v. and pf.

Kent Bugle. Obsolete (since 1815) bugle with keys similar to saxophone. Invented 1810 by Irish bandmaster Halliday and named after Duke of Kent, who took interest in it.

Kent Opera. Eng. opera company founded 1969 by Norman Platt and Roger Norrington. Regularly plays in Canterbury and Tunbridge Wells, but has toured widely in the southern counties and has visited Manchester and various fests. Casts are mixture of experienced and new singers, and repertory has extended from well-known Verdi, Mozart, and Britten to rare works by Handel (f.p. of *Atalanta* since 1736 in 1970), Telemann, and others. Staged Tippett's *King Priam* in 1984–5 season. Norrington's edns. of 3 Monteverdi operas (*The Coronation of Poppea*, *Orfeo*, and *The Return of Ulysses*) were given in 1974, 1976, and 1978. In 1984 Ivan Fischer succeeded Norrington as mus. dir.

Kentner, Louis (Philip) (*b* Karvinna, Hungary (now Cz.), 1905; *d* London, 1987). Hung.-born pianist (Brit. citizen 1946). Studied Liszt Acad., Budapest (pf. with Székely, comp. with Kodály). Recital début 1920, soon making int. reputation. Settled Eng. 1935. NY début 1956. Gave f. Hung. p. of Bartók's 2nd pf. conc., Budapest 1933, f.p. (with Ilona Kabos) of conc. for 2 pf. and perc., London 1942, and f.p. in Europe of 3rd pf. conc., London 1946. Noted player of Liszt. C.B.E. 1978.

Kenton, Stan(ley Newcomb) (*b* Wichita, Kansas, 1912; *d* Hollywood, 1979). Amer. band leader, pianist, and composer. Protagonist of 'progressive jazz'. Established reputation at ballroom in Balboa, Calif., where his *Peanut Vendor* became a hit. Wrote ballet *Homage to the Princess*, 1956, for wedding of Prince Rainier of Monaco to Amer. actress Grace Kelly. Elaborate arrs. a feature of his later style.

Keraulophon (Gr.). Horn-pipe voice. Rarely-found metal labial org. stop of 8′ pitch, resembling Fr. hn. in tone quality.

Kerll (Kerl), **Johann** (Kaspar) (*b* Adorf, Saxony, 1627; *d* Munich, 1693). Ger. organist and composer. Studied with Carissimi in Rome (and possibly with Frescobaldi). Kapellmeister, Munich 1656–73. Taught in Vienna 1674–7, becoming court organist 1677–92. Comp. operas, masses, motets, etc. Handel 'borrowed' from one of his canzonas for ch. 'Egypt was glad' in *Israel in Egypt*.

Kerman, Joseph (Wilfred) (*b* London, 1924). Amer. scholar and critic. Studied Princeton Univ. Prof. of mus., Univ. of Calif. since 1974, having previously been on staff 1951–71. Prof. of mus.

Oxford Univ. 1971–4. Books incl. *Opera as Drama* (1956, in which *Tosca* is described as 'a shabby little shocker'), *The Beethoven Quartets* (1967).

Kern, Adele (*b* Munich, 1901; *d* Munich, 1980). Ger. sop. Début Munich 1924. Frankfurt Opera 1924–9. Vienna State Opera 1929–30, Munich Opera 1937–46. CG début 1931. Salzburg Fest. 1927–35. One of singers in famous Clemens *Krauss perfs. of Strauss and Mozart in Frankfurt, Munich, and Vienna.

Kern, Jerome (David) (*b* NY, 1885; *d* NY, 1945). Amer. composer. Studied with Paolo Gallico. Wrote his first successful song in 1904. Comp. several popular musicals incl. *Oh, Boy* (1917), *Sally* (1920), *Sunny* (1925), *Show Boat* (1927), *Music in the Air* (1932), and *Roberta* (1933). *Show Boat* contained the songs 'Ol' Man River', first sung by Paul *Robeson, and 'Can't help Lovin' dat Man of Mine'. Also comp. 'Smoke Gets in your Eyes' (in *Roberta*) and other popular melodies, several being featured in films.

Kerr, Harrison (*b* Cleveland, Ohio, 1897; *d* Norman, Oklahoma, 1978). Amer. composer. Studied Cleveland 1913–20, Amer. Cons., Fontainebleau, 1921 (comp. with N. Boulanger). Various teaching and admin. posts in USA and worked as a critic. Works incl. 3 syms., vn. conc., 2 pf. sonatas, str. qt., pf. trio, vn. sonata, *Sinfonietta* for chamber orch., opera *The Tower of Kel.*

Kertész, István (*b* Budapest, 1929; *d* nr. Herzliya, Israel, 1973). Hung.-born cond. (Ger. naturalization). Studied Liszt Acad., Budapest, and Rome. On staff Budapest Acad. 1952–7, then cond. at Györ, Hung., 1953–5. Cond. Budapest State Opera 1955–7, Augsburg 1958–63, Cologne Opera from 1964, prin. cond. LSO, 1965–8 and guest cond. of most leading orchs. Brit. début 1960 (Liverpool), Amer. début 1961, CG 1965. Drowned while swimming.

Kes, Willem (*b* Dordrecht, 1856; *d* Munich, 1934). Dutch cond. and violinist. Studied Leipzig Cons. and with Wieniawski and Joachim. Leader of several Dutch orchs., first cond. Concertgebouw of Amsterdam 1888, Scottish Orch. 1895–8. Cond. Moscow Phil. Soc. 1898, dir. mus. sch. 1901–5. Dir., Koblenz orch. and mus. sch. 1905–26.

Ketèlbey, Albert (William) (Vodorinski, Anton) (*b* Birmingham, 1875; *d* Cowes, I.o.W., 1959). Eng. composer and cond. Studied TCL. Cond. London th. orchs. Comp. comic opera, *Concertstück* for pf. and orch., wind quintet, but best known for orch. works such as *In a Monastery Garden* (1915), *In a Persian Market* (1920), *Bells Across the Meadows* (1921), and *Sanctuary of the Heart* (1924).

Kettledrum. See *Drum*.

Kettledrum Mass (Haydn). See *Paukenmesse*.

Key. (1) As a principle in mus. comp., implies adherence, in any passage, to the note-material of one of the major or minor scales (see *Scale*)—not necessarily a rigid adherence (since other notes may incidentally appear), but a general adherence, with a recognition of the *Tonic (or *'key-note') of the scale in question as a principal and governing factor in its effect. For instance we speak of a passage as being 'in the key of' C major, or F minor, and also use the same terms to describe a comp. (or movement) as a whole—in this latter case implying merely that the key mentioned is that in which the piece begins and sometimes but not always (e.g. Mahler) ends and is its governing one (see *Modulation*). If a piece in several movements is so spoken of it does not necessarily mean more than that the first movement (usually also the last one) is in that key.

The element of key crept into European mus. in the early 17th cent., as the *Modes gradually fell out of use: it remained of supreme importance to the end of the 19th cent. but in the 20th cent., many composers, led by *Schoenberg, have abandoned tonality. See *Atonal*.

(2) A lever on an instr. which is depressed by finger or foot to produce a note, e.g. on a pf. by finger, on an org. by foot, on woodwind by finger (the levers covering the airholes).

Keyboard. (1) A frame, or set, of *keys presented in a continuous arr. The purpose of kbds. is to enable the 2 hands (e.g. on pf. or harmonium) or the 2 hands and 2 feet (org.) readily to control the sounds from a much larger number of str., reeds, or pipes than could otherwise be controlled. One standardized apparatus of this sort, which has been gradually developed over a long period, has come to be universally adopted: it is by no means the most convenient imaginable, but the conservatism of musicians will probably prevent its supersession unless some drastic change in the scales used in mus. (e.g. by the general adoption of *Microtones) makes such a change imperative. The unchanging span of the octave is determined by the average span of the human hand.

The earliest kbd. was, apparently, that of the org., used for perf. of sacred melodic plainsong. In those days, mus. was still modal and the longer finger-keys, as we still have them, were all that were needed. With the coming into use of the practice of *musica ficta* a B♭ was found to be desirable and space for it was made by placing a short finger-key between the A and B♮. (It appears that a few kbds. like this still existed as late as the beginning of the 17th cent.) Other finger-keys

were similarly added, and our present-day kbd. of 7 different long and broad keys and 5 short and narrow ones so came into existence. This still leaves out many notes (e.g. B♯, if required, has to be played as C, F♭ as E, etc.). The restricted no. of keys which the individual can manipulate, and the necessity of avoiding the high cost of providing a large number of extra organ pipes, str., etc., precluded the provision of further finger-keys, and the difficulty was overcome by methods of tuning, at first, partially, with Mean-tone tuning and then, fully, with Equal Temperament tuning (see *Temperament*). There have been a good many attempts at the invention of a kbd. which would be free (or largely free) from this principle of compromise, but whilst some of them have been scientifically interesting none has proved of practical value in mus. making. Various ingenious inventions, such as the *Janko kbd., have also proved ephemeral.

(2) The term is also used generally, as in 'keyboard works', to indicate that the works may be played on more than one kind of kbd. instr.

Keyboard of Light. See *Prometheus—the Poem of Fire*.

Key (Keyed) Bugle. Treble brass instr. of the *ophicleide type, introduced about 1810 but fading from the scene when the modern *cornet appeared. See also *Kent bugle*.

Keyed (Bass) Horn. Not a hn., but an improved form of *Serpent, without that instr.'s twisting shape.

Key-note. The prin. (and lowest) note of the scale out of which a passage is constructed. Same as *Tonic*.

Keys, Ivor (Christopher Banfield) (*b* Littlehampton, 1919). Eng. teacher, composer, and organist. Studied RCM (1936–8). Ass. organist Christ Church, Oxford, 1938–40, 1946–7. Dir. of mus., Queen's Coll., Belfast, prof. 1951. Prof. of mus. Nottingham Univ. 1954–68, Birmingham Univ. 1968–86. Comps. incl. cl. conc., vc. sonata, choral works. Frequent broadcaster. C.B.E. 1976.

Key-Signature. The sign, or no. of signs, written at the beginning of each staff, to indicate the *key of the comp. Use of a key-signature dispenses with the need to write *accidentals (sharps or flats) for the notes affected throughout the comp. The keys of C major and A minor require no accidentals. The 'natural' form of the minor scale determines key-signature. Major and minor key-signatures are indicated thus:

	Sharp							
Major	C	G	D	A	E	B	F♯	C♯
Minor	A	E	B	F♯	C♯	G♯	D♯	A♯
	Flat							
Major	C	F	B♭	E♭	A♭	D♭	G♭	C♭
Minor	A	D	G	C	F	B♭	E♭	A♭

The white note in each case represents the major key, the black note the minor key with the same signature (called 'Relative Minor').

It will be observed that, starting from C, the keynotes of the sharp keys rise 5 notes (a perfect 5th) each remove, and that the keynotes of the flat keys fall 5 notes (a perfect 5th) each remove.

It will also be observed that in the sharp major keys the keynote is immediately above the last sharp.

And that in the flat major keys the keynote is 4 notes below the last flat (i.e. is at the pitch of the last flat but one in the signature).

And that 3 notes down any major scale we come to the keynote of its relative minor or, conversely, 3 notes up any minor scale we come to the keynote of its relative major.

Note that keys with 6 sharps (F♯ major and D♯ minor) are (on kbd. instr.) the equivalents of the keys with 6 flats (G♭ major and E♭ minor), and that keys with 7 sharps (C♯ major and A♯ minor) are the equivalents of the keys with 5 flats (D♭ major and B♭ minor). Thus composers use either one or the other of these signatures, but it is much easier to write in D♭ with 5 flats than in C♯ with 7 sharps.

The order of the sharps in the signatures is by rising 5ths, and the order of the flats by falling 5ths.

Sharps—F C G D A E B—*Flats*

Thus, one order is the other reversed.

Khachaturian, Aram (Ilyich) (*b* Tbilisi (Tiflis), 1903; *d* Moscow, 1978). Armenian composer. Planned to be biologist, but at 19 became vc. student at Gnessin Sch., Moscow, later joining comp. class as pupil of Mikhail Gnessin. In 1929 entered Moscow Cons. as pupil of Miaskovsky. His Trio (1932) attracted the attention of Prokofiev, who arranged perf. in Paris. His 1st Sym. (1934) was a success at its f.p. in April 1935, but even greater was that of his pf. conc. (1936). Held various state posts. His 2nd Sym. and vc. conc. incurred official disapproval in 1948 and he switched to comp. of film mus. In 1950 he began to teach at Gnessin Institute and Moscow Cons. and developed as cond. of his own works, travelling to It., Eng., Latin America, and elsewhere. In 1956 his ballet *Spartacus* was acclaimed by Moscow critics as a masterpiece. His mus. is colourful and has continued the nationalist tradition of the St Petersburg sch. Prin. works:

BALLETS: *Happiness* (1939); **Gayane* (incorporating mus. from *Happiness*) (1940–2, rev. 1952; 2nd version with new plot 1957); **Spartacus* (1954, rev. 1968).

ORCH AND CHORUS: Syms.: No.1 in E minor (1934), No. 2 in A minor (1943), No. 3 (1947); *Dance Suite* (1932–3); *Poem about Stalin,* with ch. (1938); 3 *Suites* from *Gayane* (1943); *Ode in memory of Lenin* (1948); 4 *Suites* from *Spartacus* (Nos. 1–3,

1955–7, No. 4, 1967); *Ode of Joy,* mez. and ch. (1956); *Lermontov* Suite (1959).

CONCERTOS: Pf. in D♭ major (1936); Vn. in D minor (1940); Vc. in E major (1946); conc.-rhapsody for pf. (1955, rev. 1961); conc.-rhapsody for vn. (1961); conc.-rhapsody for vc. (1962).

CHAMBER MUSIC: Vn. sonata in D (1932); Trio for pf., cl., and vn. (1932).

PIANO: *Poem* (1927); 7 *Recitatives and Fugues* (1928–66); *Suite* (1932); 3 *Marches* (1929–34); sonatina in C (1958); sonata (1961).

INCIDENTAL MUSIC: *Macbeth* (1934, 1955); *King Lear* (1958).

FILMS: *Lenin* (1948–9); *Battle of Stalingrad* (1949); *Othello* (1955).

Khamma. Ballet-pantomime in 3 scenes (*légende dansée*) by Debussy, scenario by W. L. Courtney and Maud Allan. Comp. and pubd. 1911–12 with pf. acc. Prelude orch. Debussy, rest by Koechlin under composer's supervision, 1912–3, f.p. Paris 1924. First stage perf. Paris 1947.

Khovanshchina (The Khovansky Affair). Unfinished opera in 5 acts by Mussorgsky to lib. by composer and V. Stasov. Completion and orch. by Rimsky-Korsakov, prod. St Petersburg 1886, Paris and London 1913 in version (now lost) altered by Stravinsky and Ravel, Philadelphia 1928. Later completed by Shostakovich (1959).

Khrennikov, Tikhon (Nikolayevich) (*b* Elets, 1913). Russ. composer. Studied at Moscow Cons. with Shebalin. Held various official Soviet posts; as sec.-gen. of Union of Soviet Composers, denounced Prokofiev and others for *'formalism' in 1948. Became leader of Soviet Composers' Union, retaining post for over 25 years. Teacher of comp., Moscow Cons. from 1963. Works incl. 3 operas, 3 syms., vc. conc., vn. conc., 2 pf. concs., songs, and film scores.

Kidson, Frank (*b* Leeds, 1855; *d* Leeds, 1926). Eng. scholar of folk-song and dance. One of founders of Folk-Song Soc. Authority on Brit. mus. publishing 1558–1830.

Kienzl, Wilhelm (*b* Waizenkirchen, 1857; *d* Vienna, 1941). Austrian composer. Studied at Prague and Leipzig Univs. and with Liszt at Weimar. Adopted Wagnerian principles for his 9 operas and mus. plays, most successful being *Der Evangelimann* (The Evangelist) (1894).

Kiepura, Jan (*b* Sosnowiec, 1902; *d* NY, 1966). Polish ten. Studied Warsaw. Début Lwów 1924 as Faust. Sang leading operatic roles in Vienna, Berlin, Milan, Budapest, and Buenos Aires 1926–39. NY Met. 1938–41, début as Rodolfo in *La*

Bohème. Made career in films. Sang with wife, Hung. sop. Marta Eggerth (*b* 1912).

Kilpinen, Yryö (*b* Helsinki, 1892; *d* Helsinki, 1959). Finn. composer and critic. Studied Helsinki Cons. and in Berlin and Vienna. Mus. critic in Helsinki 1919–31. Taught at Helsinki Cons. State pension enabled him to compose. Wrote over 800 songs, also pf. sonatas, etc.

Kindermann, Johann Erasmus (*b* Nuremberg, 1616; *d* Nuremberg, 1655). Ger. composer and organist. By 15 was singing and playing vn. in concerts in Frauenkirche, Nuremberg. Went to It. 1635, possibly becoming pupil of Monteverdi and Cavalli. In 1640 became org. of Egidienkirche, Nuremberg, being also in demand as teacher. His *Harmonia organica* (1645) contains 25 contrapuntal pieces. Comp. over 100 pieces for wind or strings and many for str. and hpd. Perhaps the first Ger. composer to employ *scordatura.

Kinderscenen (Scenes from childhood). Suite of 13 pieces for pf. by *Schumann, Op. 15, comp. 1838. No. 7 is *Träumerei.

Kindertotenlieder (Songs of the death of children). Song-cycle of 5 songs for bar. (or cont.) and orch. or pf. by *Mahler, to poems by Rückert. Comp. 1901–4, pubd. 1905, f.p. Vienna 1905.

Kindler, Hans (*b* Rotterdam, 1892; *d* Watch Hill, Rhode Island, 1949). Dutch-born (later Amer. citizen) cellist and cond. Studied Rotterdam Cons. Solo cellist with Berlin P.O. 1910. Went to USA 1914, prin. cellist Philadelphia Orch. 1914–21. Took up cond. 1927. Founded Nat. S.O., Washington, D.C., 1931, remaining cond. until 1948.

King, Alec (Alexander) **Hyatt** (*b* Beckenham, 1911). Eng. librarian, bibliographer, and critic. Joined staff Brit. Museum 1934. Supt., mus. room at BM, 1944–76. Authority on Mozart, Handel, and mus. printing.

King Arthur, or The British Worthy. Semi-opera in prol., 5 acts, and epilogue by Purcell to lib. by Dryden, but really a play with extensive mus. Prod. London 1691, NY 1800.

King Christian II. Play by Adolf Paul for which in 1898 *Sibelius wrote incidental mus., suite from it (7 movements) being his Op. 27.

Kingdom, The. Oratorio, Op. 51, by Elgar for 4 soloists, ch., and orch. to words selected from the Bible. Comp. 1901–6. Sequel to The *Apostles. F.p. Birmingham 1906.

King, James (*b* Dodge City, 1925). Amer. tenor. Began career as bar. Teachers incl. Max Lorenz. Prof. opera début Florence 1961 (Cavaradossi in *Tosca*). Made career mainly in European opera houses, singing Strauss's Bacchus in Vienna 1963, Siegmund at Bayreuth 1965, and Calaf in Milan 1968. Sang Emperor in *Die Frau ohne Schatten* at NY Met. (1966) and CG (1967).

King Lear. Mus. works inspired by Shakespeare's play (1606) incl. (1) ov. by Berlioz, Op. 4, comp. 1831;
(2) ov. and incid. mus. by Balakirev, 1859–61;
(3) 2 movements of incid. mus. by Debussy 1904;
(4) opera by Reimann, 1978.
(5) mus. by Shostakovich, comp. 1970, for Russ. film of Shakespeare's play in B. Pasternak's trans.
Various opera composers, incl. Verdi and Britten, have contemplated but abandoned *King Lear* projects.

King of Prussia Quartets. Title given to the last 3 str. qts. written by Mozart—No. 21 in D, K575 (1789), No. 22 in B♭, K589 (1790) and No. 23 in F, K590 (1790)—commissioned by King Friedrich Wilhelm II of Prussia, a cellist (hence the prominent vc. parts). 6 were requested, but only 3 written.

King Olaf, Scenes from the Saga of. Cantata, Op. 30, by Elgar for sop., ten., and bass soloists, ch., and orch. on text by Longfellow with additions by Acworth. Comp. 1894–6, f.p. Hanley, Staffs, 1896, London (Crystal Palace) 1897.

King Priam. Opera in 3 acts by *Tippett to his own lib. based on Homer's *Iliad*. Comp. 1958–61. Prod. Coventry 1962, Karlsruhe 1963, London (concert) 1980, Canterbury (and tour) by Kent Opera 1984–5, CG 1985 (cond. E. Howarth).

King, Robert (*fl.* London 1676–1728). Eng. composer of songs and th. mus. Member of Charles II's band from 1680 remaining in royal band until 1728. Promoted public concerts in London from 1689.

King Roger (*Król Roger*). Opera in 3 acts by *Szymanowski to lib. by J. Iwaszkiewicz and composer. Comp. 1918–24. Prod. Warsaw 1926, Palermo 1949, London 1975.

King's Singers, The. Male-v. ens. of 6 singers (2 counterten., ten., 2 bar., bass) formed in 1968 and so called because orig. members, with one Oxonian exception, were choral scholars at King's College, Cambridge. Specialize in part-songs and in arrs. of various genres, incl. humorous songs. Range from Monteverdi to Noël Coward, with several works written specially for them by contemporary composers.

King Stag (Henze). See *König Hirsch*.

King, Thea (*b* Hitchin, 1925). Eng. clarinettist. Studied at RCM with F. Thurston (whom she married 1953). Prin. cl. London Mozart Players 1956–64, ECO from 1964. Member of Melos Ens. from 1974. On staff RCM from 1961. Specialist in 20th cent. Brit. mus., but has also revived 18th and 19th cent. works for cl., e.g. those by Crusell. O.B.E. 1985.

King, William (*b* Winchester, 1624; *d* Oxford, 1680). Eng. composer and organist. Organist, New Coll., Oxford, from 1664. Comp. songs, ayres, church mus.

Kinsky, Georg (*b* Marienwerder, 1882; *d* Berlin, 1951). Ger. musicologist. Teacher at Cologne Univ. 1921–32. Prepared catalogue of Beethoven's works, completed after his death by Hans Halm, pubd. 1955.

Kipnis, Alexander (*b* Zhitomir, Ukraine, 1891; *d* Westport, Conn., 1978). Russ.-born bass (Amer. citizen from 1931). Studied Warsaw, graduating as cond., then in Berlin. Sang in operetta, Berlin 1913. Hamburg Opera 1915–17, Wiesbaden 1917–22, Berlin Städtische Oper from 1919, Berlin State Opera from 1930. Left Ger. 1935. Vienna Opera 1935–8. US début, Baltimore 1923, Chicago Opera 1923–32, NY Met. 1940–6. Début at CG 1927, returning 1929–35 as Hagen, King Mark, etc. Sang at Bayreuth Fest. 1927–33, Glyndebourne (1936, Sarastro), and Salzburg. Also notable Lieder singer. Taught at Juilliard Sch., NY, till he was past 80.

Kipnis, Igor (*b* Berlin, 1930). Amer. harpsichordist and critic, son of Alexander *Kipnis. Studied Harvard Univ. Worked for radio until taking up hpd. Début 1959. Contrib. to periodicals.

Kirbye, George (*b c.*1565; *d* Bury St Edmunds, 1634). Eng. composer of motets and madrigals. Contribution to East's Psalter, 1592. His 6-part *Bright Phoebus* was incl. in *The *Triumphs of Oriana.*

Kirchner, Leon (*b* Brooklyn, NY, 1919). Amer. composer and pianist. Studied mostly in Los Angeles, with Stravinsky, Schoenberg, Toch, and Klemperer, and later with Bloch and Sessions. Taught at Univ. of S. Calif., Mills Coll., and Harvard Univ. (since 1961, becoming prof. of mus. 1966). Comp., in idiom of Berg and Schoenberg but not 12-note, incl.: *Sinfonia*, 2 pf. concs., 3 str. qts., conc. for vn., vc., 10 winds, and perc., pf. sonata, choral mus.

Kirckman, Jacob (*b* Bischweiler, nr. Strasbourg, 1710; *d* Greenwich, 1792). Ger. organist and composer. Settled in Eng. *c.*1730 to work for Tabel, hpd.-maker, and became first of line of distinguished hpd.-makers. Organist, St George's, Hanover Square. Wrote several org. pieces. Succeeded by nephew, Abraham, who extended business to pf. manufacture. Business merged with Collard, 1898.

Kirkby, Emma (*b* Camberley, 1949). Eng. soprano. Studied Classics at Oxford and taught before 1974 London début. Specialist in early mus. and has sung with Academy of Ancient Music, London Baroque, and Consort of Musicke. Amer. début 1978 and three tours of Middle East with lutenist Anthony Rooley. Repertory ranges from the Italian quattrocentro to arias by Handel, Mozart, and Haydn.

Kirkby-Lunn, Louise (*b* Manchester, 1873; *d* London, 1930). Eng. mez. Studied Manchester and RCM. Début London 1893 in Schumann's *Genoveva.* Début CG 1896. Carl Rosa Opera 1897–9, CG 1901–14, 1919–22, NY Met. 1902–3, 1906–8, 1912–14. Notable in Wagner roles. Sang Elgar's *Sea Pictures* in NY with Mahler cond. 1910.

Kirkpatrick, John (*b* NY, 1905). Amer. pianist. Studied Princeton Univ. and in Paris with N. Boulanger and Nouneberg. Member of mus. faculty, Cornell Univ. from 1946. Gave famous perf. of Ives's **Concord Sonata,* NY, Jan. 1939.

Kirkpatrick, Ralph (*b* Leominster, Mass., 1911; *d* Guilford, Mass., 1984). Amer. harpsichordist. Studied in Paris with *Landowska and *Boulanger. Début, Cambridge, Mass., 1930. Prof. of mus., Univ. of Calif. 1964, Yale Univ. 1940–76 (prof. from 1965). Biography of Domenico Scarlatti (1953) incorporated catalogue of his works which has been accepted as definitive, works being given *'K' nos. Ed. of over 60 Scarlatti sonatas, J. S. Bach's *Goldberg Variations,* etc.

Kirnberger, Johann Philipp (*b* Saalfeld, Thuringia, 1721; *d* Berlin, 1783). Ger. composer. Pupil of J. S. Bach 1739–41. Wrote many choral works and fugues for *Klavier,* also theoretical treatises. Violinist in service of Frederick the Great, 1751–4.

Kirshbaum, Ralph (*b* Denton, Texas, 1946). Amer. cellist and cond. Studied Dallas with Aronson and at Yale Univ. with Parisot, then in Paris. Début with orch. Dallas 1959. Settled in London 1971. NY début 1975. Plays in pf. trio with György Pauk (vn.) and Peter Frankl (pf.).

Kiss, The (*Hubička*). Opera in 3 acts by Smetana, comp. 1875 to lib. by E. Krásnohorská, after story by J. Mužáková (1871). Prod. Prague 1876, Liverpool 1938.

Kissentanz (Ger.). *Cushion Dance.

Kit. Pocket fiddle, about 16″ in length, used by dancing masters in the 18th and early 19th cents.

Kitezh, The Tale of the Invisible City of (Rimsky-Korsakov). See *Invisible City of Kitezh, The.*

Kithara. Ancient Gr. str. instr. shaped like lyre but plucked by fingers.

Kitchen Department. Humorous term referring to orch.'s perc. section.

Kittl, Johann Friedrich (Jan Bedřich) (*b* Orlík nad Vltavou, 1806; *d* Lissa, 1868). Ger.-Bohemian composer. Dir., Prague Cons. 1843–65. Friend of Wagner, who gave him his lib. *Die Franzosen vor Nizza* which he comp. as *Bianca und Giuseppe* (1848). Also wrote 3 other operas, 4 syms., chamber mus., songs.

Kjerulf, Halfdan (Charles) (*b* Christiania, 1815; *d* Grefsen, 1868). Norweg. composer, nationalist in feeling. Studied law but took up journalism in 1840 while studying mus. theory, eventually at Leipzig (1850–1). Returned to Norway as pf. teacher. Wrote over 100 songs, many being settings of Bjørnson, choral and pf. comps. His songs combined influence of Ger. Lieder with Norweg. folk mus., paving the way for Grieg.

Kl. Abbreviation for *Klarinette* (Ger.), i.e. *Clarinet.

Kl. Fl. Abbreviation for *kleine Flöte* (Ger.), i.e. *Piccolo.

Klafsky, Katharina (*b* Sz. János, Hungary, 1855; *d* Hamburg, 1896). Hung. sop. In ch. of Vienna Komische Oper 1874. Tuition from M. Marchesi. Sang opera at Leipzig 1876–86. London début 1882 in *Die Walküre*. Hamburg Opera 1886–95. Sang in London 1892, under Mahler, in roles of Leonore (*Fidelio*), Brünnhilde, and Isolde. Returned 1894, adding Elsa and Agathe (*Freischütz*). Married cond. Otto *Lohse 1895. Prin. sop., Damrosch Ger. Opera, NY, 1895–6.

Klagende Lied, Das (The Song of Sorrow). Cantata by *Mahler, to his own text, for sop., cont., ten., bass, ch., and orch. Orig. version in 3 parts 1880: 1. *Waldmärchen* (Forest Legend), 2. *Der Spielmann* (The Minstrel), 3. *Hochzeitstück* (Wedding Piece). Rev. 1888 into 2 parts, *Waldmärchen* being omitted. Further rev. 1893–1902. F.p. Vienna 1901. F.p. of complete orig. version: Vienna (radio) 1935. F. Eng. p. rev. version, Oxford 1914, cond. Boult, London 1956, cond. W. Goehr, orig. version, London 1970, cond. Boulez.

Klangfarbenmelodie (Ger.). Melody of tone colours. Term introduced by Schoenberg in his *Harmonielehre* (1911) to describe the contrasts in timbre which he introduced in the 3rd of his 5 *Orchestral Pieces* (1909) and which now constitute a structural element in modern comp. comparable in importance with pitch, duration, etc. Further explorations into the possibilities of melodic construction with points of tone colour were carried out by Webern.

Klappenhorn (from Ger., *Klappen*, keys). *Key Bugle.

Klarinette(n) (Ger.). *Clarinet(s).

Klaviatur (Ger.). *Keyboard.

Klavier (Clavier) (Ger.). Keyboard. Term for pf., hpd., clavichord, or any other domestic kbd. instr. In Eng. the word is chiefly used as synonym for organ manual.

Klavierauszug (Ger.). Pf. arr.

Klavierbüchlein (Little keyboard-book). Title given by J. S. Bach to 3 colls. of his kbd. mus.: (1) Pieces for the instruction of his eldest son, Wilhelm Friedemann *Bach, 1720.
(2) Similar but small coll. for his 2nd wife, Anna Magdalena, 1722.

(3) Larger coll. for his wife, 1725, incl. some vocal pieces.

Klavierstück (Ger.). Pf. piece.

Klavierstücke I–XI (Piano Pieces I–XI). 11 pf. pieces by *Stockhausen comp. between 1952 and 1956, with IX and X rev. 1961. Many new techniques of pf.-playing are introduced for perf. of these pieces. The XIth is one of the first works in *open form. It has 19 sections printed on one large sheet of paper; the player has to play any piece at random, selecting his own tempo etc. Other permutations follow. F. complete p. Darmstadt 1966 (Aloys Kontarsky).

Klavierübung (Klavier Exercise). J. S. Bach's title, borrowed from *Kuhnau, for hpd. and org. works issued in 4 sections; (a) 6 partitas or *German Suites, 1731; (b) 2 pieces for double-manual hpd., the *Italian Concerto* and Partita in B minor (or French Overture) 1735; (c) org. works incl. 'St Anne' Fugue 1739; (d) *Goldberg Variations, 1742.

Klebe, Giselher (Wolfgang) (*b* Mannheim, 1925). Ger. composer. Studied Berlin Cons. 1941–3, and with *Blacher 1946–51. Worked for Berlin Radio. Uses serialism in several comps. Prin. works:

OPERAS: *Die Räuber* (1957); *Die Tödlichen Wünsche* (1959); *Die Ermordung Cäsars* (1959); *Alkmene* (1961); *Figaro lässt sich scheiden* (Figaro seeks a divorce) (1963); *Jacobowsky und der Oberst* (1965); *Das Märchen von der Schönen Lilie* (1969); *Ein wahrer Held* (based on Synge's *Playboy of the Western World*) (1975); *Das Mädchen aus Domrémy* (1976); *Das Rendez-vous* (1977). (All dates are of f.p.)
BALLET: *Menagene* (after Wedekind) (1958).
ORCH: *Con moto; Divertissement joyeux; Die Zwitschermaschine;* 2 Nocturnes; 4 Syms; conc. for vn., vc., and orch.; vc. conc.
CHAMBER MUSIC: Va. sonata, 2 str. qts., vn. sonata, wind quintet, pf. quintet. Also choral works, pf. pieces, songs.

Kleber, Leonhard (*b* Göppingen, *c*.1495; *d* Pforzheim, 1556). Ger. organist at Pforzheim from 1521. Comp. pieces for org. and kbd. pubd. among 112 items in org. tablature (1521–4).

Klecki. See *Kletzki, Paul.*

Kleiber, Carlos (*b* Berlin, 1930). Ger.-born cond. (Austrian cit. 1980). Son of Erich *Kleiber. Studied chemistry but turned to mus., Buenos Aires 1950. Répétiteur, Gärtnerplatz, Munich, 1953. Cond. Potsdam Opera, 1954–6, Vienna Volkstheater 1956–8. Cond. Düsseldorf Opera 1956–64, Zürich Opera 1964–6, Stuttgart from 1966, Munich from 1968. Cond. *Wozzeck* at Edinburgh Fest., 1966. Bayreuth Fest. 1974–6 (*Tristan*). CG début 1974 (*Rosenkavalier*). Milan 1977 (*Otello*). Guest cond. of leading sym. orchs.

Kleiber, Erich (*b* Vienna, 1890; *d* Zürich, 1956). Austrian-born (Argentinian citizen 1938) cond.

Studied Prague Cons. and Univ. Cond., Darmstadt court th. 1912–18, Wuppertal 1919–21, Mannheim 1922–3. Gen. mus. dir. Berlin State Opera 1923–34, one of its most brilliant periods, incl. f.p. of Berg's *Wozzeck,* 1925 (after, it is said, 137 rehearsals). Amer. début 1930 with NY P.-S.O. Resigned post 1934 over *Hindemith controversy with Nazis, leaving Ger. Cond. Buenos Aires 1937–49, Amsterdam 1933–8. British concert début 1935 (LSO). Début CG 1938, working there regularly 1950–3, cond. f. Eng. stage perf. of *Wozzeck* (1952) and notable *Der Rosenkavalier* perfs. Returned to post at Berlin State Opera 1955, but resigned because of political interference before taking it up.

Klein, Kleine (Ger.). (1) Little, as in *Kleine Flöte* (little fl., i.e. piccolo), *Eine kleine Nachtmusik* (A Little Night Music).
(2) Minor (of intervals).

Kleine Nachtmusik, Eine (A Little Night Music, or Serenade). Comp. in 4 movements (K525) by Mozart (for which occasion is not known) dating from 10 Aug. 1787. It is the Serenade No. 13 in G major, scored for 2 vn., va., and bass, or small str. orch. Orig. MS. recovered in 1955, indicates that a 5th movement, a 1st minuet, was torn out.

Kleine Orgelmesse (Little Organ Mass). Nickname for Haydn's Mass No. 5 in B♭ (see also *Grosse Orgelmesse*).

Kleine Trommel (Ger.). Small drum. The *side drum; otherwise Snare Drum.

Klemperer, Otto (*b* Breslau, 1885; *d* Zürich, 1973). Ger.-born cond. and composer. Studied Frankfurt Cons. and in Berlin with Pfitzner. Later encouraged by Mahler, whom he assisted with rehearsals of 8th Sym., Munich 1910. Cond. of opera Ger. Nat. Th., Prague, 1907–10, Hamburg 1910–12, Bremen 1913, Strasbourg 1914–17, Cologne 1917–24, Wiesbaden 1924–7, Berlin 1927–33 (first at Kroll Opera then State Opera). Cond. first Berlin perfs. of *Cardillac, *Oedipus Rex, Die *glückliche Hand,* etc. Cond. Los Angeles P.O. 1933–9. Seriously ill 1939, remaining partially paralysed. Cond. Budapest Opera 1947–50, Montreal S.O. 1950–3. Began assoc. with Philharmonia Orch., London, 1951, becoming prin. cond. 1959 and cond. for life in 1964. Cond. series of famous Beethoven concerts. Cond. and prod. *Fidelio* at CG 1961, *Die Zauberflöte* 1962, and *Lohengrin* 1963. Retired 1972. Comp. 6 syms., Mass, songs, etc.

Klenau, Paul (August) **von** (*b* Copenhagen, 1883; *d* Copenhagen, 1946). Danish composer and cond. Studied Copenhagen, in Berlin with Halîř and Bruch, in Munich with Thuille, and in Stuttgart with Schillings. Cond. Freiburg Opera 1907, Stuttgart 1908–14. Champion of Delius's mus. Comp. several operas, incl. *Kjarten und Gudrun* (1924) and *Rembrandt van Rijn* (1937), 7 syms.,

str. qt., pf. pieces, and orch. work *Bank Holiday, Souvenir of Hampstead Heath* (1922).

Klenovsky, Nikolay (Semyonovich) (*b* Odessa, 1857; *d* Petrograd, 1915). Russ. composer and cond. Studied Moscow Cons. under Tchaikovsky. Ass. cond. Moscow Imperial Opera (1883–93). Dir. Tiflis Mus. Sch. from 1893. Wrote ballets, cantatas, th. mus.

Klenovsky, Paul. Pseudonym under which Sir Henry *Wood made orch. transcription (1929) of Bach's Toccata and Fugue in D minor (in order to confuse the critics). *Klen* is the Russian word for a maple tree.

Kletzki (Klecki), **Paul** (*b* Łódź, 1900; *d* Liverpool, 1973). Polish-born (later Swiss) cond. and violinist. Violinist, Łódź P.O. 1914–19. Studied and cond. in Berlin 1921–33. Taught comp., Milan, 1933–8. Guest cond. of leading Eng. orchs. after 1947, when he made début with Philharmonia. Cond., Dallas S.O. 1958–61, Orchestre de la Suisse Romande 1967–9. Frequent cond. Israel P.O. Comp. syms., pf. conc., vn. conc., 4 str. qts.

Klien, Walter (*b* Graz, 1928). Austrian pianist. Studied Frankfurt, Vienna, and Graz. Prizes at int. contests at Bolzano 1952, Paris and Vienna 1953. Int. tours. Has recorded complete solo pf. works of Brahms, Mozart, and Schubert.

Klindworth, Karl (*b* Hanover, 1830; *d* Stolpe, 1916). Ger. pianist, cond., and composer. Pupil of Liszt 1852. Worked in London as cond., pianist, teacher, and impresario 1854–68. Prof. of pf., Moscow Cons. 1868–81, settling in Berlin 1882, where he cond. Berlin P.O. and founded pf. cons. (1884). Arr. Wagner's *Ring* for pf. Critical edn. of Chopin. Wrote many pf. pieces.

Klosé, Hyacinth (Eléonore) (*b* Corfu, 1808; *d* Paris, 1880). Fr. clarinettist. Prof. of cl., Paris Cons.,1839–68. Improved method of fingering 1843. Wrote methods of cl. and sax., pieces for cl. and military band.

Kluge, Die (The Clever Girl, or The Wise Woman). Opera in 6 scenes by *Orff to his own lib. which is synthesis of different versions of folk-tale. Comp. 1941–2. Prod. Frankfurt 1943, Cleveland, Ohio, 1949, London 1959.

Knaben Wunderhorn, Des (Youth's Magic Horn). Anthology of Ger. folk poetry pubd. 1805–8, ed. by Arnim and Brentano, songs from which have been set by several composers incl. Strauss and, particularly, *Mahler, who comp. over 20 *Wunderhorn* songs for v. and pf. or orch. and incorporated *Wunderhorn* songs into his 2nd, 3rd, and 4th syms. F. Eng. p. of Mahler's *Des Knaben Wunderhorn* (10 songs for sop. and bar.) in orch. version, London, Nov. 1961, cond. B. Fairfax.

Knappertsbusch, Hans (*b* Elberfeld, 1888; *d* Munich, 1965). Ger. cond. Studied Cologne Cons.

with Steinbach. Début Mulheim 1910. Opera posts at Bochum, Elberfeld, Leipzig 1918–19, Dessau 1919–22. Cond. Bavarian State Opera, Munich, 1922–36, Vienna State Opera 1936–50. Regular cond. Bayreuth Fest. from 1951. Returned to Munich 1954. Only London appearance, *Salome,* CG 1937. Superb interpreter of Wagner (especially *Parsifal*) and Strauss.

Knecht, Justin (Heinrich) (*b* Biberach, Swabia, 1752; *d* Biberach, 1817). Ger. organist, composer, and impresario. Pioneer of annotated programme. Dir. of mus. in Biberach (as well as prof. of literature) 1771–1807. Dir. of opera and court concerts, Stuttgart, 1807–9. Returned to Biberach. His 'grand symphony' *Le Portrait musical de la nature* (*c*.1784) has a literary programme closely anticipating Beethoven's *Pastoral* Symphony which Beethoven read in an advertisement on the cover of his earliest pubd. pf. sonatas.

Kneifend (Ger.). Plucking (same as *pizzicato*).

Kneller Hall. Headquarters of *Royal Military School of Music (founded 1857) at Whitton, Twickenham, Middlesex. Former home of painter Sir Godfrey Kneller (1646–1723).

Kniplová, Naděžda (*b* Ostrava, 1932). Cz. soprano. Studied at Prague Cons. 1947–53 and Acad. of Mus. Arts 1954–8. Sang with Janáček Opera, Brno, 1959–64, then became prin. at Prague Nat. Th. Outstanding in strongly dramatic roles, e.g. Smetana's Libuše, Janáček's Emilia Marty and Kostelnička, Isolde, Tosca, Ortrud, and Renata in Prokofiev's *The Fiery Angel.*

Knipper, Lev (Konstantinovich) (*b* Tiflis, 1898; *d* Moscow, 1974). Russ. composer. Studied in Moscow with *Glière and with *Jarnach in Berlin. Works incl. 14 syms., several with choral finales, operas, symphonic poem, vn. conc., film mus., chs., songs, etc.

Knorr, Iwan (*b* Mewe, W. Prussia, 1853; *d* Frankfurt-am-Main, 1916). Ger. composer and teacher. Studied Leipzig Cons. with *Moscheles and *Reinecke. From 1886, prin. teacher of comp., Hoch Cons., Frankfurt, where he had several distinguished pupils, incl. Eng. composers who became known as 'Frankfurt group', i.e. N. O'Neill, Cyril Scott, Roger Quilter, and Balfour Gardiner. Dir. of Cons. 1908–16. Wrote operas, orch. mus., and songs.

Knote, Heinrich (*b* Munich, 1870; *d* Garmisch, 1953). Ger. ten. Studied Munich, début there 1892, CG 1901, NY Met. 1904. Regular Wagnerian ten.—esp. as Tristan and Siegfried—at CG to 1913 and the Met. up to 1908.

Knot Garden, The. Opera in 3 acts by *Tippett to his own lib. Comp. 1966–69, f.p. CG 1970. Orch. reduced for chamber ens. of 22 players by M. Bowen, 1982–3. See also *Songs for Dov.*

Knüpfer, Paul (*b* Halle, 1866; *d* Berlin, 1920). Ger. bass. Début Sondershausen 1885. Leipzig 1887–98, Berlin 1898–1920, Bayreuth Fest. 1901–6, CG 1909–14. First singer in England of Baron Ochs and Gurnemanz.

Knussen, Oliver (*b* Glasgow, 1952). Eng. composer and conductor. Began to compose at age of 6. Studied comp. privately with John Lambert 1963–9, and at Purcell Sch. Awarded fellowship at Tanglewood 1970 and studied with Gunther Schuller 1970–3. Art. dir., Aldeburgh Fest. from 1983. Prin. works:

OPERAS: *Where the Wild Things Are*, Op. 20 (1979–81); *Higglety Pigglety Pop!* (1983–4).

ORCH: Symphonies: No. 1, Op. 1 (1966–7), No. 2, Op. 7, sop. and small orch. (1970–1), No. 3, Op. 18 (1973–9); *Concerto for Orchestra*, Op. 5 (1968–70); *Choral*, Op. 8, wind, perc., dbs. (1970–2); *Ophelia Dances*, Book I, Op. 13, for 9 instr. (1975); *Coursing*, Op. 17, chamber orch. (1979, rev. 1981).

VOICE AND ENS: *Hums and Songs of Winnie-the-Pooh*, Op. 6, sop. and ens. (1970–83); Sym. No. 2, Op. 7, sop. and small orch. (Texts by Trakl and Plath) (1970–1); *Rosary Songs*, Op. 9, sop., cl., va., pf. (1972); *Océan de Terre*, Op. 10, sop. and ens. (1972–3, rev. 1976); *Trumpets*, Op. 12, sop. and 3 cl. (1975); *Songs and a Sea Interlude*, Op. 20a, sop. and orch. (from *Where the Wild Things Are*) (1979–80).

CHAMBER MUSIC: *Processionals*, Op. 2, wind quintet and str. qt. (1968–78); *Masks*, Op. 3, fl. (1969); *Fire*, Op. 4, fl., str. trio (1969); *3 Little Fantasies*, Op. 6a, wind quintet (1970, rev. 1976); *Autumnal* (*Triptych, Pt. I*), Op. 14, vn., pf. (1976–7); *Cantata* (*Triptych, Pt. III*), Op. 15 (1977).

PIANO: *Sonya's Lullaby* (*Triptych, Pt. II*), Op. 16 (1977–8).

Koanga. Opera in prol., 3 acts, and epilogue by Delius to lib. by C.F. Keary after G.W. Cable's novel *The Grandissimes* (1880). Comp. 1896–7, rev. 1898. Extracts perf. in concert version London 1899. F.p. Elberfeld 1904, cond. *Cassirer; f. Eng. p. CG 1935 cond. Beecham (with lib. rev. by Beecham and E. Agate). Concerns slaves on Mississippi plantation. See also *Calinda, La.*

Kobbé, Gustav (*b* NY, 1857; *d* Long Island, 1918). Amer. mus. critic and writer. Studied mus. in Wiesbaden (1867–72) and NY. From 1880 mus. critic for several NY papers, incl. the *Herald* for 18 years. Attended first *Parsifal* at Bayreuth 1882. Wrote 2-vol. life of Wagner (1890), and several other books. His *chef d'oeuvre* was *The Complete Opera Book*, a coll. of synopses and analyses of a large no. of operas which was on the point of completion when he was killed by a seaplane striking his sailing-boat. 1st edn. pubd. 1922, with additions by Katherine Wright. Extensive rev. 1954 ed. by Earl of Harewood, who has continued revs. up to 9th edn., 1976.

Köchel, Ludwig von (*b* Stein, nr. Krems-on-the-Danube, 1800; *d* Vienna, 1877). Austrian botanist and mineralogist with immense admiration for mus. of Mozart. Compiled chronological thematic catalogue—*Chronologisch-thematisches Verzeichnis*—of Mozart's works, giving each a 'Köchel number' (e.g. K488) by which they are now universally identified. First pubd. Leipzig 1862. Various revs. have been pubd., one being by A. Einstein, 1937. 6th edn. 1964.

Kocsis, Zoltán (*b* Budapest, 1952). Hung. pianist and composer. Studied with Kadosa and Kurtág at Liszt Acad. Won Hung. Radio Beethoven Comp. 1970. Toured USA 1971, London début 1972. Liszt Prize 1973.

Koczwara. See *Kotzwara, Franz.*

Kodály, Zoltán (*b* Kecskemét, 1882; *d* Budapest, 1967). Hung. composer and teacher. He was born and had his early education in Galánta. His father, a state railways employee, played the vn., his mother the pf., and he grew up in a mus. atmosphere. He attended the Nagyszombat Gymnasium 1892–1900, during which period his first orch. work was played by the school orch. In 1900 he entered Budapest Univ. and the Franz Liszt Acad. of Mus., where his teacher was János Koessler, who also taught *Bartók and *Dohnányi. He met Bartók after his graduation, in 1905, and embarked on his first foray as a folksong collector in Galánta. In 1906 his symphonic poem, *Summer Evening*, had its f.p.

Kodály continued his folk-song collecting between 1907 and 1914. Although he was insistent on folk mus. as a basis of nat. culture, he had a wider view of the mus. scene and travelled to Bayreuth, Salzburg, Berlin, and Paris. He taught theory at the Liszt Acad. in 1907, and took over the comp. classes from Koessler in 1908 (prof. from 1911). From that time, too, he was closely involved with the mus. curriculum in Hung. schs., and with Bartók he formed an organization for the perf. of contemporary mus. Alongside these activities he produced a steady flow of comps.

In 1923, for the 50th anniversary of the unification of Buda and Pest as the capital, he comp. *Psalmus Hungaricus*, which was soon perf. throughout Europe and America under leading conds. such as Toscanini, Mengelberg, and Furtwängler.

In 1926 he completed his opera *Háry János*, firmly rooted in folklore. Another opera, *The Spinning Room*, followed in 1932, and the orch. *Dances of Galánta* in 1933. In the same year Kodály and Bartók were requested by the Hung. Acad. of Sciences to prepare for publication all available folk mus. material. After Bartók went to the USA, Kodály took over sole editorial control. The first vol. appeared in 1951. Two important commissions were for the Amsterdam Concertgebouw Orch.'s 50th anniv., 1939 (*Variations on a Hungar-*

ian Folk Song, The Peacock) and the 50th anniv. of the Chicago S.O., 1941 (*Concerto for Orchestra*). These were in contrast to the dozens of works for children's vv. which occupied him for the last 30 years of his life. He retired from the Liszt Acad. in 1942. After World War II he travelled to Fr., Eng., the USA, and USSR to cond. his own works. A 3rd opera, *Czinka Panna,* was prod. in 1948. His sym., in memory of Toscanini, was prod. at Lucerne in 1961. He visited the USA again in 1965 and 1966.

Kodály's mus. is not as advanced in its harmonic idiom as Bartók's and is less cosmopolitan. But it has the merits of complete conviction, finished craftsmanship, and melodic inspiration. Prin. works are:

OPERAS: *Háry János (1925–6); The Spinning Room (1924–32); Czinka Panna (1946–8).

ORCH: *Summer Evening* (1906, rev. 1929–30); Suite, *Háry János* (1927); *Dances of Marosszék* (1930, arr. of work for pf. 1927); *Dances of Galánta* (1933); *Variations on a Hungarian Folk Song, The *Peacock* (1938–9); *Concerto for Orchestra* (1939–40); Sym. (1930s–61).

CHORUS AND ORCH: *Psalmus Hungaricus*, ten., ch., and orch. (1923); *Te Deum of Budavár* (1936); *Missa brevis* (1944); *At the Grave of the Martyr* (1945); *The *Music Makers*, vv., orch. (1964).

CHORUS AND ORGAN, PIANO, etc: *Pange lingua* (1929); *Hymn to King St Stephen* (1938); *Laudes Organi* (1966).

UNACC. CHORAL: *Evening* (1904); *Birthday Greeting* (1931); *Jesus and the Traders* (1934); *Ode to Ferenc Liszt* (1936); *Molnár Anna* (1936); *The Peacock* (1937); *Forgotten Song of Bálint Balassi* (1942); *Lament* (1947); *Hymn of Zrinyi* (1954); *Mohács* (1965).

CHAMBER MUSIC: Str. qts., No. 1 (1908–09), No. 2 (1916–18); Sonata for vc. and pf. (1909–10); *Duo*, vn., vc. (1914); Solo vc. sonata (1915); *Capriccio*, solo vc. (1915); Serenade, 2 vn. and va. (1919–20).
Also many folk-song arrs., children's chs., singing exercises, and transcrs. (Bach, etc.).

Koechlin, Charles (*b* Paris, 1867; *d* le Canadel, Var, 1950). Fr. composer. Began serious mus. studies only at age 22. Entered Paris Cons. 1890–7, studying with Massenet and Fauré. Wrote large amount of mus., much of it still rarely heard. Followed no 'school' or fashion, his music being influenced both by medieval procedures and by Satie, Stravinsky, etc. Bitonality and near-atonality feature in his works, some of which are marked by complex polyphony. Wrote several symphonic poems based on Kipling. One of founders, 1909, of Société Musicale Indépendante. Author of treatises, and of books on Debussy and Fauré. Prin. works:

ORCH: 7 *Stars Symphony* (on characters of film stars) (1933), *Symphony of Hymns* (1936), Sym. No. 2 (1943–4); *3 Poèmes* after Kipling (1899–

1910), *La Course de printemps,* after Kipling (1925–7), *La Loi de la jungle,* after Kipling (1939), *Les Bandar-Log,* after Kipling (1939–40); *Le Buisson ardent* (1938, 1945); *La Forêt* (1897–1907); *Partita* for chamber orch. (1945).

THEATRE: *Jacob chez Laban* (1-act 'biblical pastorale') (1896–1908); *La Forêt paienne* (ballet) (1911–25).

CHAMBER MUSIC: 3 str. qts. (1911–13, 1915–16, 1921), fl. sonata (1913), va. sonata (1906–15), ob. sonata (1911–16), vn. sonata (1916), vc. sonata (1917), bn. sonata (1919), hn. sonata (1918–25), wind trio (1924), *Primavera* for fl., vn., va., vc., harp (1936), septet for wind quintet, cor anglais, alto sax., (1937), *Epitaphe de Jean Harlow,* fl., alto sax., pf. (1937).

PIANO: *Paysages et marines* (*c.*1916); *L'Ancienne Maison de campagne* (1932–3).

Koellreutter, Hans-Joachim (*b* Freiburg, 1915). Ger. composer and flautist. Studied Berlin State Acad. (comp. with Hindemith) 1934–6, Geneva Cons. 1936–7. Taught at Brazilian Cons., Rio de Janeiro, 1937–52. Founder and dir., Free Acad. of Mus., São Paulo 1952–5, and mus. dept., Bahia Univ. 1952–62. Head of programmes, Goethe Institute, Munich, 1963–5; dir., Ger. cultural institute, New Delhi, 1965–9. Prin., New Delhi Sch. of Mus. 1966–9. Dir. of Goethe Inst., Tokyo, from 1970. Works incl. chamber sym., 4 *Pieces* for orch., 2 fl. sonatas, vn. sonata, *Música* for orch., *Concretion* for orch., *India Report* for sop., speaker, speaking ch., and orch., *Composition 70* for sitar and chamber orch.

Koenig, Gottfried (Michael) (*b* Magdeburg, 1926). Ger. composer. Studied at Brunswick Mus. Sch. 1946–7, Detmold 1947–50, and Cologne Hochschule für Musik 1953–4. Ass. to Stockhausen at Cologne elec. mus. studio 1954–64, then art. dir., elec. studio Utrecht Univ. Comps. mainly for tape and computers.

Koffler, Józef (*b* Stryj, Poland (now Ukraine), 1896; *d* Kraków, 1943 or 4). Polish composer. Studied in Vienna with Schoenberg. Prof. of comp. and theory, Lwów Cons., 1929–41. Comp. 3 syms., 15 *Variations* for str., str. trio, str. qt. Died in ghetto massacre.

Kogan, Leonid (*b* Dnepropetrovsk, 1924; *d* Moscow, 1982). Ukrainian-born violinist. Studied Moscow Cons. 1943–51. Début Moscow 1941. London début 1955, Amer. 1957. On staff Moscow Cons. from 1952. First Soviet violinist to play and record Berg conc. In trio with *Gilels (pf.) and *Rostropovich (vc.).

Kohs, Ellis (Bonoff) (*b* Chicago, 1916). Amer. composer. Studied Chicago Univ. 1933–8, Juilliard Sch. 1938–9 (comp. with Wagenaar), Harvard Univ. 1939–41 (comp. with Piston). Teacher at Univ. of S. Calif. from 1950. Comps. incl. 2 syms.; *Concerto for Orchestra*; 2 str. qts.; opera *Amerika* (after Kafka); pf. variations; *Capriccio* (for org.); *Psalm 23.*

Kokkonen, Joonas (*b* Iisalmi, Finland, 1921). Finn. composer and pianist. Studied Sibelius Acad., Helsinki, 1940–1, 1945–9, Helsinki Univ. 1940–1, 1945–8. Teacher, Sibelius Acad. since 1950 (prof. of comp. 1959–63). Wrote mus. criticism 1947–63. Works incl. 4 syms.; vc. conc.; 3 str. qts.; pf. trio; pf. qt.; *Missa a cappella; Symphonic Sketches*; opera The *Last Temptations* (1975).

Kolb, Karlmann (*b* Kösslarn, 1703; *d* Munich, 1765). Ger. organist and composer. Priest and organist, Benedictine Abbey at Asbach. Wrote organ preludes and fugues in quasi-It. style.

Kolisch, Rudolf (*b* Klamm am Semmering, 1896; *d* Watertown, Mass., 1978). Amer. violinist of Austrian birth. After childhood injury, used bow in left hand. Studied Vienna Mus. Acad. and Univ. and, after 1913, with Ševčik (vn.) and Schreker and Schoenberg (comp.). Formed Kolisch Qt. 1922, which toured Europe, Africa, and USA where its members settled in 1935. Played standard repertory from memory and championed works by Schoenberg (Kolisch's brother-in-law after 1924), Berg, and Webern. Gave f. ps. of Schoenberg's 3rd and 4th str. qts. (1927 and 1937), Berg's *Lyric Suite* (1927), Webern's Str. Trio (1928) and str. qt. (1938), Bartók's 5th str. qt. (1935) and 6th str. qt. (1941). Quartet disbanded 1941. Kolisch led Pro Arte Qt. from 1942 and taught at Univ. of Wisconsin 1944–67.

Kollo (Kollodzieyski), **René** (*b* Berlin, 1937). Ger. ten. Studied in Berlin with Elsa Varena. Début Braunschweig 1965. Düsseldorf Opera 1967–71. Sang Lohengrin at Bayreuth Fest. 1971. Leading Wagnerian roles at Salzburg, Vienna, CG (début 1976 as Siegmund), NY Met. 1977 (Siegmund), Munich, Berlin, etc.

Kol Nidrei (Kol Nidre) (All vows). (1) For vc. and orch., Op. 47, by Bruch, comp. 1881. Arr. for vc. and pf.
   (2) Setting for rabbi, ch., and orch., Op. 39, by *Schoenberg (1938), f.p. Los Angeles 1938 cond. Schoenberg. The *Kol Nidrei* is the opening prayer of the Jewish service on the eve of the Day of Atonement (*Yom Kippur*). It has tragic associations with the Sp. persecution of the Jews in the 17th cent.

Kolodin, Irving (*b* NY, 1908). Amer. mus. critic. Studied Institute of Mus. Art, NY, 1927–31. Ass. mus. critic to W. J. Henderson, NY *Sun* 1932, eventually becoming chief critic until 1950. Also critic of recordings in several publications. Author of history of NY Met., and other books.

Kolomyika. A quick Polish dance in duple time, usually with slow introduction (**dumka). Popular among the mountain peasants of Poland.

Kondracki, Michal (*b* Poltawa, Poland; now Poltava, Ukraine, 1902). Polish composer and critic. Studied Warsaw Cons. under *Szymanowski and in Paris with N. Boulanger and Dukas. Mus. critic in Warsaw 1933–40, when he settled in Rio de Janeiro. Works incl. opera, ballets, sym., pf. conc., conc. for orch., etc.

Kondrashin, Kyril (Petrovich) (*b* Moscow, 1914; *d* Amsterdam, 1981). Russ. cond. Studied Moscow Cons. with Khaikin 1932–6. Cond., Maly Opera, Leningrad, 1936–43, Bolshoy Opera, Moscow, 1943–56. Prin. cond. Moscow P.O. 1960–75. Ass. prin. cond. Concertgebouw Orch., Amsterdam, 1975–81. Cond. f.ps. of Shostakovich's 13th Sym. (1962), *The Execution of Stepan Razin* (1964), and 2nd vn. conc. (1967). Recorded all Shostakovich syms.

König Hirsch (King Stag). Opera in 3 acts by *Henze to lib. by H. von Cramer after Gozzi. Prod. Berlin 1956; rev. as *Il Re Cervo* f.p. Kassel 1963, Santa Fe 1965, BBC 1973.

König Stephan (King Stephen). Ov. and incidental mus. by Beethoven, Op. 117, comp. 1811 for prol. by Kotzebue written for opening night of Ger. th. in Budapest, 1812 (see also *Die Ruinen von Athen*).

Königin von Saba, Die (The Queen of Sheba). Opera in 4 acts by K. Goldmark to lib. by H. von Mosenthal. Prod. Vienna 1875, NY 1885, Manchester 1910.

Königskinder (The King's Children). 3-act opera by Humperdinck to lib. by 'Ernst Rosmer' (Elsa Bernstein-Porges). Orig. play with incidental mus. (Munich and London 1897, NY 1898) then converted into opera and prod. NY Met. 1910, London 1911.

Kontakte (Contacts). Comp. by *Stockhausen for pf., perc., and elec. sounds on 4-track tape, 1959–60.

Kontarsky, Alfons (*b* Iserlohn, 1932). Ger. pianist, brother of Aloys *Kontarsky. Studied Cologne Hochschule für Musik 1953–5 and in Hamburg 1955–7. Held seminars at Darmstadt summer schools 1962–9. Has appeared as pf. duo with brother since 1955, giving f. ps. of works by Berio, Bussotti, Kagel, Pousseur, Stockhausen, and Zimmermann.

Kontarsky, Aloys (*b* Iserlohn, 1931). Ger. pianist, brother of Alfons *Kontarsky. Studied Cologne Hochschule für Musik 1953–5 and in Hamburg 1955–7. Formed pf. duo with brother 1955. Gave f. complete p. of Stockhausen's *Klavierstücke I–XI*, Darmstadt 1966. Formed duo with cellist Siegfried *Palm.

Kontrabass (Ger.). Db., generally the str. instr.

Kontrabassposaune (Ger.). *Double-bass Trombone.

Kontrafagott (Ger.). *Double Bassoon.

Kontra-Punkte (Counter-points). Work by *Stockhausen, 1952–3, for 10 instr. (fl., cl., bass

cl., bn., tpt., tb., pf., harp, vn., vc.). It is a rev. of a work for orch. *Punkte* (1952), itself rev. in 1962.

Konwitschny, Franz (*b* Fulnek, N. Moravia, 1901; *d* Belgrade, 1962). Ger. cond. Studied Leipzig. Played vn. and va. in various orchs. Cond. début 1927, working in Stuttgart, Freiburg, Frankfurt, and Hanover. Cond., Leipzig Gewandhaus Orch. 1949–62, Dresden State Opera 1953–5, Berlin State Opera from 1955. Cond. *The Ring* at CG, 1959.

Konzert (Ger.). (1) Concert.
  (2) Concerto.

Konzertstück (Ger.). Concert piece, generally with the implication of 'concerted' piece, i.e. for solo instr. and orch. Term often applied to short or 1-movement concs., e.g. Weber's *Konzertstück* for pf. and orch.

Koppel (Ger.). Coupler (organ).

Korbay, Francis (Alexander) (*b* Budapest, 1846; *d* London, 1913). Hung. ten., pianist, and composer. Studied pf., comp., and singing with various teachers. Sang at Nat. Th., Budapest, 1865–8, then studied pf. with Liszt. Toured Europe. Went to USA 1871, where he resumed singing. Prof. of singing, RAM, London, 1894–1903. Comp. orch. works and songs. Made many folk-song transcrs.

Korchinska, Maria (*b* Moscow, 1895; *d* London, 1979). Russ.-born harpist. Studied Moscow Cons. Prin. harpist Bolshoy Th., 1918–24, prof. of harp, Moscow Cons., 1918–24. Settled in Eng., 1926. Took part in f.p. of Britten's *A Ceremony of Carols*, 1942.

Korchmaryov, Klimenty (Arkadyevich) (*b* Verkhne-Dneprovsk, 1899; *d* Moscow, 1958). Russ. composer. Studied Odessa Cons. Comps., mainly on revolutionary themes, incl. operas *Ivan the Soldier* (1927), *10 Days That Shook the World*; ballet *The Serf Ballerina*; choral sym., *Holland*; vn. conc., songs, etc.

Korean Temple Block. An oriental addition to the 20th-cent. dance-band drummer's equipment. A skull-shaped hollow block of wood, in several sizes giving different pitches, struck with a drum-stick. Used in some symphonic works. Similar to the *Chinese Temple Block.*

Korn, Peter (Jona) (*b* Berlin, 1922). Ger.-Amer. composer and cond. Studied Berlin Hochschule für Musik, Jerusalem Cons. (1936–8), Univ. of Calif., Berkeley (1941–2), Univ. of S. Calif. (1946–7). Comp. teachers were Rubbra, Wolpe, Schoenberg, and Toch. Founder and cond. Los Angeles New Orch. 1948–56. Teacher of comp., Trapp Cons., Munich, 1960–1, dir., Strauss Cons., Munich, from 1967. Works incl. 3 syms., *Tom Paine* ov., concertino for hn., sax. conc., vc. sonata, ob. sonata, hn. sonata, str. qt., pf. sonata, etc.

Kornett (Ger.). The modern *Cornet or the ancient *Cornett.

Korngold, Erich (Wolfgang) (*b* Brno, 1897; *d* Hollywood, Calif., 1957). Austrian-born composer (Amer. citizen 1943) and cond. Son of mus. critic Julius *Korngold. Studied Vienna with *Zemlinsky, R. Fuchs, and Grädener. Child prodigy as pianist and composer. Schnabel played a pf. sonata he wrote at 13. Cond., Hamburg Opera 1919. Prof., Vienna State Acad., 1927. His opera *Die tote Stadt* (The Dead City) was a success in Hamburg, and in Vienna and NY, where Maria Jeritza sang prin. role. Settled in USA 1935, writing mus. for many successful films until 1947. Prin. works:

STAGE: *Der Schneemann* (pantomine, orch. Zemlinsky) (1910); *Der Ring des Polykrates, Violanta* (1-act double bill, f.p. Munich 1916); *Die *tote Stadt* (simultaneous f.ps. Hamburg and Cologne, 1920); *Das Wunder der Heliane* (Hamburg, 1927); *Kathrin* (1937, f.p. Stockholm 1939); *Die stumme Serenade* (1946).

ORCH: Sym. in F$\sharp$ major (1951–2); *Schauspiel-Overtüre* (1911); *Sinfonietta* (1912); *Symphonic Serenade* for str. (1947); pf. conc. for left hand (1923); vn. conc. (1945); vc. conc. (1946).

PIANO: *Fairy-Tale Pictures* (1910); Pf. sonatas: No. 1 (1908), No. 2 (1910), No. 3 (1931).

CHAMBER MUSIC: Str. qts., No. 1 in A (1924), No. 2 in E♭ (1935), No. 3 in D (1945).

FILM MUSIC: *Give Us This Night, Captain Blood, The Prince and the Pauper, The Adventures of Robin Hood, The Sea Hawk, The Private Lives of Elizabeth and Essex, Between 2 Worlds, Devotion,* etc.

In the 1920s Korngold re-orchestrated, re-arr., and practically re-comp. (for Theater an der Wien) operettas by Strauss (incl. *Eine Nacht in Venedig*), Offenbach, and Fall.

Korngold, Julius (*b* Brno, 1860; *d* Hollywood, Calif., 1945). Austrian mus. critic, father of Erich *Korngold. Studied law. Mus. critic *Neue Freie Presse,* Vienna, 1902–34. Collab. with son on lib. of Erich's opera *Die *tote Stadt* under joint pseudonym 'Paul Schott'.

Kosakisch, Kosatcheck, or **Kosachok.** A Cossack dance, the mus. of which is in quick duple time and of ever-increasing speed, and is often in the minor.

Kosler, Zdeněk (*b* Prague, 1928). Cz. cond. Studied Prague Acad. of Arts. Début, Prague Nat. Th., 1951. Opera dir., Olomouc 1958, Ostrava 1962; permanent cond. Prague S.O. 1966; mus. dir. Berlin Komische Oper 1966–8; cond. Czech P.O. 1971; chief cond. of opera at Slovak Nat. Th., Bratislava, 1971–9; chief cond. Prague Nat. Th. from 1980.

Kossuth. Symphonic-poem in 10 tableaux by *Bartók, based on life of Lajos Kossuth (1802–94), leader of unsuccessful Hungarian uprising against Austria, 1848–9. Comp. 1903. F.p. Buda-pest 1904; f. Eng. p. Manchester 1904 (cond. Richter). Contains distorted version of Austrian national hymn.

Kostelanetz, André (*b* St Petersburg, 1901; *d* Haiti, 1980). Russ.-born cond. Settled in USA 1922. Cond. for CBS 1930. Guest cond. of NY P.O. Widely known for luscious arrs. of light mus. in which he cond. his own orch.

Kotelettenwalzer (Ger.). See *Chopsticks.*

Koto. 13-stringed Japanese psaltery, strs. being of waxed silk, tuned by movable bridges. 6' in length, 3" high and 9" wide. Rests on floor, the right end being raised by 2 small legs. Player sits on his heels, plucking the strs. with right hand and using plectra on thumb and first 2 fingers, modifying pitch with left hand. Used in ritualistic mus. and regarded since 17th cent. as Japanese nat. instr.

Kotter, Hans (*b* Strasbourg, *c.*1485; *d* Berne, 1541). Swiss organist. Wrote org. book in tablature 1513, and other works for org.

Kotzwara (Kočžwara)**, Franz** (*b* Prague, 1750; *d* London, 1791). Bohemian-born violinist, db. player, and composer. Settled in London 1790 as violinist at King's Th. Won popularity with fantasia *The *Battle of Prague,* for pf. and optional extra instrs.

Koussevitzky (Kussevitzky)**, Serge** (Sergey) (Alexandrovich) (*b* Vishny Volochek, 1874; *d* Boston, Mass., 1951). Russ.-born (Amer. citizen) cond. and db. player. Studied Moscow Cons., graduating 1894. Recognized as db. virtuoso, becoming prof. at Moscow Cons. Début outside Russia as db. soloist, Berlin 1903. Début as cond., Berlin P.O. 1908. Db. soloist début, London, 1907, cond. LSO 1908. With 1st wife, Nathalie, founded publishing firm 1909, profits going to Russ. composers. Founded and cond. Koussevitzky S.O. 1910–18. Dir., State sym. orchs. 1917, dir., Grand Opera of Moscow 1918. Left Russia for Paris, founding orch. and conducting Concerts Koussevitzky 1921–8. Guest cond. throughout Europe, introducing Russ. operas to Sp. and Fr. From 1924 to 1949 was cond. of Boston S.O., giving many f.ps. of mus. by Amer. composers. Especial champion of Sibelius. Through Koussevitzky Mus. Foundation, founded 1943 in memory of wife, commissioned many works, incl. Bartók's *Concerto for Orchestra* and Britten's *Peter Grimes.* 2nd wife Olga (from 1947) very active on behalf of foundation. Koussevitzky composed conc. for db. and other pieces for the instr.

Kovařovic, Karel (*b* Prague, 1862; *d* Prague, 1920). Cz. conductor and composer. Studied at Prague Cons. 1873–9 and had private comp. lessons with Fibich, 1878–80. Harpist at Prague Nat. Th. 1879–85. Cond. some of first concerts of Czech P.O. 1896–8. Dir. of opera Prague Nat. Th. from 1900. Cond. f. ps. of operas by Ostrčil,

Foerster, and Novák. Cond. f. Prague p. of Janáček's *Jenůfa*, 1916, having for 12 years rejected it because of a personal grudge, and rev. and reorch. parts of it. Comp. several operas.

Koželuh, Jan (Johann Anton) (*b* Velvary, 1738; *d* Prague, 1814). Cz. composer and organist. Kapellmeister, Prague Cath. from 1784. Wrote operas, church mus., bn. conc., pf. conc., etc.

Koželuh, Leopold (*b* Velvary, 1747; *d* Vienna, 1818). Cz. composer and teacher. Instructor to Viennese aristocracy. Refused to succeed Mozart at Salzburg 1781, but succeeded him as court composer in Prague 1792. Wrote operas, ballets, oratorio, syms., and pf. works. Arr. Scottish, Irish, and Welsh folk songs for George Thomson of Edinburgh. Cousin of Jan *Koželuh. Name frequently spelt in Ger. style Kozeluch.

Kraft, Anton (*b* Rokitzan, Pilsen, 1749; *d* Vienna, 1820). Cz. cellist and composer. Studied in Prague and Vienna. Haydn persuaded him to join Esterháza orch. in 1778. Haydn's vc. conc. in D was once attrib. to him. His fine playing inspired vc. part of Beethoven's triple conc.

Kraft, Nicolaus (*b* Esterháza, 1778; *d* Cheb, Cz., 1853). Cz. cellist and composer, son and pupil of Anton *Kraft. Member of Prince Karl Lichnowsky's orch. and later of Schuppanzigh's str. qt. which gave f.ps. of several Beethoven qts. Chamber musician to Prince Lobkowitz 1796. In Vienna Court opera orch. 1809–14 when he was engaged by King of Württemberg. Wrote vc. pieces.

Kraft, William (*b* Chicago, 1923). Amer. composer. Studied Columbia Univ. 1949–52 and Juilliard Sch. 1948–52. From 1955 prin. timpanist Los Angeles P.O. Jazz-influenced comps. incl. conc. for 4 percussionists and orch., *Configurations*, for 4 perc. and jazz orch., *Nonet* for brass, *Concerto grosso*, *Silent Boughs*, song-cycle for sop. and strs., *Double Trio* for prepared pf., pf., elec. guitar, tuba, and 2 perc., *Triangles*, conc. for perc. and 10 instr.

Krakoviak, Krakowiak. (1) Polish dance from Kraków district, in lively $\frac{2}{4}$ time, with distinctive syncopation.

(2) Title of Chopin's concert rondo for pf. and orch., Op. 14, comp. 1828.

Kramer, A. Walter (*b* NY, 1890; *d* NY, 1969). Amer. composer, critic, and publisher. Studied vn., va., and pf. at Coll. of City of NY. Wrote for *Musical America* 1910–22, then worked in Europe. Ed.-in-chief *Musical America* 1929–36. Man. dir., Galaxy Music Corp., 1936–56. Comp. orch. works, chamber mus., and songs.

Krämerspiegel (Shopkeeper's Mirror). Cycle of 12 songs, Op. 66, for v. and pf. by R. Strauss to poems by Alfred Kerr (1867–1948), comp. 1918. Poems contain satirical and punning references to most of leading Ger. mus. publishers with whom Strauss was in dispute over copyright. One

of the work's melodies was used again by Strauss over 20 years later as the 'Moonlight Music' in his last opera *Capriccio*.

Krasner, Louis (*b* Cherkassy, Russ., 1903). Amer. violinist. Studied New England Cons. and later in Europe. Début Vienna. Commissioned and gave f.p. of Berg's conc., Barcelona 1936. Gave f.p. of Schoenberg's conc., Philadelphia 1940. Leader, Minneapolis S.O. 1944–9. Prof. of vn., Syracuse Univ. 1949–72.

Kraus, Alfredo (*b* Canary Is., 1927). Sp. tenor. Début, Turin 1956 as Alfredo in *La Traviata*. London début in same role, Stoll Th. 1957, CG 1959, La Scala 1960, NY Met. 1966 (Duke in *Rigoletto*). Outstandingly elegant lyric tenor in such roles as Massenet's Werther and Des Grieux.

Kraus, Joseph (Martin) (*b* Miltenberg, Mainz, 1756; *d* Stockholm, 1792). Ger. composer. Cond. at Stockholm Th. 1778, Kapellmeister 1781, court Kapellmeister 1788. Wrote 4 operas, incl. *Proserpina* (1781, revived Drottningholm 1981) and *Aeneas i Carthago* (f.p. 1799; admired by Gluck and Haydn), syms., incidental mus., str. qts. His *Funeral Music for Gustavus III* (1792) has recently been revived.

Kraus, Lili (*b* Budapest, 1903; *d* Ashville, N. Car., 1986). Hung.-born pianist (Brit. subject 1948). Studied with Bartók and Kodály, Budapest Acad., and at Vienna Cons. Private study with Schnabel. World tours and soloist with leading orchs. Specialist in Mozart. First to record all Mozart pf. sonatas and first to perf. all his concs. in NY, 1966–7. Duo with Szymon *Goldberg 1935–40. Interned in Java 1942.

Kraus, Otakar (*b* Prague, 1909; *d* London, 1980). Cz.-born bar. (Brit. subject). Studied Prague and Milan privately. Début Brno 1935 as Amonasro in *Aida*. Prin. bar., Bratislava Opera 1936–9, then settled in Eng., singing with Carl Rosa Opera. Joined *English Opera Group 1946, creating Tarquinius in Britten's *Rape of Lucretia*. Netherlands Opera 1950–1. Member of CG Opera Co. 1951–73. Created Nick Shadow in Stravinsky's *The Rake's Progress* (Venice, 1951), Diomede in Walton's *Troilus and Cressida*, and King Fisher in Tippett's *The Midsummer Marriage* (both CG). Sang Alberich at Bayreuth Fest. 1960–2. O.B.E. 1973.

Krauss, Clemens (Heinrich) (*b* Vienna, 1893; *d* Mexico City, 1954). Austrian cond. Studied Vienna Cons. with Grädener and Heuberger. Opera début Brno 1913. Cond., Ger. th., Riga, 1913–14. Worked in Stettin and Graz. Ass. cond. Vienna State Opera 1922–4, earning admiration of R. Strauss of whom he became close friend and great interpreter. Dir., Frankfurt Opera 1924–9, Vienna 1929–34, Berlin 1935–7, Munich 1937–43, Vienna 1947–54. His Munich period was notable for superb standard of prods. London début CG 1934, visits 1947 and 1949 and CG

1951–3. Amer. début 1929 NY P.-S.O. Frequent cond. of Vienna P.O., Frankfurt Museum concerts. Cond. f.p. of Strauss's *Arabella* (Dresden 1933), *Friedenstag* (Munich 1938), *Capriccio*, for which he wrote part of lib. (Munich 1942), and *Die *Liebe der Danae* (Salzburg 1944 dress reh. and Salzburg 1952). Married sop. Viorica *Ursuleac.

Krebs, Johann (Ludwig) (*b* Buttlestädt, 1713; *d* Altenburg, 1780). Ger. org. and composer. Pupil of Bach at Leipzig 1726–35. Then held various org. posts. Wrote religious choral works, fl. sonatas, fl. trios, and much org. mus., some of which is heard today.

Krehbiel, Henry (Edward) (*b* Ann Arbor, Mich., 1854; *d* NY, 1923). Amer. mus. critic, author, and ed. Studied law but turned to journalism. Mus. critic *Cincinnati Gazette* 1874–80, NY *Tribune* 1880–1923. Champion of Brahms, Dvořák, and Wagner. Bitterly attacked Strauss's *Salome* and was severely critical of Mahler as composer and cond. Wrote several books. Pubd. Eng. version of *Parsifal*. Rev. and completed Eng. text of Thayer's *Life of Beethoven* (3 vols. 1921).

Krein, Alexander (Abramovich) (*b* Nizhny-Novgorod, 1883; *d* Moscow, 1951). Russ. composer. Studied Moscow Cons. Works, influenced by Jewish background, incl. *Hebrew Sketches* for cl. and str. qt., *Salome* (symphonic poem), several operas, sym., *Threnody in memory of Lenin*, and *U.S.S.R., Shock Brigade of the World Proletariat*.

Krein, Grigory (Abramovich) (*b* Nizhny-Novgorod, 1879; *d* nr. Leningrad, 1955). Russ. composer, brother of Alexander *Krein. Studied with Glière and in Leipzig with Reger. Wrote *Hebrew Rhapsody* for cl. and orch., vn. conc., str. qt., 2 pf. sonatas, 3 symphonic episodes on life of Lenin.

Kreisler, Fritz (Friedrich) (*b* Vienna, 1875; *d* NY, 1962). Austrian-born violinist and composer (Amer. citizen from 1943). Entered Vienna Cons. at age 7, studying under Auer and Hellmesberger. Paris Cons. 1885, studying with Massart (vn.) and Delibes (comp.). Amer. début 1888 in NY, followed by tour with pianist Moriz *Rosenthal. Returned to Europe and abandoned mus. career, studying medicine in Vienna and art in Rome and Paris. Joined Austrian army, becoming officer in Uhlans regiment. Resumed career as violinist 1899 in Berlin. Returned to USA 1900–1. London début May 1901. Thenceforward his brilliant technique and unmistakably personal tone put him in the forefront of int. violinists. In 1910 gave the f.p. of Elgar's conc., which is ded. to him. Recalled to Austrian army 1914, but wounded and discharged. Lived in NY 1915–24 but later returned to Europe and in 1938 became Fr. citizen. Appeared regularly as conc. soloist and solo recitalist in London, making many recordings. Returned to NY 1940, thereafter living chiefly in USA. Comp. str. qt. and many charming pieces for vn., of which the best-known are *Caprice Viennois, Liebesfreud, Liebesleid, Schön Rosmarin* and *Tambourin Chinois*. Some of his comps. he attrib. (to confuse the critics) to various 17th- and 18th-cent. composers such as *Pugnani. Also transcr. works by Dvořák, Paganini, and Tartini. Wrote cadenzas for Beethoven and Brahms concs.

Kreisleriana. Set of 8 fantasy pf. pieces by Schumann, Op. 16, comp. 1838 and ded. to Chopin (rev. 1850). Title refers to the character Kreisler in E.T.A. Hoffmann's stories.

Krejčí, Iša (*b* Prague, 1904; *d* Prague, 1968). Cz. composer and cond. Studied Prague Cons. 1923–9 (comp. with Jirák and Novák, cond. with Talich). Cond., Bratislava opera 1928–32; mus. dir. Prague Radio 1934–45; art. dir. Olomouc Opera 1945–57; cond. Prague Nat. Th. 1957–68. Style said to be comparable with that of Poulenc. Prin. works incl.: Opera, *Pozdvižení v Efesu* (Tumult in Ephesus, based on Shakespeare's *Comedy of Errors*) (1939–43); *Nonet* (1937); *Serenade* for orch. (1947–50); 4 syms.; 3 str. qts.

Křenek, Ernst (*b* Vienna, 1900). Austrian-born composer (Amer. citizen from 1945). Studied with F. *Schreker at Vienna Acad. 1916 and Berlin Cons. 1920–3. His chamber mus., neo-classical in style, was played at Donaueschingen and Nuremberg, and his scenic cantata *Zwingburg*, to a text by Franz Werfel, was prod. in Berlin, 1924, under Kleiber. In 1925–7 he was ass. to Paul Bekker as gen. man. of opera at Kassel and Wiesbaden. In 1926 he completed his opera *Jonny spielt auf* (Johnny strikes up), using jazz idiom. After rejection by several Ger. opera houses, it was staged in Leipzig in 1927 and was a sensational success, being perf. in over 100 cities and trans. into 20 languages. It made Křenek's name and fortune. He returned to Vienna in 1928 and made extensive study of 12-note technique, later writing for *Frankfurter Zeitung* 1930–3. During this time he wrote an elaborate opera, *Karl V*, using the 12-note method. In some later works he employed a free atonal technique and also applied a 'principle of rotation', in which serial variants are formed through the systematic exchange of the pitches of a given series with their adjacent pitches. He also used elec. procedures and later returned to a more lyrical style. He emigrated to USA in 1938, becoming prof. of mus. at Vassar Coll. 1939–42 and at Hamline Univ., St Paul, 1942–7. In 1948 he settled near Los Angeles, devoting his time to comp., lecture-tours, etc. After 1945 he preferred his name to be spelt simply as Krenek. Prin. works:

OPERAS: *Zwingburg*, Op. 14 (lib. by Werfel) (1922); *Der Sprung über den Schatten*, Op. 17 (1923); *Orpheus und Eurydike*, Op. 21 (lib. by Kokoschka) (1923); *Bluff*, Op. 36 (1924–5); *Jonny spielt auf*, Op. 45 (1925–6); *Der Diktator*, Op. 49 (1926); *Das geheime Königreich*, Op. 50 (1926–7); *Schwer-*

gewicht (1926–7); *Leben des Orest*, Op. 60 (1928–9); *Karl V*, Op. 73 (1930–3); *Cefalo e Procri*, Op. 77 (1933–4); *Tarquin*, Op. 90 (1940); *What Price Confidence?*, Op. 111 (1945–6); *Dark Waters* (1950); *Pallas Athene weint* (1952–5); *The Bell Tower* (1955–6); *Ausgerechnet und verspielt* (1961); *Der goldene Bock*, Op. 186 (1963); *Der Zauberspiegel* (1966); *Sardakai* (1967–9).

BALLETS: *Der vertauschte Cupido*, after Rameau (1925); *8-Column Line*, Op. 85 (1939); *Jest of Cards* (1959).

ORCH: Syms.: No. 1, Op. 7 (1921), No. 2, Op. 12 (1922), No. 3, Op. 16 (1922), No. 4, Op. 34, for wind and perc. (1925), No. 5 (1949), Sym. (unnumbered, 1947), *Little Symphony*, Op. 58 (1928), Sym. *Pallas Athene* (1954), Symphonic mus. for 9 instr., Op. 11 (1922); pf. concs.: No. 1, Op. 18 (1923), No. 2, Op. 75 (1937), No. 3 (1946), No. 4 (1950); 2-pf. conc. (1951); *Concerto grosso* No. 1, Op. 10, (1921), No. 2, Op. 25 (1924); vn. concs.: No. 1, Op. 29 (1924), No. 2 (1954); *7 Pieces*, Op. 31 (1924); *Potpourri*, Op. 54 (1927); *Symphonic Piece* for str., Op. 86 (1939); *Little Concerto* for pf., org., chamber orch., Op. 88 (1940); *I Wonder as I Wander*, variations on N. Carolina folk-song, Op. 94 (1942); *Symphonic Elegy* for str. (on death of Webern) (1946); *Brazilian Sinfonietta* for str. (1952); *Kette, Kreis und Spiegel* (1956–7); *Quaestio temporis* (1958–9); *Marginal Sounds* (1960); conc. for vn. and pf., with small orch. (1950); vc. conc. (1953); *Capriccio* for vc. and small orch. (1955); harp conc. (1951); *Horizon Circled* (1968); conc. for org. and str. (1979).

CHAMBER MUSIC: Str. qts.: No. 1, Op. 6 (1921), No. 2, Op. 20 (1923), No. 3, Op. 65 (1931), No. 4, Op. 78 (1936), No. 5, Op. 96 (1943), No. 6 (1936), No. 7 (1944); Suite for solo vc., Op. 84 (1939); org. sonata, Op. 92, No. 1 (1941); fl. and va. sonatina, Op. 92, No. 2 (1942); sonata for solo va., Op. 92, No. 3 (1944); *Pentagram* for wind quintet (1957); str. trio (1948); wind quintet (1951); solo vn. sonata (1948); va. sonata (1948); ob. sonatina; guitar suite; fl. piece in 9 phases (1959).

CHORAL: *The Seasons* (Hölderlin), Op. 35 (1925); *Lamentio Jeremiae Prophetae*, Op. 93 (1941); *The Santa Fe Time Table* (1945); *6 Motets* (Kafka) (1959); *Canon 'Igori'* (for Stravinsky's 80th birthday, 1962); *German Proper of the Mass for Trinity Sunday* (1966–7).

SONGS: *9 Songs* (1921–3); *Reisebuch aus den österreichischen Alpen* (Diary from the Austrian Alps), Op. 62, 20 songs to own words (1929); *Die Nachtigall*, Op. 68 (1931); *5 Songs* (Kafka) Op. 82 (1938); *Ballad of the Railroads* (1944); *Sestina* for sop. and 10 players (1957); *Wechselrahmen* (Change of Frames), 6 songs for sop. and pf. (1968).

PIANO: Sonatas: No. 1, Op. 2 (1919), No. 2, Op. 59 (1928), No. 3, Op. 92 No. 4 (1943), No. 4 (1948), No. 5 (1950), No. 6 (1951); 2 Suites, Op. 26 (1924); *5 Pieces*, Op. 39 (1928); completion of

Schubert's C major sonata (1921); *Echoes from Austria* (1958); 8 *Pieces* (1946); *George Washington Variations* (1950); 6 *Vermessene* (1958).

ELECTRONIC: *Spiritus intelligentiae Sanctus*, oratorio for vv. and sounds (1956); *San Fernando Sequence*; *Quintina*, for sop., tape, chamber ens. (1965).

MISCELLANEOUS: Edn. and orch. of Monteverdi's *L'incoronazione di Poppea* (Vienna 1937); perf. version of 1st and 3rd movements of Mahler's 10th sym. (with Berg and F. Schalk) (Vienna 1924).

Krenn, Werner (*b* Vienna, 1943). Austrian tenor. Member of Vienna Boys' Choir. Bassoonist in Vienna S.O. 1962–6, then turned to singing. Stage début Berlin 1966 (in Purcell's *Fairy Queen*). Brit. début 1970 (Scottish Opera). Also successful Lieder singer.

Krenz, Jan (*b* Włocławek, 1926). Polish conductor. Studied Łódź Cons. (pf., cond., and comp.). Cond. Poznań P.O. 1951–3. Worked with G. Fitelberg. Chief cond. and art. dir. Polish Radio S.O., Katowice, 1953–67. Cond., Danish Radio S.O. 1966–8. Eng. début with BBC S.O. 1961. First cond. at Warsaw Opera 1967, later perm. guest cond. Chief cond. Polish Radio and TV orchs. Orch. works by Polish composers.

Kreuz (Ger.). Cross. Ger. for the *sharp sign (♯).

Kreutzer, Conradin (*b* Messkirch, Baden, 1780; *d* Riga, 1849). Ger. composer. Pupil of Albrechtsberger in Vienna. Held several Kapellmeister posts: to King of Württemberg, at Donaueschingen (1817), Vienna (1822–7, 1829–32, 1835–40), and Cologne (1840–2). Wrote operas, incl. *Das Nachtlager von Granada* (1834), incidental mus., chamber works, and songs.

Kreutzer, Rodolphe (*b* Versailles, 1766; *d* Geneva, 1831). Fr. violinist and composer. Pupil of Stamitz. 1st vn. in *Chapelle du Roi*, 1785, and soloist at Paris Théâtre des Italiens, 1790. Two operas prod. there. Prof. of vn., Paris Cons. 1795–1826, compiling (with Baillot) the establishment's vn. method. In 1798 visited Vienna where he met Beethoven, who ded. to him his A major sonata, Op. 47, completed 1803, and known as *'Kreutzer' Sonata (it is unlikely that Kreutzer ever played it). 1st vn., Paris Opéra, from 1801, cond. there from 1816 (his career as vn. soloist being cut short by broken arm, 1810). Retired 1826. Comp. over 40 operas and ballets, 19 vn. concs., 17 str. qts., 15 trios, 3 double concs., sonatas, and many vn. pieces incl. 20 *Études ou Caprices*.

Kreutzer Sonata. (1) Nickname of Beethoven's vn. sonata in A major, Op. 47 (1803) ded. to the Fr. violinist Rodolphe *Kreutzer, who is believed never to have played it.

(2) Sub-title often given to Janáček's Str. Qt. No. 1, comp. 1923–4 and incorporating part of scrapped pf. trio of 1908–9. On the score Janáček

wrote: 'Inspired by L. N. Tolstoy's *Kreutzer-sonata*' (novel pubd. 1890).

Křička, Jaroslav (*b* Kelč, Moravia, 1882; *d* Prague, 1969). Cz. composer and cond. Studied Prague and Berlin. Prof. at Prague Cons., from 1918, later becoming dir. Comp. 2 syms., 13 operas, several str. qts., mus. for Maeterlinck's *The Blue Bird*, song-cycles, and works for children.

Krieger, Johann (*b* Nuremberg, 1651; *d* Zittau, 1735). Ger. composer and organist. Court organist, Bayreuth, 1672–7. Town mus. dir., Zittau 1681. Comp. preludes and fugues for organ much admired by Handel. Also wrote songs and church mus.

Krieger, Johann (Philipp) (*b* Nuremberg, 1649; *d* Weissenfels, 1725). Ger. composer and organist, brother of Johann *Krieger. Court organist and chamber musician at Halle 1677; Kapellmeister, Weissenfels from 1680. Wrote operas, Singspiels, sonatas, partitas, etc.

Krips, Henry (Joseph) (*b* Vienna, 1912). Austrian-born cond., brother of Josef *Krips. Studied Vienna Cons. and Univ. Guest cond. of many Brit. orchs. and SW Opera. Went to Australia 1938, becoming Australian cit. 1944. Worked for Australian radio. Cond. S. Australia S.O. 1949–72.

Krips, Josef (*b* Vienna, 1902; *d* Geneva, 1974). Austrian cond. Studied Vienna with *Weingartner. Cond. at Vienna Volksoper 1921–4, Dortmund 1925–6, Karlsruhe 1926–33, Vienna State Opera 1933–8, Belgrade Opera 1938–9. Banned by Nazis from conducting, 1939–45. Cond. first opera perf. in Vienna after war in 1945, playing major part in restoring Vienna Opera's reputation 1945–50. Re-opened Salzburg Fest. 1946. Guest cond. Eng. orchs. (Hallé, etc.) from 1947. Début CG 1947 with Vienna co. in Mozart. Cond.-in-chief LSO 1950–4, Buffalo P.O. 1954–63, San Francisco S.O. 1963–70. NY Met. début 1966.

Kroll Oper. Ger. opera house in Berlin, extant 1924–31. Was planned by Wilhelm II in 1896, the Krolls Theater, Königplatz, being purchased. Delays postponed opening until 1924. Under *Klemperer 1927–31, the Kroll was among most adventurous opera houses of world. Nazis took over th. as home of Reichstag, 1933.

Krombholc, Jaroslav (*b* Prague, 1918; *d* Prague, 1983). Cz. cond. Studied Prague Cons. with Novák and Talich. Guest cond. Prague Nat. Th. and Czech P.O. 1940. Cond., Prague Nat. Th. 1949–62, 1st cond. 1963–8, head, Prague Nat. Th. Opera 1968–70, chief cond. Nat. Th. Opera 1970–5. Chief cond. Cz. Radio 1973–8. Cond. opera in Vienna, Budapest, London (1959), Warsaw, Naples, Russia.

Krommer, Franz (*b* Kamenitz, Moravia, 1759; *d* Vienna, 1831). Moravian composer and violinist. Served in various court mus. posts, until succeed-ing Koželuh as Vienna court Kapellmeister 1818. Prolific composer of mus. for wind instrs., syms., masses, cl. conc., etc.

Krueger, Karl (*b* Atchison, Kansas, 1894; *d* Elgin, Ill., 1979). Ger.-Amer. cond. Studied Heidelberg and Vienna Univ. Studied conducting under Schalk, Weingartner, and Nikisch. Ass. cond. Vienna State Opera 1919–24. Cond., Seattle S.O. 1925–32, Kansas City P.O. 1933–43, Detroit S.O. 1943–4. Cond. several opera premières with NY Music Guild.

Krumhorn, Krummhorn (Ger.). *Crumhorn.

Krummbogen, Krummbügel (Ger.). Bent-arch, or **Stimmbogen,** Tuning-arch. Crook (of a brass instr.).

Krumpholtz, Johann (Baptist) (*b* Zlonice, nr. Prague, 1742; *d* Paris, 1790). Bohemian harpist and composer, pupil of Joseph Haydn. Originated several improvements in the harp. Comp. several works for harp. Drowned himself in Seine because of wife's infidelity.

Krumpholtz, Wenzel (*b* Budenice, nr. Zlonice, 1750; *d* Vienna, 1817). Bohemian violinist, mandolin-player, and composer, brother of Johann Baptist *Krumpholtz. Violinist in Court opera orch., Vienna, from 1796. Friend and champion of Beethoven, to whom he may have given vn. lessons. Beethoven composed a mandolin sonata for him and the vocal trio *Gesang der Mönche* in his memory.

Kubelik, Jan (*b* Michle, nr. Prague, 1880; *d* Prague, 1940). Cz.-born violinist and composer (Hungarian citizen from 1903). Studied Prague Cons. 1892–8 with Ševčik. Concert début Prague, Vienna, 1898. London début 1900. Notable virtuoso. Comp. 6 vn. concs. and *American Symphony* (1937).

Kubelik, (Jeronym) **Rafael** (*b* Býchory, 1914). Cz. cond. and composer, son of Jan *Kubelik. Studied Prague Cons. Début with Czech. P.O. 1934; accompanist to father 1935–6; cond. Czech. P.O. 1936–9, Brno Opera 1939–41, chief cond. Czech P.O. 1941–8. Left Cz. 1948. Cond. Chicago S.O. 1950–3; mus. dir. CG 1955–8 (incl. first stage perfs. in Eng. of *Jenůfa* and *Les *Troyens*); cond. Bavarian Radio S.O. 1961–79. Mus. dir. NY Met. 1973–4. Works incl. 2 syms., 4 operas, 4 str. qts., vn. conc., vc. conc., songs, chamber mus. Swiss citizen since 1966.

Kubik, Gail (Thompson) (*b* S. Coffeyville, Oklahoma, 1914; *d* Covina, Calif., 1984). Amer. composer and violinist. Studied Eastman Sch., Amer. Cons., Chicago, and Harvard Univ. (1937–8, comp. with Piston). Confidant of N. Boulanger from 1937. Comp. mus. for films, radio, and TV. Works incl. 3 syms., 2 vn. concs., folk-opera *Mirror for the Sky*, pf. sonata, *In Praise of Johnny Appleseed* for bass, ch., and orch., *Gerald McBoing Boing* (film cartoon score and concert version).

Kubla Khan, Pleasure Dome of (Griffes). See *Pleasure Dome of Kubla Khan.*

Kuhlau, Friedrich (*b* Ülzen, Hanover, 1786; *d* Copenhagen, 1832). Danish composer and pianist of Ger. birth. Studied theory and comp. in Hamburg from 1800. Went to Copenhagen 1810, becoming court musician 1813. Chorusmaster, Royal Th., 1816–17. Went to Vienna 1821 and 1825, meeting Beethoven. Wrote 45 operas, incl. *Lulu* (1824), also a pf. conc. (1810), 3 pf. qts., a large amount of pf. music, and many works for the flute, although he did not play this instr.

Kuhnau, Johann (*b* Geising, Bohemia, 1660; *d* Leipzig, 1722). Bohemian composer and lawyer. Cantor at Zittau until move to Leipzig 1682. Organist, St Thomas's, Leipzig, from 1684, cantor 1701. Bach's immediate predecessor at Leipzig. Wrote ably for clavichord and hpd., composing exercises which he called *Klavierübung*, a term later used by Bach. Among first to compose sonatas (as distinct from suites).

Kujawiak. A quick Polish dance in triple time.

Kulenkampff, Georg (*b* Bremen, 1898; *d* Schaffhausen, 1948). Ger. violinist and teacher. Studied with Willy Hess in Berlin, 1912–15. Prof. of vn., Berlin Hochschule für Musik, 1923–6. Leading soloist in Ger. between World Wars I and II, also member of pf. trio with Edwin Fischer (pf.) and Enrico Mainardi (vc.) and partnered by Georg *Solti in several sonata recitals. Succeeded Flesch at Lucerne 1943. Career cut short by paralysis. Several memorable recordings, particularly of Beethoven conc.

Kullak, Theodor (*b* Krotoschin, 1818; *d* Berlin, 1882). Ger. pianist, teacher, and composer. Pupil of *Czerny in Berlin 1842. Court pianist to King of Prussia from 1846. Founded cons. with Stern and Marx in Berlin, 1850, and in 1855 his own 'Neue Akademie der Tonkunst'. Wrote pf. conc. and many short salon pieces. Best known for his instruction book *Octave-school.*

Kullervo. (1) Symphonic poem, Op. 7, by Sibelius for sop., bar., male ch., and orch., 1892, based on Finnish legends in the *Kalevala. F.p. 1892, then withdrawn and not perf. again until 1958.
  (2) Sym. by R. *Kajanus.

Kullman, Charles (*b* New Haven, Conn., 1903; *d* New Haven, Conn., 1983). Amer. ten. of Ger. parents. Studied Juilliard Sch. and Amer. Cons., Fontainebleau. Concert début NY 1924. Opera début with Amer. Opera Co. (dir. by *Rosing), 1929, then went to Berlin, making début as Pinkerton in *Madama Butterfly* at *Kroll Oper, 1931. Berlin State Opera 1932–4. CG début 1934–5, NY Met. 1935 (appearing there regularly until 1960). Sang at Salzburg Fest., Buenos Aires, Florence, etc. Sang ten. songs in Walter's first (1936) recording of Mahler's *Das Lied von der Erde*

(recorded at public perf. in Vienna). Taught at Bloomington, Ind., after 1956.

Kunst der Fuge, Die (The Art of Fugue). Posthumous and unfinished work by J. S. Bach, comp. 1748–9, pubd. posthumously 1750, and designed to establish the possibilities of a simple subject in the various types of fugal and canonic writing.

It is not clear what medium was intended to be employed, or, indeed, whether actual perf. was in view. Modern edns. for pf. and versions for str. instr. and for orch. have appeared. Completions of the final fugue have been made by Donald *Tovey and by *Busoni in his *Fantasia contrappuntistica.*

Kunstlied (Ger.). Art-song (as distinct from *Volkslied,* folk-song).

Kunz, Erich (*b* Vienna, 1909). Austrian bass-bar. Studied Vienna Cons. Opera début Troppau 1933. Joined Glyndebourne ch. 1935. Member Vienna State Opera from 1940. Frequent guest artist at Salzburg Fest., Bayreuth Fest., NY Met. CG début 1947 with Vienna co. Notable Papageno and Beckmesser. Sang Guglielmo in *Cosi fan tutte* at Glyndebourne, 1950.

Kuolema (Death). Play by A. Järnefelt for Helsinki prod. of which in 1903 *Sibelius wrote incidental mus. incl. *Valse triste* and *Scene with cranes.*

Kupferman, Meyer (*b* NY, 1926). Amer. composer, self-taught. Teacher of comp. and chamber mus. at Sarah Lawrence Coll. since 1951. Mus., some of it highly experimental, influenced by jazz and 12-note system. Works incl. 6 operas (incl. *Dr Faustus Lights the Lights,* 1953, lib. by Gertrude Stein); 7 ballets; 4 syms.; *Concerto for Orchestra;* pf. conc.; conc. for vc. and jazz band; *Lyric Symphony;* 5 str. qts.; *Cycle of Infinities,* over 25 works of various kinds all based on same 12-note row and, principally, same theme; choral works; pf. pieces; and songs.

Kupper, Annelies (*b* Glatz, 1906). Ger. soprano. Studied in Breslau, where she taught mus. 1929–35. Her singing was heard by mus. dir. of Breslau Opera who engaged her. After 1937 she was at Schwerin and Weimar, then at Hamburg State Opera until 1946. Member of Bavarian State Opera, Munich, 1946–66. Sang Eva at Bayreuth 1944, and Danae in Strauss's *Die Liebe der Danae* at Salzburg 1952. CG début 1953 (Chrysothemis in *Elektra*).

Kurka, Robert (*b* Cicero, Ill., 1921; *d* NY, 1957). Amer. composer. Studied Columbia Univ. and at Berkshire Music Center with Milhaud. Received Guggenheim fellowships 1951, 1952. Works incl.

opera *The Good Soldier Schweik* (NY 1958, Berlin 1960), 2 syms., *Music for Orchestra, 3 Pieces for Orch.,* marimba conc., vn. conc., chamber sinfonietta, 5 str. qts., pf. trio, 5 vn. sonatas, pf. pieces, and songs.

Kurtág, György (*b* Lugoj, Romania, 1926). Hung. composer of Romanian birth. Studied at Budapest Acad. 1948–55 (comp. with Veress and Farkas). In 1957 attended Paris Cons. comp. classes of Milhaud and Messiaen. Worked as tutor at Bartók mus. sch., Budapest, 1958–63 and as coach of Nat. Philhamonia 1960–8. Prof. of pf., later of chamber mus., Budapest Acad. from 1967. Beginning as a disciple of Bartók and Kodály, he later was influenced by Webernian serialism. Works incl. va. conc. (1954), *The Sayings of Péter Bornemisza,* for sop. and pf. (1963–8), str. qt. (1959), *4 Capriccios,* sop., wind quintet, hp., perc., pf., cimbalom, str. quintet (1971), *Microludes,* str. qt. (1977), *Splitter,* pf. (1978), *8 Choruses to Poems by Dezso Tandori, Games (Játékok)* pf. studies, *Messages of the late Miss R. V. Troussova,* sop. and ens. (1980), incid. mus. for plays incl. *Hamlet.*

Kurtz, Efrem (*b* St Petersburg, 1900). Russ.-born cond. (Amer. citizen from 1944). Studied St Petersburg Cons. and Stern Cons., Berlin. Early cond. engagements with Berlin P.O., 1921–4, mus. dir. Stuttgart P.O. 1924–33, during which time he conducted much ballet in Europe. Cond. Ballet Russe de Monte Carlo 1933–42. Guest cond. leading Amer. orchs. 1933–54, chief cond. Kansas City P.O. 1943–8, Houston S.O. 1948–54. Joint cond. Liverpool P.O. 1955–7.

Kurz, Selma (*b* Biala, Silesia, 1874; *d* Vienna, 1933). Austrian sop. Studied Vienna. Opera début Hamburg 1895. Engaged by Mahler for Vienna Opera 1899, singing there until 1927, first in lyric roles, then as coloratura. Notable Zerbinetta in Strauss's *Ariadne auf Naxos.* Sang at CG 1904–7 and again in 1924 as Mimi and Violetta.

Kusser (Cousser), **Johann** (Sigismund) (*b* Pressburg, 1660; *d* Dublin, 1727). Ger. composer. Spent some years of his youth in Paris, changing name to Cousser and studying for 6 years with Lully. Lived at Stuttgart 1675–81. Kapellmeister, Brunswick opera 1690–94. His opera *Erindo* was prod. at Hamburg 1694. Dir., Hamburg Opera 1694–5, Stuttgart Opera 1700–04. Went to London and in 1710 settled in Dublin, where he was appointed 'master of the musick attending his Majesty's state in Ireland'.

Kussevitzky. See *Koussevitzky, Serge.*

Kutcher Quartet. Eng. str. qt. noted for perf. of contemporary works. Founded by Samuel Kutcher (*b* London, 1899; *d* London, 1984) in 1924. Other members were Peter Tas (2nd vn.), Raymond Jeremy (va.), and Douglas Cameron (vc.) (succeeded by John Barbirolli).

K.V. Ger. usage for the *Köchel abbreviation, from *Köchel-Verzeichnis* (Köchel Index).

Kvapil, Jaroslav (*b* Fryšták, Moravia, 1892; *d* Brno, 1959). Cz. composer, cond., and teacher. Pupil of Janáček at Brno org. sch. Prof., Brno Cons. from 1919; mus. dir. Brno Phil. Soc. 1920–45. Works incl. 4 syms., 2 vn. concs., ob. conc., pf. conc., *Burlesque* for fl. and orch., opera *Romance in May* (Prague 1950), cantata *The Lion's Heart* (Brno 1931), 5 str. qts., etc. Cond. first Cz. perf. of Bach's *St Matthew Passion* (1923).

Kynaston, Nicolas (*b* Morebath, Devon, 1941). Eng. organist. Studied with Germani in Siena and with Downes at RCM. Org. of Westminster Cath. 1960–71. Toured USA 1974. Specialist in Fr. works, notably those by Messiaen, and those by Franck.

Kyrie (Gr.). Lord. The section of the Ordinary of the *Mass which follows the Introit. Has 3 parts, *Kyrie eleison, Christe eleison, Kyrie eleison,* thrice repeated ('Lord have mercy, Christ have mercy, Lord have mercy'). In medieval times, the *Kyrie* was set as an independent movement, but after *Dufay it was incorporated as the 1st movement of a series.

Kyung-Wha Chung. See *Chung, Kyung-Wha.*

L

L. Abbreviated prefix given to nos. in the *Longo catalogue of Domenico Scarlatti's kbd. works. A later catalogue was prepared by R. *Kirkpatrick.

La. The 6th degree of the major scale, according to the system of vocal syllables derived from *Guido d'Arezzo (see *Hexachord), and so used (spelt *Lah*) in *Tonic Sol-fa, in which it is also the 1st degree of the minor scale. In many countries, however, the name has become attached (on 'fixed-doh' principles) to the note A, in whatever key this may occur.

Labbette, Dora (*b* Purley, 1898; *d* Purley, 1984). Eng. soprano. Studied GSM and with Liza Lehmann. Début 1917. Sang often in oratorios and concert works with Beecham, making speciality of Delius. Opera début Oxford, 1934. CG début, under name Lisa Perli, at CG 1935 as Mimi. Fine actress, which made memorable her perfs. of Desdemona, Mélisande, and Delius's Vreli in *A Village Romeo and Juliet*.

Labèque, Katia and Marielle (*b* Bayonne, 1950 and 1952 respectively). Fr. piano duo. Studied with their mother and then at Paris Cons. Soon established themselves as specialists in works of Messiaen, Boulez, and Berio. Also play jazz, collaborating with John McLaughlin, guitar.

Labialstimme (Ger., plural *Labialstimmen*). Flue Stop (on the org.).

Lablache, Luigi (*b* Naples, 1794; *d* Naples, 1858). It. bass of Fr. and Irish parentage. Studied Naples, début there 1812. Further study followed by 5-year engagement at Palermo. Début Scala, Milan, 1817 as Dandini in Rossini's *La Cenerentola*. Int. career followed, with appearances in Turin, Venice, Vienna (where he sang in Mozart's *Requiem* at Beethoven's funeral, 1827), Naples, and London (1830). Became great favourite in Paris and London 1830–56. Created Riccardo in Bellini's *I Puritani* (Paris 1835) and title-role in Donizetti's *Don Pasquale* (Paris 1843). Famous Bartolo and Leporello. V. had compass of 3 octaves. Taught Queen Victoria singing.

Labroca, Mario (*b* Rome, 1896; *d* Rome, 1973). It. composer, critic, and impresario. Studied with Respighi and Malipiero. Wrote 2 operas, sym., *Stabat Mater*, etc. Dir., Maggio Musicale, Florence, 1935–43. Mus. dir., Radio Italiana 1949–58. Administrator, Scala, Milan 1947–9, La Fenice, Venice, 1959–73.

Labunski, Feliks (Roderick) (*b* Ksawerynów, Poland, 1892; *d* Cincinnati, 1979). Polish-born composer, critic, and teacher (Amer. citizen from 1941). Studied Warsaw and later in Paris with Boulanger and Dukas. Founded assoc. of young Polish musicians in Paris, 1927. Head of classical mus., Polish radio, 1934–6. Went to USA 1936. Taught at Cincinnati Coll. of Mus. 1945–64. Works incl. sym., 2 str. qts., 2 pf. sonatas, choral works.

Lachner, Franz (*b* Rain am Lech, 1803; *d* Munich, 1890). Ger. cond. and composer. Most eminent of remarkable mus. family. Went to Vienna 1823, becoming friend of Schubert. Cond. at Kärntnerthor Th., 1827–34. Opera cond., Mannheim, 1834–6, Munich 1836–65 (dir. from 1852). Responsible for eminence of Munich Opera. Comp. operas, masses, oratorios, 8 syms., chamber mus., etc. Cherubini's *Médée* is usually perf. in his edn. which omits the spoken dialogue.

Lachrimae. 21 pieces for 5 viols and lute by *Dowland pubd. 1604, of which 7 pavans are entitled *Lachrimae*. The other 14 are dances such as galliards. Each of the Pavans ('sevean teares figured in sevean passionate pavans') begins with the theme of Dowland's song *Flow my tears* followed by variations.

Lachrymae. 'Reflections on a song of John Dowland' for va. and pf. by Britten, Op. 48, comp. 1950. Arr. for va. and orch. 1976, f.p. Recklinghausen 1977.

Lacrimosa. See *Requiem*.

Lacrimoso, lagrimoso (It.). Lachrymose, tearful.

Lady Macbeth of the Mtsensk District, The (*Ledi Makbet Mtsenskovo uyezda*) (Shostakovich). See *Katerina Izmaylova*.

Lady of Shalott, The. Cantata by Phyllis Tate, setting of Tennyson's poem, for ten., va., perc., 2 pf., and celesta. Comp. 1956 for 10th anniv. of BBC 3rd Programme. Also cantata by Maurice *Jacobson.

Lady Radnor's Suite. Suite in 6 movements for str. orch. by *Parry comp. 1894 for orch. cond. by amateur musician, Lady Radnor.

Lage (Ger.). Position, e.g. in str. instr., or inversion of chord.

Lah. See *La*.

Lai, Lay (Fr.). A 13th- and 14th-cent. Fr. song-form, consisting usually of 12 unequal stanzas sung to different tunes. Later examples are in several vv. Also a purely instr. piece.

Lajtha, László (*b* Budapest, 1892; *d* Budapest, 1963). Hung. composer, writer, and folk mus.

expert. In 1910 joined Bartók and Kodály in expeditions to collect folk songs, later acting independently. After war service, joined staff of Nat. Cons., Budapest. Comp. 9 syms., vc. conc., 2 masses, 10 str. qts., opera, and 3 ballets. Kossuth Prize 1951.

Lakmé. Opera in 3 acts by Delibes to lib. by Gondinet and Gille after former's *Le Mariage de Loti*. Prod. Paris and Chicago 1883, London 1885.

Lalande, Michel (Richard) **de** (b Paris, 1657; d Versailles, 1726). Fr. composer and organist, contemporary of *Lully. Taught daughters of Louis XIV, becoming Master of King's chamber mus., 1685. Dir. of royal chapel from 1714, having been sous-maître since 1683. Comp. ballets and church mus.

Lalandi, Lina (b Athens, ?). Gr.-born harpsichordist and clavichordist (Brit. citizen). Studied Athens Cons. London début 1954. Founder and art. dir., Eng. Bach Fest. Trust 1962; art. dir. Eng. Bach Fest. from 1963. O.B.E. 1975.

Lalo, Édouard (Victor Antoine) (b Lille, 1823; d Paris, 1892). Fr. composer of Sp. descent. Studied vn. and vc. at Lille Cons. and vn. at Paris Cons. from 1839, studying comp. privately. Pubd. songs 1848–9. Vn. conc. played by Sarasate 1874, who a year later gave f.p. of *Symphonie espagnole*. Violinist in str. qt. from 1855. Works incl.:

OPERAS: *Fiesque* (1866), *Le *Roi d'Ys* (1875–87), *La Jacquerie* (1891–2, completed by Coquard 1895).
BALLET: *Namouna* (1882).
ORCH: *Allegro symphonique* (1875), *Rapsodie norvégienne* (1881), Sym. in G minor (1886); concs.: vn. (1873), **Symphonie espagnole* (vn. and orch.) (1874), *Fantaisie norvégienne* (vn. and orch.) (1880), *Concerto russe* (vn. and orch.) (1883), vc. (1877), pf. (1889).
CHAMBER MUSIC: Vn. sonata, vc. sonata, str. qt., 3 pf. trios.

Lambe, Walter (b ?1450; d 1499). Eng. composer of church mus., especially motets.

Lambert, Constant (b Fulham, London, 1905; d London, 1951). Eng. composer, cond., and critic. Studied RCM with Vaughan Williams. Ballet *Romeo and Juliet* commissioned by Diaghilev and prod. Monte Carlo 1926. Series of brilliant works est. him with Walton among leading younger Eng. composers. Influenced by jazz, esp. Duke Ellington. Took leading part in est. of British ballet, and made th. orch. version of Vaughan Williams's *Job, 1931. Cond. Camargo Society ballet 1930 and ballet and opera at SW, being mus. dir. Vic-Wells ballet from its foundation in 1931 until 1947, then mus. adviser SW Ballet from 1948. Brilliant writer, his book *Music, Ho!* (1934) being an important and idiosyncratic commentary on contemporary mus. at that date. Witty conversationalist. Notable narrator in Walton's *Façade* with Edith Sitwell. Champion

of mus. of *Boyce, several of whose works he arr. Also advocate for Liszt when it was unfashionable in Eng. to admire him. Prin. works:

BALLETS: *Romeo and Juliet* (1924–5); *Pomona* (1926); *Apparitions* (orch. of Liszt) (1936); *Horoscope* (1937); *Tiresias* (1950).
ORCH: *Elegiac Blues* (1927); *Music for Orch.* (1927); pf. conc. (1931); *Aubade héroique* (1942); incidental mus. for *Hamlet*.
CHORAL: *The *Rio Grande* (1927); *Summer's Last Will and Testament* (1932–5); *Dirge* (from *Cymbeline*) for ten. and bar. solos, vv., and str. (1940).
VOCAL: 8 *Chinese Songs* for v. and 8 instr. (1926–9).
PIANO: Sonata (1928–9).

Lambert, Michel (b Vivonne, 1610; d Paris, 1696). Fr. lutenist. Master of royal chamber mus. from 1661. Comp. songs. Father-in-law of Lully.

Lambton Worm, The. Opera in 2 acts by R. Sherlaw *Johnson to lib. by Anne Ridler based on medieval legend. Prod. Oxford 1978.

Lament. Piece of elegiac mus. expressing grief, specifically mus. for bagpipes at Scottish clan funerals.

Lamentations. Lamentations of the prophet Jeremiah sung to plainchant melodies (or other settings such as the great ones by Tallis) in R.C. churches in the week before Easter. Gr. word *Threni* sometimes used.

Lamentation Symphony. Nickname for Haydn's Sym. No. 26 in D minor, 1770, because certain themes resemble the plainsong melodies sung in R.C. churches in the week before Easter. Also sometimes known, for unknown reason, as 'Christmas' Sym. (*Weihnachtssymphonie*).

Lamento (It.). Lament. In 17th-cent. opera, a tragic aria usually placed before the climax of the plot. A famous example is Monteverdi's *Lamento d'Arianna*.

Lamento d'Arianna (Ariadne's Lament). Only surviving section of Monteverdi's opera *Arianna*, 1608. Arr. by Monteverdi as 5-part madrigal *Lasciatemi morire* (Leave me to die), Book VI, 1614; this book also incl. *O Teseo mio*, reduced from 20 bars of *Lasciatemi morire*. Also arr. by Monteverdi as one of his *Selva Morale e Spirituale* (1640), *Pianto della Madonna* on the *Lamento d'Arianna: Jam moriar fili mi*, for solo v.

Lamond, Frederic (b Glasgow, 1868; d Stirling, 1948). Scot. pianist and composer. Church organist at age 12. Studied Raff Cons., Frankfurt, 1882, later with Bülow, and with Liszt 1885–6. Début Berlin 1885, followed by int. tours. Visited Russia 1896. Specially noted as Beethoven player. Prof. of pf., The Hague Cons., from 1917. Toured USA 4 times between 1922 and 1929 and taught at Eastman Sch. Later prof. of pf. Royal Scottish

Acad. of Mus. Comp. sym., pf. trio, vc. sonata, pf. pieces.

Lamotte (Lamota), **Franz** (b Vienna (or Holland), 1751; d Holland, 1781). Dutch violinist. Studied in London. Played in Vienna 1766, then toured Europe. In court orch. of Empress Maria Theresia after 1772. In London 1776–80, leaving hurriedly because of alleged scandals. His playing was admired by Mozart. Comp. vn. concs. and sonatas.

Lamoureux, Charles (b Bordeaux, 1834; d Paris, 1899). Fr. cond. and violinist. Studied vn. at Paris Cons. Played in orch. at Opéra. Ass. cond. *Société des Concerts du Conservatoire* 1872–7. Cond. Opéra-Comique 1876–7, Opéra 1877–9 (resigned latter post in dispute over tempo of aria in *Don Giovanni*). In 1881 founded *Nouveaux Concerts*, later known as *Concerts Lamoureux*. Among first to champion Wagner in France and young Fr. composers such as Lalo, Dukas, and Chabrier. Visited London 1881, and took orch. there 1896–9. Succeeded by son-in-law *Chevillard. Lamoureux Orch., under various distinguished conds., has remained among leading European orchs.

Lampe, John (Frederick) (b Saxony, c.1703; d Edinburgh, 1751). Ger.-Eng. bassoonist and composer. Settled in Eng. c.1725 to play bn. in opera orch. Comp. stage mus., songs, and hymns (to words by C. Wesley).

Lamperti, Francesco (b Savona, 1811; d Como, 1892). It. teacher of singing. Studied Milan Cons. Dir. with Masini of Teatro Filodrammatico at Lodi which attracted students from all over Europe. Prof. of singing, Milan Cons., 1850–75, pupils incl. Albani, Sembrich, Stolz, Waldmann, and Campanini. His son Giovanni Battista (b Milan, 1839; d Berlin, 1910) was his pupil and also a singing-teacher. Author of *The Technique of Bel Canto* (1905).

Lampugnani, Giovanni (Battista) (b Milan, 1706; d Milan, after 1786). It. composer. Succeeded *Galuppi as opera composer at King's Th., London, 1743. *Maestro al cembalo*, Milan, 1759–86. Comp. nearly 30 operas.

Lancashire Sol-Fa. System of sight-singing more properly called 'Old English Sol-fa', since it was universally used in Eng. from at least the early 17th cent. and its latest textbook appeared in 1879. It is a method of solmization applied to the normal staff notation; the first 3 notes of every major scale are called *fa-sol-la*, and so are the second 3 notes, the remaining note being called *mi*; the minor scale is read as if its notes were those of the relative major. In Amer. often called *Fasola*.

Lancers. Type of *quadrille dance popular in 19th-cent. Eng.

Lanchbery, John (b London, 1923). Eng. cond. and composer. Mus. dir. London Metropolitan Ballet 1947–9. Cond. SW Th. Ballet 1951–60.

Prin. cond. Royal Ballet 1960–72. Mus. dir. Australian Ballet from 1972. Arr. mus. for many ballets, incl. *House of Birds, La Fille mal gardée, The Dream, Tales of Beatrix Potter, The Merry Widow.*

Landini (Landino), **Francesco** (b Florence, 1325; d Florence, 1397). It. composer, who lost his sight as child but played org., lute, fl., and other instrs. Comp. madrigals and over 140 *ballate* (type of *virelai*).

Landini Cadence. Cadence named after Francesco *Landini (1325–97) in which the 6th degree is inserted between leading-note and the octave. Found in works of *Machaut, Desprès, Palestrina, Victoria, and Monteverdi.

Ländler (Ger.). Type of slow waltz originating in the Landel (part of Austria north of Ems river). Examples were comp. by Beethoven and Schubert, and the rhythm is employed by Mahler in his syms.

Landi, Stefano (b Rome, c.1586; d Rome, 1639). It. composer and teacher. Singer in Rome churches up to 1618 when he became choirmaster to Bishop of Padua, where he wrote his first opera, *La Morte d'Orfeo*. Returned to Rome 1620, serving Borghese and Barberini families. Sacred opera *Il Sant' Alessio* (1632), perf. at Barberini palace, had elaborate stage effects. One of musicians chosen by Pope Urban VIII in 1634 to prepare new hymn-book pubd. in Antwerp in 1643 (now lost). His *Arie*, of which he pubd. six books, are conventional.

Land of Hope and Glory. Title of finale for cont., ch., and orch. of Elgar's *Coronation Ode (1902), words by A. C. Benson. Tune is adaptation of melody of trio section of *Pomp and Circumstance March* No. 1. Also pubd. as separate song for cont. and orch., this being the version now generally and communally sung (with words different from those in *Coronation Ode*).

Land of Lost Content, The. Song-cycle by *Ireland, comp. 1920–1, of 6 poems from A. E. Housman's *A Shropshire Lad*. Orig. for high v. and pf. Titles are: 1. *The Lent Lily*, 2. *Ladslove*, 3. *Goal and wicket*, 4. *The vain desire*, 5. *The Encounter*, 6. *Epilogue*. Ireland set 3 more Housman poems under title *We'll To The Woods No More* (1926–7), No. 3 being for pf. alone.

Land of my Fathers (Hen Wlad fy Nhadau). Nat. anthem of Wales. Tune by James James, poem by Evan James of Pontypridd. Both first appeared in print in John Owen's *Gems of Welsh Melody*, 1860.

Land of Smiles, The (*Das Land des Lächelns*). Operetta in 3 acts by Lehár to lib. by L. Herzer and F. Löhner based on earlier (1923) operetta *Die gelbe Jacke* (The Yellow Jacket). F.p. Berlin 1929 (with Tauber); London 1931; Vienna (State Opera), 1938.

Land of the Mountain and the Flood. Ov. by Hamish MacCunn, comp. 1887 when he was 19.

Landon, H(oward) **C**(handler) **Robbins** (b Boston, Mass., 1926). Amer. musicologist. Studied Boston Univ. Settled in Vienna 1948, undertaking meticulous research into life and mus. of Joseph Haydn. Author of book on Haydn syms. (1955) and of *Haydn: Chronicle and Works* (5 vols., 1976–80), *Haydn: a Documentary Study* (1981), also of edn. of syms. Discovered correct attribution of *Jena Symphony*. Joint ed. of *The Mozart Companion* and author of documentary study of Beethoven (1970).

Landowska, Wanda (b Warsaw, 1877; d Lakeville, Conn., 1959). Polish-born harpsichordist and pianist. Studied Warsaw Cons. and in Berlin. Settled in Paris 1900, touring Europe and USA in recitals of baroque mus. on pf. and hpd. Head of hpd. class, Berlin Hochschule, 1912–19. First in 20th cent. to play continuo of *St Matthew Passion* on hpd. (Basle, 1919). Returned to Fr. 1919–38 as teacher and to give concerts of early mus. Falla and Poulenc comp. hpd. works for her. Author of *Musique Ancienne* (1909). Lived in NY 1940–7 and at Lakeville 1947–59.

Landré, Guillaume Louis Frédéric (b The Hague, 1905; d Amsterdam, 1968). Dutch composer and critic. Pupil of his father Willem (1874–1948) and of *Pijper. Works incl. 4 syms., *Sinfonia sacra* (in memory of his father), vc. conc., vn. conc., 3 operas, and chamber mus.

Lang, Paul Henry (b Budapest, 1901). Hung.-born musicologist and critic (Amer. citizen). Studied Budapest Acad., Heidelberg, Paris, and Cornell Univs. Chamber-mus. pianist and orch. bassoonist in Budapest. Went to USA 1928. Ass. prof. of mus. Vassar Coll., 1930–1, assoc. prof. of mus. Wells Coll., 1931–3, assoc. prof. of musicology, Columbia Univ. 1933–9, prof. 1939–69. Mus. critic, *NY Herald Tribune* 1954–66. Ed., *Musical Quarterly*. Author of several books incl. *Music in Western Civilisation* (NY, 1941).

Langdon, Michael (b Wolverhampton, 1920). Eng. bass-bar. Studied GSM, later with Alfred Jerger in Vienna and Otakar Kraus in London. Début CG 1950. Prin. bass at Royal Opera House from 1957. Notable Ochs in *Rosenkavalier*. Dir., Nat. Opera Studio, 1978. C.B.E. 1973.

Langford, Samuel (b Manchester, 1863; d Manchester, 1927). Eng. mus. critic. Studied Leipzig with C. Reinecke 1896–1900. Mus. critic, *Manchester Guardian*, 1905–27. His widow Audrey was a singing teacher in Manchester and London for 50 years after his death.

Langgaard, Rued (b Copenhagen, 1893; d Ribe, 1952). Danish composer and organist. Début as org. 1905. His first Sym. (1908–11) was perf. in Berlin, 1913. Influenced at first by Liszt and Mahler, later became disciple of Nielsen and

eventually Hindemith. In 1920s, after an Ivesian period, abandoned experimentation for a romantic style. Increasingly isolated, he became organist of Ribe Cath. in 1940. He wrote 16 syms. between 1908 and 1951, choral works, a biblical opera *Antikrist* (1916–36), and 6 str. qts.

Langlais, Jean (b La Fontenelle, 1907). Fr. organist and composer, blind from infancy. Studied Paris Cons., comp. with Dukas, orch. with Messiaen. Teacher of org., comp., and choral singing, Institut National des Jeunes Aveugles, from 1931, prof. from 1971. Teacher of org., Schola Cantorum, Paris, from 1961. Organist St Clotilde, Paris, from 1945. Works incl. 3 *Poèmes évangéliques* (1932), *Suite française* (1948), *American Suite* (1959), *Suite baroque* (1974), *Progression, 5 Pièces* (1979), and 2 org. syms. (1942, 1977).

Langridge, Philip (Gordon) (b Hawkhurst, Kent, 1939). Eng. tenor. Studied vn. at RAM and played professionally until 1964. Began singing 1962, having lessons from Bruce Boyce. Wide range of operatic roles from Handel to Britten, incl. Berlioz's Bénédict. In concert-hall is equally effective in baroque or contemporary works.

Langsam (Ger.). Slow. *Langsamer,* slower.

Lanier (Laniere), **Nicholas** (b London, 1588; d London, 1666). Eng. composer. Wrote mus. for 4 masques by Ben Jonson. Appointed master of mus. to Prince Charles in 1618, so when the prince became Charles I in 1625 Lanier became first Master of the King's Mus. Held same office under Charles II from 1660. Comp. cantatas and songs. Skilled painter who bought pictures in It. for Charles I.

Lankester, Michael (b London, 1944). Eng. cond. and composer. Studied RCM. Mus. dir. Nat. Th., 1969–75. Has cond. Surrey P.O., ECO, etc. Founder, Contrapuncti. At Britten's request in 1976, made orch. suite of ballet *The Prince of the Pagodas*, f.p. London 1979 (Proms.).

Lanner, Joseph (Franz Karl) (b Vienna, 1801; d Oberdöbling, 1843). Austrian cond. and composer. Largely self-taught. Began career by arranging potpourris of popular melodies for his ens. to play. In demand at court balls and other entertainments. Formed qt. in which Johann *Strauss I was violinist 1819–25. Appointed Kapellmeister, 2nd Bürger Regiment. In rivalry with Strauss, comp. over 100 waltzes, also quadrilles, polkas, galops, marches, and Ländler (208 in all). Arr. Weber's *Invitation to the Dance* (1819) for small orch., c.1828.

Lantins, Hugo de (fl. 1420–30). Dutch composer of sacred and secular songs.

Lanza, Mario (orig. Coccozza, Alfred Arnold) (b Philadelphia, 1921; d Rome, 1959). Amer. tenor and actor. Worked in family grocery business. Had audition with *Koussevitzky in 1942 and was awarded schol. to Tanglewood. After wartime military service, signed film contract and was chosen in 1951 for the title-role in *The Great Caruso*. His voice was heard also in *The Student Prince* (1954).

Laparra, Raoul (*b* Bordeaux, 1876; *d* Suresnes, 1943). Fr. composer. Studied Paris Cons. (*Prix de Rome* 1903), pupil of Fauré and Massenet. Wrote instr. works and several operas, most successful of which was *La Habañera* (Paris 1908, CG 1910, NY Met. 1924).

Lara, Isidore de (Cohen) (*b* London, 1858; *d* Paris, 1935). Eng. composer and pianist. Studied in Milan. Comp. several operas perf. at CG, Monte Carlo, Paris, and NY Met. They incl. *The Light of Asia* (1892), *Amy Robsart* (1893), *Messaline* (1899), *Naïl* (1910), *The Three Musketeers* (1920). Wrote many songs and organized concerts of new chamber works.

Laredo, Jaime (Eduardo) (*b* Cochabamba, Bolivia, 1941). Amer. violinist of Bolivian birth. Studied Curtis Institute, Philadelphia. Début 1952. NY début 1960. Won Queen Elisabeth of Belgians competition, 1959. London début 1961. World tours. Specialist in Bach and Handel.

Largamente (It.). Broadly. Slowish and dignified (see also *Largo*), more usually applied to style of perf. than to specific tempo.

Large, Brian (*b* London, 1937). Eng. musicologist, pianist, writer, and TV producer. Studied RAM and London Univ. Specialist in Cz. mus.; author of books on Smetana, Martinů, and Cz. opera. Joined BBC, with special responsibility for televised opera.

Larghetto (It.). The diminutive of **Largo*. Slow and dignified, but less so than *Largo*. *Larghezza*, breadth.

Largo (It.). Broad. Slow, dignified in style. *Largo di molto,* very slow and dignified, etc.

Largo (Handel). Title universally applied to the many spurious, if pleasing, instr. arrs. of the aria *Ombra mai fù* (which in fact is marked *larghetto*), from **Handel's* opera **Serse*.

Larigot (old name for Flageolet). Org. stop; same as **Nineteenth*.

Lark Ascending, The. Romance for vn. and orch. or chamber orch. by Vaughan Williams inspired by poem of that name by G. Meredith (1828–1909). Comp. 1914, rev. 1920, f.p. in arr. for vn. and pf. 1920, in orch. version 1921.

Lark Quartet (Haydn). See *Lerchenquartett*.

Larner, Gerald (*b* Leeds, 1936). Eng. critic. Educated New Coll., Oxford. Ass. lecturer in Ger., Manchester Univ. 1960–2. Joined *Guardian* staff in Manchester as ass. mus. critic 1962; chief Northern mus. critic since 1965. Trans. lib. of Wolf's *Der Corregidor* into Eng. Wrote lib. for

McCabe's *The Lion, the Witch, and the Wardrobe* 1971. Art. dir. Bowdon Fest. 1980–4.

Larrocha, Alicia de (*b* Barcelona, 1923). Sp. pianist. Concert début Madrid 1935. In late 1940s made int. reputation. London début, 1953. NY début 1955. Notable interpreter of Albéniz and Granados.

Larsson, Lars-Erik (*b* Akarp, 1908; *d* Helsingborg, 1986). Swed. composer, cond., and critic. Studied Stockholm Royal Acad. 1925–9 then in Vienna with **Berg*. Ch. master Stockholm Opera 1931. Worked as critic. Cond. for Swed. radio 1937–54, prof. of comp., Stockholm Cons., 1947–59, dir. of mus. at Uppsala Univ. 1961–5. Works incl. 3 syms. (1928, 1936, 1945), 3 concert ovs., sinfonietta for str., serenade for str., sax. conc., vn. conc., vc. conc., 12 concertinos, opera, cantata, 3 str. qts., etc.

La Rue, Pierre de (*b* ? Tournai, *c*.1460; *d* Courtrai, 1518). Flemish composer. Singer at Cambrai Cath. 1483. Returned to Netherlands *c*.1490 and in 1492 was in Burgundian court chapel. Moved to Mechelen 1508. Became abbot at Courtrai 1516. Exemplar of medieval Netherlands style of comp. Wrote 31 Masses, mostly on plainchant *cantus firmus* but some on secular tunes, e.g. 'L'Homme armé'. About 30 motets survive, also 30 secular *chansons*.

LaSalle Quartet. Amer. str. qt. formed 1949 by students from Juilliard Sch. of Mus., NY. Members are Walter Levin (*b* Berlin, 1924), a pupil of I. Galamian, Henry Meyer (*b* Dresden, 1923), studied with Enescu and Galamian, vns.; Peter Kamnitzer (*b* Berlin, 1922), studied at Juilliard Sch., va.; Lee Fiser (*b* Portland, Oregon, 1947), vc., former player in Cincinnati S.O. Fiser replaced Jack Kirstein in 1975. European tour 1954. Particularly known for perf. and recordings of Schoenberg, Zemlinsky, Berg, Webern, and for the contemporary qts. of Apostel, Pousseur, Ligeti, Kagel, Penderecki, and Lutosławski.

La Scala, Milan (Teatro alla Scala). It. opera house built in 1778 and named after Regina della Scala, wife of a Duke of Milan, who had founded a church on the site in 14th cent. Opened on 3 Aug. 1778, with opera by **Salieri*. All the great 19th-cent. It. composers wrote works for La Scala. Among f.ps. there were those of *La Gazza Ladra* (Rossini), *Lucrezia Borgia* (Donizetti), *Norma* (Bellini), *Otello* and *Falstaff* (Verdi), *Madama Butterfly* and *Turandot* (Puccini). **Toscanini* was chief cond. 1898–1902, 1906–8 and 1921–9, periods during which the greatest opera singers of the world worked in the co. Victor **de Sabata* took over dir. in 1930, continuing until 1957. In more recent times Claudio **Abbado* has been the outstanding Scala cond. Bombs almost destroyed the Scala in Aug. 1943 but by 1946 it had been rebuilt as before in time for opening concert on 11 May cond. Toscanini. Seats 3,600. Maria

*Callas was in the co. 1950–8 and Renata *Tebaldi 1949–54. Chamber th. for 600, *La Piccola Scala,* was opened in Dec. 1955.

Laserna, Blas de (*b* Corella, 1751; *d* Madrid, 1816). Sp. composer and cond. Wrote operas, *zarzuelas,* and *tonadillas.*

Lassalle, Jean Louis (*b* Lyons, 1847; *d* Paris, 1909). Fr. bar. Studied Paris Cons. and with Novelli. Opera début Liège 1869. Début Paris Opéra 1872 as Guillaume Tell (Rossini), remaining as prin. bar. until 1892. Sang at CG 1879–81 and 1888–93. NY Met. début 1892, staying in co. 6 years. Notable Sachs in de Reszke perfs. of *Die Meistersinger.* Retired 1901. Prof., Paris Cons. from 1903.

Lassen, Eduard (*b* Copenhagen, 1830; *d* Weimar, 1904). Danish cond., composer, and opera dir. Studied Brussels Cons. (*Prix de Rome* 1851). Succeeded Liszt as opera dir. at Weimar 1858–95. His opera *Landgrave Ludwigs Brautfahrt* was prod. Weimar 1857 under Liszt's sponsorship. Comp. mus. for Goethe's *Faust.*

Lasso. See *Lassus, Orlande de.*

Lass of Richmond Hill, The. Song with mus. by James *Hook and words by L. McNally. (N.B. The song refers to Richmond, Yorks., not Surrey.)

Lassú. Slow section of *csárdás.*

Lassus, Orlande (Roland) **de** (It. Orlando di Lasso) (*b* Mons, 1532; *d* Munich, 1594). Flemish composer. In boyhood and youth travelled in Sicily and Italy in service of various aristocrats. Choirmaster, St John Lateran, Rome, 1553–4. Returned to Flanders, possibly visiting Eng. and Fr. and settling in Antwerp. Pubd. first vol. of madrigals, motets, and *chansons,* 1556. Entered service of Duke of Bavaria at court in Munich, 1556, becoming Kapellmeister 1563, the year he began his *7 Penitential Psalms* (1563–70). Visited Venice 1567, Paris and Rome 1571, and Rome 1585. Wrote nearly 2,000 works, mainly motets, madrigals, masses, canzonas, *chansons,* and psalms. Ranked with Palestrina and Victoria as among supreme masters of 16th-cent. polyphonic art. Complete catalogue of works pubd. Berlin 1956 (ed. W. Boetticher).

Last Post. British Army bugle call. The *First Post* at 9.30 p.m. calls all men back to barracks and the *Last Post* at 10 p.m. ends the day. By a natural and poetical association of ideas it has become the custom to sound the same call at military funerals.

Last Rose of Summer, 'Tis the. Old Irish air, orig. *Castle Hyde,* which became *The Groves of Blarney* c.1790 by R. A. Millikin, and was incl. by Thomas Moore, to his own new words, in his *Irish Melodies* (1813). Beethoven set the air, Mendelssohn wrote a pf. fantasia on it (Op. 15, 1827), and it is sung by a sop. in Act 2 of Flotow's *Martha.*

Last Sleep of the Virgin, The (*Le Dernier Sommeil de la Vierge*). Orch. interlude from Massenet's oratorio *La Vierge* (1880), much favoured as an encore by *Beecham and the RPO.

Last Temptations, The (*Viimeiset kiusaukset*). Opera in 2 acts by *Kokkonen to lib. by L. Kokkonen, based on life of Finn. evangelist Paavo Ruotsalainen (1777–1852). Prod. Savonlinna 1977, London (Finn. Nat. Opera) 1979.

Laszlò, Magda (*b* Marosvásárhely, 1919). Hung. sop. Studied Liszt Acad., Budapest. Budapest Opera 1943–6, then settled in Italy. Created role of the Mother in *Dallapiccola's *Il prigioniero* (radio 1949, Florence 1950). Sang title-roles in Gluck's *Alceste* (1953) and Monteverdi's *L'Incoronazione di Poppea* (1962) at Glyndebourne. Created role of Cressida in *Walton's *Troilus and Cressida,* CG 1954.

Late Swallows. Title of 3rd movement of Delius's 2nd Str. Qt. (1916). Arr for str. orch. by Fenby 1963 (f.p. Houston S.O., Barbirolli, 1963).

Latham, Peter (Morton Sturges) (*b* London, 1894; *d* London, 1970). Eng. teacher and writer. Studied Oxford Univ. and RAM 1919–20. Prof. of harmony, RAM, 1938. *Gresham Prof. of Mus. 1941–64. Wrote books on Beethoven and Brahms.

Laúd. Sp. form of lute.

Lauda Sion (Praise, O Zion). One of the *Sequences allowed to remain in the liturgy of the R.C. Church when the Council of Trent (1545–63) abolished the rest. It has its traditional plainsong, but has also been set by composers. The words were written by St Thomas Aquinas (c. 1264) for the feast of Corpus Christi (on which they are still sung).

Laudi Spirituali (Spiritual songs. More correctly *Laude spirituali*). Popular devotional songs sung by the *Laudesi,* a Florentine confraternity instituted in 1233. Music was at first in unison but later in parts. 1st pubd. coll. 1485. Regarded as forerunner of oratorio.

Laudon Symphony. Haydn's own sub-title for his Sym. in C major, No. 69 in Breitkopf edn., which he ded. to the Austrian field-marshal Ernst Gideon Freiherr von Loudon (to give him his correct spelling) (1716–90).

Lauds. The 2nd of the Canonical Hours of the R.C. Church, formerly sung at sunrise.

Laurenti, Girolamo Bartolomeo (*b* Bologna, c.1644; *d* Bologna, 1726). It. violinist and composer. Wrote 6 concs. for 3 vns., also for va., vc., and org.

Lauri-Volpi, Giacomo (*b* Rome, 1892; *d* Valencia, Spain, 1979). It. ten. Trained as lawyer, but transferred to study of mus. at S. Cecilia Acad., Rome. Opera début under name Rubini at Viterbo 1919, under own name Rome 1920 (in

Massenet's *Manon*). NY Met. 1923–33. Sang Calaf in Amer. f.p. of *Turandot*, 1926. CG début 1925. Sang in Italy up to 1965 and at a Barcelona gala in 1972. Wrote several books.

Laute (Ger.). The *lute.

Lautenmacher (Ger., Fr. *luthier*). Maker of str. instrs.

Lavallée, Calixa (*b* Verchères, Quebec, 1842; *d* Boston, Mass., 1891). Fr.-Canadian composer and pianist. Studied Paris Cons. (comp. with Boieldieu). Taught at Petersilea Acad., Boston. Wrote operas, sym., oratorio, 2 str. qts., vn. sonata, etc., also Canadian nat. song. *O Canada!* (1880).

Lawes, Henry (*b* Dinton, Wilts., 1596; *d* London, 1662). Eng. composer and singer. Studied with J. Cooper (*Coprario). Gent. of Charles I's Chapel Royal. Wrote mus. for Milton's masque *Comus at Ludlow, 1634, taking part of Attendant Spirit. Reinstated in court posts 1660. Comp. anthem *Zadok the Priest* for Charles II's coronation, songs, and madrigals.

Lawes, William (*b* Dinton or Salisbury, 1602; *d* Chester, 1645). Eng. composer, brother of Henry *Lawes. Also studied with *Coprario and was one of private musicians attached to Charles I before and after he became King (1625). Comp. songs, madrigals, mus. for viols, and a large amount of mus. for the stage. Regarded as one of the greatest and most influential of Eng. composers. Killed in Royalist army at siege of Chester.

Lawrence, Marjorie (Florence) (*b* Deans Marsh, Australia, 1909; *d* Little Rock, Arkansas, 1979). Australian sop. Studied Melbourne and Paris. Opera début Monte Carlo. 1932 (Elisabeth in *Tannhäuser*). Sang at Paris Opéra 1933–6, NY Met. 1935–41. Stricken with poliomyelitis during *Die Walküre* at Mexico City 1941. Despite inability to walk unaided, continued opera career, incl. Wagnerian roles in which she excelled, and gave recitals. After retirement, prof. of v. Tulane Univ., 1956–60, prof. of v. and dir. of opera workshop, S. Illinois Univ. from 1960.

Lay. See *Lai*.

Layolle, Franciscus de (*b* Florence, 1492; *d* Lyons, *c*.1540). It. composer and organist. Organist at Florence, then settled in Lyons 1521. Taught mus. to Benvenuto Cellini. Wrote masses, motets, and madrigals.

Layton, Robert (*b* London, 1930). Eng. critic and administrator. Studied at Oxford 1949–53 under Rubbra and Wellesz, then at Stockholm and Uppsala 1953–5. On mus. staff BBC since 1959. Author of books on Berwald and Sibelius and monographs on several Scandinavian composers.

Lazarus, oder Die Feier der Auferstehung (Lazarus, or The Feast of the Resurrection). Unfinished oratorio ('Easter Cantata') by Schubert (D689), to text by A. H. Niemayer (1754–1828)

comp. 1820. What remains contains marvellous mus.

Lazzari, Sylvio (*b* Bozen, Tyrol, 1857; *d* Paris, 1944). Fr. composer. Studied Paris Cons. with Guiraud and Franck. Wrote 6 operas, sym., symphonic poems, vn. sonata, str. qt., songs, etc.

L.B.C.M. Licentiate of the Bandsman's College of Music.

L.B.S.M. Licentiate of the Birmingham School of Music.

Leader. (1) (Amer. concertmaster; Ger. *konzertmeister*). Prin. 1st vn. of sym. orch.
(2) Often used in USA for cond., e.g., 'Ormandy leads the Philadelphia Orch. in . . .'
(3) 1st vn. of str. qt. or other chamber group.

Leading Note. 7th degree of the scale, semitone below the tonic. So called because of tendency to rise, or 'lead', to the tonic. In minor keys is sometimes flattened in descent.

Leading Seventh. Chord of minor 7th on *Leading Note of major scale (e.g. in C Major, B–D–F–A).

Lead, Kindly Light. Hymn, words by John Henry Newman (1801–90), written after an illness in Sicily. Tune, *Lux benigna*, by Rev. John Bacchus Dykes, organist, first pubd. 1867, under name *St Oswald* in *Psalms and Hymns for the Church, School and Home*, ed. D. T. Barry, 1867, and a year later in appendix to *Hymns Ancient and Modern*. Another tune, *Alberta*, by W. H. Harris in *Songs of Praise*, enlarged edn., 1931.

Lear. Opera in 2 acts by *Reimann to lib. by Claus Henneberg based on Shakespeare's play *King Lear* (1606). Prod. Munich 1978 (Fischer-Dieskau as Lear). San Francisco 1981. See also *King Lear*.

Lear, Evelyn (*b* Brooklyn, NY, 1926). Amer. sop. Studied NY Univ., Hunter Coll., and Juilliard Opera Workshop. Won Fulbright scholarship to Ger. 1955. Opera début in Strauss's *Ariadne auf Naxos*, Berlin 1959. Sang Strauss's *Vier letzte Lieder* with LSO, London 1957. Sang title-role in Berg's *Lulu*, Vienna 1962 and London 1966, and Marie in *Wozzeck* in Vienna, Berlin, Munich, San Francisco, NY Met., and Milan (1971). Sang in première of Levy's *Mourning becomes Electra*, NY Met. 1967. CG début 1965 (Elvira in *Don Giovanni*). Has sung at Salzburg Fest. Notable Marschallin in *Der Rosenkavalier*, Countess in *Le Nozze di Figaro*.

Leavins, Arthur (*b* Leicester, 1917). Eng. violinist. Studied RAM. Début NZ, 1925. Member of Catterall Qt. Leader RPO, sub-leader BBC S.O., leader BBC Concert Orch.

Lebègue, Nicolas Antoine (*b* Laon, *c*.1631; *d* Paris, 1702). Fr. organist and composer. Organist, church of St Merry, Paris, 1664–1702, and court organist to Louis XIV, 1678. Comp. 2 vols. of hpd. works and 3 vols. of org. pieces (1676).

Lebewohl, Das (The Farewell). Beethoven's (therefore the correct) title for his Pf. Sonata No. 26 in E♭ major Op. 81a, usually known as 'Les Adieux'. Comp. 1809–10.

Lebhaft (Ger.). Lively. So *lebhafter*, livelier; *Lebhaftigkeit*, liveliness.

Lebrun, Ludwig August (*b* Mannheim, 1752; *d* Berlin, 1790). Ger. oboist. Member of Mannheim court orch. Composed 7 ob. concs., 12 ob. trios, fl. conc., etc. Married sop. Franziska Danzi (1756–91).

Lechner, Leonhard (*b* Austrian Tyrol, *c*.1550; *d* Stuttgart, 1606). Austrian composer. Chorister at Munich court under Lassus, an edn. of whose motets he pubd. 1579. Kapellmeister at Württemberg from 1587. Comp. masses, motets, and psalms.

Leclair, Jean-Marie (*b* Lyons, 1697; *d* Paris, 1764). Fr. composer and violinist, known as 'the elder' to distinguish him from his brother. Went to Turin as ballet-master 1722 and took up vn. Settled in Paris 1723 and played at Concert Spirituel and in opera orch. 1729–35, during which time he studied comp. Court mus. in Paris 1735–6. Wrote opera *Scylla et Glaucus* (Paris 1746, revived in concert perf., London 1979) and ballets, and many vn. works incl. concs., sonatas, trios. Murdered by his nephew outside his house. His brother, also Jean-Marie (*b* Lyons, 1703; *d* Lyons, 1777) was a violinist and composed vn. sonatas and choral works.

Lecocq, Alexandre Charles (*b* Paris, 1832; *d* Paris, 1918). Fr. composer. Studied Paris Cons. His setting of *Le *★*Docteur Miracle* (with ★Bizet's) won prize offered by Offenbach, 1856. From 1868 to 1911 produced a series of popular operettas of which most successful were *La Fille de Madame Angot* (1872) and *Giroflé-Girofla* (1874).

Lecuona, Ernesto (*b* Guanabacoa, 1896; *d* S. Cruz de Tenerife, 1963). Cuban composer and pianist. Studied at Nat. Cons., Havana, graduating in 1913. After further study with Nin, became leader of dance band, Lecuona's Cuban Boys. Lived for a time in NY, writing for musicals, films, and radio. Wrote 2 zarzuelas, *Rapsodia negra* for pf. and orch. (1943), and many songs, incl. *Andalucia*.

Ledger, Philip (Stevens) (*b* Bexhill-on-Sea, 1937). Eng. organist, cond., pianist, and harpsichordist. Studied King's Coll., Cambridge. Master of Mus., Chelmsford Cath. 1962–5; dir. of mus., Univ. of E. Anglia 1965–73; dir. of mus. and organist King's Coll., Cambridge, 1974–82. Acc. to Janet Baker, Robert Tear, etc. One of art. dirs. of Aldeburgh Fest. Prin., RSAM from 1982. C.B.E. 1985.

Ledger Lines (leger lines). Short lines added below or above the staff to accommodate notes too high or too low for the staff itself.

Leeds Festival. Mus festival, principally choral, held in Yorkshire city of Leeds since 1858 when it marked opening of town hall. Second festival, cond. by Costa, was in 1874, third in 1880 (Sullivan), after which it was held triennially until 1970. Under Sullivan festival acquired international status, with choral works commissioned from Dvořák, Massenet, Sullivan, Parry, and Stanford. When Sullivan retired, Stanford took over until 1910. Among works first perf. at Leeds festivals were Elgar's *Caractacus* (1898) and *Falstaff* (1913), Vaughan Williams's *A Sea Symphony* (1910), Holst's *Choral Symphony* (1925), Walton's *Belshazzar's Feast* (1931), Britten's *Nocturne* (1958), and Blake's *Lumina* (1970). Directors in recent years have included Earl of Harewood and John Warrack.

Leeds Piano Competition. International competition for pianists est. 1963 by Fanny Waterman and Marion Thorpe (then Lady Harewood). Held triennially. Winners have been Michael Roll, Rafael Orozco, Radu Lupu, Murray Perahia, Dmitri Alexeev, Michel Dalberto, Ian Hobson, and Jon Kimura Parker.

Leer (Ger.). Empty; applied to open str. of vn., etc.

Lees, Benjamin (*b* Harbin, Manchuria, 1924). Amer. composer. Studied Univ. of S. Calif., later with Antheil. Went to Europe 1954, returning to USA 1962. Teacher at several Amer. colleges. Prin. works:

OPERAS: *The Oracle* (1955); *The Gilded Cage* (1971).
BALLET: *Scarlatti Portfolio* (1979).
ORCH: Sym. No. 1 (1953), No. 2 (1958), No. 3 (1969); pf. conc. No. 1 (1955), No. 2 (1966); vn. conc. (1958); *Concertante breve* (1959); *Concerto for Orchestra* (1959); *Prologue, Capriccio, and Epilogue* (1961); ob. conc. (1963); conc. for str. qt. and orch. (1964); *Spectrum* (1964); Conc. for chamber orch. (1966); *Silhouettes* (1967); *Variations*, pf. and orch. (1976); Va. conc. (1977); *Portfolio* (1979); *Mobiles* (1980); double conc. for pf., vc., and orch. (1982).
VOICE(S) AND ORCH: *Visions of Poets* (Whitman), sop., ten., ch. (1961); *Medea of Corinth*, 4 soloists, wind quintet, timp. (1970); *The Trumpet of the Swan*, narrator and orch. (1972); conc. for brass, ch., and orch. (1983).
CHAMBER MUSIC: Str. Qts., No. 1 (1952), No. 2 (1955), No. 3 (1981); hn. sonata (1952); vn. sonata No. 1 (1953), No. 2 (1972); 2-pf. sonata (1951); *Collage*, wind quintet, perc., str. qt. (1973); sextet (wind quintet and pf.) (1977); 4 pf. sonatas (1949, 1950, 1956, 1963); *Odyssey*, pf. (1970); vc. sonata (1981); pf. trio (1983).

Leeuw, Ton de (*b* Rotterdam, 1926). Dutch composer. Studied in Breda, Paris, and Amsterdam (comp. with *Badings). Teacher at Amsterdam Univ. since 1963 (dir. 1971–3). Works influenced by Schoenberg, *musique concrète*, Pijper's 'germ-cell' melodic principle, and Asian mus. Has used proportional rhythmic notation to represent unlimited scale of note-values. Works incl.: opera *The Dream* (1963), radio oratorio *Job* (1956), *Symphonies of Winds*, for 29 wind instr. (1963), 2 str. qts. (1958, 1964), *Syntaxis I* for tape (1966), *Spatial Music I–IV*, *Litany of our Time* (1970), etc.

LeFanu, Nicola (Frances) (*b* Wickham Bishops, Essex, 1947). Eng. composer and teacher, daughter of Elizabeth *Maconchy. Studied Oxford Univ., and with Jeremy Dale Roberts, Wellesz, and *Petrassi. Cobbett chamber mus. prize 1968, 1st prize BBC composers competition 1971. Lecturer, Morley Coll. 1970–5, dir. of mus. Francis Holland Sch. 1975–7. Lecturer in Mus., King's Coll., London Univ. from 1977. Works incl.:

ORCH: *Preludio I*, str. (1967); *Preludio II*, str. (1976, rev. of I); *The Hidden Landscape* (1973); *Columbia Falls* (1975); *Farne* (1979).

THEATRE: *Antiworld*, dancer, with sop., bar., fl., cl., and perc. (1972); *The Last Laugh*, ballet, for sop., tape, and chamber orch. (1972); *Dawnpath*, opera, for bar., sop., male dancer, and chamber orch. (prod. London 1977).

VOCAL AND CHORAL: *Il Cantico del Cantici II* (1968); *But Stars Remaining*, sop. (1970); *Christ Calls Man Home*, unacc. SATB (1971); *Rondeaux*, ten. and hn. (1972); *Paysage*, bar. (1973); *The Valleys Shall Sing*, for ch. and wind (1973); *The Same Day Dawns*, sop. and 5 players (1974); *The Little Valleys*, for 4 unacc. sop. (1975); *For We Are the Stars*, 16 vv. (1978); *Like a Wave of the Sea*, ch. and ens. of early instrs. (1981); *The Old Woman of Beare*, sop. and 13 players (1981); *A Penny for a Song*, sop., pf. (1981); *Stranded on my Heart*, ten., ch., str. (1984).

CHAMBER AND INSTR: *Soliloquy* for ob. (1965); Variations for Ob. Qt. (1968); *Chiaroscuro* for pf. (1969); Cl. Quintet (1971); *Abstracts and a Frame*, vn. and pf. (1971); *Songs and Sketches*, vcs. (1971); *Omega*, org., (1971); *Collana* for 6 instr. (1976), *Deva*, vc. and 7 instr. (1979); *Trio*, fl., vc., perc. (1980).

Lefébure, Yvonne (*b* Ermont, Seine-et-Oise, 1900). Fr. pianist. Studied Paris Cons. with *Cortot. Prof., École Normale de Musique, Paris, from 1924, Paris Cons. 1952–67. Int. career as recitalist and soloist. Also writer and lecturer.

Le Fleming, Christopher (Kaye) (*b* Wimborne, 1908; *d* Woodbury, Devon, 1985). Eng. composer and teacher. Educated Brighton Sch. of Mus. and RSCM. Holder of many posts in sch. mus. education. Ed. of *Making Music* from 1946. Comps. incl. choral works, songs, pf. pieces.

Legato (It.). Bound together. Perf. of mus. so that there is no perceptible pause between notes, i.e.

in a smooth manner, the opposite of *staccato. Indicated by slur or *curved line. On str. instrs., legato passages are played with one stroke of the bow; in vocal mus., the legato passage is sung *portamento, in one breath. *Legato touch* in pf. playing requires holding down one key until the finger is on another. Superlative is *legatissimo*.

Legend (Ger. *Legende*). Title given to short comps. of lyrical or epic character. Well-known examples are *Dvořák's *Legends*, Op. 59 (orch. from pf. duet) and Sibelius's 4 *Lemminkäinen Legends* for orch., Op. 22.

Legende von der Heiligen Elisabeth, Die (The Legend of St Elizabeth). Oratorio by Liszt comp. 1857–62, f.p. Budapest 1865. Staged as opera-oratorio Weimar 1881 and NY Met. 1918.

Legend of Joseph (Strauss). See *Josephslegende*.

Legend of the Invisible City of Kitezh (Rimsky-Korsakov). See *Invisible City of Kitezh, The*.

Legend of Tsar Saltan, The. Opera in prol. and 4 acts by *Rimsky-Korsakov to lib. by Belsky after Pushkin's poem (1832). Prod. Moscow 1900, London 1933, NY 1937. One of orch. interludes is *Flight of the Bumble Bee*.

Leger Lines. See *Ledger lines*.

Legge, Harry (*b* Liverpool, 1914). Eng. violinist and cond. Studied Oxford Univ. and RCM. Dir., RPO 1963–73. Cond. Rehearsal Orch. and Brit. Youth Wind Orch. O.B.E. 1981.

Legge, Walter (*b* London, 1906; *d* S. Jean, Cap Ferrat, 1979). Eng. impresario, critic, and author. Joined Gramophone Co. (HMV) 1927, becoming recording manager and holding similar post with Columbia from 1938. Instrumental in putting many famous artists under recording contract. Organized Wolf and Beethoven Sonata socs. for recordings. Contributed criticisms to *Manchester Guardian* 1934–8. Ass. art. dir. CG 1938–9. Dir. of mus. ENSA 1942–5. Founded *Philharmonia Orch. 1945, administering it until 1964 when he unsuccessfully attempted to disband it. Married sop. Elisabeth *Schwarzkopf 1953.

Leggero, leggere (It.). Light. So *leggeramente* or *leggermente*, lightly, *leggerezza, leggeranza*, lightness; *leggerissimo*, as light as possible.

Leggiadro, leggiadretto (It.). Graceful. So *leggiadramente*, gracefully.

Leggiero, leggiere (It.). Light. So *leggieramente* or *leggiermente*, lightly; *leggierezza, leggieranza*, lightness; *leggierissimo*, as light as possible.

Leggio (It., from *leggere*, to read). Music desk.

Legno (It.). Wood. *Col legno*, 'with the wood', i.e. in str. playing, tapping the str. with the stick of the bow instead of using the hair, thus producing a rather bizarre sound as in finale of Berlioz's *Symphonie Fantastique. Bacchetta di legno*, wooden-headed drumstick, *strumenti* (*stromenti*) *di legno*, woodwind instrs.

Legrand, Michel (*b* Paris, 1932). Fr. composer and conductor. Studied at Paris Cons. 1943–50 (cond. and score-reading with N. Boulanger). Soon became known as brilliant orchestrator of light mus. and jazz. Cond. for Maurice Chevalier in Paris and NY 1954–5. Gained reputation with music for *Les Parapluies de Cherbourg* (1964). Comp. many film scores, among them *Un Homme et Une Femme* (1961), *The Thomas Crown Affair* (1968), *Summer of 42* (1971), and *The Go-Between* (1971).

Legrenzi, Giovanni (*b* Clusone, nr. Bergamo, 1626; *d* Venice, 1690). It. composer and choirmaster. Organist in Bergamo 1645–55, Ferrara 1656–65 (while there he wrote his first operas). At Conservatorio dei Mendicanti, Venice, 1671–81, when he became deputy choirmaster at St Mark's succeeding to the chief post in 1685. Comp. 19 operas, much instr. mus., masses, psalms, motets, church sonatas.

Lehár, Ferencz (Franz) (*b* Komáron, 1870; *d* Bad Ischl, 1948). Hung. composer. First studied with father, a military bandmaster, then Prague Cons. 1882–8. Advised by Dvořák to concentrate on comp. Joined Elberfeld opera orch. as violinist, then became ass. leader of his father's band. Cond. of various army bands 1890–1902. Cond., Theater an der Wien, Vienna, 1902. His *Wiener Frauen* was produced there Nov. 1902 and after its success he stayed in Vienna and devoted his time to comp. His operetta, *Die lustige Witwe* (The *Merry Widow*) was a colossal success not only at its Vienna première in 1905 but all over the world ever since. He was the bridge between the Strausses and Zeller and the later Oskar Straus, Fall, and Kálmán. In the 1920s the v. of Richard Tauber became indelibly associated with Lehár roles and one above all—in *Das Land des Lächelns* (The *Land* of Smiles) in 1929. He wrote a full-scale opera, *Giuditta* (1934) and several other operettas: *Der Graf von Luxemburg* (The *Count of Luxemburg*) (1909), *Zigeunerliebe* (1910), *Frasquita* (1922), *Paganini* (1925), *Der Zarewitsch* (1927), and *Friederike* (1928). Also wrote sonatas, symphonic poems, vn. conc., marches, and dances (incl. the concert-waltz *Gold and Silver*, 1902).

Lehel, György (*b* Budapest, 1926). Hung. conductor. Studied with Kadosa and Somogyi. Début 1946. Prin. cond. Budapest Radio S.O. from 1962. Brit. début, Cheltenham 1968. Kossuth Prize 1973.

Lehmann, Lilli (*b* Würzburg, 1848; *d* Berlin, 1929). Ger. sop. Childhood in Prague: studied pf. at 6 and at 12 was acc. to her mother, a sop., who also taught her singing. Début Prague 1865 as 1st Boy in *Die Zauberflöte*. Later sang at Danzig and Leipzig. Member, Berlin Opera 1870–85, singing lyric and coloratura roles. At first Bayreuth Fest.

1876 sang Woglinde, Helmwige, and Waldvogel (Wood bird) in *The Ring*. London début 1880 as Violetta in *Traviata*. Sang Isolde at CG 1884 cond. Richter. Début NY Met. 1885 as Carmen and Brünnhilde in *Die Walküre*. Was first Amer. Isolde (1886) and Brünnhilde in *Siegfried* (1887) and *Götterdämmerung* (1888). On return to Ger. in 1889 was banned from all opera by Kaiser because she had overstayed her leave. Ban lifted 1891. Excelled as Mozart singer and sang at Salzburg Fest. 1905, later becoming art. dir. Returned to Met. 1891–2 and 1898–9. Sang Isolde in Vienna 1909 and continued recitals until 1920. Was superb actress and her vocal and dramatic range covered Wagner to Bellini, Mozart, and Beethoven; also Suppé and Offenbach—in all, 170 roles in 119 operas. Taught for nearly 40 years, pupils incl. *Farrar and *Fremstad. Author and translator of several books.

Lehmann, Liza (Elizabeth Nina Mary Frederika) (*b* London, 1862; *d* Pinner, 1918). Eng. composer and sop. Successful career as concert singer ended in 1894, then devoted herself to comp. Best-known work is song-cycle *In a Persian Garden*, setting for vocal qt. (SATB) of 30 quatrains from FitzGerald's *Rubáiyát of Omar Khayyám* (f.p. London 1896).

Lehmann, Lotte (*b* Perleberg, 1888; *d* Santa Barbara, Calif., 1976). Ger.-born sop. (Amer. citizen 1945). Studied Berlin, finally with Mathilde Mallinger, who created role of Eva. Début Hamburg 1909 as 3rd Boy in *Die Zauberflöte*. Vienna début 1914. Joined Vienna Opera 1916, remaining until 1938, singing leading roles in Wagner, Strauss, Mozart, Puccini, and Beethoven. First to sing successively all 3 sop. roles in Strauss's *Der Rosenkavalier* (Sophie, Oktavian, and Marschallin), eventually becoming outstanding Marschallin of her time. Created roles of the Composer in Strauss's *Ariadne auf Naxos* (1916), Dyer's Wife in *Die Frau ohne Schatten* (1919), and Christine in *Intermezzo* (Dresden 1924). First Vienna Arabella (1933). London début 1914 as Sophie; CG début 1924 as Marschallin (her first assumption of this role) and sang there yearly until 1935 and again in 1938. Salzburg Fest. from 1926. Amer. début, Chicago, 1930, as Sieglinde in *Die Walküre*, NY Met. 1934–45. Settled in USA at Santa Barbara 1938, est. sch. of singing there. Sang last Marschallin at San Francisco 1946. Farewell recital, NY Feb. 1951. Pupils incl. Grace *Bumbry and Jeannine *Altmeyer. Gave master-classes in London 1957 and 1959. Directed prod. of *Rosenkavalier* at NY Met. 1962. Wrote several books incl. novel and poems. Salzburg street named after her.

Leibowitz, René (*b* Warsaw, 1913; *d* Paris, 1972). Polish-born Fr. composer, cond., and musicologist. Settled in Paris 1926; studied with Schoenberg in Berlin 1930–3 and with Webern in Vienna, also had lessons from Ravel. Powerful advocate of Schoenberg's 12-note system, influencing Boulez and Henze. Cond. and teacher at Darmstadt Fest. from 1949. Author of several books on dodecaphonic mus. Prolific composer (operas, syms., concs., chamber mus.).

Leichtentritt, Hugo (*b* Pleschen, 1874; *d* Cambridge, Mass., 1951). Ger. composer, teacher, and scholar. Went to USA 1889, studied Harvard Univ. 1891–4, Berlin Hochschule für Musik 1895–8, Berlin Univ. 1898–1901. Taught comp. and aesthetics at Klindworth-Scharwenka Cons., Berlin, 1901–24 and worked as critic in Berlin 1901–17. Returned to USA 1933 as lecturer at Harvard until retirement in 1940. Author of many books incl. biographies of Chopin, Busoni, and Handel, ed. of old mus., and prolific composer in all forms.

Leider, Frida (*b* Berlin, 1888; *d* Berlin, 1975). Ger. sop. Studied in Berlin and Milan. Début Halle 1915 as Venus in *Tannhäuser*. Opera at Rostock 1917–18, Königsberg 1918–19, Hamburg 1919–23, then Berlin State Opera 1923–40, esp. in Wagner roles (a great Isolde and Brünnhilde). CG début 1924, returning annually until 1938. Chicago Opera 1928–32, NY Met. 1933–4, Bayreuth 1928–38. Producer at Berlin State Opera after 1945, also taught at Hochschule für Musik.

Leigh, Walter (*b* London, 1905; *d* in action nr. Tobruk, 1942). Eng. composer. Studied Cambridge under *Dent and in Berlin with Hindemith. Wrote two light operas, *The Pride of the Regiment* (1932) and *Jolly Roger* (1933), incidental mus. (incl. *A Midsummer Night's Dream*), concertino for hpd. and str. (1936), songs, chamber mus.

Leighton, Kenneth (*b* Wakefield, 1929). Eng. composer and pianist. Studied Oxford and with Petrassi in Rome, 1951. Comp. fellowship Leeds Univ. 1953–6; teacher of comp. Edinburgh Univ. 1956–68, prof. from 1970. Works incl.:

OPERA: *Columba*, Op. 77 (1980).
ORCH: *Veris Gratia*, Op. 9, suite for ob., vc., str. (1950); Vn. Conc., Op. 12 (1952); Conc. for va. and harp, Op. 15 (1952); Vc. Conc., Op. 31 (1956); *Passacaglia, Chorale, and Fugue*, Op. 18 (1957); Pf. Concs.: No. 1, Op. 11 (1951, rev. 1959), No. 2, Op. 37 (1960), No. 3, Op. 57 (1969); *Concerto for Strings*, Op. 39 (1961); Symphonies: No. 1, Op. 42 (1964), No. 2 (*Sinfonia Mistica*), Op. 69 (1974); *Dance Suite* No. 1, Op. 53 (1968), No. 2, Op. 59 (1970); Org. Conc., Op. 58 (1970); *Dance Overture*, Op. 60 (1971).
VOICE(S) AND INSTR: *A Christmas Caroll*, Op. 21, bar., ch., str., pf. (1953); *The Birds*, Op. 28, sop., ten., ch., orch. (1954); *The Light Invisible, sinfonia sacra*, Op. 16, ten., ch., orch. (1958); *Laudes Montium*, Op. 71, bar., ch., orch. (1975); Sym. No. 2 (*Sinfonia Mistica*), Op. 69, sop., ch., orch. (1974); *Columba Mea*, Op. 78, ten., alto, ch., instr. (1978); *Animal Heaven*, Op. 83, sop., recorder, vc., hpd. (1980).

VOICE(S) AND ORGAN: *Magnificat and Nunc Dimittis*, ch., org. (1959); *Crucifixus pro Nobis*, Op. 38, ten. or sop., ch., org. (1961); *Missa Sancti Thomae*, Op. 40, ch., org. (1962); *Te Deum*, sop., bar., ch., org. (1964, with orch. 1966); *Morning Canticles*, ch., org. (1968); *Awake My Glory*, Op. 79, sop., ch., org. (1979); *Missa Cornelia*, Op. 81, treble vv., org. (1980); *These are Thy Wonders*, Op. 84, ten. or sop., org. (1981).
UNACC. VOICES: *3 Carols*, Op. 25, sop. and ch. (1948–56); *God's Grandeur*, Op 13, No. 2, ch. (1957); *Hymn of the Nativity*, sop. and ch. (1960); *Preces and Responses*, ch. (1964); *Missa brevis*, Op. 50, ch. (1967); *3 Psalms*, Op. 54, male vv. (1968); *Evening Hymn*, sop. and ch. (1979).
CHAMBER MUSIC: *Fantasia on the Name BACH*, Op. 29, va., pf. (1955); pf. quintet, Op. 34 (1959); *Nocturne*, vn., pf. (1959); *Partita*, Op. 35, vc., pf. (1959); *7 Variations* for str. qt., Op. 43 (1964); pf. trio, Op. 46 (1965); *Metamorphoses*, Op. 48, vn., pf. (1966); vc. sonata, Op. 52 (1967); *Contrasts and Variants*, pf. qt., Op. 63 (1972); *Fantasy On 'The Shining River'*, Op. 70, cl., vc., pf. (1974); *Fantasy on a Chorale*, Op. 80, vn., org. (1980); *Alleluia Pascha Nostrum*, Op. 85, vc., pf. (1981); *Fantasy-Octet 'Homage to Percy Grainger'*, Op. 87, str. (1982).
PIANO: *5 Studies*, Op. 22 (1953); *Variations*, Op. 30 (1955); *Fantasia Contrappuntistica, 'Homage to Bach'*, Op. 24 (1956); *9 Variations*, Op. 36 (1959); *Pieces for Angela*, Op. 47 (1966); *Conflicts*, Op. 51 (1967); *6 Studies*, Op. 56 (1972); *Household Pets*, Op. 86 (1981).
ORGAN: *Prelude, Scherzo and Passacaglia*, Op. 41 (1963); *Elegy* (1965); *Et Resurrexit*, Op. 49 (1966); *Improvisation* (1969); *Martyrs*, Op. 73 (1976); *Missa de Gloria*, Op. 82 (1980).

Leinsdorf, Erich (*b* Vienna, 1912). Austrian-born cond. (Amer. citizen). Studied Vienna. Ass. cond. to Bruno Walter and Toscanini at Salzburg Fest. 1934–7. Opera cond. Bologna 1936; ass. cond. NY Met. 1938 (début in *Die Walküre*), succeeded *Bodanzky as chief cond. of Ger. repertory 1939–43. Cond. Cleveland Orch. 1943–4. Served US Army. Cond. Rochester P.O. 1947–55. Dir., NY City Opera 1956. Cond. NY Met. 1957–62. Cond. Boston S.O. 1962–9. Thereafter guest cond. of leading orchs. of world.

Leise (Ger.). Soft, gentle, as in *Leise, leise*, Agathe's aria in Act 2 of Weber's *Der Freischütz. Leiser*, softer.

Leitmotiv (Leading motive). A term (often misspelt *leitmotif*) invented (1871) by F. W. Jähns, the expert on Weber, to describe a short constantly recurring mus. phrase or theme used to denote a person, thing, or abstract idea. 'Representative theme' is a good Eng. alternative. Composers throughout history have used the device in one form or another, e.g. Gluck and Mozart, Weber in *Der Freischütz*, Mendelssohn, Berlioz (the *idée fixe* in the *Symphonie Fantastique*), but it was raised to its highest and most complex form by Wagner, especially in *Der Ring des Nibelungen*, where the subtle combinations of *leitmotiv* create symphonic textures. Wagner used the term *Hauptmotiv* in 1867, but *leitmotiv* has become generally accepted. R. Strauss also developed a *leitmotiv* system in his operas.

Leitner, Ferdinand (*b* Berlin, 1912). Ger. cond. Studied Berlin with *Schnabel and Karl *Muck. Ass. to *Busch at Glyndebourne 1935. Opera cond. Berlin 1943, Hamburg 1945–6, Munich 1946–7, mus. dir. Stuttgart Opera 1947–69, Zürich 1969–84. Guest cond. in many countries. Prin. cond. Hague P.O. 1976–80.

Lejeune. See *Jeune, Claude le.*

Lekeu, Guillaume (*b* Heusy, Belg., 1870; *d* Angers, 1894). Belg. composer. Studied Paris with *Franck and *d'Indy. Died of typhoid, leaving small body of works of exceptional promise and beauty, incl. pf. sonata, vn. sonata, *Fantaisie sur deux airs populaires angevins* for orch., symphonic study on *Hamlet*, pf. trio, and vc. sonata and str. qt. both completed by d'Indy.

Lélio, ou le retour à la vie (Lélio, or the return to life). Monodrama by Berlioz, his Op. 14 *bis*, comp. 1831–2 as a sequel to *Symphonie Fantastique*. For speaker, 2 ten., bar., ch., and orch. F.p. Paris, Nov. 1832.

Lemare, Edwin (Henry) (*b* Ventnor, I.o.W., 1865; *d* Los Angeles, 1934). Eng. organist and composer. Studied with his father and at RAM. Held various org. posts, incl. St Margaret's, Westminster, 1897–1902, and gave many recitals. Visited USA 1900 and settled there holding org. posts in Pittsburgh, San Francisco, Portland (Maine), and Chattanooga. Composed 2 org. syms. and other works. *Moonlight and Roses*, his best-known comp., was adapted from an Andante for org.

Lemmens-Sherrington, Hellen (*b* Preston, 1834; *d* Brussels, 1906). Eng. sop. Studied Rotterdam and Brussels. London début in concerts, then opera at CG 1864–5. Long career in opera and oratorio, being regarded as leading Eng. sop. of her day. First prof. of singing, RMCM 1893–7. Married Nicolas Jacques Lemmens (1823–81), Belg. organist, composer, and teacher at Brussels Cons.

Lemminkäinen Legends (*Lemminkäis-sarja*). Suite for orch. Op. 22 by Sibelius containing 4 movts.:
 1. *Lemminkäinen and the Maidens of the Island* (*Lemminkäinen ja saaren neidot*) comp. 1895, rev. 1897, 1939. 2. *Lemminkäinen in Tuonela* (*Lemminkäinen Tuonelassa*) comp. 1895, rev. 1897, 1939. 3. *The Swan of Tuonela* (*Tuonelan joutsen*) comp. 1893, rev. 1897, 1900. 4. *Lemminkäinen's Return* (*Lemminkäisen paluu*) comp. 1895, rev. 1897, 1900. No. 3 was conceived as prelude to abandoned opera *The Burning of the Boat* (*Veenen luominen*) and No. 2 also had operatic origins, F.p. 1895 version, Helsinki 1896, cond. Sibelius; f.p. 1897 revision, Helsinki 1897, cond. Sibelius; f. Eng. p. of complete 1897 version, BBC 1950, cond. Cameron; f.p. of Nos. 1 and 2 outside Finland, Bournemouth 1937, cond. Wood; f. Eng. p. No. 3, London 1905, cond. Wood; f. Eng. p. No. 4, BBC Newcastle station broadcast 1925, cond. E. Clark.

Lemnitz, Tiana (*b* Metz, 1897). Ger. sop. Studied Metz. Opera début Heilbronn 1921. Aachen Opera 1922–8, Hanover 1929–33, Berlin State Opera 1934–57. CG début 1936 (Eva in *Die Meistersinger*). Wide repertory from Pamina to Jenůfa. A fine Oktavian in *Rosenkavalier*.

Léner Quartet. Hung. str. qt. formed in 1918 by 4 members of Budapest Opera Orch.—Jenö Léner, Joseph Smilovits, Sandor Roth, and Irme Hartman. Début Budapest 1919, Vienna and Paris 1920, NY 1929. Became one of leading qts. of inter-war period, making several recordings. Membership changed 1942. Disbanded on Léner's death, 1948.

Lengnick & Co. London mus. publishing firm founded 1892 by Alfred Lengnick. Limited co., 1924. Specialists in educational mus. Eng. representatives of Ger. firm Simrock.

Leningrad Philharmonic Orchestra. Orch. based in Leningrad, founded 1921 from pre-Revolutionary court orch. Prin. conds. have been Emil Cooper (1921–2), Nikolay Malko (1926–9), Alexander Gauk (1930–3), Fritz Stiedry (1934–7), and Evgeny Mravinsky since 1938, jointly with Kurt Sanderling (1941–60). Also closely ass. with it have been Arvid Yansons and Yury Temirkanov. Gave f. ps. of eight Shostakovich syms. (Nos. 1, 2, 3, 5, 6, 9, 10, and 14).

Leningrad Symphony. Sub-title of *Shostakovich's Sym. No. 7 in C major, Op. 60, comp. 1941 during Ger. siege of Leningrad. F.p. Kuibyshev 1942; f. Eng. p. London 1942 cond. Wood. Ballet made from first movement, 1961, Kirov Ballet (choreog. Igor Belsky). Theme from sym. is parodied by Bartók in *Concerto for Orchestra* (1943) in the 4th movt., 'Intermezzo interrotto'.

Lent (Fr.), **lento** (It.). Slow. So *lentando*; *lentato* (It.). slowing, slowed (same as *rallentando*); *lentement* (Fr.), *lentamente* (It.), slowly; *lenteur* (Fr.), *lentezza* (It.), slowness; *lentissimo*, very slow.

Lenya, Lotte (orig. Karoline Blamauer) (*b* Vienna, 1898; *d* NY, 1981). Austrian-born singer of mez. quality (later Amer. citizen). Went to Zürich 1914, where she studied acting, dancing, and singing. Member of *corps de ballet*, Zürich Stadttheater and made stage acting début at Schauspielhaus. Moved to Berlin 1920, where she met the playwright Bertolt *Brecht and the composer Kurt *Weill, whose wife she became.

Her distinctive singing style and accomplished acting made a major contribution to the success of the Brecht-Weill collaborations such as *Mahagonny*, and *Der Dreigroschenoper*, especially in such songs as 'Pirate Jenny', 'Surabaya Johnny' and 'Alabama Song'. With Weill, went to USA in 1933 and made new career in plays and films, incl. *From Russia with Love.*

Leo, Leonardo (*b* San Vito degli Schiavi, 1694; *d* Naples, 1744). It. composer. Studied in Naples 1709–13. Held org. posts. Wrote many operas, incl. several *opere buffe*, church mus., and concs. for vn. and for vc. Pupils incl. *Jommelli, *Pergolesi, and *Piccinni.

Leonard, Lawrence (*b* London, 1925). Eng. cond. Studied RAM and École Normale de Musique, Paris. Ass. cond. BBC Northern S.O. Assoc. cond. Hallé 1964–6; cond. and mus. dir. Edmonton S.O., Canada, 1969–74. Cond. f.p. in England of Bernstein's *West Side Story*, 1958.

Leoncavallo, Ruggiero (*b* Naples, 1857; *d* Montecatini, 1919). It. composer. Studied Naples Cons. Completed first opera, *Chatterton*, in 1876 and planned trilogy on Renaissance Italy of which only 1st part *I Medici* (1893) was written. Fame rests on successful *Pagliacci* (Milan 1892). His *La *Bohème* (1897) suffered from comparison with Puccini's, prod. 15 months earlier. Wrote series of operettas, but failed to win an audience. Last opera was *Edipo Re* (Chicago 1920).

Leonhardt, Gustav (*b* 's-Graveland, Holland, 1928). Dutch harpsichordist and organist. Studied Basle Schola Cantorum. Début Vienna 1950. Prof. of hpd., Vienna Acad. 1952–5, Amsterdam Cons. from 1954. Ed. of Bach's *Die Kunst der Fuge*, and works of Sweelinck.

Leoni, Franco (*b* Milan, 1864; *d* Hampstead, 1949). It. composer. Studied with Ponchielli. Settled in London 1891–1914 and in later years. Comp. 3 oratorios, all perf. in London, and several operas, best-known being *L'*Oracolo* (London 1905).

Leoni, Leone (*b* Verona, *c.*1560; *d* Vicenza, 1627). It. composer. Maestro di cappella, Vicenza, from 1588. Wrote motets and madrigals for double ch. Some motets had instr. acc.

Léonin (Leoninus) (*fl.* Paris, *c.*1160–80). Fr. composer. Known only from writings of Eng. theorist Anonymous IV (*fl. c.*1270), who refers to Léonin as best exponent of organum and that he compiled a large book ('magnus liber') of chants used at Paris church later rebuilt as Notre Dame. Scholarship has not determined whether any of Léonin's comps. survive, if indeed he wrote any.

Leonore. Beethoven's intended title for his opera *Fidelio* (but not used at 1805 f.p. as is sometimes supposed) and the name of its heroine. The 3 ovs. are known in Eng. as *Leonora* (see *Fidelio*).

Léonore, ou L'Amour conjugal (Leonora, or Married Love). Opera in 2 acts by *Gaveaux to text by J. N. Bouilly. Prod. Paris 1798. First setting of story used by Paër, Mayr, and Beethoven (*Fidelio*).

Leopold I, Emperor of Austria (*b* Vienna, 1640; *d* Vienna, 1705). Austrian emperor who reigned 1658–1705. Patron of mus., esp. opera. Comp. instr. sonatas, etc.

Leppard, Raymond (John) (*b* London, 1927). Eng. cond., composer, harpsichordist, and musicologist. Studied Cambridge Univ. Mus. dir. ECO since 1960. Prin. cond. BBC Northern S.O. 1973–80. Début CG 1959, Glyndebourne 1962, and SW 1965. Editorial realizations of Monteverdi's *Ballo delle Ingrate* (1958), *L'incoronazione di Poppea* (1962), *Orfeo* (1965), and *Il ritorno d'Ulisse* (1972), and of Cavalli's *Messa Concertata* (1966), *L'Ormindo* (1967), *La Calisto* (1969), *L'Egisto* (1974), *Orione* (1980), also *Magnificat* (1970). These have been criticized on the grounds that they are harmonically too rich, musicologically too imprecise, contain too many transpositions, and too much music comp. by Leppard, but there is no doubt that they popularized baroque opera and paved the way for other, more austere, editions. Also effective cond. of standard orch. repertoire. C.B.E. 1983.

Lerchenquartett (Lark Quartet). Nickname of Haydn's Str. Qt. in D, No. 11 of the *Tostquartette*; it is sometimes described as Op. 64, No. 5. Its nickname is derived from the opening. The rhythm of the last movement has given rise to another, less frequently used, nickname, the 'Hornpipe' Qt.

Leroux, Xavier Henri Napoléon (*b* Velletri, It., 1863; *d* Paris, 1919). Fr. composer. Studied Paris Cons. with Massenet. Prof. of harmony there 1896–1919. Wrote series of operas incl. *Evangéline* (1895), *La Reine Fiammette* (1903), and *Le Chemineau* (1906). Ed. periodical *Musica*.

Les Adieux (Beethoven). See *Lebewohl, Das.*

Leschetizky, Theodor (Leszetycki, Teodor) (*b* Lancut, Poland, 1830; *d* Dresden, 1915). Polish pianist, teacher, and composer. In demand as teacher at age of 14 and made successful recital tours. Dir. of pf. studies, St Petersburg Cons. 1862–78, then settled in Vienna, where est. own sch. Retired from concert-giving 1886. Developed a teaching 'method' and attracted pupils from the world over. Among them were *Paderewski, *Schnabel, and *Gabrilowitsch. Wrote 2 operas and pf. pieces.

Lesson. Term used in 17th and 18th cents. for short kbd. piece or exercise, and often synonymous with sonata.

Lesto (It.). Quick. So *lestamente,* quickly; *lestissimo,* very quickly.

Le Sueur, Jean François (*b* Drucat-Plessiel, nr. Abbéville, 1760; *d* Paris, 1837). Fr. composer. Held church posts, becoming choirmaster of Nôtre Dame, Paris, 1786, and engaging large orch. to dramatize perfs. of masses and motets. Dismissed 1788 because of opposition aroused. From 1792 wrote *grands opéras*, incl. *Paul et Virginie* (1794), *Télémaque* (1796), and *Ossian, ou Les bardes* (1804). Inspector, Paris Cons. 1795–1802. Succeeded Paisiello as Choirmaster to Napoleon, 1804. Prof. of comp., Paris Cons., from 1818. Excellent teacher, pupils incl. Berlioz. Interested in ancient Gr. mus.

Lesur, Daniel (Jean Yves) (*b* Paris, 1908). Fr. composer and organist. Studied Paris Cons. 1919–29. Ass. organist Ste Clotilde 1927–37. In 1937 founded *Jeune France* group with Messiaen, Jolivet, and Baudrier. Prof. of counterpoint Schola Cantorum 1935–64, dir. 1957–64. On mus. staff Fr. radio from 1939, mus. dir. Fr. TV (O.R.T.F.) from 1968. Many comps. incl. *La vie intérieure* for org. (1932), and ballet with Jolivet, *L'Infante et le monstre* (1938).

Let's Make an Opera. 'Entertainment for young people', Op. 45 by Britten, lib. by Eric Crozier. In 2 parts, first being preparations by children and adults to put on an opera, second being the opera itself, *The Little Sweep* (acc. for str. qt., pf. 4 hands, and perc.). Audience participates in 4 songs. Prod. Aldeburgh 1949.

Let us Garlands Bring. Song-cycle of 5 songs by *Finzi for bar. and pf. (or orch.) to words by Shakespeare. F.p. London, 12 October, 1942, on 70th birthday of Vaughan Williams, to whom it is dedicated. 1. *Come away, death* (1938); 2. *Who is Sylvia?* (1929); 3. *Fear no more the heat o' the sun* (1929); 4. *O mistress mine* (1942); 5. *It was a lover and his lass* (1940).

Letzt (Ger.). Last, e.g. *Vier letzte Lieder*, Four Last Songs (Strauss).

Leutgeb, Ignaz (Joseph) (*b* ?Salzburg, *c*.1745; *d* Vienna, 1811). Austrian hornplayer for whom Mozart wrote his 4 hn. concs. 1st hn. in archbishop's orch. at Salzburg from 1770, but was given leave to play in Paris, Vienna, and Milan. Settled in Vienna 1777 when he inherited a cheese-shop.

Levant, Oscar (*b* Pittsburgh, 1906; *d* Beverly Hills, Calif., 1972). Amer. pianist and composer. Studied comp. with Schoenberg. Settled in Hollywood in 1920s, becoming close friend and interpreter of *Gershwin. Career as wit on radio and TV and as film actor. Author of entertaining books. Wrote 2 pf. concs., str. qt., etc.

Levare (It.). To lift, or take off (past participle *levato*, plural *levati*; imperative *levate*). *Si levano i sordini*, the mutes are taken off.

Leventritt Competition. Int. competition, alternately for violinists and pianists, est. 1939 by Leventritt Foundation, NY, in memory of Edgar M. Leventritt, lawyer and patron of mus. Prin. award is series of engagements with major orchs., an honorarium, and offer of recording contract.

Levi, Hermann (*b* Giessen, 1839; *d* Munich, 1900). Ger. cond. Studied Mannheim and Leipzig (1855–8). Held cond. posts at Saarbrücken, Rotterdam, and Karlsruhe before becoming chief cond. Munich Opera 1872–96. Fine interpreter of Wagner; cond. f.p. of *Parsifal*, Bayreuth 1882, and mus. at Wagner's funeral. Rev. libs. of Mozart operas and trans. text of Berlioz's *Les Troyens*. Comp. pf. conc.

Levine, James (*b* Cincinnati, 1943). Amer. cond. and pianist. Studied Cincinnati and at Juilliard Sch. Ass. cond. to *Szell, Cleveland Orch., 1964–70. Cond. at NY Met. 1971, becoming prin. cond. 1973, mus. dir. 1975. Brit. début with WNO, Cardiff 1970 (*Aida*). Salzburg Fest. 1976. One of leading Mahler conds. of younger generation.

Levy, Marvin (David) (*b* Newark, NJ, 1932). Amer. composer and critic. Studied NY and Columbia Univ. Worked as mus. critic 1952–8. Commissioned by NY Met. in 1961 to compose opera based on O'Neill's *Mourning Becomes Electra* (f.p. 1967). Composer of 5 operas, choral works, sym., pf. conc., chamber mus.

Lewenthal, Raymond (*b* San Antonio, Texas, 1926). Amer. pianist, writer, musicologist, and ed. Studied Juilliard Sch., NY, Siena, and with Cortot. World tours. Specialist in Liszt and neglected 19th-cent. composers. Ed. pf. mus. of *Alkan.

Lewis, (Sir) **Anthony** (Carey) (*b* Bermuda, 1915; *d* Haslemere, 1983). Eng. cond., composer, ed., and teacher. Studied Cambridge Univ. and in Paris with Boulanger. On BBC mus. staff 1935–46. Prof. of Mus., Birmingham Univ. 1947–68. Prin., RAM 1968–82. Composer of hn. and tpt. concs. Founder and ed. *Musica Britannica*. Cond. of many Handel opera revivals. Ed. of Handel operas, Purcell's *Fairy Queen*, etc. C.B.E. 1967. Knighted 1972.

Lewis, Henry (*b* Los Angeles, 1932). Amer. cond., clarinettist, and db. player. Studied Univ. of S. Calif. Db. in Los Angeles P.O. Member and later cond. U.S. 7th Army S.O. 1955–7. Founder and dir. String Soc. of Los Angeles (later Los Angeles Chamber Orch.). Ass. cond. Los Angeles P.O. 1961–5, mus. dir. Los Angeles Opera Co. 1965–8. Prin. cond. NJ S.O. from 1968. NY Met. début 1972. Guest cond. LSO, RPO, Milan.

Lewis, Jeffrey (*b* Neath, 1942). Welsh composer, organist, pianist, and teacher. Studied Cardiff and with *Stockhausen, *Ligeti, and Don *Banks. Pianist, Paris Chamber Ens. 1967–8. Lecturer in 20th-cent. comp. City of Leeds Coll. of Mus. 1969–72. Lecturer, Mus. Dept., Univ. Coll. of N. Wales, Bangor, from 1972. Comps. incl. *Aurora*,

Fanfares with Variations, Mutations I (orch.), II (organ) etc.

Lewis, Mary (*b* Hot Springs, Arkansas, 1900; *d* NY, 1941). Amer. sop. Started career in Ziegfeld Follies and was offered contract at NY Met. but refused it until she had studied further. Début Vienna Volksoper 1923. Sang in Monte Carlo, Paris, Berlin, and London where she sang role of Mary in BNOC prod. of Vaughan Williams's *Hugh the Drover*, 1924. NY Met. 1926–30.

Lewis, Richard (real name Thomas Thomas) (*b* Manchester, 1914). Eng. ten. and cond. Studied privately, then at RMCM 1939–41 with Norman Allin, returning to him at RAM 1945. Began concert career in Denmark 1946. Eng. concert début Brighton 1947. Opera début Glyndebourne 1947 in Britten's *Rape of Lucretia*. Sang Peter Grimes at CG 1947 and Albert Herring with EOG 1948. Successful concert career in oratorio, esp. *Gerontius* which he sang with Barbirolli and Sargent. Created role of Troilus in Walton's *Troilus and Cressida* CG 1954 and at San Francisco 1955, and roles of Mark and of Achilles in Tippett's *The Midsummer Marriage* (1955) and *King Priam* (1962) respectively. Sang in f.p. of Stravinsky's *Canticum Sacrum*, Venice 1956. Sang Aaron in Schoenberg's *Moses und Aron* at CG 1965, in Boston (stage) 1966, and in Paris (1973). Notable Mozart singer; frequent guest artist at Glyndebourne and San Francisco. Took up cond. 1975. C.B.E. 1963.

Ley, Henry (George) (*b* Chagford, Devon, 1887; *d* Ottery-St-Mary, 1962). Eng. organist, composer, and teacher. Org. scholar, Keble Coll., Oxford; while still undergraduate appointed organist of Christ Church Cath., Oxford, 1909–26. Taught org. at RCM 1919–41. Mus. dir. (precentor) Eton Coll. 1926–45. Comp. church music, songs, etc.

Leygraf, Hans (*b* Stockholm, 1920). Swed. pianist, composer, and cond. Studied Stockholm Cons., Munich, and Switzerland. Début 1929 with Stockholm S.O. Specialist in Mozart. Composer of pf., orch., and chamber works.

Lezginka. A dance of the Mohammedan tribe the Lezghins (on the Persian border).

L.G.S.M. Licentiate of the Guildhall School of Music and Drama.

L.H. Abbreviation for Left Hand.

Lhévinne, Josef (*b* Orel, 1874; *d* NY, 1944). Russ. pianist and teacher. Studied Moscow Cons. with Safonov. Début, Moscow 1889. prof. of pf., Moscow Cons. 1902–06. NY début 1906 with Russ. S.O. Many world tours. Lived in Ger. 1907–19, settled in USA 1920. On teaching staff Juilliard Sch., NY, from 1922.

Lhévinne, Rosina (*b* Kiev, 1880; *d* Glendale, Calif., 1976). Russ. pianist and teacher, wife of Josef *Lhévinne, whom she married in 1898 on leaving Moscow Cons. Toured widely, gave many recitals with husband. Still gave recitals in mid-1960s. On staff Juilliard Sch. from 1922. Pupils incl. Van Cliburn, James Levine, and John Browning.

Liberamente (It.). Freely (i.e. with regard to tempo, rhythm, etc.).

Libretto (It.). Little book. The text of a vocal work, particularly opera. Author is 'librettist'. First known was for Peri's *Dafne* (1594–8). Among famous librettists have been *Metastasio, *da Ponte, Scribe, Romani, Piave, *Illica, *Gilbert, *Boito, and *Hofmannsthal. Some composers have written own libs., e.g. Wagner, Leoncavallo, Delius, and Tippett.

Licenza (It.). Licence, freedom (in such expressions as *Con alcuna licenza,* with some licence, i.e. freedom as to tempo and rhythm or to form of a work).

Licette, Miriam (*b* Chester, 1892; *d* Twyford, 1969). Eng. sop. Studied Milan and Paris with M. Marchesi, J. de Reszke, and Sabbatini. Début Rome 1911 as Butterfly. Member of Beecham co. 1916–20, BNOC 1922–8. Sang in CG int. seasons 1919–29.

Lichfild (Lichfield), **Henry** (*fl.* late 16th and early 17th cents.). Eng. musician, possible amateur, in service of Lady Cheney, of Toddington, nr. Luton. Composer of madrigals.

Lichnowsky, (Prince) **Karl** (*b* Vienna, 1761; *d* Vienna, 1814). Polish aristocrat who lived in Vienna. Patron of mus., maintaining str. qt. and sponsoring orch. concerts at his entertainments. Friend and patron of Mozart, then of Beethoven (whose Opp. 1, 13, 26, and 36 are ded. to him). Employed str. qt. led by Schuppanzigh which gave f.ps. of qts. by Haydn and Beethoven.

Lichnowsky, (Count) **Moritz** (*b* Vienna, 1771; *d* Vienna, 1837). Polish aristocrat, brother of Prince Karl. Intimate friend of Beethoven, whose Opp. 35, 51, and 90 are ded. to him and his wife.

Lidholm, Ingvar (*b* Jönköping, 1921). Swed. composer and cond. Comp. pupil of *Rosenberg. Studied London with *Seiber 1954 and adopted 12-note system. Head of chamber mus., Swed. Radio 1956–65, dir. of radio music planning from 1974. Works incl. conc. for str., pf. sonata, ballet, chamber mus.

Lie, Sigurd (*b* Drammen, 1871; *d* Drammen, 1904). Norweg. composer, violinist, and cond. Studied Berlin and Leipzig, 1891–4. Cond. in Bergen. Returned to Berlin for study. Works incl. sym., pf. quintet, vn. sonata, and songs.

Lié (Fr.). Bound, i.e. (1) Slurred.
   (2) Tied.

Liebe der Danae, Die (The Love of Danae). Opera in 3 acts by R. Strauss, comp. 1938–40 to lib. by J. Gregor using a draft by Hofmannsthal.

Prod. Salzburg 1952, London 1953, Los Angeles 1964 (but dress reh. was given at Salzburg 1944 in Strauss's presence, before ths. were closed by Nazi edict).

Liebermann, Rolf (*b* Zürich, 1910). Swiss composer, pupil of *Vogel. Head of orch. div., Swiss Radio 1950–7, head of mus. N. Ger. Radio, Hamburg, 1957–9, dir. Hamburg Opera 1959–73, Paris Opéra 1973–80. Champion of modern works, his Hamburg years seeing many splendid prods. of new operas. Uses 12-note system in his own works which incl.: Operas: *Leonore 40/45* (Basle 1952), *Penelope* (1954), and *Die Schule der Frauen* (1955); orchestral: *Furioso*, Sym. No. 1, Conc. for Jazz Band and Sym. Orch. (1954); also cantata, chamber mus., and songs.

Liebesgeige (Ger.) . Love-fiddle. *Viola d'amore.

Liebesliederwalzer (Love-song waltzes). Brahms's Op. 52 (containing 18 waltzes) for pf. duet with 4 vv. (SATB) *ad lib.* 1868–9. Op. 52a (1874) is minus the vocal parts. Followed in 1874 and 1877 by the *Neue Liebesliederwalzer*, also with v. parts *ad lib.*

Liebesmahl der Apostel, Das (The Love Feast of the Apostles). 'Biblical scene' for male ch. and orch. (which enters late in the work) by Wagner. F.p. Dresden 1843.

Liebesoboe (Ger.). Love-oboe, i.e. *oboe d'amore.

Liebestod (Ger.). Love-death. Title generally applied to Isolde's final aria at end of Act III of Wagner's *Tristan und Isolde* (or to orch. arr. of it, often played as concert-piece with the Prelude to Act 1). Wagner applied the term to the love duet in Act II.

Liebesträume (Love-dreams). 3 nocturnes for pf. (*c*.1850) by *Liszt, the 3rd in A♭ being the best-known. They are transcrs. of his songs *Hohe Liebe* (c.1849), *Gestorben war ich* (c.1849), and *O Liebe, so lang du lieben kannst.* (c.1845).

Liebesverbot, Das (The Ban on Love). Opera in 2 acts by Wagner to his own lib. based on Shakespeare's *Measure for Measure* (1604–5). Comp. 1835–6. Prod. Magdeburg 1836, London 1965.

Lieblich Gedackt (from Ger. *Lieblich*, 'lovely'). Org. stop, same as *Gedackt.

Lied, Lieder (Ger.). Song, songs. Lieder have existed since before 1400, but they are principally associated in the public mind with a distinctive type of Ger. solo vocal comp. that came into being as an outcome of the Romantic movement of the late 18th and early 19th cents. In this type the quality of the verse selected is very important. The treatment of the poem may be either 'verse-repeating' (strophic) or 'through-composed' (*durchkomponiert*) (i.e. either the same for every stanza or different for each), according to the lyrical or dramatic demands of the poem. The pf.

part (simple or highly elaborate) is more than a mere acc. and, as much as the vocal part, demands artistic interpretation. Some great names in the history of the Lied are *Schubert, J. *Loewe, *Schumann, *Franz, *Brahms, *Wolf, *Mahler, and *Strauss. Certain poets occur frequently in these composers' Lieder, e.g. Goethe, Dehmel, Eichendorff, Heine, Hesse, Liliencron, Mayrhofer, Mörike, Rilke, Rückert, Schack, Schiller, Trakl, Tieck. A *Lieder* recital should correctly contain only Ger. songs. A succinct appreciation of singing *Lieder* has been made by Peter *Stadlen: 'The elusive art of suggesting the dramatic content of a text by other than operatic means.'

Liederzyklus (Ger.). *Song-cycle.

Lieder eines fahrenden Gesellen (Songs of a wayfaring man). Song-cycle of 4 songs by Mahler to his own poems (based on, or imitative of, *Des *Knaben Wunderhorn*) for bar. or mez. and pf. or orch. The movements are: 1. *Wenn mein Schatz Hochzeit macht* (When my sweetheart has her wedding); 2. *Ging heut' Morgen übers Feld* (I walked this morning through the fields); 3. *Ich hab' ein glühend Messer* (I have a gleaming knife); 4. *Die zwei blauen Augen* (Her two blue eyes). Comp. 1884, later rev. F.p. Berlin 1896. Thematically linked to 1st Sym.

Liederkranz (Ger.). Song-wreath, i.e. *Song-cycle.

Liederkreis (Ger.). General term for song-cycle; used specifically by Schumann for 2 sets of songs, his 9 Heine settings, Op 24, and his 12 Eichendorff settings, Op. 39, both 1840. Term first used by Beethoven to describe *An die ferne Geliebte*.

Liedertafel (plural *Liedertafeln*) (Ger.). Song table. Name given to Ger. male-v. singing socs. which flourished in the nationalistic climate of the early 19th cent. Originally convivial occasions at which the members sat round a table with refreshments, but the aims later became more artistic. Particularly assoc. with expatriates.

Lied ohne Worte (Ger.; Fr. *Chanson sans paroles*). Song without words. Term introduced by Mendelssohn to describe pf. solo in which song-like melody progresses against acc. Pubd. in 8 books each containing 6 pieces: *Book I*, Op. 19, 1829–30; *Book 2*, Op. 30, 1835; *Book 3*, Op. 38, 1837; *Book 4*, Op. 53, 1841; *Book 5*, Op. 62, *Book 6*, Op. 67, 1843–5; *Book 7*, Op. 85, 1842; *Book 8*, Op. 102, 1842–5. Most of the titles given to these pieces were not Mendelssohn's, but the 3 *Venetian Gondola Songs* were. He also wrote a *Lied ohne Worte* for vc. and pf., Op. 109.

Lied von der Erde, Das (The Song of the Earth). Sym. for cont. (or bar.), ten., and orch. by Mahler, being settings of 6 Ger. versions by Hans Bethge (with additions by Mahler) of 8th-cent. Chinese poems. The movements are: 1. *Das Trinklied vom Jammer der Erde* (Drinking-Song of Earth's

Sorrow); 2. *Der Einsame im Herbst* (The Lonely One in Autumn); 3. *Von der Jugend* (Of Youth); 4. *Von der Schönheit* (Of Beauty); 5. *Der Trunkene im Frühling* (The Drunkard in Spring); 6. *Der Abschied* (The Farewell). Comp. 1907–09. F.p. Munich 1911, London 1914, Philadelphia 1916.

Lie Strewn the White Flocks. 'Pastoral' by Bliss for mez., ch., and orch. f.p. London 1929. Settings of poems by Jonson, Fletcher, Poliziano, Theocritus, and Robert Nichols.

Lieutenant Kijé. 5-movement symphonic suite for orch., Op. 60, by Prokofiev, derived from mus. he wrote for film of same name. Comp. 1934; suite f.p. Paris 1937.

Life for the Tsar, A. Opera in 4 acts and epilogue by ★Glinka to lib. by Baron Georgy Rosen on subject suggested by poet Zhukovsky. Prod. St Petersburg 1836, London 1887. Prague prod. of 1866 was first perf. of Russ. opera abroad. Orig. title was *Ivan Susanin*, the peasant who, by misleading Polish troops in 1613, saved life of Tsar Mikhail, founder of Romanov dynasty, at sacrifice of his own. During rehearsals Tsar Nicholas I visited Bolshoy Th., with result that the opera was ded. to him and its title changed. After 1917 revolution, subject was embarrassing to régime and various attempts to adapt mus. to new subjects were made. In 1939 S. M. Gorodetsky re-wrote Rosen's lib., re-focusing interest on leaders of uprising against Poles and restoring orig. title.

Life's Dance. Tone-poem for orch. by Delius, after Hilge Rode's play *Dansen Gaar*. 1st version 1899 as *La Ronde se déroule* (The Dance goes on), rev. 1901 as *Life's Dance*, final rev. for publication 1912. F.p. of orig., London 1899; 1st rev. Düsseldorf 1904 cond. ★Buths, final version Berlin 1912 cond. ★Fried.

Ligature. (1) The sign which in early notation (13th–16th cent.) combines several notes into one symbol:

(2) The slur which in modern notation of vocal mus. shows that the 2 or more notes it affects are to be fitted to the same syllable, or, in instr. mus., that the notes are to be phrased together.
(3) The tie or bind (see *Tie*)—a use of the word better avoided as unnecessary and confusing.
(4) The adjustable metal band which in instr. of the cl. family secures the reed to the mouthpiece. Some clarinettists use string ligature.
See *Curved Line, Various uses of*.

Ligendza, Caterina (*b* Stockholm, 1937). Swed. sop. Studied Vienna, Stuttgart, and Berlin (with Greindl). Opera début Linz 1963 (Countess in *Figaro*). Brunswick Opera 1964–5. Became nota-

ble for Wagner roles. Sang Brünnhilde (*Siegfried*), Geneva 1968. Salzburg Easter Fest. 1969, Bayreuth Fest. 1971–7 as Isolde and Brünnhilde. CG début 1972 (Senta), Vienna 1973 (Isolde), La Scala, Milan, 1970 (Arabella), NY Met. 1971 (Beethoven's Leonore).

Ligeti, György (*b* Dicsöszentmáron, 1923). Hung. composer. Studied Kolozsvár Cons., 1941–3, with Farkas and after the war at Budapest Acad. with Farkas and Veress, teaching there from 1950. Left Hungary 1956, going to work first at Cologne elec. studio, then settling in Austria. Though elec. stimulated his urge to compose, since 1958 he has written only for 'live' performers. His orch. writing uses precisely calculated textures and dense (but not thick) scoring, deriving ultimately from Webern (Ligeti's term is 'micropolyphony'). Prin. works:

OPERA: *Le ★Grand Macabre* (2 acts, f.p. Stockholm 1978).

ORCH: *Apparitions* (1958–9); ★*Atmosphères* (1961); ★*Lontano* (1967); ★*Melodien* (1971); ★*San Francisco Polyphony* (1973–4).

SOLOIST AND ORCH: Vc. conc. (1966); Double Conc. for fl. and ob. (1972).

CHORAL: *Requiem* (sop., mez., 2 ch., orch.) (1963–5); *Lux aeterna*, 16-part ch. (1966); *Clocks and Clouds* for 12-voice women's ch. and orch. (1972–3).

SMALL ORCH: *Fragment* for 11 instr. (1961); *Adventures* for 3 singers and 7 instr. (1962); *Nouvelles Aventures*, 3 singers, 7 instr. (1962–5); ★*Ramifications*, for str., or 12 solo str. (1968–9); Chamber Conc., for 13 instr. (1969–70).

CHAMBER MUSIC: 10 *Pieces* for wind quintet (1968); Str. Qt. No. 1 (*Metamorphoses nocturnes*) (1953–4), No. 2 (1968); 6 *Miniatures* for 10 wind instr. (1953, scored 1975 by F. Wanek); hn. trio (*Hommage à Brahms*) (1983).

ORGAN: *Volumina* (1961–2, rev. 1966); 2 *Studies* (1967, 1969).

2 PIANOS: 3 *Pieces* (*Monument, Selbstporträt, Bewegung*) (1976); 3 *Objekte* (1976).

MISCELLANEOUS: *Artikulation*, for tape (1958); *Poème symphonique* for 100 metronomes (1962); *Continuum* for hpd. (1968); *Horizont*, for recorder (1971).

Light. Adjective applied somewhat patronizingly and vaguely to mus. which is supposed to need less concentration than 'serious music' (another objectionable term). Thus there are also 'light' orchs. and 'light' opera. 'Light' mus. can refer to Elgar's shorter pieces or to works by composers such as Ronald ★Binge. 'Light opera' probably means ★*Merrie England* rather than *The Merry Widow*, but such classification is imprecise and unhelpful.

Light Cavalry (*Leichte Cavallerie*). Operetta by Suppé, in 2 acts, lib. by C. Costa; prod. Vienna 1866. Ov. exceedingly popular.

Lighthouse, The. Chamber-opera in 1 act by *Maxwell Davies to his own lib. Comp. 1979. Based on actual event in 1900 when the 3 keepers of the Flannan lighthouse in the Outer Hebrides unaccountably disappeared. F.p. Edinburgh 1980. London 1981, Boston 1983.

Light of Life, The (*Lux Christi*). Oratorio, Op. 29, for SATB soloists, ch., and orch. by Elgar to text by E. Capel-Cure. F.p. Worcester 1896.

Lights Out. (1) Song-cycle of 6 songs, settings of poems by Edward Thomas (1878–1917) by Ivor *Gurney, comp. 1918–25, for v. and pf.
 (2) 4 poems of Edward Thomas for bar. and pf. by R. *Holloway, Op. 24, 1974.

Lilac Time (Berté). See *Blossom Time.*

Lilburn, Douglas (Gordon) (*b* Wanganui, N.Z., 1915). N.Z. composer. Studied RCM with Vaughan Williams (Cobbett Prize 1939). Prof. of mus., Victoria Univ. Coll., Wellington, N.Z. and dir. of its elec. mus studio. Comps. incl. 3 syms. and other orch. works, str. qts., vn. sonatas, str. trio, pf. sonata, cl. sonata, song-cycles, film mus.

Lill, John (Richard) (*b* London, 1944). Eng. pianist. Studied RCM 1955–64 and with Kempff. Début London 1963. First prize Moscow Tchaikovsky competition 1970. Soloist with all leading orchs. Outstanding Beethoven player. O.B.E. 1978.

Lilliburlero. Tune of unknown origin, first appeared in print in 1686 in a book of 'lessons' for the recorder or fl., where it is styled 'Quickstep'. In the following year it achieved popularity set to satirical verses (with the mock Irish word 'Lilliburlero' as a refrain) referring to the appointment to the Lord-Lieutenant of Ireland of General Talbot, newly-created Earl of Tyrconnel, whose name is mentioned several times. It has remained a song of the Orange party to the present day, set to different words as 'Protestant Boys'. In Purcell's *Musick's Handmaid*, it appears under the title 'A New Irish Tune' as a hpd. piece: Purcell also used it as a *ground bass in mus. for the play *The Gordian Knot unty'd* (1691).

Lincoln Center for the Performing Arts. Arts centre in NY with following constituents: Metropolitan Opera House, Philharmonic Hall, Juilliard Sch., State Th. (headquarters of NY City Opera and City Ballet), Repertory Th., Film Soc., and Chamber Mus. Soc. First building to open was Philharmonic Hall, home of NY P.O. in place of Carnegie Hall, 1962. State Th. opened 1964, new Met. 1966, and Juilliard Sch. 1969.

Lincoln Portrait, A. Work for speaker and orch. by Copland, comp. 1942. Spoken words are taken from the speeches of Abraham Lincoln.

Lincoln, the Great Commoner. Song by Ives to words by Edwin Markham, for ch. and orch. 1912, for v. and pf. 1914.

Lindholm, Berit (*b* Stockholm, 1934). Swedish soprano. At Stockholm Opera Sch. 1961–3. Début Stockholm 1963 as Countess in *Figaro*. CG début 1966 as Chrysothemis in Strauss's *Elektra*. Sang Brünnhilde at Bayreuth, CG, and with Scottish Opera (1971).

Lind, Jenny (Johanna) (*b* Stockholm, 1820; *d* Malvern Wells, Worcs., 1887). Swed. sop. Studied Stockholm. Début Stockholm Opera 1838 as Agathe in *Der Freischütz*. Dissatisfied with her v., went to Paris 1841 to study with M. P. R. *García. Meyerbeer commended her to Berlin, where she sang Norma, 1844, and created leading role in Meyerbeer's *Feldlager in Schlesien* (later rev. as *L'*Étoile du Nord*). After singing in Hamburg, Stockholm, Frankfurt, Vienna (1846), and elsewhere, causing a sensation wherever she appeared, she made her London début at Her Majesty's, 1847, in *Robert le Diable*. In same year created role of Amelia in Verdi's *I Masnadieri*. Excelled in brilliant coloratura roles (*Sonnambula*, etc.). Retired from opera 1849, thereafter singing only in oratorio and concerts. Visited US 1850–2 under auspices of Barnum and acc. by Julius Benedict, the conductor, and Giovanni Belletti, the baritone who had advised her to consult García in 1841. In Boston, Mass., married the cond. Otto *Goldschmidt, returning with him to Dresden 1852–5 and then to London, where she helped him to found the *Bach Choir. Retired 1870. Prof. of singing RCM 1883. Worked for charitable causes. Her voice was remarkable for its purity and agility in cadenzas and ornamentation. Known as 'The Swedish Nightingale'.

Linda di Chamounix. Opera in 3 acts by Donizetti to lib. by Rossi based on *vaudeville La Grace de Dieu*. Prod. Vienna 1842, London 1843, NY 1847, Wexford 1983.

Lindley, Robert (*b* Rotherham, 1776; *d* London, 1855). Eng. cellist, pupil of Cervetto. Prin. cellist of opera orch. in London 1794–1851. Recital partner with *Dragonetti. First prof. of vc. RAM 1822. Comp. vc. pieces.

Linear counterpoint. Term used specifically to describe type of 20th-cent. counterpoint with emphasis on the individual strands of the fabric rather than on their harmonic implications—but all counterpoint is by nature linear.

Linke Hand (*Links*) (Ger.). Left hand.

Linley, Thomas (*b* Badminton, 1733; *d* London, 1795). Eng. composer. Taught and gave concerts in Bath. Later joint manager of oratorios at Drury Lane Th., London, which he partly owned from 1776. Wrote mus. for many plays, incl. Sheridan's *The Duenna* and *School For Scandal*, also songs, cantatas, madrigals, and elegies. Daughter Elizabeth (1754–92), sop., married Sheridan.

Linley, Thomas (*b* Bath, 1756; *d* Grimsthorpe, Lincs., 1778). Eng. composer and violinist, son of

Thomas *Linley. Pupil of Boyce and later, at Florence, of Nardini. Friend of Mozart. Wrote opera *The Cady of Baghdad* (1778), oratorio, incidental mus. (incl. *The Duenna* with his father), 6 vn. sonatas, at least 20 vn. concs. (only one survives), and songs. Drowned in boating accident.

Linz Symphony. Mozart's Sym. No. 36 in C major (K425), comp. Linz 1783 and first played there.

Lipatti, Dinu (Constantin) (*b* Bucharest, 1917; *d* Geneva, 1950). Romanian pianist and composer. Studied Bucharest Cons. 2nd prize, Vienna int. contest 1934. Studied in Paris with Cortot, Munch, Dukas, and Boulanger. On staff Geneva Cons. Superb artist, whose career was ended by leukaemia. Visited Eng. 4 times 1946–8. Comp. concertino for pf. and chamber orch. (1936), *Romanian Dances* for orch., and pf. sonata for left hand (1941).

Lipkin, Malcolm (Leyland) (*b* Liverpool, 1932). Eng. pianist and composer. Studied pf. with Gordon Green 1944–59, comp. with Seiber 1954–7, RCM 1949–53. Début, Holland 1951. Extramural lecturer, Oxford Univ. 1965–75, Kent Univ. from 1975. Prin. works:

ORCH: Symphonies: No. 1 (*Sinfonia di Roma*) (1958–65), No. 2 (*The Pursuit*) (1975–9), No. 3 (*Sun*) (1979–82); Pf. Conc. (1957); Vn. Conc. No. 2 (1960–2); Fl. Conc. (1974); *Pastorale*, hn. and str. (1963, rev. 1979); *Mosaics* (1966, rev. 1969).

CHORAL: *Psalm 96*, ch. and orch. (1969); *The White Crane*, young vv., orch. (1972).

CHAMBER MUSIC: Str. qt. (1951); Vn. sonata (1957); *Suite*, fl. and vc. (1961); str. trio (1963–4); *Interplay*, treble recorder, va. da gamba, hpd., perc. (1975); *Clifford's Tower*, fl., ob., cl., bn., hn., vn., va., vc. (1977); *Pastorale*, hn. (or ob.), pf. (1979); *Naboth's Vineyard*, recorders, vc., hpd. (1981–2).

PIANO: Sonata No. 3 (1951, rev. 1979), No. 4 (1955).

Lipp, Wilma (*b* Vienna, 1925). Austrian sop. Studied Vienna with Mildenburg and Jerger. Début Vienna 1943. Vienna State Opera from 1945, CG début 1951 (Gilda), Glyndebourne 1957 (Constanze), S. Francisco 1962 (Nannetta).

Lira (It.). (1) The *lyre.
(2) One of names indiscriminately applied in medieval times to various bowed str. instrs., e.g. *rebec and *vielle.
(3) Part of compound name of such old instr. as *lira da braccio*, offshoot of the fiddle which evolved in 2nd half of 15th cent. and in size approximated to modern va. It had 7 str., incl. 2 drones, and was used by recitalists who improvised polyphonic accs. It was played against the shoulder, like a vn. Leonardo da Vinci played it. From it developed the *lirone* or *lira da gamba*, a combination of bass viol and *lira da braccio*, held between knees like a

vc. It had drone strs., and from 9 to 14 stopped str., tuned in 4ths, 5ths, and octaves. Used in court entertainments *c*.1550–1650, and in *intermedii*.

Lira organizzata (It.). Organ lyre. Obsolete str. instr. like hurdy-gurdy, in which wooden wheel replaced bow and small org. attachment was built into body to enrich tone-colour effects. Haydn wrote 6 concs. (of which 5 survive) *c*.1786 and 9 *Notturnos* (of which 8 survive) for 2 *lire organizzate* in 1788–90 for King Ferdinand IV of Naples who enjoyed playing duets with his teacher. The 2nd and 4th movements of his Sym. No 89 in F are revs. of material used in the 5th of these concs., and the 2nd movt. of his Sym. No. 100 ('Military') originated in 3rd conc.

Lisle. See *Rouget de Lisle, Claude Joseph*.

Lisley, John (*fl.* 17th cent.). Eng. composer. Madrigal *Fair Cytherea* incl. in The *Triumphs of Oriana*.

L'Istesso (It.). See *Istesso*.

List, Eugene (*b* Philadelphia, 1918; *d* NY, 1985). Amer. pianist. Début with Los Angeles P.O. 1930. Studied in Philadelphia with Olga Samaroff. Gave f. Amer. p. of Shostakovich's 1st conc., Philadelphia 1934. Champion of *Gottschalk. Taught at Eastman Sch. of Mus., Rochester, 1964–75, then at NY Univ.

Liszt, Ferencz (Franz) (baptized as Franciscus) (*b* Raiding, Hung., 1811; *d* Bayreuth, 1886). Hung. composer and pianist. A child prodigy, he gave his first pf. recital at age 9. Went to Vienna in 1821, having lessons from Salieri and Czerny. Played in Paris 1823 and London 1824 (where he was received by George IV). Returned to Eng. in 1825 and 1826; operetta *Don Sanche* was prod. in Paris, 1825, where he lived 1823–35, becoming friend of Berlioz and Chopin and of leading literary figures and painters. His fame as a virtuoso pianist, flamboyant in style and taste, was at its height. From 1833 he lived with Countess Marie d'Agoult; of their 3 children, Cosima (*b* 1837) became the wife of *Bülow and then of *Wagner. He returned to Vienna in 1838 and to London in 1840 and 1841. Until 1847 he toured widely, incl. Russia, his mistress by now being Princess Carolyn Sayn-Wittgenstein.

In 1848 he became Kapellmeister at the Weimar court, staying until 1859. In this decade he made Weimar a pre-eminent mus. centre, conducting a vast number of works, notably by Berlioz and by his friend Wagner whom he had met in 1842. In 1850 he conducted the f.p. of *Lohengrin. These were also rich years for Liszt's own work; he wrote his *Faust* and *Dante* syms., 12 symphonic poems, and much else. From 1860 Liszt lived in Rome in the Villa d'Este, and in 1865 took minor orders, becoming the Abbé Liszt. He comp. much religious mus. at this period, incl. *The Legend of St. Elizabeth* and *Christus*. From 1869 he divided his time between Rome, Weimar, and Budapest, and his amorous adventures were still the talk of Europe. In the last 5 years of his life he concentrated on teaching, his pupils incl. *Ziloty, *Lamond, *Rosenthal, and *Weingartner, and entered a new and important compositional phase in which his harmonic innovations, always a significant feature, anticipated the 'impressionism' of Debussy, e.g. in *Nuages gris* and the *Csárdás macabre*. In 1886 he made a 'jubilee tour' to mark his 75th birthday, revisiting Paris and London.

As a pianist, Liszt was, from all reliable accounts, among the greatest, if not the greatest, there has ever been. His comps. have taken longer to win a rightful place, but they are now recognized as occupying a high place for their own virtues as well as for their undoubted influence on Wagner, R. Strauss, and subsequent composers. The pf. works are in a category of their own, the symphonic poems developed a new art-form, the syms. are compelling and imaginative, the religious works are moving and visionary, and the songs hold their own in high company. He remains a romantic enigma of mus., a genius with a touch of the charlatan, a virtuoso with the flair of an actor-manager, a man generous to colleagues and to the young. His championship of Wagner in the Weimar years, with its subsequent effect on Brahms and Schumann, thereby causing the great schism in 19th-cent. mus., had incalculable results on the art. Prin. works:

SYMPHONIES: *A* *Faust Symphony, for ten., male ch., orch. (1854-7); *Dante Symphony (1855–6, with choral *Magnificat* as 3rd movt.).

SYMPHONIC-POEMS: *Ce qu'on entend sur la montagne* ('Bergsymphonie') (What one hears on the mountain) (1848–9, orch. Raff, rev. 1850, 1854); *Tasso: lamento e trionfo* (1849, orch. Conradi, rev. 1850–1, orch. Raff, rev. 1854); *Les* *Préludes (1848, rev. before 1854); *Orpheus (1853–4); *Prometheus (1850, orch. Raff, rev. 1855); *Mazeppa (1851, orch. with Raff, rev. before 1854; based on 1840 pf. study); *Festklänge* (1853); *Héroïde funèbre* (1849–50, orch. Raff, rev. c.1854); *Hungaria* (1854); *Hamlet (1858); *Hunnenschlacht (1856–7); *Die Ideale* (1857); *Von der Wiege bis zum Grabe* (From the Cradle to the Grave) (1881–2).

MISC. ORCH: 2 *Episodes from Lenau's* *Faust: 1. *Der nächtliche Zug* (The Night Ride), 2. *Der Tanz in der Dorfschenke* (Dance in the Village Inn, also **Mephisto Waltz No. 1*) (before 1861); **Mephisto Waltz No. 2* (1880–1); *Huldigungsmarsch* (1853, rev. 1857, orig. for pf.); *3 Odes funèbres* (*Les Morts; La Notte; Le triomphe funèbre du Tasse* (1860–6); *Rákóczy March (1865); *6* **Hungarian Rhapsodies* (orch., in collab. with F. Doppler, from pf. solos. Orch. No. 1 is pf. No. 14, No. 2 (No. 12), No. 3 (No. 6), No. 4 (No. 2), No. 5 (No. 5), No. 6 (No. 9, 2nd version) (date unknown).

PIANO AND ORCH: Conc. No. 1 in E♭ (1849, collab. Raff; rev. 1853, 1856), No. 2 in A major (1839, revs. 1849–61); *Malédiction*, pf., str. (c.1840); *Fantasia on Themes from Beethoven's Ruins of Athens* (?1852); *Fantasia on Hungarian Folk Melodies* (*Hungarian Fantasia*, based on *Hungarian Rhapsody No. 14 in F minor* for solo pf.) (?1852); *Totentanz (1849, rev. 1853, 1859); **Rapsodie espagnole* (c.1863 solo pf., orch. Busoni).

OPERA: *Don Sanche* (1824–5, collab. Paer).

SACRED CHORAL: *Die* **Legende von der heiligen Elisabeth*, oratorio, sop., cont., ten., 3 bar., bass, ch., org., orch. (1857–62); *Christus, oratorio, sop., cont., ten., bar., bass, ch., org., orch. (1862–7); *Cantico del Sol di S. Francesco d'Assisi*, bar., male ch., org., orch. (1862, rev. 1880–1); *Mass*, 4 male vv., org. (1848, rev. 1859; 2nd version, 1869); *Missa solemnis*, sop., cont., ten., bass, ch., orch. (1855, rev. 1857–8); *Missa Choralis*, ch., org. (1865); *Hungarian Coronation Mass*, sop., cont., ten., bass, orch. (1867); *Requiem*, 2 ten., 2 bass, male vv., org., opt. brass (1867–8); *Psalm 13*, ten., ch., orch. (1855, rev. 1859); *Psalm 116*, male vv., pf. (1869); *Ave verum corpus*, ch., opt. org. (1871); *St Christopher*, bar., women's ch., pf., harmonium (after 1874); *Via Crucis* (1878–9); *Rosario* (1879); *Psalm 129*, bar., male vv., org. (1881); *Qui seminant in lacrimis*, mixed ch., org. (1884); *Salve Regina*, unacc. ch. (1885).

SECULAR CHORAL: *Second Beethoven Cantata*, sop., cont., ten., bass, double ch., orch. (1869–70); *An die Künstler*, 2 ten., 2 bass, male ch., orch. (1853, orch. Raff, rev. 1853, 1856); *Choruses from Herder's Entfesseltem Prometheus*, sop., cont., 2 ten., 2 bass, double ch., orch. (1850, orch. Raff, rev. 1855); *Hungaria 1848*, cantata, sop., ten., bass, male vv., orch. (1848, orch. Conradi); *Für Männergesang*, 12 songs, some with acc. (1842–59).

CHAMBER MUSIC: *Romance oubliée*, pf. qt. (1880); *La lugubre gondola*, pf. trio (1882, also pf. solo); *At Richard Wagner's Grave*, str. qt., harp (1883).

PIANO: *Étude en 12 Exercises* (1826); *24 Grandes Études* (1837); *Mazeppa (1840, orch. 1851); *6* **Études d'exécution transcendante d'après Paganini* (1838, rev. 1851 as *Grandes Études de Paganini*); *12* **Études d'exécution transcendante* (*Transcendental Studies*) (1851); *Apparitions* (1834); *Album d'un voyageur* (3 books, 1835–6); *3* **Sonetti del Petrarca* (?1839–46); *Venezia e Napoli* (c.1840, rev. 1859); **Années de Pèlerinage*, Book 1 'Switzerland', 9 pieces (1848–54, all but 2 pieces based on *Album d'un voyageur*), Book 2 'Italy', 7 pieces (1837–49), Book 3, 7 pieces (1867–77); *Harmonies poétiques et réligieuses*, 10 pieces (1845–52); *6* *Consolations (1849–50); *Grosses Konzertsolo* (?1849, arr. 2 pf. c.1855 as *Concerto pathétique*, and for pf. and orch. as *Grand Solo de Concert* ?1850); *Liebesträume—*3 Notturnos* (c.1850, transcr. of songs); *Scherzo und Marsch* (1851); *Sonata in B minor* (1852–3); *Huldigungsmarsch* (1853, arr. for orch. 1853, rev. 1857); *Berceuse* (1854, rev. 1862); *2 Concert Studies* (*Waldesrauschen, Gnomenreigen*)

(?1862–3); 2 *Légendes* (St Francis of Assisi preaching to the birds, St Francis of Paule walking on the waves) (1863); 'Weinen, Klagen, Sorgen, Zagen' prelude (1859); *Rapsodie espagnole* (c.1863); *Weihnachtsbaum*, 12 pieces (1874–6); *Nuages gris* (1881); *La lugubre gondola* (1882); *R.W.-Venezia* (1883); *Mephisto Waltz No. 3* (1883); 4 *Valses oubliées* (1881–?1885); *Csárdás macabre* (1881–2); *Mephisto Waltz No. 4* (1885); *Csárdás obstiné* (1886); 19 *Hungarian Rhapsodies* (1846–85, see also Orch.) (No. 1 in C♯, 1846; No. 2 in C♯, 1847; No. 3 in B♭; No. 4 in E♭; No. 5 *Heroïde-elégiaque* in E minor; No. 6 in D♭; No. 7 in D minor; No. 8 in F♯; No. 9 in E♭, 1st version publ. 1848, 2nd version publ. 1853; No. 10 in E; No. 11 in A minor; No. 12 in C♯; No. 13 in A minor; No. 14 in F minor; No. 15 *Rákóczy March*, 1st version publ. 1851, 2nd version publ. 1871; No. 16 in A minor, 1882; No. 17 in D minor, 1885; No. 18 in C♯, 1885; No. 19 in D minor, 1885).

PIANO TRANSCRIPTIONS: Liszt's transcr. of his own works are too numerous for listing here. A selective list follows of his transcr. of works by other composers (operatic transcr. are listed separately): J. S. BACH: *Fantasia and Fugue in G minor* (BWV 542) (1863); BEETHOVEN: Syms. Nos. 5, 6, and 7 (1837), remaining 6 (1863–4), *Septet, Op. 20* (1841); BERLIOZ: *Symphonie fantastique* (1833, finale rev. 1864–5), *Harold en Italie* (c.1836, rev. 1862), *Danse des Sylphes* (c.1860); CHOPIN: 6 *Chants Polonais* (1847–60); MENDELSSOHN: 7 *Lieder* (1840); PAGANINI: *Grand Fantasia de bravoure sur La Clochette* (on *La Campanella* from Violin Conc. in B minor, Op. 7) (1831–2, rev. as No. 3 of *Études d'exécution transcendante d'après Paganini*, 1838); ROSSINI: 12 *Soirées Musicales* (1837), Ov., *William Tell* (1838); SAINT-SAËNS: *Danse macabre* (1876); SCHUBERT: 12 *Lieder* (1837–8), *Schwanengesang* (1838–9), *Winterreise* (1839); SCHUMANN: *Widmung* (1848).

PIANO TRANSCRIPTIONS FROM OPERAS: BELLINI: *Réminiscences des Puritains* (1836), *Hexaméron* (vars. on march from *I Puritani*, collab. with Thalberg, Pixis, Herz, Czerny, Chopin) (1837), *Fantaisie sur les motifs favoris de l'opéra La Sonnambula* (1839, rev. 1840–1), *Réminiscences de Norma* (1841); DONIZETTI: *Réminiscences de Lucia di Lammermoor* (1835–6), *Réminiscences de Lucrezia Borgia* (1840); HALÉVY: *Réminiscences de La Juive* (1835); MEYERBEER: *Grande Fantaisie sur des thèmes de l'opera Les Huguenots* (1836), *Réminiscences de Robert le Diable* (1841); MOZART: *Réminiscences de Don Juan* (1841); TCHAIKOVSKY: *Eugene Onegin: Polonaise* (1880); VERDI: *Concert Paraphrase on Themes from Ernani* (1847), *Miserere du Trovatore* (1859), *Rigoletto: paraphrase de concert* (1859), *Don Carlos: Coro di festa e marcia funebre* (1867–8), *Réminiscences de Simone Boccanegra* (1882); WAGNER: *Phantasiestück on themes from Rienzi* (1859), Ov. *Tannhäuser* (1848), 2 *Pieces from Lohengrin* (1854), *Isolde's Liebestod* (1867), *Am stillen Herd* from *Die Meistersinger*

(1871), *Feierlicher Marsch zum heiligen Gral, Parsifal* (1882); WEBER: *Fantasia on Themes from Der Freischütz* (1840), Ov. *Oberon* (1843), Ov. *Der Freischütz* (1846).

SONGS (selected list): *Tre *Sonetti di Petrarca* (1838–9); *Die Loreley* (Heine) (1841); *Mignons Lied* (Goethe) (1842); *Es war ein König in Thule* (Goethe) (1842); *Oh! quand je dors* (Hugo) (1842); *Du bist wie eine Blume* (Heine) (c.1843); *Jeanne d'Arc au bûcher* (Dumas) (1845, arr. v. and orch. 1858, rev. 1874); *En ces lieux* (Monnier) (1854); *Die drei Zigeuner* (Lenau) (1860); *Go not, happy day* (Tennyson) (1879); *Verlassen* (Michell) (1880).

ORGAN: *Prelude and Fugue on the Name of Bach* (1885, rev. 1870); *Requiem* (1879); *At Richard Wagner's Grave* (1883).

Litaize, Gaston (b Ménil-sur-Belvitte, 1909). Fr. organist and composer, blind from youth. Studied Paris Cons. with M. Dupré (org.) and Busser (comp.). Organist, St François-Xavier, Paris, from 1946. Composer of org. and church mus., also pf. sonata and pf. concertino.

Litany. Christian prayer for supplication—'Deliver us, O Lord', etc.—often set to mus. Sometimes the title of instr. works, e.g. *Fricker's Litany* for double str. orch.

Literes, Antonio (b Artá, Majorca, 1673; d Madrid, 1747). Sp. composer and organist. Organist, Chapel Royal, Madrid, from 1693. Wrote church mus., operas, zarzuelas (incl. *Accis y Galatea*, 1708).

Litolff, Henry Charles (b London, 1818; d Paris, 1891). Fr. composer and pianist of Anglo-Alsatian parentage. Studied with *Moscheles. Début London 1832. Settled in Paris 1835. Cond. at Warsaw 1841–4. Became mus. publisher, Brunswick, 1851. Pioneered popular cheap edns. 1861. Returned to Paris to compose. Wrote 6 operas, operettas, oratorio, *Scenes from Goethe's Faust*, pf. solos, chamber mus., and 5 *Concerts-symphoniques* for pf. and orch. (No. 4, c.1852, contains often-played *Scherzo*).

Little Clavier-book (Bach). See *Klavierbüchlein*.

Little Night Music, A. Eng. trans. of Mozart's title *Eine *kleine Nachtmusik*. Also title of Amer. musical by Stephen *Sondheim.

Little Organ-book (J. S. Bach). See *Orgelbüchlein*.

Little Organ Mass (Haydn). See *Kleine Orgelmesse*.

'Little Russian' Symphony. Nickname for *Tchaikovsky's Sym. No. 2 in C minor (1872), so-called because of use of folk-songs from Ukraine ('Little Russia'). 2nd vers. 1879–80.

Little Sweep, The (Britten). See *Let's Make an Opera*.

Liturgy. This, properly, means the service of the Christian Eucharist, but in ordinary usage is now applied to any written and officially authorized form of service. The evolution of liturgies has had a great influence on the development of mus., especially because, for many centuries, almost the only literate and trained musicians were those of the Church and the only fully organized mus. that of its services.

Lituus. Ancient Roman cavalry tpt., made of bronze. Bell was curved and upturned to give shape of letter J. In Cantata No. 118, Bach scored for 2 *litui* (ten. tpts.).

Liuto (It.). The *Lute.

Liverpool Philharmonic Orchestra. See *Royal Liverpool Philharmonic Orchestra.*

L.L.C.M. Licentiate of the London Coll. of Mus.

Llewellyn, William (Benjamin James) (*b* Farnworth, 1925). Eng. cond., composer, and teacher. Studied RAM. Ass. mus. master, Charterhouse Sch. 1950–65, dir. of mus. from 1965. Founder and cond. Linden Singers 1950–9. Composer of hymns and songs.

Llobet, Miguel (*b* Barcelona, 1878; *d* Barcelona, 1938). Sp. guitarist and composer. Pupil of Tárrega. Settled in Paris 1902–14, making extensive tours. Visited S. America 1910 and 1912, USA 1915–17.

Lloyd, Charles (Harford) (*b* Thornbury, Glos., 1849; *d* Slough, 1919). Eng. organist and composer. Studied Oxford Univ. Organist, Gloucester Cath. 1876–82, Ch. Ch. Cath., Oxford 1882–92. Prof. of organ and comp. RCM 1887–92. Mus. dir., Eton Coll. 1892–1914. Organist, Chapel Royal from 1914. Founder Oxford Univ. Mus. Club. Wrote cantatas, church mus., motet, org. conc., etc.

Lloyd, Edward (*b* London, 1845; *d* Worthing, 1927). Eng. ten. Chorister, Westminster Abbey to 1860. Gentleman of Chapel Royal 1869–71. Had great success at Gloucester Fest. 1871 in Bach's *St Matthew Passion*, leading to outstanding career in oratorios and cantatas. Amer. début 1888. Sang ten. part at f.p. of Elgar's *King Olaf,* 1896, and was first Gerontius in1900, the year of his retirement.

Lloyd, George (*b* St Ives, Cornwall, 1913). Eng. composer. Studied vn. with Albert *Sammons and comp. with H. Farjeon. Composer of operas to libs. by his father, William Lloyd (*Iernin,* 1933–4; *The Serf,* 1936–8; and *John Socman,* 1951); 11 syms., 4 pf. concs., 2 vn. concs., pf. and vn. pieces, etc. O.B.E. 1970.

Lloyd, Jonathan (*b* London, 1948). Eng. composer. Studied comp. with E. Spira 1963–5, at RCM 1965–9 (comp. with Roxburgh, Lambert, and T. Cary). Attended Ligeti's classes at Tanglewood, 1973. Lived in Paris 1969–70. Was busker and street musician 1974–7. Works incl.:

MUSIC THEATRE: *Scattered Ruins,* sop., ens. (1973); *Musices Genus,* sop., ens. (1974).

ORCH: *Time Caught by the Tail,* str. and perc. (1969); *Cantique* (1968, rev. 1970); Va. Conc. (1979–80); *Fantasy,* vn., orch. (1980); *3 Dances* (1981–2); *Rhapsody,* vc. and orch. (1982).

VOICE(S) AND INSTR: *Everything Returns,* sop. (wordless) and orch. (1977–8); *Towards the Whitening Dawn,* ch., chamber orch. (1980); *If I Could Turn You On,* sop., chamber orch. (1981).

ENSEMBLE: *Won't It Ever be Morning?* (1980); *Waiting for Gozo* (1981); *Don't Mention the War,* 8 players (1982); *The Shorelines of Certainty,* 9 instr. (1984).

VOCAL: *Till the Wind Blows,* sop. (1969); *3 Songs,* v., va., pf. (1980).

CHAMBER MUSIC: *John's Journal,* sax., pf. (1980); Str. Quintets No. 1 (1982), No. 2, mandolin, lute, guitar, hp., db. (1982); wind quintet (1982); brass quintet (1982).

Lloyd, Richard (*b* Stockport, 1933). Eng. organist and composer. Studied Lichfield Cath. Sch. and Cambridge Univ. Sub-organist, Salisbury Cath. 1957–66, organist, Hereford Cath. and cond. 3 Choirs Fest. 1966–74, Durham Cath. from 1974. Composer of anthems etc., mus. for children and incidental mus.

Lloyd, Robert (*b* Southend-on-Sea, 1940). Eng. bass-bar. Studied London Opera Centre and with Otakar *Kraus. SW 1969. CG from 1972, singing Philip II in *Don Carlos* and the title-role in *Boris Godunov* 1983. La Scala, Milan, 1976 (*Les Troyens*). Munich Critics' Prize 1979. Frequent visitor to Aix-en-Provence opera. Sang Gurnemanz in Syberberg film of *Parsifal,* 1981. Fine interpreter of Schubert's *Winterreise.* Recorded Elgar's *Dream of Gerontius* with Boult.

Lloyd-Jones, David (Mathias) (*b* London, 1934). Eng. cond. Studied Oxford Univ. Guest cond. with many opera cos., incl. CG (début 1971, *Boris Godunov*), ENO, Wexford, Scottish Opera, and WNO, and BBC TV opera. Prin. cond. Opera North (Leeds) from 1978. Ed. full score of Mussorgsky's *Boris Godunov,* 1975, and Borodin's *Prince Igor,* 1982. Cond. f. Eng. ps. of Fauré's *Pénélope* (1970) and Haydn's *La fedeltà premiata* (1971) and f. Eng. stage p. of Prokofiev's *War and Peace* (1973). Cond. f.p. of Josephs's *Rebecca,* 1983.

Lloyd Webber, Andrew (*b* London, 1948). Eng. composer. Studied Oxford Univ., GSM, and RCM. With Tim Rice (*b* 1944) as librettist, comp. highly successful musicals, *Joseph and the Amazing Technicolor Dreamcoat* (1968), *Jesus Christ Superstar* (1970), and *Evita* (1976). Wrote *Jeeves* (1975) on text by Alan Ayckbourn, *Variations* (1978) for vc. and jazz ens. (for brother Julian *Lloyd Webber), musical *Cats* based on poems by T. S. Eliot (1981), *Song and Dance* (1983), *Starlight Express* (1984), *Phantom of the Opera* (1986), *Requiem,* sop., ten., treble., ch., orch. (1984).

Lloyd Webber, Julian (*b* London, 1951). Eng. cellist. Studied RCM, and with P. *Fournier in

Geneva, 1973. Début London 1971. Gave first London perf. of Bliss conc. at composer's request, 1972. Rodrigo wrote conc. for him, 1981. Soloist with leading Brit. orchs.

Lobe, Johann (Christian) (*b* Weimar, 1797; *d* Leipzig, 1881). Ger. composer, theorist, and flautist. Studied with Riemann. Fl. soloist, Leipzig, 1811. Played fl. and va. in Weimar court orch. until 1842, then founded sch. of mus. there. Ed., *Allgemeine Musikalische Zeitung* 1846–8. Wrote several theoretical works pub. between 1846 and 1872. Wrote 5 operas, 2 syms., chamber mus.

Lobgesang (Hymn of Praise). Symphony-cantata in B♭ (Sym. No. 2) by Mendelssohn for ch. and orch., Op. 52, in 4 movements of which only last is choral. F.p. Leipzig 1840, Birmingham 1840.

Lobkowitz, (Prince) **Joseph Franz Maximilian** (*b* Roudnice nad Labem, 1772; *d* Třeboň, 1816). Member of Bohemian aristocratic family who had a tradition of patronage of mus. Sang bass in Handel's *Alexander's Feast* in Vienna in 1812. Also violinist and cellist. On board of administrators of Vienna court theatres, 1807–14, being sole dir. of opera. Founder-member of Gesellschaft der Musikfreunde. Commissioned Haydn's Op. 77 str. qts. F.p. of Beethoven's 'Eroica' Sym. given in his home 1804. Beethoven dedicated his Op. 18 str. qts., the 3rd, 5th, and 6th Syms., the Triple Conc., the str. qt. Op. 74, and the song-cycle *An die ferne Geliebte*, to him.

Locatelli, Pietro (*b* Bergamo, 1695; *d* Amsterdam, 1764). It. violinist and composer. Pupil of *Corelli in Rome. Settled in Amsterdam where he est. concert series. A great virtuoso, he introduced new effects and techniques. Comp. 12 concerti grossi, *L'Arte del Violino,* containing 12 concs. and 24 caprices for str. qt. and continuo, 6 vn. concs., 6 str. trios, 12 solo vn. sonatas, etc.

Locke (Lock), **Matthew** (*b* Exeter, *c.*1622; *d* London, 1677). Eng. composer, esp. of th. mus. Composer-in-ordinary to Charles II, 1661. Wrote incidental mus. for Shadwell's and Davenant's versions of Shakespeare plays (e.g. *Macbeth* and *The Tempest*), many anthems, 6 suites (some for recorder), *Music for his Majesty's Sackbuts and Cornetts, Melothesia* (studies for continuo, 1673). Also wrote pamphlets defending his style.

Lockhart, James (Lawrence) (*b* Edinburgh, 1930). Scottish cond., organist, and pianist. Studied Edinburgh Univ. and RCM. Ass. organist and chorusmaster, St Giles Cath., Edinburgh, 1946–51; organist and choirmaster, St John the Divine, Kennington, 1951–3, All Souls, Langham Place, 1953–4. Apprentice cond. Yorkshire S.O. 1954–5. Ass. cond. Munster Opera 1955–6, Bavarian State Opera, Munich, 1956–7, Glyndebourne 1957–9, répétiteur Glyndebourne 1962–8. Prof. of cond. RCM 1962–72. Mus. dir. WNO 1968–73; cond. Kassel Opera from 1972. Regular accompanist to sop. Margaret Price.

Lockspeiser, Edward (*b* London, 1905; *d* Alfriston, Sussex, 1973). Eng. critic and musicologist. Studied RCM, in Paris with N. Boulanger, and in Berlin. On BBC staff 1942–51. Authority on Debussy, on whom he wrote several books. Also author of books on Berlioz, Bizet, and Tchaikovsky.

Lockwood, Normand (*b* NY, 1906). Amer. composer. Won Amer. *Prix de Rome* 1929, studying with Boulanger and Respighi. Assoc. prof. of comp., Oberlin Coll., 1933–45, afterwards teaching at several univs. Prof. of comp., Denver Univ. 1961–71. Comps. incl. 4 operas, sym., and many choral works incl. several Whitman settings.

Loco (It.). Place. Term used after a sign indicating perf. an octave higher or lower than written (*8va sopra,* or *8va bassa*) to remind the performer that the effect of that sign is now cancelled. The expression *al loco* (at the place) is often used.

Loder, Edward (James) (*b* Bath, 1813; *d* London, 1865). Eng. composer and cond. Studied at Frankfurt with Ferdinand Ries. Cond. opera in London and Manchester (with *Hallé). Comp. operas, cantata, str. qts., and many songs, incl. *The Brooklet* (set by Schubert as *Wohin?*). His opera *Raymond and Agnes* (1855) was revived in Cambridge, 1966.

Lodger, The. Opera in 2 acts by Phyllis Tate to lib. by David Franklin based on novel by Mrs Belloc-Lowndes. Prod. RAM London 1960, Manchester RMCM 1970. The lodger of the title is Jack the Ripper.

Lodoïska. Opera in 3 acts by Cherubini to lib. by Fillette-Loraux. Prod. Paris 1791, NY 1826. Also subject of operas by *Kreutzer (1791), *Storace (1794), and J. *Mayr (1796).

Loeffler, Charles (Martin Tornow) (*b* Mulhouse, Alsace, 1861; *d* Medfield, Mass., 1935). Alsatian-Amer. composer and violinist. Son of writer whose pseudonym was Tornow. Childhood in Russia, Hungary, and Switzerland. Studied vn. in Berlin and later in Paris with Massart; comp. with *Guiraud. Played in private orch. In 1881 went to USA, becoming deputy leader Boston S.O., 1882, staying until 1903, after which he concentrated on comp. Works, which reflect Fr. impressionist techniques, incl. symphonic poems, choral settings (incl. Whitman's *Beat! Beat! Drums!*), chamber mus., and songs. Many unpub. pieces.

Loeillet, Jacques (*b* Ghent, 1685; *d* Ghent, 1748). Belg. composer, brother of Jean Baptiste *Loeillet. Also flautist, oboist, and violinist. Oboist at Munich. *Maître de chapelle* to Louis XV from 1727. Wrote fl. sonatas, vn. pieces, etc.

Loeillet, Jean Baptiste (*b* Ghent, 1680; *d* London, 1730). Belg. composer, flautist, and harpsichordist. Settled in London 1705, playing in th. orch.

and teaching hpd. Introduced transverse fl. to London. Comp. many works for his instrs.

Loesser, Frank (*b* NY, 1910; *d* NY, 1969). Amer. composer. Wrote several successful Broadway musicals (*The Most Happy Fella, Guys and Dolls, How to succeed in Business Without Really Trying*) and many songs.

Loewe, Frederick (*b* Vienna, 1904). Austrian-born (later Amer.) composer. Studied pf. with Busoni and d'Albert, comp with Rezniček in Berlin. Settled in USA 1924. Wrote mus. for *Brigadoon, Paint Your Wagon,* *My Fair Lady (1956 mus. version of Shaw's *Pygmalion*), *Camelot* (mus. version of White's *The Once and Future King*), and *Gigi* (film). All these were in collab. with librettist Alan Jay Lerner (*b* NY, 1918).

Loewe, Johann (Jakob) (*b* Vienna, 1628; *d* Lüneburg, 1703). Ger. composer. Pupil of *Schütz. One of earliest Ger. composers of solo songs (1657). Wrote sym., ballets, and 2 operas (incl. *Orpheus,* 1659).

Loewe, (Johann**) Karl** (Gottfried) (*b* Löbejün, nr. Halle, 1796; *d* Kiel, 1869). Ger. composer, organist, cond., and singer. Studied mus. with father. Mus. dir. at Stettin 1821–66. Cond. at Düsseldorf and Mainz fests., 1837. Visited Eng. 1847. Developed ballad for v. and pf. as art-form, setting **Erlkönig, Edward, Tom der Reimer,* etc. His ballads, legends, Lieder, and *Gesänge,* over 500 in all, were publd. in 17 vols. 1899–1903. Also wrote 5 operas, 18 oratorios, cantatas, 4 str. qts., pf. trio, 4 pf. sonatas, etc. Entered 6-week trance, 1864, a similar event causing his death.

Loewenberg, Alfred (*b* Berlin, 1902; *d* London, 1949). Ger.-born musicologist who settled in Eng., 1934. Compiled *Annals of Opera 1597–1940* (Cambridge 1943, rev. ed. Zürich 1954 and 1978, by H. D. Rosenthal) which lists details of 4,000 opera perfs. in chronological detail.

Loewenguth Quartet. Fr. string quartet, formed in Paris in 1929. Membership has changed except for 1st vn., Alfred Loewenguth (*b* Paris, 1911; *d* Paris, 1983). Has given f.ps. of many Fr. works, but is best known for playing of Beethoven and Bartók.

Logier, Johann Bernhard (*b* Kassel, 1777; *d* Dublin, 1846). Ger.-born flautist, bandmaster, org., and pf. teacher. Went to Eng. in 1791 and settled in Dublin 1809, opening music-shop and conducting at th. In 1814 invented and patented the **Chiroplast,* evolving system of teaching based on its use in training the hands for pf.-playing. Went to Berlin for 3 years. Returned to Dublin 1829, managing a music-shop. His *Thoroughbass* (1818) was first textbook studied by Wagner. Wrote pf. conc., sonatas, etc.

Logothetis, Anestis (*b* Pyrgos, Bulgaria, 1921). Bulg.-born Gr. composer. Studied Vienna Acad. of Mus., 1945–51, and in 1957 at Cologne elec.

studio. Has employed graphic and other notation since 1959. (See illustration p. 297). Works incl. *Agglomeration* for vn. and str. (1960), *Labyrinthos* (1965), ballet *Odysseus* (1963), and *Styx* (1969) for orch. of plucked str. instr.

Logroscino, Nicola (*b* Bitonto, 1698; *d* Palermo, *c.*1765). It. composer. Wrote several comic operas, incl. *L'inganno per inganno* (Trick for Trick), 1738. Collaborated with *Piccinni. Prof. of counter-point, Palermo Cons. from *c.*1756.

Lohengrin. Opera in 3 acts by Wagner to his own lib. Comp. 1846–8. Prod. Weimar (cond. Liszt) 1850, NY 1871, London 1875. The Bridal Chorus (wedding march), adapted by innumerable organists for church weddings, occurs early in Act 3, Scene 1. Lohengrin, Knight of the Holy Grail, is the son of **Parsifal.*

Löhr, Hermann (Frederic) (*b* Plymouth, 1872; *d* Tunbridge Wells, 1943). Eng. composer. Studied RAM. Wrote popular ballads, e.g. *Where my caravan has rested* (1909) and *Little grey home in the West* (1911).

Lohse, Otto (*b* Dresden, 1858; *d* Baden-Baden, 1925). Ger. cond. and composer. Studied Dresden Cons. Cellist in Dresden court orch. 1877–9. Worked in Riga 1882–9, becoming opera cond. 1889–93. Ass. cond. to Mahler at Hamburg Opera 1893–5. Ass. cond. to W. *Damrosch, Ger. opera in NY, 1895–7. Cond. Strasbourg Opera 1897–1904 and at CG 1901–4. Cond. Cologne Opera 1904–11, Leipzig 1912–23. Married sop. Katharina *Klafsky in 1895. Wrote operetta and songs.

L'Oiseau Lyre (Lyrebird Press). Fr. firm of mus. publishers, founded in Paris 1932 by Louise Dyer, an Australian, who built up a catalogue of limited edns., incl. Byzantine liturgical mus., medieval polyphonic mus., motets by Attaignant, keyboard works by Byrd, complete edn. of Couperin, etc. Dyer worked in Oxford 1940–5, returning to Paris after the war. She died 1962, when her husband, Jeffrey Hanson, ran firm until 1971. His widow Margarita Hanson then added further vols. Recordings issued since *c.*1938, label now being part of Decca group.

Lombard, Alain (*b* Paris, 1940). Fr. conductor. Studied at Paris Cons. Cond. début 1951 with Pasdeloup Orch. Gold medal, Mitropoulos Comp. 1966. Cond., Lyons Opera 1961–5. Amer. début 1963, NY Met. 1967 (Gounod's *Faust*). Mus. dir. Strasbourg Opera from 1972, Opéra du Rhin from 1974.

Lombardi alla Prima Crociata, I (The Lombards at the First Crusade). Opera in 4 acts by Verdi to lib. by Solera. Comp. 1842. Prod. Milan 1843, London 1846, NY 1847 (first Verdi opera in USA). Fr. version under title *Jérusalem,* in 4 acts, with lib. by Royer and Vaëz, prod. Paris 1847, Milan 1850. For *Jérusalem,* Verdi wrote new orch. prelude, rearranged the order of some arias, revised others, and added some new items.

London. Eng. city, capital of Great Britain. One of main musical centres of the world, with rich and varied activities in all branches of the art. From 18th cent. has enjoyed visits from leading performers and composers. Among the latter, Handel, J. C. Bach, Mozart, Haydn, Chopin, Weber, Mendelssohn, Liszt, Berlioz, Wagner, Bruckner, Mahler, Strauss, Hindemith, Ligeti, Berio, and Stockhausen are outstanding. This summary of London music will be divided into sections, for ease of reference.

Opera. The first real operatic perf. in London was at Rutland House, 1656, when Davenant's *The Siege of Rhodes* (mus. by 5 composers) was given. Purcell's *Dido and Aeneas* was perf. at a Chelsea school in 1689. Drury Lane Th. was used for opera in the 1690s. Handel's first operatic perfs. in London after 1711 were mainly at the King's Th., Haymarket. Rival perfs. were given at Lincoln's Inn Fields and *Covent Garden. From the 1830s the Lyceum and Drury Lane staged important opera seasons. The King's (re-named Her Majesty's in 1837) was the home of It. opera, but the first London *Ring* cycle was given there in 1882. After being rebuilt smaller in 1897, Her Majesty's was used less frequently for opera, although *Beecham cond. Strauss's *Feuersnot* there in 1910 and the first version of *Ariadne auf Naxos* in 1913. The *BNOC gave seasons there after 1924. From 1931 London's second opera house was *Sadler's Wells in Rosebery Avenue which housed the Vic-Wells Opera (SW Opera from 1934) until 1939 and from 1945 to 1968 (it reopened on 7 June 1945 with f.p. of Britten's *Peter Grimes.*) The company moved to the Coliseum in 1968 and changed its name in 1974 to English National Opera. Smaller companies, e.g. Handel Opera and New Opera Co., and visiting companies continue to use Sadler's Wells. The forerunner of Sadler's Wells was the Old Vic where Lilian Baylis had first staged opera in 1900. Until 1935 Vic-Wells Opera and Vic-Wells Ballet used both the Old Vic and Sadler's Wells.

Orchestras. Public concerts in London date from 1672. Thomas Britton's weekly gathering at Clerkenwell lasted from 1678 to 1714. Subscription concerts were held at Hickford's Rooms, James Street, from 1729 to c.1752. Geminiani ran rival concerts from 1731 to 1738. The J. C. Bach-C. F. Abel concerts began in 1765 at Carlisle House, Soho Square, and moved to Hanover Square Rooms in 1775. They ceased in 1782. Concerts organized by Cramer, Clementi, and *Salomon ran from 1783 to 1793, but Salomon left to launch his own series in 1783 (it was to this series that Haydn came). In the 19th cent. concerts were given first in the Argyll Rooms, at the corner of Oxford and Argyll Streets, and it was there that the *Philharmonic Society gave its first concert on 8 March 1813. The building was demolished in 1818 and the New Argyll Rooms opened in 1820 (they burned down in 1830). The Philharmonic moved to the King's Th. in 1830, to Hanover Square Rooms 1833–68, St James's Hall 1869–93, Queen's Hall 1894–1941, Royal Albert Hall 1941–51, Festival Hall from 1951. Important orch. concerts were given at the Crystal Palace, Sydenham, cond. by August Manns 1855–1901 where the members of the orch. played continually together and were London's first permanent orch. The opening of the *Royal Albert Hall in 1871 added a hall with a capacity of 6,500 to London's musical life. It was used mainly for large-scale events until 1941 when the destruction of Queen's Hall meant that nearly all symphony concerts were given there. It has remained the home since 1941 of the Promenade Concerts, founded in 1895 by Robert Newman and Henry J. *Wood. The Queen's Hall, Langham Place, had opened in 1893 and was renowned for its acoustics. It replaced the St James's Hall, Piccadilly, built in 1858. The Richter concerts were given there from 1877 and, even though the Queen's Hall by then existed, Elgar's *Enigma Variations* had their f.p. at a Richter concert in St James's Hall in 1899. It was demolished in 1905. London's principal concert hall since 1951 has been the *Royal Festival Hall on the South Bank, with the Queen Elizabeth Hall and Purcell Room as smaller adjuncts since 1967 but not entirely replacing for recitals the usefulness since 1901 of the *Wigmore Hall (Bechstein Hall until 1917) in Wigmore Street. The latest addition is the *Barbican Concert Hall.

No other city in the world supports as many orchestras as London. The *BBC S.O. (founded 1930) and the orchestras of the Royal Opera House and ENO are independent bodies and do not, as they once would have done, share players with others. The four principal symphony orchs. are *London Symphony (founded 1904), *London Philharmonic (founded 1932), *Philharmonia (founded 1945), and *Royal Philharmonic (founded 1946). In addition there are the *English Chamber Orchestra (founded 1948, renamed 1960), *Academy of St Martin-in-the-Fields (founded 1958), *London Sinfonietta (founded 1968), and Orchestra of *St John's, Smith Square (founded 1973). Among the choirs are the *Bach Choir (founded 1876), *Royal Choral Society (founded 1871), John *Alldis Choir (founded 1962), London Choral Society (founded 1903), Monteverdi Choir (founded 1964), London Philharmonic Choir (founded 1947), London Symphony Chorus (founded 1966), and Philharmonia Chorus (founded 1957).

Colleges. The *Royal Academy of Music was founded in 1822, the *Royal College of Music in 1882, *Trinity College of Music in 1872, the *Guildhall School of Music and Drama in 1880, and the *London College of Music in 1887. In addition the Univ. of London has a thriving musical wing.

Miscellaneous. In festivals, libraries, publishing firms, and not least the churches, from Westminster Abbey, Westminster Cathedral, St Paul's Cathedral, the Temple Church, and much besides, London's music is blessed by abundance. The capital is fortunate in having and holding so much; the only cavil is that some Londoners sometimes assume that nowhere else (in Britain) has anything.

London College of Music. Mus. sch. founded (privately) 1887. Incorporated 1939. Recognized as examining body.

London Consort of Viols. Ens. formed in 1948.

London (orig. Burnstein), **George** (*b* Montreal, 1919; *d* NY, 1985). Amer. bar. of Russo-Jewish parentage. Studied Los Angeles. Opera début in A. *Coates's *Gainsborough*, Hollywood Bowl 1941, under name Geo. Burnson. San Francisco Opera 1944. Member of Bel Canto Trio, touring USA from 1947. Vienna Opera from 1949 (début as Amonasro); NY Met. 1951–66; Bayreuth début 1951 as Amfortas, appearing until 1964. Glyndebourne 1950 (Figaro), La Scala, Milan, 1952. Sang Wotan in complete *Ring*, Cologne 1962–4. Sang Mandryka in NY Met.'s first *Arabella*, 1955. Gave up opera through ill-health in 1966. Art. admin., Kennedy Center, Washington, 1968–71. Gen. dir. Music Center Opera Assoc., Los Angeles, from 1971. Début as stage director, Seattle 1973. Sang Boris Godunov at Bolshoy, Moscow, 1960.

Londonderry Air. Irish folk-tune first pubd. in 1855 in *Petrie coll. Several sets of words have been fitted to it: 'Would I were Erin's apple blossom' by A. P. Graves, 'Emer's Farewell', also by Graves, and 'Danny Boy' by F. E. Weatherly. Arr. for various combinations by *Grainger (as *Irish Tune from County Derry*).

London Mozart Players. Chamber orch. specializing in mus. of Mozart and Haydn formed by Harry *Blech. First concert, Wigmore Hall, London, 11 Feb. 1949. Developed from London Wind Players, formed by Blech in 1942. Tours to It., Switzerland, Holland, Sweden, and Ger. Many fest. appearances. Blech retired as art. dir. 1984, being succeeded by Jane *Glover.

London Opera House. Th. built in Kingsway, London, in 1911 by Oscar *Hammerstein I as home for resident opera co. After 2 seasons it closed, becoming variety th. under name Stoll. Vladimir Rosing staged an opera season in 1915 (giving f. p. in England of Tchaikovsky's *Queen of Spades*). It. opera seasons 1949 and 1952–7, Zagreb Opera visit 1955, *Porgy and Bess* 1953. Now demolished.

London Overture, A. Orch. work by *Ireland, 1936; orig. written for brass band, 1934, under title *Comedy Overture*. One of prin. themes said to be inspired by bus cond.'s call of 'Piccadilly!'

London Philharmonic Orchestra. Founded by Sir Thomas Beecham in 1932 as his answer to BBC S.O. and containing several superb players, e.g. Paul Beard, George Stratton (vn.), Anthony Pini (vc.), Gerald Jackson (fl.), Leon *Goossens (ob.), Reginald Kell (cl.), Gwydion Holbrooke (bn.), and Marie Goossens (harp). First concert, Queen's Hall, London, 7 Oct. 1932. No connection with Phil. Soc. Toured Ger. 1936. Self-governing from 1939. Sir Adrian *Boult prin. cond. 1951–7; William *Steinberg 1958–62, John *Pritchard 1962–7; Bernard *Haitink 1967–79; Sir Georg *Solti 1979–83; Klaus *Tennstedt from 1983. Played for CG opera 1933–9. Regular orch. at *Glyndebourne Opera since 1964.

London Sinfonietta. Eng. chamber orch. founded by David Atherton and Nicholas Snowman in 1968, with Atherton as first mus. dir. Specializes in 20th-cent. mus. and has given many first perfs. and first perfs. in Eng. Elgar Howarth regular cond. from 1973 and Simon Rattle works often with it.

London String Quartet. Founded 1908 by Warwick Evans, cellist, with Albert *Sammons and Thomas Petre, vns., and H. Waldo Warner, va. First public concert Bechstein Hall, London, 26 Jan. 1910. Sammons succeeded by James Levey 1917–27, in turn succeeded by John Pennington, 1927–35. Petre absent 1914–19. Warner succeeded 1929 by Philip Sainton, in turn succeeded by William Primrose 1930–5. Toured USA and Canada annually 1920–35. Set high standards. Disbanded Jan. 1935. Gave f.ps. of several British works and in 1914 perf. 3 movts. of Schoenberg's 2nd str. qt. Name acquired 1958 by qt. comprising Erich Gruenberg and Lionel Bentley (vns.), Keith Cummings (va.), and Douglas Cameron (vc.). They had been New London Quartet 1950–6. Disbanded 1961.

London Symphonies. Collective name given to Joseph Haydn's last 12 syms., Nos. 93–104 in Breitkopf ed., all written for the London impresario J. P. *Salomon and first played in London during Haydn's visits, 1791–2 and 1794–5. The last, No. 104, is usually known as the 'London', for no special or good reason. The list which follows gives the syms. in chronological order of comp., with Breitkopf numbering, according to the Haydn scholar H. C. Robbins *Landon:

No.	Date on score	F.p
96 ('Miracle')	London 1791	1791
95	London 1791	1791
93	London 1791	Feb. 1792
94 ('Surprise')	London 1791	Mar. 1792
98	London 1792(?)	Mar. 1792
97	London 1792	May 1792
. 99	(Austria 1793)	Feb. 1794
100 ('Military')	London 1794	Mar. 1794
101('Clock')	London 1794	Mar. 1794
102	London 1794	Feb. 1795
103 ('Drum Roll')	London 1795	Mar. 1795
104 ('London')	London 1795	May 1795

London Symphony, A. Sym. by *Vaughan Williams (his 2nd, first wholly orch.) comp. 1911–13, f.p. 1914, rev. 1918, 1920, 1933. Though not programmatic, contains picturesque features such as Westminster chimes, lavender-seller's cry, jingle of hansom-cabs, and street musicians.

London Symphony Orchestra. Founded 1904, self-governing from start, by players who seceded from Henry Wood's Queen's Hall Orch. because he banned the system of deputies (by which a player could unilaterally send a deputy to a concert while he took a more lucrative engage-ment). First concert Queen's Hall, London, 9 June 1904, cond. *Richter, who remained prin. cond. until 1911. Toured USA 1912 cond. Nikisch. Also assoc. with Elgar as cond. (he was prin. cond. 1911–12). For many years was regular orch. at 3 Choirs Fests. Conductors have incl. Albert *Coates and *Harty. Those appointed prin. cond. since 2nd World War have been Josef *Krips 1950–54, Pierre *Monteux 1961–4, Istvan *Kertesz 1965–8, André *Previn 1968–79, Claudio *Abbado from 1979.

Long, Kathleen (*b* Brentwood, 1896; *d* Cam-bridge, 1968). Eng. pianist. Trained RCM 1910–16. Début 1915. On staff of RCM from 1920. Specialized in Mozart and Fr. composers, e.g. Fauré *Ballade*. Player in chamber mus. with Casals, Sammons, and others. Sonata partnership with Antonio Brosa 1948–66. C.B.E. 1957.

Long, Marguérite (Marie Charlotte) (*b* Nîmes, 1874; *d* Paris, 1966). Fr. pianist and teacher. Studied Paris Cons., joining its staff 1906 and becoming prof. of pf. 1920–40. Career of over 70 years. Noted interpreter of contemporary com-posers and early champion of Debussy (whose pupil she was) and Ravel. Ravel's pf. conc. in G major is ded. to her; she gave f.p. Paris, Jan. 1932 and f.p. in England, London, Feb. 1932, both cond. composer. Also gave f.p. of Ravel's *Le Tombeau de Couperin*, April 1919. Author of book *At the piano with Debussy* (1960).

Longa (Lat.). Long. Time-valŭe of a note in medieval notation system; was intermediate of *maxima* and *brevis*. A double long was equal to 4 breves.

Long Christmas Dinner, The. Opera in 1 act by Hindemith to lib. by Thornton Wilder. Comp. 1960. Prod. Mannheim (as *Das lange Weihnachts-mahl* in Ger. trans. by Hindemith) 1961, Rome 1962. F.p. of orig. Eng. text NY Juilliard Sch. 1963.

Long drum. Ten. drum—but sometimes the name is applied to the Bass drum.

Longo, Alessandro (*b* Amantea, 1864; *d* Naples, 1945). It. pianist and composer. Studied Naples Cons., where he became prof of pf. 1897. Ed.

complete hpd. works of D. *Scarlatti in 11 vols., giving each work a Longo (*L.) no. This numbering system has been superseded by that of *Kirkpatrick.

Lontano (It.). Distant, e.g. *come da lontano*, as if from a distance, i.e. faintly. *Lontananza*, distance.

Lontano (In the distance). Work for orch. by *Ligeti, comp. 1967, f.p. Donaueschingen 1967; f. Eng. public p., Manchester 1972 (cond. Loughran).

Lopatnikoff, Nikolai (*b* Reval, Russia, 1903; *d* Pittsburgh, 1976). Russ.-born composer (Amer. citizen, 1944). Studied St Petersburg Cons., Helsinki Cons., and privately with *Toch in Berlin where he met and was influenced by Hindemith. Lived in London 1933–9. Taught in Pittsburgh 1945–69. Works incl. opera *Danton*, 4 syms., 2 pf. concs., vn. conc., 2 vn. sonatas (1st with snare drum), pf. sonata, 3 str. qts.

Lopes-Graça, Fernando (*b* Tomar, 1906). Por-tuguese composer and pianist. Studied Nat. Cons., Lisbon, 1923–31 and at Sorbonne 1937–9 (musi-cology). Private comp. study with *Koechlin in Paris, 1938. Taught piano Coimbra Mus. Institute 1932–6 and at Lisbon Acad. of Friends of Mus. 1941–54 (becoming art. dir.). Author of many books on mus., incl. biographies. Works incl. 2 pf. concs., vc. conc. (played by Rostropovich), pf. concertino, 24 pf. preludes, 4 pf. sonatas, 4 sets of Portuguese folk-songs (24 songs per set), *3 Portuguese Dances* for orch., etc.

Loppert, Max (Jeremy) (*b* Johannesburg, 1946). S. African mus. critic, settled in Eng. Studied at York Univ. Mus. critic of *Financial Times*. Contrib. to periodicals.

Lord, David (Malcolm) (*b* Oxford, 1944). Eng. composer, cond., and lecturer. Studied RAM. Pupil of Richard Rodney *Bennett. Works incl. *Incantare* for orch., hpd. conc., several song-cycles, incl. *The Wife of Winter* (comp. for Janet *Baker).

Loreley (Lorelei), **Die.** (1) Unfinished opera, Op. 98, by Mendelssohn (1847) to lib. by E. von Giebel based on Ger. legend of beautiful woman who sings on a mountain by the Rhine, luring sailors to death on the rocks below. Some fragments, incl. an *Ave Maria*, sometimes perf. in concert-hall. Operas on subject also by Ignaz Lachner (1846), Wallace (1847), Bruch (1863), Catalani (1890, rev. of *Elda*, 1880), and others.
(2) Song by Liszt for v. and pf. to Heine's poem (1841), also with orch. and transcr. for pf. solo.

Lorengar, Pilar (*b* Zaragoza, 1928). Sp. sop. Studied in Madrid, concert début in 1952. Sang at Glyndebourne 1956 (Pamina in *Die Zauberflöte*), San Francisco 1964, NY Met. 1966. Also CG (début 1955, Violetta in *La traviata*), Berlin since 1958, and Salzburg Fest.

Lorentzen, Bent (b Stenvad, 1935). Danish composer. Studied musicology at Aarhus Univ. and theory at Royal Danish Cons. until 1962. Settled in Copenhagen 1971. After Darmstadt in 1965, turned to elec. mus. His opera *Euridice* (1965) won 1970 Italia Prize. Has written much chamber and choral mus. in addition to works on tape.

Lorenz, Max (b Düsseldorf, 1901; d Salzburg, 1975). Ger. ten., specializing in Wagner. Studied Berlin. Début Dresden 1927 in *Tannhäuser*. Berlin State Opera 1929–7, Vienna State Opera 1929 and regularly from 1937. NY Met. 1931–4 and 1947–50, CG 1934 and 1937. Bayreuth Fest. 1933–44 and 1954. Salzburg Fest. 1953–5, 1961. Also a remarkable Otello.

Loriod, Yvonne (b Houilles, Seine-et-Oise, 1924). Fr. pianist. Studied Paris Cons. with *Messiaen, whom she later married. Expert in Messiaen's mus., most of which she has recorded. Prof of pf. Paris Cons. Gave first Paris perfs. of concs. by Bartók and Schoenberg and of works by Jolivet, Barraqué, Boulez, and Messiaen. NY début 1949.

Lortzing, (Gustav) **Albert** (b Berlin, 1801; d Berlin, 1851). Ger. composer, actor, singer, and librettist. Son of actors. Played pf., vn., and vc., and comp. from early youth. Married actress in 1823 and worked as actor. First opera *Ali Pascha von Janina* prod. in 1824. Leading ten. at Leipzig State Th. 1833–43. While there, his operas *Die beiden Schützen* (1837) and *Zar und Zimmermann* (1837) were successfully perf. His *Hans Sachs* (1840) and *Casanova* (1841) failed, but *Der *Wildschütz* (1842) was a triumph. In *Undine* (1845), he made use of *leitmotiv*. In 1846 he went to Vienna, returning to Leipzig 1849 for his *Rolands Knappen*. Financial troubles led him to accept Berlin post in 1850 conducting farces and vaudevilles, and largely caused his death. His last work was operetta *Die Opernprobe* (The Opera Rehearsal), 1851.

Los Angeles, Victoria de. See *De Los Angeles, Victoria*.

Los Angeles Philharmonic Orchestra. Founded 1919 with W. H. Rothwell as cond. 1919–27. Since Dec. 1964 has played in Dorothy Chandler Pavilion of Los Angeles Mus. Center. Gives summer concerts in Hollywood Bowl. Prin. cond.: Georg *Schneevoigt 1927–9, Artur *Rodzinski 1929–33, Otto *Klemperer 1933–9, Alfred *Wallenstein 1943–56, Eduard van *Beinum 1956–9, Zubin *Mehta 1962–77, Carlo Maria *Giulini 1978–84, André Previn from 1986. Toured Europe, Iran, and India under Mehta 1967.

Lost Chord, The. Song by *Sullivan, comp. 1877 in sorrow at his brother's death. Poem by Adelaide Anne Procter. Regarded as the archetypal Victorian drawing-room ballad.

Lothar, Mark (b Berlin, 1902; d Munich, 1985). Ger. composer. Wrote operas *Tyll* (1928), *Lord Spleen* (based on Jonson's *Epicoene*, as was Strauss's *Die schweigsame Frau*) (1932), *Münchhausen* (1933), *Rappelkopf* (1958). Also choral works, chamber mus., pf. pieces.

Lott, Felicity (b Cheltenham, 1947). Eng. sop. Studied RAM. Opera début with City of London Fest. and Kent Opera. ENO 1975 (Pamina), Anne in Stravinsky's *The Rake's Progress*, Glyndebourne 1977. Paris début 1976. Also concert-work and recitals. Member of *Songmakers' Almanac. One of best Eng. singers of R. Strauss.

Lotti, Antonio (b Venice, c.1667; d Venice, 1740). It. composer. Studied Venice with *Legrenzi. In St Mark's choir 1687, chief organist 1704 and *maestro di cappella* 1736. Wrote 24 operas between 1693 and 1717. Stayed in Dresden 1717–19, writing 3 operas there, and *Constantino* for Vienna. Comp. only church mus. (of high quality) after 1719. Book of madrigals (1705).

Loughran, James (b Glasgow, 1931). Scottish cond. Studied Bonn (with Peter Maag), Amsterdam, and Milan. Won first prize Philharmonia Orch. cond. competition, 1961. London début with Philharmonia Orch. 1961; assoc. cond. Bournemouth S.O. 1962–5; prin. cond BBC Scottish S.O. 1965–71; prin. cond. Hallé Orch. 1971–83 and of Bamberg S.O. 1978–83.

Louise. Opera (*roman musical*) in 4 acts by G. *Charpentier to his own lib. Completed 1896. Prod. Paris 1900, NY 1908, London 1909. Sequel *Julien* (1913).

Louis Ferdinand, Prince (Prince Friedrich Christian Ludwig of Prussia) (b Friedrichsfelde, 1772; d in battle Saalfeld, 1806). Ger. composer and pianist, nephew of Frederick the Great. Virtuoso pianist. Wrote large amount of chamber mus. Admirer of Beethoven, who dedicated 3rd pf. conc. to him.

Loure (Fr.). Type of Fr. bagpipe; also dance, like a slow jig, acc. by this instr.

Louré. Term applied in string-playing to a type of slurred staccato and formerly called *portato*. An on-string stroke is executed at moderate speed.

Lourié, Arthur (Vincent) (b St Petersburg, 1892; d Princeton, NJ, 1966). Russ.-born composer (Amer. cit. from 1947). Studied piano St. Petersburg Cons. Self-taught as composer. Settled in Paris 1923–40, then he moved to USA 1941. Friend of Stravinsky. Experimented with atonality and quarter-tones, but later adopted modal style. Works incl. 2 operas, 2 syms., several large-scale religious works, 3 str. qts. Wrote biography of *Koussevitzky (Eng. edn. 1931).

Loveday, Alan (Raymond) (b Palmerston North, N.Z., 1928). N.Z. violinist. Talent noted by Budapest Qt. on tour of N.Z. Studied under

*Sammons from 1939 and at RCM. London début 1946. Prof. of vn. RCM from 1955. Soloist with leading orchs.

Love for Three Oranges (*Lyubov k tryom apelsinam*). Opera in 4 acts by Prokofiev, Op. 33, to Fr. lib. by composer based on Gozzi's play *Fiabe dell' amore delle tre melarance* (1761). Comp. 1919. Prod. Chicago 1921, Edinburgh 1962, London 1963. Orch. suite 1923.

Love in a Village. Ballad opera (*pasticcio*) in 3 acts with mus. collected and arr. by T. Arne and comp. by him and 16 other composers. Prod. London 1762, Charleston 1766. New edn. by Arthur *Oldham, Aldeburgh Fest. 1952.

Loveland, Kenneth (*b* Sheerness, 1915). Eng. mus. critic. Mus. critic *S. Wales Daily Argus* (of which he was also for a time ed.). Lecturer on mus. Contributor to *The Times* and periodicals.

Love of the Three Kings (Montemezzi). See *Amore dei tre re, L'*.

Love-potion, The (Donizetti). See *Elisir d'amore, L'*.

Lover and the Nightingale, The (Granados). See *Maja y el ruisenor, La*.

Loveridge, Iris (Gwendoline May) (*b* London, 1917). Eng. pianist. Trained RAM, and with Cyril Smith and Kentner. Recitalist and chamber mus. player, often in duo with Evelyn *Barbirolli (ob.).

Love-song Waltzes (Brahms). See *Liebesliederwalzer*.

Love, the Magician (Falla). See *Amor brujo, El*.

Lovett, Terence (George) (*b* London, 1922). Eng. cond. Plays pf., timp., va., hn., tpt., and org. Studied RAM. Début, London 1941. Has held several posts as organist and choirmaster. Art. dir. Hull Phil. Soc. Guest cond. leading orchs.

Love went a-Riding. Song for v. and pf. (or orch.) by Frank Bridge. Comp. 1914. Poem by Mary Coleridge (1861–1907).

Löwe, Ferdinand (*b* Vienna, 1865; *d* Vienna, 1925). Austrian cond. Studied at Vienna Cons. with Krenn and Bruckner. Taught pf. and choral singing at Vienna Cons. 1883–96. Cond. Kaim Orch., Munich, 1897. Ass. cond. Vienna Opera 1898–1900. Cond. Vienna Konzertverein Orch. (now Vienna S.O.) 1900–24. Dir. Vienna Music Acad. 1912–22. Disciple and interpreter of Bruckner; one of those, who from friendliest if misguided motives, persuaded him to rev. and cut his syms. Ed. of spurious first pubd. edn. of 9th Sym. (1903), heavily cut and rev.

Lower Mordent. See *Mordent*.

L.R.A.M. Licentiate of the Royal Academy of Music.

L.R.S.M. Licentiate of the Royal Schools of Music.

L.T.C.L. Licentiate of Trinity College of Music, London.

L.T.S.C. Licentiate of the Tonic Sol-fa College.

Lualdi, Adriano (*b* Larino, 1885; *d* Milan, 1971). It. composer. Studied Venice with Wolf-Ferrari. Worked as a critic (*Giornale d'Italia*, Rome). Dir., S. Pietro Cons., Naples, 1936–43, Florence Cons. 1947–56. His operas, to his own libs., revived older It. forms. They incl. intermezzo *Il cantico* (1915), and *Guerin Meschino*, puppet opera (1920). Others were *La figlia del Re* (1914–17), *Il Diavolo nel Campanile* (1919–23), and *La Granceola* (1930). Also symphonic poems and chamber mus.

Lübeck, Vincent (*b* Padingbüttel, Hanover, 1654; *d* Hamburg, 1740). Ger. organist and composer of cantatas, org. pieces, and chorale preludes. Org. of St Nicolai, Hamburg, 1702–40, attaining widespread reputation.

Lubotsky, Mark (*b* Leningrad, 1931). Russ. violinist. Studied at Moscow Cons., completing studies under D. Oistrakh. Teacher at Gnessin Inst., Moscow, from 1967. London début 1970 in Britten's conc., which he recorded with the composer.

Lucas, Leighton (*b* London, 1903; *d* London, 1982). Eng. cond. and composer. Began career as dancer in Diaghilev Ballet, acquiring mus. knowledge by own initiative. Became ballet cond. at 19; composer of religious works and film mus. (incl. *Target for Tonight*, 1941).

Lucca, Pauline (*b* Vienna, 1841; *d* Vienna, 1908). Austrian sop. Studied Vienna. Sang in ch. at Hofoper. Début Olmütz 1859 in *Ernani*. Engaged for Berlin Opera 1861 on Meyerbeer's recommendation. Début CG 1863 as Valentine in *Les Huguenots*. Left Berlin 1872, touring USA for 2 years. Vienna Opera 1874–89. Had range of 2½ octaves to C in alt.

Luchetti, Veriano (*b* Viterbo, 1939). It. tenor. Sang at Wexford Fest. 1965 as Alfredo in *La Traviata*. Début La Scala, Milan, 1975. CG début 1973 (Pinkerton).

Lucia di Lammermoor. Opera in 3 acts by Donizetti to lib. by Cammarano based on Scott's novel *The Bride of Lammermoor* (1819). Prod. Naples 1835, London 1838, New Orleans 1841. The famous 'Mad Scene', one of the finest vehicles for a brilliant but sensitive coloratura sop., is usually perf. as Act 3, Sc. 1 (the original Sc. 1 is usually omitted, although it has been recorded). In the orig. score Lucia is acc. in this scene by glass harp, but a fl. is generally substituted.

Lucier, Alvin (*b* Nashua, New Hampshire, 1931). Amer. composer. Studied Yale Univ. 1950–6, Brandeis Univ. 1958–60, and at Darmstadt summer courses. Dir., elec. mus. studio Brandeis

Univ. 1962–9. Teacher at Wesleyan Univ. from 1970. Has worked mainly with elec. apparatus. In his *Music for a Solo Performer* (1965), 3 electrodes are attached to the performer's scalp picking up 10-cycle alpha brain waves. This signal is amplified and filtered, and directed to loudspeakers which activate sympathetic responses in perc. instrs. Various other unconventional sources of sound are used in his works.

Lucio Silla. *Dramma per musica* in 3 acts (K135) by Mozart to lib. by G. da Gamerra, altered by Metastasio. Prod. Milan 1772, Dresden 1955, London 1967. Also operas by Anfossi (1774) and J. C. Bach (1774).

Lucky Hand, The (Schoenberg). See *Glückliche Hand, Die*.

Lucrezia Borgia. Opera in prol. and 2 acts by Donizetti to lib. by Romani based on Hugo's tragedy (1833). Prod. Milan 1833, London 1839, NY 1844. At Paris prod. 1840, Hugo raised objections. The opera was withdrawn and the lib. re-written as *La Rinegata*, the action being relocated in Turkey.

Ludus Tonalis (The Play of Notes). Pf. studies in counterpoint, tonal organization, and pf. playing by Hindemith, comp. 1942, f.p. Chicago 1943. Comprises prelude, 12 fugues with 11 interludes, and postlude (inverted version of prelude).

Ludwig, Christa (*b* Berlin, 1924). Ger. sop. and mez. Parents were singers at Vienna Volksoper. Studied with her mother and Felice Hüni-Mihaček. Début Frankfurt 1946, Orlofsky in *Die Fledermaus*. Sang in opera in Darmstadt, Hanover, and Hamburg. Salzburg Fest. 1954 (Cherubino). Vienna Opera from 1955. NY Met. début 1959. CG début 1968 (Amneris). Outstanding Marschallin, Oktavian, Eboli, and Leonore in *Fidelio*. Also noted interpreter of Lieder, Mahler's orch. songcycles, Verdi *Requiem*, etc.

Ludwig II, King of Bavaria (*b* Nymphenburg, 1845; *d* Lake Starnberg, 1886). Succeeded his father, Maximilian II, in 1864. Was passionate admirer of Wagner's mus., becoming his generous patron, buying him houses, and planning to build th. in Munich to stage *Der Ring des Nibelungen*. Prime mover in Munich premières of *Tristan und Isolde* (1865), *Die Meistersinger von Nürnberg* (1868), *Das Rheingold* (1869), and *Die Walküre* (1870). Because of scandal of Wagner's affair with Cosima von Bülow, Wagner had to leave Munich, but despite breach in their friendship Ludwig continued to provide support, and helped Wagner financially in building of Bayreuth Festspielhaus and Villa Wahnfried. A fascinating historical figure, his alleged 'madness' is at the least questionable.

Ludwig, Leopold (*b* Witkowitz, 1908; *d* Lüneburg, 1979). Austrian cond. Studied Vienna. Began career at Opava, 1931. Mus. dir. Oldenburg

1936, Vienna Opera 1939–43, Berlin State Opera 1943–51. Mus. dir. Hamburg Opera 1951–70, conducting many contemporary works and taking company to Edinburgh (1952), London 1962 (f. Brit. p. of Berg's *Lulu*), and NY (1967). NY Met. 1970 (*Parsifal*). Glyndebourne 1959 (*Der Rosenkavalier*).

Luening, Otto (*b* Milwaukee, Wisconsin, 1900). Amer. composer, cond., teacher, and flautist. Studied Munich Acad. 1914–17, Zürich Cons., and privately with Busoni. Worked as flautist and accompanist, 1915. Cond. opera in Munich and Zürich 1917–20. One of founders of Amer. Grand Opera Co., Chicago, 1920. Dir., opera dept., Eastman Sch. of Mus., Rochester, 1925–8. Prof. of mus. Barnard Coll., NY, 1944–68. Co-dir. Columbia-Princeton Elec. Mus. Center from 1959. Large body of comps. incl. opera *Evangeline* (Longfellow), fl. concertino, *Kentucky Concerto* for orch., song settings of Whitman and Blake, chamber mus. incl. 3 str. qts., various sonatas, *Sonority Canon* for 2 to 37 fl., and pf. pieces. Also comp. several elec. works, e.g. *Fantasy in Space* for fl. on tape, and *Synthesis* for orch. Also elec. works in collab. with V. *Ussachevsky, incl. *A Poem in Cycles and Bells* for tape recorder and orch., and mus. for prods. of Shaw's *Back to Methuselah* and Shakespeare's *King Lear*.

Luftig (Ger.). Airy.

Luigini, Alexandre (Clément Léon Joseph) (*b* Lyons, 1850; *d* Paris, 1906). Fr. cond., violinist, and composer. Studied Paris Cons. with Massenet. Cond. Lyons th. 1877–97, then at Paris Opéra-Comique. Wrote operas, ballets (incl. *Egyptian Ballet*, 1875), orch. works, etc.

Luisa Miller. Opera in 3 acts by Verdi to lib. by Cammarano after Schiller's *Kabale und Liebe* (1784). Comp. 1849. Prod. Naples 1849, NY 1854, London 1858.

Lukáš, Zdeněk (*b* Prague, 1928). Cz. composer. Studied in Prague 1943–6. Dir., Cz. radio orch. 1953–65. Early works influenced by folk-song, but later became 12-note, aleatory, and elec. Works incl. radio operas, 4 syms., conc. for vn. and va., str. qts., and the elec. *Nezabiješ* ('You do not kill') of 1971.

Lukomska, Halina (*b* Suchedniów, 1929). Polish soprano. Studied in Poznań 1951–4, then in Warsaw. Won 's-Hertogenbosch Comp. 1956, then went to Venice for study with Toti dal Monte. Specialist in works of Webern, Boulez, Lutoslawski, and Serocki. Recorded Boulez's *Pli selon pli* with composer.

Lullaby (Fr. berceuse; Ger. Wiegenlied). Cradlesong, usually in triple rhythm. Vocal lullabies occur in mus. of all periods. There are also instrumental lullabies, such as Chopin's *Berceuse*, Op. 57 (1843–4).

Lully, Jean-Baptiste (orig. Lulli, Giovanni Battista) (*b* Florence, 1632; *d* Paris, 1687). It.-born composer (Fr. nationality from 1661). Taught himself vn. At 14 went to Fr. and worked as scullion in noble house, until prowess as dancer and mime was noted. Entered service of Louis XIV 1653, composing instr. mus. for the court ballets. Some time before 1656 he created and became leader of 'les petits violons du Roi', a band of 21 players (an offshoot of the '24 violons du roi'). 'Instrumental composer to the King' 1653–61, 'Superintendent of Mus. and chamber mus. composer' 1661–2; 'music master to Royal Family' from 1662. From 1664 collab. with Molière in series of comedy-ballets which were forerunners of Fr. opera, the last and most famous being *Le Bourgeois Gentilhomme*, in which Lully danced role of the Mufti. Having assimilated both It. and Fr. styles and tastes, from 1673 he turned to opera comp. and obtained from the King exclusive rights to arrange operatic perfs. in Paris. For the next 14 years, working with the poet Quinault, he not only wrote about 20 operas and ballets, but prod. and cond. them and trained the singers with firm discipline. He developed the formal 'French Ov.' and replaced It. *recitativo secco* with acc. recit., placing special emphasis on a style of declamation suited to Fr. language. He introduced professional female dancers into the ballet. A supreme courtier and intriguer, he nevertheless made Fr. opera a popular art. His death was caused by a gangrenous abscess which formed in his foot after he struck it with the long staff he used for beating time on the floor while conducting a *Te Deum* to celebrate Louis XIV's recovery from illness. Prin. works:

OPERAS: *Cadmus et Hermione* (1673), *Alceste* (1674), *Thésée* (1675), *Atys* (1676), *Isis* (1677), *Psyché* (1678), *Bellérophon* (1679), *Proserpine* (1680), *Persée* (1682), *Phaéton* (1683), *Amadis de Gaule* (1684), *Roland* (1685), *Armide et Rénaud* (1686), *Acis et Galathée* (1686), *Achille et Polixène* (with Colasse, 1687, prod. posthumously).

COMEDY-BALLETS with MOLIÈRE: *Le mariage forcé* (1664), *L'amour médecin* (1665), *La Princesse d'Élide* (1664), *Le Sicilien* (1667), *Georges Dandin* (1668), *Monsieur de Pourceaugnac* (1669), *Les amants magnifiques* (1670), *Le *Bourgeois Gentilhomme* (1670),

CHORAL: Motets for 2 choirs (1684), *Miserere* (1664), *Te Deum* (1677), *De Profundis* (1683), 5 *Grands Motets* (1685).

Lulu. Opera in 3 acts by Berg to his own lib. based on Frank Wedekind's *Erdgeist* (1895) and *Die Büchse der Pandora* (1901). Comp. 1929–35, but full score of Act III uncompleted. Prod. Zürich 1937. London 1962. Lulu, a *femme fatale*, sinks to prostitution and ends as a victim of Jack the Ripper. Mus. is founded on a single note-row, from which are derived *leitmotiv* assoc. with certain characters, differing from *Wozzeck* where each scene has a formal designation. After death

of Berg's widow in 1977, short score of Act III was orch. by Friedrich *Cerha and opera was given complete for first time at Paris Opéra 1979, cond. Boulez. Also Santa Fe, 1979, CG 1981.

Lumbye, Hans Christian (*b* Copenhagen, 1810; *d* Copenhagen, 1874). Danish cond. and composer of galops, marches, etc. Known as 'the Northern Strauss'.

Lumsdaine, David (*b* Sydney, N.S.W., 1931). Australian composer. Studied Sydney Univ. and N.S.W. Cons. Went to Eng. 1953 to study with *Seiber. Returned to Australia 1973 and 1976. Lecturer in mus., Durham Univ., where he inaugurated elec. studio. Prin. works:

ORCH: *Episodes* (1968–9); *Hagoromo* (1975–7); *Shoalhaven* (1982).

CHAMBER ORCH: *Mandala II* (1969); *Looking Glass Music* (1970); *Salvation Creek with Eagle* (1974); *Sunflower* (1975); *Mandala III*, pf. and ens. (1978).

BRASS BAND: *Evensong* (1975).

VOICE(S) AND CHAMBER ENS: *Annotations of Auschwitz*, sop. and ens. (1964, rev. 1970); *Easter Fresco*, sop. and ens. (1966, rev. 1971); *Aria For Edward John Eyre*, sop and ens. (1972); *Tides*, narrator, 12 vv., perc. (1979); *The Ballad of Perse O'Reilly*, ten., male ch., 2 pf. (1953–81); *What Shall I Sing?* sop., 2 cl. (1982).

CHAMBER MUSIC: *Mandala I*, wind quintet (1967); *Caliban Impromptu* (1972); *Mandala IV*, str. qt. (1983).

PIANO: *Kelly Ground* (1966); *Flights*, 2 pf. (1967); *Kangaroo Hunt*, pf. and perc. (1971); *Ruhe Sanfte, Sanfte Ruh'* (1974); *Cambewarra* (1980).

SOLO VOICE: *My Sister's Song*, sop. (1974).

TAPE: *Big Meeting*, elec. fantasy (1978); *Wild Ride to Heaven* (with N. *LeFanu), 'radiophonic adventure playground' (1980).

Lumsden, (Sir) **David** (James) (*b* Newcastle upon Tyne, 1928). Eng. organist, harpsichordist, chorusmaster, and administrator. Studied Cambridge Univ. with Boris Ord and Thurston Dart. Org., Nottingham Univ., 1954–6; dir. mus., Keele Univ., 1956–9; org., New Coll., Oxford, 1959–78; Prin., RSAM 1978–82; Prin., RAM from 1982. Authority on Eng. lute mus. K.B.E. 1985.

Lungo, lunga (It.). Long. *Lunga pausa* (1) long pause; (2) long rest.

Luogo (It.). Same as *loco.

Luonnotar. Tone-poem for sop. and orch., Op. 70, by Sibelius, to words from Finnish epic *Kalevala* telling of creation of the world. Comp. 1913.

Lupo. Family of It.-born musicians at Eng. court 1540–1640. One of them, Thomas, wrote fantasies for viols, anthems, etc.

Lupu, Radu (*b* Galati, 1945). Romanian pianist. Studied Moscow Cons. with H. Neuhaus. 1st prize Van Cliburn competition, 1966; first prize Leeds int. competition 1969. First London recital, Nov. 1969. Soloist with world's leading orchs. USA tour 1972. Settled in Eng.

Lur. (1) A prehistoric bronze tpt.
   (2) A wooden tpt.-like instr. used by herdsmen in Scandinavia as the *Alphorn, which it somewhat resembles, is in Switzerland.

Lush, Ernest (*b* Bournemouth, 1908). Eng. pianist and accompanist. Pupil of Matthay. BBC staff accompanist 1927–66.

Lusigando. A term that appears sometimes in Debussy's mus. Apparently a mistake for *lusingando.

Lusingando (It.). Flattering, i.e. play in a coaxing, intimate manner. So, too, *lusinghevole, lusinghevolmente, lusinghiero, lusingante.*

Lustigen Weiber von Windsor, Die (The Merry Wives of Windsor). Opera in 3 acts by *Nicolai to lib. by S. H. Mosenthal based on Shakespeare's comedy (1600–1). Comp. 1846–7. Prod. Berlin 1849, Philadelphia 1863, London 1864 (in It.), 1878 (in Eng.), 1907 (in Ger. at CG).

Lustige Witwe, Die (Lehár). See *Merry Widow, The.*

Lute. Fretted str. instr. of great antiquity played by plucking with the fingers (occasionally with a plectrum in earlier types). The 'long lute', with neck longer than the body, dates back at least to 2000 BC. The short lute, with neck slightly shorter than the body, dates from *c*.800 BC. It was transformed into the European lute, with distinct neck and central soundhole, probably in Spain in 14th cent. Has a round body, like halved pear, flat neck with 7 or more frets, and separate pegbox usually bent back from neck at angle. In 16th cent. had 11 str. in 6 courses, tuned to convenient pitch. Up to 6 bass courses were added in 17th cent., unalterable in pitch. In mid-17th cent., new system of tuning (called *nouveau ton*) was introduced by Denis Gaultier. Lutes were much used for solos, acc., and in ens. Their mus. was played not from notation but from *tablature which in the 16th and 17th cents. took the form of a staff with a space for each str. and small letters placed within the space to indicate the fret to be used. Small marks above the staff gave the duration of the sounds.
   Many varieties of lute were used in the 16th and 17th cents., when it was the chief domestic inst. They incl. *mandola, mandolin, angelica,* and larger, deeper lutes called *archlutes,* of which the 'long' was the *chittarone and the 'short' the *theorbo. All have the characteristic round back, differentiating them from the flat-back *guitar* family. In the 17th cent., lute music was chiefly cultivated in Fr., Ger., and Eng. (*Dowland was probably the greatest lute composer) while Sp. and It. turned to the guitar. The literature of lute mus. stretches

from 1507 to *c*.1770, among the latest composers to compose for it being Handel, J. S. Bach, Reusner, and Weiss. It came to be used in orch. mus., and there is a part for lute in Bach's *St John Passion* (1723). With the 20th-cent. revival of interest in early mus. the lute has regained considerable popularity, especially through the agency of virtuosi such as Julian *Bream.
   The term is also used generically for a large group of str. instr., e.g. fiddles, viols, vielle, etc.

Lute Harpsichord (Ger. *Lautenclavicymbel*). Hpd. with gut instead of metal strs., so-called because of lute-like sound. In 1740 J. S. Bach had one made for his use.

Lutenist (lutanist). Player of the *lute.

Luth (Fr.). The *Lute.

Luther, Martin (*b* Eisleben, 1483; *d* Eisleben, 1546). Ger. Protestant church reformer. Player of lute and fl. Est. congregational singing. Wrote treatise on mus. (1538) and words of many hymns and chorales (possibly the mus., too), best-known being *Ein' feste Burg ist unser Gott* (A safe stronghold our God is still).

Luthier (Fr., from *luth*, lute; Ger. *Lautenmacher*). A maker of str. instr., nowadays usually those of the vn. family.

Lutosławski, Witold (*b* Warsaw, 1913). Polish composer, pianist, and cond. Studied Warsaw Univ. 1932–6 and State Cons., later in Hamburg. Worked as pianist in Warsaw cafés 1939–45. His earlier works were comp. under the restraints imposed by official insistence on a style based on folk-song, but the *Concerto for Orchestra* (1950–4) is a successful example from this period. After 1956 a freer approach was allowed and the influence of Webern became apparent in his work. He began to use the 12-note system in 1958 but did not find it fruitful. In *Gry weneckie* (Venetian Games) of 1960–1, he employed *aleatory procedures within strictly defined limits. His later works, notably the 2nd Sym., combine this technique with more traditional forms such as *ostinato* and harmonic patterns. The mus. texture is all-important. Prin. works:

ORCH: *Symphonic Variations* (1938); Syms: No. 1 (1941–7), No. 2 (1965–7), No. 3 (1972–83); *Overture* for str. (1949); *Little Suite* for chamber orch. (1950, rev. 1951 for full orch.); *5 Folk-Songs* for str. (1952, from *Folk Melodies* for pf.); *Concerto for Orchestra* (1950–4); *Muzyka żałobna* (Funeral Music) for str. (1958); *3 Postludes* (1958–63); *Gry weneckie* (*Venetian Games) (1960–1); *Livre pour orchestre* (1968); *Cello Concerto* (1969–70); *Preludes and Fugue* for 13 solo strings (1972); *Mi Parti* (1976); *Variations on a Theme of Paganini,* version for pf. and orch. (1978, see 2 PIANOS); *Novelette* (1978–9); Conc. for ob., hp., and chamber orch. (1979–80); *Chain I* (1983).

VOICES AND ORCH: 2 *Fragments from a Requiem* for v., ch., and orch. (1937); *Silesian Triptych* for sop. and orch. (1951); 3 *Poems of Henri Michaux* for ch., wind, 2 pf., harp, and perc. (1963); *Paroles tissées* for ten. and 20 solo instr. (1965); *Les espaces du sommeil* (The spaces of sleep), bar. and orch. (1975)

CHAMBER MUSIC: 30 small pieces for woodwind (1943–4); wind trio (1954); *Dance Preludes* for cl. and pf. (1954, rev. 1955 for cl. and small orch., 1959 for nonet); Str. Qt. (1964); *Epitaph*, ob., pf. (1979); *Grave*, vc., pf. (1981).

2 PIANOS: *Variations on a Theme of Paganini* (1941); version for pf. and orch. (1978).

PIANO: Sonata (1934); *Folk Melodies* (1945, Nos. 9–12 rev. 1954 for 4 vn. as 4 *Silesian Folk-Songs*; 5 of them arr. for str. as 5 *Folk-Songs*, 1952); *Invention* (1983).

VOICE AND PIANO: 20 *Polish Carols* (1946); 5 Songs (1957, rev. 1958 for mez. and 30 instr.).

BRASS: *Mini Overture* (1981).

Lutto (It.). Mourning. So *luttoso* or *luttuoso*, mournful; *luttosamente*, mournfully.

Lutyens, (Agnes) **Elisabeth** (b London, 1906; d London, 1983). Eng. composer. Studied École Normale de Musique, Paris, 1922–3, RCM (with Harold *Darke) 1926–30. One of first Eng. composers to use 12-note system. Comp. nearly 200 scores for films and radio, also incidental mus. for plays. Helped to found Macnaghten-Lemare concerts, London, 1931, and founded Composers' Concourse 1954. Author of books and articles. C.B.E. 1969. Prin. works:

OPERAS: *Infidelio* (1954); *The Numbered* (1965–7); *Isis and Osiris* (1969–70); *Time off? Not a Ghost of a Chance!* (charade in 4 scenes with 3 interruptions) (1967–8); *The Goldfish Bowl* (1975); *Like a Window* (1976).

ORCH: 3 *Pieces* (1939); 5 Chamber Concs. (1939–46); 3 *Symphonic Preludes* (1942); Va. Conc. (1947); *Quincunx* (with sop. and bar.) (1959–60); *Music for Orchestra* I (1955), II (1962), III (1963), IV (1981); *Chorale* (1956); *Symphonies* for pf., wind, harps, perc. (1961); *Music for Piano and Orchestra* (1964); *Novenaria* (1967); *The Winter of the World* (1974); *Eos* (1975); *Rondel* (1976); *Concert Aria*, female v. and orch. (1976); 6 *Bagatelles* (1976); *Nox*, pf. and 2 chamber orchs. (1977); *Tides* (1978); *Echoi*, with mez. (1979); *Rapprochement* (1980); *Six* (1980); *Wild Decembers* (1980).

VOICE(S) AND INSTR: *O Saisons, O châteaux* (Rimbaud), sop. and str. (1946); *Nativity*, sop. and str. (1951); *De Amore* (Chaucer), sop., ten., ch., orch. (1957); *Catena*, sop., ten., 21 instr. (1961); *The Valley of Hatsu-se*, sop., fl., cl., vc., pf. (1965); *Akapotik Rose*, sop. and ens. (1966); *And Suddenly It's Evening*, ten. and 11 instr. (1967); *Essence of Our Happinesses*, ten., ch., orch. (1968); *A Phoenix*, sop., vn., cl., pf. (1968); *Anerca*, speaker, 10 guitars, perc. (1970); *Vision of Youth*, sop., 3 cl.,

pf., perc. (1970); *Islands*, sop., ten., speaker, ens. (1971); *Requiescat* (in mem. Stravinsky), sop., str. trio or mez., 2 cl., bass cl. (1971); *Dirge for the Proud World*, sop., counterten., hpd., vc. (1971); *The Tears of Night*, counterten., 6 sop., 3 instr. ens. (1971); *Chimes and Cantos*, bar., ens. (1972); *Laudi*, sop., 3 cl., pf., perc. (1973); *Chorale Prelude and Paraphrase*, ten., str. quintet, pf., perc. (1977); *Elegy of the Flowers*, ten. and 3 instr. groups (1978); *Cantata*, sop., instr. ens. (1979); *Cantata* (Beaudelaire), sop., cont., bar., ens. (1979); *Echoes*, cont., fl., cor ang., str. qt. (1979); *Concert Aria* ('Dialogo'), sop., ens. (1980); *Fleur du Silence*, ten., ens. (1980); *Mine Eyes, My Bread, My Spade*, ten., str. qt. (1980).

CHORAL: *Encomion*, with brass and perc. (1963); *Voice of Quiet Waters*, with orch. (1972); *Counting Your Steps*, with 4 fl., 4 perc. (1972); *The Roots of the World*, with vc. obbl. (1979).

UNACC. CHORAL: *Excerpta Tractata—Logico Philosophici* (Wittgenstein), motet (1952); *The Country of the Stars* (1963); *The Hymn of Man*, male vv. (1965), rev. for mixed vv. (1970); *Magnificat and Nunc Dimittis* (1965); *The Tyme doth Flete* (1968); *Verses of Love* (1970); *Roads*, 2 sop., counterten., ten., bar., bass (1973); *Sloth—One of the Seven Deadly Sins*, 2 counterten., ten., 2 bar., bass (1974); *It is the Hour* (1976).

STRING QUARTETS: No. 2 (1938), No. 3 (1949), No. 6 (1952), No. 12 (1981); Op. 139 (1979); Op. 158 (1982); *Plenum III* (1973); *Mare et Minutiae* (1976); *Doubles* (1978); '*Diurnal*', Op. 146 (1980).

CHAMBER ENS: Str. trio (1939); *Concertante* for fl., cl., vn., vc., pf. (1950); *Nocturnes*, vn., vc., guitar (1955); *Capricii*, 2 hp., perc. (1955); 6 *Tempi*, for 10 instr. (1957); wind quintet (1960); str. quintet (1963); wind trio (1963); *Fantasie-Trio*, fl., cl., pf. (1963); str. trio (1964); *Scena*, vn., vc., perc. (1964); *Music for Wind* (1964); *The Fall of the Leafe*, ob., str. qt. (1966); *Music for Three*, fl., ob., pf. (1966); *Horai*, vn., hn., pf. (1968); *Driving Out the Death*, ob., str. trio (1971); *Rape of the Moone*, wind octet (1973); *Plenum II*, ob., 13 instr. (1973); *Kareniana*, va., 10 instr. (1974); *Go, Said the Bird*, elec. guitar, str. qt. (1975); *Fantasia*, alto sax., 3 instr. groups (1977); *O Absalom . . .*, vn., ob., va., vc. (1977); *Trio*, cl., vc., pf. (1979); *Branches of the Night and of the Day*, hn., str. qt. (1981).

SONGS (with pf. unless otherwise stated): 2 *Songs by W. H. Auden* (1942); 9 *Songs* (Stevie Smith) (1948); 3 *Songs* (Dylan Thomas), sop., instr. (1953); *In the Temple of a Bird's Wing*, bar. (1956 and 1965); *The Egocentric*, ten. or bar. (1968); *Lament of Isis on the Death of Osiris*, solo sop. (1969); *The Supplicant*, bass (1970); *In the Direction of the Beginning*, bass (1970); *Oda a la Tormenta*, mez. (1970); *Dialogo*, ten., lute (1972); 2 *Songs* (D. H. Lawrence), unacc. v. (1974); *The Hidden Power*, 2 unacc. vv. (1974); *Of the Snow*, 3 unacc. vv. (1974); *Nocturnes and Interludes*, sop. (1976); *Variations: Winter Series—Spring Sowing*, sop. (1977); *By All These . . .*, sop., guitar (1977); *She*

Tells Her Love While Half Asleep (R. Graves), solo sop. (1979); *That Sun*, cont. (1979); *The Singing Birds*, speaker, va. (1980).

PIANO: *5 Intermezzi*(1941); *3 Improvisations*(1948); *Piano e Forte* (1958); *5 Bagatelles* (1962); *Helix* (1967); *Plenum I* (1972); *The Ring of Bone*, with opt. speaking v. or vv. (1975); *5 Impromptus* (1977); *7 Preludes* (1978); *The Great Seas* (1979); *3 Books of Bagatelles* (1979); *La Natura dell'Acqua* (1981). HPD: *Pietà* (1975).

ORGAN: *Sinfonia* (1955); *Epithalanium*, with opt. sop. (1968); *3 Short Pieces* (1969); *Plenum IV* (1974).

CHAMBER MUSIC (1 or 2 instr., classified instrumentally): *Duo No. 3*, vn., pf. (1957); *Scroll for Li-Ho*, vn., pf. (1967); *Prelude*, solo vn. (1979); *Madrigal*, ob., vn. (1977); *Morning Sea*, ob., pf. (1979); *Déroulement*, ob., guitar (1980); Sonata for solo va. (1938); *Aptote*, solo va. (1948); *Echo of the Wind*, solo va. (1981); *9 Bagatelles*, vc., pf. (1942); *Duo No. 2*, vc., pf. (1956–7); *Constants*, vc., pf. (1976); *The Tides of Time*, db., pf. (1969); *Variations*, fl. (1957); *Footfalls*, fl., pf. (1978); *Presages*, ob. (1963); *5 Little Pieces*, cl., pf. (1945); *Valediction*, cl., pf. (1954); *Tre*, cl. (1973); *Soli*, cl., db. (1980); *This Green Tide*, basset hn., pf. (1975); *Duo No. 1*, hn., pf. (1956–7); *The Dying of the Sun*, guitar (1969); *Romanza*, guitar (1977); *The Living Night*, perc. solo (1981).

Also many film, radio, and theatre scores.

Luxon, Benjamin (*b* Redruth, 1937). Eng. bar. Studied GSM. Taught physical education until becoming prof. singer 1963. Numerous recitals and concerts. Opera at Aldeburgh, Glyndebourne (début 1972 as Monteverdi's Ulysses), CG (début 1972 in Maxwell Davies's *Taverner*), ENO (début 1974 in *Don Carlos*), and other companies. Created role of Owen Wingrave in Britten's opera (BBC TV 1971 and CG 1973).

Lvov, Alexey (Fyodorovich) (*b* Reval, 1798; *d* nr. Kovno, 1870). Russ. composer, cond., and violinist. Served in army, becoming general, then in 1837 succeeded father as dir. of St Petersburg court choir. Led str. qt. Wrote 3 operas, vn. conc., 24 caprices, church mus., and Imperial nat. anthem, *God Save the Tsar* (1833), quoted by Tchaikovsky in *1812 Overture*.

Lyadov, Anatoly (Konstantinovich) (*b* St Petersburg, 1855; *d* Novgorod, 1914). Russ. composer. Pupil of Rimsky-Korsakov at St Petersburg Cons., where he later became prof. of comp. Researched Russ. folk mus. with *Balakirev and *Lyapunov. His tone poems for orch. incl. *The Enchanted Lake* (*Volshebnoye ozero*) (1909), *Baba Yaga* (1904), and *Kikimora* (1910). Collab. in Borodin's *Paraphrases* (*Chopsticks version). Orig. choice to comp. mus. for ballet *The Firebird*, but because he did not begin work on it, it was passed to *Stravinsky (some sources maintain that yet another composer was offered the commission before Stravinsky).

Lyapunov, Sergey (Mikhaylovich) (*b* Yaroslavl, 1859; *d* Paris, 1924). Russ. composer. Studied Moscow Cons. 1878–83. Ass. dir. Imperial choir, St Petersburg, 1884–1902. Worked with *Lyadov and *Balakirev on folk-song research. Prof., St Petersburg Cons. 1910–18. Ed. correspondence between Balakirev and Tchaikovsky. Works incl. 2 syms., 2 pf. concs., vn. conc., many songs, and pf. pieces.

Lydian Mode. See *Modes*.

Lyke-Wake Dirge. 15th-cent. anonymous Eng. poem set by *Britten in his *Serenade* for ten., hn., and str. (1943), by *Stravinsky in his *Cantata* (1951–2) and by Whittaker for ch. and orch. (1924).

Lympany, Moura (*b* Saltash, 1916). Eng. pianist. Studied RCM and Liège, and with Matthay. Public début 1928, Harrogate. Int. career. Gave f. London p. of Khachaturian's pf. conc. C.B.E. 1979.

Lyra (Lira). (1) The *Lyre.
(2) Early Ger. name for *hurdy-gurdy; see *lira*.

Lyra organizzata. See *Lira organizzata*.

Lyra Viol. Small bass *viol.

Lyre. Ancient Gr. instr., like small harp, in which strings were fixed to a cross-bar between 2 arms and plucked by fingers or plectrum.

Lyre-Bird Press. See *L'Oiseau-Lyre*.

Lyric. (1) Strictly, vocal perf. with *lyre; hence *lyric drama* = opera of all kinds (Fr. *drame lyrique*), *lyric stage* = operatic stage.
(2) Short poem, not epic or narrative; composers such as Grieg adapted this meaning to mus., e.g. *Lyric Piece, Lyric Suite*.
(3) Vocal description, e.g. *lyric tenor, lyric soprano*, somewhere between 'light' and 'heavy' vocal weight.
(4) The words of a song in a 'musical' or of a popular 20th-cent. song.

Lyric Suite. (1) Orch. by Grieg (1904) of 4 of his *6 Lyric Pieces* (Book 5), Op. 54 (1891) (*Shepherd's Boy, Norwegian March, Nocturne*, and *March of the Dwarfs*).
(2) Work for str. qt. in 6 movements by *Berg, comp. 1925–6, f.p. Vienna 1927. 2nd, 3rd and 4th movements arr. for str. orch. 1928, f.p. Berlin 1929. Research has lately disclosed that the *Lyric Suite* was a manifestation of Berg's love for Hanna Fuchs, wife of a Cz. industrialist, whom he met 1925. In addition to quotations from Wagner's *Tristan*, Zemlinsky's *Lyric Symphony*, and his own *Wozzeck*, Berg used the notes representing Hanna's and his initials (H(B nat.), F, A, and B) in the note-row which is the basis of the work. The 6th movement, *Largo desolato*, exists also in version with mez. voice as setting of S. George's trans. of Baudelaire's 'De profundis clamavi'. F. Eng. p. of suite with vocal finale, BBC broadcast 1979.

Lyrische Symphonie (Lyric Symphony). Zemlinsky's Op. 18, being seven songs after poems by Rabindranath Tagore (*b* Calcutta, 1861; *d* Calcutta, 1941) in Ger. trans. by the composer, for sop., bar., and orch. Comp. 1922–3. 7 poems are: 1. *Ich bin friedlos* (I am restless), 2. *Mutter, der junge Prinz muss an unsere Türe vorbeikommen* (Mother, the young Prince is to pass our door), 3. *Du bist die Abendwolke* (You are the evening cloud), 4. *Sprich zu mir Geliebter!* (Speak to me, my love), 5. *Befrei mich von den Banden deiner süsse Lieb!* (Free me from the bonds of your sweetness, my love!), 6. *Vollende denn das letzte Lied und lass uns auseinandergehn* (Then finish the last song and let us leave), 7. *Friede, mein Herz* (Peace, my heart). In the **Lyric Suite*, which is dedicated to Zemlinsky, Berg in the 4th movt. quotes the principal theme from No. 3 of the *Lyrische Symphonie*, which occurs at the words 'Du bist mein Eigen' ('You are my own'). F.p. Prague 1924, cond. Zemlinsky; f. Eng. p. 1977, BBC broadcast, cond. Süsskind.

Lysenko, Mykola (*b* Hrynky, 1842; *d* Kiev, 1912). Ukrainian composer. Studied Kiev Univ. 1860–4 and in St Petersburg with Rimsky-Korsakov 1874–6. Expert in Ukrainian folk-song, publishing 240 popular songs (1868–1911). Comp. several operas, incl. *Taras Bulba*, cantatas, songs, etc.

Lysy, Alberto (Ivan) (*b* Argentina, 1935). Ukrainian-Argentine violinist and cond. Studied in Argentina, Paris, and London. 1st prize, Queen Elisabeth competition, Brussels, 1955. Later studied with Menuhin. Founded chamber orch. in Buenos Aires, 1965.

Lyttelton, Humphrey (*b* Eton, 1921). Eng. jazz trumpeter and band-leader. Prof. career began 1947. Formed own band 1948. Also writer and broadcaster.

M

M. Surnames beginning M', Mc, or Mac, are all treated, in accordance with most British reference books (though not with Amer. dictionaries), as though spelt Mac.

Ma (It.). 'But', as in *ma non troppo*, 'but not too much'.

Ma, Yo-Yo (*b* Paris, 1955). Fr cellist of Chinese parents. Gave first recital at age of 6. Studied at Juilliard Sch., NY, from 1962 with L. Rose. In 1970s achieved international eminence as soloist with world's leading orchs.

Maag, Peter (*b* St Gall, Switz., 1919). Swiss cond. and pianist. Studied Zürich and Geneva Univs. and with Furtwängler and Cortot. Cond. Düsseldorf Opera 1952–4, Bonn Opera 1954–9. Chief cond. Vienna Volksoper 1964–7; mus. dir. Parma Opera from 1971, Turin Opera from 1974. Brit. débuts 1959 (CG and Glyndebourne), Amer. 1959 (Minneapolis S.O.), NY. Met. 1972. Has conducted many unfamiliar operas and championed 20th cent. works.

Maayani, Ami (Hay) (*b* Ramat-Gan, Israel, 1936). Israeli composer and cond. Studied architecture, Haifa, and founded Technion S.O. Studied mus. at Jerusalem Acad. 1950–3 and Columbia Univ., NY (1964–5, elec. mus. with V. *Ussachevsky). Studied comp. privately with Paul Ben-Haim 1956–60. Cond. of Israel Youth Orch. Comps. incl. 2 harp concs., vn. conc., vc. conc., va. conc., 2-pf. conc., *Qumran*, 'symphonic metaphor' for orch., *Mismorim*, for high v. and orch., etc.

Maazel, Lorin (Varencove) (*b* Neuilly, 1930). Amer. cond. and violinist. Studied Pittsburgh Univ. Cond. at NY World Fair and Hollywood Bowl 1939 when a child, leading Amer. orchs., incl. NY P.O., NBC S.O., Chicago, and Cleveland, from 1941. Violinist in Pittsburgh S.O. from 1948. Cond. in It. from 1953. Cond. Bayreuth Fest, 1960, 1968, 1969; mus. dir. Deutsche Oper 1965–71, Berlin Radio S.O. 1965–71. Opera débuts at La Scala, Milan, and Vienna 1966. CG, 1978. Ass. prin. cond. New Philharmonia 1970–2; cond. and mus. dir. Cleveland Orch. 1972–82. Dir., Vienna Opera 1982–6 (first Amer. to hold post) but left amid controversy in 1984.

Mácal, Zdeněk (*b* Brno, 1936). Cz. conductor. Studied under Jílek at Brno Cons. 1951–6 and at Janáček Acad. 1955–60. Cond. Moravian P.O. (Olomouc) 1963–7. Won Besançon int. cond. competition 1965. Début with Czech P.O. 1966, taking orch. on tour to W. Ger. 1968. Settled in Switzerland 1969. Brit. début Bournemouth S.O.

1969. Cond. Cologne Radio S.O. 1970–4. Cond. Sydney S.O. from 1985. Amer. début Chicago S.O. 1972.

McAllister, Rita (Margaret Notman) (*b* Mossend, Lanarks., 1946). Scottish writer and composer. Studied Glasgow Univ. and RSAM (comp. with Anthony Hedges, Robin Orr, and Frederick Rimmer). Lecturer in mus., Edinburgh Univ. Composer of str. qt., song-cycles, cantata, etc. Authority on Prokofiev and other 20th-cent. Russ. composers.

Macbeth. (1) Opera in 4 acts by Verdi, his 10th, to lib. by Piave based on Shakespeare's tragedy. Comp. 1846. Prod. Florence 1847, NY 1858. Rev. for Paris 1865 in Fr. trans., this version now being generally used. Glyndebourne 1938.

(2) Symphonic poem Op. 23 by R. Strauss, comp. 1887–8, rev. 1889–90, f.p. Weimar 1890 cond. Strauss.

(3) Opera in prol. and 3 acts by Bloch to Fr. lib. by Edmond Fleg, after Shakespeare. Comp. 1903–9, prod. Paris 1910.

(4) Opera by L. Collingwood, lib. selected from Shakespeare. Prod. London 1934.

McBride, Robert (*b* Tucson, Ariz., 1911). Amer. composer. Studied Arizona Univ. 1928–35, comp. with *Luening. Woodwind player in Tucson S.O. 1928–35. Taught theory and wind instr., Bennington Coll. 1935–46. Composer-arranger Triumph Films, NY, 1946–57. Teacher of theory, wind instr., and comp. at Arizona Univ. from 1957. Works incl. *Mexican Rhapsody, Punch and the Judy, Jazz Symphony* (ballet), *Panorama of Mexico, Hill Country Symphony* (all for orch.); *Workout*, ob. and pf.; ob. quintet; *String Foursome* for str. qt; *Lament for the Parking Problem*, tpt., hn., tb.

McCabe, John (*b* Huyton, 1939). Eng. composer, pianist, and critic. Studied Manchester Univ., RMCM (comp. with *Pitfield), Munich Music Acad., and privately with Harold Genzmer. As pianist specializes in 20th-cent. Eng. mus. and Haydn. Pianist-in-residence Univ. Coll., Cardiff, 1965–7. Dir., London Coll. of Mus. from 1983. C.B.E. 1985. Prin. comps.:

OPERAS: *The Play of Mother Courage* (1974); *The Lion, The Witch, and The Wardrobe* (1968).
BALLETS: *Mary, Queen of Scots* (1975); *The Teachings of Don Juan* (1973).
ORCH: Sym. for 10 wind instr. (1964); Syms.; No. 1 (*Elegy*) (1965), No. 2 (1970–1), No. 3 (*Hommages*) (1978); *Variations on a Theme by Hartmann* (1964); *Concertante Variations on a Theme of Maw* (1970); *The *Chagall Windows* (1974); *Sonata on a Motet*

for Strings (1976); 2 *Suites* from ballet 'Mary, Queen of Scots' (1976); *The Shadow of Light* (1979); *Concerto for Orchestra* (1982).

CONCERTOS: Pf., No. 1 (1966), No. 2 (1970), No. 3 (1976); Vn., No. 1 (1959), No. 2 (1980); Cl. (1978); *Concerto funèbre*, va. and chamber orch. (1962); Chamber Conc., va., vc., and orch. (1965); *Concertante*, hpd. and chamber ens. (1965); *Metamorphoses*, hpd. and orch. (1968); ob. d'amore (1972).

VOICE AND ORCH: *Notturni ed Alba*, for sop. and orch. (1970); *Voyage*, 5 soloists, boys' ch., ch., and orch. (1972); *Time Remembered*, sop. and ens. (1973); *Stabat Mater*, sop., ch., orch. (1976); *Reflections on a Summer Night*, ch. and orch. (1976).

CHAMBER MUSIC: *Partita* for str. qt. (1960); 3 *Pieces*, cl. and pf. (1964); str. trio (1965); *Fantasy* for brass qt. (1965); *Movements* for cl., vn., vc. (1964, rev. 1966); *Partita* for vc. (1966); *Nocturnal* for pf. and str. qt. (1966); *Rounds* for brass quintet (1967); *Canto* for guitar (1968); ob. qt. (1968); conc. for pf. and wind quintet (1969); Str. Qt. No. 2 (1972), No. 3 (1979); *The Goddess Trilogy*, hn. and pf. (1973–5).

PIANO: *Variations* (1963); 5 *Bagatelles* (1964); *Fantasy on a Theme of Liszt* (1967); *Intermezzi* (1968); *Capriccio* (1969); *Sostenuto* (1969); *Gaudi* (1970); *Aubade* (1970).

ORGAN: *Sinfonia* (1961); *Prelude* (1964); *Johannis-Partita* (1964); *Elegy* (1965); *Miniconcerto*, organ, perc., and audience (485 penny whistles) (1966).

VOCAL: *Great Lord of Lords* (1966); *Hymn to God the Father* (1966); *Canticles for Salisbury* (1966); *The Morning Watch* (1968); *Behold a Silly Tender Babe* (1975); *Visions* (1984).

McCaldin, Denis (*b* Nottingham, 1933). Eng. cond., writer, and teacher. Studied Nottingham and Birmingham Univs., intending to be scientist. Dir. of mus., Lancaster Univ. from 1971. Guest cond. leading orchs.

McCartney, Paul (*b* Liverpool, 1942). Eng. songwriter, guitarist, pianist, and organist. Member of the *Beatles pop group 1960–70; formed new group Wings 1971. Comp. many songs (some with John Lennon) incl. *Eleanor Rigby*, *Yesterday*, etc. Mus. for several films. Over 200,000,000 recordings of his comps. sold. M.B.E. 1965.

McCormack, John (*b* Athlone, 1884; *d* Dublin, 1945). Irish-born ten. (Amer. citizen 1917). Without previous instruction, won gold medal at Nat. Irish Fest. 1902, then studied in It. Opera début Savona 1906. London début in concert 1907, later that year at CG as Turiddù in *Cavalleria Rusticana*. NY début, Manhattan Opera 1909 as Alfredo in *Traviata*, same role 1910 NY Met. Member Boston Opera 1910–11, Chicago 1912–14. Then gave up opera and devoted himself to concerts and recitals. Famous for singing of Irish and sentimental ballads, but his beautiful phras-

ing and pure tone in operatic roles can be heard on recordings. Made papal Count, 1928.

McCracken, James (*b* Gary, Indiana, 1926). Amer. ten. Acted in Broadway plays and sang on radio before début NY Met. 1953. Sang opera in Zürich and elsewhere until return to Met. 1963 as Otello in Verdi's opera, a role with which he became closely identified throughout world. CG début 1964.

MacCunn, Hamish (*b* Greenock, 1868; *d* London, 1916). Scottish composer and cond. Studied with Parry at RCM 1883–6. Prof. of harmony RAM 1888–94 and at GSM from 1912. Cond. Carl Rosa Opera after 1898 and later for Beecham co. Wrote several operas, incl. *Jeanie Deans* (1894) and *Diarmid* (1897), cantatas, incl. *The Wreck of the Hesperus* (1905), concert-ovs., *Land of the Mountain and the Flood* (1887) and *The Ship o' the Fiend* (1888), part-songs, songs, pf. pieces.

McDonald, Gerald (*b* Wallasey, 1913). Eng. mus. administrator. Studied in Dresden and with Imogen Holst. Regional dir. Arts Council 1948–56, gen. man. RLPO 1956–64. Head of Mus. (North), BBC 1964–9, gen. man. New Philharmonia Orch. 1969–74. Administrator, Musicians' Benevolent Fund, 1974–8. Administrator, Nat. Opera Studio 1978–84. Member of several mus. committees, trusts, etc. O.B.E. 1981.

Macdonald, Hugh (John) (*b* Newbury, 1940). Eng. lecturer and musicologist. Studied Cambridge Univ. On mus. staff Cambridge Univ. 1966–71, Oxford Univ. from 1971. Specialist in Berlioz. Cond. Cambridge Phil. Soc. 1969–71. Prof., Glasgow Univ., from 1980.

MacDonald, Malcolm (*b* Bedford, 1916). Eng. composer, critic, teacher, and jazz pianist. Studied RCM. Lecturer, Cape Town Univ. 1948–54, prof. RAM from 1954. Works incl. 2 syms., sinfonietta, hpd. conc., *Cuban Rondo*, etc.

MacDonald, Malcolm (Calum) (*b* Nairn, 1948). Scottish critic and composer. Studied Cambridge Univ. Composer of songs and pf. pieces. Author of many articles and of books on Havergal Brian, J. H. Foulds, and Schoenberg.

MacDowell, Edward (Alexander) (*b* NY, 1860; *d* NY, 1908). Amer. composer and pianist. Studied pf. as child, having occasional lessons from Teresa *Carreño. Entered Paris Cons. 1876, Frankfurt Cons. 1879, studying pf. with Heymann and comp. with *Raff. Teacher of pf., Darmstadt Cons. 1881. In 1882 visited Liszt at Weimar; on Liszt's recommendation, *First Modern Suite* for pf. and first pf. conc. were pubd. From 1885 to 1888 lived at Wiesbaden. Returned to USA 1888, settling in Boston. Soloist in f.p. of 2nd pf. conc., NY 1889. First head of mus. dept., Columbia Univ., NY, 1896–1904, resigning amid controversy. Injured when knocked down in street, and was insane for last 3 years of his life. His mus. is romantic in style and charmingly melodic. The MacDowell Colony in Peterboro, New Hampshire, where composers and other artists can work peacefully, was founded in his memory. Prin. works:

ORCH: Symphonic poems *Hamlet* and *Ophelia* (1885), *Lancelot and Elaine* (1886), *Lamia* (1887–8), Suite No. 1 (1888–93), No. 2 (*Indian*) (1891–5).

CONCERTOS: Pf., No. 1 in A minor (1882), No. 2 in D minor (1884–6).

PIANO: *1st Modern Suite* (1880–1), *2nd Modern Suite* (1882–3); *Forest Idyls* (1884); *Idyls* (1887, rev. as *6 Idyls After Goethe*, 1901); *12 Studies* (1890); Sonatas: *Tragica* (1893), *Eroica* (1895), *Norse* (1900), *Keltic* (1900); *12 Virtuoso Studies* (1894); *10 Woodland Sketches* (1896, No. 1 is *To a Wild Rose*); *8 Sea Pieces* (1898); *6 Fireside Tales* (1902); *10 New England Idyls* (1902).

Also many songs, part-songs, arrangements, and works pubd. under pseudonym Edgar Thorn.

Mace, Thomas (*b* Cambridge, 1612 or 1613; *d* ?Cambridge, *c*.1706). Eng. writer on mus. Wrote *Musick's Monument* (1676), a book about psalmody, lute-playing, the viol, etc.

Macero, Teo (*b* Glens Falls, NY, 1925). Amer. composer, arranger, cond., and saxophonist. Studied Juilliard Sch. 1947–53. Composer of many film and TV scores, also *In Retrospect* for orch., *C* for alto sax., vn., va., and orch. (1957), *Polaris* for orch., *Dylan* (musical).

McEwen, (Sir) **John** (Blackwood) (*b* Hawick, 1868; *d* London, 1948). Scottish composer and teacher. Studied RAM 1893, under Prout, Corder, and Matthay. Prof. of harmony and comp., RAM, 1898–1924, prin. 1924–36. Knighted 1931. Benefactor of chamber concerts. Works incl. *Solway Symphony*, va. conc., ov. *Grey Galloway*, many str. qts. (incl. *Biscay*), choral mus., str. quintet, pf. pieces, songs, etc.

Macfarren, (Sir) **George** (Alexander) (*b* London, 1813; *d* London, 1887). Eng. composer and teacher. Studied RAM with Cipriani Potter, Prof., RAM 1837–87. Cond. at CG from 1845. Prof. of mus., Cambridge Univ., 1875. Prin., RAM 1875–87. Knighted 1883. Blind by 1860, dictating to amanuensis. Works incl. 12 operas (*Don Quixote*, 1846, *Robin Hood*, 1860, *She Stoops to Conquer*, 1864), 9 syms., oratorios, cantatas, ov. *Chevy Chase* (1836), pf. conc., vn. conc., sonatas, str. qts., and much church mus. Also wrote textbooks on harmony and articles for *Grove's Dictionary*, etc. Ed. works by Purcell and Handel, and colls. of Eng., Scottish, and Irish songs.

McGuire, Edward (*b* Glasgow, 1948). Scottish composer. Works incl. sym., trilogy for chamber ens. (*Rebirth, Interregnum, Liberation*), symphonic poem *Calgacus*, and *Rant* for solo vn., *Life-Songs*, solo vv., str.

Mácha, Otmar (*b* Ostrava, 1922). Cz. composer. Studied Prague Cons. and Mus. Acad. Worked at Radio Prague 1945–62. Works incl. oratorio *Testament of J. A. Comenius* (1952–5), operas *Infidelity Unmasked* (1956–7) and *The Lake Ukereve* (1960–3), symphonic poem *Night and Hope* (1959), *Variants* for orch. (1968), vn. sonata, bn. sonata.

Machaut (Machault), **Guillaume de** (*b* Reims, *c*.1300; *d* Reims, 1377). Fr. composer, cleric, poet, and diplomat. Secretary to John, Duke of Luxembourg from *c*.1323 to 1346. Later in service of King of Navarre, King of Cyprus, Duke of Berry, and others. Canon of churches at Reims, Verdun, and S. Quentin. Comp. motet for election of Archbishop of Reims, 1324. Outstanding practitioner of *Ars Nova and among first to comp. polyphonic setting of poetry in fixed forms (*ballade, rondeau,* and *virelai*), to write in 4 parts, and to compose integrated setting of entire Ordinary of the Mass. Also among last to compose in the medieval forms of *Lai and *Dit. His most important works are probably the *Messe de Notre Dame* for 4 vv. and the *Voir Dit* (Tale of Truth), a collection of letters, lyrics, and song-settings (*ballades* and *rondeaux*) written in praise of a woman (Péronne d'Armentières). Machaut's works have appeared in 3 complete edns., by Ludwig (1926, 1954), Schrade (1956), and Sylvette Leguy (Paris, from 1977).

Machicotage. (1) Extemporary ornamentation of plainsong by the priest. Machicots were members of the lower clergy who were singers (Lat. *macicoti*; It. *maceconchi*).

(2) Addition of an improvised 2nd part to a plainsong.

(3) Singing of inferior quality.

Mächtig (Ger.). Mighty, powerful.

McIntyre, Donald (*b* Auckland, N.Z., 1934). N.Z. bar. Studied GSM. Opera début, Cardiff (WNO) 1959. Member SW Opera 1960–7, CG début 1967 (Pizarro). Bayreuth début 1967 as Telramund. In 1973 became first British singer to sing Wotan in Bayreuth *Ring* cycle and sang role in 1976 centenary cycle. Wotan in CG *Ring* cycle 1974. NY Met. début as Wotan 1974. Guest singer Vienna, Hamburg, Milan. O.B.E. 1977. C.B.E. 1985.

Mackenzie, (Sir) **Alexander** (Campbell) (*b* Edinburgh, 1847; *d* London, 1935). Scottish composer, violinist, cond., and teacher. Studied Sondershausen Cons. 1857–62, RAM 1862–5. In Edinburgh 1865–79 as violinist, cond., etc. Lived in Florence 1879–88. Prin., RAM 1888–1924. Cond., Philharmonic Soc. 1892–9, giving f.Eng.p. of Tchaikovsky's 6th sym. (1894). Knighted 1895, K.C.V.O. 1922. Works incl. 5 operas (incl. *The Cricket on the Hearth*, 1900), oratorios, cantatas (incl. *The Dream of Jubal*, 1889), 3 *Scottish Rhapsodies*, vn. conc., chamber mus., and songs.

Mackerras, (Sir) (Alan) **Charles** (*b* Schenectady, NY, 1925). Australian cond. and oboist. Studied

N.S.W. Cons. (Sydney). Prin. ob. Sydney S.O. 1943–6. Went to Eng. 1946. Studied cond. with Talich. Prague Acad., 1947–8. Cond., SW Opera 1948–53. Prin. cond. BBC Concert Orch. 1954–6. CG from 1963 (début cond. *Katerina Izmaylova*). First cond., Hamburg State Opera 1966–70. Mus. dir. SW Opera (ENO from 1974) 1970–8; prin. cond. Sydney S.O. 1982–5. Mus. dir. WNO from 1987. Cond. f.p. in England of a Janáček opera, *Káťa Kabanová*, SW 1951, following with several other Janáček operas, some of which he has ed. Awarded Janáček Medal, 1978. Arr. mus. by Sullivan for ballet *Pineapple Poll* and by Verdi for *The Lady and the Fool*. Guest cond. leading sym. orchs. Has cond. and ed. operas by Handel, J. C. Bach, and Gluck. His *Nozze di Figaro* at SW 1965 was remarkable for addition of ornamentation and for 18th cent. appoggiaturas. C.B.E. 1974. Knighted 1979.

McKie, (Sir) **William** (Neil) (*b* Melbourne, Victoria, 1901; *d* Ottawa, 1984). Australian organist and cond. Studied RCM. Dir. of mus., Clifton College, 1926–30, Melbourne city organist 1931–8, Magdalen College, Oxford, 1938–41, organist and master of choristers, Westminster Abbey 1941–63, Dir. of mus. for coronation of Queen Elizabeth II, 1953. Knighted 1953.

MacMillan, (Sir) **Ernest** (Campbell) (*b* Mimico, Ontario, 1893; *d* Toronto, 1973). Candian cond., organist, and composer. Concert organist from age 10. A.R.C.O. at age of 13, F.R.C.O. at 17. Studied Edinburgh with Niecks and Hollins, then Paris. At Bayreuth 1914 and interned throughout war, gaining his Oxford D.Mus. while prisoner. Prin., Toronto Cons. of Mus. 1926–42, dean of mus. Toronto Univ. 1927–52. Cond., Toronto S.O. 1931–56. Composed choral works and arr. Canadian folk-songs. Knighted 1935 (first Canadian 'for services to mus.').

MacMillan, (Sir) **Kenneth** (*b* Dunfermline, 1929). Scottish dancer, choreog., and dir. Studied SW Ballet Sch. Joined SW Th. Ballet 1946. Choreog., Royal Ballet, 1965. Ballet dir., Deutsche Oper, Berlin, 1966–9. Dir., Royal Ballet 1970–77, prin. choreog. from 1977. Choreog. incl. *Somnambulism* (1953), *Rite of Spring* (1962), *Romeo and Juliet* (1965), *Song of the Earth* (1965), *Checkpoint* (1970), *7 Deadly Sins* (1973), *Manon* (1974), etc. Knighted 1983.

Macnaghten, Anne (Catherine) (*b* Whitwick, Leics., 1908). Eng. violinist. Studied Leipzig Cons. 1926–9 and in London 1929–34 with André Mangeot. Founder and leader Macnaghten Str. Qt. 1932–40 and co-founder in 1931 with Iris Lemare and E. Lutyens of Macnaghten concerts at which works by young Brit. composers, notably Britten, were introduced.

McNaught, William (Gray) (*b* London, 1849; *d* London, 1918). Eng. writer, teacher, and choral cond. Studied RAM. Ass. inspector of mus., Board of Education, 1883–1901. Authority on tonic sol-fa. Ed., *Musical Times*, 1909–18.

McNaught, William (*b* London, 1883; *d* London, 1953). Eng. mus. critic, son of W. G. *McNaught. Worked for several papers, incl. *Glasgow Herald*. Ed., *Musical Times*, 1944–53.

Maconchy, (Dame) **Elizabeth** (*b* Broxbourne, 1907). Eng. composer of Irish parentage. Studied RCM with Charles Wood and *Vaughan Williams, and in Prague with Jirák from 1929 where her pf. concertino was perf. by Prague P.O., 1930. In the same year her suite *The Land* was played at the London Proms. Her ob. quintet won *Daily Telegraph* chamber mus. prize, 1933. She has concentrated on chamber mus., inspired by Bartók's example. Her mus. is contrapuntal and tends to have short concise thematic material, but a freer, more passionate style has developed in later works. Cobbett Medal for chamber mus. 1960, C.B.E. 1977. D.B.E. 1987. Nicola *LeFanu is her daughter. Prin. works:

OPERAS: 3 1-act operas, *The Sofa* (1956–7), *The Departure* (1960–1), *The Three Strangers* (Hardy) (1958–67) (1st perf. as trilogy, Middlesbrough 1977); *The Birds* (1967–8); *The Jesse Tree*, masque (1970); *The King of the Golden River* (1975).

ORCH: Suite, *The Land* (1930); ov. *Proud Thames* (1953); *Concertino* for pf. and orch. (1930); *Dialogue* for pf. and orch. (1940); *Serenata Concertante* for vn. and orch. (1963); *Concertino* for bn. and str. (1959); *Variazioni Concertante* (1965); *Music for brass and woodwind* (1966); 3 *Cloudscapes* (1968); 3 *Poems by Gerard Manley Hopkins* for high v. and chamber orch. (1964–70); *Ariadne* (C. Day Lewis) for sop. and orch. (1970); *Epyllion* for vc. and 15 str. (1975); *Sinfonietta* (1975–6); *Romanza*, va., str. (1979); *Little Symphony* (1981); *Tribute*, vn. and ens. (1982–3); *My Dark Heart*, sop. and ens. (1982); *Music for Strings* (1983).

CHORAL: *And Death Shall Have No Dominion*, ch. and brass (1969); cantata, *Samson and the Gates of Gaza* (1964); *Héloise and Abélard*, dramatic cantata for sop., ten., and bar. soloists, ch., and orch. (1979); *Sirens' Song*, unacc. (1974); 2 *Epitaphs*, unacc. women's ch. (1975); 4 *Miniatures*, unacc. (1978); *The Leaden Echo and the Golden Echo*, ch., alto fl., va., hp. (1978); *Creatures*, ch. (1979).

SONG-CYCLE: *Sun, Moon, and Stars*, sop. and pf. (1978).

CHAMBER MUSIC: Str. Qts. No. 1 (1933), No. 2 (1937), No. 3 (1938), No. 4 (1939–43), No. 5 (1948), No. 6 (1950), No. 7 (1955–6), No. 8 (1966), No. 9 (1969), No. 10 (1971–2), No. 11 (1976), No. 12 (1979); ob. quintet (1933); *Reflections*, ob., cl., va., and harp (1961); *Notebook*, hpd. (1965–6); 3 *Bagatelles*, ob. and hpd. (1972); 3 *Songs*, ten. and harp (1974); 3 *Pieces*, harp (1976); *Contemplation*, vc. and pf. (1978); *Colloquy*, fl., pf. (1978–9); *Fantasia*, cl., pf. (1979); str.

trio (1980); *Piccola Musica,* str. trio (1981); *Trittico,* 2 ob., bn., hpd. (1981); wind quintet (1982); *Tribute,* vn. and 8 wind (1983). Also songs and pf. pieces.

McPhee, Colin (*b* Montreal, 1901; *d* Los Angeles, 1964). Canadian-born Amer. composer and pianist. Studied Peabody Cons. until 1921, then in Paris with Le Flem, 1924–6 and in NY with *Varèse. Lived in Bali 1934–6, studying native mus. and using its procedures in his orch. work *Tabuh-Tabuhan* (1936). Taught at Univ. of Calif. 1960–64. Other works incl. pf. conc. (1923), *Balinese Ceremonial Music,* 3 syms., and conc. for wind orch. Arr. Britten's *Variations on a Theme of Frank Bridge* for 2 pf., 1942.

Madama Butterfly. Opera orig. in 2 acts by Puccini, comp. 1901–3, to lib. by Giacosa and Illica based on Belasco's play (1900) which in turn was taken from a story by J. L. Long (possibly based on a real event). Prod. Milan 1904. New version in 3 acts prod. Brescia 1904 (3 months later), London 1905, Washington (in Eng.) 1906, NY Met. 1907. Version usually perf. today dates from Paris 1906 prod. for which Puccini made further cuts and revs. 1978 WNO prod. restored over 400 measures of 1904 score.

Madame Chrysanthème. Ballet in 1 act to mus. by Rawsthorne, lib. and choreog. by Ashton. Prod. London 1955.

Madame Sans-Gêne. Opera in 3 acts by Giordano to lib. by Simoni after play by Sardou and Moreau. Prod. NY Met. and Turin 1915.

Madeira (orig. Browning), **Jean** (*b* Centralia, Ill., 1918; *d* Providence, Rhode Island, 1972). Amer. mez. Studied Juilliard Sch. Opera début 1943, Chautauqua in *Martha.* Appeared at San Carlo and on European tour in title-role of *Menotti's *The Medium.* Début at NY Met. 1948 in *Götterdämmerung* (First Norn). Member of Vienna Opera 1955 (singing Carmen, Amneris, Azucena, etc.). CG début 1955 as Erda. Also sang in Paris, Bayreuth, Salzburg, Milan, and Buenos Aires. Created Circe in Dallapiccola's *Ulisse,* Berlin 1968. A memorable Klytemnestra in Strauss's *Elektra.*

Maderna, Bruno (*b* Venice, 1920; *d* Darmstadt, 1973). It. composer and cond., among leaders (with *Berio) of the It. *avant-garde.* Studied Milan Cons., Siena Acad., and S. Cecilia Acad., Rome (until 1940). Comp. pupil of Malipiero and others, studied cond. with H. *Scherchen. After service in World War II, was encouraged by Virgil Thomson and met *Boulez. Taught at Venice Cons. 1947–50 and at Darmstadt summer courses (from 1951). With Berio, founded elec. mus. studio of It. Radio at Milan, 1955, later becoming mus. dir. Milan Radio. Brilliant cond. of 20th-cent. mus. Cond. many modern operas in Europe. Visited USA 1965 to conduct *Nono's *Intolleranza* at Boston and sym. concerts in Chicago and NY. His early works were influenced by Bartók and

Stravinsky. He adopted serialism in 1951 and Webernian features entered his work. He also used elec. media, usually in combination with live perf. However complex his mus., his native It. lyricism was always present. Prin. works:

THEATRE PIECE: *Hyperion* (Venice 1964), composite work i.e. *Dimensioni III + Aria da Hyperion + 2-track tape; Hyperion II* (*Dimensioni III* + cadenza for fl. + *Aria da Hyperion*); *Hyperion III* (*Hyperion + Stele per Diotima*); *Dimensioni IV* (*Dimensioni III + Stele per Diotima*); *Satyricon* (1973).

ORCH: *Serenata* for 11 instr. (1946, rev. 1954); *Introduzione e Passacaglia* (1947); *Quadrivium* (1948); Conc. for 2 pf. and chamber orch. (1948); Studi per 'Il Processo' di Kafka, for reciter, sop., and small orch. (1949); fl. conc. (1954); *Composizione in 3 tempi* (1954); *Serenata II* for 11 instr. (1957); pf. conc. (1959); vn. conc. (1969); conc. for ob., chamber ens., tape *ad lib* (1962, rev. 1965); *Dimensioni III* for sop., fl., and orch. (1963); *Aria da Hyperion* for sop., fl., and orch. (1964); *Stele per Diotima* (1965); ob. conc. (1967); *Music of Gaiety* (based on virginals pieces by Byrd, Farnaby, Dowland, and Philips) (1969); *Juilliard Serenade (Free Time I)* (1970); *Venetian Journal* for ten. and chamber orch. (1971); *Giardino Religioso* (1972); *Aura* (1972); *Biogramma* (1972).

TAPE: *Musica su 2 dimensioni,* fl. and 2-track tape (1952, rev. 1958); *Notturno* (1956); *Syntaxis* (2-track) (1957); *Continuo* (1958); *Dimensioni II* (2-track) (1960); *Tempo libero I* (1971); *Ages* (1972).

CHAMBER MUSIC: Str. Qt. (1955); *Aulodia per Lothar,* ob. d'amore, guitar ad lib (1965); *Widmung* for vn. (1967); *Solo* (1971); *Dialodia,* 2 fl., recorder, ob. (1972); *Y después,* guitar (1972).

Madetoja, Leevi (*b* Uleåborg, 1887; *d* Helsinki, 1947). Finn. composer and cond. Studied Helsinki Cons. (pupil of Sibelius), Paris (1910–11, pupil of d'Indy), and Vienna (1911–12). Cond., Helsinki P.O. 1912–14. Prof. of mus., Helsinki Cons. 1916–39. Comp. 2 operas, 3 syms., symphonic poems, cantatas, etc.

Madrigal (It. *madrigale;* orig. *matricale*—pastoral in the mother-tongue). Vocal comp., of It. origin, for several vv., usually unacc. but sometimes with instr. acc. Texts usually secular (amorous, satirical, or allegorical), but there are *madrigali spirituali.* Madrigals were first sung in It. towards the end of the 13th cent. and early examples survive by Giovanni da Cascia and Jacopo da Bologna. The form was revived in a different style in the 16th cent. by It. composers and by the Flemish Arcadelt, Verdelot, and Willaert. It became more complex and experimental in the hands of*Lassus, *Palestrina, and A. *Gabrieli and achieved its finest flowering in the works of Donati, Marenzio, Gesualdo, and, especially, Monteverdi. In the 17th cent. it was superseded by the cantata.

The singing of It. madrigals was imported to Eng. by It. composers such as *Ferrabosco the elder who worked at Elizabeth I's court. Nicholas Yonge, of St Paul's Cath., formed a madrigal choir and in 1588 pubd. *Musica Transalpina*, a coll. of It. madrigals to Eng. words. Eng. composers such as *Byrd, *Morley, and later *Weelkes and *Wilbye, wrote superb madrigals, though they did not always call them by that name. In the 19th cent., mock-madrigals were composed by *Sullivan and *German.

See also *Fellowes, E. H.*

Madrigal Comedy. Short drama set to mus. as series of secular vocal pieces (madrigals or some other vocal form). First known example was Vecchi's *L'Amfiparnaso* (1594), followed by Banchieri's *La pazzia senile* (1598).

Madrigale. See *Madrigal.*

Madrigali guerrieri e amorosi (Madrigals of love and war). Monteverdi's 8th book of madrigals, 1638, which contains 58 items, some purely instr., some for 8 vv. with 2 vn. and basso continuo. Contains whole of *Il ballo delle ingrate*, also separate extracts from it, and whole of *Il *combattimento di Tancredi e Clorinda*, with separate extracts from it.

Maelzel (Mälzel), **Johann Nepomuk** (*b* Ratisbon, 1772; *d* at sea, 1838). Ger. inventor of mechanical mus. devices. Settled in Vienna 1792. Constructed *Panharmonicon, a mechanical orch. for which his friend Beethoven wrote his *Battle Symphony* (1813). Made mus. chronometer based on Stöckel's invention and, in 1814, a metronome, based on Winkel. The second movement of Beethoven's 8th sym. begins with a theme said to derive from a canon extemporized by Beethoven at a supper in honour of Maelzel, the tickings of the chronometer being represented by staccato 16th-notes, i.e. 'Ta-ta-ta-ta . . . lieber Maelzel'.

Maestoso (It.). Majestic, dignified, hence *allegro maestoso*.

Maestro (It.). Master. Title given in Italy to celebrated composers, conds., and teachers, e.g. *Maestro Verdi, Maestro Toscanini, Maestro Martini*. The tendency has grown in USA (and has spread) to use it as a synonym only for conds., e.g. 'the maestro'. *Maestro di cappella* was the mus. dir. of a chapel or of an aristocratic mus. est.; *maestro al cembalo* was the musician who, in 17th and 18th cents., directed perfs. from the hpd. or other continuo instr.

Maestro di Cappella, Il (The Chorus Master). Intermezzo by Cimarosa, comp. *c*.1786–93, for bar. and orch. Ov. is that of Cimarosa's opera *L'Impresario in angustie*, prod. 1786.

Maestro di Musica, Il (The Music Master). Comic opera in 1 act, being altered version of *Orazio*, opera by P. Auletta to lib. by A. Palombo.

Prod. Naples *c*.1737. Often wrongly attrib. *Pergolesi.

Magaloff, Nikita (*b* St Petersburg, 1912). Russ. pianist (later Swiss citizen). Studied Paris Cons., pf. with Philipp and comp. with Prokofiev. Began career in duo with *Szigeti (vn.), then soloist with orchs. and recitalist in Europe and USA. Prof. of pf. Geneva Cons. 1949–59.

Magelone, Die schöne (The fair Magelone). 15 songs or romances for solo v. and pf. by Brahms, Op. 33, settings of extracts from the novel *Die schöne Magelone* by Ludwig Tieck (1773–1853). Comp. 1861–8.

Maggini, Giovanni (Paolo) (*b* Botticino-Marino, 1580; *d* Brescia, *c*.1630). It. maker of vns., vas., vcs., and dbs. valued nearly as highly as instrs. by *Stradivari and *Guarneri. Introduced many improvements, particularly in way the wood was cut.

Maggiolata (It.). May Song, or Spring Song—either traditional or comp.

Maggiore (It.). Major.

Maggot. Old Eng. word meaning 'fanciful idea', used by 16th- and 17th-cent. composers in titles of instr. pieces, often country dances, e.g. 'My Lady Winwoods Maggot'. Revived in 20th-cent. by Peter *Maxwell Davies in his *Miss Donnithorne's Maggot*.

Magic Flute, The (Mozart). See *Zauberflöte, Die*.

Magic Fountain, The ('Watawa'). Opera in 3 acts by Delius to lib. by comp. and Jutta Bell (?1857–1934). Comp. 1894–5. F. (concert) p. BBC broadcast recorded in London, July 1977 and relayed on 20 Nov. 1977.

Magnard, Albéric (*b* Paris, 1865; *d* Baron, 1914). Fr. composer. Studied Paris Cons. 1886–8 under Massenet, then became pupil of d'Indy. Comps. are of strong structure, somewhat austere in effect. Wrote 3 operas (*Yolande* 1891, *Guercoeur* 1903, *Bérénice* 1909), 4 syms., *Chant funèbre*, for orch., str. qt., songs, pf. pieces. Died when his house was set on fire when he refused to surrender after shooting dead 2 German soldiers who had entered his property. Almost all his MSS. were burned with him.

Magne, Michel (*b* Lisieux, 1930; *d* Cergy-Pontase, Val d'Oise, 1984). Fr. composer of *avant-garde* proclivities. His *Symphonie humaine* (1955) for 150 perfs. calls for inaudible 'infrasounds' to produce psychological reaction through powerful low frequencies. Wrote mus. for ballet *Le Rendezvous manqué* (1957).

Magnificat (Lat.). Canticle of the Virgin Mary ('My soul doth magnify the Lord') as it appears in St Luke's Gospel. The Lat. name is first word of Vulgate trans. (Magnificat anima mea Dominum). Part of R.C. Vespers and of Anglican

Evensong (where mus. setting is followed by *Nunc Dimittis). Sung to plainchant in R.C. service and to Anglican chant in latter, but there are many comp. settings for church and concert perf., e.g. by Dunstable, Dufay, Lassus, Palestrina, Monteverdi, Bach, Schütz, and Vaughan Williams.

Mahler, Fritz (*b* Vienna, 1901; *d* Winston-Salem, N. Carolina, 1973). Austrian-born cond. and composer (Amer. citizen 1939). Nephew of Gustav*Mahler. Studied with Berg, Schoenberg, and Adler at Vienna Univ. Settled in USA 1936. Taught cond. Juilliard Sch. 1938–53. Cond. Erie (Penn.) S.O. 1947–53, Hartford S.O. 1953–64. Wrote symphonic poem, chamber mus., and songs.

Mahler, Gustav (*b* Kalist, Bohemia, 1860; *d* Vienna, 1911). Austrian composer, cond., and pianist. Began to learn pf. at age 6, giving public recital in 1870. Entered Vienna Cons. 1875, studying pf. under J. Epstein, harmony under R. Fuchs, and comp. with Franz Krenn. Became friendly disciple, but not pupil, of *Bruckner, helping to make pf. duet arr. of 3rd Sym. (1878). While at Cons. comp. and played in perfs. of his own pf. quintet and vn. sonata. On leaving Cons. in 1878 comp. cantata *Das klagende Lied*, entering it in 1881 for Beethoven Prize but it was rejected. Began career as cond. 1880 at Hall, Upper Austria, followed by posts at Laibach (Ljubljana), Olmütz (1883), and Kassel 1883–5. While in the Kassel post he had an unhappy love-affair recorded in his song-cycle *Lieder eines fahrenden Gesellen*. Moved to Prague, 1885, and the next year to Leipzig as 2nd cond. to *Nikisch. While there he was invited by Weber's descendants to construct an opera from the fragments of *Die drei Pintos*. This, when prod. in 1888, was very successful. That year he went to Budapest Opera as chief cond. There his genius as cond. and administrator had full rein for the first time. In 1889 he conducted the f.p. of his first Sym., then simply described as 'symphonic poem'.

In 1891 Mahler became chief cond. of Hamburg Opera, where he built up a co. of remarkable singers (whom he coached also to be singer-actors), and introduced many new works. He took the co. to London in 1892, his only visit, for perfs. of Wagner's *Ring* and *Tristan*, and Beethoven's *Fidelio*. His 2nd Sym. (*Resurrection*) was completed 1894 and perf. in Berlin 1895. For the rest of his life Mahler divided his time between comp. in the summer and cond. in the winter. His mus. met at first with hostility, but its quality was recognized by his contemporary Richard Strauss. In 1897, having converted from Judaism to Roman Catholicism, he became dir. of the Vienna Court Opera, inaugurating a glorious decade during which he set standards still scarcely surpassed and revolutionized the production and lighting of operas in collaboration with gifted colleagues. In 1902 he married Alma Schindler,

also a musician, by whom he had 2 daughters (the elder died in 1907, aged 4). Between 1896 and 1907, when he resigned his post after controversy, he comp. his Syms. 3 to 8, the song-cycle *Kindertotenlieder*, and other songs with orch. Each of the syms. was on a huge scale, but perfs. were becoming more frequent throughout Europe, especially through the championship of *Mengelberg.

Mahler made his Amer. début on 1 Jan. 1908 conducting *Tristan* at the NY Met. In 1909 he was appointed cond. of the reorganized NY P.O. In 1910 in Munich he cond. the first 2 perfs. of his 8th Sym. (*Symphony of a Thousand*), returning to NY 2 months later. From 1907 he lived under the shadow of death from a heart ailment. This led in 1911 to a severe blood infection which caused his premature death on 18 May. He left 3 large posthumous works, the song-sym. *Das Lied von der Erde* and Syms. 9 and 10. *Das Lied* and the 9th were f.p. in 1911 and 1912 respectively cond. by Bruno*Walter in Munich and Vienna. The 10th was long thought to be unfinished and only 2 movements were pubd. and played until the Eng. scholar Deryck *Cooke discovered in 1960 that the work was complete in short score and made a performing version.

Mahler's greatness as a cond. was never contested. But his comps. for many years were regarded with fanatical admiration by a handful of disciples and admirers and equally fanatical scorn by a larger section of musicians. However the championship of certain conds. and critics led gradually in the late 1950s to a fervent revival of interest. His works were frequently recorded and entered the repertories of the world's leading orchs. to public acclaim. His mus. appealed both to those elements who cherished its romantic eloquence and to the *avant-garde* who recognized that it bridged the divide between the old and the new. Deeply personal in expression, the extreme chromaticism of works such as the 9th Sym. anticipates the innovations of Schoenberg. The unconventional form of the syms., their juxtaposition of popular elements with mystic passages, the *concertante* use of solo instrs., the complex and subtle instr. polyphony, the contrasts of irony, pathos, childlike simplicity, and psychological insight, all appealed to later 20th-cent. composers; and audiences found in his mus. a cogent and comprehensive expression of the anxieties and complexities of modern life. He championed the younger generation in his own lifetime and became their idol after his death. Prin. works:

SYMPHONIES: No. 1 in D major (1884–8, rev. 1893, 1896 reduced from 5 to 4 movements, and 1897–8; excluded movement, *Blumine*, restored in some 20th-cent. perf.). F.p. Budapest 1889, f.p. in England 1903. No. 2 in C minor (*Resurrection*; 1888–94, rev. 1910), for sop., cont., ch., and orch. F.p. Berlin 1895, f.p. in

England 1931. No. 3 in D minor (1895–6), for cont., women's and boys' chs., and orch. F.p. Krefeld 1902, f.p. in England 1947. No. 4 in G major (1899–1900, rev. 1910), sop. solo in finale. F.p. Munich 1901, f.p. in England 1905. No. 5 in C♯ minor (1901–2, rev. 1904–10). F.p. Cologne 1904, f.p. in England 1945 (*Adagietto* only 1909). No. 6 in A minor (1903–5, rev. 1908), f.p. Essen 1906, f.p. in England 1950 (broadcast relay 1947). No. 7 in B minor (1904–5, rev. 1909), f.p. Prague 1908, f.p. in England 1913. No. 8 in E♭ major (1906–7), for 8 soloists, ch., boys' ch., and orch. F.p. Munich 1910, f.p. in England 1930. No. 9 in D major (1909–10). F.p. Vienna 1912, f.p.in England 1930. No. 10 in F♯ major (1910). F.p. of *Adagio* and *Purgatorio* Vienna 1924, f.p. in England *Adagio* 1948, *Adagio* and *Purgatorio* 1955. F.p. of Cooke version, London 1960, rev. 1964, final rev. 1972. Note that Mahler himself cond. the f.ps. of the first 8 syms. (Strauss did not conduct f.p. of No. 2, as often stated).

SONG-SYMPHONY: *Das*★*Lied von der Erde* (The Song of the Earth) for cont. (or bar.), ten., and orch. (1907–9). F.p. Munich 1911; f.p. in Eng. 1914; f.p. in Amer., Philadelphia 1916.

CANTATA: *Das* ★*klagende Lied* (The Song of Sorrow) for sop., cont., ten., bass, ch., and orch. (1878–80). Orig. in 3 parts. Rev. 1888 to 2 parts. Further rev. between 1893 and 1902. F.p. Vienna 1901, f.p. in England 1956. F.p. of complete 1880 version Vienna 1935, f.p. in England 1970.

SONG-CYCLES: ★*Lieder eines fahrenden Gesellen* (Songs of a Wayfarer) for v. and pf./orch. (1884, rev. c.1892, 1896). F.p. Berlin 1896, f.p. in England 1927. ★*Kindertotenlieder* (Songs of the Death of Children) for v. and orch./pf. (1901–4). F.p. Vienna 1905, f.p. in England 1913 (pf.), 1924 (orch.).

SONGS: *3 Songs* for ten. and pf. (1880); *5 Songs* for v. and pf. (1880–3), later (1892) pubd. as Book I of *Lieder und Gesänge aus der Jugendzeit* (Songs of Youth). Books II and III (comp. 1888–91) are 9 settings from *Des* ★*Knaben Wunderhorn*; *Lieder aus Des Knaben Wunderhorn*, 12 settings for v. and orch./pf. (1888–99); 3 songs from *Des Knaben Wunderhorn*: *Wir geniessen die himmlischen Freuden* (1892; incorporated into finale of 4th Sym. 1899), *Revelge* (1899), *Der Tamboursg'sell* (1901); *5 Lieder nach Rückert* for v. and orch./pf.: 1. *Ich atmet' einen linden Duft* (1901), 2. *Liebst du um Schönheit* (1902), 3. *Blicke mir nicht in die Lieder* (1901), 4. *Ich bin der Welt abhanden gekommen* (1901), 5. *Um Mitternacht* (1901). F.p. Vienna 1905 (excluding No. 2).

CHAMBER MUSIC: Vn. sonata (1876); pf. quintet in A minor (1876); pf. qt. in A minor (1876).

ARRANGEMENTS: J. S. Bach's Suite for Orch. in 4 movements (1st and 2nd from Suite No. 2, 3rd and 4th from Suite No. 3). F.p. NY 1909; Schubert's Str. Qt. in D minor (*Death and the Maiden*), for str. orch., c.1894; Beethoven's Str.

Qt. in F minor, Op. 95, for str. orch. (f.p. Vienna, Jan. 1899) and Str. Qt. in C♯ minor, Op. 131, for str. orch.; Bruckner's 3rd Sym. for pf. 4 hands (1878).

OPERA: Completion of Weber's *Die* ★*drei Pintos*. F.p. Leipzig 1888, f.p. in England 1962

Maid as Mistress, The (Pergolesi). See *Serva padrona, La*.

Maid of Orleans, The. Opera in 2 acts by Tchaikovsky, comp 1878–9 to his own lib. based on Schiller's play about Joan of Arc. Prod. St Petersburg 1881, London 1978.

Maid of Pskov, The (*Pskovityanka*). Opera in 4 acts by ★Rimsky-Korsakov to his own lib. after play by Mey (1860). Comp. 1868–72. Prod. St Petersburg 1873; Moscow 1898, rev. version 1876–7, 3rd version 1891–2, prod. London 1913. Also known under title *Ivan the Terrible,* bestowed by Diaghilev, Paris 1909.

Maid of the Mill, The (Schubert). See *Schöne Müllerin, Die*.

Mai-Dun. Symphonic rhapsody for orch. by ★Ireland comp. 1921. Title refers to prehistoric Dorset fortification, Maiden Castle.

Maillart, Aimé (Louis) (*b* Montpellier, 1817; *d* Moulins, 1871). Fr. composer. Studied Paris Cons. under Halévy. Comp. several operas, best-known being *Les Dragons de Villars* (1856), and cantatas.

Mainardi, Enrico (*b* Milan, 1897; *d* Munich, 1976). It. cellist and composer. Pupil of H. ★Becker. Soloist with leading orchs. Gave master classes from 1933 at S. Cecilia Acad., Rome, Salzburg Mozarteum, and Lucerne Cons. Wrote 4 vc. concs., solo vc. sonatas, etc. Recorded *Don Quixote* with Strauss conducting (1933).

Maine, Basil (Stephen) (*b* Norwich, 1894; *d* Sheringham, 1972). Eng. author, critic, organist, and composer. Studied Cambridge Univ. under Wood and Stanford. Ass. organist Durham Cath. Mus. critic, *Daily Telegraph,* 1921–6, *Morning Post* 1926–37. Wrote several books, inc. 2-vol. life and works of Elgar (1933). Comp. orch. and choral mus. Narrator or 'orator' in such works as Honegger's *Le Roi David* and Bliss's *Morning Heroes*. Closely assoc. with Norwich Fest. Ordained C. of E., 1939.

Mainzer, Joseph (*b* Trier, 1801; *d* Salford, 1851). Ger. singing teacher, also mining engineer, priest, composer, and critic. Became priest 1826, later abbé. Taught singing at Trêves, later Brussels. In Paris from 1834 where he pubd. several mus. textbooks. Went to London 1841, then Edinburgh, settling in Manchester 1847. There he est. singing courses based on ★Wilhem system. His *Singing for the Million* (1841) had large sale. Founded *Musical Times and Singing-Class Circular* 1842, taken over by Novello 1844 as *Musical*

Times. His methods were challenged by those of *Hullah. Comp. 2 operas.

Maio, Gian (Francesco) **de** (*b* Naples, 1732; *d* Naples, 1770). It. composer. Organist at Naples royal chapel. Visited Vienna 1764. Wrote 20 operas and much church mus.

Maisky, Mischa (*b* Riga, 1948). Soviet cellist. Studied Moscow Cons. Début with Leningrad P.O. 1965; London début 1976. Winner, Cassado competition, Florence 1973.

Maître de Chapelle (Fr.). Equivalent of Ger. *Kapellmeister.*

Maîtrise. A Fr. choir sch.

Maja y el Ruisenor, La (The Love-sick Girl and the Nightingale). No. 4 of the *Goyescas* by Granados orig. for pf., later incorporated as song into Scene 2 of opera *Goyescas* and frequently heard as separate concert aria with orch.

Major Bass. Organ stop of 16′ pitch, generally an *Open Diapason.*

Major Common Chord. A common chord incl. the major 3rd.

Major Flute. Loud org. stop of 8′ or 16′ length and pitch.

Major Scale. See *Scale.*

Makrokosmos. 12 fantasy-pieces after the Zodiac for amplified pf. by *Crumb, comp. 1972. They are studies in *avant-garde* pf. technique, each being assoc. with a sign of the Zodiac and with a friend of the composer's who was born under that sign.

Makropulos Affair, The (*Věc Makropulos*; literally 'The Makropulos Thing', hence variations in trans. title, e.g. 'The Makropulos Case', 'The Makropulos Secret'). Opera in 3 acts by Janáček to his own lib. based on play (1922) of same name by Karel Čapek (1890–1938). Comp. 1923–5. F.p. Brno 1926, London 1964, San Francisco 1966.

Maksymiuk, Jerzy (*b* Grodno, 1936). Polish conductor, composer, and pianist. Studied at Warsaw Cons. Cond., Teatr Wielki, Warsaw, 1970–2. Cond. Polish Chamber Orch. Cond. BBC Scottish S.O. from 1983. Comp. ballet, *Capriccio* for pf. and orch. (1969), str. trio, and pf. pieces for children.

Mal (Ger.). Time, in such contexts as *Erste Mal*, first time; *2 Mal* (*Zweimal*), twice, etc.

Malagueña (Sp.). (1) Sp. dance of fandango variety from Málala and Murcia, exported to Mexico by Sp. settlers.

(2) Sp. gipsy song involving improvisation and cadenzas and sung by amorous youths with guitar accompaniment. Instr. malagueñas occur in Chabrier's *España* (1883), Ravel's *Rapsodie espagnole* (1907), and Albéniz's *Iberia* (1906–9).

Malbrouck s'en va-t-en guerre (Malbrouck goes off to the war). 18th-cent. Fr. nursery song. In Britain the tune is sung to either 'For he's a jolly good fellow', or 'We won't go home until morning'. Sung to various different sets of words, it has enjoyed great European popularity. It is usually stated that 'Malbrouck' refers to the 1st Duke of Marlborough, but the name is found in medieval literature.

Malcolm, George (John) (*b* London, 1917). Eng. harpsichordist, pianist, cond., and composer. Studied Oxford Univ. and RCM. Master of the Music, Westminster Cath. 1947–59. On staff RAM. Frequent recitalist. Assoc. with Britten's mus. C.B.E. 1965.

Malcuzyński, Witold (*b* Warsaw, 1914; *d* Palma, Majorca, 1977). Polish pianist. Studied with *Paderewski. Settled Paris 1939, début there 1940. NY début 1942. Worldwide tours. Specialized in Chopin, Liszt, etc.

Male Voice Choir (or **Chorus**). One (usually) of men only but it may be of boys and men.

Male Voice Quartet. 4 male vv., either alto, first and 2nd ten., and bass ('with alto lead'), or first and 2nd ten. and first and 2nd bass ('with tenor lead').

Malgoire, Jean-Claude (*b* Avignon, 1940). Fr. conductor and oboist. Studied at Paris Cons. In 1966 founded La Grande Écurie et la Chambre du Roy which specializes in baroque mus., mixing modern instr. with restored models.

Malibran (*née* García), **Maria** (Felicitá) (*b* Paris, 1808; *d* Manchester, 1836). Sp. mez. Studied with her father, Manuel *García. Sang in Paër's *Agnese* in Naples at age 5. First public perf. Paris 1824. Opera début London 1825 as Rosina in Rossini's *Il barbiere di Siviglia.* Went to NY 1826 singing leading roles in her father's It. opera co. While there married François Eugène Malibran, but the union was short-lived. Début Paris Opéra 1828 in Rossini's *Semiramide.* Triumphs followed in London, Naples, Rome, Bologna, Venice, Lucca, and Milan. Sang title-role in Donizetti's *Maria Stuarda* 1835. In 1836 married Belg. violinist Charles de *Bériot with whom she had lived since 1830. Fell from horse in London, April 1836, her injuries leading to her death in Sept. when she collapsed after singing a duet at a Manchester fest. Her v. was notable for its colour and range, and was described as 'like the costliest gold, but it had to be mined, forged, and stamped like metal under the hammer to make it malleable'. Her lively temperament, intensity as an actress, and exciting life made her a legend. Her younger sister was Pauline *Viardot.

Malimba. See *Marimba.*

Malinconia, malinconico (It.). Melancholy. So *malinconoso, malinconioso, malinconicamente*, in melancholy fashion. Walton marked the slow movement of his First Sym. 'con malincolia' (sic).

Malipiero, Gian Francesco (b Venice, 1882; d Treviso, 1973). It. composer. Studied Vienna Cons. 1898–9, then in Venice and Bologna under Bossi. Settled in Venice 1904–15, but spent some months in Berlin in 1908–10 attending lectures by Bruch. In this period, in the Marciana Library, Venice, he discovered and transcr. the almost forgotten works of Monteverdi, Galuppi, Tartini, Stradella, etc. This determined him to rebel against the 'operatic tyranny' of It. mus. life. In 1913 he met *Casella, who became his colleague in the struggle. Became prof. of comp., Parma, 1921–3. Then settled at Asolo. Taught comp. at Liceo B. Marcello, Venice, from 1932, becoming dir. 1939–52. Pubd. complete edn. of Monteverdi 1926–42 which stimulated present revival of interest. Also ed. many vols. of Vivaldi's complete works. Author of books on Vivaldi, Monteverdi, and Stravinsky. He destroyed most of his mus. written before 1914, but thereafter he was a prolific composer and wrote many operas. His mus., naturally influenced by the early It. composers, also shows traces of Debussy's impressionism and, in the 1920s, the angularity of Janáček. The later works border on atonality, but he rejected serialism. Prin. works:

OPERAS: L'Orfeide (triptych: La Morte delle maschera, 1921–2, Sette canzoni (1918–9), Orfeo, 1919–20); S. Francesco d'Assisi (1920–1); Tre Commedie Goldoniane (triptych: La bottega da caffè, 1922, Sior Todero Brontolon, 1922, Le baruffe chiozzote, 1920); Filomela e L'infatuato (1925); Merlino mastro d'organi (1926–7); Il Mistero di Venezia (triptych: Le Aquile di Aquileia, 1928, Il finto Arlecchino, 1925, I Corvi di S. Marco, 1928); Torneo Notturno (1929); I Trionfi d'amore (triptych: Castel smeraldo, Mascherate, Giochi olimpici, comp. 1930–1. No. 2 perf. 1937 as Il festino); La Favola del figlio cambiato (1932–3); Giulio Cesare (1934–5); Antonio e Cleopatra (1936–7); Ecuba (1940); La Vita è sogno (1940–1); I Capricci di Callot (1941–2); L'Allegra brigata (1943); Vergilii Aeneis (1943–4); Mondi celesti e infernali (1948–9); Il Figliuol prodigo (1952); Donna Urraca (1953–4); Il Capitan Spavento (1954–5); Venere prigioniera (1955); Rappresentazione e festa di Carnasciale e della Quaresima (1961); Don Giovanni (1962); Le Metamorfosi di Bonaventura (1963–5); Don Tartufo Bacchettone (1966); Il Marescalco (1960–8); Gli eroi di Bonaventura (1968); Uno dei dieci (1970); L'Iscariota (1970).

BALLETS, etc.: Pantea (1917–19); Stradivario (1948); El Mondo Novo (1950–1).

ORCH: Syms.: No. 1 ('in 4 movements like the 4 seasons', 1933), No. 2 (Elegiaca, 1936), No. 3 (delle Campane, 1944–5), No. 4 (In Memoriam, 1946), No. 5 (Concertante, in Eco, 1947), No. 6, for str. (1947), No. 7 (delle Canzoni, 1948), No. 8 (Sinfonia brevis, 1964), No. 9 (dell' ahimè, 1966), No. 10 (Atropo, 1967), No. 11 (delle cornamuse,

1970); Sinfonia in un tempo (1950); Sinfonia dello Zodiaco (1951); Impressioni dal Vero I (1910–11), II (1915), III (1921–2); Pause del Silenzio I (1917), II (1925–6); Concerti (1931); 4 Invenzioni (1933), Vivaldiana (1952).

VOICES AND ORCH: La Principessa Ulalia (1924); La Cena (1927); La Passione (1935); Missa pro mortuis (1938); La festa della Sensa (1950); Magister Josephus (1957).

INSTR. AND ORCH: Variazioni senza Tema, pf. and orch. (1923); Vn. Conc. No. 1 (1932), No. 2 (1963); Pf. Conc. No. 1 (1934), No. 2 (1937), No. 3 (1948), No. 4 (1950), No. 5 (1958), No. 6 (1964); Vc. Conc. (1937); Triple Conc. (1938); Dialogo, 2 pf. (1956); Fl. Conc. (1968).

VOICES AND CHAMBER ENS: De profundis (1937); Universa Universis (1942); Mondi celesti (1948); Ave Phoebe dum queror (1964).

CHAMBER MUSIC: Str. Qt. No. 1 (1920), No. 2 (1923), No. 3 (1931), No. 4 (1934), No. 5 (1950), No. 6 (1947), No. 7 (1950), No. 8 (1963–4) (No. 5 based on material from opera I Capricci di Callot, 1941–2); Sonata for vn., vc., and pf. (1927); vc. sonatina (1942); wind quintet (1956).

Also songs and pf. pieces.

Malipiero, Riccardo (b Milan, 1914). It. composer. Studied Milan Cons. and Turin Cons. 1930–7 and at Venice with his uncle G. F. *Malipiero. Adopted 12-note system 1945 and helped to organize first Int. Congress of 12-note mus., Milan, 1949. Works incl. opera, vn. conc., wind quintet, 6 Poems of Dylan Thomas for sop. and 10 instr., 3 syms., vc. conc., 3 str. qts., pf. quintet, ob. sonata, and conc. for ballerina and orch.

Malizia (It.). Malice. The scherzo of Walton's first sym. is marked presto, con malizia.

Malko, Nikolay (Andreyevich) (b Brailov, 1883; d Sydney, N.S.W., 1961). Russ.-born cond. (Amer. citizen 1946). Studied St Petersburg Cons. with Rimsky-Korsakov and Glazunov, and with *Mottl in Munich. Cond. opera and ballet, St Petersburg 1908–18. Prof. Leningrad Cons. 1918–26, cond. Leningrad P.O. 1926–9. Prof. Moscow Cons. 1927–33. Went to Eng. Settled in Chicago 1940. Cond. Yorkshire S.O. 1954. Sydney S.O. 1956–61. Cond. f.p. of Shostakovich's 1st and 2nd Syms., Leningrad 1926 and 1927.

Mallinger (orig. Lichtenegger), **Mathilde** (b Zagreb, 1847; d Berlin, 1920). Croatian sop. Studied Zagreb, Prague, Vienna. Début as Norma, Munich 1866. Created role of Eva in Die Meistersinger von Nürnberg, Munich 1868. Berlin Opera 1869–82, prof. of singing Prague Cons. 1890–5, Berlin Eichelberg Cons. from 1895. Taught Lotte *Lehmann.

Malovec, Josef (b Hurbanovo, 1933). Cz. composer. Studied Bratislava Acad. 1951–3 and Prague Acad. 1953–7. Worked for Cz. radio from 1957, helping establish elec. studio 1965. Works incl.

Scherzo for orch., *Concert Music* (1967), *Orthogenesis* (tape, 1967), *Tmel* (synthesized and concrete sounds on tape, 1968), *Tabu* (elec. sounds on tape, 1970).

Mamelles de Tirésias, Les (The Breasts of Tiresias). *Opéra-bouffe* in 2 acts by Poulenc to lib. based on play by Apollinaire. Prod. Paris 1947, Brandeis Univ. 1953, Aldeburgh 1958, Leeds 1978, London (SW) 1978.

Ma mère l'Oye (Mother Goose). Suite in 5 movements by Ravel based on fairy-tales by Péricault. Orig. for 4 hands (1 pf.) (1908–10), orch. 1911 and prod. as ballet (to scenario by Ravel), Paris 1912. There are differences between the 2 versions. The 5 movements of piano suite are (1) *Pavane de la Belle au Bois dormant* (Sleeping Beauty's Pavan), (2) *Petit Poucet* (Tom Thumb), (3) *Laideronette Impératrice des Pagodes* (Empress of the Pagodas), (4) *Les Entretiens de la Belle et la Bête* (Conversations of Beauty and the Beast), (5) *Le Jardin féerique* (The Fairy Garden). For the ballet Ravel added a *Prélude*, the *Danse du Rouet* and 4 extensive interludes.

Man. (1, It.) Short for *mano*, hand.
(2, Ger.) Short for *Manuale*, manual (of organ); Man. I = Great; II, Swell; III, Choir; IV, Solo (but occasionally another numeration is used, based on position, i.e. I, Choir; II, Great; III, Swell; IV, Solo).

Manchega. An especially lively type of **seguidilla* danced in the La Mancha province of Spain.

Manchester Camerata. Chamber orchestra founded in Manchester in 1972 under auspices of BBC Radio Manchester. Maximum strength 38 players. Became autonomous organization in 1979. Main series in Manchester but plays throughout North West of England and has visited France, Norway, and Hongkong. Prin. conds.: Frank Cliff 1972–7; Szymon Goldberg 1977–80; Manoug Parikian 1980–4; Nicholas Braithwaite from 1984. London début 1983, cond. Braithwaite (Croydon 1976, cond. Goldberg). Plays for opera at Buxton Fest.

Manchester School. Title given to group of composers—*Maxwell Davies, *Birtwistle, *Goehr, and *Ogdon—who studied in Manchester (RMCM and Univ.) under Richard *Hall in late 1950s and gave concerts there.

Mancinelli, Luigi (*b* Orvieto, 1848; *d* Rome, 1921). It. cond., composer, and cellist. Studied Florence. Th. orch. cond. Rome 1874. Dir. Liceo Musicale, Bologna, 1881–6. Cond. opera Drury Lane, London, 1887, CG 1888–1905; cond. f.ps. in England of Verdi's *Falstaff* and Puccini's *Tosca*. Mus. dir. Madrid Th. Royal 1887–93. Chief cond. It. opera at NY Met. 1893–1903. Cond. Teatro Colón, Buenos Aires, 1908–13. Comp. operas *Ero e Leandro*, *Paolo e Francesca*, and *Midsummer Night's Dream*, also choral works and church mus.

Mancini, Francesco (*b* Naples, 1672; *d* Naples, 1737). It. composer. Studied Naples. Maestro, royal chapel there. Wrote over 20 operas, of which *Idaspe Fedele* was the first opera to be sung in London wholly in It. (1710). Dir., Cons. di S. Maria di Loreto 1720–35.

Mancini, Henry (Nicole) (*b* Cleveland, Ohio, 1924). Amer. composer, cond., and arranger. Studied Juilliard Sch. 1942–3. Guest cond. leading sym. orchs. Composer of numerous film scores, incl. *Breakfast at Tiffany's*, with its hit-song *Moon River*.

Mandola, mandora, mandore (from Gr. *Pandoura*). Ancient instr. (possibly as early as 9th cent.), a small ancestor of the *lute. Popular in Sp. and It., reaching Eng. at end of 14th cent. Had 9 frets and up to 6 str. Played with plectrum and used for popular mus.-making. Ancestor of *mandolin.

Mandolin(e). Plucked str. instr. of lute family, of It. orig., usually with 8 str. tuned in pairs and played with plectrum, generally in a sustained tremolo. Used in informal mus.-making, but occurs in several famous scores, e.g. *Alexander Balus* (Handel, 1747), *L'Amant jaloux* (Grétry, 1778), *Don Giovanni* (Mozart, 1787), *Otello* (Verdi, 1887), 7th Sym. and *Das Lied von der Erde* (Mahler), *Serenade* (Schoenberg), *5 Pieces* (Webern), *Agon* (Stravinsky), etc. Beethoven wrote some pieces for mandolin and pf., and Vivaldi several concs.

Mandoline. Poem by Verlaine set for v. and pf. by Debussy, 1882, as no. 3 of *Fêtes galantes (orig. version), and by Fauré, 1891, as No. 1 of 5 *Mélodies*, Op. 58.

Mandora. See *Mandola*.

Manduell, John (*b* Johannesburg, 1928). S. African-born Eng. administrator and composer. Studied RAM. On staff of BBC 1956–68 (chief planner, Mus. Prog. 1964–8). Dir. of Mus., Lancaster Univ. 1968–71. Prin., RNCM from 1972. Dir., Cheltenham Fest. since 1969, having been programme adv. 1961–7. Works inc. ov. *Sunderland Point*, str. qt., etc. C.B.E. 1982.

Mandyczewski, Eusebius (*b* Czernowitz, 1857; *d* Vienna, 1929). Romanian musicologist and cond. Studied Vienna Cons. with Nottebohm and Fuchs. Cond. Vienna Singakademie 1880, and archivist *Gesellschaft der Musikfreunde*. On staff Vienna Cons. from 1897. Ed. the Lieder in complete Schubert ed. 1897, 3 vols. of Haydn syms., works by Beethoven and Brahms. Wrote songs and pf. pieces.

Manfred. Verse-drama by Byron (1817) on which are based (1) Ov. and 15 items of incidental mus. by Schumann, Op. 115 (1848–9); (2) Sym. (unnumbered) by Tchaikovsky, Op. 58 (1885).

Manfredini, Francesco (b Pistoia, 1684; d Pistoia, 1762). It. violinist and composer. At Monaco court 1711. Maestro di capella Pistoia Cath. from 1727. Wrote several *concertini da camera* (1704), 12 *sinfonie da chiesa* (1709), concs. for 2 vn. and continuo (1718).

Manfredini, Vincenzo (b Pistoia, 1737; d St Petersburg, 1799). It. composer, son of F. *Manfredini. Court post in Russia 1758–69, returning to It. Comp. ballets, operas, 6 syms., and kbd. sonatas.

Mangeot, André (Louis) (b Paris, 1883; d London, 1970). Eng. violinist and impresario of Fr. birth. Studied Paris Cons. Settled in London, becoming Brit. citizen. Played in Queen's Hall Orch. under Wood and CG orch. under Richter (1908). Founded International String Quartet 1919, specializing in Brit. works and contemporary mus. Gave f. Eng. p. of Fauré's str. qt. 1925. Ed. 17th cent. Eng. works for str. (with Peter Warlock).

Manhattan School of Music. Mus. coll. in NY City, founded 1917, permanent charter 1925. Pres. was John *Brownlee 1958–69, succeeded by George Schick. Moved into buildings vacated by *Juilliard School, 1962.

Mani (It., plural of *mano*). Hands.

Manica (It.). Shift (on vn., etc.; see *Position*).

Manichord. See *Monochord*.

Manico (It.). Fingerboard (vn., etc.).

Manieren (Ger.). *Ornaments, or graces.

Mann, William (Somervell) (b Madras, 1924). Eng. mus. critic. Studied Cambridge Univ. and with Seiber (comp.) and Ilona Kabós (pf). Ass. mus. critic *The Times* 1948–60, chief mus. critic 1960–82. Author of books on operas of R. Strauss and Mozart. Many trans. of libs. and song-texts.

Männergesangverein (Ger.). Male singing society, i.e. male v. ch. Developed from *Liedertafel.

Manners, Charles (orig. Southcote Mansergh) (b London, 1857; d Dublin, 1935). Irish bass and impresario. Studied Dublin, RAM, and Florence. Joined D'Oyly Carte Opera 1881, created role of Private Willis in *Iolanthe* 1882. Carl Rosa co., then CG from 1890. Amer. début 1893. Married sop. Florence Moody 1890 and with her est. *Moody-Manners Opera Co., 1898.

Mannes College of Music. Mus. coll. in NY City founded 1916 as Mannes Mus. Sch. by violinist and cond. David Mannes (b NY, 1866; d NY, 1959) and his wife Clara (1869–1948). Charter 1960.

Mannes, Leopold (Damrosch) (b NY, 1889; d Vineyard Haven, Mass., 1964). Amer. pianist, composer, teacher, and inventor. Son of David Mannes and nephew of Walter *Damrosch.

Teacher of comp. at *Mannes Sch., ass. dir. 1939, president from 1951. Founded pf. trio 1949. Gave up mus. for period in 1920s while with Leopold Godowsky jr. he invented Kodachrome photographic colour process. Wrote orch. and chamber mus.

Mannheim School. Name given by modern musicologists to group of 18th-cent. Ger. composers based on Mannheim and assoc. with the court of the Elector of Pfalzbayern (1724–99). Their importance, shared to some extent with similar progressives in Vienna, Italy, and Bohemia, was in laying foundation of the sym. as it was to be developed by Haydn and Mozart. They were headed by Johann W. *Stamitz (1717–57), followed by Ignaz Holzbauer (1711–83, in Mannheim from 1753), F. X. *Richter (1709–89, in Mannheim from 1747), *Cannabich (1731–98), and Stamitz's sons Karl (1745–1801) and Anton (1754–1809). The elder Stamitz joined the Mannheim orch. in 1745, soon becoming cond. He founded a new style of perf. suited to his works. Features of this style incl. melodic prominence of vns., extended crescendi and precise dynamics, tremolando, and replacement of improvised continuo by written-out parts.

Manning, Jane (Marian) (b Norwich, 1938). Eng. sop., expert in contemporary mus. Studied RAM and Switzerland. Début London 1964 in songs by Webern, Messiaen, and Dallapiccola. Has given f.ps. of numerous works by Eng. composers.

Manns, (Sir) August (Friedrich) (b Stolzenberg, 1825; d Norwood, 1907). Ger.-born cond. (naturalized Eng.). After studies, was prin. clarinettist in Danzig military band. In 1848 became first violinist in *Gung'l's orch., Berlin. Bandmaster, Königsberg and Cologne 1851–4. Went to London 1854 as ass. cond. of Crystal Palace band. In 1855 became cond. and augmented band to sym. orch. From 1855 to 1901, when orch. was disbanded, Manns's Crystal Palace concerts were most enterprising concerts in Eng., where many works received their f.ps. in England. Manns cond. first London perf. of mus. by Elgar. Instituted Saturday popular concerts 1856. Cond. Handel Fest. 1883–1900. Knighted 1903.

Manon. Opera in 5 acts by *Massenet to lib. by Meilhac and Gille, after Prévost's novel *Manon Lescaut* (1731). Prod. Paris 1884, Liverpool and NY 1885, CG 1891, NY Met. 1895. Massenet wrote 1-act sequel *Le Portrait de Manon* (1894). Operas on same subject by *Auber (1856), *Puccini (1890–2), Balfe (*The Maid of Artois*, 1836), and Henze (*Boulevard Solitude*, 1951).

Manon Lescaut. Opera in 4 acts by Puccini to lib. by Giacosa, Illica, G. Ricordi, Praga, and Oliva, after Prévost's novel. Comp. 1890–2. Prod. Turin 1893, CG and Philadelphia 1894, NY 1898 (Met. 1907).

Manowarda, Josef von (b Kraków, 1890; d Berlin, 1942). Austrian bass. Début Prague 1913. Member, Vienna Opera 1919–42, Berlin Opera 1934–42. Salzburg Fest. from 1922. Bayreuth 1931, 1934, 1939, 1942. Outstanding King Mark (*Tristan*) and Gurnemanz (*Parsifal*).

Mantovani, (Annunzio Paolo) (b Venice, 1905; d Tunbridge Wells, 1980). It.-born cond. and violinist. Studied TCL. Formed hotel orch., Birmingham, 1923. Recitalist in London. Broadcasting orch. from 1927. Mus. dir. for many musicals, esp. those by Noël Coward. Famous for 'singing strings' sound, heard chiefly in arrs. by Ronald *Binge.

Mantra. Work for 2 amplified, ring-modulated pf. by *Stockhausen, comp. 1969–70. F.p. 1970, London 1971. Fully notated. Pianists also play perc. instr. (wood-block and little bells). Title refers to Indian word for a mystical repetition, a 'sound which makes one see'.

Manual. Any of the org. kbds. provided for the hands (as opposed to pedal-kbd.). Hpds. have 1st and 2nd manuals (kbds.).

Manuale (Ger.). Manual (of organ). See *Man.*

Manualkoppel (Ger.). Manual coupler, i.e. (usually) Swell to Great.

Manuel (really Lévy), **Roland** (Alexis) (sometimes Roland-Manuel or Manuel-Lévy) (b Paris, 1891; d Paris, 1966). Fr. composer and critic. Pupil of Roussel and Ravel. Comp. operettas, ballets, pf. conc., etc. Wrote 3 books on Ravel. On staff Paris Cons. from 1947.

Manzoni Requiem. Title sometimes given to Verdi's *Requiem*, which was comp. in memory of It. novelist and poet Alessandro Manzoni. F.p. Milan 1874, London 1875.

Manzuoli, Giovanni (b Florence, c.1720; d Florence, 1782). It. castrato. Sang first in It., then in Madrid 1749–53. Sang in London 1764 and 1765, where he instructed the child Mozart, then settled in Florence. Ended career in Milan, 1771, when he created title-rôle in Mozart's *Ascanio in Alba* (K111). Retired to Florence to teach.

Maraca (plural *maracas*). Lat.-Amer. perc. instr. made from a pair of dried Cuban gourds, with beans or beads inside. Shaken by handle to produce a rattling effect. (Sometimes made of other materials with lead shot inside, to give a stronger effect). Usually played as a pair. Used by dance-bands, also in concert works by 20th-cent. composers such as Varèse, Prokofiev, Bernstein, Arnold, McCabe, etc.

Marais, Marin (b Paris, 1656; d Paris, 1728). Fr. composer. Studied with Lully. Virtuoso player of viola da gamba in royal band. Became cond. of Paris Opéra orch. Wrote operas (incl. *Alcione*, 1706), 5 vols. of pieces for viol, chamber mus., etc.

Marazzoli, Marco (b Parma, c.1602 or c.1608; d Rome, 1662). It. composer, singer, and harpist. Singer in papal chapel 1637–62. With V. *Mazzocchi, wrote what is believed to be first comic opera, *Chi soffre, speri* (Rome 1639, rev. of *Il falcone*, 1637), also other operas, oratorios, cantatas, etc.

Marcando; marcato (It.). Marking; marked, i.e. each note emphasized. *Marcatissimo* is the superlative.

Marcello, Alessandro (b Venice, 1669; d Venice, 1747). It. composer and mathematician, brother of Benedetto *Marcello. Comp. cantatas, concs. for fls. and vns., and for ob. and fl.

Marcello, Benedetto (b Venice, 1686; d Brescia, 1739). It. composer. Pupil of Gasparini. Also studied law, and held important State posts. Wrote operas, oratorios, cantatas, instr. concs., and settings of 50 psalms for vv. with instr. acc.

March (Fr. *Marche*, Ger. *Marsch*, It. *Marcia*). Form of mus. to accompany the orderly progress of large group of people, especially soldiers; one of earliest known mus. forms. Military marches are of 4 kinds: funeral (4/4 time), slow (usually 4/4), quick (2/4 or 6/8), and double-quick. The march entered art mus. in 17th cent. in the works of *Couperin and *Lully, but there are marches in virginals pieces by Byrd. Marches occur in the operas of Mozart (e.g. *Die Entführung, Figaro, Così fan tutte*, and *Zauberflöte*); Schubert wrote *Marches militaires* and Beethoven incorporated a *funeral march into his *Eroica* sym., as did Chopin into a pf. sonata. Famous operatic marches were written by Meyerbeer, Wagner, and Verdi. It was further developed in the sym. by Berlioz, Mahler, Tchaikovsky, and Elgar. Military marches for concert perf. by sym. orch. were written by Elgar (*Pomp and Circumstance*) and R. Strauss. Some of the best military marches were written in the 19th cent. by *Sousa, Johann Strauss I, and *Lanner.

Marchal, André (b Paris, 1894; d St Jean de Luz, 1980). Fr. organist, blind from birth. Studied Institut des Jeunes Aveugles and Paris Cons. Organist S. Germain-des-Prés, Paris, 1915–45, then S. Eustache 1945–63. Began career as recitalist 1923, undertaking world tours. Noted for improvisations.

Marchand, Louis (b Lyons, 1669; d Paris, 1732). Fr. organist and composer. Organist, Nevers Cath. at age of 14. Organist, royal chapel 1708–14. Banished from Fr. High reputation in Fr. as kbd. virtuoso. On tour of Ger. in 1717, he was involved in projected hpd. competition with Bach in Dresden, but withdrew at the last minute, afraid of failure. Returned to Fr. as teacher. Works incl. kbd. pieces, opera, cantata, airs, and 3 *Cantiques spirituels* (texts by Racine). Teacher of *Daquin.

Marchant, (Sir) **Stanley** (b London, 1883; d London, 1949). Eng. organist. Studied RAM. Ass.

organist, St Paul's Cath. 1903, organist 1927–36. Prin., RAM 1936–49; prof. of mus., London Univ. 1937–49. Knighted 1943. Wrote church mus.

Marchesi, Blanche (b Paris, 1863; d London, 1940). Fr. sop., daughter of Mathilde*Marchesi. Début Prague 1900, Brünnhilde in *Walküre*. Joined *Moody-Manners co. Settled in London to teach.

Marchesi de Castrone (orig. Graumann), **Mathilde** (b Frankfurt, 1821; d London, 1913). Ger. mez. and teacher. Studied Vienna with *Nicolai, Paris with *García (1845). Concert début, Frankfurt 1844. Sang in London, 1849. Married It. bar. and teacher Salvatore Marchesi (1822–1908) in 1852. Prof. of singing Vienna Cons. 1854–61 and 1869–78, Cologne Cons. 1865–8. Taught at own sch. in Paris 1861–5 and from 1881. Wrote vocal method and 24 books of exercises. Pupils incl. Calvé, Eames, Mary Garden, and Melba.

Marcovici, Silvia (b Bacau, Romania, 1952). Romanian-born violinist. Studied at Bacau and Bucharest Cons. Pupil of S. Gheorghiu. Soloist with Hague Residentie Orch. in 1967. In 1969 won Thibaud-Long comp. in Paris, Enescu comp., Bucharest 1970. London début 1970 (LSO). Chosen by Stokowski as soloist at his 90th birthday concert in 1971. Emigrated to Israel in 1976, settling later in Ger.

Marenzio, Luca (b Coccaglio, Brescia, 1553/4; d Rome, 1599). It. composer and singer. Probably a choirboy in Brescia Cath.; later in employ of Cardinal Madruzzo in Rome in 1570s. From 1578 in employ of Cardinal Luigi d'Este. Pubd. books of madrigals in 1580s, achieving widespread popularity. In 1588 went to Florence to serve Medici family. Was at Pol. court in Warsaw in 1596–7. Early madrigals and *villanelle* were noted for detailed illustration of the texts. In 1590s his style became more chromatic and dissonant as his choice of texts became more serious. His earlier works were popular in Eng., where they were pubd. in *Musica Transalpina and influenced Wilbye, Weelkes, and others.

Margot-la-Rouge ('A Night in Paris'). Unpubd. opera in 1 act by Delius to libretto by 'Rosenval' (Berthe Gaston-Danville), comp. 1901–2. Vocal score by Ravel 1902 (pubd. Paris c.1905). See *Idyll*. F.p. (in orch. by Fenby) BBC studio broadcast 1979; f. stage p. (in orig. Delius orch.) St. Louis 1983; f. London stage p. 1984.

Maria di Rohan. Opera in 3 acts by Donizetti to lib. by Cammarano. Prod. Vienna 1843, London 1847, NY 1849.

Maria Golovin. Opera in 3 acts by *Menotti to his own lib. Prod. Brussels and NY 1958, London 1976.

Maria Stuarda. Opera in 3 acts by Donizetti to lib. by G. Bardari based on Schiller's play. Prod. as

Buondelmonte, Naples 1834, with orig. title Milan 1835, NY (concert) 1964, NY City Opera 1972, London 1966 (St Pancras Fest.),1973 (SW).

Mariani, Angelo (b Ravenna, 1821; d Genoa, 1873). It. cond. and composer. Studied with Rossini in Bologna. Début as opera cond. Messina 1844. Court cond., Copenhagen 1847–8. Cond., Genoa 1852–73. Cond. It. premières of *Lohengrin* and *Tannhäuser*, and many important Verdi perfs. Comp. requiem, cantatas, songs.

Marienleben, Das (The Life of Mary). Settings by Hindemith, Op. 27, for sop. and pf. of 15 poems by R. M. Rilke, comp. 1922–3, f.p. Frankfurt 1923. New and rev. version, worked on from 1936–48, f.p. Hanover 1948. 4 songs orch. by Hindemith 1938, 2 more 1959.

Mariés de la Tour Eiffel, Les (The newly-weds of the Eiffel Tower). Ballet in 1 act with mus. by 5 of Les *Six (excl. Durey). Lib. by Cocteau, choreog. by Börlin. Prod. Paris 1921.

Marimba. Lat.-Amer. perc. instr. of African origin. It consists of strips of wood of different length with (tuned) resonators underneath, the whole fixed in a frame and struck with drumsticks—in fact, a super-xylophone large enough for perf. by 4 players (or *Marimberos*), standing or sitting side by side. Now made with bars of rosewood and tubular metal resonators which are struck with soft-headed hammers held by the player(s). Grainger scored for the marimba in the suite *In a Nutshell* before 1916. *Milhaud wrote a conc. for marimba and vibraphone (1947) and *Creston a conc. for marimba (1940). It now frequently occurs in orch. works.

The S. African original, known to Afrikaans-speaking Europeans as the *Kaffir Piano*, is called the *Malimba* by natives.

Marinetti, Filippo Tommaso (b Alexandria, 1876; d 1944). It. apostle of *Futurism. Advocated 'noise-makers' of all kinds in mus.

Marini, Biagio (b Brescia, 1597; d Venice, 1665). It. violinist and composer. Held court posts in It. and Ger. Wrote vn. concs., ballets, etc.

Marinuzzi, Gino (Giuseppe) (b Palermo, 1882; d Milan, 1945). It. cond. and composer. Studied Palermo Cons. Début as cond. in Catania. Cond. at Palermo, Milan, Madrid, Buenos Aires, and Rio. Dir., Liceo Musicale, Bologna, 1915–18. Cond. f.p. of Puccini's *La Rondine*, Monte Carlo 1917. Cond., Chicago Opera 1919–21, Rome Opera 1928–34, Scala, Milan, 1934–44. Début CG 1934. Wrote 3 operas, requiem, and cantata.

Mario, Giovanni (Matteo) (Cavaliere de Candia) (b Cagliari, 1810; d Rome, 1883). It. ten. Army career took him to Paris, 1836, where he was persuaded to become opera singer because of exceptional beauty of v. Début Paris Opéra 1838 in *Robert le Diable*. It. Opera in Paris, 1840. London début, Her Majesty's, 1839, singing there until

1846. CG 1847–67. With Giulia *Grisi, his lifelong companion after 1839, *Tamburini, and *Lablache sang in f.p. of Donizetti's *Don Pasquale*, Paris 1843. Handsome in appearance and fine actor. Retired 1871.

Mariotte, Antoine (*b* Avignon, 1875; *d* Izieux, Loire, 1944). Fr. composer. Studied Paris with d'Indy. Prof. of pf., Lyons Cons. 1902–20, dir. Orléans Cons. 1920–36. Wrote several operas incl. *Salomé* (1908), based like Strauss's on Wilde play. Dir., Opéra-Comique, Paris, 1936–8.

Maritana. Opera in 3 acts by W.V. *Wallace to lib. by E. Fitzball (with interpolated lyrics by Alfred Bunn) after play *Don César de Bazan* by D'Ennery and Dumanoir. Prod. London 1845, Philadelphia 1846, NY 1848.

Mark, Peter (*b* NY City, 1940). Amer. violist and cond. Studied Columbia Univ. and Juilliard Sch. Prin. violist, Juilliard Orch. 1960–3, Chicago Lyric Opera 1964–6, ass. prin. violist Los Angeles P.O. 1968–9. Art. dir. and cond. Virginia Opera Assoc. from 1975. Solo violist in f.p. of conc. by his wife Thea *Musgrave.

Markevitch, Igor (*b* Kiev, 1912; *d* Antibes, 1983). It. cond., composer, and writer of Russ. birth. Studied Paris 1926 with *Boulanger. Guest cond. leading European orchs. Mus. dir. Stockholm S.O. 1952–5, Montreal S.O. 1955–60. US début Boston S.O. 1955. Cond., Lamoureux Orch. 1957–61, Spanish Radio-TV orch. 1965–8; dir., Monte Carlo Opera 1968. Fine interpreter of Stravinsky. Composer of pf. conc., cantata *Paradise Lost*, ballet scores, etc.

Markiert (Ger.). Marked, i.e. clearly accented, or brought out. Used in connection with, for instance, the emphasis given to a melody above its acc.

Markig (Ger. 'vigorous'). Directive frequently found in Bruckner scores, e.g. *sehr markig* in finale of 8th Sym.

Marriage, The (*Zhenitba*). (1) Unfinished opera by Mussorgsky to his own lib. based on Gogol's comedy (1842). 1 act completed 1868. Concert perf. at Rimsky-Korsakov's house 1906, stage (with pf. acc.) St Petersburg 1909, 1st full prod. in Rimsky's rev., Petrograd 1917.
(2) Opera in 1 act by Martinů to his own lib. after Gogol. Amer. TV (NBC) 1953; stage prod. Hamburg 1954.

Marriage of Figaro, The (Mozart). See *Nozze di Figaro, Le*.

Marriner, (Sir) Neville (*b* Lincoln, 1924). Eng. cond. and violinist. Studied RCM. Taught at Eton Coll. 1948. Member of Martin Str. Qt. 1949. Prof. of vn. RCM 1949–59. Violinist in Philharmonia Orch. 1952, prin. 2nd vn. LSO 1956–68. Founder, *Academy of St Martin-in-the-Fields, 1958; dir. 1958–78. Cond. Los Angeles Chamber Orch.

from 1968. Début as opera cond. RNCM Manchester (*Bohème*) 1977. Prin. cond. Minnesota Orch. 1979–86, cond. S.W. German Radio Orch. from 1983. C.B.E. 1979. Knighted 1985.

Marschalk, Max (*b* Berlin, 1863; *d* Poberowa-d-Ostsee, 1940). Ger. mus. critic and composer. Friend of R. Strauss and Mahler. Critic for Berlin *Vossische Zeitung* from 1895. Wrote incidental mus. to plays (incl. some by his brother-in-law Gerhardt Hauptmann), orch. works, and songs.

Marschner, Heinrich (August) (*b* Zittau, 1795; *d* Hanover, 1861). Ger. composer and cond. Studied Leipzig. Went to Vienna 1817 and met Beethoven. Success of his opera *Heinrich IV und d'Aubigné*, prod. by Weber at Dresden 1820, led to his appointment there as co-cond. with Weber. Appointed mus. dir. 1824, resigning on Weber's death 1826. Kapellmeister, Leipzig, 1827, where his *Der *Vampyr* (1828) was successful. In Dec. 1829 *Der Templer und die Jüdin*, based on Scott's *Ivanhoe*, was prod. Court Kapellmeister, Hanover, 1831–59. Most famous opera, *Hans Heiling*, prod. Berlin 1833. 8 other operas followed, none successful. Wrote incidental mus. to Kleist's *Prinz von Homburg*, also 7 pf. sonatas, pf. trios, songs, etc. Occupies place between Weber and Wagner in history of Romantic opera.

Marseillaise, La. Fr. nat. anthem (first line 'Allons, enfants de la patrie'). Words and mus., by Claude Joseph *Rouget de Lisle, written on 24 April, 1792, under title *Chant de guerre pour l'armée du Rhin* (War song for the Rhine army). Received present title when sung by battalion of Marseilles troops as they entered Paris. Quoted by Schumann in *Faschingsschwank aus Wien* and *Die beiden Grenadier*, by Elgar in *The Music Makers*, and by Tchaikovsky in his *1812* ov. Elaborately arr. for soloists, ch., and orch. by Berlioz.

Marsh, Roger (*b* Bournemouth, 1949). Eng. composer. Studied York Univ. with *Rands. Ran mus.-th. group 'Clap'. Univ. of Calif., San Diego, from 1976. Works incl.: *Dum's Dream* for str., singer, actor (1973); *Cass*, mus. th. (1970); *Calypso*, mus. th. (1973); *Scènes de Ballet*, mus. th. (1974); *Serenade* for amplified db. (1974); *Deadpan's Romance*, wind quintet (1975); *Not a Soul but Ourselves*, 4 vv. with amplification (1977); *Variations*, tb. and elec. (1979); *Bits and Scraps*, SATB, technician, light (1979); *Point to Point*, 2 ob., 2 cl., 2 hn., 2 bn. (1979); *2 Movements*, 2 fl., 2 cl., hp., str. qt. (1979); *Music for Ensemble* with 4 vv. (1980); *Still (as far as may be)*, ens. (1980); *The Wormwood and the Gall*, mez. and ens. (1981); *Delilah*, sop. and sax. (1982); *Words of Love*, bar., 2 ob., bn., hpd. (1982); *Spit and Blow*, tuba (1983); *Songs of Devotion*, sop., cl., guitar (1983–4); *Samson*, ch. (1984).

Marshall, Margaret (*b* Stirling, 1949). Scottish soprano. Studied RSAM and with Hans *Hotter. 1st prize Munich comp. 1974. London début

1975, Edinburgh Fest. 1978. Opera début Florence 1978 (Euridice in Gluck's *Orfeo*), CG 1980 (Countess in *Figaro*), La Scala, Milan, and Salzburg 1982 (Fiordiligi in *Così fan tutte*). Amer. début (concert) 1980.

Marteau sans maître, Le (The hammer without a master). Work by *Boulez for cont., alto fl., va., guitar, vibraphone, xylorimba, and perc. Comp. to text by René Char 1952–4, rev. 1957. F.p. Baden-Baden June 1955, cond. Rosbaud, Paris 1956, cond. Boulez, London 1960, cond. Boulez.

Martelé (Fr.). Hammered—referring to the manner of playing bowed instr. by a series of short, sharp blows with the bow upon the str. The point of the bow is to be used for this process unless the heel is indicated by the expression *Martelé du talon* (see also *Détaché*).

Martellando; martellato (It.). Same as *Martelé*, though the words are sometimes applied to pf. playing and even singing.

Martenot, Maurice (*b* Paris, 1898; *d* Paris, 1980). Fr. musician and inventor. Studied vc. and comp. at Paris Cons. Prof. at École Normale de Musique, Paris, and dir. of École d'Art Martenot, Neuilly. Gave demonstration of his elec. mus. instr. the *Ondes Martenot, at the Paris Opéra on 20 April 1928.

Martha, or Richmond Fair (*Martha, oder Der Markt von Richmond*). 4-act opera by Flotow to lib. by F. W. Riese after V. de Saint-Georges's ballet-pantomime *Lady Henriette* for which Flotow had comp. some mus. Makes use of 'The Last Rose of Summer'. Prod. Vienna 1847, London 1849, NY 1852.

Martin, Frank (*b* Geneva, 1890; *d* Naarden, Holland, 1974). Swiss composer, pianist, and harpsichordist. Studied Geneva with Lauber. Studied in Rome 1921–3. Taught at Geneva Cons. Dir., Technicum moderne de musique, Geneva, 1933–9. Taught Cologne Cons. 1952–8. Works of high quality, notable for delicate colouring, contrapuntal skill, and expressive nature. Used 12-note system very freely in late works. Prin. comps.:

OPERAS: *Der Sturm* (The *Tempest*) (1952–5); *Monsieur de Pourceaugnac* (1961–2).
BALLETS: *Die blaue Blume* (1936); *Fairy-Tale of Cinderella* (1941).
ORCH: *Symphonie burlesque sur les thèmes savoyards*, (1915); *Rythmes* (1926); *Guitare* (1933); *Petite Symphonie Concertante* (1946); Concerto for 7 winds, timp., and str. (1949); *Études* for str. (1956); *Passacaille* for str. (1963); *Les 4 éléments* (1963); *5 Ballades*: alto sax., str., and pf. (1938); fl. and str. (1939); pf. (1939); tb. (1940); vc. and small orch. (1949).
CONCERTOS: Pf. conc. No. 1 (1934), No. 2 (1968–9); vn. conc. (1951); hpd. conc. (1952); vc. conc. (1966); *Triptych*, vn. and orch. (1973–4).

VOICE AND ORCH: *Der Cornet*, for cont. and small orch. (1943); *Sechs Monologe aus Jedermann* (Hofmannsthal), bar. or cont. (1943).
CHORAL: *Mass* (1922–6); *Le vin herbé*, secular oratorio on Tristan legend (1938–41); *In terra pax*, oratorio (1944); *Golgotha*, oratorio (1945–8); *Pilate* (1964); *Requiem* (1971–2).
CHAMBER MUSIC: Pf. quintet (1919); str. trio (1936); Str. Qt. No. 1 (1936), No. 2 (1967); Vn. Sonata No. 1 (1913), No. 2 (1931–2).

Martinelli, Giovanni (*b* Montagnana, 1880; *d* NY, 1969). It. ten. Played in regimental band, where his v. was noticed by bandmaster. Studied Rome. Début Milan 1910 in Rossini's *Stabat Mater*. Engaged by Puccini to sing Dick Johnson in European première of *La Fanciulla del West* (1911). London début CG 1912 (*Tosca*). US début Philadelphia 1913, NY Met. 1913 (*Bohème*). Member of NY Met. 1913–46, singing in 36 operas.

Martinet, Jean-Louis (*b* Ste-Bazeille, 1912). Fr. composer. Studied Paris Cons. 1938–45, teachers incl. Roger-Ducasse, Koechlin, Messiaen, and Munch. Instructed in Schoenberg theories by *Leibowitz, 1945. Vienna 1949. Works incl. symphonic poem *Orphée, Variations* for str. qt., 7 *Poems by René Char*, vocal qt. and orch., 2 *Images* for orch., Sym. (1962–3).

Martini, Giovanni (Battista) (Giambattista; known as 'Padre Martini') (*b* Bologna, 1706; *d* Bologna, 1784). It. composer and theorist. Entered monastery 1722; maestro di cappella San Francesco, Bologna, 1725. Took minor orders 1725, ordained priest 1729 and devoted much time to scientific aspects of mus., amassing library of 17,000 books. Pupils incl. J. C. Bach, Grétry, Mozart, and Jommelli. Wrote church mus., instr. sonatas, and theoretical books.

Martini, Giovanni (Paolo) (Martini il Tedesco, 'Martini the German'; real name Johann Paul Aegidius Schwarzendorf) (*b* Freistadt, 1741; *d* Paris, 1816). Ger. organist and composer. After service with King Stanislaus, settled in France, changing name to Martini. Held various court posts, was th. cond., and taught at Paris Cons. Wrote operas, church mus., and songs, of which best-known is *Plaisir d'amour*.

Martino, Donald (James) (*b* Plainfield, NJ, 1931). Amer. composer. Studied Syracuse and Princeton Univs. and in Italy 1954–6. Comp. pupil of *Babbitt, *Sessions, and *Dallapiccola. Teacher at various Amer. univs. and chairman of comp. dept., New England Cons. Some of mus. uses 12-note technique and dense polyphonic textures. Works incl. *Quodlibets* for fl., *Contemplations* for orch., pf. fantasy, cl. trio, pf. conc., sym., and triple conc. for cl., bass cl., and contrabass cl.

Martinon, Jean (*b* Lyons, 1910; *d* Paris, 1976). Fr. cond., violinist, and composer. Studied Lyons Cons. and Paris Cons. 1923–9 (comp. with Roussel and cond. with Désormière and Munch). Prisoner-of-war for 2 years during which he comp. several works. Cond. f.p. of one of these in Paris, which led to post at Bordeaux. Ass. to Munch with LPO 1946. Cond. Radio Eireann Orch. 1948–50. Mus. dir. Lamoureux Orch., 1951–8, Israel P.O. 1958–60, Chicago S.O. 1963–9 (Amer. début Boston 1957), French Radio Orch. 1968–75, Hague Residentie 1975–6. First Frenchman to win Mahler Medal. Wrote 4 syms., opera, oratorio, 2 vn. concs., vc. conc., 2 str. qts., etc.

Martinů, Bohuslav (Jan) (b Polička, 1890; d Liestal, Switz., 1959). Cz. composer and violinist. Vn. lessons at 6; began composing at 10. Studied Prague Cons. 1906–10 with Suk. Violinist, Czech P.O. 1918–23, whose cond. *Talich performed Martinů work in Prague 1923. Went to Paris 1923 to study with Roussel. Stayed until 1941, when settled in USA where he composed 5 syms. Returned to Europe 1953, living in Fr. and Switz. Prolific composer in all mus. forms. Remained essentially Cz. despite long exile. His works are uneven and flawed, but the best, such as the opera *Julietta* and the syms., are progressive and full of rhythmical energy and imagination. Basically diatonic, but with wide, sometimes dissonant, harmonic range. Prin. works:

OPERAS: *The Three Wishes* (film, 1929); *The Miracles of Mary* (1933–4); *Comedy on the Bridge* (radio, 1935); *Theatre Behind the Gate* (1936); *Julietta* (1936–7); *What Men Live By* (TV, 1952); *The *Marriage* (TV, 1952); *Mirandolina* (1954); *Ariadne* (1958); *The Greek Passion* (1956–9).

BALLETS: *Ištar* (1918–22); *Who is the Most Powerful in the World?* (1922); *Revolt* (1925); *The Butterfly that Stamped* (1926); *Kitchen Revue* (1927); *Špalíček* (*The Chap Book*, singing ballet) (1931–2); *The Strangler* (1948).

ORCH: *The Angel of Death*, sym.-poem (1910); *Half-Time* (1924); *La Bagarre* (*Tumult*) (1926); *Le jazz* (1928); *Serenade* (1930); Sinfonia Concertante, 2 orch. (1932); *Invence* (1934); *Concerto Grosso* (1937); *Double Concerto*, for 2 str. orch., pf., timp. (1938); *Memorial to Lidiče* (1943); *Intermezzo* (1950); *The Rock* (1957); *3 Estampes* (1958); Syms.: No. 1 (1942), No. 2 (1943), No. 3 (1944), No. 4 (1945), No. 5 (1946), No. 6 (*Fantaisies symphoniques*) (1951–3).

CONCERTOS: Pf., No. 1 (1925), No.2 (1934), No. 3 (1948), No. 4 (*Incantations*) (1955–6), No. 5 (*Fantasia Concertante*) (1957), Concertino, left hand (1926), Concertino (1938), 2 pfs. (1943); vn. (1943), 2 vns., No. 1 (1937), No. 2 (1950); Vc., No. 1 (1930, rev. 1955), No. 2 (1944–5), Concertino (1924); Misc., str. qt. and orch. (1931), 2 concertinos, pf. trio, str. (1933), hpd. (1935), fl., vn. (1936), *Concerto da camera*, vn., pf., perc., str. (1941), Sinfonia Concertante, ob., bn., vn., vc. (1949), Rhapsody, va. (1952), vn., pf. (1953), ob. (1955).

CHORAL: *Czech Rhapsody* (1918); *The Epic of Gilgamesh* (1954–5); *Mikeš of the Mountains* (1959).

CHAMBER MUSIC: Nonet, wind quintet, pf. qt. (1924–5), Nonet, wind quintet, str. trio, db. (1959); Pf. Quintet (1911); Str. Quintet (1927); wind quintet (1930); Pf. Quintet No. 1 (1933), No. 2 (1944); Pf. Qt. (1942); Ob. Qt. (1947); Str. Trios, No. 1 (1923), No. 2 (1934); Pf. Trios, No. 1 (1930), No. 2 (1950), No. 3 (1951); Vn. Sonatas, No. 1 (1927), No. 2 (1931), No. 3 (1944); Vc. Sonatas, No. 1 (1939), No. 2 (1941), No. 3 (1952); Va. Sonata (1955); Fl. Sonata (1945); Cl. Sonatina (1956); Tpt. Sonatina (1956); Str. Qts., No. 1 (1918), No. 2 (1925), No. 3 (1929), No. 4 (1937), No. 5 (1938), No. 6 (1946), No. 7 (*Conc. da camera*) (1947).
Many kbd. pieces and songs.

Martín y Soler, Vicente (b Valencia, 1754; d St Petersburg, 1806). Sp. composer. Went to Italy 1780, Vienna 1785, and St Petersburg 1788 as dir. of It. opera. Wrote 20 operas, several to libs. by da Ponte, incl. *Una cosa rara* (1786) from which Mozart quoted in the supper scene of *Don Giovanni* and two to libs. by Catherine II of Russia. In London 1794–6, returning to Russia as teacher.

Martirano, Salvatore (b Yonkers, NY, 1927). Amer. composer. Studied Oberlin Cons. 1947–51, Eastman Sch. 1952, Florence 1952–4 (with Dallapiccola). Before Oberlin, was Marine bandsman and in dance bands. Teacher at Illinois Univ. since 1963. Works incl. Mass (unacc.); *Oooo That Shakespeherian Rag*; vn. sonata; wind sextet; str. qt.; opera *The Magic Stones*; *Ballad* for amplified night-club singer and instr. ens.; *L's GA* for gas-masked politico, helium bomb, 3 16mm. movie projectors, 2-channel tape (text is Lincoln's Gettysburg Address; the gas, when inhaled by the actor, changes the sound of his v.); *Election Night Address*.

Marttinen, Tauno (b Helsinki, 1912). Finnish composer. Studied Viipuri Institute of Mus. and Sibelius Acad. Dir., Hämeenlinna Institute of Mus. Works incl. 5 syms.; opera *The Cloak* (Gogol); 2 pf. concs., vn. conc., 3 Kalevala cantatas; ballets, vc. conc., etc.

Martucci, Giuseppe (b Capua, 1856; d Naples, 1909). It. cond., pianist, and composer. Studied Naples Cons. Prof. of pf. there 1880–7. Toured Europe 1875. Dir., Liceo Musicale, Bologna, 1886–1902, Naples Cons. 1902–9. Est. orch. concerts at which he introduced many modern works to It. audiences. Cond. f.p. in Italy of Wagner's *Tristan und Isolde*, Bologna 1888. Comp. 2 syms., 2 pf. concs., pf. quintet, 2 pf. trios, vc. sonata, many pf. pieces. Made many transcrs. of classical works.

Martyrdom of St Magnus, The. Chamber opera (mus. th.) in 1 act by *Maxwell Davies to his own lib. adapted from 'Magnus' by George Mackay Brown. For ten., 2 bar., bass, and sop., and chamber ens. Prod. St Magnus Cath., Kirkwall, Orkney, 1977, London 1977, Liverpool 1978.

Martyre de Saint-Sébastien, Le (The Martyrdom of St Sebastian). Mus. by Debussy comp. in 1911 for 5-act mystery-play (*mystère*) by D'Annunzio perf. Paris in that year. For sop., 2 cont., ch., and orch. Symphonic fragments (4 movements) f.p. in Eng. 1915, cond. Wood.

Martzy, Johanna (*b* Temesvar, 1924; *d* Rüschli-kon, Switz., 1979). Hung. violinist. Studied Budapest Acad. 1932–42. Soloist with Budapest P.O., cond. Mengelberg, 1943. European tour 1947. US début 1957.

Marx, Joseph (*b* Graz, 1882; *d* Graz, 1964). Austrian composer. Studied musicology at Graz Univ. Dir., Vienna Acad. of Mus. 1922–7. Noted for his 120 songs, but also wrote *Romantic* pf. conc., *Autumn Symphony*, pf. qt., vc. sonata, choral works, etc.

Mary, Queen of Scots. (1) Opera in 3 acts by Thea *Musgrave to her own lib. based on Amalia Elguera's play *Moray*. Prod. Edinburgh 1977, Stuttgart and Norfolk, Virginia, 1978, Bielefeld 1984.
(2) Ballet with mus. by John *McCabe, prod. Glasgow 1975.

Marziale (It.). Martial.

Masaniello. Name usually given in Britain to Auber's opera in 5 acts *La Muette de Portici* (The Dumb Girl of Portici) to lib. by Scribe and Delavigne. Prod. Paris 1828, London 1829, NY 1831. Perf. in Brussels in 1830 led to Belgian revolt (plot being based on Neapolitan uprising against Spanish oppressors, 1647).

Mascagni, Pietro (*b* Leghorn, 1863; *d* Rome, 1945). It. composer and cond. Studied Milan Cons. with Ponchielli, having already had sym. and choral works performed. Left Cons. to join touring opera co. as cond. Settled as pf. teacher at Cerignola. In 1889 won first prize in competition sponsored by publisher Sonzogno with 1-act opera *Cavalleria Rusticana*. The abundant success of this work overshadowed his remaining operas, and the assertion that he is a one-opera composer (*verismo at that) has only recently been chal-lenged. In his later years he associated himself with Mussolini's Fascist régime. Prin. comps.:

OPERAS: *Pinotta* (1880); *Guglielmo Ratcliff* (1885); *Cavalleria Rusticana* (1888); *L'*Amico Fritz* (1891); *I Rantzau* (1892); *Silvano* (1895); *Zanetto* (1896); *Iris* (1898); *Le maschere* (1900); *Amica* (1905); *Isabeau* (1911); *Parisina* (1913); *Lodoletta* (1917); *Il piccolo Marat* (1921); *Nerone* (1934).
CHORAL: Cantata for Leopardi centenary (1898); Requiem in memoriam Re Umberto (1900); *Inno del Lavro* (1928); *Inno del Avanguardisti* (1929).

Mascarade (Fr.). In earlier use this means *Masque and in later use Masquerade, i.e. Masked Ball.

Maschera, Florentio (*b c*.1540; *d* Brescia, *c*.1584). It. composer and organist. Organist Brescia Cath.

1557–84. Vol. of instr. *canzone* for 4 vv., 1584, and other org. and kbd. comps.

Mascheroni, Edoardo (*b* Milan, 1852; *d* Ghirla, Como, 1941). It. cond. and composer. Début Brescia 1880. Opera cond., Rome, 1885–92, introducing Beethoven's *Fidelio* to Italy; Scala, Milan, 1891–4, cond. f.ps. of Catalani's *La Wally* and Verdi's *Falstaff*. Toured Europe and S. America. Wrote 2 operas (libs. by Illica), choral works, and songs.

Maschinenpauken (Ger.). Mechanically-tuned kettledrums. See *Drum*.

Mask, Maske. Old spellings of *Masque. Some-times found attached to, for instance, a virginals piece, where it probably implies a dance of a suitable character for use in a masque.

Maskarade (Masquerade). Opera in 3 acts by *Nielsen to lib. by V. Andersen based on play by Holberg. Comp. 1904–6. Prod. Copenhagen 1906.

Masked Ball, A (Verdi). See *Ballo in maschera, Un*.

Mask of Time, The. Work for sop., mez., ten., bar., ch., and instr., in two parts, by *Tippett. Comp. 1981–3. F.p. Boston, Mass., April 1984, cond. Sir Colin Davis. F. European p. London, July 1984, cond. Andrew Davis.

Masnadieri, I (The Robbers). Opera in 4 acts by Verdi to lib. by Maffei from Schiller's play *Die Räuber* (1781). Comp. 1846–7. Prod. London 1847 (with Jenny Lind; only Verdi opera written for London); NY 1860. Revived It. Radio 1951 and by WNO 1977, Cardiff and elsewhere.

Masnelli, Paolo (*b* Verona, *fl*.1578–1609). It. composer. Court organist, Mantua, 1585–92, Verona Cath. *c*.1596. Wrote several books of madrigals.

Mason, Colin (*b* Northampton, 1924; *d* London, 1971). Eng. mus. critic. Studied TCL and Budapest Acad. Authority on Bartók. Mus. critic *Manchester Guardian* 1950–64, *Daily Telegraph* from 1964. Ed. *Tempo* 1964–71. Active in promotion of contemporary works. Ed. suppl. *Cobbett's Cyclo-pedia of Chamber Music* 1963.

Mason, Daniel (Gregory) (*b* Brookline, Mass., 1873; *d* Greenwich, Conn., 1953). Amer. com-poser, writer, and teacher. Pupil of d'Indy, 1913. Joined mus. faculty Columbia Univ., becoming prof. 1929. Retired 1942. Wrote several books. Comps. incl. 3 syms. (No. 3 *A Lincoln Symphony*), qt. on Negro themes, *Elegy* for pf., pf. qt., etc.

Masonic Music by Mozart. Mozart, a Freemason in a Vienna Lodge, comp. several works for masonic purposes, the chief of which are: *Maurerischer Trauermusik* (Masonic funeral mu-sic), (K477, 1785), cantata, *Die ihr des unermesslichen Weltalls Schöpfer ehrt* (K619, 1791); song, *Die ihr einen neuem Grade* (K468, 1785); cantata, *Dir, Seele* *des Weltalls* (K429, 1783); choruses: *Ihr unsere neuen Leiter* (K484, 1785), *Lasst uns mit geschlungnen Händen* (K623a, 1791), *Laut verkünde unsere Freude* (K623, 1791); song, *O heiliges Band* (K148, 1772); cantata, *Sehen, wie dem starren Forscherange* (K471, 1785); ch., *Zerfliesset heut', geliebte Brüder* (K483, 1785).

Masque (or **Mask** or **Maske**). An aristocratic ceremonial entertainment in the 17th cent., consisting of a combination of poetry, vocal and instr. mus., dancing, acting, costume, pageantry, and scenic decoration, applied to the representation of allegorical and mythological subjects. It was much cultivated in It., from which country Eng. seems to have learnt it, then carrying it to a very high pitch of artistic elaboration. It developed from the *intermedii* and from mystery plays. In Elizabethan times, among the authors employed was Ben Jonson, a supreme master of the Eng. masque; he sometimes enjoyed the collab. of Inigo Jones as designer of the decorations and machinery. Among composers of masque mus. were *Campion, *Coprario, *Lanier, and the younger *Ferrabosco. From a literary point of view the most famous masque is Milton's *Comus* (1634); for this the mus. was supplied by Henry *Lawes, but the finest masques of this period had music by his brother William. Masques continued under the Puritan régime of the Commonwealth and Protectorate, some being arr., by authority, for entertainment of distinguished foreign visitors. After the Restoration, masque episodes were popular in plays, and music for them was composed by John Blow, Pelham Humfrey, Louis Grabu, and Henry Purcell. A late example is Arne's *Alfred* (1740), written for perf. in the Prince of Wales's garden: from it comes the song *Rule, Britannia!*

In the 20th cent. Vaughan Williams described his ballet *Job* as a 'masque for dancing', to indicate that 19th-cent. type of choreog. would not be appropriate. Lambert's *Summer's Last Will and Testament* is described as a masque.

Masques et Bergamasques (Masks and Bergomasks). Divertissement by Fauré to scenario by R. Fauchois, comp. 1919, prod. Monte Carlo 1919. Suite for orch., Op. 112, 4 movements, f.p. Paris 1919, London 1920.

Mass. Owing to the importance the R.C. Mass holds in the minds of worshippers and the opportunities it offers for mus. participation it has exercised a large influence upon the development of mus. High Mass is sung, Low Mass is spoken. The Proper of the Mass (i.e. the parts which vary from season to season and day to day) has naturally usually been left to its traditional plainsong treatment. The 5 passages that are frequently set for ch., or for ch. and soloists, are: (a) *Kyrie* (Lord have mercy), (b) *Gloria in excelsis Deo* (Glory be to God on high), (c) *Credo* (I believe), (d) *Sanctus*, with *Benedictus* properly a part of it,

but in practice often separated (Holy, Holy ... Blessed...), (e) *Agnus Dei* (O Lamb of God). These are, properly, the congregational element in the Ordinary, or Common of the Mass, i.e. the invariable part. Innumerable mus. settings have been provided by hundreds of composers of all European nations. The earliest polyphonic setting was probably that by *Machaut in 14th cent. In the 15th cent. *Dufay and others introduced secular tunes as a *cantus firmus*, e.g. the folk song *L'Homme armé*. A high point was reached at the end of the 16th cent., when the unacc. choral contrapuntal style of comp. reached its apogee (Palestrina in It., Byrd in Eng., Victoria in Sp., etc.). In the 17th and 18th cents. the development of solo singing and increased understanding of the principles of effective orch. acc. led to great changes in the style of mus. treatment of the Mass, and the settings of the late 18th-cent. and early 19th-cent. composers (Haydn, Mozart, Weber, Schubert, etc.), however musically effective, have not the devotional quality of the settings of the late 16th and early 17th cents. The practice had grown up of treating the 5 passages above mentioned as the opportunity of providing an extended work in oratorio style, two outstanding examples of this being the Mass in B minor of J. S. Bach (1724–49) and the Mass in D of Beethoven (1819–22). Many impressive settings have been comp. since Beethoven, e.g. by Bruckner, and in the 20th cent. by Stravinsky, Vaughan Williams, Rubbra, and many others.

In large-scale settings the above-mentioned 5 passages tended to become subdivided. The great setting by Bach is as follows: (a) *Kyrie eleison* (Lord, have mercy), *Christe eleison* (Christ, have mercy), *Kyrie eleison* (Lord, have mercy); (b) *Gloria in excelsis Deo* (Glory be to God on high), *Laudamus te* (We praise Thee), *Gratias agimus tibi* (We give Thee thanks), *Domine Deus* (Lord God), *Qui tollis peccata mundi* (Who takest away the sins of the world), *Qui sedes ad dexteram Patris* (Who sittest at the right hand of the Father), *Quoniam tu solus sanctus* (For Thou only art holy), *Cum Sancto Spiritu* (With the Holy Spirit); (c) *Credo in unum Deum* (I believe in one God), *Patrem omnipotentem* (Father almighty), *Et in unum Dominum* (And in one Lord), *Et incarnatus est* (And was incarnate), *Crucifixus* (Crucified), *Et resurrexit* (And rose again), *Et in Spiritum Sanctum* (And (I believe) in the Holy Spirit), *Confiteor unum baptisma* (I confess one baptism); (d) *Sanctus* (Holy), *Hosanna in excelsis* (Hosanna in the highest), *Benedictus qui venit* (Blessed is he that cometh); (e) *Agnus Dei* (O Lamb of God), *Dona nobis pacem* (Give us peace). See also *Missa* and *Requiem*.

Massart, Joseph (Lambert) (*b* Liège, 1811; *d* Paris, 1892). Belg. violinist. Pupil of *Kreutzer in Paris. Prof. of vn. Paris Cons. 1843–90. Pupils incl. *Wieniawski and *Kreisler.

Massenet, Jules (Émile Frédéric) (*b* Montaud, St Étienne, 1842; *d* Paris, 1912). Fr. composer.

Entered Paris Cons. at 11, becoming pupil of A. Thomas. Won *Grand Prix de Rome*. Spent 3 years in Rome; returned to Paris 1866, his first (1-act) opera being prod. at Opéra-Comique 1867. His oratorios est. his name until the opera *Hérodiade* (a version of the Salome story) in 1881, but his greatest success came in 1884 with *Manon*. He was prof. of advanced comp. at Paris Cons. 1878–96. Among his later successes was *Don Quichotte*, prod. Monte Carlo 1910, with Chaliapin in the title-role. Massenet used Wagner's *leitmotiv* device, but translated it into his melodious and agreeable style, a style considered by some to be saccharine but which has won admiration in the later 20th cent. for its stylishness, craftsmanship, sense of th., and understanding of the human v. Prin. works:

OPERAS: *La Grand' Tante* (1867); *Le Roi de Lahore* (1877); **Hérodiade* (1881); **Manon* (1883); *Le*Cid* (1885); **Esclarmonde* (1889); *Le Mage* (1891); **Werther* (1891); **Thaïs* (1894); *Le Portrait de Manon* (1894); *La *Navarraise* (1894); *Amadis* (c.1895); *Sapho* (1897); **Cendrillon* (1899); *Grisélidis* (1901); *Le *Jongleur de Notre Dame* (1901); *Chérubin* (1902); *Ariane* (1906); *Thérèse* (1907); *Bacchus* (1909); **Don Quichotte* (1908–9); *Roma* (1911); *Panurge* (1912); *Cléopâtre* (1912).

BALLETS: *Le Carillon* (1892); *Cigale* (1904); *Espada* (1908).

ORATORIOS AND CANTATAS: *David Rizzio* (1863); *Marie-Magdeleine* (1873, rev. as opera 1906); *Eve* (1875); *Narcisse* (1877); *La Vierge* (1880); *Biblis* (1886); *La Terre Promise* (1900).

ORCH: *Scènes hongroises* (1871); **Scènes pittoresques* (1874); *Scènes napolitaines* (1876); *Scènes alsaciennes* (1881); *Marche solennelle* (1897); *Fantaisie*, vc. and orch. (1897); pf. conc. (1903).

Also about 200 songs, some with orch.

Mass in D (*Missa Solemnis*). For sop., cont., ten., and bass soloists, ch., org., and orch. by Beethoven, Op. 123, comp. 1819–22. F.p. complete, St Petersburg, April 1824; f.p. (incomplete) to Ger. words, Vienna May 1824 in first part of concert which incl. f.p. of 9th Sym.; complete but private perf. London 1832; public, but probably incomplete, London 1839; first complete public perf. in London 1846.

Mässig (Ger.). (1) Moderate, moderately, *mässiger*, more moderate and *mässigen*, to moderate.

(2) In the style of (e.g. *marschmässig*, in march style).

Mass of Christ the King. Choral work by **Williamson for sop., mez., ten., and bass soloists, ch., and orch., comp. 1977–8, f.p. (incomplete) Gloucester Fest. 1977, (complete) Westminster Cath. 1978.

Mass of Life, A (*Eine Messe des Lebens*). Choral work by Delius for SATB soloists, double ch., and orch. to Ger. text selected by F. **Cassirer from

Nietzsche's *Also sprach Zarathustra*. Comp. 1904–5. F.p. of Part 2 only, Munich 1908; f. complete p. London 1909 (in Eng.) cond. Beecham. In 1898 Delius wrote unpubd. setting of the 'Midnight Song' from *Zarathustra* for bar., male ch., and orch. (perf. London 1899).

Mass of Pope Marcellus (Palestrina). See *Missa Papae Marcelli*.

Masson, Diego (*b* Tossa, Sp., 1935). Fr. conductor. Studied at Paris Cons. 1953–9, also comp. with Leibowitz 1955–9 and Maderna 1964, and cond. with Boulez 1965. Worked as perc. player in Paris in 1960s, particularly at Domaine Musical, and founded his ens. Musique Vivante in 1966. Took part in several Stockhausen f.ps. and recorded Boulez's *Domaines*. Mus. dir. Marseilles Opéra. London début 1971 (SW).

Masson, Paul Marie (*b* Sète, 1882; *d* Paris, 1954). Fr. mus. historian, pupil of d'Indy and Koechlin. Lecturer, mus. history, Fr. Institute in Florence 1910–14. Founded Fr. Institute, Naples, 1919. Taught at Paris Univ. 1931–52. Wrote books on Berlioz and Rameau and ed. madrigals of **Gesualdo.

Master Class. Form of teaching in which celebrated performer instructs a group of pupils in front of other pupils or a paying audience. Master classes have become a popular feature at festivals and on television, but there is sometimes doubt as to whether the pupils benefit from what can, in effect, become a solo perf. by the teacher.

Master of Music. Degree awarded at some Brit. and Amer. univ., according status between Bachelor and Doctor of Mus.

Master of the King's (Queen's) Music. Title of the only surviving mus. post in the British royal household; carries honorarium and no fixed duties. The post originated in reign of Charles I (office being held by Nicholas Lanier) and meant the head of the sovereign's private band which accompanied him or her wherever he or she went. In 1660 Charles II est. a band of 24 players of str. instr. Since 1893 the post has been given to some eminent musician, usually a composer, who will write a fanfare, march, or larger work for some royal or state occasion, and is an influential figure in the mus. world generally (mus. equivalent of the Poet Laureate). Holders of the post since 1660 (some dates conjectural) are: Nicholas Lanier, 1660; Louis Grabu, 1666; Nicholas Staggins, 1674; John Eccles, 1700; Maurice Greene, 1735?; William Boyce, 1755; John Stanley, 1779; William Parsons, 1786; William Shield, 1817–29; Christian Kramer, 1834; George Frederick Anderson, 1848–70; William George Cusins, 1870–93; Walter Parratt, 1893–1924; Edward Elgar 1924–34; Walford Davies, 1934–41; Arnold Bax, 1942–53; Arthur Bliss, 1953–75; Malcolm Williamson from 1975.

Master Peter's Puppet Show (*El Retablo de Maese Pedro*). 1-act opera by *Falla to lib. by composer based on incident in Cervantes's *Don Quixote* (Part 2, Ch. 26). For singers, puppets, and chamber orch. Comp. 1919–22. F.p. (concert) Seville, Mar. 1923; stage (private) Paris, June 1923; Paris, Nov. 1923.

Mastersingers of Nuremberg, The (Wagner). See *Meistersinger von Nürnberg, Die*.

Masterson, Valerie (*b* Birkenhead, 1937). Eng. sop. Studied Liverpool, RCM, and Milan. Début Salzburg Landesth. 1963. D'Oyly Carte Opera Co. 1966–70. Member of SW (later ENO) from 1970. CG début 1974 (*Rheingold*). Paris début 1978. Amer. début San Francisco 1980 (*La traviata*). Combines brilliant coloratura with rich dramatic qualities, hence her particular success as Violetta (*La traviata*). Also admired as Handel singer (Cleopatra in ENO *Julius Caesar* 1979 and in CG *Semele* 1982).

Masur, Kurt (*b* Brieg, Silesia, 1927). Ger. conductor. Studied Breslau, 1942–4, and Leipzig Cons. 1946–8. Cond., Erfurt 1951–3, Leipzig City Th. 1953–5, Dresden P.O. 1955–8, Schwerin 1958–60. Chosen by Felsenstein as mus. dir., Berlin Komische Oper 1960, staying until 1964. Returned to Dresden P.O. 1964–7; cond., Leipzig Gewandhaus Orch. from 1970. Eng. début 1973 (New Philharmonia).

Mata, Eduardo (*b* Mexico City, 1942). Mexican cond. and composer. Studied Mexico Nat. Cons. of Mus. (comp. with Chávez), later at Berkshire Music Center, USA. Cond. and mus. dir. Mexican Ballet Co. 1963–4, Guadalajara S.O. 1965–6, Orch. Phil. U.N.A.M., Mexico City from 1966; prin. cond. Phoenix S.O., Arizona, 1972–8, Dallas S.O. from 1977. Guest cond. of European orchs. Comps. incl. 3 syms., ballet suite *Debora*, str. qt., pf. sonata, *Trio to Vaughan Williams*, etc.

Matačić, Lovro von (*b* Sušak, 1899; *d* Zagreb, 1985). Yugoslav cond. Studied Vienna, where he was member of *Sängerknaben*. Début Cologne Opera 1919; cond. opera Ljubljana 1924–6, Belgrade 1926–31, Zagreb 1932–8, returning to Belgrade as dir., 1938. Chief cond. Dresden Opera 1956–8 and at Berlin jointly with Konwitschny. Guest cond. Vienna and Milan 1958, Chicago 1959. Chief cond. Frankfurt Opera 1961; cond. Monte Carlo Opera until 1978.

Matassins, Mattachins. The dance also known as *Bouffons.

Matelotte (from Fr. *matelot*, sailor). Dutch sailors' dance like a hornpipe, perf. in wooden shoes, the dancers' arms being interlaced behind their backs.

Materna, Amalie (*b* St Georgen, 1844; *d* Vienna, 1918). Austrian sop. Début Graz 1864 as soubrette, then sang in operetta in Vienna. Member, Vienna Court Opera 1869–97. Chosen by Wagner as Brünnhilde for first Bayreuth *Ring* 1876 and as

Kundry in *Parsifal* 1882. Sang at Wagner's London concerts, 1877, and NY Met. 1885. Joined W. Damrosch's Ger. opera co., NY 1894. Taught after retirement, but last sang in public in 1913 at Wagner centenary concert in Vienna.

Mather, Bruce (*b* Toronto, 1939). Canadian composer. Studied Toronto Royal Cons. 1953–9 with *Beckwith, Paris 1959–62 with Messiaen and Milhaud. Teacher of comp. McGill Univ., Montreal, since 1966. Works incl. *Cycle Rilke*, ten. and guitar, *Symphonic Ode* for orch., *Ombres* for orch., *Musique pour Rouen* for 12 str., sonata for 2 pf., etc.

Mathias, William (*b* Whitland, Dyfed, 1934). Welsh composer and pianist. Studied Univ. Coll. of Wales, Aberystwyth, RAM (comp. with Berkeley, pf. with P. Katin). Bax Soc. prize 1968. Lecturer in mus., Univ. Coll. of N. Wales, Bangor, 1959–68, senior lecturer in comp. Edinburgh Univ. 1968–70, prof. of mus. Univ. Coll. of N. Wales from 1970. Art. dir. N. Wales Mus. Fest. C.B.E. 1985. Prin. works:

OPERA: *The Servants* (1980).

ORCH: *Divertimento* str. (1958); *Music for Strings* (1961); *Serenade, Invocation and Dance* (1962); *Concerto for Orchestra* (1966); Syms.: No. 1 (1966), No. 2 (*Summer Music*) (1982–3); *Sinfonietta* (1967); *Celtic Dances* (1972); *Laudi* (1973); *Vistas* (1975); *Requiescat* (1977); *Dance Variations* (1977).

CONCERTOS: Pf. No. 1 (1955), No. 2 (1961), No. 3 (1968); harp (1970); hpd., str., perc. (1971); cl. (1975); hn. (1984); organ (1984).

VOICE(S) AND ORCH. OF PIANO: *Ave Rex*, mixed ch. and orch. (1969); *Elegy for a Prince*, bar. and orch. (1972); *A Vision of Time and Eternity*, cont., pf. (1972); *This Worldes Joie*, soloists, ch., orch. (1974); *A May Magnificat*, double ch. (1977–8); *Shakespeare Songs*, ch., pf. (1978); *Lux Aeterna*, sop., mez., cont., ch., boys' ch., org., orch. (1981–2); *Psalm 67* (*Let the People Praise Thee, O God*), ch., org. or orch. (1981); *Angelus*, women's vv. (1983); *Let Us Now Praise Famous Men*, ch., orch. (1984).

CHURCH: *Festival Te Deum* (1965); *Magnificat and Nunc Dimittis* (1970); *Missa brevis*, No. 1 (1973), No. 2 (1984); *Te Deum* (1981); *Tantum Ergo*, ch., org. (1983).

CHAMBER MUSIC: Vn. sonata, No. 1 (1962), No. 2 (1984); wind quintet (1963); Pf. sonata, No. 1 (1964), No. 2 (1979); str. qt. No. 1 (1968), No. 2 (1982).

ORGAN: *Invocations*; *Partita*; *Variations on a Hymn-Tune* ('*Braint*'); conc. (1984).

Mathieson, Muir (*b* Stirling, 1911; *d* Oxford, 1975). Scottish cond. and composer. Studied RCM. Occasional opera cond. at SW but prominent as cond. of film mus. Worked for Sir Alexander Korda, film producer, 1931–9. Mus. dir. Govt. film units 1940–5, then for J. Arthur Rank films. Responsible for persuading Bliss,

Vaughan Williams, Walton, Benjamin, Britten, and Bennett to compose for films. O.B.E. 1957.

Mathilde di Shabran. *Opera buffa* in 2 acts by Rossini to lib. by Ferretti, who rewrote an earlier lib. 3 nos. comp. by Pacini. F.p. cond. by Paganini. Prod. Rome 1821, Paris 1857.

Mathis der Maler (Matthias the Painter). Opera in 7 scenes by *Hindemith to his own lib. based on life of Matthias Grünewald (*c.*1460–1530) and his altar-piece at Isenheim. Comp. 1933-5. Prod. Zürich 1938, London (concert) 1939, Edinburgh 1952. Boston Univ. 1956. Nazis banned Ger. première in 1935. Also Sym. for orch. in 3 movements: (1) *Engelkonzert* (Angels' Concert), (2) *Grablegung* (Burial), (3) *Versuchung des heiligen Antonius* (Temptation of St. Anthony). F.p. Berlin 1934, cond. Furtwängler.

Mathis, Edith (*b* Lucerne, 1938). Swiss sop. Studied Lucerne Cons. Début Lucerne 1956. Has sung at most leading opera houses and fests. Cologne Opera 1959–62; Deutsche Oper, W. Berlin, 1963. Glyndebourne début 1962 (Cherubino in *Figaro*), CG 1970 (Susanna in *Figaro*). Specialist in Mozart roles and songs.

Matin, Le; Midi, Le; Soir, Le (Morning, Afternoon, Evening). Nickname for 3 Haydn syms., Nos. 6–8 in Breitkopf edn., Hob. I. 6–8. (respectively in D, C, and G), comp. *c.*1761. The last is also known as *Le Soir et la tempête* (Evening and Storm).

Matrimonio segreto, Il (The Secret Marriage). Opera buffa in 2 acts by Cimarosa to lib. by G. Bertati after the comedy *The Clandestine Marriage* (1766) by Colman and Garrick. Prod. Vienna 1792, London 1794, NY 1834.

Matsudaira, Yoritsune (*b* Tokyo, 1907). Japanese composer. Studied with *Tcherepnin, winning Weingartner Prize 1936. Works incl. 2-pf. conc. (1946), *Ancient Japanese Dance* (1953), *Metamorphosis* on old Japanese melody (1954), *Circulating Movements*, for 2 chamber orchs. (1971), 2 str. qts., etc.

Mattachins. See *Bouffons*.

Mattei, Stanislao (*b* Bologna, 1750; *d* Bologna, 1825). It. priest, composer, and teacher. Pupil and ass. of Padre *Martini, succeeding him as maestro di cappella at San Francesco, Bologna. Prof. of counterpoint at Liceo from 1804. Pupils incl. Rossini and Donizetti. Wrote 8 masses, a Passion, 28 syms., much church mus., and harmony textbook.

Matteis, Nicola (*fl.* late 17th cent.). It. violinist and composer who settled in London 1672. Wrote and pubd. vn. solos 1685–8 and guitar text-book. Also wrote *Ode on St Cecilia's Day* and 2 books of songs.

Matthay, Tobias (Augustus) (*b* London, 1858; *d* High Marley, Haslemere, 1945). Eng. pianist,

composer, and teacher. Studied RAM, joining staff 1876 and becoming prof. of pf. 1880–1925. Gave up career as concert pianist to teach. Opened pf. sch. in London 1900. Pupils incl. Myra Hess, Irene Scharrer, Harriet Cohen, and York Bowen. Evolved own method of teaching, based on close observation of physical and psychological aspects of pf.-playing. Comp. much mus. and wrote several books on the pf.

Mattheson, Johann (*b* Hamburg, 1681; *d* Hamburg, 1764). Ger. composer, singer, harpsichordist, and theorist. Pupil of Hanff. Entered opera ch. 1690, singing tenor roles 1697–1705 during which time he wrote 5 operas and met Handel, with whom he fought a duel after an argument during a perf. of Mattheson's opera *Cleopatra* in 1704. Mus. dir. Hamburg Cath. 1715–28. Comp. church cantatas. Wrote 8 operas, 24 oratorios and cantatas, 12 fl. sonatas, and much else. Also wrote important books, full of advanced views and much historical material. One of his operas was *Boris Goudenow* (Hamburg, 1710).

Matthews, Colin (*b* London, 1946). English composer. Studied Nottingham Univ., comp. with A. Whittall and N. *Maw. Awards for comp. incl. BBC chamber mus. prize 1970, and Ian Whyte award 1975. Taught at Sussex Univ. 1972-3 and 1976-7. Author of study of Mahler and authority on Berg. Collab. with D. *Cooke on perf. version of Mahler's 10th sym. Worked for Britten in composer's last years. Prin. works:

ORCH: *Fourth Sonata* (1974–5); *Night Music* (1976–7); *Little Suite* No. 1 (1979), No. 2 (1979); *Sonata No. 5 (Landscape)* (1979–80); vc. conc. (1983–4); *Night's Mask*, chamber orch. (1984).

INSTR: *Ceres*, 3 fl., guitar, perc., 2 vc., db. (1972); *Specula*, fl., keyed perc., hp., va. (1976–7); *Rainbow Studies*, fl., ob., cl., bn., pf. (1977–8).

VOICE AND INSTR: *Un colloque sentimental*, v. and pf. (1971–8); *5 Sonnets: to Orpheus*, ten., hp. (1975–6); *Shadows in the Water*, ten., pf. (1978–9).

UNACC. VOICES: *Second-hand Flames*, 5 vv. (1982).

CHAMBER MUSIC: *Partita*, vn. (1975); *Str. Qt. No. 1* (1979); *Little Suite*, hp. (1979); *ob. qt.* (1981); *Divertimento*, double str. qt. (1982).

PIANO: *5 Studies* (1974–6); *Suite* (1977–9).

Matthews, David (*b* London, 1943). Eng composer and writer, brother of Colin *Matthews. Studied comp. with A. Milner. Worked with Britten and helped D. *Cooke on perf. version of Mahler's 10th Sym. Author of book on mus. of *Tippett (1980). Prin. works:

ORCH: *Little Concerto*, chamber orch. (1971); Syms.: No. 1 (1975, rev. 1978), No. 2 (1976–9), No. 3 (1984–5); Vn. Conc. (1979–82); *White Nights*, fantasy for vn. and small orch. (1980); *Serenade*, chamber orch. (1982).

INSTR: *Introit*, 2 tpt., str. (1981).

VOICE(S) AND INSTR: *Stars*, ch. and orch. (1970); *3 Songs*, sop. and orch. (1971).

CHAMBER MUSIC: Str. Qts., No. 1 (1970, rev. 1980), No. 2 (1976, rev. 1980), No. 3 (1977–80), No. 4 (1980); *Fantasia*, va. (1970); *Fantasia*, vc. (1971); *Songs and Dances of Mourning*, vc. (1976).

Matthews, Denis (*b* Coventry, 1919). Eng. pianist. Studied RAM 1935–40, pf. with H. Craxton and comp. with Alwyn. Début, London (Prom) 1939. Soloist with all leading orchs. Noted Mozartian and brilliant lecturer. Gave f.p. of Rubbra's pf. conc. 1956. Prof. of mus., Newcastle upon Tyne Univ. 1972–84. C.B.E. 1975.

Mattinata (It.). A Morning Song, or a piece with that assoc., i.e. the same as *aubade* (Fr.), *alborada* (Sp.), and *Morgenlied* (Ger.).

Matton, Roger (*b* Granby, Quebec, 1929). Canadian composer. Studied Montreal and in Paris with Boulanger. Teacher of comp., Laval Univ., Quebec, since 1957. Works incl. sax. conc., conc. for 2 pf. and perc. and for 2 pf. and orch.

Mauceri, John (*b* NY, 1945). Amer. conductor. Studied at Yale Univ. and Tanglewood. Opera début Wolf Trap Fest. 1973. Mus. dir. Washington Opera 1980–2, Scot. Opera from 1987. European opera début Spoleto 1974 (Menotti's *Tamu-Tamu*). NY City Opera début 1977 (Boito's *Mefistofele*), NY Met. 1976 (*Fidelio*). Brit. opera début 1974 (WNO *Don Carlos*), Royal Opera 1983 (Manchester, *Madama Butterfly*), concert début 1976 (SNO).

Maultrommel (Ger.). *Jew's harp.

Maurel, Victor (*b* Marseilles, 1848; *d* NY, 1923). Fr. bar. Studied Marseilles and Paris Cons. Début Paris Opéra 1868 in *Les Huguenots*. Sang in St Petersburg, Cairo, and Venice before appearing at La Scala, Milan, 1870. London début CG 1873 in *Un Ballo in Maschera*, singing there until 1904, particularly in Wagner. NY début 1873 in *Aida*. Returned to Paris Opéra 1879. Went into operatic management 1883. Sang in f.p. of Massenet's *Hérodiade* 1881, created role of Iago in Verdi's *Otello*, Milan 1887, and title-role in *Falstaff*, Milan 1893. Appeared as actor for short time, then settled NY as teacher 1909. Designed sets for Gounod's *Mireille*, NY Met. 1919. Wrote 4 books on singing.

Maurerische Trauermusik (Masonic Funeral Music). Work in C minor by Mozart (K477) scored for 2 ob., cl., 3 basset hn., double bn., 2 hn., and str. Comp. in July 1785 for installation of a master (a ritual which includes funerary imagery) and perf. again in Nov. 1785 at memorial service for two of Mozart's lodge brothers.

Mauresco (Sp.), **Mauresque** (Fr.). Moorish (see also *Moresca*). Elgar wrote a *Sérénade mauresque*.

Má Vlast (My Country). Cycle of 6 symphonic poems by Smetana, comp. 1874–9. They are: 1. *Vyšehrad* (The High Citadel), 2. *Vltava* (River Moldau), 3. *Šárka* (leader of Bohem. Amazons), 4.

Z Českych Luhů a Hájů (From Bohemia's Meadows and Forests), 5. *Tabor* (stronghold of the Hussites), 6. *Blánik* (Valhalla of the Hussite heroes: a mountain in S. Bohemia).

Mavra. Opera in 1 act by Stravinsky to lib. by Kochno after Pushkin's poem *The Little House at Kolomna*. Comp. 1921–2. Prod. Paris 1922, London (broadcast) and Philadelphia 1934, Edinburgh 1956, London (stage) 1978.

Maw, Nicholas (*b* Grantham, 1935). Eng. composer. Studied RAM 1955–8 and with N. Boulanger and Max Deutsch in Paris 1958–9. One of the generation of 'modern romantics' whose mus., while contemporary in some of its procedures, remains attached to traditional forms and outlook. Prin. works:

OPERAS: *One-Man Show* (2 acts, 1964, rev. 1966); *The *Rising of the Moon* (1967–70).

ORCH: *Sinfonia* (1966); *Sonata*, str. and 2 hn. (1967); *Concert Music* (derived from *Rising of the Moon*, 1972); *Serenade* (1973, rev. 1977); *Odyssey* (1973–9); *Summer Dances* (1981); *Toccata* (1982); *Morning Music* (1982).

VOICE(S) AND ORCH: *Nocturne*, mez. and chamber orch. (1958); *Scenes and Arias*, sop., mez., cont. (1961–2, rev. 1966); *La Vita Nuova* (The New Life), sop., chamber ens. (1979).

VOICE(S) AND PIANO etc: *The Voice of Love*, mez. (1966); *6 Interiors*, ten. and guitar (1966).

VOCAL: *5 Epigrams* (1960); *Our Lady's Song* (1962); *Corpus Christi Carol* and *Balulalow* (1964); *5 Irish Songs* (1972); *Te Deum* (1975); *Nonsense Songs* (1976); *The Ruin*, with hn. obbl. (1980).

CHAMBER MUSIC: Fl. sonatina (1957); *Chamber Music*, ob., cl., hn., bn., pf. (1962); Str. Qt. No. 1 (1965), No. 2 (1982); *Epitaph, Canon in mem. Stravinsky*, fl., cl., harp (1971); *Life Studies* I-VIII, 15 str. (1973–6); qt. for fl. and str. (1981); *Night Thoughts*, fl. (1982).

Maxwell Davies, (Sir) **Peter** (*b* Salford, 1934). Eng. composer, cond., and teacher. Studied Manchester Univ. and RMCM (comp. with Richard Hall) at same time as Birtwistle, Goehr, and Ogdon (all members of *Manchester School). In 1957 won It. Govt. scholarship and studied in Rome with *Petrassi. His *Prolation* won Olivetti Prize 1958 and was f.p. ISCM fest., Rome 1959. Mus. dir Cirencester Grammar Sch. 1959–62. Studied Princeton Univ. 1962–4, with Sessions. Resident composer Adelaide Univ. 1966. In 1967 was co-dir. of chamber ens., Pierrot Players, formed to perf. contemporary works; this was reorganized 1970 as The *Fires of London, for which many of his works have been written. Since 1970 he has lived intermittently in Orkney, where the landscape and solitude have had an undoubted effect on his music, notably in the chamber opera *The Martyrdom of St Magnus* and the large-scale sym. Mus. dir., Dartington Hall summer sch. 1979–84. C.B.E. 1981. Knighted 1987.

Maxwell Davies soon became one of the most important of the Eng. so-called *avant-garde*. Like Britten, he has enjoyed writing for specific performers and his wide-ranging imagination has devised striking sounds, freakish perhaps but always springing from a genuine mus. impulse. Rhythms are sometimes complex, vocal lines angular. He developed *music theatre*, staged pieces for a single performer, as in the remarkable *Eight Songs for a Mad King*. His music is marked also by a strong dramatic impulse which found a full outlet in the opera *Taverner*. He has been inspired by the ability to combine and contrast the music of medieval times with his own idiom, and has also made much use of the 1920s fox-trot rhythm for nostalgic purposes. Prin. works:

OPERAS: *Taverner (1962–70); The *Martyrdom of St Magnus (1976–7); The Two Fiddlers (children's opera) (1978); The *Lighthouse (1979).

THEATRE PIECES: Notre Dame des Fleurs, sop., mez., counterten., ens. (1966); *Vesalii Icones (Images from Vesalius), dancer, vc., ens. (1969); Eight *Songs for a Mad King, male v., ens. (1969); *Blind Man's Buff, sop., mez., mime, and stage band (1972); *Miss Donnithorne's Maggot, mez., ens. (1974); Le *Jongleur de Notre Dame, mime, bar., ens., children's band (1978); Cinderella (for children) (1980); The Medium, mez. (1981); The Rainbow (for children) (1981); The No. 11 Bus, mez., ten., bar., 2 dancers, mime, and ens. (1983–4).

BALLET: Salome (1978).

ORCH: Prolation (1958); 5 Klee Pictures (1959, rev. 1976); 1st *Fantasia on an In Nomine of John Taverner (1962); 2nd Fantasia (1964); *St Thomas Wake (1969); Worldes Blis (1969); Sym. No. 1 (1973–6), No. 2 (1980), No. 3 (1984); A Mirror of Whitening Light (1977); Dances from 'Salome' (1979), vn. conc. (1986).

VOICE(S) AND ORCH. OR CHAMBER ENS: 5 Motets, SCTB soloists, double ch., instr. (1959); *O Magnum mysterium, cycle of carols, ch., instr., org. (1960); Te Lucis ante Terminum, ch. and chamber orch. (1961); Frammenti di Leopardi, cantata for sop., cont., and instr. (1962); Veni Sancte Spiritus, sop., cont., and bass soloists, ch., orch. (1963); Ecce Manus Tradentis, ch. and instr. (1965); *Revelation and Fall, sop. and 16 instr. (1965); The Shepherd's Calendar, young vv. and instr. (1965); *Missa super 'L'Homme Armé', speaker and ens. (1967–8, rev. 1971); *From Stone to Thorn, mez., chamber ens. (1971); *Hymn to St Magnus, sop., chamber ens. (1972); Fool's Fanfare, sop., ens. (1972); Tenebrae super Gesualdo, mez., guitar, chamber ens. (1972); *Stone Litany, mez. and orch. (1973); Fiddlers at the Wedding, mez., chamber ens. (1973–4); My Lady Lothian's Lilt, mez., ens. (1975); Anakreontika, Gr. songs for mez. and instr. (1976); The Blind Fiddler, sop. and instr. (1976); Kirkwall Shopping Songs, children's vv., instr., pf. (1979); Black Pentecost, mez., bar., instr. (1979); Solstice

of Light, ten., ch., org. (1979); Into the Labyrinth, ten, and orch. (1983).

CHAMBER ENS: Alma Redemptoris Mater, 6 wind instr. (1957); St Michael, sonata for 17 wind instr. (1957); Ricercar and Doubles, 8 instr. (1959); Sinfonia, chamber orch. (1962); 7 In Nomine (1963–5); Shakespeare Music (1964); *Antechrist (1967); Stedman Caters (1968); Eram quasi agnus, motet for instr. (1969); Points and Dances from 'Taverner' (1970); Canon in Memory of Igor Stravinsky (1972); Renaissance Scottish Dances (1973); Psalm 124 (1974); Ave Maris Stella (1975); Runes from a Holy Island (1977); Our Father Whiche in Heaven Art (1977); Dances from 'The Two Fiddlers' (1978); A Welcome to Orkney (1980); The Bairns of Brugh (1981); Image, Reflection, Shadow (1982); Sinfonia Concertante (1982); Sinfonietta Accademica (1983).

SOLO VOICE(S) AND ONE INSTR: Shall I Die for Mannis Sake?, sop., alto, pf. (1965); Dark Angels, sop., guitar (1974); The Yellow Cake Review, 6 cabaret songs, v. and pf. (1980).

VOICES ONLY (SATB unless specified): 4 Carols (1962); The Lord's Prayer (1962); Ave, Plena Gracia, with opt. org. (1964); 5 Carols, women's vv. (1966); Ave Rex Angelorum, with opt. org. (1976); Westerlings (1977); Songs of Hoy (1981); Seven Songs Home (1981); Lullabye for Lucy (1981).

CHAMBER MUSIC: Sonata, tpt., pf. (1955); cl. sonata (1956–7); Sextet (1958); Str. Qt. (1961); Solita, fl. with mus. box (1966); Hymnos, cl., pf. (1967); Stedman Doubles, cl., perc. (1968); Bell Tower (Turris Campanarum Sonantium), perc. (1971); Ara Coeli: Lullaby for Ilian Rainbow, guitar (1972); The Door of the Sun, va. (1975); The Kestrel paced round the Sun, fl. (1975); The Seven Brightnesses, cl. in B♭ (1975); 3 Studies for Percussion (1975); Nocturne, alto fl. (1979); Little Quartets, str., No. 1 (1980), No. 2 (1981); Sonatina, tpt. (1981); Hill Runes, guitar (1981); 2 Gesualdo Motets, brass quintet (1982); The Pole Star, brass quintet (1982); 4 Tallis Voluntaries, brass quintet (1982); Sea Eagle, hn. (1982); Birthday Music for John, fl., va., vc. (1983); sonata for vn. and cimbalom (1984).

PIANO: 5 Pieces (1956); 5 Little Pieces (1967); Sub tuam protectionem (1970); Ut Re Mi (1971); Stevie's Ferry to Hoy (1976); 4 Lessons for 2 Keyboards (1978); Sonata (1980–1).

ORGAN: 3 Preludes (1976); Sonata (1982).

BRASS BAND: March: The Pole Star (1982); 4 Tallis Voluntaries (1982); 2 Gesualdo Motets (1982).

REALIZATIONS: Purcell: Fantasia on a Ground and 2 Pavans, chamber ens. (1968); Fantasia on One Note, instr. (1973); Gabrieli: Canzona, wind and str. (1969); Buxtehude: Cantata: Also hat Gott die Welt geliebet, sop., fl., vn., vc., hpd. (1971); J. S. Bach: Prelude and Fugue in C♯ minor, instr. (1972); Prelude and Fugue in C♯ major, instr. (1974); Dunstable: Veni Sancte Spiritus, instr. (1972); Kinloch: Kinloch His Fantassie, instr. (1976); Anon.: Scottish 16th cent.: 4 Instrumental

Motets, instr. (1973–7), *Renaissance Scottish Dances*, instr. (1973).
MISC: *The Devils*, mus. for K. Russell film (1971); *The Boy Friend*, mus for K. Russell film and arrs. of Wilson's songs from musical (1971).

May, Florence (*b* London, 1845; *d* London, 1923). Eng. pianist. Pupil of Brahms, several of whose works she introduced to Eng. Author of his biography (1905, new edn. 1948).

Maybrick, Michael (*b* Liverpool, 1844; *d* Buxton, 1913). Eng. bar. and composer. Studied Leipzig Cons. Under pseudonym 'Stephen Adams' wrote popular ballads, e.g. *Star of Bethlehem* and *The Holy City*.

Mayer, (Sir) Robert (*b* Mannheim, 1879; *d* London, 1985). Ger.-born businessman and patron of mus. who settled in London 1896 and became Eng. cit. Founder (1923), Robert Mayer children's concerts, founder and chairman, Youth and Music. Knighted 1939, C.H. 1973, created K.C.V.O. on his 100th birthday, 5 June 1979. His first wife Dorothy (*née* Moulton Piper) (*b* Crouch End, London, 1886; *d* Henham, Essex, 1974) was one of the first sopranos to sing mus. by Schoenberg and Stravinsky in Britain before 1914. She also wrote biographies of Marie-Antoinette and Angelika Kaufman and of Spohr (London 1959).

Mayer-Lismann, Else (Mitia) (*b* Frankfurt, 1914). Ger. musician and lecturer. Studied Hochs Cons., Frankfurt. Settled in Eng. Art dir. Mayer-Lismann Opera Workshop. M.B.E. 1984.

Maynard, John (*b* St Albans, 1577; *d* after 1615). Eng. lutenist and song-writer. His *The XII Wonders of the World*, settings of poems by Sir John Davies, was pubd. 1611. These satirical songs have accompaniments for lute and bass viol.

May Night (*Mayskaya Noch*). Opera in 3 acts by Rimsky-Korsakov to his own lib. based on story by Gogol. Prod. Moscow 1880, London 1914.

Mayr, Richard (*b* Henndorf, Austria, 1877; *d* Vienna, 1935). Austrian bass-bar. Studied medicine Vienna Univ., but became singer on Mahler's advice, studying at Vienna Cons. Début Bayreuth 1902 (Hagen). Vienna Opera 1902–35, début under Mahler in *Ernani*. Most famous role was Ochs in Strauss's *Der Rosenkavalier*, written with him in mind though he did not create it, but sang at Vienna première 1911. CG début 1924 (Ochs), NY Met. 1927 (Pogner). Created role of Barak in Strauss's *Die Frau ohne Schatten*, Vienna 1919. Also renowned Gurnemanz in *Parsifal*, Rocco in *Fidelio*, and Sarastro (*Zauberflöte*). Favourite singer at Salzburg Festivals.

Mayr, (Johannes) Simon (*b* Mendorf, Bavaria, 1763; *d* Bergamo, 1845). Ger.-born composer. Studied in Bergamo and Venice where his oratorios found favour. First opera *Saffo* (1794) was successful and was followed by 67 others until 1824, his popularity in Italy being immense

until eclipsed by Rossini's. Maestro di cappella, S. Maria Maggiore, Bergamo, 1802; prof. of counterpoint at institute 1805. Wrote only church mus. after 1816. Taught Donizetti. His best operas are said to be *La Lodoïska* (1795, rev. 1799), *L'Amor Coniugale* (1805, to same plot as Beethoven's *Fidelio* and f.p. 4 months earlier), *Il ritorno di Ulisse* (1809), and *Medea in Corinto* (1813). Wrote life of Haydn. Also comp. instr. works, e.g. 2 pf. concs.

Mayuzumi, Toshiro (*b* Yokohama, 1929). Japanese composer. Studied Tokyo and Paris Cons. Organizer of modern mus. group *Ars Nova Japonica*, and has worked in Tokyo Radio elec. studio. Works combine Japanese sources with *avant-garde* Western methods. Wrote mus. for film *The Bible* (1965). Other orch. comps. are *Essay* for str., *Bacchanale*, *Mandala* sym., *Microcosmos*, *Fireworks*, *Samsara*, *Texture*, *Tonepleromas 55*, *Phonologie symphonique*, *Sphénogrammes*, *The Birth of Music*, xylophone concertino, perc. conc.; operas: *The Temple of the Golden Pavilion*, *Minoko*; ballet: *Bugaku Olympics*; cantatas: *Nirvana sym.*, *Pratidesana*; elec. tape: *Aoi-no-ue* (Princess Hollyhock), *Campanology*, *Olympic Campanology*, *3 Hymns*, *Variations sur 7*.

Mazas, Jacques Féréol (*b* ?Lavour, 1782; *d* Béziers, 1849). Fr. violinist and composer. Studied Paris Cons. under Baillot. Tours of Europe 1811–29. Dir., mus. sch., Cambrai 1837–41. Wrote 2 operas, qts., trios, and many vn. solos, also methods for vn. and va.

Mazeppa. (1) Pf. pieces by *Liszt, 1st 1840, 2nd No. 4 of *Études d'exécution transcendante* (1851); and symphonic poem for orch. (1851) based on Hugo's story (also for 2 pf. 1855, and pf. 4 hands 1874).
(2) Opera in 3 acts by Tchaikovsky to lib. by composer and Burenin after Pushkin. Comp. 1881–3. Prod. Moscow 1884, Liverpool 1888, Boston 1922. Mazeppa (1644–1709) was Russ. historical character.

Mazurka. A traditional Polish country dance (orig. sung as well as danced). Originated in Mazovia, near Warsaw, inhabitants being Mazurs. It spread in the early 18th cent. to Ger. and then to Paris, and early in the 19th to Brit. and the USA. It is in triple time with a certain accentuation of the 2nd beat of each measure and an ending of the phrases on that beat; dotted notes are a feature. It is not a fast dance, and a certain aristocratic pride of bearing, sometimes combined with a touch of abandon, helps to differentiate it from the waltz. Its place in concert mus. was est. by *Chopin, who wrote *c*.60 for pf. These are in a greatly refined style and the tempo and rhythm are sometimes changed from those that are traditional.
The *Polka-Mazurka* differs from the Polka in being in triple time and from the Mazurka in having an accent on the 3rd beat of the measure.

Mazurok, Yury (*b* Krasnik, Poland, 1931). Polish baritone. Studied with Sveshikovaya at Moscow Cons. and privately until 1963. Joined Bolshoy Th., 1963. First prize Montreal int. singing comp. 1967. CG début 1975 (Renato in *Un Ballo in Maschera*). Amer. début S. Francisco 1977 (Renato), Vienna 1979 (Escamillo in *Carmen*). Notable singer of role of Onegin.

Mazzocchi, Domenico (*b* Civita Castellana, 1592; *d* Rome, 1665). It. composer and lawyer. Wrote opera (1626), oratorio *Querimonia di S. Maria Maddalena* (Plaint of St Mary Magdalene, 1631), and pubd. book of madrigals (1640) in which signs < and > for crescendo and diminuendo, *f* for *forte*, *p* for *piano*, and *tr* for trill first appear.

Mazzocchi, Virgilio (*b* Civita Castellana, 1597; *d* Civita Castellana, 1646). It. composer, brother of Domenico *Mazzocchi. Maestro di cappella, St John Lateran, Rome, 1628–9, when he moved to similar post at St Peter's. With *Marazzoli, wrote what is said to be first comic opera, *Chi soffre, speri* (Rome 1639, rev. of *Il falcone*, 1637). Also wrote vocal mus.

M.D. = *Main Droite* (Fr.) or *Mano Destra* (It.), i.e. Right Hand. Sometimes, also, used as abbreviation of Musical Director.

Me. See *Mi*.

Meale, Richard (Graham) (*b* Sydney, N.S.W., 1932). Australian composer. Studied N.S.W. State Cons. (pf., hp., and cl.—he never formally studied comp.). From 1955 gave recitals of contemporary pf. mus. and in 1961 visited Spain, developing interest in work of the poet Lorca. Up to this point his comps. had been of the Bartók-Hindemith genre; thereafter he followed Messiaen and Boulez, with a further influence from Indonesian mus. Programme planner for A.B.C. 1962–8. Senior Lect., Mus. Dept., Adelaide Univ. from 1969. M.B.E. 1971. Prin. works:

ORCH: Fl. Conc. (1959); *Homage to Garcia Lorca*, 2 str. orch. (1964); *Images* (*Nagauta*) (1966); *Nocturnes*, vibraphone, hp., celesta, orch. (1967); *Very High Kings* (1968); *Clouds Now and Then* (1969); *Soon It Will Die* (1969); *Evocations*, ob., chamber orch., vn. obbl. (1973); *Viridian*, str. (1979).
INSTR: *Divertimento*, vn., pf., vc. (1959); fl. sonata (1960); *Las Alboradas*, fl., hn., vn., pf. (1963); *Intersections*, fl., va., vib., pf. (1965); *Cyphers*, fl., va., vib., pf. (1965); wind quintet (1970); *Interiors/Exteriors*, 2 pf., 3 perc. (1970); *Incredible Floridas*, fl., cl., vn., vc., pf., perc. (1971); *Plateau*, wind quintet (1971); *Fanfare*, brass (1978); Str. Qt. No. 1 (1974), No. 2 (1980).
PIANO: *Sonatina patetica* (1957); *Orenda* (1959); *Coruscations* (1971).

Measure. (1) Old Eng. term, now adopted in USA and reintroduced into Britain in 19th cent. by John *Curwen, indicating time-content of notational space between one bar-line and the next, e.g. '2 beats in the bar'.
(2) The bar-line itself. Note that the Eng. 'bar' is the same as Amer. 'measure'; Amer. 'bar' means Eng. 'bar-line'.
(3) A stately Eng. dance of 15th and 16th cents. ('trod a measure' is a frequent phrase in Elizabethan drama).

Meck, Nadezhda von (*b* nr. Smolensk, 1831; *d* Wiesbaden, 1894). Russ. patroness of Tchaikovsky, whom she never met. Gave him annual grant of 6,000 roubles to devote himself to comp. Their correspondence was pubd. in USSR 1934–6. 4th Sym. ded. to her. In 1880 and 1881 Debussy worked for her as a pianist.

Médée (*Medea*). Opera in 3 acts by Cherubini to lib. in Fr. by F. B. Hoffmann based on Euripides. Prod. Paris 1797, Berlin 1800, London 1865. Spoken dialogue of orig. set to mus. by F. Lachner 1854 and by Arditi for London prod. 1865. F.p. in England of orig. score Durham 1967, Univ. of Hartford, Conn., 1970. Operas on same subject by several composers, incl. Kusser (1692), M. A. Charpentier (1693), Mysliveček (1764), J. A. Benda (1775), Mayr (1813), and Milhaud (1938). Also ballet by S. Barber (1946).

Medesimo (It.). Same, e.g. *Medesimo movimento*, The same speed.

Medial Cadence. One in which leading chord is inverted instead of being in root position.

Mediant. The 3rd degree of the major or minor scale. So called because it is midway between the tonic and the dominant.

Mediation. Inflexion in *plainchant occurring at the end of first section of a psalm-tune.

Medicean Edition. See *Plainsong*.

Medium, The. Opera in 2 acts by *Menotti to his own lib. Comp. 1945. Prod. Columbia Univ. 1946, London 1948.

Medley. Similar to *pot-pourri: a collection of parts or passages of well-known songs or pieces arranged so that the end of one merges into the start of the next.

Medtner, Nicolas (Nikolay Karlovich) (*b* Moscow, 1880; *d* London, 1951). Russ. composer and pianist. Studied Moscow Cons. (pf. with Safonov, comp. with Arensky and Taneyev). Prof. at Moscow Cons. 1909–10 and 1914–21. Left Russia 1921, living in Ger. and France and touring as virtuoso pianist. Amer. début 1924 with Philadelphia Orch. Wrote much pf. mus.; was influenced by Ger. romanticism. Wrote book, 1935, opposing modern innovations and affirming faith in tonality. Wrote 3 pf. concs., several pf. sonatas, many genre pieces for pf., e.g. series called *Fairy-Tales*, and many songs. Settled in Eng. 1935. Patronized by Maharajah of Mysore.

Meet My Folks! 'Theme and relations', Op. 10, by *Crosse, comp. 1964, being settings of poems by Ted Hughes for speaker, children's ch., perc. band, ob., cl., bn., hn., tpt., vc., pf., and percussionists. F.p. Aldeburgh Fest. 1964.

Mefistofele (Mephistopheles). Opera in prol., 4 acts, and epilogue by *Boito to his own lib., based on both parts of Goethe's *Faust*. Prod. Milan 1868. Rev. version prod. Bologna 1875, London 1880.

Megaphone. A large speaking tpt. Also a device introduced by Edison for listening at a distance of some miles without the use of wires or electricity—practically an improved ear-tpt. on a large scale.

Mehta, Zubin (*b* Bombay, 1936). Indian cond., violinist, and pianist. Son of Mehli Mehta, founder of Bombay S.O. and at one time violinist in Hallé Orch. Studied Vienna State Acad. of Mus. 1954–57. Won first prize, Liverpool int. conductors' competition 1958, this leading to guest engagements throughout world. Amer. début 1970 (Philadelphia Orch.). Mus. dir. Montreal S.O. 1961–7; mus. dir. Los Angeles P.O. 1962–77; mus. dir. New York P.O. from 1978; mus. dir. Israel P.O. from 1977. Salzburg Fest. début 1962, NY Met. 1965, CG 1977. Frequent guest cond. Vienna P.O.

Méhul, Étienne Nicolas (*b* Givet, nr. Mezières, 1763; *d* Paris, 1817). Fr. composer. Organist at convent at age 10. Taken to Paris 1778 by rich amateur who recognized his talent, studying under Edelmann. Befriended by *Gluck who advised him to compose for the stage. His *Euphrosine et Coradin* (1790) won him fame and imparted new dramatic force to opéra comique. 30 other stage-works followed in next 17 years, most famous being *Joseph* (1807) in which his strong dramatic sense and lyrical vein are found at their best. Taught at Paris Cons. 1793–1815. Fortunes declined after fall of his patron Napoleon. Also wrote ballets, cantatas, songs, a Mass, and syms. His operas incl.: *Euphrosine et Coradin* (1790), *Stratonice* (1792), *Le Jeune Sage et le vieux fou* (1793), *Le Jeune Henri* (1797), *Ariodant* (1799), *Les Deux Aveugles de Tolède* (1806), *Uthal* (1806), *Joseph* (1807), *Le Prince troubadour* (1813), *L'Oriflamme* (1814).

Meistersinger (Mastersingers). Middle-class Ger. literary and mus. movement of 15th and 16th cents. cultivated by craftsmen's guilds and representing continuation of aristocratic *Minnesinger of preceding 2 centuries. Movement declined in 17th cent., the Ulm school being disbanded in 1839 and its last survivor dying in 1876. The conduct of a mastersingers' guild was very much as depicted by Wagner in his opera *Die *Meistersinger von Nürnberg*. Rigid and pedantic rules governed the weekly meetings (after church on Sunday); competitions were held and prizes awarded; members were promoted into various classes: *Schüler* (apprentice), *Schulfreund* (friend), *Sänger* (singer), *Dichter* (poet), *Meister* (master). Title *Dichter* was awarded for new poem (*Lied*, *Gesang*), *Meister* for new melody (*Ton*, *Weise*). Several of the characters in Wagner's opera were historical personages, e.g. Konrad Nachtigall and especially Hans Sachs (1494–1576). Some attractive songs by Sachs survive, but generally Meistersinger melodies are dull and suffer from a surfeit of coloratura.

Meistersinger von Nürnberg, Die (The Mastersingers of Nuremberg). Opera in 3 acts by Wagner to his own lib. based on Wagenseil and other sources. Gives accurate and heartwarming picture of medieval guild of *Meistersinger, several of whom, notably Hans Sachs, actually lived. Comp. 1862–7. Prod. Munich 1868, London 1882, NY Met. 1886.

Melartin, Erkki Gustav (*b* Käkisalmi, 1875; *d* Pukinmäki, 1937). Finn. composer and pianist. Studied Helsinki Cons., Vienna, and elsewhere. Prof. at Helsinki Cons., of which he was dir. 1911–36. Wrote opera *Aino*, 8 syms., symphonic poems, ballet, vn. conc., 4 str. qts., 400 pf. pieces, over 300 songs.

Melba, (Dame) **Nellie** (Mrs Helen Porter Armstrong (*née* Mitchell)) (*b* Richmond, nr. Melbourne, 1861; *d* Sydney, N.S.W., 1931). Australian sop. As child, studied pf., organ, and theory, but sang in churches and at local concerts. Studied Paris with M. *Marchesi. Début in opera in Brussels 1887 as Gilda in *Rigoletto*, CG 1888 as Lucia, Paris 1889 as Ophélie. Her London triumphs date from her Juliette (Gounod) in 1889 and she appeared regularly at CG until 1914 (except 1909) and then in 1919, 1922–4 (BNOC), and 1926. Début Scala, Milan, 1893 (Lucia), and NY Met. same year. Her Met. appearances were 1893–7, 1898–9, 1900–1, 1904–5, 1910. In 1897–8 toured USA with own co. and was member of Manhattan Opera Co. for several seasons from 1907. Also sang with Chicago Opera. Final operatic appearance CG 1926 as Mimi (recording exists). V. notable for purity, freshness, and brilliance of ornamentation in coloratura roles. Finest parts were Gilda, Mimi, Violetta, Desdemona, Nedda, and Marguérite. In 1896 in NY inadvisedly sang the *Siegfried* Brünnhilde. At CG her supremacy enabled her to dictate casting of operas in which she sang. Her stage name was adopted in tribute to Melbourne. The ice-cream sweet *pêche Melba* and Melba toast are named after her. D.B.E. 1918, G.B.E. 1929.

Melchior, Lauritz (*b* Copenhagen, 1890; *d* Santa Monica, Calif., 1973). Danish-born ten. (Amer. citizen 1947). Studied Copenhagen, making début there as bar. in *Pagliacci*, 1913. Début as ten. (*Tannhäuser*) 1918, at suggestion of Mme. Charles *Cahier. Studied 1921–3 with Biegel in London, Grenzebach in Berlin, Anna *Mildenburg in Munich, and Karl Kittel in Bayreuth.

Début London CG as Siegmund in *Die Walküre* opposite F. *Leider, then 1926–9. Studied Wagner roles at Bayreuth, singing there 1924–31. Amer. début NY Met. 1926, continuing there until 1950. One of most famous Wagnerian *Heldentenors*, singing Tristan over 200 times and appearing often as Siegfried, Lohengrin, Siegmund, and Parsifal.

Melisma (Gr. 'song'; plural *melismata*). A group of notes sung to a single syllable, as opposed to coloratura. Used in plainsong and in other song. *Melismata* is title of vocal pieces (madrigals, etc.) pubd. 1611 by Thomas *Ravenscroft.

Melkus, Eduard (*b* Baden, Austria, 1928). Austrian violinist. Studied Vienna Univ. and Acad. of Mus. Début Vienna 1944. Teaches vn. and va., Vienna Hochschule für Musik. Founder, Vienna Capella Academica, specializing in 18th-cent. works on authentic instr.

Mellers, Wilfrid (Howard) (*b* Leamington, 1914). Eng. composer, critic, and teacher. Studied Cambridge and Birmingham Univs., and privately with *Wellesz and *Rubbra. Lecturer at Cambridge 1945–8, Birmingham Univ. 1948–60, Pittsburgh Univ. 1960–3. Prof. of mus., York Univ., 1964–81. Interested in bridging gap between symphonic mus., jazz, pop, and folk mus. Has written books on Couperin and Amer. mus. Works incl. cantatas, song-cycles, chamber mus., and songs. O.B.E. 1982.

Mellophone. Brass instr. of semi-conical bore, coiled in circular shape and played with a cup mouthpiece. Has 3 piston valves. Sometimes used as substitute for French hn., being easier to play but not so rich in tone.

Melodia. Org. stop of *Hohlflöte* type popular in USA, of 8' length and pitch.

Melodic Minor Scale. See *Scale.*

Mélodie (melody). Term applied to Fr. solo song with acc., counterpart of the Ger. *Lied.*

Melodien (Melodies). Work for orch. by *Ligeti, comp. 1971, f.p. Nuremberg 1971.

Melodrama. Dramatic comp., or part of play or opera, in which words are recited to a mus. commentary. Popularized late in 18th cent. Where one or two actors are involved, 'monodrama' or 'duodrama' is term used. J. A. *Benda's *Ariadne auf Naxos* (1774) and *Medea* (1775) are early examples. Mozart used melodramatic monologues in *Zaide* (1780). *Fibich wrote a trilogy *Hippodamia* (1888–91). Famous operatic examples occur in the dungeon scene of Beethoven's *Fidelio*, the Wolf's Glen in Weber's *Der Freischütz*, Gertrude's aria in Marschner's *Hans Heiling*, and the Prologue to Strauss's *Ariadne auf Naxos*. Other examples are R. Strauss's *Enoch Arden* (1898), Honegger's *Jeanne d'Arc au bûcher* (1935), Bliss's *Morning Heroes* (1930), and Vaughan Williams's *An Oxford Elegy* (1949). The word has also come to mean an over-dramatic play, hence the adjective 'melodramatic', but in a musical connotation the orig. meaning is conveyed.

Melodramma (It.). 17th-cent. term for opera. Nothing to do with *melodrama.

Melody (from Gr. 'Melos'). A succession of notes, varying in pitch, which have an organized and recognizable shape. Melody is 'horizontal', i.e. the notes are heard consecutively, whereas in *harmony notes are sounded simultaneously ('vertical'). The mus. of many primitive races still remains purely melodic, as does European folk-song and also plainsong. Many apparently simple folk melodies will be found, on examination, however, to be highly organized, e.g. as regards the use at different pitch levels of some simple, brief *motif, the adroit use of a high note as a point of climax, etc.; many such melodies will be found to be cast in some definite form, such as Simple Ternary form.

*Rhythm is an important element in melody, whether it be the prose rhythm of primitive mus., plainsong, and the comps. of some modern composers, or the metrical rhythm of most other mus. Indeed this element is so much a governing factor in the effect of a melody that if, while the notes of a popular melody are left intact, the rhythm is drastically altered, it becomes difficult to recognize the melody. The rhythm of many melodies is extraordinarily subtle and repays close study.

Once harmony had become an element in mus. it began to influence melody in this way—that melodic passages are often found to be based on the notes of a chord (with or without added decorative or intermediate notes).

It is difficult to define 'originality' in melody. Apparently it lies mainly in mere detail, since, on critical examination, what we accept as an orig. melody is often found closely to resemble some previous and quite well-known melody. It is often difficult to see what has led to the popularity of a particular melody, or what it is that gives some melodies durability while others prove to be merely ephemeral: however, it will generally be found that the long-lived melodies possess the valuable quality of logical organization.

Racial and nat. feeling expresses itself strongly in melody, particular scales, intervals, and rhythms being typical of the mus. of particular races or nations.

The word is also sometimes used as the title for a small, simple piece, e.g. Rubinstein's *Melody* in F.

Melophone. Wind instr. with free-beating reeds, air being supplied by bellows operated by right hand and concealed in body of guitar or vc. Invented 1837 by Leclerc of Paris.

Melos Ensemble. Eng. instr. ensemble formed 1950 by Cecil *Aronowitz (va.), Gervase de Peyer (cl.), Richard Adeney (fl.), and Terence Weil (vc.) as a group of up to 12 players (str. quintet, wind quintet, harp, and pf.). Took part in f.p. of Britten's *War Requiem* (1962). Amer. début 1966.

Melos Quartet of Stuttgart. Ger. string qt. founded in 1965. Won Geneva int. comp. 1966. Recorded all Beethoven qts. 1968–70. Personnel unchanged in first 20 years of existence.

Melusina, The Fair (*Märchen von die schönen Melusine*). Ov. in C major by Mendelssohn, Op. 32, comp. 1833 and prompted by Conradin Kreutzer's opera *Melusine*.

Membranophone. Term for mus. instr. which produce sound from tightly stretched membranes, either struck (as in drums) or 'singing' (as the kazoo). One of four classifications of instr. devised by C. Sachs and E. M. von Hornbostel and pubd. in *Zeitschrift für Ethnologie*, 1914. Other categories are *aerophones, *chordophones, and *idiophones, to which *electrophones have been recently added.

Memento Vitae (Memory of Life). Conc. for orch. in homage to Beethoven by *Musgrave, comp. 1969–70, f.p. Glasgow 1970, cond. Loughran.

Memorial to Lidiče. Work for orch. by Martinů f.p. NY 1943; comp. in memory of Cz. village annihilated in Nazis' reprisal.

Mendelssohn (Mendelssohn-Bartholdy), **Fanny Cäcilie** (*b* Hamburg, 1805; *d* Berlin, 1847). Ger. amateur pianist and composer, sister of Felix *Mendelssohn. Published 6 of her songs with her brother's, and (in her own name) 2 books of *Lieder ohne Worte* for pf., also oratorio, songs, and partsongs. Married painter Wilhelm Hensel in 1829.

Mendelssohn (Mendelssohn-Bartholdy), (Jakob Ludwig) **Felix** (*b* Hamburg, 1809; *d* Leipzig, 1847). Ger. composer, pianist, organist, and cond. Grandson of Moses Mendelssohn, philosopher, and son of banker Abraham who added Bartholdy to his surname when he became Protestant Christian. Felix was 2nd of 4 children, eldest being Fanny *Mendelssohn, almost as good a pianist as her brother. His first pf. lessons were from his mother and in Berlin he was taught harmony by Karl Zelter. Boy prodigy as pianist, making public début at 9. In 1819 his setting of Ps. 19 was sung by Berlin Singakademie. In 1821 Zelter took him to Weimar to visit Goethe, a warm friendship developing between the 72-year-old poet and the boy of 12, who was already a prolific composer. His comic opera, *Die Hochzeit des Camacho* was completed 1825 and produced 1827. In 1826, at age 17, he comp. the ov. to *A Midsummer Night's Dream*, adding the remainder of the incidental mus. 16 years later. Attended Berlin Univ. 1826–9, and finally determined upon mus. as a profession. In Mar. 1829, he cond. Bach's St Matthew Passion at the Singakademie (its

first perf. since Bach's death in 1750), one of his many services to the Bach revival. Visited Eng. 1829, giving one of first perfs. there of Beethoven's 'Emperor' conc. From the outset he received adulation from Eng. public. Before leaving, toured Scotland and was inspired by scenery to write *Hebrides* ov. Toured Ger., Austria, and It. in next 2 years, composing 2 syms. and publishing 1st book of *Lieder ohne Worte*. Further visits to London 1832 and 1833 (when he cond. f.p. of his *Italian* Sym.). Appointed cond., Lower Rhine Mus. Fest., Düsseldorf 1833–6 and cond. of Leipzig Gewandhaus Orch. 1835–46. Married 1837 and in next few years wrote several of his finest works, incl. *Lobgesang*, the *Variations Sérieuses*, and vn. conc. Organized new cons. of mus. at Leipzig, becoming dir. when it opened in 1843 as well as teaching pf. and comp., with Schumann as associate. Made 8th visit to Britain 1844, and returned in 1846 to cond. f.p. of oratorio *Elijah* at Birmingham Fest. Last (10th) visit was in 1847, when he conducted *Elijah* in London, Manchester, and Birmingham, and played for Queen Victoria and Prince Albert. Severe overwork, combined with the shock of his sister Fanny's sudden death in May 1847, led to his own death in Nov. of that year.

Mendelssohn's gifts were phenomenal. He was a good painter, had wide literary knowledge, and wrote brilliantly. He was a superb pianist, a good violist, an exceptional organist, and an inspiring cond. He had an amazing mus. memory. He was generous to other musicians, and keen to raise standards of popular taste. His genius as a composer led Bülow to describe him as the most complete master of form after Mozart. In him, a classical upbringing was combined with romantic inclination, imparting to his work a poetic elegance which has caused it to be regarded as superficial because of its lack of impassioned features. The popularity of his work in the 19th cent. was followed by a severe reaction, partly caused by a feeling that his life had been too comfortably easy, but the pendulum has swung again and the best qualities of his music, its craftsmanship, restraint, poetry, inventive orchestration, and melodic freshness are now highly valued. Prin. works:

THEATRE: *Die *Hochzeit des Camacho*, Op. 10, comic opera (1825); incidental mus. to *A *Midsummer Night's Dream*, Op. 61 (1842); *Son and Stranger (Die Heimkehr aus der Fremde), operetta, Op. 89 (1829); *Lorelei*, unfinished opera (1847).

ORCH: 13 early syms. for str.; Syms: No. 1 in C minor, Op. 11 (1824), No. 2 (*Lobgesang) in B♭, Op. 52 (1840), No. 3 in A minor, Op. 56 (*Scotch) (1830–42), No. 4 in A, Op. 90 (*Italian) (1833); No. 5 in D minor, Op. 107 (*Reformation) (1830–2); ov. *Ruy Blas*, Op. 95 (1839), ov. *A *Midsummer Night's Dream*, Op. 21 (1826), ov. *Hebrides* (*Fingal's Cave (Fingals Höhle)), Op. 26 (1830, rev. 1832); *Meeresstille und Glückliche Fahrt*

(*Calm Sea and Prosperous Voyage), Op. 27 (1832); *Die schöne Melusina* (Fair *Melusina), Op. 32 (1833).

CONCERTOS, etc: Pf.: No. 1 in G minor, Op. 25 (1832), No. 2 in D minor, Op. 40 (1837); *Capriccio brillant* in B minor, Op. 22 (1832), *Rondo brillant* in E♭, Op. 29 (1834), *Serenade and Allegro giocoso* in B minor, Op. 43 (1838); Vn., in E minor, Op. 64 (1844); Conc. in A minor for pf. and str. (op. posth.) (1822); Conc. in D minor, vn. and str. (op. posth.) (1822); Conc. in E, 2 pf. and orch. (op. posth.) (1823); Conc. in A♭, 2 pf. and orch. (1824).

CHORAL: *Die *erste Walpurgisnacht* (The First Walpurgis Night), Op. 60 (1831, rev. 1842); Oratorios: *St Paul*, Op. 36 (1834–6); *Elijah*, Op. 70 (1846, rev. 1846–7); *Christus*, Op. 97, unfinished (1847); *Lobgesang* (Hymn of Praise, Sym. No. 2 in B♭), Op. 52 (1840); *Lauda Sion*, Op. 73 (1846); *Hear My Prayer* (1844); 9 settings of Psalms.

CHAMBER MUSIC: Str. Qts.: No. 1 in E♭, Op. 12 (1823), No. 2 in A minor, Op. 13 (1827), No. 3 in D, No. 4 in E minor, No. 5 in E♭, Op. 44 nos. 1, 2 and 3 (1837–8), No. 6 in F minor, Op. 80 (1847); *4 Pieces* for str. qt., Op. 81: *Andante* in E major (1847), *Scherzo* in A minor (1847), *Capriccio* in E minor (1843), *Fugue* in E♭ (1827); Pf. Qts: No. 1 in C minor, Op. 1 (1822), No. 2 in F minor, Op. 2 (1823), No. 3 in B minor, Op. 3 (1824–5); va. sonata in C minor (1824); cl. sonata in E♭ (1824); vn. sonata in F minor, Op. 4 (1825); *Variations concertantes* for pf. and vc., Op. 17 (1829); Str. Quintets: No. 1 in A, Op. 18 (1831), No. 2 in B♭, Op. 87 (1845); Octet in E♭, for str., Op. 20 (1825); scherzo from Octet arr. for orch.; vc. sonatas: No. 1 in B♭, Op. 45 (1838), No. 2 in D, Op. 58 (1843); Pf. Trios: No. 1 in D minor, Op. 49 (1839), No. 2 in C minor, Op. 66 (1845); *Lied ohne Worte* in D for vc. and pf., Op. 109 (1845); sextet in D, Op. 110 (1824); *Concertstück*, No. 1 in F minor for cl., corno di bassetto, and pf., Op. 113 (1833), No. 2 in D minor, Op. 114 (1833).

PIANO: *Capriccio* in F♯ minor, Op. 5 (1825); sonatas: E major, Op. 6 (1826), G minor, Op. 105 (1821), B♭, Op. 106 (1827); *7 Characteristic Pieces*, Op. 7 (1827); *Rondo capriccioso*, Op. 14; *Lieder ohne Worte*, Book 1, Op. 19 (1829–30), II, Op. 30 (1835), III, Op. 38 (1837), IV, Op. 53 (1841), V, Op. 62, VI, Op. 67 (1843–5), VII, Op. 85 (1842), VIII, Op. 102 (1842–5); *Fantasy*, Op. 28 (1833); *3 Capriccios*, Op. 33 (1833–5); *Variations sérieuses* in D minor, Op. 54 (1841), *Variations*, Op. 82 (1841), Op. 83 (1841); *Allegro brillant*, pf. duet, Op. 92 (1841); *3 Preludes and Studies*, Op. 104 (1836–8); *Capriccio* in E, Op. 118 (1837).

VOICE AND PIANO: 12 Songs, Op. 8 (1830); 12 Songs, Op. 9 (1829); 6 Songs, Op. 19a (1830); 6 Songs, Op. 34 (1834–7); 6 Songs, Op. 47 (1839); 6 Songs, Op. 57 (1839–42); 6 Songs, Op. 71 (1845–7); 3 Songs, Op. 84 (1831–9); 6 Songs, Op. 86 (1826–47); 6 Songs, Op. 99 (1841–5); 2 Sacred Songs, Op. 112 (1835).

PART-SONGS: 6 for SATB, Op. 41 (1834); 6 SATB, Op. 48 (1839); 6 TB, Op. 50 (1837–40); 6 SATB, Op. 59 (1837–43); 6 2-part songs, Op. 63 (1836–44); 4 TB, Op. 75 (1837–44); 4 TB, Op. 76 (1840–7); 3 2-part songs, Op. 77 (1836–47); 6 SATB, Op. 88 (1839–47); 4 TB, Op. 100 (1839–44); 4 TB, Op. 120 (1837–47); these are settings mainly of Heine, Goethe, Eichendorff, Fallersleben, Uhland, and Scott; *Festgesang*, male vv. and brass (1840).

ORGAN: 3 Preludes and Fugues, Op. 37 (1833–7); 6 Sonatas, Op. 65 (1839–44); *Andante and Variations* in D (1844).

Ménestrel (Fr.). Minstrel. Type of Fr. public mus. entertainer in 14th cent., orig. called *ménestrier*, the profession being known as *ménestrandie*. Spreading over the channel to Eng., the term became 'minstrel'. The minstrels (in effect professional musicians) formed a guild *c*.1350. See also *Jongleurs*, *Meistersinger*, and *Minnesinger*.

Mengelberg, (Josef) **Willem** (*b* Utrecht, 1871; *d* Zuort, Switz., 1951). Dutch cond. Studied Cologne Cons. (cond. under F. *Wüllner). Mus. dir., Lucerne 1891. Appointed permanent cond. of *Concertgebouw Orch. of Amsterdam 1895, remaining until 1945 and making it one of the great orchs. of the world. He particularly championed works of *Mahler and *Strauss in early years of 20th cent., winning friendship and admiration of both composers, who went to Amsterdam to conduct the orch. in their own works. Strauss ded. *Ein Heldenleben* to Mengelberg and the orch. In 1920 Mengelberg held a fest. in Amsterdam at which all Mahler's syms. and other major works were perf., the first such proclamation of faith in the composer. Cond. NY P.O., 1921–9. Prof. of mus., Utrecht Univ. from 1933. Frequent guest cond. of Eng. orchs. In 1945, because of alleged collaboration with the Nazi conquerors of Holland, was forbidden by Dutch govt. to 'exercise his profession in public in any matter whatever for a period of 6 years 1945–51'. He died in exile in the 6th year of this 'sentence', the justice of which is now questioned.

Menges, Herbert (*b* Hove, 1902; *d* London, 1972). Eng. cond. of Ger. parentage. First public appearance as violinist at 4, then studied pf. with Mathilde Verne and A. de Greef and comp. at RCM. Mus. dir. and composer to Old Vic Theatre 1931–50. Cond. SW, 1941–4. Mus. dir. and cond. Brighton P.O. from 1925, introducing many rare Eng. contemporary works. Dir. of mus., Chichester Fest. Th. from 1962. O.B.E. 1963.

Menges, Isolde (*b* Hove, 1893; *d* Richmond, Surrey, 1976). Eng. violinist of Ger. parentage, sister of Herbert *Menges. Studied with Auer, St Petersburg. London début 1913. Toured USA 1916–19. Founded Menges Qt. 1931. Prof. of vn., RCM from 1931.

Mennin (orig. Mennini), **Peter** (b Erie, Penn., 1923; d NY, 1983). Amer. composer. Studied at Oberlin Cons. and Eastman Sch. of Mus. First recipient of Gershwin Memorial Award. Taught comp., Juilliard Sch., 1947–58. Dir., Peabody Cons., Baltimore, 1958–62. President, Juilliard Sch. from 1962. Comps., somewhat severe in style, won many awards. They incl. 8 syms. (1941–1973; No. 4 (*The Cycle*) employs ch.); pf. conc., vc. conc., *Sinfonia* for chamber orch., *Concertato*, *Moby Dick* (1952), *Sinfonia* for large orch., cantata *The Pied Piper of Hamelin*, 2 str. qts., org. sonata, pf. sonata, songs, etc.

Meno (It.). Less, as in *meno mosso*, less moved, i.e. slower.

Menotti, Gian Carlo (b Cadegliano, It., 1911). It.-born composer, librettist, and cond., mainly resident in USA and Scotland. Taught as child by mother and wrote 2 operas before he was 15. Studied Milan Cons. 1924–7, then, on Toscanini's advice, at Curtis Institute, Philadelphia, under Rosario Scalero, 1928–34 (taught there 1948–55). His tendency as composer was always towards opera and his first adult essay, *Amelia Goes to the Ball*, was cond. by *Reiner in 1937 and later at NY Met. As with all his operas, he wrote his own lib. First outstanding success was in 1946 with *The Medium*, but this was eclipsed in 1950 by *The Consul*, dealing with the plight of refugees at the mercy of heartless bureaucracy. *Amahl and the Night Visitors* was the first opera to be written for TV in America. His works have achieved considerable popularity and his intention to bring opera nearer to the Broadway theatregoer has been achieved if at some cost in originality of expression. But of his dramatic effectiveness and melodic gift there can be no doubt. Founded Fest. of Two Worlds at Spoleto, It., 1958. Wrote lib. for *Barber's opera *Vanessa* (1957). Works incl.:

OPERAS: *Amelia Goes to the Ball* (Amelia al Ballo) (1934–7); *The Old Maid and the Thief* (1939); *The Island God* (1942, withdrawn); *The *Medium* (1945); *The *Telephone* (1946); *The *Consul* (1949); *Amahl and the Night Visitors* (1951, TV); *The *Saint of Bleecker Street* (1954); *Maria Golovin* (1958); *The Last Savage* (1963); *The Labyrinth* (TV, 1963); *Martin's Lie* (1964); *Help! Help! the Globolinks* (1968, children); *The Most Important Man* (1971); *Tamu-Tamu* (1973); *The Hero* (1976); *The Egg* (1976).

BALLETS: *Sebastian* (1944); *Errand into the Maze* (1947); *The Unicorn, the Gorgon, and the Manticore* (1956).

CANTATAS: *The Death of the Bishop of Brindisi* (1963); *Landscapes and Remembrances* (1976).

INSTRUMENTAL: Pf. Conc. in F (1945); *Apocalypse* for orch. (1951); Vn. Conc. in A minor (1952); Triple Conc. a Tre, for 9 soloists (1970); Sym. *The Halcyon* (1976).

Mensural Music. In the 13th to 16th cents. the contrast to *musica plana* (plainsong). It is poly-

phonic mus. in which every note has a strictly determined value, distinct from the free rhythm of Gregorian chant.

Mensural Notation. System of mus. notation est. c.1250 by Franco of Cologne and used until 1600. All shapes of notes and pauses had definite time values, in contrast with system of preceding epoch (modal notation) in which pattern of series of ligatures was key to required values. Basis of modern system.

Menuet (Fr.), **Menuett** (Ger.). See *Minuet*. The spelling *Menuetto*, used by Beethoven, is incorrect.

Menuhin, Hephzibah (b San Francisco, 1920; d London, 1981). Amer. pianist, sister of Yehudi *Menuhin. Début, San Francisco 1928. Soloist in concs. and frequent recitalist with her brother. Settled in Australia 1938, but continued to tour.

Menuhin, (Sir) Yehudi (b NY, 1916). Amer.-born violinist and cond. Child prodigy. First public recital San Francisco 1924. Studied with A. *Busch and G. *Enescu. Début with orch. San Francisco 1926, NY 1927. In 1929 played concs. by Bach, Beethoven, and Brahms in one programme with Berlin P.O. cond. *Walter, in Berlin, Dresden, and Paris. London début 1929, LSO cond. F. Busch. In 1932 recorded Elgar's conc., cond. by composer, and played work under his baton in Paris 1933. First recitals with sister Hephzibah in NY, London, and Paris 1934, followed by world tour of 73 cities. His career and talent continued beyond the 'prodigy' years. Bartók wrote the solo vn. sonata for him (1944). Gave many concerts for troops during World War II. After war continued his career as most famous of modern vn. virtuosi, but settled in Eng. and also began to conduct in 1957 (fest. at Gstaad). Art. dir. Bath Fest. 1959–69, conducting many concerts with own chamber orch. US début as cond. 1966. Founded Menuhin Sch. of Mus., now at Stoke d'Abernon, Surrey, 1963. Did much to encourage Western interest in Indian mus. Hon. K.B.E. 1965. Brit. citizen from 1985. O.M. 1987.

Mephisto Waltzes (*Mephistowalzer*). Mephisto is abbreviation for Mephistopheles. 4 works by Liszt. No. 1, orig. for orch. as No. 2 (*Der Tanz in der Dorfschenke*) of *2 Episodes from Lenau's *Faust* (before 1861), was transcr. for pf. solo and pf. duet (1881); No. 2, orig. for orch., transcr. pf. solo and duet (1881); No. 3 for pf. (1883) orch. Riesenauer; No. 4 for pf. (1885, pubd. 1952).

Mer, La (The Sea). 3 symphonic sketches for orch. by Debussy comp. 1903–5, f.p. Paris 1905; London 1908 (cond. Debussy). Movements are named *De l'Aube à midi sur la mer* (From dawn to noon on the sea), *Jeux de vagues* (Play of the waves), and *Dialogue du vent et de la mer* (Dialogue of the wind and the sea).

Merbecke (Merbeck, Marbeck, Marbecke), **John** (b Windsor, c.1510; d Windsor, c.1585). Eng.

composer and organist. Chorister, St George's Chapel, Windsor, 1531, organist 1541. Condemned to death as heretic 1543, but pardoned. In 1550 wrote first setting of prayer-book liturgy as authorized by 1549 Act of Uniformity. Compiled first biblical concordance in Eng. and wrote theological pamphlets. Also comp. mass and motets.

Mercadante, (Giuseppe) **Saverio** (Raffaele) (*b* Altamura, 1795; *d* Naples, 1870). It. composer. Pupil of Zingarelli, Naples 1816–20. Early works were instr. and choral, but turned to opera in 1819 and wrote nearly 60 up to 1856. With *Il giuramento* (1837), he threw off the Rossinian idiom of his earlier works and developed greater dramatic power in the orch. in the style of Meyerbeer, but his works have failed to hold the stage except for occasional perfs. in Italy and in concert versions in Vienna. Maestro di cappella Novara Cath., 1833. Dir., Naples Cons., 1840–70. Wrote 17 masses, orch. fantasies, songs, etc. Operas incl. *Maria Stuarda, Elisa e Claudio* (1821); *Amleto* (1822); *Don Chisciotte* (1829); *Francesca da Rimini* (1830–1); *I briganti* (1836); *Il bravo* (1839); *La Vestale* (1840); and *Violetta* (1853). Blind from 1862.

Mercure, Pierre (*b* Montreal, 1927; *d* Avallon, 1966). Canadian composer. Studied Quebec, later in Paris with Boulanger and Tanglewood with Dallapiccola. Bassoonist, Montreal S.O. 1947–52. Worked as producer of TV programmes for CBC Fr. network 1952–66. Worked with *musique concrète* and elec. methods.

Meriläinen, Usko (*b* Tampere, Finland, 1930). Finn. composer. Studied Sibelius Acad., Helsinki, and with Vogel in Switz. Chorusmaster at Finnish Opera. Works incl. 4 syms., 2 pf. concs., *Concerto for Orchestra*, str. qt., etc.

Merkel, Gustav (*b* Oberoderwitz, 1827; *d* Dresden, 1885). Ger. composer and organist. Court organist, Dresden, from 1864 and prof., Dresden Cons. from 1861. Wrote 9 org. sonatas, many choral preludes, and other works.

Merrick, Frank (*b* Clifton, Glos., 1886; *d* London, 1981). Eng. pianist and composer. Studied with Leschetizky in Vienna 1898–1901 and 1905. First public appearance, Clifton 1895; London début 1903. Diploma of Honour, Rubinstein Competition, St Petersburg, 1910. Prof. of pf., RMCM 1911–29. On staff RCM 1929–56, TCL 1956–75. Comps. incl. 2 pf. concs. and 'completion' of Schubert's 'Unfinished' Sym., also settings of Esperanto poems. Espoused cause of many unfashionable composers and of Brit. composers, e.g. Ireland, Bax, Rawsthorne, etc. C.B.E. 1978.

Merrie England. Light opera in 2 acts by *German to lib. by Basil Hood, introducing Queen Elizabeth I, Raleigh, and other Elizabethan characters. Prod. London 1902.

Merrill (orig. Miller), **Robert** (*b* Brooklyn, NY, 1917). Amer. bar. Studied with his mother, Lillian Miller, and later with Margolis in NY. Début Trenton 1944. Won Met. Auditions of Air, 1945, making début there in Dec. 1945 as Germont *père* in *La traviata*. Sang in Toscanini opera recordings. Long career at Met. in roles such as Figaro, Rigoletto, Iago, and Scarpia. CG début 1967 (Germont *père*).

Merry Widow, The (*Die lustige Witwe*). Operetta in 3 acts by Lehár to lib. by V. Léon and L. Stein after Meilhac's comedy *L'Attaché*. Prod. Vienna 1905 (first Widow was Mizzi Günther), London (Lily Elsie) and NY 1907. Merry Widow's name is Hanna Glawari.

Merry Wives of Windsor, The (Nicolai). See *Lustigen Weiber von Windsor, Die.*

Mersenne (Mersennus), **Marin** (*b* La Soultière, Maine, France, 1588; *d* Paris, 1648). Fr. theologian, mathematician, and mus. theorist. Wrote *Harmonie universelle* (2 vols. 1636–7). Valuable source of information on contemporary instr.

Merulo (orig. Merlotti), **Claudio** (*b* Correggio, 1533; *d* Parma, 1604). It. organist, publisher, and composer. Organist, Brescia 1556, St Mark's Venice, 1557–84. Wrote motets, madrigals, and sacred songs, also opera in madrigal-style *La tragedia* (Venice 1574). Org., ducal chapel, Parma, from 1584.

Messa di Voce (It.). Placing of the voice. Practice in *bel canto* of singing a crescendo then a diminuendo on a held note. Not to be confused with *mezza voce.*

Messager, André (Charles Prosper) (*b* Montluçon, 1853; *d* Paris, 1929). Fr. composer, organist, and cond. Studied Paris, teachers incl. Saint-Saëns. Organist, St Sulpice, 1874. Cond., Paris Opéra-Comique 1898–1903, 1919–20. Cond. f.p. of Debussy's *Pelléas et Mélisande* (1902), which is ded. to him. Art. dir. CG 1901–6, dir. and chief cond. Paris Opéra 1907–15. Cond. Société des Concerts du Cons., 1908–19 (touring Argentina 1916, USA 1918). Wrote several successful light operas. Works incl.:

OPERAS: *La Béarnaise* (1885), *La Basoche* (1890), *Madame Chrysanthème* (1893), *Les p'tites Michu* (1897), *★Véronique* (1898), *Fortunio* (1907), *Béatrice* (1914), *★Monsieur Beaucaire* (1919).
BALLETS: *Les ★deux pigeons* (1886), *Le Chevalier aux fleurs* (1897).
Also wrote sym. and pf. pieces.

Messa per i defunti (Mass for the Dead). See *Requiem.*

Messchaert, Johannes (*b* Holland, 1857; *d* Zürich, 1922). Dutch bar. Studied under Wüllner and Stockhausen and became outstanding interpreter of Christus in Bach's *St Matthew Passion.* Sang bass part in Elgar's *Dream of Gerontius,*

Düsseldorf 1902. Taught in Berlin from 1911 and in Zürich from 1920.

Messe des Morts (Mass of the Dead). See *Requiem*. For that by Berlioz, see *Grand' Messe des Morts*.

Messiaen, Olivier (Eugène Prosper Charles) (*b* Avignon, 1908). Fr. composer, organist, and teacher. Studied Paris Cons. 1919–30, studying comp. with (among others) Caussade, Dupré, and Dukas. In his youth he studied Indian and Greek mus. rhythms, plainchant, and folk mus. He also notated the songs of all French birds, classifying them by region. Several of his works quote and make great use of birdsong. In 1931 he became organist of L'Église de la Trinité, Paris, holding the post ever since. In 1936 he became a teacher at the École Normale de Musique and Schola Cantorum, and founded *Jeune France*, a group of young musicians, with Jolivet, Daniel Lesur, and Baudrier. He was imprisoned by the Germans for 2 years during the war, but on release, 1942, he was appointed a teacher at Paris Cons. (harmony, then analysis from 1947 and comp. from 1966). His pupils have incl. Boulez, Stockhausen, Barraqué, Xenakis, Amy, Sherlaw Johnson, and Goehr. His 2nd wife, the pianist Yvonne Loriod, has exercised great influence on his work.

Messiaen's mus., which is among the most influential and idiosyncratic of the century, is compounded from his deep Catholic faith, his celebration of human love, and his love of nature. He gave a new dimension of colour and intensity to org. mus., making special use of acoustic reverberations and contrasts of timbres. His harmony, rich and chromatic, derives from Debussy's use of 7ths and 9ths and modal progressions of chords. In his orch. works he makes use of the *ondes Martenot* in the vast *Turangalîla-symphonie* and of exotic perc. instrs., giving an oriental effect. Birdsong is also a major feature. His treatment of rhythm is novel, involving irregular metres, some of them originating in ancient Gr. procedures. Messiaen also acknowledges the supremacy of melody. Prin. works:

OPERA: *Saint François d'Assisi* (lib. by comp., f.p. Paris 1983) (1975–83).

ORCH: *Le Banquet eucharistique* (1928); *Les *Offrandes oubliées* (1930); *Hymne au Saint Sacrément* (1932); *L'*Ascension* (1933); *Turangalîla-symphonie* (1946–8); *Réveil des oiseaux* (1953); *Oiseaux exotiques* (1955–6); *Chronochromie* (1960); *7 Hai-Kai* (1962); *Couleurs de la cité céleste* (1963); *Et exspecto resurrectionem mortuorum* (1964); *Des canyons aux étoiles* (1970–4).

VOCAL AND CHORAL: *2 Ballades de Villon*, v. and pf. (1921); *3 Mélodies*, sop. and pf. (1930); *Mass*, 8 sop. and 4 vn. (1933); *Vocalise*, sop. and pf. (1935); *Poèmes pour Mi*, sop. and pf. (1936) with orch. (1937); *O sacrum convivium* (1937); *Chants de terre et de ciel* (1938); *3 Petites Liturgies de la présence divine*, women's ch., pf., ondes

Martenot, and orch. (1944); *Harawi, chant d'amour et de mort*, sop. and pf. (1945); *5 *Rechants*, 12 unacc. vv. (1949); *La *Transfiguration de Notre Seigneur Jésus-Christ*, ten., bar., ch., and orch. (1965–9).

PIANO: *8 Préludes* (1929); *Fantaisie burlesque* (1932); *Pièce pour le tombeau de Paul Dukas* (1935); *Visions de l'Amen*, 2 pf. (1943); *Rondeau* (1943); *20 *Regards sur l'Enfant Jésus* (1944); *Cantéyodjayâ* (1948); *4 Études de rythme* (1949–50); *Catalogue d'oiseaux* (1956–8); *La Fauvette des jardins* (1972).

ORGAN: *Variations écossaises* (1928); *Le Banquet céleste* (1928); *Diptyque* (1930); *Apparition de l'Église éternelle* (1932); *L'*Ascension* (1934); *La *Nativité du Seigneur* (1935); *Les *Corps glorieux* (1939); *Messe de la Pentecôte* (1950); *Livre d'orgue* (1951); *Verset pour la fête de la dédicace* (1960); *Méditations sur le mystère de la Sainte Trinité* (1969).

MISC. INSTR: *Thème et Variations*, vn. and pf. (1932); *Fêtes des belles eaux*, 6 ondes Martenot (1937); *2 Monodies en quart de ton*, ondes Martenot (1938); *Quatuor pour la fin du temps*, vn., cl., vc., pf. (1940); *Le Merle noir*, fl. and pf. (1951); *Timbres-durées, musique concrète* (1952); *Le Tombeau de Jean-Pierre Guézec*, hn. (1971).

Messiah. Oratorio by Handel to lib. selected from scriptures by Charles Jennens. Comp. between 22 Aug. and 14 Sept. 1741, though parts are adaptations from other works by Handel. F.p. Dublin, 13 April 1742; London, 23 March 1743; Boston, Mass., 25 Dec. 1818 (extracts in NY 1770). There is no single definitive version, Handel having altered, rewritten, and added numbers for various perfs. It became the custom in the 19th cent. to perf. *Messiah* with grossly inflated forces, but in the mid-20th cent. various performing edns. restored the work nearer to its original proportions and reverted to the correct tempo and rhythm for many nos. Mozart composed additional accs. for *Messiah* for an occasion when no org. was available to provide the figured bass, and these are still frequently used.

Messing (Ger.). Brass. So *Messinginstrumente*, brass instr.

Mesto (It.). Mournful, sad. So *Mestizia*, sadness.

Mesure (Fr.). (1) Measure, bar.
(2) Time; e.g. *à la mesure* = *a tempo*.

Metallophone. Percussion instr. comprising series of tuned metal bars arr. in a single or double row. *Orff scored for it in some of his comps. Far Eastern versions influenced development of *glockenspiel and *vibraphone.

Metamorphosen. Study in C minor for 23 solo str. by R. Strauss, comp. 1945 as a lament for the destruction of the Ger. cultural world in which he had lived. Quotes from funeral march of Beethoven's *Eroica* Sym. F.p. Zürich 1946 cond.

Paul Sacher; f. Eng. p. London, Dec. 1946 (Boyd Neel Orch.).

Metamorphoses after Ovid, Six. Work for solo ob., Op. 49, by Britten, comp. 1951. Movements are entitled *Pan, Phaeton, Niobe, Bacchus, Narcissus,* and *Arethusa.*

Metamorphosis of Themes by Weber, Symphonic (Hindemith). See *Symphonic Metamorphosis of Themes by Weber.*

Metamorphosis. Term used to describe manner in which composer may change tempo, rhythm, and notes of a theme yet preserve its essential and recognizable characteristics. Employed by Liszt in his symphonic poems and by Elgar and Franck in syms. Hindemith's *Symphonic Metamorphosis of Themes by Weber and Britten's 6 *Metamorphoses after Ovid* are modern examples of the device. Strauss's use of the term in his *Metamorphosen refers to Goethe, not to mus. form.

Metastasio (orig. Trapassi), **Pietro Antonio Domenico Bonaventura** (*b* Rome, 1698; *d* Vienna, 1782). It. poet and librettist. Pubd. first work at 14 and later enjoyed protection of the singer Marianna Benti-Bulgarelli. Lived in Vienna as court poet from 1730 and devoted himself to providing composers with opera libs., mainly on classical subjects. They were set over 800 times by different composers. Some texts from his vast output were used up to 70 times. *Artaserse* was set by 40 composers. Among those who set his libs. were Galuppi, Gluck, Handel, Hasse (who set nearly all), Jommelli, Koželuh, Mercadante, Meyerbeer, Mozart, Paisiello, Piccinni, Spontini, etc. Gluck's opera reforms were directed against the highly formal, artificial, and conventional nature of Metastasio's works, with the development of the plot being halted continually for displays of vocal agility. Among Metastasio's libs. were *Didone abbandonata, La Clemenza di Tito,* and *Il Rè Pastore.*

Metre. Term used of regular succession of rhythmical impulses, or beats, in poetry and mus., e.g. $\frac{3}{4}$ and $\frac{6}{8}$ being described as different kinds of metres. Rhythm is no longer accepted as a sufficiently precise definition, *metre* being considered as the basic pulse and rhythm as the actual time-patterns of the notes within a measure. E.g., in $\frac{3}{4}$ the 3 beats—strong, weak, weak—are metrical, while the time-values of the notes actually heard are the rhythm.

Metrical Psalm. A psalm versified in a regular syllabic metre which thus can be sung to a hymn-tune. Brought to Britain by Calvinists fleeing to Eng. and Scotland from Geneva. Famous treasury of Eng. sacred tunes is Sternhold and Hopkins's metrical psalter (London 1562). It was followed by other such psalters (Este's 1592, Ravenscroft's 1621, Playford's 1677, Tate and Brady's 1696).

Metric Modulation. Term and technique introduced by Amer. composer Elliott *Carter for changing the rhythm (not necessarily the metre) from one section to another.

Metronome. Apparatus for sounding an adjustable number of beats per minute and therefore for fixing the tempo of a comp. An early form, called *chronomètre,* was available at end of 17th cent. and further experiments followed. That most commonly used is a clockwork model patented by *Maelzel, who appropriated the idea from the Dutch inventor D. N. Winkel and est. a metronome factory in Paris, 1816. Consists of steel rod, about $7\frac{1}{2}''$ long by $\frac{1}{8}''$ wide, pierced near top through which comes the pivot on which the rod oscillates. This rod, governed by a double pendulum, is suspended by a pivot in front of a wooden case and held perpendicular. By means of a weight, the pendulum may be made to oscillate between 40 and 208 times in a minute. Maelzel's graduated scale, fixed to the case, gives speed of oscillation. A spiral spring keeps the instrument beating for a considerable period. A composer who wants 78 quarter-note (crotchet) beats in 1 minute will write 'M.M. (Maelzel metronome) ♩ = 78'. It should be mentioned that some composers' metronome markings are suspect. Eds. of early works have in many cases added metronome marks which they think are feasible. Elec. metronomes have been marketed by several firms, and there is a pocket-metronome, about the size of a watch, consisting merely of an adjustable pendulum.

The ticking of Maelzel's metronome is supposed to have inspired the theme of the 2nd movement of Beethoven's 8th sym. Several 20th-cent. composers have incorporated the ticking of actual metronomes into their scores, e.g. *Ligeti's symphonic poem for 100 metronomes and Gordon *Crosse's *Play Ground.*

Metropolitan Opera House. Chief Amer. opera house, now a constituent of NY's *Lincoln Center for the Performing Arts. Opened Sept., 1966, with Barber's *Antony and Cleopatra.* Seating capacity 3,800. Orig. 'Met.' opened 1883, with Gounod's *Faust.* After first season, Leopold Damrosch was appointed art. dir., but died before his first season was over and was succeeded by Anton Seidl and by Walter Damrosch, son of Leopold, who remained until 1890–1, giving all operas in Ger. Singers at the Met. in the period up to 1903 incl. Nilsson, Materna, Sembrich, Nordica, Eames, the de Reszkes, Calvé, Melba, Plançon, Maurel, and Scotti. In 1903 Heinrich Conried became manager, engaging Caruso, Fremstad, Farrar, and Chaliapin. In 1907 he brought Mahler as cond., but resigned in 1908 and was followed by the joint direction of Andreas Dippel and Giulio Gatti-Casazza who engaged Toscanini as cond. Dippel resigned in 1910 and Gatti-Casazza remained until 1935. An outstanding occasion was the f.p. in 1910 of Puccini's *La Fanciulla del West,* with Caruso, Destinn, and Toscanini. Toscanini resigned in 1914–15 and was followed by a group of conductors among whom Bodanzky, Serafin, and Wolff were outstanding. During Gatti-Casazza's régime operas by Strauss, Janáček, Respighi, and others had their first Amer. performances. Gigli, Ponselle, Pinza, Flagstad, Leider, Melchior, Muzio, Jeritza, and Tibbett were among the principal singers. Gatti-Casazza's successor was Herbert Witherspoon, who died almost immediately and the management passed to Edward Johnson, a member of the company since 1922. In his 15 years he encouraged Amer. singers, e.g. Warren, Peerce, Tucker, Traubel, Thebom, and strengthened the conducting by engaging Stiedry, Walter, Busch, Szell, Reiner, and others. From 1950 to 1972, Rudolf Bing was manager. In his régime stage techniques were modernized and theatrical producers engaged. He extended the season from 30 to 45 weeks. Great singers in his era incl. Callas, Tebaldi, Price, Merrill, de los Angeles, Bergonzi, and Siepi. Bing was succeeded by Goeran Gentele, who was killed before taking office, though not before he had appointed the Met.'s first mus. dir. Rafael Kubelik. The manager from 1973 was Schuyler Chapin. He appointed James Levine mus. dir. in 1975. Broadcasting from the Met. began in 1931. Since 1932 the Saturday matinées have been relayed nationally.

Mewton-Wood, Noel (*b* Melbourne, 1922; *d* London, 1953). Australian pianist. Studied at Melbourne Cons. and RAM, later with Schnabel. London début 1940. Regarded as one of greatest pianists of his day. Brilliant exponent of Bliss's conc., Tippett's 1st sonata, and of works by Busoni and Britten. Acc. Pears in song-cycles by Tippett. Gave f.p. of rev. version of Britten's pf. conc. 1946.

Meyer, Kerstin (Margareta) (*b* Stockholm, 1928). Swedish mez. Début Stockholm 1952 as Azucena in *Il trovatore*, then studied in Salzburg and Italy. Guest singer in opera Vienna, Venice, Hamburg, Berlin, since 1956. Sang in Eng. from 1960, esp. with Barbirolli and Hallé (Angel in *Gerontius*, Mahler, Chausson, etc.). Débuts CG (Dido in Berlioz's *Les Troyens*) and NY Met. 1960, Bayreuth 1962. Frequent appearances at Glyndebourne (début 1961 in *Elegy for Young Lovers*). Striking singing-actress, notably in modern operas. Created leading roles in operas by Maw, Goehr, Schuller, Searle, Henze, and Ligeti (*Le grand macabre*, 1978). Hon. C.B.E. 1985.

Meyer, Krzysztof (*b* Kraków, 1943). Polish composer, pianist, and writer. Studied Kraków and Amer. Cons., Fontainebleau. Prof. Kraków High School of Mus. Works incl. opera, 5 syms., 5 concs., 5 str. qts., pf. sonatas, etc.

Meyerbeer, Giacomo (really Jakob Liebmann Beer) (*b* Berlin, 1791; *d* Paris, 1864). Ger. composer who worked mainly in Paris. After receiving legacy from relative named Meyer converted his name into Meyerbeer. Child prodigy pianist,

playing Mozart conc. in public at age 7. Studied counterpoint with Vogler at Darmstadt 1810–12, at which time he wrote 2 operas and and an oratorio. His comic opera was a failure in Vienna, where he was urged by Salieri to study vocal methods in It. He fell under Rossini's spell in 1815 and wrote 6 It. operas between 1817 and 1824, all successful, especially *Il Crociato in Egitto*. Weber advised him to turn to Ger. opera, but after the Paris première of *Il Crociato* in 1826 he concentrated on Fr. opera, spending the next few years assimilating Fr. history and character. He collaborated with the librettist Scribe and their first opera, *Robert le Diable*, in 5 acts and on a grand scale, was an unprecedented success. This was followed by *Les Huguenots* and *Le Prophète*. He was *Generalmusikdirektor* in Berlin 1842–9, during which time he wrote *Ein Feldlager in Schlesien* for Jenny *Lind, later incorporating some of its nos. into *L'Étoile du Nord*. The success of Meyerbeer's pageant-like operas irked Wagner (who nevertheless learned from them in early works like *Rienzi) and Meyerbeer, born of Jewish parentage, was bitterly attacked in Wagner's pamphlet *Das Judentum in der Musik* in spite of the fact that Meyerbeer had assisted him early in his career. He returned to Paris in 1863 to supervise rehearsals of his longest opera, *L'Africaine*, on which he had been working for nearly 25 years but he became ill and died. It had been customary to deride Meyerbeer for an eclecticism which lacked sufficient inner conviction to give his operas life beyond their day and away from the spectacular dramatic productions they received in Paris. Revivals of his operas, however, have revealed virtues which were his alone, and, as with so many other figures in mus. history, it would be rash to write him off as forgotten. Prin. works:

OPERAS: *Jephtas Gelübde* (1812), *Wirth und Gast* (1813, rev. 1820 as *Alimelek*), *Romilda e Costanza* (1817), *Semiramide Riconosciuta* (1819), *Emma di Resburgo* (1819), *Margherita d'Anjou* (1820), *L'esule di Granata* (1822), *Il Crociato in Egitto* (1824), *Robert le Diable* (1831), *Les *Huguenots* (1836), *Ein Feldlager in Schlesien* (1844, rev. 1847 as *Vielka*), *Le *Prophète* (1849), *L'*Étoile du Nord* (1854), *Le Pardon de Ploërmel* or *Dinorah* (1859), *L'*Africaine* (1837–64).
Also wrote oratorio, marches, songs, and church mus.

Meyerowitz, Jan (orig. Hans-Hermann) (*b* Breslau, 1913). Ger.-born composer (Amer. citizen since 1951). Studied Berlin Hochschule für Musik 1930–3 with *Zemlinsky and in Rome 1933–7 with *Casella and *Respighi. Settled in USA 1946, teaching at Tanglewood, Brooklyn, and in NY. Works incl. 7 operas, e.g. *Esther* (1957); choral works incl. *The Glory Around His Head* (1955), *Stabat Mater*, *e.e. cummings Cantata* (1949–56), *Emily Dickinson Cantata* (1948), *Robert Herrick*

Cantata (1948–54); Sym. *Midrash Esther* (1957); fl. conc., vc. sonata, songs, etc.

Mezzo, mezza (It.). Half. *Mezza voce,* half-voice, i.e. half the vocal (or instr.) power possible. (Not to be confused with *★Messa di voce.*) *Mezzo-forte,* half-loud, i.e. neither loud nor soft.

Mezzo-Soprano (It.). Half-soprano. Female (or artificial male) v. midway between sop. and cont. Several operatic roles written for sops. are traditionally sung by and better suited to mezzos, e.g. Dorabella in *Così fan tutte,* Carmen, Oktavian in *Der Rosenkavalier,* the Composer in *Ariadne auf Naxos.* Occasionally a singer will describe herself as 'mezzo-contralto', meaning a little lower in range than mez.

mf. = *Mezzo forte,* Half-loud.

M.G. = *Main gauche* (Fr.). Left hand.

Mi. (1) The 3rd degree of the major scale, according to the system of vocal syllables derived from Guido d'Arezzo (see *Hexachord*), and so used (spelt *Me*) in ★Tonic Sol-fa, in which it is also the 5th degree of the minor scale. In many countries, however, the name has become attached (on 'fixed-doh' principles) to the note E, in whatever key it may occur.
(2) ★Messiaen's intimate name for his first wife, the violinist Claire Desnos, for whom he wrote his ★*Poèmes pour Mi.*

Miaskovsky. See *Myaskovsky, Nikolay.*

Micheau, Janine (*b* Toulouse, 1914; *d* Paris, 1976). Fr. sop. Studied Toulouse and Paris. Début Paris 1933. Paris Opéra from 1936, creating title-roles of ★Milhaud's *Médée* (1940) and Manuela in his *Bolivar* (1950). CG 1937 (Micaela in *Carmen*), San Francisco 1938, Chicago 1956. Prof. of singing, Paris Cons. from 1960. Notable Mélisande and Micaela.

Michelangeli, Arturo Benedetto (*b* Brescia, 1920). It. pianist. Studied Brescia and Milan Cons. 1st prize Geneva Int. Mus. Competition 1939. Eng. début 1946. Remarkable artist, but appearances infrequent.

Michelangelo Buonarroti, Suite on Verses of. 11 settings by Shostakovich, Op. 145, for bass and pf., comp. 1974, f.p. Leningrad 1975. Orch. version, Op. 145a, 1974, f.p. Moscow 1975.

Michelangelo Sonnets (Britten). See *Seven Sonnets of Michelangelo.*

Mi contra Fa. The ★tritone (interval of 3 whole tones), from F up or down to B, difficult to sing, thus giving rise to the saying 'Mi contra fa diabolus est in musica' ('Mi against fa [the Hexachord system names for these notes] is the devil in music').

Microtone. All intervals which lie between the semi-tones of the 12-note, equal-tempered tuning system. Several 20th-cent. composers have exper-imented in microtones and quarter-tones. Joseph Yasser proposed a scale of 19 notes per octave and Adriaan Fokker 31 per octave, but little mus. has been written using these temperaments because instrs. are not designed to play them. Elec. instrs., however, enable division of intervals other than the octave in equal intervals, as in ★Stockhausen's *Gesang der Jünglinge.* Among the earliest composers to employ microtones were ★Ives, ★Bartók, and ★Bloch but as incidental features. More systematic use was devised by A. ★Hábá, J. ★Carrillo, and H. Partch.

Middelschulte, Wilhelm (*b* Werne, 1862; *d* Werne, 1943). Ger. organist and composer. Studied Berlin. Organist, Lukaskirche, Berlin, 1888–91, Chicago R.C. Cath. 1891–5, St James's Ch., Wisconsin, 1899–1919. Wrote several org. works.

Middle C. The note C found at approx. middle of pf. kbd., commonly tuned to 256 Hz. The pitch represented by note on 1st ledger line below treble staff, or 1st above bass staff.

Midi, Le (Haydn). See *Matin, Le.*

Midsummer Marriage, The. Opera in 3 acts by ★Tippett to his own lib. Comp. 1946–52. Prod. London 1955, San Francisco 1983. *Ritual Dances* from Act II are often perf. as concert piece and were f.p. before opera was prod. (Basle, 1953, Liverpool 1954).

Midsummer Night's Dream, A. Play (1593–4) by Shakespeare which has attracted several composers. (1) *The Fairy Queen,* 1691, adaptation (by E. Settle?) of Shakespeare for which ★Purcell wrote incidental mus. Shakespeare's text is not quoted.
(2) ★Mendelssohn composed an Ov. in E major, Op. 26, in 1826 when he was 17, adding additional items of incidental mus., Op. 61, for a prod. of the play at Potsdam in Oct. 1843 these being: 1. *Scherzo* (entr'acte after Act 1). 2. *Melodrama.* 2a. *Fairy March* (Act 2). 3. *You spotted snakes* (2 sop. and ch.) (Act 2). 4. *Melodrama* (Act 2). 5. *Intermezzo* (entr'acte after Act 2). 6. *Melodrama* (Act 3). 7. *Nocturne* (entr'acte after Act 3). 8. *Melodrama* (Act 4). 9. *Wedding March* (after end of Act 4). 10. *Melodrama.* 10a. *Funeral March* (Act 5). 11. *Bergomask Dance* (Act 5). 12. *Melodrama.* 12a. *Finale* (Act 5).
(3) Incidental mus. by ★Orff commissioned by Nazis when Mendelssohn's mus. was banned. 1st version 1939 (f.p. Frankfurt 1939; withdrawn), 2nd version 1944 (withdrawn), 3rd version 1952 (f.p. Darmstadt 1952), 4th version 1964 (f.p. Stuttgart 1964).
(4) Opera in 3 acts by ★Britten to lib. (Shakespeare's text) abbreviated by composer and Peter Pears. Prod. Aldeburgh 1960, San Francisco and CG 1961, NY 1963, Glyndebourne 1981.

Mighty Handful (Russ., *Moguchaya kuchka*). Term coined by critic V. Stasov and applied to the 5 Russ. composers Balakirev, Borodin, Cui, Mussorgsky, and Rimsky-Korsakov who were consciously nationalist in their approach to mus. Sometimes known as 'the *Five' or the 'Mighty Five'.

Mignon. Opera in 3 acts by Ambroise Thomas to lib. by Barbier and Carré based on Goethe's novel *Wilhelm Meisters Lehrjahre* (1795–6). Prod. Paris 1866, London 1870, New Orleans 1871, NY 1883.

Mignone, Francisco (*b* São Paulo, 1897; *d* Rio de Janeiro, 1986). Brazilian composer, cond., and pianist. Studied in São Paulo and Milan. Prof. of pf. and harmony Rio Cons. from 1934. Works incl. operas, ballets, orch. mus., and smaller pieces.

Migot, Georges Elbert (*b* Paris, 1891; *d* Levallois, 1976). Fr. composer. Studied Paris Cons. with Widor and d'Indy. Curator of Paris Cons. museum of instrs. 1949–61. Influenced by Asian mus. and Fr. medieval polyphony. Prolific composer of 13 syms., several operas, ballets, oratorios, *Requiem*, etc. Also painter and writer.

Mihalovici, Marcel (*b* Bucharest, 1898). Romanian-born composer. Studied Bucharest and Paris (1919–25). Settled in Paris. Teacher at Schola Cantorum 1959—62. Husband of pianist Monique *Haas. Works incl. operas *Phèdre* (1948–9), *Die Heimkehr* (1954–5), *Krapp* (1959–60), ballets, 5 syms., mus. for Eliot's *Murder in the Cathedral*, 3 str. qts., sonatas for several instr. (incl. cl., bn., va.).

Mihály, András (*b* Budapest, 1917). Hung. composer. Studied Budapest Acad. 1933–8. Teacher of chamber mus. Budapest Acad. from 1950. Founder and cond. Budapest Chamber Ens. 1968. Works incl. 3 syms., vc. conc., pf. conc., vn. conc., opera *Together and Alone* (1965), 2 str. qts., choral works, etc.

Mikado, The, or The Town of Titipu. Operetta comp. 1884–5 by Sullivan to lib. by Gilbert. Prod. London, NY, Chicago, and Sydney, N.S.W., 1885.

Mikrokosmos. 153 'progressive pieces for pianoforte' by Bartók comp. between 1926 and 1939 and pubd. in 6 vols. 7 pieces (Nos. 69, 113, 123, 127, 135, 145, 146) transcr. by Bartók for 2 pf. 7 pieces (Nos. 102, 117, 137, 139, 142, 151, 153) transcr. by Tibór Sérly for orch. 5 pieces (Nos. 102, 108, 116, 139, 142) transcr. by Sérly for str. qt.

Milán, Luis de (*b* Valencia, *c.*1500; *d* Valencia, *c.*1561). Sp. composer, poet, and player of the *vihuela*, for which he wrote many pieces. Also wrote songs with *vihuela* acc., a book of them being pubd. 1536.

Milanov (orig. Kunc), **Zinka** (*b* Zagreb, 1906). Yugoslav sop. Studied Zagreb, then with *Ternina. Début Ljubljana 1927 in *Trovatore*. Prin. sop., Zagreb Opera 1928–35, singing 350 perfs. all in Croatian. Salzburg Fest. 1937. NY Met.

début 1937, appearing there regularly until 1966, excluding 1947–50.

Milanova, Stoika (*b* Plovdiv, Bulgaria, 1945). Bulgarian violinist. Studied Moscow Cons. with D. *Oistrakh. 1st prize City of London int. competition 1970, also Flesch prize. London début 1970. Hongkong Fest. with Hallé Orch. 1976. Recitals with Radu Lupu.

Mildenburg, Anna von (*b* Vienna, 1872; *d* Vienna, 1947). Austrian operatic sop. Studied with Rosa Papier. Début Hamburg 1895 under *Mahler, whose mistress she was for a time and about whom she wrote a valuable book of memoirs. Became eminent in Wagner: Bayreuth (Kundry) 1897, CG (Isolde) 1906. Sang at Vienna Opera in Mahler's directorship and was regular member of co.1908–16. Outstanding Klytemnestra in Strauss's *Elektra*. Stage dir. Nat. Th., Munich, 1921–6. Taught in Berlin 1938. Married the writer Hermann Bahr, 1909, with whom she wrote *Bayreuth und das Wagner-Theater* (1910).

Mildmay, Audrey (*b* Herstmonceux, 1900; *d* London, 1953). Eng. sop. Sang with Carl Rosa and SW. Married John *Christie of *Glyndebourne, 1931, who built opera house for her and launched famous summer operatic fest. 1934. She sang Susanna (*Figaro*), Zerlina (*Don Giovanni*), and Norina (*Don Pasquale*) at Glyndebourne. Edinburgh Fest. was her idea.

Milford, Robin (*b* Oxford, 1903; *d* Lyme Regis, 1959). Eng. composer. Studied RCM under Holst, Vaughan Williams, and R. O. Morris. Taught mus. in schools. Wrote oratorios, *A Prophet in the Land* (1931) and *The Pilgrim's Progress*, sym., vn. conc., ballets, and songs.

Milhaud, Darius (*b* Aix-en-Provence, 1892; *d* Geneva, 1974). Fr. composer and pianist. Entered Paris Cons. 1909, studying with Gédalge, Widor, and d'Indy. Attaché at Fr. legation, Rio de Janeiro, 1917–19, meeting Claudel, poet-diplomat, who was to write libs. for several of his works. Returned to Paris 1919, becoming known as one of Les *Six who owed allegiance to Satie and Cocteau. Visited USA 1922 as pianist in his own works. Left Fr. 1940, settling in USA, teaching at Mills Coll., Oakland, Calif., 1940–71 and in summers at Aspen, Colorado. Also taught at Paris Cons. 1947–71. Extremely prolific composer, despite handicap of precarious health from late 1920s when rheumatic condition necessitated use of wheelchair. Dominating feature of his mus. is use of *polytonality. Experimented with many instr. combinations and also with tape. Prin. works:

OPERAS: *Les Malheurs d'Orphée* (1925); *Le Pauvre Matelot* (1926); *Christophe Colomb* (1928); *Maximilien* (1930); *Médée* (1938); *Bolivar* (1943); *David* (1952); *La Mère Coupable* (based on 3rd play of Beaumarchais's Figaro trilogy) (1964–5); *St Louis* (1970).

467 MILLS

BALLETS: *L'Homme et son désir* (1918); *Le *Boeuf sur le toit* (1919); *Les *Mariés de la Tour Eiffel* (1921); *La *Création du monde* (1923); *Le Train bleu* (1924); *La Bien-Aimée* (after Schubert and Liszt) (1928); *La Mort d'un tyran* (1933); *Mme Miroir* (1948); *Jeux de printemps* (Imagined Wing) (1944); *The Bells* (1946); *Les Rêves de Jacob* (1949); *Vendange* (1952).

THEATRE: *Agamemnon*, incidental mus. to Claudel adaptation of Aeschylus (1913–14); *Protée*, incidental mus. to drama by Claudel (1913–19); *Les Choëphores*, Claudel, after Aeschylus (1915); *Les Euménides*, Claudel, after Aeschylus (1917–22); *L'Annonce faite à Marie*, incidental mus. to Claudel drama (1932); *Le Jeu de Robin et Marion*, mystery play after *Adam de la Halle (1951); *L'Opéra des gueux*, arr. of *The Beggar's Opera* (1937).

ORCH: 6 syms. for small orch. (*Le Printemps, Pastorale, Serenade*, 10 str. instr., 10 wind instr., 4 vv., ob., vc.) (1917–22); *Saudades do Brazil* (1920–1, orig. for pf.); *Suite provençale* (1937); *Suite française* (1945); Syms. Nos. 1–12, comp. 1940–62 (No. 3 *Hymnus ambrosianus* with ch.); va. conc. (1927); 2 vc. concs. (1935, 1946); cl. conc. (1941); harp conc. (1954).

PIANO AND ORCH: 5 concs; *5 Études* (1920); *Le Carnaval d'Aix* (1926); Conc. for 2 pf. (1942).

VIOLIN AND ORCH: *Concertino de printemps* (1934); 3 concs. (1927–58) (No. 3 *Concerto Royal*).

MISC: Conc., perc. and small orch. (1930); Suite for harmonica (or vn.) and orch. (1942); *L'Apothéose de Molière*, hpd. and str. (1948); conc. for *marimba, vibraphone, and orch. (1947); *Concertino d'hiver*, tb. and str. (1953).

CHAMBER MUSIC: 18 str. qts., comp. 1912–62 (Nos. 14 and 15 can be played separately or together as an octet, 1949); *La *Cheminée du roi René*, suite (1939); str. trio (1947); str. septet (1964); sonatinas for vn. and va., fl. and pf., cl. and pf.; sonatas for va., and for vn. and hpd.; *Elégie* for vc. and pf. (1945).

PIANO: Sonata No. 1 (1916), No. 2 (1949); *Saudades do Brazil* (1920–1, also orch.); *L'Album de Madame Bovary* (1934); *Le Candélabre à sept branches* (1951); *Scaramouche for 2 pf. (1939); *Paris*, suite of 6 pieces for 4 pf. (1948).

VOCAL: *Machines agricoles*, v. and 7 instr. (1919); *Catalogue des fleurs*, v. and chamber orch. (1920); Sym. for vocal qt., ob. and vc. (1923); *Pacem in terris*, ch. and orch. (1963).

Also many songs and music for about 30 films, 1929–59, incl. *Madame Bovary* (dir. J. Renoir, 1933) and *Péron et Evita* (1958).

Militärtrommel (Ger.). *Side drum.

Military band. This term is used in Britain to describe either an actual army (or naval or airforce) band or for one on the same model, i.e. comprising both brass and woodwind instr. The composition of such bands varies widely in different countries, and even in different regimental or other units of the same country. One common Brit. combination is as follows: (a) 1 picc. (or fl., or both); 1 ob.; 1 small cl., 12–14 ordinary cl., 2 bass cl.; 1 alto and 1 ten. sax; 2 bn. (b) 4 hns., 2 bars., 2 euphoniums, 4 bombardons. (c) 4 cornets; 2 tpt.; 3 tb. (d) 2 drummers with a variety of perc. instr. Sometimes, when conditions of perf. allow, 1 or 2 str. db. may appear, as an alternative to the same number of bass wind instr. Bands in USA vary from the above scheme merely in detail.

The score and parts of the military band, unlike those of the brass band, employ the ordinary orch. system of notation. The term 'wind band' is used in USA.

Military, The. Nickname of Haydn's Sym. in G, No. 100 in Breitkopf edn., comp. 1794 in London. So called because of 'military' instrs. and solo tpt.-call in 2nd movement.

Milkina, Nina (*b* Moscow, 1919). Russ.-born pianist. Studied Paris Cons. and with Marguérite Long, Harold Craxton, and T. Matthay. Début Paris, with Lamoureux Orch. Specialist in Mozart and 18th-cent. chamber mus. Settled in Eng.

Miller, Edward Jay (*b* Miami, 1930). Amer. composer. Studied Miami, Berlin (with *Blacher), and Tanglewood. Teacher of comp. at Hartt Coll. 1959–71, Oberlin Coll. from 1971. Works incl. *Reflections at the Bronx Zoo* for orch. and opera *The Young God*.

Miller, (Alton) **Glenn** (*b* Clarinda, Iowa, 1904; *d* between London and Paris, 1944). Amer. trombonist, band-leader, composer, and arranger. Played in various bands from 1921 until joining Dorsey brothers' orch. 1934. Devised reed section of cl. and 4 sax. while with Ray Noble 1935. Formed own band 1937; this became one of best-known and most popular in the world because of its characteristic sound, exemplified in recordings such as *Moonlight Serenade, Chatanooga Choo-Choo, In the Mood, American Patrol*, etc. Disbanded 1942 when Miller joined US Army. In 1944 assembled service band and went to Eng. same year. Disappeared on flight to Paris, Dec. 1944, aircraft never being found. Band continued under other leaders, notably Ray McKinley (1956–65).

Millöcker, Karl (*b* Vienna, 1842; *d* Baden, 1899). Austrian composer and cond. Studied Vienna Cons. Cond. posts at Graz and Vienna, where he was cond. and composer at Theater an der Wien from 1869. Prolific composer of operettas, best-known of which are *Der tote Gast* (1865), *Der *Bettelstudent* (1882), *Gasparone* (1884), *Der arme Jonathan* (1890).

Mills, Charles (*b* Asheville, N. Carolina, 1914; *d* NY, 1982). Amer. composer. Played in jazz bands from age 17. Studied NY with Copland, Sessions, and Harris. Winner of several prizes. Commissioned by *Mitropoulos to compose work for NY P.O., 1951. Prin. works incl. 4 syms., pf. conc., fl. conc., *Theme and Variations* for orch., ob. concertino, and many chamber works, some involving jazz groups.

Milner, Anthony (Francis Dominic) (*b* Bristol, 1925). Eng. composer. Studied comp. with *Seiber, 1944–8, and RCM 1945–7. Taught at Morley Coll. 1946–62. Dir. and harpsichordist, London Cantata Ens., 1954–65. Teacher at RCM from 1961 and at King's Coll., London, 1966–71. Lecturer in mus., Goldsmith's Coll., London Univ. from 1971. Visited USA as lecturer 1965–7. Also writer on mus. Works mainly choral, with strong religious (R.C.) basis, incl.:

ORCH: *Variations* (1958); *Divertimento* for str. (1961); *Chamber Sym.* (1968); *Sym. No. 1* (1972), *No. 2* for ten., ch., and orch. (1978); conc. for symphonic wind band (1979); conc. for str. (1982).

CHORUS AND ORCH: *Salutatio angelica* (1948); *The*City of Desolation* (1955); *St Francis* (1956); *The Water and the Fire* (1960–1); *Break to be Built, O Stone* (1962); *Festival Te Deum* (1967); *Roman Spring* (1969); *Motet for Peace* (1973); *Emmanuel Cantata* (1975).

UNACC. CHORUS: *Mass* (1951); *Benedic anima mea Dominum* (1954); *The *Harrowing of Hell* (1956); *Cast Wide the Folding Doorways of the East* (1963); *Ashmansworth* (1963); *The Leaden Echo and the Golden Echo* (1974).

VOICE AND INSTR: *The Song of Akhenaten*, sop. and chamber orch. (1957); *Our Lady's Hours*, sop. and pf. (1957); *Midway*, mez. and chamber orch. (1974).

CHAMBER MUSIC: Ob. qt. (1953); wind quintet (1964); str. qt. (1975).

Milnes, Rodney (*b* Stafford, 1936). Eng. critic and author, specialist in opera. Studied Oxford Univ. Worked in journalism before specializing in mus. Opera critic, *Spectator*, from 1970. Assoc. ed. *Opera* from 1976, ed. from 1986.

Milnes, Sherrill (*b* Downers Grove, Ill., 1935). Amer. bar. Studied Drake and Northwestern Univs. and with Rosa *Ponselle, among others. Opera début Boston Opera Co., 1960 (Masetto in *Don Giovanni*). Member Goldovsky Opera Co. 1960–5, NY City Opera 1964–7; prin. bar. NY Met. from 1965 (début as Valentin in Gounod's *Faust*). Guest singer at world's leading opera houses. London début 1969. CG début 1971 (Renato in *Un ballo in maschera*). Has cond. opera recordings.

Milstein, Nathan (*b* Odessa, 1904). Russ.-born violinist (naturalized Amer.). Pupil of Ysaÿe and Auer. Début Odessa 1920. Toured Russia in duo with *Horowitz. Début in USA 1929 with St Louis Orch., thereafter settling there. Authority on Romantic composers. Ed. of vn. mus.

Milton, John (*b* Stanton St John, nr. Oxford, *c.*1563; *d* London, 1647). Eng. composer of madrigals, viol mus., and psalms. Contributed 'Fair Orian' to The *Triumphs of Oriana*. Father of poet John Milton (1608–74).

Mime. (1) Acting in dumb-show (or the actor in such) sometimes acc. by mus.
(2) The Nibelung dwarf, brother of Alberich in Wagner's *Der Ring des Nibelungen*.

Mimodrama. Play or drama in which action is carried on in dumb-show, often to mus. Differs from ballet because movements are not formalized.

Minaccevole; minaccevolmente (It.). Menacing; menacingly. So also *minacciando, minaccioso, minacciosamente.*

Mines of Sulphur, The. Opera in 3 acts by Richard Rodney Bennett to lib. by Beverley Cross. Comp 1963. Prod. London (SW) 1965 cond. C. Davis.

Minim. See *Half-note.*

Minimalists. Term applied to group of composers, e.g. Steve *Reich and Philip *Glass, in whose music there is the minimum of material which is repeated to maximum effect.

Minkus, Léon (really Aloisius Ludwig) (*b* Vienna, 1826; *d* Vienna, 1917). Austrian composer of ballet mus. Collab. with Delibes on *La Source*, Paris 1866. Settled in Russia and wrote mus. for many Petipa ballets in St Petersburg, incl. *Don Quixote* (1869) and *La Bayadère* (1877). From mus. point of view, had misfortune to be contemporary of Tchaikovsky.

Minneapolis Symphony Orchestra. See *Minnesota Orchestra.*

Minnelied (Ger.). Love song.

Minnesinger (Ger.). 'Singer(s) of love'. Ger. equivalent of troubadours, flourishing in 12th- and 13th-cent. guilds. Mainly of aristocratic orig. in contrast to *Meistersinger* who were of merchant class. Among the most celebrated *Minnesinger* were Walther von der Vogelweide (*d* 1230), Neidhardt von Reuenthal (*c.*1180–1240), Heinrich von Meissen (Frauenlob, *d* 1318), Hermann, the Monk of Salzburg (*c.*1350–1410), and Oswald von Wolkenstein (*c.*1377–1445). Wagner's *Tannhäuser* and Strauss's *Guntram* are operas dealing with the *Minnesinger* class.

Minnesota Orchestra. Name since 1968 of Minneapolis S.O., USA, giving regular series of subscription concerts in Minneapolis and St Paul. Founded 1903 by Emil Oberhoffer who was cond. until 1922, followed by Bruno *Walter 1922–3, Henry *Verbrugghen 1923–31, Eugene *Ormandy 1931–6, Dimitri *Mitropoulos 1937–49, Antal *Dorati 1949–60, Stanislaw *Skrowaczewski 1960–80, Neville *Marriner 1979–86, Edo de Waart from 1986.

Minor (It. *Minore*; Fr. *mineur*). Opposite of major, applied to *scale, key, chord, and intervals.

Minor Common Chord. Common chord of which the 3rd is minor.

Minor Intervals. See *Interval*.

Minor Scale. See *Scale*.

Minstrels. (1) See *Menéstrel*.

(2) Black-faced entertainers, 'nigger minstrels', popular in USA (though not with genuine blacks) from about 1830s whose songs and humour were based on those of Negroes. Debussy's *Minstrels* in his *Préludes* (Book 1, No.12), refers to these mus.-hall troupes.

Minton, Yvonne (Fay) (*b* Sydney, N.S.W., 1938). Australian mez. Studied Sydney Cons. and in London (with H. Cummings and Joan *Cross). Won international vocalist comp. at 'sHertogenbosch 1961. Opera début 1964 (Lucretia in Britten's opera). CG début 1965. Created role' of Thea in Tippett's *The Knot Garden* (1970). Cologne Opera from 1969. Chicago 1970, NY Met. 1973 (Oktavian), Bayreuth 1974 (Brangäne). Australian Opera 1972–3. Many concert appearances, notably with Chicago S.O. and Solti. C.B.E. 1980.

Minuet (Eng.), **Menuet** (Fr.), **Menuett** (Ger.), **Minuetto** (It.). Dance in triple time, orig. as Fr. rustic dance and adapted by the court in the 17th cent. So called because of small, dainty step (*menu* = small) which is characteristic. Soon taken up by composers of art mus. from *Lully onwards and became one of optional movements of the *Suite. It also occurred in ovs. by Bach and Handel. In 18th cent. it was used in syms. (and other forms) by Wagenseil, Haydn, Mozart, and others, becoming the standard 3rd movement until supplanted from Beethoven onwards by the *scherzo. Normally in A B A form, the B section being a contrasting minuet called 'trio' because some Fr. composers wrote it in 3-part harmony or reduced the performers to 3. Note that, although Beethoven and other composers used it in their scores, the word *Menuetto* does not exist in any language.

Minute Waltz. Nickname for Chopin's Waltz in D♭, Op. 64, No. 1, comp. 1847, on the assumption that it can be played in 1 minute—but only if played too fast.

Miracle. Nickname of Haydn's Sym. in D major, No. 96 in Breitkopf edn., comp. London 1791. So called in error because it used to be said that at its f.p. in London on 11 Mar. 1791 the audience rushed forward at the end to congratulate the composer, thereby escaping injury when a chandelier collapsed on to their vacated seats. Research has est. that this incident occurred during Haydn's 2nd visit to London, at a concert on 2 Feb. 1795 and that the sym. which had been played, and which therefore really deserves the nickname, was Haydn's No. 102 in B♭.

Miracle in the Gorbals. Ballet in 1 act, mus. by Bliss, lib. by M. Benthall, choreog. R. Helpmann.

Prod. London 1944. The Gorbals is a notorious slum district of Glasgow.

Miracle Plays, Mysteries, and Moralities. The custom of teaching Bible stories by means of sacred dramas (often in church) is venerable. These dramas were known as *Miracle Plays* (or, simply, *Miracles*), another name, given by writers on the subject (apparently first in the 18th cent.), being *Mystery*. Of similar character were the plays which, personifying virtues and vices, taught moral lessons, e.g. *Moralities*. Religious plays of such types as these are recorded as early as the 4th cent. In Eng., there are records of them from the 11th to the 16th cents., some of the finest being perf. in York and Chester. Even today there are traces of them in the rural perfs. of mummers in the N. of Eng. (e.g. the play of St George and the Dragon).

Corpus Christi (June) was in some cities a great occasion for plays in the streets (at Chester 24 such played in a single day, moving to different locations, with all 24 given at each). Some of the plays involved a good deal of singing, and contained the seeds of the future masque, oratorio, and opera. In the 20th cent. several composers have based works on the old mystery plays, notably Stravinsky and Britten (whose *Noye's Fludde* is a fine example). Vaughan Williams described his opera based on Bunyan's *The *Pilgrim's Progress* as a morality.

Miraculous Mandarin, The (*A csodálatos mandarin*). Pantomime in 1 act, Op. 19, by Bartók to scenario by Menyhért Lengyel, f.p. in Cologne 27 Nov. 1926. Orch. suite f.p. Budapest 1928. Comp. 1918–19, rev. 1924 and 1926–31. Censorship dogged the early history of this work, which was not perf. in Budapest until 1946, the year after Bartók's death.

Mireille. Opera in 3 (orig. 5) acts by *Gounod to lib. by Carré based on Mistral's poem *Mirèco* (1859). Prod. Paris and London 1864, Chicago 1880.

Mirliton. Generic term applied to acoustical devices, many of folk origin, which modify tonal characteristics of other instruments by means of vibration of their membrane, as in comb and paper.

Miroirs (Mirrors). Set of 5 epoch-making pf. pieces by Ravel, comp. 1905, entitled *Noctuelles*, *Oiseaux tristes*, *Une Barque sur l'océan*, *Alborado del Gracioso*, *La Vallée des cloches*. In 1908 Ravel scored *Une Barque sur l'océan* for orch., followed in 1912 by *Alborado*.

Mirror Canon, Mirror Fugue. Canon or fugue in which the parts (or vv.) and intervals appear in the score simultaneously both the right way up and upside down, as if a mirror lay between them.

Mirror on which to Dwell, A. Cycle of 6 songs for sop., picc., 2 fl., ob., cor anglais, E♭ cl., bass cl., perc., pf., vn., va., vc., db. by *Carter to poems by Elizabeth Bishop, comp. 1975, f.p. NY Feb. 1976, London Nov. 1976. Titles are: 1. *Anaphora*, 2. *Argument*, 3. *Sandpiper*, 4. *Insomnia*, 5. *View of the Capitol from the Library of Congress*, 6. *O Breath*.

Miserere. Ps. 51 (50 in R.C. numeration). In the R.C. Church it is sung in the service of *Lauds. It has frequently been set by composers. A famous operatic setting occurs in Act 4 of Verdi's *Il Trovatore*, for sop., ten., ch., and orch.

Miserly Knight, The (*Skupoy rytsar*). Opera in 3 scenes by *Rakhmaninov, a setting of Pushkin's poem. Comp. 1905, prod. Moscow 1906.

Missa (Lat.). *Mass. Thus one finds *Missa brevis*, short mass; *missa cantata*, sung mass; *missa ad fugam* or *missa ad canones*, mass in fugal or canonic style; *missa sine nomine*, mass without a name, i.e. comp. (in 15th and 16th cents.) with orig. material and not, as was customary, on an existing plainsong or secular melody.

Missa in tempore belli (Mass in time of war) (Haydn). See *Paukenmesse*.

Missa Papae Marcelli (Mass of Pope Marcellus). Mass for 6 vv. by Palestrina comp. *c*.1561. The Pope Marcellus II, who resigned after only a few weeks, showed a desire to promote a reform in church mus. and this Mass is traditionally assoc. with the circumstance. But the romantic legend that has grown around the occurrence has no historical basis.

Missa pro defunctis (Mass for the dead). See *Requiem*.

Missa solemnis (Lat., 'Solemn Mass'). (1) Mass in which all sections—apart from the readings of the Epistle and the Gospel—are sung either in polyphony or plainchant. Term is also applied to elaborate ceremonial setting.
(2) See *Mass in D* (Beethoven).

Missa super L'homme armé. Work for speaker or (male or female) singer and chamber ens. by *Maxwell Davies, comp. 1967–8, rev. 1971. F.p. London 1968, rev. Perugia 1971. See *Homme armé, L'*.

Miss Donnithorne's Maggot. Th. piece by *Maxwell Davies for mez. and chamber ens. (incl.4 metronomes, football rattle, bosun's whistle, chamois leather rubbed on glass). Text by Randolph Stow. F.p. Adelaide, S. Australia, 1974, with Mary Thomas (mez.), cond. composer.

Miss Julie. (1) Opera in 2 acts by Ned *Rorem to lib. by Kenward Elmslie after the play by Strindberg (1889), comp. 1964, prod. NY 1965.
(2) Ballet in 2 acts, based on Strindberg. Choreog. MacMillan, mus. by *Panufnik. Prod. Stuttgart 1970.
(3) Opera in 2 acts by W. *Alwyn to his own lib. based on Strindberg. Comp. 1961–76. F.p. (broadcast) 1976.

(4) Opera by Bibalo, to lib. based on Strindberg, comp. 1973, orch. rev. 1983–4.

Mistero, misterio (It.). Mystery. *Misterioso*, mysteriously; *misteriosamente*, in a mysterious manner.

Misura (It.). Measure. (1) in the Eng. sense of 'bar'.
(2) In the general sense of regularity. So *alla misura*, in strict time; *senza misura*, without strict time. And so, too, *misurato*, measured, i.e. strictly in time.

Mitchell, Donald (Charles Peter) (*b* London, 1925). Eng. publisher, critic, and author. Man. dir., Faber Music 1965–71, chairman from 1977. Visiting Fellow, Sussex Univ. 1970, prof. of mus. 1971–6. Founder and co-ed., *Music Survey* 1947–52; mus. critic for *Musical Times* 1953–7, *Daily Telegraph* 1959–64; ed. *Tempo* 1958–62. Joint ed. *Benjamin Britten* (1952), *The Mozart Companion* (with H. C. Robbins Landon, 1956). Ed. *Gustav Mahler* by Alma Mahler (Eng. edn.). Author of *Gustav Mahler: The Early Years* (1958 rev. ed. 1979) and *The Wunderhorn Years* (1975); *The Language of Modern Music* (1963); *Benjamin Britten, 1913–76: Pictures from a Life* (with J. Evans, 1978); *Britten and Auden in the Thirties* (1981).

Mitchell, Howard (*b* Lyons, Nebraska, 1911). Amer. cond. and cellist. Studied Peabody Cons., Baltimore, and at Curtis Institute, Philadelphia, 1930–5 with Felix Salmond. Prin. cellist, Nat. S.O., Washington, 1933–41, then ass. cond. 1941–9, cond. and mus. dir. 1949–70. Mus. dir. Nat. Orch. of Uruguay from 1970.

Mitchinson, John (*b* Blackrod, Lancs., 1933). Eng. ten. Studied RMCM, graduating 1955. Founder-member of BBC Northern Singers, 1953. Sang in concert perf. *Don Giovanni*, *Chelsea Opera Group, 1955. Successful career in concert hall and opera house (roles incl. Peter Grimes). Notable interpreter of Mahler's *Das Lied von der Erde*, Stravinsky's *Oedipus Rex*, and Tristan in Wagner's opera.

Mitridate, Rè di Ponto (Mitridates, King of Pontus). Opera seria (K87) in 3 acts by Mozart to lib. by V. A. Cigna-Santi, after Racine. Prod. Milan, 1770.

Mitropoulos, Dimitri (*b* Athens, 1896; *d* Milan, 1960). Gr.-born cond., pianist, and composer (Amer. citizen from 1946). Studied Athens Cons. and with *Busoni in Berlin. Répétiteur, Berlin State Opera 1921–5. Cond., Paris S.O. 1932–6. US début with Boston S.O. 1937. Cond. Minneapolis S.O. (now *Minnesota Orch.) 1937–49, NY P.O. 1949–58. Début NY Met. 1954. (*Salome*). Cond. f.p. of Barber's *Vanessa* NY Met. 1958 and at Salzburg Fest. 1958. Fine exponent of 20th-cent. mus. Wrote opera and orch. works. Int. competition for young cond. named in his memory. Died after heart attack while rehearsing Mahler's 3rd Sym.

Mitte (Ger.). Middle, e.g. *Auf der Mitte des Bogen*, In the middle of the bow.

Mixed Chorus, Mixed Voices. Body containing male and female vv.

Mixed Media. Term for theatrical works, events, or 'happenings' in which several forms of art are merged, e.g. mus., dance, film, elec. devices, etc. *Avant-garde* composers such as Cage, Berio, Xenakis, Stockhausen, and Reich have created mixed media works.

Mixer. Elec. device which combines several signals and routes them to one or more channels corresponding to tracks on a magnetic tape, or to a loudspeaker.

Mixolydian Mode. See *Modes*.

Mixture Stop. Org. stop in which each finger-key (or pedal-key) played operates on a group of pipes corresponding to some of the higher harmonics of the note of that key. The group may be of from 2 to 7 pipes and the stop is then spoken of as having that number of *Ranks* (indicated in order specifications in Roman figures). It cannot be used alone, but adds brightness and richness when combined with stops of normal pitch in 'Full Organ', etc. See also *Sesquialtera*.

M.K. Abbreviation for *Manualkoppel* (Ger.), i.e. Manual Coupler (in org. mus.—followed by an indication of the particular manuals to be coupled).

Mlada. Opera in 4 acts by Rimsky-Korsakov to his own lib. based on lib. for earlier scheme for opera-ballet to be written in collab. with Borodin, Cui, and Mussorgsky, with ballet mus. by *Minkus. Prod. St Petersburg 1892.

Mládí (Youth). Suite in 4 movements for wind sextet by Janáček, comp. 1924. For fl./picc., ob., cl., hn., bn., and bass cl. F.p. Brno 1924, f.p. in England, London 1926.

Mlynarski, Emil (Simon) (*b* Kibarty, Lithuania, 1870; *d* Warsaw, 1935). Polish composer, violin-ist, and cond. Studied St Petersburg Cons. 1880–9, vn. with Auer, comp. with Lyadov. Int. career as violinist. Ass. cond. Warsaw Opera 1897–1903, cond., Warsaw P.O. 1901–5, dir. Warsaw Cons. 1904–7 and 1919–22. Cond. Scottish Orch., 1910–16. Cond., Bolshoy Th. Orch., Moscow, 1914–17. Dir., Warsaw Opera 1919–28. Teacher of cond., Curtis Institute 1929–31. Wrote opera, sym., and 2 vn. concs.

M.M. (1) See *Metronome*.
(2) Abbreviation for Master of Music (sometimes M.Mus.).

M.Mus. See *Master of Music*.

Moby Dick. (1) Cantata for 2 ten., 2 basses, male ch., and orch. by *Herrmann to text selected by W. Clark Harrington from Herman Melville's novel (1851). Comp. 1936–8, f.p. NY 1940.
(2) Symphonic poem by Douglas *Moore (1929).
(3) 'Concertato' for orch. by *Mennin (1952).

Modal. Pertaining to the *modes; style of comp. in which the modes are used.

Modes. (1) Names for each of the ways of ordering a scale, i.e. *major mode* and *minor mode*.
(2) The scales which dominated European mus. for 1,100 years (approx. AD 400 to AD 1500) and strongly influenced composers for another hundred years (up to *c*. 1600). They have since reappeared from time to time in the work of some composers, especially in the 20th cent. Throughout that total period of 1,500 years the plainsong of the Church, which is entirely 'modal', has continued to accustom the ears of fresh generations to the melodic effect of the Modes. But the description 'Church Modes' or 'Ecclesiastical Modes' is wrong, since their use was general.

The available mus. material at the time when the Modes became accepted was that which may be nowadays conveniently represented by the white keys of the pf. or org., the notes of which constitute (with slight differences of tuning) the scale worked out scientifically in the 4th cent. BC by Pythagoras and the Gr. thinkers of his time. In the 2nd cent. AD the Greeks were using this scale in 7 different ways: Gr. influence was strong in the early Christian Church and changes in the modal system developed among singers as a practical measure. In the 5th cent. 4 modes were adopted (Authentic Modes) and at the time of Pope Gregory (*c*.540–604) 4 more were added (Plagal) and later 4 more, making 12. In the Authentic Modes, the 5th note (the Dominant), was much used as a reciting-note in plainsong, and the first (the Final), as a cadence-note, to close a passage. The Authentic Modes may be re-created by playing on the pf. octave scales of white notes beginning respectively on D, E, F, and G. A melody played in one of the modes and then in another will alter in some of its intervals and hence in its general effect, as opposed to a melody played in our 12 major or minor scales, which are all alike as to intervals.

The *Plagal Modes* were merely new forms of the others, being the same 4 taken in a compass lying not between Final and Final of the corresponding authentic modes but between their Dominant and Dominant, the Final, on which the cadences fell, thus coming in the middle. In order to avoid having the Reciting Note at the very top or bottom of the series of notes a new one was chosen, lying 3 notes below the original, and this was now regarded as the Dominant. The whole series was now as follows (A = Authentic and P = Plagal):

Mode I (A) Range D-D with Dominant A

II (P)	„	A-A	„	„	F
III (A)	„	E-E	„	„	C†
IV (P)	„	B-B	„	„	A
V (A)	„	F-F	„	„	C
VI (P)	„	C-C	„	„	A
VII (A)	„	G-G	„	„	D
VIII (P)	„	D-D	„	„	C†

Nearly a thousand years after Gregory a Swiss monk, Henry of Glarus, or Henricus Glareanus, brought forth, in a book called *Dodecachordon* (1547), a theory that there should, historically, be 12 modes instead of 8. He added modes on A and C (none on the unsuitable B), with their Plagal forms, so that the table above was complemented as follows:

IX (A)	Range	A-A	with Dominant		E
X (P)	„	E-E	„	„	C
XI (A)	„	C-C	„	„	G
XII (P)	„	G-G	„	„	E

Glareanus gave his 12 modes what he thought to be their orig. Gr. names and these (though incorrect) have become accepted:

I. Dorian	VIII. HypoMixolydian
II. HypoDorian	IX. Æolian
III. Phrygian	X. HypoÆolian
IV. HypoPhrygian	XI. Ionian
V. Lydian	XII. HypoIonian
VI. HypoLydian	
VII. Mixolydian	

It should be clearly understood that the difference between the various modes is not one of pitch but of the order in which fall the tones and semitones. Any mode could be taken at another than its original pitch (i.e. transposed), but in that case its intervals remained as before. Thus the whole series could be set out as beginning on C, when the Dorian and Lydian (to take two examples) would appear as follows:

The Authentic Modes shown uniformly with C as final (with the semitones marked)
I. Dorian.

V. Lydian.

With the development of harmonized music the modal system in time tended to disintegrate: the two Authentic Modes added by Glareanus (the Ionian and Æolian) were felt to be the most suited to harmony and have remained as our 'major'

†The Dominants of the two modes so marked (one of them Authentic and the other Plagal) would normally be B, but this being found an unsuitable note C was adopted instead.
It will be noted that the odd-numbered Modes are the Authentic ones and the even-numbered the Plagal.)

and 'minor' scales. The other modes, however, are in use in plainsong, some folk-song, and occasionally in the work of certain composers such as Vaughan Williams, Bartók, and Kodály.

Modinha. Type of song (not folk song) popular in Portugal and Brazil in the 18th and 19th cents.

Mödl, Martha (*b* Nuremberg, 1912). Ger. sop., orig. mez. Studied Nuremberg. Opera début Remscheid 1942 as Cherubino. Düsseldorf Opera 1945–9 as mez., Hamburg Opera from 1949, also Vienna State Opera. CG 1949–50 (début as Carmen) and 1953; début NY Met. 1956. Sang as dramatic sop. from 1950; Kundry (*Parsifal*) at Bayreuth 1951, followed by other Wagner roles incl. Brünnhilde and Isolde. Sang in 1981 Salzburg f.p. of Cerha's *Baal*.

Moderato (It., 'restrained', 'moderate'). Direction used either alone, as in Elgar's Vc. Conc., or as qualification of another direction, e.g. *allegro moderato* (a bit slower than *allegro*). Fr. *modéré*.

Modo (It.). (1) Manner, e.g. *In modo di*, in the manner of.
(2) Mode (see *Modes*).

Modulation. The changing from one key to another in the course of a section of a comp. by evolutionary mus. means (not just by stopping and starting anew in another key) and as a part of the work's formal organization. The simplest and most natural modulations are to the related keys (or attendant keys) i.e. to the relative minor or major, to the ★dominant and its relative major or minor and to the ★subdominant and its relative minor or major. The ★tonic major and minor are also related keys, modulation from one to the other being simple, but they are not usually so described. *Chromatic modulation*, found frequently in Wagner, Franck, and Strauss, in general means altering a chord by means of a chromatic change. It can also be achieved by moving basses up or down major or minor 3rds. *Enharmonic modulation* covers the use of chords altered by ★enharmonic means, e.g. turning a dominant 7th chord to a Ger. 6th. Modulation becomes less of a feature in atonal mus. because of the enlargement of the scale. First composers to use modulation may have been Obrecht and Desprès. Chromatic modulation occurs in madrigals of ★Gesualdo and ★Monteverdi. John Bull's organ fantasia *Ut, re, mi, fa, sol, la* modulates a whole tone upward successively into different keys. With J. S. Bach, modulation became integral part of ★fugue.

Modulator. (1) Elec. device by which frequency or amplitude of a waveform can be changed.
(2) Diagram used in teaching of ★tonic sol-fa on which note-names are ranged in order perpendicularly.

Modus Lascivus. The Ionian mode, the same as the major scale of C.

Moeran, E(rnest) **J**(ohn) (*b* Heston, Middx., 1894; *d* Kenmare, Co. Kerry, 1950). Eng. composer of Irish descent. Studied RCM and with John Ireland. Collected folksongs in Norfolk, where he lived for several years. Mus. first heard in London 1923. Comps., which are predominantly lyrical, incl.:

ORCH: *In the Mountain Country* (1921); Rhapsodies Nos. 1 and 2 (1924); *Whythorne's Shadow* (1931); *Lonely Waters* (1932); Sym. in G minor (1934–7); *Overture for a masque* (1944); *Sinfonietta* (1944); *Serenade in G* (1948).
CONCERTOS: Vn. (1942); *Rhapsody* for pf. and orch. (1943); Vc. (1945).
CHAMBER MUSIC: Str. qt.; vn sonata; sonata for 2 unacc. vns. (1935); ob. qt. (1946); vc. sonata (1947); *Prelude* for vc. and pf. (1948).
PIANO: 3 Pieces (1919); *Theme and Variations* (1920); *On a May Morning, Stalham River, Toccata* (1921); *3 Fancies* (1922); *2 Legends* (1923); *Bank Holiday, Summer Valley* (1925); *Irish Love Song* (1926); *White Mountain* (1927); *Prelude and Berceuse* (1933).
SONG-CYCLE: *Ludlow Town*, 4 Housman Songs for bar. and pf. (1920).

Moeschinger, Albert Jean (*b* Basle, 1897). Swiss composer, pianist, and teacher. Studied Berne Cons., Leipzig Cons., and Munich Cons. 1917–24. Prof. of theory and comp. Berne Cons. 1937–43. Comp. incl. 5 syms., *Variations and Fugue on a Theme of Purcell* for str. and timp. (1933), cantata *The Little Mermaid* (1947), vn. conc. (1934, rev. 1950), tpt. conc. (1954), 5 pf. concs. (1964), hpd. conc. (1967), conc. for ballerina, sax., and chamber orch. (1968), ballet *Amor und Psyche* (1954), and much chamber mus.

Moevs, Robert Walter (*b* La Crosse, Wisconsin, 1920). Amer. composer and pianist. Studied Harvard Univ. with *Piston and at Paris Cons. 1947–51 (comp. with *Boulanger). On mus. staff Rutgers Univ. from 1964. Chairman, Dept. of Mus. from 1974. Influenced by Boulez and describes his method of comp. as 'systematic chromaticism', a modified serial technique. Works incl. ballet *Endymion*, *3 Symphonic Pieces*, pf. conc., *Cantata sacra*, and other choral works incl. *A Brief Mass* (ch., org., vibraphone, guitar, db., 1968), str. qt., sonata for solo vn., pf. sonata, etc.

Moffo, Anna (*b* Wayne, Penn., 1932). Amer. sop. Studied Curtis Institute and in Rome. Opera début, Spoleto 1955 as Norina in Donizetti's *Don Pasquale*. Début Chicago Lyric Opera 1957 (Nannetta in Verdi's *Falstaff*), NY Met. 1959 (Violetta in *La traviata*), CG 1964 (Gilda in *Rigoletto*).

Mohaupt, Richard (*b* Breslau, 1904; *d* Reichenau, Austria, 1957). Ger. composer and cond. Held opera posts in Ger. until forced to leave. His opera *Die Wirtin von Pinsk* was prod. Dresden

1938 and banned by the Nazis after 2 perfs. Lived in USA 1939–55. Sym. and vn. conc. f.p. by NY P.O. His operas *Bremer Stadtmusikanten* and *Der grüne Kakadu* were prod. at Bonn (1949) and Hamburg (1958) respectively.

Moise (Rossini). See *Mosè in Egitto*.

Moiseiwitsch (Moiseivich), **Benno** (*b* Odessa, 1890; *d* London, 1963). Russ.-born pianist (Brit. nationality from 1937). Studied at Odessa and became pupil of *Leschetizky in Vienna, 1904. First appeared in Eng. at Reading, 1908, London 1909. Continental tours, then settled in Eng. 1914. Expert in classical repertory but noted above all for his playing of mus. of Rakhmaninov, regarded as surpassed in its day only by composer himself.

Moldau. Ger. title for *Vltava* in Smetana's *Má Vlást*.

Moldenhauer, Hans (*b* Mainz, 1906). Amer. musical scholar of Ger. birth. Pupil of H. Rosbaud in Mainz. Emigrated to USA 1938. Founded Spokane Cons. 1942 (pres. since 1946). Creator and dir. of Moldenhauer Archive, large coll. at Spokane of MSS., letters, documents, etc., relating especially to Webern about whom he wrote the authoritative study *Anton von Webern: Chronicle of his Life and Work* (NY and London 1978, Ger. trans. 1979).

Molinari, Bernardino (*b* Rome, 1880; *d* Rome, 1952). It. cond. Studied Rome Cons. Cond. Augusteo, Rome, 1912–43. Frequent guest cond. Europe and USA. Expert in 20th-cent. mus., esp. *Respighi and *Malipiero.

Molinari-Pradelli, Francesco (*b* Bologna, 1911). It. cond. Studied with B. *Molinari in Rome. Mainly cond. of opera, at Scala, Milan, from 1946. CG from 1955, NY Met. from 1966.

Molinaro, Simone (*b* Genoa, *c.*1565; *d* Genoa, 1615). It. composer. Maestro di cappella, Genoa Cath., from *c.*1602. Wrote motets, masses, madrigals, canzonets, church mus., but principally works for lute. Ed. some of *Gesualdo's madrigals, 1613.

Molique, Wilhelm Bernhard (*b* Nuremberg, 1802; *d* Cannstadt, Stuttgart, 1869). Ger. violinist and composer. Studied under Spohr. Member of orch. at Theater an der Wien, then leader of Munich court orch. 1820–6. Cond. royal orch., Stuttgart, 1826–49. Settled in Eng. 1849–66 as soloist and teacher. Wrote 6 vn. concs., 8 str. qts., sym., oratorio, vc. conc., vn. solos, etc.

Moll (Ger.). Minor, in the sense of key, e.g. *A moll*, A minor; *Moll Ton*, or *Moll Tonart*, minor key.

Molnár, Antal (*b* Budapest, 1890). Hung. composer, musicologist, and violist. Va.-player in Waldbauer Quartet and Dohnányi Pf. Qt. In 1919 became teacher of harmony, Budapest Acad. until

1959. Author of several books incl. studies of Bartók and Kodály, whose mus. he fervently championed. Comp. 3 concs. (vc., vn., harp), wind quintet, 3 str. qts., and stage 'legend' *Savitri (1912).

Molter, Johann-Melchior (b Tiefenort, 1696; d Durlach, 1765). Ger. composer. Kapellmeister, court of Baden 1722–53; dir. of church mus., Eisenach, 1733. Returned to Baden post 1743–65. Comp. over 165 syms., 44 concs., 66 sonatas, etc.

Molto (It.). Much, very, e.g. *allegro molto*, very quickly.

Momente (Moments). Comp. by *Stockhausen for sop. solo, 4 ch. groups, and 13 instrumentalists. The first 'Donaueschingen' version dates from 1961–4, the 2nd 'Europa' from 1972.

Moment-Form. Type of work devised by *Stockhausen, the 'moment' being a short part of a comp. having its own mus. characteristic. What occurs within this moment may be regarded as more important than the succession between moments, which may be indeterminate as in Stockhausen's *Momente (1961–4).

Moment Musical (Fr.). Musical moment. Title popular in 19th cent. for short pf. pieces, e.g. Schubert's 6 *Moments musicaux* (D780), completed 1828.

Mompou, Federico (b Barcelona, 1893; d Barcelona, 1987). Sp. (Catalan) pianist and composer. Studied Barcelona Cons. and from 1911 in Paris with Philipp. Returned to Barcelona 1914–21 when he wrote most of his works, mainly pf. pieces in what he called *primitivista* style (no bar-divisions, key-signatures, or cadences). Lived in Paris 1921–41, again returned to Barcelona and composed further pf. works and songs, religious settings for ch. and orch., and mus. for guitar.

Monckton, Lionel (b London, 1861; d London, 1924). Eng. composer. Studied Oxford Univ. Mus. critic, *Daily Telegraph*, for brief period. Composer of popular light operas, e.g. *A Country Girl, The Arcadians, The Quaker Girl, Our Miss Gibbs*, etc.

Mond, Der (The Moon). Opera in 3 acts by *Orff to his own lib. after Grimm. Comp. 1937–8, rev. 1945. Prod. Munich 1939, NY 1956.

Mondo della luna, Il (The World on the Moon). Opera in 3 acts by Haydn to lib. by Goldoni (set previously by Galuppi and also by Paisiello, Piccinni, and others). Prod. Esterháza 1777, London (incomplete) 1951. Restored by Robbins Landon and prod. Holland Fest. 1959.

Mondonville, Jean Joseph Cassanéa de (b Narbonne, 1711; d Belleville, Paris, 1772). Fr. violinist and composer. Prominent in Paris from 1734; dir. Royal Chapel 1744 and of Concert Spirituel 1755–62. Active on Fr. side in 'Querelle

des *Bouffons', 1752–4. Comp. *Titan et l'Aurore* (1753) and 6 other operas, 3 oratorios, vn. sonatas, etc.

Money, David (b London, 1912). Eng. pianist, teacher, and critic. Studied RCM and with Louis Kentner, Kathleen Long, and George Reeves. Début London 1935. Specialised as accompanist. On mus. staff *Daily Telegraph*, 1946–84.

Moniuszko, Stanisław (b Ubiel, Lithuania, 1819; d Warsaw, 1872). Polish composer. Studied Warsaw 1827–30 and in Berlin 1837–9. org. at Wilno 1840–58. Lived in Warsaw from 1858. Cond. Warsaw Opera and prof. at Cons. Regarded as foremost Polish 19th-cent. composer after *Chopin. His opera *Halka* is regarded as first Polish nat. opera (2-act version 1846–7, rev. in 4 acts 1857 and prod. Warsaw 1858). Wrote other operas, none as successful. Composed symphonic poem *Bajka* (Fairy Tale), 7 masses, a *Requiem* (1890), and over 300 songs.

Monk, William (Henry) (b London, 1823; d London, 1889). Eng. composer and organist. Choirmaster King's College, London, 1847, organist 1849, prof. of vocal mus. 1874. Ed., 1861, of *Hymns Ancient and Modern.* Wrote mus. of hymn *Abide with me* ('Eventide').

Monn, Georg (Matthias) (b Vienna, 1717; d Vienna, 1750). Austrian organist and composer. Organist, Karlskirche, Vienna. Wrote 21 syms., 7 hpd. concs., and a vc. conc. of which *Schoenberg made an edition in 1911–12.

Mono. Abbreviation for *monophonic with special meaning in gramophone recording when long-playing records first appeared. Mono records were recorded on one channel requiring only one loudspeaker as opposed to *stereophonic 2-channel recording. Gradually stereo ousted mono, but certain transfers from the pre-LP recording era can only be made in mono.

Monochord (Gr.). One string. (1) Scientific instr. consisting of soundbox over which is stretched a single string which can be divided at any point by a movable bridge, the position of which can be exactly determined by scale of measurements on the surface across which it moves. By altering the ratios in which the str. is vibrating, different notes of the *harmonic series may be prod. Used in Ancient Egypt and Ancient Gr. and is still used by modern acousticians.
(2) In later medieval times, monochords were made with 2 or 3 str., capable of emitting intervals and chords. These were ancestors of *clavichord, sometimes called in It. *monocordo.*

Monocordo (It.). One string. Term used in str. playing to indicate when certain passage or whole piece is to be perf. entirely on one str. Orig. with *Paganini in his 'Napoleon' Sonata for G str.

Monodrama (Gr.). Single play. Stage work involving only one character, e.g. Schoenberg's *Erwartung, and Poulenc's La *Voix humaine.

Monody, Monodic. Term sometimes used as synonym of *monophonic mus. or for acc. solo song, but properly it is a particular kind of acc. solo song which developed *c.*1600 as a reaction against 16th-cent. polyphonic style. It is distinguished by recit.-like v.-part and figured-bass acc. The members of *Bardi's Camerata in Florence wrote in monodic style, Caccini publishing a coll. of monodies, *Le nuove musiche*, in 1602. By 1613 it was adopted for instr. mus. e.g. in trio sonatas of Rossi and Marini.

Monophony, Monophonic (Gr.). One sound. Mus. which has a single melodic line of notes without harmonies or melody in counterpoint, as opposed to *polyphony and *homophony. Oldest type of mus., being only type perf. in Ancient Gr., early church mus. (Gregorian etc.), and mus. of *Minnesinger, *Meistersinger, etc. All this mus. was in monophonic notation, which is a term covering several systems. For special 20th-cent. application, see *Mono*.

Monothematic (Gr.). Having only one theme, and therefore applied to comp. or movements based on one subject, e.g. a figure. Finales of several Haydn syms. are examples of monothematic construction.

Monotone (Gr.). Recitation of liturgical text on unaltered pitch as in prayers, psalms, etc.

Monsieur Beaucaire. Operetta in prol. and 3 acts by Messager to book by Frederick Lonsdale and lyrics by Adrian Ross, based on story by Booth Tarkington. Prod. Birmingham, London, and NY 1919, Paris 1925.

Monsigny, Pierre Alexandre (*b* Fauquembergues, nr. St Omer, 1729; *d* Paris, 1817). Fr. composer. Not educated for mus. profession, though learned vn. Worked in noble household from 1749 and took comp. lessons after hearing Pergolesi's *La serva padrona*. After 5 months wrote operetta *Les Aveux indiscrets* (1759) which brought immediate fame. Wrote 12 more comic operas, incl. *La Belle Arsène* (1773) and, said to be his finest, *Le Déserteur* (1769). Ceased composing 1777 at height of popularity, possibly unwilling to compete with *Grétry. Succeeded Piccinni as Inspector at Paris Cons., 1800–02.

Montagnana, Domenico (*b* Lendinara, *c*.1687; *d* Venice, 1750). It. vn.-maker. Pupil of Goffriller in Venice; lived in Cremona and Venice. Also made vas. and vcs. His instr. are scarce and very valuable.

Monte, Philippe de (*b* Mechlin, 1521; *d* Prague, 1603). Flemish composer. In Naples 1542–51 and England 1554–5. Kapellmeister to Austrian emperors at Vienna and Prague from 1568. Visited It. and Eng. Comp. over 1200 madrigals and similar works, also masses and motets.

Montéclair, Michel Pinolet de (*b* Andelot, 1667; *d* St Denis, 1737). Fr. composer, teacher,

and db. player. From 1699 db. player at Paris Opéra. Wrote opera-ballet *Les Festes de l'été*, 1716, and other stage works; cantatas, motets, trio sonatas, etc., and a vn. method.

Montella, Giovanni Domenico (*b* Naples, 1570; *d* Naples, 1607). It. composer of madrigals and church mus. Lutenist in Naples. Some of his madrigals have texts like *villanelle*. He was a master of counterpoint and used experimental harmonies.

Montemezzi, Italo (*b* Vigasio, 1875; *d* Vigasio, 1952). It. composer. Intended for engineering career, but in Milan decided to become musician and at 3rd attempt was admitted to Milan Cons. His first opera was prod. Turin 1905, but he achieved fame in 1913 with *L'*amore dei tre re*, a work in *verismo style but influenced by Debussy also. Lived in USA 1939–49. Prin. works:

OPERAS: *Giovanni Gallurese* (Turin 1905), *Hellera* (Turin 1909), *L'*amore dei tre re* (Milan 1913), *La nave* (Milan 1918), *La notte di Zoraima* (Milan 1931), *L'incantesimo* (NY radio 1943).

ORCH: Symphonic poems *Paolo e Virginia* (1929), *Italia mia!* (1944).

Monteux, Pierre (*b* Paris, 1875; *d* Hancock, Maine, 1964). Fr.-born cond. (Amer. citizen from 1942). Studied vn. at Paris Cons. Played va. in orch. of Paris Opéra-Comique. Early years as cond. with Diaghilev's Ballet Russe in Paris, when he cond. f.ps. of Stravinsky's *Petrushka (1911) and *Rite of Spring (1913), Debussy's *Jeux (1913) and Ravel's *Daphnis et Chloé (1912). Cond. Paris Opéra 1913–14, incl. f.p. of Stravinsky's The *Nightingale. Cond. NY Met. 1917–19, Boston S.O. 1919–24 (introducing much modern mus.). Cond. Orchestre Symphonique de Paris 1929–38. Cond. San Francisco S.O. 1935–52. NY Met. 1953–6. Prin. cond. LSO 1961–4. Outstanding interpreter of Fr. and Russ. mus., but of much else besides.

Monteverdi, Claudio (*b* Cremona, 1567; *d* Venice, 1643). It. composer. Chorister, Cremona Cath., and pupil of *Ingegneri. At 16, when he was already a fine organist and viol player, he pubd. some sacred madrigals. Entered service of Duke of Mantua as viol player and singer of madrigals. Went with Duke on military expeditions to Danube and Flanders, 1595 and 1599. Heard and was influenced by Florentine operas of the *Camerata, notably Peri's *Euridice*, 1600. His own first opera, *La favola d'Orfeo* was prod. in 1607, notable in history of mus. because for the first time the acc. was for a full (by the standards of the time) orch. The following year his *Arianna* was perf. at a ducal celebration in Mantua; only the *Lamento*, which was immediately popular, survives. He left Cremona after the death of the Duke in 1612 and in 1613 became Master of Mus. of the Venetian Republic. For St Mark's, Venice, he composed a superb stream of sacred works which spread his fame throughout Europe. He received a visit from *Schütz and his works were studied by M. *Praetorius in Ger., *Mersenne in Fr., and *Tomkins in Eng. 12 of the operas he had written in Mantua were destroyed there in 1630 when it was sacked by Austrian troops. In the same year the plague ravaged Venice; the combination of these catastrophes probably accounts for Monteverdi's admission to holy orders in 1632. When the first opera house, San Cassiano, was opened in Venice in 1637, Monteverdi's interest in opera was re-kindled and for the remaining 6 years of his life he comp. a series of works of which only 2 survive.

Monteverdi's place in the history of Renaissance mus. can be justly compared to Shakespeare's in literature. Working from traditional beginnings, he transformed every genre in which he worked by imaginative use of available styles rather than by revolutionary means. His madrigals cover a period of 40 years, from publication of the 1st book in 1589 to the 8th in 1638 (the 9th was pubd. posthumously in 1651). He soon introduced instr. accs., and chromatic modulations, and the dramatic nature of the mus. foreshadows the solo cantata and operatic recit., culminating in Il combattimento di Tancredi e Clorinda (1624) which is a miniature opera in style, acc. by str. and employing descriptive effects.

His sacred mus. veered between elaborate traditional polyphony and an advanced concerted style in which elements from his secular madrigals and operas lend colour and drama to the text, as in the famous Vespers comp. for Mantua in 1610. The operas take the Florentine *melodramatic and monodic form and embellish it with all that he learned from It. madrigalists and Fr. composers. They are, in effect, the first mus. dramas, making use of what came to be known as *leitmotiv and deploying many startling dramatic devices. They are also the first operas in which the characters are recognizably human rather than symbolic figures. Above all, the melodic genius and fertility of his mus. and its harmonic adventurousness are what make it so attractive and 'contemporary' in the 20th cent. Naturally, the scores present many musicological problems; their solution by various eds. has caused considerable disagreement among students of the period. Prin. works:

OPERAS AND BALLETS: La *favola d'Orfeo (1607); *Arianna (1608, lost); Il ballo delle Ingrate (1608); Tirsi e Clori (1616); Favola di Peleo e di Theti (1617, lost); Il matrimonio d'Alceste con Admeto (1618, lost); Andromeda (1619, lost); Commento d'Apollo (1620, lost); La finta Pazza Licori (1627, lost); Mercurio e Marte (1628, lost); Adone (1639, lost); Le nozze d'Enea con Lavinia (1641, lost); Il *Ritorno d'Ulisse in patria (1640); L'*incoronazione di Poppea (1642).

SACRED: Madrigali spirituali, 4 vv. (1583); *Vesperae (1610); Masses for 4 vv., and psalms (1650);

Selva morale e spirituale (1641) for varying numbers of vv. with varied instr. acc. in most cases; and a large number of motets, etc.

SECULAR VOCAL: Canzonette for 3 vv. (1584); Madrigali: Book I for 5 vv. (1587), II for 5 vv. (1590), III for 5 vv. (1592), IV for 5 vv. (1603), V for 5 vv., some with instr. acc. (1605), VI for 5 vv., some with instr. acc.; includes *Lamento d'Arianna, (1614), VII for vv. from 1 to 6, with instr. acc., incl. Lettera amorosa (1619), VIII *Madrigali guerrieri e amorosi (Madrigals of Love and War) for vv. from 1 to 8 with instr. acc., incl. Il *Combattimento di Tancredi e Clorinda of 1624 (1638), IX Madrigali e Canzonette for 2 to 3 vv., 4 with basso continuo (1651); 10 *Scherzi musicali for 1 or 2 vv., all with basso continuo (1632); 15 Scherzi musicali for 3 vv., unacc. (1607).

Montgomery, Kenneth (Mervyn) (b Belfast, 1943). Irish cond. Studied RCM. Début Glyndebourne 1967. Staff cond. SW 1967–70. Ass. cond. Bournemouth S.O. and Sinfonietta from 1970; dir. Bournemouth Sinfonietta 1973–5. Mus. dir. Glyndebourne Touring Opera 1975–6. Cond. Oberon at Wexford, 1972; cond. Strauss's Ariadne and Capriccio for Netherlands Opera 1972 and 1975. Prin. cond. Netherlands Radio Orch. from 1976. CG début 1975 (Le Nozze di Figaro).

Mont Juic. Orch. suite of Catalan dances in 4 movements by *Britten (Op. 12) and Berkeley (Op. 9). Comp. 1937. Authorship of individual parts never disclosed. 3rd movement is a Lament sub-titled Barcelona, July 1936. F.p. BBC concert 8 Jan. 1938.

Montoya, Carlos (b Madrid, 1903). Sp. guitarist whose skill in *flamenco style achieved its recognition on a par with classical style. Played in cafés at age 14. In 1928 toured Europe with dancer La Argentina. First solo recitals 1948. Comp. and arr. mus. for flamenco guitar but could not read mus.

Montreal Symphony Orchestra. Canadian orch., the successor of several previous organizations. From 1897 to 1907 an orch. with this name was cond. by Joseph Goulet, a Belg. violinist who lived in Montreal from 1890. Douglas Clarke, dean of faculty of mus., McGill Univ., in 1930 formed sym. orch. which survived until 1941 and introduced many important works and soloists to Canada. A rival orch., sharing some of the players, was formed in 1935 as Les Concerts Symphoniques, sometimes cond. by Wilfrid *Pelletier and after 1941 by the Belg. Désiré *Defauw. In 1954 orch. was re-named Orchestre Symphonique de Montréal—Montreal S.O. Conds. after Defauw: O. Klemperer 1950–3; I. Markevich 1955–60; Z. Mehta 1961–7; F.-P. Decker 1968–75; R. Frühbeck de Burgos 1975–6; Charles Dutoit from 1978.

Montsalvatge, Xavier (b Gerona, 1912). Sp. composer. Studied Barcelona Cons. 1923–36.

Wrote opera *El gato con botas* (Puss in Boots) (1947), *Mediterranean Symphony* for orch. (1949), 3 *Divertimenti* for pf. (1941), *Concerto breve* for pf. and orch., *Poema concertante* for vn., and orch. (1952), and 5 *Canciones negras* for sop. and pf. (1945).

Moody, Fanny (*b* Redruth, 1866; *d* Dundrum, Co. Dublin, 1945). Eng. sop. Studied with Mme Sainton-Dolby. Début London 1885; stage début with Carl Rosa Opera, Liverpool, 1887. Married Charles *Manners 1890, with whom she formed *Moody-Manners Opera Company. Sang at CG and was first Eng. Tatiana in Tchaikovsky's *Eugene Onegin*.

Moody-Manners Opera Company. Touring opera co. formed 1898 by Charles *Manners and his wife Fanny *Moody and disbanded 1916. At its peak was split into 2 cos., one of 175 members, the other of 95.

Moog, Robert (Arthur) (*b* Flushing, NY, 1934). Amer. audio-engineer and inventor. Studied Columbia Univ. and Cornell Univ. Pres., Moog Mus. Inc., Williamsville, NY. Invented and patented Moog *synthesizer (1965), manufactured by his co., which greatly increased options open to composers of elec. mus.

Moonlight and Roses. See *Lemare, E. H.*

Moonlight Sonata. Popular nickname of Beethoven's Pf. Sonata No. 14 in C♯ minor, Op. 27 No. 2, comp. 1800–1. The nickname originated in review by poet Heinrich Rellstab (1799–1860) in which he wrote that the first movement reminded him of moonlight on Lake Lucerne—a misleading approach to a movement with almost the character of a funeral march.

Moór, Emanuel (*b* Kecskemét, Hung., 1863; *d* Chardonne, 1931). Hung. composer, pianist, and cond. Studied Budapest and Vienna. Toured Europe and USA 1885–7 as pianist and cond. Wrote 4 operas, 8 syms., 3 pf. concs., 2 vc. concs., 4 vn. concs., triple conc., harp conc., va. conc., much chamber mus., and over 500 songs. Invented *Duplex-Coupler pf., 1921, with 2 kbds. tuned octave apart.

Moore, Douglas (Stuart) (*b* Cutchogue, NY, 1893; *d* Greenport, NY, 1969). Amer. composer, organist, and teacher. Studied with Horatio Parker at Yale and later in Paris with d'Indy, Boulanger, and Bloch. Ass. prof. of mus. Columbia Univ., NY, 1926, becoming head of mus. dept. 1940 and MacDowell Prof. of Mus. 1943–62. Works steeped in Amer. legends and history. Wrote 2 books. Prin. comps.:

OPERAS: *The *Devil and Daniel Webster* (1938), *The Emperor's New Clothes* (1948), *The Ballad of Baby Doe* (1956), *Carrie Nation* (1966).
ORCH: *Pageant of P.T. Barnum* (1924), **Moby Dick* (1929), *Village Music* (1941), *Symphony in A* (1945), *Farm Journal* (1947).

CHAMBER MUSIC: Vn. sonata (1929), str. qt. (1933), cl. quintet (1946), pf. trio (1953).
CHORAL: *Simon Legree* (1938), *Prayer for the United Nations* (1943).

Moore, Gerald (*b* Watford, 1899; *d* Penn, Bucks, 1987). Eng. pianist, known as one of the finest of accompanists. Spent boyhood in Canada. First recorded for HMV 1921. Accompanist to tenor John *Coates from 1925. From early 1930s emerged as sensitive accompanist to leading singers. After 1945 closely assoc. with Kathleen *Ferrier, Elisabeth *Schwarzkopf, Victoria *de los Angeles, Janet *Baker, Dietrich *Fischer-Dieskau, and others. Made many records. Wrote several books, incl. *The Unashamed Accompanist* (1943, rev. 1957) and *Am I Too Loud?* (1962). Frequent broadcaster. C.B.E. 1954. Retired from concerts 1967 but continued to record and lecture.

Moore, Grace (*b* Nough, Tenn., 1898; *d* Copenhagen in air crash, 1947). Amer. sop. After singing in cafés, night-clubs, and revues went in 1926 to Fr. to study for 2 years with Richard Barthélemy. Début Paris and Nice 1927 with Amer.-Ger. Opera Co. NY Met. 1928 as Mimi, appearing at Met. 1928–32, 1935–46. CG 1935. Paris Opéra-Comique 1928, 1938, 1946. Sang *Louise* in Paris after study with *Charpentier. Appeared in several films, some with Jan *Kiepura, incl. *One Night of Love, New Moon*, and *Love Me Forever*.

Moore, Jerrold Northrop (*b* Paterson, NJ, 1934). Amer. musicologist. Studied at Yale Univ. Settled in Eng. 1970, becoming a leading authority on Elgar and the history of gramophone recording. Joint ed. of Elgar Complete Edition. Ed. *Music and Friends: Seven Decades of Letters to Adrian Boult* (1979). Author of *An Elgar Discography* (1963), *Elgar: a Life in Photographs* (1972), *Elgar on Record* (1974), *A Voice in Time: the Gramophone of Fred Gaisberg* (1976), *Spirit of England: Edward Elgar in his World* (1984), and *Edward Elgar: a Creative Life* (1984). Trustee of Elgar's Birthplace.

Moore, Thomas (*b* Dublin, 1779; *d* Devizes, 1852). Irish poet and musician. Studied Trinity Coll., Dublin, 1793–8. Self-taught musically. In 1802 began to write words and mus. of songs pubd. 1807–8 as *Irish Melodies*. By 1834, 10 sets of these melodies and folk-song arrs. had been pubd., the last 2 being harmonized by *Bishop. Among the most enduring of his songs were *The Last Rose of Summer* (incorporated into Flotow's *Martha*), *The Harp that Once in Tara's Halls*, and *The Minstrel Boy*, the words of which he set to traditional tunes. His *Lalla Rookh* (1817) with its 4 interpolated poems (e.g. *Paradise and the Peri*), became the basis of several mus. comps. (by Spontini, Rubinstein, Stanford, Schumann, and Bantock).

Moraes, Joao de Silva (*b* Lisbon, 1689; *d* Lisbon, 1747). Portuguese composer of religious mus.

Morales, Cristóbal de (*b* Seville, *c.*1500; *d* Málaga, 1553). Sp. composer. Chapelmaster, Ávila Cath., 1526–31. Member of Papal Choir, Rome, 1535–45. While in It. comp. most of his church mus. which ranks him with Victoria and Palestrina as a master of polyphony. Returned to Toledo 1545–7, chapelmaster at Málaga Cath. 1551–3.

Moralities. See *Miracle Plays.*

Moralt, Rudolf (*b* Munich, 1902; *d* Vienna, 1958). Ger. cond. Ch. trainer Munich Opera 1919–23. Held opera posts in Ger. and Austria. Cond. at Vienna State Opera 1940–58.

Morasco. See *Moresca.*

Morbido; morbidezza (It.). Soft, gentle; softness, gentleness. (Not morbid, or morbidity.)

Morceau (Fr.). Piece. So *Morceau symphonique,* Symphonic piece. (For *Morceau d'ensemble* see *Ensemble.*)

Morceaux en forme de poire, Trois (3 Pear-shaped pieces). Work for pf., 4 hands, by *Satie, 1903, containing, title notwithstanding, 6 items. Orch. version by R. Désormière.

Mordent (from It. *mordere,* to bite). Mus. *ornament shown by a sign over the note. There are Upper and Lower Mordents.

In Ger. *Mordent* means only the Lower Mordent. Examples are:

Upper Mordent   Upper Mordent
(in German   with inflected note
Pralltriller)

Lower Mordent   Lower Mordent
(in German simply   with inflected note
Mordent)

In the case of the Upper Mordent these 'crushed in' notes are the main note itself and the note above; if the latter is to be inflected in any way the necessary sign (♯ ♭ ♮ × ♭♭) appears *above* the mordent sign.

In the case of the Lower Mordent the 'crushed in' notes consist of the note itself and the note below; if this latter is to be inflected in any way the necessary sign appears *below* the Lower Mordent sign (the interval is generally that of a semitone).

There is a confusion of terminology. The terms 'Mordent' and 'Inverted Mordent' are very commonly used for the two forms, but some call the first one shown above the 'Mordent' and the second one the 'Inverted Mordent', and others reverse these titles. The one way of avoiding all misunderstanding is always to use the words

'Upper' and 'Lower'. In addition to these 2 forms, others were used by earlier composers but in modern edns. those are set out in full. See also *Acciaccatura.*

Moreau, Jean-Baptiste (*b* Angers, 1656; *d* Paris, 1733). Fr. composer, organist, and choirmaster. After holding church posts went to Paris 1686, composing divertissements for the court. Wrote incidental mus. for Racine's *Esther* (1689) and *Athalie* (1691).

Morendo (It. 'dying'). Instruction for the mus. to die away gradually, often used by Verdi (also by Beethoven, at end of slow movt. of str. qt. Op. 74).

Moresca (Moresco), **Morisca** (Morisco). A Moorish dance. Apparently the name (which was common from the 15th to 17th cents.) did not carry any fixed implications as to rhythm or style. Often it was applied to any rough-and-ready grotesque dance employing animal costumes, etc. In *Arbeau's *Orchésographie* (1588–9), it is said that some performers blacked their faces to resemble Moors and wore bells on their legs; this has led to speculation that the Eng. *Morris dance" is a derivation.

Moresque (Fr.). Same as *Moresca.

Morgenblätter (Morning leaves, or morning newspapers). Title of waltz, Op. 279, by Johann Strauss II comp. for Vienna Press Ball (1864).

Morhange, Charles Henri. Real name of *Alkan.

Mörike-Lieder (Songs of Mörike). 53 songs by Hugo *Wolf for solo v. and pf. to poems by the Ger. poet Eduard Friedrich Mörike (1804–75), comp. 1888, incl. *Elfenlied, Gesang Weylas, Der Feuerreiter,* and *An die Geliebte.* 11 of them were later orchestrated.

Morillo, Roberto Garcia (*b* Buenos Aires, 1911). Argentinian composer and critic. Studied with J. J. Castro and in Paris 1926–30. Taught at Nat. Cons., Buenos Aires; mus. critic of *La Nacion.* Author of books on Mussorgsky and Rimsky-Korsakov. Works incl. 2 syms., pf. conc., *3 Paintings of Paul Klee* for orch., pf. qt., str. qt., mimodrama *The Fall of the House of Usher,* 3 pf. sonatas.

Morison, Elsie (Jean) (*b* Ballarat, 1924). Australian sop. Studied Melbourne and RCM (with Clive Carey). Début London 1948 in *Acis and Galatea.* In SW Opera Co. 1948–54 and at CG 1953–62, also many concert appearances in oratorio, etc. Sang Blanche in Eng. première of Poulenc's *Dialogues des Carmélites,* CG 1958, and Anne in f. Brit. p. of Stravinsky's *The Rake's Progress* by Glyndebourne at Edinburgh Fest. 1953. Wife of Rafael *Kubelik.

Morlacchi, Francesco (*b* Perugia, 1784; *d* Innsbruck, 1841). It. composer. Studied in Perugia and with Zingarelli in Loreto. Wrote cantata for Napoleon's coronation as King of It. in Milan 1805. Comp. 8 opera buffa 1807–10, then went to Dresden as cond. of It. opera there, remaining until his death. Wrote many operas, incl. *Il nuovo barbiere di Siviglia* (Dresden, 1816), and much church mus. Morlacchi's absences in It. caused Weber, appointed Kapellmeister at Dresden, 1817, to overwork.

Morley, Thomas (*b* ?Norwich, 1557; *d* London, 1602). Eng. composer. Pupil of *Byrd. Mus.B., Oxford Univ., 1588. Organist, St Paul's Cath. *c*.1589–92. Almost certainly worked as a government spy. Gentleman of Chapel Royal 1592. In 1598, granted by Elizabeth I exclusive licence for 21 years to print song-books of all kinds and mus. paper. Thus he pubd. not only his own mus. but that of his contemporaries. Pubd. and ed. *The Triumphs of Oriana* (1601), to which he contributed *Arise, awake* for 5 vv. and *Hard by a crystal fountain* for 6 vv. Was one of great masters of Eng. madrigal. Probably friend of Shakespeare: setting of *It was a lover and his lass* for *As You Like It* may have been for orig. prod., 1599. Specialized in balletts. Also wrote church mus., incl. Burial Service; lute songs, and *A Plaine and Easie Introduction to Practicall Musicke* (1597). Among his works and publications were: *Canzonets* for 3 vv. (1593), *Madrigals* for 4 vv. (1594), *1st Book of Balletts*, 5 vv. (1595), *1st Book of Canzonets*, 2 vv. (1595), *Canzonets*, 4 vv. (selected from 'best It. authors' but incl. 2 by Morley) (1597), *Madrigals*, 5 vv. (selected from 'best It. authors') (1598), *1st Book of Consort Lessons*, 6 instr. (1599), *1st Book of Ayres*, lute and bass viol (1600), *The *Triumphs of Oriana*, 5 and 6 vv. 'by divers several authors' (1601).

Morley College. Non-vocational adult education centre in London, founded 1889. Has flourishing and adventurous mus. dept., dirs. of which have incl. Holst (from 1907), Goldsbrough (from 1924), Arnold Foster (from 1928), Tippett (from 1940), Fricker (from 1953), Gardner (from 1965), Graubart (from 1969).

Morning Heroes. Sym. for orator, ch., and orch. by Bliss, f.p. Norwich Festival 1930. Comp. in memory of his brother, killed in 1914–18 war in which Bliss also served. Texts used are Iliad, Whitman, Li-Tai-Po, Wilfred Owen, and Robert Nichols.

Mornington, Garrett Colley Wesley, 1st Earl of (*b* Dangan, Co. Meath, 1735; *d* London, 1781). Irish composer and landowner, father of Arthur Wellesley, first Duke of Wellington, (surname changed to Wellesley after Mornington's death). Self-taught in mus. Founded Dublin Acad. of Mus. Prof. of mus., Dublin Univ. 1764–74. Excelled in composing glees. Wrote church mus., incl. fine setting of the Burial Service, and an unpublished cantata, *Caractacus*.

Moro, Giacomo (*fl.* 16th–17th cents.). It. composer and Servite monk. Wrote much church mus. incl. collections of *concerti ecclesiastici* (1604, rev. 1613).

Moross, Jerome (*b* Brooklyn, NY, 1913; *d* Miami, Flor., 1983). Amer. composer. Belonged to 'young composers' group', NY 1934–6. Went to Hollywood 1938 to write film mus. Works incl.: *Paul Bunyan* (ballet, 1934), *Frankie and Johnnie* (ballet, 1938), *Susanna and the Elders* (ballet-opera, 1940), *The Eccentricities of Davy Crockett* (ballet-opera, 1945), *Gentlemen, Be Seated!* (opera, 1955–6), sym. (1941–2), *Suite* for chamber orch. (1934), sonata for db. and pf.

Morris, Gareth (Charles Walter) (*b* Clevedon, 1920). Eng. flautist. Studied privately with R. Murchie, then at RAM. Début as soloist, London 1939. Played with Boyd Neel Orch. and in Dennis Brain Wind Quintet. Prof. of fl., RAM, from 1945. Prin. fl., Philharmonia Orch. 1948–72. Always played wooden fl.

Morris, Morrice. A type of Eng. folk dance for men, assoc. with Whitsuntide and perf. to the acc. of pipe and tabor. The dancers wear bells on their ankles: sometimes they are dressed to represent characters (the Queen of the May, the Fool, etc.). The mus. is usually in duple or quadruple time. Some Eng. villages possess Morris troupes whose origin goes back to an unknown antiquity. Conjecture that the dance derives from the *moresca is unsubstantiated.

Morris, R(eginald) **O**(wen) (*b* York, 1886; *d* London, 1948). Eng. teacher and composer. Studied Oxford Univ. and RCM. On staff RCM 1920–6. Dir. of theory and comp. Curtis Institute, Philadelphia, 1926–8; rejoined RCM 1928. Author of several textbooks incl. *Contrapuntal Technique in the 16th Century* (1922). Had many distinguished pupils. Comp. sym. (1935), vn. conc., vc. suite, str. qts., songs, and folk-song arrs. Brother-in-law of *Vaughan Williams. Compiled crosswords for *The Times*.

Morris, Wyn (*b* Trlech, 1929). Welsh cond. Studied RAM and Salzburg Mozarteum. Founder-cond., Welsh S.O. 1957–60. Cond., Royal Choral Soc. 1968–70, Huddersfield Choral Soc. 1969–74. Specialist in mus. of Mahler. Cond. f.p. final rev. of Cooke perf. version of Mahler's 10th Sym., 1972.

Morrison, (Stuart) Angus (*b* Maidenhead, 1902). Eng. pianist. Studied RCM, joining teaching staff 1926. Début, London 1923. Also played in trio with Jean Pougnet (vn.) and Anthony Pini (vc.). Champion of Fr. and Eng. composers, friend of Walton, Lambert, etc. Played solo pf. part in f.p. (broadcast) of Lambert's *Rio Grande*, 1928. C.B.E. 1979.

Mortari, Virgilio (*b* Passirana di Lainate, Milan, 1902). It. composer. Studied Milan Cons. with

Bossi and Pizzetti. Wrote 4 operas, conc. for str. qt. and chamber orch., pf. conc., *Stabat Mater*, etc. With *Casella, wrote book on modern orch. technique (1950). On staff of Venice Cons. 1933–40; prof. of comp. Rome Cons. 1940–73.

Mort de Cléopâtre, La (The Death of Cleopatra). Lyric scene for sop. or mez. and orch. by Berlioz, comp. 1829 as entry for *Prix de Rome* but no prize was awarded. Part of a larger cantata, *Cléopâtre*, the rest being destroyed.

Mortimer, Harry (Henry) (*b* Hebden Bridge, Yorks., 1902). Eng. brass-band conductor and trumpeter. Member of celebrated brass-band family. Cornet-player at 7. Trumpeter in Hallé Orch. (under Harty) 1926–30, Liverpool P.O. 1930–4, BBC Northern Orch. 1935–42. Cond. several championship brass bands, incl. Foden's, Fairey Aviation, Munn and Felton's, Morris Motors, and Black Dyke Mills. Brass and military bands supervisor, BBC 1942–64. C.B.E. 1984.

Moscheles, Ignaz (*b* Prague, 1794; *d* Leipzig, 1870). Ger.-Bohemian pianist, composer, and teacher. Studied Prague Cons. and in Vienna with Albrechtsberger and Salieri. Made pf. score of *Fidelio*, 1814, under Beethoven's supervision. After success of his *Variations*, Op. 32, in 1815 he toured Europe for 10 years, visiting London 1821 and 1823. Gave pf. lessons to *Mendelssohn 1824. Settled in London 1826. Cond. f. (private) London p. of Beethoven's *Missa Solemnis*, 1832; and 9th Sym. 1837 and 1838 at Philharmonic Soc. Founded series of chamber concerts and played Bach and Scarlatti on hpd. Prof. of pf. at new Leipzig Cons. 1846–70. Comp. 8 pf. concs. and numerous other works. Trans. Schindler's biography of Beethoven into Eng., 1841.

Mosè in Egitto (Moses in Egypt). Opera (*azione tragica-sacra*) in 4 acts (orig. 3) by Rossini to lib. by A. L. Tottola. Prod. Naples 1818 (the well-known 'Prayer' being added for 1819 revival), Vienna 1821 (in Ger.), London 1822 (in It. as *Pietro l'Eremita* (Peter the Hermit)), CG 1833 (in Eng. as *The Israelites in Egypt* with adds. from Handel's *Israel in Egypt*), NY 1832. 4-act version with Fr. lib. by Balocchi and de Jouy and mus. substantially rev., prod. Paris 1827 under title *Moïse et Pharaon*. This version prod. CG (under title *Zora*) 1850, NY 1860.

Moser, Hans Joachim (*b* Berlin, 1889; *d* Berlin, 1967). Ger. musicologist, singer, teacher, and historian. Son of Andreas Moser, violinist. Studied Berlin. Prof. of musicology, Halle Univ. from 1922, Heidelberg from 1925. Dir. State Acad. for Sch. and Church Mus., Berlin, 1927–33. Prof. of musicology, Jena Univ. 1947; dir., Berlin Cons. 1950–60. Arr. Weber's *Euryanthe* with new text, Berlin 1915; ed. Handel's *Orlando* (1922); ed. works of Weber with A. Sandberg. Author of many books of mus. history and biography, incl. *Musiklexikon* (1932–5, 1955, suppl. 1963), *Ge-*

schichte der deutschen Musik (3 vols., 1920–4), *J. S. Bach* (1935), *Heinrich Schütz* (1936, rev. 1954), *Gluck* (1940), *Handel* (1941), *Weber* (1941), *Goethe and Music* (1949), *Buxtehude* (1957). Also composer.

Moses und Aron (Moses and Aaron). Opera in 3 acts (3rd act lib. only) by Schoenberg to his own lib. Comp. 1930–2. Prod. (concert) Hamburg 1954, stage Zürich 1957, Berlin 1959, London CG 1965, Boston 1966, Paris 1975. Schoenberg in 1951 said that the 3rd act could be spoken, but Scherchen in Berlin had it spoken to mus. taken from Act 1. Most perfs. keep to 2 completed acts. Act 2 contains *Dance Before the Golden Calf*.

Mosonyi, Mihály (Brand, Michael) (*b* Boldogasszonyfalva, Hung., 1815; *d* Pest, 1870). Hung. composer, teacher, and writer. Studied mus. in Pozsony from 1832 while earning living as copyist. From 1835 to 1843 was pf. teacher to aristocratic family and comp. str. qts. and pf. pieces. Moved to Pest 1842 as teacher of pf. and comp. and also played db. in orch. In 1856 became friend of Liszt and in 1859 began to comp. in national style and took Hung. name of Mosonyi. Among his later works are cantatas and operas on Hung. themes. First to use cimbalom in symphonic work. Also admirer and champion of Wagner.

Mosso (It.). Moved, e.g. *più mosso*, More moved, i.e. quicker.

Mossolov, Alexander (Vasilyevich) (*b* Kiev, 1900; *d* Moscow, 1973). Russ. composer. Studied Moscow Cons. with Myaskovsky and Glière. Early songs had newspaper advertisements as texts. Was among first proponents of 'Soviet realism' under name 'constructivist music', e.g. ballet *The Factory* (1927), which employed metal sheet, shaken in the orch., for realistic effects (perf. also as concert piece under names 'Music of the Machines' or 'Iron foundry'). This was criticised in Russia as 'decadent'. Mossolov was back in favour during 1941–5 war with patriotic works. Wrote 6 syms., 2 pf. concs., vc. conc., vn. conc., chamber mus., and songs.

Mosto, Giovanni Battista (*b* Udine, before 1550; *d* Karlsburg, 1596). It. composer. Maestro di cappella, Padua Cath., 1580–9 and 1595–6. Wrote 6 books of madrigals and church mus.

Moszkowski, Moritz (*b* Breslau, 1854; *d* Paris, 1925). Polish-Ger. pianist and composer. Studied Dresden. Début Berlin 1873, London 1886. Wrote opera, vn. conc., pf. conc., and many songs, but chiefly known for his lighter pf. pieces, esp. his *Spanish Dances* for pf. duet. Retired to Paris 1897.

Motet. A form of short unaccompanied choral comp. which eventually superseded *conductus, although both were in use from 13th to early 16th cents. In 13th, 14th, and 15th cents. the motet was exclusively sacred and was based on a pre-existing melody and set of words to which other melodies and words were added in counterpoint. *Machaut, *Desprès, *Ockeghem, and others were masters of the motet. *Dufay introduced secular melodies as the *cantus firmus of the motet. By the 16th cent., the motet reached its apogee as a sacred comp., with the madrigal as its secular counterpart. Palestrina wrote about 180 motets. Victoria, Morales, Tallis, Byrd, Bull, and Taverner were great composers of motets, sometimes called Cantiones Sacrae. J. S. Bach wrote motets (incl. Singet dem Herren), 4 of them for 8 vv. Soon the term came to be loosely applied by composers, sometimes to works with acc. and even to works for solo v. and acc. In some cases, e.g. Parry's Songs of Farewell, the words are not ecclesiastical. Generally today the term signifies a church choral comp., with Lat. words not fixed in the Liturgy. In 1951–2 Bernard Naylor wrote 9 motets to Eng. texts as a cycle for the 9 major church festivals.

Mother, The (Matka). Opera in 10 scenes by A.*Hába to his own lib. Prod. Munich 1931, rev. version Florence 1964. First opera to employ quarter-tones.

Mother Goose (Ravel). See Ma Mère l'oye.

Motif (Fr.; Eng. motive; Ger. motiv). The shortest intelligible and self-existent melodic or rhythmic figure (e.g. the first 4 notes of Beethoven's 5th Sym.). Every 'theme' or 'subject' perhaps has several motifs, and almost every mus. passage will be found to be a development of some motif. But the word has, in mus. analysis, been used as a synonym for 'theme'; and Wagner's extension of it to *leitmotiv has further complicated the issue. The adjective 'motivic' is an invention of analytical writers, functional but ugly and better avoided.

Motion. (1) Term which denotes the course upwards or downwards of a melody or melodies. In the combination of any 2 'voices' or 'parts' of a comp., if they proceed in the same direction (notationally considered), they are said to be in Similar Motion, if in opposite directions, in Contrary Motion. If one part holds (or repeats) a note and the other part moves up or down from it, that is Oblique Motion. Similar Motion in which the parts proceed by the same intervals (numerically considered) is Parallel Motion.
(2) In the shaping of a single part progress of one note to an adjacent note by step is called Conjunct Motion and progress by some other note by leap Disjunct Motion.

Moto (It.). Motion. Con moto, with motion, i.e. quickly. Moto perpetuo (It.). Perpetual motion. See Perpetuum mobile.

Motor Rhythm. 20th-cent. term for the type of rhythm which is as though mechanized, i.e. like the sound of an engine. The ugly adjective

'motoric' has, alas, been coined as descriptive of this kind of comp. or passage of comp.

Mottl, Felix (b Unter-Sankt-Veit, nr. Vienna, 1856; d Munich, 1911). Austrian cond. and composer. Studied Vienna Cons. Appointed as one of Wagner's assistants at first Bayreuth Fest., 1876, becoming one of group of young admirers in Wagner's circle. Cond. Karlsruhe Opera 1881–1903, setting high standards. Cond. first complete perf. of Berlioz's Les Troyens (on 2 consecutive evenings), Karlsruhe 1890. Cond. Bayreuth Fest. 1886–92. Cond. CG 1898–1900, NY Met. 1903. Cond. Munich Opera 1903–11. Comp. 3 operas, str. qt., songs, etc. Ed. vocal scores of all Wagner's works, made reduced orch. score for some of the operas. Orchestrated Wagner's 5 Wesendoncklieder. Also ed. Berlioz works. Collapsed while conducting Tristan and died a few days later.

Motto Theme. A theme which recurs, sometimes transformed, throughout the course of a comp., e.g. in Beethoven's 5th, Tchaikovsky's 4th and 5th, and Elgar's 1st Syms. It is akin to Wagner's leitmotiv, Berlioz's idée fixe, and Liszt's metamorphosis of themes.

Moule-Evans, David (b Ashford, Kent, 1905). Eng. composer, cond., and teacher. Studied RCM under Howells and Sargent. Prof. of harmony, counterpoint, and comp., RCM, from 1945. Works incl. Concerto for Strings (1928), ov. Spirit of London (1942), Vienna Rhapsody (1943), Sym. (1944), chamber mus., and songs.

Mount of Olives (Beethoven). See Christus am Ölberge.

Mouret, Jean Joseph (b Avignon, 1682; d Charenton, 1738). Fr. composer. Worked in Paris from 1707. Dir., Concert Spirituel 1728–34. Wrote operas, ballets, divertissements, and instr. works.

Moussorgsky. See Mussorgsky, Modest.

Mouth Organ. See Harmonica.

Mouthpiece (Fr. bec (woodwind); embouchure (brass)). Part of a woodwind or brass instr. which is inserted in the player's mouth or to which he applies his lips in order to produce a sound.

Mouton, Jean (b Holluigue, c.1459; d St Quentin, 1522). Fr. composer. Served at courts of Louis XII and François I. Wrote at least 15 masses, over 100 motets, and chansons. Teacher of *Willaert. His music has great technical polish, excellent contrapuntal mastery, and flowing polyphony, but perhaps lacks brilliance of Desprès.

Mouvement (Fr., abbreviated to Mouvt.). Movement, either in the sense of motion, or a section of a large comp., such as a sym. (see Movement). Sometimes (as in Debussy), the word is used to indicate a return to the orig. speed after some tempo deviation. Mouvement perpétuel is the Fr. equivalent of *perpetuum mobile.

Movable-doh. A term applied to that system of sight-singing in which *Doh* is the name applied to the keynote of every major scale, *ray* to the 2nd note, *me* to the 3rd, and so on—as distinct from the *Fixed-doh* system in which C is, in every key in which it occurs, called *doh*, D called *ray*, and so on. (See *Sight-Reading, Tonic Sol-fa*.)

Movement. The primary, self-contained sections of a large comp. (sym., conc., sonata, suite, etc.), so called because each movement of a work usually has a separate tempo indication. Some comps. are in one movement, e.g. Sibelius's 7th Sym., and in many the movements are joined to play continuously. The word sometimes occurs in the title of a work, e.g. Stravinsky's *Symphony in 3 Movements* and his *Movements* for pf. and orch.

Movements. Work in 5 short sections for pf. and orch. by Stravinsky, comp. 1958–9. F.p. NY 1960. Used as mus. for ballet to choreog. by Balanchine, prod. NY, 1963.

Movimento (It.). Motion, as distinct from movement in the structural sense. *Doppio movimento* means 'at double the preceding speed'.

Mozart, (Johann Georg) **Leopold** (*b* Augsburg, 1719; *d* Salzburg, 1787). Ger. composer and violinist. Played in orch. of Prince-Archbishop of Salzburg, becoming court composer and Kapellmeister 1762. Father of 2 prodigiously talented children, Wolfgang and Anna, to whose training and exploitation he devoted much time. Comp. many types of mus., incl. famous *Toy Symphony* (simplified and reduced version of a *Cassation* in G) and author of influential vn. method, 1756.

Mozart, Wolfgang Amadeus (baptized Johannes Chrysostomus Wolfgangus Theophilus) (*b* Salzburg, 1756; *d* Vienna, 1791). Austrian composer, kbd. player, violinist, violist, and cond. Son of Leopold *Mozart, Kapellmeister to Prince-Archbishop of Salzburg, Mozart showed exceptional musical precocity, playing the klavier at 3 and composing at 5. His elder sister Maria Anna (1751–1829) was also a brilliant kbd. player and in 1762 Leopold decided to present his children's talents at various European courts. They first visited Munich and Vienna in 1762. Wolfgang was now able to play the vn. without having had formal teaching. In 1763 a longer journey began, from Munich, Augsburg, Frankfurt, and other cities to Cologne, Brussels, and Paris. They spent a fortnight at Louis XV's court at Versailles. In Apr. 1764 they arrived in London and were received by George III. While in London, Wolfgang studied with *Abel, comp. with J. C. *Bach, and singing with the castrato *Manzuoli. He wrote his first 3 syms. in London. After visits to Holland and Switzerland, the Mozart family returned to Salzburg in Nov. 1766. Further visits to Vienna were made in 1767 and 1768 and Mozart comp. 2 operas, *La finta semplice* and

Bastien und Bastienne. In Dec. 1769, Leopold took Mozart to It. where the boy's genius was everywhere acclaimed. He was taught by *Martini and met Nardini, *Jommelli, and Burney. In Rome he heard Allegri's *Miserere* and wrote it out from memory. His opera *Mitridate, Rè di Ponto* was successfully prod. in Milan in Dec. 1770. Two further visits to It. speedily followed, but the new prince-archbishop of Salzburg was less well-disposed towards the Mozarts and in 1777 Mozart left on a tour with his mother, Leopold not being well enough to go. They visited Munich, Augsburg, Mannheim (where he heard the famous orch.) and arrived in Paris in 1778. Mozart's mother died there in July of that year. No longer a *Wunderkind*, Mozart had less appeal for the Parisians, who were engrossed in the Gluck-Piccinni controversy. Unable to obtain a court post, Mozart returned to Salzburg where he spent the next 2 years as court and cath. org. amid growing hostility to the archbishop. In 1780 the Elector of Bavaria commissioned an opera from Mozart (*Idomeneo*), prod. in Munich, Jan. 1781. On Mozart's return to Salzburg he had a final confrontation with the archbishop and resigned. He went to Vienna, where he married Constanze Weber in Aug. 1782, a few days after the first perf. of his opera *Die Entführung aus dem Serail*. The last 9 years of his life were a juxtaposition of financial troubles with an astonishing outpouring of masterpieces in almost every genre. In 1785 he frequently played the va. in str. qts. with Dittersdorf and Haydn. To the latter, who regarded Mozart as the greatest composer he knew, Mozart dedicated 6 str. qts. in the autumn of 1785, when he also began work on *Le nozze di Figaro*. He frequently appeared as soloist in his own kbd. concs. Although *Figaro* was rapturously received in Vienna in 1786, it was taken off after 9 perfs., but was the rage of Prague when prod. there in 1787. During his visit to the Bohemian capital, Mozart's Sym. in D (K504, No. 38) received its f.p., thereafter being known as the 'Prague Sym'. He was subsequently commissioned to write an opera for Prague for the following autumn. The result was *Don Giovanni*, written in a few months while the 2 str. quintets in C major and G minor and *Eine kleine Nachtmusik* were also composed. In the same year Leopold Mozart died at Salzburg. The new opera was a success in Prague, but initially failed in Vienna, where it was prod. with some extra numbers in May 1788. A month later Mozart began to compose the first of his 3 last syms., completing them between 26 June and 10 Aug. In 1789, under severe financial pressure, he played a conc. in Dresden on the way to Berlin. He visited Leipzig, playing Bach's org. at St Thomas's. In Berlin King Friedrich Wilhelm II, a cellist, commissioned 6 str. qts. of which only 3 were written. In the autumn Emperor Joseph II of Austria commissioned a new comic opera, *Così fan tutte*, which was prod. early in 1790. Joseph died shortly afterwards, but Mozart's hope of being appointed by Leopold II Kapellmeister in place of Salieri was not fulfilled. In 1791 he was approached by the actor-manager Schikaneder with a view to composing a fairy-tale opera on a lib. concocted by Schikaneder. *Die Zauberflöte* was almost completed by July, the month in which Mozart received a commission to compose a *Requiem* for an anonymous patron (Count F. von Walsegg who wished to pass it off as his own). Mozart deferred work on it to compose an adaptation of Metastasio's *La clemenza di Tito* for Leopold II's coronation as King of Bohemia in Prague in Sept. This prod. was supervised by Mozart, who returned to Vienna, wrote the cl. conc., cond. the f.p. of *Die Zauberflöte*, and then resumed work on the *Requiem*. But ill-health which had been overtaking him for some time now became critical and he died on 5 Dec., leaving the *Requiem* to be completed by his pupil Süssmayr. He received a cheap funeral with others who had died at the same time, and the location of his grave remains unknown. The circumstances of Mozart's death and the unseemly and unnecessary haste with which one of Vienna's most famous men was buried have given rise to many sensational theories, none proved but all giving some ground for believing that things were not quite as they seem.

The extent and range of Mozart's genius are so vast and so bewildering that any concise summing-up of his achievement must risk being trite. He took the mus. small-change of his day, learned from childhood in the courts of Europe, and transformed it into a mint of gold. His sense of form and symmetry seems to have been innate and was allied to an infallible craftsmanship which was partly learnt and partly instinctive. In his operas he not only displayed hitherto unequalled dramatic feeling, but widened the boundaries of the singer's art through contact with some of the greatest vv. of his day and, with his amazing insight into human nature, at once perceptive and detached, he created characters on the stage who may be claimed in their context as the equal of Shakespeare's. His music was supranational, combining It., Fr., Austrian, and Ger. elements. Not by revolutionary deliberation but by the natural superiority of the mus. he wrote, he changed the course of the sym., the pf. conc., the str. qt., the sonata, and much more besides. Perhaps the only element missing from his mus. is the worship of Nature which Beethoven and later 19th-cent. composers were to supply. There are brilliance and gaiety on the surface of Mozart's mus., but underneath a dark vein of melancholy which gives his works (*Così fan tutte* in particular) an ambivalence which is continually fascinating and provocative. 'Mozart *is* music', a critic said, and most composers since 1791 have agreed. A selective list of prin. works follows. Some of the dates, which are *Köchel's, are conjectural:

OPERAS: *Apollo et Hyacinthus*, intermezzo (K38, 1767);*Bastien und Bastienne* (K50, 1768); *La *finta semplice* (K51, 1768); *Mitridate, Rè di Ponto* (K87, 1770); *Ascanio in Alba* (K111, 1771); *Il sogno di Scipione* (K126, 1772); *Lucio Silla* (K135, 1772); *La *finta giardiniera* (K196, 1774); *Il *Rè Pastore* (K208, 1775); *Zaide* (K344, 1780); *Thamos, König in Ägypten* (K345, 1780, incid. music); *Idomeneo, Rè di Creta* (K366, 1780); *Die *Entführung aus dem Serail* (K384, 1781–2); *L'*Oca del Cairo* (K422, 1783); *Lo sposo deluso* (K430, 1783); *Der Schauspieldirektor* (The *Impresario) (K486, 1786); *Le *nozze di Figaro* (K492, 1786); *Don Giovanni* (K527, 1787); *Così fan tutte* (K588, 1790); *Die *Zauberflöte* (The Magic Flute) (K620, 1791); *La *Clemenza di Tito* (K621, 1791).

BALLET MUSIC: *Les *Petits Riens* (K app. 10, 1778); for *Idomeneo* (K367, 1780).

SYMPHONIES (numbered according to Breitkopf and Härtel edn.): No. 1 in E♭ (K16, 1764); No. 4 in D (K19, 1764); No. 5 in B♭ (K22, 1765); No. 6 in F (K43, 1767); No. 7 in D (K45, 1768); No. 8 in D (K48, 1768); No. 9 in C (K73, 1771); No. 10 in G (K74, 1770); No. 11 in D (K84, 1770); No. 12 in G (K110, 1771); No. 13 in F (K112, 1771); No. 14 in A (K114, 1771); No. 15 in G (K124, 1772); No. 16 in C (K128, 1772); No. 17 in G (K129, 1772); No. 18 in F (K130, 1772); No. 19 in E♭ (K132, 1772); No. 20 in D (K133, 1772); No. 21 in A (K134, 1772); No. 22 in C (K162, 1773); No. 23 in D (K181, 1773); No. 24 in B♭ (K182, 1773); No. 25 in G minor (K183, 1773); No. 26 in E♭, ov. for *Thamos* (K184, 1773); No. 27 in G (K199, 1773); No. 28 in C (K200, 1773); No. 29 in A (K201, 1774); No. 30 in D (K202, 1774); No. 31 in D (*Paris, K297, 1778); No. 32 in G, probably ov. to *Zaide* (K318, 1779); No. 33 in B♭ (K319, 1779); No. 34 in C (K338, 1780); No. 35 in D (*Haffner, K385, 1782); No. 36 in C (*Linz, K425, 1783); No. 37 in G (only introduction, rest by M. Haydn) (K444, 1783); No. 38 in D (*Prague, K504, 1786); No. 39 in E♭ (K543, 1788); No. 40 in G minor (K550, 1788); No. 41 in C (*Jupiter, K551, 1788); also various others, some only fragmentary, and some probably of doubtful authenticity.

MISC. ORCH: *Cassations*: B♭ (K99, 1769); *Kontretänze* (Country Dances): B♭ (K123, 1770), Set of 6 (K462, 1784), *Das Donnerwetter* (K534, 1788), *La Bataille* (K535, 1788), Set of 2 (K565, 1788), *Der Sieg vom Helden Koburg* (K587, 1789), Set of 2 (K603, 1791), E♭ (K607, 1791), Set of 5 (K609, 1791), G major (K610, 1791); *German Dances*: Set of 6 (K509, 1787), Set of 6 (K536, 1788), Set of 6 (K567, 1788), Set of 6 (K571, 1789), Set of 12 (K586, 1789), Set of 6 (K600, 1791), Set of 4 (K602, 1791), Set of 3 (K605, 1791), C major (K611, 1791); *Divertimenti*: No. 1 in E♭ (K113, 1771), No. 2 in D (K131, 1772), D (K136, 1772), B♭ (K137, 1772), F (K138, 1772), No. 3 in E♭ (K166, 1773), No. 4 in B♭ (K186, 1773), No. 5 in

C (K187, ?1773), No. 6 in C (K188, 1776), No. 7 in D (K205, 1773), No. 8 in F (K213, 1775), E♭ (K226, 1775), B♭ (K227, 1775), No. 9 in B♭ (K240, 1776), No. 10 in F (K247, 1776), No. 11 in D (K251, 1776), No. 12 in E♭ (K252, 1776), No. 13 in F (K253, 1776), No. 14 in B♭ (K270, 1777), No. 15 in B♭ (K287, 1777), F (K288, 1777), No. 16 in E♭ (K289, 1777), No. 17 in D (K334, 1779); *Serenades*: G (K63, 1769), No. 1 in D (K100, 1769), No. 2 in F (*Kontretanz*) (K101, ?1776), No. 3 in D (K195, 1773), No. 4 in D (K203, 1774), No. 5 in D (K204, 1775), *Serenata notturna*, No. 6 in D for 2 orch. (K239, 1776), No. 7 in D (*Haffner*, K250, 1776), No. 8 in D (*Notturno* for 4 orch., K286, 1776–7), No. 9 in D (*Posthorn*, K320, 1779), No. 10 in B♭ for 13 wind instr. (K361, 1784), No. 11 in E♭ for wind (K375, 1781), No. 12 in C minor for wind (K388, 1782), No. 13 in G for str., *Eine *kleine Nachtmusik* (K525, 1787); *Maurerische Trauermusik* (*Masonic Funeral Music) (K477, 1785); *Ein musikalischer Spass* (A *musical joke) (K522, 1787); *Sinfonia Concertante* in E♭ for ob., cl., bn., hn. (K297b, 1778, considered doubtful attribution by some scholars); also Marches, Minuets, Gavottes.

CONCERTOS: PIANO: No. 1 in F (arr. of sonata-movements by Raupach and Honauer, K37, 1767), No. 2 in B♭ (arr. of sonata-movements by Raupach and Schobert, K39, 1767), No. 3 in D (arr. of sonata-movements by Honauer, Eckart, and ?C.P.E. Bach, K40, 1767), No. 4 in G (arr. of sonata-movements by Honauer and Raupach, K41, 1767), No. 5 in D (K175, 1773), No. 6 in B♭ (K238, 1776), No. 8 in C (K246, 1776), No. 9 in E♭ (K271, 1771), No. 11 in F (K413, 1782–3), No. 12 in A (K414, 1782), No. 13 in C (K415, 1782–3), No. 14 in E♭ (K449, 1784), No. 15 in B♭ (K450, 1784), No. 16 in D (K451, 1784), No. 17 in G (K453, 1784), No. 18 in B♭ (K456, 1784), No. 19 in F (K459, 1784), No. 20 in D minor (K466, 1785), No. 21 in C (K467, 1785), No. 22 in E♭ (K482, 1785), No. 23 in A (K488, 1786), No. 24 in C minor (K491, 1786), No. 25 in C (K503, 1786), No. 26 in D, *Coronation* (K537, 1788), No. 27 in B♭ (K595, 1791); 2 PIANOS: E♭ (K365, 1779); 3 PIANOS: F major (K242, 1776); Concert Rondo in D (K382, 1782), in A (K386, 1782).

VIOLIN: No. 1 in B♭ (K207, 1775), No. 2 in D (K211, 1775), No. 3 in G (K216, 1775), No. 4 in D (K218, 1775), No. 5 in A (K219, 1775, with alternative Adagio in E, K261, 1776), *Rondo* in C (K373, 1781); 2 VIOLINS: Concertone in C (K190, 1773); VIOLIN AND VIOLA: Sinfonia Concertante in E♭ (K364, 1779); BASSOON: B♭ (K191, 1774); CLARINET: A major (K622, 1791); FLUTE: No. 1 in G (K313, 1778), No. 2 in D transcr. from ob. conc. in C (K314, 1778); *Andante* in C (K315, 1778); FLUTE AND HARP: C major (K299, 1778); HORN AND STRINGS: No. 1 in D (K412, 1782), No. 2 in E♭ (K417, 1783), No. 3 in E♭ (K447, 1783), No. 4 in E♭ (K495, 1786),

No. 5 in E♭, fragment (K494a, 1786); *Concert Rondo* for hn. and orch. in E♭ (K371, 1791); OBOE: C major (K314, ?1778, transcr. for fl. as conc. No. 2 in D).

CHURCH MUSIC: *Kyrie* in F (K33, 1766), *Missa brevis* in G (K49, 1768), in D minor (K65, 1769), in C (K115, 1773), in F (K116, 1771), in F (Mass No. 6) (K192, 1774), in D (K194, 1774), in C (Mass No. 10) (K220, 1775), in C (K258, 1776), in C (Mass No. 13) (K259, 1776), in B♭ (K275, 1777); Mass in C, *Dominicus* (K66, 1769), No. 4 in C minor, *Waisenhausmesse* (K139, 1768), No. 7 in C, *Missa in honorem S S^{mae} Trinitatis* (K167, 1773), in C (K257, 1776), in C, *Missa longa* (K262, 1776), No. 16 in C, *Coronation* (K317, 1779), in C major, *Missa solemnis* (K337, 1780), No. 18 in C minor, unfinished (K427, 1782–3); *Regina Coeli* (K127, 1772); Motet, *Exsultate, jubilate* for sop., orch., and organ (K165, 1773); *Dixit Dominus* (K193, 1774); *Litaniae Lauretanae* (K195, 1774); *Litaniae de venerabili altaris Sacramento* (K243, 1776); *Vesperae de Dominica* (K321, 1779); *Kyrie* in D minor (K341, 1780–1); *Vesperae solennes de Confessore* (K339, 1780); Motet, *Ave verum corpus* (K618, 1791); *Requiem Mass* in D minor (unfinished) (K626, 1791).

CHORUS AND ORCH: *Die Schuldigkeit des ersten Gebotes*, pt. I of sacred drama (K35, 1767); *Grabmusik*, Passion cantata (K42, 1767); *La Betulia liberata*, oratorio (K118, 1771); *Davidde Penitente*, cantata, mainly based on Mass in C minor, K427 (K469, 1785); *Die Maurerfreude*, cantata (K471, 1785); *Eine kleine Freimaurer-Kantate* (K623, 1791).

UNACC. VOICES: *God is our Refuge*, sacred madrigal (K20, 1765); *5 Riddle Canons* (K89a, 1770); numerous *Canons* comp. between 1782 and 1788, also various secular trios, qts., and chs.

SOLO VOICE AND ORCH: (mainly concert arias): *Per pietà, bell' idol mio*, sop. (K78, c.1766); Scena and aria, *Misera, dove son? Ah, non son'io che parlo*, sop. (K369, 1781); Scena and rondo (extra number for *Idomeneo*) *Non più, tutto ascoltai. Non temer, amato bene*, sop. (K490, 1786); Scena and rondo, *Ch'io mi scordi di te. Non temer amato bene*, sop. with pf. obbl. (K505, 1786); Scena and aria, *Bella mia fiamma. Resta, oh caro*, sop. (K528, 1787); aria, *Un bacio di mano*, for Anfossi's *Le gelosie fortunate*, for bass (K541, 1788); rondo, extra aria for Susanna in *Figaro*, *Al desio di chi t'adora*, sop. (K577, 1789); *Un moto di gioia*, sop., extra number for Susanna in *Figaro* (K579, 1789); *Schon lacht der holde Frühling*, sop. for *Paisiello's *Il Barbiere di Siviglia* (K580, 1789); *Vado, ma dove?*, sop., for Martin's *Il burbero di buon core* (K583, 1789); *Rivolgete a lui lo sguardo*, bass, orig. for *Così fan tutte* (K584, 1789); *Per questa bella mano*, bass (K612, 1791).

STRING QUARTETS: No. 1 in G (K80, 1770), No. 2 in D (K155, 1772), No. 3 in G (K156, 1772), No. 4 in C (K157, 1772–3), No. 5 in F (K158, 1772–3), No. 6 in B♭ (K159, 1773), No. 7 in E♭ (K160, 1773), No. 8 in F (K168, 1773), No. 9 in A (K169,

1773), No. 10 in C (K170, 1773), No. 11 in E♭ (K171, 1773), No. 12 in B♭ (K172, 1773), No. 13 in D minor (K173, 1773), Nos. 14–19 'Haydn Quartets': No. 14 in G (K387, 1782), No. 15 in D minor (K421, 1783), No. 16 in E♭ (K428, 1783), No. 17 in B♭ (*Hunt*, K458, 1784), No. 18 in A (K464, 1785), No. 19 in C (*Dissonanzen*, K465, 1785), No. 20 in D (*Hoffmeister*, K499, 1786), Nos. 21–23 (*'King of Prussia* Quartets'): No. 21 in D (K575, 1789), No. 22 in B♭ (K589, 1790), No. 23 in F (K590, 1790); *Adagio and Fugue* in C minor, fugue identical with K426 for 2 pf. of 1783 (K546, 1788).

STRING QUINTETS: No. 1 in B♭ (K174, 1773), No. 2 in C minor, arr. of *Serenade No. 12* for wind, K388 (K406, 1786), No. 3 in C (K515, 1787), No. 4 in G minor (K516, 1787), No. 5 in D (K593, 1790), No. 6 in E♭ (K614, 1791).

CLARINET QUINTET: A major (K581, 1789); CLARINET TRIO, E♭ for cl., va., pf. (K498, 1786).

FLUTE QUARTETS: No. 1 in D (K285, 1777), No. 2 in G (K285a, 1777), No. 3 in C (K285b, 1777), No. 4 in A (K298, 1778); FLUTE (or vn.) SONATAS, with hpd: No. 1 in B♭ (K10, 1764), No. 2 in G (K11, 1764), No. 3 in A (K12, 1764), No. 4 in F (K13, 1764), No. 5 in C (K14, 1764), No. 6 in B♭ (K15, 1764).

HORN QUINTET: E♭ (K407, 1782).

OBOE QUARTET: F major (K370, 1781).

PIANO QUARTETS: No. 1 in G minor (K478, 1785), No. 2 in E♭ (K493, 1786).

PIANO AND WIND QUINTET (pf., ob., cl., hn., bn.): E♭ (K452, 1784).

PIANO TRIOS: No. 1 in B♭ (K254, 1776), No. 2 in G (K496, 1786), No. 3 in B♭ (K502, 1786), No. 4 in E (K542, 1788), No. 5 in C (K548, 1788), No. 6 in G (K564, 1788); in D minor/major, completed by Stadler (K442, 1783).

MISC. CHAMBER WORKS: *Adagio and Rondo* in C minor for glass armonica, fl., ob., va., vc. (K617, 1791); *Adagio* for cor anglais and str. (K580a, 1789); *Adagio in Canon* in F for 2 basset hn. and bn. (K410, 1783); *Adagio in F* for 2 cl. and 3 basset hns. (K411, 1783); *12 Duets* for 2 basset hns. (K487, 1786); *Duo* for vn. and va., No. 1 in G (K423, 1783), No. 2 in B♭ (K424, 1783); *5 Divertimenti* for 2 cl. and bn. (K229, 1783); *Minuet* in D, 2 vns., 2 hns., bass (K64, 1769); *7 Minuets with Trio*, 2 vn. and bass (K65a, 1769); *Adagio* in C for glass armonica (K356, 1791).

SONATAS: BASSOON AND CELLO: B♭ (K292, 1775); PIANO: No. 1 in C, No. 2 in F, No. 3 in B♭, No. 4 in E♭, No. 5 in G, No. 6 in D (K279–284, 1774, No. 6, 1775), No. 7 in C (K309, 1777), No. 8 in A minor (K310, 1778), No. 9 in D (K311, 1778), No. 10 in C, No. 11 in A, No. 12 in F, No. 13 in B♭ (K330–333, 1778), No. 14 in C minor (K457, 1784), No. 15 in C (K545, 1788), No. 16 in B♭ (K570, 1789), No. 17 in D (K576, 1789); VIOLIN AND PIANOFORTE: No. 1 in C (K6, 1762–4), No. 2 in D (K7, 1763–4), No. 3 in B♭ (K8, 1763–4), No. 4 in G (K9, 1764), Nos. 5–10, K10–15 (see *flute sonatas*), No. 11 in E♭, No. 12 in G, No. 13

in C, No. 14 in D, No. 15 in F, No. 16 in B♭ (K26–31, 1766), No. 17 in C (K296, 1778), No. 18 in G, No. 19 in E♭, No. 20 in C, No. 21 in E minor, No. 22 in A, No. 23 in D (K301–306, 1778), No. 24 in F (K376, 1781), No. 25 in F (K377, 1781), No. 26 in B♭ (K378, 1779), No. 27 in G major/minor (K379, 1781), No. 28 in E♭ (K380, 1781), No. 29 in A (K402, 1782, completed by Stadler), No. 30 in C (K403, 1782, unfinished), No. 31 in C (K404, 1782, unfinished), No. 32 in B♭ (K454, 1784), No. 33 in E♭ (K481, 1785), No. 34 in A (K526, 1787), No. 35 in F (K547, 1788). Also sonata movt. in C minor (K396, 1782, completed by Stadler).

STRING TRIOS: B♭, 2 vn. and bass, (K266, 1777), *Divertimento* in E♭, vn., va., vc. (K563, 1788). Also 6 *Fugue* arrs. from J. S. and W. F. Bach, with orig. introductions (K404A, 1782).

PIANO (4 HANDS): Sonatas: in B♭ (K358, 1774), D (K381, 1772), F (K497, 1786), C (K521, 1787); *Fugue* in G minor (K401, 1782); *Andante and Variations* (K501, 1786).

2 PIANOS: *Fugue* in C minor (K426, 1783, arr. for str., with short *Adagio* as preface, 1788), Sonata in D (K448, 1781).

SOLO PIANO (except Sonatas): *Minuet and Trio* in G, *Minuet* in F, *Allegro* in B♭, *Minuet* in F, *Minuet* in F (K1–5, 1761–2), 8 *Variations on 'Laat ons juichen'* (air by C. E. Graaff) in G (K24, 1766), 7 *Variations on 'Wilhelmus van Nassouwe'* (K25, 1766), 12 *Variations on a Minuet by Fischer* (K179, 1774), *Andantino* in E♭ (K236, 1790), 9 *Variations on 'Lison dormait'* from Dezède's *Julie* (K264, 1778), 12 *Variations on 'Ah, vous dirai-je, maman'* (K265, 1778), 8 *Variations on a March in Grétry's 'Mariages Samnites'* (K352, 1781), 12 *Variations on 'La Belle Françoise'* (K353, 1778), 12 *Variations on 'Je suis Lindor'* in Beaumarchais's *'Le Barbier de Séville'* (K354, 1778), *Minuet* in D (K355, c.1786), *Fantasia and Fugue* in C (K394, 1782), *Capriccio* in C (K395, 1778), *Fantasia* in D minor (K397, 1782), 6 *Variations on Paisiello's 'Salve tu, Domine'* (K398, 1783), *Suite* in C (K399, 1782), 1st movement of Sonata in B♭ (K400, 1782), *Kleiner Trauermarsch* in C minor (K453a, 1784), 10 *Variations on Unser dummer Pöbel meint* from Gluck's *La rencontre imprévue* (K455, 1784), *Fantasia* in C minor (K475, 1785), *Rondo* in D (K485, 1786), *Rondo* in F (K.494, 1786), 12 *Variations on an Allegretto* in B♭ (K500, 1786), *Rondo* in A minor (K511, 1787), *Allegro and Andante* (K533, 1788, often used with *Rondo*, K494, as finale to make 'Sonata No. 18'), *Adagio* in B minor (K540, 1788), 9 *Variations on a Minuet by Duport* (K573, 1789), *Gigue* in G (K574, 1789), 8 *Variations on Schack's 'Ein Weib ist das herrlichste Ding'* (K613, 1791).

ORGAN: Sonatas with orch: C major (K263, 1776), C major (K278, 1777), C major (K329, 1779); 14 Sonatas for org. and str., comp. between 1767 and 1780.

MECHANICAL ORGAN: *Adagio and Allegro* in F minor (K594, 1790), *Fantasia* in F minor (K608, 1791), *Andante* in F (K616, 1791).

SONGS (v. and pf.): Mozart wrote about 40 solo songs and Lieder, of which the best-known are: *Die Zufriedenheit* (K349, 1780), *Ah, spiegarti, O Dio* (K178, 1772), *Oiseaux, si tous les ans* (K307, 1777), *Komm, liebe Zither* (with mandolin) (K351, 1780), *An die Hoffnung* (K390, 1782), *Gesellenreise* (K468, 1785), *Der Zauberer* (K472, 1785), *Die betrogene Welt* (K474, 1785), *Das Veilchen* (K476, 1785), *Lied der Freiheit* (K506, 1786), *Die Alte* (K517, 1787), *Die Verschweigung* (K518, 1787), *Das Lied der Trennung* (K519, 1787), *Als Luise* (K520, 1787), *Abendempfindung* (K523, 1787), *An Chloe* (K524, 1787), *Des kleinen Freidrichs Geburtstag* (K529, 1787), *Das Traumbild* (K530, 1787), *Die kleine Spinnerin* (K531, 1787), *Sehnsucht nach dem Frühlinge* (K596, 1791), *Das Kinderspiel* (K598, 1791), *Eine kleine deutsche Kantate, 'Die ihr des unermesslichen Weltalls'* (K619, 1791).

ADDITIONAL ACCOMPANIMENTS TO WORKS BY HANDEL: *Acis and Galatea* (K566, 1788), *Messiah* (K572, 1789), *Alexander's Feast* (K591, 1790), *Ode for St Cecilia's Day* (K592, 1791).
See *Masonic Music by Mozart.*

Mozart and Salieri. Opera in 2 acts by Rimsky-Korsakov to his own lib. based on Pushkin's poem (1830). Prod. Moscow 1898, London (concert) 1927, Forest Park, Penn., 1933.

Mozartiana. Sub-title of Tchaikovsky's Suite No. 4 for Orch. comp. 1887, the 4 movements consisting of arrs. of Mozart's (1) *Gigue* for pf. (K574), (2) *Minuet* for pf. (K355), (3) *Ave verum corpus* (K618) in orch. arr. by Liszt, (4) *Variations* for pf. on *Unser dummer Pöbel meint* from Gluck's *La rencontre imprévue* (K455).

mp. *Mezzo piano,* half-soft.

Mravinsky, Evgeny (Alexandrovich) (*b* St Petersburg, 1906). Russ. cond. Studied St Petersburg Cons. Prin. cond., Leningrad P.O. since 1938. Mus. dir., Kirov Th. Ballet 1932–8. Prof., Leningrad Cons. Cond. f.ps. of Shostakovich's 5th, 6th, 8th, 9th, and 10th Syms. and other works.

M.S. *Mano sinistra* (It.), left hand.

Muck, Karl (*b* Darmstadt, 1859; *d* Stuttgart, 1940). Ger. cond. and pianist. Studied Leipzig Cons. Chorus master Zürich, then posts as opera cond. at Salzburg, Brno, and Graz. Cond., Deutsches Landestheater, Prague, 1886. Cond. first Moscow and St Petersburg perfs. of Wagner's *Ring*, 1889. Cond. Berlin Opera 1892–1912 (chief cond. from 1908), in that time cond. 103 different operas, 35 of them new. CG London 1899. Bayreuth Fest. (*Parsifal*) 1901–30. Joint cond. Vienna P.O. 1903–6. Cond. Boston S.O. 1906–8, becoming chief cond. 1912–18. Outcry against him when USA entered war led to his internment. Cond. Hamburg P.O. 1922–33.

Mudarra, Alonso (*b* Palencia diocese, Sp., *c.*1510; *d* Seville, 1580). Sp. composer of mus. for *vihuela*. Pubd. vol. of *vihuela* pieces 1546.

Mudd, John (*b* London, 1555; *d* Peterborough, 1631). Eng. composer. Matriculated, Cambridge Univ. 1573. Organist, Peterborough Cath. 1583–1631. Wrote church mus., anthems, etc.

Mudd, Thomas (*b* London, *c.*1560; *d* after 1619). Eng. composer. Studied Cambridge Univ. 1578, being Fellow of Pembroke Coll. up to 1590. Became rector in Kent, 1592. Wrote church mus. and dances for viols, etc.

Mudge, Richard (*b* Bideford, 1718; *d* ?Bedworth, Warwicks., 1763). Eng. composer and clergyman, known principally for 6 concerti grossi, pub. 1749, tpt. conc., etc. Modern edns. of concerti arr. by G. *Finzi.

Mudie, Michael (Winfield) (*b* Manchester, 1914; *d* Brussels, 1962). Eng. cond. Studied RCM. Cond. of opera with Carl Rosa 1935–9, SW 1946–53. Cond. f.p. in England of Verdi's *Simon Boccanegra*, 1948. Retired 1953 because of ill-health.

Muette de Portici, La (Auber). See *Masaniello.*

Muffat, Georg (*b* Megève, Alsace, 1653; *d* Passau, 1704). Ger. composer and organist. Organist of Strasbourg Cath. until 1675, to Bishop of Salzburg *c.*1687. Organist and later Kapellmeister to Bishop of Passau from 1690. Wrote many org. works, concerti grossi, etc.

Muffat, Gottlieb (*b* Passau, 1690; *d* Vienna, 1770). Ger. composer and organist, son of Georg *Muffat. Dir. of operas and chamber mus., Vienna court, from 1717. Wrote org. mus., hpd. works, etc. Handel borrowed some of his themes.

Muffling (of drums). A way of muting kettle-drums (e.g. at a funeral) by placing a cloth over the surface. Nowadays it is usual to use sponge-headed drumsticks instead.

Mugnone, Leopoldo (*b* Naples, 1858; *d* Naples, 1941). It. cond. and composer. Cond. at Teatro alla Fenice, Naples, 1874. Cond. f.p. of Mascagni's *Cavalleria rusticana*, Rome 1890, and Puccini's *Tosca*, Rome 1900. Cond. La Scala, Milan, from 1891. London CG 1905–6, 1919, and 1925. Début USA 1920. Comp. operas.

Mühlfeld, Richard (*b* Salzungen, 1856; *d* Meiningen, 1907). Ger. clarinettist. Joined Grand Duke's orch. at Meiningen as violinist. Self-taught clarinettist, becoming prin. cl., Meiningen Orch., 1879, and at Bayreuth 1884–96. Brahms's cl. works (trio, Op. 114, quintet, Op. 115, and 2 sonatas, Op. 120) were written for him.

Mukle, May (Henrietta) (*b* London, 1880; *d* London, 1963). Eng. cellist. Studied RAM. Long career as soloist and chamber mus. player. Works written for her by Vaughan Williams and Holst.

Muldowney, Dominic (b Southampton, 1952). Eng. composer and cond. Studied Southampton Univ. with Jonathan Harvey and in London with Birtwistle, then at York Univ. with Bernard Rands and David Blake. Mus. dir. Nat. Th. from 1976. Prin. works:

THEATRE: *An Heavyweight Dirge* (1971); *Klavier-Hammer* (1973); *Da Capo al Fine*, tape for ballet (1975); *Earl of Essex's Galliard* for 3 actors, dancer, and instr. (1976); ballet *Macbeth* (1979); realization *The Beggar's Opera* (1982).

ORCH: *Driftwood to the Flow*, str. (1972); *Music at Chartres*, chamber orch. (1974); *Perspectives*, full orch. (1975); Conc., 4 vn. and str. (1980); pf. conc. (1983); saxophone conc. (1984).

CHAMBER ENSEMBLE: *Love Music for Bathsheba Everdene and Gabriel Oak* (1974); *Solo/Ensemble* (1974); *3-part Motet* for 11 instr. (1976); *12 Shorter Chorale Preludes of Bach* arr. for 8 woodwind instr. (1976); *10 Longer Chorale Preludes of Bach* arr. for 8 woodwind instr. (1976); *Variations after Sweelinck* (1977); *Double Helix* (1977); *Entr'acte* (1977).

CHAMBER MUSIC: *In a Hall of Mirrors*, alto sax., pf. (1979); Pf. Trio (1980); Str. Qt. No. 1 (1973), No. 2 (1980).

VOCAL AND CHORAL: *Bitter Lemons* for women's vv. (1970); *Cantata* for soloists, speakers, 2 vc. and perc. (1975); *Procurans Odium*, sop. and 8 instr. (1977); *Five Psalms*, sop., ten., ch., wind, tape (1979); *5 Theatre Poems* (Brecht), mez. and ens. (1980–1); *From Little Gidding* (Eliot), bar., treble, pf. (1980); *In Dark Times* (Brecht), sop., alto, ten., bass, ens. (1981); *The Duration of Exile*, mez., ens. (1983); *A Second Show*, cont., harp, vn., alto sax., tape (1983).

PIANO: *A Little Piano Book*, 24 pieces (1979).

Mulè, Giuseppe (b Termini Imerese, 1885; d Rome, 1951). It. composer. Studied Palermo Cons. Wrote 7 operas (incl. *Dafni*, 1928), orch. and chamber mus.

Müller-Hartmann, Robert (b Hamburg, 1884; d Dorking, 1950). Ger.-born composer, teacher, and critic (Brit. citizen from 1948). Studied Stern Cons., Berlin. Worked as mus. critic on several papers. Taught at Bernuth Cons., Hamburg; lecturer, Hamburg Univ. 1923–33; mus. adv., N. German Radio, 1931–3. Settled in Eng., 1933, becoming friend of Vaughan Williams, whose The **Pilgrim's Progress* he partially trans. into Ger. Works incl. Sym. (1927), ov., *Leonce and Lena* (1922), *Variations on a Pastoral Theme* (1925), Sinfonietta (1943), *Craigelly Suite* (1944), chamber mus., pf. pieces, and songs.

Müller, Maria (b Litoměřice, 1898; d Bayreuth, 1958). Cz. soprano. Studied in Vienna with E. Schmedes. Début Linz 1919 (Elsa). NY Met. début 1925 (Sieglinde), singing each season until 1934–5. Sang in Berlin and regularly at Bayreuth 1930–44. CG début 1934 (Eva). Sang Jenůfa and

Strauss's Helen. One of most radiant singers of Eva in *Die Meistersinger*.

Müller von Asow, Erich (b Dresden, 1892; d Berlin, 1964). Ger. musicologist. Studied with Riemann. Dir., contemporary mus. fest., Dresden, 1917. Ed. of 5-vol. edn. of Mozart family's correspondence, 1942. Author of books on Schütz, Handel, and Reger. Ed., thematic catalogue of R. Strauss's works (1959–74, continued by A. Ott and F. Trenner). Ed. of mus. dictionaries.

Müller, Wenzel (b Tyrnau, 1767; d Baden, nr. Vienna, 1835). Austrian composer and conductor. Child prodigy as instrumentalist. Joined th. orch. at Brno 1782 as violinist and comp. Singspiel. Became Kapellmeister at Leopoldstädter Th., Vienna, 1786, staying until 1830. Prolific composer of Singspiels, incl. *Die Schwestern von Prag* (1794) and *Das lustige Beilager* (1797). From 1807 to 1813 was also cond. of Ger. opera in Prague. Songs from his works attained—and several retain—widespread popularity.

Mulliner Book. MS. coll. of Eng. mus. containing 131 comps., mainly for kbd. but also for cittern, made by Thomas Mulliner c.1560. Pubd. in modern notation 1951, ed. Denis Stevens, rev. 1962.

Mullings, Frank (Coningsby) (b Walsall, 1881; d Manchester, 1953). Eng. ten. Studied Birmingham. Début Coventry 1907 as Faust. Denhof Co. 1913, Beecham Co. 1916–21, BNOC 1922–9. First to sing Parsifal in Eng. (1919). Noted singer of Otello and Tristan. Later taught at Birmingham Sch. of Mus. 1927–46 and RMCM 1944–9.

Mumma, Gordon (b Framingham, Mass., 1935). Amer. composer. Studied hn. and pf. Co-founder, Co-operative Studio for Elec. Mus., Ann Arbor, 1958–66. From 1966 composer with Merce Cunningham Dance Co. Among first to use live elec. mus. processes, devising a computerized system which he calls cybersonics. Comps. incl. *Swarm*, for vn., concertina, bowed crosscut saw, and cybersonic modification; and other similar works.

Munch, Charles (b Strasbourg, 1891; d Richmond, Virginia, 1968). Fr. cond. and violinist. Studied vn. at Strasbourg and Berlin and with **Flesch. Prof. of vn., Strasbourg Cons., 1919–25 and leader of Strasbourg orch.; prof. Leipzig Cons. 1925–32 and leader of Gewandhaus Orch. Début as cond. Paris 1932. Founder and cond., Orchestre de la Société Philharmonique 1935–8. London début 1938. Cond., Société des Concerts du Conservatoire 1938–46 and prof. of cond. Paris Cons. US début Boston 1946. Cond. Boston S.O. 1949–62; dir., Berkshire Mus. Center 1951–62. Toured Europe, Far East, and Australia with Boston S.O. Organized Orchestre de Paris 1967.

Münchinger, Karl (b Stuttgart, 1915). Ger. cond. Studied Leipzig Cons. Cond. Hanover S.O.

1941–3. Founder-cond. *Stuttgart Chamber Orch., 1945, with which he has made many int. tours. London début 1949. Recorded Bach's Brandenburg Concertos three times—in mono, stereo, and quadraphonic sound.

Mundharmonika (Ger.). Mouth harmonica, i.e. mouth organ.

Mundy, John (b c.1555; d Windsor, 1630). Eng. composer and organist, son of William Mundy. Organist St George's Chapel, Windsor for over 40 years. Wrote pieces for viols and madrigals, incl. *Lightly she tripped* for 5 vv. in The *Triumphs of Oriana*. His kbd. fantasia *Faire Wether* has descriptions of lightning and thunder.

Mundy, William (b c.1529; d London, 1591). Eng. composer. Singer in Chapel Royal. Comp. motets and anthems, incl. *O Lord, the maker of all things*.

Munich Philharmonic Orchestra. Orch. in Munich, Bavaria, founded 1924 on basis of former *Kaim Orch. (1893–1923). Cond. have incl. Pfitzner, Rosbaud, and Kempe (1967–76).

Munrow, David (John) (b Birmingham, 1942; d Chesham Bois, 1976). Eng. player of recorder, crumhorn, etc., and specialist in early mus. and its instr. Founder-dir. of Early Music Consort, 1967; lecturer in history of early mus., Leicester Univ. from 1967. Prof. of recorder, RAM, from 1969. Frequent broadcaster. Comp. and arr. mus. for films and TV. Author of *Instruments of the Middle Ages and Renaissance*, 1976.

Muradeli, Vano (b Gori, Tiflis, 1908; d Tomsk, 1970). Russ. (Georgian) composer. Studied Tiflis Cons. and with Myaskovsky at Moscow Cons. His opera *The Great Friendship* (Moscow 1947) precip-itated the denunciation by Soviet officials in 1948 of 'formalism', distortion of history, and lack of melody in the mus. not only of Muradeli but of Shostakovich and Prokofiev. He was reinstated in the Khruschev era, becoming deputy in Supreme Soviet and recipient of Order of Lenin, 1967. Wrote 2 syms. and opera *October*.

Murder in the Cathedral (Pizzetti). See *Assassinio nella cattedrale*.

Murdoch, William (David) (b Bendigo, Aus-tralia, 1888; d Holmbury St Mary, Surrey, 1942). Australian pianist. Studied Melbourne Univ. and RCM. Settled in Eng. 1905 and made reputation as chamber mus. player, especially in assoc. with Albert *Sammons, violinist. Prof. of pf. at RAM 1930–6. Wrote books on Brahms and Chopin, and arr. Bach's works for pf. Was pianist in f.p. of Elgar's Pf. Quintet (1919).

Muris, Johannes de (Jehan des Murs) (b Lisieux diocese, c.1300; d c.1350). Fr. mus. theorist. Wrote treatise *Musica speculativa* at Sorbonne, Paris, 1323, and 4 other treatises, incl. one on counter-point. Opposed the innovations of the *ars nova*.

Murray, Ann (b Dublin, 1949). Irish-born mez. Studied RMCM with Frederic R. *Cox and at London Opera Centre. Opera début with Scottish Opera as Alceste (Snape Maltings, 1974). CG début 1976 (Cherubino). NY début 1979 (in *La Clemenza di Tito*). Notable Béatrice in Berlioz's opera, Buxton Festival 1980. Song recitalist and oratorio singer.

Murrill, Herbert (Henry John) (b London, 1909; d London, 1952). Eng. composer, organist, and administrator. Studied RAM and Oxford Univ. Taught comp. at RAM 1933–52. Dir. of Mus. BBC, 1950–2. Wrote jazz opera *Man in Cage* (1929), ballet *Picnic* (1927), 2 vc. concs., str. qt., and incidental mus. for plays.

Mus. Abbreviation for 'Music', as in B.Mus. (Bachelor of Music), D.Mus. (Doctor of Music).

Musette. (1) Type of Fr. bagpipe popular in court circles in 17th and 18th cents. Was bellows-blown and had 4 or 5 drones enclosed in cylinder. Used in orch. by Lully.
(2) Variety of gavotte in which persistent drone bass suggests the above instr. Vaughan Williams's ob. conc. (1944) has a *musette* in 2nd movement.

Musgrave, Thea (b Barnton, Midlothian, 1928). Scottish composer and cond. Studied Edinburgh Univ. 1947–50 with Mary Grierson and Hans Gál and in Paris 1952–4 with Nadia Boulanger. Lecturer in mus., London Univ. 1959–65. Taught at Univ. of California 1970. Her mus. developed from early diatonicism to a more chromatic idiom and to use of serialism; from various elements she has forged a mature style capable of rich expressiveness as in her opera *Mary, Queen of Scots*. In her orch. works, solo instr. are often given virtuoso opportunities; and in her cl. conc. the soloist moves about the orch. to play with different sections in the manner of a jazz improvisation. Prin. comps.:

OPERAS: *The Abbot of Drimock*, 1-act (1955); *The Decision*, 3 acts (1964–5); *The *Voice of Ariadne* (1972–3); **Mary, Queen of Scots*, 3 acts (1976); *A Christmas Carol* (1978–9); *An Occurrence at Owl Creek Bridge*, radio opera (1981); *Harriet Tubman, the Woman Called Moses* (1983–4).
BALLETS: *A Tale for Thieves* (1953); *Beauty and the Beast* (1968–9); *Orfeo*, with dancer (see Chamber Music below).
ORCH.: *Obliques* (1958); *Themes and Interludes* (1962); *Sinfonia* (1963); *Festival Overture* (1965); **Nocturnes and Arias* (1966); *Concerto for Orches-tra* (1967); cl. conc. (1967); *Night Music* (1969); **Memento Vitae* (homage to Beethoven) (1969–70); hn. conc. (1971); va. conc. (1973); *Space Play* (1974); *Peripateia* (1981).
CHORAL AND VOCAL: *Triptych*, ten. and small orch. (1959); *The Phoenix and the Turtle*, ch. and orch. (1962); *The Five Ages of Man*, ch. and orch. (1963); *Rorate coeli*, unacc. (1974, rev. 1976); *The Last Twilight*, ch., brass, perc. (1980); *The Lord's Prayer*, ch. and org. (1984).

CHAMBER MUSIC: Str. qt. (1958); *Colloquy*, vn. and pf. (1960); Trio, fl., ob., pf. (1960); *Serenade* (1961); Chamber Conc. No. 1 (1962), No. 2 (1966), No. 3 (1966); *Soliloquy*, guitar and prerecorded tape (1969); Impromptu No. 1, fl., ob. (1967), No. 2, fl., ob., cl. (1970); *Elegy*, va., vc. (1970); *Orfeo I*, fl., tape (1975, orch. vers. fl. and 15 str., *Orfeo II*, 1975).

Musica Antiqua (Lat.). Old music. Coll. of 190 pieces of mus. compiled and ed. by John Stafford Smith and pubd. 1812. Ranges from ancient chants by Merbecke to Norman *chansons*, and masques from time of James I of Eng.

Musica ficta (Lat.). Feigned music. **Musica falsa** (It.). False music. In early mus., the sharpening or flattening of certain notes, conventionally prescribed or permitted in modal mus. (see *Modes*) to avoid certain awkward intervals, etc. Its prevalence in mus. up to and incl. that of the 16th cent. requires considerable knowledge of performing practice of the period on the part of modern eds. In most modern edns. the necessary alterations are written in.

Musica figurata (It.), **Figuralmusik** (Ger.). The term has 2 meanings: (1) Contrapuntal mus. in which the various melodic strands move more or less independently, shorter notes in one v. against longer in others—as distinct from mere 'note against note' counterpoint; (2) Decorated melody in plainsong, etc., as distinct from the more sober type (such decorated plainsong is also known as *musica colorata*, coloured music).

Musical America. American monthly mus. magazine founded as a weekly in 1898. Among eds. have been J. C. Freund, Deems Taylor, Oscar Thompson, and Everett Helm. Absorbed by *High Fidelity*, 1965.

Musical Box. Toy in which pins on a rotating barrel pluck the teeth of a comb. These teeth are graduated in length, thus providing a scale of notes from which tunes can be produced. (Multiple sets of pins produce several tunes.) Mechanism usually activated by lifting of lid.

Musical Comedy (Musicals). Type of musical entertainment, 20th cent. development of operetta, which relies for its popular success on a succession of catchy and easily memorable tunes, either as songs, duets, or choruses. Some early Eng. examples date from end of 19th cent., e.g. Lionel Monckton's *The Runaway Girl* (1898), but perhaps the first of the kind were Osmond Carr's *In Town* (1892) and Sidney Jones's *A Gaiety Girl* (1893), both staged by George Edwardes at the Prince of Wales Th., London. These were followed by Leslie Stuart's *Florodora* (1899), *The Arcadians* (Monckton, 1909), and *The Maid of the Mountains* (Fraser-Simson, 1916). The outstanding success of the First World War was Norton's *Chu Chin Chow* (1916). After 1918 American shows began to visit London and the names became familiar of

Youmans (*No, No, Nanette*, 1924), Jerome Kern (*The Cabaret Girl*, 1922, *Sunny*, 1925, *Show Boat*, 1927), Gershwin (*Oh Boy*, 1917, *Lady, Be Good*, 1924, *Funny Face*, 1927, *Girl Crazy*, 1930, *Strike up the Band*, 1930), Rodgers and Hart (*The Girl Friend*, 1926, *Evergreen*, 1930, *On Your Toes*, 1936, *Pal Joey*, 1940), Cole Porter (*Gay Divorce*, 1932, *Nymph Errant*, 1933, *Anything Goes*, 1934). Emigré European composers such as Victor Herbert, Rudolf Friml (*Rose Marie*, 1924, *The Vagabond King*, 1925), and Sigmund Romberg also contributed to the transatlantic successes. Romberg's shows incl. *The Student Prince* (1924), *The Desert Song* (1926), and *New Moon* (1928).

In England two native composers dominated the musicals of the 1930s, Noël Coward with *Bitter-Sweet* (1929) and *Operette* (1938), and Ivor Novello with *Glamorous Night* (1935), *Careless Rapture* (1936), and *The Dancing Years* (1939). Scarcely less popular were Vivian Ellis's *Mr Cinders* (1929), *Jill Darling* (1934), and *Under Your Hat* (1938), while Noel Gay's *Me and My Girl* (1937) made 'The Lambeth Walk' almost a national song for a time. After the Second World War, the 1930s type of musical comedy lingered on with Ellis's *Bless the Bride* (1947), Novello's *King's Rhapsody* (1949), Wilson's *The Boy Friend* (1953), and Julian Slade's *Salad Days* (1954). But the death-knell of this genteel kind of affair was sounded by the record-breaking *Oklahoma!* (1943) of Rodgers and Hammerstein, first of an amazing series of shows from this duo: *Carousel* (1945), *South Pacific* (1949), *The King and I* (1951), *Flower Drum Song* (1958), and *The Sound of Music* (1959). The stronger construction of these musicals attracted into the popular th. such choreographers as Agnes de Mille, Jerome Robbins, and George Balanchine. Comparable with them were Irving Berlin's *Annie Get Your Gun* (1946) and *Call Me Madam* (1950), Porter's *Kiss Me Kate* (1948, based on *The Taming of the Shrew*), and *Can-Can* (1953), and (a new team) Frederick Loewe's and Alan Jay Lerner's *Brigadoon* (1947), *Paint Your Wagon* (1951), *★My Fair Lady* (1956, based on Shaw's *Pygmalion*), and *Camelot* (1960).

A tougher vein was exploited by Leonard *★Bernstein with *On the Town* (1944), *Wonderful Town* (1953), and *West Side Story* (1957). The lyrics of the last-named were written by Stephen Sondheim, who later comp. some of the best musicals of the 1970s in *Company* (1970), *A Little Night Music* (1973), and *Pacific Overtures* (1976). The Brit. challenge to the Amer. dominance after 1946 was best represented by Lionel Bart's *Fings ain't wot they used t'be* (1959) and *Oliver!* (1960, based on *Oliver Twist*), Bricusse's and Newley's *Stop the World—I Want to Get Off* (1961), *Charlie Girl* (1965, Taylor and Heneker), but it was left to Andrew *★Lloyd Webber and Tim Rice to chart a new course with *Joseph and the Amazing Technicolor Dreamcoat* (1968), *Jesus Christ Superstar* (1970), *Evita* (1976, a life of Eva Peron), and *Cats* (1981, based on T. S. Eliot poems). Other significant musicals of the second half of the 20th cent. have been Frank Loesser's *Guys and Dolls* (1950), *The Most Happy Fella* (1956), and *How to Succeed in Business Without Really Trying* (1961), Adler's and Ross's *The Pajama Game* (1954) and *Damn Yankees* (1955), Jule Styne's *Funny Girl* (1964), Herman's *Hello Dolly!* (1964), Bock's *Fiddler on the Roof* (1964), Leigh's *Man of La Mancha* (1965, based on *Don Quixote*), Kander's *Cabaret* (1966, based on Isherwood's *Goodbye to Berlin*), MacDermot's *Hair* (1967, a 'rock' musical which incorporated elec. sounds), and Marvin Hamlisch's *Chorus Line* (1975) and *Jean Seberg* (1983).

Musical Glasses. See *Glass Armonica*.

Musical Joke, A (*Ein musikalischer Spass*). Divertimento in F for 2 hn. and str. qt. by Mozart (K522) comp. Vienna, 1787, as satire on composers and perfs. of popular mus.

Musical Offering, The (*Das musikalische Opfer*). Coll. of 13 comps. by Bach (BWV 1079) in various contrapuntal forms, all using a theme given to Bach for extemporization by King Frederick the Great of Prussia in Potsdam in 1747. Some are for kbd., 2 for fl., and others for no particular medium. Nos. 1–8 constitute the actual offering, the remainder having been added later. Modern performing edns. exist and various composers have orchestrated certain items, e.g. Webern *Ricercare*. The pieces are: 1. *Ricercare a 3*, 2. *Canon perpetuus*, 3. *Canon a 2 violini in unisono*, 4. *Canon a 2 per motum contrarium*, 5. *Canon a 2 per augmentationem*, 6. *Canon a 2 per tonos*, 7. *Canon a 2*, 8. *Canon a 2 quaerendo invenietis*, 9. *Canon perpetuus*, 10. *Canon a 4*, 11. *Fuga canonica*, 12. *Trio sonata*, 13. *Ricercare a 6*.

Musical Switch. A medley constructed out of snatches of popular tunes dovetailed into each other so that one tune is 'switched', after a few measures, to another.

Musical Times. Eng. monthly mus. magazine founded 1844. Eds. have incl. W. McNaught (father and son), Martin Cooper, Harold Rutland, Andrew Porter, and Stanley Sadie.

Musica Mensurata (Lat.). Measured music. Medieval system of notation, necessitated by invention of figured mus. to denote relative duration and pitch of each note of plainchant to be sung.

Music and Letters. Eng. mus. quarterly founded 1920 by A. H. Fox Strangways, who was ed. until 1937. Succeeded by Eric Blom 1937–50, Richard Capell 1950–4, Blom 1954–9, J. A. Westrup 1959–76, Denis Arnold and Edward Olleson 1976–80, Edward Olleson and Nigel Fortune from 1981.

Musica Reservata (Lat.). Reserved music. (1) Term coined in early 16th cent., possibly for expressive style of composers such as Després and for its method of perf., but exact meaning is unknown. One view applies it to mus. employing exceptional reserve in use of ornamentation and another theory is that it meant mus. reserved for what would now be called 'highbrows'.

(2) Name of London ens. formed 1960 to perform early mus. in authentic manner.

Musica Transalpina. First printed coll. of It. (i.e. transalpine) madrigals with Eng. words, compiled and pubd. in London by Nicholas Yonge in 2 vols., 1588 and 1597 (both It. and Eng. words were given). Had great influence on Eng. composers. Vol. I contained 57 pieces, incl. examples by Marenzio, Palestrina, Byrd, de Lassus, and others; 2nd vol. of 24 pieces incl. Ferrabosco, Marenzio, Venturi, etc.

Music Centre. Really a place, e.g. a hall, on which mus. activity is centred, but the term has been appropriated by commerce for piece of equipment in which stereo record-player, cassette-player, recording equipment, and sometimes radio are all assembled into single item of domestic furniture.

Music Drama. Term used by Wagner after *Lohengrin* to describe his operas in order to emphasize that the mus., dramatic, and scenic elements were on equal terms—a fusion of the arts as Gluck had proposed. Yet the old It. description of opera was *dramma per musica*.

Music for a While. Song by *Purcell, part of his incidental mus. to Dryden's play *Oedipus*, 1692.

Music Hall. Strictly, the place where a particular type of variety entertainment was held, often attached to a public house or containing a bar where customers could drink while they listened and watched; but the term also means the entertainment itself. It flourished in Brit. from c.1850 to 1914. Among the most famous London music-halls were the Surrey (Southwark), the Bedford (Camden Town), the Metropolitan (Edgware Road), and Collins's (Islington). By 1870 there were said to be 200 in London and 300 elsewhere. Many 'acts' were performed; musically the halls' importance lay in the association of a popular song with a particular performer, e.g. Charles Coborn and *Two Lovely Black Eyes*, Eugene Stratton and *Lily of Laguna*, Albert Chevalier and *My Old Dutch*, Harry Champion and *Any Old Iron*, Harry Lauder and *Roamin' in the gloamin'*, Vesta Victoria and *Waiting at the Church*, Florrie Forde and *Down at the ol' Bull and Bush*, Will Fyffe and *I Belong to Glasgow*, and Ella Shields and *Burlington Bertie from Bow*. After 1914 the consumption of food and drink in the auditorium was forbidden and the music-hall gave way to the variety theatre and its stars like Gracie Fields and Hetty King. Something of the music-hall spirit survives in North of England working-men's clubs. It is an irony that while the songs and their singers have acquired a kind of immortality in Eng. theatrical folklore, the names of the composers are scarcely remembered, with the exception of Leslie Stuart, who wrote for Eugene Stratton. Thousands of music-hall songs, for example, were comp. by Joseph Tabrar, yet for one whose melodies reached more lips than Mozart's and Beethoven's, the reward has been almost total obscurity.

Musicians' Benevolent Fund. British mus. charity founded in 1921 orig. as fund in memory of the ten. Gervase *Elwes. Maintains 3 residential homes for elderly and retired musicians, and helps many other musicians in various ways.

Musicians' Company. See *Worshipful Company of Musicians.*

Musicians' Union. Brit. trade union formed in 1921 by amalgamation of Nat. Orch. Assoc. of Professional Musicians (1891) and Amalgamated Musicians' Union (1893). Objective is to improve pay and conditions of professional musicians.

Music Makers, The. Ode, Op. 69, for cont. or mez., ch., and orch. by Elgar, to poem by A. O'Shaughnessy (1844–81), in which several self-quotations occur (e.g. from *Enigma Variations*, first Sym., Vn. Conc., etc.). Comp. 1911–12, with earlier sketches. F.p. Birmingham 1912. Also set for vv. and orch. by Kodály, 1964.

Musicology (Ger. *Musikwissenschaft*). Mus. scholarship. A 20th-cent. word taken into the Eng. language (from the Fr. *Musicologie*), but the Ger. term *Musikwissenschaft* was coined by J. B. Logier in 1827. It may be said to cover all study of mus. other than that directed to proficiency in perf. or comp. Thus, a musicologist is one who is a specialist in some mus. study.

Among the divisions of musicology are acoustics; the physiology of v., ear, and hand; the psychology of aesthetics and, more directly, of mus. appreciation and education; ethnology so far as it bears on mus. (incl. folksongs, folk dances, etc.); rhythm and metrics; modes and scales; the principles and development of instrs.; orchestration; form; theories of harmony; the history of mus.; the bibliography of mus.; terminology—and so forth.

The International Mus. Soc. (IMS, 1900–14) had as its purpose the promotion of musicological study, and its post-war successor made its purpose clear in its name—'Société Internationale de Musicologie' (SIM, founded 1928, publishes journal *Acta Musicologica*). There are also nat. musicological socs. in many countries. A Brit. musicological soc. (The Royal Mus. Assoc.) has existed since 1874, and the Amer. Musicological Soc. was founded in 1934: both socs. publish journals.

Music Review, The. Brit. mus. quarterly, founded 1940. Ed. Geoffrey Sharp until 1974, when A. F. Leighton Thomas took over.

Music Theatre. A type of comp., sometimes quasi-operatic but more usually a concert piece,

for which a semi-staged presentation is necessary. It developed after about 1950, esp. in USA and Ger. An Eng. example is *Maxwell Davies's Eight *Songs for a Mad King. The term is better avoided, for a precise definition is impossible.

Musikalische Opfer, Das (Bach). See *Musical Offering, The.*

Musique Concrète (Fr.). Concrete music. Mus. prepared from recorded sounds, either natural (e.g. birdsong) or man-made (traffic, instr. etc.). Term originated by Pierre *Schaeffer in 1948 to differentiate between mus. assembled from concrete sound objects and mus. based on the abstract medium of notation. Strictly, *musique concrète* should not be modified electronically but the distinction between it and electronically synthesized sound has been increasingly blurred until the term elec. mus. covers the whole process.

Mussorgsky, Modest (Petrovich) (*b* Karevo, Pskov, 1839; *d* St Petersburg, 1881). Russ. composer. Showed mus. talent as a child but was destined for an army career. In 1857 he met Balakirev in St Petersburg and studied with him, resigning his commission the next year. His early songs and pf. pieces show little sign of his later achievement, but by 1864 he was writing fine songs. He started and abandoned 2 operas, but began work in 1868 on *Boris Godunov*, which he rev. when it was rejected by the Imperial Th. On its prod. in 1874 it pleased audiences but not musicians, who resented its unconventional methods and unusual style in which speech-inflexion governed the vocal lines. Over the next few years Mussorgsky worked on 2 operas, but his heavy drinking, a habit acquired at cadet school, sapped his capacity for concentrated work. He was one of the group of 5 Russ. composers of nationalist tendencies known as the *'Mighty handful'. After his death his works were completed and 'improved' by Rimsky-Korsakov and others, but in the 20th cent. his realistic and progressive qualities have been recognized and his orig. scores have been restored where possible. Prin. comps.:

OPERAS: *Salammbô* (unfinished, 1863–6); *The *Marriage (1 act only finished) (1868); *Boris Godunov* (1868–9, rev. 1871–2, rev. 1873); *Mlada* (projected 4-act opera-ballet of which Cui, Rimsky-Korsakov, and Borodin were to compose the other 3 acts, 1872); *Khovanshchina (1873, 5th act unfinished); *Sorochintsy Fair (1874–80, unfinished).

ORCH.: *Night on the Bare Mountain (1867).

PIANO: *Souvenir d'Enfance* (1857); *Intermezzo* (1861, orch. and expanded 1867); *Memories of Childhood* (1865); *Pictures at an Exhibition (1874).

SONGS: Many solo songs and 3 song-cycles: *The Nursery* (7 songs) (1868–72); *Sunless* (6 songs) (1874); *Songs and Dances of Death (4 songs) (1875–7). (The famous *Song of the Flea dates from 1879.)

Mustel Organ. Kbd. 'cabinet organ' invented by V. Mustel (1815–90).

Muta (It., plural *mutano*). Change, e.g. of kettle-drum tuning. *Muta D in C* means Change tuning from D to C (no connection with the word 'mute'). Also used in connection with change of crook in brass instr.

Mutation Stop. Org. stop sounding not at normal or octave pitch, but at pitch of one of the non-octave harmonics. See *Quint, Twelfth, Seventeenth, Nineteenth, Flat Twenty-first*.

Mute. A mechanical device used to reduce the tonal vol. of an instr. and usually indicated by the term *con sordini*. (1) In bowed instr. a small clamp to be placed on the bridge. (2) In brass instr. a pear-shaped stopper to be pushed into the bell or, in the case of the hn., putting the hand in the bell. It is impossible to mute woodwind instr. (3) With the kettledrums muting was formerly effected by placing a cloth over the parchment heads but it is usual now to employ sponge-headed drumsticks instead. (4) In the pf. the sound is muted by the left (soft) pedal. The mute should not be confused with the damper.

Muti, Riccardo (*b* Naples, 1941). It. conductor. Studied Naples (pf.) and Milan (cond. with Votto). Cantelli Prize 1967. Opera début Florence 1966 in work by Paisiello. Salzburg Fest., 1971, Vienna 1973, CG début 1977 (*Aida*). Chief cond., (New) Philharmonia Orch. 1973–82. Art. dir., Florence Fest. from 1977. Prin. guest cond., Philadelphia Orch. from 1977, prin. cond. from 1981. Mus. dir. La Scala, Milan, from 1986.

Muzio, Claudia (*b* Pavia, 1889; *d* Rome, 1936). It. sop. Daughter of ass. stage manager at CG and NY Met. Studied Turin and Milan. Début Messina 1910 as Gilda. CG 1914, NY Met. 1916–22 and 1933–4, Chicago 1922–31. Created role of Giorgetta in Puccini's *Il Tabarro*, NY 1918. Notable interpreter of Violetta, Desdemona, and Tosca.

Myaskovsky, Nikolay (Yakovlevich) (*b* Novo-georgyevsk, 1881; *d* Moscow, 1950). Russ. composer. Studied with *Glière, Lyadov, and Rimsky-Korsakov. Prof. of comp. Moscow Cons., 1921–50, pupils incl. Kabalevsky, Khachaturian, and Shebalin. One of composers denounced by Soviet officials in 1948 for *'formalism'. Wrote 27 syms., the 1st in 1908, the last being perf. posthumously.

No. 19 is for military band. Also comp. symphonic poems *Nevermore* (after Poe's *The Raven*) and *Alastor* (after Shelley), sinfonietta, vn. conc. (1938), vc. conc. (1944–5), 13 str. qts. (No.1 1929–30, No. 13 1949), 9 pf. sonatas, and many songs.

My Country (Smetana). See *Má Vlast*.

Myers, Rollo (Hugh) (*b* Chislehurst, 1892; *d* Chichester, 1985). Eng. writer on mus. Studied Oxford Univ. and Paris. Mus. critic for *Times* then *Daily Telegraph* 1920–34. BBC 1935–44. British Council officer in Paris 1944–5. Ed. *The Chesterian* 1947. Author of books on 20th-cent. mus. generally and on Satie and Debussy in particular. Trans. Strauss-Rolland correspondence (London, 1968).

My Fair Lady. Musical version of G. B. Shaw's play *Pygmalion* (1912) with music by Frederick *Loewe and words by Alan Jay Lerner (*b* NY, 1918). F.p. NY 1956, London 1958, and has been in performance somewhere in the world almost ever since. Roles of Eliza Doolittle and Prof. Higgins created by Julie Andrews and Rex Harrison, the latter successfully employing a type of *Sprechstimme* for his songs. Film version 1964.

My Lady Nevells Booke (My Lady Nevill's Book). Coll. of 42 virginals pieces by Byrd transcr. in 1591 by John Baldwin of Windsor for the use of Lady Nevell, or Nevill, believed by Dr. E. H. *Fellowes to have been Rachel, wife of Sir Edward Nevill. Modern ed. by Hilda Andrews, 1926.

Mysliveček, Josef (*b* Ober-Sárka, 1737; *d* Rome, 1781). Bohemian composer. Studied Venice. His first opera *Medea* was a big success in Parma, 1764, followed by *Il Bellerofonte*, Naples 1767. Went to Vienna and Munich 1772. In 1773 he composed *La Clemenza di Tito* for Venice. Mozart admired his pf. sonatas and praised his oratorio *Abramo ed Isacco*, Munich 1777. Comp. 27 operas, 6 oratorios, and instr. works of all kinds.

Mysteries. See *Miracle Plays*.

Mystic Trumpeter, The. (1) Scena, Op. 18, by Holst for solo v. (usually sop.) and orch. to words by Whitman, comp. 1904, rev. 1912, f.p. 1905 (rev. version f.p. 1913).

(2) Setting of same text for vv. and orch. by Harty, 1913.

(3) Symphonic fantasy after Whitman for orch. by F. S. Converse, 1904.

N

Nabokov, Nicolai (Nicolas) (*b* Lubcha, nr. Minsk, 1903; *d* NY, 1978). Russ.-born composer (Amer. citizen from 1939). Studied in Yalta, 1913–20, and at Stuttgart Acad. of Mus., 1920–1, Berlin Hochschule für Musik, 1921–3, and Sorbonne, 1923–6. Lived in Paris and Ger. 1926–33. Ballet-oratorio *Ode* prod. by Diaghilev's ballet co., 1928. Settled in USA 1933, teaching at various colls. and univs. Worked for US Government in Berlin 1945–7; sec.-gen., Congress for Cultural Freedom 1951–66. Art. dir., Berlin Fest. of the Arts 1963–6. Prin. comps.:

OPERAS: *The Holy Devil* (lib. by S. Spender, 1958; rev. as *The Death of Rasputin*, 1959); *Love's Labour's Lost* (lib. by Auden and Kallman, 1970).
BALLETS: *Ode, or Meditation at Night on the Majesty of God, as revealed by Aurora Borealis* (ballet-oratorio for SATB, ch., and orch., 1928); *Union Pacific* (1933); *Vie de Polichinelle* (1934); *The Last Flower* (1941); *Don Quixote* (1964–5); *The Wanderer* (1966).
ORCH: *Symphonie lyrique*, No. 1 (1930), No. 2 (Biblical) (1940), No. 3 (A Prayer) (1967); symphonic suite, *The Last Flower* (1957); pf. conc. (1932), fl. conc. (1948), vc. conc. (1953), *Studies in Solitude* (1962); *Variations on a Theme by Tchaikovsky*, vc. and orch. (1968).
CHORAL: *Collectionneur d'échos*, cantata (1933); *Job*, cantata (1933); *The Return of Pushkin*, sop., orch. (1948); *La vita nuova*, sop., ten., orch. (1951); *4 Poems by Pasternak*, bar., orch. (1961); *6 Poems by Anna Akhmatova*, sop., orch. (1966).

Nabucco (Nabucodonosor, Nebuchadnezzar). Opera in 4 acts by Verdi to lib. by T. Solera written for and rejected by Nicolai. Comp. 1841. Prod. Milan 1842, London 1846, NY 1848.

Nach (Ger.). After, in the manner of, according to, towards, to. Hence *Nach und nach*, bit by bit; *nach Es*, now tune to E♭; etc.

Nachschlag (Ger., 'after stroke'). (1) The 2 notes that end the turn closing a shake. See *Trill*.
(2) Any ornamental note or notes added after another note; such notes decorate the following note, but take their time-value from the preceding note, and are therefore classified as an 'after-stroke'.

Nachspiel (Ger.). Afterplay. The equivalent of *postlude.

Nachtanz (Ger.). After-dance. Term applied to the 2nd of the two dance tunes which were commonly paired from the 15th to the 17th cents., i.e. Pavan and Galliard, Passamezzo and Saltarello, Sarabande and Gigue, etc. (The Saltarello, especially, is known by this name.)

Nachthorn (Ger.). Org. stop, same as *Cor de nuit*.

Nacht in Venedig, Eine (A Night in Venice). Operetta in 3 acts by Johann Strauss II to lib. by 'F. Zell' (Camillo Walzel) and Genée. Prod. Berlin 1883, NY 1889, London 1944.

Nachtmusik (Ger.). Night-music. A serenade, such as Mozart's Serenade in G, *Eine *kleine Nachtmusik*.

Nachtstück (Ger.). Night-piece. (1) The Ger. equivalent of *Nocturne.
(2) A piece which conveys the impressions or feelings of night, such as the central (3rd) movement of Bartók's *Concerto for Orchestra*.

Nacht und Träume (Night and Dreams). Song for v. and pf. by Schubert (D827) to poem by Matthäus von Collin (1779–1824), comp. 1825.

Naderman, François (Joseph) (*b* Paris, 1781; *d* Paris, 1835). Fr. harpist, pupil of Krumpholz. Harpist at Paris Opéra and from 1816 in royal chapel. Prof. of harp, Paris Cons., from 1825. Wrote 2 concs., 7 sonatas, and other pieces for harp.

Nail Fiddle (Nail Violin, Nail Harmonica). 18th-cent. instr. consisting of a semicircular board with nails, graduated in size, fastened around the curve: it was held in the left hand and bowed with the right.

Naldi, Romolo (*b* ? Bologna, *c*. 1550; *d* Rome, 1612). It. priest who lived in Rome and Bologna. Comp. book of madrigals (1589), book of motets (1600), and other pieces.

Namensfeier (Name Day). Concert ov. in C major by Beethoven, Op. 115, comp. 1814 for name-day festivities of Emperor Francis II of Austria. F.p. 1815, pubd. 1825.

Names of the Notes and Rest Values. The Eng. names of the longer notes are based upon the old Lat. names of the early Middle Ages. The earlier It. names are similar. The Fr. names stand alone as being purely descriptive of the appearances. The Ger. names are arithmetical, and the Amer. practically a trans. of them. The Amer. and Ger. names require no remembering, being logically descriptive of time-values. They are undoubtedly the best, and the Amer. names are now largely adopted in the Commonwealth.

NAMES OF THE NOTES AND REST VALUES
ENGLISH, ITALIAN, FRENCH, GERMAN, AND AMERICAN

	English	Italian	French	German	American
breve	breve	breve	carrée (square) or brève	Doppeltakt-note (double measure note)	double whole-note
semibreve	semibreve	semibreve	ronde (round)	Ganze Takt-note (whole measure note)	whole-note
minim	minim	minima or bianca (white)	blanche (white)	Halbe (half) or Halbenote or Halbe Taktnote	half-note
crotchet	crotchet	semiminima or nera (black)	noire (black)	Viertel (quarter)	quarter-note
quaver	quaver	croma	croche (hook)	Achtel (eighth)	eighth-note
semiquaver	semi-quaver	semi-croma	double-croche (double-hook)	Sechzehntel (sixteenth)	sixteenth-note
demisemiquaver	demisemi-quaver	biscroma	triple-croche (triple-hook)	Zweiund-dreissigstel (thirty-second)	thirty-second note
hemidemisemiquaver	hemidemi-semiquaver	semi-biscroma	quadruple-croche (quadruple-hook)	Vierund-sechzigs-tel (sixty-fourth)	sixty-fourth note

(The word 'Rest' is in It. *Pausa*; Fr. *Silence,* or *Pause*; Ger. *Pause*.)

Nänie (Ger., from Lat. *Naenia*, 'dirges'). Ode by Brahms, Op. 82, for ch. and orch., comp. 1880–1, to text by Schiller.

Nanino, Giovanni Bernardino (*b* Vallerano, *c*.1560; *d* Rome, 1623). It. composer, studied with his brother G. M. *Nanino. Maestro di cappella, S. Luigi de' Francesi, Rome, 1591–1608, and later at S. Lorenzo in Damaso. One of first to use org. in acc. to church comps. Wrote 3 books of madrigals (1588, 1599, 1612), 4 vols. of motets (1610–18), and other works.

Nanino, Giovanni Maria (*b* Tivoli, *c*.1545; *d* Rome, 1607). It. composer. Studied Rome and sang ten. at S. Maria Maggiore there, becoming maestro di cappella in 1567. Maestro di cappella S. Luigi de' Francesi, Rome 1575–7. Tenor in Sistine Chapel ch. from 1577, becoming maestro di cappella 1586. Est. Rome's first public sch. of mus. to be run by an Italian, being helped by his brother G. B. *Nanino and Palestrina. Wrote madrigals, motets, canzonets, etc. Regarded as one of greatest contrapuntists of his time.

Napoleon, Ode to (Schoenberg). See *Ode to Napoleon Buonaparte*.

Napoli, Jacopo (*b* Naples, 1911). It. composer. Studied at Cons. S. Pietro in Naples, of which he later became dir. 1954–62. Dir. Milan Cons. 1969–72, Rome Cons. 1972–6. Comp. comic operas incorporating Neapolitan songs. His *Masaniello* (1953) won a prize in La Scala, Milan, competition.

Napolitana (It.), **Napolitaine** (Fr.). A light and simple type of madrigal, presumably of Neapolitan origin, and much like the *Villanella*. During the 20th cent. a certain type of mus.-hall song also took the name 'Napolitana': it usually had verses in the minor and chs. in the major.

Nápravník, Eduard (Franzevich) (*b* Beišt, Bohemia, 1839; *d* Petrograd, 1916). Bohemian composer and cond. Studied Prague. Went to St Petersburg 1861 to conduct prince's orch., succeeding Lyadov as cond. of Imperial Russ. Opera 1869. Raised standards and cond. over 4,000 opera perfs., incl. f.ps. of Mussorgsky's *Boris Godunov*, Rimsky-Korsakov's *The Maid of Pskov*, and of 3 operas by Tchaikovsky. Cond. sym. concerts 1870–82. Wrote 4 operas, incl. *Francesca da Rimini* (1902), 4 syms., 3 str. qts., songs, etc.

Nardini, Pietro (*b* Leghorn, 1722; *d* Florence, 1793). It. violinist and composer. Studied at Padua with *Tartini. Solo violinist at court of Stuttgart, 1762–5; dir. of mus. to Duke of Tuscany 1770. Wrote 16 vn. concs., vn. sonatas, str. qts., etc.

Nares, James (*b* Stanwell, Middx., 1715; *d* London, 1783). Eng. organist and composer. Chorister in Chapel Royal with Pepusch. Organist, York Minster 1735–56, Chapel Royal 1756, master of the children 1757–80. Wrote 3 hpd. methods and comp. org. pieces, catches and glees, anthems, etc.

Narrator (It. *testo*, 'witness'). Singer or speaker in oratorios, cantatas, and sometimes operas who tells the basic story of the work, normally in recit. Among the first works to use a narrator was *Monteverdi's dramatic madrigal *Il combattimento di Tancredi e Clorinda* (1624). In the Passion settings of the 17th and 18th cents. the narrator is often called the Evangelist, e.g, in Bach's *St Matthew Passion*. Narrators are used in many 20th-cent. works, e.g. Stravinsky's *The Soldier's Tale*, Vaughan Williams's *An Oxford Elegy*, and Honegger's *Le Roi David*. The Male and Female Ch. in Britten's opera *The Rape of Lucretia* (1946) act as narrators.

Narváez, Luis de (*b* 1500; *d* c.1555). Sp. player of *vihuela* for which he wrote many pieces. Said to have introduced variation-form into Sp. mus.

Nascimbeni, Maria Francesca (*b* Ancona, 1657–8). It. composer, lived in Ascona. Pupil of Lazarini. Comp. madrigals, canzonas, and motets.

Nash, Heddle (*b* London, 1894; *d* London, 1961). Eng. ten. Chorister, Westminster Abbey. Studied London and Milan with Borgatti. Début Milan 1924 as Almaviva in Rossini's *Il barbiere di Siviglia*. Sang opera in London at Old Vic and SW from 1925. Sang with BNOC 1926–9; CG 1929–39, 1947–8; Glyndebourne 1934–8. Outstanding in Mozart and Rossini tenor roles, and a famous David in Wagner's *Die Meistersinger*. Also had successful career in oratorio, e.g. *Messiah*, and was one of finest interpreters of Elgar's *Gerontius*, which he recorded 1944.

Naso, nasetto (It.). Nose, little nose. The point of the vn. bow.

National Anthems. Songs or hymns adopted by certain nations to be perf. on official occasions and to represent them at int. events, e.g. when a competitor is awarded a medal in the Olympic Games. They are the mus. equivalent of the flag. Among the best-known (with author and composer, where both are known) are: Austria (since 1919): *Land der Berge, Land am Strome* (Preradović; Mozart, adapted from last part of *Kleine Freimaurer-Kantate*, K623); (before 1919): *Gott erhalte unsern Kaiser* (Haschka; J. Haydn, 1797); Belgium: *Après des Siècles d'esclavage,* known as *La *Brabançonne* (Dechet; F. van Campenhout, 1830); Chile: *Dulce patria, recibe los votos* (Pintado, rev. 1847 by Lillo; Carnicer, 1828); Denmark: *Kong Kristian* (Ewald; Rogart, 1779); E. Germany: *Auferstanden aus Ruinen* (Becher; Eisler, 1949); France: *Allons, enfants de la patrie,* known as *La *Marseillaise* (R. de Lisle 1792, words and mus.); Germany (before 1945): *Deutschland, Deutschland über Alles* (Fallersleben; J. Haydn); Great Britain: *God Save the King* (Queen); Greece: *Segnorizo apo tin Kopsi* (Solomós; Mantzaros, 1828); Israel: *Kol od balevav* (known as *Hatikvah* (N. H. Imber, 1878; mus. trad., arr. S. Cohen); Italy: *Fratelli d'Italia* (Mameli; Novaro, 1847); Netherlands: *Wilhelmus von Nassouwe* (Marnix, c.1570; mus. in A. Valerius, *Gedenck-Clanck*, 1626); Norway: *Ja, vi elsker dette landet* (Bjørnson, 1864; *Nordraak); Poland: *Jeszcze Polska nie zgineta* (Wybiski; Oginski, c.1795); USA: *The Star-spangled Banner* (F. Scott Key, 1814; mus. by John Stafford Smith comp. for *To Anacreon in Heaven*); USSR: *Gimn Sovetskovo Soyuza* (Mikhalov and Registan; Alexandrov, 1943); West Germany: *Einigkeit und Recht und Freiheit* (to Haydn's tune, since 1950).

National Broadcasting Company. See *NBC*.

National Conservatory of Music of America. Mus. coll. founded in NY and Washington in 1885 by Mrs Jeannette M. Thurber with charters from NY State and the US Congress. *Dvořák was dir., 1892–5. Tuition free until 1915.

National Federation of Music Societies. Brit. organization founded 1935 by Sir George *Dyson with general aim of improving and advancing education by promoting 'art and the practice and the public performance' of mus. About 1,100 mus. socs. belong to the Federation, which aids them financially.

National Gallery Concerts. Famous series of weekday lunchtime concerts given in Nat. Gallery, London, during World War II from 10 Oct. 1939 to 10 Apr. 1946 (a total of 1,698 concerts). Est. by Dame Myra *Hess, who herself played many times. Several works f.p. at these concerts. Proceeds (nearly £16,000) went to Musicians' Benevolent Fund.

Nationalism in Music. A mus. movement which began during the 19th cent. and was marked by emphasis on nat. elements in mus. such as folk-songs, folk dances, folk rhythms or on subjects for operas and symphonic poems which reflected nat. life or history. It burgeoned alongside political movements for independence, such as those which occurred in 1848, and as a reaction to the dominance of Ger. mus. Haydn was an early 'nationalist' in his use of folk-song in many works. Chopin, by his use of Polish dance rhythms and forms, e.g. the mazurka and the *Krakowiak*, was a nationalist and wrote a *Fantasia on Polish Airs* in 1828. In Russ., Glinka's *A Life for the Tsar* (1836) began the nationalist movement, which was sustained by Cui, Mussorgsky, Balakirev, Rimsky-Korsakov, etc. Liszt expressed the Hungarian spirit in his works, and this spirit was later intensified by Bartók and Kodály. Smetana, Dvořák, and Janáček were leading nationalists in Bohemia; in Norway, Grieg; Finland, Sibelius; Spain, Falla, Albéniz, and Granados; England, Holst and Vaughan Williams; USA, Copland, Gershwin, Ives, and Bernstein; Brazil, Villa-Lobos.

National Opera Studio. Training sch. for opera singers, providing one-year courses for advanced post-graduate trainees. Dir., Michael *Langdon. Established in 1978 as replacement for London Opera Centre, founded 1963 and administered in collab. with Royal Opera house. First dir. was H. *Procter-Gregg, succeeded in 1964 by James *Robertson. The Centre took over the work of the National Sch. of Opera, directed since 1948 by Joan *Cross and Anne Wood.

National Symphony Orchestra. Amer. orch. founded in Washington D.C., 1931 by Hans Kindler, who was cond. until 1948, when Howard Mitchell succeeded him. In 1970 Mitchell was succeeded by Antal Dorati. In 1977 *Rostropovich was appointed cond. Since 1971 concerts given in Kennedy Center for the Performing Arts.

National Training School of Music. Mus. coll. founded in Kensington, London, 1873 (although the idea originated with Prince Albert, who died in 1861). Opened 1876, with Sullivan as prin., until succeeded by Stainer in 1881. Absorbed in 1882 by *Royal College of Music, which opened 1883.

National Youth Orchestra of Great Britain. Sym. orch. for children aged between 13 and 19 founded in 1947 by Ruth Railton (now Dame Ruth King). Assembled in Bath 1947 under conductorship of Reginald Jacques. Players selected by audition, the orch. assembling in school holidays for rehearsal and study under guest cond. Very high standard achieved and many players have 'graduated' into leading sym. orchs.

Nativité du Seigneur, La (The Birth of the Saviour). 9 meditations in 4 books for organ by *Messiaen, comp. 1935.

Natural. (1) A note that is neither raised ('sharpened') nor lowered ('flattened').

(2) The sign ♮, which, after a note has been raised by a sharp or double-sharp, or lowered by a flat

or double-flat, restores it to its orig. pitch. After a double-sharp or double-flat the change to a single one is sometimes indicated ♮♯ or ♮♭ (at other times by the single accidental).

(3) Type of *harmonic in str.-playing.

Naturale (It.). Natural. Direction to perf. to return to a natural style after performing in some unusual way, e.g. falsetto, or muted.

Natural Harmonics. *Harmonics produced from an open str., as distinct from artificial harmonics produced from a stopped str.

Natural Keys. Keys with no sharp or flat in the signature, i.e. C major and A minor.

Natural Trumpet (Ger. *Naturtrompete*). A tpt. without *crooks which can produce only notes of the harmonic series of its fundamental note. From 17th cent. to late in the 19th, crooks were used, i.e. additional lengths of tubing which lowered the pitch of the fundamental note and thus of the whole harmonic series. However, crooks could not be very quickly changed, removed, or inserted. In his *Pastoral Symphony* (1921), *Vaughan Williams requires use of the natural tpt.

Nature, Life, and Love. Cycle of ovs. by Dvořák, comprising *Amid Nature* (V přírodě), *Carneval* (Karneval), and *Othello*, comp. 1891–2.

Natürlich (Ger.). Natural (in same sense as given under *Naturale*).

Naumann, Johann Gottlieb (b Blasewitz, Dresden, 1741; d Dresden, 1801). Ger. composer. Studied in It. with Tartini and Martini. Court composer of sacred mus., Dresden, 1764. In It. 1765–8 when he wrote several operas incl. *La Clemenza di Tito* (1769) and *Armida* (1773). Kapellmeister, Dresden 1776. Went to Stockholm 1777 to reform Court orch. and to conduct opera. Was guest opera cond. and comp., Copenhagen, 1785–6, returning to Dresden as Oberkapellmeister. Comp. 24 operas, 13 oratorios, 21 masses, 18 syms., chamber mus., etc. Comp. so-called 'Dresden Amen', from his Threefold Amen.

Navarra, André (b Biarritz, 1911). Fr. cellist. Studied Toulouse and Paris Cons. and privately. Played in str. qt. 1929–35. Début as soloist Paris, 1931. Eng. début 1950 Cheltenham in Elgar conc. with Barbirolli. World tours as soloist with orch. Recorded Elgar conc. with Barbirolli 1957. Prof. of vc., Paris Cons., from 1949.

Navarraise, La (The Girl from Navarre). Opera (lyric episode) in 2 acts by Massenet to lib. by Jules Claretie and Henri Cain. Prod. CG 1894, Paris 1895, NY Met. 1895.

Naylor, Bernard (b Cambridge, 1907; d England, 1986). Eng. composer, cond., and organist, son of E. W. *Naylor. Studied RCM with Vaughan Williams and Holst. Cond. Winnipeg Phil. Orch., 1932–6. Organist, Queen's Coll., Oxford, 1936–9.

Founder-cond. Little Sym. Orch., Montreal, 1942–7. Lecturer, Oxford Univ. 1950–2, Reading 1953–9. Settled in Canada 1959. Composer of choral and vocal works, incl. *Sonnets from the Portuguese* (E. B. Browning) for v. and str. qt. His *Stabat Mater* was perf. at 3 Choirs Fest. 1961. The 9 *Motets* (1952) are a cycle for the 9 major church festivals.

Naylor, Edward (Woodall) (*b* Scarborough, 1867; *d* Cambridge, 1934). Eng. organist, composer, and musicologist. Studied RCM. Held several org. posts in London. Wrote church mus. and songs. Opera *The Angelus* won Ricordi prize for Eng. opera (prod. CG 1909, revived 1921). Books incl. *Shakespeare and Music* (1896, rev. 1931) and analysis of *Fitzwilliam Virginal Book* (1905).

NBC Symphony Orchestra. Orch. created in NY in 1937 by the NBC specially for Toscanini, who had just left the NY P.O. Made many recordings. When Toscanini retired in 1954, orch. was disbanded by the NBC but continued for another decade as co-operative enterprise under name 'Symphony of the Air'.

NBC Television Opera. Opera co. formed by NBC in NY in 1949 with Peter Herman Adler as mus. dir. Gave first Amer. perfs. of Britten's *Billy Budd* and Prokofiev's *War and Peace*. Commissioned Menotti's *Amahl and the Night Visitors* and gave f.p. of Martinů's *The Marriage*. Has toured in over 50 Amer. cities.

Neaman, Yfrah (*b* Sidon, Lebanon, 1923). Lebanese-born violinist. Studied Paris Cons. Début Paris 1939. Settled in Eng. as base for int. career. Head of Str., GSM.

Neapolitan School. Term applied, with little real justification, to 18th-cent. school of comp. said to have originated in Naples or been cultivated by composers who studied there. Among these were A. Scarlatti, Porpora, Pergolesi, Jommelli, Anfossi, Piccinni, Paisiello, and Cimarosa, most of whom were active outside Naples and It.

Neapolitan Sixth. A chromatic chord. It is a major common chord on the flattened supertonic in its 1st inversion e.g. in key C it comprises F–A♭–D♭. Reason for its name is unknown, since it occurs in 17th-cent. mus. before the so-called Neapolitan sch. existed, e.g. in mus. by Carissimi, Corelli, and Purcell (in *King Arthur*).

Neary, Martin (Gerard James) (*b* London, 1940). Eng. organist, harpsichordist, and cond. Studied Cambridge Univ. Organist, St Margaret's, Westminster, 1965–71, Winchester Cath. from 1972. Prof. of org. TCL from 1963. Ed. of org. works.

Neate, Charles (*b* London, 1784; *d* Brighton, 1877). Eng. pianist and composer. Pupil of John Field. Début CG 1800. Founder-member of Phil. Soc., London, 1813. Visited Beethoven in Vienna, 1815. First to play Beethoven's 5th ('Emperor')

pf. conc. in London, at Philharmonic Soc. concert, 8 May 1820. Wrote pf. sonatas.

Nebuchadnezzar (Verdi). See *Nabucco*.

Neck. The projecting portion of a str. instr. such as a vn. or lute, which carries the fingerboard and terminates in the peg-box.

Nedbal, Oskar (*b* Tabor, 1874; *d* Zagreb, 1930). Cz. composer, cond., and violist. Pupil of Dvořák. Member of Bohemian Str. Qt. 1891–1906. Cond. Czech P.O. 1896–1906, taking it to London 1902, then Tonkünstler Orch., Vienna, 1906–19. Dir., Bratislava Opera from 1923. Wrote opera, operettas, ballets.

Neefe, Christian Gottlob (*b* Chemnitz, 1748; *d* Dessau, 1798). Ger. musician who taught *Beethoven at Bonn. Studied under Hiller. Court org., Bonn, 1782, becoming Kapellmeister 1783. Cond. opera at Dessau 1796. Wrote 8 operas, concs., church mus., etc.

Neel, (Louis) **Boyd** (*b* Blackheath, 1905; *d* Toronto, 1981). Eng. cond. Qualified as naval officer and doctor of medicine, but turned to mus., founding Boyd Neel Str. Orch. 1933 which rapidly achieved an int. reputation for its perfs. of Eng. and other mus. for str., notably of the baroque era, which was at that time rarely played with chamber forces. Played at Salzburg Fest. 1937, giving f.p. of Britten's specially commissioned *Variations on a Theme of Frank Bridge*. Cond. Robert Mayer Children's Concerts 1946–52. Dean of Toronto Royal Cons., 1953–70. Boyd Neel Orch. renamed Philomusica of London 1957. C.B.E. 1953.

Negro Spiritual. See *Spiritual*.

Neidlinger, Gustav (*b* Mainz, 1912). Ger. bass-bar. Studied Frankfurt. Opera début Mainz 1931. Hamburg Opera 1936–50, Stuttgart Opera from 1950. Bayreuth Fest. 1952–75. London début 1955, CG 1963, NY Met. 1972 (Alberich). Renowned for singing of Alberich, Pizarro, and similar roles.

Nell. Poem by Lecomte de Lisle set for v. and pf. by Fauré (Op. 18 No. 1, 1880).

Nelson. Opera in 3 acts by Lennox *Berkeley to lib. by Alan Pryce-Jones. Prod. London (SW) 1954.

Nelson Mass (*Nelsonmesse*). Nickname for Haydn's Mass No. 9 in D minor (*Missa in angustiis*) (Mass in time of peril), comp. 1798. A legend says that the work celebrates Nelson's victory at Aboukir Bay in 1798, another that Nelson heard it perf. at Eisenstadt in 1800.

Nelsova, Zara (*b* Winnipeg, 1917). Canadian-born (later naturalized Amer.) cellist. Studied in London and with Feuermann and Casals. Début at age 12 with LSO, cond. Sargent. Amer. début, NY 1942. Worldwide tours. On staff Juilliard

Sch., NY, from 1962. Gave f.p. of Hugh Wood's vc. conc., London 1969.

Nenia (It. 'Dirge'). In Ancient Rome, a funeral song in praise of the dead. Schiller's *Nänie* were set by Goetz (1874), Brahms (1880–1), and Orff (1956). Term has also been used by Birtwistle in his *Nenia on the death of Orpheus* (1970).

Nenna, Pomponio (*b* Bari, *c*.1550; *d* Rome, 1613). It. composer influenced by *Gesualdo. Pubd. several books of madrigals, for 5 vv. 1582–1608 and 1618 (posth.), for 4 vv. 1613. Active mainly in Naples and Rome.

Neo-Bechstein Piano. Semi-elec. pf. dating from 1931, based on research by W. Nernst of Berlin. Str. are set in vibration by hammers, but blow required is very light ($\frac{1}{20}$ that given on ordinary pf). No sound-board, the vibrations being amplified through a loudspeaker. Vol. or tone controlled by pedal acting on the amplifier.

Neo-Classicism. Term applied to 20th-cent. mus. trend which developed in the 1920s, when several composers wrote works in 17th- and 18-cent. forms and styles as a reaction against the excessive orchestration of the late 19th-cent. romantics. Prokofiev's *Classical Symphony* (1916–17) and R. Strauss's *Ariadne auf Naxos* (1912) can be claimed as neo-classical, but the movement began in earnest with Stravinsky *(Capriccio* for pf. and wind, pf. conc., *Pulcinella*, vn. conc., *Oedipus Rex*, etc.) and Hindemith. In Eng. Vaughan Williams's vn. conc. (orig. *Concerto Accademico*) of 1925 was neo-classical in style, though, because for most composers the model was Bach, neo-baroque might be a more accurate description. (Prokofiev's *Classical Symphony*, being a pastiche of Haydn, is truly named.)

Nera (It.). Black. Crotchet or Quarter-note.

Neri, Massimiliano (*b* ? Brescia, ?1615; *d* Bonn, 1666). It. composer. Organist at St Mark's, Venice 1644–64. Court organist, Cologne, 1664. Wrote motets, *Sonate e canzone* (1644), and instr. sonatas (1651).

Nerone (Nero). (1) Opera in 4 acts by *Boito to his own lib. Begun in 1877 and still incomplete when Boito died in 1918. Completed by Toscanini, Tommasini, and Smareglia and prod. Milan 1924, Rome 1928.
  (2) Opera in 3 acts by Mascagni to lib. by Targioni-Tozzetti after comedy by P. Cossa (1872). Prod. Milan 1935.

Neruda, Wilma (Wilhelmina) (*b* Brno, 1839; *d* Berlin, 1911). Bohem. violinist. Début Vienna 1846. Toured Ger. as prodigy; London début 1849. Many tours of Europe and Russia. Married the Swed. composer *Norman 1864, playing under name Norman-Neruda. Regular visitor to Eng. after 1869. In 1888 married Sir Charles *Hallé with whom she gave many recitals, touring S. Africa and Australia. Retired 1895

when Hallé died, but resumed playing 1898, touring USA 1899. Lived in Berlin from 1900.

Nesbet, John (*d* ? 1488). Eng. composer of church mus. and songs, about whom little is known except that he was a member of Christ Church Cathedral Priory, Canterbury, in the 1470s.

Nessler, Victor (*b* Baldenheim, 1841; *d* Strasbourg, 1890). Ger. composer and cond. Studied theology, but success of his opera *Fleurette* (1864) decided him on wholly mus. career. Ch. master, Leipzig, 1870–9, becoming cond. at Caroltheater there 1879. Had great success with operas *Der Rattenfänger von Hameln* (The Pied Piper of Hamlin) (1879) and *Der Trompeter von Säckingen* (1884).

Nesterenko, Evgeny (*b* Moscow, 1938). Russ. bass. Studied Leningrad 1963 (début as Gremin in *Eugene Onegin*). Among finest Russ. basses, a notable Boris, and also excellent in It. repertory. Joined Bolshoy Opera, Moscow, 1971. Sang Boris with Bolshoy company in Milan 1973, Vienna 1974, NY Met. 1975. Début at CG 1978 (Don Basilio). Noted interpreter of Shostakovich's 14th Sym.

Neues vom Tage (News of the Day). Comic opera in 3 parts by Hindemith to lib. by Marcellus Schiffer. Comp. 1928–9. Prod. Berlin 1929. Rev. (mus. and text) by Hindemith 1953, prod. Naples 1954, Cologne 1956, Santa Fe (in Eng.) 1961.

Neukomm, Sigismund, Chevalier von (*b* Salzburg, 1778; *d* Paris, 1858). Austrian composer. Chorister, Salzburg Cath. 1788–93. Studied under Michael and Joseph Haydn. Kapellmeister at St Petersburg Ger. Th. 1806. Settled in Paris 1809, entering service of Talleyrand. Lived in Brazil 1816–21, thereafter in Paris and London. Wrote around 1,300 works, all now forgotten, in many forms.

Neumann, Angelo (*b* Vienna, 1838; *d* Prague, 1910). Austrian ten. and impresario. Début 1859. Sang at Vienna Court Opera 1862–76. Man. of Leipzig Opera 1876–82, Bremen Opera 1882–5, Prague Landestheater 1885–1910 (among conds. he engaged there was Mahler). Formed touring co. based on Leipzig to give Wagner's operas, especially *Der Ring des Nibelungen*, in London, Paris, Rome, St Petersburg, etc.

Neumann, František (*b* Přerov, 1874; *d* Brno, 1929). Cz. conductor and composer. Studied at Leipzig Cons. Worked in various Ger. and Cz. opera houses 1903–19. On *Janáček's recommendation, appointed cond. Brno Nat. Th. 1919–29. Collab. closely with Janáček and cond. f.ps. of *Káťa Kabanová* (1921), *The Cunning Little Vixen* (1924), *Šárka* (1925), and *The Makropulos Affair* (1926), also f.ps. of operas by Novák and Ostrčil. His 8 operas incl. *Die Brautwerbung* (Linz, 1901),

Liebelei (Frankfurt, 1910), *Herbststurm* (Berlin, 1919), and *Beatrice Caracci* (Brno, 1922).

Neumann, Václav (*b* Prague, 1920). Cz. cond. and violist. Studied Prague Cons. Violist in Smetana Qt. and Cz. P.O. Deputy cond. Cz. P.O. 1948. Cond. Prague S.O. 1956–63, Prague P.O. 1963–4, Komische Oper, Berlin, 1956–64, Leipzig Gewandhaus Orch. and Leipzig Opera 1964–7; chief cond. Czech P.O. from 1968. Mus. dir. Stuttgart Opera 1970–3. Cond. Felsenstein's famous Berlin production of Janáček's *The Cunning Little Vixen*, 1956.

Neum(e)s (from Gr. *neuma*, 'gesture' or 'sigh'). System of mus. notation from 7th to 14th cents. Orig. generating forms were grave and acute accents with a horizontal line, but developed into elaborate system for plainsong manuals of the church. Gave precise indication of pitch, but at first were merely approximate indications to singer of shape of the melody.

Neusidler, Hans (*b* Pressburg, 1508; *d* Nuremberg, 1563). Ger. lutenist and composer of dances and songs for lute.

Nevada, Mignon (*b* Paris, 1886; *d* Long Melford, 1971). Eng. sop., daughter of Amer. sop. Emma Nevada (1859–1940) with whom she studied. Opera début Rome 1907 as Rosina in *Il barbiere di Siviglia*, CG 1910 with Beecham. Also sang in Milan, Paris, and other opera houses.

Neveu, Ginette (*b* Paris, 1919; *d* San Miguel, Azores, in air crash, 1949). Fr. violinist. Studied Paris Cons. and with Enescu and Carl Flesch. Début with Paris Colonne Orch. 1926. Won Wieniawski Prize, Warsaw Int. Competition, 1935. Amer. début 1937, Eng. 1945. Brilliant interpreter of Sibelius conc.

Nevin, Ethelbert Woodbridge (*b* Edgeworth, Penn., 1862; *d* New Haven, Conn., 1901). Amer. composer and pianist. Studied Pittsburgh, Dresden, and Berlin. Appeared as soloist in concs. in Pittsburgh and wrote popular songs and pf. pieces despite intermittent ill-health. *Narcissus* (1891) and *The Rosary* (1898) were his most popular pf. piece and song respectively, the latter achieving a sale of 6 million copies in 30 years.

New England Conservatory of Music. Mus. sch. in Boston, Mass., founded in Feb. 1867 by Eben Tourjée (*b* Warwick, R.I., 1834; *d* Boston, Mass., 1891) in assoc. with Robert Goldbeck. Within 10 years it was largest mus. sch. in the USA with over 14,000 graduates. After Tourjée, dirs. were Carl Faelton (1891–7), George W. Chadwick (1897–1931), Wallace Goodrich (1931–42), Harrison Keller (1942–66), and Gunther Schuller from 1966. Cons. has Afro-Amer. dept. and courses in jazz and ragtime. Members of Boston S.O. are among teaching staff.

New England Holidays. Sym. (unnumbered) by *Ives for orch., comp. 1904–13. Movements entitled 1. *Washington's Birthday*. 2. *Decoration Day*. 3. *Fourth of July*. 4. *Thanksgiving and/or Forefathers' Day* (with ch.).

Newlin, Dika (*b* Portland, Oregon, 1923). Amer. musicologist and composer. Studied U.C.L.A. and Columbia Univ., and privately with *Sessions and *Schoenberg. Est. mus. dept. at Drew Univ., Madison, NJ, 1952. Prof. of mus., North Texas State Univ. from 1965. Has written on Mahler, Bruckner, and Schoenberg. Trans. Schoenberg's *Style and Idea* (1950). Composer of 12-note chamber mus.

Newman, Ernest (orig. William Roberts) (*b* Everton, 1868; *d* Tadworth, 1959). Eng. mus. critic and author. Began career as bank employee, writing on economics and mus. Wrote first book, *Gluck and the Opera*, in 1895 and *A Study of Wagner* in 1899. On staff Birmingham Midland Institute of Mus. 1903–5. Mus. critic *Manchester Guardian* 1905–6, *Birmingham Post* 1906–19, *Observer* 1919–20, *Sunday Times* 1920–58. Authority on Wagner, of whom he wrote 4-vol. biography (1928–47) in addition to *Wagner as Man and Artist* (1914, rev. 1924), *Fact and Fiction about Wagner* (1931), and *Wagner Nights* (1949). Also wrote studies of Elgar (1906), Wolf (1907), and Strauss (1908); *The Unconscious Beethoven* (1927), *The Man Liszt* (1934), *Opera Nights* (1943), *Wagner Nights* (1949), *More Opera Nights* (1954), and other books. Trans. most of Wagner's libs., incl. perf. versions of *Tannhäuser* and *Die Meistersinger*.

Newman, Robert (*b* 1859; *d* London, 1926). Eng. bass and impresario. Studied RAM. After singing career, became man. of Queen's Hall, London, 1893 and started Promenade concerts in assoc. with Henry J. *Wood in 1895.

Newmarch, Rosa (Harriet) (*née* Jeaffreson) (*b* Leamington, 1857; *d* Worthing, 1940). Eng. writer on mus. Went to Russia in 1897, working under Stasov at Imperial Public Library and meeting leading Russ. composers. On return to Eng. did much to spread the fame of these composers and from 1908 to 1927 wrote programme notes for the Promenade Concerts. Wrote several books and translated libs. of Russ. operas. Also early advocate of Sibelius and Janáček (whose *Sinfonietta*, 1926, is ded. to her).

New Music (Ger. *Neue Musik*). Term which periodically recurs in the history of mus., e.g. (1) *Ars nova* of 14th cent.

(2) *Nuove musiche* of 17th cent. when new monodic style transformed the art. In 1602 G. Caccini pubd. *Le nuove musiche* (The New Musics) containing arias and madrigals with monodic recitative.

(3) The mus. of Liszt, Wagner, and their followers from *c.*1850, compared with the 'traditional' Brahms.

(4) In 20th cent., atonal and elec. mus.

New Opera Company. Formed in Cambridge in late 1950s as part-amateur, part-professional co., began to give short London seasons at SW in 1957, making a speciality of rare, modern, or Eng. operas. Among works they have staged are Benjamin's *A Tale of Two Cities,* Vaughan Williams's *Sir John in Love,* Egk's *Der Revisor,* Dallapiccola's *Il prigioniero,* Schoenberg's *Erwartung,* Prokofiev's *Love for 3 Oranges,* Henze's *Boulevard Solitude,* Szymanowski's *King Roger,* Martinů's *Julietta,* and Shostakovich's *The Nose.*

New Philharmonia Orchestra. See *Philharmonia Orchestra.*

News of the Day (Hindemith). See *Neues vom Tage.*

New Symphony Orchestra. London orch. founded 1905. Beecham became cond. 1906, succeeded by Landon Ronald in 1908. In 1920 name changed to Royal Albert Hall Orch., which later disbanded.

Newton, Ivor (*b* London, 1892; *d* Bromley, 1981). Eng. pianist, principally accompanist. Worked with many celebrated artists, e.g. Melba, Gerhardt, Gigli, McCormack, Flagstad, Chaliapin, Casals, Ysaÿe, Menuhin, etc. C.B.E. 1973.

New World, From the (*Z nového svéta*). Subtitle given by Dvořák to his 9th (5th in the old numbering) Sym. in E minor, Op. 95, comp. 1893 and f.p. NY Dec. 1893 cond. Anton Seidl. Some themes are regarded as in the spirit of Amer. Negro folk tunes but none is directly quoted, though the resemblance of one to 'Swing low, sweet chariot' is often noticed. On the other hand, the Bohemian element is equally strong. The main theme of the *largo* has been made into a Negro spiritual to the words 'Goin' Home'. Dvořák himself hoped to write an opera based on Longfellow's *Hiawatha* and he said that the *largo* was a study for it.

New York City Opera. Opera co. founded 1943 as part of NY City Center of Music and Drama. 1st prod. in Feb. 1944, Laszlo Halász being mus. dir. until 1951, succeeded by Joseph Rosenstock 1952–5, Erich Leinsdorf 1956, Julius Rudel 1957–79, Beverly *Sills from 1979. Moved to NY State Theatre in Lincoln Center 1966. Follows adventurous policy, presenting unusual and modern operas. Has nurtured many fine singers, best known of whom are the sop. Beverly Sills and the ten. Placido Domingo.

New York Philharmonic Orchestra. America's oldest sym. orch., founded 1842 as Phil. Soc. of NY. Up to 1892 the conds. incl. Leopold Damrosch and Theodore Thomas. Since then the usual rule has been for there to be a 'permanent' or prin. cond. with some guest conds., the post being one of the most highly prized in the mus. world: 1891–8, Anton Seidl; 1898–1902, Emil Paur; 1902–3, Walter Damrosch; 1903–6, guest cond.

incl. Wood, Weingartner, R. Strauss, and F. Steinbach; 1906–9, Vasily Safonov; 1909–11, Gustav Mahler; 1911–21, Josef Stransky; 1921–9, Willem Mengelberg; 1928–36, Arturo Toscanini (jointly with Mengelberg 1928–9); 1936–42, John Barbirolli; 1943–7, Artur Rodzinski; 1947–9, Bruno Walter; 1949–50, Leopold Stokowski and Dimitri Mitropoulos; 1950–8, Dimitri Mitropoulos; 1958–69, Leonard Bernstein; 1971–7, Pierre Boulez; 1978– , Zubin Mehta. Bernstein in 1969 became cond. laureate for life. The orch. merged in 1928 with the *New York Symphony Orchestra, becoming the Philharmonic-Symphony Orchestra of New York, but is now simply the NY P.O.

New York Symphony Orchestra. Founded by Leopold Damrosch, 1878, who was cond. until his death in 1885. Succeeded by his son Walter until merger with *New York Philharmonic Orchestra in 1928.

Nicholls, Agnes (*b* Cheltenham, 1877; *d* London, 1959). Eng. sop. Studied RCM 1894–7. Opera début London 1895 at Purcell's *Dido.* CG, 1901–24, with Denhof, Beecham, and BNOC cos. Sang Sieglinde in *Die Walküre* and Brünnhilde in *Siegfried* in first Eng. *Ring* at CG in 1908 under Richter. Successful career in oratorio, singing in f.p. of Elgar works. Wife of cond. Sir Hamilton *Harty.

Nicholson, George (*b* Durham, 1949). Eng. composer and pianist. Studied at York Univ. with Rands and Blake. Has had several comps. commissioned by BBC and by various contemporary mus. groups. Member of chamber group Nomos. Works incl.:

THEATRE: *The Arrival of the Poet in the City,* melodrama for actor and 7 instr. (1982–3).
ORCH: *Recycle,* 11 instr. (1975—6); *1132* (1976); *The Convergence of the Twain,* chamber orch. (1978); *Chamber Concerto,* 13 players (1979–80).
VOCAL: *Colloque sentimental,* sop., hp. (1976); *Rondeau,* sop. (1977); *Settings,* sop., pf. (1977); *Hallel,* sop., org. (1979); *Alla Luna,* sop., cl., pf. (1981); *Aubade,* sop., 5 players (1981).
CHAMBER MUSIC: *Overture,* 7 wind instr. (1976); str. qt. (1976–7); brass quintet (1977); *The Seventh Seal,* va. (1977); *Nodus,* cl., pf. (1978); *Winter Music,* cl., hp., perc. (1978); *N'est-ce pas ...?,* vn. (1979); *Slide Show,* tb. (1981); *So Low,* db. (1981); *Ancient Lights,* fl., cl., bass cl., vn., va., vc., pf. (1982); *Movements,* 7 instr. (1982–3); pf. sonata (1983).

Nicholson (Nicolson), **Richard** (*b c.*1570; *d* Oxford, 1639). Eng. composer and organist. Organist and choirmaster Magdalen Coll., Oxford. First prof. of mus., Oxford Univ., 1626. Wrote madrigals, motets, and *Joan, quoth John, when will it be?* a madrigal cycle for 3 vv. which has been called the first song-cycle. Contrib. 5-part madrigal *Sing shepherds all* to The *Triumphs of Oriana.*

Nicholson, (Sir) **Sydney** (Hugo) (*b* London, 1875; *d* Ashford, Kent, 1947). Eng. organist and composer. Organist, Carlisle Cath. 1904–8, Manchester Cath. 1908–18, Westminster Abbey 1918–27. Founder-dir. Sch. of Eng. Church Mus., 1927, which became *Royal School of Church Music 1945. Wrote church mus. and org. pieces. Knighted 1938.

Nicodé, Jean Louis (*b* Jerczik, 1853; *d* Lange-brück, 1919). Ger. composer, cond., and pianist. Studied Berlin. Prof. Dresden Royal Cons. 1878–85, cond. Dresden Phil. 1885–8. Concentrated on comp. after 1900 and wrote sym. ode in 6 movements *Das Meer* (1889), *Gloria! ein Sturm und Sonnenlied*, ch. and orch. (1905), and other works.

Nicolai, (Karl) **Otto** (Ehrenfried) (*b* Königsberg, 1810; *d* Berlin, 1849). Ger. composer and cond. Studied in Berlin and Rome. Kapellmeister and singing master of Kärntnerthor Th., Vienna, 1837, returning to Rome 1838, where he comp. several operas in It. style. Kapellmeister, Vienna Court Opera 1841–7, founding Phil. concerts 1842. Credited with being first to insert Beethoven's *Leonora No. 3* ov. into *Fidelio* as entr'acte (1841). Dir., Berlin Opera 1847, where his most successful opera, *Die *Lustigen Weiber von Windsor,* was prod. 2 months before his death. Also wrote 2 syms., pf. conc., str. qt., etc.

Nicolini (Nicolino Grimaldi) (*b* Naples, 1673; *d* Naples, 1732). It. castrato cont. Sang in It. 1694–1708, then went to London where he achieved enormous success 1708–11 and 1714–18. Sang in many of Handel's operas and created roles of Rinaldo and Amadigi.

Niedermeyer, (Abraham) **Louis** (*b* Nyon, Switz., 1802; *d* Paris, 1861). Swiss composer, pupil of Moscheles in Vienna and of Zingarelli in Naples. Wrote unsuccessful operas for Paris. Took over sch. of church mus. now known as École Niedermeyer. Wrote mass and other religious works.

Niederschlag (Ger.). (1) Down-beat (up-beat being *Aufschlag).
(2) In str. playing, down-stroke of the bow (also called *Niederstrich).

Nielsen, Carl (August) (*b* Nørre-Lyndelse, 1865; *d* Copenhagen, 1931). Danish composer, violinist, and cond. Showed mus. talent as child and became military trumpeter at 14 at Odense. Formed str. qt. in 1882. Entered Royal Cons., Copenhagen, 1884, studying theory with Rosenhoff and mus. history with Gade. Joined th. orch. as violinist, 1886, and was violinist in Royal Opera orch. 1889–1905. Made some appearances as cond., and became a cond. at Royal Th., Copenhagen, 1908–14. Conducted Copenhagen Mus. Soc. 1915–27. On staff of Royal Danish Cons. from 1915, becoming dir. 1931. Visited Berlin 1921, London 1923, and Paris 1926 to conduct his own works.

For many years his mus. was little known outside Denmark, but after World War II the power and originality of his syms. spread to other countries. The 5th Sym. contains an early aleatory feature, when the side-drummer is instructed to improvise so as to drown the rest of the orch. His First Sym. of 1891–2 is one of earliest examples of 'progressive tonality', i.e. it begins in one key and ends in another. Prin. comps.:

OPERAS: *Saul and David* (1898–1901); *Maskarade (1906).

INCIDENTAL MUSIC: *Snefrid* (1893); *Hr. Oluf han rider* (Master Oluf Rides) (1906); *Ebbe Skammelsen* (1925); *Amor og Digterer* (Love and the Poet) (1931).

ORCH: Syms.: No. 1 in G minor (1891–2), No. 2 (*The *Four Temperaments*) (1901–2), No. 3 (*Sinfonia espansiva*) with sop. and bar. (1910–11), No. 4 (*Det uudslukkelige*, The *Inextinguishable) (1915–16), No. 5 (1921–22), No. 6 (*Sinfonia semplice*) (1924–5); *Little Suite* for str. (1888); *Helios,* ov. (1903); *The Dream of Gunnar* (Saga-Drøm) (1908); vn. conc. (1911); *Franz Neruda in memoriam,* speaker, orch. (1918); *Pan and Syrinx,* pastorale (1917); *7 Pieces from 'Aladdin'* (1918–19); fl. conc. (1926); *En Fantasirejse til Faerøerne* (An Imaginary Trip to the Faroe Islands), rhapsody (1927); cl. conc. (1928).

CHORAL: *Hymnus Amoris,* sop., ten., bar., bass, children's ch., male ch., mixed ch., and orch. (1896); *Søvnen* (Sleep), ch. and orch. (1904); *Fynsk Foraar* (Springtime on Fyn), sop., ten., bass-bar., ch., and orch. (1921); *Hyldest til Holberg* (Homage to Holberg), solo vv., ch., orch. (1922); *Hymne til Kunsten* (Hymn to Art), sop., ten., ch., wind instr. (1929); *3 Motets,* unacc. ch. (1929); various occasional cantatas, incl. one for the 50th anniv. of Danish Cremation Union (1931).

CHAMBER MUSIC: Str. Qts.: in D minor (1882–3), in F (1887), No. 1 in G minor (1888), No. 2 in F minor (1890), No. 3 in Eb (1898), No. 4 in F (1906); Str. Quintet in G (1888), Wind Quintet (1922); Vn. sonatas: in G (1881–2), No. 1 in A (1895), No. 2 (1912); *Ved en ung Kunstners Baare* (At the bier of a young artist), str. qt. and db. (1910); *Prelude and Theme with Variations,* solo vn. (1923); *Serenata in vano,* cl., bn., hn., vc., db. (1914).

PIANO: *2 Characteristic Pieces* (c.1882–3); *5 Pieces* (1890); *Symphonic Suite* (1894); *6 Humoresque-Bagatelles* (1894–7); *Festive Prelude to the New Century* (1899); *Chaconne* (1916); *Theme with Variations* (1916); *Suite* (1919); *Tre Klaverstykker* (3 Pieces) (1928); *Piano Music for Young and Old,* 24 5-finger pieces (1930).

VOICE AND PIANO: *5 Poems by J. P. Jacobsen* (1891); *6 Songs and Verses by J. P. Jacobsen* (1891); *6 Songs* (Holstein) (1894); *7 Strophic Songs* (1905–7); *Tove,* 3 songs for Holstein's play (1906–8); *Willemoes,* 5 songs for L.C. Nielsen's play (1907–8); *Hymn to Denmark* (1917); *3 Songs from 'Aladdin'* (1918); *20 Popular Melodies* (1917–21);

Balladen om Bjørnen (Ballad of the Bear) (1923); *10 Little Danish Songs* (1923–4).

ORGAN: *29 Short Preludes* (or for harmonium) (1929); *2 Preludes* (1930); *Commotio* (1931).

Nielsen, Riccardo (*b* Bologna, 1908). It. composer. Studied with Carlo Gatti in Milan. Earlier works in neo-classical idiom, later in 12-note; incl. radio opera *La via di Colombo* (NY 1953), *L'incubo*, monodrama (Venice 1948), 2 syms., conc. for orch., vn. conc., pf. concs., chamber mus.

Niemann, Albert (*b* Erxleben, 1831; *d* Berlin, 1917). Ger. ten. Début Dessau 1849 in minor operatic roles, then studied there and in Paris. Sang in various Ger. opera cos. until joining Berlin Opera 1866–88. Sang Wagner roles of Tannhäuser (Paris 1861), Siegmund (Bayreuth 1876). London début, as Siegmund, 1882. NY Met. 1886–8 (first Amer. Tristan and Siegfried).

Niente (It.). Nothing. Term used (especially by Vaughan Williams) to indicate that the sound is gradually to fade out of earshot.

Nietzsche, Friedrich Wilhelm (*b* Röcken, 1844; *d* Weimar, 1900). Ger. philosopher, poet, and amateur composer. Friend and ardent disciple of Wagner but turned against him and denounced his influence in 3 pamphlets, the last and most effective of them being *Der Fall Wagner* (1888). Instead, championed Bizet. Wrote songs, pf. pieces, and choral mus. His epic prose-poem *Also sprach Zarathustra* (1883–5) inspired mus. from R. Strauss, Mahler, and Delius.

Nigg, Serge (*b* Paris, 1924). Fr. composer. Studied Paris Cons. 1941–6, pupil of Messiaen. In 1945–8 studied 12-note technique with R. Leibowitz. Later reacted against atonality and turned to more romantic idiom. Works incl. symphonic poems *Timour* (1944), *Pour un poète captif* (1950); 2 pf. concs., vn. conc., fl. conc., vn. sonata, 2 pf. sonatas, *Jérôme Bosch Symphony* (1960), etc.

Nightingale. Imitative toy instr. used in an oratorio by A. Scarlatti, in Leopold Mozart's *Toy Symphony*, and in Crosse's *Play Ground*.

Nightingale, The (Russ. *Solovey*; Fr. *Le Rossignol*). Opera in 3 acts by Stravinsky to lib. by composer and S. Mitusov, based on Hans Andersen. Comp. 1908–9, 1913–14. Prod. Paris and London 1914, NY Met. 1926. Also *Song of the Nightingale* (*Le Chant du Rossignol*) sym.-poem in 3 parts based on mus. from the opera, 1917. F.p. Geneva 1919; f.p. in England, London 1920; *Songs of the Nightingale and Chinese March* for vn. and pf., transcr. Stravinsky and S. Dushkin, 1932.

Night on the Bare Mountain (*Ivanova noch na lisoy gore,* St John's Night on the Bare Mountain). Orch. work by Mussorgsky inspired by witches' sabbath in Gogol's story *St John's Eve.* Comp. 1867 for orch., rev. as choral piece for inclusion in opera *Mlada*, 1872, again rev. as choral introduc-

tion to Act 3 of *Sorochintsy Fair*, 1874. This final version was freely rev. and orch. by Rimsky-Korsakov, 1908, and it is this version which is well-known, though it is scarcely accurate to describe it as by Mussorgsky.

Night Ride and Sunrise. Tone poem for orch., Op. 55, by *Sibelius, comp. 1907, f.p. St Petersburg 1909 (cond. Ziloti), f.p. in England Hastings 1930.

Nights in the Gardens of Spain (Falla). See *Noches en los jardines de España.*

Nijinsky (Nizhinsky), **Vaclav** (*b* Kiev, 1889; *d* London, 1950). Russ. dancer. Entered St Petersburg ballet sch. 1898, graduated 1907. Joined Maryinsky Th. Danced with Pavlova in Fokine's *Pavillon d'Armide* (1907). Met *Diaghilev and became prin. attraction in Paris seasons of Ballet Russe. Noted for his dancing in *Les Sylphides* (1909), *Shéhérazade* (1910), *Spectre de la Rose* and *Petrushka* (1911), *Daphnis and Chloë* (1912). Resigned from Maryinsky co. 1911 because his costume in *Giselle* was considered indecent. Choreographer for Diaghilev prods. of *L'Après-midi d'un Faune* (1912), *Jeux* (1913), and *Le Sacre du Printemps* (1913). His marriage led to break with Diaghilev. Estab. own co. 1914 but it failed. Rejoined Diaghilev 1916, choreographing *Till Eulenspiegel*. Last solo perf. St Moritz 1919. Spent last years in mental hospitals. One of the greatest artists in history of ballet. His sister Bronislava Nijinska (properly Nijinskaya) (*b* Minsk, 1891; *d* Los Angeles, 1972) also created roles in Diaghilev ballets (*Carnaval*, 1910 and *Petrushka*, 1911). Returned to Russ. 1914 but left 1921 to rejoin Diaghilev co. as dancer, prod., and choreographer. Created *Renard* (1922), *Les Noces* (1923), *Les Biches* and *Le train bleu* (1924). Worked as choreog. for Paris Opéra, Teatro Colón in Buenos Aires, and with Ida Rubinstein co. (*Le Baiser de la Fée, Boléro,* 1928, *La Valse,* 1929). Later worked for Max Reinhardt in Berlin and opened ballet sch. in Los Angeles 1938. Guest choreog. for various cos. in 1940s. Prod. *Les Biches* (1964) and *Les Noces* (1966) for Royal Ballet at CG.

Nikisch, Artur (*b* Lébényi Szent-Miklós, 1855; *d* Leipzig, 1922). Hung. cond. and violinist. Child prodigy pianist. Entered Vienna Cons. at 11, staying until 1873. Played vn. in orch. at laying of Bayreuth foundation stone, May 1872. Violinist, Vienna Court Opera Orch. 1874–7. Engaged by A. *Neumann as ch. master, Leipzig Opera, 1877, 2nd cond. there 1878, 1st cond. 1879–89 (with Mahler as 2nd cond. 1886–8). Cond. Boston S.O. 1889–93. Dir. Budapest Opera 1893–5. Cond. Leipzig Gewandhaus Orch. and Berlin P.O. from 1895. Frequent guest cond. in Eng. and USA. Took LSO on 1st Amer. tour 1912. Cond. opera at CG 1907, 1912 (Holbrooke's *Children of Don*), and 1913–14 (*The Ring*). Cond. much Eng. mus. incl. Elgar's First Sym. and f.p. of Butterworth's *Shropshire Lad* Rhapsody (Leeds 1913). Comp. chamber mus. and cantata.

Nilsson, (Märta) Birgit (*b* Karup, 1918). Swed. sop. Entered Stockholm Acad. 1941 to study with Joseph Hislop. Opera début Stockholm 1946 as Agathe in *Der Freischütz*. Sang variety of roles in Stockholm, esp. Wagner, Verdi, Puccini, and Strauss. Glyndebourne 1951 (Electra in *Idomeneo*). Sang Brünnhilde in *Der Ring des Nibelungen*, Munich 1955, and Strauss's Salome. Sang Isolde and Sieglinde at Bayreuth 1957, being acknowledged as Flagstad's successor as leading Wagnerian sop. Outstanding Turandot at Scala, Milan, 1958. CG début (Brünnhilde) 1957, San Francisco 1956, NY Met. 1959 (Isolde). Added Dyer's Wife in Strauss's *Die Frau ohne Schatten* to her repertoire in 1975. Retired from stage 1982.

Nilsson, Bo (*b* Skelleftehamn, Sweden, 1937). Swed. composer, largely self-taught. Serialist and has used elec. and *avant-garde* techniques. Works incl. *Frequenzen*, chamber ens. (1956), *20 Clusters* for picc., ob., and cl. (1958–9), cantata *And the hands of his eyes were slowly turned back* (1959), *Entrée* for orch. and tape (1962–3), *Szene* I, II, and III for chamber ens. (1960–2), *Versuchungen* for orch. in 3 groups (1963), *Nazm* for reciter, solo vv., ch., jazz group, orch. all amp. (1973), *Taqsim-Caprice-Maqam*, ens. (1974), *Szene IV*, jazz sax., ch. (1975), *Madonna*, mez., ens. (1977), etc.

Nilsson, Christine (*b* Sjöabol, 1843; *d* Stockholm, 1921). Swed. sop. Studied Stockholm and Paris. Début Paris 1864 as Violetta, London 1864. Sang opera regularly in London until 1881 and gave farewell concert there in 1891. NY 1870–4 and 1883–4 (sang Marguérite in Gounod's *Faust* on opening night of NY Met. 1883).

Nimphes des Bois (Fr. 'Wood Nymphs'). Title of poem by Jehan Molinet which is combined with the Latin Requiem as text for the six-part motet-chanson *La Déploration de la mort de Johannes (Jehan) Ockeghem* by Josquin *Desprès. Written and composed 1497 (Ockeghem died on 6 Feb., 1497). Text refers to several contemporary composers, incl. Josquin himself. Requiem chant is used as *cantus firmus* to principal setting.

Nimrod. 9th (*adagio*) of Elgar's *Enigma Variations*. So called because it is a portrait of Elgar's friend A. J. Jaeger (Jäger is Ger. for hunter: Nimrod was 'mighty hunter' in Old Testament). Enshrines a day when the two men discussed Beethoven slow movements and is often used as a commemorative separate item.

Nimsgern, Siegmund (*b* St Wendel, 1940). Ger. bass. Studied at Saarbrücken. Between 1967 and 1971 won singing comps. at 's Hertogenbosch, Cologne, Munich, and Berlin. Member of Saarbrücken Staatstheater 1971–4, then Deutsche Oper-am-Rhein. Brit. début 1972 (concert perf. of *La Damnation de Faust*, cond. Boulez), CG 1973 (Amfortas). Amer. début San Francisco 1974 (Jokanaan in *Salome*), NY Met. 1978 (Pizarro).

Nin (y Castellanos), **Joaquín** (*b* Havana, 1879; *d* Havana, 1949). Cuban pianist, composer, and musicologist. Studied Barcelona and later in Paris with Moszkowski and d'Indy. Prof. of pf., Schola Cantorum, 1905. Worked in Berlin 1908–10. Specialized as pianist in old and modern Sp. mus. Ed. several vols. of early Sp. mus. Wrote pf. works, songs, guitar pieces, etc.

Nin-Culmell, Joaquín (Maria) (*b* Berlin, 1908). Ger.-born Amer. composer and pianist, son of Joaquín *Nin. Studied Schola Cantorum, and Paris Cons. (with Dukas). Also studied pf. privately with Cortot and Viñes and comp. with Falla. Professional pianist 1930–50, cond. since 1940, and teacher in Amer. colls. Comps. incl. *48 Tonadas* for pf., vc. conc., pf. conc., choral mus., pf. quintet, etc.

Nineteenth. Org. mutation stop. Length and pitch 1⅓′, pitch being thus a 19th (2 octaves and a 5th) above normal.

Ninth. *Interval of 9 steps, if bottom and top notes are counted. Chord of the 9th is common chord plus the 7th and 9th.

Ninth Symphony. Although several composers published 9 syms., e.g. Mahler, Bruckner, Dvořák, and Vaughan Williams, this term to the general mus.-lover means one work, Beethoven's Sym. No. 9 in D minor, the 'Choral'.

Nobile (It.). Noble.

Nobilissima Visione (Most noble vision). Choreographic legend in 1 act and 5 scenes, lib. and mus. by Hindemith based on life of St Francis of Assisi. Choreog. Massine, who danced in f.p. London (CG) 1938. Danced in USA under title *Saint Francis*. Also orch. suite in 3 movements.

Nobilmente (It.). Nobly, in a noble style. Directive closely, almost exclusively, assoc. with mus. of Elgar, who first used it in a pubd. score in the pf. transcription of 'Nimrod' in the *Enigma Variations* (1899), but not in full score. First used in pubd. orch. score in *Cockaigne* concert-ov., 1901. Though widely regarded as symbol of Elgar's 'ceremonial' manner, it should be noted that he did not apply it to the *Pomp and Circumstance* marches, nor to the *Coronation Ode*, but used it for themes of a particular emotional intensity, as in the Vn. and Vc. Concs., and the syms. Vaughan Williams also used the term in his *Coastal Command* film mus., 1942.

Noble, Dennis (*b* Bristol, 1899; *d* Jávea, Spain, 1966). Eng. bar. Chorister Bristol Cath. Heard by Percy *Pitt singing in cinema and offered CG audition. Début there 1924. Sang there regularly until 1938 and also in 1947. Also with BNOC and Carl Rosa. Sang bar. part in f.p. of Walton's *Belshazzar's Feast*, Leeds 1931.

Noble, (John) **Jeremy** (*b* London, 1930). Eng. musicologist and critic. Studied Oxford Univ. Wrote mus. criticism for *The Times* 1960–3, *Sunday Telegraph* 1972–6. Assoc. prof. State Univ. of NY at Buffalo 1966–70 and from 1976. Specialist in Renaissance mus.

Noble, John (*b* Southampton, 1931). Eng. bar. Studied Cambridge Univ. Abandoned career as physicist 1954 when he sang Pilgrim in Vaughan Williams's *The Pilgrim's Progress* at Cambridge. Since then has had successful career in oratorio and opera, with tours of Europe and USSR.

Noble, Thomas (Tertius) (*b* Bath, 1867; *d* Rockport, Mass., 1953). Eng. organist and composer. Studied at RCM with Parratt, Frederick Bridge, and Stanford. Ass. organist, Trinity Coll., Cambridge, 1890–2. Organist, Ely Cath. 1892–8, York Minster 1898–1912, St Thomas's Church, NY, 1912–47. Comps. incl. anthems, hymns, cantata, and org. pieces.

Noces, Les (Russ. *Svadebka*; Eng. 'The Wedding'). 'Choreographic scenes with song and music' by Stravinsky (words adapted by composer from popular sources) for mixed ch., 4 soloists, 4 pf., and 17 perc. instr., in 4 scenes: *The Blessing of the Bride, The Blessing of the Bridegroom, The Bride's Departure from her Parents' Home,* and *The Wedding Feast.* 1st version 1917 unfinished (scored for full wind, str. octet, with cimbalom, hps., perc., and harmonium. Completed 1971 by R. Craft and C. Matthews). 2nd version 1919, for perc., harmonium, cimbalom, and pianola. Prod. Paris 1923, choreog. Nijinskaya, cond. Ansermet. Later choreog. Béjart.

Noches en los Jardines de España (Nights in the Gardens of Spain). Symphonic impressions for pf. and orch. by Falla, comp. 1909–16, f.p. Madrid 1916; f.p. in England, London 1921 (soloist Falla); f.p. in Amer., Boston, Mass., 1924. Movements are: 1. *En el Generalife.* 2. *Danza lejana* (Dance in the distance). 3. *En los jardines de la Sierra de Córdoba.*

Nocturne (Fr., 'pertaining to night'). A comp. which suggests a nocturnal atmosphere, e.g. Haydn's *Notturnos* for *lira organizzata, Mozart's Serenata Notturna,* but more specifically a short pf. piece of romantic character. First to use the title for this genre was John *Field, followed by *Chopin. An expressive melody in the right hand is accompanied in the left by broken chords.

Nocturne. Song-cycle for ten., 7 obbl. instr., and str. orch., Op. 60, by Britten, comp. 1958. Settings of 8 poems about night by Shelley, Tennyson, Coleridge, Middleton, Wordsworth, Owen, Keats, and Shakespeare. The opening poem is acc. by str. only; each succeeding setting is dominated by an obbl. instr. (bn., harp, hn., timp., cor anglais, and fl. and cl.), and the finale is for the full complement. Ded. to Mahler's widow. F.p. Leeds 1958.

Nocturnes. Symphonic triptych for orch., and in the last movement women's ch., by Debussy, comp. 1897–9. The 3 movements are *Nuages* (Clouds), *Fêtes* (Festivals), and *Sirènes* (Sirens). F.p. (Nos. 1 and 2), Paris 1900, f. complete p. Paris 1901. F.p. in England, London 1909, cond. Debussy. Arr. for 2 pf., 4 hands, by Ravel 1909.

Nocturnes and Arias. (1) Orch. work by *Musgrave comp. 1966, f.p. Zürich, cond. N. Del Mar.
(2) Settings by *Henze of poems by I. Bachmann for sop. and orch. Comp. 1957. F. p. Donaueschingen (Gloria Davy; H. Rosbaud).

Node (of a vibrating string). Point of rest between two vibrating portions.

Noël (Fr.), **Nowell** (Eng.). A popular Christmas song or carol. In Eng. several 15th-cent. carols begin with the word 'Nowell' and *Busnois (*c.*1430–92) wrote a work for 4 vv. with the word 'Noël' as the sole text. In the 17th cent. the name 'noël' was given to organ pieces to be played during the Christmas services and based on Christmas melodies.

Noire (Fr.). The crotchet or Amer. quarter-note.

Nola, Domenico da (*b* Nola, Naples, early 16th cent.; *d* Naples, 1592). It. composer. Between 1541 and 1564 pubd. books of motets, madrigals, *villanelles*, etc. Choirmaster, Ch. d'Annunziata, Naples, 1563–88.

None. The 6th of the Canonical Hours of the R.C. Church. Properly it takes place at 3 p.m. (i.e. the '9th hour').

Nonet (Eng.), **nonette** (Fr.), **nonett** (Ger.), **nonetto** (It.). Comp. for 9 solo instr. or 9 vv. Famous examples are by Spohr, Rheinberger, Stanford, Ravel (3 *Poèmes de Mallarmé* for v. and 9 instr.), and Webern (*Concerto*, Op. 24).

Non-Harmonic Note. Term in harmonic analysis meaning a note not part of the chord with which it sounds and therefore requiring explanation, e.g. *passing-note or *appoggiatura.

Nonnengeige (Ger.). Nun's fiddle. The *Tromba Marina.

Non Nobis Domine (Not unto us, O Lord). Vocal canon, said to be by *Byrd, sung at the end of banquets or other festive occasions as a kind of 'grace after meat'.

Nono, Luigi (*b* Venice, 1924). It. composer. Law student at Padua Univ. but turned to mus., studying in Venice with *Malipiero and later with *Maderna and H. *Scherchen. Early works showed Webern's influence; later works became dominated by his commitment to Communist political and social causes and themes. What may be called the 'protest' element in his mus., expressed by heavy use of perc. and by use of pre-recorded tape, has not entirely obscured a characteristically Italian lyricism, such as may be found in his early works and in *Liebeslied*. Prin. comps.:

OPERAS: *Intolleranza 1960* (1960–1); *Al gran sole carico d'amore* (1974–5, rev. 1977).

ORCH: *Variazioni canoniche* (1950), *Composizione I* (1951), *Due espressioni* (1953), *Composizione II* (1959), *Per Bastiana Tai-Yang Cheng*, orch. and tape (1967).

INSTRUMENTAL: *Polifonica-Monodia-Ritmica*, 7 players (1951), *Canti per tredici* (1955), *Incontri*, 24 instr. (1955), *Varianti*, vn., str., woodwinds (1957).

CHORUS AND ORCH: *Epitaffio per García Lorca* (1951–3), *Il mantello rosso*, ballet for sop., bar., ch., and orch. (1953), *La victoire de Guernica* (1954), *Liebeslied* (1954), *Il canto sospeso* (1956), *La terra e la compagna*, sop., ten., ch., and instr. (1958), *Coro di Didone* (1958), *Canciones a Guiomar I*, sop., 6-part women's ch., and instr. (1962), *II*, 12-part women's ch. and instr. (1963), *Ricorda cosa ti hanno fatto in Auschwitz*, solo vv. and tape (1966), *Non consumiamo Marx*, vv. and tape (1969), *Un volto e del mare*, vv. and tape (1969), *Voci destroying Muros*, women's ch. and orch. (1970), *Y entonces comprendio*, 6 women's vv., ch., and tape (1970), *Ein Gespenst geht um in der Welt*, sop., ch., and orch. (1971).

UNACC. VOICES: 'Ha venido', sop. solo and 6-part sop. ch. (1960), *Sarà dolce tacere*, 8 vv. (1960), *Siamo la gioventù del Vietnam* (1973).

VOICE AND ORCH: *Canti di vita e d'amore (Sul ponte di Hiroshima)*, sop., ten., and orch. (1962); *La fabbrica illuminata*, mez. and tape (1964); *Como una ola de Fuerza y Luz*, sop., pf., orch., tape (1972).

TAPE: *Omaggio a Vedova* (1960), *Music for Die Ermittlung* (Weiss) (1965), *Contrappunto dialettico alla mente* (1968), *Musiche per Manzu* (1969), *Für Paul Dessau* (1974), *Notturni-albe* (1974), *Sofferte onde serene* (1976).

Noonday Witch, The (The Mid-day Witch, Cz. *Polednice*). Symphonic poem for orch., Op. 108, by Dvořák, comp. 1896.

Noras, Arto (Erkki) (*b* Turku, 1942). Finn. cellist. Studied Paris Cons. with *Tortelier. 2nd prize Tchaikovsky Competition, Moscow, 1966. Soloist with leading orchs. Exponent of Walton and Bliss concs. Gave f.p. of conc. by *Sallinen.

Norcome (Norcombe, Norcum), **Daniel** (*b* 1576; *d* Windsor, before 1626). Eng. lutenist and composer. Contrib. 5-part madrigal *With Angel's Face* to The *Triumphs of Oriana*. Lutenist at Danish court 1599–1601.

Nordheim, Arne (*b* Larvik, Norway, 1931). Norweg. composer. Studied Oslo Cons. Worked as mus. critic 1960–8. Since 1968 has concentrated on elec. mus. not only in the concert-hall but by providing 'accompaniment' for an Oslo sculpture. Works incl.:

BALLET: *The Tempest* (1979).

ORCH: *Canzona* (1960); *Floating* (1970); *Katharsis*, suite (1962); *Epitaffio*, orch. and magnetic tape (1963); *Greening* (1973); *Tenebrae*, vc., orch. (1982).

CHAMBER MUSIC: *Epigram*, str. qt. (1955); str. qt. (1956); *Aftonland*, song-cycle for v. and chamber ens. (1957); *Partita*, va., hpd., perc. (1963).

CHORAL: *Eco* (text by S. Quasimodo) for sop. solo, children's ch., mixed ch., and orch. (1967).

ELECTRONIC: *Favola*, musical play for TV, sop., ten., ch., orch., and elec. sound (1965); *Evolution*, elec. and concrete sound on tape (1966); *Colorazione*, Hammond organ and perc., 2 tape-recorders, amplifiers, loudspeakers (1968); *Solitaire*, elec. and concrete sound on tape (1968); *Partita II*, electric guitar (1969); *Lux et tenebrae* (1970); *Pace* (1970); *Osaka-Music* (1970); *Dinosauros*, for accordion and elec. sounds (1970).

Nordica (really Norton), **Lillian** (*b* Farmington, Maine, 1857; *d* Batavia, Java, 1914). Amer. soprano. Studied Boston. Début NY 1877, London 1878, under name Lilly Norton. Lessons in Milan 1878 were followed by début (as 'Nordica') in *Don Giovanni* (Elvira), 1879. Paris début as Marguérite 1882, CG 1887 (Violetta), singing there regularly until 1893. NY Met. début 1890, joining co. 1893. First Amer. to sing at Bayreuth (Elsa in *Lohengrin* 1894). Became noted singer of Isolde, Brünnhilde, and Kundry in USA and Europe from 1895 to her death. Her technique enabled her to follow Brünnhilde one night with Violetta the next night.

Nordoff, Paul (*b* Philadelphia, 1909; *d* Herdecke, Ger., 1977). Amer. composer and teacher. Studied Philadelphia Cons. and Juilliard Sch., NY. Head of comp., Philadelphia Cons. 1938–43, prof. of mus., Bard Coll., 1949–58. Specialist in mus. as therapy for handicapped children. Works incl. 2 syms., 2 pf. concs., vn. conc., operas, ballets for Martha Graham, chamber mus.

Nordraak, Rikard (*b* Christiania, 1842; *d* Berlin, 1866). Norweg. composer. Advocate of Norweg. nationalism and influenced Grieg. Wrote Norweg. nat. anthem *Ja, vi elsker dette landet* ('Yes, we love this land') (1863–4).

Norfolk Rhapsody. Orch. work in E minor by Vaughan Williams comp. 1906 and rev. in early 1920s. Based on 3 folk-songs collected in Norfolk in 1905 by composer. F.p. London 1906. 2 other *Norfolk Rhapsodies*, in D minor and G minor, were written and f.p. in Cardiff 1907, the orig. plan being a 'Norfolk Symphony', but they were withdrawn in 1914.

Nørgård, Per (*b* Gentofte, 1932). Danish composer. Studied Copenhagen Cons. with Holmboe, then in Paris with Boulanger. Worked as mus. critic in Copenhagen and teaches at Copenhagen Cons. and at Århus Cons. since 1965. Works make use of complex contrapuntal techniques and of some aspects of serialism. In 1959 developed 'the infinite row', a 12-note series which expands, it is said, to infinity, and has combined this with rhythms expressed in graphic notation. Works incl.:

OPERAS: *The Labyrinth* (1963); *Gilgamesh* (1971–2).
ORCH: 4 syms.; *Constellations*, conc. for 12 solo str. or 12 str. groups (1958); *Lyse Danse* (1959); *Fragment VI* for 6 orch. groups (1959–61); *Iris* (1967); *Luna* (1968); *Voyage into the Golden Screen*, chamber orch. (1968); *Lilá*, 11 instr. (1972); *Jousting*, small orch. (1975); *Twilight* (1977); *Illumination* (1984).
BALLET: *Le Jeune Homme à marier* (Scenario by Ionesco) (1964).
CHORAL: *Babel*, oratorio (1964); *Libra*, ten., guitar, 2 mixed ch., and 2 vibraphones or 2 pf. (1973); *Singe die Gärten*, 8 vv., 8 instr. (1974), Sym. No. 3, ch., orch. (1972–5); *Frostsalmer*, 16 vv. (1976).
CHAMBER MUSIC: *Quartetto brioso* (str. qt.) (1958); 2nd str. qt. in 3 spheres (1965); 3rd str. qt. *Inscape* (1969); wind quintet (1970); *Spell* for cl., vc., pf. (1973); *Nova genitura*, sextet (1975); *Solo Intimo*, vc., pf. (1983); *Ode to Plutonium*, sop., vc. (1984).

Norma. Opera in 2 acts by Bellini to lib. by Romani after play by Soumet. Prod. Milan 1831, London 1833, New Orleans 1836, NY 1841. The heroine, Norma, is a Druid priestess.

Norman, Frederick (Vilhelm Ludwig) (b Stockholm, 1831; d Stockholm, 1885). Swed. composer and cond. Studied Leipzig Cons. Cond. Royal Orch., Stockholm, 1859–79. Prof. of comp., Royal Swed. Acad. Married violinist Wilma *Neruda, 1864. Wrote 4 syms., pf. conc., and much chamber mus.

Norman, Jessye (b Augusta, Georgia, 1945). Amer. sop. Studied Peabody Cons., 1967, Univ. of Michigan 1967–8. Opera début, Deutsche Oper, Berlin, 1969 (Elisabeth in *Tannhäuser*), It. 1970 (Scala, Milan, 1972), CG 1972 (Cassandra in *Les Troyens*). US début, Hollywood Bowl 1972, NY Met. 1983. Noted Lieder singer and interpreter of such works as Berlioz's *Les Nuits d'été*. Settled in Eng.

Norrington, Roger (Arthur Carver) (b Oxford, 1934). Eng. cond. Studied Cambridge Univ. and RCM. Professional tenor 1962–70. Mus. dir. *Kent Opera 1966–84, Schütz Choir of London, London Str. Players, and London Baroque Ens. Prin. cond. Bournemouth Sinfonietta from 1985. Ed. Monteverdi's *L'incoronazione di Poppea, Orfeo*, and *Il Ritorno d'Ulisse in patria* (Kent Opera, 1974, 1976, 1978). SW début 1971, Amer. début 1974. O.B.E. 1980.

Norris, Geoffrey (b London, 1947). Eng. musicologist and author. Studied Durham, Liverpool, and Leningrad. Lecturer, RNCM 1975–6. Specialist in Russ. composers. Author of books on Rakhmaninov and Shostakovich., Mus. critic for *Times* and *Daily Telegraph*. Deputy ed., *New Oxford Companion to Music* from 1983.

Northcott, Bayan (Peter) (b Harrow-on-the-Hill, 1940). Eng. mus. critic and composer. Studied Oxford and Southampton Univs. Mus. critic *New Statesman* 1973–5, *Sunday Telegraph* from 1975. Author of book on A. Goehr.

North Country Sketches. Orch. work by *Delius, comp. 1913–14, in 4 movements: 1. *Autumn* (The wind soughs in the trees). 2. *Winter landscape*. 3. *Dance*. 4. *The march of Spring* (Woodlands, meadows, and silent moors). F.p. London 1915.

Northern Sinfonia. Chamber orch. based at Newcastle upon Tyne and serving north-eastern area of Eng., though it regularly plays in London. Founded as freelance orch. in 1958 by Michael Hall; became first permanent chamber orch. in Brit. 1961. Has made several overseas tours, played for opera, and made several recordings. Conductors have been: Hall 1958–64, Rudolf Schwarz 1964–73 (jointly with Boris Brott 1964–7); Christopher Seaman 1973–9; Tamás Vasáry and Ivan Fischer 1979–82; Richard Hickox from 1982. N. Marriner was ass. cond. 1971–3. Title changed to Northern Sinfonia of England in 1982.

North, Roger (b ? Tostock, Suffolk, c. 1651; d Rougham, Norfolk, 1734). Eng. author, lawyer, and musician. M.P. and Attorney-Gen. under James II but in 1688 retired to country life at Rougham. Wrote many essays on mus. His reminiscences span from the time of consorts of viols heard in his boyhood to Purcell and the It. 'invasion' of early 18th cent. They are specially valuable for their detailed discussion of performing practice in his lifetime.

Northumbrian Bagpipes. See *Bagpipe*.

Nose, The (*Nos*). Opera in 3 acts by Shostakovich, Op. 15, to lib. by E. Zamyatin, G. Yunin, A. Preys, and composer, after Gogol. Comp. 1927–8. Prod. Leningrad 1930; London, SW, New Opera Co. 1973.

Nota Cambiata (It.). Exchanged note. See *Changing Note*.

Notation and Nomenclature. The methods of writing down mus. so that it can be performed. These are devices for which the human being long felt no need, and although every race has its mus. they are still unknown to the larger part of the world's population. They are apparently purely European in origin and even in Europe thousands of tunes existed which were transmitted by one generation to another without achieving the dignity of being recorded on paper until the folk-song collectors came on to the scene.

The naming of notes by letters of the alphabet goes back as far as the Ancient Greeks; the Romans also possessed an alphabetical system. In both cases, however, this nomenclature served rather the purposes of scientific discussion than those of performance.

An early (7th-cent.) system of notation was that of *neums (neumes). Our conventional signs for the turn and the trill are derived from details of neum notation. The present exactitude in pitch indication has been effected by adding to the one line of the early neum notation. Plainsong now uses a *staff of 4 lines, and other mus. one of 5 lines. The *clef derives from neum notation: attached to the Staff it fixes the pitch of one of its lines as middle C or some other note, from which all the others may be deduced.

Proportional notation of an exact character (i.e. as to the time values) began in the 10th cent. when the primitive developments of polyphony brought about its necessity. Definite notes, of different shapes according to their intended proportionate length, were devised, from which our present series of semibreve (whole-note), minim (half-note), etc. is derived. *Bar lines became common only during the 16th and 17th cents. (the earliest use dates from 1448): they were at first casually drawn as aids to the eye— the idea of making them of equal time-value coming later. They first arose in choral scoring to demonstrate the coincidence of the different vv., and were originally not present in the independent vocal parts for the use of singers.

Adjustments to and changes in traditional staff notation have increased in the 20th cent., particularly since c.1950 when total serialism, aleatory procedures, etc. have required a parallel development of notational signs, resulting in some confusion where individual composers have devised their own methods which may use terms employed by another composer for a different effect. Some mus. cannot be written at all in conventional notation. The subject is too large for more than an outline to be given here, but some of the changes can be mentioned briefly.

With the arrival of atonal and 12-note mus., conventional pitch notation, with its selection of accidentals, tended to become unworkable, but no new system has been generally adopted, and makeshift adaptation of conventional methods has been favoured by performers. Systems of microtonal notation devised by A. *Hába and J. Carillo have not lasted.

Traditional notation is little use in pulseless mus. and in mus. in which different and often complicated rhythms progress simultaneously at different speeds. To cope with notating these durations, *proportionate notation has been employed, whereby durational proportions are transmuted into the graphic equivalent of notes spaced out horizontally along the staff according to their durations.

For graphic notation, see the separate entry under Graphic scores. Mention may be made here of 2 explicit new notational systems which have not yet found acceptance. Equiton uses only 2 staff lines per octave. The 12 chromatic notes are notated with alternating black and white note-heads and without accidentals. Note-heads appear below, on, and above each staff line; and those between the staff-lines occur close to lower or upper line and centred between the lines. Those close to the lines have ledger lines drawn through them. Notation of durations is proportionate. Klavarscribo uses a staff in which lines and spaces run vertically, being grouped according to the black and white keys of the keyboard. No accidentals are needed. Black-and-white note-heads are used for easy identification with corresponding keys. The mus. is read from top to bottom. Notation of durations is proportionate and bar-lines are horizontal.

Below is a selection of some of the generally accepted new notational symbols:

Note. (1) A single sound of a given mus. pitch and duration; in Amer. called a *tone*.

(2) A written sign representing (1).

(3) A finger-key of the pf., organ, accordion, etc. to produce a sound of particular pitch.

Note-row (Amer. 'tone-row'). In 12-note mus., the order in which the composer decides to arrange the 12 notes within the octave, this order acting as the basis for the comp. (almost like a motto-theme). Strictly no note should be repeated before the row comes to an end, but the rhythm in which they are presented may be. Also, any note in the row may appear an octave higher or lower than it did originally and the whole row can be used at any higher or lower level. But successive composers have broken the rules.

Notes Inégales (Fr. 'unequal notes'). Rhythmic convention whereby certain divisions of the beat move in alternately long and short values even when written as equal. Inequality was normal feature of musical teaching in 17th and 18th cent. in France. Its use in baroque performance in modern times is subject of much controversy.

Note values.

1 whole-note (semibreve)   𝅝

equals

♩   ♩

2 half-notes (minims)

or

♩   ♩   ♩ ♩

4 quarter-notes (crotchets)

or

♪   ♪   ♫   ♫♫

8 eighth-notes (quavers)

or

♪ ♪ ♫   ♫♫   ♫♫♫

16 sixteenth-notes (semiquavers)

or

♫♫♫   ♫♫♫♫   ♫♫♫♫♫♫♫

32 thirty-second notes (demisemiquavers).

After this follow 64th notes (hemidemisemi-quavers) and, occasionally, notes of 128 to the whole-note.

A dot after a note increases its value by half; thus ♩. = ♩ ♪ (but see exception mentioned under *Dot, Dotted Note*). A double dot after a note increases its value by a half plus a quarter; thus ♩‥ = ♩ ♪ ♪. A third dot has very occasionally been used; thus ♩... = ♩ ♪ ♪ ♪

Notre Dame (Our Lady). Romantic opera in 2 acts by F. *Schmidt to lib. by composer and Leopold Wilk after Hugo. Comp. 1902–4. Prod. Vienna 1914. The Intermezzo is a popular concert-piece.

Nottebohm, (Martin) **Gustav** (*b* Lüdenscheid, Westphalia, 1817; *d* Graz, 1882). Ger. composer and musicologist. Studied Berlin and Leipzig, having a few lessons from Schumann and Mendelssohn. Settled in Vienna 1846, became friend of Brahms, and wrote some minor works, but is known for his valuable research into Beethoven's sketchbooks embodied in three books, pubd. 1872 and 1887 (posth.). Also pubd. thematic catalogues of works of Beethoven (1868)

and Schubert (1874). One of first authorities in textual criticism.

Notturni ed Alba (Nocturnes and Dawn). Song-cycle for sop. and orch. in 5 movements, to words from medieval Lat. texts, by *McCabe. F.p. Hereford Fest. 1970. Perf. as ballet, Westfalen, 1976.

Notturnino (It.). A miniature *nocturne.

Notturno. See *Nocturne.*

Novachord. Patented elec. kbd. instr. invented by Laurens Hammond. It has 6-octave kbd. like that of a pf. Chords and not just single notes can be played. Tone is varied by manual controls and vol. is controlled by pedals, which also sustain notes.

Novák, Jan (*b* Nová Říša na Moravě, 1921). Cz. composer. Studied Brno Cons. 1940–6. In 1947–8 studied with Copland in Tanglewood and Martinů in NY. Settled Brno 1948, but emigrated to Denmark 1968–70, thereafter to It. The neo-classical style of his early works gave way in 1958 to employment of jazz elements and 12-note techniques. Works incl.: *Passion Play* (1965), ob. conc. (1952), 2-pf. conc. (1955), *Philharmonic Dances*, orch. (1955–6), *Variations on a Theme of Martinů*, orch. (1959, pf. version 1949), *Concentus Eurydicae*, guitar, str. (1971), *Dido*, speaker, mez., male vv., orch. (1967), *Orpheus et Eurydice*, sop., va. d'amore, pf. (1971), *Voces latinae*, ch., drum, pf., db. (1975), and pf. pieces.

Novák, Vítězslav (*b* Kamenice, Cz., 1870; *d* Skuteč, 1949). Cz. composer. Studied Prague Cons. 1889–92 (comp. with Knittl and Dvořák). Prof. of comp. Prague Cons. 1909–39, influencing and teaching many Cz. composers. His early works were Brahmsian in style but he became more nationalist under the influence of Janáček. Works incl.:

OPERAS: *Karlštejn* (1914–15); *Lucerna* (The Lantern) (1919–22); *Dĕdův odkaz* (Grandfather's Legacy) (1922–5).

ORCH: Serenade in F (1894); pf. conc. (1895); *3 Bohemian Dances* (1897); *V Tatrách* (In the Tatras), symphonic poem (1902); *Slovak Suite* (1903); *South Bohemian Suite* (1936–7); *De Profundis* (1941); *St Wenceslas Triptych* (1941).

CHORAL: *6 Men's Choruses* (1906); *Bouře* (The Storm), sea fantasy for soloists, ch., and orch. (1908–10); *Svatební Košile* (The Spectre's Bride), soloists, ch., and orch. (1912–13); *Podzimní symfonie* (Autumn Sym.), ch. and orch. (1931–4); *Májová symfonie* (May Sym.), soloists, ch., and orch. (1943); *Hvĕzdy* (Stars), female vv. and orch. (1949).

CHAMBER MUSIC: Pf. Trios: G minor (1892), D minor (1902); Pf. Qt. (1894, rev. 1899); Pf. Quintet (1896, rev. 1897); Str. Qts.: in G (1899), in D (1905), in G (1938); vc. sonata (1941).

PIANO: *Variations on a Theme of Schumann* (1893); *Sonata eroica* (1900); *Exotikon* (1911); 6 Sonatinas (1919–20).

Novelette (Eng.), **Novellette** (Ger.). A term introduced by Schumann as a compliment to the Eng. soprano Clara *Novello as the title for his 8 pf. pieces Op. 21, 1838. They have no individual titles but each, says the composer, is to be taken as the mus. equivalent of a romantic story. A few other composers have adopted the term: it has no special connotation as to form.

Novello, Clara (Anastasia) (*b* London, 1818; *d* Rome, 1908). Eng. soprano, daughter of Vincent *Novello. Studied in Paris. Sang at Worcester Fest. 1833 and in Mendelssohn's *St Paul* in Birmingham 1837. Mendelssohn engaged her for Leipzig Gewandhaus concerts, leading to triumphs in Ger. Went to Milan 1839 to study for operatic stage, making her début at Bologna in 1841 in Rossini's *Semiramide*. Rossini chose her as sop. soloist in f. It. p. of his *Stabat Mater* in 1841. Gave up career on marriage in 1843 to It. Count, but resumed it in 1849. On return to Eng. in 1851, became leading oratorio singer in choral fests. Retired 1861.

Novello, Ivor (Davies, David Ivor) (*b* Cardiff, 1893; *d* London, 1951). Welsh composer, actor, playwright, and impresario, son of choral cond. Clara Novello-Davies (1861–1943). Composer of *Keep the Home Fires Burning*, one of the most popular songs during 1914–18 war. Wrote, comp., and acted in successful mus. comedies, e.g. *Glamorous Night* (1935), *Crest of the Wave* (1937), *The Dancing Years* (1939), *King's Rhapsody* (1942), and *Perchance to Dream* (1945). Acted in Shakespeare.

Novello, Vincent (*b* London, 1781; *d* Nice, 1861). Eng. organist, publisher, and composer of It. origin. Organist, Portuguese Embassy chapel, London, 1797–1822. Founded publishing house *Novello and Co. 1811. Founder-member of Phil. Soc. Comp. sacred mus. and ed. classics. Pubd. 5 vols. of 17th cent. It. church mus. under title *The Fitzwilliam Music*, 1825, and 5 vols. of Purcell's sacred mus., 1826–9. In 1829 organized fund to assist Mozart's widow, going to Salzburg to give her the money and collect material for biography of Mozart which he never wrote. Diaries of this journey pubd. 1955 as *A Mozart Pilgrimage*. Also helped to prepare way for Bach revival in Eng.

Novello and Co. Eng. music publishers, founded in London 1811 by Vincent *Novello. His son Alfred, from 1829 to 1857, followed by Henry Littleton (1823–88), made the business extremely successful by issuing standard edns. of the classics, particularly choral works. Most Eng. Victorian oratorios and cantatas were pubd. by Novello, incl. those by *Elgar. Its house magazine, *The *Musical Times*, remains one of the most respected

publications. Business was purchased by Granada, 1970.

Novotná, Jarmila (*b* Prague, 1907). Cz. soprano. Studied in Prague with *Destinn and in Milan. Début Prague 1925 as Mařenka in *The Bartered Bride*. Sang at Vienna Opera 1933–8, and was a distinguished Oktavian in Strauss's *Der Rosenkavalier* in Vienna and Salzburg. Created title role in Lehár's *Giuditta*, with Tauber as ten., 1934. Amer. début S. Francisco 1939 as Butterfly. NY Met. 1940–56. Sang in Vienna and Salzburg after Second World War.

Nowak, Leopold (*b* Vienna, 1904). Austrian musicologist. Prof. at Vienna Univ. Dir., mus. division, Vienna Nat. Library 1946–54. Author of books on Liszt, Haydn, and Bruckner. Ed., following R. *Haas in 1954, of complete works of Bruckner.

Nowak, Lionel (*b* Cleveland, 1911). Amer. composer and pianist. Studied Cleveland Institute of Mus. 1929–36, with Sessions and Q. Porter. Composer and mus. dir. Humphrey-Weidman Dancers 1938–42, since when he has held teaching posts. Wrote several ballets, ob. sonata, ob. qt., 3 vc. sonatas, etc.

Noye's Fludde. Setting by Britten, Op. 59, of Chester miracle play for adults' and children's vv., children's ch., chamber ens., and children's orch. F.p. Aldeburgh Fest. (Orford Church) 1958.

Nozze di Figaro, Le (The Marriage of Figaro). *Commedia per musica* in 4 acts (K492, 1786) by Mozart to lib. by da Ponte after Beaumarchais's comedy *La Folle Journée, ou Le Mariage de Figaro* (1778). Prod. Vienna 1786, London 1812, NY 1824.

Nuance (Fr.). Shade, distinction, gradation. A word frequently used by writers on mus. to imply those delicate differences of intensity and speed which largely constitute the character of a perf.

Nuits d'été, Les (Summer Nights). 6 songs, Op. 7, by Berlioz to poems by Théophile Gautier. Comp. 1840–1, rev. 1843 and 1856. Orig. for mez. or ten. with pf. acc. Berlioz orchestrated *Absence* in 1843, and the rest in 1856. The songs are: 1. *Villanelle*. 2. *Le Spectre de la rose*. 3. *Sur les lagunes*. 4. *Absence*. 5. *Au Cimitière*. 6. *L'Île inconnue*. A problem arises in performing these songs: usually one singer (sop. or mez.) is engaged, but it is a rare v. which can encompass them all. The pubd. version for v. and pf. is marked 'for mez. or ten.', but in orchestrating the songs Berlioz rewrote them in some respects, also transposing the first 3. He also specified the v. for each song as follows: 1. Mez. or ten. 2. Cont. 3. Bar., cont., or mez. 4. Mez. or ten. 5. Ten. 6. Mez. or ten.

Numbers. Term used for self-contained item in a musical or opera (because each piece of this kind is separately numbered in the score). A 'numbers opera' is an opera in which these divisions occur, as opposed to Wagner's later operas, for example, where each act is written continuously without internal divisions or pauses.

Number Systems. J. *Rousseau introduced a system of numerical notation in which the first 8 numerals are substituted for the 8 notes in the scale. Nos. are popular among 20th-cent. composers, because of the concept of 'parameters', in which mus. sounds are regarded as the sum of several components (pitch, duration, intensity, timbre, and position in space). What is called the Fibonacci series (each no. the sum of the previous 2) has been used to control these components by such composers as Křenek, Stockhausen, and Nono.

Nunc Dimittis. The Song of Simeon in St Luke's Gospel (Lord, now lettest thou thy servant depart in peace). It is a part of the service of Compline in the R.C. Church and of that of Evensong in the Anglican Church. It has its traditional plainsong in the former, and is often sung to an Anglican chant in the latter. It has also been set innumerable times by church composers, usually as an adjunct to a *Magnificat.

Nun's Fiddle. The *Tromba Marina.

Nuove Musiche. See *New Music*.

Nursery Suite. 7-movement orch. suite by Elgar, f.p. London 1931, and ded. to the then Duchess of York and her daughters Princess Elizabeth (later Queen Elizabeth II) and Princess Margaret Rose. Ballet with choreog. by N. de Valois, London 1932.

Nusch-Nuschi, Das. 1-act opera by Hindemith, Op. 20, for Burmese marionettes to lib. by Franz Blei. Prod. Stuttgart 1921.

Nussbaum, Der (The Nut tree). Song for v. and pf. by R. Schumann, to poem by Julius Mosen

(1803–67), being No. 3 of cycle *Myrthen*, Op. 25 (1840).

Nut. (1) On a str. instr., the slight ridge over which the str. pass on leaving the pegs. On a *ukelele and similar instr. a moveable nut is placed on the fingerboard which can shorten all str. equally and thus raise the pitch.

(2) Device at the heel of the bow of a vn., etc., which adjusts the tension of the bow-hairs.

Nutcracker (Russ. *Shchelkunchik*, Fr. *Casse-Noisette*). Ballet in 2 acts and 3 scenes with mus. by *Tchaikovsky, Op. 71, comp. 1891–2, choreog. by Ivanov, and lib. by Petipa based on Hoffmann's *Der Nüssknacker und der Mäusekönig* (The Nutcracker and the King of the Mice). Prod. St Petersburg 1892, London (complete) 1934. Has been choreog. also by Balanchine, Cranko, Nureyev, etc. Orch. suite of 8 numbers, Op. 71a, arr. Tchaikovsky, 1892.

Nymphs and Shepherds. Song by *Purcell, part of his incidental music for Shadwell's play *The Libertine*, 1692. Often sung by sop., but made famous in choral version recorded by Manchester schoolchildren's choirs cond. *Harty in 1929.

Nystedt, Knut (*b* Oslo, 1915). Norweg. composer. Studied Oslo and in USA with Copland. Wrote orch. and choral mus. and 4 str. qts.

Nystroem, Gösta (*b* Silvberg, 1890; *d* Särö, 1966). Swed. composer. Studied Copenhagen and later in Paris with d'Indy. Mus. critic in Sweden 1932–47. Wrote 6 syms. (incl. No. 4, *Sinfonia Shakespeariana*, 1952), 2 concs. for str., opera, ballet, vn. conc., va. conc., Sinfonia Concertante for vc. and orch., and many songs.

NZ. Neue Zeitschrift für Musik. Ger. bi-monthly periodical, orig. *Neue Leipziger Zeitschrift für Musik*, founded in Leipzig by Schumann in 1834. Edited by Schumann until 1844. Present title adopted 1979.

O

O, od (It.). Or.

Oakeley, (Sir) **Herbert** (Stanley) (*b* Ealing, 1830; *d* Eastbourne, 1903). Eng. organist and composer. Studied Oxford and Leipzig. Prof. of mus., Edinburgh Univ., 1865–91. Wrote church mus. Knighted 1876.

Obbligato (It.; Fr. *obligé*; Ger. *obligat*). Indispensable. Adjective attached to the name of an instr., e.g. 'vc. obbligato', where the instr.'s part is obligatory, and special or unusual in effect. To use the term in the opposite sense of optional or *ad libitum* is wrong, as is the frequently-encountered spelling *obligato*.

Oberhoffer, Emil (*b* Munich, 1867; *d* San Diego, Calif., 1933). Ger. pianist and cond. Studied in Paris with Philipp. Settled in USA at St Paul, Minn., 1897 as cond. of local mus. soc. His efforts led in 1903 to formation of Minneapolis S.O., which he cond. until 1922. See *Minnesota Orch.*

Oberlin College (Oberlin, Ohio). Amer. coll. est. 1833, with cons. of mus. 1865.

Oberlin, Russell (*b* Akron, Ohio, 1928). Amer. counterten. Studied Juilliard Sch., NY. Soloist with NY Pro Musica Antiqua 1953–9. Début CG 1961 as Oberon in Britten's *A Midsummer Night's Dream.*

Oberon, or The Elf-King's Oath. Opera in 3 acts by Weber to Eng. lib. by J. R. Planché, after W. Sotheby's trans. (1798) of Wieland's poem *Oberon* (1780), which is based on the 13th-cent. Fr. *chanson de geste, Huon de Bordeaux.* Prod. London, CG 1826, cond. Weber; Leipzig 1826; NY 1828. Other operas on subject by Kunzen (*Holger Danske*, 1789) and P. Wranitzky (*Oberon, König der Elfen*, 1789).

Obertas(s). A nat. Polish round dance of rather wild character, in quick triple time.

Oberto, Conte di San Bonifacio (Oberto, Count of Bonifacio). Opera in 2 acts by Verdi to lib. by A. Piazza, rev. with additions by T. Solera. Comp. 1837–8, being Verdi's first opera to be prod. (Milan 1839). Chicago 1903 (concert version), London 1965 (concert), NY 1978.

Oberwerk (Ger.). Upper-work, i.e. Swell Org. (Abbreviated to 'Obw' or 'O.W.')

Oblique motion. See *Motion.*

Oboe. Org. reed stop of 8′ pitch, imitative of instr. whose name it bears.

Oboe family. The ob. is a woodwind instr. blown through a double reed and with a compass from the B♭ below middle C upwards for over 2½ octaves. Standard orch. instr., also in chamber mus. and military bands. It is the note A sounded on the oboe to which the rest of the orchestra tune their instr. Many concs. have been written for its solo use, e.g. by Vivaldi, Albinoni, R. Strauss, Vaughan Williams, Martinů, etc. Derives from the *shawm and the *curtal. Known in Fr. and Eng. in the 17th cent. as *hautbois* and *hautboy*. There also exist: (1) *Oboe d'amore* (ob. of love): pitched a minor 3rd below normal oboe. Has pear-shaped bell, which gives it its mellow and individual tone-colour, and is midway in size between ob. and cor anglais. Was favoured by Bach, but subsequently neglected. In 20th cent, has been used by R. Strauss in *Symphonia Domestica*, Holst in *Somerset Rhapsody*, Ravel in *Boléro*, and John McCabe has written a conc. for it (1972). (2) *Oboe da caccia* (hunting ob.): obsolete predecessor of cor anglais. See also *cor anglais, bassoon, Heckelphone, shawm.*

Oborin, Lev (Nikolayevich) (*b* Moscow, 1907; *d* Moscow, 1974). Russ. pianist. Studied Moscow Cons., where he taught from 1928, becoming prof. 1935. Won first Warsaw int. Chopin comp. 1927. Many successful pupils, incl. *Ashkenazy.

Obraztsova, Elena (Vasilyevna) (*b* Leningrad, 1937). Russ. mez. Studied Leningrad. Opera début Moscow 1963 (Marina in *Boris Godunov*). Has sung in Milan, Hamburg, Vienna, etc. NY Met. (with Bolshoy Co.) 1975. San Francisco 1975 (Azucena).

Obrecht (Obertus), **Jacob** (*b* Bergen-op-Zoom, *c*.1451; *d* Ferrara, 1505). Flemish composer. Kapellmeister, Utrecht, *c*.1474; worked in Cambrai and Bruges 1484–91; Kapellmeister, Antwerp Cath., 1491. Visited It. several times. Wrote much church mus., incl. masses, motets, etc., and secular songs. Forerunner of Josquin *Desprès. Used secular *cantus firmus* in his masses, e.g. *Missa super Maria Zart.* Used number symbolism in his works, cabalistic significance having been discovered in many of his structures, e.g. the number of *tactus* in his *Missa 'Sub tuum praesidium'* is 888, the symbol of Christ. Some of his works are deliberately imitative of other composers. The 'boundless exuberance', as one scholar has put it, of his music ranks it with the greatest of its time.

Obukhov, Nikolay (*b* Kursk, 1892; *d* Paris, 1954). Russ. composer. Pupil of Tcherepnin and Steinberg, and, after settling in Paris in 1918, of Ravel. Developed elec. instr., *croix sonore*, for which he comp. works. Invented new system of notation and 12-note system independent of

Schoenberg's. Devoted most of his life to mystical choral work *Le Livre de vie*, soloists, ch., 2 pfs., and orch., (begun in 1916).

Obw. Abbreviation for **Oberwerk* (i.e. Swell Org. in Ger. org. mus.).

O.C. Abbreviation for *Organo corale* (It.), choir org.

Oca del Cairo, L' (The Goose of Cairo). Unfinished *opera buffa* in 2 acts (K422) by Mozart 1783 to lib. by Varesco; prod. Paris 1867, London 1870. Several modern edns., incl. one by **Redlich.

O Canada! Canadian nat. song, especially popular among Fr.-Canadians. The mus., by Calixa **Lavallée, comp. 1880, was orig. a hymn in honour of St John the Baptist.

Ocarina (It. 'Little goose'). Small keyless wind instr., shaped rather like an egg with holes for fingers and invented *c*.1860. Made of earthenware or metal. Mainly used as a toy and sometimes nicknamed 'sweet potato' (as in once-popular song *Sweet Potato Piper*).

Oceanides, The (*Aallottaret*). Symphonic poem for orch. by Sibelius, Op. 73, comp. 1914. F.p. Norfolk, Conn., 1914, cond. Sibelius.

Ochsenkuhn, Sebastian (*b* Nuremberg, 1521; *d* Heidelberg, 1574). Ger. lutenist in service of Rhenish Electors. Wrote tablature book for lute (1558) containing Fr. and Ger. secular songs.

Ockeghem (Okeghem), **Johannes** (Jean) (*b c.* 1410; *d* ? Tours, 1497). Fr.-Flemish composer. In about 1445 was a singer in Notre Dame, Antwerp, and in 1446 was member of chapel of Duke of Bourbon at Moulins, nr. Dijon. About 7 years later was at Fr. court, where he stayed for the rest of his life, serving three successive kings. Travelled on court missions to It. and Sp. Leading composer of period between Dufay and Josquin Desprès, but only 14 Masses, fewer than a dozen motets, and about 20 *chansons* survive, enough to show his stature. Style noted for contrapuntal richness. His *Missa 'Fors seulement'* was one of first parody Masses, based on one of his own *chansons*. His *Missa pro Defunctis* is earliest surviving requiem, Dufay's having been lost. His *chansons* were the 'popular songs' of his day. After he died, Molinet's commemorative poem **Nimphes des Bois* was set to mus. by Desprès.

O Come, all ye Faithful. See *Adeste Fideles*.

Octandre (Plant with 8 stamens). Work for small orch. (woodwind, brass, db.) by Varèse, comp. 1923, f.p. NY 1924.

Octave. Interval of 8 notes, counting bottom and top notes. Notes an octave apart have same letter-names. Interval from, say, D to next D above is *perfect octave*; from D up to D♭ and from D up to D♯ are *diminished* and *augmented* octaves respectively. Also *double octave*, 2 octaves; *at the octave*,

to be perf. octave higher than written; *in octaves*, to be perf. with each note doubled one or more octaves above or below.

Octave Coupler. Device on org. or hpd. with which note struck is doubled an octave higher.

Octave Flute (It. **ottavino*). **Piccolo.

Octave quint. Organ stop same as **Twelfth.*

Octaves graves, Octaves aiguës. In Fr. org. mus. mean respectively the sub- and super-octave couplers.

Octave Signs.

8va or 8	*8va bassa or 8va sotto*
Ottava, i.e. perform an octave higher than written.	Perform an octave lower than written (*sotto* = under).
loco	*con 8*
Place, i.e. (after playing an octave higher or lower) resume the playing as written.	Play the passage not in single notes, as marked, but in octaves (the added line of octaves will be above if the passage occurs in the treble of a pf. piece, and below if in the bass).

Octavin (Fr.). The 'Fifteenth' stop of the org. So *Octavin harmonique*, Harmonic Piccolo.

Octet (Fr. *Octuor, Octette*; It. *Ottetto*; Ger. *Oktett*). Any combination of 8 performers or any piece of mus. comp. for such. The normal str. octet is for 4 vn., 2 va., 2 vc., as in Mendelssohn's. Schubert's Octet is for 2 vn., va., vc., db., cl., bn., and hn. That by Stravinsky is for wind instr.

Octo-bass. A str. db. 10′ high invented by the great Paris *luthier* J. B. Vuillaume in 1849 and recommended by Berlioz. The stopping was controlled by levers operated by the left hand and the feet; the instr. was bowed in the normal way. It had a range of 2 octaves and a 5th. Failed to catch on but a conc. written for it in 1984.

Octuor. See *Octet*.

Od (It.). Or.

Ode. In literature, a lyrical poem. In Ancient Greece an ode was recited to mus. acc. In its mus. sense, the term often means a ceremonial work, e.g. Purcell's *Ode for St Cecilia's Day* and Elgar's *Coronation Ode*, but sometimes the term is used for works with particular significance to the composer, e.g. Elgar's *The Music Makers* and Stravinsky's Ode: *Elegiacal Chant*.

Ode for St Cecilia's Day. (1) Title of 4 choral works by **Purcell, 2 comp. in 1683, another probably of that date, a 4th in 1692. All except one (Lat.) have Eng. texts.
  (2) Choral work by Handel, 1739, being setting of Dryden's poem (1698).
  (3) Cantata by Hubert **Parry, 1889.
  (4) There are many other works with this title.

Ode to Death. Setting for ch. and orch., Op. 38, by Holst of text by Whitman. Comp. 1919. F.p. Leeds Fest. 1922, London 1923.

Ode to Napoleon Buonaparte. Setting by Schoenberg, Op. 41, of Byron's poem (1814) for str. qt., pf., and reciter (whose part is rhythmically notated at approx. pitch). Comp. 1942. Version (Op. 41b) for str. orch., pf., and reciter f.p. NY 1944.

O.E. Abbreviation for *Organo espressivo* (It. Swell Organ).

Oedipus Rex (King Oedipus). Opera-oratorio in 2 acts by Stravinsky to lib. by J. Cocteau trans. into Lat. by J. Daniélou and based on Sophocles. Comp. 1926–7. Prod. Paris 1927 (as oratorio), London 1928 (broadcast), 1936 (concert). F.p. on stage Vienna 1928. Boston 1928 (concert), NY 1931 (stage).

Oestvig, Karl (Aagaard) (*b* Oslo, 1889; *d* Oslo, 1968). Norweg. ten. Studied Cologne Cons. Opera début Stuttgart 1914. Vienna State Opera 1919–27. Created role of Emperor in Strauss's *Die Frau ohne Schatten*. Also fine Wagnerian singer.

Offenbach, Jacques (*b* Deutz, nr. Cologne, 1819; *d* Paris, 1880). Ger.-Fr. composer, cond., and cellist. Orig. surname Eberst, Wiener, or Levy: took name Offenbach because family came from Offenbach-am-Main. Son of cantor of Cologne synagogue. Studied Paris Cons. 1833–7, also playing vc. in Opéra-Comique orch. Cond. at Théâtre Français, 1849–55. From 1853 began to compose operettas, writing no fewer than 90 in the next quarter-cent. Man. of Théâtre Comte, renaming it Bouffes-Parisiens. The best of his lighter works, *La Belle Hélène, Orphée aux Enfers* (*Orpheus in the Underworld), etc., symbolize the Fr. 2nd Empire, but his fame rests equally securely on his sole grand opera *Les Contes d'Hoffmann* (The *Tales of Hoffmann), on which he worked for many years. It was prod. after his death in a version rev. and largely orchestrated by *Guiraud. Among his chief works are:

OPERAS: *Die Rheinnixen* (Vienna 1864); *Les Contes d'Hoffmann* (1881).
BALLET-PANTOMIME: *Le Papillon* (1860).
OPERETTAS: *Barbe-bleue* (1866); *La *Belle Hélène* (1864); *Les Bergers de Watteau* (1865); *Daphnis et Chloé* (1860); *Les Deux Aveugles* (1855); *Dragonette* (1857); *La Fille du tambour-major* (1879); *Geneviève de Brabant* (1859, rev. 1875); *La *Grande Duchesse de Gérolstein* (1867); *Madame Favart* (1878); *Le Mariage aux lanternes* (1857); *Monsieur Choufleuri* (1861); *Orphée aux enfers* (1858, rev. 1874); *La *Périchole* (1868); *Princesse de Trébizonde* (1869); *Robinson Crusoé* (1867); *La *Vie parisienne* (1866, see also *Gaîté parisienne*); *Pomme d'api* (1873); *Whittington and his Cat* (1874).

Offertory (Fr. Offertoire; Lat. Offertorium). The Offertory of the Mass consists of an *Antiphon, a part of the Proper of the Mass, sung just after the Credo, while the priest is preparing the bread and wine and offering them upon the altar. The plainsong setting is generally insufficient to occupy the time, so a motet or org. voluntary may be interpolated.

Offrandes oubliées, Les (The Forgotten Offerings). Work for orch. by *Messiaen, comp. 1930, f.p. Paris 1931. In 3 parts, *The Cross, The Sin, The Eucharist*.

Ogdon, John (Andrew Howard) (*b* Mansfield, 1937). Eng. pianist and composer. Studied RMCM (with Gordon Green) and with Denis Matthews and Egon Petri. As a student gave f. ps. of works by Goehr, Maxwell Davies, and himself. Played Brahms's 1st conc. with Barbirolli, 1956, when still a student; début with Hallé Orch. 1957, London (Prom) 1959. Joint first prize (with *Ashkenazy), Moscow Tchaikovsky competition 1962 (prize not shared; 2 first prizes awarded). Brilliant exponent of Liszt, Busoni, Alkan, in addition to wide repertory of concs. NY début 1963. Composer of pf. conc., etc.

Ogiwara, Toshitsugu (*b* Osaka, 1910). Japanese composer. Studied with *Tcherepnin. Works incl. str. qts. and orch. pieces.

O God, our Help in Ages Past. Hymn, words (based on Psalm 90) by Isaac Watts (1674–1748), first pubd. in his *Psalms of David* (1719) with first words 'Our God, our help' which were altered to 'O God' by John Wesley in *Collection of Psalms and Hymns* (1737). Tune (attrib. William *Croft) first appeared anonymously, set to Psalm 42, in 1708 *Supplement* to Tate and Brady Psalms. Known as *St Anne*, Croft being organist of St Anne's, Soho, in 1708. First line of tune is stock 18th-cent. phrase and is found in J. S. Bach's org. fugue in E♭ which is therefore known in Eng. as 'St Anne Fugue'. Has claim to be most popular of all hymns, and is especially assoc. with Remembrance Day services.

Ogura, Roh (*b* Moji, 1916). Japanese composer. Has written 2 syms., opera, vn. conc., pf. conc., str. qts., etc.

Ohana, Maurice (*b* Casablanca, 1914). Fr. composer and pianist. Studied Paris Schola Cantorum (1937–40) and S. Cecilia Acad., Rome (1944–6). Mainly self-taught in composition. Works, in avant-garde idiom, incl. 2 operas, guitar conc., tpt. concertino, *Silenciaire* for 6 percussionists, and *Tombeau de Claude Debussy* for sop., zither, pf., and chamber orch.

Ohlsson, Garrick (*b* Bronxville, 1948). Amer. pianist. Studied Juilliard Sch., NY. Winner of Busoni Competition, It., 1966, Montreal Competition, 1968, Warsaw Int. Chopin Competition, 1970. Has pursued int. career as soloist and recitalist.

Oiseaux exotiques (Exotic birds). Orch. work by *Messiaen for pf., 2 cl., xylophone, glockenspiel, perc., small wind orch., comp. 1955–6. F.p. Paris 1956, Loriod (pf.) R. Albert (cond.).

Oistrakh, David (*b* Odessa, 1908; *d* Amsterdam, 1974). Russ. violinist and cond. Studied Odessa Mus. Sch. Played Glazunov conc. with composer conducting, Kiev 1926. Moscow début 1928, joining staff of Cons. 1934. 1st prize Brussels Int. Competition, 1937. Début Paris and London 1953, USA 1955. Dedicatee and first performer of both Shostakovich vn. concs., No. 1 (1955); No. 2 (1967). One of greatest violinists of his day.

Oistrakh, Igor (*b* Odessa, 1931). Russ, violinist, son of David *Oistrakh. Studied with his father at Moscow Cons. Début 1948. Frequently appeared as joint recitalist with his father, also in Bach's double vn. conc. and in Mozart's Sinfonia Concertante, with father as violist. Won Wieniawski Competition, Poland, 1952. On staff Moscow Cons. from 1958.

Okeghem. See *Ockeghem, Johannes.*

Oker (Okeover), **John** (*b* ? London, after 1590; *d* Wells, *c.* 1663). Eng. composer and organist. Organist Wells Cath., 1619–39 and again after 1660. Gloucester Cath., 1640–4. Wrote fancies for viols, and other instr. pieces.

Oklahoma! Amer. musical with mus. by Richard Rodgers and lyrics by Oscar Hammerstein II which is generally held to have pioneered new type of musical show. Prod. NY 1943, London 1947. Contains songs *O, What a Beautiful Morning* and *The Surrey with the Fringe on Top*, among others equally good.

Oktave (Ger.). Octave. So *Oktavflöte*, octave flute, i.e. *piccolo; *Oktavkoppel*, octave coupler.

Olczewska, Maria (orig. Berchtenbreitner, Marie) (*b* Ludwigsschwaige, nr. Donauwörth, 1892; *d* Klagenfurt, 1969). Ger. mez. Studied in Munich. Began career in operetta. Heard by *Nikisch, who engaged her for Leipzig Opera 1916. Sang at Hamburg Opera 1917–20, Vienna 1921–3, Munich 1923–5. Member of Vienna State Opera 1923–30, being a notable Oktavian in *Der Rosenkavalier.* Sang at CG 1924–32, Chicago Opera 1928–32, NY Met. 1933–5. Prof., Vienna Acad. from 1947. Fine Wagnerian singer and of roles such as Amneris in *Aida.*

Old Hall Manuscript. Early 15th-cent. coll. of church mus. found in the library of St Edmund's Coll., Old Hall, Herts., first described in 1903 and pubd. 1933–8. Now in the Brit. Library. It offers a valuable opportunity of studying the choral style of a period *c.*1415. Comprises 140 folios of church mus. by composers of the Chapel Royal.

Oldham, Arthur (*b* London, 1926). Eng. composer, ch.-master, and pianist. Studied RCM with Howells and privately with *Britten. Mus. dir.

Ballet Rambert. Adapted Arne's *Love in a Village* for Aldeburgh Fest., 1952. Works incl. ballets (*Bonne-Bouche* 1952), choral works, *Divertimento* for str. etc. Ch.-master of Scottish Opera 1966–74, LSO Chorus 1969–76.

Old Hundredth (Amer. Old Hundred). Metrical psalm tune of uncertain origin. Its name indicates that it was set to the 100th psalm in the 'old' version of the metrical psalms, i.e. Sternhold and Hopkins as distinct from Tate and Brady. The edn. of this version in which it first appeared was Daye's of 1560–1, where it was set to the words 'All people that on earth do dwell' by W. Kethe. But the history of the tune goes back to Marot and Béza's Genevan Psalter of 1551, in which it is attached to the 134th psalm. An even earlier form of the tune appears in the Antwerp collection *Souter Liederkens* (1540). A ceremonial arr. of the tune for ch., congregation, orch., organ, and 'all available trumpets' was made by Vaughan Williams for the coronation of Elizabeth II, 1953. (It was also perf. at his funeral in Westminster Abbey, 1958.)

Old King Cole. Ballet for orch. and ch. (ad lib.) by Vaughan Williams to lib. by Mrs E. Vulliamy, prod. Cambridge 1923. Based on Eng. folk dances; score incorporates some folk-songs.

Oldman, Cecil (Bernard) (*b* London, 1894; *d* London, 1969). Eng. musicologist. Joined Brit. Museum staff 1920, becoming Prin. Keeper of Printed Books 1947–59. Expert on bibliography of Mozart, Beethoven, and Haydn. C.B. 1952.

Old Vic. Familiar name for S. London th. properly the Royal Victoria Hall, Waterloo Road. Built 1818 as Royal Coburg Hall, being renamed 1833 and becoming mus.-hall. Bought in 1880 by Emma Cons, a social reformer, who renamed it Royal Victoria Coffee Hall and staged operatic excerpts. In 1898 her niece Lilian *Baylis took over and, with courageous single-mindedness, developed the th. as a home for cheap-seat Shakespeare and opera, the latter being given twice a week and on alternate Saturday matinées. In 1931 the opera was transferred to new SW Th.

Ole (Sp.). A gipsy type of *Seguidilla also known as *Polo* or *Romalis.*

Oliphant (from Fr. *cor d'olifant*, elephant's horn). Hole-less type of cow-horn made of ivory, introduced into the W. from Byzantium in medieval times. Became symbol of royalty, owing to rich carving and decoration.

Oliver, Stephen (*b* Liverpool, 1950). Eng. composer. Studied Oxford Univ. with *Leighton and elec. mus. with Sherlaw *Johnson. Taught for 2 years at Huddersfield Sch. of Mus. Prolific composer of operas and mus. th. *Perseverance* calls for rock group, dance band, and skiffle group. Works incl.:

VOICE(S): *Sirens*, bar., pf. (1972); *Magnificat and Nunc Dimittis* (1976); *Exchange*, counterten., ten., bar., pf. (1978); *The Child from the Sea*, treble, ch., orch. (1980); *A String of Beads*, ch., orch. (1980); *Trinity Mass*, unacc. (1981); *Beauty and the Beast*, solo vv. and orch. (1984).

THEATRICAL (incl. OPERA): *Slippery Soules*, Christmas drama (1969); 3 Mini-Operas (*Paid Off, Time Flies, Old Haunts*) (1973); *Sufficient Beauty* (1973); *A Fur-Coat for Summer* (1973); *Perseverance* (1973–4); *Past Tense* (1974); *Cadenus Observed* (solo bar., 1974); **Tom Jones* (1974–5); *Bad Times* (1975); *The Great McPorridge Disaster* (1976); *The Waiter's Revenge* (1976); *The Girl and the Unicorn*, children's opera (1978); *The Duchess of Malfi* (1971–7); *The Dreaming of the Bones* (1979); *Nicholas Nickleby* (1980); *Sacha* (1982); *Blondel* (1983); *Britannia Preserv'd* (1984).

ORCH: *The Boy and the Dolphin* (1974); *Luv* (1975); Sym. (1976).

INSTR. AND CHAMBER: *Music for the Wreck of the Deutschland*, pf. quintet (1972); *Ricercare*, cl., vn., vc., pf. (1973); *Bad Times*, bar., str. qt. (1975); *The Elixir*, bar., cl., ch. (1976); guitar sonata (1978); *The Key to the Zoo*, spkr., 2 ob., bn., hpd. (1980); *Ricercare II* (1981).

ARR: Peri's *Euridice* (1600), for 13 solo vv., ch., and 8 players (1980).

Olivera, Mercedes (*b* Montevideo, 1919). Uruguayan pianist and harpsichordist. Début Montevideo 1932. London début 1946.

Olivero, Magda (*b* Saluzzo, 1912). It. sop. Opera début Turin 1933. Retired 1941 on marriage, but returned 1950–1. London 1952 (Mimì in *La Bohème*). Sang in USA 1966–77, making her Met. début in 1975 as Tosca. Notable singing-actress in such roles as Liù, Violetta, Mimì.

Oliveros, Pauline (*b* Houston, 1932). Amer. composer. Worked at San Francisco Tape Centre 1961–6. Worked with David Tudor, pianist, and Elizabeth Harris, dancer-choreog., 1963–6. Dir., tape mus. centre, Mills Coll., 1966; teacher of elec. mus., Univ. of California, San Diego, from 1967. After 1963 her works used mixed media and she prefers live elec. perf. to prepared tape. Has written a trio for fl., pf., and page-turner (1961) and a work for orch., ch., elecs., and lights called *To Valerie Solonas and Marilyn Monroe in recognition of their desperation* (1970).

Olsen, Ole (*b* Hammerfest, 1850; *d* Oslo, 1927). Norweg. composer. Studied Leipzig 1870–4. Inspector of mus., Norweg. military acad. 1887–1903. Wrote operas, oratorios, sym.

Olympians, The. Opera in 3 acts by *Bliss to lib. by J. B. Priestley. Prod. London 1949.

O magnum mysterium (O great mystery). Cycle of 4 carols for mixed ch. with instr. sonatas and fantasia for org. by *Maxwell Davies. Written for Cirencester Grammar Sch., 1960.

O'Mara, Joseph (*b* Limerick, 1861; *d* Dublin, 1927). Irish ten. and impresario. Studied Milan. Début London 1891 in *Ivanhoe*. Sang at CG, then became prin. ten. of *Moody-Manners co., 1902–10. Formed O'Mara Co. 1912. Retired 1926.

Omar Khayyám. Work for cont., ten., bass soloists, ch., and orch. by Bantock to text drawn from Edward FitzGerald's *Rubaiyát of Omar Khayyám* (1859). In 3 parts (Birmingham 1906, Cardiff 1907, Birmingham 1909, then perf. complete in London and Vienna 1912).

Omphale's Spinning-wheel (Saint-Saëns). See *Rouet d'Omphale, Le*.

Oncina, Juan (*b* Barcelona, 1925). Sp. ten. Studied Barcelona, making début there 1946. Sang in It. 1946–52, specializing in Rossini and Donizetti roles. Glyndebourne 1952–61.

Ondeggiando, ondeggiante, ondeggiamento (It.). Undulating, i.e. *tremolo or *vibrato, or (also) any swaying effect.

Ondes Martenot. Elec. instr. developed by Maurice *Martenot, a Fr. musician, who patented it in 1922 and produced it in 1928. Looks like a *spinet, with a kbd. of 5 octaves but can produce only one note at a time. Uses oscillating valves like *theremin, but is operated by a wire across the kbd., the player producing the desired pitch by manipulating the wire which moves a variable condenser, the kbd. serving as a guide. The signal is amplified through a loudspeaker. Tone-colour and timbre are obtained by pressing a button, and vol. is controlled by a key. The instr. is used in *Messiaen's *Turangalîla Symphony and in *Honegger's *Jeanne d'Arc au bûcher.

Ondine. See *Undine*.

Ondine (Ravel). See *Gaspard de la nuit*.

Ondříček, František (*b* Prague, 1857; *d* Milan, 1922). Cz. violinist and composer. Studied Prague Cons. and Paris Cons. (with Massart). Début Paris 1882, followed by tours. Gave f.p. of Dvořák's vn. conc., Prague 1883. Settled in Vienna 1907, forming qt. Prof. of vn. Vienna Cons. 1911–19, Prague Cons. 1919–22. With Mittelmann, wrote vn. method (1908). Composed vn. conc. and other vn. pieces.

Onegin, Sigrid (*b* Stockholm, 1889; *d* Magliaso, Switz., 1943). Swed. cont. Studied Frankfurt, Munich, and Milan. Début Stuttgart 1912 (with Caruso), creating role of Dryad in Strauss's *Ariadne auf Naxos* in 1st season. London début 1913 (under name Lilli Hoffmann-Onegin). Munich Opera 1919–22, Berlin 1926–33, NY Met. 1922–4, CG 1927, Bayreuth 1933–4. V. of much power and range. Notable as Lady Macbeth, Fricka, Herodias, Orfeo, and Brangäne.

O'Neill, Norman (*b* London, 1875; *d* London, 1934). Eng. composer and cond. Studied London with *Somervell and in Frankfurt with *Knorr (see *Frankfurt Group*). Treasurer, Royal Phil. Soc. 1918–34. Teacher of harmony and comp., RAM 1924–34. Mus. dir. Haymarket Th. for many years, composing incidental mus. for Maeterlinck's *The Blue Bird* (1909) and Barrie's *Mary Rose* (1920). Also wrote orch. works and chamber mus.

One-step. Amer. dance in simple duple time and rather more vigorous than the *fox-trot. Became popular *c.* 1910.

Ongarese (It.). Hungarian.

On Hearing the first Cuckoo in Spring (Delius). No. 1 of *2 Moood Pictures* for small orch. comp. 1911–13, f.p. Leipzig 23 Oct. 1913, cond. Nikisch, f.p. in England 1914 (cond. Mengelberg). Main theme based on No. 14 ('In Ola Valley') of Grieg's *Norwegian Folk Tunes*, Op. 66.

Onslow, Georges (Louis) (*b* Clermont-Ferrand, 1784; *d* Clermont-Ferrand, 1853). Fr. pianist and composer (Brit. father, Fr. mother). Studied pf. in London with J. L. Dušek and Cramer and comp. in Paris with Reicha. Settled in Fr., giving pf. recitals and lessons. Wrote 3 comic operas, 4 syms., 35 str. qts., 34 str. quintets, and other chamber works.

On this Island. 5 songs for high v. and pf. by Britten, Op. 11, to poems by W. H. Auden. Comp. 1937. F.p. BBC broadcast 1937.

Onward, Christian Soldiers. Hymn with words by the Rev. S. Baring-Gould, first pubd. 1868 in appendix to *Hymns Ancient and Modern*, with tune by J. B. *Dykes adapted from slow movt. of Haydn's Sym. No. 53. Became popular when set by *Sullivan in 1871 as 'St Gertrude', pubd. in *The Hymnary* (ed. Barnby), but first pubd. in *Musical Times*. Holst set same words in 1924.

On Wenlock Edge. Song-cycle by Vaughan Williams to 6 poems from A. E. Housman's *A Shropshire Lad* (1896) for ten., str. qt., and pf. F.p. 1909. Also arr. by composer for ten. and orch. (f.p. 1924). First item of cycle is the poem *On Wenlock Edge*.

Op. (plural **opp.**). Abbreviation for *opus.

Open. (1) Applied to bowed or plucked instr., a str. which is allowed to vibrate throughout its full length, i.e. not 'stopped' by a finger pressed on it.
  (2) Of a hn., not 'stopped' by the placing of the hand inside the bell.

Open Diapason. The chief manual stop of the org., 8′ in length, contrasted with the 'stopped diapason'.

Open Form. A structural procedure whereby the sequence and/or construction of parts of a notated work are variable. First employed by *Ives, *Cowell, and *Grainger, but developed as indeterminacy by *Cage and Earle *Brown. In Boulez's 3rd pf. sonata, for example, the 5

movements may be played in any order except the 3rd which must stay central.

Open Harmony. Harmony in which the notes of the chords are widely spread.

Opening cuts. Phrase used in operatic parlance, meaning that passages of an opera which are usually omitted are being performed.

Oper (Ger.). Opera. Also refers to an opera co., e.g. Vienna Staatsoper (Vienna State Opera—co. implied).

Opera. Monthly magazine covering news and reports of all operatic matters founded 1950 by Earl of Harewood, who was ed. until 1953, when he was succeeded by Harold *Rosenthal.

Opera (It., work, but actually plural of Lat. *opus*, a work; Fr. *Opéra*; Ger. *Oper*). The term is an abbreviation of *opera in musica*. Opera is a drama set to mus. to be sung with instr. acc. by singers usually in costume. Recit. or spoken dialogue may separate the *numbers, but the essence of opera is that the mus. is integral and is not incidental, as in a 'musical' or play with mus.
  Although literary dramas and *sacre rappresenta-ʒione* were its precursors in some respects, opera is generally said to have originated in Florence towards the close of the 16th cent. (see *Camerata*) with the earliest examples by *Peri and *Caccini. Recit. was the dominant feature, but with *Monteverdi, whose operatic career extended from 1607 to 1642, opera developed rapidly, borrowing elements from the madrigal and from the ornate Venetian church mus. The aria became an important element, and in *L'incoronazione di Poppea*, the insight shown into the humanity of the characters anticipated 19th-cent. developments. *Cavalli followed Monteverdi's lead, but a more formal approach was reintroduced by A. *Scarlatti, who comp. 115 operas between 1679 and 1725. He introduced instr. acc. for recit. in 1686. During the 17th cent. opera was pioneered in Fr. by *Lully and *Rameau and in Ger. by *Schütz and *Keiser. But the next great figure in operatic history was *Handel, whose operas were mostly comp. for London (between 1711 and 1741) in the It. *opera seria* style. His glorious solo arias were written for the brilliant techniques and skills of the great *castrato* singers of his day and for equally fine sops.; in addition, he imparted a lengthened degree of dramatic tension to the form both in arias and recits. It was left to J. C. *Bach in his London operas of the 1760s to restore the ch. to a place in opera, as was done also by *Gluck, whose operas were written between 1741 and 1779. Gluck's *Orfeo*, written for Vienna in 1762, is a revolutionary opera because it exploits to the full the mus. and dramatic possibilities of the lib. Gluck scrapped the *da capo* aria, which was a primary cause of holding up the dramatic development of the plot, and in his preface to *Alceste* (1767) he wrote of reducing

mus. to its true function 'which is that of seconding poetry in the expression of sentiments and dramatic situations of a story'. Although *opera seria* was to reach its culmination with Mozart's *Idomeneo* (1781), Gluck's reforms effectively killed it off, even if fashion still prevented him from carrying out his theories fully.

*Haydn's operas, mostly written for Esterháza, are rich in mus. content but were eclipsed by the works of genius with which *Mozart ended the 18th cent., operas which brought the orch. into the forefront of the art, giving it a whole new dimension. Moreover they were works which defied classification under the old headings of *opera seria* and *opera buffa*. After *Don Giovanni* almost anything was possible.

The beginning of the 19th cent. was given a post-Mozartian sparkle by the brilliance, wit, and zest of *Rossini's comic operas, and a generation of remarkable singers was served by Rossini, *Bellini, and *Donizetti. In Ger. the romantic movement, with its interest in folklore and fantasy, found an operatic spokesman in *Weber, whose *Der Freischütz*, *Oberon*, and *Euryanthe* opened the way for the colossal transformation wrought by *Wagner, who in his maturity dispensed with the established *numbers opera and converted recit. and aria into a seamless, continuous, and symphonic web of mus., with the orch. almost an extra character on the stage. He preferred the term 'music drama' to 'opera', wrote his own libs., and viewed opera as an amalgam of all the arts. In one sense his operas were a reaction against the spectacular 'singers' operas' of *Meyerbeer which he had seen in his Parisian youth. Meyerbeer was Ger., but it is with Paris that he is assoc., enjoying success while the much more talented *Berlioz had little operatic success in his lifetime, though his *Les Troyens* is now recognized as a major masterpiece. The operas of Massenet, Gounod, Bizet, and Saint-Saëns dominated Fr. mus. in the latter half of the 19th cent. But next to Wagner the outstanding figure was *Verdi, also born in 1813, who learned much from Donizetti and refined and developed his art, keeping to a numbers-opera format, from *Oberto* of 1837–8 to the magical *Falstaff* of 1889–92.

Nationalist opera was principally an E. European development, beginning with *Glinka's *A Life for the Tsar* in 1836 and continuing with *Mussorgsky's *Boris Godunov* and Borodin's *Prince Igor*. Tchaikovsky's operas, of which *Eugene Onegin* is the best known, were not overtly nationalist, however. *Smetana in Bohemia with *Dalibor* and *The Bartered Bride* est. a Cz. operatic tradition which reached its apogee in the first quarter of the 20th cent. with the powerful, realistic, and orig. operas of *Janáček.

In Ger. the greatest post-Wagnerian figure in opera was Richard *Strauss, whose first opera, *Guntram*, was prod. 1894 and his last, *Capriccio*, in 1942. He was continually trying to find new ways of reconciling words and mus., several of his works having the advantage of fine libs. by the Austrian poet Hofmannsthal. Other major operas from Ger. and Austria in the 20th cent. were written by *Berg (*Wozzeck* and *Lulu*), Schoenberg, Pfitzner, Korngold, Einem, Orff, and Henze.

After Verdi in It. came the *verismo* (reality) movement, in which operas, often but not necessarily in contemporary settings, strove to present the harsh realities of the situations with which they dealt. In many cases these derived from the realistic novels of Fr. literature in the late 19th cent., e.g. Zola, but like all such categorizations, *verismo* is hard to define and it could easily be said that Verdi's *La traviata* is *verismo*. However, the term is generally applied to the works of *Mascagni, *Leoncavallo, *Montemezzi, *Leoni, and, though he is a special case, to *Puccini, whose operas achieved and have retained a wide popularity because of their mus. and dramatic colour and immediate appeal. *La Bohème* in particular is among the most frequently perf. of all operas, with *Madama Butterfly* running it close.

Opera in Eng. was for many years mainly an imported commodity. Only *Purcell's short *Dido and Aeneas* (1689) and the ballad-opera *The *Beggar's Opera* (1728) were of any quality among native products, although Balfe's *The Bohemian Girl* (1843) achieved popularity. *Sullivan wrote a grand opera (*Ivanhoe*) but won immortality through the light operas written in collab. with Gilbert in which his flair for parody and pastiche could be exploited to the full. *Vaughan Williams comp. 5 operas which have excellent mus. qualities but are still held to be dramatically weak. *Britten, with *Peter Grimes* in 1945, showed that Eng. had at last produced a natural operatic composer, as was shown by the eagerness with which these works were also staged abroad. He wrote several operas which needed only a chamber orch. and also developed a genre which he called 'church parables'. These are midway between opera and medieval morality play. The example of Britten was followed by Tippett, Bennett, Walton, Maxwell Davies, Oliver, Tavener, and many others.

In the USA, native opera took even longer than in Brit. to find its feet. *Gershwin's *Porgy and Bess* has a claim to be the first successful Amer. opera. Operas by the It.-born *Menotti and by *Barber followed the European tradition, and qualities of exuberance, raciness, and wit which the Americans bring to mus. have been channelled most effectively into the genre of 'musical' such as *Oklahoma!* and *Kiss Me Kate*.

Some great composers have written only one opera, the supreme examples being *Beethoven, whose *Fidelio* is regarded by many as the greatest of all operas, and *Debussy (*Pelléas et Mélisande*), while others have written none, e.g. Brahms, Bruckner, Elgar, Mahler, Ives, and Rubbra. Yet opera remains for most composers the greatest and most attractive challenge. With the development of mechanical and elec. techniques and the advance of the stage producer to an importance comparable with that of the cond., the staging of operas has grown more exciting and controversial, and has been exploited in the works of Henze, Maxwell Davies, *Ginastera, and others. It has also become more expensive. Finance was a contributory cause of Britten's development of chamber operas, and has also led to the emergence of *music theatre, a genre in which works of quasi-operatic character, sometimes involving only one singer or reciter, can be perf. either with a minimum of stage trappings (costumes, etc.) or with none at all but purely as a concert performance. A remarkable example of mus. theatre at its best is Maxwell Davies's 8 *Songs for a Mad King. Yet even here it can be argued that 20th-cent. mus. theatre is merely a reversion to Monteverdi's Il combattimento di Tancredi e Clorinda.

The term opera not only covers the form of mus. composition but the whole business of performing opera. Thus it embraces the famous opera houses and cos. of It. in Milan, Rome, Naples, and Venice, of other parts of Europe in Vienna, Salzburg, Berlin, Dresden, Frankfurt, Munich, Bayreuth, and Paris, of Russia in Moscow and Leningrad, in the USA in NY and Chicago, and in Eng. in London. Two prin. cos. work in London, the Royal Opera at CG, and ENO at the Coliseum. Outside London there is the summer fest. at *Glyndebourne, Sussex, but opera is provided on almost an all-the-year-round basis by the regional cos., Scottish Opera (based in Glasgow), WNO (Cardiff) and Opera North (Leeds). These cos. also tour. There are also many other cos., e.g. Kent Opera, which provide excellent perfs. and reflect the immense development of operatic life in Britain since 1945. All these activities, except Glyndebourne, are heavily subsidized. Commercial sponsorship of opera has become a valuable and necessary contribution to its continuance.

Opéra-ballet. Stage work, especially assoc. with Campra and Rameau in Fr. in the late 17th and early 18th cents., in which equal or nearly equal importance is given to singing and dancing.

Opera buffa (It.; Fr. Opéra bouffe). Comic opera, the opposite of *opera seria. Began as use of a comic subject involving characters drawn from everyday life. Examples are Mozart's Le nozze di Figaro, Rossini's Il barbiere di Siviglia, and Donizetti's Don Pasquale.

Opéra comique (Fr.). Comic opera. By no means the Fr. equivalent of opera buffa, and it has changed its meaning several times. It now means opera in which there is spoken dialogue, but the subject-matter ought to be light-hearted and treated thus. Beethoven's Fidelio and Bizet's Carmen are technically opéras comiques but cannot be classified as such.

Opéra-Comique, Paris. The 2nd opera house of Paris, orig. housing Fr. mus. works with spoken dialogue. It has had a chequered history: opened 1715, closed 1745, reopened 1752. Moved to the rue Favart 1782 (still sometimes being known as the *Salle Favart). Closed 1801, amalgamated with a rival co. Works by Méhul, Boïeldieu, and Auber were produced there in the first half of the 19th cent. as well as Donizetti's La Fille du régiment (1840). Later, Offenbach's Tales of Hoffmann and Delibes's Lakmé had their f.ps. there. The building was burned down in 1887, the co. finding haven elsewhere until 1898 when the present th. opened. Debussy's Pelléas et Mélisande was given its f.p. in the new th. in 1902. In 1959 administration of the Opéra-Comique and the Paris Opéra was merged under A. M. Julien, succeeded 1962 by *Auric, 1969–71 by Nicoly. The th. closed in 1972 and reopened 1973 as Opéra Studio de Paris under dir. of L. Erlo. Opéra Studio moved to Lyons 1976, and Opéra-Comique, dir. by R. Liebermann, opened with old name of Salle Favart.

Opera North. Opera company based in Leeds, Yorkshire, formed in 1978 as northern arm of English National Opera at the London Coliseum. F.p. November 1978, Grand Th., Leeds, Saint-Saëns's Samson et Dalila. Mus. dir. David Lloyd-Jones. As financial independence grew, co. altered name from English National Opera North to Opera North in 1981. Gives regular seasons in Manchester, York, Nottingham, etc. Commissioned Wilfred Josephs's Rebecca 1983. Gave f. Eng. p. of Křenek's *Jonny spielt auf, 1984.

Opera-Oratorio. Term used by Stravinsky to describe his *Oedipus Rex, which is designed to be presented on the stage but in the static manner of a concert perf. of an oratorio.

Opéra, Paris. See Paris Opéra.

Opera Seria (It.). Serious opera. In the 17th and 18th cents., opera seria was the chief operatic genre, becoming very formal and complex, with elaborate display arias. Mythological subjects were the norm, and most of these were written for various composers by the librettist *Metastasio. The last and greatest examples of the form were Mozart's Idomeneo (1781) and La clemenza di Tito (1791).

Operetta (It.; Fr. opérette). Little opera. Strictly a play with ov., songs, entr'actes, and dances, but the term has become synonymous with 'light opera', e.g. Offenbach's La Belle Hélène and Strauss's Die Fledermaus, and 'musical comedy', e.g. Coward's Bitter-Sweet.

Opernball, Der (The Opera Ball). Operetta in 3 acts by *Heuberger to lib. by Léon and Waldeberg after the farce Les Dominos roses by Delacour and

Henniquin. Prod. Vienna 1898, NY 1909. Contains the song *Im Chambre séparée*.

Oper und Drama (Ger.). Opera and Drama. Long essay by *Wagner, written in Zürich 1850–1, in which he expounded his theories on mus. drama, speech-origins, etc.

Ophicleide. (1) Obsolete keyed brass instr. of conical bore and played with cup mouthpiece. Was a development of the *serpent and existed in alto, bass, and double-bass sizes, but only the bass was much used. Was used in military bands and is also incl. in early scores of Mendelssohn, Berlioz, Verdi, and Wagner. Superseded by the bass tuba.
(2) Org. stop like *Tuba*.

Op. Posth. Posthumous work, i.e. work pubd. after composer's death. See *Opus*.

Opus (Lat.). Work. Word used, followed by a number, e.g. Opus 50, for the numbering of a composer's works. This numbering gives a rough idea of the order in which works were comp., but can be misleading. Sometimes the Opus no. is allotted by the composer, sometimes by the publisher. Some composers, e.g. Mozart, Haydn, did not number their works; some, e.g. Elgar, gave some works Opus nos. and not others; some, e.g. R. Strauss, did likewise but also reallotted Opus nos. so that much confusion arises in his case. Dvořák allowed early works to be given late Opus nos. by his publisher. In many cases an Opus no. covers a group of works, in which case the numbering is subdivided, e.g. Op. 59, No. 3, or in a style often used, Op. 59/3. In other cases, 2 versions of the same work exist and the composer uses letters after the number to differentiate them, e.g. Op. 49a, Op. 49b. Although the Latin plural of Opus is Opera, it has become customary to write 'opuses', to avoid confusion, just as in Italian 'opera' has become a singular noun with the plural *opere*.

Oracolo, L' (The Oracle). Opera in 1 act by F. *Leoni to lib. by C. Zanoni from a story 'The Cat and the Cherub' by C. B. Fernald. Prod. CG 1905, NY Met. 1915.

Oration. 'Concerto elegiaco' for vc. and orch. by Frank *Bridge, comp. 1930.

Oratorio. (1) Strictly, a mus. setting of a religious lib. for solo singers, ch., and orch., in dramatic form but usually perf. without scenery or costumes in concert-hall or church. The form originated in plays given in the Oratory of S. Philip Neri, Rome, in the mid-16th cent., the mus. form developing *c*.1600. The first oratorio was Cavalieri's *La rappresentazione di anima e di corpo* (The Representation of Soul and Body), a *morality set to music and perf. in costume. Later oratorios, in concert-form, were written by *Carissimi, A. *Scarlatti, *Schütz, *Handel (esp. *Messiah*, the most popular of all oratorios),

*Haydn, *Spohr, *Beethoven, and *Mendelssohn (*Elijah*). Elgar wrote 3 oratorios (but *The Dream of Gerontius* is not an oratorio).
(2) The term is also applied to works similar to these cited above but on a non-religious subject, e.g. Handel's *Semele*, *Tippett's A *Child of our Time*. Stravinsky's *Oedipus Rex* is described as an *opera-oratorio.

Orb and Sceptre. Coronation march by *Walton, comp. for coronation of Elizabeth II, 1953 and f.p. in Westminster Abbey, cond. Boult, 2 June 1953.

Orchésographie. Treatise on dancing by Thoinot *Arbeau, written in Fr. and pubd. 1588–9. Important source of information on ancient dances and their tunes. They are described in a dialogue with his pupil Capriol, hence the title *Capriol Suite* for *Warlock's work based on several of the dance tunes.

Orchestra (Fr. *orchestre*, Ger. *Orchester*). A mixed body of instrumentalists for the perf. of symphonic and other works. There are various types of orch., e.g. symphony orchestra, a body of (usually) over 90 players able to play elaborate works; chamber orchestra, small version of above (from, say, 15 to 45 players); string orchestra, strings only; theatre orchestra, medium-size orch. used for musicals, etc., and often incl. saxs.

The orch. has changed and developed over the centuries, the standard version today comprising str., woodwind, brass, and perc. In the 17th cent. the orch. was a haphazard affair, often incl. viols, fls., obs., cornetts, tbs., drums, and hpd. In the 18th cent., with instr. improvements, vns. ousted viols. Accs. were realized by the harpsichordist or org. from a figured bass. From *c*.1800, the orch. became more elaborate and composers more skilled in its use, obtaining tone-colour by subtle combinations and by solo passages. In Beethoven's 1st Sym. (1800) the orch. consisted of: Vns., div. into 1st and 2nd sections, vas., vcs., dbs., fls., obs., cls., bns., tpts., hns., timp. Later composers added the harp and Berlioz enlarged the woodwind, brass, and perc. departments, as did Wagner and Liszt. Towards the end of the 19th and in the 20th cents., composers enlarged the orch. enormously, and we have the marvellously rich, exotic, and grandiose orch. works of Strauss, Mahler, Elgar, Havergal Brian, Ravel, Stravinsky, and many more. Huge brass sections are often a feature of their scores, with triple or quadruple woodwind (i.e. 3 or 4 of each instr.). Later in the 20th cent. even more variety in orch. use is encountered, with reversions to small combinations of instr., works scored for solo instr. and wind or brass instr. only, exotic perc. effects, and of course the addition of elec. instr., tape-recorded and synthesized effects.

The lay-out of the standard sym. orch. is normally as shown in the accompanying diagram, but certain works call for special seating arrange-

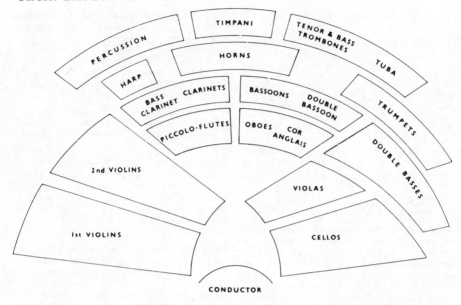

ments and some conds. have individual preferences.

Orchestral Employers' Association. British advisory and consultative committee of which the members are the managers of the prin. London and provincial sym. and opera orchs. Acts as advisory and consultative body on matters of common interest and represents its members in negotiations with Musicians' Union on pay and conditions, and in representations to the Govt. Works in assoc. with *Arts Council.

Orchestral oboe. Org. stop.

Orchestral Pieces, Five (*Fünf Orchesterstücke*). Work for large orch. by Schoenberg, Op. 16, comp. June–Aug. 1909, rev. 1922 and 1949 (reduced to normal-sized orch.). F.p. Berlin (Nos. 1, 2, and 4), Jan. 1912, cond. Schoenberg; f. complete p. London 1912, cond. Wood (also cond. Schoenberg in London 1914). Arr. for chamber orch. 1925 by Felix Greissle and for 2 pf. by Webern.

Orchestral Set. Name of 2 orch. works by *Ives. No. 1 is usually known as *Three Places in New England, 1908–14; No. 2, comp. 1909–15, has 3 movements: 1. *An Elegy to our Forefathers*; 2. *The Rockstrewn Hills Join in the People's Outdoor Meeting*; 3. *From Hanover Square North at the end of a Tragic Day (1915), the Voice of the People again Rose*.

Orchestration. (1) The art of scoring mus. for an orch. or band. Many composers show special skill in this, e.g. Haydn, Mozart, and Beethoven, while Berlioz, Wagner, Mahler, Elgar, Strauss, Ravel, Rimsky-Korsakov, and Britten are all masters of the art.
  (2) Arr. of a work for orch. which was comp. for another medium, e.g. Ravel's orchestration of his own *Ma Mère l'Oye*, written for pf. duet.

Orchestre de la Société des Concerts du Conservatoire. Fr. symphony orch. inaugurated by *Habeneck on 5 Feb. 1828, with Beethoven's *Eroica* Symphony, and comprising over 80 past and present students of the Conservatoire. Habeneck was succeeded by Girard (1849), Tilmant (1861), and Hainl (1864). Towards the end of the century Messager was cond. and after 1945 Munch and Cluytens were associated with it. Disbanded 1967 and succeeded by the Orchestre de *Paris.

Orchestre de la Suisse Romande. Orch. based on Geneva founded 1918 by Ernest *Ansermet, who was cond. until 1966. His successors have been Paul *Kletzki 1967–9, Wolfgang *Sawallisch 1970–80, Horst *Stein 1980–5, and Armin Jordan from 1985.

Ord, Boris (Bernhard) (*b* Bristol, 1897; *d* Cambridge, 1961). Eng. organist, choirmaster, and composer. Studied RCM and Cambridge Univ. Organist and choirmaster, King's Coll., Cambridge, 1929–57, popularizing through radio the famous Christmas Eve Fest. of Nine Lessons and Carols; lecturer in mus., Cambridge Univ. 1936–58; cond. Cambridge Univ. Mus. Soc. 1938–54.

Wrote one carol, *Adam lay y-bounden* (1957). C.B.E. 1958.

Ordinario (It.). Ordinary, normal, e.g. *tempo ordinario*.

Ordre (Fr.). Term synonymous with *suite used by *Couperin and his contemporaries.

Orel, Alfred (*b* Vienna, 1889; *d* Vienna, 1967). Austrian musicologist. Librarian, music div., Austrian Nat. Library 1918–40 and of Vienna Univ. musicological institute. Worked with R. *Haas from 1934 on collected works of Bruckner. Wrote books on Beethoven, Bruckner, Mozart, Schubert, Wolf, and Brahms, and ed. coll. of Bruckner's letters and other documentary sources.

Orfeo ed Euridice (Orpheus and Eurydice). Opera (*azione teatrale per musica*—theatrical action for mus.) in 3 acts by Gluck to lib. by Calzabigi based on mythological legend. Prod. Vienna 1762, London 1770, NY 1863. Title-role sung at f.p. in Vienna by alto castrato Gaetano *Guadagni. For Parma prod. 1769, male sop. sang role. Fr. version, *Orphée*, to trans. by Moline with title-role transposed for high ten. prod. Paris 1774. (Some mus. from ballet *Don Juan* recurs, and other new mus. was added.) Orfeo is now generally sung by mez. but sometimes by bar. Ed. by Berlioz prod. Paris 1859 (with Viardot as Orpheus). See also *Favola d'Orfeo* (Monteverdi) and *Orpheus*. Many composers have written works on the Orpheus legend.

Orff, Carl (*b* Munich, 1895; *d* Munich, 1982). Ger. composer, teacher, and cond. Studied Munich Acad., leaving to join army 1914. Worked in opera houses and returned to Munich 1920 for further study with Kaminsky. In 1924 founded the Günther School, Munich, where his life-long interest in children's mus. education began. About this time he made edns. of several operas by Monteverdi, incl. *L'incoronazione di Poppea*, comp. cantatas and an *Entrata* for orch. 'after William Byrd'. In 1937, when his *Carmina Burana* was f.p., he disowned all his previous works, though some were later rev. and restored. From then he comp. exclusively for the stage, though not conventionally (*Carmina Burana*, for example, is usually given in a concert version). His mature style is dry and staccato, with much use of perc. and the content of the mus. based on rhythmic patterns and their variations. Harmony is reduced to basic elements, and melody is nearer to rhythmic speech than to the 'expressive' ideal of other composers. Prin. works:

STAGE: *Trionfi*—*Trittico Teatrale* (Triumphs—theatrical triptych): 1. *Carmina Burana* (Songs of Beuren), *cantiones profanae* (1935–6); 2. *Catulli Carmina* (Songs of Catullus), *ludi scaenici* (1943); 3. *Trionfo di Afrodite* (Triumph of Aphrodite), *concerto scenico* (1950–1). Der *Mond* (The Moon), *ein Kleines Welttheater* (1937–8, rev. 1945); Die *Kluge* (The Clever Girl) (1941–2);

Die *Bernauerin* (1944–5); *Astutuli* (1945–6); *Antigonae* (1947–8); *Comoedia de Christi Resurrectione*, an Easter play (1955); *Oedipus der Tyrann* (1957–8); *Ludus de Nato Infante Mirificus*, a Christmas play (1960); *Ein Sommernachtstraum* (A *Midsummer Night's Dream), incidental mus. for Shakespeare (1939, rev. 1944 (withdrawn) and 1952); *Prometheus* (1963–7); *De temporum fine comoedia* (1969–71).

CHORUS AND ORCH: *Die Sänger der Vorwelt* (The Singer of Former Times) (1955); *Nänie und Dithyrambe* (1956); *Rota* (1972).

EDUCATIONAL: *Das Schulwerk, Musik für Kinder*, 5 vols. (1930–54).

ARRANGEMENTS: Monteverdi: *L'Incoronazione di Poppea* (1925, rev. 1940); *Lamenti* (triple bill, prod. Schwetzingen 1958, of *Lamento d'Arianna*, 1925, rev. 1940, *La Favola d'Orfeo*, 1925, rev. 1931, 1940, *Il Ballo delle Ingrate*, 1925, rev. 1940).

Organ (Ger. *Orgel*; Fr. *orgue*; It. *organo*). Kbd. instr. operated by air blown by a bellows through pipes to sound the notes. Often known as 'the king of instruments' because of its normal large size, although it is made in various sizes. The phrase was coined by *Machaut, who was probably referring also to the organ's versatility.

The principles of construction, in primary outline, are:

(1) A row of Pipes, graduated as to size (and hence as to pitch), is placed in a corresponding row of holes in a Windchest, which is fed by a Bellows.

Under each hole in the Windchest is a Pallet, i.e. a type of hinged cover which can be opened and closed.

The pallets are operated, in the older orgs., by a series of rods, called Stickers, and these are connected with the kbd. of the instr. by levers called Backfalls and rods called Trackers: thus on depressing a finger-key a current of air is admitted to its particular pipe, and on releasing it the current of air is then cut off. In many modern organs, instead of the Sticker-Backfall-Tracker action there are the tubes of a *Pneumatic Action* or the wires of an *Electric Action*.

What has been described is a theoretical org. of only one row of pipes. But in practice the Windchest has several such rows, the pipes being some of wood and some of metal, some of normal pitch and some of a pitch an octave below or above that pitch, etc., some being simple ('flue') pipes and others supplied with a vibrating tongue of metal called a Reed, and so on. The Pallets extend, *from front to back*, under each of these rows, so admitting air to, or excluding it from, the pipes related to one finger-key of the organ, whilst *from side to side* of the Windchest, under each row of pipes, runs a board with holes in it, called a Slider; when slid into one position the holes in this board coincide with those under the pipes and so permit the pallets to operate as regards that row; when slid into another position they no longer coincide, and so cut off the operation of the pallets in admitting air. The sliding is accomplished (mechanically, pneumatically, or electrically) by connexion with handles or other devices; these are the Drawstops, Stop-Keys, etc., respectively, each of which operates one row of pipes—called a Register or Stop (we speak of an organ of '20 stops', of '100 stops', etc.).

A kbd. operated by the hands is called a Manual and one operated by the feet, a Pedal-Board. All orgs. nowadays possess both types of kbd. When an instr. contains any considerable number of stops, differentiation in their use is made easier by their being distributed over 2, 3, or 4 manuals (occasionally more). These are banked up stepwise before the player. The chief manual is that of the Great Organ, which contains a variety of stops, incl. especially many of robust tone. Above it is that of the Swell Organ, the pipes belonging to which are enclosed in a Swell Box—with Venetian shutters which by means of a Swell Pedal can be opened or closed, so increasing or diminishing the volume of tone. Below the Great Organ manual, in a 3-manual organ, is that of the Choir Organ which contains softer stops, intended originally in a church, chiefly for the acc. of the choral body. If there is a 4th manual (above the Swell manual) it is that of the Solo Organ (with special stops of the character indicated by that name), and there may also be an Echo Organ, with very soft stops.

(2) The two varieties of stop are respectively called Flue Pipes and Reed pipes. Both are graduated in size, the larger producing the lowest notes and the smaller the highest. The normal pitch of an organ (the same, properly, as that of a pf.) is the product of any set of open-ended flue pipes of which the largest (representing C two lines below the bass staff) is 8′ long, the length of the remaining pipes of the set diminishing by half as each octave is ascended. The tone from the stops with these pipes of normal size can be reinforced by that from others of abnormal size, with their pipe for low C 4′ or 2′ long (so that the whole stop concerned gives an effect respectively 1 or 2 octaves higher than the normal) or, on the other hand, 16′ or even 32′ long (so that the stop concerned gives an effect respectively 1 or 2 octaves lower than normal). There are also stops of other lengths which give intermediate pitches reinforcing some of the natural harmonics of the normally pitched stops: these are called Mutation Stops or, if several rows (Ranks) of them are operated in chorus as though they made one, *Mixture stops. The chief stops on the Pedal Organ are pitched an octave below those of the manuals (i.e. whereas the chief stops of the manuals are 8′ stops, those of the Pedal are 16′ stops).

Besides 'open-ended flue pipes' there are flue pipes which have a stopper at the top ('End-plugged' is a term used in various entries in this dictionary), which lowers their pitch by an octave. The chief manual stop of the organ is the 8′ *Open Diapason: but there is generally also a Stopped Diapason, also, from its pitch, spoken of as an 8′ stop although, in actual physical length, 4′. (These stops are also to be found in the pedal department.)

By a system of *Couplers the Pedal organ can have one or more of the manuals connected with it. Some of the organ's stops are imitative of other instrs. such as the Flute, the Orchestral Oboe, Clarinet, and Trumpet (the last 3 being Reed Stops), and the Gamba (a String-Toned stop, supposed to reproduce the tone of the old viola da gamba). Stops presumably intended to be imitative are the Vox Humana (a reed stop) and the Vox Angelica or Voix céleste (with 2 flue pipes to each note slightly out of tune with each other, so producing a somewhat mysterious effect—or, if only one, by the drawstop simultaneously bringing into action some normally tuned soft stop). The Tremulant is not a stop, though operated by the player by similar means: it causes a slight fluctuation of the tone.

History: the org. is the oldest kbd. instr. The first was built by Ktesibios, a Gr. engineer living in Alexandria, in the 3rd cent. BC. This was called the *hydraulis, and wind pressure was stabilized by the use of water. During the 4th cent. AD bellows replaced the hydraulic mechanism (creating the pneumatic org.), and thereby increasing the vol. of sound. In the medieval org., pipes were of the 'flute' type (voiced with a lip, like the recorder); instead of the hydraulis kbd. (levers, each with a return mechanism, which were depressed by fingers to play notes), there was a series of tongues or sliders which were pulled or pushed manually; 2 players were often required, seated at the same manual; pipes sometimes outnumbered sliders by 10 to 1 and each note was prod. by a simultaneous 'mixture' of different pipes, producing a variety of timbre and pitch—there were unisons (basic pitch), octaves (octave higher), and quints (1 or more octaves plus a 5th higher).

During the 13th and 14th cents. the fashion for building very large instrs. was succeeded by a trend to smaller varieties, with the clumsy slider movement being replaced by the more flexible and sensitive kbd. One of the most popular types of org. from the 13th to the 16th cent. was the portative org. (organetto), so called because it could be carried. There were usually 2 rows of pipes giving a range of up to 2 octaves. The player provided his own air supply, using the right hand for the kbd. and the left for the bellows. The portative org. was monophonic, suited to playing a solo dance-tune. The 'great' church org. gained additional kbds. to offer variety of tone, that at Halberstadt, Ger., built in 1361, having 3 manuals and a pedal kbd. It had 20 bellows worked by 10 men. When the wind pressure was strong, the player had to use the full power of his arm to hold down a key. Between the cath. and the portative orgs. in size was the positive, which could be used in church and for chamber mus. It required 2 or 3 sets of bellows and someone else to operate them so that the player could use both hands on the kbd. Though not portable, the positive could be easily moved, smaller versions often standing on a table. In Eng. it became known as the 'chair' org., corrupted into 'choir' org.

At the close of the Middle Ages, several improvements occurred in construction of large church orgs., making them less unwieldy. By the beginning of the 16th cent. the kbd. had been altered to make it as responsive as that of smaller orgs; registration for each kbd. could be controlled by stops which worked in a similar way to the slider mechanism; in addition to open and stopped 'flue' pipes, there were 'reed' pipes employing a single vibrating tongue and a resonator; stops were contrasted, many of them being designed to imitate instr., and couplers were used to join manual to manual or manual to pedals. Further improvements were added over the course of the next century. Pedals were not introduced into Eng. org.-building until nearly the end of the 18th cent. In Paris, 1867, electricity was first used to activate the key action. Since that time every kind of refinement has been introduced to make orgs. capable of a wider and subtler range of tone-colour. The elec. org. was introduced in 1935. See also *Regal*.

Organistrum. The *Hurdy-Gurdy.

Organ Solo Mass. Mozart's Mass in C, K259 (1776). So named because there is an important org. solo in the Benedictus.

Organum. An early form of melodic harmonization which flourished from c.900 to 1200. In plainchant the melody was harmonized by addition of 1, 2, or 3 parts, usually parallel.

Orgelbüchlein (Little Organ Book). Unfinished coll. of 46 short chorale preludes for org. by Bach (164 were intended), written for instruction and for pedalling practice.

Orgue de Barberie. Small mechanical organ played by turning a handle. At one time frequently heard in Eng. streets.

Orgue expressif (Fr.). *Harmonium.

O'Riada, Seán (Reidy, John) (*b* Cork, 1931; *d* London, 1971). Irish composer. Studied Univ. Coll., Cork, under Fleischmann 1948–52. Ass. mus. dir. Radio Éireann 1954–5, mus. dir. Abbey Th., Dublin, 1955–62. Lect., Univ. Coll., Cork, 1963–71. Works incl. 2 ballets; *The Banks of Sullane*, sym. essay (1956); *Nomos No. 4*, pf., orch. (1957–8); *Requiem for a Soldier*, sop., ten., bar., ch., org. (1968).

Orlando. Opera in 3 acts by Handel to It. lib. by G. Bracciotti based on Ariosto's 16th-cent. poem *Orlando furioso* (Mad Orlando). Prod. London 1733.

Orlando Paladino. Opera in 3 acts by Haydn to lib. by N. Porta based on version by P. Guglielmi (1771) of Ariosto's *Orlando furioso*. Prod. Esterháza 1782.

Orloff, Vladimir (*b* Odessa, 1928). Russ.-born cellist. Studied Bucharest Cons. Prof., Vienna Acad. 1967, Toronto Univ. from 1971. Début, Bucharest 1947. First prize Bucharest Int. Competition, 1947, Warsaw Int. competition 1955.

Ormandy, Eugene (Blau, Jenö) (*b* Budapest, 1899; *d* Philadelphia, 1985). Hung.-born cond. (Amer. citizen since 1927). Entered Budapest Royal Acad. of Mus. at 5 to study vn. as pupil of Hubay. Toured Europe as child prodigy until 1914. Head of master classes, Budapest Cons. 1919. Went to USA 1920, becoming leader and later cond. of orch. at Capitol cinema, NY. Cond. Minneapolis S.O. 1931–6; Philadelphia Orch. 1936–80. Hon. K.B.E. 1976.

Ornaments (Fr. *agréments*; It. *fioriture*; Ger. *Verzierungen, Manieren*). Embellishments and decorations of a melody as expressed through small notes or special signs. Further detail will be found under *Acciaccatura, *Appoggiatura, *Mordent, *Gruppetto, and *Trill. In early vocal mus. and opera, embellishments were improvised by the singers, some of whom carried them to ridiculous lengths. In the 19th and early 20th cent. this improvised ornamentation became almost unknown (except in jazz), but since the 1950s it has been restored to some perf. of oratorios and operas, incl. (under Charles Mackerras) the operas of Mozart.

Ornstein, Leo (*b* Kremenchug, 1892). Russ.-born composer and pianist (Amer. citizen). Given pf. lessons by father, a cantor. Studied Imperial Cons., St Petersburg, 1900–07. Settled in USA 1907, studying in NY, where he made début 1911. Became leading soloist in Amer. and Europe. Introduced pf. mus. of Schoenberg to USA. Retired from public perf. in 1935 to devote time to comp. Taught in Philadelphia and founded Ornstein Sch. of Mus. (retiring 1953). His early works (c.1913) were regarded as extremely discordant and innovatory. Prin. comps. incl.: *Lysistrata Suite* for orch. (1930), *Nocturne and Dance of the Fates*, orch. (1936), vn. sonata (1917), pf. conc. (1923), *Hebraic Fantasy*, vn. and pf. (1929), str. qt. (1940), vc. sonata (1916); and for pf.: *Wild Men's Dance* (1912), *Impressions of Chinatown* (1917), *Poems of 1917* (1919), 20 *Waltzes* (1955–68), *Tarantella* (1958), and 4 sonatas.

Orozco, Rafael (*b* Córdoba, 1946). Sp. pianist. Studied Cordoba, Madrid Cons., and Siena Acad. with *Weissenberg. Won Leeds Int. pf. competition 1966. Int. career.

Orpharion. Development of the *cittern very popular in Eng. in 16th and 17th cent. Had 15 frets and wire strings. Bridge was fixed and the str. ran over a small metal saddle into the bridge and were fastened to small metal pegs driven into lower side of bridge. Orig. had 6 courses but a 7th was added *c*.1600. Specified as alternative to lute in several books of lute tablature.

Orphée aux enfers (Offenbach). See *Orpheus in the Underworld*.

Orpheus. (1) Symphonic poem by Liszt, comp. 1853–4 as introduction to his Weimar prod. of Gluck's *Orfeo.

(2) Ballet in 3 scenes to mus. by Stravinsky, comp. 1947, choreog. Balanchine, prod. NY 1948, Hamburg 1962. Other versions choreog. Cranko, Georgi, and others.

Orpheus Britannicus. The 'British Orpheus', i.e. Purcell. Title given to 2 posthumous vols. of Purcell's vocal mus. pubd. by H. Playford (1698–1702), also to vol. of his songs pubd. by J. Walsh (1735). *Britten and Pears realized and ed. 18 of these solo songs for v. and pf. and 6 duets for high and low vv. and pf. They also made a Suite of Songs for high v. and orch. and arr. 3 songs for high v. and orch.

Orpheus in the Underworld (*Orphée aux Enfers*). *Opéra-féerie* by Offenbach to lib. by Crémieux and Halévy. Comp. in 2 acts 1858, rev. in 4-act version 1874. Prod. Paris (2-act version) 1858; NY 1861; London 1865 (adapted by Planché as *Orpheus in the Haymarket*).

Orr, Charles (Wilfred) (*b* Cheltenham, 1893; *d* Painswick, 1976). Eng. composer and writer on mus. Studied GSM. Wrote mainly songs, incl. 24 settings of Housman. Also *A Cotswold Hill-Tune* for str.

Orr, Robin (Robert Kemsley) (*b* Brechin, 1909). Scottish composer, organist, and teacher. Studied RCM, Cambridge Univ., and privately with Casella and Boulanger. Ass. lecturer in mus., Leeds Univ., 1936–8; organist, St John's Coll., Cambridge, 1938–51; prof. of comp., RCM, 1950–6; prof. of mus., Glasgow Univ., 1956–65; prof. of mus., Cambridge Univ., 1965–76; chairman, Scottish Opera, 1962–76. Works incl. operas *Full Circle* (1967) and *Hermiston* (1975), 3 syms. (1965, 1971, 1978), chamber mus., and songs. C.B.E. 1972.

Orrego-Salas, Juan (Antonio) (*b* Santiago, Chile, 1919). Chilean composer. Studied comp. privately with H. Allende and in 1944–6 in Amer. with P. H. Lang, R. Thompson, and Copland. Dir., Lat.-Amer. centre, Indiana Univ., from 1961. Mus. uses Sp. rhythms and melodic contours, 12-note melodies (though no strict dodecaphonic system), and irregular rhythmic patterns. Exotic orchestration a feature. Works incl. 4 syms., pf. conc., choral works to Sp. texts, str. qt., pf. sonata, etc.

Orrey, Leslie (Gilbert) (*b* Hawnby, Yorks., 1908; *d* Bath, 1981). Eng. pianist, cond., and writer. Studied RCM and Durham Univ. Lecturer and head of mus. dept., Goldsmiths' College, London

Univ., 1945–69. Author of books on harmony, opera, programme mus., Bellini, and Gluck.

Orthel, Léon (*b* Roosendaal, 1905). Dutch composer and pianist. Studied The Hague and Berlin Acad. Teacher of pf., Royal Cons., The Hague, 1941–71, and of comp., Amsterdam Cons. 1949–71. Works incl. 6 syms., chamber mus., and songs.

Ortiz, Cristina (*b* Bathia, Brazil, 1950). Brazilian pianist. Studied with Tagliaferro in Paris and Serkin in Philadelphia. Recital début NY 1971, London début 1973 (with LSO). Winner of prizes in int. competitions. Soloist with leading orchs.

Ortiz, Diego (*b* Toledo, *c*.1510; *d* ? Naples, *c*. 1570). Sp. composer of church and lute mus. Chapelmaster to Duke of Alba at Sp. court in Naples, 1557–70. Author of celebrated treatise on art of playing divisions (variations) on bass viol (1553).

Orton, Richard (Henry) (*b* Derby, 1940). Eng. composer and teacher. Studied comp. at Birmingham Univ. and at Cambridge Univ. Lect. in mus., York Univ., from 1967, becoming dir. of elec. mus. studio there. His *Mug Grunt* (1972) is a piece of wordless mus.-th.

O Salutaris Hostia (O saving victim). R.C. hymn sung at Benediction and some other services to plainsong melody or one of many comp. settings.

Osanna. It. form of 'Hosanna'.

Osborne, Charles (*b* Brisbane, 1927). Australian critic and writer. Studied pf. and singing. Ass. ed. *London Magazine* 1957–66; ass. literary dir., Arts Council 1966–71, literary dir. from 1971. Author of books on Verdi's (1969), Mozart's (1978), and Puccini's (1982), operas and ed. of coll. of Verdi's letters (1971), *Dictionary of Opera* (1983). Contrib. to many periodicals.

Osborne, George (Alexander) (*b* Limerick, 1806; *d* London, 1893). Irish pianist. Self-taught till age 18. Went to Paris 1826 studying under Pixis, Fétis, and *Kalkbrenner, becoming friend of Chopin, Berlioz, Hallé, etc. Settled as teacher in London 1843. Comp. chamber mus., pf. pieces, and 33 vn. duos in collab. with de Bériot.

Osborne, Nigel (*b* Manchester, 1948). Eng. composer. Studied Oxford Univ. with Wellesz and Leighton, later in Poland with Rudziński. While in Poland worked with live elec. mus. group. Won Swiss Radio prize 1971 with cantata *7 Words*. Lecturer in mus., Nottingham Univ. from 1978. Works incl. *Heaventree*, unacc. ch. (1973); *Remembering Esenin*, vc. and pf. (1974); *Musica da camera*, vn., tape, audience (1975); *Prelude and Fugue* for chamber ens. (1975); *Chansonnier*, ch. and ens. (1975); *The Sickle*, sop. and ens. (1975); *Passers By*, bass recorder and vcs. (1976); *I am Goya*, bar. and 4 instr. (1977); vc. conc. (1977); *In Camera*, for 13 instr. (1979); *Songs* *from a Bare Mountain*, unacc. ch. (1979); *Madeleine de la Ste-Baume*, sop., db. (1979); *Poem without a Hero*, sop., mez., ten., bass., live elec. (1980; rev. 1981 with instr. ens. added); *Gnostic Passion*, 36 unacc. vv. (1980); *Mythologies*, fl., cl., tpt., hp., vn., vc. (1980); fl. conc. (1980); *The Cage*, ten. and ens. (1981); pf. sonata (1981); *For a Moment*, vc. and women's ch. (1981); *Choralis* I, II, and III, 6 vv. unacc. (1981–2); *Sinfonia*, orch. (1982); *Fantasia*, ens. (1983); *Alba*, mez., instr. ens., computer-generated tape (1984); *The Electrification of the Soviet Union*, opera (1986–7).

Oscillator. That part of electrical generator which produces a repetitive waveform. The term is sometimes used to mean the whole generator.

Ossia (It. *o sia*, 'it may be'). (1) Term used in the sense of 'or else' to indicate an alternative version of a mus. passage, e.g. composer's simplified alternative for a difficult section, or ed.'s emendation of composer's text where it is presumed to be wrong.
(2) Used in opera titles in the sense of 'or', e.g. *Il dissoluto punito, ossia Il Don Giovanni*.

Osten, Eva Plaschke von der (*b* Heligoland, 1881; *d* Dresden, 1936). Ger. sop. Studied Dresden, début there 1902. Prin. sop., Dresden Opera, 1902–27. Created role of Oktavian in Strauss's *Der Rosenkavalier* 1911, also being first to sing it at CG 1913. First to sing Kundry in Eng. Member Ger. Opera Co., USA, 1923–4. Wife of Friedrich Plaschke (1875–1951), bass-bar. at Dresden and later stage dir. (e.g. for 1933 première of Strauss's *Arabella*).

Ostinato (It.). Obstinate, persistent. A persistent mus. phrase or rhythm. A basso ostinato is a figure in the bass which is persistently repeated.

Ostrčil, Otakar (*b* Prague, 1879; *d* Prague, 1935). Cz. composer and cond. Studied with *Fibich 1895–1900. Chief cond. Prague Nat. Opera 1920–35. Champion of Cz. operas and of contemporary opera generally. Cond. f.p. of Janáček's *Excursions of Mr Brouček*, Prague 1920. Comp. 6 operas, sym., symphonic poems.

Osud (Fate). Opera in 3 acts by Janáček to lib. by composer adapted by Fedora Bartošová. Comp. 1903–6. F.p. Brno (broadcast) 1934. F. stage p. Brno 1958. F. public p. in Eng. (concert) London 1983. F. Eng. stage p. London (ENO) 1984.

Otello (Othello). (1) Opera in 4 acts by Verdi to lib. by Boito based on Shakespeare's tragedy *Othello, the Moor of Venice* (1604–5). Comp. 1884–6. Prod. Milan 1887, NY 1888, London 1889, NY Met. 1894.
(2) Opera (*Otello, ossia Il Moro di Venezia*) in 3 acts by Rossini to lib. by di Salsa. Prod. Naples 1816, London 1822, NY 1826.

Ôter (Fr.). To take off. *Ôtez les sourdines*, take off the mutes. In org. mus. *ôter* means to discontinue use of a stop.

Othello. Ov. for orch. Op. 93, by Dvořák, comp. 1891–2 as 3rd of cycle of 3 ovs. called *Nature, Life, and Love*, the others being *Amid Nature* and *Carneval*. See also *Otello*.

Othmayr, Kaspar (*b* Amberg, 1515; *d* Nuremberg, 1553). Ger. composer. Studied Heidelberg Univ. Wrote secular songs, motets, etc.

Ottava (It., sometimes abbreviated '8va'). Octave. Indications to play a passage an octave higher are *all'ottava* (at the octave), *ottava alta* (high octave), and *ottava sopra* (octave above). Indications to play an octave below written pitch are *ottava bassa* (low octave), and *ottava sotto* (octave below).
An expression meaning 'play in octaves' is *coll' ottava* (with the octave).

Ottavino (It.). Modern name for small fl., known in other countries as *piccolo.

Otterloo, (Jan) **Willem van** (*b* Winterswijk, 1907; *d* Melbourne, Australia, 1978). Dutch cond., cellist, and composer. Cellist, Utrecht municipal orch., ass. cond. 1933, chief cond. 1937. Cond., Residentie Orch., The Hague, 1949–73; Melbourne S.O. 1967–73; Düsseldorf S.O. 1974–7. Wrote sym., orch. suites, chamber mus., org. pieces.

Ottoni (It.). Brass instrs.

Our Hunting Fathers. Symphonic song-cycle for high v. and orch., Op. 8, by Britten to text devised by W. H. Auden. F.p. Norwich Fest. 1936. F. London p. 1937.

Our Man in Havana. Opera in 3 acts by Williamson to lib. by Sidney Gilliat based on Graham Greene's novel. Prod. London 1963.

Ours, L' (Haydn). See *Bear Symphony*.

Ouseley, (Sir) **Frederick** (Arthur) **Gore** (*b* London, 1825; *d* Hereford, 1889). Eng. organist, composer, pianist, and clergyman. Child prodigy musician. Studied Oxford Univ. Succeeded to baronetcy 1844. Ordained as clergyman 1849. Precentor, Hereford Cath., 1855. Prof. of mus., Oxford Univ. 1855–89 (instituted formal exams. for degrees of Mus.B. and Mus.D.). Founded St Michael's Coll., Tenbury, 1854, with special emphasis on church mus. Wrote oratorios, church mus., org. pieces, and an opera (1834) on Metastasio's libretto *L'Isola disabitata*. Ed. sacred works of O. Gibbons.

Ousset, Cécile (*b* Tarbes, 1936). French pianist. Gave first recital aged 5. Studied Paris Cons. with Marcel Ciampi and won first prize in pf. on graduation at age 14. Brit. début Edinburgh Fest. 1980. Int. concert career.

Overblow. To blow a woodwind instr. so hard that its notes are stepped up from basic pitch. This is usually an octave but the cl. overblows a 12th.

Overstrung. When the str. of a pf. are set at two differing levels and crossing, to give greater length of str.

Overtone. Any note of the harmonic series except the fundamental.

Overture (from OFr. *ouverture*, opening). (1) Piece of instr. mus. which precedes opera, oratorio, or play. *Lully est. the *French Overture* in a 3-movement style of slow—fast (fugal)—slow (concluding section). The *Italian Overture*, introduced by A. *Scarlatti, also had 3 movements, quick–slower–quick (see *Symphony*). Gluck was the first to give ovs. a thematic connection with what followed. Weber's ovs. were orchestral synopses of the opera. But in It. opera, ovs. were still used as a way of stopping the audience talking and giving latecomers a chance to reach their seats. Thus one of Rossini's ovs. did duty for 3 of his operas (incl. *Il barbiere di Siviglia*). Wagner preferred the term *Vorspiel* (Prelude). In the 20th cent., operatic ovs. have become rare, composers often bringing up the curtain immediately. Strauss's orch. introduction to *Der Rosenkavalier* is almost an ov., as is the sextet which opens *Capriccio*. For his comic opera *Die schweigsame Frau* he wrote a *potpourri*, a medley of tunes from the opera in the style of the composers of light operas, e.g. Sullivan.

(2) Term sometimes used as equivalent of *Suite (by Handel and Bach) or *Symphony (Haydn's London programmes 1791).

(3) See *Concert Overture*.

Overture, Scherzo, and Finale. Orch. work by Schumann, Op. 52, comp. 1841, rev. 1845.

O.W., in Ger. org. mus. = *Oberwerk*, i.e. swell org.

Owen Wingrave. Opera in 2 acts by Britten, Op. 85, to lib. by Myfanwy Piper based on Henry James. Comp. for BBC TV (16 May 1971) and later rev. for first stage perf. at CG 10 May 1973. Santa Fe 1973.

Owl and the Pussy-Cat. The. (1) Setting for speaker, fl., vc., and guitar by *Searle (1951) of poem by Edward Lear (1870).

(2) Setting for v. and pf. by Stravinsky (1966).

Oxford Elegy, An. Work for narrator, small mixed ch., and chamber orch. by Vaughan Williams, with text adapted from Matthew Arnold's poems *The Scholar Gipsy* (1853) and *Thyrsis* (1867), comp. 1949. Some of text is spoken, some sung by ch., also wordless part for ch. F. public p. Oxford 1952.

Oxford Symphony. Nickname for Haydn's Sym. No. 92 in G (Hob. I:92) because it was perf. when Haydn received hon. doctorate at Oxford Univ. in 1791. Comp. 1789 with no thought of Oxford.

Oxford University. Eng. university which has awarded degrees in music since 1499 (B.Mus. and D.Mus.). William Heather (Heyther) founded lectureship in music in 1627, the holder of the post of choragus eventually becoming known as professor. Post of choragus re-established 1848. Professorship was long regarded as sinecure. Profs. of mus. since 1797: William Crotch (1797–1847), H. R. Bishop (1848–55), F. A. Gore Ouseley (1855–89), John Stainer (1889–1900), Hubert Parry (1900–08), Walter Parratt (1908–18), Hugh Allen (1918–46), J. A. Westrup (1947–71), Joseph Kerman (1971–4), Denis Arnold from 1975. The Faculty of Music was created in 1944, largely thanks to Allen.

Ox Minuet (Ger. *Ochsenmenuett*). Minuet attrib. J. Haydn but comp. by his pupil I. X. von Seyfried (1776–1841) who introduced it into his opera *Das Ochsenmenuett* (1823), compiled mainly from Haydn's works. Based on legend that Haydn wrote a minuet for a butcher who gave him an ox in return.

Ozawa, Seiji (*b* Hoten, Manchuria, 1935). Japanese cond. Studied Toho Sch. of Mus., Tokyo, and in Berlin with *Karajan. Won Koussevitzky scholarship 1960. Début Tokyo, N.H.K. Orch. Ass. cond. to Bernstein, NY P.O. 1961–2 and 1964–5. Cond. Ravinia Park Fest., Chicago, 1964–8; Toronto S.O. 1965–9; San Francisco S.O. 1970–6; Boston S.O. from 1973. London début 1965 (LSO). Opera début Salzburg 1969 (*Così fan tutte*), CG 1974 (*Eugene Onegin*). Cond. f.p. of Messiaen's *St Francis of Assisi* (Paris, 1983).

Ozim, Igor (*b* Ljubljana, Yugoslavia, 1931). Yugoslav violinist. Studied Ljubljana Acad., RCM, and privately with Max Rostal. Début Ljubljana 1947. Carl Flesch medal 1951. World tours. Has given f.ps. of several contemporary concertos.

P

P. Abbreviated prefix to numbers in the *Pincherle catalogue of Vivaldi's works.

p. Abbreviation of *piano* (It., soft), hence *pp*, *ppp*, and sometimes even quieter (Verdi optimistically uses *pppp* in his *Requiem*, also Elgar in *Enigma Variations*).

P. In Fr. org. mus., this abbreviation sometimes means *Pédales* (pedals) and sometimes *Positif* (choir org.).

Pachelbel, Johann (*b* Nuremberg, 1653; *d* Nuremberg, 1706). Ger. organist and composer. Held several important org. posts. His comps. influenced Bach. Works incl. *Hexachordum Apollinis* (1699), 6 sets of airs and variations for hpd.; 78 chorale preludes (1693), incl. *Ein' feste Burg*, *Nun komm der Heiden Heiland*, *Vom Himmel hoch*, etc.; *Aria Sebaldina*, variations in F minor for hpd.; *Canon and Gigue* in D for 3 vns. and continuo; *Chaconne and 13 variations* for hpd., etc. His church music, for long disregarded, has been highly revalued, particularly his sacred concertos and his 13 settings of the *Magnificat*.

Pachelbel, Wilhelm Hieronymus (*b* Erfurt, 1686; *d* Nuremberg, 1764). Ger. organist and composer, son and pupil of Johann *Pachelbel.

Pachmann, Vladimir de (*b* Odessa, 1848; *d* Rome, 1933). Russ. pianist. Studied Vienna Cons. Début Odessa 1869, then retired for 8 years' further study; reappeared in public but then retired again for 2 years. From age of 32 became popular and successful recitalist, especially in mus. of Chopin. Début USA 1891. Eccentric platform-manner, often making remarks to the audience in praise of himself or in disparagement of other pianists.

Pacific 231. 'Mouvement symphonique' for orch. by Honegger, 1923. F.p. Paris 1924, f.p. in England, Manchester 1924. *Pacific 231* is a locomotive.

Pacini, Giovanni (*b* Catania, 1796; *d* Pescia, 1867). It. composer and teacher. His first opera was unperformed, but his second was prod. in Milan in 1813; he comp. 90 in all, mostly in the Rossini comic manner, although *Saffo* (1840) was more serious. *Maria Tudor* (1843) was revived at Camden Fest. 1983. Also wrote quantities of church mus. and a *Dante Symphony*. Founded mus. sch. at Viareggio, moving to Lucca.

Paderewski, Ignacy Jan (*b* Kurylówka, 1860; *d* NY, 1941). Polish pianist, composer, and statesman. Studied at Warsaw Mus. Institute 1872–8, becoming pf. teacher there 1879–83. Studied in Vienna with Leschetizky 1884–7. Début Paris 1888, London 1890, NY 1891. Became one of the most famous int. pianists. Began composing at age 6. Up to 1899 he wrote mainly pf. solos, incl. the *Tatra Album* (1885), based on songs and dances of the Polish Tatra mountain-dwellers. In the 1890s he comp. a vn. sonata, the 6 *Humoresques de Concert* for pf. (no. 1 of which is the famous Minuet in G), a pf. conc. in A minor, and the *Polish Fantasy* for pf. and orch. His opera *Manru* (1900) had its f.p. in Dresden 1901 and was given at the NY Met. in 1902. In 1903 he wrote a pf. sonata, 12 songs to Fr. poems by Mendès, and a set of Variations for pf. His Sym., avowedly patriotic, was completed in 1907 and f.p. Boston, Mass., 1909. In 1910 he spoke at the unveiling of a monument in Kraków and thereafter symbolized Polish aspirations. During the 1914–18 war he worked ceaselessly for the Polish cause. When Poland was created an independent nation in 1919 he became Prime Minister and Foreign Minister of the first govt. but retired a year later after disagreement with other politicians. In 1922 he resumed his recitals, raising large amounts of money for war victims. He sponsored several competitions and est. scholarships. In 1936 he appeared in a film, *Moonlight Sonata*, and in 1936-8 supervised a complete Chopin edn. pubd. in Warsaw. He died when Poland was again enslaved.

Padiglione (It.). Pavilion, tent. Hence, the bell of a wind instr. *Padiglione cinese*, Turkish Crescent or *Jingling Johnny.

Padovana (It.). See *Pavan*.

Paean. Song of triumph or praise (orig. to Apollo).

Paer, Ferdinando (*b* Parma, 1771; *d* Paris, 1839). It. composer. Orig. violinist but gave it up for comp. First opera prod. Parma 1791, then went as cond. to Venice where he wrote several more light operas. Worked in Vienna 1797–1802. Became Kapellmeister at Dresden 1802 and wrote *Leonora*, on same plot as Beethoven was to use in *Fidelio*. In 1807 went to Paris as cond. of Opéra-Comique and *maître de chapelle* to Napoleon I. Succeeded Spontini 1812 as dir. of Théâtre des Italiens. Dismissed 1827, becoming cond. of royal chamber mus. 1832. Wrote 53 operas incl. *La Didone abbandonata* (1810), *L'oriflamme* (1814), and *Le Maître de chapelle* (1821), also oratorios, masses, cantatas, and numerous instr. works.

Paganini, Niccolò (b Genoa, 1782; d Nice, 1840). It. violinist and composer. Regarded as greatest of all vn. virtuosos. Studied with father and later with other teachers. Made first tour at 13 and comp. difficult pieces for himself to play. During a love affair in 1801–4 he took up the guitar, for which he composed 6 str. qts. with a guitar part, and other works. Returned to platform 1805 with sensational success. Dir. of mus. to Princess of Lucca 1805–9. Milan début 1813, Vienna 1828, Paris and London 1831. In Paris in 1833 commissioned va. conc. from Berlioz, the result being *Harold in Italy*, but he never played it. From 1834 he made few appearances: for some years he had been suffering from cancer of the larynx which killed him in 1840. He left a fortune and was generous to colleagues in need. Owned vns. by Stradivarius, Guarnerius, and Amati, also Stradivarius va. and db. His Mephistophelean appearance led to stories that his virtuosity stemmed from diabolical powers; he was a skilled showman and although his feats as a virtuoso are no longer regarded as unique or unapproachable, he pioneered the use of harmonics, tuned his instr. to obtain special effects, used several styles of bowing, and exploited staccato and pizzicato as never before. His intonation was unfailingly accurate. Works incl.:

VN. CONCS.: No. 1 in E♭ (usually played in D) (?1817), No. 2 in B minor, with *Rondo à la clochette* (1826), No. 3 in E major (1826), No. 4 in D minor (1830), No. 5 in A minor (1830), and the so-called No. 6 in E minor (comp. c.1815) (and others lost).

VN. AND ORCH.: *Le Streghe* (Witches' Dance) based on air by Süssmayer; Variations on *God Save the King*; *Moto perpetuo, allegro de concert*; Variations on *Non più mesta* (*La Cenerentola*); Variations on the air *Di tanti palpiti* (*Tancredi*).

VC. AND ORCH: *Variations on Theme of Rossini* for 2 vc.

SOLO VN.: *24 Caprices* (c.1805); Variations on *Le Carnaval de Venise*; *Duo in C*; Recitative and Variations on 3 airs for the 4th string.

CHAMBER MUSIC: 12 sonatas for vn. and guitar; 6 qts. for vn., va., guitar, and vc.; vn. sonata with vn. and vc. acc.; *Terzettos* for vn., vc., guitar.

Paganini Transcriptions. There are several transcrs. by other composers of Paganini comps. and several comps. based on the theme of his *Caprice* No. 24 in A minor (e.g. Brahms's *Variations on a Theme of Paganini* for pf., 1862–3; Rakhmaninov's *Rhapsody on a Theme of Paganini*, for pf. and orch., 1934; Blacher's *Variations on a Theme of Paganini*, for orch., 1947; Lutoslawski's *Variations on a Theme of Paganini*, for 2 pf., 1941; Rochberg's *50 Caprice-Variations*, for solo vn. 1970). Schumann wrote *12 Études de Concert* based on Paganini's *Caprices* in 2 sets, Op. 3, 1832, Op. 10, 1833. Liszt wrote a *Grande Fantaisie de Bravoure sur la clochette* (1831–2), on a theme from vn. conc. No. 2 in B minor, Op. 7, and *6 Études*

d'exécution transcendante d'après Paganini (1838, rev. 1851 as *Grandes Études d'après les caprices de Paganini*, No. 3 being *La campanella*).

Pagliacci (Strolling players, or Clowns). Opera in 2 acts by *Leoncavallo to his own lib. Prod. Milan 1892, CG and NY 1893. Customarily perf. in double bill with *Mascagni's *Cavalleria rusticana*, the result being colloquially known as 'Cav and Pag'.

Paik, Nam June (b Seoul, 1932). Korean composer. Studied Tokyo Univ. and in Ger. with Fortner. Worked at Cologne elec. studio of W. Ger. Radio. Assoc. with NY Avant-Garde Fest. since 1964. Teacher of intermedia and videosynthesis at Calif. Institute of Arts, Los Angeles, from 1970. Has written vc. sonata and *Variations on a Theme by Saint-Saëns*, also comps. such as *Hommage à John Cage* for 2 pf. which are destroyed during the perf., 3 tape recorders, eggs, and motorbike, and *Étude* for pf. also involving destruction of 2 pf., 'cutting John Cage's necktie, and shampooing him without advance warning', etc.

Paine, John Knowles (b Portland, Maine, 1839; d Cambridge, Mass., 1906). Amer. composer, organist, and teacher. Studied in Ger. Became instructor in mus., Harvard Univ. 1862, ass. prof. of.mus. 1873, prof. 1875 (the first Amer. prof. of mus.). Pupils incl. D. G. Mason, J. A. Carpenter, and Richard Aldrich. Wrote 2 operas, 2 syms., choral works incl. Mass in D (1866–7), and chamber mus.

Paisiello, Giovanni (b Taranto, 1740; d Naples, 1816). It. composer. In youth wrote mainly church mus., but discovered flair for opera buffa and wrote his first comic operas for Bologna 1764. Settled in Naples as rival of Piccinni, then of Cimarosa. Went to St Petersburg 1776 as court cond. and master of It. opera to Catherine the Great, while there composing his *Il *barbiere di Siviglia* (1782) which had such great success in It. that Rossini's later setting encountered resentment. Returned to Naples 1784 as court cond. to Ferdinand IV. Sided with Napoleon in 1799 and went to Paris 1802 to organize and direct the mus. of his chapel. On return to Naples, remained out of favour with Bourbons and died in relative poverty. Wrote over 100 operas, many of them accomplished and pleasant, 12 syms., 6 pf. concs., comic cantatas, and other works. Prin. operas were: *Don Chisciotte* (1769), *Achille in Sciro* (1778), *La serva padrona* (1781), *Il *barbiere di Siviglia* (1782), *Il re Teodoro in Venezia* (1784), *La Molinara* (1789), *Nina* (1789), *Didone abbandonata* (1794), *Proserpina* (1803).

Palestrina. Opera (*Musikalische Legende*) in 3 acts by *Pfitzner to his own lib. Comp. 1912–15. Prod. Munich 1917, London (Abbey Opera) 1981. Based on untrue legend that Palestrina comp. the *Missa Papae Marcelli* to persuade the Council of Trent not to ban polyphonic mus.

Palestrina, Giovanni Pierluigi da (*b* Palestrina, nr. Rome, *c*.1525; *d* Rome, 1594). It. composer who took his name from his birthplace. Chorister at S. Maria Maggiore, Rome, in 1537. Studied in Rome *c*.1540. Organist and choirmaster, Palestrina, 1544. In 1550 the Bishop became Pope Julius III and in 1551 summoned Palestrina to Rome as choirmaster of Cappella Giulia, a nursery for Sistine Choir. The following year Palestrina published his first book of Masses. In 1555 a new Pope, Paul IV, dismissed Palestrina and two others from the Sistine Choir because they were married. Palestrina was appointed maestro di cappella of St John Lateran in 1555 in succession to *Lassus. For this church he wrote his *Lamentations*. He resigned in 1560 over dissatisfaction with the way the choirboys were fed, becoming choirmaster of S. Maria Maggiore in 1561. He pubd. his first book of motets 2 years later. In 1567 he resigned to enter service of Cardinal Ippolito d'Este, having become dissatisfied with the papal reforms of church mus. which rendered 2 of his masses unliturgical because they contained words foreign to the mass. In addition, others of his masses incl. secular songs, such as *L'*Homme armé*. The cardinal kept a mus. establishment at his palace in Tivoli (the Villa d'Este). In 1571 Palestrina became dir. of the Cappella Giulia. Over the next few years he lost both his sons and his wife through epidemics and decided to become a priest. But after a few weeks he changed his mind and married again, his new wife being the rich widow of a fur merchant. Palestrina formed a partnership with one of the men in the business and made a fortune which enabled him in the last 13 years of his life to publish 16 colls. of his mus.

Palestrina's mus. is marked by flowing, smooth lines and a rich beauty of sound in the way vv. are blended. He had neither the range nor the inventiveness of Byrd and Lassus, but the skill with which his sacred works are based on the secular madrigal gives his mus. special characteristics which are greatly admired. His works incl.:

MASSES: 4 for 8 vv.; 22 for 6 vv. (incl. *Missa Papae Marcelli* and *Hexachord Mass*); 39 for 4 vv.; 29 for 5 vv. (incl. *L'Homme armé*).
MOTETS: 6 for 12 vv. (incl. *Stabat Mater*); 56 for 8 vv.; 2 for 7 vv.; 34 for 6 vv.; 79 for 5 vv.; 67 for 4 vv.; 29 settings for 4 vv. from the *Song of Solomon*.
CANTIONES SACRAE: 2 for 8 vv.; 4 for 4 vv.
MAGNIFICATS: 35 on the 8 tones.
OTHER WORKS: Hymns for 4 vv.; Offertories for 5 vv.; Lamentations for 4 vv.; Psalms for 12 vv.; Litanies; Antiphon; Sacred Madrigals for 5, 4, and 3 vv.; Secular Madrigals.

Pallavicino, Benedetto (*b* Cremona, 1551; *d* Mantua, 1601). It. monk, composer of madrigals and motets. Among first to write for as many as 12 and 16 vv. Choirmaster at Mantua 1596–1601, preceding Monteverdi.

Pallavicino, Carlo (*b* Salò, Lake Garda; *d* Dresden, 1688). It. composer. Began career in Venice; became Kapellmeister at Dresden, dividing his time between both cities. Wrote over 20 operas, all but one prod. Venice. Also wrote church mus.

Palm, Siegfried (*b* Wuppertal, 1927). Ger. cellist. Studied privately. Cellist in Lübeck municipal orch. 1945–7, N.W. Ger. Radio S.O. 1947–62, Cologne Radio S.O. 1962–7. Member, Hamann Qt. 1951–62. Soloist with leading orchs. since 1962. Dir. of mus., vc. class, Cologne Nat. College of Mus. from 1962. Dir., Deutsche Oper, Berlin, 1977–81. Has developed cello technique to suit *avant-garde* works. Was first to play works by Penderecki, Xenakis, Zillig, Ligeti, Zimmermann, and Blacher. Penderecki wrote *Capriccio per Siegfried Palm* (1968).

Palmer, Felicity (Joan) (*b* Cheltenham, 1944). Eng. sop. Studied GSM and at Munich Hochschule für Musik. Sang in professional choirs, notably John Aldiss Ch. Soloist with orchs., and recitalist. Won Kathleen Ferrier Memorial Prize 1970. Opera début, Kent Opera (Dido) 1971, then with ENO at Coliseum. Amer. début Houston Opera 1973. Specialist in Fr. songs (notably Messiaen and Poulenc) and admired in Gluck's *Armide*.

Palmer, Robert (*b* Syracuse, NY, 1915). Amer. composer. Studied Eastman Sch. 1934–9 (with Hanson) and later with Harris and Porter. Teacher of comp. at Cornell Univ. since 1943. Influenced by Quincy *Porter and Bartók. Works incl.:

ORCH: *Concerto for Orchestra* (1944); *Symphonic Variations* (1945); Sym. No. 1 (1953), No. 2 (1966); *Centennial Overture* (1966); pf. conc. (1968–70); *Symphonia Concertante*, 9 instr. (1972); *Organon II*, str. (1975).
CHORAL: *Abraham Lincoln Walks at Midnight* (1948); *Slow, Slow, Fresh Fount* (1953); *Nabuchodonosor*, oratorio (1960–4); *Portents of Aquarius*, ch., org. (1975).
CHAMBER MUSIC: Str. Qts. Nos. 1–4 (1939–59); pf. sonatas No. 1 (1938–46), No. 2 (1942–8); pf. qt. No. 1 (1947), No. 2 (1974); pf. quintet (1950); va. sonata (1951); wind quintet (1951); cl. quintet (1952); pf. trio (1958); vc. sonata (1976).

Palmgren, Selim (*b* Pori, 1878; *d* Helsinki, 1951). Finn. composer, pianist, and cond. Studied Helsinki Cons. 1895–9, then in Ger. and It. and with Busoni. Held cond. posts in Finland 1902–12. Toured USA 1921 as accom. to his wife, who sang his songs. Taught at Eastman Sch. 1923–6. Prof. of harmony, Sibelius Acad., Helsinki, 1936–51. Wrote 2 operas, 5 pf. concs., songs, and many short pf. pieces.

Palotache (*Palotás*). Hung. type of instr. piece in dance style (2 beats to the measure), derivative of the *verbunkos.

Pammelia (from Gk., all honey). First coll. of vocal rounds, catches, and canons pubd. in Eng.

(by T. Ravenscroft, 1609, 2nd edn. 1618). Part 2 (*Deuteromelia*) also pubd. 1609. No composers' names given.

Panassié, Hugues (*b* Paris, 1912; *d* Montauban, 1974). Fr. mus. critic and specialist in jazz. Founded 'Hot Club de France' 1932. Lectured on jazz at Sorbonne 1937. Author of several books on jazz, dictionary of jazz (Paris 1954, London 1956), and biography of Louis *Armstrong.

Pandiatonicism. Term coined by Amer. musicologist *Slonimsky to describe the free use in chord-formation of the 7 degrees of the *diatonic scale, e.g. the added 6th in jazz.

Pandora, Pandore. See *Cittern*.

Pandorina. Small type of wire-strung lute.

Panerai, Rolando (*b* Campi Bisenzio, 1924). It. bar. Studied Florence and Milan. Début Naples 1947. Leading bar. in several It. opera houses and at fests., notably in role of Rossini's Figaro. CG début 1960. Sang Falstaff at CG 1984.

Panharmonicon. Mechanical orch. invented by *Maelzel in 1805. Beethoven wrote his *Battle Symphony* (1813) for it.

Panizza, Ettore (*b* Buenos Aires, 1875; *d* Milan, 1967). Argentinian cond. of It. descent. Studied Milan. Début Rome 1899. Cond. at CG, 1907–14, 1924. Ass. cond. to Toscanini at La Scala, Milan, 1921–9. Cond., La Scala, 1930–2, 1946–8. NY Met. 1934–42. Colón, Buenos Aires, 1921–67. Wrote 4 operas, ed. Berlioz's treatise on orchestration (1913). Cond. f.p. of d'Erlanger's *Tess* at CG 1909.

Pannain, Guido (*b* Naples, 1891; *d* Naples, 1977). It. musicologist, author, and composer. Studied Naples Univ. Prof. of mus. history, Naples Cons. 1915–61. Wrote 3 operas, vn. conc., and other works, but best-known for historical books. Wrote *Modern Composers*, pubd. in Eng. 1932. Mus. critic for various journals 1920–57.

Panormo, Vincenzo (*b* Monreale, nr. Palermo, 1734; *d* London, *c*.1813). Sicilian maker of vns. who worked in Paris, London, and Dublin. Went to London 1772, then to France, returning to Eng. in 1789. Most of his instrs. were unsigned. One of his two sons, George Lewis Panormo (*d* *c*.1850) made guitars and vn. bows.

Pan-Pipes (Pandean Pipes, Syrinx). Instr. of classical antiquity, ancestor of the fl. Series (4 to 12 or more) of short vertical pipes of wood, cane, or pottery fixed side by side and graduated in length to give the pitches of the different notes. The player blows across the open ends. The ancient Greeks credited the god Pan with its invention. Used by Papageno in Mozart's *Die Zauberflöte*.

Pantaleon. (1) Large dulcimer invented by Pantaleon Hebenstreit (1667–1750).

(2) Term used by Ger. writers in late 18th cent. to describe a small square piano.

Pantomime (from Gk., 'all imitating'). (1) Play in which artists use dumb show.

(2) Mimed episode in larger work, e.g. in Ravel's ballet *Daphnis et Chloé* when story of Pan and Syrinx is mimed.

(3) Type of Eng. stage show usually presented at the Christmas period, loosely based on a fairystory, containing songs, and in former times concluding with harlequinade.

Pantonality. Term coined by R. *Réti in 1958 to describe extension of tonality in late19th cent., as developed by Debussy, Wagner, and others, whereby the mus. cannot be said to be 'in' a key but moves in and out of discernible key centres without becoming atonal. Thus it applies to mus. by Bartók, Hindemith, Stravinsky, and others.

Pantoum (Fr., from Malay *pantum*). Type of verse quatrain of Malayan origin adapted in Fr. verse by Victor Hugo. The term was used by Ravel to describe 2nd movement (scherzo) of his Pf. Trio (1914).

Panufnik, Andrzej (*b* Warsaw, 1914). Polishborn composer and cond. (Brit. citizen from 1961). Studied Warsaw Cons. 1934–6, then studied cond. with Weingartner in Vienna 1937–8. Completed studies in Paris and London. Cond. Kraków P.O. 1945–6, Warsaw P.O. 1946–7. Guest cond. leading orchs. Left Poland in protest against political regimentation 1954, settling in Eng. Cond. CBSO 1957–9, resigning to concentrate on comp. His mus. has extraordinary intensity and power. His works up to 1944 were destroyed during the Warsaw uprising of that year. Some of the 'revisions' of pre–1944 works are reconstructions. Prin. comps.:

BALLET: *Miss Julie* (Stuttgart 1970).

ORCH: *Tragic Overture* (1942, rev. 1945, 1955); *Lullaby* for 29 str. and 2 harps (1947, rev. 1955); *Nocturne* (1947, rev. 1955); Symphonies: *Sinfonia Rustica* (1948, rev. 1955), *Sinfonia Elegiaca* (1957, rev. 1966), *Sinfonia Sacra* (1963), *Sinfonia di Sfere* (1975), *Sinfonia Mistica* (1977), *Sinfonia Votiva* (1981); *Heroic Overture* (1952, rev. 1969); *Rhapsody* (1956); *Polonia* (1959); *Autumn Music*, chamber orch. (1962, rev. 1965); pf. conc. (1962, rev. 1970, re-composed 1972); *Landscape*, str. (1962, rev. 1965); *2 Lyric Pieces* (1963); *Katýn Epitaph* (1967, rev. 1969); vn. conc., with str. (1971); *Metasymphonia,* organ and orch. (1978); Concertino, timp., perc., str. (1980); *A Procession for Peace* (1982–3).

VOCAL: *5 Polish Peasant Songs*, sop., fls., and cls. (1940, rev. 1945, 1959); *Hommage à Chopin*, sop. and pf. (1949, rev. 1955, orch. version 1966); *Song to the Virgin Mary*, unacc. ch. (1964); *Universal Prayer*, cantata (1968–9); *Thames Pageant*, cantata (1969); *Invocation for Peace*, trebles, 2 tpt., 2 tb. (1972); *Winter Solstice,* soloists, ch., brass, timp. (1972); *Night Thoughts*, v. and pf. (1977).

CHAMBER MUSIC: *Triangles*, 3 fl., 3 vc. (1972); *Sinfonia Concertante*, fl., harp, str. (1973); *Prelude and Transformations*, str. qt. No. 1 (1976), *Messages*, No. 2 (1980).

PIANO: 12 Miniature Studies (1947, rev. 1955, 1964); *Reflections* (1969).

Panzéra, Charles (*b* Hyères, 1896; *d* Paris, 1976). Swiss bar. Studied Paris Cons. Opera début Opéra-Comique 1919 in Massenet's *Werther*. Later was celebrated Pelléas. Noted recitalist and interpreter of Fr. song. Prof. of singing, Paris Cons., 1949. Also taught at Juilliard Sch., NY. Author of *L'Art de chanter* (1945).

Papaïoannou, Yannis (Andreou) (*b* Cavala, Greece, 1911). Gr. composer. Studied Hellenic Cons. 1929–34. Primarily self-taught as comp., but had lessons from Honegger in Paris 1939. Taught comp. Hellenic Cons. 1954. Pioneer in Gr. of *avant-garde* resources. Adopted total-serial methods in his syms. from 1963 and has used other techniques. Influenced by tribal mus. and Byzantine chant. Works incl. 5 syms. (1946–64), pf. conc., conc. for orch., *Hellas,* symphonic poem after Shelley, str. qt., pf. sonata, guitar suite, ob. qt., and cantatas to texts by C. Cavafy.

Papier, Rosa (*b* Baden, nr. Vienna, 1858; *d* Vienna, 1932). Austrian mez. Sang at Vienna Opera but throat infection forced retirement 1891, whereupon she became celebrated teacher. Prof. of singing, Vienna Cons. Her son was Bernhard *Paumgartner. She was instrumental in securing Mahler's appointment to Vienna Opera in 1897.

Papillons (Butterflies). 12 short dance pieces for pf. solo, Op. 2, by Schumann, comp. 1829–31, inspired by masked-ball scene at end of Jean-Paul Richter's *Flegeljahre* (Age of Indiscretion).

Papineau-Couture, Jean (*b* Montreal, 1916). Canadian composer. Studied Montreal and with Quincy Porter in Boston, 1940. Worked later with Nadia Boulanger in Montecito, Calif. Taught at Quebec Cons. (Montreal section) 1946–51, then at Univ. of Montreal (dean 1968–73). Active in promoting Canadian contemporary mus. Prolific composer, works incl. pf. conc., vn. conc., str. qts., and *Paysage* (Landscape) for 8 narrators, 8 singers, and instr. ens. (1968).

Parade. 'Ballet réaliste' in 1 act with mus. by *Satie to lib. by Cocteau, choreog. Massine, décor Picasso. Prod. Paris 1917 (Diaghilev's Ballet Russe, cast incl. Lopokova and Massine).

Paradies (Paradisi), (Pietro) **Domenico** (*b* Naples, 1707; *d* Venice, 1791). It. composer and harpsichordist. Studied with Porpora. Settled in London 1747 as teacher. Wrote several operas and 12 hpd. sonatas.

Paradis, Maria Theresia von (*b* Vienna, 1759; *d* Vienna, 1824). Austrian pianist, blind from childhood, also org., composer, and singer. Visited most European capitals, incl. London. Mozart's pf. conc. in B♭ major (K456, 1784), was written for her. She comp. in a specially devised notation and founded a mus. sch. for girls.

Paradise and the Peri (*Das Paradies und die Peri*). Part 2 of T. Moore's poem *Lalla Rookh* (1817), the Peri being a benign spirit in Persian mythology seeking re-admission to Paradise. 3 comps. based on it, by (1) Schumann, Op. 50, cantata for soloists, ch., and orch., based on free trans., f.p. Leipzig 1843.

(2) Sterndale Bennett, fantasy-ov., Op. 42, comp. 1862.

(3) J. F. Barnett, cantata for soloists, ch., and orch., 1870.

Paradise Lost. (1) Opera in 2 acts by *Penderecki to lib. by Christopher Fry adapted from Milton's poem (1658–64, pubd. 1667). Prod. Chicago, 1978, Stuttgart 1979.

(2) Dramatic cantata by Christopher Steel, Op. 34, for sop., ten., and bass soloists, ch., and orch. Comp. 1966. F. public p. Gloucester Fest. 1974.

Parameter. Orig. mathematical term, in musical connotation refers to 'dimension' of a sound, its pitch, loudness, duration, rhythm, and (controversially) timbre.

Paraphrase. (1) Compositional process in polyphonic works of 15th and 16th cent., involving quotation in one or more vv. of a plainchant melody, usually one that has been altered rhythmically or melodically.

(2) In 19th cent., term applied to works based on existing melodies or comps., especially as a vehicle for virtuosity. Thus, Liszt's many 'paraphrases' for pf. of arias from It. operas.

(3) Scottish paraphrases are metrical versions of scriptural passages sung to psalm tunes in the Church of Scotland.

Paraphrases. Collection of pf. duets (24 variations and 14 other pieces) based on *Chopsticks, by Borodin, Rimsky-Korsakov, and others incl. Liszt.

Paray, Paul (*b* Le Tréport, 1886; *d* Monte Carlo, 1979). Fr. cond. and composer. Studied Paris Cons. Ass. cond. Lamoureux Orch. from 1920, prin. cond. from 1923. Cond. Monte Carlo Orch. 1928–32, Orch. of Concerts Colonne, Paris, 1932–52 (excluding war years), Detroit S.O. 1952–63. Wrote syms., ballet, oratorio *Jeanne d'Arc*, Mass, etc.

Pardessus de viole. Type of *viol, smaller than the treble.

Parepa-Rosa, Euphrosyne (*b* Edinburgh, 1836; *d* London, 1874). Scottish sop. Début Malta 1855. CG début 1857 as Elvira in *I Puritani*. Sang in Handel fests. of 1862 and 1865. Toured USA 1865 with Carl Rosa, whom she married 1867.

Had range of $2\frac{1}{2}$ octaves. Prin. sop. Carl Rosa Opera Co. Career in oratorio also.

Parergon (Gr., 'supplementary work'). Term used by R. Strauss in title of his *Parergon zur Symphonia Domestica,* Op. 73, for pf. (L.H.) and orch., 1925, comp. for Paul Wittgenstein and using theme from earlier *Symphonia Domestica.*

Paride ed Elena (Paris and Helen). Opera in 5 acts by Gluck to lib. by Calzabigi. Prod. Vienna 1770, Manchester (RMCM) 1963 (in Eng. trans. by Arthur Jacobs).

Parikian, Manoug (*b* Mersin, Turkey, 1920). Turkish-born violinist (Brit. citizen). Studied TCL. Leader Liverpool P.O. 1947–8, Philharmonia Orch. 1949–57. Début as conc. soloist, Liverpool 1947, London 1949. Prof. of vn., RCM, 1954–6, RAM from 1959. Frequent appearances as soloist, giving f.p. of works by Goehr, Rawsthorne, Musgrave, Hamilton, Wood, Crosse, and Maconchy. Mus. dir., Manchester Camerata 1980–4.

Paris, Alain (*b* Paris, 1947). Fr. cond. Studied pf., solfège, mus. history, 1951–65, harmony and cond. at École Normale de Musique, Paris, 1965–8, then studied cond. with *Fourestier and *Paray. Guest cond. of leading orchs. since 1975.

Paris Conservatoire de Musique. Free sch. of mus. est. in Paris 1795 incorporating 2 previous schs. Among dirs. have been Sarrette, Cherubini, Auber, Thomas, Dubois, Fauré, and Rabaud. For its distinguished teachers and pupils, see this dictionary *passim.* Since 1911 has been in rue de Madrid.

Paris Opéra. Premier opera house of Fr., its official title being *Académie de Musique, Paris.* Opened 1671. Controlled by *Lully 1672–87. Destroyed by fire 1763, also the next building 1781. In 1794 moved to rue de Richelieu as Théâtre des Arts, then to rue Favart 1821 and to rue Lepeletier 1822. Great period in its history followed, with operas by Meyerbeer, Auber, and Hérold and commissioned works from Rossini (*Guillaume Tell*), Verdi (*Don Carlos* and *Les Vêpres siciliennes*). New th. opened 1875. Accommodates 2,600 people and has large stage (100′ wide and 112′ deep). See also *Opéra-Comique.*

Paris, Orchestre de. Fr. sym. orch. founded in 1967 when the Orchestre de la Société des Concerts du Conservatoire (founded in 1828) was disbanded. First cond. was Munch (1967), succeeded by Karajan (1969), then Solti (1971) and Barenboim (1976).

Paris Symphonies (Haydn). Set of 6 syms. by Joseph Haydn, Nos. 82–87 (Hob. I:82–7), comp. 1785–6 and commissioned by Comte d'Ogny, one of backers of a Masonic Parisian concert society, 'Le Concert de la Loge Olympique'. F.ps., Paris 1787. The works are: No. 82 in C, *L'Ours* (The *Bear); No. 83 in G minor, *La *Poule* (The

Hen); No. 84 in E♭; No. 85 in B♭, *La *Reine* (The Queen); No. 86 in D; No. 87 in A. Haydn's next 5 syms., Nos. 88–92, were also written for Paris.

Paris Symphony. Nickname of Mozart's Sym. No. 31 in D (K297), comp. in Paris, 1778, where it was f.p. at the Concert Spirituel on Corpus Christi Day, 18 June 1778.

Paris: The Song of a Great City. Nocturne for orch. by Delius, 1899. F.p. Elberfeld 1901 cond. *Haym, Liverpool and London 1908, cond. Beecham. Used for ballet by F. Ashton, SW 1936 (Fonteyn and Helpmann).

Parish-Alvars, Elias (*b* Teignmouth, 1808; *d* Vienna, 1849). Eng. harpist, pianist, and composer. Lived mainly in Vienna from 1834. Important contributor to the development of harp-playing. Wrote many works for harp, incl. 2 concs.

Parker, Charlie (*b* Kansas City, 1920; *d* NY, 1955). Amer. jazz alto and ten. saxophonist and composer. Became full-time professional musician on leaving school in 1935. Worked mainly in Kansas City 1935–9 with blues and jazz groups. First visited NY 1939. Joined Earl Hines's band 1942 and Billy Eckstine band 1944. Led own group 1945, worked with Dizzy Gillespie (trumpeter) and began to make recordings. In 1946 worked in Los Angeles, returning to NY 1947. His greatest period was 1947–51, when he made over half his surviving records and visited Europe three times. His last years were shadowed by drug addiction and alcoholism. Parker was one of the most influential figures in jazz and a leader in the development of bop in the 1940s. His outstanding achievement was his improvisation.

Parker, Horatio (William) (*b* Auburndale, Mass., 1863; *d* Cedarhurst, NY, 1919). Amer. composer, organist, and teacher. Studied with his mother and then at Munich Cons. with Rheinberger 1881–4. Held org. posts in NY, and taught at Nat. Cons. when Dvořák was dir. Organist and mus. dir. Trinity Church, Boston, from 1893. Prof. of mus., Yale Univ., 1894–1919. Taught *Ives. His oratorio *Hora Novissima* (1893) was the first work by an Amer. to be perf. at a 3 Choirs Fest. (Worcester 1899). His *Wanderer's Psalm* was perf. Hereford 1900, Part 3 of *Legend of St Christopher* at Worcester 1902, complete work Bristol 1902. Also wrote 2 operas, sym., symphonic poem, chamber mus., ch. works, org. pieces, and songs.

Parker-Smith, Jane (*b* Northampton, 1950). Eng. organist. Studied RCM 1967–71 (org., pf., and hpd.). London début Westminster Cath. 1970. Prom début 1972. Studied in Paris 1973 with Jean Langlais, later with Kynaston. Won Nat. Organ Competition, 1974. Many foreign tours as recitalist.

Parkhouse, David (*b* Teignmouth, 1930). Eng. pianist. Studied RCM. Player in many chamber-music ens.

Parkin, Eric (*b* Stevenage, 1924). Eng. pianist. Studied TCL. Début London 1948. Specialist in mus. of John Ireland.

Parlando, Parlante (It.). Speaking. (1) In vocal mus., a directive for the tone of the v. to approximate to speech.
(2) In instr. mus., it calls for an expressive freedom greater than is implied by *cantabile*.

Parlato (It.). Spoken.

Parma, Ildebrando da. See *Pizzetti, Ildebrando*.

Parody. The only true use of the term applies to the 18th- and 19th-cent. parodies of the popular or most talked-about operas of the day, e.g. that of Wagner's *Tristan* prod. in Munich 1865 and called *Tristanderl und Süssholde*. Examples of parodies of one composer by another or of a type of composition are to be found in Bartók's *Concerto for Orchestra* (where Shostakovich is the target), Britten's *Midsummer Night's Dream* (Italian 19th cent. opera), and Walton's *The Bear* (various).

Parody Mass (Lat. *Missa parodia*). Misleading term for a 15th- and 16th-cent. Mass which incorporated material derived from a motet, *chanson*, or madrigal. There was nothing of 'parody' about this practice, merely the use of already existing material.

Paroles tissées (Woven words). Work for ten. and 20 solo instr. by *Lutosławski, comp. 1965. Text by Jean-François Chabrun. Commissioned and first sung by Peter *Pears.

Parratt, (Sir) **Walter** (*b* Huddersfield, 1841; *d* Windsor, 1924). Eng. organist and composer. Pupil of his father. Held organist post at age of 11. Organist, Magdalen Coll., Oxford, 1872–82, St George's Chapel, Windsor, 1882–1924. Prof. of org. RCM 1883–1923. Prof. of mus., Oxford Univ., 1908–18, dean of mus., London Univ. from 1916. Knighted 1892, K.C.V.O. 1921. Master of the Queen's (King's) Mus. 1893–1924. Bach specialist. Some comps.

Parris, Robert (*b* Philadelphia, 1924). Amer. composer, pianist, harpsichordist, and teacher. Studied Juilliard Sch. 1946–8 with P. Mennin, later at Tanglewood with Ibert and Copland, and in Paris with Honegger at École Normale, 1952–3. Ass. mus. critic, *Washington Post*, 1959–63. Since 1963 on staff of George Washington Univ. Works incl. pf. conc., va. conc., conc. for 5 kettledrums, vn. conc., 2 syms., cantata *The Hollow Men* (1949), chamber mus., and songs.

Parrott, Andrew (*b* Walsall, 1947). Eng. conductor. Began cond. at Oxford; dir. mus. Merton Coll. and research into perf. practice of 16th and 17th cent. mus. Founded Taverner Choir 1973 and later Taverner Consort and Players. Prom. début 1977 with Monteverdi Vespers, RFH 1979. Gave f.p. in London of Bach's Mass in B minor with period instr.; also perfs. of *St Matthew Passion*

and *Brandenburg* concs. with authentic instr. Has cond. ECO, London Bach Orch., and Concerto Amsterdam. Assoc. with Tippett and recorded his mus. for *The Tempest*, 1983

Parrott, (Horace) **Ian** (*b* London, 1916). Eng. composer and teacher. Studied RCM. Lecturer, Birmingham Univ. 1947–50, prof. of mus., Univ. Coll., Aberystwyth, 1950–83. Author of books on orchestration and Elgar. Comp. operas (incl. *The Black Ram*, 1951–3), 3 syms., symphonic poem *Alamein*, pf. conc., cor anglais conc., ob. qt., pf. trio, choral works, etc.

Parry, (Sir) (Charles) **Hubert** (Hastings) (*b* Bournemouth, 1848; *d* Rustington, Sussex, 1918). Eng. composer, teacher, and writer. Studied Oxford Univ. (co-founder of Mus. Club) with Sterndale Bennett and Macfarren. Entered business 1871 but 3 years later gave it up for mus. Studied pf. with E. Dannreuther, who introduced his pf. conc., 1880. His choral works, especially *Blest Pair of Sirens* (1887), est. him, with Stanford, in the forefront of Brit. composers at a time when Brahms and Bach were the admired models. He wrote prolifically in several genres (even composing an unprod. opera, *Guinevere* 1885–6), and exerted a beneficial influence on Eng. mus. through his educational work. He joined staff of RCM 1883, becoming dir. 1894 until death. Prof. of mus., Oxford Univ. 1900–08. Knighted 1898, baronet 1903. His *Songs of Farewell* are masterpieces of *a cappella* writing and his settings of English poetry, in the sets known as the *English Lyrics*, are extremely felicitous. In 1916 he wrote the unison setting of Blake's 'Jerusalem' which has become a nat. song like Elgar's 'Land of Hope and Glory'. The scorn poured on Parry's choral works by Bernard Shaw put them into critical purdah for many years, but the best of them are re-emerging, to be regarded with delighted surprise, notably *The Soul's Ransom* and the *Nativity Ode*. His chamber music, too, amply rewards exploration. Wrote several books, among them *Studies of the Great Composers* (1886), *The Evolution of the Art of Music* (1896), *Style in Musical Art* (1911), *J. S. Bach* (1909). Prin. comps.:

OPERA: *Guinevere* (1885–6).

INCIDENTAL MUSIC: *The Birds* (1883); *The Frogs* (1891); *Hypatia* (1893); *Agamemnon* (1900); *The Clouds* (1905); *The Acharnians* (1914).

ORCH: Syms. No. 1 in G (1878–82), No. 2 in F ('Cambridge') (1883), No. 3 in C ('English') (1889), No. 4 in E minor (1889), No. 5 in B minor (orig. *Symphonic Fantasia*) (1912); *Allegretto scherzando* in E♭ (1867); *Intermezzo religioso* (1868); Pf. conc. in F♯ (1878–9); *Suite Moderne* (1886); *Suite* for str. in E minor (1892); *Overture to an Unwritten Tragedy* (1893); *Lady Radnor's Suite*, str. (1894); *Symphonic Variations* (1897); *Elegy for Brahms* (1897); *From Death to Life*, sym.-poem (1914); *An *English Suite*, str. (1921, posth.).

ORATORIOS AND SACRED: *Magnificat and Nunc Dimittis* (1864); *Te Deum in E♭* (1873); **Judith*, SATB soloists, ch., orch. (1888); **Ode on St Cecilia's Day*, sop., bass, ch., org. (1889); **Job*, sop., ten., 2 basses, ch., orch. (1892); *King Saul*, SATB soloists, ch., orch. (1894); *Te Deum* (1900); *The Love that casteth out fear*, ch., orch. (1904); *The Soul's Ransom*, sinfonia sacra, sop., bass, ch., orch. (1906); *Te Deum in D* (Coronation) (1911); *An Ode on the Nativity*, sop., ch., orch. (1912).

MOTETS AND ANTHEMS: *De Profundis*, sop., 12 vv., orch. (1891); *Crossing the Bar* (1903); *Voces clamantium*, sop., bass, ch., orch. (1908); *Beyond these voices there is peace*, sop., bass, ch., orch. (1908); **Songs of Farewell* (*My soul, there is a country*, 1916, *I know my soul hath power*, 1916, *Never weatherbeaten sail*, 1916, *There is an old belief*, 1916, *At the round earth's imagin'd corners*, 1917, *Lord, let me know mine end*, 1918); *I Was Glad*, with processional music (1902, Coronation).

SECULAR CHORAL: *Scenes from Shelley's *Prometheus Unbound*, cont., ten., bass, ch., orch. (1880); *The Glories of Our Blood and State*, ch., orch. (1883, rev. 1914); **Blest Pair of Sirens*, ch., orch. (1887); *L'Allegro ed Il Penseroso*, sop., bass, ch., orch. (1890); *Choric Song from The Lotus Eaters*, sop., ch., orch. (1892); *Invocation to Music*, sop., ten., bass, ch., orch. (1895); *Ode to Music*, sop., ten., bass, ch., orch. (1901); *War and Peace*, SATB soloists, ch., orch. (1903); *The Pied Piper of Hamelin*, ten., bass, ch., orch. (1905); *A Vision of Life*, sop., bass, ch., orch. (1907, rev. 1914); *The Chivalry of the Sea*, ch., orch. (1916); *England*, unison song (1916); **Jerusalem*, choral song, unison vv., orch. (1916).

CHAMBER MUSIC: Nonet in B♭ for wind (1877); Str. Quintet in E♭ (1884); Pf. Qt. in A (1879); Str. Qts., No. 1 in G minor (1867), No. 2 in C minor (1868), No. 3 in G (1878–80); Pf. Trios, No. 1 in E minor (1878), No. 2 in B minor (1884), No. 3 in G (1884–90); *3 Movements*, vn., pf. (1863); *2 Duettinos*, vc., pf. (1868); *Romance in D*, vn. (1866–8); *Allegretto pastorale* in G, vn., pf. (1870); *6 Freundschaftslieder*, vn., pf. (1872); *Fantasie-sonata* in B minor, vn., pf. (1878); Vc. sonata in A (1883); *Partita in D minor*, vn., pf. (1877–86); Vn. sonata in D (?1888–9); *12 Short Pieces*, vn., pf. (1895); *Suite in D*, vn., pf. (1907); *Suite in F*, vn., pf. (1907).

PIANO: *Andante* in C (1867); *Sonnets and Songs Without Words*, Set I (1869), II (1875), III (1877); *7 Charakterbilder* (1872); *Variations on an Air by Bach* (1873–5); Sonatas, No. 1 in F (1877), No. 2 in A (1878); *Theme and 19 Variations* in D minor (1878–85); *10 Shulbrede Tunes* (1914); *Suite, Hands Across the Centuries* (1918).

SONGS: Over 40 part-songs (1864–1918); over 100 songs for v. and pf., 74 of them in 12 sets of **English Lyrics*.

Parry, John (*b* Bryn Cynan, *c*.1710; *d* Ruabon, 1782). Welsh harpist. Although blind, became most distinguished player of his time in Brit. From 1734 to death was in service of Williams Wynn family at Wynnstay, Ruabon. His playing impressed Handel, and the Prince of Wales (later George III) became his patron. After he had played at Cambridge 1757, the poet Thomas Gray was inspired to complete his ode *The Bard*. Composed for the harp and the guitar. In collab. with Evan Williams, another harpist, pubd. first coll. of Welsh melodies (1742), later adding two more coll. under his own name. These contributed to the popularity of the harp melody in the late 18th cent.

Parry, Joseph (*b* Merthyr Tydfil, 1841; *d* Penarth, 1903). Welsh composer. Studied RAM. Prof. of mus., Univ. Coll., Aberystwyth 1873–9, becoming lecturer in mus. at Univ. Coll. of S. Wales, Cardiff, 1888–1903. Wrote 5 operas, 3 oratorios, cantatas, and hymn-tunes, incl. the superb **Aberystwyth*, to which are usually sung the words 'Jesu, Lover of my Soul'. Tune appeared in *Ail Lyfr Tonau ac Emynau*, 1879.

Parry, Wilfrid (*b* Birmingham, 1908). Eng. pianist and accompanist. Studied TCL. BBC staff accompanist 1961. Member of several chamber ens.

Parsifal. Sacred fest. drama (*Bühnenweihfestspiel*) in 3 acts by Wagner to his own lib. His last opera, composed 1878–82, f.p. Bayreuth 1882, NY Met. 1903, CG 1914. (Concert perfs., London 1884, NY 1886.) Wagner wanted *Parsifal* to be perf. nowhere but at Bayreuth, and the Bayreuth Fest. had a copyright on the work until 31 Dec. 1913. Nevertheless this was infringed by the NY Met. and in Zürich in 1903 and by perfs. in Boston, Mass., and other Amer. cities 1904–5, in Amsterdam 1905, and in Buenos Aires and Rio 1913.

Parsley, Osbert (*b* 1511; *d* Norwich, 1585). Eng. composer and singer. Singer in Norwich Cath. choir for over 50 years, according to tablet there in his memory. Wrote church mus. for Eng. and Latin rites, incl. two 4-part morning services, *Magnificat* and *Nunc Dimittis*, and anthem. Also wrote for viols.

Parsons, Geoffrey (Penwill) (*b* Sydney, N.S.W., 1929). Australian pianist and accompanist. Studied N.S.W. State Cons. Toured Australia with Essie Ackland 1948 and with Peter *Dawson 1949. Went to London 1950 as accompanist to Dawson and settled there. World tours as accompanist to leading singers, e.g. Janet Baker, Nicolai Gedda, Elisabeth Schwarzkopf, and Hans Hotter.

Parsons, Robert (*b* Exeter, *c*.1530; ? *d* Newark, 1570). Eng. composer of church mus. and of pieces for viols. Richness of harmony and contrapuntal ingenuity placed him high among his contemporaries. Gentleman of Chapel Royal 1563. Drowned in River Trent.

Part (Fr. *Partie* or *voix*; Ger. *Part* or *Stimme*; It. *parte* or *voce*). (1) The mus. from which a particular perf. or singer in an ens. works, e.g. bass part, ob. part. One speaks of 'score and parts', to denote the full score (containing all the parts) and the individual parts.

(2) Individual line of notes to be perf. by any instr. or v., or group of instrs. or vv., thus, Fugue in 4 parts, etc.

(3) A division of a large comp., e.g. Part I of *The Dream of Gerontius*. See also *colla parte*.

Pärt, Arvo (*b* Paide, 1935). Estonian composer. Worked for Estonian radio 1957–67. Studied at Tallinn Cons., graduating 1963. Early works influenced by Shostakovich, but later adopted strict serialism and eventually collages. Works incl.: *Nekroloog*, orch. (1960); *Stride of the World*, oratorio (1960); Syms. No. 1 (1964), No. 2 (1966), No. 3 (1971); *Collage teemal BACH* (1964); *Pro et contra*, vc., orch. (1966); *Credo*, pf., ch., orch. (1968); *Song for the Beloved*, cantata (1975); *Dies Irae*, ch., org., instr. (1976); *Arbos*, chamber ens. (1977); *Tabula Rasa*, 3 vn., str., prepared pf. (1977); *Missa Sillabica*, vv. and instr. (1977); *Fratres*, str. and perc. (1977–83), vn. and ens. (1980), 12 vc. (1980–2); *De Profundis*, male vv., org., perc. (1980); *Summa*, ten., bar., instr. (1980); conc. for vn., vc., and chamber orch. (1980); *Cantus in Memory of Benjamin Britten*, str. and bell (1980); *Wenn Bach bienen gezüchtet hätte* (If Bach had kept bees), two versions, hpd. and elec. or hpd. and str. (1980); *St John Passion*, ten., bass, solo vv., ch., org., and instr. (1982).

Part Books (Ger. *Stimmbücher*). MS. or printed books of 15th and 16th cents. containing mus. for an individual v. in a polyphonic comp.

Partch, Harry (*b* Oakland, Calif., 1901; *d* San Diego, 1974). Amer. self-taught composer and inventor. Comp. several large works before he was 25 but destroyed them. Wandered over USA during depression as hobo. In 1943, while a lumberjack, he received Guggenheim award enabling him to develop 20 instrs. he had invented. He used system of intonation with 43 notes to octave; instrs. incl. the 'marimba eroica', 'chromelodeon', etc. Research assoc., Wisconsin Univ. 1944–7. Works incl. *Windsong, Barstow, 2 Settings from Finnegans Wake*, and *And on the 7th Day Petals Fell in Petaluma*.

Parthenia (Gk. 'Maidenhood'). Title of 1st book of kbd. mus. printed in Eng. 1611 containing 21 pieces by Byrd, Bull, and Gibbons—'*Parthenia, or the Maidenhead of the first music that ever was printed for the virginals.*' Reprinted 1613 and several other times in 17th cent. Reprints 1847, in facsimile by O. E. Deutsch, 1943, and edn. by Thurston Dart, 1961. A companion work, *Parthenia inviolata* (pun on 'Inviolated' and 'set for the viol') was pubd. shortly after *Parthenia* containing 20 anon. pieces for virginals and bass viol. Only known copy in NY Public Library.

Partials. Constituents of the notes of the *harmonic series, the main (fundamental) note being the first partial and the remainder the upper partials.

Particell (Ger.). Short *score.

Partie. See (1) *Part*; (2) *Suite*.

Partimento (It.). Division. Practice in 17th and 18th cents. of improvising melodies above a written bass. In Eng. viol-playing, 'divisions' on a ground were a form of *partimento* technique.

Partita (It.). Strict mus. meaning of this term is a variation, the total comp. being *partite*. But the ungrammatical custom of applying *Partita* to a composite work such as a suite has developed from the 6 Partitas in Bach's *Klavierübung* (1731). Bach's 3 suites for solo vn. are actually termed on the autograph score *Partia*.

Partition (Fr.). *Score.

Partito (It.). Divided.

Partitur (Ger.), **Partitura** (It.). *Score.

Partos, Ödön (*b* Budapest, 1907; *d* Tel Aviv, 1977). Hung.-Israeli composer and violist. Studied Budapest Cons. with Hubay and Kodály. Worked in Berlin 1928–33, Budapest, 1933–6. Settled in Palestine 1938 as violist in Tel Aviv orch. Played in orch. until 1956. Dir., Tel Aviv Acad. of Mus. from 1951. Comps. incl. *Yizkor* (In Memoriam), va. and str. (1946); *Choral Fantasia on Yemenite Jewish Themes* (1946); 3 va. concs. (1949, 1957, 1962); vn. conc. (1958); *Arabesque*, ob. and chamber orch. (1975); *Improvisation*, 12 harps (1960); *Ballade*, pf. qt. (1977); works for str. qt., and songs.

Partridge, Ian (*b* Wimbledon, 1938). Eng. ten. Studied RCM and GSM. Début Bexhill 1958. Lieder recitalist and specialist in Eng. songs. CG début 1969 (*Les Troyens*). Often acc. at pf. by his sister Jennifer (*b* New Malden, 1942).

Part-Song. Strictly any song written for several vocal parts, but in practice, a comp. for male, female, or mixed vv. (usually but not necessarily unacc.) which is not contrapuntal like the *madrigal but has the melody in the highest part with accompanying harmonies in the other vv. Either through-composed (*Durchkomponiert*) or strophic (verse-repeating). Is a particularly Eng. genre, developing in popularity with growth of choral socs. in early 19th cent., so there are many examples by Pearsall, Barnby, Stanford, Elgar, Delius, Warlock, and many others. But examples exist by Schubert, Schumann, Mendelssohn, Brahms, etc.

Part-Writing (Ger. *Stimmführung*; Amer. voice-leading). The organization of a comp. so that each individual part is blended into a euphonious whole.

Pas (Fr.). (1) A step in dancing and ballet, e.g. *Pas seul*, solo dance, *pas de deux*, dance for 2, *pas d'action*, dramatic ballet scene.

(2) Not, as in *pas trop vite*, not too fast.

Pas d'acier, Le (Prokofiev). See *Age of Steel, The*.

Pasdeloup, Jules Étienne (*b* Paris, 1819; *d* Fontainebleau, 1887). Fr. cond. Studied Paris Cons., later joining staff and becoming cond. of students' orch., 1851. In 1861 founded Concerts Populaires and cond. many works by contemporary Fr. composers, also much Wagner. After his death concerts continued for a time under name Concerts Pasdeloup.

Pashley, Anne (*b* Skegness, 1937). Eng. sop. Studied GSM. Début with Handel Opera Soc. in *Semele*. Soloist with leading orchs. and guest singer at CG, ENO, Scottish Opera, WNO, Aldeburgh Fest. Also Olympic athlete.

Pasodoble (Sp.). Double step. 20-cent. Sp. dance in quick 2/4 time. The Tango-pasodoble in *Walton's *Façade* is a parody (using 'I do like to be beside the seaside').

Pasquini, Bernardo (*b* Massa da Valdinievole, Tuscany, 1637; *d* Rome, 1710). It. composer, organist, and harpsichordist. Organist of S. Maria Maggiore, Rome, and influenced by mus. of his predecessor there, *Palestrina. Played hpd. continuo in opera house orch. with Corelli as first violinist. Wrote operas and oratorios and dir. concerts for Queen Christina of Sweden.

Passacaglia. See *Chaconne*.

Passage. Section of a comp. which perhaps has no structural significance, e.g. a pizzicato passage, which may last only 2 bars. 'Passage-work' is often applied to brilliant display for the soloist.

Passamezzo, Pass'e mezzo (It.). Dance in quicker tempo. It. dance of 16th and 17th cents. similar to *pavan but faster and less serious. Examples by Byrd and Philips are in *Fitzwilliam Virginal Book.

Passecaille (Fr.). Passacaglia. See *Chaconne*.

Passepied (Fr.; Eng. 'Paspy'). Pass-foot. Lively dance in $\frac{3}{8}$ or $\frac{6}{8}$ said to have originated among sailors of Basse-Bretagne and introduced to Paris in late 16th cent. by street dancers, becoming popular at courts of Louis XIV and Louis XV. Examples in Fr. operas of the period, e.g. by *Campra. The term was incorrectly applied by Debussy to a 2-in-a-measure piece.

Passing-Notes. Harmonic term to describe note which forms a discord with the chord with which it is heard but is melodically placed between two non-discordant notes.

Passion Music. The practice of setting to mus. the Passion of Christ, for perf. during Holy Week, has 2 connected origins—the old mysteries (see *Miracle Plays*) and (a more direct and obvious source) a very ancient Holy Week practice of reading or reciting in church, in a more or less dramatic fashion, the story of the Passion of Christ. It is known to have existed in the 4th cent.; by the 8th its character was determined as follows: a priest recited, in Lat., the story of the Passion from one of the Gospels, in a speaking voice except for the words of Christ, which he gave out to a traditional plainsong. By the 12th cent. 3 of the clergy took part, a ten. as Narrator, a bass as Christ, and an alto as the Crowd (Turba). By the 15th cent. Passions of more musically elaborate character became common. The Reformation brought a further development. The Ger. (Lutheran) reformers, acting on their principle that the people should be able to follow the words of the service, adapted it to the Ger. language.

In the 16th cent., unacc. polyphonic settings of the complete Lat. text of the Passion were based on a plainchant *cantus firmus*. Among many such settings were those of *Obrecht, Daser, Ruffo, Lassus, Victoria, and Byrd. One of the earliest settings by an Eng. composer was that by Richard *Davy.

Outstanding examples of the Ger. type of Passion are the settings of *Schütz (1585–1672). He adopted a type of recit. derived from the new It. style but which also had considerable affinity with the old plainsong. The 4-part chs. are acc. by str. The various characters are allotted to different vocal soloists and the works can be designated as 'oratorio Passions'. In the 17th cent. the 'Passion oratorio' developed, in which the biblical text was replaced by a metrical paraphrase, as in *Keiser's *Der blutige und sterbende Jesus* (1704). But Bach, in his great *St John* and *St Matthew* Passions, combined both types of setting, making use of biblical text, paraphrases, chorales, arias, and imparting to the mus. a startlingly dramatic quality. In the 19th cent. oratorios on biblical subjects replaced the strict Passion settings, but *Penderecki in the 20th cent. had remarkable success with his *St Luke Passion* (1963–6).

Passione, La. Nickname for Haydn's Sym. in F minor, No. 49 in Breitkopf edn., comp. 1768. Begins with *adagio* suggestive of Passion mus.

Pasta (orig. Negri), **Giuditta** (*b* Saronno, nr. Milan, 1797; *d* Blevio, nr. Lake Como, 1865). It. sop., among greatest of opera singers. Studied Milan. Début Brescia 1815, London 1817, both unsuccessful. Further study with Scappa was followed by successful début 1819 in Venice. Caused sensation in Paris, 1821–2, where the immense range of her v. and her dramatic gifts were matched by poignancy of expression, though she was an uneven artist. Sang regularly in London, Paris, and St Petersburg 1824–37. Created role of Amina in Bellini's *La sonnambula*, Milan 1831, and title-roles in Bellini's *Norma*, (Milan 1831, London 1833) and *Beatrice di Tenda* (Venice 1833) and in Donizetti's *Anna Bolena*, Milan 1830.

Pasticcio (It.). Pie, pasty. (1) A dramatic entertainment with songs, ensembles, dances, and other items assembled from the works of several composers, thus giving the audience a medley of their favourite tunes. Popular in 18th cent., e.g. *Thomyris* (1707).

(2) An opera in which each act is by a different composer, e.g. *Muzio Scevola* (1721) by Amadei, Bononcini, and Handel.

(3) Instr. comp. containing different sections or items by different composers, e.g. Diabelli's *Väterlandischer Künstlerverein* (1823–4), containing variations by 50 composers; the *Hexaméron (1837), and L'*Éventail de Jeanne* (1927).

Pastiche (Fr.). Imitation. Not the same as *pasticcio, being a work deliberately written in the style of another period or manner, e.g. Prokofiev's *Classical Symphony*, Strauss's *Ariadne auf Naxos,* and Stravinsky's *Pulcinella*. Although *pastiche* has a meaning as 'medley', it is invariably applied musically in the sense outlined above.

Pastoral, Pastorale. (1) Type of instr. or vocal comp., generally in $\frac{6}{8}$ or $\frac{12}{8}$, which suggests rustic or bucolic subject, often by imitation of shepherd's pipe. A 20th-cent. use of the term is *Bliss's Pastoral, *Lie Strewn the White Flocks.*

(2) Stage piece dealing with legendary or pastoral subject. Began as a play but in Fr. pastorals were set to mus. as an early form of *opéra-ballet* and were at height of popularity in 17th and 18th cents. Handel's *Acis and Galatea* is an example.

Pastorale (Fr.). *Pastoral.

Pastorale d'été (Summer Pastoral). Symphonic poem for small orch. by Honegger, comp. 1920. F.p. Paris 1921.

Pastoral Sonata. Publisher's name for Beethoven's Pf. Sonata No. 15 in D major, Op. 28, comp. 1801 (presumably because of rustic rhythm in finale).

Pastoral Symphony. (1) Sym. No. 6 in F major, Op. 68, by Beethoven, comp. 1807–8, f.p. Vienna 1808. A 'programme symphony' in which birdsong and a storm are represented. Each movement has a title, viz., 'Awakening of happy feelings on arriving in the country', 'By the brook', 'Joyous gathering of country folk—storm', 'Shepherd's song; happy and thankful feelings after the storm'.

(2) 3rd Sym. by Vaughan Williams comp. 1916–21, rev. 1950–1, f.p. London 1922. Last movement has wordless solo for sop. (or cl.).

(3) Short orch. movement in Handel's *Messiah,* depicting calm of first Christmas Eve.

Pastor Fido, Il (The Faithful Shepherd). Opera in 3 acts by Handel to lib. by Rossi based on Guarini's pastoral play (1585). Prod. London 1712, NY 1952. Also opera by *Salieri (1789).

Pastourelle (Fr.). Light Fr. song of pastoral type, popular in 18th cent.

'Pathetic' Symphony. Subtitle, authorized by composer, of *Tchaikovsky's Sym. No. 6 in B minor, Op. 74. After f.p. in St Petersburg 1893, Modest Tchaikovsky suggested title 'Tragic' but composer demurred, immediately agreeing to *Pathetic*. No reason in Eng. why Fr. title *Symphonie Pathétique* should be used. Note that Russ. word *patetichesky* means 'passionate' or 'emotional' rather than 'pathetic'.

Pathétique Sonata (Pathetic Sonata). Beethoven's Pf. Sonata No. 8 in C minor, Op. 13, comp. 1798–9 and entitled by him, in Fr., *Grande sonate pathétique.*

Patience, or Bunthorne's Bride. Operetta by *Sullivan to lib. by Gilbert. Prod. London 1881, St Louis 1881, NY 1882. Satire on 'aesthetic' movement.

Patterson, Paul (b Chesterfield, 1947). Eng. composer. Entered RAM 1964 to study tb., then comp. with R. Stoker. Private study with Richard Rodney *Bennett. Dir. of contemporary mus., Warwick Univ. 1974–80. Prof. of comp. and dir. elec. studies, RAM, from 1975. Works, some using elec. tape and *aleatory methods, incl.:

ORCH: Tpt. conc. (1969); *Concertante* (1969); *Partita* (1970); *Piccola Sinfonia* (1971); *Symphonic Study II* (1971); hn. conc. (1971); *Fiesta Sinfonica* (1972); *Sonors* (1972); *Fusions* (1974); *Strange Meeting* (1975); *The Circular Ruins* (1975); cl. conc. (str. orch.) (1976); *Wildfire* (1976); *Concerto for Orchestra* (1981); *Sinfonia for Strings* (1982).

ENSEMBLE: Wind quintet (1967); wind trio (1968); *Comedy* for 5 winds (1972); *Conversations,* cl. and pf. (1974); *Diversions,* saxophone qt. (1976); *Floating Music* (1974); *Intersections* (1973); *Syntony; Rebecca,* speaker and ens.; *Cracowian Counterpoints,* 14 instr. (1977); *Deception Pass,* brass (1980); *At the Still Point of the Turning World,* octet (1980); *Duologue,* ob., pf. (1984).

VOCAL: *Kyrie,* ch. and pf. (2 players) (1972); *Timepiece,* 6 male vv. (1973); *Gloria,* ch. and pf. (2 players) (1973); *Requiem,* ch. and orch. (1975); *Spare Parts,* 6 male vv. (1977); *Brain Storm,* 4 vv. and elec. (1978); *Voices of Sleep,* sop., ch., orch. (1979); *Sing Praises!* ch. and orch. (1980); *The Canterbury Psalms,* ch. and orch. (1981; ch., brass, and org. 1984); *Mass of the Sea,* SATB soloists, ch., and orch. (1983; rev. for sop., bass, ch., and orch. 1983–4).

PIANO: *3 Portraits* (1984).

Patter-Song. Comic song, prevalent in opera, which is a rapid iteration of words, the mus. merely being lightly supportive. Examples exist in Haydn, Mozart, and Rossini operas; there are many in the Sullivan operettas (e.g. 'My name is John Wellington Wells', from *The Sorcerer*). Usually solos, but *Ruddigore* has a patter-trio.

Patti, Adelina (b Madrid, 1843; d Craig-y-Nos Castle, Wales, 1919). It. sop. Daughter of singers. Taken to NY as child, making début there 1850.

Studied singing with brother-in-law, M. Strakosch. Stage début NY 1859 as Lucia; London CG 1861 as Amina in *Sonnambula,* Paris 1862. Rapidly recognized as leading sop. of day and *Grisi's successor. V. had great range, flexibility, and purity of tone. Essentially a coloratura sop., but sang dramatic roles such as Leonora in *Trovatore* and Violetta in *Traviata.* 1st London *Aida* (1876). In 25 consecutive CG seasons sang over 30 roles by Donizetti, Bellini, Rossini, Verdi, Meyerbeer, etc. Zerlina in *Don Giovanni* was her only Mozart role. CG farewell 1895; sang last operas in Monte Carlo and Nice 1897. Toured N. and S. Amer. and the world's capitals. Highest-paid singer of her day. Farewell concert, London 1906, followed by provincial tour. Retired to her castle in Wales but gave charity concert in 1914. Buried in Paris.

Patzak, Julius (*b* Vienna, 1898; *d* Rottach, 1974). Austrian ten. Studied Vienna Univ. and Sch. of Mus. Intended to be cond. but turned to singing, making début Reichenberg Opera 1926, as Radamès in *Aida.* Munich Opera 1928–45, Vienna Opera 1945–60, CG début 1938 as Tamino. Outstanding Florestan in *Fidelio* and Palestrina in title-role of Pfitzner's opera. Superb singer of Lieder, oratorio, etc.

Pauk, György (*b* Budapest, 1936). Hung. violinist. Studied Budapest Liszt Acad. of Mus. with Weiner and Kodály. Won Paganini competition, Genoa 1956, Munich competition, 1957, Thibaud competition, Paris 1959. Eng. début 1961. Prof. of vn. RMCM 1964. Soloist with leading orchs. and member of trio, often with Peter *Frankl (pf.) and Ralph *Kirshbaum (vc.).

Pauke(n) (Ger.). Kettledrum(s). See *Drum.*

Paukenmesse (Kettledrum Mass). Popular subtitle for Haydn's Mass No. 7 in C major, comp. 1796 and named by composer *Missa in tempore belli* (Mass in time of war).

Paukenwirbel Symphonie (Drum-roll Symphony). Nickname for 11th of Haydn's 'London' Syms., No. 103 in E♭ major in Breitkopf edn., because it opens with a roll on the kettledrums.

Paul Bunyan. (1) Choral operetta by Britten in 2 acts and prol. to text by Auden. F.p. Columbia Univ., NY, May 1941. Then withdrawn until rev. in 1974 and publication as Op. 17. First complete perf. in England, BBC broadcast, Feb. 1976; f. stage p. Aldeburgh, June 1976; f. professional Amer. p., St Louis 1984.

(2) Ballet for puppets and solo dancer by W. Bergsma, 1937, prod. San Francisco 1939; also orch. suite 1937, rev. 1945.

Paulus (Mendelssohn). See *St Paul.*

Pauly, Rose (orig. Rose Pollak) (*b* Eperjes, 1894; *d* Tel Aviv, 1975). Hung. sop. Studied Vienna with *Papier. Début Vienna 1918. Cologne Opera 1922–7, Berlin 1927–31, Vienna 1922–38, NY

Met. 1938–40. CG début 1938. Notable Elektra. Retired to Israel.

Paumgartner, Bernhard (*b* Vienna, 1887; *d* Salzburg, 1971). Austrian cond., composer, and musicologist. Son of Hans Paumgartner and Rosa *Papier. Studied Vienna Univ. and with Bruno Walter. Cond. at Vienna Opera, but became one of leading organizers of Salzburg Fest., often conducting there. Dir. Salzburg Mozarteum 1917–38, 1945–59. Founded Salzburg Mozart Chamber Orch. Visited USA 1965. Comp. operas, ballet, and other works. Wrote books on Mozart (1927), Schubert (1945), and J. S. Bach (1950).

Paur, Emil (*b* Czernowitz, Bukovina, 1855; *d* Mistek, Moravia, 1932). Austrian cond., composer, and violinist. Entered Vienna Cons. 1866, studying vn. with Hellmesberger and comp. with Dessoff. Played in Vienna Opera Orch. from age 15. Began cond. career at Kassel 1876, becoming cond. of Mannheim opera and concerts 1880. Cond. Leipzig Stadttheater 1891–3, Boston S.O. 1893–8, NY P.O. and dir. Nat. Cons. of Mus. 1898–1902. NY Met. 1899–1900 (Wagner), CG 1900. Cond. Pittsburgh S.O. 1904–10. Succeeded Muck at Berlin Opera 1912, but stayed only 2 months. Comp. sym., vn. conc., and chamber works.

Pausa (It.). Rest (*not* Pause, which is *fermata).

Pause (Eng.). (1) The sign ⌒, which means that the note or rest so indicated must be held longer than usual (at performer's discretion). Placed over a bar line, it means a short silence. The Fr. term is *point d'orgue.*

(2) In the phrase General Pause (G.P.) it means the whole orch. is briefly silent.

(3) *Lunga pausa,* a long pause.

Pause (Ger.). (1) A pause, as in Eng.

(2) Rest.

(3) Interval of a concert.

Pause (Fr.). (1) Pause.

(2) Rest, especially a whole-note rest and a measure rest.

Pavan (Fr. *Pavane;* It. *Pavana;* old forms incl. *Pavin, Pavyn, Paven,* etc.). The Pavan was a dance of It. orig., popular in the 16th and 17th cents., and as the name sometimes appears as *Padovana* it is assumed that its orig. home was Padua. It was in simple duple time, and of stately character. In Italy the Pavan gave way to the Passamezzo by the mid-16th cent., but was given a new lease of life by its treatment by Eng. composers, e.g. Byrd, Dowland, Bull, and Philips. It was usually paired with the *Galliard and their assoc. was the orig. of the *suite. Some 19th- and 20th-cent. composers have written works to which they gave the name *Pavan,* e.g. Fauré's *Pavane,* *Ravel's *Pavane pour une infante défunte,* and the *Pavan* in Vaughan Williams's *Job.*

Pavane. Work by *Fauré, Op. 50, for orch. with optional mixed ch. Comp. 1887, f.p. Paris 1888.

Pavane pour une infante défunte (Pavan for a dead Infanta). Pf. piece by *Ravel comp. 1899 (f.p. 1902), orch. by composer 1910 (f.p. Paris 1910). Recalls Sp. court custom of solemn ceremonial dance at time of royal mourning.

Pavarotti, Luciano (*b* Modena, 1935). It. ten. Studied Mantua. Won int. competition at Reggio Emilia 1961, making opera début there later that year as Rodolfo in *La Bohème*. Rapid success. CG début 1963 (Rodolfo), Glyndebourne 1964 (Idamante in *Idomeneo*). Toured Australia 1965 with Joan *Sutherland. Début Milan 1966, San Francisco 1967, NY Met. 1968.

Pavillon (Fr.). Pavilion. The bell of a brass instr. e.g. tpt., hn., etc. So called because of tent-like shape. The direction to brass-players 'pavillons en l'air' means hold the bells high (in order to increase vol.).

Pavillon Chinois (Fr.). See *Jingling Johnny*.

Paxton, Stephen (*b* London, 1735; *d* London, 1787). Eng. cellist and composer of glees, catches, masses, and some fine works for vc.

Payne, Albert (*b* Leipzig, 1842; *d* Leipzig, 1921). Ger.-born son of Eng. mus. publisher in Leipzig. Studied Leipzig Cons. and in Paris. Entered father's firm 1862. Began publication of cheap edns. of miniature chamber mus. scores, 1886. Sold out to E. *Eulenburg 1892.

Payne, Anthony (Edward) (*b* London 1936). Eng. composer and critic. Studied Durham Univ. 1958–61. Illness halted his creative work 1961–5, but his *Phoenix Mass* was start of new phase. Mus. critic *Daily Telegraph* from 1965. Author of book on Schoenberg (1968) and authority on 20th-cent. Eng. composers, particularly Bax and Bridge. Works incl.:

INSTRUMENTAL: *Contrapuncti*, str. (1958, rev. 1979); *Conc. for Orch.* (1974); *The World's Winter*, sop., fl., ob., cl., hn., harp, str. trio (1976); *Fire on Whaleness*, brass band and perc. (1976); *The Stones and Lonely Places Sing*, chamber ens. (1979); *The Song of the Clouds*, ob., 2 hns., str., perc. (1979–80); *A Day in the Life of a Mayfly*, fl., cl., pf., vn., vc., perc. (1981); *Spring's Shining Wake*, orch. (1981); *Songs and Dances*, str. (1984).
CHORAL: *Phoenix Mass*, ch., 3 tpt., 3 tb. (1965–9, with add. 1972); *2 Songs Without Words*, male v. quintet (1970); *A Little Passiontide Cantata*, unacc. ch. (1974); *First Sight of Her and After*, 16 solo vv. (1975); *A Little Whitsuntide Cantata*, unacc. ch. (1977); *A Little Ascensiontide Cantata*, unacc. ch. (1977); *The Sea of Glass*, ch., organ (1977).
CHAMBER MUSIC: *Paraphrases and Cadenzas*, cl., va., pf. (1969); *Sonatas and Ricercars*, wind quintet (1970); str. qt. (1978); *Footfalls Echo in the Memory*, vn., pf. (1978); *Evening Land*, v. and pf. (1981).

PIANO: *Paean* (1971).
ORGAN: *Reflections in the Sea of Glass* (1983).

Paz, Juan Carlos (*b* Buenos Aires, 1901; *d* Buenos Aires, 1972). Argentinian composer and critic. Founded Grupo Renovación 1930 and Agrupación Nueva Música 1944. Moved from tonal style to use of 12-note method and then to 'open forms'. Comps. incl. tone poems, concs., and chamber mus.

Peabody Conservatory. Sch. of mus. at Baltimore, Maryland, USA, which also houses library and art gallery. Founded 1857, but opening delayed until 1868. Confers degrees of B.Mus., M.Mus., and Doctor of Musical Arts.

Peacock Variations. *Variations on a Hungarian Folk-Song 'The Peacock'* for orch. by Kodály, comp. 1938–9, commissioned for 50th anniv. of Concertgebouw Orch. of Amsterdam, 1939.

Pears, (Sir) Peter (*b* Farnham, 1910; *d* Aldeburgh, 1986). Eng. ten. and organist. Studied RCM. Organist, Hertford Coll., Oxford. Dir. of mus., Grange Sch., Crowborough, 1933–4. Had lessons from E. *Gerhardt. In BBC Singers 1934–7, New Eng. Singers 1936–8. Went to USA with friend Benjamin *Britten 1939, returning 1942. Stage début London 1942 as Hoffmann in *The Tales of Hoffmann*. SW Opera 1943–6, EOG from 1946. Closely assoc. with mus. of Britten, giving f.ps. of many works (e.g. *Serenade*, *Nocturne*, *Seven Sonnets of Michelangelo*, *Holy Sonnets of John Donne*, etc.) and creating several of Britten's operatic roles, e.g. title-roles in *Peter Grimes* and *Albert Herring* and Male Chorus in *The Rape of Lucretia*, Captain Vere in *Billy Budd*, Essex in *Gloriana*, Quint in *The Turn of the Screw*, Flute in *A Midsummer Night's Dream* (of which he was co-librettist with Britten), Madwoman in *Curlew River*, Sir Philip Wingrave in *Owen Wingrave*, Aschenbach in *Death in Venice*. Created Pandarus in Walton's *Troilus and Cressida*, CG 1954. Notable singer of Schubert, Bach (Evangelist), and of Vašek in *The Bartered Bride*. Writer on mus. and ed. (with Britten) of Purcell. NY Met. début 1974 (Aschenbach). C.B.E. 1957. Knighted 1978.

Pearsall, Robert (Lucas) (*b* Clifton, 1795; *d* Wartensee, 1856). Eng. composer. Studied as lawyer but turned to mus. when in Ger., 1825. Thereafter lived mainly abroad and bought castle of Wartensee on Lake Constance. Wrote madrigals in 16th-cent. style. Comp. many part-songs, incl. *O Who will o'er the Downs so Free?* His setting for 8 solo vv. and 5-part chorus of the Ger. macaronic carol *In dulci jubilo* was made in 1834 and pubd. in 1836. Also comp. *Requiem* 1853–6.

Pearson, H. H. See *Pierson, Henry Hugo*.

Peasant Cantata (*Bauernkantate*). Light-hearted cantata by Bach, 1742, to lib. by Picander. It is Cantata No. 212, *Mer hahn en neue Oberkeet*, for sop., bass, hn., fl., str., and continuo.

Pêcheurs de perles, Les (The Pearl Fishers). 3-act opera by Bizet to lib. by Cormon and Carré. Prod. Paris 1863, London 1887 (under title *Leila,* the heroine's name), Philadelphia 1893. Action set in Ceylon (Sri Lanka).

Ped. Abbreviation for *pedal. In pf. mus., means that the sustaining pedal is to be depressed until its release is indicated. In org. mus., means that mus. is to be played on the *pedal-board.

Pedal. (1) In *harmony, a note sustained below changing harmonies and called a *pedal-point* or *pedal-bass.* If sustained but not in the bass, it is an *inverted pedal.*
(2) Lowest, i.e. fundamental, note of *harmonic series, esp. in brass instrs.
(3) Lever operated by the foot, as in harp, hpd., kettledrum, organ, and pf.

Pedal-Board. Kbd. played with the feet, as on an org. Also found (rarely) in hpd., clavichord, and pf.

Pedal Clarinet. Same as db. cl., a very rare form of cl., used mainly in military bands.

Pédalier (Fr.). *Pedal-board or *pedal-piano.

Pedalpauken (Ger.). Mechanically-tuned kettle-drums.

Pedal-Piano. Pf. fitted with pedal kbd. in addition to manual. Used by orgs. for practice at home. Schumann and Alkan comp. for it.

Pedal-Point. See *Pedal (1).*

Pedrell, Felipe (*b* Tortosa, 1841; *d* Barcelona, 1922). Sp. composer and musicologist. Chorister, Tortosa Cath. Believed that a nation should base its mus. on its folk-song. Ed. early Sp. church and secular mus., and complete works of *Victoria (Leipzig, 1902–13). Taught at Madrid Cons. 1895–1903, pupils incl. *Albeniz, *Granados, and *Falla. Comp. several operas, orch. works, and church mus.

Peel, Gerald (Graham) (*b* Pendlebury, 1877; *d* Bournemouth, 1937). Eng. composer. Studied with Ernest Walker. Wrote many songs incl. settings of Housman's *A Shropshire Lad* poems.

Peele, George (*fl.* 16th cent.). Eng. composer of madrigals.

Peerce, Jan (orig. Jacob Pincus Perelmuth) (*b* NY, 1904; *d* New Rochelle, NY, 1984). Amer. ten. Trained as violinist, played and sang in dance-bands. Sang at Radio City Music Hall 1933–9. Opera début Philadelphia 1938 (Duke in *Rigoletto*). NY Met. début 1941 (Alfredo in *La traviata*), becoming regular member of co. and singing several times in Toscanini's NBC opera broadcasts.

Peer Gynt. Play by Ibsen for which Grieg comp. 23 items of incidental mus., Op. 23, 1874–5, f.p. Christiania, Feb. 1876. Later arr. for pf., 4 hands, then as 2 orch. suites: No. 1 (Op. 46, 1874–5, rev.

1888): 1. *Morning,* 2. *Death of Aase,* 3. *Anitra's Dance,* 4. *In the Hall of the Mountain King*; No. 2 (Op. 55, 1874–5, rev. 1891 and 1892): 1. *Abduction of the Bride* and *Ingrid's Lament,* 2. *Arabian Dance,* 3. *Peer Gynt's Homecoming,* 4. *Solvejg's Song.* Additional items sometimes perf. are *Wedding March, Solvejg's Cradle Song, Prelude, Dance of the Mountain King's Daughter.* Incidental mus. also comp. by *Saeverud, 1947 (2 orch. suites pubd.). Also opera by *Egk (Berlin 1938).

Peerson, Martin (*b* ? nr. Ely, *c*.1572; *d* London, 1651). Eng. composer of church mus. and part-songs. Also wrote for viols and virginals. Organist of St Paul's Cath., London, from *c*.1624.

Peeters, Flor (*b* Thielen, 1903; *d* Antwerp, 1986). Belg. organist and composer. Studied at Lemmens Institute, Mechelen (Malines), 1919–23 (org. with Depuydt) and worked privately with M. Dupré. Organist Mechelen Cath. from 1923. Prof. of org., Lemmens Institute 1925–52, Royal Cons., Ghent, 1931–48, and Royal Flemish Cons., Antwerp, 1948–68 (dir. from 1952). Ed. early Flemish, Dutch, and Eng. org. works and wrote 3-vol. org. method (*Ars Organi,* 1952). World tours as org. recitalist. Comps. incl.:

ORGAN: *Variations and Finale* (1929); *Toccata, Fugue, and Hymn on Ave Maris Stella* (1931); *Flemish Rhapsody* (1935); *Passacaglia and Fugue* (1938); *Sinfonia* (1940); Conc. (1944); *Lied Symphony* (1948); *3 Preludes and Fugues* (1950); organ and pf. conc. (1951); *Hymn Preludes for Liturgical Year* (1959–64); 6 *Lyrical Pieces* (1966); *10 Inventions* (1969); *10 Preludes on Old Flemish Songs* (1972); *Introduzione, fugato con corale supra 'Pro Civitate'* (1976).
VOICE(S) AND ORGAN: *Mass for St Joseph* (1929); *Speculum vitae,* sop. (1935); *Jubilate Deo* (1936); *Te Deum* (1945); *Missa festiva* (1958); *Entrata festiva* (1959); *Magnificat* (1962); *Canticum gaudii* (1971–2).

Peg (Ger. *Wirbel*; Fr. *cheville*; It. *bischero*). Movable wooden pin set in head of instr. of vn. family and used to adjust the tension of the str.

Pelléas et Mélisande. (1) Opera (*drame lyrique*) in 5 acts, 12 *tableaux,* by Debussy, comp. 1893–5 and 1901–2, being a nearly complete setting of the text of Maeterlinck's play of this name (1892). Prod. Paris 1902, NY 1908, London 1909.
(2) Symphonic poem after Maeterlinck, Op. 5, by Schoenberg, comp. 1902–3 and f.p. 1905 (Vienna). F.p. in England 1930.
(3) Incidental mus. to Maeterlinck's play by Sibelius, Op. 46, comp. 1905 for prod. in Helsinki. Suite of 9 items for small orch. pubd. 1905.
(4) Incidental mus. to Maeterlinck's play by Fauré, Op. 80, comp. 1898 for London prod. (cond. Fauré). Suite of 4 items for orch. pubd. 1900 and f.p. 1901 (also arr. for pf. solo, and pf., 4 hands).

Pellegrini, Vincenzo (*b* Pesaro, late 16th cent.; *d* Milan, *c*.1631). It. composer. Wrote masses and other church mus., canzonets and instr. pieces. Maestro di cappella, Milan Cath. 1611–31.

Pelletier, Wilfrid (*b* Montreal, 1896; *d* NY, 1982). Canadian cond. Studied in Paris. Ass. cond. Montreal Opera Co., then of NY Met. 1917, becoming cond. there 1932–50. Initiated Met. Auditions of the Air. Cond. Ravinia Park, Chicago, and San Francisco Opera. Dir. Montreal Cons. 1942–61. Cond. Quebec S.O. 1951–66.

Penderecki, Krzysztof (*b* Debica, 1933). Polish composer. Studied Kraków High Sch. for Mus. with Malawski until 1957, then with Wiechowicz. Won all 3 prizes at Warsaw autumn fest. 1959. Teacher at Kraków High Sch. for Mus. from 1958, dir. from 1972. Teacher at Yale Sch. of Mus. from 1975. After 1960 abandoned Boulez-influenced style and was one of first *avant-garde* composers to experiment with sounds such as sawing wood, rustling paper, typewriters, knocking, hissing, screeching, etc., and various orig. effects obtained from conventional instr. by unconventional means, in particular microtonal glissandi and dense clusters. In choral mus., the singers are asked to articulate consonants rapidly, to hiss and to whistle. Nevertheless these freakish effects are put to artistic use and his *St Luke Passion* (1966) was an immediate success with a wide public. Prin. works:

OPERAS: The *★Devils of Loudun* (Diably z Loudun) (1968–9), *★Paradise Lost* (1976–8).
ORCH: *Emanations*, 2 str. orch. (1958); *Anaklasis*, 42 str., perc. (1960); *★Threnody for the Victims of Hiroshima* (Tren ofiarom Hiroszimy) 52 str. (1960); *Fonogrammi,* fl. and chamber orch. (1961); *Polymorphia*, 48 str. (1961); *Fluorescences* (1961); *Canon*, 52 str., 2 tapes (1961); *Sonata* for vc. and orch. (1964); *Capriccio*, ob. and str. (1965); *De natura sonoris* (Of the nature of sound) I (1966), II (1971); *Pittsburgh Overture* for wind (1967); *Capriccio*, vn. and orch. (1967); *Prélude*, for wind, perc., and dbs. (1971); vc. conc. No. 1 (1971–2), No. 2 (1981–2); *Partita*, hpd., 5 elec. amplified solo instr. and orch. (1971–2); *Actions*, jazz ens. (1971); Sym. No. 1 (1973), No. 2 (1980); *The Dream of Jacob* (1974).
CHORUS AND ORCH: *From the Psalms of David*, ch. and chamber ens. (1958); *Strophes* (Strofy) for sop., narrator, 10 instr. (1959); *Dimensions of Time and Silence* (Wymiary czasu i ciszy), ch. and chamber ens. (1960); *Stabat Mater*, 3 ch. (1963); *Cantata in honorem Almae Matris Universitatis Iagellonicae*, ch. and orch. (1964); *★St Luke Passion*, narrator, soloists, ch., and orch. (1963–6); *Dies Irae*, soloists, ch., and orch. (1967); *★Utrenja*: Part I, *The Entombment of Christ*, soloists, ch., and orch. (1969–70), Part II, *The Resurrection of Christ*, soloists, ch., and orch. (1970–1); *Kosmogonia*, soloists, ch., and orch. (1970); *Canticum Canticorum Salomonis* (Song of Songs), ch., chamber

orch., and dance pair (1971–2); *Ecloga VIII* (Virgil), 6 male vv. (1972); *Magnificat*, bass, boys' vv., ch., orch. (1974); *Te Deum*, solo vv., ch., orch. (1979).
CHAMBER MUSIC: Str. qt, No. 1 (1960), No. 2 (1968); *Capriccio per Siegfried Palm*, vc. (1968).
TAPE: *Psalmus* (1961); *Brigade of Death* (1963).

Pénélope. (1) Opera (*drame lyrique*) in 3 acts by *★Fauré to lib. by René Fauchois. Prod. Monte Carlo and Paris 1913, London, 1970.
(2) Opera semi-seria in 2 parts by Liebermann to text by H. Strobel. Prod. Salzburg 1954. Other operas on Penelope legend are by Monteverdi (*Il *★ritorno d'Ulisse in patria*), Cimarosa, Galuppi, Piccinni, and Jommelli.

Penillion. Type of Welsh traditional singing in which improvised or set poems are sung in counterpoint to well-known melody played by harpist. Also title of orch. work by Grace *★Williams, comp. 1955.

Pennario, Leonard (*b* Buffalo, NY, 1924). Amer. pianist. Public début at 7, played with Dallas S.O. at 12. Served in World War II; on resumption of career played in trio with Heifetz (vn.) and Piatigorsky (vc.). Many tours as conc. soloist.

Penny for a Song, A. Opera in 2 acts by Richard Rodney Bennett to lib. by Colin Graham from play by John Whiting. Prod. London (SW) 1967.

Pentatonic Scale (from Gr. *pente*, five). Scale of 5 notes widely found in folk mus. (Scottish, Chinese, Negro, etc.) and found as early as 2000 BC. Can be easily prod. by playing 5 black keys only of pf., beginning with F♯. The tune of *Auld Lang Syne* is pentatonic.

Pentland, Barbara (Lally) (*b* Winnipeg, 1912). Canadian composer. Studied Winnipeg and Montreal 1921–9, Paris 1929–30, Juilliard Sch. 1936–9, and Tanglewood 1941, 1942 (comp. with Copland). Taught theory and comp. Toronto Cons. 1943–9, Univ. of B.C., Vancouver, 1949–63. Works incl. 4 syms., 3 str. qts., pf. conc., vn. sonata, etc.

Pépin, Clermont (*b* St Georges de Beauce, 1926). Canadian composer. Studied Quebec, Montreal, Curtis Institute, Toronto Cons., and in Paris 1949–51 with Honegger, Jolivet, and Messiaen. Teacher of comp., Montreal. Works incl. 4 syms., 2 pf. concs., 4 str. qts., symphonic poem *Guernica*, ballets *The Gates of Hell* and *The Phoenix*.

Pepping, Ernst (*b* Duisburg, 1901; *d* Berlin, 1981). Ger. composer. Studied in Berlin 1922–6 with Gmeindl. Prof. of comp. Berlin Hochschule 1953–68. Works incl. 3 syms., pf. conc., 2 org. concs., 4 pf. sonatas, and a large number of choral works incl. *Missa, Dona nobis pacem* (1949) and *Passionsbericht des Matthäus* (1950).

Pepusch, Johann Christoph (*b* Berlin 1667; *d* London, 1752). Ger.-born composer, cond., and organist. Mainly self-taught; expert in theory and history. Settled in London 1704. Played vn. and cembalo in Drury Lane orch. One of founders of *Academy of Ancient Music. Organist and composer to Duke of Chandos 1715–20. From 1715 comp. mus. for operas and masques at Drury Lane and Lincoln's Inn Th. Orchestrated folk tunes and comp. ov. for Gay's The *Beggar's Opera (1728) and for its sequel Polly (1729). Wrote treatise on harmony (1730) and other theoretical books.

Per (It.). By, through, for, in order to, etc., e.g. per stromentati, for instrs.

Peragallo, Mario (b Rome, 1910). It. composer. Pupil of *Casella. Works, in advanced style, incl. 5 operas, scenic cantata, conc. for orch., pf. conc., vn. conc. (Rome prize 1954), str. qts.

Perahia, Murray (b NY, 1947). Amer. pianist and cond. Studied Mannes Coll., NY. Winner Leeds Int. pf. competition 1972. Soloist with leading orchs. Frequently conducts from kbd. in perfs. of Mozart concs. First London recital 1973.

Percival, Allen (Dain) (b Bradford, Yorks., 1925). Eng. teacher and author. Studied Cambridge Univ. with Ord and Dart. Prin., GSM 1965–77. Chairman, Stainer and Bell. C.B.E. 1975.

Percussion. Name for family of instrs. (perhaps the most ancient in existence) which are usually played by striking a resonating surface with a stick or the hand, or by a pedal. The pf. may be used percussively (as in Orff, Stravinsky, Bartók, etc.) but is not classified as a perc. instr., nor is the celesta. The instr. are divided into those of definite pitch—*kettledrum, *tubular bells, *glocken-spiel, *vibraphone, *xylophone, *marimba—and those of indefinite pitch—*triangle, *gong, *cas-tanets, *whip, *rattle, *anvil, *bass drum, ten. *drum, *side drum, *tabor, *tambourine, *bongo, and *cymbals. Various unusual devices such as iron chains, motor horns, tin sheet, come into the perc. section of an orch.

Perdendo, perdendosi (It.; Fr. se perdant). Losing, i.e. gradually dying away.

Perfall, Karl, Freiherr von (b Munich, 1824; d Munich, 1907). Ger. opera-house administrator, cond., and composer. Civil servant until 1850. Studied mus. Leipzig 1848–9. Cond. Munich Liedertafel 1850, oratorio soc. 1854–64. Intendant of Munich court mus. 1864–7, court th. 1867–93. Despite the composer's hostility, was champion of Wagner's music and over 700 Wagner perfs. were given in Munich during his intendancy. Wrote operas, cantatas, and songs.

Perfect Cadence. See Cadence.

Perfect Fool, The. Comic opera in 1 act by Holst, Op. 39, to lib. by composer. Comp. 1918–22. Prod. London, CG 1923 cond. E. Goossens;

Wichita 1962. Also separate orch. suite of ballet mus., f.p. 1920.

Perfect Intervals. See Interval.

Perfect Time. See Common Time.

Perfect Pitch. See Absolute Pitch.

Performing Right Society. Brit. assoc. of composers, authors, and mus. publishers founded 1914 for the purpose of collecting royalties for the non-dramatic public perf. and broadcasting of members' works. (Often incorrectly described as the Performing Rights Society.)

Pergolesi, Giovanni Battista (b Jesi, nr. Ancona, 1710; d Pozzuoli, nr. Naples, 1736). It. composer, violinist, and organist. Studied Naples 1725. Principally talented as composer of comic operas, the first of which, Salustia, was a failure in Naples in 1732. In 1733 he comp. Il prigioner superbo, now forgotten except for its intermezzo La *serva padrona, which has remained popular. His Stabat Mater (1736) for male sop., male alto, and orch. is still perf. After his early death from tuberculosis, many works were and still are falsely ascribed to him, such as the comic opera Il maestro di musica, concs., and songs. Stravinsky in *Pulcinella 're-composed' material by Pergolesi, but even there some of the attributions are false.

Peri, Jacopo (b Rome, 1561; d Florence, 1633). It. composer, pupil of Malvezzi. Dir. of mus. at Medici court and later at court of Ferrara. One of group of poets and musicians assoc. in Florence with Jacopo Corsi and Count *Bardi in last quarter of 16th cent. (see Camerata), and whose interest in reviving elements of Gr. drama led to comp. in monodic style of what is regarded as the first opera or mus.-drama, Dafne (1594–8), followed by Euridice (1600). He later wrote other operas, some in collab., ballets, madrigals, etc., only a few of which survive.

Péri, La (The Peri). Ballet (poème dansé) by Dukas, choreog. Clustine, f.p. Paris 1912. Orch. suite from mus.

Périchole, La. Opéra-bouffe by Offenbach to lib. by Meilhac and Halévy after Mérimée's Le Carrosse du Saint Sacrément. Orig. in 2 acts (1868), rev. in 3 acts (1874). Prod. Paris 1868, NY 1869, London 1870.

Périgourdine. Old Fr. dance to mus. in compound duple time which was sung by the dancers. Its native home was Périgord.

Perkowski, Pyotr (b Oweczacze, Ukraine, 1901). Polish composer and cond. Studied Warsaw Cons. and with Szymanowski and Roussel (in Paris). Founded assoc. of young Polish musicians in Paris, 1927. Dir. Torun Cons. 1935–9. Prof. of comp., Warsaw State Acad. 1946–70 with interval 1950–6 when he was dean of Wrocław Acad. of Mus. Cond. Polish Radio Orch. 1956–8. Works incl. syms., concs., ballets, radio opera, and *Szkice torunskie* (Torun Sketches) for orch. (1938).

Perle, George (*b* Bayonne, NJ, 1915). Amer. composer. Studied De Paul Univ. 1934–8 and later with Křenek. Prof. of mus., Queens Coll., City Univ. of NY, since 1961, having held teaching posts at other univs. since 1949. Author of important book on *Serial Composition and Atonality* (1962). Authority on music and life of Alban Berg. As a composer evolved his own serialist method. Works incl. *Hebrew Melodies* for vc. (1945), 6 str. qts., 3 wind quintets, vc. conc. (1966), *3 Movements* for orch. (1960), *6 Bagatelles* for orch., etc.

Perlemuter, Vlado (*b* Kowno (Kaunas), 1904). Fr. pianist of Polish birth. Studied with Moszkowski and Cortot. Learned all Ravel's pf. mus. between 1925 and 1927 and played it to the composer. His other specialization is Chopin. Prof. of pf., Paris Cons. from 1950.

Perlman, Itzhak (*b* Tel Aviv, 1945). Israeli violinist. Studied Tel Aviv Acad. of Mus. and Juilliard Sch. Recital on Amer. radio at age 10, Carnegie Hall 1963, with leading orchs. from 1964. London début 1968. Assoc. in chamber mus. with Barenboim, Ashkenazy, Zukerman, etc. Plays seated because of polio.

Perosi, Lorenzo (*b* Tortona, 1872; *d* Rome, 1956). It. composer and priest. Studied Milan Cons. Maestro di cappella, St Mark's, Venice, 1894, ordained 1895, maestro di cappella, Sistine Chapel 1898–1915. Had remarkable success Milan 1897 with oratorio-trilogy. This was followed by 8 other oratorios before 1904 which had a spectacular but short-lived success. Also comp. 33 masses, many other religious choral works, and several symphonic poems.

Pérotin (known as Perotinus Magnus) (*c*.1160–1240). Fr. composer. Choirmaster of chapel on site of present Notre Dame Cath., Paris, and leader of what became known as Notre Dame Sch. Wrote liturgical mus. in style known as *Ars antiqua and improved mus. notation.

Perpetual Canon. A *canon so arr. that each v., having arrived at the end, can begin again, and so continue indefinitely.

Perpetuum Mobile (Lat.; It. *moto perpetuo*). Perpetually in motion. Title often given to type of instr. comp. based on rapid, repetitive note-patterns.

Perséphone. Melodrama in 3 scenes by Stravinsky to lib. by André Gide, choreog. Jooss, for narrator, ten., ch., children's ch., and orch. Comp. 1933–4. Prod. Paris 1934, concert version London 1934. In ballet version, performer of Perséphone must recite and dance.

Persiani (*née* Tacchinardi), **Fanny** (*b* Rome, 1812; *d* Paris, 1867). It. sop. Taught by her father, a ten.

Début Leghorn 1832. Created title-role in *Lucia di Lammermoor*, which Donizetti wrote for her, 1835. London début 1838. At CG 1847–9, helping to establish it as Royal It. Opera. Sang in Paris 1837–48. V. of great range and brilliance and capable of virtuoso ornamentation.

Persichetti, Vincent (*b* Philadelphia, 1915). Amer. composer, cond., and teacher. Studied Philadelphia Cons. and Curtis Institute. Taught by Roy Harris (comp.), Fritz Reiner (cond.), and Olga Samaroff (pf.). Teacher of comp. at Philadelphia Cons. 1942–62 and Juilliard Sch. from 1947. Publishing executive and lecturer. Prolific and fluent composer in wide range of styles. Works incl. 9 syms., 12 pf. sonatas, 4 str. qts., septet *King Lear*, cantatas, songs, etc. Wrote *Twentieth-Century Harmony* (NY, 1961).

Pert, Morris (*b* Edinburgh, 1947). Scottish composer. Studied at Edinburgh Univ. and RAM (comp. with A. Bush, perc. with Blades). Won Royal Phil. Soc. award for orch. work *Xumbu-Ata* (1970). Worked for 2 years with Japanese percussionist Stomu Yamash'ta, then formed own experimental mus. group 'Suntreader'. Works comp. since 1971 incl.:

ORCH: *Sun Dragon*; Sym. in 1 movement; Sym. No. 2 (The Beltane Rites), 1979.

ENSEMBLE: *Akhenaten*; *Alpha Centauri*; *Cernunnos*; *Chromosphere*; *Eoastrion Luminos (a)*, basset horn or cl. and pf.; *Omega Centauri*; cl. sonata; *The Ancient Pattern*.

BALLETS: *Diary*; *Earth Dances*; *Continuum*.

VOCAL: *Epitaphs*, sop.; *5 Songs from the Japanese*, sop.; *4 Japanese Verses*, sop.; *2 Medieval Latin Lyrics*, SATB; *2 Medieval Love Songs*, 2-part ch., pf., perc.

PIANO: *Luminos (b)*; *Sonores*; *Suilven Moon Voyage in Space*; *Fragmenti II* (hpd.).

TAPE: *Ionosphere*; *Magnificat N.G.C. 6853*; *Theta Orionis*.

Perti, Giacomo Antonio (*b* Bologna, 1661; *d* Bologna, 1756). It. composer. After working in Venice and Modena in his youth, returned to Bologna, where he was a choirmaster 1690–1756. Wrote 26 operas but later devoted himself to religious works, especially oratorios, cantatas, and masses. Also wrote sonatas for vn. and vc. and other instr. works.

Pertile, Aureliano (*b* Montagnana, 1885; *d* Milan, 1952). It. ten. Début Vicenza 1911 followed by further study. NY Met. 1921–2. CG 1927–31. Leading ten. Scala, Milan, 1921–37, where he was greatly admired by Toscanini. Retired 1940. Prof. of singing, Milan Cons., 1945–52.

Pes (Lat.). Foot. (1) Name for the ten. in Eng. mus. MSS. of 13th and 14th cents., also for 2 lower parts in *Sumer is icumen in* (as ground bass).

(2) Synonym for *podatus,* a melodic figure in the old *neume notation.

PESANTE

Pesante (It.). Weighing, i.e. heavy or heavily as in *allegro pesante,* implying that the whole passage is to be perf. with weight, as opposed to *allegro marcato,* which means that individual notes or groups of notes are to be emphasized.

Peter and the Wolf (*Petya i volk*). Symphonic fairy-tale for narrator and orch., Op. 67, by Prokofiev to his own lib. F.p. Moscow Children's Theatre Centre 1936, f.Eng.p. London 1941. The boy Peter's fooling of a wolf is narrated and brilliantly illustrated by solo orch. instrs.; the work is delightful in itself and a wonderful way of instructing children (and others) how to identify orch. instr.

Peter Grimes. Opera in prol. and 3 acts by *Britten, op. 33, to lib. by Montagu Slater (1902–56) based on poem 'The Borough' (1810) by George Crabbe (1754–1832). Comp. 1944–5. F.p. London, SW, 7 June 1945; Tanglewood, Mass. 1946; CG 1947.

Peters, Carl Friedrich (*b* Leipzig, 1779; *d* Sonnenstein, Bavaria, 1827). Ger. mus. publisher who bought Kühnel and Hoffmeister's business (est. 1800) in 1814 and pubd. first complete edns. of Bach and Haydn. On his death business was continued by others, notably, after 1863, by Max Abraham who developed the 'Peters Edition' of inexpensive classic scores and est. the Peters Library, opening it to the public in 1894. He enriched the firm's catalogue with works by Brahms, Grieg, Bruch, and Wagner. His nephew, Henri Hinrichsen, assumed control on Abraham's death in 1900, expanded the catalogue, and was joined in partnership by his sons in 1931 and 1933. One of these, Max, settled in London 1937 where he est. Peters Edition 1938. His brother Walter (1907–69) settled in USA 1936 where he est. C. F. Peters Corp. 1948, publishing many important Amer. composers. Leipzig house passed into other hands 1939, but Peters Edition was restored to Hinrichsen family in 1948. Firm of Peters Edition became state-owned company in Leipzig, also the Peters Library. Hinrichsen interest divided into 3 equal partners in London, NY, and Frankfurt. Peters Frankfurt acquired Belyayev Edition in 1971.

Peter Schmoll und Seine Nachbarn ('Peter Schmoll and his Neighbours'). Opera (*Singspiel*) in 2 acts by Weber, lib. Joseph Türk based on novel by C. G. Cramer (1798–9). Dialogue now lost. Comp. 1801–2. Prod. Augsburg 1803 (and possibly Munich 1807). Revived Lübeck 1927 with new dialogue by K. Eggert. Reconstructed version by H. Hasse prod. Freiburg 1943. Version based on idea of R. Lauckner by W. W. Göttig published 1963.

Petite Flûte (Fr.). Little flute, i.e. the *Piccolo.*

Petite Messe solennelle (Little Solemn Mass). Setting of Mass by Rossini for sop., cont., ten., and bar. soloists, ch., 2 pf., and harmonium,

1863. Arr. 1867 for full orch. by composer. The 'petite' does not refer to the work's size but is Rossini's too modest evaluation of its importance.

Petite Suite (Little Suite). Work for pf. 4 hands by Debussy comp. 1886–9 (arr. for pf. solo by Durand 1906). 4 movements are *En bateau* (In a boat), *Cortège* (Funeral Procession), *Menuet,* and *Ballet.* Orch. version by Busser, 1907 (also version for small orch. by Mouton, 1909).

Petite Symphonie (Little Symphony). Work in 4 movements for 9 wind instr. (2 each of obs., cls., hns., and bns., and 1 fl.) by *Gounod, comp. 1885 for Paul Taffanel, Fr. flautist, and f.p. by *Société de Musique de la Chambre pour Instruments à Vent,* Paris 1885.

Petite Symphonie Concertante (Little concertante symphony). Work by Frank *Martin for harp, hpd., pf., and 2 str. orchs. F.p. Zürich 1946.

Petits Riens, Les (The Little Nobodies). Ballet mus. by Mozart (K Anh. 10) comp. in Paris, June 1778, for a perf. of a ballet-divertissement *Les Petits Riens* with lib. and choreog. by the Parisian ballet-master Jean Noverre. Mus. lost until 1872, when found in library of Paris Opéra.

Petrarch Sonnets, Three (Liszt). See *Sonetti di Petrarca.*

Petrassi, Goffredo (*b* Zagarolo, 1904). It. composer. Educated at choir school. Worked in Rome mus. store and was given harmony lessons in his free time. Studied S. Cecilia Acad., Rome, 1928–32, where he became prof. of comp. 1939–59. Dir., La Fenice, Venice, 1937–40. Comps. in neo-classical style, using 12-note method in later works. Prin. works:

OPERAS: *Il Cordovano* (1944–8); *La Morte dell' Aria* (1950).
BALLETS: *La Follia di Orlando* (1942–3); *Ritratto di Don Chisciotte* (1945).
ORCH: *Divertimento* (1930); *Ouverture da concerto* (1931); *Passacaglia* (1931); *Concertos for Orchestra,* No. 1 (1933–4), No. 2 (1951), No. 3 (*Récréation Concertante*) (1952–3), No. 4, str. (1954), No. 5 (1955), No. 6 (*Invenzione concertata*), brass, str., perc. (1956–7), No. 7 (1961–2, rev. 1964), No. 8 (1970–2); pf. conc. (1936–9); fl. conc. (1960); *Estri,* for 15 instr. (1966–7).
CHAMBER MUSIC: *Sonata da camera* (1948); *Dialogo angelico,* 2 fl. (1948); *Musica a due,* 2 vc. (1952); str. qt. (1956–7); str. trio (1959); *Ala,* fl. and hpd. (1972).
CHORAL: *Salmo 9,* ch. and orch. (1934–6); *Magnificat,* sop., ch., and orch. (1939–40); *Coro di morti,* male ch., 3 pf., brass, perc. (1940–1); *Noche oscura,* cantata (1950–1); *Orationes Christi,* ch., brass, va., vc. (1974–5).

Petri, Egon (*b* Hanover, 1881; *d* Berkeley, Calif., 1962). Ger. pianist of Dutch ancestry. Son of H. V. Petri, violinist and composer. Studied with Carreño and Busoni. Recitalist from 1902, with int. reputation. Prof. of pf. RMCM, 1906–10. Settled in Berlin, 1921, as pf. prof. at Berlin Hochschule für Musik until 1925. Lived in Poland 1925–39. Début USA 1932. Pianist-in-residence, Cornell Univ. 1940–6, Mills Coll., Oakland, from 1947. Returned to Europe to teach in Basle 1957. Specialist in Liszt and Busoni. Collab. with Busoni in edn. of Bach.

Petrić, Ivo (b Ljubljana, 1931). Yugoslav composer. Studied Ljubljana Acad. 1950–8. Influenced in early works by *Bartók, turned to new types of sound after encountering mus. of *Lutosławski, *Ligeti, and *Penderecki. Works incl. *Goga* Sym. (No. 1) (1954); *Concerto grosso* (1955); fl. conc. (1955); Sym. No. 2 (1957), No. 3 (1960); cl. conc. (1958); *Symphonic Mutations* (1964); *Musique Concertante*, pf., orch. (1971); *Dialogues concertantes*, vc., orch. (1972); *3 Images*, vn., orch. (1973); *Nocturnes et Jeux* (1973); *Gemini Conc.*, vn., vc., orch. (1975); *Jeux*, v. and harp (1965); *Jeux II*, vocal and instr. sounds on tape (1966); *Intégrals en couleur*, chamber ens. (1968); str. qt. (1969); *3 Satires after Kriloff* for ch. and ens. (1970); *Meditations*, pf. trio (1971); *Capriccio*, vc., 8 instr. (1973); *Summer Music*, fl., pf. (1973); *Autumn Music*, vn., pf. (1974); 3 wind quintets (1953, 1959, 1974); Sonata, vn. (1976); *Winter Music*, cl., pf. (1977).

Petridis, Petro (b Nigdé, Turkey, 1892; d Athens, 1978). Gr. composer. Studied law at Sorbonne, Paris, and comp. briefly with Roussel (1919–20). Worked as mus. critic and lecturer. Works, influenced by folk and Byzantine church mus., incl. 5 syms., 2 pf. concs., conc. for 2 pf., vn. conc., oratorio *St Paul*, opera *Zefyra*.

Petrie, George (b Dublin, 1789; d Dublin, 1866). Irish painter, violinist, and collector of folk-songs. Published standard coll. of Irish folk-songs 1855, new edn. ed. *Stanford, 3 vols. 1902–5 (containing 1,582 songs).

Petrovics, Emil (b Nagybecskerek, Yugoslavia, 1930). Hung. composer. Studied Liszt Cons., Budapest, with Farkas and Kodály. Mus. dir. Petőfi Th., Budapest, 1960–4. Teacher of comp. Liszt Cons. since 1969. Works incl. operas *C'est la Guerre, Lysistrata,* and *Crime and Punishment*; fl. conc., str. qt., wind quintet, oratorio *The Book of Jonah*.

Petrushka. (The title *Pétrouchka* is merely the Fr. transliteration of the Russ. and should properly be used only in Fr.) Ballet (burlesque) in 4 tableaux with mus. by Stravinsky, comp. 1910–11 to lib. by Benois, choreog. by Fokine. Prod. Paris (Diaghilev Ballet) 1911, London 1911, NY 1916. Nijinsky created title-role, Karsavina the Ballerina. Orch. suite f.p. Paris (cond. Monteux) 1914; re-orch. 1947 as suite in 4 parts with 15 movements. 3 movements (*Russian Dance, In Petrushka's Cell,* and *Shrove-tide Fair*) arr. for pf. by Stravinsky, 1921. Version for 2 pf. arr. Babin

exists, also Suite of 5 pieces arr. for pf. by Szántó, 1922.

Pettersson, Allan (b Stockholm, 1911; d Stockholm, 1980). Swed. composer and violist. Studied Stockholm Cons. 1930–9 (vn., va., and counterpoint). Studied comp. with *Blomdahl and later with Honegger and Leibowitz 1951–2. Violist, Stockholm P.O. 1940–50. Comps. incl. 16 syms., conc. for vn. and str. qt., vn. conc., 3 concs. for str. orch., 7 sonatas for 2 vn., song-cycle *Vox Humana* for soloists, ch., and orch., songs, etc.

Petto, Voce di (It.). Chest v.

Petzold, Johann Christoph (b Glatz, 1639; d Bautzen, 1694). Ger. trumpeter and violinist; employed civic musicians in Leipzig and Bautzen. Wrote prolifically for wind instr.

Peuerl (Bäurl or Beurlin), **Paul** (b Stuttgart, 1570; d 1625). Austrian composer and organist. Credited with invention of Ger. variation-suite form. Wrote songs, instr. pieces, and organ works.

Pevernage, Andreas (b Harelbeke, nr. Courtrai, 1543; d Antwerp, 1591). Flemish composer of religious mus. and of madrigals (*Harmonia Celeste* 1583). Choirmaster Antwerp Cath. from 1585.

Peyer, Gervase de (b London, 1926). Eng. clarinettist and cond. Studied RCM. Début, broadcast of Mozart conc. while at school. Founder member, Melos Ens. Prin. cl., LSO, 1955–71. Dir. LSO wind ens. Ass. cond. Haydn Orch.

Pezzo (It., plural *pezzi*, 'piece'). A comp., the word sometimes being used as part of the title, e.g. *Pezzo concertante, Tre pezzi*.

Pfeife (Ger.). Fife, fl. org. pipe.

Pfitzner, Hans (Erich) (b Moscow, 1869; d Salzburg, 1949). Ger. composer and cond. Studied with his father (violinist and mus. dir., Frankfurt municipal th.) and at Hoch Cons., 1886–90. Taught pf. Coblenz Cons. 1892–3. Cond. Mainz mus. th. 1894–6. Taught comp. and cond. Stern Cons., Berlin, from 1897. First cond. Theater des Westens, Berlin, from 1903. Municipal mus. dir. and dir. of Cons., Strasbourg, from 1908, becoming mus. dir. Strasbourg Opera 1910–16. Taught in Berlin 1920–9. Prof. of comp., Munich Acad. 1930–3. Influenced by Wagner and Schopenhauer. Well-known as writer on mus. and determined critic of modern tendencies. Mahler cond. two of his operas in Vienna, but his chief success was with *Palestrina* (Munich 1917) which has remained in the repertory in Ger. and has won many admirers beyond its frontiers. The Nazis upheld his mus. as in the best Ger. tradition and contrasted it with the 'degeneracy' of Strauss. After the 1939–45 war he was found in penury in a Munich home for the aged by the president of the Vienna P.O. who took him to Vienna where he was supported by the orch. His mus. is romantic in a Wagner-Strauss idiom; his songs in particular are beautiful. Prin. works:

OPERAS: *Der arme Heinrich* (1891–3); *Die Rose vom Liebesgarten* (1897–1900); *Christelflein* (1906, rev. 1917); **Palestrina* (1912–15); *Das Herz* (1931).

ORCH: *Scherzo* (1888); *Kleine Symphonie* (1939); *Fantasie* (1947); pf. conc. (1922); vn. conc. (1923); vc. conc. No. 1 (1935), No. 2 (1944); Sym. in C♯ minor (adapted from 2nd str. qt.) (1932); Sym. in C (1940).

INCIDENTAL MUSIC: *Das Fest auf Solhaug* (Ibsen) (1889–90); *Das Käthchen von Heilbronn* (Kleist) (1905).

CHORAL: *Der Blumen Rache,* ballad for alto, women's ch., and orch. (1888); *Columbus,* 8-part unacc. ch. (1905); *Rundgesang zum Neujahrsfest,* bass, ch., and pf. (1901); *Von deutscher Seele,* cantata for 4 soloists, ch., and orch. (1921, rev. 1937); *Das dunkle Reich* (1929).

CHAMBER MUSIC: Str. qt. No. 1 (1902–3), No. 2 (1925), No. 3 (1942); pf. trio (1896); pf. quintet (1908); vc. sonata (1890); pf. sextet (1945).

Over 90 Lieder with pf. acc. and songs with orch.

Phaedra. (1) Dramatic cantata by Britten, Op. 93, for mez. and small orch., being setting of extracts from Racine's *Phèdre* trans. by Robert Lowell. Comp. 1975. Ded. to Dame Janet Baker, who gave f.p. Aldeburgh 1976.

(2) Monodrama for mez. and orch. by G. Rochberg (text drawn from Lowell by Gene Rochberg). F.p. NY, 1976, by Neva Pilgrim with Syracuse S.O., cond. D. Loebel.

Phaëton. Symphonic poem, Op. 39, by Saint-Saëns, comp. 1873. Also opera by Lully (Paris, 1683).

Phagotum. Instr. invented *c*.1520 by Canon Afranio of Ferrara (*c*.1489–*c*.1565), being a kind of bellows-blown bagpipe. Nothing to do with bn. (fagott), the only feature in common being use of parallel bores.

Phalèse, Pierre (*b* ? Louvain, *c*.1510; *d* ? Louvain, *c*.1574). Dutch composer and founder (*c*.1545) of firm of publishers which existed until 1674.

Phantasie (Ger.). Fantasy, fancy, hence *Phantasiestück* (more commonly spelt *Fantasiestück*), 'fantasy piece'. See *Fantasia*.

Phantasy. Same as Fantasy, but this spelling was preferred by W. W. *Cobbett when he est. his prize in 1906 for works comp. in this form. Hence the large number of Eng. works with this word in their title, e.g. *Phantasy Quintet* by Vaughan Williams, *Phantasy Quartet* by Britten.

Philadelphia Orchestra. Amer. sym. orch. founded 1900 by Fritz Scheel, who remained cond. until 1907. Succeeded by Karl Pohlig 1907–12. The orch.'s fame and style (rich and virtuoso) were est. under the conductorship 1912–38 of Leopold Stokowski, who also introduced many new and adventurous works to Amer. audiences

(e.g. Mahler's 8th Sym., 1916, and works by Schoenberg). Eugene Ormandy was co-cond. 1936–8 and succeeded Stokowski, occupying the post for the next 40 years and consolidating the orch.'s position as among the world's greatest. Riccardo Muti prin. cond. from 1981.

Philharmonia Orchestra. Eng. sym. orch. founded 1945 by Walter *Legge primarily to make recordings for the Gramophone Co. Among those who cond. it on records and in the concert-hall were Karajan, Klemperer, Toscanini, Furt-wängler, Strauss, Giulini, Cantelli, Dobrowen, etc. Became principally assoc. with Klemperer, who was made 'conductor for life'. In 1964, after Legge had attempted to disband it, orch. became self-governing body under title New Philharmonia, the 'New' being dropped in 1977. Maazel assoc. prin. cond. 1971–3; Riccardo Muti prin. cond. 1973–82; Giuseppe Sinopoli from 1984.

Philharmonic Society (of London). See *Royal Philharmonic Society*.

Philidor (real name Danican). Fr. family of musicians over several generations, *c*.1600–1800. Best-known was François André (*b* Dreux, 1726; *d* London, 1795), famous as composer (pupil of Campra) and as chess-player. Visited London annually to play chess from 1745 and heard Handel's operas. Settled in Paris 1754, composing successful comic operas, e.g. *Tom Jones* and *L'amant déguisé*. His father, André (*b* Versailles, *c*.1647; *d* Dreux, 1730) was an oboist and composer. Compiled coll. of Fr. court mus. from reign of Henri III to end of 17th cent., some of which is in Versailles Municipal Library, and a large part, formerly at St Michael's College, Tenbury, is now in the Bibliothèque Nationale, Paris.

Philipp, Isidor (*b* Budapest, 1863; *d* Paris, 1958). Hung.-born pianist and teacher (Fr. citizen). Lived in Paris from age 3. Studied at Paris Cons. with Mathias and Saint-Saëns. Recitalist and soloist with orchs. London début 1890. Prof. of pf., Paris Cons., 1893–1934, with long list of illustrious pupils. Lived in NY 1941–55. Wrote books on pf. technique, comp. works for pf. and for orch., and arr. mus. by Bach, Massenet, and Mendelssohn for 2 pf.

Philippot, Michael Paul (*b* Verzy, 1925). Fr. composer. Studied Paris Cons. 1945–7 and privately with *Leibowitz 1945–9. Sound engineer, Fr. radio and TV 1949–59. Dir., *Groupe de Recherches Musicales* 1959–61. Mus. dir., Fr. radio and TV 1964. Works incl. sonata, pf. trio, *musique concrète* on tape, etc.

Philips, Peter (*b c*.1561; *d* Brussels, 1628). Eng. composer and organist. Choirboy, St Paul's Cath., London, 1574. First comp., a keyboard pavan, 1580. Fled country 1582 because he was Roman Catholic. Settled in Antwerp 1590 as court organist, later organist of Chapel Royal, Brussels. Was arrested 1593 and accused of conspiracy to assassinate Elizabeth I, but was exonerated and released. Comp. motets, madrigals, masses, and psalms, all of high quality and interest.

Phillips, Montague (Fawcett) (*b* London, 1885; *d* Esher, 1969). Eng. composer and organist. Studied RAM. Org. and choirmaster, Esher church, for many years. Wrote sym., 2 pf. concs., and light opera *The Rebel Maid* (1921).

'Philosopher, The' (*Der Philosoph*). Nickname of Haydn's Sym. No. 22 in E♭ (Hob. I:22) comp. 1764. Known by this title in Haydn's lifetime in reference to opening *adagio*. Haydn said he had once written a sym. in which God speaks to an unrepentant sinner: this could be the work. A 2nd version, omitting the *adagio*, was printed in Paris by Venier in 1773.

Phoebus and Pan (Eng. title for *Der Streit zwischen Phoebus und Pan*, 'The Strife between Phoebus and Pan'). Cantata by J. S. Bach (BWV 201), comp. ?1729, to lib. by Picander (based on Ovid) satirizing hostile mus. critic. Sometimes staged as opera.

Phoenix Mass. Choral work by *Payne for mixed ch., 3 tpt., and 3 tb., comp. 1965–9 with 39 bars added to *Agnus Dei* in 1972.

Phoneuma. Very soft org. stop of *Dulciana* tone and *Quintatön* effect.

Phonograph. Same as gramophone and used in USA. The term was devised by Edison for his recording machine, the record or wax cylinder being called a *phonogram*.

Phrase. Short section of a comp. into which the mus., whether vocal or instr., seems naturally to fall. Sometimes this is 4 measures, but shorter and longer phrases occur. It is an inexact term: sometimes a phrase may be contained within one breath, and sometimes sub-divisions may be marked. In notation, phrase-marks are the slurs placed over or under the notes as a hint of their proper punctuation in perf. (see *Curved line, various uses of*). The art of phrasing by a perf. is often instinctive and is one of the features by which a supreme artist may be distinguished from one of lesser inspiration, whether cond., singer, or instrumentalist.

Phrygian Mode. The 3rd of the ecclesiastical *modes, represented by white keys of pf. beginning on E.

Piacevole (It.). Agreeable.

Piangendo, piangente (It.). Weeping; **piangevole, piangevolmente.** Plaintive; plaintively.

Piano (It.). Soft, quiet. (1) Instruction to play softly (abbreviation *p*, or *pp*, *pianissimo*, very softly). Opposite of *forte*, loud.
 (2) Eng. term for kbd. instr. whose full name is *pianoforte* (It.), soft-loud. This instr. is, with regard to its str. and hammers, a descendant of the *dulcimer, and, to its kbd., a descendant of the *harpsichord and *clavichord. The modern pf. has an iron frame and is either *grand* (str. horizontal) or *upright* (str. vertical). It normally has 88 keys, with a standard compass of 7⅓ octaves, but some models by Bösendorfer have a compass of 8 octaves.

Although there are other claimants to the invention of the instrument, it is generally accepted that the earliest instr. of its type was made in Florence, *c*.1698–1700, by Bartolomeo *Cristofori, who prod. what he called a *gravicembalo col piano e forte*, i.e. a 'harpsichord with loudness and softness': for the hpd.'s plucking of the str. he had substituted the blows of a series of hammers, and it was this that gave the players of his instr. their new power of control of degrees of force. The Cristofori pfs. had a range of 4 to 4½ octaves.

Cristofori's idea was taken up in Ger. by the org.-builder Gottfried Silbermann, who in 1726 made 2 pfs. which he submitted to Bach, whose opinion of them was unfavourable and perhaps led to the improvements which apparently were introduced. In 1747 Bach, on a visit to the court of Frederick the Great at Potsdam, played the Silbermann pfs. there. All pfs. up to this point were of the hpd. shape—rather like what we now call the grand pf., with the str. horizontal and in line with the relevant finger-keys. The first pf. in clavichord shape, known as the square pf., was made by Frederici of Gera, but he was closely followed by one of Silbermann's apprentices, Johannes Zumpe, who went to London and introduced there the popular rectangular form of the instr. Further impetus to the pf. was given by J. C. Bach, when he settled in London, and by *Clementi. Developments in the 'action' of the instr. were made by Backers, John Broadwood, and Stodart. Broadwood made changes in the square pf. In Fr., Érard made the square, and grand pfs., while the Austrian Andreas Stein found a way of giving extra lightness of touch to the grand. The first Amer.-built pfs. were by J. Behrent in Philadelphia, 1775.

The *Upright Pianoforte*, in which the str. run perpendicularly, was developed by John Isaac Hawkins of Philadelphia (1800) and Robert Wornum, jun., of London (1811, perfected 1829): the existing model is largely founded on that of Wornum. From the middle of the 19th cent. it superseded the square form, but was itself almost ousted in the 20th cent. by the 'baby', i.e. small-sized, grand.

Hawkins also introduced the iron frame. One advantage was the possibility of using str. at higher tension than the wooden frame allowed, so making possible the use of thicker wire, producing a fuller tone. The tension of a single str. today may be 180–200 lb., the varying stress of the different sizes of str. being more or less equally distributed by *Overstringing*, i.e. by one group of str. passing more or less diagonally over another: this principle as applied to the pf. dates from c.1835, but there had previously been occasional overstrung clavichords.

18th-cent. hpds. had more than 1 str. to each note and Cristofori's pf. had 2 throughout: the modern pf. has 1 string for a few of the very lowest notes, 2 for the middle register, and 3 for the highest (on account of the decrease of resonance with the shorter str.): the lowest str. are wrapped with a copper coil to increase their mass without too greatly decreasing their flexibility.

The *Sound-board* of a pf. (lying behind the str. in an upright and below them in a grand) fulfils the same function as the body of a vn.: without it the tone of the instr. would be very faint and thin. The *Sustaining Pedal*, when depressed, removes the whole series of dampers from the str.: thus any note or chord played can be given some duration, even though the finger or fingers have been removed from the keys, and also the harmonics of the str. sounded are enriched by the sympathetic resonance of those derived from other freely-vibrating str., resulting in a fuller tone. (It is a mistake to call this pedal the 'Loud Pedal' as it is as much used in soft passages as in loud.) This pedal must of course normally be lifted at a change of harmony, as otherwise confusion will result. There is in most instr. manufactured in the USA and Canada a *Sostenuto Pedal*. It ingeniously enables the player to make (within limits) a selection as to the notes he wishes to be held over. It was introduced by the Steinway firm and perfected in 1874. The *Soft Pedal* may act in one of several ways: (a) In grands by moving the kbd. or set of hammers sideways, so as to leave unstruck 1 str. of each note (see *Corda*); (b) In uprights by moving the whole set of hammers nearer to the str., so that the force of their blows is diminished, or by interposing a piece of felt between hammer and str. (a crude method now little used).

Experiments in the construction of the pf. have been frequent; these have included pfs. with double kbd.; pfs. with indefinitely prolonged sounds (by means of a revolving wheel or other imitation of the vn. bow, or of a current of air tending to keep the str. in vibration, or by some electrical device); pfs. with tuning-forks in place of str. (incapable of getting out of tune); combinations of the pf. principle with that of some other instr. (e.g. fl., organ, hpd., clavichord); quarter-tone pfs. (see *Microtone*); various applications of electricity, etc. See *Keyboard* for experimental kbds.; see *prepared piano*; see *Aliquot* and *Duplex* scaling.

The pf. is, of course, principally used as a solo instr., or as the solo instr. in a conc. with orch., or in chamber mus. (pf. trio, pf. qt., etc.). But many composers in the 20th cent. have used it as an orch. instr., e.g. Stravinsky in *Petrushka*, Vaughan Williams in *Sinfonia Antartica*, Bartók in *Music for Strings, Percussion, and Celesta*, and numerous other works. Stravinsky's *Les Noces* is scored for 4 pf. used as perc. instrs. Later composers, from *Cage onwards, have conjured new sounds from the pf. by making adjustments to the str. (see *prepared piano*), having them plucked by hand, or used as resonators.

Since its first appearance, the pf. has called forth executants of varying styles and techniques. C. P. E. Bach was among the first to develop the new methods of playing so different from those required for hpd. and clavichord, followed by *Clementi. Absolute evenness of touch was his ideal, inculcated also in his pupil *Cramer. The Viennese-made pf. was lighter, with less sonorous tone, than the heavier English type. Mozart's playing was attuned to the Viennese action. His most famous pupil was *Hummel. But Beethoven used an Eng. pf., suitable to his energetic and dynamic playing. He was the first fully to profit by the opportunities afforded by the sustaining pedal. His example was followed by Schubert, Schumann, *Chopin, and Mendelssohn, whose works would be unimaginable on a pedal-less instr. John *Field developed the 'singing touch' of legato playing and his exploitation of the *Nocturne* influenced Chopin whose playing and comps. for the pf. opened up new possibilities of tone-colour. *Liszt was the first of the virtuosi whose technique rivalled Paganini's on the vn., expanding it beyond all previous bounds, and pointing the way to the harmonic experiments of Debussy and Ravel and even to the percussive effects of Stravinsky and Bartók. Other great 19th-cent. executants were Rubinstein, Thalberg, and Bülow, while among the great composer-pianists born in the 19th cent. were Busoni, Rakhmaninov, and Bartók. The 20th cent. has been rich in superb virtuosi. One need name only Arthur Rubinstein, Arrau, Horowitz, and Richter as exemplars.

Pianoforte (It.). 'Soft-loud'. The *piano.

Pianola. Patented name (by the Aeolian Corp.) for one of the group of pfs. known as 'player-pianos'. These instr. are fitted with a mechanism by which the keys are depressed not by the fingers but by air-pressure supplied through bellows and pedals or by electricity. The air-pressure is applied through perforations on a paper roll which unwinds and which are arranged so that a comp. is played. It is not necessary for the perforations to be restricted to the number of notes which can be played by 2 (or 4) hands. In some cases the rolls incorporate perforations made mechanically from a perf. by an eminent pianist or musician, the instr. then reproducing this perf. (hence the name reproducing piano). Historic rolls of this kind preserve, for example, the playing of their own mus. by Mahler and Debussy.

Piano Quartet. Group of 4 players—usually pianist, violinist, violist, and cellist—or work written for them to perform.

Piano Quintet. Group of 5 players—usually pianist, 2 violinists, violist, cellist—or work written for them, but one of the most famous works, Schubert's 'Trout' quintet, is for pf., vn., va., vc., and db.

Piano Score. Score in which the orch. parts and vocal parts (if any) are reduced to a pf. part.

Piano Signs For 'Spreading' of Chords

('Arpeggioed', i.e. harp-fashion)

WRITTEN   PLAYED

Instead of attacking the notes of the chord simultaneously, play them from the bottom upwards, holding each as struck. (Occasionally in early mus. the notes are to be played from the top downwards and the question as to which is intended is sometimes a difficult one.)

Sometimes the wavy line is not continuous between the two staves, and then it is to be understood that the composer intends the arpeggio effect to go on in the two hands simultaneously.

It is to be noted that all spread chords should be so played as not to destroy the rhythm of the passage.

Piano Trio. Group of 3 players—pianist, violinist, cellist—or work written for them to perform.

Piatigorsky, Gregor (b Ekaterinoslav, 1903; d Los Angeles, 1976). Russ.-born cellist (Amer. citizen from 1942). Studied Moscow Cons. Prin. cellist Moscow opera orch. and then (1924) Berlin P.O. under Furtwängler until 1928. Became internationally known as soloist and chamber mus. player. Amer. début 1929. Taught at Curtis Institute and Boston Univ. Dedicatee and first performer of Walton's vc. conc. (1957).

Piatti (It.). *Cymbals.

Piatti, Alfredo (Carlo) (b Bergamo, 1822; d Crocetta di Mozzo, nr. Bergamo, 1901). It. cellist and composer. Studied with Zanetti and at Milan Cons. 1832–7 with Merighi. Début Milan 1837, Paris and London 1844. Annual visitor to London, being particularly assoc. with the Monday and Saturday Popular Chamber Concerts 1859–98. Lived in London from 1846. Piatti prize for cellists at RAM is in his memory. Wrote 2 vc. concs., 6 vc. sonatas, other chamber works, and ed. vc. sonatas by other composers.

Piave, Francesco Maria (b Murano, 1810; d Milan, 1876). It. poet and librettist. Wrote the libs. for 10 Verdi operas—*Ernani, I due Foscari, Macbeth, Il corsaro, Stiffelio, Aroldo, Rigoletto, La traviata, Simon Boccanegra,* and *La forza del destino.* Also wrote libs. for Balfe, Mercadante, and Ricci.

Pibroch (Gaelic *piobaireachd*). Type of Scot. Highland bagpipe mus. in the form of variations.

Picardie, Tierce de (Fr.). Picardy third. See *Tierce de Picardie.*

Piccaver, Alfred (b Long Sutton, Lincs., 1884; d Vienna, 1958). Eng. ten. Studied NY. Début Prague 1907, then further study in Milan and Prague. Leading ten. at Vienna Opera 1910–37, Chicago 1923–5, CG 1924. Noted for smooth legato and noble phrasing. Returned to London 1937–55, giving some lessons, but went back to Vienna as guest for re-opening of State Opera 1955 and remained to teach.

Picchettato, picchiettato, picchiettando (It.). Knocked, knocking. In the playing of bowed instr., detaching the notes (See also *Spiccato*).

Picchi, Giovanni (*fl.* early 17th cent.). It. organist and composer. Pubd. book of hpd. pieces (1620), canzoni with str. and wind, and other works.

Piccinini, Alessandro (b Bologna, 1566; d c.1638). It. composer and instrumentalist at courts of Modena and Ferrara. Wrote text-book on lute.

Piccinni, Niccolò (b Bari, 1728; d Passy, 1800). It. composer. Studied Naples 1742–54. First opera, *Le donne dispettose* was success in Naples, 1755. His most popular opera buffa, *La cecchina, ossia La buona figliuola,* 1760, based on Richardson's *Pamela,* was perf. throughout Europe. In 1776 moved to Paris to write Fr. operas at instigation of Marie Antoinette, who became his singing pupil. His first Fr. opera was *Roland* (1778). This was perf. in the midst of the celebrated Gluck-Piccinni feud, engineered by the composers' supporters. The dir. of the Paris Opéra arranged for each to compose *Iphigénie en Tauride.* Gluck's version came first, 1779, and eclipsed Piccinni's of 1781. After Gluck left Paris, *Sacchini became a rival. Piccinni became a teacher at the École Royale de Chant 1784, but returned to Naples on the outbreak of the Revolution. There he was suspected of political intrigue and lived for 4 years under virtual house arrest. Returned to Paris 1798 but his star had waned. His operas, no rivals to Gluck's, nevertheless have excellent qualities. They incl. *Il curioso del suo proprio danno*

(1756), *La Cecchina* (1760), *L'Olimpiade* (1761), *Alessandro nelle Indie* (1758, rev. 1774), *Didon* (1783), *Pénélope* (1785), *La serva onorata* (1792).

Piccolo (from It. *flauto piccolo*, little flute; also known as octave flute, It. *ottavino*). Small fl. pitched octave higher than concert fl., used in orch. and military band. Famous picc. parts occur in Beethoven's *Egmont* ov. and in Sousa's march *The Stars and Stripes Forever*. Also organ stop, metal or wood, of 2′ length and pitch.

Pick-Mangiagalli, Riccardo (b Strakonice, 1882; d Milan, 1949). Bohemian-born composer of partly It. descent; naturalized It. Studied Milan Cons. Dir., Milan Cons. 1936–49. Wrote operas, symphonic poems, chamber mus., and songs.

Pictures at an Exhibition (*Kartinki s vystavki*). Pf. comp. by Mussorgsky, 1874, being mus. representation of 10 pictures at a memorial exhibition for Russ. artist Victor Hartmann, who died in 1873, with a 'promenade' as linking passage. Orch. versions by Ravel, Henry Wood, Stokowski, Ashkenazy, Elgar Howarth (brass and perc.), and others. The titles of the pieces are: *The Gnome, The Old Castle, Tuileries, Bydlo* (Polish farm cart), *Unhatched chickens, Samuel Goldenberg and Shmuyle, Market-place at Limoges, Catacombs, Baba-yaga* (*The Hut on Fowl's Legs*), *The Great Gate of Kiev.*

Pied en l'air (Fr.). Foot in the air. A particular motion in the *Galliard.

Pieltain, Dieudonné Pascal (b Liège, 1754; d Liège, 1833). Belg. violinist and composer. At Paris Concert Spirituel 1778–83 and in London 1783–93. Wrote concs., sonatas, qts., etc.

Pieno, piena (It.). Full. *Organo pieno*, full organ; *coro pieno*, full choir (contrasted with passages for smaller ens.); *a voce piena*, with full v.

Pierné, (Henri Constant) **Gabriel** (b Metz, 1863; d Ploujean, Finistère, 1937). Fr. composer, organist, and cond. Studied Paris Cons. from age 8 (organ with Franck, comp. with Massenet). Organist, Ste-Clotilde, 1890–8. Ass. cond., Concerts Colonne 1903, becoming prin. cond. 1910–34. Works incl. ballet *Cydalise et le Chèvre-pied* (Cydalise and the Satyr), 1923, from which comes the 'Entry of the Little Fauns'; oratorio *La Croisade des Enfants* (The Children's Crusade), 1902, pf., conc., incidental and chamber mus.

Pierrot Lunaire (Moonstruck Pierrot). Melodrama for female v., pf., fl., piccolo, cl., bass cl., vn., va., and vc., Op. 21, by Schoenberg, comp. 1912, f.p. Berlin 1912, London 1923. Cycle of '3 times 7' songs—in *Sprechgesang*—to poems by Albert Giraud trans. from Fr. into Ger. by O. E. Hartleben. The titles are: I, *Mondestrunken, Colombine, Der Dandy, Eine blasse Wäscherin, Valse de Chopin, Madonna, Der kranke Mond.* II, *Die Nacht, Gebet an Pierrot, Raub, Rote Messe, Galgenlied, Enthauptung, Die Kreuze.* III, *Heimweh, Gemeinheit,*

Parodie, Der Mondfleck, Serenade, Heimfahrt, O alter Duft.

Pierrot Players. Instr. ens. founded 1967 by *Maxwell Davies and Harrison *Birtwistle for perf. of contemporary mus., particularly their own. Title adopted because of frequent perf. of Schoenberg's *Pierrot Lunaire*. Re-organized 1970 as *Fires of London.

Pierson (orig. Pearson), **Henry Hugo** (b Oxford, 1815; d Leipzig, 1873). Ger. composer and teacher of Eng. origin. Studied at Cambridge Univ. then in Ger. Prof. of mus., Edinburgh Univ., 1844, resigning after a few months to return to Ger. Wrote several operas, prod. Brno and Hamburg, oratorios, incl. *Jerusalem* (London 1852), music for Goethe's *Faust, Part II* (Hamburg 1854), part-song *Ye Mariners of England*, and other pieces. His songs are regarded as of considerable interest and originality

Piffaro, Piffero (It.). In 16th cent., generic term for any kind of pipe. Specifically a rustic wind instr. of the *shawm family. When Handel wrote *pifa* above his 'Pastoral Symphony' in *Messiah* he was referring to the *piffero.*

Pijper, Willem (b Zeist, 1894; d Leidschendam, 1947). Dutch composer. Studied harmony and comp. with J. Wagenaar, 1911–16. Mus. critic in Utrecht 1918–23. Prof. of comp. Amsterdam Cons. 1925–30. Dir., Rotterdam Cons. 1930–47. Most prominent Dutch composer of his generation. Works incl. 3 syms. (1918, 1921, 1926); 6 *Symphonic Epigrammata*; pf. conc., vn. conc., vc. conc., 4 str. qts., and other chamber mus.

Pilarczyk, Helga (b Schöningen, Brunswick, 1925). Ger. sop. Studied Hamburg and Hanover. Début Brunswick 1951 as mez. Member of Hamburg Opera from 1953. Glyndebourne (Composer in Strauss's *Ariadne auf Naxos*) and CG 1958. Specialist in 20th-cent. roles such as Salome, Marie (*Wozzeck*), and Lulu.

Pilgrim's Progress, The. There have been several mus. settings based on the allegory by John Bunyan (Part I 1674–9, II 1684). The best-known are: (1) Opera (Morality) in 4 acts by *Vaughan Williams to his own adaptation of Bunyan, with Christian's name altered to Pilgrim. Comp. between 1925 and 1951. Prod. CG 1951, Cambridge 1954. Act IV, Sc. 2 is The *Shepherds of the Delectable Mountains*, which had been prod. as a separate 'pastoral episode' in London in 1922. Vaughan Williams also comp. incidental mus. (some of it later incorporated into the opera) for BBC prod. of *The Pilgrim's Progress* in 1943. His 5th Sym. (1938–43) uses themes from the opera, which at that time he did not expect to finish.
(2) Oratorio for soloists, ch., and orch. by *Bantock, 1928.
(3) Oratorio by Robin *Milford.

Pilkington, Francis (b c.1565; d Chester, 1638). Eng. composer. Chorister, Chester Cath. from

1602, later clergyman, and precentor of the cath. from 1623. Wrote songs with lute or viola da gamba (1605), 2 sets of madrigals (1614 and 1624), and religious part-songs. Contrib. 5-part madrigal *When Oriana Walked to Take the Air* to *The *Triumphs of Oriana*.

Pincé (Fr.). Pinched. *Pizzicato. Also formerly a type of *mordent.

Pincherle, Marc (*b* Constantine, Algeria, 1888; *d* Paris, 1974). Fr. musicologist. Studied at Sorbonne. After 1918 taught history of vn. at École Normale de Musique, Paris. Editor-in-chief *Monde musical* 1925–7, *Musique* 1927–30. Specialist in Fr. and It. mus. of 17th and 18th cent. His 1948 book on Vivaldi was a pioneering study and was followed by another in 1955 (Eng. trans. 1957).Wrote 2 books on Corelli (1933, 1954), and books on Kreisler and Roussel.

Pineapple Poll. Ballet in 1 act and 3 scenes, lib. and choreog. by John Cranko to mus. by Sullivan arr. by *Mackerras. Prod. SW 1951. Story taken from W. S. Gilbert's Bab Ballad 'The Bumboat Woman's Story'. Also concert suite.

Pines of Rome (*Pini di Roma*). One of 3 symphonic poems by *Respighi about Rome. Comp. 1923–4 (f.p. Rome 1924, London 1925). Score incl. nightingale on a gramophone record. 4 sections are : *Villa Borghese, A Catacomb, Janiculum*, and *Appian Way*.

Pini, Anthony (*b* Buenos Aires, 1902). Eng. cellist. Prin. cellist LPO 1932–9, RPO 1947–63, CG 1964. Soloist with leading orchs. Prof of vc. RCM. Member of several quartets and chamber ensembles.

Pini-Corsi, Antonio (*b* Zara, 1858; *d* Milan, 1918). It. bar. Début Cremona 1878. Chosen by Verdi to create role of Ford in *Falstaff*, Milan 1893. Sang at CG 1894–6, 1902–3; NY Met. 1899–1914. Created roles of Schaunard in Puccini's *La Bohème* (Turin, 1896) and of Happy in *La fanciulla del West* (NY, 1910).

Pinkham, Daniel (*b* Lynn, Mass., 1923). Amer. composer, harpsichordist, organist., and cond. Studied comp. at Harvard with *Piston, later with Boulanger, Copland, and Honegger. Has held various teaching posts. Works incl. 2 syms., pf. conc., vn. conc., chamber opera *The Garden of Artemis*, arr. (with additions) of *The Beggar's Opera* (1956), *Wedding Cantata, Christmas Cantata, Requiem*, organ conc. (1970), *Signs of the Zodiac* for orch., etc.

Pinnock, Trevor (David) (*b* Canterbury, 1946). Eng. harpsichordist. Studied RCM 1964–7. Début as soloist London 1971. Played with Galliard Harpsichord Trio 1966–72, English Concert from 1973.

Pinto, George Frederic (Saunders) (*b* Lambeth, 1785; *d* Camden Town, 1806). Eng. violinist,

composer, and pianist. Wrote 5 pf. sonatas and 3 vn. sonatas. The pf. sonatas, written when he was 16, have been ed. by N. *Temperley and revived (1979) by John *McCabe, who has shown them to be works of extraordinary merit, which could easily be mistaken for mature Schubert.

Pinza, Ezio (*b* Rome, 1892; *d* Stamford, Conn., 1957). It. bass. Studied Bologna. Début Soncino, 1914. After army service, made Rome début 1920 as King Mark in *Tristan*. Sang at Scala, Milan, 1921–4, NY Met. 1926–48, CG 1930–9. Repertory of nearly 100 roles. A great Don Giovanni. His noble voice and fine looks were matched by dramatic ability. After his operatic career, appeared in musicals and films, notably in *South Pacific* on Broadway (1949).

Piobaireachd. See *Pibroch*.

Pipe. (1) Hollow cone or cylinder in which air vibrates to produce a sound, e.g. in an org. or a blown wind instr.
(2) A simple woodwind instr. without any mechanism such as bamboo pipes, or the 3-holed pipe used in Eng. folk dances together with the tabor.
(3) The *bagpipe.

Piqué (Fr.). Pricked. A bowed instr. term, same as *Spiccato*.

Pique Dame (Queen of Spades). (1) Operetta by Suppé, 1862.
(2) For Tchaikovsky opera, see *Queen of Spades*.

Piquiren (Ger.). To play *Spiccato*.

Pirata, Il (The Pirate). Opera in 2 acts by Bellini to lib. by Romani. Prod. Milan 1827, London 1830, NY 1832.

Pirates of Penzance, The, or The Slave of Duty. Operetta by Sullivan to lib. by Gilbert. Prod. Paignton, Devon, and NY 1879, London 1880.

Pirouette (Fr.). Spinning-top. (1) Funnel-shaped reed shield, made in variety of shapes, used on *shawm and *rackett against which player could press his lips while taking projecting part of reed into his mouth. Helped to avoid lip-fatigue and protected reed.
(2) In dancing, one or more turns of the body on one leg, with the point of the working leg usually touching knee of supporting leg.

Pisador, Diego (*b* Salamanca, 1509–10; *d* after 1557). Sp. vihuela player and composer for his instr. Pubd. *Libro de musica de vihuela* (1552).

Pisk, Paul (Amadeus) (*b* Vienna, 1893). Austrian-born composer and musicologist. Studied Vienna (comp. with *Schreker and *Schoenberg, musicology with Adler). Worked as mus. critic in Vienna. Settled in USA 1937, becoming prof. of mus. Redlands Univ., Calif., dir of sch. of mus. 1948–50; prof. of mus., Univ. of Texas, Austin, 1951–63, Washington Univ., St Louis 1963–72.

Wrote *Life and Works of Schütz* (1972). Works incl. *3 Ceremonial Rites* for orch., str. qt., cantata *Die neue Stadt*, etc.

Piston. (1) A type of valve in brass instr., bored with passages which, when it is depressed within its casing, deflect the air-stream passing through it into the valve tubing. First valve lowers pitch a tone, 2nd a semitone, 3rd 3 semitones. If a 4th valve is added, it is adjusted to lower pitch 2 tones and a semitone, or a perfect 4th. New harmonic series can be prod. from these valves singly or in combination.

(2) (Fr.). Abbreviation for *cornet-à-pistons*, the *cornet.

Piston, Walter (Hamor) (*b* Rockland, Maine, 1894; *d* Belmont, Mass., 1976). Amer. composer. Studied Harvard Univ. and in Paris with Boulanger. Joined mus. faculty at Harvard 1926, becoming prof. of mus. 1944–60. Author of 3 important textbooks, *Harmony* (1941), *Counterpoint* (1947), *Orchestration* (1955). Prin. works:

ORCH: *Concerto for Orchestra* (1933); Syms.: No. 1 (1937), No. 2 (1943), No. 3 (1948), No. 4 (1951), No. 5 (1956), No. 6 (1955), No. 7 (1960), No. 8 (1965); *Sinfonietta* (1941); vn. conc. No. 1 (1939), No. 2 (1960); pf. concertino (1937); *Symphonic Suite* (1948); va. conc. (1957); double pf. conc. (1959); *3 New England Sketches* (1959); *Variations* for vc. and orch. (1967); cl. conc. (1967); *Ricercare* (1968); *Fantasia*, vn. and orch. (1970); fl. conc. (1971); conc. for str. qt., woodwind, perc. (1976).

BALLET: *The *Incredible Flutist* (1938), also orch. suite (1938).

CHAMBER MUSIC: Fl. sonata (1930); ob. suite (1931); str. qts., No. 1 (1933), No. 2 (1935), No. 3 (1947), No. 4 (1951), No. 5 (1962); pf. trio No. 1 (1935), No. 2 (1966); vn. sonata (1939); fl. quintet (1942); pf. quintet (1949); wind quintet (1956); str. sextet (1964); pf. qt. (1964); *Duo*, vc., pf. (1976).

Pitch. The location of a sound in the tonal scale, depending on the speed of vibrations from the source of the sound, fast ones producing a high pitch and slow ones a low. The rate of vibration per second is the note's 'frequency'. By int. agreement of 1939, renewed and extended in 1960, the present-day standard of 'concert-pitch' to which instr. are tuned is that in which the A directly above middle C has 440 (double) vibrations per second (440 Hz), which makes middle C 261.6 Hz. This replaced the standard of 435 (diapason normal) fixed in Paris in 1859 and confirmed in Vienna in 1885. Before then, a variety of pitches existed. In Eng. in the 16th cent., domestic kbd. pitch was about 3 semitones lower than today's pitch and the church mus. pitch over 2 semitones higher. Between 1700 and 1850, the note A varied between 415 and 429. Pitch can now be measured electronically, but

still the most common way is by a tuning-fork. See *A*.

Pitch Names of the Notes

English	C	D	E	F	G	A	B
German	„	„	„	„	„	„	H
French	ut or do	ré	mi	fa	sol	la	si
Italian	do	re	„	„	„	„	„

Note that Eng. B♭ = Ger. B; and that Eng. B = Ger. H.

Pitchpipe. Small wooden pipe of square section, about 18 in. in length, with whistle mouthpiece, used in 18th and 19th cents. Leather-covered wooden stopper can be inserted to shorten pipe and thus raise the pitch. On the stem of the stopper the various notes were marked. Principally used in churches that had neither organ nor band of musicians.

Pitfield, Thomas (Baron) (*b* Bolton, 1903). Eng. composer and teacher, also poet, artist, and craftsman. Studied RMCM 1923–7, joined staff 1947, becoming prof. of comp. and later at RNCM until 1973. Pupils incl. A. Goehr, Maxwell Davies, and McCabe. Comps. incl. pf. conc., cantata *A Sketchbook of Women*, songs, and chamber mus.

Pitt, Percy (*b* London, 1869; *d* London, 1932). Eng. cond. Studied Leipzig and Munich 1886–91. Ass. cond. CG 1902, mus. dir. Grand Opera Syndicate (CG) 1907–24. Assoc. with Beecham Opera Co. 1915–18. Art. dir., BNOC 1920–4, mus. dir. BBC 1924–30. Also composer of sym., symphonic poem, incidental mus., etc.

Pittsburgh Symphony Orchestra. US orch., founded 1895, first concert 27 Feb. 1896, cond. Frederic Asker. Prin. conds., 1898–1904, Victor *Herbert; 1904–10, Emil Paur. Guest conds. incl. R. Strauss in 1903–4 season and Elgar in 1906–7. Disbanded March 1910, re-formed 1926. Cond. Antonio Modarelli 1930–7. Reorganized 1937 by *Klemperer. Prin. cond. 1938–48, Fritz *Reiner; 1952–76, William *Steinberg; 1976–85, André *Previn. Toured Europe and Middle East 1963, Japan and Korea 1972 with Steinberg; Europe 1978 with Previn. Moved into new hall, Heinz Hall for Performing Arts, 1971.

Pitz, Wilhelm (*b* Breinig, 1897; *d* Aachen, 1973). Ger. ch.-master, cond., and violinist. Violinist, Aachen City Orch., 1913–33. Ch.-master Aachen Opera 1933–61, also mus. dir., Aachen Choral Soc. Cond., Aachen Opera from 1946. Ch.-master

Bayreuth Fest., 1951–71. First ch.-master, Philharmonia Ch. 1957–71, establishing very high standards for conds. such as Klemperer, Karajan, Giulini, and Barbirolli. Hon. O.B.E. 1970.

Più (It.). More. *Più lento*, slower; *più mosso*, more movement, i.e. quicker, etc.

Piva (It.). (1) Bagpipe.
(2) 16th-cent. dance step.

Pixis, Johann Peter (*b* Mannheim, 1788; *d* Baden–Baden, 1874). Ger. pianist, teacher, and composer. After concert career became teacher in Munich, Vienna, Paris (from 1823), and Baden-Baden from 1840. Wrote operas, sym., pf. conc., and joined Chopin, Liszt, Czerny, Thalberg, and Herz as contributor to the *Hexaméron*.

Pizzetti, Ildebrando (*b* Parma, 1880; *d* Rome, 1968). It. composer and teacher, sometimes known as 'Ildebrando da Parma'. Studied Parma Cons. 1895–1901, becoming pupil of Tebaldini who interested him in It. Renaissance and Baroque mus. Taught at Parma Cons. until 1908, moving to Cherubini Institute, Florence (dir. 1917–24). Dir. Milan Cons. 1924–36, prof. of comp. S. Cecilia Acad., Rome, 1936–58. Though associated briefly with It. *avant-garde* of his day (Malipiero, Casella, etc.), he later advocated a return to 'tradition'. His mus. character was divided between a deeply religious vein, which is reflected in his operas (at the other extreme from those of Puccini) and a hedonistic vein which found expression in collab. with d'Annunzio, for whose plays he wrote incidental mus. Toscanini cond. 2 of his operas in Milan. His choral works are especially fine. Prin. comps.:

OPERAS: *Fedra* (1909–12); *Debora e Jaele* (1915–21); *Lo straniero* (1922–5); *Fra Gherardo* (1925–7); *Orséolo* (1931–5); *L'Oro* (1938–42); *Vanna Lupa* (1947–9); *Ifigenia* (1950); *Assassinio nella Cattedrale* (1957); *Il calzare d'argento* (1961); *Clitennestra* (1961–4).
ORCH: *Per l'Edipo Re di Sofocle* (1903); suite, *La pisanella* (1913); *Sinfonia del fuoco* (1914); *Concerto dell' estate* (1928); *Rondò Veneziano* (1929); pf. conc. (*Canti della Stagione Alta*) (1930); vc. conc. (1933–4); sym. (1940); vn. conc. (1944); *Preludio a un altro Giorno* (Prelude to Another Day) (1952); harp conc. (1958–60).
CHORUS and ORCH: *Agamemnon* (1931); *Epithalamium* (1939); *Cantico di Gloria 'Attollite Portas'* for 3 ch., 24 wind instr., 2 pf., perc. (1948); *Vanitas Vanitatum*, cantata (1958).
UNACCOMPANIED VOICES: *2 canzoni corali* (1913); *Canto d'amore* (1914); *Requiem* (1922–3); *De profundis* (1937); *2 composizioni corali* (1961).

Pizzicato (It., abbreviated to *pizz*; Fr. *pincé*). Pinched. Direction that notes on str. instr. are to be prod. by plucking, not bowing, the str. An early use occurs in Monteverdi's *Il combattimento di Tancredi e Clorinda* (1624), but Tobias Hume in *Harke, harke*, one of his 'Musicall Humors' from

The First Part of Ayres (1605, *Musica Britannica* IX, 116), written for bass viol and lyra viol, instructs the performers to 'play 9 letters (i.e. notes) with your fingers'. In his vn. conc. (1910), Elgar uses the direction *pizzicato tremolando*, meaning that the players should 'thrum' rapidly with the fingers across the str.

P.K. (Ger.). Abbreviation used in org. mus. for *Pedalkoppel* (pedal-coupler), followed by indication of the particular manual to be coupled to the pedal.

Pk. (Ger.). Abbreviation found in orch. scores for *Pauken*, kettledrums. See *Drum*.

Plagal Cadence. Cadence with subdominant preceding the tonic, normally both in root position. Known also as 'Amen cadence', because it was used for the Amen of hymns in the 15th and 16th cents. Use revived by Hindemith.

Plainchant. Same as *Plainsong*.

Plainsong. The large body of traditional ritual melody of the Western Christian Church, in its final form called Gregorian chant. Comprises single line of vocal melody, properly (but not always nowadays) unacc. in free rhythm, not divided into bar-lengths. Has own system of notation, employing stave of 4 lines instead of 5. The word is a trans. of *Cantus planus*—in contradistinction to *Cantus figuratus* (florid song, implying a counterpoint added to the traditional melody) or *Cantus mensuratus* (measured song, implying the regularity of rhythm assoc. with harmonic mus.). The Eastern (or 'Greek') branch of the Christian Church and the Jewish Synagogue have similar bodies of melodic ritual song, but the term *Plainsong*, as ordinarily used, does not incl. them.

Plainsong rhythm is the free rhythm of speech; it is a prose rhythm, which of course arises from the unmetrical character of the words to be recited—psalms, prayers, and the like.

In character, plainsong falls into two essentially distinct groups—the responsorial (developed from recitation of psalms round a 'dominant'), and antiphonal (developed as pure melody).

Plainsong developed during the earliest centuries of Christianity, influenced possibly by the mus. of the Jewish synagogue and certainly by the Gr. modal system (see Modes). A major reform was instituted in the 6th cent. at, it is said, the request of Pope Gregory.

Further reform was attempted at the end of the 16th cent., but the results were disastrous. *Palestrina was charged with the work of revising the plainsong of the Gradual, Antiphonal, and Psalter, but died almost immediately after accepting the commission. Felice Anerio and Soriano undertook the work, and their edn. was pubd. by the Medicean Press in 2 vols., 1614–15. This *Medicean Edition*, as it is called, with its addition and suppression of melismata, its altered melodies, and its new ones, became the basis for many cheaper performing edns. In the 18th cent. there was a fashion for introducing grace notes and passing notes into the plainsong (called in Fr. *Machicotage*). In the 19th cent. there was another cry for reform and the famous Ratisbon (Regensburg) edns. appeared—unfortunately based on the *Medicean Edition*. Years of controversy followed, for the Benedictine monks of Solesmes, in Fr., had long been at work in the most scientific spirit, photographing and collating innumerable manuscripts, in all the libraries of Europe. They pubd. their Gradual in 1883 and their Antiphonal in 1891. The Ratisbon edn. had had papal privileges conferred upon it, but in 1903 these expired and in the same year Pius X was chosen Pope and he at once issued his famous *Motu Proprio* on church mus., laying down, among other things, the importance of plainsong and the necessity of taking it from early and pure sources.

Among the reforms of the Solesmes monks (who, temporarily driven from France by anticlerical legislation in 1901, carried on their work for some years in Eng.) was the introduction of a lighter and more rhythmic manner of perf.

Planché, James Robinson (*b* London, 1796; *d* London, 1880). Eng. writer for the th. Trans. many opera libs. (incl. those of operas by Rossini, Bellini, Offenbach, Mozart, etc.). Made Eng. version of Weber's *Der Freischütz* and was librettist for *Oberon*.

Plançon, Pol (Henri) (*b* Fumay, 1851; *d* Paris, 1914). Fr. bass. Opera début Lyons 1877, Paris 1880. Paris Opéra 1883–93, CG 1891–1904, NY Met. 1893–1908. V. of great range and flexibility, capable of trills like a sop. Famous Mephistopheles in Gounod's *Faust*. Created roles in Massenet operas.

Planets, The. Suite for orch. by Holst, his Op. 32. Comp. 1914–16. 7 movements based on astrological assocs.: 1. *Mars, the Bringer of War*; 2. *Venus, the Bringer of Peace*; 3. *Mercury, the Winged Messenger*; 4. *Jupiter, the Bringer of Jollity*; 5. *Saturn, the Bringer of Old Age*; 6. *Uranus, the Magician*; 7. *Neptune, the Mystic* (with wordless female ch.). F.p. (semi-private) 1918; excl. nos. 2 and 7, 1919; complete 1920.

Planquette, ** (Jean) **Robert (*b* Paris, 1848; *d* Paris, 1903). Fr. composer, Studied Paris Cons. Began career by writing songs for the 'cafés-chantants', then turned to comic opera. Wrote about 20 operettas, most popular being Les *cloches de Corneville* (1877). Also *Rip Van Winkle* (1882), *Surcouf* (1887, as *Paul Jones* 1889), and *Panurge* (1895).

Plaqué (Fr.). Indication that notes of a chord should be played simultaneously, not as an arpeggio.

Platti, Giovanni (*b* ? Venice, *c*.1700; *d* Würzburg, 1763). It. composer, violinist, oboist, and singer. Court chamber musician to Bishop of Bamberg. Comp. sonatas and concs. for hpds. and other chamber works.

Playera (Sp.). Sp. *seguidilla* of Andalusian orig. which is sung and danced.

Player-Piano. See *Pianola*.

Playford, John (*b* Norfolk, 1623; *d* London, 1686). Eng. mus. publisher. Began business in 1647. In 1650 he registered *The English Dancing Master* (pubd. 1651), source-book of folk mus., followed by many other important publications. On his death Purcell wrote an elegy. His son Henry (1657–*c*.1720) pubd. works by Purcell, also *Orpheus Britannicus,* and later founded concerts in London and Oxford.

Play of Daniel, The. Medieval liturgical drama which exists in several versions, only the Beauvais version having survived with mus. complete. Comp. between 1227 and 1234 for perf. at Beauvais Cath. during matins probably on 1 Jan. In 2 parts, 1st dealing with Daniel at Belshazzar's court, 2nd with Daniel's trials at the court of Darius. Several modern edns., incl. one by David Wulstan.

Pleasure Dome of Kubla Khan, The. Symphonic poem by *Griffes based on Coleridge's poem. Orig. pf. piece, comp. 1912; orch. 1917, f.p. Boston S.O. 1919.

Plectrum. Small thin piece of horn, wood, tortoiseshell, metal, ivory, or other material used to pluck the str. of certain str. instrs. such as zither, mandolin, lyre, lute, banjo, etc. On the hpd. it is a part of the mechanism.

Pleeth, William (*b* London, 1916). Eng. cellist. Studied London Violoncello Sch. and Leipzig Cons. Début Leipzig 1932, London 1933. Frequent soloist with orchs. but principally chamber mus. player. Cellist in Blech Quartet 1936–41, Allegri Quartet 1953–67. Prof. of vc., GSM, from 1948. Pupils incl. Jacqueline *du Pré.

Plein Jeu (Fr.). Full play. (1) Type of org. mixture stop incl. only unison, octave, and 12th. (2) Full org. in Fr. mus.

Pleyel, Ignaz (Joseph) (*b* Ruppersthal, Vienna, 1757; *d* Paris, 1831). Austrian composer, violinist, pianist, and founder of pf. firm. Pupil for 5 years of Joseph Haydn and also studied Rome. Became choirmaster at Strasbourg Cath. 1789. Cond. concerts in London 1791–2. Set up as mus. dealer in Paris 1795, founding pf. factory 1807. Very prolific composer of 29 syms., 45 str. qts., 18 fl. qts., 2 vn. concs., 4 vc. concs., 2 pf. concs., 6 pf. sonatas, etc. His son Camille (1788–1855) became his partner in 1821 and they were joined by *Kalkbrenner in 1824. Camille was succeeded by Auguste Wolff. After Wolff's death, his son-in-law Gustave Lyon (1857–1936) assumed control. In 1961 firm was merged with Gaveau-Érard, but still made pianos under name Pleyel. Merged firm bought by Schimmel of Brunswick, 1976.

Pli selon pli (Fold upon fold). 'Portrait of Mallarmé' for sop. and orch. by Boulez. In 5 sections, some involving choice of order by cond. Comp. 1957–62 but liable to continuous rev. First Brit. perf. Edinburgh, Aug. 1965, cond. Boulez.

Plötzlich (Ger.). Suddenly.

Plowright, Rosalind (*b* Worksop, 1949). Eng. sop., formerly mez. Studied RMCM with F. R. *Cox, making opera début 1968 in J. C. Bach's *Temistocle*. Sang Donna Elvira with Glyndebourne Touring Opera 1977. Won Sofia int. comp. 1979. ENO début 1979 (Miss Jessel in *The Turn of the Screw*), CG 1980 (Ortlinde). Amer. concert début 1982 (Philadelphia), opera San Diego 1982. Fine singer of Desdemona, Donizetti's Queen Elizabeth I, and Strauss's Danae and Ariadne. Sang Aida at CG 1984, Elena in *The Sicilian Vespers*, ENO 1984, and title-role in Cherubini's *Médée*, Buxton Fest. 1984.

Ployer, Barbara von (*fl.* 1770–90). Austrian pianist. Pf. and comp. pupil of Mozart, who in 1784 wrote for her his pf. concs. No. 14 in E♭ (K449) and No. 17 in G (K453) of which she gave f.ps. in Vienna. Also played the sonata in D for 2 pf. (K448) with Mozart. Daughter of Court Councillor Gottfried Ignaz von Ployer, from 1780 agent of Salzburg Court in Vienna.

Pneuma (Gr.). Breath, breathing. Term applied to the florid passages sung to a single vowel at the end of certain pieces of plainsong. Such final vocalises were also known as *Jubili*, indicating their intention as expressions of pious joy.

Pneumatic Action. See *Organ*.

Pochette (Fr.; It. *sordino*). Pocket. Small type of vn. formerly used by 17th-cent. dancing-masters, and known in Eng. as a kit.

Poco (It.). A little, rather, e.g. *poco lento*, rather slow. *Poco a poco* means little by little, so *poco a poco animando*, becoming livelier by degrees. *Pochetto, pochettino*, very little, very little indeed, *pochissimo*, the least possible.

Podatus. See *Pes*.

Poem. Literary term introduced into music by Liszt with the expression 'symphonic poem' to apply to his narrative orch. works. Famous individual works bearing this title are the *Poem* by *Fibich, a movement from his orch. serenade *At Twilight* (*V Podvečer*), and the *Poème* for vn. and orch., 1896, by Chausson.

Poème de l'amour et de la mer (Poem of Love and the Sea). Work for v. (usually mez.) and orch. (or pf.) in 3 parts by Chausson, to words by Maurice Bouchor. Comp. 1882–90, rev. 1893,

f.p. Brussels 1893, f.p. in England, London 1919 (with orch.).

Poèmes pour Mi (Poems for Mi). Song-cycle by *Messiaen, to his own poems, for sop. and pf. (1936); for sop. and orch. (1937). 'Mi' was composer's intimate name for his first wife, the violinist Claire Deslos. F.p. Paris 1937.

Poem of Ecstasy (*Poema ekstasa*; Fr. *Le Poème d'extase*). Orch. work by *Skryabin, Op. 54, comp. 1905–8 and f.p. NY 1908, London 1910. Inspired by his theosophical ideas on love and art.

Poem of Fire (Skryabin). See *Prometheus, the Poem of Fire*.

Poet and Peasant (*Dichter und Bauer*). Play in 3 acts (1846) by K. Elmar, for which ov. and incidental mus. were comp. by *Suppé.

Poet's Echo, The. Setting by Britten for high v. and pf., Op. 76, of 6 poems (in Russ.) by Pushkin, comp. 1965 for *Vishnevskaya and *Rostropovich, who gave f.p. in Moscow Cons. Dec. 1965.

Poglietti, Alessandro (*b* ?Tuscany; *d* Vienna, 1683). Austrian composer of It. birth. Court organist Vienna 1661–83. Comp. works for org. and hpd. Killed in siege of Vienna.

Pogorelich, Ivo (*b* Belgrade, 1958). Yugoslav pianist, son of db. player. Began lessons at age of 7, and went to study in Moscow 1970. Won Casagrande competition at Terni 1978 and 1st prize in Montreal int. comp. 1980. His failure to reach the final rounds of the 1980 Int. Chopin Comp. in Warsaw led to resignation from the jury of Martha *Argerich and to the launching of his career. Settled in Eng. 1982.

Pohjola's Daughter. Symphonic fantasia for orch., Op. 49, by Sibelius comp. 1906 and based on legend from the *Kalevala*. F.p. St Petersburg 1906.

Pohl, Carl Ferdinand (*b* Darmstadt, 1819; *d* Vienna, 1887). Ger. musicologist and organist. Archivist and librarian of Vienna Society of the Friends of Music (*Gesellschaft der Musikfreunde*) 1866–87. Began huge biography of Haydn of which he completed only Vol. I (pubd. in 2 parts 1875, 1882). Wrote book on *Mozart and Haydn in London* (1867), living in London 1863–6 while engaged on reseach, and treatise on glass armonicas (1862) (he was grandson of first maker of them).

Pohl, Richard (*b* Leipzig, 1826; *d* Baden-Baden, 1896). Ger. mus. critic and ardent champion of Wagner. Worked in Dresden (1852–4) and Weimar (1854–64). Wrote books on Wagner, Liszt, and Berlioz.

Poi (It.). Then, e.g. (after some direction for the repetition of a passage) *poi la coda*, then the Coda.

Point. (1) The tip of the bow of vn., etc., opposite to that held by the hand. (2) Same as *pedal. (3) See *pointing.

Point d'orgue (Fr.). Organ-point. (1) *Pedal.
(2) The pause-sign, ⌢.
(3) A cadenza in a conc., so-called because of pause sign indicating where it begins.

Pointillist(e). A term used in painting (meaning the use, by Seurat and other Post-Impressionists, of separate dots of pure colour instead of mixed pigments) and borrowed by writers on mus. to describe passages where the notes seem to be in 'dots' rather than in melodic phrases, e.g. in the mus. of Webern.

Pointing. In Anglican chant, the allotting of syllables to the notes on which they are to be sung (as in psalms and canticles). First attempt to present pointing in printed form was by Robert Janes, organist of Ely Cath., in 1837.

Poisoned Kiss, The, or The Empress and the Necromancer. Opera (romantic extravaganza) by Vaughan Williams to lib. by Evelyn Sharp (1869–1955) derived from Richard Garnett's *The Poison Maid* and Nathaniel Hawthorne's *Rapaccini's Daughter.* Comp. 1927–9, rev. 1934–5, 1936–7, 1956–7. Prod. Cambridge and London 1936, NY 1937. Spoken dialogue rev. by Ursula Vaughan Williams in 1957 and subsequently. All characters have botanical names, e.g. Amaryllis and Persicaria.

Polacca (It.). *Polonaise.

Polacco, Giorgio (*b* Venice, 1875; *d* NY, 1960). It. cond. Studied St Petersburg, Venice, and Milan. Début London 1891. Cond. Milan, Genoa, Rome, and in St Petersburg, where he won fame as a Wagnerian. Engaged for 3 seasons in Buenos Aires and 7 in Rio de Janeiro. Amer. début at San Francisco 1905. NY Met. 1912–17, Chicago Opera 1918–30. CG début 1913.

Poldowski. Pseudonym of Lady (Irene) Dean Paul (*b* Brussels, 1880; *d* London, 1932), daughter of the violinist *Wieniawski. Composed popular ballads, sometimes singing them to her own pf. accompaniment.

Poliphant. Eng. instr. of early 17th cent., strung with wire and evidently mixing the qualities of harp, lute, and theorbo. Had 37 str.

'Polish' Symphony. Nickname for Tchaikovsky's Sym. No. 3 in D, Op. 29, because finale is in *polonaise rhythm. Comp. 1875.

Polka. Bohem. dance which originated in the early 19th cent. and quickly spread throughout Europe. It was a round dance in quick duple time, with steps on the first 3 half-beats of the measure and a sort of rest on the 4th. Introduced to Prague 1837, Vienna and St. Petersburg 1839, Paris 1840, and London 1844. The mus. bears some resemblance to that of the Schottische, and a particular kind was, in fact, called *Schottische bohème* (or *Polka tremblante*). One of the first uses of the Polka in art-mus. was by *Smetana in *The Bartered Bride.*

Pollak, Anna (*b* Manchester, 1912). Eng. mez. Studied Holland and Manchester. Began career as actress, then studied singing with Joan *Cross, who engaged her for SW 1945. Début London 1945 as Dorabella in Mozart's *Così fan tutte.* Created role of Bianca in Britten's *The Rape of Lucretia,* of Ruth in Berkeley's opera of that name, and Lady Nelson in Berkeley's *Nelson.* Sang at Glyndebourne and CG. Prin. mez. SW 1945–62, guest artist 1962–8. O.B.E. 1962.

Pollarolo, Carlo Francesco (*b* Brescia, 1653; *d* Venice, 1723). It. composer. Pupil of Legrenzi. 2nd organist, St Mark's, Venice, 1690, vice-maestro di cappella there 1692–1722. Comp. 85 operas and 13 oratorios.

Pollini, Bernhard (orig. Baruch Pohl) (*b* Cologne, 1838; *d* Hamburg, 1897). Ger. impresario, formerly ten. (début in *I Puritani,* Cologne 1857). Later, bar. with It. Opera Co. of which he became man. Dir. of It. opera St Petersburg and Moscow. Dir., Hamburg Opera 1876–97, engaging Mahler as cond. in 1891.

Pollini, Maurizio (*b* Milan, 1942). It. pianist and conductor. Début at age of 9. Studied with Carlo Vidusso. Left Milan Cons. 1959, won Warsaw Chopin Comp. 1960. Since then has appeared in Europe and USA as recitalist and concerto soloist, working often with conductor Claudio *Abbado. Has wide repertory, from Bach to *avant-garde* works such as Boulez's 2nd sonata. Has played complete pf. mus. of Schoenberg and was soloist in f.p. of Nono's *Como una ola de fuerza y luz,* Milan 1972. Like Ashkenazy, Barenboim, Perahia, and others, has often conducted from keyboard. Opera début as cond. Pesaro 1981 in Rossini's *La donna del lago.*

Pollitzer, Adolf (Adolphe) (*b* Budapest, 1832; *d* London, 1900). Hung. violinist and teacher. Studied in Vienna and Paris (with Alard). Settled in London 1851. Led opera orch. under Costa for many years and led orch. of New Philharmonic Soc. Prof. of vn., London Acad. of Mus. from 1861, becoming principal 1890. Wrote vn. caprices and ed. works of Alard and Vieuxtemps. In 1877–8 gave private vn. lessons to Elgar.

Polly. Ballad opera in 3 acts written 1729 by Gay, with mus. arr. by *Pepusch and Arnold. Sequel to The *Beggar's Opera.* Prod. London 1777, NY 1925. Rev. version with text by Clifford Bax and mus. arr. Frederic Austin prod. London 1922. Another modern version by John Addison (Aldeburgh 1952).

Polo. Andalusian folk-song (and dance) in moderate $\frac{3}{8}$ with syncopations and vocal coloraturas on words such as 'Ole' and 'Ay'. Example comp. by M. *García in his opera *El criado fingido* was quoted by Bizet in prelude to Act IV of *Carmen*. No. 7 of Falla's *7 Spanish Popular Songs* is a polo.

Polonaise (Fr.), **Polonäse** (Ger.), **Polacca** (It.). A nat. Polish dance, in simple triple time and of moderate speed; it should, perhaps, more properly be described as a stately ceremonial procession rather than a dance, and probably originated among the aristocracy in 16th cent. Certain rhythms are characteristic, such as the frequent division of the first beat of the measure with accentuation of its 2nd half, the ending of phrases on the 3rd beat of the measure, etc. Many composers, incl. Bach, Handel, Mozart, Beethoven, and Schubert have written polonaises; Chopin's 13 examples, in which he found an outlet for his patriotic feeling, are outstanding.

Polonia. (1) Concert-ov. by Wagner, comp. 1836. F.p. Palermo 1881, London 1905.
(2) Symphonic prelude for orch., Op. 76, by Elgar, f.p. 1915.
(3) Suite for orch. by *Panufnik, comp. and f.p. 1959. Polonia means Poland.

Polovtsian Dances. Sequence of choral and orch. pieces forming ballet scene in Act 2 of *Borodin's opera *Prince Igor*. The Polovtsy were nomadic invaders of Russia who, in the opera, capture Igor.

Polska. Scandinavian dance in simple triple time, so-called because of its Polish origin (it derives from the Mazurka). Dates from the union of Swedish and Polish crowns in 1587.

Polstertanz (Ger.). Pillow dance. Same as *Kissentanz* or *Cushion Dance.

Polyphony (Gr.). Many sounds. Mus. in which several simultaneous v. or instr. parts are combined contrapuntally, as opposed to monophonic mus. (single melody) or homophonic mus. (one melodic line, the other parts acting as acc.). In historical terms, polyphonic era is defined as 13th–16th cents., but polyphony survived beyond 1700.

Polyrhythm. Several different rhythms perf. simultaneously, as in many 20th-cent. works. Mozart combined 3 different dance-rhythms simultaneously in *Don Giovanni*.

Polytonality. The simultaneous use of more than one key in different contrapuntal strands, an effect found in works by Holst, Milhaud, Bartók, and others. The use of only two keys is *bitonality.

Pommer. Type of *shawm, forerunner of the ob. Often taken as meaning a large (lower-pitched) instr., but antiquarian authorities apply the term indiscriminately.

Pommier, Jean-Bernard (*b* Béziers, 1944). Fr. pianist. Studied Paris Cons. 1958–61. Won first prize, int. competition *Jeunesses Musicales* 1960, thereafter soloist with world's leading orchs. Amer. début 1973–4. Has acted as conductor/

soloist with Northern Sinfonia and other ensembles.

Pomp and Circumstance. Title given by Elgar (quoting Act 3 of Shakespeare's *Othello*) to set of 5 marches for sym. orch., Op. 39: No 1 in D major and No. 2 in A minor, f.p. Liverpool 1901; No. 3 in C minor, f.p. London 1904; No. 4 in G major, f.p. London 1907; No. 5 in C major, f.p. London 1930. Trio section of No. 1, slightly altered, became finale, with words by A. C. Benson beginning *'Land of Hope and Glory', of *Coronation Ode* 1902.

Ponce, Manuel (*b* Fresnillo, 1882; *d* Mexico City, 1948). Mexican composer. Studied in Mexico City, Berlin, and Bologna. Lived in Paris 1925–33. Taught at Nat. Cons., Mexico City, 1909–15, 1917–22, becoming dir. 1934–5. Founded mus. journal, 1936–7, and was first Mexican composer to carry out research on Creole and Meztiso folklore, which, together with Fr. composers such as Dukas, influenced his mus. Wrote many works for guitar, incl. 24 Preludes, 5 sonatas, and *Concierto del sur* (1941), also 2 pf. concs., vn. conc., and over 100 songs and 100 pf. pieces.

Ponchielli, Amilcare (*b* Paderno, 1834; *d* Milan, 1886). It. composer. Studied Milan Cons. 1843–54. Organist at Cremona. First opera, *I promessi sposi*, prod. Cremona 1856 and in rev. version at Milan 1872. Comp. ballet and several operas of which only La *Gioconda* (Milan 1876) has held its place. Choirmaster Bergamo Cath., 1881. Taught comp. Milan Cons. from 1880.

Pons, Lily (orig. Alice Joséphine) (*b* Draguignan, 1898; *d* Dallas, Texas, 1976). Fr.-born sop. (Amer. citizen 1940). Studied Paris. Opera début, Mulhouse 1928 as Lakmé. Recommended to *Gatti-Casazza of NY Met. where she made début as Lucia 1931, singing there regularly to 1940. CG 1935 as Rosina. Made several films.

Ponselle (orig. Ponzillo), **Rosa** (*b* Meriden, Conn., 1897; *d* Green Valley, Baltimore, 1981). Amer. sop. First sang in cinemas and in vaudeville act with her sister Carmella. Studied NY with W. Thorner and Romani. At Caruso's suggestion was engaged for Leonora in *La forza del destino*, NY Met. 1918. Sang at Met. 1918–37, CG 1929–31. One of greatest sops. of cent. in such roles as Norma, Violetta, Rachel (*La Juive*), and the *Trovatore* Leonora. Retired at height of powers and taught at Baltimore, becoming art. dir. of civic opera.

Ponticello (It.). Little bridge. Bridge of a str. instr. The direction *sul ponticello* means 'play with the bow as close as possible to the bridge' to produce a special 'metallic' tone-quality. In *bel canto* singing it means the join between the chest and head registers.

Poole, Geoffrey (*b* Chingford, Essex, 1949). Eng. composer. Studied at Univ. of E. Anglia 1968–

70, Southampton Univ. 1970–1 (with A. Goehr and J. Harvey), Leeds Univ. 1973–5 (with A. Goehr). Lect. in mus., Manchester Univ., from 1977. Works incl. *Wymondham Chants*, chamber ch. (1970); *Algol of Perseus*, pf. trio (1973); *Visions*, orch. (1974–5); *Piano Pictures*, pf. (1974–7); *Harmonice Mundi*, pf. quintet (1977–8); *Chamber Concerto* (1979); *TEN*, pf. (1981); *Prelude to the Net and Aphrodite*, orch. (1982); str. qt. (1983–4).

Poot, Marcel (*b* Vilvoorde, Belgium, 1901). Belgian composer. Studied Brussels Cons. and Antwerp Cons. 1916–23, also with Paul Gilson and Dukas. One of Gilson pupils who founded *Les Synthétistes*, 1925, champions of new ideas. Taught at Brussels Cons. 1938–66, dir. from 1949. Worked as critic for 20 years. Wrote 5 syms., oratorio, ballet, 2 pf. concs., cl. conc., symphonic poem *Charlot* (Charlie Chaplin).

Pop. Abbreviation for 'popular'. Earlier meaning meant concerts appealing to a wide audience. The London Popular Concerts were founded by *Benedict in 1858 and continued until 1898. Since the late 1950s, however, *pop* has had the special meaning of non-classical mus., usually in the form of songs, perf. by such artists as the Beatles, the Rolling Stones, Abba, etc. Thus 'pop groups' (performers of pop, usually singer(s), guitars, drums, sometimes sophisticated elec. effects), and 'pop festivals'.

Popp, Lucia (*b* Bratislava, 1939). Cz.-born Austrian sop. Studied Bratislava Music Acad. Prin. sop., Vienna State Opera, guest singer CG (from 1966, début as Oscar in Verdi's *Un ballo in maschera*), Salzburg (from 1963), NY Met. 1967 (Queen of the Night), and other leading opera houses. Also concert career.

Popper, David (*b* Prague, 1843; *d* Baden, Vienna, 1913). Bohem. cellist, pupil of Goltermann at Prague Cons. Played in orch., then from 1863 rose to leading position among world's cellists. Prin. cellist, Vienna Opera 1868–73. Member of Hubay Qt. Taught at Budapest Acad. from 1896. Composed 4 vc. concs., *Requiem* for 3 vc. and orch. (1892), str. qt., suites for vc., and many short vc. pieces incl. the *Dance of the Elves*.

Porgy and Bess. Opera in 3 acts by Gershwin to lib. by Du Bose Heyward and I. Gershwin after play *Porgy* by Du Bose and Dorothy Heyward. Prod. Boston, Mass., and NY 1935, London 1952, NY Met. 1985, Glyndebourne 1986.

Porpora, Nicola Antonio (*b* Naples, 1686; *d* Naples, 1768). It. composer and singing teacher. Studied Naples. Earliest operas prod. in Naples (from 1708). Taught in Naples 1715–21, producing many brilliant graduates. As teacher, held posts in several It. cities, in Ger., and in Austria. Went to London 1733 to est. opera in rivalry to Handel but was no match for him. Returned to Venice and Vienna (where Haydn was for a time

his pupil). Died in poverty. Wrote 48 operas, oratorios, syms., 12 vn. sonatas, etc.

Portamento (It.). Carrying. With the v. or a bowed instr., the carrying of the sound from note to note smoothly and without any break, hence very *legato* and momentarily sounding the pitches in between any 2 indicated by the notation. See *Curved Line, Various uses of*.

Portando, Portato (It.). Carrying, carried. The same as *portamento

Portative Organ. Medieval org. small enough to be carried by the player.

Port de voix (Fr.). Carrying of the voice. A vocal *portamento. 1 or 2 obsolete 'graces' also bore this name, either as it stands or with some added adjective.

Porter, Andrew (*b* Cape Town, 1928). Eng. mus. critic. Studied Oxford Univ. Mus. critic *Manchester Guardian* 1949, *Financial Times* 1953–74, *New Yorker* from 1972. Ed., *Musical Times*, 1960–7. Authority on opera and contrib. to many periodicals and dictionaries. Trans. several opera libs. for perf., incl. Verdi's *Otello, Falstaff, Don Carlos*, and *Rigoletto* and Wagner's *Der Ring des Nibelungen* (for ENO). Responsible for rediscovery and subsequent performance of 1st version of Verdi's *Don Carlos*.

Porter, Cole (*b* Peru, Ind., 1891; *d* Santa Monica, Calif., 1964). Amer. composer and lyricist, successful in long series of Broadway musicals and films, e.g. *Gay Divorce* (1932, filmed as *The Gay Divorcee*, 1934), *Anything Goes* (1934), *Kiss Me, Kate* (1948). His individual songs, marked by witty lyrics, incl. *Begin the Beguine, Let's Do It, Night and Day, Miss Otis Regrets*, and many others equally good and cherished. In 1919 he studied in Paris with D'Indy.

Porter, Quincy (*b* New Haven, 1897; *d* Bethany, Conn., 1966). Amer. composer and violist. Studied Yale Univ., and at Schola Cantorum, Paris, with d'Indy 1920–1. Also with *Bloch in NY. Taught at Cleveland Institute, 1922–28 and 1931–2. Prof. of mus., Vassar Coll., 1932–8, dean of mus. faculty, New England Cons., 1938–42, dir. 1942–6. Prof. of mus., Yale Univ., 1946–65. Works incl. 2 syms. (1934, 1964), va. conc. (1948), *Concerto concertante* for 2 pf. and orch. (1954), *New England Episodes* (1958), 10 str. qts., and other chamber mus.

Porter, Walter (*b* c.1595; *d* London, 1659). Eng. composer. Member of Choir of Chapel Royal 1617–44, master of choristers, Westminster Abbey, 1639–44. Said to have been pupil of Monteverdi. Pubd. madrigals and airs with instr. acc. and interludes (1632).

Portsmouth Point. (1) Orch. ov. by *Walton after an etching by Rowlandson (1756–1827).

Comp. 1925. F.p. Zürich 1926, London 6 days later.

(2) Orch. work by Lord *Berners c.1920 of which score is lost; pubd. as pf. solo.

Portunal, Portunalflöte (Ger.). An org. stop of open wooden pipes wider at the top than the bottom. It has a smooth tone.

Pos. (1) In Fr. org. mus., *Positif* (i.e. Choir Org.).
(2) In str. mus., *Posizione* (It.), *Position* (Fr.), *Position.

Posaune (Ger.). (1) Tb., but tpt. in biblical sense of 'the last tpt'.
(2) Org. reed stop of 8′ or 16′ pitch.

Posément (Fr.). Steadily, sedately.

Positif (Fr.). Choir org.

Position. (1) In the playing of str. instr., term used for specifying the moving of left hand up or down the finger-board so that the fingers may produce different sets of notes, e.g. first position, 'nearest the pegs', 2nd etc. progressively further from pegs.
(2) How far the slide should be pushed out in tb. playing (first position is least extended).
(3) Lay-out of a chord in harmony to determine which note comes at the bottom, so that one speaks of a chord in 'root position'.

Positive Organ. Type of small org. which could be placed on floor or table in contrast with *portative organ.

Posthorn. Brass instr. without valves or keys which can produce only the notes of one *harmonic series. Made straight, oblong-coiled, or circular-coiled, and once used by postillions for signalling. Mozart's *Serenade* No. 9 in D (K320, 1779) is nicknamed *Posthorn*.

Posthorn Galop. Solo (with acc.) for posthorn comp. by cornet-player Koenig, 1844.

Postlude. Piece played at the end, i.e. opposite of *prelude.

Postnikova, Viktoria (*b* Moscow, 1944). Russ. pianist. Studied Central Mus. Sch., Moscow, 1950–62, Moscow Cons., 1962–5 (with Yakov Flier). Prizewinner, Chopin Competition Warsaw 1965; 2nd prize, Leeds Int. Pf. Competition 1966. London début 1967. Soloist with world's leading orchs.

Poston, Elizabeth (*b* Highfield, Herts., 1905; *d* Stevenage, 1987). Eng. composer and pianist. Studied RAM. On BBC staff 1940–5, becoming dir. of European Service. Authority on and arranger of folk-songs and carols. Composer of incidental mus. for radio, choral mus., chamber mus., and songs.

Pothier, Joseph (*b* Bouzemont, nr. St Dié, 1835; *d* Conques, Belg., 1923). Fr. Benedictine monk, Abbot of Solesmes 1898–1923. Leading figure in reformation and restoration of plainsong, and author of scholarly works on subject.

Pot-Pourri (Fr.). Rotten-pot. Mus. application of this horticultural term is to a medley of tunes strung together without development. R. Strauss called the ov. to his *Die schweigsame Frau* a 'pot-pourri'.

Potter, (Philip) **Cipriani** (Hambley) (*b* London, 1792; *d* London, 1871). Eng. composer, pianist, cond., and teacher. Pupil of *Crotch. Début as pianist 1816 with Phil. Soc., London. Went to Vienna 1817 to study comp. with A. Förster and was advised by Beethoven. Prof. of pf., RAM from 1822, prin. 1832–59. Introduced 3 Beethoven pf. concs. (Nos. 1, 3, and 4) to Eng. at Phil. concerts. Wagner praised one of his 9 syms. Wrote 3 pf. concs. and much other mus., including '*Enigma' Variations* for pf. (*c.*1825) composed 'in the style of five eminent artists'.

Pougnet, Jean (*b* Mauritius, 1907; *d* Ferring, Sussex, 1968). Eng. violinist and violist. Studied RAM 1918–25. Début London 1923. Leader LPO 1942–5. Then career as soloist.

Pouishnoff, Leff (Nicolas) (*b* Odessa, 1891; *d* London, 1959). Russ.-born pianist and composer. Début at age 5. Studied St Petersburg Cons. London début 1912, USA 1923. Settled in W., becoming noted interpreter of Romantic mus.

Poule, La (The Hen). Nickname for Haydn's Sym. in G. minor, No. 83 in Breitkopf edn., comp. 1785. A 19th-cent. accretion, purporting to describe 'clucking' 2nd subject of 1st movement.

Poulenc, Francis (*b* Paris, 1899; *d* Paris, 1963). Fr. composer and pianist. Taught pf. by his mother and began composing at age of 7. At 15 studied with Ricardo Viñes, who encouraged his ambition to compose and introduced him to *Satie, *Casella, *Auric, and others. In 1917 his *Rapsodie nègre* brought his name to notorious prominence in Paris as one of a number of composers—*Les Nouveaux Jeunes*—encouraged by Satie and Cocteau. Even so, his technical knowledge was still scanty and in 1920 he studied harmony for 3 years with *Koechlin, but never studied counterpoint nor orchestration. His knowledge of form was instinctive. In 1920, a mus. critic, Henri Collet, selected 6 of *Les Nouveaux Jeunes* and called them *Les *Six*, Poulenc being among them. They gave concerts together, one of their articles of faith being to draw inspiration from 'Parisian folklore' i.e. street musicians, mus.-halls, circus bands. This milieu is faithfully reflected in Poulenc's settings of Cocteau's *Cocardes*. These caught the ear of Stravinsky who recommended Poulenc to Diaghilev, the result being the ballet *Les Biches* (1923), in which he expressed brittle 20s sophistication, a faithful understanding of the jazz idiom, and (in the *adagietto*) the romantic lyricism that was increasingly to dominate his work. Perhaps his finest achievements are contained in his many songs for v. and pf., particularly those written after 1935 when he began to acc. the great Fr. bar. Pierre *Bernac. His settings of Apollinaire and of his friend Paul Eluard are particularly good, covering a wide emotional range. He comp. 3 operas, the biggest being *Les Dialogues des Carmélites* (1953–6), based on events of the Fr. Revolution, and his religious works have a tuneful ecstatic joy such as one finds elsewhere only in Haydn. Of his instr. works, the organ conc. (1938) is highly original in its treatment of the solo instr. His mus., eclectic yet strongly personal in style, is essentially diatonic and melodious, embroidered with 20th-cent. dissonances. It has wit, elegance, depth of feeling, and a bitter-sweetness which derives from the mixture in his personality of gaiety and melancholy. Prin. works:

OPERAS: *Les *Mamelles de Tirésias* (1944); *Les *Dialogues des Carmélites* (1953–6); *La *Voix humaine* (1958).
BALLETS: *Les *Biches* (1923); contribution to *L'*Eventail de Jeanne* (1927); *Les Animaux modèles* (1941).
ORCH: *Suite, Les Biches* (1940, rescored); *Suite, Les Animaux modèles* (1942); *Sinfonietta* (1947).
CONCERTOS: *Concert champêtre,* hpd. or pf. and orch. (1927–8); *Aubade,* 'concerto choréographique', pf. and 18 instr. (1929); 2 pf. and orch. (1932); org., str., and timp. (1938); pf. and orch. (1949.
CHAMBER MUS.: 2-cl. sonata (1918); sonata for cl. and bn. (1922); sonata for tpt., tb., hn. (1922); trio for ob., bn., pf. (1926); pf. sextet (1932–40); vn. sonata (1942–3); vc. sonata (1940–8); str. qt. (1946, but destroyed); fl. sonata (1947); ob. sonata (1961); cl. sonata (1962).
VOICE AND INSTR.: *Rapsodie nègre,* bar., pf., str. qt., fl., cl. (1917); *Le Bestiaire,* v., fl., cl., bn., str. qt. (1919); *Le Bal masqué,* cantata for bar. (or mez.) and chamber ens. (1932); *La Dame de Monte Carlo,* sop. and orch. (1961).
CHORAL: *7 Chansons,* unacc. ch. (1936); *Mass in G,* unacc. ch. (1937); *Sécheresses,* ch. and orch. (1937); *4 Motets pour un temps de pénitence,* unacc. ch. (1938–9); *Salve Regina,* unacc. ch. (1941); *Figure humaine,* cantata for unacc. double ch. (1943); *Un soir de neige,* cantata for 6 unacc. vv. (1944); *Chansons françaises,* unacc. ch. (1945); *Stabat Mater,* sop., ch., orch. (1950); *Ave verum corpus,* 3 female vv. (1952); *Gloria,* sop., ch., orch. (1959); *7 Répons des ténèbres,* male ch. and orch. (1962).
PIANO: *3 mouvements perpétuels* (1918); *5 Impromptus* (1920); *10 Promenades* (1924); *Suite, Napoli* (1925); *Pastourelle* (1927); *2 Nouvellettes* (1927–8); *8 Nocturnes* (1929–38); *12 Improvisations* (1932–42); *Suite française* (1935); *Les Soirées de Nazelles* (1936); *Intermezzo* in A♭ (1944); *Improvisation in D: Hommage à Edith Piaf* (1960).

PIANO AND NARRATOR: *Histoire de *Babar le petit éléphant* (1940–5).
PIANO (4 HANDS): *Sonata* (1918).
2 PIANOS: *Sonata* (1953); *Elégie* (1960).
SONGS: *Le Bestiare au cortège d'Orphée* (Apollinaire, 6 songs) (1919); *Cocardes* (Cocteau, 3 songs) (1919); *5 Poèmes de Ronsard* (1924–5); *Chansons gaillardes* (17th-cent. anon., 8 songs) (1926); *Airs chantés* (Moréas, 4 songs) (1927–8); *3 Poèmes de Louise Lalanne* (Apollinaire pseudonym, 3 songs) (1931); *4 Poèmes* (Apollinaire) (1931); *5 Poèmes* (Jacob) (1931); *8 Chansons Polonaises* (1934); *4 Chansons pour enfants* (Jaboune) (1934–5); *5 Poèmes* (Eluard) (1935); *Tel jour, telle nuit* (Eluard) (1936–7); *3 Poèmes* (Vilmorin) (1937); *2 Poèmes* (Apollinaire) (1938); *Miroirs brûlants* (Eluard, 2 songs) (1938); *La Grenouillère* (Apollinaire) (1938); *Ce doux petit visage* (Eluard) (1938); *Bleuet* (Apollinaire) (1938); *Fiançailles pour rire* (Vilmorin, 6 songs) (1939); *Banalités* (Apollinaire, 5 songs) (1940); *Chansons villageoises* (Fombeure, 6 songs) (1942, also with chamber orch.); *Métamorphoses* (Vilmorin, 3 songs) (1943); *2 Poèmes* (Aragon) (1943); *Montparnasse; Hyde Park* (Apollinaire) (1945); *Le Pont; Un Poème* (Apollinaire) (1946); *3 Chansons de F. Garcia Lorca* (1947); *Main dominée par le coeur* (Eluard) (1947); *Calligrammes* (Apollinaire, 7 songs) (1948); *La Fraîcheur et le feu* (Eluard, 7 songs) (1950); *Parisiana* (Jacob, 2 songs) (1954); *Rosemonde* (Apollinaire) (1954); *Le Travail du peintre* (Eluard, 7 songs) (1956); *La Courte Paille* (Carême) (1960).

Poulton, Diana (*b* Storrington, 1903). Eng. lutenist and historian. Studied with A. Dolmetsch. Co-ed. of lute mus. of *Dowland. Prof. of lute RCM from 1971. Wrote *Life of Dowland* (1972).

Pound, Ezra (*b* Hailey, Idaho, 1885; *d* Venice, 1972). Amer. poet, mus. critic, and composer. Studied Hamilton Coll., Clinton, NY and Univ. of Penn. Went to It. 1908, Eng. 1908–20, Paris 1920–4, It. 1924–45. Committed to Amer. mental hospital, 1946–58. Returned to It. 1958. Principally known as poet, but wrote mus. criticism regularly in Eng. from 1908. Especially interested in mus. of medieval troubadours. Wrote 1-act opera *Le Testament de Francois Villon* (1920–1); *Hommage à Froissart* for vn. (1926); *Cavalcanti* (unfinished opera, 1920s).

Poussé (Fr.). Pushed. Up-bow (in str. playing), contrasted with *tiré* (pulled), down-bow.

Pousseur, Henri (*b* Malmédy, Belg., 1929). Belg. composer. Studied Liège Cons. and Brussels Cons. 1947–53. Taught mus. at Brussels sch. 1950–60. Influenced by Webern, Boulez, Stockhausen, and Berio. Comp. his first elec. work in Cologne, 1954. Has written many articles on contemporary mus. and trans. Berg's writings into Fr. Has taught at Darmstadt. Prof. of mus., State Univ. of NY at Buffalo, 1966–8. Prof. of comp., Liège Cons., from 1971. Works incl.:

OPERAS: *Votre Faust* (1961–7); *Die Erprobung des Petrus Hebraïcus* (1974).

ORCH: *Phonèmes couleurs croisées* (1967); *Les Ephémérides d'Icare II* (1970); *Icare apprenti* (1970); *L'Effacement du Prince Igor* (1971).

ELECTRONIC AND TAPE: *Scambi* (1957); *Rimes pour différentes sources sonores* (1958–9); *3 Visages de Liège* (1961).

CHAMBER MUSIC: *Quintet in mem. Anton Webern* (1955); *Répons* (1960, re-composed 1965); *Ode*, str. qt. (1960–1); *Madrigal II*, fl., vn., viola da gamba, cembalo; *Madrigal III*, cl., vn., vc., 2 perc., pf. (1962).

PIANO(s): *Mobile*, 2 pf. (1956–8); *Caractères* (1961); *Apostrophes et 6 Réflexions* (1964–6).

VOICES AND INSTR.: *Miroir de votre Faust*, pf., sop. ad lib. (1964–5); *Mnemosyne 1*, monody for v. or instr. or ch. (1968); *Chronique berlinoise*, bar., pf. quintet (1976); *Chronique illustrée*, bar., orch. (1976); *Tales and Songs from the Bible of Hell*, vv., tape, and live elec. (1979); *Agonie*, elec. vv. (1981).

Powell, Mel (*b* NY, 1923). Amer. composer and pianist. Pianist and arr. for Benny Goodman and Glenn Miller bands. Studied comp. with Wagenaar and J. Schillinger in NY 1937–9 and with Toch in Los Angeles 1946–8. Worked in NY 1950–7. On comp. faculty Yale Univ. 1958–69, est. elec. mus. studio there 1960. Dean of Mus., Calif. Institute of Arts from 1969. His works, even those using elec. means, retain strong traditional features. Works incl. *Filigree Setting*, str. qt. (1959); *Haiku Setting*, v. and pf. (1961); *Events*, tape (1963); *Stanzas* for orch. (1965); *Analogs 1–4*, tape (1966); *Immobiles 1–4*, tape and/or orch. (1967); *Immobile 5*, tape and orch. (1969); *Setting*, vn., tape, wind (1972).

Power, Lionel (*d* Canterbury, 1445). Eng. composer. Supposed colleague of *Dunstable. Wrote 2 treatises on mus. theory and much church mus., incl. *Salve Regina* and *Mater ora filium*. Many works incl. in *Old Hall MS.

pp, ppp, etc. Abbreviations for *Pianissimo*, very soft.

P.R. In Fr. org. mus., abbreviation for *Positif-Récit*, i.e. Choir-Swell (Swell to Choir coupler).

Practical Cats. Work for speaker and orch. by Rawsthorne, settings of 6 poems from T. S. Eliot's *Old Possum's Book of Practical Cats* (1939). F.p. Edinburgh Fest. 1954.

Praeger, Ferdinand (Christian Wilhelm) (*b* Leipzig, 1815; *d* London, 1891). Ger. pianist. Settled in London 1834, becoming London correspondent of Schumann's *Neue Zeitschrift für Musik*, 1842. Champion of Wagner, partly instrumental in engaging him to conduct in London 1855. His book, *Wagner as I Knew Him* (1885, Ger. edn. 1892) was withdrawn because of inaccuracies. Wrote symphonic poems and chamber mus.

Praeludium (Lat.). Prelude. Title of popular orch. work by *Järnefelt, first played in Eng. 1909.

Praetorius. Latinized form of Schulz or Schultz adopted by several Ger. musicians in 16th and 17th cents. Among them are: **Hieronymus Praetorius** (*b* Hamburg, 1560; *d* Hamburg, 1629). Comp. church mus., wedding songs, etc., much of it pubd. in 5 vol. *Opus musicum novum et perfectum* (1622–5). **Michael Praetorius** (*b* Kreuzberg, 1571; *d* Wolfenbüttel, 1621). Prolific composer and important mus. historian. Began career as organist, 1604, to Duke of Brunswick. His *Syntagma musicum* (1614–20, 3 vols.) is a wide survey of mus., the 2nd vol. being a prime source of information on mus. instr. of the time.

Prague Symphony. Nickname of Mozart's Sym. No. 38 in D (K504) comp. 1786 and f.p. during Mozart's visit to Prague in 1787. In 3 movements.

Pralltriller (Ger.). Upper Mordent. See *Mordent*.

Pratella, Francesco Balilla (*b* Lugo, 1880; *d* Ravenna, 1955). It. composer. Studied in Pesaro with *Mascagni. Dir., Lugo Mus. Acad. 1910–26, Liceo Musicale G. Verdi, Ravenna, 1927–45. His first opera *Lilia* won prize in Sonzogno contest 1903. In 1910, joined futurist movement of Marinetti and Russolo and wrote manifesto of futurist musicians. Wrote *Musica futurista* for orch. 1912. Also wrote symphonic poems, chamber mus., and songs.

Pratt, Stephen (*b* Liverpool, 1947). Eng. composer. Studied at Reading Univ. and Liverpool Univ. (comp. with Hugh Wood and privately to 1975). Lect. in mus., Liverpool Inst. of Higher Education. Works incl. pf. sonata (1974–5); *Concert*, chamber ens. (1973–5); *Nonet* (1976); *Star and Dead Leaves*, fl., pf. (1977); *Winter's Fancy*, cl., pf. (1978–9); *Some of their Number*, orch. (1978); *Between the Lines*, chamber ens. (1982); hn. trio (1980–3); *Salve Regina*, ch. (1982).

Prausnitz, Frederik (*b* Cologne, 1920). Ger.-born cond. (Amer. citizen). Studied Juilliard Sch. NY. Début Detroit S.O. 1944. On staff Juilliard Sch. in various capacities 1947–61. Guest cond. Brit. and European orchs. from 1957. Cond., New Eng. Cons. S.O., Boston, 1961–9, Syracuse S.O. 1971–4, chief cond. Peabody Institute, Baltimore, from 1976. Has cond. f. Amer. ps. of works by Dallapiccola, Gerhard, Lutyens, Schoenberg, Stockhausen, Varèse, and Webern.

Precentor (Lat.). First singer. Ecclesiastical official, in charge of vocal mus. in Anglican caths.

Preciosa. Ger. play about a gipsy by P. A. Wolff for which Weber in 1820 comp. ov., 4 chs., song, 3 melodramas, and dances.

Precipitato, Precipitoso, etc. (It.). Impetuously.

Pre-Classical. Term applied to composers such as C. P. E. Bach who are considered to be later than baroque and leading to the 'classical' style of Haydn, Mozart, etc.

Prelude. A piece of mus. which precedes something else, e.g. preceding a fugue; forming first movement of a suite; orch. introduction to opera. Also a self-contained short piece for pf., as those by Chopin, Rakhmaninov, Debussy, etc.

Préludes. 2 books of pf. pieces by Debussy. *Book I* (1910): (1) *Danseuses de Delphes* (Dancing Women of Delphi), suggested by a pillar in the Louvre on which are sculptured 3 Bacchantes; (2) *Voiles* (Sails); (3) *Le Vent dans la plaine* (The wind in the plain); (4) *Les Sons et les parfums tournent dans l'air du soir* (Sounds and perfumes in the evening air); (5) *Les Collines d'Anacapri* (The hills of Anacapri); (6) *Des Pas sur la neige* (Footsteps on the snow); (7) *Ce qu'a vu le vent d'Ouest* (What the west wind saw); (8) *La fille aux cheveux de lin* (The girl with the flaxen hair), suggested by a poem of Leconte de Lisle; (9) *La Sérénade interrompue* (The interrupted serenade), Spanish in its idioms; (10) *La Cathédrale engloutie* (The submerged cathedral), based on the legend of the cath. of Ys, with its bell-tolling and chanting under the sea; (11) *La Danse de Puck* (Puck's dance); (12) *Minstrels*—Negro or music-hall type. *Book II* (1912–13): (1) *Brouillards* (Mists); (2) *Feuilles mortes* (Dead leaves); (3) *La Puerta del Vino*—name of famous gate of Alhambra; (4) *Les Fées sont d'exquises danseuses* (Fairies are exquisite dancers); (5) *Bruyères* (Heaths); (6) *General Lavine—eccentric*—Paris mus.-hall performer; (7) *La Terrasse des audiences du clair de lune* (Terrace of Moonlight Audiences); (8) *Ondine*—the water-spirit maiden of the early 19th-cent. story of de la Motte Fouqué; (9) *Hommage à S. Pickwick Esq., P.P.M.P.C.*—with a touch of the Brit. nat. anthem; (10) *Canope* (Canopic vase), ancient Egyptian cinerary urn; (11) *Les Tierces alternées* (Alternating 3rds); (12) *Feux d'artifice* (Fireworks).

Préludes, Les (The Preludes). Symphonic poem by Liszt, comp. 1848, rev. before 1854. Title from one of Lamartine's *Nouvelles Méditations poétiques.*, but mus. was orig. comp. as ov. to *Les Quatre Eléments*, 4 male chs. with words by J. Autran and orch. by Conradi. Liszt's preface to rev. score states that life is treated as a series of preludes to the unknown after-life.

Preludio (It.). Prelude.

Preparation. Device in harmony whereby effect of discord is lessened: the note in a chord which causes the chord to be discordant is sounded in the preceding chord where it is not a cause of discord, i.e. prepared discord. If this course is not followed, the discord is unprepared.

Prepared Piano. A pf. in which the strs. have been 'doctored' in various ways to produce abnormal tone-qualities. Introduced by *Cage for his *Bacchanale* (1938).

Pressando, pressante (It.), **pressant** (Fr.). Pressing on, *accelerando.* Sometimes the Fr. infinitive *presser* is used.

Prestant. Org. stop, same as *Principal in Brit. and Amer. instr.

Presto (It.). Quick. *Prestezza*, quickness; *prestamente*, quickly; *prestissimo*, very quick; *prestissimamente*, very quickly.

Preston, Simon (John) (*b* Bournemouth, 1938). Eng. org., teacher, harpsichordist, and cond. Studied Cambridge Univ. Sub-organist Westminster Abbey 1962–7. Cond. Oxford Bach Ch. 1967–8. Organist, Christ Church, Oxford, 1970–81; organist and master of the choristers, Westminster Abbey, from 1981.

Prêtre, Georges (*b* Waziers, 1924). Fr. cond. Studied Paris Cons. Conducting pupil of *Cluytens. Dir. of mus., opera houses of Marseilles, Lisle, and Toulouse 1946–55. Mus. dir. Opéra-Comique 1956–9; cond. f. Paris p. of Strauss's *Capriccio*, 1956. London début 1961, NY Met. 1964. Regular guest cond. at Paris Opéra (mus. dir. 1970–1), Milan, Chicago, Vienna, etc. Conductor at CG for Callas's *Tosca* 1965 and often conducted for her in the theatre and recording studio. Cond. f.ps. of Poulenc's *La Voix humaine* (1959) and *Gloria* (1959).

Previn, André (George) (orig. Andreas Ludwig Priwin) (*b* Berlin, 1929). Amer. (naturalized 1943) pianist, cond., and composer. Educated Berlin Cons. and Paris Cons. Once a jazz pianist, he later worked as composer and arranger of film mus. in Hollywood. Studied conducting with Monteux in 1951. Début as cond., St Louis S.O. 1963. Cond.-in-chief, LSO, 1968–79; settled in Eng. where he won popular following as presenter of mus. on TV. Champion of Eng. mus., notably Walton and Vaughan Williams (whose 9 syms. he recorded). Cond. Houston S.O., 1967–9, Pittsburgh S.O., 1976–85, mus. dir. RPO 1985–7, mus. dir. Los Angeles P.O. from 1986. Comps. incl. vc., vn., and guitar concs., chamber mus., and works for solo pf., mus. for 'play for actors and orch', by Tom Stoppard, *Every Good Boy Deserves Favour*, prod. London 1978 (with LSO).

Previtali, Fernando (*b* Adria, 1907; *d* Rome, 1985). It. cond. and composer. Studied Turin Cons. (vc., pf., comp.). Cond. Florence orch. and fest. 1928–36. Cond. It. Radio Orch. 1936–53, S. Cecilia Orch. from 1953. Guest cond. European orchs. from 1948. Amer. début, Cleveland Orch. 1955. Noted for radio opera perfs. Author of books on mus. Wrote ballet and other works.

Prey, Hermann (*b* Berlin, 1929). Ger. bar. Studied Berlin State Mus. Acad. Joined Hamburg Opera 1953. Guest singer Berlin and Vienna Operas from 1956. Salzburg Fest. from 1959 (Guglielmo in *Così fan tutte*, Papageno, etc.). Eng. début 1965

(Edinburgh Fest.), CG since 1973 (début as Rossini's Figaro). Amer. début in Lieder 1952, NY Met. 1960 (Wolfram in *Tannhäuser*). Especially fine exponent of Lieder. Founder (1976), of annual Schubert fest. at Hohenems.

Pribaoutki (Song games). For v., fl., ob., cor anglais, cl., bn., and str. qt. by *Stravinsky comp. 1914 to Russ. popular texts. F.p. London 1918, cond. Goossens. Items are: 1. *L'Oncle Armand* (*Kornillo*), 2. *Le Four* (*Natashka*), 3. *Le Colonel*, 4. *Le Vieux et le lièvre* (The Old Man and the Hare).

Price, Leontyne (*b* Laurel, Miss., 1927). Amer. sop. Studied Juilliard Sch., NY, singing Mrs Ford in Verdi's *Falstaff* in student prod. Chosen by Virgil Thomson to sing in revival of *Four Saints in Three Acts* in NY and Paris, 1952. Sang Bess in Gershwin's *Porgy and Bess*, 1953–4. Recital début NY 1954. Opera débuts at San Francisco 1957, 1958–9, Chicago 1959, Vienna 1958 (as Aida), CG 1958–9, Salzburg 1960 (Donna Anna), Milan 1960, NY Met. 1961 (Leonora in *Il Trovatore*), Rome 1967, Paris 1968. One of finest Verdi sops. of her day. Also noted exponent of mus. of Samuel Barber (sang Cleopatra in NY Met. première of his *Antony and Cleopatra*, 1966).

Price, Margaret (Berenice) (*b* Blackwood, Wales, 1941). Welsh sop. Studied TCL. Opera début as Cherubino with WNO 1962 and at CG 1963. Guest singer, especially in Mozart roles, in leading opera houses. Glyndebourne début 1968 (Constanze in *Die Entführung*). Amer. début San Francisco 1969, Paris 1973. Has recorded role of Isolde with C. Kleiber. Noted Lieder singer. C.B.E. 1982.

Prick-song. Old Eng. term (prick = mark) for mus. which was written down, i.e. 'pricked' instead of being extemporized or traditional (as plainchant).

Priestman, Brian (*b* Birmingham, 1927). Eng. cond. Studied Birmingham Univ. and Brussels Cons. Ass. cond. Yorkshire S.O. 1952–4, mus. dir. Royal Shakespeare Th., Stratford-upon-Avon, 1960–3. Cond. Edmonton S.O. 1964–8, Baltimore S.O. 1968–9, Denver S.O. 1970–8. Prin. cond. N.Z. Broadcasting Corporation 1973–6, Miami P.O. 1978–80. Prof. of mus., Univ. of Cape Town Coll. of Mus. from 1981.

Prigioniero, Il (The Prisoner). Opera in prol. and 1 act by *Dallapiccola, comp. 1944–8, to lib. by composer after Villiers de L'Isle Adam's *La Torture par l'espérance* (1883) and Charles Coster's *La Légende d'Ulenspiegel et de Lamme Goedzak*. F.p. It. radio 1949. Prod. Florence 1950, NY 1951, London 1959.

Prima Donna (It.). First lady. Orig. the chief woman singer in an opera cast, but term has been generalized to mean a leading woman singer. Thus, for orig. meaning, one has to use term *prima donna assoluta*, 'the absolute first lady'. The

same process has occurred in ballet with *prima ballerina assoluta*.

Prima Donna. Comic opera in 1 act by A. Benjamin to lib. by Cedric Cliffe. Comp. 1933, prod. London 1949, Philadelphia 1955.

Primo, Prima (It.). First. Hence *primo*, top part in pf. duets; *primo uomo*, prin. male singer in opera (orig. the leading castrato); *prima vista*, first sight; *tempo primo*, same tempo as at beginning; *come prima*, as at first; *prima volta*, first time.

Primrose, William (*b* Glasgow, 1903; *d* Provo, Utah, 1982). Scottish-born violist and violinist (Amer. cit. 1955). Studied vn. at GSM and with *Ysaÿe. Changed to va. and played in London Str. Qt. 1930–5. Settled in USA 1937. Prin. va. NBC S.O. 1938–42. Many appearances as soloist. Commissioned Bartók's va. conc. and gave f.p. Played in several chamber-mus. ens. C.B.E. 1953.

Prince Igor. Opera in 4 acts, with prol., by *Borodin to his own lib. after an outline by Vladimir Stasov. Begun in 1869 and left unfinished in 1887. Completed by Rimsky-Korsakov and Glazunov; prod. St Petersburg 1890, London 1914, NY 1915.

Prince of the Pagodas, The. Ballet in 3 acts by Britten, Op. 57, choreog. John Cranko, comp. 1956, f.p. CG 1957. 'Pas de six', Op. 57a, pubd. separately for orch. 1957. Inspired by a visit to the Far East. Orch. suite, *Prelude and Dances from The Prince of the Pagodas*, arr. N. Del Mar, f.p. 1963; orch. suite (approved by Britten), arr. M. Lankester, f.p. 1979. Another suite has been compiled by A. Previn.

Princess Ida, or Castle Adamant. Operetta in 3 acts by Sullivan to lib. by Gilbert. Comp. 1883. Prod. London and Boston, Mass., 1884. 'Respectful operatic perversion of Tennyson's *The Princess*'.

Principal. (1) Leading player of orch. section, e.g. 'prin. cl.', 'prin. hn.', etc.

(2) Singer who takes main parts in opera—'prin. ten.', meaning ten. who sings prin. roles, not the chief tenor.

(3) Open diapason org. stop of 4' length on manuals or 8' on pedal.

Principale (It.). (1) Great Org.

(2) Type of 17th- and 18th-cent. tpt. part.

Printemps (Spring). Symphonic suite for orch. and ch. by Debussy, comp. 1887. Definitive version re-orch. Busser 1913 without ch., f.p. Paris 1913. Not to be confused with *Rondes de printemps* (see *Images*).

Prinz von Homburg, Der (The Prince of Homburg). Opera in 3 acts by Henze to lib. by Bachmann after play by Kleist. Prod. Hamburg 1960, London 1962.

Prise de Troie, La (The Capture of Troy). Part I (Acts 1 and 2) of Berlioz's opera Les *Troyens.

Prisoner, The (Dallapiccola). See *Prigioniero, Il.*

Pritchard, (Sir) **John** (Michael) (*b* London, 1921). Eng. cond. Studied pf., vn., org. Cond., Derby Str. Orch., 1943–5. Répétiteur at Glyndebourne 1947, becoming ch. master 1949 and cond. *Don Giovanni, Così fan tutte,* and *Figaro* 1951. Prin. cond. Glyndebourne 1967, mus. dir. 1969–77. CG début 1952. Cond. f.ps. of Britten's *Gloriana* (1953) and Tippett's *The Midsummer Marriage* (1955) and *King Priam* (1962). Guest cond. at leading European opera houses. Prin. cond. RLPO 1957–63, LPO 1962–7. BBC S.O. from 1981. Opera début Chicago 1969, San Francisco 1970, NY Met. 1971. Cond. Cologne Opera from 1978. C.B.E. 1962. Knighted 1983. Hamburg Shakespeare Prize 1975.

Prix de Rome. Prizes awarded annually since 1803 by Institut de France to candidates selected by competition from comp. students at Paris Cons. First prize (*Grand Prix de Rome*) entitles winner to live in Rome for 4 years at Villa Medici (Fr. Acad.) while engaging in study and creative work. 2nd prize is a gold medal. Exam. takes place *en loge* (in isolation); candidates must set to mus. a cantata on a given subject. Jury's verdict must be ratified by entire Académie des Beaux-Arts. Among winners have been Berlioz (1830), Gounod (1839), Bizet (1857), Massenet (1863), Debussy (1884), and Charpentier (1887). Ravel's failure to win was subject of famous scandal. Belg. awards prize of same name and does not insist upon residence in Rome. An Amer. Prix de Rome was instituted in 1905, the winner to reside at the Amer. Acad. in Rome. No award was made until 1921 (Sowerby). Fr. competition suppressed 1968; promising young composers etc. now sent to Rome on teachers' recommendations.

Pro Arte Quartet. Belgian str. qt., founded 1912 by graduates from Brussels Cons. Début Brussels 1913, achieving reputation for perfs. of contemporary mus. Eng. début 1925, USA 1926. Perf. annually in Cambridge for a week 1932–8. Title passed to faculty qt. of Univ. of Wisconsin at Madison. Austrian str. qt. of same name founded in Salzburg, 1973

Pro Cantione Antiqua. Eng. vocal ens. formed in 1968 by Mark Brown, Paul *Esswood, and James Griffett to perf. mus. of medieval, Renaissance, and baroque eras. Début Westminster Cath., 1968, cond. by Colin Mawby.

Procesión del Rocio, La (The Procession of Rocio). Symphonic poem in 2 parts by Turina, 1913. (The Rocio is a place of pilgrimage near Seville.)

Procter, Norma (*b* Cleethorpes, 1928). Eng. cont. Studied with Roy Henderson and Paul Hamburger. Specialist in concert works and oratorio (Mahler, Britten, Elgar, etc.). Sang Gluck's Orfeo at CG 1961.

Procter-Gregg, Humphrey (*b* Kirkby Lonsdale, 1895; *d* Grange-over-Sands, 1980). Eng. teacher, opera producer, composer, and trans. Studied Cambridge Univ. and RCM (with Stanford). Supervised college opera prods. Worked at Scala, Milan. Stage manager and designer, BNOC, Carl Rosa, and CG touring cos. 1922–33. Founder and head of mus. dept., Manchester Univ. 1936, becoming first prof. of mus. 1954–62. Responsible for BBC studio opera 1941–5, providing several new trans. Dir., Carl Rosa Opera 1957–8. Dir., London Opera Centre 1963–4. Wrote pf. mus., songs, and sonatas. Ed. book of memoirs about Beecham. C.B.E. 1971.

Prodaná Neveštá (Smetana). See *Bartered Bride, The.*

Prodigal Son, The. There are several mus. comps. on this theme, among them: (1) *L'Enfant Prodigue,* ballet by Prokofiev, Op. 46, 1928–9, choreog. Balanchine, prod. Paris 1929.

(2) *The Prodigal Son,* parable for church perf., by Britten, Op. 81, to lib. by W. Plomer, prod. Aldeburgh (Orford) 1968, NY 1969.

(3) *L'Enfant Prodigue,* cantata for sop., ten., bar., by Debussy, 1884, with which he won *Prix de Rome.*

(4) *The Prodigal Son,* oratorio by Sullivan, perf. Worcester Fest. 1869.

Programme Music. Instr. mus. which tells a story, illustrates literary ideas, or evokes pictorial scenes. Though the term originated with Liszt, illustrative mus. has existed for as long as mus. itself. Beethoven's *Pastoral Symphony* is a wellnigh perfect example of mus. which is both illustrative and satisfying purely as mus. In the 19th cent., composers such as Berlioz, Liszt, Tchaikovsky, and R. Strauss lent the full resources of the sym. orch. to this form of mus. art in works such as the *Symphonie fantastique, Romeo and Juliet,* and *Don Quixote.* The precept, once widely propagated, that 'absolute mus.' was, *ipso facto,* superior to 'programme mus.' is now, happily, outdated.

Progression. The motion of one note to another note or one chord to another chord, in logical progression.

Progressive Tonality. Beginning a symphonic movement in one key and ending it in another, as in certain works of *Nielsen and *Mahler.

Prohaska, Felix (*b* Vienna, 1912). Austrian cond. Studied in Vienna. Taught at Graz Cons., 1936–9. Cond. of opera in Duisburg 1939–41, Strasbourg 1941–3, Prague 1943–5. Cond. and teacher, Vienna, 1946–55; chief cond. Frankfurt Opera 1955–61; dir., Hochschule für Musik, Hanover, from 1961.

Prohaska, Jaro (*b* Vienna, 1891; *d* Munich, 1965). Austrian bass-bar. Studied Vienna. Member of Vienna Boys' Choir 1898–1906. Opera début Lübeck 1922. Nuremberg Opera 1925–31, Berlin State Opera 1931–52, Bayreuth Fest. 1933–44. Famous interpreter of Wagnerian roles of Sachs, Wotan, and Amfortas. Retired 1959. Dir., opera school of West Berlin Musikhochschule 1952–9, having taught there from 1947. Hermann *Prey among his pupils.

Prokofiev, Sergey (Sergeyevich) (*b* Sontsovka, 1891; *d* Moscow, 1953). Russ. composer and pianist. Was taught pf. at age 3 by his mother, who encouraged him to compose (he wrote an opera at age 9). Studied with *Glière 1902. Entered St Petersburg Cons. 1904, studying harmony and counterpoint with Lyadov and orch. with Rimsky-Korsakov. Later studied pf. with Anna Essipova and cond. with Tcherepnin. Comp. and pubd. several works while student, incl. 2 pf. sonatas and first pf. conc. Visiting London in 1914 he met Diaghilev, who commissioned a ballet from him (the war upset this plan and the mus. survives as the *Scythian Suite, Ala and Lolly*). In 1917 he comp. his first sym., the *Classical*, a superb 20th-cent. reincarnation of Haydn. After its f.p. in Petrograd in 1918 he left Russia for USA, appearing in NY as solo pianist in his own works. His opera *Love for Three Oranges* was commissioned by Chicago Opera, perf. 1921. From 1920 he made his home in Paris, writing 3 ballets for Diaghilev, and having several of his works perf. at the orch. concerts cond. *Koussevitzky, another Russ. exile. Never fully at home in the W., Prokofiev returned to Russia in 1933, choosing an inopportune moment when the doctrine of 'socialist realism' in the arts had just been propounded. He found an outlet for his particular gifts in film mus.—brilliant scores for *Lieutenant Kijé* and *Alexander Nevsky*—and ballet (*Romeo and Juliet* and, later, *Cinderella*), In 1941 he began work on his most ambitious opera, *War and Peace*, and in 1944 wrote his richest and most heroic sym., the 5th. In spite of its success, he was among those in 1948 condemned for *'formalism' and was compelled to 'confess' his shortcomings in an open letter to the Union of Soviet Composers.

Though regarded as impossibly dissonant and *avant-garde* in his youth, Prokofiev can now be seen as in the direct line of Russ. comps., embodying the bold and colourful strokes of 19th-cent. nationalists into a 20th-cent. style strongly marked by its brittle wit and capacity for pungent dramatic characterization. Like Walton and Poulenc, he was fundamentally a romantic melodist and his style is formed like theirs from a reconciliation of the two strains in his personality, the tough, astringent modernist and the lyrical traditionalist. He was successful in a wide range of works: *War and Peace* is a great opera on the largest scale, the syms. and concs. are fine mus., at least 3 of his ballets are masterpieces, the pf. sonatas are crucial to the 20th-cent. pf. repertory; and in *Peter and the Wolf* he created the most enduring, touching, and

instructive of young persons' guides to the orch. Prin. works:

OPERAS: *Maddalena*, Op. 13 (1911, rev. 1913, completed in pf. score but only Scene 1 orch. Scenes 2–4 orch. Downes, 1979); The *Gambler (Igrok)*, Op. 24 (1915–17, 2nd version 1927–8); *Love for Three Oranges (Lyubov k tryom apelsinam)*, Op. 33 (1919); The *Fiery Angel (Ognenniy angel)*, Op. 37 (1919–23, rev. 1926–7); *Semyon Kotko*, Op. 81 (1940); The *Duenna (Betrothal in a monastery)*, Op. 86 (1940–1); *War and Peace (Voyna i mir)*, Op. 91 (1941–2, 1946–7, and rev. up to 1953); *The Story of a Real Man (Povest' o nastoyashchem cheloveke)*, Op. 117 (1947–8).

BALLETS: *The Buffoon (*Chout)*, Op. 21 (1915, rev. 1920); *Age of Steel (Le Pas d'acier)*, Op. 41 (1925–6); The *Prodigal Son (L'Enfant prodigue)*, Op. 46 (1928–9); *Sur le Borysthène*, Op. 51 (1930–1); *Romeo and Juliet*, Op. 64 (1935–6); *Cinderella*, Op. 87 (1940–4); The *Stone Flower*, Op. 118 (1948–53).

ORCH: Symphonies: No. 1 (*Classical*), Op 25 (1916–17, f.p. 1918), No 2 in D minor, Op. 40 (1924, f.p. 1925), No. 3 in C minor, Op. 44 (1928, f.p. 1929), No. 4 in C, Op. 47 (1929–30, f.p. 1930, 2nd version, Op. 112, 1947), No. 5 in B♭, Op. 100 (1944, f.p. 1945), No. 6 in E♭ minor, Op. 111 (1947, f.p. 1947), No. 7 in C♯ minor, Op. 131 (1951–2, f.p. 1952); *Sinfonietta*, Op. 5/48 (1909, 1929); *Esquisse automnale*, Op. 8 (1910); *Scythian Suite*, Op. 20 (1914); *Overture for 17 instr.*, Op. 42 (1926); *Divertimento*, Op. 43 (1929); *Symphonic Song*, Op. 57 (1933); Suite, *Lieutenant Kijé*, Op. 60 (1934); *Egyptian Nights*, Op. 61 (1934); *Peter and the Wolf*, narrator and orch., Op. 67 (1936); *Russian Overture*, Op. 72 (1936); Suite, *1941*, Op. 90 (1941).

CONCERTOS: Piano: No. 1 in D♭, Op. 10 (1911–12), No. 2 in G minor, Op. 16 (1912–13, rev. 1923), No. 3 in C, Op. 26 (1917–21), No. 4 in B♭, Op. 53, left hand (1931), No. 5 in G, Op. 55 (1932); Violin: No. 1 in D, Op. 19 (1916–17), No. 2 in G minor, Op. 63 (1935); Cello: No. 1 in E minor, Op. 58 (1934, rev. 1938), No. 2 in E minor (1950–1) rev. as *Sinfonia Concertante*, Op. 125 (1952).

CHAMBER MUSIC: *Overture on Hebrew Themes*, Op. 34, cl., pf., str. qt. (1919; orch. version 1934); quintet, wind and str., Op. 39 (1924); Str. Qt. No. 1, Op. 50 (1930), No. 2, Op. 92 (1942); sonata for 2 vns., Op. 56 (1932); vn. sonata No. 1, Op. 80 (1938–45), No. 2 (from Op. 94) (1944); fl. sonata, Op. 94 (1943); solo vn. (or unison vns.) sonata, Op. 115 (1947); vc. sonata, Op. 119 (1949).

CHORAL WORKS: *Seven, They are Seven*, ten., ch., and orch., Op. 30 (1917–18, rev. 1933); *Mass Songs*, Op. 68, for ch. (1936); *Cantata on 20th Anniversary of October Revolution*, Op. 74, for orch., band, perc., 2 ch. (1937); *Songs of Our Days*, Op. 77, ch. and orch. (1937); *Alexander Nevsky*, Op. 78, mez., ch., orch. (1939); *Tale of*

Boy Who Remained Unknown, Op. 93, ch. and orch. (1944); *Winter Bonfire*, reciters, boys' ch., orch. (1949–50); *On Guard For Peace*, oratorio (1950).

PIANO: Sonatas: No. 1 in F minor, Op. 1 (1909), No. 2 in D minor, Op. 14 (1912), No. 3 in A minor, Op. 28 (1907–17), No. 4 in C minor, Op. 29 (1908–17), No. 5 in C, Op. 38 (1923, rev. as Op. 135, 1952–3), No. 6 in A minor, Op. 82 (1940), No. 7 in B♭, Op. 83 (1939–42), No. 8 in B♭, Op. 84 (1939–44), No. 9 in C, Op. 103 (1947), No. 10 (unfinished); *4 Études*, Op. 2 (1909); *4 Pieces*, Op. 3 (1907–11); *4 Pieces*, Op. 4 (1908–13); *10 Pieces*, Op. 12 (1908–13); *Sarcasms*, Op. 17 (1912–14); **Visions fugitives*, Op. 22 (1915–17); *Tales of the Old Grandmother*, Op. 13 (1918); *2 Sonatines*, Op. 54 (1931); *10 Pieces from Romeo and Juliet*, Op. 76 (1937).

SONGS: *The Ugly Duckling*, Op. 18 (1914); *5 Poems*, Op. 23 (1915); *5 Songs to words of Anna Akhmatova*, Op. 27 (1916); *5 Melodies Without Words*, Op. 35 (1920); *7 Songs*, Op. 79 (1939).

FILM AND THEATRE MUSIC: *Lieutenant Kijé* (1934); *Queen of Spades*, Op. 70 (1936); *Eugene Onegin*, Op. 71 (1936); *Boris Godunov*, Op. 74 (1936); *Alexander Nevsky* (1938); *Ivan the Terrible* (1942–5).

Prolation. (1) Division in medieval mensural notation of the whole-note (semibreve) into 3 smaller time-units (major prolation) or 2 (minor).

(2) Work for orch. by *Maxwell Davies, 1959.

Promenade Concerts. Literally, concerts at which the audience can walk about, but in modern usage concerts at which a section of the audience stands. First Eng. promenade concerts were held in London 1838 under title 'Promenade Concerts à la Musard' (Musard was the leader). Later concerts on similar lines were promoted by *Jullien, *Balfe, Mellon, and others. In 1895 Robert Newman began new series at Queen's Hall, cond. Henry *Wood. These still continue. They have been sponsored by BBC since 1927, since when majority of concerts have been given by BBC S.O. After Wood died in 1944, Malcolm Sargent became prin. cond. in 1948, but after his death in 1967 no single cond. dominated. The 'Proms', held in the Royal Albert Hall and other venues for 8 weeks from mid-July each year are in effect an enormous mus. fest., embracing semi-staged opera perfs. and chamber mus. Several orchs. take part, each concert is broadcast, and several are televised. The Last Night has become a traditional feature of Brit. life, especially the 2nd half in which the audience enthusiastically join in the perfs. of Elgar's **Land of Hope and Glory*, Parry's **Jerusalem*, and Wood's **Fantasia on British Sea-Songs*. Various other orchs., e.g. the Hallé, CBSO, and SNO, give their own series of promenade concerts.

Prometheus. Symphonic poem by Liszt. Orig. comp. (and orch. by Raff) 1850 as prelude to a setting of chs. from Herder's *Prometheus Unbound*. Re-scored by Liszt 1855.

Prometheus, Die Geschöpfe des (The Creatures of Prometheus). Ballet by Beethoven, Op. 43, comp. 1800–1 (ov., introduction, and 16 nos.), f.p. Vienna 1801, choreog. Salvatore Viganò. Beethoven used 2 themes from the finale of the ballet in other works, *viz.* 1. A theme in G major appears as No. 11 of the 12 *Kontretänze* for orch., WoO 14. 2. A theme in E♭ major is used as No. 7 of the 12 *Kontretänze*, WoO 14; as the theme of the Piano Variations (**Eroica*) Op. 35; and as the main theme of the finale of Symphony No. 3 (**Eroica*) Op. 55.

Prometheus, the Poem of Fire (*Prometei, Poema Ognya*). Symphonic poem in F♯ by Skryabin, Op. 60, for orch. with pf., optional ch., and 'kbd. of light' (projecting colours on to screen). Comp. 1908–10, f.p. Moscow 1911, London 1913, NY 1914 (this perf. used 'kbd. of light').

Prometheus Unbound, Scenes from Shelley's. Work by Hubert *Parry for soloists, ch., and orch. to text by Shelley. F.p. Gloucester 1880.

Prophète, Le (The Prophet). Opera in 5 acts by *Meyerbeer to lib. by Scribe. Prod. Paris and London 1849, New Orleans 1850.

Proportion. Conception in medieval mus. theory of relationship between vibration nos. of notes and also between their time-signatures in mensural notation expressed by fractions.

Proportionate (proportional) **Notation.** In 20th-cent. mus. a graphic method of indicating durations, i.e. instead of traditional notation, the horizontal spacing of symbols represents the intended length of durations.

Proporz, Proportz (Ger.). Same as **Nachtanz*.

Prosa, Prose. In the Christian church service, the earliest sequences (types of hymn sung to special melodies) were in prose, and this term is sometimes still used instead of sequence.

Proses Lyriques (Lyrics in prose). 4 songs for v. and pf. by Debussy to his own texts. Comp. 1892–3. Titles are: *De Rêve* (Of a dream), *De Grève* (About the Shore), *De Fleurs* (About flowers), *De Soir* (About evening).

Protest Song. Term which gained currency (first in USA) in 1960s for song which voiced feelings of protest about some social injustice, real or imagined, or about some int. event which aroused strong emotions, e.g. Amer. part in Vietnam war. Among the prin. singers of the genre were Bob Dylan and Joan Baez.

Prout, Ebenezer (*b* Oundle, 1835; *d* London, 1909). Eng. composer, organist, theorist, and teacher. Largely self-taught. Organist in Islington 1861–73; pf. teacher Crystal Palace Sch. of Art 1861–85. Taught theory RAM from 1879 and at

GSM from 1884. Prof. of mus. Dublin Univ. 1894–1909. Comp. large no. of works in many forms, ed. Handel's *Messiah*, but best known for his mus. textbooks.

Provenzale, Francesco (*b* Naples, *c.*1626; *d* Naples, 1704). It composer and teacher. Wrote first opera, *Il Ciro*, for Naples 1653. For its Venice prod. a year later, *Cavalli wrote additional mus. Became choirmaster to City of Naples in 1665 and was teacher at a Naples Cons. from 1663–75, these posts leading to a diminution of his operatic activities. Head of mus. staff at Cons. of S. Maria della Pietà dei Turchini, 1675–1701. Forerunner of Neapolitan sch. of operatic and vocal composers.

Prozess, Der (The Trial). Opera by *Einem, Op. 14, to lib. by Blacher and H. von Cramer after novel by Kafka (1925). Prod. Salzburg 1953.

Prozession (Procession). Comp. by *Stockhausen, 1967, for tam-tam, va., electronium, pf., 2 microphones and controls, 2 filters: 6 players. The players are instructed to play 'events' from other Stockhausen works, i.e. *Mikrophonie I, Gesang der Jünglinge, Kontakte, Momente, Telemusik, Solo,* and *Klavierstücke I–XI.*

Prussian Quartets (Mozart). See *King of Prussia Quartets.*

Pryor, Gwenneth (Ruth) (*b* Sydney, N.S.W., 1941). Australian pianist. Studied N.S.W. State Cons. of Mus. London début 1965. Soloist in concs. of Malcolm Williamson.

Ps. Short for Ger. *Posaunen,* i.e. tbs.

Psalm. Hymn acc. by harp or other str. instrs. But by the term is generally understood the Old Testament Book of Psalms. In Christian church services these are sung antiphonally to various chants. Verse paraphrases of the psalms are known as metrical psalms. There are countless settings of individual psalms by composers from Bach to Britten (and by earlier and later composers).

Psalmody. Study of the psalms or of the tunes used for metrical psalms.

Psalmus Hungaricus. Work for ten., ch., org., and orch. by Kodály, Op. 15, based on text of Psalm 55 in paraphrase of 16th-cent. Hung. poet Mihály Végh. Commissioned for 50th anniv. of union of Buda and Pest. F.p. Budapest 1923, Zürich 1926, Cambridge 1927.

Psalter. A collection of Eng. verse paraphrases of the psalms, intended to be sung. Miles Coverdale pubd. a coll. in 1539. The Sternhold and Hopkins coll. appeared in 1549 and was completed by 1564. Other famous psalters were those by John Day, Este, Ravenscroft, Playford, and Tate and Brady.

Psaltery. Medieval str. instr., played by plucking with a plectrum or the fingers, trapeze-shaped, and usually strung horizontally over a sound-board. Had sweet, pure tone. Can be played with bow. Tavener scores for 4 bowed psalteries in *Toward the Son* (1982).

Psaume (Fr.). *Psalm.

Puccini, Giacomo (*b* Lucca, 1858; *d* Brussels, 1924). It. composer. 5th of a line of It. church musicians. Organist at local church. Entered Milan Cons. 1880, studying comp. with Bazzini and Ponchielli. Showed bias towards symphonic works, but Ponchielli sensed his pupil's operatic potentiality and persuaded him to enter Sonzogno 1-act opera competition with *Le Villi*. Rejected by the jury, the work was admired by Boito and prod. Milan, 1884. It was heard by Verdi's publisher, Ricordi, who commissioned an opera from Puccini. *Edgar,* when it appeared in 1889, was a failure, but Ricordi's faith was justified in 1893 by *Manon Lescaut,* in which the mature Puccini is already evident in the ardent and profuse melodic mastery which distinguishes the work. Strangely, Puccini's next opera, *La Bohème,* prod. Turin 1896, was at first less successful than *Manon,* but it soon became what it remains, probably the most popular and generally beloved opera ever written, a masterpiece of characterization, sentiment, and craftsmanship. Power of characterization also marked his next opera, *Tosca,* based on a Sardou play. *Madama Butterfly* was his most successful psychological character-study and requires exceptional vocal and histrionic skill from the sop. who sings the heroine. The work was a failure at its Milan première, but Puccini re-cast it in 3 acts for Brescia 3 months later, where it was acclaimed as a triumph and has since almost rivalled *Bohème* in popularity. *Butterfly* was set in Japan and was based on a play by Belasco, who was author of the Amer. melodrama *The Girl of the Golden West* which became Puccini's next opera (*La fanciulla del West*). This was prod. at the NY Met. in 1910 but has never attained a popularity equal to its predecessors although on closer acquaintance the mus. is revealed as of very high quality. Similar re-assessment is due to *La rondine* (Monte Carlo 1917). Nothing illustrates Puccini's instinctive theatrical skill more remarkably than the success with which he achieved the difficult feat of combining 3 contrasting 1-act operas in *Il trittico* (Triptych): a thriller in *Il tabarro,* a sentimental tragedy in *Suor Angelica,* and a comedy in *Gianni Schicchi.* For his next opera Puccini selected a lib. inspired by Gozzi's play *Turandot.* But he died of cancer before he could complete the duet which was planned as the climax of the work. It was completed skilfully by *Alfano and the opera has held its place despite this anti-climax because of the superb mus. earlier in the opera and because the part of the cruel Princess Turandot is a glorious gift to dramatic sops.

Puccini lacks the nobility of Verdi, but few opera composers can rival him in dramatic flair and skill. He is sentimental but it is a sentimentality to which millions are glad to respond. His sense of characterization was highly developed and his genius for orchestration enabled him with a few notes to hold an audience in the palm of his hand. Most of his operas contain a heroine in whom there are elements of the 'little girl', and there is a streak of sadistic cruelty which also marred the personality of the man himself. He continued to develop as an artist and to respond to contemporary influences, from Debussy to Schoenberg. Prin. works:

OPERAS: *Le *Villi (The Wilis)* (first, one-act, version, 1883; 2-act version, 1884); **Edgar* (4-act version, 1884–8; 3-act version 1892, rev. 1901, 1905); **Manon Lescaut* (1890–2); *La *Bohème* (1894–5); **Tosca* (1898–9); **Madama Butterfly* (2-act version, 1901–3; 3-act version, 1904; further cuts and rev., 1906); *La *fanciulla del West* (1908–10); *La *rondine* (The Swallow) (1914–16); *Il *trittico* (*Il *tabarro, *Suor Angelica, *Gianni Schicchi*) (1913–18); **Turandot* (1920–6, last scene completed by Alfano).

CHORAL: *Messa di Gloria* in A, for sop., ten., bar., ch., and orch. (1880).

ORCH: *Preludio sinfonico* (1876); *Capriccio sinfonico* (1883).

CHAMBER MUSIC: *Crisantemi*, str. qt. (1890); *3 Minuets*, str. qt. (1892, nos. 1 and 3 rev. 1898).

Pugnani, Gaetano (*b* Turin, 1731; *d* Turin, 1798). It. violinist and composer. Travelled widely 1754–70, staying for long spells in Paris and London. Returned to Turin as orch. leader and teacher. His pupils incl. *Viotti. Comp. operas, cantatas, ballets, vn. conc., 20 vn. sonatas, 6 str. qts., and other works. A *Praeludium and Allegro* said to have been arr. from Pugnani by the violinist *Kreisler was admitted by Kreisler in 1935 to be entirely his own work.

Pugno, (Stéphane) **Raoul** (*b* Montrouge, N. Fr., 1852; *d* Moscow, 1914). Fr.-It. pianist, organist, and composer. Studied Paris Cons. Organist St Eugène, Paris, 1872–92. Prof. of harmony, Paris Cons. 1892–6, of pf. 1896–1901. Frequently played in duo with violinist *Ysaÿe. Wrote 4 comic operas, 6 ballets, oratorio, and pf. pieces.

Pulcinella. Ballet, with song, in 1 act by Stravinsky, comp. 1919–20, to lib. and choreog. by Massine. For sop., ten., bass, and small orch. Prod. Paris 1920. The mus., comprising 18 items, is a re-comp. of works by *Pergolesi, though at least one item is a false attrib. Also suite of 8 movements for small orch., c.1922, rev. 1947. The *Suite italienne* for vc. and pf. (1932) comprises 5 movements from *Pulcinella*, and the version for vn. and pf. (c.1933) has 6.

Pulitzer Prize. Prizes in Amer. journalism, letters, and mus. awarded since 1943 under will of the publisher Joseph Pulitzer (1847–1911). Administered by Columbia Univ., NY. Mus. prize (for comp.) incl. award of $500, and earlier a travelling scholarship of $1,500 was given to a student to enable him or her to study in Europe. Since 1970 mus. critics have been eligible for award for criticism.

Pult (Ger., plural *Pulte*). Orch. mus. stand (shared by 2 performers, such as violinists, playing the same part). *Pultweise*, deskwise, i.e. in order of the players' desks.

Punch and Judy. Opera in 1 act by Birtwistle, lib. by Stephen Pruslin (prod. Aldeburgh 1968).

Punta (It.). Point. *A punta d'arco,* with the point of the bow.

Punto coronato, Punto d'organo (It.). The pause sign ⌢.

Punto, Giovanni (Stič, Jan Václav or Stich, Johann Wenzel) (*b* Zehušice, 1746; *d* Prague, 1803). Bohemian horn-player and violinist. Studied in Prague, Munich, and Dresden (under Hampel). Assumed It. name 1766 and in 1768 began European travels, visiting Eng. in 1770 and 1777. At Mainz court 1769–74. Met Mozart in Paris 1778. Worked in Paris 1782–7 and 1789–99. When he visited Vienna in 1800, Beethoven wrote his hn. sonata, Op. 17, for him. Acclaimed as virtuoso of highest order. Wrote 11 hn. concs. (pubd. c.1787– c.1806), 24 hn. qts., 20 hn. trios, 56 hn. duos, other chamber works, and a book of hn. exercises (1795).

Purcell, Daniel (*b* London, c.1660; *d* London, 1717). Eng. organist and composer, brother of the great Henry *Purcell. Organist, Magdalen Coll., Oxford, 1688–95, St Andrew's, Holborn, 1713–17. In 1695 succeeded his brother as composer of incidental mus. for plays. Prolific writer of other works.

Purcell, Edward (Cockram) (really Edward Purcell Cockram) (*d* 1932). Eng. composer best known for song *Passing by.*

Purcell, Henry (*b* London, 1659; *d* London, 1695). Eng. composer and organist. Son of Thomas Purcell, one of the King's musicians. Boy chorister of Chapel Royal. Studied with *Humfrey and *Blow. In 1674 he was appointed tuner of Westminster Abbey org. and at 18, in 1677, he succeeded Matthew Locke as 'composer to the King's violins' (a str. band of 24 players). He succeeded Blow as organist of Westminster Abbey in 1679. In the following year he pubd. the superb Fantasias for strs., written for his private enjoyment and not for the royal band. From 1680 Purcell began to compose the long series of 'welcome odes' and other official choral pieces, his music by far transcending the doggerel of the words. In that year, too, he comp. the first of the incidental mus. he wrote for the London th., for plays by Dryden, Congreve, Shadwell, Brady,

Behn, etc. In 1682 he became one of the 3 organists of the Chapel Royal and in 1683 pubd. his sonatas in 3 parts (2 vn., and bass, with organ or hpd.), in the preface to which he admitted that he had attempted a 'just imitation of the most fam'd Italian masters'. In 1685 his anthem *My Heart is Inditing* was comp. for the coronation of James II and 4 years later he was involved in the coronation of William III. In 1689 his only opera, *Dido and Aeneas*, was perf. at Josias Priest's boarding-school for girls at Chelsea. In the last few years of his life, Purcell was increasingly prolific, composing some of his greatest church mus. such as the *Te Deum* and *Jubilate in D*. In 1695, for Queen Mary's funeral, he comp. an anthem (*Thou knowest, Lord, the Secrets of our Hearts*), 4 canzonas for brass, and 2 elegies, which are among his most masterly works and were used for his own funeral later the same year.

Purcell's position as among the greatest of Eng. composers was acknowledged in his lifetime, but it was not until the bicentenary of his death that this judgment came to be accepted by later generations. The work of the Purcell Soc. and of composers such as Holst and Vaughan Williams helped to rehabilitate him, and Benjamin Britten of a later generation paid him the compliment of imitation and also restored many of his works to the concert-hall, aided by the 20th-cent. revival of interest in perf. the mus. of Purcell's time in authentic style. Purcell's brilliance of invention, his sense of drama, and the 'common touch' which endeared him to his contemporaries (both musicians and non-musicians) give his mus. freshness and immediacy. In *Dido and Aeneas*, he comp. the first great Eng. opera and set a new standard of sensitivity to words and word-rhythms in addition to displaying rare depths of emotion. Yet it is in the instrumental works that the real genius of Henry Purcell dwells. Prin. works:

OPERA: *Dido and Aeneas* (1689).

SEMI-OPERAS: *The Prophetess, or The History of *Dioclesian* (1690); *King Arthur, or The British Worthy* (1691); *The *Fairy Queen* (1692); *The Indian Queen* (1695); *The Tempest, or The Enchanted Island* (?1695. See Weldon, John).

INCIDENTAL MUSIC: *Theodosius, or The Force of Love* (1680); *Amphitryon* (1690); *Distressed Innocence* (1690); *The Indian Emperor* (1691); *The Libertine* (?1692); *The Double Dealer* (1693); *Timon of Athens* (1694); *The Comical History of Don Quixote* (1694–5); *The Married Beau* (1694); *Abdelazer* (1695); *The Mock Marriage* (1695); *Bonduca, or The British Heroine* (1695); *The Spanish Friar* (1694–5). (See also *Songs from Theatre Music*, below.)

CHORAL: *Behold, I Bring you Good Tidings*, Christmas anthem (1687); *Come ye sons of art*, ode for Queen Mary's birthday (1694); *Elegy on the death of Queen Mary* (1695); *Jehovah, quam multi*, motet; *Jubilate Deo in D* (1694); *Let God arise* (1679); *Magnificat and Nunc Dimittis* in G minor; *My*

Beloved Spake (c.1680); *My Heart is Inditing*, anthem (1685); *Now Does the Glorious Day Appear*, ode for Queen Mary's birthday (1689); *O God, thou art my God*, anthem (1682); *O God, thou has cast us out*, anthem (1682); *O Lord God of hosts*, anthem (1682); *O Sing unto the Lord* (1688); *Ode for St Cecilia's Day* (1683–92); *Rejoice in the Lord Alway*, the *Bell anthem* (1685); *Remember not, Lord, our offences*, anthem (1682); *Te Deum in D* (1694); *They that go Down to the Sea in Ships*, anthem (1685); *Thou knowest, Lord, the Secrets of our Hearts*, anthem (*Queen Mary's Funeral Music*, 1695); *Thy Word is a Lantern*, anthem (c.1694).

SONGS FROM THEATRE MUSIC: *Cinthia frowns whene'er I woo her* (*Distressed Innocence*, 1690); *O Let me Weep; Turn then thine Eyes* (*The Fairy Queen*, 1692); *I Sighed and owned my Love* (*The Fatal Marriage*, 1694); *I Attempt from Love's Sickness to Fly* (*The Indian Queen*, 1695); *Fairest Isle, all Isles Excelling; Shepherd, Leave Decoying* (*King Arthur*, 1691); *Nymphs and Shepherds* (*The Libertine*, ?1692); *No, Resistance is but Vain* (*The Maid's Last Prayer*, 1693); *Man is for the Woman Made* (*The Mock Marriage*, 1695); *Music for a while* (*Oedipus*, 1692); *My Dearest, my Fairest*; *Sweeter than Roses* (*Pausania*, 1695); *Arise ye Subterranean Winds; Halcyon Days; See, see, the Heavens Smile* (*The Tempest* ?1695).

SONGS: *Ah Cruel Nymph; Fly Swift, ye Hours; The Father brave; I Lov'd fair Celia* (1694); *I Vowed to Die a Maid; If Music be the food of Love* (3 versions 1692, 1693, 1695); *Lord, What is Man?* (1693); *Love Arms himself in Celia's Eyes* (1695); *Love, thou art Best; Lovely Albina* (1695); *Morning Hymn; Now that the Sun hath Veiled his Light* (*Evening Hymn*, 1688); *Queen's Epicedium; Sleep, Adam, sleep* (1683); *Tell me some Pitying Angel* (*The *Blessed Virgin's Expostulation*, 1693); *What a Sad Fate is Mine; When Night her Purple Veil*.

INSTRUMENTAL: *Strings, without continuo: Chacony in G minor*, 4 parts; *3 Fantasias*, 3 parts (1680); *9 Fantasias*, 4 parts (1680); *Fantasia upon 1 note*, 5 parts; *In Nomine*, 6 parts; *In Nomine*, 7 parts; *Pavan in G minor*, 4 parts. *Strings, with continuo: Fantasia on a ground in D*, 4 parts; *Overtures in G*, 4 parts; *in D minor*, 4 parts; *in G minor*, 5 parts; *12 Sonatas of 3 parts* (1683); *10 Sonatas of 4 parts* (pubd. 1697); *Sonata in G minor; Suite in G major; Sonata in D for tpt., strs., continuo; Symphoniae sacrae*, viol and organ; *Trumpet Tune and Air. Brass: March and Canzona* for 4 tbs. (*Queen Mary's Funeral Music*, 1695).

KEYBOARD: Suites for hpd. (pubd. 1696): No. 1 in G, No. 2 in G minor, No. 3 in G, No. 4 in A minor, No. 5 in C, No. 6 in D, No. 7 in D minor, No. 8 in F; *Musick's Handmaid* (1689) in 2 parts (No. 9 of part 2 is *New Irish tune in G*, *Lillibulero*); *Air in D minor; Fanfare in B♭; Ground in D minor; Hornpipe in E minor; Pavans in A minor and G; Round in D; Toccata in A minor*.

ORGAN: Voluntary on the Old 100th; Voluntary in G.

Purgatory. Opera in 1 act by *Crosse, Op. 18, to lib. based on play by W. B. Yeats. Prod. Cheltenham 1966. For ten., bar., women's ch., and orch. Also opera by *Weisgall.

Puritani di Scozia, I (*I Puritani*; The Puritans of Scotland). Opera in 3 acts by Bellini to lib. by C. Pepoli after play *Têtes rondes et cavaliers* by F. Ancelot and X. B. Saintine derived from Scott's *Old Mortality* (1816). Prod. Paris and London, 1835, Philadelphia 1843, NY 1844.

Putnam's Camp. 2nd movement of Ives's *Three Places in New England* for orch., sometimes played separately.

Puyana, Rafael (*b* Bogota, 1931). Colombian harpsichordist. Studied New Eng. Cons. of Mus. and with W. *Landowska 1951–7. European tour 1955, NY début 1957, London, 1966. Dir., early mus. dept. of summer sch. at Santiago de Compostela, Sp., from 1961. Several works written for him, e.g. by Evett, McCabe, Mompou, Orbon.

Pygott, Richard (*fl.* early 16th cent.). Eng. composer. Trained choristers in Wolsey's chapel choir 1517–29. Gentleman of Chapel Royal, 1524–53. Wrote mainly church mus.

Pylkkänen, Tauno (Kallervo) (*b* Helsinki, 1918; *d* Helsinki, 1980). Finnish composer. Studied Helsinki and in Fr. and It. Worked for Finn. Radio 1942–61. Art. dir. Finnish Nat. Opera 1960–70. Wrote nearly a dozen operas in a style described as Finnish *verismo*, sym., vc. conc., and song-cycles.

Pyne, James (Kendrick) (*b* Bath, 1852; *d* London, 1938). Eng. organist and composer. Studied org. with his father and later with S. S. Wesley. Organist at Bath church at age of 11. Organist, Chichester Cath. 1873, St Mark's, Philadelphia, 1875, Manchester Cath. 1876–1908. Prof. of org., RMCM from 1893. Dean of Faculty of Mus., Manchester Univ. 1908. Wrote church mus. and Lancashire dialect songs.

Pyne, Louisa (Fanny) (*b* 1832; *d* London, 1904). Eng. sop. Studied with Sir G. *Smart. Opera début Boulogne 1849, thereafter singing regularly in London. Toured USA 1854–6. Co-director with William Harrison of Pyne-Harrison Opera Co., which gave seasons in London (incl. CG) 1858–64. Retired 1868 and became teacher.

Q

Quadrat (Ger.). Natural sign (♮).

Quadrille. Type of square dance popular at court of Napoléon I in early 19th cent. In 5 sections (4 of 32 bars each and finale), varying in time-signature from ⁶⁄₈ to ²⁄₄, the mus. being selected from popular tunes, operatic arias, and sometimes sacred works. Elgar composed a series of quadrilles for use by the band which he cond. for staff dances at a lunatic asylum (1879–84).

Quadruple Counterpoint. Counterpoint in which 4 vv. are concerned, which are capable of changing places with each other, thus making 24 positions of the v. parts possible.

Quadruple-Croche (Fr.). Quadruple-hook. Hemidemisemiquaver, or 64th note.

Quadruplet. A group of 4 notes, of equal time-value, written to be played in the time of 3. See *Irregular rhythmic groupings*.

Quadruple Time. See *Time-signature*.

Quail. Toy instr. which imitates the cry of the quail; used in 'toy symphonies'. Beethoven imitated the quail in his *Pastoral* Symphony but using normal instrs.

Quantz, Johann Joachim (*b* Oberscheden, Hanover, 1697; *d* Potsdam, 1773). Ger. flautist and composer. Began mus. training 1708. In 1718 was oboist in Polish King's orch. in Dresden and Warsaw, becoming flautist after study with Buffardin. Studied counterpoint with Gasparini in Rome, 1724. Engaged 1728 as teacher in Dresden of Crown Prince Frederick of Prussia; in 1741, when Frederick became King, entered royal service as court composer, chamber musician, and dir. of royal concerts. Added 2nd key to fl. and invented sliding tuning device. Wrote comprehensive method on fl.-playing (1752 and many subsequent edns.). Comp. 300 fl. concs. and 200 other comps. involving fl., mostly for the use of his royal patron.

Quartal. Medieval or modern term for harmony in which chords are constructed on basis of superimposed 4ths.

Quarter Note. The note ♩ as a time-value, called in Eng. the crotchet, although the Amer. usage is gaining wider currency. Quarter-note rests are notated 𝄽 or ❜.

Quarter-Tone. An interval of half a semitone (24 quarter-tones to the octave). Introduced into Western mus. in 20th cent. but poses special problems of notation. Some composers who have written in quarter-tones have built special pfs., e.g. Hans Barth and Alois Hába. Boulez, Stockhausen, and other *avant-garde* serial composers have used quarter-tones.

Quartet (Fr. *quatuor*; Ger. *Quartett*; It. *Quartetto*). A comp. for 4 vv. or instr. or the 4 singers or performers who sing or play such comps. (e.g. Chilingirian Qt.). In the case of perfs., qt. usually implies a str. qt., i.e. 2 vn., va., vc. But there are also pf. qt. (pf. and 3 bowed instr.), ob. qt. (ob. and 3 bowed instr.), etc. In opera, a qt. is for 4 solo vv. (e.g. in the last act of *Rigoletto*). The vocal qt. for unacc. vv. has existed since mid-15th cent.

Quartetto Italiano. It. string quartet formed in 1945, making début at Carpi as Nuovo Quartetto Italiano. Noted for playing its repertory from memory, each piece being most carefully prepared. Outstanding in Debussy, Ravel, and Beethoven. Frequent international tours. Members are Paolo Borciani (*b* Reggo Emilia, 1922), Elisa Pegreffi (*b* Genoa, 1922), Piero Farulli (*b* Florence, 1920; he replaced Lionello Forzanti in 1946), and Franco Rossi (*b* Venice, 1921).

Quartettsatz (Quartet movement). Title given to a movement in C minor by Schubert (D703, 1820) intended for str. qt. which was never completed.

Quartfagott (Ger.). Medieval bn. pitched a 4th lower than normal.

Quartflöte (Ger.). Small fl. tuned 4th above concert fl.

Quasi (It.). As if, almost. Thus, *sonata quasi fantasia*, sonata almost like a fantasia.

Quattro (It.). Four. *Quattro mani*, four hands; *quattro voci*, four vv.

Quattro pezzi sacri (Four Sacred Songs). Composite title for 4 short works for ch. and orch. by Verdi (1888–97): *Ave Maria, Stabat Mater, Te Deum, Laudi alla Vergine Maria*.

Quattro Rusteghi, I (The Four Rustics). Opera in 3 acts by Wolf-Ferrari, lib. by Pizzolato based on Goldoni's comedy. Prod. Munich 1906, London (SW) 1946 (as *The School for Fathers*), NY 1951.

Quatuor pour la fin du temps (Quartet for the end of time). Qt. by *Messiaen for pf., cl., vn., and vc., comp. 1940 while Messiaen was in Silesian prisoner-of-war camp Stalag 8A, where it had its f.p., 15 Jan., 1941.

Quaver (Fr. *croche*; Ger. *Achtelnote*; It. *croma*). The 8th-note, notated ♪ (rest notated 𝄾): half value of *quarter-note.

Queen Mary's Funeral Music. Mus. comp. by Purcell for the Westminster Abbey funeral on 5 Mar. 1695 of Queen Mary, wife of William III, who died of smallpox on 28 Dec. 1694. The mus. comprised two of the sentences from the burial service, which he had set at least 12 years earlier; the anthem *Thou knowest, Lord, the Secrets of our Hearts,* specially comp.; 2 canzonas for slide tpts. and tbs.; and a March originally written for a scene in Shadwell's *The Libertine* (?1692), an adaptation of the Don Juan legend. Some of the mus. was perf. in the Abbey in Nov. 1695 for Purcell's funeral.

Queen of Sheba, The (Goldmark). See *Königen von Saba, Die.*

Queen of Spades, The (Russ. *Pikovaya Dama*; Fr. *Pique Dame*). Opera in 3 acts by Tchaikovsky to lib. by M. Tchaikovsky after Pushkin's novel (1834). Prod. St Petersburg 1890, NY Met. 1910, London 1915.

Queen's Hall. Prin. London concert-hall, in Langham Place, opened 1893 and destroyed by bombing 1941. First home of Henry Wood Promenade Concerts and scene of many illustrious perfs.

Queffélec, Anne (*b* Paris, 1948). Fr. pianist. Studied Paris Cons. 1st prize, Munich Competition, 1968, finalist Leeds Pf. Competition, 1969. Soloist with leading orchs. and recitalist.

Queler, Eve (*b* NY, 1936). Amer. cond. and pianist. Studied Mannes Coll. of Mus., NY and with Joseph Rosenstock. Cond. and vocal coach for NY City Opera. Founded Opera Orch. of NY 1967.

Querelle des Bouffons. See *Bouffons, Querelle des.*

Querflöte (Ger.). Transverse fl.

Queue (Fr.). Tail. Tail or stem of a note, or tail-piece of vn., vc., etc. *Piano à queue* (Fr.). Grand pf.

Quick-Step. Lively march in $\frac{2}{4}$, also known as quick march (*c.*108 steps to the minute). Also a fast version of the foxtrot.

Quiet City. Work by Copland for tpt., cor anglais, and str. Orig. incidental mus. to play by Irwin Shaw. Prod. NY 1939; as orch. work f.p. 1941.

Quilico, Louis (*b* Montreal, 1929). Canadian bar. Studied Quebec Cons. and in NY. Début with NY City Opera 1953, San Francisco 1955, CG 1961, NY Met. 1972. Continued to sing regularly at Met. Teacher at Univ. of Toronto from 1971.

Quilisma (Lat.). Most important of decorative *neumes, something like the trill.

Quilter, Roger (*b* Brighton, 1877; *d* London, 1953). Eng. composer. Studied with *Knorr at Frankfurt. Wrote highly distinguished songs, chiefly settings of Shakespeare, Tennyson (*Now Sleeps the Crimson Petal*), Herrick (cycle, *To Julia*),

and others. Wrote opera *Julia* (London 1936), *A Children's Overture,* incidental mus. to children's play *Where the Rainbow Ends,* and some chamber mus.

Quinault, Jean-Baptiste Maurice (*b* Verdun, 1687; *d* Gien, 1745). Fr. composer, actor, and singer. Wrote ballets, *divertissements,* and *intermèdes* for Fr. theatre 1714–32, incl. incid. music for Molière's *Le bourgeois gentilhomme.*

Quinault, Pierre (*b* Paris, 1635; *d* Paris, 1688). Fr. dramatist and poet. Valet to the poet Tristan l'Hermite, who gave him literary education. Studied law. Secretary to Duc de Guise from 1665. Became court poet 1668. In 1671, with part of divertissement *Psyché,* began 15-year collab. as librettist with Lully. Also wrote verses for mus. by other composers.

Quinet, Marcel (*b* Binche, 1915). Belg. composer. Studied Mons Cons. and Brussels Cons. Teacher at latter from 1943. Works include sym., 3 pf. concs., va. conc., *Dialogues* for 2 pf. and orch., str. qt., chamber opera, and pf. pieces.

Quint. Org. stop sounding a note a 5th higher than key depressed. When on the pedal it is a $10\frac{2}{3}'$ stop designed to be used in conjunction with 16' stop, producing effect of 32' stop. *Quintadena* and *quintatön* are types of org. stop which sound not only the note of the key depressed but also the note a 12th higher. Also the 4th partial tone of a bell when it is tuned a 5th above the strike note.

Quinte (Fr.). (1) Interval of a 5th.
 (2) Obsolete Fr. name for va. (orig. ten. viol with 5 str., pitched 5th lower than vn.).

Quintet (Fr. *quintette, quintuor*; Ger. *Quintett*; It. *quintetto*). Comp. for 5 instr. or vv., or the singers or players who perform such comps. In vocal music usually 2 sop., alto, ten., and bass (there are many 5-part madrigals). A str. quintet is usually 2 vns., 2 va., and vc., but sometimes (as in most of quintets by Boccherini and in those by Schubert and Vaughan Williams) for 2 vns., va., and 2 vc. A pf. quintet is usually for pf., 2 vns., va., vc., but note that Schubert's 'Trout' Quintet is for pf., vn., va., vc., db. There are also cl. quintets, ob. quintets, etc. The customary wind quintet is for fl., ob., hn., cl., bn., but Elgar's wind quintets are for 2 fl., ob., cl., bn. There are also operatic quintets, the most famous occurring in Act 3 of Wagner's *Die Meistersinger von Nürnberg.*

Quintfagott (Ger.). Bn. pitched 5th lower than normal.

Quintole (quintuplet). Group of 5 notes, or notes and rests, of equal time-value, written to be played in the time of 4 or 3. See *Irregular rhythmic groupings.*

Quintuple Counterpoint. Counterpoint in which 5 vv. are concerned, which are capable of changing places with each other, so making 120 positions of the v. parts possible.

Quintuplet. See *Quintole.*

Quintuple Time. When there are 5 beats to a measure, with prin. accents on 1st, and 3rd or 4th beats according to whether the 5 are a compound of $\frac{2}{4}$ and $\frac{3}{4}$ or of $\frac{3}{4}$ and $\frac{2}{4}$. Famous examples are in Chopin's pf. sonata in C minor, Op. 4, Wagner's *Tristan und Isolde,* Act III, Sc. 2, and Tchaikovsky's 6th Sym. (2nd movement).

Quodlibet (Lat.). What pleases. Light-hearted comp. comprising several popular tunes or fragments of tunes ingeniously put together, e.g. finale of Bach's *Goldberg Variations,* where 2 popular melodies of the day, *Ich bin so lang nicht bei dir g'west* (I've been away from you so long) and *Kraut und Rüben* (Cabbage and turnips), are combined within the harmonic outline of the theme.

R

R. (1) Abbreviation for right, e.g. R.H., right hand, in pf. mus.

(2) Abbreviation for Responsorium in church mus. (Gregorian chant).

(3) Abbreviation for *ripieno* in early orch. mus.

(4) Abbreviation for *clavier de récit,* the swell manual, in Fr. org. mus.

(5) Abbreviation for *ritardando,* found particularly in Elgar's scores.

(6) In catalogues of works of *Vivaldi, abbreviation for Rinaldi or for Ryom (latter usually in form RV).

Raabe, Peter (*b* Frankfurt-am-Oder, 1872; *d* Weimar, 1945). Ger. cond., composer, and scholar. Cond. opera at Königsberg, Elberfeld, Amsterdam 1894–9. Cond., Kaim Orch., Munich and Mannheim, 1903–7. Court cond., Weimar 1907, curator Liszt Museum from 1910. Dir. of mus. Aachen 1920–34. Succeeded R. Strauss as president of Reichsmusikkammer, 1935–45. Chairman, editorial board of Liszt complete edn. Wrote 2-vol. book on Liszt. Comp. songs and pf. pieces.

Raaff, Anton (*b* Gelsdorf, Bonn, 1714; *d* Munich, 1797). Ger. ten. Studied Munich and Bologna. Sang in It. 1738–42, Ger. 1742–9, Lisbon 1753–5, Madrid 1755–9. In Mannheim from 1770 and Munich from 1779. Went to Paris with Mozart, 1778. Mozart wrote role of Idomeneo for him, 1781.

Rabaud, Henri (Benjamin) (*b* Paris, 1873; *d* Paris, 1949). Fr. composer, cond., and teacher. Studied Paris Cons., pupil of Massenet. Won *Prix de Rome* 1894 with cantata *Daphné.* Cond. Paris Opéra 1908–18 (dir. 1914–18), Boston S.O. 1918–19. Prof. of harmony, Paris Cons., dir. 1920–41. Wrote 8 operas, incl. *L'Appel de la mer* (*Riders to the Sea) 1924, 2 syms., symphonic poems, oratorio *Job,* vc. concertino, str. qt., etc. Wrote vc. method. Orch. Fauré's *Dolly* suite.

Rabin, Michael (*b* NY, 1936; *d* NY, 1972). Amer. violinist, son of violinist in NY P.O. Studied Juilliard Sch., NY. Prof. début 1947. Brilliant and sensitive artist whose untimely death ended int. career.

Race, Steve (*b* Lincoln, 1921). Eng. pianist, composer, writer, and broadcaster. Studied RAM. Career as jazz pianist followed by success as popular presenter of mus. on radio and TV. Comp. *Variations on a Smoky Theme* for orch., film mus., and *Cyrano de Bergerac* for radio.

Rachmaninov. See *Rakhmaninov, Sergey.*

Racket (Ger. *Rackett*). Renaissance woodwind instr., forerunner of bn., developed in Ger. in late 16th cent., when it was called *Raggett.* Had narrow cylindrical bore of 9 parallel channels drilled in wooden or ivory cylinder and connected alternately top and bottom. Existed in 4 types: ten., bass, quint bass, great bass. Ten. was 4½″ high, great bass just over 12″. During latter part of 17th cent., bass racket was redesigned, with wider expanding conical bore, coiled crook inserted at side, central bulbous bell, and new disposition of finger-holes. This instr., in effect a narrow-bore bn., is known as the baroque racket. Modern versions of both Renaissance and Baroque racket available, former with a plastic reed.

Radcliffe, Philip (Fitzhugh) (*b* Godalming, 1905; *d* nr. Dunkirk, 1986). Eng. musicologist and composer. Educated Cambridge Univ. Lecturer in Mus., Cambridge Univ. 1947–72. Composer of str. qt., songs, mus. for Gr. plays. Author of books on Mendelssohn, Schubert pf. sonatas, etc.

Raddoppiare (It.). To double. Hence *raddoppiamento,* doubling.

Radetzky March. March comp. 1848 by Johann Strauss the elder. Radetzky was Austrian field-marshal.

Radford, Robert (*b* Nottingham, 1874; *d* London, 1933). Eng. bass. Studied RAM with Randegger. Opera début CG 1904 as Commendatore in *Don Giovanni.* Sang Hagen and Hunding in Eng. *Ring* under Richter at CG 1908. Member of Beecham and BNO cos. First Eng. Boris Godunov. Equally successful in oratorio etc., singing at major choral fests. Taught at RAM after 1928.

Radical Bass. Same as fundamental bass; roots of various chords.

Radical Cadence. Any cadence of which the chords are in root position, i.e. the roots of the chords in the bass.

Raff, (Joseph) Joachim (*b* Lachen, Switz., 1822; *d* Frankfurt, 1882). Ger. composer. School-teacher who taught himself pf., vn., and comp. Encouraged by Mendelssohn and Liszt. Orchestrated some of Liszt's works at Weimar. Espoused cause of 'music of the future'. Pf. teacher, Wiesbaden, from 1856. Dir., Hoch Cons., Frankfurt, 1877–82. Taught Amer. composer *MacDowell. Prolific and attractive composer whose mus. has enjoyed a modest revival after being almost forgotten except for celebrated *Cavatina* for vn. and pf. Comps. incl. several operas; oratorio; 11 syms., incl. No. 3 *Im Walde* (In the Forest), No. 5 *Lenore,* No. 7 *In den Alpen* (In the Alps), No. 9 *Im Sommer* (In Summer); pf. conc., 2 vn. concs., 2 vc. concs., numerous chamber works, songs, transcrs., etc.

Rāga. Indian melodic type, first mentioned in 5th cent. AD. Various rāga systems have developed over the centuries. A rāga comprises an unchangeable series of notes presented as an ascending and descending scale, some notes being used only in the ascending part, others only in the descending. Rāgas are assoc. with moods, e.g. loneliness, bravery, eroticism, and with particular times of day or year, or with certain ceremonial occasions.

Ragtime. Early type of jazz, particularly for solo pf., and comp. rather than improvised. Famous exponent and composer of it was Scott *Joplin. Popular from *c.*1895–1920, when other forms of jazz took over, but it had a revival in 1970s, when Joplin's mus. was used for the film *The Sting.* Stravinsky comp. *Ragtime* for 11 instr. (1918) and *Piano-Rag Music* (1919). A *Rag* is a ragtime comp. To *rag* is to play in ragtime.

Railton, (Dame) **Ruth** (*b* Folkestone, 1915). Eng. pianist and cond. Début Liverpool 1936. Dir. of mus. at several schs. Founder and mus. dir. Nat. Youth Orch. and Nat. Junior Mus. Sch. 1947–65. O.B.E. 1954, D.B.E. 1966.

Railway Music. Many comps. have reflected interest in railways and railway engines. Perhaps the earliest is Berlioz's *Le chant des chemins de fer,* 1846, which exists in 2 versions: as No. 3 of his 6 *Feuillets d'album,* Op. 19, for v. and pf., and for v. and orch. The cantata version was written for the opening of the Fr. Northern Railway and was perf. at Lille on 14 June, 1846. The text was by Jules Janin. Other works worthy of note are J. Strauss's *Excursion Train Polka,* Honegger's *Pacific 231,* A. Butterworth's *Trains in the Distance,* Lumbye's *Copenhagen Steam Railway Galop,* and Villa-Lobos's *Little Train of the Caipira.* Britten's song *Midnight on the Great Western,* from *Winter Words,* Op. 52, is also memorable. The first piece of *musique concrète* by Schaeffer in 1948 was an assemblage of railway noises called *Étude aux chemins de fer.* There are also Vivian Ellis's light orch. piece *Coronation Scot,* commemorating the L.M.S. 1937 'crack' engine, and the delightful Amer. song *Chattanooga Choo-Choo* by Gordon and Warren. Possibly the film mus. by Britten for *Night Mail* should also count as railway mus.

Raimann, Rudolf (*b* Veszprém, Hung., 1861; *d* Vienna, 1913). Hung. composer. Wrote 15 operas and operettas, incl. *Enoch Arden* (1905), and songs and pf. pieces.

Raimondi, Pietro (*b* Rome, 1786; *d* Rome, 1853). It. composer and cond. Studied Naples. Dir., Naples royal ths. 1824–32, taught comp. Royal Cons. 1825–32, Palermo Cons. 1832–52, maestro di cappella, St Peter's, Rome, 1852. Famous contrapuntist. Wrote 3 oratorios (1847–8) to be perf. simultaneously (as they were on tripartite stage in Rome, 1852). Wrote 64-v. fugue for 16 4-part choirs, also about 50 operas, 21 ballets, and many other fugues capable of intricate combinations. Posterity, heartlessly, has preferred on the whole to attend to one work at a time, but to none by Raimondi.

Raimondi, Ruggero (*b* Bologna, 1941). It. bass. Studied in Rome. Opera début Spoleto 1964, Glyndebourne 1969 (as Don Giovanni), NY Met. 1970 (Colline in *La Bohème*), CG 1972 as Silva in *Ernani* and Fiesco in *Simon Boccanegra*). Member of Scala, Milan, Co. from 1970.

'Raindrop' Prelude. Nickname for Chopin's Prelude in D♭, Op. 28, No. 15 (1839), on unauthenticated supposition that the repeated note A♭ represents raindrops.

Rainier, Priaulx (*b* Howick, Natal, 1903; *d* Besse-en-Chandesse, 1986). S. African composer and violinist. Entered S. African College of Mus. as vn. student 1913. Won vn. scholarship to RAM 1920 and settled in London. Worked as violinist and only concentrated on comp. after grant in 1935. Studied in Paris with Boulanger to 1939. Prof. of comp., RAM, 1943–61. Prin. works:

ORCH: *Sinfonia da Camera,* str. (1947); *Ballet Suite* (1950); *Phala-Phala,* dance conc. (1960–1); vc. conc. (1964); *Aequora Lunae* (1966–7); *Trios and Triads,* 10 trios and perc. (1969–73); *Ploërmel,* winds and perc. (1973); vn. conc. (*Due canti e finale*) (1977); *Concertante,* ob., cl., orch (1981).

VOCAL: *3 Greek Epigrams,* sop. and pf. (1942); *Dance of the Rain,* ten. and guitar (1961); *Ubunzima,* ten. or sop., guitar (1973); *Cycle for Declamation* (Donne), solo sop., ten., or bar. (1954); *The Bee Oracles* (E. Sitwell), ten. or bar., fl., ob., vn., vc., hpd. (1969); *Vision and Prayer,* ten. and pf. (1973); *Prayers from the Air,* ten., harp (1974–5).

CHAMBER MUSIC: Str. Qt. (1939); *Suite* for cl. and pf. (1943); va. sonata (1945); *6 Pieces* for fl., ob., cl., hn., bn. (1954); *Pastoral Triptych,* ob. solo (1960); *Quanta,* ob. and str. trio (1961–2); str. trio (1965–6).

KEYBOARD: *Barbaric Dance Suite,* pf. (1949); *Quinque,* hpd. (1971); *Gloriana,* org. (1972); *Primordial Canticles,* org. (1974).

Raisa, Rosa (orig. Rose Burchstein) (*b* Bialystok, Poland, 1893; *d* Pacific Palisades, Calif., 1963). Polish-born sop. Child singer. Fled from pogrom in Poland to It. Taught by Eva Tetrazzini and by Marchisio at Naples Cons. Opera début Parma 1913 (Leonora in Verdi's *Oberto*), then at Scala, Milan. Sang Aida at Chicago Opera 1913, becoming member of co. 1917–32, 1933–6. CG début 1914. Created role of Asteria in Boito's *Nerone,* Milan, 1924, and was chosen by Puccini to be first Turandot (Milan 1926). Much admired as Marschallin, Norma, and Tosca. Retired 1938 and taught in Chicago.

Rajah's Diamond, The. Opera for TV by
*Hoddinott to lib. by Myfanwy Piper based on
story in R. L. Stevenson's *New Arabian Nights*
(1882). F.p. BBC TV 1979.

Rajna, Thomas (*b* Budapest, 1928). Brit. pianist
and composer of Hung. birth. Studied with
*Kodály and *Veress at Liszt Acad., Budapest,
1944–7. Settled in London 1947, studying under
*Howells for comp. and A. Morrison for pf. at
RCM. Taught at GSM 1963–7, Univ. of Surrey
1967–70. Senior lect. in mus., Univ. of Cape
Town, from 1970. Specialist in Stravinsky's pf.
mus. Comps. incl. pf. conc., chamber mus., and
songs.

Rakastava (The Lover). Comp. by *Sibelius, Op.
14, orig. 3 songs for unacc. male ch. with text
from Book 1 of *Kanteletar*. 1. *Where is my Beloved?*
2. *My Beloved's Path*. 3. *Good Evening, my Little Bird*.
Comp. 1893, f.p. Helsinki 1894. Version for male
ch. and str. 1894 (unpubd.). Version for unacc.
mixed ch., 1898. Rewritten version for str. orch.,
triangle, and timp., 1911, in 3 movements: 1. *The
Lover*. 2. *The Path of the Beloved*. 3. *Goodnight—
Farewell*.

Rake's Progress, The. (1) Opera in 3 acts and
epilogue by *Stravinsky to lib. by W. H. Auden
and Chester Kallman based on Hogarth's 8
engravings (1735). Comp. 1948–51. Prod. Venice
1951, NY Met. and Edinburgh 1953 (by Glyndebourne co.).
  (2) Ballet in 6 scenes with mus. by Gavin Gordon,
choreog. N. de Valois, prod. London 1935.

Rakhmaninov, Sergey (Vasilyevich) (*b* Semyon-
ovo, Starorussky, 1873; *d* Beverly Hills, Calif.,
1943). Russ. composer, pianist, and cond. Entered
St Petersburg Cons. 1882; studied pf. with
Nikolay Zverev in Moscow, 1885, and began to
compose in 1886. Entered Ziloti's pf. class at
Moscow Cons. 1888, also studying counterpoint
with Taneyev and harmony with Arensky. In
1890 he began to compose his first pf. conc.,
completing it a year later. In the summer of 1892
he wrote the Prelude in C♯ minor which became
his most celebrated comp. His first opera *Aleko*
was staged at the Bolshoy, Moscow, in 1893 and
praised by Tchaikovsky. It was a success, unlike
his first Sym. which received a disastrous perf.
under Glazunov in St Petersburg in 1897.
Rakhmaninov withdrew the work, which was
never again played in his lifetime. In 1897–8 he
became 2nd cond. of the Moscow Private Russian
Opera Co., forming a lifelong friendship with the
co.'s then unknown bass *Chaliapin. His first
professional visit abroad was to London in 1899,
where he played 'the' Prelude and cond. his orch.
fantasy *The Rock*. At this time he lost faith in his
power of comp., but was helped by hypnosis
treatment from Dr Nikolay Dahl, also an amateur
musician, who had many talks on mus. with his
patient. A few months later Rakhmaninov began
his 2nd pf. conc., which was a great success at its

f.p. and has remained immensely and rightly
popular. Thenceforward Rakhmaninov comp.
fluently. He worked simultaneously on 2 operas,
The Miserly Knight and *Francesca da Rimini*, both
of which he cond. at the Bolshoy where he was
cond. 1904–6. Worried by political unrest in
Russia, he moved to Dresden in 1906, beginning
work on a 2nd Sym., the f.p. of which he cond.
on a visit to St Petersburg in 1908. His first visit
to USA followed in 1909, where he was soloist in
the f.p. of his 3rd pf. conc. in NY. He returned to
live in Russia, conducting several Moscow Phil.
concerts in the 1912–13 season and completing
his choral sym. *The Bells*. In 1917 he left Russia
for ever and began a new career as int. concert
pianist, making America his base. This reduced
the time he had for comp. and it was not until
1926 that he completed the 4th pf. conc. he had
begun in 1914. The work was played 1927 but
was not, and never has been since, a success. After
he signed a letter in 1931 attacking the Soviet
régime his mus. was banned in Russia until 1933.
In 1934 he comp. one of his finest works, the
Rhapsody on a Theme of Paganini, which was
followed in 1936 by the 3rd Sym. In 1938 he was
in London to play at Henry Wood's jubilee
concert and gave his last London recital in Mar.
1939. He comp. the *Symphonic Dances* for orch. in
1940. Despite failing health he embarked on an
arduous Amer. tour in the winter of 1942–3,
giving the proceeds to war relief. After playing
in Knoxville, Tennessee, on 15 Feb. he became
seriously ill and died on 28 Mar.
  Rakhmaninov was one of the greatest of pianists,
as is proved by his recordings not only of his own
concs. but of other composers' mus., incl. sonatas
with the violinist Kreisler. The vigour and
attention to detail of his cond. are also preserved
on records. But it is as a composer that his name
will live longest. He was the last of the colourful
Russian masters of the late 19th cent., with their
characteristic gift for long and broad melodies
imbued with a resigned melancholy which is
never long absent. His operas have failed to hold
the stage, mainly because of defects in their libs.,
but recordings have enabled their splendid mus.
to be appreciated. Three of the 4 pf. concs. are an
ineradicable part of the romantic repertory, and
the syms., though long overshadowed by the pf.
works, have gained esteem and popularity. The
songs are at last being recognized as among
Russia's best. In his later years his style grew
subtler, as can be heard in the *Corelli Variations*
for pf., the *Paganini Rhapsody*, the last set of songs,
and the *Symphonic Dances*. But his masterpiece is
The Bells, in which all his powers are fused and
unified. Prin. works:
OPERAS: *Aleko (1892); The *Miserly Knight (Skupoy
rytsar) Op. 24 (1903–5); *Francesca da Rimini,
Op. 25 (1900, 1904–5); Monna Vanna (1907, one
act in pf. score).
ORCH: *Scherzo* in D minor (1887); *Prince Rostislav
(Knyaz Rostislav)* (1891); *The Rock (Utyos)*, Op. 7

(1893); *Caprice bohémien (Kaprichchio na tsigan-skiye temi,* Capriccio on gipsy themes), Op. 12 (1892–4); Symphonies: No. 1 in D minor, Op. 13 (1895), No. 2 in E minor, Op. 27 (1906–7), No. 3 in A minor, Op. 44 (1935–6, rev. 1938); *The *Isle of the Dead (Ostrov myortvikh),* Op. 29 (1909); *Symphonic Dances,* Op. 45 (1940).

PIANO AND ORCH: Concertos: No. 1 in F♯ minor, Op. 1 (1890–1, rev. 1917), No. 2 in C minor, Op. 18 (1900–1), No. 3 in D minor, Op. 30 (1909), No. 4 in G minor, Op. 40 (1914–26, rev. 1941); *Rhapsody on a Theme of Paganini,* Op. 43 (1934).

CHORAL: *6 Choruses,* Op. 15, women's or children's ch. (1895–6); *Spring (Vesna),* Op. 20, cantata, bar., ch., and orch. (1902); *Liturgy of St John Chrysostom,* Op. 31 (1910); *The *Bells (Kolokola),* Op. 35, sym. for sop., ten., bar., ch., and orch. (1913); *All-Night Vigil (Vsenoshchnoye bdeniye),* Op. 37, soloists and ch. (1915); *3 Russian Songs,* Op. 41, ch. and orch. (1926).

CHAMBER MUSIC: 2 movements for str. qt. (1889, also arr. for orch. by Rakhmaninov, 1891); *Trio élégiaque,* No. 1 in G minor, pf., vn., vc. (1892); *2 Pieces* for vc. and pf., Op. 2 (1892); *2 Pieces* for vn. and pf., Op. 3 (1893); *Trio élégiaque,* No 2 in D minor, Op. 9 (1893); 2 movements for str. qt. (?1896); Vc. sonata in G minor, Op. 19 (1901).

PIANO: *3 Nocturnes* (1887–8); *4 Pieces* (?1888); *Prelude* in F (1891); *5 Morceaux de Fantaisie,* Op. 3 (No. 2 is Prelude in C♯ minor, also arr. for 2 pf., 1938) (1892); *7 Morceaux de Salon,* Op. 10 (1893–4); *6 Moments Musicaux,* Op. 16 (1896); *Variations on a theme of Chopin,* Op. 22 (1902–3); *10 Preludes,* Op. 23 (No. 1 in F♯ minor, No. 2 in B♭ major, No. 3 in D minor, No. 4 in D major, No. 5 in G minor, No. 6 in E♭ major, No. 7 in C minor, No. 8 in A♭ major, No. 9 in E♭ minor, No. 10 in G♭ major) (1903, except No. 5 in 1901); *13 Preludes,* Op. 32 (No. 1 in C, No. 2 in B♭ minor, No. 3 in E major, No. 4 in E minor, No. 5 in G major, No. 6 in F minor, No. 7 in F major, No. 8 in A minor, No. 9 in A major, No. 10 in B minor, No. 11 in B major, No. 12 in G♯ minor, No. 13 in D♭ major) (1910); *Études tableaux,* Op. 33 (No. 1 in F minor, No. 2 in C, No. 3 in E♭ minor, No. 4 in E♭ major, No. 5 in G minor, No. 6 in C♯ minor (1911) (3 Études of Op. 33 were withdrawn by composer before publication: orig. No. 4 in A minor (pubd. as Op. 39, No. 6), orig. No. 3 in C minor and orig. No. 5 in D minor (both pubd. 1948)); *Études tableaux,* Op. 39 (No. 1 in C minor, No. 2 in A minor, No. 3 in F♯ minor, No. 4 in B minor, No. 5 in E♭ minor, No. 6 in A minor, No. 7 in C minor, No. 8 in D minor, No. 9 in D major (1916–17, except No. 6, pubd. 1911, rev. 1916); *Oriental Sketch* (1917); *Variations on a Theme of Corelli (La folia)* (1931); Sonatas: No. 1 in D minor (1907), No. 2 in B♭ minor (1913, rev. 1931).

PIANO DUET: *Romance* in G (?1893); *6 Duets,* Op. 11 (1894).

2 PIANOS: *Russian Rhapsody* in E minor (1891); *Fantaisie-tableaux (Suite* No. 1), Op. 5 (1893), *Suite* No. 2, Op. 17 (1900–1).

SONGS: *6 Songs,* Op. 4 (1890–3); *6 Songs,* Op. 8 (1893); *12 Songs,* Op. 14 (1894–6); *12 Songs,* Op. 21 (1902; No. 1 1900); *15 Songs,* Op. 26 (1906) (No. 7 is *To the Children, K detyam); Letter to K. S. Stanislavsky* (1908); *14 Songs,* Op. 34 (1912; No. 7 1910; No. 14 is *Vocalise,* rev. 1915); *6 Songs,* Op. 38 (1916).

Also several transcr., incl. *Scherzo* from Mendelssohn's *Midsummer Night's Dream* and 3 movts. of J. S. Bach's *Partita* No. 3 for solo vn. (all 1933).

Rákóczy March. Hung. march-tune dating from c.1809 by unknown composer (possibly János Bihari, gipsy violinist) and named in honour of Prince Francis Rákóczy, leader of the Hung. revolt against Austria, 1703–11. Liszt played it at recitals in Hungary, where its patriotic assocs. brought it into high popularity. Berlioz arr. it as *Marche hongroise,* 1846, and added it to his *Scenes from Faust* when he remodelled it as *La Damnation de Faust.* Also occurs in Johann Strauss's *Zigeuner-baron.*

Ralf, Torsten (*b* Malmö, 1901; *d* Stockholm, 1954). Swed. ten. Studied Stockholm and Berlin. Opera début Stettin 1930. Sang opera in Frankfurt 1933–5, Dresden 1935–44. Created Apollo in R. Strauss's *Daphne,* 1938. Sang at CG 1935–9 and 1948, NY Met. 1945–8. Notable Parsifal, Walther, and Radamès.

Rallentando (It.). Slowing down, gradually. Abbreviated to *rall.* in scores. Virtually the same as *ritardando.*

R.A.M. *Royal Academy of Music, London.

Rameau, Jean-Philippe (*b* Dijon, 1683; *d* Paris, 1764). Fr. composer, harpsichordist, and organist. Self-taught in harmony and counterpoint. Visited It. 1701. Organist, Clermont-Ferrand 1702–5, Paris 1705–8, Dijon 1709–14, Lyons 1714–15, and then Clermont-Ferrand again, where he worked on his important *Traité de l'harmonie,* pubd. in Paris 1722, in which he set out the then novel doctrines of inversions of chords and principles of chord-progression. This was followed by other textbooks on harmony between 1726 and 1752, and by his dissertation on methods of acc. for hpd. and org. (1732). He taught the hpd. in Paris and wrote many works for the instr. In 1730 he came under the patronage of Le Riche de la Pouplinière. In 1733, at the age of 50, his first opera, *Hippolyte et Aricie,* met with no success, but he persevered and wrote over 20 operas and opera-ballets, incl. *Castor et Pollux* and *Les Indes galantes.* These works, though controversial because of their novel use of colourful orchestration, bold harmonies, and use of recit., est. Rameau as *Lully's successor in the field of Fr. opera. His champions opposed those of *Pergolesi in the *Querelle des *Bouffons.* In 1745 he was appointed chamber mus. composer to the King. Prin. works:

OPERAS AND OPERA-BALLETS (+ = opera-ballet): *Hippolyte et Aricie* (1733, rev. 1742); *Les *Indes galantes* (1735); **Castor et Pollux* (1737); *Dardanus* (1739); +*Les Fêtes d'Hebé* (1739); +*Les Fêtes de Polymnie* (1745); *Le Temple de la gloire* (1745); +*La Princesse de Navarre* (1747); + *Les Fêtes de l'Hymen et de l'Amour* (1747); +*Zais* (1748); + *Pygmalion* (1748); *Nais* (1748); *Zoroastre* (1749); +*Platée* (1749); *Acante et Céphise* (1751); +*La guirlande* (1751); *Daphne et Eglé* (1753); *Lysis et Delia* (1754); *La Naissance d'Osiris* (1754); *Zéphire* (1757); *Nélée et Mithis* (1757); *Le Retour d'Astrée* (1757); +*Anacréon* (1757); *Les Surprises de l'amour* (1759); *Les Sybarites* (1760); *Les Paladins* (1760); *Abaris ou Les Boréades* (1764).

CANTATAS AND SACRED WORKS: *Thétis* (1718); *Aquilon et Orinthié* (1719); *Les Amants trahis* (1721); *Orphée* (1721); *L'Impatience* (1715–22); *Le Berger fidèle* (1728); *Pour la fête de St-Louis* (1740); *Deus Noster Refugium* (before 1716); *In Convertendo* (1718); *Quam dilecta* (c.1720).

CHAMBER MUSIC: *5 Pièces de clavecin en concert* for hpd., va. da gamba, baroque vn. (1741); *5 Concerts* for hpd., vn., fl. (1741).

HARPSICHORD: (pubd. in 3 vols. of suites in Rameau's lifetime): 1. *Prelude*, 2. *Allemande 1, 3. Allemande 2, 4. Courante, 5. Gigue, 6. Sarabande 1, 7. Sarabande 2, 8. La Vénétienne, 9. Gavotte, 10. Menuet, 11. Menuet en rondeau, 12. Allemande, 13. Courante, 14. Gigue en rondeau, 15. 2nd Gigue en rondeau, 16. Le Rappel des oiseaux, 17. Rigaudon 1, 18. Rigaudon 2, 19. Double, 20. Musette en rondeau, 21. Tambourin, 22. La Villageoise* (rondeau), *23. Les Tendres Plaintes* (rondeau), *24. Les Niais de Sologne, 25. Doubles I des Niais, 26. Doubles 2 des Niais, 27. Les Soupirs, 28. La Joyeuse, 29. L'Ollette* (rondeau), *30. L'Entretien des Muses, 31. Les Tourbillons* (rondeau), *32. Les Cyclopes* (rondeau), *33. Le Lardon* (menuet), *34. La Boiteuse, 35. Allemande, 36. Courante, 37. Sarabande, 38. Les Trois Mains, 39. Fanfarinette, 40. La Triomphante, 41. Gavotte* (with 6 doubles), *42. Les Tricotets* (rondeau), *43. L'Indifférente, 44. Menuet 1, 45. Menuet 2, 46. La Poule, 47. Les Triolets, 48. Les Sauvages, 49. L'Enharmonique, 50. L'Egyptienne, 51. La Dauphine, 52. La Laivri* (rondeau), *53. L'Agaçante, 54. La Timide* (rondeau), *55. La Timide* (rondeau), *56. L'Indiscrète* (rondeau).

Ramifications. Work for str. orch. or 12 solo str. by *Ligeti, comp. 1968–9, f.p. (str. orch. version) Berlin, April 1969, cond. Gielen; (solo str. version) Saarbrücken, Oct. 1969, cond. Janigro.

Ramm, Friedrich (*b* Mannheim, 1744; *d* after 1808). Ger. oboist. Played in Bavarian electoral court orch. 1758–1808 and was friend of Mozart and Beethoven.

Rampal, Jean-Pierre (Louis) (*b* Marseilles, 1922). Fr. flautist. Studied Marseilles and Paris. Solo flautist at Paris Opéra 1956–62 and in Orchestre de l'Association des instruments à vent. Founded French Wind Quintet 1945 and Paris Baroque

Ens. 1953. Toured worldwide after 1945 as soloist in recitals and with orch. Prof. of fl. Paris Cons. Ed. of much early fl. mus. Author of *Ancient Music for the Flute* (1958).

Ranalow, Frederick (Baring) (*b* Dublin, 1873; *d* London, 1953). Irish bar. Studied RAM with *Randegger. Successful oratorio singer and prominent member of Beecham Opera Co. as Figaro, etc. Sang part of Macheath in revival of *The Beggar's Opera*, 1920, over 1,600 times.

Randegger, Alberto (*b* Trieste, 1832; *d* London, 1911). It.-born singing teacher, composer, and cond. Cond. opera in Italy 1852–4, settled in London 1855 becoming prof. of singing, RAM, 1868, and later also at RCM. Cond. Carl Rosa Opera 1879–85, Drury Lane and CG 1887–98. Cond., Norwich Fest. 1881–1905. Wrote operas, cantatas, church mus., etc.

Rands, Bernard (*b* Sheffield, 1935). Eng. composer. Studied at Univ. of Wales, then lived in It. where he studied with *Dallapiccola, *Boulez, and *Maderna, and later with *Berio. Spent 2 years in Amer. at Princeton and Univ. of Illinois, Urbana. Member of mus. faculty York Univ. from 1974. Founder-member of mus.-th. ens., C.L.A.P. Worked in elec. mus. studios in various cities. His mus., *avant-garde* in style, and sometimes aleatory, is notable for its richly colourful sonorities. Won Pulitzer Prize 1984 with *Canti del Sole*. Works incl.:

ORCH: *Per Esempio* (1968); *Agenda* (1969–70); *Wildtrack 1* (1969), *2* (1973), *3* (1974–5); *Mésalliance*, pf. and orch. (1972); *Ology* (17-piece jazz orch.) (1973); *Aum*, harp and orch. (1974); *Serenata 75b*, fl., chamber orch. (1976).

MUSIC THEATRE: *Serena*, singing actress, 2 mimes, and ens. (1972, rev. 1977–8).

INSTR. ENS: *Actions for Six* (1962–3); *Formants 2* (1969–70); *Tableau* (1970); *déjà* (1972); *'as all get out'* (1972); *étendre* (1974); *Scherzi* (1974); *Cuaderna*, str. qt. (1975); *Madrigali* (1977); *Obbligato*, str. qt. and tb. (1980).

VOICE AND INSTR: *Ballad 1*, mez. (1970); *Canti Lunatici*, sop. and ens. (1980), and orch. (1981); *Canti del Sole*, ten. and orch. (1983); *Metalepsis 2*, mez. (1971); *Deja 2*, sop. and ens. (1980); *Ballad 4*, 8vv. and ens. (1980).

EDUCATIONAL MUSIC: Sound Patterns 1–5, for various combinations, with vv.

INSTR: *Tre espressioni*, pf. (1960); *Espressione IV*, 2 pf. (1964); *Espressione Va* and *Vb*, pf. (1969–70); *Formants I*, harp (1965); *Memo 1*, db. (1971), *2*, tb. (1973), *3*, vc. (1974), *4*, organ (1975), *5*, pf. (1975); *Response*, db. and tape (1973); *Ballad 2*, v. and pf. (1970), *Ballad 3*, sop. and tape (1973).

Rangström, Türe (*b* Stockholm, 1884; *d* Stockholm, 1947). Swed. composer, teacher, and critic. Mainly self-taught, but studied comp. with *Pfitzner. Cond., Göteborg Orch. Soc. 1922–5. Wrote 4 syms. (No. 1 in memoriam Strindberg),

3 operas, symphonic poems, concs., chamber-mus., songs with orch., etc.

Rank. Each separate set of org. pipes, particularly mixture stops.

Ránki, Dezsö (b Budapest, 1951). Hung. pianist. Studied Bartók Cons. 1964–9, and Budapest Acad. 1969–73. Liszt Prize 1973.

Rankin, Nell (b Montgomery, Alabama, 1926). Amer. mez. Studied in NY, début there 1947. Zürich Opera 1949. NY Met. as Amneris in *Aida* 1951, remaining regular member of co. CG 1953.

Rankl, Karl (b Gaaden, 1898; d St Gilgen, 1968). Austrian-born cond. and composer. Studied comp. with Schoenberg and Webern. Cond. Vienna Volksoper 1922–5. Cond. opera at Reichenberg and Königsberg, 1925–8, then ch.-master to Klemperer at Kroll Opera, Berlin, 1928–31. Graz Opera 1932–7, Prague 1937–9 (conducting f.p. of Křenek's *Karl V*). Settled in Eng. 1939. Mus. dir. new CG Opera Co. 1946–51. Prin. cond. Scottish Orch. 1952–7. Mus. dir. Elizabethan Opera Trust, Sydney, N.S.W., 1958–60. Wrote 8 syms., oratorio, and opera *Deirdre of the Sorrows* (Fest. of Britain prizewinner, 1951, but not prod.).

Rant. Old Eng. 17th-cent. dance of the jig variety. It originated in Scotland and North of England. Four examples occur in Playford's *The Dancing Master* (1657 and 1665 revisions).

Ranz des vaches (Kuhreigen, Kuhreihen). Cow-procession. A type of Swiss Alpine melody, sung or played on the *Alphorn to call the cows scattered over the mountain-side. Every district has its own version, some of which (with modifications) have been introduced into comps., e.g. Rossini's *William Tell* ov., Beethoven's *Pastoral* sym., Berlioz's *Symphonie fantastique*, Schumann's *Manfred*, Strauss's *Don Quixote* and *Ein Heldenleben*. Walton's *Façade* contains a parody of a *Ranz des vaches*.

Rape of Lucretia, The. Opera in 2 acts by Britten to lib. by Ronald Duncan after André Obey's *Le viol de Lucrèce*. F.p. Glyndebourne, 1946. Britten's first chamber opera, comp. for English Opera Group. Rev. 1947.

Raphael, Günter (b Berlin, 1903; d Herford, 1960). Ger. composer. Studied Berlin Hochschule 1922–5. Teacher Leipzig Cons. 1926–34. Works banned by Nazis. Taught at Duisburg 1949–53 and Cologne 1956–8. Wrote 5 syms., vn. conc., requiem, and much chamber mus.

Rappresentazione (It.). Representation, staged action. Type of staged oratorio, precursor of opera.

Rappresentazione di anima e di corpo, La (The Representation of the soul and the body). Staged oratorio by *Cavalieri to text by Manni. Sometimes described as first opera. Prod. Rome 1600.

Rapsodie espagnole (Spanish Rhapsody). (1) Orch. work in 4 sections by *Ravel, 1907: *Prélude, Malagueña, Habañera, Feria*. The *Habañera* was orig. written for 2 pf., 1895–7 as No. 1 of the *Sites auriculaires*.
(2) Work for pf. by Liszt, comp. 1863, arr. for pf. and orch. by Busoni.

Raptak (Rektah). A whirlwind type of dance which appears in Delibes's opera *Lakmé*.

Rasch; rascher (Ger.). Quick; quicker.

Rasi, Francesco (b Arezzo, 1574; d after 1620). It. singer and composer. Pupil of *Caccini. Sang in Peri's *Euridice,* Florence 1600, and at court of Mantua for 20 years until 1620. Almost certainly created title-role in Monteverdi's *Orfeo,* 1607. Wrote cantatas, songs, madrigals, and chamber mus.

Rasiermesserquartett (Razor Quartet). Nickname of Haydn's Str. Qt. in F minor, Op. 55, No. 2 (Hob. III:61). The story is that Haydn exclaimed in 1787 when shaving 'I'd give my best quartet for a new razor', and was taken at his word by a visitor, the London mus.-publisher Bland. This qt. was Haydn's side of the bargain.

Raskin, Judith (b NY, 1928; d NY, 1984). Amer. sop. Studied Juilliard Sch. Opera début NBC 1957 as Susanna, NY Met. 1962. Glyndebourne 1963 (Pamina in *Die Zauberflöte*). Sang with NY City Opera and other Amer. cos. Also concert soloist.

Rasoumovsky (Razumovsky), **Count** (later Prince) **Andrey** (Kyrilovich) (b St Petersburg, 1752; d Vienna, 1836). Russ. mus. patron. Admiral in Russ. navy, then ambassador in various capitals, culminating in Vienna 1792–1812. Friend of Beethoven, whose three Op. 59 qts. are ded. to him. From 1808 played 2nd vn. in his own qt., trying out Beethoven's chamber mus. for composer.

Rasoumovsky (Razumovsky) **Quartets.** Beethoven's Str. Qts. Nos. 7, 8, and 9, Op. 59, Nos. 1, 2, and 3, in F major, E minor, and C major, comp. 1806 and so called because of ded. to Count Rasoumovsky, Russ. ambassador in Vienna, who was a keen qt. player. Each qt. contains a Russ. theme; in two cases these are folk-tunes.

Rataplan. Onomatopoeic word for sound of a drum. Used as name for solos and ens. in operas by Donizetti, Meyerbeer, and Verdi (*La forza del destino*).

Ratchet (Ger. *Ratsche*). Rattle. Percussion instr. of indefinite pitch. A cogwheel is either revolved by means of a handle against one or several tongues of wood or metal, or twirled so that the tongues strike the cogs. Is used by Strauss in *Till Eulenspiegel*, Ravel in his orch. of Mussorgsky's *Pictures at an Exhibition*, and Walton in his *Façade* ballet suite No. 1. But of course any instr.

producing a rattling noise, such as pebbles shaken in a dried gourd, is a rattle.

Rathaus, Karol (*b* Tarnopol, Poland, 1895; *d* NY, 1954). Polish-born composer. Pupil of *Schreker. Taught at Berlin Hochschule 1925–33. Settled in Paris 1932–4, London 1934–8, then NY, becoming prof. of comp. at Queens Coll. Wrote opera, ballet, 3 syms., and chamber mus. Rev. and restored Mussorgsky's orig. orch. for *Boris Godunov*, NY Met. 1953. Amer. citizen from 1946.

Ratsche (Ger.). See *Ratchet*.

Rattle. See *Ratchet*.

Rattle, Simon (*b* Liverpool, 1955). Eng. cond. Studied RAM 1971–5. Played perc. in Merseyside Youth Orch. at age of 8 and later in RLPO. Founded and cond. Liverpool Sinfonia 1970–2. Other early cond. experiences with Liverpool Mozart Orch., Merseyside Youth Orch., and at RAM. First prize John Player int. cond. award 1974, leading to 2-year contract with Bournemouth S.O. and Sinfonietta. Festival Hall début 1975. Cond. Glyndebourne Touring Opera 1975, Glyndebourne Fest. from 1977. Worked with London Sinfonietta and Eng. Mus. Th., 1976. Ass. cond. BBC Scottish S.O. 1977–80, ass. cond. RLPO 1977–80. Prin. cond. CBSO from 1980. Cond. f. Eng. public p. of Janáček's *Osud*, London 1983 (concert). C.B.E. 1987.

Ratz, Erwin (*b* Graz, 1898; *d* Vienna, 1973). Austrian musicologist. Studied with Adler at Vienna Univ. 1918–22, and was private pupil of Schoenberg 1917. Founder with Schoenberg, Berg, and Pisk of the *Society for Private Performances, 1918. Also studied comp. with Webern. For many years taught theory at Vienna Acad. of Mus. In 1955 became ed. of Mahler critical edn. and pres. of International Gustav Mahler Soc.

Rautavaara, Einojuhani (*b* Helsinki, 1928). Finnish composer. Studied comp. with Merikanto at Sibelius Acad. 1948–52, with Persichetti at Juilliard Sch., NY, 1955–6, with Copland and Sessions at Tanglewood 1955–6, with Vogel in Ascona 1957, and with Petzold in Cologne 1958. Dir., Käpylä Mus. Sch., Helsinki, 1965–6, lect. in mus. Sibelius Acad. from 1966. Works incl. 5 operas, ballet, 4 syms., *Requiem in Our Time* (1953), vc. conc., pf. conc., fl. conc., str. qts., bn. sonata, and songs.

Rauzzini, Venanzio (*b* Camerino, 1746; *d* Bath, 1810). It. composer, male sop., and teacher. Début Rome 1765. Sang in f.p. of Mozart's *Lucio Silla*, Milan 1772. Mozart wrote *Exsultate, jubilate* for him. Settled in Eng. 1774. Wrote 5 operas for London and 5 for Munich, also chamber mus. and songs. Became singing teacher in London and Bath, pupils incl. Braham, Storace, Kelly, and

Elizabeth Billington. Haydn was his guest in 1794.

Ravel, Maurice (Joseph) (*b* Ciboure, 1875; *d* Paris, 1937). Fr. composer and pianist. Born in Basque region but spent childhood in Paris. Entered Paris Cons. 1889, studying pf. with Bériot and comp. with Fauré, and remaining for 16 years. By 1895 he had already developed a personal style of comp., but his unconventional harmonies offended academic ears in spite of the classical basis of his work. He competed for the *Prix de Rome* in 1901, 1902, 1903, and 1905. At the last attempt he was eliminated in the preliminary test. The ensuing outcry led to the resignation of Dubois as dir. of the Cons. He had already written several works now acknowledged as masterpieces, incl. the str. qt., *Shéhérazade*, and the *Miroirs* for pf. Though a brilliant orchestrator, several of his works were first written for pf. His outstanding achievement in orch. writing is the ballet *Daphnis et Chloé*, comp. for *Diaghilev and f.p. in 1912. In 1911 his comic 1-act opera *L'Heure espagnole* had not been a success, but was later welcomed for the brilliant piece it is. After service in the 1914–18 war, Ravel captured the savage flavour of the end of an era in his *La Valse*. Fragile health in the last 17 years of his life reduced the no. of his comps. but not the quality. To the late years belong his fascinating opera, to a lib. by Colette, *L'Enfant et les sortilèges*, 2 pf. concs., his popular *Boléro* (orginally a ballet score), chamber works, and the *Don Quixote* songs. He occasionally cond. his own works, but held no official posts and had very few pupils, though one of them (for 3 months) was *Vaughan Williams.

Ravel is conveniently classified with Debussy, but their dissimilarities are more striking and significant. He had more respect for classical forms than Debussy and was nearer to the ethos of Saint-Saëns than to that of Massenet. Satie, Chabrier, Strauss, Mussorgsky, the orientalism learned from the 1889 int. Exposition, and jazz were influences on him. Dance rhythms frequently occur in his works. His harmonies, often 'impressionist' in technique, extended the range of tonality by the exploitation of unusual chords and by the use of bitonality. His melodies sometimes have a modal tendency. Repetition, sequences, and variation are preferred to regular development. The charge that he was a miniaturist in his choice of forms can be sustained, but there is nothing small about the invention. That artificiality which led Stravinsky to call him 'a Swiss clock-maker' can also be perceived, but perhaps this is part of the price he paid for the exceptional clarity of his thought and of his scoring. He was one of the great innovators in writing for the pf. Prin. works:

OPERAS: *L'*Heure espagnole* (The Spanish Hour) (1907–9); *L'*Enfant et les sortilèges* (The Child and the Spells) (1920–5).

BALLETS: *Daphnis et Chloé (1909–12); *Boléro (1928); Fanfare for L'*Eventail de Jeanne (1927).
ORCH: Shéhérazade, ov. (1898); Menuet antique (1929, orch. version of pf. piece); *Pavane pour une infante défunte (1910, arr. from the pf. version); *Alborada del gracioso (1918, orch. version of No. 4 of Miroirs for pf.); *Rapsodie espagnole (1907); *Ma Mère l'oye (1911, orch. version of 4-hands pf. work); *Valses nobles et sentimentales (1912, orch. version of pf. work); *Daphnis et Chloé, Suite No. 1 (1911), Suite No. 2 (1913); Le *Tombeau de Couperin (1919, orch. version of pf. work); La *Valse (1919–20); pf. conc. for left hand (1929–30); pf. conc. in G (1929–31).
CHAMBER MUSIC: Str. Qt. in F (1902–3); Introduction and Allegro, harp, str. qt., fl., cl. (1905); Pièce en forme d'Habañera, vn. and pf. (version of Vocalise, 1907); pf. trio (1914); Le Tombeau de Claude Debussy, vn. and vc. (1920); sonata for vn. and vc. (1920–2); Berceuse sur le nom de Gabriel Fauré, vn. and pf. (1922); *Tzigane, vn. and pf. (1924, version for vn. and orch. 1924); Rêves, v. and pf. (1927); vn. sonata (1923–7).
VOICE AND ORCH: Manteau de fleurs (1903); Shéhérazade (1903); Le Noël des Jouets (1905, 2nd version 1913); 5 Máelodies populaires grecques (5 Popular Greek Melodies) (1904–6); 3 Poèmes de Stéphane Mallarmé, v. and chamber ens. (1913); 2 Mélodies hébraïques (?1919); Ronsard à son âme (1924); Chansons madécasses, v., fl., vc., pf. (1926); *Don Quichotte à Dulcinée (1932–3).
VOICE AND PIANO: Un Grand Sommeil noir (1895); Sainte (1896); 2 Épigrammes (1898); Manteau de fleurs (1903); Le Noël des jouets (1905); Les Grands Vents venus d'outre-mer (1906); 5 Mélodies populaires grecques (1904–6); *Histoires naturelles (1906, orch. version by M. Rosenthal); Sur l'herbe (1907); Vocalise en forme d'Habañera (1907; also version for vn. and pf.); Tripatos (1909); 2 Mélodies hébraiques (1914); 3 Chansons (1916); 7 Chants populaires (1910–17; No. 4, Chanson hébraique, orch. Delage); Ronsard à son âme (1924); Rêves (1927); *Don Quichotte à Dulcinée (1932–3).
UNACC. VOICES: 3 Chansons (1915; also v. and pf.).
PIANO: Menuet antique (1895); *Pavane pour une infante défunte (1899); *Jeux d'eau (1901); Sonatine (1905); *Miroirs (1905); *Ma Mère l'oye (4 hands) (1908–10); *Gaspard de la Nuit (1908); Menuet sur le nom d'Haydn (1909); *Valses nobles et sentimentales (1911); À la manière de (1) Borodin (2) Chabrier (1913); Le *Tombeau de Couperin (1914–17).
2 PIANOS: Sites auriculaires (1895–7, unpubd. but No. 1, Habañera, was incorporated in Rapsodie espagnole 1907); Frontispiece (1918). (*Ma Mère l'oye is for 1 pf., 4 hands.)
TRANSCRIPTIONS ETC. OF OTHER COMPOSERS: Chabrier: Menuet pompeux, orch. (1920); Debussy: Nocturnes, 2 pf. (1909), Prélude à l'après-midi d'un faune, 2 pf. (1910), Sarabande, orch. (1920), Danse, orch. (1923); Delius: vocal score of opera

Margot-la-Rouge (1902); Mussorgsky: *Khovansh-china, completed and orch. by Ravel and Stravinsky (lost), Tableaux d'une Exposition (*Pictures at an Exhibition), orch. 1922; Satie, Le Prélude du fils des étoiles, orch. 1913; Schumann: Carnaval, orch. 1914 (unpubd.).

Ravenscroft, John (d c.1708). Eng. violinist and composer who lived in Italy. May have been pupil of Corelli. Wrote 12 sonatas for 2 vns. and violone and 6 for 2 vns. and continuo.

Ravenscroft, Thomas (b c.1582; d c.1633). Eng. composer and publisher. Studied Cambridge Univ. Chorister, St Paul's Cath., London. Ed. of important psalter, The Whole Booke of Psalmes (1621), in which he comp. 55 of the 105 settings. Pubd. Pammelia (Musick's Miscellanie), 1609 (1st coll. of 100 rounds, catches, and canons), and its successor Deuteromelia, 1609, coll. of 31 songs and rounds, incl. 'Three blind mice'. Also comp. anthems.

Ravinia. Park in Highland Park, Ill., a suburb of Chicago, Ill. Venue for summer season of opera by Ravinia Opera Co., 1911–31. Singers drawn from NY Met. and Chicago Opera. Summer fest. organised there since 1936, comprising concerts, recitals, operas in concert form, popular mus., etc. with Chicago S.O. as mainstay.

Ravvivando; ravvivato (It.). Quickening; quickened.

Rawsthorne, Alan (b Haslingden, 1905; d Cambridge, 1971). Eng. composer and pianist. Began as dental student then turned to mus. Entered RMCM 1926, studying pf. with F. Merrick and comp. with T. Keighley. Went abroad 1930, continuing pf. study with E. Petri. Taught at Dartington Hall 1932–4, settled in London 1935, concentrating on comp. His mus., overshadowed by that of his contemporary fellow Lancastrian Walton, has style, structural strength, and impeccable craftsmanship. C.B.E. 1961. Prin. works:

ORCH: Syms.: No. 1 (1950), No. 2 (Pastoral) (1959), No. 3 (1964); Symphonic Studies (1939); *Street Corner Overture (1944); *Cortèges, fantasy ov. (1945); Concerto for Strings (1949); Concertante Pastorale (1951); Hallé, ov. (1958); Improvisations on a Theme of Constant Lambert (1961); Concerto for 10 Instruments (1961); Divertimento (1962); Elegiac Rhapsody, str. (1964); Theme, Variations, and Finale (1967); Triptych (1969).
BALLET: *Madame Chrysanthème (1955).
CONCERTOS: Piano: No. 1, orig. version (1939) with str. and perc., rev. with full orch. (1942), No. 2 (1951); 2 pf. (1968); Vn.: No. 1 (1948), No. 2 (1956); Vc. (1966); Ob., str. (1947); Cl., str. (1936).
VOICES AND INSTR.: A Canticle of Man, bar., ch., fl., str. (1952); *Practical Cats, speaker and orch. (1954); Medieval Diptych, bar. and orch. (1962); Carmen Vitale, sop., ch., and orch. (1963); Tankas

of the 4 Seasons, ten. and chamber ens. (1965); *The God in the Cave,* ch. and orch. (1967).

CHORAL: *Canzonet,* sop. and unacc. ch. (part of *A *Garland for the Queen,* 1953); *4 Seasonal Songs,* unacc. ch.; *Lament for a Sparrow,* ch. and harp (1962); *The Oxen,* unacc. ch.; *A Rose for Lidiče,* sop. and unacc. ch. (1956).

CHAMBER MUSIC: Str. Qts.: No. 1 (*Theme and Variations*) (1939), No. 2 (1954), No. 3 (1965); pf. trio (1962); cl. qt. (1948); ob. qt. (1970); quintet (pf., cl., hn., vn., vc.) (1971); quintet (pf., ob., cl., hn., bn.) (1963); pf. quintet (1968); vn. sonata (1959); va. sonata (1935, rev. 1954); vc. sonata (1949); *Theme and variations* for 2 vn. (1938); *Elegy* (guitar) (1971).

PIANO: *4 Bagatelles* (1938); *4 Romantic Pieces* (1953); *Sonatina* (1949); *Ballade* (1967); Suite, *The Creel,* pf. duet (1942); *Theme and 4 Studies* (1971).

Also scores for 22 films.

Rawsthorne, Noel (*b* Birkenhead, 1924). Eng. organist. Studied RMCM. Organist, Liverpool Cath. 1955–80.

Razor Quartet (Haydn). See *Rasiermesserquartett.*

R.C.M. See *Royal College of Music, London.*

R.C.O. See *Royal College of Organists.*

Re. The 2nd degree of the major scale, according to the system of vocal syllables derived from Guido d'Arezzo (see *Hexachord*), and so used (spelt *Ray*) in Tonic Sol-fa (also in that system the 4th degree of the minor scale; see *Tonic Sol-fa*). In many countries the name has become attached (on 'fixed-doh' principles) to the note D, in whatever key this may occur.

Read, Ernest (*b* Guildford, 1879; *d* London, 1965). Eng. cond. and teacher. Studied RAM 1896–1906. Founder, London Junior Orch. 1926; and Ernest Read Concerts for children, which still continue. Prof. of cond. RAM 1919–50. Author of books on mus. training. C.B.E. 1956.

Read, Gardner (*b* Evanston, Ill., 1913). Amer. composer. Studied at Eastman Sch., Rochester, 1933–7. Won NY Phil. orch. contest, 1937, with first sym. Studied in Europe with *Pizzetti and in Amer. with *Copland. Teaching posts at several Amer. univs. Comps. incl. 4 syms., opera *Villon, The Golden Journey to Samarkand* (choral), vc. conc., pf. quintet, str. qts., pf. and organ works.

Reading, John (*b* Lincoln, *c.*1645; *d* Winchester, 1692). Eng. composer and organist. Vicar-choral, Lincoln Cath., 1667, master of choristers 1670; organist, Winchester Cath. 1675, Winchester College from 1681. Wrote song *Dulce domum* (Sweet home) for Winchester College.

Real. Term used in certain special senses as opposite to tonal, e.g. in *fugue *real answer* is when the answer exactly reproduces the subject (except for a 5th displaced), the fugue being a *real*

fugue. In *sequence, if the intervals within a sequence are unaltered, the result is called a *real sequence.*

Realism. Musically this term is applied to (1) operas where the plot or characters are said to be 'true to life' (*verismo*) as distinct from remote. (2) The attitude required by Soviet bureaucracy from Russian composers, meaning that their mus. should be optimistic, easily comprehended, and 'of the people'.

Realize. To give full artistic life to mus. left by the composer in a sparse condition, e.g. to fill out the continuo bass line of a 17th- or 18th-cent. comp., to write in ornamentation, to interpret vague directions as to the manner of perf. Thus one speaks of Britten's 'realizations' of Purcell, etc., rather than his 'arrangements', and of Leppard's 'realizations' of Venetian operas compared with 'editions' by Harnoncourt, Glover, etc.

Reaney, Gilbert (*b* Sheffield, 1924). Eng. musicologist. Studied Sheffield Univ. 1942–3, 1946–52, later at Sorbonne. Taught at Reading and Birmingham Univs. before becoming assoc. prof. (1960) and prof. (1963) at U.C.L.A. Authority on medieval and Renaissance mus. and theory, particularly on Machaut.

Rebec (ribible, rubible). One of the first bowed str. instr., which probably originated in Moslem countries (as *rebab* or *rabab*) and was introduced to Europe in 8th cent. AD. It had rounded back carved out of the solid wood, with flat soundboard added. After 15th cent., no. of str. varied from 1 to 5. In Renaissance there were several sizes and pitches of rebec, e.g. sop., ten., and bass. The ten. and bass were probably played gamba-wise, held between knees. Smaller versions were known as *ribecchino* (It.) or *rubechette* (Fr.).

Rebel, François (*b* Paris, 1701; *d* Paris, 1775). Fr. composer and violinist, son of Jean-Féry *Rebel. Member of Paris Opéra orch. at 13. Music for 18 stage works in collab. with Francoeur 1726–60. Joint cond. Paris Opéra 1733–44, later becoming manager. Superintendent of mus. to Louis XV. Wrote cantatas, etc.

Rebel, Jean-Féry (*b* Paris, 1666; *d* Paris, 1747). Fr. composer and violinist. Pupil of *Lully. One of the '24 violons du Roi' from 1705. Chamber-composer to king, 1726. Violinist and cond., Paris Opéra. Wrote sonatas and pieces for solo vn.

Rebikov, Vladimir (Ivanovich) (*b* Krasnoyarsk, Siberia, 1866; *d* Yalta, 1920). Russ. composer. Studied Moscow Cons. and Berlin. Early works suggest influence of Tchaikovsky, but soon exploited whole-tone scale, new harmonies, and novel forms, e.g. in his pf. pieces, *Mélomimiques,* in which mus. and mime are combined. Wrote operas (incl. *The Christmas Tree,* 1902) and 'psychological dramas', orch. works, and many pf. pieces, incl. *Rythmodéclamations*.

Recapitulation. That section of a comp. in sonata form and its variants in which the themes, or some of them, presented in the exposition are repeated, more or less in their orig. form.

Re cervo, Il (Henze). See *König Hirsch*.

Rechants, Cinq. 5 pieces by Messiaen for 12-v. ch., one of 3 Messiaen works inspired by Tristan and Isolde legend (the others being *Harawi* and *Turangalîla*). Comp. 1949. F.p. Bordeaux 1950.

Récit (Fr.). (1) Short for *Recitative*.
(2, not abbreviation). Swell Org.

Recital. Term denoting a mus. perf. by soloists or duettists, e.g. an organ recital, song recital (by 1 or 2 singers), pf. recital, sonata recital. Orig. referred only to singers, but was applied *c.*1840 to Liszt's concert perfs.

Recitative (It. *recitativo*). Form of declamatory speech-like singing used especially in opera or oratorio and free in rhythm. Serves for dialogue or narrative (as a means of advancing the plot), whereas the subsequent *aria* is often static or reflective. In 17th- and 18th-cent. opera, especially *opera seria,* the distinction between recit. and aria was clear, but with Mozart's much more expressive and inventive use of recitative (as in *Don Giovanni*), the convention began to break up. Types of recit. are: *recitativo accompagnato* or *stromentato* (It., acc. or instr. recit.), introduced *c.*1663, in which the v. is acc. by instr.; *recitativo secco* (It., dry recit.), in which the notes and metre of the singing followed the verbal accents, accompanied only by occasional hpd. chords, perhaps with a vc. or other instr. taking the bass line.

Recorder (Fr. *flûte à bec*; Ger. *Blockflöte*; It. *flauto diretto*; Sp. *flauta de pico*). Woodwind instr. of ancient lineage, made without reed. Forerunner of the fl., but end-blown through a whistle-mouthpiece. In medieval times, the recorder was known under the Lat. name *fistula*, hence 'fipple-flute'. It had 7 finger-holes in front and a thumb-hole behind, and a beak-shaped mouthpiece. The antiquity of the instr. is hard to determine because its playing position is so like that of similar instr. (other whistle types), that contemporary illustrations are of little help. But it has been est. as being in existence in the 12th cent., although the word 'recorder' first appeared in a document in 1388. A recorder tutor was pub. in Venice, 1535. By the 15th cent. there were several sizes of recorder. Praetorius lists 8, i.e. great bass, quint bass, bass, ten., alto, 2 sop., sopranino. Thus, recorder consorts were a common feature of Renaissance mus. life. The instr. has been widely revived in the 20th cent. both as an easy instr. for children and as part of the revival in performing early mus. on authentic instr. Some modern composers

have written for it e.g. Britten, Arnold Cooke, and Rubbra. The most common size today is the descant (sop.), but there are also sopranino, treble (alto), ten., and bass.

Recte et Retro (Lat.). In the right way and backwards. Another name for the *canon cancrizans* in which the theme of a canon is perf. normally in counterpoint with itself perf. backwards.

Redford, John (*b c.*1485; *d* London, 1547). Eng. composer, organist, poet, and playwright. Organist St Paul's Cath., London, from *c.*1530. Comp. anthems and org. mus.

Redlich, Hans (Ferdinand) (*b* Vienna, 1903; *d* Manchester, 1968). Austrian-born cond., composer, and scholar. Studied at univs. of Vienna, Munich, and Frankfurt. Opera cond. Berlin 1924–5, Mainz 1925–9. Settled in Eng. 1939 (Eng. citizen from 1947), lecturer in mus. Cambridge Univ. 1942–55, Birmingham Univ. 1949–55, Edinburgh Univ. 1955–62. Prof. of mus., Manchester Univ. 1962–8. Ed. of operas and masses by Monteverdi, of Mozart's *L'Oca del Cairo*, and of works by Handel. Comp. vocal works. Author of books on Mahler, Bruckner, Berg, Monteverdi, and Wagner operas.

Redowa. Bohemian dance usually in quick $\frac{3}{4}$ time. It resembles the Polish dance, the Mazurka. See *Rejdovačka*.

Reed. Sound-producing agent (of thin cane, plastic, or metal) of various mouth-blown wind instr., such as ob. and harmonica, certain org. pipes, etc. A reed which vibrates *against* an air slot is a *Beating Reed*; one which vibrates *through* such a slot (i.e. from one side to the other) is a *Free Reed*. Reeds may be either single, as in cl. family, or double (in the latter the two halves of the mouthpiece itself being pieces of reed vibrating against each other, see *Oboe*). On an org., the *reed stop* controls pipes which have reeds.

Reed-Cap Instruments. From the late 15th cent. some woodwind instr. were made with a reed-cap which kept the reed from direct contact with the player's lips. The player blew through a slit in the top of the cap to activate the reed. Most reed-cap instr. cannot overblow and have a restricted compass.

Reed-Organ. Name for kbd. instr. using free-beating reeds and no pipe, as the *harmonium* and the *American org*. Also for *accordion* and *harmonica*. See also *Regal*.

Reed, William (Henry) (*b* Frome, 1876; *d* Dumfries, 1942). Eng. violinist, composer, and author. Studied RAM under Sauret. Violinist in London orchs. Leader, LSO 1912–35. Taught at RCM. Close friend of *Elgar*, about whom he wrote 2 books. Comp. orch. works, incl. *The Lincoln Imp* (1921), vn. conc., va. rhapsody, 5 str. qts., songs, etc. Long assoc. with 3 Choirs Fest.

Reel. Dance common in Scotland, parts of England, and Ireland, for 2 or more couples. The mus. is rapid and smoothly flowing and generally in simple quadruple time. The *Highland Fling* is a particularly vigorous form of the Scottish reel. Scandinavian countries have similar dances. In N. Amer., the *Virginia Reel,* said to be the same as the Eng. dance *Sir Roger de Coverley,* was probably introduced by Eng. settlers.

Reeve, Stephen (*b* London, 1948). Eng. composer. Worked as journalist, contrib. to jazz magazines. Studied sitar and Indian mus. 1968–9, then studied in Liège 1971–3, becoming pupil of *Pousseur. Won Arts Council award 1972 for *Poème: Couleurs du Spectre* for light projection and orch. Other works incl. *The Kite's Feathers* (1969–70) for mez. and chamber ens., *Colour Music* (1970), woodwind qt., *Mode* (1970–1), 4 perc. and 15 obbligati, *La Chasse de la flamme* (1972), pf., *Summer Morning by a lake full of colours* (1974), orch., *Ardeurs de la flamme ouverte* (1974–5), vc. and pf., *Strophe* (1975), 4 guitars, . . . *aux régions éthérées . . .*(1975–6), 3 chamber groups.

Reeves, Sims (orig. John) (*b* Shooters Hill, 1818; *d* Worthing, 1900). Eng. ten. Taught by father. Début as bar., Newcastle upon Tyne 1838, then studied in Paris and Milan, singing as ten. at La Scala, Milan, 1846, London 1846 (Dec.). First sang in oratorio, Norwich Fest. 1848 and thereafter appeared more often on concert-platform than in opera. Particularly assoc. with Handel Fests.

Refice, Licinio (*b* Patrica, Rome, 1883; *d* Rio de Janeiro, 1954). It. composer and priest. Taught at sch. of church mus. in Rome 1910–50 and was choirmaster S. Maria Maggiore 1911–47. Comp. 2 operas, church mus., choral symphonic poems, requiem, etc.

Reformation Symphony. Mendelssohn's Sym. No. 5 in D minor, Op. 107, comp. 1830–2. Written for tercentenary of Augsburg Confession of 1530 but not perf. until 1832 in Berlin. The first and last movements quote the 'Dresden Amen' and the Lutheran chorale *Ein' feste Burg.*

Refrain. That part of a song which recurs at the end of each stanza. Refers to both words and mus. Corresponds to poetic 'burden'. In popular 20th-cent. mus., 'chorus' is used as synonym.

Regal. Small portable 1-manual org. popular from 15th to 17th cents. Had reed pipes of type known as 'beating reeds' (reeds which vibrate against an air slot). Variety known as Bible Regal folded in two like a book.

Regards sur l'enfant Jésus, Vingt (20 looks at the Child Jesus). 20 pieces for solo pf. by Messiaen, comp. 1944. F.p. Paris 1945 (Loriod).

Reger, (Johann Baptist Joseph) **Max** (imilian) (*b* Brand, 1873; *d* Leipzig, 1916). Ger. composer, pianist, organist, and teacher. Organ pupil in Sonderhausen and Wiesbaden 1890–5. Lived in Munich from 1901, teaching at Acad. of Mus. 1905–6. Dir. of mus. Leipzig Univ. 1907–8, prof. of comp. Leipzig Cons. 1907–16. Cond., Meiningen Orch. 1911–14. Toured Europe and Russia as organist. Was opponent of 'programme' mus. and comp. only in 'absolute' forms. Master of polyphony and developed complex harmonic procedures. Prolific composer, chief works incl.:

ORCH: *2 Romances,* vn., orch. (1900); *Variations and Fugue on a Theme of Beethoven* (1915, arr. of 2-pf. work 1904); *Sinfonietta* in A (1904–5); *Serenade* in G (1905–6); *Variations and Fugue on a Theme of J. A. Hiller* (1907); Vn. Conc. in A (1907–8); *Symphonic Prologue for a Tragedy* in A minor (1908); Pf. Conc. in F minor (1910); *Comedy Overture* (1911); *Concerto in Olden Style* (1912); *Romantic Suite, after Eichendorff* (1912); *4 Böcklin Tone-Pictures* (1913); *Ballet Suite* in D (1913); *Variations and Fugue on a Theme of Mozart* (1914, arr. for 2 pf. 1914)

CHORAL: *Hymne an den Gesang,* male ch., orch. (1898); *7 Male Choruses* (1899); *4 Cantatas* (1903–5); *10 Gesänge,* male vv. (1904, 1909); *Psalm 100,* ch., orch., org. (1908–9); *Geistliche Gesänge,* 5 vv. (1912); *Die Weihe der Nacht,* male vv., orch. (1911); *Römischer Triumphgesang,* male vv., orch. (1912).

CHAMBER MUSIC: 6 str. qts. (1888–9, 1900 (2), 1903–4, 1909, 1911); 2 pf. quintets (1897–8, 1901–2); 2 pf. qts. (1910, 1914); str. sextet (1910); cl. quintet (1915); 7 vn. sonatas (1905); 3 vc. sonatas (1898, 1904, 1910); 3 cl. sonatas (1900 (2), 1908–9).

PIANO: *12 Waltz-Caprices,* duet (1892); *7 Waltzes* (1893); *Lose Blätter* (1894); *6 Morceaux* (1898); *7 Fantasie-Stücke* (1898); *7 Charakterstücke* (1899); *6 Intermezzi* (1900); *7 Silhouettes* (1900); *12 Blätter und Blüten* (1900–2); *10 Pieces* (1901–3); *Variations and Fugue on a Theme of J.S. Bach* (1904); *Aus meinen Tagebuch* (35 little pieces) (1904–12); *Variations and Fugue on a Theme of Beethoven,* 2 pf. (1904, orch. 1915); *4 Pieces* (1901–6); 4 Sonatinas (1905, 1908); *Introduction, Passacaglia, and Fugue,* 2 pf. (1906); *Variations and Fugue on a Theme of Mozart,* 2 pf. (1914, arr. of orch. work); *Variations and Fugue on a Theme of G. P. Telemann* (1914); *Träume am Kamin,* 12 little pieces (1915).

ORGAN: *3 Pieces* (1892); *Chorale Fantasia 'Ein' feste Burg'* (1898); *Fantasia and Fugue* in C minor (1898); Sonatas, No. 1 in F♯ (1899), No. 2 in D minor (1901); *Fantasia and Fugue on BACH* (1900); *6 Trios* (1900); *5 Easy Preludes and Fugues* (1904); *12 Pieces* (1901); *12 Pieces* (1902); *52 Easy Chorale Pieces* (1902); *10 Pieces* (1903); *Variations and Fugue on an Original Theme in F♯* (1903); *13 Chorale Preludes* (1901–3); *12 Pieces* (1904); *4 Preludes and Fugues* (1904); *Introduction, Passacaglia, and Fugue* in E minor (1913); *9 Pieces* (1913); *30 Little Chorale Preludes* (1914); *Fantasia and Fugue* in D minor (1916); *7 Pieces* (1915–16).

VOCAL: *An die Hoffnung,* alto and orch. or pf. (1912); *Hymnus der Liebe,* bar. or alto, and orch. (1914); *12 Sacred Songs,* v. and pf. or org. or harmonium (1914); also over 250 solo songs, 12 of them with orch. acc.

Reggae. Rhythmic mus. indigenous to black culture of Jamaica and originating in mid-1960s; extremely eclectic, being drawn from African religious mus. and cult drum mus., Christian black revival songs, and liturgical mus. of Rastafarian sect. Words usually relate news, social gossip, and political comment. Reggae spread into commercialized jazz field, being known first as 'Rudie Blues', then 'Ska', later 'Blue Beat', and 'Rock Steady'.

Register. (1) Set of org. pipes belonging to a particular stop.

(2) To 'register' a piece of mus. is to select the stops to be employed in its various sections; hence, 'registration', the art of selecting and using stops in playing organ and harpsichord.

(3) The part of the compass of an instr. having a distinctive tonal quality, e.g. *chalumeau* register of cl.

(4) Part of vocal compass, e.g. chest v., high register, etc.

Rehfuss, Heinz (Julius) (*b* Frankfurt, 1917). Ger.-Swiss bass-bar. and singing teacher. Member of Zürich Stadttheater 1940–52. Wide repertory of operatic roles and noted for singing of oratorio. Settled in USA. Taught at various schs. of mus.

Reich, Steve (*b* NY, 1936). Amer. composer; one of the *minimalists. Studied Juilliard Sch. 1958–61 and Mills College, Oakland, 1962–3 (comp. with Berio and Milhaud). Worked with San Francisco tape mus. centre 1964–5, then est. own elec. studio in NY. Though influenced to some degree by African and Asian mus., his works deal exclusively with very gradual changes in time. They incl.: *Pitch Charts* (1963), *Music,* for 3 or more pf. or pf., tape (1964), *Piano Phase,* 2 pf. (1967), *My Name Is,* 3 or more tape recorders, performers, audience (1967), *Pendulum Music,* microphones, loud-speakers, amplifiers, performers (1968), *Pulse Music,* for instr. invented by composer (1968–9), *Piano Store,* for store full of pfs. (1969), *Phase Patterns,* 4 electric organs (1970), *Drumming,* 4 pairs of tuned bongos, 3 marimbas, 3 glockenspiels, male and female vv. (1971), *Clapping Music,* 2 musicians (1972), *Six Pianos,* 6 pf. (1973), *Music for Mallet Instruments, Voices and Organ* (1973), *Music for Pieces of Wood,* claves (1973), *Music for 18 Musicians* (1975).

Reich, Willi (*b* Vienna, 1898; *d* Zürich, 1980). Austrian musicologist and critic. Studied with *Berg and Webern. Settled in Switzerland 1938. Wrote books on Berg, Mozart, Haydn, Wolf, Wagner, Bruckner, Mahler, and Schoenberg.

Reicha, Antonín (*b* Prague, 1770; *d* Paris, 1836). Bohemian composer and flautist. Flautist in Bonn Elector's orch., 1785–94, becoming friend of Beethoven. Lived in Hamburg 1794–9, Paris 1799–1802, Vienna 1802–8, 1808 Paris, becoming prof. of comp. at Paris Cons. from 1818 (pupils incl. Liszt and Gounod). Wrote 16 operas, 2 syms., *Scènes italiennes* for orch., octet for str. and wind, 24 wind quintets, 20 str. qts., 24 hn. trios, 12 vn. sonatas, and numerous other chamber works. Remembered almost exclusively for his frequently-played wind quintets, nearly the first of their kind.

Reichardt, Johann Friedrich (*b* Königsberg, 1752; *d* Giebichenstein, 1814). Ger. composer, cond., and writer. Court composer and cond. to Frederick the Great and Frederick II, 1775–94. Instituted many reforms. Visited London and Paris 1785 and again some years later. Dismissed from court post for sympathy with Fr. Revolution. Cond. Kassel Opera 1808. Wrote at least 12 operas, *Singspiele,* setting of Milton's *Morning Hymn,* over 1500 songs (incl. setting of *Erlkönig,* highly praised by Mendelssohn), and much chamber mus. Author of several books on comp.

Reichmann, Theodor (*b* Rostock, 1849; *d* Marbach, Bodensee, 1903). Ger. bar. Studied Berlin, Prague, and Milan. Début Magdeburg 1869. Sang opera in Berlin, Munich, and Hamburg, joining Vienna Opera 1882–9, 1893–1902. Created Amfortas in *Parsifal,* Bayreuth 1882. London début 1882, CG 1884, 1892, NY Met. 1889–91. Last appearance Munich 1902, as Sachs.

Reichwein, Leopold (*b* Breslau, 1878; *d* Vienna, 1945). Ger. cond. Karlsruhe Opera 1909–13, Vienna Opera 1913–21; dir. concerts of Vienna Musikfreunde 1921–6, mus. dir. Bochum 1926. Cond. f. Ger. p. of Vaughan Williams's 4th sym. (Bochum, Jan. 1937). Took his own life when accused of being member of Austrian Nazi Party.

Reid Concerts. On foundation of chair of mus. at Edinburgh Univ., 1839, through bequest by Gen. John Reid (really Robertson) (1721–1807), Reid's stipulation of annual concert on the anniv. of his birth was observed. Under *Oakeley the observance was widened, and *Tovey est. the Reid concerts and orch. in 1917, writing his celebrated programme-notes for them.

Reigen, Reihen (Ger.). Round dance, or simply dance. *Elfenreigen,* elf dance, *gnomenreigen,* gnome dance.

Reilly, Tommy (*b* Guelph, Ontario, 1919). Canadian-born mouth-org. player, self-taught. Studied vn. at Leipzig Cons., 1937–9, being interned on outbreak of World War II. Has transcr. mus. by Bach, Mozart, Smetana, and Chopin for his instr. Works written for him by Spivakovsky and Jacob. Soloist with leading orchs.

Reimann, Aribert (*b* Berlin, 1936). Ger. composer and pianist. Studied in Berlin with *Blacher (comp.) and Rausch (pf.). Exceptional accompanist, often with *Fischer-Dieskau. Comps. influenced by Berg, Webern, and the mus. of India. Abandoned serialism in 1967. Has set texts by Shakespeare and Shelley. Prin. works:

OPERAS: *Ein Traumspiel* (A Dream Play), after Strindberg, (1964); *Melusine* (1970); *Lear* (1978); *Gespenstersonate* (1984).

BALLET: *Stoffreste* (1957), rev. as *Die Vogelscheuchen* (The Scarecrows), lib. by Günter Grass (1970).

ORCH: *Rondes* for str., (1968); *Loqui*, (1969); suite, *Ein Traumspiel*, (1965); suite, *Die Vogelscheuchen*, (1972); pf. conc. No. 1, (1961), No. 2, (1972); vn. conc. (1959).

VOCAL: *Ein Totentanz*, bar. and chamber orch. (1960); *Hölderlin-Fragmente*, sop. and orch. (1963); *Inane*, sop. and orch. (1968); *Zyklus*, bar. and orch. (1971); *Epitaph*, ten. and 7 instr. (1965); *5 Poems of Paul Celan*, bar. and pf. (1960); *3 Shakespeare Sonnets*, bar. and pf. (1964); *Lines* (Shelley), sop. and 14 str. (1973); *Wolkenloses Christfest* (Cloudless Christmas), requiem for bar., vc., and orch. (1974); *Verrà la Morte* (Death Shall Come), cantata, sop., ten., and bar., 2 ch., and orch. (1966); *Lear*, sym. for bar. and orch. (1980); *Unrevealed*, bar. and str. qt. (1980).

CHAMBER MUSIC: Pf. sonata (1958); *Canzoni e Ricercare*, fl., va., vc. (1961); *Reflexionen*, 7 instr., (1966); vc. sonata, (1963); *Invenzioni* for 12 players, (1979).

Reine, La (The Queen). Nickname of Haydn's Sym. in B♭, No. 85 in Breitkopf edn., comp. 1785, being abbreviation of 'La Reine de France'. No. 4 of the *'Paris'* syms. and much admired by Marie Antoinette.

Reinecke, Carl (Heinrich Carsten) (*b* Altona, 1824; *d* Leipzig, 1910). Ger. pianist, violinist, composer, cond., and teacher. Pupil of his father. Début as violinist 1835. Orch. violinist but then devoted himself to pf., making int. reputation. After teaching in Cologne, Barmen, and Breslau, settled in Leipzig, becoming cond. of Gewandhaus Orch. 1860–95 and prof. of pf. and comp. at Cons. 1860–92, dir. 1892–1902. Wrote 5 operas, oratorio, cantatas, 3 syms., 4 pf. concs., harp conc., much chamber mus., and pf. pieces. Wrote over 40 cadenzas for pf. concs. by other composers.

Reiner, Fritz (*b* Budapest, 1888; *d* NY, 1963). Hung.-born cond. Studied Budapest Acad. and also graduated in law at Univ. Chorusmaster Budapest Opera 1909. Cond. Budapest Volksoper 1911. Chief cond., Dresden Opera 1914–22. Cond. Cincinnati S.O. 1922–31. Head of orch. and opera depts., Curtis Institute, Penn., 1931–41. Cond., Pittsburgh S.O. 1938–48. NY Met. 1949–53. Cond., Chicago S.O. 1953–63. London début with LSO, 1924. CG 1936–7. Famed interpreter of R. Strauss, Wagner, Bartók.

Reiner, Karel (*b* Žatec, 1910; *d* Prague, 1979). Cz. composer and pianist. Studied in Prague, and comp. privately with A. *Hába (1929–30) and

Suk (1930–1). Pianist specializing in contemporary mus., 1931–8, 1945–7; worked at *avant-garde* th. in Prague 1935–8. Also critic and ed. of mus. magazines. Holder of govt. posts 1951–70. Under influence of Hába experimented in quarter-tone writing, later adopting free atonal style. Prolific composer, works incl. sym., pf. conc., vn. conc., 3 pf. sonatas, str. qts., db. sonata, and over 250 other chamber comps.

Reinhardt, Delia (*b* Elberfeld, 1892; *d* Arlesheim, 1974). Ger. sop. Début Wrocław 1913. Munich Opera 1917–24, Berlin Opera 1924–32. Sang at CG 1924–9, NY Met. 1922–4. A famous Oktavian in *Der Rosenkavalier*, also won acclaim for her Eva, Pamina, and Desdemona.

Reinhardt, Django (Jean Baptiste) (*b* Liberchies, 1910; *d* Fontainebleau, 1953). Belg. jazz guitarist. Burned in fire 1928, mutilation of left hand causing him to devise new fingering method. Worked with the singer Jean Sablon and the violinist Stephane *Grappelli. Founder-member with Grappelli of Quintet du Hot Club de France, 1934. Visited London 1946 and toured USA as soloist with *Ellington's orch. Can claim to have been first really great European jazz musician.

Reining, Maria (*b* Vienna, 1903). Austrian sop. Vienna Opera 1931–3, 1937–55. CG début 1938 (Elsa). Toscanini's choice for Eva in Salzburg 1937 *Meistersinger*. Famous for Strauss roles of Marschallin, Arabella, and Ariadne. Chicago 1938.

Reinken (Reincken), **Johann Adam** (Jan Adams) (*b* Wilshausen, Alsace, 1623; *d* Hamburg, 1722). Ger. organist and composer. Pupil of Scheidemann. Bach, while at Lüneburg 1700–3, several times walked to Hamburg to hear Reinken play at St Catherine's, where he had been organist since 1663. Was still active as organist at age 99.

Reiss, Albert (*b* Berlin, 1870; *d* Nice, 1940). Ger. ten. Orig. actor until Pollini discovered his vocal ability in 1897. Member of NY Met. co. 1901–20. CG 1902–5, 1924–9. One of finest interpreters of David in *Die Meistersinger* and of Mime in *Der Ring des Nibelungen*. Created Nick in *La fanciulla del West*, 1910.

Reizenstein, Franz (*b* Nuremberg, 1911; *d* London, 1968). Ger.-born composer, pianist, and cond. Studied in Berlin with *Hindemith. Settled in London 1934, pupil of *Vaughan Williams at RCM. Taught at RAM from 1958, RMCM (pf.) from 1965. Works incl. 2 radio operas, oratorio *Genesis*, cantata *Voices of Night*, 2 pf. concs., 2 vn. concs., vc. conc., much chamber mus. Frequently played in various chamber ens. Composed 2 of best *Hoffnung concert *pastiches*, *Let's Fake an Opera* and *Concerto popolare* (both 1958).

Rejdovačka or **Rejdovák.** Bohemian dance in duple time, somewhat like the Polka but considered to be a variant of the *Redowa.

Rejoice in the Lord Alway. Anthem by H. Purcell known as *Bell Anthem.

Rektah. See *Raptak*.

Relâche (theatrical term denoting 'No show' or 'Theatre closed'). 'Ballet instantanéiste' in 2 acts and cinematographic entr'acte by René Clair, with music by *Satie to lib. by F. Picabia, choreog. Börlin. Prod. Paris 1924.

Related. Term used for one key's harmonic distance from, or closeness to, another. 'Related keys' is an unspecific term, since all keys are related in some way.

Relative. Term used to indicate connection between a major and a minor key having same key signature, e.g. A minor is the *relative minor* of C major, and C major the *relative major* of A minor.

Remedios, Alberto (*b* Liverpool, 1935). Eng. tenor. Studied RCM. Opera début 1957 at SW (Tinca in *Il tabarro*). CG début 1965 as Dimitri in *Boris Godunov*. Scored major success as Walther in *The Mastersingers* at SW 1968, under *Goodall. Frankfurt Opera 1968–70. Sang Siegmund and Siegfried in SW *Ring* cycles cond. by Goodall, with Rita *Hunter as Brünnhilde. NY Met. début 1976 (Strauss's Bacchus).

Reményi (orig. Hoffmann), **Eduard** (*b* Miscolcz, Hung., 1828; *d* San Francisco, 1898). Hung. violinist. Studied at Vienna Cons. 1842–5. Début Pest 1846, London 1848. Was in USA 1848–52. Toured Europe 1852–3 with Brahms as accompanist. Friend of Liszt at Weimar. Visited London 1854, becoming court solo violinist to Queen Victoria 1854–9. Austrian court violinist, 1860. Many world tours. Wrote vn. conc. and other pieces. The 'gipsy' element in some of Brahms's music is probably attributable to his time with Reményi. Died while playing in a concert.

Remettre (Fr.). To put back. The imperative *remettez* in Fr. org. mus. means to bring into use some stop that has been temporarily out of action.

Remoortel, Edouard van (*b* Brussels, 1926; *d* Paris, 1977). Belg. cond. Studied Brussels Cons. 1945–9, Geneva Cons., and with Josef Krips.

Chief cond., Belg. Nat. Orch. 1951. Cond. St Louis S.O. 1958–62. Monte Carlo Opera 1965–9.

Renaissance (Fr., 'rebirth'). In mus. parlance, the Renaissance period is that between 'medieval' and 'baroque', i.e. from early 15th to early 17th cents.

Renard (The Fox). 1-act *histoire burlesque chantée et jouée* (burlesque in song and dance) by Stravinsky to his own lib. after Russ. folk-tales in Fr. trans. by C. F. Ramuz. Comp. 1915–16. Prod. Paris 1922, NY 1923.

Renaud, Maurice (*b* Bordeaux, 1861; *d* Paris, 1933). Fr. bar. Studied Paris and Brussels. Opera début Brussels 1883. Member Brussels Opera 1883–90, Paris 1890–1902, CG 1897–1904, NY Manhattan Opera 1906–10, Met. 1910–12. Created several Wagner roles in Fr. Fine actor and master of make-up.

Renn, Samuel (*b* Kedleston, Derbyshire, 1786; *d* Manchester, 1845). Eng. organ-builder. Apprenticed *c*. 1800 to his uncle James Davis and became his foreman 1808, supervising many installations. On Davis's retirement, Renn took over his Lancashire business and traded as Renn & Boston. Built 100 organs 1822–45. By standardizing dimensions of pipes etc., he reduced costs. Built Chester Cath. organ 1829 and St Philip's, Salford. His nephew James Kirtland took over business when Renn died, being joined in 1846 by F. W. Jardine. The title Jardine & Co. was adopted 1867 and the firm survived until 1976.

Rennert, Günther (*b* Essen, 1911; *d* Salzburg, 1978). Ger. producer and intendant. Film producer 1933. Worked in opera, at Felsenstein's prompting, at Wuppertal, Frankfurt, and Mainz 1935–9, Königsberg 1939–42, Berlin 1942–4, Munich 1945. Intendant, Hamburg Opera 1945–56, making it leading Ger. co. of its day and staged such 20th cent. operas as *Peter Grimes*, *Wozzeck*, *Lulu*, and *The Rake's Progress*. Artistic counsellor and head of prod., Glyndebourne 1959–67. Guest producer CG, NY Met., and other leading opera houses.

Rè Pastore, Il (The Shepherd King). *Dramma per musica* in 2 acts (K208) by Mozart to lib. by Metastasio. Prod. Salzburg 1775, London 1954. Lib. also used by Hasse, Gluck, and several others.

Repeat Marks (for passages).

:‖ means return to :‖ or, if that does not occur, to the beginning of the piece.	D.C. or *Da Capo*, literally 'From the head', i.e. return to the beginning.	D.S. or *Dal Segno*, i.e. from the sign, meaning the return to the mark :§:.	A.S. (rare) or *Al Segno*, i.e. to the sign. Usually the expression is *D.C. al Segno e poi la Coda*, i.e. 'From the beginning to the :§: and then the Coda'.	*Bis* means perform the passage twice.

To avoid needless writing or engraving (especially in orchestral mus.) the repetition of a short passage is often indicated as below:

Sometimes when a section is marked to be repeated it ends in a way suitable for the return to the beginning, and, having been repeated, ends in a way suitable to proceed to the next section (or to close the whole composition if nothing more follows). The two endings are then shown thus:

Or instead of the '1' there may be used the expression '1ma Volta', or 'Prima Volta', or '1st Time'.

Instead of the '2' there may be used the expression '2da Volta', or 'Seconda Volta', or '2nd Time'.

When a return to the opening of the piece, or of some section of it, is indicated but only a part is to be repeated and then the piece brought to an end, the word *Fine* (end) shows where to stop.

For instance, a Minuet is often followed by another Minuet called ★Trio, after which the first Minuet is to be repeated and then an end to be made. In this case the word 'Fine' is placed at the end of the first Minuet to indicate that this is the place to conclude when performing the repetition.

Repeat Marks (for notes).

There is a 'catch' in (c) and (d), the convention not being quite logical. In (c) (3 examples are given) the time-value to be filled is that of *one* of the notes shown (in this case half-note); in (d) the time-value to be filled is that of *both* of the notes shown (in this case eighth notes).

Note. If *Tremolo* (or *Trem.*) is added to any of the above or similar signs the notes concerned should be repeated very rapidly and without any attention to the exact number of repetitions attained during the time-value available.

Répétiteur (Fr.; It. *maestro collaboratore*). Rehearser. Member of mus. staff of opera house who coaches singers in their roles and also sometimes acts as chorusmaster, and prompter in perfs. Word is generally used in Eng., otherwise 'coach'. Many distinguished opera conds. have learned their craft as *répétiteurs*. 'Repet' is orch. players' term for the inside 1st vn. next to the leader.

Répétition (Fr.). Repetition, i.e. Rehearsal. The *répétition générale* is final dress rehearsal.

Repiano. See *Ripieno*.

Reports, rapports (from Fr. *rapporter,* to carry back). In 17th-cent. mus. parlance, 'report' was equivalent of 'imitation'. It meant the re-introduction, by one v. or part, of a melodic phrase just heard from another.

In the Scottish Psalter of 1635 some tunes are

headed 'Heere are some Psalmes in Reports'. These are subjected to motet or anthem-like treatment.

Reprise (Fr.). Repeat. In comp., a return to the first section after an intervening and contrasting section. In the works of Rameau, Couperin, etc., the term means a short refrain at the end of a movement and intended to be repeated.

Reproducing Piano. See *Pianola*.

Requiem. The R. C. Mass for the Dead (Lat. *Missa pro defunctis*) beginning 'Requiem aeternam' (Rest eternal). Text follows that of normal Mass but with Gloria and Credo omitted and Dies Irae added. There are many mus. settings, from the traditional plainsong to elaborate versions more suitable for concert perf. than for liturgical use, e.g. those by Berlioz and Verdi. Other notable settings are by Palestrina, Mozart (incomplete), Fauré, and Dvořák. A typical disposition of the text in these large settings is: 1. *Requiem aeternam*; *Kyrie eleison*; 2. *Dies Irae* (Day of Wrath) divided into *Tuba mirum* (Hark, the trumpet), *Liber scriptus* (A book is written), *Quid sum miser* (How wretched am I), *Rex tremendae* (King of glory), *Recordare* (Remember), *Ingemisco* (Sadly groaning), *Confutatis* (From the accursed), *Lacrimosa* (Lamentation); 3. *Domine Jesu Christe* (Lord Jesus Christ); 4. *Sanctus* (Holy); 5. *Agnus Dei* (Lamb of God); 6. *Lux aeterna* (Eternal light); 7. *Libera me* (Deliver me). This is Verdi's scheme: there are several variations of it. Not all Requiem settings follow the Lat. text. Brahms's *Ein *Deutsches Requiem* uses texts from the Ger. Bible. Delius's *Requiem* is a setting of a text by H. Simon and was described as 'pagan'. Hindemith's setting of Whitman's poem 'When Lilacs Last in the Dooryard Bloom'd' is of the character of a Requiem. Britten's *War Requiem* uses the Lat. Mass interspersed with poems by Wilfred Owen. Geoffrey Burgon's *Requiem* also uses several sources. The term is occasionally used in other contexts as in Britten's *Sinfonia da Requiem* for orch.

Rescue opera. Type of opera, or *opéra comique*, popular in Fr. after the Revolution, in which the hero or heroine is saved from some dire fate by human heroism. The most famous rescue opera is Beethoven's *Fidelio* (1805), based on a real-life incident previously used as libretto by *Gaveaux in 1798 (*Léonore, ou l'amour conjugal*).

Resnik, Regina (*b* NY, 1922). Amer. mez. Studied NY with Rosalie Miller. Concert début as sop. Brooklyn Acad. of Mus. 1942, opera début 1942 NY (Lady Macbeth). NY City Opera 1944, joined Met. 1944. Guest appearances San Francisco, Chicago, and Bayreuth (Sieglinde 1953). Changed to mez., 1955. CG début 1957 (Carmen). Interpreter of Amneris, Carmen, and Klytemnestra. Début as opera dir., Hamburg 1971 (*Carmen*).

Resolution. The satisfactory following of a discordant chord (or of the discordant note in such a chord) with a concord or less acute discord.

Resoluto, risoluto (It.). Resolute.

Resonance. (1) Sympathetic vibration of bodies capable of producing sounds as soon as a pitch similar to that of the body or one of its overtones is heard.
(2) The rebound of vibration-waves from a solid structure such as walls of a hall or church.
(3) Transmission of vibrations from the str. of a str. instr. to a sounding-board.

Respighi, Ottorino (*b* Bologna, 1879; *d* Rome, 1936). It. composer, cond., str.-player, pianist, and teacher. Studied vn. and comp. in Bologna, 1891–1901. Went to St Petersburg 1900 as first va. in opera orch. and from 1901 studied with *Rimsky-Korsakov, then in Berlin with *Bruch, 1902. From 1903 to 1908 pursued career as violinist and violist and was pianist at Berlin singing-sch. 1908–9. Prof. of comp. at Liceo di S. Cecilia, Rome, 1913; dir. 1923–5. His mus., though based on classical forms, was influenced by the brighter colours of Rimsky-Korsakov and Strauss, and his symphonic poems are notable for their brilliant and luscious scoring. In his operas he reacted against Puccinian 'realism', but they are more impressive orchestrally than vocally. Some of his most tender and exquisite work is to be found in his shorter vocal pieces. Prin. works:

OPERAS: *Re Enzo* (1905); *Semirama* (1910); *Belfagor* (1921–2); *La campana sommersa* (The Sunken Bell) (1923–7); *Maria Egiziaca* (1929–32); *La Fiamma* (1930–3); *Lucrezia* (1935).

BALLET: *La *Boutique fantasque* (The Fantastic Toyshop) adapted from mus. by Rossini (1919).

ORCH: *Notturno* (1905); *Sinfonia drammatica* (1913–14); *Fountains of Rome* (*Fontane di Roma*) (1914–16); *Old Airs and Dances for Lute,* transcr. for orch., 1st series (1917), 2nd series (1924); *Pines of Rome* (*Pini di Roma*) (1923–4); *Rossiniana* (from Rossini pf. pieces) (1925); *Vetrate di Chiesa* (Church Windows), 4 symphonic impressions (1925); *Trittico Botticelliano* (1927); *The *Birds* (*Gli uccelli*) (1927); *Feste Romane* (Roman Festivals) (1928).

CONCERTOS etc.: Pf. conc. (1902); *Concerto in the Old Style,* vn. (1908); *Concerto Gregoriano,* vn. (1921); *Adagio con variazioni,* vc. (1920); conc. for ob., hn., vn., db., pf., and str. (1933).

VOICE AND ORCH: *Aretusa,* mez. and orch. (1911); *La primavera,* soloists, ch., and orch. (1918–9); *Il Tramonto,* v. and str. qt. (1914); *Deità silvane,* sop. and pf. (1917), high v. and chamber ens. (1925); *Lauda per la natività del Signore,* sop., cont., ten., ch., orch. (1928–30).

CHAMBER MUSIC: Str. Qt. (1907); vn. sonata (1917); Doric str. qt. (1924).

TRANSCRIPTIONS: Monteverdi: *Orfeo,* (1935); *Lamento d'Arianna,* (1908); Marcello: *Didone,* cantata, (1935); Rossini: *Soirées musicales* for ballet

La Boutique fantasque, (1919); J. S. Bach: *Prelude and Fugue* in D, for orch. (1930); 3 Organ Chorals, for orch. (1931); *Passacaglia* in C minor, for orch. (1934); Vitali: *Chaconne,* for vn., str., org. (1909).

Responses. In Anglican church, the replies of the choir (or congregation) to the versicles of the priest. Usually in plainsong. Tallis, Byrd, Gibbons, etc. wrote superb harmonized versions.

Responsorio. Type of motet in which a soloist and the choir sing responsively—in Eng. a variety of 'Solo Anthem'.

Rest. (1) Musical silence.
(2) Notation of absence of sound in performer's part for a length of time corresponding to a given number of beats or measures, e.g. 4 measures' rest or an 8th-note rest. Notation of rests is as shown:

The ○ rest hangs down; the ♩ rest remains on the surface. (Imagine the rest of greater value is the heavier.)
The ♩ rest (▮) turns to the right (Mnemonic: cRotchet—Right; or quaRter Note—Right); the rest (ɤ) turns to the left.
In addition to the above there is the Double-note rest, occupying the whole space between two lines— ▬.
Also, the Whole-note rest is used as a whole-measure rest, irrespective of the actual time-value of the measure.
A silence of several measures is often indicated thus (or in some similar way):

```
        15                    15
┌─────────────────┐   ┌─────────────────┐
├────────■────────┤   ├──────▬▬▬────────┤
└─────────────────┘   └─────────────────┘
```

Rests can be dotted and doubly dotted, as notes are, and with the same effect: this, however, is less commonly done.
See also *Note values.*

Restez (Fr.). Remain, i.e. linger on a note rather than hurry off it; in str. mus., remain in the same position for the duration of a passage.

Resultant Bass. Org. stop; same as *Quint.

Resultant Tone. When 2 loud notes are heard together they produce a 3rd sound, the resultant tone, corresponding to the difference between the 2 vibration nos.: this (low in pitch) is called a 'difference tone'. They also produce a 4th sound, high and faint, corresponding to the sum of the 2 vibration numbers. This is a 'summation tone'.

Resurrection Symphony. Sub-title of *Mahler's Sym. No 2 in C minor (1888–94, rev. 1910)

because finale is setting for sop. and alto soloists, ch., and orch. of the 'Resurrection' (*Aufersteh'n*) chorale by Klopstock (1724–1803).

Retablo de Maese Pedro, El (Falla). See *Master Peter's Puppet Show.*

Retardando (It.). Same as *Ritardando.

Retardation. In harmony, the same as *suspension, but with the discord resolved by rising a degree.

Retenant; retenu (Fr.). Holding back; held back (immediately, like *ritenuto, not gradually, like *rallentando).

Rethberg (orig. Sättler), **Elisabeth** (orig. Lisbeth) (*b* Schwarzenburg, 1894; *d* NY, 1976). Ger.-born sop. (later Amer. citizen). Studied Dresden Cons. (pf., later turned to singing). Début Dresden 1915 in *Zigeunerbaron*. Début NY Met. 1922, staying with co. until 1942, CG 1925, 1934–9. Created title-role in Strauss's *Die ägyptische Helena,* Dresden 1928. A notable Aida, Marschallin, Elsa, and Sieglinde. Many concert appearances. Retired 1942.

Réti, Rudolph (*b* Užice, Serbia, 1885; *d* Montclair, NJ, 1957). Serbian-born musicologist, pianist, and composer. Studied Vienna Cons. One of founders of I.S.C.M., Salzburg, 1922. Settled in USA 1938. Wrote opera, orch. mus., and other pieces, but best known for books *The Thematic Process in Music* (NY, 1951) and *Tonality, Atonality, Pantonality* (NY, 1958). Gave f.p. of Schoenberg's *3 Piano Pieces,* Op. 11, in 1911.

Return of Lemminkäinen (Sibelius). See *Lemminkäinen Legends.*

Reubke, Julius (*b* Hausneindorf, 1834; *d* Pillnitz, 1858). Ger. pianist and composer, son of org.-builder Adolf Reubke (1805–75). Pupil of Liszt. Wrote org. sonata on Ps. 94, pf. sonata, and pf. solos.

Reusner, Esajas (*b* Löwenberg, Silesia, 1636; *d* Cöllnam-Spree, 1679). Ger. lutenist and composer. Court lutenist in various Ger. towns. Wrote dance suites and many songs.

Reutter, Hermann (*b* Stuttgart, 1900; *d* Heidenheim an der Brenz, 1985). Ger. composer and pianist. Studied privately 1907–20, Munich Acad. of Mus. 1920–3. Began career as pf. accompanist to Sigrid Onegin and Karl Erb. Taught comp. Stuttgart 1932–6, dir., Berlin Hochschule 1936–45, prof. of comp. Stuttgart Acad. 1952–6, dir. 1956–66, prof. of mus., Munich Acad. from 1966. Prolific composer, especially of Lieder (over 200), in which expressive vocal line is supported by elaborate pf. part. Friend of Hindemith. Comp. several operas, incl. *Saul* (1928, rev. 1947), *Der verlorene Sohn* (The Prodigal Son) (1929), *Doktor Johannes Faust* (1935, rev. 1955), *Odysseus* (1942), *Don Juan und Faust* (1950), *The Bridge of San Luis Rey* (1953), *The Death of Empedocles* (1965);

ballets; sym. for str. (1960); choral works, incl. *Pandora* (text by Goethe); 4 pf. concs.; and instr. works.

Reveille (from Fr. *réveil,* wakening). The military signal beginning the day (in the Brit. army pronounced 'revelly' or 'revally').

Revelation and Fall. Work for sop. and 16 instr. by *Maxwell Davies to text from Georg Trakl's *Offenbarung und Untergang.* Comp. 1965. F.p. London 1968 (Mary Thomas, mez.) cond. composer.

Revenge, The Choral ballad, setting of Tennyson's poem, by Stanford, Op. 24, f.p. Leeds Fest. 1886.

'Revolutionary' Study. Nickname for Chopin's pf. Étude in C minor, Op. 10, No. 12 (1831), supposedly because it expressed his patriotic fury on hearing that Warsaw had been captured by the Russians; however, the story is unsupported by evidence.

Revue. Form of entertainment comprising a series of scenes, without a plot, and sketches, dances, songs, and ballet. Evolved in Fr. in early 19th cent. as purveyor of satire, later becoming more spectacular and including *tableaux vivants.* In 20th cent. became more sophisticated, with personalites like Mistinguett (1873–1956), Maurice Chevalier (1888–1971), and Josephine Baker (1906–75), whose erotic dancing in a 1925 revue caused a scandal. In Brit., revue did not really take root until early in 20th cent. The producer and impresario C. B. Cochran imported Fr. artists, notably Alice Delysia. His revues, with those of André Charlot, dominated the London stage in the 1920s. Noël Coward and Ivor Novello wrote songs for Charlot and Cochran, and Coward later wrote his own revues (e.g. *Tonight at 8.30*). Brit. revue stars incl. Gertrude Lawrence, Beatrice Lillie, Jessie Matthews, Jack Buchanan, and Leslie Henson. Berners comp. his ballet *Luna Park* for Cochran's 1930 revue and Walton his *The First Shoot* for Cochran's *Follow the Sun* (1935–6). 'Intimate' revues by Herbert and Eleanor Farjeon brought fame to Hermione Baddeley and Hermione Gingold. Later developments of revue were the shows which featured Michael Flanders and Donald Swann (*At the Drop of a Hat,* etc.) and the wittily satirical *Beyond the Fringe* (1961). In the USA, revue developed from vaudeville. Its most successful form was in the *Follies* produced by Florenz Ziegfeld annually from 1907 until the mid-1920s.

Revueltas, Silvestre (*b* Santiago Papasquiaro, 1899; *d* Mexico City, 1940). Mexican composer and violinist. Studied in Mexico then at Chicago Mus. Coll. 1918–20 and 1922–4. Free-lance violinist and cond. until 1928 when *Chávez appointed him assoc. cond. of Mexico S.O., a post he held until 1935. Taught vn. and chamber mus. at Mèxico Nat. Cons. Went to Sp. for Civil War. Picturesque and colourful comps., influenced by but not directly quoting Mexican folk-mus. Used atonalism from 1930. Works incl. *Esquinas* (1930), *Colorines* (1932), *Janitzeo* (1933), *Sensemayá* (1938) symphonic poems; 8 x *Radio,* chamber orch. (1933); *Planos,* 'geometric dance', chamber orch. (1934); *Homenaje a Garcia-Lorca,* chamber orch. (1935–6); 3 str. qts., songs, and film mus.

Reyer, Ernest (orig. Rey, Louis Etienne) (*b* Marseilles, 1823; *d* Le Levandou, 1909). Fr. composer and critic. Studied in Marseilles and continued to compose while civil servant in Algiers. Went to Paris 1848, taking up mus. as career. His early operas were praised by Berlioz and his 2-act *Erostate* was perf. at Baden-Baden at same time as *Béatrice et Bénédict* (1862). Planned opera on Nibelungen legends, but postponed project because of work as critic. Championed Berlioz, Wagner, Bizet, Franck, etc. Eventually the Nibelung opera appeared, *Sigurd* (Brussels and CG 1884, Paris 1885). This was followed by *Salammbô,* based on Flaubert's novel (Brussels 1890, Paris 1892, NY Met. 1901). Also wrote choral works and songs.

Reynish, Timothy (John) (*b* Axbridge, 1938). Eng. cond. and hn.-player. Studied Cambridge Univ. and privately with Aubrey Brain and Sir Adrian Boult. Prin. hn. with Northern Sinfonia, SW, and CBSO, 1959–71. Guest cond. leading Brit. orchs. 3rd prize Mitropoulos competition, NY, 1971. On staff RNCM.

Reynolds, Anna (*b* Canterbury, ?1931). Eng. mez. Studied RAM. Opera début at Parma 1960. Has sung at La Scala, Milan, Bayreuth (1970–6), NY Met., CG, etc., and in concert works. Glyndebourne 1962 (Geneviève in *Pelléas*).

Reznìček, Emil Nikolaus von (*b* Vienna, 1860; *d* Berlin, 1945). Austrian composer and cond. Studied Leipzig Cons. Cond. of various military bands and th. orchs. Court cond. Mannheim 1896–9. Settled in Berlin 1902, founding series of orch. concerts and teaching at Klindworth-Scharwenka Cons. from 1906. Mus. dir. Warsaw Phil. and Imperial Opera 1907–9. Returned to Berlin. Taught at Hochschule from 1920. Visited London 1907 and cond. f.p. of *Harnham Down* by Vaughan Williams. Wrote several operas incl. *Donna Diana* (1894, rev. 1908, 1933) and *Till Eulenspiegel* (1902), requiem, 4 syms., and other orch. works, 3 str. qts., pf. pieces.

rf, rfz. = *Rinforzando.*

R.H. Right Hand.

Rhapsody. Strictly, from the ancient Gr. usage, the recitation of parts of an epic poem. In mus. the term has come to mean a comp. in one continuous movement, often based on popular, nat., or folk melodies. Thus Liszt's *Hungarian Rhapsodies,* Stanford's *Irish Rhapsodies,* Vaughan Williams's *Norfolk Rhapsody.* Delius's *Brigg Fair,* variations on an Eng. folk-song, is subtitled *An English Rhapsody,* and Rakhmaninov's variations on a caprice by Paganini are called **Rhapsody on a Theme of Paganini.* Brahms used the term for works for solo pf. and for his *Alto Rhapsody,* a setting for v., male ch., and orch. of verses by Goethe. Gershwin used the term for his **Rhapsody in Blue* and Chabrier's *España* is a Sp. rhapsody.

Rhapsody in Blue. Work for pf. and orch. by *Gershwin, among first to combine jazz with symphonic procedures. Orch. by *Grofé. F.p. NY 12 Feb. 1924, Gershwin (pf.) and Paul Whiteman's Orch.

Rhapsody on a Theme of Paganini. Work for pf. and orch. by Rakhmaninov, Op. 43, comp. and f.p. 1934 (Baltimore), f.p. in Eng., Manchester 1935. Contains 24 variations on Paganini's violin Caprice No. 24 in A minor.

Rheinberger, Josef (Gabriel) (*b* Vaduz, Liechtenstein, 1839; *d* Munich, 1901). Ger. organist, pianist, cond., and composer. Organist at Vaduz church at age 7. Studied Munich Cons. Taught at Munich Cons. 1859–65 and 1867–1901. Organist, St Michael's, Munich, 1860–6, choral cond. in Munich and coach at court opera. Prolific composer of operas, syms., chamber mus., and choral works but remembered almost exclusively through his elaborate and challenging organ comps. which incl. 2 concs., 20 sonatas, 22 trios, 12 *Meditations,* 24 fughettos, and 36 solo pieces.

Rheingold, Das (The Rhine Gold). Prol. in 1 act by Wagner, to his own lib., to his tetralogy *Der *Ring des Nibelungen.* Comp. 1853–4. Prod. separately Munich 1869, London 1882, NY Met. 1889; first prod. as part of *The Ring,* Bayreuth 1876.

'Rhenish' Symphony. Name given to *Schumann's Sym. No. 3 in E♭ major (No. 4 in order of comp.), comp. 1850, f.p. 1851. The 4th of its 5 movements was inspired by the installation of a cardinal at Cologne on the Rhine.

Rhosymedre (Lovely). Hymn-tune by J. D. Edwards (1805–85), on which Vaughan Williams based the 2nd of his *3 Preludes* for org., founded on Welsh hymn-tunes, 1920.

Rhythm (in the full sense of the word) covers everything pertaining to the *time* aspect of mus. as distinct from the aspect of pitch, i.e. it incl. the effects of beats, accents, measures, grouping of notes into beats, grouping of beats into measures, grouping of measures into phrases, etc. When all these factors are judiciously treated by the performer (with due regularity yet with artistic purpose—an effect of forward movement—and not mere machine-like accuracy) we feel and say that the performer possesses 'a sense of rhythm'. There may be 'free' or 'strict' rhythm.

The human ear seems to demand the perceptible presence of a unit of time (the BEAT); even in the 'Free Rhythm' of *Plainsong or of *Recitative this can be felt, though in such mus. the grouping into measures is not present.

Apart from such mus. as that just mentioned it will be found that the beats fall into regular groups of 2s or 3s, or of combinations of these (as a group of 4 made up of 2 + 2, or a group of 6 made up of 3 + 3). Such groups or combinations of groups are indicated in our notation by the drawing of bar-lines at regular intervals, so dividing the mus. into MEASURES (or 'bars'). The measures, in their turn, can be felt to build up into larger groups, or PHRASES (4 measures to a phrase being a very common but not invariable combination; cf. *Phrase*).

It is chiefly ACCENT that defines these groupings, e.g. taking the larger groupings, a 4-measure phrase is normally accentuated something like this:

and if the beats are in any part of the music subdivided into what we may call shorter beat-units sub-accentuations are felt, as

Where the measures have 3 beats an accented note is followed by 2 unaccented:

$\frac{3}{4}$ ♩ ♩ ♩ | ♩ ♩ ♩ |

and similarly in a 3-measure phrase the first measure will be more heavily accentuated than the 2 following measures

$\frac{2}{4}$ ♩ ♩ | ♩ ♩ | ♩ ♩ |

It will be seen, then, that what we may call the official beat-unit of a composition is a convention, there being often present smaller units and always present larger units, both of which may be considered beats.

Another example of Free Rhythm may be seen in much of the choral mus. of the polyphonic period (madrigals, motets, etc.): these may be said (in literary terms) to be in 'prose rhythm', as opposed to the 'verse rhythm' of most tunes for marching and dancing.

Just as the traditional conception of tonality dissolved at the beginning of the 20th cent., so the organization of rhythm became more elaborate, irregular, and surprising. It can be divided into 2 categories (1) *Metrical,* with irregular groups of short units, (2) *Non-metrical,* where there is no perceptible unit of measurement and no 'traditional' tempo. Metrical rhythms predominated at the start of the century, but the different uses possible are illustrated by the contrast between Schoenberg's works *c.*1908–15, where constantly changing tempi and freer use of changing time signatures make the rhythmic structure highly complex, and Stravinsky's of the same period, where there are similar constant changes of time signature but the irregularities are much more clearly defined. *Syncopation has also invaded all types of mus. Although syncopated rhythm can be found in the earliest music, in the 20th cent. it has stemmed mainly from jazz.

Non-metrical rhythm can be discerned in Wagner and its possibilities were outlined by Busoni, who wrote of the tense silence between movements being in itself mus. and more 'elastic' than sound. *Messiaen in the late 1930s developed 'ametrical' rhythm and described in a treatise (1944) that the techniques he used were 'augmented or diminished rhythms', 'retrograde' rhythms, and 'polyrhythm'. Since 1940 composers such as *Babbitt, *Boulez, and *Messiaen have developed these tendencies, though some find the results 'static' rather than conveying the sense of impetus which is the function of rhythm. Further revolutionary attitudes to rhythm have developed since the 1950s, with the increasing use of *indeterminacy. Composers such as *Cage, *Stockhausen, *Carter, and *Xenakis have written works which leave the choice of duration and tempo to the performer. With the introduction of elec. and scientific techniques into comp., there seems no limit to the expansion and intricacy of rhythmic procedures in mus.

Rhythmicon. Kbd. perc. instr. using photo-electric cell and developed by Theremin and the Amer. composer *Cowell in 1931 in order to demonstrate the combination of complex rhythms. Cowell wrote his *Rhythmicana* for it.

Ribible or **Rubible.** The *rebec.

Ricci, Federico (b Naples, 1809; d Conegliano, 1877). It. composer. Studied Naples Cons. under Bellini and Zingarelli. Comp. 19 operas, some in collab. with his brother Luigi *Ricci. One of his solo efforts was La Prigione di Edimborgo (1838, based on Scott's The Heart of Midlothian, 1818). Also wrote masses and cantatas.

Ricci, Luigi (b Naples, 1805; d Prague, 1859). It. composer. Studied Naples Cons. with Zingarelli. From 1836 choirmaster of Trieste Cath. Wrote some 30 operas, some in collab. with his brother Federico *Ricci, incl. Crispino e la comare (Venice 1850, Wexford 1979), also masses, songs, etc.

Ricci, Ruggiero (b San Francisco, 1918). Amer. violinist. Pupil of Persinger and Kulenkampff. Début San Francisco at age 10, NY 1929, London 1932. Brilliant int. career. Interpreter of many contemporary concs., such as those by *Ginastera (1963), written for him, Einem, and Schurmann. Special interest in Paganini, whose rediscovered 4th conc. he introduced in 1971. First to record the 24 Caprices in their orig. form. Teacher at Juilliard Sch. from 1975.

Ricciarelli, Katia (b Rovigo, 1946). It. sop. Studied Marcello Cons., Venice. Opera début Mantua 1969. Won Parma competition 1970. Leading roles in It. opera at world's greatest opera houses. Amer. début 1972 (Chicago), CG 1974 (La Bohème), 1984 (Aida).

Ricercare (Ricercar, Ricercata) (It., Eng. 'research', Fr. 'recherché'). To seek out. As noun, applied musically in 16th to 18th cents. to (a) an elaborate contrapuntal instr. comp. in fugal or canonic style (a famous example being that by Bach in Das musikalische Opfer), and (b) more loosely to any type of prelude (usually contrapuntal in style).

Ricercata (It., past participle of verb ricercare, and used as a noun in same sense). See Ricercare.

Rich, John (b London, c.1692; d London, c.1761). Eng. theatrical producer and manager. Manager of Lincoln's Inn Fields Th., where he introduced The *Beggar's Opera to London (1728). Built first CG Th., 1732.

Richard Coeur de Lion (Richard the Lion-hearted). Opera in 3 acts by *Grétry to lib. by Sedaine. Prod. Paris 1784, London 1786, Boston 1797. Beethoven comp. 8 Vars. on the Romance 'Un fièvre brûlante' from 'Richard Coeur de Lion', for pf., c.1795 (WoO 72).

Richard III. Play by Shakespeare (1593) for which incidental mus. was composed by Edward *German (1889). Mus. for film of play comp. by *Walton, 1955. Symphonic poem by Smetana, 1858. The nickname 'Richard III' was given to the young Richard Strauss in Ger., indicating that although he was regarded as a successor to Wagner, there could be no Richard II.

Richards, Bernard (Roland) (b Coulsdon, 1913). Eng. cellist. Studied with *Feuermann. Career mainly in chamber mus. with Int. Str. Qt., Martin Str. Qt., Richards Pf. Qt., and Amici Qt. Teacher at GSM.

Richardson, Alan (b Edinburgh, 1904; d London, 1978). Scottish composer and pianist. Studied RAM 1929–30 and was pupil of H. Craxton. Was acc. to Carl *Flesch 1936–9. Married Janet *Craxton, the oboist. Comp. pf. sonatinas, bn. sonata, va. sonata, fl. sonatina, and a large body of works for ob.

Richardson (really Heybourne), **Ferdinand** (b c. 1558; d Tottenham, Middx., 1618). Eng. composer, pupil of *Tallis. Wrote 8 works for *Fitzwilliam Virginal Book.

Richettato (It.). Same as *Spiccato.

Richter, Franz Xaver (b Holleschau, Moravia, 1709; d Strasbourg, 1789). Bohemian composer. Choirmaster at Kempten, Swabia, 1740–50. Bass singer and violinist at Mannheim court from 1747. Choirmaster Strasbourg Cath. 1769–89. One of leaders of *Mannheim sch. Wrote c. 70

syms., 6 str. qts., 6 kbd. concs., chamber mus., oratorio, church mus., etc.

Richter, Hans (b Györ, Hung., 1843; d Bayreuth, 1916). Austro-Hung. cond. Choirboy in Vienna Court Chapel. Studied Vienna Cons., 1860–5 (pf., hn., vn., and comp.). Hn.-player, Kärntnerthor Th., Vienna, 1862–6. Worked with Wagner at Tribschen, 1866–7, making fair copy of score of *Die Meistersinger*. Recommended by Wagner to von Bülow as chorusmaster, Munich Opera, 1868–9. Cond. Brussels première of *Lohengrin*, 1870. Cond., Budapest Opera 1871–5, Vienna Opera 1875–99 (mus. dir. 1893–7). Cond. Vienna P.O. and dir., Musikfreunde Gesellschaft 1875–98. Chosen by Wagner to conduct first complete *Ring*, Bayreuth 1876. Went to London as co-cond. with Wagner 1877, thereafter giving annual series of Richter Concerts in London. London opera début, Drury Lane 1882 (f. ps. in England of *Tristan* and *Meistersinger*), CG 1884 and 1903–10 (cond. first *Ring* sung in English, 1908). Permanent cond. Hallé Orch., Manchester, 1899–1911. Prin. cond. LSO, 1904–11. Cond. Birmingham Fest. 1885–1909 (incl. f.p. of Elgar's *The Dream of Gerontius* 1900). Champion of Elgar, also cond. f.ps. of *Enigma Variations* (1899) and First Sym. (1908, ded. to him). Cond. f.p. of Brahms's 2nd and 3rd Syms. and Bruckner's 8th. Retired 1912, last appearance as cond. of *Meistersinger* at Bayreuth. Championed several Eng. composers besides Elgar and during his Hallé years introduced mus. of Bartók and Sibelius. Organized and rehearsed private orch. for f.p. of Wagner's *Siegfried Idyll* on staircase at Tribschen, 1870, playing tpt. (not hn., as often stated).

Richter, Karl (b Plauen, 1926; d Munich, 1981). Ger. organist, harpsichordist, and cond. Studied Leipzig. Organist, Thomaskirche, Leipzig, 1947–50. Joined staff of Munich Acad., 1951, becoming prof., 1956. Founder-cond. Munich Bach Choir. Specialist in Bach.

Richter, Svyatoslav (Teofilovich) (b Zhitomir, 1915). Russ. pianist. Boy prodigy. Début Odessa 1934. Studied Moscow Cons. 1937–42, pf. pupil of Neuhaus. Of exceptional virtuosity, he soon won int. recognition. Specialist in works of Prokofiev, givings f.ps. of 7th and 9th pf. sonatas and conducting f.p. of *Symphony-Concerto* for vc. and orch. (1952, *Rostropovich soloist). London début 1961; Amer. début Chicago and NY 1960–1. Equally impressive in concs., solo recitals, and chamber mus. Has played at Aldeburgh Fest. in assoc. with *Britten and Rostropovich.

Richter-Haaser, Hans (b Dresden, 1912; d Braunschweig, 1980). Ger. pianist, cond., and composer. Début 1928. Cond. Detmold Orch., 1945–7. Prof. of pf., N.W. Ger. Mus. Acad. from 1947. Frequent world tours as pianist. Composer of sym., pf. concs., and other works.

Rickenbacher, Karl Anton (b Basle, 1940). Swiss cond. Studied W. Berlin Cons., 1962–6. Début

R.I.A.S., Berlin. Ass. cond., Zürich Opera, 1966–9. Cond., Freiburg 1969–74. Guest cond. of leading European orchs. Cond., BBC Scottish S.O. 1977–80.

Ricketts, Frederick Joseph. See *Alford, Kenneth J.*

Ricordi. It. (orig. Sp.) family of mus. publishers, founded in Milan 1808. Pubd. operas and other works of Bellini, Rossini, and Donizetti. Under Giulio Ricordi (1840–1912), the firm prospered, especially through his championship of Verdi and friendship with Verdi, and later Puccini. Succeeded by his son Tito (1865–1933). London branch est. 1824–8, re-est.1875; Paris 1888; NY 1911 (now closed).

Ridderbusch, Karl (b Recklinghausen, 1932). Ger. bass. Studied Duisburg Cons. as protégé of Rudolf Schock and later with Clemens Kaiser-Breme in Essen. Opera début Münster 1961, Essen 1962, Düsseldorf 1965, Vienna 1968. Bayreuth début 1967, Salzburg Easter Fest. 1968. Début NY Met. 1967 (Hunding), CG 1971 (Fasolt, Hunding, and Hagen). Leading exponent of Wagnerian bass roles, also in choral works by Mozart, Beethoven, etc.

Riddick, Kathleen (b Epsom, 1907). Eng. cond. and cellist. Studied GSM and at Salzburg with *Malko. Formed Riddick Str. Orch., 1938, and Surrey P.O. Champion of Eng. mus.

Riddle, Frederick (Craig) (b Liverpool, 1912). Eng. violist. Studied RCM, later on staff there. LSO 1933–8, LPO 1938–52, RPO from 1953. Fine player of Walton conc., of which he made first recording (1937). Prof. of va., RMCM, 1964.

Riders to the Sea. (1) Opera in 1 act by Vaughan Williams, being an almost verbatim setting of J. M. Synge's play (1904). Comp. 1925–32. Prod. London (RCM) 1937, Cambridge 1938, Cleveland, Ohio, 1950, SW 1953, Naples 1959.
(2) Opera in 1 act, under title *L'Appel de la mer*, by *Rabaud, based on Synge's play, prod. Paris 1924.

Řídký, Jaroslav (b Liberec, 1897; d Poděbrady, 1956). Cz. composer. Studied Prague Cons., with Foerster, 1919–23. Harpist, Czech P.O. 1924–38. Cond., Czech Phil. Ch., 1925–30. Taught comp. at Prague Acad. of Music 1929–56. Wrote 7 syms., 5 str. qts., concs., songs, etc.

Ridout, Alan (John) (b West Wickham, Kent, 1934). Eng. composer. Studied RCM, later with Fricker, Tippett, and Badings. Lecturer, Cambridge Univ., 1963–75, prof. RCM from 1960. Works incl. 8 operas, 6 syms., *Christmas Oratorio*, chamber mus., song-cycles, etc.

Ridout, Godfrey (b Toronto, 1918; d Toronto, 1984). Canadian composer. Studied Toronto Cons., pupil of Healey Willan. Teacher at Toronto Univ. from 1948, becoming senior prof. Works incl. *Esther* (dramatic sym); *Cantiones mysticae,* No. 1 for sop. and orch., No. 2 for sop., tpt., str.; chamber mus.; songs.

Riefling, Robert (*b* Oslo, 1911). Norweg. pianist. Studied Oslo, Hanover, and Berlin (with Fischer and Kempff). Début Oslo 1925. Prof., Royal Danish Cons., Copenhagen, 1967–73, Norwegian Mus. H.S., Oslo, from 1973. Many tours of Europe and USA. Specialist in contemporary Scandinavian works by Valen, Saeverud, etc.

Riegger, Wallingford (Constantin) (*b* Albany, Georgia, 1885; *d* NY, 1961). Amer. composer and cond. As boy learned vn. and vc. Entered Cornell Univ. 1904, transferring to Institute of Mus. Art (later Juilliard Sch.) 1905. Studied in Munich and Berlin 1907–10, making cond. début with Blüthner Orch., 1910. Returned to USA as cellist in St Paul S.O., Minnesota. Returned to Ger., 1913–17, as opera cond. and cond. of sym. concerts. On return to USA he held teaching posts at various univs. until settling in NY, 1923. Wrote several scores for Amer. choreographers, 1930–41. Under several pseudonyms made hundreds of arrs. of various kinds of choral mus. to supplement income. Began composing in a 19th-cent. style; but under influence of the Schoenberg 12-note method became more adventurous. His use of atonality was always individual. Strong rhythmic drive and contrapuntal forms also characterize his mus. Prin. works:

ORCH: Syms. No. 1 (1944), No. 2 (1945), No. 3 (1946–7), No. 4 (1957); *Dichotomy* (1931–2); *Little Black Sambo* (1946); *Music for Orchestra* (1951); *Festival Overture* (1957).
DANCE: *Bacchanale* (1930); *Evocation* (1933); *New Dance* (1935); *Candide* (1937); *Case History No...* (1937); *Pilgrims' Progress* (1941).
SOLOIST WITH ORCH: *Variations* for pf. and orch. (1952–3); *Variations* for vn. and orch. (1959); *Introduction and Fugue* for vc. and wind (1960); conc. for pf. and woodwind quintet (1953).
VOCAL: *La Belle Dame sans merci* (1923); *From Some Far Shore* (1946); *The Dying of the Light* (1954); *Who Can Revoke?* (1948).
CHAMBER MUSIC: Str. Qts: No.1 (1938–9), No. 2 (1948), No. 3 (1945–7); *Romanza* for str. qt. (1954); pf. quintet (1951); pf. trio (1930); vn. sonatina (1947); woodwind quintet (1952).
PIANO: *Blue Voyage* (1927); *4 Tone Pictures* (1932); *New and Old* (1944).

Riemann, (Karl Wilhelm Julius) **Hugo** (*b* Gross-Mehlra, 1849; *d* Leipzig, 1919). Ger. musicologist, teacher, and composer. Studied Leipzig Cons. Lecturer on mus., Leipzig Univ. 1878. Taught pf., etc., Hamburg Cons. 1881–90, Wiesbaden Cons., 1890–5. Returned to Leipzig 1895, prof. from 1901. Dir., Institute of Mus. Science 1908. Extremely prolific scholar and ed. of many learned symposiums, etc., trans. many scholarly works. Prin. achievement was his *Musiklexikon*

(dictionary of mus.), (1882 and subsequent edns.). Comp. 2 str. qts. and other chamber works.

Rienzi (orig. *Cola Rienzi, der letzte der Tribunen,* Cola Rienzi, the last of the Tribunes). Opera in 5 acts by Wagner to his own lib. based on Bulwer Lytton's novel (1835) and Mary Russell Mitford's play (1828). Comp. 1838–40. Prod. Dresden 1842, NY 1878, London (in Eng.) 1879.

Ries, Ferdinand (*b* Bonn, 1784; *d* Frankfurt, 1838). Ger. pianist, composer, and cond., son of Franz Anton *Ries. Pupil of his father and of Beethoven in Vienna 1801–5. Toured Europe and Scandinavia as pianist. Lived in London 1813–24 as pianist and teacher. Worked in Ger., esp. Frankfurt, from 1824. Cond. at 8 of Lower Rhine fests. 1825–37. With Wegeler, wrote *Biographical Notices of Beethoven,* 1838. Comp. 3 operas, 2 oratorios, 18 syms., 9 pf. concs., 26 str. qts., 128 vn. sonatas, 14 pf. sonatas, etc.

Ries, Franz Anton (*b* Bonn, 1755; *d* Godesberg, 1846). Ger. violinist. Leader of Bonn electoral court orch. 1779–94. Friend and teacher of Beethoven. Attended unveiling of Beethoven statue in Bonn, 1845, at age of 89.

Ries, Hubert (*b* Bonn, 1802; *d* Berlin, 1886). Ger. violinist and teacher. Son and pupil of Franz Anton *Ries, also pupil of *Spohr. Settled in Berlin 1824. In court orch. from 1825 (leader 1836). Dir. of Phil. Soc. 1835. Taught at Royal Orch. Sch. 1851–72. Wrote vn. sch., 2 vn. concs., and other works.

Rieti, Vittorio (*b* Alexandria, Egypt, 1898). It. composer (Amer. citizen from 1944). Studied pf. in Milan and comp. with Casella, Respighi, and Malipiero in Rome. Lived in Paris from 1925. Wrote ballets for Diaghilev and mus. for plays and films of Louis Jouvet. Settled in USA 1939. Taught at various Amer. colleges. Works, often influenced by Stravinsky and Les *Six, incl. 14 ballets, 7 operas, 5 syms., 3 pf. concs., 2-pf. conc., hpd. conc., 2 vc. concs., triple conc. (pf., vn., va.), 4 str. qts., woodwind quintet, pf. pieces, and songs.

Rietz, Julius (*b* Berlin, 1812; *d* Dresden, 1877). Ger. cellist, composer, and cond. In Berlin th. orch. from 1828; ass. cond. to Mendelssohn at Düsseldorf Opera in 1834, succeeding him 1835. Cond., Leipzig Opera 1847–54, dir. Gewandhaus concerts and teacher of comp., Leipzig Cons., 1848–60. Court cond. Dresden from 1860, also dir., Dresden Cons. Wrote 3 operas, operetta, 3 syms., 4 concs., *Konzertstück* for ob., str. qt., etc. Ed. complete works of Mendelssohn.

Riff. Jazz term meaning a short, repetitive, but not improvised, instr. passage, e.g. the beginning of *In the Mood.*

Rigaudon (Fr.), **Rigadoon** (Old Eng.). Ancient Provençal type of dance, in simple duple or quadruple time, similar to the *bourrée. Rameau used the rigaudon in nearly all his operas and there are 2 in Fux's *Concentus musicus* (1701). It occurs in suites by Couperin, Lalande, Telemann, Muffat, and others. Also used by Grieg in *Holberg Suite* (1884), Saint-Saëns, MacDowell, and by Ravel in *Le Tombeau de Couperin*.

Righini, Vincenzo (*b* Bologna, 1756; *d* Bologna, 1812). It composer, teacher, and conductor. Début as ten. in Parma 1775. Joined opera co. in Prague 1776, composing *Il Convitato di Pietra (Don Giovanni)* for it, (Haydn later cond. it at Esterháza.) Dir., It. Opera in Vienna from 1780. In much demand as singing teacher. Kapellmeister, Mainz electoral court 1787. Comp. oratorio *Der Tod Jesu* at this time, also highly praised *Missa Solemnis* (1790), the latter perf. at Coronation of Leopold II in Frankfurt. Court cond. and dir. of It. Opera, Berlin, from 1793. His operas incl. a setting of Goldoni's *La Vedova Scaltra* (1778), later set by Wolf-Ferrari (1931). Beethoven comp. 24 vars. for pf. on Righini's arietta *Venni amore* in 1790–1 (WoO 65).

Rignold, Hugo (Henry) (*b* Kingston-on-Thames, 1905; *d* Hampstead, 1976). Eng. cond. and violinist. Studied vn. at Winnipeg in Canada, RAM 1920. Worked as violinist in jazz bands, sym. orchs., and str. qts. Cond. Cairo S.O. 1944, CG ballet 1947, Liverpool P.O. 1948–54, Cape Town Orch. 1956. Mus. dir., Royal Ballet 1957–60; cond. CBSO 1960–8.

Rigoletto. Opera in 3 acts by Verdi to lib. by Piave based on V. Hugo's play *Le Roi s'amuse* (1832). Orig. title was *La maledizione* (The Curse). Comp. 1850–1. Prod. Venice 1851, London 1853, NY 1855.

Rig Veda (Holst). See *Hymns from the Rig Veda*.

Rihm, Wolfgang (*b* Karlsruhe, 1952). Ger. composer. Studied theory and comp. at Karlsruhe. Studied with Stockhausen 1973 and Huber 1974. Lecturer at Karlsruhe Musikhochschule from 1973. Works incl.:

CHAMBER OPERA: *Faust und Yorick* (1976).
BALLET: *Tutuguri* (1981–2).
ORCH: Syms. No. 1 (1969), No. 2 (1972–3), No. 3 *Ein imaginäres Requiem*, sop., bar., ch., orch. (1976); *Dis-Kontur* (1976); *Cuts and Dissolves*, conc. for 29 players (1977); *La Musique Creuse Le Ciel*, 2 pf., orch. (1977–9); *5 Abgesangsszene* (1979); *Erste Abgesangsszene* (1979); Conc. for 2 vas. (1979–83); *Walzer* (1979–81); *Doppelgesang*, va., vc., orch. (1980); *Tutuguri I–VII* (1981–2); *Zeichen*, bass fl., bass cl., orch. (1981–2); *2nd Doppelgesang*, cl., vc., orch. (1981–3); *Monodram*, vc., orch. (1982–3); *Schwarzer und Roter Tanz*, fragment from *Tutuguri* (1982–3).
VOICE(S) AND INSTR: *Hervorgedunkelt*, mez., ens. (1974); *2nd Abgesangsszene*, vv., orch. (1979); *4th Abgesangsszene*, vv., orch. (1979–80); *3rd Abgesangsszene*, bar., orch. (1980); *5th Abgesangsszene*, mez., bar., orch. (1979–81); *Umhergetrieben*,

aufgewirbelt, Nietzsche fragments for bar., mez., ch., and fl. (1981); *Wölfli-Lieder*, bar., pf., ens. (1981–2).
ENSEMBLE: *Music-Hall Suite* (1979); *Ländler*, 13 str. (1979); *Nature-Morte—Still Alive*, 13 str. (1979–80); *Chiffre I*, pf., 7 instr. (1982); *Gebild*, tpt., perc., str. (1982–3); *Silence to be Beaten (Chiffre II)*, ens. (1983); *Chiffre III*, 12 players (1983).
CHAMBER MUSIC: *Paraphrase*, vc., perc., pf. (1972); Str. qt. (1979–81); *Ohne Titel* (str. qt.) (1981–3); pf. trio (1981); *Canzona*, 4 va. (1982); *Fremde Szene I*, vn., vc., pf. (1982), *II (Charackterstück)*, vn., vc., pf. (1983); *III*, vn., vc., pf. (1983).
VOICE AND PIANO: *4 Songs of Paul Celan* (1973); *Hölderlin-Fragmente* (1977); *Neue Alexanderlieder* (1979); *Lenz-Fragmente* (1980); *Wölfli-Liederbuch* (1980–1).
KEYBOARD: *Contemplatio*, org. (1967); *2 Fantasies*, org. (1967); *Fantasie*, org. (1968); *Siebengestalt*, org., tam-tam (1974); *Ländler*, pf. (1979); *'Bann, Nachtschwärmerei'*, org. (1980); *Piano Piece No. 7* (1980).

Riisager, Knudåge (*b* Port Kunda, Estonia, 1897; *d* Copenhagen, 1974). Danish composer. Studied political science, Copenhagen Univ. 1916–21. Studied orch. with Roussel in Paris and counterpoint with Grabner in Leipzig, 1932. Worked in Danish Finance Ministry 1925–47. Dir., Royal Danish Cons. 1956–67. Leader of Denmark's progressive composers and noted ballet composer. Wrote 5 syms., 6 str. qts., pf. sonatas, sinfonietta, syms. for str., etc. Best-known ballets incl. *Land of Milk and Honey* (1942), *Qarrtsiluni* (1942), *The Phoenix* (1946), *Etude* (1948), and *The Lady from the Sea* (1960).

Riley, Howard (*b* Huddersfield, 1943). Eng. pianist and composer. Studied Univ. of Wales and York Univ. Prof. GSM from 1970. Comps. incl. str. qts., str. trio, etc.

Riley, Terry (Mitchell) (*b* Colfax, Calif., 1935). Amer. composer and saxophonist. Studied San Francisco State Coll., 1955–7, and Univ. of Calif., Berkeley, 1960–1. Frequent tours of Europe as performer of his own works, which 'take the form of charts of repeated patterns and series, which must assume a form during rehearsal and performance'. Comps. incl. *Keyboard Studies* for amplified or elec. instr., 1965; *Dorian Reeds*, for sop. sax., tape, time-lag and feedback system, 1966; *Untitled Organ*, amplified reed organ, 1966; *Poppy Nogood and the Phantom Band*, sop. sax., tape, time-lag and feedback system, 1968; *Rainbow in Curved Air*, elec. kbd. instrs., 1970. Since 1970 has been interested in Indian music.

Rimbault, Edward (Francis) (*b* London, 1816; *d* London, 1876). Eng. organist and scholar. From 1832 organist at Soho and other London churches. Wrote history of org. (with E. J. Hopkins) (1855, rev. 1877), ed. coll. of Catholic chants, Morley's *1st Book of Ballets*, Tallis's *Parthenia*, Gibbon's 3-

part *Fantasies*, 2 colls. of Christmas carols, etc. Comp. mus. for the stage.

Rimmer, Frederick (William) (*b* Liverpool, 1914). Eng. composer, organist, and teacher. Studied Cambridge Univ. Senior lecturer in mus. Homerton Coll., Cambridge, 1948–51. Lecturer in mus., Glasgow Univ. 1951–66, prof. 1966–80. Organist, Glasgow Univ. 1954–66. Composer of org. works and church mus.

Rimmer, John (Francis) (*b* Auckland, N.Z., 1939). New Zealand composer and teacher. Works incl. *O Magnum Mysterium*; str. trio *Abstract as White*; and many works employing elec. media.

Rimsky-Korsakov, Nikolay (Andreyevich) (*b* Tikhvin, 1844; *d* Lyubensk, 1908). Russ. composer and cond. Born into aristocratic family and had conventional mus. education. Ambition to be sailor; entered Corps of Naval Cadets 1856 in St Petersburg, where he had pf. lessons and attended opera and concerts. Nationalist works of Glinka deeply impressed him and he met and was influenced by Balakirev. Wrote part of a sym., though ignorant of names of chords and of rules of part-writing. Away at sea 1862–5. Completed sym. 1865, first of importance by Russ. composer. In 1865–8 wrote *Sadko* and *Antar*, both later rev. In 1869 was entrusted with completion of *Dargomyzhsky's opera The Stone Guest* and in 1872 completed his own opera *The Maid of Pskov*. In 1871, while still a naval lieutenant and still unlearned in harmony and counterpoint, was appointed prof. of practical comp. and instrumentation, St Petersburg Cons. Taught himself in secret. Inspector of Naval Bands, 1873–84. For several years as part of his self-education prod. 'academic' comps. incl. str. qt., pf. quintet, pf. fugues, etc. His editing of *100 Russian Folk-Songs*, 1876–7, led him to a new, more attractive phase in his own works, incl. the operas *May Night* and *Snegurochka* (The Snow Maiden). From 1874–81 was dir. of the Free School of Mus. After 1882 much occupied with administration, cond., and rev. and orchestration of *Khovanshchina* and other works by *Mussorgsky. When Borodin died in 1887, completion and orch. of *Prince Igor* was undertaken by Rimsky-Korsakov and his pupil *Glazunov. He interrupted this to write 2 of his most colourful works, the *Spanish Caprice* and *Sheherazade*. Thereafter, influenced by the first Russ. perfs. in 1888–9 of Wagner's *Ring*, devoted himself to opera. For a time, neurasthenic illness robbed him of the will to work, but he resumed creative work in the 1890s and in 1896 made his version of Mussorgsky's *Boris Godunov* which, though it is now partly discredited, preserved this opera until scholars restored the composer's orig. In 1905, having shown sympathy with revolutionary students, was temporarily removed from his professorship at St Petersburg Cons. and a 2-month ban imposed on perf. of his works. This clash with authority is reflected in his last and

satirical opera, *The Golden Cockerel*, which was banned by the govt. and not prod. until after his death. In 1906, rev. *Boris Godunov*, and in 1907 cond. in Paris at Diaghilev's concerts of Russ. mus.

Less talented than his colleagues in the nationalist school, Rimsky-Korsakov excelled them all in the art of clear and colourful orchestration, and to us today his mus. seems to epitomize the brilliance and pageantry of Tsarist Russia. Lately the splendour of his operas has been re-discovered. His influence on his most distinguished pupil, *Stravinsky, can be discerned above all in *The Firebird*. Wrote textbooks on harmony and orchestration, also autobiography. Prin. comps.:

OPERAS: *The *Maid of Pskov* (Ivan the Terrible) (1868–72, rev. 1876–7, rev. 1891–2); *May Night* (1878–9); *Snow Maiden* (*Snegurochka*) (1880–1, rev. c. 1895); *Mlada* (1889–90); *Christmas Eve* (1894–5); *Sadko* (1894–6); *Mozart and Salieri* (1897); *Boyarina Vera Sheloga* (comp. 1877 as prol. to *Maid of Pskov*, reconstructed as 1-act opera 1898); *The *Tsar's Bride* (1898); *The *Legend of Tsar Saltan* (1899–1900); *Servilia* (1900–1); *Kashchey the Immortal* (1901–2); *Pan Voevoda* (1902–3); *Tale of the *Invisible City of Kitezh* (1903–5); *The *Golden Cockerel* (1906–7).

ORCH: Syms.: No. 1 in E♭ minor (1861–5, rev. in E minor 1884), No. 2 (*Antar*, 1868, rev. 1876 and 1897, symphonic suite 1903), No. 3 in C (1866–73, rev. 1885–6); *Overture on 3 Russian Themes* (1866, rev. 1879–80); *Fantasia on Serbian Themes* (1867, reorch. 1886–7); *Sadko*, symphonic picture (1867, rev. 1869, 1891; see also opera); conc. for tb. and military band (1877); *Sinfonietta on Russian Themes* (1879 for str. qt.; rev. and orch. 1880–4); *Skazka* (Legend) (1879–80); pf. conc. (1882–3); *Fantasia on Russian Themes*, vn. and orch. (1886); *Spanish Caprice* (1887); *Sheherazade* (1888); *Russian Easter Festival Overture* (1888); *Dubinushka* (1905).

CHORAL: *Alexey the Man of God*, ch. and orch. (1877); *Svitezyanka*, cantata (1897); *Song of Oleg the Wise*, cantata (1899); *From Homer* (1901).

CHAMBER MUSIC: Str. qt. (1875); str. sextet (1876); pf. quintet (pf. and wind) (1876); *Allegro in B♭* for str. qt. (1899)

TRANSCRIPTIONS etc.: Borodin: *Prince Igor*, orch. and completed (with Glazunov), prod. 1890; Mussorgsky: *Boris Godunov*, re-orch. 1896, rev. 1906, *Khovanshchina*, rev. and orch. 1882–5; Dargomyzhsky: *The *Stone Guest*, orch. and completed 1870–1, rev. 1902.

Also songs, chs., folk-song arrs. and pf. pieces.

Rinaldo. (1) Opera in 3 acts by Handel (his first in Eng.) to lib. by Rossi after sketch by Aaron Hill from Tasso (1562). Prod. 1711.

(2) Cantata, Op. 50, by Brahms for ten., male ch., and orch. (1863–8).

Rinaldo di Capua (b Capua or Naples, c. 1705; d ?Rome, c. 1780). It. composer of about 30 operas, composed mainly for Rome after 1737 (*La Zingara* and *La donna superba* prod. Paris 1752–3). Only fragments of his works remain because son sold scores as waste paper.

Rinck, Johann Christian Heinrich (b Elgersburg, Thuringia, 1770; d Darmstadt, 1846). Ger. organist and composer. Studied at Erfurt 1786–9. Organist at Giessen from 1790, Darmstadt from 1805. Wrote many works for org., motets, pf. sonatas, and vc. sonatas. Also wrote org. sch. (re-ed. by Dienel 1881).

Rinforzando; rinforzato (It.). Reinforcing; reinforced, i.e. stress is applied to individual notes or chords. So *rinforza, rinforzamente*; reinforcement. Abbreviation *rf, rfz*.

Ring des Nibelungen, Der (The Nibelung's Ring). 4 operas (mus. dramas) by Wagner, to his own libs., which he called a 'stage festival for 3 days with a preliminary evening' (*Ein Bühnenfestspiel für drei Tage und einen Vorabend*). The cycle, often referred to as 'the tetralogy', is based on versions of the Scandinavian saga of the Niebelungs involving gods and mortals. Among the characters in the operas are Wotan, Alberich, Siegfried, Mime, Siegmund, Loge, Brünnhilde, Fricka, Hagen, Gutrune, Sieglinde, Freia, Fasolt, Fafner, Donner, and the Valkyries. The 4 operas, with details of their f.ps., are: *Das Rheingold* (The Rhine Gold), prol. in 1 act, comp. 1853–4, prod. Munich 1869, Bayreuth (as part of complete *Ring*) 1876, London 1882, NY 1889; *Die Walküre* (The Valkyrie), 3 acts, comp. 1854–6, prod. Munich 1870, Bayreuth (as part of complete *Ring*) 1876, NY (incomplete) 1877, London 1882; *Siegfried*, 3 acts, comp. 1856–7, 1864–71, prod. Bayreuth (as part of complete *Ring*) 1876, London 1882, NY 1887; *Götterdämmerung* (Twilight of the Gods), 3 acts, comp. 1869–74, prod. Bayreuth (as part of complete *Ring*) 1876, London 1882, NY Met. 1888. Writing and comp. of *The Ring* occupied Wagner intermittently from 1848 to 1874.

The first complete *Ring* cycle, sung in Ger., at *Bayreuth was cond. Hans Richter on 13, 14, 16, and 17 Aug., 1876. The first cycle to be perf. in London was at Her Majesty's, cond. Anton Seidl, on 5, 6, 7, and 9 May 1882. Seidl also cond. first cycle at NY Met. on 4, 5, 8, and 11 March 1889 (although there had been perfs. of the cycle excluding *Das Rheingold* in 1887–8, also under Seidl). First CG cycle in June 1892, cond. Mahler, but given out of sequence. First cycle in Eng. trans. at CG cond. Richter, 1908, and in Brit. provinces by *Denhof Co. in Edinburgh 1910, cond. *Balling (Leeds, Manchester, Glasgow 1911, Hull, Leeds, Liverpool 1912). No further perfs. in provinces until Scottish Opera cycle (in Ger.) in Glasgow, Dec. 1971. F. ps. of new Eng. trans. by Andrew Porter for ENO 1970–3, complete cycle, London, July–Aug. 1973.

Rinuccini, Ottavio (b Florence, 1563; d Florence, 1621). It. poet. Wrote earliest opera libs. for *Peri (*Dafne* and *Euridice*), *Monteverdi (*Arianna*), *Gagliano, and *Caccini.

Rio Grande, The. Work by C. *Lambert for ch., orch., and solo pf., comp. 1927, f.p. BBC broadcast 1928; in public, Manchester 1929. Setting of poem by Sacheverell Sitwell.

Ripieno (It.). Replenished, supplementary. (1) The term is used in older mus. to make a distinction between passages to be played by the full body and others to be played by a group of soloists, or *Concertante* (see *Concerto*). The term is in this sense still used in Eng. brass bands, generally misspelt Ripiano or Repiano. Also used of a supplementary choral body, e.g. the boys' vv. in Bach's *St Matthew Passion* are the *ripieno* ch.

(2) In It. organ mus., Mixture.

Ripley, (Maud) Gladys (b Essex, 1908; d Chichester, 1955). Eng. cont., largely self-taught. Leading exponent of oratorio roles and of Angel in Elgar's *Dream of Gerontius*. Also sang in opera.

Rippon, Michael (George) (b Coventry, 1938). Eng. bass. Studied Cambridge Univ. Opera début CG 1969. Has sung at Glyndebourne and in other leading houses. Fine exponent of solo role in Walton's *Belshazzar's Feast* and of Maxwell Davies's *8 Songs for a Mad King* and Henze's *El Cimarrón*.

Ripresa (It.; Fr. *reprise*). (1) Repeat, of a section of a comp.

(2) Recapitulation section of a movement in *Sonata form.

(3) Revival, of opera, etc.

Rise and Fall of the City of Mahagonny (*Aufstieg und Fall der Stadt Mahagonny*). Opera in 3 acts by Weill to lib. by Brecht. Prod. Leipzig 1930, London 1963, NY 1970. Comp. 1927–9; developed from 'Songspiel' *Mahagonny* (1927).

Rising of the Moon, The. Opera in 3 acts by *Maw to lib. by Beverley Cross. Prod. Glyndebourne 1970, Graz (Ger. trans. by M. Vogel) 1978.

Risoluto; risolutamente (It.). Resolute; resolutely. So the superlative *risolutissimo*. **Risoluzione,** resolution.

Rispetto (It., plural *rispetti*). A type of It. folksong with 8 lines to the stanza. Title used for mus. by Wolf-Ferrari, Malipiero, and others.

Ristič, Milan (b Belgrade, 1908; d Belgrade, 1982). Yugoslav composer. Studied Belgrade Acad. 1929–32, 1935–7, and at Prague Cons. 1937–9 (comp. with A. Hába). Mus. staff of Belgrade Radio from 1950, dir. from 1963. Composer of 7 syms., vn. conc., pf. conc., 7 *Bagatelles* for orch., cl. conc., *Concerto for Orchestra*, etc.

Rit. Short for *ritardando.

Ritardando, ritardare, ritardato (It.). Holding back, to hold back, held back (gradually, i.e. same as *rallentando). Abbreviated to 'Rit.' (but see also *Ritenuto). **Ritardo** (It.). The act of holding back (i.e. of gradually diminishing the speed).

Ritchie, Margaret (Mabel) (*b* Grimsby, 1903; *d* Ewelme, Oxon., 1969). Eng. sop. Early education in Austria. Studied RCM. Leading Eng. exponent of Schubert Lieder. Sang in opera at Glyndebourne, CG, EOG, etc. First to sing wordless sop. role in Vaughan Williams's *Sinfonia Antartica* (1953), also in film mus. (1948). Created roles of Lucia and Miss Wordsworth in Britten's *Rape of Lucretia* and *Albert Herring*, 1946 and 1947.

Ritenuto (It.). Held back, i.e. slower (immediately, not gradually as with *ritardando and *rallentando). Sometimes abbreviated to *Rit.*, or *riten*. Also *ritenendo, ritenente*, holding back.

Rite of Spring, The (*Vesna svyashchennaya* (Spring the sacred), Fr. *Le Sacre du printemps*). Ballet (pictures from pagan Russia) in 2 parts, mus. by Stravinsky, lib. Roerich, choreog. Nijinsky. Comp. 1911–13. Prod. Paris and London 1913, Boston and NY 1924 (concert version). Part I: *The Adoration of the Earth*, Part II: *The Sacrifice*. Arr. for pf. 4 hands by composer, 1913. F.p. (cond. Monteux) on 29 May 1913 at Théâtre des Champs-Elysées was occasion of celebrated riot.

Ritmo (It.). Rhythm, as in *ritmo di tre battute*, rhythm of 3 measures. **Ritmico** (It.). Rhythmic.

Ritornel (Fr. *ritournelle*; It. *ritornello*; Ger. *Ritornell*). A return (*ritornello* is a little return). (1) The refrain in 14th and 15th-cent. madrigal-type comps.
(2) An It. folk-song, each stanza of 3 lines, the last line rhyming with the first.
(3) The repetition of the instr. introduction to a song, and hence also the instr. introduction itself.
(4) In the classical conc., the return of the full orch. after a solo passage, same as *tutti.
(5) Synonym for *Da capo.

Ritorno d'Ulisse in patria, Il (Ulysses's return to his native land). Opera in prol. and 5 acts by *Monteverdi to lib. by G. Badoaro. Prod. Venice 1640. Revived in fragmentary concert-form Brussels 1925, Paris (d'Indy version) 1925, London (d'Indy version broadcast in Eng.) 1928, Florence (Dallapiccola stage version) 1942, Wuppertal (Křenek edn.) 1959, Glyndebourne (Leppard edn.) 1972, Washington 1974. F. stage p. in Britain was in London, 1965.

Ritter, Alexander (*b* Narva, Estonia, 1833; *d* Munich, 1896). Ger. violinist, composer, and cond. Studied Leipzig Cons. 1849–51. Married Wagner's niece Franziska, 1854, and joined Liszt circle at Weimar. Cond., Stettin Opera 1856–8. Worked at theatre in Würzburg 1863–82. Violinist in Meiningen Orch. under von Bülow, 1882–6 where he met R. Strauss and influenced him to follow Lisztian precepts. Wrote 2 operas, incl. *Der faule Hans* (1885), 6 symphonic poems, str. qt., etc.

Ritter, Hermann (*b* Wismar, 1849; *d* Würzburg, 1926). Ger. violist. Introduced the richer-toned *viola alta* which Wagner used at Bayreuth. Taught va. at Würzburg from 1879. Formed str. qt. comprising vn., va. alta, va. tenore, and va. bassa, in 1905. Wrote about vas. and other str. instr., also biography of Schubert.

Ritual Dances. 4 dances for ch. and orch. in Tippett's opera *The Midsummer Marriage* which are often played separately as a concert work. 3 occur in Act 2: *The Earth in Autumn* (The Hound chases the Hare); *The Waters in Winter* (The Otter pursues the Fish); *The Air in Spring* (The Hawk swoops on the Bird). In Act 3 occurs the 4th dance *Fire in Summer* (celebration of carnal love). F.p. Basle 1953, Liverpool 1954 (before f.p. of opera).

Ritual Fire Dance. One of dances in Falla's ballet *El *Amor Brujo* popularized in composer's pf. arr. and played with exceptional brilliance by Arthur Rubinstein. Also arr. for other instr., eg. vc.

Riverso, Al. See *Rovescio, Al.*

Rivier, Jean (*b* Villemomble, 1896). Fr. composer. Studied Paris Cons., where he taught comp. 1948–66. Comp. 7 syms., comic opera *Vénetienne*, *Requiem*, vn. conc., pf. conc., conc. for brass, timp., and str.

Rk. Rank, with reference to the *Mixture stops of an org.

R.M.C.M. *Royal Manchester College of Music.

R.N.C.M. *Royal Northern College of Music, Manchester.

Robbins Landon, H. C. See *Landon, H. C. Robbins.*

Robert le diable (Robert the Devil). Opera in 5 acts by *Meyerbeer to lib. by Scribe. Prod. Paris 1831, London 1832, NY 1834.

Roberto Devereux, conte di Essex. 3-act opera by Donizetti to lib. by Cammarano after Ancelot's play *Elisabeth d'Angleterre*. Prod. Naples 1837, London 1841, NY 1849.

Roberton, (Sir) Hugh (Stevenson) (*b* Glasgow, 1874; *d* Glasgow, 1952). Scottish chorusmaster. Founder and cond. of Glasgow Orpheus Choir, 1906–51, which made several overseas tours and won innumerable competitions. Choir voluntarily disbanded 1951 when Roberton retired, but was later re-formed by younger members as Glasgow Phoenix Choir, with Sir Hugh as hon. pres. Arr. Scottish folk-songs, etc. Knighted 1931.

Roberts, Bernard (*b* Manchester, 1933). Eng. pianist. Studied RCM. Début London 1957. Member of Parikian-Fleming-Roberts Trio. Prof. of pf. RCM.

Robertson, Alec (*b* Southsea, 1892; *d* Midhurst, 1982). Eng. organist, chorusmaster, critic, and broadcaster. Worked for the Gramophone Co. 1920–30. Head of mus. talks, BBC, 1940–52. Authority on plainchant. Author of monographs and books on Schubert, Dvořák, etc. Ed. of several reference books. Reviewer of records in *Gramophone* for nearly 50 years (its music ed. 1952–72).

Robertson, James (*b* Liverpool, 1912). Eng. cond. Studied Cambridge Univ., Leipzig Cons., and RCM. Chorusmaster, Carl Rosa Opera 1938–9; on staff Glyndebourne 1937–9; dir. and cond. SW Opera 1946–54; cond. N.Z. Nat. Broadcasting Orch. 1954–7; Carl Rosa Opera 1958; guest cond. SW Opera 1958–63; mus. dir. N.Z. Opera 1962–3; dir., London Opera Centre 1964–78. C.B.E. 1969.

Robertson, Leroy (*b* Fountain Green, Utah, 1896; *d* Salt Lake City, 1971). Amer. composer. Studied in Boston and with Bloch in Europe. Taught at Brigham Young Univ. 1925–48, prof. of mus. Utah Univ. 1948–62. Comps. incl. *Punch and Judy Overture* (1945), vn. conc. (1948), *The Book of Mormon,* oratorio (1953), str. qt., pf. quintet, etc.

Robertson, Rae (*b* Ardersier, Inverness, 1893; *d* Los Angeles, 1956). Scottish pianist. Studied Edinburgh Univ. and RAM (pf. with Matthay). Began career as solo pianist but formed famous 2-pf. duo with his wife Ethel *Bartlett and toured world. Britten wrote 3 works for them.

Robeson, Paul (Leroy) (*b* Princeton, NJ, 1898; *d* Philadelphia, 1976). Amer. bass and actor. Studied as lawyer, but in 1922 entered professional th. as actor in O'Neill plays. Won int. renown in Kern's musical *Show Boat* (1927) when he sang 'Ol' Man River'. Famous as singer of Negro spirituals. Appeared in films (*Sanders of the River,* etc.) and was a notable Othello. Career halted in 1950s when he fell into disfavour in USA because of alleged Communist sympathies.

Robinson, Douglas (*b* Leeds, 1913; *d* Leeds, 1984). Eng. organist and choirmaster. Organist, Christ Church, Harrogate, 1946. Chorusmaster, CG Opera, 1946–74; Lyric Opera, Chicago, 1976. Chorusmaster, Huddersfield Choral Soc., 1972.

Robinson, Forbes: (*b* Macclesfield, 1926; *d* London, 1987). Eng. bass. Studied in Milan. Opera début CG 1954. Prin. bass, CG. Created title-role in Tippett's *King Priam*, 1962. Took speaking part of Moses in Schoenberg's *Moses und Aron,* 1965. Guest singer with WNO, notably as Claggart in Britten's *Billy Budd* and as Boris Godunov.

Robinson, Stanford (*b* Leeds, 1904; *d* Brighton, 1984). Eng. cond. Studied RCM. On BBC staff 1924–66. Chorusmaster BBC 1924–32, founding BBC Singers, BBC Choral Soc. Ch. Cond., BBC Th. Orch. 1932–46. Opera dir., assoc. cond. BBC S.O. 1946–9; cond. BBC Opera Orch. 1949–52;

chief cond. Queensland S.O. 1968–9. CG début 1937 (*Die Fledermaus*). O.B.E. 1972.

Robinson, Thomas (*fl.* 1589–1609). Eng. composer of mus. for lute and other instr. Wrote textbook *The Schoole of Musicke* (1603, modern edn. Paris 1971).

Robles, Marisa (*b* Madrid, Spain, 1937). Sp.-born harpist. Studied Madrid Cons. Début 1953 with Nat. Orch. of Sp. Prof. of harp, Madrid Royal Cons., 1958. Settled in Eng. 1959. London début 1963. Prof. of harp RCM from 1971. Harp tutor Nat. Youth Orch. of G.B. Soloist with leading orchs.

Rocca, Lodovico (*b* Turin, It., 1895; *d* Turin, 1986). It composer. Studied with Orefice at Milan Cons. Dir., Turin Cons. 1940–66. Comps. incl. opera *Il Dibuk* (The Dybbuk) (1934), symphonic poems, choral works, and chamber mus.

Rochberg, George (*b* Paterson, NJ, 1918). Amer. composer. Studied comp. with Leopold Mannes and Georg Szell at Mannes Sch. of Mus., NY, 1939–42 and with Rosario Scalero at Curtis Institute, 1945. Teacher, Curtis Institute, 1948–54; chairman, mus. dept., Pennsylvania Univ. 1961–8, prof. of mus. from 1968. Influenced by Schoenberg and Mahler, his mus. developed an individual type of serialism but later returned to tonality. Author of many critical articles. Works incl.:

OPERA: *The Confidence Man* (1982).

ORCH: Syms. No. 1 (1948–57, in 3 movts; withdrawn 1977; restored to 5 movts. 1977), No. 2 (1955–6), No. 3, double ch., chamber ch., soloists, orch. (1966–9), No. 4 (1976); *Night Music* (1948); *Cheltenham Concerto* (1958); *Time-Span I* (1960, withdrawn), *II* (1962); *Zodiac* (1965); *Music for the Magic Theater* (1965–9); *Imago Mundi* (1973); Vn. conc. (1974); *Transcendental Variations,* str. (based on 3rd movt. of 3rd str. qt.) (1975); ob. conc. (1983).

SOLO VOICE AND ORCH: *David the Psalmist,* ten. (1954); *4 Blake Songs,* sop. and ens. (1961); *Music for 'The Alchemist',* sop. and 11 players (1965); *Tableaux,* sop., 2 actors' vv., ch., and 12 players (1968); *Sacred Song of Reconciliation,* bass-bar. (1970); *Phaedra,* mez. (1973–4).

ENSEMBLE: *Chamber Symphony,* 9 instr. (1953); *Cantio Sacra,* (transcr. of org. mus. by Scheidt) (1954); *Serenate d'Estate,* 6 instr. (1955); *Apocalyptica,* wind band (1964); *Black Sounds,* winds and perc. (1965); *Fanfares,* brass (1968).

CHAMBER MUSIC: Str. qts., No. 1 (1952), No. 2, with sop. (1959–61), No. 3 (1972), No. 4 (1977), No. 5 (1978), No. 6 (1978), No. 7, with bar. (1979); *Duo Concertante,* vn., vc. (1953); *Dialogues,* cl., pf. (1956); *La Bocca della Verità,* ob., pf. (1958–9, vn., pf. 1962); Pf. Trio (1963); *Contra Mortem et Tempus,* vn., fl., cl., pf. (1965); *50 Caprice-Variations* (after Paganini), solo vn. (1970); *Electrikaleidoscope,* amp. ens. of fl., cl., vc., pf., elec. pf. (1972); *Ricordanza*, vc., pf. (1972); *Ukiyo-e*, harp (1973); Pf. Quintet (1975); *Slow Fires of Autumn*, fl., hp. (1978); va. sonata (1979); *Duo*, ob., bn., (orig. version 1946) (1979); *Trio*, cl., hn., pf. (1980); Str. Quintet (1982).

VOICES: *3 Psalms*, unacc. (1954); *Passions According to the 20th Century*, singers, jazz quintet, brass, perc.,pf., tape (1967); *Behold, My Servant*, unacc. (1973).

SOLO VOICE AND INSTR: *Songs of Solomon*, v., pf. (1947); *3 Cantes flamencos*, high bar. (1969); *11 Songs to Poems by Paul Rochberg*, v., pf. (1969); *Songs in Praise of Krishna*, mez., pf. (1970); *Fantasies*, v., pf. (1971); *Songs of Inanna and Dumuzi*, alto, pf. (1977).

PIANO: *Variations on an Original Theme* (1941); *2 Preludes and Fughettas* (1946); *12 Bagatelles* (1952); *Sonata-Fantasia* (1956); *Nach Bach*, hpd. or pf. (1966); *Carnival Music* (1969); *Partita Variations* (1976); *Book of Contrapuntal Pieces* (1979).

Roche, Jerome (Lawrence Alexander) (*b* Cairo, 1942). Eng. musicologist. Studied at Cambridge Univ. 1959–62, 1964–7. Lecturer, Durham Univ. 1967. Studied at Cini Foundation, Venice, 1973. Authority on 17th cent. Italian sacred music. Author of book on Palestrina, ed. *Dictionary of Early Music* (with E. Roche).

Rock. Species of popular mus. originating in USA (as rock'n'roll) in early 1950s and spreading throughout world. Perf. by 'groups', e.g. of v(v)., guitars, often electronically amplified, and drums. There are sub-species such as *folk rock, jazz rock,* and *punk rock.* Rock was used in stage works such as *Hair, Tommy,* and *Jesus Christ Superstar.* Lyrics often refer to social themes.

Rock of Ages, Cleft for Me. Hymn, words by Rev. Augustus Montague Toplady (1740–78), Vicar of Broadhembury, Devon, first pubd. in *Gospel Magazine,* ed. Toplady, in 1776. Tune by Richard Redhead, from *Church Hymn Tunes, Ancient and Modern,* 1853.

Rococo (from Fr. *rocaille,* fancy rock-work in architecture). In visual arts term is applied to the delicate, diverting style of Watteau and his contemporaries. Mus. application refers to the decorative style e.g. of F. Couperin, and of certain works by Rameau and J. C. Bach. Musically it is a vague term, almost synonymous with *galant* and the 18th cent. and referring to works which are no longer baroque and not yet classical.

Rode, (Jacques) **Pierre** (Joseph) (*b* Bordeaux, 1774; *d* Château de Bourbon, Damazon, 1830). Fr. composer and violinist, pupil in Paris of Viotti. Début, Paris 1790. Prof. of vn., Paris Cons., from 1795 and solo violinist at the Opéra 1799. Violinist to Napoleon, 1800. Settled in St Petersburg 1803–8. Beethoven wrote vn. sonata in G, Op. 96, for him. Skill declined and he abandoned public concerts. Wrote 13 vn. concs., 12 études, 24 caprices, str. qts., and vn. method.

Rodelinda. Opera in 3 acts by Handel to lib. by Salvi rev. by Haym. Prod. London 1725; Northampton, Mass., 1931.

Rodeo. Ballet in 1 act by Copland, 1942, choreog. and lib. by Agnes de Mille. Sub-titled 'The Courting at Burnt Ranch' and set (like *Billy the Kid*) in America's Wild West. Uses traditional songs. Prod. 1942. Suite of 4 movements for orch. 1943.

Rodgers, Richard (*b* Hammels Station, Long Is., 1902; *d* NY, 1979). Amer. composer. Studied Columbia Univ. 1919–21 and Institute of Mus. Art, (later Juilliard Sch.), NY 1921–3. With Lorenz Hart as lyric-writer, wrote successful Broadway musicals *Connecticut Yankee* (1927), *On Your Toes* (1936), *Babes in Arms* (1937), *The Boys from Syracuse* (1938), and *Pal Joey* (1940). With Oscar *Hammerstein II, wrote *Oklahoma!* (1943), *Carousel* (1945), *South Pacific* (1949), *The King and I* (1951), and *The Sound of Music* (1959). Many of these made into films. Wrote mus. for TV documentary *Victory at Sea.* Among the songs he composed are 'There's a Small Hotel', 'My Funny Valentine', 'The Lady is a Tramp', 'Bewitched, bothered, and bewildered', 'Blue Room', 'O What a Beautiful Morning', 'Some Enchanted Evening', 'The Sound of Music', etc.

Rodrigo, Joaquin (*b* Sagunto, 1901). Sp. composer. Blind from age 3. Studied with Dukas in Paris from 1927 and encouraged by Falla. Won Sp. nat. prize 1925 for orch. work *Cinco Piezas Infantiles.* Prof. of mus. history, Madrid Univ. from 1946. Works incl. symphonic poem *Per la flor del Uiri blau* (1934), *Concierto de Aranjuez,* guitar and orch. (1939), *Concierto heroico,* pf. and orch. (1943), *Concierto de estio,* vn. and orch. (1944), *Concierto en modo galante,* vc. and orch. (1949), *Concierto serenata,* harp and orch. (1954), *Fantasia para un gentilhombre,* guitar and orch. (1955), *Concierto Andaluz,* 4 guitars and orch. (1967), *Concierto-madrigal,* 2 guitars and orch. (1968), *Concierto pastoral,* fl. and orch. (1978), *Concierto como un divertimento,* vc. and orch. (1979–81), and choral works.

Rodzinski, Artur (*b* Spalato (Split), Dalmatia, 1892; *d* Boston, Mass., 1958). Polish-born cond. (Amer. citizen from 1933). Studied Vienna Cons. with Schalk. Début Lwów 1921. Cond. opera and concerts in Warsaw 1921–5. Ass. cond. Philadelphia Orch. 1926–9. Cond. Los Angeles P.O. 1929–33, Cleveland Orch. 1933–43, NY P.O. 1943–7, Chicago S.O. 1947–8. Trained and selected players for Toscanini's N.B.C. Orch., 1937. Cond. Amer. première of Shostakovich's *The Lady Macbeth of the Mtsensk District,* Cleveland 1935. Cond. Prokofiev's *War and Peace,* Florence 1953 (f.p. outside Russia).

Rogé, Pascale (*b* Paris, 1951). Fr. pianist. Studied Paris Cons. Début Paris 1969, London 1969. First prize Marguérite Long-Jacques Thibaud int.

competition 1971. Specialist in works of Ravel, Liszt, Bartók, etc. Soloist with leading orchs.

Roger-Ducasse, Jean (Jules Aimable) (*b* Bordeaux, 1873; *d* Taillan-Médoc, 1954). Fr. composer and teacher. Studied Paris Cons. under Fauré (comp.) and de Bériot (pf.). Prof. of comp., Paris Cons. 1935–40. Works incl. comic opera *Cantegril* (1931), mime-drama *Orphée* (1913), *Suite française*, orch. (1907), pf. qt., str. qt., motets, and songs. Completed and orch. Debussy's *Rhapsody* for sax. and orch. (1919).

Rogers, Benjamin (*b* Windsor, 1614; *d* Oxford, 1698). Eng. composer and organist. Organist, Christ Church Cath., Dublin, 1639–41; lay clerk St George's, Windsor, 1641–4. Organist, Eton College Chapel 1660–4, lay clerk again at Windsor 1662; organist and choirmaster Magdalen College, Oxford, 1664–86. Comp. chamber and kbd. works and church mus., incl. *Hymnus eucharisticus* (1660) still sung from top of Magdalen College tower at dawn each May Day.

Rogers, Bernard (*b* NY, 1893; *d* Rochester, 1968). Amer. composer. Studied Institute of Mus. Art, NY, 1919–21, and Cleveland Institute (comp. with Bloch). Went to London and Paris 1927–9 to study with F. Bridge and N. Boulanger. Chief critic, *Musical America*, 1913–24. Taught at Eastman Sch. 1929–67. Works incl. operas *The Warrior* (1944), *The Veil* (1950), *The Nightingale* (1954), 5 syms., oratorio *The Passion* (1942), *The Musicians of Bremen*, narrator and 13 instr. (1958), *Variations on a Song of Mussorgsky* for orch. (1960), vn. sonata (1962), 2 str. qts., and *Dirge for 2 Veterans*, ch. and pf. (1967).

Rogg, Lionel (*b* Geneva, 1936). Swiss organist and harpsichordist. Studied pf. with N. Magaloff. Début as organist, Geneva 1961, thereafter world career as recitalist. Prof. Geneva Cons. from 1960. Recorded all J. S. Bach's organ works.

Rohrflöte (Rohr Flute) (Ger.). Reed flute. Org. stop of 4′ length and 8′ pitch; metal end-plugged pipes with narrow tube through plug. Reed of cl., ob., etc. is Rohrblatt.

Rohrwerk, Rohrstimmen (Ger.). Reed dept. of the org.

Roi David, Le (King David). 'Psaume dramatique' (dramatic psalm) in 5 parts (28 nos.), by Honegger for narrator, sop., mez., ten., ch., and orch. F.p. Mézières, 1921. Rev. and re-orch. 1923, into 3 parts (27 nos.). F.p. Winterthur 1923 (in Ger.), f.p. in England, London 1927. Also orch. suite of 4 nos.

Roi d'Ys, Le (The King of Ys). Opera in 3 acts by *Lalo to lib. by Blau. Prod. Paris 1888, New Orleans 1890, London 1901.

Roi malgré lui, Le (King despite himself). Opera in 3 acts by *Chabrier to lib. by de Najac and Burani (rev. by Richepin). Prod. Paris 1887. Rev. version by A. Carré, 1929.

Roland-Manuel. See Manuel, Roland.

Roldán, Amadeo (*b* Paris, 1900; *d* Havana, 1939). Cuban composer and cond. Studied Madrid Cons. Settled in Cuba 1921 where he was active as cond. and violinist. Cond. Havana P.O. from 1932. Prof. of comp., Havana Cons. from 1935. Interested in African influence on Cuban mus. His works make liberal use of Afro-Cuban rhythms and themes. Works incl. *Overture on Cuban Themes* (1925), *La Rebambaramba*, Afro-Cuban ballet (1928), *Ritmicas I–IV*, wind quintet, pf. (1930), *Ritmicas V–VI*, perc. (1930), 3 *Toques* for orch., *Negro Poem* for str. qt., etc.

Rolfe Johnson, Anthony (*b* Tackley, Oxon, 1940). Eng. ten. Took up singing 1967 after being farmer. Studied GSM. Ch. and small roles, Glyndebourne 1972–6. Won John Christie Award. Opera appearances with ENO, WNO, and Eng. Mus. Th. Notable Mozart and Handel singer. Sang Aschenbach in Britten's *Death in Venice* for Scottish Opera, 1983. Also sings Lieder, *Dream of Gerontius*, Bach Passions, etc.

Roll (Ger. *Wirbel*). Rapid succession of notes on a drum, becoming almost a continuous sound.

Rolland, Romain (*b* Clamecy, 1866; *d* Vézelay, 1944). Fr. writer and musicologist. Studied in Paris and Rome. Prof. of mus. hist., Sorbonne, 1903–13. Lived in Switzerland 1913–39. Author of books on Beethoven and Handel. His huge novel, *Jean-Christophe* (1904–12), concerns the life of a composer and won him the Nobel Prize for literature. Friend of R. Strauss (their interesting correspondence has been pubd.).

Roller, Alfred (*b* Vienna, 1864; *d* Vienna, 1935). Austrian stage designer and painter. Studied painting at Vienna Acad. In 1890s helped to found Vienna Sezession with Schiele, Kokoschka, and Klimt. Prof. at Vienna School of Art 1900, dir. 1909–34. Engaged by Mahler at Vienna Court Opera, 1903, to provide new sets for *Fidelio, Don Giovanni, Tristan und Isolde,* and *Das Rheingold* and *Die Walküre*. These revolutionized stage design. Worked closely with Max Reinhardt at Salzburg Fest. Chief designer Vienna Opera 1903–9, 1918–34, and at Burgtheater 1918–34. Designed orig. prods. of Strauss's *Elektra* and *Der Rosenkavalier* (Dresden 1909 and 1911) and *Die Frau ohne Schatten* (Vienna 1919).

Rolling Stones. Eng. rock group formed in London 1962. Orig members were Mick (Michael Philip) Jagger (*b* 1944) v., Keith Richard (*b* 1944) v. and guitar, Brian Jones (1944–69) guitar and harmonica, Charlie (Charles Robert) Watts (*b* 1942) drums, and Bill Wyman (*b* 1941) bass guitar. Jones's place was taken in 1969 by Mick Taylor, who was succeeded in 1974 by Ron Wood. By 1964 Jagger and Richard were composing most of their material and the group attracted a large following notwithstanding, perhaps because of, its rebellious mode of dress and behaviour. Their songs included *Satisfaction, Mother's Little Helper,* and *Let's Spend the Night Together.* Jagger increasingly became a cult figure among the *avant-garde* of the pop world.

Rollschweller (Ger.). The 'General Crescendo' pedal of an org. which gradually brings out all the stops.

Romalis *(Ole, Polo)* (Sp.). Type of **Seguidilla.*

Roman, Johan Helmich *(b* Stockholm, 1694; *d* Haraldsmåla, nr. Kalmar, 1758). Swed. composer. In 1714 studied under Pepusch and Ariosti in London. Returned to Stockholm 1720, becoming Kapellmeister 1729. Wrote 7 sinfonias, 13 trio sonatas, Swed. Mass, 12 fl. sonatas, and vn. solos.

Roman Carnival, The (Berlioz). See *Carnaval Romain, Le.*

Romance (It. *Romanza,* Ger. *Romanze).* Title with no strict formal application—composers use it as they fancy, vocally or instrumentally. Generally it implies a specially personal or tender quality. Mozart called the slow movement of his pf. conc. No. 20 in D minor (K466) a 'Romance'. Schumann wrote *Drei Romanzen.* Vaughan Williams used the term several times: his *The Lark Ascending* for vn. and orch. is a 'Romance' (1914), he wrote a *Romance* for harmonica, str., and pf. (1951), and the slow movement of the 5th Sym. (1943) is entitled *Romanza.* Elgar wrote a *Romance* for bn. and the 13th 'Enigma' var. is *Romanza.*

Romanesca (It.), **Romanesque** (Fr.). (1) Probably a kind of **galliard danced in the Romagna.
(2) A certain melody much used in the 17th cent. as a **ground bass.
(3) A type of song (e.g. by Monteverdi).

Roman Festivals (Respighi). See *Feste Romana.*

Romani, Felice *(b* Genoa, 1788; *d* Moneglia, 1865). It. poet and librettist. Wrote over 100 opera libs. for Mayr, Rossini, Bellini, Donizetti, etc. Among best-known are those of *Norma, La sonnambula, L'Elisir d'amore, Lucrezia Borgia,* and *Il Turco in Italia.*

Romanian Rhapsodies. 2 works for orch., No. 1 in A and No. 2 in D, by **Enescu, Op. 11.

Romantic(ism). Term used to describe literature, written mainly in the 2 decades 1830–1850, and applied to mus. written in the period *c.*1830 to *c.*1900. It is a vague term, for there are 'romantic' elements in all mus. of all ages. However, the composers generally classified as Romantic are of the period of Weber, Schubert, Schumann, Chopin, Liszt, Berlioz, Wagner, etc., in whose mus. emotional and picturesque expression appeared to be more important than formal or structural considerations. Thus Romanticism became the antithesis of Classicism. In literature

the works of Byron, Scott, Wordsworth, Goethe, Hugo, Gautier, and Balzac were the heart of the Romantic movement and composers such as Berlioz and Liszt were particularly influenced by Byron and Scott. The supernatural element in Romantic literature is reflected musically in works such as Weber's *Der Freischütz,* and the *Witches' Sabbath* movement of Berlioz's *Symphonie fantastique.* However, Chopin, an essentially Romantic composer, was not influenced by literary models; and many movements in works by 'Classical' composers such as Haydn, Mozart, Beethoven, and others, have Romantic leanings. As in so many branches of mus., distinctions between one category and another are blurred, thus nationalism, impressionism, and post-romanticism all impinge upon Romanticism.

'Romantic' Symphony. (1) Bruckner's sub-title for his Sym. No. 4 in E♭ major (1874, rev. 1878, 1879–80, 1881, 1886).
(2) Sub-title of Sym. No. 2 by Howard Hanson (1930).

Romanza. See *Romance.*

Rombando (It.). Humming.

Romberg, Andreas Jakob *(b* Vechta, Münster, 1767; *d* Gotha, 1821). Ger. violinist and composer. Played at Concert Spirituel, Paris, 1784. Tours of Europe 1784–96 and member (with Beethoven and Ries) of Bonn electoral court orch. 1790–3. Lived in Hamburg 1801–15. Court cond., Gotha, from 1815. Wrote 8 operas and operettas, choral mus., 10 syms., incl. *Toy Symphony,* 20 vn. concs., 19 str. qts., etc.

Romberg, Bernhard *(b* Dinklage, 1767; *d* Hamburg, 1841). Ger. cellist and composer, cousin of Andreas **Romberg with whom he toured in Europe 1784–96 and played in Bonn electoral court orch. 1790–3. Taught at Paris Cons. 1800–3. Court cond., Berlin, 1815–19. Visited Russia and Eng. Wrote 5 operas, 5 syms., 10 vc. concs., and chamber works.

Romberg, Sigmund *(b* Szeged, Hung., 1887; *d* NY, 1951). Hung.-born composer. Studied in Vienna with **Heuberger. Went to USA 1909, settling eventually in NY and becoming Amer. citizen. Wrote succession of popular operettas, incl. *Maytime* (1917), *The Student Prince* (1924), *The Desert Song* (1926), *New Moon* (1928), and *Up in Central Park* (1945).

Romeo and Juliet. Several mus. comps. have been based on this Shakespeare tragedy (1594–5). Among them are: (1) *Roméo et Juliette,* dramatic sym., Op. 17, for sop., ten., bass, ch., and orch. by **Berlioz, 1838–9.
(2) *Roméo et Juliette,* opera in 5 acts by **Gounod to lib. by Barbier and Carré. Prod. Paris, London, and NY, 1867.
(3) *Romeo and Juliet (Romeo i Dzhulietta),* fantasy-ov. for orch. by **Tchaikovsky, 1869 (f.p. 1870),

rev. 1870 and 1880 (f.p. 1886). Also duet for sop., ten., and orch., partly based on fantasy-ov., 1893, completed by Taneyev.

(4) *Romeo and Juliet (Romeo i Dzhulietta)*, ballet in prol., 3 acts, and epilogue by *Prokofiev, Op. 64, to lib. by Lavrovsky, Prokofiev, and Radlov, choreog. Psota. Comp. 1935–6. Prod. Brno 1938. Also Symphonic Suite No. 1, Op. 64b (7 movements), 1936, No. 2, Op. 64 c (7 movements), 1937, No. 3, Op. 101 (6 movements), 1944.

(5) *Romeo und Julia*, opera by Sutermeister to his own lib. Prod. Dresden 1940. (There are also operas on this subject by *Zandonai, *Zingarelli, and *Blacher. See also *Bellini's I *Capuleti e i Montecchi.)

Rome Prize (French, Belgian, American). See *Prix de Rome.*

Ronald, (Sir) Landon (orig. Russell, Landon Ronald) (b London, 1873; d London, 1938). Eng. cond., composer, pianist, and administrator. Son of Henry *Russell. Studied RCM. CG coach under Mancinelli 1891, becoming cond. of Augustus Harris's touring opera co. Toured USA as *Melba's accompanist, 1894. CG début as cond. 1896 (*Faust*). Cond. mus. comedy in London 1898–1902. Guest cond. LSO 1904–7 and later of Berlin P.O. and other leading orchs. Permanent cond. Royal Albert Hall Orch. 1909–14, Scottish Orch. 1916–20. Prin., GSM 1910–38. Wrote mus. criticism. Friend and interpreter of Elgar, who ded. *Falstaff* to him. Wrote operetta and orch. mus. but remembered chiefly through his song *Down in the Forest,* one of nearly 200. Knighted 1922.

Ronde (Fr.). Round. (1) The *whole-note or *semibreve.

(2) A round dance to vocal acc. by the dancers.

Rondeau (Fr.).Mus. form so called because of its circle of recurrence. (1) Type of medieval song (also *rondel*) sung by troubadours in which sections of both words and mus. recurred.

(2) Instr. form in 17th and later cents. in which the first section recurs. See *Rondo.*

Rondeña. A kind of *fandango of southern Sp. (named after Ronda in Andalusia), with the same harmonic peculiarity as the *malagueña.

Rondes de printemps (Debussy). See *Images.*

Rondine, La (The Swallow). Opera in 3 acts by Puccini to lib. by Adami trans. from Ger. lib. by Willner and Reichert. Comp. 1914–16. Prod. Monte Carlo 1917, NY 1928, London 1965.

Rondo (It., properly spelt *rondò*). Round. Form of comp., usually instr., in which one section intermittently recurs. By Mozart's day it was the usual form for the last movement of a conc. or sonata. Frequent pattern is A B A C A D A etc., A being the recurring rondo theme and B, C, and D contrasting episodes. Mozart and Beethoven combined this with sonata form into a *sonata-*rondo.* Strauss's *Till Eulenspiegel* is designated a rondo. The term is also sometimes used in opera for an aria with a slow section followed by a faster one.

Ronger, Florimond. See *Hervé.*

Röntgen, Julius (b Leipzig, 1855; d Utrecht, 1932). Dutch composer, pianist, and cond. Studied Leipzig Cons. Accompanist to distinguished singers. Teacher at Amsterdam Mus. Sch. 1878. Cond. Maatschappij concerts, Amsterdam, 1886–98. Dir. Amsterdam Cons. 1918–24. Comp. operas, 21 syms., concs., chamber mus., songs, etc.

Rooley, Anthony (b Leeds, 1944). Eng. lutenist and specialist in early mus. Studied guitar at RAM 1965–8, becoming teacher there, of guitar and lute, 1969–71. Founded (with James Tyler) the Consort of Musicke 1969. Author of several articles on lute and aspects of early mus. Frequently partners the sop. Emma *Kirkby.

Root. The note from which a chord originates, the lowest note when the chord is in its 'basic' position, e.g. in chord of C major (common chord) C–E–G, the root is C.

Rootham, Cyril (Bradley) (b Bristol, 1875; d Cambridge, 1938). Eng. organist and composer. Studied RCM and Cambridge Univ. Organist, St John's College, Cambridge, from 1901. Lecturer in mus. Cambridge Univ. from 1913. Wrote opera, choral works incl. *For the Fallen* (1915), 2 syms., str. qts., songs, etc.

Ropartz, Joseph Marie Guy- (b Guingamp, 1864; d Lanloup, 1955). Fr. composer, cond., and teacher. Studied Paris Cons. under Massenet and later privately with Franck. Dir., Nancy Cons. 1894–1919, cond. Strasbourg orch. 1919–29. Wrote operas, 5 syms., choral mus., 6 str. qts., etc.

Roper, (Edgar) Stanley (b Croydon, 1878; d London, 1953). Eng. organist and composer. Chorister, Westminster Abbey. Ass. organist, Westminster Abbey 1917, organist, Chapels Royal 1919. Prin., TCL 1929–44. Wrote and ed. church mus.

Rore, Cipriano (Cyprian) **de** (b Machelen, nr. Ghent, or Mechelen, 1516; d Parma, 1565). Flemish composer. Pupil of *Willaert in Venice. Held various It. church and court posts, succeeding Willaert as choirmaster of St. Mark's, 1563. Comp. *St John Passion* (1557) and many highly esteemed motets and madrigals.

Rorem, Ned (b Richmond, Indiana, 1923). Amer. composer and author. Studied in Chicago, at Curtis Institute, Penn., 1943, and later at Juilliard Sch., NY, (comp. with Wagenaar). Worked in NY as copyist to Virgil Thomson. Lived in Morocco and Paris 1949–58, and in 1951–5 wrote *The Paris Diary of Ned Rorem,* entertaining journal, pubd. 1966. Recipient of several awards and fellowships.

Prof. of mus., Buffalo Univ. 1959–61, prof. of comp. Utah Univ. 1965–7. Studied in Fr. with Honegger, 1951–2. The influence of Poulenc is discernible in his many songs, of which he is the foremost Amer. composer. His orch. works are colourful and he sometimes uses a modified serial technique. Has written several other books, incl. *Critical Affairs, A Composer's Journal* (1970). Prin. comps.:

OPERAS: *A Childhood Miracle* (1952); *The Robbers* (1956); *Last Day* (1959); *The Anniversary* (1962); *Fables* (5 very short operas) (1970); **Miss Julie* (1964); *Bertha* (1968–9); *Three Sisters Who Are Not Sisters* (1969); *Hearing* (1976).

ORCH: 3 syms. (1950, 1955, 1957); 3 pf. concs.; *Lento*, str. (1950); *Design* (1954); *Pilgrims*, str. (1958); *Eagles* (1958); *11 Studies* (1959); *Ideas* (1961); *Lions* (1964); *Water Music,* cl., vn., small orch. (1967); *Air Music* (1974); *Assembly and Fall* (1975); *Sunday Morning* (1977).

VOICE AND ORCH: *6 Irish Poems* (1950); *6 Songs* (1953); *Poèmes pour la paix* (1956); *Sun*, sop. and orch. (1966); *Gloria* (1970); *Ariel* (1971); *Last Poems of Wallace Stevens* (1972); *Serenade on 5 English Poems* (1976).

CHORAL: *Laudemus Tempus Actum,* ch. and orch.; *Letters from Paris*, ch. and orch. (1966); *The Poets' Requiem*, sop., ch., and orch. (1955–6); *Little Prayers*, sop., bar., ch., orch. (1973); *Missa brevis*, sop., ten., ch. (1974); *3 Christmas Choruses*, ch. (1978).

SONG-CYCLES (with pf.): *Flight for Heaven*, bar. (1950); *Cycle of Holy Songs* (1951); *King Midas* (1960–1); *Poems of Love and the Rain* (1962–3); *Hearing* (1965–6); *War Scenes* (1969); *To Jane* (1974); *Women's Voices* (1976); *A Journey* (1976); *After Long Silence*, mez. and ob. (1982).

CHAMBER MUSIC: Vn. sonata (1949); *Day Music* and *Night Music*, vn. and pf.; *11 Studies for 11 Players* (1959); *Lovers*, hpd., ob., vc., perc. (1964); *Ariel*, sop., cl., pf. (1971); *Sky Music*, harp (1976); *Romeo and Juliet*, harp, guitar (1977).

SONGS: Among nearly 300 songs for v. and pf. are: *Alleluia* (1946); *The Lordly Hudson* (1947); *Little Elegy* (1949); *Rain in Spring* (1949); *The Tulip Tree, Sally's Smile, Clouds* (1953); *Youth, Day, Old Age, Night* (1954); *Look Down, Fair Moon* (1957).

Rosa, Karl (Carl) (August Nikolaus) (really Karl Rose) (*b* Hamburg, 1842; *d* Paris, 1889). Ger. cond., violinist, and impresario. Studied Leipzig Cons. and Paris Cons. Leader of orch. in Hamburg, 1863–5. London début 1866, in USA 1866–71. In NY 1867 married sop. Euphrosyne Parepa and became manager and dir. of opera co. headed by his wife. After her death in 1874 formed *Carl Rosa Opera Co., based in Eng. from 1875.

Rosa, Salvator (*b* Arenella, Naples, 1615; *d* Rome, 1673). It. painter, writer, and lutenist. Wrote *La Musica*, satire on church mus., pubd. posthumously. Most or all of songs attrib. to him are by other composers.

Rosalia. Name sometimes given to harmonic real *sequence (because It. popular song *Rosalia, mia cara* began with this device). An example is Diabelli's theme set by Beethoven and others.

Rosamunde, Fürstin von Cypern (Rosamund, Princess of Cyprus). Play by Helmina von Chézy (1823) for which *Schubert wrote ov., 3 entr'actes, 2 ballet pieces, and some vocal nos. The ov. played at the f.p. was that already comp. for *Alfonso und Estrella and pubd. under that title as Op. 69 (D 732). What we know as the *Rosamunde* ov. (D 644) was written in 1820 for melodrama by Hoffmann called *Die *Zauberharfe* (The Magic Harp).

Rosbaud, Hans (*b* Graz, 1895; *d* Lugano, 1962). Austrian cond. and pianist. Studied Frankfurt. Cond. and dir., mus. sch., Mainz 1923–30; chief cond. Frankfurt radio orch. 1928–37; Münster Opera 1938–41; Strasbourg Opera 1941–4; Munich P.O. 1945–8; S.W. Ger. Radio Orch. 1948–62; Zürich Tonhalle Orch. 1950 (mus. dir. from 1957). Chief cond. Aix-en-Provence Fest. 1947–59. Frequently cond. at Donaueschingen. Cond. f.p. (radio and stage) of Schoenberg's *Moses und Aron (1954 and 1957). Renowned interpreter and champion of 20th-cent. mus. Cond. f.p. of Bartók's 2nd pf. conc., with composer as soloist, 1933.

Rose. Sound-hole cut to aid resonance in the lute, guitar, mandolin, etc. So-called owing to ornamental flower-like shape.

Rosé, Arnold (Josef) (*b* Jassy, Romania, 1863; *d* London, 1946). Austrian violinist. Studied Vienna Cons. Début Leipzig Gewandhaus 1879. Leader of Vienna Court Opera Orch. and of Vienna P.O. for 57 years (1881–1938), also led orch. at Bayreuth Fest. Formed and led Rosé Qt. from 1883. It gave f.ps. of works by Reger and Schoenberg. Taught at Vienna State Acad. until 1924. Brother-in-law of Mahler. Fled to Eng. 1938.

Rose, Bernard (William George) (*b* Little Hallingbury, Herts., 1916). Eng. organist, cond., and teacher. Studied RCM 1933–5 and Cambridge Univ. Organist Queen's College, Oxford, 1939–57, Magdalen College, Oxford, 1957–81.

Rose, Leonard (*b* Washington D.C., 1918; *d* White Plains, NY, 1984). Amer. cellist. Studied Curtis Institute, Penn., with *Salmond 1934–8. Member of N.B.C. Orch., under Toscanini. Prin. cellist Cleveland Orch. 1939–43, NY P.O. 1943–51, then successful solo career. Teacher at Curtis Institute 1951–62 and at Juilliard Sch. from 1947.

Roseingrave, Thomas (*b* Winchester, 1688; *d* Dunleary, Ireland, 1766). Irish organist and composer, son and pupil of Daniel Roseingrave (*d* 1727, organist of Gloucester, Winchester, and Salisbury caths. and of St Patrick's and Christ Church caths., Dublin). Studied in Italy, where he knew both Scarlattis. Organist, St George's,

Hanover Sq., 1725–52. Wrote opera, cantatas, extra numbers for D. Scarlatti's opera *Narciso* in London 1720, hpd. pieces, etc.

Rosen, Charles (*b* NY, 1927). Amer. pianist and author. Studied Juilliard Sch. 1934–8 (between the ages of 7 and 11) and with M. Rosenthal. Début NY 1951. Prof. of mus., State Univ. of NY from 1971. Author of *The Classical Style* (1971) and *Schoenberg* (1975). Noted for his playing of Bach's *Goldberg Variations*, the late Beethoven sonatas, and Debussy. Has given important perfs. of Schoenberg, Webern, Carter, and Boulez.

Rosenberg, Hilding (Constantin) (*b* Bosjökloster, Sweden, 1892; *d* Stockholm, 1985). Swedish composer, pianist, and cond. Studied in Stockholm and later in Ger. and Austria. Taught pf. and theory, Stockholm, 1916–30. Cond., Royal Swedish Opera 1932–4. Comps. reflect Scandinavian nationalist tendencies, also influence of Schoenberg. Prin. works incl.:

OPERAS: *Resa till Amerika* (Voyage to America) (1932); *Marionetter* (1939); *Lycksalighetens ö* (Island of Felicity) (1945); *Josef och hans bröder* (Joseph and his Brethren, after T. Mann) (1945–8); *Hus med dubbel ingäng* (House with two entrances) (1969).
ORCH: 8 syms. (1919–74); sym. for wind (1968); *Orpheus in town* (ballet and orch. suite) (1938); pf. conc. (1950); 2 vn. concs. (1924, 1951); *Riflessioni 1–3* for str. (1959–60); *Symphonic Metamorphoses 1–3* (1964); tpt. conc. (1928); vc. conc. (1939); va. conc. (1942); *Louisville Concerto* (1955).
CHORAL: *Den Heliga Natten* (The Holy Night) (1936); *Huvudskalleplats* (Calvary) (1938); *Hymnus* (1965).
VOCAL: *Åt jordgudinnan* (To The Earth Goddess), mez. or bar. and 6 instr. (1960); *Dagdrivaren* (The Sluggard), bar., orch. (1962).
CHAMBER MUSIC: 12 str. qts.; 3 vn. sonatas.

Rosenkavalier, Der (The Knight of the Rose). Opera in 3 acts by Richard Strauss, his Op. 59, to lib. (comedy for mus.) by Hugo von Hofmannsthal. Comp. 1909–10. Prod. Dresden 1911; London and NY Met. 1913. Among the famous characters in this opera are the Marschallin (wife of the field-marshal), Oktavian, Sophie, Baron Ochs, and Faninal. For silent film (first shown 1926) with altered plot, Strauss arr. much of the mus. of the opera for chamber orch. (1925) as accompaniment. He cond. for the film in Dresden and London but did not use this reduced score, which was not perf. until recorded in 1980.

Rosenmüller, Johann (*b* Oelsnitz, *c.* 1619; *d* Wolfenbüttel, 1684). Ger. composer and organist. Studied Leipzig. Organist, Nikolaikirche, Leipzig, 1651–5. Taught in Venice for nearly 20 years. Court cond., Wolfenbüttel from 1682. Wrote dance suites, sonatas, and church mus.

Rosenstock, Joseph (*b* Kraków, 1895; *d* NY, 1985). Polish-born cond. and pianist (Amer. citizen 1949). Studied Kraków Cons. and Vienna Cons. Cond., Darmstadt Opera 1922–5, Wiesbaden 1925–7, Mannheim 1930–3; mus. dir. Jewish Kulturbund, Berlin, 1933–6. Début NY Met. 1929 (*Rosenkavalier*). Cond. in Tokyo after 1938. Settled in USA 1946. Cond., NY City Opera 1948–55 (dir. from 1952); mus. dir. Cologne Opera 1958–61. Returned to USA 1961, conducting at NY Met. and San Francisco Opera.

Rosenthal, Harold (David) (*b* London, 1917; *d* London, 1987). Eng. critic and author. Archivist, Royal Opera House, CG, 1950–6. Ed., *Opera* 1953–86. Books incl. *Two Centuries of Opera at Covent Garden* (1958). Co-ed., *Concise Oxford Dictionary of Opera* (2nd edn., 1979). Revised Loewenberg *Annals of Opera* 1978; supplement (1940–80), 1985. Autobiography *My Mad World of Opera* (1983). O.B.E. 1983.

Rosenthal, Manuel (*b* Paris, 1904). Fr. composer and cond. Studied at Paris Cons. 1918–23 and with Ravel (1926–30). Cond. of many Fr. orchs.; mus. dir. Fr. Nat. Radio Orch. 1944–7. Cond. Seattle S.O. 1949–51. Works incl. oratorio *St Francis of Assisi* (1936–9), orch. suite *Joan of Arc* (1936), sym. (1949), mass (1953), operas, and chamber mus. Arr. of ballet *Gaîté parisienne* (1938) from Offenbach themes. Orch. transcrs. of works by Ravel.

Rosenthal, Moriz (*b* Lemberg, 1862; *d* NY, 1946). Ukrainian pianist. Studied with Joseffy in Vienna 1875 and with Liszt in Weimar and Rome 1877. Début Vienna 1876. Studied philosophy, Vienna Univ. 1880–6. Began foreign tours 1887, making int. reputation as one of the great pianists 'in the grand manner'. London début 1895. Taught at Curtis Institute, Penn. Settled in NY 1939.

Roses from the South (*Rosen aus dem Süden*). Waltz, Op. 388, by Johann Strauss II. Occurs in operetta *Das Spitzentuch der Königin* (The Queen's Lace Handkerchief), 1880.

Rosetti, Francesco. See *Rössler, Franz Anton*.

Rosiers, Charles (*b* Liège, 1640; *d* Cologne, 1725). Flemish violinist. Vice-Kapellmeister, electoral court at Bonn. Wrote 14 sonatas for vn. and ob., motets, guitar method, and *Pièces choisies à la manière italienne*, for various instr. (1691).

Rosing, Vladimir (*b* St Petersburg, 1890; *d* Los Angeles, 1963). Russ.-born ten. (later Amer. citizen). Pupil of Jean *de Reszke. Début St Petersburg 1912 as Lensky in *Eugene Onegin*. London concert début 1913. Settled in London. Dir. and sang in opera season at London Opera House 1915 (sang Herman in Eng. première of Tchaikovsky's *Queen of Spades*). Gave notable series of recitals in London and elsewhere 1916–21. Toured USA 1922. Dir., opera dept., Eastman

Sch. of Mus. 1923. Dir., Amer. Opera Co., 1927–9. In 1936, with Albert *Coates, organized Brit. Mus.-Drama Opera Co., which survived for one season at CG. Settled in Los Angeles from 1939, becoming ass. dir. S. California Opera Assoc. Prod. opera for NY City Opera.

Rosselli, Francesco (b c.1510; d after 1577). It. composer, but may have been Fr. (François Roussel). Choirmaster St Peter's, Rome, 1548–50. Wrote motets, madrigals, and songs.

Rossellini, Renzo (b Rome, 1908; d Monte Carlo, 1982). It. composer and critic. Wrote several operas, incl. *Una sguàrdo dal ponte* (based on A. Miller's play *A View from the Bridge*, prod. Rome 1961), ballets, orch. works, chamber mus., and scores for films dir. by his brother Roberto Rossellini, incl. *Rome, Open City* (1945). Art. dir. Monte Carlo Opera, 1973–82.

Rössel-Majdan, Hildegard (b Moosbierbaum, Austria, 1921). Austrian cont. Studied in Vienna. Career in oratorio and concerts, Vienna 1948–51. Member, Vienna State Opera from 1951.

Rosseter, Philip (b 1567 or 8; d London, 1623). Eng. composer and lutenist. Wrote half of *Booke of Ayres* (1601) with *Campion, also works for broken consort, etc. Lutenist at court of James I, 1603. Managed company of boy actors (Children of Whitefriars) 1609–17.

Rossetto, Steffano (b Nice, fl. 1560–80). It. composer of madrigals and motets. Court organist, Munich, 1579–80. Choirmaster at Novara, then in service of Medicis in Florence, composing 17-part *Lamento d'Olimpia* 1567.

Rossi, Lauro (b Macerata, 1812; d Cremona, 1885). It. composer and cond. Pupil in Naples of *Zingarelli. Cond. in Rome and Milan 1832–4. Dir. It. opera co. in Mexico 1835–9. Cond. opera in Havana, Cuba, 1839–42, New Orleans 1842–3. Dir., Milan Cons., 1850–70, Naples Cons. 1870–8. Wrote nearly 30 operas, oratorio *Saul*, church mus., etc.

Rossi, Luigi (b Torre Maggiore, 1598; d Rome, 1653). It. composer, singer, and organist. Church organist in Rome by 1633 and by 1640 was regarded as one of Italy's outstanding musicians. First opera perf. Rome 1642, lasting seven hours. Went in 1646 to Paris where he comp. and sang in *Le mariage d'Orphée et d'Euridice*, said to be first It. opera given in Paris (1647). Wrote oratorio, many cantatas, and other church mus.

Rossi, Mario (b Rome, 1902). It. cond. Deputy cond., Augusteo Orch., Rome, 1926–36. Taught cond. at S. Cecilia Acad., Rome, 1931–6. Cond., Maggio Musicale Fiorentino, 1936–44, Turin Radio Orch. 1946–69. Advocate of contemporary music.

Rossi, Salomone (b Mantua, c.1570; d Mantua, c.1630). It. composer at court of Mantua 1587–

1628, where he was colleague of Monteverdi. Wrote 7 books of madrigals, and other secular and sacred vocal mus. Pioneer of trio sonata form.

Rossignol, Le (Stravinsky). See *Nightingale, The*.

Rossi-Lemeni, Nicola (b Istanbul, 1920). It. bass of mixed It. and Russ. parentage. Abandoned law for mus., 1943. Opera début Venice 1946 as Varlaam in *Boris Godunov*. Regular appearances at La Scala, Milan, 1947–60. CG début 1952, San Francisco 1951–3, NY Met. 1953–4. Sang in f. It. p. of Britten's *Billy Budd* (Florence 1965) and in f.p. of Pizzetti's *L'Assassinio nella cattedrale* (Milan 1958).

Rossini, Gioachino Antonio (b Pesaro, 1792; d Paris, 1868). It. composer, son of town trumpeter and a singer. As child, apprenticed to blacksmith, sang in churches, and played hpd. in ths. Entered Bologna Acad. 1806 and while a student wrote opera *Demetrio e Polibio*. In 1810 Venetian impresario commissioned him to write comic opera (*La cambiale di matrimonia*), and in 1812 his *La pietra del paragone* was produced at the Scala, Milan. 2 operas prod. in Venice, 1813, est. his reputation outside It.—*Tancredi*, an *opera seria*, and *L'Italiana in Algeri*, an *opera buffa*. In 1814 was engaged as mus. dir. of both Neapolitan opera houses and for San Carlo wrote *Elisabetta, Regina d'Inghilterra*, in which he replaced *recitativo secco* with recits. acc. by str. Other operas for Naples were *Otello* and *Il barbiere di Siviglia*, a failure at first but soon to be hailed as an outstanding *opera buffa*. These were followed by *La Cenerentola*, *La gazza ladra*, and *Mosè in Egitto*. In 1822 married sop. Isabella Colbran, who had created several of his sop. roles, incl. in 1823 *Semiramide*, the last opera of his It. cycle.

In 1822 Rossini visited Vienna, where he met Beethoven; this was followed by a trip to London. In 1824 settled in Paris as dir. of the Théâtre Italien, and wrote 3 operas for Paris, incl. *Guillaume Tell* (1829). Appointed composer to King Charles X in 1825 and after success of *Tell* was commissioned by Govt. to write 5 operas in 10 years. But the 1830 revolution dethroned Charles, and the new govt. set aside the commissions. Rossini left Paris for Italy in 1836 and for the next 19 years composed only three religious works and some occasional pieces. The likely reason is his prolonged neurasthenic ill-health which followed the intensive work on *Guillaume Tell*. In Bologna became hon. pres. of the Liceo Musicale and reformed its teaching methods, but left the town in 1848. In 1855 he and his 2nd wife settled in Paris where, for the remaining 13 years of his life, Rossini was the centre of artistic and intellectual life. He also began to compose again, the *Petite Messe solennelle* in 1863 and the 150-odd piano pieces, songs, and ensembles which called *Péchés de vieillesse* (Sins of Old Age) (1857–68). Many of these were first perf. at the Rossinis' 'Samedi Soirs'. He was buried in Paris (at his funeral Beethoven's Funeral March from Op. 26 was played by an ens. of instr. invented by Adolphe *Sax and many of the greatest singers of the day were soloists, incl. *Patti and *Nilsson). In 1887 he was reinterred in Florence.

Rossini's comic operas have perpetuated his name. Their wit, speed, and grace, their bubbling fun and entirely appropriate orchestration, are perennially fresh. Several of them were written within the space of a fortnight: although there is nothing slipshod about them, the impression of spontaneity remains. Nevertheless his serious works, *Guillaume Tell, Tancredi,* and *Semiramide,* contain superb mus., and although *Otello* has yielded to Verdi's masterpiece, it is still worth hearing. His 2 late religious works are masterpieces, and the sparkling str. sonatas (str. qts.) of his youth testify to his grounding in the classics of Haydn and Mozart. Prin. works:

OPERAS: *Demetrio e Polibio (1806); La cambiale di matrimonio (1810); L'equivoco stravagante (1811); L'inganno felice (1812); Ciro in Babilonia (1812); La *scala di seta (1812); La pietra del paragone (1812); L'occasione fa il ladro (1812); Il *signor Bruschino (1813); *Tancredi (1813); L'*Italiana in Algeri (1813); Aureliano in Palmira (1813); Il *Turco in Italia (1814); Sigismondo (1814); *Elisabetta, Regina d'Inghilterra (1815); Torvaldo e Dorliska (1815); Il *barbiere di Siviglia (1816); La gazzetta (1816); *Otello (1816); La *Cenerentola (1817); La *gazza ladra (1817); Armida (1817); Adelaide di Borgogna (1817); *Mosè in Egitto (1818, rev. as Moïse 1827); Adina (1818); Ricciardo e Zoraide (1818); Ermione (1819); Edoardo e Cristina (1819); La donna del lago (1819); Bianca e Faliero (1819); Maometto II (1820); *Mathilde di Shabran (1821); Zelmira (1822); *Semiramide (1823); Il viaggio a Reims (1825); Le *Siège de Corinthe (1826, rev. and amplification of Maometto II); Le *Comte Ory (1828); *Guillaume Tell (1829).

CANTATAS: Il pianto d'armonia (1808); La morte di Didone (1811); Partenope (1819); Il vero omaggio (1823); Il pianto delle Musi per la morte di Lord Byron (1823); Il serto votivo (1829).

SACRED MUSIC: Messa di gloria (1820); Stabat Mater (1842); *Petite Messe solennelle (1863).

MISCELLANEOUS: Inno dell' Indipendenza (1815); Soirées musicales, songs and duets incl. La Danza (1835); Regata Veneziana, song-cycle (1857).

INSTRUMENTAL: Introduction and Variations for cl. and orch. (1809); Andante con variazioni in F, ob. and harp; Prelude, Theme, and Variations, hn. and pf.; Str. sonatas (sonatas a quattro), 2 vn., vc., db. (1804), No. 1 in G, No. 2 in A, No. 3 in C, No. 4 in B♭ major, No. 5 in E♭, No. 6 in D. In 1808 Rossini transcribed 5 of these sonatas as wind qts. which are given here in relation to the numbers of the str. versions: No. 1 in F, No. 2 in G, No. 4 in B♭, No. 5 in F, No. 6 in D. The str. No. 3 has no wind version. A 6th wind qt. (in F, two movts.) has no str. equivalent.

Rössler, Franz Anton (b Leitmeritz, Bohemia, c. 1750; d Ludwigslust, Ger., 1792). Bohemian-born Ger. composer and cond. Played db. in orch. of Prince Öttingen-Wallerstein from 1773, becoming cond. 1785. Court cond., Ludwigslust, from 1789. Italianized name to Francesco Antonio Rosetti. Wrote operas, requiem, oratorios, over 30 syms., concs., and chamber mus.

Rostal, Max (b Teschen, 1905). Austrian-born violinist, composer, and teacher. Studied with *Rosé and *Flesch. Leader Oslo P.O. 1927. Ass. to Flesch 1927–30. Prof., Berlin State Acad. 1930–3. Settled in Eng. 1934 (becoming Brit. citizen). Prof. GSM 1944–58. Prof. Cologne State Acad. and Berne Cons. from 1957. Noted exponent of contemporary mus. and much sought after as teacher. C.B.E. 1977.

Rostropovich, Mstislav (Leopoldovich) (b Baku, 1927). Russ. cellist, pianist, and cond. Studied Moscow Cons. 1943–48. Début 1942. Prof. of vc., Moscow Cons. from 1956. One of great cellists of his day, for whom Prokofiev, Shostakovich, and Britten (all of whom were his friends) wrote works. Also pf. accompanist to his wife, the sop. Galina *Vishnevskaya. London début 1956. Art. dir., Aldeburgh Fest. from 1977. Début as cond., Moscow Bolshoy 1968 (Eugene Onegin). Cond. début in London 1974 (New Philharmonia). Cond. Nat. S.O., Washington, from 1977. Out of favour with Soviet authorities from 1970 because of public defence of dissident novelist Solzhenitsyn and was denied exit from USSR for foreign engagements for over a year until he cond. opera in Vienna. Left USSR with wife 1974, ostensibly for 2 years, but never returned. In 1978 they were deprived of Soviet citizenship. Hon. K.B.E. 1987.

Roswaenge (orig. Rosenving-Hansen), **Helge** (b Copenhagen, 1897; d Munich, 1972). Danish ten. Début 1921. Member Cologne Opera 1927–30, Berlin State Opera 1930–44. Sang at Vienna Opera from 1936, CG 1938 (Florestan), Salzburg 1933–9. Sang Parsifal at Bayreuth 1934–6.

Rota (Lat.). Wheel. (1) Term occasionally used for *round, as in Reading Rota, i.e. *Sumer is icumen in, thought to have been comp. by a monk of Reading Abbey.
(2) Hurdy-gurdy.

Rota, Nino (b Milan, 1911; d Rome, 1979). It. composer. Wrote oratorio at age of 11 and opera at 14. Studied comp. with Casella and Pizzetti and at Curtis Institute, Penn. Taught at Liceo Musicale, Bari, from 1939, becoming dir. 1950. Comp. 10 operas, 3 syms., concs. for pf., tb., vc., bn., pf., db., and horn., chamber mus., and film scores.

Roth, Daniel (b Mulhouse, 1942). Fr. organist and composer. Studied Paris Cons. Deputy organist Sacré Coeur, Paris, 1963–72, organist from 1972; prof. of org., Marseilles Cons. from

1973. Recitals in USA and Europe. Comps. for org. and choir.

Rothenberger, Anneliese (*b* Mannheim, 1924). Ger. sop. noted for Mozart and R. Strauss operatic roles and for singing of operetta. Studied at Mannheim Musikhochschule. Début Koblenz 1943. Member Hamburg State Opera 1946–56. Joined Deutsche Oper 1956. Vienna début 1957. Glyndebourne début 1959 (Sophie), NY Met. 1960 (Zdenka).

Rothmüller, Marko (*b* Trnjani, 1908). Yugoslav bar. Studied Zagreb Acad. and Vienna Cons. (comp. with Berg). Opera début Hamburg 1932 in *Der Freischütz*. Zagreb Opera 1932–4, Zürich Opera 1935–47, CG 1939 and 1948–55, NY City Opera 1948–52, Met. 1959–65. First stage Wozzeck in Eng. (CG 1952, cond. Kleiber).

Rothwell, Evelyn. See *Barbirolli, Evelyn*.

Rothwell, Walter Henry (*b* London, 1872; *d* Los Angeles, 1927). Eng. cond., composer, and pianist. Studied Vienna Cons. under Epstein, Fuchs, Bruckner, etc. Toured Europe as pianist, but abandoned kbd. for cond.'s rostrum when he became ass. to Mahler at Hamburg, 1895. Cond. Savage Opera Co. in USA, incl. perfs. of *Parsifal* in English. Cond. Amer. première of *Madama Butterfly* (in Eng.) 1906. Cond. St Paul S.O. 1908–14, Los Angeles P.O. 1919–27. Wrote pf. conc., chamber mus., and songs.

Rott, Hans (*b* Vienna, 1858; *d* Vienna, 1884). Austrian composer and organist. Studied at Vienna Cons. (Bruckner for org., Krenn for comp.). Close friend of Mahler, whose methods are anticipated in Rott's Symphony in E (1878–80). Became insane 1880.

Rotte (or rote). Name applied in Middle Ages to various instr., such as harp, lyre, crwth, and hurdy-gurdy. (Variant of *chrotta, crot*, etc.)

Rouet d'Omphale, Le (Omphale's Spinning-Wheel). First symphonic poem by Saint-Saëns, his Op. 31, comp. 1871–2. Omphale was mythical queen to whom Hercules was slave (wearing woman's dress) for 3 years, spinning wool for her.

Rouget de Lisle, Claude Joseph (*b* Lons-le-Saunier, 1760; *d* Choisy-le-roi, 1836). Fr. army engineer, poet, and composer. While stationed in Strasbourg, wrote on 25 April 1792 words and music of *Chant de guerre pour l'armée du Rhin*. This was perf. so often by Marseilles Volunteer Battalion it eventually became known as *La Marseillaise*. Sanctioned as national song in 1795, fell out of favour, restored to respectability 1830, adopted as Fr. nat. anthem 1879.

Roulade (Fr.). One of Fr. vocal ornaments, much like **divisions*.

Rouleau, Joseph (Alfred) (*b* Matane, Quebec, 1929). Fr.-Canadian bass. Studied Montreal and Quebec, later in Milan. Début New Orleans 1955.

Opera appearances in world's leading opera houses. CG from 1957. Sang Grand Inquisitor in first Fr.-language perf. of Verdi's *Don Carlos* at CG, 1983.

Round. Short unacc. vocal 'perpetual canon' at the unison or octave in which the vv. enter in turn. Popular in Eng. after 16th cent. Famous examples are *Three Blind Mice* and *London's Burning*.

Round Dance. (1) A dance in which the performers turn round.
  (2, a more common use of the term) A dance in which they move round in a circle, i.e. a ring dance.

Roundelay (Fr. *rondelet*). Country songs or ballads common in 14th cent. So called because of constant recurrence of first verse.

Rounseville, Robert (*b* Attleboro, Mass., 1914; *d* NY, 1974). Amer. ten. Studied in NY. Sang in night-clubs, on radio, and in musicals under name Robert Field. Studied at Berkshire Music Center opera dept.; joined NY City Opera 1948, singing Pelléas in Debussy's opera opposite Maggie Teyte. Sang Hoffmann in Beecham film version of opera, 1950. Created role of Tom Rakewell in Stravinsky's *The Rake's Progress*, Venice 1951. Returned to Broadway mus. stage, singing in Bernstein's *Candide* and in *Man of La Mancha*.

Rousseau, Jean-Jacques (*b* Geneva, 1712; *d* Ermenonville, 1778). Swiss philosopher, composer, and writer on mus. While working as copyist, devised new system of mus. notation which he published in *Dissertation sur la musique moderne* (Paris, 1743). Wrote *opéra-ballet, Les muses galantes* (1747), and very successful pastoral opera *Le Devin du village* (Fontainebleau 1752). Took It. side in *Querelle des *Bouffons* and attacked Fr. mus. in his *Lettre sur la musique française* (1753). Pubd. *Dictionnaire de Musique* (1768). Left unfinished opera *Daphnis et Chloé* and wrote about 100 songs.

Rousseau, Samuel Alexandre (*b* Neuve-Maison, 1853; *d* Paris, 1904). Fr. composer and organist. Studied org. with **Franck at Paris Cons. Won *Prix de Rome* 1878. Choirmaster, Ste Clotilde. Worked as mus. critic. Comp. operas, org. pieces, church mus.; pieces for harp, etc.

Roussel, Albert (*b* Tourcoing, 1869; *d* Royan, 1937). Fr. composer. Despite showing mus. tendencies as a child, began career as naval officer, his service in Indo-China leaving profound impression. Resigned commission 1894 to study mus. Worked with Gigout and from 1898 to 1909 at Schola Cantorum under d'Indy. Prof. of counterpoint, Schola Cantorum, 1909–14. Served in Fr. army 1914–18, thereafter devoting himself to comp. and living secluded life because of ill-health. Once free of d'Indy influence, Roussel developed a neo-classical style in which strong Stravinskyan rhythms and daring harmonies were blended with a rich, sometimes orientally exotic, orch. palette and expressive melodies. His 3rd and 4th syms. represent him at his most individual, but his ballet *Bacchus et Ariane* is his best-known work. Prin. comps.:

OPERA-BALLET: *Padmâvatî* (1914–18, prod. 1923).

OPERA: *Le Testament de la tante Caroline* (1932–3).

BALLETS: *Le *Festin de l'araignée* (1912); **Bacchus et Ariane* (1930); *Aeneas* (1935).

INCIDENTAL MUSIC: *Le Marchand de Sable qui passe* (1908); *La Naissance de la lyre* (1923–4).

ORCH: Syms: No. 1 (*Le Poème de la forêt*) (1904–6), No. 2 in B♭ (1919–21), No. 3 in G minor (1930), No. 4 in A (1934); *Prelude to Tolstoy's Resurrection* (1903); *Pour une fête de printemps* (1920); 2 suites from *Bacchus et Ariane* (1930); Suite in F (1926); pf. conc. (1927); *Petite Suite* (1929); *Sinfonietta*, str. (1934); *Rapsodie flamande* (1936); vc. concertino (1936).

VOICE(S) AND ORCH: *La Ménace* (1908); *Madrigal aux muses* (1923); *Psalm 80*, ten., ch., and orch. (1928).

CHAMBER MUSIC: pf. trio (1902); *Divertissement*, pf. and 5 wind (1906); vn. sonata No. 1 (1907–8), No. 2 (1924); *Serenade*, fl., harp, str. trio (1925); *Joueurs de flûte*, fl. and pf. (1924); Trio for fl., va., vc. (1929); str. qt. (1932); *Andante and Scherzo*, fl., pf. (1934); str. trio (1937).

PIANO: *Rustiques* (1904–6); *Suite* (1909–10); Sonatina (1912); *3 Pieces* (1933).

SONGS: 4 *Poèmes d'Henri de Régnier* (1903); 4 *Poèmes d'Henri de Régnier* (1907); *Flammes* (1908); 2 *Songs from the Chinese* (1907–8); 2 Songs (*Light, Farewell*) (1918); 2 Songs (*Le Bachalier de Salamanque, Sarabande*) (1919).

Routh, Francis (John) (*b* Kidderminster, 1927). Eng. composer, organist, pianist, and author. Studied Cambridge Univ. and RAM 1951–3. Founder, Redcliffe Concerts of Brit. mus., 1963. Works incl. sym., vc. conc., pf. conc., double conc., org. sonatina, etc. Author of books on the org., contemporary mus., Stravinsky, etc.

Roux, Gaspard le (*b* Paris, *c*.1660; *d c*.1705). Fr. composer. Wrote hpd. suites and pieces, motets, airs, etc.

Rovescio, Al (It.). In reverse. Term which refers either to a passage that can be played backwards as well as forwards, or to a form of canon in which every descending interval in the leading v. is imitated by an ascending one, and *vice versa*.

Row. See *Note-row*.

Rowicki, Witold (*b* Taganrog, Russia, 1914). Polish cond. and composer. Studied Kraków Cons. Début as cond. 1933. Chamber mus. performer 1932–45. Founder and mus. dir. Katowice Radio S.O. 1945–50. Chief cond. Warsaw P.O. (now Nat. P.O.) since 1950. Dir., Teatr Wielki opera centre from 1965. Cond. Bamberg S.O. 1983–6.

Rowley, Alec (*b* London, 1892; *d* Weybridge, 1958). Eng. composer, pianist, and organist.

Studied RAM. Wrote 2 pf. concs., ob. conc., *English Suite* for str., *Serenata* for str., *The Boyhood of Christ* (suite for str.), choral works, chamber mus., and songs. Also much educational mus.

Roxburgh, Edwin (*b* Liverpool, 1937). Eng. composer, cond., and oboist. Studied RCM and Cambridge Univ. Later had lessons from Nono, Dallapiccola, and Boulanger. Prin. oboist, SW Opera Orch. 1964–7. Prof. of comp. and dir. 20th cent. dept., RCM, from 1967. Cond. and dir. 20th-Cent. Ens. of London. Works incl. *Variations* for orch. (1963), *The Tower*, ballet (1964), *The Rock*, oratorio (1979), *Chamber Music* (Joyce), ten., perc., harp (1972), *Night Music*, sop., perc., orch. (1969), *How Pleasant to Know Mr Lear*, narrator, orch. (1971), str. qt. (1961), *Images*, ob., pf. (1967), *Nebula II*, wind quintet (1974).

Roxolane, La. Nickname of Haydn's Sym. No. 63 in C major, (Hob. I:63), comp. *c*.1780. Uses material from earlier mus., incl. incidental mus. for the play *Soliman II* whose heroine was Roxolane.

Royal Academy of Music. College of mus. in London instituted in Tenterden Street, 1822; Royal charter 1830. Lodging and boarding of students discontinued after 1853, when first board of professors was appointed. Moved to Marylebone Road 1912. Wide range of activities: premises incl. concert-hall (Duke's Hall), lecture hall, opera th., and library. About 700 students, with teaching staff of 150. Prins.: William Crotch (1822–32), Cipriani Potter (1832–59), Charles Lucas (1859–66), Sterndale Bennett (1866–75), G. A. Macfarren (1876–87), A. C. Mackenzie (1888–1924), J. B. McEwen (1924–36), S. Marchant (1936–49), R. S. Thatcher (1949–55), Thomas Armstrong (1955–68), Anthony Lewis (1968–82), David Lumsden (from 1982). RAM is supported by Govt. grant, subscriptions, donations, and fees. (The name Royal Acad. of Mus. was also given to an operatic venture started successfully in London in 1719 under directorship of Handel, Bononcini, and Ariosti but which collapsed in 1728.)

Royal Albert Hall. Large, all-purpose, oval-shaped hall in London (South Kensington) built in memory of Prince Consort (*d* 1861) and formally opened March 1871. Seating capacity 10,000. Venue for many occasions incl. balls, pageants, fest. of remembrance, Miss World competition, etc., but best known as concert hall and especially, since destruction of Queen's Hall (1941), as home of Henry Wood Promenade Concerts. Formerly acoustically notorious for echo, but this has been largely eliminated by special installations.

Royal Ballet. Name bestowed by Royal charter in 1956 on former SW Ballet (CG), SW Theatre Ballet (SW), and SW Ballet School. Originated in Acad. of Choreographic Art, formed by Ninette de Valois in London, 1926. This sch. moved in 1931 to newly-built SW Th. under direction of Lilian Baylis. Became Vic-Wells Ballet, dir. by Constant *Lambert and with *Ashton and de Valois as leading choreogs. Visited Paris 1937, Holland 1940. Became resident co. at CG from 1946, opening with famous prod. of *The Sleeping Beauty*. Second co. (orig. SW Opera Ballet) formed 1946. Many eminent dancers worked for prin. co., incl. Fonteyn (from 1934), Dolin, Helpmann, Turner, Somes, Grey, Shearer, Massine, Nerina, Beriosova, Blair, Nureyev, Sibley, Park, and Collier. Choreogs. have incl. Massine, Balanchine, Cranko, Tudor, and MacMillan. NY début 1949. Art. dirs.: de Valois 1931–63, Ashton 1963–70, MacMillan 1970–77; Morrice from 1977.

Royal Choral Society. London choir of about 850 vv. which originated in choir formed and cond. by Gounod for opening of *Royal Albert Hall, 1871. Taken over by Barnby, 1872. Name at first was Royal Albert Hall Choral Soc., present name adopted 1888. Barnby was succeeded in 1896 by J. F. Bridge. Sir Malcolm Sargent had long assoc. as cond. from 1929.

Royal College of Music. London mus. college, successor to *National Training School for Music. Founded by Prince of Wales (later Edward VII) in 1882 and opened 1883, when it received Royal charter. Orig. housed in building occupied by Nat. Training Sch., new building in Prince Consort Road was opened 1894. Large concert-hall added 1901 and later an opera th. (Parry Theatre). Further extensions 1964 and 1973. Has superb mus. library and valuable coll. of historical instr. Governed by pres. and council, with dir., board of professors, graduates, and donors. Dirs.: George Grove 1883–94; Hubert Parry 1894–1918; H. P. Allen 1918–37; G. Dyson 1937–52; E. Bullock 1953–60; K. Falkner 1960–74; D. Willcocks 1974–84; M. Gough Matthews from 1984.

Royal College of Organists. Formed 1864 in London, among aims being to provide examinations and certificates to safeguard standards among organists and also to encourage comp. and study of sacred mus. Orig. housed in Bloomsbury, since 1894 in Kensington Gore in building vacated by RCM. Royal charter 1893.

Royal Festival Hall. Concert-hall built in London (by London County Council) on S. Bank of River Thames as part of Fest. of Brit. 1951. Designed by R. H. Matthew, with org. by Harrison and Harrison, Durham. Seating capacity 3,200. Prin. home of London orch. concerts. Queen Elizabeth Hall and Purcell Room are part of S. Bank concert-hall 'complex'.

Royal Hunt of the Sun, The. Opera in 2 acts by *Hamilton to his own lib. based on play by Peter Shaffer. Comp. 1967–9. Prod. London 1977.

Royal Irish Academy of Music. Mus. college founded in Dublin, 1848, reorganized 1856. Governed by 24 governors and secretary.

Royal Liverpool Philharmonic Orchestra and Society. Soc. founded 1840 since when it has promoted orch. concerts. Opened Phil. Hall 1849, among finest in Europe; destroyed by fire 1933 and replaced 1939 by present fine building. Title 'Royal' bestowed 1957. First cond. was John Russell, succeeded in 1843 by violinist Zeugheer Herrmann, who stayed until his death in 1865. He was followed by Alfred Mellon 1866–87, Julius Benedict 1867–79, Max Bruch 1880–3, Charles Hallé 1883–95, Frederic Cowen 1895–1913. Guest conds. were engaged until the appointment of Malcolm Sargent 1942–8, succeeded by Hugo Rignold 1948–54, Efrem Kurtz and John Pritchard 1955–7, John Pritchard 1957–63, Charles Groves 1963–77, Walter Weller 1977–80, David Atherton 1980–3, Marek Janowski 1983–6, Libor Pešek from 1987. First tour abroad 1966.

Royal Manchester College of Music. Mus. college founded in Manchester 1893, with title Royal from inception. Royal charter 1923. Founded on initiative of Sir Charles *Hallé, Prin. 1893–5. Successors: A. Brodsky 1895–1929, R. J. Forbes 1929–53, F. R. Cox 1953–70, J. Wray 1970–2. From 1957 gave 4 diplomas. Premises were in Ducie Street, Manchester. In 1972 merged with Northern Sch. of Mus. to become *Royal Northern College of Music, Manchester.

Royal Military School of Music. Founded 1856 at Kneller Hall, Twickenham, Middlesex, for training of army instrumentalists and bandmasters.

Royal Musical Association. Organization founded by Stainer and Pole in London in 1874 'for investigation and discussion of subjects connected with the art, science, and history of music'. Incorporated 1904, prefix 'Royal' since 1944. Papers, etc., read to the Assoc. are pubd. in its *Proceedings*.

Royal Northern College of Music, Manchester. Coll. of mus. opened in Manchester 1972 by amalgamation of Royal Manchester Coll. of Mus. and Northern Sch. of Mus. Housed in new building on Oxford Road containing concert-hall, opera th., recital room, tutorial rooms, etc. Financed by 4 local authorities and governed by court and council. Prin. since inception: John *Manduell.

Royal Opera House. See *Covent Garden*.

Royal Philharmonic Orchestra. Sym. orch. founded 1946 by Sir Thomas Beecham, who remained prin. cond. until his death in 1961. Regular orch. at Glyndebourne Fest. 1947–63. Tour of USA 1950 (first Brit. orch. to visit Amer. since LSO 1912). Rudolf *Kempe became ass. cond. 1960, chief cond. 1961–3, art. dir. from

1964 (cond. for life from 1970). Antal *Dorati was appointed cond.-in-chief 1975–8, Walter Weller 1980–5. André Previn from 1985. No connection with *Royal Philharmonic Society.

Royal Philharmonic Society. Founded in London, Jan. 1813 for encouragement of orch. and instr. concerts and immediately promoted annual series of concerts. First concert 8 Mar. 1813. Concerts were given at first in Argyll Rooms, then successively at New Argyll Rooms, King's Th., Hanover Sq. Rooms, St. James's Hall, Queen's Hall, Royal Albert Hall, Royal Fest. Hall. Commissioned Beethoven's 9th Sym. (though f.p. in Vienna) and gave the first Eng. perf. under Smart on 21 Mar. 1825. Sent Beethoven £100 on his death-bed and waived claim to its return when it was found among his effects. Since 1871 a replica of Schaller's bust of Beethoven, presented to the Soc. in that year by Mme. F. Linzbauer, has been placed at the front of the platform at every Phil. concert. To commemorate centenary of Beethoven's birth in 1870 a Gold Medal was struck by the Soc. in 1871 and is presented sporadically, at the recommendation of the dirs., to distinguished musicians (composers and executants), being among the most coveted mus. awards. Most of the world's leading musicians have appeared on the Soc.'s platform. Prefix 'Royal' granted 1912.

Royal School of Church Music. Founded as Sch. of Eng. Church Mus. 1927 by S. H. *Nicholson and members of Church Mus. Soc. Royal charter 1945. Main training centre opened 1929 at College of St Nicolas; successively at Chislehurst, Canterbury, and Croydon (since 1953).

Royal Schools of Music. See *Associated Board of the Royal Schools of Music.*

Royal Scottish Academy of Music and Drama. Mus. college in Glasgow, originating from Glasgow Athenaeum Sch. of Mus., founded 1890. In 1929, a Scottish Nat. Acad. of Mus. was formed to combine with univ. faculty of mus., the Prin. combining office with that of univ. prof. of mus. Prefix 'Royal' 1944. Drama sch. added 1950, present title dating from 1968. Separate Prin. appointed 1953. Prins.: W. G. *Whittaker 1929–41; Ernest *Bullock 1941–52; H. Havergal 1953–69; K. Barritt 1969–76; D. Lumsden 1978–82; Philip Ledger from 1982.

Royal Society of Musicians of Great Britain. Soc. for relief of infirm and distressed musicians and their dependants, founded 1738. Royal charter 1790.

Rozhdestvensky, Gennady (Nikolayevich) (*b* Moscow, 1931). Russ. cond., son of cond. Nikolay Anosov (1900–62); took his mother's surname. Studied pf. Moscow Cons. Ass. cond. Bolshoy Th., 1951, on cond. staff there 1956–60. Chief cond. USSR Radio and TV Orch. 1960–5 and 1970–4; prin. cond. Bolshoy 1965–70. Cond. Russian première of Britten's *Midsummer Night's Dream* (1965). Toured USA 1973 as cond., Leningrad

P.O. London début 1956, CG début 1970 (*Boris Godunov*). Mus. dir., Stockholm P.O. from 1975. Chief cond. BBC S.O. 1978–81. Cond. Vienna S.O. 1981–3.

Rózsa, Miklós (*b* Budapest, 1907). Hung.-born composer (later Amer. citizen). Studied Leipzig Cons. 1925–9. Settled in Paris 1932, then in London, studying at TCL 1936–40. Mus. dir. and composer for Korda films 1936–42. Emigrated to USA 1940. Comp. for M.G.M. 1948–62. Taught at Univ. of S. Calif., 1945–65. Influenced by folk mus. His film mus. is rich and the essence of 'Hollywood'; his other works combine dissonance and strong rhythms. Prin. comps. are *Concerto for Strings,* pf. conc., vn. conc., vc. conc., str. qt., *Sinfonia Concertante* for vn., vc., and orch., pf. quintet, str. trio, pf. sonata, motet *The Vanities of Life,* etc. Film scores incl. *Knight Without Armour* (1937), *The Thief of Bagdad* (1940), *The Jungle Book* (1942), *Double Indemnity* (1944), *The Lost Weekend* (1945), *Spellbound* (1945), *Double Life* (1948), and *Ben Hur* (1959).

Rubato, or Tempo rubato (It.). Robbed time. A feature of perf. in which strict time is for a while disregarded—what is 'robbed' from some note or notes being 'paid back' later. When this is done with genuine artistry and instinctive mus. sensibility, the effect is to impart an admirable sense of freedom and spontaneity. Done badly, rubato merely becomes mechanical. The question of rubato in Chopin is particularly contentious, since its use in his mus. may be dangerously open to abuse. Accounts of his playing (and of Mozart's) suggest that he kept the left-hand in strict time, and added rubato with the right.

Rubbra, Edmund (*b* Northampton, 1901). Eng. composer and pianist. Worked at 14 as railway clerk. Private comp. lessons from Cyril *Scott. Studied at Reading Univ. 1920–1, comp. with Holst, pf. with E. Howard-Jones, at RCM 1921–5, comp. with Holst and Morris. Taught, wrote mus. criticism, and comp. mus for a travelling th. group. Recognition came with perf. of first Sym. (1935–7). Lecturer in mus., Oxford Univ. 1947–68, prof. of comp., GSM from 1961. Served in army 1941–5 and was ordered to form pf. trio with which he gave concerts to Servicemen and women throughout Brit. and, later, Ger. C.B.E. 1960. Contrib. to several works of reference, reviewer, etc. His prolific output covers all forms except for the th., and he is in the mould of Holst and Vaughan Williams, although folk-song as such plays no part in his work. His use of modal harmony and his large amount of religious mus. are in a particularly Eng. tradition, and his syms. have a mus. substance and spiritual grandeur which have still not been fully appreciated. Prin. works:

ORCH: Syms.: No. 1, Op. 44 (1935–7), No. 2, Op. 45 (1938, rev. 1951), No. 3, Op. 49 (1939), No. 4, Op. 53 (1941), No. 5, Op. 63 (1947–8), No. 6,

Op. 80 (1954), No. 7, Op. 88 (1957), No. 8 (*Hommage à Teilhard de Chardin*), Op. 132 (1966–8), No. 9 (*Sinfonia Sacra*, 'the Resurrection') for sop., cont., bar., ch., and orch., Op, 140 (1971–2), No. 10 (Chamber sym.), Op. 145 (1974), No. 11, Op. 153 (1978–9); *Festival Overture*, Op. 62; *Improvisations on Virginal Pieces by Giles Farnaby*, Op. 50; Ov., *Resurgam*, Op. 149; pf. conc., Op. 85 (1956); va. conc., Op. 75 (1952); vn. conc., Op. 103 (1959); *Improvisation*, vn. and orch., Op. 89; *Sinfonia Concertante*, pf. and orch., Op. 38; *Soliloquy*, vc. and small orch., Op. 57; orchestrations of Brahms's *Variations on a Theme of Handel* and of Rakhmaninov's Prelude in G minor.

CHORUS AND ORCH: *The Dark Night of the Soul*, Op. 41, No. 1 (solo cont.); *Song of the Soul*, Op. 78; *The Morning Watch* (Vaughan), Op. 55; *Cantata di Camera* (Carey and Spenser), Op. 111, solo ten.; Suite, *In Die et Nocte Canticum*, Op. 129; *Inscape* (G. M. Hopkins), Op. 122; *Advent Cantata*, Op. 136, solo bar.; *Veni, Creator Spiritus*, Op. 130.

UNACC. CHOIR: *5 Madrigals* (Campion), Op. 51; *5 Motets* Op. 37 (No. 3 is Donne's *Hymn to God the Father*); *Missa Cantuariensis*, Op. 59; *Missa in honorem Sancti Dominici*, Op. 66; *9 Tenebrae Motets*, Op. 72; *3 Motets*, Op. 76; *Agnus Dei*, Op. 143; *3 Greek Folk Songs*, Op. 151; *Prayer for the Queen*, Op. 152.

CHAMBER MUSIC: Str. Qts.: No. 1 in F minor, Op. 35 (1934, rev. 1956), No. 2 in E♭, Op. 73 (1952), No. 3, Op. 112 (1962–3), No. 4, Op. 150 (1976–7); pf. trio No. 1, Op. 68, No. 2, Op. 138; *Lyric Movement*, pf. and str. qt., Op. 24; *4 Easy pieces*, vn. and pf., Op. 29; vn. sonatas: No. 1, Op. 11, No. 2, Op. 31, No. 3, Op. 133; *Phantasy*, 2 vn. and pf., Op. 16; Suite, *The Buddha*, Op. 64, fl., ob., vn., va., vc.; *Variations on a Phrygian Theme*, solo vn., Op. 105; *Meditations on a Byzantine Hymn*, solo va., Op. 117; *Improvisation*, solo vc., Op. 124; *Pezzo Ostinato*, harp, Op. 102; vc. sonata, Op. 60; ob. sonata, Op. 100; *Fantasia on a Theme of Machaut*, Op. 86, recorder, str. qt., hpd.; sonatina, Op. 128, treble recorder and hpd.

KEYBOARD: *8 Preludes* for pf., Op. 131; *Introduction and Fugue* for pf., Op. 19; *9 Pieces* for pf., Op. 74: 1. *Question and Answer*, 2. *Pipe Tune*, 3. *Hurdy Gurdy*, 4. *Slow Dance*, 5. *Catch me if you can*, 6. *Peasant Dance*, 7. *Cradle Song*, 8. *The Donkey*, 9. *The Shining River*; *Prelude and Fugue*, Op. 69, for pf.; *Introduction, Aria, and Fugue* for hpd. (or pf.), Op. 104.

SONGS: *Amoretti* (5 Spenser Sonnets), ten. and str. qt., Op. 43; *5 Spenser Sonnets*, ten. and str. orch., Op. 42; *4 Medieval Latin Lyrics*, bar. and str., Op. 32; *The Jade Mountain*, high v. and harp, Op. 116; *3 Psalms*, low v. and pf., Op. 61.

Rubens, Paul (Alfred) (*b* London, 1875; *d* Falmouth, 1917). Eng. composer. Studied law at Oxford Univ. Wrote some nos. for *Floradora* (1899) and then devoted himself entirely to comp.

of light operas, e.g. *Miss Hook of Holland* (1907), *The Balkan Princess* (1910), *Tonight's the Night* (1915), etc.

Rubible. The **rebec*.

Rubini, Giovanni-Battista (*b* Romano, 1794; *d* Romano, 1854). It. ten. Studied Bergamo. Début Pavia 1814. Sang in Naples 1815–31 and had sensational success in Paris 1825–6 in Rossini operas. Divided time between Paris and London 1831–43. Toured with Liszt 1843. Retired, immensely rich, 1845. Especially notable for his singing of Donizetti and Bellini, where his gift for broad cantabile and an exceptionally high range excelled. His tremolo, apparently remarkable, was imitated by lesser artists and reduced to vocal 'sob' which disfigures much It. singing.

Rubinstein, Anton (Grigorevich) (*b* Vekhvatinets, 1829; *d* Peterhof, 1894). Russ. pianist and composer. Taught by his mother, then by Villoing. Début Moscow 1839, European tour 1840–3. Studied comp., Berlin 1844–6. Returned to Russia 1848, then went to Ger. 1854 with many of his own comps. Settled in St Petersburg 1858 as court pianist and cond. Founded St Petersburg Cons. 1862 (dir. until 1867, then 1887–90). Cond. Vienna P.O. 1871–2. Toured USA 1872–3. Visited Eng. several times between 1841 and 1886. Farewell recitals 1886–7. One of greatest pianists of his day and a prolific composer, whose work had insufficient individuality to survive, in spite of memorable perfs. He considered that Russ. composers should imitate Western models. Remembered for his *Melody in F* for pf. Other works incl. 20 operas (incl. *The Demon*, 1871), 6 syms., incl. the 'Ocean', 5 pf. concs., vn. conc., 2 vc. concs., 10 str. qts., and much other chamber mus., also pf. pieces and songs.

Rubinstein, Arthur (Artur) (*b* Łódź, 1887; *d* Geneva, 1982). Polish-born pianist (Amer. citizen 1946). Child prodigy, giving recital in Warsaw at age 5. Studied there with Rozycki, then taken by sister to Berlin to play for Joachim, who, with 3 others, paid for his mus. training in Berlin (pf., comp., and theory). Played Mozart conc. cond. Joachim, Berlin 1900. Began extensive overseas tours. First visited USA 1906 (Philadelphia and NY). London début 1912. Settled in Paris but was in London 1914 and, speaking 8 languages fluently, became wartime interpreter. Gave recitals for charity with violinist **Ysaÿe*. Had great success in Spain 1916, becoming noted exponent of Falla's mus. Played frequently in USA 1919–27 but did not gain full success there until 1937. Settled in Hollywood 1939. Among greatest pianists of 20th cent., a master in the classics, in Chopin, and in 20th-cent. repertory. Played with almost undiminished power and skill up to his 90th birthday. Last London recital 30 April, 1976. Hon. K.B.E. 1977.

Rubinstein, Nikolay (Grigorevich) (*b* Moscow, 1835; *d* Paris, 1881). Russ. pianist and composer, brother of Anton *Rubinstein. Studied in Berlin 1844–6. Founded Moscow Cons. 1866, remaining dir. until his death. Notable teacher, pupils incl. Taneyev and Ziloti. Gave f.p. of Balakirev's *Islamey*. Tchaikovsky's Pf. Trio in A minor was composed in his memory.

Ruckers. Antwerp firm of hpd. and virginals makers between 1579 and 1667, the founder being Hans Ruckers (c.1550–1598). Over 100 Ruckers instr. still exist. The aim of the hpds. made between 1580 and 1650 was to offer the player some contrast of tone or register. The single-manual instr. had a short-octave compass of 4 octaves from C and had 2 sets of str., respectively 8′ and 4′. Ruckers also made 2-manual hpds., probably as transposing device to help accompanists. Hans Ruckers was helped and succeeded by his sons Jan (1578–1643) and Andries (1579–c.1645).

Ruddigore, or The Witch's Curse. Operetta by Sullivan to lib. by Gilbert. Prod. London and NY 1887.

Rudel, Julius (*b* Vienna, 1921). Austrian-born cond. (Amer. citizen from 1944). Studied Vienna Acad. Settled in USA 1938, attending Mannes Coll., NY. Cond. small opera socs. in NY and elsewhere, then ass. cond. NY City Opera 1944, art. dir. there 1957–79 (prin. cond. from 1979). Mus. dir., Kennedy Center, Washington D.C., 1971–5. Début as cond. at NY Met. 1978. CG début 1985. Champion of contemporary works and of lighter stage works by Austrian and Amer. composers. Cond. Buffalo P.O. 1978–85.

Rudersdorff, Hermine (*b* Ivanovsky, 1822; *d* Boston, Mass., 1882). Russ.-born Ger. sop. Pupil of Bordogni. Sang in opera in Ger. 1841–54. London début 1854. Lived in Eng. until 1865, winning reputation in oratorio. Visited USA 1869 and settled as teacher in Boston. Mother of Amer. actor Richard Mansfield.

Rudhyar, Dane (pseudonym of Daniel Chennevière) (*b* Paris, 1895; *d* San Francisco, 1985). Fr.-born composer (Amer. citizen 1926). Studied Paris (Sorbonne and Paris Cons.). Went to USA 1916 with group of dancers and settled there 1917. Deep interest in Indian theosophy. Comp. orch. tone-poems, ballets, and pf. pieces. Also poet and painter. Author of books on Debussy and Hindu mus.

Rudziński, Witold (*b* Siebiez, Lithuania, 1913). Polish composer. Studied at Vilna Univ. and Cons. (1928–37) and at Institut Grégorien, Paris, 1938–9 (also with Boulanger and Koechlin). Taught at Vilna Cons. 1939–42 and Lódź Cons. 1945–7. Cond. Warsaw Opera and P.O. 1948–9. Prof., Warsaw Cons. from 1957. Author of books on Bartók (1964) and ed. of letters of Moniuszko (1954–70). Works incl. operas, oratorios, 2 syms., pf. concs., chamber mus.

Rudziński, Zbigniew (*b* Czechowice, 1935). Polish composer. Studied Warsaw State Coll. of

Mus. 1956–62. Mus. dir. Warsaw documentary film studio 1960–7. Works incl. sym. for bass ch. and orch. (1969), str. trio (1964), sonata for 2 str. qts., pf., and timp. (1960), *Requiem* (1971), pf. sonata (1975).

Rue, Pierre de la (*b* ?Tournai, c.1460; *d* Courtrai, 1518). Flemish composer. At Burgundian court 1492–1516. Follower of *Després. Wrote 47 masses, many motets, and *chansons*.

Rueda. Sp. round dance in quintuple time, popular in Castile.

Ruffo, Titta (orig. Ruffo Cafiero Titta) (*b* Pisa, 1877; *d* Florence, 1953). It. bar. Studied Rome and Milan. Opera début as Herald in *Lohengrin*, Rome 1898. CG 1903. Amer. début Philadelphia 1912, then Chicago 1912–14, 1919–26, NY Met. 1922–9. Superb singer of Verdi.

Ruffo, Vincenzo (*b* Verona, c.1510; *d* Sacile, Udine, 1587). It. composer. Choirmaster Verona Cath. from 1554, Milan Cath. from 1563, Pistoia 1574–9, Milan from 1580. Wrote much church mus. and pubd. several books of madrigals containing at least 260 examples.

Rugby. 'Mouvement symphonique' No. 2 for orch. by Honegger, 1928. F.p. Paris 1928, f.p. in England, London 1929.

Ruggles, Carl (Charles Sprague) (*b* East Marion, Mass., 1876; *d* Bennington, Vermont, 1971). Amer. composer. Earned living as youth as violinist in Boston th. orchs. Studied comp. privately with J. K. *Paine. Studied Harvard Univ. with Paine 1903–7. Cond. Winona, Minn., S.O. 1912–17. Thereafter concentrated on comp., but taught at Univ. of Miami 1938–43. His mus. is uncompromisingly dissonant and employed atonal principles long before their general acceptance. Wrote few works, being slow and conscientious worker, discarding many attempts. Prin. comps.:

ORCH: *Men and Angels*, (1920: *Men* destroyed; *Angels* for 6 tpt., rev. 4 tpt., 3 tb., 1938); *Suntreader* (1926–31), rev. as *Men of Men and Mountains*; *Men and Mountains*, small orch. (1924), rev. large orch. 1936, rev. 1941 (comprises *Men*; *Lilacs* for str.; *Marching Mountains*); *Portals* for 13 str. (1925), rev. str. orch. 1929, further rev. 1941 and 1952–3; *Organum* (1944–7).

VOICE AND ORCH: *Vox clamans in deserto*, sop. and small orch. (1923, comprises *Parting at Morning* (Browning), *Son of Mine* (Meltzer), *A Clear Midnight* (Whitman)).

SONG: *Toys*, v. and pf. (1919).

CHAMBER MUSIC: *Mood*, vn. and pf. (c. 1918).

PIANO: *Evocations*, 4 chants (1935–43, rev. 1954), No. 2 orch. 1942, others later.

Ruhe (Ger.). Peace, rest. *Ruhig*, peaceful; *Ruhelos*, peace-less, restless.

Ruhepunkt; Ruhezeichen (Ger.). Rest-point; rest-sign, i.e. the sign ⌒.

Rührtrommel (Ger.). Tenor drum.

Ruimonte (Rimonte), **Pedro** (b ? Saragossa, c.1507; d after 1618.). Sp. composer of madrigals and *villancicos. Held court post at Brussels 1598–1614.

Ruinen von Athen, Die (The Ruins of Athens). Ov. and incidental mus. by Beethoven, Op. 113, comp. 1811 for an epilogue by Kotzebue written for first night of Ger. th. in Budapest, 1812. (See also *König Stephan.*) In 1922–4, Strauss and Hofmannsthal ed. and arr. *Die Ruinen von Athen* and included parts of *Die Geschöpfe des *Prometheus.*

Rule, Britannia! Song by *Arne to words by James Thomson, f.p. in masque *Alfred* at Maidenhead, 1 Aug. 1740. Handel quoted it 6 years later in his *Occasional Oratorio*. Beethoven introduced it into his *Battle Sym. (*Wellington's Victory*) and wrote 5 pf. variations in D on it (pubd. 1804). Wagner wrote an ov. based on it (1836). It has been suggested that it is the 'hidden theme' behind Elgar's *Enigma Variations* (Elgar quoted it in *The Music Makers*).

Rule of the Octave (It. *Regola dell' ottava*). Formula for harmonization of the ascending and descending scale in the bass.

Ruler of the Spirits, The (*Der Beherrscher der Geister*). Concert-ov., Op. 27, by Weber, 1811, being rev. of ov. to incomplete opera *Rübezahl.*

Rullante, Tamburo (It.). Rolling drum, i.e. tenor drum.

Rumba. Cuban dance in $\frac{8}{8}$ time which extended into world of jazz c.1930. Orig. perf. by instr. ens. with singer uttering meaningless phrases and syllables. Arthur Benjamin wrote a *Jamaican Rumba* and rumba rhythm has been used by other composers, e.g. Tippett and McCabe.

Rumford, (Robert) **Kennerley** (b Hampstead, 1870; d North Stoke, Oxford, 1957). Eng. bar. Pupil of Henschel and Blume. Début under Henschel 1893. Gave many popular recitals with his first wife, Clara *Butt.

Rummel, Christian (b Brichsenstadt, Bavaria, 1787; d Wiesbaden, 1849). Ger. pianist, violinist, clarinettist, cond., and composer. Cond., court orch. at Wiesbaden 1815–42. Wrote concs., chamber mus., and pf. pieces.

Rummel, Walter (b Berlin, 1887; d Bordeaux, 1953). Ger. pianist and composer. Pupil of Godowsky. Settled in Paris and became associate of Debussy. Wrote str. qt., vn. sonata, *Invocation to Wagner* for vn. and orch., over 40 songs, etc.

Runciman, John F. (b 1866; d London, 1916). Eng. critic and author. Mus. critic, *Saturday Review,* 1894–1916. Wrote books on Purcell and

Wagner. Outspoken views involved him in several libel suits.

Running Set. Eng. folk dance still in use in Appalachian mountains of USA. Also title of orch. work by Vaughan Williams (1933) based on traditional tunes assoc. with this dance.

Rusalka. (1) 3-act opera by Dvořák to lib. by Kvapil. Comp. 1900. Prod. Prague 1901, Chicago 1935, London 1950. Rusalka is a watersprite.

(2) 4-act opera by *Dargomyzhsky to his own lib. after Pushkin (1832). Prod. St Petersburg 1856, London 1931.

Ruslan and Lyudmila. Opera in 5 acts by Glinka to lib. by V. F. Shirkov and V. A. Bakhturin based on poem by Pushkin (1820). Comp. 1837–42. Prod. St Petersburg 1842, London 1931, NY 1942 (concert).

Russell, Henry (b Sheerness, 1812; d London, 1900). Eng. composer, singer, and organist. Studied singing in Italy. Organist at Rochester, NY, for several years between c.1835 and 1840. Returned to Eng. 1841 and gave popular entertainments at which he sang his own songs, among them 'Cheer, Boys, Cheer' and 'A Life on the Ocean Wave', accompanying himself at the piano. Wrote singing treatise. Had 2 sons, one being Landon *Ronald, the other Henry Russell (b London, 1871; d London, 1937), impresario and singing teacher who presented opera at CG in 1904 and was dir. of Boston, Mass., Opera Co. 1909–14.

Russian Bassoon. Old form of *serpent with bn. shape. Made of wood in 3 or 4 detachable sections, ending in brass bell. 6 finger-holes and 3 or 4 keys.

Russian Easter Festival Overture. Ov. by Rimsky-Korsakov, comp. 1888, based on Russ. Orthodox Church melodies.

Russian Quartets (*Die Russischen Quartette*). Name given to Haydn's 6 str. qts., Op. 33 (Hob. III:33), 1781, ded. to Grand Duke Paul of Russia. Also known as *Gli Scherzi*, from the character of their minuets, and as *Jungfernquartette* (Maiden qts.).

Russo, William (b Chicago, 1928). Amer. composer. Studied in Chicago and privately with Jirák, 1955–7. Trombonist and composer-arranger for Stan Kenton orch., 1950–4. Dir., Russo Orch., NY, 1958–61 and London Jazz Orch. 1962–5. Teacher and dir. Rock Theater, Peabody Institute, from 1970. Comps. incl. 2 syms., ballet *Les Deux Errants* (1955), opera *John Hooton* (1961), vc. conc. (1962), *The Civil War,* rock cantata (1968), *David,* rock cantata (1968), *Liberation,* rock cantata (1969).

Russolo, Luigi (b Portogruaro, 1885; d Cerro di Laveno, 1947). It. composer and painter. Theorist of *futurism movement, for which he also comp.

In *L'arte dei rumori* (1913), advocated use of variety of sounds and noises as materials for comp. and invented instrs. for which he developed graphic notation (1926). These were stored in Paris and destroyed during Second World War.

Rust, Friedrich Wilhelm (*b* Wörlitz, nr. Dessau, 1739; *d* Dessau, 1796). Ger. composer, violinist, cond., lutenist, and kbd.-player. Studied in Potsdam with F. Benda and C. P. E. Bach. Returned to Dessau where he promoted concerts and founded an opera theatre. Court mus. dir., Dessau, from 1775. Wrote vn. sonatas, operas, concs., and pf. sonatas regarded as precursors of Beethoven's.

Rust, Wilhelm Karl (*b* Dessau, 1787; *d* Dessau, 1855). Ger. organist and pianist, son of F. W. *Rust. Friend of Beethoven. Taught in Vienna 1807–27. Wrote pf. and organ pieces.

Rustic Wedding (*Ländliche Hochzeit*). Title of sym. in 5 movements by K. Goldmark, 1876.

Rustle of Spring (*Frühlingsrauschen*). Title of pf. piece (No. 3 of 6, Op. 32, pubd. 1909) by Sinding, extremely popular and exists in many arrs. Comp. 1896.

Rute, ruthe (Ger.). Rod. Type of birch brush used to beat the bass drum to obtain special effect. Called for by R. Strauss, Mahler in 7th sym., etc.

Ruth. Opera in 1 act by L. Berkeley to lib. by E. Crozier based on *Book of Ruth*. Prod. London 1956. Also title of various 19th-cent. oratorios.

Rutland, Harold (*b* London, 1900; *d* London, 1977). Eng. pianist, composer, adjudicator, and critic. Studied GSM, Cambridge Univ., and RCM. Worked for BBC 1940–56. Ed., *Musical Times* 1957–60. Authority on John Ireland. Examiner TCL from 1959.

Rutter, John (*b* London, 1945). Eng. composer. Studied Cambridge Univ. Dir. of mus., Clare Coll., Cambridge. Special interest in composing for young people and for amateurs. Works incl.: *Bang!* (opera, 1975), *Partita,* orch. (1975–6), *The Falcon,* ch., semi-ch., boy's ch., and orch. (1969), *Fancies,* ch. and orch. (1971), *Gloria,* ch., brass, perc., org. (1974), *5 Childhood Lyrics,* unacc. ch. (1973), anthems, carols, and church mus.

Ruy Blas. Ov. by Mendelssohn, Op. 95, comp. 1839 for a Ger. perf. of Victor Hugo's play of that name (1838).

Ruyneman, Daniel (*b* Amsterdam, 1886; *d* Amsterdam, 1963). Dutch composer. Studied Amsterdam Cons. 1913–16. Helped to found Netherlands Soc. for Development of Modern Mus. 1918. Cond. of student mus. soc., Groningen Univ. 1924–9. Founder and dir., Netherlands Soc. for Contemporary Mus. 1930–62. Constant experimenter with new sonorities. Works incl. opera *The Brothers Karamazov,* sym., vn. conc., pf. conc., and str. qt. Influenced by Javanese mus.

Ryom, Peter (*b* 1937). Danish musicologist. Catalogued works of Vivaldi (1973), superseding earlier catalogues by Fanna, Pincherle, and Rinaldi.

Rysanek, Leonie (*b* Vienna, 1926). Austrian sop. Studied Vienna Cons. with Alfred Jerger. Opera début Innsbruck 1949 as Agathe in *Der Freischütz*. Munich State Opera from 1952, Vienna State Opera from 1954. CG début 1953 (Strauss's *Danae*), NY Met. 1959 (Lady Macbeth). Bayreuth Fest. from 1951 in several roles. Notable singer of R. Strauss roles (Empress in *Die Frau ohne Schatten,* etc.).

Rzewski, Frederic (Anthony) (*b* Westfield, Mass., 1938). Amer. composer and pianist. Studied Harvard Univ. (counterpoint with R. Thompson). Professional pianist from 1960. Taught at Cologne courses for new mus., 1963, 1964, 1970. Co-founder, Musica Elettronica Viva studio, Rome. Returned to NY 1971. Disciple of Cage and Stockhausen. Has written works involving dancers, film, tape, etc.

S

S. (1) Abbreviation for *segno, *sinistra, *subito.
(2) Abbreviation for *schola* (choir) in liturgical books.
(3) Abbreviation for *Schmieder in catalogue of works of J. S. Bach.

Sabbatini, Galeazzo (*b* Pesaro, 1597; *d* Pesaro, 1662). It. composer. Mus. dir. to Duke of Mirandola 1630–9. Comp. madrigals and motets. Wrote treatise on figured bass.

Sabrá, Wadí (*b* Beirut, 1876; *d* Beirut, 1952). Lebanese composer and organist. Studied in Beirut and at Paris Cons. (1893). Organist of several Paris churches 1893–1910. Founded mus. sch. in Lebanon. Returned to Paris 1919 and worked on problems of Arab scale, having special pf. purpose-built by Pleyel. Dir., Nat. Cons., Beirut, 1925. Proposed universal scale uniting Eastern and Western systems. Comp. operas, oratorios, Lebanese folk-song settings, etc.

Sacchini, Antonio (Maria Gasparo) (*b* Florence, 1730; *d* Paris, 1786). It. composer, influenced by Gluck's reforms. Studied in Naples. Active in Rome 1762–9. Worked in London 1772–81, writing 17 operas which won him popularity. Settled in Paris 1782 where he enjoyed even greater vogue. Piccinni's most formidable rival in It. Wrote over 40 operas, incl. *Semiramide, Armido e Rinaldo,* and *Oedipe à Colonne,* 2 syms., 6 str. qts.

Sacher, Paul (*b* Basle, 1906). Swiss cond. Studied Basle Univ. and Cons. Founded Basle Chamber Orch. 1926, Schola Cantorum Basiliensis 1933. Cond. Zürich Collegium Musicum (chamber orch.) from 1941. Dir., Basle Acad. of Mus. 1954–69. Cond. at Glyndebourne 1954–63 (début in Stravinsky's *The Rake's Progress*). NY début 1955. Among works commissioned for his Basle and Zürich chamber orchs. are Bartók's *Divertimento* and *Music for Strings, Percussion and Celesta,* and works by Berio, Fortner, Henze, Hindemith, Honegger, Ibert, Křenek, Malipiero, Martin, Strauss, Stravinsky, and Tippett.

Sachs, Curt (*b* Berlin, 1881; *d* NY, 1959). Ger.-born musicologist. Studied Berlin. Prof. of musicology, Berlin Univ. and curator of state coll. of mus. instrs. Left Ger. 1934, settling first in Paris, then USA. Author of books on instrs., rhythm and tempo, history of dance, etc.

Sachs, Hans (*b* Nuremberg, 1494; *d* Nuremberg, 1576). Ger. shoemaker and poet, foremost of Nuremberg Mastersingers. Wrote over 4,000 master-sch. poems and nearly 2,000 narrative and dramatic poems. His master-songs were pubd. in *Das Singebuch des Adam Puschmann* ed. Münzer

(1906). Immortalized by Wagner in *Die Meistersinger von Nürnberg* (1862–7).

Sackbut. (1) Early Eng. name for tb. Origin of name unknown (sometimes occurs as *shagbolt*). Used from last years of 15th cent. Most common size was tenor in B♭ which could cope with alto, ten., or bass parts. Adaptable to different pitches. Little different from modern tb. except that modern instr. has bell with greater flare. Matthew *Locke's *Music for His Majesty's Sackbuts and Cornetts* dates from 1661.
(2) Name of mus. periodical founded by Philip *Heseltine, 1920.

Sackman, Nicholas (*b* London, 1950). Eng. composer. Studied Nottingham Univ., then Leeds Univ. (with A. Goehr). Teaches in London. Works incl. *Ensembles and Cadenzas* (1972) for chamber ens.; *From this moment a change* (1973), chamber ens.; *A Pair of Wings* (1970–3), 3 solo sop. and chamber ens.; *Ellipsis* (1976), orch. incl. pf., prepared pf., elec. org., sax.; *Doubles Group 1 and Group 2* (1977), for chamber ens.; str. qt. (1979); *And the World a Wonder Waking,* mez., 8 instr. (1981); *Holism,* vn., vc. (1982); pf. sonata (1984).

Sacra rappresentazione (It.). 'Sacred representation'. Type of staged oratorio, precursor of opera, popular in Italy up to mid-16th cent.

Sacred and Profane. 8 settings of medieval lyrics for unacc. vv. by Britten, Op. 91, comp. 1974–5: 1. *St. Godric's hymn.* 2. *I mon waxe wod.* 3. *Lenten is come.* 4. *The long night.* 5. *Yif ic of luve can.* 6. *Carol.* 7. *Ye that pasen by.* 8. *A death.* F.p. Snape 1975.

Sacred Harmonic Society. Eng. choral soc. est. 1832 for perf. of sacred mus. Gave concerts at Exeter Hall 1834–80, then evicted by YMCA, who bought the hall and objected to 'oratorios for amusement'. Dissolved 1889.

Sacred Service (*Avodath Hakodesh*). Setting by Bloch of Jewish Sabbath morning service for bar., ch., and orch. Hebrew text follows 5 traditional chief liturgical sections with additions chosen by Bloch. Comp. 1930–3 after request in 1930 for setting for use in Reform Synagogue, NY. F.p., Turin 1934.

Sacre du printemps, Le. Fr. title for Stravinsky's *The *Rite of Spring.*

Sadaï, Yizhak (*b* Sofia, 1935). Bulgarian composer. Studied Tel Aviv Acad. of Mus. 1951–6 under Partos and Haubenstock-Ramati. Teacher in Jerusalem since 1960 and at Tel Aviv Univ. since 1966. Works incl. *Prélude à Jerusalem* for 3 reciters, ch., and orch. Since being influenced by

Pierre Schaeffer in 1966, many of his works have used tape.

Sadie, Stanley (John) (b Wembley, 1930). Eng. critic, writer, and editor. Studied Cambridge Univ. with Dart, Cudworth, and Hadley. On mus. staff of *The Times* 1964–79. Ed., *Musical Times* from 1967. Ed., *New Grove Dictionary of Music* (6th edn. of Grove's *Dictionary of Music and Musicians*) 1970 (pubd. 1980). Author of books on Handel, Mozart, and Beethoven. C.B.E. 1982.

Sadko. Opera (*opera-bylina*) in 7 scenes by Rimsky-Korsakov to lib. by composer and Belsky. Comp. 1894–6. Prod. Moscow 1898, NY Met. 1930, London 1931. Developed from 'symphonic picture' for orch., *Sadko*, comp. 1867, rev. 1869 and 1891.

Sadler's Wells. Th. in N. London (Rosebery Avenue). Named because in 1683 a Mr Sadler discovered a well in his garden with supposedly medicinal properties and enlarged his buildings and grounds to accommodate customers, for whom he also provided entertainment. In 1765 a th. was built on the site. Various entertainments were given there before it fell into disuse. In 1925 a public appeal raised £70,000 in 5 years to restore the th. as a home for opera and drama like the Old Vic. It opened, with a capacity of 1,650, in Jan. 1931 under management of Lilian *Baylis. Opera and ballet alternated with Shakespeare prods., between SW and Old Vic, but from 1934–5 the opera was based at SW. In next 5 years, several operas had their f.ps. and f.ps. in England (incl. Rimsky-Korsakov's *Snow Maiden* and the orig. *Boris Godunov*), and many famous Eng. singers and conds. worked there. During war, co. concentrated on touring but was built up again under directorship of Joan Cross. For return to its London home in June 1945 the co. produced a new opera by Benjamin Britten, *Peter Grimes*. In 1947, Norman Tucker became co-dir. (dir. 1954–66), and post-war mus. dirs. incl. James Robertson 1946–54, Alexander Gibson 1957–9, Colin Davis 1959–65, Charles Mackerras 1970–8, Charles Groves 1978–9, Mark Elder from 1979. Since 1950 new operas by Berkeley, Gardner, Richard Rodney Bennett, Malcolm Williamson, and Gordon Crosse have been prod. at SW and the co. has often toured the provinces. Its Janáček perfs. est. the composer in the Brit. public's favour, and there have been famous prods. of *Così fan tutte*, *Rusalka*, *Simon Boccanegra*, and many other operas. Stephen Arlen was dir. 1966–72, succeeded by the Earl of Harewood, whose tenure ended in 1985 when he was succeeded by Peter Jonas (b London, 1947). Arlen pioneered the co.'s move from the Rosebery Avenue th. to the London Coliseum and in 1974 the co.'s name was changed from SW Opera to *English National Opera. A feature of Arlen's management was the engagement of Reginald Goodall to conduct Wagner's *Mastersingers* and later the complete *Ring* in a new Eng. trans. by Andrew Porter, and with Rita Hunter as Brünnhilde. A separate opera co., ENO North, based in Leeds, was founded Nov. 1978, with David Lloyd-Jones as mus. dir. Its name was changed to *Opera North in 1981. For SW Ballet, see *Royal Ballet*.

Sádlo (Zátvrzský), **Miloš** (b Prague, 1912). Cz. cellist. Studied vn. and taught himself the vc. Adopted name of his teacher K. P. Sádlo. Début as soloist 1929, London 1937. Studied at Prague Cons. 1938–40 and with Casals in 1955. Member of Prague Qt. (1931–3) and other chamber groups incl. Prague Trio (1966–73). Taught at Prague Acad. from 1950. Gave modern première of Dvořák's A major conc., which he edited.

Saeta. Andalusian folk-song sung during Lent or Feast of the Nativity to acc. street processions.

Saeverud, Harald (Sigurd Johan) (b Bergen, 1897). Norweg. composer. Studied Bergen Cons. 1915–20 and Berlin Hochschule für Musik 1920–1. Studied cond. in Berlin, 1935, with C. Krauss. Mus. critic in Bergen 1929–40. Works incl. 9 syms. (1920–65), *Overtura appassionata* for orch. (1920), *50 Variazioni piccole* for chamber orch. (1931), ob. conc. (1938), incidental mus. to *Peer Gynt* (1947, 2 orch. suites 1947), 2 pf. concs., vn. conc. (1956), bn. conc. (1963), str. qt. (1969).

Safonov (Safonoff), **Vasily** (Ilyich) (b Itsyursk, Caucasus, 1852; d Kislovodsk, 1918). Russ. pianist and cond. Pupil of Leschetizky in St Petersburg, where he made début 1880. Taught at St Petersburg Cons. 1881–5 and at Moscow Cons. 1885–1905 (dir. from 1889). Began career as cond. 1889. NY début 1904, cond. NY P.O. 1906–9. Dir., Nat. Cons., NY, 1906–9. London début with LSO 1906. Returned to Russia 1911. Notable advocate of Tchaikovsky's mus.

Saga, En (Sibelius). See *En Saga*.

Sainete (Sp. 'Farce', 'titbit'). Sp. form of late 18th-cent. comic opera, usually employing scenes of low life. Among notable composers of *Sainetes* was *Soler.

St Anne. Eng. hymn-tune of disputed orig. but probably comp. by William *Croft, who pubd. it in 1708. Usually sung to words 'O God, our help in ages past'. J. S. Bach's Fugue in E♭ for org. (last item of *Klavierübung*, Book 3, 1739) begins with same notes and is known in Eng. as *St Anne Fugue*.

'St Anthony' Variations (Brahms). See *Variations on a Theme by Haydn*.

Saint-Foix, Marie Olivier Georges du Parc Poulain, Comte de (b Paris, 1874; d Aix-en-Provence, 1954). Fr. musicologist. Studied at Schola Cantorum. Author, with T. de *Wyzewa, of life of Mozart in 5 vols., 1912–46 (last 3 vols. by Saint-Foix alone). Wrote book on Mozart's syms. (1932, Eng. edn. 1947).

Saint François d'Assisi (St Francis of Assisi). Opera (*scènes franciscaines*) in 3 acts and 8 tableaux by Messiaen to his own lib. Comp. 1975–83. F.p. Paris, Dec. 1983, cond. Ozawa.

Saint-George, George (*b* Leipzig, 1841; *d* London, 1924). Eng. violinist and player of viola d'amore. Studied in Dresden and Prague. Settled in London 1862, manufacturing instr. and giving recitals on viola d'amore and *crwth. His son Henry (*b* London, 1866; *d* London, 1917) was also an expert on str. instr., ed. *The Strad* for 4 years, and wrote book on the bow (1895). Taught at TCL.

St James's Hall. Chief concert-hall in London 1858–1905, in Regent St. Capacity 2,127 people. Home of chamber concerts known as 'Monday Pops' 1859–98 and 'Saturday Pops' 1865–98, Phil. Soc. concerts, Richter concerts, etc. Superseded by Queen's Hall and subsequently demolished.

St John Passion (*Johannespassion*; properly in Eng. *The Passion According to St John*). Setting by Bach (BWV245) for solo vv., ch., and orch. of the Passion of Christ narrated in St John's Gospel, with interpolations. F.p. Leipzig, Good Friday 1723, f.p. in England 1872. There are also *St John Passion* settings by Selle (1623), *Schütz (1666), and *Telemann (1741).

St John's Night on the Bare Mountain (Mussorgsky). See *Night on the Bare Mountain*.

St John's, Smith Square. London church built between 1713 and 1728. Converted into concert-hall 1969 and used often for broadcasts of chamber mus. and chamber ensembles. Orch. of St John's, Smith Square, founded by John Lubbock, 1973.

St Louis Symphony Orchestra. Second oldest sym. orch. in USA, founded in St Louis, Missouri, March 1881. Complement of about 100 musicians. Since 1968 has played in Powell Symphony Hall. Prin. conds. have incl. Joseph Otten, Alfred Ernst, Max Zach, Rudolph Ganz, Vladimir Golschmann (1931–58), Edouard van Remoortel, Eleazar Carvalho, Walter Süsskind, Jerzy Semkow, and Leonard Slatkin.

St Ludmila. Oratorio, Op. 71, by Dvořák, comp. 1885–6 and f.p. Leeds Fest. 1886. Text by Vrchlický. For sop., cont., 2 ten., bass, ch., and orch.

St Luke Passion. Oratorio by *Penderecki for narrator, sop., bar., bass, boys' ch., 3 mixed ch., and orch. Comp. 1963–6. Commissioned by W. Ger. Radio (Cologne). F.p. Münster Cath. 1966.

St Matthew Passion (*Matthäuspassion*; properly in Eng. *The Passion According to St Matthew*). Setting by Bach (BWV244) for solo vv., ch., and orch. of the Passion of Christ from St Matthew's Gospel with interpolations by Picander. F.p. Leipzig, Good Friday 1727; revived by Mendelssohn, Berlin 1829 (see *Bach Revival*), f.p. London 1854 (incomplete), 1870 (complete, cond. Barnby). There are other settings of the *St Matthew Passion*, incl. those by R. *Davy and *Schütz (1665).

St Nicolas. Cantata, Op. 42, by Britten, text by Eric Crozier, for solo ten., ch., women's semi-ch., 4 boy singers, str., pf. duet, perc., and org. Comp. 1947–8. F.p. Aldeburgh 1948.

Saint of Bleecker Street, The. Opera in 3 acts by *Menotti to his own lib. Prod. NY 1954, Milan 1955, London (TV) 1956.

Sainton, Prosper (Philippe Cathérine) (*b* Toulouse, 1813; *d* London, 1890). Fr. violinist. Studied Paris Cons., 1831–4, with Habeneck. Prof., Toulouse Cons. 1840–5. Settled in London 1845, becoming prof. at RAM, leader of Phil. Soc. orch. 1846–54, CG orch. 1847–71. Wrote 2 vn. concs. and several vn. pieces. Retired 1883.

Sainton-Dolby, Charlotte (Helen) (*b* London, 1821; *d* London, 1885). Eng. cont. Studied RAM. Début as soloist London 1842. Sang at Leipzig Gewandhaus concerts 1845–6. Mendelssohn wrote cont. part in *Elijah* for her. Married violinist Prosper *Sainton 1860. Opened singing sch. in London 1872. Comp. 4 cantatas.

St Paul (*Paulus*). Oratorio by Mendelssohn, Op. 36, for SATB soloists, ch., and orch., comp. 1834–6, f.p. Düsseldorf 1836 cond. composer.

St Paul's Suite. Suite for str. orch., Op. 29 No. 2, by Holst, comp. 1912–13. Written for sch. orch. of St Paul's Girls' Sch., Hammersmith, where Holst was dir. of mus. from 1905. 4 movements are *Jig, Ostinato, Intermezzo*, and *Finale: the *Dargason* (in which the tune *Greensleeves* is used as a counterpoint).

Saint-Saëns, (Charles) **Camille** (*b* Paris, 1835; *d* Algiers, 1921). Fr. composer, pianist, and organist. Showed mus. aptitude as child almost comparable with Mozart's. Gave pf. recital in Paris 1846. Entered Paris Cons. 1848, studying org. with Benoist and comp. with Halévy. Organist, Eglise Ste-Merry, Paris, 1853–7, Madeleine 1857–77. In 1852 met and became friends with Liszt, by whom he was much influenced. Wrote his first syms. c.1848 and 1850 (unpubd.) and became pf. prof. at École Niedermeyer 1861–5 (his pupils incl. Fauré and Messager). Wrote first opera 1864–5 and began work on *Samson et Dalila* in 1868. In 1871 was co-founder of Société Nationale de Musique, formed to encourage development of Fr. instr. sch. To this end wrote a series of excellent symphonic poems. By this time was in demand as solo pianist and organist, and was soloist at the f.p. of his 5 pf. concs. between 1865 and 1896. First visit to Eng., 1871, to play Albert Hall org. Liszt prod. *Samson et Dalila* at Weimar 1877, Parisian impresarios regarding the biblical subject as too serious (not prod. at the Opéra until 1892). His best sym., No. 3 in C minor (the

'Organ') was ded. to Liszt's memory and f.p. in London, 1886. In later life Saint-Saëns travelled widely and stayed often in Algeria, some of his later works reflecting local colour. Visited USA in 1915. Last visited Eng. 1913 to conduct *The Promised Land* at Gloucester Fest. Wrote coronation march for Edward VII in 1902.

Saint-Saëns's output was prolific and extended for most of his 86 years. Elegance of form and line, beautiful harmonies and chords were more important to him than emotional feeling or technical adventure, and his mus. has therefore been condemned for its superficiality and facility. Nevertheless these very qualities, to which may be added graceful melodic invention, have ensured the survival of a large amount of his work. It is not insignificant that he was admired by Ravel, another emotionally undemonstrative composer. His best features are to be found in *Samson et Dalila*, the 3rd Sym., and the pf. concs. Hon. C.V.O. 1902. Prin. comps.:

OPERAS: *La Princesse jaune* (1872); *Le Timbre d'argent* (1877); *Etienne Marcel* (1879); *Samson et Dalila* (1868–77); *Henri VIII* (1883); *Proserpine* (1887); *Ascanio* (1890); *Phryné* (1893); *Les Barbares* (1901); *Hélène* (1904); *L'ancêtre* (1906); *Déjanire* (1911).

ORCH: Syms: No. 1 in E♭ (1853), No. 2 in A minor (1859), No. 3 in C minor, with org. (1886) (2 other syms., 2nd and 3rd in order of comp., 1852 and 1859, were withdrawn by the composer); symphonic poems: *Le *Rouet d'Omphale* (1871–2); *Phaëton* (1873), *Danse macabre* (1874), *La *Jeunesse d'Hercule* (1877); *Marche héroïque* (1871); *Suite Algérienne* (1880); *Une Nuit à Lisbonne* (1880); *Jota Aragonesa* (1880); *Ouverture de fête* (1910).

INSTR. AND ORCH: Pf. Concs.: No. 1 in D (1858), No. 2 in G minor (1868), No. 3 in E♭ (1869), No. 4 in C minor (1875), No. 5 in F (1896); Vn. Concs.: No. 1 in A major (1859), No. 2 in C (1858, pubd. 1879), No. 3 in B minor (1880); Vc. Concs.: No. 1 in A minor (1872), No. 2 (1902); Miscellaneous: *Introduction and Rondo Capriccioso*, vn. (1863, pubd. 1870), *Romance*, vn. (1874), *Morceau de Concert*, vn. (1880), *Caprice Andalou*, vn. (1904); *Allegro appassionato*, pf. (1884); *Rapsodie d'Auvergne*, pf. (1884); *Africa*, fantasy, pf. (1891); *Tarantelle*, fl., cl. (1857); *Romance*, fl. or vn. (1871); *Odelette*, fl. (1920); *Romance*, hn. or vc. (1874); *Carnaval des Animaux*, 2 pf. and orch. (1886).

CHORUS AND ORCH: *Mass* (1856); *Oratorio de Noël* (1858); *Les Noces de Prométhée* (1867); *Psalm 18* (1865); *Le Déluge* (1875); *Requiem* (1878); *La Lyre et l'harpe* (1879); *Hymne à Victor Hugo* (1881); *Le Feu céleste* (1900); *Psalm 150* (1907); *The Promised Land* (1913); *Hail, California* (1915); *Hymne à la Paix* (1919).

CHAMBER MUSIC: Str. Qt. No. 1 (1899), No. 2 (1918); pf. quintet (1865); pf. trio No. 1 in F (1863), No. 2 in E minor (1892); pf. qt. (1875); *Septet*, pf.,

str., tpt. (1881); vn. sonata No. 1 in D minor (1885), No. 2 in E♭ (1896); *Wedding-Cake*, caprice-valse, pf. and str. (1886); *Havanaise*, vn. and pf. (or orch.) (1887); vc. sonata No. 1 (1872), No. 2 (1905); *Cavatina*, ten. tb. and pf. (1915); *Elegy* No. 1, vn. and pf. (1915), No. 2 (1920); ob. sonata, cl. sonata, bn. sonata (1921).

PIANO: *6 Bagatelles* (1855); *6 Études* (1877); *6 Études* (1899); *6 Fugues* (1920).

2 PIANOS: *Variations on a Theme of Beethoven* (1874); *Polonaise* (1886); *Caprice Arabe* (1884); *Caprice héroïque* (1898).

ORGAN: *Bénédiction nuptiale* (1859); *3 Preludes and Fugues* (1894); *Marche réligieuse* (1897); *3 Fantaisies* (1857, 1895, 1919).

St Thomas Wake. Foxtrot for orch by *Maxwell Davies on a Pavan by John Bull. Scored for large orch., with many exotic instr., contrasting Bull's tune with 20th-cent. dance-band foxtrot, and inspired by composer's memories of air raid on Manchester 1940. F.p. Dortmund 1969, cond. composer.

Saite (Ger., plural *Saiten*). String, thus *Saiteninstrumente*, str. instr.

Salas, Juan Orrego. See *Orrego-Salas, Juan*.

Salazar, Adolfo (*b* Madrid, 1890; *d* Mexico City, 1958). Sp. composer and critic. Pupil of Falla. Mus. critic Madrid *El Sol* 1918–36. Settled in Mexico 1939 as teacher. Wrote orch. mus. Author of books on Sp. mus., ballet, and Bach.

Salicional. Org. stop of soft tone, 8′ length and pitch (sometimes 16′). *Salicet* is of 4′ length and pitch.

Salieri, Antonio (*b* Legnago, 1750; *d* Vienna, 1825). It. composer and cond. Studied at San Marco singing sch., Venice. Taken to Vienna 1766 as protégé of Gassmann. Début as cond. Vienna Court Opera 1770 and in next 4 years had 9 operas prod. Returned to It. 1778. Court cond. Vienna 1788–1824 (of choral concerts only after 1790). Was hostile to Mozart, but there is no truth in legend that he poisoned him (as is depicted in Rimsky-Korsakov's *Mozart and Salieri*). Taught Beethoven, Schubert, and Liszt. Wrote over 40 operas, incl. *Tarare* (1787), *Falstaff* (1798), and *Prima la musica, poi le parole* (1786), 4 oratorios, much church mus., and many vocal and instr. pieces.

Salignac, Thomas (orig. Eustace Thomas) (*b* Générac, Gard, 1867; *d* Paris, 1945). Fr. ten. Studied Marseilles Cons. and Paris Cons. Début Paris Opéra-Comique 1893, NY Met. 1896–1903, CG 1897–9, 1901–4, Paris 1905–13. Dir., Nice Opera 1913–4. Created roles in operas by Milhaud, Massenet, etc. Notable Don José in *Carmen*. Prof. of singing, Fontainebleau 1923–32.

Salinas, Francisco de (*b* Burgos, 1513; *d* Salamanca, 1590). Sp. organist and theorist. Blind from age 10. Served in Italy as organist to Sp.

viceroy in Rome and Naples 1538–61. Prof., Salamanca Univ. 1567–87. Pubd. *De musica libri septem*, 1577.

Salle Favart. Colloquial name for Paris Opéra-Comique th., which is in the Rue Favart and was for a time known as Théâtre de la rue Favart.

Sallinen, Aulis (Heikki) (*b* Salmi, Finland, 1935). Finn. composer. Studied Sibelius Acad. 1955–60 (comp. with Merikanto and Kokkonen). Manager, Finnish Radio S.O. 1960–70. Teacher, Sibelius Acad. from 1965. Comps. incl. 5 syms. (1971, 1972, 1975, 1979, 1986), *Funeral Music*, orch. (1962), vn. conc. (1968), vc. conc. (1976), *Shadows*, prelude for orch. (1982), 5 str. qts., operas *The Horseman* (1976), *The Red Line* (1978), and *The King Goes Forth to France* (1983), *Chorali* for wind, perc., harp, and celesta (1970), *Dies Irae*, sop., bass, male ch., orch. (1978), and *The Beaufort Scale*, chamber ch. (1984).

Salmenhaara, Erkki (*b* Helsinki, 1941). Finn. composer. Studied Sibelius Acad., Helsinki, 1957–64 (comp. with Kokkonen) and privately with *Ligeti in Vienna 1963. Mus. critic in Helsinki 1963–73, lecturer Helsinki Univ. from 1963. Works incl. 4 syms., *Requiem profanum, Information Explosion* (elec.).

Salmhofer, Franz (*b* Vienna, 1900; *d* Vienna, 1975). Austrian composer and cond. Studied comp. with Schreker at Vienna Acad. Cond., Hofburg Th. 1929–39; dir. Vienna Staatsoper 1945–55 and of Volksoper 1955–63. Comp. operas, ballets, 2 syms., tpt. conc., vc. conc., chamber mus., and songs.

Salmond, Felix (*b* London, 1888; *d* NY, 1952). Eng. cellist. Studied RCM 1905–9. Cellist in London Str. Qt. and other chamber mus. ens. Soloist in f.p. of Elgar's Vc. Conc., 1919. Début NY 1922, settling in USA. Formed Trio of NY 1937. Taught at Curtis Institute 1925–42 and Juilliard Sch. 1924–52. Pupils included Leonard *Rose.

Salome. (1) Opera in 1 act by Richard Strauss, being setting of Hedwig Lachmann's Ger. trans. of Wilde's Fr. play *Salomé*. Prod. Dresden 1905, NY Met. 1907, London 1910.
(2) Opera, based on Wilde's play, by Mariotte. Prod. Lyons 1908, Paris 1910.
(3) Drama without words, *La tragédie de Salomé*, by F. Schmitt. Prod. Paris 1907, rev. 1910.
(4) Ballet choreog. Flemming Flindt, mus. by *Maxwell Davies, prod. Stockholm 1978.

Salomon, Johann Peter (*b* Bonn, 1745; *d* London, 1815). Ger.-born violinist and impresario. Played in Bonn court orch. 1758–65. Violinist and composer in royal orch. at Rheinsberg 1765–80. Settled in London 1781, winning special fame as qt. player. Began to organize concerts and introduced Haydn and Mozart syms. at series in 1786. Brought Haydn to Eng. 1791 and 1794

(hence name 'Salomon symphonies' for Haydn's last 12). Suggested *The Creation* to Haydn. Friend of Beethoven. Co-founder Phil. Soc. of London 1813, leading orch. at first concert. Comp. operas, oratorio, vn. concs. Buried in Westminster Abbey.

Salomon, Karel (*b* Heidelberg, 1897; *d* Beit Zayit, nr. Jerusalem, 1974). Ger.-Israeli composer, bar., and cond. Studied with Wulfrum and R. Strauss. Cond. in Hamburg 1920–6. Settled in Palestine 1933. Mus. dir., Jerusalem Univ., then of Palestine Radio 1936. Mus. dir. Israel radio 1948–57. Works incl. opera *David and Goliath*, 2 syms., pf. conc., vc. conc., glockenspiel conc., chamber mus., etc.

Salomon Symphonies (Haydn). See *London Symphonies*.

Salon Music. Term applied, often pejoratively, to mus. of light character which aims to please rather than to be profound, suitable for perf. in a salon. Elgar's lighter works are sometimes called 'salon music' by those who wish to disparage them.

Saltando; saltato (It.). Leaping, leapt. Term used in str. playing, meaning with a springing bow, i.e. same as *Spiccato.

Saltarello (modern It. *salterello*). Lively dance of Sp. and It. provenance in varying meters ($\frac{6}{8}$, $\frac{3}{4}$, $\frac{3}{8}$, $\frac{9}{8}$), incorporating jumps. In 16th cent. was the after-dance (*Nachtanz*) to a *pavan or *passamezzo, the mus. often being indistinguishable from a galliard. Mendelssohn called the finale of his 'Italian' Sym. a *saltarello*.

Saltbox. Traditional handy instr. used when joyous mus. was to be extemporized, domestically or publicly. The lid was flapped up and down and the side battered with a rollingpin.

Salter, Lionel (Paul) (*b* London, 1914). Eng. pianist, harpsichordist, composer, critic, and cond. Studied Cambridge Univ. and RCM. Pupil of C. Lambert (comp.) and A. Benjamin (pf.). Ass. cond. BBC Th. Orch. 1945–6. Mus. supervisor, BBC European service 1948. Head of Mus., BBC TV 1956. Head of TV Opera 1963, Ass. Controller of Mus. 1967–74. Translator of opera libs., ed. of early mus. for perf. Critic for *The Gramophone* since 1948, contrib. to many mus. books. Authority on jazz.

Salut d'amour (*Liebesgruss*) (Love's greeting). Short piece by Elgar, Op. 12, orig. written as pf. solo 1888, orch. 1889, also arr. for vn. and pf. and for many other combinations.

Salve Regina (Hail, Queen). One of 4 Antiphons to Virgin Mary, probably written in 11th cent. Polyphonic settings became numerous in 15th and 16th cents.

Salviucci, Giovanni (*b* Rome, 1907; *d* Rome, 1937). It. composer. Studied with Respighi and Casella. Comp. 4 symphonic poems (1927–31), orch. suite *Campagna romana* (1929), *Sinfonia Italiana* (1932), etc.

Salzburg Festival. Fest. held annually in Austrian town where Mozart was born. Mus. coll. known as *Mozarteum* est. there 1880. In 1877, first of 8 Mozart fests. up to 1910 was held there with Richter, Mottl, Mahler, Strauss, Muck, and Schalk among conds. In 1917, Hofmannsthal, Strauss, Max Reinhardt, and Schalk became dirs. of planned new fest. The 1921 fest. was devoted to orchestral and chamber works and the *Requiem*. Several operas were perf. in 1922. In 1927 Festspielhaus was opened as opera house, and old riding school (*Felsenreitschule*) was converted into th. Singers engaged were the best from Vienna and Munich, conds. incl. Krauss, Strauss, and Walter. Repertory mainly Mozart and Strauss, with Beethoven's *Fidelio*, Verdi's *Falstaff*, and Wagner's *Die Meistersinger*. Toscanini cond. there 1934–7; followed by Furtwängler, Böhm, etc. After war, fest. resumed 1946. Strauss's *Die *Liebe der Danae*, which reached dress-rehearsal stage in 1944, had f.p. there 1952. New operas by Einem, Orff, Henze, Nono, Blacher, Liebermann, Egk, etc. prod. there. Fest. also incl. sym. concerts, chamber mus., recitals, plays. Karajan art. dir. 1957–60 and from 1964. New Festspielhaus opened 1960, seating 2,160. Has largest stage in world, 135′ wide, 70′ deep, and 120′ high. In 1967 Karajan est. an Easter Fest. at which he prod. Wagner operas.

Salzédo, Carlos (*b* Arcachon, Fr., 1885; *d* Waterville, Maine, 1961). Fr.-born harpist and composer (Amer. citizen from 1923). Studied Paris Cons. 1896–1901 (pf. with de Bériot, harp with Hasselmans). Solo harpist Monte Carlo 1905–9, NY Met. 1909–13. Founded Salzédo Harp Ens. 1917. Taught at Curtis Institute and Juilliard Sch. Est. harpists' colony at Camden, Maine, 1931. Wrote harp sonata, harp concs., and other works for harp. Devised new effects on instr.

Salzedo, Leonard (Lopès) (*b* London, 1921). Eng. composer, violinist, and cond. Studied RCM 1940–4. Violinist in LPO, RPO, etc., 1947–66. Mus. dir., Ballet Rambert 1966–72. Prin. cond. Scottish Th. Ballet 1972–4. Comp. 7 str. qts., perc. conc., tpt. conc., brass sextet, part-songs, etc.

Salzman, Eric (*b* NY, 1933). Amer. composer, critic, and impresario. Studied Columbia and Princeton Univs. (comp. with Luening, Sessions, and Babbitt) and in Rome 1956–8 with *Petrassi. Mus. critic in NY 1958–66. Mus. dir. NY radio station 1962–3, 1968–71. Organized concerts of new mus. in NY and multi-media mus. th. ens., *Quog*, 1970. Many of his works involve elecs.

Samazeuilh, Gustave (*b* Bordeaux, 1877; *d* Paris, 1967). Fr. composer and critic. Studied with d'Indy at Schola Cantorum and with Chausson and Dukas. Wrote criticism for several papers,

incl. *La Revue musicale*. Trans. lib. of Wagner's *Tristan und Isolde* and Strauss's *Capriccio* into Fr. Wrote book on Dukas, and autobiography. Comp. symphonic poems, chamber mus., and songs.

Samba. Brazilian dance in two forms: rural samba, African-influenced, and urban samba known as the 'samba-carioca', developed from the maxixe, a type of tango. Also a song-form. Modern dance-form, closer to maxixe, has simple $\frac{2}{4}$ rhythm. Popularized in Brit. in 1940 by Edmundo Ros.

Saminsky, Lazare (*b* Vale-Hotzulovo, Odessa, 1882; *d* Port Chester, NY, 1959). Russ.-born composer. Pupil of Rimsky-Korsakov at St Petersburg Cons. 1906–10. Dir., Tiflis Cons. 1917–18. Left Russ. and settled in NY 1920. Mus. dir., Temple Emanu-El, NY, 1924–58. Expert on Jewish mus. and on Hassidic mystical songs. Wrote 5 syms., *The Daughter of Jephta* (cantata-pantomime), and many pieces for Hebrew worship.

Samisen. Japanese 3-str. guitar, without frets, with strs. of waxed silk played by plectrum called 'batsi'. Wrongly applied to perc. instr. in Puccini's *Madama Butterfly* and Massenet's *Iris*.

Sammarco, Mario (*b* Palermo, 1868; *d* Milan, 1930). It. bar. Studied in Palermo and Milan. Début Palermo 1888, CG 1904 (as Scarpia), NY 1908–10, Chicago 1911–12. Sang role of Alec in *Tess* with *Destinn in title-role, CG 1909.

Sammartini, Giovanni-Battista (*b c.*1700; *d* Milan, 1775). It. composer and organist. Leading Milan composer of his day; choirmaster of eight churches. Pioneer of sonata form and teacher of Gluck, 1737–41. Said to have comp. 2,000 works in all genres, incl. some notable syms. and str. qts.

Sammartini (San Martini), **Giuseppe** (*b* Milan, 1695; *d* London, 1750). It. composer and oboist, brother of Giovanni *Sammartini. Settled in Eng. 1728, becoming oboist at the opera. Chamber-mus. dir. to Princess of Wales. Comp. instr. works, incl. concs., concerti grossi, trio sonatas, etc.

Sammons, Albert (Edward) (*b* London, 1886; *d* Southdean, 1957). Eng. violinist, mainly self-taught. Heard in 1908 by *Beecham while playing in restaurant orch. and became leader of Beecham Orch. First vn. of London Str. Qt. 1908–17. Became concert soloist, memorable as interpreter of Elgar conc. Gave f.p. of Delius conc. (ded. to him) 1919. Prof. of RCM. Author of book on technique. In 25-year partnership with the pianist William *Murdoch gave f.ps. of many British sonatas, notably Ireland's No. 2 (1917). C.B.E. 1944.

Samson. Oratorio by Handel to text compiled from Milton's works, f.p. London 1743.

Samson et Dalila (Samson and Delilah). Opera in 3 acts by Saint-Saëns to Fr. lib. by Lemaire based on Bible. Prod. Weimar 1877 (in Ger.), NY 1892 (concert), CG 1893 (concert), 1909 (stage). F.p. in Fr., Rouen 1890, Paris 1892.

Samuel, Harold (*b* London, 1879; *d* Hampstead, 1937). Eng. pianist. As a child played in public houses. Studied RCM, pupil of Dannreuther and Stanford. Début, London 1894. Became specialist in kbd. mus. of Bach, playing it practically complete in a series of recitals spread over a week (first in London 1921, then in NY 1924, and several times elsewhere). Toured USA almost every year after 1924. Wrote mus. comedy, incidental mus., songs, etc. Prof. of pf. RCM for many years.

San Carlo, Naples, Teatro di. It. opera house ranking next to Scala, Milan. Opened Nov. 1737, destroyed by fire 1816 and replaced in 6 months by present building, seating 3,500. Extensive alterations 1844, modernized stage 1929. Rossini wrote several operas for San Carlo, incl. *Otello*, and Donizetti's *Lucia di Lammermoor* and Verdi's *Luisa Miller* had their premières there. Co. visited CG 1946.

Sanchez de Fuentes, Eduardo (*b* Havana, 1874; *d* Havana, 1944). Cuban composer and writer. Studied Havana Cons. Studied Cuban folklore and collected folksongs. President, Nat. Acad. of Art and Letters 1930–42. Wrote 5 operas (incl. one based on Tennyson's *Enoch Arden*), ballet, choral works, songs, etc.

Sancta Civitas (Holy City). Oratorio by Vaughan Williams, comp. 1923–5, f.p. Oxford 1926. Text from *Revelation*, with additions from Taverner's Bible (1539) and other sources. For bar., ten., ch., boys' ch., and orch.

Sanctus (Holy). One of 5 main parts of the Mass. Settings by innumerable composers.

Sanderling, Kurt (*b* Arys, E. Prussia, 1912). Ger. conductor. Répétiteur at Berlin State Opera, 1931. Left Ger. 1936, becoming cond. Moscow Radio S.O. 1937–41. Cond., Leningrad P.O. 1941–60 (jointly with Mravinsky), East Berlin S.O. from 1960, Dresden Staatskapelle 1964–7. Eng. début 1970 (with Leipzig Gewandhaus Orch.). Notable interpreter of classics and of Mahler and Shostakovich.

Sanders, John (Derek) (*b* Wanstead, 1933). Eng. organist and cond. Studied RCM and Cambridge Univ. Ass. organist, Gloucester Cath. 1958–63. Organist, Chester Cath. 1963–7, Gloucester Cath. from 1967. Cond. 3 Choirs Fest. Comp. a *Te Deum*.

Sanderson, Sibyl (*b* Sacramento, 1865; *d* Paris, 1903). Amer. sop. Studied San Francisco and Paris Cons. (with Massenet, v. lessons from Marchesi and Sbriglia). Début (as Ada Palmer) The Hague 1888 in *Manon*. Massenet wrote *Esclarmonde* and

Thaïs for her to exploit the extraordinary range of her v. (g–g‴). Saint-Saëns wrote *Phryné* for her. CG début 1891, NY Met. 1895 but was never as successful as in Paris. Fine actress and very beautiful.

Sándor, György (*b* Budapest, 1912). Hung.-born pianist (later Amer. citizen). Studied Budapest with Kodály (comp.) and Bartók (pf.). Toured Europe 1930–8, settled in USA 1939. London début 1937. Soloist in f.p. of Bartók's 3rd conc., Philadelphia 1946. Has recorded all Bartók's and Kodály's pf. mus. and all Prokofiev's solo pf. works. Made pf. transcr. of Dukas's *L'apprenti sorcier*.

San Francisco Opera Co. Founded 1922 by Gaetano Merola, who was dir. until 1953, then succeeded by Kurt Herbert Adler. Ranks with Chicago in importance after NY Met. Opera house, seating 3,252, opened Oct. 1932. Among 20th-cent. works staged for the first time in USA are Strauss's *Die Frau ohne Schatten*, Poulenc's *Les Dialogues des Carmélites*, and Britten's *A Midsummer Night's Dream*.

San Francisco Polyphony. Work for orch. by *Ligeti, comp. 1973–4; f.p. San Francisco 1975 cond. Ozawa.

San Francisco Symphony Orchestra. Founded 1911 under sponsorship of Mus. Assoc. of San Francisco. Conds.: Henry Hadley 1911–15; Alfred Hertz 1915–29; Basil Cameron and Issay Dobrowen 1930–2; Dobrowen 1932–4; Pierre Monteux 1935–52; Enrique Jorda 1954–63; Josef Krips 1963–70; Seiji Ozawa 1970–6; Edo de Waart from 1977. Since 1980 has played in Louise M. Davies Symphony Hall.

Sanguine Fan, The. Ballet by Elgar, Op. 81, comp. 1917 to scenario by Ina Lowther based on a fan design drawn in sanguine (blood-red crayon) by Charles Conder showing Pan and Echo with 18th-cent. figures in background. Ballet was f.p. Chelsea 1917 at a matinée to raise money for war charities. After 2 perfs. and a recording of excerpts in 1920, the mus. was unperf. until a recording in 1973. Revived as ballet, choreog. Ronald Hynd, London 1976.

Sankey and Moody. Joint Amer. compilers of hymn-tune colls. popular in late Victorian years. Ira David Sankey (1840–1908) was an evangelistic singer from 1871 when he joined forces with D. L. Moody and toured with him in USA and Brit. until 1899. *Sacred Songs and Solos* was pubd. 1873. Moody did not write the words of any hymns. Sankey wrote many tunes and collected as many others.

Sanromá, Jesús Maria (*b* Carolina, Puerto Rico, 1902; *d* San Juan, 1984). Puerto Rican pianist, pupil of Schnabel in Berlin. Pianist with Boston S.O. 1925–43. Taught at New Eng. Cons. Head of Mus. Dept., Puerto Rico Univ., from 1951.

Santa Cruz, Domingo (*b* La Cruz, Valparaiso, Chile, 1899). Chilean composer. Studied Santiago and Madrid. Held govt. posts 1921–7; taught mus. history and analysis, Santiago Nat. Cons. 1928–53 (dean from 1932), prof. of comp. Chile Univ. 1942–8, vice-rector 1944–9. Founded many of leading Chilean mus. institutions, incl. Bach Soc. and nat. sym. concerts. Works incl. 4 syms., choral works, 3 str. qts., wind quintet, pf. pieces, etc.

Santa Fe Opera. Opera co. in Santa Fe, New Mexico, founded 1957 by John Crosby. Orig. theatre destroyed by fire 1967, rebuilt 1968. 2-month annual summer fest., theatre being partially in open-air. Adventurous policy, operas receiving f.ps. there including Floyd's *Wuthering Heights* (1958), Berio's *Opera* (1970), and Villa-Lobos's *Yerma* (1971). F.p. since 17th cent. of Cavalli's *Egisto*. F.Amer.ps. of Berg's *Lulu* (both incomplete and complete versions), Henze's *Boulevard Solitude* and *The Bassarids*, Strauss's *Daphne*, Shostakovich's *The Nose*, Britten's *Owen Wingrave*, and Stephen Oliver's *Duchess of Malfi*.

Santa María, Tomás de (*b* Madrid, *c*.1516–20; *d* Ribadavia, 1570). Sp. organist and monk. Wrote works for *vihuela* and other instr.; and a treatise (1565) on playing kbd. or *vihuela* fantasias.

Santini, Fortunato (*b* Rome, 1778; *d* Rome, 1861). It. musician and priest. Collected, copied, and scored early classics of It. church mus.—the resulting valuable library of about 4,500 MSS. and 1,100 printed items now being at Münster Episcopal Seminary. Comp. requiem, motets, etc.

Santley, (Sir) **Charles** (*b* Liverpool, 1834; *d* London, 1922). Eng. bar. and composer. Studied in Milan and in London (with *García). Opera début Pavia 1857 (as Doctor in *La Traviata*), London (concert) 1857, CG 1859. Sang with various Eng. opera cos. Sang Valentine in Eng. première of *Faust*, 1863 (for 1864 revival Gounod added 'Avant de quitter ces lieux' specially for him). Sang at Scala, Milan, 1865–6. First sang Don Giovanni 1868 (Manchester). Sang title-role in Italian in *Der fliegende Holländer*, first London prod. of any Wagner opera (1870). Carl Rosa Co., 1875–6. Notable singer of oratorios etc. (especially *Elijah*), appearing at Leeds Fests., 3 Choirs (1863–1906), Birmingham Fest., Handel Fest. Knighted 1907, year of his golden jubilee. CG farewell 1911 but sang in 1915 at concert for Belgian relief. Wrote books on singing, and autobiography. Comp. mass and other church mus.

Santoro, Claudio (*b* Manáos, Brazil, 1919). Brazil. composer and violinist. Studied Rio and in Paris (with Boulanger). Co-founder Brazilian S.O., playing vn. in it 1941–7. Teacher at various Brazil. institutions, mus. dir. Brasilia cultural foundation 1962–7. Mus. dir., Teatro Novo, Rio, 1968–9. Prof. of comp., Heidelberg-Mannheim Hochschule für Musik, 1970. Comp. many scores

for radio, TV, and films. Other works incl. 8 syms., 3 pf. concs., 2 vn. concs., 5 vn. sonatas, 6 str. qts., *Ode to Stalingrad* (1947), oratorio *Berlin, 13th August* (1961–2), and songs.

Sanz, Gaspar (*b* Calanda, 1640; *d* Madrid, 1710). Sp. guitarist and composer. Author of book on guitar-playing (1674).

Sanzogno, Nino (*b* Venice, 1911; *d* Milan, 1983). It. cond., composer, and violinist. Studied Venice, vn. with Guarneri, and comp. with *Malipiero. Later studied cond. with *Scherchen in Brussels. Cond. La Fenice Orch., Venice. Cond. at La Scala, Milan, from 1939, being esp. assoc. with 20th-cent. works (cond. f.p. in Italy of Walton's *Troilus and Cressida*, 1956). Mus. dir. Scala, 1962–72. Composer of va. and vc. concs., and chamber mus.

Sapellnikov (Sapelnikoff), **Vasily** (*b* Odessa, 1867; *d* San Remo, It., 1941). Russ. pianist and composer. Studied under Sophie Menter, St Petersburg Cons. Début Hamburg 1888, London 1889. Teacher Moscow Cons. 1897–9. Left Russia 1923, settling in Ger. and It. Wrote opera and pf. mus.

Sapieyevski, Jerzy (*b* Lódź, 1945). Polish-born composer and cond. Studied engineering but turned to mus. at Sopot Cons. Formed own experimental ens. 1966. Settled in USA 1967. Teacher at several Amer. univs. Works incl. double pf. conc., conc. for va. and winds, *Summer Overture*, etc.

Sarabande (Sp. Zarabanda). Dance form in 17th and 18th cents. Originated in Lat. America, appearing in Sp. in early 16th cent. Was banned by Philip II in 1583 because it was regarded as loose and ugly, 'exciting bad emotions'. Introduced to Fr. and Eng. in early 17th cent., where a stately version, in slow triple time, was preferred to the lively Sp. original. Sarabandes became a standard movt. of the *suite in instr. works by Purcell, J. S. Bach, and Handel. In 20th cent. it has been revived by Debussy, Satie, Vaughan Williams (in *Job*), and Britten (in *Simple Symphony*).

Sarangi. Indian 3-str. viol with 4-cornered, wooden, skin-covered soundbox, wide finger-board, and 10 or more sympathetic understr. Tone like va. Used to acc. dancing. 4th str. sometimes added, tuned in unison with highest of other 3 at middle C. Name sometimes applied to other Indian bowed instr.

Sarasate y Navascuéz, Pablo Martín Melitón de (*b* Pamplona, 1844; *d* Biarritz, 1908). Sp. violinist and composer, known as Pablo de Sarasate. Studied Paris Cons. 1856–9 with *Alard, then had int. success. London début 1861. Had sweet tone and pure style. Lalo comp. *Symphonie espagnole* for him, Bruch his 2nd conc. and *Scottish fantasy*, and Saint-Saëns his 1st and 3rd concs. and *Introduction and Rondo Capriccioso*. Comp. several vn. pieces, incl. *Zigeunerweisen* and *Jota Aragonesa, Carmen Fantasy* (with orch.), and transcr. Sp. folk mus.

Sardana. Nat. Catalonian dance, perf. to acc. of the *fluvial*, Sp. equivalent of pipe and tabor. It is in sections, partly in compound duple and partly in simple duple time. Participants link hands in a large ring, as in the **farandole*.

Sargent, (Sir) (Harold) **Malcolm** (Watts) (*b* Ashford, Kent, 1895; *d* London, 1967). Eng. cond., organist, pianist, and composer. Organist, Melton Mowbray church 1914–24. Pf. pupil of **Moiseiwitsch* 1919–21. Mus.D., Durham, 1919. Cond. his own *Impression of a Windy Day* at London Promenade concert 1921. On staff RCM as teacher of cond. from 1923. Cond. opera for BNOC (Vaughan Williams's *Hugh the Drover*, London 1924, Holst's *At the Boar's Head*, Manchester 1925). Mus. dir. Courtauld-Sargent Concerts 1929–40. Cond. of many choral socs., incl. Royal Choral Soc. (from 1928), Huddersfield Choral Soc. (from 1932), Liverpool Welsh Choral Union (from 1941), Leeds Phil. Soc. (from 1947). Prin. cond. Hallé Orch. 1939–42, Liverpool P.O. 1942–8, BBC S.O. 1950–7, chief cond., Henry Wood Promenade Concerts 1948–67. Cond. many f.ps. of Brit. works, incl. Walton's *Belshazzar's Feast* (Leeds 1931) and *Troilus and Cressida* (CG 1954). Frequently cond. D'Oyly Carte Opera Co. Guest cond. of int. orchs. and ambassador for Eng. mus. Arr. carols and authentic tune of *Rule, Britannia!* Orchestrated Brahms's *Vier ernste Gesänge* and *Nocturne* from Borodin str. qt. No. 2. Knighted 1947.

Šárka (Smetana). See *Má Vlast*. Also operas by Fibich and Janáček.

Sarnia. 'An Island Sequence' of 3 pieces for pf. solo by Ireland, comp. 1940–1 and descriptive of the Channel Island. Pieces entitled 1. *Le Catioroc*, 2. *In a May Morning*, 3. *Song of the Springtides*. F.p. 1942 by Clifford Curzon.

Sarod. Indian str. instr., bowed or plucked, usually with 6 strs. and 12 to 15 sympathetic str.

Sarrusophone. Double-reed woodwind instr., although made of brass, invented 1856 by Fr. bandmaster named Sarrus. Made in 9 sizes (in keys E♭, B♭, and C) from sop. to db. Saint-Saëns and Delius (e.g. in *Songs of Sunset, Dance Rhapsody No. 1, Fennimore and Gerda, Arabesk, Song of the High Hills, Requiem, Eventyr*) have scored for db. sarrusophone (usually played by double bn.).

Sarti, Giuseppe (*b* Faenza, 1729; *d* Berlin, 1802). It. composer, cond., and organist. Pupil of **Martini* in Bologna. Organist, Faenza Cath. 1748–52; cond. of It. opera and court cond. in Copenhagen 1753–65 and 1768–75. Wrote 20 It. and Danish operas in Denmark. Dir., Ospedaletto Cons., Venice, 1775–9; choirmaster Milan Cath. 1779–84 (teacher of Cherubini); court cond. to Catherine II of Russia 1784–7, dir., Ukraine mus. sch. 1787–91, dir. St Petersburg Cons. from 1793. Made scientific study of acoustics. Wrote over 70 operas, incl. one with text by Empress Catherine. At Don Giovanni's supper-party in last scene of his opera, Mozart quotes the air *Come un agnello* (Like a lamb) from Sarti's *Fra i due litiganti* (Between Two Litigants). Also choral mus. and many other works which have proved ephemeral.

Sartorio, Antonio (*b* Venice, 1630; *d* Venice, 1680). It. composer. Opera *Gl' amori infruttuosi di Pirro* prod. in Venice 1661. Moved to Hanover 1665 as cond. at court of Duke of Brunswick-Lüneburg. Stayed until 1675, but visited Venice each year to enlist musicians for the court orch. and to comp. an opera for the carnival. On return to Venice became deputy choirmaster of S. Marco, 1676. Noted for his laments and tpt. arias. Wrote 15 operas and cantatas and sacred vocal mus.

Sass, Sylvia (*b* Budapest, 1951). Hung. sop. Studied Budapest. Opera début 1971 (Frasquita in *Carmen*). Brit. début Scottish Opera, Glasgow, 1975 (Desdemona in Verdi's *Otello*). London CG 1976 (*I Lombardi*), NY Met. 1977 (Tosca). Had lessons from **Callas*, whose dramatic gifts she emulates. Fine singer of Judith in Bartók's *Duke Bluebeard's Castle*.

S.A.T.B. Soprano, Alto, Tenor, Bass; meaning either a mixed ch. or 4 soloists.

Satie, Erik (Eric Alfred Leslie) (*b* Honfleur, 1866; *d* Paris, 1925). Fr. composer and pianist, son of Fr. father and Scottish mother. Moved to Paris 1878. Studied Paris Cons. 1879–86 with little success. Worked as pianist in 1888 at Montmartre cabaret. In same year wrote his *Gymnopédies* for pf. Met Debussy in 1890. In 1891 joined Catholic Rosicrucian sect and comp. several works for it. Shortly afterwards seemed almost to have retired from comp., writing fewer than 10 works in 12 years. In 1905 entered Schola Cantorum as pupil of d'Indy and Roussel, leaving in 1908. From about 1910 became something of a cult among young composers attracted by the eccentric, humorous titles of some of his works, e.g. *Trois Morceaux en forme de poire* (Three Pear-shaped Pieces). Strongly influenced group of young composers known as Les **Six*. Meeting with Cocteau in 1915 led to Diaghilev ballet *Parade* (1917), in which jazz rhythms are used and the instrumentation incl. typewriter, steamship whistle, and siren. Later, was assoc. with Surrealists and Dadaists. Satie's importance lay in directing a new generation of Fr. composers away from Wagner-influenced impressionism towards a leaner, more epigrammatic style. His harmony is often characterized by unresolved chords, which may have influenced Debussy (or he may have learned the device from Debussy—nobody knows). Melody is simple, sometimes slightly archaic, and scoring economical, with few *tutti* passages. *Socrate* is the most ambitious of his works, most of which are comparatively short, the majority being for solo pf. He anticipated many later *avant-garde* trends; e.g. in *Gnossiennes* (1890) there are no bar-lines and the score contains verbal instructions bearing little relation to the mus. But beware—behind the clown's mask is a serious composer. Prin. comps.:

STAGE: *Le Fils des étoiles*, incidental mus. (1891, prelude re-orch. Ravel 1913); *Geneviève de Brabant*, marionette opera (1899); *Le Piège de Méduse*, lyric comedy (1913); **Parade*, ballet (1917); *Mercure*, ballet (1924); **Relâche*, ballet (1924).

ORCH: *En Habit de cheval* (1911); *Cinq Grimaces* (1914); *Trois petites pièces montées* (1919, also for pf. 4 hands, 1920); *La belle excentrique* (1920); *Jack-in-the Box* (1900, unperf. pantomime, orch. Milhaud 1926).

CHORAL: *Messe des Pauvres*, with organ or pf. (1895, orch. version by D. Diamond 1960); *Socrate*, 4 sop. and small orch. (1918).

PIANO: 3 *Sarabandes* (1887–8, orch. Caby); 3 **Gymnopédies* (1888, nos. 1 and 3 orch. Debussy 1896, no. 2 orch. H. Murrill and by Roland-Manuel); 3 *Gnossiennes* (1890, orch. Lanchbery; no. 3 orch. Poulenc 1939); *Trois Préludes* from *Le Fils des étoiles* (1891, orch. Roland-Manuel); *Valse, Je te veux* (c. 1900, arr. for v. and orch., also arr. for orch. by C. Lambert); 9 *Danses gothiques* (1893); 4 *Préludes* (1893, nos. 1 and 3 orch. Poulenc, 1939); *Prélude de la porte héroique du Ciel* (1894, orch. Roland-Manuel 1912); 2 *Pièces froides* (1897); 3 *Nouvelles pièces froides* (pre-1910); *Le Poisson rêveur* (1901; version for pf. and orch. by Caby); 3 **Morceaux en forme de poire*, for 4 hands (1903; orch. Désormière); 12 *Petits chorals* (c.1906); *Passacaille* (1906); *Prélude en tapisserie* (1906); *Aperçus désagréables*, for 4 hands (1908–12); 2 *Rêveries nocturnes* (1910–11); *En Habit de cheval*, version for 4 hands (1911); 3 *Véritables Préludes flasques (pour un chien)* (1912); 3 *Descriptions automatiques* (1913); 3 *Embryons desséchés* (1913); 3 *Croquis et agaceries d'un gros bonhomme en bois* (1913); 3 *Chapitres tournés en tous sens* (1913); 3 *Vieux Séquins et vieilles cuirasses* (1913); *Enfantines* (9 pieces) (1913); 6 *Pièces de la période 1906–13*; 21 *Sports et divertissements* (1914); *Heures séculaires et instantanées* (1914); 3 *Valses du précieux degoûte* (1914; orch. Greenbaum). *Avant-dernières pensées* (1915); *Parade*, suite for 4 hands from ballet (1917); *Sonatine bureaucratique* (1917); 5 *Nocturnes* (1919); *Premier Menuet* (1920).

VOICE AND PIANO: 3 *Mélodies de 1886*; 3 *Poèmes d'Amour* (1914); 3 *Mélodies* (1916); *Ludions* (5 songs) (1923).

VIOLIN AND PIANO: *Choses vues à droit et à gauche (sans lunettes)* (1914).

Satyricon. Comedy ov. by **Ireland, comp. 1946, headed by quotation from the *Satyricon* of Petronius.

Satz (Ger.). 'Setting'. Term used in several different ways, e.g.: (1) Movement, as in Schubert's qt. movement (*Quartettsatz*). (2) Setting or comp. (*Tonsatz*). (3) Theme or subject, i.e. *Hauptsatz*, first subject or main theme. (4) Texture. (5) Style.

Saudades (Portuguese). Term expressive of the haunting sense of sadness and regret for days gone by. It has been used (e.g by Milhaud and Warlock) as a title for pieces of instr. or vocal mus.

Sauer, Emil von (*b* Hamburg, 1862; *d* Vienna, 1942). Ger. pianist and composer. Pupil of Liszt and N. Rubinstein. Int. tours from 1882, Eng. début 1894. Dir. of pf. master-classes Vienna Cons. 1901–7 and after 1915. Comp. pf. concs., pf. sonatas, 33 studies, etc. Ed. Brahms's pf. works.

Sauguet, Henri (real name Jean Pierre Poupard) (*b* Bordeaux, 1901). Fr. composer. Studied with **Canteloube, later with **Koechlin. Became disciple of **Satie. Best known for his ballets and has also comp. *musique concrète*. Most considerable work is his Stendhal opera *La Chartreuse de Parme* (1927–36, prod. Paris 1939). Wrote 5 other operas; 25 ballets, incl. *Paul et Virginie*, *Les Mirages*, and *La Dame aux Camélias*; 3 pf. concs., 4 syms., *Symphonie expiatoire*, in memory of innocent war victims, vn. conc., etc.

Saul and David (*Saul og David*). Opera in 4 acts by **Nielsen to lib. by Einar Christiansen. Comp. 1898–1901. Prod. Copenhagen 1902, Glasgow (BBC concert perf.) 1959, London (stage) 1977.

Sauret, Emile (*b* Dun-le-Roi, 1852; *d* London, 1920). Fr. violinist (pupil of de Bériot) and composer. Began European tours at age of 8. Amer. début 1872. Played sonatas with Liszt. Taught in Berlin 1880–9. Prof. of vn., RAM 1890–1903, Chicago Mus. Coll. 1903–6, TCL from 1908. Wrote vn. conc., over 100 vn. pieces, and *Gradus ad Parnassum* for vn. (1894).

Sausage Bassoon. Name for the **racket (Ger. *Wurstfagott*).

Sautillé (Fr.). Springing. Type of bowing on vn., va., vc., and db. like **spiccato*, the bow lightly rebounding off the str.

Savile, Jeremy (*fl*.1651–65). Eng. composer of songs and part-songs. Remembered for *Here's a health unto his Majesty*.

Savitri. (1) Chamber opera in 1 act, Op. 25, by Holst to his own lib. taken from the Sanskrit *Mahabharata*. 3 characters, Savitri (sop.), Satyavan (ten.), Death (bar.), with acc. of 2 fl., cor anglais, and str. Comp. 1908. Prod. London (students) 1916, (professional) 1921, Chicago 1934.
   (2) 'Legend' for stage by Molnár (1912).

Savoy Operas. Name by which the operettas of Gilbert and Sullivan are known because from *Iolanthe* (1882) onwards they were prod. at the

Savoy Th., London, built specially for them. The performers were known as 'Savoyards'.

Sawallisch, Wolfgang (*b* Munich, 1923). Ger. cond. and pianist. Studied in Munich. Début as cond. at Augsburg Stadttheater 1947–53, beginning as répétiteur, leaving as first Kapellmeister. Gen. mus. dir., Aachen 1953–7, Wiesbaden 1957–9, Cologne 1959–63. Cond. at Bayreuth Fest. 1957–61. Gen. mus. dir. Hamburg P.O. 1961–73. Cond. Orch. de Suisse Romande 1970–80. Gen. mus. dir., Bavarian State Opera, Munich, 1971–86. Amer. début 1964, CG 1972. Fine accompanist (to H. Prey, etc.).

Saw, Musical. Hand-saw played for novel entertainment by holding it between the knees and playing with a vn. bow, the left hand altering the pitch of the note by bending the saw.

Sax, Adolphe (Antoine Joseph) (*b* Dinant, 1814; *d* Paris, 1894). Belg. instr.-maker. Studied fl. and cl. at Brussels Cons. About 1840 invented new brass instr., *saxophone, which he registered in 1846. Also invented the *saxhorn family of instr.

Saxhorn. Type of brass wind instr. of wide semiconical bore, using cup mouthpiece and played with valves, invented by A. *Sax *c.*1845. There are 7 varieties (deep bass to high treble), i.e. 2 sop., alto, ten., B♭ bass, E♭ bass, and BB♭ bass (BB signifies wider bore). They are transposing instrs.: those in Brit. brass bands are the E♭ ten. (ten. hn.) and B♭ bar. (bar. hn.), both closely related to the *flügelhorn. Nomenclature for the group is somewhat confused, e.g. in the 4 higher instrs.:

(a) Sopranino saxhorn in E♭ (or F), also called sop. saxhorn or (mistakenly) sop. flügelhorn, or flügelhorn piccolo. Little different from E♭ cornet.
(b) Sop. saxhorn in B♭ (or C), also called alto saxhorn or (mistakenly) alto flügelhorn. Little different from B♭ cornet.
(c) Alto saxhorn in E♭ (or F), also called saxhorn, or ten. saxhorn, or ten. hn., or alto, or althorn in E♭ (or F).
(d) Ten. in B♭ (or C), also called bar., or bar. saxhorn, or althorn in B♭.

The 3 lower saxhorns are whole-tube instrs., the 4 higher are half-tube instrs. The 3 lower instrs. are classified with tubas, e.g.

(e) Bass saxhorn in B♭ (or C), almost identical with *euphonium.
(f) Bass saxhorn in E♭ (or F), almost identical with E♭ bass tuba, otherwise E♭ bombardon.
(g) Double-bass saxhorn in B♭ (or C), almost identical with B♭ bass tuba but with complete range at bottom.

These are not always used as transposing instr.: sometimes the bass clef is used, sometimes the treble clef showing the notes an octave higher than if the bass clef had been used. In each case, middle C represents the octave of the fundamental note.

Saxophone. Family of wind instrs. invented by A. *Sax *c.*1840, having metal body. Played with a single beating reed, like cl., but conical in bore, like ob. Complete family is of 8 sizes, alternately in E♭ and B♭, i.e. sopranino in E♭, sop. in B♭, alto in E♭, ten. in B♭, bar. in E♭, bass in B♭, contrabass in E♭, subcontrabass in B♭. All are transposing instr., written in the treble clef, the most commonly used being the alto and ten. The sax.'s tone is extremely flexible and variable, blending well with either woodwind or brass, capable of a fl.-like softness, str.-like richness, and metallic stridency. It is a standard feature of jazz big bands, where a section of saxs. takes the place of a sym. orch.'s str. section (e.g. in Glenn Miller's and Tommy Dorsey's bands). But it has also been effectively used in symphonic mus. Berlioz, Meyerbeer, Bizet, Massenet, Saint-Saëns, and others all scored for the sax. Strauss used 4 saxs. in *Symphonia Domestica* (though he intended saxhorns), and he would have been preceded by Elgar, whose desire for 4 in *Caractacus* was thwarted only by economic considerations. Debussy, Ibert, Milhaud, Villa-Lobos, and Eric Coates have written conc.-like works for sax. and orch. Vaughan Williams uses it brilliantly in *Job*, and in his 6th and 9th Syms., and innumerable other 20th-cent. composers have called upon it. The idea that it is mainly a jazz instr. and so not quite decent in symphonic mus. is therefore as inaccurate as it is snobbish.

Sax(o)tromba. *Sax's modification of the *saxhorn *c.*1850 with a more cylindrical bore somewhere between tb. and saxhorn. Seldom used.

Saxton, Robert (*b* London, 1953). Eng. composer. Studied with E. Lutyens 1970–4, at Cambridge Univ. with Robin Holloway, at Oxford Univ. with Sherlaw Johnson, and with Berio. Works incl.:

ORCH: *Choruses to Apollo* (1980); *Traumstadt* (1980); *Ring of Eternity* (1982–3); *Concerto for Orchestra* (1984).
ENSEMBLE: *Reflections of Narziss and Goldmund*, 2 chamber groups, hp., pf. or celesta (1975); *Canzona*, fl., ob., cl., hn., hp., str. trio (1978); *Processions and Dances*, 11 instr. (1981); *Piccola Musica per Luigi Dallapiccola*, fl., ob., va., vc., pf. or celesta (1981).
VOICE(S) AND INSTR: *La Promenade d'Automne*, sop., fl., cl., perc., pf., str. trio (1972); *Where Are You Going To, My Pretty Maid?*, arr. for sop., fl., cl., hp., guitar, vn., vc. (1973); *What does the song hope for?*, sop., fl., ob., cl., pf., str. trio, tape (1974); *Brise Marine*, sop., pf., tape (1976); *Cantata on Poems of Hölderlin*, ten., counterten., pf. (1979); *Cantata No. 2*, ten., ob., pf. (1980); *Cantata No. 3*, 2 sop. and tape delay (1981); *Eloge*, sop., fl., ob., cl., hn., pf., str. qt. (1980).
UNACC. CHORUS: *Chaconne*, double ch. (1981).

CHAMBER MUSIC: *Krystallen*, fl., pf. (1973); *Echoes of the Glass Bead Game*, wind quintet (1975); *Poems for Mélisande*, fl., pf. (1977); *Arias*, ob., pf. (1977); *Study for a Sonata*, fl., ob., vc., hpd. (1977); *Toccata*, vc. (1978); *Chiaroscuro*, perc. (1981); *Fantasiestück*, accordion (1982).

PIANO: *Ritornelli and Intermezzi* (1972); *2 Pieces* (1976); *Sonatas for 2 Pianos* (1977); *Sonata (in memory of Belá Bartók)* (1981).

Saygun, Ahmed Adnan (*b* Izmir, 1907). Turkish composer. Studied Paris Cons. and Schola Cantorum, Paris, 1928–31, with d'Indy. Returned to Turkey to hold various teaching posts, from 1946 at Ankara State Cons. Works incl. operas, 4 syms., 3 str. qts., wind quintet, vn. sonata, vc. sonata, etc.

Sbriglia, Giovanni-Battista (*b* Naples, 1832; *d* Paris, 1916). It. ten. and teacher. Début Naples 1853, NY 1860. Settled in Paris as teacher 1875, pupils incl. the *de Reszkes, *Nordica, *Plançon, and Sibyl *Sanderson.

Scala di seta, La (The Silken Ladder). Opera in 1 act by Rossini to lib. by Rossi after Planard. Prod. Venice 1812, London 1954.

Scala Enigmatica (Lat.). Enigmatic scale. Term applied to arbitrary scale used by Verdi in his *Ave Maria* (1897), the first of his *Quattro pezzi sacri*. Scale, which sounds like whole-tone scale, is C-D♭-E-F♯-G♯-A♯-B-C.

Scala, La. See *La Scala.*

Scale (from It. *scala*, 'staircase', 'ladder'; Ger. *Tonleiter*; Fr. *gamme*). A series of single notes progressing up or down stepwise. Thus, a series of notes within an octave used as the basis of comp. Scales are arbitrary, and the no. in use throughout the world is incalculable.

For the older European scales, used in the Church's plainsong and in folk song, see *Modes*. Two of these ancient Modes remained in use by composers, when the other 10 were almost abandoned, and these are our Major and Minor Scales—the latter, however, subject to some variations in its 6th and 7th notes. Taking C as the keynote these scales (which have provided the chief material of music from about AD 1600 to 1900) run as follows:

Major Scale (Semitones 3–4 and 7–8—the two halves thus being alike).

Minor Scale—'Harmonic' Form (Semitones 2–3, 5–6, 7–8; there is the interval of the Augmented Second, 6–7).

Minor Scale—'Melodic' Form (Semitones 2–3, 7–8 ascending; 6–5, 3–2 descending; this avoids the interval of the augmented 2nd while allowing the Leading Note to retain its function of 'leading' to the Tonic).

The Major and Minor scales are spoken of as DIATONIC SCALES, as distinct from a scale using nothing but semitones, which is the CHROMATIC SCALE, for which 2 different notations are employed:

Chromatic Scale (in 'melodic' notation—sharps upwards, flats downwards; this notation economizes accidentals),

Chromatic Scale (in 'harmonic' notation).

This scale when begun on other notes is 'harmonically' notated according to the same principles; for instance, beginning on D it reads:

The scheme is: the notes of the major scale, plus those of the harmonic minor scale, plus the minor 2nd and augmented 4th.

A scale comprising the same notes as the Chromatic Scale is the *DODECAPHONIC SCALE, in which the 12 notes are considered to be all of equal status and are so treated, whereas the Chromatic Scale beginning on any particular note is considered to comprise the Diatonic Scale of that note 'coloured' (this is the literal meaning of 'chromatic') by the addition of the extra semitones.

Scales with smaller intervals than the semitone have been introduced. See *Microtone.*

The WHOLE-TONE SCALE is free of semitones and thus allows of only 2 different series, each with 6 notes:

The Whole-tone Scale.

An extremely widespread scale is the 5-note or PENTATONIC SCALE (common in Scottish, Chinese, and other music):

The Pentatonic Scale (commonest order of the intervals).

The Scottish Highland Bagpipe is tuned to a scale that cannot be represented in orthodox notation. It is roughly that of the white notes of the piano with the C and F about a quarter of a tone sharp.

Scalero, Rosario (*b* Moncalieri, Turin, 1870; *d* Settimo Vittone, Turin, 1954). It. violinist, composer, and teacher of vn. and of comp. Pupil of Sivori in Genoa and Wilhelmj in London. Taught in Fr. and It. before going to USA in 1919. Head of vn. class, Mannes Sch., NY, 1919–28, Curtis Institute from 1928. Pupils incl. *Barber, *Menotti, and L. *Foss. Wrote vn. conc., chamber mus., songs, etc.

Scapino. Comedy ov. by Walton, comp. 1940 to commission from Chicago S.O. who gave f.p. in Apr. 1941, cond. Frederick Stock. F. Eng. p. London, Nov. 1941. Rev. 1950. Score is subtitled 'after an etching from Jacques Callot's *Balli di Sfessania, 1622'. Scapino was comic valet in *commedia dell' arte* and the hero of Molière's *Les Fourberies de Scapin*.

Scaramouche. (1) Suite for 2 pf., 1939, by *Milhaud. Based on incidental mus. for play *The Flying Doctor*, 1937, prod. in Paris at Théâtre Scaramouche, hence title.
   (2) Ballet in 3 scenes, mus. by Sibelius (1913), lib. by P. Knudsen, choreog. E. Walbom. Prod. Copenhagen 1922.

Scarbo (Ravel). See *Gaspard de la nuit*.

Scarlatti, Alessandro (*b* Palermo, 1660; *d* Naples, 1725). It. composer, specially important in development of opera and considered founder of so-called Neapolitan sch. Taken to Rome 1672, said to have studied with *Carissimi, and wrote first opera there 1679. Engaged by Queen Christina of Sweden, then living in Rome, as cond., 1680–4, for her private th. Court cond., Naples, 1684–1702. Alternated between Rome and Naples for rest of life, in various court and church appointments. Contribution to opera was liberation of dramatic expression. Est. the *da capo* aria, first in *Teodora* (1692), the opera in which orch. ritornello is supposedly used for the first time. The so-called 'It. ov.' was introduced in 1696 in a revival of *Dal male il bene*. In 1685, in *L'Olimpia vendicata*, occurs the first recorded instance of acc. recit. His greatest opera is reckoned to be *Mitridate Eupatore* (1707), comp. for Prince Ferdinando de' Medici. In his late Rome years, the general enthusiasm for opera, stimulated by Scarlatti, overcame all ecclesiastical objections. His 115 operas incl. only one comic opera, *Il trionfo dell' onore* (Naples 1718). About 70 survive, wholly or in part, of which revivals show superb craftsmanship and lofty invention. He also wrote some 20 oratorios, 10 masses, several settings of *Stabat Mater*, etc., over 40 motets, over 600 solo cantatas with basso continuo and 60 with other instr., some 30 chamber cantatas for 2 vv., 28 serenatas, several madrigals, 12 chamber concs., various sonatas, and hpd. pieces, incl. variations on *La Folia*. Father of Domenico *Scarlatti.

Scarlatti, (Giuseppe) **Domenico** (*b* Naples, 1685; *d* Madrid, 1757). It. composer and harpsichordist, son of A. *Scarlatti. Thought to have been pupil of his father and after 1708 of Pasquini and Gasparini in Venice, where he met Handel. In 1709, according to one biographer, Handel's patron, Cardinal Ottoboni, arranged a hpd.-playing contest between Handel and Scarlatti which was a tie, Handel being adjudged a better organist. Maestro di cappella to Queen of Poland, composing operas for her private th. in Rome. Mus. dir., St Peter's, Rome 1715–19. Court harpsichordist to King of Portugal and teacher of Princess Maria Barbara in Lisbon 1719–28; returned to Italy on leave 1725–9; accompanied Maria Barbara to Spain on her marriage to the Sp. Crown Prince in 1729. Stayed in Madrid for rest of his life. Domenico did for kbd.-playing what his father did for opera, by imparting to it a hitherto unsuspected freedom of style. Introduced many new technical devices (rapid repetitions, crossed hands, double-note passages, etc.) and the 550 single-movement sonatas he wrote in Sp. are exercises (*esercizi*) as well as innovatory comps. foreshadowing sonata form. Also comp. 14 operas, masses, *Stabat Mater* for 10 vv., *Salve Regina*, cantatas, at least 12 concerti grossi, 17 sinfonias, and org. fugues. His works have been catalogued by R. *Kirkpatrick, superseding the *Longo catalogue begun in 1906.

Scarlatti, Giuseppe (*b* Naples, *c*.1718; *d* Vienna, 1777). It. composer, nephew of D. *Scarlatti. Comp. 30 operas for Turin, Venice, Lucca, Naples, Florence, and Rome, then moved to Vienna where his subsequent operas incl. *La clemenza di Tito* (1757).

Scat Singing. Jazz term meaning the interpolation of nonsense words and syllables and other vocal effects, introduced in 1920s by Cab Calloway and Louis Armstrong.

Scemando (It.). Diminishing, in vol. of tone. Same as *diminuendo*.

Scena (It.). Scene. Prin. meaning of this term is an elaborate concert aria for v. and orch. in several sections, like the cantatas of Haydn, A. Scarlatti, etc. Examples are Beethoven's *Ah! perfido*, Bliss's *The Enchantress*, Barber's *Andromache's Farewell*, and Britten's *Phaedra*. Other meanings are (1) a scene, subdivision of an act in opera; (2) solo operatic movement, less formal than an aria e.g. Leonore's *Abscheulicher!* in Beethoven's *Fidelio*.

Scenes and Arias. Setting of medieval love-letters for sop., mez., cont., and orch. by *Maw, comp. 1962, rev. 1966. F.p. London, 1962, cond. N. Del Mar.

Scenes from Childhood (Schumann). See *Kinderscenen*.

Scenes from Comus. Work for sop. and ten. soloists and orch. by Hugh *Wood, comp. 1962-5, commissioned by BBC and f.p. Promenade Concert, London, 1965, cond. Norman Del Mar. Text from Milton's masque *Comus* (1634).

Scenes from Goethe's Faust (Schumann). See *Faust, Scenes from Goethe's*.

Scenes from the Bavarian Highlands (Elgar). See *Bavarian Highlands, Scenes from the.*

Scenes from the Saga of King Olaf (Elgar). See *King Olaf, Scenes from the Saga of.*

Scènes historiques (Historical Scenes). Fr. title given by Sibelius to 2 suites of orch. pieces. No. 1 (Op. 25) dates from 1899 and comprises *All' Overtura, Scène*, and *Festivo* (rev. 1911). No. 2 (Op. 66) dates from 1912 and comprises *The Chase, Love-Song*, and *At the Drawbridge.*

Scènes pittoresques (Picturesque Scenes). Orch. work by Massenet, comp. 1874.

Schack (orig. Žák), **Benedikt** (*b* Mirotice, 1758; *d* Munich, 1826). Bohem. ten., composer, flautist, and cond. Court cond., then joined *Schikaneder's co. 1786 as ten., singing with it in Salzburg, Vienna, Graz, and Munich until 1805. Created role of Tamino in Mozart's *Die Zauberflöte*, 1791, playing the fl. himself. Said to be one of group who sang parts of Mozart's *Requiem* to composer on his death-bed. Wrote several operas and church mus.

Schaeffer, Boguslaw (Julian) (*b* Lwów, 1929). Polish composer, mainly self-taught, and pianist. Studied Kraków State Coll. of Mus. 1949-53, where he has taught since 1963. First comp. 1946 in neo-classical style but with atonal leanings. Wrote atonal chamber mus. 1946-8. First composer in E. Europe to use 12-note system for orch. work (*Nocturne*, 1953). In 1955 discovered note-less composing of mus., e.g. in *Study in Diagram* for pf. (1955-6) only intervals, directions of linear motion, and articulations are used. In 1958 wrote *Tertium datur* with geometrical constructions written in graphical notation. Since 1959 his orch. scores have all been for unusual combinations of instr. Has written several jazz comps. since 1962 and elec. pieces since 1964. Many of his works inspired by paintings and literature. Uses 'synectic' method of comp., i.e. performers themselves decide what they understand by special signs and graphics. Has written books on new mus. (1958, 1969), *Sounds and Signs* (1969), and *Introduction to Composition* (1976, Eng. trans.). Prin. works:

STAGE: *Quartet*, 4 actors (1966); *TIS MW2*, ens. (1963); *Scenario*, actor (1963); *Audiences I-V*, actors (1964); *Fragment*, vc. and 2 actors (1968), also db. and 2 actors (1980); *Autogenic Composition*, sop., fl., vc., pf., and 4 actors (1980).

ORCH: Sym.: No. 1 (*Little Symphony: Scultura*) (1960), No. 2 (*Codes*), small orch. (1961), No. 3 (*Musica ipsa*), orch. of deep instr. (1962), No. 4 (*Collage*) (1964), No. 5 (1967), No. 6 (*Texts*) (1971), No. 7 (*Symphony in 9 movements*) (1973), No. 8 (*Tentative music for 159 instr.*) (1973), No. 9 (*Gravesono*), wind and perc. orch. (1977), No. 10 (*Maah*), with tape (1979); *Three Short Pieces*, small orch. (1951); *Music for Strings: Nocturne* (1953); *Monosonata*, 6 str. qts. (1959); *Equivalenze sonore*, perc. orch. (1959); *Topofonica*, 40 instr. (1960); *Harmonies and Counterpoints*: No. 1 (*Warsaw Overture*) (1975), No. 2 (*Romuald Traugutt*), ov. (1976); *Kesukaan*, str. (1978); *Five Introductions and An Epilogue*, small orch. (1981).

CONCERTOS: Piano, No. 1 (*Quattro movimenti*) (1957), No. 2 (1967); Hpd., No. 1 (*Tertium datur*) (1958), No. 2 (*Musica*) (1961); Vn. (1963); Vc. (*Concerto breve*) (1959); Db. (*Jangwa*) (1979); fl. (1963); alto sax. (*S. alto*).

CHAMBER ENS: *Extremes*, 10 instr. (1957); *Azione a due*, pf., 12 instr. (1961); *Imago musicae*, vn., 9 instr. (1961); *Mare*, pf., 9 instr. (1971); *Matan*, 5 perc. (1980).

CHAMBER MUS: Str. Qts.: No. 1 (*Music*) (1954), No. 2 (1957), No. 3 (*Concerto*) (1959), No. 4 (1964), No. 5 (1971), No. 6 (1973); pf. trio (1969); *Andante*, str. sextet (1947); str. trios, No. 1 (*Four Pieces*) (1962), No. 2 (*Estratto*) (1971); *Sonatina*, 2 vn. (1946); *Neues*, 3 vn. (1972); *Essentials*, 3 vn. (1981); oboe qt., ob., str. (1966); sax. qt. (1980); Octet, fl., ob., cl., bn., hn., tpt., tb., db. (1980); *2 Pieces*, vn., pf. (1964); *Duodrama*, alto sax., perc. (1981).

3 PIANOS: *Concerto* (1972).

2 PIANOS: *Concerto* (1951); *15 Elements* (1971); *blueS I*, with tape (1972); *blueS III* (1978); *4H/1P* (4 hands) (1966).

PIANO: *Models*: No. 1 (1956), No. 2 (1957), No. 3 (1961), No. 4 (1963), No. 5 (1965), No. 6 (1970), No. 7 (1971), No. 8 (1972), No. 9 (1976), No. 10 (1977); *Sonatina* (1952); *Study in Diagram* (1955-6); *8 Pieces* (1958); *3 Studies* (1958); *Non-stop* (8 hours) (1960); *Contours* (1963); *Emotiographs* (1966).

ORGAN: *Tsiyur*, with tape (1979).

INSTR: *2 Studies*, solo fl. (1953); *Sound Forms*, solo alto sax. (1961); *Constructions*, solo vibraphone (1962); *5 Short Pieces*, harp (1964); *Conglomeration*, solo perc. (1970); *Heraklitiana*, 12 alternative perfs. and tape (fl., alto sax., perc., vibraphone, pf., prepared pf., hp., vc., db., actor, painter, composer) (1970); *Project* for an instr. and tape (10 versions: ob., bass cl., bn., alto sax., tuba, vc., db., pf., perc., sop.) (1970); *Variants*, ob. (1971); *Interview*, vn. (1972); *Free Form No. 2 (Evocazioni)*, db. (1972); *aSa*, clavichord (1973); *aDieu*, tb. (1973); *Self-expression*, vc. (1978); *Monologue*, bass cl. (1980); *Euphony*, db. (1981).

VOICE(S) AND INSTR: *Guillaume Apollinaires Poetries*, sop., orch. (1949); Cantata (*Audiogram*), 60 vv., orch. (1966); *Howl* (after Ginsberg), 3 actors, orch. (1966); *Te Deum*, vv., orch. (1979).

JAZZ ENS: *Three Comps. for MJQ* (1961); *Music for MI*, vibraphone, sop., jazz ens., orch. (1963); *Collage and Form*, orch. (1963); *Jazz Concerto*, jazz ens. (12 instr.) and orch. (1969); *blueS II*, ens. (1972).

ELECTRONIC: *Sym.* (1964–6); *Assemblages* (1966); *Monodrama* (*Ritsos, Seferis*) with voice of I. Jun (1968); *Theme*, computer mus. (1970); *Missa elettronica*, boys' ch. and tape (1975); *Poetries* (C. Adler) (1968); *Miserere*, sop., ch., orch., tape (1978); *Cantata* (1980).

Schaeffer, Pierre (*b* Nancy, 1910). Fr. composer. Trained as radio technician and has worked mostly for RTF, Paris. In 1942 founded acoustical experiments studio. Began experiments in 1948 with comps. based on assemblage of recorded sounds. For these he coined the term *musique concrète*, his first being *Étude aux chemins de fer*, made from the sounds of railway trains. This and 4 other works were broadcast from Paris on 5 Oct. 1948. In 1949 he began to collaborate with the composer Pierre Henry. In 1951 RTF est. a studio under Schaeffer's dir., the first to be devoted to elec. mus. Dir. of research, RTF 1959. Prin. comps. incl. *Symphonie pour un homme seul* (collab. Pierre Henry, 1949–50, rev. 1966), *Orphée 53* (with Henry, for vn., hpd., 2 singers, and tape, 1951–3), *Sahara d'aujourd'hui* (collab. Henry, 1957), *Études aux objets* (1959, rev. 1966–7).

Schafe Können Sicher Weiden (Sheep may safely graze). Recit. and air by Bach, with obbl. for 2 recorders, in secular cantata *Was mir behagt ist nur die munter Jagd!* (What I enjoy is only the merry chase!) (BWV208, ?1713). Several arrs. of it have been made, among them one by Walton as 7th no. of his ballet *The Wise Virgins* (No. 5 in orch. suite), 1940, and one by Barbirolli for cor anglais and str., c.1937.

Schafer, R. Murray (*b* Sarnia, Ontario, 1933). Canadian composer, teacher, and writer. Studied pf., hpd., and theory at Toronto Royal Cons., 1945–55, and comp. with J. Weinzweig at Toronto Univ. 1954–5. Went to Vienna 1956, then worked in Eng. Returned to Canada 1962 founding '10 Centuries Concerts'. Composer-in-residence Simon Fraser Univ., Vancouver, from 1965, founding elec. studio. Works incl. *Loving/ Toi*, music th. (1963–6), *Requiems for the Party Girl*, sop. and 9 instr. (1966), *Gita*, ch., 8 brass, and tape (1967), *Son of Heldenleben*, orch. and tape (1968), *Patria II*, th. piece (1969), *Music for the Morning of the World*, mez., 4-track tape (1970), str. qts. No. 1 (1970), No. 2 (*Waves*) (1976), *Enchantress*, mez., fl., 8 vc. (1971, rev. 1972), *Arcana*, v., ens. (1972), *East*, chamber orch. (1972),

Patria I (*The Characteristics Man*), music th. (1972), *Patria II* (*Requiems for the Party Girl*), music th. (1972), *North White*, orch. (1973), *Adieu, Robert Schumann*, alto, orch. (1976), *Hymn to Night*, sop. and orch. (1976), *Cortège*, orch. (1977), *Apocalypsis*, music th. (1977). Books and articles incl. *Ezra Pound and Music* (1977) and *British Composers in Interview* (1963).

Schale; Schalen (Ger.). *Cymbal; cymbals.

Schalk, Franz (*b* Vienna, 1863; *d* Edlach, 1931). Austrian cond. Studied under Bruckner. Cond. in Liberec 1888, Graz 1889–95, Prague 1895–8, Berlin 1899–1900, Vienna Opera 1900–29 (joint dir. with R. Strauss 1919–24). CG 1898, 1907, and 1911 (3 *Ring* cycles); NY Met. 1898–9. Co-founder of Salzburg Fest. Ed. several Bruckner syms., making cuts and, in the deplorable case of No. 5, recomposing parts and adding instr. Cond. f.p. of Strauss's *Die Frau ohne Schatten* (Vienna, 1919). Joint ed. with Křenek of *Adagio* and *Purgatorio* movts. from Mahler's 10th sym. and cond. their f.p., Vienna 1924.

Schallbecken (Ger.). *Cymbals.

Schallplatte (Ger.). Sound plate. Gramophone record.

Schalmey, Schalmei. Another name for the *shawm.

Scharf (Ger.). Sharply—in various contexts, such as *scharf betont*, given out with emphatic accent. *Schärfe*, sharpness, definiteness, precision.

Scharrer, Irene (*b* London, 1888; *d* London, 1971). Eng. pianist. Pupil of *Matthay at RAM from 1900. Thereafter high reputation as player. First visited USA 1925. London début 1904, last appearance there 1958. Cousin of Myra *Hess.

Scharwenka, (Franz) **Xaver** (*b* Samter, Posen, 1850; *d* Berlin, 1924). Ger. pianist, cond., and composer. Studied at Kullak Acad., Berlin, where he taught 1868–73. Début Berlin 1869. European tours from 1874. Visited London on occasions between 1879 and 1899. Founded cons. in Berlin 1881 (merged with Klindworth Cons. 1893). Lived in USA 1891–8, founding cons. in NY. Returned to Ger. and was co-dir. Klindworth-Scharwenka Cons. 1898–1914. Opened new sch. in Berlin 1914. Comps. incl. opera, sym., 4 pf. concs., 2 pf. sonatas, church mus., chamber mus., and many songs. Ed. Schumann's pf. works.

Schauspieldirektor, Der (Mozart). See *Impresario, The*.

Scheherazade. See *Sheherazade*.

Scheibler, Johann Heinrich (*b* Montjoie, nr. Aix-la-Chapelle, 1777; *d* Crefeld, 1837). Ger. silk manufacturer with interest in acoustics. Experimented in measurement of pitch and in 1834 at Stuttgart proposed 440 vibrations for A at 69°F, adopted as 'Stuttgart pitch'. Invented 'Aura', first mouth harmonica, 1816. Writings on subject pubd. 1838.

Scheidemann, Heinrich (*b* Wöhrden, Holstein, *c*.1596; *d* Hamburg, 1663). Ger. organist and composer. Pupil of *Sweelinck in Amsterdam 1611–14. Organist, St Catherine's, Hamburg, from 1629. Comp. org. mus., hpd. pieces, and songs.

Scheidt, Samuel (*b* Halle, 1587; *d* Halle, 1654). Ger. organist and composer. Pupil of *Sweelinck in Amsterdam. Organist, Moritzkirche, Halle, from *c*.1603; organist and choirmaster to Margrave of Brandenburg in Halle from *c*.1609, becoming court cond. 1619. Best known in his day for his vocal works, incl. *cantiones sacrae* for 8 vv. (1620) and 70 *Symphonien auf Concerten-Manier* with 3 vv. and basso continuo (1644). Most important was his book of org. mus., *Tabulatura nova* (1624, 3 vols.) proposing staff notation for org. instead of *tablature and containing psalms, hymns, chorales, mass, etc.

Schein, Johann Hermann (*b* Grünhain, Saxony, 1586; *d* Leipzig, 1630). Ger. composer. Chorister, Dresden court chapel from 1599. Court Kapellmeister, Weimar, from 1615. Cantor of Thomas Sch., Leipzig, from 1616. One of first Ger. musicians to benefit from It. influence. Wrote nearly 100 chorale melodies and harmonizations, sacred songs in It. style, *villanelles*, madrigals, *Venus Kräntzlein* (new secular songs, 1609), motets, dance suites, wedding-songs, etc.

Schelle, Schellen (Ger.). Bell, bells. Also *Schellenbaum* (bell-tree), *Jingling Johnny; *Schellengeläute* (bell-ringing), sleigh-bells; *Schellentrommel* (bell-drum), *tambourine. *Schellbecken* is Ger. for cymbals.

Schelling, Ernest Henry (*b* Belvidere, NJ, 1876; *d* NY, 1939). Amer. pianist, composer, and cond. Child prodigy. Studied in Paris, later becoming pupil of Moszkowski, Leschetizky, and Paderewski. After service in 1914–18 war, became cond. Baltimore S.O. 1935–8. Cond. of NY P.O. children's concerts from 1924. Works incl. sym., conc. for vn. and pf., vn. sonata, and pf. pieces.

Schelomo (Hebrew, Solomon; Eng. transliteration is *Shelomo*, but Ger. version more often used). Rhapsody for vc. and orch. by Bloch, based on Book of Ecclesiastes, authorship of which is attrib. to Solomon. Comp. 1916, f.p. NY 1916.

Schemelli Hymn Book. Coll. of 954 hymns and 69 tunes (*Musikalisches Gesangbuch*) pubd. 1736 by Georg Christian Schemelli (*b* Herzberg, *c*. 1676; *d* Zeitz, 1762), cantor of Zeitz castle, and ed. by J. S. Bach, who comp. three of the tunes and provided or improved the figured basses.

Schenk, Johann Baptist (*b* Wiener Neustadt, 1753; *d* Vienna, 1836). Austrian composer and teacher. Comp. syms. as a boy. Went to Vienna

1773 to study with Wagenseil. By 1777 was composing religious works for St Stephen's Cath. and wrote incid. mus. and Singspiels in 1780s. His masterpiece in this genre *Der Dorfbarbier* was perf.1796. Helped Beethoven with counterpoint and comp. exercises in 1793 and had been friend of Mozart. Also wrote cantatas, 10 syms., concs., and 5 str. qts.

Schenk, Otto (*b* Vienna, 1930). Austrian producer and actor. Studied at Reinhardt Seminar and Vienna Univ. First opera prod. was *Die Zauberflöte* for Salzburg Landestheater 1957. Moved to forefront with Vienna Fest. prods. of Einem's *Dantons Tod* and Berg's *Lulu*, 1962. Prod. Janáček's *Jenůfa* at Vienna Opera 1964. NY Met. début 1970 (*Fidelio*), Scala, Milan, 1974 (*Le Nozze di Figaro*), and CG 1975 (*Un Ballo in maschera*). Two of his most successful prods. were of Weber's *Der Freischütz* (Vienna 1972) and Strauss's *Der Rosenkavalier* (Munich 1975).

Schenker, Heinrich (*b* Wisniowczyk, Galicia, 1868; *d* Vienna, 1935). Austrian pianist, writer, and teacher. Pupil of Bruckner. Ed. Beethoven's pf. sonatas, Handel's org. works, and C. P. E. Bach's kbd. music. Wrote several theoretical books. Inventor of famous system of analysis based on theory that one type of mus. structure was basis of all masterpieces from Bach to Brahms.

Scherchen, Hermann (*b* Berlin, 1891; *d* Florence, 1966). Ger. conductor and violist. Mainly self-taught. Violist in Berlin P.O. 1907–10. Worked with Schoenberg 1910–12, making début as cond. 1911. Cond. Riga S.O. 1914. Founded Berlin soc. for new mus., 1918. Cond. Frankfurt Museum concerts 1922–4. Dir., Musikkollegium, Winterthur, 1922–47. Mus. dir. at Königsberg 1928–31. Left Ger. 1933, making Switzerland his base and conducting at mus. courses and summer classes. Ardent champion of 20th-cent. mus., especially that of Schoenberg and Webern. Cond., Zürich Radio Orch. 1944–50. Opened elec. studio at Gravesano, 1954. Amer. début, Philadelphia 1964. Wrote *Handbook of Conducting* (1929) and *The Nature of Music* (1946). Cond. f.ps. of operas by Nono, Dallapiccola, Henze, and Dessau.

Scherchen-Hsiao, Tona (*b* Neuchâtel, 1938). Swiss composer. Studied at Peking Cons. and Shanghai Cons., then with Messiaen and Ligeti. Works incl. *Wai* (1966) mez., str. qt., and perc., *Shen* (1968) for 6 perc., *Khouang* (1966–8) orch., *Tzi* (1969–70) unacc. ch., *Tao* (1971) alto and orch., *Tjao-Houen* (1973) chamber orch., *Lien* (1973) va., *Vague T'ao* (1974–5) orch., *L'Invitation au Voyage* (1976–7), chamber orch., *Oeil de chat* (1976–7) orch., *Lǒ* (1978–9) tb., 12 str. (1978–9) *Ziguidor*, wind quintet (1977). Has won several comp. prizes in Paris. Daughter of H. *Scherchen.

Scherz (Ger.). Fun, joke. *Scherzend, Scherzhaft*, jocular. **Scherzando, scherzante, scherzevole, scherzevolmente** (It., from *scherzare*, 'to joke'). Jokingly, playfully (superlative *scherzantissimo*).

Scherzetto, scherzino (It.). A short *scherzo*.

Scherzi, Gli (Haydn). See *Russian Quartets*.

Scherzi musicali (Musical Jokes). 2 sets of madrigal-like songs, influenced by Fr. style, by Monteverdi. First set (1607) for 3 vv. contains 15 songs, the 2nd (1632) for 1 or 2 vv. with basso continuo contains 10.

Scherzo (It., plural *scherzi*). Jest, joke. Name for a movement in orch. mus., but the term was first applied in 17th cent. to vocal mus., e.g. Monteverdi's *Scherzi musicali*. Generally it is the 3rd (or 2nd) movement of a sym. or str. qt., etc., the liveliest movement, usually but not necessarily the most light-hearted. It is the successor to the 18th-cent. Minuet and Trio, which was developed almost to *scherzo* pitch by Haydn. A movement in S. Storace's 2nd pf. quintet (1784) is a scherzo. Beethoven was the real creator of the scherzo (as early as the Op. 1 pf. trios), investing the movement with a rough, almost savage humour, with marked rhythm, generally in $\frac{3}{4}$ time. The contrasting section is known as the Trio, but not all scherzos have trios. Chopin called 4 of his pf. works *Scherzo*, but they are marked more by vigour and intensity than by anything in the nature of a jest.

Scherzoso; scherzosamente (It.). Playful; playfully, i.e. like a *scherzo*.

Schibler, Armin (*b* Kreuzlingen, 1920). Swiss composer. Studied comp. with W. Burkhard in Zürich, 1940–5, and at Darmstadt summer courses 1949–53 with Adorno, Fortner, Leibowitz, and Křenek. Composer of concs. for a wide variety of instr. Other works incl. operas, syms., str. qts., oratorios, and mus. with narrator.

Schicksalslied (Song of Destiny). Setting by Brahms, Op. 54, for ch. and orch. of part of a poem by Hölderlin. Comp. 1871.

Schickele, Peter (*b* Ames, Iowa, 1935). Amer. composer. Studied Fargo, N. Dakota, and Juilliard Sch., NY (comp. with Persichetti). Taught at Juilliard Sch. Wrote film scores, songs for Joan Baez, and formed chamber-rock group, 1967–70. Works incl. *The Civilian Barber* for orch. (1953), *A Zoo Called Earth* (1970), *The Birth of Christ*, ch. (1960), 3 pf. sonatinas, 4 *Rags* (1972), str. trio (1960), etc. Has writen series of humorous works under pseudonym 'P. D. Q. Bach', including operas *The Stoned Guest* and *The Abduction of Figaro* (1984).

Schiff, Andras (*b* Budapest, 1953). Hung. pianist. Studied Liszt Acad., Budapest, and privately with George Malcolm. Début Budapest 1972, then worldwide tours. Prizes in Tchaikovsky comp., Moscow 1974, Leeds 1975.

Schikaneder, Emanuel (Johann) (really Johannes Joseph) (*b* Straubing, 1751; *d* Vienna, 1812). Ger. th. manager, librettist, singer, and actor. Was singer and actor in troupe of strolling players before becoming manager of Kärntnerthor Th., Vienna, and later of Theater an der Wieden then. For latter, persuaded Mozart to write mus. for his lib. *Die Zauberflöte* (1791) and himself played Papageno. In 1801 was partner in opening Theater an der Wien, managing it until 1806. Other libs. by him were set by Schack, *Paisiello, *Süssmayr, etc. His *Vestas Feuer*, 1805, was begun by Beethoven, but eventually set by Weigl.

Schiller, Allan (*b* Leeds, 1943). Eng. pianist. Studied RMCM and Moscow Cons. Début Leeds (with Hallé) 1954. Member of various chamber mus. ensembles.

Schillinger, Joseph (*b* Kharkov, 1895; *d* NY, 1943). Russ.-born composer, teacher, and writer. Studied St Petersburg Cons. (comp. with Tcherepnin). Taught comp. Kharkov State Acad. 1918–22; comp. for Leningrad State Acad. Th. 1925–28. Settled in USA 1928, teaching comp., mathematics, and art history at various institutions. Taught *Gershwin. Pubd. manual of new tone progressions. Comp. *Airphonic Suite* for theremin (1929), also vn. sonata, *Symphonic Rhapsody* (1927), *North Russian Symphony*, accordion and orch. Writings incl. *Kaleidophone, New Sources of Melody and Harmony* (NY 1940), *Schillinger System of Musical Composition* (NY 1941–6, 2 vols.), and *Mathematical Basis of the Arts* (NY 1948).

Schillings, Max von (*b* Düren, 1868; *d* Berlin, 1933). Ger. composer, administrator, and cond. Studied in Bonn and Munich. Ass. stage cond. 1892 and from 1902 chorusmaster at Bayreuth Fest. Cond., court orch. and opera, Stuttgart 1908–18, gen. mus. dir. Stuttgart Opera 1911–18. Intendant Berlin State Opera 1919–25. Visited USA 1924 and 1931 with Ger. Opera Co. Comp. 4 operas, incl. *Mona Lisa* (1915), several monodramas, vn. conc., choral works, chamber mus., and songs, incl. the *Glockenlieder* with orch. (1908). Married sop. Barbara *Kemp.

Schindler, Anton (*b* Meedl, Moravia, 1795; *d* Bockenheim, Frankfurt, 1864). Austrian violinist and cond., remembered as friend and biographer of Beethoven. Leader and cond. at Josephstadt Th., Vienna, 1822, Kärntnerthor Th., 1825. Cond. all Beethoven's syms. under composer's supervision 1823–4. Choirmaster, Münster Cath., 1831–5, mus. dir. and choirmaster, Aachen 1835–40. Met Beethoven 1814, becoming kind of secretary 1816, living in his house 1822–4, and caring for him in his last illness 1826–7. Published biography of Beethoven (Münster 1840, many subsequent edns.), but despite its immense value, there are many inaccuracies and scholarship has convicted him of forgeries in the Beethoven conversation-books. Wrote 2 masses and chamber mus.

Schindler, Kurt (*b* Berlin, 1882; *d* NY, 1935). Ger.-born composer, organist, and cond. Pupil of Wolf and Thuille. Studied Berlin and Munich

Univs. Ass. cond. Stuttgart Opera 1902, Würzburg 1903. Ass. cond. NY Met. 1905–8. Formed MacDowell Ch. 1909, renaming it Schola Cantorum in 1912. With this choir he performed many contemporary works and revived old mus., especially by Sp. composers. Organist, Temple Emanu-El, NY, 1912–25. Comp. choral pieces and wrote books on Russian song, Sp. choral mus., etc.

Schiøtz, Aksel (b Roskilde, Denmark, 1906; d Copenhagen, 1975). Danish ten. Studied languages at Copenhagen Univ. and became teacher. In 1939 made opera début and in 1942 début as recitalist. Eng. début, 1946, singing in Britten's *Rape of Lucretia* at Glyndebourne. Toured USA 1948. Noted Lieder singer. Illness halted career 1950; later resumed it as bar. Taught at Minnesota Univ. 1955–8, Royal Cons. of Mus., Toronto, 1958–61, Colorado Univ. 1961–8. Returned to teach in Denmark 1968. Danish knighthood 1947.

Schipa, Tito (b Lecce, 1888; d Wickersham, NY, 1965). It. ten. Studied in Milan. Opera début Vercelli, 1910, as Alfredo in *La Traviata*. Rome 1914, Milan 1915. Created role of Ruggero in Puccini's *La Rondine*, Monte Carlo 1917. Member, Chicago Opera 1919–32. NY début 1920. Sang at NY Met. 1932–5 and 1940–1. Sang in It. until 1952. Last stage appearances Buenos Aires and Lecce 1954. Concert tour of Russia 1957. Superb and elegant lyric ten., with impeccable phrasing, in such operas as *Don Pasquale*, *Il barbiere di Siviglia*, *Don Giovanni*, *Rigoletto*, etc. Taught in Rome and wrote operetta (1935).

Schippers, Thomas (b Kalamazoo, Michigan, 1930; d NY, 1977). Amer. cond. Studied Curtis Institute, Philadelphia, 1944–5. Début NY 1948. Closely assoc. with *Menotti and cond. f.p. in NY of *The Consul* 1950 and f.p. in London 1951, also première of *Amahl and the Night Visitors* (TV 1951). Cond. NY City Opera 1952–4, cond. f.p. of Copland's *The Tender Land* and Menotti's *The Saint of Bleecker Street*, 1954. Cond. Cherubini's *Medea* for Callas, Milan 1962. Débuts NY Met. and Scala, Milan, 1955. Cond. f.p. of Barber's *Antony and Cleopatra* 1966. Cond. Spoleto Fest. 1958–76. Bayreuth Fest. 1963 (*Die Meistersinger*). CG début 1968. Cond. Cincinnati S.O. from 1970 to his death.

Schirmer, G., Inc. Firm of NY mus. publishers founded 1861 by Gustav Schirmer (1829–93) and B. Beer. Schirmer gained full control 1866, and later his sons joined him as partners. Publishers of many leading Amer. composers, incl. Creston, Barber, Harris, Schuman, Menotti, and Bernstein. *The Musical Quarterly* was launched by the firm in 1915. Schirmer Music Co. of Boston, founded 1921 by a nephew of G. Schirmer, is a separate firm and publishes many of the *avant-garde* Amer. composers in addition to Copland, Del Tredici, R. Thompson, Piston, and Rorem.

Schiske, Karl (b Raab, 1916; d Vienna, 1969). Hung.-born composer. Studied at Vienna Mus. Acad., where he became prof. of comp. 1952. Works incl. 5 syms., chamber conc., 2 concs. for str., vn. conc., pf. conc., Mass, cl. sextet, wind quintet, 2 str. qts., pf. trio, vn. sonata, songs, and pf. mus.

Schlagen (Ger.). To strike; hence *Schlägel*, drumstick; *Schlaginstrumente*, perc. instr.

Schlagobers (Whipped cream). 'Gay Viennese ballet' in 2 acts by R. Strauss, Op. 70, to his own lib., choreog. Kröller. Comp. 1921–2. Prod. Vienna and Breslau 1924.

Schleifer. (1) *Ländler.*
(2) Old ornament in instr. mus., the essential feature of which was the filling in of an interval between 2 melodic notes with a kind of slide.

Schleppend (Ger.). Dragging. Often found in Mahler's scores in the negative, *Nicht schleppend*, i.e. don't let the tempo drag.

Schlesinger, Kathleen (b Hollywood, Belfast, 1862; d London, 1953). Irish musicologist who made special study of ancient (especially Gr.) mus. instr. Wrote book on modern orch. instr. (1910).

Schlesinger, Maurice (b Berlin, 1798; d Baden-Baden, 1871). Fr. mus. publisher of Ger. descent. Settled in Paris c. 1820 and started own business 1821. Issued scores by Meyerbeer, Moscheles, Weber, Hummel, complete edns. of pf. works of Beethoven (whom he knew), and pubd. his str. trios, qts., and quintets, and early works by Mendelssohn, Liszt, and Berlioz. Pubd. about 40 of Chopin's works. Established the weekly *Gazette musicale de Paris* 1834 (later *Revue et gazette musicale*, ceased publication 1880). From 1840 to 1842 employed Wagner to make pf. arrs. of scores by Donizetti, Halévy, and others. Sold business 1846 and retired.

Schlick, Arnolt (b ?Heidelberg, c.1460; d ?Heidelberg, after 1521). Ger. composer, organist, and lutenist. Born blind. Wrote works for org. and lute, and important treatise on orgs. and org.-building (1511).

Schlick, Johann Konrad (b Münster, c.1759; d Gotha, 1825). Ger. cellist and composer. In ducal orch. at Gotha from 1776. Comp. syms. and many chamber works.

Schlumpf, Martin (b Aarau, Switz., 1947). Swiss composer and pianist. Studied in Berlin. Works incl. songs with orch., fl. trio, *5 Pieces for Orch.*, str. qt., etc.

Schlusnus, Heinrich (b Braubach, 1888; d Frankfurt, 1952). Ger. bar. Studied Frankfurt and Berlin. Concert début Frankfurt 1912; in opera Nuremberg 1915–17. Sang at Berlin State Opera 1917–45, also Chicago 1927–8, Bayreuth 1933 (Amfortas in *Parsifal*). Leading Verdi bar. of his day in Ger., but at his finest in Lieder (especially Schubert).

Schlüssel (Ger.). Clef. See *Notation*.

Schluss-Satz. (Ger.). Coda. See *Satz*.

Schlusszeichen (Ger.). Close-sign. The double-bar with pause which indicates the end of a repeated section after which the movement ends.

Schmachtend (Ger.). Yearning, longing.

Schmedes, Erik (*b* Gjentofte, Copenhagen, 1868; *d* Vienna, 1931). Danish ten. Studied Berlin, Vienna, Dresden, and Paris (with Artôt). Opera début as bar., Wiesbaden 1891–4. Début as lyric ten. Nuremberg 1894. Dresden 1894–7. Engaged by Mahler for Vienna Opera, making début as Siegfried 1898 and remaining there until 1924. NY Met. 1908–9. Bayreuth 1899–1902. One of great Wagnerian tens. of Mahler régime.

Schmelzer, Johann Heinrich (*b* Scheibbs, *c*.1620–3; *d* Prague, 1680). Austrian composer. Chamber musician at Vienna court from 1649, becoming Kapellmeister 1679. Comp. opera-ballets, chamber mus., esp. trio sonatas, and vocal works.

Schmetternd (Ger.). In hn.-playing, blared, i.e. notes prod. as stopped (with hand inserted in the bell), combined with hard blowing. Normal Brit. indication is + together with *ff*.

Schmid, Erich (*b* Balsthal, Switz., 1907). Swiss cond. Studied Frankfurt 1927–30, Berlin (with Schoenberg) 1930–1. Mus. dir. Glarus, Switz., 1934–49; cond. Tonhalle Orch., Zürich, 1949–57, Beromünster Radio Orch. 1957–72. Champion of 20th-cent. mus. Made orch. arr. of Debussy's pf. duet *Six épigraphes antiques*.

Schmidt, Bernhard. See *Smith, 'Father'*.

Schmidt, Franz (*b* Pressburg (Pozsony; now Bratislava), 1874; *d* Perchtoldsdorf, Vienna, 1939). Austrian composer, pianist, cond., and cellist. Studied Vienna Cons. (comp. with Bruckner, theory with Fuchs). Pf. pupil of Leschetizky. Cellist in Vienna P.O. 1896–1911. Taught pf. Vienna Acad. of Mus. from 1914, prof. of comp. 1922, dir. 1925–7, rector of Hochschule für Musik 1927–31. Regarded in Austria as composer in tradition of Bruckner. Works incl.:

OPERAS: **Notre Dame* (1902–4); **Fredigundis* (1916–21).
ORCH: Syms.: No. 1 in E major (1896–9), No. 2 in E♭ major (1911–13), No. 3 in A major (1927–8), No. 4 in C major (1932–3); *Zwischenspiel* (Intermezzo) from *Notre Dame* (1902–4); *Variations on a Hussar Song* (1930–1); *Chaconne* in C♯ minor (1931, orch. of 1925 organ work); *Concertante Variations on a Theme of Beethoven*, pf. (left-hand) and orch. (1923); pf. conc. in E♭ (left-hand) (1934).

CHORAL: *Das Buch mit sieben Siegeln* (The Book with Seven Seals), oratorio (1935–7); *Deutsche Auferstehung*, cantata, soloists, ch., org., orch. (1938–9).
CHAMBER MUSIC: Pf. Quintet (1926); Cl. Quintet No. 1 in B major (1932), No. 2 in A major (1938), both scored for cl., vn., va., vc., and pf. left-hand; Str. Qt. No. 1 in A major (1925), No. 2 in G major (1929); Quintet in G, pf. left-hand, 2 vn., va., vc. (1926); *3 Little Fantasy-Pieces* on Hung. nat. melodies, vc. and pf. (1892).
ORGAN: Fantasy and Fugue in D (1924); Prelude and Fugue in E♭ (1924); *Chaconne* in C♯ minor (1925); *4 Little Choral-Preludes* (1926); *Solemn Fugue* (1937).

Schmidt, Joseph (*b* Bavideni, Bukovina, 1904; *d* Zürich, 1942). Romanian ten. Studied Berlin Cons. Made name as radio singer and on gramophone records. Small stature prevented his operatic career. Settled Switz. 1939.

Schmidt, Ole (*b* Copenhagen, 1928). Danish cond., composer, and pianist. Studied Copenhagen RAM 1947–55. Début as cond. 1955. Royal Opera, Copenhagen, 1958–65, chief cond. Hamburg S.O. 1970–1, Danish Radio S.O. from 1971. Guest cond. of world's leading orchs. Comps. incl. 2 syms., pf. conc., 2 concs. for accordion, hn. conc., vn. conc., tuba conc., guitar conc., 5 str. qts., and ballets.

Schmidt-Isserstedt, Hans (*b* Berlin, 1900; *d* Hamburg, 1973). Ger. cond. and composer. Studied Heidelberg, Münster, and Berlin (with Schreker). Cond. in Wuppertal, then Rostock 1928–31, Darmstadt 1931–3, and at Hamburg State Opera 1935–42. Dir., Deutsches Opernhaus, Berlin, 1942–5. Founded N. Ger. Radio S.O. (Hamburg Radio S.O.) in 1945, remaining cond. until 1971. Toured Eng. with it 1951 (first foreign orch. to play in rebuilt Free Trade Hall, Manchester). Prin. cond. Stockholm P.O. 1955–64. Cond. Glyndebourne 1958 (*Le Nozze di Figaro*) and CG 1962 (*Tristan*). Frequent guest cond. of Brit. orchs. Comp. comic opera, orch. mus., and songs.

Schmieder, Wolfgang (*b* Bromberg, 1901). Ger. musicologist. Archivist, Breitkopf and Härtel, Leipzig; head of mus. div. of Frankfurt State Library 1942. Compiled thematic catalogue of Bach's mus. (Leipzig 1950) which provides standard method of numbering his work. See *BWV*.

Schmitt, Aloys (*b* Erlenbach, 1788; *d* Frankfurt, 1866). Ger. pianist, organist, and composer. Court organist Hanover 1825–9. Comp. operas, oratorio, sym., 4 pf. concs., chamber mus. His son Georg Aloys Schmitt (*b* Hanover, 1827; *d* Dresden, 1902) was also a pianist and composer. Wrote 3 operas, chamber mus., etc., and ed. and completed (1901) Mozart's Mass in C minor.

Schmitt, Florent (*b* Blâmont, Nancy, 1870; *d* Neuilly-sur-Seine, 1958). Fr. composer. Studied

Paris Cons. with Fauré and Massenet. Won *Grand Prix de Rome* 1900. Dir., Lyons Cons. 1922–4. Frequent writer on mus. (in *Le Temps*, etc.). Mus. is rich in orch. colouring, often exotically scored. Works incl.:

ORCH: *Feuillets de Voyage* (1903–13, orch. from pf. duet); *La tragédie de *Salomé*, sym.-poem (1910, rev. of 1907 mimodrama); *Légende*, va. (or vn. or sax.) and orch. (1918); *Antony and Cleopatra*, 6 symphonic episodes (1919–20); *Salammbô*, 6 symphonic episodes (1925); *Symphonie concertante*, pf. and orch. (1931); Sym. (1958).

MIMODRAMA: *La tragédie de *Salomé* (1907, rev. as sym.-poem 1910).

VOICE(S) AND ORCH: Psalm 47 (46 in Vulgate), sop., ch., and orch. (1904); 4 *Poèmes de Ronsard* (1940).

CHAMBER MUSIC: pf. quintet (1901–8); vn. sonata (1918–19); sax. qt. (1943); str. trio (1944); fl. qt. (1944); qt. for 3 tb. and tuba (1946); str. qt. (1947–8); sextet, 6 cl. (1953); *Chants alizés*, wind quintet (1952–5); *Suite*, fl., pf. (1954–8).

Also many pf. pieces and songs.

Schnabel, Artur (*b* Lipnik, 1882; *d* Axenstein, Switz., 1951). Austrian pianist, composer, and teacher. (Amer. cit. from 1944). Pupil of Leschetizky. Public début at age 8. Became one of world's most respected and admired pianists, famous for his Beethoven and Schubert interpretations. Devoted his career to music which was 'better than it could be performed'. Leschetizky had told him, 'You will never be a pianist; you are a musician'. Notable recordings. Taught at Berlin Hochschule 1925–33 and later in Switzerland. Ed. Beethoven pf. sonatas and, with *Flesch, the Mozart and Brahms vn. sonatas. Settled in USA 1939–45, before returning to Switz. Rarely played 20th–cent. mus. but comp. in atonal style: works incl. 3 syms., 5 str. qts., and pf. conc. Wrote 3 books.

Schnabel, Karl Ulrich (*b* Berlin, 1909). Ger. born pianist (Amer. citizen 1944), son of Artur *Schnabel. Studied in Berlin. Début Berlin 1926. Settled USA 1938, teaching at Dalcroze Sch. of Mus., NY. Wrote *Modern Technique of the Pedal* (1950).

Schnarre (Ger.). Rattle. *Schnarrtrommel*, sidedrum. *Schnarrsaite*, rattle-string, i.e. the snare. But the *Schnarrwerk* of an organ is the reed department.

Schnebel, Dieter (*b* Lahr, 1930). Ger. composer. Studied Freiburg 1949–52. Entered Lutheran church; teacher of religion in Frankfurt 1963–70. Believes in theory that mus. can only be saved through abandonment. Hence works incl. nonmus. sounds and noises, and his *Nostalgie (Visible Music II)*, 1962, is for cond. only. Has written books on K. Stockhausen (1963–71) and Kagel (1970).

Schnéevoigt, Georg (*b* Viipuri, 1872; *d* Malmö, 1947). Finn. cond. and cellist. Studied Leipzig.

Cellist in Helsinki P.O. for 8 years, then toured Europe as soloist. Cond. début Riga 1901. Cond. Kaim Orch., Munich, 1904–8. Formed new sym. orch. in Helsinki 1912 which in 1914 became Helsinki City Orch. Cond. Helsinki City Orch. 1916–41 (jointly with *Kajanus 1916–32). Cond. in Stockholm 1915–24, Oslo P.O. 1919–27, Riga Opera 1928–32, Los Angeles P.O. 1927–9, Malmö 1930–47.

Schneider, Alexander (*b* Vilna, 1908). Russ.-born violinist (later Amer. citizen). Studied Frankfurt Cons. Leader, Frankfurt S.O. 1925–33. 2nd vn. Budapest Qt. 1932–44, and 1955–64. Settled USA 1933. Helped *Casals to found Prades Fest. 1950 and Casals Fest., Puerto Rico, 1957. Member of several chamber ens.

Schneider, (Johann Christian) **Friedrich** (*b* Alt-Waltersdorf, 1786; *d* Dessau, 1853). Ger. composer, cond., organist, and teacher. Studied Leipzig Univ. Organist, St Thomas's, Leipzig, from 1812; court cond. Dessau from 1821. Cond. of many Ger. choral fests. Wrote 16 oratorios, 7 operas, 23 syms., many choruses and songs, 7 pf. concs., much church and chamber mus. His perf. of Beethoven's 5th pf. conc. in Leipzig, in Dec. 1810 is thought to have been work's f.p.

Schneiderhan, Wolfgang (*b* Vienna, 1915). Austrian violinist. Studied in Vienna. Toured Europe at age of 11. Lived in Eng. 1929–32. Leader Vienna S.O. 1932–6, then played in opera orch. Leader Vienna P.O. 1937–51. Founded and led Schneiderhan Quartet 1937–51. Prof. of vn. Salzburg Mozarteum 1938–56. On staff Lucerne Cons. from 1949. Frequent soloist with leading orchs.

Schneider-Siemssen, Günther (*b* Augsburg, 1926). Austrian designer. Worked on first prod. in Bremen of Wagner's *Ring* (from 1954) and later at CG (1962–4), Salzburg Easter Fest. (1967–70), and NY Met. Notable collab. with Karajan at Salzburg incl. *Boris Godunov* (1965), *Tristan und Isolde* (1972), and *Die Frau ohne Schatten* (1974). Aims for realistic effects with modern methods, incl. subtle use of lighting.

Schnell; schneller (Ger.). Quick, Quicker. *Schnelligkeit*, Speed.

Schnittke (Schnitke), **Alfred.** See *Shnitke, Alfred*.

Schnorr von Carolsfeld, Ludwig (*b* Munich, 1836; *d* Dresden, 1865). Ger. ten. Studied Dresden, Leipzig, and Karlsruhe (with Devrient). Opera début Karlsruhe 1855. Prin. tenor Karlsruhe 1858–60, Dresden Opera 1860–5. Wagner, having heard him sing Lohengrin, asked him to create role of Tristan at Munich, 1865, with his Danish wife Malvina Schnorr von Carolsfeld (*b* Copenhagen, 1825; *d* Karlsruhe, 1904) as Isolde. Ludwig died 6 weeks after *Tristan* première and Malvina became singing teacher.

Schobert, Johann (*b* *c*.1735; *d* Paris, 1767). Silesian composer and harpsichordist. Moved to Paris, *c*.1760, becoming court harpsichordist. Composer of variety of works in so-called Mannheim style, influencing Mozart's early kbd. works. Died with his family after eating poisonous fungi.

Schock, Rudolf (*b* Duisburg, 1915; *d* Gürzenich, 1986). Ger. ten. Studied Cologne and Hanover. Opera début Duisburg, then sang chiefly in Berlin, Hamburg, and Munich, joining Vienna Opera 1953. CG 1949. Many appearances at Salzburg and Bayreuth Fests.

Schoeck, Othmar (*b* Brunnen, Switz., 1886; *d* Zürich, 1957). Swiss composer and cond. Studied Zürich Cons. and Leipzig Cons. (with *Reger). Mainly self-taught. Choral cond. 1909–17, then cond. St Gallen sym. concerts 1917–44. Noted for lyrical vocal comps. Works incl. 5 operas, incl. *Penthesilea* (1924–5), *Elegie*, v. and chamber orch. (1922–3), *Lebendig begraben*, low v. and orch. (1926), *Notturno*, bar., str. qt. (1931–3), several song-cycles with pf. acc., vc. conc., hn. conc., vn. conc., and chamber mus.

Schoenberg (orig. Schönberg), **Arnold** (*b* Vienna, 1874; *d* Los Angeles, 1951). Austrian-born composer, cond., and teacher (Amer. citizen from 1941). One of most influential figures in history of mus. Learned vn. and vc. as boy. Mainly self-taught in theory, but had lessons in counterpoint from *Zemlinsky, 1894. Began composing when youth; str. qt. and songs perf. 1897. Earned living scoring other composers' operettas and in 1901 became cond. of Wolzogen's *Überbrettl* (satirical cabaret; Wolzogen was librettist of R. Strauss's *Feuersnot). In 1899 comp. *Verklärte Nacht* and in 1900 began work on *Gurrelieder*, both being in romantic post-Wagnerian style. On strength of Part I of *Gurrelieder*, obtained teaching post and scholarship at Stern Cons., Berlin, on recommendation of Strauss. While there comp. tone-poem *Pelleas und Melisande*. Returned to Vienna in 1903. At rehearsal of his chamber mus. by Rosé Qt., met Mahler. Among his students at this time were men who became lifelong disciples—Webern, Berg, Wellesz, Erwin Stein. In Schoenberg's comps. of 1903–7, chromatic harmony was explored to its limits and tonal structures became ever more elusive until, in 1909, he arrived at atonality with the *3 Pieces* for pf., Op. 11, and the song-cycle *Das Buch der hängenden Gärten*. Perfs. of these works met with vehement hostility, and with equally vehement acclaim from his supporters. In 1911 he pubd. his masterly book *Harmonielehre*. At this time, also painted in striking 'expressionist' style. In 1912 comp. *Pierrot Lunaire* for actress Albertine Zehme, a work for reciter (in *Sprechstimme*) and chamber ens. Its Vienna perf. was the occasion of further hostility, but the f.p. there of the early-style *Gurrelieder* was a success. The *5 Orchestral Pieces* were first played

complete in London, 1912. In 1918 founded in Vienna a Soc. for Private Mus. Perfs. from which critics were excluded, no programme was announced in advance, and applause was forbidden. Wrote little between 1913 and 1921, and when next completed works appeared in 1923—the *5 Piano Pieces*, Op. 23 and the *Serenade*, Op. 24—they introduced to the world the 'method of comp. with 12 notes', which was Schoenberg's technique for organizing atonal mus. *Suite* for pf., Op. 25, was first work wholly in 12-note method. Side-by-side with this revolutionary procedure, Schoenberg also returned to a strict use of traditional forms. In 1925 was invited to Berlin to teach comp. at the Prussian Acad. of Arts, remaining until 1933 when dismissed by Nazis and left Ger. Reconverted to Judaism in Paris in 1933, and emigrated to USA. Settled in Los Angeles and taught at Univ. of Calif. 1936–44. At this time announced his preference for spelling of his name Schoenberg instead of Schönberg. In the next 18 years comp. inconsistently in 12-note or tonal styles, dismaying his followers but not himself, for he said that all composers had varied their styles to suit their creative needs and purposes. Also rev. earlier works, wrote several religious pieces, and returned to two major undertakings he had abandoned in Europe, the oratorio *Die Jakobsleiter*, which remained unfinished, and the opera *Moses und Aron*, of which only two of the 3 acts were completed and which, when prod. after his death, was revealed as a deeply moving experience, although he wrote only a few bars for Act 3 in 1951.

Schoenberg's mus., full of melodic and lyrical interest, is also extremely complex, taking every element (rhythm, texture, form) to its furthest limit and making heavy demands on the listener. But more and more listeners find the effort worth making. His greatness lies not only in his own mus. but in his artistic courage and in his powerful and continuing influence on 20th-cent. mus. He is likely to remain always a controversial, revered, and revolutionary musician. He was also a talented painter. Prin. works:

STAGE: *Erwartung, Op. 17, monodrama (1909); *Die *glückliche Hand*, Op. 18, drama with mus. (1910–13); *Von Heute auf Morgen, Op. 32, opera (1928–9); *Moses und Aron (1930–2, 1951).

ORCH.: *Verklärte Nacht, Op. 4 (orig. str. sextet 1899, arr. for str. orch. 1917, rev. 1943); *Pelleas und Melisande, Op. 5 (1902–3); *Kammersymphonie (Chamber Symphony) No. 1, Op. 9, for 15 solo instr. (1906, arr. for orch. 1922; new version Op. 9b, 1935; arr. by Webern for 5 instr. 1922); *5 *Orchestral Pieces (Fünf Orchesterstücke)*, Op. 16 (1909, rev. 1922 and 1949; arr. for 2 pf. by Webern); *3 Little Pieces* for chamber orch. (1910); *Variations*, Op. 31 (1926–8); *Accompaniment to a Film Scene (Begleitungsmusik zu einer Lichtspielszene)* Op. 34 (1929–30); vc. conc. (after conc.

for clavicembalo by *Monn) (1932–3); conc. for str. qt. and orch. (after Handel's Concerto Grosso Op. 6 No. 7) (1933); *Suite* for str. (1934); Vn. conc., Op. 36 (1934–6); *Second Chamber Symphony*, Op. 38a (1906–16, 1939); pf. conc., Op. 42 (1942); *Theme and Variations*, Op. 43a for band (1943), Op. 43b for orch. (1943).

VOICE(S) AND INSTR: *Gurrelieder*, 5 soloists, narrator, ch., and orch. (1900–3, 1910–11); *Lied der Waldtaube* (Song of the Wood Dove) from *Gurrelieder*, mez. and chamber orch. (1922); *6 Songs with Orchestra*, Op. 8 (1903–4, also with pf.); *Herzgewächse*, Op. 20, high sop., celesta, harmonium, harp (1911); *Pierrot Lunaire*, Op. 21, speaker and chamber ens. (1912); *4 Songs*, Op. 22, v. and orch. (1913–16); *Die *Jakobsleiter*, oratorio (unfinished) for 6 soloists, speaking ch., ch., and orch. (1917–22, scoring completed by W. Zillig); *Kol Nidre*, Op. 39, rabbi, ch., and orch. (1938); *Ode to Napoleon Buonaparte*, Op. 41, str. qt., pf., reciter (1942), Op. 41b for str. orch., pf., reciter (1944); *Genesis Prelude*, Op. 44, ch. and orch. (1945); *A *Survivor from Warsaw*, Op. 46, narrator, male ch., and orch. (1947); *Moderne Psalmen*, Op. 50c, mixed ch., speaker, orch. (1950).

UNACC. CHORUS: *Friede auf Erden* (Peace on Earth), Op. 13 (1907); *4 Pieces*, Op. 27 (No. 4 with acc. of mandoline, cl., vn., vc.) (1925); *3 Satires*, Op. 28 (No. 3, *Der neue Klassizismus* (The new classicism) with va., vc., pf.) (1925); *3 German Folk-Songs* (1928); *6 Pieces*, Op. 35, male ch. (1929–30); *Birthday Canons*, 3 vv. (1943); *3 Folk-Songs*, Op. 49 (1948); *Dreimal tausend Jahre*, Op. 50a (1949); *De Profundis*, Op. 50b (1950). Also many other canons, 1905–49.

CHAMBER MUSIC: Str. Qt. in D (1897); Str. Qt. No. 1 in D minor, Op. 7 (1905), No. 2 in F♯ minor, with sop. v. in 3rd and 4th movements, text by S. George (1907–8), No. 3, Op. 30 (1927), No. 4, Op. 37 (1936); *Verklärte Nacht*, Op. 4, str. sextet (1899; orch. version 1917); *Serenade*, Op. 24, for cl., bass cl., mandoline, guitar, vn., va., vc., and bar. in 4th of 7 movements (1920–3); *Weihnachtsmusik (Christmas Music)*, 2 vn., vc., harmonium, pf. (1921); wind quintet, Op. 26 (1923–4); *Suite* (Septet), Op. 29, pf., picc., cl. (or fl.), bass cl. (or bn.), vn., va., vc. (1924–6); str. trio, Op. 45 (1946); *Phantasy*, Op. 47, vn. and pf. (1949).

PIANO: *3 Pieces*, Op. 11 (1909, rev. 1924; No. 2 orch. Busoni 1909); *6 Little Pieces*, Op. 19 (1911); *5 Pieces*, Op. 23 (1920–3); *Suite*, Op. 25 (1921); *2 Piano Pieces*, Op. 33a (1928), Op. 33b (1931).

ORGAN: *Variations on a Recitative*, Op. 40 (1941).

SONGS WITH PIANO: *2 Songs*, Op. 1 (1897); *4 Songs*, Op. 2 (1899); *6 Songs*, Op. 3 (1899–1903); *Cabaret Songs* (1901); *8 Songs*, Op. 6 (1903–5); *2 Ballads*, Op. 12 (1907); *2 Songs*, Op. 14 (1907-8); *2 Songs* (1909, pubd. 1966); *Das *Buch der hängenden Gärten*, Op. 15, 15 songs for sop. (1908–9); *German Folk-Songs* (1930); *3 Songs*, Op. 48 (1933).

ARRS. OF OTHER COMPOSERS: Bach: *2 Chorale-Preludes* arr. for large orch. (1922) (1. *Komm, Gott, Schöpfer, Heiliger Geist*; 2. *Schmücke dich, O liebe Seele*); *Prelude and Fugue* in E♭ (org.) arr. for large orch. (1928). Brahms: Pf. Qt. No. 1 in G minor, Op. 25, arr. for orch. (1937). Loewe: *Der Nöck*, ballad, arr. for orch. (?1910). J. Strauss II: *Kaiserwalzer* (Emperor Waltz), arr. for fl., cl., str. qt., pf. (1925).

BOOKS: *Harmonielehre* (Treatise on harmony) (Vienna 1911, 2nd edn. 1922, abridged Eng. trans. by D. Adams, NY 1948; complete Eng. trans. by R. E. Carter 1978); *Style and Idea* (NY 1950, enlarged edn. London 1972); *Structural Functions of Harmony* (NY 1954).

See also *Atonal*; *Serialism*; *Klangfarbenmelodie*.

Schöffler, Paul (*b* Dresden, 1897; *d* Amersham, 1977). Ger.-born Austrian bar. Studied Dresden, Berlin, and Milan. Opera début Dresden 1925. Member, Dresden Opera 1925–37, then Vienna Opera until early 1970s. CG début 1934 (as Donner), singing there each year to 1939 and 1949–53. NY Met. 1949–53, Bayreuth 1943, 1944, 1956. Outstanding in Verdi roles, but best known for his Wagner parts (Sachs, Wotan, Dutchman) and as Strauss's Barak in *Die Frau ohne Schatten*. Sang role of Jupiter in Strauss's *Die Liebe der Danae* (Salzburg 1952) and created title-role in Einem's *Dantons Tod* (Salzburg 1947). Settled in Eng.

Scholes, Percy (Alfred) (*b* Leeds, 1877; *d* Vévey, Switz., 1958). Eng. mus. critic, organist, teacher, and lexicographer. Active in 'music appreciation' movement. Founded *Music Student* (1908; now *Music Teacher*). Wrote on mus. for *The Observer*, 1920–7, and *Radio Times* (1923–9). Compiled and ed. *Oxford Companion to Music* (1938 and subsequent edns.), *Concise Oxford Dictionary of Music* (1952 and subsequent edns.), and *The Mirror of Music 1844–1944* (1947, 2 vols.). Wrote books on *God Save the King* (1942), opera, Eng. mus., Puritans and mus., etc. O.B.E. 1957.

Schollum, Robert (*b* Vienna, 1913). Austrian composer, cond., and teacher. Studied New Vienna Cons. 1927–32 and at Vienna State Acad. of Music (comp. with J. Marx). Cond. and teacher since 1933. Teacher at Vienna Hochschule from 1959. Follower of Schoenberg's 12-note technique, but not strict after *c*.1967. Works incl. 5 syms., 2 vn. concs., octet, etc.

Schönbach, Dieter (*b* Stolp, 1931). Ger. composer and cond. Studied in Detmold 1949–57 and later with *Fortner. Dir. of Bochum elec. studio since 1959. Formed multi-media team 1967. Comps. incl. pf. conc., multi-media opera, several works named *Canzona da Sonar*, for various instr. groups, incl. prepared pf., tape, etc.

Schonberg, Harold C. (*b* NY, 1915). Amer. mus. critic and author. Studied NY Univ. Mus. critic, *NY Sun* 1946–50, *NY Times* 1950 (senior critic

1960–80). Pulitzer Prize for criticism 1971. Author of books on pianists, conds., and composers.

Schöne Melusine, Die (Mendelssohn). See *Melusina, The Fair*.

Schöne Müllerin, Die (The Fair Maid of the Mill). Song-cycle by Schubert, D795, comp. 1823, for male v. and pf. to 20 poems by Wilhelm Müller (1794–1827) from *Gedichte aus den hinterlassenen Papieren eines reisenden Waldhornisten* (1821). Songs are: *Das Wandern* (Wandering); *Wohin?* (Where to?); *Halt*; *Danksagung an den Bach* (Grateful address to the millstream); *Am Feierabend* (After the day's work); *Der Neugierige* (Curiosity); *Ungeduld* (Impatience); *Morgengruss* (Morning greeting); *Des Müllers Blumen* (The Miller's Flowers); *Tränenregen* (Rain of Tears); *Mein* (Mine); *Pause*; *Mit dem grünen Lautenbande* (With the Lute's green ribbon); *Der Jäger* (The Huntsman); *Eifersucht und Stolz* (Jealousy and Pride); *Die liebe Farbe* (The beloved colour); *Die böse Farbe* (The hated colour); *Trockne Blumen* (Dry flowers); *Der Müller und der Bach* (The Miller and the Millstream); *Des Baches Wiegenlied* (The Millstream's lullaby).

Schönherr, Max (*b* Marburg, 1903; *d* Vienna, 1984). Austrian cond. and composer. Studied Graz Cons. Cond. opera at Graz, then at Volksoper and Theater an der Wien, Vienna. Cond. Vienna Radio 1931–68. Specialist in Johann Strauss, Lehár.

Schönzeler, Hans-Hubert (*b* Leipzig, 1925). Ger.-born cond. and musicologist (naturalized Eng. 1947). Studied N.S.W. State Cons., Sydney. Cond. 20th-Cent. Ens., London, 1957–61; Western Australian S.O. 1967. Specialist in Bruckner, on whom he has written a book (1970). Cond. f.p. of original version (1884–7) of Bruckner's Sym. No. 8 in BBC broadcast 1973.

School for Fathers. Eng. title of Dent's trans. of Wolf-Ferrari's *I *Quattro rusteghi*.

Schoolmaster, The (Haydn). See *Schulmeister, Der*.

Schools of Music. See under names of individual schools and colleges.

Schöpfung, Die (Haydn). See *Creation, The*.

Schorr, Friedrich (*b* Nagyvárád, 1888; *d* Farmington, Conn., 1953). Hung.-born bass-bar. (later Amer. citizen). Studied Vienna. Sang minor operatic roles at Chicago 1912, later same year sang Wotan in *Die Walküre* at Graz. Sang at Prague Opera 1916–18, Cologne 1918–23, Berlin 1923–31, CG 1924–33, Bayreuth 1925–31, NY Met. 1924–43. Singer of great nobility and rich tone, the outstanding Wagnerian bass of the inter-war years.

Schott, B., und Söhne (Schott and Sons). Firm of Ger. mus. publishers est. at Mainz 1780 by Bernhard Schott (1748–1809), succeeded in 1817 by his sons. London branch founded 1835, also branches in Paris, Leipzig, Rotterdam, and NY. Acquired Eulenburg 1957. Publishes much contemporary music, e.g. Tippett, Maxwell Davies, Goehr, etc. Publisher of Hoboken's Haydn catalogue.

Schottishe (Ger. plural). Scottish. Type of ballroom round dance similar to polka, introduced to Eng. in 1848 and known as 'German polka'. No connection with *Écossaise* and none with Scotland.

Schrammel Quartet. Viennese instr. combination for perf. of light mus.—2 vn., guitar, and accordion (replacing the G cl.). Called after Joseph Schrammel (1850–93), leader of a qt. of this kind and composer of waltzes etc. for it. Originally a trio, formed 1878, qt. from 1886.

Schrecker, Bruno (*b* Frankfurt, 1928). Ger.-born cellist. Studied RCM and with Casals. Member Oromonte Str. Trio and Pf. Trio, Allegri Qt.

Schreier, Peter (Max) (*b* Meissen, 1935). Ger. ten. and cond. Studied Dresden Hochschule 1956–60. Début Dresden 1961 (Dresden co. 1959–63); Berlin Staatsoper since 1963. London SW 1966 (Ferrando in *Così fan tutte* in Hamburg co. visit), NY Met. 1968 (Tamino). Specialist in Lieder and Mozart roles. Recital début London 1978. Début as cond. 1969.

Schreierpfeifen (Ger.). Crying fife. Renaissance reed-cap woodwind instr., member of shawm family, made in 4 sizes (bass, 2 ten., alto). Sometimes known as *Schryari*. Were used in military bands outdoors. None extant.

Schreker, Franz (*b* Monaco, 1878; *d* Berlin, 1934). Austrian composer and cond. Studied Vienna, under R. Fuchs. Founded and cond. Vienna Phil. Ch. 1908–20. Taught comp. at Vienna Acad. Cond. at Volksoper. Dir., Berlin Hochschule für Musik 1920–32. His mus. is powerful and expressionist, his biggest success being with the opera *Der *ferne Klang* in 1912 which influenced Berg's *Wozzeck*. Among his other operas were *Das Spielwerk und die Prinzessin* (1909–12, rev. 1920), *Die Gezeichneten* (1913–15), *Der Schatzgräber* (1915–18), *Irrelohe* (1919–24), *Christophorus* (1924–7), *Der singende Teufel* (1924–8), and *Der Schmied von Gent* (1929–32). In 1908 he composed a ballet-pantomime based on Wilde, *Der Geburtstag der Infantin*, for str. orch., producing a *Suite* from it scored for full orch. in 1923. Wrote chamber sym., works for str., and about 50 songs.

Schröder-Devrient, Wilhelmine (*b* Hamburg, 1804; *d* Coburg, 1860). Ger. sop. Studied with her parents. Began career as actress. Opera début Vienna 1821 as Pamina in *Die Zauberflöte*. In 1822 sang Leonore in *Fidelio* in presence of Beethoven in Vienna. Sang in Dresden 1823–47, Paris 1830–32, London 1832, 1833, 1837. Wagner was so overwhelmed by her singing that he vowed to dedicate his life to creating a new kind of opera. She created 3 Wagner roles: Adriano in *Rienzi* (1842), Senta in *Der fliegende Holländer* (1843), and Venus in *Tannhäuser* (1845). Retired 1847. Schumann's song *Ich grolle nicht* was dedicated to her. Also sang in Rossini, Bellini, and Gluck. Though her vocal technique was apparently flawed, her dramatic powers made her interpretations unforgettable.

Schubart, Christian Friedrich Daniel (*b* Sontheim, 1739; *d* Stuttgart, 1791). Swabian organist, composer, and poet. Court opera dir., Stuttgart, from 1787. Spent 10 years in prison 1777–87, ostensibly for insulting a duke's mistress but probably for 'free-thinking' writings. Works incl. operetta, cantatas, and songs. Wrote words of Schubert's songs *Die Forelle, An mein Klavier, An den Tod*, and *Grablied auf einen Soldaten*.

Schubert, Franz (*b* Dresden, 1808; *d* Dresden, 1878). Ger. violinist and composer. Played in Dresden court orch. 1823–73 (leader from 1861). Comp. works for vn. and orch. and popular vn. piece *L'Abeille* (The Bee).

Schubert, Franz (Seraph Peter) (*b* Vienna, 1797; *d* Vienna, 1828). Austrian composer. Son of impoverished school-master, who was his first teacher. In 1808 admitted as boy sop. to imperial chapel, living in the Konvikt. Played vn. in sch. orch., for which he wrote his First Sym. (1813). Became pupil of *Salieri for theory, 1812. Left Konvikt when v. broke 1813, and worked as ass. schoolmaster to father, but continued to compose prolifically. Frequently attended opera in Vienna and wrote his first opera, *Des Teufels Lustschloss* in 1814, the first of many stage works, none of which was successful. On 19 October 1814 set Goethe's poem *Gretchen am Spinnrade*, his first masterpiece and the song that, it is inaccurately but understandably said, gave birth to the *Lied*. This released a flood of inspiration. In 1815 Schubert comp. 144 songs, incl. 8 in one day in Oct. In addition, comp. a sym., 2 Masses, and other works. Altogether wrote over 600 songs, of which about 200 are different settings of poems he had already set—he set some poems (particularly those by Goethe and Schiller) up to 6 times.

In 1817 he abandoned teaching and lived in Vienna with one or other of his friends, among whom the poet Mayrhofer was the closest. They talked, drank, discussed the questions of the day, and made mus. in coffee-houses and at their homes. Schubert also met at this time the bar. Michael *Vogl, one of the outstanding opera singers of the day, who became the foremost interpreter of his songs, often acc. by the composer. Apart from church mus., the first public concert of Schubert's mus. was in March 1818, at which were perf. (on 2 pf.) the ovs. he had written in imitation of Rossini, whose operas were all the rage in Vienna from 1816. In 1818

spent summer as teacher to the 2 daughters of Count Johann Esterházy at summer estate at Zseliz, where he heard Slav and gipsy folk-mus. On return to Vienna, Schubert lived with Mayrhofer and Hültenbrenner, latter acting as factotum, assembling Schubert's MSS. His *Singspiel, Die Zwillingsbrüder*, received 6 perfs. in Vienna in June 1820, with Vogl singing the roles of the twin brothers; and in Aug. his incidental mus. for *Die Zauberharfe* was used at the Theater an der Wien. Other works comp. in this period were the 'Trout' Quintet, written at Steyr, Upper Austria, during holiday in 1819 with Vogl, the oratorio *Lazarus*, setting of *Psalm 23, Wanderer Fantasy*, and the *Quartettsatz*. In 1821 Diabelli pubd. song *Erlkönig*, the first mus. by Schubert to appear in print. Others followed. In 1820–1, the Schubert circle of friends changed as some members left Vienna. Among new associates were painters Leopold Kupelwieser and Moriz von Schwind, and musician Franz Lachner.

In 1821 sketched his 7th Sym., in E major, but left it unorch. (several musicians have 'completed' it, among them J. F. Barnett, 1884, Felix Weingartner, 1935, and Brian Newbould, 1977). The following year, comp. an 8th Sym. in B minor, but completed only 2 movements in full and 130 bars of a scherzo. However, the 'Unfinished' Sym. is a complete work of art in itself as it stands. Schubert heard Weber conduct *Der *Freischütz* and *Euryanthe* in Vienna and himself wrote several stage works between 1821 and 1823, the operas *Alfonso und Estrella* and *Der häusliche Krieg*, and incidental mus. for *Rosamunde, Fürstin von Cypern*, a play by Helmina von Chézy (librettist of *Euryanthe*) which ran for 2 perfs.

Ill-health began to trouble Schubert in 1823; while in hospital that year comp. some of the songs of the song-cycle *Die schöne Müllerin*. At Zseliz in 1824 with the Esterházy family, wrote A minor str. qt. and *Grand Duo* for pf. duet. In the summer of 1825, joined Vogl for a 5-month tour of Austria, composing all the time. At Gmunden and Gastein said to have comp. a sym. of which no trace has been found, but modern scholarship tends to take the view that this is the 'Great' C major Sym. (No. 9), usually ascribed to 1828 but now thought to date from 1825. Scholarship is equally divided over what personal contact there was between Schubert and Beethoven, but incontrovertibly Schubert was a torchbearer at Beethoven's funeral in 1827 and had earlier visited him on his deathbed.

The last 2 years of Schubert's short life are fully documented in *Schubert: The Final Years* by John Reed (1972). To them belong the song-cycle *Winterreise,* the Eb pf. trio, *Moments musicaux* and 3 pf. sonatas, many songs, and Str. Quintet in C major. All Schubert's mus., even the happiest, has a tinge of sadness; the works of his last years, when illness increasingly afflicted him, are at an extreme of poignancy. In Mar. 1828 gave a public concert of his works in Vienna. It made a profit for him, but none of the city's mus. critics attended. Died on 19 Nov. 1828 and was buried near to Beethoven at Währing. Both composers were later exhumed and reburied in the Central Cemetery of Vienna.

Many of the works by Schubert which we hold most dear were not perf. until several years after his death. As a composer of songs he has no equal in fertility of melodic invention, but all his work is so graced with melody of the most seraphic kind that there was at one time a tendency to regard him as an 'undisciplined' composer for whom form meant little. How wrong a judgement this was can be realized simply by studying the great chamber works and late pf. sonatas alone. He ranks among the very greatest of composers in all forms except opera, and concs. (of which he wrote none), and the listener has a lifetime of discoveries among his vast output. His works were catalogued by O. E. *Deutsch and are now given Deutsch (D) nos. Prin. comps.:

OPERAS: *Des Teufels Lustschloss* (1813–14, D84); *Die Bürgschaft* (fragment, 1816); *Alfonso und Estrella* (1821–22, D732); *Der häusliche Krieg* (1823; orig. title *Die Verschworenen* (The Conspirators)); *Fierabras* (1823, D796).

OPERETTAS: *Claudine von Villa Bella* (1815, D239); *Die Freunde von Salamanka* (1815); *Fernando* (1815); *Der vierjährige Posten* (1815); *Die *Zwillingsbrüder* (1819, D647).

STAGE MUSIC: *Die *Zauberharfe* (The Magic Harp), melodrama (1820, D644); *Rosamunde, Fürstin von Cypern* (1823, entr'actes, ballet mus., Romanza for sop., Shepherd's Song, and choruses, D797).

ORCH: Symphonies: No. 1 in D (1813, D82), No. 2 in B♭ (1814–15, D125), No. 3 in D (1815, D200), No. 4 in C minor ('Tragic', 1816, D417), No. 5 in B♭ (1816, D485), No. 6 in C major (1818, D589), No. 7 in E major (1821, unscored by Schubert), No. 8 in B minor (*Unfinished', 2 movements only, 1822, D759), No. 9 in C major ('Great', 1825, D944); Overtures: in B♭ (1812, D11), in C major (D591) and D major (D590) (both 'in Italian style', 1817), in D (1817, D556), in E minor (1819, D648); *5 German Dances* (1813, D90); *5 Minuets with 6 Trios* (1813, D89); *Rondo* in A major, vn. and orch. (1816, D438).

CHURCH MUSIC: Masses: F major (1814, D105 with 2nd Dona nobis 1815, D185), G major (1815, D167), C major (1816, D452), A♭ (1819–22, D678), B♭ (1815, D324), E♭ (1828, D950), *Deutsche Messe* (1826–7, D872); *Lazarus*, oratorio (1820, D689); *Hymn to the Holy Spirit*, male vv. and wind (1828, D964); *Kyrie* in D minor (1812, D31), B♭ (1813, D45), D minor (1813, D49), F major (1813, D66); *Salve Regina*, sop., orch., organ (1812, D27); *Psalm 23*, women's vv. (1820, D706); *Tantum ergo* in C (1822, D739), in D (1822, D750).

VOICES AND ORCH: *Cantata in honour of Spendou* (1816, D472); *Prometheus* (1816, lost, D451); *Namensfeier* (1813, D80).

VOICES (unacc. or with pf./guitar): *An die Sonne* (1816, D439); *Die Advokaten* (1812, D37); *Begräbnislied* (1815, D168); *Cantata for Vogl's birthday* (1819, D666); *Cantata for Salieri's jubilee* (1816, D441); *Christ ist erstanden* (1816, D440); *Coronach* (1825, D836); *Das Leben ist ein Traum* (1815, D269); *Der Entfernten* (c.1816, D331); *Der Geistertanz* (1816, D494); *Der Tanz* (1825, D826); *Frühlingsgesang* (1822, D740); *Gebet* (1824, D815); *Geist der Liebe* (1822, D747); *Gesang der Geister über den Wassern* (Song of the Spirit over the Waters) (1817, 2 versions, D538, 1821 with orch. D714); *Gondelfahrer* (1824, D809); *Gott der Weltschöpfer* (c.1815, D986); *Gott im Ungewitter* (c.1815, D985); *Gott in der Natur* (1822, D757); *Grab und Mond* (1826, D893); *Hymne an den heiligen Geist* (1828, D964); *Hymne an den Unendlichen* (1815, D232); *Im Gegenwärtigen Vergangenes* (c.1821, D710); *Jünglingswonne* (?1822, D983); *Lebenslust* (1818, D609); *Mondenschein* (1826, D875); *Nachthelle* (1826, D892); *Nur wer die Sehnsucht kennt* (1819, D877/4); *Punschlied* (1815, D277); *Ständchen* (1827, D920); *Trinklied* (1815, D148); *Verschwunden sind die Schmerzen* (1813, D88).

CHAMBER MUSIC: String Quartets: No. 1 in B♭ (1812, D18), No. 2 in C (1812, D32), No. 3 in B♭ (1813, D36), No. 4 in C (1813, D46), No. 5 in B♭ (1813, D68), No. 6 in D (1813, D74), No. 7 in D, (1814, D94), No. 8 in B♭ (1814, D112), No. 9 in G minor (1815, D173), No. 10 in E♭ (1813, D87), No. 11 in E (1816, D353), No. 12 in C minor (*Quartettsatz) (1820, D703), No. 13 in A minor (1824, D804), No. 14 in D minor (*Death and the Maiden, 1824, D810), No. 15 in G (1826, D887); String Quintet (2 vn., va., 2 vc.), C major (1828, D956); Piano Quintet, A major (*Die Forelle* (*Trout), 1819, D667); Quartet for guitar, fl., va., vc. (arr. of Notturno by Matiegka) (1814 D96); Piano Trios: No. 1 in B♭ (1827, D898), No. 2 in E♭ (1827, D929), *Notturno* in E♭ for pf. trio (1825, D897), sonata for pf. trio in B♭ (1812, D28); Sonatas: vn. and pf. in A (1817, D574), *arpeggione (or vc.) and pf. in A minor (1824, D821); Sonatinas: vn. and pf., No. 1 in D (1816, D384), No. 2 in A minor (1816, D385), No. 3 in G minor (1816, D408); Octet in F (2 vn., va., vc., db., cl., bn., hn.) (1824, D803). Miscellaneous: *Adagio and Rondo Concertante*, pf., vn., va., vc. (1816, D487), *Fantasia* in C, vn, and pf. (1827, D934); *Rondo brillant* in B minor, vn. and pf. (1826, D895); *Introduction and Variations on Trock'ne Blumen*, fl. and pf. (1824, D802); *Minuet and Finale* in F for wind octet (1813, D72).

2 PIANOS: *Divertissement à la hongroise* (1824?, D818), *Fantasia* in F minor (1828, D 940), Sonata in B♭ (1818, D617), Sonata in C (*Grand Duo) (1824, D813), *Introduction and Variations on an Original Theme* in B♭ (c.1818, D603), *2 Marches*

caractéristiques in C (1826, D886), *3 Marches militaires* (No. 1 in D, No. 2 in G, No. 3 in E♭, 1822, D733, also for orch.); also polonaises, rondos, ovs., and sets of variations.

PIANO: Sonatas: No. 1 in E (1815, D157), No. 2 in C (1815, D279, unfinished), No. 3 in E (1816, D459), No. 4 in A minor (1817, D537), No. 5 in A♭ (1817, D557), No. 6 in E♭ (1817, D568), No. 7 in F♯ minor (1817, D570/1 unfinished), No. 8 in B (1817, D575), No. 9 in A minor (1817, D537), No. 10 in C (1818, D613 unfinished), No. 11 in F minor (1818, D625), No. 12 in C♯ minor (1819, D655 unfinished), No. 13 in A (1819, D664), No. 14 in A minor (1823, D784), No. 15 in C (1825, D840), No. 16 in A minor (1825, D845), No. 17 in D (1825, D850), No. 18 in G (1826, D894), No. 19 in C minor (1828, D958), No. 20 in A (1828, D959), No. 21 in B♭ (1828, D960); *Allegretto* in C minor (1827, D915); *Fantasia* in C (*Wanderer, 1822, D760; version for pf. and orch. by Liszt); 11 *Impromptus* (1828): No. 1 in C minor, No. 2 in E♭, No. 3 in G♭, No. 4 in A♭ (D899), No. 5 in F minor, No. 6 in A♭, No. 7 in B♭, No. 8 in F minor (D935), No. 9 in E♭ minor, No. 10 in E♭, No. 11 in C (D946); *Klavierstück* in A (1818, D604); 12 *Ländler* (1823, D790); 6 *Moments musicaux* (1823–8, D780): No. 1 in C, No. 2 in A♭, No. 3 in F minor, No. 4 in C♯ minor, No. 5 in F minor, No. 6 in A♭; 3 *Klavierstücke* (1828, D946): No. 1 in E♭ minor, No. 2 in E♭, No. 3 in C; *Rondo* in D (1818, D608); 2 *Scherzos* (1817, D593); *Hungarian Melody* (1824, D817); *Valses nobles* (1827, D969); 13 *Variations in A minor on a theme of Anselm Hüttenbrenner* (1817, D576); 12 *Waltzes* (1815–21, D145); 36 *Waltzes* (1816–21, D365).

SONG-CYCLES: *Die *schöne Müllerin* (1823, D795); *Winterreise* (1827, D911); *Schwanengesang* (1828, D957, publisher's coll., not conceived as cycle). See individual entries for names of component songs.

SONGS: It is impossible to list all Schubert's songs. A selection of the best known is given here, with poet's name:

Abendstern (Mayrhofer, 1824, D806), *Die abge-blühte Linde* (Széchényi, 1817, D514), *Alinde* (Rochlitz, 1827, D904), *Allein, nachdenklich wie gelähmt* (Petrarch, 1818, D629), *Die Allmacht* (Pyrker, 1825, D852), *Am Bach im Frühling* (Schober, 1816, D361), *Am Grabe Anselmos* (Claudius, 1816, D504), *Am See* (Bruchmann, 1823, D746), *An den Frühling* (Schiller, 1815, D245), *An den Mond* (Goethe, 1815, D296), *An die Entfernte* (Goethe, 1822, D765), *An die Freude* (Schiller, 1815, D189), *An mein Klavier* (Schubart, c. 1816, D342), *An die Laute* (Rochlitz, 1827, D905), *An die Leier* (Bruchmann, 1822, D737), *An die Musik* (Schober, 1817, D547), *An die Nachtigall* (Holty, 1815, D196), *An die unterge-hende Sonne* (Kosegarten, 1816, D457), *An eine Quelle* (Claudius, 1817, D530), *An schwager Kronos* (Goethe, 1816, D369), *An Sylvia* (Shake-speare, 1826, D891), *Auf dem Wasser zu singen*

(Stolberg, 1823, D774), *Auf der Bruck* (Schulze, 1825, D853), *Auf der Donau* (Mayrhofer, 1817, D553), *Auflösung* (Mayrhofer, 1824, D807), *Ave Maria* (Ellen's Song, W. Scott, trans. Storck, 1825, D839), *Bei dir Allein* (Seidl, 1826, D866/2), *Beim Winde* (Mayrhofer, 1819, D669), *Berthas Lied in der Nacht* (Grillparzer, 1819, D653), *Der blinde Knabe* (Cibber, 1825, D833, 2nd version), *Die Bürgschaft* (Schiller, 1815, D246), *Cronnan* (Ossian, 1815, D282), *Delphine* (Schütz, 1825, D857), *Des Fischers Liebesglück* (Leitner, 1827, D933), *Du bist die Ruh'* (Rückert, 1823, D776), *Der Einsame* (Lappe, 1825, D800), *Epistel* (Collin, 1822, D749), *Erlkönig* (Goethe, 1815, D328), *Die erste Liebe* (Fellinger, 1815, D182), *Der Fischer* (Goethe, 1815, D225), *Fischerweise* (Schlechta, 1826, D881), *Die Forelle* (Schubart, 1817, D550), *Frühlingsglaube* (Uhland, 1820, D686), *Frühlings-lied* (Anon, 1816, D398), *Ganymed* (Goethe, 1817, D544), *Geheimes* (Goethe, 1821, D719), *Geheimnis* (Mayrhofer, 1816, D491), *Die Götter Griechen-lands* (Schiller, 1819, D677), *Grablied* (Kenner, 1815, D218), *Gretchen am Spinnrade* (Goethe, 1814, D118), *Gruppe aus dem Tartarus* (Schiller, 1817, D583), *Harfenspieler I—Wer sich der Einsamkeit ergibt* (Goethe, 1816, D478); *II—An die Türen will ich schleichen* (Goethe, 1816, D479); *III—Wer nie sein Brot* (Goethe, 1816, D480), *Heidenröslein* (Goethe, 1815, D257), *Heimliches Lieben* (Klenke, 1827, D922), *Heiss' mich nicht reden* (Goethe, Mignon Song, 1826, 2nd version D877/2), *Hektors Abschied* (Schiller, 1815, D312), *Hermann und Thurnelda* (Klopstock, 1815, D322), *Herrn Josef Spaun* (Collin, 1822, D749), *Der Hirt auf dem Felsen* (The *Shepherd on the Rock) with cl. obbl. (Müller and von Chézy, 1828, D965), *Horch, horch, die Lerch* (Shakespeare, 1826, D889), *Im Abendrot* (Lappe, 1824, D799), *Im Frühling* (Schulze, 1826, D882), *Im Haine* (Bruchmann, 1822, D738), *Iphigenia* (Mayrhofer, 1817, D573), *Jäger, ruhe von der Jagd* (W. Scott, 1815, D838), *Die junge Nonne* (Craigher, 1825, D828), *Der Jüngling am Bache* (Schiller, 3 versions, 3rd, 1819, D638), *Der Jüngling an der Quelle* (1821, D300), *Der Jüngling und der Tod* (Spaun, 1817, D545), *Kennst du das Land?* (Goethe, 1815, D321), *Der König in Thule* (Goethe, 1816, D367), *Lachen und Weinen* (Rückert, 1823, D777), *Licht und Liebe* (Collin, 1816, D352), *Die Liebende schreibt* (Goethe, 1819, D673), *Liebhaber in allen Gestalten* (Goethe, 1817, D558), *Lied eines Schiffers an die Dioskuren* (Mayrhofer, 1816, D360), *Das Mädchen* (Schlegel, 1819, D652), *Das Mädchen aus der Fremde* (Schiller, 1814, D117), *Meeresstille* (Goethe, 1815, D216), *Mignon und der Harfer* (Goethe, 1826, D877/1), *Minnelied* (Holty, 1816, D429), *Miriams Siegesgesang* for sop. and ch. (Grillparzer, 1828, D942), *Morgenlied* (Werner, 1820, D685), *Der Musensohn* (Goethe, 1822, D764), *Nacht und Träume* (Collin, 1822, D827), *Nachtgesang* (Kosegarten, 1815, D314), *Nachtvio-len* (Mayrhofer, 1822, D752), *Nähe des Geliebten* (Goethe, 1816, D162), *Normans Gesang* (W. Scott, trans. Storck, 1825, D846), *Nunmehr, da Himmel, Erde* (Petrarch, 1818, D630), *Nur wer die Sehnsucht Kennt* (Goethe, Mignon song, 5 versions. 5th, 1826, D877/4), *La pastorella* (Goldoni, 1817, D528), *Der Pilgrim* (Schiller, 1823, D794), *Prometheus* (Goethe, 1819, D674), *Rastlose Liebe* (Goethe, 1815, D138), *Raste, Krieger* (Scott, 1825, D837), *Die Rose* (Schlegel, 1822, D745), *Das Rosenband* (Klopstock, 1815, D280), *Der Sänger* (Goethe, 1815, D149), *Schäfers Klagelied* (Goethe, 1814, D121), *Der Schiffer* (Mayrhofer, 1817, D536), *Schlummerlied* (Mayrhofer, 1817, D527), *Der Schmetterling* (Schiegel, 1815, D633), *Schwestergruss* (Bruchmann, 1822, D762), *Sehnsucht* (Schiller, 1813, D52), *Sei mir gegrüsst* (Rückert, 1822, D741), *Seligkeit* (Holty, 1816, D433), *So lasst mich scheinen* (Goethe, Mignon song, 2 versions, 2nd, 1826, D877/3), *Sprache der Liebe* (Schlegel, 1816, D410), *Ständchen* (*Horch, horch, die Lerche*) (Grillparzer, 1827, D921), *Die Sterne* (Leitner, 1828, D939), *Suleika's Songs I—Was bedeutet die Bewegung* (Goethe, 1821, D720), *II— Ach, um deine feuchten Schwingen* (Goethe, 1821, D717), *Der Tod und das Mädchen* (*Death and the Maiden*) (Claudius, 1817, D531), *Totengräbers Heimweh* (Craigher, 1825, D842), *Trost im Liede* (Schober, 1817, D546), *Über Wildemann* (Schulze, 1826, D884), *Dem Unendlichen* (Klopstock, 1815, D291), *Der Vater mit dem Kind* (Bauernfeld, 1827, D906), *Versunken* (Goethe, 1821, D715), *Die Vögel* (Schlegel, 1820, D691), *Der Wanderer* (Lübeck, 1816, D493), *Der Wanderer an den Mond* (Solde, 1826, D870), *Wanderers Nachtlied* (Goethe, 2 settings, 2nd 1822, D768), *Wehmut* (Collin, 1823, D772), *Wiegenlied* (Anon., 1815, D498), *Wiegenlied* (Seidl, 1826, D867), *Der zürnende Barde* (Bruckmann, 1823, D785), *Der Zwerg* (Collin, 1822, D771).

Schuch, Ernst von (*b* Graz, 1846; *d* Kötzschenbroda, nr. Dresden, 1914). Austrian cond. Studied in Graz, Vienna, and Breslau, learning vn. and pf. Début as cond., Breslau 1867. Cond. Dresden Court Opera 1872–1914 (gen. mus. dir. from 1889). Ennobled by Austrian emperor 1898. Raised standards at Dresden, making it among world's leading opera houses. During his 42-year régime, Dresden had 51 world premières of operas and 117 other operas were added to the Dresden repertory. Cond. f.ps. of Strauss's *Feuersnot* (1901), *Salome* (1905), *Elektra* (1909), and *Der Rosenkavalier* (1911). NY Met. 1900. Married Clementine Schuch-Proska (orig. Procházka) (1850–1932), leading coloratura sop. at Dresden 1873–1904.

Schuh, Willi (*b* Basle, 1900; *d* Zürich, 1986). Swiss mus. critic and author. Studied in Berne and Munich. Mus. critic of *Neue Züricher Zeitung* 1928–65; teacher at Zürich Cons. 1930–44. Ed. Busoni and Wagner letters. Friend of and authority on R. Strauss, who appointed him his official biographer. First vol., *Richard Strauss:*

Jugend und frühe Meisterjahre 1864–98, pubd. Zürich 1976 (Cambridge 1982, trans. Mary Whittall).

Schulhoff, Erwin (*b* Prague, 1894: *d* Wülzbourg concentration camp, 1942). Cz. pianist and composer. Studied in Prague, Vienna, Leipzig, Cologne, and Berlin. Worked with A. *Hába on microtones and also influenced by jazz. Wrote 6 syms., opera, 2 ballets, pf. conc., conc. for str. qt. and wind orch.

Schuller, Gunther (*b* NY, 1925). Amer. composer, cond., and hn.-player, son of violinist in NY P.O.. Studied Manhattan Sch. of Mus. Prin. hn., Cincinnati S.O. 1943–5. Joined NY Met. orch. in 1945, playing in it until 1959. Taught hn. Manhattan Sch. 1950–63. Assoc. prof. of mus., Yale Univ. 1964–7, president, New England Cons. 1967–77, supervising contemporary mus. concerts at Tanglewood since 1965. Influenced by Webern and Stravinsky but with great interest in jazz, his comps. drawing on jazz elements being among the most successful and convincing yet written. Commissioned by Hamburg Opera to compose *The Visitation* (Hamburg 1966). Joint art. dir., Berkshire Music Center 1970–85. Author of books on jazz and hn. technique. Guest cond. of leading Amer. and Brit. orchs. Prin. comps.:

OPERAS: *The Visitation* (1966); *The Fisherman and his Wife* (1970).
BALLET: *Variants* (1961, choreog. Balanchine).
ORCH: Sym. (1965); *Symphony for Brass and Percussion* (1950); *Symphonic Tribute to Duke Ellington* (1955); *Contours* (1956); Concertino for jazz qt. and orch. (1959); *7 Studies on Themes of Paul Klee* (1959); *Spectra* (1960); *American Triptych* (1965); *Shapes and Designs* (1968); *Concerto for Orchestra* (1965–6); *Contrasts*, woodwind quintet and orch. (1961); *Colloquy*, 2 pf. (1966); *Museum Piece* for Renaissance instr. and orch. (1970); hn. conc. No. 1 (1944), No. 2 (1977); vc. conc. (1945); *Fantasia Concertante* for 3 tb.; *Capriccio* for tuba; pf. conc. (1962); db. conc. (1968); vn. conc. (1976); *Deaï*, 2 orch. (1978).
CHAMBER MUSIC: Vc. sonata (1947); qt. for 4 db. (1947); hn. trio (1948); ob. sonata (1948–51); *Conversations* for jazz qt. and str. qt.; *5 Pieces* for 5 hn.; 2 str. qts.; woodwind quintet (1958); Fantasy Quartet for 4 vc. (1959).
VOCAL: *5 Shakespeare Songs*, bar. and orch.

Schulmeister, Der (The Schoolmaster). Nickname for Haydn's Sym. No. 55 in E♭ (Hob. I: 55) comp. 1774. Dotted figure in slow movement suggests admonishing finger of schoolmaster, and scholars believe Haydn authorized title.

Schuman, William (Howard) (*b* NY, 1910). Amer. composer and administrator. As youth composed jazz arrs. and studied at sch. of commerce. Abandoned this for serious mus. studies with Max Parsin and Charles Haubiel and at Juilliard Summer Sch. In 1933 enrolled for teacher's course at Columbia Univ., attended Salzburg Mozarteum summer course 1935 where he began work on First Sym. This he submitted for advice to Roy Harris, who gave him private lessons. His 2nd Sym. was eventually played in Boston under *Koussevitzky, who became his champion. Henceforward composed prolifically, and became prof. at Sarah Lawrence Coll., Larchmont. In 1945 became president of Juilliard Sch., holding this post until 1961; president of Lincoln Center for Performing Arts, 1961–9.

His syms. are a major feature of Amer. mus. His mus. has a firm melodic basis, large in gesture and conception, with strong contrapuntal element and motor rhythms, some derived from jazz. He has comp. in most forms, incl. ballets for Antony Tudor and Martha Graham, and been much honoured by Amer. institutions. Prin. works:

OPERA: *The Mighty Casey* (baseball opera, 1951–3, rev. as cantata *Casey at the Bat*, 1976).

BALLETS: *Undertow* (1945); *Night Journey* (1947); *Judith* (1949); *Voyage for a Theater* (1953); *The Witch of Endor* (1965).

ORCH: Symphonies: No. 1 (1935; withdrawn), No. 2 (1937, withdrawn), No. 3 (1941), No. 4 (1941), No. 5 (*Symphony for Strings*) (1943), No. 6 (1948), No. 7 (1960), No. 8 (1962), No. 9 (*Le Fosse ardeatine*) (1968), No. 10 (*American Muse*) (1976); *American Festival Overture* (1939); pf. conc. (1942); *William Billings Overture* (1944), *Circus Overture* (1944 for small orch., 1945 for large); *New England Triptych* (1956); vn. conc. (1947, rev. 1954, 1959); *Song of Orpheus*, vc. and orch. (1961); *Orchestra Song* (1963); *To Thee Old Cause* (1968); *In Praise of Shahn* (1969); *Voyage* (1972).

CHORAL: *Pioneers!* (1937); *This is Our Time* (1940); *Te Deum* (1944); *Carols of Death* (1958).

CHAMBER MUSIC: String Quartets: No. 1 (1936, withdrawn), No. 2 (1937), No. 3 (1939), No. 4 (1950); *Amaryllis*, str. trio (1964).

PIANO: *Voyage* (1953, orch. 1972); *3 Piano Moods* (1958).

Schumann, Clara (Josephine) (née Wieck) (*b* Leipzig, 1819; *d* Frankfurt, 1896). Ger. pianist and composer, wife of Robert *Schumann. Daughter and pupil of F. *Wieck. Début aged 9. Toured Ger. 1831 and elsewhere in Europe from 1832. Overcame fierce parental opposition to marriage to Schumann 1840, becoming his foremost interpreter. Toured Russia 1844. First visit to Eng. 1856, often thereafter to 1888. Lived in Berlin 1856–63. Head of pf. faculty, Hoch Cons., Frankfurt, 1878–92. Championed Brahms in his youth and remained lifelong friend. Last public perf. 1891. Comp. pf. conc. (in A minor), pf. trio, many pf. pieces, several songs, and cadenzas for concs. by Mozart and Beethoven. Had distinguished pupils. Was renowned for the breadth and integrity of her playing.

Schumann, Elisabeth (*b* Merseburg, 1888; *d* NY, 1952). Ger.-born sop. (Amer. citizen from 1944). Studied Berlin, Dresden, and Hamburg. Opera début Hamburg 1909, remaining member of co. until 1919. NY Met. 1914–15, début as Sophie in *Der Rosenkavalier*, one of her most famous and effective roles. Vienna Opera 1919–37; CG 1924–31. Toured USA 1921 in recitals with R. Strauss as accompanist. One of best-loved and most admired singers of her day, notable interpreter of Strauss Lieder and of such Mozart *soubrette* roles as Susanna, Zerlina, Despina, Blonde. Also memorable Adèle in *Fledermaus*. Left Austria 1938 and settled in USA, teaching for a brief spell at Curtis Institute.

Schumann, Robert (Alexander) (*b* Zwickau, 1810; *d* Endenich, 1856). Ger. composer, pianist, cond., and critic. Studied law at Leipzig and Heidelberg Univs., but main interests were mus. and Romantic literature, e.g. Jean-Paul Richter. In 1828 met Clara Wieck, to whose father Friedrich he went for pf. lessons in 1829, lodging with him and beginning to compose. In 1832 permanently injured hand by device he had invented to keep 4th finger immobile while practising. Was already contributing mus. criticism to Ger. papers and in 1831 called attention to Chopin's genius. Depressed by mus. situation in Ger., founded 'David Club' in 1834 to fight artistic philistines, and periodical *Neue Zeitschrift für Musik*, which he ed. for 10 years. In writings and comps., gave himself dual personality: Florestan for his impetuous self and Eusebius for his contemplative side. In 1838 visited Vienna and discovered MS. of Schubert's 'Great' C major sym., which he sent to Mendelssohn. Married Clara Wieck 1840 after long opposition from her father, this being followed by outpouring of songs and song-cycles. In 1841 concentrated on syms., in 1842 on chamber mus., and in 1843 choral works. Taught comp. at Leipzig Cons. Toured Russia with Clara, 1844. On return had severe attack of depression. Moved to Dresden in search of quiet, living there until 1850. In 1846 Clara gave f.p. of his pf. conc. and Mendelssohn cond. f.p. of 2nd Sym. In 1850 moved to Düsseldorf in hope of earning more by conducting, but was not a success. Met 20-year-old Brahms in 1853, acclaiming him in article 'New Paths'. The next year his mental health failed and he threw himself into Rhine, but was saved and taken to private asylum where he lived another 2 years.

Schumann was one of the greatest composers for pf., enriching its literature with a series of poetic works in which classical structure and Romantic expression are combined. His vocal and chamber mus. is of comparable quality, with the freshness, vitality, and lyricism which also characterize the orch. works. His orchestration is sometimes criticised for its thickness and lack of fluency, and various attempts have been made to 'improve' the scoring, e.g. by Mahler, but the present-day tendency is to prefer the spontaneity of Schumann's own. His songs, particularly his song-cycles, are among the glories of Lieder. His works contain many musical quotations and allusions and a number of his themes have been shown to be musical cryptograms. Prin. comps.:

OPERA: *Genoveva*, Op. 81 (1847–9).

INCIDENTAL MUSIC: *Manfred*, Op. 115 (Byron) (1848–9).

ORCH: Symphonies: No. 1 in B♭ (*Frühling*, *Spring*), Op. 38 (1841), No. 2 in C, Op. 61 (1845–6), No. 3 in E♭ (*Rhenish*), Op. 97 (1850), No. 4 in D minor (begun 1841, 2nd in order of comp., rev. 1851), Op. 120; *Overture, Scherzo, and Finale*, Op. 52 (1841, rev. 1845); *Overture to Shakespeare's Julius Caesar*, Op. 128 (1851); *Overture on Goethe's Hermann and Dorothea*, Op. 136 (1851).

CONCERTOS, etc.: Pf. conc. in A minor, Op. 54 (1st movement written as *Fantasie* 1841, rest added 1845); *Konzertstück*, 4 hn., in F, Op. 86 (1849); *Introduction and Allegro appassionato*, pf., Op. 92 (1849); vc. conc. in A minor, Op. 129 (1850); *Fantasy* in C, vn., Op. 131 (1853); *Concert-Allegro and Introduction* in D minor, pf., Op. 134 (1853); vn. conc. in D minor, Op. 2 posth. (1853).

CHAMBER MUSIC: String Quartets: Op. 41, No. 1 in A minor, No. 2 in F, No. 3 in A (1842); pf. qt. in E♭, Op. 47 (1842); pf. quintet in E♭, Op. 44 (1842); Piano Trios: No. 1 in D minor, Op. 63 (1847), No. 2 in F, Op. 80 (1847), No. 3 in G minor, Op. 110 (1851); Vn. Sonata No. 1 in A minor, Op. 105 (1851, No. 2 in D minor, Op. 121 (1851); *Adagio and Allegro* in A♭, hn. (or vn. or vc.) and pf., Op. 70 (1849); *Fantasiestücke*, cl. (or vn. or vc.) and pf., Op. 73 (1849); *Fantasiestücke*, pf., vn., vc., Op. 88 (1842); 3 *Romanzen*, ob. (or vn. or cl.) and pf., Op. 94 (1849); *Märchenbilder*, va. (or vn.) and pf., Op. 113 (1851); 5 *Pieces in Folk Style*, vc. (or vn.) and pf., Op. 102 (1849); *Märchenerzählungen*, pf., cl. (or vn.), and va., Op. 132 (1853); pf. accs. to 6 vn. partitas by J. S. Bach (1854).

PIANO: *Abegg Theme with Variations*, Op. 1 (1830); *Papillons*, Op. 2 (1829–31); 12 *Concert Studies on Paganini Caprices*, Set I, Op. 3 (1832), Set II, Op. 10 (1833); 6 *Intermezzi*, Op. 4 (1832); *Impromptus on a Theme by Clara Wieck*, Op. 5 (1833, rev. 1850); 18 *Davidsbündlertänze*, Op. 6 (1837, rev. 1850); *Toccata* in C, Op. 7 (1830); *Allegro* in B minor, Op. 8 (1831); *Carnaval: Scènes mignonnes sur 4 notes*, Op. 9 (1834–5); Sonatas: No. 1 in F♯ minor, Op. 11 (1833–5), No. 2 in G minor, Op. 22 (1833–8), No. 3 in F minor, Op. 14 (1835, rev. 1853); 8 *Fantasiestücke*, Op. 12 (1838); *Études symphoniques* (Symphonic Studies), Op. 13 (1834–7, rev. 1852); *Kinderscenen*, Op. 15 (1838); *Kreisleriana*, Op. 16 (1838, rev. 1850); *Fantasy* in C, Op. 17 (1836); *Arabeske* in C, Op. 18 (1839); *Blumenstück* in D♭, Op. 19 (1839); *Humoreske* in

B♭, Op. 20 (1839); 8 *Novelletten*, Op. 21 (1838); 4 *Nachtstücke*, Op. 23 (1839); *Faschingsschwank aus Wien*, Op. 26 (1839); 3 *Romanzen*, Op. 28 (1839); *Album für die Jugend*, Op. 68, Book I containing 18 pieces, Book II, 25 (1848); *Waldscenen*, Op. 82 (1848–9); *Bunte Blätter*, Op. 99 (1852); 3 *Fantasiestücke*, Op. 111 (1851); 3 pf. sonatas 'für die Jugend', Op. 118 (1853); *Albumblätter*, Op. 124 (1832–45); 7 *Piano Pieces in the form of fugues*, Op. 126 (1853); 5 *Gesänge der Frühe*, Op. 133 (1853).

PIANO DUETS: 6 *Impromptus*, Op. 66 (1848), *Ball-Scenen*, Op. 109 (1851).

ORGAN: 6 *Fugues on the Name of Bach*, Op. 60 (1845).

CHORUS AND ORCH: *Das Paradies und die Peri* (*Paradise and the Peri*), Op. 50 (1843); *Requiem für Mignon*, Op. 98b (1849); *Nachtlied*, Op. 108 (1849); *Der Rose Pilgerfahrt*, Op. 112 (1851); *Mass*, Op. 147 (1852); *Requiem*, Op. 148 (1852); *Scenes from Goethe's *Faust* (1844–53).

PART-SONGS: Mixed: 5 *Lieder*, Op. 55 (1846); *Romanzen und Balladen*, 4 vols., Opp. 67, 75, 145, 146 (1846–9); Women's: *Romanzen*, 2 vols., Opp. 69, 91 (1849); Men's: 6 *Lieder*, Op. 33 (1840); 5 *Hunting-Songs*, with 4 optional hn., Op. 137 (1849).

SONGS AND SONG-CYCLES: *Liederkreis* (Heine), Op. 24 (1840); *Myrthen*, cycle of 26 songs, Op. 25 (1840); *Lieder und Gesänge*, I, Op. 27 (1840), II, Op. 51 (1842), III, Op. 77 (1840 and 1850), IV, Op. 96 (1850); 12 *Gedichte*, Op. 35 (1840); 6 *Gedichte*, Op. 36 (1840); 12 *Gedichte aus Liebesfrühling*, Op. 37 (1840); *Liederkreis* (Eichendorff), Op. 39 (1840); *Frauenliebe und -Leben*, song-cycle, Op. 42 (1840); *Romanzen und Balladen*, I, Op. 45 (1840), II, Op. 49 (1840), III, Op. 53 (1840), IV, Op. 64 (1841 and 1847); *Dichterliebe*, song-cycle, Op. 48 (1840); *Liederalbum für die Jugend*, Op. 79 (1849); 3 *Gesänge*, Op. 83 (1850); 6 *Gesänge*, Op. 89 (1850); 6 *Gedichte*, Op. 90 (1850); 3 *Gesänge*, Op. 95 (1849); 9 *Lieder und Gesänge aus Wilhelm Meister*, Op. 98a (1849); 7 *Lieder*, Op. 104 (1851); 6 *Gesänge*, Op. 107 (1851–2); 4 *Husarenlieder*, Op. 117 (1851); 3 *Gedichte*, Op. 119 (1851); 5 *Heitere Gesänge*, Op. 125 (1851); 5 *Lieder und Gesänge*, Op. 127 (1850–1); *Gedichte der Königin Maria Stuart*, Op. 135, (1852); 4 *Gesänge*, Op. 142 (1852).

Schumann-Heink (orig. Rössler), **Ernestine** (b Lieben, 1861; d Hollywood, Calif., 1936). Cz.-born cont. (Amer. citizen from 1908). Studied in Graz and Dresden, teachers incl. F. Wüllner. Début Graz 1876 in Beethoven's 9th Sym.; opera début Dresden 1878 as Azucena in *Il Trovatore*. Member Hamburg Opera 1883–98. CG début 1892 as Erda. Bayreuth 1896–1914 (excl. 1904). Amer. début Chicago 1898 as Ortrud, NY Met. 1899. Sang mainly in USA until retirement 1932. Created role of Klytemnestra in Strauss's *Elektra*, Dresden 1909. Repertory of 150 roles. Voice of power and range allied to exceptional dramatic skill.

Schuppanzigh, Ignaz (*b* Vienna, 1776; *d* Vienna, 1830). Austrian violinist and cond. Friend of Beethoven, whom he taught vn. and va. Member of Prince *Lichnowsky's qt. 1794–5. Formed his own str. qt. 1804–5. Leader of Count *Rasoumovsky's qt. 1808–14, giving f.p. of several Beethoven qts. Member of Vienna court opera orch. from 1824, conducting there from 1828. Comp. some vn. pieces.

Schuricht, Carl (*b* Danzig, 1880; *d* Corseaux-sur-Vévey, Switz., 1967). Ger. cond. Studied Berlin Hochschule für Musik 1901–3. Cond. posts in Mainz, Dortmund, etc. Chief cond., Wiesbaden 1911–44 where he championed Delius, Ravel, Stravinsky, and Schoenberg. Guest cond. of many orchs. Settled Switzerland 1944.

Schurmann, Gerard (*b* Kertosono, Indonesia, 1928). Indonesian-born Dutch composer and cond. Settled in Eng. 1941. Studied comp. with *Rawsthorne. Cond. Dutch radio, Hilversum. Works incl. *6 Studies of Francis Bacon*, orch., (1968), *Variants*, orch. (1970), pf. conc. (1972–3), vn. conc. (1975–8), fl. sonatina (1968), *Contrasts*, pf. (1973), wind quintet (1963, rev. 1976), *Chuench'i*, v. and pf. (7 songs from Chinese, trans. Waley) (1966, also with orch. 1967), *The Double Heart*, cantata (1976), *Piers Plowman*, SCTB, ch., orch. (1979–80), *Duo*, vn., pf. (1984).

Schütz, Heinrich (*b* Köstritz, 1585; *d* Dresden, 1672). Ger. composer and organist, one of greatest of Bach's predecessors. Studied law, but patron, impressed by his mus. ability, sent him in 1609 to study in Venice with G. Gabrieli until 1612. Court organist, Kassel, 1613. Kapellmeister, Dresden electoral court, 1617. Spent 3 periods as court cond. in Copenhagen 1633–45. In Dresden with court orch. from 1645. Comp. first Ger. opera, *Dafne*, 1627 (mus. destroyed by fire 1760). Revisited It. 1628–9. His special importance lies in his grafting of It. choral and vocal style on to Ger. polyphonic tradition. Wrote magnificent settings of Passions, Christmas oratorio, *7 Words from Christ on the Cross*, etc. Works pubd. in 16 vols. 1885–94, ed. *Spitta, with suppl. vol. 1927, contents as follows: 1. 4 Passions, *Resurrection* oratorios, and *Sieben Worte Jesu Christi am Kreuz*; 2 and 3. Psalms and Motets, 1619; 4. *Cantiones sacrae*, 4 vv., 1625; 5. *Symphoniae sacrae*, Pt. I, 1629; 6. *Geistliche Concerte*, 1–5 vv., 1636 and 1639; 7. *Symphoniae sacrae*, Pt. II, 1647; 8. *Musicalia ad chorum sacrum*, 1648; 9. It. madrigals, Venice 1611; 10 and 11. *Symphoniae sacrae*, Pt. III, 1630; 12–15. Motets, concs., arias, psalms, etc; 16. Psalms for 4 vv. Suppl.: Christmas oratorio: *Die Historia von der freuden und gnadenreichen Geburt Gottes und Mariens Sohns* (1664, lost until 1908).

Schwanda the Bagpiper (*Švanda Dudák*). Opera in 2 acts by *Weinberger to lib. by Kareš and

Max Brod after folk-tale by Tyl. Prod. Prague 1927, NY Met. 1931, CG 1934.

Schwanendreher, Der (The Swan-turner). Conc. for va. and small orch. by Hindemith based on Ger. folk-songs, the soloist being (in composer's words) one 'who comes among merry company and performs the music he has brought from afar: songs grave and gay and, to conclude, a dance'. Movements are entitled: (1) *Zwischen Berg und tiefem Tal* (Between mountain and deep valley); (2) *Nun laube, Lindlein, laube* (Now shed your leaves, little linden); (3) *Seid ihr nicht der Schwanendreher?* (Is it not the swan-turner?). F.p. Amsterdam 1935, Hindemith (soloist), Mengelberg (cond.).

Schwanengesang (Swan Song). Coll. of 14 song-settings by Schubert (D957) issued after his death as a 'cycle' by publisher Haslinger; comp. 1827–8. The poets are Heine, Rellstab, and Seidl. The songs, in pubd. order, are: *Liebesbotschaft* (Love-message), *Kriegers Ahnung* (Warrior's presentiment), *Frühlingssehnsucht* (Longing for Spring), *Ständchen* (Serenade), *Aufenthalt* (Staging-post), *In der Ferne* (In the distance), *Abschied* (Farewell), *Der Atlas* (Atlas), *Ihr Bild* (Her Portrait), *Das Fischermädchen* (The Fisher Girl), *Die Stadt* (The Town), *Am Meer* (By the Sea), *Der Doppelgänger* (The ghostly double), *Die Taubenpost* (The Pigeon-post).

Schwarz, Rudolf (*b* Vienna, 1905). Austrian-born cond. (Brit. citizen from 1952). Studied in Vienna. Violist in Vienna P.O. Ass. cond. Düsseldorf Opera 1923, later at Karlsruhe 1927–33. Mus. dir. Jüdischer Kulturbund, Berlin, 1936. Spent some years in Belsen camp after 1940. Released 1945 and settled in Eng. Cond. Bournemouth Municipal Orch. 1946–51, CBSO 1951–57. Chief cond. BBC S.O. 1957–62. Prin. cond. Northern Sinfonia Orch. 1964–73. C.B.E. 1973.

Schwarzendorf. See *Martini, G. P.*

Schwarzkopf, Elisabeth (*b* Jarocin, nr. Poznán, 1915). Ger. sop. Studied Berlin Hochschule für Musik and with Maria Ivogün. Opera début 1938, Berlin, as Flower Maiden in *Parsifal*. Vienna début 1942 as Zerbinetta in Strauss's *Ariadne auf Naxos*, remaining there in coloratura roles until 1948. Salzburg début 1947 as Susanna. CG début 1947 as Elvira in *Don Giovanni*. Settled in Eng. 1948, member of CG co. 1948–51. Milan début 1948, San Francisco from 1955. NY Met. 1964 (Marschallin). Created role of Anne Trulove in Stravinsky's *The Rake's Progress* 1951. Walton wrote Cressida for her, but she never sang it on stage. Famous in Strauss roles such as Marschallin. One of greatest sops. of her generation, superb interpreter of Lieder, especially Wolf. Major asset was her intelligent and considered approach to each song, sometimes resulting in lack of spontaneity, but this defect many times outweighed by rare insight. Was wife of Walter *Legge, who produced many of her recordings.

Schwebung (Ger.). Fluctuation. (1) The 'beats' between 2 notes nearly but not quite in tune. (2, Org.) The *tremulant.

Schweigen (Ger.). Silence, or to be silent. *Schweigt*, *tacet*; *Schweigezeichen* ('silence-sign'), *rest.

Schweigsame Frau, Die (The Silent Woman). Opera in 3 acts by R. Strauss to lib. by Stefan Zweig after Ben Jonson's *Epicoene* (1609). Comp. 1933–4. Prod. Dresden 1935, NY 1958, CG 1961, Glyndebourne 1977.

Schweitzer, Albert (*b* Kaysersberg, Alsace, 1875; *d* Lambaréné, Gabon, 1965). Fr. (Alsatian) organist and Bach scholar (also theologian and medical missionary). Studied Strasbourg, Paris, and Berlin and with *Widor. Organist, Strasbourg Bach concerts from 1896 and Paris Bach concerts from 1906. Ed. Bach's org. works (first 5 vols. (1912–14) with Widor, remainder (1954–67) with Nies-Berger). Biography of Bach (in Fr. 1905, rewritten in Ger. 1908; Eng. trans. by E. Newman, 1911). Wrote book on Fr. and Ger. orgs. 1906. Worked as medical missionary in Fr. Congo, returning 1922 to give org. recitals to raise money for mission. Nobel Peace Prize 1952. Hon. O.M. 1954.

Schweizerpfeife (Ger.). Swiss pipe. Renaissance name for military fife or *Feldpfeife* (Field pipe).

Schwellen (Ger.). To swell, i.e. to increase in vol. of tone (*crescendo). *Schweller*, the *swell of an org., *Schwellwerk*, Swell Org.; *Schwellkasten*, Swell Box.

Schwer (Ger.). (1) Heavy (in style).
(2) Difficult. *Schwermütig, Schwermutsvoll*. Heavy-hearted.

Schwindend (Ger.). Diminishing (in tone, i.e. *diminuendo).

Schwung (Ger.). Swing. Term beloved of critics when describing an idiomatic perf. of, for example, *Die Fledermaus*. Also *Schwungvoll*, full of go, vigorous.

Scimone, Claudio (*b* Padua, 1934). It. conductor. Studied with Mitropoulos and others. Founded chamber ens. I Solisti Veneti, 1959, to specialize in 18th cent. It. instr. mus. and contemporary works by Bussotti, Donatoni, Malipiero, etc. Teacher at Venice Cons. 1961–7, Verona 1967–74, and dir., Padua Cons., from 1974.

Sciolto, scioltamente (It.). Untied. Loosely, i.e. in a free and easy manner. The noun is *scioltezza*.

Sciutti, Graziella (*b* Turin, 1932). It. sop. Studied Rome. Opera début Aix-en-Provence 1951 as Lucy in Menotti's *The Telephone*. Glyndebourne 1954–9, début as Rosina, and 1977 when she produced and sang Poulenc's *La voix humaine*. CG 1956–62. Scala, Milan, since 1956. Amer. début S. Francisco 1961 (Susanna). Outstanding in soubrette roles (Despina, Norina, etc.).

Scivolando (It.). Sliding, i.e. *glissando.

Scontrino, Antonio (*b* Trapani, Sicily, 1850; *d* Florence, 1922). It. composer and db. player. Studied Palermo Cons. and in Munich. Played in opera orch. in London 1874–5. Taught in Milan 1875–91, Florence from 1892. Wrote 5 operas, syms., 3 str. qts., church and chamber mus., etc.

Scordatura (It.). Mistuning. Abnormal tuning of a str. instr. in order to obtain special chordal effects and changes of tonal quality. Prevalent in vn. mus. (e.g. of Heinrich Biber), of 17th and 18th cents., possibly originating with lute. Paganini and Bériot in 19th cent. tuned G string of vn. up a tone to increase vol. and to make certain passages easier. In *andante* movement of Schumann's Pf. Qt., the C string of the vc. is tuned down to B♭ to increase the compass. Mahler in the scherzo of his 4th sym. has a solo vn. tuned up a tone to represent the 'dance of death'. Other 20th cent. examples of *Scordatura* occur in Kodály's sonata for unacc. vc., Stravinsky's *Firebird*, and Bartók's *Contrasts* (finale).

Score. A mus.-copy which shows in ordered form the parts allotted to the various performers, as distinct from 'parts' which show only that of one performer. Thus to speak of *score and parts* means a comprehensive copy, used by the cond., and separate copies for individual instrs. and singers. A *full score* shows all the parts separately displayed. A *vocal score* gives all the v. parts of a choral work or opera with the orch. parts reduced to a pf. part. *Short score* is a stage in comp. where the composer may write out his mus. giving indications (but not full details) of scoring and harmonization. Mahler's 10th Sym. was left mainly in short score. *Piano score* is a reduction to a pf. part of *all* the parts of a work. A *Miniature, study,* or *pocket score* is a full score issued in a handy size for study or for following a work at a concert. Conds. who know a work very well (and have good eyesight) sometimes use a miniature score.

Scoring. (1) The art and process of orchestrating a comp.
(2) Taking the separate parts of a work and assembling them in a score, e.g. where only the parts have been preserved.

Scorrendo, scorrevole (It.). Scouring. (1) Gliding from note to note, i.e. *glissando.
(2) In a flowing style.

Scotch Snap (Catch). A rhythmic figuration in which a dotted note is preceded by a note of shorter value. It is a feature of the *Strathspey and is found in some Scottish songs. It seems to be not earlier than 18th-cent., and of unknown origin. Occurs in the mus. of composers, e.g. Rossini, who have never been within hailing distance of Scotland.

Scotch Symphony. Mendelssohn's Sym. No. 3 in A minor, Op. 56, begun 1830 and completed

1842. Inspired by visit to Holyrood, Edinburgh, and ded. to Queen Victoria. F.p. Leipzig, March 1842, f. Eng. p. London, June 1842.

Scott, Anthony (Leonard Winstone) (*b* Datchet, 1911). Eng. composer, organist, and organ-restorer. Studied RCM (comp. with Howells, org. with Ley) and privately with Finzi. Organist, Lambourn, Berks., 1953–71. Works incl. org. pieces, part-songs, vn. conc., pf. sinfonia, 2 1-act operas.

Scott, Cyril (Meir) (*b* Oxton, 1879; *d* Eastbourne, 1970). Eng. composer, poet, and pianist. Studied in Frankfurt at age of 12 and again at 16 under *Knorr. Settled in Liverpool 1898 as pf. teacher. Composed *Heroic Suite*, cond. Richter in Liverpool and Manchester 1900, and First Sym. perf. in Darmstadt same year. Pf. quintet perf. London 1901 and 2nd Sym. (later rev. as *3 Symphonic Dances*) cond. Wood 1903. Through terms of publisher's contract, wrote many short pf. pieces in impressionist style which earned him title of 'English Debussy' and reputation as miniaturist. Other works incl. vn. sonata (1908–10), notable for constant changes of time-signature, *La Belle Dame sans merci* for ch. and orch. (1915–16), opera *The Alchemist* (prod. Essen 1925), 2 other operas, sym. *The Muses*, (1939), 2 pf. concs. (1913–14, 1958), 3 vn. concs. (1927, 1935), 2-vn. conc., vc. conc., *The Ballad of Fair Helen of Kirkconnel*, for bar. and orch., 4 str. qts., 3 pf. sonatas, and 2 str. trios. Also wrote poetry and philosophical and medical books. Taught *Rubbra comp.

Scott, Marion (Margaret) (*b* London, 1877; *d* London, 1953). Eng. writer on mus. Studied RCM 1896–1904 (vn., pf., comp., etc.). Formed str. qt. Founded Soc. of Women Musicians, 1911. Wrote mus. criticism for *Christian Science Monitor* 1919–33. Noted for research on Haydn, especially the str. qts. Wrote books on Beethoven and Mendelssohn.

Scotti, Antonio (*b* Naples, 1866; *d* Naples, 1936). It. bar. Studied Naples. Opera début Malta 1889 as Amonasro in *Aida*. Sang for 9 seasons in It., Sp., Russia, and S. America. Sang Sachs at Scala, Milan, 1898. CG début as Don Giovanni 1899, singing there regularly until 1910. Amer. début, Chicago 1899. NY Met. 1899–1933. First to sing Scarpia in London and NY. During years at Met. was heard frequently as Scarpia, Sharpless, Falstaff, Iago, and Rigoletto. Fine actor in addition to having v. of rare beauty but not of unusual power. For 4 years, 1919–23, managed and financed touring opera co.

Scottish Chamber Orchestra. Chamber orch. with headquarters in Queen's Hall, Edinburgh, and serving all Scotland. Founded 1974 with Roderick *Brydon as art. dir. R. *Leppard prin. guest cond. from 1978. Played for Scottish Opera, when appropriate, up to 1979. Has toured abroad, appearing at Aix-en-Provence 1978, 1980, 1981.

Scottish Fantasy. Fantasia on Scottish Folk Tunes for vn. and orch. by Bruch, comp. 1879–80, f.p. Hamburg 1880 (Sarasate). In 4 movements, last being an *Allegro guerriero* (warlike). Scottish tune featured in each movement: *Auld Rob Morris, The Dusty Miller, I'm a doun for lack of Johnnie,* and *Scots wha hae wi'Wallace bled.*

Scottish National Orchestra. Prin. prof. sym. orch. of Scotland, based in Glasgow and giving regular series of concerts in Glasgow, Edinburgh, and other Scottish towns. Formed 1891 as Scottish Orch., with George *Henschel as cond. 1891–95. His successors were Willem *Kes (1895–8), Max *Bruch (1898–1900), Frederic *Cowen (1900–10), Emil *Mlynarski (1910–16), Landon *Ronald (1916–20), Julius *Harrison (1920–3). From 1923 to 1933 there was no regular cond. except in 1926 when Václav *Talich was in charge. *Barbirolli was cond. 1933–6, followed by *Szell 1936–9, W. *Braithwaite 1940–6, and Walter *Süsskind 1946–52. Reorganized 1950 as Scottish Nat. Orch., with players on annual contracts and much enlarged schedule. Karl *Rankl became cond. 1952–7, Hans *Swarowsky 1957–9, Alexander *Gibson 1959–84, and Neeme *Järvi from 1984. During Gibson's régime the orch. increased its repertory, gave many f.ps., toured abroad, and played in the pit for *Scottish Opera. Stockhausen's *Gruppen, and several works by Henze received first Brit. perfs. from Gibson and SNO, and Scottish composers received particular encouragement. Schoenberg's vn. conc. had first Brit. public perf. in 1960.

Scottish Opera. Opera co. based in Glasgow but giving seasons in Edinburgh, Aberdeen, and elsewhere in Scotland, also paying regular visits to Eng. provinces. Has played in London, at Edinburgh Fest., and made several tours abroad. Founded 1962 by Alexander *Gibson, first season being of 2 operas, *Madama Butterfly* and *Pelléas et Mélisande,* in King's Th., Glasgow. With Peter Hemmings as administrator from 1963, co. began to build a reputation for striking productions, with excellent sets and lighting; singers were mainly Brit. but with several int. artists who worked with the co. for long spells, e.g. Helga *Dernesch. Contemporary works were perf., notably of Britten, and operas were commissioned from Scottish composers, e.g. Wilson's *Confessions of a Justified Sinner.* In 1969, Berlioz's *Les Troyens* was perf., with Janet Baker as Dido, and in 1966, with *Die Walküre*, the co. began to build a *Ring* cycle, culminating in 1971 in Glasgow with the first Brit. perf. of the *Ring* outside London for about 40 years. In 1975 the co. moved into the re-equipped and re-furbished Th. Royal, Glasgow, as its permanent headquarters, setting the seal on the finest and most important operatic development in Britain since the foundation of Glyndebourne. In 1976 Hemmings was appointed dir. of Australian Opera and was succeeded by Peter Ebert, former chief prod. of Scottish Opera. He resigned in 1980. His successor was John *Cox, appointed in 1982, who handed over to Richard Mantle in 1985. In addition to the SNO, orchs. playing regularly for the co. were the BBC Scottish S.O., the Scottish Chamber Orch., and the Scottish Philharmonia, but in 1980 the company formed its own orch. Scottish Opera is a remarkable example of the flowering of Scottish mus. life since 1945, especially under the aegis of Sir Alexander Gibson. John *Mauceri succeeded Gibson as mus. dir. in 1987.

Scotto, Renata (b Savona, 1933). It. sop. Studied Milan. Opera début Milan 1953. Member of Scala Co. since 1953. London début (Stoll) 1957. At Edinburgh Fest., 1957, replaced Callas in *La Sonnambula* at very short notice. CG début 1962, NY Met. 1965 (as Butterfly on both occasions). Specially successful in Puccini and Verdi.

Scozzese (It.). Scottish.

Scriabin. See *Skryabin, Alexander*.

Scribe, (Augustin) **Eugène** (b Paris, 1791; d Paris, 1861). Fr. dramatist and librettist. Most prolific librettist of his day, complete works comprising 76 vols. Among composers for whom he wrote libretti were Adam, Auber (38), Bellini (*Sonnambula*), Boieldieu (*La dame blanche*), Cherubini, Ciléa (*Adriana Lecouvreur*), Donizetti (5, incl. *L'Elisir d'Amore* and *La Favorite*), Gounod, Halévy (6, incl. *La Juive*), Hérold, Macfarren, Meyerbeer (5, incl. *L'Africaine*, *Les Huguenots*, and *Le Prophète*), Offenbach, Rossini (2, incl. *Le Comte Ory*), Suppé, Verdi (*Vêpres siciliennes* and *Un ballo in maschera*), and Zandonai.

Sculthorpe, Peter (Joshua) (b Launceston, Tasmania, 1929). Australian composer and pianist. First pf. lesson at age 8. Studied at Melbourne Univ. Cons. of Mus. and later at Oxford with Wellesz and Rubbra, 1957–60. Teacher at Sydney Univ. from 1963. Composer-in-residence Yale Univ., 1966; visiting prof., Sussex Univ., 1972–3. O.B.E. 1977. Set out to be 'Australian' composer in sense that Copland expressed something peculiarly American and Bloch depicted biblical wilderness. Rejected atonality and serialism as inappropriate to his task, and concentrated on rhythmic procedures and orch. sonorities. Influenced also by Balinese melodies and rhythms. Prin. works:

ORCH: *Irkanda IV*, vn., str., perc. (1961); *The 5th Continent*, speaker and orch. (1963); *Sun Music I* (1965), III (1967), IV (1967), V (*Ketjak*) (1969); *From Tabuh Tabuhan*, str. and perc. (1968); *Love 200*, rock band, 2 singers, orch. (1970); *Music for Japan* (1970); *Overture for a Happy Occasion* (1970); *Rain* (1970); *Love 200*, rock band and chamber orch. (1970); *Love 201*, rock band and chamber orch. (1971); *Lament for Strings* (1976); *Port Essington*, str. trio and str. orch. (1977).

CHAMBER MUSIC: Solo vn. sonata (1954); *The Loneliness of Bunjil*, str. trio (1954); *Irkanda I*, solo vn. (1955), II, str. qt. (1959), III, pf. trio (1961);

va. and perc. sonata (1960); *Red Landscape* (7th str. qt.) (1966); *Tabuh Tabuhan*, wind quintet and perc. (1968); Str. Qt. Mus. (8th str. qt.) (1969); *Dream* (1970); *How the Stars were made*, perc. ens. (1971); 9th str. qt. (1975); *Alone*, vn. (1976); *Little Serenade*, str. qt. (1977).

PIANO: Sonatina (1954); *3 Haiku* (1966); *Night Pieces* (1971); *Landscape*, pf. with tape echo and pre-recorded tape (1971); *Koto Music I and II*, amplified pf. and pre-recorded tape loop (1973–6).

VOCAL AND CHORAL: *Sun Music II*, vv. and perc. (1966); *Morning Song for the Christ Child*, unacc. ch. (1966); *Autumn Song*, unacc. ch. (1968); *Ketjak*, 6 male vv. with tape echo (1972); *The Song of Tailitnama*, v., 6 vc., and perc. (1974); *Eliza Fraser Sings*, sop., fl., pf. (1978).

STAGE: *Ulterior Motifs* (1956); *Sun Music*, ballet (1968); *Rites of Passage* (1972–3).

Scythian Suite (Ala and Lolly). Work for orch. in 4 movts. by Prokofiev, his Op. 20. Comp. 1914–15. F.p. Petrograd 1916 cond. Prokofiev, f.Eng.p. London 1920, cond. Coates.

Sdrucciolando (It.). Sliding, i.e. *glissando*.

Sea, The. Suite for orch. by Frank Bridge, comp. 1910–11 and pubd. by Carnegie Trust.

Sea Drift. Setting by Delius for bar., ch., and orch. of extract from Whitman's *Out of the cradle endlessly rocking*. Comp. 1903–4. F.p. Essen 1906, Sheffield 1908 (cond. Wood), London 1909 (cond. Beecham).

Sea Fever. Setting for v. and pf. by *Ireland, 1913, of poem by John Masefield beginning 'I must down to the seas again', but the song begins 'I must go down . . .'

Sea Interludes, Four. Concert work Op. 33a by Britten of the descriptive mus. in his opera *Peter Grimes* (1945). Comprises *Dawn* (Act I), *Sunday Morning* (Act II), *Moonlight* (Act III), and *Storm* (Act I); the *Passacaglia* (Act II) Op. 33b is often added. F.p. Cheltenham, 1945.

Seaman, Christopher (b Canterbury, 1942). Eng. cond. Studied King's Coll., Cambridge and GSM (conducting). Timpanist, Nat. Youth Orch., LPO 1964–7. Ass. cond. BBC Scottish S.O. 1968–70, prin. cond. 1971–7. Prin. cond. Northern Sinfonia 1973–9. Chief guest cond., Utrecht S.O. Cond., Gelders Orch., Arnhem, from 1980. Chief cond., Robert Mayer children's concerts.

Sea Pictures. Song-cycle, Op. 37, for cont. or mez. and orch. (or pf.) by Elgar to 5 poems by Noel, C. A. Elgar, E. B. Browning, Garnett, and Lindsay Gordon. F.p. Norwich 1899 (with Clara Butt); 4 of the songs were sung in London 2 days later by Butt with Elgar playing pf. acc.

Searle, Humphrey (b Oxford, 1915; d London, 1982). Eng. composer and writer on mus. Studied Oxford Univ. and RCM (comp. with R. O. Morris and Ireland), and in Vienna with Webern, 1937–8. Worked for BBC mus. dept. 1938–40 and 1946–8. Prof. of comp. RCM from 1965. C.B.E. 1968. Expert on mus. of Liszt, about which he wrote book (1954, rev. 1967). In own works used version of 12-note technique and showed predilection for unusual forms. Several settings of poems by Edith Sitwell. Works incl.:

OPERAS: *Diary of a Madman* (1958); *Photo of the Colonel* (1963–4); **Hamlet* (1964–8).

BALLETS: *Noctambules* (1956); *The Great Peacock* (1957–8); *Dualities* (1963).

ORCH: Symphonies: No. 1 (1953), No. 2 (1956–8), No. 3 (1958–60), No. 4 (1961–2), No. 5 (1964); Piano Concertos: No. 1 (1944), No. 2 (1955); Suites No. 1 for str. (1942), No. 2 (1943); *Night Music* (1943); *Poem* for 22 str. (1950); concertante, pf., str., perc. (1954); *Hamlet Suite* (1968); Sinfonietta (1968–9); *Zodiac Variations* (1970); *Labyrinth* (1971).

CHORUS AND ORCH: **Gold Coast Customs* (1947–9); *The River-run* (Joyce), speaker and orch. (1951); *The Shadow of Cain*, speakers, male ch., and orch. (1952); *Jerusalem*, speakers, ten., ch., orch. (1970); *Dr Faustus*, solo vv., ch., orch. (1977).

VOICE AND ORCH: *3 Songs of Jocelyn Brooke*, high v. and ens. (1954); *Oxus*, ten. and orch. (1967); *Contemplations*, mez. and orch. (1975); *Kubla Khan*, ten., orch. (1973).

UNACC. CHORUS: *The Canticle of the Rose* (1965).

CHAMBER MUSIC: Bn. quintet (1945); *Intermezzo* for 11 instr. (1946); qt. for cl., bn., vn., va. (1948); *The *Owl and the Pussy-Cat*, speaker, fl., vc., guitar (1951); vc. fantasia (1972); *Five*, guitar (1974); *Il Penseroso e L'Allegro*, vc., pf. (1975).

SONG-CYCLE: *Les fleurs du mal*, ten., hn., pf. (1972).

SONG: *Counting the Beats*, high v. and pf. (1963).

PIANO: Sonata (1951); *Suite* (1955); *Prelude on Theme by Rawsthorne* (1965).

Seasons, The (*Die Jahreszeiten*). (1) Secular oratorio by Joseph Haydn (Hob. XXI:3) to Ger. text by G. van Swieten based on Eng. poem (1726–30) by James Thomson (1700–48). F.p. Vienna 1801.
(2) 1-act ballet by Glazunov, Op. 67 (1899).
(3) Sub-title of Spohr's Sym. No. 9 (1849–50).

Sea Symphony, A. Sym. (his first) by Vaughan Williams for sop., bar., ch., and orch., to text taken from poems by Whitman. Comp. 1903–9. F.p. Leeds Fest. 1910, cond. composer.

Sebastiani, Johann (*b* nr. Weimar, 1622; *d* Königsberg, 1683). Ger. composer. Settled in Königsberg 1650, becoming cantor of cath. 1661. Court Kapellmeister of Brandenburg 1663–79. His major work was a *St Matthew Passion*, comp. *c.*1663, scored for soloists, 5-part ch., and 2 vns., 4 viols, and continuo, and the earliest setting known to incl. chorales. Also comp. *Funeral Songs* for 5 vv. and continuo (1663–80), and many occasional pieces.

Sec (Fr.). Dry. Direction for note to be played and released sharply; in perc. playing, indication that

the note should be damped, i.e. not allowed to ring on.

Secco (It.). Dry. See *Recitative*.

Sechter, Simon (*b* Friedberg, 1788; *d* Vienna, 1867). Ger.-Bohem. composer, organist, and teacher of theory. Studied Vienna with Koželuh. Court organist, Vienna 1824; prof., Vienna Cons. 1851–63. Taught Bruckner. Wrote comic opera, str. qts., org. pieces, etc. Schubert, just before his death, had one lesson from him.

Sechzehntel or Sechzehntelnote (Ger.). Sixteenth or sixteenth-note (semiquaver).

Second. (1) As noun: interval in melody or harmony, being 2 steps in major or minor scale. *Minor second* is a semitone, e.g. C up to D♭; *major second* is 2 semitones, e.g. C up to D; *augmented second* is 3 semitones, e.g. C up to D♯.
(2) As adjective: term denoting perf. of lower-pitched part, such as 2nd vn., 2nd tb.

Second Inversion. In lay-out of a chord, that in which the 5th becomes the bass.

Secondo (It.). Second. Lower of the 2 parts in pf. duet, higher being **primo*.

Second Viennese School. Somewhat imprecise generalization, usually understood to mean the group of composers who worked in Vienna between 1910 and 1930 under the moral leadership of Schoenberg (e.g. Berg, Webern, Skalkottas); their common ground being adoption of the 12-note method of comp.

Secret Marriage, The (Cimarosa). See *Matrimonio segreto, Il*.

Secret of Susanna, The (Wolf-Ferrari). See *Segreto di Susanna, Il*.

Secret, The (*Tajemství*). Opera in 3 acts by **Smetana to lib. by E. Krásnohorská. Prod. Prague 1878, Oxford 1956.

Sedlák. Same as **Furiant*.

Seefried, Irmgard (*b* Köngetried, Bavaria, 1919). Ger. sop. of Austrian parentage. Studied Augsburg and Munich. Début Aachen 1939 where she remained until 1943. Vienna Opera from 1943. Sang Composer in *Ariadne auf Naxos* in Vienna 1944 in honour of Strauss's 80th birthday. Début CG 1947, NY Met. 1953. Outstanding in Strauss and Mozart, one of most appealing artists of her time. Wife of violinist Wolfgang **Schneiderhan, Henze's *Ariosi* for sop., vn., and orch. (1963) being comp. for them. Last stage appearance, as Káťa Kabanová, Vienna 1976. Also noted for singing of Lieder, etc.

Seele (Ger.). Soul. (1) Feeling. *Seelenvoll*, soulful.
(2) The soundpost of a bowed instr.

Segal, Uri (*b* Jerusalem, 1944). Israeli conductor. Studied vn. and cond. Rubin Cons., Jerusalem, cond. at GSM 1966–9. Won 1969 Mitropoulos

Comp., NY. Cond. début Copenhagen 1969. Brit. début 1970 (BBC Welsh S.O.). Amer. début with Chicago S.O. at Ravinia Park Fest. 1972. Opera début Santa Fe 1973 (*Der fliegende Holländer*). Prin. cond. Bournemouth S.O. 1980–2.

Segerstam, Leif (*b* Vasa, Finland, 1944). Finn. cond. and composer. Studied Sibelius Acad. 1952–63 (comp. with Englund and Kokkonen) and Juilliard Sch. 1963–5, (comp. with Overton and Persichetti). Cond. Finnish Nat. Opera 1965–8 (dir. 1973–4), Stockholm Royal Opera 1968–72, Deutsche Oper, Berlin, 1971–3, and guest cond. of many Amer. and European orchs. Works incl. vn. conc., 12 str. qts., *Pandora* (essay for orch. and 9 dancers), songs, etc.

Segno (It.). The 'sign' (see *Dal segno, Al segno*).

Segovia, Andrés (*b* Linares, 1893; *d* Madrid, 1987). Sp. guitarist and composer. Studied Granada Mus. Institute, specializing in guitar. Début in Granada 1909. More than any other man responsible for revival of interest in guitar as 'classical' instr. Works specially comp. for him by Castelnuovo-Tedesco, Ponce, etc. Transcr. works by Bach and others for guitar. Continued world tours well into his 80s. Wrote pieces for guitar.

Segreto di Susanna, Il (Susanna's Secret). Opera in 1 act by *Wolf-Ferrari to lib. by Golisciani. Prod. (as *Susannas Geheimnis*) Munich 1909, NY and CG 1911. The secret is that Susanna smokes: what her jealous husband smells is not a lover's cigarette smoke.

Segue (It.). Follows. Direction that next section is to follow without a break.

Seguidilla. Andalusian dance, found as early as 16th cent., in simple triple time, similar to the bolero but quicker. The participants interpolate vocal passages called *coplas*, which are in short lines of alternately 5 and 7 syllables, with assonance (agreement of vowels) rather than rhyme. Castanets, and usually guitar, are used for acc. Many regional variants.

Seguidillas Gitanas. See *Playera*.

Sehnsucht (Ger.). Longing, yearning (noun). Adjectives are *sehnsuchtsvoll, sehnsüchtig*. Several Lieder, e.g. by Schubert and Strauss, bear the title *Sehnsucht*.

Seiber, Mátyás (György) (*b* Budapest, 1905; *d* Kruger Nat. Park, S. Africa, in car crash, 1960). Hung.-born composer and cellist. Studied Budapest Acad. 1919–24 (vc. with Shiffer, comp. with Kodály). Settled in Ger. where he played in th. orchs. and taught jazz at Frankfurt. Went to Eng. 1935, working for publisher. Taught at Morley Coll. from 1942. Co-founder of Committee (now Soc.) for Promotion of New Mus., 1942. Founder and cond., Dorian Singers, 1945. Great influence as teacher. Eclectic in style, his mus. is distinguished by fastidious craftsmanship and imagi-

nation. Works incl. cantata *Ulysses* (1946–7), *3 Fragments from Joyce's Portrait of the Artist as a Young Man* for ch. (1956–7), *Missa brevis* (1924), *Fantasia Concertante*, vn. and str. (1943–4), cl. concertino (1954), *Elegy,* va. and str. (1953), *Tre Pezzi*, vc. and orch. (1956), *4 Greek Folk-Songs,* sop. and str. (1942), 3 str. qts. (1924, 1934–5, 1948–51), *Permutazione a cinque*, wind quintet (1958), vn. sonata (1960), pf. pieces, and film mus. (notably for Orwell's *Animal Farm*).

Seidl, Anton (*b* Budapest, 1850; *d* NY, 1898). Hung. cond. Studied Leipzig Cons. In 1872 went to Bayreuth where he made first copy of score of *Der Ring des Nibelungen* for Wagner and, in 1876, assisted at first fest. Cond., Leipzig Opera 1879–82. Toured Ger., Holland, Eng., and It. 1882 as cond. of Neumann's Wagner co. Cond. first *Ring* cycle in London, 1882 (Her Majesty's Th.). Cond. Bremen Opera 1883–5. Cond. of Ger. opera at NY Met. from 1885, cond. f. Amer. ps. of *Meistersinger* (1886), *Tristan* (1886), and complete *Ring* (1889). Cond. NY P.O. 1891–8. Cond. f.p. of Dvořák's *New World* Sym., 1893. CG début 1897.

Seinemeyer, Meta (*b* Berlin, 1895; *d* Dresden, 1929). Ger. sop. whose early death was tragic loss. Studied Berlin. Opera début Berlin 1918. Sang at Berlin Opera 1918–25. NY début 1923. Dresden 1925–9. CG début 1929 (as Sieglinde, Elsa, and Eva). Notable Verdi singer.

Seite (Ger.). Side, e.g. page of book, end of drum, and side of gramophone record.

Seixas, (José) **Carlos de** (*b* Coimbra, 1704; *d* Lisbon, 1742). Portuguese composer, organist, and harpsichordist. Organist at Coimbra and, after 1720, at Royal Chapel, Lisbon. Wrote hpd. sonatas and conc., org. pieces, orch. works, and church mus.

Sekles, Bernhard (*b* Frankfurt, 1872; *d* Frankfurt, 1934). Ger. composer, cond., and teacher. Studied Hoch Cons., Frankfurt. Cond. at Heidelberg 1893–4 and Mainz 1894–5. Taught at Hoch Cons., Frankfurt, from 1896 (co-dir. from 1916, dir. 1923–33). Works incl. operas, sym., symphonic poem, chamber mus., songs, etc.

Selle, Thomas (*b* Zörbig, nr. Bitterfeld, 1599; *d* Hamburg, 1663). Ger. composer. Studied at Leipzig Univ. Kantor in various NW Ger. towns from 1624 to 1641 when he became civic dir. of church mus. in Hamburg. Wrote much vocal mus., incl. *St John Passion* (1641, enlarged 1643), the first Passion to incl. instr. interludes, and *St Matthew Passion* (1636). His own catalogue of his works listed 282 comps.

Sellick, Phyllis (Doreen) (*b* Newbury Park, Essex, 1911). Eng. pianist. Studied RAM 1925–7. Début Harrogate 1933 (Grieg conc.). Duettist with husband, Cyril *Smith. O.B.E. 1971.

Sellinger's Round, Variations on an Elizabethan Theme. Composite work for str. orch.

comprising 6 variations on Elizabethan tune 'Sellinger's Round' comp. to celebrate Coronation of Elizabeth II 1953 and f.p. at Aldeburgh Fest. that year, cond. Britten. Composers were Oldham, Tippett, L. Berkeley, Britten, Searle, and Walton. Tippett expanded his contribution into his *Divertimento* (1953–4), the tune appearing in all 5 movements.

Sembrich, Marcella (orig. Prakseda Marcelina Kochánská) (*b* Wiśniewczyk, 1858; *d* NY, 1935). Polish sop. Child pianist and violinist. Liszt urged her to study singing. Studied Vienna 1875–6 and Milan (with Lamperti). Début Athens 1877 in *I Puritani*. Dresden Opera 1878–80. London début (CG) 1880 as Lucia di Lammermoor, returning each season to 1884 and in 1895. NY Met. début 1883. Member of Met. co. 1898–1909. Sang in concerts to 1917. V. of beauty and brilliance, controlled by superb technique. Taught at Curtis Institute and Juilliard Sch. from 1924. Became Amer. cit.

Semele. Secular oratorio by Handel to text adapted from Congreve's lib. for Eccles's opera *Semele* about Semele's love for Jupiter. F.p. London 1743. Contains arias *Sleep, why dost thou leave me?* and *Where'er you walk*. Revived CG 1982.

Semibiscroma (It.). 64th note or hemidemisemiquaver.

Semibreve (o). The Whole-Note, half the time-value of the *breve and double the value of the half-note or minim.

Semichorus. Half-chorus. In some choral works, e.g. Elgar's *Dream of Gerontius* and Vaughan Williams's *Sea Symphony*, special antiphonal effect is created by contrasting small group of singers (semich.) with full body, or the semich. alone is used for certain passages.

Semicroma (It.). 16th note or semiquaver.

Semidemisemiquaver ( ) or **Hemidemisemiquaver.** The 64th note, i.e. $\frac{1}{64}$ the time-value of the whole-note or semibreve.

Semiminima (It.). The quarter-note or crotchet.

Semi-opera. Term denoting type of Eng. Restoration drama in which there were extensive mus. episodes, similar to *masques, perf. only by subsidiary characters. Form was developed by Betterton with *The Tempest*, 1674, an adaptation of Shakespeare's play with mus. by Humfrey, Locke, and others. Another example was *King Arthur*, text by Dryden (1684) and mus. by Purcell (1691). Purcell was also involved in *Dioclesian* (1690), *The Fairy Queen* (1692, rev. 1693), and *The Indian Queen* (1695). Only *King Arthur* was specifically devised as a semi-opera, the others being Betterton versions of earlier plays. Daniel Purcell, John Eccles, and D'Urfey also wrote semi-operas, but early in the 18th cent. the form was superseded by It. opera.

Semi-Perfect Cadence. Perfect cadence with 3rd or 5th of tonic in highest part.

Semiquaver ( ). The 16th-note, i.e. $\frac{1}{16}$ the time-value of the whole-note or semibreve.

Semiramide. Opera in 2 acts by Rossini to lib. by Rossi after Voltaire's *Sémiramis* (1748). Prod. Venice 1823, London 1824, New Orleans 1837. Also subject of about 40 other operas, incl. those by Porpora, Vivaldi, Hasse, Gluck, Galuppi, Paisiello, Salieri, Meyerbeer, and Respighi. With exception of Respighi's, all were settings of text by *Metastasio.

Semitone. Half a tone. Smallest interval in European mus. On pf., interval between any note and the next, up or down. There are three types of semitone: *diatonic* (same as a minor 2nd); *chromatic* (difference between major 2nd and minor 2nd); and *enharmonic* (doubly diminished 3rd). Diatonic semitone has ratio of 16/15, and two chromatic semitone intervals are recognized ('lesser semitone' of 25/24 and 'greater semitone' of 135/128). These intervals occur between values of chromatic-scale notes conventionally accepted as 'just' or 'perfect'.

Semkow, Jerzy (*b* Radomsko, Poland, 1928). Polish cond. Studied Kraków and Leningrad Cons. (1951–3). Ass. cond. Leningrad P.O. 1954–6; cond. Bolshoy Opera and Ballet, 1956–8; prin. cond. Warsaw Opera 1959–62; cond. Royal Opera, Copenhagen, 1966–76. London début 1968 (LPO), CG 1970 (*Don Giovanni*). Amer. début Cleveland 1970–1. Mus. dir. St. Louis S.O. 1976–9. Art. dir. RAI Rome from 1979.

Semplice; semplicità (It.). Simple, simplicity. *semplicemente*, simply; *semplicissimo*, extremely simple.

Sempre (It.). Always; e.g. *sempre legato*, the whole passage or comp. to be played smoothly.

Senaillé, Jean-Baptiste (*b* Paris, *c*.1688; *d* Paris, 1730). Fr. violinist and composer. Pupil in It. of T. A. *Vitali. From 1720 member of Louis XV's court orch. Introduced It. methods to Fr. sch. of vn.-playing. Comp. numerous vn. sonatas, incl. 50 for solo vn.

Senesino (orig. Francesco Bernardi) (*b* Siena, *c*.1680; *d* Siena, by 1759). It. male mez. Pupil of Bernacchi in Bologna. Sang in Dresden, 1717–20. Handel heard him and engaged him for London, where he sang with Handel's co. 1720–8 (singing in 32 operas, 13 by Handel) and 1730–3 when he joined Porpora's rival co. until 1736. Returned to Italy after having made fortune. Created leading roles in 17 Handel operas. Voice was considered more beautiful even than Farinelli's.

Senfl, Ludwig (*b* Zürich or Basle, *c*.1486; *d* Munich, *c*.1543). Swiss-born composer. Studied under Isaac, following him as cond. of the Imperial chapel, Vienna. Court cond., Munich,

1530–40. Leading Ger. composer of his day, composing Lieder, motets, masses, and other works remarkable for expressive qualities.

Sensibile; sensibilità (It.). Sensitive; sensitivity (the *nota sensibile* is the *leading note).

Senza (It.). Without, hence *senza sordino*, or *senza sordini*, without mute(s), of str. instr. In pf.-playing, *senza sordini* means without dampers, i.e. use the right pedal, which throws the dampers out of action and leaves the strs. to vibrate freely.

Séparé (Fr.). Separated. In Fr. org. mus., uncoupled.

Septet (Fr. *septette, septuor*; It. *settimino, septetto*; Ger. *Septett*). Any combination of 7 performers (usually instr.), or any piece of mus. for such, e.g. Beethoven's *Septet* in E, Op. 20, for vn., va., hn., cl., bn., vc., and db.

Septième (Fr.). Seventh. Org. stop, same as *Flat Twenty-first*.

Septimole, Septolet. See *Septuplet*.

Septuor. See *Septet*.

Septuplet. Group of 7 notes of equal time-values written where a group of 4 or 6 notes is suggested by time-signature. See *Irregular rhythmic groupings*.

Sequence. (1) In mus. construction, the more or less exact repetition of a passage at a higher or lower level of pitch. If the repetition is of only the melody it is called a MELODIC SEQUENCE; if it is of a series of chords it is a HARMONIC SEQUENCE. If the intervals between the notes of the melody are to some extent altered (a major interval becoming a minor one and so forth, as is practically inevitable if the key is unchanged) it is called a TONAL SEQUENCE; if there is no variation in the intervals (usually achieved by altering not merely the pitch of the notes but also the key) it is called a REAL SEQUENCE. If there are several repetitions, some of them Tonal and some Real, the result is a MIXED SEQUENCE. A Harmonic Real Sequence is sometimes called *Rosalia* (some authorities, however, require as an additional qualification for this description a rise of one degree of the scale at each repetition).

(2) In ecclesiastical use the term Sequence is applied to a type of hymn which began as one of the many forms of interpolation in the original liturgy of the Western Christian Church. As the traditional plainsong did not provide for such interpolations, special melodies were composed. In the Church's service Sequences follow (whence the name) the Gradual and Alleluia. The earliest Sequences were in prose, not, as later, in rhymed verse, and the term 'Prose' is still sometimes used instead of 'Sequence'. The following are examples of the Sequence: *Dies Irae* (now a part of the Requiem), *Veni Sancte Spiritus*, *Lauda Sion*, and *Stabat Mater dolorosa*.

(3) The It. composer *Berio uses the title *Sequence* (*Sequenza*) for a series of works for solo instr. and v.

Sequencer. Elec. device enabling a succession of several sounds (together with modifications in each) to be pre-set.

Sequenza (Sequence). Title given by *Berio to series of short aleatory virtuoso works for solo instr. e.g. harp, vn., tb., pf., ob., fl., va., perc., and female v. Nos. II, VI, and VII were later arr. with orch. and called *Chemins I, II*, and *IV* respectively.

Serafin, Tullio (*b* Rottanova di Cavarzere, Venice, 1878; *d* Rome, 1968). It. cond. Studied Milan Cons. Played vn. in orch. of La Scala, Milan. Début as cond. Ferrara 1898. Turin 1903, Rome 1906, then cond. at Scala 1909–14 and at subsequent intervals to 1946–7. CG 1907, 1931, 1959, 1960. NY Met. 1924–34, cond. f. Amer. ps. of *Turandot* and *Simon Boccanegra*. Chief cond. and art. dir., Rome Opera, 1934–43 and from 1962. Chicago Opera 1956–8. Cond f.ps. in Italy of Strauss's *Der Rosenkavalier*, Berg's *Wozzeck*, and Britten's *Peter Grimes*. Encourager of *Callas in early years.

Seraglio, The (Mozart). See *Entführung aus dem Serail, Die*.

Serebrier, José (*b* Montevideo, 1938). Uruguayan composer, cond., and teacher. Studied at Curtis Institute, Minnesota Univ. (cond. with Dorati), Tanglewood (with Copland), and Maine. Mus. dir., Amer. Shakespeare Fest. 1962–4. Taught at Eastern Michigan Univ. 1966–8. Cond., Amer. S.O. 1962–6. Composer-in-residence with Cleveland Orch. 1968–70. Works incl. sonatas for solo vn. and solo va., sym. for perc., sax. qt., sym., *Partita* for orch., *Variations on a Theme from Childhood* for tb. and str. qt. or orch., *Erotica*, for sop., tpt., woodwind quintet, *Nueve* for db. and orch., etc.

Serenade (Fr.). Evening music. Properly, open-air evening mus. (opposite of *aubade*) such as song by lover outside beloved's window (as by Don Giovanni in Mozart's opera), but a term extended to other meanings. The instr. serenade was developed towards the end of 18th cent. as type of work similar to cassation and divertimento, particularly by Mozart (e.g. his *Eine kleine Nachtmusik*). It was scored for small ens. and sometimes for wind instr. alone, and written in several movements (midway between sym. and suite). Beethovens's serenades were chamber works. Other fine examples are those by Brahms, Dvořák, Tchaikovsky, Elgar, and Strauss. In Ger., *Nachtmusik* implies the instr. form and *Ständchen* the vocal.

Serenade for Tenor, Horn, and Strings. Song-cycle by Britten, Op. 31, being prol. and epilogue (for unacc. hn.) enclosing 6 settings of poems on theme of evening by Cotton, Tennyson, Blake,

Anon. (Lyke-Wake Dirge), Jonson, and Keats. F.p. London 1943 (Pears, D. Brain, cond. W. Goehr).

Serenade to Music. Setting by Vaughan Williams for 16 solo vv. (4 sop., 4 cont., 4 ten., 4 bass) and orch. of passage from Shakespeare's *The Merchant of Venice*, comp. for Sir Henry Wood's golden jubilee as a cond., London, Oct. 1938. Orig. singers were Stiles Allen, Isobel Baillie, Elsie Suddaby, Eva Turner, Margaret Balfour, Muriel Brunskill, Astra Desmond, Mary Jarred, Parry Jones, Heddle Nash, Frank Titterton, Walter Widdop, Norman Allin, Robert Easton, Roy Henderson, and Harold Williams. Also arr. for 4 soloists and orch., for ch. and orch., or for orch. (1940).

Serenata (It.). Serenade. (1) Instr. serenade, as Mozart's *Serenata Notturna* (1776, K239).

(2) 18th-cent. term for dramatic cantatas which might also be called 'semi-operas', such as Handel's *Acis and Galatea*. In 16th cent. meant a satirical polyphonic comp. of the *villanelle* type. Term first appeared in print in 1560 as the title of one of Alessandro Stiggio's 6-part madrigals.

Serenata Notturna (Nocturnal Serenade). Title of Mozart's Serenade No. 6 in D (K239) for 2 small orchs., comp. 1776.

Seria (It.). Serious; e.g. *opera seria*, serious (or tragic) opera—as distinct from *opera buffa*, comic opera.)

Serialism, Serial Technique, Serial Music. Terms applied to the 20th-cent. revolution in comp. whereby traditional melodic, harmonic, rhythmic, and tonal rules and conventions were replaced. Serial mus. is that in which a structural 'series' of notes governs the total development of the comp. It originated in *Schoenberg's atonality, leading to his system of composing with 12 notes (1923). This system is based on use of a series of intervals (note-row) involving in turn all 12 notes of the chromatic scale in any order selected by the composer. In its strictest application, no note should be repeated until the other 11 have appeared and the order of the *series* remains unaltered throughout the work, with certain permitted modifications. Schoenberg later broke his own rules and other modifications were introduced by *Berg and *Webern. While the *series* in Schoenberg's hands remained comparable with a theme, in Webern's it was more subtly pervasive and often not perceptible as a given sequence of 12 notes. The next stage in *serialism* was foreshadowed in 1944 by *Messiaen in his *Technique de mon langage musical*, in which he wrote about serialization of durations. By the 1950s several components (parameters) of a work were being serialized by, for example, Babbitt, Boulez, and Stockhausen. With the introduction of elec. media, the scope for serial permutations became much enlarged, in relation to time. By the end of the 1960s, many composers renounced

serialism as too restrictive; others, incl. Boulez, questioned its continued necessity because *aleatory developments and new sounds available through elec. means achieve by synthesis the ends of serialism. Whatever the future of serialism, it remains a development which radically altered the tenets of mus. comp.

Serinette (from Fr. *serin*, canary). Small hand org. reproducing 10–13 high-pitched notes and formerly used to teach canaries to sing.

Serkin, Peter (*b* NY, 1947). Amer. pianist, son of Rudolf *Serkin. Studied with his father at Curtis Institute, 1958–64. Début 1959, playing in NY same year. Subsequent career as conc. soloist and chamber mus. performer.

Serkin, Rudolf (*b* Eger, Bohemia, 1903). Austrian-born pianist. Studied in Vienna (pf. with R. Robert, comp with Marx and Schoenberg). Début Vienna 1915. Played in chamber mus. and sonata recitals with the violinist Adolf *Busch, whose son-in-law he became. Amer. début with Busch 1933. Settled in USA, joining teaching staff at Curtis Institute 1939, becoming dir. 1968–76. One of greatest pianists of his time, especially but not exclusively in classics. Art. dir. of Marlboro music festivals in Vermont.

Sérly, Tibór (*b* Losonc, 1900; *d* London, 1978). Hung.-born composer, cond., and str. player. Taken to USA in 1905. Studied Budapest Cons. 1922–4 (vn. with Hubay and comp. with Bartók and Kodály). Played va. in Cincinnati S.O. and NBC S.O. 1927–37. Settled in NY as teacher, 1937. Comp. va. conc., 2 syms., chamber mus., etc. Completed last few bars of Bartók's 3rd pf. conc. and completed Bartók's va. conc. from composer's sketches, 1945.

Sermisy, Claude de (Claudin) (*b c*.1490; *d* Paris, 1562). Fr. composer and priest. Singer at Fr. Chapel Royal from 1508, and attended Field of the Cloth of Gold 1520. Wrote over 200 *chansons*, many Masses, motets, etc.

Serocki, Kazimierz (*b* Torun, Poland, 1922; *d* Warsaw, 1981). Polish composer and pianist. Studied Lódź 1947–51, and in Paris with Boulanger 1947–8. In 1949, with Baird and Krenz, formed 'Group 49'. Concert pianist until 1952. Co-founder, Warsaw fest. of modern mus., 1956. Began in neo-classicist, folk-influenced style of comp., wrote Webern-type serial mus. in 1950s, developing use of aleatory procedures. Works incl. syms. (No. 2 with sop., bar., ch., and orch.), tb. conc., *Segmenti* for 19 instr., *Symphonic Frescoes: Forte e piano*, 2 pf. and orch., *Niobe*, 2 narrators, ch., and orch.

Serov, Alexander (Nikolayevich) (*b* St Petersburg, 1820; *d* St Petersburg, 1871). Russ. composer and critic. Studied law and became civil servant, but also studied mus. In 1851 began career as mus. critic, becoming keen Wagnerian in 1858 and antipathetic to new Russ. Sch. Wrote 6 operas, orch. works, and religious pieces.

Serpent. Obsolete bass member of *cornett family, 8′ long and roughly S-shaped, hence the name. Made of wood, sometimes of metal; had 6 fingerholes and sometimes keys. First introduced in Fr. towards end of 16th cent., where it was used in church to double male vv. Became popular military-band instr. and was in use in Eng. church bands to mid-19th cent. (mentioned by Thomas Hardy).

Serpette, (Henri Charles Antoine) **Gaston** (*b* Nantes, 1846; *d* Paris, 1904). Fr. composer. Pupil at Paris Cons. of Thomas (*Prix de Rome* 1871). Wrote 17 operettas, incl. *La Petite Muette* (1877).

Serré (Fr.). Tightened. With increasing tension and speed, as in It. *stringendo*.

Serse (*Xerxes*). Opera in 3 acts by Handel to text from a lib. by Minato written for Cavalli in 1654 and rev. for Bononcini 1694. Prod. London 1738, Northampton, Mass., 1928. Contains in Act I aria *Ombra mai fù* for Serse, male sop., praising a tree that gives him shade. It is marked *larghetto*, but the tune, in countless spurious arrs., has become known as 'Handel's *Largo*'.

Serva padrona, La (The maid as mistress). Intermezzo (to *Il prigioner superbo*) in 2 parts by Pergolesi to lib. by Federico; prod. Naples 1733, London 1750, Baltimore 1790.

Service. In mus. sense, elaborate and continuous setting of the canticles from the Anglican prayer-book for morning and evening services, or Communion service. The terms *Short Service* and *Great Service* were used in 16th and early 17th cents. to distinguish between normal daily service and that for an elaborate special occasion. Tye, Tallis, Byrd, Gibbons, Tomkins, Weelkes, etc. all comp. fine services. Later examples are by Walmisley, S.S. Wesley, Stanford, Vaughan Williams, Howells, etc.

Sesquialtera (Lat.). One and a half. (1) Org. mixture stop properly of 2 ranks (12th and 17th) but sometimes of 3–5 ranks.
(2) Relationship of 3 : 2 in mensural mus.

Sessions, Roger (Huntington) (*b* Brooklyn, NY, 1896; *d* Princeton, NJ, 1985). Amer. composer and teacher. Wrote opera at age of 13. Harvard Univ. 1910–15, Yale Univ. 1915–17 (comp. with H. *Parker). Mus. faculty Smith Coll., Northampton, Mass., 1917–21, studying privately with Bloch. Became ass. to Bloch at Cleveland Institute of Mus., 1921–5. Lived in Florence, Rome, Berlin 1927–33. His first sym. (1927) perf. Boston 1927 and at ISCM Fest., Geneva, 1929. Taught Boston Univ. 1933–5, Princeton Univ. 1935–45; prof. of mus., Univ. of Calif., Berkeley, 1945–51; prof. of mus., Princeton, 1953–65. Taught at Juilliard Sch. from 1965. Pupils incl. Babbitt, Imbrie, and Diamond. Sessions's mus. has been described as

'constructively eclectic', drawing on the chief 20th-cent. influences but retaining a serious individual stamp. Author of several books, and tireless champion of contemporary mus. Prin. works:

OPERAS: *The Trial of Lucullus* (1947); *Montezuma* (1941–63).
ORCH: Symphonies: No. 1 (1927), No. 2 (1944–6), No. 3 (1957), No. 4 (1958), No. 5 (1964), No. 6 (1966), No. 7 (1967), No. 8 (1968); vn. conc. (1935, with orch. without vns. and with 5 cl.); *Idyll of Theocritus*, sop. and orch. (1954); pf. conc. (1956); *Divertimento* (1959); *Rhapsody* (1970); Conc. for vn., vc., and orch. (1971); *Concertino* (1972).
CHAMBER MUSIC: String Quartets No. 1 (1936), No. 2 (1951); solo vn. sonata (1953); str. quintet (1958); *6 Pieces* for vc. (1966); *Canons*, str. qt. (1971).
CHORAL: *Turn, O Liberated*, ch. and 2 pf. or orch. (1944); Mass (1955); *When Lilacs Last in the Dooryard Bloom'd*, soloists, ch., and orch. (1970).
PIANO: 3 sonatas (1930, 1946, 1965); *From my Diary* (1939); *5 Pieces* (1975).

Set. Term normally applied to *atonal mus., meaning a small group of notes (a cell or a unit) which the composer or the analyst of the work concerned deems to be of structural significance, e.g. the notes B-C-F in the 4th of Webern's *5 Movements* for str. qt. In a serial work the series or part of it may be considered as the set. And so can the opening notes of Beethoven's 5th Sym.!

Seter, Mordecai (*b* Novorossiysk, Russ., 1916). Russ.-born Israeli composer. Studied at École Normale, Paris (comp. with Dukas and Boulanger). Teacher at Israeli Acad. of Mus. since 1952. Mus. influenced by Jewish liturgical chants and serialism. Works incl. *Sabbath Cantata* (1940–7); *Ricercar*, str. (1953–6); *Variations* for orch. (1959); *Midnight Vigil*, oratorio (1962); *The Daughter of Jephthah*, orch. (1965); *Jerusalem*, sym. for ch. and orch. (1966, rev. 1967–8); and 4 str. qts. (1975–7).

Ševčík, Otakar (*b* Horazdowitz, Bohemia, 1852; *d* Pisek, 1934). Cz. violinist and teacher. Studied Prague Cons. 1866–70; début Vienna 1873. Settled in Russia. Taught Imperial Russ. Mus. Sch., Kiev, 1875–92. Taught at Prague Cons. 1892–1906. Dir., vn. master-sch., Vienna Acad. of Mus. 1909–19. Returned to Prague 1919. Among his pupils were Kubelik and Marie Hall. Developed special intonation and bowing techniques, set out in detail in his pubd. method.

Seven Deadly Sins, The (*Die sieben Todsünden der Kleinbürger*). Ballet with songs, for sop., male ch., and orch., in prol., 7 scenes, and epilogue by *Weill to lib. by Brecht, choreog. Balanchine. Prod. Paris 1933. New Balanchine choreog. NY 1958.

Seven Last Words of our Saviour from the Cross, The (*Die sieben letzten Worte unseres Erlösers am Kreuz*). Work by Haydn commissioned by Cadiz Cath. 1785 as orch. interludes to separate the sermons on Good Friday. Pubd. in Vienna as *7 sonate, con un' introduzione, ed al fine un terremoto* (7 sonatas, with an introduction, and at the end an earthquake). In 1787 arr. by Haydn for str. qt. as Op. 51, Nos. 1–7 (qts. Nos. 50-6), and also arr. by him as cantata with soloists and ch. (*c.*1796).

Seven Sonnets of Michelangelo. Song-cycle, Op. 22, for ten. and pf. by Britten, comp. 1939–40, f.p. 1942. It. settings of sonnets 16, 31, 30, 55, 38, 32, and 24.

Seventeenth. Org. *mutation stop; length and pitch 1⅗', sounding 2 octaves and a 3rd (i.e. 17th) above normal.

Seventh. Interval in melody or harmony when 2 notes, major or minor, are 7 steps apart (counting bottom and top notes). A up to G♯ is *major seventh*; A up to G♮ is *minor seventh*; A up to G♭ is *diminished seventh*.

Séverac, (Joseph Marie) **Déodat de** (*b* St Félix de Caraman, 1872; *d* Céret, 1921). Fr. composer. Studied at Toulouse Cons. and at Schola Cantorum, Paris, under Magnard and d'Indy 1896–1907. Mus. (esp. his songs) evoke atmosphere of his native Provence. Wrote 3 operas, 4 symphonic poems, chamber works, pf. pieces, and songs.

Severn Suite. 5-movement suite for brass band, Op. 87, by Elgar, comp. 1930 (using sketches from as far back as 1879) for Crystal Palace competitive band fest. (Brass band orch. from Elgar's piano score by H. Geehl. Rev. edn. (restoring orig. key of C major) by G. Brand, 1983.) Ded. to Bernard Shaw. Arr. for orch. by composer 1932. Arr. for org. as sonata No. 2, Op. 87a, by I. *Atkins, 1933 (this omits a movt. and contains mus. comp. by Atkins).

Sevillana. (1) Seville variety of the Sp. *seguidilla* folk-dance.
(2) Orch. work, Op. 7, by Elgar, f.p. Worcester 1884, London 1884 (first Elgar work perf. in London).

Sextet (Fr. *sextette* or *sextuor*; It. *sestetto*; Ger. *sextett*). Performing group of 6 instrumentalists or singers, or work written for them to perform, e.g. Brahms's str. sextets. Schoenberg's *Verklärte Nacht* (1899) was orig. a str. sextet. Janáček's *Mládí* (1924) is a wind sextet. Strauss's opera *Capriccio* (1940–1) opens with a str. sextet. The most famous operatic sextet is in Donizetti's *Lucia di Lammermoor*.

Sextolet. See *Sextuplet*.

Sextuor. See *Sextet*.

Sextuplet. Group of 6 notes of equal time-values written where a group of 4 notes is suggested by time-signature. See *Irregular rhythmic groupings*.

Seyfried, Ignaz Xaver, Ritter von (*b* Vienna, 1776; *d* Vienna, 1841). Austrian composer. Pupil of Mozart and Koželuh for pf. and of Haydn for comp. Close friend of Mozart. Cond at *Schikaneder's ths. 1797–1826. Wrote over 100 stage works, biblical dramas, church mus., and chamber works. Arr. Mozart pf. pieces as *Ahasuerus* (1823) and Haydn themes as Singspiel *Das Ochsenmenuette* (1823). Cond. 1806 revival of Beethoven's *Fidelio* in Vienna.

sf, sfz. Abbreviation for *sforzando, sforzato*.

Sfogato (It.). Airy, evaporated. Light and easy in style. *Soprano sfogato* is a light sop. Term used by Chopin indicating need for delicate touch in his mus.

Sforzando, Sforzato (It.). Reinforced. Direction that a note or chord be strongly accented or played in a 'forced' manner. Usually found in abbreviation *sf.* or *sfz*. Beethoven made much use of it.

sfp. *Sforzando* followed immediately by *piano*.

Sgambati, Giovanni (*b* Rome, 1841; *d* Rome, 1914). It. composer, cond., and pianist. Had Eng. mother. Pf. pupil of Barbieri and of Liszt (in Rome). Settled in Rome 1860. Founded orch. and chamber concerts in Rome 1866, introducing Ger. classics to It. audiences. Toured Ger., Eng., It., Fr., and Russia as pianist and cond. Founder Liceo Musicale, Rome, and pf. prof. Wagner persuaded Schott to publish Sgambati's 2 pf. quintets. Rich melodic gift and one of few It. composers of 19th cent. interested in instr. mus. Wrote 2 syms., *Requiem Mass*, pf. conc., str. qt., pf. pieces, and songs.

Shacklock, Constance (*b* Sherwood, Notts., 1913). Eng. mez. Studied in Nottingham and at RAM. Professional début 1944. Member CG co. 1946–56, singing Amneris, Brangäne, Oktavian, and Carmen. Also sang in oratorio, notably as Angel in Elgar's *Gerontius* with Barbirolli. Sang opera in Berlin with Kleiber. Prof of singing, RAM, from 1968. O.B.E. 1970.

Shaffer, Elaine (*b* Altoona, Penn., 1925; *d* London, 1973). Amer. flautist. Studied Curtis Institute. Prin. flautist, Houston S.O., and soloist with leading orchs. Married cond. Efrem *Kurtz.

Shafir, Shulamith (*b* Odessa, 1923). Russ.-born pianist. Studied Palestine, It. with *Schnabel, and in London with Solomon. Début 1934. Settled in Eng. 1935 and pursued successful career as conc. soloist and recitalist.

Shake. Early Eng. name for *Trill.

Shakers (Shaking Quakers). Name for members of the United Society of Believers in Christ's Second Appearing, a religious celibate community founded in the USA after 1774 by Ann Lee (1736–84), formerly of Manchester in Eng. They developed their own hymnology, incl. spirituals and dance, and in the 1840s two tunebooks were pubd. giving details of Shaker mus. theory, notation, and tunes. When a Shaker had a religious seizure which resulted in a hymn or dance-tune, a scribe wrote down the tune in a primitive letteral notation. The words of the songs were sometimes in Eng., at others were nonsense, or derived from Indian or Negro speech. *Copland quotes the Shaker tune *Simple Gifts* in his *Appalachian Spring*. Shakers are now almost extinct, but their mus. has been collected and is studied.

Shakespeare and Music. The influence of William Shakespeare (*b* Stratford-upon-Avon, 1564; *d* Stratford, 1616) upon composers, from his own time until today, is of such magnitude that a short entry is essential. *Morley comp. songs for the f.ps. of some of the plays. Since then nearly every composer of note has set a Shakespeare song—among the greatest being Schubert's *Who is Sylvia?* Incidental mus. to the plays ranges from Mendelssohn's and Orff's for *A Midsummer Night's Dream* to Walton's for *Macbeth*. Walton and Shostakovich are among those who have written mus. for Shakespeare films. In categories of their own are Berlioz's dramatic sym. and Tchaikovsky's fantasy-ov. *Romeo and Juliet*, Elgar's symphonic study *Falstaff*, and Vaughan Williams's *Serenade to Music* (a setting of words from *The Merchant of Venice*). Operas based on Shakespeare are many. Chief among them are Verdi's *Falstaff*, *Otello*, and *Macbeth*; Britten's *A Midsummer Night's Dream*; Berlioz's *Béatrice et Bénédict* (*Much Ado About Nothing*); Vaughan Williams's *Sir John in Love* (*Merry Wives of Windsor*); and Wagner's *Das Liebesverbot* (*Measure for Measure*). Purcell's *The Fairy Queen* is a masque based on *A Midsummer Night's Dream* although no word of Shakespeare's text is set. Bellini's *I Capuleti e i Montecchi* is based on *Romeo and Juliet* but not on Shakespeare's version. Walton's *Troilus and Cressida* is also *not* based on Shakespeare's play.

Shakespeare, William (*b* Croydon, 1849; *d* London, 1931). Eng. ten., pianist, composer, and teacher. Church organist at 13. Studied with *Molique, then at RAM, Leipzig Cons., and Milan (with Lamperti). From 1875 was concert and oratorio singer in Eng. Prof. of singing, RAM, from 1878. Cond. RAM concerts and others. Comp. sym. and other works. Wrote books on singing.

Shakuhachi. Japanese end-blown long fl., dating from *c*.14th cent., made in several types, one having 4 fingerholes, another 7.

Shalyapin. See *Chaliapin, Fyodor*.

Shankar, Ravi (*b* Varanasi, Uttar Pradesh, 1920). Indian sitar-player and composer. Trained by his brother Uday Shankar, with whose troupe of musicians and dancers he worked. Dir. of instr. ens., India Radio, 1949–56. Founder-dir., Kinnara

Sch. of Mus., Bombay, 1962. Toured Europe and N. Amer. giving sitar recitals which led to awakening of interest in Indian mus. Wrote 2 concs. for sitar and orch. (1971, 1976), ballet scores, and film mus. On staff Calif. Institute of Mus.

Shanty (Chanty). Sailors' work-song, originating in days of sailing ships, sung while pulling together on a rope and helping to secure rhythmic unanimity. 'Shanty man', placed apart, sang the tune, the rest joining in ch. Tune and words are traditional. Famous examples are *Shenandoah*, *The Rio Grande*, *What shall we do with a drunken sailor?*, etc.

Shapero, Harold (*b* Lynn, Mass., 1920). Amer. composer. Jazz pianist and arranger in his teens. Began serious study of mus. 1936 with N. Slonimsky at Boston. Harvard Univ. 1938–41 (comp. with Piston and Křenek). Later studies were with Boulanger and Hindemith. Prof. of mus., Brandeis Univ. since 1952 (chairman, mus. dept., 1966–9). Works comp. in classical forms with harmonic idiom based on Copland and occasional use of 12-note system. Works incl. pf. sonatas, tpt. sonata, str. qt., sym., *Hebrew Cantata*, and pieces for synthesizer.

Shaporin, Yury (*b* Glukov, 1887; *d* Moscow, 1966). Russ. composer. Studied Petrograd Cons. (comp. with Glazunov and Tcherepnin). Comp. in traditional idiom. Works incl. opera, *The Decembrists* (1920–53), sym., patriotic cantatas, pf. sonata, and songs.

Sharp. (1) As noun, the sign (♯) which, placed by a note, raises its pitch by a semitone. A sharp in the key signature affects all notes on corresponding degree of scale. See *Inflection of Notes*. (In Amer. usage a note is 'sharped'; in Eng. 'sharpened'.)
(2) As adjective, describes singing or playing which departs from correct intonation upwards (opposite of flat, downwards).

Sharp, Cecil (James) (*b* Denmark Hill, London, 1859; *d* Hampstead, 1924). Eng. folk-song and folk-dance collector and ed., organist, and writer. Studied mus. at Cambridge Univ. Trained as lawyer and practised as such in Australia. Organist, Adelaide Cath., 1889–92. Prin., Hampstead Cons. of Mus. 1896–1905. In 1899 began systematic coll. of Eng. folk-dances and in 1903 began to collect folk-songs. Though not first in the field, his proselytizing and energy inspired others to emulate him. Founded English Folk Dance Soc., 1911. With M. *Karpeles, collected folk-songs in Appalachian mountains of N. Amer., 1916–18. Pubd. many arrs. and colls. of folk-songs and dances (some in collab. with G. Butterworth, Vaughan Williams, C. L. Marson, etc.). Wrote *English Folk Song* and other books. After his death Cecil Sharp House, in London, was built as headquarters of amalgamated *English Folk Dance and Song Society.

Sharpe, Cedric (*b* London, 1891; *d* Steyning, 1978). Eng. cellist and composer. Pupil of W. H. Squire at RCM. Prin. cellist, LSO, and in other London orchs. Noted chamber-mus. player. Prof. of vc., RAM 1928–66. Wrote orch. works and songs.

Sharp mixture. Org. *Mixture stop of high-pitched pipes and bright tone.

Shaw, Geoffrey (Turton) (*b* London, 1879; *d* London, 1943). Eng. composer and organist. Brother of Martin *Shaw. Trained in St Paul's Cath. choir and at Cambridge Univ. Organist, St Mary's Ch., Primrose Hill. Inspector of sch. mus. Campaigner for better church mus. Wrote orch. and choral works, and ed. song colls. (with his brother).

Shaw, George Bernard (*b* Dublin, 1856; *d* Ayot St Lawrence, 1950). Irish playwright, essayist, and mus. critic. Taught mus., esp. singing, by his mother. Wrote mus. criticism—arguably the most brilliant in the language—for London periodicals, the *Star* and the *World*, from 1888 to 1894 having earlier (from *c.* 1876) 'ghosted' for music critic of *The Hornet*. Adopted pseudonym 'Corno di Bassetto', until 1890. Early champion of Wagner's mus. and one of first to put political interpretation on *The Ring* (in *The Perfect Wagnerite*, 1898). Criticisms reprinted in *London Music* 1888–9, *Music in London* 1890–94 (3 vols.), and *How to become a Musical Critic* (ed. Laurence 1960). Friend of Elgar, whose *Severn Suite* is ded. to Shaw. His play *Arms and the Man* was basis of operetta *The Chocolate Soldier* (*Der tapfere Soldat*, 1908) by O. Straus, and his *Pygmalion* became Loewe's musical *My Fair Lady* (1956). Composers of music for films based on Shaw plays incl. Honegger (*Pygmalion*, 1938), Walton (*Major Barbara*, 1941), Auric (*Caesar and Cleopatra*, 1945), and Richard Rodney Bennett (*The Devil's Disciple*, 1959).

Shaw, Martin (Edward Fallas) (*b* London, 1875; *d* Southwold, 1958). Eng. composer, organist, and cond. Studied RCM. Organist, St Martin-in-the-Fields, 1920–4. Campaigner for better church mus. and for Eng. opera. Co-ed. with Vaughan Williams of hymn-book *Songs of Praise* (1925, rev. 1931) and *Oxford Book of Carols* (1928). Comp. ballad-opera *Mr Pepys* (1926), anthems, hymns, songs, etc. O.B.E. 1955.

Shaw, Robert (*b* Red Bluff, Calif., 1916). Amer. cond., particularly of choirs. Studied Pomona Coll. Founder and cond. Collegiate Chorale, NY, 1941–54. Cond., Robert Shaw Chorale 1948–66. Taught at Juilliard Sch. Cond. San Diego S.O. 1953–7. Ass. cond. Cleveland Orch., 1956–67. Cond. Atlanta S.O. from 1967. One of most gifted of choral conductors and trainers. At Cleveland he created a remarkable chorus, as fine in Verdi as in Haydn or Mozart. Was first professional conductor to give perfs. in USA of Bach's Mass in B minor and Handel's *Messiah* with small forces.

Shaw, (Harold) **Watkins** (*b* Bradford, Yorks., 1911). Eng. writer, teacher, and musicologist. Studied Oxford Univ. and RCM. Lecturer, Worcester Coll. of Education 1949–71. Hon. librarian, St Michael's Coll., Tenbury Wells, from 1948. Keeper, Parry Room Library, RCM 1971–80. Specialist in church mus. and Handel's *Messiah* (of which he made celebrated edn., 1965). Hon. gen. ed., Church Mus. Soc. 1956–70. O.B.E. 1985.

Shawe-Taylor, Desmond (Christopher) (*b* Dublin, 1907). Irish mus. critic and author. Studied Oxford Univ. Wrote mainly literary criticism until 1939, then contrib. mus. criticism to *The Times, New Statesman* (1945–58) etc. Mus. critic, *Sunday Times*, 1958–83. Specialist in opera. Author of book on CG. Ed. (with E. Sackville-West) of *The Record Guide* (1951, rev. 1955 with A. Porter and W. S. Mann; suppl. 1956). C.B.E. 1965.

Shawm (from Lat. *calamus*, 'reed'; Eng. *shawm, shalm*; Fr. *chalemie*, Ger. *schalmei*). Woodwind instr., double-reeded forerunner of the ob., made in 7 sizes from sopranino to great bass, with keys. Some shawms were described as *bombards*. Had piercing brilliance of tone, with great carrying power outdoors. In Middle Ages, had broad cane reed controlled by player's lips. On largest sizes, reed was placed on end of crook (as in bn.); on smaller, it was placed on a staple inside a *pirouette. All shawms had a number of vent-holes, placed between little-finger hole and end of bell. Modern reproductions have been made for perf. of early mus.

Shchedrin, Rodion (Konstantinovich) (*b* Moscow, 1932). Russ. comp. Studied Moscow Cons. 1950–55 (comp. with Shaporin) and taught comp. there 1964–9. Specialist in Russian folk mus. of the various regions. Some of his later works use Western *avant-garde* processes formerly frowned upon in Soviet Union. Prin. comps. incl. 2 syms. (1958 and 1965, the 2nd subtitled *25 Preludes for Orchestra*); 2 pf. concs.; 4-act ballet *Little Hump-Backed Horse* (*Konyok-gorbunok*) (1959); 3-act opera *Not Love Alone* (*Ne tol'o linbov*) (1961); Conc. for Orch., No. 1, *Naughty Limericks* (*Ozornyye chastushki*) (1963); No. 2, *Chimes* (*Zvoni*) (1967); 24 Preludes and Fugues for pf. (1963–70); oratorio *Poetoria*, for poet, woman's v., ch., and orch. (1968); 1-act ballet *Carmen* (1968), transcr. from Bizet; 3-act opera *Anna Karenina* (1972); cantata *Lenin Lives* (*Lenin zhiryot*) (1972); songs, etc.

Shcherbachov, Vladimir (Vladimirovich) (*b* Warsaw, 1889; *d* Leningrad, 1952). Russ. composer. Studied St Petersburg Cons. and with Lyadov. Prof. of comp. at Leningrad Cons. 1923–31, and in Tbilisi 1931–4. Wrote 5 syms., oratorios, opera, film mus., and pf. suite on poems by Alexander Blok.

Shebalin, Vissarion (*b* Omsk, 1902; *d* Moscow, 1963). Russ. composer. Studied Moscow Cons. with Myaskovsky. Prof. of comp., Moscow Cons., from 1935, dir. 1942–8. Relieved of post in 1948 when, like Shostakovich and Prokofiev, was condemned for *formalism. Completed Mussorgsky's opera *Sorochintsy Fair* 1930. Wrote 5 syms. between 1925 and 1962, choral symphonic poem *Lenin*, opera *The Taming of the Shrew* (1946–56), vn. conc., hn. concertino, 9 str. qts., pf. trio, pf. mus., and songs.

Sheep may safely graze (Bach). See *Schafe können sicher weiden*.

Sheherazade. (1) Symphonic suite for orch., 'after the Thousand and One Nights' by Rimsky-Korsakov, Op. 35, comp. 1888, f.p. St Petersburg, 1889.
(2) *Shéhérazade*, ov. for orch. by Ravel, comp. 1898, f.p. Paris 1899, unpubd.
(3) Song-cycle for v. and orch. by Ravel to poems by Tristan Klingsor (pseudonym of Léon Leclère), comp. 1903, f.p. Paris 1904. Songs are: 1. *Asie* (Asia), 2. *La flûte enchantée* (The magic flute), 3. *L'Indifférent* (The indifferent one).

Shelley, Howard (Gordon) (*b* London, 1950). Eng. pianist. Studied RCM 1967–71 and with H. Craxton, Kendall Taylor, Lamar Crowson, and Ilona Kabos. Début London 1971, followed by int. career. Pf. duettist with wife, Hilary Macnamara, and recitalist with Malcolm Messiter (ob.) and Jane Manning (sop.). Has recorded 1-pf. version of Vaughan Williams's conc.

Shepherd, Arthur (*b* Paris, Idaho, 1880; *d* Cleveland, 1958). Amer. composer. Studied New England Cons., pupil of Chadwick. Teacher, Salt Lake City, 1897–1908 and New England Cons. 1908–17; assoc. cond. Cleveland Orch. 1920–6. Prof. of mus., Western Reserve Univ., 1927–50. Works incl. 2 syms., 4 str. qts., pf. quintet, choral mus., vn. conc., 2 pf. sonatas, etc.

Shepherd Fennel's Dance. Orch. piece by Balfour *Gardiner, 1910, based on Hardy's story *The Three Strangers* (from *Wessex Tales*, 1888).

Shepherd, John (*b* c.1515; *d* c.1560). Eng. composer and organist. Organist, Magdalen Coll., Oxford, 1542–3 and 1545–7. Member of Chapel Royal in Mary's reign. Wrote 4 Masses, incl. *Western Wynde Mass* and *French Mass*, also *Haec dies*, many motets, anthems, etc.

Shepherd on the Rock, The (*Der Hirt auf dem Felsen*). Song by Schubert (Oct. 1828, D965) for sop. and pf. with cl. obbl., setting of words by Müller and H. von Chézy put together, presumably, by the sop. Anna Milder who commissioned the song.

Shepherds of the Delectable Mountains, The. Pastoral episode in 1 act by Vaughan Williams to his own lib. based on Bunyan's *The Pilgrim's Progress* (1678, 1684). Prod. London 1922. Incorporated, with final section omitted, into morality *The *Pilgrim's Progress* (1951) as Scene 2 of Act IV.

Sheppard, Honor (*b* Leeds, 1931). Eng. sop. Studied RMCM. Member of Deller Consort. Specialist in Purcell and other mus. of 17th and 18th cents.

Shera, Frank (Henry) (*b* Sheffield, 1882; *d* Sheffield, 1956). Eng. teacher, writer, and composer. Studied RCM and Cambridge Univ. Dir. of mus., Malvern Coll., 1916–28; prof. of mus., Sheffield Univ., 1928–48. Wrote *Miniature Symphony*, chamber mus., etc. Author of books on Debussy and Ravel (1925) and Elgar (1931).

Sheridan, Margaret (*b* Castlebar, 1889; *d* Dublin, 1958). Irish sop. Studied RAM and Milan. Début Rome 1918 as Mimi in *La Bohème*, CG 1919 and 1925–30; Scala, Milan, 1921–4. Also sang with Chicago Opera.

Sheriff, Noam (*b* Ramat-Gan, Israel, 1935). Israeli composer. Studied Hebrew Univ., Jerusalem (philosophy) and at Berlin Hochschule für Musik 1960–2 (comp. with *Blacher). Private study 1949–57 with P. *Ben-Haim. Founder and cond. Hebrew Univ. S.O. 1955–9. Teacher of orchestration, Jerusalem Acad. of Mus. from 1966 and Tel Aviv Nat. Acad. from 1967. Works incl. *Songs of Degrees*, orch. (1959); pf. sonata (1962); *Metamorphoses on a Galliard*, orch. (1966); *Chaconne*, orch. (1968); *Cain*, choreog. drama with elec. mus. on tape (1969); *Sonata*, chamber orch. (1973); str. qt. (1973); harp quintet (1975–6); *The Story of Deborah*, choreog. movement for ch., brass, perc., synthesizers (1976); va. sonata (1976).

Sherlaw Johnson, Robert. See *Johnson, Robert Sherlaw.*

Sherman, Alec (*b* London, 1907). Eng. cond. and violinist. Joined BBC S.O. as violinist, 1930. Founder and cond. New London Orch. from 1941. Co-cond., SW Ballet 1943–5. Cond. in Portugal and at weekly concerts at Cambridge Th., London, 1945–9. Husband of pianist Gina *Bachauer.

Shield, William (*b* Swalwell, Co. Durham, 1748; *d* London, 1829). Eng. composer, pupil of *Avison. Violinist in travelling orchs. and theatre cos. Giardini heard him at Scarborough and advised him to go to London. Played in orch. at King's Th., Haymarket, 1773–91, first as violinist, then as prin. va. Wrote first opera, *The Flitch of Bacon*, in 1778, the forerunner of 35 more. In most of his operas about one-third of the mus. was borrowed or arr. from other sources. In his first opera for CG, *Rosina* (1782), the ov. ends with a tune orchestrated to suggest bagpipes which later became popular as *Auld Lang Syne*. (He may well have heard the tune in Northumbria.) The song *The Plough Boy*, often thought to be a folk-song and popularized in the 20th cent. by *Pears and *Britten, was comp. by Shield for *The Farmer* (1787), with a piccolo solo as part of the acc. Master of the King's Mus. 1817–29, composing in 1818 the last of Eng. court odes.

Comp. str. qts., str. trios, vn. duets, and wrote text-books on harmony (1800) and thoroughbass (1815).

Shifrin, Seymour (*b* Brooklyn, NY, 1926; *d* Boston, 1979). Amer. composer. Studied comp. privately with W. Schuman, with O. Luening at Columbia Univ., and with *Milhaud in Paris. Teacher at Univ. of Calif., Berkeley, 1952–66 (prof. of mus. from 1964); and prof. of mus., Brandeis Univ. from 1966. Mus., in intensely chromatic style, uses highly contrasted material. Works incl. 5 str. qts., chamber sym., *Satires of Circumstance* (Hardy) for mez. and chamber ens., vc. sonata, etc.

Shimizu, Osamu (*b* Osaka, 1911). Japanese composer. Studied Tokyo Music Acad. On staff Tokyo Radio. Works incl. several operas and ballets, 3 syms., *Olympic Hymn* 1964, several cantatas, chamber mus., and songs.

Shinner, Emily (*b* Cheltenham, 1862; *d* London, 1901). Eng. violinist, pupil of Joachim. Début London 1881. Founded first all-female str. qt., 1887.

Shirley, George (Irving) (*b* Indianapolis, 1934). Amer. ten. Studied Wayne State Univ. Début with Turnau Opera Players, Woodstock, NY, 1959. Won Metropolitan Opera Auditions 1960–1. NY Met. début 1961 as Ferrando in *Così fan tutte*, subsequently opera perfs. in Buenos Aires 1964, Glyndebourne 1966 (Tamino), CG and Scottish Opera (Pelléas) 1967, Netherlands Opera and Monte Carlo 1976. Noted singer of Pelléas in Debussy's opera.

Shirley-Quirk, John (Stanton) (*b* Liverpool, 1931). Eng. bar. Studied Liverpool Univ. and with Roy Henderson. Début 1961. Noted Lieder singer and also active in opera. Created several roles in operas of Britten incl. all 7 bar. roles in *Death in Venice* (1973). Has sung Eugene Onegin with Glyndebourne and in Henze's *Elegy for Young Lovers* with Scottish Opera. NY Met. début 1974 (*Death in Venice*). Outstanding interpreter of choral works by Elgar, Tippett, Britten, etc. C.B.E. 1975.

Shnitke (Schnitke, Schnittke), **Alfred** (Garriyevich) (*b* Engels, USSR, 1934). Russ. composer. Private lessons in Vienna 1946–8. Studied at Moscow Cons. 1953–61, then teacher of counterpoint and comp. there 1961–72. Also worked in Moscow Experimental Studio of Elec. Mus. Influenced by 12-note composers, also by Stockhausen, Cage, and Ligeti, but after 1966 gave dramatic, programmatic basis to his works, using quotations and pastiche. Has written articles on aspects of Shostakovich's work. Prin. works:

OPERA: *The 11th Commandment* (*Odinnadtsataya Zapoved*) (1962).

BALLETS: *The Labyrinth* (*Labirinti*) (1971); *Yellow Sound* (*Zhyoltïy zvuk*), mime, 9 musicians, tape, lighting (1974).

ORCH: Syms. No. 1 (1969–72), No. 2 (*St Florian*), chamber ch., and orch. (1979); Concertos, Pf. (1960), Vn. No. 1 (1957, rev. 1962), No. 2 (1966), No. 3 (1978), No. 4 (1981–2), Ob. and hp. with str. (1970); *Poem of the Cosmos* (1961); *Music for Chamber Orch.* (1964); *Music for Piano and Chamber Orch.* (1964); *Pianissimo* (1968); *Concerto Grosso*, 2 vn., hpd., 21 str. (1977); *Passacaglia* (1979–80).

CHORAL: *Nagasaki*, oratorio, mez., ch., orch. (1958); *Songs of War and Peace*, cantata (1959); *Voices of Nature*, women's ch., vib. (1972); *Minnesang*, for 52 vv. (1980–1); *'Seid Nüchtern und Wachet...' History of Dr Johann Faust*, cantata, counterten., cont., ten., bass, ch., org., orch. (1982).

CHAMBER MUSIC: Str. Qts., No. 1 (1966), No. 2 (1981); Vn. sonatas, No. 1 (1963), No. 2 (1968); *Dialogue*, vc., fl., ob., cl., hn., tpt., pf., perc. (1965); *Serenade*, cl., pf., perc., vn., db. (1968); *Canon in memory of Stravinsky*, str. qt. (1971); *Hymn*, vc., hp., timp. (1974); *Cantus perpetuus*, hpd., perc. (1975); *Prelude in memory of Shostakovich*, 2 vn. (1975); *Moz-Art à la Haydn*, 2 vn., 11 str. (1977); vc. sonata (1978); Septet, fl., 2 cl., str. qt. (1982); *Sound and Fury*, perc., org. (1983).

PIANO: *Prelude and Fugue* (1963); *Improvisation and Fugue* (1965).

ORGAN: *2 Little Pieces* (1981).

TAPE: *The Stream* (*Potok*) (1969).

Shofar (Heb.). Wind instr. made of ram's horn, used in Jewish synagogue rituals, sounding only natural scale. Elgar employs it in *The Apostles* (1903), simulated by brass.

Shore, Bernard (Alexander Royle) (*b* London, 1896; *d* Hereford, 1985). Eng. va.-player. Studied RCM (org. with Alcock, va. with Bent, comp. with Dunhill). Studies interrupted by war; on return to RCM studied va., hn. (with Borsdorf), and cond. (with Boult). Also had va. tuition from *Tertis. Joined Queen's Hall Orch. 1922; début as soloist 1925. Prin. va. BBC S.O. 1930–40. Prof. of va., RCM. Mus. dir., Rural Mus. Schools Assoc. Inspector of Schools and Staff Inspector, Ministry of Education 1948–59. Composer of vn. pieces and songs. Author of notable character-studies of conds. in *The Orchestra Speaks* (1938), also *Sixteen Symphonies* (1949). C.B.E. 1955.

Short Octave and **Broken Octave.** Devices for avoiding expenditure on the lowest and biggest (and consequently most costly) pipes of the organ, and as they were adopted also in domestic kbd. instrs. such as virginals, spinet, and clavichord, the economic motive probably operated in their case also.

(1) Where the SHORT OCTAVE device was adopted the lowest octave incl. only 9 notes instead of 13 (C, D, E, F, G, A, B♭, B, and C) and these were distributed over 6 long finger-keys and 3 short ones, the omitted notes being those which in the

days before equal *temperament were not likely to be needed in the bass.

(2) Where the BROKEN OCTAVE device was adopted the arrangement was generally the following or something like it. The lowest octave was complete from C to C, except that the lowest C♯ was replaced by a more useful note, the A from below. This device was still to be seen in some Eng. organs at the beginning of the 19th cent.

Short Score. See *Score.*

Short Service. See *Service.*

Shostakovich, Dmitry (Dmitryevich) (*b* St Petersburg, 1906; *d* Moscow, 1975). Russ. composer and pianist. Had pf. lessons from his mother at age 9 and later at Glasser Sch. of Mus. 1916–18. Entered Petrograd Cons. 1919, encouraged and helped by Glazunov, and studied pf. with Nikolayev and comp. with M. Steinberg. Completed pf. course in 4 years and made several concert appearances. Gained 'honourable mention' in Int. Chopin Comp., Warsaw, 1927. His diploma work, the 1st Sym., was perf. in Leningrad and Moscow in 1926 and earned the composer world fame at the age of 20. As a convinced believer in Russ. socialism, he sought ways in which his mus. could serve the state. Prompted by the cond. Malko, he wrote for the stage and films, in the next decade producing his opera *The Nose*, the ballets *The Age of Gold* and *The Bolt*, and several cinema scores. These works, particularly *The Nose*, reflect the then-permitted influence of Western *avant-garde* music. His opera *The Lady Macbeth of the Mtsensk District* and ballet *Bright Stream* had both been successfully prod. when on 28 Jan. 1936 the opera was savagely attacked in the official Soviet newspaper *Pravda* for 'leftist distortion', 'petty-bourgeois sensationalism', and 'formalism' in an article headed 'Chaos instead of Music' (*Sumbur vmesto muzyki*). This article is said to have been written by Stalin himself, who had hated the opera. Another article attacking the ballet *Bright Stream* appeared in *Pravda* 10 days later. It almost seemed that Shostakovich's career was at an end, and he withdrew his 4th Sym. after initial rehearsals. His response was his 5th Sym. (1937), described by an unidentified commentator as 'A Soviet artist's practical creative reply to just criticism', a work which became and has remained one of his most popular. Significantly he avoided the stage for many years and between 1938 and 1953 wrote 5 more syms. and 4 str. qts. He taught comp. at Leningrad Cons. 1937–41 and was a fire-fighter during Ger. siege of Leningrad in 1941. From these experiences came his 7th Sym. (the *Leningrad*), which had a tremendous wartime success not only in USSR but in Eng. and USA. His pf. quintet (1940) won the Stalin Prize. In 1943 he settled in Moscow, becoming prof. of comp. at the Cons. In 1948, with other leading Russ. composers, he was again in disgrace following

the notorious Zhdanov decree against *'formalism' and 'anti-people art'. He was relieved of his Moscow professorship and did not resume the post until 1960. He made an official recantation, but his published works from 1948 to 1953 (when Stalin died) were chiefly film music and patriotic cantatas, exceptions being the *24 Preludes and Fugues* for pf. The first Vn. Conc. (1947–8, rev. 1955), the 4th str. qt., and the song-cycle *From Jewish Folk Poetry* were all withheld from performance until after Stalin's death, and the arrival, under Khruschev, of a relatively and temporarily more liberal political and cultural climate.

In 1953 the 10th Sym. appeared, a masterpiece which is one of several highly personal works using the motif DSCH (based on the initials of his name). This sym. inaugurates the great final period of his career, 22 years in which he comp. some of his finest mus.—the 10th to 15th Syms., the 6th to 15th str. qts., 2 vc. concs., *The Execution of Stepan Razin* to a text by the poet Yevtushenko, the 2nd vn. conc., the vn. and va. sonatas, and the *Suite on Verses of Michelangelo*. He visited England in 1958 and 1974, becoming a close friend and admirer of *Britten. In 1969 he had a severe heart attack and was in fragile health thereafter.

Many consider that Shostakovich is the greatest 20th-cent. composer. In his 15 syms., 15 qts., and in other works he demonstrated mastery of the largest and most challenging forms with mus. of great emotional power and technical invention. Nearly all the significant features of his mus. are present in the 1st Sym.: sectionalized structures, with themes built up into a mosaic, and frequent use of solo instr. in their highest and lowest registers. All his works are marked by emotional extremes—tragic intensity, grotesque and bizarre wit, humour, parody, and savage sarcasm. He frequently uses quotation, of himself and others. After his illness his mus. seemed preoccupied with death, and the great final works have an extraordinary and alarming power and tension. His admiration for, and knowledge of, Mahler is evident in his symphonic works, and he follows the Mahlerian precedent of juxtaposing the banal and the sublime. His student days in the decade following the Revolution were a time of comparative liberalism in Leningrad and it is evident from his 1st Sym. that he had studied the Western *avant-garde* of the time (Berg, Hindemith, and Křenek). The influence of Berg's *Wozzeck*, perf. in Leningrad, 1927, may be discerned in the *Lady Macbeth* opera, No one can know whether Shostakovich became disillusioned with the Soviet system and whether the intensifying darkness and bitterness of his work reflects a spiritual misery connected with external events (his attributed memoirs, published in the West in 1979, suggest that he was and it does). What is certain is that the tensions within him, whatever their cause, produced a succession of masterpieces. Prin. works:

OPERAS: The *Nose (Nos), Op. 15 (1927–8); The Lady Macbeth of the Mtsensk District (Ledi Makbet Mtsenskovo uyezda), Op. 29 (1930–2) rev. 1956 as *Katerina Izmaylova, Op. 29/114; Moscow, Cheryomushki, musical comedy (ov. and 39 nos.), Op. 105 (1958); The *Gamblers (Igroki), Op. 63 unfinished (1941; concert perf. Leningrad 1978).

BALLETS: The *Age of Gold (Zolotoy vek), Op. 22 (1927–30); The *Bolt (Bolt), Op. 27 (1930–1); Bright Stream (Svetytoly ruchey), Op. 39 (1934–5); The Dreamers, mus. drawn chiefly from The Age of Gold and The Bolt, with some new material (1975).

ORCH.: (except for syms. and concs., listed separately): Scherzo in F# minor, Op. 1 (1919); Theme with Variations, Op. 3 (1921–2); Scherzo in Eb, Op. 7 (1924); Prelude and Scherzo for str. octet or str. orch., Op. 11 (1924–5); Tahiti Trot (*Tea for Two), Op. 16 (1928); 2 Scarlatti Pieces, transcr. for wind, Op. 17 (1928); Suite, Age of Gold, Op. 22a (1929–32); Suite, The Bolt (Ballet Suite No. 5), Op. 27a (1931); Suite, Golden Mountains, Op. 30a (1931); *Hamlet, suite of 13 movements, for small orch., Op. 32a (1932); Suite for Jazz Orch., No. 1 (1934), No. 2 (1938); 5 Fragments, for small orch., Op. 42 (1935); Fragments from Maxim Film-Trilogy (assembled by L. Atoumian), Op. 50a (1938, 1961); Suite from Pirogov (assisted by Atoumian), Op. 76a (1947); Suite from Young Guards (assisted by Atoumian), Op. 75a (1947–8, 1951); Suite from Meeting on the Elbe, Op. 80a (c.1948); Ballet Suite No. 1 (1949), No. 2 (1951), No. 3 (1952), No. 4 (1953); Fragments from The Memorable Year 1919 (assisted by Atoumian), Op. 89a (1951, ?1955); Festival Overture, Op. 96 (1954); Fragments from The Gadfly (assisted by Atoumian), Op. 97a (1955); Suite in 5 scenes from Katerina Izmaylova (1956); Novorossiysk Chimes (1960); Suite from 5 Days, 5 Nights (assisted by Atoumian), Op. 111a (1961); Overture on Russian and Kirghiz Folk Themes, Op. 115 (1963); Suite from Hamlet (film mus.) (assisted by Atoumian), Op. 116a (1964); Chamber Symphony (arr. of 8th Str. Qt. for str. by Barshay); Symphony for Strings (arr. of 10th Str. Qt.); Funeral-Triumphal Prelude, Op. 130 (1967); October, symphonic poem, Op. 131 (1967).

SYMPHONIES: No. 1 in F minor, Op. 10 (1924–5), f.p. Leningrad, cond. Malko, 1926; No. 2 in B major (October) with ch. (text by A. Bezymensky), Op. 14 (1927), f.p. Leningrad, cond. Malko, 1927; No. 3 in Eb (First of May) with ch. (text by S. Kirsanov), Op. 20 (1929), f.p. Leningrad, cond. A. Gauk, 1930; No. 4 in C minor, Op. 43 (1935–6) (withdrawn during rehearsal), f.p. Moscow, cond. Kondrashin, 1961; No. 5 in D minor (A *Soviet Artist's Practical Creative Reply to Just Criticism), Op. 47 (1937), f.p. Leningrad, cond. Mravinsky, 1937; No. 6 in B minor, Op. 54 (1939), f.p. Leningrad, cond. Mravinsky, 1939; No. 7 in C major (*Leningrad), Op. 60 (1941), f.p. Kuibyshev, cond. S. Samosud, 1942;

No. 8 in C minor, Op. 65 (1943), f.p. Moscow, cond. Mravinsky, 1943; No. 9 in Eb, Op. 70 (1945), f.p. Leningrad, cond. Mravinsky, 1945; No. 10 in E minor, Op. 93 (1953), f.p. Leningrad, cond. Mravinsky, 1953; No. 11 in G minor (The Year 1905), Op. 103 (1957), f.p. Moscow, cond. N. Rachlin, 1957; No. 12 in D minor (1917), Op. 112 (1961), f.p. Moscow, cond. Kondrashin, 1961; No. 13 in Bb minor (*Babi-Yar), Op. 113, for bass, bass ch., and orch. (poems by Y. Yevtushenko) (1962), f.p. Moscow, V. Gromadsky (bass), cond. Kondrashin, 1962; No. 14, for sop., bass, str., and perc., Op. 135 (11 poems by Lorca, Apollinaire, Küchelbecker, and Rilke) (1969), f.p. Leningrad, G. Vishnevskaya (sop.), M. Reshetin (bass), cond. Barshay, 1969; No. 15 in A major, Op. 141 (1971), f.p. Moscow, cond. M. Shostakovich, 1972.

CONCERTOS: Pf.: No. 1 in C minor, pf., tpt., str., Op. 35 (1933), No. 2 in F, Op. 102 (1957); Vn.: No. 1 in A minor, Op. 77 (1947–8, f.p. 1955 and orig. pubd. as Op. 99), No. 2 in C# minor, Op. 129 (1967); Vc.: No. 1 in Eb, Op. 107 (1959), No. 2 in G, Op. 126 (1966).

SOLO VOICE(S) AND ORCH: 2 Fables of Krylov, Op. 4, mez. (also with pf., 1922); Suite, The Nose, Op. 15a, ten., bar. (1927–8); 6 Romances on Words by Japanese Poets, Op. 21, ten. (1928–32); 8 English and American Folksongs, low v. (1944); From Jewish Folk-Poetry, Op. 79, sop., cont., ten. (1963) (with pf. 1948); 7 Romances on Poems of Alexander Blok, Op. 127, suite for sop. and pf. trio (1967); 6 Romances on Verses of English Poets, Op. 140, bass (1971) (with pf., Op. 62, 1942); 6 Poems of Marina Tsvetayeva, Op. 143a, cont. (1973), (with pf., Op. 143, 1973); Suite on Verses of *Michelangelo Buonarroti, Op. 145a, bass, 1974 (with pf., Op. 145, 1974).

CHORUS AND ORCH. (excl. syms.): Poem of the Motherland, cantata, Op. 74, mez., ten., 2 bar., bass soloists (1947); The Song of the Forests, oratorio, Op. 81, ten., bass soloists, and children's ch. (1949); The Sun Shines over our Motherland, cantata, Op. 90, with children's ch. (1952); Fragments from the 1st Echelon, Op. 99a (1956); The *Execution of Stepan Razin (Kazn' Stepana Razina), cantata, Op. 119, bass soloist (1964).

UNACC. CHORUS: 10 Poems on Texts by Revolutionary Poets, SATB, Op. 88 (1951); 2 Russian Folksong Adaptations, SATB, Op. 104 (1957); Loyalty, 8 ballads for male ch., Op. 136 (1970).

VOICE AND PIANO: 2 Fables of Krilov, Op. 4, mez. (1922); 4 Romances on Verses of Pushkin, Op. 46, bass (1936); 6 Romances on Verses of English Poets, Op. 62, bass (1942); Vow of the People's Commissar, bass and ch. (1942); 2 Songs (texts by Svetlov), Op. 72 (1945); Homesickness (1948, arr. by composer 1956); From Jewish Folk-Poetry, Op. 79, sop., cont., ten. (1948); 2 Romances on Verses by Lermontov, Op. 84, male v. (1950); 4 Songs to words by Dolmatovsky, Op. 86 (1951); 4 Monologues on Verses of Pushkin, Op. 91, bass (1952); 5 Romances (Songs of our Days), Op. 98, bass (1954);

6 Spanish Songs, Op. 100, sop. (1956); *Satires (Pictures of the Past)*, 5 Romances, Op. 109, sop. (1960); *5 Romances on texts from Krokodil Magazine*, Op. 121, bass (1965); *Preface to the Complete Collection of my Works, and Brief Reflections apropos this Preface*, Op. 123, bass (1966); *Spring, Spring* (Pushkin), Op. 128, bass (1967); *6 Poems of Marina Tsvetayeva*, Op. 143, cont. (1973); *Suite on Verses of *Michelangelo Buonarroti*, Op. 145, bass (1974); *4 Verses of Capitan Lebyadkin*, Op. 146, bass (texts by Dostoyevsky) (1974).

CHAMBER MUSIC: Str. Qts.: No. 1 in C, Op. 49 (1938), No. 2 in A, Op. 68 (1944), No. 3 in F, Op. 73 (1946), No. 4 in D, Op. 83 (1949. also arr. for 2 pf. by composer), No. 5 in B♭, Op. 92 (1953), No. 6 in G, Op. 101 (1956), No. 7 in F♯ minor, Op. 108 (1960), No. 8 in C minor, Op. 110 (1960, arr. for str. orch. by Barshay as *Chamber Symphony*), No. 9 in E♭, Op. 117 (1964), No. 10 in A♭, Op. 118 (1964, arr. for str. orch. by Barshay as *Symphony for Strings*), No. 11 in F minor, Op. 122 (1966), No. 12 in D♭, Op. 133 (1968), No. 13 in B♭ minor, Op. 138 (1970), No. 14 in F♯ major, Op. 142 (1972–3), No. 15 in E♭ minor, Op. 144 (1974); Pf. Trio No. 1, Op. 8 (1923), No. 2 in E minor, Op. 67 (1944); *2 Pieces (Prelude and Scherzo)* for str. octet, Op. 11 (1924–5); Pf. Quintet in G minor, Op. 57 (1940).

PIANO: Sonatas: No. 1, Op. 12 (1926), No. 2 in B minor, Op. 61 (1942); *8 Preludes*, Op. 2 (1919–20); *5 Preludes* (1920–1); *3 Fantastic Dances*, Op. 5 (1922); *10 Aphorisms*, Op. 13 (1927); *Polka (Age of Gold)* (1935, arr. for 4 hands 1962); *24 Preludes*, Op. 34 (1932–3) (No. 14, orch. Stokowski); *Children's Notebook*, Op. 69 (1944–5); *24 Preludes and Fugues*, Op. 87 (1950–1); *7 Dances of the Dolls* (1952–62).

2 PIANOS: *Suite in F♯ minor*, Op. 6 (1922); *Polka (Age of Gold)* (1962); *Prelude and Fugue No. 15 from Op. 87* (?1963); *Concertino*, Op. 94 (1953); *Tarantella from The Gadfly* (?1963).

INCIDENTAL MUSIC FOR PLAYS: *The Flea (Klop)* (Mayakovsky), Op. 19 (1929); *Rule Britannia!* (Pyotrovsky), Op. 28 (1931); *Hamlet* (Shakespeare), Op. 32 (1931–2); *The Human Comedy* (Sukotkin, after Balzac), Op. 37 (1933–4); *Salute to Spain* (Apinogenov), Op. 44 (1936); *King Lear* (Shakespeare), Op. 58a (1940).

FILM MUSIC: *New Babylon*, Op. 18 (1928, score missing: suite reconstructed by *Rozhdestvensky, 1976); *Alone*, Op. 26 (1930–1); *Golden Mountains*, Op. 30 (1931, lost, new version 1936); *Encounter*, Op. 33 (1932); *Love and Hate*, Op. 38 (1934); *Maxim's Youth (The Bolshevik)*, Op. 41 (i) (1934–5); *Girl Companions*, Op. 41 (ii) (1934–5); *The Tale of the Priest and his worker Balda*, Op. 36 (1936, not released); *Maxim's Return*, Op. 45 (1936–7); *Volochayev Days*, Op. 48 (1936–7); *Vyborg District*, Op. 50 (1938); *Friends*, Op. 51 (1938); *The Great Citizen (Part I)*, Op. 52 (1938); *Man at Arms*, Op. 53 (1938); *The Great Citizen (Part II)*, Op. 55 (1939); *Zoya*, Op. 64 (1944); *Simple Folk*, Op. 71 (1945); *Pirogov*,

Op. 76 (1947); *Young Guards*, Op. 75 (1947–8); *Michurin*, Op. 78 (1948); *Meeting on the Elbe*, Op. 80 (1948); *The Fall of Berlin*, Op. 82 (1949); *Belinsky*, Op. 85 (1950); *The Memorable Year 1919*, Op. 89 (1951); *Song of a Great River*, Op. 95 (1954); *The Gadfly*, Op. 97 (1955); *The 1st Echelon*, Op. 99 (1956); *Five Days—Five Nights*, Op. 111 (1960); *Cheryomushki* (1962); *Hamlet*, Op. 116 (Shakespeare, trans. Pasternak, 1963–4); *A Year Like a Life*, Op. 120 (1965); *Sofya Perovoskaya*, Op. 132 (1967); *King Lear*, Op. 137 (1970).

ARRS. OF OTHER COMPOSERS: Scarlatti: *2 Scarlatti Pieces* for wind orch., Op. 17 (1928); Mussorgsky: *Boris Godunov*, re-orch., Op. 58 (1939–40, f.p. 1959); *Khovanshchina*, ed. and orch., Op. 106, (1959, for film version, f. stage p. 1960), *Songs and Dances of Death* (orch. 1962); Davidenko (1899–1934): *2 Choruses*, arr. for ch. and orch., Op. 124 (1962); Schumann: vc. conc., re-orch. (1963); Youmans: * Tea for Two, orch. as *Tahiti Trot*, Op. 16 (1928).

Shostakovich, Maxim (*b* Leningrad, 1938). Russ. cond. and pianist, son of Dmitry *Shostakovich. Studied Leningrad Cons. and privately (cond.) with Gauk and *Rozhdestvensky. Début, Moscow S.O. 1965. Toured Europe, Japan, USA, and Mexico. London concert début 1968 (LPO). Prin. cond., USSR Radio and TV S.O. 1971–81. Début as opera cond., London 1979 (The *Nose). Cond. f.ps. of D. Shostakovich's *October*, 1967, Sym. No. 15, 1972, and *Suite on Verses of Michelangelo* (orch. version), 1975. Solo pf. in f.p. of Pf. Conc. No. 2, 1957. Cond. many recordings of his father's works. Settled USA 1981. Cond. New Orleans S.O. from 1986.

Shropshire Lad, A. Book of poems by A. E. Housman (1859–1936) pubd. 1896 which had profound influence on many Eng. composers. Settings of the poems (to the poet's dislike) by, among others, Vaughan Williams (*On Wenlock Edge, Along the Field*), John *Ireland (*Land of Lost Content*), Ivor *Gurney, Graham *Peel, *Somervell, Frank Lambert, C. W. *Orr, and George *Butterworth. Butterworth's song-cycle retained the name *A Shropshire Lad*, and he later based an orch. rhapsody (1913) of the same title on a theme from the song *Loveliest of trees*.

Shrubsole, William (*b* Canterbury, 1760; *d* London, 1806). Eng. composer and organist. Organist, Bangor Cath. 1782–4 and Lady Huntingdon's Chapel, Clerkenwell, 1784–1806. Wrote hymn-tune *Miles Lane* (pubd. anonymously 1799), sung to words 'All hail the power of Jesu's name' by E. Perronet (1762–92), and others. Subject of famous essay (1943) by Vaughan Williams.

Shuard, Amy (*b* London, 1924; *d* London, 1975). Eng. sop. Studied TCL and with Eva *Turner. Opera début Johannesburg 1949 as Aida. Member SW Opera 1949–55. CG 1954 till death. Fine dramatic sop. in roles such as Turandot, Elektra,

Santuzza, and Aida. Sang at Bayreuth 1965. First Eng.-born sop. to sing Brünnhilde at CG, 1964. Sang Káťa Kabanová and Jenůfa in first Eng. stage perfs. Vienna 1961, Milan 1962. C.B.E. 1966.

Shudi (Tschudi), **Burkat** (Burkhardt) (*b* Schwanden, Switz., 1702; *d* London, 1773). Swiss-born hpd.-maker who settled in Eng. 1718. Founded own business 1742 to which in 1772 his son-in-law John *Broadwood succeeded. Among those who bought his instrs. were Frederick the Great, Maria Theresia, Haydn, Handel, Gainsborough, and Reynolds. From 1769 Shudi hpds. had the 'Venetian swell', enabling volume to be varied by movement of louvres worked by a foot-pedal.

Shumsky, Oscar (*b* Philadelphia, 1917). Amer. violinist and conductor. Début with Stokowski and Philadelphia Orch. 1925. Studied with Auer from 1925 and at Curtis Inst. 1928–38 (with Auer and Zimbalist). Joined NBC S.O. under Toscanini 1938 and became leader of Primrose Qt. Début as cond. 1959. On staff of Juilliard Sch., NY, from 1953. After virtually abandoning concert-platform for 30 years, he returned in the early 1980s to clamorous critical acclaim.

Shylock. 6 items of incidental mus. by Fauré, Op. 57, for a verse-drama (based on Shakespeare's *Merchant of Venice*) by Edmund Haraucourt. F.p. Paris 1889.

Si (Fr.). The note B (see *Pitch names of the notes). *Si bémol*, B♭, *Si dièse*, B♯. Also 7th degree of major scale according to d'Arezzo system. In *Tonic sol-fa it has been changed to *Te*.

Sibelius, Jean (orig. Johan Julian Christian) (*b* Hämeenlinna (Tavastehus), 1865; *d* Järvenpää, 1957). Finn. composer, the nat. mus. v. of his country. In boyhood was called Janne by his friends and later adopted first name of an uncle, Jean Sibelius. Comp. as a child before he had technical instruction. Learned pf. and vn., hoping to become virtuoso of latter. Studied comp. in text-books. Entered Helsinki Univ. as law student 1885, taking special courses in mus. at Cons. and abandoning law in 1886. Studied comp. with Wegelius and vn. with Csillag at Helsinki Cons. 1886–9, being encouraged also by *Busoni, in Berlin 1889–90 (comp. with A. Becker), and at Vienna Cons. 1890–1 (comp. with K. Goldmark and R. Fuchs). Taught vn. and theory, Helsinki Mus. Institute 1892–7. Inspired by nationalist feeling sweeping Finland in protest at Russ. domination, comp choral sym. for soloists, male ch., and orch., *Kullervo*, based on Finn. nat. epic *Kalevala*. This had great success in Helsinki, 1892, but was withdrawn and not perf. again until after composer's death, when it was found to contain, amid immaturities, many indications of the later Sibelius. In the period 1893–7 he wrote the 4 Kalevala *Legends* about the hero Lemminkäinen and in 1892 the highly original tone-poem *En Saga*, a theme of which was taken

from a student str. octet. In 1897 the Finnish state voted Sibelius an annual pension (increased in 1926) to enable him to concentrate solely on comp. His tone-poem *Finlandia*, which became almost a nat. emblem, dates from 1899, the year of his first visit to It. He had by then completed his First Sym., which blends Sibelian originality with a Slav romanticism derived from Tchaikovsky. The 2nd Sym. (1902), while still classical in outline, contains more of Sibelius's individual use of short themes gradually building into a larger whole, his fondness for ostinati, and his predilection for long, atmospheric str. passages (often inevitably likened to the Finnish wind) and for unusual and effective grouping of instr., esp. woodwind. The vn. conc. was written in 1903, its warm middle movement reflecting the It. visit, and rev. 1905 when Strauss cond. it in Berlin. The 3rd Sym., often regarded as traditional but one of the most original of the 7, followed in 1904–7. It is ded. to *Bantock, one of his earliest Eng. champions. Sibelius first visited Eng. in 1905, conducting the 2nd Sym. in Liverpool. In Nov. 1907 *Mahler visited him in Helsinki and they had a famous conversation in which they expressed their contrasted views of the sym. For Mahler it was 'the world—it must embrace everything'; for Sibelius, it was the 'profound logic creating a connection between all the motifs' and the 'severity of style' which were the attractions. His 4th Sym. (1911) is indeed the antithesis of the Mahlerian symphony, epigrammatic, austere (but not lacking passion), economically scored, the whole work severely concentrated. Its introspective character, like that of the str. qt. *Voces Intimae* of 1908–9, is possibly attributable to his fear that a throat ailment from which he suffered at that period might be cancer. In 1914 he visited the USA, conducting at the Norfolk Fest., Conn., and taking a new symphonic poem, *The Oceanides*. On return to Finland he was isolated by World War I but celebrated his 50th birthday by composing the 5th Sym., later much rev. This work, in the heroic key of E♭ major, is among his most popular works, summing up all the familiar Sibelian characteristics and possessing a strong emotional power. After the war he revisited London in 1921 and in 1923 completed his 6th Sym., the most 'pastoral' and elusive of the set, with modal harmonies and a flavour of his admiration for Palestrina. In 1924 he finished the 7th Sym., compressed into 1 movement but with the conventional 4 symphonic movements easily recognizable. This was followed by incid. mus. for *The Tempest*. Another tone-poem, *Tapiola*, commissioned by the NY Sym. Soc., appeared in 1926. He wrote some male chs., and some pieces for vn. and pf., and 2 pieces for org. in 1931. Thereafter, though he is said to have written and destroyed an 8th Sym., he never pubd. another note in the remaining 26 years of his life. Yet despite this silence he remained a dominating figure, elevated to heroic status in his own country, in Eng., and the USA, but not in Ger. or Fr. In Eng. in the 1930s he was regarded by many composers as almost the only worthwhile figure in contemporary mus. and this effectively closed Eng. ears to Schoenberg, Berg, Webern, and to a large extent Stravinsky, until a rearguard action was fought on their behalf coincident with Sibelius's death. His reputation then suffered an exaggerated relapse, but a more balanced view of his highly original and rewarding style, particularly in the syms., now prevails. His mastery of the orch. has overshadowed the beauty of his choral works and his songs. Like Elgar, he wrote a good deal of lighter music of high worth and his incidental mus. is among the finest in existence. The picture of him as an ascetic, bleak figure is not supported by the facts of his far from austere life, nor is the mus. the 'cold, forbidding' art which some writers have portrayed. His place in symphonic development is assured, particularly if he is regarded as complementary to Mahler and the late romantics rather than as the antithesis. Prin. works:

ORCH: Symphonies: No. 1 in E minor, Op. 39 (1898–9, f.p. Helsinki 1899, f.p. in England, London 1903), No. 2 in D, Op. 43 (1901–2, f.p. Helsinki 1902, f.p. in England, Manchester 1905), No. 3 in C, Op. 52 (1904–7, f.p. Helsinki 1907, f.p. in England, London 1908), No. 4 in A minor, Op 63 (1911, f.p. Helsinki 1912, f.p. in England, Birmingham 1912), No. 5 in E♭, Op. 82 (1914–15, rev. 1916 and 1919, f.p. Helsinki 1915, 1916 version, Helsinki 1916, 1919 version Helsinki 1919, f.p. in England, London 1921), No. 6 in D minor, Op. 104 (1923, f.p. Helsinki 1923, f.p. in England, Gloucester 1925), No. 7 in C, Op. 105 (1924, f.p. under title *Fantasia sinfonica*, Stockholm 1924, f.p. in England, London 1927); Symphonic poems: *Kullervo*, sop., bar., male ch., and orch., Op. 7 (1892, f.p. Helsinki 1892, f.p. in England, Bournemouth 1970), *En Saga*, Op. 9 (1892, rev. 1901), *The Wood Nymph (Skogsrået)*, Op. 15 (1895), *Spring Song (Vårsång)*, Op. 16 (1894), *Tiera*, brass and perc., (1898), *Finlandia*, Op. 26 (1899, rev. 1900, orig. 6th tableau of 'Press Celebration' mus. from which *Scènes historiques* were also taken), *Pohjola's Daughter* (symphonic fantasia), Op. 49 (1906), *Night Ride and Sunrise*, Op. 55 (1907), *Luonnotar*, Op. 70, sop. and orch. (1910–13), *The Dryad*, Op. 45, No. 1 (1910), *The *Bard*, Op. 64 (1913, rev 1914), *The *Oceanides*, Op. 73 (1914), *Tapiola*, Op. 112 (1925–6); Suites, etc: *Karelia*, ov., Op. 10, suite Op. 11 (1893), *Rakastava*, str., triangle, and timp., Op. 14 (1911, see also UNACC. VOICES); *Lemminkäinen* (4 Legends), Op. 22 (1893–7), No. 3 is The *Swan of Tuonela; King Christian II*, Op. 27 (1898), *Scènes historiques* I, Op. 25 (1899, rev. 1911), II, Op. 66 (1912), *Romance* in C for str., Op. 42 (1903), *Valse triste*, Op. 44 (1904, being rev. of item of incidental mus. to *Kuolema), Scene with cranes,*

Op. 44 (1906, being rev. of Nos. 3 and 4 of *Kuolema*), Vn. Conc., Op. 47 (1903, f.p. Helsinki 1904, rev. 1905, f.p. Berlin 1905, f.p. in England, London 1907), *Autumn Evening*, Op. 38 No. 1 (1907, orch. of song), *Dance Intermezzo*, Op. 45 No. 2 (1907, orch. of pf. piece), *Pelléas et Mélisande*, Op. 46 (1905), *Belshazzar's Feast*, Op. 51 (1906–7), *Pan and Echo*, Op. 53 (1906), *Swanwhite*, Op. 54 (1908–9), *In Memoriam*, funeral march, Op. 59 (1909), *2 Pieces (Canzonetta and Valse romantique)*, Op. 62 (1911, for rev. version of *Kuolema)*, *2 Serenades*, vn. and orch., D major and G minor, Op. 69 (1912–13), *2 Pieces*, vn. (or vc.) and orch., *Cantique and Devotion*, Op. 77 (1914), *2 Humoresques*, vn. and orch., Op. 87 (1917), *4 Humoresques*, vn. and orch., Op. 89 (1917, 2 with str. only), *Valse lyrique*, Op. 96 No. 1 (1920), *Valse chevaleresque*, Op. 96 No. 3 (1920), *Suite mignonne*, fl. and str., Op. 98 No. 1 (1921), *Suite champêtre*, str., Op. 98 No. 2 (1921), *Andante festivo*, str. (1922, orig. str. qt.), *Suite caractéristique*, harp and str., Op. 100 (1922), *The *Tempest*, Suites I and II, Op. 109 (1925).

THEATRE MUSIC: *Karelia* (1893, unpubd.); *King Christian II* (A. Paul) Op. 27 (1897–8); *Kuolema* (Death) (A. Järnefelt) Op.44 (1903, 6 'scenes' for str., bass drum, and church bell); *Pelléas et Mélisande* (Maeterlinck), Op. 46 (1905); *Belshazzar's Feast* (H. Procopé), Op. 51 (1906); *Swanwhite* (Strindberg), Op. 54 (1908); *The Lizard (Ödlan)* (Lybeck), Op. 8, for vn. and str. quintet (1909, unpubd.); *2 Songs for 'Twelfth Night'* (Shakespeare), Op. 60, v. and guitar (or pf.) (1909); *Scaramouche* (Knudsen and Bloch), Op. 71 (1913); *Everyman* (Hofmannsthal), Op. 83 (1916, unpubd.); *The *Tempest* (Shakespeare), Op. 109 (1925).

VOICE(S) AND INSTR: *Kullervo*, Op. 7 (see ORCHESTRAL); *The Rapids-Shooter's Brides (Koskenlaskijan morsiamet)*, Op. 33, bar. or mez., and orch. (1897); *Song of the Athenians (Atenarnes sång)*, Op. 31 No. 3, boys' and men's vv., wind, and perc. (1899); *Impromptu*, Op. 19, women's ch. and orch. (1902, rev 1910); *The Origin of Fire (Tulen synty)*, Op. 32, bar., male ch., and orch. (1902, rev. 1910); *The Liberated Queen (Vapautettu Kuningatar)*, Op. 48, cantata (1906); *Luonnotar* (see ORCHESTRAL); *Scout March*, Op. 91 No. 2, ch. and orch. (?1917); *Song of the Earth (Jordens sång)*, Op. 93, cantata (1918); *Väinö's song (Väinön virsi)*, Op. 110 (1926); *Masonic Ritual Music*, Op. 113, male vv., pf., organ (1927); *Karelia's Fate*, male ch. and pf. (1930).

UNACC. VOICES: *Rakastava* (The Lover), Op. 14, male vv. (1893, see also ORCHESTRAL); *Natus in curas*, Op. 21 No. 2, male vv. (1896); *10 Songs for Mixed Chorus*, Op. 23 (1897, from *Cantata for University Ceremonies of 1897*); *Carminalia* (1899); *Nostalgia (Kotikaipaus)*, 3 women's vv. (1902); *9 Partsongs*, Op. 18, male vv. (1893–1904); *2 Partsongs*, Op. 65, mixed ch. (1911–12); *3 Songs for American Schools*, children's vv. (1913); 5

Partsongs, Op. 84, male vv. (1914–15); *In the moonlight (Kuntamolla)*, male vv. (1916); *Fridolin's Folly, The roaring of a wave, Jonah's voyage, One hears the storm outside*, male vv. (1917–18); 2 *Partsongs*, Op. 108, male vv. (1925); *Introductory Antiphons*, mixed ch. (1925); *The way to school*, children's vv. (1925); *You are mighty, O Lord*, mixed ch. (1927).

CHAMBER MUSIC: 2 *Pieces*, Op. 2, vn. and pf. (1888, rev. 1912); *Malinconia*, Op. 20, vc. and pf. (1901); Str. Qt. in D minor (*Voces Intimae*), Op. 56 (1908–9); 4 *Pieces*, Op. 78, vn. (or vc.) and pf. (1915–19); 6 *Pieces*, Op. 79, vn. and pf. (1915); sonatina in E, Op. 80, vn. and pf. (1915); 5 *Pieces*, Op. 81, vn. and pf. (1915); 5 *Danses Champêtres*, Op. 106, vn. and pf. (1925); 4 *Pieces*, Op. 115, vn. and pf. (1929); 3 *Pieces*, Op. 116, vn. and pf. (1929).

PIANO: 6 *Impromptus*, Op. 5 (1893); sonata in F, Op. 12 (1893); 10 *pieces*, Op. 24 (1894–1903); 6 *Finnish Folksongs* (1903); *Kyllikki* (3 Lyric Pieces), Op. 41 (1904); *Dance Intermezzo*, Op. 45 No. 2 (1904); 10 *Pieces*, Op. 58 (1909); 3 sonatinas, Op. 67, F♯ minor, E major, B♭ minor (1912); 2 *Rondinos*, Op. 68 (1912); 10 *Pensés Lyriques*, Op. 40 (1912–14); 4 *Lyric Pieces*, Op. 74 (1914); 5 *Pieces*, Op. 75 (1914); 13 *Pieces*, Op. 76 (c.1914); 10 *Pieces*, Op. 34 (1914–16); 5 *Pieces*, Op. 85 (1916); *Mandolinato* (1917); 6 *Pieces*, Op. 94 (1919); 6 *Bagatelles*, Op. 97 (1920); 8 *Pieces*, Op. 99 (1922); 5 *Romantic Pieces*, Op. 101 (1923); 5 *Pieces*, Op. 103 (1924); *Morceau romantique* (1925); 5 *Esquisses*, Op. 114 (1929).

ORGAN: 2 *Pieces*, Op. 111 (1925–31).

SONGS (VOICE AND PIANO): 7 *Songs of Runeberg*, Op. 13 (1891–2); 7 *Songs*, Op. 17 (1894); 6 *Songs*, Op. 36 (1899); 5 *Songs*, Op. 38 (1903–4, No. 1, *Autumn Evening*, with orch. 1907); *Extinct (Erloschen)* (1906); 6 *Songs*, Op. 50 (1906); 2 *Songs*, Op. 35 (1907–8); 8 *Songs*, Op. 57 (1909); 8 *Songs*, Op. 61 (1910); 5 *Christmas Songs*, Op. 1 (1895–1913); 6 *Songs*, Op. 72 (1907–15); 6 *Songs*, Op. 86 (1916); 6 *Songs*, Op. 88 (1917); 6 *Songs*, Op. 90 (1917).

Siciliano (a) (It.), **Sicilienne** (Fr.). Sicilian. Type of dance, song, or instr. piece, presumably of Sicilian origin, in compound duple or quadruple time and with a swaying rhythm, often in minor key. Usually pastoral in character and popular in 18th cent. 'Pastoral symphony' in Handel's *Messiah* is *alla siciliana*. Style uncommon after 18th cent., but Fauré used siciliano as 3rd entr'acte of his incidental music to *Pelléas et Mélisande* (1898).

Sicilian Vespers, The (Verdi). See *Vêpres siciliennes, Les*.

Side-Drum (snare-drum). Small cylindrical drum with parchment at each end, one having str. (snares) across it to add a rattling effect and thus increase brilliance of tone, other end being left for use of 2 drumsticks. Famous passage for side-drum occurs in first movement of *Nielsen's 5th sym., where player is instructed to improvise in order to drown the sound of the rest of the orch.

Sieben Letzten Worte, Die (Haydn). See *Seven Last Words, The*.

Siège de Corinthe, Le (The Siege of Corinth). Opera by Rossini to Fr. lib., prod. Paris 1826, London 1834, NY 1835. Rev. of earlier opera *Maometto II*, prod. Naples 1820, with It. lib. by C. della Valle.

Siege of Rhodes, The. Opera with mus. (lost) by Locke, H. Lawes, H. Cooke, C. Coleman, and G. Hudson to lib. by W. D'Avenant. Prod. London 1656. Said to be first Eng. opera.

Siegfried. Mus. drama in 3 acts by Wagner to his own lib., being 3rd part of Der *Ring des Nibelungen*. Comp. 1856–7, 1864–71. F.p. Bayreuth 1876, London 1882, NY Met. 1887.

Siegfried Idyll. Comp. for orch. by Wagner, comp. 1870 as birthday gift for his wife Cosima and f.p. on Christmas morning 1870, her 33rd birthday, and twice later in same day. F.p. by about 15 musicians, incl. Hans *Richter (who learned tpt. specially for the occasion), cond. Wagner, standing outside Cosima's bedroom in their villa at *Tribschen on shore of Lake Lucerne. Orig. scoring was for a few str., fl., ob., 2 cl., tpt., 2 hn., and bn., but Wagner later scored it for larger orch. Material is based on themes from unfinished str. qt., comp. 1864 when Wagner met Cosima, *motifs* from opera *Siegfried*, on Act III of which he was working in 1869 when their son Siegfried was born, and a lullaby he had noted (or comp.) in 1868. MS. ded. stated: 'Tribschen Idyll, with Fidi's Bird-Song and Orange Sunrise, presented as a Symphonic Birthday Greeting to his Cosima by her Richard, 1870.' 'Fidi' was domestic name for Siegfried, the 'orange sunrise' referred to memory of how the sunrise lit up the orange wallpaper on the morning of his birth. The Idyll was never intended for public perf., but financial hardship compelled Wagner to sell it in 1877 and it was pubd. 1878.

Siegfrieds Tod (Siegfried's Death). Proposed opera by *Wagner, lib. of which he wrote in 1848. From it developed the scheme for a 4-opera cycle on the legend of Siegfried and the Nibelung's Ring. *Siegfrieds Tod*, much rev., eventually became *Götterdämmerung* (f.p. Bayreuth 1876).

Siegmeister, Elie (b NY, 1909). Amer composer. Studied Columbia Univ. from 1924 (comp. with S. Bingham and private lessons with *Riegger), Paris 1927–32 (comp. with Boulanger), and Juilliard Sch., NY, 1935–8. Worked in NY as cond., pianist, and teacher. Founded Amer. Ballad Singers 1939 and toured with them for 5 years to promote Amer. folk mus. Joined teaching faculty at Hofstra Coll. (now Univ.) near NY, 1949, becoming prof. of mus. and composer-in-residence 1966. Author of several books. Works incl. opera *The Plough and the Stars* (1963–9), 5 syms., 3 vn. sonatas, 2 str. qts., pf. conc., vn. conc., cl. conc., fl. conc., choral works, sextet for brass and perc., etc.

Siems, Margarethe (*b* Wrocław, 1879; *d* Dresden, 1952). Ger. sop. Studied with Orgeni. Opera début Prague 1902. Member of Dresden Opera 1908–22. CG début 1913. Created Strauss roles of Chrysothemis in *Elektra*, Marschallin in Rosenkavalier, and Zerbinetta in *Ariadne auf Naxos* (first version, 1912). Taught in Berlin 1920 and in Dresden and Wrocław until 1940. Sang in concerts after Second World War and taught in Dresden.

Siepi, Cesare (*b* Milan, 1923). It. bass. Self-taught. Opera début at Schio, near Vicenzo, 1941 as Sparafucile in *Rigoletto*. Member of Scala, Milan, co. from 1946. CG début 1950 (Colline in *La Bohème*), NY Met. 1950 (Philip II in *Don Carlos*), Salzburg Fest. 1953–8. Memorable Don Giovanni, singing it with Furtwängler on several occasions. Member of Met. co. for 24 years.

Siesta. Comp. for small orch. by Walton, f.p. London 1926. Perf. as ballet *pas de deux*, choreog. Ashton, London 1936, and with new choreog. by Ashton 1972.

Sifflöte (Ger.). Whistle-flute. High-pitched org. stop (2′ or 1′).

Sight-Reading, Sight-Singing. The reading or singing of mus. at first sight in order to perform it. Various methods of sight-singing have been used through the centuries, from d'Arezzo's *Hexachords* in the 11th cent. to *Tonic sol-fa. Most Eng.-speaking countries now use systems based on *movable doh* or *fixed doh.

Signal horn. Another name for *bugle.

Signature. A 'sign' placed at the opening of a comp. or of a section of a comp., indicating the key (Key Signature) or the value of the beat and the no. of beats in each measure (Time Signature). The key signature consists of one or more sharps or flats; the time signature usually of figures resembling a fraction, e.g. $\frac{3}{4}$.

Signature-Tune. A term which gained currency in the 1920s with the growing popularity of dance-bands, especially when broadcasting. As a means of quick identification, each band began and ended its perf. with a tune, known as the 'signature tune'. Most bands used one tune, e.g. Jack Payne's *Say it with music,* but some used one tune at the beginning and another 'to sign off', e.g. Henry Hall played *It's just the time for dancing* at the start and *Here's to the next time* at the end. Individual variety artists introduced their acts with a signature-tune; and if one wished to be facetious, one could say that the *leitmotiv* of characters in Wagner's *Ring* are their 'signature-tunes'.

Signor Bruschino, Il; ossia il figlio per Azzardo. Opera in 1 act by Rossini to lib. by Foppa after Fr. comedy by de Chazet and Ourry. Prod. Venice 1813, NY Met. 1932, Orpington 1960.

Sigurd. Opera in 5 acts by *Reyer to lib. by Du Locle and Blau. Prod. Brussels and CG 1884, New Orleans 1891. Lib. is based on Nibelung legend which supplied basis of Wagner's *Ring* tetralogy.

Sigurd Jorsalfar (Sigurd the Crusader). Play by Bjørnson for which Grieg wrote 5 items of incidental mus., Op. 22, for Oslo perf. celebrating dramatist's 70th birthday, 1872. Titles are: 1. *Borghild's Dream* (intermezzo), 2. *Trial of Strength*, 3. Song: *The Northern people will wander*, 4. *Ceremonial March*, 5. *The King's song*. Nos. 1, 2, and 4 arr. for orch. as Op. 56 and rev. 1892 (also arr. for pf. 2 hands and 4 hands). No. 2 also arr. for vn. and pf., 1874.

Siki, Béla (*b* Budapest, 1923). Hung.-born pianist. Studied Budapest Univ. and Franz Liszt Acad. with Dohnányi and at Geneva Cons. with Lipatti. Début Budapest 1945. Won Liszt competition 1943. Settled in USA. Int. concert career. Prof. of pf., Univ. of Washington, Seattle, from 1965. Much in demand as juror for pf. comps.

Sikorski, Kazimierz (*b* Zürich, 1895). Polish composer. Studied Chopin Sch., Warsaw, and in Paris. Prof. of comp., Warsaw State Cons., 1928. Dir., Lódź Cons. from 1947. Works incl. 4 syms., 3 str. qts., hn. conc., choral mus., etc.

Sikorski, Tomasz (*b* Warsaw, 1939). Polish composer and pianist. Studied Warsaw State Coll. of Mus., 1956–62 (comp. with his father K. *Sikorski, pf. with Drzewiecki). Concert pianist, esp. in contemporary works. Comps. incl. *Concerto breve* for pf., 24 winds, 4 percussionists, pf. sonata, *Diafonia* for 2 pf., radio opera *Sinbad the Sailor,* and *Music from afar* for ch. and instr. Possibly first Polish *minimalist.

Silbermann. Ger. firm of org.-builders, hpd. and pf. manufacturers, founded in Strasbourg by Andreas Silbermann (*b* Klein-Bobritzsch, 1678; *d* Strasbourg, 1734) and his brother Gottfried (*b* Klein-Bobritzsch, 1683; *d* Dresden, 1753). Gottfried settled in Freiburg, building cath. org. there in 1714 and 46 other orgs., incl. Dresden court church. Was first Ger. pf.-maker. Andreas built Strasbourg Cath. org. and 29 others. Business carried on by descendants.

Silent Woman, The (R. Strauss). See *Schweigsame Frau, Die.*

Silja, Anja (*b* Berlin, 1940). Ger. sop. Opera début Brunswick 1955. Notable Wagnerian (Bayreuth from 1960). CG 1967 (*Fidelio*). Amer. début Chicago 1968 (Senta), NY Met. 1972. Remarkable singer-actress, especially in Wagnerian roles, as Strauss's Salome and Elektra, and as Berg's Marie and Lulu.

Silk, Dorothy (*b* King's Norton, 1883; *d* Alve-church, 1942). Eng. sop. Studied in Vienna. Notable singer of Bach and of Eng. mus., esp. works of Holst, Vaughan Williams, etc. Gave enterprising series of chamber concerts 1921–6 in which she sang works by the then rarely-performed Schütz and others.

Silken Ladder, The (Rossini). See *Scala di seta, La*.

Sills, Beverly (orig. Belle Silverman) (*b* Brooklyn, NY, 1929). Amer. sop. Studied NY. Child performer on radio and later in Gilbert and Sullivan. Opera début Philadelphia 1947. NY City Opera 1955 as Rosalinde in *Die Fledermaus*, beginning long assoc. with co. Sang Cleopatra in Handel's *Giulio Cesare* 1966. Milan début 1969 in *Siege of Corinth*, CG as Lucia di Lammermoor 1970, NY Met. 1975 (*Siege of Corinth*). Outstanding in coloratura roles. Dir., NY City Opera from 1979.

Siloti, Alexander. See *Ziloti, Alexander*.

Silver Band. Brass band with instr. coated with substance giving impression of silver.

Silveri, Paolo (*b* Ofena, nr. Aquila, 1913). It. bar. Studied Florence and Rome. Opera début as bass, Rome 1939. Bar. from 1944. CG début 1946, member of co. 1947–9. NY Met. 1950–3. Sang ten. role of Verdi's Otello, Dublin 1959. Outstanding as Falstaff, Scarpia, etc. Teacher in Rome from 1970.

Silverstein, Joseph (*b* Detroit, 1932). Amer. violinist and cond. Studied Curtis Institute 1945–50. Violinist in Houston S.O. and Philadelphia Orch., then leader Denver S.O. Joined Boston S.O. 1955, becoming leader 1961 and ass. cond. 1971. Frequent soloist and chamber-mus. player. Teacher at New England Cons.

Silvestri, Constantin (*b* Bucharest, 1913; *d* London, 1969). Romanian-born cond., pianist, and composer (Brit. citizen from 1967). Studied Bucharest Cons. Career as pianist until 1935, then coach and cond. Bucharest Opera 1935–60 (mus. dir. from 1955). Cond., Bucharest P.O. 1946. Prof. of cond. Bucharest Acad. of Mus. 1949. Cond. Bournemouth S.O. 1961–9. Wrote orch. and chamber mus.

Similar Motion. When any 2 vv. or parts of a comp. proceed notationally in the same direction they are in *similar motion*. If the procession is by the same intervals (numerically considered), it is called *parallel motion*.

Simile, Simili (It.). The same. Composer's direction in score to indicate that phrase, etc., is to be perf. in same manner as parallel preceding phrase, thus avoiding copying expression marks at each repetition.

Simionato, Giulietta (*b* Forlì, 1910). It. coloratura mez. Studied Rovigo. Winner of Bel Canto Competition, Florence 1933. Regular member of Scala, Milan, co. 1939–66. Sang at first Edinburgh Fest. 1947. CG début 1953 (Adalgisa, Amneris, and Azucena, all with *Callas), NY Met. 1959–63; Chicago from 1954. Voice of wide range and agility enabling her to sing brilliant Rossini, Bellini, and Donizetti roles. Retired 1966.

Simmes, William (*fl.* 1607–16). Eng. composer of viol fantasies, anthems, etc.

Simon, Abbey (*b* NY, 1922). Amer. pianist. Studied Curtis Institute, Penn., from age 8. Recital début NY 1940. Lived in Europe 1949–59. Int. career as conc. soloist. Teacher at Indiana Univ.

Simoneau, Léopold (*b* Quebec City, 1918). Canadian ten. Studied NY. Opera début Montreal 1941 as Hadji in *Lakmé*. Paris Opéra and CG 1947–9, Glyndebourne 1951 (Idamante in *Idomeneo* and Don Ottavio in *Don Giovanni*) and other seasons. Chicago Opera 1954. NY Met. 1963. Guest singer at Vienna Opera, Milan, Salzburg Fest., etc. Noted Mozartian. Art. dir. L'Opéra du Quebec 1971–2.

Simone Boccanegra. Opera in prol. and 3 acts by Verdi to lib. by Piave and Montanelli, based on play *Simón Boccanegra* by Gutiérrez. Comp. 1856–7. Prod. Venice 1857. Lib. rev. by Boito 1880, Verdi revising the score and composing new council chamber scene (Act I, Sc. 2). Prod. Milan 1881, NY Met. 1932, London (SW) 1948.

Simonov, Yury (Ivanovich) (*b* Saratov, 1941). Russ. cond. Studied Leningrad Cons. 1956–68. Won 5th int. cond. competition, Rome, 1968. Cond. Kislovodsk Phil. Soc. 1967–9, ass. cond. Leningrad P.O. 1968–9, Bolshoy Opera, Moscow, 1969, chief cond. from 1970. Teacher at Moscow Cons. from 1975.

Simple Symphony. 4-movement work for str. orch. (or str. qt.), Op. 4, by Britten, based on themes he wrote in 1923, 1924, 1925, and 1926 and re-scored in 1933. Movements are named: *Boisterous Bourrée, Playful Pizzicato, Sentimental Saraband, Frolicsome Finale*. F.p. Norwich, 1934.

Simple Time (duple, triple, quadruple, etc.). Time in which each beat in a measure has a simple note value, e.g. $\frac{3}{4}$ means 3 quarter-note (crotchet) beats in a measure, $\frac{4}{2}$ means four half-notes (minims) in a measure. Each beat has two equal subdivisions. See also *Compound Time* and *Time Signature*.

Simpson (Sympson), **Christopher** (*b* ?Westonby, Yorks., *c*.1605; *d* ?Holborn, London, 1669). Eng. composer, author, and player of viola da gamba. Wrote fancies, divisions, etc., for str. Author of important treatises, e.g. *The Division Violist* (1659), *Principles of Practical Music* (1665).

Simpson, Robert (Wilfred Levick) (*b* Leamington, 1921). Eng. composer, musicologist, and author. Pupil of *Howells 1942–6. On BBC mus.

staff 1951–80. Author of *Carl Nielsen, Symphonist* (1952) and *The Essence of Bruckner* (1967). Awarded Nielsen Medal (1956) and Bruckner Medal (1962). Works firmly based in tonality, with Beethoven as model for organic unity. Prin. works:

ORCH: Syms.: No. 1 (1951), No. 2 (1956), No. 3 (1962), No. 4 (1972), No. 5 (1972), No. 6 and No. 7 (1977), No. 8 (1979); pf. conc. (1967); vn. conc. (1959); *Allegro deciso*, str.; *Canzona* for brass (1958).

INCIDENTAL MUSIC: *The Pretenders* (Ibsen), *Samson Agonistes* (Milton).

BRASS BAND: *Energy*, symphonic study (1971).

CHAMBER MUSIC: Str. Qts.: No. 1 (1952), No. 2 (1953), No. 3 (1954), No. 4 (1973), No. 5 (1974), No. 6 (1975), No. 7 (1977), No. 8 (1979); *Variations and Fugue*, recorder and str. qt. (1959); Trio, cl., vc., pf. (1967); cl. quintet (1968); horn qt. (1976).

PIANO: *Variations and Finale on a Theme of Haydn* (1948); pf. sonata (1946).

Simpson, Thomas (b Milton-next-Sittingbourne, Kent, 1582; d after 1630). Eng. composer and viol player. Around 1610 was in Heidelberg court orch., and from 1622 to 1625 in Copenhagen royal orch. Pubd. 3 collections of consort music, incl. 53 of his own works.

Simrock, Nikolaus (b Mainz, 1751; d Bonn, 1832). Ger. publisher. Played hn. in Bonn court orch. with Beethoven. Founded publishing firm 1793 in Bonn, issuing many of Beethoven's works. Business continued by son and grandson. Firm moved to Berlin 1870. Publishers of Brahms's mus. Branches opened in London and Paris. Sold to Benjamin, of Hamburg, 1929.

Sin' (It.). Abbreviation of *sino*, until, e.g. *sin' al segno*, until the sign.

Sinatra, Frank (Francis Albert) (b Hoboken, NJ, 1915). Amer. singer (light bar.) and actor. Radio début 1938. Sang with Harry James Band (1939) and Tommy Dorsey Band (1940–2). Solo career from 1942, with radio shows. Inspired excitement among 'bobbysoxers' of 1940s unequalled until advent of Elvis Presley and Beatles. Had successful career as 'straight' film actor, e.g. *From Here to Eternity* (1952), *Von Ryan's Express* (1965), and *The Detective* (1968). Resumed vocal career and made international tours in 1970s. Secret of his artistry was his emphasis on significance of a song's lyrics.

Sinclair, George (Robertson) (b Croydon, 1863; d Birmingham, 1917). Eng. organist and cond. Studied Royal Irish Acad. of Mus. Ass. organist, Gloucester Cath. 1879. Organist and choirmaster, Truro Cath., 1880–9. Organist, Hereford Cath., 1889–1917, cond. at 3 Choirs Fest. 1891–1912. Cond. Birmingham Choral Union 1899–1917. Friend and champion of Elgar, who incl. him as the 11th (G.R.S.) of *Enigma Variations* (though the mus. is really about Sinclair's bulldog Dan).

Sinclair, Monica (b Evercreech, Somerset, 1926). Eng. mez. Studied RAM and RCM. Opera début, Carl Rosa 1948. CG from 1949. Glyndebourne 1954. Created role of Mme Popova in Walton's *The Bear*, 1967.

Sinding, Christian (b Kongsberg, Norway, 1856; d Oslo, 1941). Norweg. composer and pianist. Studied in Leipzig (1874–8), Berlin, Dresden, and Munich (1880–2). Lived in Oslo from 1882 apart from spell as teacher at Eastman Sch., NY, 1921–2. Life pension from Norweg. Govt. 1910. Works incl. operas, 4 syms., 3 vn. concs., pf. conc., pf. quintet, str. qt., over 200 songs, and many pf. pieces, incl. famous *Rustle of Spring* (*Frühlingsrauschen*), one of 6 *Pieces*, Op. 32 (1896).

Sinfonia (It.). Symphony. (1) Symphony.

(2) Bach's term for his 3-part inventions.

(3) Name given in Baroque period to orch. piece which served as 3-movement introduction to opera, suite, or cantata, i.e. an early form of ov. Operatic *sinfonia* standardized c.1690 by A. Scarlatti into so-called 'Italian overture'.

(4) In 20th cent., often means a chamber orch., e.g. Northern Sinfonia, English Sinfonia.

Sinfonia Antartica (Antarctic Symphony). Title given by *Vaughan Williams to his 7th sym. for orch., sop. solo, and women's ch., f.p. Manchester 1953. Work based on mus. composed 1947–8 for film *Scott of the Antarctic*, about Capt. Scott's last expedition to S. Pole, 1910–12. Score contains part for wind-machine.

Sinfonia Concertante. Term preferred to conc. by Haydn, Mozart, and others, for comp. for more than one solo instr. and orch., e.g. Mozart's for vn. and va. In 20th cent. Walton, Williamson, and others have used the term even where only one solo instr. is employed, to imply that solo part is more closely integrated with orch. than in a 'display' conc.

Sinfonia da Requiem. Orch. work in 3 movements, Op. 20, by Britten, comp. 1940 in memory of his parents. F.p. NY 1941, London 1942. Commissioned by Japanese Govt. to celebrate (spurious) 2,600th anniversary of Mikado's dynasty in 1940, and furiously rejected because of work's reference to terms from R.C. liturgy, e.g. *Dies Irae*.

Sinfonia Eroica (Beethoven). See *Eroica Symphony*.

Sinfonia Espansiva (Expansive Symphony). Subtitle of Nielsen's 3rd Sym., Op. 27, comp. 1910–11. F.p. Copenhagen 1912, cond. Nielsen; f. Eng. p. 1937 (broadcast), London (public) 1962. Sop. and bar. solo vv. used.

Sinfonia Sacra. Sym. by *Panufnik, comp. 1963, f.p. Monte Carlo, cond. Frémaux 1964.

Sinfonia Semplice (Simple Symphony). Sub-title of Nielsen's 6th sym., Op. posth., comp. 1924–5.

F.p. Copenhagen 1925, cond. Nielsen; f.p. in England 1954.

Sinfonietta (It.). Little symphony. (1) Short, and perhaps light, sym., e.g. those by Moeran, Roussel, and Janáček, whose *Sinfonietta* (1926) has a special brass ens. of 9 tpts., 2 ten. tubas, and 2 bass tpts., with 2 pairs of timpani. In finale 12 tpts. are used.
  (2) Small sym. orch., such as Bournemouth Sinfonietta, London Sinfonietta, etc.

Singakademie (Ger.). Singing-school. Choir founded in Berlin 1791 by *Fasch. Mendelssohn cond. it in 1829 revival of Bach's *St Matthew Passion*. Name has been appropriated by other choirs.

Singing. Mus.-making by the human v. either solo or with others. Styles of singing and methods of v. prod. have varied over the centuries. In 14th and 15th cents., use of *falsetto* was favoured, hence high range of much mus. of that era; in 17th and 18th cents., the *castrati* imparted special brilliance, purity, and flexibility to operatic roles, qualities inherited by the *bel canto* singers of early 19th cent. opera (Bellini, Donizetti, Rossini, etc.). In the 19th cent. the growing expressive and dramatic nature of mus., e.g. the works of Beethoven, Berlioz, Verdi, Wagner, etc., led to a new style of singing in which vocal characterization was regarded as of more importance than mere technical agility. In 20th cent., with jazz, *Sprechstimme*, and a host of effects required by *avant-garde* composers, the demands on singers' virtuosity and versatility became even heavier. At the same time, revival of interest in early and baroque mus. restored styles of earlier centuries.

Singing Saw. Ordinary handsaw held between player's knees and played on by a vn. bow (or, more rarely, struck with a drumstick); its blade is meanwhile bent, under a lesser or greater tension, by the player's left hand, so producing different pitches.

Singspiel (Ger.). Song-play. Type of opera, Ger. equivalent of *dramma per musica*, which developed *c*.1700, term orig. being applied to all operas. From *c*.1750, *Singspiel* implied an opera with spoken dialogue, comparable to Eng. ballad-opera and Fr. *opéra comique*, e.g. those by Hiller and Benda. Zenith was reached with Mozart's *Die Entführung aus dem Serail*, 1782 and *Die Zauberflöte*, 1791. Beethoven's *Fidelio* is technically a *Singspiel*, but term generally implies a comic or light subject.

Sinigaglia, Leone (*b* Turin, 1868; *d* Turin, 1944). It. composer. Pupil of Mandyczewski in Vienna and Dvořák in Prague, 1900–1. Rare among It. composers of his day in writing no opera. Wrote mainly instr. works, incl. orch. variations, *Romanza* for vc. and orch., chamber mus., choral pieces, and songs.

Sinistra (It.). Left (hand).

Sink-a-Pace (from Fr. *cinque-pace*). Name by which orig. 5-step form of *Galliard was known.

Sino (It.). Until. *Sin' al fine,* until the end; *sin' al segno,* until the sign, etc.

Sinopoli, Giuseppe (*b* Venice, 1946). It. composer and conductor. Studied Venice Cons. and graduated in medicine from Padua Univ. 1971. Attended Darmstadt summer courses 1968 and studied cond. with Swarowsky in Vienna 1972. Founded Bruno Maderna Ens., Venice, 1975, to play contemporary mus. CG début 1983 (Puccini's *Manon Lescaut*). Works incl. opera *Lou Salome* (1981), pf. conc. (1974–5), *Symphonic Imaginaire* for 3 solo vv., 10 children's vv., 3 ch., 3 orch. (1972–3), pf. sonata (1973–5), str. qt. (1977). Prin. cond. Philharmonia Orch. from 1984.

Sir John in Love. Opera in 4 acts by Vaughan Williams to his own lib. based on Shakespeare's *The Merry Wives of Windsor* (1600–01), with interpolations from other Elizabethan dramatists. Comp. 1924–8. Score quotes several folk-songs, incl. *Greensleeves,* which is sung by Mrs. Ford in Act III. Prod. London (RCM) 1929, NY (Columbia Univ.) 1949, London (SW) 1946. See also *In Windsor Forest*.

Sir Roger de Coverley. Eng. country dance to tune of uncertain orig. (being variant of *The Maltman,* a Scottish tune sometimes called *Roger the Cavalier*). First printed by Playford, 1685. Arrs. by Grainger, Bridge, etc.

Sistrum. Ancient type of rattle used in worship of goddess Isis, comprising rings or bells which jingled on a metal frame when shaken by handle. Sometimes called for by 19th-cent. composers.

Sitar. Indian long-necked lute, with 18 movable frets and wooden body. Orig. had 3 str., but 4 to 7 now common (5 melody and 2 drone if the latter). Nine to 13 or more sympathetic under-str. increase resonance. Played with plectrum worn on right forefinger or with finger-nails. Popularized outside India in 1950s by virtuosity of Ravi *Shankar.

Sivori, (Ernesto) **Camillo** (*b* Genoa, 1815; *d* Genoa, 1894). It. violinist and composer. Pupil of *Paganini, who wrote sonatas for him. Played in Paris 1827, London 1828, thereafter touring Europe extensively. Visited N. and S. Amer. 1846–50. Retired 1870. Had amazing technique but small tone. Wrote vn. concs., vn. pieces, *Souvenir de Norma,* etc.

Six Épigraphes Antiques (6 Ancient Inscriptions). Set of pf. duets by Debussy, comp. 1914. 1. *Pour invoquer Pan, dieu du vent d'été* (To invoke Pan, god of the summer wind); 2. *Pour un tombeau sans nom* (For a nameless tomb); 3. *Pour que la nuit soit propice* (That night may be propitious); 4. *Pour la danseuse aux crotales* (For the dancing girl with castanets); 5. *Pour l'égyptienne* (For the Egyptian girl); 6. *Pour remercier la pluie du matin* (To thank the morning rain). Orch. versions by Rudolf Escher and Erich Schmid.

Six-Four Chord. 2nd *inversion of a chord, e.g. C major chord with G in bass.

Six, Les (Fr.). The Six. Name applied by Fr. mus. critic Henri Collet in 1920 to group of young Fr. composers who, under influence of *Satie and Cocteau, had achieved notoriety for their advanced ideas. They were Auric, Durey, Honegger, Milhaud, Poulenc, and Tailleferre. However, they soon went their separate ways and did not long operate as a group.

Sixteenth Note. The note ♪ (semiquaver). Its rest is notated ♪.

Sixth. Interval in melody or harmony, encompassing 6 degrees of the major or minor scale, counting bottom and top notes. *Major 6th* is distance, for instance, from C up to A, *minor 6th* (semitone less) from C up to A♭, *augmented 6th* (semitone more) from C up to A♯. See *Neapolitan 6th.*

Sixty-Fourth Note. The note ♪ (hemidemisemiquaver). Rest is notated ♪.

Sizzle Cymbal. Cymbal with 5 or 6 small jingles (sizzlers) loosely attached to its upper surface. Played with special type of side-drumstick.

Skalkottas, Nikolaos (Nikos) (*b* Chalkis, 1904; *d* Athens, 1949). Greek composer and violinist. Studied at Athens Cons. 1914–20 and from 1921–33 in Berlin, being comp. pupil of Weill, Jarnach, and, most important, Schoenberg (1927–31). Studied vn. with Willy Hess, 1921–3. Returned to Gr. 1933, where his mus. attracted little attention and he comp. mainly in secret, working as back-desk orch. violinist. Collected Greek folk mus. After his death, committee was formed to promote interest in and publication of his mus., much of which was written in the 12-note system, but after 1938 was often freely atonal. Works incl.:

ORCH: *Symphonic Suite* No. 1 (1929, rev. 1935), No. 2 (1944, orch. 1946–9); Conc. for wind (1929); conc. for pf. and vn. (1929–30); pf. concs.: No. 1 (1931), No. 2 (1937–8), No. 3 for 10 winds and perc. (1939); *36 Greek Dances* (1933–6); *9 Greek Dances* for large wind orch. (transcr. from *36 Greek Dances*, 1936); vc. conc. (1937–8); *The Maid and Death,* ballet suite (1938); vn. conc. (1937–8); conc. for vn., va., large wind orch. (1939–40); *10 Sketches* for str. (1940); db. conc. (1942–3); *Little Suite* for str. (1942); *The Return of Ulysses* (1942–3); conc. for 2 vn. (1944–5); *5 Short Greek Dances* (1946); *Classical Symphony* in A, for wind (1947); *Sinfonietta* in B♭ (1948); *Ballet Suite* (1948); *The Sea,* ballet (1949); Pf. Concertino in C (1949).

CHORAL, etc.: *The Unknown Soldier* (1949); *The Mayday Spell,* narrator, sop., dancers, orch. (1944–9).

CHAMBER MUSIC: Str. Qt. (1923–24); Str. Qts.: No. 1 (1928), No. 2 (1929), No. 3 (1935), No. 4 (1940); Easy Str. Qt. (1929); Str. Trio (1923–4); sonata, solo vn. (1925); Vn. Sonatinas, No. 1 (1928), No. 2 (1929), Nos. 3 and 4 (1935); vn. sonata No. 1 (1928), No. 2 (1940); Octet, 4 woodwind and str. qt. (1931); *Piece* for 8 woodwind or double str. qt. (1931); pf. trio (1936); *March of the Little Soldiers,* vn. and pf. (1937–8); *Rondo,* vn. and pf. (1936); *Little Chorale and Fugue,* vn. and pf. (1936); *8 Variations on a Greek Theme,* pf. trio (1938); *Suite,* vc. and pf. (1938); vc. sonata (1938); concertino, ob. and pf. (1939); *Duo,* vn. and pf. (1938); *Largo,* vc. and pf. (1941–2); Qt. for pf. and winds, No. 1 (1941–3), No. 2 (1941–3); concertino, tpt. and pf. (1940–2); *Sonate concertante,* bn., pf. (1943); *Little Suite,* vn. and pf., No. 1 (1946), No. 2 (1949); *Echo,* harp (1947); *Duo,* vn. and vc. (1947); *Bolero,* vc. and pf. (1945); *Little Serenade,* vc. and pf. (1945); vc. sonatina (1949); *Tender Melody,* vc. and pf. (1949).

VOICE(S) AND PIANO: *Sometime* (1939); *The Moon* (1942); *16 Songs* (poems by Evelpidis) (1941).

PIANO: *Greek Suite* (1924); *Suite* for 2 pf. (1924); *Sonatina* (1927); *15 Little Variations* (1927); *10 Canons* (1936); *32 Pieces* (1940); *Piano Suites,* No. 1 (1936), Nos. 2, 3, and 4 (1940); *4 Études* (1940).

Sketch (Ger. *Skizze;* Fr. *esquisse*). (1) Short piece, usually for pf. and often pictorial in intention, e.g. 'Woodland Sketch'.
(2) Composer's preliminary jottings out of which work is built, of great fascination to mus. scholars as showing workings of composer's mind (e.g. Beethoven's sketchbooks show how a comp. went through many stages over several years).

Skram, Knut (*b* Hjörundfjord, 1937). Norweg. bar. Studied Wiesbaden and Rome. Sang with Norwegian Opera, Oslo, from 1964. Glyndebourne from 1969. Also Lieder singer (esp. Strauss).

Skrowaczewski, Stanislaw (*b* Lwów, 1923). Polish-born cond. and composer (Amer. cit. from 1963). Studied at Lwów Acad., Kraków Cons., and in Paris with Boulanger. Early career as pianist until injury. Comp. 4 syms., str. qt., film scores, and songs, but became known as cond.: Wrocław P.O. 1946–7, Katowice Nat. P.O. 1949–54, Kraków P.O. 1955–6, Warsaw Nat. P.O. 1957–9. Amer. début Cleveland Orch. 1958. Mus. dir. Minneapolis (later Minnesota) S.O. 1960–79. Prin. cond. Hallé Orch. from 1984.

Skryabin, Alexander (Nikolayevich) (*b* Moscow, 1872; *d* Moscow, 1915). Russ. composer and pianist, son of a lawyer and his wife who was a brilliant pianist. Prodigy pianist; enrolled in Moscow Cadet School but studied pf. with N. S. Zverev. Entered Moscow Cons. 1888, studying pf. with Safonov and comp. with Taneyev and Arensky. While at the cons., attracted notice of the publisher Belayev who issued his early comps. under generous terms and in 1896 sponsored Skryabin's tour of Europe as pianist in his own works. Prof. of pf., Moscow Cons., 1898–1903, an occupation with which he became increasingly bored. Settled in Switz. 1903 when former pupil settled annuity on him. Toured USA 1906–7 and found new publisher and champion in *Koussevitzky. Since 1905 he had been under the influence of Mme. Blavatsky's theosophy and mystical influences; regarded his works from that date as preparation for a 'supreme ecstatic mystery' which would accompany a final cataclysm. Toured Russ. 1910 with Koussevitzky's orch. and in 1911 perf. his works with Mengelberg and Concertgebouw Orch. of Amsterdam. Visited London 1914 for perf. of his *Prometheus* under Wood and to play his pf. conc. and give recitals. Toured Russ. 1914 then became ill, dying from septicaemia from tumour on his lip.

Skryabin's early works are strongly flavoured by Chopin and Liszt. As he developed his personal theories he grew harmonically bolder in his pf. works, using chords built of 4ths and sometimes of 2nds, sometimes achieving what has been called 'impressionist atonality'. In his sym.-poem, *Prometheus,* and 7th pf. sonata, he developed the 'mystic' chord, a series of 4ths—C, F♯, B♭, E, A, and D. This extreme chromaticism was combined with a strong feeling for classical form. His obsession with extra-mus. ideas has tended to divert attention from the undoubted excellent qualities of his mus. Prin. works:

ORCH: Syms.: No. 1 in E, with ch. (1899–1900, f.p. 1900), No. 2 in C minor (*c.* 1901, f.p. 1903), No. 3 in C, *Bozhestvennaya poema* (*Divine Poem, 1902–4, f.p. 1905); Sym.-Poems: *Poema ekstasa* (*Poem of Ecstasy, 1905–8, f.p. 1908), *Prometei—Poema ogyna* (*Prometheus—The Poem of Fire, 1908–10, f.p. 1911); Pf. Conc. in F♯ minor (1896).

PIANO: Sonatas: No. 1 in F minor (1892), No. 2 in G♯ minor (*Fantasy*) (1892–7), No. 3 in F♯ minor (1897), No. 4 in F♯ (1903), No. 5 in F♯ (1907), No. 6 in G (1911), No. 7 in F♯ (*White Mass*) (1911), No. 8 in A (1913), No. 9 in F (*Black Mass*) (1913), No. 10 in C (1913); 24 *Études*; 85 *Preludes*; *Concert Allegro* in B♭ minor; Waltzes, Impromptus, Mazurkas, etc.

Sladen, Victoria (*b* London, 1910). Eng. sop. Studied Berlin, Vienna, and London. Opera début London 1942. Member SW opera co. 1943–50, CG 1947–8, 1950–2.

Slancio (It.). Dash. Impetuosity, outburst, thus *con slancio,* with impetuosity.

Slargando, Slargandosi (It.). Slowing. Same as *rallentando.*

Slatkin, Leonard (*b* Los Angeles, 1944). Amer. cond. and pianist. Studied Juilliard Sch. and with Süsskind. Début with Youth S.O. of NY, 1966. Mus. dir. New Orleans P.O. and of St Louis S.O. from 1979. London début 1974 (RPO). Guest cond. of leading Amer., Brit., and European orchs.

Slavonic Dances. 2 sets of dances by *Dvořák in folk-mus. style but 'original' in melody. Written for pf. duet, Nos. 1–8, Op. 46, in 1878, Nos. 9–16, Op. 72, in 1886. All orch. by Dvořák, in which form they are now usually heard.

Slavonic Rhapsodies. 3 comps. for orch. by Dvořák, Op. 45, comp. 1878, in vein of folk-mus. but all 'original': No. 1 in D, No. 2 in G minor, No. 3 in A♭.

Sleeping Beauty, The (*Spyashchaya krasavitsa*). Ballet in prol. and 3 acts with mus. by *Tchaikovsky to lib. by Petipa and Vsevolojsky, based on Perrault's fairy-tale, choreog. Petipa. Comp. 1888–9. Prod. St Petersburg 1890, London 1921 (under title The Sleeping Princess). Last act sometimes perf. separately as *Aurora's Wedding.* Additions to orig. choreog. by Ashton, 1968, and MacMillan 1973.

Slentando (It.). Becoming slower; same as *rallentando.*

Slezak, Leo (*b* Krásná Hora, 1873; *d* Egern am Tegernsee, 1946). Austro-Cz. ten. Studied with J. de Reszke in Paris 1908–9. Sang in ch. of Brno Opera, making début there 1896 as Lohengrin. Berlin Royal Opera 1898–9. Engaged by Mahler for Vienna Opera 1901, remaining until 1927 (when he was made hon. member and made occasional guest appearances until 1933). CG début 1900 (Lohengrin) and 1909 (Otello). NY Met. 1909–13 (singing Herman in Amer. première of Queen of Spades under Mahler, 1910). Guest singer in world's leading opera houses. Man of towering height with dramatic power and sense of humour to match. Fine Lieder singer. On retirement wrote several books and appeared in Austrian films as comedian. His son Walter was in several Hollywood films and in *Die Fledermaus* at NY Met.

Slide. (1) In vn.-playing, expressive means of passing from one note to another, usually at distance of a 3rd or 4th. Paganini introduced virtuoso slide by executing chromatic passages, singly or in 3rds, with the same fingers.
(2) Device fitted to wind instr. to adjust the pitch by altering length of vibrating air-column. Mainly used on tb.
(3) An ornament; when 2 or more notes approach main note by conjunct *motion.

Slide Trumpet. Mechanism, as in the tb., was fitted to tpts. as early as 15th cent. Bach probably meant this instr. when he scored for *tromba da tirarsi*. At beginning of 19th cent. new device was invented with springs to bring back slide to normal position. This lacked agility and became obsolete on invention of valve tpt.

Slobodskaya, Oda (*b* Vilno, 1888; *d* London, 1970). Russ. sop. Studied St Petersburg. Opera début there 1918 in *Queen of Spades* (Lisa). Left Russia for Paris 1922. London début 1931 (CG 1932). Appeared in operetta in London 1930–2 as Odali Careno. Sang in first London stage perf. of Delius's *Koanga* 1935. Created role of Prasha in Stravinsky's *Mavra*, 1922.

Slonimsky, Nicolas (*b* St Petersburg, 1894). Russ.-born Amer. cond., composer, and lexicographer. Studied pf. and comp. at St Petersburg Cons. Settled in USA 1923, becoming Amer. citizen 1931. Cond. concerts of Amer. mus. in Europe 1931–2, incl. *Ives's Three Places in New England, and cond. f.ps. in USA of works by Varèse (world premières), Riegger, Cowell, and Chávez. Comps. used atonal, polytonal, and quarter-tone effects. Founder and cond., Boston Chamber Orch., 1927–34. Ed. of complete rev. of *Baker's Biographical Dictionary of Musicians* (5th, 6th, and 7th edns. 1958, 1978, 1984). Author of *Music Since 1900* (chronological list of major mus. events throughout world), contrib. to many dictionaries and encyclopaedias.

Slonimsky, Sergey (*b* Leningrad, 1932). Russ. composer, nephew of Nicolas *Slonimsky. Studied Moscow (comp. with Shebalin) 1943–5, Leningrad Mus. Sch. (comp. with Arapov) 1945–50, Leningrad Cons. (comp. with Evlakhov) 1950–5. Teacher of comp., Leningrad Cons. from 1959. Collector of folk mus., which has influenced his works. Comps. incl. operas, syms., chamber mus., cantatas, song-cycles, ballet, and *Choreographic Miniatures* for orch. (1963).

Slur. Curved line used in musical notation to group together notes. Most common indication is that notes concerned are to be played or sung smoothly (*legato*). For a str.-player, this signifies that the notes should be taken in one stroke of the bow, for a wind-player or singer that they should be taken in one breath. If notes within slur have dots above or below, this means they are to be played slightly detached. Slur also used in vocal mus. to indicate that one syllable is to be sung to several notes.

Smallens, Alexander (*b* St Petersburg, 1889; *d* Tucson, Arizona, 1972). Russ.-born cond. Taken to USA 1890, Amer. citizen from 1919. Studied Institute of Mus. Art, NY, and Paris Cons., 1909–11. Ass. cond., Boston Opera House 1911–14; cond. Chicago Opera 1919–23, mus. dir. Philadelphia Civic Opera 1924–31. Ass. cond., Philadelphia Orch. 1927–34. Mus. dir. Radio City Music Hall, NY, 1947–50. Long assoc. with contemporary mus. Cond. f.ps. of Prokofiev's *Love for 3 Oranges* (Chicago 1921), de Koven's *Rip Van Winkle*, Thomson's *Four Saints in Three Acts*, and Gershwin's *Porgy and Bess* (1935; also cond.

revival 1942 and int. tour 1956). Cond. f. Amer. ps. of Strauss's *Feuersnot* (1927) and *Ariadne auf Naxos,* (1928) and of Rimsky-Korsakov's *Invisible City of Kitezh.*

Smalley, Roger (*b* Swinton, Manchester, 1943). Eng. composer and pianist. Studied RCM 1961–5 and later with Stockhausen. Specialized as pianist in contemporary mus. Co-founder, 1969, of Intermodulation, instr. ens. for scores involving live elecs. (disbanded 1976). Uses elec. and aleatory techniques in comps. On staff Univ. of W. Australia from 1976. Author of articles on contemporary mus. Prin. works:

ORCH: *Beat Music*, with amplified instr. (1971); *Gloria tibi Trinitas I* (1965); *Variations*, str. (1964–7); *Strata*, 15 solo str. (1971); *Konzertstück*, vn. and orch. (1980); Sym. (1979–81).

VOCAL: *Elegies* (4 Rilke poems), sop., ten., orch. (1965); *The Crystal Cabinet*, unacc. ch. (1967); *Missa brevis*, 16 solo vv. (1967); *The Song of the Highest Tower*, sop., bar., ch., orch. (1968); *William Derrincourt*, bar., male vv., chamber ens. (1977).

INSTR. ENS.: *Melody Study* I and II (1970); *Missa Parodia I*, pf. solo, II, pf. nonet (1967); *Pulses*, brass and perc. (1969); *Monody*, pf. and elecs. (1972); *Transformation*, pf. and live elecs.; *Zeitebenen*, 4 players and prepared tape (1973).

CHAMBER MUS.: Str. sextet (1965); 6 *Modular Pieces*, 4 fl. (1976–7); str. qt. (1979); *Movement*, fl., pf. (1980).

PIANO: Pf. pieces I–V (1962–3); *Accord*, 2 pf. (1975).

Smallman, (Frederick) **Basil** (Rowley) (*b* Croydon, 1921). Eng. teacher, pianist, and cond. Studied Oxford Univ. Lecturer in mus., Nottingham Univ., 1950–64, prof. of mus. Liverpool Univ. from 1965.

Smanioso (from It. *smania,* 'frenzy'). With furious excitement; also *smaniato* and *smaniante.*

Smareglia, Antonio (*b* Pola, 1854; *d* Grado, 1929). It. composer. Studied Milan Cons. 1873–7. Wrote 9 operas in Wagnerian style, most famous being *Nozze Istriane* (Trieste 1895), and symphonic poem *Eleonora* (1877). Blind from 1903.

Smart, (Sir) **George** (Thomas) (*b* London, 1776; *d* London, 1867). Eng. cond., composer, organist, violinist, and teacher. Chorister in Chapel Royal. Violinist, *Salomon's concerts. Knighted 1811. Organist, Chapel Royal from 1822, composer to Chapel Royal from 1838. One of founders of Phil. Soc., London, 1813, and one of its conds. 1813–44. Cond. f.p. in England of Beethoven's 9th Sym., 1825. Weber died while staying at Smart's London home, 1826. Cond. many Eng. choral fests. Cond. f.ps. in England of Beethoven's *Christus am Ölberge* (London 1814) and Mendelssohn's *St Paul* (Liverpool, 1836). Was cond. at Manchester fest. 1836 on occasion of *Malibran's fatal collapse. Dir. of mus. for coronations of William IV (1830) and Victoria (1837). Notable singing teacher. Wrote church mus., ed. O. Gibbons's madrigals and Handel's *Dettingen Te Deum.*

Smetáček, Václav (*b* Brno, 1906; *d* Prague, 1986). Cz. conductor and oboist. Studied Prague Cons. 1922–30 (oboe with Skuhrovský, cond. with Doležil and Dědeček). Founded Prague Wind Quintet 1928, playing in it until 1955. Oboist in Czech P.O. 1930–33. Cond., Prague Radio Orch., 1934–43. Prof. of oboe and cond., Prague Cons. and Prague Acad., 1945–66. Eng. début 1938. Noted interpreter of operas of Smetana and Janáček.

Smetana, Bedřich (*b* Litomyšl, 1824; *d* Prague, 1884). Bohem. composer, pianist, and cond., regarded as the founder of Czech mus. Played in str. qt. at age 5, pf. recital at 6, and wrote first comp. at 8. Settled in Prague in 1843, working as teacher to aristocratic family while having lessons from J. Proksch. Heard Liszt play and became close friend. Took part in fighting at barricades during abortive 1848 nationalist uprising. Set up mus. sch. but in 1856 went to Sweden as dir. of Göteborg Phil. Soc. Visited Liszt in Weimar and comp. 3 symphonic poems on Lisztian lines, incl. *Wallenstein's Camp* (1858–9). Returned to Prague 1861 but, through financial instability, toured Europe as concert pianist until 1863, coinciding with reawakening of Cz. nationalist fervour after Austria's defeat by Hungary. Became cond. of a Prague choral soc. and critic for daily newspaper. His patriotic opera *The Brandenburgers in Bohemia,* was prod., after much controversy, at Prague Provisional Th. (est. 1862) in 1866 and won him public success. Smetana was appointed cond. of the th. and dir. f.p. of *The Bartered Bride* (1866), which was a triumph. For laying of foundation-stone of permanent Prague Nat. Th. in 1868 he comp. the opera *Dalibor.* This was failure and was criticized as insufficiently nationalist because of Wagnerian influences on score. Resigned conductorship of Provisional Th. in 1874 because of total deafness, the result of venereal disease. Over next 5 years comp. his cycle of 6 symphonic poems *Má Vlast* (My Country) and in 1876 wrote his E minor str. qt. subtitled 'From My Life', in which the high-pitched note heard in finale represents the noise in his head which he experienced continually during onset of deafness. Living in isolation in the country, he comp. choral pieces and 2 operas *The Kiss* and *The Secret.* During 1880s nat. celebrations marked his achievement and his opera *Libuše* was chosen to inaugurate Prague Nat. Th. in 1881. Encouraged, comp. last opera, *The Devil's Wall,* but this was a failure in 1882, though it contains some of his best mus. He worked on *Viola,* an adaptation of Shakespeare's *Twelfth Night* which had occupied him for many years, but wrote only 363 bars before he became insane and died in asylum.

Smetana was buried as a nat. hero. With *The Bartered Bride* he wrote the incomparable masterpiece of folk-opera. His other operas had to wait until many years after his death for a proper appreciation of their virtues. Inevitably there was a Germanic influence on his work, since he grew up under Austrian domination of Czech culture, but although Janáček and later composers are more truly 'Czech', the ground was furrowed by Smetana, and his mus. has freshness and strength which ensure its popularity. Prin. works:

OPERAS: *The Brandenburgers in Bohemia (Branibori u Čechách)* (1863); *The *Bartered Bride (Prodaná Nevěstá)* (1863–6, rev. 1869 and 1870); **Dalibor* (1865–7, rev. 1870); *Libuše* (1869–72); *The *Two Widows (Dvě vdovy)* (1873–4, rev. 1877, 1882); *The *Kiss (Hubička)* (1875); *The *Secret (Tajemství)* (1877–8); *The Devil's Wall (Čertova Stěna)* (1879–82); *Viola* (unfinished, 1874, 1883–4).

ORCH: *Triumph Symphony* in E (1854); symphonic poems: *Richard III* (1858), *Wallenstein's Camp* (1858–9), *Hakon Jarl* (1861); *Festival Overture* (1868); **Má Vlast* (1874–9); *Carnival in Prague* (1883).

CHAMBER MUSIC: Pf. Trio in G minor (1855, rev. 1857); Str. Qts.: No. 1 in E minor (*Z mého života,* Eng. **From my Life,* Ger. *Aus meinem Leben*) (1876); No. 2 in D minor (1882–3); *From my Home,* duets for vn. and pf. (1880).

VOCAL: Male vv.: *The Three Horsemen* (1882), *The Renegade* (1864), *The Farmer, Peasant Song* (1868), *Sea Song* (1877), *The Dower,* Prayer (1880). Female vv.: *3 Choruses* (1878). Mixed vv.: *Song of the Czechs,* cantata with orch. (1878), *Our Song* (1883).

PIANO: *6 Characteristic Pieces* (1848), *Album Leaves* (1851), *Sketches* (1856–7), *3 Polkas, 3 Poetical Polkas* (1855), *Memories of Bohemia* (1859–60), *At the Seashore* (1862), *Dreams* (1874–5), *14 Czech Dances* (1877–9, orch. by others).

Smetana Quartet. Cz. string quartet formed in 1945 by students of J. Micka at Prague Cons. Début Prague, Nov. 1945. First va. player was Václav *Neumann, who left in 1946 to pursue cond. career. Other changes in personnel have also occurred. First tour abroad (Poland) 1950. London début 1955, NY 1957. Quartets by Dvořák, Janáček and Smetana are basis of repertory. Many recordings.

Smeterlin, Jan (*b* Bielsko, 1892; *d* London, 1967). Polish-born pianist. Studied in Vienna; pupil of Godowsky. Amer. début 1930. Int. reputation as Chopin player. Settled in Eng.

Smit, Leo (*b* Philadelphia, 1921). Amer. composer and pianist. Studied Curtis Institute 1930–2. Comp. studies with N. Nabokov, 1935. Worked as pianist with Balanchine ballet 1936–7 and NY City Sym. 1947–8. Taught at various colleges and univs. Prof. Fred Hoyle, Eng. astronomer, wrote lib. for his opera *The Alchemy of Love* (1969). Works incl. ballet *Virginia Sampler* (1947), 2 syms., pf. conc., *Academic Graffiti* for v. and chamber ens. (text by Auden), chamber mus., etc.

Smith, Alice Mary (*b* London, 1839; *d* London, 1884). Eng. composer. Pupil of Macfarren. Wrote 2 syms., 5 cantatas (incl. *Ode to the Passions,* Hereford Fest. 1882), 3 str. qts., 4 pf. qts., cl. conc., and many songs.

Smith, Cecil (*b* Chicago, 1906; *d* London, 1956). Amer. mus. critic. Studied with *Piston at Harvard Univ. Taught at Chicago Univ. 1929–46. Mus. critic, *Chicago Tribune* 1936–42. Ed., *Musical America* 1948–51. Worked in Eng. from 1951 as mus. critic, *Daily Express.* Contributor to *Opera,* etc.

Smith, Cyril (James) (*b* Middlesbrough, 1909; *d* East Sheen, 1974). Eng. pianist. Studied RCM. Played at Henry Wood Promenade Concert 1929. Prof. of pf. RCM from 1934. Fine interpreter of Rakhmaninov. Well-known as pf. duettist with wife, Phyllis *Sellick. On their visit to USSR 1956, had stroke which deprived him of use of one hand, but continued to play duets for 3 hands, several works being specially comp. for them (by Bliss, Arnold, Jacob, etc.). O.B.E. 1971.

Smith, David (Stanley) (*b* Toledo, 1877; *d* New Haven, Conn., 1949). Amer. composer, teacher, and cond. Studied with H. *Parker at Yale, then in Munich and Paris. Joined Yale Univ. mus. faculty 1916, succeeding Parker as dean, 1920–46. Cond., New Haven S.O. Wrote 4 syms. and other orch. works, cantatas, 10 str. qts., str. sextet, songs, etc.

Smith, 'Father' (really Bernhard Schmidt) (*b* c.1630; *d* London, 1708). Ger.-born org.-builder. Went to Eng. 1666 after Restoration, when use of org. was renewed in churches. With 2 nephews, built orgs. for St Margaret's, Westminster (1675), St Paul's Cath. (1697), Temple Church (1684), Banqueting Hall, Whitehall (1699), Durham Cath. (1683), Sheldonian Th., Oxford, etc. Organist, St Margaret's, Westminster, from 1676.

Smith (Schmidt), **John Christopher** (*b* Anspach, 1712; *d* Bath, 1795). Ger.-born composer and kbd. player. Went to Eng. as child, becoming pupil of Handel, Pepusch, and Roseingrave. In Europe 1745–8. Organist, Foundling Hospital Chapel from 1754; played org. at Handel oratorio perfs. Wrote 10 operas (incl. *The Tempest*), oratorio *Paradise Lost* and others, songs, hpd. suites, and ovs. for Garrick productions at Drury Lane.

Smith, John Stafford (*b* Gloucester, 1750; *d* London, 1836). Eng. composer, ten., and organist. Taught by father (organist of Gloucester Cath.) and Boyce. Chorister, Chapel Royal 1761, Gentleman, Chapel Royal from 1784, organist from 1802, master of choristers 1805–17. Pubd. *Musica Antiqua,* 1812, coll. of Eng. mus. from 12th to 18th cents. Wrote church mus., canons, glees, etc. Wrote song *To Anacreon in Heaven* from which *The Star-Spangled Banner* was adapted.

Smith, Julia (*b* Denton, Texas, 1911). Amer. composer and pianist. Studied Juilliard Sch. (comp. with R. Goldmark, orch. with Wagenaar) and NY Univ. Taught at various colleges of mus., then devoted herself from 1946 to comp. and playing. Works incl. 6 operas, pf. conc., str. qt., etc.

Smith, Nicholas (Richard Norman) (*b* Manchester, 1948). Eng. cond. Studied Birmingham Univ. and N.S.M. Taught RNCM, Manchester, 1973–5. Prin. cond. Northern Chamber Orch. from 1971.

Smith, Ronald (*b* London, 1922). Eng. pianist and composer. Studied RAM and privately in Paris. Début, London 1942. Specialist in mus. of *Alkan, about whom he has written books. Some orch. comps.

Smith, Russell (*b* Tuscaloosa, Alabama, 1927). Amer. composer. Studied Columbia Univ. 1948–53, later with Copland. Teacher at various colleges. Ed. for Ricordi in NY 1961–5 and H. W. Gray 1965–66. Composer-in-residence Cleveland Orch. 1966–7, New Orleans P.O. 1969–70. Also writer on mus. Comps. incl. opera, 2 pf. concs., ballet *Antigone, Anglican Mass,* chamber mus., etc.

Smith, William Charles (*b* London, 1881; *d* Bromley, 1972). Eng. musicologist, authority on Handel. Had large Handel coll. and wrote books about him. On staff British Museum 1900–44, being Assistant Keeper of Printed Books 1920–44. Specialist in mus. bibliography, esp. of 17th and 18th cents., with interest in Eng. mus. engravers and publishers of the period.

Smith Brindle, Reginald (*b* Bamber Bridge, Lancs., 1917). Eng. composer and author. Studied Univ. College of N. Wales, Bangor, 1946–9, S. Cecilia Acad., Rome, 1949–52 (comp. with Pizzetti). Studied privately with Dallapiccola in Florence 1949 and 1952–3. Worked for It. radio 1956–61. Taught at Univ. Coll., Bangor, 1967–70. Prof. of mus., Surrey Univ., from 1970. Mus. influenced by It. *avant-garde* sch. of Berio, Maderna, Nono, etc. Books incl. *Serial Composition* (1966), *Contemporary Percussion* (1970), *The New Music* (1975). Prin. works:

OPERA: *Antigone* (1969).

ORCH.: Sym. (1954); *Variations on a Theme of Dallapiccola* (1955); *Epitaph for Alban Berg,* str. (1955); *Symphonic Variations* (1957); *Cosmos* (1959); *Via Crucis,* str. (1960); *Homage to H. G. Wells* (1960); cl. conc. (1960); *Creation Epic* (1964); *Apocalypse* (1970); *Interface* (1972); *Fons bonitatis II* (1973).

CHORUS AND ORCH.: *Gráfico de la Petenera* (1956); *Extremum Carmen* (1961); *Worlds Without End,* speaker, vv., orch., tapes (1973).

UNACC. CHORUS: *Vivo sin Vivir* (1968); *Discoveries* (1970); *Windhover* (1971).

VOICE AND INSTR.: *Genesis Dream* (1962); *3 Japanese Lyrics* (1966); *Amalgam* (1968).

CHAMBER MUSIC: *String Quartet Music* (1958); *Concerto for 5 instr. and perc.* (1960); *Tre dimensione*, harp, vibraphone, hpd. (1965); *Segments and Variants*, wind quintet (1965); *In memoriam Jan Palach*, elec. organ (1969); *Tubal Cain's Legacy*, tb., pf. (1973); *The Walls of Jericho*, tuba, tape (1975); *Conc. on Cum Jubilo*, brass quintet (1975).

GUITAR: *Variants* (1970); *Trio*, 3 guitars (1970); *Concerto breve*, 8 guitars and perc. (1970); *Memento* (1973); *Conc. de Angelis*, 4 guitars (1973, arr. 3 guitars 1974); *November Memories* (1974); *Do not go gentle* (1974); *4 Poems of Lorca* (1975); *Guitar Cosmos* (1976).

ELECTRONIC: *February Run*, tape (1971); *3 Pieces*, tape (1971).

Smorzando (It., abbreviation *Smorz.*, past participle *Smorzato*). Extinguishing. Gradually dying away.

Smyth, (Dame) **Ethel** (Mary) (*b* Footscray, Kent, 1858; *d* Hook Heath, Woking, 1944). Eng. composer and cond. Studied Leipzig Cons. and in Berlin with Herzogenberg. Came into prominence with Mass in D, perf. London 1893. First 3 operas were prod. in Ger. Active in militant campaign for women's suffrage and was jailed 1911. Comp. *March of the Women* as their battlesong and cond. it in Holloway Jail with toothbrush. D.B.E. 1922. Music was Ger.-influenced but with breezy Eng. quality typical of her personality. Her operas *The Wreckers* and *The Boatswain's Mate* contain mus. of considerable quality. Wrote highly entertaining autobiography. Prin. works:

OPERAS: *Fantasio* (1892–4); *The Forest* (*Der Wald*) (1899–1901); *The* ★*Wreckers* (1903–4); *The* ★*Boatswain's Mate* (1913–14); *Fête galante* (1923); *Entente Cordiale* (1925).

ORCH: *Serenade* in D (1890); *On the Cliffs of Cornwall* (prelude, Act II, *The Wreckers*) (1928); conc. for vn., hn., orch. (1927).

CHORAL: Mass in D (1891, rev. 1925); *March of the Women* (1911); *The Prison* (1930).

CHAMBER MUSIC: Str. quintet (1884); str. qt. (1902–12); vc. sonata (1887); vn. sonata (1887); pf. sonatas; organ preludes; songs (some with orch.).

Snare Drum. See *Side drum.*

Snegurochka (Rimsky-Korsakov). See *Snow Maiden, The.*

Snow Maiden, The (*Snegurochka*). Opera and prol. in 4 acts by Rimsky-Korsakov to his own lib. based on Ostrovsky's play (1873). Comp. 1880–1, rev. *c.*1895. Prod. St Petersburg 1882, NY Met. 1922, London 1933.

Soap Opera. Nothing to do with opera. Term to describe long-running, often daily or several-times-weekly serial on TV and radio, e.g. (in Britain) *Crossroads, Coronation Street, The Archers*. Genre originated in USA on commercial radio and was sponsored by a firm—soap manufacturer, for instance—wishing to advertise its product. Irreverently, one could claim *The Ring* as the biggest soap opera in the world.

Soave; soavità (It.). Suave; suavity (or gentle; gentleness). *Soavemente,* suavely.

Sociable Songs. Title given by ★Warlock to 3 settings of anonymous poems for male vv. and pf., comp. 1924–5, pubd. 1926. Titles are: 1. *The Toper's Song,* 2. *One more river,* 3. *The Lady's Birthday.*

Society for the Private Performance of Music (*Verein für Musikalische Privataufführungen*). Society founded in Vienna in Nov. 1918 by ★Schoenberg, with Berg, Ratz, and Paul A. Pisk. Aim was presentation of 'all modern mus. from that of Mahler and Strauss to the newest' under best possible conditions. Subscribers only admitted; critics were excluded. Comps. frequently perf. twice. Much organizational work undertaken by Berg. Dissolved 1922. Among composers whose mus. was played were Schoenberg, Berg, Webern, Mahler, Stravinsky, Skryabin, Debussy, Marx, Wellesz, Bartók, Ravel, and Suk. The pianist on several occasions was Rudolf Serkin. Prague branch under presidency of ★Zemlinsky 1921–4.

Socrate (Socrates). Symphonic drama in 3 parts for 4 sop. and orch. by ★Satie to lib. by Plato (trans. by V. Cousin). Parts are entitled 1. *Portrait de Socrate,* 2. *Les bords de l'Ilussus,* 3. *Mort de Socrate.* Comp. 1918. F.p. Paris 1920; f.p. in England BBC broadcast 1949.

Söderström, Elisabeth (*b* Stockholm, 1927). Swed. sop. Studied singing at Royal Swedish Acad. of Mus. Opera début Drottningholm 1947 while still student. Joined Stockholm Royal Opera 1950. Salzburg début 1955, Glyndebourne 1957 (Composer in *Ariadne auf Naxos*), NY Met. 1959–60, CG 1960. Notable Strauss singer, but wide repertory of roles, including Janáček roles of Emilia Marty in *The Makropoulos Affair,* Káťa Kabanová, and Jenůfa. Is also accomplished singer of Britten's vocal music in addition to his operatic roles. Hon. C.B.E. 1985.

Soft Pedal. Pf. pedal, operated by left foot, which reduces vol. by causing fewer than normal number of str. to be struck or by bringing the hammers nearer the str. before they start to move.

Soggetto (It.). Subject, meaning, in a mus. sense, the subject of a fugue.

Soh. See *Sol.*

Sohal, Naresh (*b* Harsipind, Punjab, 1939). Indian composer. Studied science and mathematics at Punjab Univ., but as interest lay in composing Western mus. went to Eng. 1962, studying with Jeremy Dale Roberts. Research on micro-intervals under A. Goehr. Works incl. *Asht Prahar* for orch. (1965), *Aalaykhyam I* (1970–1) and II (1971–2) for chamber orch., *Indra-Dhanush* (1973) for orch., harmonica conc. (1966), *Dhyan I*, vc. and small orch. (1974), *Inscape*, ch., fl., perc. (1979), *The Wanderer*, bar., ch., orch (1981), brass quintet No. 1 (1983), No. 2 (1984), *Undulation*, vc. (1984), *Shades IV*, va. (1984), other chamber mus., songs, and choral works.

Soirées musicales (Musical Evenings). Coll. of songs and duets by *Rossini, pubd. 1835. *Britten orch. 5 of these (1936) under same title, others were orch. by *Respighi in ballet *La *Boutique fantasque*. 12 were transcr. for pf. by Liszt, 1837.

Soir (et la Tempête), Le (The Evening (and the Storm)). Nickname of Haydn's Sym. No. 8 (Hob. I:8) c.1761, Nos. 6 and 7 being known respectively as *Le *Matin* (Morning) and *Le Midi* (Noon) (Hob. I:6 and 7).

Sokoloff, Nikolay (Grigorovich) (*b* nr. Kiev, 1886; *d* La Jolla, Calif., 1965). Russ.-born cond. and violinist (later Amer. citizen). Studied Yale Univ. Violinist in Boston S.O. Cond. San Francisco P.O. 1916, first cond. of Cleveland Orch., 1918–33, cond. Seattle S.O. 1938–40.

Sol. The 5th degree (dominant) of major scale and so used (spelt *soh*) in *Tonic Sol-fa. In many countries, where *fixed-doh* principles apply, it means the note G in any key, thus *sol dièse* is G♯ in Fr.

Solares, Enrique (*b* Guatemala City, 1910). Guatemalan composer and pianist. Studied Guatemala Nat. Cons. 1933–5 and Brussels Cons. 1936, later privately with Křička in Prague 1936–9 and Casella in Rome 1939–42. Piano teacher at Guatemala Nat. Cons. 1943–8. Entered Guatemalan diplomatic service 1948. Adopted 12-note procedures in 1968. Works incl. pieces for guitar, *Partita* for str., *4 Short Pieces* for orch., *12 Microtransparencias* for pf. (1969–70).

Soldaten, Die (The Soldiers). Opera in 4 acts by B. A. *Zimmermann to lib. by composer after J. M. Reinhold Lenz, comp. 1958–60, rev. 1963–4. For orch., singing and speaking vv., elecs., and *musique concrète*, with ballet, mime, film, and lighting effects. Prod. Cologne 1965, Edinburgh 1972. Also orch. suite.

Soldier's Tale, The (Stravinsky). See *Histoire du Soldat, L'*.

Soleil des eaux, Le (The sun of the waters). Music by Boulez orig. comp. for radio play by René Char (1948). Rev. 1950 as cantata for sop., ten., bass, chamber orch. Rev. 1958 for sop., ten., bass. ch., and orch. Rev. 1965 for sop. and ch. F.p. 1965 version, Berlin 1965.

Solemn Melody. Comp. for org. and str. by Walford *Davies, 1908.

Solenne, solennemente, solennita (It.); **solennel (le), solennellemente** (Fr.); **Solemnis, solennis** (Lat.). Solemn, solemnly, solemnity.

Soler, Antonio (*b* Olot, nr. Gerona, 1729; *d* El Escorial, 1783). Sp. composer, organist, and friar. Studied Montserrat from age 6. Choirmaster at Lérida. Became monk 1752, entering Escorial monastery as organist 1753. Wrote theoretical treatise 1762. Disciple of D. Scarlatti and wrote 120 keyboard sonatas. Also comp. several quintets for org. and str. qt., church mus., etc.

Solesmes. Fr. village near Le Mans where the monks of the Benedictine monastery became famous for their work on restoration of liturgical mus. Order founded 1833 by Dom Prosper Gueranger. Important publications on nature of plainsong issued in 1883, 1891, and 1896. When Pope Pius X in 1904 est. commission to prepare new official edn. of plainchant, the Solesmes Benedictines were appointed eds. This edn. was known as Vatican Edn. (but some authorities on the subject strongly criticize its interpretation of Gregorian rhythm). In 1901, because of their non-compliance with Law of Associations, the monks were expelled from Solesmes and moved to I.o.W. and later to Quarr Abbey, near Ryde. Returned to Solesmes 1922.

Solfeggio (It., plural *solfeggi*; Fr. *solfège*). Term for method of sight-reading or vocal exercise in which names of the notes are used as in *fixed-doh* system, e.g. *do* for C, *sol* for G, etc. Fr. term *solfège* is also used to cover all rudimentary mus. instruction.

Soli (It.). Alone; plural of *solo, but 'solos' in general usage today.

Sollberger, Harvey (*b* Cedar Rapids, Iowa, 1938). Amer. composer, cond., and flautist. Studied Iowa Univ. 1956–60. Teacher at Columbia Univ. from 1965. Works influenced by *Babbitt's use of 12-note system but gradually with a less rigid application. Works incl. fl. qt., mus. for Sophocles's *Antigone* (with elec. tape), str. trio, etc.

Solmization. System of designating notes by the sol-fa syllables in any of the various methods used since Guido d'Arezzo in 11th cent., as in the It. *do, re, mi, fa,* etc. and Tonic sol-fa *doh, ray, me, fah,* etc.

Solo (It.). Alone. A vocal or instr. piece or passage perf. by one performer, i.e. a solo song is for one singer, with or without acc. The solo instr. in a conc. might also be acc. by a solo passage for one of the orch. players. The word *soloistic* is sometimes used to denote a composer's use of the individual qualities of an instr., but its use is to be regretted.

Solomon. Oratorio by Handel to text adapted from Bible by unknown author. F.p. London 1749 (comp. 1748).

Solomon (orig. Solomon Cutner) (b London, 1902). Eng. pianist. Pupil of Mathilde *Verne. Début at 8, playing Tchaikovsky's first conc. at Queen's Hall, London. Amer. début 1926. Gave f.p. of Bliss's pf. conc., NY World Fair 1939. Brilliant career as conc. soloist, recitalist, and chamber-mus. player of exceptional sensitivity cut short by incapacitating illness 1955. C.B.E. 1946.

Solomon, Yonty (b Cape Town, 1938). Brit. pianist of S. African birth. Studied at Cape Town Univ. 1953–8. Moved to London 1963 to study with Myra *Hess. Has given f.ps. of works by Richard Rodney Bennett, W. Josephs, and Merilaainen. Wide repertory from Bach to Ives (Concord Sonata).

Solo Organ. Manual on some orgs., with solo stops such as cl., tuba, fl., etc.

Solo Pitch. Tuning of instrs. rather higher than normal pitch in order to obtain greater brilliance of tone.

Solo Stop. Any org. stop used solo against acc. of softer stops played on a different kbd. Some stops are more suitable than others for solo use.

Solti, (Sir) Georg (b Budapest, 1912). Hung.-born cond. and pianist (Brit. citizen since 1972). Studied Budapest, pupil of Kodály, Bartók, and Dohnányi. Ass. at Budapest Opera 1930. Début as cond. Budapest 1938 (Le Nozze di Figaro). Assisted Toscanini at Salzburg Fest. 1936 and 1937. Left Hungary for Switz. 1939, earning living as pianist. Mus. dir. Munich Opera 1946–52, Frankfurt Opera 1952–61, CG 1961–71 (his tenure there being a decade of particular distinction). Mus. dir. Chicago S.O. from 1969, LPO 1979–83. Cond., Orchestre de Paris 1971–5. Amer. début, San Francisco Opera 1953, NY Met. 1960. Glyndebourne début 1954 (Don Giovanni), CG 1959 (Der Rosenkavalier). Cond. f. Eng. perf. of Schoenberg's Moses und Aron (1965). Cond. f.p. of Tippett's 4th Sym. (Chicago) (1977). Fine cond. of Wagner, Strauss, Mahler, Elgar, etc. Cond. first complete studio recording of Wagner's Ring. Cond. Bayreuth Fest. Ring, 1983. Hon. K.B.E. 1971.

Sombrero de tres picos, El (Falla). See Three-cornered Hat, The.

Somers, Harry (Stewart) (b Toronto, 1925). Canadian composer, pianist, and guitarist. Studied Toronto (comp. with Weinzweig) 1945–9, Paris (with Milhaud) 1949–50. Worked as taxi-driver, copyist, radio commentator, and later as teacher. In some works tonal and atonal materials are juxtaposed in the manner of Ives. Works incl. operas, notably Louis Riel, syms., ballets, sonatas, str. qts., and Voiceplay (for singer-actor, male or female, any range).

Somervell, (Sir) Arthur (b Windermere, 1863; d London, 1937). Eng. composer. Studied Cam-

bridge Univ. (comp. with Stanford), Berlin, and RCM (comp. with Parry). Teacher at RCM 1894–1901. From 1901, inspector of mus. to Board of Education and Scottish Education Dept. (chief inspector 1920–8). Prolific composer, his song-cycle Maud being of high quality. Possibly first to set Housman Shropshire Lad poems (1904). Knighted 1929. Works incl. sym., Normandy (symphonic variations for pf. and orch., 1912), Highland Concerto (pf. and orch., 1921), vn. conc. (1932), cl. quintet, 2 Masses, Ode on the Intimations of Immortality (Leeds Fest. 1907), song-cycles Maud and A Shropshire Lad, solo songs, etc.

Sommer, Raphael (b Prague, 1937). Cz. cellist. Studied Jerusalem and Paris Cons. (with Tortelier). Won Casals Int. Competition 1961 and other prizes. Prof. of vc., RMCM 1967–71, RNCM from 1972. Soloist with leading orchs.

Sommer, Vladimir (b Dolní Jiřetín, 1921). Cz. composer. Studied Prague Cons. 1942–6 and Prague Acad. of Mus. 1946–50. Worked for Prague Radio and as mus. critic. Taught at Charles Univ. in Prague from 1960. Works incl. syms., str. qts., vn. conc., vc. conc., and The Black Man, tone-poem for ten., bass, orch.

Son and Stranger (Die Heimkehr aus der Fremde, The Homecoming from Abroad). Operetta in 1 act by *Mendelssohn, Op. 89, to lib. by K. Klingemann, comp. 1829 for family perf. in celebration of his parents' silver wedding, Dec. 1829. F.public p. Leipzig 1851, f.Eng.p. (in trans. by H. F. *Chorley) 1851.

Sonata (It., sounded, from suonare, to sound; Fr., Ger. Sonate). Instr. comp. for pf., or for other instr(s). with pf. acc., e.g. vc. sonata, fl. sonata, in several movements (sometimes in one, as in Liszt's B minor pf. sonata). Formal features of the sonata are found in other instr. comps., such as sym., qt., trio, but the term sonata is usually reserved for works involving not more than 2 performers. The sonata originated in the 16th cent., when it meant anything not sung but played. During early part of 17th cent., comps. for instr. ens., which were div. into 5 or more contrasting sections were known as sonatas. From these the baroque sonata developed, having 3–6 movements like a suite, and taking 2 forms, the sonata da camera ('chamber sonata', often for 2 or more players with kbd. acc., in dance rhythms) and sonata da chiesa ('church sonata', of more serious character). The earliest sonatas for kbd. alone are by Salvatore and Kuhnau, and these reached their apogee with D. Scarlatti and C. P. E. Bach. Later in that century, the Viennese classical sonata of Haydn, Mozart, and Beethoven, usually but not invariably in 3 movements, marked the greatest period in the development of the form, leading to the superb romantic era. Like the orch. sym., the sonata remains the most important form for 1 or 2 instr., and the majority of important 20th-cent. composers have written them. Most sonatas are written in *sonata-form or a version of it. The Haydn/Mozart sonata is usually in 3 movements, allegro–andante–allegro. Beethoven introduced the minuet (later scherzo), as 3rd movement, but in his Op. 111 pf. sonata he anticipated the 1-movement sectional structure adopted by later composers. The last movement of a 3- or 4-movement sonata is often in sonata or *rondo form, or is sometimes a set of variations. Some 20th-cent. composers have revived 18th-cent. application of term to works for several instr., e.g. Walton's *Sonata for Strings* and C. Matthews's *Sonata* for orch. The fact is that a sym. is a sonata for orch., a str. qt. a sonata for 4 str. instr., etc.

Sonata da Camera (It.). Chamber sonata. Baroque type of sonata, the term originally indicating place (i.e. court, chamber), rather than type, of perf. Had several dance-like movements for 2 or 3 str. players with kbd. acc. Corelli standardized the form as a suite consisting of introduction, followed by 3 or 4 dances.

Sonata da Chiesa (It.). Church sonata. Like the *sonata da camera,* but of a more serious character appropriate to ecclesiastical surroundings. The standard Corelli *sonata da chiesa* is in 4 movements, slow–fast–slow–fast.

Sonata Form. Type of mus. construction (sometimes known as compound binary form) normally used in first movement of a *sonata, sym., or conc. (and in other types of work). Used also in other movements. Regular sonata form implies 3 sections: 1. *Exposition* (containing first subject, in tonic key, and 2nd subject, in dominant, and sometimes further subjects), often repeated and followed by 2. *Development* (in which the material of the Exposition is worked out in a kind of free fantasia), and 3. *Recapitulation* (in which the Exposition is repeated, though often with modification, and with the 2nd subject now in the tonic). The Recapitulation has a coda, a peroration of moderate length though some composers, incl. Beethoven, extend it into what amounts to a 2nd Development section. The basis of sonata form is key relationships.

Sonata Rondo. Movement designed as combination of sonata and rondo form (e.g. finale of Beethoven's 8th Sym.). Outline is: *Exposition* (A B A, i.e. first subject in tonic: rondo theme; 2nd subject in dominant or another key; first subject in tonic), *Development* (C), *Recapitulation* (A B A, i.e. rondo first subject in tonic; 3rd episode, with 2nd subject now in tonic; rondo theme leading to coda). There are many variants.

Sonatina (It.; Fr. *sonatine*). Little sonata. A short sonata, usually lighter and easier (but several 20th-cent. sonatinas, e.g. by Ravel, Milhaud, Busoni, etc. are technically difficult).

Sondheim, Stephen (Joshua) (*b* NY, 1930). Amer. composer and lyric-writer. Studied Williams College, Mass. Wrote lyrics for *Bernstein's *West Side Story* (1957) and for Jule Styne's *Gypsy* (1959). Comp. successful musicals incl. *A Little Night Music* (1973), *Company* (1970), *Pacific Overtures* (1976), and *Sweeney Todd* (1979), writing words and mus.

Sonetti di Petrarca, Tre (3 Petrarch Sonnets). 3 songs by Liszt (1839) which he later transcr. for pf. as Nos. 4–6 of the *Seconde Année (Italie)* of *Années de pèlerinage* (1837–49).

Song. Short vocal comp., acc. or solo. Song is the natural human means of mus. self-expression (as it is for most birds). There are various types of song—the individual folk-song, the part-song for a group of vv., the art-song for the trained performer. Today a 'song recital' generally means an evening of Eng. songs (mus. settings of poems), Ger. *Lieder, or Fr. *mélodies*. In opera the term *aria* or air is preferred to 'song' for a solo vocal item. Many composers, Berlioz, Mahler, Strauss, Elgar, Britten, Shostakovich, etc.—have written songs with orch., and the term is sometimes applied to a large-scale piece, e.g. *Song of the Earth* (Mahler) and *Song of Destiny* (Brahms).

Probably prehistoric man uttered some sort of song, and the origins of folk-songs are beyond discovery (though not beyond speculation!). Synagogue and church were among the official institutions where song developed, through chants and hymns, some of the latter being adaptations of folk and popular songs. With 12th-cent. minstrels and troubadours, the love-song and ballad developed, to be followed in the 14th and 15th cents. by songs of the Ger. *Minnesinger and *Meistersinger. By the end of the 15th cent., following the revolution of *Ars Nova, song colls., many of them polyphonic settings, were pubd. in several countries. In Eng. in the 16th and 17th cents. the lute-songs, exemplified by Dowland and the madrigals of Weelkes and Byrd, in Sp. the lute-songs of Milán, and in It. the madrigals of Monteverdi and others all played a significant role in the growth of elaborate song-writing. Ger. developed the *Lied*, beginning with Hassler and Abert, and continuing through Mozart and Beethoven to the great flowering of Schubert, who more than any composer made the song a mus. form into which as much emotional and dramatic expression could be poured as into a sym. Some of his songs are *strophic,* i.e. repeating the tune in successive stanzas, others are 'through-composed' (*durchkomponiert*), i.e. developing freely from start to finish. Schubert was followed by Schumann, Brahms, Wolf, Loewe, Marx, Mahler, Strauss, Pfitzner, and others. In Fr., Duparc, Debussy, and especially Fauré developed the *chanson* in as distinctive and complex a fashion as the great Germans developed the *Lied*. Indeed, in the 19th and 20th cents., composers in Eng., Sp., USA, Russia, Hungary, etc. have added masterpieces to the world's treasury of song. Nor should the immense world of 'popular song', from 19th-cent. mus.-hall songs to today's 'pop' songs be forgotten, ignored, or under-rated. Brave the man who will make a didactic value-judgment between *Dives and Lazarus, Gretchen am Spinnrade,* and *Smoke gets in your eyes.*

Song-cycle (Ger. *Liederkreis*). Set of songs grouped into an artistic unity by the composer in a particular order and referring to a particular theme—love, death, jealousy, nature, etc.—or telling a story, or both. Examples are Beethoven's **An die ferne Geliebte,* Schubert's **Winterreise,* Schumann's **Frauenliebe und -Leben,* Mahler's **Kindertotenlieder,* Berlioz's *Les *Nuits d'été,* Elgar's **Sea Pictures,* Vaughan Williams's **On Wenlock Edge,* Britten's **Nocturne,* etc. Some of the above are with pf. acc., some with chamber ens., and some with orch. Coprario's *Funeral Teares* (1606) is one of the earliest, if not the earliest, song-cycles.

Song-form. Another, if misleading, name for ordinary **ternary* form as generally applied in an instr. slow movement.

Song for the Lord Mayor's Table, A. Cycle of 6 songs for sop. and pf. by **Walton to words collected by Christopher Hassall from poems by Blake, Thomas Jordan, Charles Morris, Wordsworth, and 2 anon. 18th-cent. poets. Written for City of London Fest. 1962. F.p. Schwarzkopf 1962. Re-scored for sop. and orch. 1970. F.p. City of London Fest. 1970 with Janet Baker.

Songmakers' Almanac, The. Eng. ensemble who give song-recital programmes devoted to a particular theme, often literary, in which songs are perf. with complementary readings (e.g. Scott's influence on composers; Schubert in 1827, etc.). Founded 1976 (début London, August) with art. dir. Graham **Johnson and Felicity **Lott (sop.), Ann **Murray (mez.), Anthony **Rolfe Johnson (ten.), and Richard Jackson (bar.). Fest. appearances Aldeburgh, King's Lynn, Buxton, Edinburgh, etc.

Song of Destiny (Brahms). See *Schicksalslied.*

Song of the Earth, The (Mahler). See *Lied von der Erde, Das.*

Song of the Flea. Song for v. and pf. by Mussorgsky, 1879, setting of Mephistopheles's song in Goethe's *Faust.* Also set by Beethoven, in 6 *Lieder,* Op. 75, No. 3.

Song of the High Hills, The. For orch. and ch. (wordless) by Delius, with solo parts for sop. and ten. from ch. Comp. 1911, f.p. London 1920, cond. Coates.

Songs and Dances of Death (*Pesni i plyaski smerti*). Cycle of 4 songs for v. and pf. by Mussorgsky, 1875–7, to poems by Golenischev-Gutuzov. Titles are: 1. *Trepak, Death and the Peasant.* 2. *Cradle Song, the Child breathes gently.* 3.

Death the Serenader, Soft is the Night. 4. *Field Marshal Death, War Rumbles.* Orch. by Shostakovich, 1962.

Songs for a Mad King, Eight. Th. piece by **Maxwell Davies for male actor-singer and chamber ens. (incl. railway whistle, dijeridu, chains). Text by Randolph Stow and King George III. Has 8 movements. F.p. London 1969.

Songs for Dov. Cycle of songs for ten. and small orch. (with 6 perc. players) by **Tippett, 1970, the texts written by himself. Based on songs for the character Dov in Tippett's 3rd opera *The *Knot Garden.* F.p. Cardiff 1970, Gerald English and London Sinfonietta, cond. Tippett.

Songs my Mother Taught Me. Song for high v. and pf. by Dvořák, to words by Heyduk, being No. 4 of his *Gipsy Songs,* Op. 55 (1880).

Songs of a Wayfarer (Mahler). See *Lieder eines fahrenden Gesellen.*

Songs of Farewell. (1) 6 unacc. secular motets by **Parry, comp. 1916–18 to texts from the Bible, Donne, Vaughan, J. Davies, Campion, and Lockhart. Nos. 1–5 f.p. London 1916, No. 6 f.p. Oxford 1918, f. complete p. Oxford 1919 (cond. Hugh **Allen in each case).
(2) 5 settings of Whitman for double ch. and orch. by Delius, comp. 1930, f.p. London 1932 cond. Sargent. One of works written with help of E. **Fenby.

Songs of Gurra (Schoenberg). See *Gurrelieder.*

Songs of Sunset. Delius's settings of poems by Ernest Dowson for mez., bar., ch., and orch. 1906–8. F.p. London 1911 cond. Beecham.

Songs of the Fleet. Five settings of poems by Henry Newbolt (1862–1938) for bar., ch., and orch. by **Stanford, Op. 117, f.p. Leeds Fest. 1910. No. 3 is *The Middle Watch.*

Songs of the Sea. Five settings of poems by Henry Newbolt (1862–1938) for bar., male ch., and orch. by **Stanford, Op. 91, f.p. Leeds Fest. 1904.

Songs of Travel. Song-cycle for v. and pf. by Vaughan Williams to 9 poems by Robert Louis Stevenson from his *Songs of Travel.* F.p. London 1904. Incl. *The Vagabond, The Roadside Fire, Whither must I wander?* and *Bright is the Ring of Words,* all often sung separately. 9th song not perf. until 1960. F.p. as cycle, May 1960 (BBC).

Songs on the Death of Children (Mahler). See *Kindertotenlieder.*

Songs without Words (Mendelssohn). See *Lieder ohne Worte.*

Sonnambula, La (The Sleepwalking Girl). Opera in 2 acts by Bellini to lib. by Romani. Prod. Milan and London 1831, NY 1835.

Sonnleithner, Joseph (*b* Vienna, 1766; *d* Vienna, 1835). Austrian art-collector and impresario.

Manager of Vienna court ths. 1804–14 and of Theater an der Wien until 1807. Trans. opera libs., incl. Beethoven's *Fidelio*. Friend of Grillparzer and Schubert. One of founders of Gesellschaft der Musikfreunde (1812).

Sonnleithner, Leopold Edler von (*b* Vienna, 1797; *d* Vienna, 1873). Austrian connoisseur, son of Ignaz Sonnleithner (*b* Vienna, 1770; *d* Vienna, 1831, who was a doctor and amateur bass singer). Friend of Schubert, preserving many of his songs and, with others, pubd. *Erlkönig*, etc. Aided *Jahn with material for life of Mozart.

Sonore (Fr.), **sonoro** (It.). Sonorous; so *sonorité* (Fr.) and *sonorità* (It.), sonority; *sonoramente* (It.), sonorously.

Sons bouchés (Fr.). Stopped notes in hn. playing.

Sontag, Henriette (orig. Gertrud Walburga) (*b* Koblenz, 1806; *d* Mexico City, 1854). Ger. sop. First public appearance at age 6. Studied Prague Cons. Opera début 1821 in Boieldieu's *Jean de Paris*. Sang in Vienna from 1822. At Weber's request created title-role in *Euryanthe*, 1823. Sang sop. part in f.p. of Beethoven's 9th Sym., Vienna 1824. Berlin début 1825, Paris 1826, London 1828, all in Rossini roles in which she excelled, her voice being exceptionally clear and reaching E *in alt* with ease. Retired from stage on marriage to Count Rossi, but continued concert work. Returned to opera 1849, toured USA 1852, died of cholera in Mexico.

Sonzogno, Edoardo (*b* Milan, 1836; *d* Milan, 1920). It. publisher. Firm founded at end of 18th cent.; he began publication of Fr. and It. mus. in 1874. Est. series of competitions for new operas 1883, 2nd contest in 1889 being won by Mascagni with *Cavalleria Rusticana*. Last contest 1903.

Sonzogno, Giulio Cesare (*b* Milan, 1906; *d* Milan, 1976). It. composer, studied with *Pick-Mangiagalli. Mainly instr. mus., incl. symphonic poems, *Il Negro* for vc. and orch., some songs.

Sopra (It.). On, above. *Sopra una corda,* on 1 str. (of vn., etc.); for pf. application see *Corda; come (di) sopra,* as above.

Sopranino (It.). Little soprano. Name given to size of instr. higher than sop., e.g. sopranino recorder, sopranino sax., sopranino flügelhorn, etc.

Soprano (from It. *sopra,* 'above'). (1) The highest register of female (or artificial male) v. A boy sop. is known as a *treble. Normal female range is from middle C upwards for 2 octaves. The male sop. was a *castrato*, used in opera and church mus. in 17th and 18th cents. In the opera house, many sub-divisions of the term *soprano* exist, e.g. dramatic, lyric, coloratura, soubrette, character, etc.

(2) Sop. clef is obsolete clef, with middle C on bottom line of staff.

(3) The term is also used for high instr. register, e.g. soprano cornet, soprano sax. (See also *sopranino*).

See also *Mezzo-soprano*.

Sor (orig. Sors), **Fernando** (orig. Ferdinando) (*b* Barcelona, 1778; *d* Paris, 1839). Sp. guitarist and composer. Studied at Montserrat. Virtuoso of guitar, teaching in Paris, London, and elsewhere. Played his 'concertante' for guitar and vn., va., and vc. at Phil. Soc. concert in London, 1817. Wrote many pieces for guitar, an opera, ballet *Cendrillon*, perf. in London 1822, syms., and str. qts.

Sorabji, Kaikhosru Shapurji (orig. Leon Dudley Sorabji) (*b* Chingford, Essex. 1892). Eng.-born composer, pianist, and writer. Son of Parsi father and Sp.-Sicilian mother. Self-taught as composer. Played his pf. works in London and Paris 1921 and Vienna 1922, but thereafter discouraged public perf. of his mus. until relenting in mid-1970s, though he remained something of a cult figure. Wrote music criticism notable for acerbity and wit, also for championship of then unfashionable composers, e.g. Mahler and Szymanowski. Works are of great complexity, the *Opus clavicembalisticum* for pf. being in 3 parts with 12 subdivisions, incl. a theme with 44 variations, and lasting over 2 hours. Other works, demanding elaborate forces, incl. syms., organ syms., 5 pf. concs., pf. sonatas, etc.

Sorcerer, The. Operetta by Sullivan to lib. by Gilbert. Prod. London 1877, NY 1879.

Sorcerer's Apprentice, The (Dukas). See *Apprenti sorcier, L'*.

Sordino, sordina (It., plural *sordini*). A mute for an instr. Thus, *con sordini,* with mutes, means put the mutes on. Other phrases are *sordini alzati* or *sordini levati,* mutes raised (taken off). On the pf., *sordini* means the dampers; *senza sordini* is without dampers, meaning that the sustaining pedal is to be depressed.

Sordun (Ger.). (1) See *Sourdine*.

(2) Org. stop of muffled tone (8′ and 16′).

Soriano (Suriano), **Francesco** (*b* Soriano, 1549; *d* Rome, 1621). It. composer and singer. Chorister, St John Lateran, at 15. Pupil of Palestrina. Dir. of mus. for Gonzaga family in Mantua, 1581–6. Choirmaster at 3 Rome churches: S. Maria Maggiore 1587–99, 1601–3, St John Lateran 1599–1601, St Peter's 1603–20. Wrote church mus. and madrigals.

Sorochintsy Fair (*Sorochintskaya Yarmarka*). 3-act unfinished opera by Mussorgsky to composer's lib. based on Gogol's story. Begun 1874. Mussorgsky completed only the prelude, the market scene and part of the next, most of Act 2, a scene based on his *Night on the Bare Mountain*, an instr. episode, and 2 songs. Ed. 1904 and 1912 by Lyadov and Karatygin: version from these edns.

prod. Moscow 1913. Completion by *Cui prod. St Petersburg 1917; by *Tcherepnin prod. Monte Carlo 1923, NY Met. 1930, London 1934. Completion by Shebalin pubd. 1933. Sometimes spelt *Sorochints Fair* or called *The Fair at Sorochinsk.*

Sospirando, sospirante, sospirevole, sospiroso (It.). Sighing, i.e. plaintive in style.

Sospiri (Sighs). Comp. for str., harp, and org., Op. 70, by Elgar, f.p. London 1914. Also arr. for vn. and pf.

Sostenuto (It.). Sustained. Direction that notes must be sustained to their full value in a smooth flow; it can also be interpreted as meaning that a passage is to be played at a slower but uniform speed. Also *sostenendo,* sustaining.

Sotin, Hans (b Dortmund, 1939). Ger. bass. Studied at Dortmund Cons. Début Essen 1962 (*Der Rosenkavalier*). Hamburg Opera from 1964, becoming prin. bass and singing Wotan in *Das Rheingold* and *Die Walküre.* Glyndebourne début 1970 (Sarastro), Chicago 1971, NY Met. 1972 (Fafner), Bayreuth 1972, CG 1974 (Hunding), and La Scala 1976 (Ochs).

Sotto Voce (It.). Below the voice. In an undertone or barely audible (as in an aside). Applied to vocal and instr. perf.

Soubasse (Fr.). Contra-bourdon org. stop (32′).

Soubrette (Fr.). Light sop. taking rather pert roles in opera and operetta such as Despina in *Così fan tutte,* Blonde in *Die Entführung aus dem Serail,* Adèle in *Die Fledermaus,* etc.

Sound-board. (1) Wooden board on pf. (and other kbd. instr.) placed behind the str. in an upright instr., below them in a grand, to amplify the vol. of sound.

(2) In an org., the upper portion of wind chest on which pipes sound.

Sound-holes. The holes, shaped like an f, cut in the belly of a vn. and related instr. to assist resonance. In lutes, guitars, etc., the holes are more ornamental and are called 'roses'.

Soundpost. Piece of wood fixed inside a vn. and other str. instr., vertically connecting upper and lower surfaces and helping to support pressure of str. on the bridge. Thus the vibrations of the str. are distributed over the body of the instr.

Sourdine (Fr.). Mute. (1) Mute, used in same sense as *sordino. Mettez* (put on), *ôtez* (take off) *les sourdines.*

(2) Fr. name for early form of bn. (Ger. *Sordun,* It. *sordone*), also known as *courtaut.* Appeared first in 16th cent. and was made in several sizes from bass to descant. Had no bell, the sound coming from lateral hole at top near the crook. Had 12 finger-holes, some also having 2 keys.

Souris, André (b Marchienne-au-Pont, Belgium, 1890; d Paris, 1970). Belg. composer and cond.

Studied Brussels Cons. 1911–18. Cond., Belgian Radio-TV Orch. 1937–46. Dir., mus. dept. Brussels Seminary of Arts 1944–8, and of Marchienne Acad. of Mus. 1949. Founded journal *Polyphonies* in Paris, 1947. Prof. of harmony, Brussels Cons., 1949–64. Works incl. *Symphonies* for orch. (1939), cantata *Le marchand d'images* (1954–65), wind trio, etc.

Sousa, John Philip (b Washington D.C., 1854; d Reading, Penn., 1932). Amer. composer and bandmaster. As youth played vn. in th. orchs. Cond., US Marine Corps band 1880–92. Formed own military band 1892 which became very popular and toured Europe 4 times between 1900 and 1905 and the world in 1910–11. It was a victim of the 1931 Depression. Best known for his superb marches, of which he comp. nearly 100, among them *The Stars and Stripes Forever, The Washington Post, El Capitán, Semper Fidelis, Liberty Bell, King Cotton, Hands across the Sea,* etc. Also wrote several operettas, incl. *El Capitán* (1895), *The Queen of Hearts,* and *Victory.*

Sousaphone. Amer. helical form of bass tuba made to circle the player's body, with a large bell turned up through 2 right angles to face forward and terminating in a flange 2′ wide. Made first in 1898 for Sousa's band, the earliest model having bell which opened directly upward. New version dates from 1908. Also used in jazz.

Souster, Tim (Andrew James) (b Bletchley, 1943). Eng. composer. Studied Oxford Univ. 1961–5, at Darmstadt summer courses, and privately with R. R. Bennett, 1965. BBC mus. producer 1965–7. Composer-in-residence, King's Coll., Cambridge, 1969–71. Teaching ass. to *Stockhausen, Cologne, 1971–3. Co-founder, 1969, of elec. group Intermodulation. Research fellow in elec. mus., Keele Univ. 1975–7. Also writer on mus. Works incl. *Titus Groan Music* for wind quintet, tape, elec. apparatus; *Pelvic Loops* for 2-track tape; *Chinese Whispers* for perc. and 3 synthesizers; *Triple Music II* for 3 orch. (1970); *Music for Eliot's 'Waste Land'* (1970); *World Music* (1971–4); *Eastern Arts* (1975).

Soutenu (Fr.). Sustained; used in same way as *sostenuto.*

Souvenirs de Bayreuth (Memories of Bayreuth). 'Fantaisie en forme de quadrille sur les thèmes favoris de l'Anneau du Nibelung de Richard Wagner', for pf. duet (4 hands) by Fauré and Messager. Pubd. 1930. Arr. for pf. solo by Samazeuilh.

Souzay, Gérard (really Tisserand, Gérard Marcel) (b Angers, 1920). Fr. bar. Studied Paris Cons. and with Pierre *Bernac. Recital début 1945. NY début 1950. Occasional appearances in opera, début NY City Center as Monteverdi's Orfeo, 1960. Sang the Count in *Le Nozze di Figaro,* NY Met. 1965, but best-known for fine singing of Fr. songs and Ger. Lieder. Accompanist since 1954, Dalton Baldwin.

Soviet Artist's Practical Creative Reply to Just Criticism, A. Sub-title of Shostakovich's 5th Sym., provided by an anonymous commentator in 1937 after the Soviet hierarchy had criticized 'formalist' tendencies in the composer's opera *The Lady Macbeth of the Mtsensk District* and ballet *Bright Stream.*

Sowerby, Leo (*b* Grand Rapids, Mich., 1895; *d* Port Clinton, Ohio, 1968). Amer. composer and organist. Studied in Chicago and 3 years in Italy as first Amer. *Prix de Rome* fellow for mus., 1921–4. Taught comp., Amer. Univ., Chicago, 1925–62. Founded College of Church Musicians, Washington, 1962. Prolific composer of org. mus. but wrote in most genres except opera. Works incl. 5 syms., 2 pf. concs., choral works, vn. conc., vc. conc., org. sym., 2 org. concs., *Symphonia Brevis* for org., several cantatas, and over 300 songs.

Soyer, Roger (Julien Jacques) (*b* Paris, 1939). Fr. bass. Studied at Paris Cons. Début Paris Opéra 1962–3 season. Sang Pluto in Monteverdi's *Orfeo*, Aix Fest. 1965. Amer. début 1968, Miami (*Roméo et Juliette*). Wexford Fest. 1968. In much demand internationally as Don Giovanni.

Spagnoletti, Paolo (really Paolo Diana) (*b* Cremona, 1768; *d* London, 1834). It. violinist. Studied Naples Cons. Went to London 1802, playing in various orchs. One of first associates of Phil. Soc., 1813. Leader of orch. at King's Th. from 1817. Wrote vn. pieces and songs.

Spagnoletto, spagnoletta, spagniletta, spagnicoletta. Old round dance, probably related to the *Pavan.

Spanisches Liederbuch (Spanish Songbook). 44 songs for v. and pf. by *Wolf, comp. 1889–90, being Ger. trans. by Paul von Heyse (1830–1914) and Emanuel Geibel (1815–84) of Sp. poems pubd. 1852 as *Spanisches Liederbuch.*

Spanish Caprice. Orch. work by Rimsky-Korsakov, Op. 34, comp. 1887, often known by mixed It.-Fr. title *Capriccio espagnol.*

Spanish Hour, The (Ravel). See *Heure espagnole, L'.*

Spanish Lady, The. Title of projected opera in 2 acts by Elgar, Op. 89, to lib. by Barry Jackson based on Jonson's *The Devil is an Ass* (1616). Begun 1932. 2 songs, ed. P. M. Young, pubd. 1955, and suite for str., ed. Young, 1956.

Spanish Rhapsody (Ravel). See *Rapsodie espagnole.*

Spanish Symphony (Lalo). See *Symphonie espagnole.*

Sparta, sparto; spartita, spartito (It.). *Score.

Spartacus (*Spartak*). Ballet in 4 acts, mus. by *Khachaturian, lib. by Volkov, choreog. Jacobson. Comp. 1954, rev. 1968. Four suites, Nos. 1–3 (1955–7), No. 4 (1967). Prod. Leningrad 1956,

Moscow 1958. Extract from mus. used as theme mus. for Brit. TV series *The Onedin Line.*

Spassapensieri (It.). *Jew's harp.

Speaker-Keys. Keys fitted to reed wind instr. to facilitate production of harmonics. They open hole(s) which break continuity of air column. Obs. have two and cls. one.

Speaks, Oley (*b* Canal Winchester, Ohio, 1874; *d* NY, 1948). Amer. bar. and composer. Of his 200 songs, best-known are *The Road to Mandalay* and *When the Boys Come Home.*

Specht, Richard (*b* Vienna, 1870; *d* Vienna, 1932). Austrian mus. critic and writer. Studied architecture in Vienna but turned to mus. on advice of Brahms. Mus. critic of *Die Zeit* from 1895. Wrote for *Die Musik* 1908–15. Co-founder *Der Merker* 1909, directing it until 1919. Author of books on Mahler (1906, rev. 1913), Johann Strauss (1909), Richard Strauss (1920–1), Furtwängler (1922), Brahms (1928), Beethoven (1931), and Puccini (1931).

Species. Name given to each of 5 types of process in strict counterpoint. The species are: 1. Added voice (i.e. the counterpoint melody) proceeds at same pace as *cantus firmus (1 note to a measure). 2. Added voice proceeds at 2 or 3 times pace of *cantus firmus.* 3. Added voice proceeds at 4 or 6 times pace of *cantus firmus.* 4. Added voice proceeds (as in 2) at rate of 2:1, but 2nd note is tied over to 1st note of following measure (syncopation). 5. Added voice uses mixture of processes of other 4 species and also introduces shorter notes (florid counterpoint).

Spectre de la rose, Le. 1-act ballet, choreog. Fokine, set to mus. of Weber's *Aufforderung zum Tanz* (*Invitation to the Dance*), Op. 65, 1819, and danced by Karsavina and Nijinsky, Monte Carlo 1911. Also poem by T. Gautier set by Berlioz as No. 2 of song-cycle *Les *Nuits d'Été* (1840–1).

Spectre's Bride, The (*Svatebni košile*, The Wedding Shift). Cantata by Dvořák, Op. 69, comp. 1884, to text by K. J. Erben, f.p. (in Eng.) Birmingham Fest. 1885. Same text set by Novák 1913, as his Op. 48.

Speer, Daniel (*b* Breslau, 1636; *d* Göppingen, 1707). Ger. musician, cantor in various towns. Wind-player at Göppingen. Wrote songs, incl. *Die lustige Tafelmusik* (Jolly table-music) for 3 vv. and 4 instr., 1685, *Musikalisch-Turkischer Eulenspiegel* (1688), and sonatas for tbs., tpts., timp., and continuo.

Spells. Setting of poems by Kathleen Raine for sop., ch., and orch. by Richard Rodney *Bennett, comp. 1974, f.p. Worcester Fest. 1975. (2nd and 5th movements arr. as *Love Spells* for sop. and orch. (1974). F. p. London 1978.

Spem in alium nunquam habui. Motet by *Tallis in 40 parts for 8 5-v. choirs.

Spencer, Robert (*b* Ilford, 1932). Eng. lutenist, guitarist, and singer. Studied GSM and Dartington Sch. of Mus. Member of Julian Bream Consort from 1960. Formed duo with wife, Jill Nott-Bower, sop. Ed. of Elizabethan duets for guitars, etc.

Spendiarov (Spendiaryan), **Alexander** (*b* Kakhovka, Crimea, 1871; *d* Erevan, 1928). Armenian composer and conductor. Studied St Petersburg with Rimsky-Korsakov. Wrote early orch. works in Russ. oriental style, but made name with 2 series of *Crimean Sketches* in which he used local tunes and rhythms. Went to Armenia 1924, where he wrote opera *Almast*, prod. Moscow 1930.

Sphaerophon. Single-voiced elec. instr. developed by a German, Jong Mager, about 1924. Had oscillating radio valves, the frequency being altered by means of a variable condenser.

Spianato, spianata (from It. *spiana*, carpenter's plane). Planed, levelled, smoothed.

Spiccato (It.). Separated. In playing of bowed str. instr., form of staccato bowing in which the bow is allowed to bounce on the str.; prod. by rapid movements with restricted (central) portion of the bow. Same as *Saltando. See also Sautillé.

Spider's Feast, The (Roussel). See *Festin de l'araignée, Le*.

Spiegl, Fritz (*b* Zurndorf, 1926). Austrian-born flautist, writer, and broadcaster. Prin. flautist RLPO 1948–63. Expert on mus. curiosities, also on misuse of Eng. language. Ed. of old mus.

Spiel; Spielen (Ger.). Play; To play. So *Spielend*, playing, playful; *Volles Spiel*, Full Org.; *Spieler*, player.

Spiering, Theodore (*b* St Louis, 1871; *d* Munich, 1925). Amer. violinist and cond. Pupil of Joachim in Berlin 1892. Member of Chicago S.O. 1892–6. Founded str. qt. in Chicago, 1893–1905. Went to teach at Stern Cons., Berlin, 1905, returning to USA as leader of NY P.O., 1909. Cond. last concerts of Mahler's last NY season, 1910–11 when Mahler became mortally ill. Taught NY College of Mus. 1914–16.

Spies, Claudio (*b* Santiago, 1925). Chilean-born composer (Amer. citizen from 1966). Settled in USA 1942. Studied in Boston, Mass., 1943 with Boulanger and at Harvard Univ. 1947–50 (comp. with Hindemith, Piston). Taught at Harvard 1954–7, Swarthmore College 1958–64, and Princeton Univ. from 1970. Friend of and influenced by Stravinsky, becoming 12-note practitioner after 1959. Works incl. several song-cycles, also *Ensembles* for orch., *Viopiacem* for va. and hpd. or pf., *5 Orchestral Songs* for sop. and orch., *Times 2* for 2 hns., etc. Author of articles on Stravinsky's works.

Spinet (Fr. *épinette*; It. *spinetta*). Small type of early kbd. instr. of hpd. family in which str. ran diagonally in front of player or more or less parallel to kbd. as on virginals. Often made in uneven 6-sided shape with kbd. on longest side. Normally one set of str. and 4-octave compass. The name 'spinet' is indiscriminately applied to a no. of plucked kbd. instr. First mentioned 1496. A theory is that it was named after Giovanni Spina, an instr.-maker active in late 15th cent., another that the name derives from its thorn-like plectra, *spinetta* being diminutive of *spina*, a thorn. The 19th-cent. square pf. is often incorrectly called a spinet.

Spink, Ian (*b* London, 1932). Eng. teacher and authority on Eng. lute-songs. Studied TCL. Lecturer in mus. Sydney Univ., NSW, 1962–9. Head of mus. dept., Royal Holloway Coll., London Univ. from 1969, dean, Faculty of Arts 1973–5, dean, Faculty of Mus., London Univ. from 1974. Ed. Stainer and Bell edn. of *English Lute-Songs* vols. 17, 18, and 19, *English Song 1625–60* in *Musica Britannica*, xxxiii, etc.

Spinner, Leopold (*b* Lwów, 1906; *d* London, 1980). Austrian composer and teacher. Studied in Vienna 1926–30 with Pisk and 1935–8 with Webern. Though influenced by Webern, his works are on a larger scale. They incl.: Sym. (1934), *Passacaglia* for chamber orch. (1936), pf. conc. with chamber orch. (1947), *Concerto for Orchestra* (1957), *Ricercata*, orch. (1965), str. qt. (1934), vn. sonata (1936), str. qt. No. 1 (1941), No. 2 (1952), pf. sonata (1943), pf. trio (1950), quintet for cl., bn., hn., guitar, db. (1961), cl. sonata (1961), vc. sonatina (1973), cantata *Lebenslauf* (Hölderlin), sop., ch., orch. (1955), and songs.

Spinnerlied (Ger.). Spinning Song.

Spinto (It.). Pushed, urged on. Term used of certain variety of v., particularly sop. or ten., e.g. *soprano lirico spinto*, meaning a v. which has been 'pushed' into more forceful singing. Butterfly is an example of a *spinto* sop. role.

Spirito; Spiritoso (It.). Spirit, spirited.

Spirit of England, The. Settings by Elgar, Op. 80, for sop. or ten. soloist, ch., and orch. of 3 poems by Binyon, (1) *The 4th of August*, (2) *To Women*, (3) *For the Fallen*. Comp. 1915–16. F.p. of (1) Birmingham 1917, of (2) and (3) Leeds 1916, of complete work London 1917.

Spiritual. Folk-hymn which developed during Amer. religious revival of *c*.1740 and took its name from 'spiritual song', the term by which publishers distinguished it from hymns and metrical psalms. Negroes attended revivalist meetings and their characteristic adaptations of spirituals became the religious folk-songs of the Amer. Negro, e.g. *Swing low, sweet chariot, Go down Moses, Deep River*, etc. Became prominent *c*.1871 in concerts by Fisk Jubilee Singers, but even better known in 20th cent. through singing of Paul Robeson and Marian Anderson. Dvořák was deeply touched by Negro spirituals, though their influence on his Amer. works is arguable; and Tippett used some very effectively as chorales in his oratorio *A *Child of Our Time*.

Spisak, Michal (*b* Dabrowa Górnicza, 1914; *d* Paris, 1965). Polish composer. Studied Warsaw and in Paris 1937 with Boulanger. Settled in Fr. Works incl. bn. conc., *Divertimento* for 2 pf. and orch., pf. conc., 2-pf. conc., chamber mus., pf. pieces.

Spitfire Prelude and Fugue. 2 items from film mus. for *The First of the Few* by Walton (1942) rearr. for full orch. F.p. Liverpool 1943. Title refers to Spitfire fighter aircraft used by RAF in Battle of Britain, 1940 (the film told story of its designer, R. J. Mitchell).

Spitta, Julius August Philipp (*b* Wechold, Hoya, 1841; *d* Berlin, 1894). Ger. mus. scholar and writer. Studied at Göttingen, then taught in various towns incl. Leipzig. Prof. of mus. history, Berlin, 1875–94 and permanent secretary to Berlin Acad. of Arts. Dir., Berlin Hochschule für Musik, 1875–94. Contrib. to several dictionaries, histories, etc. Wrote 2-vol. life of Bach (1873, 1880, Eng. trans. 1884–5) and history of Ger. romantic opera. Ed. organ works of Buxtehude, (1876–7), complete works of Schütz (1885–94) and selected works of Frederick the Great (1889).

Spitze (Ger.). Point. Hence, in str. playing, *an der Spitze*, at the point (of the bow).

Spitzflöte (Ger.). Point-flute. Metal org. stop of slightly conical shape; 8′, 4′, or 2′ length and pitch.

Spivakovsky, Tossy (*b* Odessa, 1907). Russ.-born violinist (later Amer. citizen). Studied in Berlin with W. Hess, making début there 1917. Toured Europe 1920–33, settled in Australia 1933–41. Went to USA 1941. Developed new techniques of playing.

Spleen. Poem by Verlaine set for v. and pf. by Debussy, 1887–8, as no. 6 of *Ariettes oubliées* and by Fauré, 1889, as No. 3 of his Op. 51.

Spofforth, Reginald (*b* Southwell, Notts., 1770; *d* Brompton, London, 1827). Eng. composer of glees, the 2 most popular being *Hail, smiling morn* (No. 6 of *Six Glees*, 1810) and *How calm the evening* (pubd. *c*.1796).

Spohr, Ludwig (Louis) (*b* Brunswick, 1784; *d* Kassel, 1859). Ger. composer, violinist, and cond. Child prodigy as violinist and composer. At 14 member of Duke of Brunswick's court orch. Toured Russ. 1802, meeting Clementi and Field. From 1805 toured Ger. as violinist and cond., composing operas and oratorios. Vienna début 1812, becoming leader of orch. at Theater an der Wien until 1815. London début at Philharmonic

Soc. concert 1820 as solo violinist in his own 8th conc., thereby inaugurating Spohr vogue in Eng. Was one of first conds. to use baton. Appointed court cond. for life at Hesse-Kassel 1822 (gen. mus. dir. from 1847). Completed vn. method 1831. Early champion of Wagner, conducting *Der fliegende Holländer* at Kassel 1843 and *Tannhäuser* 1853. Spohr's operas were successful in their day (and *Faust* was successfully revived in London, 1984), but it is the melodic charm of his chamber mus. and his vn. concs. which has principally led to a moderate revival of interest in his work. Prin. comps.:

OPERAS: *Der Zweikampf mit der Geliebten* (1811), *Faust* (1813, rev. 1852), *Zemire und Azor* (1819), *Jessonda* (1823), *Der Alchymist* (1830).
ORATORIO: *The Last Judgment* (1825–6).
ORCH: Symphonies: No. 1 in E♭, No. 2 in D minor, No. 3 in C minor, No. 4 (*Die Weihe der Töne*, The Power of Sound), No. 5 in C minor, No. 6 in G (*Historical Symphony*), No. 7 in C (Double Symphony, *Irdisches und Göttliches in Menschenleben*), No. 8 in G minor, No. 9 in B minor (*The Seasons*); 6 ovs.; Waltzes.
CONCERTOS: 15 for vn. (1802–44), No. 8 in A minor being sub-titled *Gesangszene*, 'in the form of a vocal scena'; 4 for cl.; potpourris for vn., vc., and orch.; conc. for str. qt.
CHAMBER MUSIC: 34 str. qts.; 4 double str. qts.; 7 str. quintets; octet in E major (str. and wind); septet for pf. and wind; nonet in F for str. qt., fl., ob., cl., bn., hn.; pf. and wind quintet; 3 pf. trios; str. sextet; sonatas, etc.

Spontini, Gaspare (Luigi Pacifico) (*b* Majolati, Ancona, 1774; *d* Majolati, 1851). It. composer. Studied Naples Cons. Some church mus. earned him opera commission for Rome, 1796. 5 other operas followed. Went to Paris 1803, meeting with barely moderate success until the triumph of *La Vestale* in 1807. Became cond. of It. Opera in Paris 1810, improving standards and giving f. Paris p. of Mozart's *Don Giovanni* in its orig. form. Dismissed 1812, but reinstated 1814. Cond., Berlin Court Opera 1819. There, too, his tenure was stormy and controversial, partly because his quick temper and pompous manner made him hard to work with, and partly because he continued to promote his own Italianate works in the face of the new enthusiasm for Ger. romantic opera engendered by the success of Weber's *Der Freischütz*. When his royal patron died in 1840, Spontini was dismissed in 1841 but generously treated. Thereafter he lived chiefly in Paris until returning to his native village, to whose poor he left all his property. Operas incl.: *Li puntigli delle donne* (1796), *L'eroismo ridicolo* (1798), *Il finto pittore* (1800), *La fuga in maschera* (1800), *La finta filosofa* (1799), *Milton* (1804), *La *Vestale* (1807), *Fernand Cortez* (1809), *Olympie* (1819), *Nurmahal* (1822), *Alcidor* (1825), *Agnes von Hohenstaufen* (1829). Fest. pageant: *Lalla Rookh*

(1821). Most of Spontini's operas were rev. several times. Some have been perf. in It. since 1945.

Sprechgesang, Sprechstimme (Ger.). Spoken song, speech-song. Type of vocal perf. between speech and song. First used by *Humperdinck in first version of his opera *Königskinder* (1897), where singers were told to approximate the pitches but were doubled by instr. playing exact pitches. *Schoenberg used the idea in his *Gurre-lieder* (1900–11), in *Die *glückliche Hand* (1910–13), and especially in *Pierrot Lunaire* (1912) and in his opera *Moses und Aron* (1930–2). Berg used the device in *Wozzeck*, and many others have used it since. Schoenberg was liberal in his attitude to manner of perf., as his recording of *Pierrot Lunaire* shows. In general usage, *Sprechgesang* is the term for the vocal technique, *Sprechstimme* for the v.-part employing it. A well-known example of *Sprechgesang* is that of Rex Harrison (and his successors) as Prof. Higgins in *My Fair Lady*.

Springer (Norweg.). (1) Norweg. folk-dance in $\frac{3}{4}$ time, used in their mus. by Grieg and Svendsen.

(2) (Ger. *Nachschlag*). Ornament in which an extra note, indicated in smaller mus.-type, takes part of the preceding note's time-value, i.e. the opposite of *appoggiatura.

Spring Sonata (*Frühlingssonate*). Nickname given by someone other than Beethoven to his Sonata in F, Op. 24, for vn. and pf. (1801) – the name is not inappropriate.

Spring Song (*Frühlingslied*). Unauthorized name for Mendelssohn's *Lied ohne Worte*, No. 30 in A, Op. 62, No. 6.

Spring Symphony, A. Choral work, Op. 44, by Britten for sop., cont., and ten. soloists, ch., boys' choir, and orch. Setting of poems by Herrick, Auden, Barnefield, Peele, Blake, Beaumont, Fletcher, Nashe, Vaughan, Spenser, Clare, Milton and Anon. F. p. Amsterdam 1949, f. London p. 1950.

'Spring' Symphony. Title given to Schumann's Sym. No. 1 in B♭ major (1841).

Spugna, Bacchetta di (It.). Sponge-headed drumstick.

Square Piano. Rectangular form of *piano invented in London in 18th cent. and later made by the firm of Broadwood. Several restored instr. are now used to play mus. of the period.

Squillante, squillanti (It.). Clanging. (Applied to cymbals, it means that they should be suspended and struck with drumsticks.)

Squire, William Barclay (*b* London, 1855; *d* London, 1927). Eng. mus. scholar and critic. Studied Frankfurt and Cambridge Univ. Became solicitor but then joined staff of Brit. Museum 1885, in charge of printed mus. until 1920. Mus. critic of various London journals 1890–1904. Wrote libs. Hon. sec., Purcell Soc., and contrib. to

Grove's Dictionary. Ed. works by Purcell, Byrd, Palestrina, Handel, etc., also *Fitzwilliam Virginal Book (with Fuller Maitland).

Squire, William Henry (*b* Ross, 1871; *d* London, 1963). Eng. cellist and composer. Studied RCM. Début London 1890. Played in CG orch. 1894–7, Queen's Hall Orch. 1897–1901. Prof. of vc., RCM 1898–1917 and GSM 1911–17. Wrote vc. conc. and songs. Recorded Elgar conc. with Harty.

Staatskapelle (Ger.). Literally 'State chapel', but any est. mus. institution such as an orch., deriving from the time of princely courts. Thus, the 400-year-old Dresden orch. is known still as *Staatskapelle Dresden*.

Staatsoper (Ger.). State opera-house or co.

Stabat Mater Dolorosa (Lat.). A grief-stricken mother was standing. Devotional poem about Virgin Mary's vigil by Christ's Cross, used as sequence in R.C. liturgy since 1727 to plainchant melody. Text once attrib. Jacopo de Benedetti, known as Jacopone da Todi (*c*.1228–1306). Among the many comp. settings are those by Palestrina, Pergolesi, Haydn, Rossini, Verdi, Dvořák, Stanford, Szymanowski, Berkeley, and others.

Stäbchen (Ger.). Little staff. *Triangle beater.

Stabile, Mariano (*b* Palermo, 1888; *d* Milan, 1968). It. bar. Studied in Rome. Opera début Palermo 1911 as Marcello in Puccini's *Bohème*. Sang title-role in Verdi's *Falstaff* at La Scala, Milan, in 1921 under Toscanini, this becoming his most famous and successful role: he sang it until 1961 and his perf. is regarded as unsurpassed. Sang at CG 1926–31, Glyndebourne 1936–9. Returned to London at Cambridge and Stoll Th.s' opera seasons 1946–8. Salzburg Fest. 1935–9. Repertory of over 60 parts.

Staccato (It.). Detached. Method of playing a note (shown by a dot over the note) so that it is shortened—and thus 'detached' from its successor—by being held for less than its full value. Superlative is *staccatissimo*. For signs used to indicate degrees of staccato see diagram p. 687.

Stade, Frederica von (*b* Somerville, NJ, 1945). Amer. mez. Studied Mannes Coll. of Mus., NY. Opera début with NY Met. 1970. Sang Cherubino at Paris Opéra 1973 and Glyndebourne. CG début 1975 (Rosina in *Il barbiere di Siviglia*). Guest singer at Milan, NY City Opera, Holland Fest., etc. Exceptional Oktavian in *Der Rosenkavalier*.

Staden, Johann (*b* Nuremberg, 1581; *d* Nuremberg, 1634). Ger. organist and composer. Held various court organist posts. Wrote much church mus., also secular instr. pieces and songs.

Stader, Maria (*b* Budapest, 1911). Hung.-born Swiss sop. Studied at Karlsruhe, Zürich, and Milan. Celebrated singer of Mozart and Strauss. Teacher at Zürich Mus. Acad. Retired 1969.

MEZZO-STACCATO (shorten the note by about ¼)	STACCATO (shorten the notes by about ½)	STACCATISSIMO (shorten the notes by about ¾)
Written		

The sign $\bar{\cdot}\ \bar{\cdot}\ \bar{\cdot}$ (i.e. a combination of accent marks and staccato marks) indicates a combination of pressure with a slight detachment.

Stadlen, Peter (*b* Vienna, 1910). Austrian-born pianist, cond., and mus. critic (Brit. citizen since 1946). Studied Vienna Hochschule für Musik 1929–33 (pf. with Kreutzer). Career as pianist from 1934, specializing in Viennese classics and 2nd Viennese Sch. Gave f.ps. of Webern's Pf. Variations (1937), Křenek's *Bagatelles* for pf. duet, with composer (1936). Soloist in European f.p. of Schoenberg conc. (Darmstadt 1948). Settled in Eng. 1939. Master classes in modern pf. works, Darmstadt 1948–51. Schoenberg Medal 1952. Mus. lecturer, Reading Univ., 1965–9. Mus. critic, *Daily Telegraph*, from 1960 (chief critic 1977–86). Author of monographs on Beethoven's metronome marks, decline of serialism, Schoenberg and *Sprechgesang*, and Schindler's Beethoven forgeries.

Stadler, Anton (*b* Bruck an der Leitha, 1753; *d* Vienna, 1812). Austrian clarinettist and basset-hn. player. Member of Vienna court orch. 1787–99. Friend of Mozart, who greatly admired his playing of the 'basset clarinet' (a cl. with a downward extension of 4 semitones) and wrote for him the Cl. Trio in E♭ (K498, 1786), the Cl. Quintet in A (K581, 1789), and the Cl. Conc. in A (K622, 1791), as well as other pieces such as the cl. and basset-horn obbligati in *La Clemenza di Tito* which Stadler played at the f.p. in Prague, 1791. The quintet and conc. were pubd. in altered form to suit a normal cl., but in the 20th cent. Alan *Hacker has played the orig. versions to good effect. Stadler and Mozart played together in f.p. of Mozart's E♭ quintet (K452), Vienna 1784.

Stadlmayer, Johann (*b* Freising, Bavaria, *c*.1575; *d* Innsbruck, 1648). Ger. composer and choirmaster at several courts until settling in Innsbruck 1607. Wrote large amount of church mus. (masses, motets, cantatas, psalms, etc.).

Städtische Oper (Ger.). City or municipal opera-house or co.

Stadtpfeifer (Ger.). Town piper. Musician(s) in employ of town council. Term used since late 14th cent. in European cities. Duties of these musicians incl. perf. at official festivities, weddings, baptisms, royal visits, etc. They had exclusive right to provide mus. in the city boundaries.

Staempfli, Edward (*b* Berne, 1908). Swiss composer and pianist. Studied at Cologne 1929–30 and with Dukas in Paris 1930–1. Interest in 12-note mus. stimulated by hearing f.p. of Berg vn. conc. 1936. Settled in Berlin 1954. Works incl. 3 syms., 4 pf. concs., 3 vn. concs., opera *Medea*, oratorios, 6 str. qts., cl. qt., etc.

Staff (Stave, plural staves). The system of parallel lines on and between which the notes are written, from which mus. is played, the pitch being determined by the *clef written at the beginning of the staff. Normally of 5 lines, but plainsong uses a staff of 4 lines. In medieval tablature a 6- or even 7-line staff was used. 'Staff notation' means ordinary notation as distinct from Tonic Sol-fa, etc. See also *Great Staff*.

Staggins, Nicholas (*d* Windsor, 1700). Eng. composer and violinist. Appointed Master of the King's Band (i.e. Master of the King's Musick) by Charles II in 1674. First prof. of mus. Cambridge Univ., 1684. Wrote songs.

Stagione (It.). Season. Term used with reference to opera. *Stagione lirica* is the opera season at It. ths.; a *Stagione* th. is one which stages a seasonal repertory.

Stainer and Bell. Eng. firm of mus. publishers, founded 1907 by group of composers to publish Brit. music (there was no Mr Stainer nor Mr Bell). Publisher of Carnegie coll. of modern Brit. works from 1917. Also pubd. Eng. madrigalists, lute-song writers, works of Byrd, etc.

Stainer, Jacob (*b* Absam, nr. Hall, Tyrol, ?1617; *d* Absam, 1683). Austrian violin-maker. Apprenticed to Ger. violin-maker who lived in It. Oldest surviving example of his work is dated Absam 1638. Court employee from 1658. Last vn. dated 1682. Also made viols, cellos, and double basses. Though admired for 150 years, Stainer's violins were superseded in 19th cent. by those made in Cremona which produced a greater volume of sound.

Stainer, (Sir) John (*b* London, 1840; *d* Verona, 1901). Eng. composer, organist, teacher, and scholar. Chorister, St Paul's Cath., 1849–54. Studied Oxford Univ. Organist, St Paul's 1872–88. Prof. of org. and harmony, Nat. Training Sch. of Mus., and prin. from 1881. Prof. of mus., Oxford Univ., from 1889. Wrote books on harmony and about *Dufay. His *Early Bodleian Music* (1901) is one of first serious studies of medieval music. Comp. much church mus., incl. *Sevenfold Amen*, and oratorios and cantatas of which the best-known is The *Crucifixion* (1887). Knighted 1888.

Stamitz (orig. Stamic), **Anton** (Johann) (orig. Jan Antonín) (*b* Německý Brod, 1750; *d* ?Paris, after 1789). Member of Cz. family of musicians who settled in Ger. and adopted Ger. form of surname. Son of Johann Wenzel *Stamitz. Went with brother Karl to Paris in 1770 and settled there as comp., violinist, and viola player. Wrote 12 syms., various concs., str. qts., etc.

Stamitz (orig. Stamic), **Johann Wenzel** (orig. Jan Václav Antonín) (*b* Německý Brod, Bohemia, 1717; *d* Mannheim, 1757). Bohem.-born violinist and composer. Studied with his father. Played vn. at coronation of Karl VII 1742 and was heard by Elector of Mannheim who made him court violinist and mus. dir. in 1745. Raised the orch. there to standards which became famous throughout Europe and influenced composers such as Haydn and Mozart. Visited Paris 1754–5, playing at Concert Spirituel. As composer, greatly expanded sonata-form principles in the sym., giving new importance to development section. Wrote 58 syms., 15 vn. concs., vn. sonatas, and much else.

Stamitz (orig. Stamic), **Karl** (orig. Karel) (*b* Mannheim, 1745; *d* Jena, 1801). Ger. composer and violinist, son of Johann Wenzel *Stamitz. Violinist in Mannheim orch. 1762–70. Went to Paris with brother in 1770 and to London 1777–9. Returned to Ger. as cond. at Jena. Also visited Russ. Wrote operas, over 50 syms., 38 sinfonie concertanti (for vn. and va., etc.), concs. for various instr. (incl. vn., vc., va. d'amore, bn., cl., fl., hpd.), and chamber mus.

Ständchen (Ger.). Serenade. Songs by Schubert, R. Strauss, etc., carry this title.

Standford, Patric (John) (*b* Barnsley, 1939). Eng. composer. Studied GSM with *Rubbra. Awarded Mendelssohn Schol. 1964 and went to It. to study with Gianfrancesco Malipiero and Lutosławski,

1964–5. Prof. of comp. GSM from 1967; has also taught at Goldsmith's Coll and Chetham's Sch. of Mus., Manchester. Awarded City of Geneva's Ansermet Prize 1983 for his 3rd Sym. Works incl.:

OPERA: *Villon* (1972–84).

ORCH: Syms., No. 1 (*The Seasons*) (1971–2), No. 5 (1984); *A Christmas Carol Symphony* (1965); *Saracinesco*, sym.-poem (1966–8); *Suite* (1966); *Notte*, poem for chamber orch. (1968); *Celestial Fire*, ballet suite (1969); *Antitheses* (in memoriam Sir John Barbirolli), 15 str. (1971); *Reflections*, ballet suite (1980); *Folksongs for Strings* (1982).

CONCERTOS: Vc. Conc. (1974); Vn. Conc. (1975); Sym. No. 4 (*Taikyoku*) for 2 pf. and 6 perc. (1975–6); Pf. Conc. (1979); *Dialogues*, cimbalom and orch. (1981).

CHORAL & VOCAL: Syms., No. 2 (*Christus-Requiem*), oratorio, 4 male soloists, narrator, ch., children's ch., org., orch. (1971–2), No. 3 (*Towards Paradise*), ch. and orch. (1973, rev. 1982); *Stabat Mater* (1966); *3 Motets in memory of Benjamin Britten* (1977); *Psalm Dances*, sop., alto, basses, orch. (1977); *Mass*, ch. and brass (1980); *Ave Maris Stella*, women's vv. (1981)

CHAMBER MUSIC: Str. Qt. No. 1 (1964), No. 2 (1973); *Bagatelles*, str. qt. (1969); pf. trio (1970); solo vn. sonata (1971).

PIANO: *Variations* (1969); sonata (1979).

Stanford, (Sir) Charles Villiers (*b* Dublin, 1852; *d* London, 1924). Irish composer, cond., organist, and teacher. Studied Cambridge Univ. 1870. Organist, Trinity College, Cambridge, 1873–92. Studied in Leipzig with Reinecke and in Berlin with Kiel 1874–6. Cond., Cambridge Univ. Mus. Soc. from 1873, winning it high reputation and giving f. Eng. ps. of works by Brahms. Tennyson asked him to write incidental mus. for his play *Queen Mary*, 1876. Prof. of comp., RCM, 1883–1924, pupils incl. Vaughan Williams, Bliss, Howells, Ireland, Holst, Gurney, etc. Prof. of mus., Cambridge Univ., 1887–1924. Cond., Bach Choir 1885–1902, also cond. of orch. concerts and opera at RCM. Cond. of several Leeds Fests. after 1901. Knighted 1901. Prolific composer, whose best work is to be found in his operas, choral mus., and songs rather than in his orch. and chamber mus., where his admiration for Brahms tended to become paramount. One of prin. figures in late 19th-cent. 'renaissance' of Brit. mus. Ed. and arr. colls. of Irish traditional tunes. Chief works:

OPERAS: *The Veiled Prophet of Khorassan* (1877); *Savonarola* (1884); The *Canterbury Pilgrims* (1884); *Lorenza* (unpubd.); *Shamus O'Brien* (1896); *Much Ado About Nothing* (1900); *The *Critic* (1915); The *Travelling Companion* (1919).

ORCH: Syms.: No. 1 in B♭ (1875), No. 2 in D minor (*Elegiac*) (1882), No. 3 in F minor (*Irish*) (1887), No. 4 in F (1888), No. 5 in D (*L'Allegro ed il Pensieroso*) (1894), No. 6 in E♭ (1905), No. 7

in D minor (1911); *Overture in the Style of A Tragedy* (1904); *6 Irish Rhapsodies*; cl. conc. (1902); vc. conc.; 3 pf. concs.; 2 vn. concs.

CHORAL: Oratorios: *The Three Holy Children* (1885), *Eden* (1891); *Requiem* (1897); *Te Deum* (1898); *Stabat Mater* (1907); *Magnificat in G*; *The *Revenge*, choral ballad (1886); *Phaudrig Crohoore* (1896); *The Last Post* (1900); 5 *Songs of the Sea*, bar., male ch., and orch. (1904); 5 *Songs of the Fleet*, bar. and ch. (1910).

CHAMBER MUSIC: 8 str. qts., 2 str. quintets, 2 pf. trios, 2 pf. qts., pf. quintet, 2 vn. sonatas, 2 vc. sonatas, cl. sonata.

Also organ preludes, songs, partsongs (incl. *The *Blue Bird*), anthems, and church services (notably that in B♭, Op. 10, 1879 with additions 1910).

Stanley, (Charles) **John** (*b* London, 1712; *d* London, 1786). Eng. composer and organist, blinded at age 2. Pupil of Maurice *Greene from age 7. Organist of various London churches, incl. the Temple, from 1734. Wrote 6 cantatas, 1748, oratorio *Jephtha* 1751–2. The 6 concs. for str., with org. or hpd., Op. 10, have considerable appeal, influenced by Handel, and he also wrote 30 org. voluntaries, fl. solos, etc. Succeeded Boyce as Master of the King's Musick, 1779.

Star Clusters, Nebulae, and Places in Devon. Work for mixed double ch. and brass by David *Bedford, comp. 1971; arr. Bram Wiggins, 1974, for mixed double ch. and brass band.

Starer, Robert (*b* Vienna, 1924). Austrian-born composer (Amer. citizen since 1957). Studied Vienna State Acad. and after 1938 at Jerusalem Cons. Went to NY 1947, studying at Juilliard Sch., joining teaching faculty 1949. Teacher at Brooklyn College 1963 (prof. from 1966). Works incl. 2 operas, 3 syms. (1950, 1951, 1969), 3 pf. concs. (1947, 1953, and 1972), va. conc., vc. conc., vn. and vc. conc., *Concerto a tre* (cl., tpt., tb., and str.) (1954), *Kohelet* (Hebrew text) for soloists, ch., and orch. (1952), *Joseph and his Brothers* (1966), ballet *The Dybbuk* (1960), and ballets for Martha Graham.

Stark (Ger.). Strong, loud; so *stärker*, stronger, louder. **Stark anblasen, stark blasend.** Strongly blown (wind instr.).

Starker, János (*b* Budapest, 1924). Hung.-born cellist (Amer. citizen). Studied Liszt Acad., Budapest. Début age of 10. Prin. cellist Budapest Opera and P.O., 1945–6. Settled in USA 1948. Prin. cellist Dallas S.O. 1948–9, NY Met. opera orch. 1949–53, Chicago S.O. 1953–8. Prof. of vc., Indiana Univ., from 1958. Soloist with leading orchs. since 1958. Invented a vc. bridge.

Starlight Express, The. Incidental mus. by Elgar, Op. 78, to play by Violet Pearn based on Algernon Blackwood's *Prisoner in Fairyland.* Prod. London 1915. Contains songs for sop. and bass

soloists. Quotes themes from *Wand of Youth. Cowbells and wind-machine used in score.

Starokadomsky, Mikhail (*b* Brest-Litovsk, 1901; *d* Moscow, 1954). Russ. composer and organist. Studied Moscow Cons. (comp. with Myaskovsky, org. with Goedicke). Wrote opera and light operas, also orch. works in neoclassical style, incl. *Concerto for Orchestra*, vn. conc., org. conc., oratorio, str. qts., pf. pieces, and songs.

Star-Spangled Banner, The. Nat. anthem of USA, officially adopted under Senate Bill in 1931 but long used as such before that. Words written by Francis Scott Key (1779–1843) of Baltimore on 15 Sept. 1814, after he had seen defence of Fort McHenry, near Baltimore, against Brit. bombardment. First appeared in *Baltimore Patriot*, 20 Sept. 1814. Metre of poem indicates it was written to tune of *To Anacreon in Heaven* by Eng. composer J. Stafford *Smith which was then popular in Amer. as official song of Anacreontic socs. there.

Starzer, Josef (*b* Vienna, c.1726; *d* Vienna, 1787). Austrian composer and violinist. Violinist in orch. of Burgtheater, Vienna, 1752–7. Court composer St Petersburg 1760–70. Returning to Vienna in 1768, became popular composer of ballets, of which he wrote over 20. Also comp. divertimenti.

Stasov (Stassov), **Vladimir** (Vasilyevich) (*b* St Petersburg, 1824; *d* St Petersburg, 1906). Russ. critic. Worked in art div. of Imperial Public Library from 1857. Champion of Russ. nationalism in arts, esp. mus. Wrote monographs on Mussorgsky, Borodin, Cui, Rimsky-Korsakov, Dargomizhsky, Glinka, and others. Coined phrase 'mighty handful' (*moguchaya kuchka*) later applied to Russ. nationalist composers known as 'The Five'.

Stave. Same as *Staff.*

Stavenhagen, Bernhard (*b* Greiz, 1862; *d* Geneva, 1914). Ger. pianist and cond. Studied with Kiel, Rudorff, and Liszt. Mendelssohn pf.-playing prize 1880. Settled in Weimar 1885, becoming court pianist 1890 and Kapellmeister 1895. Dir., Munich Acad. of Mus., 1901–4. Returned to Weimar, but left to cond. Geneva subscription concerts from 1907. Wrote 2 pf. concs., pf. pieces, etc.

Steber, Eleanor (*b* Wheeling, W. Virginia, 1916). Amer. sop. Studied in Boston and NY, giving recitals and becoming church soloist in NY. Won Metropolitan Auditions of the Air 1940, making début at Met. in Dec. 1940 as Sophie in *Der Rosenkavalier*. Member of Met. co. until 1963, being highly successful in Mozart and Strauss, also in Puccini and as Marie in *Wozzeck*. Created title-role in Barber's *Vanessa* 1958. Sang with Glyndebourne at Edinburgh Fest. 1947. Bayreuth 1953. Sang title-role in f. Amer. p. of *Arabella* (NY

Met. 1955) and gave f.p. of Barber's *Knoxville: Summer of 1915* (1948) which she commissioned. After retirement from stage, gave Lieder recitals (in London in 1964) and taught at Cleveland Institute of Mus., New England Cons., and Juilliard Sch.

Steel Band. Type of instr. ens. in the Caribbean, 'instruments' being old oil drums whose heads are indented, etc., so that each head will produce several notes. Used extensively in calypso mus.

Steel, Christopher (*b* London, 1939). Eng. composer. Studied RAM 1957–61 (comp. with *Gardner) and in Munich from 1961. Taught mus. at Cheltenham College, 1963–6, ass. dir. of mus. Bradfield College 1966–8, dir. from 1968. Has written several works for amateur enjoyment in addition to orch. mus. and choral pieces. Chief comps.: 4 syms. (3rd being *A Shakespeare Symphony* for bar., ch., and orch., 1965), conc. for str. qt. and orch. (1966), org. conc., *Odyssey* (suite for brass band, 1973), *Mass* in 5 movements for sop., ten., ch., and orch. (1964), *Gethsemane*, cantata (1964), *Mary Magdalene*, cantata (1966), *Paradise Lost*, cantata for sop., tenor, bass, ch., and orch. (1966), *Passion and Resurrection according to St Mark*, sop., ten., bass soloists, ch., and orch. (1979), pf. sonatinas, cl. sonatina, *Divertimento* for wind quintet, pf. trio, str. qt., *6 Pieces* for org., org. sonata, fl. trio, etc.

Stefano, Giuseppe di. See *Di Stefano, Giuseppe*.

Stefan, Paul (*b* Brno, 1879; *d* NY, 1943). Austrian critic and scholar. Studied at Brno (then Brünn) and Vienna Univ. Pupil of Schoenberg. Mus., art, and literary critic of Vienna newspaper *Die Stunde* for many years, also foreign correspondent for 28 years of *Neue Züricher Zeitung* and other newspapers. Co-founder of ISCM. Left Austria 1938, settling eventually in USA. Author of books on Vienna Opera (1932), Schoenberg (1924), Mahler (1910 and many other edns.), Schubert (1928), Hofmannsthal, Max Reinhardt, Bruno Walter (1936), Toscanini (1935). Ed. E. T. A. Hoffmann's mus. writings.

Steffani, Agostino (*b* Castelfranco, 1654; *d* Frankfurt, 1728). It. composer, diplomat, and priest. Chorister, then taken to Munich 1667 and educated at Elector's expense. Went for further studies in Rome, returning to Munich 1675 as court organist. Became priest 1680. Wrote 6 operas for Munich 1680–8. Court Kapellmeister, Hanover, 1688, where he wrote 9 operas. Became successful diplomat and was made Bishop of Spiga *in partibus infidelium* 1706. Wrote 3 operas for Düsseldorf 1703–9. Left Hanover 1711, being succeeded by Handel. Worked in It. 1722–5. His operas were much admired in their day (and *Tassilone* (1709) was revived in 1980s), and his church mus., particularly the *Stabat Mater*, and chamber duets are worth exploration.

Steg (Ger.). Bridge (of vn., etc.). *Am Steg*, same as *Sul ponticello*, i.e. bow on (near) the bridge.

Stehle, Sophie (*b* Hohenzollern-Sigmaringen, 1838; *d* Schloss Harterode, Hanover, 1921). Ger. sop. Début Munich Opera 1860. Created roles of Fricka in Wagner's *Das Rheingold*, Munich 1869, and of Brünnhilde in *Die Walküre*, Munich 1870.

Steibelt, Daniel (*b* Berlin, 1765; *d* St Petersburg, 1823). Ger. pianist and composer. From 1790 to 1797 was fashionable teacher and pianist in Paris, where his opera *Romeo and Juliet* was prod. 1793. From 1797 to 1808 he was often in London, as well as in Vienna, 1799, where he was involved in an improvisation contest with Beethoven and came off much the worse. In Paris, 1800, he cond. Haydn's *The Creation* with additions and alterations of his own. Wrote ballets for London, 1804–5. Court cond. to Emperor Alexander in St Petersburg 1808, succeeding Boieldieu as cond. of Fr. opera there in 1810. Wrote 8 pf. concs., over 160 vn. sonatas, and a pf. method.

Stein, Erwin (*b* Vienna, 1885; *d* London, 1958). Austrian-born cond., ed., and critic, later Eng. citizen. Pupil of Schoenberg 1906–10 and active as opera cond. Ed. for Universal Edition in Vienna 1924–38. Settled in London 1938, joining Boosey and Hawkes. Ed. Schoenberg's letters. Associate and friend of Britten. Book of essays, *Orpheus in New Guises*, 1953. Daughter **Marion** (*b* Vienna, 1927) is pianist, dir., Aldeburgh Fest. and Leeds pf. competition, and wife of (1) Earl of Harewood, (2) Jeremy Thorpe.

Stein, Fritz (Wilhelm) (*b* Gerlachsheim, Baden, 1879; *d* Berlin, 1961). Ger. musicologist and cond. Studied Leipzig Cons. Mus. dir., later prof., Jena Univ. 1906–14, 1915–18, court cond., Meiningen 1914–15, prof. of mus. Kiel Univ. 1928–33, dir., Berlin Hochschule für Musik 1933–45. While at Jena found in library parts of sym. which he pubd. in 1911 as 'an unknown sym. of Beethoven's youth'. This became known as *Jena Symphony*. In 1957 Robbins Landon discovered it was the work of Friedrich Witt.

Stein, Horst (*b* Elberfeld, 1928). Ger. conductor. Studied at Cologne Hochschule für Musik, then cond. in Wuppertal. Cond. at Hamburg Opera 1951, Berlin State Opera 1955–61, Mannheim 1963–70, Vienna 1970–2. Gen. mus. dir. Hamburg State Opera from 1972. Cond., Orchestre de la Suisse Romande 1980–5, Bamberg S.O. from 1986. Regular cond. at Bayreuth Fest.

Stein, Richard Heinrich (*b* Halle, 1882; *d* S. Brigida, Canary Is., 1942). Ger. composer. Studied Berlin Hochschule. Lived in Spain 1914–19, then Berlin. Settled in Canary Is. 1933. Experimented with quarter-tones in pf. comps. from 1906. Wrote books on Grieg and Tchaikovsky.

Steinbach, Emil (*b* Lengenrieden, Baden, 1849; *d* Mainz, 1919). Ger. cond. and composer, elder brother of Fritz *Steinbach. Studied Leipzig Cons. 1867–9 and with H. *Levi. Court cond., Darmstadt 1872–7, then at Mainz 1877–1909. Cond. at CG 1893. Wagner interpreter; cond. f. public p. of *Siegfried Idyll*, 1877. Wrote orch. works and songs.

Steinbach, Fritz (*b* Grünsfeld, Baden, 1855; *d* Munich, 1916). Ger. cond. and composer. Studied with his brother Emil *Steinbach and at Leipzig Cons. 1873. 2nd cond. at Mainz 1880–6. Taught in Frankfurt 1883–6. Cond. Meiningen Orch. 1886–1902, taking it on tour (incl. England) 1902. Guest cond. NY P.O. 1906. Cond. Gürzenich concerts, Cologne (succeeding Wüllner) and dir., Cologne Cons. from 1902. Famous as Brahms interpreter, also cond. several Elgar works in Ger. Wrote chamber mus. and songs.

Steinberg, Maximilian (*b* Vilna, 1883; *d* Leningrad, 1946). Russ. composer. Studied with Rimsky-Korsakov (his father-in-law from 1908), and Glazunov. Prof. of comp. St Petersburg Cons. from 1908, becoming dir. 1934. Pupils incl. *Shostakovich. Comps. incl. 4 syms. (1907, 1909, 1928, 1933), ballets, choral works, str. qts., etc.

Steinberg, William (*b* Cologne, 1899; *d* NY, 1978). Ger.-born cond. (Amer. citizen). Ass. cond. to Klemperer at Cologne Opera 1920. Cond., German Th. in Prague 1925–9. Mus. dir. Frankfurt Opera 1929–33 (cond. f.p. of Schoenberg's *Von Heute auf Morgen* 1930); mus. dir. Jewish Culture League, Ger., 1933–6. In Palestine 1936–8. Settled in USA 1938. Ass. cond. NBC S.O. 1938–41. Cond. Buffalo P.O. 1945–52, Pittsburgh S.O. 1952–76. Prin. cond. LPO 1958–62, Boston S.O. 1969–72, prin. guest cond. NY P.O. 1964–8.

Steiner, Max(imilian Raoul) (*b* Vienna, 1888; *d* Hollywood, Calif., 1971). Austrian-born composer (Amer. citizen). Studied in Vienna. Cond. musical comedies in London 1905–11. Settled in USA 1914. Worked in NY as orchestrator and cond. of musicals. Went to Hollywood 1929 and wrote mus. for many successful films, incl. *The Informer*, *Now, Voyager*, *Gone With the Wind*, and *Since You Went Away*.

Steinitz, (Charles) **Paul** (Joseph) (*b* Chichester, 1909). Eng. organist and choral cond. Studied RAM, later joining teaching staff. Organist, St Bartholomew the Great, Smithfield, 1949–61. Founder and cond., London Bach Soc. from 1946. Famous for perfs. of Bach's *St Matthew Passion* in Ger. with forces near to Leipzig orig. O.B.E. 1985.

Steinspiel (Ger.). Stone-play. Perc. instr. specially made for *Orff's operas *Antigone* and *Oedipus Tyrannus*. Shaped like a kbd., it is an arr. of varying-sized stone bars, which are struck by beaters held in the player's hand.

Steinway and Sons. NY firm of pf. manufacturers founded 1853 by Henry Engelhardt Steinway (orig. Steinweg) (*b* Wolfshagen, 1797; *d* NY, 1871)

and his sons Charles and Henry, who in 1851 had gone to NY from Hamburg where they were involved in the Steinweg firm which eventually became Grotrian-Steinweg. At 1855 NY World Fair, Steinway prod. iron-framed pf. of much greater sonority than had hitherto been heard. A 3rd son, Theodore, joined the firm in the 1860s and developed the concert-grands which made the firm world-famous. Branch opened in London 1875 by 4th son, William, and factories est. in Hamburg 1880. Amer. factory moved to Long Island to site which became known as Steinway. Firm sold to CBS in 1972.

Stendendo (It.). Extending, i.e. spacing out the notes (same as *rallentando*).

Stendhal (orig. Marie-Henri Beyle) (*b* Grenoble, 1783; *d* Paris, 1842). Fr. writer. Wrote life of Rossini (1824), an entertaining but inaccurate book.

Stenhammar, Wilhelm Eugen (*b* Stockholm, 1871; *d* Stockholm, 1927). Swedish pianist, composer, and cond. Studied in Stockholm and Berlin. Mus. dir., Stockholm Phil. 1897–1900, 2nd cond. Royal Th., Stockholm, 1900–1, cond. Göteborg S.O. 1906–22. Wrote 2 operas, 2 syms., 2 pf. concs., vn. conc., *2 Sentimental Romances* for vn. and orch. (1910), chamber mus., etc.

Steppes of Central Asia, In the (Borodin). See *In the Steppes of Central Asia*.

Steptoe, Roger (Guy) (*b* Winchester, 1953). Eng. composer, pianist, and teacher. Studied at Reading Univ. and RAM 1974–6 (comp. with Alan Bush). Composer-in-residence Charterhouse Sch. 1976–9. Works incl.:

OPERA: *King of Macedon* (1978–9).
ORCH: *2 Miniatures* (1977); *Sinfonia Concertante*, vn., va., vc., str. (1981); ob. conc., str. (1982).
VOICE AND ORCH: *The Inheritor*, bar. (1979).
CHAMBER ENS: Str. qt. (1976); cl. quintet (1980); Sonata No. 1 (*Aurora*), str. qt., pf., cl., tpt. (1982), No. 2, 2 hns., pf. (1982).
BRASS: *Ceremonial Fanfare* (for Aberdeen) (1981); Sonata No. 3 (*The Knight of the Sun*), brass quintet (1982); *Dance Music* (rev. 1982).
VOCAL: *5 Songs*, ten., pf. (1977); *Aspects*, high v., pf. (1978); *The Looking Glass*, sop., ob., pf. (1980); *A Little Music*, bar., pf. (1981); *5 Chinese Lyrics*, sop., pf. (1982).
CHORAL: *The Jumblies*, cantata for children (1975); *King of Glory, King of Peace*, ch., org. (1980).
CHAMBER MUSIC: *2 Impromptus*, cl. (1976); *From Hyperion*, ob., pf. (1977); *Study*, vn. (1978); pf. sonata (1979); *Equinox*, pf. (1981); *2 Impromptus*, vc., guitar (1981); *Study No. 2*, guitar (1981); *Dance Suite*, str. qt., cl., ob. (1984).

Sterbend (Ger.). Dying away.

Sterling, Antoinette (*b* Sterlingville, NY, 1850; *d* London, 1904). Amer. cont. Studied in NY, Baden (with Viardot-García), Cologne (with Marchesi), and London (with García). Returned to USA 1871 but went to London 1873 where she became very popular as singer of ballads (Sullivan's *The Lost Chord*, 1877, was written for her).

Stern, Isaac (*b* Kremenets, 1920). Russ.-born Amer. violinist, taken as infant to San Francisco. Studied with Blinder and Persinger. Début 1935 (recital) and 1936 with San Francisco S.O. NY début 1937. Int. career as conc. soloist, also fine chamber-mus. player, esp. in assoc. with Eugene Istomin (pf.) and Leonard Rose (vc.).

Stern, Julius (*b* Breslau, 1820; *d* Berlin, 1883). Ger. violinist, cond., composer, and teacher. Studied Berlin, Dresden, and Paris. Founded Sternscher Gesangverein, Berlin, 1847 (disbanded 1912). In 1850, with Kullak and Marx, founded conservatory in Berlin.

Steso (It., 'Spread out'). Slow.

Stesso, stessa, stessi, stesse (It.). Same.

Steuermann, Eduard (*b* Sambor, nr. Lwów, 1892; *d* NY, 1964). Polish-born pianist and composer (Amer. citizen). Studied in Berlin (pf.with Busoni, theory with Schoenberg, comp. with Humperdinck). Pianist in f.ps. of Schoenberg's *Pierrot Lunaire* 1912 and of several other Schoenberg works with pf. part. Also gave f.p. of Berg's sonata. Pianist for Schoenberg's Society for Private Musical Performances. Taught pf. at Lwów and at Kraków Cons. (1932–6). Settled in USA 1936, teaching and playing in NY. Taught at Philadelphia Cons. 1948–52 and at Juilliard Sch. 1952–64. Tireless champion of 12-note mus., especially Schoenberg's, several of whose orch. works he transcr. for pf. Gave series of concerts of contemporary mus. in NY. Works incl. cantata to text by Kafka, *Variations* for orch., *Suite* for chamber orch., song-cycles, str. qts., etc.

Stevens, Bernard (*b* London, 1916; *d* Great Maplestead, Essex, 1983). Eng. composer. Studied Cambridge Univ. and RCM 1937–40 (with Jacob, R. O. Morris, Benjamin). Prof. of comp., RCM, from 1948. Works incl. *Symphony of Liberation* (1945), vn. conc., vc. conc., chamber mus., songs, film mus.

Stevens, Denis (William) (*b* High Wycombe, 1922). Eng. musicologist, critic, violinist, and cond. Studied Oxford Univ. with Wellesz. Worked as mus. critic in Calcutta and Oxford. Played vn. and va. in Philharmonia Orch. 1946–9. On BBC mus. staff as producer specializing in Renaissance and Baroque mus. 1949–54. Cond., Ambrosian Singers 1956–60. Prof., RAM 1956–61, prof. of musicology, Columbia Univ., NY, 1964–74 and visiting prof. at other Amer. univs. Ed. of Monteverdi's *Vespers* (1961) and *Orfeo* (1967), author of books on Tudor church mus. and Thomas Tomkins, ed. of Eng. madrigals, Tudor org. mus., etc. C.B.E. 1984.

Stevens, Halsey (*b* Scott, NY, 1908). Amer. composer and writer. Studied at Syracuse Univ. 1926–31 and with Bloch in Calif. 1944. Held various univ. teaching posts from 1935, becoming prof. and chairman of mus. dept. at Univ. of S. California Sch. of Mus. from 1948. Author of *Life and Music of Béla Bartók* (NY 1953 and later edns.). Prolific composer, works incl. syms., vc. conc., choral pieces (many unacc.), songs, and much chamber mus.

Stevens, Horace (Ernest) (*b* Melbourne, Victoria, 1876; *d* Melbourne, 1950). Australian bass. Chorister, St Paul's Cath., Melbourne. London début 1919. Fine reputation in oratorio and opera (esp. Wagner). Frequently sang in USA.

Stevens, Paul (James) (*b* London, 1923). Eng. composer. Studied GSM, Paris Cons., and Berlin Hochschule für Musik. Works incl. several syms., song-cycle *The Infinite Heart*, solo songs, and pf. mus.

Stevens, Richard (John Samuel) (*b* London, 1757; *d* London, 1837). Eng. composer and organist. Organist, Temple Church from 1786 and Charterhouse from 1796. Gresham Prof. of Mus. 1801. Wrote hpd. sonatas, songs, glees (e.g. *Ye spotted snakes*), and ed. church mus. by Eng. and It. composers.

Stevens, Risë (*b* NY, 1913). Amer. mez. Studied at Juilliard Sch. and in Vienna (with Gutheil-Schoder). Début in NY 1931 in *The Bartered Bride*. Sang in Prague 1936–8, also in Vienna and Buenos Aires. NY Met. début 1938, Glyndebourne 1939 and 1956 (Cherubino and Dorabella). Member of Met. co. for many years but sang in Vienna, Milan, San Francisco. Outstanding as Carmen, Oktavian, Delilah, and Orlofsky (in *Die Fledermaus*). Appeared in films. Gen. man., Met. Nat. Touring Co. 1964. Dir. of Opera, Mannes College 1973–8.

Stevenson, Ronald (*b* Blackburn, 1928). Scottish pianist and composer. Studied RMCM 1945–8 and S. Cecilia Acad., Rome, 1955. Taught comp. at Cape Town Univ. 1963–5. Mus. influenced by Busoni and Scottish folk mus. Self-confessed aim is for an 'epic music . . . absorbing elements from East and from Africa, as well as from Western culture'. Works incl. *Prelude, Fugue, and Fantasy on Busoni's Faust* for pf. (1949–59); *Passacaglia on DSCH* for pf. (1961–2); *Jamboree for Grainger* for orch. (1961); *Weyvers o' Blegburn* (Weavers of Blackburn), for boy's broken v., weak amateur ten., amateur ch., and pf. (to Lancashire dialect) (1961); hpd. sonata (1968); Pf. Conc. No. 1 (*Faust Triptych*) (1960), No. 2 (*The Continents*) (1972); *Peter Grimes Fantasy*, pf. (1971); *Border Boyhood*, song-cycle, ten., pf. (1970); *9 Haiku*, sop., ten., pf./harp (1971); *Ben Dorain*, choral sym. (1973); vn. conc. (*The Gipsy*) (1973).

Stewart, Thomas (James) (*b* San Saba, Texas, 1928). Amer. baritone. Studied Juilliard Sch., NY.

Opera début as student NY 1954 (*Capriccio*). After singing at NY City and Chicago Operas, went for further study in Europe. Sang in Berlin 1960 (Escamillo). CG début 1960, Bayreuth 1960–75, NY Met. 1966 (Ford in *Falstaff*), San Francisco 1971 (Onegin). Particularly impressive in Wagner.

Stich, Johann Wenzel. See *Punto, Giovanni.*

Stich-Randall, Teresa (*b* West Hartford, Conn., 1927). Amer. sop. Studied pf. at age 3. Entered Hartford Sch. of Mus. 1938, Columbia Univ. Sch. of Mus. 1942. While at Columbia sang in Amer. premières of Thomson's *The Mother of us all* and Bloch's *Macbeth*. In 1949 chosen by Toscanini to sing in NBC perfs. of *Aida* and *Falstaff*. Went to Europe 1951; won Lausanne int. competition for opera singers. Salzburg Fest. 1952. Début Vienna Opera 1952 as Violetta in *La Traviata*. Chicago Opera 1955, NY Met. 1961 (as Fiordiligi). First American to be made an Austrian *Kammersängerin*, 1962.

Sticker. Light wooden rod in org. which operates the pallet.

Stiedry, Fritz (*b* Vienna, 1883; *d* Zürich, 1968). Austrian-born cond. (Amer. citizen). Studied at Vienna Cons. Recommended by Mahler to *Schuch, who engaged him at Dresden Opera 1907–8. 2nd cond. Kassel court opera 1913; first cond. Berlin Opera 1914–23; cond. Vienna Volksoper 1924–5, (cond. f.p. of Schoenberg's *Die glückliche Hand*, Vienna 1924); Berlin Städtische Oper 1928–33. Mus. dir., Leningrad P.O. 1934–7. Went to USA 1938. Cond., New Opera Co., NY, 1941, Chicago 1945–6, NY Met. 1946–58, being prin. Wagner cond. but, as in Berlin, cond. major Verdi prods. Cond. Glyndebourne 1947 (*Orfeo*, with Ferrier), CG 1953–4 (*The Ring* and *Fidelio*). Guest cond. of leading sym. orchs. Retired to Zürich.

Stierhorn (Ger., 'Bull horn'). Giant medieval bugle horn used in war. Straight tubes with exact conical bore and no bell flare. Wagner requires them off-stage in *Die Walküre*, Act 2, and in *Götterdämmerung*, Acts 2 and 3. 3 special instrs. were made, in C, D♭, and D, played by trombonists.

Stiffelio. Opera in 3 acts by Verdi to lib. by Piave after play *Le Pasteur* by E. Souvestre and E. Bourgeois. Comp. 1850. Prod. Trieste 1850 and later staged, because of censorship problems, under title *Guglielmo Wellingrode*. Revived at Parma 1968. Rev. as *Aroldo*, 1856–7, with new lib. by Piave and newly composed 4th act. Prod. Rimini 1857, NY 1863.

Stignani, Ebe (*b* Naples, 1904; *d* Imola, 1974). It. mez. Studied Naples Cons. Début Naples (San Carlo) 1925 as Amneris in *Aida*. Engaged by Toscanini for Scala, Milan, 1925–6, where her Eboli in Verdi's *Don Carlos* and other mez. roles

were considered the finest of the day. CG début 1937, San Francisco 1938. V. of immense range in top register. Last appearance 1958 (as Azucena) in London.

Stile antico (It.). Old style. Term to describe church mus. written after *c*.1600 in an archaic style, in imitation of Palestrina, by Soriano, Anerio, and Allegri. Its antithesis was *Stile moderno*.

Stile Concertante (It.). In concerto-like style. Style of baroque mus. in which instr. are treated as rivals in conc.-like fashion.

Stile Concitato (It.). In excited style. Style of baroque mus. in which dramatic expression and excitement were paramount, e.g. in Monteverdi's *Il combattimento di Tancredi e Clorinda*, 1624.

Stile Rappresentativo (It.). In representational style. Term used by early It. composers of opera and oratorio to describe their new device of recit., in which human speech was represented dramatically as in Peri's *Euridice* (1600) and Monteverdi's *Arianna* (1608).

Stiles Allen, Lilian (*b* London, 1896; *d* Tunbridge Wells, 1982). Eng. sop. Studied GSM and in Vienna. Noted for oratorio perfs. but also sang Brünnhilde and other dramatic sop. roles. One of orig. 16 singers in Vaughan Williams's *Serenade to Music* 1938. Teacher after retirement, pupils incl. Julie Andrews, popular mus. comedy and film actress (*My Fair Lady, The Sound of Music*, etc.).

Still, Robert (*b* London, 1910; *d* Bucklebury, Berks., 1971). Eng. composer. Studied Oxford Univ. under Ernest Walker, RCM under C. H. Kitson, and privately with Hans Keller. Taught at Eton Coll. Author of essay on Mahler from psycho-analytical standpoint (1960). Works incl. 4 syms., pf. conc., vn. conc., 5 str. qts., 3 pf. sonatas, vn. sonata, cl. quintet, pf. quintet, cl. trio, ob. qt., quintet for 3 fl., vn., and vc., motets, orch. fantasy *The Delphic Oracle, Elegy* for ten. (or bar.), ch., and orch., songs, org. voluntaries.

Still, William Grant (*b* Woodville, Miss., 1895; *d* Los Angeles, 1978). Amer. composer and cond. Studied Wilberforce Coll. 1911–15 and at Oberlin Cons. 1917–18 and 1919–22. Studied privately with *Varèse 1922–5 and with G. W. Chadwick at New England Cons. 1922. Played vn., vc., and ob. in orchs. and worked in 1920s as orchestrator for Paul Whiteman's band and for Broadway musicals and radio shows. Worked for CBS from 1935. Works incl. 5 syms., first being *Afro-American Symphony* (1930), several operas and ballets, *Pages from Negro History* for orch. (1943), chamber mus.

Stimme (Ger., plural *Stimmen*). Voice. (1) The human v.

(2) Instr. part and org. stop. Part-writing or v.-leading in Ger. is *Stimmführung*.

Stimmung (Ger.). Mood. (1) Atmosphere or mood, hence *Stimmungsbild*, mood picture, title given to short comp. evoking particular mood, e.g. Strauss's *5 Stimmungsbilder*, Op. 9, for pf., 1883–4.
(2) Tuning.

Stimmung (Tuning). Comp. by K. *Stockhausen, 1968, for 6 unacc. singers (2 sop., 1 alto, 2 ten., 1 bass) vocalizing without words for 75 mins.

Stinguendo (It.). Extinguishing, i.e. fading out.

Stirando, stirato; stiracchiando, stiracchiato (It.). Stretching, stretched, i.e. making the mus. last out. Same as *ritardando.

Stochastic (from Gr., 'point of aim' or 'target'). Term first used by Swiss 18th-cent. mathematician Bernoulli regarding mathematical laws of probability. Applied by *Xenakis to mus. procedures whereby overall sound contours are determined but inner details are left to chance or worked out mathematically by composer or by computer, i.e. *Chance in stochastic works is restricted to the comp. process, the result being fully notated for the performer.

Stock, Frederick (August) (*b* Jülich, Prussia, 1872; *d* Chicago, 1942). Ger.-born cond., violinist, and composer. Studied Cologne Cons. 1886–90 (with Wüllner, Humperdinck, etc.). Violinist in Cologne orch. 1890–5. Went to USA as violinist in Chicago S.O. Became ass. cond. to Theodore Thomas 1899, succeeding him 1905 and remaining cond. until his death. Gave f.p. of several Amer. works and introduced many modern works to Amer. audiences. Commissioned Walton's *Scapino* ov., 1940. Wrote 2 syms., vn. conc., chamber mus., etc.

Stockhausen, Julius (*b* Paris, 1826; *d* Frankfurt, 1906). Fr.-born Ger. bar., son of harpist-composer and his singer wife. As child learned several instr. Studied at Paris Cons. and in London with García. Sang in *Elijah* at Basle, 1848, and joined Paris Opéra-Comique 1857. Gave f. public p. of Schubert's *Die schöne Müllerin*, Vienna, May 1856. Dir., Hamburg Phil. Concerts and Choir 1863–7. Many recital tours. Cond., Sternscher Gesangverein, Berlin, 1874–8 (see *Stern, Julius*); teacher at Hoch Cons., Frankfurt, 1878–80 and 1883–4. Wrote 2-vol. singing method, 1886–7. Regarded as one of finest interpreters of Schubert's *Winterreise* and other Lieder. Brahms ded. songs to him.

Stockhausen, Karlheinz (*b* Mödrath, nr. Cologne, 1928). Ger. composer, regarded as leader of elec. *avant-garde*. Son of village schoolmaster. Began to learn pf. at 5, also vn. and ob. Worked after 1945 as farmhand, also played pf. in dancebands. Studied at Cologne Musik-Hochschule 1947–51 (pf. and theory) and Cologne Univ. 1952. Studied comp. 1950 with Frank *Martin and began his own analytical studies of Schoenberg, Bartók, and Webern. At Darmstadt int.

summer school 1951 met Messiaen and Boulez. At this time he wrote his *Kreuzspiel* for pf., ob., bass cl., and perc. Lived in Paris 1952–3, studying with Messiaen. Worked in *musique concrète* studios of Fr. Radio and experimented with use of elec. tone generators. In 1953 returned to Cologne, becoming assistant to Herbert *Eimert in elec. mus. studio of W. Ger. Radio. Became dir. of the studio in 1963. From 1954 to 1956 studied phonetics and acoustics with W. Meyer-Eppler at Bonn Univ., this enabling him to have a complete understanding of his mus. material through ability to produce an infinite number of sounds and their permutations and to analyse them scientifically. In 1954 became ed. of new magazine for serial mus., *Die Reihe*, founded by Eimert. Gave first lecture-concerts in USA 1958 and since then has toured frequently as lecturer and cond. of small ens. Pupils from all over the world went to study with him and in 1957 he was appointed head of comp. courses at Darmstadt. Visiting prof. at several Amer. univs. Founded, 1963, Cologne Course for New Mus., teaching comp. until 1968. Prof. of comp., Cologne Musik-Hochschule from 1971. Collected writings pubd. in several vols.

Few composers of the 20th-cent. 'New Music' can approach Stockhausen in the length and extent of his studies for his task. The first and strongest influence on his development was the mus. of Webern. Through detailed and profound analysis of Webern's mus., he realized how much further he could take Webern's techniques. He evolved the theory of 'parameters' or dimensions of sound: pitch, intensity, duration, timbre, and position in space. As Webern had serialized pitches, so Stockhausen in his early works serialized each parameter. Webern's method of composing with small 'cells' of *motifs* was developed by Stockhausen into what he called 'group composition', a group being a slice of mus. time (the larger groups are called 'moments'). How various groups are inter-related decides the formal design of a work. The culmination of this period came in 1961–4 with *Momente*. The next step was a new attitude to mus. mobility, whereby the order of self-contained groups could be varied so that mus. continuity could be altered. The 11th (1956) of his series of pf. works *Klavierstücke* is in mobile form, the groups being playable in any order the performer selects. In *Zyklus* (1959) for solo percussionist, the performer may start at any of its 17 pages and go on until he returns to his starting-point (he may read from left to right or turn over the score and go from right to left). The element of *chance in these works means that no 2 perfs. are ever likely to be identical. In elec. mus., Stockhausen explored the spatial parameter (and transferred the same procedures to live mus. in his *Gruppen* for 3 orchs.). He began to specify the procedures—placing and use of microphones, etc.—for producing sounds, sometimes, as in *Carré*, calculating beforehand the basic materials and forms but leaving realization of details to someone else. In *Prozession* (1967), the mus. events are taken from various of his earlier comps.

The whole concept of elec. mus. is still so strange to ears accustomed to the disciplines of instr. comp. that the majority of audiences find it beyond their ken. But Stockhausen has an enormous following. He is constantly re-examining his theories, restructuring his comps., and exploring new media, in contrast to Boulez who seems to have remained where he was 20 years earlier. He has reached a wide audience with such works as *Gesang der Jünglinge*, which combines elec. sounds with the v. of a boy sop. altered by echo-effects, filters, etc., and the Orient-inspired *Stimmung*, in which for 75 minutes 6 singers take up elec. tones coming from concealed speakers and create a trance-like but ever-shifting vocalization. Prin. works:

OPERA: *Donnerstag aus Licht* (Milan 1981); *Samstag aus Licht* (Milan, 1984) (2 parts of projected opera cycle, *Licht*, one for each day of the week).
ORCH: *Formel* (1951); *Punkte* (1952, rev. 1962; rev. as **Kontra-Punkte* for 10 instr. 1952–3); *Spiel* (1952, rev. 1973); **Gruppen*, for 3 orch. (1955–7); *Carré*, for 4 orch. and 4 choirs (1959–60); *Stop* (1965; Paris version 1969 for 18 players in 6 groups; London version 19 instrs., 1973); *Fresco*, for 4 orch. groups (1969); *Trans* (1971); *Inori* (*Adorations*), soloist and orch. (1973–4); *Jubiläum* (1977); Scenes from *Licht* (Part I, *Der Jahreslauf*, dancers and orch. 1977; Part 2 *Michaels Reise um die Erde*, tpt. and ens. 1978; Part 3, *Michaels Jugend*, sop., ten., bass, tpt., basset horn, tb., modulated pf., 3 dancers, tape, 1978–9; Part 4, *Michaels Heimkehr*, as Part 3 except that ch. and orch. replace tape, 1979).
CHAMBER ENSEMBLE: *3 Lieder*, for high v. and chamber orch. (1950); *Kreuzspiel*, ob., bass cl., pf., and perc. (1951); *Percussion trio*, pf. and perc. (1952, rev. 1974); **Kontra-punkte*, for 10 instr. (1952–3, rev. of *Punkte* for orch.); *Zeitmasse*, for 5 winds (1955–6); *Refrain*, pf., celesta, perc. (1959); **Momente*, sop., 4 ch. groups, 13 instr. (1961–4, another version 1972); *Adieu*, wind quintet (1966); **Aus den sieben Tagen*, 15 comps. for ens. (1968); *Für Dr. K*, sextet (1969); *Für Kommende Zeiten*, 17 texts for intuitive mus. (1968–70); *Ylem*, for 19 players or singers (1972); *Tierkreis* (*Zodiac*) (1975–7); *In Freundschaft*, fl., cl., ob., tpt., vn., va. (1977).
ELECTRONIC: *Electronic Study I* (1953), II (1954); **Gesang der Jünglinge*, on tape (boy's v.) (1955–6); **Kontakte*, pf., perc., elec. sounds (1959–60), also for elec. sounds (1959–60), and *Originale* (1961), mus. th. piece with *Kontakte*; *Mikrophonie I*, tam-tam and elecs. (1964), II for ch., Hammond organ, and elecs. (1965); *Mixtur* for 5 orch. and elecs. (1964), reduced scoring (1967); *Solo*, melody instr. with feedback (1965–6); *Telemusik*, on tape (1966); **Hymnen*, tape and concrete mus. (1966–7), tape and concrete mus. with 4 soloists (1966–7), with orch. (1969, much shorter version); **Prozession*, tam-tam, pf., elecs. (1967); *Kurzwellen* (*Short-wave*), tam-tam, pf., elecs. (1968); *Spiral*, soloist with short-wave receiver (1969); *Sirius*, elecs. with 4 soloists (1975).
VOICES: *Chöre für Doris*, unacc. mixed ch. (1950); *Choral*, unacc. ch. (1950); **Stimmung*, 6 singers (1968); '*Am Himmel wandre Ich . . .*', 12 Indian songs (1972); *Atmen gibt das Leben . . .*, mixed ch. (1974, rev. as 'choral opera' 1977).
PIANO(S): **Klavierstücke*: I–IV (1952–3), V (1954–5), VI (1954–5), VII (1954–5), VIII (1954), IX (1954–5, rev. 1961), X (1954–5, rev. 1961), XI (1956); *Pole*, 2 pf. and 2 short-wave receivers (1969–70); *Expo*, 3 pf. (1969–70); **Mantra*, 2 pianists and elecs. (1969–70); *Klavierstücke XIII* (part of *Samstag aus Licht* (1984)).
SOLO PERCUSSION: **Zyklus* for 1 percussionist (1959).
CHAMBER MUSIC: Sonatina for vn. and pf. (1951); *Laub und Regen*, cl. and va. (1974); *Harlekin*, cl. (1975); *Der kleine Harlekin*, cl. (1975); *Amour*, 5 pieces, cl. (1976).

Stoker, Richard (*b* Castleford, Yorks., 1938). Eng. composer. Studied Huddersfield Sch. of Mus. and RAM, later with L. Berkeley and Boulanger. Prof. of comp., RAM, from 1963. Works incl. operas (incl. *Thérèse Raquin*, after Zola), cantata *Ecce Homo*, sextet, wind quintet, org. sonatas, str. qts., etc.

Stokowski, Leopold (*b* London, 1882; *d* Nether Wallop, Hants., 1977). Eng.-born cond. and organist, son of Polish father and Irish mother, who became Amer. citizen 1915. Studied Oxford Univ. and RCM. Organist, St James's, Piccadilly, 1900, then St Bartholomew's NY, 1905–8. Returned to London and cond. orch. concerts, but settled in USA shortly afterwards. Cond. Cincinnati S.O. 1909–12, Philadelphia Orch. 1912–38 (last 2 years jointly with **Ormandy). Made Philadelphia one of world's finest orchs. and introduced many major works to USA, e.g. Mahler's 8th Sym., Berg's *Wozzeck*, Stravinsky's *Rite of Spring*, Schoenberg's *Gurrelieder*, etc. Also championed new Amer. mus., incl. that of Ives. Cond. f.ps. of 3 Rakhmaninov works, Sym. No. 3, Pf. Conc. No. 4, and *Rhapsody on a Theme of Paganini*. Appeared in films and cond. mus. for Disney's *Fantasia*, 1940, in which mus. and cartoons were allied. Founder and cond. All-American Youth Orch. 1939–41; chief guest cond. NBC Orch. 1941–44; founder and cond. NY City S.O. 1944–5; chief guest cond. NY P.O. 1946–50; cond. Houston S.O. 1955–61, Amer. S.O. of NY 1962–72. Returned to Eng. 1972, frequently conducting LSO. Made transcrs. of Bach (for large sym. orch.). Was a master of sound and put his stamp on every orch. he cond. Opinions differed on quality of that stamp, for he took unusual liberties (which included alterations to the composer's scoring) in order to obtain effects he required, but that he was a superb cond.

can scarcely be denied. He was active to the day of his death.

Stoltzer, Thomas (*b* Schweidnitz, Silesia, *c*.1480–5; *d* Ofen, 1526). Ger. composer. Kapellmeister to King of Hungary from 1522. Wrote church mus. and a few secular songs.

Stolz, Robert (*b* Graz, 1880; *d* Berlin, 1975). Austrian composer, pianist, and cond. Son of mus. teacher and pianist, and great-nephew of Teresa *Stolz. Studied at Vienna Cons. with R. Fuchs and later with Humperdinck. Toured Europe as pianist, playing Mozart at age 7. First comp. pubd. in Berlin, 1891. Succeeded Bodanzky as chief cond., Theater an der Wien, Vienna, 1905–17. Cond. f.p. of Straus's *Der tapfere Soldat* (1908). Wrote over 60 operettas, over 100 film scores, and some 1,500 songs (incl. *Im Prater blüh'n wieder die Bäume*). Lived in Paris 1938–40 and in USA 1940–6, returning to Austria 1946–50. Wrote music for ice revues 1952–71. While in USA, composed scores for Hollywood films, winning 2 'Oscars'. His most successful operettas were *Der Tanz ins Glück* (Waltz into Happiness) 1921 and *Wo die kleinen Veilchen blühen* (Wild Violets) 1932; wrote extra mus. for *Im Weissen Rössl* (White Horse Inn). Active as cond. in his 90s.

Stolz, Teresa (orig. Terezie Stolzová) (*b* Elbekosteletz, 1834; *d* Milan, 1902). Cz. sop. Studied Prague, Trieste, and Milan (with Lamperti). Opera début at Tiflis 1857. It. début at Turin 1863. Became mistress of cond. Mariani. Milan début 1865. Intimate friend of Verdi. Sang Elisabeth in *Don Carlos*, Milan 1868, first It. Aida, 1872; created sop. role in Verdi's *Requiem*, 1874. Retired from opera 1877, concerts 1879. Voice of great range, dramatic expression, and flexibility.

Stolze, Gerhard (*b* Dessau, 1926; *d* Garmisch-Partenkirchen, 1979). Ger. ten. Studied in Dresden, where he made début 1949. Bayreuth Fest. from 1951. Début Vienna 1957, CG 1960. Splendid character-ten. e.g. as Mime in *The Ring* (recorded with Solti), Herod in *Salome*.

Stone Flower, The (*Kamenny tsvetok*). Ballet in prol. and 3 acts by Prokofiev, Op. 118, lib. by M. Mendelson and Lavrovsky, choreog. Lavrovsky, comp. 1948–53. Prod. Moscow 1954. New choreog. by Grigorovich, Leningrad 1957.

Stone Guest, The (*Kamenny Gost*). Opera in 3 acts by Dargomyzhsky, a setting of Pushkin's drama (1830) on same story as *Don Giovanni*. Begun 1866 and left almost finished. Orch. by Rimsky-Korsakov, ov. by Cui. Prod. St Petersburg 1872, Florence 1954.

Stone Litany. 'Runes from a House of the Dead' for mez. and orch. by *Maxwell Davies. F.p. Glasgow 1973 by Jan de Gaetani (mez.), SNO, cond. *Gibson.

Stop (as noun). (1) Row of pipes on org. (registers), all operated by handles or draw-stops placed near the player. Both the pipes and the handles are called *stops*.
(2) Hpd. mechanism for similar purpose as org. stop, i.e. to vary tone-colour, simulate sounds of other instr., etc.

Stop (verb). (1) on str. instr., 'stopping' means the placing of the fingers on a str., thereby determining length of portion of str. which is to vibrate. Thus double-stopping, triple stopping, means this action on 2, 3 str. at once.
(2) In hn.-playing, the insertion of a hand into the bell of the hn. to alter pitch and tone-quality of a note.
(3) In orgs.: to block passage of air through one end of pipe (i.e. end-stopped pipe), thereby producing note an octave lower than would otherwise be sounded.

Storace, Anna (Selina) (orig. Nancy) (*b* London, 1765; *d* Dulwich, 1817). Eng. sop., daughter of It. father. Début as singer, Haymarket Th., London, 1774. Became pupil of Rauzzini, singing in 1777 at CG in oratorio and at Hereford Fest. Went to Venice 1778 to study with Sacchini. Sang in Florence 1780, Parma 1781, and Milan 1782. Engaged as prin. sop. at Imperial Th., Vienna, 1784. Created role of Susanna in Mozart's *Le Nozze di Figaro*, 1786. Returned to Eng., 1787, singing in It. comic operas. For her farewell perf. in Vienna, Mozart comp. concert aria *Ch'io mi Scordi di te* (K505) for sop., pf., and orch., and played kbd. part himself. She sang in her brother Stephen *Storace's *The Haunted Tower*, 1789, thereafter confining herself to comic roles in Eng. works. Sang at Handel Fest. 1791. Became mistress of ten. *Braham, bearing him a son, and touring Europe with him. CG 1801–8. Died very wealthy.

Storace, Stephen (*b* London, 1762; *d* London, 1796). Eng. composer, brother of Anna *Storace. Child violinist. Studied in Naples from 1776. Joined his sister in It. when she arrived in 1778 and went with her to Vienna, where 2 of his operas, *Gli sposi malcontenti* (1785) and *Gli equivoci* (1786, with lib. by da Ponte), were prod. Friend of Mozart. Returned to Eng. 1787. Wrote series of dialogue-operas in which he incorporated popular airs and adapted other composers' mus. Among them were *The Haunted Tower* (1789), *No Song, No Supper* (1790), *The Siege of Belgrade* (1791), *The Pirates* (1792), *The Prize* (1793), *Cherokee* (1794), etc. His last full-scale opera, *Dido, Queen of Carthage*, was prod. at King's Th. in May 1792. Many of his scores were lost in the Drury Lane fire of 1809, but *The Pirates* was reconstructed in 1975 by Richard Vardigans from vocal score and MS. lib. *Gli equivoci*, based on Shakespeare's *Comedy of Errors*, was revived in 1975 and showed that Storace's contemporary reputation was deserved.

Storchio, Rosina (*b* Venice, 1876; *d* Milan, 1945). It. soprano. Studied at Milan Cons., making her début there as Micaela in *Carmen*. Sang Sophie in *Werther* at La Scala 1895. Created title-role of *Madama Butterfly* 1904. Sang in Barcelona 1898–1923 and in Buenos Aires 1904–14. NY début 1921.

Stornello (It., plural *Stornelli*). A traditional type of Tuscan folk-song often improvised by a *Stornellatore* (masc.) or *Stornellatrice* (fem.). The stanza has 3 lines each of 11 syllables.

Straccinato (It.). Stretched out, i.e. *ritardando*.

Stradella, Alessandro (*b* Montefestino, 1644; *d* Genoa, 1682). It. composer. Taught singing in Venice and Rome. From 1658 was in service of Queen Christina of Sweden in Rome, composing motets for her. Wrote operas, oratorios, cantatas, all notable for richness of expression and instr. acc. Was murdered. Flotow's opera *Alessandro Stradella* (Hamburg 1844) is a romanticized and inaccurate account of events leading to his death.

Stradivari (Stradivarius). Family of vn.-makers of Cremona, N. Italy. The greatest of them was Antonio Stradivari (*b* 1644; *d* Cremona, 1737), apprenticed as youth to Nicola *Amati, continuing connection with Amati's workshop to 1684. Inserted his own label into vn. 1666 (signing himself, as always afterwards, by Maltese cross and initials A. S. enclosed within double circle). After 1684, his work developed experimentally towards perfection of design and balance, leading in 1690 to invention of the 'Long Strad'. 1700–20 was Stradivari's 'golden period' during which he prod. a series of magnificent instr., inc. vcs. and vas., and those made in the last 17 years of his life show no decline in craftsmanship. He made his last vn. in 1737 at age 92. It is calculated in the standard work on Stradivari by the Hill brothers (1902, rev. 1909) that he made 1116 instruments after 1666 of which over 600 are still in existence. Many are known by names e.g. La Pucelle, Viotti, Alard, Messie, Rode, etc. He paid vigilant attention to detail and personally designed pegs, fingerboards, tailpieces, inlaid patterns, and bridges; he designed the cases and also made bows. His application of the varnish was unsurpassed, soft in texture and shading from orange to red. The tone of the instrs. varies, of course, but is generally a sop. tone compared with the more cont. *Guarneri. Stradivari was assisted by his sons Francesco (*b* Cremona, 1671; *d* 1743) and Omobono (*b* Cremona, 1679; *d* 1742) and by Carlo Bergonzi. These instruments bore the label 'sotto la disciplina d'Antonio Stradivari' but in many cases these were later unscrupulously removed and a label substituted attributing the instr. to Stradivari himself. Hence the controversies over the authenticity of certain 'Strads', highly important in view of the high prices the genuine instr. can fetch.

Strambotto (It.). 'Rustic Song'. It. Renaissance poetical form, often set to mus. on the lines of

the *Frottola. Poem had 8 lines, rhyming abababcc; and the mus. setting was usually strophic, with only 2 lines set to mus. and repeated for each remaining pair. See also *Rispetto*.

Straniera, La (The Foreigner). Opera in 2 acts by Bellini to lib. by Romani. Prod. Milan 1829, London 1832, NY 1834.

Stransky, Josef (*b* Humpolec, Bohemia, 1872; *d* NY, 1936). Bohemian cond. Studied medicine, qualifying as doctor in Prague 1896. While at univ. also studied mus., becoming comp. pupil of Fuchs, Bruckner, and Dvořák in Vienna. Prin. cond., Landestheater, Prague, 1898, Hamburg 1903–10. Also cond. in Berlin, Dresden, London, Amsterdam, etc. Succeeded Mahler as cond. NY P.O. 1911, holding post until 1921. Retired 1925, going into art-dealing business. Wrote operas and other works, and adapted Berlioz's *Béatrice et Bénédict*. Figures in R. Strauss's opera *Intermezzo* as Stroh; he was the cond. for whom Strauss was mistaken by an importunate lady, thereby nearly precipitating Strauss's divorce.

Strascicando; strascinando; strascinato (It.). Dragging; dragged (e.g. heavily slurring notes in bowing, singing *portamento*, etc.).

Stratas, Teresa (orig. Anastasia Strataki) (*b* Toronto, 1938). Canadian sop. of Gr. parentage. Studied Toronto Royal Cons. and in NY. Opera début Toronto 1958 as Mimi in *La Bohème*. Won NY Met. opera auditions 1959, making her début at Met. in Oct. 1959. Excellent Mozart singer in roles such as Despina. Sang Lulu in f. complete p. of opera, Paris 1979, and is an impressive Salome.

Strathspey. Slow dance of Scotland, as the reel is its quick dance. Mus. is in simple quadruple time, with many dotted notes and some use of the *Scotch Snap. Appeared in mid-18th cent.

Stratton, George (Robert) (*b* London, 1897; *d* London, 1954). Eng. violinist and cond. Studied GSM. Leader, LSO 1933–52, occasionally conducting it. Leader and founder, Stratton Qt. 1925–42. Prof. of vn., RCM, from 1942. Wrote book on playing of chamber mus. O.B.E. 1954.

Straube, Karl (*b* Berlin, 1873; *d* Leipzig, 1950). Ger. organist, cond., and teacher. Had Eng. mother. Studied in Berlin (organ with H. Reimann). Toured Ger. giving org. recitals 1894–7, winning high reputation. Organist, Thomaskirche, Leipzig (Bach's post) from 1902 and cond. of Leipzig Bach Soc. Prof. of org., Leipzig Cons., from 1907. Cantor of Thomasschule from 1918. Cond. several Bach Fests. 1904–23 and 1925 Handel Fest. which led to formation of Handel Soc. Friend of Reger and champion of his mus., as of that of other 20th-cent. composers, incl. Vaughan Williams and Holst. Ed. choral works of Bach and Handel, and organ works by Bach and Liszt.

Straus, Oscar (b Vienna, 1870; d Bad Ischl, 1954). Austrian-born composer (Fr. citizen from 1939). Studied in Vienna and with Bruch in Berlin. Cond. of th. orchs. in Ger. 1895–1900, then pianist for Wolzogen's Überbrettl in Berlin, for which he comp. several pieces. Wrote orch. and chamber mus., but best known for operettas comp. between 1904 and 1926. Most successful of these were *Ein Walzertraum* (A Waltz Dream), Vienna 1907; *Der tapfere Soldat,* based on Shaw's *Arms and the Man* (1894), Vienna 1908, NY as *The *Chocolate Soldier* 1909; and *Der letzte Walzer* (The Last Waltz), Vienna 1920. Left Berlin 1927, living mainly in Paris and USA until after 1945. His last success was with the music for the film *La Ronde,* 1950.

Strauss, Eduard I (b Vienna, 1835; d Vienna, 1916). Austrian composer and cond., youngest son of Johann *Strauss I. Début as cond. 1862, succeeding brother Johann *Strauss II at St Petersburg 1865. In 1872 took over conductorship of court balls which Johann had held since 1863. Took Strauss orch. to London 1885, disbanded it 1901. Wrote over 300 dances, many of them polkas. In 1907 burned all original MSS. of Strauss family because he believed world no longer deserved to possess them. Thus many waltzes have been preserved only in pf. reductions.

Strauss, Eduard (Leopold Maria) **II** (b Vienna, 1910; d Vienna, 1969). Austrian cond., nephew of J. Strauss III. Début 1949. Cond. Vienna S.O. in recordings and toured with Vienna Johann Strauss Orch.

Strauss, Franz Joseph (b Parkstein, 1822; d Munich, 1905). Ger. hn.-player and composer. Prin. hn., Munich Court opera orch. 1847–89. Taught at Munich Acad. until 1896. Cond. semi-professional orch. 1875–96. Though disliking Wagner's mus., played in several Wagner premières and was consulted by composer on Siegfried's hn.-call. Wrote hn. conc., works for hn. and pf., etc. The composer Richard *Strauss was his son by his 2nd wife.

Strauss, Johann I (b Vienna, 1804; d Vienna, 1849). Austrian composer, cond., and violinist, founder of the 'Strauss Waltz Dynasty', and known as Johann Strauss I to distinguish him from his son. Studied vn. and played va. in 1819 in *Lanner's qt. With Lanner until 1825, when he began to compose his own waltzes. In 1826 appeared with 14-piece orch. at the 'Swan' in the Rossau suburb of Vienna and captivated public. With larger orch. engaged for 6 years at the 'Sperl', in the Leopoldstadt. Among those who heard him there were Chopin, Wagner, and Hans Christian Andersen. Also appointed Kapellmeister of first Bürger-regiment, responsible for mus. at court fêtes and dances. Toured Ger. and other parts of Europe from 1833. Visited London 1838, giving 72 concerts and playing at festivities in honour of Victoria's coronation. In 1840 intro-

duced the quadrille to replace the galop. Successive tours were triumphal processions for Strauss. Visited Eng. again 1849, and died of scarlet fever shortly after return to Vienna. Comp. 251 works, 152 of which were waltzes, but his fame in this respect was eclipsed by his eldest son and his *Radetzky March* (1848) is by far the strongest survivor of his life's work.

Strauss, Johann II (b Vienna, 1825; d Vienna, 1899). Austrian composer, cond., and violinist, eldest son of Johann *Strauss, and deservedly known as 'the Waltz King'. Because his father did not want his sons to choose mus. as career, worked as bank clerk but learned vn. secretly and studied comp. with Drechsler. In 1844 formed own orch. of 24 and appeared as cond. of his own and his father's waltzes. When his father died, amalgamated both orchs. and toured Austria, Poland, and Ger. In 1855 engaged to direct summer concerts in Petropaulovsky Park, St Petersburg, for 10 years. Cond. of Austrian court balls 1863–72. Comp. nearly 400 waltzes which have come to epitomize Viennese gaiety and sentiment. Visited Paris 1867, London 1867, USA 1872. Turned to stage 1871, when first of a series of successful operettas was produced at the Theater an der Wien, the most famous being *Die Fledermaus* (1874). Of his waltzes, the *Blue Danube* (1867), *Roses from the South* (1880), the great *Emperor Waltz* (1888), and *Tales from the Vienna Woods* (1868) are beloved wherever mus. is played, as are his polkas and other dances. Was friend and admirer of Wagner, who, like Brahms and other composers incl. Schoenberg, were what we should now call 'fans' of Strauss, recognizing a supreme master of a genre who comp. with style, elegance, taste, and wit. Prin. works:

OPERETTAS: *Indigo und die vierzig Räuber* (1871); *Der Karneval in Rom* (1873); *Die *Fledermaus* (1874); *Cagliostro in Wien* (1875); *Prinz Methusalem* (1877); *Blindekuh* (1878); *Das Spitzentuch der Königin* (1880); *Der lustige Krieg* (1881); *Eine *Nacht in Venedig* (1883); *Der *Zigeunerbaron* (1885); *Simplicuis* (1887); *Ritter Pázmán* (1892); *Fürstin Ninetta* (1893); *Jubuka* (1894); *Waldmeister* (1895); *Die Götten der Vernunft* (1897).

BALLET: *Cinderella* (1899; completed as *Aschenbrödel* by J. Bayer, f.p. Berlin 1901, f.Eng.p. Manchester 1979).

WALTZES: *Abschied von St Petersburg*, Op. 210; *Accelerationen*, Op. 234; *An der schönen blauen Donau* (On the beautiful *Blue Danube*), Op. 314; *Architektenball-Tänze*, Op. 36; *Cagliostro*, Op. 370; *Erinnerung an Covent Garden*, Op. 139; *Freuet euch des Lebens*, Op. 340; *Frühlingsstimmen* (Voices of Spring), Op. 410; *Geschichten aus dem Wienerwald* (*Tales From the Vienna Woods), Op. 325; *Grossfürstin Alexandra*, Op. 181; *Hofballtänze*, Op. 298; *Juristenballtänze*, Op. 177; *Kaiser-Walzer* (Emperor Waltz) Op. 437; *Kronungslieder*, Op. 184; *Künstlerleben*, Op. 316; *Der Kuss*, Op. 400; *Lagunen*, Op. 411; *Liebesliederwal-*

zer, Op.114; *★Morgenblätter* (Morning Papers), Op. 279; *Nordseebilder*, Op. 380; *O schöner Mai*, Op. 365; *Rathausballtänze*, Op. 438; *Rosen aus dem Süden* (*★Roses* from the South), Op. 388; *Schneeglockchen*, Op. 143; *Seid umschlungen Millionen*, Op. 443; *Wein, Weib und Gesang* (Wine, Woman and Song), Op. 333; *Wiener Blut* (Vienna Blood), Op. 354; *Wiener Bonbons*, Op. 307; *Wo die Zitronen blüh'n*, Op. 364.

POLKAS: *Aesculap*, Op. 130; *Annen*, Op. 117; *Armenball*, Op. 176; *Aurora*, Op. 165; *Bürgerball*, Op. 145; *Champagne*, Op. 211; *Damenspende*, Op. 305; *Demolierer*, Op. 269; *Electropher*, Op. 297; *Explosionen*, Op. 43; *Figaro*, Op. 320; *Juristenball*, Op. 280; *Lagerlust*, Op. 431; *Leichtes Blut*, Op. 319; *Pizzicato Polka* (with Josef Strauss); *Tritsch, Tratsch*, Op. 214; *Unter Donner und Blitz* (Thunder and Lightning), Op. 324.

Also, marches, galops, and *Perpetuum Mobile*, Op. 257.

Strauss, Johann (Maria Eduard) **III** (*b.* Vienna, 1866; *d* Berlin, 1939). Austrian composer and cond. Son of Eduard Strauss I. Became a civil servant (accountant), but success of his operetta *Katze und Maus* (1898) caused him to follow family tradition. Conducted imperial court balls in Vienna 1901–05, relinquishing post after criminal conviction for debt.

Strauss, Josef (*b* Vienna, 1827; *d* Vienna, 1870). Austrian composer, 2nd son of Johann *★Strauss I. Became architect, but studied mus. secretly and cond. in place of his brother Johann in 1853. Formed own orch. and comp. waltzes, etc., for it, writing 283 pieces. Polkas more often played today than his waltzes, but the latter incl. *Dynamiden*, Op. 173 (1865), borrowed by R. Strauss for one of waltz-themes in opera *Der Rosenkavalier*, and *Dorfschwalben aus Österreich* (*Village Swallows*), Op. 164.

Strauss, Richard (Georg) (*b* Munich, 1864; *d* Garmisch-Partenkirchen, 1949). Ger. composer, cond., and pianist. Son of Franz *★Strauss, hn.-player in Munich court orch. Had pf. lessons at 4 and began composing at 6. Vn. lessons at 8. Studied theory with F. Meyer 1875, but went to no mus. acad., having normal education, ending at Munich Univ. At 16 wrote first sym. and str. qt., both being perf. in Munich, 1881. In 1882 *Serenade* for wind perf. in Dresden, leading to commission from *★Bülow for Meiningen Orch. 2nd Sym. perf. NY 1884. Ass. cond. to Bülow at Meiningen 1885, succeeding him after a month. Left Meiningen 1886, visited It., and became 3rd cond. at Munich Opera. His *Aus Italien* perf. Munich 1887. Ass. cond. to Levi at Bayreuth 1889. 3rd cond. Weimar Opera 1889. Success of symphonic poem *Don Juan* est. him as most important young composer in Ger. and natural successor to Wagner, whose widow took great interest in his career. Married sop. Pauline de *★Ahna 1894 and wrote many songs for her,

appearing as her accompanist. First opera *Guntram* failure at Weimar 1894. Ass. cond., Munich Opera 1894, chief cond. 1896–8. Cond. Berlin P.O. 1894–5. Series of tone-poems—*Till Eulenspiegel, Also sprach Zarathustra, Don Quixote*, and *Ein Heldenleben*—between 1895 and 1899 confirmed his stature as master of the orch. 2nd opera *Feuersnot* success in Dresden and Vienna, 1901 and 1902. Visited Eng. 1903, USA 1904. F.p. of *Symphonia Domestica* in NY. Operas *Salome* (1905) and *Elektra* (1909) caused sensations through their supposedly 'obscene' treatment of biblical and classical subjects. In latter Strauss first collab. with Austrian poet Hugo von *★Hofmannsthal, who was to be librettist of 5 more of his operas, beginning in 1911 with the 18th-cent. comedy *Der Rosenkavalier*. This work was a triumph at its Dresden première, went straight into the repertory of world's leading opera houses, and has stayed there. Since 1898 Strauss had been cond. of Berlin Royal Opera, living in the capital, but after 1908 lived in villa at Garmisch and was in constant demand as cond. of his own works. Completed his last full-scale orch. work, *Eine Alpensinfonie*, in 1915. Resigned Berlin post 1918 and became joint dir., Vienna Opera, 1919–24. His opera *Die Frau ohne Schatten* and ballet *Schlagobers* produced there 1919 and 1924. Opera *Intermezzo*, to his own lib. representing incident in his own marriage, prod. Dresden 1924. During comp. of *Arabella*, Hofmannsthal died, 1929. In 1933 new Nazi régime in Ger. appointed Strauss (without consultation) pres. of Reichsmusikkammer, but removed him in 1935 because of disapproval of his collab. with Jewish librettist Stefan *★Zweig on opera *Die schweigsame Frau*, which was banned after 4 perfs. Thereafter Strauss was tolerated by régime but kept under surveillance because of Jewish daughter-in-law. Visited London 1936, receiving Gold Medal of Royal Phil. Soc. and conducting at CG. 1-act operas *Friedenstag* and *Daphne* prod. 1938. During World War II lived mostly in Vienna and comp. operas *Die Liebe der Danae* and *Capriccio*. In 1943 reverted to instr. comps., writing 2nd hn. conc., wind sonatinas, ob. conc., and 'poem for 23 strings' *Metamorphosen*, inspired by destruction of Ger. opera houses in bombing raids. Moved to Switzerland 1945–9, not returning to Garmisch until officially cleared of complicity in Nazi régime. Visited London 1947, conducting own works and attending perfs. cond. by Beecham. His last work completed 23 Nov., 1948, was a song *Malven* (Knobel), ded. to Maria *★Jeritza.

Strauss, like his friend and contemporary Mahler, had immense dual reputation as composer and cond. He was a master of several mus. forms. No sym. orch. can reasonably exist without having in its repertory his series of magnificent tone-poems, in which brilliance of scoring and vividness of representational detail are matched by satisfying mus. construction. Of his 15 operas at least half are regularly in the repertories of the

STRAUSS

major opera houses. They provide superb singing roles, particularly for women's vv., of which, through his marriage to a sop., he had a profound understanding. In *Der Rosenkavalier* alone, he wrote parts for 3 sop. in which many a 20th-cent. reputation has been made and which have contributed to making it the most popular opera written in the 20th cent., with the probable exception of *Madama Butterfly*. In *Elektra* he approached the atonal and neuro-psychological world of Schoenberg and Berg, but turned aside to what Stravinsky called the 'time-travelling' of *Der Rosenkavalier* and *Ariadne auf Naxos*, the latter being one of several operas in which Strauss treated subjects from classical mythology, investing them with 20th-cent. traits e.g. *Die ägyptische Helena, Daphne,* and *Die Liebe der Danae.* His last opera, a 'conversation piece', *Capriccio,* has also become popular. Strauss's mus. is in the Ger. 19th-cent. tradition deriving from Mendelssohn, Liszt, and especially Wagner. However, his love for Mozart, of whose mus. he was a fine cond., is also reflected in many works, leading to a curious but satisfying blend of 18th-cent. elegance and Wagnerian richness as in *Rosenkavalier, Ariadne,* and *Capriccio,* and particularly in the superb instr. works of his last years. His natural gift for counterpoint leads to complex and interweaving textures in all his works, which has led his critics to complain of 'note-spinning' for its own sake (a charge that has some justification), but the former tendency to 'write off' Strauss operas comp. between 1919 and 1940 is gradually being reversed as their virtues become apparent. Though he wrote some concs., his big display pieces are for full orch. and for vv. His unacc. choral works are in a class of their own, and he wrote many first-rate Lieder, some with orch. A song such as *Morgen,* for example, is a perfect blend of melody and expression of the text, while its style epitomizes the highly-developed melodic conversational-recit. which was Strauss's lifelong preoccupation in his operas and which even forms part of the subject-matter of *Capriccio.* His last work, the *Vier letzte Lieder* (*4 Last Songs*) for sop. and orch. is a remarkable and moving summing-up of his life's work as well as a testament to all that the late-romantic style had meant to the art of mus. Prin. works:

OPERAS (with dates of f.p. and cond.'s name): *Guntram,* Op. 25, Weimar, 1894 (Strauss); *Feuersnot,* Op. 50, Dresden, 1901 (Schuch); *Salome,* Op. 54, Dresden, 1905 (Schuch); *Elektra,* Op. 58, Dresden, 1909 (Schuch); *Der Rosenkavalier,* Op. 59, Dresden, 1911 (Schuch); *Ariadne auf Naxos,* Op. 60, Stuttgart, 1912 (Strauss); rev. version, Vienna, 1916 (Schalk); *Die *Frau ohne Schatten,* Op. 65, Vienna, 1919 (Schalk); *Intermezzo,* Op. 72, Dresden, 1924 (Busch); *Die *ägyptische Helena,* Op. 75, Dresden, 1928 (Busch); *Arabella,* Op. 79, Dresden, 1933 (Krauss); *Die *schweigsame Frau,* Op. 80, Dresden,

1935 (Böhm); *Friedenstag,* Op. 81, Munich, 1938 (Krauss); *Daphne,* Op. 82, Dresden, 1938 (Böhm); *Die *Liebe der Danae,* Op. 83, dress rehearsal only Salzburg, 1944 (Krauss); Salzburg, 1952 (Krauss); *Capriccio,* Op. 85, Munich, 1942 (Krauss).

BALLETS AND OTHER STAGE WORKS: *Josephslegende,* Op. 63 (1913–14); *Der Bürger als Edelmann* (*Le *Bourgeois Gentilhomme*), incidental mus. for Molière-Hofmannsthal play, Op. 60 (1912–17); *Schlagobers,* Op. 70 (1921–2); *Des Esels Schatten,* children's mus. play (1947–8, completed from sketches by K. Haussner), Ettal 1964, London 1970.

ORCH: *Serenade* in Eb, for 13 wind instr., Op. 7 (1881–2); *Suite* in Bb, for 13 wind instr., Op. 4 (1883–4); Symphonies: No. 1 in D minor (1880, unpubd.), No. 2 in F minor, Op. 12 (1883–4), *Symphonia Domestica,* Op. 53 (1902–3), *Eine *Alpensinfonie,* Op. 64 (1911–15); *Aus Italien,* symphonic fantasy, Op. 16 (1886); Symphonic poems: *Macbeth,* Op. 23 (1887–8, rev. 1889–90), *Don Juan,* Op. 20 (1888), *Tod und Verklärung,* Op. 24 (1888–9), *Till Eulenspiegels lustige Streiche,* Op. 28, (1894–5), *Also sprach Zarathustra,* Op. 30 (1896), *Don Quixote,* Op. 35 (1896–7), *Ein *Heldenleben,* Op. 40, (1897–8); *Festliches Präludium,* orch. and organ, Op. 61 (1913); *Suite, Le *Bourgeois Gentilhomme,* Op. 60, (1918); *Dance Suite* (after Couperin) (1922); Sonatina No. 1 in F, for 16 wind instr. (1943), No. 2 in Eb, for 16 wind instr. (1944–5); *Metamorphosen,* for 23 solo str. (1945).

CONCERTOS etc: Hn. Conc. No. 1 in Eb, Op. 11 (1882–3), No. 2 in Eb (1942); Vn. Conc. in D minor, Op. 8 (1881–2); *Burleske* in D minor, pf. and orch. (1885–6, rev. 1890); *Parergon zur Symphonia Domestica,* pf. (left hand) and orch., Op. 73 (1925); *Panathenäenzug,* pf. (left hand) and orch., Op. 74 (1927); oboe conc. (1945–6); *Duett-Concertino,* cl., bn., str., and harp (1947).

CHAMBER MUSIC: Str. Qt., Op. 2 (1879–80); Pf. Qt., Op. 13 (1883–4); Vc. Sonata, Op. 6 (1881–3); Vn. Sonata, Op. 18 (1887–8).

PIANO: Sonata in B minor, Op. 5 (1881); 5 *Stimmungsbilder,* Op. 9 (1883–4).

CHORAL: *Wandrers Sturmlied,* Op. 14, ch. and orch. (1884); *Der Abend* and *Hymne,* Op. 34, for unacc. ch. (1897); *Taillefer,* Op. 52, sop., ten., bar., ch., and orch. (1903); *Deutsche Motette,* Op. 62, sop., alto, ten., bass, and unacc. ch. (1913, rev. 1943); *Die Tageszeiten,* Op. 76, 4 songs for male ch. and orch. (1928); *Die Göttin im Putzzimmer,* unacc. ch. (1935); *An den Baum Daphne,* unacc. ch. (1943).

SONG-CYCLES: *Krämerspiegel,* Op. 66, v. and pf. (1918); *Vier letzte Lieder* (4 Last Songs) for high v. and orch. (1948).

SONGS (with pf. and/or orch.): Strauss wrote over 200 songs, publishing them in groups. Listed below alphabetically is a selective group of the best-known, with opus numbers where applicable. The sign † means that an orch. acc. (not necessarily by Strauss) exists: *Allerseelen*, Op. 10 No. 9 (1885), *All' mein Gedanken*, Op. 21 No. 1 (1888), †*Das Bächlein* (1933), †*Befreit*, Op. 39 No. 4 (1898), †*Cäcilie*, Op. 27 No. 2 (1894), *Du meines Herzens Krönelein*, Op. 21 No. 2 (1888), *Einerlei*, Op. 69 No. 3 (1918), *Einkehr*, Op. 47 No. 4 (1900), †*Freundliche Vision*, Op. 48 No. 1 (1900), *Gefunden*, Op. 56 No. 1 (1903–6), *Hat gesagt*, Op. 36 No. 3 (1897), †*Die Heiligen drei Königen*, Op. 56 No. 6 (1906), †*Heimkehr*, Op. 15 No. 5 (1886), †*Heimliche Aufforderung*, Op. 27 No. 3 (1894), †*Ich wollt' ein Sträusslein binden*, Op. 68 No. 2 (1918), †*Liebes-hymnus*, Op. 32 No. 3 (1896), †*Mein Auge*, Op. 37 No. 4 (1897), †*Meinem Kinde*, Op. 37 No. 3 (1897), †*Morgen*, Op. 27 No. 4 (1894), †*Muttertanderlei*, Op. 43 No. 2 (1899), *Die Nacht*, Op. 10 No. 3 (1885), *Nachtgang*, Op. 29 No.3 (1895), *Nichts*, Op. 10 No. 2 (1885) †*Das Rosenband*, Op. 36 No. 1 (1897), †*Ruhe, meine Seele*, Op. 27 No. 1 (1894), †*Säusle, Liebe Myrthe*, Op. 68 No. 3 (1918), *Schlechtes Wetter*, Op. 69 No. 5 (1918), †*Ständchen*, Op. 17 No. 2 (1887), *Der Stern*, Op. 69 No. 1 (1918), †*Traum durch die Dämmerung*, Op. 29 No. 1 (1895), †*Waldseligkeit*, Op. 49 No. 1 (1901), †*Wiegenlied*, Op. 41 No. 1 (1899), *Wozu noch, Mädchen*, Op. 19 No. 1 (1887–8), †*Zueignung*, Op. 10 No. 1 (1885).

Stravaganza, La (The Extraordinary). Title of Vivaldi's Op. 4, 12 vn. concs., pubd. Amsterdam *c*.1714.

Stravinsky, Igor (Fyodorovich) (*b* Oranienbaum, 1882; *d* NY, 1971). Russ.-born composer, cond., pianist, and writer (Fr. citizen 1934, Amer. citizen 1945). Son of prin. bass at Imperial Opera, St Petersburg. Went to St Petersburg Univ. 1901 to study law but increasingly spent time in mus. pursuits. Spent much time at Rimsky-Korsakov's house, becoming his pupil in 1903. Began first sym., 1905, also pf. sonata. When his short orch. pieces *Fireworks* and *Scherzo fantastique* were played in St Petersburg in 1909, they were heard by *Diaghilev, who had by then formed the famous Ballets Russes in Paris. He invited Stravinsky to compose a ballet on the legend of *The Firebird*, Lyadov having failed to meet his deadline, for 1910 season. Its success made Stravinsky world-famous, and was followed by *Petrushka* (1911) and by *The Rite of Spring* (1913), the f.p. of the latter causing a riot. By then, Stravinsky was regarded as the leader of the mus. *avant-garde*. With the Russ. Revolution of 1917, resulting in confiscation of his property, and the financial troubles of the Diaghilev co., Stravinsky thought of forming a small touring th. co. to present inexpensively mounted productions. The result was *The Soldier's Tale* (*L'Histoire du Soldat*), for chamber ens.; it also enabled him to combine 2 of his main interests, Russ. folk-rhythms and Amer. jazz. His ballet *Pulcinella*, composed for Diaghilev in 1919–20, was a 're-composition' of mus. attrib. to Pergolesi and initiated the 'neo-classical' phase in Stravinsky's career. His last

overtly Russ. works of this period were the ballet *Les Noces* and the opera *Mavra*. Settling in Fr., he wrote a series of works in which the spirit of the 18th cent. is invoked but with unmistakably 20th-cent. harmonic and rhythmic flavouring. The pf. conc., in which he played the solo part, the *Capriccio* for pf. and orch., the vn. conc., the ballet *Apollo Musagetes*, the Sym. in C major and, most of all the Hogarthian opera *The Rake's Progress* (1951), are the finest flowers of this facet of Stravinsky's art. On the other hand, the opera-oratorio *Oedipus Rex* (1926–7), for which Cocteau wrote the text, is 19th cent. and Verdian in its heroic melodies. In 1939 he settled in the USA, moving eventually to Los Angeles where the climate suited one who had contracted tuberculosis in 1936–7. His first major 'American' work was the *Symphony in 3 Movements* of 1945. Yet another turning-point was the ballet *Orpheus* (1947), which had led Stravinsky to study of Monteverdi, and a meeting with the young Amer. cond. Robert *Craft, who (besides an enthusiasm for Stravinsky) combined interest in the Baroque period with intense sympathy for the 2nd Viennese Sch. of Schoenberg, etc. Stravinsky had lately shown awareness of serialism, particularly as practised by Webern, and, spurred by Craft, his work now began to reflect these new interests, as in the *Canticum Sacrum* of 1955, the *Threni* of 1958, the ballet *Agon*, and *Movements* for pf. and orch. In 1962 he was invited to return to Russ., a triumphant tour ending in his reception by the then Soviet leader Khruschev at the Kremlin. In his final years he wrote short, bare works, many of them religious in feeling and form, at the opposite pole from the opulence of his early successes. He is buried in Venice near to Diaghilev, as he wished.

Stravinsky's place as a seminal figure in 20th-cent. mus. and individually as a great composer seems assured. Though it used to be said he 'changed his skin' every few years, and though he did, superficially at any rate, alter his style more than once, he remained fundamentally himself throughout his life. Like his antithesis Strauss, he was a time-traveller, at home in centuries other than his own. Yet when he touched Pergolesi, Gesualdo, and Tchaikovsky, they became Stravinskyan re-creations. Where the prin. features of Strauss's mus. are complex harmonic and contrapuntal textures, the overriding feature of Stravinsky from first to last is rhythm. It is rhythm, in many wonderful forms from the primitive (*Les Noces*) to the sophisticated (*Rite of Spring*), which is the mainspring of his work. With the great Diaghilev ballets he took part in a golden age in assoc. with some of the most extraordinary talents of the century, not only Diaghilev but Nijinsky, Picasso, Bakst, Fokine, and others. Later Cocteau, Auden, and Dylan Thomas came within his orbit. The sense of th. and of the dance is never wholly absent from even his most austere works, such as the *Mass* of 1948, nor his delight in childlike fun (the *Circus Polka, Jeu de cartes,* etc.), and his sardonic humour. It seems appropriate that almost his last work was a setting of Lear's *The Owl and the Pussycat.* His critics once used to write of a 'soulless' mus., bare of expression and emotion. As he recedes from us and his mus. comes into perspective, the wrongheadedness of this judgment provokes either mirth or anger. Prin. works:

OPERAS: *The *Nightingale* (1908–9, 1913–14); **Mavra* (1921–2); **Oedipus Rex* (1926–7, also can be perf. as oratorio); *The *Rake's Progress* (1948–51).

THEATRE PIECES: **Renard,* burlesque (1915–16); *L'*histoire du soldat (The Soldier's Tale)* (1918); **Perséphone,* melodrama for ten., ch., and orch. (1933–4); *The *Flood,* mus. play (1961–2).

BALLETS: The **Firebird (Zhar-Ptitsa)* (1909–10); **Petrushka* (1910–11); The **Rite of Spring (Vesna Svyashchennaya)* (1911–13); *Les*Noces* (1914–17, and revisions); **Pulcinella* (after Pergolesi) (1919–20); **Apollo Musagetes* (1927–8); *The Fairy's Kiss (Le *baiser de la fée)* (after Tchaikovsky) (1928); **Jeu de cartes* (1936); **Circus Polka* (1942); **Orpheus* (1947); **Agon* (1953, 1956–7).

ORCH: Symphonies: No. 1 in E♭ (1905–7), Sym. in C (1938–40), **Symphony in 3 Movements* (1942–5); *Scherzo Fantastique* (1907–8); **Fireworks* (1908); *Suite, The Firebird* (first version 1911, 2nd version 1919, 3rd version 1945); *Song of the Nightingale,* symphonic poem from mus. of the opera (1917), *Ragtime,* 11 instr. (1918); *Suites for small orch.,* No. 1 (1917–25), No. 2 (1921); *Symphonies of Wind Instruments* (1920, rev. 1945–7); *Suite from Pulcinella,* chamber orch. (c.1922, rev. 1947); *Divertimento* (arr. from *The Fairy's Kiss*) (1934, rev. 1949); *Preludium* (orig. for jazz band 1936–7, orch. 1953); Conc. for chamber orch. **Dumbarton Oaks* (1937–8); *Danses Concertantes* (1941–2); *4 Norwegian Moods* (1942); *Ode* (1943); *Scherzo à la Russe* (1943–4, version for Paul Whiteman Band 1944); **Circus Polka* (1944, orch. of pf. piece 1942); Conc. in D for str. (1946); *Tango,* for 19 instr. (1953, orch. of pf. piece 1940); *Greetings Prelude* (1955); *Monumentum pro Gesualdo di Venosa ad CD annum,* 3 Gesualdo madrigals recomposed for instr. (1960); *Variations* (in memoriam Aldous Huxley) (1963–4).

SOLO INSTR. AND ORCH: Conc. for pf. and wind instr. (1923–4); *Capriccio,* pf. and orch. (1928–9); Vn. Conc. (1931); **Ebony Concerto,* cl. and chamber orch. (1945); **Movements,* pf. and orch. (1958–9).

VOICES AND INSTR: *The King of the Stars,* cantata, male ch. and orch. (1911–12); **Symphony of Psalms,* ch. and orch. (1930); *Babel,* cantata, narrator, male ch., and orch. (1944); *Mass,* mixed ch. and double wind quintet (1944–8); **Cantata,* sop., ten., female ch., and chamber ens. (1951–2); **Canticum Sacrum ad honorem Sancti Marci Nominis,* ten., bar., ch., and orch.

(1955); **Threni,* sop., alto, 2 tens., bass, basso profundo, ch., and orch. (1957–8); *A Sermon, A Narrative, and a Prayer,* cantata, alto, ten., speaker, ch., and orch. (1960–1); **Abraham and Isaac,* bar. and chamber orch. (1962–3); *Introitus* (T. S. Eliot in memoriam), tens., basses, chamber ens. (1945); *Requiem Canticles,* alto, bass, ch., and orch. (1965–6).

UNACC. VOICES: *Saucers: 4 Russian Peasant Songs,* unacc. female vv. (1914–17, rev. for equal vv., 4 hn., 1954); *Pater Noster,* mixed ch. (1926); *Credo,* mixed ch. (1932, 1949, 1964); *Ave Maria,* mixed ch. (1934,1949); *Little Canon,* 2 tens. (1947); *The Dove Descending,* mixed ch. (1962).

CHAMBER MUSIC: *3 Pieces,* cl. (1919); *Concertino* for str. qt. (1920), arr. for 12 instr. (1952); *Octet* for fl., cl., 2 bn., 2 tpt., ten. tb., bass tb. (1922–3, rev. 1952); *Duo Concertant,* vn. and pf. (1931–2); *Suite Italienne* (arr. from *Pulcinella*), vn. or vc. and pf. (1932); *Elegy,* vn. con sordini (1944); *Septet,* cl., hn., bn., pf., vn., va., vc. (1952–3); *Epitaphium,* fl., cl., hp. (1959).

PIANO: Sonata in F♯ minor (1903–4); *4 Studies* (1908); *3 Easy Pieces,* duet (1914–15); *5 Easy Pieces,* duet (1916–17); *Piano Rag-Music* (1919); *Sonata* (1924); *Serenade* in A (1925); Conc., 2 solo pf. (1931, 1934–5); *Tango* (1940, arr. for 19 instr. 1953); **Circus Polka* (1942, arr. for orch. 1944); *Sonata,* 2 pf. (1943–4).

SONGS WITH PIANO OR OTHER INSTR.: *Faun and Shepherdess,* song suite, mez. and orch. (1906); *Pastorale,* sop. and pf. (1907); *2 Melodies,* mez. and pf. (1907–8); *2 Verlaine Poems,* bar. and pf. (1910, with orch. 1951); *2 Balmont Poems,* high v. and pf. (1911, with chamber orch. 1954); *3 Japanese Lyrics,* sop. and pf. (1912–13); **Pribaoutki,* v. and instr. (1914); *Cat's Cradle Songs,* alto and 3 cls. (1915–16); *Berceuse,* v. and pf. (1917); *3 Shakespeare Songs,* mez., fl., cl., va. (1953); *In Memoriam Dylan Thomas,* ten., str. qt., 4 tbs. (1954); *Elegy for J.F.K.* [J. F. Kennedy, President of USA], bar., 3 cls. (1964); *The *Owl and the Pussycat,* v. and pf. (1966).

ARRANGEMENTS: Chopin: *Nocturne* in A♭ and *Valse brillante* in E♭, orch. for *Les Sylphides* (1909); Bach: *Vom Himmel hoch,* mixed ch. and orch. (1955–6); *2 Preludes and Fugues* from the '48', str., woodwind (c.1969); Gesualdo: *Tres sacrae cantiones,* reconstructed parts (1957 and 1959); Sibelius: *Canzonetta,* Op. 62a (orig. for str., 1911), arr. for 4 hns., 2 cls., harp, db. (1963); Wolf: *2 Sacred Songs* from *Spanisches Liederbuch,* mez. and 9 instr. (1968). Other works: *Song of the Volga Boatmen,* orch. (1917); *La Marseillaise,* for solo vn. (1919); *The Star-Spangled Banner,* for orch. and optional ch. (1941).

Stravinsky, Svyatoslav (Soulima) (*b* Lausanne, 1910). Swiss-born pianist, son of Igor **Stravinsky.* Studied Paris with I. Philipp and N. Boulanger. Stravinsky wrote the Conc. for 2 solo pf. (1931–5) for Soulima and himself to play and they gave f.p. in Paris, 1935. Settled in USA.

Street Corner. Ov. for orch. by Rawsthorne, f.p. 1944. Version for wind band by R. O'Brien.

Street Piano. Instr. used by vagrant musicians, being a mechanical type of pf. By turning a handle to operate a barrel-and-pin mechanism, a selection of tunes is available. Sometimes called *piano-organ.*

Streich (Ger.). Stroke (of bow). *Streichquartett,* string quartet, *Streichstimmen,* string-toned stops (org.), etc.

Streich, Rita (*b* Barnaul, 1920; *d* Vienna, 1987). Ger. sop., studied in Berlin with Erna Berger, Maria Ivogün, and Willi Domgraf-Fassbänder. Opera début Aussig 1943. Berlin State Opera 1946–50, Berlin City Opera 1950–3, Vienna State Opera from 1953. London début 1954, San Francisco 1957, Glyndebourne 1958. Outstanding in Mozart and Strauss (Queen of the Night, Constanze, Pamina, Zerbinetta, Sophie, Verdi's Gilda, etc.).

Strepitoso (It.). 'Noisy', 'loud'. Direction to play forcefully, with the implication of headlong excitement. Elgar used it as an expression mark. Liszt's *Tasso* begins *allegro strepitoso.*

Strepponi, Giuseppina (*b* Lodi, 1815; *d* Busseto, 1897). It. sop. and 2nd wife of Giuseppe *Verdi. Studied Milan Cons. 1830–4. Opera début Trieste 1835 in Rossini's *Mathilde di Shabran.* Sang in Vienna, Rome, Venice, etc., before Milan début 1842 in Donizetti's *Belisario.* Instrumental in getting Verdi's first opera *Oberto* staged at Milan, 1839. Created Abigaille in *Nabucco,* Milan, 1842. Retired from stage 1846 to live with Verdi. Married him 1859.

Stretta (It.). Drawn together, tightening (feminine of *stretto). Passage at end of It. operatic aria, ens., or act where tempo is quickened for final climax.

Stretto (It.). Drawn together. (1) Quicker tempo. (2) In fugue: when entry of the answer occurs before subject is completed, overlapping with it. This is a way of increasing excitement, as in a 4-part fugue when all 4 vv. enter in *stretto.*

Strich or **Bogenstrich** or **Anstrich** (Ger.). A stroke (with a bow); hence *mit breitem Strich,* with the breadth of the whole bow, and so forth. So also *Strichart,* manner of bowing; *Aufstrich,* up-bow; *Niederstrich,* down-bow.

Strict Canon. *Canon in which intervals of the imitating v. are same as those of v. imitated.

Strict Counterpoint. See *Counterpoint.*

Striggio, Alessandro (*b* Mantua, *c.*1540; *d* Mantua, 1592). It. composer. Prin. composer at court of Medicis in Florence in 1560s, writing *intermedi* for ceremonial occasions. Visited Eng. as political emissary 1567. Wrote madrigals for Ferrara 1584. Returned to Mantua 1584. Skilled instrumentalist, playing lira da gamba and

descant viol. Unusual for his time in composing little sacred mus.

String(s). The sound-producing agent of certain instr., i.e. thin strands of wire or gut vibrated on vn., va., vc., db., etc. by bow, on pf. by hammers, and on hpd., harp, guitar, etc. by plucking. But *strings,* meaning str. instr., is taken as referring in an orch. to the vns., vas., vcs., and dbs. A *string orchestra* comprises these only. A *string quartet* is 2 vn., va., vc.; *string trio,* vn., va., vc.

Stringendo (It.). Squeezing. Direction that intensity of the mus. is to be increased, by quickening the tempo (as when approaching a climax).

String Quartet. Group of 4 players (almost always 2 vn., va., vc.) or comp. written for them to play. Like the sym. in orch. mus., the str. qt. in chamber mus. has become the highest medium for a composer's thought. Form first developed at beginning of 18th cent. with A. Scarlatti, Tartini, etc., but achieved its flowering with Haydn, Mozart, Beethoven, and Schubert. Since then most composers have written str. qts., and the 19th and 20th cent. produced many superb qts. of performers, e.g. the Joachim, Brodsky, Bohemian, Léner, Griller, Amadeus, Gabrieli, Vermeer, etc.

String Quintet. Group of performers (2 vn., 2 va., vc.; or 2 vn., va., 2 vc.; or 2 vn., va., vc., db.) or work written for them. Great examples are those by Mozart and Schubert.

String-toned stops. Org. stops whose tone quality resembles that of str. instr., e.g. *Gamba.*

String Trio. Group of 3 players (usually 2 vn. and vc., or vn., va., vc.) or comp. written for them to perf. Trios for 2 vn. and vc. were derived from baroque trio sonata. Haydn seems to have been the first to write for vn., va., and vc. and was emulated by Boccherini. Mozart's Divertimento (K563) is a notable example and there are others by Beethoven. An unusual combination of instr. is Dvořák's *Terzetto* for 2 vn. and va. (1887). In the 20th cent. trios for vn., va., and vc. have been written by Webern (1927), Schoenberg (1945), Dohnányi, Hindemith, Roussel, Moeran, and L. Berkeley. In 1938 Vaughan Williams wrote a double str. trio (2 vn., 2 va., 2 vc.), revised it in 1942, and rewrote it 1946–8 as *Partita* for str.

Strisciando (It.). Trailing. Smooth, correct It. term for what is usually called *glissando.*

Strohfiedel (Ger.). Xylophone. (*Stroh* = straw, on ropes of which the wooden blocks of the instr. formerly rested).

Stromento (It., old form of *strumento*). Instrument, *Stromento a corde,* str. instr.; *stromenti d'arco,* bowed instr.; *stromenti di legno,* woodwind instr.; *stromenti d'ottone,* brass instr.; *stromenti a percossa,* perc. instr.; *stromenti a fiato,* wind instr.; *stromenti* *da tasto,* kbd. instr. Also, *recitativo stromentato,* acc. recit.

Strophic (from Gk. *strophe*). Term applied to song in which the same mus. is repeated, perhaps with very minor change, for each successive stanza of setting of a poem, in manner of folksong. The opposite, where the mus. progresses, is called 'through-composed' (Ger. *Durchkomponiert*). In general, the strophic song is simple and lyrical, the through-composed more dramatic or complex.

Stuart, Leslie (really Thomas Barrett) (*b* Southport, 1864; *d* Richmond, Surrey, 1928). Eng. composer and organist. Organist, Salford Cath., and Church of the Holy Name, Manchester. Went to London 1895 where he became composer of such popular songs as *Soldiers of the Queen* (1895), *Little Dolly Daydream* (1897), *Lily of Laguna* (1898), and operettas *Florodora* (1899), *The Belles of Mayfair* (1906), etc.

Stück (Ger.). Piece, as in **Konzertstück,* concert piece.

Stucken, Frank Valentine van der (*b* Fredericksburg, Texas, 1858; *d* Hamburg, 1929). Amer. cond. and composer. Studied vn. in Brussels 1866–76, then comp. in Leipzig with Grieg and Reinecke. Returned to USA 1884 conducting NY Arion Soc. (male ch.) until 1895. Cond. Cincinnati S.O. 1896–1907 (gave f.p. in USA of Mahler's 5th Sym., Mar. 1905). Dir., Cincinnati Coll. of Mus. 1895–1903. Thereafter spent much time in Ger. Wrote opera, orch. works, etc.

Stuckenschmidt, Hans Heinz (*b* Strasbourg, 1901). Ger. critic, author, and composer. Studied with Schoenberg and cond. concerts of new mus. in Hamburg, 1923–4. Mus. critic in Berlin 1929–34, when removed by Nazis, and in Prague 1937–41. Head of new mus. dept., Berlin radio, 1946. Returned to Berlin mus. criticism 1947. Prof. of mus. history, Berlin Tech. Univ. from 1948 (emeritus from 1967). Author of books on Busoni, Stravinsky, Ravel, Blacher, and David. His major biography of Schoenberg appeared in 1974 (Eng. trans. 1978).

Study. See *Étude.*

Sturm und Drang (Ger., 'Storm and stress'). Term applied to period, roughly 1760–80, in Ger. literature and mus. when emotionalism was at height. Specially applied to works comp. by Joseph **Haydn at that time, particularly syms. (roughly nos. 40–59), and str. qts. These works are marked by new and audacious formal and harmonic features. Also used to describe much kbd. mus. by C. P. E. Bach.

Stuttgart Chamber Orchestra. Founded by Karl **Münchinger, first concert 18 Sept. 1945. Tours to France, Britain, and Spain 1949, Central and S. Amer. 1952, USA 1954, Far East 1955, and Russsia 1959. Has made many recordings, notably of Bach's Brandenburg Concs. and his choral works. Orch. augmented in 1966 to 45 players to form Stuttgart Klassische Philharmonie.

Style Galant (Fr.). **Galanter Stil** (Ger.). See *Galant.*

Su (It., other forms incl. *sul, sull', sulla, sulle,* etc.).
(1) On, near. *Sul G* (in vn. playing), on the G str.
  (2) Up, e.g. *arcata in su,* up-bowed.

Sub-bourdon. Org. pedal end-plugged stop of 16' length and 32' pitch.

Subdominant. 4th degree of major or minor scale, e.g. F in key of C. So called because it is the same distance below the tonic as the **dominant is above it (not because it is the note below the dominant or less important).

Subito (It.). Suddenly. Quickly, immediately, as in *volti subito* (abbreviated to *V.S.*), turn over at once; *attacco subito,* go on without a break. Sometimes *subitamente* is used.

Subject. (1) Term in mus. analysis meaning a motif, phrase, or melody which forms a basic element in the construction of a comp. Thus, in sonata-form, one has the first and 2nd subjects, sometimes more. These are introduced in the exposition, then developed and recapitulated.
  (2) In **fugue, the melodic theme which is stated at the beginning, reappearing at various places and pitches during the comp. The answer is the imitation of the subject.

Submediant. 6th degree of major or minor scale, e.g. A in key of C major, A♭ in key of C minor, lies midway between tonic and subdominant in the same way as the **mediant is midway between tonic and dominant.

Sub-Octave Coupler. Coupler on pedal organ which duplicates notes played an octave lower on same stop.

Subotnick, Morton (*b* Los Angeles, 1933). Amer. composer and clarinettist. Studied Mills Coll. 1957–9 (comp. with Milhaud). Played cl. in orchs., then became mus. dir. Lincoln Center Repertory Th., 1967. Est. elec. mus. studio at Pittsburgh Univ. On staff Calif. Institute of the Arts, 1969. Mainly concerned with elec. mus., using synthesizer designed for him by D. Buchla. His *Silver Apples of the Moon* (1967) was first elec. work comp. for records. At NY toyshop, devised panels of buttons for shoppers to push which enabled instant creation of elec. works.

Sucher (orig. Hasselbeck), **Rosa** (*b* Velburg, Bavaria, 1849; *d* Eschweiler, Aachen, 1927). Ger. sop., outstanding in Wagnerian roles. Studied Munich. Sang in Berlin and Leipzig, where she married cond. Josef Sucher (1843–1908). London début (Drury Lane) 1882. 1st London Isolde and Eva. CG 1892 (Brünnhilde), Bayreuth 1886–96, Berlin 1888–98, NY Met. 1895. Retired Berlin 1903. Taught singing in Vienna after 1908.

Suchoň, Eugen (*b* Pezinok, 1908). Cz. composer. Studied Bratislava and Prague Cons. (1931–3, comp. with Novák). Teacher in Bratislava 1933–74. Author of textbooks on harmony. Works incl. opera *Krútňava* (Whirlpool), *Serenade* for wind quintet, *Rhapsodic Suite* for pf. and orch. Adopted serialism from 1959.

Suddaby, Elsie (*b* 1898; *d* Radlett, 1980). Eng. sop. Trained as pianist but turned to singing, making big reputation in oratorio. One of orig. 16 soloists in Vaughan Williams's *Serenade to Music*, 1938.

Sugár, Rezsö (*b* Budapest, 1919). Hung. composer. Studied Budapest Acad. of Mus. 1937–42 (comp. with Kodály). Teacher of comp., Bartók Cons., Budapest, 1949–69, Budapest Acad. from 1969. Works incl. *Concerto for Orchestra*, *Rhapsody* for vc. and pf., *Heroic Song*, cantata, and str. qts.

Suggia, Guilhermina (*b* Oporto, 1888; *d* Oporto, 1950). Portuguese cellist. Taught as child by father. Prin. cellist of Oporto orch. at age 12. In 1904 went to Leipzig to study under Klengel. Début at Gewandhaus cond. Nikisch, followed by tours. Studied in 1906 with Casals. Resumed int. career 1912 and settled in London. Subject of highly dramatic portrait by Augustus John, 1923. Came out of retirement to play at Edinburgh Fest. 1949.

Suisse Romande, Orchestre de la. See *Orchestre de la Suisse Romande.*

Suite (Fr., Eng.; Old Fr. *Ordre*; Old Eng. *Lesson*; Old Ger. *Partita* or *Partia*; Old It. *sonata da camera*). A following. Orig. a piece of instr. mus. in several movements, usually in dance-style. During 17th and 18th cents. was one of most important forms of instr. mus. During Baroque period, typical *Suite* would have framework of Allemande, Courante, Sarabande, and Gigue, with frequent interpolations of Minuet, Gavotte, Passepied, Bourrée, Musette, and Rigaudon. The various movements were usually based on one key, though modulations occurred within individual movements. Nearly all movements were in simple binary form. Fr. kbd. suites sometimes contained up to 18 movements, but these were not necessarily all intended to be perf. at once: the composer left it to the player to make a selection. In importance the suite was superseded by the sonata and the sym., and the title was given to works of a lighter type, e.g. Grieg's *Holberg* and Elgar's *Wand of Youth* Suites, and assemblages of movements from opera or ballet scores, e.g. Ravel's *Daphnis et Chloé* suites. 20th-cent. neo-classic composers revived the term (Stravinsky for example).

Suite Bergamasque (Bergomask suite). Pf. suite by Debussy containing 4 movements, *Prélude, Menuet, *Clair de Lune,* and *Passepied.* Comp. 1890, rev. 1905. Orch. version of Nos. 1, 2, and 4 by G. Cloez, No. 3 by *Caplet.

Suite on Verses of Michelangelo (Shostakovich). See *Michelangelo Buonarroti, Suite on Verses of.*

Suitner, Otmar (*b* Innsbruck, 1922). Austrian conductor. Studied pf. at Innsbruck Cons. and Salzburg Mozarteum, also cond. with C. *Krauss. Mus. dir., Ludwigshafen 1957. Chief cond. Dresden Opera and State Orch. 1960–4. Gen. mus. dir., Deutsche Staatsoper, Berlin, from 1964.

Suk, Josef (*b* Křečovice, 1874; *d* Benešov, 1935). Cz. composer and violinist. Studied Prague Cons. 1885–92 (comp. with Stecker and Dvořák, chamber mus. with Wihan). 2nd vn. in Bohemian Str. Qt. 1892–1933. Married Dvořák's daughter (*d* 1905). Prof. of comp., Prague Cons. 1922–35. Early works influenced by Dvořák, but later developed a more complex harmonic and polyphonic style, sometimes near to atonality. Works incl.:

ORCH: *Serenade* in E♭, for str. (1892); Sym. in E (1899); *Pohádka*, suite (1899–1900); *Fantastic Scherzo* (1903); *Praga* (Prague), symphonic poem (1904); Sym., *Asrael* (1905–6); *Pohádka léta* (A Summer's Tale) (1907–9); *Zrání* (Harvest Time), symphonic poem (1912–17); *War Triptych*, Op. 35, No. 1 *Svatý Václave* (Oh, St Wenceslas), *Meditation on an old Bohemian Chorale* (1914), No. 2 *Legend of the Dead Victors* (1919), No. 3 Sokol ceremonial march, *V nový život* (Towards a New Life, 1919–20); *Fantasia* in G minor, vn. and orch. (1902).

CHORAL: *10 Songs* for women's ch. (1899); *4 Songs* for male ch. (1900).

VOICE(S) AND PIANO/ORCH: *Chant d'Amour*, v. and pf. (1892); *O matince* (About Mother), 5 songs for v. and pf. (1907); *Životem a snem* (Life and Dreams), v. and pf. (1909); *Epilogue*, sop., bar., bass, ch., and orch. (1920–9).

CHAMBER MUSIC: 2 str. qts. (1896, 1911); pf. qt., pf. quintet, pf. trio; *4 Pieces* for vn. and pf.; *Ballad,* vn. and pf.; *Meditation on old Bohemian Chorale* Op. 35a (1914), arr. for str. qt. from orch. work.

Suk, Josef (*b* Prague, 1929). Cz. violinist, grandson of Josef *Suk. Studied Prague Cons. Début Prague 1951. Won Cz. State Prize 1964. Soloist in concs. with world's leading orchs. London début 1964.

Sul, sull', sulla, sui, sugli, sulle (It.). See *Su.*

Šulek, Stjepan (*b* Zagreb, 1914). Yugoslav composer, cond., and violinist. Studied Zagreb Acad. of Mus. 1923–36. Teacher of comp., Zagreb Acad. since 1945. Works incl. 7 syms., 3 pf. concs., vn. conc., va. conc., cantata, pf. sonata, and incidental mus. for Shakespeare's *The Tempest* and *Coriolanus.*

Sul G (Sul IV) (It.). Term used in vn. mus. meaning on the G (4th) str.

Suliotis, Elena (*b* Athens, 1943). Gr. sop. Studied Buenos Aires and Milan. Opera début, Naples 1964. Milan début 1966, CG 1969. Outstanding in dramatic roles (Lady Macbeth, etc.). Vocal problems caused early end to career.

Sullivan, (Sir) **Arthur** (Seymour) (*b* Lambeth, 1842; *d* Westminster, 1900). Eng. composer, cond., and organist. Son of Irish bandmaster at Sandhurst. Chorister, Chapel Royal, 1854. First comp., an anthem, pubd. 1855. First holder of Mendelssohn Scholarship, RAM, 1856, becoming pupil of Goss and Sterndale Bennett. Went to Leipzig Cons. where his teachers incl. Rietz, David, and Moscheles. Returned to Eng. 1861 and became organist, St Michael, Chester Sq. In 1862 his mus. for Shakespeare's *The Tempest* was played under Manns at Crystal Palace and made Sullivan's name. Ballet *L'Île enchantée* prod. CG 1864 and cantata *Kenilworth* Birmingham Fest. later same year. To 1864 also belongs comp. of *Irish Symphony*. Prof. of comp. RAM 1866, in which year he wrote vc. conc. for Piatti. Went with *Grove to Vienna in 1867 to recover Schubert's *Rosamunde* mus. and to examine MS. of 'Great' C major Sym. In 1866 wrote light opera *Cox and Box,* first of works in genre which was to ensure Sullivan's lasting fame.

For a time, however, Sullivan persisted with oratorio (*The Prodigal Son,* Worcester 1869) and incidental mus. to Shakespeare. However in 1871 met playwright William Schwenck Gilbert (1836–1911) and collaborated in unsuccessful light opera *Thespis,* following it in 1872 with tune for hymn 'Onward, Christian Soldiers'. *Festival Te Deum* followed, then another Birmingham oratorio, *The Light of the World* (1873). By now much in demand as cond. and administrator, and was also friend of royalty. In 1875 another collaboration with Gilbert, engineered by Richard D'Oyly Carte, resulted in successful curtain-raiser *Trial by Jury.* This led to D'Oyly Carte's leasing of Opéra-Comique Th. especially to produce operas by Gilbert and Sullivan. *The Sorcerer* (1877) justified the risk, running for 175 nights, but this was eclipsed by the 700-night run of *H.M.S. Pinafore* (1878). Despite copyright pirates, these works were in demand throughout the Western world, particularly in USA. *The Pirates of Penzance* (1879) continued run of success, followed by *Patience* (1881). During run of *Patience,* D'Oyly Carte opened his new th., the Savoy, and the operas became known as the Savoy operas and the cast 'Savoyards'. Sullivan was knighted 1883. It is a tragic irony that Sullivan and some of his friends felt that the success of the operettas was beneath the dignity of the dir. of the Nat. Training Sch. for Mus., 1876–81; they were happier with *The Martyr of Antioch* (Leeds 1880) and *The Golden Legend* (1886) than with *Iolanthe* (1882), *Princess Ida* (1883), and *The Mikado* (1885). These were followed by further 'hits': *Ruddigore* (1886), *The Yeomen of the Guard* (1888), and *The Gondoliers* (1889). During run of the last-named, the 2 partners quarrelled (supposedly over a new carpet at the Savoy Th.). *Haddon Hall* (1892) was comp.

to a lib. by S. Grundy. Reconciliation with Gilbert led to *Utopia Limited* (1893) and *The Grand Duke* (1896). During quarrel, Sullivan's only 'grand opera', *Ivanhoe,* to a lib. by Julian Sturgis, was prod. in 1891 at new Eng. Opera House built by D'Oyly Carte. Had 160 perfs., but costly venture failed and th. became a mus.-hall. By then, Sullivan's health was beginning to rebel against the strain he put on it. He was cond. of the Phil. Soc. 1885–7, frequently cond. at the Hallé Concerts in Manchester, was cond. of the Leeds Fest. from 1883, and continued to write th. mus., anthems, etc. In his last years his path crossed that of the rising Elgar. He died on St Cecilia's Day 1900 at comparatively early age of 58.

Sullivan's 'serious' work, by which he set such store, survives in the occasional ch. from *The Golden Legend* and the infrequent revivals of his sym. and incidental mus. and of *Ivanhoe.* These show talent, not quite as much, it could be argued, as in his hymn-tunes and in his popular ballads, such as *My dearest heart* and *The *Lost Chord* (written in 1877 on the death of his brother and given a further lease of fame by the Amer. comedian Jimmy 'Schnozzle' Durante in his song 'The guy who found the Lost Chord'). But in the Savoy operettas there is genius. In them Sullivan's melodic felicity, light-fingered orchestration, and truly astonishing gift for pastiche and parody (Handel, Verdi, Donizetti, Wagner—all are paid the compliment of witty imitation) found their proper outlet and gave England a unique type of mus. entertainment and cult. Sometimes parody seems to have taken over completely and one longs to call out 'Will the real Sullivan stand up?' At other times, Gilbert's cruelties and facetiousness become oppressive; also the stylized, unchanging ritual of the D'Oyly Carte prods. became wearisome except to devotees, of whom there are millions, seemingly versed in every phrase of both mus. and lib. With such a following, Sullivan's fame seems secure for as long as one dares to foretell. Prin. works:

OPERA: **Ivanhoe* (1890).

OPERETTAS (Where no librettist is given, Gilbert is implied): **Cox and Box* (Burnand, 1866); *Contrabandista* (Burnand, 1867); **Thespis* (1871, lost); **Trial by Jury* (1875); *The Zoo* (Stevenson, 1875); *The *Sorcerer* (1877); **H.M.S. Pinafore* (1878); *The *Pirates of Penzance* (1879); **Patience* (1880–1); **Iolanthe* (1882); **Princess Ida* (1883); *The *Mikado* (1884–5); **Ruddigore* (1886); *The *Yeomen of the Guard* (1888); *The *Gondoliers* (1889); *Haddon Hall* (Grundy, 1892); **Utopia Limited* (1893); *The Chieftain* (Burnand, 1894); *The *Grand Duke* (1895–6); *The Beauty Stone* (Pinero and Comyns Carr, 1898); *The Rose of Persia* (Hood, 1899); *The *Emerald Isle* (Hood, 1900, mus. completed by *German).

INCIDENTAL MUSIC: Shakespeare: *The Tempest* (1862); *The Merchant of Venice* (1871); *The Merry Wives of Windsor* (1874); *King Henry VIII* (1877);

Macbeth (1888); *The Foresters* (Tennyson, 1892); *King Arthur* (Comyns Carr, 1894).

ORCH: Sym. in E (*Irish*) (1864–6); Ov., **In Memoriam* (1866); *Overture Di Ballo* (1870); *Imperial March* (1893); Vc. Conc. (1866).

CHORAL: Oratorios: *The *Prodigal Son* (1869); *The Light of the World* (1873, rev. 1890); *The Martyr of Antioch* (1880, rev. as opera 1898); Cantatas: *Kenilworth* (1864); *On Shore and Sea* (1871); *The *Golden Legend* (1886).

Also songs, chamber mus., ballads, hymns, anthems, organ pieces.

Sul Ponticello (It.). On the bridge. Instruction to the player of the vn., va., vc., and db. that he is to take the bow as near as possible to the bridge to produce a rather metallic but mysterious sound-effect.

Sul Tasto (It.). On the touch. Direction to player of vn., etc., to take the bow over the fingerboard, giving a rich, mellow sound. *Sulla tastiera* (on the fingerboard) means the same.

Sumer is Icumen In (Old Eng.). Summer is coming in. Eng. comp., dating supposedly from *c.*1240, sometimes known as the Reading Rota because the MS. originated at Reading Abbey. The conjectural author was a monk of Reading, **John of Fornsete. An infinite canon at the unison for 4 ten. vv., with 2 basses repeating a ground bass or *pes*, also in canon at the unison. Can claim to be the earliest extant canon, 6-part comp., example of ground bass, and mus. setting of both sacred (Latin) and secular words.

Summation Tone. Acoustical phenomenon whereby, when 2 loud notes are sounded, another note, higher than orig. 2, may also be heard, corresponding to sum of their vibrations.

Summer Night on the River. Title of 2nd of *2 Mood Pictures* for small orch. by Delius, comp. 1911 and f.p. in Leipzig 1913, London 1914. First piece is **On hearing the first cuckoo in Spring* (1912). Not to be confused with Delius's 2 chs. *To be sung of a summer night on the water*, 1917.

Summer's Last Will and Testament. Work by C. **Lambert for solo bar., ch., and orch., comp. 1935, f.p. London 1936. Setting of 5 lyrics from play of same name (1593) by Thomas Nashe, movements being entitled *Intrata, Drinking Chorus, King Pest* (rondo burlesca for orch.), *Madrigal, Sarabande.*

Sumsion, Herbert (Whitton) (*b* Gloucester, 1899). Eng. organist, cond., and composer. Pupil of **Brewer at Gloucester 1915–17, acting as ass. organist Gloucester Cath. 1916–17 and again 1919–22. Organist, Christ Church, Lancaster Gate, London, 1922–6. Prof. of harmony and counterpoint, Curtis Institute, Philadelphia, 1926–8. Organist and choirmaster Gloucester Cath. 1928–67, cond. at 3 Choirs Fests. within that period. Dir. of mus., Cheltenham Ladies College, 1935–68. Wrote org. mus., church services, etc. C.B.E. 1961.

Sunderland (née Sykes), **Susan** (*b* Brighouse, 1819; *d* Brighouse, 1905). Eng. sop. Sang in Halifax Choral Society. Début as soloist, Bradford 1838. Studied in London and then returned north to become known as 'Yorkshire's Queen of Song', remaining for 25 years leading singer of extracts from oratorio and of popular songs. Expressive voice of great power. London début 1849 in *Messiah*, continuing as soloist in oratorios there until 1856. Sang at opening of Leeds Town Hall and first Leeds Fest. Retired 1864. Had she been fully trained her career might have been of int. celebrity. Remembered still through 'Mrs Sunderland' competitive fest. held in her memory.

Suo (It.). Its own, e.g. *Suo loco*, indicating a return to 'its own place' after transposition of vocal or instr. part up or down an octave, etc.

Suolahti, Heikki (*b* Helsinki, 1920; *d* Helsinki, 1936). Finn. composer. Studied Helsinki Cons. Youth of great promise. Wrote *Sinfonia piccola* (1935), vn. conc., *Agnus Dei*, and left large works unfinished.

Suor Angelica (Sister Angelica). Opera in 1 act by Puccini to text by Forzano. Part 2 of *Il*Trittico*. Comp. 1917. Prod. NY Met. 1918, Rome and Chicago 1919, London 1920.

Super-Octave Coupler. Coupler on an org. which duplicates notes played an octave higher on same stop.

Supertonic. 2nd degree of the scale, lying whole tone above tonic, e.g. note D in key of C (major or minor) lying immediately above tonic (1st degree).

Supervia, Conchita (*b* Barcelona, 1895; *d* London, 1936). Sp. mez. and mezzo-cont. Studied Barcelona. Début at 14 in Buenos Aires, singing Carmen in Rome 1911. First Rome Oktavian in *Rosenkavalier*, 1911. Chicago Opera 1915–16 and 1932–3, CG 1934–5. Sang Rossini roles of Isabella in *L'Italiana in Algeri*, Rosina in *Il barbiere di Siviglia*, and Angelina in *La Cenerentola* in orig. keys, dating from appearances with **Gui in Turin, 1925. Created title-role in Lehár's *Frasquita* (1922). Singer of vivacious originality, with distinctive timbre.

Suppé, Franz von (*b* Split (Spalato), 1819; *d* Vienna, 1895). Austrian composer, born in Dalmatia, of Belg. descent. Name is Ger. form of Francesco Ezechiele Ermenegildo, Cavaliere Suppé-Demelli. Studied Padua Univ., later at Vienna Cons. with Sechter and Seyfried. Relative of Donizetti, who helped him. Became cond. at Josephstadt Th., Vienna, 1841, later in Pressburg and Baden, *c.*1862 at Theater an der Wien, and 1865–95, at Leopoldstadt Th., Vienna. Comp. serious works, incl. *Requiem* (1855), but fame rests on series of tuneful operettas (about 30 in

number). These incl. *Pique Dame (Die Kartensch-
lägerin) (1862); Die schöne Galatea (The *Beautiful
Galathea) (1865), Leichte Cavallerie (*Light Cavalry) (1866), Banditenstreiche (The Jolly Robbers)
(1867), and *Boccaccio (1879). The famous Poet
and Peasant ov. (1846) is part of the incidental
mus. to Elmar's play Dichter und Bauer.

Supprimez (Fr.). Suppress. In Fr. org. mus. it
means 'put out of use' the stop in question.

Surinach, Carlos (b Barcelona, 1915). Sp.-born
composer and cond. (Amer. citizen 1959). Studied
Barcelona, Düsseldorf, Cologne, and Berlin. Cond.
Barcelona P.O. 1944, and in Paris 1947–50. Settled
in USA 1951 and wrote scores for dancers, e.g.
Martha Graham and Pearl Lang. In 1954 transcr.
for orch. those movements of Albéniz's Iberia
which Arbós left unfinished. Works incl. ballet
David and Bathsheba (NY 1960, staged in London
1961 as A Place in the Desert), Sinfonietta flamenca,
Conc. for Orch., Passacaglia Symphony, pf. concertino, guitar sonatina, songs, etc.

Sur la touche (Fr.). On the fingerboard. Direction
in str. playing to bow over the fingerboard.

Sur le chevalet (Fr.). On the bridge. Direction in
str. playing to bow on or near the bridge, same as
*Sul ponticello.

Surprise Symphony. Nickname of Haydn's Sym.
in G major, No. 94 (Hob. I: 94)., comp. London
1791, so called because of sudden forte drumbeat
in slow movement. In Ger., sym. is known as mit
dem Paukenschlag (With the drumstroke).

Sursum Corda (Lift up your hearts). (1) Work
for str., brass, and org., Op 11, by Elgar, f.p.
Worcester Cath. 1894. Comp. for visit of Duke of
York (later King George V) to Worcester.
(2) No. 7 of Liszt's Troisième année (pubd. 1883)
of the Années de pèlerinage for solo pf.

Survivor from Warsaw, A. For narrator, male
ch., and orch. by Schoenberg, Op. 46, comp. Aug.
1947. Eng. text by Schoenberg, Fr. version by R.
Leibowitz, Ger. by Maquet Peter. F.p. Albuquer-
que, New Mexico, 1948, f.p. in England 1951.

Susanna's Secret (Wolf-Ferrari). See Segreto di
Susanna, Il.

Susato, Tylman (b ?Cologne, c.1500; d ?Antwerp,
c.1561). Ger. mus. publisher and composer. Town
musician in Antwerp 1529–49, where in 1543 he
est. a printing firm. Pubd. over 50 vols. of church
mus. and chansons. His songs and instr. dances are
attractive.

Suspended Cadence. Delay before final cadence
of a comp. so that performer in conc. (or,
formerly, aria) may insert cadenza.

Suspension. Opposite of *anticipation: a note in
a chord is held over (sounded slightly late) as a
momentary discordant part of the combination
which follows; it is then resolved by falling a

degree to a note which forms a real part of the
2nd chord. When 2 notes are held over it is called
a double suspension. In many 20th-cent. works
suspensions are often left unresolved.

Süsskind, (Jan) **Walter** (b Prague, 1918; d
Berkeley, Calif., 1980). Cz.-born cond. and pianist
(Eng. citizen). Studied Prague Acad. of Mus. with
Suk, Hába, and Szell. Début as cond., Ger. Opera,
Prague, 1934–8. Pianist in London Czech Trio
1938–42. Prin. cond. Carl Rosa Opera, 1943–5.
Cond., Scottish Orch. 1946–52, Victorian S.O. of
Melbourne, 1953–5, Toronto S.O. 1956–65, St
Louis S.O. 1968–75. Guest cond. of many Brit.
orchs. and opera cos.

Süssmayr, Franz Xaver (b Schwanenstadt, 1766;
d Vienna, 1803). Austrian composer. Studied
Vienna with Salieri and Mozart. Cond. at Nat.
Th., Vienna, 1792, 2nd cond., court th. 1794.
Wrote several operas, oratorios, masses, etc.
Assisted in completion of Mozart's Requiem
(K626).

Sustaining Pedal. Pf. pedal, often erroneously
called 'loud pedal', operated by right foot to
prolong sound by holding off the dampers.
Beethoven, as a player, was said to make telling
use of this pedal, which is much exploited by
Romantic composers.

Susurrando, susurrante (It.). Whispering.

Sutermeister, Heinrich (b Feuerthalen, 1910).
Swiss composer. Studied Basle and Munich Acad.
1934–5. Worked as répétiteur at Berne Stadttheater. Influenced by Verdi's last works and by *Orff,
determined to write melodic 20th-cent mus.
Works incl.:

OPERAS: *Romeo und Julia (after Shakespeare;
1939); Die Zauberinsel (The Magic Island, after
Shakespeare's Tempest; 1942); Niobe (1946);
Raskolnikoff (after Dostoyevsky; 1945–7); Der
rote Stiefel (The Red Shoe; 1951); Titus Feuerfuchs
(1957–8); Die schwarze Spinne (The Black Spider;
1948–9); Seraphine (after Rabelais; 1959); Madame Bovary (after Flaubert; 1966–7); Das Gespenst
von Canterville (The Canterville Ghost (after
Wilde), 1966).

ORCH: Suite, Romeo und Julia (1940); Die Alpen
(1948); Divertimento No. 1 for str. (1936), No.
2 for orch. (1959–60); Serenade (1970); 3 pf.
concs. (1944, 1954, 1961–2); vc. conc. (1954–5).

CHORAL: 8 Cantatas (1938–1966); Requiem, sop.,
bar., ch., and orch. (1952); Te Deum (1975).
Also songs with pf./orch., pf. pieces, etc.

Suthaus, Ludwig (b Cologne, 1906; d Berlin,
1971). Ger. ten. Studied Cologne. Opera début
Aachen 1928 as Walther in Die Meistersinger.
Stuttgart Opera 1933–41, Berlin 1941–9, 1948–
65, Vienna 1948–71, CG 1952–3. Bayreuth from
1943. Amer. début San Francisco 1953. Mainly
sang Wagnerian roles, especially Tristan and
Siegmund.

Sutherland, (Dame) **Joan** (*b* Sydney, N.S.W., 1926). Australian sop. Studied Sydney and RCM. Début Sydney 1947 in Purcell's *Dido and Aeneas*. CG 1952, joining co. Created role of Jenifer in Tippett's *The Midsummer Marriage* 1955 and was New Prioress in f.p. in England of Poulenc's *Carmelites*. Sang Gilda and under guidance of Richard Bonynge developed dramatic coloratura possibilities of her v., scoring enormous success as Lucia in Donizetti's opera, CG 1959. Thereafter sang many *bel canto* roles in works specially revived for her. Also fine Handel singer. Took own opera co. to Australia 1965. C.B.E. 1961. D.B.E. 1979.

Suzuki, Shin'ichi (*b* Nagoya, 1898). Japanese vn. teacher. Son of maker of violins. Studied vn. with Kō Andō in Nagoya and in Berlin 1921–8 with K. Klingler. Founded Suzuki Qt. 1928. Founded Tokyo Str. Orch. which introduced baroque mus. to Japanese listeners. Pres. of Teikoku Mus. Sch. from 1930 and put into practice his belief that any child could reach a high standard of ability as a violinist by adapting external stimuli. Taught vn. from 1950 at Sainō Kyōiku Kenkyū-kai, Matsumoto. Visited USA 1964, Eng. 1973.

Svanholm, Set (*b* Västeras, 1904; *d* Stockholm, 1964). Swed. ten., orig. bar. Studied Stockholm Cons., teaching singing there 1929 after spell as church organist. Studied singing with Forsell and made début as bar., 1930. Resumed training, then made ten. début in 1936. Sang first Wagner roles 1937. Salzburg Fest. 1938. Bayreuth 1942, NY Met. 1946–56, CG 1948–57. In 1940s and 1950s was world's leading Wagnerian ten., in demand as Siegfried and Tristan and frequently singing with *Flagstad. First Peter Grimes in Stockholm. Intendant, Stockholm Opera 1956–63.

Svegliando; svegliato (It.). Awakening; awakened, i.e. brisk, alert.

Svendsen, Johan (Severin) (*b* Christiania, 1840; *d* Copenhagen, 1911). Norweg. composer, cond., and violinist. Studied Leipzig Cons. 1863–7. Went to Paris 1868, playing in orch. there. Met Liszt at Weimar 1870. Sym. played at Leipzig, 1871. Became close friend of Wagner and played in orch. at laying of Bayreuth foundation-stone, 1872. Returned to Norway as cond. and teacher, 1872–7. First visit to London 1870. Court cond. Copenhagen from 1883. Works incl. 2 syms., vc. conc., vn. conc., *Carnaval à Paris, 4 Norwegian Rhapsodies, Romance* for vn. and orch., and chamber mus. and songs.

Svetlanov, Yevgeny (Fyodorovich) (*b* Moscow, 1928). Russ. cond. and composer. Studied Moscow Cons. Cond. Moscow Radio 1953. Cond., Bolshoy Th., Moscow, 1954–62, chief cond. 1962–5. Cond. USSR State S.O. from 1965. Has comp. symphonic poems, cantata, sonatas, songs.

Sviridov, Georgy (Vasilyevich) (*b* Fatezh, 1915). Russ. composer and pianist. Studied Leningrad Cons. 1936–41 (comp. with Shostakovich). First secretary, Soviet Union of Composers since 1968. Works mainly comprise songs, settings of Blok and Pasternak, and some of Russ. trans. of Burns and Shakespeare, also *Emotional Oratorio* (1959).

Svoboda, Josef (*b* Časlav, 1920). Cz. stage designer. Studied architecture Prague Art Coll. 1945–50. Chief designer and tech. dir., Prague Nat. Th. 1951–6. Influenced by Appia and Craig, developed concept of 'psychoplastic stage', concentrating on 'inner meaning' of work. Has made inspired use of modern lighting techniques, incl. laser beams in his 1970 *Zauberflöte* in Munich. Other celebrated opera designs were seen at CG in Strauss's *Die Frau ohne Schatten*, 1966, Debussy's *Pelléas*, 1969, *The Ring*, 1974–6, at Munich in Zimmermann's *Die Soldaten*, 1969, and in Verdi's *Sicilian Vespers*, Hamburg, 1969, and London, 1984.

Swan of Tuonela, The. 'Symphonic legend' by *Sibelius, orig. comp. as prelude to unfinished opera, 1893, but pubd. as Op. 22, No. 3, one of the 4 *Lemminkäinen Legends* for orch. Rev. 1897 and 1900. F.p. Helsinki 1896, f.p. in England 1905. Tuonela is Finnish Hades. Cor anglais solo depicts swan.

Swan Lake (*Lebedinoye ozero*; Fr. *Le lac des cygnes*). Ballet in 4 acts, mus. by Tchaikovsky, comp. 1875–6, to lib. by Begitchev and Geltser, choreog. Reisinger, prod. Moscow 1877. Later choreog. Petipa and Ivanov (St Petersburg 1895).

Swan Song (Schubert). See *Schwanengesang*.

Swarowsky, Hans (*b* Budapest, 1899; *d* Salzburg, 1975). Hung. cond. Studied in Vienna with Schoenberg. Cond. posts in Stuttgart, Berlin, Hamburg, and Zürich. Cond. Polish P.O. in Kraków, 1944–6. Dir. Graz Opera 1947–9. Cond. SNO 1957–9. Ed. Fr. versions of Gluck's *Alceste* and *Orphée*. Wrote parts of lib. of Strauss's *Capriccio* (incl. the Sonnet) but his part in this was suppressed by C. Krauss, the official librettist.

Swarthout, Gladys (*b* Deepwater, Missouri, 1900; *d* Florence, 1969). Amer. mez. Studied in Chicago, and with Mugnone. Début Chicago 1924. NY Met. 1929–45, singing variety of roles incl. Carmen and Mignon.

Swayne, Giles (Oliver Cairnes) (*b* Stevenage, 1946). Eng. composer and cond. Studied Cambridge Univ. and RAM (1968), also with N. Maw. Cond. course at Siena, 1968. Opera *répétiteur* at Wexford Fest. 1972 and 1973 and Glyndebourne 1973–4. Teacher at Bryanston Sch. and St Paul's Girls' Sch. Won Lancaster Univ. composer's prize, 1974. Studied with Messiaen after 1976. Works incl.:

ORCH: *Orlando's Music* (1974); *Pentecost Music* (1977); Sym. (1983); *Song for Haddi*, chamber ens. (1983); *Naaotwa's Song* (1984).

CHAMBER MUSIC: Str. Qts., No. 1 (1971), No. 2 (1977); *4 Lyrical Pieces,* vc. and pf. (1971); Trio, fl., ob., pf. (1972); *Canto,* for guitar (1972), pf. (1973), vn. (1973), cl. (1975), vc. (1981); *Duo,* vn. and pf. (1975); *Suite,* guitar (1976); *Freewheeling,* va., baryton, vc. (1980).

OPERA: *Le Nozze di Cherubino* (1983–4).

VOCAL: *3 Shakespeare Songs,* mixed ch. (1969); *The Good Morrow,* Donne cycle of 5 songs, mez. and pf. (1971); *Cry,* 28 amplified solo vv. (1978); *Count-Down,* 16-pt. ch. and 2 perc. players (1981); *Magnificat,* unacc. ch. (1982).

PIANO: *Synthesis,* 2 pf. (1974); *Phoenix Variations* (1968–79).

ORGAN: *Paraphrase on a theme of Tallis* (1971); *Riff-Raff* (1983).

Sweelinck, Jan Pieterszoon (b Deventer or Amsterdam, 1562; d Amsterdam, 1621). Dutch composer, organist, harpsichordist, and teacher. Succeeded father as organist of Old Church, Amsterdam, c.1580, remaining in post until death. First composer to give independent part to the pedal and to write fully worked-out fugues, thus pioneering and establishing form to be used by Bach. Taught most of great N. Ger. school of organists and was of immense influence. Wrote over 250 vocal works and 70 for keyboard. Set the entire psalter. Keyboard works show Eng. and It. influences.

Swell. Mechanical device on org. and certain other kbd. instr., e.g. hpd., for increasing (and lessening) the vol. of sound.

Swell Organ (Swell). Section of organ in which the pipes are enclosed in a *Swell Box.* Player can increase or diminish vol. of sound by means of *Swell Pedal* which opens and closes a Venetian shutter. Manual controlling this is placed above *Great Org. and is known as *Swell Manual.* On some modern orgs. 'swell' effect may be obtained also on Choir and Solo manuals.

Swieten, Gottfried, Baron van (b Leiden, 1733; d Vienna, 1803). Dutch-born Austrian patron of mus. Went to Vienna 1745 when his father became empress's physician. Held diplomatic posts in Brussels, Paris, and London, and was ambassador to Berlin 1770–7. Prefect of Imperial Lib., Vienna, 1778–1803. Wrote light operas, but remembered for commissioning works from C. P. E. Bach, Haydn, and Mozart. Introduced Mozart to mus. of Bach and Handel 1782–3. Mozart made his arrs. of Handel oratorios and other vocal works for private concerts van Swieten founded. Wrote or adapted texts of Haydn's *Seven Last Words* (ch. version 1796), *The Creation* (1798), and *The Seasons* (1801). Helped the young Beethoven, who dedicated his 1st Sym. to him.

Swing. See *Jazz.*

Sydney Symphony Orchestra. Orch. based in Sydney, N.S.W. Began in 1934 as broadcasting orch. (A.B.C.) also giving public and schools concerts. Title of Sydney S.O. adopted permanently in 1945. Prin. conds. have incl. Joseph Post, Nikolay Malko, Dean Dixon, Moshe Atzmon, Willem van Otterloo, and Sir Charles Mackerras. Gives over 160 concerts a year.

Sygietynski, Tadeusz (b Warsaw, 1896; d Warsaw, 1955). Polish cond. Studied Lwów, Leipzig (with Reger), and Vienna (with Schoenberg). Founded state dance ens. 1949 to popularize Polish folk-dance and with it toured Europe and USA. Arr. Polish folk-songs.

Sylphides, Les (The Sylphs). Ballet in 1 act, orig. called *Chopiniana,* arr. to mus. of Chopin, choreog. Fokine. Prod. St Petersburg 1907 (Pavlova among dancers). This first version used 5 pieces orch. by Glazunov: *Polonaise* in A, Op. 40 No. 1, *Nocturne* in F, Op. 15 No. 1, *Mazurka* in C♯ minor, Op. 50 No. 3, *Waltz* in C♯ minor, Op. 64 No. 2, and *Tarentella* in A♭, Op. 43. Rev. version by Fokine prod. St Petersburg 1908 with additional pieces orch. by Maurice Keller. This comprised *Polonaise* in A, Op. 40 No. 1 (in most Western versions *Prelude* in A, Op. 28 No. 7), *Nocturne* in A♭, Op. 32 No. 2, *Waltz* in G♭, Op. 70 No. 1, *Mazurka* in D, Op. 33 No. 2, *Mazurka* in C, Op. 67 No. 3, *Prelude* in A, Op. 28 No. 7, *Mazurka* in C♯ minor, Op. 50 No. 3, *Grand Waltz* in E♭, Op. 18 No. 1. Later Fokine choreographed *Mazurka* in C, Op. 33 No. 3 as alternative to Op. 67 No. 3. Revived by Diaghilev, Paris 1909. Extra items were scored by Tcherepnin and Lyadov, and Stravinsky rescored the *Nocturne* in A♭, Op. 32 No. 2 and the *Grand Waltz* in E♭, Op. 18 No. 1. One of most popular ballets in repertory. Eng. versions have used Chopin arrs. by Roy Douglas, Gordon Jacob, Malcolm Sargent, and others.

Sylvia, ou La Nymphe de Diane. Ballet in 3 acts, mus. by Delibes, lib. by Barbier and de Reinach, choreog. Mérante. Prod. Paris 1876, London 1911. New choreog. by Ashton CG 1952.

Sympathetic Strings. Those str. on a bowed, plucked, or hammered instr. which vibrate (and thereby sound a note) in sympathetic resonance with the note sounded near them by some other agent. Certain instr., e.g. viola d'amore, were strung with sympathetic str., tuned to certain pitches, which vibrated because of proximity to bowed str. above them and thus enriched the tone.

Symphonia. (1) Gr. word taken into Lat. and sometimes used by composers instead of 'symphony'. Thus R. Strauss's *Symphonia Domestica* is correct title given by composer, not *Sinfonia Domestica* (It.).

(2) Name given in medieval period to hurdy-gurdy, first str. instr. to which kbd. principle was applied. Perhaps so called because it was used in polyphonic mus., a master of polyphony being then sometimes called a *symphoneta* (Gr.).

Symphonia Domestica (Domestic Symphony). Orch. tone-poem by R. Strauss, Op. 53, comp. 1902–3, f.p. NY 1904, f.Eng.p. London 1905. Depicts a day in the life of the Strausses, with themes representing wife Pauline, their baby son, and himself, but is also a sectional sym. in one movement not solely dependent on programme for mus. effectiveness.

Symphonic Dances. Orch. work in 3 movements by Rakhmaninov, Op. 45, comp. 1940, f.p. Philadelphia 1941.

Symphonic Metamorphosis of Themes by Carl Maria von Weber. Orch. work by Hindemith, comp. 1940–3, f.p. NY 1944. Originated in sketches (1940) for ballet for Massine on Weber themes, using *Turandot* ov. The Weber themes used are: 1st movt. (*Allegro*), No. 4 (*All'Ongarese*) of *Eight Pieces* for pf. duet, 1818–19; 2nd movt. (*Turandot Scherzo*), theme from ov. to incid. mus. for Schiller's trans. of Gozzi's *Turandot, Prinzessin von China*, 1809; 3rd movt. (*Andantino*), No. 2 of *6 Petites Pièces faciles*, pf. duet, 1801; 4th movt. (*Marsch*), No. 7 of *Eight Pieces* for pf. duet, 1818–19.

Symphonic Poem (Ger. *Sinfonische Dichtung*). Descriptive term first applied by *Liszt to his 13 one-movement orch. works which, while on a symphonic scale, were not 'pure' syms. because they dealt with descriptive subjects taken from classical mythology, Romantic literature, recent history, or imaginative fantasy e.g. *Prometheus, Mazeppa, Les Préludes*, etc. In other words, they were 'programmatic'. Other composers followed his line, e.g. Smetana (*Wallenstein's Camp*, etc.), Tchaikovsky (*Francesca da Rimini*, etc.), Saint-Saëns (*Le Rouet d'Omphale*, etc.), Franck (*Le chasseur maudit*, etc.), and many others. Richard Strauss, who carried pictorialism a stage further, preferred the term *Tondichtung* for his works in this form (*Don Juan*, etc.). This is usually translated as 'tone-poem', but it has been well suggested that 'sound-poem' comes nearer to the intention. Most late 19th- and early 20th-cent. composers wrote symphonic poems though they did not always so describe them, e.g. Delius's *In a Summer Garden*. Elgar used designation 'concert-ov.' for what are in effect 3 symphonic poems, *Froissart, Cockaigne*, and *In the South*, and he called *Falstaff* a *symphonic study. Later 20th-cent. composers have shown less interest in the form, but it still survives in such works as Birtwistle's *The Triumph of Time* (1972).

Symphonic Study. Term used by various composers in different ways. Schumann called his 1837 set of pf. variations *Études symphoniques*; Elgar applied the term to his symphonic poem *Falstaff*, presumably to show that it was an 'in depth' character-study; Rawsthorne described an orch. set of variations as *Symphonic Studies*.

Symphonie espagnole (Spanish Symphony). Orch. work for vn. and orch. by Lalo, Op. 21,

comp. 1874, written for and first played by *Sarasate in 1875.

Symphonie Fantastique (Fantastic Symphony). Orch. work, Op. 14, in C major by Berlioz, comp. 1830 when he was 26, and f.p. Paris, 5 Dec. 1830. F.Eng.p. Manchester, cond. Hallé, 9 Jan. 1879. F. complete London p., cond. W. Ganz, April 1881. One of most remarkable Romantic comps. and forerunner of the programme-syms. and symphonic poems of Liszt, Mahler, Strauss, Tchaikovsky, and others. Sub-titled 'Episode in the Life of an artist', it was inspired by Berlioz's then unrequited love for the Irish actress Harriet Smithson, whom he later married. This is symbolized in the mus. by a melody (*idée fixe*) which acts as a motto-theme recurring in various guises, like a Wagnerian leitmotiv, in each of the 5 movements. A theme in the 1st movement was taken from a song Berlioz wrote when he was 12 and the *March to the Scaffold* was taken from his unfinished opera *Les Francs Juges* (1826). Berlioz rev. the *Symphonie Fantastique* in Rome, 1831–2, and made other re-touchings before publication 1846. Titles of the movements are: 1. *Rêveries, passions* (Dreams, Passions). 2. *Un bal* (A ball). 3. *Scène aux champs* (Scene in the fields). 4. *Marche au supplice* (March to the Scaffold). 5. *Songe d'une nuit du Sabbat* (Witches' Sabbath). Arr. for pf. by Liszt, 1833. See also *Lélio*.

Symphonie funèbre et triomphale ('Funereal and triumphal symphony'). Work by Berlioz, sometimes known as *Grande Symphonie funèbre et triomphale*, composed 1840 to commission by French Government to mark tenth anniversary of 1830 Revolution. Originally scored for large military band and perf. out of doors. Berlioz in 1842 added parts for optional str. orch. and later also for chorus to patriotic text by A. Deschamps. In 3 movements: 1. *Marche funèbre* in F minor; 2. *Oraison funèbre* in G; 3. *L'Apothéose* in B♭. Probably comp. from earlier sketches.

Symphonie Liturgique. Honegger's Sym. No. 3, comp. 1945–6. F.p. Zürich 1946.

Symphonie sur un chant montagnard français (Symphony on a French mountain song). D'Indy's Op. 25, sub-titled *Symphonie Cévenole* because the theme comes from the Cévennes region. Specified as 'for orch. and pf.'. Comp. 1886, f.p. Paris, Lamoureux concert 1887.

Symphony (from Gk., 'a sounding together'; Ger. *Sinfonie*, Fr. *Symphonie*, It. *Sinfonia*, Gk.-Lat. *Symphonia*). A term which has had several meanings over the centuries: (1) In 17th and 18th cents., *Sinfonia* meant what we should now call an 'overture' to an opera, etc., i.e. a short instr. piece often consisting of 3 short sections or movements in quick-slow-quick form.

(2) It was also used of an orch. interlude, e.g. the 'Pastoral' sym. in Handel's *Messiah*, in a vocal work. Some 20th-cent. composers have revived

this archaic usage of the term, e.g. Stravinsky in his *Symphonies of Wind Instruments* (1920).

(3) As the word is now generally used, it means a large-scale orch. comp. (usually in 4 movements but often in 1, 3, or 5, occasionally in 2), a *Sonata for orch., the first movement and others being in sonata-form. It is reserved by composers for their most weighty and profound orch. thoughts, but of course there are many light-hearted, witty, and entertaining syms. The movements of the Classical and early Romantic sym. were usually an opening allegro, followed by a slow movement, then a minuet or scherzo, finally another allegro or rondo. Frequently the slow movement is placed 3rd, sometimes last. Early composers of the 18th-cent. 4-movement sym. were Sammartini, Wagenseil, Gossec, J. C. and C. P. E. Bach, Boyce, and especially the composers of the Mannheim School, Stamitz, Cannabich, Richter, and others, who made innovations in dynamics, expanded the development of themes, and broadened the harmonic idiom. The average 18th-cent. sym. orch. comprised str., double woodwind (cls. later), hns., and a continuo instr., usually hpd. The sym. was brought to a new peak by Joseph Haydn, who wrote 107, and was the first composer to demonstrate what later composers also seized upon, namely that the word 'symphony' should not imply rigidity of form or material. Some of Haydn's syms. have 6 movements; some utilize mus. he wrote for plays; some themes are based on folk-songs; most have slow introductions; many movements are monothematic; rondos, variations, and minuets are used; wit and humour are deployed; rare keys are explored; deep emotions are aroused. Haydn's example was followed and improved upon by Mozart, especially in his 3 last syms. of 1788, and these in turn led to even further marvels from Haydn in his last 12 syms. written for his 2 visits to Eng.

Taking over from Haydn and Mozart, Beethoven raised the sym. to a new plane of emotional expression, his 3rd Symphony (*Eroica*, 1803–4) ending the 18th cent. at a stroke and striding forward into an age when democracy, revolution, and ethics were to become influential factors in art, while at the same time effecting a mus. revolution by its enlarged dimensions, boldness of harmony, subtlety of key relationships, and general scope. In the *Pastoral Symphony*, No. 6 (1807–8), Beethoven reconciled perfectly the claims of 'absolute' and 'descriptive' mus., and in the 9th (1817–23) he introduced human vv. into the finale in a setting of Schiller's *Ode to Joy*. The floodgates were now open. Schubert's syms. bridged the way to the Romantic period. The syms. of Mendelssohn and Schumann combine classical outlines with romantic feeling and some pictorialism, as in the former's *Scotch* and *Italian* syms. and the latter's *Spring* and *Rhenish*. Brahms's 4 syms. eschew pictorial associations and uphold the virtues of classical design (though they are

deeply romantic in essence and also formally unusual in places) as an antidote to the growing craze for Lisztian symphonic poems and the operas of Wagner (who wrote only one early sym. but was contemplating others when he died). Berlioz's *Symphonie Fantastique* (1830) is one of the most remarkable works in the genre, frankly programmatic, brilliantly orchestrated, and opening up horizons which were not further explored until the picturesque late-19th-cent. syms. of Tchaikovsky. Yet the epitome of the Romantic sym., imbued still with classical principles while on a huge architectural scale, is to be found in the 9 syms. of Bruckner. Berlioz's pioneering was taken a stage further by Mahler, whose 10 syms. not only bridge the 19th and 20th cents. but also form a 'transition passage' of their own between 19th-cent. mus. idioms and the new 20th-cent. preoccupation with the dissolution of tonality. The crisis of the sym. in the early years of the 20th cent. is exemplified by the contrasting approaches of Sibelius and Mahler. The former expressed his faith in compression, concentration, and 'absolute' mus. whereas Mahler said that 'the symphony must embrace everything'. In Sibelius, especially in the 4th and 7th syms., symphonic thought and processes are elliptical and pared to essentials. In Mahler, vv. are used in 4 of the syms., philosophical and religious theories are at the root of their inspiration, and wildly juxtaposed thematic material is brought into cohesive unity by sheer force of conviction, the instrumentation being exotic and multiple. The two attitudes, regarded as mutually exclusive, are in fact not incompatible and a compromise has governed the development of the 20th-cent. sym., often within the works of the same composer, e.g., compare the severe 'classicism' of Vaughan Williams's 4th Sym. with the programmatic 7th, *Sinfonia Antartica*; compare Shostakovich's 5th Sym. with his 13th and 14th.

From time to time throughout the 20th cent. composers and pundits have pronounced the sym. dead but it shows an encouraging refusal to lie down. Nielsen (6), Vaughan Williams (9), Bax (7), Shostakovich (15), Ives (4), W. Schuman (9), Rubbra (11), and many others show that the sym. has not lost either its attraction or challenge for composers. Argument frequently occurs over whether certain works designated 'symphony' really merit the description, e.g. Stravinsky's *Symphony in 3 Movements* (1945), Messiaen's *Turangalîla* (1946–8), etc. An answer to this is that no mus. form can be regarded as immutable. The 18th-cent. composer (with the likely exception of Haydn) would scarcely recognize some 20th-cent. syms. in form, but there is more to a sym. than its title. It implies an attitude of mind, a certain mental approach by the composer, and in this respect the 4 syms. of Tippett and the three large-scale syms. by Maxwell Davies, as well as many others comp. since 1960, suggest that, for some considerable time to come, reports of the demise of the sym. will prove to have been exaggerated.

(4) In the USA 'symphony' also means 'symphony orchestra'.

(5) Sym. concert means, pedantically, a concert at which a sym. is played, but it is generally used to mean a concert by a sym. orch., whatever it is playing.

Symphony in 3 Movements. Orch. work by *Stravinsky comp. 1942–5 and f.p. NY P.O. cond. Stravinsky 1946. F.Eng.p. 1946, cond. Ansermet (broadcast). Work's genesis is of special interest; first movement began, in 1942, as pf. conc. or conc. for orch. with *concertante* pf. part, inspired by film on China's 'scorched earth' tactics. 2nd movement was written as acc. for apparition of Virgin Mary in film *Song of Bernadette,* an abortive project where Stravinsky was concerned. 3rd movement influenced by wartime newsreels.

Symphony of a Thousand. Nickname, not wholly approved by the composer, for Mahler's Sym. No. 8 in E♭ major, comp. 1906–7, f.p. Munich 1910 (cond. Mahler), because of the huge forces employed to perf. it. It is, however, not necessary to use 1,000 people, although at the f.p. more than that number were on the platform. F.Eng.p. London 1930 (Wood).

Symphony of Psalms. Work for mixed ch. and orch. in 3 movements by *Stravinsky, Lat. text being drawn from the Psalms 39, 40, and 150. Comp. 1930 to commission from Boston S.O. for 50th anniversary. F.p. Brussels 1930, cond. Ansermet; f.p. in USA 6 days later, Boston, cond. Koussevitzky; f.p. in England London 1931, cond. Stravinsky.

Syncopation. Device used by composers in order to vary position of the stress on notes so as to avoid regular rhythm. Syncopation is achieved by accenting a weak instead of a strong beat, by putting rests on strong beats, by holding on over strong beats, and by introducing a sudden change of time-signature. First used at time of *Ars Nova,* and exploited to fullest capabilities by jazz musicians, often in improvisation. Stravinsky, Bartók, etc. also employ syncopation with dramatic effect.

Synthesizer. Term for system of elec. apparatus which can be used to control or produce sounds (usually from a kbd.). Used by composers of elec. mus. Its invention, by Robert Moog in 1965, revolutionized elec. comp. by speeding up the process and doing away with drudgery of assembling and splicing small sections of tape. The first synthesizer was built from voltage-controlled and selected non-voltage-controlled components. It could play itself in mobile sound patterns which might be recurrent or non-repetitive and could also, by use of a device called a 'sequencer', memorize long and complex mus. structures and play them live without recording

or tape editing. (It is possible to reproduce instr. mus. on a synthesizer, as was convincingly demonstrated in 1969 by the success of Walter Carlos's commercial recording 'Switched-on Bach'.) Its numerous functions are controlled by punched paper tape. A means of producing mobility is by an 'envelope shaper', a device to control the shape of a sound or other parameter. It has controls which est. the time of attack, sustain, decay, and end of a sound. An initial drawback was that most synthesizers could perform only one note at a time. Since 1976, however, polyphonic synthesizers have been developed. See also *Electronic music.*

Syrinx. For solo fl., by Debussy, comp. 1913 for Louis Fleury who gave f.p. Paris 1913. Syrinx was the Gr. term for the *panpipes, instr. played by the mythical god Pan (half-goat, half-man).

Szabó, Ferenc (*b* Budapest, 1902; *d* Budapest, 1969). Hung. composer. Studied Liszt Acad. of Mus., Budapest, 1922–6 (comp. with Kodály, etc.). Lived in Russia and Ger. 1932–45. Prof. of comp. Liszt Acad. 1945–67 (dir. from 1958). Works incl. Conc. for Orch., oratorio, ballets, 2 str. qts., solo vn. sonatas, etc.

Szántó, Theodor (*b* Vienna, 1877; *d* Budapest, 1934). Austrian-born Hung. pianist. Studied in Budapest. Rev. version of Delius's pf. conc. (1906–7) is ded. to him; gave f.p. at Promenade Concert in London 1907.

Székely, Endre (*b* Budapest, 1912). Hung. composer, cond., and critic. Studied Budapest Acad. Active in Hung. Communist party mus. work. Dir., Municipal Th., Budapest. Prolific writer about mus. Comp. choral works, *Musica notturna* for pf. and chamber ens., songs, etc.

Székely, Zoltán (*b* Kocs, 1903). Hung.-born violinist (Amer. citizen from 1960). Studied Budapest with Hubay and Kodály. Founded Hungarian Str. Qt., 1935. Gave f.p. in Amsterdam, 1938, of Bartók's Vn. Conc. No. 2, which is ded. to him. Settled in USA 1949. Taught at Amer. univ.

Szelényi, Istvan (*b* Zólyom, 1904; *d* Budapest, 1972). Hung. composer, pianist, writer, and teacher. Studied Liszt Acad. of Mus., Budapest. Prof. of pf., Hung. Gymnasium, 1948–51, ed., *New Review of Music,* Hungary, 1951–6, prof. of comp., Bartók Cons., Budapest, from 1945 (dir. from 1956), Liszt Acad. 1956–72. Works incl. sym., 3 str. qts., 6 sonatas, oratorios, etc. Wrote biography of Liszt.

Szell, Georg (*b* Budapest, 1897; *d* Cleveland, Ohio, 1970). Hung.-born cond., pianist, and composer (Amer. citizen 1946). Studied with Reger. Solo pianist at age 10 with Vienna S.O. and at 17 cond. Berlin P.O. in one of his own comps. Cond., Strasbourg Stadttheater 1917, on recommendation of R. Strauss. Cond., Deutsches

Landtheater, Prague, 1919–21, Darmstadt 1921–2, Düsseldorf 1922–4, Berlin 1924–9. Returned to Prague 1930–6. Cond., Scottish Orch. 1936–9. Amer. début 1931, St Louis S.O. Settled in USA 1939, teaching at Mannes Sch. Cond. NY Met. 1942–5. Cond. Cleveland Orch. 1946–70, making it one of the finest in world and taking it on int. tours. Cond. at post-1946 Salzburg Fests., e.g. premières of Liebermann's *Penelope* (1954) and Egk's *Irische Legende* (1955). Noted for his Wagner, Strauss, Mahler, and the classics but outstanding in modern scores. Many stories are told of his amazing memory for mus. and mus. detail and of his caustic wit.

Szenkar, Eugen (*b* Budapest, 1891; *d* Düsseldorf, 1977). Hung. cond. Studied Budapest Acad. Cond. Deutsches Landtheater, Prague, 1911–13, Budapest Volksoper 1913–15, Salzburg Mozarteum 1915–16, Altenburg 1916–20, Frankfurt Opera 1920–3, Berlin Volksoper 1923–4, Cologne Opera 1924–33. Left Ger. for Russia 1933. Cond., Brazilian S.O., Rio, 1939. Returned to Mannheim Opera 1950–1, Düsseldorf Opera 1952–6.

Szervánszky, Endre (*b* Budatétény, 1911; *d* Budapest, 1977). Hung. composer. Studied Liszt Acad. of Mus., Budapest, 1923–8, 1931–6. Prof. of comp. Budapest Cons. 1942–8 and at Liszt Acad. from 1948. Authority on, and influenced by, mus. of Bartók. Works incl. Conc. for Orch., cl. conc., fl. conc., *Serenade* for cl. and orch., *Variations* for orch., 2 str. qts., vn. sonata, 2 wind quintets, *Dark Heaven* (Requiem) (1963), songs, etc.

Szeryng, Henryk (*b* Warsaw, 1918). Polish-born violinist, Mexican citizen since 1946. Studied with Hess, Flesch, Thibaud, and comp. for six years with Boulanger. Début 1933. Settled in Mexico 1946 where he taught. Int. career as virtuoso violinist.

Szidon, Roberto (*b* Porto Alegre, Brazil, 1941). Brazilian pianist. Studied Porto Alegre and NY. Début Porto Alegre at age 9. Int. career as soloist. Settled in Ger.

Szigeti, Josef (*b* Budapest, 1892; *d* Lucerne, 1973). Hung.-born violinist (Amer. citizen 1951). Studied Budapest RAM with Hubay. Début Berlin 1905, followed by world tours. London début 1907, living there until 1913 and giving f.p. of Harty's vn. conc. 1909. Taught at Geneva Cons. 1917–24. Settled in USA 1926 after Philadelphia début 1925. Wide repertory from Bach to modern composers such as Prokofiev, Bartók, and Bloch, whose conc. he championed. Retired to Switz. 1960. Wrote cadenzas and made many transcriptions for vn. and pf., including one of Elgar's *Serenade* for pf. (1932).

Szokolay, Sándor (*b* Kúnágota, 1931). Hung. composer. Studied Budapest Acad. (comp. with Szabó and Farkas). Worked for Hung. radio 1957–61. Teacher at Budapest Acad. from 1966. Works incl. operas *Hamlet* (1966–8), *Vérnász* (Blood Wedding, after Lorca, 1962–4), vn. conc., pf. conc., tpt. conc., *Déploration,* in memoriam Poulenc, ch. and orch. (1964), etc.

Szöllösy, András (*b* Szászváros, 1921). Hung. composer and writer. Studied Budapest Acad. (with Kodály) and S. Cecilia Acad., Rome (with Petrassi). Ed. writings of Bartók and Kodály. Works incl. 5 Concs. for Orch., *Music for Orchestra,* 3 pieces for fl. and pf., hpd. conc., etc.

Szymanowski, Karol (*b* Tymoshovka, Ukraine, 1882; *d* Lausanne, 1937). Polish composer. Boyhood spent in Ukraine, where many Poles owned land. Showed early mus. promise and because of leg injury which compelled a sedentary life, studied much mus. and conceived lifelong enthusiasm for Chopin. Studied theory with Neuhaus and wrote 9 pf. preludes in 1900. In 1901 went to Warsaw to study comp. with Noskowski. Moved to Berlin 1905, attracted by brilliance of Strauss and others, and wrote first sym. there. With 3 compatriots (Fitelberg, Różycki, and Szeluta) formed 'Young Poland in Music' soc., the Berlin P.O. giving a concert of their works. Left Berlin 1908, returning to Tymoshovka, his mus. being championed by other Polish musicians, e.g. the pianist Arthur Rubinstein, the cond. Fitelberg, and his sister Stanislawa, for whose sop. v. he wrote many of his songs. Another Polish virtuoso, the violinist Paul Kochánsky, was inspiration of the 1st vn. conc. and other works. Family home was destroyed in 1917 and for four years Szymanowski abandoned music while he wrote a long novel *Efebos* (the manuscript was destroyed in Warsaw in 1939). Left Russia 1920 for Warsaw, but visited Paris, London, and NY, taking part in concerts of modern mus. Back in Poland, wrote several works inspired by folklore. Became dir., Warsaw Cons. 1926, revolutionizing teaching methods. F.p. in 1928 of his *Stabat Mater* was his first big Polish triumph. Resigned directorship 1929 because of tuberculosis but became rector of Warsaw Acad. (which replaced Cons.) in 1930, resigning in 1932 after a dispute. Completed 2nd vn. conc. 1933, f.p. being given by Kochánsky shortly before he died. In 1933–4, Szymanowski toured Europe as solo pianist in his *Symphonie Concertante,* but continued ill-health weakened him and he died in a sanatorium.

Szymanowski is typical of many 20th-cent. composers who searched for some key to the liberation of what they felt to be their individual characteristics. Through his works can be traced the influence of the Ger. school of Strauss, etc., from which he was released by admiration for Debussy and the Fr. 'impressionist' composers. From them he took what he needed, experimenting further with atonality, polytonality, microtones, elaborate rhythms, and declamatory passages. The return to Poland awakened his latent nationalism—inspired by Chopin—as he studied his native mus., particularly the songs and dances of the Tatra mountaineers, which led to the *Mazurek* for pf. and the colourful, exotic ballet *Harnasie*. His opera *King Roger* is among his best works, a notable example of modern romanticism, and the vn. concs. are particularly rewarding. The *Stabat Mater* is an especially beautiful setting. Prin. comps.:

OPERAS: *Hagith,* Op. 25 (1912–13); **King Roger (Król Roger),* Op. 46 (1918–24).

BALLETS: *Mandragora,* Op. 43 (1920); *Harnasie,* Op. 55 (1923–31).

ORCH: Symphonies: No. 1 in F minor, Op. 15 (1907), No. 2 in B♭, Op. 19 (1909–10), No. 3 for ten. (or sop.), male ch., and orch. (*Song in the Night* to Cz. trans. of 13th-cent. Persian text), Op. 27 (1914–16), No. 4, *Symphonie Concertante,* pf. and orch. (1931–2); Violin Concertos: No. 1, Op. 35 (1916), No. 2, Op. 61 (1932–3); Concert Ov. in E, Op. 12 (1904–5, rev. 1912, 1913).

VOICE(S) AND ORCH: *Penthesilea,* sop. and orch., Op. 18 (1908, reorch. 1912); *Love Songs of Hafiz,* Op. 26, v. and orch. (1914, incl. orch. of Nos. 1, 4, & 5 of Op. 24, 1911, for v. and pf.); *Demeter,* alto, women's ch., and orch., Op. 38 (1917, reorch. 1924); *Agawa,* sop., ch., and orch., Op. 39 (1917); *Stabat Mater,* sop., cont., bar., women's ch., and orch., Op. 53 (1926); *Veni Creator,* sop., ch., and orch., Op. 57 (1930); *Litany of the Virgin Mary, (Litania do Marii Panny),* sop., women's ch., and orch. (1930–33).

CHAMBER MUSIC: Vn. Sonata in D minor, Op. 9 (1904); String Quartets: No. 1, Op. 37 (1917), No. 2, Op. 56 (1927).

VIOLIN AND PIANO: *Romance,* Op. 23 (1910); *Notturno e Tarantella,* Op. 28 (1915); 3 *Myths* (*Mity*) (The **Fountain of Arethusa, Narcissus, Dryads and Pan*), Op. 30 (1915); 3 *Paganini Caprices,* transcr., Op. 40 (1918); *Berceuse d'Aitacho Enia,* Op. 52 (1925).

PIANO: 9 *Preludes,* Op. 1 (1900); *Variations in B♭ minor,* Op. 3 (1903); 4 *Studies,* Op. 4 (1902); Sonatas: No. 1 in C minor, Op. 8 (1904), No. 2 in A minor, Op. 21 (1911), No. 3, Op. 36 (1917); *Variations on a Polish Theme,* Op. 10 (1904); *Fantasy in F minor,* Op. 14 (1905); *Métopes,* 3 poems (The *Sirens' Isle, Calypso, Nausicaa*), Op. 29 (1915); 12 *Studies,* Op. 33 (1916); 3 *Masques* (*Maski*), Op. 34 (*Shéhérazade, Tantris the clown, Don Juan's Serenade*) (1916); *Mazurek* (1925); 4 *Polish Dances,* Op. 47 (1926); 20 *Mazurkas,* Op. 50 (1924–5); 2 *Mazurkas,* Op. 62 (1934).

VOICE AND PIANO: 12 *Songs,* Op. 17 (1907); 6 *Songs,* Op. 20 (1909); *Love Songs of Hafiz,* 1st cycle of 6, Op. 24 (1911); 6 *Songs of the Fairy Princess,* Op. 31 (1915); 4 *Songs* to poems by Tagore, Op. 41 (1918), 6 *Songs of the Infatuated Muezzin,* Op. 42 (1918); 2 *Basque Songs,* Op. 44 (1921); *Slopiewnie,* 5 songs, Op. 45 (1921); 3 *Lullabies,* Op. 48 (1922); 20 *Children's Rhymes* (*Rymy dzieciece*), Op. 49 (1923); 4 *Songs* to words by Joyce, Op. 54 (1926); 12 *Kurpian Songs,* Op. 58 (1930–3).

T

t. Tonic sol-fa symbol for 7th degree of scale, pronounced *te*.

Tabachnik, Michel (*b* Geneva, 1942). Swiss cond. and composer. Studied Geneva Cons. Ass. cond. to Boulez for 4 years. Début Royan Fest. Guest cond. with European and Brit. orchs. Cond., Gulbenkian Orch., Lisbon, 1973–5. Art. dir. Ensemble Inter-Contemporain, Fr., 1976–7, Cond. Lorraine P.O. from 1975.

Tabarro, Il (The Cloak). Opera in 1 act by Puccini to lib. by Adami, after Didier Gold's play *La Houppelande* (1910). Part 1 of *Il *trittico*. Comp. 1913–6. Prod. NY Met. 1918, Rome and Chicago 1919, London 1920.

Tabla. Indian small hand-drum with single head but double body of 2 truncated cones. Played with fingers. Usually wedged in crook of right knee of seated player. Some Western composers have scored for it, e.g. Berio and Cowell.

Tablature. System of writing down mus. to be perf. other than by use of notes. Instead figures, letters, and similar signs were used. There were systems of org. and lute tablature in which the symbols represented the position of the player's fingers, not the pitch. Diagrammatic notation used today in popular mus. for guitar, ukelele, etc. is type of tablature.

Tabor. Small drum used in medieval times to accompany folk-dancing, usually played in conjunction with end-blown pipe. Performer struck drum with one hand, holding pipe in the other.

Tacet (Lat.). It is silent. Indication that particular performer or instr. has no part to play for considerable time. *Tacet al fine* means he has no more to play.

Tactus (Lat.). Term used in 15th and 16th cents. to designate a specified 'beat', either a unit of time, or the cond.'s beat. For a considerable period, the *tactus* was the equivalent of the whole-note.

Taddei, Giuseppe (*b* Genoa, 1916). It. bar. Opera début Rome 1936. London début 1947, Salzburg 1948, CG 1960. Famous as Scarpia in *Tosca*, and in buffo roles.

Tafelmusik (Ger.). Table-music. Mus. to be sung or played during or after a meal. Telemann wrote a fine example of *Tafelmusik* 1733, in 3 sections, each with 6 movements, for various groups of instr. In *Der Rosenkavalier*, the off-stage band in Act III is described to Baron Ochs as *Tafelmusik*.

Tagliabue, Carlo (*b* Mariano Comense, 1898; *d* Monza, 1978). It. bar. Opera début Lodi 1922 as Amonasro. Sang at Scala, Milan, 1930–53. CG 1938 and 1946, NY Met 1937–9. Noted Verdi bar., also sang Wagner parts in It.

Tagliavini, Ferruccio (*b* Reggio Emilia, 1913). It. ten. Studied Parma and Florence. Opera début Florence 1939. Leading It. lyric ten. during World War II, then Buenos Aires 1946–7, NY Met. 1947–54, CG 1950. Excelled in *bel canto* roles, such as Nemorino, Duke of Mantua, etc.

Tahiti Trot (Shostakovich). See *Tea for Two*.

Taille (Fr.). Old name for middle v., particularly ten., and for instr. of similar register, e.g. *taille de basson*, ten. ob., or *taille*, va. In Bach's cantatas, *taille* is taken to mean ten. ob. (*oboe da caccia*).

Tailleferre, Germaine (*b* Parc St Maur, nr. Paris, 1892; *d* Paris, 1983). Fr. composer and pianist, one of *Les *Six*. Studied Paris Cons. Pupil of Ravel. Comps. incl. pf. conc., harp concertino, conc. for 2 pf., v., and orch., conc. for bar., pf., and orch., str. qts., vn. sonata, ballets, etc.

Tajo, Italo (*b* Pinerolo, 1915). It. bass. Studied in Turin. Opera début Turin 1935 as Fafner. Sang at first Edinburgh Fest., 1947, with Glyndebourne Co. San Francisco 1948–56, CG 1950, NY Met. 1948–50. Outstanding in Donizetti buffo roles. After 1966 taught at Cincinnati Cons.

Takács, Jenö (*b* Cinfalva, 1902). Austrian composer, pianist, and teacher. Studied comp. in Vienna with Gál and Marx. Taught at Cairo Cons. 1927–32, 1934–6, Univ. of Philippines, Manila, 1932–4. Visit to USA as pianist 1938. Dir., Pécs Cons. 1942–8. Taught at Univ. of Cincinnati from 1970. Deeply interested by folk mus. of many nations. Works incl. *Tarantella* for pf. and orch., chamber mus., and many pf. pieces.

Takemitsu, Toru (*b* Tokyo, 1930). Japanese composer, mainly self-taught except for study with Kiyose 1948–50. Organized experimental workshop for painters and composers in Tokyo, 1951. Art. dir. of Space Theatre at Osaka Exposition 1970. His mus. uses *avant-garde* procedures and much of it is on tape. Influenced at first by Schoenberg, Messiaen, and Schaeffer's *musique concrète*. Much concerned, like Ligeti, with timbre. Works incl. *Relief statique* on tape (1955), *Requiem* for str. (1957), *Music of Tree*, orch. (1961), *Coral Island*, sop. and orch. (1962), *The Dorian Horizon*, 17 str. (1966), *November Steps* No. 1, shakuhachi, biwa, orch. (1967), *Asterism*, pf. and orch. (1968), *Cassiopeia*, perc. and orch., *Crossing*, 12 women's vv., guitar, harp, pf., vibraphone, and 2 orchs. (1969). *Eucalypts I*, fl., ob., harp, str. (1970), *Winter*, orch. (1971), *Corona*, 22 str. (1971). *Gitimalay (Bouquet of Songs)*, marimba and orch. (1975), *Quatrain*, vn., vc., cl., pf., and orch. (1975), *A Flock descends into the pentagonal garden*, orch. (1977), *Rain Spell*, ens. (1982), *Orion*, vc., pf. (1984), *Star Isle*, orch. (1984), conc. for guitar, oboe d'amore, orch. (1984), and pf. works incl. *Far away, Piano distance, Undisturbed Rest*.

Takt (Ger.). (a) 'Time' (b) 'Beat' (c) 'Measure' (i.e. bar). So **im Takt**, 'in time' (= 'A tempo'); **ein Takt wie vorher zwei**, 'one beat as previously two' (one beat allowed as much time as two beats previously).

Among compounds and derivatives of Takt, are: Taktart, 'time-species'—duple, triple, etc.; taktfest ('time-firm'), 'in steady time'; Takt halten, 'to hold (keep) time'; taktieren, 'to beat time'; Taktschlag ('time-stroke'), 'beat'; Taktzeichen ('time-sign'), 'signature'; Taktwechsel, 'time-change'; taktmässig ('time moderated'), generally meaning the same as *'Tempo commodo'; Taktmesser (time-measure), 'metronome'; Taktnote ('bar-note'), 'semibreve'; Taktpause, 'measure-rest' (i.e. bar-rest); Taktstock ('time-stick'), 'baton'; Taktstrich ('bar-stroke'), 'bar-line'; taktig, 'bar-ish', in such connexion as 3-taktig, 'three-bar-ish', i.e. having 3-bar (3-measure) phrases.

Tal (orig. Gruenthal), **Josef** (*b* Pinne, 1910). Polish-born Israeli composer and pianist. Studied Berlin Hochschule 1928–30. Settled in Palestine 1934. Prof. of pf. and comp., Jerusalem Cons. 1937. Dir., Israel Acad. of Mus. 1948–52. Chairman, musicology dept., Hebrew Univ. from 1965. Dir., Israel elec. mus. centre from 1961. Works incl. several choral works to Heb. texts, 3 syms., 6 pf. concs. (Nos. 4, 5, and 6 with tape), va. conc., hpd. conc. with tape, woodwind quintet, elec. ballets, 6 operas (incl. *Ashmedai* and *Die Versuchung*, 1973–4), ob. sonata, and *5 Instructive Compositions in Dodecaphonic Technique* for pf.

Tala. Indian term for rhythm, being a fixed time-span for mus., repeated in cycles, and articulated by hand-beats, drum-beats, or by a percussive *idiophone.

Tale of Two Cities, A. Opera in 3 acts by A. Benjamin to lib. by Cedric Cliffe after Dickens. Comp. 1949–50 and awarded a Fest. of Britain prize (1951) but not prod. until 1957 (London, SW). San Francisco 1960.

Tales from the Vienna Woods (*Geschichten aus dem Wienerwald*). Waltz, Op. 325, by Johann Strauss II. Comp. 1868.

Tales of Hoffmann, The (*Contes d'Hoffmann, Les*). Opera in prol., 3 acts, and epilogue by *Offenbach to lib. by J. Barbier and M. Carré based on stories *Der Sandmann, Geschichte von verlorenen Spiegelbilde*, and *Rat Krespel* by E.T.A. *Hoffmann. Left incomplete at Offenbach's death (many numbers unfinished, sketches only of others). At f.p. the

Giulietta act was omitted and Guiraud provided revisions, recitatives (in place of the correct spoken dialogue), and some of the orchestration. In 1893, Giulietta act was restored as Act 2, where it is placed in the largely corrupt Choudens edn. of 1907. New edn. by Fritz Oeser (1980) attempts to interpret Offenbach's final intentions, with acts in the order: 1, Olympia; 2, Antonia; 3, Giulietta. F.p. Paris 1881, NY 1882, London 1907. Famous *Barcarolle*, orig. written for *Die Rheinnixen* (1864), occurs in Giulietta act as orch. intermezzo before epilogue.

Talich, Václav (*b* Kroměříž, Moravia, 1883; *d* Beroun, 1961). Cz. cond. and violinist. Studied Prague Cons. 1897–1903 under Ševčik, later studying cond. with Nikisch. Leader, Berlin P.O. 1903–4. Taught vn. in Tiflis 1905–07. Cond. Ljubljana P.O. 1908, then opera at Plzeň (Pilsen) 1912–15. Chief cond., Cz. P.O. 1919–41, during which the orch. became world-famous through tours and records. Re-orch. substantial parts of Janáček's operas, *Káťa Kabanová* and *The Cunning Little Vixen*. Art. dir. and cond. Prague Nat. Opera 1935–45; dismissed 1945, restored to post 1947, again removed 1948 and restored 1954. Founded Slovak P.O. of Bratislava 1949–52. Retired 1956.

Tallis, Thomas (*b* c.1505; *d* Greenwich, 1585). Eng. composer and organist. Organist, Waltham Abbey from *c*. 1538 to 1540. Lay clerk, Canterbury Cath. 1540–2. Gentleman of the Chapel Royal 1540–85, serving under Henry VIII, Edward VI, Mary, and Elizabeth I, and organist jointly with *Byrd. In 1575 Elizabeth granted Tallis and Byrd letters patent giving them 21-year monopoly for printing mus. and mus. paper. In that year they pubd. 34 *Cantiones sacrae* in 5 and 6 parts (16 by Tallis and 18 by Byrd). Tallis wrote some pieces for kbd. and viols, but is mainly known for church mus. of great contrapuntal ingenuity and technical dexterity. In this respect his masterpiece is perhaps the 40-part motet *Spem in alium, in the opening section of which 20 vv. enter successively with theme in imitation. The other 20 then enter with new material and, after passages for varying numbers of vv., all 40 combine for the ending. Of special interest, too, is the use of modulation in the 2 *Lamentations* from near the end of his long career. The tune known as *Tallis's Canon* was one of 9 which Tallis comp. for Archbishop Parker's metrical *Whole Psalter*, 1567, where it is attached to Ps. 67. In 1732 it was linked with Bishop Ken's Winchester evening hymn, 'Glory to thee, my God, this night'. Another tune written for this psalter was that used by Vaughan Williams in 1910 as the basis of his *Fantasia on a Theme by Thomas Tallis* for str.

Talma, Louise (*b* Arcachon, 1906). Fr.-born Amer. composer. Studied NY 1922–30 (with H. Brockway) and Columbia Univ. 1923–33, and in summers in Fr. with I. Philipp and N. Boulanger

1926–39. Teacher since 1928 at Hunter Coll., NY, becoming prof. of mus. 1952. Winner of several prizes and scholarships. Works incl. opera *The Alcestiad*,1955–8, (Frankfurt 1962), oratorio *The Divine Flame, Dialogues* for pf. and orch., vn. sonata, str. qt., *All the days of my life*, ten., cl., vc., pf., and perc. (1965), *Voices of Peace*, ch. and str. (1973), *Summer Sounds*, cl., str. qt. (1973), and *Textures*, pf. (1978).

Talon (Fr.). Heel. The nut end of the bow of a str. instr.

Talvela, Martti (Olavi) (*b* Hiitola, 1935). Finn. bass. Sang at Royal Opera, Stockholm, 1961–2, Bayreuth, 1962 (Titurel), then at Deutsche Oper, Berlin, Hamburg, Vienna, Milan, CG (Gurnemanz, 1973), etc. Salzburg Fest. from 1962. Art. dir. Savonlinna Opera Fest., Finland, 1972–80.

Tamagno, Francesco (*b* Turin, 1850; *d* Varese, 1905). It. ten. Studied Turin Cons. and sang in ch. of Turin Opera, 1870. Opera début 1873 in Donizetti's *Poliuto*. Sang at Scala, Milan, from 1877. Toured S. America 1880, then sang in Lisbon and Madrid. Chosen by Verdi to create title-role in *Otello* in Milan 1887, his famous 'trumpet tone' being ideally suited. London début 1889 at Lyceum in *Otello*, CG 1895. Chicago 1889–90. NY Met. (as Otello) 1890, 1894–5. Retired 1902.

Tamberlik, Enrico (*b* Rome, 1820; *d* Paris, 1889). It. ten. Studied Rome and Naples, making opera début at Naples 1841 in Bellini's *I Capuleti e i Montecchi*. CG 1850 in *Masaniello*, then regularly until 1864. NY 1873–4. Created Alvaro in Verdi's *La forza del destino*, 1862, St Petersburg. First Eng. Manrico in *Il trovatore*. Noted as Rossini's Otello and as Florestan in *Fidelio*. Some authorities say he was Romanian, orig. Nikita Torna.

Tambour (Fr.). Drum. Hence, *tambour de Basque*, tambourine; *tambour militaire*, side-drum.

Tambourin (Fr.). (1) Small 2-headed medieval drum, i.e. the tabor.
(2) Old Provençal dance, orig. acc. by pipe and tabor. Rameau's operas contain several *tambourins*, and he wrote kbd. pieces in the style of the dance.

Tambourine. Type of perc. instr. of Arab orig. but known in Europe before 1300. Small, shallow, single-headed drum; 'jingles' (circular metal discs) are inserted into its wooden frame. It can be played by (a) hitting the head with knuckles, clenched fist, or back of the hand, or by striking it on the player's knee; (b) shaking it so that the jingles rattle; (c) rubbing a thumb along the edge to cause a tremolo from the jingles; (d) playing near rim with fingers or sticks. Mozart used the tambourine in his *German Dances* (K571, 1787) and it was also used by Weber and Berlioz, and often since then, especially in scenes of revelry, etc.

Tambura (also *tanbura, tanpura*). Long-necked Indian lute, unfretted and round-bodied. 4 wire str. all played open and together as drone acc. Plucked with fingers.

Tamburin (Ger.), **tamburino** (It.). Usually the *tambourine, but sometimes the tabor.

Tamburini, Antonio (*b* Faenza, 1800; *d* Nice, 1876). It. bar. Played hn. as child and sang in Faenza opera ch. at 12. Opera début Cento 1818. Sang in main It. opera houses 1824–32. London début 1832, Paris 1832–43 during period of Rubini, Lablache, Grisi, and Viardot. Created Ernesto in Bellini's *Il Pirata* 1827, Valdeburgo in *La Straniera* 1829, Riccardo in *I Puritani* 1835, and Malatesta in Donizetti's *Don Pasquale* 1843. Was also noted Don Giovanni. Retired 1855, but five years later in Nice sang Rossini's Figaro.

Tamburo (It.). Drum. Thus *tamburo Basco*, tambourine; *tamburo grande* or *grosso* (or *gran tamburo*), bass drum; *tamburo militare* and *tamburo piccolo*, side drum; *tamburo rullante*, ten. drum.

Tamburone (It.). Bass drum.

Taming of the Shrew, The (*Der widerspenstigen Zähmung*). Opera in 4 acts by *Goetz to lib. by J. V. Widmann based on Shakespeare's play. Comp. 1868–72. Prod. Mannheim 1874; London 1879; NY 1886.

Tamir, Alexander. See *Eden and Tamir*.

Tam O'Shanter. (1) Concert-ov. by Malcolm *Arnold, Op. 51 (1955) based on the poem by Burns.
(2) Symphonic ballad for orch. by George *Chadwick (1911).
(3) Mackenzie's *Scottish Rhapsody* No. 3 for orch. (1911).

Tampon (Fr.). Drumstick. *Tampon double* is 2-headed stick used to produce roll on bass drum (imitating thunder, etc.).

Tam-tam. The gong, especially one of indefinite pitch. Nothing to do with *tom-tom.

Tancredi. Opera (*melodramma eroico*) in 2 acts by Rossini to lib. by Rossi after Tasso's *Gerusalemme liberata* (1575) and Voltaire's *Tancrède* (1760). Prod. Venice 1813, London 1820, NY 1825.

Taneyev, Alexander (Sergeyevich) (*b* St Petersburg, 1850; *d* Petrograd, 1918). Russ. composer. Studied with Rimsky-Korsakov. Wrote operas, 3 syms., 3 str. qts., pf. pieces, etc.

Taneyev, Sergey (Ivanovich) (*b* Govt. of Vladimir, 1856; *d* Dyudkovo, 1915). Russ. composer and pianist. Studied Moscow Cons. 1866–75 (pf. with N. Rubinstein, comp. with Tchaikovsky). Début as pianist, Jan. 1875, in Brahms's D minor pf. conc. Gave f. Moscow p. of Tchaikovsky's B♭ minor conc. Dec. 1875. Toured with violinist Auer 1876. Prof. of instrumentation Moscow Cons. 1880, then of pf. and later of comp. 1883–

7, dir., 1885–9, prof. of counterpoint 1888–1906. Opponent of nationalist sch. in Russia. Student of works of Ockeghem, Desprès, and Lassus. Wrote books on theory. Completed vocal version of Tchaikovsky's *Romeo and Juliet*. Wrote 4 syms. (No. 1 in E minor, 1874; No. 2 in B♭, 1877–8, orch. Blok 1974; No. 3 in D minor, 1884; No. 4 in C minor, 1898), *Overture on Russian Themes*, choral works, 9 str. qts., much other chamber mus., and songs.

Tangent (from Lat. *tangere*, to touch). Part of *clavichord, a small metal 'tongue', which touches a str. when key is struck and produces sound. Remains in contact with str. while note sounds.

Tanglewood. Estate near Lennox, Mass., which in 1937 was offered to the Boston S.O. so that it could establish the Berkshire Music Center for instruction in conducting, opera and instrumental perf., and composition. The summertime Berkshire Fest., directed by the incumbent cond. of the Boston S.O. and his guests, has over the years accommodated thousands of students and enthusiasists.

Tango. Argentinian dance, possibly imported into America by African slaves, perf. by couples at slow walking pace to mus. in simple duple time and with dotted rhythm like *habañera*. Became popular ballroom dance after 1907. Some composers have used the tango in their works, e.g. Walton, in his suite *Façade*, and Stravinsky.

Tango, Egisto (*b* Rome, 1873; *d* Copenhagen, 1951). It. cond. Studied Naples. Début 1896. NY Met. début 1909 in *Werther*. Cond. in Vienna (Volksoper) and for 7 years in Budapest. Cond. f.p. of Bartók's *Duke Bluebeard's Castle*, Budapest 1918. Settled in Copenhagen 1925.

Tannhäuser und Der Sängerkrieg auf Wartburg (Tannhäuser and the Singing Contest at the Wartburg, usually abbreviated to *Tannhäuser*). Opera (*Handlung*) in 3 acts by Wagner to his own lib. Comp. 1843–5. Prod. Dresden 1845, NY 1859, CG 1876. Rev. of 1861, known as 'Paris version', prod. Paris 1861 (occasion of Jockey Club riot), NY 1889, CG 1896. Paris version is now usually perf., but Dresden version was used at CG 1984.

Tansman, Aleksander (*b* Łódź, 1897). Polish-born Fr. composer and pianist. Studied Łódź Cons. 1902–14, Warsaw Univ. 1915–19. Settled in Paris 1919 except for spell in USA 1940–6, when he wrote film mus. in Hollywood. Works incl. 8 syms., 2 pf. concs., va. conc., vn. conc., vc. conc., cl. conc., guitar concertino, oratorio *Isaiah the Prophet*, Conc. for Orch., *Resurrection* for orch., ob. concertino, fl. concertino, 8 str. qts., vc. sonata, etc. Wrote book on Stravinsky.

Tanto (It.). So much, as much, too much. *Non tanto*, not too much, don't overdo it! (e.g. Allegro non tanto). *Tantino* means A very little.

Tantum ergo (Lat. 'Therefore we before Him bending, this great sacrament revere', in Eng.

version). Opening words of last section of St Thomas Aquinas's Corpus Christi hymn *Pange lingua*. Used in services other than that of Corpus Christi and especially in that of Benediction. Has own plainsong, but has often been set by composers.

Tanz, Tänze (Ger.). Dance, dances. *Tänzchen*, little dances.

Tap Box. See *Chinese Wood Block*.

Tapfere Soldat, Der (Straus). See *Chocolate Soldier, The*.

Tapiola. Tone-poem for orch., Op. 112, by *Sibelius, comp. 1926 to commission by NY Sym. Soc. who gave f.p. in NY 1926, cond. W. Damrosch. F.p. in England London 1928. Tapio was god of Finnish forests.

Tarantella (It.), **Tarantelle** (Fr.). Neapolitan dance in $\frac{6}{8}$ time which probably takes its name from Taranto, in the heel of Italy, or from a spider common there, the tarantula, whose bite is mildly poisonous. The music is of great rapidity with an approach to the *perpetuum mobile*. The saltarello is a similar type. Chopin, Rossini, Liszt, and Mendelssohn are among composers who have used the *tarantella* in their works.

Taras Bulba. (1) Rhapsody for orch. by Janáček, comp. 1915–18, f.p. Brno 1921, f. Eng. p. 1928. Bulba was historical Ukrainian Cossack leader; Janáček based this work on story about him by Gogol. The 3 movements are: 1. *Death of Andrea* (*Smrt Andrijova*). 2. *Death of Ostap* (*Smrt Ostapova*). 3. *Capture and Death of Taras Bulba* (*Proroctví a smrt Tarase Bulby*).

(2) Opera by Argentinian composer Berutti (1895).

Tarbouka. Flower-pot-shaped drum from N. Africa, used by Berlioz in the Slave Dance in *Les Troyens*.

Tardo, tarda (It.). Slow. So *tardamente*, slowly; *tardando, tardantemente*, slowing (gradually); *tardato*, slowed (gradually).

Tarógató. Hung. single-reed, conical-bore woodwind instr. similar to sax., with cl. mouth-piece, which is sometimes used for 2nd of the shepherd's tunes in Act 3 of Wagner's *Tristan und Isolde*. Wagner specifies a *Holztrompete* (wooden tpt.), but while at Budapest Opera (1888–91) Mahler used the tarógató and this was also adopted at Bayreuth by Richter. Orig. tarógató was a wooden cornett, sounding only natural notes, used for military signals.

Tarr, Edward (Hankins) (*b* Norwich, Conn., 1936). Amer. trumpeter and musicologist. Studied trumpet in Boston (1953) and Chicago (1958–9) and musicology in Basle (1959–64). Specialist in reviving of early trumpet works on modern and old instr. Works written for him by Kagel and Stockhausen. Founded Edward Tarr Brass

Ensemble 1967. Taught in Cologne 1968–70 and in Basle from 1972. Has edited many baroque works for modern perf., notably trumpet works of Torelli.

Tárrega, Francisco (*b* Villarreal, 1852; *d* Barcelona, 1909). Sp. guitarist and composer. Studied Madrid Cons. Gave recitals in Paris and London 1880, being acclaimed as 'Sarasate of the guitar'. Prof. of guitar, Madrid Cons. Wrote many guitar preludes, and transcr. works by Granados, Albéniz, Beethoven, and Chopin.

Tartini, Giuseppe (*b* Pirano, Istria, 1692; *d* Padua, 1770). It. violinist, composer, teacher, and inventor. Studied law at Padua Univ., though learned vn. as child. Fled from Padua 1710 because of disapproval of his marriage. Took refuge in monastery at Assisi where he studied comp. and acoustics, invented new vn. bow, and gave vn. recitals. Returned to Padua, forgiven, 1715. Played as orch. violinist; became first vn. at Cappella del Santo, Padua, 1721–3. Kapellmeister of Count Kinsky's band, Prague, 1723–5, playing also in Vienna. On return to Padua founded, 1728, school of vn.-playing, becoming known as 'Master of Nations' and numbering many subsequently celebrated violinists among his pupils. Was teaching up to 1768. Discovered *resultant tones', which he then called *terzo suono* (3rd sound), though it was left to *Helmholtz to explain them years later. Wrote several treatises and comp. some religious vocal mus. and *canzone* in addition to 42 vn. sonatas, 12 sonatas for vn. and vc., 135 vn. concs., vc. concs., and concs. for other instr. incl. cls., obs., and tpt. Celebrated *'Devil's Trill' sonata was almost certainly composed after 1745, but no autograph exists.

Taste, Tasten (Ger.). Key(s) of kbd. instr., etc.

Tastiera (It.). Same meanings as *Tasto*, below. Thus *sulla tastiera = sul tasto*.

Tasto, tasti (It.). (1) Key(s) (i.e. of kbd. instr.). In early mus. with figured bass, *Tasto solo* means 'Play the key alone', i.e. only the bass line, without adding chords.
(2) The fingerboard of a bowed str. instr. *Sul tasto* (on the fingerboard) means 'bow over the fingerboard'. See also *Tastiera*.

Tate, Jeffrey (*b* Farnham, Surrey, 1943). Eng. conductor. Studied medicine at Cambridge Univ. and qualified as doctor. Turned to mus. 1970, joining Else *Mayer-Lismann's Opera Workshop as pianist. Worked at London Opera Centre. Répétiteur CG 1971. Ass. to Boulez on 1976 Bayreuth *Ring*. Cond. début Gothenburg 1978 (*Carmen*), CG 1982 (*Die Zauberflöte*), NY Met. 1983 (*Lulu*). Dir., Cologne Opera 1984. Prin. cond. ECO from 1985, CG from 1986.

Tate, Nahum (*b* ? Dublin, 1652; *d* London, 1715). Irish-born poet and playwright, poet laureate from 1692. Wrote lib. of Purcell's *Dido*

and Aeneas and collab. with Nicholas Brady (*b* Bandon, Co. Cork, 1659; *d* Richmond, Surrey, 1726) in metrical version of Psalms (pubd. 1696).

Tate, Phyllis (Margaret Duncan) (*b* Gerrards Cross, 1911; *d* Hampstead, 1987). Eng. composer. Studied RAM 1928–32. Imaginative and skilled composer, writing especially well for vv. and small ens. Works incl.:
OPERAS: The *Lodger* (1959–60); *Dark Pilgrimage* (1963).
ORCH: Sax. conc. (1944); *Panorama*, str. (1977).
VOICE(S) AND INSTR(S): The*Lady of Shalott*, ten. and chamber ens. (1956); *Nocturne,* SATB soloists, str. qt., db., bass cl., celesta (1946); *Apparitions*, ten., harmonica, pf. quintet (1968); *A Victorian Garland*, sop., cont., hn., pf.; *Scenes from Kipling*, bar. and pf. (1978).
CHORAL: *Choral Scene from The Bacchae*, mixed ch. and optional org. (1953); *A Secular Requiem*, mixed ch., org., orch. (1967); *Serenade to Christmas*, mez., ch., and orch. (1972); *St Martha and the Dragon*, narrator, soloists, ch., orch. (1976); *All the World's a Stage*, ch., orch. (1977); *Compassion*, ch., orch. (or org.) (1978).
CHAMBER MUSIC: *The Rainbow and the Cuckoo*, ob., str. trio (1975); cl. and vc. sonata (1947); *Air and Variations*, vn., cl., pf. (1958); *Seasonal Sequence*, va., pf. (1977).
PIANO: *Explorations around a Troubadour Song* (1974); *Lyric Suite*, 2 pf. (1973).

Tátrai Quartet. Hung. string quartet formed in 1946 from soloists of Budapest Municipal Orch. Won 1948 Bartók Comp. Toured Europe 1952. Has recorded complete cycles of Beethoven and Bartók qts.

Tattermuschová, Helena (*b* Prague, 1933). Cz. sop. Member of Prague Nat. Opera co. Studied Prague Acad. of Mus. Opera début Ostrava 1954. At Prague Opera since 1956. Many tours abroad. Exponent of sop. roles in Janáček operas.

Tattoo. The mus. of bugles and drums, recalling soldiers to their barracks at night. In the Brit. Army it begins with the *First Post*, lasts about 30 minutes, and ends with the *Last Post*. Another meaning is a display by the army, involving mock battles, etc., as at the Aldershot Tattoo.

Tauber, Richard (orig. Seiffert) (*b* Linz, 1892; *d* London, 1948). Austrian-born ten., cond., and composer (later Brit. citizen from 1940). Studied Freiburg and Frankfurt. Début Chemnitz 1913 as Tamino in *Zauberflöte*. Dresden Opera 1913–25, Vienna Opera 1926–38. CG 1938–9 but had often sung in Eng. before then in operettas. Superb Mozart and Lieder singer, also known for his perfs. in operetta, especially those of Lehár, such as *Das Land des Lächelns* (The Land of Smiles), *Paganini*, etc. Also wrote musicals, e.g. *Old Chelsea*. Made last appearance at CG autumn 1947, singing Ottavio in *Don Giovanni* with colleagues of Vienna Opera on their visit to London although he had serious lung trouble which led to death a few months later.

Taubert, (Karl Gottfried) **Wilhelm** (b Berlin, 1811; d Berlin, 1891). Ger. composer and pianist. Studied in Berlin. Mus. dir., Berlin Royal Opera 1845–8, court cond. 1845–69. Wrote operas (incl. *Macbeth* 1857), 4 syms., chamber mus., and nearly 300 songs.

Taubman, Howard (b NY, 1907). Amer. mus. critic and author. Studied Cornell Univ. Ass. mus. critic, *New York Times* 1930–55, chief mus. critic 1955–60, drama critic 1960–66. Wrote biography of Toscanini (1951).

Tauriello, Antonio (b Buenos Aires, 1931). Argentine composer, pianist, and cond. Studied Argentine Nat. Cons., pf. with Gieseking and comp. with Ginastera. Cond. ballet at Teatro Colón, Buenos Aires. Cond. of 'Ritmus' perc. ens. Opera coach and répétiteur, Chicago Lyric Opera, NY City Opera, etc. Works incl. Rabelais opera *Les Guerres Picrocholines,* 2 pf. concs., *Canti* for vn. and orch., *Serenade* for orch., *Aria* for fl. and ens.

Tausig, Karl (b Warsaw, 1841; d Leipzig, 1871). Polish pianist and composer. Pupil of Liszt at Weimar from 1855. Début Berlin 1858, where he settled 1865, founding pf. sch. Wrote pf. pieces and concs. and made many arrs. of Bach organ works and of mus. by other composers (Wagner, Schubert, Schumann, Weber, etc.).

Tausky, Vilem (b Prerov, Cz., 1910). Cz.-born cond. and composer (Eng. citizen). Studied Brno Univ., Janáček Cons., Brno, and Prague. Cond. at Brno Opera 1929–39. Settled in Eng. Mus. dir., Carl Rosa Opera 1945–9. Guest cond. CG, SW, BBC from 1950. Art. dir. Phoenix Opera from 1967. Dir. of opera GSM from 1966. Cond. f. Eng. p. (BBC) of Janáček's *Osud,* 1972. Cond. f. Eng. p. of Suppé *Requiem,* 1984. Works incl. ob. conc., harmonica concertino, *Divertimento* for str. C.B.E. 1981.

Tavener, John (Kenneth) (b London, 1944). Eng. composer and organist. Studied RAM 1961–5 (comp. with L. Berkeley and privately with D. Lumsdaine, 1965–7). Organist, St John's, Kensington, from 1960. Teacher of comp., TCL from 1969. Mus. of rich imaginative and eclectic resource, e.g. cantata *The Whale,* and of profound religious spirit, as in *Ultimos ritos* and *Celtic Requiem,* in which children's games are linked to the idea of death. Convert to Gr. Orthodox Church. Prin. works:

OPERAS: *Thérèse* (1973–6); *A Gentle Spirit* (after Dostoyevsky), sop., ten., and small ens. (1976).
ORCH: Pf. conc. (1962–3); Chamber Conc. (1965, rev. 1968); *Grandma's Footsteps,* 5 mus. boxes, chamber ens. (1967–8); *In Memoriam Igor Stravinsky,* 2 alto fl., organ, bells (1971); *Variations on 3 Blind Mice* (1972); *Palintropos,* pf. and

orch. (1978–9); *Towards the Son: Ritual Procession,* tb., 4 gongs, 4 bowed psalteries, perc., str. (1982).
CHORAL: *The Cappemakers,* 2 narrators, 10 soloists, male ch., orch. (1964, rev. for stage 1965); *The *Whale,* mez., bar., mixed ch., orch., tape (1965–6); *Introit for March 27,* sop., alto, ch., orch. (1967–8); **Celtic Requiem,* sop., ch., orch. (1969); *Coplas,* SATB soloists, ch., tape (1970); *Responsorium in memory of Annon Lee Silver,* 2 sop., ch., 2 fl. (1971); *Requiem for Father Malachy,* ten., ch., org., str. qt. (1973, rev. 1979); **Ultimos Ritos,* SATB soloists, ch., 5 speakers, orch. (1972); *Canticle of the Mother of God,* sop., unacc. ch. (1976); *Kyklike Kinésis,* sop., vc., ch., pf., str. (1978); *Liturgy of St John Chrysostom,* unacc. ch. (1978); *Akhmatova: Requiem,* sop., bar., orch. (1979–80); *Risen!* ch., orch., pf., organ, str. (1980); *Funeral Ikos,* ch. (1981); *Ikon of Light,* ch., str. trio (1984).
VOICE AND ORCH: *3 Holy Sonnets of Donne,* bar. and orch. (1962); *Cain and Abel,* cantata, SATB soloists and orch. (1965); *In Alium,* sop., orch., tape (1968); *6 Russian Folk Songs,* v. and ens. (1978); *The Immurement of Antigone,* monodrama for sop. and orch. (1978).
CHAMBER MUSIC: *Greek Interludes,* fl. and pf. (1979); *Mandelion,* organ (1981); *Trisagion,* brass quintet (1981).
CHAMBER MUSIC WITH VOICES: *3 Sections from T. S. Eliot's 4 Quartets,* ten., pf. (1963–4); *3 Surrealist Songs,* mez., tape, pf. (1967–8); *Canciones espanolas,* 2 sops. or counterten. and ens. (1972); *6 Russian Folk Songs,* sop. and ens. (1978); *6 Abbasid Songs,* ten. and flutes (1979); *Sappho: Lyrical Fragments,* 2 sop., str. (1980).
VOICE AND PIANO: *Last Prayer, Lamentation, and Exaltation,* sop. and handbells or pf. (1977).
PIANO: *Palin* (1977; expanded as *Palintropos* with orch.).

Taverner. Opera in 2 acts by *Maxwell Davies to his own lib. drawn from 16th-cent. letters and documents concerning life of composer John *Taverner, with 14 singing roles, ch., and boys' ch. Comp. 1962–8, rev. 1970, 1983. Prod. London CG 1972, cond. E. Downes; Boston 1984.

Taverner, John (b c. 1490; d Boston, Lincs., 1545). Eng. composer and organist. Organist of Cardinal Coll. (now Christ Church), Oxford, 1526–30. One of great polyphonic masters of 16th-cent. Eng. mus. Wrote 8 Masses, incl. one based on secular song *The Western Wynde* (36 variations, 9 in each of 4 movements). His Mass *Gloria tibi Trinitas* was fount of the **In nomine* form for str.; this came about because the instr. comps. by Taverner called *In nomine* are transcrs. of the passage in the Benedictus of his Mass which sets the words *In nomine Domini.* Other composers followed his example and used the same title. Also wrote 3 Magnificats and several motets. Taverner was link between medieval mus. and Renaissance. Maxwell Davies's opera **Taverner* is based on legend about his life.

Taylor, Charles (*b* Manchester, 1911). Eng. violinist. Studied RMCM (pupil of Catterall). Founder and leader, Taylor Str. Qt., 1934–50. Leader, orch. of Royal Opera, CG, 1952–76. O.B.E. 1972.

Taylor, (Joseph) **Deems** (*b* NY, 1885; *d* NY, 1966). Amer. composer, critic, and author. Studied NY Univ. Mus. critic, *New York World* 1921–5. Orch. works well received; commissioned by NY Met. to write opera *The King's Henchman* (1926–7), this being followed by *Peter Ibbetson* (1930–1). Became mus. adviser to CBS 1936 and well-known for narrations of NY Met. broadcasts and NY P.O. concerts. Spoke narration in Disney's *Fantasia*. Popular orch. works incl. *Through the Looking Glass* (1922) and *Marco Takes a Walk* (1942).

Taylor, Samuel Coleridge-. See *Coleridge-Taylor, Samuel.*

Tchaikovsky (Chaykovsky), **Boris** (Alexandrovich) (*b* Moscow, 1925). Russ. composer and pianist. Studied Moscow Cons. (comp. with Shostakovich, Shebalin, and Myaskovsky). Works, several based on folk mus., incl. syms., opera *The Star* (1949), *Fantasia on Russian Folk Themes* for orch. (1950), *Capriccio on English Themes*, for orch. (1954), cl. concertino (1957), Sinfonietta, str. qts., pf. trio, vn. sonata, pf. quintet, and film scores.

Tchaikovsky (Chaykovsky), **Pyotr** (Ilyich) (*b* Votkinsk, 1840; *d* St Petersburg, 1893). Russ. composer and cond. Studied law before entering St Petersburg Cons. (comp. with A. Rubinstein) 1863–5. Went to Moscow 1866, becoming prof. of harmony at new Cons. under directorship of N. Rubinstein. During first 2 years there wrote First Sym. and opera *Voyevoda*. In 1868 met nationalist group of young Russ. composers headed by Rimsky-Korsakov and was stirred by their enthusiasm, as is shown by his 2nd Sym., but later came to be regarded by them as cosmopolitan rather than truly Russ. From 1869 to 1875 wrote 3 more operas and first pf. conc. and was mus. critic of *Russkiye vedomosti* 1872–6, going to first Bayreuth Fest. 1876. In 1877 married one of his pupils, separating from her 9 weeks later and coming near to mental collapse, psychological result of fatal step for a man of homosexual tendencies. At this time was taken under patronage of wealthy widow, Nadezhda von Meck, who out of admiration gave him yearly allowance which enabled him to abandon teaching and devote himself wholly to comp. She and Tchaikovsky never spoke to each other, though they corresponded voluminously. 4th Sym. is ded. to her. Went to Switz. and It., composing opera *Eugene Onegin*, prod. by students of Moscow Cons. 1879, with moderate success. By 1880, his works were popular in Russia (thanks to advocacy of N. Rubinstein), and in Brit. and USA but still met with hostility in Paris and Vienna. In 1885 bought country house,

first of several, at Klin, living in hermit-like isolation. There, wrote *Manfred* and in 1887 made début in Moscow as cond. of rev. version of opera *Vakula the Smith* under title *Oxana's Caprice*. In 1888 toured Ger., Fr., and London as cond., returning to Ger. and Eng. in 1889. Ballet *Sleeping Beauty* prod. 1890, after which Tchaikovsky went to Florence to work on opera *Queen of Spades*, prod. St Petersburg 1890. Year ended with sudden rupture of relationship with Mme von Meck; illness had dictated her decision, which wounded Tchaikovsky deeply. Visited USA with great success 1891, and in Jan. 1892 heard Mahler conduct *Eugene Onegin* at Hamburg. Ballet *Nutcracker* comp. 1891–2, and work started on a 6th Sym. In that year, again visited Vienna and in 1893 went to Eng., where hon. doctorate of mus. was conferred on him by Cambridge Univ. During 1893 wrote 6th Sym., having abandoned sym. begun in 1891–2 and re-worked it as a 3rd pf. conc., eventually retaining only one movement (2nd and 3rd orch. from the surviving sketches by Taneyev after Tchaikovsky's death). F.p. of the sym. was only moderately successful, though Tchaikovsky was convinced it was his best work. It is usually stated that 4 days later he felt ill and drank a large glassful of unboiled water (possibly with deliberate intent) and developed cholera, which led to his death. But in 1979 the Russian scholar Alexandra Orlova revealed some substantiation for the theory that the composer's death was suicide by poison, ordered by a private court of his former law-student colleagues to prevent revelation of a homosexual scandal involving the aristocracy. Not all specialists on the composer accept the validity of this research.

Few composers are more popular with audiences than Tchaikovsky; the reasons are several and understandable. His music is extremely tuneful, luxuriously and colourfully scored, and filled with emotional fervour directed to the heart rather than to the head (though the notion that Tchaikovsky's syms. are lacking in symphonic thinking and structure does not bear serious consideration). Undoubtedly the emotional temperature of the mus. reflected the man's nature. He was doubly afflicted: by repressed homosexuality (hence his disastrous attempt at marriage) and by the tendency to extreme fluctuations between elation and depression, each success being followed by a period of introspective gloom and melancholy which stemmed from psychological defects rather than from 'typical Russian melancholy'. This showed itself also in his attitude to his visits abroad. As soon as he left Russia he was ill with homesickness; once back, he was restlessly planning to be off again.

In 19th-cent. Russ. mus., Tchaikovsky stands alone. His *Romeo and Juliet* was ded. to Balakirev, one of the 'Five', but he never identified himself with out-and-out nationalism. He succumbed to the influence of neither Brahms nor Wagner, but greatly admired the Fr. mus. of Bizet and Saint-Saëns. This can be linked with his lifelong passion for Mozart, and many passages in Tchaikovsky's mus. are as delicately detailed and coloured as works by Bizet and Mozart. The other element of his nature, the fate-laden, Byronic, emotional impact of the last 3 syms., is traceable in many episodes in the operas, notably *Eugene Onegin*. None of his operas was a success on its first appearance, but *Onegin* and *Queen of Spades* are now widely perf. and admired, and adventurous cos. have explored the others, which, however, are marred by dramatic defects. The true theatrical Tchaikovsky is to be found in the ballets, a supreme combination of melodic inventiveness, grand sweep, and constant freshness. Nor should the superb songs be forgotten: in them, in miniature, the soul of Tchaikovsky is enshrined as surely as in the great syms., concs., and orch. masterpieces. Prin. works:

OPERAS: *Voyevoda*, Op. 3 (*Dream on the Volga*) (1867–8); *Undine* (destroyed) (1869); *Oprichnik (The Life Guardsman)* (1870–2); *Vakula the Smith*, Op. 14 (*Vakula kuznets*) (1874, rev. 1885–7 as *Cherevichki* (The Little Shoes) or *Oxana's Caprice*); *Eugene Onegin* (*Evgeny Onyegin*), Op. 24 (1877–8); *The *Maid of Orleans* (*Orleanskaya Deva*) (1878–9, rev. 1882); *Mazeppa* (1881–3); *The Sorceress* (*Charodeyka*) (1885–7); *Queen of Spades* (*Pikovaya Dama*), Op. 68 (1890); *Yolanta*, Op. 69 (1891).

BALLETS: *Swan Lake* (*Lebedinoye ozero*), Op. 20 (1875–6); *The *Sleeping Beauty* (*Spyashchaya krasavitsa*), Op. 66 (1888–9); *Nutcracker (Shchelkunchik)*, Op. 71 (1891–2).

ORCH: Symphonies: No. 1 in G minor, Op. 13 (*Winter Daydreams*) (1866, rev. 1874), No. 2 in C minor, Op. 17 (*Ukrainian* or *Little Russian*) (1872, rev. 1879–80), No. 3 in D, Op. 29 (*Polish*) (1875), No. 4 in F minor, Op. 36 (1877–8), No. 5 in E minor, Op. 64 (1888), No. 6 in B minor, Op. 74 (*Pathetic*) (1893); Concertos, etc.: Piano: No. 1 in B♭ minor, Op. 23 (1874–5), No. 2 in G, Op. 44 (1879–80, rev. 1893 Ziloti), *Concert Fantasy*, Op. 56 (1884): Vn. Conc. in D, Op. 35 (1878), *Sérénade mélancolique*, vn., Op. 26 (1875), *Valse-Scherzo*, vn., Op. 34 (1877); *Variations on a Rococo Theme*, vc., Op. 33 (1876), *Pezzo capriccioso*, vc., Op. 62 (1887); Symphonic fantasies: *The *Tempest*, Op. 18 (1873), *Francesca da Rimini*, Op. 32 (1876); *Slavonic March*, Op. 31 (1876); *Serenade*, str., Op. 48 (1880); *1812, Ceremonial Overture*, Op. 49 (1880); *Manfred Symphony*, Op. 58 (1885); Ov., *The Storm*, Op. 76 (1864); symphonic poem *Fate*, Op. 77 (1868); Fantasy Overtures: *Hamlet*, Op. 67a (1888), *Romeo and Juliet* (1869, rev. 1870 and 1880); *Italian Caprice*, Op. 45 (1880); Symphonic ballad, *Voyevoda*, Op. 78 (1891); Suites: No. 1 in D, Op. 43 (1878–9), No. 2 in C, Op. 53 (1883), No. 3 in G, Op. 55 (1884, *Theme and Variations* movement often perf. separately), No. 4 *Mozartiana*, Op. 61

(1887), *Nutcracker*, Op. 71a (1892). (N.B. The 'Sym. No. 7 in E♭' and the 'Pf. Conc. No. 3 in E♭, are compilations by other hands. The sym. was begun by Tchaikovsky in 1891–2, but abandoned. He scored first movement as pf. conc., Taneyev later adding *andante* and *finale* from sketches of the sym. S. Bogatyryov (1890–1960) prod. perf. version of orig. sym. from same sketches. Taneyev also completed vocal duet version (1893) of part of *Romeo and Juliet* ov. for sop., ten., and orch.).

CHAMBER MUSIC: Str. Qts.: No. 1 in D, Op. 11 (contains *Andante cantabile* often played separately) (1871), No. 2 in F, Op. 22 (1874), No. 3 in E♭ minor, Op. 30 (1876); Pf. Trio in A minor (in memory of a great artist), Op. 50 (1881–2); *Souvenir de Florence*, str. sextet, Op. 70 (1887–90, rev. 1891–2).

PIANO: *Valse Caprice*, Op. 4 (1868); *Capriccio*, Op. 8 (1870); *3 Pieces*, Op. 9 (1870); *Nocturne* and *Humoreske*, Op. 10 (1871); *6 Pieces*, Op. 19 (1873); *6 Pieces on 1 Theme*, Op. 21 (1873); Sonata in G, Op. 37 (1878); *The Seasons*, 12 characteristic pieces (1875–6); *Children's Album*: 24 Pieces, Op. 39 (1878); *12 Pieces*, Op. 40 (1878); *6 Pieces*, Op. 51 (1882); *Dumka*, Op. 59 (1886); *18 Pieces*, Op. 72 (1893; the 10th of these, *Scherzo-Fantaisie* in E♭ minor, exists in orch. sketch of 1891–2 and is presumed to have been intended as scherzo of projected sym. Incorporated by Bogatyryov in '7th Sym.', see above); Sonata in C♯ minor (posth.).

CHORAL: *Liturgy of St John Chrysostom*, Op. 41 (1878); *Russian Vesper Service*, unacc., Op. 52 (1881–2).

SONGS: Tchaikovsky's songs were pubd. in the following groups (no. of songs, Op. no. and date): 6, Op. 6, 1869; 6, Op. 16, 1872; 6, Op. 25, 1874; 6, Op. 27, 1874; 6, Op. 28, 1874; 6, Op. 38, 1877; 7, Op. 47, 1879; 16 for children, Op. 54, 1883; 6, Op. 57, 1883; 12, Op. 60, 1886; 6, Op. 63, 1888; 6, Op. 65, 1888; 6, Op. 73, 1893. Among the best-known are: *Again as before*; *As they kept on saying*; *At the ball*; *Behind the window*; *Cradle Song*; *Deception*; *Don Juan's Serenade*; *Evening*; *Exploit*; *In the early Spring*; *My spoiled darling*; *Night*; *No, only he who has known* (*None but the lonely heart*) (Op. 6 No. 6); *Not a word, my friend*; *Over the golden cornfields*; *Reconciliation*; *To forget so soon*; *Wait*; *Why did I dream of you?*

Tchaikowsky, André (*b* Warsaw, 1935; *d* Oxford, 1982). Polish-born pianist and composer. Studied Warsaw and Paris Cons. Début Paris 1948. Leading recitalist. Settled in Eng. Comps. incl. pf. conc., str. qt., cl. sonata. Bequeathed skull to Royal Shakespeare Co. for use in perfs. of *Hamlet* (début 1984).

Tcherepnin, Alexander (Nikolayevich) (*b* St Petersburg, 1899; *d* Paris, 1977). Russ.-born composer and pianist (Amer. citizen 1958), son of Nikolay *Tcherepnin. Studied with his father and at St Petersburg Cons. with Lyadov and

Sokolov, and later at Tiflis with Hartmann. Went to Paris 1921 and studied comp. at Cons. Earned int. reputation as pianist and in 1923 wrote ballet, *Ajanta's Frescoes,* for Pavlova, who prod. it at CG. His first sym. (Paris 1927) caused protests because of its dissonance. Wrote several more ballets and scored Mussorgsky's unfinished opera, *The Marriage.* Visited USA 1926. Prof. of pf. and comp. at De Paul Univ., Chicago, 1949–64. In tours of Far East 1934–7 taught young Chinese and Japanese composers. Mus. influenced by Georgian and Oriental folk-mus. and by his formulation of 9-note scale, leading to complex chords. Comp. 3 operas (one to libretto by Hofmannsthal), 4 syms., 6 pf. concs., harmonica conc., *The Story of Ivan the Fool* (cantata after Tolstoy, using elec. devices, 1968), chamber mus., and pf. pieces.

Tcherepnin, Nikolay (*b* St Petersburg, 1873; *d* Issy-les-Moulineaux, nr. Paris, 1945). Russ. composer. Studied St Petersburg Cons. with Rimsky-Korsakov 1895–8, after abandoning law studies. Cond. of Belyayev concerts 1901 and at Maryinsky Th. Cond. for Diaghilev Ballet 1909–14. Principal, Tiflis Cons. 1918–21. Settled in Paris 1921, with son Alexander *Tcherepnin. Wrote operas, ballets, orch. works, and pf. conc. Completed *Mussorgsky's *Sorochintsy Fair* (prod. Monte Carlo 1923).

T.C.L., T.C.M. *Trinity College of Music, London.

Te. In *Tonic sol-fa, spoken name for 7th degree of scale, written *t.

Te Deum Laudamus (We praise thee, O God). Ecclesiastical canticle, or hymn of thanksgiving, the words of which were probably written in 5th cent. Adopted by both R.C. and Anglican churches. Has traditional plainsong melody, but has been set by innumerable composers, incl. Purcell, Handel, Berlioz, Verdi, Dvořák, Bruckner, Vaughan Williams, Britten, Walton, often on highly elaborate scale for soloists, ch., and orch. as well as more simply.

Tea for Two. Song by*Youmans, comp. for musical *No, No, Nanette* (1925). In 1928 orch. version was made by Shostakovich in, it is said, 45 mins. at the request of the cond. *Malko who wanted something extra to perf. at a concert of Shostakovich's mus. at Moscow Cons. on 25 Nov. 1928. The cond. Aleksandr Gauk included it as an entr'acte in Shostakovich's ballet *The Age of Gold.* Shostakovich gave the arrangement the title *Tahiti Trot (Taiti trot)* because this was the Russ. name for the song, which enjoyed great popularity in the USSR when it was new.

Tear, Robert (*b* Barry, Glamorgan, 1939). Welsh ten. Choral scholarship to King's, Cambridge, where he read mus. but took degree in Eng. Studied singing with Julian Kimbell. In 1960 appointed lay vicar, St Paul's Cath., and worked with Ambrosian Singers. Operatic début with English Opera Group 1963 as Quint in Britten's *Turn of the Screw.* CG début as Lensky in *Eugene Onegin.* Created role of Dov in Tippett's *The Knot Garden,* 1970. Has sung with Scottish Opera in Verdi and Mozart. Sang The Painter in f.p. of complete *Lulu,* Paris 1979. C.B.E. 1984.

Tebaldi, Renata (*b* Pesaro, 1922). It. sop. Studied Parma. Opera début 1944 as Elena in Boito's *Mefistofele.* Chosen by Toscanini for re-opening of Scala, Milan, 1946, and sang there 1949–54 and 1959. CG début 1950. NY Met. 1955 (as Desdemona), singing there regularly afterwards until 1973. Chicago 1955–69. V. of power and beauty, esp. in Verdi and Puccini roles.

Tedesco, Tedesca (It., plural *tedeschi, tedesche*). German. Found in the term *alla tedesca,* 'in the Ger. style', which has had several meanings. Beethoven indicated a Ger. waltz by it, others mean a Ger. dance of any kind. In his tuba conc., 1954, Vaughan Williams's *Rondo alla tedesca* means a rondo as in a Ger. comp.

Teil or **Theil** (Ger.). Part, in the sense of portion or section. So *Teilen* or *Theilen,* to divide.

Te Kanawa, (Dame) **Kiri** (*b* Gisborne, Auckland, N.Z., 1944). N.Z. soprano. Studied at London Opera Centre and with Vera Rosza. Opera début in Rossini's *La Donna del Lago,* Camden Fest. 1969, then as Flower Maiden in *Parsifal* at CG 1970. First major CG role was Countess in *Le Nozze di Figaro* 1971. Amer. début, San Francisco 1972. Glyndebourne 1973 (Countess). NY Met. début 1974 (Desdemona). Chosen by bridegroom to sing at wedding of Prince of Wales and Lady Diana Spencer in St Paul's Cath., 1981. Fine lyric sop., especially in Mozart, Verdi, and the Strauss roles of Arabella and Marschallin. O.B.E. 1973. D.B.E. 1982.

Tel Aviv Quartet. Israeli str. qt. founded in 1962, making an international tour every year since then. Strong modern representation in repertory. 2nd vn. has changed three times, otherwise personnel remains the same as at first concert.

Telemann, Georg Philipp (*b* Magdeburg, 1681; *d* Hamburg, 1767). Ger. composer and organist. Self-taught by study of scores (esp. those of Lully and Campra). Organist, Neuekirche, Leipzig, 1704, having already written several operas. Kapellmeister at Eisenach 1708–12, moving then to Frankfurt. In 1721 he went to Hamburg as Kantor of the Johanneum and mus. dir. of the 5 main churches. When in 1722 an attempt was made to prevent his taking part in operatic performances, he retaliated by applying for the vacant post of Kantor at the Thomaskirche, Leipzig. He was appointed, in preference to J. S. Bach, but Hamburg retained him by increasing his salary and appointing him mus. dir. of the Opera. Extremely prolific composer, skilled in counterpoint and of great facility, but his mus.

has surface charm rather than depth. The best of it, however, is delightful. Among his voluminous output, which incl. 600 ovs. in the It. style, 44 Passions, 12 complete services, and 40 operas, are the following:

OPERAS: *Pimpinone* (1725); *Der geduldige Sokrates* (1721).

ORATORIOS: *Der Tag des Gerichts* (The Day of Judgement), *Die Tageszeiten* (The Times of Day), *Der Tod Jesu* (The Death of Jesus), *Die Auferstehung Christi* (The Resurrection of Christ), *St Luke Passion* (1728, 1744), *St Mark Passion* (1759), *St Matthew Passion* (1730).

CANTATAS: *Cantata oder Trauer-Musik eines kunsterfahrenen Kanarien-Vogels* (Funeral Music for a sweet-singing canary); *Der Schulmeister* (The Schoolmaster); *Die Landlust* (The Joy of Country Life); *In dulci jubilo*.

ORCH: *Tafelmusik* (Table Music) I, II, and III; Suite, *Don Quichotte*, str. and b.c.; *La Lyra*, suite in E♭, str. and b.c.; Concertos; 3 tpt., drums, 2 ob., str., b.c.; in G for vn., str., b.c.; A minor for concertino vn., str., b.c.; C major, 2 vn., str.,; E minor, fl., str.; E minor, 2 fl., vn., str.; E minor, ob., str.; A major, ob. d'amore, str.; A minor, treble recorder, viola da gamba, str.; D major for D tpt., str.; D major, hn., str.; C major, 4 vn.; G major, 4 vn.; 12 12-part qts. Also many trio sonatas, suites, fl. qts., etc.

Telephone, The. Opera in 1 act by *Menotti to his own lib. Prod. NY 1947, London 1948.

Tel jour, telle nuit (Such a day, such a night). Song-cycle by Poulenc to 9 poems by Paul Eluard. Comp. 1936–7, f.p. by Pierre Bernac acc. Poulenc. Titles are: *Bonne Journée, Une Ruine coquille vide, Le Front comme un drapeau perdu, Une Roulotte couverte en tuile, À Toutes brides, Une Herbe pauvre, Je n'ai envie que de t'aimer, Figure de force brûlante et farouche, Nous avons fait la nuit*.

Teller (Ger.). Plate (e.g. of cymbal).

Telmányi, Emil (b Arad, Hung. (now Romania), 1892). Hung. violinist and cond. Studied Budapest Acad. of Mus. with Hubay and Popper. Début, with Berlin P.O. 1911, when he gave f.p. on Continent of Elgar conc. Thereafter leading soloist and chamber-mus. player. London début 1923 on visit with *Nielsen, whose works he played and conducted. Founded own str. quintet. Cond. concerts in Europe, opera in Budapest. Invented special Vega (arched) bow for perf. of Bach's vn. works. Transcr. and arr. works by Handel, Beethoven, Brahms, etc. Settled in Copenhagen 1919. On staff Åarhus Cons. from 1940.

Tema (It.). Theme, as in *Tema con variazioni*, Theme and Variations.

Temperament. Adjustment in tuning (i.e. 'tempering') of mus. intervals away from 'natural' scale so that such pairs of notes as B♯ and C, or C♯ and D♭, are combined instead of being treated individually. This leaves neither note accurate but sufficiently so for the ear to accept it. In kbd. instr. this avoids unmanageable number of finger-keys. The pf., organ, and other fixed-pitch modern instr., are tuned to *equal temperament*, in which each semitone is made an equal interval, making it easy to play in any key and to modulate. Before Equal Temperament (which was introduced for pfs. in Eng. in 1846 and for organs a little later), the commonest system was *mean-tone temperament*, which left certain keys tolerable, others less so, and some unusable. The untempered scale is known as *just intonation*. Instr. such as the vn. family can have no system of temperament, the player determining the pitch and checking it by ear. Some 20th-cent. composers have restored 12-note scale to *just intonation*. Others have used microtonal scales in just relationship. Still more have used 'prepared' instr. producing unexpected pitches, or elec. systems, or computers.

Temperley, Nicholas (b Beaconsfield, 1932). Eng. musicologist, composer, and pianist. Studied RCM and Cambridge Univ. Ass. lecturer in mus., Cambridge Univ. 1961–6. Ass. prof., Yale Univ. 1966; assoc. prof. Univ. of Illinois 1967 (prof. and chairman of musicology dept. from 1972). Has written organ pieces. Ed. of *Pinto's pf. sonatas. Author of *The Music of the English Parish Church* (1979, 2 vols.). Ed. *Loder's opera *Raymond and Agnes* (prod. 1966) and Berlioz's *Symphonie Fantastique* (new Berlioz edn., xvii, Kassel 1972, a collation of 14 versions).

Tempest, The. Play by Shakespeare (his last, 1612–13) for which various composers have written songs and incidental mus. Among works connected with the play are: (1) *The Tempest*, incidental mus. Op. 109, by *Sibelius, comp. 1925, in 34 parts for soloists, ch., harmonium, and orch. F.p. Copenhagen 1926. 2 orch. suites, with Prelude, No. 1 of 9 items, No. 2 of 9; f.Eng.p. of *Prelude*, Hastings 1930, of Suite 1 Leeds 1934;
(2) Symphonic-fantasy for orch., Op. 18 by Tchaikovsky, 1873;
(3) Opera *Der Sturm* (1952–5) by Frank *Martin, prod. Vienna 1956;
(4) Opera by *Sutermeister *Die Zauberinsel* (The Magic Island), prod. Dresden 1942;
(5) Incidental mus. by John *Weldon for Restoration version of play, c. 1712;
(6) Symphonic prelude *The Magic Island* by *Alwyn, 1953.

Temple Block. See *Korean Temple Block*.

Templeton, Alec Andrew (b Cardiff, 1909; d Greenwich, Conn., 1963). Welsh-born pianist and composer, born blind. Studied RCM and RAM. After career in London as radio entertainer, settled in USA 1936. Wrote orch. and pf. works, but best-known for his witty 'skit', *Bach Goes to Town*, a jazzed-up pastiche of Bach.

Templeton, John (*b* Riccarton, Kilmarnock, 1802; *d* New Hampton, 1886). Scot. ten. Sang in churches as youth. Studied in London, making opera début at Drury Lane 1831. Chosen by *Malibran to sing opposite her in *La sonnambula*, 1833, subsequently doing so on several occasions and becoming known as 'Malibran's ten.'. Had repertory of 80 roles. Toured USA 1845–6. Retired 1852.

Tempo, Tempi (It.). Time(s). The speed at which a piece of mus. is perf. The anglicized 'tempos' is an acceptable plural, like 'concertos'. Among the many mus. terms containing the word are the following: *a tempo*, resume orig. speed; *tempo a piacere*, please yourself what speed; *tempo comodo*, at a convenient or moderate speed; *tempo di ballo*, in dance time, or a movement in dance style; *tempo di gavotta*, in gavotte tempo; *tempo di minuetto*, in minuet time; *tempo giusto*, in exact time, or at speed the style of the mus. demands; *tempo maggiore*, same as *alla breve* (take the half-note as your beat unit); *tempo minore*, *tempo ordinario*, ordinary time, moderate speed, same speed as before; *tempo primo*, resume orig. speed; *tempo rubato*, see *rubato*; *tempo wie vorher* (Ger.), same as *tempo primo*.

Temps (Fr.). Time, same as *tempo* but also used in the sense of 'beat'.

Ten. Short for (1) *Tenor, (2) *tenuto*.

Tender Land, The. Opera in 2 acts by *Copland to lib. by H. Everett. Prod. NY 1954, Cambridge 1962.

Tenducci, Giusto Ferdinando (*b* Siena, *c.*1736; *d* Genoa, 1790). It. male sop. Went to London 1758, being hailed as Guadagni's successor. In Dublin 1765–8, where he married a pupil. Sang at Handel Fests. 1784 and 1791. Mozart wrote song for him (lost). Wrote hpd. sonatas and treatise on singing. Last appearance 1785 as Orfeo (Gluck).

Tenebroso (It.). Dark. Gloomy.

Tenendo (It.). Sustaining, e.g. *tenendo il canto*, sustaining the melody.

Tenero (It.). Tender. So *teneroso*, *teneramente*, tenderly; *tenerezza*, tenderness.

Tennstedt, Klaus (*b* Merseburg, 1926). Ger. conductor and violinist. Studied Leipzig Cons. Leader of theatre orch. at Halle 1948, becoming ch. cond. On cond. staff, Dresden Opera, 1958–62; cond. Schwerin State Orch. 1962–71. Worked in Scandinavia from 1971, then in W. Ger. as mus. dir. Kiel Opera. Amer. début 1974 (Boston S.O.), London 1976 (LSO). Prin. guest cond. Minnesota Orch. Prin. cond. N. Ger. Radio S.O. 1979–82. Prin. cond. LPO 1983–7. NY Met. début 1983 (*Fidelio*). Fine interpreter of Mahler.

Tenor (from It. *tenore*, 'holding'). (1) Highest normal male v., its name deriving from medieval

times when it was the v. which carried the plainsong or other *cantus firmus* while other vv. sang a counterpoint. There are various categories of ten., e.g. *tenor di forza*, heroic ten., as for Verdi's Otello; *tenor di grazia*, lyrical ten., as Nemorino in *L'elisir d'amore*; *tenor robusto*, powerful ten., as Manrico in *Il trovatore*; *tenor spinto*, forceful lyric ten., as Rodolfo in *La Bohème*; *Heldentenor* (Ger.), heroic, powerful ten., as in Wagner and some Strauss roles; *Countertenor*, male alto.
(2) Name given to certain instr. deemed to be equivalent in range, etc., of ten. v., e.g. ten. sax., ten. tuba, etc.
(3) The va.

Tenor Clef. Type of clef, almost obsolete but still sometimes used for vc., ten. tb., bn., in which middle C is indicated on 2nd line down of staff.

Tenor Cor. The mellophone, instr. of hn.-like character but easier to play, used in some bands as substitute for hns.

Tenuto (It.). Held. Direction to hold note to its full value, sometimes even longer.

Ternary. In 3 parts or sections. *Ternary Form* is the form of a movement in 3 sections, the 3rd being an exact or near-exact repetition of first. Term still applies if first section is stated twice, making 4 sections but only 3 where subject-matter is concerned.

Ternina, Milka (*b* Vezisce, 1863; *d* Zagreb, 1941). Croatian sop. Studied Zagreb and Vienna (1880–2 with Gänzbacher). Opera début while student at Zagreb, 1882. Sang opera at Leipzig 1883–4, Graz 1884–6, Bremen 1886–9, Munich 1890–99. Excelled in Wagnerian roles. London début, concert 1895. CG début 1898 (Isolde), singing regularly to 1906. Was first London Tosca, 1900, and first NY Tosca 1901. Amer. début 1896 with Damrosch's German Opera Co. in Boston, Mass., as Brünnhilde. NY Met. 1900–4. Bayreuth 1899 as Kundry in *Parsifal*, but banned from Bayreuth after 1903 when she sang in 'pirate' *Parsifal* in NY. One of greatest singers of her day and type, forced by illness to retire, 1906.

Terry, Charles Sanford (*b* Newport Pagnell, 1864; *d* Westerton of Pitfodels, Aberdeen, 1936). Eng. historian and mus. scholar. Chorister, St Paul's Cath. Prof. of history, Aberdeen Univ. 1903–30. Became interested in life and time of Bach, becoming leading authority of day on subject. Wrote life of Bach (1928, rev. 1933) and of J. C. Bach (1929), ed. Bach's chorales in 3 vols. (1915–21), also Mass in B minor, and arr. *Coffee Cantata* for stage under title *Coffee and Cupid* (1924; perf. by BNOC).

Terry, (Sir) Richard (Runciman) (*b* Ellington, Northumberland, 1865; *d* London, 1938). Eng. organist, cond., composer, and scholar. Organist and choirmaster St John's Cath., Antigua, 1892,

Downside Abbey 1896–1901. While at Downside revived church mus. by early Eng. composers, reviving Byrd's Masses for 5 and 3 vv. and works by Tallis, Taverner, etc. Organist and dir. of mus., Westminster Cath. 1901–24, where he raised standard of choral singing to new height, continued to revive Tudor mus., Palestrina, and others. Works specially written for Westminster Cath. choir by Howells, Stanford, Holst, Bax, and Vaughan Williams. Knighted 1922. Wrote 5 masses, *Requiem*, motets, etc. Ed. *Westminster Hymnal* 1912, and 2 vols. of Shanties.

Terschak, Adolf (*b* Hermannstadt, 1832; *d* Breslau, 1901). Ger. flautist. Studied Vienna Cons. Many tours as solo flautist, playing his own works, of which there are over 150.

Tertis, Lionel (*b* West Hartlepool, 1876; *d* Wimbledon, 1975). Eng. violist, son of Russ. father and Polish mother, both naturalized Britons. Studied TCL (pf. first study, vn. 2nd, later concentrating on vn. with Carrodus), Leipzig Cons., and RAM. Took up va. at 19 to play in str. qt. Prof. of va. RAM 1901. Prin. va. Queen's Hall Orch. 1900–04. Prin. va. Beecham Orch. 1909. Gave f.ps. of many works for va. written for him or as a result of his artistry. Devoted life to cause of va., then the 'Cinderella' of str. instr. Played in several str. qts. Dir. of ens. class, RAM 1924–9. Designed Tertis Model viola, 16¾″ long. Arr. and ed. many works for va., incl. Elgar vc. conc., Delius vn. sonatas, Brahms cl. sonatas. Many distinguished pupils. Last played in public at age of 87. C.B.E. 1950.

Terzetto (It.). Generally applied to a comp. for any combination of 3 vv., but also used sometimes (instead of trio) for instr. comps., e.g. Dvořák's *Terzetto* for 2 vn. and va., Op. 74 (1887) and Holst's *Terzetto* for fl., ob., and va. (1925).

Teschemacher, Margarete (*b* Cologne, 1903; *d* Bad Wiessee, 1959). Ger. sop. Opera début Cologne 1924 (as Micaela in *Carmen*). Mannheim Opera 1928–30, Stuttgart 1930–5, Dresden 1935–46. Created title-role in Strauss's *Daphne* and was first Dresden *Capriccio* Countess. Joined Düsseldorf Opera 1948–52. CG début 1931. Admired in Strauss and as Jenůfa.

Tess. Opera in 4 acts by F. d'Erlanger to lib. by Illica, based on Hardy's novel *Tess of the d'Urbervilles* (1891). Prod. Naples 1906 and CG 1909 (with *Destinn as Tess).

Tessarini, Carlo (*b* Rimini, *c.* 1690; *d* ?Amsterdam, after 1766). It. violinist and composer, possibly pupil of Corelli. Violinist at St Mark's, Venice, 1720, later at Brno (Brünn). Wrote many vn. sonatas and concerti grossi.

Tessitura (It.). Texture. Term which indicates prevailing or average position of a comp.'s notes in relation to compass of v. or instr. for which it was written, high, low, or medium.

Testore, Carlo Giuseppe (*fl.* 1690–1720). It. violin-maker, pupil of Grancino. Sometimes criticized for hasty construction. Instr. often branded with emblem of an eagle. His two sons, Carlo Antonio and Paolo Antonio, also made vns.

Tetrachord (Gr. 'Four string'). Succession of four notes contained within compass of a perfect fourth. In Ancient Gr. mus. a tetrachord consisted of 4 notes descending through a perfect fourth in the order tone-tone-semitone (A–G–F–E) and joined together to form a series of eight-note modes. The modern diatonic scale is divisible into two tetrachords (C–D–E–F, and G–A–B–C).

Tetrazzini, Eva (*b* Milan, 1862; *d* Salsomaggiore, 1938). It. sop., sister of Luisa *Tetrazzini. Studied Florence. Opera début 1882 as Marguérite in Gounod's *Faust*. First to sing Desdemona in Verdi's *Otello* in NY (1888). CG début 1890. Retired on marriage to cond. Campanini.

Tetrazzini, Luisa (*b* Florence, 1871; *d* Milan, 1940). It. sop. Studied Florence and with her sister Eva. Opera début Florence 1890 as Inez in Meyerbeer's *L'Africaine*. Sang for several years in Argentina. Major success at San Francisco 1904. CG 1907, sensational acclaim for her Violetta (*La traviata*), Lucia, and Gilda (*Rigoletto*); sang there 1908–12. NY début 1908, Met. 1911. Concert appearances only after 1918 until 1934. Brilliant coloratura technique.

Teutsch. Mozart's (and Old Ger.) way of spelling *Deutsch* (Ger.) as in *Teutsche Tänze* (Ger. Dances).

Teyte, (Dame) **Maggie** (orig. Margaret Tate) (*b* Wolverhampton, 1888; *d* London, 1976). Eng. sop. Studied RCM and in Paris with J. *de Reszke, 1903–07. Début Monte Carlo 1907 as Tyrcis in Offenbach's *Myriam et Daphné*. Sang Mélisande in Debussy's opera, Paris, 1908, having studied role with composer. London opera début 1910 (Cherubino). Sang with BNOC from 1922. Amer. début 1911, Chicago (Cherubino). In inter-war years appeared also in mus. plays (*Monsieur Beaucaire, Tantivy Towers*, etc.). Sang Eva in *Die Meistersinger* with CG touring co., 1938. Sang her last Mélisande, NY, 1948. Last operatic role, Belinda in Purcell's *Dido and Aeneas*, London 1951 (with *Flagstad). Superb interpreter of songs by Debussy, Fauré, Hahn, etc. D.B.E. 1958.

Thaïs. Opera in 3 acts by Massenet to lib. by L. Gallet after the novel by Anatole France (1890). Prod. Paris 1894, NY 1907, CG 1911.

Thalben-Ball, (Sir) **George** (Thomas) (*b* Sydney, N.S.W., 1896; *d* Wimbledon, 1987). Australian-born organist and composer. Studied RCM. Settled in Eng. Organist, Temple Church, London, 1923, City of Birmingham, 1949. C.B.E. 1967. Knighted 1982.

Thalberg, Sigismond (*b* Geneva, 1812; *d* Posillipo, 1871). Swiss-born Austrian pianist and composer. Studied Vienna (theory with Sechter, pf. with Hummel). Public début 1826. London début 1830, followed by tour of Ger., playing his own conc. and other works. Paris 1835, where he studied with Pixis and Kalkbrenner. London 1836, after which he and Liszt were regarded as 2 greatest rival virtuosi. Toured USA 1856 with Vieuxtemps, entering opera management. Wrote 2 operas, pf.conc., and many pf. works and songs. Contrib. to *Hexameron, 1837.

Thamos, König in Ägypten (Thamos, King of Egypt). Play by Tobias von Gebler for which Mozart comp. incidental mus. (K345) for prod. by Schikaneder's co. in Salzburg, 1780. Mozart had written 2 chs. for this play in Vienna in 1773 and these were rev.

Thayer, Alexander Wheelock (*b* South Natick, Mass., 1817; *d* Trieste, 1897). Amer. writer, the biographer of Beethoven. Studied Harvard Univ., working in library there after graduation. While student, determined to write life of Beethoven and went to Ger., Austria, and Bohemia 1849–52 to begin coll. of material. Over next decade spent much time interviewing people who had known Beethoven and examining documents. Book, entitled *Ludwig van Beethovens Leben*, was written in Eng., trans. into Ger. by H. Deiters of Bonn, and pubd. in Berlin, Vol. I (1770–96) in 1866, Vol. II (1797–1806) in 1872, Vol. III (1807–16) in 1879. Vol. IV was unfinished when he died and was completed by *Riemann and pubd. in 1907. Riemann pubd. Vol. V in 1908 and rev. of Vols. II and III in 1910–11. Eng. edn. in 3 vols. by H. E. Krehbiel was pubd. in NY, 1921, and by E. Forbes, pubd. in Princeton 1964, rev. 1967.

Theater an der Wien. Vienna th. built by *Schikaneder and opened 1801. Held 1,230 people. F.ps. of Beethoven's *Fidelio* (1805) and Strauss's *Die Fledermaus* (1874), given there, also Viennese premières of several Rossini operas. Home of Vienna State Opera 1945–54 while Staatsoper was being rebuilt. Bought by city of Vienna 1961, renovated, and reopened 1962.

Theatre Organ. Org., also called cinema org., installed in cinemas in 1920s and 1930s to provide mus. during breaks in the programme. Usually a *unit org., with special effects. In 17th and 18th cents., the term applied to organs used in theatrical entertainments, operas, and concerts.

Thebom, Blanche (*b* Monessen, Penn., 1918). Amer. mez. of Swed. parents. Studied with Edyth Walker. Concert début NY 1941. NY Met. début 1944 as Fricka, singing with this company until 1966–7. Glyndebourne 1950 (Dorabella). CG 1957 (Dido in *Les Troyens*). Later sang in operetta. Art. dir., Atlanta opera co. 1967.

Theil (Ger.). See *Teil*.

Theile, Johann (*b* Naumburg, Saxony, 1646; *d* Naumburg, 1724). Ger. composer. Studied Leipzig Univ. and with *Schütz at Weissenfels. Settled in Hamburg 1675, then Kapellmeister at Wolfenbüttel 1685 and Merseburg 1689. Wrote much church mus. of great contrapuntal skill and some church operas.

Thievish Magpie, The (Rossini). See *Gazza ladra, La*.

Thematic Material. The themes, subjects, motifs, rhythmic figures, from which a comp. is constructed.

Theme. Succession of notes which play important part in construction of a comp. Same as *subject*, but also refers to part of a subject. In *Theme and Variations*, means the mus. statement on which variations are built. *Theme-song* is an unspecific term with several meanings, e.g. in a mus. play or film, a theme-song is a song which recurs several times, or has a special significance in a plot, or is the song from which the play takes its title. Also, tune assoc. with a variety artist and played when he or she comes on to the stage to perform is called his or her 'theme song', like *signature-tune*.

Theodora. Oratorio by Handel to lib. by T. Morell. F.p. London 1750.

Theodorakis, Mikis (*b* Chios, Gr., 1925). Gr. composer. Studied Athens and Paris Cons. Lived in Paris 1954–61. Works incl. oratorios, ballets, sym., pf. conc., *7 Songs of Lorca*, and mus. for film *Zorba The Greek*.

Theorbo (Fr. *théorbe*, Ger. *Theorb*, It. *tiorba*; possibly from Arabic *tarab*). Renaissance instr., a larger type of *lute (but not so large as *chittarone). Used as accompanying instr., but solo repertory exists. Resonant lower register, caused by longer fingerboard and greater str. length. Probably developed in It.; first mentioned 1544. Had between 14 and 16 courses, plus extra bass str. Gut str. Often used for continuo instead of organ and hpd. in Eng. 17th-cent. songs. Handel scored for it in *Esther* (1732) and *Athalia* (1733). Modern revivals for early mus. perf.

Theremin. 'Space-controlled' elec. instr. developed by the Russian, Lev Theremin (*b* St Petersburg, 1896), and first publicly demonstrated in the Soviet Union 1920. Introduced to USA 1927. 'Space-controlled' means that it is played by movements of the hands, which do not touch the instr. The theremin is built like a radio receiver, with an antenna protruding from the right and a metal loop on the left. The mus. is prod. by 2 high-frequency circuits, employing oscillating (thermionic) valves, one being at constant frequency while that of the other is altered when the player moves his hand through the air in front of the antenna. The resultant oscillation is called 'heterodyning' ('beating together'), and the heterodyne frequency can be made audible by amplification through a loudspeaker. Vol. is controlled by a switch and by the movement of the player's left hand over the metal loop. Sounds similar to the human v. or to those of about 7 instr. can be prod. Plays only one note at a time; range of 5 octaves. First comp. to use instr. was Pashchenko's *Symphonic Mystery*, for theremin and orch., Leningrad, 1924. Martinů wrote a *Fantasy* for theremin, str. qt., ob., and pf.

Theresienmesse (Theresa Mass). Nickname of Haydn's Mass No. 10 in B♭, comp. 1799, referring to consort of Emperor Francis II of Austria.

These Things Shall Be. Cantata for bar. (or ten.) solo, ch., and orch. by *Ireland, text taken from *A Vista* by J. A. Symonds. Comp. 1936–7, f.p. 1937.

Thespis, or The Gods Grown Old. 'Grotesque opera' by Sullivan to lib. by Gilbert (their first collab.). Score now lost. Prod. London 1871.

Thibaud, Jacques (*b* Bordeaux, 1880; *d* in air crash near Mt. Cemet, Fr. Alps, 1953). Fr. violinist. Studied Paris Cons. Soloist many times in 1898 with Colonne Orch., Paris. Thereafter world tours. Member of pf. trio with Cortot and Casals. Taught at École Normale de Musique, Paris.

Things to Come. Korda film (1935) based on H. G. Wells's futuristic novel *Shape of Things to Come* (1933) for which Bliss wrote the mus. and from which he later arr. an orch. suite, the March being especially well known.

Third (noun). Melodic and harmonic interval, reckoned as taking 3 steps in scale (major or minor) counting bottom and top notes, thus, *major third* (C up to E) or *minor third* (C up to E♭) or *diminished third* (C♯ up to E♭).

Third Inversion. In harmony, when determining lay-out of a chord, that inversion in a 4-note chord in which 4th note becomes the bass is the *Third Inversion*, e.g. in chord G–B–D–F, the form F–G–B–D or F–B–G–D, etc.

Third Stream. Term coined in 1950s by Gunther *Schuller to describe mus. in which the styles of both jazz and concert works are combined.

Thirty-Second Note. Demisemiquaver, notated ♪, with rest notated as ♪.

This Day (Vaughan Williams). See *Hodie*.

This Have I Done for my True Love. Work for unacc. ch., Op. 34, by Holst, comp. 1916. Setting of traditional carol.

Thomas, (Charles Louis) **Ambroise** (*b* Metz, 1811; *d* Paris, 1896). Fr. composer. Studied Paris Cons. (*Prix de Rome* 1832). Wrote some ballets for Paris Opéra, but from 1840 concentrated on operas for Opéra-Comique, achieving greatest success with *Mignon (1866) and *Hamlet (1868). Prof. of comp. Paris Cons. from 1856, dir. from 1871. Other stage works incl. *Raymond* (1851), *Le *Carnaval de Venise* (1857), and *Françoise de Rimini*

(1882). Also wrote choral works, *Fantasia* for pf. and orch., chamber mus., and songs.

Thomas, Arthur Goring (*b* Ratton Park, Sussex, 1850; *d* London, 1892). Eng. composer. Studied Paris 1873–7 with Durand, RAM with Sullivan and Prout, later orchestration with Bruch. Opera *Esmeralda* commissioned by Carl Rosa, 1883, followed by *Nadeshda* (1885), both being perf. also in Ger. Wrote other operas, orch. works, and cantata *The Swan and the Skylark* (orch. by Stanford). Became insane 1891.

Thomas, Jess (*b* Hot Springs, S. Dakota, 1927). Amer. ten. Opera début San Francisco 1957 as Malcolm in Verdi's *Macbeth*. Career then mainly in Ger., Baden 1958 (Lohengrin), Bayreuth 1961 (Parsifal), also Vienna Opera and Milan. NY Met. début 1962 (Walther in *Die Meistersinger*). CG début 1969 (Walther).

Thomas, Michael Tilson (*b* Hollywood, Calif., 1944). Amer. cond. and pianist. Studied Univ. of S. Calif., then at Bayreuth, 1966, and Berkshire Mus. Center 1968–9. Ass. cond. Boston S.O. 1969. Mus. dir. Buffalo P.O. 1971–9. London début with LSO 1970, prin. cond. LSO from 1988.

Thomas, Theodore (*b* Esens, Hanover, 1835; *d* Chicago, 1905). Ger.-born cond. (Amer. citizen). Taken to USA in 1845. Played vn. and hn. Played vn. in *Jullien's orch. 1853, in NY P.O. 1854. Leader of NY Acad. of Mus. Orch., 1856, taking over at short notice as cond. for perf. of *La Juive* in 1858. Formed own orch. 1862 and gave concerts in many inland cities which had never before heard an orch., always incl. some unfamiliar work. Dir., Philadelphia Centennial Concerts 1876. Cond., NY P.O. 1877–8; dir., Cincinnati Coll. of Mus. 1878–9; cond. NY P.O. 1879–91. First cond. Chicago S.O. 1891–1905. Always progressive in his taste, introduced many modern works to USA, e.g. f.p. of R. Strauss's F minor Sym. in NY 1884.

Thomé, François Luc Joseph (*b* Port Louis, Mauritius, 1850; *d* Paris, 1909). Fr. composer. Studied Paris Cons. Wrote ballets, operetta, and pf. piece, *Simple Aveu* (Simple avowal), known in many and various arrs.

Thompson, Oscar (*b* Crawfordsville, Ind., 1887; *d* NY, 1945). Amer. critic, author, and ed. Entered journalism, graduating to criticism. Critic for *Musical America* 1919, becoming ed. 1936–43. Mus. critic *NY Evening Post* 1928–34, *NY Sun* from 1937. Taught at Curtis Institute, Penn., and Columbia Univ. Wrote book on Debussy. Ed.-in-Chief, *International Cyclopedia of Music and Musicians* (1st-3rd edns.).

Thompson, Randall (*b* NY, 1899; *d* Boston, Mass., 1984). Amer. composer and teacher. Studied Harvard. After holding various teaching posts, became prof. of mus., Univ. of Calif. at Berkeley, 1937. Dir., Curtis Institute, 1939–41.

Head of mus. dept., Virginia Univ., 1941–6. Prof. of mus., Princeton Univ. 1946–8, Harvard Univ. 1948–65. Comp. 3 syms., opera, many choral works, incl. *St Luke Passion*, unacc. *Requiem* and *Americana*, and str. qt. *The Wind in the Willows*.

Thomson, Bryden (*b* Ayr, 1928). Scottish conductor. Studied RSAM and conducting with Hans Schmidt-Isserstedt and Igor Markevich. Ass. to Ian *Whyte with BBC Scottish Orch. Cond. opera at Oslo and Stockholm. Prin. cond. BBC Northern S.O. 1968–73; mus. dir. Ulster Orch. 1977–85; chief guest cond. Trondheim S.O.; prin. cond. BBC Welsh S.O. from 1979.

Thomson, César (*b* Liège, 1857; *d* Bissone, nr. Lugano, 1931). Belg. violinist. Studied with Vieuxtemps, Wieniawski, and Massart. Leader of orch. in Berlin, 1879. Prof. of vn., Liège Cons., 1883–97, Brussels Cons., 1898–1914, Paris Cons., 1914–24, Ithaca Cons., NY, and Juilliard Sch., NY, 1924–7. Ed. works of Tartini, Corelli, and Vivaldi.

Thomson, George (*b* Limekilns, Dunfermline, 1757; *d* Leith, 1851). Scot. publisher and educationist. Secretary, board of trustees for encouragement of arts and manufactures in Scotland 1780–1830. Collected folk-songs. Commissioned Haydn, Pleyel, and Beethoven to compose accs. for Scottish and Welsh songs. Haydn made 187 Scots settings for Thomson (and a further 221 for another Edinburgh publisher) and Beethoven 126. Those by Haydn pubd. in Vols. 3 and 4 of Scottish Songs (1802, 1805), 4 in Vol. 5 (1818), 12 in Vol. 6 (1841) and some in 2nd edn. of Vol. 2 (1803). Of those by Beethoven, 26 were in Vol. 5 and 13 in Vol. 6. Of Haydn's Welsh songs, 20 were in Vol. 1 (1809), 17 in Vol. 2 (1811), and 4 in Vol. 3 (1814); of Beethoven's, 26 in Vol. 3. In 1818–20, Beethoven wrote variations on a dozen Scot. melodies, pubd. by Thomson, and in 1825 Weber arr. 10 Scots songs for him. In view of Haydn's age, some scholars believe many of his arrs. must have been done by pupils or associates.

Thomson, Virgil (*b* Kansas City, 1896). Amer. composer, critic, and organist. Mus. child prodigy. Studied Harvard Univ., and in Paris with Boulanger 1921–22 and in NY with Scalero 1923–4. Wrote criticism for *Vanity Fair*. Lived in Paris 1925–32, associating with *Les Six* and Gertrude Stein. Returned to NY permanently 1940, becoming mus. critic of *Herald-Tribune* until 1954. Wrote several successful film scores and much incidental mus., esp. for Shakespeare plays. Influenced by Debussy and Satie. Inveterate champion of 20th-cent. mus. Works incl.:

OPERAS: *Four Saints in Three Acts* (1928); *The Mother of us all* (1947); *Lord Byron* (1961–8).

ORCH: 3 syms. (1928, 1931, 1972, 3rd being transcr. of 2nd Str. Qt., 1932); *Suite* (*Portraits*) Nos. 1 and 2 (1944); vc. conc. (1949).

CHAMBER MUSIC: 3 str. qts.; *5 Portraits* for 4 cl. (1929); *4 Portraits*, vn. and pf. (1931); *7 Portraits*, vn. (1928).

VOCAL: *Capital, Capitals*, 4 male vv. and pf. (1927). Also 4 pf. sonatas and other works, songs, etc.

Thorborg, Kerstin (*b* Venjan, 1896; *d* Falun, Dalarna, 1970). Swed. mez. Studied Stockholm; début Royal Opera Stockholm 1924 as Ortrud. Stockholm Opera 1924–30, Prague 1932–3, Berlin 1933–5, Vienna 1935–8. Salzburg Fests. 1935–7. CG début 1936 in Wagner's *Ring*, and until 1939. NY Met. 1936–50. Mainly Wagner and Strauss operatic roles. Soloist in famous 1936 Bruno Walter recording in Vienna of Mahler's *Das Lied von der Erde*.

Thoroughbass. See *Basso continuo*.

Three Choirs Festival. Name for the annual meeting of the 3 (Cath.) Choirs of Gloucester, Hereford, and Worcester, held by rotation in these cities. First was held probably in 1715 with aim of alleviating poverty of widows and orphans of clergy in the 3 dioceses. Early meetings lasted 2 days, and in 18th cent. mus. of Handel was frequently perf. In 1737 William Boyce was engaged for Worcester as chief cond. of fest. *Messiah* was first oratorio to be perf. complete in the caths. (Hereford 1759, Worcester 1761, Gloucester 1769). In 19th cent., 'star' singers became chief attractions and the mus. of Mendelssohn the staple fare. In 1875 the church authorities at Worcester refused use of the cath. because the perfs. could not be equated with the idea of worship. In the 2nd half of the 19th cent. the fests. became a leading forum for Eng. oratorios etc., from Sullivan's *The Prodigal Son* (1869) to Parry's *Job* in 1892. In 1878 one of the orch. violinists was a local man, Edward Elgar (a Catholic), who was to become the prin. figure at the fests. from 1902 to 1933, although few of his works were specially written for the 3 Choirs. Exceptions were *Froissart* (1890), *Lux Christi* (1896), and the *Te Deum and Benedictus* (1897). The organists at this period, Ivor Atkins (Worcester), G. R. Sinclair (Hereford), and Herbert Brewer (Gloucester) were Elgar's friends, Sinclair being immortalized as G.R.S. in the *Enigma Variations*. Elgar cond. *Gerontius* at Worcester, 1902; thereafter his conducting of his own major works was the foundation of the programmes each year. Other composers who came to be assoc. with the 20th-cent. fests. were Coleridge Taylor, Walford Davies, Vaughan Williams (several of whose works had f.ps. at the fests., e.g. *Tallis Fantasia, 5 Mystical Songs* and *Hodie*), Holst (*Choral Fantasia*), Bliss, Howells, Finzi, etc. Sibelius's *Luonnotar* had f.p. at Gloucester in 1913, and Kodály's *Psalmus Hungaricus* was cond. by the composer there in 1928. There were no fests. 1914–19 but they resumed at Worcester in 1920. A similar break occurred 1939–45. Since 1945 the programmes, both sacred and secular, have been much expanded and a more adventurous policy has been followed. For many years the LSO led by W. H. Reed provided the chief orch. support, but the

RPO and CBSO have lately been engaged. Works by John McCabe, Geoffrey Burgon, Philip Cannon, Malcolm Williamson, Jonathan Harvey, Gordon Crosse, Maxwell Davies, Christopher Steel, and others have been commissioned or performed, and the programmes have been broadened to include Mahler's 8th Sym., David Fanshawe's *African Sanctus*, and Walton's *Belshazzar's Feast* (for many years regarded as too 'barbaric' for these surroundings).

Threepenny Opera, The (Weill). See *Dreigroschenoper, Die.*

Threnody. Dirge.

Three-Cornered Hat, The (*El sombrero de tres picos*; Fr. *Le Tricorne*). 1-act ballet with mus. by Falla, choreog. by Massine, and scenario by Martinez Sierra based on P. A. de Alarcon's story *El sombrero de tres picos* (1874). F.p. London 1919 (Diaghilev Ballet Russe). Rev. version of pantomime by Sierra and Falla, *El corregidor y la molinera*, Madrid 1917. Same plot as *Wolf's opera Der *Corregidor.

Three Places in New England. Orch. work (with optional org.) by *Ives, also known as *Orchestral Set No. 1.* Comp. 1908–14. Movements are 1. *Boston Common: Colonel Shaw and his Colored Regiment.* 2. *Putnam's Camp.* 3. *The Housatonic at Stockbridge.* F.p. NY 1931, f.p. in England, London 1960.

Threni (id est LamentationesJeremiae Prophetae) (That is to say, the lamentations of the Prophet Jeremiah). Setting of biblical words for 6 soloists (sop., cont., 2 ten., bass, basso profundo), mixed ch., and orch. by *Stravinsky. Comp. 1957–8. F.p. Venice 1958, f.p. in England, London 1959.

Through-composed (Ger. *Durchkomponiert*). See *Durch* and *Strophic.*

Thuille, Ludwig (Wilhelm Andreas Mario) (*b* Bozen, Tyrol, 1861; *d* Munich, 1907). Ger. composer. Studied at Innsbruck and Munich (1879–81), pupil of Rheinberger. Prof., Munich Sch. of Mus. from 1883. Friend of R. Strauss, who cond. several of his early works. Wrote 3 operas: *Theuerdank* (1893–5), *Lobetanz* (1896), and *Gugeline* (1898–1900), also works for orch., and ch. and orch., pf. quintet, sextet for wind and pf., vc. sonata, vn. sonata, org. sonata.

Thule, the Period of Cosmography. Madrigal for 6 vv. by *Weelkes pubd. 1600; one of most remarkable examples of mus. settings of ostensibly unmus. words.

Thunder Machine. Theatrical contraption for imitating sound of thunder, required by some composers in their scores, e.g. Strauss for *Eine Alpensinfonie.*

Thunder Stick, Bull Roarer, Whizzer (Ger. *Schwirrholz*, 'whirlingwood'; Fr. *planchette ronflante,* 'roaring board'). Instr. in use among Amer.

Indians, Australian aborigines, natives of Central Africa, etc. A thin, flat piece of wood, swung to produce a whirring noise, rising or falling in pitch with changing speed of motion.

Thurston, Frederick (*b* Lichfield, 1901; *d* London, 1953). Eng. clarinettist. Studied RAM (pupil of Charles Draper). Prin. cl. BBC S.O. 1930–46 and other orchs. Prof. of cl., RCM. C.B.E. 1952. Several Eng. composers (e.g. Bliss, Howells, Bax) wrote works for him.

Thus Spake Zoroaster (Strauss). See *Also sprach Zarathustra.*

Tibbett, Lawrence (Mervil) (*b* Bakersfield, Calif., 1896; *d* NY, 1960). Amer. bar. Began career as actor, then sang in light opera. Studied NY with Frank la Forge. Opera début NY Met. 1923 as monk in *Boris Godunov.* Made name as Ford in Verdi's *Falstaff,* NY Met. 1925. Sang at Met. until 1950, creating bar. roles in Taylor's *The King's Henchman* and *Peter Ibbetson* and Gruenberg's *Emperor Jones.* Outstanding Iago in *Otello* and in other Verdi roles, e.g. Amonasro, Simon Boccanegra, Rigoletto, and Germont *père,* and such Puccini roles as Jack Rance, Gianni Schicchi, and Scarpia. Outstanding success in Gershwin's *Porgy and Bess.* CG début 1937 as Scarpia. Made several films. Equally popular as concert singer.

Tibia. Org. stop, not brilliant but full-toned. Varieties are: *Tibia Major* (8′ or 16′ length and pitch); *Tibia Minor* (4′ or 8′); *Tibia Plena* (8′, loud); *Tibia Profunda* (16′); *Tibia Dura* (4′, hard in tone); *Tibia Clausa* (4′).

Tichatschek (orig. Tichaček), **Joseph** (*b* Ober-Weckelsdorf, 1807; *d* Blasewitz, 1886). Bohem. ten. Abandoned medicine for mus. Studied in Vienna. In ch. at Kärntnerthor Th., 1830. Prin. ten. at Graz and Vienna. Début Dresden 1837, remaining there to 1872. Coached by *Schröder-Devrient. Created roles of Rienzi (1842), and Tannhäuser (1845). Sang in London 1841.

Tie (or bind). Curved line placed over note and its repetition to indicate that the 2 shall be perf. as one unbroken note of their combined time-value. Thus *tied note.*

Tief (Ger.). Deep, low, thus *tiefgespannt,* deep-stretched, i.e. of a drum, so as to give a low sound.

Tiefland (Lowland). Opera in prol. and 3 acts by d'*Albert, to text by R. Lothar after Catalan play by Guimerá. Prod. Prague 1903, NY (revised version) 1908, CG 1910.

Tierce (Fr. noun). Third. (1) Interval of a 3rd, major or minor.
(2) 4th of series of natural harmonics.
(3) Org. stop of same pitch as similarly-named harmonic.

Tierce de Picardie (Fr.). Picardy third. Term applied to major 3rd used at end of a comp. which is otherwise in a minor key, thus converting expected minor chord into major, e.g. in key of C minor the expected chord C–E♭–G becomes C–E♮–G. Commonly used up to end of 18th cent. Reason for name unknown.

Tiersot, (Jean-Baptiste Elisée) **Julien** (*b* Bourg-en-Bresse, 1857; *d* Paris, 1936). Fr. musicologist and composer. Pupil of Massenet and Franck at Paris Cons. from 1876. Worked in library at Paris Cons. 1883–1921. Authority on Fr. folk-songs, many of which he ed.; author of books on Berlioz, Gluck, and Rousseau. Wrote orch. and choral works.

Tietjen, Heinz (*b* Tangier, 1881; *d* Baden-Baden, 1967). Ger. cond., producer, and opera dir. Cond. and producer at Trier 1904–7, intendant 1907–22. Intendant at Breslau 1922–4, Berlin City Opera 1925–30, Berlin State Opera 1927–45. Art. dir., Bayreuth Fest. 1931–44 (cond. *The Ring* and other operas). Intendant Berlin City Opera 1948–54, Hamburg 1954–9. Prod. CG 1950 and 1951. Last cond. at Bayreuth 1959.

Tietjens, Thérèse (Carolina Johanna Alexandra) (*b* Hamburg, 1831; *d* London, 1877). Ger. sop. Studied Hamburg and Vienna. Opera début Altona 1849 as Lucrezia Borgia. Frankfurt Opera 1850–6, Vienna 1856–9. London début 1858, thereafter settling in Eng. Sang in NY 1874 and 1876. One of great opera and oratorio singers of her day, famous as Norma and Donna Anna. Was first to sing Marguérite in Gounod's *Faust* in London (1863), also created several Verdi roles for London.

Till Eulenspiegel. Tone-poem for orch., Op. 28, by R. Strauss, full title being *Till Eulenspiegels lustige Streiche, nach alter Schelmenweise—in Rondeauform—für grosses Orchester gestetzt* (Till Eulenspiegel's merry pranks, in the manner of an old rogue—in rondo form—set for full orchestra). Comp. 1894–5, f.p. Cologne 1895 cond. Wüllner. Strauss abandoned idea of opera on the subject 1893–4. Till's adventures were first told in a 15th-cent. book and remain part of Ger. folklore. Other composers who have treated the subject incl. Alpaerts (symphonic poem), Blockx (opera, 1900), Jeremiáš (opera, 1949), Rezniček (opera, 1902), and M. Steinberg (ballet). Strauss's score has been basis of several ballets, incl. one by Nijinsky (1916).

Tilney, Colin (*b* London, 1933). Eng. harpsichordist. Studied at Cambridge Univ., hpd. with Mary Potts, and later with Leonhardt in Amsterdam. Soloist and ens. performer since 1960s. Amer. début 1971. Plays kbd. works on most appropriate instr., using clavichords and early pianos (historical and modern replica). Ed. of Forqueray's hpd. mus. Has recorded *Parthenia* and complete kbd. works of Locke.

Tilson Thomas, Michael. See *Thomas, Michael Tilson.*

Timbales. Pair of single-headed cylindrical drums, usually assoc. with Latin-Amer. dance

orch. but also used by composers of modern orch. mus., e.g. Lipkin in *Interplay* (1975), who uses six instead of timpani.

Timbre (Fr.; Ger. *Klangfarbe*). Tone-colour; that which distinguishes the quality of tone or v. of one instr. or singer from another, e.g. fl. from cl., sop. from mez., etc.

Timbrel. Medieval tambourine. Also Hebrew instr. in biblical times, thought to be similar to tambourine.

Time. Fundamental rhythmical patterns of mus., e.g. $\frac{3}{8}$ time = 3 8th-notes to the measure. One speaks of waltz time ($\frac{3}{4}$) and march time (usually $\frac{2}{4}$), and more generally of 'quick time'.

Time Signature. Sign placed after the clef and *key signature at the beginning of a piece of music, or during the course of it, to indicate the time or metre of the music. Normally it comprises two numbers, one above the other, the lower defining the unit of measurement in relation to the whole-note, the upper indicating the number of those units in each measure (bar). Thus the time-signature $\frac{3}{4}$ indicates three quarter-notes (crotchets) to the measure, one of $\frac{6}{8}$ that there are six eighth-notes (quavers) in the measure. But see also *Compound Time* and *Simple Time*.

Timpani (It.). See *Drum.*

Tinctoris, Johannes (*b* Braine l'Allend, *c.* 1435; *d* ?1511). Franco-Flemish theorist and composer. Entered service of King of Naples *c.*1472 as tutor to King's daughter. His treatise *Terminorum musicae diffinitorium* (Treviso, 1495) was probably written in 1472. It contains 299 definitions of terms then in use. His *Liber de arte contrapuncti* (1477) contains principles of consonance and dissonance and discussions on counterpoint. Comp. several masses and secular songs. Was also painter, lawyer, and mathematician.

Tinel, Edgar (*b* Sinaai, Belg., 1854; *d* Brussels, 1912). Belg. composer and pianist. Studied Brussels Cons. Dir., Institute for Church Mus., Malines, 1881. Prof. of counterpoint, Brussels Cons., 1896, dir. 1909. Wrote mainly religious works, pf. sonata, etc.

Tinsley, Pauline (Cecilia) (*b* Salford, 1928). Eng. sop. Studied NSM, Manchester, and Opera Sch., London. Opera début as Desdemona in Rossini's *Otello*, London 1951. Thereafter guest singer with many opera cos., e.g. CG (début 1965), ENO, Scottish Opera, WNO, etc. Well known for Verdi roles such as Lady Macbeth, also for Janáček and Strauss (Elektra).

Tintagel. Orchestral tone-poem by Bax, comp. 1917–19. F.p. London, 1920. Quotes motif from Wagner's *Tristan und Isolde.*

Tin-Whistle. 6-holed keyless wind instr. made of metal. Also called penny-whistle.

Tiomkin, Dimitri (*b* St Petersburg, 1894; *d* London, 1979). Russ.-born composer and pianist (Amer. citizen). Studied St Petersburg Cons. Toured Europe as pianist. NY début 1926. Settled in USA 1929 and became prolific composer of film scores, incl. those for *Lost Horizon, High Noon, The Guns of Navarone,* and many more.

Tippett, (Sir) **Michael** (Kemp) (*b* London, 1905). Eng. composer. Studied RCM (comp. with Charles Wood, cond. with Boult and Sargent). Became schoolmaster and cond. choral soc.; in 1920 studied counterpoint and fugue with R. O. Morris. Mus. dir., Morley College, 1940–51, dir. of Bath Fest. 1969–74. Imprisoned during 1943 for failure to comply with conditions of his conscientious exemption from military service. C.B.E. 1959. Knighted 1966. C.H. 1979. O.M. 1983.

Tippett's life is his mus. A late developer, he did not achieve any kind of recognition until 1935 with his first str. qt. The work which made his name more familiar was the Conc. for Double Str. Orch. (1938–9). His oratorio *A Child of Our Time,* comp. 1939–41, was among the first of his works which reconcile personal vision with expression of 'collective' feeling. After 6 years of work he completed his first opera, *The Midsummer Marriage* in 1952. Though not successful until its revival over 20 years later, this opera marks the culmination of Tippett's early lyrical style, a style that is complex in its madrigalian, contrapuntal, inter-weaving but which repays close study. He entered a tougher middle phase in 1962 with the opera *King Priam* and the 2nd pf. sonata, works of rhetoric and drama. This period culminated in the *Concerto for Orchestra* and the elaborate choral work *The Vision of St Augustine.* With the opera *The Knot Garden* (1969) Tippett entered a 3rd period in which he fused his 2 earlier periods, the 'lyrical' and the 'disjunct', as they have been called, and also extended his bounds by reference to popular and serious mus., past and present, e.g. 'blues', quotations from Monteverdi, and a tighter control of form as shown in the 3rd pf. sonata and the 4th sym. Yet, like all great composers, Tippett has remained essentially himself, and the flowing lines of the Double Conc. are still discernible in *King Priam,* just as the exuberant, life-enhancing lyricism of *The Midsummer Marriage* spills over into the pf. conc., the *Corelli Fantasia,* and the 4th sym. Some of his determinedly popular passages in recent years may come to sound increasingly self-conscious, but this is part of the price one pays for Tippett's open-eyed, even naive outlook on the world expressed in mus. of exceptional technical sophistication. Prin. works:

OPERAS: The **Midsummer Marriage* (1946–52); **King Priam* (1958–61); The **Knot Garden* (1966–9); The **Ice Break* (1973–6).

ORCH: Symphonies: No. 1 (1944–5, f.p. 1945), No. 2 (1956–7, f.p. 1958), No. 3, sop. and orch. (1970–2, f.p. 1972), No. 4 (1976–7, f.p. 1977); Conc. for Double Str. Orch. (1938–9); **Fantasia on a Theme of Handel,* pf. and orch. (1939–41); *Little Music,* for str. (1946); *Suite in D for the Birthday of Prince Charles* (1948); **Ritual Dances from The Midsummer Marriage* (1952–3); *Divertimento on Sellinger's Round* (1953–4); Pf. Conc. (1953–5); **Fantasia Concertante on a Theme of Corelli* for str. (1953); *Concerto for Orchestra* (1962–3); Conc. for str. trio and orch. (1978–9).

CHORAL: A **Child of Our Time,* SATB soloists, ch., and orch. (1939–41); *The Source* and *The Windhover,* unacc. ch. (1942); *Plebs angelica,* unacc. double ch. (1943); *The Weeping Babe,* sop. and mixed ch. (1944); *Crown of the Year,* women's ch. and chamber ens. (1958); *Magnificat and Nunc Dimittis* (1961); The **Vision of St Augustine,* bar., ch., and orch. (1963–5); *The Shires Suite,* ch. and orch. (1965–70); The **Mask of Time,* sop., mez., ten., bar., ch., and orch. (1981–3).

VOICE AND ORCH/INSTR: **Boyhood's End,* ten. and pf. (1943); The **Heart's Assurance* (1950–1); *Songs for Achilles,* ten. and guitar (1961); *Songs for Ariel,* v. and pf. (or hpd.) (1962); **Songs for Dov,* ten. and small orch. (1970).

CHAMBER MUSIC: String Quartets: No. 1 (1934–5, rev. 1943), No. 2 (1941–2), No. 3 (1945–6), No. 4 (1977–8); *4 Inventions* for descant and treble recorders (1954); Sonata for 4 hn. (1955); *The Blue Guitar,* guitar (1983).

PIANO: Sonatas: No. 1 (1936–7, rev. 1942, 1954), No. 2 (1962), No. 3 (1972–3), No. 4 (1984).

ORGAN: *Preludio al Vespro di Monteverdi* (1946).

BRASS: *Festal Brass with Blues* (1983); *Suite in D for the Birthday of Prince Charles* (arr. B. Bowen, 1983).

EDITIONS (in collab. with W. Bergmann): J. S. Bach: songs, *Amore traditore,* cantata for bass, *If thou art near, Come sweet death,* and *Jesu, in thy love;* Handel: *Lucretia,* cantata for sop.; Humfrey: *A Hymne to God the Father;* Purcell: *Come ye sons of art,* sop., 2 altos, bass, ch., orch., *Ode for St Cecilia's Day* (1692), sop., 2 altos, ten., bar., bass, ch., and orch., *Golden Sonata,* 2 vns. and basso continuo; and songs and duets.

Tirana. Sp. song-dance popular in Andalusia, usually with rhythmic guitar acc. in $\frac{6}{8}$ time.

Tirasse (Fr.). Coupler of organ—generally a pedal coupler. So *Tirasse du Positif, du Récit, du Grand Orgue,* mean respectively Choir to Pedal, Swell to Pedal, Great to Pedal. These may be abbreviated to *Tir. P., Tir. R.,* and *Tir. G.O. Tirasse G.P.R.* means that all 3 couplers are to be used.

Tiresias. Ballet in 3 scenes, lib. and mus. by **Lambert, choreog. Ashton. Prod. London 1951.

Tirésias, Les mamelles de (Poulenc). See *Mamelles de Tirésias, Les.*

Tirimo, Martino (*b* Larnaca, Cyprus, 1942). Cyprus-born pianist. Studied RAM, Vienna Acad. Début London 1965. Won Geneva int. pf. competition 1972. Specialist in Schubert sonatas.

Tishchenko, Boris (Ivanovich) (*b* Leningrad, 1939). Russ. composer. Studied with Salmanov and Shostakovich. Teacher at Leningrad Cons. Works incl. ballets, 5 syms., pf. conc., 2 vc. concs. (No. 1 orch. by Shostakovich 1969, No. 2 for soloist with 48 vc. and 2 db.), conc. for fl. and pf., harp conc., vn. conc., chamber mus., songs, film mus.

Ti Tzu. Chinese fl., played transversely. 6 fingerholes and extra hole covered with membrane which vibrates to give characteristic reedy tone.

Tjeknavorian, Loris (*b* Broudjerd, Persia, 1937). Persian composer, violinist, and conductor of Armenian descent. Studied Vienna Acad. of Mus. 1954–60. Dir., Teheran music archives 1961. Composer-in-residence, Concordia Univ., Minnesota, 1966. Ass. prof. of music, Moorhead State Coll., 1966–9. Prin. cond., Teheran Opera 1972. Mus. dir., London Percussion Virtuosi. Eng. début as cond., Manchester 1974, London 1975. Works incl. *Requiem for the Massacred* for over 60 percussion instrs. (1975), operas, piano concerto, violin concerto, and over 30 film scores. Settled in Eng.

Toccata (It.). Touched. One of oldest names for kbd. piece (org., hpd., etc.), orig. a short movement, often merely a prelude, in which the player's 'touch' was displayed through rapidity and delicacy. But note that Monteverdi's first opera *Orfeo*, 1607, begins with a *Toccata* for baroque tpts. Later the toccata form was combined with a ricercare, and Bach wrote several toccatas and fugues. Bach also comp. hpd. toccatas in several movements. Several 20th-cent. composers have used the term *toccata* for movements of orch. works, e.g. Vaughan Williams for first movement of pf. conc. and 4th movement of 8th Sym. First printed source for use of word is G. A. Casteliono's *Intabolatura de leuto de diversi autori* (1536). Earliest printed keyboard toccatas were by S. Bertoldo (1591).

Toch, Ernst (*b* Vienna, 1887; *d* Santa Monica, Calif., 1964). Austrian-born composer and pianist (Amer. citizen from 1940). Studied at Mannheim and Frankfurt. Taught comp. at Mannheim 1913–29, privately in Berlin 1929–32. Went to Eng. 1933, writing mus. for BBC 1934; then to USA 1934, teaching in NY 1934–6. Went to Hollywood, composed some film scores, and became prof. of comp., U.C.L.A., 1940–8. Wrote 7 syms. (1950–64), also choral sym. *To My Fatherland*; *The Chinese Flute*, sop. and chamber orch. (1922, rev. 1949); *Big Ben*, variations for orch. (1934); vc. conc., 2 pf. concs., pf. sonata, pf. quintet, and 13 str. qts.

Tod Jesu, Der (The Death of Jesus). Passion-cantata by *Graun to text by Ramler. Berlin 1755, London 1877. Annually perf. in Berlin far into 20th cent.

Tod und das Mädchen, Der (Death and the Maiden). Song by Schubert (1817, D531), to poem by Claudius, which is also used as theme for variations in 2nd movement of Str. Qt. No. 14 in D minor (1824, D810).

Tod und Verklärung (Death and Transfiguration). Orch. tone-poem, Op. 24, by R. Strauss depicting a man's death-bed visions. Comp. 1888–9; f.p. Eisenach 1889, cond. Strauss.

Toëschi, Carlo Giuseppe (*b* Ludwigsburg, 1731; *d* Munich, 1788). It. composer and violinist. Pupil of *Stamitz. Violinist in *Mannheim orch. from 1752, leader from 1759. Dir. of mus., Munich, 1780. Wrote over 60 syms. and other instr. works.

Togli (It.). Take away, used in org. mus. for the shutting off of any stop, etc.

Togni, Camillo (*b* Gussago, 1922). It. composer. Studied Siena 1939–42 with *Casella, earlier privately at Brescia 1935–40 (pf. with Michelangeli). Active as pianist in contemporary mus. 1950–5. At Darmstadt summer courses 1951–7. Worked at Milan elec. studio from 1961. Adopted 12-note system 1940. Works incl. settings of T. S. Eliot for ch. and orch., fl. sonata, *Recitative* on tape, etc.

Tomášek, Václav Jan (*b* Skuč, Bohem., 1774; *d* Prague, 1850). Bohem. composer, organist, and pianist. Studied at Chrudim and Iglau. Became teacher in Prague. Wrote operas, 3 syms., 2 pf. concs., vocal scenas, 7 pf. sonatas, *Hungarian Dances* for pf., 42 *Eclogues* for pf., etc.

Tomasi, Henri Frédien (*b* Marseilles, 1901; *d* Avignon, 1971). Fr. composer and cond. Studied Paris Cons. with d'Indy. Mus. dir., Fr. Indo-China radio 1930–5. Dir., Monte Carlo Opera 1946–50. Wrote 8 operas, incl. *Le silence de la mer* (1959), 10 ballets, *Tam Tam* for sop., male ch., and orch., and 16 concs. for different instr. (incl. sax., guitar, tb., harp, and db.).

Tomasini, Luigi (*b* Pesaro, 1741; *d* Eisenstadt, 1808). It. violinist. Member of Haydn's orch. for Prince Esterházy from 1757 at Eisenstadt, becoming leader 1761. Later dir. of chamber mus., Haydn composing qts. with his playing in mind. Wrote vn. concs., qts., and 24 divertimenti for *baryton.

Tombeau (Fr.). Tomb, tombstone. Fr. 17th-cent. composers' term for memorial works, revived by several 20th-cent. composers, notably by Ravel in Le *Tombeau de Couperin* (1914–17).

Tombeau de Couperin, Le (The Tomb of Couperin). Suite for solo pf. by Ravel of 6 movements each ded. to memory of friends who died in World War I, comp. 1914–17: 1. *Prélude*, 2. *Fugue*, 3. *Forlane*, 4. *Rigaudon*, 5. *Menuet*, 6. *Toccata*. F.p. Paris 1919. Nos. 1, 3, 5, and 4 (in that order) orch. by Ravel 1919, f.p. 1920. Prod.

as ballet, Paris 1920, choreog. Berlin, later choreog. Balanchine, NY 1975.

Tom Jones. (1) Opera in 3 acts by Stephen *Oliver to his own lib. based on Fielding's novel (1749). Prod. Snape 1976 (Eng. Music Th.), Nottingham and London 1976.
   (2) Comic opera in 3 acts by *German, lib. by A. M. Thompson and R. Courtneidge based on Fielding. Prod. Manchester and London 1907.

Tomkins, Thomas (*b* St David's, Pembroke, 1572; *d* Martin Hussingtree, Worcs., 1656). Welsh composer, grandson of organist of Worcester Cath. and one of large family of musicians. Thought to have studied with Byrd. Organist, Worcester Cath. 1596–1646, Chapel Royal from 1621. Comp. mus. for Charles I's coronation 1625. Wrote mus. for consorts, pavans and galliards (incl. *Sad Pavan for these distracted times*), 95 anthems, and services, but his finest work is to be found in his polyphonic madrigals *Songs of 3, 4, 5, and 6 parts*, pubd. 1622. These incl. *Above the stars, Music divine, Oft did I marle, See, see, the shepherd's queen, When David heard that Absalom was slain*, and *When I observe*. His sacred works were pubd. posthumously in *Musica Deo sacra* (1668).

Tomlinson, Ernest (*b* Rawtenstall, 1924). Eng. composer, organist, and cond. Studied Manchester Univ. and RMCM. Organist, 3rd Church of Christ Scientist, London, 1948–58. Comp. sym. for jazz and sym. orch., conc. for 5 sax. and orch., incidental mus., elec. mus.

Tommasini, Vincenzo (*b* Rome, 1878; *d* Rome, 1950). It. composer. Studied in Rome and in Berlin with Bruch. Wrote operas and orch. works but is remembered for his arr. of mus. by D. Scarlatti for Diaghilev ballet The *Good-humoured Ladies* (*Le donne di buon umore*), (comp. 1916, prod. Rome 1917, suite 1920).

Tom-Tom. Type of drum, imitative of African small hand-played drums, used in Western dance-bands from 1920s and sometimes in orch. works. May or may not be tuned. Not the same as *tam-tam.

Ton (Fr.). Pitch, key, mode, tone, crook, sound, note; e.g. *donner le ton*, to give the pitch; *ton de cor*, horn crook.

Ton (Ger.). Pitch, key, mode, note, sound, mus., e.g. *Tonfarbe*, tone-colour; *Tonkunst*, tonal art (i.e. mus.), *Tondichtung*, tone-poem.

Tonada (Sp.). Tune or air; used as title of works by some Sp. composers.

Tonadilla (Sp.). (1) Diminutive of *Tonada*.
   (2) Cantata with vocal solos, usually incl. choral and instr. movements. Such works were used as satirical intermezzi in the th.; their popularity was est. by Luís Misón, Sp. fl. virtuoso and cond. (who from c.1757 wrote over 100), and others.

Form revived by Granados. Originally a topical solo song, with guitar acc., added to Sp. theatrical interludes.

Tonal. (1) Opposite to *real* in such technicalities as *Answer* and *Sequence*. See *Fugue*.
   (2) Of keys, as in *tonal* basis.
   (3) Of *tonality, i.e. the opposite of *atonal, as in *tonal* comp.

Tonality. Key, meaning particularly observance of a single tonic key as basis of comp., thus, *bitonality*, use of 2 keys at once; *polytonality*, use of several keys at once; *atonality*, loyalty to no key.

Tonart (Ger.). Mode, scale, or key.

Tondichter (Ger.). Sound-poet, i.e. composer.

Tondichtung (Ger.). Tone-poem; term preferred to *symphonic poem* by R. Strauss.

Tone. (1) Mus. sound, as in analysis to show that a vn. note has several different *tones*.
   (2) Interval of major 2nd, e.g. C-D, E-F♯.
   (3) Quality of sound, as in 'sweet *tone*', 'harsh *tone*', 'dry *tone*'.
   (4) Plainsong melody, as in Gregorian tone.
   (5) Amer. usage for 'note', hence *12-tone mus.* and *tone-row* instead of 12-note and note-row.

Tone-Cluster. Amer. term for *cluster, i.e. group of notes on pf. played by placing the forearm flat on the keys.

Tone-Colour. See *Timbre*.

Tone-Poem. See *Symphonic Poem*.

Tone Roads. Name of 2 works by *Ives. No. 1 for small orch., comp. 1911; No. 3 for chamber orch., comp. 1915.

Tonguing. Use of the tongue to articulate certain notes in playing of wind instr. Thus, single-, double-, and triple-tonguing refer to increasingly fast playing. *Flutter-tonguing* (Ger. *Flatterzunge*) is used chiefly by flautists, but occasionally by clarinettists and trumpeters, for a trilling effect required by composers from R. Strauss and Mahler to the present day.

Tonic. First degree of the major or minor scale. The 'key-note' from which the key takes its name, as Key of A etc.

Tonic Sol-Fa. Eng. system of sight-singing and notation first mooted by D. Sower in 1832, developed by Sarah Ann Glover (1785–1867) as *Norwich Sol-fa*, and pioneered by John Curwen (1816–80) in the 1840s. Based on *movable-doh* system of *Solmization. Notes of major scale are named (in ascending order) *doh, ray, me, fah, soh, lah, te,* where *doh* is the tonic, other notes being thus related to tonic of the moment, not fixed in pitch. Minor is treated as mode of the major, first note being *lah,* 2nd *te,* 3rd *doh,* etc. In notation notes are written as d, r, m, f, s, l, t. Sharps and flats are indicated by change of vowel, sharps to 'e', flats to 'a' (pronounced 'aw'). E.g. *doh* sharpened is *de*; *me* flattened is *ma*. Double dots (:) separate beat from beat; single dots are used when a beat has to be divided into a half-beat, commas to divide half-beats into quarters. Horizontal lines show that notes are held; blanks indicate rests.

Tonkunst (Ger.). 'Sound art'. Music.

Tono (It., plural *toni*). Tone—in all the various senses of the English word (see *Tone*). Also mode, key.

Tono (Sp.). Type of part-song or madrigal, of 2 or 3 stanzas, sung before play in 17th cent.

Tonreihe (Ger.). *Note-row.

Tonus Peregrinus (Lat.). Foreign tone. (1) Medieval term for minor scale.
(2) Plainsong for Psalm 114 (*When Israel went out of Egypt*).

Torelli, Giuseppe (*b* Verona, 1658; *d* Bologna, 1709). It. violinist and composer. Attached to Church of San Petronio, Bologna, 1686–95. Visited Vienna. Leader of band at court of Margrave of Brandenburg-Anspach, 1697–99. Returned to Bologna 1701. Comp. mus. for str. and continuo, incl. 12 concerti grossi, Op. 8 (1708), guitar conc., tpt. concs., suites for tpt., str., and continuo, etc.

Tornada (Sp.). Type of refrain in many of the folk-songs of Catalonia.

Tórroba, Federico Moreno (*b* Madrid, 1891; *d* Madrid, 1982). Sp. composer of zarzuelas, guitar works, flamenco conc., etc. Dir., Royal Acad. des Beaux Arts de Madrid.

Tortelier, Paul (*b* Paris, 1914). Fr. cellist, cond., and composer. Studied Paris Cons., winning first vc. prize 1930 (playing Elgar conc.). Prin. vc. Monte Carlo Orch. 1935–7; 3rd cellist, Boston S.O. 1937–40; prin. cellist Société des Concerts du Conservatoire, Paris, 1946–7, then solo career with world's leading orchs. Eng. début (in Strauss's *Don Quixote*), London 1947. Lived in Israel 1955–6. Prof. of vc., Paris Cons., from 1956. Works incl. 2 vc. concs., conc. for 2 vc., *Israel Symphony*, vc. sonata, *Suite* for unacc. vc. Also chamber-mus. player with wife Maud Martin Tortelier (*b* 1926) cellist, daughter Maria de la Pau (*b* 1950) pianist, and son Yan Pascal (*b* 1947) violinist and cond.

Tosca. Opera in 3 acts by Puccini to lib. by Giacosa and Illica based on Sardou's play *La Tosca* (1887). Comp. 1898–9. Prod. Rome and London 1900; NY Met. 1901.

Toscanini, Arturo (*b* Parma, 1867; *d* NY, 1957). It. cond. and cellist. Entered Parma Cons. 1876, studying vc. and comp. Engaged as cellist in opera orch. for S. American tour, 1886 and in Rio de Janeiro replaced regular cond., conducting *Aida* from memory. In It. later that year cond.

Catalani's *Edmea* in Turin. Played vc. in f.p. of Verdi's *Otello*, Milan 1887. Cond. Turin municipal orch. and opera in various It. cities. Cond. f.p. of *Pagliacci* in Milan (Teatro dal Verme), 1892, f.p. of Puccini's *La Bohème*, Turin 1896. Cond. f. ps. in Italy of *Götterdämmerung*, Turin 1895, and of *Siegfried*, Milan 1899. Début at La Scala 1896 as cond. of 4 orch. concerts; opera début there 1898 in *Die Meistersinger* as prin. cond. under management of *Gatti-Casazza. Stayed till 1903, resigning after demonstration when he refused to allow ten. an encore in a Verdi opera. Returned 1906–8. Went to NY Met. with Gatti-Casazza 1908, making début in *Aida*. Cond. f.p. of Puccini's *La fanciulla del West* 1910, and f. ps. in USA of several operas, incl. *Boris Godunov* (1913). Cond. Verdi's *Requiem* at Met. 1909 and Beethoven's 9th Sym. there 1913. Returned to It. 1915 and again became chief cond. at La Scala 1921–9, one of its golden periods. Friction with Fascists led to his departure. Cond. part of NY P.O. seasons 1926–28 (orch. becoming Phil.-Sym. Orch. of NY, 1928), prin. cond. 1928–36. Took orch. on European tour 1930. Cond. at Bayreuth 1930 and 1931, at Salzburg 1934–7 (famous perfs. of *Falstaff*, *Fidelio*, and *Die Meistersinger*). Début with Vienna P.O. 1933. Refused to cond. in Ger., It., and Austria under Nazi and Fascist régimes. Cond. inaugural concerts of Palestine S.O. (now Israel P.O.), 1936. NBC formed new orch in NY for him which he cond. 1937–54, giving public concerts and many famous concert perfs. of operas. Guest cond. in London of BBC S.O. 1935 and 1937–9, with whom he recorded Beethoven's *Pastoral Symphony*, 1938, and of Philharmonia Orch. 1952 in Brahms series. Returned to La Scala 1946, conducting a concert of It. operatic music and, in subsequent years, several other concerts. Last appearance as cond. NY June 1954. Encouraged Amer. composers, especially Barber and Hanson. Always cond. from memory, but not only because he was extremely short-sighted. Tyrannized orchs., but drilled them to remarkable standards. Regarded by many Amer. critics as beyond criticism, but, like all conds., had his limitations, far outweighed in his case by virtues of clarity, expressiveness, and ens. Outstanding in It. opera, but also in Wagner and in a limited range of composers of symphonic mus. from Haydn to his own day.

Toselli, Enrico (*b* Florence, 1883; *d* Florence, 1926). It. pianist and composer. Studied with Martucci and Sgambati. Wrote operetta, symphonic poem, chamber mus., and songs, incl. the well-known *Serenata* (1900).

Tosti, (Sir) (Francesco) **Paolo** (*b* Ortano sul Mare, Abruzzi, 1846; *d* Rome, 1916). It.-born composer and singing-teacher. Studied Naples, 1858. Became singing-teacher to future Queen of It. Visited Eng. 1875, appointed royal singing-master 1880. Took Eng. nationality 1906 and was knighted 1908. Wrote songs and duets to It., Fr., and Eng. texts. His *Good-bye* extremely popular.

Tosto (It.). (1) Rapid; so *piuttosto,* more rapid. But *più tosto,* or *piùt-tosto,* as ordinary It. expressions mean rather, in either sense of this word. Superlative is *tostissimo,* very rapid, *tostissama-mente,* very rapidly.
  (2) 'Immediately.'

Tost Quartets. Name given to 12 str. qts. by Haydn, 1788–90 (Hob. III 57–68; or Op. 54, Nos. 1–3, Op. 55 Nos. 1–3, Op. 64 Nos. 1–6). So-called because of ded. to Viennese violinist Johann Tost.

Total Serialism. Comp. which treats all mus. parameters serially, not only pitch but time-values, vol., etc.

Totentanz (Dance of Death). Work by Liszt for pf. and orch., being variations on *Dies irae.* Comp. 1849, rev. 1853, 1859. Also arr. Busoni (1918).

Tote Stadt, Die (The Dead City). Opera in 3 acts by Erich *Korngold to lib. by 'Paul Schott' (himself and his father J. Korngold) based on Ger. trans. by S. Trebitsch of G. Rodenbach's play *Le Mirage,* itself adapted from his novella *Bruges la Morte* (1892). Prod. Hamburg and Cologne (joint premières) 1920; Vienna and NY 1921.

To The Children (*K detyam*). Song for v. and pf. by Rakhmaninov, Op. 26, No. 7 (1906), a setting of poem by Khomyakov. F.p. Moscow 1907 by Ivan Grizunov.

Touch (Ger. *Anschlag*). (1) Applied to kbd. instr., the weight required to bring keys into effect. Applied to performers it means the manner of pressing or striking the keys and is one of the most subtle and indefinable facets of the art of pf.-playing.
  (2) (Old Eng.). Sound. Also used in 16th and 17th cents. to mean *toccata, e.g. a *touch* by Byrd.

Touche (Fr.). Fingerboard—of vn., etc., e.g. *sur la touche,* bow over the fingerboard.

Tourel (orig. Davidovich), **Jennie** (*b* ?St Petersburg, 1900; *d* NY, 1973). Probably Russian-born mez. (Amer. citizen 1946). Studied Paris with Anna El-Tour (whose name is an anagram of Tourel, although the singer denied choosing her stage name for that reason). Opera début, Paris 1931 in *Prince Igor.* Sang in Paris until 1940. NY Met. début 1937. Settled in USA 1940. NY Met. 1943–7. Created Baba the Turk in Stravinsky's *The Rake's Progress,* 1951. Taught at Juilliard Sch. Last stage appearance Chicago 1973.

Tournemire, Charles (Arnould) (*b* Bordeaux, 1870; *d* Arcachon, 1939). Fr. organist and composer. At age of 11, org. of St Pierre, Bordeaux, later of St Seurin. Went to Paris Cons., studying pf. with Bériot and winning *premier prix* for org. in Widor's class. Org. of Ste Clotilde, Paris, from 1898. Prof. at Paris Cons. from 1919. Deeply influenced by Franck and Widor. Comp. 4 operas

(3 unpubd.), 8 syms. (last 3 unpubd.), songs, choral works, chamber mus., and many works for org., incl. *L'Orgue mystique* (1927–32), which lasts as long as the entire org. mus. of J. S. Bach.

Tournier, Marcel (*b* Paris, 1879; *d* Paris, 1951). Fr. harpist. Studied Paris Cons., where he became harp prof. 1912. Wrote many works for harp.

Tours, Berthold (*b* Rotterdam, 1838; *d* London, 1897). Dutch-born violinist, teacher, organist, and mus. ed. Studied Brussels and Leipzig. Spent 2 years in Russia. Settled in London 1861, as orch. violinist, writer, and teacher. Organist, Swiss Church, Holborn, 1862. Mus. adviser and ed. to Novello from 1878. Made pf. reduction of Beethoven's Mass in C, Mendelssohn's *Elijah,* etc. Wrote hymns and anthems, pf. pieces, and songs. Author of vn. primer.

Tourte, François (*b* Paris, 1747; *d* Paris, 1835). Fr. maker of vn. bows, one of a family, and known as 'the Stradivari of the bow'. Developed between 1782 and 1790 the modern bow, known as 'Tourte bow'. Selected Pernambuco wood which he set in permanent curvature by subjection to moderate heat. Determined true length and curvature, tapered it towards point, and determined height of point and nut. Invented method of fixing hairs on face of nut by means of movable metal band.

Tovey, (Sir) **Donald** (Francis) (*b* Eton, 1875; *d* Edinburgh, 1940). Eng. pianist, composer, cond., teacher, and writer. Began to compose at 8. Studied with Parratt, later with Parry. Oxford Univ. 1894–8. Pianist with Joachim 1894. Played own works at London chamber concerts 1900–1. Prof. of Mus., Edinburgh Univ. from 1914. Est. Reid orch. concerts 1917, for which he wrote celebrated programme-notes (pubd. in 6 vols. as *Essays in Musical Analysis,* 1935–8). Wrote opera *The Bride of Dionysus* (1918), vc. conc. (for Casals, 1935), much chamber mus. Made conjectural completion of unfinished fugue in Bach's *Die *Kunst der Fuge.* Many books and articles on mus. subjects. Knighted 1935.

Toward the Unknown Region. Song for mixed ch. and orch. by Vaughan Williams to words by Whitman from *Whispers of Heavenly Death* (1870). Comp. 1905–7. F.p. Leeds Fest. 1907. Set simultaneously in friendly competition by Holst, whose setting was judged (by the composers themselves) as inferior, and suppressed.

Toye. Light 16th- and early 17th-cent. comp. for virginals or lute.

Toye, Francis (John) (*b* Winchester, 1883; *d* Florence, 1964). Eng. mus. critic and author. Pupil of E. J. Dent. Wrote for various Eng. papers and journals, incl. *Morning Post* 1925–37. Author of books on Verdi (1931) and Rossini (1934). Lived later years in It. Comp. songs. Dir., Brit. Institute, Florence 1936–9. C.B.E. 1954.

Toye, Geoffrey (*b* London, 1889; *d* London, 1942). Eng. cond. and composer, brother of Francis *Toye. Studied RCM, then became Lloyds marine underwriter but combined career as cond. of opera and th. mus. Cond. f.p. of orig. version of Vaughan Williams's *London Symphony*, 1914. Cond., Beecham Opera Co. and D'Oyly Carte Opera Co. Manager, SW Opera 1931–4; man. dir., CG 1934–6. Wrote sym., songs, and popular ballet The *Haunted Ballroom* (1934).

Toy Symphony (Ger. *Kindersymphonie*). Simple sym. in which toy instr. are used, in addition to str. and pf. Most popular example, formerly attrib. to Joseph Haydn, is by Leopold Mozart, with toy instr. probably added by M. Haydn. Several others exist, e.g. by A. Romberg, and by Malcolm Arnold (1957).

Tr. Abbreviation for (1) trill or *tremolo, tremolando*, (2) trumpet.

Trabaci, Giovanni Maria (*b* Monte Pelusio, *c*.1575; *d* Naples, 1647). It. organist and composer. Organist at Naples churches 1597–1614, becoming choirmaster of royal chapel of Sp. viceroys in Naples 1614–47. Wrote motets, madrigals, and org. pieces.

Tracker. Rod (thin flat strip of wood) in mechanism of org. which connects kbd. to pallets. *Tracker action* is the operating of this linking-system, later succeeded by pneumatic or electric action, or by tracker-pneumatic action, a combination of both.

Tradotto (It.), **traduit** (Fr.). (1) Translated.
(2) Arranged (see *Arrangement*).
(3) Transposed.

Traduzione (It.), **traduction** (Fr.). (1) Translation.
(2) *Arrangement.
(3) Transposition.

Traetta, Tommaso (Michele Francesco Saverio) (*b* Bitonto, 1727; *d* Venice, 1779). It. composer. Studied in Naples 1738–48. Opera *Il Farnace* prod. with success at Naples 1751. Wrote 43 operas in all, 2 of them for Vienna. Succeeded Galuppi as Russ. Empress Catherine II's court composer 1768–75. Visited London without success. Also wrote choral works and instr. divertimenti.

Tragic Overture (*Tragische-ouvertüre*). Concert-ov. by Brahms, Op. 81, comp. 1880–1 and f.p. Breslau 1881. No particular tragedy is depicted.

Tragic Symphony. Schubert's own title for his Sym. No. 4 in C minor (D417), comp. 1816. Mahler orig. intended to call his 6th Sym. (1903–5) the 'Tragic', but changed his mind.

Trainé (Fr.). Dragged, slurred, lingering.

Trampler, Walter (*b* Munich, 1915). Ger.-born violist (Amer. citizen 1944). Studied Munich State Acad. Member Strub Qt., violist in Ger. Radio S.O. Went to USA 1939. Founding member of New Mus. Qt. 1947–56. Sometimes played with Budapest Qt. as extra va. for Mozart str. quintets and in Juilliard Qt. Prof., Juilliard Sch. from 1962. Soloist and chamber-mus. player. Commissioned and gave f.ps. of Berio's *Chemins* II and III (1969). Gave f.p. of va. conc. by Bainbridge (1978).

Tranchell, Peter (Andrew) (*b* Cuddalore, India, 1922). Eng. composer. Studied Cambridge Univ. (org. and pf. with B. Ord and H. Darke). Music lecturer Cambridge Univ. from 1950; dir. of mus. Gonville and Caius Coll. from 1960. Comp. opera *The Mayor of Casterbridge* (1951), mus. comedy *Zuleika*, several 'concert entertainments', incl. *The Mating Season* (based on P. G. Wodehouse, 1962, rev. 1969), anthems, etc.

Tranquillo (It.). Tranquil. So *tranquillamente*, tranquilly; *tranquillità, tranquillezza*, tranquillity.

Transcendental Studies (Liszt). See *Études d'exécution transcendante*.

Transcription. (1) Arr. of mus. comp. for a performing medium other than orig. or for same medium but in more elaborate style.
(2) Conversion of comp. from one system of notation to another.

Transfiguration de Notre Seigneur Jésus-Christ, La. Work in 14 movements to texts from the Bible, the Missal, and St Thomas Aquinas by *Messiaen for ten., bar., ch., pf., and orch. Comp. 1965–9. F.p. Lisbon, 1969, cond. Baudo.

Transfigured Night (Schoenberg). See *Verklärte Nacht*.

Transition. (1) Modulation from one key to another, particularly of a sudden and abrupt nature.
(2) Transition passage is one which acts as link between 2 more substantial passages (in sym., conc., etc.).

Transposing Instruments. Instruments which are not notated at their true pitch but (mechanically and without any effort on the player's part) produce the effect of that pitch. For example, the cl. is made in several sizes, the B♭ and A being the most often used because these keys reduce the difficulty of playing in the flat and sharp keys, respectively, by reducing the number of flats or sharps with which the player has to cope. In the B♭ instr., that key is to its player the 'natural key' (as C is to the pianist): the player faced with music in (say) the key of E♭ finds the music written in the key of F, i.e. there are 2 flats fewer to consider. Similarly with the A instrument a piece written in the key of B is notated in the key of D, i.e. there are 3 sharps fewer to consider. Thus music for the B♭ cl. is notated a tone higher than it is to sound and music for the A cl. a minor 3rd higher. Many players, with improved mechanism and developed technique, use the B♭ instrument for all keys, making the transposition mentally. On the rare C cl. the note sounded is the note written; the E♭ cl. transposes 1½ tones higher than written note; the bass clarinet in B♭ an octave and a tone lower.

The transposing instruments are as follows: (a) Bass Fl.; (b) Cor Anglais, Ob. d'Amore, Ob. in E♭, Heckelphone, Sarrusophone (c) Cl. in B♭ and A, Bass Cl., High Cl. in E♭ and D, Alto Cl. in E♭ and F, Basset Hn., Pedal Cl. (d) Saxophones (e) Cornets (f) French Hns. (g) Tpts. (h) Saxhorns (i) Kettledrums (up to Mozart's period, but excluding Handel).

Transposition. Changing of the pitch of a comp. without other change, e.g. the raising of the pitch of a piece in the key of C to that of key D, or its lowering to the key of B or A.

Transverse Flute. Side-blown fl., distinguished from recorder, which is end-blown and therefore held pointing downwards.

Trascinado (It.). Dragging. Holding back, same as *rallentando.

Trattenuto (It.). (1) Held back. (2) Sustained.

Tratto (It.). Dragged (used in the negative, *non tratto*, not dragged).

Traubel, Helen (b St Louis, 1899; d Santa Monica, Calif., 1972). Amer. sop. Studied St Louis, making début with St Louis S.O. 1926. Created role of Mary in W. Damrosch's *The Man Without a Country*, NY Met. 1937. Notable Met. success as Sieglinde, 1939. Leading Wagnerian sop. at Met. after Flagstad left, 1941–53. Left over disagreement about singing in night clubs. Wrote detective stories.

Trauer (Ger.). Mourning, grief. Hence, *Trauermarsch*, funeral march; *Trauermusik*, funeral mus.; *traurig*, heavily, mournfully.

Träumerei (Reverie). Pf. piece by Schumann, No. 7 of his *Kinderscenen*, Op. 15, 1838.

Trauermusik (Mourning Music). Work for va. (or vn. or vc.) and str. by Hindemith comp. (1936) in a few hours on death of King George V for perf. at concert the next day. Last of 4 short movements uses chorale *Vor deinen Thron tret ich hiermit* (The Old Hundredth).

Trautonium. Elec. instr. first exhibited in Berlin in 1930 by Friedrich Trautwein (b Würzburg, 1888; d Düsseldorf, 1956). Similar to *theremin, but with extra devices enabling the player to obtain the correct notes of the tempered scale and a variety of tone-colour. Hindemith wrote conc. for it in 1931.

Travelling Companion, The. Opera in 4 acts by Stanford to lib. by Henry Newbolt, based on story by Hans Andersen, comp. 1919, prod. Bristol, 1926.

Travers, John (b c.1703; d London, 1758). Eng. composer and organist. Chorister, St George's Chapel, Windsor, studying with M. Greene and Pepusch. Organist St Paul's CG, 1726, Chapel Royal 1737. Wrote psalm-settings for v. with kbd. continuo, services, and org. voluntaries.

Travesti (Fr.; Eng. 'trousers-role', 'breeches-part', Ger. *Hosenrolle*). Term to describe operatic roles which, though male characters, are sung by women, e.g. Romeo in Bellini's *I Capuleti e i Montecchi*, Cherubino in Mozart's *Le Nozze di Figaro*, Prince Orlofsky in J. Strauss's *Die Fledermaus*, Oktavian and the Composer in R. Strauss's *Der Rosenkavalier* and *Ariadne auf Naxos*.

Traviata, La (The Wayward One, or The Woman Gone Astray). Opera in 3 acts by Verdi to lib. by Piave based on Dumas *fils*'s play *La Dame aux camélias* (1852), based in turn on his partly autobiographical novel of the same name (1848). Comp. 1852–3. Prod. Venice 1853, London and NY 1856.

Travis, Roy (Elihu) (b NY, 1922). Amer. composer. Studied Juilliard Sch. 1947–50 (comp. with Wagenaar), Columbia Univ. 1950–1, and Paris Cons. 1951–2 (comp. with Milhaud). Teacher in NY 1952–7, then at Univ. of Calif. from 1957, working since 1969 in elec. studio. Comps. incl. opera *The Passion of Oedipus* (1965), *African Sonata* for pf., *Collage* for orch., pf. conc., septet, conc. for fl., pre-recorded African instr., and synthesizer.

Treatise on Orchestration (*Grande Traité de l'instrumentation et d'orchestration modernes*). Berlioz's historic book on orch. scoring pubd. in Paris in 1843 as his Op. 10. 2nd edn. (1855) incl. suppl.: *Le Chef d'orchestre, théorie de son art*. Trans. into several languages. (Eng. 1855). Ed. and enlarged by R. Strauss 1904–5, in Ger.

Trebelli (orig. Gillebert), **Zélia** (b Paris, 1838; d Étretat, 1892). Fr. mez. Studied singing with Wartel. Opera début Madrid 1859 as Rosina in *Il barbiere di Siviglia*, followed by brilliant success in Ger. London début 1862, CG 1868–71, 1881–2, 1888. Particularly admired in *travesti roles.

Treble. (1) Highest v. in choral singing, term today usually being applied to children, adult equivalent being *soprano.

(2) Upper part of comp., opposite in pitch of bass.

(3) Applied as adjective to certain high-pitched instr. e.g. treble recorder, treble viol.

Treble Clef. The sign 𝄞 (derived from old letter G) which indicates that the line on which it is placed is the G a 5th above middle C. Used for high-pitched instr., for high vv., and for right-hand pf. parts. For ten. v., treble clef is modified to indicate that notes are sounded octave lower than written.

Tremblay, George (Amédée) (b Ottawa, 1911; d Tijuana, Mexico, 1982). Canadian composer. Studied with Schoenberg 1936. In 1965 founded

Los Angeles Sch. for Discovery and Advancement of New Serial Techniques. Works incl. 3 syms. (3rd being based on all-interval row and its 288 permutations), 4 str. qts., ob. qt. etc.

Tremblay, Gilles (*b* Arvida, Quebec, 1932). Fr.-Canadian composer. Studied Montreal Cons. and in Paris, 1954–61, with Messiaen, Y. Loriod, and Martenot, also Fr. radio elec. studio. His mus. concentrates on wind and perc. and incl. *Sonorization* (elec. sounds on 24 tape channels), *Cantique de durées* for orch., *Kékoba*, ondes Martenot, *Champs* I, II, and III (I pf., 2 perc., II wind, brass, perc., pf., db., III wind, brass, perc., str.), *Solstices*, woodwind, perc., db., *Fleuves*, orch., and pf. works.

Tremolando (It.). Trembling. With **tremolo* effect.

Tremolo (It.). Shaking, trembling. (1) In playing of str. instr., the rapid reiteration of a note or chord by back-and-forth strokes of the bow; also, on other instr. as well as str., the very rapid alternation between 2 notes. Note that *tremolo* is the rapid iteration or alternation of *notes*, whereas **vibrato* is fluctuation of *pitch*.

Tremulant. Mechanical org. device, operated by a stop-knob, which varies the wind-pressure and thus imparts a 'wobbling' effect to the note being sounded.

Trepak. Lively Russ. popular dance in $\frac{2}{4}$ time, introduced by some Russ. composers, e.g. Mussorgsky, into their works. Famous example is in Tchaikovsky's *Nutcracker*.

Triad. Chord of 3 notes, basically a 'root' and the notes a third and a fifth above it, forming two superimposed thirds, e.g. C–E–G ('common chord' of C major). If lower third is major and the upper minor, the triad is major. If lower third is minor and the upper major, the triad is minor. If both are major the triad is *Augmented*. If both are minor, the triad is *Diminished*.

Trial. Term applied at Paris Opéra-Comique to ten. of dramatic rather than vocal powers who specializes in comedy. Named after Antoine Trial (*b* Avignon, 1737; *d* Paris, 1795).

Trial by Jury. Operetta in 1 act (styled 'dramatic cantata') by Sullivan, lib. by Gilbert, the only one of their works sung throughout (i.e. no spoken dialogue). Prod. London 1875.

Triangle. Perc. instr. of indefinite pitch, made of metal shaped into a triangle and struck with metal stick to give tinkling sound. Much used by composers to intensify excitement, e.g. in 3rd movement of Brahms's 4th Sym. Liszt's Pf. Conc. No. 1 in E♭ has important part for triangle.

Tribschen (Triebschen). Villa near Lucerne, Switz., on Vierwaldstätter lake, where Wagner lived from 1866 until 1872 when he moved to Bayreuth. On its staircase on Christmas Day 1870,

Siegfried Idyll was f.p. (orig. title *Tribschen Idyll*). (The spelling *Triebschen*, although incorrect, was Wagner's own.)

Tricorne, Le (Falla). See *Three-Cornered Hat, The*.

Trill (shake). Ornament comprising rapid alternation of main note and note above, normally slurred, and assoc. with cadences. Occurs instrumentally and vocally. Is indicated by *tr* 〰 and ✛ Wavy line often indicates length of trill.

Trillo del Diavolo (Tartini). See *Devil's Trill*.

Trimble, Lester Albert (*b* Bangor, Wisconsin, 1923). Amer. composer. Studied Carnegie Inst. of Technology 1944–8, at Tanglewood 1947 with Milhaud, and in Paris 1948 with Milhaud, Honegger, and N. Boulanger. Mus. critic *NY Herald Tribune* 1951–9. Prof. of mus., Univ. of Maryland 1963–7 and at Juilliard Sch. 1971–3. Works incl. opera *Boccaccio's Nightingale*, 3 syms., *Sonic Landscape* for orch., *4 Fragments from The Canterbury Tales* for sop. and ens.

Trinity College of Music, London. Mus. coll. incorporated as Trinity Coll., London, 1875, developed from mus. soc. founded 1872. In 1874 complete system of testing by examination, both of teachers and their pupils, was organized at centres throughout Brit. and Ireland and, from 1876, at centres in S. Africa and other places then under Brit. rule. Today TCL examiners visit nearly 40 countries. Now part of Univ. of London. Awards graduate diploma (GTCL).

Trinklied (Ger.). Drinking song.

Trio (It.). Three. (1) Any body of 3 performers together, or piece of mus. written for them to perform, e.g. **string trio*, usually vn., va., vc., *piano trio*, usually pf., vn., vc. The comp. called a trio is usually in sonata form and in 3 movements.
 (2) The central section of a minuet, scherzo, or march, usually in gentler contrast to the first section and its repeat. So called because formerly it was written in 3-part harmony, as for a trio.
 (3) A vocal trio may be acc. or unacc. In the 16th cent. the minor-key sections of the mass were often written for 3 vv.; there were also 3-part canzonets. In opera, the simultaneous combination of 3 vv. is a *trio*, a famous example being that for 3 sop. in Act 3 of Strauss's *Der Rosenkavalier*, but there are of course many examples of trios for 3 different types of v.
 (4) For the org. a *trio* is intended for manuals and the pedals, each in a different registration for contrast (and, of course, played by one performer).

Trionfi (It.). Triumphs. Theatrical triptych by **Orff comprising **Carmina Burana*, **Catulli Carmina*, **Trionfo di Afrodite*.

Trionfo di Afrodite (Triumph of Aphrodite). Scenic conc. by **Orff, the 3rd part of his trilogy **Trionfi*. Comp. 1950–1, to Lat. and Gr. texts by

Catullus, Sappho, and Euripides. For soloists, ch., and orch. Prod. Milan 1953.

Trio Sonata. Comp. prevalent in late 17th and early 18th cents. (Baroque period), usually for 2 vn. and vc. or bass viol, with kbd. continuo. The most important genre of Baroque chamber mus. Towards the end of the 17th cent. the form diverged into the *sonata da chiesa and the *sonata da camera. Among the most celebrated examples of the trio sonata are the 48 by Corelli, 12 by Purcell, 28 by Handel, 14 by François Couperin, and 12 by Vivaldi.

Triple Concerto. Conc. for 3 solo instr. and orch. or ens. Beethoven's is for pf., vn., and vc., but there are other combinations, e.g. Tippett's for vn., va., and vc.

Triple Counterpoint. That concerning 3 vv. or parts which are capable of changing places with one another, so making 6 positions of the parts possible.

Triple-croche (Fr.). Triple-hook. 32nd note, or demisemiquaver.

Triplet. Group of 3 notes, or notes and rests, equal in time-value, written where a group of 2 notes is suggested by time-signature. Usually indicated by adding numeral 3 above each group.

Triple Time. Where the primary division is into 3 beats. Usually indicated by figure 3 (in simple time) or 9 (in *compound time) as upper digit of a *time-signature, e.g. $\frac{3}{4}$ or $\frac{9}{8}$.

Tristan. Preludes for pf., orch., and tape by *Henze. Comp. 1973. F.p. London, 1974 (Homero Francesch, C. Davis).

Tristan und Isolde. Mus. drama (*Handlung*, action) in 3 acts by Wagner to his own lib., based on G. von Strassburg's *Tristan*, c. 1210, and ultimately on Arthurian legend. Comp. 1857–9. Prod. Munich 1865, London 1882, NY Met. 1886. The Prelude to Act I and Isolde's *Liebestod* (Love Death) are often perf. as concert item.

Tritone. Interval of augmented 4th which comprises 3 whole tones, e.g. from F up or down to B. Difficult to sing, and in medieval times its use was prohibited. There was saying, involving the Hexachord names for the notes, *Mi contra fa diabolus est in musica*, 'Mi against fa is the devil in music', hence the frequent use of the tritone in comps. to suggest evil.

Trittico, Il (The Triptych). Set of 3 1-act operas for perf. on one evening by Puccini, comprising *Il*tabarro (The Cloak) (1913–6), *Suor Angelica (Sister Angelica) (1917), *Gianni Schicchi (1917–8). Prod. NY Met. 1918, Rome and Chicago 1919, London 1920.

Triumphlied (Song of Triumph). Setting by Brahms, his Op. 55, for ch. and orch. of text from *Revelation*. Comp. 1871, f.p. 1872, to celebrate Prussia's defeat of Fr.

Triumph of Neptune, The. Eng. pantomime in 10 scenes, mus. by *Berners, lib. by S. Sitwell, choreog. Balanchine. Prod. London 1926. Orch. suite (1926–7), arr. Berners, longer suite arr. R. Douglas.

Triumphs of Oriana, The. Coll. of Eng. madrigals in 5 and 6 parts by various composers, ed. by *Morley in honour of Elizabeth I and dated 1601 but issued only after her death in 1603. Modelled on It. *Trionfo di Dori* 1592. In first edn. 24 composers were incl., as follows; Michael Este (*Hence Stars*); Daniel Norcome (*With Angel's Face*); John Mundy (*Lightly she Tripped*); Ellis Gibbons (*Long live fair Oriana*); John Benet (*All Creatures now are Merry-minded*); John Hilton (*Fair Oriana, beauty's Queen*); George Marson (*The Nymphs and Shepherds danced*); Richard Carlton (*Calm was the Air*); John Holmes (*Thus Bonny-boots*); Richard Nicholson (*Sing shepherds all*); Thomas Tomkins (*The Fauns and Satyrs*); Michael Cavendish (*Come gentle Swains*); William Cobbold (*With Wreaths of Rose and Laurel*); Thomas Morley (*Arise, awake*); John Farmer (*Fair Nymphs*); John Wilbye (*The Lady Oriana*); Thomas Hunt (*Hark, did ye ever Hear so Sweet a Singing?*); Thomas Weelkes (*As Vesta was from Latmos Hill descending*); John Milton (*Fair Orian*); Ellis Gibbons (*Round about her Chariot*); G. Kirbye (*Bright Phoebus*) (*With Angel's Face*); Robert Jones (*Fair Oriana*); John Lisley (*Fair Cytherea*); Thomas Morley (*Hard by a Crystal Fountain*); Edward Johnson (*Come blessed Bird*); Giovanni Croce (*Hard by a Crystal Fountain*). To these in later edns. were added: Thomas Bateson (*When Oriana walked to Take the Air* and *Hark, hear you not?*) and Francis Pilkington (*When Oriana walked to Take the Air*). There were 2 issues of first edn.: in the first Kirbye's madrigal has the words *With Angel's Face*, already set by Norcome, and in the 2nd the same mus. is set to *Bright Phoebus*.

For 20th-cent. Eng. composers' similar tribute to Elizabeth II, 1953, see *Garland for the Queen*.

Troilus and Cressida. Opera in 3 acts by *Walton to lib. by Christopher Hassall based on Chaucer and other sources (but not Shakespeare). Comp. 1948–54. Prod. CG 1954, San Francisco and NY 1955, Milan 1956; rev. and prod. CG 1963; further rev., with Cressida's role altered to mez., 1972–6, prod. CG 1976.

Tromba. (1) (It.). Trumpet.
(2) 8' organ stop.

Tromba da Tirarsi (It.). Drawing-out trumpet. Slide tpt., probably invented in 14th cent., and required by Bach in 7 of his cantatas.

Tromba Marina (It.). Marine trumpet. Not a tpt., but a type of *monochord, developed in 12th cent. Had 3-sided body about 4' long, tapering towards pegbox. Single str. (2 after 15th cent.) and played with bow. Produced only natural harmonics (hence assoc. with tpt. tone): player's left thumb lightly touched str(s)., his right hand drawing bow across str(s). Reason for 'marine' in title remains obscure (possibly corruption of Marian).

Tromba Spezzata (It.). Broken trumpet, i.e. *Trombone.

Tromboncino, Bartolomeo (*b* Verona, *c*.1470; *d* ?Venice, after 1535). It. composer, prolific composer of *frottole. Was at Mantua 1487–1501. In 1499 he murdered his wife and her lover. He was pardoned, but fled from Mantua in 1501 and for the next 6 years was in service of Lucrezia Borgia in Ferrara. In 1521 he settled in Venice.

Trombone (from It., large trumpet). (1) Nontransposing brass instr., derived from*sackbut, of semi-cylindrical bore and cup-mouthpiece, generally equipped with slide which serves to extend length of the tube. In any one of the 7 recognized slide positions, the 7 fundamental notes of harmonic series can be prod. a semitone apart. A few pedal notes can also be prod.: the first tones of the harmonic series in various positions. Tbs. make a noble sound and have been used by composers for dramatic effect, e.g. by Mozart in *Don Giovanni* and by Beethoven in his 5th sym., (their first use in sym.). Several tb. concs. have been written. In baroque times they were confined to church mus. but are now standard in military and brass bands, and have been effectively used in jazz (several brilliant solo players incl. Tommy Dorsey and Glenn Miller). Members of the tb. family are: *Treble*: required in scores by Purcell and Bach; *Alto*: much used in baroque mus. but later replaced by ten. Britten uses one in *The Burning Fiery Furnace*: *Tenor*: the most generally used, notated in either ten. or bass clef, with chromatic range from E below bass stave upwards for about 2½ octaves; *Bass*: compass is a 4th below that of ten.; *Tenor-bass*: ten. with a mechanism which allows for extra length of tubing for conversion to bass; *Double-bass* or *Contrabass*: octave in pitch below ten., sometimes required by Wagner; *Valve*: with valves in place of a slide. made in ten. and bass sizes.

(2) Org. stop, type of *tuba* or *tromba*, 16′ pitch, generally on pedal.

Trombonino (It.). Alto trombone.

Trommel (Ger.). Drum, thus *kleine Trommel*, sidedrum; *grosse Trommel*, bass drum; *Trommelschlägel*, drumstick.

Trompete (Ger.). *Trumpet.

Trompette (Fr.). *Trumpet, hence *trompette à coulisse*, slide tpt.; *trompette à pistons*, normal tpt.; *trompette basse*, bass tpt.; *trompette cromatique*, valve tpt.

Tronco, Tronca (It.). Broken off short, truncated (used of a note, especially in singing).

Trope. (1) Interpolations in plainsong words, resulting either in mus. melisma on one note or a fragment of new melody. Practice flourished from 9th to 15th cent., was abused, and finally banned by Tridentine reform. Survived only as the *sequence (trope set to final melisma of Alleluia).

(2) Term used by *Hauer to describe 44 pairs of unordered hexachords which are basis of his version of 12-note technique.

Troppo (It.). Too much. Found usually in such directions as *allegro ma non troppo*, fast but not too fast.

Troubadours. See *Minstrels*.

Trouble in Tahiti. 1-act opera by Leonard Bernstein, to own lib. Prod. Brandeis Univ. June 1952, cond. Bernstein; NY 1958.

Troutbeck, John (*b* Blencowe, Cumberland, 1832; *d* Westminster, 1899). Eng. translator and clergyman. Studied Oxford Univ. Precentor, Manchester Cath. 1865–9, minor canon, Westminster Abbey from 1869. For Novello's, trans. Bach *Passions*, *Christmas Oratorio*, *Magnificat*, etc., Beethoven *Mount of Olives*, Brahms *Song of Destiny*, Dvořák *Spectre's Bride*, *St Ludmilla*, Gounod *Redemption*, Weber *Jubilee Cantata*. His opera trans. incl. Mozart's *Così fan tutte* and *Die Entführung aus dem Serail*, Wagner's *Der fliegende Holländer*, and Gluck's *Orfeo*, *Iphigenia in Tauris*, and *Iphigenia in Aulis*.

'Trout' Quintet. Nickname of pf. quintet in A major by Schubert (D667), so called because 4th of 5 movements is set of variations on his song *Die Forelle* (The *Trout, 1817, D550). Comp. 1819.

Trout, The (*Die Forelle*). Song for v. and pf. by Schubert comp. 1817 (D550) to words by *Schubart. Exists in 4 versions, differing in only minor ways; last version (1821) has 5-measure pf. prelude. Used as theme for variations in *andantino* (4th) movement of his pf. quintet in A major (1819, D667), which is therefore known as the *'Trout' Quintet.

Trouvères. See *Minstrels*.

Trovatore, Il (The Troubadour). Opera in 4 acts by Verdi to lib. by Cammarano (with part of 3rd act and all 4th act completed after Cammarano's death by L. E. Bardare). Based on play *El trovador* by Gutiérrez. Comp. 1851–2. Prod. Rome 1853, NY and London 1855.

Trowell, Brian (Lewis) (*b* Wokingham, 1931). Eng. musicologist. Studied Cambridge Univ. with Thurston *Dart. Lecturer in mus. at Birmingham Univ., 1957–62, and King's Coll., London, 1964–5. Head of radio opera, BBC, 1967–70. Returned to King's Coll. 1970 as reader, becoming prof. 1974. Authority on 15th cent.

Eng. mus. and on opera of all periods. Has written important articles on Elgar.

Troyanos, Tatiana (b NY, 1938). Amer. mez. Studied Juilliard Sch., NY, graduating 1963, and with Hans Heinz. Joined NY City Opera (début in Britten's *Midsummer Night's Dream*, 1963), then NY Met. Went to Ger. to sing with Hamburg Opera, Aix-en-Provence Fest., 1966 (Composer in Strauss's *Ariadne*). Salzburg Fest. 1969. CG début 1969 (Oktavian), La Scala 1977 (Adalgisa).

Troyens, Les (The Trojans). Opera in 5 acts by Berlioz to his own lib. from Virgil's *Aeneid*. Comp. 1856–8. To achieve a staging, Berlioz in 1863 divided it into two operas: Acts I and II became *La Prise de Troie* (The Capture of Troy) in 3 acts; Acts III, IV, and V became *Les Troyens à Carthage* (The Trojans at Carthage) in 5 acts with prelude not in orig. score, this part being perf. in Paris 4 Nov. 1863. First prod. of whole work but with the 2 parts on successive evenings, Karlsruhe, 6–7 Dec. 1890, cond. F. Mottl, likewise in Glasgow 18–19 March 1935, cond. E. Chisholm. F.p. on one evening, London, CG 1957, cond. Kubelik, (but cut by 20 mins), f.p. complete on one evening, sung in Eng., Glasgow (Scottish Opera) May 1969, cond. Gibson, f.p. complete on one evening, sung in Fr., London CG Sept. 1969, cond. C. Davis.

Trumpet. (1) Metal wind instr. of cylindrical bore, which in last quarter of its length widens into a moderate-sized bell. Cup-shaped mouthpiece. Since mid-19th cent. fitted with 3 valves which admit air to additional lengths of tubing, making available harmonic series at 6 pitches. Either a transposing instr. in B♭ (which may be switched to A) with compass from e upwards for nearly 3 octaves, or non-transposing in C (a tone higher). Used in orch. and jazz bands, also in military and brass bands (though sometimes replaced by cornet). Medieval tpts. without slides, valves, or finger-holes, were restricted to 'natural' notes of harmonic series. Straight tpt. of that time was over 6′ long, made in jointed metal sections, often with flared bell. Known as buisine. Shorter tpts. were called *claro* or *clarion*. In Renaissance, new methods of metalworking greatly improved sound quality, and the brilliant, high-pitched effects required from the baroque tpt. by Monteverdi and others were obtained from the *clarino*. Mutes in that day were inserted so far into the bell that they raised pitch by whole tone. Members of tpt. family are: *bass trumpet*: rare, sounding in C an octave lower than normal valved tpt.; *piccolo trumpet*; pitched octave higher, and sometimes has 4 valves; *Bach trumpet*: 19th-cent instr., in D, specially made (with valves) to play high tpt. parts in works of Baroque period. Ravel, Stravinsky, and Britten have included it in certain scores, and Maxwell Davies wrote a sonata for it. See also under *Crook*.

(2) Org. reed stop, 8′ pitch.

Trumpet Marine (Marine Trumpet). See *Tromba marina*.

Trumpet Tune or **Voluntary.** Piece which, while not comp. for a tpt., imitates its sound, as on tpt.-like org. stop. Title *Trumpet Voluntary* was given by Henry Wood to his transcr. of a kbd. piece for organ, brass, and kettledrums. This piece was mistakenly attrib. to Purcell, but is now known to be by Jeremiah *Clarke.

Tryon, Valerie (Ann) (b Portsmouth, 1934). Eng. pianist. Studied RAM and with Jacques Février in Paris. Début London 1953. Specialist in Liszt.

Tsar's Bride, The (*Tsarskaya nevesta*). Opera in 3 acts by Rimsky-Korsakov to lib. adapted from L. A. Mey's play (1849) with extra scene by I. F. Tumenev. Comp. 1898. Prod. Moscow 1899, Seattle 1922, London 1931.

Tschaikowsky (Ger.). See *Tchaikovsky, Pyotr*.

Tschudi. See *Shudi, Burkat*.

Tuba. (1) Type of bass brass instr. played in vertical position in contrast to horizontal position of tpt., tb., etc. Term covers several kinds of brass-band instr., e.g. *euphonium, but term tuba usually means the standard orch. *bass tuba* in F (invented 1835) with compass from f an octave below bass clef upwards for about 3 octaves. Vaughan Williams comp. a conc. for bass tuba, 1954. There is a French 6-valve tuba which can cover four octaves and play Wagner contrabass parts. The *contrabass tuba* has become standard in orchestras since the 1940s, where it is known as the 'double C' (CC) tuba. This is a whole tone higher than the 'double B♭' (BB♭), with either 3 or 4 valves, which is generally used in bands. Most of tuba family are of semi-conical bore, with from 3 to 5 valves, and cup mouthpiece. The *tenor tuba* is rare, but is required by Strauss in *Don Quixote*, and in Brit. is identical with *euphonium*. Brass and military band tubas, sometimes called 'basses' are in E♭ (same as double-bass tuba). See also *sousaphone* and *Wagner tuba*.

(2) Sonorous organ stop, like *trumpet*, 8′, 16′, or 4′ pitch.

Tuba mirum (Hark, the trumpet). Part of the Requiem Mass, being a section of the *Dies Irae*. Verdi's setting is especially fine.

Tubb, Carrie (Caroline Elizabeth) (b London, 1876; d London, 1976). Eng. sop. Studied GSM. Principally known for work in oratorio, etc., but sang in opera (*Elektra, Hänsel und Gretel* etc.) at CG 1910 and later in Beecham co. Taught at GSM for over 30 years from 1930.

Tubin, Eduard (b Kallaste, 1905; d Stockholm, 1982). Estonian composer and conductor. Studied comp. at Tartu Acad., 1924–30. Cond. Vanemuine Th. Orch., Tartu, 1930–44. Keen interpreter of Stravinsky, Bartók, and Kodály. Settled in Swed. 1944. His mus. is strongly melodic and attractively scored. Comps. incl.:

ORCH: Syms., No. 1 (1934), No. 2 (1937), No. 3 (1942), No. 4 (1943), No. 5 (1946), No. 6 (1954), No. 7 (1958), No. 8 (1966), No. 9 (1970), No. 10 (1973); Vn. Conc. No. 1 (1941), No. 2 (1945); Db. Conc. (1948); Conc. for chamber orch. (1963).

VOCAL: *5 Hasjasoidu Songs*, bar. and orch. (1975); also 2 operas (1967, 1970).

CHAMBER MUS: Vn. sonata No. 1 (1936), No. 2 (1949), No. 3 (1963); pf. sonata (1950).

Tubular Bells. Orch. instr. in form of suspended tubes, tuned to the diatonic scale, struck by hammer held by player. Set of tubular bells sometimes spans an octave. Vaughan Williams wrote for them in finale of his 8th Sym., 1953–5.

Tucker, Norman (*b* Wembley, 1910; *d* Ruislip, 1978). Eng. pianist, opera administrator, and translator. Studied Oxford Univ. and RCM (pf. with H. Samuel and theory with R. O. Morris). Promising career as Mozart pianist cut short by manual disability. Co-dir., SW Th., 1947–54, dir. 1954–66. Under his aegis Janáček operas were brought into the Eng. repertory and (at that time) rare Verdi operas such as *Simon Boccanegra*, *Don Carlos*, and *Luisa Miller*. Nurtured Eng. singers such as Peter Glossop and Amy Shuard and conds. Colin Davis, Charles Mackerras, and Alexander Gibson. Trans. *Simon Boccanegra* and *Luisa Miller*, Janáček's *Káťa Kabanová*, *Excursions of Mr Brouček*, Einem's *Visit of the Old Lady*, and other works. C.B.E. 1956.

Tucker, Richard (orig. Reuben Ticker) (*b* Brooklyn, NY, 1913; *d* Kalamazoo, 1975). Amer. ten. Sang in synagogues as cantor, then studied NY with P. Althouse. Opera début NY Met. 1945, becoming prin. ten. there in It. and Fr. operas. CG début 1958 as Cavaradossi in *Tosca*. Sang opposite Callas at Verona in her It. début, 1947. Sang in Toscanini concert-opera perfs.

Tucket. Old Eng. term for fanfare or flourish.

Tuckwell, Barry (Emmanuel) (*b* Melbourne, 1931). Australian hn.-player. Hn.-player in Sydney S.O. 1947–50. Settled in Brit. 1951. Hallé 1951–3, SNO 1953–4, Bournemouth S.O. 1954–5, LSO 1955–68. Prof. of hn., RAM 1963–74. Formed Tuckwell Wind Quintet. Soloist in concs. and chamber works. O.B.E. 1965.

Tudor, Antony (orig. William Cook) (*b* London, 1908; *d* NY, 1987). Eng. choreog., dancer, and teacher. Studied with Rambert 1928, then with others. Joined Ballet Rambert 1930. Founded Dance Th. with A. de Mille 1937. Formed London Ballet 1938. Worked in NY 1940–50 as dancer and choreog. Royal Swed. Ballet 1949–50, NY City Ballet 1951–2. Dir. NY Met. Opera Ballet Sch. 1950. Joined teaching staff, Juilliard Sch. Dir., Royal Swed. Ballet 1963–4. Ass. dir., Amer.

Ballet Th. 1974. One of foremost and most perceptive 20th-cent. choreogs. Ballets (composers in parentheses) incl. *Dark Elegies* (Mahler) 1937, *Judgement of Paris* (Weill) 1938, *Gala Performance* (Prokofiev) 1938, *Romeo and Juliet* (Delius) 1943, *Lady of the Camellias* (Verdi) 1951, *Shadowplay* (Koechlin) 1967, *Knight Errant* (R. Strauss) 1968.

Tudor Church Music. Name of famous critical edn. of mus. by Brit. composers of 16th and 17th cents. pubd. in 10 vols., 1929, with appendix 1948, under editorship of Percy Buck, E. H. Fellowes, Sylvia Townsend Warner, and A. Ramsbotham. Vols. contain: 1. Taverner Masses. 2. Byrd Services, etc. 3. Taverner motets. 4. Gibbons services and anthems. 5. Whyte. 6. Tallis. 7. Byrd Graduals. 8. Tomkins services, etc. 9. Byrd masses, etc. 10. Merbecke, Aston, and Parsley.

Tudor, David (*b* Philadelphia, 1926). Amer. pianist, organist, and composer. Studied in Philadelphia and NY (with S. Wolpe). Organist, St Mark's, Philadelphia 1938–43, Swarthmore Coll. 1944–8. Taught pf. in NY 1948. Musician with Merce Cunningham Dance Co. from 1953. Began assoc. with ★Feldman and ★Cage 1948–9. Member 1951–3 of Cage's elec. studio project. Helped Cage in 1960s to pioneer 'live' elec. mus., as distinct from pre-recorded. Took part as pianist in f.p. of several Cage works, incl. *Music of Changes*, pf. conc., and *Atlas Eclipticalis with Winter Music*. Gave f.p. of ★Bussotti's *5 Piano Pieces for David Tudor* and f. Amer. p. of Boulez's 2nd pf. sonata. Also plays bandoneon, performing works written for it by Kagel. Expertise in elec. works has pioneered many techniques for composers. His own works use visual forces, e.g. light systems, laser projections, dance TV, etc. They incl.: *Fluorescent Sound*, *Rain Forest*, *Assemblage*, *Video/Laser* I, II, and III, *4 Pepsi Pieces*, and many 'collaborative realizations' of mus. by Cage, Oliveros, etc.

Tudway, Thomas (*b* c.1650; *d* Cambridge, 1726). Eng. composer and organist. Chorister, Chapel Royal, under Blow, 1660. Org., King's Coll., Cambridge, 1670–1726. Prof. of mus., Cambridge Univ., from 1705 (he was suspended from his university posts from July 1706 to March 1707 for making uncomplimentary puns about Queen Anne). Wrote church mus. and compiled (1714–20) 6 MS. vols. of Eng. church mus. from Reformation to Restoration.

Tunder, Franz (*b* Bannesdorf, 1614; *d* Lübeck, 1667). Ger. organist and composer. Organist, Marienkirche, Lübeck, from 1641. Founded Lübeck *Abendmusiken* (Musical Evenings) of church mus. played by str. and brass. Succeeded by son-in-law Buxtehude. Wrote org. works, church cantatas, etc.

Tune. (1) As noun. Melody.
(2) Upper part of any simple comp.

(3) As verb. To est. correct intonation of an instr., e.g. to tune a pf. so that it is 'in tune'.

Tuning. Adjustment of pitch in any instr. so that it corresponds to accepted norm. Str. players tune their instrs. just before playing by simple adjustments to the str., but kbd. instr. need lengthy professional attention.

Tuning-Fork. 2-pronged metal instr., invented 1711 by the trumpeter John Shore (b c. 1662; d London, 1752; noted for his playing of Purcell and Handel). When set in vibration, it produces a sound wherewith to check the pitch of instr. and to give the pitch to singers. Gives a 'pure' tone, without upper harmonics.

Tuominen, Harri Olavi (b Kuusankoskc, 1944). Finnish composer and cond. Studied in Helsinki, Prague, and Budapest. Comp. chiefly choral works.

Turandot. (1) Opera in 3 acts by Puccini to lib. by Adami and Simoni after Gozzi's play (1762). Comp. 1920–6. His last work, the final scene being completed by *Alfano. Prod. Milan 1926, NY Met. 1926, London 1927.

(2) Opera in 2 acts by Busoni to his own lib. after Gozzi, prod. Zürich 1917. Based on incidental mus. to the play comp. 1911.

(3) Incidental music by Weber, comprising an ov. and 6 instr. items, to Schiller's trans. of Gozzi's play, prod. Stuttgart, Sept. 1809. Hindemith used a theme from it in his *Symphonic Metamorphosis of Themes by Weber.

Turangalîla Symphonie (Sanskrit, Turanga, 'the passage of time, movement, rhythm', and lîla, 'play in the sense of divine action on the cosmos, also the play of creation, destruction, life and death, also love'). Sym. in 10 movements by *Messiaen for large orch. incl. ondes Martenot, pf., and section of pitched and unpitched perc. Largest of 3 works inspired by Tristan and Isolde legend (the others being 5 *Rechants and *Harawi). Commissioned by *Koussevitzky, comp. between July 1946 and Nov. 1948. F.p. Boston S.O. cond. Bernstein, 1949. F.p. in England BBC broadcast, cond. W. Goehr, 1953; public, 1954. Movements entitled: Introduction, Chant d'amour 1, Turangalîla 1, Chant d'amour 2, Joie du sang des étoiles, Jardin du sommeil d'amour, Turangalîla 2, Développement de l'amour, Turangalîla 3, Final. Basis of complete ballet, choreog. Petit, Paris 1968, and choreog. Vesak, San Francisco 1971. In 1960 at Hamburg 3 movements were used for ballet, choreog. Van Dyk.

Turbae (Lat.). Crowds. Name given to the chs. in oratorios and Passions in which the crowd participate in the action, e.g. in Bach's St Matthew Passion.

Turca, Alla (It.). In the *Turkish style.

Turchi, Guido (b Rome, 1916). It. composer, pupil of Pizzetti. On staff of Rome Cons. from

1941 (prof. of comp. from 1959). Dir. Parma and Florence Cons., 1967–72. Authority on Bartók. Works incl. opera The Good Soldier Schweik, Concerto breve for str. (in memoriam Bartók), 5 Comments on Bacchae of Euripides for orch., fl. trio, etc.

Turco in Italia, Il (The Turk in Italy). Opera in 2 acts by Rossini to lib. by Romani. Prod. Milan 1814, London 1821, NY 1826.

Tureck, Rosalyn (b Chicago, 1914). Amer. pianist and cond. Studied with Chiapusso 1929–31, then at Juilliard Sch. Début, Chicago 1923, NY 1935. Toured Europe from 1957, specializing in playing Bach on the modern pf. Formed Tureck Bach Players, London, 1959. First woman to cond. NY P.O., 1958. Prof. at Juilliard Sch. from 1972. Author of several books.

Turina (y Perez), **Joaquin** (b Seville, 1882; d Madrid, 1949). Sp. composer, cond., and pianist. Studied in Seville and Madrid, later at Schola Cantorum, Paris, 1905–13 (comp. with d'Indy). Cond. ballet in Sp.; prof. of comp., Madrid Cons., from 1931. Wrote mus. criticism. Works, nationalist in style, incl.:

OPERAS: Margot (1914); Jardín de oriente (1923).

ORCH: La *procesión del Rocio (1913); Danzas fantásticas (1920); Sinfonia Sevillana (1920); Ritmos (1928); pf. conc. (1931).

CHAMBER MUSIC: Str. qt. (1911); La oración del torero for str. qt. (also str. orch.) (1925); 2 vn. sonatas (1929, 1934); Circulo, pf. trio (1942).

PIANO: Sonata romántica (1909); 3 Andalusian Dances (1912); Mujeres espanoles (2 sets, 1917, 1932); Jardines de Andalucia (1924); 5 Tarjetas postales (1930); 5 Siluetas (1932).

VOICE AND PIANO: Poema en forma de cancionces (1918); Saeta en forma de salve; Triptico (1929).

GUITAR: Sonata (1931); sonatina; Fandanguillo (1926); Hommage a Tárrega (1932); Sevillana (1923).

Turini, Francesco (b Prague, c.1589; d Brescia, 1656). Bohem.-born It. composer. Studied Venice and Rome. Organist Brescia Cath. 1620–56. Wrote church mus., madrigals, and instr. sonatas (among the earliest trio sonatas).

Turkish Music. Name given in 18th cent. to mus. for cymbals, triangles, and bass drum, the typical instr. of Turkish military bands, several of which visited Austria. Thus Mozart introduced 'Turkish' effects into his opera Die Entführung aus dem Serail, K384 (1782) and called the finale of his pf. sonata No. 11 in A, K331 (1778) a rondo alla turca.

Turn. See Gruppetto.

Turner, (Dame) **Eva** (b Oldham, 1892). Eng. sop. Studied RAM. Joined ch., Carl Rosa Opera, 1916, singing with them to 1924. Went to Milan 1924 for audition with Toscanini. Début at Scala, Milan, 1924, as Freia in Das Rheingold. Thereafter est. as leading dramatic sop. in It. and Wagnerian repertory, particularly as Brünnhilde and as Puccini's Turandot (although she did not create the role). Sang with BNOC, then CG 1928–30, 1933, 1935–9, 1947–8. Member of Chicago Opera. Prof. of singing, Oklahoma Univ. 1950–9. Taught in London from 1959. One of orig. 16 soloists in Vaughan Williams's *Serenade to Music* 1938. D.B.E. 1962.

Turner, Walter James (*b* Shanghai, 1889; *d* London, 1946). Australian writer on mus., and poet. Mus. critic, *New Statesman* 1916–40. Wrote books on Beethoven, Wagner, Mozart, and aesthetics.

Turn of the Screw, The. Opera in prol. and 2 acts, Op. 54, by Britten to lib. by Myfanwy Piper based on Henry James's story (1898). Prod. Venice and London 1954, NY 1958. The 'screw' is represented by a theme and 15 variations, interludes between the 16 scenes. Scored for chamber orch.

Turnovsky, Martin (*b* Prague, 1928). Cz. cond. Studied Prague Acad. of Mus. Début 1952, Prague S.O. Cond., Brno State P.O. 1960–3, Pilsen Radio Orch. 1963–7, Dresden Staatskapelle 1967–8. Mus. dir. Norwegian Opera, Oslo 1975–80, Bonn Opera from 1981. Guest cond. leading European orchs.

Turski, Zbigniew (*b* Warsaw, 1908; *d* Warsaw, 1979). Polish composer and cond. Studied Warsaw. Mus. dir., Warsaw Radio 1936–9, cond. Baltic P.O. 1945–6. Works incl. 3 syms., 2 vn. concs., opera, str. qts., etc.

Tutti (plural of It. *tutto*, other forms *tutta, tutte*). All. (1) *Tutti*, meaning 'everybody', is loosely used. A *tutti* is a passage, e.g. in conc., where the orch. (but not necessarily or even usually the whole orch.) plays without the soloist. 'The opening tutti' is a phrase often used in this connection.

  (2) *Tutte le corde*, 'all the str.': In pf. mus., means 'cease to play Una *Corda*'. *Tutto il cembalo* means the same.

Tuukkanen, Kalervo (*b* Mikkeli, 1909; *d* Helsinki, 1979). Finn. composer and cond. Début as choral cond. 1930. Works incl. 5 syms., 3 sym.-poems, 2 vn. concs., vc. conc., opera, and songs.

Tuxen, Erik (*b* Mannheim, 1902; *d* Copenhagen, 1957). Ger.-born Danish cond. (Danish parentage; settled in Denmark 1916). Studied Copenhagen, Paris, Vienna, and Berlin. Cond. Danish State Radio Orch. 1936–41. Guest cond. of leading orchs. in USA and Europe.

Tveitt, Geirr (*b* Kvam, 1908; *d* Oslo, 1981). Norweg. composer and pianist. Studied Leipzig Univ. and Vienna State Acad., also privately with Honegger, Schmitt, and Villa-Lobos. Toured as pianist. Works incl. 6 pf. concs., 4 operas, 3 ballets, 2 concs. for Hardanger fiddle, sym., and 4 str. qts.

Twelfth. Org. stop of the *Mutation kind. Length and pitch 2⅔' sounding an octave and a 5th (i.e. a 12th) above normal.

Twelve-Note Composition (Ger. *Zwölftonmusik*). System of comp. in which all 12 notes within octave (7 white and 5 black notes of pf.) are treated as 'equal', in an ordered relationship where no group of notes predominates in any major/minor key system. One of first, if not the first, to devise such a system was J. M. *Hauer, but it is generally assoc. with *Schoenberg, whose 'method of composing with 12 notes which are related only to one another' was developed gradually 1920–25 and first used by him partially in his Op. 23 and Op. 24 (the *5 Piano Pieces* and *Serenade*) and throughout his Op. 25 (the *Suite* for pf.). In the Schoenberg method, all pitches are related to a fixed order of the 12 chromatic notes, this order providing the work's basic shape. The fixed order is called a note-row (or series or set). No note is repeated within a row, which therefore comprises 12 different notes and no other. The note-row is not a theme but a source from which the comp. is made. It can be transposed to begin on any of the 12 pitches, and it may appear in retrograde, inversion, and retrograde-inversion. Since each of these transformations may also be transposed, each note-row can have 48 related pitch successions. Schoenberg's foremost contemporary disciples were *Berg and *Webern, but it should be noted that their application of his theory differs considerably from his own, particularly in the case of Webern, who explored the possibility of 'cellular' comp., i.e. self-contained structures within the note-row. From his type of serialism, later composers progressed to *total serialism.

Certain composers, e.g. Dallapiccola, Frank Martin, and Stravinsky, have used 12-note technique but have retained not only their marked individuality of style but a relationship in their work to the major/minor system of tonality. Other composers who do not subscribe to Schoenbergian tenets have used all 12 notes without repeating any one note. Examples of this are to be found in Walton, Britten, Hindemith, and Shostakovich.

Argument will no doubt continue about which composer was the first to use 12-note technique. Medieval candidates may be found, and Skryabin's 'mystic chord' is a pointer. Hauer's system pre-dated Schoenberg's; and the Ger. critic Herbert Eimert has written that Jef Golyscheff comp. 'the first unequivocal 12-note music' in 1914.

Twilight of the Gods (Wagner). See *Götterdämmerung*.

Two Widows, The (*Dvě vdovy*). Comic opera in 2 acts by Smetana to lib. by Emanuel Züngel adapted from *Les Deux Veuves* by Félicien Mallefille. Comp. 1873–4, rev. 1879 and 1882, prod. Prague 1874, Wexford 1978.

Tye, Christopher (*b* *c.*1505; *d* Doddington-cum-Marche, 1573). Eng. composer. Lay clerk at King's College, Cambridge, 1537, having taken Mus.B. in 1536 after 10 years' study and teaching. Choirmaster, Ely Cath. 1543–61; Mus.D., Cambridge, 1545. Thought to have been teacher of Edward VI. In 1553 pubd. *The Acts of the Apostles*, trans. into Eng. metre, for 4 vv., with lute. Ordained 1560 and in 1561 became rector of Doddington-cum-Marche, Isle of Ely. Wrote anthems in popular and tuneful style, several motets, services, and masses, incl. a 'Western Wynde' mass, and the *Euge bone* mass. Also instr. *In nomines.*

Tympanon. Medieval name for *dulcimer.

Tympanum, Tympana. The kettledrum(s) as spelt in medieval documents (sometimes *tymbal*), but the modern spelling *timpani* is now standard.

Tyson, Alan (*b* Glasgow, 1926). Scottish musicologist. Studied Oxford Univ. (1947–51). Visiting prof. of mus., Columbia Univ., NY, 1969 and Univ. of Calif. at Berkeley 1977–8. Authority on Beethoven. Pubd. Clementi thematic catalogue 1967.

Tzigane (Gipsy). Concert rhapsody for vn. and pf. by Ravel, comp. 1924; also orch. version, 1924.

U

Überbrettl. Type of cabaret est. in Berlin 1901–2 by the writer Ernst von Wolzogen (librettist of Strauss's *Feuersnot*), in assoc. with the poets Bierbaum and Wedekind. Their aim was to raise standard of variety theatre by mimes, poems recited with mus., etc. Mus. contributions from such composers as Oscar Straus, Zemlinsky, and Schoenberg (whose *Pierrot Lunaire* of 1912 demonstrates the surviving influence of the cabaret).

Uccelli, Gli (Respighi). See *Birds, The.*

Uhde, Hermann (*b* Bremen, 1914; *d* Copenhagen, 1965). Ger. bass-bar. Studied Bremen. Opera début Bremen 1936 as Titurel in *Parsifal*. Freiburg Opera 1938–40, Munich 1940–2, Hamburg 1949–50, Munich again after 1951. Bayreuth Fest. 1951–7. CG début 1953 as Mandryka in *Arabella*, and 1954–60. NY Met. 1955–61. Created Creon in Orff's *Antigonae*, Salzburg 1949. Particularly fine as Wagner's Dutchman.

Uhl, Alfred (*b* Vienna, 1909). Austrian composer. Studied Vienna Hochschule für Musik (comp. with F. Schmidt). Teacher there from 1945. Works incl. 48 cl. studies, *Konzertante sinfonie*, cl. and orch., *4 Capriccios* for orch., *Gilgamesch*, oratorio, str. qts., etc.

Uhl, Fritz (*b* Vienna, 1928). Austrian ten. Studied Vienna State Acad. of Mus. 1947–52. Opera début Graz 1952. Munich Opera 1956, Vienna from 1961. Bayreuth 1957, Salzburg Fests. 1968–72.

Uilleann Pipes (*uilleann*, 'elbow'). Irish bagpipes, played by wind supplied by bellows held under player's arm.

Ukelele (ukulele) (from Hawaiian 'leaping flea'). Small 4-str. instr. like a guitar, of Portuguese orig. and introduced by the Portuguese to Sandwich Island *c.*1877. Patented in Hawaii 1917, where it became very common, its popularity spreading to USA and Europe. Easy to learn, with special notation. Played by strumming with fingers. Eng. popularity much aided by its assoc. with the Lancashire comedian George Formby (1905–61).

Ukrainian Symphony. One of nicknames for Tchaikovsky's Sym. No. 2 in C minor, Op. 17, 1872 (the other being 'Little Russian') owing to use of Ukrainian folk-tunes in 1st and 4th movements.

Ulster Orchestra, The. Sym. orch. of N. Ireland. Founded 1966 to give regular concert series in Belfast and in other towns in province. First recording 1979 (music by Harty to mark his centenary). Prin. conds.: M. Miles 1966–7; S. Comissiona 1967–9; E. Cosma 1969–74; A. Francis (ass. cond. from 1969) 1974–7; B. Thomson 1977–85; V. Handley from 1985. Orch. has toured England and has added several more works by Harty and Bax to its list of recordings.

Ultimos Ritos (Last Rites). Oratorio by *Tavener for sop., alto, ten., and bass soloists, 5 priests (speakers), ch., large orch., Comp. 1972. F.p. Haarlem 1974, f.p. in England, Winchester and London 1975.

Ulysses. (1) Cantata by *Seiber, 1946–7, based on text from Joyce's novel of same name (1922).
   (2) Opera (*Ulisse*) by *Dallapiccola, 1959–68, to his own lib. based on Homer.

Umstimmen (Ger.). To tune in some special way (see *Scordatura*). So the noun *Umstimmung*.

Unanswered Question, The (or A Contemplation of a Serious Matter). Orch. work by *Ives, comp. 1906, for tpt., 4 fl. (or 2 fl., ob., cl.), str., and pf.

Unda Maris (Wave of the sea). Org. stop much like *Voix céleste*.

Undine (Ondine). Ballet in 3 acts and 5 scenes by Henze, choreog. Ashton. Prod. London 1958, Munich, Berlin, 1959.

Unessential Note. A passing note, suspension, appoggiatura, etc., whereas an essential note is an actual note of a chord.

'Unfinished' Symphony. There are many unfinished syms. (e.g. by Tchaikovsky, Mahler, Elgar, Shostakovich) but this title is generally taken to refer only to Schubert's No. 8 in B minor (1822, D759). His 7th in E was also left incomplete. No one knows why the 8th was left unfinished—2 movements were completed and sketches exist for the scherzo. Romantic solutions have been invented, but the truth seems to be that Schubert either forgot about it or abandoned it because he could not find comparable inspiration for the 3rd and 4th movements. F.p. Vienna, Dec. 1865, cond. Herbeck. Among 'completions' of the sym. are those by G. Abraham (1971) and B. Newbould.

Ungar, Ungarisch (Ger.). Hungarian.

Unger, Caroline (*b* Vienna, 1803; *d* Florence, 1877). Austrian cont. Studied in Milan and Vienna (with Vogl and Aloysia *Weber). Opera début Vienna 1821 as Dorabella in *Così fan tutte*. In 1824 in Vienna sang in f.p. of Beethoven's 9th Sym. (it was she who turned the deaf Beethoven to face the audience after the 9th so that he could see applause). Sang for several years in It., creating roles in Donizetti operas and Bellini's *La straniera*.

Paris début 1833, winning high praise from Rossini. Retired on marriage 1843.

Unger, Georg (*b* Leipzig, 1837; *d* Leipzig, 1887). Ger. ten. The first Wagner *Heldentenor*. Created role of Siegfried at first Bayreuth Fest. 1876. Sang in London 1877 at Wagner's concerts in Royal Albert Hall, although he frequently failed to appear. Sang at Leipzig Opera until 1881.

Unger, Gerhard (*b* Bad Salzungen, Thuringia, 1916). Ger. tenor. Studied at Eisenach. Opera début Weimar 1947. Berlin Deutsche Staatsoper 1952–61, Stuttgart from 1961. Wide repertory of character parts, e.g. Captain in *Wozzeck*, Skuratov in *From the House of the Dead*, and Wagner's Mime and David, which he has sung in most of the world's leading opera houses.

Unger, Heinz (*b* Berlin, 1895; *d* Toronto, 1965). Ger.-born cond. Cond. Berlin P.O. 1919–33, Leningrad Radio Orch. 1934–6. Spent some years in Eng., guest cond. of leading orchs. Settled Toronto 1948.

Ungherese (It.). Hungarian.

Unison. Sounding of the same note by all perf., e.g. *Unison singing*, everyone singing the same tune but not in harmony.

Uniti (It.). United. Term used to revoke a direction such as **Divisi*.

Unit Organ. Type of org., sometimes called extension org., which, to save space, has various stops which 'borrow' pipes from each other, e.g. pipes of 8' stop may also be used for 4' stop by a connexion which draws on them an octave higher throughout. Cinema orgs. are unit orgs.

Universal Edition. Publishing house formed in Vienna 1901 by amalgamation of several privately-owned businesses. In 1904 bought Munich firm of Aibl which brought in many R. Strauss works. Other firms were absorbed and after Alfred Kalmus joined the firm in 1909 the catalogue was extended to include a large number of contemporary composers (Delius, Bartók, Mahler, Schoenberg, Webern, Zemlinsky, Szymanowski, and Janáček among them). Since the Second World War the firm has published works by Berio, Birtwistle, Boulez, Dallapiccola, Einem, Kagel, Kurtag, Ligeti, Shostakovich, and Stockhausen. Universal Edn. (London) was founded by Kalmus in 1937 and is an independent house.

Universal Prayer. Cantata by **Panufnik* to poem by Pope for sop., cont., ten., and bass soloists, 3 harps, org., and mixed ch. F.p. NY (Cath. of St John the Divine) cond. Stokowski, 1970.

Un poco (It., sometimes shortened to *un po'*; Fr. *un peu*). A little (often in the sense of 'rather').

Unprepared Suspension. Effect similar to **suspension* but without **preparation*, i.e. the sounding in a chord of a concordant note which is to remain (in the same 'part') in next chord as a discordant note.

Unterwerk (Ger.). Under work. **Choir Organ.*

Up-Beat. Upward movement of cond.'s baton or hand, especially to indicate beat preceding barline.

Upper Mordent. See *Mordent*.

Upper Partials. 2nd, 3rd, 4th, and higher tones in harmonic series which are at fixed intervals above fundamental.

Uppman, Theodore (*b* Pao Alto, Calif., 1920). Amer. bar. Studied Curtis Institute, Penn., with Steuart Wilson, Univ. of Calif. with C. Ebert. Opera début Stanford Univ., 1946 as Papageno. San Francisco Opera 1948, later NY City Opera as Pelléas. Created role of Billy Budd in Britten's opera, CG 1951. Début, NY Met., 1953 (Pelléas). Sang Billy Budd in f. Amer. stage perf. Chicago, 1970.

Upright Piano. Pf. in which str. are upright, (vertical), not, as in grand pf., horizontal. First built by Hawkins of Philadelphia, 1800.

Urhan, Chrétien (*b* Montjoie, 1790; *d* Paris, 1845). Fr. violinist and composer. Pupil of LeSueur. Joined Paris Opéra orch. 1816, becoming leader 1831. Comp. str. qts., pf. pieces, etc.

Ursuleac, Viorica (*b* Cernauti, Romania, 1894; *d* Ehrwald, Tyrol, 1985). Romanian sop. Studied Vienna and Berlin with Lilli Lehmann. Opera début Agram 1922; Frankfurt Opera 1927–30, Vienna 1930–4, Berlin 1935–7, Munich 1937–44. Salzburg Fest. 1930–4 and 1942. R. Strauss's favourite sop. in 1930s. Created roles of Arabella, Maria in *Friedenstag*, and Countess in *Capriccio*. Also sang Danae at Salzburg dress rehearsal of *Die Liebe der Danae* 1944. Married to cond. Clemens **Krauss*. CG début 1934. Had 83 roles in her repertory and sang 506 perfs. of 12 Strauss roles during her career.

Urtext (Ger.). Orig. text, meaning an edn. of a score giving, or purporting to give, composer's intentions without later editorial additions—much needed in case of **Bruckner*, for example.

Ussachevsky, Vladimir (*b* Hailar, Manchuria, 1911). Manchurian-born composer of Russ. parentage. Settled in USA 1930. Studied Pomona Coll., Calif., Eastman Sch. 1935–9 (with Hanson), and Columbia Univ. 1947–8. Taught at Columbia Univ. from 1947. Co-dir., Columbia-Princeton elec. mus. centre from 1959. Up to 1951 wrote mus. with Russ. romantic flavour, then experimented with tape-recorder comp. Since then has comp. mainly elec. mus., incl. scores for radio, TV, and films.

Ut. Keynote of major scale, according to system of vocal syllables derived from d'Arezzo, now generally replaced by *do* (*doh* in *Tonic Sol-fa). In many countries, incl. France, *ut* and *doh* have become attached to C in whatever key this may occur.

Utility Music. See *Gebrauchsmusik*.

Utopia Limited, or The Flowers of Progress. Operetta by Sullivan to lib. by Gilbert. Prod. London 1893, NY 1894.

Utrecht Te Deum and Jubilate. Setting by Handel, 1712–13, to celebrate Peace of Utrecht and f.p. in St Paul's Cath., London, 7 July, 1713.

Utrenja. Choral work by *Penderecki (1969–71) in 2 parts, both commissioned by W. Ger. Radio (Cologne). Part I, *The Entombment of Christ*, sop., cont., ten., bass, and basso profundo soloists, 2 mixed ch., and orch. F.p. Altenberg Cath. 1970. Part II, *The Resurrection of Christ*, for same forces plus boys' ch. F.p. Münster Cath. 1971. 'Utrenja' is the Russ. Orthodox matins.

V

Va. Short for viola.

Vactor, David van (*b* Plymouth, Ind., 1906). Amer. composer and flautist. Studied Vienna Acad. 1928–9, Paris Cons. (fl. with Marcel Moyse), and École Normale (comp. with Dukas). Flautist in Chicago S.O. 1931–43, flautist and ass. cond. Kansas City P.O. 1943–6, cond. Knoxville S.O. 1947–72 and prof. of mus. Univ. of Tennessee 1947–71. Composer of syms., vn. conc., va. conc., str. qts., *Walden* for ch. and orch., and many works involving fl.

Valdengo, Giuseppe (*b* Turin, 1914). It. bar. Studied Turin. Opera début Parma 1936 as Rossini's Figaro. Milan 1939. NY City Centre Opera 1946–8, Met. 1946–54, Glyndebourne 1955. Sang Iago and Falstaff in Toscanini's NBC opera broadcasts.

Valen, Fartein (Olav) (*b* Stavanger, 1887; *d* Haugesund, 1952). Norweg. composer. Spent early years in Madagascar. Studied Oslo Cons. 1906–9 and Berlin Hochschule für Musik 1909–11 (comp. with Bruch) and stayed in Berlin until 1916. Mus. librarian Oslo Univ. 1927–39. Came under influence of Schoenberg in 1913, and evolved own system of atonal polyphony. Wrote 5 syms. (5th unfinished), vn. conc., pf. conc., 2 str. qts., *Sonette di Michelangelo* for orch., 2 pf. sonatas, organ works, etc.

Valkyrie, The (Wagner). See *Walküre, Die*.

Vallas, Léon (*b* Roanne, Loire, 1879; *d* Lyons, 1956). Fr. musicologist and historian. Abandoned medicine for mus. Lecturer, history of mus., Lyons Univ. from 1908. Author of books on Debussy and Franck (both trans. into Eng.), and on d'Indy.

Vallée d'Obermann (Obermann Valley). Pf. work by Liszt, No. 6 of *Première Année (Suisse)* of *Années de pèlerinage* (1848–54).

Valois, (Dame) **Ninette de** (orig. Edris Stannus) (*b* Baltiboys, Ireland, 1893). Irish dancer, choreog., and administrator. Studied with Cecchetti. Danced at CG in opera ballet 1919 and with Ballets Russes 1923–6. Opened London Acad. of Choreog. Art 1926 (closed 1931) and began collab. with Lilian Baylis at Old Vic. First choreog. for Mozart's *Les Petits Riens*, 1928. Dir., Vic-Wells Ballet (later SW Ballet) 1931, running SW Ballet sch. at same time. Founded SW Opera Ballet (later SW Theatre Ballet) 1946 (became Royal Ballet 1956). Resigned as dir., Royal Ballet, 1963. Among ballets she choreog. are *La Création du monde* (Milhaud, 1931), *Job* (Vaughan Williams, 1931), *The Haunted Ballroom* (Toye, 1934), *The Rake's Progress* (Gordon, 1935), *The Gods go a-begging* (Handel-Beecham, 1936), *Checkmate* (Bliss, 1937), *The Prospect before us* (Boyce-Lambert, 1940), and *Don Quixote* (Gerhard, 1950). C.B.E. 1947, D.B.E. 1951.

Valse. See *Waltz*.

Valse, La (The Waltz). *Poème chorégraphique* for orch. by Ravel. Begun 1906–14, completed 1919–1920. F.p. Paris 1920. Also prod. as 1-act ballet, Paris 1928, Monte Carlo 1929, choreog. by Nijinskaya for Ida Rubinstein. Other versions by Balanchine 1951, Ashton 1958. Versions for solo pf. and 2 pf. by Ravel, for 4 hands by L. Garban.

Valses Nobles et Sentimentales (Noble and Sentimental Waltzes). Work for solo pf. by Ravel, comp. and f.p. 1911 (arr. for 4 hands by L. Garban). Orch. by Ravel 1912 for ballet *Adélaïde, ou Le Langage des fleurs* to lib. by Ravel, choreog. Clustine, prod. Paris 1912 (later lib. and choreog. Lifar 1938, Ashton 1947, MacMillan 1966, Hynd 1975).

Valse Triste (Sad Waltz). Waltz by *Sibelius, Op. 44, orig. comp. for str. 1903 as one of 6 items of incidental mus. to play *Kuolema* (Death) by Arvid Järnefelt, in Helsinki. Rev. for orch. 1904. Also arr. for pf.

Valve (Fr. *piston*; Ger. *Ventil*; It. *pistone*). Mechanism invented c.1813 by the horn-player Heinrich Stölzel and improved in 1818 in collaboration with Friedrich Blühmel, whereby all the notes of the chromatic scale were made available to brass instr. Pitch altered by increasing or decreasing length of tube through which wind must go to produce sound (except normal *trombones, for which slide is sufficient). 2 types in use, *piston*, in which piston works up and down in casing, and *rotary*, a 4-way stop-cock turning in cylindrical case and governed by a spring. Credit for the first type of valve must go to Charles Clagget, an Irishman, who patented an invention in 1788 which enabled pitch to be altered by means of a lever.

Valve Instruments. Brass instrs. which have *valves, i.e. all except certain *trombones.

Valverde, Joaquin (*b* Badajoz, 1846; *d* Madrid, 1910). Sp. composer, cond., and flautist. Played fl. in th. orchs. 1859–71, then cond. 1871–91. Wrote *zarzuelas and songs incl. the popular *Clavelitos* (Carnations).

Vamping. Improvised acc. to a song or instr. solo, often by pianist who cannot read notation but 'plays by ear'.

Vampyr, Der (The Vampire). Opera in 2 acts by Marschner to lib. by Wohlbrück. Comp. 1827. Prod. Leipzig 1828, London 1829.

Van Allan, Richard (*b* Clipstone, Notts., 1935). Eng. bass. Studied Birmingham Sch. of Mus. with D. Franklin. Glyndebourne ch. 1964 (John Christie Award 1966). CG début 1971. Created Jowler in Maw's *The Rising of the Moon* (Glyndebourne 1970). Has sung with ENO, WNO, Paris Opéra, and at Wexford Fest. Sang Ochs in *Der Rosenkavalier* for first time at San Diego 1976.

van Beinum. See *Beinum, Eduard van.*

van Biene. See *Biene, August van.*

Van Dam, José (*b* Brussels, 1940). Belg. bass. Studied in Brussels. Sang minor roles at Paris Opéra and Opéra-Comique 1961–5. Geneva Opera 1965–7, singing in f.p. of Milhaud's *La mère coupable* (1966). Deutsche Oper, Berlin, from 1967. CG début 1973 as Escamillo, a role he has sung with much success in all leading opera houses. Created title-role in Messiaen's *St Francis of Assisi*, Paris 1983.

Vandernoot, André (*b* Brussels, 1927). Belg. cond. Studied Brussels Cons. and Vienna Acad. Mus. dir., Belg. Nat. Orch. 1954, Brussels Théâtre Royal de la Monnaie orch. from 1960.

van der Stucken. See *Stucken, Frank V. van der.*

van Dieren. See *Dieren, Bernard van.*

Vanhal. See *Wanhal, Johann Baptist.*

Van Kampen, Christopher (Francis Royle) (*b* Pinner, 1945). Eng. cellist. Studied King's Coll., Cambridge, and RAM 1966–9. Début with Bournemouth S.O. 1967 in Elgar conc. Prin. vc., RPO 1970–3, London Sinfonietta. Soloist with leading orchs.

Van Rooy, Anton (ius Maria Josephus) (*b* Rotterdam, 1870; *d* Munich, 1932). Dutch bass-bar. Studied with J. Stockhausen in Frankfurt. Sang Wotan at Bayreuth 1897 and thereafter at every fest. until 1902, also Sachs in 1899 and Dutchman 1901 and 1902. Sang Wagner roles at CG 1898–1913 (except one season) and NY Met. 1898–1908 (except one season). Sang Amfortas in unauthorized *Parsifal*, NY 1903, and was banned from Bayreuth. Finest male Wagnerian of his generation, and equally good in Lieder. Retired 1913.

van Wyk. See *Wyk, Arnold van.*

Varady, Julia (*b* Oradia, 1941). Romanian sop. Studied Budapest Cons. Cluj State Opera 1960–70, Frankfurt 1970–2, Munich from 1972. Brit. début Edinburgh Fest., 1974 as Gluck's Alcestis. Outstanding Vitellia in *La clemenza di Tito* and other dramatic roles.

Varella-Cid, Sergio (*b* Lisbon, 1935). Portuguese pianist. Studied with father, later in London with Harold *Craxton and Ilona Kabos. Début 1942. Protégé of *Moiseiwitsch. Int. career.

Varèse, Edgard (*b* Paris, 1883; *d* NY, 1965). Fr.-born composer and cond. (Amer. citizen from 1926). Studied in Turin, Schola Cantorum, Paris, 1904 (comp. with d'Indy, theory with Roussel), and Paris Cons. with Widor. Lived mainly in Berlin 1907–15, active as cond. Went to NY 1915. Founder-cond. New S.O. 1919 to perform modern mus.; resigned because of pressure to popularize programmes. With Salzedo, founded International Composers' Guild 1921, devoted to new mus., which lasted until 1927, when (with Slonimsky, Ives, Cowell, and Chávez) founded Pan-American Assoc. of Composers. Returned to Paris 1928–32, then taught at Amer. colleges. Founded ch. to perform early mus. in NY 1940. Began to experiment with tape and elecs. 1953. Tireless experimenter with unusual sounds and instr. combinations, many of his works being patterns of rhythm and accents. Most of his early works, in a romantic idiom, are lost or destroyed. Prin. comps.:

ORCH: *Amériques* (1918–21); *Hyperprism*, small orch. and perc. (1923); *Octandre*, small orch. (1923); *Intégrales*, woodwind, brass, perc. (1924–5); *Arcana* (1925–7); *Ionisation*, perc. (1929–31); *Déserts* (with optional tapes) (?1950–4).

VOICE AND ORCH: *Offrandes*, sop., small orch. (1921); *Ecuatorial*, bass v. and orch. (1933–4); *Nocturnal*, sop., bass ch., orch. (1961, unfinished; ed. and completed 1973 by Chou Wen-chung).

INSTRUMENTAL: *Density 21.5*, solo fl. (1936).

ELECTRONIC: *Good Friday Procession in Verges* (1955–6); *Poème electronique* (1957–8).

Varga, Tibór (*b* Györ, 1921). Brit. violinist of Hung. birth. Studied Budapest Acad. 1931–8 with Hubay and Flesch. Début 1931. Prof. of vn., Detmold Acad. 1949–55. Founded chamber orch. 1954. Settled in Switzerland 1955. Founder of Sion Fest. 1964.

Variant. (1) Name for differing versions of same piece of mus.
(2) Sudden changes from major to minor.
(3) Differing versions of folk-songs, the tune often slightly altering from region to region.

Variation. Piece of mus. which is a varied version of a well-known tune or of an orig. theme specially comp. as basis for variations. Some variations follow the orig. tune closely, others make the briefest reference to it, sometimes harmonically rather than thematically. Popular form with composers from 16th cent., 'divisions on a ground' being the same as 'variations on a theme'. In some comps., one movement takes the form of a theme with variations, e.g. the finale of Beethoven's *Eroica* sym., and movements of several Haydn syms. Among famous sets of variations are Beethoven's on a waltz by Diabelli,

Brahms's on a theme by Haydn, Schumann's *Études symphoniques*, Strauss's *Don Quixote*, Elgar's *Enigma*, Rakhmaninov's *Rhapsody on a theme of Paganini*, and Britten's *Variations on a Theme of Frank Bridge*.

Variations. 6 works comp. between 1958 and 1966 in which *Cage took *indeterminacy to remarkable limits. Some of them consist of transparent plastic sheets inscribed with lines and circles, and instructions explaining how these can be 'performed' by any number of players using any means. In Var. V the performer is merely supplied with a description of previous perfs., involving actions as well as sounds.

Variations and Fugue on a Theme by Purcell (Britten). See *Young Person's Guide to the Orchestra*.

Variations on 'America' (*Variations on a National Hymn, 'America'*). Orig. work for organ by *Ives comp. 1891 or 1892. Arr. for orch. by William Schuman 1964 and for concert band by Schuman and W. Rhoads.

Variations on a Theme by Haydn. Orch. comp., 1873, by Brahms, Op. 56a, or in version for 2 pf., Op. 56b. Often called the 'St Anthony' Variations, because the theme is called the 'St Anthony Chorale'. Brahms took the theme from a suite in B♭ for military band (*Feld-partita*) by Haydn but research has shown that the theme was borrowed by Haydn. However, since Brahms named the work 'Variations on a Theme by Haydn' there seems no good reason to discard this title for a musicological nicety.

Variations on a Theme of Frank Bridge. Work for str. orch. Op. 10, by Britten comp. 1937 for Salzburg Fest. Theme is taken from *Bridge's *Idyll* No. 2 for str. qt. Arr. for 2 pfs., 1942, by Colin McPhee for ballet *Jinx*.

Varnay, Astrid (*b* Stockholm, 1918). Swed.-born sop. of Austro-Hungarian parentage, resident in USA since childhood. Studied with her mother and H. Weigert. Opera début NY Met. 1941 as last-minute deputy for Lotte *Lehmann as Sieglinde in *Die Walküre*. Stayed at Met. until 1956, becoming leading Wagnerian and Strauss sop. CG 1948–9, 1951, 1958–9, and 1968. Bayreuth 1951–67. Exciting Wagnerian singer. Late in career sang mez. roles, e.g. Strauss's Klytemnestra, and made deep impression as Kostelnička in Janáček's *Jenůfa*.

Varsoviana, Varsovienne. A dance originating in France during 1850s, a slow, genteel type of *mazurka. Popular at balls in the Tuileries. Named from Fr. form of 'Warsaw'.

Varviso, Silvio (*b* Zürich, 1924). Swiss cond. Studied Zürich Univ. and in Vienna with Krauss. 1st cond., Basle Opera 1950–62. Leading opera cond. at int. fests. NY Met. début 1961, CG 1962, Glyndebourne 1962 (*Rosenkavalier*). Prin. cond. Stockholm Royal Opera 1965–71. Mus. dir.,

Württemberg Opera, Stuttgart, 1972–8. Bayreuth Fest. 1969–74 (*Die Meistersinger*). Mus. dir. Paris Opéra from 1981.

Vásáry, Tamás (*b* Hungary, 1933). Hung. pianist and cond. Studied Liszt Acad., Budapest, with Hernadi and Kodály. Début at age 8. Taught theory, Liszt Acad. Swiss resident from 1958. London début 1961, NY 1962. World tours. Specialist in Liszt. Joint cond., Northern Sinfonia 1979–82.

Vasilenko, Sergey (*b* Moscow, 1872; *d* Moscow, 1956). Russ. composer. Studied Moscow Cons. Prof. of comp., Moscow Cons. 1906–41, 1943–56. Wrote 5 operas (incl. *Christopher Columbus*, 1933), 5 syms., symphonic poems, ballets, balalaika conc., 3 str. qts., songs, etc.

Vaudeville (Fr., either from *vaux de vire* or *voix de ville*). (1) In late 16th cent., song with amorous words as sung in the valleys (*vaux*) near Vire or catches sung in the streets of towns.
(2) In 18th cent., the term came to mean a song with different verses sung in turn by different singers, and this meaning was incorporated into operatic terminology, e.g. a 'vaudeville finale', as in Mozart's *Die Entführung aus dem Serail*.
(3) In 19th cent., meant short comedies interspersed with popular songs, as in Fr. revues.
(4) In late 19th and 20th cents., a synonym for a variety show or mus.-hall, particularly in USA.

Vaughan, Denis (*b* Melbourne, Victoria, 1926). Australian cond., organist, and musicologist. Studied Melbourne Univ. and at RCM (org. with Thalben-Ball, db. with E. Cruft). Org. and kbd. recitalist in Europe and USA 1948–56. Played db. in Beecham's RPO from 1949. Operatic work at Glyndebourne, Munich, Bayreuth, and in It. Ass. cond. to Beecham 1954–7. Made special study of Verdi's and Puccini's autographs, noting discrepancies in printed scores, etc.

Vaughan, Elizabeth (*b* Llanfyllin, Montgomery, 1937). Welsh soprano. Studied RAM (with Olive Groves) and won 1959 Ferrier schol. Sang Abigaille with WNO 1960. CG début 1961, where she has sung Mimi, Tosca, Liù, Tytania, and Violetta. NY Met. début 1972 (Donna Elvira). A particularly fine Butterfly.

Vaughan Williams, Ralph (*b* Down Ampney, Glos., 1872; *d* London, 1958). Eng. composer, cond., and organist. Studied at Cambridge Univ. and RCM, teachers incl. Parry, Charles Wood, Alan Gray, and Stanford; later in Ger. with Bruch and in Paris 1908 with Ravel. Organist, St Barnabas, S. Lambeth, 1897. Began collecting Eng. folk-songs 1902. Mus. ed., *English Hymnal*, 1906. Cond. Leith Hill (Dorking) Fest., 1905–53. Prof. of comp. RCM 1919–39. Cond., Bach Choir, London, 1920–7. O.M. 1935.

One of leaders, with Holst and others, of 20th-cent. revival of Eng. mus. in wake of Elgar. Early works mainly songs, such as the famous *Linden*

Lea and Silent Noon, and chamber mus. Deeply influenced by revival of interest in Eng. 16th-cent. composers and by his own folk-song collecting. Studied for 3 months with Ravel when 36 and thereafter produced series of major works, incl. *Fantasia on a Theme by Thomas Tallis* for str., *On Wenlock Edge*, song-cycle on Housman's 'Shropshire Lad' poems, and *A London Symphony* (1913). Served in 1914–18 war although over military age and after war was active in every phase of Eng. mus. life as cond. of amateur choral fests., teacher, writer, and of course composer. Lived at Dorking, Surrey, 1929–53, then returned to London. Gave constant encouragement to young musicians; had strong prejudices, about which he wrote entertainingly in various essays.

Vaughan Williams's mus. is strongly individual, with the modal harmonies characteristic of folk-song composers, yet owing something to Fr. influence of Ravel and Debussy. He wrote works in almost every genre, from operas and syms. to choral works for amateurs as well as for highly professional choirs, concs. for neglected instrs. such as harmonica and tuba, a suite for pipes, etc. He believed that a composer should 'make his art an expression of the whole life of the community', but he was paradoxically a very personal composer rather than a state laureate. His operas have not so far held the stage, except for *Riders to the Sea*, but all are spasmodically revived, for they contain fine mus. His 9 syms. range from the choral *Sea Symphony* (Whitman text) and the picturesque *London* to the programmatic *Antartica* and the sternly 'absolute' Nos. 4, 5, 6, and 9. A wide range of orch. colour is deployed in these works and in his large-scale choral works such as *Sancta Civitas*. The basis of his work is melody, rhythm sometimes being unsubtle, but its visionary quality, as in the masque *Job* and the 5th and 9th syms., its broad humanity, and its appeal at several levels make it a remarkable expression of the nat. spirit in mus. just as the man himself personified all that was best in the liberal 19th-cent. tradition of which he was a scion. Prin. works:

OPERAS: *Hugh the Drover* (1910–14, rev. 1924 and 1956); *The *Shepherds of the Delectable Mountains* (1921–22); *Sir John in Love* (1924–8); *Riders to the Sea* (1925–32); *The *Poisoned Kiss* (1927–9, rev. 1934–7, 1956–7); *The *Pilgrim's Progress* (1925–36, 1944–51).

ORCH: Symphonies: *A *Sea Symphony*, sop., bar., ch., and orch. (1903–9), *A *London Symphony* (1911–13), *A *Pastoral Symphony* (1916–21), No. 4 in F minor (1931–4), No. 5 in D (1938–43), No. 6 in E minor (1944–7), *Sinfonia Antartica* (1949–52), No. 8 in D minor (1953–5), No. 9 in E minor (1956–7, rev. 1958); *In the Fen Country* (1904, rev. 1905, 1907, 1908, 1935); *Norfolk Rhapsody* (1906, rev. c.1921); Aristophanic Suite, *The *Wasps* (1909, orig. incidental mus.); *Fantasia on a Theme by Thomas Tallis*, str. qt. and

double str. orch. (1910, rev. 1913, 1919); *Charterhouse Suite* (1923, orch. of 6 pf. pieces); *English Folk Songs*, suite for military band (1923, arr. full orch. Jacob 1942, brass band Jacob 1956); *Sea Songs* (1942, version of march for bands 1923); *The Running Set* (1933); *Fantasia on Greensleeves* (arr. from *Sir John in Love* by Greaves, 1934); *2 Hymn-Tune Preludes* (1936); *Serenade to Music* (1940, orch. version of ch. work); *Partita*, double str. orch. (1946–8); *5 Variants of *Dives and Lazarus*, str. and harps (1939); Suite, *Story of a Flemish Farm* (1945; see Film Music); *Concerto grosso*, str. (1950); *Prelude on an old carol tune* (1953); *Prelude on 3 Welsh Hymn Tunes*, brass band (1954); *Variations*, brass band (1957; arr. for orch. Jacob 1959); *Flourish for Glorious John* (1957, 'Glorious John' being affectionate name for *Barbirolli).

CONCERTOS, etc: The *Lark Ascending*, Romance, vn. and orch. (1914, rev. 1920); *Flos Campi*, suite for va., ch., and orch. (1925); vn. conc. in D minor, with str. (1924–5); pf. conc. in C (1926–31, rev. 1946 for 2 pf. with some new material); Suite for va. and small orch. (1934); ob. conc. in A minor, with str. (1943–4); *Fantasia on Old 104th Psalm Tune*, pf., ch., and orch. (1949); Romance in D♭, harmonica, str., pf. (1951); tuba conc. in F minor (1954).

BALLETS, etc: *Old King Cole*, with optional ch. (1923, also suite); *On Christmas Night*, masque (1925–6); *Job, a Masque for Dancing* (1927–30); *The Bridal Day*, masque (1938–9, rev. 1952–3); *The First Nowell*, nativity play for soloists, ch., orch. (1958).

CHORUS AND ORCH: *Toward the Unknown Region* (1905–7); *A *Sea Symphony*; *5 Mystical Songs*, bar., optional ch., and orch. (1911); *Fantasia on Christmas Carols*, bar., ch., and orch. (1912); *Lord, Thou hast been our refuge* (1921); *Sancta Civitas*, ten., bar., ch., orch. (1923–5); *In Windsor Forest* (cantata from *Sir John in Love) (1931); *Benedicite*, sop., ch., orch. (1929); *The 100th Psalm* (1929); *Magnificat*, cont., fl., women's ch., orch. (1932); *Five Tudor Portraits*, choral suite, mez., bar., ch., orch. (1935); *Dona nobis pacem*, sop., bar., ch., orch. (1936); Festival Te Deum (1937); *Serenade to Music* (1938); Epithalamion, bar., ch., orch. (1957, based on Bridal Day); Thanksgiving for Victory, sop., speaker, ch., orch. (1944); An *Oxford Elegy, speaker, ch., orch. (1949); Folk Songs of the 4 Seasons, women's ch. and orch. (1949); The Sons of Light (1950); The Old 100th Psalm Tune (1953); *Hodie (This Day), Christmas cantata, sop., ten., bar., ch., and orch. (1953–4).

VOCAL: *3 Elizabethan Songs* (1890–1902); *5 English Folk Songs* (1913); *O clap your hands* (1920); *O vos omnes* (1922); Mass in G minor, unacc. double ch. (1920–1); Services in D minor (1939); *6 Choral Songs in time of War* (1940); *Valiant for Truth* (1940); *The Souls of the Righteous* (1947); *Prayer to the Father of Heaven* (1948); *3 Shakespeare Songs* (1951); *O taste and see* (1952); *Silence and

Music (1953); *Heart's Music* (1954); *A *Vision of Aeroplanes* (1956); and many folk-song arrs.

VOICE AND ENSEMBLE: **On Wenlock Edge*, ten., str. qt., pf. (1908–09); *4 Hymns*, ten., pf., va. (or str. and va.) (1914); *Merciless Beauty*, v. and str. trio or pf. (1921).

SONGS (excluding above): *Linden Lea* (1901); *Silent Noon* (1903); *Orpheus with his lute* (1901 and new setting 1925); *The House of Life*, 6 Rossetti sonnets, v. and pf. (1903); **Songs of Travel*, 9 Stevenson poems for v. and pf. (1904, 3 orch. by composer 1905, rest by R. Douglas 1960); *Dreamland* (1905); *Buonaparty* (1908); *2 Poems by Seumas O'Sullivan* (1925); *3 Songs from Shakespeare* (1925); *4 Poems by Fredegond Shove* (1925); *3 Poems by Whitman* (1925); *Along the Field*, 8 Housman songs, v. and vn. (1926); *7 Songs from 'The Pilgrim's Progress'* (1952); *In the Spring* (1952); *10 Blake Songs*, v. and ob. (1957); *3 Vocalises*, sop. and cl. (1958); *4 Last Songs* v. and pf. (1954–8); and many folk-song arrs.

CHAMBER MUSIC: Str. Qts.: No. 1 in G minor (1908, rev. 1921), No. 2 in A minor (1942–4); *Phantasy Quintet* (1912); *Suite de Ballet*, fl. and pf. (1920); *6 Studies in English Folk-Song*, vc. (or vn., va., cl.) and pf. (1926); *Suite for Pipes* (1938–9); *Household Music*, str. qt. or alternatives (1940–1); vn. sonata in A minor (1954).

PIANO: *Suite of 6 short Pieces* (1920, arr. for str. as *Charterhouse Suite*); *Hymn-Tune Prelude on 'Song 13' by O. Gibbons* (1928); *6 Teaching Pieces* (1934); *Introduction and Fugue* (2 pf.) (1946); *The lake in the mountains* (1947).

ORGAN: *3 Preludes on Welsh Hymn-Tunes* (1920); *Prelude and Fugue* in C minor (1930); *Wedding Tune for Ann* (1943); *2 Organ Preludes* (1956).

FILM MUSIC: *49th Parallel* (1940–1); *Coastal Command* (1942); *The People's Land* (1941–2); *The Flemish Farm* (1943); *Stricken Peninsula* (1944); *The Loves of Joanna Godden* (1946); *Scott of the Antarctic* (1947–8); *Dim Little Island* (1949); *Bitter Springs* (1950); *The England of Elizabeth* (1955); *The Vision of William Blake* (1957).

Vautor, Thomas (*b* c.1580). Eng. composer, one of last of madrigal sch. Pubd. madrigal coll., 1619, for vv. and viols., incl. *Sweet Suffolk Owl*.

Vazsonyi, Bálint (*b* Budapest, 1936). Hung. pianist and writer. Studied Liszt Acad., Budapest, Vienna Acad. 1957–8, and Florida State Univ. 1960. Début Budapest 1948. Soloist with leading orchs. Author of books on Dohnányi and Schumann's pf. mus. Settled in London.

Vc. Short for violoncello.

Veasey, Josephine (*b* Peckham, London, 1930). Eng. mez. Studied with Audrey Langford and sang in CG chorus 1949–50. CG début as soloist 1955 (Shepherd Boy in *Tannhäuser*). Sang major Wagner roles at CG under Solti régime, also Dorabella, Berlioz's Dido, Eboli, Oktavian, and Herodias. Glyndebourne 1969 (*Werther*). NY Met. 1968. Created Emperor in Henze's *We Come to the River*, CG 1976. Successful career on concert-platform in Verdi *Requiem*, Berlioz's *Nuits d'Été*, etc. Retired from opera 1982.

Vecchi, Orazio (*b* Modena, 1550; *d* Modena, 1605). It. composer and priest. Choirmaster, Modena Cath., 1584–6 and 1593–1605, and court choirmaster there from 1598. Wrote madrigals, masses, motets. His *L'*Amfiparnaso*, comp. 1594 and prod. Modena 1594, is the first known example of a madrigal-comedy.

Vega, Aurelio de la (*b* Havana, 1925). Cuban-born Amer. composer. Studied music privately 1942–6 in Havana and 1947–9 with *Toch in Calif. and at Havana Institute 1950–5. Dean of mus. sch., Oriente Univ., Santiago de Cuba, 1953–9. Dir., elec. studio, San Fernando Valley State Coll., Calif., from 1960. Mus. critic in Havana 1950–7. Style has progressed from influence of Berg to that of Boulez, and later to *avant-garde*. Works incl. *Overture to a Serious Farce* (1950), str. qt. in memory of Berg, woodwind quintet, Symphony, *Vectors* (mono tape), *Interpolation*, cl. and tape, *Toccata* for pf., etc.

Végh, Sándor (*b* Koloszvár, 1905). Hung. violinist. Studied in Budapest. Founded Hungarian Trio 1931, founder and 2nd vn. Hungarian Qt. 1935. Prof. of vn., Budapest Hochschule 1940; founder and leader Végh Qt. 1940. Left Hung. 1946, teaching in Switz. and Ger. Végh Qt. famous for Bartók interpretations. Has given some of the most successful televised *master classes.

Veloce, velocemente (It., superlatives *velocissimo*, *velocissimamente*). With speed, very fast.

Venetian Games (*Gry weneckie*; *Jeux vénétiens*). Work for orch. by *Lutosławski, comp. 1960–1. First in which he used *aleatory procedures.

Venice. Italian city, capital of region of Veneto. Its importance as a musical centre dates from 1527 when the Netherlands composer *Willaert was appointed choirmaster of S. Marco Cath. Through his influence, Venice became centre of madrigal composition in private houses and academies. Under Zarlino, choirmaster from 1564, an instr. ens. was formed (1568) which, augmented, performed at large fests. Use of choral and instr. forces by dividing them into groups placed in different galleries of the cath. (*cori spezzati*) led to the dominating splendour of Venetian church mus. 1575–1610, notably under G. *Gabrieli and A. *Gabrieli. In 1612 *Monteverdi was appointed choirmaster and remained for 30 years. He revivified the city's musical life, introducing younger composers, e.g. Cavalli and Grandi. The plague of 1630 ended the dominance of S. Marco in Venetian music-making and the balance was tipped towards operas, of which Monteverdi provided several masterly examples and was followed by Cavalli. Refusal of the authorities after 1642 to raise the salary of the choirmaster led to a decline in standard, halted only by Legrenzi, who achieved an increase in the size of the choir and orch. (to 36 and 34 respectively).

After 1700 Venetian musicians made their living in the *ospedali*, charitable institutions for the sick and orphaned where mus. was taught and perf. in the chapels. From this milieu arose the next great sch. of Venetian composers, Vivaldi, Porpora, Sarti, Galuppi, Jommelli, and Albinoni. Visitors to Venice included Gasparini, A. Scarlatti, and Handel.

Galuppi excelled in *opera buffa* and collab. with the playwright Goldoni from 1749. Opera thrived again after the opening of the Teatro La *Fenice in 1792 with a work by Paisiello. No Venetian sch. now existed, but f.ps. were given at La Fenice of operas by Cimarosa, Rossini (*Tancredi*, 1813), Meyerbeer (*Il Crociato in Egitto*, 1824), Bellini (*I Capuleti e i Montecchi*, 1830), and Donizetti (*Maria di Rudenz*, 1838). Several Verdi operas were commissioned for La Fenice, notably *La Traviata*, 1853.

In the 20th cent. La Fenice has been the birthplace of Dallapiccola's *Marsia* (1948), Stravinsky's *The Rake's Progress* (1951), Britten's *The Turn of the Screw* (1954), Prokofiev's *The Fiery Angel* (1955), Nono's *Intolleranza* (1960), and Bussotti's *Lorenzaccio* (1973). It has also staged the Venetian Malipiero's operas. These operas were given at the annual fest. of contemporary mus. held between 1948 and 1973. Stravinsky also comp. several choral and instr. works for Venice 1956–60 and was buried there near *Diaghilev. The fascination of Venice for composers is epitomized by Britten's opera *Death in Venice* (1973) and it was in Venice that the dying composer wrote some of his 3rd str. qt. (1975). And not the least of Venice's claims to musical fame is that Richard Wagner died there on 13 Feb., 1883.

Veni Creator Spiritus (Come Holy Ghost). Whitsuntide hymn generally attrib. Hrabanus Maurus, 9th-cent. Archbishop of Mainz, and sung liturgically to harmonized adaptation of plainsong melody. Set by several composers. Mahler's setting for soloists, ch., and orch. forms Part I of his 8th Sym. (1906–7).

Veni Sancte Spiritus (Come Holy Spirit). *Sequence of R. C. liturgy for Whitsunday sung to traditional plainsong. Text ascribed to Pope Innocent III and Stephen Langton. Settings include those by Dufay, Desprès, Willaert, Palestrina, and Victoria.

Venite (Come). Ps. 95 (Ps. 94 in Vulgate) chanted as canticle at Anglican matins to words 'O come, let us sing unto the Lord'. Settings by several composers, incl. Mendelssohn.

Vent (Fr.). Wind. *Instruments à vent*, wind instruments.

Ventil (Ger.), **Ventile** (It.). Valve. *Ventilhorn* (Ger.), *corno ventile* (It.), valve horn.

Venus and Adonis. Opera in prol. and 3 acts by *Blow to lib. by unknown author. Prod. London c.1684. Revived Glastonbury 1920, Cambridge, Mass., 1941.

Vêpres Siciliennes, Les (The Sicilian Vespers). Opera in 5 acts by Verdi to Fr. lib. by Scribe and Duveyrier, comp. 1854, prod. Paris 1855, London and NY 1859. Trans. into It. as *I vespri siciliani*. Lib. was orig. written by Scribe for Donizetti, 1839, as *Le duc d'Albe* (prod. 1882).

Veracini, Francesco Maria (*b* Florence, 1690; *d* Florence, 1768). It. violinist and composer. Début Venice 1711. In Dresden 1717–22 where high salary caused resentment among other musicians. Visited London 1714, 1733–8, 1741–5. His 4 operas incl. *La Clemenza di Tito* (perf. in London, 1737). Wrote oratorios, cantatas, over 40 vn. sonatas, songs, and church music. One of finest violinists of his time, with interest in special effects and with a romantic streak.

Verbrugghen, Henri (*b* Brussels, 1873; *d* Northfield, Minn., 1934). Belg. violinist and cond. Studied Brussels Cons. with Ysaÿe, Hubay, and Gevaert. Member, Scottish Orch. 1893, Lamoureux Orch., Paris, 1894–5. Leader, Queen's Hall Orch., 1902–5, Scottish Orch. from 1903. Cond., summer concerts Llandudno 1895–7, Colwyn Bay 1898–1902. Cond., Glasgow Choral Union 1911. Dir., State Cons. of N.S.W., Sydney, and cond., Sydney S.O. 1915–22. Cond. Minneapolis S.O. 1923–31. Soloist in f. Eng. p. of Sibelius's vn. conc., London, 1907, cond. Wood.

Verbunkos. Hung. soldiers' dance, used from c. 1775 to attract recruits for the army. Danced, to gipsy mus., by uniformed hussars. Survived after introduction of conscription in 1849 as ceremonial dance with two or more sections, similar to those of *csardás. Used by Liszt in his *Hungarian Rhapsody No. 2*, and by Bartók and Kodály.

Verdelot, Philippe (*b* Verdelot, Orange, ?1470–80; *d* before 1552). Fr. composer. Spent most of his life in It. Choirmaster in Florence from 1522, part of time at cath. Visited Rome 1523. Wrote much church mus. but best known for madrigals, composed before first madrigal publications c. 1530.

Verdi, Giuseppe (Fortunino Francesco) (*b* Le Roncole, nr. Busseto, Parma, 1813; *d* Milan, 1901). It. composer. Son of innkeeper. Taught by local organist. Local grocer, who liked mus., recognized his mus. ability and offered to pay for him to go to Milan Cons., but authorities would not admit him, partly because of poor pf.-playing. Studied in Milan privately for 2 years. Returned to Busseto, where he continued studies, directed town's mus. activities, and married grocer's daughter. Completed opera *Rocester* (now lost) in 1836, but *Oberto* was prod. at La Scala, Milan, in 1839 with some success, followed by comic opera,

Un giorno di regno (1840), a failure. Between 1838 and 1840, Verdi's wife and 2 children died. Prostrate with grief, vowed to abandon comp., but was persuaded to compose *Nabucco* (1841); its triumphant success made him most prominent of young It. composers. Thereafter wrote series of operas, some more successful than others at their premières, but each eagerly sought by impresarios. In 1847 he comp. *I masnadieri* for Her Majesty's, London, with Jenny Lind and Lablache heading the cast. In 1849 he bought a farming estate at Sant' Agata, near Busseto, to which he returned whenever possible. In the sensitive political climate of 19th-cent. It., Verdi's libs. (e.g. for *Rigoletto*, *Un ballo in maschera*, etc.) frequently caused trouble with the censors, especially when they dealt with historical events which could be interpreted as referring to contemporary political events, Verdi's sympathies for It. independence from Austria being well known. In 1860, after the It. war of independence, he was elected a Deputy in first It. nat. parliament, resigning 5 years later. His next 3 operas were written for perf. outside It., *La forza del destino* for St Petersburg, 1862, *Don Carlos* for Paris, 1867, and *Aida* for Cairo, 1871. 16 years were to pass before the next opera, but in 1874 the great *Requiem*, comp. in memory of the poet Manzoni, was perf. in Milan. It was an immediate success. Verdi cond. 15 perfs. of it in Paris in 1874 and 1875, 4 in Vienna, and 3 in London. In 1879, his publisher Ricordi suggested Shakespeare's *Othello* as an operatic subject, and *Boito, with whom Verdi's relations had hitherto been cool, submitted a draft lib. The work (*Otello*) was f.p. in Milan in 1887 and was acclaimed as the supreme achievement not only of its composer but of It. opera. In 1889 Boito suggested a further collaboration, on *Falstaff*. Its prod. at Milan in 1893, though a personal triumph, was not such a success as that of *Otello* and it has taken until recent times for this masterpiece of comic opera to become a popular favourite. In 1859 Verdi had married the sop. Giuseppina Strepponi, with whom he had lived for a decade before that. Her death in 1897 marked the end of Verdi's composing career. He died at Sant' Agata, leaving most of his money to a home for elderly musicians which he had founded in Milan.

Verdi's stature as one of the 2 or 3 greatest opera composers is unchallengeable. Though his technical mastery continually developed and was refined, and his powers of characterization became more subtle and expressive, the essential Verdi—direct, noble, and intense—remained unchanging from *Nabucco* to *Falstaff*. There was no 'change of style' in *Otello*: the lib. drew from Verdi his greatest mus., but it is still recognizably the work of the composer of *Il trovatore* and *Simon Boccanegra*. In recent years the earlier works have been revived and have revealed their considerable merits—the comic *Un giorno di regno*, for example, is particularly fine. In operas like *Rigoletto*, *La*

traviata, and *Aida*, Verdi put on to the stage operatic characters who are as real as the characters in Shakespeare. His 3 Shakespeare operas are major achievements and his failure to compose *King Lear*, though he toyed with the idea for many years, must ever be regretted. Prin. works:

OPERAS: **Oberto, Conte di San Bonifacio* (1837–8); *Un *giorno di regno* (1840); **Nabucco* (1841); *I *Lombardi alla prima crociata* (1842), adapted to Fr. lib. as *Jérusalem*, with rev. and some new mus., 1847; **Ernani* (1843); *I *due Foscari* (1843–4); **Giovanna d'Arco* (1844); *Alzira* (1845); **Attila* (1845–6); **Macbeth* (1846–7, rev. 1865); *I *masnadieri* (1846–7); *Il *corsaro* (1847–8); *La *battaglia di Legnano* (1848); **Luisa Miller* (1849); **Stiffelio* (1850), adapted to new lib., with some new mus., as **Aroldo* (1856–7); **Rigoletto* (1850–1); *Il *trovatore* (1851–2, rev. 1857); *La *traviata* (1852–3); *Les *Vêpres siciliennes* (1854); **Simon Boccanegra* (1856–7, lib. and mus. rev. 1880–1); *Un *ballo in maschera* (1857–8); *La *forza del destino* (1861–2); **Don Carlos* (1866, rev. as 4-act work, with some new music, 1882–3); **Aida* (1870); **Otello* (1884–6); **Falstaff* (1889–92).

CHORAL: *Inno delli nazioni* (Hymn of the Nations), ten., ch., orch. (1862); *Libera me*, sop., ch., orch. (1868–9, incorp. into *Requiem*, 1874); *Pater Noster*, unacc. ch.; *Ave Maria*, sop. and str. (1879–80); *Requiem* (1873–4); **Quattro pezzi sacri: Ave Maria*, unacc. ch. (1888–9); *Stabat Mater*, ch. and orch. (1895–7); *Laudi alla Vergine Maria*, women's ch. (1888–9); *Te Deum*, sop., ch., and orch. (1895–7).

CHAMBER MUSIC: Str. Qt. in E minor (1873).

SONGS: *6 Romances* (1838); *L'esule* (The Exile); *La seduzione*; *Notturno: Guarda che bianca luna* (Nocturne: See the pale moon) (1839); *Chi i bei di m'adduce ancora* (Who will bring back the beautiful days?) (1842); *6 Romances* (1845); *Il poveretto* (The beggar) (1847); *Suona la tromba* (Sound the trumpet) (1848); *L'Abandonée* (The forsaken woman) (1849); *Fiorellin che sorge appena* (The little flower that rises) (1850); *La preghiera del poeta* (The poet's prayer) (1858); *Il brigidin* (The rosette) (1863); *Tu dici che non m'ami* (You say you do not love me) (1869).

Verdoppeln (Ger.). To double. *Verdoppelt*, doubled; *Verdoppelung*, doubling.

Verein (Ger.). Society, as in *Musikverein*, mus. soc.

Veress, Sándor (*b* Kolozsvár, 1907). Swiss composer of Hung. birth. Studied Budapest RAM 1924–30 (pf. with Bartók, comp. with Kodály), later with Lajtha on folk mus. 1923–35. Helped Bartók on folk mus. research 1937–40. Taught at Budapest State Acad. 1943–8. Teacher of comp., Berne Cons. from 1950, prof. of musicology, Berne Univ. from 1968 (dir. of dept. from 1971). Has taught in USA and Australia and was a regular juror at Llangollen int. eisteddfod. Works incl. ballet *The Magic Flute* (1937), vn. conc. (1939), *Homage to Paul Klee*, 2 pf., str., (1952), pf. conc. (1952), Sym. (1940), *Sinfonia Minneapolitana* (1952–4), conc. for str. qt. and orch. (1960–1), 2 str. qts., 2 vn. sonatas, cl. trio (1972) etc.

Veretti, Antonio (*b* Verona, 1900; *d* Rome, 1978). It. composer. Studied Bologna. Taught at Rome Cons. until 1943. Dir., Cons. Rossini, Pesaro, 1950–2, Cagliari Cons. 1953–5, and Florence 1956–70. Wrote operas, ballets, *Sinfonia italiana* for orch. (1929), pf. conc. (1949), choral and chamber works, and film mus.

Verhallend (Ger.). Dying away.

Verismo (It.). Realism. Term applied to 'realistic' sch. of It. opera in which (following Zola in literature) subjects treated were usually contemporary and down-to-earth, e.g. Mascagni's *Cavalleria rusticana*, Giordano's *Fedora*, Puccini's *Il tabarro*, etc. But, like all such terms, it is imprecise and has acquired a slight pejorative tinge. Also, some *verismo* operas are not truly *verismo*, and where does one draw the line—is Verdi's *La traviata* not *verismo*? But the opera-lover understands the Mascagni type of work by this term.

Verklärte Nacht (Transfigured Night). Str. sextet (2 vn., 2 va., 2 vc.) Op. 4, by Schoenberg, based on poem by Richard Dehmel (from *Weib und Welt*). Comp. 1899. F.p. Vienna 1902, f.p. in England 1914. Version for str. orch. by Schoenberg 1917, rev. 1943. Used as mus. for 1-act ballet *Pillar of Fire*, choreog. A. Tudor, prod. NY Met. 1942.

Verlierend (Ger.). Losing itself, i.e. dying away.

Verlöschend (Ger.). Extinguished, i.e. dying away.

Vermeer Quartet. Amer. str. qt. founded 1969 by its 1st vn., Shmuel Ashkenasi, with 3 colleagues from professorial staff N. Illinois Univ. Orig. members were Pierre Menard (2nd vn.), Nobuko Imai (va., succeeded 1978 by Jerry Horner and 1980 by Bernard Zaslav), and Marc Johnson (vc.). First European tour 1972–3. London début 1974.

Vermeulen, Matthijs (*b* Helmond, 1888; *d* Laren, 1967). Dutch composer, studied with *Diepenbrock. Wrote on mus. for various papers 1907–56. Based works on medieval techniques. Wrote 7 syms., str. qt., *The Flying Dutchman* for orch., *The Soldier* (setting of Rupert Brooke), etc.

Verne (orig. Wurm), **Adela** (*b* Southampton, 1877; *d* London, 1952). Eng. pianist. Sister of Mathilde *Verne. After brilliant int. career as pianist, taught at pf. sch. founded by sister.

Verne (orig. Wurm), **Mathilde** (*b* Southampton, 1868; *d* London, 1936). Eng. pianist, pupil of Clara Schumann. Organized chamber concerts in London. Founded sch. of pf.-playing in Kensington, pupils incl. *Solomon.

Véronique. Operetta in 3 acts by Messager to lib. by Van Loo and Duval. Prod. Paris 1898, London 1903, NY 1905.

Verrall, John (Weedon) (*b* Britt, Iowa, 1908). Amer. composer. Studied Minneapolis Coll. of Mus. 1928–31, RCM, London, 1929–30 (pf. with Merrick, theory with Morris), Liszt Cons., Budapest (comp. with Kodály), and Minneapolis Univ. 1932–4. Later studied with Harris and Copland. Teacher at Washington Univ. from 1948. Works incl. operas, 4 syms., pf. conc., va. conc., 7 str. qts., etc.

Verrett, Shirley (*b* New Orleans, 1931). Amer. mez. capable of singing sop. roles (e.g. Norma and Lady Macbeth). Studied Juilliard Sch. Recital début NY 1958, operatic début Yellow Springs, Ohio, 1957 (*Rape of Lucretia*), then NY City Opera 1958 under name Shirley Carter. Sang title-role in *Carmen*, Spoleto 1962, and thereafter elsewhere with much success. CG début 1966 (Ulrica in *Un ballo in maschera*). Début NY Met. 1968 as Carmen.

Verschiebung (Ger.). Shoving away. Soft pedal.

Verschwindend (Ger.). Disappearing, i.e. dying away.

Verse. (1) Term used in Anglican church mus. meaning a passage for solo v. (or several solo vv.) as contrasted with full ch., thus *verse anthem*, an anthem in which solo v. and full ch. are contrasted.

(2) Biblical verse in Gregorian chant.

Verset (Fr.). Verse. Short org. piece, replacing sung verse of psalm in R. C. service.

Versetzung (Ger.). Transposition. *Versetzungszeichen*, accidental.

Versicle. In the Roman or Anglican service a short verse spoken or chanted by the priest and responded to by the congregation (or ch.).

Verstovsky, Alexey (Nikolayevich) (*b* Seliverstovo, 1799; *d* Moscow, 1862). Russ. composer. Studied in St Petersburg. Official of Imperial Opera, Moscow, from 1825, becoming dir. of all Moscow theatres 1842–60. Wrote operas which were eclectic forerunners of Russ. nationalist style, particularly the once-popular *Askold's Tomb* (1835).

Verzierungen (Ger.). Embellishments.

Vesalii Icones (Images of Vesalius). Th. piece by *Maxwell Davies for dancer, solo vc., and ens. (incl. motor horn, anvil, saucepan, knife-grinder, out-of-tune pf.). Comp. 1969. F.p. London 1969, cond. composer. Its 14 dances are based on the anatomical drawings by the physician Vesalius in his *De humani corporis fabrica* (1543), with the 14 Stations of the Cross superimposed on the Vesalian images.

Vesperae Solennes de Confessore (Solemn Vespers of the Confessor). Work for 4 vv., ch., orch., and org. by Mozart (K339) comp. 1780.

Vespers. 7th of Canonical Hours of R. C. Church, also known as Evensong. Famous large-scale setting by *Monteverdi (1610).

Vespers of 1610 (Monteverdi). See *Vespro della Beata Vergine*.

Vespro della Beata Vergine (Vespers of the Holy Virgin). A collection of psalms and hymns by Monteverdi comp. 1610 for perf. in small surroundings at Mantua and comprising *Audi coelum, verba mea*, solo v. and 6 vv.; *Ave, Maris stella*, 8 vv.; *Dixit Dominus Domino meo*, 6 vv.; *Domine ad adjuvandum*, 6 vv.; *Duo Seraphim*, 3 vv.; *In illo tempore*, 6 vv.; *Laetatus sum*, 6 vv.; *Lauda Jerusalem*, 7 vv.; *Laudate pueri*, 8 vv.; *Magnificat*, 6 vv.; *Magnificat*, 7 vv.; *Nigra sum*, solo v.; *Nisi Dominus*, 10 vv.; *Pulchra es*, 2 vv. (all with basso continuo); *Sancta Maria, ora pro nobis* (sonata) for solo v. with 8 instr. (2 cornets, 2 vn., 2 tb., one of which can be replaced with viola da braccio, and double tb.). This last item can be perf. separately. There are several modern eds. of the *Vespers*, e.g. by Harnoncourt, W. Goehr, Redlich, Norrington, etc.

Vestale, La. Opera by Spontini in 3 acts, comp. 1807, to lib. by de Jouy (originally written for Boieldieu and later refused by Méhul). F.p. Paris 1807. Milan 1824, London 1826, Philadelphia 1828. Revived for *Ponselle (NY Met. 1925) and *Callas (Scala, Milan, 1955).

Vestris (*née* Bartolozzi), **Lucia Elizabeth** (*b* London, 1797; *d* London, 1856). Eng. cont. Opera début London 1815. Sang at It. Opera, Paris, and King's Th., London, 1821–5. Wife of Auguste Armand Vestris, one of celebrated ballet family, who was ballet master at King's Th. 1809–17. Sang in Eng. f.ps. of several Rossini operas at King's Th. 1821–4. Frequently sang in Dublin, 1824–47. Created Fatima in Weber's *Oberon*, 1826. Became manager of CG 1839–42, having previously managed Olympic Th. 1831–8 and subsequently the Lyceum 1847–55, with her 2nd husband Charles Matthews. Sang male roles, incl. Don Giovanni.

Veyron-Lacroix, Robert (*b* Paris, 1922). Fr. harpsichordist. Studied Paris Cons. Début Fr. radio 1949. Frequent tours with flautist Jean-Pierre *Rampal. Prof. of harpsichord, Paris Cons., from 1967.

Viadana (really Grossi), **Lodovico** (*b* Viadana, Mantua, *c.* 1560; *d* Gualtieri, 1627). It. composer. Choirmaster Mantua Cath., 1594–7, Cremona 1601–8, Fano Cath. 1610–12. Franciscan monk from 1586. Wrote *concerti ecclesiastici* for vv. and org., masses, madrigals, etc.

Viardot-García, Pauline (*b* Paris, 1821; *d* Paris, 1910). Fr. mez. of Sp. parentage. Daughter of Manuel García and sister of Maria *Malibran and Manuel *García. Studied singing with parents, pf. with Liszt, comp. with Reicha. Concert début Brussels 1837, stage début London 1839, as Rossini's Desdemona, Paris 1839. Married Louis Viardot, manager of Théâtre Italien, Paris, 1840. Created role of Fidès in Meyerbeer's *Le Prophète*, 1849. Famous in Mozart roles and as Gluck's *Orphée* (Paris 1859) and *Alceste* (1861). Retired from stage 1863 and wrote plays, painted, and comp. Friend of Schumann and Turgenev. Sang Dalila privately to Saint-Saëns. Taught singing at Paris Cons. 1871–5, pupils incl. Désirée Artôt.

Vibraharp. Same as *vibraphone.

Vibraphone (colloquial, 'vibes'). Perc. instr. similar to *marimba. Tuned metal bars, laid out like pf. kbd., are struck by the players holding small padded hammer in each hand. Beneath bars are resonators fitted with lids which constantly open and close electrically, giving pulsating sound to any of the metal bars when struck by the player. Compass f–f′′′. Used first in jazz (Lionel Hampton a celebrated player), then frequently in symphonic and operatic works, e.g. by Berg in *Lulu*, Vaughan Williams, McCabe, Britten, Milhaud, Henze, Messiaen, Tippett, and Boulez.

Vibrato (It.). Vibrated. Undulation of pitch of a note, prod. in str. instr. by controlled vibration of player's finger stopping the str. and in wind instr. by breath-control. In singing the greatest skill is needed in use of *vibrato* or it becomes wobble. Not the same as *tremolo.

Vicentino, Nicolà (*b* Vicenza, *c.*1511; *d* Rome, 1572). It. composer. Studied in Venice, pupil of *Willaert. Ded. to revival of ancient Gr. modes; built 6-kbd. 'archiorgano' to illustrate his system and wrote madrigals. Pubd. *The Ancient Music reduced to Modern Practice*, Rome 1555.

Vickers, Jon (Jonathan Stewart) (*b* Prince Albert, Saskatchewan, 1926). Canadian ten. Studied Toronto Royal Cons. Sang with Toronto S.O. Opera début Canadian O.C., Toronto, 1954 (Duke in *Rigoletto*). CG début 1957 (Riccardo in *Un ballo in maschera*), Bayreuth 1958 (Siegmund), San Francisco 1959, NY Met. 1960, Milan 1961. Outstanding Tristan, Peter Grimes, Florestan, Aeneas (*Les Troyens*), Siegmund, etc.

Victoria, Tomás Luis de (*b* Avila, *c.*1548; *d* Madrid, 1611). Sp. composer. Went to Rome 1565 as student for priesthood (ordained 1575) and was possibly a pupil of Palestrina. Organist and choirmaster S. Maria di Monserrato, Rome, 1569–71; choirmaster Collegium Romanum 1571–3, Collegium Germanicum 1573–8. Chaplain at Church of S. Girolamo della Carità 1578–85, working with *Neri, founder of oratorio. Returned to Spain 1595. (Because of long residence in It., name is often spelt in It. form, *Vittoria*.) Organist and choirmaster, convent of Descalzas Reales, Madrid, 1596–1611. With

Palestrina, regarded as one of supreme contrapuntists of his age, his mus. having a dramatic vigour and colour which reflect his nationality. Wrote only church mus., incl. settings of all hymns of R. C. liturgical year. Works pubd. in complete modern edn. by Pedrell (Leipzig 1902–1913). The 8 vols. comprise: I, 44 motets; II, 10 Masses; III, 18 Magnificats and a Nunc Dimittis; IV, 5 Masses; V, 34 hymns and *Officium Hebdomadae Sanctae*; VI, 5 Masses; VII, 10 psalms, 10 settings of Marian antiphons, 3 other works; VIII, Biography, bibliography, and 5 other works. Among greatest works are motets *Vexilla regis, O magnum mysterium, O quam gloriosam, O vos omnes*; *Requiem* (1583 and 1603).

Victory. Opera in 3 acts by Richard Rodney Bennett to lib. by Beverley Cross based on novel by Joseph Conrad. Prod. London (CG) 1970.

Victory, Gerard (really Alan Loraine) (*b* Dublin, 1921). Irish composer and cond. Mus. producer, Radio Telefis Eireann 1948–67, dir. of mus. from 1967. Works incl. opera *Héloise and Abelard, Jonathan Swift, Homage to Petrarch* for str., str. qts., *Miroirs* for orch., etc.

Vida breve, La (Short Life). 2-act opera by *Falla to lib. by Carlos Fernández Shaw. Comp. 1904–5. Prod. Nice (in Fr.) 1913; Madrid (in Sp.) 1914; NY Met. 1926; Edinburgh 1958.

Vide (Fr.). Empty. Thus *corde à vide* means open string.

Vielle (Fr.). Medieval name for various instr., e.g. hurdy-gurdy and fiddle.

Vielle à roue (Fr.). Wheel fiddle, i.e. the *hurdy-gurdy.

Vienna Boys' Choir (Ger. *Wiener Sängerknaben*). Choir of Vienna Seminary Sch., founded 1498, formerly providing mus. for chapel of Austrian imperial court. Present-day ch. gives secular concerts.

Vienna Philharmonic Orchestra (Ger. *Wiener Philharmoniker*). Austrian orch. founded in Vienna 1842, first cond. being Otto *Nicolai 1842–8. The concerts were interrupted by the 1848 revolution. A few were given under Karl Eckert between 1854 and 1857, but a regular season of 8 concerts did not occur until 1860. Orch. soon recognized as one of world's greatest, a reputation it has maintained. Among prin. conds. after Nicolai were Dessov (1860–75), *Richter (1875–98), Mahler (1898–1901), Hellmesberger (1901–3), Weingartner (1907–27), Furtwängler (1927–8), Krauss (1929–33), Furtwängler and Walter (1933–8), Furtwängler (1938–54), Karajan (1956), Abbado (from 1971). Orch. is self-governing and plays for *Vienna State Opera. Many other conds., notably Karl *Böhm, have been assoc. with it and have made recordings with it. Richard Strauss wrote to the orchestra in 1942: 'Only he who has *conducted* the Vienna Philharmonic players knows what they are! But that will remain our very own secret!'

Vienna State Opera (Ger. *Wiener Staatsoper*). Prin. Austrian opera house and co., one of leading opera organizations of world. Orig. Vienna Court Opera (*Wiener Hofoper*). The first opera was perf. in Vienna in 1633 (Bartolaia's *Il Sidonio*). Opera then became est. as regular court entertainment and special th. built. Theater bei der Hofburg was opened 1748. Gluck was court Kapellmeister 1754–70, 10 of his operas being written for Vienna. Towards end of 18th cent., Burgtheater lost ground to Theater am Kärntnerthor (built 1708), where *Salieri became cond. Mozart's *Die Entführung aus dem Serail* (1782), *Le Nozze di Figaro* (1786), and *Così fan tutte* (1790) all had f.ps. at Burgtheater, while *Don Giovanni* had its first Vienna perf. there (with additions) in 1788. In 1842 Donizetti was both court composer and cond. Court opera's first permanent cond. was Karl Eckert (1854–60) who introduced Wagner's operas to the city. New theatre, Die Oper am Ring, opened 1869. *Richter became cond. in 1875 and shared directorship with Jahn from 1880 to 1896, the co. in this period having singers of the quality of Materna, Reichmann, Winkelmann and van Dyck. In 1897 Mahler became dir. and initiated the most glorious decade in the history of the th., with a great singing–acting co. incl. Gutheil-Schoder, Mildenburg, Selma Kurz, Schmedes, Mayr, and Slezak, and *Roller as designer. Mahler was succeeded by Weingartner 1907–11 and Hans Gregor 1911–18. In 1918 Court Opera became State Opera, with Schalk and R. Strauss as joint dirs. 1919–24, Schalk continuing alone until 1929. The singers now included Lotte Lehmann, Elisabeth Schumann, Jerger, Piccaver, and Jeritza, who were joined in the 1930s by Tauber, Kern, Ursuleac, Kiepura, Schorr, Olszewska, Dermota, etc. Krauss was cond. 1929–34, Weingartner 1934–6, Walter 1936–8. After an interregnum, Karl Böhm became dir. in 1943 until the th. was bombed in March 1945. For 10 years, with Böhm, Josef Krips, and Krauss as conds. the State Opera played in the Theater an der Wien and the Volksoper, and visited London in 1948. Böhm again became dir. 1955 and the rebuilt th. (capacity 2,200) opened in 1955 with *Fidelio*. Böhm resigned 1956, being succeeded by Karajan 1956–64. The postwar vocal galaxy incl. Gueden, Schwarzkopf, Reining, Seefried, Welitsch, Hotter, Patzak, Schöffler, and Weber. In the 1970s Bernstein, Böhm, Karajan, and Mehta cond. famous perfs. In 1982 Lorin *Maazel, an American, was appointed dir., with a contract until 1986, but he left in 1984 after a controversial period of musical politics which his predecessors Mahler and Strauss would have recognized as characteristically Viennese. It may be fairly said that the history of the Vienna Opera is one of spectacular triumphs, petty politics, a fairly conservative policy towards new mus., and glorious singing.

Vienna Symphony Orchestra (Ger. *Wiener Symphoniker*). Orch. founded in 1900 as Wiener

Konzertverein Orchester. In 1921 it merged with Verein Wiener Tonkünstler (formed 1907 under Oskar Nedbal) and became Wiener Sinfonie-Orchester. It assumed present name in 1933, with over 120 players. Administered by Gesellschaft der Musikfreunde, Wiener Konzerthausgesellschaft, Bregenz Fest., and Austrian Radio. First cond. was Ferdinand *Löwe, 1900–24. In 1934 became Vienna's main broadcasting orch. and in 1938 was taken over by city as its municipal orch. Has had series of famous guest conds. and has made many recordings.

Vie parisienne, La (Parisian Life). *Opéra-bouffe* in 4 acts by Offenbach to lib. by Meilhac and Halévy. Prod. Paris 1866; NY 1869. See *Gaîté parisienne.*

Vier ernste Gesänge (Four Serious Songs). Song-cycle for low v. and pf., Op. 121, by Brahms, comp. 1896 to biblical texts. 1. *Denn es gehet dem Menschen*; 2. *Ich wandte mich und sahe an alle*; 3. *O Tod, O Tod, wie bitter bist du*; 4. *Wenn ich mit Engelszungen redete.* Inspired by his emotion over Clara *Schumann's final illness. Orch. version by Malcolm *Sargent.

Vier letzte Lieder (Four Last Songs). Songs for high v. and orch. by R. Strauss, his last works, comp. 1948. 5th song left unfinished. In order of comp.: 1. *Im Abendrot* (In the Sunset) (Eichendorff), 2. *Frühling* (Spring), 3. *Beim schlafengehen* (Falling asleep), 4. *September.* (Poems of 2, 3, and 4 by Hesse). Title of cycle given by publisher after Strauss's death. Strauss favoured order 3, 4, 2, 1. F.p. London 1950, Flagstad and Philharmonia Orch., cond. Furtwängler.

Vierne, Louis (Victor Jules) (*b* Poitiers, 1870; *d* Paris, 1937). Fr. organist and composer, born blind. Studied Paris Cons. with Franck and Widor. Organist, Nôtre Dame de Paris 1900–37. Prof. of org., Schola Cantorum, Paris, from 1912. Toured Europe and USA as org. recitalist. Wrote 6 org. syms. and shorter pieces for org., also mass, str. qt., vc. sonata, and an orch. sym. (1907–8). Died playing org. at Nôtre Dame.

Viertel(note) (Ger.). Quarter-note (the crotchet).

Vierundsechzigstel(note) (Ger.). 64th note (the hemidemisemiquaver).

Vieuxtemps, Henri (Joseph François) (*b* Verviers, 1820; *d* Mustapha-lez-Alger, Algeria, 1881). Belg. violinist and composer. Played conc. with orch. at age of 6. Became pupil of de Bériot in Paris from 1828. Toured Ger. 1833 and studied counterpoint with Sechter in Vienna. Revived interest (1834) in Beethoven's vn. conc. Studied comp. with Reicha in Paris, 1835. Visited Russia 1838, USA 1844. Court violinist and prof. of vn., St Petersburg 1846–52. Prof. of vn., Brussels Cons. 1871–3. Regarded as one of greatest violinists of his day. Wrote 7 vn. concs., vn. sonata, 3 str. qts., many vn. pieces, and cadenzas

for Beethoven conc. Had 2 brothers, one a pianist, the other—Jules Joseph Ernest Vieuxtemps (*b* Brussels, 1832; *d* Belfast, 1896)—a cellist who played in CG orch. and became prin. vc., Hallé Orch.

Vignoles, Roger (Hutton) (*b* Cheltenham, 1945). Eng. pianist. Studied Cambridge Univ. 1962–6. Début London 1967. Répétiteur CG 1969–71. Accompanist to Rita Streich, Gwyneth Jones, John Shirley-Quirk, etc.

Vihuela. Sp. Renaissance instr. of guitar type. Word was used generically for all str. instrs., so further identification was necessary, e.g. *vihuela de arco*, bowed vihuela, *vihuela de penole*, plectrum-plucked vihuela, *vihuela de mano*, finger-plucked vihuela. Main period of popularity 1530–80. Luis de Milán's book on the *vihuela de mano* (1536) is a teaching manual containing first solo songs printed in Sp. Larger than guitar, usually with 6 courses, and up to 10 frets. Superseded by guitar c.1700. Mus. notated in tablature.

Village Romeo and Juliet, A (*Romeo und Julia auf dem Dorfe*). Opera in 6 *tableaux* by Delius to Ger. lib. by composer based on short story *Romeo und Julia auf dem Dorfe* from coll. of *Novellen* entitled *Die Leute von Seldwyla* (1856) by Gottfried Keller (1819–90). Comp. 1900–1. Prod. Berlin 1907, cond. Cassirer, London CG 1910, cond. Beecham. The intermezzo between scenes 5 and 6 was rewritten and extended in 1906 to cover the scene-change and became known in the concert-hall as the 'Walk to the Paradise Garden'. Suite for orch. arr. Fenby (1948).

Villa-Lobos, Heitor (*b* Rio de Janeiro, 1887; *d* Rio de Janeiro, 1959). Brazilian composer. First mus. lessons from father, who taught him vc. Had harmony lessons 1907, otherwise self-taught, earning living by playing in cafés etc. Played vc. in Rio opera and sym. orchs., absorbing influences from Russ. nationalists, Stravinsky, and Strauss, under whose baton he played in 1920. Befriended by *Milhaud when latter was Claudel's secretary at Fr. embassy, and by Arthur Rubinstein, 1921, who played his pf. mus. Spent 1923–4 in Europe and 1927–30 in Paris where he was influenced by Satie and Milhaud and by fashionable neo-classicism. Result was series of works called *Bachianas Brasileiras* in which Baroque forms were re-created with Brazilian 'local colour'. Returning to Brazil 1930, held series of official teaching posts. Founded Conservatório Nacional de Canto Orfeónico 1942 and Brazilian Acad. of Mus., 1945. Visited USA 1944 as cond. of own mus. Extremely prolific composer, with expected sharp variations in quality. Though his mus. suggests the folk idiom, he rarely, if ever, quoted a folk-song, relying instead on colour and rhythm to give Brazilian flavour. Melodist and romantic, he used the popular *chôro* form as a basis for series of works for various combinations of instr. and vv. with specific nationalist intent. Prin. works incl.:

OPERAS: *Izath* (1912–14); *Yerma* (1955–6).

*CHÔROS: No. 1, guitar (1920), 2, fl., cl. (1924), 3, 7 winds, male ch. (1925), 4, 2 hn., tb. (1926), 5, pf. (1926), 6, orch. (1926), 7, 5 winds, vn., vc. (1924), 8, 2 pf., orch. (1925), 9, orch. (1929), 10, orch., ch. (1925), 11, pf., orch. (1928), 12, orch. (1929), 13, 2 orchs., band (1929), 14, orch., band, ch. (1928).

*BACHIANAS BRASILEIRAS: 1, 8 vc. (1930), 2, *The Little Train of the Caipira,* chamber orch. (1930), 3, pf., orch. (1938), 4, pf. (1930–6) or orch. (1941), 5, v. and vcs. (1938), 6, fl., bn. (1938), 7, orch. (1942), 8, orch. (1945), 9, unacc. ch. or str. (1944).

ORCH: Symphonies: 1 (1916), 2 (1917), 3 and 4 (1919), 5 (1920)—the syms. 3, 4, and 5 are a World War I trilogy, subtitled respectively 'A guerra', 'A Vitória', and 'A Paz'—6 (1944), 7 (1945), 8 (1950), 9 (1951), 10 (1952), 11 (1955), 12 (1957); *Suite Suggestive* No. 1 (1929); 4 Suites, *Descrobimento di Brasil* (Discovery of Brazil) (1936–7, 1942); *New York Skyline* (1940); Vc. concs., 1 (1915), 2 (1953); 5 pf. concs. (1945–54); guitar conc. (1951); harp conc. (1953); harmonica conc. (1955).

PIANO: *Suite Infantil* Nos. 1 and 2 (1912, 1913); *A Prole do Bebê* Nos. 1 and 2 (The Baby's Family) (1918, 1921); *Rudepoema* (1921–6, also for pf. and orch.); *Saudades das Selvas Brasileiras* (1927). CHAMBER MUSIC: 17 str. qts. (1915–57); 3 pf. trios (1911–18); 4 vn. sonatas (1912–23); *Berceuse* (1915); Nonet (1923); *Sextetto mistico* (1945). GUITAR: 12 Études (1928); 15 Preludes (1940).

Villancico (from Sp. *villano,* rustic). (1) 16th-cent. choral comp., like cantata, generally on subject of Christmas, for soloists, ch., and str. and/or org.

(2) Madrigalian setting for 3 to 5 vv. of Sp. verse-form called *villancico.*

Villanella (It.; Fr. *villanelle*). Street song popular in 16th cent., also a type of part-song less complicated than madrigal. The first song in Berlioz's cycle *Les Nuits d'été* is entitled *Villanelle.*

Villi, Le (The Wilis). Opera in 1 act by Puccini to lib. by Fontana based on folk-legend. Comp. 1883. Prod. Milan 1884. Rev. version in 2 acts prod. Turin 1884, Manchester (in Eng.) 1897, NY Met. 1908.

Villotta (It.). Plebeian 16th-cent. song, later known as *villanella.*

Vinay, Ramón (*b* Chillán, Chile, 1912). Chilean ten. Studied Mexico. Opera début (as bar.) Mexico City 1931 as Alfonso in *La Favorite.* Tenor début 1943 as Don José in *Carmen.* NY City Opera 1945–6, 1948; NY Met. 1946–61; CG 1950, 1953–60; Bayreuth 1952–7. Superb Otello (Verdi), coached in role by Toscanini with whom he made famous recording. Resumed bar. roles 1962, singing Telramund, Iago, Falstaff, and Scarpia. Remarkable actor. Sang last act of *Otello,* Santiago 1969. Producer until 1972.

Vincent, John (*b* Birmingham, Alabama, 1902; *d* Santa Monica, Calif., 1977). Amer. composer and teacher. Studied New England Cons. with Chadwick, under Piston at Harvard 1933–5, then for 2 years with N. Boulanger in Paris. Head of mus. dept. W. Kentucky State Univ. 1937–45 and succeeded Schoenberg as prof. of comp. U.C.L.A. 1946–69. Employed 'paratonality' in his mus., i.e. diatonic element predominating in polytonal or atonal passages. Wrote comic opera *Primeval Void* (1969–71), prod. Vienna 1973, Sym. in D (1954), *Nude Descending the Staircase,* xylophone and str. (1972), *Stabat Mater,* sop. and male vv. (1969), *Mary at Calvary,* sop., ch., and org. (1976), 2 str. qts. (1936, 1967), and songs.

Vincent, Robert (William) (*b* Medan, Sumatra, 1941). Eng. organist and harpsichordist. Studied Oxford Univ. and GSM. Prof. of org., GSM from 1967. Organist and choirmaster St Martin-in-the-Fields 1967–77, Manchester Cath. 1977–80.

Vinci, Leonardo (*b* Strongoli, *c.* 1690; *d* Naples, 1730). It. composer. Studied in Naples. Choirmaster. Monk from 1728. Between 1719 and 1730 wrote 35 operas, incl. *Ifigenia in Tauride* (Venice 1725), some in Neapolitan dialect.

Viñes, Ricardo (*b* Lérida, 1875; *d* Barcelona, 1943). Sp. pianist. Studied in Barcelona and later in Paris with de Bériot and Godard. Champion of contemporary composers, being among first pianists to play works of Debussy, Ravel, and others. Introduced much Russ. pf. music to France (incl. Mussorgsky's *Pictures at an Exhibition* and Balakirev's *Islamey*) and was dedicatee of Falla's *Nights in the Gardens of Spain,* Ravel's *Oiseaux tristes,* and Debussy's *Poissons d'Or.* In 1936 gave f.ps. of works by *Messiaen.

Viol. Type of bowed str. instr., made in various sizes. Developed in Renaissance period, then superseded by vn. family, now revived for perf. of early mus. Origins obscure, but probably developed from efforts to apply bow to plucked instr. during 2nd half of 15th cent. in Spain. Term 'viol' was used generically, like *vihuela in Sp. Consort of viols mentioned in Eng. records of King's Musick for 1540. Shape of viol varied much during first century of existence. Documentation of 1556 says that Fr. viols had 5 str. tuned in 4ths, whereas It. viols had 6. All viols were played held downwards, larger sizes between the legs, smaller resting on knees. Eng. composers from Byrd to Purcell wrote superb series of works for viols, a consort (or chest) normally comprising 2 trebles, 2 tenors, and 2 basses. Viol had flat back, frets, and C-shaped sound-holes. Bow held in underhand grip with fingers controlling tension of horse-hair. Prin. types of viol are: *Division viol*: smaller version of bass viol suitable for agile playing of *divisions (variations); *Lyra-viol*: instr. specially built for virtuoso viol players who practised double- and triple-stopping, pizzicato, etc.; mus. written in tablature. Tobias

Hume's *First Part of Ayres*, 1605, is lyra-viol mus. See also *baryton, viola d'amore, viola da braccio, viola da gamba*.

Viola (Fr. *alto* or *taille*; Ger. *Bratsche*). (1) Bowed 4-str. instr., sometimes known as *alto* or *tenor* because of its lower pitch compared with vn., to which it is closely related. Tuned to c, g, d′, a′. Va. section standard in all orchs.; one va. is standard component of str. qt. Also used as solo instr., several concs. and conc.-type works having been written for it. *Viola pomposa* was rare 18th-cent. type with a higher 5th str. See also *Tertis, Lionel*.
(2) Org. stop of 8′ length and pitch.
(3) Generic It. term for str. instrs. in Renaissance and baroque periods, incl. *viole da gamba* (leg viols), i.e. members of the *viol family; and *viole da braccio* (arm viols), the forerunners of the vn. family.

Viola Alta (It.; Ger. *Altgeige*). High viola, i.e. large va. with 5 str. introduced by H. Ritter in 1876 and used by Wagner at Bayreuth. Cumbersome to play.

Viola Bastarda. Continental equivalent of Eng. *division* *viol.

Viola da Braccio (It.). Arm-viol. First known use of term in 1543 as generic description of str. instr. played on the arm (e.g. *rebec, Renaissance fiddle, and *lira da braccio*) but later meaning members of *violin family.

Viola da Gamba (It.). Leg-viol. (1) Strictly, every *viol was a *viola da gamba* because of the way it was held for perf., but term applies mainly to bass viol because it was held between the knees like the modern vc.
(2) Org. stop. See *Gamba*.

Viola d'Amore (It.). Love-viol. Bowed str. instr. of the *viol family but without frets and played under the chin. Larger than modern *viola, with 7 bowed gut str. and 7 sympathetic str. (which give the instr. its name) which vibrate to the sound of the stopped strs. Particularly beautiful sound. Used by Baroque composers, and in 19th cent. by Meyerbeer and Berlioz. Specially required by Janáček in his operas *Káťa Kabanová* and *Věc Makropoulos* and his 2nd str. qt.

Viola Pomposa. Instr. of vn. family with 5 str. used in Baroque works for high vc. passages. Larger than va.

Viole (Fr.). (1) *Viol.
(2) *Viola.

Violin (Fr. *Violon*; It. *Violino*; Ger. *Geige* or *Violine*). Bowed 4-str. instr., prin. and treble member of its family (va., vc., and db. being the others). Tuned g d′ a′ e″; compass of over 3½ octaves. Standard feature of every orch., where vns. are divided into '1sts' and '2nds', corresponding to higher- and lower-pitched parts. Str. qt. has 2 vn.

(1st and 2nd). Emerged independently of the *viol, to which it is not related. A 3-str. vn. is represented in paintings at Ferrara 1508–9. At some time in It. before 1550 the 4-str. instr. was invented and was regarded as the instr. for dancing whereas the viol was the courtly instr. Earliest printed vn. mus. is 2 dances incl. in the *Balet comique de la royne* of 1581. Undoubtedly the vn. was perfected by one man, Andrea *Amati of Cremona, from whom the king of Fr. ordered 38 str. instrs. in 1560. For account of later development of instr., see *Stradivari*. Vn. is made from wood, with 2 f-shaped sound holes. Str., made of gut or metal, are stretched along upper surface (belly). Sound from the str. when touched by *bow is transmitted by upright bridge which supports the str. and which they cross at fractionally less than a right angle. Str. are held in place by tailpiece, cross bridge, and continue over ebony fingerboard attached to upper surface of neck. At extreme end they cross nut, or saddle, and enter a pegbox where they are attached to, and tuned by, 4 pegs. Among the most expressive of instr., the vn. has inspired a treasury of great mus. and great performers. The *violino piccolo* (It., little violin) was a small, higher-pitched instr. used in Baroque period in such works as Bach's Brandenburg Conc. No. 1. The vn. bow used to be convex, but since late 18th cent. has been concave, with increased tension.

Violinbogen (Ger.). Vn. bow.

Violino. (1) (It.). *Violin.
(2) Org. stop of 4′ (sometimes 8′) length and pitch.

Violins of Saint-Jacques, The. Opera in 3 acts by *Williamson to lib. by William Chappell after novel by Patrick Leigh Fermor. Prod. London (SW) 1966.

Violin-Steg (Ger.). Vn. bridge.

Violoncello (It., usually abbreviated to 'cello'; Ger. *Violoncell*; Fr. *violoncelle*). Bowed 4-str. instr., one of *violin family, originating in early 16th cent. Played between performer's knees. Tuned to C G d a; compass of over 3 octaves. All sym. orchs. contain vc. section, and one vc. is part of every str. qt. Noble sound of instr. has been well catered for in concs., those by Dvořák and Elgar in particular exploiting its expressive capabilities to the full.

Violone. An imprecise term dating from 1520. In 16th and 17th cents. the double-bass *viol was often called the *violone*, but some writers used the term to mean ordinary bass viol, and Corelli and Handel used it as synonym for vc. Also meant the db. Many *violones* had 6 str., were fretted and tuned like viol. Probably used for bass part of consort mus.

Viotti, Giovanni Battista (*b* Fontanetto, Piedmont, 1755; *d* London, 1824). It. composer and violinist. Son of blacksmith who played hn. and taught him mus. Studied Turin and with *Pugnani, touring Ger. and Russia with him, 1780. Played in Concert Spirituel, Paris, 1782, becoming accompanist to Marie Antoinette. Visited London 1792, making début in Feb. 1793 at Salomon concert and playing in Haydn's benefit concerts 1794 and 1795, and at It. opera at King's Th., 1795–8. Returned to London 1801, becoming wine merchant. Active in formation of Phil. Soc. 1813. Dir., It. Opera in Paris 1819–22. Died impoverished after commercial misfortunes. Reckoned as greatest classical player of his day and founder of modern sch. of classical playing. Wrote 29 vn. concs., of which No. 22 in A minor is especially important, 21 str. qts., 21 str. trios, many vn. duets, 18 vn. sonatas with bass, pf. concs., fl. qts., and other pieces.

Virdung, Sebastian (*b* Amberg, Oberpfalz, *c*.1465). Ger. priest, member of court mus. staff at Heidelberg from 1495. Author of oldest-known book on mus. instrs., *Musica getutscht und ausgezogen* (Basle 1511), with illustrations. Repubd. in facsimile 1882 and 1931. Wrote songs. *Musica getutscht* is principally a tutor for kbd. instrs., lute, and recorder.

Virelai (*chanson balladée*). Medieval Fr. song, probably of Sp. origin, consisting of refrain alternating with (usually) 3 stanzas. Est. as common Fr. poetic and mus. form by Machaut; continued in use throughout 15th cent. (by Dufay, Ockeghem, and Busnois). The word derives from old Fr. *virer*, to turn or twist, thus suggesting a dance origin.

Virginal(s). This word (not of Eng. origin) was used in Eng. as generic term for all types of plucked kbd. instr., but also had specific meaning. First mentioned *c*.1460, name being used in Fr. and Ger. Typical virginals of oblong shape with one set of strs., parallel to kbd. (Differed from hpd. in shape of soundbox, placing of strs.—at right angles on hpd.—and existence of 2 bridges.) Kbd. on Flemish virginals was set to right or left, in others it was centrally placed. Double virginals had 2 kbds. Much fine mus. written for virginals by Byrd, Bull, Morley, Farnaby, etc. See *Fitzwilliam Virginal Book*. Origin of name obscure, but probably comes from instrument's association with female performers or possibly from its tone (like a young girl's voice).

Virtuoso (It.). (1) As noun: a performer of exceptional skill with particular reference to technical ability.
(2) As adjective: a performance of exceptional technical accomplishment. There is sometimes an implication that a virtuoso performance excludes emotional and expressive artistry, or subdues it to technical display, but a true virtuoso is both technician and artist.

Visconti (di Modrone), (Count) **Luchino** (*b* Milan, 1906; *d* Rome, 1976). It. producer, designer, and writer. Came of family with long assoc. with Scala, Milan. Began career as stage and film dir. and went into opera because of admiration for Maria *Callas, for whom he prod. *La Vestale* in 1954. Later he staged, for Callas, *La Sonnambula*, *La Traviata*, *Anna Bolena*, and *Iphigénie en Tauride*, all at La Scala. His first opera prod. outside It. was the memorable *Don Carlos* at CG, 1958, where he later prod. *Il Trovatore, La Traviata*, and *Der Rosenkavalier*. His last opera prod. was *Manon Lescaut* at Spoleto, 1972. Among his protégés were the designers Sanjust and Zeffirelli. Wrote lib. for Mannino's opera *Il Diavolo in giardino* (Palermo 1963) and scenario of Henze's ballet *Maratona* (1956). Directed film of Mann's *Death in Venice* (1971) in which he made use of Mahler's mus. Productions notable for authentic period style, attention to detail and characterization, and visual taste.

Vishnevskaya, Galina (*b* Leningrad, 1926). Russ. sop. Studied with V. Garina 1942–52. Sang at Leningrad Operetta Th. from 1944, then opera début, Leningrad, 1950 in Strelnikov's *Kholopka*. Joined Bolshoy Opera 1952. NY Met. 1961 (début as Aida), CG 1962 (Aida). Fine dramatic singer. Wife of *Rostropovich, whom she married 1955 and with whom she left USSR. Sop. part of Britten's *War Requiem*, 1962, written for her, but she did not sing at f.p. in Coventry. Gave f.p. of Britten's *The Poet's Echo*, Moscow 1965. Shostakovich dedicated his 7 *Romances*, Op. 127, to her (f.p. Moscow 1967) and she sang soprano part in f.p. of his 14th Sym., Leningrad 1969. Sang title-role in first recording of orig. version of Shostakovich's *The Lady Macbeth of the Mtsensk District*. Retired from opera 1982 (Paris, *Eugene Onegin*). Autobiography *Galina* (1984).

Vision of Aeroplanes, A. Motet for mixed ch. and org. by Vaughan Williams on text from Ezekiel, Ch. 1. F.p. Cornhill, London 1956.

Vision of Judgement, The. Oratorio by *Fricker, his Op. 29, to text compiled by him from 8th-cent. poem by Cynewulf. For sop. and ten. soloists, ch., and orch. Comp. for 1958 Leeds Fest., where its f.p. was cond. by John Pritchard.

Vision of St Augustine, The. Setting of Lat. text for bar., ch., and orch. by *Tippett, comp. 1963–5. F.p. London 1966 by Dietrich Fischer-Dieskau, LSO and LSO Ch. cond. Tippett.

Visions de l'Amen. Suite in 7 movements for 2 pf. by *Messiaen, comp. 1943. F.p. Paris, 1943 (Loriod and Messiaen).

Visions fugitives (Fleeting Visions). 20 pieces for solo pf. by Prokofiev, Op. 22, comp. 1915–17. F.p. Petrograd, 1918 (Prokofiev).

Visit of the Old Lady, The (*Der Besuch der alten Dame*). Opera in 3 acts by von *Einem to lib. by Dürrenmatt based on his own play. Prod. Vienna 1971, Glyndebourne, 1973.

Vitali, Giovanni Battista (b Bologna, 1632; d Modena, 1692). It. composer and violinist. Held court post at Modena from 1674. One of pioneers of sonata. Wrote *sonate de chiesa*, sonatas for 2 vn. with bass, etc.

Vitali, Tomaso Antonio (b Bologna, 1663; d Modena, 1745). It. violinist and composer, son of G. B. *Vitali. Studied in Bologna. Chamber musician in Modena. Wrote sonatas (1693–5) and famous Chaconne for vn. with figured bass (though this is of doubtful attrib.).

Vitry, Philippe de (b Paris, 1291; d Paris, 1361). Fr. composer, poet, and theorist. Held court posts and became Bishop of Meaux in 1351. Wrote 4 treatises on *Ars Nova. Some motets survive. May have originated isorhythmic motet.

Vittoria. See *Victoria, Tomás Luis de.*

Vivace, vivacemente (It.). Vivacious, from *vivacità, vivacezza,* vivacity. Fast and lively. *Vivacissimo,* very fast. Composers (e.g. Schubert) often use *vivace* as an indication of mood rather than tempo. In 18th cent. it often meant something between *allegro* and *largo.*

Vivaldi, Antonio (b Venice, 1678; d Vienna, 1741). It. composer and violinist. Son of violinist in orch. of St Mark's, Venice, under *Legrenzi. Taught by father. Entered church, becoming priest 1703, though after 2 years never said Mass because of congenital chest complaint. Taught vn. at orphanage (Ospedale della Pietà) from 1703 and gave recitals. Pubd. trio sonatas, Op. 1, 1705 and vn. sonatas, Op. 2, 1709. First opera, *Ottone in villa,* prod. Vicenza 1713; first Venetian opera, *Orlando finto pazzo,* 1714. Was also operatic impresario in Venice and cond. and played vn. in opera perfs. Spent 3 years in service of Landgrave of Hesse-Darmstadt in Mantua, probably 1719–1721. Between 1722 and 1725, wrote operas for Mantua, Vicenza, Milan, and Rome. His famous Op. 8, incl. *Le quattro stagioni* (The Four Seasons), was pubd. 1725. By this time, Vivaldi was known and admired throughout Europe. In 1734 first collaborated with librettist Goldoni (1709–93). In 1737 prod. of a new Vivaldi opera at Ferrara was forbidden by papal authorities on ground that Vivaldi was a priest who did not say Mass and had a relationship with a woman singer. In 1738, visited Amsterdam, where his mus. had been pubd. since 1711, for royal th. centenary celebrations—his reputation stood higher in Fr., Holland, and Eng. in his lifetime than it did in Venice. Despite intermittent disputes over the years, Vivaldi was still maestro at the Pietà and was still writing cantatas for perf. there in 1740. In 1741 he decided to leave Venice for Vienna, presumably in search of some court appointment, but died there, being buried in a pauper's grave.

Among contemporaries who appreciated Vivaldi was J. S. Bach, who transcr. 10 Vivaldi concs. as hpd. or org. concs. Like Bach himself, Vivaldi's mus. fell out of favour for many years, but the 20th cent., in particular since the revival of interest in authentic methods of performing baroque mus., has seen it re-est. Once regarded merely as the composer of works for str., his genius as an opera composer is now recognized (he said he wrote 94, but fewer than 50 are extant) as well as the Venetian splendour of his church mus. No composer did more to establish the vc. as a solo instr., and he displayed a keen interest in the use of unusual instr.: it is the infinite variety and invention of his work that has made it so beloved 300 years after his birth. There have been several catalogues of his work, the most recent (Leipzig 1974) by Peter Ryom (works are numbered with the prefix RV = *Ryom-Verzeichnis*). Prin. works:

OPERAS: *Bajazet* (*Tamerlano*) (1735); *Catone in Utica* (1737); *Dorilla in Tempe* (1726); *Ercole sul Termodonte* (1723); *Farnace* (1727); *La fida ninfa* (1732); *Il Giustino* (1724); *Griselda* (1735); *L'incoronazione di Dario* (1716); *L'Olimpiade* (1734); *Orlando finto pazzo* (1714); *Orlando furioso* (1727); *Ottone in villa* (1713); *Rosilena ed Oronta* (1728); *Rosmira* (1738); *Il Teuzzone* (1719); *Tito Manlio* (1719); *La verità in cimento* (1720).

PUBLISHED WORKS IN HIS LIFETIME: Op. 1, 12 Sonatas for 2 vn. and basso continuo (1705); Op. 2, 12 Sonatas for vn. and basso continuo (1709); Op. 3, L'*estro armonico* (Harmonic inspiration), 12 concs. for various combinations (4 vn., 4 vn. and vc., etc.) (1711); Op. 4, *La *stravaganza* (The extraordinary), 12 vn. concs. (c.1714); Op. 5 (2nd part of Op. 2), 4 sonatas for vn. and 2 sonatas for 2 vn. and basso continuo (1716); Op. 6, 6 vn. concs. (1716–21); Op. 7, 2 ob. concs. and 10 vn. concs. (1716–21); Op. 8, *Il cimento dell' armonia e dell' inventione* (The Contest between Harmony and Invention), 12 vn. concs., the first 4, in E, G minor, F, and F minor being known as The *Four Seasons* (Le quattro stagioni) (1725); Op. 9, *La cetra* (The lyre), 11 vn. concs. and 1 for 2 vn. (1727); Op. 10, 6 fl. concs. (c.1728); Op. 11, 5 vn. concs., 1 ob. conc. (1729); Op. 12, 5 vn. concs. and 1 without solo (1729); Op. 13, *Il pastor fido* (The Faithful Shepherd), 6 sonatas for musette, viella, recorder, ob. or vn., and basso continuo (1737, doubtful authenticity).

The rest of Vivaldi's instr. output is so vast that it can only be summarized:

10 sonatas for vc. and basso continuo; 28 sonatas for vn. and basso continuo; 4 sonatas for fl. and basso continuo; sonatas for 2 vn. and basso continuo; concs. for various instr. (fl., ob., recorders, vns., bn., etc.) and basso continuo; over 60 concs., sinfonias, and sonatas for str. and basso continuo; 170 concs. and sinfonias for vn., orch., and basso continuo; 7 concs. for viola d'amore; 28 vc. concs.; mandolin conc.; 9 fl. concs.; 2 recorder concs.; 14 ob. concs.; over 40

bn. concs.; many concs. for 2 vn., 2 vc., 2 mandolins, 2 ob., 2 hn., 2 tpt., etc.

SACRED MUSIC: Mass; *Kyrie* for double ch.; 3 *Glorias*; 2 *Dixit Dominus*; 3 *Laudate pueri*; 2 *Magnificat*; 3 *Salve Regina*; *Stabat Mater*; **Juditha triumphans* (oratorio, Venice 1716); also many secular cantatas, etc.

Vivo (It.). Lively; *vivissimo* is the superlative.

Vl. Short for violin in orch. scores. In this and other dictionaries, vn. is used.

Vlach Quartet. Cz. str. qt. formed by Josef Vlach (*b* Ratměřice, 1923) with 3 colleagues in the Cz. Chamber Orch. Concert début Prague 1951. Va. player has changed three times. Won Liège int. comp. 1955 which led to world tours.

Vlad, Roman (*b* Cernăuti, 1919). Romanian composer and writer. Studied Cernăuti Cons., then studied in Rome with Casella until 1941. Comp. in 12-note idiom from 1943. Taught at Dartington summer sch., 1954 and 1955. Art dir., Accademia Filarmonica Romana 1955–8, Maggio Musicale, Florence, from 1964. Prof. of comp., Perugia Cons. from 1968. Contributor to several periodicals; author of book on Stravinsky (Eng. trans. 1967). Works incl. opera *Storia di una mamma* (1950–1), ballets *La strada sul caffè* (1944), *La dama delle camelie* (1945), *Sinfonia all' antica*, orch. (1947–8), *Variazioni concertanti*, pf. and orch., based on series of 12 notes in Mozart's *Don Giovanni*, *Serenata* for str., *De Profundis*, sop., ch., and orch. (1949), etc.

Vltava (Smetana). See *Má Vlast*.

Vn. Abbreviation for violin.

Vocalise. A wordless vocal exercise or concert piece sung to one or more vowels. One of first concert pieces was Ravel's *Vocalise en forme d'habañera*. There are also *Vocalise*, for v. and pf. by Rakhmaninov, Op. 34, No. 14, comp. 1912, rev. 1915, and *3 Vocalises* for sop. and cl. by Vaughan Williams (1958).

Vocal Score (abbreviated to V.S.). Score of a comp. which gives all the v.-parts of a work but with the orch. parts reduced to a pf. acc.

Voce, voci (It.). Voice, voices. *Colla voce*, with the voice, i.e. direction to the accompanist closely to follow the singer's fluctuations of tempo, etc.

Voce di petto; Voce di testa (It.). Chest voice; head voice.

Voces Intimae (Friendly Voices). Sibelius's subtitle for his Str. Qt. in D minor, Op. 56, comp. 1909.

Vogel, Edith (*b* Czernowitz, 1912). Austro-Hung. pianist and teacher. Studied Vienna Acad. Début Vienna at age 10. Settled in Eng. Taught at GSM and Dartington summer schs.

Vogel, Jaroslav (*b* Pizeň, 1894; *d* Prague, 1970). Cz. conductor, composer, and writer. Studied in Prague, vn. with Ševčik and comp. with Novák, also in Munich and in Paris (1912–13) with d'Indy. Opera cond. in Ostrava 1919–23, returning as chief cond. 1927–43. Cond., Prague Nat. Th. 1949–58, chief cond. Brno State P.O. 1959–62. In Ostrava his perfs. of operas by Janáček, Smetana, and Novák were renowned. Wrote 3 operas. Also notable for his extensive study of Janáček's life and works (Prague 1958, abridged Eng. trans. 1962; rev. by K. Janovický, Eng. trans. 1981). Cond. first complete recording of a Janáček opera (*Jenůfa*, 1952).

Vogel, Vladimir (*b* Moscow, 1896; *d* Zürich, 1984). Russo-Ger.-born composer, Swiss citizen since 1954. Studied in Berlin with Tiessen and Busoni. Taught at Klindworth-Scharwenka Cons. 1929–33, then settled in Switzerland. Several large-scale works using speaking ch. and *Sprechstimme*. Style a compound of Berg's 12-note technique and Busoni neo-classicism. Works incl.: *4 Études* for orch. (1930–2), *Tripartita* for orch. (1934), vn. conc. (1937), vc. conc. (1954), *Epitaph for Alban Berg*, pf. (1936), *Thyl Claes*, sop., 2 speakers, speaking ch., orch. (1938–42), *Flucht*, oratorio for soloists, 4 *Sprechstimmen*, speaking ch., orch. (1963–4), *Goethe Aphorisms*, sop., str. (1955), chamber mus., etc.

Vogelweide, Walther von der (*b* c.1170; *d* ?Würzburg, c.1230). Ger. singer and composer, one of greatest of Ger. **Minnesinger*. About 8 of his melodies have survived. Mentioned by Wagner in *Die Meistersinger von Nürnberg*, Act I, when the hero, Walther, tells the Masters that he is a pupil of Vogelweide. 'A good Master', says Sachs.

Vogl, Heinrich (*b* Au, nr. Munich, 1845; *d* Munich, 1900). Ger. ten., outstanding in Wagnerian parts. Studied Munich with Lachner. Opera début Munich 1865 as Max in *Der Freischütz*. Took over role of Tristan after death of Schnorr von Carolsfeld. Created Loge in *Rheingold* 1869 and Siegmund in *Walküre* 1870. Sang at Bayreuth 1876–97, incl. roles of Tristan and Parsifal. London début 1882 (1st London Loge and Siegfried). NY Met. 1890 (singing 6 Wagner tenor roles in the season). Wrote opera, 1899. Wife was sop. Therese Thoma (*b* Tutzing, 1845; *d* Munich, 1921), who studied at Munich Cons. and made début in Munich 1866, singing there until 1892. Created role of Sieglinde 1870. London 1882 (1st London Brünnhilde). For some years was only Ger. Isolde.

Vogl, (Johann) Michael (*b* Ennsdorf, nr. Steyr, Austria, 1768; *d* Vienna, 1840). Austrian bar. Educated at monastery. Sang at Vienna Court Opera 1795–1822. Met Schubert c.1817 through Schober and became first singer of many of his Lieder. Sang twins (who never appear on stage together) in Schubert's *Singspiel*, *Die Zwillingsbrüder*, 1820. Travelled with Schubert, 1819, to

Upper Austria, and again in 1823 and 1825. First to sing *Winterreise* cycle, 1827. Created role of Pizarro in Beethoven's *Fidelio* in the 1814 revision.

Vogler, Georg Joseph (Abbé Vogler) (*b* Pleichach, nr. Würzburg, 1749; *d* Darmstadt, 1814). Ger. composer, theorist, organist, and teacher. Studied in Bologna with Martini. Ordained priest in Rome 1773. Returned to Mannheim 1775 and founded mus. sch. Became 2nd Kapellmeister and wrote operas. After visits to Paris (1780) and London (1783) to propagate his theories of musical performance, he became court cond. at Munich 1784–6. Travelled widely from 1786. Court mus. dir. Stockholm 1786, founding mus. sch. there. Travelled again from 1799. Taught in Vienna 1803–4. Court cond., Darmstadt 1807. Invented 'simplifications system' for org., demonstrating it in Eng., Denmark, and Holland on portable 'orchestration'. Famous for his 'storm' effects in org. recitals. Wrote 10 operas, cantata, much church mus., pf. concs., many theoretical works, 32 org. preludes in every key (with analysis), arr. 12 Chorales by J. S. Bach. Pupils incl. Aloysia Weber (singing), Meyerbeer, Weber, Danzi, etc. (comp.). Subject of poem *Abt Vogler* by Robert Browning (1812–89) containing line 'The rest may reason and welcome; 'tis we musicians know'.

Voice. (1) Means of producing sounds in humans and animals using 2 vibrating agents called vocal cords. The various kinds of human v., e.g. *soprano, *tenor, *bass, etc., are described under their individual entries.
(2) Separate strand of mus. in counterpoint or harmony, also known as 'part'. A fugue is in several vv. or parts, whether these are sung or played.
(3) As verb, meaning to adjust org.-pipe at construction stage so that it meets required standards of pitch, etc.

Voice of Ariadne, The. Opera in 3 acts by Musgrave, to lib. by A. Elguera based on James's *The Last of the Valerii*. Comp. 1972–3. F.p. Snape Maltings, 1974, NY 1977.

Voix (Fr.). Voice or voices.

Voix Céleste (Fr.). Heavenly voice. Org. stop, 8′ pitch, with 2 pipes to each note, tuned slightly apart and producing effect not unlike str. of orch.

Voix humaine, La (The Human Voice). Lyric tragedy in 1 act by Poulenc to text by Cocteau (a monodrama for sop. and orch.). Comp. 1958. Prod. Paris 1959, NY (concert) 1960, Edinburgh (concert) 1960, Glyndebourne (stage) 1976.

Volante (It.). Flying. Swift, light. In vn. playing, a certain bow-stroke in which the bow has to bounce from the str. in a slurred staccato.

Volkmann, (Friedrich) **Robert** (*b* Lommatzsch, Saxony, 1815; *d* Budapest, 1883). Ger. composer. Studied Leipzig 1836 and encouraged by Schumann. Taught in Prague 1839–41, in Pest 1841–1854, and in Vienna 1854–8. Prof. of comp., Budapest Acad. from 1875. Wrote 2 syms., vc. conc., *Sappho* for sop. and orch., many songs, and large amount of chamber mus.

Volkonsky, Andrey (Mikhaylovich) (*b* Geneva, 1933). Swiss-born Russ. composer, pianist, cond., and harpsichordist. Studied Geneva Cons. 1944–5 (pf. with Lipatti) and Paris Cons. 1946–7 (comp. with Boulanger). Further study at Moscow Cons. 1950–4. Influenced by Schoenberg, Boulez, Berio, etc. and encountered difficulties from Soviet authorities because of modern trend of his works. Founded *Madrigal*, early mus. ens. of Moscow Phil. Emigrated to Israel 1973. Works incl. Conc. for Orch., cantata *Dead Souls*, *Serenade to an Insect* for chamber orch., str. qts., pf. sonata, and music-theatre pieces.

Volkslied (Ger.). Folk-song, but often extended to incl. nat. and popular song which is properly covered by term *Volkstümliches Lied*.

Volles Werk (Ger.). Full Org.

Volonté (Fr.). Will. *A volonté,* at one's own pleasure, i.e. *ad libitum*.

Volta (It.). (1) 'Time', in sense of *prima volta*, 1st time.
(2) Quick dance in triple time, also known as 'Lavolta', resembling galliard. A Lavolta is danced in Britten's *Gloriana* (1953).

Volti (It.). Turn, as in *volti subito* (abbreviated to V.S.), turn over page quickly (found in orch. parts).

Voluntary. (1) Org. solo at beginning and end of Anglican church service, sometimes but not necessarily extemporized.
(2) In 16th cent., applied to extemporized instr. comp. See also *Trumpet Tune* or *Voluntary*.

Von Heute auf Morgen (From One Day to the Next). Comic opera in 1 act, Op. 32, by *Schoenberg to lib. by Max Blonda (Gertrud Schoenberg). Comp. 1928–9. Prod. Frankfurt 1930, London (concert) 1963. Orch. score requires saxs., mandoline, guitar, banjo, and flexatone.

Vonk, Hans (*b* Amsterdam, 1942). Dutch cond. Studied Amsterdam Cons. (comp. and conducting). Cond. lessons from *Scherchen. Ass. cond. Dutch Nat. Ballet 1965. Ass. cond. Concertgebouw Orch., Amsterdam, 1969–72. Début with Netherlands Opera 1971 (mus. dir. from 1976). London début 1974 (RPO). Amer. début 1974 (San Francisco). Cond., Dutch Radio Orch. from 1972. Prin. cond. Netherlands Opera. Assoc. cond., RPO 1977.

Von Stade, Frederica. See *Stade, Frederica von.*

Vorbereiten (Ger.). To prepare (applied to the registration of org. mus., often in the form of *bereite vor,* mentioning a stop). *Vorbereitung,* preparation.

Vorhalt (Ger.). (1) Suspension.
(2) Retardation.
(3) Long appoggiatura.
(4) Syncopation.

Voříšek, Jan (*b* Vamberk, Bohemia, 1791; *d* Vienna, 1825). Bohem. composer. Played org., pf., and vn. at 8 and was sent to Prague to study with Tomášek. Went to Vienna 1813, becoming friend of Hummel, Meyerbeer, and Moscheles. Pianist and cond. of Gesellschaft der Musikfreunde from 1818. Organist, Imperial Chapel, 1822. Wrote sym., church mus., pf. conc., pf. sonata, *Impromptus* for pf., etc.

Vorschlag (Ger.). Forestroke. *Kurzer Vorschlag* (short forestroke), *Acciaccatura; Langer Vorschlag* (long forestroke), *Appoggiatura.

Vorspiel (Ger.). Foreplay. Ov. or prelude, used by Wagner in relation to his operas.

Vostřák, Zbyněk (*b* Prague, 1920). Cz. composer and cond. Studied Prague Cons. 1939–43 and at Darmstadt courses 1965–6, attending lectures by Boulez, Stockhausen, etc. Taught at Prague Cons. 1945–8. Cond. opera and, from 1963, Prague contemporary mus. ens. Worked at Prague Radio elec. studios from 1967. Works incl. comic opera, *3 Shakespeare Sonnets* for bass and chamber orch., *The Balance of Light,* 2-track tape; *Sextant* for wind quintet, etc.

Vox (Lat.). Voice. Thus *vox humana* (human voice), org. reed stop of 8′ pitch, supposedly but not actually like human v.

Vranický. See *Wranitzky, Anton.*

Vronsky, Vitya (*b* Evpatoria, Crimea, 1909). Russ.-born pianist, later Amer. citizen. Studied Kiev, Berlin (with Petri and Schnabel), and Paris (with Cortot). Married Victor *Babin 1933, forming celebrated pf. duo and settling in USA.

V.S. (1) *Vocal score.
(2)*Volti subito,* turn over quickly.

Vuillaume, Jean Baptiste (*b* Mirecourt, 1798; *d* Paris, 1875). Fr. maker of str. instr. Went to Paris 1818, where est. own business 1828. Made fine vns. and vcs.

Vulpius, Melchior (*b* Wasungen, Henneberg, *c.*1570; *d* Weimar, 1615). Ger. composer and cantor. Comp. chorales, *cantiones sacrae, St Matthew Passion* (1613), and ed. mus. compendium.

Vuoto, Vuota (It., 'empty'). Applied musically (1) to indicate a general pause, i.e. measure in which all parts have 'rest'; or (2) as indication to violinist to play on open str. (*corda vuota*).

Vycpálek, Ladislav (*b* Prague, 1882; *d* Prague, 1969). Cz. composer. Studied Prague Univ., then privately with Novák 1908–12. Chief mus. librarian, Prague Univ. 1922–42. Specialist in folk mus. Works incl. *Czech Requiem* (1940); cantata *On the Final Affairs of Man* (1920–2, denounced in 1950 by Communist authorities as 'subjective and mystical'); sonata for mez., vn., pf. 'in praise of violin' (1927–8); song-cycles, etc.

Vyšehrad (Smetana). See *Má Vlast.*

Vyshnegradsky, Ivan (*b* St Petersburg, 1893; *d* Paris, 1979). Russ. composer. Studied St Petersburg Univ. with Sokolov, 1911–14. Disciple of Skryabin; explored microtones and used 'ultrachromatic scales'—quarter-tone, 6th-tone, etc.— until his work became pantonal. Went to Ger. to meet *Hába. Settled in Fr., where Pleyel built quarter-tone, 3-manual pf. to his design. Comp. after 1936 exclusively for pfs. tuned microtone apart. Works incl. *Ainsi parlait Zarathoustra* (Thus spake Zarathustra) for orch., 24 *Preludes* for 2 pf., 5 *Variations sans thème et conclusion* for orch. in quarter-tones, etc.

Vyvyan, Jennifer (*b* Broadstairs, 1925; *d* London, 1974). Eng. sop. Studied RAM and with Roy Henderson. Joined Glyndebourne ch. Solo part in EOG *Beggar's Opera,* 1948. Went to Switzerland to study with Carpi, 1950 and won Geneva int. comp. 1951. Joined SW Opera 1952, singing Mozart roles. Created Penelope Rich in Britten's *Gloriana,* CG 1953. Sang Electra in Mozart's *Idomeneo,* Glyndebourne 1954. Created Governess in Britten's *The Turn of the Screw,* Venice 1954, Tytania in *A Midsummer Night's Dream,* Aldeburgh 1960, and Mrs Julian in *Owen Wingrave,* TV 1971, CG 1973. Also successful career in concert works, particularly Elgar oratorios and Howells's *Hymnus Paradisi.*

W

W. Abbreviation for *Werk(e)* (Ger., works(s)), the same as Opus. In Kinsky's Beethoven catalogue, *WoO signifies *Werk ohne Opuszahl*, 'work without opus number.'

Waart, Edo de (*b* Amsterdam, 1941). Dutch cond. and oboist. Studied Amsterdam. Prin. oboe, Concertgebouw Orch. of Amsterdam, 1963. Winner, Mitropoulos Competition NY 1964. Ass. cond., Concertgebouw Orch. 1966. Prin. cond., Rotterdam P.O. 1973–7; prin. guest cond. San Francisco S.O. from 1975, cond. 1977–85. Cond. Minnesota Orch. from 1986. British début Folkestone (RPO) 1969, CG 1976 (*Ariadne auf Naxos*). Amer. opera début Santa Fe 1971.

Wachet auf (Wake up!, often trans. as 'Sleepers, awake'). Church cantata No. 140 by J. S. Bach, 1731, based on Lutheran chorale. Also choral-prelude for organ (BWV 645) by J. S. Bach. 'Wach' auf' is ch. in Act 3 of Wagner's *Die Meistersinger*, sung to words by orig. Hans Sachs.

Wachtelpfeife (Ger.). Quail-pipe. Instr. imitative of quail used in Toy Sym. attrib. Leopold Mozart. Beethoven, in ob. part in 2nd movement of *Pastoral* Sym., uses this term where imitation of quail is required.

Wächter, Eberhard (*b* Vienna, 1929). Austrian bar. Studied Vienna. Opera début Vienna Volksoper 1953. Member of Vienna State Opera from 1954. CG début 1956 (Count in *Figaro*). Bayreuth Fest. from 1958. NY Met. from 1961.

Waddington, Sidney (Peine) (*b* Lincoln, 1869; *d* Uplyme, Devon, 1953). Eng. composer and teacher. Studied London, Frankfurt, and Vienna. Choirmaster at St Mary's, Bayswater, 1894–1905. Prof. of harmony RCM from 1905. Wrote pf. conc., choral works, chamber mus., etc. Admired as teacher by Vaughan Williams, who ded. the opera *Sir John in Love* to him. Cond. f.p. (private) of Vaughan Williams's *Hugh the Drover*, 1924.

Waelrant, Hubert (*b* Tongerloo, *c*.1516–7; *d* Antwerp, 1595). Flemish composer. Ten. in choir of Antwerp Cath. Founded mus. sch. in Antwerp, 1547. Taught system of *solmization*. Mus. publisher. Wrote madrigals, *chansons*, church mus.

Wagenaar, Bernard (*b* Arnhem, 1894; *d* York, Maine, 1971). Dutch-born composer (Amer. citizen from 1927). Son of Johan *Wagenaar. Studied with his father and at Utrecht Cons. Went to USA 1920, joining NY P.O. as violinist 1921–3. Taught at NY Juilliard Sch. 1925–68. Works incl. 4 syms. (2nd and 3rd first cond. by Toscanini, No. 1 by Mengelberg) 1926, 1931,

1935, 1949; triple conc. (fl., harp, vc.) 1937; *Sinfonietta*, 1929; *Song of Mourning*, orch., 1944; *5 Tableaux*, vc. and orch., 1952; vn. conc., 1940; 4 str. qts., vn. sonata, song-cycle, etc.

Wagenaar, Johan (*b* Utrecht, 1862; *d* The Hague, 1941). Dutch composer and organist. Studied Berlin with Herzogenberg, 1889. Organist, Utrecht Cath. 1887–1919 (famous Bach player). Dir., Utrecht Mus. Sch. 1904–18, The Hague Cons. 1918–38. Wrote 2 operas, symphonic poem *Saul and David*, vn. and pf. pieces, songs.

Wagenseil, Georg Christoph (*b* Vienna, 1715; *d* Vienna, 1777). Austrian composer and pianist. Studied comp. with Fux. Court composer, Vienna, from 1739, becoming mus.-master to Empress Maria Theresia. Wrote 16 operas (incl. *La Clemenza di Tito*, 1746), at least 30 syms., hpd. concs., harp concs., chamber mus.

Wagenseil, Johann Christoph (*b* Nuremberg, 1633; *d* Altdorf, 1708). Ger. writer and librarian. In 1697 pubd. his *Nuremberg Chronicles*, containing treatise on the Meistersinger from which Wagner drew much of the background (and several of the characters) for his opera *Die Meistersinger von Nürnberg*.

Wagner, Cosima (*née* Liszt) (*b* Bellaggio, Lake Como, 1837; *d* Bayreuth, 1930). Of Franco-Hungarian birth, being daughter of *Liszt and Countess Marie d'Agoult. Educated in Fr. Went to Ger. and in 1857 married Hans von Bülow, pianist and cond., by whom she had 2 children. First met Richard Wagner in Paris 1853; declared love for each other in Berlin 1863. Went to Munich 1864 to be near Wagner. Daughter, Isolde, born to them 1865. Lived with Wagner at Tribschen, Lucerne, from 1868. Another daughter, Eva, born 1867. Divorced from von Bülow 1869. Son, Siegfried, born to her and Wagner 1869. Married Wagner 1870. Moved with him to Bayreuth 1872 and was active in preparations for 1876 festival. After Wagner's death in 1883, became mus. dir. of Bayreuth Fest., handing over to her son Siegfried in 1908. Became blind 1920. Her Diaries, covering years 1869–83, are invaluable source of information on Wagner's life and thought.

Wagner, Johanna (*b* Seelze, nr. Hanover, 1826; *d* Würzburg, 1894). Ger. sop. Illegitimate child of army officer and singer, adopted by R. Wagner's brother. Engaged at Dresden, where Wagner was cond., 1843. Created role of Elisabeth in *Tannhäuser* 1845. Studied with Viardot in Paris 1846–8. Sang in Berlin 1850–62, then lost v. but became actress. London début 1856. Resumed singing in 1870s. Sang alto part in Beethoven's 9th Sym. at Bayreuth stone-laying ceremony 1872. Created First Norn in *Götterdämmerung*, 1876. Taught in Munich 1882–4.

Wagner, Peter Josef (*b* Kürenz, Trèves, 1865; *d* Fribourg, 1931). Ger. musicologist. Studied at Trèves and in Berlin with *Spitta. On staff Fribourg Univ. from 1893, prof. of mus. history 1902, and rector 1920–1. Specialist in plainsong, Palestrina, madrigals, etc.

Wagner, (Wilhelm) **Richard** (*b* Leipzig, 1813; *d* Venice, 1883). Ger. composer, cond., poet, and author. One of the handful of composers who changed the course of mus. Went to sch. in Dresden and attended Thomasschule, Leipzig, 1830–1. Deeply interested in literature as youth. Mus. inclination intensified by hearing *Schröder-Devrient in Bellini. Wrote sym. 1832 and later that year made first attempt at opera, *Die Hochzeit*, which he destroyed. Choral cond. at Würzburg 1833 and in 1834 completed opera *Die Feen*. Became cond. of orch. at th. in Lauchstädt and later in 1834 mus. dir. of th. at Magdeburg. His 2nd opera *Das Liebesverbot*, based on Shakespeare's *Measure for Measure*, prod. there 1836. Married actress Minna Planer. Ass. cond. at Riga 1837–9. Went to Paris 1839. Wrote *Rienzi* 1838–40 and *Der fliegende Holländer* 1841. Lived in poverty in Paris, doing mus. hack-work and writing articles. In 1842 returned to Dresden, where *Rienzi* was prod. with great success. *Der fliegende Holländer* equal success in 1843, leading to Wagner's appointment as court opera cond. Cond. legendary perfs. of Beethoven's 9th Sym. and works by Mozart, Weber, and Gluck. *Tannhäuser* prod. at Dresden 1845. Began project for series of operas based on Nibelungen sagas, completing lib. of *Siegfrieds Tod*, 1848. Sided with revolutionaries in 1849 uprising in Dresden. Fled to Liszt at Weimar after police issued warrant for his arrest, eventually settling in Zürich where he wrote series of essays, incl. the important *Oper und Drama* in which he expounded his theory of *music drama, the unification of mus. and drama superseding all other considerations (such as singers' special requirements in the way of display arias). Also continued to write text of his Nibelung operas and comp. mus. of *Das Rheingold* and *Die Walküre*. In permanent financial straits, was helped by Julie Ritter and by Ger. merchant Otto Wesendonck, with whose wife Mathilde Wesendonck he had affair. Under the influence of this emotional experience he wrote lib. and mus. of *Tristan und Isolde* (1857–9), interrupting *Siegfried* after completing Act 2. In 1855 visited London as cond. of Phil. Soc. concerts. Wife Minna left him (not for first time) in 1858 because of Wesendonck affair but rejoined him in 1859. Cond. in Paris 1860 and rev. *Tannhäuser* for perf. at Opéra in 1861; but tried to withdraw it after riots instigated by Jockey Club. Allowed to re-

enter Ger., except Saxony. Heard *Lohengrin* (comp. 1846–8) in Vienna and hoped for prod. there of *Tristan*, but it was abandoned after 77 rehearsals as 'unperformable'. Amnesty granted from Saxony 1862. At work on *Die Meistersinger von Nürnberg* from 1862. Fled Vienna 1864 because of pressing debts, but while in Stuttgart was 'rescued' by young King Ludwig of Bavaria, a passionate admirer of Wagner's mus., who became his patron and invited him to Munich, where *Tristan* was prod. 1865, cond. by Hans von Bülow, with whose wife Cosima, Wagner had been in love since 1863. Work resumed on Nibelung operas under stimulus of Ludwig's enthusiasm. Opposition to Wagner in Munich political circles led to his departure from Munich and his settling at the villa of *Tribschen, Lucerne, where Cosima, having borne him 2 daughters, joined him in 1868. Minna having died in 1866 and Cosima's marriage being annulied in 1869 (the year in which she gave birth to Wagner's son Siegfried), Wagner and Cosima were married in 1870. *Das Rheingold* and *Die Walküre* prod. in Munich 1869 and 1870, *Die Meistersinger* in 1868. In 1871 persuaded *Bayreuth municipal authority to grant land for erection of th. specially designed for staging of *Der Ring des Nibelungen*; foundation-stone laid 1872. Toured Ger. to seek artists and raise funds for first Bayreuth Fest. Settled into new home, *Wahnfried, at Bayreuth 1874, where he completed *Götterdämmerung*, 4th opera in *Ring* project begun in 1848. Bayreuth th. opened August 1876 and *Ring* perf. complete under Hans *Richter, supervised in every detail by Wagner. In 1877 cond. series of concerts at Royal Albert Hall, London, to raise funds to cover Bayreuth deficit, and then began work on *Parsifal*, which he had first contemplated in 1857 (completed 1882, perf. in July at Bayreuth). From 1878, suffered series of heart attacks, fatal one occurring in Venice on 13 Feb. 1883. Buried at Wahnfried.

Wagner's mus., richly expressive, intensely illustrative, and on the grandest scale, dominated the 19th cent. and split the mus. world into opposing factions. His influence, good and bad, on countless other composers is still a prime factor a century after his death. He wrote the texts of all his operas, reading copiously in the sources of the legends he selected as subjects and writing a prose sketch, then the poem (lib.) before he comp. any of the mus., though it is clear that certain ideas came to him ready-clothed in mus. He was inspired by the Ger. Romantic spirit of Weber's operas, and to some extent by the grandiose operatic aims of Meyerbeer, whom he despised. In Liszt he found a fellow-spirit from whom he learned much, as he did from Berlioz. But he surpassed them all in the single-mindedness with which he pursued his dream of an art form in which mus. and drama should be one and indivisible, his *Zukunftsmusik* (mus. of the future). With the chromaticism of *Tristan* he took tonality to its limits and beyond, and opened the way for the Schoenbergian revolution. Philosophical and psychological undertones contribute immensely to the spell of the *Tristan* mus. Wagner brought to a fine art the use of *Leitmotiv* to depict not only characters but their emotions, and wove them into an orch. texture of such richness that the orch. assumed an extra dimension in operatic terms. His operas also required a new technique of singing and a new breed of singers with the intelligence to convey the subtleties of his art. The idea that 'bawling' was all that Wagner needed has long been disproved by generations of singers by whom his music has been shown to be as singable as *bel canto*. In a sense Wagner was a dead-end, since he was a unique genius. The sheer mastery of *The Ring*, the sustaining of such an imposing achievement at a white-heat of inspiration for something like 15 hours of mus., is among the most amazing artistic achievements of the human spirit. But opera could never be the same after him: he made it the vehicle for the expression of the most complex emotional and psychological issues, but, being first and foremost a musician, these are still secondary to the hypnotic power of the mus., at least for those (and they number millions) who fall under its sway. Prin. works:

OPERAS AND MUSIC DRAMAS: *Die *Feen* (The Fairies) (1833–4); *Das *Liebesverbot* (Forbidden Love) (1835–6); **Rienzi* (1838–40); *Der *fliegende Holländer* (The Flying Dutchman) (1841); **Tannhäuser* (1843–5, rev. 1861); **Lohengrin* (1846–8); *Der *Ring des Nibelungen* (The Nibelung's Ring): *Das *Rheingold* (The Rhine Gold) (1853–4), *Die *Walküre* (The Valkyrie) (1854–6), **Siegfried* (1856–7 and 1864–71), **Götterdämmerung* (Twilight of the Gods) (1869–74, some ideas composed as **Siegfrieds Tod* many years earlier); **Tristan und Isolde* (1857–9); *Die *Meistersinger von Nürnberg* (The Mastersingers of Nuremberg) (1862–7); **Parsifal* (1878–82).
ORCH: Sym. in C (1832); **Siegfried Idyll* (1870); Concert Ov. in D minor (1831), in C (1832); **Christopher Columbus*, ov. (1835); **Rule, Britannia*, ov. (1836–7); **Polonia*, ov. (1836); **Faust*, ov. (1840, rev. 1855); **Huldigungsmarsch* (1864); **Kaisermarsch* (1871); *Centennial March* (1876).
CHORAL: *Weihegruss* (1843); *An Webers Grabe* (1844); *Das *Liebesmahl der Apostel* (The Love Feast of the Apostles), orch. with male ch. (1843).
PIANO: Sonata in B♭ (1831); *Lied ohne Worte* (1840); Album Sonata in A♭ (1853); *Albumblätter* in A♭ and C (1861).
SONGS: *7 Songs from Goethe's Faust* (1832); *Der Tannenbaum* (1838); *Les deux grenadiers* (1839–40); *Les adieux de Marie Stuart* (1840); *5 Gedichte von Mathilde Wesendonck* (5 *Wesendonck Songs), v. and pf. (1857–8; orch. Mottl; arr. Henze for high v. and chamber orch., 1979); *Kinder-Katechismus* (1873).

WRITINGS: *My Life* (1865–80); *German Opera* (1851); *Art and Revolution* (1849); *Judaism in Music* (1850); *Opera and Drama* (1850–1); *The Music of the Future* (1860); *Religion and Art* (1880); *On Conducting* (1869).

Wagner, Roger (*b* Le Puy, 1914). Fr.-born choral cond. (later Amer. citizen). Son of organist of Dijon Cath. Taken to USA at age of 7. Organist and choirmaster, Church of St Ambrose, Los Angeles, at 12. Studied in Paris with M. Dupré. Mus. dir., St Joseph's Church, Los Angeles, 1937. Founded Roger Wagner Chorale 1947, which toured widely and won high reputation as one of the finest Amer. choirs. Dir., choral mus., U.C.L.A. from 1959. Authority on Desprès.

Wagner, (Helferich) **Siegfried** (*b* Tribschen, Lucerne, 1869; *d* Bayreuth, 1930). Ger. composer and cond. Only son of Richard *Wagner and Cosima *Wagner (then von Bülow). Educated as architect, but turned to mus. Studied with Humperdinck. Ass. cond. Bayreuth 1894, cond. perfs. there 1896. Succeeded mother as art. dir., Bayreuth Fest. from 1908, producer from 1901. Married Englishwoman Winifred Williams (1894–1980) who dir. Bayreuth 1930–44. Wrote 13 operas, incl. *Der *Bärenhäuter* (1899), *Der Kobold* (1904), and *Der Schmied von Marienburg* (1920), symphonic poems, vn. conc. (1915), and sym. (1925).

Wagner, Wieland (*b* Bayreuth, 1917; *d* Munich, 1966). Ger. opera producer and designer. Son of Siegfried *Wagner. Studied in Bayreuth and Munich. Worked among stage staff at pre-1939 Bayreuth Fests. and designed scenery for *Parsifal*, 1939. With his brother Wolfgang *Wagner became art. dir. of Bayreuth Fest. 1951 and revolutionized Wagner prods., causing intense controversy. Scrapped representational productions, substituting settings with little scenery, emphasis on lighting, and all-purpose circular platform. Many of Wagner's stage directions were ignored. Also prod. operas by other composers at Hamburg, Stuttgart, etc.

Wagner, Wolfgang (*b* Bayreuth, 1919). Ger. opera impresario and producer. Son of Siegfried *Wagner. With his brother Wieland *Wagner was co-dir. of Bayreuth Fest. 1951–66, mainly concerned with administration. Succeeded brother as art. dir., 1966. Though less controversial a producer than Wieland, caused controversy by choice of other producers, e.g. Patrice Chéreau for centenary *Ring*, 1976.

Wagner-Régeny, Rudolf (*b* Szász-Régen, Romania, 1903; *d* E. Berlin, 1969). Ger. composer, cond., and pianist. Studied Leipzig Cons. 1919–20, Berlin Hochschule für Musik 1920–3. Chorusmaster, Berlin Volksoper 1923-5, worked with Laban's dance co. 1927–30. Dir. Rostock Hochschule für Musik, 1947–50, prof. of comp. East Berlin Acad. of Arts 1950–68. Influenced by

Weill-Brecht works, later by 12-note procedures. Works incl. 9 operas (incl. *Die Bürger von Calais* 1936–8 and *Das Bergwerk zu Falun* 1958–60), 3 ballets (incl. *Tristan*, 1958), pf. conc., ch. works, etc.

Wagner Tuba. Brass instr. invented by Wagner as compromise between hn. and tb. to give special tone-colour in orchestration of *Der Ring des Nibelungen* (for Hunding in *Die Walküre*, for example). Look more like hns. than tubas. The 4 used in the *Ring* are 2 tenors in B♭, with 3 valves plus extra for correcting intonation of lowest octave and 2 basses in F. Played by 5th–8th hns. Wagner had the idea for the tubas after seeing some instruments in Sax's workshops in 1853 which may have been saxhorns. Possibly the tubas used at Bayreuth in 1876 were made in Berlin. They did not survive after 1939. In any case they were replaced in 1890 by a set made in Mainz. CG used brass band instruments until 1935 when Beecham obtained a set from Mainz. Wagner tubas were used also by Bruckner, R. Strauss, and Stravinsky in *The Rite of Spring*.

Wahnfried. Name of villa at Bayreuth into which Wagner and his wife moved in April 1874 and where they are buried. Now a museum housing valuable archives. Name chosen by Wagner (orig. Wahnfriedheim) from Hesse town of Wahnfried because he liked its mysticism, the word meaning 'Peace from Wahn' (*Wahn* = madness, illusion, etc.). Above portal he engraved: *Hier, wo mein Wähnen Frieden fand—Wahnfried Sei dieses Haus von mir benannt* (Here where my illusion found peace, be this house named by me Peace from Illusion).

Wait(s) (Old Eng.). Watchman. (1) Musicians in medieval Eng. who acted as town watchmen, marking the hours of the night by sounding instr. By 16th cent. they formed town bands, each having its *'signature tune', thus *London Waits, Chester Waits*, etc. Some waits were renowned for singing, and this originated application of term to groups who sang hymns and carols in the streets at Christmas.
(2) Old Eng. name for *shawm, much used by waits. Other name for shawm was *wayte-pipe*.

Wakefield, (Augusta) **Mary** (*b* Sedgwick, nr. Kendal, 1853; *d* Grange-over-Sands, 1910). Eng. cont. Studied with Randegger and Henschel and later in Rome, where she also studied pf. with Sgambati. Sang at Gloucester Fest. 1880. Est. competitive fest. at Sedgwick 1885, moving it to Kendal 1886, where it still flourishes and has given rise to many similar events. Lecturer from 1890. Ed. *Ruskin on Music* (1894).

Walcha, Helmut (*b* Leipzig, 1907). Ger. organist, blind since age of 16. Studied Leipzig 1922–7, ass. organist, Thomaskirche 1926–9. Organist, Frankfurt Friedenskirche 1929, prof. of org. Hoch Cons. from 1933, and at State Mus. Sch. from

1938. Organist, Dreikönigskirche from 1946. Famous Bach interpreter, preferring to play on orgs. resembling those of Bach's day. Ed. of Handel org. concs. Comp. 25 chorale preludes for org. Author of book on Reger.

Waldflöte (Ger.). Woodland Flute. Org. stop like *Clarabella, but often of 4′ length and pitch, and with inverted mouth.

Waldhorn (Ger.). Forest horn. The hunting hn., i.e. 'natural' hn. without valves.

Waldscenen (Woodland Scenes). 9 pieces for solo pf. by R. Schumann, Op. 82, comp. 1848–9.

Waldstein Sonata. Beethoven's pf. sonata No. 21 in C major, Op. 53, comp. 1804 and so called because of ded. to his patron Count Ferdinand Waldstein (*b* Dux, Bohemia, 1762; *d* Vienna, 1823). Orig. slow movement, replaced by present *adagio*, was pubd. separately as *Andante favori* (WoO 57).

Waldteufel, Emil (*b* Strasbourg, 1837; *d* Paris, 1915). Fr. (Alsatian) composer and pianist. Studied Paris Cons. Court pianist and dir. of court balls from 1865. Cond. at CG promenade concerts 1885. Wrote over 250 dances, especially waltzes, incl. *España* (1886, after Chabrier), *Estudiantina* (1883), and *Les Patineurs* (Skaters) (1882).

Walker, Alan (*b* Scunthorpe, 1930). Eng. musicologist and writer. Studied at GSM and Durham Univ., also privately with H. Keller, 1958–60. Prof. of harmony, GSM, 1958–60. BBC mus. prod. 1961–71. Prof. of mus., McMaster Univ., Hamilton, Ontario, from 1971. Authority on Liszt, 1st vol. of large-scale biography pubd. 1983. Has also written extensively on Schumann, and musical criticism.

Walker, Edyth (*b* Hopewell, NY, 1867; *d* NY, 1950). Amer. mez. Studied in Dresden with Orgeni. Opera début in Meyerbeer's *Le Prophète*, Berlin 1894, after concert appearance at Leipzig. Member of Vienna Opera 1895–1903. NY Met. 1903–6 (début as Amneris), Hamburg 1906–12, singing sop. and mez. parts, Munich 1912–17. CG début 1900 (1st London Elektra 1910). Sang Kundry at Bayreuth 1908. Often sang Isolde and Brünnhilde. Taught at Amer. Cons., Fontainebleau, 1933–6, then privately in NY.

Walker, Ernest (*b* Bombay, 1870; *d* Oxford, 1949). Eng. composer and scholar. Studied Oxford Univ. Mus. dir., Balliol College, Oxford, 1900–25, running series of chamber concerts. Wrote *Stabat Mater*, chamber mus., and songs. Author of several books, incl. *A History of Music in England* (1907, 1924, and 1952, with Westrup).

Walker, Frank (*b* Gosport, 1907; *d* Tring, 1962). Eng. musicologist and author. Worked for General Post Office, but devoted all spare time to meticulous biographical research from orig. sources. Wrote superb biographies of Hugo Wolf

(1951, 2nd edn. 1968 with new material suppressed in 1st edn.; Ger. trans. 1953), and Verdi (1962, It. trans. 1964).

Walker, Robert (*b* Northampton, 1946). Eng. composer. Chorister at St Matthew's, Northampton. Studied at Cambridge Univ. (organ scholar, Jesus Coll.). Org. and schoolmaster for 5 years in Grimsby, then freelance composer. Lives in Elgar's Sussex cottage 'Brinkwells'. Works incl. *Variations on a Theme of Elgar*, orch. (1982), Chamber Sym. (1981), *Pavan* for vn. and str. (1975), *Requiem*, ten., ch., orch. (1976), *Canticle of the Rose*, sop., bar., ch., orch. (1980), str. qt. (1982), *The Sun Used to Shine*, ten., hp., str. (1983), pf. quintet (1984), and church mus.

Walk to the Paradise Garden, The. Intermezzo for orch. before last scene of Delius's opera *A ★Village Romeo and Juliet* and frequently played as concert item. The 'Paradise Garden' was the village inn. Orig. intermezzo, comp. 1900–1, was re-written and extended in 1906 to cover scene-change in projected Berlin f.p., and it is this version that is now so well-known.

Walküre, Die (The Valkyrie). Opera (mus. drama) in 3 acts by ★Wagner to his own lib., being 2nd opera of *Der Ring des Nibelungen*. Comp. 1854–6. F.p. Munich 1870, NY 1877 (incomplete), London 1882; f.p. as part of complete cycle, Bayreuth 1876. The Valkyrie of the title is Brünnhilde.

Wallace, Ian (*b* London, 1919). Eng. bass-bar. Studied singing but began career in law. Opera début London 1946 as Schaunard in *Bohème*. New London Opera Co. 1946–9. Sang with Glyndebourne co. at Edinburgh Fest. 1948 (Masetto in *Don Giovanni*) and at Glyndebourne 1952–6, 1959–61. Successful buffo singer in such roles as Don Magnifico in *La Cenerentola* and Malatesta in *Don Pasquale*, also in Gilbert and Sullivan. Many appearances in popular musicals and as member of radio panel games. O.B.E. 1983.

Wallace, Lucille (*b* Chicago, 1898; *d* London, 1977). Amer. harpsichordist and pianist. Studied in Chicago, at Vienna Univ., and in Paris with Boulanger and Landowska, later with Schnabel in Berlin. Did much to revive interest in kbd. mus. of D. Scarlatti and Couperin. Wife of Clifford ★Curzon from 1931.

Wallace, (William) Vincent (*b* Waterford, 1812; *d* Château de Haget, nr. Vieuzos, 1865). Irish composer. Played org. and vn. as boy. Led orch. in Dublin th. Emigrated to Australia 1835, opening music coll. in Sydney (which failed) and then touring as violinist and pianist in Chile, Argentina, Cuba, and USA, where he was lionized. Returned to London 1845 where he composed successful opera ★*Maritana*. Operas *Lurline* (1847) and *The Amber Witch* (1861) were successful, as was his pf. mus.

Wallace, William (*b* Greenock, 1860; *d* Malmesbury, 1940). Scottish composer and writer. Studied in Glasgow and Vienna as ophthalmic surgeon, holding hospital posts in Glasgow and London. Abandoned career for mus. (resuming it only in 1914–18 war). Entered RAM 1889. Hon. Sec., Phil. Soc. 1911–13. Wrote 6 symphonic poems, *The Passing of Beatrice* (1892) being said to be first Brit. work in the genre. Others included *Wallace* (1905) and *Villon* (1909). Also comp. sym., suite *The Lady from the Sea* (after Ibsen, 1892), songs, etc. Prof. at RAM. Wrote *Richard Wagner as he lived* (1925).

Wallenstein, Alfred (*b* Chicago, 1898; *d* NY, 1983). Amer. cellist and cond. Début as cellist, Los Angeles 1912. Later played in San Francisco S.O. from 1916 and Los Angeles P.O. Prin. cellist, Chicago S.O. 1922–9, NY P.O. 1929–36 (under Toscanini). Became radio cond. Cond. Los Angeles P.O. 1943–56. Taught at Juilliard Sch. from 1968.

Waller, 'Fats' (Thomas Wright) (*b* NY, 1904; *d* Kansas City, 1943). Amer. jazz pianist, organist, and composer. Studied pf. with Carl Bohm and later with Leopold Godowsky, while working from age of 14 as organist in Harlem film th. Encouraged by jazz pianist James P. Johnson. Made nearly 500 records, wrote about 400 copyright works, and many more without copyright. Comp. mus. comedy *Hot Chocolates*, 1929, and the songs *Honeysuckle Rose*, c.1928, and *Ain't Misbehavin'*, 1929. His amusing vocal style masked the serious and influential qualities of his piano-playing.

Wallerstein, Lothar (*b* Prague, 1882; *d* New Orleans, 1949). Cz.-born composer, pianist, and opera producer (later Amer. citizen). Studied Prague, Munich, and Geneva. Taught pf., Geneva Cons. Cond., Poznań opera 1910–14. Chief producer, Breslau opera 1918–22, Frankfurt 1924–6, Vienna 1927–38 (in which period prod. 65 operas), Salzburg Fest. 1926–37. Guest producer Milan, Buenos Aires. Went to USA, 1941, working at Met. until 1946. Collab. with R. Strauss in Vienna 1930 in 're-working' of Mozart's *Idomeneo*.

Wallfisch, Peter (*b* Breslau, 1924). Ger.-born pianist. Studied Jerusalem Acad. of Mus. and in Paris with Marguérite Long. Settled in Eng. Prof. of pf., RCM. Worldwide tours as recitalist. Bartók Prize 1948.

Wally, La. Opera in 4 acts by ★Catalani to lib. by Illica after W. von Hillern's novel *Die Geyer-Wally* (1875). Prod. Milan 1892, NY Met. 1909, Manchester 1919.

Walmisley, Thomas Attwood (*b* London, 1814; *d* Hastings, 1856). Eng. composer. Studied comp. with ★Attwood, his godfather. Organist, Croydon church 1830, Trinity and St John's Colleges, Cambridge, 1833. Prof. of mus., Cambridge Univ., 1836. Also brilliant mathematician. Comp.

anthems, installation odes, and famous Services in B♭ (1834) and D minor (c.1855). One of first to give mus. lectures with practical examples. Pioneer in Eng. appreciation of J. S. Bach.

Walond, William (b 1725; d Oxford, 1770). Eng. organist at Oxford Univ. Wrote org. voluntaries and setting of Pope's *Ode on St Cecilia's Day* (1758).

Walsh, John (b ?1665 or 6; d London, 1736). Eng. mus. publisher, est. off the Strand, London, by c.1690. Pubd. Handel's works from 1711. Succeeded by son John (1709–66).

Walsh, Stephen (b Chipping Norton, 1942). Eng. mus. critic. Studied Cambridge Univ. Ass. mus. critic, *Observer*, 1966–86. Mus. critic, *The Listener*, 1965–7. Author of books on Schumann Lieder and Bartók's chamber music. Senior lecturer in music, Cardiff Univ., from 1976.

Walsworth, Ivor (b London, 1909; d ?, 1978). Eng. composer. Studied RAM. Works incl. 5 syms., concs., pf. qt., songs, and elec. mus.

Walter (orig. Schlesinger), **Bruno** (b Berlin, 1876; d Beverly Hills, Calif., 1962). Ger.-born cond. and pianist. Studied at Stern Cons., Berlin; decided to become cond. after attending Bülow concert. Coach and ass. cond., Cologne Opera, 1893–4, Hamburg 1894–8 as ass. to Mahler, Riga 1898–1900, Berlin 1900–01, Vienna 1901 (with Mahler till 1907)–1912, Munich Opera (gen. mus. dir. in succession to Mottl) 1913–22. Disciple of Mahler and cond. f.ps. of *Das Lied von der Erde*, Munich 1911, and 9th Sym., Vienna 1912. Cond. f.p. of Pfitzner's *Palestrina* 1917. Cond. Berlin Municipal Opera 1925–9, Leipzig Gewandhaus Orch. 1929–33. Mus. dir., Vienna Opera 1936–8. Assoc. with Salzburg Fest. 1922–37. Emigrated to Fr., taking Fr. citizenship, 1938, and then moving to USA., where he became Amer. citizen. Début NY Met. 1941. London début 1909, Phil. Soc. concerts, CG 1910 (Smyth's *The Wreckers*, Wagner's *Tristan*). From 1924 to 1931, cond. regularly at CG, incl. memorable perfs. of *Der Rosenkavalier, Die Fledermaus*, and *Le Nozze di Figaro*. Amer. début 1923, NY Sym. Orch. After World War II returned to London to cond. LPO 1946 and at 1st Edinburgh Fest., 1947, cond. legendary perf. of *Das Lied von der Erde* with Kathleen Ferrier and Peter Pears. Accompanied Ferrier at recitals and recorded *Das Lied von der Erde* with her in Vienna. Prin. cond. NY P.O. 1947–9. Cond. at NY Met. 1941–6, 1951 (*Fidelio*), 1955–7, 1958–9. Last visit to Eng., 1955. One of greatest conds., especially of Beethoven, Bruckner, Schubert, and Mahler. His warm, expansive approach was at opposite pole to Toscanini's precision and brilliance. Wrote biography of Mahler (1936, Eng. edns. 1937 and 1958) and autobiography (1946).

Walters, Gareth (b London, 1928). Eng. composer. Studied RAM, Paris Cons., and Siena. Mus.

prod., BBC from 1957. Works incl. *Sinfonia breve, Divertimento* for str., hpd. suites, etc.

Walters, Jess (b Brooklyn, NY, 1918). Amer. bar. Studied privately. Début 1935, Brooklyn Acad. of Mus. Opera début NY New Opera Co. 1941 as Macbeth. Prin. bar. at CG 1947–60, Netherlands Opera 1960–5. Prof. of v., Univ. of Texas, Austin, from 1965.

Walther, Johann (b Kahla, Thuringia, 1496; d Torgau, 1570). Ger. composer. Bass singer at Torgau 1524, then singing posts in Saxony. Friend of Martin Luther, advising him on establishing Ger. mass. Pubd. Protestant hymn-book, 1524. Wrote secular songs and instr. pieces.

Walther, Johann Gottfried (b Erfurt, 1684; d Weimar, 1748). Ger. organist and composer. Organist at Erfurt 1702–7, Weimar from 1707. Became friend of his cousin J. S. Bach while Bach was in Weimar 1708–14. Wrote kbd. conc. and org. works. Compiled mus. dictionary 1732.

Walthew, Richard (Henry) (b London, 1872; d East Preston, Sussex, 1951). Eng. composer. Studied GSM and RCM (pupil of Parry). Dir., Passmore Edwards Settlement 1900–04. Prof. of mus., Queen's Coll., 1907. Dir., GSM opera class from 1905. Works incl. cantata *The Pied Piper*, pf. conc., chamber mus., songs.

Walton, Bernard (b Manchester, 1917; d London, 1972). Eng. clarinettist. Studied RCM. Prin. cl. LPO 1937–40 and from 1966; Philharmonia Orch. 1948–66. Prof. of cl., RCM from 1954. Founder-member Music Group of London, 1966.

Walton, (Sir) William (Turner) (b Oldham, 1902; d Ischia, 1983). Eng. composer. Son of choirmaster and singing-teacher. Chorister at Christ Church Cath. Sch., Oxford, 1912–18, during which time wrote anthems and songs. Wrote Pf. Qt. 1918. 'Adopted' as a brother by Osbert, Sacheverell, and Edith Sitwell, 1919, living with them in London and It. Comp. first version of *Façade*, instr. accs. to recited poems by Edith Sitwell, in 1921, f.p. London (privately) 1922. Str. qt. played at Salzburg 1923. Made jazz arrs. for Savoy Orpheans, 1923. Public perf. of *Façade* 1923 caused furore. Comedy ov. *Portsmouth Point* perf. at Zürich 1926. Came into wider prominence in 1929 with va. conc., f.p. at Promenade concert with Hindemith as soloist. This was followed at 1931 Leeds Fest. by dramatic cantata *Belshazzar's Feast*. In 1934 First Sym. was perf. without finale, which was added 1935. Next large-scale work was vn. conc. commissioned by Heifetz, 1939. Wrote mus. for film of Shaw's *Major Barbara*, 1940, followed by several other wartime film scores, best-known being that for *The First of the Few* (1942), story of building of Spitfire fighter aircraft, and Olivier's *Henry V* (1944). Next major work was str. qt., 1947. From 1948 to 1954 was engaged on large-scale opera, *Troilus and Cressida*, prod. CG 1954. Followed by vc. conc. for *Piatigorsky, 2nd Sym., *Variations on a Theme of Hindemith*, a 1-act 'extravaganza' *The Bear*, based on Chekhov, and shorter works. From 1948 lived in Ischia. Knighted 1951. O.M. 1968.

Walton's mus., although it was at first regarded in Eng. as that of an *enfant terrible* because of *Façade* and the 'jazz-age' influence on his early works, remained remarkably consistent. It is fundamentally lyrical and romantic, with two basic ingredients: a pungent, spiky rhythmic impetus, with wide intervals and tangy harmonies, and a brooding melancholy. It is as if two influences were perpetually at war in his nature: the 20th-cent. Stravinsky–Prokofiev strain and the 19th-cent. Elgar. His true qualities can be discerned in *Façade*, a masterpiece which never 'dates', because it is musically so good and true. Almost alone among later Eng. composers, he successfully wore the Elgarian pomp-and-circumstance mantle, as in his 2 Coronation Marches, much of the film mus., and parts of *Belshazzar's Feast*, but the finest of his works—the 3 concs., the 1st Sym., the *Hindemith Variations*, *Belshazzar*, *The Bear*, and parts of *Troilus and Cressida*—have a powerful individuality in which the opposing strains are successfully reconciled. All his mus. is fastidiously fashioned and it has a Mediterranean luxuriousness which is reconciled to the robust qualities of a composer whose place in the history of 20th-cent. Eng. mus. is high and important. Prin. works:

OPERAS: *Troilus and Cressida (1948–54, rev. 1972–6); The *Bear (1967).

BALLETS: The *Wise Virgins (transcr. of J. S. Bach) (1940); The Quest (1943); *Façade (1929, 1931, 1935, 1940, 1972).

ENTERTAINMENT: *Façade, reciter and instr. ens. (1921, rev. 1926, 1928, 1942, 1951, 1978); Façade 2 (1979, after rev.).

ORCH: Symphonies: No. 1 in B♭ (1931–5), No. 2 (1959–60); Concertos: Va. in A minor (1928–9, rev. 1961), Vn. in B minor (1938–9, rev. 1943), Vc. (1956), Sinfonia Concertante for orch. with pf. (1927, rev. 1943); *Portsmouth Point (1925); *Siesta (1926); *Façade, Suite No. 1 (1926), No. 2 (1938); Coronation March, *Crown Imperial (1937, rev. 1963); Suite, The *Wise Virgins (1940); Music for Children (1940, orch. of Duets for Children); Comedy Ov., *Scapino (1940, rev. 1950); *Spitfire Prelude and Fugue (1942); 2 Pieces for Strings from Henry V (1944); Sonata for Strings (1972, arr. of str. qt. 1947); Coronation March, *Orb and Sceptre (1953); Finale, presto giocoso, of Variations on an Elizabethan Theme (*Sellinger's Round) (1953); *Johannesburg Festival Overture (1956); Partita (1957); Variations on a Theme of *Hindemith (1962–3); *Capriccio Burlesco (1968); Improvisations on an Impromptu of Benjamin *Britten (1969); Varii Capricci (1976, orch. of 5 Bagatelles for guitar); Prologo e Fantasia (1981).

CHORUS AND ORCH: *Belshazzar's Feast, bar., ch., and orch. (1929–31); *In Honour of the City of London, ch. and orch (1937); Coronation Te Deum, 2 ch., 2 semi ch., boys' ch., org., orch., military brass (1952–3); Gloria, cont., ten., bass, ch., and orch. (1960).

SONG-CYCLES: *Anon in Love, 6 songs for ten. and guitar (1959; for ten. and small orch. 1971); A *Song for the Lord Mayor's Table, 6 songs for sop. and pf. (1962; sop. and orch. 1970).

VOCAL (unacc. except where stated): A Litany (Drop, drop, slow tears) (1916); Make we Joy now in this Fest (1931); Set me as a Seal upon thine Heart (1938); Where does the Uttered Music Go? (1946); What Cheer? (1961); The Twelve, with org. (1965); Missa brevis, double ch. and organ (in Gloria only); All This time (1970); Jubilate Deo, with organ (1972); Cantico del Sole (Song of the Sun (1973–4); Magnificat and Nunc Dimittis, with org. (1975).

CHAMBER MUSIC: Pf. Qt. (1918–19; rev. 1976); Str. Qt. (2 movements 1919, central scherzo added 1922); Toccata in A minor, vn. and pf. (1925); Str. Qt. (1946-7; version for str. orch. entitled Sonata 1972); Vn. sonata (1949); 2 Pieces for vn. and pf. (1951); 5 Bagatelles, guitar (1971–2; transcr. for orch. as Varii Capricci 1976); Passacaglia, vc. (1980).

SONGS: The Winds (1918?); Tritons (1918?); 3 Songs by E. Sitwell (1930, rev. of songs written in 1923).

PIANO: Duets for Children (duet 1940; orch. as Music for Children).

ORGAN: 3 Pieces from Richard III (1955).

BRASS BAND: The First Shoot (1980–1, re-scoring of ballet written for revue, 1935).

FILMS: As You Like It (1936), Dreaming Lips (1937), Stolen Life (1938), Major Barbara (1940), Next of Kin (1941), The Foreman Went to France (1941), The First of the Few (1942), Went the Day Well? (1942), Henry V (1944), Hamlet (1947), Richard III (1955), The Battle of Britain (1969), Three Sisters (1970).

THEATRE INCID. MUSIC: The Son of Heaven (L. Strachey) (1925), The Boy David (Barrie) (1936), Macbeth (1941).

Waltz (Ger. *Walzer*; Fr. *Valse*). Dance in $\frac{3}{4}$ time probably deriving from Ger. *Ländler* which came into prominence in last quarter of 18th cent. both among composers and in the ballroom. Where the latter was concerned, the waltzes of the Viennese composers Johann *Strauss I and *Lanner were popular throughout Europe. Beethoven, Schubert, and Hummel wrote waltzes. Weber's *Invitation to the Dance is in waltz rhythm and is the first 'sophisticated' treatment of the waltz. Chopin's waltzes are fine examples. In symphonic mus. the 2nd movement of Berlioz's *Symphonie fantastique* and 3rd movement of Tchaikovsky's 5th sym. are outstanding. Tchaikovsky also wrote great waltzes in his operas and ballets; and those by Johann Strauss II, Richard Strauss (*Der Rosenkavalier*), Ravel, and others are deservedly cherished.

Waltz, Gustavus (*fl.* 1732–59). Eng. bass of Ger. birth. Sang in Arne's Eng. opera season at Little Haymarket Th., 1732. Sang small part in f.p. of Handel's *Deborah*, 1733. Went with Handel to Oxford in July 1733, singing in 4 of his oratorios and in anthems. Member of Handel's opera co. 1733–6. Rejoined Handel for oratorio season 1738–9, singing title-role in f.p. of *Saul*, and in f.p. of *Israel in Egypt*. In later part of career sang mainly in lighter works by Lampe and Arne. Sang in chorus at Foundling Hospital perfs. of *Messiah* 1759. Story that he was once Handel's cook is unverified, as is Handel's alleged remark in 1745 that 'Gluck knew no more of counterpoint than my cook Waltz'.

Wälzel, Camillo (pseudonym F. Zell) (*b* Magdeburg, 1829; *d* Vienna, 1895). Ger. librettist. Trans. Fr. comedies. Wrote texts, often collab. Richard Genée, for operettas by Suppé, Johann Strauss II, Millöcker, and others.

Wand, Günter (*b* Elberfeld, 1912). Ger. conductor and composer. Studied Cologne Cons. under Jarnach (comp.) and Paul Baumgartner (pf.). Held cond. posts at Wuppertal and Detmold. Cond., Cologne Opera 1938–44, Salzburg Mozarteum Orch. 1944–5. Mus. dir. Cologne Opera 1945–8, cond. Cologne Gürzenich concerts 1946–74. London début 1951 (LSO). Cond. Berne S.O. from 1974. Prin. cond. North German Radio S.O. (Hamburg) from 1982. Comps. incl. cantata, ballet, and songs.

'Wanderer' Fantasy. Nickname for Schubert's Fantasia in C for pf. (1822, D760), so called because the adagio section, or movement, is variations on a passage from his song *Der Wanderer* (1816, D493). Liszt arranged it for pf. and orch. some time before 1852 and for 2 pfs. after 1851.

Wandering Scholar, The. Chamber opera in 1 act, Op. 50, by Holst to lib. by Clifford Bax founded on incident in Helen Waddell's *The Wandering Scholars* (1927). Comp. 1929–30. Prod. Liverpool 1934.

Wand of Youth, The. 2 orch. suites by Elgar, Opp. 1a and 1b, arr. and orch. in 1907 and 1908 respectively from material written by Elgar as a child of 12 for a family play. Some themes used again in mus. for The **Starlight Express*.

Wangenheim, Volker (*b* Berlin, 1928). Ger. cond. and composer. Studied Berlin Hochschule für Musik. Chief cond. Berlin Mozart Orch. 1950–9, mus. dir., city of Bonn from 1957 (gen. mus. dir. from 1963), chief cond. Ger. Nat. Youth Orch. from 1969. Cond., Bournemouth Sinfonietta 1977. Prof. of cond., Cologne Hochschule für Musik from 1972. Works incl. sym.

Wanhal, Johann Baptist (Vanhal, Jan Křtitel) (*b* Nové-Nechanise, Bohemia, 1739; *d* Vienna, 1813). Bohemian composer, violinist, and org.

Pupil of **Dittersdorf. Became teacher in Vienna in 1760s, pupils incl. Pleyel. Was in Italy 1769–71. After spell in Hungary returned to Vienna 1781, playing vc. in quartet with Haydn, Dittersdorf, and Mozart. Many of his works were prod. by Haydn at Esterháza. Wrote over 70 syms., 100 str. qts., 60 masses, concs., and many chamber works.

War and Peace (*Voyna i Mir*). Opera in prol. and 13 scenes by Prokofiev, Op. 91, to lib. by composer and Mira Mendelson based on Tolstoy's novel (1869). Comp. 1941–2, 1946–7, 1948–53. F.p. (cut) concert version Moscow 1945. First stage prod. (sc. 1–8 only) Leningrad 1946; 2nd version 11 scenes, Leningrad 1955; Florence 1953, Moscow 1957, London 1972, Boston 1974.

Ward, David (*b* Dumbarton, 1922; *d* Dunedin, N.Z., 1983). Scottish bass. Studied RCM and with **Hotter. SW ch. 1952. Sang Count Walter in Verdi's *Luisa Miller* SW 1953. Prin. bass, SW 1952–9, CG from 1960. Bayreuth Fest. 1960–2. Début NY Met. 1963. Many appearances as Wotan with Scottish Opera, with CG in the 1964 *Ring*, and in 6 *Ring* cycles at Buenos Aires, 1967. The nobility and dignity of his performance were impressive. Also outstanding concert singer. C.B.E. 1972.

Ward, John (*b* Canterbury, 1571; *d* London, 1638). Eng. composer. Wrote set of madrigals 1613, fantasias for viols, pieces for virginals, services, etc.

Ward, Robert (*b* Cleveland, 1917). Amer. composer and cond. Studied Eastman Sch. of Mus. with **Hanson and Juilliard Sch., later with **Copland at Berkshire Mus. Center. Taught at Juilliard Sch. 1946–56 and Columbia Univ. 1946–8. Managing ed. Galaxy Music (Publishers) 1956–66. Won Pulitzer Prize 1962 with opera *The Crucible*. Pres., N. Carolina Sch. of Arts, 1967–75. Works incl. operas *He Who Gets Slapped* (1956) and *The Crucible*, 5 syms., pf. conc., *Yankee Overture*, choral mus., and songs.

Warfield, William (*b* Helena, Arkansas, 1920). Amer. bar. Studied Eastman Sch. of Mus. Sang in revues. Recital début NY 1950. Sang Porgy in European tour of Gershwin's *Porgy and Bess* with wife, Leontyne **Price, as Bess, and later with NY City Opera and in Vienna.

Warlock, Peter (really Heseltine, Philip) (*b* London, 1894; *d* London, 1930). Eng. composer, critic, and author. Pubd. his mus. under pseudonym Peter Warlock. Studied mus. at Eton, then helped by van **Dieren and Delius. Founded and co-ed. periodical *The Sackbut* 1920 and wrote book on Delius 1923. Friend of Cecil Gray, E. J. Moeran, and Constant Lambert. Edited much 16th and 17th cent. music in collab. with **Mangeot. His songs alternate between lyricism of Delius and roistering spirit reminiscent of first Elizabethan age. His personality veered between extrovert, heavy-drinking joviality and neurotic introspection. Eventually (it may be presumed, despite the open verdict at the inquest) took his own life. Sensitive critic and writer. His mus., especially his songs and part-songs, is of high merit. Prin. works:

ORCH: *An Old Song* (1917); *Serenade for Delius on his 60th birthday*, str. (1921–2); **Capriol*, suite for str. (1926: for full orch. 1928).

CHORUS AND ORCH: *3 Carols* (1923).

VOICE AND ENSEMBLE: *The *Curlew*, song-cycle, ten., fl., cor anglais, str. qt. (1920–1, rev. 1922); *Corpus Christi*, sop., bar., str. qt. (1919–23); *Sorrow's Lullaby*, sop., bar., str. qt. (1927).

CHORUS AND KEYBOARD: **Sociable Songs*, male vv., pf., (1924–5); *What Cheer? Good cheer!*; *Where Riches is everlastingly*, ch., org. (1927); *The bailey beareth the bell away*, 2 vv., pf. (1918–28); *Lullaby*, women's trio, pf. (1918–28); *The First Mercy*, 3 vv. and pf. (1927–8); *The Five Lesser Joys of Mary*, ch., org. (1929).

UNACC. VOICES: *Cornish Christmas Carol* (1918); *As dewe in Aprylle* (1918); *Corpus Christi*, cont., ten., ch. (1919); *The Full Heart* (1917–22); *3 Dirges of Webster* (1923–5, No. 3 is *The Shrouding of the Duchess of Malfi*, male vv.); *The Spring of the Year* (1925); *Bethlehem Down* (1927).

SOLO SONGS: *3 Saudades* (1916–17), *The bailey beareth the bell away* (1918), *There is a lady* (1919), *Balulalow* (1919), *Captain Stratton's Fancy* (1920), *Mr Belloc's Fancy* (1921–30), *Piggesnie* (1922), *6 Peterisms*, sets 1 and 2 (1922), *Sleep* (1922), *Tyrley Tyrlow* (1922), *Milkmaids* (1923), *Candlelight* (12 nursery rhymes) (1923), *Peter Warlock's Fancy* (1924), *Twelve Oxen* (1924), *Yarmouth Fair* (1924), *3 Belloc Songs* (1926), *Sigh no more, ladies* (1927), *Passing by* (1928), *The Passionate Shepherd* (1928), *The Cricketers of Hambledon* (1928), *The Frostbound Wood* (1929), *Bethlehem Down* (1927–30), *The Fox* (1930), and others.

Warner, H. Waldo (*b* Northampton, 1874; *d* London, 1945). Eng. violinist, violist, and composer. Studied GSM from 1888. Prof. of va., GSM, 1893–1920. Violist of London Str. Qt. from its foundation 1907 until 1928. Prin. va. leading London orchs. Wrote opera and over 100 songs, but best mus. is for chamber groups, e.g. pf. trio (won **Cobbett Prize*), str. qt., va. sonata, etc.

Warner, Sylvia Townsend (*b* London, 1893; *d* Maiden Newton, Dorset, 1978). Eng. novelist, musicologist, and composer. Specialist in 16th-cent. notation and Tudor church mus. One of eds. of Carnegie Trust coll. of Tudor church mus. Wrote chamber mus., song-cycle, etc.

Warrack, Guy (Douglas Hamilton) (*b* Edinburgh, 1900; *d* Englefield Green, 1986). Scottish cond. and composer. Studied Oxford Univ. and RCM. On staff RCM 1925–35, conducting class at RCM from 1945. Cond. BBC Scottish Orch. 1935–45, SW Ballet 1948. Wrote film mus. and works for orch., incl. *Variations* (1924) and sym. (1932).

Warrack, John (Hamilton) (*b* London, 1928). Eng. critic and author, son of Guy **Warrack*. Studied ob. at RCM. Mus. critic *Daily Telegraph* 1954–61, *Sunday Telegraph* 1961–72. Art dir. Leeds Fest. from 1978. Author of books on Weber and Tchaikovsky. Co-ed. *Concise Oxford Dictionary of Opera* (1964, 2nd edn. 1979).

Warren (orig. Warenoff), **Leonard** (*b* NY, 1911; *d* NY, 1960). Amer. bar. of Russ. parentage. Studied NY and Milan. Won NY Met. Auditions of Air 1938. Opera début NY Met. 1939 as Paolo in Verdi's *Simone Boccanegra* (though he had sung excerpts from operas there in 1938). Became leading bar. at Met. and elsewhere in such roles as Iago and Rigoletto. Died on stage of NY Met. during perf. of Verdi's *La forza del destino*.

War Requiem. Choral work, Op. 66, by Britten, interpolating 9 poems by Wilfred Owen (1893–1918) into liturgical Mass. Comp. 1961 and f.p. in new Coventry Cath. May 1962. Sop., ten., and bar. soloists, ch., boys' ch., and orch. Owen poems are acc. by chamber orch., sometimes, but not necessarily, under 2nd cond. F.p. was cond. by Meredith Davies, with Britten cond. of chamber orch. F. London p., Westminster Abbey, Nov. 1962.

Wasps, The. Incidental mus. for ten. and bar., male ch., and orch. comp. by Vaughan Williams for Cambridge Univ. prod., 1909, of Aristophanes's play. Orch. suite of 5 movements (1912), incl. frequently played ov.

Wassail. Old Eng. term for jovial and convivial song which often occurs in Christmas carols.

Watanabe, Akeo (*b* Tokyo, 1919). Japanese cond. Studied Tokyo Acad. of Mus. and at Juilliard Sch. Cond., Tokyo P.O. 1948–54; founder and cond. Japan P.-S.O. 1956–66; mus. dir. Kyoto S.O. from 1970; prof. of cond. Tokyo Univ. of Arts 1962–7. Guest cond. of European and Amer. orchs.

Water Carrier, The (Cherubini). See *Deux Journées, Les*.

Waterhouse, William (*b* London, 1931). Eng. bassoonist. Studied RCM under A. Camden, then joining Philharmonia Orch. In CG orch. 1953–5, prin. bn. Italian-Swiss Radio Orch., Lugano, 1955–8. Prin. bn. LSO 1958–64, BBC S.O. from 1964. Joined Melos Ensemble 1959. Prof. of bn. RMCM 1966–72, later at RNCM.

Waterman, Fanny (*b* Leeds, 1920). Eng. pf. teacher. RCM 1940–3. Founder and joint chairman, Leeds Int. Pf. Competition from 1963. O.B.E. 1970.

Water Music. Instr. suite by Handel, the origin of which is unknown. The legend that Handel wrote it for a royal water party in 1715 to restore himself to favour with King George I is attractive but unsubstantiated. (The King had been Elector of Hanover when Handel had effectively deserted his post as Kapellmeister at Hanover in order to visit Eng., where he settled.) However, it is documented that Handel provided mus. for a royal journey up the Thames on 17 July 1717. No complete autograph score of the mus. exists and contemporary edns. differ in several respects. Some of the movements in autograph exist in earlier versions, so dating the mus. is impossible. About 20 numbers were written, scored for tpts., hns., obs., bns., fls., recorders, and str. Best-known of modern orchestrations is that by *Harty.

Water Music. Work by *Cage (1952) in which pianist has to make the visual element a major feature of the perf., being provided with radio, whistles, water containers, a pack of cards, and a score mounted like a poster.

Water Organ. See *Hydraulus*.

Watkins, Michael Blake (*b* Ilford, 1948). Eng. composer. Studied with Lutyens and Richard Rodney Bennett; made special study of guitar and lute with Michael Jessett. His Double Conc. won Menuhin comp. prize 1975. Works incl.:

ORCH: *Proem* (1972); Double Conc. (*After Psallein*), ob., guitar, orch. (1972); *Concertante*, 11 players (1973); *Clouds and Eclipses*, guitar, str. (1973); hn. conc., str. and opt. hp. (1974); *Dreams* (1975); vn. conc. (1977); *étalage* (1979); *Sinfonietta* (1982).

ENS: *Psallein*, guitar with guitar ens. of 6 players, clavichord, perc. (1971); *The Magic Shadow-Show*, vc. and ens. (1980).

VOICE(S) AND INSTR: *Those Dancing Days Are Gone*, ten., vn., cl., guitar (1969); *Invocation*, ten., lute (1972); *Before the Beginning of Years*, sop., ten., pf. (1972); *Youth's Dream and Time's Truth*, ten., tpt., harp, str. (1973); *Solarium*, school ch., orch. (1974); *All That We Read in Their Smiles* (5 Songs), ten., hn., pf. (1977); *The Spirit of the Universe*, sop. and ens. (1978); *The Bird of Time*, ten., ob. (1979); *The Spirit of Night*, ten., guitar (1980).

CHAMBER MUSIC: *Synthesis*, pf. (1969); *Cavatina*, vc. (1972); guitar qt. (4 guitars) (1972); *Solus*, guitar (1975); *The Wings of Night*, vn. (1975); *The Spirit of the Earth*, guitar (1978); str. qt. (1979); quintet, cl., vn., va., vc., pf. (1981); ob. qt. (1984).

BRASS: *Aubade*, brass band (1973); *From the High Towers*, 2 tpt., hn., ten. tb., tuba (1976).

Watson, Henry (*b* Burnley, 1846; *d* Salford, 1911). Eng. organist, teacher, composer, and collector. Studied Cambridge Univ. Organist, Congregational Church, Withington, Manchester. Founded and cond. Manchester Vocal Union. On orig. teaching staff of RMCM 1893 as choirmaster. Collected over 5,000 mus. books and scores with intention of founding free reference library. Gave them in 1899 to Manchester Corporation and they form nucleus of Henry Watson Mus. Library, part of Manchester Central Reference Library. Gave coll. of rare instr. to RMCM (now at RNCM).

Watson, Sydney (*b* Denton, Manchester, 1903). Eng. cond., organist, pianist, and composer. Studied Oxford Univ. and RCM. Organist, New College, Oxford, 1933–8. Mus. dir. Winchester College, 1938–46, Eton College, 1946–55. Lecturer in mus. Christ Church, Oxford, 1955–70. Cond. f.p. of Walton's *The Twelve* at Christ Church Cath., 1965. Prof. of org. RCM 1946–71. Cond. Oxford Orch. Soc., Petersfield Fest. 1946–64, Oxford Bach Choir 1955–70. O.B.E. 1970.

Watts, André (*b* Nuremberg, 1946). Amer. pianist. Studied Peabody Institute, Baltimore, with Fleischer. Début 1955 with Philadelphia Orch. Soloist with NY P.O. cond. Bernstein 1963. London début 1966. World tours after 1967. Superb player of Liszt and Brahms.

Watts, Helen (Josephine) (*b* Milford Haven, 1927). Welsh cont. Joined Glyndebourne and BBC choruses. Toured USSR with EOG 1964. Début USA 1967. Sings in opera but mainly in oratorio, e.g. Elgar, Bach, Beethoven, Handel. C.B.E. 1978.

Wat Tyler. Opera in 3 acts by Alan Bush to lib. by Nancy Bush. Awarded prize in Fest. of Britain 1951 but not prod. in Eng. until 1974. F.p. Leipzig 1953.

Wayenberg, Daniel (*b* Paris, 1929). Dutch pianist and composer. Studied pf. with Marguérite Long. Played in private houses 1939–46; public début Paris 1949. Amer. début, NY 1953. Has comp. ballet, sym., and conc. for 3 pf.

Wayte. See *Wait*. Also an old name for the hautboy.

Weber, (Maria) **Aloysia** (Louise) (*b* Zell or Mannheim, *c*.1760; *d* Salzburg, 1839). Austrian soprano. Had singing lessons from Mozart, 1777–8, in Mannheim. He fell in love with her and took her, with her father (also a singer) on concert tours. Later that year, in Munich, she rejected him. Vienna début 1779, remaining there until 1792, having married actor Joseph Lange, in 1780. Mozart wrote several arias for her and the part of Mme. Herz in *Der Schauspieldirektor*. Sang Donna Anna in f. Vienna p. of *Don Giovanni*, 1788. Her sister Constanze (1762–1842) became Mozart's wife in 1782.

Weber, Ben (*b* St Louis, 1916; *d* NY, 1979). Amer. composer. Abandoned medicine for mus. Studied Chicago, and encouraged by Schoenberg. On staff NY College of Mus. from 1966. Works incl. *Symphony on Poems of William Blake* for bar. and chamber ens., vn. conc., pf. conc., chamber mus., songs, etc. One of first Amer. composers to use 12-note technique, but generally with strong tonal associations.

Weber, Carl Maria (Friedrich Ernst) **von** (*b* Eutin in Oldenburg, 1786; *d* London, 1826). Ger. composer, cond., and pianist. Son of town musician and theatrical impresario and his 2nd wife, a singer and actress. Taught as boy by Michael *Haydn in Salzburg, then by court organist, Kalcher, in Munich. By 1800 had already composed opera, mass, and pf. works. Went to Vienna in 1803 as pupil of *Vogler, through whose influence became Kapellmeister at Breslau municipal th. 1804–6. Worked in Karlsruhe 1806–7, where he wrote 2 syms. Court secretarial post Stuttgart 1807–10, where he was encouraged by Kapellmeister, *Danzi. While there wrote incidental mus. to *Turandot,* opera *Silvana,* and other works. Banished from Stuttgart because of suspected embezzlement, went to Mannheim, where he was befriended by Gottfried *Weber (no relation), then to Darmstadt, where he met Vogler again and took lessons from him in company with *Meyerbeer. At this time wrote comic opera *Abu Hassan,* pf. conc., and vn. sonatas. Travelled to Munich 1811, where he wrote bn. conc. for court wind-player, and to Prague, where his pf. improvisations were acclaimed. Appointed dir., Prague Opera, 1813–16. Court Kapellmeister, Dresden, 1817, with commission to est. Ger. opera alongside It. variety. Wrote Mass in E♭ 1818 and worked on opera *Der Freischütz.* Work continually frustrated by opposition from It. opera dir., Morlacchi. Weber rehearsed operas exhaustively, making himself responsible for every aspect of prods., and, in his operatic theories, anticipating those of his disciple Wagner. *Freischütz* was prod. in Berlin, to tumultuous acclaim, in 1821 and was taken up throughout Ger., making Weber the most popular composer of the day. At the same time, he was at work on a comic opera *Die drei Pintos,* which he never finished and which was subsequently prepared for perf. by Mahler. He interrupted work on it to compose an opera commissioned by the Vienna Kärntnerthor Th. for 1822–3 season. This was *Euryanthe,* prod. Vienna, Oct. 1823. While in Vienna, Weber met Beethoven, with whom he had been in correspondence. By now, Weber's health was seriously undermined by tuberculosis. In 1824, the manager of CG, Kemble, commissioned an opera from Weber, who agreed to set Planché's Eng. lib. *Oberon.* Went to London 1826, staying with Sir George *Smart in Great Portland St., supervising rehearsals at CG and conducting several concerts. After *Oberon* première, became increasingly ill and died 7 weeks later in Smart's house. Body taken to Moorfields Chapel. In 1844, on instigation of the Dresden Kapellmeister Richard Wagner, coffin was shipped back to Ger. and buried in Dresden Catholic cemetery on 15 Dec. after funeral oration by Wagner and the perf. of Wagner's *Hebt an den Sang (An Webers Grabe)* for unacc. male ch.

Weber's place in history of Ger. mus. is that of a liberator, setting it free from It. influences and showing how the shape of folk tunes could be adapted for operatic and other purposes. Marschner and Lortzing were his immediate successors, Wagner his culmination. In his instr. and vocal works, his virtuosity, startling effects achieved without use of unusual instrs., and formal and technical innovations stimulated Chopin, Liszt, Berlioz, and in due course Mahler. According to Debussy, the sound of the Weber orch. was achieved by 'scrutiny of the soul of each instrument'. Though handicapped by the weakest of libs. (by the eccentric poetess Helmina von Chézy), *Euryanthe* contains mus. of outstanding subtlety and strength; while the powerful atmospheric spell of the 'nature' mus. in *Freischütz* is created by the poetic establishment of a mood. For some time Weber was regarded as more important as an influence on others than for his own achievement. Today his rightful place as a master is acknowledged. Prin. works:

OPERAS: *Peter Schmoll und seine Nachbarn* (1801–2); *Silvana* (1808–10); *Abu Hassan* (1810–11); *Der *Freischütz* (1817–21); *Euryanthe* (1822–3); *Die *drei Pintos* (begun 1820); *Oberon* (1825–6).

THEATRE MUSIC: Ov. and 6 nos. for *Turandot* (1809); Ov. and 11 nos. for *Preciosa* (1820); and many other items for plays.

CHURCH MUSIC: Mass in E♭ *(Grosse Jugendmesse)* (1802); Mass in E♭ (1818); Mass in G (1819).

CHORAL: *Der erste Ton,* reciter, ch., orch. (1808); *Kampf und Sieg,* SATB soloists, ch., orch. (1815); *Jubel-Kantate,* SATB soloists, ch., orch. (1818).

ORCH: Syms: No. 1 in C (1807), No. 2 in C (1807); Ov., *The *Ruler of the Spirits (Der Beherrscher der Geister)* (1811); *Jubel-Ouvertüre* (Jubilee Overture) (1818); *Andante und Rondo Ungarese,* va. and orch. (1809, rev. for bn. 1813); Pf. Concs: No. 1 in C (1810), No. 2 in E♭ (1812), *Konzertstück* in F minor, pf. (1821); cl. concertino (1811); Cl. concs.: No. 1 in F minor (1811), No. 2 in E♭ (1811); Bn. conc. in F (1811, rev. 1822); horn concertino (1815); *Romanza Siciliana,* fl. and orch. (1805); *Grand Potpourri,* vc. and orch. (1808).

CHAMBER MUSIC: Pf. Qt. (1809); cl. quintet (1815); Trio, fl., vc., pf. (1819); 6 *Progressive Sonatas,* vn. and pf. (1810); *Grand Duo Concertant* in E♭, pf. and cl. (1816); *Divertimento,* guitar and pf. (1816).

PIANO: 6 *Variations on Original Theme* (1800); 12 *Allemandes* (1801); *Écossaises* (1802); 7 *Variations on Original Theme* (1808); *Momento capriccioso* (1808); *Grande Polonaise* (1808); Sonatas: No. 1 in C (1812), No. 2 in A♭ (1816), No. 3 in D minor (1816), No. 4 in E minor (1822); 7 *Variations on a Theme from Méhul's Joseph* (1812); 7 *Variations on a Gipsy Song* (1817); *Rondo brillante* (1819); *Invitation to the Dance (Aufforderung zum Tanz)* (1819); *Polacca brillante* (1819).

PIANO DUETS: 6 *Petites pièces faciles* (1801); 6 *Pieces* (1809); 8 *Pieces* (1818–19).

SONGS: A selection of Weber's many songs: *Wiedersehn* (1804); *Serenade* (1809); *Trinklied* (1809); *Wiegenlied* (1810); *Leyer und Schwerdt* (Lyre and Sword) Vol. I, 4 songs (1814), Vol. II,

6 songs for 4 male vv. (1814), Vol. III (1816); *Die Temperamente beim Verluste der Geliebten* (1816); *Elfenlied* (1819); *Das Licht im Thale* (1822); also many canons and part-songs.

ARRS: *God Save the King*, 3 versions, for male vv., (?1818), male vv. (?1818), and SATB and wind (1819); *10 Scottish National Songs*, v. with fl., vn., vc., pf.

Weber, Dionys (*b* Welchau, 1766; *d* Prague, 1842). Ger.-Bohemian composer. Pupil of *Vogler. Wrote operas, qts. for 4 hns., dances, etc. Founder and dir. Prague Cons. 1811.

Weber, Gottfried (*b* Freinsheim, 1779; *d* Kreuznach, 1839). Ger. composer and theorist. Settled Mannheim 1802 as lawyer. Friend of C. M. von *Weber. Comp. songs, church mus., and chamber works. Wrote several textbooks, incl. a study of the authenticity of Mozart's *Requiem* (1826). His most important theoretical work was the *Versuch einer geordneten Theorie der Tonsetzkunst* (Mainz, 1817–21, 1832, Eng. trans. 1851) in which he proposed a new and easier system of terminology and figuration. In 1832 he became general state prosecutor in Darmstadt.

Weber, Ludwig (*b* Vienna, 1899; *d* Vienna, 1974). Austrian bass. Studied Vienna. Opera début Vienna Volksoper 1920. Sang in opera at Elberfeld 1925–7, Düsseldorf 1927–30, Cologne 1930–3, Munich 1933–45, Vienna from 1945. CG début 1936, appearing there to 1939, then 1947, 1950–1. Bayreuth Fest. 1951–60. One of greatest 20th-cent. basses in Wagner and Strauss roles. Created role of Holsteiner in Strauss's *Friedenstag*, 1938.

Webern, Anton (Friedrich Wilhelm von) (*b* Vienna, 1883; *d* Mittersill, 1945). Austrian composer and cond. Early tuition from his mother, a pianist. (Most of his works were written in her memory.) Studied at Klagenfurt with Edwin Komauer, composing first works in 1899. Entered Vienna Univ. 1902, studying musicology with Guido *Adler. Studied comp. with Pfitzner but became pupil of *Schoenberg 1904–08. Ed. works of 15th-cent. Dutch composer Heinrich Isaac. Became close friend of *Berg. Was operetta cond. at Bad Ischl (1908), Teplitz (1910), Danzig (1910–11), Stettin (1911–12), and Prague 1917. In Vienna 1918–22 was active in Schoenberg's Soc. for Private Perfs., and cond. Vienna workers' sym. concerts 1922–34. Cond. and mus. adviser, Austrian Radio 1927–38. Visited London 5 times to conduct for BBC (1929, 1932, 1933, 1935, 1936). Music proscribed by Nazis as 'cultural Bolshevism' although Webern was sympathetic to their cause (as is reflected in texts of his cantatas). Worked as publisher's proof-reader during war. Accidentally shot by Amer. sentry, 1945. (See *The Death of Anton Webern: a drama in documents* by Hans Moldenhauer, NY 1961.) Largely ignored except by the BBC in his lifetime, Webern's mus. became a rallying-point for

the post-1945 generation of European composers, such as Stockhausen, Boulez, and Maderna (and for some of the older generation, e.g. *Stravinsky and Eimert). They were attracted by the way in which his mus., through its sheer concentration, opened up a new and more complete *serialism based on the est. of the relationship between a particular note and a particular quality of sound. Even in the earliest works to which he gave an opus no. there is preoccupation with the inter-relationship of symmetrical structures. From 1908 until the late 1920s Webern wrote in a free atonal style. A characteristic of many of the works of this period is their epigrammatic brevity. The 4th of his *6 Pieces* for orch. has only 6 bars. Timbre plays an important role, also str. effects such as *col legno* and *sul ponticello*. In his vocal mus., the extremes of range are contrasted, with fragmented instr. accs. In this period he wrote his last atonal work, the *5 Canons*, Op. 16, and adopted 12-note technique from his Op. 18, *3 Songs*. His last group of works, 1928–45, is marked on the one hand by a simplification of the contrapuntal texture and on the other by an increasingly complex use of the note-row. The row is often broken down to 3 or 6 notes, and the resulting structures are related by imitation, inversion, retrograde-inversion, palindromic devices, etc. The Sym. of 1928 has a theme and variations as its 2nd of 2 movements, the theme and each variation being symmetrical. He comp. an important set of Pf. Variations, and 3 cantatas in which the beauty of the vocal writing is a reminder of how much Webern derived from the medieval masters whose work he had studied. Although the post-war *avant-garde* admired his mus. for its technical innovations, such as serialization of durations and dynamic levels, it should not be forgotten that Webern's place is in the romantic tradition, as his choice of texts implies, and that his homage to classical forms, such as the passacaglia and the canon, is an unwavering feature of his work. He remained, too, a lifelong admirer of Wagner's operas and he was apparently a superb cond. of Schubert, Mahler, and Brahms. Prin. works:

ORCH: *Im Sommerwind,* idyll (1904); *3 Studies on a Ground* (1908; f.p. 1978); *Passacaglia,* Op. 1 (1908); *5 Movements,* Op. 5 (orig. for str. qt., arr. for str. 1929); *6 Stücke* (*6 Pieces*), Op. 6 (1909–10, rev. for smaller orch. 1928); *5 Stücke,* Op. 10 (1911–13); *5 Stücke,* Op. 11–13, f.p. 1969, pubd. 1971); Symphony, Op. 21, for cl., bass cl., 2 hn., harp, vns., vas., vcs. (1928); *Concerto for 9 instruments,* Op. 24, for fl., ob., cl., hn., tpt., tb., vn., va., pf. (1931–4); *Variations,* Op. 30 (1940). Also *5 Stücke,* 1913, related to Op. 6 and Op. 10; *8 Fragmente,* 1911–13, related to Op. 10.

CHORAL: *Entflieht auf Leichten Kähnen* (Flight to Light boats), Op. 2, double canon for unacc. ch. (1908); *2 Goethe Lieder,* Op. 19, ch., guitar, celesta, vn., cl., bass cl. (1926); *Das *Augenlicht*

(Eyesight), Op. 26, ch. and orch. (1935); *Erste Kantate* (1st Cantata), Op. 29, sop., ch., orch. (1938–9); *Zweite Kantate* (2nd Cantata), Op. 31, sop., bass, ch., orch. (1941–3).

VOICE AND INSTR: *Siegfrieds Schwert* (Siegfried's Sword), ballad for ten. and orch. (1903, f.p. 1978); *2 Lieder* (Rilke), Op. 8, v. and cl., hn., tpt., celesta, harp, vn., va., vc. (1910); *3 Lieder*, sop. and small orch. (1913–14); *4 Lieder*, Op. 13, sop. and orch. (1914–18); *6 Lieder* (Trakl), Op. 14, high v., cl., bass cl., vn., vc. (1917–21); *5 Geistliche Lieder* (5 Spiritual Songs), Op. 15, high sop., fl., cl., bass cl., tpt., harp, vn., va. (1917–22); *5 Canons* (Latin texts), Op. 16, high sop., cl., bass cl. (1923–4); *3 Folk-Songs,* Op. 17, v., cl., bass cl., vn. or va. (1924); *3 Lieder*, Op. 18, v., E♭ cl., guitar (1925).

VOICE AND PIANO: *2 Songs* (Avenarius) (1900–1); *3 Gedichte* (1899–1903); *8 frühe Lieder* (1901–4); *3 Lieder* (Avenarius) (1903–4); *5 Dehmel Lieder* (1906–8); *5 Lieder aus der siebente Ring* (George), Op. 3 (1907–8); *5 Stefan George Lieder*, Op. 4 (1908–9); *4 Lieder*, Op. 12 (1915–17); *3 Gesänge* (Jone), Op. 23 (1934); *3 Lieder* (Jone), Op. 25 (1934–5).

CHAMBER MUSIC: Str. qt. in 1 movement (1905); *Langsamer Satz,* str. qt. (1905); pf. quintet in 1 movement (1906); *5 Movements* for str. qt., Op. 5 (1909, scored for str. orch. 1929); *4 Pieces,* Op. 7, vn. and pf. (1910); *6 Bagatelles,* Op. 9, str. qt. (1913); *3 Little Pieces,* Op. 11, vc. and pf. (1914); vc. sonata (1914); *Movement* for str. trio (1925); Str. Trio, Op. 20 (1926–27); Qt., Op. 22, vn., cl., ten. sax., pf. (1930); Str. Qt., Op. 28 (1936–8).

PIANO: *Kinderstück* (1924); *Variations,* Op. 27 (1935–6).

ARRS. OF OTHER COMPOSERS: Bach: *Ricercare* from *The Musical Offering* for chamber orch. Schoenberg: Nos. 2 and 6 of *6 Orchester-Lieder,* Op. 8, arr. for v. and pf.; *Kammersymphonie,* Op. 9, arr. for fl. (or 2 vn), cl. (or va.), vn., vc., pf. (1922); *5 Orchestral Pieces,* Op. 16, arr. for 2 pf.; Prelude and Interludes from *Gurrelieder,* arr. 2 pf., 8 hands (1910). Schubert: *Deutsche Tänze vom Oktober 1824,* arr. for orch.; *Rosamunde Romanze, Ihr Bild, Der Wegweiser, Du bist die Ruh',* and *Tränenregen,* arr. for v. and small orch. Wolf: *Lebe wohl, Der Knabe und das Immelein,* and *Denk es, O Seele,* arr. for v. and full orch.

Webster, (Sir) **David** (Lumsden) (*b* Dundee, 1903; *d* London, 1971). Scots-born impresario and opera administrator. Studied Liverpool Univ. 1921–4. Began career as department store gen. manager in Liverpool, taking major part in city's cultural activities, and becoming chairman, Liverpool Phil. Soc. 1940–5. Gen. administrator, Royal Opera House, CG 1944–70, presiding over post-war development of opera at CG, finding and encouraging many Brit. singers. Knighted 1960, K.C.V.O. 1970.

Wechseln (Ger.). To change. **Wechselnote,** *Changing Note.

Weckerlin, Jean-Baptiste (Théodore) (*b* Gebweiler, Alsace, 1821; *d* Trottberg, 1910). Fr. composer and scholar. Studied Paris Cons. (comp. with Halévy). Librarian, Paris Cons., 1876–1905. Wrote operas, oratorios, cantatas, and over 300 songs. Ed. several colls. of old Fr. songs and mus.

Weckmann, Matthias (*b* Niederdorla, Thuringia, ?1619; *d* Hamburg, 1674). Ger. composer and organist. Chorister at Dresden court chapel; pupil of Schütz. Went to Denmark and on return became organist, St James's, Hamburg, 1655. Founded concert soc. to promote new works. Wrote org. toccatas, songs, etc.

We Come to the River (*Wir erreichen den Fluss*). Opera (actions for music) in 2 parts and 11 scenes by Henze to lib. by Edward Bond (Ger. version by Henze). Prod. London 1976, Berlin 1976.

Wedding Day at Troldhaugen. Pf. piece by Grieg, No. 6 of his *Lyric Pieces* (Book 8), Op. 65 (1897), later orch. Grieg's villa, built in 1885 outside Bergen, was called Troldhaugen.

Wedding March. Many court composers have written marches for the weddings of royal and aristocratic brides, but Brit. brides have for long favoured entry into the church to the strains of the bridal ch. from Wagner's *Lohengrin* and exit to the wedding march which is the 6th no. of Mendelssohn's incidental mus. to Shakespeare's *A Midsummer Night's Dream.* The vogue for the Mendelssohn began in 1847 and received a boost in 1858 when Queen Victoria's daughter, the Princess Royal, used it at Windsor. Its supremacy was dented in 1960 by the Duchess of Kent, who left York Minster to the *Toccata* from Widor's 5th Sym. for org., her example being widely followed. Various more bizarre mus. selections are occasionally reported.

Wedding, The (Stravinsky). See *Noces, Les.*

Wedekind, Frank (*b* Hanover, 1864; *d* Munich, 1918). Ger. playwright and musician. 2 of his plays, *Erdgeist* (Earth Spirit) 1895 and *Die Büchse der Pandora* (Pandora's Box) 1901 were adapted by *Berg as lib. for his *Lulu.* Wrote songs with lute acc. His sister Erika (1868–1944) was leading sop. at Dresden Opera 1894–1909, singing Eva, Mimi, Butterfly, Violetta, etc.

'Wedge' Fugue. Nickname of Bach's org. fugue in E minor (BWV 548), comp. between 1727 and 1736. So called because of shape of subject, which proceeds in gradually widening intervals.

Weelkes, Thomas (*b* c.1576; *d* London, 1623). Eng. composer and organist. Book of madrigals in 3, 4, 5, and 6 vv. pubd. 1597, followed in 1600 by 2 further books, one of 5-part madrigals, the other of 6-part. Organist, Winchester College, 1598. Wrote 6-part madrigal *As Vesta was from Latmos hill descending* for The *Triumphs of Oriana,* 1601. Took Mus.B., Oxford Univ., 1602. Organist, Chichester Cath. from c.1601–2. His *Ayres or*

Phantasticke Spirites for 3 vv. was pubd. 1608, and shows a lighter, satirical side to his art. One of greatest of Eng. madrigalists, with daring harmonies and imaginative expression. *O Care, wilt though despatch me,* *Thule, *the period of cosmography,* and *Like two proud armies* are among the finest examples of their kind. Wrote much church mus., incl. many anthems (notably *Hosanna to the Son of David*), and instr. pieces for viols, In Nomines, pavans, etc. Wrote 3-part song, *Death hath Deprived me of my Dearest Friend,* in memory of *Morley. Buried in St Bride's, Fleet Street.

Weerbeke, Gaspar van (*b* Oudenaarde, *c.*1440; *d* after 1517). Flemish composer. Spent his time in service of ducal chapel in Milan, papal chapel in Rome, and at Burgundian court. Wrote cycles of motets to replace normal movts. of the Mass (e.g. *Kyrie* and *Gloria*). Was connected with Dufay and his circle.

Wegelius, Martin (*b* Helsingfors (Helsinki), 1846; *d* Helsinki, 1906). Finn. cond. and teacher. Studied Vienna and Leipzig. Cond. Helsingfors opera 1878. First dir., Helsinki Cons. 1882, pupils incl. Sibelius, Järnefelt, and Palmgren. Wrote vocal works and books on science of mus.

Weidt, Lucie (*b* Troppau, 1880; *d* Vienna, 1940). Austrian soprano, whose father was a conductor and composer. Studied with Rosa Papier. Member of Vienna Opera 1902–27, taking over *Mildenburg's roles under Mahler régime. Celebrated Leonore in *Fidelio*. First Vienna Marschallin. Sang Brünnhilde at NY Met. 1910–11 season and in Buenos Aires 1912. Created role of the Nurse in Strauss's *Die Frau ohne Schatten,* Vienna 1919.

Weigl, Joseph (*b* Eisenstadt, 1766; *d* Vienna, 1846). Austrian composer, son of prin. cellist in Haydn's orch. at Esterháza. Pupil of Salieri. Held court posts in Vienna and comp. over 30 Ger. and It. operas, popular in their day, and much other mus.

Weigl, Karl (*b* Vienna, 1881; *d* NY, 1949). Austrian-born composer, cond., and teacher (Amer. citizen 1943). Studied Vienna Acad. 1898–1902 (comp. with Fuchs) and Vienna Univ. (musicology with Adler). Comp. lessons from *Zemlinsky. Ass. coach at Vienna Opera under Mahler, 1904–6. Taught theory and comp. at New Vienna Cons. 1918–28. Prof. of music theory, Vienna Univ. 1931–8. Went to USA 1938. Taught in NY, Boston, and Philadelphia. Wrote 6 syms. (1908–47), 8 str. qts. (1903–49, 2nd uses viola d'amore), vn. conc., vc. conc., pf. conc., 2 vn. sonatas, songs, etc. Wrote memories of Mahler (1947, 1948).

Weihe des Hauses, Die (Beethoven). See *Consecration of the House, The.*

Weihnachtslied (Ger.). Christmas carol.

Weihnachts Oratorium (Bach). See *Christmas Oratorio.*

Weikl, Bernd (*b* Vienna, 1942). Austrian baritone. Sang with Hanover Opera 1968–70, Düsseldorf 1970–2. Salzburg 1971 (Melot). CG début 1975 (Rossini's Figaro), NY Met. 1977 (Wolfram in *Tannhäuser*). Outstanding Mandryka in Strauss's *Arabella.*

Weill, Kurt (*b* Dessau, 1900; *d* NY, 1950). Ger.-born composer (Amer. citizen from 1943). Studied Berlin Hochschule für Musik 1918–19 (comp. with Humperdinck) and privately 1921–4 with Busoni. Opera coach at Dessau 1918–21 and th. cond. at Lüdenscheid. Founded new sch. of popular opera which attracted wide attention in Ger. and also attracted implacable hostility of Nazi régime when it achieved power. First opera *Der Protagonist,* Dresden 1926. In 1927 collab. with Bertolt *Brecht in radio cantata about Lindbergh's flight across the Atlantic and in 'Songspiel' *Mahagonny* which in 1929 they reworked into 3-act opera *Rise and Fall of the City of Mahagonny,* a satire on Amer. life. His outstanding success came in Berlin in 1928 with updated version of *The* **Beggar's Opera* called *Die Dreigroschenoper* (The Threepenny Opera) containing satirical topical references to Ger. life at the time and evoking by its jazzy and harsh but brilliant scoring the atmosphere of that particular period even for those who did not experience it. Brecht's lyrics and the singing of Lotte *Lenya, who became Weill's wife, were significant factors in its success. Driven from Ger. in 1933, Weill went to Paris, then to London, and finally to NY in 1935. In America he wrote several successful Broadway musicals, lacking the pungency of his Ger. operas but of high merit nonetheless. The evocative melody 'September Song' was written for *Knickerbocker Holiday.* After his death, *The Threepenny Opera* was given an Eng. lib. by Marc *Blitzstein and ran successfully in NY. Weill's music, like Coward's on another level, captures the flavour of an era and also successfully fuses jazz with classical elements. Prin. works:

OPERAS, MUSICALS, etc. (librettist in parentheses): *Der Protagonist* (Kaiser) (1925); *Die* *Dreigroschenoper (Hauptmann, Brecht) (1928); **Rise and Fall of the City of Mahagonny* (*Aufsteig und Fall der Stadt Mahagonny*) (Brecht) (1927–9); *Der Zar lässt sich photographiern* (The Tsar has his photograph taken) (Kaiser) (1927); *Happy End* (Hauptmann, Brecht) (1929); *Der Jasager* (Brecht) (1930); *Die Bürgschaft* (Neher) (1930–1); *Der Silbersee* (Kaiser) (1932–3); *Marie galante* (Deval) Paris (1933); *A Kingdom for a Cow,* London (1935); *Johnny Johnson* (Green) NY (1936); *Knickerbocker Holiday* (Maxwell Anderson) NY (1938); *Lady in the Dark* (M. Hart, I. Gershwin) NY (1940); *One Touch of Venus* (Perelman-Nash) NY (1943); *Down in the Valley*

(Sundgaard) NY (1945-8); *Street Scene* (Rice) NY (1946); *Lost in the Stars* (Anderson) NY (1949).

BALLET: *Seven Deadly Sins* (*Die sieben Todsünden*), sop., male ch., orch. (1933).

ORCH: Syms: No. 1 (1921), No. 2 (1933–4); *Quodlibet*, Op. 9 (1923); Vn. conc., wind ens., Op. 12 (1924); *Der neue Orpheus,* Op. 16, sop., vn., orch. (1925); *3 Walt Whitman Songs,* bar. and orch. (1940); *Kleine Dreigroschenmusik* (Suite from *Threepenny Opera*).

CHORAL: *Recordare,* unacc. ch.; *Der Lindberghflug,* radio cantata, ten., bar., bass, ch., orch. (1927); *The Ballad of the Magna Carta,* soloists, ch., orch. (1939).

CHAMBER MUSIC: Str. Qt., Op. 8 (1923).

SONGS: *Das Berliner Requiem; September Song; Ballade vom ertrunken Mädchen; Happy end; Bilbao Song; Surabaya Johnny; Matrosen Tango; Havanalied; Alabama Song; Der Silbersee; Lied der Fennimore;* etc.

14 MSS. of Weill compositions were discovered in NY in 1983. All date from before 1921 and are available for study at the Weill/Lenya Research Center, NY. They include an orch. suite in E, an *Intermezzo* for pf., a song-cycle to 12th-cent Jewish texts, and 3 *Lieder* to Ger. Romantic texts.

Weinberger, Jaromír (*b* Prague, 1896; *d* St Petersburg, Florida, 1967). Cz. composer. Studied in Prague and with Reger in Leipzig. Taught at Ithaca Cons., NY, in 1922, then worked in Prague, Vienna, etc. Settled in USA 1939. Prolific composer of operas, orch. works, religious mus., songs, etc., but achieved success with 2 works, the opera *Švanda Dudák* (*Schwanda the Bagpiper*) (1927) and the *Variations and Fugue on Under the Spreading Chestnut Tree* for orch. (1939, rev. 1941).

Wein, Der (The Wine). Concert aria for sop. and very large orch. by Berg, comp. 1929. Text poem by Baudelaire in Ger. trans. by S. George. F.p. Königsberg 1930 cond. Scherchen.

Weiner, Leó (*b* Budapest, 1885; *d* Budapest, 1960). Hung. composer and teacher. Studied Budapest 1901–06, later in Berlin, Vienna, Paris, and Leipzig. Prof. of comp., Budapest State Acad. 1908–60. Famous teacher of chamber mus. Ed. Beethoven's pf. and vn. sonatas. Wrote symphonic poem, 2 vn. concs., 3 str. qts., th. mus., and *Suite on Hung. Folk Dances* (1931) for orch.

Weingarten, Joseph (*b* Budapest, 1911). Hung.-born pianist (Brit. citizen). Studied Liszt Acad., Budapest, pupil of Kodály, Dohnányi, and Weiner. Member Budapest Trio. Settled in London as recitalist and chamber mus. player.

Weingartner, (Paul) **Felix** (*b* Zara, 1863; *d* Winterthur, 1942). Austrian cond., composer, and writer. Studied philosophy Leipzig Univ. 1881–3, mus. at Leipzig Cons. Pupil of Liszt at Weimar 1883. Opera cond., Königsberg 1884, Danzig 1885–7, Hamburg 1887–9, Mannheim 1889–91, Berlin 1891–8, Vienna (after Mahler) 1907–11, Hamburg 1912–14, Darmstadt 1914–19, Vienna Volksoper 1919–24, Boston 1912–13. His orch. appointments included Berlin royal concerts 1891–1907, Vienna P.O. 1907–27, Basle 1927–33. Dir., Basle Cons. 1927–35. Guest cond., London orchs. from 1898 and at CG 1939. NY concert début 1905. Comp. several operas, 7 syms., symphonic poems, concs. (vn., vc.), choral works, 5 str. qts., etc. Wrote autobiography and several other books, incl. treatise on cond. and on interpretation of Beethoven syms.

Weinzweig, John (Jacob) (*b* Toronto, 1913). Canadian composer. Studied Toronto Univ. 1934–7, Eastman Sch. 1938. Prof. of comp., Toronto Royal Cons. from 1939 and at Toronto Univ. from 1952. Co-founder, Canadian League of Composers. First Canadian to use 12-note procedures. Has written mus. for films and radio in addition to sym. (1940), vn. conc., 4 *Divertimenti,* harp conc., pf. conc., vn. sonata, vc. sonata, pf. suites, 3 str. qts., and *Around the stage in 25 minutes during which a number of instruments are struck,* for 1 percussionist (1970).

Weir, Gillian (Constance) (*b* Martinborough, N.Z., 1941). N.Z. organist and harpsichordist. Studied RAM 1962–5. Début London 1965. Worldwide reputation as recitalist.

Weir, Judith (*b* Aberdeen, 1954). Scottish composer. Studied with *Tavener and played in Nat. Youth Orch. of Great Britain. Worked on computer mus., Mass. Inst. of Technology 1973. Studied with Robin *Holloway at Cambridge 1973–6, also at Tanglewood with Schuller and Messiaen. On staff of Glasgow Univ. from 1979. Works incl.:

OPERA: *A Night at the Chinese Opera* (1986–7).

ORCH: *Wunderhorn* (1978); *Isti Mirant Stella* (1981); *Ballad,* with bar. solo (1981); *The Ride Over Lake Constance* (1983–4).

ENS. (also with VOICE): *25 Variations,* sop. and 6 players (1976); *Black Birdsong,* bar., fl., ob., vn., vc. (1977); *Between Ourselves,* 7 players (1978); *Hans the Hedgehog,* speaker, 2 ob., bn., hpd. (1978); *King Harald sails to Byzantium,* 6 players (1979); *Thread!,* narrator, 8 players (1981).

CHAMBER MUSIC: *Out of the Air,* wind quintet (1975); *Harmony and Invention,* hp. (1978, rev. 1980); *Pas de Deux,* vn., ob. (1980); *An mein Klavier,* pf. (1980); *Several Concertos,* fl., vc., pf. (1980); *vc. sonata* (1980); *Pleasant Dreams,* db. and tape (1983); *A Serbian Cabaret,* pf. qt. (1983–4).

PIANO: *The Art of Touching the Keyboard* (1983).

Weisgall, Hugo (*b* Ivančice, 1912). Cz.-born Amer. composer and cond. Settled in USA 1920. Studied Johns Hopkins Univ. and Curtis Institute (comp. with Scalero, cond. with Reiner). Private study with *Sessions. Cond., Baltimore Str. Sym. 1937–9, and other Baltimore organizations 1949–60. Chairman of faculty, Cantors' Institute, NY, from 1951. Teacher at Juilliard Sch. 1957–70, prof. Queens Coll., NY from 1960. Works incl. 9 operas (9 *Rivers from Jordan, 6 Characters in Search of an Author, Purgatory,* etc.), cantata *A Garden Eastward,* ballet, songs, radio mus.

Weiss, Adolph (*b* Baltimore, 1891; *d* Van Nuys, Calif., 1971). Amer. composer and bassoonist. Studied Columbia Univ., then in Berlin 1924–7 with Schoenberg, being first Amer. to learn 12-note method. Bassoonist, Russian S.O. 1907, NY P.O., NY S.O., Chicago S.O. 1916–21, and Rochester S.O. 1921–4. Cond. San Francisco Opera 1933 and Los Angeles P.O. 1951. Wrote tpt. conc., bn. conc., wind quintet, *Tone Poem* for bass and perc., etc.

Weiss, Sylvius Leopold (*b* Breslau, 1686; *d* Dresden, 1750). Ger. lutenist and composer. Worked in Rome, Dresden, and Prague. Associate of *Fux. Wrote works for lute.

Weissenberg, Alexis (*b* Sofia, 1929). Fr. pianist of Bulgarian birth. Studied in Sofia, then at Juilliard Sch. 1946 with Samarov. Début with NY P.O., cond. Szell 1947. First prize Leventritt Competition 1948. London début 1974. World-wide tours and appearances with leading orchs.

Weldon, George (*b* Chichester, 1906; *d* Cape Town, 1963). Eng. cond. Studied RCM. Prin. cond. CBSO 1943–51; assoc. cond. (to Barbirolli) Hallé Orch. from 1952.

Weldon, John (*b* Chichester, 1676; *d* London, 1736). Eng. composer and organist. Pupil of Purcell. Organist, New College, Oxford 1694, Chapel Royal 1708, St Martin-in-the-Fields 1714. Wrote 4 operas, masque, anthems, songs, and mus. for *The Tempest.* (Scholars believe that the music for *The Tempest* usually attrib. Purcell may be by Weldon).

Welitsch (orig. Veličkova), **Ljuba** (*b* Borissovo, 1913). Bulgarian sop. Violinist as child, then studied singing in Vienna. Opera début Sofia 1936. Sang in opera at Graz 1937–40, Hamburg 1941–3, Munich 1943–6, Vienna 1946–58. CG début 1947, then 1948–52. Sang Amelia in *Un Ballo in Maschera* with Glyndebourne co. at Edinburgh Fest. 1948. NY Met. 1948–52. Exciting singer-actress, memorable as Salome, which she sang in Vienna 1944 for Strauss's 80th birthday, and in Eng. at CG 1949. Also a fine Tosca, Aida, and capricious Musetta.

Weller, Walter (*b* Vienna, 1939). Austrian cond. and violinist. Studied Vienna Hochschule. Violinist in Vienna P.O. from 1956, becoming leader 1961–9. Founder and leader Weller Str. Qt. from 1958, touring Europe and USA. Studied cond. with Krips and Szell. Cond. début Vienna P.O. 1968, Vienna Opera 1969. Prin. cond. RLPO 1977–80. Prin. cond. RPO 1980–5. Guest cond. Scottish Opera, SNO, and other Brit. orchs.

Welles Raises Kane. Mus. 'portrait of Orson Welles' (actor and film producer) by *Herrmann, based on mus. he wrote for Welles's films 'Citizen Kane' and 'The Magnificent Ambersons'. Comp. 1942, f.p. NY cond. composer, 1942.

Wellesz, Egon (*b* Vienna, 1885; *d* Oxford, 1974). Austrian-born composer, cond., scholar, and teacher (Eng. naturalized). Studied Vienna Univ. 1895–1908 with G. Adler and New Vienna Cons. 1911–15. Lessons from Schoenberg 1905–6; attended Mahler rehearsals at Vienna Opera. Taught at Vienna Univ. 1913–38 (prof. of history of mus. from 1929). Went to Eng. 1938, joining faculty of mus. at Oxford Univ. as lecturer. Reader in Byzantine Mus. 1948–56. Pupils incl. *Rubbra. Authority on Byzantine mus. and Gregorian chant. Several books on these and other subjects. First biographer of Schoenberg, 1921. C.B.E. 1957. Works, some in idiom of Schoenberg and medieval mus., but in later years reverting to diatonicism, incl.:

OPERAS: *Die Prinzessin Girnara,* Op. 27 (1921, rev. 1928); *Alkestis,* Op. 35 to Hofmannsthal lib. (1922–3); *Scherz, List, und Rache* (Joke, Cunning, and Revenge), Op. 41 (1926–7); *Die Bakchantinnen* (The Bacchantes), Op. 44 (1929–30); *Incognita* (1951).

BALLETS: *Die Opferung des Gefangenen* (The Prisoner's Sacrifice), opera-ballet, Op. 40 (1924–5); *Persisches Ballett* (Persian Ballet), Op. 30 (1920); *Achilles auf Skyros,* Op. 32 (1921); *Die Nächtlichen* (The Night People), Op. 37 (1923); *Das Wunder der Diana,* Op. 18 (1924).

ORCH: Syms. No. 1, Op. 62 (1945), No. 2, Op. 65 (1948), No. 3, Op. 68 (1951), No. 4 (*Symphonia austriaca*), Op. 70 (1952), No. 5, Op. 75 (1956), No. 6, Op. 95 (1965), No. 7, Op. 102 (1967–8), No. 8, Op. 110 (1970), No. 9, Op. 111 (1971); *Vorfrühling,* Op. 12 (1912); *Suite* for vn. and chamber orch., Op. 38 (1924); pf. conc., Op. 49 (1934); *Prosperos Beschwörungen,* Op. 53 (1936); vn. conc., Op. 84 (1961); *Symphonischer Epilog,* Op. 108 (1969–70).

VOICE AND INSTR: *Gebete der Mädchen zu Maria,* sop., women's ch., orch., Op. 5 (1910); 6 *George Lieder,* mez., pf., Op. 22 (1917); *Amor Timido,* sop., orch., Op. 50 (1933); *Sonnets of E. B. Browning* (in Rilke trans.), sop. and str., Op 52 (1934); *The Leaden Echo and the Golden Echo,* sop., vn., vc., pf. (1944); 5 *Lieder aus Wien,* bar., pf., Op. 82 (1959); 4 *Songs of Return,* sop., chamber orch., Op. 85 (1961); *Duineser Elegie,* sop., ch., chamber ens., Op. 90 (1963).

CHORAL: *Mitten im Leben,* Op. 45, sop., ch., orch. (1932); *Mass in F minor* (1934), in C (1937); *Missa brevis* (1936); *Mirabile mysterium,* Christmas cantata, sop., bar., ch., orch., Op. 101 (1967); *Canticum sapientiae,* bar., ch., orch., Op. 104 (1968).

CHAMBER MUSIC: Str. Qts. 1–9 (1912–66); Octet, cl., bn., hn., str. quintet, Op. 67 (1948–9); cl.

quintet (1959); str. trio, Op. 86 (1962); str. quintet, Op. 109 (1970).

PIANO: *3 Sketches*, Op. 6 (1911); *4 Eclogues*, Op. 11 (1912); *5 Epigrams*, Op. 17 (1914); *5 Idylls*, Op. 21 (1916); *5 Dance Pieces*, Op. 42 (1926); *5 Studies in Grey*, Op. 106 (1969).

Wellington's Victory (Beethoven). See *Battle Symphony*.

Well-Tempered Klavier (Bach). See *Wohltemperierte Klavier, Das*.

Welsh, Moray (Meston) (*b* Haddington, 1947). Scottish cellist. Studied York Univ. and Moscow Cons. (with *Rostropovich). London début 1972. Taught at RNCM. Soloist with leading orchs. and member of pf. trio with Anthony Goldstone (pf.) and Ralph Holmes (vn.).

Welsh National Opera. Opera co. based in Cardiff and founded in 1946. Soon built fine reputation for its perfs. of such rare Verdi operas as *Nabucco*, *I Lombardi*, and *Les Vêpres siciliennes*. Has semi-professional ch. and professional orch. Tours widely, giving seasons in Birmingham, Manchester, Liverpool, Leeds, etc. In joint venture with *Scottish Opera, embarked on cycle of Janáček operas, first in Brit. Its Britten prods. have won great admiration, especially *Billy Budd* and *Midsummer Night's Dream*. Has visited London and toured abroad (e.g. Barcelona). Mus. dirs. incl. Charles Groves 1961–3, Bryan Balkwill 1963–7, James Lockhart 1968–73, Richard Armstrong 1973–86, Charles Mackerras from 1987. Gave early opportunities to sops. Gwyneth Jones, Elizabeth Vaughan, and Margaret Price. First Brit. opera co. to stage Berg's *Lulu* (before 3rd act completion).

Welte-Mignon Reproducing Piano. Type of *pianola using photo-electric cell, developed by Edwin Welte, 1904. His uncle, Emil Welte (1841–1923), est. branch of Freiburg family business of making pneumatic mus. instrs. in NY in 1865 and developed paper roll used with pneumatic action. On these rolls are preserved historic perfs. of pf.-playing by Mahler and others.

Wenzinger, August (*b* Basle, 1905). Swiss cellist, cond., and teacher. Studied Basle Univ. 1926, Cologne Univ. 1927–9. Prin. vc. Bremen S.O. 1929–34, Basle orch. 1934–70. Teacher of viola da gamba and ornamentation at Basle Schola Cantorum from 1934. Prof. of mus., Basle Acad., from 1936. Expert in perf. of early mus.

Werle, Lars Johan (*b* Gävle, 1926). Swed. composer. Studied Uppsala Univ. 1948–51 and privately with Bäck. Mus. prod., Swedish Radio, 1958, head of chamber mus. from 1968. Works incl. Zola opera *Dreams about Thérèse* (1964), ballet *Zodiac* (1966), *Pentagram* for str. qt.

Werner, Gregor Joseph (*b* Ybbs, 1693; *d* Eisenstadt, 1766). Austrian composer. Kapellmeister to Prince Paul, then to Prince Nikolaus

Esterházy 1728–66, Haydn becoming his assistant in 1761. Wrote oratorios, over 40 masses, sonatas, fugues, etc.

Werner, Sven Erik (*b* Copenhagen, 1937). Danish composer. Studied Copenhagen Univ. Worked for Danish radio 1964–70. Dir., Odense Acad. of Mus. from 1974. Works incl. opera *The Holy Communion*, mass for TV, etc.

Wert, Giaches de (Jakab von) (*b* ?Weert, nr. Antwerp, 1535; *d* Mantua, 1596). Flemish composer. Boy chorister in It., becoming choirmaster Mantua 1565 and holding ducal court post. Pubd. several books of madrigals, 1558–95, canzonets, and motets.

Werther. Opera in 4 acts by Massenet to lib. by Edouard Blau, Paul Milliet, and Georges Hartmann based on Goethe's novel *The Sorrows of Young Werther* (*Die Leiden des jungen Werthers*, 1774). Prod. (in Ger.) Vienna 1892, Paris 1893, Chicago, NY, and London 1894.

Wesendonck, Mathilde (*b* Elberfeld, 1828; *d* Villa Traunblick, Altmünster, 1902). Ger. amateur poet and wife of Otto Wesendonck (*b* Elberfeld, 1815; *d* Berlin, 1896), a wealthy merchant. They befriended *Wagner and put house at his disposal in Zürich 1857 where he wrote part of *Tristan und Isolde* and set 5 of Mathilde's poems to mus. as the *Wesendonck Songs*. She was Wagner's mistress at this time, the inspiration of Isolde and Sieglinde. Spelling Wesendonk adopted by son some years later.

Wesendonck Songs, 5 (*Fünf Gedichte von Mathilde Wesendonck*). Set of 5 songs for v. and pf. by Wagner to poems written by his mistress Mathilde *Wesendonck. Comp. Zürich 1857–8. Orch. by Mottl under Wagner's supervision. Arr. for vn. and pf. 1872 by H. Léonard (1819–90). Arr. Henze for high v. and chamber orch. (1979). *Träume* arr. by Wagner for vn. and orch. Titles of songs are 1. *Der Engel* (The Angel) 1857, 2. *Stehe still!* (Stand still!) 1858, 3. *Im Treibhaus* (In the greenhouse) 1858, 4. *Schmerzen* (Agonies) 1857, 5. *Träume* (Dreams) 1857. Themes from *Tristan* occur in Nos. 3 and 5, which are designated 'studies for Tristan'. Often called *Wesendonck-Lieder*. Spelling Wesendonck is accurate; form Wesendonk was not adopted by family until some years after the songs were written.

Wesley, Charles (*b* Bristol, 1757; *d* London, 1834). Eng. org., harpsichordist, and composer. Son of the Methodist Charles Wesley who wrote hymns *Jesu, Lover of my Soul* and *Hark, the herald angels sing*. Child prodigy, pupil of Boyce; held church organist posts in London and wrote keyboard concs., etc. in his teens. Did not fulfil youthful promise.

Wesley, Samuel (*b* Bristol, 1766; *d* London, 1837). Eng. composer and organist, brother of Charles *Wesley. Child prodigy; wrote part of oratorio at 8 and pubd. hpd. tutor at 11. Became R.C. 1784. One of earliest Eng. Bach enthusiasts, playing important part in *Bach revival. Cond., Birmingham Fest. 1811. Regarded as greatest organist of his day, but career interrupted by recurring illness stemming from injury to skull after fall in 1787. Wrote masses, motets (*In exitu Israel* the best-known), services, anthems, songs, glees, syms., org. concs. (one based on *Rule, Britannia!*), chamber mus., and many kbd. pieces.

Wesley, Samuel Sebastian (*b* London, 1810; *d* Gloucester, 1876). Eng. composer, organist, and cond., illegitimate son of Samuel *Wesley. Chorister, Chapel Royal, 1820. Organist of several London and suburban churches 1826–32, also th. cond. Organist, Hereford Cath. 1832–5, Exeter Cath. 1835–41, where est. as country's leading org. and church musician. Organist, Leeds Parish Church 1842–9, Winchester Cath. 1849–65, Gloucester Cath. from 1865. Prof. of org., RAM from 1850. Advocate of and tireless fighter for improvements in standards of Anglican church mus., publishing tract on need for reform, 1849. Comp. splendid anthems (notably *Thou wilt keep him in perfect peace*), 5 Services (that in E major, 1845, being the finest), hymns (incl. the famous *Aurelia*), glees, songs, and pf. mus. Cond. f.p. of Bach's *St. Matthew Passion* at a Three Choirs Fest. (Gloucester 1871). His genius as an organist was such that church authorities overlooked his often questionable conduct in personal and professional affairs.

Westergaard, Peter (*b* Champaign, Ill., 1931). Amer. composer. Studied Harvard Univ. 1949–53 (comp. with Piston) and Princeton Univ. 1955–6 (comp. with Sessions, theory with Babbitt), later in Paris and Detmold (with Fortner). Taught at Columbia Univ. 1958–66 and Princeton from 1968. Works incl. cantata to text by Dylan Thomas (1958), *5 Movements* for orch., chamber works.

Western Wynde. Eng. 16th-cent. secular tune used as *cantus firmus* in Masses by *Taverner, *Tye, and John *Shepherd which are therefore known as 'Western Wynde' Masses. The use of secular tunes in sacred mus. was eventually banned by the R.C. church, not surprisingly when one considers that the anonymous and beautiful words to which congregations were accustomed to hearing this tune sung were:

Western wynde, when wilt thou blow,
The small raine down can raine.
Christ, if my love were in my armes
And I in my bedde again!

Westrup, (Sir) **Jack Allan** (*b* London, 1904; *d* Headley, Hants., 1975). Eng. teacher, scholar, writer, and cond. Studied Oxford Univ. Founder-member, Oxford Univ. Opera Club. Ed. Monteverdi's *Orfeo* for perf. while undergraduate (1925) and *L'incoronazione di Poppea* (1927). Also ed.

Locke's *Cupid and Death*. Taught classics, Dulwich College, 1928–34. Ass. mus. critic, *Daily Telegraph*, 1934–40, lecturer in history of mus., RAM 1938–40. Ed., *Monthly Musical Record*, 1933–45. Lecturer in mus. King's College, Newcastle upon Tyne, 1941–4, prof. of mus., Birmingham Univ., 1944–46, Oxford Univ. 1947–71. Ed., *Music and Letters* from 1959. Pres., R.M.A. 1958–63. Cond. Oxford Univ. Orch. 1954–63, Oxford Bach Ch. and Orch. Soc. 1970–1. Contrib. to many mus. dictionaries, ed. of encyclopaedias. Author of books on Purcell, Handel, Liszt, Bach cantatas, and Schubert chamber mus. While at Oxford after 1947 cond. many opera perfs., incl. *Idomeneo, Les Troyens, Macbeth, Hans Heiling, The Secret, L'Enfant et les Sortilèges*, and *Incognita*. One of most practical of scholars. Knighted 1960.

West Side Story. Amer. musical on modernized version of Romeo and Juliet story with mus. by Leonard Bernstein, lib. by Stephen Sondheim. Prod. Washington and NY 1957, London 1958.

Wetz, Richard (*b* Gleiwitz, 1875; *d* Erfurt, 1935). Ger. composer and cond. Studied Leipzig Cons., then with *Thuille in Munich. Th. cond., then cond. of various choirs in Erfurt 1906–25. Taught comp. in Weimar. Wrote books on Bruckner, Liszt, and Beethoven. Wrote 2 operas, 3 syms., many choral works, 2 str. qts.

Wexford. Town in Eire where autumn opera fest. has been held in highly convivial atmosphere since 1951. Has made speciality of reviving It. operas of *bel canto* sch. or once-popular operas such as *Tiefland*. Good record of discovering rising star singers. Founded by Dr T. J. Walsh (art. dir. 1951–66). Other dirs. B. Dickie 1966–74, T. Smillie 1974–8, A. Slack 1979–81, E. Padmore from 1982.

Whale, The. Cantata by *Tavener for mez. and bar., speaker, ch., organ, tape, orch., on text assembled from various sources by composer. Comp. 1965–6 and f.p. 1968 at inaugural concert of London Sinfonietta.

Whelen, Christopher (*b* London, 1927). Eng. composer and cond. Studied Oxford Univ. and Birmingham Sch. of Mus. Conducting début, Bournemouth 1948, becoming ass. cond. Bournemouth S.O. 1948–52. Mus. dir., Old Vic 1952–5; ass. cond. CBSO, 1955–7. Composer of radio and TV operas and many scores for stage and radio plays, especially Shakespeare.

When Lilacs last in the Dooryard Bloom'd. (1) 'Requiem for those we love' for mez., bar., ch., and orch. by *Hindemith to text by Whitman (Ger. trans. by Hindemith). Comp. April 1946 in memory of F. D. Roosevelt and Americans killed in World War II. F.p. NY 1946.
(2) Cantata for sop., bar., ch., and orch. by *Sessions, f.p. at Univ. of Calif., Berkeley, 1971.

Where the Wild Things Are. Fantasy opera in 9 scenes, Op. 20, by Oliver Knussen to lib. by Maurice Sendak and composer, based on children's book by Sendak. Comp. 1979–83. F.p. Brussels 1980. F. concert p. of rev. version London 1982 (both incomplete); f. stage p. (complete) London 1984 (by Glyndebourne co.).

Whettam, Graham (Dudley) (*b* Swindon, 1927). Eng. composer, mainly self-taught. First professional perf. of his work 1950; ob. conc. at Proms 1953. Chairman, Composers' Guild 1971, being specially concerned with matters of copyright. Gregynog Arts Fellowship 1978. Pubd. own comps. from 1970s. Several early works withdrawn and disowned. Many works f.p. abroad. Prin. mature comps.:

OPERA: *The Chef who wanted to rule the world* (1969).
ORCH: *Introduction and Scherzo impetuoso* ('Benvenuto Cellini') (1960); cl. conc. (1959); *Variations*, ob., bn., str. (1961); vc. conc. (1962); *Sinfonia contra timore* (1962), *Sinfonia intrepida* (1976), *Sinfonia drammatica* (1978); *Sinfonietta stravagante* (1964); Sinfonia concertante, fl., ob., cor anglais, bn., hn., hpd., str. (1966); *The Masque of the Red Death*, 2 scenes for dancing after E. A. Poe (1968); *Hymnos*, str. (adapted from 2nd str. qt.) (1978).
INSTRUMENTAL: *Fantasy* for 10 wind (1960, rev. 1975); *Hymnos*, 8 vc. (adapted from 2nd str. qt.) (1978); Conc. for 10 wind (1979).
CHORAL: *The Wounded Surgeon plies the Steel* (T. S. Eliot) (1959); *Magnificat and Nunc Dimittis*, choir and organ (1961); *Then spake Solomon*, choir, organ, 3 tpt., 3 tb., timp. (1962); *Do not go gentle into that good night* (D. Thomas), 5 solo vv. or 5-pt. ch. (1965); *Celebration*, cont., ch., organ, orch., and brass band (1975).
CHAMBER MUSIC: *A Little Suite*, brass quintet (1974); *Quintetto Concertato*, fl., ob., cl., bn., hn. (1979); *Music for Brass*, sextet (1964); Sextet, fl., ob., cl., bn., hn., pf. (1970); ob. qts., No. 1 (1960), No. 2 (1973); str. qts., No. 1 (1967), No. 2 (1978), No. 3 (1980); *Prelude, Allegro, and Postlude*, fl., ob., pf. (1955); Trio, ob., cl., bn. (1975); hn. trio (1976); cl. sonatina (1965); *Duo declamando*, hn., pf. (1972); *Duo*, ob., vc. (1974); solo vn. sonatas, No. 1 (1957), No. 2 (1972).
BRASS BAND: *Partita* (1975); *Invocation* (1977).
SONGS: 2 Songs (1958); *3 Yeats Songs* (1966, rev. 1973).
PIANO: *6 Little Dances* (1958); *Prelude, Scherzo, and Elegy* (1964); *Prelude and Scherzo Impetuoso* (1967); *Night Music* (1969).
ORGAN: *Partita* (1962); *Triptych* (1965).

Whip (slapstick) (Fr. *fouet*; Ger. *Holzklapper*; It. *frusta*). Instr. in form of wooden clapper, comprising two pieces of wood hinged at base to form handle. The pieces are struck together rapidly. Used by Mahler (7th Sym.), Ravel (Pf. Conc. in G), and Britten (several works).

Whistle. (1) As verb. Sound produced by emitting breath through small aperture in pursed lips, pitch being controlled by shaping of the mouth as resonating chamber. Some people can whistle through their teeth. Some professional whistlers have appeared on concert platform. Bing Crosby was a mellifluous whistler. Harty, at rehearsal, did not sing or hum phrases to the orch. to indicate how he wished them to be played but whistled in perfect pitch and tune.
(2) As noun. Term for various primitive wind instr., e.g. tin-whistle.

White, Eric Walter (*b* Bristol, 1905; *d* London, 1985). Eng. writer on mus. and arts administrator. Worked for League of Nations 1929–33. From 1942 to 1971 worked for Council for Encouragement of Mus. and Arts and its successor (1946), the Arts Council. Author of books on Stravinsky and Britten (1948, rev. 1970, 1983) and of *A History of English Opera* (1983).

White, Felix Harold (*b* London, 1884; *d* London, 1945). Eng. composer. Taught pf. by mother, otherwise self-taught. Played in LPO 1933–5 and on CG mus. staff at same period. Prolific composer of works of all kinds, especially songs and part-songs, and translator of Hindemith's operas *Cardillac* and *Mathis der Maler*.

White, Maude Valérie (*b* Dieppe, 1855; *d* London, 1937). Eng. composer. Studied RAM (comp. with Macfarren). Wrote popular songs to Eng., Fr., and Ger. texts.

White Peacock, The. Orch. work by *Griffes, being orch. version of No. 1 of his *4 Roman Sketches*, Op. 7, for pf. after poems of William Sharp. Comp. 1915–16.

White (Whyte), **Robert** (*b c.*1538; *d* Westminster, 1574). Eng. composer and organist. Possibly pupil of *Tye, since the Ellen Tye he married was the older composer's daughter. Mus.B., Cambridge, 1560. Choirmaster, Ely Cath., 1562. Organist, Chester Cath., then from 1570, organist and choirmaster, Westminster Abbey. Died of plague, as did wife and 3 children. One of finest Eng. composers of his time. Wrote mainly church mus., making brilliant use of imitation. Works incl. *Magnificat*, 2 *Lamentations*, 20 motets, and 4 anthems.

White, Willard (*b* St Catherine, Jamaica, 1946). West Indian bass-baritone. Studied at Jamaica Sch. of Mus. Won schol. to Juilliard Sch., NY, 1968 and took part in *Callas masterclasses. Début with NY City Opera 1974 (Colline). ENO début 1976 (Seneca in *L'Incoronazione di Poppea*). Glyndebourne début 1978 (*Die Zauberflöte*). Sang Hunding in ENO's 1983 *Rhinegold*. Concert career incl. bass parts in Elgar's *Dream of Gerontius* and Shostakovich's 13th Sym.

Whitehill, Clarence (*b* Marengo, Iowa, 1871; *d* NY, 1932). Amer. bar. Studied in Chicago; advised by *Melba to go to Paris. Opera début Brussels 1898, followed by Paris Opéra-Comique. Then studied with J. Stockhausen in Frankfurt. Sang at Bayreuth 1904, 1908–9, Cologne Opera 1903–08. NY Met. 1909–10, then joined Chicago Opera, returning to Met. 1914–32. CG 1905–16 (incl. Eng. *Ring* under Richter, 1908). One of finest interpreters of Wagner roles of Amfortas, Sachs, and Wotan. Also memorable Golaud in Debussy's *Pelléas et Mélisande*. Created title-role in Delius's *Koanga*, Elberfeld 1904.

Whiteman, Paul (*b* Denver, 1890; *d* Doylestown, Penn., 1967). Amer. jazz band director. Violist in Denver S.O. from 1912 and San Francisco S.O. from 1915. Formed Paul Whiteman Orch. 1920, larger than usual jazz band, which bridged gap between jazz and other forms of mus. by what he called 'symphonic jazz'. Orch. contained several great jazz musicians, e.g. Bix Beiderbecke (trumpet), Joe Venuti (vn.), Tommy Dorsey (tb.), Eddie Lang (guitar). Commissioned Gershwin's *Rhapsody in Blue*, giving f.p. Feb. 1924. Most Whiteman orchestrations were by *Grofé.

Whittaker, William (Gillies) (*b* Newcastle upon Tyne, 1876; *d* Orkney Isles, 1944). Eng. composer, cond., organist, and scholar. Abandoned science for mus. Studied Armstrong College, Newcastle upon Tyne, joining its staff as, successively, instructor, lecturer, and reader in mus. Devoted most of his life to promoting mus. activities, particularly choral singing, in N.E. of Eng. Specialist in cantatas of J. S. Bach (his 2-vol. book on them was pubd. posthumously, 1959). Championed mus. of his friends Holst and Vaughan Williams, also of Debussy, Satie, and Poulenc. Founder and cond., Newcastle Bach Ch. 1915. Cond. Newcastle and Gateshead Choral Union 1919–29. With Newcastle Bach Ch., gave first complete perf. for 3 centuries of Byrd's *Great Service*, 1924 (Newcastle Cath. and St Margaret's, Westminster). First Gardiner Prof. of Mus., Glasgow Univ., 1929–41, Prin., Scottish Nat. Acad. of Mus. (now RSAM) 1929–38, 1939–41. E.N.S.A. mus. adviser to Scottish Command, 1942–4. In 1930 rediscovered at Uppsala Univ., Sweden, sonatas of Eng. composer, William *Young (*d* 1671) and gave their f.p. in Brit.

Whittaker's work as cond. and scholar overshadowed his creative work, but perf. of several of his works in his centenary year revealed an orig. and compelling composer, ahead of his time, whose mus. deserves further and widespread exploration. In addition, his many arrs. of North Country folk-songs, pipe-tunes, and ballads, and of works by Bach, Purcell, Gluck, etc., have their own high value. Prin. works:

BALLET: *The Boy who didn't like fairies*, fl., str., pf., perc.

ORCH: Prelude, *The Coephori of Aeschylus* (1921); *3 Mood Pictures* (orig. for pf.) (1923); pf. conc., with str.

CHORUS AND ORCH: *A Lyke-Wake Dirge* (1924); *The Coelestial Sphere* (1923); *A Festal Psalm* (1932); Choruses (women's) from *The Coephori*; *Southward Bound*; *Ode*, male ch.

VOICE AND ORCH: *To the Beloved*, sop.

CHORAL: Psalm 139 (1925); *Candle Gate* (1929); *The Concertina* (1929); *I said in the noontide of my days* (1930); *Chorus of Spirits from Prometheus* (1931); *Where neither moth nor rust* (1931); *4 Poems by Bridges*; *The wind and the rain*; *Jocelyn*; *The Ship of Rio*; and other works still in MS.

CHAMBER MUSIC: *Among the Northumbrian Hills*, pf. and str. qt. (1921); *Phantasie* qt. (1929); *Phantasie* qt., pf., and str. (1929); *Phantasie* str. trio (1930); wind quintet (1930); va. suite (1932); vn. sonatina (1928); fl. suite (1925); *Suite of North Country Folk-Tunes*, pf. and str. qt.; *Swedish Impressions*, sextet for pf. and wind.

PIANO: *A Day in the Country* (1916); *3 Mood Pictures* (1918, orch. 1923); *4 Short Pieces* (1924); *5 Short Sketches* (1926); *A Short Suite* (1930); *By Running Water*.

SONGS: *The Ship of Rio* (1919); *Dream Song* (1919); *4 Songs of the Northern Roads* (1919); *2 Song Carols* (1921); *Bog Love* (1924); *Stay in Town* (1924); *2 Lyrics from the Chinese* (1925); *Michael's Song* (1926); *Gay Robin is seen no more* (1936).

Whittall, Arnold (Morgan) (*b* Shrewsbury, 1935). Eng. musicologist. Studied mus. at Cambridge Univ. 1956–62. Univ. posts at Nottingham 1964–9, Cardiff 1969–75, and King's Coll., London, from 1976. Expert in analysis of works by Schoenberg, Britten, Webern, and other 20th cent. composers. Author of study of Britten and Tippett.

Whole Consort. See *Consort*.

Whole-Note. The semibreve ○.

Whole-Tone. Interval of 2 semitones, e.g. from C up to adjacent D. *Whole-tone scale* progresses entirely in whole-tones instead of partly in whole-tones and partly in semitones as in major and minor scales and modes. The scale is obtained by taking every other note of the 12-semitone chromatic (or equal-tempered) scale, thus only 2 whole-tone scales are possible, one beginning on C, the other on C♯ (but since there is no keynote each scale can begin on any note). Used by Debussy, Vaughan Williams, Glinka, and others for chords and short passages.

Whyte, Ian (*b* Dunfermline, 1901; *d* Glasgow, 1960). Scottish cond. and composer. Studied RCM (comp. with Stanford and Vaughan Williams). Mus. dir., BBC (Scotland) 1931–46. Formed BBC Scottish Orch. 1935, conducting it after 1945 in adventurous programmes. Wrote operas, 2 syms., symphonic poems *Edinburgh* and *Tam o'Shanter*, ballet *Donald of the Burthens*, concs. (pf., vn., va.), choral works, and songs.

Whythorne (Whithorne), **Thomas** (*b* Ilminster, 1528; *d* London, 1596). Eng. composer. Travelled in It. Pubd. secular songs in 3, 4, and 5 parts, 1571, also duos, with option for vv. or instrs., and works for viols. Wrote autobiography, rediscovered 1955 and pubd. 1961.

Wich, Günther (*b* Bamberg, 1928). Ger. conductor. Studied fl. at Freiburg 1948–52, then became cond. Début 1952 at Freiburg, becoming chief cond. of opera 1952–9. Chief cond. Graz Opera 1959–61, Hanover 1961–5, Deutsche Oper-am-Rhein, Düsseldorf, from 1965. Prof. of cond., Essen Hochschule 1969–73. CG début 1968 (*Die Zauberflöte*). Champion of contemporary opera. First to cond. Schoenberg's 1-act operas as triple bill (Hanover 1963).

Wicks, Allan (*b* Harden, Yorks., 1923). Eng. organist and cond. Studied Oxford Univ. Sub-organist York Minster, 1947–54; organist and choirmaster Manchester Cath. 1954–61, Canterbury Cath. from 1961. One of first brilliant Eng. players of Messiaen's org. mus.

Widdicombe, Gillian (*b* Aldham, Suffolk, 1943). Eng. mus. critic. Studied RAM and Gloucester Cath. Worked for BBC 1966, Glyndebourne Fest. 1969 (administration). Contributor to *Financial Times*, *Observer*, etc.

Widdop, Walter (*b* Norland, Halifax, 1892; *d* London, 1949). Eng. ten. Opera début BNOC 1923 as Radames in *Aida*. CG 1924 (*Siegfried*), 1928–33, 1935, 1937–8. Fine oratorio singer, but better-known for Wagner roles such as Siegmund and Lohengrin. Sang Tristan to Flagstad's Isolde. Sang in Barcelona (1927), Amsterdam, and Ger.

Widerspenstigen Zähmung, Der (Goetz). See *Taming of the Shrew, The.*

Widor, Charles-Marie (Jean Albert) (*b* Lyons, 1844; *d* Paris, 1937). Fr. organist and composer. Studied at Brussels under Lemmens. Organist, St Sulpice, Paris 1870–1933. Succeeded Franck as prof. of org., Paris Cons., 1890, prof. of comp. from 1896. Mus. critic of *L'Estafette* for many years. Famous as improviser. Ed. complete org. works of Bach (with *Schweitzer). Wrote treatise on modern orchestration, 1904. Comp. 3 operas, ballet, 2 syms. with org., symphonic poems, 2 pf. concs., vc. conc., 10 org. syms., shorter org. pieces, and choral works.

Wieck, (Johann Gottlob) **Friedrich** (*b* Pretzsch, nr. Torgau, 1785; *d* Loschwitz, nr. Dresden, 1873). Ger. music teacher. Abandoned theology for mus., being self-taught. Settled in Leipzig where he gave lessons, est. a piano factory, and founded a lending library. Moved to Dresden 1844, where he became one of most famous of piano teachers. Pupils inc. *Bülow, Robert *Schumann, and his daughter (by his first wife) Clara, who married Schumann. Wrote book *Klavier und Gesang* (1853, rev. 1878).

Wiegenlied (Ger.). Cradle song. Lullaby or *Berceuse*. Title given to songs by Wolf, Strauss, and many others.

Wiegold, Peter (*b* Ilford, 1949). Eng. composer. Studied Univ. Coll. of Wales, Aberystwyth, 1967–72, then at Durham Univ. with David Lumsdaine until 1975. Taught at TCL 1975–6. Music organizer, City Univ., London, 1976. Founder and dir., Gemini Ens. Plays elec. instr. for London Sinfonietta. Works incl. *Rain Has Fallen* (Joyce), for sop., ch., orch. (1972), *The Dancing Day*, for brass quintet (1973), *Night Visitors*, tape (1975), *The Soft Complaining Flute*, fl. and tape (1977), *Prelude V*, str. qt. (1981), and *Saving the Sun*, for tenor (playing gong) and tape (1980).

Wieniawski, Henryk (*b* Lublin, 1835; *d* Moscow, 1880). Polish violinist and composer. Entered Paris Cons. at age 8. Gave first concert 1848, toured Poland and Russia, returned to Cons. Appointed solo violinist to Tsar, 1860; taught at St Petersburg Cons. 1862–9. Toured USA with A. Rubinstein 1872. Prof. of vn., Brussels Cons. 1875–7. Wrote 2 vn. concs., mazurkas, études, caprices, and other pieces. Regarded by many good judges as one of the greatest violinists after Paganini.

Wieniawski, Józef (*b* Lublin, 1837; *d* Brussels, 1912). Polish pianist, brother of Henryk *Wieniawski. Studied Paris Cons. (with Alkan), then with Liszt at Weimar 1855–6. Taught at Moscow Cons. 1866, at Brussels Cons 1878–1912. Toured with his brother. Wrote pf. conc., str. qt., 24 studies, etc.

Wigmore Hall. London concert hall in Wigmore Street, opened 1901 as Bechstein Hall (architect, Collcutt). Capacity 543. Used often for recitals by artists making their débuts or London débuts.

Wihan, Hanuš (*b* Politz, 1855; *d* Prague, 1920). Bohem. cellist. Studied Prague Cons., then played in Berlin concerts. Prin. cellist Munich court orch. from 1880 and cellist in King Ludwig's qt., which played at Wagner's Bayreuth home. Prof. of vc., Prague Cons. from 1887. Est. Bohemian Str. Qt. 1892, eventually becoming its cellist for 20 years. Gave f.p. of R. Strauss's vc. sonata 1883 and was dedicatee of Dvořák's vc. conc. 1895, although he did not give the first performance, when the soloist was Leo Stern.

Wilbraham, John (*b* Bournemouth, 1944). Eng. trumpeter. Studied RAM. Trumpeter in New Philharmonia Orch. 1966–8, RPO 1968–72, BBC S.O. from 1972. Brilliant player of Baroque mus.

Wilbye, John (*b* Diss, 1574; *d* Colchester, 1638). Eng. composer. Took post at Hengrave Hall, near Bury St Edmunds, 1593, remaining there for rest of his life and becoming wealthy landowner after 1613. Wrote some sacred motets but chiefly known as among greatest of Eng. madrigal sch. Absorbed It. influence of Marenzio, and incorporated solo-song features into his madrigals similar to lute air. Pubd. 2 books of madrigals, 1598 and 1609. Seems to have written nothing after 1614. Among best-known of his madrigals are: *Adieu,* *sweet Amaryllis; All Pleasure is of this Condition; Down in a Valley; Draw on, Sweet Night; Flora gave me Fairest Flowers; Lady, your Words do Spite Me; Softly, softly; Stay, Corydon; Sweet Honey-Sucking Bees; Unkind, O Stay thy Flying; Weep, Weep mine Eyes.*

Wild, Earl (*b* Pittsburgh, Penn., 1915). Amer. pianist. Studied with *Petri and others. Played conc. with Toscanini 1942. Since then, int. career. Renowned Liszt player. Some comps., incl. ballet and oratorio. London début 1973.

Wilde, David (Clark) (*b* Stretford, Lancs., 1935). Eng. pianist and cond. Studied with *Reizenstein 1945–7, then with Elinson at RMCM 1948–53, in 1963 with Nadia *Boulanger. BBC staff accompanist, Glasgow, 1959–62. Prof. of pf., RAM 1965–7, RMCM 1967–9. Recitals throughout Europe and USA. Liszt and Bartók specialist.

Wildschütz, Der (The Poacher). Opera in 3 acts by Lortzing to his own lib. after Kotzebue's comedy *Der Rehbock.* Prod. Leipzig 1842, Brooklyn 1856, London 1895.

Wilhelmj, August (*b* Usingen, 1845; *d* London, 1908). Ger. violinist and teacher. Studied Wiesbaden 1849, début 1854. Leipzig Cons. 1861–4 with F. *David. World tour 1878–82. Led orch. at first Bayreuth Fest. 1876 and for Wagner's concerts in London 1877. Taught at Blasewitz, Dresden, 1886–94. Prof. of vn. GSM from 1894. Comp. str. qt. and works for vn. and orch. Wrote cadenzas for classical vn. concs. Arr. Bach melody as *Air on the G string* and Wagner's *Träume* for vn. and small orch.

Wilhem (Bocquillon), **Guillaume Louis** (*b* Paris, 1781; *d* Paris, 1842). Fr. teacher. Studied Paris Cons. Organized teaching of sight-singing in Paris schs. from 1835 and instituted male-v. choirs throughout Fr. Wrote textbooks on *fixed-doh. System was later adapted by *Hullah for Eng. usage.

Wilkinson, Marc (*b* Paris, 1929). Fr.-born Australian composer and cond. Studied comp. with Varèse and Messiaen, and at Columbia Univ. and Princeton Univ. Comp. and mus. dir., Royal Shakespeare Co., then mus. dir., Nat. Th. 1966–74. Many scores for films and plays.

Wilkinson (Wylkynson), **Robert** (*b* c.1450; *d* ?Eton, 1515 or later). Eng. composer. Some church mus. survives in MS. at Eton College Library, 2 *Salve Regina* settings, a 13-part creed, and *O Virgo prudentissima.*

Wilkinson, Stephen (*b* Eversden, Cambridge, 1919). Eng. cond. Studied Christ Church Cath., Oxford, and with Thomas *Armstrong. Org. scholar, Queen's Coll., Cambridge. Studied hpd. with Boris *Ord and singing with George Parker. Dir., Hertfordshire Rural Mus. Sch., 1951–2. Joined BBC 1953. Cond., BBC Northern Singers

from 1962. Founder and cond. William Byrd Singers of Manchester since 1970.

Wilkomirska, Wanda (*b* Warsaw, 1931). Polish violinist. Studied Łódź Cons. and in Budapest and France (with Szeryng). Début at age 7. Soloist after 1946 with leading orchs., making speciality of .modern concs., esp. those by Szymanowski and Britten. Has toured internationally since 1955. Gave f.p. of Penderecki's *Capriccio,* 1967. Settled in West, 1983.

Wilkomirski, Józef (*b* Kalisz, 1926). Polish cond., composer, and writer. Studied Łódź and Warsaw. Works incl. sinfoniettas, symphonic poems, conc. for 4 harps, sonatas, and songs.

Willaert, Adriaan (*b* Bruges or Roulaers, c.1490; *d* Venice, 1562). Flemish composer. Went to Paris to study law but took up mus. Went to Rome 1515 and was then in service of cardinal at Ferrara until 1520, having visited Hungary 1517–19 with his employer. Appointed choirmaster, St Mark's, Venice, 1527. Founded singing sch. there and established the foundations of the 'Venetian School' of which he was a major figure. One of first madrigal composers. Wrote much church mus., some of it for double ch. (because of 2 orgs. and 2 choirs at St Mark's), his motets being his finest works.

Willan, Healey (*b* Balham, 1880; *d* Toronto, 1968). Eng.-born composer, organist, and teacher. Studied at choir school in Eastbourne, and was organist at several churches. Went to Toronto 1913, becoming head of theory dept. at Cons. Vice-prin. 1920–36. Prof. of mus., Toronto Univ. 1938–50, univ. organist 1932–65. Authority on plainsong. Prolific composer: 2 syms. (1936, 1948), pf. conc. (1944), opera *Deirdre* (1946), chamber mus., *Coronation Suite* (1953), org. pieces, and *11 Liturgical Motets* (1928–37).

Willcocks, (Sir) David (Valentine) (*b* Newquay, 1919). Eng. cond., organist, composer, and teacher. Studied RCM and King's College, Cambridge. Organist, Salisbury Cath., 1947–50. Worcester Cath. 1950–7. Cond. City of Birmingham Ch. 1950–7, Bradford Festival Choral Soc. 1955–74. Dir. of mus., King's College, Cambridge, 1957–73, univ. organist 1958–74, cond. Cambridge Univ. Mus. Soc. 1958–73, lecturer Cambridge Univ. 1957–74. Mus. dir., Bach Ch. from 1960. Cond. f.p. in Italy (Milan) of Britten's *War Requiem,* 1963. Dir., RCM 1974–84. C.B.E. 1971. Knighted 1977. Expert cond. of Eng. mus. by Vaughan Williams, Britten, Howells, etc., of which he has made many recordings. Comp. church mus., arr. carols, etc.

Williams, Alberto (*b* Buenos Aires, 1862; *d* Buenos Aires, 1952). Argentinian composer, conductor, pianist, and teacher. Studied in Buenos Aires then at Paris Cons. 1882–9. Founded concert series 1892 and others subsequently. Founder and dir. Buenos Aires Cons. 1893–1941. Conducted

Berlin P.O. in his works 1900. Influenced by European mus. at first, he moved to a more nationalist stance and later to a wider style. Wrote 9 syms. (1907–39), orch. suites, 3 vn. sonatas, and songs.

Williams, Charles Lee (*b* Winchester, 1853; *d* Gloucester, 1935). Eng. organist and composer. Ass. organist, Winchester Cath. 1865–70. Organist, Llandaff Cath. 1876–82, Gloucester Cath. 1882–97. Stalwart of 3 Choirs Fest. Wrote cantatas and church mus.

Williams, Christopher à Becket (*b* Dorchester, 1890; *d* Chandler's Ford, Hants., 1956). Eng. composer and writer. Wrote Mass in G, vn. concertino, vn. and vc. sonatas, and pf. pieces.

Williams, Grace (Mary) (*b* Barry, S. Wales, 1906; *d* Barry, 1977). Welsh composer. Studied RCM (pupil of Vaughan Williams) and with Wellesz. Works incl. *Penillion* for orch. (1955), *Fantasia on Welsh Nursery Tunes, Sea Sketches* for str. (1944), vn. conc. (1950), tpt. conc., opera *The Parlour* (1961), 2 syms., *Fairest of Stars*, sop. and orch., etc.

Williams, John (*b* Melbourne, Victoria, 1941). Australian guitarist. Studied RCM and with *Segovia. Début, London 1955. Concs. written for him by Stephen *Dodgson and others. Duo with Julian *Bream. Founder of ens. 'Sky' which plays jazz and pop in addition to works in classical style. Prof. of guitar, RCM, 1960–73. O.B.E. 1980.

Williams, Joseph. Eng. mus. publishing business, founded 1808. Inc. as Joseph Williams Ltd. 1900. Specialized in Eng. and Elizabethan mus. Taken over by Galliard in 1962 and later by Stainer & Bell.

Williams, Peter (Frederic) (*b* Wolverhampton, 1937). Eng. musicologist and organist. Studied Cambridge Univ. 1955–62. His research on 18th and 19th cent. Eng. org. mus. was supervised by T. *Dart. Studied hpd. with Leonhardt from 1964. Lect. in mus. Edinburgh Univ. from 1962. Author of history of the organ (1980) and book on Bach's org. mus. (1970), besides many papers on org. mus. and technique.

Williams, Ralph Vaughan. See *Vaughan Williams, Ralph.*

Williamson, Malcolm (Benjamin Graham Christopher) (*b* Sydney, N.S.W., 1931). Australian composer, pianist, organist, and cond. Entered Sydney Cons. at 11 to study pf., hn., and comp. (with Eugène Goossens). Went to London 1953 to study with *Lutyens and Erwin *Stein. Played org. at church and pf. in nightclub to support himself. Lecturer in mus., Central Sch. of Speech and Drama, London, 1961–2. Bax Memorial Prize 1963. Org. work commissioned for opening of Coventry Cath., 1962. Perf. as soloist in his own org. and pf. concs. Emulated Britten in writing

works for children. Composer-in-residence, Westminster Choir Coll., Princeton, 1970–1. His style, influenced by Messiaen, Britten, jazz, and popular mus., is individualistic, essentially melodic, versatile in approach, and technically accomplished. Succeeded *Bliss as Master of the Queen's Music, 1975. Prin. works:

OPERAS: *Our Man in Havana* (1962–3); *The *Violins of Saint-Jacques* (1966); *English Eccentrics* (1964); *The *Happy Prince* (1964–5); *Julius Caesar Jones* (1965); *Dunstan and the Devil* (1967); *The *Growing Castle* (1968); *Lucky-Peter's Journey* (1969); *The Red Sea* (1971–2).

BALLETS: *The Display* (1963–4); *Sun into Darkness* (1965–6); *BigfellaTootsSquoodge and Nora* (1967).

ORCH: Syms., No. 1 (*Elevamini*) (1956–7), No. 2 (*Pilgrim på havet*) (1968), No. 4 (1977), No. 5 (*Aquerò*) (1979–80); *Santiago de Espada*, ov. (1957); *Sinfonia Concertante*, 3 tpt., pf., str. (1958–62); Suite, *Our Man in Havana* (1963); Suite, *The Display* (1964); *Sinfonietta* (1965–7); *Concerto Grosso* (1964–5); *Symphonic Variations* (1965); *Epitaphs for Edith Sitwell*, str. (also org.) (1966); *A Word from Our Founder* (1969); *2 Pieces* for str. from *The Bridge That Van Gogh Painted* (1975); *The Bridge That Van Gogh Painted*, str. (1975, orig. pf.); *Fiesta* (1978); *Ochre* (1978, also for org. and str.); *Fanfarade* (1979); *Ode for Queen Elizabeth*, str. (1980).

CONCERTOS: Pf., No. 1 (1957–8), No. 2, with str. (1960), No. 3 (1962); Organ (1961); Vn. (1964–5); 2 pf. and str. (1972); hp. and str. (*Au Tombeau du Martyr Juif Inconnu*) (1973–6); *Lament* (in memory of Lord Mountbatten) (1979–80).

SOLO VOICE AND ORCH: *Hasselbacher's Scena* (*Our Man in Havana*), bass (1963); *6 English Lyrics*, low v. and str. or pf. (or ch. and pf.) (1966); *Hammarskjöld Portrait*, sop., str. (1974); *Les Olympiques*, mez., str. (1976); *Josip Broz Tito*, bar. and orch. (or pf.) (1980–1).

CASSATIONS (Audience and Orch. or Pf.): *The Moonrakers* (1967); *Knights in Shining Armour* (1968); *Genesis* (1971); *The Stone Wall* (1971); *The Winter Star* (1973); *The Glitter Gang* (1973–4); *La Terre des Rois* (1974); *The Valley and The Hill* (1977).

CHORUS AND ORCH: Concert Suite, *Our Man in Havana*, sop., ten., bass, ch., orch. (1963); *The Brilliant and the Dark*, women's ch., orch. (1966); Sym. No. 3 (*The Icy Mirror*), sop., mez., 2 bar., ch., orch. (1972); *Ode to Music*, ch., echo ch., orch. (or pf.) (1972–3); *Jubilee Hymn*, ch. and orch. (or pf.) (1977); *Mass of Christ the King*, 2 sop., ten., bar., ch., echo ch., orch. (1975–8).

CHORUS AND ORGAN OR PIANO: *Adoremus*, Christmas cantata, alto, ten., ch., org. (1959); *Dawn Carol* (1960); *Ascendit Deus* (1961); *Tu es Petrus*, speaker, ch., org. (1961); *Agnus Dei*, sop., ch., org. (1961); *Dignus est Agnus*, sop., ch., org. (1961); *Procession of Psalms*, ch. and org. or pf. (1961); *Easter Carol* (1962); *Jesu, Lover of My Soul*, solo qt., double ch., org. (1962); *12 New*

Hymn Tunes (1962); *Harvest Thanksgiving*, ch., org. (1962); *Wrestling Jacob*, sop., ch., org. (1962); *The Morning of the Day of Days*, sop., ten., ch., org. (1962); *Te Deum*, vv. and pf. or org. (1963); *An Australian Carol*, ch., org. (1963); *Epiphany Carol* (1963); *6 Christmas Songs for the Young*, vv. and pf. with opt. perc. (1963); *Mass of St Andrew*, vv., pf. or org. (1964); *6 Evening Hymns*, vv., pf., or org. (1964); *A Psalm of Praise (Psalm* 148), vv., org. (1965); *I will lift up mine eyes (Psalm* 121), ch., echo ch., org. (1970); *Cantate Domino (Psalm* 98), ch., org. (1970); *In Place of Belief*, ch., pf. duet (1970); *Te Deum*, ch., org., opt. brass (1970–1); *6 Wesley Songs for the Young*, vv. and pf. (1971); *O Jerusalem, The King of Love, Who is the King of Glory, and Together in Unity*, ch., congregation, org. (1972); *Canticle of Fire*, ch., org. (1973); *The World at the Manger*, sop., bar., ch., org. or pf. duet (1973); *Communion Hallelujahs*, children's ch., male ch., org. (1974–5); *16 Hymns and Processionals*, vv., pf. or org. (1975); *This is My Father's World*, ch., org. (1975); *Love Chorales*, vv., pf. or org. or guitar (1975); *Dove Chorales*, vv., pf. or org. (1975); *Above Chorales*, vv., pf. or org. (1975); *Mass of St James*, vv., pf. or org. (1975); *20 Psalms of the Elements*, ch., congregation, org. (1975); *This Christmas Night*, ch., pf. (1977); *Kerygma*, ch., org. (1979); *Little Mass of St Bernadette*, unbroken vv. and org. or instr. (1980); *Mass of St Margaret of Scotland*, congregation, opt. ch., org. (1977–80); *Mass of the People of God*, vv., org. (1980–1).

UNACC. CHORUS: *2 Motets* (1954); *Dawn Carol* (1960); *Symphony for Voices*, cont., ch. (1960–2); *Planctus*, male vv. (1962); *English Eccentrics*, choral suite (1964); *A Young Girl* (1964); *A Canon for Stravinsky* (1967); *Sonnet* (1969); *Love, the Sentinel* (1972); *The Musicians of Bremen*, 2 counterten., ten., 2 bar., bass (1971–2); *3 Choric Hymns* (No. 2, 1980, Nos. 1 and 3, 1947).

VOICE(S) AND INSTR: *A Vision of Beasts and Gods*, high v., pf. (1958); *Celebration of Divine Love*, high v., pf. (1963); *3 Shakespeare Songs*, high v., guitar or pf. (1964); *A Christmas Carol*, low v., pf. (1964); *6 English Lyrics*, low v. and pf. (1966); *From a Child's Garden* (R. L. Stevenson), song-cycle for high v., pf. (1967–8); *The Death of Cuchulain* (Yeats), 5 male vv., perc. (1968–71); *Pietà*, sop., ob., bn., pf. (1973).

CHAMBER MUSIC: Incidental mus. to *The Merry Wives of Windsor*, chamber ens. (1964); *Variations*, vc., pf. (1964); Conc. for wind quintet and 2 pf. (8 hands) (1964–5); *Serenade*, fl., pf., vn., va., vc. (1967); *Pas de Quatre*, fl., ob., cl., bn., pf. (1967); Pf. Quintet (1968); *Partita on Themes of Walton*, va. (1972); Pf. Trio (1975–6).

BRASS: *Canberra Fanfare*, brass, perc. (1973); *Adelaide Fanfare*, brass, org. (1973); *Konstanz Fanfare*, brass, perc., org. (1980); *Richmond Fanfare*, brass, perc., org. (1980); *Fontainebleau Fanfare*, brass, perc., org. (1981).

PIANO(s): Sonatas, No. 1 (1955–6), No. 2 (1957, rev. 1970–1); *Travel Diaries* (1960–1); *5 Preludes* (1966); Sonata for 2 pf. (1967); *Haifa Watercolours* (1974); *The Bridge That Van Gogh Painted and the French Camargue* (1975).

ORGAN: *Fons Amoris* (1955–6); *Résurgence du Feu (Pâques 1959)* (1959); Sym. (1960); *Vision of Christ Phoenix* (1961, rev. 1978); *Elegy—J.F.K.* (1964); *Epitaphs for Edith Sitwell* (1966, or str.); *Peace Pieces* (1970–1); *Little Carols of the Saints* (1971–2); *Mass of a Medieval Saint* (1973); *Fantasy on 'This is My Father's World'* (1975); *Fantasy on 'O Paradise!'* (1975); *The Lion of Suffolk (for Benjamin Britten)* (1977).

William Tell (Rossini). See *Guillaume Tell.*

Willis, Henry (*b* London, 1821; *d* London, 1901). Eng. org. builder. Invented special manual and pedal couplers. Founded own business, London 1845. Built or renewed many cath. orgs. incl. that in St Paul's Cath., London, and also those in St George's Hall, Liverpool, and the Royal Albert Hall, London.

Wills, Arthur (*b* Coventry, 1926). Eng. organist and composer. Organist, Ely Cath. from 1958, prof. of org., RAM from 1964. Works incl. org. sonata, org. conc., preludes and fugues, and choral works.

Wilson, Catherine (*b* Glasgow, 1930). Scottish sop. Studied RAM and RMCM. Opera début SW. Leading roles with EOG, ENO, WNO, and Scottish Opera (Governess in *Turn of the Screw*, Marschallin in *Rosenkavalier*, etc.). Has sung at Glyndebourne, Cologne, Santa Fe, and Geneva.

Wilson, John (*b* Faversham, Kent, 1595; *d* Westminster, 1674). Eng. composer, singer, lutenist, and viol-player. Set some of Shakespeare's songs, and is thought to be the 'Jack Wilson' who acted and sang in Shakespeare's co. Court musician to Charles I 1635; prof. of mus., Oxford Univ., 1656–61; court musician to Charles II 1660; Gentleman of Chapel Royal 1662. Wrote catches, church mus., and fantasies for lute.

Wilson, Marie (*b* London, 1903). Eng. violinist. Studied RCM, later prof. of vn. there. Formed and led own str. qt. One of orig. members of BBC S.O., frequently leading it. Returned to solo work 1944.

Wilson, (Sir) (James) Steuart (*b* Bristol, 1889; *d* Petersfield, 1966). Eng. ten. and administrator. Studied King's College, Cambridge, then with *Henschel and Jean de Reszke. Came into prominence singing Tamino in *Zauberflöte*, Cambridge 1910, and Vaughan Williams's *On Wenlock Edge* 1911. Lung damaged in 1914–18 war but resumed career. Involved in Glastonbury Fest. opera ventures. Founder-member of English Singers (specialists in Elizabethan and folk-songs), sang with BNOC, and famous as Evangelist in Bach's *St Matthew Passion* and as Elgar's Gerontius. Taught at Curtis Institute, Penn., 1939–42; overseas mus. dir. BBC 1942–5, mus. dir., Arts

Council, 1945–8; head of mus., BBC 1948–9; deputy gen. administrator, CG 1949–55. Prin., Birmingham Sch. of Mus., 1957–60. Knighted 1948. With A. H. Fox Strangways, made singing trans. of Schubert Lieder.

Wilson, Thomas (Brendon) (*b* Trinidad, Colorado, 1927). Scottish composer. Studied Glasgow Univ. Lecturer, Glasgow Univ. 1957–72, Reader from 1972. Works incl.:

OPERAS: *Confessions of a Justified Sinner* (1976); *The Charcoal Burners* (1968).
BALLET: *Embers of Glencoe* (1973).
ORCH: Syms.: No. 1 (1956), No. 2 (1965), No. 3 (1982); *Toccata* (1960); *Variations* (1961); *Touchstone, a Portrait* (1967); *Concerto for Orchestra* (1967); *Threnody* (1970); *Pas de Quoi*, str. (1964); *Ritornelli*, str. (1972); *Refrains and Cadenzas*, brass band (1973); pf. conc. (1984).
CHORAL: *Missa pro mundo conturbato*, ch., perc., harp, str. (1970), *Sequentiae passionis*, ch., orch., tape (1971), *Te Deum*, ch. and orch. (1971), *Songs of Hope and Expectation*, ch., piano, elec. org., hpd. (1977).
CHAMBER MUSIC: 4 str. qts.; vn. sonata (1961); *Fantasia*, vc. (1964); pf. trio (1966); *Sinfonia for 7 instr.* (1968); *Concerto da camera* (1965); *Canti notturni* (1972); vc. sonata (1973); *Complementi*, cl., vn., vc., pf. (1973); *Cancion*, guitar (1977).
VOICE AND INSTR: *Carmina sacra*, high v., harp, str. (1964); *One foot in Eden*, mez. (1977).
CHURCH: Mass in D minor, unacc. (1955); *Missa brevis*, unacc. (1955); *Ave Maria* and *Pater Noster*, unacc. (1966); *A Babe is born*, ch. and org. (1968); *Ubi caritas et amor*, male ch. and perc. (1976).
PIANO: Sonata (1964); Sonatina (1954).

Wimberger, Gerhard (*b* Vienna, 1923). Austrian composer. Studied Salzburg 1937–41, 1945–7 (comp. with J. N. *David, cond. with Krauss). Coach at Vienna Volksoper 1947–8. Theatre cond., Salzburg, 1948–51. Teacher at Mozarteum, Salzburg, from 1963. Works incl. operas, pf. conc., mus. comedy *Dame Kobald, Chronique* for orch., cantatas, *Resonances* for 3 orch. groups (1966), *Hero und Leander*, dance-drama (1963), *Multiplay*, 23 players (1974).

Wind-Band. In medieval times, bands of roving pipers who later received official recognition as 'town pipers', providing mus. for civic occasions. In modern usage, the term denotes a band of mixed wind instr., often with perc., and is more often called a 'military band' to distinguish it from the 'brass band' in which no woodwind is used. In USA 'wind band' denotes a military band. Haydn's *Wind-band Mass* (*Harmoniemesse*), 1802, is named because the wind instr. are prominent in the scoring, not because they are the only instr. used.

Wind Chest. Box-like construction which receives the wind from an org.'s bellows and supplies it to the pipes when the pallets are opened. See *Organ*.

Windgassen, Wolfgang (*b* Andemasse, 1914; *d* Stuttgart, 1974). Ger. ten. Studied with his father, Fritz Windgassen, prin. ten., Stuttgart Opera 1923–44. Opera début Pforzheim 1941 as Alvaro in Verdi's *La forza del destino*. Stuttgart Opera 1945–53, Vienna from 1953. Bayreuth Fest. 1951–71 (début as Parsifal). CG début 1955, NY Met. 1957. Outstanding singer of Parsifal, Tristan, Siegfried, and other Wagner roles, though not a *Heldentenor* of traditional kind. Art. dir. Stuttgart Opera 1972–4.

Wind Instruments. Those mus. instrs. in which sound is produced by vibrations of a column of air set in motion by the perf.'s blowing. Two main categories are woodwind (not all made of wood) and brass (not all made of brass), e.g. fl., picc., ob., cl., bn., among former; hn., tpt., tb., tuba, among latter. An org. is not a wind instr. in the sense defined here, since the air is mechanically impelled.

Wind Machine. Device to simulate sound of wind, a barrel-shaped framework being covered with silk or other fabric and rotated by a handle. Friction with wood or cardboard produces sound which can be varied in pitch by pace at which handle is turned. Used by several composers, e.g. by Strauss in *Don Quixote* and *Eine Alpensinfonie* and by Vaughan Williams in *Sinfonia Antartica*.

Wind Quintet. Composition for five wind instr., or the performers who play it. Usual combination is fl., ob., cl., bn., and hn., but there are several exceptions (Elgar's were written for 2 fl. and no hn.). Among composers of wind quintets are Reicha, Danzi, Schmitt, Françaix, Carter, Milhaud, Nielsen, Fricker, Henze, Gerhard, Stockhausen, and Schoenberg.

Winkelmann, Hermann (*b* Brunswick, 1849; *d* Vienna, 1912). Ger. ten. Studied Hanover. Opera début Sondershausen 1875. Sang Wagner roles in Vienna and created Parsifal at Bayreuth 1882. London début 1882; was first London Tristan and Walther. Concert début USA 1884. Vienna Opera 1883–1906 (first Vienna Tristan and Otello).

Winter Journey (Schubert). See *Winterreise*.

Winterreise (Winter Journey). Song-cycle for male v. and pf. by Schubert (D911), settings of 24 poems by Wilhelm Müller (pubd. 1823 and 1824). Comp. (1827) and pubd. (1828) in 2 instalments, each of 12 songs. The titles of the individual songs, in Schubert's (not Müller's) selected order are: I. *Gute Nacht* (Good Night), *Die Wetterfahne* (The Weathervane), *Gefrorne Tränen* (Frozen Tears), *Erstarrung* (Frozen Rigidity), *Der Lindenbaum* (The Lime-Tree), *Wasserflut* (Flood), *Auf dem Flusse* (On the River), *Rückblick* (Backward Glance), *Irrlicht* (Will-o'-the-Wisp), *Rast* (Rest), *Frühlingstraum* (Dream of Spring), *Einsamkeit* (Loneliness); II. *Die Post* (The Post), *Der greise Kopf* (The hoary head), *Die Krähe* (The Crow), *Letzte*

Hoffnung (Last Hope), *Im Dorfe* (In the Village), *Der stürmische Morgen* (The Stormy Morning), *Täuschung* (Delusion), *Der Wegweiser* (The Signpost), *Das Wirtshaus* (The Inn), *Mut* (Courage), *Die Nebensonnen* (Phantom Suns), *Der Leiermann* (The Hurdy-Gurdy Man).

Winter Words. Song-cycle of 8 poems by Thomas Hardy set for high v. and pf., Op. 52, by Britten. F.p. Leeds Fest. 1953 (in Harewood House). Title taken from Hardy's last pubd. vol. of poetry, 1928. The songs are: 1. *At day-close in November*, 2. *Midnight on the Great Western*, or *The journeying boy*, 3. *Wagtail and Baby*, 4. *The little old table*, 5. *The Choirmaster's burial*, or *The tenor man's story*, 6. *Proud songsters, thrushes, finches, and nightingales*, 7. *At the railway station, Upway*, or *The convict and boy with the violin*, 8. *Before life and after*.

Wirbel (Ger.). Whirl. Drum roll.

Wirbeltrommel (Ger.). Ten. drum.

Wire Brush. Variety of drumstick with head consisting of several stiff wires. Produces 'brushing' or 'swishing' sound from side-drum or cymbals. Used mainly in jazz, but also by many 20th-cent. composers.

Wirén, Dag (Ivar) (*b* Noraberg, 1905; *d* Stockholm, 1986). Swed. composer. Studied Stockholm 1926–31, then in Paris 1932–4. Mus. critic, *Svenska Morgonbladet* 1938–46. From 1944 used 'Metamorphosis technique', i.e. construction of a work from a single 'cell' or set of cells. Works incl. 5 syms. (1938–64), vn. conc. (1946), pf. conc. (1950), vc. conc. (1936), *Serenade for Strings*, Op. 11 (1937), Sinfonietta, 5 str. qts., and radio opera, *Blått, gult, rött* (1940), inspired by Churchill's 'blood, tears, sweat' speech.

Wise, Michael (*b* ?Salisbury, *c*.1648; *d* Salisbury, 1687). Eng. singer, organist, and composer. Chorister, Chapel Royal 1660, lay clerk St George's Windsor, 1663. Organist and choirmaster, Salisbury Cath., 1668–85, choirmaster St Paul's Cath., 1687. Killed in quarrel with night watchman after argument with his wife. Wrote anthems, services, and catches.

Wise Virgins, The. Ballet in 1 act by Walton, music being his arr. of 9 items from the church cantatas of J. S. Bach selected by Constant Lambert. Scenario based on parable of Wise and Foolish Virgins in *St Matthew XXV*. Choreog. by Frederick Ashton, designs by Rex Whistler. Prod. London (SW) 1940 with Fonteyn as the Bride. Orch. suite 1940, of 6 movts.: 1. What God hath done is rightly done (*Was Gott thut, das ist wohlgetan*, BWV 99); 2. Lord, hear my longing (*Herzlich thut mich verlangen*, BWV 727); 3. See what His love can do (*Seht was die Liebe tat*, from BWV 85); 4. Ah! how ephemeral (*Ach wie flüchtig, ach wie nichtig*, BWV 26); 5. Sheep may safely graze (*Schafe können sicher weiden*, from BWV 208); 6. Praise be

to God (*Gelobet sei der Herr, mein Gott*, from BWV 129).

Wishart, Peter (Charles Arthur) (*b* Crowborough, 1921; *d* Frome, Som., 1984). Eng. composer. Studied in Paris with Boulanger. Lecturer in mus., Birmingham Univ. 1950–9, prof., GSM from 1961, King's Coll., London, 1972–7, prof. of music, Reading Univ. 1977–84. Works incl. operas *The Clandestine Marriage, Klytemnestra, Two in the Bush*, and *The Captive*; 2 syms., 2 vn. concs., *Te Deum, 5 Pieces* for str., and choral works.

Wiszniewski, Zbigniew (*b* Lwów, 1922). Polish composer. Studied Łódź Univ. and Cons. Violinist in Polish Dance Co. Orch. 1955–7. Mus. dir., Polish Radio from 1957. Works incl. radio opera *Nefru; Kammermusik* 1–4; oratorio *Genesis*; 3 *Postludes* (on tape).

Witt, (Jeremias) **Friedrich** (*b* Niederstetten, 1770; *d* Würzburg, 1836). Ger. composer and cellist. Court cond., Würzburg, from 1802. Wrote operas, oratorios, and much instr. mus. Comp. so-called **Jena Symphony*, at one time erroneously attrib. to Beethoven.

Wittgenstein, Paul (*b* Vienna, 1887; *d* Manhasset, NY, 1961). Austrian pianist, pupil of **Leschetizky. Lost right arm in World War I, so developed remarkable left-hand technique. Commissioned concs. or similar works for left-hand pianist from several composers, incl. Ravel (conc.), R. Strauss (*Parergon zur Symphonia Domestica* and *Panathenäenzug*), Prokofiev (4th conc.), Schmidt (*Conc. Vars.*), and Britten (*Diversions*). Settled in NY 1939 (Amer. citizen from 1946).

Wittich, Marie (*b* Giessen, 1868; *d* Dresden, 1931). Ger. sop. Studied Würzburg. Sang in Düsseldorf etc., then joined Dresden Opera 1889–1914. Bayreuth 1901–10, CG 1905–6. In Dresden 1905 created role of Strauss's Salome, though not without protest about its 'indecency'.

Woelfl, Joseph (*b* Salzburg, 1773; *d* London, 1812). Austrian composer and pianist. Chorister, Salzburg Cath. 1783–6. Taught by Leopold Mozart and Michael Haydn. In Warsaw 1791–4, Paris 1801–06, then London. Wrote syms., 7 pf. concs., 12 str. qts., 20 pf. trios, 22 vn. sonatas, 36 pf. sonatas, 4 operas, and 2 ballets.

Wohltemperierte Klavier, Das (The Well-tempered Klavier). Title given by Bach to his 24 Preludes and Fugues for kbd., Cöthen 1722, in all the major and minor keys, and also applied to 2nd set of 24 composed in Leipzig, 1744, the 2 sets often being known simply as 'the 48'. Bach's object was to demonstrate the advantages of the then new equal **temperament. Pubd. 1800–1.

Wolf. (1) Jarring sound which sometimes occurs from bowed str. instrs. when body of instr. resonates to a particular note.

(2) Out-of-tune effect on old orgs. (before equal *temperament) when playing in certain extreme keys.

Wolf, Hugo (b Windischgraz, 1860; d Vienna, 1903). Austrian composer. Taught rudiments of mus. by his father, a leather-dealer. Entered Vienna Cons. 1875 (fellow-pupil of Mahler). Expelled 1877 (unjustly) and made bare living by teaching pf. 2nd cond. at Salzburg 1881, but gave up after 3 months. Mus. critic. in Vienna 1884–7, making enemies by his fanatical praise of Wagner and dislike of Brahms. From 1888, when he discovered the poetry of Mörike, poured out dozens of songs, incl. the *Spanish Songbook*, in which the art of the Lied reached one of its most sophisticated and intricately-wrought stages, with the pf. part no longer simple acc. but an integral part of the song. The concentrated characterization of each song is unequalled in Lieder, demanding the utmost artistry from the performers, psychological as well as vocal and instr. For 3 years from 1892 to 1894, Wolf wrote nothing except the orch. arr. of the *Italian Serenade*, but his fame gradually spread and in Berlin a 'Hugo Wolf Society' was founded. Even Vienna began to capitulate late in 1894. In 1895 he wrote an opera based on *The Three-Cornered Hat* which he called *Der Corregidor*. In the spring of 1896, he wrote the 24 songs of the *Italian Songbook* (Vol. II). In 1897 he began his Michelangelo settings and a 2nd opera, *Manuel Venegas*. But in the autumn his mind gave way, the outcome of venereal disease, and he was taken to an asylum. Though he seemed to be 'cured' in 1898 he tried to drown himself in Oct. of that year and spent his last years insane in a mental hospital. Prin. works:

SONGS (mostly with pf. acc., but some with orch.): *12 Lieder aus der Jugendzeit* (1877–8); *6 Songs for Woman's Voice*; 6 Poems of Scheffel, Mörike, Goethe, and Kerner; 4 Poems of Heine, Shakespeare, and Byron; 6 Poems by Gottfried Keller; 3 Ibsen Songs; 3 Poems by Reinick (1877–87); *53 *Mörike-Lieder* (1888); *20 Eichendorff-Lieder* (1880–88); *51 Goethe-Lieder* (1888–9); *Spanisches Liederbuch* (44 songs) (1889–90); *Italienisches Liederbuch*, Vol. I (22 songs) (1890–1); *Italienisches Liederbuch*, Vol. II (24 songs) (1896); 3 Poems by Michelangelo (1897). Among the best-loved Wolf songs (selectively chosen) are: *An die Geliebte*; *Abschied*; *Anakreons Grab*; *Begegnung*; *Denk es, O Seele*; *Einsame*; *Elfenlied*; *Der Feuerreiter*; *Gebet*; *Gesang Weylas*; *Heimweh*; *Im Frühling*; *In dem Schatten meiner Locken*; *Jägerlied*; *Kennst du das Land?*; *Lebewohl*; *Schlafendes Jesuskind*; *Der Tambour*; *Verborgenheit*; *Das verlassene Mägdlein*.
ORCH: *Penthesilea*, symphonic poem (1883); *Italienische Serenade* (1892, orch. of work for str. qt. 1887).
CHAMBER MUSIC: Str. Qt. in D minor (1879–80); Serenade in G for str. qt. (1887; arr. for str. orch. 1892 as *Italienische Serenade* (*Italian Serenade*)).

CHORAL: 6 Eichendorff chs., unacc. (1881) *Christ-Nacht*, soloists, ch., orch. (1886–9); *Elfenlied* ('You spotted snakes', from *Midsummer Night's Dream*), sop., ch., orch. (c.1890, arr. from song for v. and pf., 1888, but not same as *Elfenlied* in *Mörike-Lieder*); *Der Feuerreiter* (The Fire-rider) (Mörike song 1888 arr. ch and orch. 1892); *Dem Vaterland* (song for v. and pf. 1888, arr. for male ch. and orch. 1888–91).
OPERAS: *Der *Corregidor* (1895); *Manuel Venegas* (1897, incomplete).

Wolff, Albert (Louis) (b Paris, 1884; d Paris, 1970). Fr. cond. and composer. Studied Paris Cons. Chorusmaster Opéra-Comique, Paris, 1908, cond. from 1911, mus. dir. 1921–4, th. dir. 1945–6. Cond. first Paris perf. of Ravel's *L'Enfant et les sortilèges*, 1926, and f.p. of Poulenc's Les *mamelles de Tirésias*, Paris 1947. Cond. Fr. repertoire at NY Met. 1919–21. CG début 1937 (Debussy's *Pelléas*). Cond., Concerts Lamoureux 1928–34, then Concerts Pasdeloup. Fine interpreter of Roussel. Wrote opera *L'Oiseau bleu* (NY 1919).

Wolff, Christian (b Nice, 1934). Fr.-born Amer. composer. Studied classics Harvard Univ., 1951–63, and taught classics there later. Self-taught in comp., being influenced by Cage, Tudor, Feldman, Varèse, and Cardew. Works, some written in special notation, incl. pieces for *prepared piano, magnetic tape, and for 'various combinations of players using, in many cases, any instruments or objects'. He aimed to eliminate the 'monarchical authority' of the conductor.

Wolf-Ferrari, Ermanno (b Venice, 1876; d Venice, 1948). It. composer, son of Ger. father and It. mother. Studied in Munich with Rheinberger 1893–5. Returned to Venice 1895. Dir., Liceo Benedetto Marcello 1903–9. Taught at Salzburg Mozarteum from 1939. Wrote mainly operas, being adept at light works based on Goldoni comedies, elegantly scored and immediately appealing. Some were produced in Ger. before It. Prin. works:

OPERAS: *Cenerentola* (1900); *Le donne curiose* (1903); *I *quattro Rusteghi* (1906); *Il *segreto di Susanna* (1909); *I *gioielli della Madonna* (1911); *L'amore medico* (1913); *Gli amanti sposi* (c.1916); *La veste di cielo* (c.1917–25); *Sly* (1927); *La vedova scaltra* (1931); *Il Campiello* (1936); *La dama boba* (1939); modern rev. of *Idomeneo* (Mozart), Munich 1931. Also wrote oratorios, chamber sym., vn. conc., vc. conc., chamber mus., *Suite* for bn., 2 hn., and str., etc.

Wolfrum, Philipp (b Schwarzenbach am Wald, 1854; d Samaden, Grisons, 1919). Ger. organist, composer, and teacher. Studied in Munich with Rheinberger and Franz Wüllner and became close friend of Humperdinck. Taught at Bamberg 1879–84, dir. of mus. Heidelberg Univ. (prof. from 1898). Founded Heidelberg Bach Choir 1885. Cond. all *Reger's works comp. between

1898 and 1916 and often gave Bach recitals at 2 pf. with Reger. Revived many Bach cantatas. Cond. first Ger. perfs. of several of Elgar's choral works. Comps. incl. *Ein Weihnachtsmysterium*, for ch. and orch. (1903), str. qt., vc. sonata, pf. trio, 3 org. sonatas.

Wolpe, Stefan (b Berlin, 1902; d NY, 1972). Ger.-born composer (Amer. citizen from 1944). Studied Berlin Hochschule für Musik 1919–24. Private tuition from Busoni, Scherchen, and Webern (1933–4). Wrote th. mus. for Brecht in 1920s and was ardent radical socialist, writing works on political themes. Went to Austria 1933, then to Palestine 1934–8 (prof. of comp. at Cons.), finally to USA. Taught at various colls. in NY 1938–52. Head of mus. dept., Long Island Univ., 1957–68, prof. of comp. Mannes College, 1968. Most of his later works employ serial technique based on small pitch cells rather than on 12-note rows. Also influenced by Jewish mus. traditions and harmonies. Works incl. 2 operas, ballet *The Man from Midian* (1942), incid. music for plays by G. von Wangenheim and Brecht, sym., several cantatas, tpt. conc., chamber mus. for various combinations, and songs.

Wolstenholme, William (b Blackburn, 1865; d London, 1931). Eng. composer, pianist, and organist, blind from birth. Studied Worcester College for Blind. Helped by Elgar, who also gave him vn. lessons. Organist, St Paul's, Blackburn, 1888–1903, All Saints, St John's Wood, London, 1926. Wrote chiefly for org.

Woman without a Shadow, The (Strauss). See *Frau ohne Schatten, Die*.

Women's Love and Life (Schumann). See *Frauenliebe und -Leben*.

WoO. Werk ohne Opuszahl (Work without opus number). Applied, for example, to Beethoven's works in Kinsky's catalogue and to those of Richard Strauss in Asow's catalogue.

Wood Block. See *Chinese Wood Block*.

Wood, Charles (b Armagh, 1866; d Cambridge, 1926). Irish composer and teacher. Studied with T.O. Marks, organist, Armagh Cath., then at RCM 1883–7 as comp. pupil of Stanford. Taught harmony at RCM from 1888, later becoming prof. Cond. Cambridge Univ. Mus. Soc. 1888–94. Org. scholar Gonville and Caius, Cambridge, 1889–94. Lecturer in harmony and counterpoint, Cambridge Univ., 1897–1924, prof. of mus. from 1924. Pupils incl. *Vaughan Williams. Wrote mus. for Gr. plays, opera *The Pickwick Papers* (1922), *Ode to the West Wind* (1894), *Dirge for Two Veterans* (1901), 3 str. qts., partsongs, solo songs incl. *Ethiopia Saluting the Colours* (Whitman), and much church mus. incl. over 30 anthems and several services. Wrote the chimes for the clock of Gonville and Caius Coll.

Woodcock, Robert (fl. c.1720–34). Eng. composer. Wrote 12 concs. for fl. and str., c.1728–30.

Wood Dove, The (*Holoubek*). Symphonic poem for orch., Op. 110, by Dvořák, comp. 1896.

Wooden Prince, The (*A fából faragott Királyfi*). Ballet in 1 act by Bartók to scenario by Bela Balázs comp. 1914–17 and f.p. Budapest 12 May, 1917. Orch. suite f.p. Budapest 1931.

Woodforde-Finden, Amy (b Valparaiso, Chile, 1860; d London, 1919). Eng. composer of songs, remembered for the *Indian Love Lyrics* (poems by 'Laurence Hope', Adela Florence Nicolson, 1865–1904), incl. *Pale hands I loved beside the Shalimar*, which were pubd. privately in 1902.

Woodgate, Leslie (b London, 1902; d London, 1961). Eng. organist and chorusmaster. Studied RCM. Organist of various London churches. Joined BBC 1928; Chorusmaster, BBC Singers, from 1934. Wrote some choral pieces and textbooks. O.B.E. 1959.

Wood, Haydn (b Slaithwaite, Yorks., 1882; d London, 1959). Eng. composer and violinist. Pupil of Arbós, Stanford, and César Thomson. Won Cobbett Prize with Phantasy Qt., also wrote pf. conc., vn. conc., 9 orch. rhapsodies, 7 song-cycles, and about 200 songs. It is on these last that his fame chiefly depends, for they incl. *Love's Garden of Roses* (1914), *A Brown Bird Singing* (1922), and *Roses of Picardy* (1916) which gained poignancy from its associations with World War I. (He pronounced Haydn with the 'Hay' as in hay-making, not as in the composer after whom he was named).

Wood, (Sir) Henry (Joseph) (b London, 1869; d Hitchin, 1944). Eng. cond. and organist. Taught by his mother, and was deputy church organist at age of 10. Organist, St John's Fulham, 1887. Studied RAM under Prout and García, intending to be composer. Obtained post as cond. with Rousbey touring opera co., 1889. Helped Sullivan to rehearse *Ivanhoe* 1890. Cond. for Carl Rosa, 1891, then for Lago's It. Opera at Olympic Th. Cond. f.p. in England of *Eugene Onegin*, 1892. Taught singing until 1894, when he was mus. adviser to Mottl's Wagner concerts at new Queen's Hall. In 1895 engaged by Robert Newman as cond. of his new series of *Promenade concerts in London. These he built from rudimentary beginnings to be a premier feature of Eng. mus. life, retaining conductorship until year of his death. After 1896 cond. no more opera but devoted himself to concert work not only in London but in many provincial cities and at all the leading fests. (Birmingham, Leeds, Sheffield, Norwich, etc.). Waged war on 'deputy' system, whereby orch. players could send deputy to a concert while they took a more remunerative engagement, and did as much as any Eng. cond. to raise standards of playing. Tireless champion of contemporary mus. List of works of which he gave f.ps. and f.ps. in England is long and honourable. Tchaikovsky, Sibelius, Strauss, Skryabin, and Debussy were championed by him before their present popularity. Cond. first complete perf. of Schoenberg's *5 Orchestral Pieces* in 1912, the f.ps. in England of Mahler's 1st, 4th, 7th, and 8th syms. and *Das Lied von der Erde*, and introduced the mus. of Janáček to Eng. Every major Eng. composer of his lifetime was perf. at the Proms, and he helped the careers of many Brit. singers and instrumentalists. At his golden jubilee concert, 1938, 16 leading Brit. singers took part in Vaughan Williams's **Serenade to Music*, ded. to Wood. Made several orch. transcriptions, incl. Mussorgsky's *Pictures from an Exhibition* and Bach's *Toccata and Fugue* in D minor (under the name P. **Klenovsky*) and arr. **Fantasia on British Sea Songs* perf. on last night of every Prom Season, with audience participation (orig. written for Trafalgar centenary concert 1905). Knighted 1911. C.H. 1944.

Wood, Hugh (Bradshaw) (*b* Parbold, Lancs., 1932). Eng. composer. Studied at Oxford Univ., then in London with W. S. Lloyd Webber, Anthony Milner, Iain Hamilton, and Mátyás Seiber. Prof. of harmony RAM 1962–5, teacher at Morley Coll., London, 1958–67. Research fellow in comp., Glasgow Univ., 1966–70; lecturer in mus., Liverpool Univ., 1971–3. His mus., while reflecting a variety of influences from Tippett and Messiaen to *avant-garde* techniques, is consistent in its shapeliness, lyricism, and expressive concentration. Prin. works:

ORCH: Vc. Conc., Op. 12 (1965–9); Chamber Conc., Op. 15 (1971, rev. 1978); vn. conc., Op. 17 (1970–72); Sym. (1979–82).
VOICE AND ORCH: **Scenes from Comus*, Op. 6, sop., ten., orch. (1962–5).
CHAMBER MUSIC: Str. Qts.: Str. Qt. in B♭ (1959); No. 1, Op. 4 (1960–2), No. 2, Op. 13 (1969–70), No. 3 (1976–8); Pf. trio (1984); *Variations*, Op. 1, va. and pf. (1958); Trio, Op. 3, fl., va., pf. (1961); Quintet, Op. 9, cl., hn., vn., vc., pf. (1967).
SONGS: *Logue Songs*, Op. 2 (1959); *The Horses* (Ted Hughes), Op. 10 (1967); *The Rider Victory* (Edwin Muir), Op. 11 (1968); *Song-Cycle to Poems of Neruda*, Op. 19, high v., chamber ens. (1973–4).
PIANO: *3 Pieces*, Op. 5 (1961).
ORGAN: *Capriccio*, Op. 8 (1968).

Woodward, Roger (Robert) (*b* Sydney, N.S.W., 1942). Australian pianist. Studied N.S.W. Cons., Sydney, 1952–62, and Warsaw State Acad. Débuts Warsaw and London 1967. Won 23rd Int. Chopin Comp., Warsaw, 1968. Rapid rise to leading place among exponents of *avant-garde* mus. of Boulez, Barraqué, Cage, Xenakis, Stockhausen, Takemitsu, etc. O.B.E. 1980.

Woodwind. Name for wind instrs. orig. and usually made of wood, either blown directly by

mouth (fl. and recorder) or by means of a reed (cl. and ob.). Saxs. are classified as woodwind. *Double woodwind*, in descriptions of a composer's scoring for orch., means 2 players of each standard type of woodwind instr., e.g. fl., ob., cl., bn. (this being usual Beethoven or Schubert orch.). *Triple woodwind* means 3 of each, one player normally taking an extra member of the family of his instrument, e.g. picc. with fl., cor anglais with ob., bass cl. with cl., double bn. with bn. *Quadruple woodwind* means 4 of each, as in Strauss, Mahler, and other composers for very large orch.

Wooldridge, David (Humphry Michael) (*b* Deal, 1931). Eng. cond., composer, and writer. Studied RAM and Vienna Acad. Staff cond., Bavarian State Opera, 1954–5, guest cond. Amer. orchs. 1957–68, mus. dir. Beirut S.O. 1961–5, cond. Cape Town Orch. 1965. Works incl. va. conc., *Partita* for orch., and film mus. Author of *Conductors' World* (1970).

Wordsworth, William (Brocklesby) (*b* London, 1908). Eng. composer. Studied with **Tovey* in Edinburgh. His 2nd Sym. won Edinburgh Fest. Int. Competition 1950. Mus. in idiom unfashionable in 1960s and 1970s but of expressive emotional range, melodic attraction, fine craftsmanship, and consistent integrity. Lived many years in Surrey, then moved in 1960s to Scottish Highlands (in which he anticipated Maxwell Davies) and helped to form Scottish branch of Composers' Guild. Prin. works:

ORCH: Syms.: No. 1 in F minor (1944), No. 2 in D (1947–8), No. 3 in C (1951), No. 4 in E♭ (1953), No. 5 in A minor (1959–60), No. 6 (1976–7); Divertimento in D (1954); *Highland Overture* (1964); Concs.: pf. in D minor (1946), vn. in A (1955); vc. (1963).
CHORAL: *In No Strange Land* (1951); *A Song of Praise* (1956); *2 Seasonal Songs* (1971).
CHAMBER MUSIC: Str. Qts.: No. 1 (1941), No. 2 (1944), No. 3 (1947), No. 4 (1950), No. 5 (1957), No. 6 (1964); *4 Lyrics*, ten. and str. qt. (1941); str. trio (1945); pf. qt. (1948); pf. trio (1949); ob. qt. (1949); cl. quintet (1952); pf. quintet (1959); *The Solitary Reaper*, sop., cl., pf. (1973); vc. sonata (1937); vn. sonata (1944); *Theme and Variations*, ob. and pf. (1954); va. sonatina (1961); *Prelude and Scherzo*, ob. and pf. (1974).
PIANO: Sonata in D minor (1939); *Cheesecombe Suite* (1945–6); *Ballade* (1949); *Valediction* (1967).
VOICE AND PIANO: *4 Songs*, high v. (1936); *3 Songs*, medium v. (1938); *4 Sacred Sonnets* (Donne), low v. (1944); *4 Blake Songs*, high v. (1948); *Ariel's Songs*, medium v. (1968).

Working-out. The Development section in **Sonata Form*.

Worshipful Company of Musicians. Ancient London guild. Royal charter 1604, revoked 1632, renewed 1950. Offers prizes for chamber mus. comps. and awards Collard Fellowship and other scholarships.

Wotquenne, Alfred (b Lobbes, 1867; d Antibes, 1939). Belg. musicologist. Studied Brussels Cons. Librarian, Brussels Cons. 1894–1918. Among his works are a bibliographical study of *Galuppi (1899, enlarged 1902), catalogue of 17th-cent. It. opera and oratorio libs. (1901–14), thematic catalogue of works of Gluck (1904) and of C. P. E. Bach (1905). The prefix Wq. is used for numbering of C. P. E. Bach's works.

Wozzeck. (1) Opera in 3 acts of 5 scenes each by Berg, Op. 7, to lib. by Berg based on play *Wozzeck* by Georg Büchner (1836). Comp. 1917–22. Prod. Berlin 1925 (cond. Kleiber), Philadelphia and NY 1931, London 1952 (also cond. Kleiber). Play is often named as 'Woyzeck' since contemporary (1830s) newspaper account of the original incident came to light giving this spelling (Büchner's MS. was presumed to read 'Wozzeck'). Important feature of the opera is that each scene is in a strict mus. form e.g. Act I Sc. 1–5, suite, rhapsody and hunting song, march and lullaby, passacaglia (21 variations on a note-row), rondo; Act II Sc. 6–10, sym. in 5 movements: sonata-allegro, fantasia and fugue on 3 themes, largo, scherzo, rondo; Act III Sc. 11–15, theme and variations, pedal-point, a rhythm, 6-note chord, key (D minor), equal movement in 8ths *quasi toccata* (this act being 6 "inventions").
(2) Opera by Gurlitt (1926).

Wq. Abbreviated prefix to numbers in the *Wotquenne catalogue of C. P. E. Bach's works.

Wranitzky (Vranický), **Anton** (Antonín) (b Neureisch, now Nová Říše, 1761; d Vienna, 1820). Moravian composer and violinist, brother of P. *Wranitzky. Pupil of Albrechtsberger, Mozart, and Haydn. Court cond. for Prince Lobkowitz in Vienna from 1797, becoming orch. dir. of court theatre 1807–20. Wrote 15 syms., 15 vn. concs., and much church and chamber mus. His daughter Karoline (1790–1872) was a sop. who created role of Agathe in Weber's *Der *Freischütz*.

Wranitzky (Vranický), **Paul** (Pavel) (b Neureisch, now Nová Říše, 1756; d Vienna, 1808). Moravian composer and violinist. Studied Vienna. Violinist in Esterháza orch. under Haydn. Leader of Vienna court opera orch., 1790–1808. Comp. operas (incl. *Oberon*, 1789), ballets, 51 syms., 60 str. qts., 25 str. quintets, and many other works. Cond. f.p. of Beethoven's 1st Sym., Vienna, 2 April 1800.

Wreckers, The. Opera in 3 acts by Ethel Smyth to lib. by 'H. B. Laforestier' (Harry Brewster). Comp. 1903–4. Prod. Leipzig, 1906; London 1909.

Wright, Denis (b London, 1895; d 1967). Eng. composer, cond., and adjudicator. Studied RCM. Head of BBC brass-band broadcasts from 1936. Author of books on brass-band scoring. Composer and arranger for brass band. O.B.E. 1959.

Wright, Kenneth (Anthony) (b East Tuddenham, Norfolk, 1899; d London, 1975). Eng. composer

and administrator. 1st BBC dir. in Manchester 1922, ass. to Percy Pitt 1923–30 and Boult 1930–7 at BBC, ass. dir. of mus. 1937, overseas mus. dir. 1940–3, dep. dir. of mus. 1944–7. Head of TV Mus. 1951–9. Composer of mus. for brass bands, films, songs, etc. O.B.E. 1953.

Wu, Enloc (Ruth) (b Shanghai, 1946). Chinese pianist. Studied Hongkong and RCM. London début 1967. Taught at RCM from 1970. World tours as recitalist.

Wührer, Friedrich (b Vienna, 1900; d Mannheim, 1975). Austrian pianist and teacher. Studied at Vienna Acad. 1915–20 (pf. with F. Schmidt, comp. with Marx, cond. with Löwe). Toured Europe and USA as concert pianist 1923. Taught pf. at Vienna Acad. 1922–32, 1939–45, Mannheim 1934–6, 1952–8, Kiel 1936–9, Salzburg Mozarteum 1948–51, Munich 1955–68. One of best and most influential of teachers. Gave many perfs. of pf. works by Schoenberg, Berg, Webern, Bartók, and Stravinsky. Comp. str. qts., pf. pieces, and songs.

Wüllner, Franz (b Münster, 1832; d Braunfels, 1902). Ger. cond., composer, and pianist. Studied Brussels, Cologne, Leipzig, and Munich with, among others, Brahms, Joachim, and Jahn. Prof. of pf., Munich Cons. 1856. Mus. dir., Aix-la-Chapelle 1858. Court cond., Munich, 1864, succeeding Bülow 1871 as cond. of Munich Opera. Cond. premières of *Das *Rheingold*, Munich 1869, and *Die *Walküre*, Munich 1870. Court cond. and dir. of Cons., Dresden, 1877. Dir., Cologne Cons. from 1884 and cond. of Gürzenich concerts there. Cond. f.ps. of R. Strauss's *Till Eulenspiegel* (1895) and *Don Quixote* (1898). Cond. early Ger. perfs. of works by Elgar. Wrote choral and chamber mus.

Wüllner, Ludwig (b Münster, 1858; d Berlin, 1938). Ger. ten., also bar., and actor, son of Franz Wüllner. Studied philology Munich and Berlin. Taught at Münster Acad. 1884–7. Studied mus. Cologne 1887–9. Actor at Mannheim 1889–95. Lieder singer from 1896. Sang Elgar's Gerontius in Düsseldorf 1901 and 1902 and at f.p. in London 1903. Toured USA 1908 and 1909–10. Gave f.p. in NY of Mahler's *Kindertotenlieder*, cond. Mahler, 1910.

Wulstan, David (b Birmingham, 1937). Eng. cond. and teacher. Studied Oxford Univ. Cond., The Clerkes of Oxenford, specialists in Early and Tudor Eng. mus. Comp. carols.

Wunderhorn, Des Knaben. See *Knaben Wunderhorn, Des*.

Wunderlich, Fritz (b Kusel, 1930; d Heidelberg, 1966). Ger. ten. Studied with Margarete von Wintenfeldt, 1950–5. Début as soloist with Freiburg Bach Choir, c.1951. Opera début Freiburg 1954 as Tamino in *Zauberflöte*. Sang with Stuttgart Opera 1955–8, Frankfurt 1958–60,

Munich Opera from 1960 and also at Vienna from 1962, becoming recognized as fine Mozart ten. Aix-en-Provence Fest. 1958, Salzburg Fest. 1959. CG début 1965 (Don Ottavio), Edinburgh Fest. 1966. Created role of Tiresias in Orff's *Oedipus der Tyrann* (1958). Outstanding exponent of Henry in Strauss's *Die schweigsame Frau* and Leukippos in *Daphne*. Recorded ten. songs of Mahler's *Das Lied von der Erde* with Klemperer. Superb singer of operetta. Died in fall, at height of recognition as one of greatest of Ger. lyric tens. for many years.

Wunsch (Ger.). Wish. So *Nach Wunsch,* according to one's wish, same as *ad libitum.*

Wuorinen, Charles (*b* NY, 1938). Amer. composer, cond., and pianist. Studied Columbia Univ. (comp. with Luening, Ussachevsky, and Beeson). Taught at Columbia 1964–71 and Mannes Coll. from 1971. Co-founder Group for Contemporary Mus., 1962. Prolific composer of works in many genres, incl. elec. Tonal up to *c.*1960, then 12-note technique as propounded by Babbitt. Works incl. syms., *Symphonia sacra, Evolutio transcripta* for chamber orch. (1961), Octet, 2 pf. concs., 4 chamber concs., str. trio, *Time's Encomium* (elec., 1969), *Contrafactum* for orch. (1969), cantata *A Message to Denmark Hill* (1970), str. qt. (1971), tuba conc., masque *The Politics of Harmony* (1968), conc. for amplified vn., *The W. of Babylon* (1975), baroque burlesque for 8 soloists, narrator, and orch., Sym. for 24 perc. (1976), pf. sonata No. 2 (1976).

Wurlitzer. Amer. firm of org.-builders founded 1856, particularly assoc. with th. and cinema orgs. of period 1920–40. Now specializes in elec. orgs. and electric pfs.

Wurm, Marie (*b* Southampton, 1860; *d* Munich, 1938). Eng. pianist, composer, and teacher. Studied Stuttgart Cons. with Clara Schumann, Joachim, and Raff, then at RAM with Sullivan, winning Mendelssohn Prize. Sister of Mathilde and Adela *Verne but retained orig. spelling of name. Formed women's orch., Berlin 1899. Wrote pf. conc., opera, str. qt., and vc. sonata. Retired to Ger. to teach in Berlin and Munich.

Wuthering Heights. Opera (lyric drama) in prol. and 4 acts by *Herrmann to lib. by Lucille Fletcher adapted from Emily Brontë's novel (1847). Comp. 1940–52. F.p. Portland, Oregon, 1982. Also opera by Carlisle *Floyd (1958).

Wyk, Arnold van (*b* Calvinia, Cape Province, 1916; *d* Cape Town, 1983). S. African composer. Studied Stellenbosch Univ. and RAM. On BBC staff 1939–44. Taught at Cape Town Univ. 1949–60, Univ. of Stellenbosch from 1961. Works incl. 2 syms., *Christmas Cantata, 5 Elegies* for str. qt., song-cycle, pf. mus.

Wyner, Yehudi (*b* Calgary, 1929). Canadian-born Amer. composer, pianist, cond., and teacher. Studied Juilliard Sch., Yale and Harvard (with Piston). Taught in NY before joining Yale mus. faculty 1964–77. Mus. dir., Turnau Opera Co., Woodstock, NY, 1962–4. Wrote liturgical mus. for Jewish synagogue, also *Partita* for pf., pf. sonata, *Serenade* for 7 instr., *Passover Offering, Torah Service* for ch., 4 brass, and db., *Da camera* (pf. conc.), *Cadenza!* cl., hpd.

Wynne, David (*b* Hirwaun, Glam., 1900; *d* Pencoed, Mid-Glamorgan, 1983). Welsh composer. Studied Univ. Coll., Cardiff, and Bristol Univ. Taught comp. at Cardiff Coll. of Mus. and Drama from 1961. Works incl. 5 syms., 2 pf. concs., vn. conc., va. conc., str. qts., sonatas, song-cycles, etc.

Wyss, Sophie (*b* Neuveville, 1897; *d* Bognor Regis, 1983). Swiss sop. Settled in Eng. 1925. Gave f.ps. of several works by Brit. composers, incl. Britten's *Our Hunting Fathers* (1936) and *Les Illuminations* (1940).

Wyttenbach, Jürg (*b* Berne, 1935). Swiss pianist, cond., and composer. Studied Berne Cons. 1948–55 (comp. with Veress), Paris Cons. 1955–7 (pf. with Lefébure), and Lower Saxony Sch. of Mus. 1958–9. Taught Biel Mus. Sch., 1958–67, Berne Cons. 1960–7, and Basle Acad. of Mus. from 1967. Specialist in contemp. mus. as cond. and pianist. Comps., some in aleatory and serial techniques, incl. *Divisions* for pf. and 9 str., *Nachspiel* for 2 pf., *Contests* for musicians, *Exécution ajournée* (Jokes for musicians).

Wyzewa (Wyzewski), **Théodore de** (Teodor de) (*b* Kalusik, 1862; *d* Paris, 1917). Fr. writer and mus. critic. Taken to Fr. 1869. Founded *Revue Wagnérienne*, Paris 1884, which was important in symbolist movement. Authority on Mozart, writing in collab. with Georges de Saint-Foix the first 2 vols. of a 5-vol. biography (pubd. Paris 1908–9). Ed. 20 of Clementi's pf. sonatas (1916).

X

Xenakis, Iannis (*b* Braila, Romania, 1922). Romanian-born Gr. composer (Fr. nat. since 1965). Parents moved back to Gr. in 1932. Began mus. study 1934 with Kundurov. Graduated from Athens Polytechnic 1947 with engineering degree. Went to Paris 1947, studying with Honegger and Milhaud, later with Messiaen 1950–1. Also studied in Switz. with Scherchen. Worked as architect with Le Corbusier 1948–59; designed Philips pavilion for 1958 Brussels Exhibition. Est. School of Mathematical and Automated Music, Paris 1966 and at Indiana Univ. where he also taught after 1967. Although he has used elecs., most of Xenakis's works employ traditional human forces, but embody his concept of **stochastic* music. This mathematical term, as applied to mus., is a theory of probability: that the results of chance will reach a determinate end. In contrast to the *aleatory processes of *Cage and others, Xenakis works to retain the composer's domination of his material, and calculates the events in his mus. himself or by means of a computer, e.g. speeds of glissandi, density of sonorities, etc. Xenakis converts the printout from the computer either into a score for conventional instr. or into an elec. comp. In 2 works, *Duel* and *Stratégie*, he used his 'theory of games' to introduce an aleatory element into perf., but the rules of the games are strictly predetermined. Prin. works:

BALLETS: *Kraanerg*, orch. and tape (1968–9); *Antikhthon* (1971).

THEATRE MUSIC: *Oresteia*, ch. and chamber ens. (1965–6).

ORCH: *Metastasis* (After-standstill), 61 players (1953–4); *Pithoprakta*, 50 players (1955–6); *Achoripsis*, 21 players (1956–7); *ST/10*, 10 players (1956–62); *Atrées*, 10 instr. (1958–62); *Analogiques A and B*, str., tape (1959); *Duel*, 2 orch. (1959); *Syrmos*, 18 str. (1959); *ST/48*, 48 instr. (1959–62); *Stratégie*, 2 orch. and 2 cond. (1959–62); *Akrata*, 16 wind instr. (1964–5); *Terrêtektorh*, orch. deployed among audience (1966); *Polytope* (Many-placed), 4 small orch. (1967); *Nomos gamma*, orch. deployed among audience (1967–8); *Synaphai*, pf., orch. (1969); *Eridanos*, 8 brass, 10 str. (1973); *Erikhthon*, pf., orch. (1974); *Noomena* (1975); *Empreintes* (1975); *Ionchaies* (1977); *Palimpsest*, pf., ens. (1982).

TAPE: *Diamorphoses*, 2-track (1957–8); *Conret PH*, 2-track (1958); *Analogique B*, 2-track (1958–9); *Orient–Occident*, 2-track (1960); *The Thessaloniki World Fair*, 1-track (1961); *Bohor*, 4-track (1962); *Hibiki-hana-ma*, 12-track (1969–70); *Persepolis*, 8-track (1971); *Polytope de Cluny*, 8-track, lighting (1972); *Polytope II*, tape, lighting (1974); *Bohor II*, 4-track (1975); *Diatope*, 4 or 8-track (1977).

CHAMBER AND ENS.: *ST/4*, str. qt. (1956–62); *ST/10*, cl., bass cl., 2 hn., hp., perc., str. qt. (1956–62); *Morsima-Amorsima*, pf., vn., vc., db. (1956–62); *Amorsima-Morsima*, cl., bass cl., 2 hn., hp., tpt., tb., 2 perc., vn., vc. (1962); *Atrées*, fl., cl., bass cl., hn., tpt., tb., 2 perc., vn., vc. (1962); *Herma*, pf. (1960–4); *Eonta*, 2 tpt., 3 tb., pf. (1963–4); *Nomos Alpha*, vc. (1965–6); *Anaktoria*, cl., bn., hn., str. qt., db. (1969); *Persephassa*, 6 perc. (1969); *Aroura*, 12 str. (1971); *Charisma*, cl., vc. (1971); *Linaia-Agon*, hn., tb., tuba (1972); *Mikka*, vn. (1972); *Evryali*, pf. (1974); *Gmeeoorh*, org. (1974); *N'shima*, 2 mez., 2 hn., 2 vc. (1975); *Phlegra*, 11 instr. (1975); *Psappha*, perc. (1975); *Theraps*, db. (1975–6); *Epeï*, cor anglais, cl., tpt., 2 tb., db. (1976); *Khoaï*, hpd. (1976); *Retours-Windungen*, 12 vc. (1976); *Dmaathen*, ob., perc. (1976); *Kottos*, vc. (1977); *Tetras*, str. qt. (1983).

CHORAL: *Polla ta dhina*, children's vv., wind, perc. (1962); *Hiketides*, 50 women's vv., 10 instr. or orch. (1964); *Oresteia*, ch., ens. (1965–6); *Medea*, male vv., orch. (1967); *Nuits*, unacc. (1967–8); *Cendrées*, ch., orch. (1973–4); *Hélène*, mez., women's vv., 2 cl. (1977); *Akanthos*, sop., ens. (1977).

Xylophone (Gr.). Wood sound. (1) Perc. instr. consisting of graduated tuned wooden bars, arr. as on pf. kbd., and played by being struck with small hard or soft hammers held in the hands. Compass from middle C upwards for 4 octaves. Orig. found in Africa and in Javanese orch. in 14th cent. First mentioned in Europe in 1511 as 'wooden clatter', later being known as strawfiddle (*Strohfiedel*) because the bars lay on straw. First used in orch. 1874, by Saint-Saëns in *Danse macabre*, its sound being particularly apt for representation of rattling skeletons. Since then regular feature of perc. section, most 20th-cent. composers making use of it, e.g. Mahler in 6th Sym., Puccini in *Madama Butterfly*, Strauss in *Salome*, Walton in *Belshazzar's Feast*, Stravinsky, Vaughan Williams, etc.

(2) Perc. organ stop of 8' pitch, played electrically to duplicate sound of xylophone.

Xylorimba. Perc. instr.—combination of xylophone and *marimba—with compass of about 5 octaves.

Y

Yamash'ta, Stomu (Yamashita, Tsutomu) (*b* Kyoto, 1947). Japanese percussionist and composer. Studied Kyoto Music Acad. and Art Acad. College of Mus., Boston. Percussionist in Kyoto P.O. and Osaka P.O. 1961. Début as soloist in Milhaud conc. with Osaka P.O. 1963. Played with jazz quintet in USA. Aldeburgh Fest. 1970 when he scored success in Henze's *El Cimarrón*. Remarkable virtuoso perf. Founder-member of Red Buddha Th. Composer of film scores and works for own perf.

Yaniewicz. See *Janiewicz, Feliks*.

Yankee Doodle. Popular Amer. tune with confused history of both words and mus., the 2 words of the title being still unexplained as to orig. Earliest printed version of tune, under this title, in Vol. I of Aird's *Selection of Scotch, English, Irish, and Foreign Airs for the Fife, Violin, or German Flute* (Glasgow, *c*.1775). Many sets of humorous or nonsense words fitted to it since. Anton Rubinstein wrote pf. variations on tune, and Vieuxtemps's *Caprice burlesque,* vn. and pf., is based on it. It is used, altered, in theme in finale of Dvořák's *New World* Sym.

Yansons, Arvid (*b* Liepaya, Latvia, 1914; *d* Manchester, 1984). Latvian cond. Studied vn. Début as cond., Riga 1944 in ballet. Assoc. cond., Leningrad P.O. from1948, became joint cond. with Mravinsky. Chief guest cond., Hallé Orch. from 1965. His son Mariss is cond. Oslo P.O.

Yardumian, Richard (*b* Philadelphia, 1917; *d* Bryn Athyn, Pa., 1985). Amer. composer, of Armenian parentage. Mainly self-taught, but helped by Virgil Thomson, Stokowski, and Ormandy. Works incl. syms., vn. conc., pf. conc., str. qt., *Armenian Suite, Cantus animus et Cordis* for str., *Chorale Prelude,* etc.

Yeomen of the Guard, The, or The Merryman and his Maid. Operetta by Sullivan to lib. by Gilbert. Prod. London and NY 1888.

Yepes, Narciso (*b* Lorca, 1927). Sp. guitarist. Studied Valencia, later with Enescu and Gieseking. Début Madrid 1947. Uses (since 1961) 10-str. guitar of his own creation. Specialist in Sp. mus. from 15th to 20th cents. Has recorded complete lute works of Bach.

Yevgeny Onyegin (Tchaikovsky). See *Eugene Onegin*.

Yodel. Eng. spelling of *Jodel.* See *Jodelling*.

Yolanta (Iolanta). Lyric opera in one act by Tchaikovsky to lib. by M. Tchaikovsky after V.

Zotov's trans. of H. Hertz's *King René's Daughter.* Comp. 1891. F.p. St Petersburg 1892.

Yon, Pietro Alessandro (*b* Settimo Vittone, 1886; *d* NY, 1943). It. organist and composer. Studied Milan Cons., then studied pf. in Venice and Rome. Deputy organist at Vatican. Organist, St Patrick's Cath., NY. Works incl. masses, motets, org. sonatas, and 10 *Divertimenti* for org.

Yonge, Nicholas (*b* Lewes, Sussex, ? ; *d* London, 1619). Eng. musician, possibly a singer in choir of St Paul's Cath., London. Introduced It. madrigal into Eng. when he published *Musica transalpina* (2 vols., 1588 and 1597), coll. of It. madrigals, by Marenzio, Palestrina, Lassus, and others, in Eng. trans. 1st vol. contained 57, 2nd had 24.

Youll, Henry (*b* ?Newark; *fl.* 1608). Eng. musician of whom little is known except that he pubd. a vol. of 3-part canzonets and balletts, 1608.

Youmans, Vincent (*b* NY, 1898; *d* Denver, 1946). Amer. composer. Worked as mus. publisher 1918. Wrote successful musical comedies from 1921, having enormous success on both sides of Atlantic with *No, No, Nanette* (1924). Illness forced retirement 1933.

Young, (Basil) **Alexander** (*b* London, 1920). Eng. ten. Studied RCM and in Vienna. Opera début in Strauss's *Ariadne auf Naxos,* Edinburgh 1950. Wide repertory in opera, Lieder, and songs. Chosen by Stravinsky to sing Tom Rakewell in recording of *The Rake's Progress,* 1964 (he had sung the role in 1953 in work's f.p.—BBC studio perf.—in Eng.). Head of Sch. of Vocal Studies, RNCM, from 1973. Fine singer of Handel opera and Ferrando in *Così fan tutte.* Founder and cond., Jubilate Choir, Manchester, 1977.

Young, Douglas (*b* London, 1947). Eng. composer. Studied RCM. 1966–70, comp. with A. Milner. Wrote 2 ballets, *Pasiphae* and *Charlotte Brontë,* for Royal Ballet. Has also written works for schools and amateurs. Formed his own ensemble, Dreamtiger, 1973. Influenced by Carter and Boulez. Prin. works:

ORCH: *Sinfonietta* (1968–70); *Departure* (1970); *Aubade* (1972–3); pf. concertino (1972–4); *3 Regions from Terrain* (1974); *La lugubre gondola (after Liszt),* vc., small orch. (1974); *Sea Change* (1976); *Circus Band Et Al (after Ives)* (1977); *Virages—Region I,* vc. conc. (1978); *William Booth Enters Heaven (after Ives)* (1980); *2nd Night Journey Under the Sea,* va., 11 str. (1980); *3rd*

Night Journey Under the Sea (1980–2); *Rain, Steam, and Speed* (1981).

BALLETS: *Pasiphae* (1969); *Charlotte Brontë* (1973–4).

CHORAL: *The Listeners* (cantata, text by De La Mare), narrator, sop., -women's vv., chamber orch. (1967); *Of Birds and Beasts*, ch. and orch. (1970); *Sir Patrick Spens*, ch. and orch. (or 2 pf.) (1970); *Canticle* (Auden), unacc. (1970–1); *Vers d'un voyage vers l'hiver*, 12 solo vv. (1975–7); *Mrs Blow and Her Animals*, narrator, sop., women's vv., small orch. (1975–6); *Care Charmer Sleep*, unacc. (1972–6); *2 Carols*, women's vv. (1977); *Journey Between Two Worlds*, ch., rock group, steel band, orch. (1979); *The Hunting of the Snark*, narrator, ch., pf., small orch. (1981–2).

VOCAL: *4 Nature Songs*, v., pf. (1964–77); *To Blossoms*, mez. or bar., pf. (1964); *Caterpillar Scene from 'Alice'*, narrator, sop., pf. (1968); *Not Waving But Drowning* (S. Smith song-cycle), sop., pf. (1970); *Landscapes and Absences*, sop., fl. (1972–3); *Realities* (Yeats), sop., ens. (1973–4); *Poem 66*, sop., pf., perc. (1975); *3 Scottish Nursery Rhymes*, sop., cl. (1982); *Chamber Music* (Joyce), sop., guitar (1976–82).

CHAMBER MUSIC: Sonata for str. trio (1968); *Essay*, str. qt. (1971); *Compasses*, cl., str. trio (1972–7); *Studies for Virages*, vc. (1974); *Enfantines (after Satie)*, vn. or fl., vc. (1976); *Croquis et Agaceries (after Satie)*, fl., vc., pf. (1976); *10 Préludes de la Porte Héroique du Ciel* , vc., pf. (1977); *Trajet/inter/lignes*, fl. (picc.) (1978–80); *Storm in Miniature*, 5 recorders (1979); *Slieve League*, vn., vc. (1979); *Jeu d'éclair II*, vc., perc. (1980–2); *Fantômes*, str. trio (1980–1); *Sports et Divertissements (after Satie)*, narrator, cl., str. trio, pf. (1981); *Arabesque brève*, vc. (1982); *Jeu d'éclair I*, vc., pf. (1982); *Symbols of Longevity*, cl. in B♭ (1982).

PIANO: *Le Tombeau de Barraqué* (1974); *Columba* (1977); *Dream-landscapes* (1982).

Young, La Monte (*b* Bern, Idaho, 1935). Amer. composer. Studied U.C.L.A. and Berkeley, later under Stockhausen at Darmstadt, 1959. Founded Theatre of Eternal Music, 1962. Method of composition may be deduced from his directions for perf. of certain of his works: *Composition 1960* #2 is building a fire in front of the audience; #5 is releasing butterflies; *Composition 1961* is 'draw a straight line and follow it'. Has also 'written' *The Tortoise, his dreams and journeys*, a continuing perf. (since 1964) for vv., mixers, amplifiers, drones, and loudspeakers (but no tortoise).

Young Lord, The (Henze). See *Junge Lord, Der*.

Young, Percy (Marshall) (*b* Northwich, 1912). Eng. author, teacher, organist, and composer. Studied Cambridge Univ. and Trinity Coll., Dublin. Mus. adviser, Stoke-on-Trent, 1937–44; Wolverhampton Coll. of Technology, 1944–65. Author of over 50 books, subjects incl. Handel, Elgar, Sullivan, Sir George Grove, and Vaughan

Williams. Ed. various letters of Elgar. Arr. suite from Elgar's unfinished opera *The Spanish Lady*. Wrote va. conc., pf. conc., choral works, etc.

Young Person's Guide to the Orchestra, The. Orch. work (or for speaker and orch.), Op. 34, by Britten which is sometimes known (against the composer's wishes) only by its sub-title *Variations and Fugue on a Theme of Purcell*. Written for documentary film (1946), *The Instruments of the Orchestra* (commentary written by Eric *Crozier), in which narrator described the uses and characteristics of various sections of the orch., these being illustrated by Britten's variations. Theme is from Purcell's incidental mus. to the play *Abdelazer* (1695). F.p. of orch. version, Liverpool 1946.

Young, Victor (*b* Chicago, 1900; *d* Palm Springs, 1956). Amer. composer and violinist. Studied Warsaw Cons., playing vn. with Warsaw P.O. Returned to Chicago 1914. After radio career, went to Hollywood 1935 to compose film mus. Songs incl. *Sweet Sue, Love Letters*, and *Indian Summer*.

Young, William (*d* Innsbruck, 1662). Eng. composer, viol player, and flautist. Worked on Continent, in Italy and Austria. At Innsbruck his playing enchanted Queen Christina of Sweden in 1655. There in 1653 he pubd. earliest set of (21) sonatas for 3, 4, and 5 parts (for 3 vns., va., bass viol, and continuo, the Purcell type of *trio-sonata). Returned to Eng. 1661 and became member of King's band.

Youth's Magic Horn, The. See *Knaben Wunderhorn, Des*.

Yradier, Sebastián (*b* Sauciego, Alava, 1809; *d* Vitoria, 1865). Sp. composer and singing teacher at Madrid Cons. Wrote many popular songs, e.g. *La paloma* (The Dove). His *El Arreglito: chanson havanaise* was adapted by Bizet as the Habañera in Act 1 of *Carmen*.

Ysaÿe, Eugène (*b* Liège, 1858; *d* Brussels, 1931). Belg. violinist, cond., and composer. Studied at age 5 with his father, then at Liège Cons. with Massart, later with Wieniawski (from 1873) and Vieuxtemps (from 1876). Leader of Bilse's orch., Berlin, 1879–81. Toured Russia and Scandinavia with Anton Rubinstein 1882. Lived in Paris 1883–6, forming close ties with Franck, Chausson, Fauré, Saint-Saëns, and Debussy. Prof. of vn., Brussels Cons., 1886–98. Founded and cond. Ysaÿe concerts, Brussels. London début 1889. Amer. début 1894. Many tours from 1899. Played many new works, incl. Franck vn. sonata (ded. to him) and Elgar conc. (but never in Eng.). Cond. Cincinnati S.O. 1918–22. One of most remarkable virtuosi of his day, with powerful tone. Wrote 6 vn. concs., several solo vn. sonatas, *Variations on a Theme of Paganini*, and other pieces. Also wrote opera in Walloon dialect.

Ysaÿe, Théophile (*b* Verviers, 1865; *d* Nice, 1918). Belg. pianist and composer, brother of Eugène *Ysaÿe. Studied Liège Cons. and in Paris with Franck. Prof. of pf., Geneva Acad. of Music 1889–1900. Wrote sym., *Fantasy on Walloon Songs* for orch., 2 pf. conc., *Requiem*, etc.

Yun, Isang (*b* Tongyong, S. Korea, 1917). Korean-born composer. Studied Western mus. in Korea and Japan. Studied vc. and theory, Osaka Cons., 1935–7, and harmony and comp., Tokyo Univ. 1941–3. After teaching in Korea, went to Paris Cons. 1956–7 and Berlin 1958–9 (studying with Blacher). Settled in Berlin 1963–7. Taught in Hanover 1970–1 and at Berlin Hochschule für Musik from 1970 (prof. 1971). Became Ger. citizen 1971. Scrapped early works up to 1959 when he began to use Darmstadt total serial procedures into which he injected sounds and rhythms of Korean mus. Works incl. operas *Dream of Liu-Tung*, *Butterfly Widow*, and *Geisterliebe*; *Colloides sonores* for str. orch., *Loyang* for chamber ens., *Fluctuations* for orch., vc. conc., fl. conc., conc. for ob., hp., small orch., str. qts., octet, and many pf. pieces.

Z

Z. Abbreviated prefix to numbers in the Zimmerman catalogue of Henry *Purcell's works.

Zabaleta, Nicanor (*b* San Sebastián, 1907). Sp. harpist. Studied Madrid Cons. Début Paris 1925. Soloist with world's orchs. Has revived much forgotten harp mus. and commissioned works from modern composers, e.g. Křenek and Milhaud.

Zaccaria, Nicola (*b* Piraeus, 1923). Gr. bass. Studied Athens. Début Athens 1949. Opera appearances at Milan, Genoa, and many fests. Scala, Milan, 1953–74. CG début 1957.

Zacconi, Ludovico (*b* Pesaro, 1555; *d* Fiorenzuola, 1627). It. theorist. Studied with A. *Gabrieli in Venice. Became monk. Went to Vienna *c.*1585, then had court post in Munich, 1590, under dir. of Lassus. Returned to Italy 1596. Wrote major theoretical book *Prattica di musica* (Vol. 1, Venice 1592, Vol. 2, Venice 1622). Wrote canons and organ works.

Zacharewitsch, Michael (*b* Ostrov, 1879; *d* London, 1953). Russ.-born violinist (Brit. citizen from 1915). Début Odessa 1894 in Tchaikovsky conc., cond. by composer. Later studied in Prague with Ševčik. Eng. début 1903; settled in Eng. 1909. Wrote treatise on violin playing, 1934. Wrote vn. conc. *Dunkirk 1940* (1945).

Zachau (Zachow), **Friedrich Wilhelm** (*b* Leipzig, 1663; *d* Halle, 1712). Ger. composer and organist. As child, learned vn., ob., hpd., and org. Organist, Liebfrauenkirche, Halle, 1684–1712. Handel from age of 7 was his pupil. Wrote church and org. mus.

Zacher, Gerd (*b* Meppen, 1929). Ger. composer and organist. Studied Lippstadt 1941–8, Detmold Acad. 1949–52, and at Darmstadt summer courses with Messiaen, Boulez, and Stockhausen. Cantor and organist in Santiago, Chile, 1954–7; organist and mus. dir., Luther Church, Hamburg, 1957–70, prof. Inst. of Church Music, Essen, from 1970. Has given f.ps. of organ works by Kagel, Ligeti, and Yun. Works incl. *The Prayers of Jonah in the Fish's Belly*, sop., org. (1963), *Text* for org., *St Luke Passion* for ch., *Ré* for org., etc.

Zadok the Priest. No. 1 of 4 anthems comp. Handel for coronation of George II, 1727, and perf. at every Eng. coronation since then. Henry *Lawes had set the same text for the coronation of Charles II, 1660.

Zádor, Jenö (Eugene) (*b* Bátaszék, 1894; *d* Hollywood, 1977). Hung.-born composer (Amer. cit.). Studied Vienna Cons. with Heuberger and

in Leipzig with Reger. Taught at New Vienna Cons. 1922–8. Settled in USA 1939, working in Hollywood as orch. of over 120 film scores. Composed 12 operas (incl. *The Island of the Dead*, 1925, and *Christopher Columbus*, 1939), ballet *The Machine-Man* (1934), orch. works, wind quintet, and songs.

Zaide. Unfinished opera in 2 acts (K344, 1780) by Mozart to lib. in Ger. by Schachtner. Prod. in version with extra mus. by A. André, Frankfurt 1866, London 1953. Mozart left finale incomplete and did not give the work a title. Plot is similar to *Die Entführung aus dem Serail* and lib. was probably based on Friebert's operetta *Das Serail*.

Zamba (Sp.). Argentinian scarf dance in $\frac{6}{8}$ time, with guitar introduction to vocal section. Originated in Peru.

Zambra (Sp.). Moorish dance, perf. with clasped hands to woodwind mus.

Zampa, ou la fiancée de marbre (Zampa, or the Marble Bride). Opera in 3 acts by *Hérold to lib. by Mélesville. Prod. Paris 1831, London and Boston, Mass., 1833.

Zandonai, Riccardo (*b* Sacco, Trentino, 1883; *d* Pesaro, 1944). It. composer. Studied at Rovereto 1893–8 and with Mascagni in Pesaro. Dir., Pesaro Cons. 1940–3. Wrote operas in *verismo* style successful at time. Works incl.:

OPERAS: *Il grillo del Focolare* (1908); *Conchita* (1911); *Melenis* (1912); *Francesca da Rimini* (1914); *La via della finestra* (1919, rev. in 2 acts 1923); *Giulietta e Romeo* (1922); *I Cavalieri di Ekebu* (1925); *Giuliano* (1928); *La farsa amorosa* (1933).
ORCH.: *Il ritorno di Ulisse*, symphonic poem; vn. conc.; *Serenata medievale*.
CHORAL: *Ave Maria*; *Alla patria*.

Zanelli (Morales), **Renato** (*b* Valparaiso, 1892; *d* Santiago, 1935). Chilean baritone, later tenor. Started business career and was advised to study singing after he had sung at a party. Début Santiago 1916 as Valentine in Gounod's *Faust*. NY Met. début 1919–20 season as Amonasro. In It., 1923, was advised to change to tenor and made début at Naples 1924 in *Les Huguenots*. Sang his first Otello, Turin 1926, following it with Lohengrin. CG début 1928 (Otello). Later sang Tristan and Siegmund in It. Regarded as best Otello since *Tamagno.

Zanotti, Camillo (*b* Cesena, *c.* 1545; *d* Prague, 1591). It. composer. Vice-Kapellmeister at court of Rudolf II in Prague from 1587. Wrote masses, motets, and madrigals in 5, 6, and 12 parts (pubd. 1587–90).

Zapateado (Sp.). Sp. solo dance, in triple time, in which rhythm is marked by stamping of the heels, frequently in syncopation.

Zareska, Eugenia (b Rava Ruska, nr. Lwów, 1922; d Paris, 1979). Ukrainian-born mez. (later Brit. citizen). Studied Lwów Cons., then Milan and Salzburg. Début Milan 1941 as Dorabella in *Così fan tutte*. London début 1947 (Rosina in *Il barbiere di Siviglia*), CG 1948–9, 1952–3, 1957–8. Glyndebourne 1948. Guest singer at many fests. Fine Lieder singer. Taught singing in Paris.

Zarlino, Gioseffe (b Chioggia, 1517; d Venice, 1590). It. theorist. Singer, later organist, Chioggia Cath. 1536–41. Became Franciscan monk in 1537. Studied with Willaert in Venice 1541 and became choirmaster of St Mark's 1565. Wrote 3 important treatises (1558, 1571, and 1588). Suggested equal *temperament for kbd. instr. Wrote church mus.

Zar und Zimmermann (Tsar and Carpenter). Opera in 3 acts by *Lortzing to his own lib. after play by Mélesville, Merle, and De Boirie (1818). Prod. Leipzig 1837, NY 1851, London 1871 (as *Peter the Shipwright*).

Zarzuela (Sp. from *ʒarʒa*, 'bramble bush'). Idiomatic Sp. form of opera in which mus. is intermingled with spoken dialogue. Name comes from entertainments perf. in 17th cent. at royal palace of La Zarzuela, near Madrid, for Philip IV and court. First known composer of zarzuelas was Juan Hidalgo, c.1644. In 18th cent., popularity of the form was challenged by *tonadillas, which were racier and more satirical. Despite brief revival, the zarzuela languished until nat. movement of 19th cent. when desire to create a Sp. nat. opera led to comp. of numerous zarzuelas by such composers as Barbieri, Arieta, Bretón, and Vives. Some were in 3 acts, with serious subjects. In the 20th cent., Alonso and Tórroba have written large-scale zarzuelas, and the form, always flexible, has been expanded to embrace features from operetta and jazz.

Zarzycki, Alexander (b Lwów, 1834; d Warsaw, 1895). Polish pianist and composer. Studied Paris 1856–61. Dir. of Warsaw Cons. 1879–88. Wrote pf. conc., many pf. pieces, and songs.

Zauberflöte. Metal organ stop, 8′ pitch, with stopped pipes and hole pierced in such a place that note heard is 3rd harmonic, not the 2nd (octave).

Zauberflöte, Die (The Magic Flute). Opera in 2 acts by Mozart (1791, K620) to lib. by E. Schikaneder after the story *Lulu* by Liebeskind in Wieland's collection of Oriental fairy-tales *Dschinnistan* (1786). Prod. Vienna 1791, London 1811, NY 1833.

Zauberharfe, Die (The Magic Harp). Melodrama by G. E. Hoffmann for which Schubert comp. ov. and other items in 1820 (D644). Prod. Vienna 1820. Ov. now known as *Rosamunde*.

Zecchi, Carlo (b Rome, 1903; d Salzburg, 1984). It. pianist and conductor. Studied at Rome Cons., later going to Berlin to study with Schnabel and Busoni. Début as pianist, Berlin 1920. Career as soloist ended 1939 when he formed duo with cellist Mainardi. From 1938 studied conducting and launched new career 1947. Taught in Rome and Salzburg. Ed. D. Scarlatti kbd. works.

Zedda, Alberto (b Milan, 1928). It. conductor and musicologist. Studied Milan Cons. (cond. with Giulini). Début Milan 1956. Taught at Cincinatti Coll. of Mus. 1957–9. Cond. at Deutsche Oper, Berlin, 1961–3, then NY City Opera. Prod. critical edn. of Rossini's *Il barbiere di Siviglia* (Milan 1969) which he cond. at CG 1975 (it was recorded by Abbado). Co-ed., complete edn. of Rossini's works.

Zednik, Heinz (b Vienna, 1940). Austrian tenor. Studied in Vienna; début Graz 1963. Vienna Opera début 1965. Has appeared in Paris, Montreal, Moscow, and Munich where his roles have incl. David in *Die Meistersinger*, Jacquino in *Fidelio*, and The Painter in *Lulu*. Sang Loge and Mime at Bayreuth Fest. centenary *Ring* 1976. One of most admired of contemporary character tenors.

Zeffirelli (Corsi), **Franco** (b Florence, 1923). It. producer and designer. Began as actor, but became ass. to *Visconti. First opera prod., *La Cenerentola*, Scala, Milan, 1953. CG début with *Lucia di Lammermoor*, 1959. Other CG prods. incl. *Falstaff* (1961), *Don Giovanni* and *Alcina* (1962), and *Tosca* (1964). Glyndebourne 1961 (*L'Elisir d'Amore*). Amer. début, Dallas with *La Traviata* (1958) for *Callas. NY Met. début *Falstaff* (1964). Designed Barber's *Antony and Cleopatra* (1966), first opera at new Met. Prods. notable for Romantic realism.

Zeitlin, Zvi (b Dubrovna, USSR, 1923). Russ.-born Amer. violinist. Studied Juilliard Sch. and Hebrew Univ., Jerusalem. Début with Palestine S.O. 1940. Amer. début NY 1951, London 1961. Soloist with leading orchs. Authority on concs. of Nardini. Prof. of vn., Eastman Sch., head of vn. dept., Mus. Acad. of West, Santa Barbara, Calif.

Zeitmass (Ger.). Time-measure, i.e. Tempo. *Zeitmesser*, metronome. Stockhausen comp. *Zeitmasse* for 5 wind instr., 1955–6.

Zelenka, Jan Dismas (b Lounovice, 1679; d Dresden, 1745). Bohemian composer and db. player. Studied in Prague and Vienna (comp. with Fux 1716). Db. player in Dresden from 1710. Studied in It. with Lotti, 1716. Returned to Dresden 1719 and became court church composer 1735. Wrote 20 masses, 3 oratorios, and quantities of smaller works.

Zell, F. See *Wälzel, Camillo.*

Zeller, Karl (*b* St Peter-in-der-Au, Austria, 1842; *d* Baden, Vienna, 1898). Austrian composer. Wrote chiefly operettas incl. *Joconde* (1876), *Capitän Nicoll* (1880), *Der Vagabund* (1886), *Der Vogelhändler* (1891), *Der Obersteiger* (1894), and *Der Kellermeister* (prod. 1901 completed by J. Brandl).

Zelter, Carl Friedrich (*b* Berlin, 1758; *d* Berlin, 1832). Ger. composer and teacher. Studied vn. and theory (with Fasch). Dir., Berlin Singakademie from 1800. Founded Liedertafel, Berlin, 1809, and Royal Institute for Church Mus. 1820. Friend and teacher of Mendelssohn, allied with him in Bach revival. Wrote oratorio, operas, cantatas, and Lieder.

Zémire et Azor. *Comédie-ballet* in 4 acts by Grétry to lib. by Marmontel after La Chaussée's *Amour par Amour* (1742). Prod. Fontainebleau 1771, London 1776 (revived by Beecham, Bath 1955). Other operas on this subject (Beauty and the Beast) by Tozzi, Spohr, and Garcia.

Zemlinsky, Alexander (von) (*b* Vienna, 1871; *d* Larchmont, NY, 1942). Austrian composer and conductor. Studied at Vienna Cons. with A. Door for pf. 1887–90, and J. Fuchs for comp. 1890–2. Joined Vienna Society of Musicians 1893, having several chamber works played, some of which pleased Brahms. Met Schoenberg 1893, and gave him lessons in counterpoint and introduced him to Wagner's mus. Cond. amateur orch. Polyhymnia in which Schoenberg played vc. Schoenberg said that Zemlinsky was the man he had to thank 'for practically all my knowledge of technique and the problems of composition'. Zemlinsky's sister Mathilde became Schoenberg's first wife in 1901. Cond. at Carltheater, Vienna, 1900–3, Theater an der Wien 1903–4, Volksoper 1904–11 (at Court Opera 1907–8). Encouraged by Mahler, who helped to revise and conducted the opera *Es war einmal.* Gave comp. lessons to Alma Schindler, who became Mahler's wife. Arr. Mahler's 6th sym. for pf. (4 hands), pubd. 1906. Cond. of opera at Deutsches Landestheater, Prague, 1911–27, where he cond. f.ps. of 3 of Schoenberg's *6 Songs with Orchestra*, Op. 8, in 1914, and the monodrama *Erwartung* in 1924, also many other important new works. Pres. of Prague branch of *Society for Private Performance, 1921–4. Taught comp. at Ger. Acad. of Mus., Prague, from 1920. Ass. cond. to Klemperer at Kroll Opera 1927–31. Taught at Berlin Hochschule für Musik 1927–33. Fled to Vienna 1933, to USA via Prague 1938.
Zemlinsky's mus. was greatly admired by Schoenberg and it had a high reputation generally in the early years of the cent. In later years it was almost forgotten, but since *c.* 1975 has enjoyed a gradual and accelerating climb back to favour. It has a flavour of Wagner–Strauss and remains determinedly tonal. Zemlinsky did not follow

Schoenberg into atonality and his mus. offers much to those who enjoy Mahler. The *Lyrische Symphonie* is avowedly inspired by *Das *Lied von der Erde* and is none the worse for it, while the 2nd str. qt. owes much to early Schoenberg and repays the debt with interest. His Maeterlinck settings are very attractive and the Wilde-based opera *Der Zwerg* is a masterpiece of concentrated lyric drama. Prin. works:

OPERAS: *Sarema* (*c.*1895); *Es war einmal* (1897–9); *Der Traumgörge* (1903–6); *Kleider machen Leute* (*c.*1908, rev. 1921); *Eine florentinische Tragödie* (Wilde, trans. Meyerfeld) (1915–16); *Der *Zwerg* (Klaren, after Wilde's *The Birthday of the Infanta*) (1920–1); *Der Kreidekreis* (1932); *König Kandaules* (1935–6, complete in short score).
BALLET: *Das gläserne Herz* (after Hofmannsthal's *Der Triumph der Zeit*) (1900–1).
INCIDENTAL MUSIC: *Cymbeline* (1914).
ORCH: Syms., No. 1 in D minor (1892), No. 2 in B♭ (1897); *Suite* (*c.*1894); *Die Seejungfrau* (1902–3); *Sinfonietta* (1934).
CHURCH: *Psalm 83*, ch., orch. (1900); *Psalm 23*, vv., orch. (1910); *Psalm 13*, vv., orch. (1935).
VOICE(S) AND INSTR: *Waldgespräch* (Eichendorff), sop., 2 hns., hp., str. (1895–6); *Der alte Garten* (Eichendorff), v., orch. (1895); *Die Riesen* (Eichendorff), v., orch. (1895); *Orientalisches Sonett*, v., pf. (1895); *Nun schwillt der See so bang*, v., pf. (1896); *Süsse Sommernacht*, v., pf. (1896); *Frühlingsglaube* (Uhland), vv., str. (1896); *Frühlingsbegräbnis* (Heyse), sop., alto, ten., bass. ch., orch. (1896); *Lieder* (Heyse, Liliencron), 2 books, v., pf. (1894–6); *Gesänge* (Heyse, Liliencron), 2 books, v., pf. (*c.* 1896); *Walzer-Gesänge nach toskanischen Volksliedern* (Gregorovius), v., pf. (1898); *Irmelin Rose und andere Gesänge* (Dehmel, Jacobsen), v., pf. (1898); *Turmwächterlied und andere Gesänge* (Jacobsen, Liliencron), v., pf. (1898–9); *Ehetanzlied und andere Gesänge* (Bierbaum, Morgenstern), v., pf. (*c.* 1900); *Es war ein alter König* (Heine), v., pf. (1903); *Schmetterlinge* (Liliencron), v., pf. (1904); *Ansturm* (Dehmel); v., pf. (1907; *Auf See* (Dehmel), v., pf. (1907); *Jane Grey* (Ammann), v., pf. (1907); *6 Gesänge* (Maeterlinck), mez. or bar., pf. (1910–13, and with orch.); *Lyrische Symphonie* (Tagore), sop., bar., orch. (1922–3); *Symphonische Gesänge*, v., orch. (1929); *6 Lieder* (Morgenstern, Goethe), v., pf. (1934); *12 Lieder* (George, Kalidasa, Goethe), v., pf. (1937).
CHAMBER MUSIC: *Serenade* in A, vn., pf. (1892); *Suite* in A, vn., pf. (*c.* 1893); str. quintet in D minor (2 vn., 2 va., vc.) (*c.* 1895); Trio for cl. or va., vc., pf. (1895); Str. Qts., No. 1 in A (*c.* 1895, f.p. 1896), No. 2 (1913–15), No. 3 (1924), No. 4 (*Suite*) (1936).
PIANO: *Ländliche Tänze* (1892); *Fantasien über Gedichte von Richard Dehmel* (1898).

Zenatello, Giovanni (*b* Verona, 1876; *d* NY, 1949). It. ten., orig. bar. Studied Verona. Opera début Naples 1898 (Silvio in *Pagliacci*); as ten.

1899 (Canio in *Pagliacci*). La Scala, Milan, 1903–7. Created role of Pinkerton in *Madama Butterfly* 1904. CG 1905–6, 1908–9, 1926; NY (Manhattan) 1907, Boston Opera 1909–14, Chicago 1912–13. Retired 1930 and taught. Famous singer of title-role in Verdi's *Otello*. Helped to launch Verona open-air opera 1913.

Zender, (Johannes Wolfgang) **Hans** (*b* Wiesbaden, 1936). Ger. cond. and composer. Studied pf. and comp. Frankfurt (1956–9) and Freiburg (with Fortner) (1959–63). Ass. cond., Freiburg Opera 1959. Studied comp. in Rome 1963 under B. A. *Zimmermann. Prin. cond., Bonn opera 1964–8; gen. mus. dir. Kiel 1969–71. Prin. cond. Saar Radio S.O. 1971–84. Mus-dir. Hamburg Opera from 1984. Cond. *Parsifal* at Bayreuth 1975. London début 1977. Comps. incl. *Zeitströme* (Time Stream) (1974), Cantos I–V for vv. and instr., elec. works.

Zeugheer, Jakob (J. Z. Herrmann) (*b* Zürich, 1803; *d* Liverpool, 1865). Swiss-born violinist and cond. Formed str. qt. in Munich after hearing Schuppanzigh Qt. in Vienna, 1823. Toured Europe and settled in Liverpool 1830. Cond., *Gentlemen's Concerts, Manchester, 1831–8, Liverpool Phil. Soc. 1843–65. Wrote 2 syms., vn. conc., str. qt., songs, etc.

Ziani, Marc Antonio (*b* Venice, *c.*1653; *d* Vienna, 1715). It. cond. and composer. Choirmaster at Mantua until 1686, becoming deputy court cond., Vienna 1700, court cond. 1712. Wrote over 40 operas, many oratorios, etc. Nephew of P. A. *Ziani.

Ziani, Pietro Andrea (*b* Venice, 1616; *d* Naples, 1684). It. organist and composer. Organist in Venice from 1640. Choirmaster, Bergamo 1657–9. Held court cond. post in Vienna 1662–8. 2nd organist, St Mark's, Venice, from 1669. At Naples from 1676, becoming choirmaster 1680. Wrote 30 operas, oratorios, and other church mus.

Zich, Jaroslav (*b* Prague, 1912). Cz. composer, son of Otakar *Zich. Studied with his father and Foerster. Wrote mainly chamber mus. and songs.

Zich, Otakar (*b* Králové Městec, 1879; *d* Oubenice, 1934). Cz. composer and scholar. Prof. at Prague Univ. Expert on Slavonic folk-song. Wrote operas and choral ballads. Author of books on aesthetics, the dance, and Cz. folk-songs.

Zichy, Géza, (Count Vazóny-Keö) (*b* Sztára, Hung., 1849; *d* Budapest, 1924). Hung. pianist, composer, opera intendant, and lawyer. Lost right arm as boy but studied with Liszt and became proficient left-hand player. President, Hung. Nat. Acad. of Mus. until 1892. Intendant, Budapest Nat. Opera 1891–4, dir. Nat. Cons. of Mus. 1895–1918. One of his first acts at Budapest Opera 1891 was to dismiss Mahler, who retaliated some years later by successfully defying royal wish for a Zichy opera to be staged in Vienna. Wrote 5 operas (incl. *Rakoczy* trilogy), pf. conc., pf. studies for left hand, and songs.

Žídek, Ivo (*b* Kravaře, 1926). Cz. tenor. Studied in Ostrava, making début there as Werther, 1945. Joined Prague Nat. Th. 1948. Vienna Opera début 1957, NY 1966 (concert perf. of *Jenůfa*). Sang at Edinburgh, Leeds, and Wexford fests. Best in light tenor roles.

Ziehen (Ger.). To draw out.

Ziehharmonika (Ger.). *Accordion.

Ziehn, Bernard (*b* Erfurt, 1845; *d* Chicago, 1912). Ger.-born teacher and theorist. Studied Erfurt and taught at Mühlhausen. Taught in Chicago 1868–71. Wrote several important books on harmony and counterpoint, and treatise on classical ornamentation.

Ziehrer, Karl Michael (*b* Vienna, 1843; *d* Vienna, 1922). Austrian self-taught composer and cond. of dance orchestra. Formed orch. 1863 and toured Ger. and Austria as bandmaster 1870–95. Mus. dir., Austrian court balls from 1908, last holder of the post. Wrote 24 operettas, 70 marches, and over 120 waltzes.

Zigeunerbaron, Der (The Gipsy Baron). Operetta in 3 acts by Johann Strauss II to lib. by Schnitzer, altered from Jokai's libretto on his story *Saffi*. Prod. Vienna 1885, NY 1886, London (amateur) 1935.

Zigeunerlieder (Gipsy Songs). 11 songs by Brahms, his Op. 103 (1887) for vv. and pf. Texts are verses by Hugo Conrat adapted from prose versions of Hung. folk poems by a Fräulein Witzl.

Zilcher, Hermann (*b* Frankfurt, 1881; *d* Würzburg, 1948). Ger. composer and pianist. Studied Hoch Cons., Frankfurt. Toured as accompanist to singers. Prof. of pf. and comp., Munich Acad. from 1908; dir., Würzburg Cons. 1920–44. Wrote 2 operas, 5 syms., 3 vn. concs., 2 pf. concs., several song-cycles, incidental mus., chamber works.

Zillig, Winfried (*b* Würzburg, 1905; *d* Hamburg, 1963). Ger. composer, conductor, and writer. Studied law at Würzburg Univ. and mus. at Cons. Went to Vienna 1925 to study with Schoenberg and followed him to Berlin to study at the Prussian Acad. of Arts 1926–8. Répétiteur Oldenburg 1928–32. Cond. at Düsseldorf 1932–7, 1946–7; chief cond. Essen Opera 1937–40. Mus. dir. Poznán Opera 1940–3. Chief cond. Hesse Radio, Frankfurt, 1947–51, where he promoted 20th cent. mus., incl. f. European p. of Schoenberg's vn. conc. Freelance cond. 1951–9. Dir. of mus., Hamburg Radio, 1959–63. His mus. is nearer to Berg than Schoenberg. Wrote 7 operas, incl. *Troilus and Cressida* (1949, rev. 1963), vn. conc., 2 str. qts., and choral mus. Completed scoring of Schoenberg's oratorio *Die Jakobsleiter* (f.p. in Zillig version, Vienna 1961), and prepared vocal score of *Moses und Aron*.

Ziloti (Siloty), **Alexander** (*b* nr. Kharkov, 1863; *d* NY, 1945). Russ. pianist and cond. Studied Moscow Cons. 1876–81 (pf. with N. Rubinstein, comp. with Tchaikovsky). Pupil of Liszt at Weimar 1883–6. Début Moscow 1880, Leipzig 1883. Prof. of pf., Moscow Cons. 1887–90. Extensive tours, incl. Eng. and USA 1898–9. Cond., Moscow P.O. 1901–2; formed own orch. in St Petersburg. Left Russia 1919, settled in NY. Taught at Juilliard Sch. 1924–42. Arr. concs. by Bach and Vivaldi.

Zimbalist, Efrem (*b* Rostov, 1889; *d* Reno, Nevada, 1985). Russ.-born violinist and violist (later Amer. citizen). Studied St Petersburg Cons. with *Auer. Début Berlin 1907 in Brahms conc. Tours of Europe. London début 1907. Amer. début, Boston 1911. Settled in USA 1914. Dir., Curtis Institute, Philadelphia, 1941–68, having taught there from 1928. *Shumsky was one of his pupils. Retired as player 1949, but returned to give f.p. of Menotti conc., NY 1952, and played Beethoven conc. in Philadelphia 1955. On jury Tchaikovsky comp., Moscow, 1962 and 1966. Wrote *American Rhapsody*, vn. conc., etc.

Zimbalon. See *Cimbalom*.

Zimbelstern (Ger.). A toy organ-stop, prevalent in N. Europe *c*.1500–1800. It comprised a revolving star near the top of the organ-case with a set of tuned or untuned bells attached to a wind-blown driving-wheel behind the case. It was an effect often used on feast days. There is a Zimbelstern on the org. of the chapel of St John's Coll., Cambridge.

Zimmer, Jan (*b* Ružomberok, 1926). Cz. pianist and composer. Studied Bratislava Cons., Budapest, and Salzburg. On staff Bratislava radio, 1945–8; prof., Bratislava Cons. 1948–52. Works incl. 10 syms., pf. concs., conc. grosso, opera *Oedipus Rex*, chamber mus., and film scores.

Zimmerman, Franklin Bershir (*b* Wauneta, Kansas, 1923). Amer. musicologist. Studied Univ. of S. Calif. and at Oxford Univ., teachers incl. H. Stevens, Wellesz, and Westrup. Taught at Univ. of S. Calif. 1959–64; prof. of mus. Dartmouth Coll. 1964–7, Kentucky Univ. 1967, Pennsylvania Univ. from 1968. Specialist in Eng. baroque mus., especially Purcell. Has pubd. analytical catalogue of Purcell's mus. (London 1963), *Henry Purcell, His Life and Times* (London 1967), and other works.

Zimmermann, Agnes (Marie Jacobina) (*b* Cologne, 1847; *d* London, 1925). Ger.-born pianist and composer, taken to Eng. as child. Studied RAM with Potter. Début London 1863, Leipzig 1864. European tours. Comp. pf. sonatas, vn. sonatas, and songs. Ed. pf. works of Mozart,

Beethoven, and Schumann. Gave f. Eng. p. of Beethoven's transcr. of his vn. conc. for pf., 1872.

Zimmermann, Bernd Alois (*b* Bliesheim, nr. Cologne, 1918; *d* Königsdorf, 1970). Ger. composer. Studied at Bonn, Königsdorf, and Berlin Univs. while earning living as labourer and dance-band player. Studied comp. with Jarnach, and with Fortner and Leibowitz at Darmstadt. Taught history of mus. theory, Cologne Univ., 1950–2, comp. at Cologne Hochschule from 1958. Works covered whole field of mid-20th cent. comp. techniques from serialism to elecs. Opera *Die Soldaten* a 'pluralistic' work, because it uses mixed-media resources and combines conventional orch. with elecs. Made much use of quotations, referring to this method as 'collage'. Prin. works:

OPERA: *Die *Soldaten* (The Soldiers) (1958–60, rev. 1963–4).

ORCH: Sym. in 1 movement (1947, rev. 1953); Conc. for str. (1948); vn. conc. (1950); ob. conc. (1952); *Canto di Speranza* (1952, rev. 1957); *Contrasts* (1953); tpt. conc. (1954); *Dialogues*, 2 pf., orch. (1960, rev. 1965); vc. conc. (1965–6); *Photoptosis* (1968); *Stille und Umkehr* (1970).

CHORAL: *Lob der Torheit*, burlesque cantata (1948); *Die Soldaten*, vocal sym. from opera, 6 solo vv., orch. (1959); *Requiem for a young poet*, speaking and singing ch., elecs., orch. (1967–9).

CHAMBER MUSIC: Vn. sonata (1950); *Tempus loquendi*, 3 fl. (1963).

Zimmermann, Louis (*b* Groningen, 1873; *d* Amsterdam, 1954). Dutch violinist and composer. Studied Leipzig Cons. and Brussels (with Ysaÿe). Member, Concertgebouw Orch., 1899–1904. Taught vn. at RAM 1904–11. Leader, Concertgebouw Orch. from 1911. Soloist in modern concs. Wrote vn. conc., chamber mus., and cadenzas for Beethoven, Brahms, and Mozart concs.

Zimmermann, Udo (*b* Dresden, 1943). Ger. composer. Studied at Dresden Hochschule für Musik 1962–8. Three times recipient of E. Germany's Mendelssohn schol. Has worked as producer at Dresden Opera. Works incl. 4 operas, timpani conc. (1965), *Dramatic Impression of the Death of J. F. Kennedy*, vc., orch. (1963), *Sinfonia come un grande lamento* (1970), str. qt. (1974), and settings of Neruda and Różewicz for v. and pf.

Zingarelli, Niccolò Antonio (*b* Naples, 1752; *d* Torre del Greco, 1837). It. composer and violinist. Studied Naples, held court posts, then went to Milan, writing operas for La Scala from 1785. Haydn produced 2 of his operas at Esterháza. In Paris 1790. Choirmaster Milan Cath. 1792, Loreto 1794, St Peter's, Rome, 1804–11. Dir., Naples RCM from 1813, choirmaster Naples Cath. 1816. Prolific composer, writing over 30 operas up to 1811 when he concentrated on church mus. Best-known opera *Giulietta e Romeo*, 1796.

Zingaro, zingara (It.). Gipsy. *Alla zingarese,* in gipsy style; *zingaresca,* gipsy song.

Zinman, David (*b* NY, 1936). Amer. cond. Mus. dir. Netherlands Chamber Orch. 1965–77. Chief cond. Rochester P.O. from 1974. Chief cond., Rotterdam P.O. 1979–82.

Zipoli, Domenico (*b* Prato, 1688; *d* Santa Catalina, nr. Córdoba, Argentina, 1726). It. organist and composer. Studied Florence 1707–9, Naples 1709 to study with A. Scarlatti, but quarrelled and went to Rome in same year. Organist at Jesuits' Church 1715–17. Wrote hpd. suites, kbd. sonatas, org. fugues, etc. Went to Argentina 1717, becoming organist of Jesuits' church in Córdoba.

Zither. Folk instr., descendant of medieval psaltery, prevalent in Austrian Tyrol and Bavaria. Consists of flat wooden soundbox over which are stretched 4 or 5 melody str. and up to 37 acc. str. Melody str., nearest to player, are stopped on fretted fingerboard with fingers of left hand and plucked by plectrum on right thumb. Acc. str. are plucked by fingers of either hand. Used for 'local colour' in operetta scores. Gained great popularity in Eng. after World War II when film *The Third Man* had as theme mus. a zither tune written and played by Anton Karas.

Zitternd (Ger.). Trembling. Same as *tremolando.*

Zivoni, Yossi (*b* Tel Aviv, 1939). Israeli violinist. Studied Tel Aviv and Brussels Cons. Winner of several vn. competitions. World tours as soloist and chamber music player. Prof. of vn. RMCM, 1968–72.

Znamenny. Russ. liturgical chant as used from 11th to 17th cents. Name derived from *znamya* (sign or neume). Underwent many changes. System included over 90 different signs for single notes.

Zögernd (Ger.). Delaying, i.e. *Rallentando.*

Zöllner, Heinrich (*b* Leipzig, 1854; *d* Freiburg, 1941). Ger. composer and teacher. Studied Leipzig Cons. 1875–7. Cond., Cologne Male Voice Ch., 1885. Lived in USA 1890–8. Mus. dir., Leipzig Univ. 1898, prof. of comp., Leipzig Cons. from 1902. Cond., Antwerp Opera 1907–14. Went to Freiburg as teacher 1914. Works incl. 10 operas (incl. *Faust,* 1887), choral works, 5 syms., 5 str. qts.

Zoppa, Alla (It. *zoppo, zoppa,* lame, limping). Mus. application is in the sense of *syncopation,* or with a *Scotch snap.*

Zorian, Olive (*b* Manchester, 1910; *d* London, 1959). Eng. violinist. Studied RMCM and RAM. Formed Zorian String Quartet 1942, giving perfs. of contemporary works notably those by Bartók, Bliss, and Britten. (F.p. of Britten's 2nd Qt. 1945.) Played concs. with leading orchs. Leader, EOG orch. 1952–7.

Zortziko (Zortzico). Basque folk dance in ⅝ time, like the *Rueda* except that the 2nd and 4th beats are almost always dotted notes. Formed 3rd figure in *aurresku* communal dance.

Zu 2 (Ger.). (1) 2 instr. to play the same part.
(2) All the instr. in question (e.g. first vns.) to divide into 2 parts.

Zug (Ger.). The action of pulling; thus org. stop knob, or pf. pedal (which pulls down some mechanism). *Zugposaune,* slide tb., *Zugtrompete,* slide tpt.

Zukerman, Pinchas (*b* nr. Tel Aviv, 1948). Israeli violinist and cond. Studied Israel Cons., Tel Aviv Acad. of Mus., and Juilliard Sch. Leventritt Award 1967. Début with NY P.O. 1969. Eng. début 1969 Brighton Fest. but he had appeared on television and made a recording in 1968. World-wide reputation as soloist and as chamber mus. player with Barenboim, Perlman, etc. Superb exponent of Elgar conc. Also plays va. Began to be soloist/director in baroque music 1971. Debut as cond., London 1974 (New Philharmonia). Mus. dir. St Paul Chamber Orch., Minnesota, from 1980.

Zukofsky, Paul (*b* Brooklyn, NY, 1943). Amer. violinist, conductor, composer, and teacher. Began to play vn. age 4, and made public début at 6. Studied with I. Galamian. Début as soloist with orch., New Haven S.O. 1953. First NY recital 1956. London début 1969. Specialist in 20th cent. mus., particularly that demanding new techniques. Has given f.ps. of concs. and similar works by Sessions, Wuorinen, I. Hamilton, Babbitt, and Crumb.

Zumpe, Herman (*b* Oppach, 1850; *d* Munich, 1903). Ger. cond. and composer. Studied Leipzig Cons. Helped Wagner in preparing first *Ring,* 1873–6. Cond. Salzburg, Würzburg, Hamburg Opera 1884–6, Stuttgart 1891–5, Munich 1900–3. CG 1898 (Wagner). Wrote operas, operettas, and sym.

Zumpe, Johannes (*fl.* 1735–83). Ger. employed by Shudi, London hpd. maker, who in 1761 began manufacture of *square pianos, though it is not known certainly if he invented them.

Zumsteeg, Johann Rudolf (*b* Sachsenflur, 1760; *d* Stuttgart, 1802). Ger. composer, friend of Schiller. Studied vc. and comp., becoming cond. and opera dir. at Stuttgart 1793. Wrote narrative ballads which anticipate those by Löwe, Zelter, and Schubert. Also wrote operas.

Zürich. Swiss city with long musical tradition. Main orch. is the Tonhalle, founded 1868. Its cond. have incl. Friedrich Hegar (1868–1906), Volkmar Andrae (1906–49), and Erich Schmid (1949–57) jointly with Hans Rosbaud (1950–62), Rudolf Kempe (1965–72), and Charles Dutoit (1967–71). Among smaller ensembles the Collegium Musicum was cond. by Paul Sacher from

1941. At the opera house, *Parsifal* had its first authorised stage perf. outside Bayreuth in 1913. Operas given f. stage p. in Zürich incl. Berg's *Lulu* (1937), Hindemith's *Mathis der Maler* (1938), and Schoenberg's *Moses und Aron* (1957). First European perf. of Gershwin's *Porgy and Bess* given there in 1945.

Zurück (Ger.). Back again. *Zurückgehend,* going back (i.e. to orig. tempo); *zurückhaltend,* holding back (i.e. *rallentando*).

Zweig, Stefan (*b* Vienna, 1881; *d* Petrópolis, Brazil, 1942). Austrian novelist and playwright who wrote lib. of *Die schweigsame Frau* for Richard Strauss and supervised libs. of *Friedenstag* and *Daphne*. Further collaboration with Strauss forbidden by Nazis because he was Jewish. Correspondence with Strauss pubd. (Frankfurt 1957, Eng. trans., Univ. of Calif., 1977).

Zweiunddreissigstel, Zweiunddreissigstelnote (Ger.). 32nd, 32nd note (the demisemiquaver).

Zwerg, Der (The Dwarf). Opera in 1 act by *Zemlinsky to lib. by G. C. Klaren based on Wilde's *The Birthday of the Infanta*. Comp. 1920–1. F.p. Cologne 1922, (cond. Klemperer), f.Brit.p. Edinburgh Fest. 1983 (by Hamburg Opera in double bill with Zemlinsky's *Eine florentinische Tragödie,* also based on Wilde, f.p. Stuttgart, 1917). In the 1983 Hamburg prod. and subsequent recording of *Der Zwerg,* a new lib. by Adolf Dresen is sung.

Zwillingsbrüder, Die (The Twin Brothers). Operetta (Singspiel) in 1 act by Schubert (D647, 1819) to lib. by G. E. Hoffmann, adapted from Fr. Prod. Vienna 1820.

Zwischenspiel (Ger.). Between-play. Any comp. having the character of an interlude or intermezzo, e.g. (1) Org.-playing between the stanzas of a hymn.
  (2) Episodes of a fugue.
  (3) Solo portions between the *tuttis* of a conc.

Zwölftonmusik (Ger.). 12-note mus.

Zyklus (Cycle). Work for solo percussionist by *Stockhausen, 1959, involving random choice and improvisation, and notated in graphics, dynamics of notes being indicated by their size.

Zylis-Gara, Teresa (*b* Vilnius, 1935). Polish sop. Studied Łódź Acad. of Mus. Début Kraków 1956. Career with leading opera houses, in major roles, especially Mozart. Glyndebourne début 1965 (Oktavian), CG 1968 (Violetta), Salzburg 1968, NY Met. from 1968 (Donna Elvira).